Handbook of
North American Indians

Handbook of North American Indians

WILLIAM C. STURTEVANT

General Editor

VOLUME 15

Northeast

BRUCE G. TRIGGER

Volume Editor

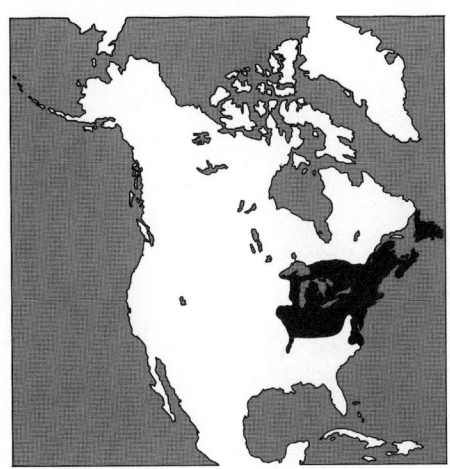

SMITHSONIAN INSTITUTION

WASHINGTON

1978

For sale by the Superintendent of Documents,
U.S. Government Printing Office, Washington, D.C. 20402.
Stock Number: 047-000-00351-2

Library of Congress Cataloging in Publication Data

Handbook of North American Indians.

    Bibliography: pp. 807-890
    Includes index.
    CONTENTS:

                v. 15 Northeast.

    1. Indians of North America. 2. Eskimos.
I. Sturtevant, William C.

E77.H25   970′.004′97   77-17162

Northeast Volume Planning Committee

Bruce G. Trigger, Volume Editor

William C. Sturtevant, General Editor

Elisabeth Tooker, Coordinator for Six Nations chapters

Gordon M. Day

William N. Fenton

James E. Fitting

Ives Goddard

Nancy Oestreich Lurie

John Witthoft

Contents

This map is a diagrammatic guide to the coverage of this volume rather than an authoritative depiction of tribal ranges. Sharp boundaries have been drawn and no territory is unassigned. Tribal units are sometimes arbitrarily defined, subdivisions are not mapped, no joint or disputed occupations are shown, and different kinds of land use are not distinguished. Since the map depicts the situation at the earliest periods for which evidence is available, the ranges mapped for different tribes often refer to quite different periods, and there may have been many intervening movements, extinctions, and changes in range. Boundaries in the western half of the area are especially tentative for these early dates. The tribal boundaries to the north and west also do not correspond precisely with the ecological boundaries used to define the Northeast for the purposes of this volume (see "Introduction"). Not shown are groups that came into separate political existence later than the map period for their areas.

For more specific information see the maps and text in the accompanying chapters.

Key to Tribal Territories

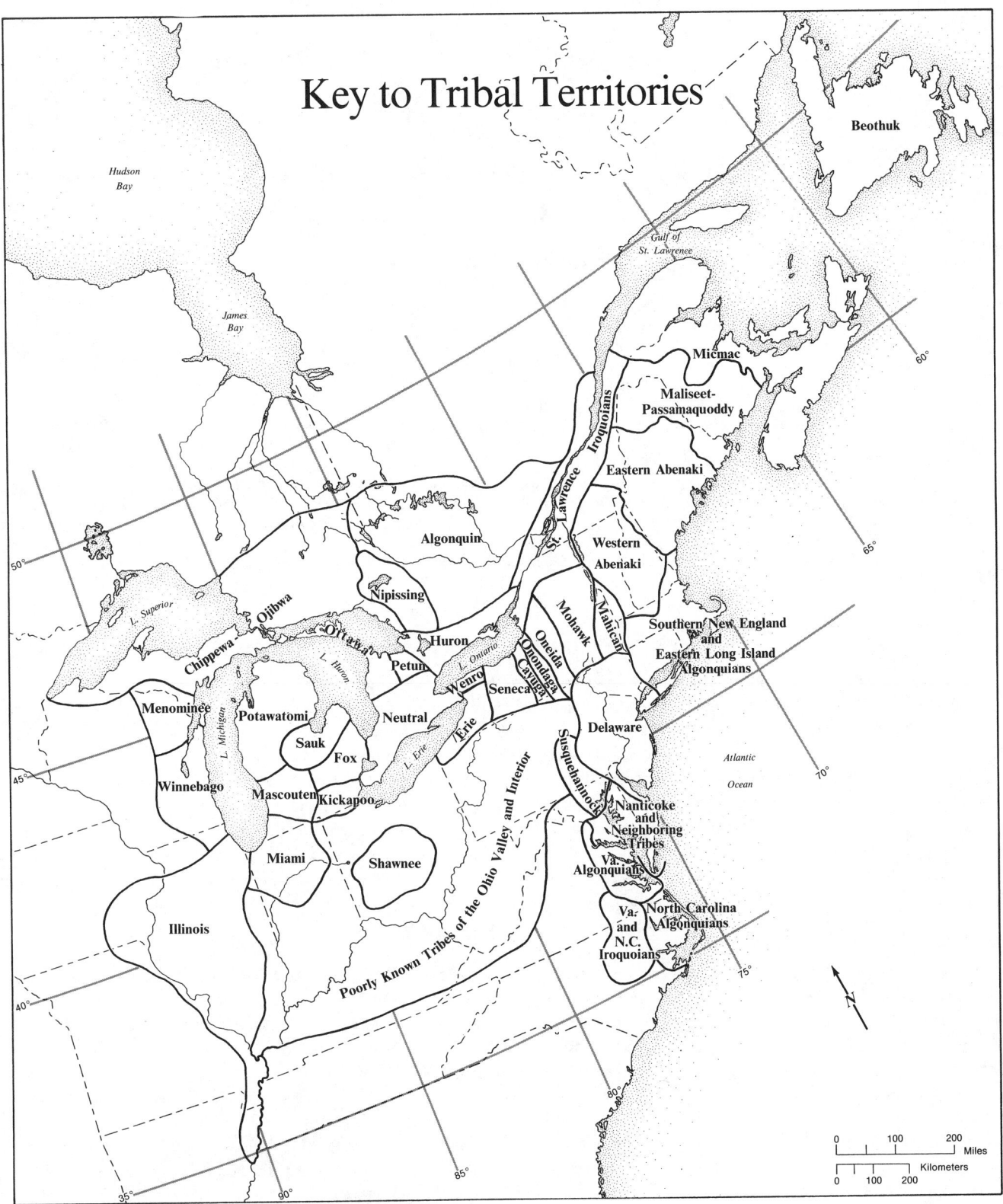

Hudson Bay

James Bay

Gulf of St. Lawrence

Beothuk

Micmac

Maliseet-Passamaquoddy

Eastern Abenaki

Western Abenaki

Algonquin

St. Lawrence Iroquoians

Nipissing

L. Superior

Ojibwa

Chippewa

Ottawa

Huron

Mohawk

Mahican

Southern New England and Eastern Long Island Algonquians

Petun

L. Ontario

Oneida

Menominee

Potawatomi

L. Michigan

L. Huron

Wenro

Onondaga

Cayuga

Seneca

Neutral

Erie

L. Erie

Delaware

Atlantic Ocean

Sauk

Fox

Susquehannock

Winnebago

Mascouten

Kickapoo

Nanticoke and Neighboring Tribes

Miami

Shawnee

Va. Algonquians

Va. and N.C. Iroquoians

North Carolina Algonquians

Illinois

Poorly Known Tribes of the Ohio Valley and Interior

60°

65°

50°

45°

70°

40°

75°

80°

85°

90°

35°

N

0   100   200
Miles

Kilometers

0   100   200

Technical Alphabet

Consonants

		bilabial	labiodental	dental	alveolar	alveopalatal	velar	back velar	glottal
stop	vl	p		t	t		k	q	ʔ
	vd	b		d	d		g	ġ	
affricate	vl			θ̂	c	č			
	vd			δ̂	ʒ	ǯ			
fricative	vl	φ	f	θ	s	š	x	x̣	h
	vd	β	v	δ	z	ž	γ	γ̇	
nasal	vl	M		N			Ŋ		
	vd	m		n			ŋ	ŋ̇	
lateral	vl				ɬ				
	vd				l				
semivowel	vl	W				Y			
	vd	w				y			

vl = voiceless; vd = voiced

Other symbols include: λ (voiced lateral affricate), ƛ (voiceless lateral affricate), ʕ (voiced pharyngeal fricative), ḥ (voiceless pharyngeal fricative), r (medial flap, trill, or retroflex approximant). Where in contrast, r is a flap and R is a continuant.

Modifications indicated for consonants are: glottalization ($i̓$, $k̓$, etc.), retroflexion (ṭ), palatalization (t^y, k^y, n^y, l^y), labialization (k^w), aspiration (t^h), length (t·). For vowels: length (a·), three-mora length (a:), nasalization (ą), voicelessness (A). The commonest prosodic markings are, for stress: á (primary) and à (secondary), and for pitch: á (high), à (low), â (falling), and ǎ (rising); however, the details of prosodic systems and the uses of accents differ widely from language to language.

Vowels

	front	central	back
high	i (ü)	ɨ	u (ɨ)
	ɪ		ʊ
mid	e (ö)	ə	o
	ɛ		ɔ
		ʌ	
low	æ	a	a

Unparenthesized vowels are unrounded if front or central, and rounded if back; ü and ö are rounded; ɨ is unrounded. The special symbols for lax vowels (ɪ, ʊ, ɛ, ɔ) are generally used only where it is necessary to differentiate between tense and lax high or mid vowels. ɨ and a are used for both central and back vowels, as the two values seldom contrast in a given language.

Words in Indian languages cited in italics in this volume are of two types. Those in Massachusett, Narragansett, and Huron are in the standard, if not necessarily consistent, orthographies formerly used for these now extinct languages. Italic words in other Indian languages are written in phonemic transcription. That is, the letters and symbols are used in specific values defined for them by the structure of the sound system of the particular language. However, as far as possible, these phonemic transcriptions use letters and symbols in generally consistent values, as specified by the standard technical alphabet of the *Handbook*. Deviations from these standard values as well as specific details of the phonology of each language (or references to where they may be found) are given in an orthographic footnote in each tribal chapter. In the chapters "Eastern Algonquian Languages" and "Iroquoian Languages" this footnote specifies conventions for the use of italics different from those described here.

No italicized Indian word is broken at a line end except when a hyphen would be present anyway as part of the word. Words in italicized phonemic transcription are never capitalized. Pronunciations or phonetic values given in the standard technical alphabet without regard to phonemic analysis are put in square brackets ([]) rather than in italics. The glosses, or conventionalized translations, of Indian words are enclosed in single quotation marks.

Indian words recorded by nonspecialists or before the phonemic systems of their languages had been analyzed are often not written accurately enough to allow respelling in phonemic transcription. Where phonemic retranscription has been possible the citation of source has been modified by the label "phonemicized" or "from." Words that could not be phonemicized have in some cases been "normalized"—rewritten by mechanical substitution of the symbols of the standard technical alphabet. Words that have not been normalized sometimes contain letters used according to the values of other technical alphabets or traditional orthographies. The most common of these are c for the *Handbook*'s š; ch for š (in French sources) or for x or h (in Dutch and German sources); eñ for ę; j for ž, ʒ, or y; oñ for ǫ; tc and tj for č; ' for ʔ; and ' for h (or nondistinctive aspiration). 8 is used to transcribe a digraph, open at the top in its written form, used in early French sources with the values of French ou (phonetic u or w). The iota subscript in Huron (as in ͵a) represents y or γ; it has sometimes been transcribed as a hook beneath the following vowel (ą, ę). In the transcriptions of words in Beothuk, Mahican, Massachusett, Nanticoke, Narragansett, and Powhatan the letters have approximately their English values. All nonphonemic transcriptions give only incomplete, and sometimes imprecise, approximations of the correct pronunciation.

Nontechnical Equivalents

Correct pronunciation, as with any foreign language, requires extensive training and practice, but simplified (incorrect) pronunciations may be obtained by ignoring the diacritics and reading the vowels as in Italian or Spanish and the consonants as in English. For a closer approximation to the pronunciation or to rewrite into a nontechnical transcription the substitutions indicated in the following table may be made.

technical	nontechnical	technical	nontechnical	technical	nontechnical
æ	ae	M	mh	Y	yh
β	bh	N	nh	$\check{z}$	zh
c	ts	η	ng	$\mathfrak{z}$	dz
$\check{c}$	ch	N	ngh	$\check{\mathfrak{z}}$	j
δ	dh	$\mathfrak{o}$	o	$\mathfrak{q}$	'
$\hat{\delta}$	ddh	θ	th	$\acute{k}, \acute{p}, \acute{t}$, etc.	k', p', t', etc.
ε	e	$\hat{\theta}$	tth	$a\cdot, e\cdot, k\cdot, s\cdot$, etc.	aa, ee, kk, ss, etc.
γ	gh	ϕ	ph	$\mathfrak{q}, \mathfrak{e}$, etc.	an, en, etc.
$\not{l}$	lh	$\check{s}$	sh	k^y, t^y, etc.	ky, ty, etc.
λ	dl	W	wh	k^w	kw
$\acute{\lambda}$	tlh	x	kh		

English Pronunciations

The English pronunciations of the names of tribes and a few other words are indicated parenthetically in a dictionary-style orthography in which most letters have their usual English pronunciation. Special symbols are listed below, with sample words to be pronounced as in nonregional United States English. Approximate phonetic values are given in parentheses in the standard technical alphabet.

ŋ: thing (η)
θ: thin (θ)
ð: this (δ)
zh: vision ($\check{z}$)
ă: bat (æ)

ä: father (a)
ā: bait (ey)
e: bet (ε)
ē: beat (iy)

ə: about, gallop (ə)
ĭ: bit (ι)
ī: bite (ay)
ô: bought ($\mathfrak{o}$)

ō: boat (ow)
ŏŏ: book (υ)
ōō: boot (uw)
u: but (Λ)

ˈ(primary stress), ˌ (secondary stress): elevator (ˈeləˌvātər) (éləvèytər)

Conventions for Illustrations

Map Symbols

●   Indian settlement

■   Non-Indian town

Mountain range, peak

— - — - —   National boundary

- — - — -   State or province boundary

- - - - - -   County boundary

River or stream

Mahican   Tribe

Neponset   Tribal subdivision

Boston   Settlement, site, reservation

Merrimack R.   Geographical feature

Toned areas on tribal maps represent estimated territory.

Credits and Captions

Credit lines give the source of the illustrations or the collections where the artifacts shown are located. The numbers that follow are the catalog or inventory numbers of that repository. When the photographer mentioned in the caption is the source of the print reproduced, no credit line appears. "After" means that the *Handbook* illustrators have redrawn, rearranged, or abstracted the illustration from the one in the cited source. All maps and drawings not otherwise credited are by the *Handbook* illustrators. Measurements in captions are to the nearest millimeter if available; "about" indicates an estimate or a measurement converted from inches to centimeters. The following abbreviations are used in credit lines:

Amer.	American	Ind.	Indian
Anthr.	Anthropology, Anthropo-logical	Inst.	Institute
		Instn.	Institution
Arch.	Archives	Lib.	Library
Arch(a)eol.	Arch(a)eology, Arch(a)eological	Mus.	Museum
		NAA	National Anthropological Archives
Assoc.	Association		
Co.	County	NCFA	National Collection of Fine Arts
Coll.	Collection(s)		
Dept.	Department	Nat.	Natural
Div.	Division	Natl.	National
Ethnol.	Ethnology, Ethnological	opp.	opposite
fol.	folio	pl(s).	plate(s)
Ft.	Fort	Soc.	Society
Hist.	History	U.	University
Histl.	Historical		

Metric Equivalents

10 mm = 1 cm	10 cm = 3.937 in.	1 in. = 2.54 cm
100 cm = 1 m	1 m = 39.37 in.	1 ft. = 30.48 cm
1,000 m = 1 km	10 m = 32.81 ft.	1 yd. = 91.44 cm

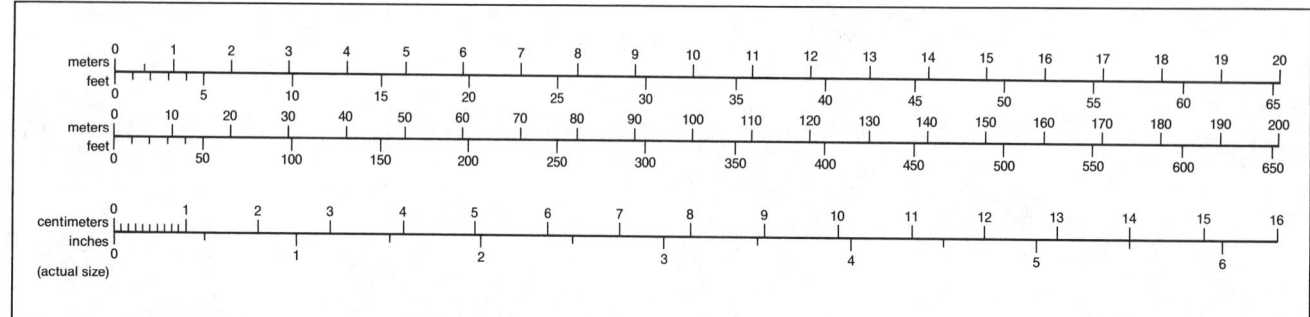

Preface

This is the second to be published of a 20-volume set planned to give an encyclopedic summary of what is known about the prehistory, history, and cultures of the aboriginal peoples of North America who lived north of the urban civilizations of central Mexico. Volumes 5–14 treat the other major culture areas of this region.

Some topics relevant to the Northeast area are excluded from this volume because they are more appropriately discussed on a continent-wide basis. Readers should refer to volume 1, Introduction, for general descriptions of anthropological and historical methods and sources and for summaries for the whole continent of certain topics regarding social and political organization, religion, and the performing arts. Volume 2 contains detailed accounts of the different kinds of Indian and Eskimo communities in the twentieth century, especially during its third quarter, and describes their relations with one another and with the surrounding non-Indian societies and nations. Volume 3 gives the environmental and biological backgrounds within which Native societies developed, summarizes the early and late human biology or physical anthropology of Indians and Eskimos, and surveys the earliest prehistoric cultures. (Therefore the Paleo-Indian or Early Man period in the Northeast receives major treatment in volume 3 rather than in this volume.) Volume 4 contains details on the history of Indian-White relations. Volume 16 is a continent-wide survey of technology and the visual arts—of material cultures broadly defined. Volume 17 surveys the native languages of North America, their characteristics and historical relationships. Volumes 18 and 19 are a biographical dictionary; included in the listing are many Northeast Indians. Volume 20 contains an index to the whole, which will serve to locate materials on Northeast Indians in other volumes as well as in this one.

Preliminary discussions on the feasibility of this *Handbook* and alternatives for producing it began in 1965 in what was then the Smithsonian's Office of Anthropology. A history of the early development of the *Handbook* will be found in volume 1. Detailed planning for the Northeast volume was undertaken at a meeting of the General Editor and the Volume Editor with a specially selected Planning Committee (listed on p. v) held in Montreal, November 13–14, 1970. At that time a tentative table of contents was drawn up, and qualified specialists on each topic were listed as potential authors. The chapter headings in the final volume largely reproduce the list decided upon at that meeting, and about two-thirds of the authors were those first invited. Inevitably, some replacements had to be made as people were unable to accept invitations or later found that they could not meet their commitment to write. Charles Callender and Elisabeth Tooker deserve special thanks for writing on short notice several chapters, in addition to those originally assigned them, when the authors first chosen were unable to complete them. The final chapter was to have been the work of Joseph R. Caldwell. His untimely death occurred before he was able to begin writing it. It is also sad to record the death of Marian White, who contributed three chapters to this volume. One of her last projects was to organize the chapter on the Cayuga, when no one else was willing to undertake this task.

One organizational anomaly deserves comment: among the several recognized, distinct, and surviving Southern New England peoples, only one group has a separate chapter devoted to it, the others being discussed together in the two chapters on Southern New England Indians. This is because for the Narragansett alone it was both possible to secure such a chapter and practical to treat them separately.

At the time they were invited, contributors were sent a prospectus prepared by the Volume Editor containing descriptions of each of the topics to be covered and a "Guide for Contributors" prepared by the General Editor describing the general aims and methods of the *Handbook* and the editorial conventions. One convention has been to avoid the present tense, where possible, in historical and cultural descriptions. Thus a statement in the past tense, with a recent date or approximate date, may also hold true for the time of writing. As they were received, the manuscripts were reviewed by the General Editor, the Volume Editor, and usually one or more referees (frequently including a member of the Planning Committee). Suggestions for changes and additions often resulted. The published versions frequently reflect more editorial intervention that is customary for academic writings, since the encyclopedic aims and format of this publication made it necessary to attempt to eliminate duplication, avoid gaps in coverage, prevent contradictions, impose some standardization of organization and terminology, and keep within strict constraints on length. Where the evidence seemed so scanty or obscure as to allow different authorities to come to differing conclusions, authors have been permitted to elaborate whichever view they prefer, but the editors have endeavored by cross-referencing to draw readers' attention to alternative interpretations in other chapters. Ives Goddard has provided much editorial assistance for many sections of this volume, in matters relating to history and ethnography as well as to linguistics.

When planning the chapters dealing with the Six Nations of the Iroquois, it was clear to the Planning Committee that the cross-cutting nature of tribal and theme chapters would make the coordination of this section especially difficult. After the various manuscripts were received, Elisabeth Tooker was persuaded to take on the difficult task of editing and coordinating these chapters. Her efforts to ensure even and thorough coverage, to eliminate unnecessary duplication, and to meld these papers into an integrated coverage of the Iroquois required a vast amount of work and have contributed greatly to the usefulness of the volume. This has also resulted in even greater editorial intervention and standardization of these chapters than has occurred elsewhere in the volume.

The first manuscript submitted was received on January 25, 1972, and the last on June 6, 1977; the first final acceptance of an author's manuscript was on April 4, 1972, and the last on June 6, 1977. Edited manuscripts were sent from the Washington office to authors for their final approval between August 27, 1974, and June 16, 1977. These dates for all chapters are given in the list of Contributors. Late dates may reflect late invitations as well as late submissions.

Linguistic Editing

All cited words in Indian languages were referred to consultants with expert knowledge of the respective languages and, as far as possible, rewritten by them in the appropriate technical orthography. The consultants and the spelling systems are identified in an orthographic footnote to each tribal chapter; these footnotes were drafted by the Linguistic Editor.

Statements about the genetic relationships of Indian languages have also been checked with linguist consultants, to ensure conformity with recent findings and terminology in comparative linguistics and to avoid conflicting statements within this *Handbook*. In general, only the less remote genetic relationships are mentioned in the individual tribal chapters, and it was not possible to evaluate here the evidence for the controversial claim that Beothuk has a genetic relationship to Algonquian. The three chapters on the Eastern and Central Algonquian languages and the Iroquoian languages treat more

remote relationships, and further information will be found in volume 17.

The Linguistic Editor served as coordinator and editor of these efforts by linguist consultants. A special debt is owed to these consultants, many of whom took time from their own research to check words with native speakers, for all provided advice and assistance without compensation. Michael K. Foster, Marianne Mithun, and Hanni J. Woodbury are particularly to be thanked for the extensive additional fieldwork they undertook in response to the editors' inquiries.

Synonymies

Toward the end of each tribal chapter (or, sometimes, in an early chapter of a set covering closely related tribal groupings) is a section called Synonymy. This describes the various names that have been applied to the groups and subgroups treated in that chapter (or set of chapters), giving the principal variant spellings used in English and, frequently, in French, and often the names applied to the groups in neighboring Indian languages. A number of the synonymies have been expanded or reworked by the editors, particularly the Linguistic Editor, most frequently simply by adding names from the literature and from other manuscripts submitted for the *Handbook* (from which they have then been deleted) and names and analyses provided by linguist consultants. Where a synonymy is wholly or substantially the work of the Linguistic Editor, a footnote specifying authorship is given. These sections should assist in the identification of groups mentioned in the earlier historical and anthropological literature. They should also be examined for evidence on changes in the identifications and affiliations of groups, as seen by their own members as well as by neighbors and by outside observers.

Radiocarbon Dates

Authors were instructed to convert radiocarbon dates into dates in the Christian calendar. Such conversions normally have been made from the dates as originally published, without taking account of changes that may be required by developing research on revisions of the half-life of carbon 14, long-term changes in the amount of carbon 14 in the atmosphere, and other factors that may require modifications of absolute dates based on radiocarbon determinations.

Binomials

The scientific names of plant and animal genera and species, printed in italics, have been checked by the General Editor to ensure that they reflect modern usage by biological taxonomists. Scientific plant names have been brought into agreement with those accepted by Gray and Fernald (1950), while zoological nomenclature has been revised in consultation with Smithsonian staff in the appropriate departments.

Bibliography

All references cited by contributors have been unified in a single list at the end of this volume. Citations within the text, by author, date, and often page, identify the works in this unified list. Wherever possible the *Handbook* Bibliographer has resolved conflicts between citations of different editions, corrected inaccuracies and omissions, and checked direct quotations against the originals. The bibliographic information has been verified by examination of the original work or from standard reliable library catalogs (especially the National Union Catalog and the published catalog of the Harvard Peabody Museum Library). The unified bibliography lists all and only the sources cited in the text of the volume, except personal communications. The sections headed Sources at the ends of most chapters provide general guidance to the most important sources of information on the topics covered.

Illustrations

Authors were requested to submit suggestions for illustrations: photographs, maps, drawings, and lists and locations of objects that might be illustrated. To varying degrees most complied with this request. Yet considerations of space, balance, reproducibility, and availability required modifications in what was submitted. In addition the *Handbook* Illustrations Researchers and Scientific Illustrators provided much original material from research they conducted in museums and other repositories and in the published literature. Most of the contemporary illustrations earlier than 1860, and caption information about them, derive from the files of a long-term research project of the General Editor on such depictions. All maps were prepared by the *Handbook* Cartographer or Scientific Illustrators, who redrew some submitted by authors and compiled many new ones using information from the chapter manuscripts and from other sources. The base maps for all are authoritative standard ones, especially U.S. Geological Survey sheets and Canadian Department of Mines and Minerals Topographic Quadrangle maps. When possible, the hydrography has been reconstructed for the date of each map. Layout and design of the illustrations have been the responsibility of the Chief Scientific Illustrator, who has worked in consultation with the Illustrations Researchers. Captions for illustrations and maps usually were composed by the Illustrations Researcher, Scientific Illustrators, or the General Editor. However, all illustrations, including maps and drawings, and all captions have been approved by the Volume Editor and the

authors of the chapters in which they appear, and authors frequently have participated actively in the selection process and in the improvement of captions.

We are indebted to Donnelly Cartographic Services (especially Sidney P. Marland, III, resident manager) for their meticulous care in converting the map artwork into final film.

Acknowledgements

The *Handbook* editorial staff for this volume at the Smithsonian in Washington has consisted of the following persons:

General Editor: William C. Sturtevant (1966-)
Linguistic Editor: Ives Goddard (1970-)
Editorial Assistants: Betty T. Arens (1972-); Carol H. Blew (1969-1972)
Coordinator: Diane Della-Loggia (1976-)
Manuscript and Copy Editor: Diane Della-Loggia (1972-)
Bibliographer: Lorraine Jacoby (1972-)
Bibliographic Assistants: Caroline Ladeira (1976-); Mark Passen (1974-1976)
Chief Scientific Illustrator: Jo Ann Moore (1972-)
Scientific Illustrator: Brigid Melton Sullivan (1975-1976)
Cartographer: Judith Crawley Wojcik (1975-)
Illustrations Researcher: Laura J. Greenberg (1976-)
Illustrations Researcher: Joanna Cohan Scherer (1970-1976)
Assistant Illustrations Researcher: Nancy Henderson (1973-1975)
One-year Research Assistants: Paula Rabkin (1975-1976); Laura Conkey (1974-1975); Nancy Stasulis (1973-1974); Susan Golla (1973-1974); William L. Merrill (1972-1973)
Summer Research Assistant: Ira Jacknis (1973-1975)
Secretaries: Alice Nance Boarman (1975-); Filomena Chau (1975); Gloria Harman (1974-1975); Rosemary De Rosa (1973-1974); Marianna Koskouras (1969-1973).

In the Center for the Study of Man, Smithsonian Institution, administrative support for the *Handbook* has been provided by: the Director, Sol Tax (1968-1976); the Program Coordinator, Samuel L. Stanley (1968-1976); the Administrative Officer, Sherrill Berger (1975-); the Administrative Assistant, Jennifer Burdick Stephens (1968-1975); and Secretaries Lydia Ratliff (1972-), Melvina Jackson (1974-), and Rebecca Noah (1973-1974). Other Smithsonian staff who have provided crucial support and assistance include S. Dillon Ripley, Secretary (1965-); David Challinor (1972-) and Sidney R. Galler (1965-1970), Assistant Secretaries for Science; Charles Blitzer (1968-), Assistant Secretary for History and Art; Porter Kier (1976-), Director, National

Museum of Natural History and Director, Center for the Study of Man; James F. Mello (1976-), Assistant Director, National Museum of Natural History; Catherine J. Kerby (1976-), Assistant to the Director, National Museum of Natural History; Stephen Kraft (1971-), Managing Designer, Smithsonian Institution Press; Victor E. Krantz (1972-) of the Smithsonian Photographic Laboratory (especially for photographing objects); and Jack F. Marquardt (1972-) and Carolyn S. Hahn (1972-) of the Smithsonian Libraries. The Department of Anthropology, National Museum of Natural History, Smithsonian Institution, released the General Editor from part of his curatorial and research time.

Preparation and publication of this volume have been supported by federal appropriations made to the Smithsonian Institution, in part through its Bicentennial Programs.

The Volume Editor, Bruce G. Trigger, acknowledges the secretarial assistance of Jeanette Fernandez at McGill University, Montreal, from 1970 to 1975. He also acknowledges the editorial assistance given to him by the members of the Planning Committee and by David A. Baerreis, Charles A. Bishop, Douglas W. Boyce, T.J. Brasser, Charles Callender, Fred Eggan, C.D. Ellis, Christian F. Feest, Raymond D. Fogelson, James B. Griffin, Peter B. Hammond, William C. Noble, David Beers Quinn, James F. Pendergast, Robert E. Ritzenthaler, E.S. Rogers, Helen C. Rountree, Irving Rouse, Bert Salwen, Dean R. Snow, James A. Tuck, Wilcomb E. Washburn, Sylvia Warner, and Erminie Wheeler-Voegelin. Part of the editorial work on this volume was done while the Volume Editor was the recipient of a Killam Award and later a Leave Fellowship of the Canada Council and sabbatical leave from McGill University.

September 6, 1977   William C. Sturtevant
                                  Bruce G. Trigger

Introduction

BRUCE G. TRIGGER

The aim of this volume is to describe the history, cultural background, and present circumstances of the Indian peoples of the northeastern United States and southeastern Canada. Because of the lack of any single, uniform set of ethnographies covering this area (such as may be found for the Southeast in Swanton 1946, *The Indians of the Southeastern United States*), the Planning Committee for this volume decided that the tribal sketches should be as detailed as possible; hence more space has been assigned to these chapters than is the case with some other volumes of the Handbook.

Since the concept of culture areas has fallen increasingly into disrepute as an analytical device, the Northeast is regarded primarily as an editorial convenience. This area has been delimited on the north and west by ecological boundaries. The northern line is congruent with the southern margin of the boreal forest that stretches in a broad belt across Canada and Alaska and whose hunting bands are described in volume 6. In spite of the presence of much coniferous forest and a native band organization not greatly different from that found in the boreal forest, the Atlantic Provinces of Canada have been included in the Northeast. This decision is justified by the maritime orientation of the subsistence economies of this area, which is clearly different from that of the boreal forests, and also by the well-documented and long-standing cultural connections between this area and the rest of the Northeast. Such an arrangement draws within the compass of the Northeast all those northern groups whose subsistence economies are distinguished from those of the boreal forest by any degree of dependence on more intensive forms of subsistence, such as horticulture (however limited), the importing of agricultural produce from farther south, gathering wild rice, or the intensive exploitation of marine or lacustrine resources. Associated with these "enriched economies" are varying degrees of greater social and economic complexity, culminating in the Powhatan and other small states or chiefdoms found in the southeastern corner of the region. The western border is that between the Eastern Woodlands, which in the historic period were occupied by horticulturalists, and the Prairies, which were the locale of equestrian hunting groups. The earlier riverine extensions of Eastern Woodland economies up the western tributaries of the Mississippi River are reserved for discussion in volume 13.

While both these boundaries have demonstrably shifted as a result of climatic changes, they are nevertheless of long-term significance. By contrast, the boundary between the Northeast and Southeast is more arbitrary. It can be argued that the Eastern Woodlands constitutes a single culture area or at least a single zone of variation. Nevertheless, the societies of the southeastern United States are characterized as a group by a greater dependence on agriculture, denser population, more social stratification and political complexity, and more markedly matrilineal organization (such as the Crow kinship system) than are found among the peoples to the north. The boundary here drawn runs along the southern margin of the Ohio watershed (an area largely depopulated before adequate historical and ethnographic records became available) and is extended to the coast in such a way as to include in the Northeast all the Eastern Algonquian- and Iroquoian-speaking peoples (except the Cherokee).

The Northeast represents the northerly limits of diffusion of significant cultural elements of Mesoamerican origin. Mesoamerican influence is strikingly apparent in the horticultural complex, but other definite or presumed influences can be traced in most aspects of northeastern life and some may be of considerable antiquity. While all these features appear to have arrived through the Southeast, they became elements in a total pattern sufficiently distinct to constitute another reformulation of nuclear American influence. While nourished by ideas from the south, economic and environmental conditions in the Northeast were sufficiently different and the stimuli from farther south sufficiently diffuse and indirect that these southern influences never overrode the internal dynamic of the Northeast or detracted from the distinctiveness of the cultural pattern that developed there.

Archeological data are currently accumulating at a rapid pace and while it is hoped (perhaps vainly) that the outline of Northeastern culture history presented here will remain valid in general terms, it is clear that any detailed account will soon be out of date. The prehistory of the Northeast prior to A.D. 1000 therefore is treated succinctly in three chronologically successive papers, which each survey the whole region. Further and more detailed coverage of the Paleo-Indian period can be found in volume 3. After A.D. 1000, which for most areas represents the point at which archeological cultures can be associated satisfactorily with the ancestors of specific historic groups, regional essays provide a more detailed coverage of the archeological record.

All these papers reflect the conceptual changes that have come about in North American archeology since the 1960s. These have involved a movement away from cultural chronology as an end in itself and from mechanical tracing of interconnections among different regions by means of trait diffusion. In their place there is a growing interest in explaining the development of cultures by tracing how they have evolved as functionally integrated systems interrelated with specific natural environments.

The archeological record reveals the changing nature of the cultures of the Northeast in prehistoric times. There is no longer any basis for the once cherished beliefs that these cultures were in a state of equilibrium until they were disturbed by European contact and that this equilibrium constituted a baseline from which ideal Indian culture can be described. While changes were speeded up and dislocations introduced by European contact, the internal dynamism of the Northeast and the ability of its inhabitants to employ new ideas to sustain internal development over many thousands of years cannot be doubted.

Although European explorers and fishermen frequented the coasts of the Northeast more or less continuously after 1497, they had less impact on the Indians of this area during the sixteenth century than the Spanish had farther south. It also appears likely that the Northeast escaped the worst epidemics and depopulation that followed the penetration of the Southeast by Spanish expeditions. Because of this, even along the Eastern seaboard, the Indian cultures of the Northeast remained relatively undisturbed into the seventeenth century.

It is also clear, however, that the effects of European contact penetrated into the interior far ahead of Europeans themselves and there, prior to the arrival of Whites, played an important role in transforming Indian political organization and intertribal relations. Larger tribal units and confederacies developed to protect hunting territories and trade routes from encroachment, as a growing demand for furs pitted tribes against one another in new forms of economic competition. Contrary to what an older generation of anthropologists assumed, it now seems extremely unlikely that the earliest European accounts of any ethnic group in the Northeast describe a way of life that is totally uninfluenced by European contact. It is certain that many cultures had been radically transformed prior to such descriptions.

The geography of the Northeast played a major role in shaping the nature of Indian-White interaction. Trading for furs between the two groups was of some economic importance throughout the Northeast, but especially in the north. There the growing season is short and the soil tends to be poor, while there was an abundance of fur-bearing animals and river systems that facilitated transporting pelts to coastal markets. In this area the fur trade remained until the nineteenth century the basis of relations between Indians and Whites. Farther south, principally in what is now the United States, expanding European settlements and an abundance of good soil soon led Whites to covet the Indians' land and wherever possible to seize it from them.

Important as this geographical difference has been in the history of Indian-White relations, a set of geographical divisions of even more long-term significance has been used to organize this volume. This is the tripartite division into Coastal, Saint Lawrence Lowlands, and Great Lakes-Riverine.

The Coastal zone embraces the Atlantic Provinces of Canada and the seaboard of the United States as far south as North Carolina. Most of this region was separated from the interior by the Appalachian Mountains. In historic times it was occupied by Eastern Algonquian speakers, in addition to the problematical Beothuk in Newfoundland and some Iroquoian-speaking groups in the far south. The different Eastern Algonquian languages appear to have constituted a single continuum of variation along the coast. Population densities and reliance on agriculture increased southward and political organization varied from hunting bands in the north to rudimentary states in the extreme south.

The Indians of the East Coast were the first in the Northeast to come into intimate contact with Europeans and to be affected by European colonization. Most groups lacked the time and opportunity to reorganize themselves to cope with the combined onslaught of European epidemics and political pressures and were decimated or dispersed westward. To a large degree, this happened before these groups had been adequately described by Europeans. Not unexpectedly, the largest numbers who survive in situ live in Maine and the adjacent Maritime Provinces, where the pressure of White colonization was less severe. The extermination of the insular Beothuk is a separate story that invites at least superficial comparison with the fate of the Tasmanians.

The Saint Lawrence Lowlands embraces southern Ontario, upper New York State, and most of the Saint Lawrence and (for convenience) the Susquehanna valleys. In historic times this was the homeland of the Northern Iroquoian-speaking peoples. These tribes shared a similar cultural pattern based on a combination of intensive horticulture and fishing and characterized by large, often fortified villages, prisoner sacrifice, similar shamanistic rituals, and a matrilineal kinship system (although without Crow kin terms). The Iroquoians were once believed to have pushed north relatively recently, driving a wedge between the Central and Eastern Algonquians. However, later archeological, linguistic, and other evidence indicates that the northern Iroquoian culture had developed in situ around the Lower Great Lakes.

The Iroquoian-speaking peoples were sufficiently remote from the earliest centers of European trade and permanent settlement that they did not succumb to European encroachment. The fur trade nevertheless led to a hitherto unprecedented competition for furs that, by 1660, had led the five Iroquois tribes to disperse and in part to absorb all the other Iroquoian tribes except the Susquehannock, who were ultimately dispersed by their European neighbors. Until the fall of New France in 1760, the Iroquois were able to maintain a large degree of autonomy by balancing rival European powers against one another. Afterward the Iroquois quickly became subject to British and American suzerainty and their homeland was overrun by White settlement. Nevertheless, the lessons that the Iroquois had learned in their dealings with Europeans enabled many of them to retain their traditions and a sense of identity on reservations, most of which are located within the Iroquoian homeland.

The Great Lakes-Riverine area comprises the rest of the Northeast. It was inhabited by Central Algonquian- and Siouan-speaking groups, most of whom depended to varying degrees on horticulture and all of whom shared patrilineal kinship systems. Except in the Ottawa Valley and around Lake Nipissing, this area was not penetrated by French traders until the latter half of the seventeenth century, and for a long time afterward these traders had to resort to devious means to circumvent the opposition of the Iroquois. Even before Europeans began to penetrate this area, events connected with the fur trade had resulted in Indian wars that led to the tribes of southeastern Michigan being driven westward and to the dispersal of the original tribes of the Ohio Valley by the Iroquois. With the proliferation of European settlement along the East coast, tribes and tribal remnants from that area sought refuge in the midwest, further complicating intertribal relations. As European encroachment continued, the Great Lakes-Riverine area became a theater for notable pan-tribal efforts to resist European domination, the best-known of which were those led by Pontiac and Tecumseh. While some once-important groups have disappeared, others, indigenous to the area or coming as refugees, continue to live on reservations on both sides of the Canada-United States border.

The groups included in this volume are those who now live in the Northeast or who have lived there during the most significant or best-documented period of their history. Hence various groups of Northeastern origin who now live in Oklahoma (the Wyandots) or in Mexico (some Kickapoo) are included; on the other hand, those Chippewa who adapted to life in the boreal forest or on the plains prior to significant documentation are dealt with in the volumes for those areas.

The space allotted to each group generally reflects the amount of information concerning them, although to maintain an acceptable balance it has been necessary to slight the best-documented groups. It is hoped that the cultural descriptions of the better-documented groups (like the Huron) will complement descriptions of closely related but less well-known ones (like Neutral, Petun). Authors generally have been encouraged to develop their chapters along the lines best suited to their data, provided that certain basic categories are covered for each Indian group.

The production of this volume, which has brought together information about all the Indian groups of the Northeast, has emphasized as never before the complexity of the Indian history of this area since European contact. Repeatedly major geographical dislocations of Indian groups are observed as well as the formation of larger tribal units in response to early European contact, their disintegration as a result of mounting White pressures, and the recombination of refugees to form new, heterogeneous, and often surprisingly resilient groupings. This is not a process that can be explained briefly or without some repetition in the various tribal articles.

This survey has served to draw attention to the many gaps that exist in a current understanding of the ethnography and history of the Indians of the Northeast. In some cases the gaps appear irremediable, but it is hoped that this publication may encourage research along hitherto neglected lines. While ethnohistorical methods of research must largely replace ethnographical ones in order to deal effectively with the past, it can no longer be claimed that the ethnology of the Northeast is a worked-out field. What has been accomplished in this volume demonstrates exactly the contrary. More research along ethnohistorical lines should also result in greater awareness of the studies of Indian history and ethnology carried out in the nineteenth century. This work was reflected in Hodge's (1907-1910) *Handbook,* but much of it has unwarrantedly been lost sight of by more recent generations of anthropologists.

While an effort has been made by authors to indicate the current state of Indian groups, it is manifestly impossible to deal adequately with the complex and rapidly changing situation in a reference work. Further discussions of current social and political movements are presented in volume 2. What appears here must be considered not as a full account of the Indians of the Northeast but as background for understanding a future that Indians are once again determined to shape for themselves.

History of Research

ELISABETH TOOKER

The relatively few Indians in the mid-twentieth century living on small and scattered reservations in the Northeast belie the importance of these peoples not only in the shaping of the unique national experiences of the United States and Canada, but also in the development of anthropology in both countries. As Hallowell (1960:23) has noted, an intimate association "prevailed, until recently, between American anthropology and the study of the aborigines of this country, a fact which gave a distinctive coloring to the early history of anthropology here as compared with its development in countries where no comparable conditions existed." After Europeans had discovered the New World, the Indian inhabitants of the continent and their ways of life became the subject of considerable curiosity. Not only were the reports of the New World avidly read in the Old and various articles made by the Indians collected for the "cabinets" of the time, forerunners of the present-day museum, but also interest was excited by those Indians brought back to Europe. Indians were depicted in the various literary and visual arts, and provided material for historical and philosophical speculations—interests that continue. The same concerns have long been evident in America, but for anthropologists as well as other Whites of the continent, Indians have not been merely strange and unfamiliar peoples living in exotic, faraway places, but also neighbors, sometimes friendly and sometimes hostile, whose presence cannot be ignored and whose history is a part of the history of all those living on the continent. As one result, American anthropologists have expended considerable effort in gaining knowledge of Indian life from the Indians themselves—data that have often challenged the speculations of those lacking this experience and have given direction to the intellectual interests of those who have.

Contact

Research on Indian cultures and history of the Northeast may properly be said to have begun with the first European exploration of the area, and more particularly with the sixteenth-century explorers, who, as did later ones, included in their reports accounts of the Indians they met as well as description of the flora, fauna, and other natural resources they found in the lands 'they "discovered." Although in the sixteenth century Euro-

pean exploration of the Northeast lagged behind that of many other parts of the New World (the climate of the region was similar to that of Europe and the region offered few resources not already available there) and although the earliest of these expeditions obtained little information on Indians, later sixteenth- and seventeenth-century ones were to provide invaluable data, and sometimes the best data on the native peoples living along the Atlantic coast. The record of Giovanni da Verrazano's 1524 voyage (Wroth 1970) contains the most extensive early description of the Indians of this area, but later accounts contain information of greater ethnographic value. Important among these are the descriptions of Jacques Cartier's second and third voyages (Cartier 1924), which contain virtually all that is known of Saint Lawrence Iroquoian language and culture. When Samuel de Champlain explored the Saint Lawrence early in the seventeenth century, he found the territory that had been inhabited by these Iroquoians occupied by Algonquian speakers. Of comparable importance are the drawings of John White (Hulton and Quinn 1964) and the other records of Sir Walter Raleigh's expeditions (Quinn 1955) including the descriptions accompanying Theodor De Bry's engravings (Hariot 1588) of John White's drawings—material that constitutes much of what is known about some North Carolina Algonquians.

Increased White exploration and settlement of the continent after the sixteenth century produced both profound changes in the lives of the Northeastern Indians and a more extensive literature on them, including the best accounts of certain Indian groups. A notable example is that of the Beothuk. Virtually all that is likely to be known about these Indians of Newfoundland, probably the first Northeastern Indians to be met by Europeans in the fifteenth century and the Indians most affected by the extensive fishing on the Grand Banks in the sixteenth century, is to be found in the historical documents (Howley 1915). A somewhat comparable instance is that of the Hurons. The best descriptions of Huron culture are to be found in the accounts of Champlain (1922–1936, 3) and Sagard-Théodat (1939) and especially in the *Jesuit Relations* (JR 7:34). Other important seventeenth-century accounts include the descriptions of various eastern Algonquian peoples written by Jesuit (JR) and Recollect (Le Clerq 1910) missionaries and by the jurist, Lescarbot (1907–1914). Neither did the French ignore the study of

Indian languages, and an extensive, although at the time largely unpublished, literature on them was produced, particularly by the Jesuits (Hanzeli 1969).

But if in New France missionaries provided the most extensive descriptions of Indian life and culture, in the English colonies the earliest comparable seventeenth-century accounts were often written by men important in establishing and governing the new settlements, such as John White and John Smith. For example, undoubtedly the best description of the Indians of New England is Roger Williams's (1643) *Key into the Language of America,* a phrase and guide book for those who would travel in the country of the Narragansetts. Other ethnographic information on New England Indians is contained in the various reports of the colonies to their sponsors in England, such as that known as Mourt's *Relation* (Mourt 1963), as well as in other accounts including those by William Wood (1634) and Thomas Morton (1637). Although the English Protestant missionaries were less interested in Indian culture than the French Catholic ones, they too were concerned with the languages of the Indians, most notably John Eliot who produced what became a famous translation of the Bible into Massachusett (Pilling 1891:127-184), and with the progress the Indians were making toward Christianity and civilization, as related, for example, in Gookin's account (MHSC ser. 1, 1:141-226).

Seventeenth-century descriptions of the Indians of the Middle Colonies are of a similar character. Important information on the Delawares is contained in a letter written in 1683 by William Penn (1912) to the Free Society of Traders. Probably the best account of the Indians of New York City and Long Island was written by Daniel Denton (1845), an early settler. Valuable seventeenth-century Dutch descriptions of the eastern Iroquois include one probably written by Van den Bogaert (1909), a surgeon at Fort Orange, and one written by Megapolensis (1909), a minister. Also of special interest is Lindeström's (1925) account of the Delaware Indians of New Sweden. In the Carolina area, Lederer's (1672) and especially Lawson's (1709) accounts contain useful information.

As the involvement of the Upper Great Lakes Indians in the fur trade increased so also did French exploration and knowledge of that region, and the accounts written by traders such as Perrot (1911) and Radisson (1885), the Jesuits (JR; Charlevoix 1761) and others such as Bacqueville de la Potherie (1911) and Deliette (1934), although not so detailed as might be wished, provide valuable data on these Indians.

In histories of the European exploration and settlement of the North American continent Indians necessarily figured prominently. Among these are the histories of New France written by Lescarbot (1907-1914), Sagard-Théodat (1866), Le Clerq (1881), Du Creux (1951-1952), Charlevoix (1866-1872), and Lafitau (1724). The histo-

ries of Virginia include those by Beverley (1705), Strachey (1953), and Stith (1747). New Englanders, ever conscious of their divine mission, produced a number such as those by William Bradford (1952), Nathaniel Morton (1910), William Hubbard (1865), Increase Mather (1677), Cotton Mather (1702), Benjamin Church (1716), and Samuel Penhallow (1726). And in New York, Colden (1747) compiled a history of Iroquois-White relations.

Late Eighteenth and Early Nineteenth Centuries

All these various types of accounts continued to appear after the American War of Independence. The interest of the English-speaking colonists in the once French-controlled territory in the Great Lakes region began after the

Fig. 1. A plate from Lafitau (1724), comparing North and South American Indian and Classical Mediterranean dress and ornament. Nos. 1 and 2 are identified as an Iroquois and Huron man and woman in contemporary dress (both were copied, with changes, from Bacqueville de la Potherie 1722); nos. 3 and 4 supposedly show the same in ancient dress (derived from illustrations in Du Creux 1664). Nos. 5 and 7 are Classical necklaces, compared with no. 6, a North American Indian necklace with shell pendant. No. 8 is an Iroquoian wampum bracelet. No. 10, identified as a Northern Indian tobacco bag, is copied from a De Bry (1590:pl. XVI) engraving of a Carolina Algonquian bag. Nos. 9, 11, 12 represent Island Carib leg bands and gorget.

French and Indian War and intensified after the American Revolution. The Rev. David Jones (1774) described his trips there in 1772 and 1773, Carver (1778) gave an account of his exploration of the area after the French and Indian War, and Long (1791) and Henry (1901) described the country there. Accounts by missionaries detailing their work and describing Indian life and customs continued to be written; examples of particular interest include those by Loskiel (1794), Heckewelder (1819), Zeisberger (1910), H. Jackson (1830, 1830a), and Finley (1840). Halkett (1825) wrote the history of missionary activity, and Flint (1833) wrote the history of the land west of the Alleghenies.

At the same time, there was developing a somewhat different attitude toward the Indians and hence toward writings about them, an approach to the study of Indian life and history that in the last decades of the nineteenth century became an integral part of the newly emerging scientific and academic discipline of anthropology. As did their nineteenth-century counterparts in England, those Americans who made such studies were interested in establishing evolutionary stages; the idea of progress was to win out over that of degeneration during the nineteenth century. But Indian customs also interested them for other reasons. The establishment of the new country independent of England increased interest in the uniqueness of the American experience and in American history, not as an appendage to English history but as separate from it. As what the New World had that the Old World did not included the Indians, Indians became one of the focuses around which Americans constructed their national identity.

This concern with the Indian expressed itself not only in the popular literature of the time (Hallowell 1957, 1957a) but also in the activities of the local historical societies (some of whom acquired extensive manuscript holdings on Indian history and culture) and of the scientific societies that became increasingly important in the eighteenth and nineteenth centuries. One such was the American Philosophical Society in Philadelphia, soon to become the first capital of the United States. Reorganized and enlarged in 1768, it endeavored to duplicate in America the place the Royal Society of London had as a national scientific society and to demonstrate that Americans could carry out scientific work of the quality done in England and on the continent. To this end, members of the Society (like other educated Americans) explored many and diverse subjects including the history, cultures, and languages of the Indian. Because these interests were shared by the United States government as it developed its own policy respecting Indians and methods for implementing these policies, the federal government supported some research on the Indians. Pursuit of these joint interests was facilitated during the eight years that Thomas Jefferson was concurrently president of the American Philosophical Society (1797-1814) and pres-

ident of the United States (1801-1809). Jefferson organized a committee of the Society to study the customs, languages, history, and archeology of the Indians (Chinard 1943:269-270). Jefferson himself contributed to the studies brief pieces in what were to become the four subfields of American anthropology: archeology, physical anthropology, linguistics, and social (cultural) anthropology. In 1784 Jefferson had excavated a mound using an approach and methods that came into more general use a century later (Lehmann-Hartleben 1943:163). He collected vocabularies (most of which unfortunately were destroyed) in order to explore the possible relationships between Indians and Asians (Pilling 1891:260-261). He observed the physical characteristics of Indians sufficiently to enable him to argue that they were not degenerate or inferior as Buffon, the noted naturalist of the time, had argued or as Ulloa had stated (Chamberlain 1907:500-504; Jefferson 1787). He also outlined in a letter of instruction to Meriwether Lewis in 1803 those ethnographic topics on which information should be collected (Chamberlain 1907:505-506) and himself wrote some descriptions of the Indians of Virginia (Jefferson 1787).

Jefferson was not alone in his interest in the archeological remains to be found on the North American continent in the nineteenth-century, and a number of others published their observations, particularly of the mounds and other earthworks located along the Mississippi River and its tributaries. Although at least some of the seventeenth and eighteenth-century French explorers, missionaries, and traders may have known of the existence of these large archeological sites, they had not mentioned them in their writings. Consequently, those whose knowledge of the region rested solely on written accounts were unaware these sites existed. This quickly changed as numbers of White settlers began moving across the Alleghenies and into the valleys of the Ohio and its tributaries to clear the land, finding extensive earthworks in many of the places most suitable for their own settlements. As more of this land was settled, more of these mounds were found and White fascination with them increased, a fascination that was only in part mere wonder at the spectacular size of some of these earthworks. In Europe, interest in exploring archeological remains was increasing, and exploration of these monuments of the New World reassured Americans both of their continuing interest in matters that concerned educated Europeans and of the unique history of the American continent.

To a number of writers, these archeological remains were testimony that the history of the continent before Columbus was not that of the Indians alone. They argued that the Indians neither were numerous enough nor had the political organization or inclination to build these works, and that consequently they must have been constructed by some Old World people. Egyptians, Hebrews, Tartars, Phoenicians, Picts, and Hindus were among those mentioned as possible builders, just as in earlier discussions they had been thought responsible for the original peopling of the continent (Huddleston 1967). The controversy that began in the 1780s with speculations such as those by Noah Webster (G.H. Smith 1931), Ezra Stiles (1783), and Benjamin Smith Barton (1798) and continued for 100 years regarding the identity of the "Mound Builders" was of such importance that virtually every major scientific group concerned with Indians and Indian history took up the question. The first association to do so was the American Philosophical Society. Later the American Antiquarian Society (organized at Worcester, Massachusetts, in 1812) became interested in this subject. It published, for example, Caleb Atwater's (1820) important synthesis of information on the mounds.

Meanwhile, the American Philosophical Society, in part as consequence of Jefferson's interest in languages, turned more of its attention to American Indian linguistics. Benjamin Smith Barton (1787), a member of the Society, published in a volume dedicated to Jefferson a compilation of Indian vocabularies and some classification of them (for a modern review of this book see Haas 1970). Of greater importance was the work of Peter Stephen DuPonceau, president of the Society from 1828 to 1844. In the first decades of the nineteenth century, linguists such as Friedrich von Schlegel and Wilhelm von Humboldt proposed typologies based on grammatical similarities. In this intellectual climate, DuPonceau's (1819, 1838) suggestion that Indian languages were characterized by what he called "polysynthesis" attracted considerable notice.

The classification of the differences as well as the similarities of the various Indian languages was studied by Albert Gallatin (1836) in a publication of the American Antiquarian Society. He offered the most comprehensive classification of Indian languages up to that time as well as a survey of the history and ethnology of the Indians then known to Whites. Gallatin, who had been Jefferson's secretary of the treasury, also encouraged others to study the Indians and was the key figure in founding the American Ethnological Society in 1842. Six years later, this society published Gallatin's (1848) revised classification of North American Indian languages.

The American Ethnological Society also encouraged Squier and Davis in their extensive survey of the mounds and hoped to publish the results, but the completed manuscript was so lengthy that the newly established Smithsonian Institution was asked to publish it. The survey appeared as the first volume of the series, *Smithsonian Contributions to Knowledge* (Squier and Davis 1848). Later important studies of the mounds—Squier's (1849) survey of New York State, Whittlesey's (1852) of

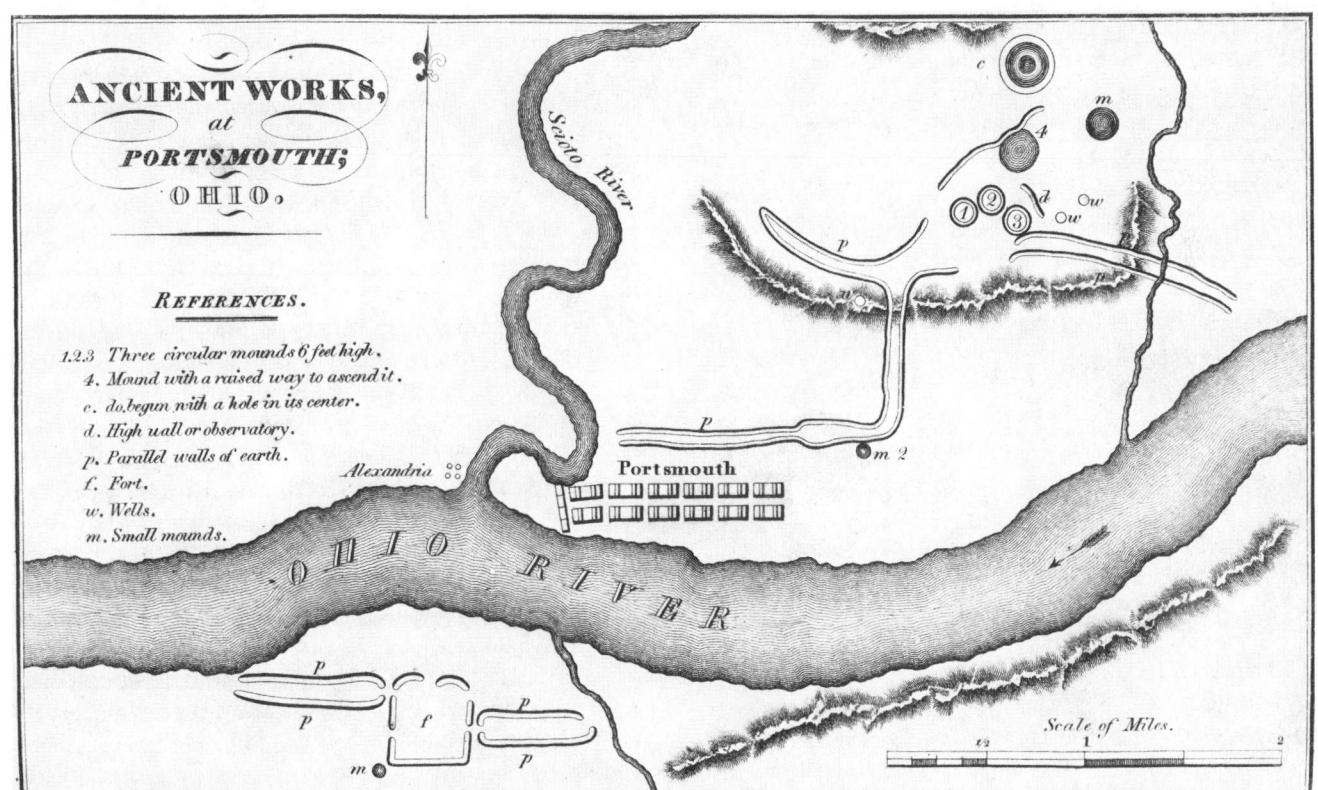

Dept. of Anthr., Smithsonian: Atwater 1820:151.

Fig. 2. Map of the mounds and ancient earthworks at Portsmouth, Ohio, engraved for the first volume of the *Transactions* of the American Antiquarian Society from surveys by Caleb Atwater, whose descriptions (1820:151-156) were quite accurate but who speculated that these and similar constructions were the work of migrating Hindus (Willey and Sabloff 1974:16).

Ohio, Lapham's (1855) of Wisconsin, and Haven's (1856) general summary—appeared in this series.

The Smithsonian also encouraged other types of surveys, on occasion by the device of circulars (see Gibbs 1867), continuing earlier government support that underwrote Jedidiah Morse's (1822) survey of Indian conditions in 1820, which overshadowed Ezekiel Sanford's (1819) compendium; Lewis Cass's (1823) questionnaire distributed while he was governor of Michigan Territory; and Schoolcraft's (1851–1857) encyclopedic potpourri of miscellany.

In the third decade of the nineteenth century, interest in relatively recent history of Indians led to the publication of a number of biographies such as Drake's (1832), Thatcher's (1832), and McKenney and Hall's (1933–1934) collections of biographical sketches; Stone's lives of Joseph Brant (1838), Red Jacket (1841), and Uncas and Miantonomi (1842); Benjamin Drake's biographies of Black Hawk (1839) and Tecumseh (1841); and Black Hawk's (1955) autobiography. Given the popularity of biography at the time, a popularity that had been long accorded captivity narratives (Vail 1949; Barbeau 1950), it may be no accident that the first volume of what was to become Francis Parkman's life work, *France and England in North America,* was *The Conspiracy of Pontiac* (1851).

Mid- and Late Nineteenth Century

Although these biographies contained some information on the cultures of various Indian peoples, the coverage was both scanty and spotty, a fact that became apparent to Lewis Henry Morgan when he and other young men reorganized a secret society they had formed into what they called "the New Confederacy of the Iroquois." This was a society whose organization they planned to model

left, U. of Rochester Lib.; right, Ill. State Histl. Lib., Springfield.

Fig. 3. left, Lewis Henry Morgan (b. 1818, d. 1881) at about the time of publication of his *League of the. . .Iroquois* (Morgan 1851), a work he dedicated to his principal collaborator in Iroquois research, Ely S. Parker (b. 1828, d. 1895), *to·nihokæ·ʔwęh,* Tonawanda Seneca, shown at right as photographed about 1863.

after that of the League of the Iroquois and one of whose purposes was "to encourage a kinder feeling towards the Indian." To learn more about the Iroquois, Morgan and others of the "New Confederacy" sought out Indians living on nearby reservations in New York State as well as authorities such as Schoolcraft. Of all those Indians Morgan met, his acquaintance with Ely S. Parker, a young Seneca Indian and interpreter (later to become commissioner of Indian affairs in the Grant administration) proved most valuable. From information provided by Parker and others, Morgan (1847) wrote a series of letters addressed to Albert Gallatin published in the *American Whig Review.* Morgan then turned to fulfilling a request to collect Indian materials for New York State's Natural History Cabinet. At the time, interest in such collections was growing, and after he had visited Connecticut's Indian collection in Hartford, the governor of New York State decided Albany ought to have a similar one. Morgan provided not only a large collection of Indian articles but also a description of them, which was published by the state (Morgan 1850, 1852). These descriptions and the previously published "Letters to Gallatin" slightly expanded and edited were republished by Morgan as his *League of the Ho-dé-no-sau-nee or Iroquois* (1851), the first modern ethnography of an Indian group. This book remains the best single ethnography of the Iroquois and is of such quality that later students of Iroquois culture and society such as J.N.B. Hewitt, Arthur C. Parker, A.A. Goldenweiser, Frank G. Speck, and William N. Fenton have found it necessary only to provide more extended discussion of particular matters mentioned in it, not a comprehensive ethnography that would supersede it.

In 1856 Morgan's interest in kinship and social organization was rekindled while attending a meeting of the American Association for the Advancement of Science (an organization founded in 1848 to further the work of the few professional scientists of the time and others interested in science), and he was to spend the rest of his life in the study of the subject. What Morgan had discovered was that the kinship terminology of the Iroquois and other Indians was organized on a different "plan" from that used in civil and canon law. This discovery suggested to Morgan, as the similarity of grammatical forms and structure of Indian languages (DuPonceau's "polysynthesis") had suggested to Gallatin (1836:142), a common origin of Indians, a question then still being debated. This observation together with the pertinent data Morgan had collected from questionnaires sent out by himself and by the Smithsonian and Secretary of State Lewis Cass (Morgan 1859, 1862), and from Indians on his trips to the West was published in his *Systems of Consanguinity and Affinity of the Human Family* (1871), a work that established the study of kinship systems as a subject of significance in anthropology. Six years later Morgan published *Ancient Society*

(1877), one of the most important studies of social evolution. In 1880, the year before he died, he served the American Association for the Advancement of Science as its president, the first anthropologist so honored.

The second half of the nineteenth century also witnessed the publication of an increasing number of books on American history, some of which took Indians as their subject. Among these are DeForest's (1851) history of the Connecticut Indians, Ruttenber's (1872) history of the Indians of the Hudson valley, Harvey's (1855) of the Shawnee, and Warren's (1885) of the Ojibwa. Some local histories, such as Clark's (1849) history of Onondaga County, New York, and Prime's (1845) history of Long Island, contain valuable data. A few Indians, such as George Copway (1850) and Peter Jones (1861), both Ojibwas; Peter D. Clarke (1870), a Wyandot; and Elias Johnson (1881), a Tuscarora, also wrote histories of their tribes. The noted Catholic historian John Gilmary Shea (1855) wrote a history of the Catholic missions and edited various historical writing including the *Library of American Linguistics,* among whose 13 volumes are to be found Bruyas's (1863) study of the Mohawk language, Maillard's (1864) Micmac grammar, and an Onondaga dictionary (Shea 1860). Three decades later, in order to provide illustration for his observation that Indians had a literature worthy of attention, Daniel G. Brinton published the *Library of Aboriginal American Literature* (1882–1890). Included in one of the eight volumes of this series are the texts and translations of Iroquois Condolence ceremony speeches as edited by Horatio Hale (1883a), longest of Hale's publications on the Iroquoians (Chamberlain 1897).

Interest in the Indian also led to the founding in 1879 of the Bureau of Ethnology (later, the Bureau of American Ethnology) with John Wesley Powell as its director. Under Powell's direction, the BAE became the center of anthropological research during the remaining decades of the century. Powell, himself a geologist, brought together at the BAE a number of men who, although like him trained in other disciplines, became the first group of professional anthropologists in the United States. Powell also encouraged and published (in the Annual Reports and Bulletins of the BAE) work such as Hoffman's studies of the Midewiwin society (W.J. Hoffman 1891) and the Menominee (W.J. Hoffman 1896), Jenks's (1900) study of the use of wild rice, and Pilling's (1888, 1891) bibliographies of works on Iroquoian and Algonquian languages. Work of members of the BAE staff, like Mooney's (1894) survey of the eastern Siouan tribes, Hewitt's (1903–1928) studies of Iroquois cosmology, and Powell's (1881) description of Wyandot social and political organization, was also published.

The interests of the BAE were not limited to ethnography. At the time, the identity of the Mound Builders remained an open question, and the BAE was forced by Congress to undertake research on the subject. The task

NAA, Smithsonian.
Fig. 4. J.N.B. Hewitt (b. 1859, d. 1937) (Tuscarora), ethnologist on the staff of the Bureau of American Ethnology, photographed with a group of Iroquois visiting the Smithsonian. rear, left to right, William Sandy (Cayuga), Hewitt, Alexander Hill (Onondaga), Andrew John (Seneca); front, left to right, William Henry Fishcarrier (Cayuga), Robert David (Cayuga). Andrew John was from the Cattaraugus Reservation, a former president of the Seneca Nation, and a collaborator in Hewitt's and other Smithsonian research. The others were from the Six Nations Reserve; Hewitt published their portraits, taken on this occasion, in his work on Iroquoian cosmology (Hewitt 1903–1928, 1:pls. 64–67). Photograph by DeLancey Gill, Dec. 1901.

was given to Cyrus Thomas, who finally settled the issue, establishing that the Mound Builders had indeed been Indians (C. Thomas 1887, 1887a, 1889, 1894).

But closer to what Powell envisioned as the true aim of the Bureau was the "mapping of North America," an extensive survey of the Indian peoples of the country. As Powell regarded linguistic classification as critical (McGee 1897a:372–381) to such an endeavor, he revised and enlarged a circular he had previously written (Powell 1877, 1880), and engaged the BAE staff (Sturtevant 1959; Darnell 1971) in revising Gallatin's (1836, 1848) earlier classification. The results, which became known as the "Powell map" (Powell 1891), incorporated linguistic work done since Gallatin's survey, such as Hale's (1883, 1883b) studies that demonstrated Tutelo a Siouan language and confirmed Barton's and Gallatin's (1836: 91–92) earlier suggestion as to the possible relationship between the Cherokee and Iroquois languages.

While Powell was building the BAE into a center of anthropological research, Frederic Ward Putnam was similarly engaged in furthering the growth of anthropological museums, which he envisioned should be connected with university departments of anthropology, thus furthering the acceptance of anthropology as a proper subject in the university curriculum. It was for these activities more than his excavations, such as those of shell heaps in New England and mounds in the Midwest, that he became best known. In 1874, eight years after it had been founded, Putnam became curator of the Peabody Museum of American Archaeology and Ethnology (a position he held until his retirement in 1909) and professor at Harvard in 1887. In 1873 he had been appointed permanent secretary of the American Association for the Advancement of Science, holding that position for 25 years until becoming its president in 1898. To these tasks, Putnam added three others of particular significance: from 1891 to 1894, chief of the Department of Ethnology of the Columbian Exposition, building collections that were to become the nucleus of the Field Museum in Chicago; from 1894 to 1903, Curator of Anthropology at the American Museum of Natural History in New York, greatly strengthening anthropological activities there; and from 1903 to 1909, Professor of Anthropology and Director of the Anthropological Museum at the University of California in Berkeley.

The activities of men such as Powell and Putnam were part of the more general interest in and growth of science that also led in the last two decades of the nineteenth century to a proliferation of professional societies, including anthropological ones. By 1882, the American Association for the Advancement of Science had attained such a size that it was reorganized into sections, anthropology becoming Section H. In 1879 the Anthropological Society of Washington had been founded, and in 1888, this society published the first issue of the *American Anthropologist* (old series). Growing interest in the subject led to a reorganization of this journal separate from that of the Anthropological Society of Washington and more national in scope, and in 1899, publication of the new series began. In 1902 the American Anthropological Association was founded.

The increasing interest in science led not only to the growth of museums and professional societies, but also to changes in the college curriculum and to a university system based on the German model and in part staffed by those trained in Germany. By the end of the 1880s, courses in anthropology were being offered by Daniel G. Brinton at the University of Pennsylvania and Franz Boas (who had come to the United States earlier in the decade from Germany) at Clark University, and in 1890 by Putnam at Harvard. By the end of the century, courses in anthropology had been added to the curriculum at a few other universities (MacCurdy 1899; see also Starr 1892).

Early Twentieth Century

As this work progressed, interest in the question, "How did *we* get to where we are now?" decreased. With it came a lessening of faith in the belief that by classifying various phenomena the evolution of man and his institutions would be revealed, much as comparable classifications had revealed evolutionary sequences in other natural sciences. In the nineteenth century, this interest in progress and in discovery of those classifications that would reveal it dominated comparative studies in ethnology, linguistics, and archeology. In the last decade of the nineteenth century and early decades of the twentieth, coincidentally with the introduction of anthropology into the university curriculum, anthropological perspectives changed. During this period, Franz Boas became the dominant figure in American anthropology, and although he himself did little work among the Northeastern Indians (Boas 1909), Boas profoundly influenced the course of anthropological work in the area, training at Columbia University many of those who became professional anthropologists in the early twentieth century. However, the number of anthropologists remained small, and as much of the methodology that came to be regarded as characteristic of American anthropology at the time was worked out informally in discussion and by correspondence (Kluckhohn 1939:335–336), the essential features of the anthropology identified with Boas have remained relatively difficult even for his students to describe. Nevertheless, it may not be in error to suggest that in the early decades of the twentieth century the question of paramount importance became "How did each of the many peoples of the world get to where they are now?" With this change in question, evolution was rejected as an explanatory concept; and studies of the past, although still more profoundly influenced by the methods of natural science than by those of history, became not so much studies of the development of civilization as histories of particular peoples and geographic areas. These utilized not only information from the historical documents and archeological remains but also ethnographic and linguistic data (the methodology employed is best outlined in Sapir 1916). "Culture"—not only as "a precipitate of history" but also as "an affair of the mind" (Fenton 1962:298)—became a key concept. In fact, Boas (1911a, 1938) titled his popular book on culture and race *The Mind of Primitive Man*. The similarity of fundamental psychological processes of all peoples ("psychic unity") was emphasized and the notion that there are innate differences in mental capabilities among "races" rejected. The result was both an emphasis on "cultural relativism," differences between cultures and the validity of these differences, and an emphasis on "universals," the essential similarities of both culture and individuals, a dual emphasis that is only seemingly contradictory (Lounsbury 1968:201, 207).

This change in anthropological perspective affected all areas of anthropological inquiry. In linguistics, Boas's rejection of evolutionary interpretations (such as that which dominated Powell 1880) led him to develop various ideas regarding the nature and study of language (see especially Boas 1911) that gave direction to much of American anthropological linguistic work in the first half of the twentieth century. These were further developed by his student, Edward Sapir, and by the Germanic philologist and Indo-European scholar, Leonard Bloomfield. Of particular importance in this work was Bloomfield's study of Central Algonquian languages (for evaluations see Sapir 1931 and Hockett 1948a, and for a selection of Bloomfield's writings see Hockett 1970). The linguistic studies made during the first decades of the century also produced an interest in revising Powell's classification, notably by reducing the number of linguistic stocks (Powell's map had 58) through the postulation of deeper genetic relationships (Darnell 1971a). The result was Sapir's (1929) classification of North American Indian languages, which remained basic until the 1960s.

In ethnology, studies of the evolution of culture traits were replaced by studies of the geographic distribution of these inventions, studies that were concerned both with the influence of environment on culture change and with inferring history from the spatial distribution of culture traits. Boas (1887, 1887a) early argued that museum collections should be arranged by geographic provenience and by tribe rather than according to a typological classification that would disclose evolutionary development. But, although it was Otis T. Mason's use of this typology that Boas (1887) attacked in arguing for an arrangement by tribe and "geographical province," it was also O.T. Mason (1896, 1907) who provided the first relatively detailed delineation of the culture areas of North America, a concept usually associated with the name of Clark Wissler. Wissler succeeded to Boas's position at the American Museum of Natural History, New York, and in a number of publications (Wissler 1914, 1917, 1923, 1926) provided a culture-area classification for North America as well as studies of the geographical distribution of certain culture traits. Kroeber (1939) later published a more extensive classification of culture areas, and Driver and Massey (1957) a more detailed study of trait distributions. Special studies of particular complexes, like E.W. Voegelin's (1944) study of mortuary customs and Witthoft's (1949a) of the Green Corn ceremony, have also appeared.

The growing body of archeological data led, as had the growing body of ethnologic data, to an increased concern with matters of classification and with geographical distribution. Such concern is evident in Moorehead's (1910) and Holmes's (1919) surveys of North American lithic materials and in Holmes's (1903) study of the pottery of the Eastern United States. As they had in ethnology, these studies also led to a consideration of culture areas, the most notable being that by Holmes (1914).

In the years that followed, local archeological work expanded, more studies of the archeological remains of states and regions in the Northeast were undertaken, surveys of work accomplished published, and state and regional societies founded to foster these activities. As this work progressed and the archeological data accumulated, the need for a more adequate taxonomic system to order them became apparent. The Midwestern Taxonomic method, also known as the McKern Classification (McKern 1939; Griffin 1943:341-372), provided such a typology for the organization of data into progressively more inclusive categories of culture complexes. Elsewhere in North America, interest in archeological chronologies had increased and consequently interest in stratigraphy and in excavating stratified sites. But in the Northeast where relatively few such sites were to be found, the Midwestern Taxonomic method came to be regarded as a means for ascertaining temporal sequences although not originally designed to do so.

In the early decades of the twentieth century the BAE continued its activities, and museums such as the Heye Foundation (Museum of the American Indian) and the American Museum of Natural History, New York, spurred by the realization that old Indian technologies were falling into disuse, added to their collections by increasing their support of ethnographic fieldwork; however, support for anthropological work increasingly came from the universities. In Canada, it was particularly furthered by the Anthropological Division in the Geological Survey of the National Museum of Canada. It was founded in partial emulation of the BAE in 1910 with Edward Sapir as its director to continue and expand the work earlier done by the Committee on the Northwestern Tribes of Canada of the British Association for the Advancement of Science and to support work of both Canadian and American anthropologists.

One result of this support in both the United States and Canada was the publication of a number of ethnographic studies, many of which were written by students of Boas, but not all; for example, Marius Barbeau and Diamond Jenness received their training at Oxford, as did Wilson Wallis who later attended Boas's seminars at Columbia. It was common practice at the time for graduate students enrolled elsewhere to attend some of Boas's classes at Columbia. Important among these studies, which provided basic information unavailable earlier, are Speck's numerous publications on the Eastern Algonquians and Iroquois (Hallowell 1951), Goldenweiser's (1912, 1914, 1914a) on the Iroquois, Barbeau's (1915, 1960) on the Wyandot, M.R. Harrington's (1913, 1921) on various Northeastern groups including the Delaware, Radin's (1923) on the Winnebago, William Jones's (1913, 1915, 1917-1919, 1939) on various Central Algonquians, Truman Michelson's on the Fox (Cooper 1939a), Alanson Skinner's on Central Algonquians (Harrington 1926), Landes's (1937, 1938, 1968) and Jenness's (1935) on the Ojibwa, and Wallis and Wallis on the Micmac (1955) and Maliseet (1957).

Although primarily concerned with the collection of basic ethnographic data, the ethnographic work done during this period did provide some evidence disproving

Fig. 5. Frank G. Speck (b. 1881, d. 1950) interviewing Josiah Montour, *àxkó·kšəš* 'little snake' (b. 1872), one of the last speakers of the Munsee variety of Delaware at Six Nations Reserve, Ont. The results of this interview in Montour's house were published by Speck (1946a). Photograph by William N. Fenton, Nov. 1945.

Fig. 6. Alanson Skinner (b. 1885, d. 1925), left, with Amos Oneroad, Dakota, in a Menominee cornfield at Keshena, Wis. Photograph by Huron H. Smith, Sept. 1922.

various sequences proposed by nineteenth-century evolutionists. For example, the evolutionists' contention that matrilineality preceded patrilineality was found not always to be the case, and in at least some instances the reverse was indicated by the data (Swanton 1905; Speck 1922:84). The sequence that came under particular attack in studies of Indians of the Northeast was the evolutionists' claim that the "simplest" hunting societies either owned land communally or had no notion of property ownership, a claim that was rejected by Speck, who argued that the family hunting band owned the territory it used and that this form of organization was pre-Columbian. As a result, Speck's (1915d:305) early paper suggesting that the family group was "the earliest fundamental social unit of the Algonkian" and had a definite claim of ownership to its hunting territory was followed by a number of other studies of the matter (the most important of which include Speck 1922, 1928e; Speck and Eiseley 1939; Cooper 1939).

Mid-Twentieth Century

The perspective developed by Boas and his students did not remain the only one in the next decades of the century. Questions and concerns more prominent in nineteenth-century anthropological studies reemerged, in part influenced by the work of British anthropologists (anthropology in England had been relatively little affected by that done in the United States) and in part because old questions remained unanswered. Also, the work done in the early decades of the century fostered

more extensive inquiries into certain matters and so led to the development of particular methodologies designed to answer these questions. In linguistics, for example, there was a great increase in the number of specialized descriptive studies of Iroquoian and Algonquian languages, which led to both better understanding of their historical relations and insights of a general theoretical interest. The result in all subfields was not only the accumulation of more data, but also specialization within the discipline and the emergence of various and sometimes contradictory interpretations of the data, a diversity that has been encouraged by the increase in the number of people engaged in anthropological studies in recent years.

One such area of both continuing and renewed interest has been that of social organization and kinship—in part the result of the influence of A.R. Radcliffe-Brown, who in turn was influenced by the work of W.H.R. Rivers, whose work in its turn was influenced by Lewis H. Morgan. Various studies of Central Algonquian kinship systems have been made, and these indicate a relationship of various systems of kinship terminology with certain marriage practices, most particularly cross-cousin marriage, and descent, most particularly patrilineal clans (Tax 1955; Eggan 1955:485–551, 1966; Callender 1962). However, these explanations poorly account for the Iroquois data (Lounsbury 1964:1079); in fact, it was the lack of such relationships between Iroquois kinship terminology and Iroquois marriage and descent practices at the time that led Morgan to study other such systems. For this reason, among others, some have turned to other methods of studying kinship terminology. One is Lounsbury (1964), who has provided a semantic analysis of Seneca terminology.

Another subject of continuing concern has been the influence of ecology on social organization and culture. For example, Hallowell (1949) suggested that the size of the winter hunting territory among Northern Algonquians (and by extension other Algonquians) depended on the abundance of game in the area rather than on the size of the hunting group. Caldwell (1958) in his study of Eastern Woodlands archeological cultures paid considerable attention to utilization of the environment, a concern with ecological factors evident in a number of other archeological studies such as Ritchie's (1965) survey of New York State archeology and Fitting's (1970) of Michigan.

These archeological studies have also paid attention to developmental stages of the sort suggested by Ford and Willey (1941) in their survey of eastern archeology (for a later summary see Willey 1966), the chronology of which has been clarified by application of carbon-14 dating. In ethnological studies, this interest in developmental sequences has led to a revival of evolutionary interpretations of the development of the Algonquian hunting band. Jenness (1935:4-7) found evidence for band ownership of hunting territories rather than for family ownership among the Parry Island Algonquians, and suggested, contrary to Speck's interpretation, that the family hunting territory developed as the fur trade became important. Subsequently, Leacock (1954) offered a similar interpretation of the data on the Northern Algonquian and Hickerson (1962, 1967) on the Chippewa.

At the same time, there appeared a number of studies of the psychological characteristics of various Northeastern Indian groups and of their persistence and change. These were in part inspired by Hallowell's (1946, 1951a, 1952) studies of the Ojibwa, which suggested a persistence of basic personality characteristics. These include studies of the Chippewa by Barnouw (1950), Caudill (1949), Friedl (1956), Boggs (1958), and James (1961); of the Menominee by George Spindler (1955) and Louise Spindler (1962), and of the Tuscarora and other Iroquois by Wallace (1952, 1959).

These studies were an outgrowth of earlier anthropological interest in psychology, an interest that was in part responsible for the publication of some life histories, such as those edited by Radin (1920, 1926c), Michelson (1925b), and Lurie (1961). These autobiographies have provided an important supplement also to the more traditional biographies such as those on Pontiac (Peckham 1947), Teedyuscung (Wallace 1949), Tecumseh (G. Tucker 1956), and Handsome Lake (Wallace 1969).

Students of Northeastern Indian cultures have long used ethnographic data in the historical documents, that is, done what in recent decades has come to be called "ethnohistory." The term "ethnohistory" has acquired several different meanings; in anthropology, it most commonly refers to the use of data in the historical documents on peoples such as the American Indians. For example, Speck used such data when they were available in various of his studies of Algonquians (Hallowell 1951:68). Other studies of this type include those by Willoughby (1907, 1935:276-300) on the Virginia and New England Indians, Rainey (1936) on the Indians of Connecticut, Flannery (1939) on the Coastal Algonquians, and Kinietz (1940) on the Indians of the Upper Great Lakes. In the 1930s, interest in acculturation greatly increased, with the result that more studies of culture change, often combining data on contemporary Indian life with those in the historical documents, appeared. Examples of this type of study include Keesing's (1939) on the Menominee, Joffe's (1940) on the Fox, Stern's (1952) on the Chickahominy, Hickerson's (1962, 1970) on the Chippewa, Wallace's (1969) on the Seneca, and Trigger's (1976) on the seventeenth-century Hurons. Ethnographic study of contemporary Indians has also been used to help interpret the scantier data in the earlier documents, a method Fenton (1949, 1957:21-22) has termed "upstreaming," and a method in part comparable to the "direct historical approach," that is, using data in the historical documents to identify archeological sites. Interest in culture change also has led to an interest in contemporary culture change including the "action anthropology" of the Fox Project (Gearing, Netting, and Peattie 1960; Gearing 1970) as well as descriptions of contemporary Indian life such as Slotkin's (1952) and Spindler and Spindler's (1971) studies of Menominee and Shimony's (1961) of the Iroquois. Traditional kinds of history of particular tribes such as Hagan's (1958) history of the Sauk and Fox, Gibson's (1963) of the Kickapoo, Anson's (1970) of the Miami, and Weslager's (1972) of the Delaware continue to be published.

Sources

An excellent review of the development of American anthropology in the nineteenth century is given in Hallowell (1960). Anthropological work in Canada about the same time is discussed by D. Cole (1973). The history of archeology in America is surveyed in Willey and Sabloff (1974) and work in the Northeast in particular in Guthe (1952), Haag (1961), and Brose (1973). The Mound Builder controversy is considered in Silverberg (1968). Lounsbury (1968) has provided a very useful history of linguistic concerns, and Haas (1969), a survey of nineteenth-century American typological interests.

A review of the literature on and state of knowledge of North American Indians toward the end of the nineteenth century was assembled by Winsor (1884-1889, 1). Some assessment of anthropological knowledge of the Northeast a half-century later is given in Johnson (1946), Fenton (1948, 1957), and Griffin (1952b) and of the discipline as a whole in Kroeber (1953).

Prehistory: Introduction

JAMES E. FITTING

Thomas Jefferson was one of the first systematic investigators of archeological materials in the Northeast; his work in Virginia was careful and his conclusions were well documented (Brose 1973; Stoltman 1973a). Jefferson's interpretations were couched in the terms of the intellectual understanding of his time and all archeological interpretations since have been bound not only by the raw archeological data but also by the chronological reference points and scholarly emphasis of the period.

The organization of the chapters on archeology presented in this volume reflects the accumulation of several centuries of research as well as the near revolutionary development of exact dating techniques applicable to the area. The chronological framework, which escaped archeologists for so many years in the Northeast, has since 1949 been fairly well established and archeologists do not anticipate any surprises as great as those when the first radiocarbon dates placed man's occupation of the area hundreds, and even thousands, of years earlier than was expected.

Prior to the development of radiocarbon dating, models for archeological interpretations were ethnographic, geographical, or typological. Many archeologists in the nineteenth century, and some in the twentieth, applied the direct historic approach to all archeological remains. Where different types of archeological materials were present, presumed correlations with historic tribal divisions were used to explain these differences. Some suspected, quite correctly, that there might be a great deal of time depth in the Northeast and that the uniform application of the direct historic approach might be obscuring the importance of the differences that did exist. As an alternative, a geographical model was developed, which dealt with the distribution of similar artifact styles over space. It was found that such similarities were often very local and could be used to define culture areas. This system shifted the emphasis from specific sites to groups of sites and to differences and similarities in artifact style. This shift in emphasis from individual site descriptions to regional comparisons was the basis for the development of the Midwestern Taxonomic system—a system that attempted to use the percentage of similarities in archeological materials from different sites to determine the degree of relationship of these sites. This system (McKern 1939) was designed to deal with differences and similarities of artifact assemblages without taking into account

variations in time and space. Time and space relationships were to be considered only after formal degrees of similarity and difference had been established.

The Midwest Taxonomic system came into widespread use through the work of Fay-Cooper Cole, Thorne Deuel, William Ritchie, and James B. Griffin. Even as it was used, however, archeological knowledge advanced to the point where, through stratigraphic excavation, local developmental sequences became known. Culture change over time had been amply documented in New York, Ohio, and Illinois decades before the development of radiocarbon dating. Summary interpretations (Ford and Willey 1941; Griffin 1946, 1952b) continued to be couched in the terminology of the Midwestern Taxonomic system but were decidedly concerned with cultural history.

Following the development of radiocarbon dating in the late 1940s, problems of chronology could be solved and the challenge became the study not so much of cultural succession as of cultural adaptation and change. Caldwell's (1958) imaginative synthesis of Eastern prehistory was one such example and paved the way for later studies with even more dependence on environmental correlates.

Griffin (1960a, 1961) next called attention to the correlations that existed in the Northeast between climatic and cultural change. This approach to investigation and interpretation has proved most productive and plays an important role in the organization of the archeological contributions to this volume; however, the interpretations found in the following chapters are not based totally on patterns of environmental change, for much is useful in all of the earlier approaches and has been incorporated when appropriate.

The period of major climatic change following the retreat of the glaciers is covered first. Between 9000 B.C. and 3000 B.C. the land forms and environmental associations in the Northeast underwent a series of dramatic changes. This period saw the first sparse settlement and man was not well entrenched in the area until after the development of essentially modern environmental associations, which occurred around 3000 B.C.

After 3000 B.C. there is a spectacular increase in both the quantity and the complexity of archeological materials. The elaboration of mortuary associations, particularly after 2000 B.C., has received particular attention. There are also indications that cultivated plants were present by 1000 B.C. in southern areas, with a slow spread northward after that date. This time period has been designated as the Late Paleo-Indian (R.J. Mason 1962), the Archaic (Ritchie 1969a), and Middle and Late Archaic (Griffin 1967). The introduction of ceramics has been conventionally used to separate Late Archaic from Early Woodland, but archeological investigations have shown that this trait had little impact on life-styles. Radiocarbon dating has also demonstrated that it has little chronological significance. Ceramics were manufactured in the southern parts of the region by at least 1500 B.C. but did not reach the northern portions until the beginning of the Christian era.

There are a number of indications of climatic change around 300 B.C. that correlate with the development of Adena, Hopewell, and Lake Forest Middle Woodland cultures (Griffin 1960a, 1961; Baerreis and Bryson 1965). Cleland (1966:28) has called this the "Hopewell episode" and has suggested that it lasted from 300 B.C. to A.D. 300. The cultural climaxes of this time do not simply disappear and it is easier to mark the beginning of Adena and Hopewell than it is their termination dates.

The third of the following chapters on regional cultural development covers the time from 300 B.C. until approximately A.D. 1000. It includes the Hopewell episode and most of what Baerreis and Bryson (1965) have called the Scandic (A.D. 300-A.D. 800) and Neo-Atlantic (A.D. 800-A.D. 1300) episodes: the former a period of climatic deterioration and the latter a favorable episode that saw some of the most elaborate cultural development ever found in the Northeast. This embraces what has traditionally been called Middle Woodland and early Late Woodland.

Following A.D. 1000, and in some cases preceding it, it is possible to use the direct historic approach to deal with the prehistoric archeology of ethnographically known groups. There is variation in the times at which these identifications become possible and in the certainty of the identifications, but after A.D. 1000 the archeology of the subareas used in this volume relates to the historic and ethnographic interpretations for these areas. Hence, this period will not be treated in terms of the Northeast as a whole but in terms of specific groupings of historic cultures. The widespread and rapid population dislocation that followed, and in interior areas even preceded, European contact often makes the identification of these cultures with specific historically attested tribes very difficult.

Although the archeology of the Northeast has been divided into four analytical segments, new names have not been given to them. The archeological literature of the area is already full of names of historical importance for regional archeological interpretation. These names and the relationships that they imply will be used in the specific archeological chapters. The overall organization reflects the major time periods of cultural development as they are now known throughout the entire area.

Post-Pleistocene Adaptations

ROBERT E. FUNK

The oldest cultures in the northeastern area that have been revealed by archeological research were adapted to a succession of floral and faunal environments that were determined by the climatic changes accompanying and following the retreat of the Wisconsin continental ice. The ice commenced withdrawal from its maximum position about 15,000 B.C. Thereafter palynological and paleontological data document a changing series of plant and animal associations that only by 3000 B.C. had attained essentially modern forms. It should come as no surprise that concomitant changes took place in aboriginal cultures.

These cultures are meagerly represented in the archeological record in comparison to the considerable mass of information available for the period of 3000 to 1000 B.C. (the Late Archaic period). The paucity of data relates in part to the usual loss of archeological resolution that results from the operation of natural processes over long periods of time. But it must also be a consequence of the low density of aboriginal populations possessing simple technologies in the relatively unfavorable environment of late glacial and early postglacial times.

Paleo-Indians, about 10,500–6000 B.C.

The period 10,500–6000 B.C. witnessed the initial human penetration and settlement of the Northeast. The environment of the Paleo-Indians or Early Hunters was the tundra or park-tundra adjoining the southern edge of the Wisconsin ice sheet. It was a constantly changing environment. When the ice began to withdraw from the terminal moraine, the tundra and fringing spruce woodlands followed it northward. The northern limit of the broadleaf forest accordingly expanded from the south. After the last of the Canadian ice had disappeared (about 6000 B.C.), the floral and faunal zones had stabilized in essentially their modern locations and composition.

The oldest cultural assemblages of this period have been compared to the Clovis (Llano) and Folsom big-game hunters of the Plains. There are general resemblances to both groups. The eastern and western manifestations have in common the fluted bifacial projectile point style, a repertory of unifacial chipped stone tools, and a primary dependence on now extinct megafauna for sustenance.

In the East some writers visualize two stages or periods of Paleo-Indian: Early Paleo-Indian, represented by all the Clovis-like points and associated assemblages, and Late Paleo-Indian, represented by a variety of non-Clovis fluted points and a separate group of stemmed or lanceolate, usually parallel-flaked points allied to "Plano" forms of the Plains (Wormington 1957; R.J. Mason 1962; Williams and Stoltman 1965). Plano manifestations are actually very rare in the Northeast; their geographic center lies to the south and west of this area.

The fluted-point hunters probably entered the Northeast from the south and west following upon the glacial retreat. They could have been established south of the ice border prior to 15,000 B.C. but were unable to enter those areas north of the Cary-Port Huron moraine until after retreat of the ice from the moraines about 12,000 B.C.

The few available radiocarbon dates in conjunction with geochronological data suggest that in New York and New England the northeastern Paleo-Indian time period extended from about 10,500 to 8000 B.C. In the West the antiquity of fluted points seems not to exceed 9500 B.C.

South of the glacial end moraines in western Pennsylvania, excavations sponsored by the University of Pittsburgh at the deeply stratified Meadowcroft Rockshelter have yielded Paleo-Indian materials of as yet undetermined affiliation, radiocarbon dated between 14,225 B.C. and 11,300 B.C. (Adovasio et al. 1975). These occupations may have been coeval with the earliest stages of ice recession, when the glacier covered nearly all of New York State.

Early Paleo-Indian Manifestations, 10,500–8000 B.C.

In New York State evidence for Early Paleo-Indian occupations in the form of scattered finds of characteristic fluted points was reported by Ritchie (1957). At that time only two Paleo-Indian campsites were known for glaciated parts of the Northeast. Bull Brook in northeastern Massachusetts (Byers 1954, 1955, 1956; D.F. Jordan 1960) and Reagen, a Late Paleo-Indian site, in northwestern Vermont (fig. 1) (Ritchie 1953, 1957). Sites of major significance discovered in later years include the Davis site on Lake Champlain (Ritchie 1965:16–30); the Potts site near Phoenix (ibid.); West Athens Hill near Catskill, New York (fig. 2) (Funk and Johnson 1964; Funk 1967a; Ritchie 1969:xv–xvi; Ritchie and Funk 1973); Port Mobil on Staten Island (fig. 3) (Ritchie 1969:xvii–xviii);

16

Debert in Nova Scotia (fig. 4) (G.F. MacDonald 1966, 1968); Kings Road near Coxsackie (Funk, Weinman, and Weinman 1969; Ritchie 1969:xvi–xvii); Dutchess Quarry Cave in Orange County (Funk et al. 1969; Funk, Walters, and Ehlers 1969; Funk, Fisher, and Reilly 1970; Guilday 1968, 1969); and Wapanucket 8 in Massachusetts (Robbins and Agogino 1964).

Paleo-Indian manifestations in Ohio were summarized by Prufer and Baby (1963), and those in Indiana were described by Dorwin (1966). Fluted-point components, as opposed to scattered finds, have not been discovered or reported in these states. The data for the Upper Great Lakes were summarized by Quimby (1960), but later discoveries in Michigan, including investigations at the Barnes, Hi-Lo, and Holcombe sites (fig. 6), were reported by Fitting (1963, 1965a, 1970:34–57; Fitting, DeVisscher, and Wahla 1966). Important sites farther south are Williamson, in Virginia (McCary 1951; Benthall and McCary 1973); Shoop, in central Pennsylvania (Witthoft 1952); Wells Crater, in Tennessee (Dragoo 1973); Shawnee-Minisink, in eastern Pennsylvania (McNett and McMillan 1974), the Flint Run complex in Virginia (Gardner 1974); and the Plenge site, New Jersey (Kraft 1974).

Early Paleo-Indian assemblages from Michigan to Nova Scotia exhibit remarkable consistency in tool forms apart from projectile points (figs. 3, 5). Almost universally present are biface knives, biface preforms, end scrapers, side scrapers, flake knives, and other unifaces. In shape, size, and mode of retouch the unifaces are usually easily distinguished from unifaces of later cultures. Also, many end scrapers and some side scrapers bear small projections or "graving spurs" on the working edges, and there occasionally appear small tools with several spurs, reminiscent of denticulates in the Mousterian industries of Europe. Very few of the known sites have produced tools of the "rough stone" category, such as hammerstones, anvilstones, pitted stones, or abraders. Polished stone tools and bone tools are unknown, and ornamental items very rare.

The overall uniformity in fluted point assemblages is generally assumed to be the result of a highly conservative way of life, attuned to the requirements of a specialized subsistence pattern dependent on the ubiquitous megafauna of the late Pleistocene environment. A fairly rapid spread of the fluted point users is suggested by the data, with subsequent maintenance of great mobility resulting from their focal economic adaptation. Detailed study of the materials elicits a degree of variability among assemblages. This variability could be the result of temporal change (evolution), geographical variation (stylistic drift), functional variation, or a combination of these factors.

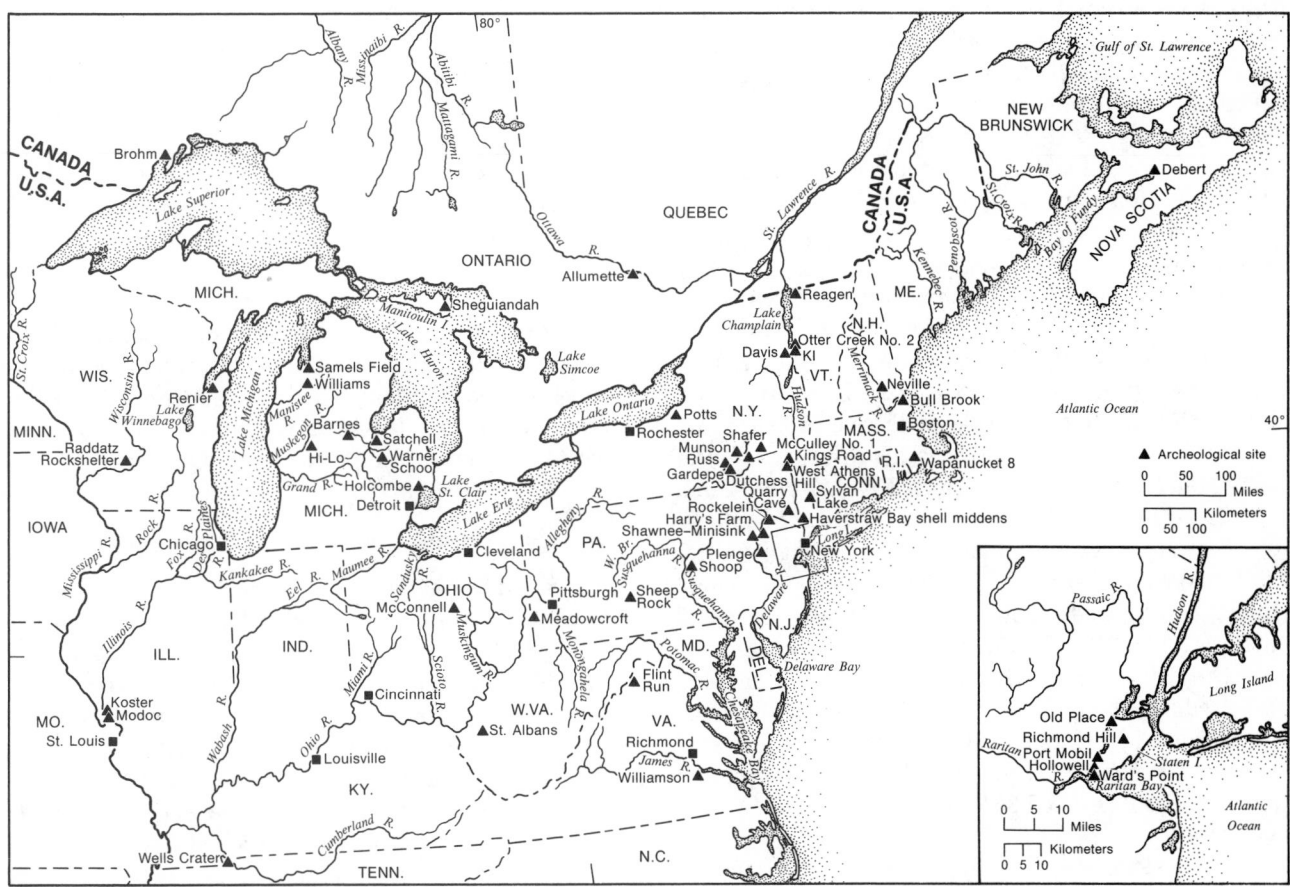

Fig. 1. Paleo-Indian and Archaic sites.

N.Y. State Mus., Albany.

Fig. 2. Fluted points from West Athens Hill. Materials: 1, western New York Onondaga flint; 2, 5-8, Normanskill flint; 3, dark gray chalcedony; 4 is plastic replica of original made of black Normanskill flint. Length of 1, 5 cm, rest same scale.

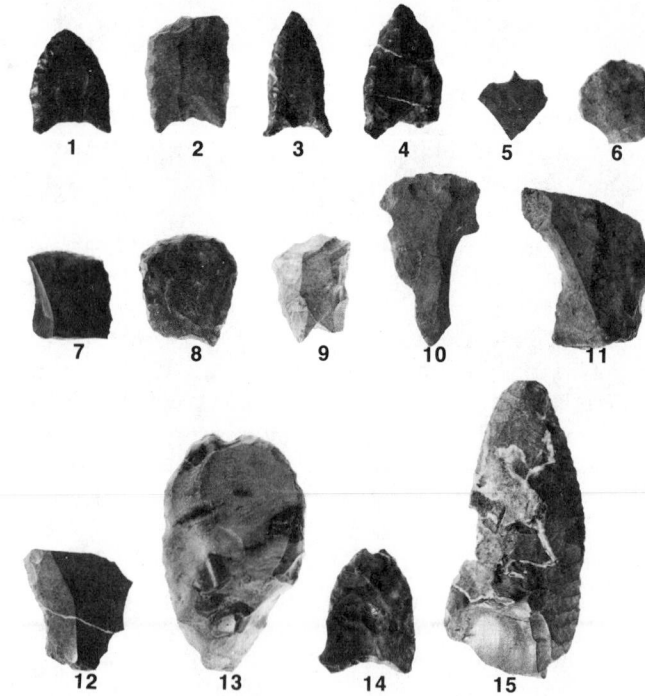

N.Y. State Mus., Albany.

Fig. 3. Paleo-Indian artifacts from the Port Mobil site, Staten Island, N.Y.: 1-4, fluted points; 5, graver on flake; 6-10, end scrapers; 11, concave scraper; 12-13, side scrapers; 14-15, retouched flake knives. Materials are yellow jasper except 8, 11, 13, which are probably Normanskill flint. Length of 1, 2.8 cm, rest same scale.

Most sites in the Northeast are located on hills or rises where good drainage, meaning a dry living floor, was an important consideration. At West Athens Hill and the Williamson site good sources of flint were key determinants of site selection. In the rare cases where rockshelters or caves, such as Dutchess Quarry Cave, were utilized, temporary protection from wind, cold, or precipitation was doubtless the principal motive. Other factors are suggested by reconstruction of the Paleo-Indians' ecological setting. For example, in a tundra or park-tundra setting, elevated locations would have provided good vantage points for observing the movements of game in adjoining valleys (Funk 1972).

Fluted point groups in the Plains depended heavily on large mammals, nearly all of which are now extinct, for food, clothing, and raw materials for tools. Among these animals were the mammoth, Pleistocene horse, and bison (*Bison antiquus*). In the Northeast, there is evidence that the caribou (genus *Rangifer*) was the principal prey of Early Man (Fitting, DeVisscher, and Wahla 1966; Funk et al. 1969; Funk, Fisher, and Reilly 1970), although the total data argue for the contemporaneity of man, mastodon, moose-elk, caribou, and other Pleistocene fauna (Funk, Fisher, and Reilly 1970). It is wise to recall Ritchie's (1956, 1957:7) admonition that Early Man may have been a forager as well as big-game hunter, making use of edible plants and small animals. The Shawnee-Minisink site in the upper Delaware Valley has provided evidence that fishing was practiced by the Early Hunters; this component is dated 8640 B.C. (McNett and McMillan 1974).

Internal settlement data for Paleo-Hunter sites are meager but can provide clues to the size of occupying groups, the intensity of occupation, and the organization of activities. The larger sites such as Shoop, Bull Brook, or West Athens Hill may have been occupied for several seasons by one or more bands. They were probably the loci of multiple activities carried on by several households. Smaller sites such as Potts and Kings Road were probably special-purpose sites occupied by smaller groups engaged in a more limited range of activities.

Some writers have suggested analogies between Paleo-Indian groups and caribou-hunting tribes recorded in ethnographic literature. Among the latter are the Barren-Ground Eskimos of Keewatin (Birket-Smith 1929) and the Montagnais-Naskapi Indians of Quebec and Labrador (Rogers 1963).

Late Paleo-Indian Manifestations, 8000-6000 B.C.

Prufer and Baby (1963) distinguish several kinds of Plano points (fig. 6) in Ohio, and describe a number of surface sites. In the western Great Lakes, Late Paleo-Indian manifestations are grouped by Quimby (1960) under an "Aqua-Plano" tradition. Fitting (1970:58-59) finds this term, which implies both prairie and lake associations, unsatisfactory and prefers the cultural designation "Satchell complex," after the type site in Michigan. Similar materials have been excavated from sites on the Canadian side of Lake Huron (Lee 1954, 1955, 1956; Greenman and Stanley 1940, 1943; Greenman 1948).

18

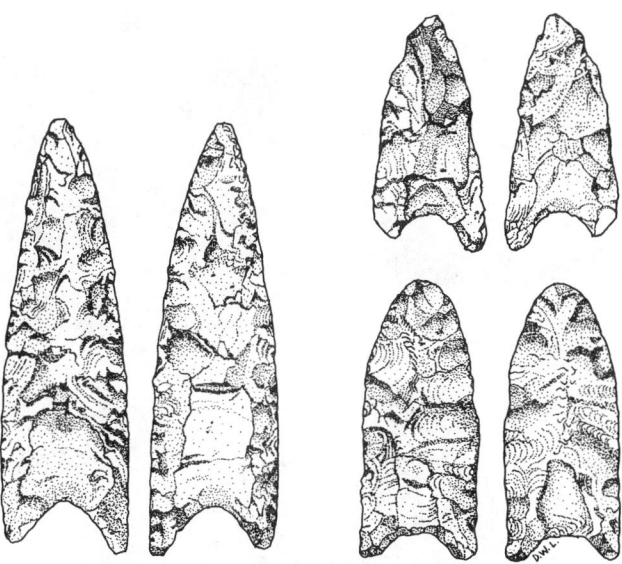

Natl. Mus. of Canada, Ottawa.

Fig. 4. Characteristic indented-base fluted points from the Debert site. Length of left 11.3 cm, rest same scale.

Also of Late Paleo-Indian age is the Eden-Scottsbluff cremation burial at the Renier site in Wisconsin (Mason and Irwin 1960) and the Samels Field site in Michigan.

East of Ohio, scattered Plano points were reported for the Upper Ohio Valley (Mayer-Oakes 1955), but these styles are very rare in New York and New England (Ritchie 1940:71; Funk and Schambach 1964; Ritchie 1965:16–18). Like Fitting (1968b), Ritchie (1965:32–33, 1969a:212–213) invokes an unfavorable early postglacial environment, dominated by coniferous forest elements of low carrying capacity for game, to explain the paucity of Plano traces.

Ritchie (1953, 1957) has reported on the unique Late Paleo-Indian assemblage from the Reagen site on the Missisquoi River in northwestern Vermont (fig. 5). In addition to a wide assortment of uniface scrapers and graving tools, the assemblage comprises fluted and un-fluted pentagonoid, unfluted lanceolate (Plano-like), un-fluted trianguloid, and weakly stemmed points. The Reagen point styles are seen rarely in other collections, as at the Williamson site (McCary 1951) and the Plenge site (Kraft 1974). Like the Brohm site on the north shore of Lake Superior (MacNeish 1952b; Fitting 1970:57), the Reagen site may represent the terminal phases of the fluted point tradition in the Northeast, at a time when the prevalent styles in some areas related to the Plano tradition.

Archaic Occupations to 3000 B.C.

Many writers have discussed the events leading to the disappearance of the Paleo-Indian cultures, and the subsequent debut of Archaic groups, in the eastern parts of North America (for example, Griffin 1952, 1964; Dragoo 1959; Fowler 1959; R.J. Mason 1962; Coe 1964;

Williams and Stoltman 1965; Willey 1966; Ritchie 1965, 1969, 1971; Ritchie and Funk 1973; Fitting 1970; Tuck 1974). While the Paleo-Indian tradition is generally equated with the hunting of big game in the late glacial period, Archaic groups are believed to represent hunting-fishing-gathering adaptations to the biotic milieu associated with early postglacial climatic conditions. Since the big-game animals of the tundra and spruce woodland were generally extinct in the area by 8000 B.C., Archaic peoples came to depend heavily on the white-tailed deer, black bear, elk or wapiti, many smaller mammals, birds, turtles, fish, and shellfish, plus nuts, seeds, and other plant foods in the forests and streams of the area. Their sites are more numerous and in a general sense larger and richer in occupation debris than those of the preceding era, reflecting not only larger, denser populations but also a more abundant and reliable subsistence base provided by the deciduous forests with their higher carrying capacity (Butzer 1971:144–150). Groups living in tidewater areas eventually learned to harvest creatures of the sea (Ritchie 1969a; Salwen 1970; Brennan 1974).

As a consequence of the new way of life, territoriality and regional diversity are more evident in Archaic assemblages than in Paleo-Indian ones, becoming most pronounced in Late Archaic times.

It is generally agreed that Archaic cultures evolved from Late Paleo-Indian expressions of the Southeast and Midwest, since there is growing evidence for transitional manifestations. It is very unlikely that new migrations from Asia were represented. Projectile-point styles and even assemblages of the earliest Archaic have been identified and were generally coeval with the Plano groups on the Plains (R.J. Mason 1962; Williams and Stoltman 1965).

Although a correlation is apparent during this transitional period among changing environment, changing economic adjustments, and changing material culture, implying a linked series of causal relationships, the specific factors determining change in projectile-point styles or other artifact traits remain obscure.

A minority of eastern archeologists favor the view that the Archaic tradition arose independently of the Paleo-Indian tradition, although they believe there was some interaction between the two. In part this hypothesis is based on the evidence for contemporaneity of notched points with Late Paleo-Indian styles in the Plains. Also, on some deep stratified Midwestern sites Archaic artifacts have been recovered in or below levels containing Paleo-Indian items (Logan 1952; Fowler 1959). In this view, both traditions developed from an older, very generalized culture carried into the New World by Asian immigrants who manufactured simple ovate, bifacially flaked points.

Following Fowler (1959) the eastern Archaic is arbitrarily divided into three subperiods: the Early Archaic,

Ritchie 1953:fig. 89.

Fig. 5. Late Paleo-Indian artifacts from the Reagen site, northern Vermont. 1-3, talc pendants; 4-7, lanceolate pentagonoid points; 8-9, stemmed points; 10-11, trianguloid points; 12, pentagonal point; 13, eared triangular point; 14, combined graver and spoke-shave scraper; 15-16, stemmed end scrapers; 17-20, simple end scrapers; 21-23, side scrapers; 24-25, knives from retouched flakes; 26-27, knives with single shouider; 28, ovate knife; 29, lanceolate knife. Materials are chiefly flints and jaspers of unknown source. Fluting scars on 4, 5, 28 chalked for photography. Length of 29 about 10.5 cm, rest same scale.

8000-6000 B.C.; the Middle Archaic, 6000-4000 B.C.; and the Late Archaic, 4000-1500 B.C.

On the southern borders of the Northeast culture area, the generally favorable postglacial environment supported small but widely distributed human populations from the beginning of Early Archaic times, as in the Southeast proper. Important evidence bearing on the whole sequence was provided by the Modoc Rockshelter in southern Illinois, which contained 28 feet of stratified deposits and the remains of Indian occupations commencing about 8000 B.C. as dated by radiocarbon (Fowler 1959). Deeply buried Archaic living floors at the Koster site, on the Illinois River, have been dated as far back as 5100 B.C. (Houart 1972). The distribution of Early Archaic projectile points in Illinois has been analyzed by Luchterhand (1970), who relied mainly on surface finds. Less information is available on Early to Middle Archaic occupations of Indiana and Ohio.

For New York, New England, and adjoining areas, Ritchie (1965, 1969, 1969a, 1971) has repeatedly noted the absence or extreme rarity of Early or Middle Archaic remains comparable to those of the Ohio and Mississippi valleys and the Southeast in general. Quimby (1960), in his synthesis of Upper Great Lakes prehistory, postulated a vaguely defined Early Archaic based on sparse surface finds of Southeastern point types. Fitting (1970:65-67) described the thin distribution in southern Michigan of early Southeastern types such as Big Sandy and Cypress Creek, defined in Tennessee (Lewis and Lewis 1961), the Modoc Side-Notched type of Illinois (Fowler 1959), and bifurcated-base forms (Fitting 1964a). Until 1966, no Archaic assemblages in Pennsylvania, New York, New England, and the Upper Great Lakes could be confidently assigned an age as great as 3000 B.C.

Further investigations have begun to close this gap between the Paleo-Indian occupations and the well-

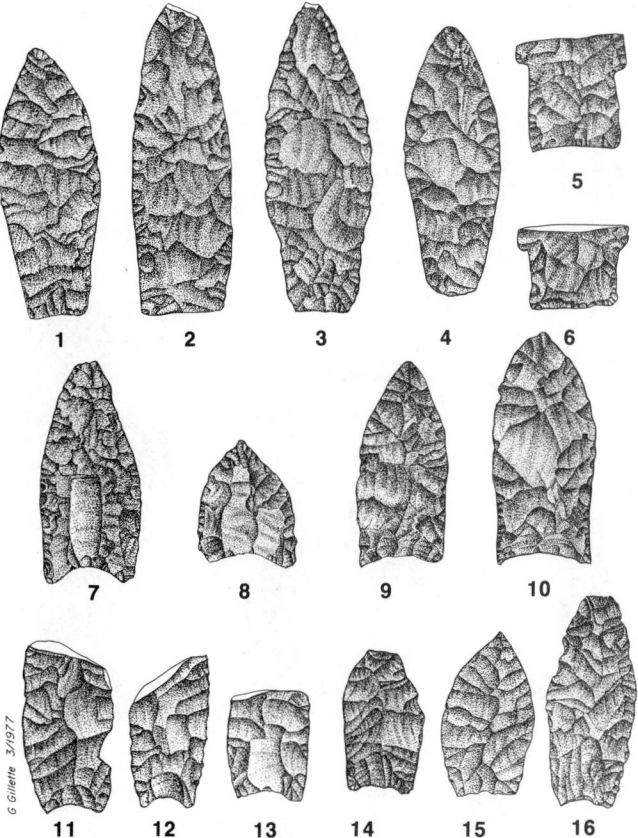

1-10, after Prufer and Baby 1963:figs. 21, 23; 11-16, after Fitting, De Visscher, and Wahla 1966: fig. 6. drawings by G. Gillette.

Fig. 6. Paleo-Indian projectile point styles from Michigan and Ohio. 1-4, lanceolate points from the Sawmill site, Erie Co., Ohio; 5-6, square stemmed points from the Sawmill site; 7-8, fluted points from the Mathewson site, Hardin Co., Ohio; 9-10, unfluted lanceolate points from the Mathewson site; 11-16, projectile points from the Holcombe site, Macomb Co., Mich. Note short channel or thinning flake scars on 12-14, 16. Length of 1, 7 cm, rest same scale.

documented Late Archaic manifestations. The lowest level of the deep stratified Sheep Rock Rockshelter in Huntingdon County, Pennsylvania (Michels and Smith 1967; Michels and Dutt 1968), lacking culturally diagnostic artifacts, was dated 6920 B.C. ± 320 years (M-1909).* The next higher level was dated 5100 B.C. ± 250 years (M-1908) and contained two Kirk Corner-Notched points; this type is assigned an age of about 7000 B.C. in the Southeast (Coe 1964; Broyles 1966, 1971). The middle levels produced a bifurcated-base point, some untyped broad stemmed points, and some untyped corner-notched points, all of which could broadly be considered Early to Middle Archaic in age. The upper levels of the site ranged from Late Archaic to Late Woodland in age and affiliation.

Amateur archeologists working on Staten Island have excavated a number of sites with old Archaic living

* Radiocarbon dates cited in this chapter are given as reported by the testing laboratories, uncorrected for secular variation in production of carbon 14 as determined by calibration with the bristlecone pine chronology (Rippeteau 1973, 1974; Damon et al. 1974).

floors, some of which have been radiocarbon dated between 5310 and 7410 B.C. (Ritchie and Funk 1971, 1973). Associated projectile point types (fig. 7) include Kirk Corner-Notched, Kirk Stemmed, Hardaway Side-Notched, Palmer Corner-Notched, LeCroy Bifurcated Base, Kanawha Stemmed, and Stanly Stemmed, all of which are of Early to Middle Archaic provenience in the Southeast (Kneberg 1956; Coe 1964; Broyles 1966, 1971). Artifacts from the deepest occupation levels at the Ward's Point site were dated 6300 B.C. ± 140 years (I-5331) and 5310 B.C. ± 125 years (I-4512). Unfortunately, on all the Staten Island sites several of the point styles occurred together on one level, whereas in Southeastern sites they occurred individually in separate levels. This suggests some mixture of components on the Staten Island sites.

Two dates of about 5400 B.C. have been obtained for basal levels of the stratified Harry's Farm site, on the Delaware River in New Jersey; a fragmentary broad stemmed point similar to the Kirk Stemmed type was in one of these levels (Kraft 1975). A date of 5570 B.C. was reported for the deep, stratified Rockelein site on the Delaware River in northernmost New Jersey. Bifurcated-base points and points similar to the Kirk Corner-Notched type were found in the same level as the hearth. In higher levels a group of Morrow Mountain-like points was dated 3330 B.C. (Dumont 1974).

Also on the upper Delaware River, Early Archaic materials have been recovered in place above a Paleo-Indian level at the Shawnee-Minisink site near East Stroudsburg, Pennsylvania; the artifacts include bifurcated-base, side-notched, and corner-notched points; end scrapers; and large bifaces (McNett and McMillan 1974).

Basal levels of the stratified Neville site in Manchester, New Hampshire, produced points resembling the Stanly Stemmed and Morrow Mountain types (defined on the Piedmont by Coe 1964) and radiocarbon dates ranging from about 3400 to 5800 B.C. The Stanly-like points have been designated Neville points (Dincauze 1971).

The lowest levels of the stratified Sylvan Lake Rockshelter near Poughkeepsie, New York, contained a small assortment of broad side-notched, broad stemmed, and triangular points and other items (fig. 8) dated 3720 B.C. ± 75 (Dic 208), 4030 B.C. ± 120 (I-2599), and 4610 B.C. ± 100 (Y-1655) (Funk 1965, 1976). In the same general region (the lower Hudson Valley) dates of 3700, 3900, and 5000 B.C. were obtained on the lower levels of oyster-shell middens on Haverstraw Bay, unfortunately without diagnostic artifact associations (Brennan 1962, 1972, 1974).

A fall-winter campsite, the McCulley No. 1 site on Charlotte Creek in east-central New York, yielded broad-side-notched Otter Creek points (Ritchie 1961), scrapers, and other tools (fig. 9), dated 3780 B.C. ± 110 years

N.Y. State Mus., Albany.

Fig. 7. Early Archaic artifacts from the Ward's Point site, Staten Island, N.Y.: 1-2, Kirk stemmed points; 3, broad stemmed point; 4, damaged bifurcated-base point; 5-6, LeCroy bifurcated-base points; 7-9, Kanawha stemmed points; 10, small stemmed point or drill; 11-12, side scrapers (12 is convergent scraper); 13, small spoke-shave scraper; 14, end scraper; 15, flake tool with two retouched edges forming a beak; 16, flake knife; 17, ovate biface knife; 18, small oval chopper; 19, large stemmed chopper; 20, bifacially chipped and partially ground celt. Materials: 1-2, rhyolite; 3, 5, 7, 10, siltstone; 4, 6, 8, 9, 12, 16-17, gray flint; 11, 13-15, Normanskill flint; 18-19, sandstone; 20, felsite. Length of 1, 4.8 cm, rest same scale.

(I-5524) (Funk and Hoagland 1972). A very similar assemblage from lowest levels of the Shafer site near Breakabeen, New York (fig. 10), has been dated 4340 B.C. ± 100 years (Dic 218) (Wellman and Hartgen 1974).

Excavations in the upper Susquehanna Valley have provided the first clear evidence for Early to Middle Archaic populations in upstate New York. The basal occupation on the stratified Gardepe site near Wells Bridge has one carbon-14 reading of 7430 B.C. ± 100 years (Dic 261) on hearth charcoal; a bifurcated-base point from the same level may have been associated. Another enigmatic component, so far consisting only of notched pebble netsinkers and flint chips, has been dated 5090 B.C. ± 120 years (Dic 248RR) in the basal zone of the Munson site, West Oneonta (Funk and Rippeteau 1976). Further work during the summer of 1975 at the Russ site near Wells Bridge (fig. 11) disclosed several buried living floors that produced characteristic Early to Middle Archaic artifacts, including Kirk Stemmed and Kirk Corner-Notched points, broad-bladed indented-base stemmed points similar to the Neville type, various untyped forms, and tool assemblages that include unusual varieties of end scrapers, side scrapers, and chopperlike tools. The Neville-like points were radiocarbon-

dated 5930 B.C. ± 145 years (Dic-474), 6010 B.C. ± 215 years (Dic-473), and 6270 B.C. ± 420 years (Dic-475).

The oldest dates so far available for the Archaic in Canada range from about 3600 to 5500 B.C., obtained from sites of varying affiliation in coastal Labrador (Harp and Hughes 1968:44; James A. Tuck, personal communication 1974). The situation there is not strictly comparable with that in upstate New York or New England, because different ecologies are involved.

Despite the influx of new data on artifact assemblages and radiocarbon dates, it should be noted that the bulk of information on the Early to Middle Archaic comes from the southern and coastal parts of the Northeast. This distribution conforms to quantitative studies of the occurrence of characteristic projectile point types in surface collections in New York State (Funk and Rippeteau 1976).

The apparent south-to-north gradient in the incidence of Early to Middle Archaic traces in the Northeast is in accordance with hypotheses proposed by Fitting (1968b) and Ritchie (1969a, 1971). Both postulate that substantial Archaic colonization north of the Ohio Valley and equivalent latitudes was correlated with the northward advance of deciduous forests into regions formerly occupied by predominantly coniferous forests, during the

22

Fig. 8. Artifacts of the Archaic stage from deep levels of the Sylvan Lake Rockshelter. 1-14, from lower levels of stratum 2, represent Vosburg Laurentian occupation: 1-6, Beekman triangle points. 7, Brewerton eared triangle point; 8, Brewerton eared-notched point; 9-10, Vosburg points; 11, large side-notched point; 12, large triangular point or knife; 13, large corner-notched point; 14, ovate or trianguloid biface. 15-18 from deep pocket of stratum 2: 15, point with squated tangs and rubbed base and notches reminiscent of Otter Creek and Brewerton eared-notched types; 16, broad stemmed point similar to Neville type; 17, point or knife fragment; 18, chipped slate knife. 19-28 from stratum 3: 19, Otter Creek-like point; 20, side-notched point displaying some attributes of Otter Creek type (rubbed base and notches); 21, Beekman triangle point; 22, Brewerton eared-notched point; 23, untyped stemmed point; 24, biface knife; 25, end scraper; 26, grooved pebble hammerstone; 27-28, bone awls. Materials: 1, 3-5, 7-9, 11-12, 15-16, 19-21, 24, gray to black flint (Normanskill variety?); 2, 10, 13-14, 23, 25, quartzite; 17-18, 22, slate. Length of 1, 4.0 cm, rest same scale.

Hypsithermal climatic episode. Prior to that time (8000-5000 B.C.) the coniferous forests with their low carrying capacity for deer and other game constituted an unfavorable environment for hunters and gatherers (Butzer 1971:144-150). Although this population-resources model has been disputed by some archeologists, there is no denying the extreme paucity of Early to Middle Archaic manifestations relative to Late Archaic materials in upstate New York and New England. It seems clear that sampling factors alone do not account for the difference.

Floral and faunal remains associated with some of the Middle Archaic components confirm the existence of essentially modern conditions—Ritchie's (1969a:32) "oak-chestnut-deer-turkey biome"—at the time of occupation. The deer, raccoon, turkey, and other deciduous-forest species were present in the refuse from early levels at Sheep Rock (Guilday and Parmalee 1965), Sylvan Lake (Funk 1965, 1976), and the Haverstraw Bay shell middens (Brennan 1962, 1972, 1974). Charred butternuts were found in hearths at the McCulley No. 1 site and were associated with the lowest level at the Munson site.

A tentative reconstruction of the northeastern Archaic sequence from 8000 to 3000 B.C. (fig. 12) would begin in Pennsylvania, on Staten Island, in the southern tier of upstate New York, and westward to southern Michigan, with sparsely distributed Early Archaic groups using projectile-point styles similar to those of the Southeast. The types would have included Palmer, Kirk, Cypress Creek (related to Kirk), and various bifurcated-base forms, collectively dated between 7410 and 5310 B.C. on Staten Island (Ritchie and Funk 1971). Presumably each type occupied its own time level and was shared by all contemporary human groups on a regional or areal basis (despite the seeming coexistence of several types in the Staten Island sites). Further, some of the sequences of types may represent evolutionary lineages, for example, the development of the bifurcated-base form through several individual types, ending in the Stanly Stemmed

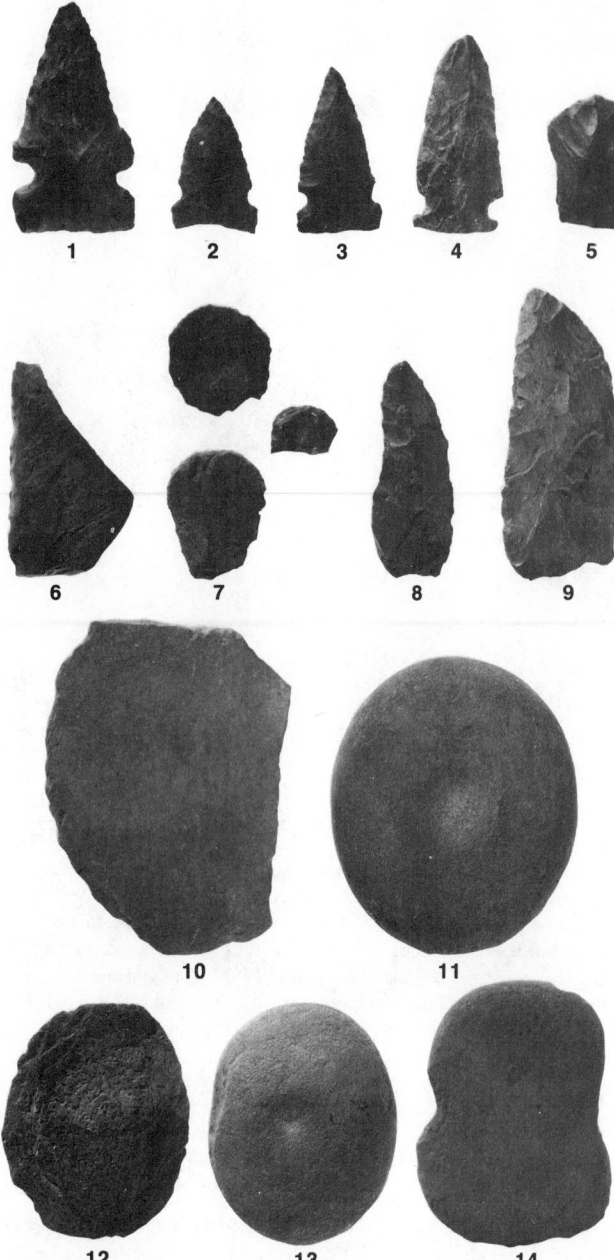

Fig. 10. Excavations at the Shafer site, Schoharie Co., N.Y. Upper occupation zone (Lamoka phase) and lower occupation zone ("Early Laurentian") are visible in the long profile, as are hearth features containing stone slabs.

Fig. 9. The late Archaic (Early Laurentian) assemblage from the McCulley No. 1 site. 1-3, Otter Creek points; 4, Brewerton side-notched point; 5, bifacially retouched flake knife; 6, side scraper; 7, end scraper; 8, lanceolate knife; 9, biface preform; 10, crescentic edge "chopper"; 11, anvil stone; 12, ovate bifacially chipped "chopper"; 13, bipitted "nutting" stone; 14, net sinker. Materials: 1-9, eastern Onondaga flint; 10-11, 13-14, sandstone; 12, gray-wacke. Length of 1, 7.5 cm, 2-9 same scale; width of 14, 10.8 cm, 10-13 same scale.

type, as hinted by the Saint Albans site data (Broyles 1966, 1971).

Tool kits in the Southeastern sites include biface knives, heavy bifacial "choppers," drills, and uniface end and side scrapers; all but the biface "choppers" occur on

Staten Island. Projectile points heavily predominate in the assemblages of both areas, probably reflecting a hunting emphasis, in contrast to the predominance of unifaces on most Paleo-Indian sites (where most hunting gear may have been lost or discarded at kill sites, outside the main camps). Refuse remains in deep levels at Sheep Rock Rockshelter (Michels and Dutt 1968) indicate some reliance of Early Archaic peoples on local fish and shellfish resources. It seems likely the unifaces and biface knives signify the continuance of the same activities (woodworking, boneworking, butchering) imputed to them in Early Hunter assemblages. These elements persisted through the full period of Archaic occupancy in the Northeast. A different note is struck by the "choppers"—large, roughly chipped sandstone or argillite tools, probably used in hide working (see fig. 7, nos. 18-19)—on the Staten Island sites and the ground stone celts (woodworking tools) at Sheep Rock and in the Staten Island assemblages (fig. 7, no. 20). These items appear to be lacking in the comparable Southeastern inventories, so may have occurred earlier in the Northeast than elsewhere. Ground stone tools such as grooved axes are rare on the Southeastern sites and are first recorded about 5000 B.C. with the possible exception of a "hematite adz" at Graham Cave, dating to about 7700 B.C.

In the formal characteristics and frequency of hearths, the relative abundance of fire-shattered stones (perhaps reflecting the practice of stone-boiling food), and the predominance of projectile points in most assemblages, the Staten Island sites are typical of Archaic sites in general and in contrast to the great majority of eastern Paleo-Indian sites. In Early and Middle Archaic times, seasonal rounds were doubtless as much a part of economic life as in Late Archaic times.

Early Archaic traces identified by means of projectile-point types are of extremely low incidence in upstate New

24

N.Y. State Mus., Albany.

Fig. 11. View of north profile of section W6S39 at the Russ site, Locus 2, Delaware Co., N.Y. Plow zone, living floors, and Feature 27 are marked by tags. Feature 27 occurred in a deep occupation zone that produced artifacts of Early Archaic affiliation, dated between 5930 and 6270 B.C.

York, New England, and the western Great Lakes, as a probable consequence of unfavorable early Holocene environmental conditions. Of this group, bifurcated-base points are by far the most numerous. By 6000 B.C. ameliorating conditions in the regions mentioned may have permitted moderately extensive occupancy by small populations using these points, which have been radiocarbon dated between 6200 and 6800 B.C. in West Virginia (Broyles 1966, 1971).

The next horizon suggested by the data is represented by the Stanly Stemmed points on Staten Island; the probably related small, broad stemmed Neville points and tapered-stemmed Morrow Mountain-like Stark points from the Neville site, New Hampshire (Dincauze 1971); and the Russ site, New York; the Morrow Mountain-like points from the Rockelein site, New Jersey (Dumont 1974); and the small assortment of stemmed and corner-notched points from middle levels at Sheep Rock Rockshelter in Pennsylvania (Michels and Smith 1967; Michels and Dutt 1968). These types probably date to the Middle Archaic period, between 6000 and 4000 B.C., despite the relatively late age reading of 3330 B.C. at Rockelein.

Though reasonably common throughout New Hampshire and other New England states, the Neville and Stark types seem rare in New York, Connecticut, and Pennsylvania, where there are some specimens in collections. A restricted surface site in the Mohawk Valley has produced a number of Neville points, side scrapers, and biface knives. At the Sylvan Lake Rockshelter, a small broad stemmed point resembling the Neville type (fig. 8, no. 16) was positioned near a hearth dated 4610 B.C. ± 100 years (Y-1655) (Funk 1976). The lithic tool kit associated with Neville and Stark points in New Hampshire included thin biface knives, drills on reworked

points, and retouched flake scrapers including end scrapers. The Stark assemblage also included atlatl weights and grooved axes. Again, the prevalance of projectile points is interpreted to signify continued emphasis on the chase, though the location of Neville site on a major falls of the Merrimack River suggests fishing may have been an important activity.

Some "firsts" for this time level, in terms of present data, include the utilization of marine shellfish (Brennan 1974) and the introduction of the notched stone netsinker.

In the next time period of 4000 to 3000 B.C., larger broad side-notched points, often with concave base, squared tangs, ground base, and ground notches, seem to have predominated. These are exemplified by the side-notched points from the Shafer and McCulley No. 1 sites (fig. 9, nos. 1-4) and from lower levels at Sylvan Lake (fig. 8, nos. 15, 19, 20) and by similar points from Archaic levels in the Dutchess Quarry Cave (Funk et al. 1969:fig. 4, items 19, 20). These points are either identical with or very similar to Otter Creek points, the diagnostic type of the Vergennes phase of the Laurentian tradition (Ritchie 1961:40-41, 1965:84-87, 1968).

The broad side-notched styles, especially the Otter Creek type, strongly resemble the Raddatz points of Wisconsin, found in deep levels of the stratified Raddatz Rockshelter where they are radiocarbon dated 3241 B.C. and estimated to range in age from 4500 to 1800 B.C. (Wittry 1959a). There are also morphological affinities with Big Sandy points, described on the basis of work in Tennessee (Lewis and Lewis 1961); Graham Cave Side-Notched, defined in Missouri (Logan 1952); and similar styles from deep levels of other sites in the Midwest (Fowler 1959).

As with older types, there is good reason to believe that these points diffused into the Northeast from a hearth in the Southeast and Midwest. Impressionistically, they are associated with the Laurentian tradition in the minds of many archeologists. Yet the basic style to which Otter Creek, Big Sandy, Raddatz, and other forms belong is older, in the South, than any dated Laurentian component. There appears to have been a south-to-north time slope, as no Laurentian site that meets the definition (Ritchie 1969:79-83, 1971) has been radiocarbon dated to an age greater than about 3300 B.C. This widely distributed projectile-point form appears to have been integrated into a number of regionally diversified complexes. Because of the considerable time depth, it does not strictly qualify as a horizon style (Willey and Phillips 1958:31-32). By 3000 B.C. in the Northeast, Otter Creek points, and certain other chipped stone types, were part of assemblages into which gouges, plummets, ground slate points and knives, and other classic Laurentian traits had been introduced.

Funk (1965, 1976) has argued that the Vergennes phase, hence the Laurentian tradition, ranged in age as

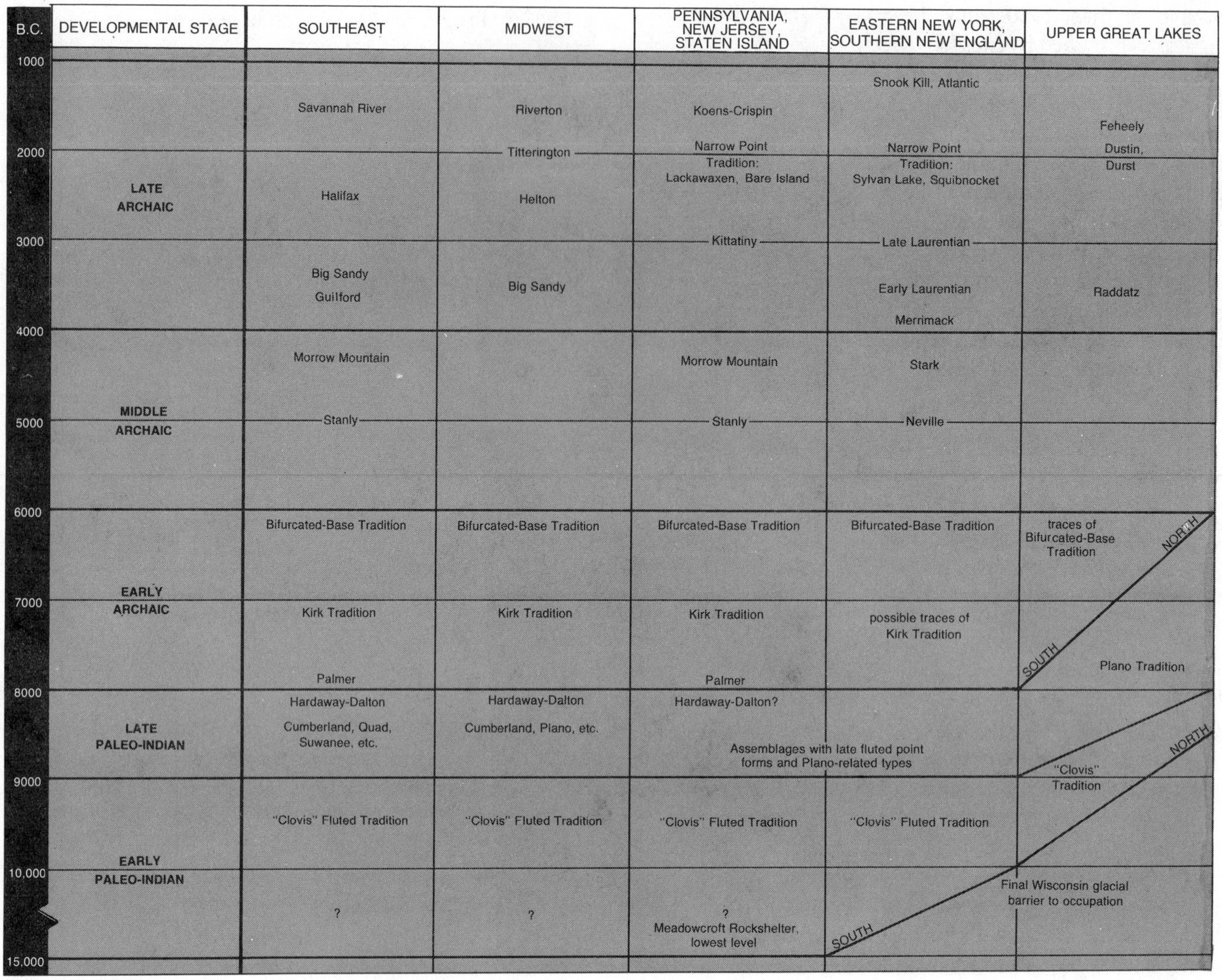

B.C.	DEVELOPMENTAL STAGE	SOUTHEAST	MIDWEST	PENNSYLVANIA, NEW JERSEY, STATEN ISLAND	EASTERN NEW YORK, SOUTHERN NEW ENGLAND	UPPER GREAT LAKES
1000					Snook Kill, Atlantic	
2000	LATE ARCHAIC	Savannah River	Riverton — Titterington —	Koens-Crispin Narrow Point Tradition: Lackawaxen, Bare Island	Narrow Point Tradition: Sylvan Lake, Squibnocket	Feheely Dustin, Durst
3000		Halifax	Helton	— Kittatiny —	— Late Laurentian —	
4000		Big Sandy Guilford	Big Sandy		Early Laurentian Merrimack	Raddatz
5000	MIDDLE ARCHAIC	Morrow Mountain —Stanly—		Morrow Mountain — Stanly —	Stark —Neville—	
6000		Bifurcated-Base Tradition	Bifurcated-Base Tradition	Bifurcated-Base Tradition	Bifurcated-Base Tradition	traces of Bifurcated-Base Tradition
7000	EARLY ARCHAIC	Kirk Tradition	Kirk Tradition	Kirk Tradition	possible traces of Kirk Tradition	
8000	LATE PALEO-INDIAN	Palmer Hardaway-Dalton Cumberland, Quad, Suwanee, etc.	Palmer Hardaway-Dalton Cumberland, Plano, etc.	Palmer Hardaway-Dalton?		Plano Tradition
9000				Assemblages with late fluted point forms and Plano-related types		"Clovis" Tradition
10,000	EARLY PALEO-INDIAN	"Clovis" Fluted Tradition	"Clovis" Fluted Tradition	"Clovis" Fluted Tradition	"Clovis" Fluted Tradition	Final Wisconsin glacial barrier to occupation
15,000		?	?	? Meadowcroft Rockshelter, lowest level		

Fig. 12. Paleo-Indian and Archaic cultures of the Northeastern area. The sequence in the Southeast is shown for comparative purposes, and major Late Archaic cultures after 3000 B.C. are included. The schematic nature of the chart has obscured some controversial details. Note that many cultures—Big Sandy, Kirk, Palmer—are named after projectile point types, even though frequently much is known about other cultural traits.

far back as 4000 B.C. This estimate was based largely on stratigraphic data for eastern New York and on typological affinities of Otter Creek points with Big Sandy and other Middle Archaic point types of the Southeast. Ritchie (1969:84-89) suggested an age of 2500-3500 B.C. In the absence of authentic Otter Creek points and other salient Laurentian traits in deep levels at Sylvan Lake, Ritchie (1971) suggested that these materials represent a Middle Archaic horizon, unrelated to the Laurentian tradition except possibly as a donor of some chipped stone elements. Similarly, he has stated (William A. Ritchie, personal communication 1971) that in the absence of gouges, plummets, and other Laurentian "core" traits, the McCulley site assemblage cannot be considered an expression of the Vergennes phase, despite the occurrence of Otter Creek points. The same can be said of the basal assemblage at the Shafer site (Wellman and Hartgen 1974).

Whether or not demonstrable Laurentian manifestations can be traced back to 4000 B.C., there is accumulating evidence that the Vergennes phase had an antiquity in excess of 3000 B.C., as indicated by a determination of 3290 B.C. on human bone from the Vergennes component at Allumette Island in the upper Ottawa Valley, Quebec (Clyde C. Kennedy, personal communication 1970), and by a date of 3120 B.C. ± 210 years (I-6349) for the Otter Creek No. 2 site in western Vermont (Ritchie and Funk 1973:340). The probable genetic relationship of the Vergennes phase to subsequent Laurentian complexes of the Late Archaic period is discussed in "Regional Cultural Development 3000 to 300 B.C.," this volume.

In this period of 4000-3000 B.C. hunting continued to draw heavily on male energies, though women must have contributed much to the larder through gathering of wild plant foods; the earliest clear-cut evidence for the harvesting of mast foods and the use of pitted "nutting stones" is provided by sites like McCulley No. 1. Also, the oldest bone and antler pools so far recovered in the Northeast were in lower Archaic levels at Sylvan Lake and Dutchess Quarry Cave, associated with Otter Creek–like points. Characteristic on this general time level are the exploitation of marine shellfish (Brennan 1962, 1972, 1974; Salwen 1970) and the manufacture and use of polished stone woodworking tools. The taking of freshwater fish and shellfish is evinced by fish bones and mussel shells in the lowest cultural levels at Sylvan Lake, demonstrating a continued exploitation of inland aquatic resources from Early to Middle Archaic times.

In the two millennia following 3000 B.C., numerous Late Archaic phases have been defined in New York, New England, and other parts of the Northeast. During this period the evidences of occupancy (such as number and size of sites and amount of refuse) are quantitively far greater than those of the Early and Middle Archaic periods. It is almost as if an "explosion" had occurred in population and/or intensity (stability) of occupation, and it is possible that this change was largely in response to environmental change, even though the climatic, floral, and faunal environment of the Northeast had evolved to an essentially modern configuration at least one to two millennia before (Funk and Rippeteau 1976).

Regional Cultural Development, 3000 to 300 B.C.

JAMES A. TUCK

To summarize the Northeastern cultures traditionally assigned to the late Archaic, Early Woodland, and in some areas "Transitional" periods requires the formulation of some broad constructs to unify the many particular archeological assemblages revealed by over a century of excavations. Using whole cultural traditions (Goggin 1949:17) means not considering merely one or two aspects of technology or even an entire technology but instead combining the study of technology with what can be inferred about subsistence and settlement patterns, art, aesthetics, religion, and whatever other cultural data have been recovered by archeologists. Thus may be defined a number of widespread cultural patterns. In many cases, these Late Archaic cultural traditions seem coterminus with what were, at the time of European contact, equally broad environmental zones as these have been defined by Dice (1943), Braun (1950), Kendeigh (1961), and others. For the most part, the traditions described herein take their names from these ecological zones.

It is likely that these environmental differences are one factor—perhaps even a major factor—responsible for the observed differences among the cultural manifestations. A second factor was communication or exchange networks, which often followed drainage patterns, ecological zones, or other natural features.

The Mixed Prairie-Hardwood Area of the Midwest

Important to Late Archaic and subsequent cultural development is the mixed prairie-hardwood forest of western Indiana, Illinois, and points south and west (fig. 1). The area is characterized by extensive grasslands interrupted by stands of oak and hickory trees. It is an excellent area for deer and elk, along with beaver, bear, raccoon, fox, squirrels, and other mammals, birds (notably the wild turkey, passenger pigeon, and migratory birds), and fish and shellfish. There is considerable evidence that this biome has existed since prior to 3000 B.C. (Winters 1969). In terms of interaction and exchange, this area might be lumped with an "interior riverine" or Mississippi drainage physiographic area.

The best known Late Archaic (actually Middle to Late Archaic) cultural manifestation in this area is the Helton culture known from the important Koster site in southern Illinois and several stations in Indiana (Kellar

1956:45–49), notably the McCain site (R.K. Miller 1941). In every case the distinctive stone and bone components of this assemblage have been found within the mixed prairie-hardwood zone.

Struever's excavations at the Koster site revealed an intensive Helton culture occupation estimated at between 5000 and 3000 B.C. (Stuart Struever, personal communication 1972) but probably near the recent end. Preliminary data indicate that hunting, fishing, and collecting all figured in the economy of the Helton people, and specialized tools and weapons for all three modes of subsistence have been found. These include distinctive side-notched projectile points of two types. The first type resembles and clearly is related to the Big Sandy points of the southern Mississippi basin from the fourth and fifth millennia B.C. These are virtually identical to projectile points used slightly later by the earliest occupants of the Lake Forest zone to the north. Therefore, the upper Mississippi Valley may have been a "staging area" from where took place the first intrusive Archaic occupation into the beech-maple-hemlock Lake Forest area surrounding much of the Great Lakes. Slightly higher in the Helton culture level at the Koster site, hence presumably more recent, but still associated with the earlier varieties, are a number of long, narrow projectile points called Helton points. These range from unnotched to examples with well-defined broad side notches (see R.K. Miller 1941 for examples of both types). The association of these two types is not fortuitous, for it recurs elsewhere, notably at the McCain site in Indiana.

Subsistence and settlement patterns for this culture have yet to be precisely defined. Deer, small mammals, turkey, and migratory birds were clearly hunted. Fishing is indicated by refuse bone, notably catfish of various sizes and ages (Stuart Struever, personal communication 1972), as well as by fishhooks cut from deer phalanges found throughout Horizon 6 at the Koster site. Channel-grooved metates and irregular manos were doubtless used to grind nuts and perhaps other vegetable food. The entire pattern may have been similar to the Riverton culture settlement system suggested by Winters (1969).

Other diagnostics of this cultural complex include a suggestion of wattle-and-daub houses with thatched roofs, large roasting pits, and racks for smoking or drying fish. Chipped stone, in addition to the projectile points

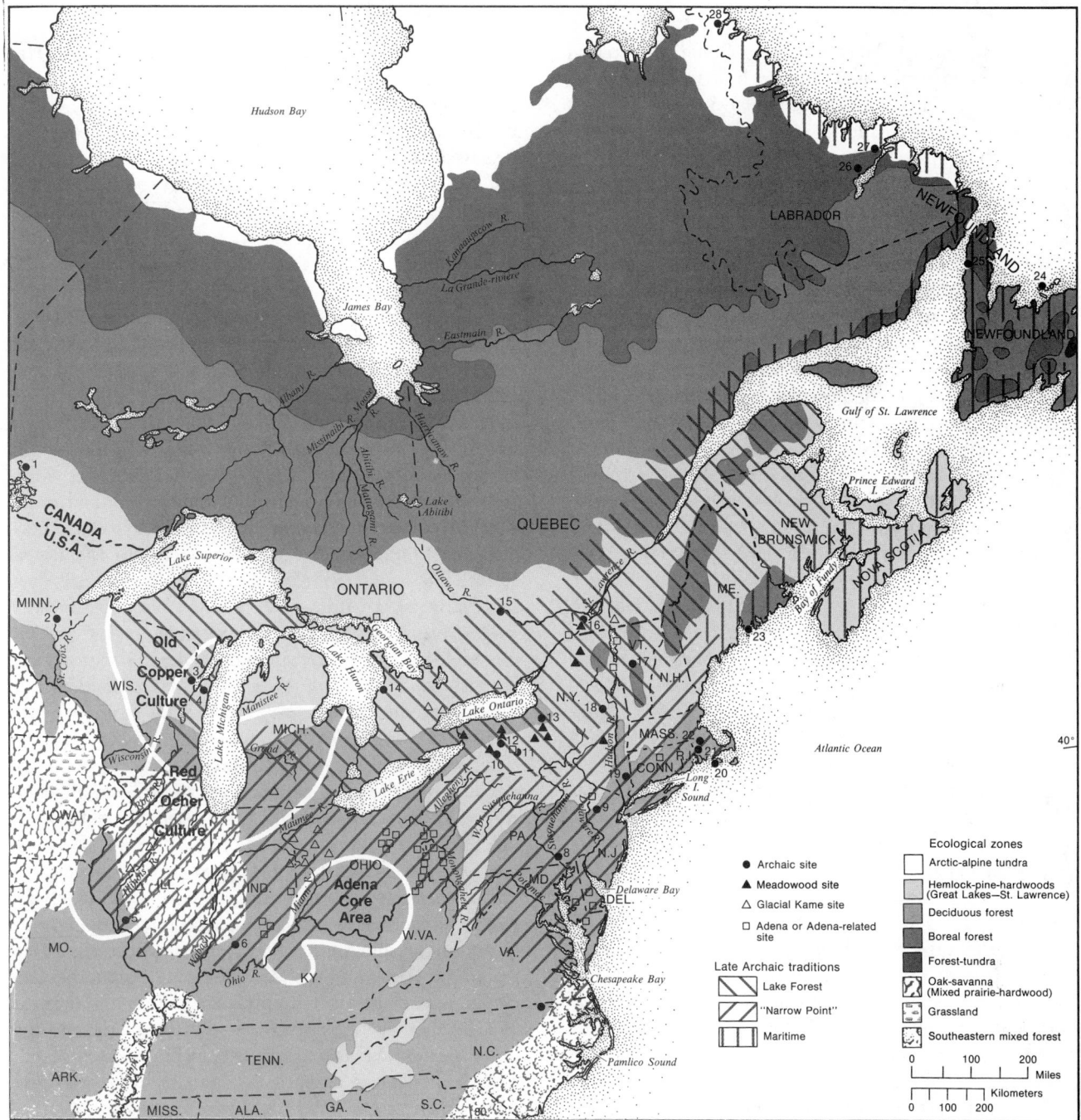

Fig. 1. Approximate archeological culture areas and Archaic sites. 1, Eaka; 2, Petaga Point; 3, Oconto; 4, Renier; 5, Koster; 6, McCain; 7, Gaston; 8, Kent-Halley; 9, Miller Field; 10, Scaccia; 11, Lamoka Lake; 12, Morrow; 13, Brewerton; 14, Inverhuron; 15, Morrison's and Allumette Islands; 16, Pointe-aux-Buissons; 17, KI; 18, Bent; 19, Sylvan Lake Rockshelter; 20, Hornblower II; 21, Bear Swamp; 22, Wapanucket; 23, Nevin or Blue Hill; 24, Twillingate Island; 25, Port au Choix; 26, Lake Milville; 27, Hamilton Inlet; 28, Saglek Bay. Ecological zones after Kendeigh 1974.

described above, includes end scrapers and drills with bases like the projectile points, small flake perforators or gravers, and various knife varieties. Both full-grooved and three-quarter-grooved axes of various sizes are also known and are occasionally made from hematite. Limestone and hematite plummets are also common, with a single biconical perforation in one end. These intergrade with rough perforated pebbles, which as a group may

have served as weights for bolas or some similar bird hunting device.

Outstanding and distinctive is the Helton culture bone component, here described from the Koster site but virtually duplicated at the McCain site (R.K. Miller 1941) and elsewhere (Kellar 1956) in the prairie-hardwood area. Crutchlike bone pins, flat pins or pendants, all decorated with chevron or other rectilinear designs, bird-bone beads, antler flakers, bone awls (some with spatulate ends), and turtle shell cups or bowls comprise the distinctive elements of these assemblages.

Interments were made in small cemeteries near the edge of the village and consisted of flexed burials in shallow graves generally unaccompanied by mortuary offerings. No physical anthropological data are presently available.

The origin of some elements of the Helton culture, notably projectile points, seems to lie farther south in the Mississippi drainage. Grooved axes (Webb 1946: 271-272; Webb and Haag 1947) and many of the distinctive bone artifacts also have cognates to the south, suggesting some sort of historical relationship; but its precise nature and the direction of time slope, if any, remains to be determined.

The Helton culture is supplanted by the little-known Titterington culture (Titterington 1950) comprising a variety of large lanceolate and stemmed projectile points seemingly unrelated to those in the earlier Helton culture; drills from reworked stemmed points; conical antler points; some perforated stones (perhaps related to the plummetlike stones from earlier complexes); and, from burials in Illinois-Missouri, bannerstones or atlatl weights, quite unlike anything from earlier cultures.

Following this the Riverton culture (Winters 1969) appears in the Wabash and other interior river valleys. Its artifact complex seems to reflect the blending of a midwestern and southern tradition with a lithic tradition derived from the east.

The Great Lakes–Lake Forest Archaic

The Great Lakes–Lake Forest tradition is found primarily in the Great Lakes drainage systems. It is usually associated with beech-maple-hemlock and maple-basswood forests, often with a fair amount of oak, walnut, butternut, and pine. Two principal factors seem to account for the development of a distinctive "Great Lakes" or "Lake Forest" Archaic: a biome distinguishable from the boreal forest to the north and the mixed hardwood forest to the south, and a communication or exchange network comprising the Great Lakes drainage rather than adjacent interior-riverine drainages.

Neither the name "Great Lakes Archaic" nor "Lake Forest Archaic" is entirely suitable, since the tradition is precisely coterminus with neither. The term "Great Lakes–Saint Lawrence," which most accurately describes the forest type, is too cumbersome. Therefore, following James B. Griffin (personal communication 1972) and Papworth (1967) the term "Lake Forest" will be used here, despite its poor fit with the cultural remains.

Differences between the fauna of the boreal forest and the Lake Forest areas were of some economic importance. Differential distribution of raccoon, cottontail rabbit, gray squirrel, and Virginia deer, which are more common in the Lake Forest than the Boreal Forest (Hall and Kelson 1959), and caribou and moose, which are more common in the Boreal Forest, no doubt accounts in part for different adaptive patterns in the two areas. Not nearly so clear a distinction can be made when comparing the Lake Forest area with adjacent southern regions where opposum, lynx, and porcupine have differential distributions but were probably not economically significant to the extent that they would radically alter hunting patterns from one area to the other.

Fish may present a more significant distinction between the Lake Forest and more southerly regions. Both in historical and Archaic times there seem to have been differences in methods of taking fish as well as in fish species. While hook-and-line fishing was known throughout the Northeast in early historic times, harpoons and leisters were restricted to the Great Lakes and more northern areas, while the simple spear was found in the south. Hauled seines and gill nets seem also to have been confined to the Great Lakes drainage and the Boreal Forest (Rostlund 1952:296, 293, 291). This fact is even more striking in Late Archaic times, when hook-and-line fishing, usually with bone hooks manufactured from deer phalanges, was common south of the Lake Forest region, for instance at Lamoka Lake, New York (Ritchie 1932), the Koster site, Illinois, and in the shell mounds of the Southeast (Webb 1946:287, 89-90) while the "Laurentian" and "Old Copper" cultures of the Lake Forest Archaic seem to have confined their fishing implements primarily to harpoon, leister points, and the gaff, which need not be used with hook and line. Admittedly, copper fishhooks are known from the Upper Great Lakes but few of these can be assigned with absolute certainty to the Late Archaic. Exceptions are one specimen from Oconto (Ritzenthaler and Wittry 1952), another from the Inverhuron site, and a third from Eaka, a Shield Archaic component (James V. Wright, personal communication 1973). Whether this is somehow related to a dependence upon species such as northern pike, which were probably more easily taken by spearing than by hook and line, remains uncertain but is a suggestive possibility. The change in fishing technology from hook and line to leister and harpoon may have been one adaptive feature responsible for the apparent increase in population in the Lake Forest area around 3000 B.C.

Evidence now seems to indicate clearly that there was not only a distinctive set of resources but also a distinctive culture type, or whole cultural tradition, in the Lake Forest zone and Great Lakes–Saint Lawrence drainage from about 3000 to after 1000 B.C. that was internally homogeneous and at the same time distinct from surrounding cultural traditions. Various elements of the Lake Forest Archaic doubtless have disparate origins, although the distinctive adaptive pattern of hunting, fishing, and collecting, of course, developed in the Lake Forest area from which it takes its name. The earliest manifestation of this tradition consists of a lithic assemblage including: large, thick, more or less parallel-sided projectile points with concave bases (usually ground), well-defined side notches, and squared tangs; end scrapers with similar bases and possibly made on broken points (fig. 2); expanded base drills; and occasionally bifacial "knives." Projectile points of nearly identical form are found throughout the area and are known by various type designations. The fact of their near identity and close dating (at least as presently understood) across this wide area bespeaks a rapid dispersal of this lithic complex, if not of people, into the Lake Forest area; and the large number of reported stations, especially when compared to the very limited earlier Middle Archaic remains, suggests an actual movement of people into the Lake Forest area sometime slightly prior to 3000 B.C.

These northern projectile point forms are virtually identical to Godar points from the Koster site in southern Illinois (T.G. Cook, personal communication 1972), Graham Cave notched points from Missouri (Scully 1951:8), and the true Middle or Late Archaic Big Sandy points (Lewis and Kneberg 1961:36, 37) from Tennessee, Arkansas (Schambach 1970:134–138), and elsewhere in the southern Mississippi drainage, where they may have had their origin. (These points must be distinguished from those superficially similar but smaller and unrelated so-called Big Sandy points dated to about 7000 B.C. in Alabama—De Jarnette, Kurjack, and Cambron 1962.) With the chipped stone assemblage the resemblance between the Lake Forest Archaic and cultures to the

south ceases; further adjustment and elaboration must be found within the Lake Forest area.

Around 3000 B.C. there seem to be two indigenous industrial developments taking place in this area. In the east a ground-stone industry including axes, adzes, gouges, ulus, ground slate knives or spears combined with the chipped-stone complex common to most of the Lake Forest area formed what Ritchie (1965:79ff.) has termed "Laurentian." A western equivalent centered in the native copper-producing areas of the Upper Great Lakes has long been known as the "Old Copper Culture" (McKern 1942; Ritzenthaler and Wittry 1952; Baerreis, Daifaku, and Lundsted 1954). Although the invalidity of the Old Copper culture concept has been pointed out on several occasions it is nonetheless true that *part* of an Old Copper *industry* (cf. Miles 1951), is of Late Archaic provenience. Objects such as awls, "crescents," gouges, socketed and tanged spear points, adzes, "spuds," and beads (fig. 3) are associated with chipped-stone forms nearly identical (in form and in time) with Laurentian; and many of the copper forms appear to be functional equivalents of the ground-stone artifacts in Laurentian.

Evidence for the subsistence base of the Lake Forest Archaic rests heavily upon inference from implement types. Ritchie (1969a:92) postulates that "hunting seems clearly to have constituted the primary subsistence activity" of Laurentian, since "high chipped stone projectile-point frequencies characterize all sites and phases of the Laurentian tradition". Recent discoveries in Vermont at two Vergennes phase stations (the "classic" early Laurentian expression in the East) provide support for

after Ritchie 1965:pls. 26–27, 29, 32–33.
Fig. 2. Lake Forest Archaic artifacts. a, Ground slate double-edged knive or point, KI site, Rutland Co., Vt.; b, Otter Creek projectile point, KI site; c-d, Brewerton scrapers; e, Brewerton eared-notched projectile point; f, Brewerton side-notched projectile point; g, Brewerton stone gouge. Length of a, 6.9 cm, rest same scale.

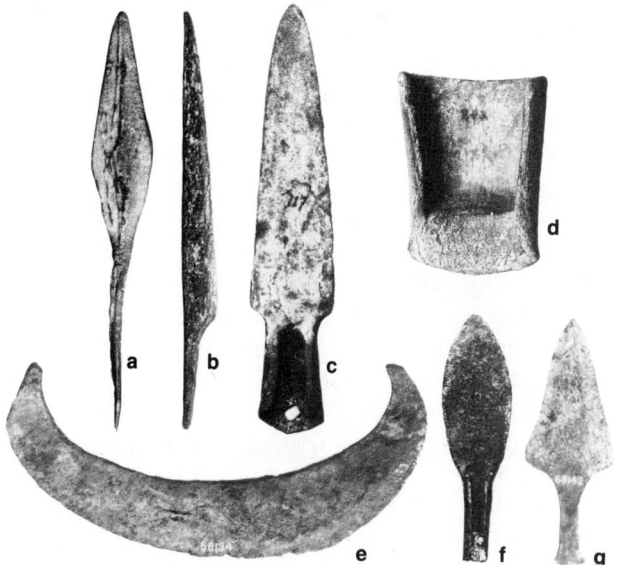

Field Mus. of Nat. Hist., Chicago.
Fig. 3. Old Copper culture tools of copper. a, spearpoint with tang; b, knife; c, f, socketed spearpoints; d, socketed ax or "spud"; e, crescent-shaped knife; g, spearpoint with flat tang. Length of a about 19.5 cm, rest same scale; sizes of b and d are estimated. (See also Quimby 1960:fig. 24-28.)

this assumption (Ritchie 1968). The first preserved faunal remains from a site of this culture consisted almost entirely of the remains of Virginia deer, black bear, and beaver (William A. Ritchie, personal communication 1972), the presumed quarry of all eastern (and, by extension, western) Lake Forest Archaic peoples. Fishing supplemented the red meat obtained by hunting and the taking of birds as suggested by some bird-bone artifacts from, for instance, the Brewerton sites in New York (Ritchie 1940:46, 80). Notable, but not surprising, is the low frequency of mortars, pestles, and other implements for the preparation of vegetable foods when Lake Forest assemblages are compared to those from the oak-hickory-chestnut area where these trees contributed significantly to the subsistence economy.

In the western reaches of the Lake Forest area (the Old Copper homeland) there is even less direct evidence for subsistence patterns, since most known stations are cemetery sites and the few living sites excavated, for instance, that at Petaga Point, Minnesota (Bleed 1969), contained no preserved faunal remains. However, the percentages of weapon categories remain about the same as in the east, and probably subsistence activities were roughly similar.

Little evidence for settlement pattern or social organization exists among the Lake Forest Archaic people, but a small circle of post molds at the KI site in Vermont (Ritchie 1965:85) suggests at least a temporary shelter framed with poles and covered with bark or skins. Almost certainly small, mobile bands, probably with a well-defined territory, constituted the local unit. Seasonal movements within the territory were probably determined by the locations of various subsistence resources— mammals, fish, birds, plant food—as they became available.

As for technology, the chipped stone industry— notched projectile points, end and side scrapers, drills and knives—was restricted and utilitarian. The copper and ground-stone industries show considerable geographic variation although their distributions clearly overlap (cf. Kennedy 1967), and there is considerable functional similarity between artifacts of the two different raw materials. The stone and copper artifacts also indicate the presence of industries involving productions in perishable materials. Gouges, axes, and adzes bespeak a well-developed woodworking technology, probably including dwelling frames, wooden bowls, weapons, perhaps dugout canoes, and a host of similar objects. Fine-eyed needles and bone and copper awls suggest the manufacture of tailored clothing and footwear. Heavy bone needles from the Brewerton sites are similar to snowshoe needles recently in use, and snowshoes would certainly have had an adaptive advantage in the Lake Forest zone.

Objects of personal adornment, decoration, and recreation are not common in the Lake Forest Archaic (even at Morrison's Island, in the Ottawa valley, most grave offerings were utilitarian), although they become increasingly common after about 1500-1000 B.C. During the Laurentian and Old Copper periods there were decorated bone whistles, occasionally preserved by favorable conditions (Ritzenthaler and Wittry 1952:211, 213; Kennedy 1967:108), and simple bone and copper beads. The use of red ocher in ceremonials and perhaps as body paint is also indicated.

The culture history of the Lake Forest Archaic is not completely understood and perhaps never will be because of destruction of sites by various agents. After about 3000 B.C. there seems to have been a number of regional variations—at least in the artifact complex—mostly of a fairly minor nature and probably indicating little basic change in subsistence. Owing to the lack of excavated habitation sites in the west and to Ritchie's long and intensive investigations in New York and its environs, the eastern variations are much better known than their western counterparts. In the extreme eastern portion of the Lake Forest, the classic Vergennes complex or phase gives way to the Vosburgh phase, dated about 2500 B.C. (Ritchie 1958:67). Vosburgh is characterized by distinctive corner-notched points, a diminution in the percentages of ground slate points and other polished stone tools, and a persistence of other chipped-stone implement types from the earlier Vergennes phase (Ritchie 1965:83-87). In central New York State, and perhaps in southern Ontario, the Vergennes complex evolved into a broadly similar complex typified by Brewerton side- and corner-notched and eared triangle projectile points, a much diminished ground slate industry, and a persistence of earlier chipped-stone scrapers and knives. In the west changes seem to reflect the same minor alterations in the tool kit but in this area there is a somewhat greater suggestion of local or regional evolution of implement styles toward the succeeding Early Woodland forms.

The Maritime Area

The coastal portions of northern New England, the Maritime provinces of Canada, Newfoundland, and Labrador may be regarded as a distinct culture area during Late Archaic times (Tuck 1970, 1971a). Despite the fact that this area transects several biotic provinces, there is considerable homogeneity in the resources important to man throughout this area. Caribou were the dominant cervid, with the possible exception of moose or elk in the south. Black bear, beaver, fox, and smaller mammals are also present over much of the area. The most important resources are those connected in one way or another with the sea, and it is the exploitation of these resources that give the Late Archaic culture of this area its distinctive flavor. Sea mammals including seals (harp, ringed, harbor, gray, and bearded seals), walrus (cf. Mansfield 1963; Scheffer 1958), porpoises, and various whales are all available throughout this area, although the precise species of seal vary with the particular region. Finally, sea birds form a distinctive resource as do marine and anadromous fishes.

Within this area there developed a distinctive cultural tradition that is best known from the second and third millennia B.C., although evidence from the Strait of Belle Isle region in southern Labrador suggests beginnings earlier than 5000 B.C. (McGhee and Tuck 1975). Known originally from the "great boneless cemeteries" of Maine and the Maritime Provinces, cemeteries or habitation sites have been recognized in Maine, New Brunswick, Nova Scotia, Newfoundland and Labrador, and eastern Quebec (Snow 1969; Sanger 1971; Bourque 1975; Tuck 1976a; McGhee and Tuck 1975). A great deal has been inferred about the people responsible for these sites, whose way of life has been called the Maritime Archaic tradition, because in every area where it is known at least a part (and in most cases a major part) of the culture was oriented toward the sea.

The uniformity of the material culture over this area is evidenced by chipped stone, ground stone, bone artifacts (where they have been preserved), and magical or decorative objects such as concretions and quartz pebbles, red ocher, and the general pattern of burial ceremonialism. In addition, there must have been similar, although not identical, exploitative patterns over this vast area.

The subsistence base was formed by the birds, fish, and mammals mentioned above, with local variations such as the harpooning of swordfish in the southern Maritimes and New England (perhaps a transference of an older sea mammal technique); the availability of some moose or wapiti in the same area; and some variations in the birds, fish, and sea mammals locally available. Overall, however, an exploitative pattern not unlike that reconstructed from findings in Newfoundland and Labrador (Tuck 1971a; Fitzhugh 1972) was probably found over the entire area. Early spring was probably spent on the coast where seals and other sea mammals were available on the pack and landfast ice, especially in the north and surrounding the Gulf of Saint Lawrence where the harp seals could be taken in almost unlimited quantities. The summers were probably also spent on or near the coast, where sea mammals would continue to be available, albeit in somewhat diminished quantities, but where fish—especially Atlantic salmon—plant foods, and various nesting and moulting birds could have been taken. At the first snow, there was a retreat from the coast to favored hunting locations, especially to crossing places of caribou, where these animals could be easily slaughtered as they crossed streams or lakes. During the remainder of the winter, single caribou, beaver, or other mammals provided red meat for the diet until spring when a return to the coast signaled the beginning of another cycle.

The technology of this tradition includes implements and weapons (fig. 4) for all the above economic pur-

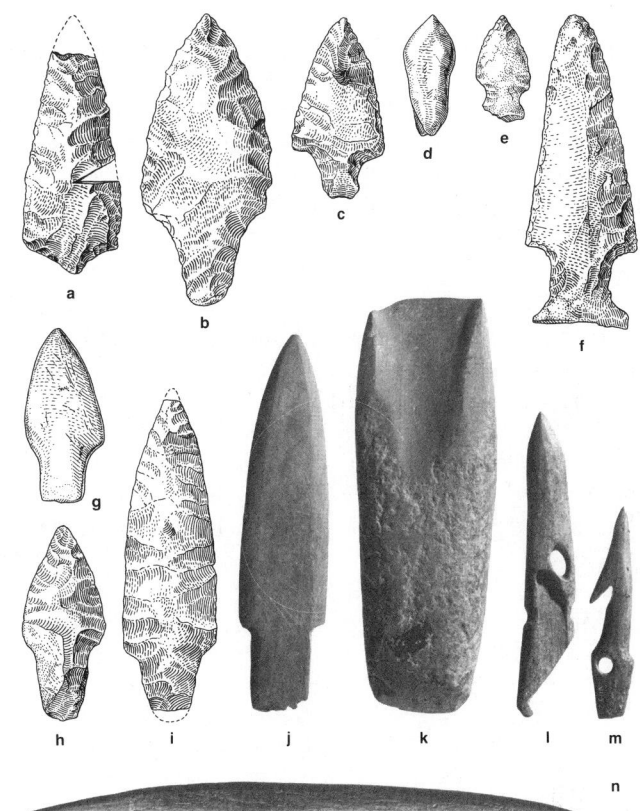

Newfoundland Mus.: a, HeCi-6:1, 2; b, HdCk-8:1; c, GcBk-5:52; d, GcBk-9:5; e, GcBk-13:114; f, GcBk-13:555; g, GcBi-7:491; h, GcBi-22:12; i, GcBi-22:325. Dept. of Anthr., Memorial U. of Newfoundland, St. John's: j-n.

Fig. 4. Maritime Archaic artifacts. Points from Labrador: a, Early Maritime Archaic, about 4500 B.C. gray chert, Ballybrack Hill-5; b, Middle Maritime Archaic, about 4000 B.C., Ramah chert, Nain; c-d, Sandy Cove phase, about 3500 B.C., c, gray chert, d, ground slate, Groswater Bay, Hamilton Inlet; e-f, Black Island 2, about 2000 B.C., rhyolitic chert, Groswater Bay; g-i Rattlers Bight phase, about 1800 B.C., g, ground slate; h-i, Ramah chert, Groswater Bay. From Port au Choix, Newfoundland; j, ground slate spear or lance; k, ground slate gouge; l, bone toggling harpoon; m, bone barbed harpoon; n, bone leister point. Length of b 7.7 cm, rest same scale.

suits—toggling and barbed harpoons, slate and bone spears and lances, barbed bone leister points and bird dart tips—as well as for processing the catch. In the last category are chipped-stone knives, bone knives, beamers, and fleshers. All this, of course, implies hide- and bone-working industries; the latter, at least, is confirmed by the weapons, tools, and decorative objects from Port au Choix, Newfoundland, and the Blue Hill site in Maine (Douglas S. Byers, personal communication 1969). Stone was manufactured into spears and lances as well as into axes, adzes, and gouges, which in turn bespeak a heavy woodworking industry, the products of which probably included frames for shelters, weapon and tool handles, boats, dugout canoes, and wooden bowls.

Art, aesthetics, magic, and religion are particularly well represented in Port au Choix material, from the Nevin site in Maine, and to a lesser extent from other cemeteries throughout Maine and the Atlantic provinces.

Hunting magic consisted of the wearing of charms and amulets made from the feet and bills of diving birds, the claws and teeth of seals, bears, caribou, fox, or beaver and less easily interpreted objects of crystal, stone, and bone. All imply a well-developed magico-religious system on the North Atlantic coast that was also expressed in the spectacular burial ceremonialism. The lavish use of red ocher, inclusion of both utilitarian and esoteric grave offerings (often in great quantities), and possibly some orientation of the cemeteries toward the east may be the earliest manifestation of a "basic core of religiousity" found throughout the Northeast.

In almost all respects this tradition is distinct from those in surrounding areas—the Shield Archaic in the boreal forest, the Lake Forest Archaic of the Great Lakes, and Late Archaic cultures of southern New England. Contacts with other areas occurred of course; but as with other regional traditions, cultural exchange within an area was much greater than that between areas.

The history of the Maritime Archaic tradition is less well known than that of some contiguous traditions but enough is known to make some educated guesses. A series of carbon-14 dates clearly establishes the Maritime Archaic in the north by the end of the fourth millennium B.C. A series of second millennium B.C. dates from Port au Choix and Twillingate Island, Newfoundland, and from Maine and the Maritimes places the florescence of this tradition during the second millennium B.C., after which it disappears as a cultural entity and its relationship to succeeding cultures is somewhat unclear. While the earliest manifestations of this complex may be in Maine and the Maritime provinces, their antiquity in this area remains to be demonstrated, probably because rising sea level has obliterated seashore living sites. Fitzhugh's (1972) Sandy Cove complex from Lake Melville, dated prior to 3000 B.C., seems to be a full-blown Maritime Archaic habitation component containing typical chipped- and ground-stone artifacts. Moreover, red ocher is common at the type site; and distinctive Ramah chalcedony, a translucent, pebbly-grained gray silicate, was utilized extensively. Saglek Bay material fills the chronological gap between this early manifestation and the later complexes dated during the second millennium B.C., when the Maritime Archaic burial florescence seems to have taken place.

The second millennium B.C. saw a southward wasting of Maritime Archaic peoples. From 1940 B.C. at Saglek Bay to 1800 B.C. at Hamilton Inlet, to 1280 B.C. at Port au Choix, Newfoundland, there is a clearly indicated north-south time slope with the Indian peoples retreating southward, perhaps as a result of environmental change combined with the press of a northern Pre-Dorset Eskimo population that made its appearance in northern Labrador by at least 1880 B.C. only 60 years after the latest Maritime Archaic determination for the same stratified site.

South of the Saint Lawrence a similar fate seems to have befallen these people, for they are replaced after 1000 B.C. by what appear to be groups of interior hunters who moved to the coast and began to utilize the resources there, most conspicuously shellfish. These people may have had their origin in the Canadian Shield, from where they slowly spread to the open pine and spruce forest of Maine and the Atlantic provinces. Furthermore, there is growing evidence that the Shield Archaic tradition can be traced forward in time to the present-day Algonquian-speaking peoples of the Northeast—Micmac, Maliseet, Abenaki—in an essentially unbroken sequence. The movement to the coast of these Algonquian speakers either occurred after the Maritime Archaic peoples vacated the area or, alternatively, may have been partly responsible for their demise. Continuity between the recent inhabitants of the Maritimes and the older "shell mound" people was long ago recognized, as was the distinctiveness of these cultures from the underlying Maritime Archaic complexes (Moorehead 1922:143-145, 149-150). Recent researches have not demonstrated any relationship between the Maritime Archaic people and later Algonquians.

The Mixed Forest Areas of the Northeast

South of the Great Lakes-Saint Lawrence formation, home of the Lake Forest Archaic people, the flora and fauna of the Northeast are remarkably homogeneous. Including even the mixed prairie-hardwood area, the oak-hickory-chestnut-deer-turkey biome was the environment of Late Archaic peoples on both the Atlantic coastal and interior riverine drainages. Adaptive patterns, and to a certain extent artifact types and varieties, are similar in both major physiographic areas. Some likenesses are probably a result of convergence, but others clearly bespeak persistent contact between the coastal and interior areas, via the many rivers whose headwaters nearly meet in the Appalachian Mountains.

The Atlantic Coast

The northeastern portion of the Atlantic coastal plain is a narrow strip of flat land extending southward from New Hampshire. In the south, the change to the Piedmont is abrupt and marked by a fall of several hundred feet, while elsewhere the low hills of New England rise slowly, almost imperceptably, to the north.

Mammals important to man include the Virginia deer, black bear, raccoon, opossum, woodchuck, eastern and New England cottontail rabbits, otter, gray squirrel, red and gray foxes, and perhaps the wolf. Fowl included the wild turkey, grouse, passenger pigeon; the migrating waterfowl of the eastern flyway were available in the fall and spring; and resident populations of sea birds no doubt also added to the larder. The sea provided fish species ranging from alewives to swordfish, all of which were at least occasionally taken; sea mammals—seals, porpoise, and occasionally small whales—were utilized; and shellfish provided at times a sizable percentage of the protein diet of coastal peoples. Freshwater and anadromous species of fish were also utilized, including the common and short-nosed sturgeon, shad, eels, suckers, chain pickerel, and walleyed pike.

This biome seems to have been one of the most conducive to human utilization of any area of the Northeast. Moreover, its resources set it apart considerably from surrounding areas to the north, northwest, and to a lesser extent to the west and south. These differences in environment seem to have been roughly paralleled throughout the Late Archaic by similar differences in the culture complexes found in them.

There is an increasing body of data indicating that at least a moderate-sized population was already living on the northern fringes of the coastal plain during Middle (Dincauze 1971) or even Early Archaic (Ritchie and Funk 1971) times. Moreover, although its locus is in the northern extreme of the coastal plain, Dincauze (1971) provides reasonably sound evidence that the dominant Late Archaic culture—the so-called Narrow Stemmed Point tradition—was the product of an in-place evolution dating back to Middle Archaic times. Clear stratigraphic evidence for such an evolution is presently lacking from the Middle Atlantic states, but on typological grounds, based upon mixed surface collections, a similar evolution is more than likely. Finally, there is some evidence that the narrow stemmed Halifax points of the North Carolina coast (Coe 1964:108–110) may be a southern expression of this unnamed cultural tradition.

The economic patterns within this area are becoming fairly well known although a major question still exists as to whether there was a year-round coastal adaptation and a small complimentary interior adaptation or whether coastal and inland stations represent seasonal camps of the same people. Ritchie's (1969) Martha's Vineyard data do not reliably indicate a winter Archaic occupation at any site; and even if such were the case, the insular location of these stations might present a special case. Data from "upriver" sites that are cognates of the coastal stations will most likely show a predominance of winter sites away from the coast, with the summer sites occurring in the shell heaps surrounding the tidal marshes, ponds, and bays of the Atlantic coastal plain from New Hampshire to North Carolina.

Regardless of seasonality, the people of this tradition undoubtedly were grouped in the small, mobile bands so often postulated for late Archaic peoples. Also, regardless of whether a coastal/inland movement took place annually, each group probably moved seasonally within its own territory. The subsistence base was clearly the Virginia deer with lesser amounts of meat taken from the other species of birds, fish, and mammals mentioned above (cf. J. Watters's summaries of faunal remains in Ritchie 1969a).

Nonperishable remains from the Late Archaic in southern New England and the Middle Atlantic states do not suggest an elaborate technology. The lithic complex consisted predominantly of several varieties of narrow, thick-bladed projectile points with broad side notches or a thick stem, nearly always made from quartz and known by various names; triangular projectile points or knives (fig. 5), choppers, hammerstones, and polished adzes; and at least one cylindrical pestle (Ritchie 1969a:216). Bone work seems even less elaborate than the stone industry of these people, despite excellent bone preservation in coastal shell middens. For instance, Ritchie (1969) found only splinter and deer ulna ("pistol grip") awls associated with his Squibnocket complex, the southern New England version of the Late Archaic on the coastal plain.

Art and ornamentation are virtually unknown from this period on the coast, unless such crafts were confined to now-disintegrated substances such as wood, bark, or skins. Similarly, there is little evidence of magical or religious beliefs for this period with the probable exception of Robbins's (1960) discovery of the mortuary complex at the Wapanucket site in eastern Massachusetts.

The culture history of the Late Archaic on the coastal plain is imperfectly known; what follows is based upon excavations from southern New England and may not precisely represent the situation in the Middle Atlantic states.

Dincauze's (1971) hypothesis that these cultures were derived from a resident Middle Archaic base, while not accepted by all researchers, seems to account best for the

after Ritchie 1969:pls. 12, 43.
Fig. 5. Atlantic Coast artifacts. a, Arkosite chopper from Vincent site; from Hornblower II site: b, plummet or sinker; c–e, Squibnocket Triangle quartz projectile points; f–i, Wading River quartz points. Length of a 7.5 cm, rest same scale.

emergence of Late Archaic cultures along the Atlantic coast. With the basic economy established prior to 3000 B.C., the primary cultural changes during the following three millennia seem to consist, with two notable exceptions, of the development of local variants of the same general tradition. Ritchie's Squibnocket complex and Wading River component and Funk's (1965) Sylvan Lake complex are three such regional expressions.

The two exceptional events mentioned above appear to be brief incursions of other cultures or peoples during the second and third millennia B.C. First, there seems to have been an incursion of Laurentian or Lake Forest Archaic traits or people into southern New England sometime before 2000 B.C. Their presence at the base of the stratigraphic colum on Martha's Vineyard (Ritchie 1969) was first interpreted to indicate their temporal priority over all other Late Archaic cultures; but other evidence, including a date of 2690 B.C. associated with narrow stemmed points from the Bear Swamp site in Rhode Island (Staples and Athearn 1969:5) and Dincauze's sequence in the Merrimack valley, clearly indicates that people of this indigenous tradition were in coastal southern New England both before and after the appearance of typical Laurentian forms on the coast. Moreover, Laurentian-like notched points appear in Dincauze's (1971:196) Neville site in a position suggesting a date of 2500–2000 B.C.

A second unusual case is evidenced most clearly at the Hornblower II site on Martha's Vineyard (Ritchie 1969:19, 32–34), where the stratigraphy of a narrow-stemmed-point-producing shellheap is interrupted by an assemblage including broad-bladed projectile points and other elements attributable to the so-called Transitional period. In addition to the distinctive artifact complex, the absence of evidence of shellfish over large areas of the intrusive cultural stratum further serves to distinguish it from under- and overlying strata. Immediately above this horizon there reappeared the typical shell midden, containing narrow stemmed and triangular points, which some evidence suggests persisted until after the advent of the first ceramics in southern New England.

While migration theories for which a point of origin, route of movement, time slope, and destination cannot be clearly demonstrated must be advanced with caution, it seems hard to explain these two anomalies in the southern New England sequence without invoking some unusual dispersion of people or ideas and artifacts that were later supplanted by traditional cultural forms.

The Interior-Riverine Area

The "narrow stemmed point" cultures are not unique to the coast (although they may have developed there), for elements of these complexes, especially the distinctive projectile points, comprise portions of several local or regional Late Archaic cultures of the interior of the Northeast.

A more or less continuous distribution of projectile point forms and other lithic elements cognate to the coastal series is found from the Hudson valley (Funk 1965:146–148) and southern New York State (Ritchie 1961:29, 37–38) through Ohio and into Michigan and as far west as Illinois (Binford and Papworth 1963:105; Winters 1969:41). Although found in several cultural assemblages, the narrow-bladed, thick stemmed, and sometimes broadly side-notched forms with a broken or unfinished base are constant throughout. The adaptive pattern seems common across this area but certain elements of artifactual assemblages from various regions show marked dissimilarities, probably reflecting varying degrees of communication among peoples of different drainage systems.

Most distinctive is Ritchie's (1932) Lamoka culture (fig. 6), the first Archaic component to be isolated, which contains, in addition to characteristic Lamoka points, the distinctive beveled adz, thousands of notched pebble net sinkers, hollow mortars and manos, and an elaborate bone industry—with fishhooks, gorges, socketed deer astragali, flakers, daggers, notched pendants, and occa-

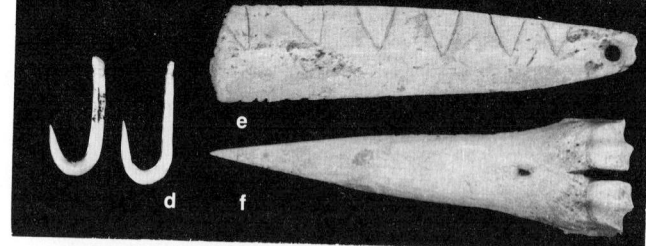

after Ritchie 1965:pls. 12, 14, 17, 19, 21.

Fig. 6. Interior Riverine artifacts, Lamoka phase. a–c, Chipped stone points; d, bone fishhooks; e, antler pendant; f, bone awl; g, mortar with deep concave surface, pestle on top. Length of a 5 cm; b–f, same scale; length of g 44 cm—not to same scale.

sional traces of painted red stripes. The bone work has no known parallels in the immediate area but there are some cognate forms in the Kentucky and Tennessee shellmounds. Moreover, the Lamoka Lake-type station has yielded ample evidence of houses framed with upright poles, probably the first clear indication of a central-based wandering community pattern in the Northeast.

Between the coast and the western New York center of the Lamoka Lake culture there is a continuous distribution of cognate lithic artifacts. Although lacking most of the Lamoka diagnostics (for example, the beveled adz and elaborate bone industry) these people were undoubtedly akin to the loosely related interior riverine cultures. Occasionally there is more than a scatter of projectile points upon which to base these conclusions. Funk's (1965) Sylvan Lake complex, described on the basis of excavations at the Sylvan Lake Rockshelter, includes: "Sylvan stemmed" projectile points (small thick points clearly related to Lamoka, Normanskill, and Wading River points), Lamoka points, expanded base drills, bannerstones (notched at Sylvan Lake, drilled at other probably related stations such as the Bent site—Ritchie 1965:127), ovate knives, antler flakes, and evidence of a winter hunting economy. Fishing and collecting of nuts are in evidence at other stations. The Kent-Halley site on Bare Island in Pennsylvania (Kinsey 1959) presents a similar assemblage, with the addition of certain traits, such as steatite vessels presumably borrowed from adjacent areas to the south.

Ritchie's River phase (1965:124–130) should also be equated with this tradition. The best-known component of this phase, the Bent site in the Mohawk valley, has produced literally thousands of narrow stemmed projectile points that are identical to many specimens from western New York. In addition to specific artifact similarities, large fire beds presumably used to roast acorns in order to remove the tannic acid indicate extensive use of vegetable foods, as with other manifestations of this tradition.

To the west of New York one of the most completely described cultures related to this poorly defined interior riverine adaptation is the Riverton culture of the Wabash valley in eastern Illinois (Winters 1969). It is firmly dated between 1600 and 1000 B.C.; hence, it is one of the latest manifestations of this tradition and clearly indicates the east-to-west time slope of narrow stemmed projectile points. The points of this assemblage, called Merom expanding stem and Trimble side-notched (Winters 1969:41–42), are morphologically similar to eastern variants and are probably related. Other elements of the assemblages, not surprisingly, show affinities with Mississippi Valley cultures.

The immediate area of exploitation by Riverton culture people in eastern Illinois was prairie interspersed with stands of oak-hickory forest at the time of European exploration, and Winters (1969:7–10) has offered convincing evidence that conditions were essentially the same 3,500–3,000 years ago. Bird and mammal remains indicate a typical "Carolinean Biotic Province" fauna, which is also not vastly different from that found by early visitors to the Midwest.

The settlement and subsistence system inferred for the Riverton culture revolves around at least three seasonal camps: a spring-summer occupation of river banks where shellfish, fish, turtles, and migratory birds might be taken; a fall camp (such as the Koster site in southern Illinois) where acorns, hickory nuts, and other vegetable foods were gathered; and winter hunting camps where deer and other mammals and birds were hunted (Winters 1969).

In addition to the stone projectiles mentioned above the technology of the Riverton people included: flaking tools, awls, scrapers, abraders, sewing and weaving tools, gravers, drills and unusual micro-perforators, chisels, and other fabricating implements suggesting hide and skin working, woodworking, as well as bone and stone working (which products are directly represented in Riverton culture shell middens); additional weapon parts such as conical antler points; knives, net weights, an antler spoon, shredders, nutting stones and manos, used in food preparation or acquisition; bone beads, shell and animal tooth pendants, "cloud blower" smoking pipes, flutes, and box turtle rattles.

The origin of this culture remains unclear for as Winters has said (1969:107), it "certainly cannot be traced to any earlier Archaic occupation of the Wabash Valley on the basis of present evidence." He suggests an intrusion of shellfish gatherers from the "Mid-Continent tradition" (Lewis and Kneberg 1959) of the Mississippi drainage. The lack of relationships with the distinctive Helton culture, seemingly confined to the same prairie-hardwood zone, has been remarked upon by Winters and others, although the intervening and little-known Titterington culture may provide some links between the two. Similarly, there is little evidence of the relationship of these people to succeeding Early Woodland peoples.

The Susquehanna Tradition and "Transitional" Cultures of the Late Archaic

The so-called Transitional cultures of parts of the Northeast were first defined by Witthoft (1949:10–11) as characterized by steatite bowls; early ceramic vessels of similar form; heavy thick soapstone gorgets; and broad, stemmed projectile points and drills. The area of dispersion of these traits, now recognized for many parts of the Northeast, seems to center on the coast of the Middle Atlantic states and to radiate there from along the coast and major river systems. From one of these, the Susquehanna, is derived another name for these related complexes, the Susquehanna tradition.

Sites are located along the major rivers and their tributaries; although known, in the early stages coastal stations are not common. After 300 or 400 years had passed, later Susquehanna tradition peoples on the coast (for example, Ritchie's Orient phase) had added shellfish as a significant dietary item. Red meat—especially that of the deer—probably continued to comprise a major portion of the diet of these peoples as it had done in this region during the earlier Late Archaic period, although Witthoft (1953:14) has postulated "a very distinct and marked change in every detail of material culture and way of life from earlier times in the Susquehanna Valley." The change in artifact forms is clear, but in view of the relatively stable environment throughout the Late Archaic period and the limited dietary evidence that is available, there seems no profound change in the way of life between these two cultures. Nevertheless, the rapid spread of Susquehanna tradition artifacts clearly implies some adaptive advantage; and the use of heavy and not easily transportable soapstone bowls may indicate a somewhat more sedentary existence.

Technology, on the other hand, shows evidence of considerably more change, with the replacement of narrow stemmed projectile points by larger, heavier, broad-bladed forms (cf. Ritchie 1961:53–54; Witthoft 1953:7–16). These were clearly used with the atlatl, for bannerstones or spearthrower weights are more common in the Northeast at this time than during any other period (Cross 1941–1956, 1:81–90; Regensberg 1970–1971; Kraft 1970:101–103). Soapstone bowls, oval to rectangular in plan, with flat bottoms and lug handles at each end (fig. 7) (cf. Ritchie 1959; Kraft 1970:105–112) also represent a technological innovation that must have greatly simplified vegetable food preparation, formerly carried out by the laborious stone-boiling technique in wooden or bark vessels. A final innovation is the appearance of plain, thick, poorly made ceramics, Marcey Creek Plain (Manson 1948:223–226; Kraft 1970:113–120), tempered with crushed steatite and fashioned to duplicate the earlier soapstone bowls. It is this local ceramic industry that makes sites of this culture truly "transitional," if the single criterion of the presence or absence of ceramics is accepted as characterizing, respectively, Woodland or Archaic cultures. (Stimulus from the Southeast for these ceramics is possible and even likely, but the invention of ceramics has often been repeated and may easily be indigenous to the Northeast and elsewhere in the New World.)

Art, ornamentation, and decoration have left little trace in Susquehanna tradition sites; but the use of red and yellow ocher in burial rituals (see Ritchie 1959; Dincauze 1968) implies possible use in daily life, and elaborately carved bannerstones and a single pointed bone pendant from the Hornblower II site on Martha's Vineyard (Ritchie 1969:34) combine to suggest that aesthetics was not neglected. Mortuary ceremonialism was well developed during this time, including both local and northern elements, and it is almost certain that hunting magic and other simple contagious magic had its place among these people.

The culture history of the Susquehanna tradition is complex and not yet fully understood. There seems little doubt that many elements, if not the entire complex, have their ultimate origin in the Southeast, where Savannah River broad points and soapstone bowl fragments have been dated at 1944 ± 250 B.C. at the Gaston site in North Carolina (Coe 1964:97) and similar broad-bladed projectile points have been dated to the fourth millennium B.C. in Florida (Bullen and Bryant 1965).

Koens-Crispin, Snook Kill, and Lehigh broad points (fig. 8), which may differ from one another only in the material from which they are made (Witthoft 1953; Kraft 1970), seem to be the earliest northern representatives of this tradition. R. Alan Mounier's (personal communica-

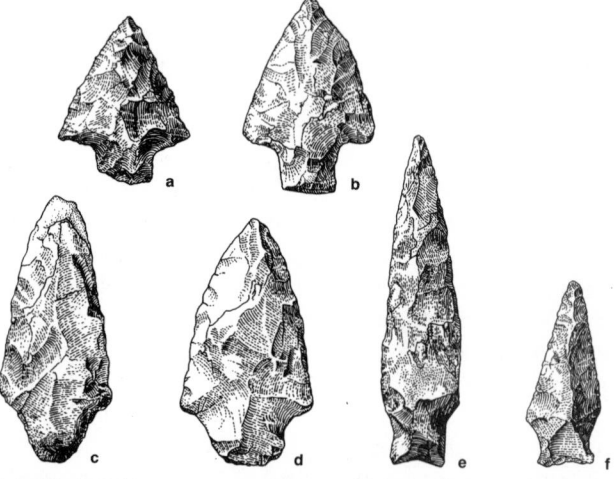

Dept. of Anthr., Smithsonian, Archeol.: a, 234215; b, 303905; c-d, 197329; e, 172839; f, 303905.

Fig. 8. Artifacts of the "Transitional cultures" of the Atlantic Coast. Broad, stemmed spearpoints: a, Lehigh Broad, Village site, Montgomery Co., N.Y.; b, Snook Kill, Great Bend, Susquehanna R., Va.; c-d, Koens-Crispin, Woodbury, N.J.; e-f, Orient fish tail, e, Northumberland Co., Pa., f, Great Bend, Susquehanna R., Va. Length of b 6.9 cm, rest same scale.

Dept. of Anthr., Smithsonian, Archeol.: 342083.

Fig. 7. Transitional or terminal Archaic reconstructed soapstone bowl with lug handles, Buck Mt., Buckingham Co., Va. Height 17.2 cm.

tion 1973) date of 1880 B.C. for related artifacts in New Jersey indicates their early position. Kraft's 1720 B.C. date for Snook Kill points conflicts with Ritchie's (1965:135) 1470 B.C. date. The more northerly position of Ritchie's date does not seem to account for this discrepancy, and the question of absolute chronology must await future clarification.

Following the initial appearance of these artifacts, there is evidence of a series of locally evolved descendent cultures that persisted for the better part of a millennium. A variety of clearly related projectile points, knives, and scrapers with consistently similar hafting modifications provides the best evidence of stylistic change, although "bannerstones," steatite vessels, milling stones, and mullers may one day provide a more complete basis of comparison.

The end of this local evolution is typified by the quartz Orient Fishtail points (Ritchie 1961:39), "serpent-head shaped" points (Witthoft 1953:22), and Hudson valley fishtail points. An essentially similar assemblage accompanies these projectile points, with the addition of two varieties of ceramics. The flat-bottomed Marcey Creek vessels have been reported from New Jersey (Kraft 1970:138), while on Long Island and elsewhere in the North a new style, Vinette I and related types (Ritchie 1959:37-39, 66-67), was introduced from the north. These conoidal-based pots, coil-made and malleated with a cord-wrapped paddle on both the interior and exterior surfaces, clearly represent a disparate ceramic tradition from the older and more southerly Marcey Creek bowls, although they may have been stimulated by them. Friable as they were, the Vinette techniques probably produced a more acceptable and durable form of ceramics than the older flat-bottomed molded bowls. It is a case of technology catching up with a new medium—an oft-repeated feature of technological development. Orient components have been dated at 1220 ± 120 B.C. at Miller Field (Kraft 1970:136) and between 1043 and 763 B.C. on Long Island (Ritchie 1965:164), a reasonably compatible series of dates.

In summary, then, this tentatively named Susquehanna River tradition arrived in the Northeast via the coastal plain during the early second millennium B.C., where it flourished until after 1000 B.C., meanwhile adopting or inventing the use of ceramic vessels and thereby marking the arbitrary transition from Archaic to Woodland cultures.

Early Woodland Culture

The definition of Early Woodland cultures in the Northeast has been one of the most perplexing, but perhaps least important, questions facing prehistorians for several decades. Presently the only clear criterion for distinguishing Terminal Archaic cultures from Early Woodland cultures is the presence of ceramics in the latter; however,

even this has not always been clear, for many Early Woodland sites are cremation burials containing no ceramics as part of the mortuary offerings. The distinctions between Early and Middle Woodland are somewhat more numerous but unhappily no less confusing (cf. R.J. Mason 1970).

There seem to be two indigenous Early Woodland cultures in the Northeast in addition to a somewhat different development in northern New England and the Maritime area of eastern Canada. These two locally evolved cultures appear to have had separate origins; but they held certain elements in common, notably thick, plain ceramics and an elaborate ritual system involving lavish burial practices. These cultures might properly be called "transitional" since they represent the people who produced the first ceramics in this area.

The first of these Late Archaic-Early Woodland cultures seems indigenous to the Lake Forest area and is a lineal descendent of the Lake Forest Archaic. Living sites of this period are extremely rare. No recognized living sites of the so-called Late Archaic Glacial Kame culture have been recognized. Burials pertaining to this manifestation have been found in both the Lake Forest and Prairie Peninsula zones, but such sites probably represent a religious "overlay" on existing indigenous cultures. The diagnostic artifact of these red-ocher-covered burials is the "sandal-sole" shell gorget (fig. 9), although copper adzes, round and rectangular shell gorgets, discoidal shell beads, galena nodules, and copper awls are regularly found in sites attributed to this somewhat equivocal culture (Cunningham 1948). In its eastern extremity, Ritchie (1965:134) reports a broken projectile point "suggesting the Meadowood type," which provides a positive link between this and the presumably later Meadowood culture of the Early Woodland in New York, Ontario, and Quebec. The Glacial Kame culture remains undated, although dates older than 1000 B.C. are suspected on the negative evidence of the lack of pottery associated with Glacial Kame burials.

The second related manifestation of this Late Archaic-Early Woodland period, and probably the one which most clearly demonstrates the continuity during the late second and early first millennia B.C., is the so-called Old Copper culture in the western Great Lakes (Baerreis, Daifaku, and Lundsted 1954; Ritzenthaler 1946; Ritzenthaler and Wittry 1952). Sites of this complex are also primarily cemeteries and little is indicated of the actual lifeway of these late Archaic-Early Woodland people.

The eastern equivalent of the late Old Copper and Glacial Kame cultures (perhaps a slightly later variant) is Ritchie's (1965:179-200) Meadowood phase, described on the basis of several cemeteries and small habitation sites throughout northern and western New York State. Additional sites are also known from adjacent southeastern Ontario and southern Quebec (Levesque, Osborne, and Wright 1964). Particularly important is the Pointe-

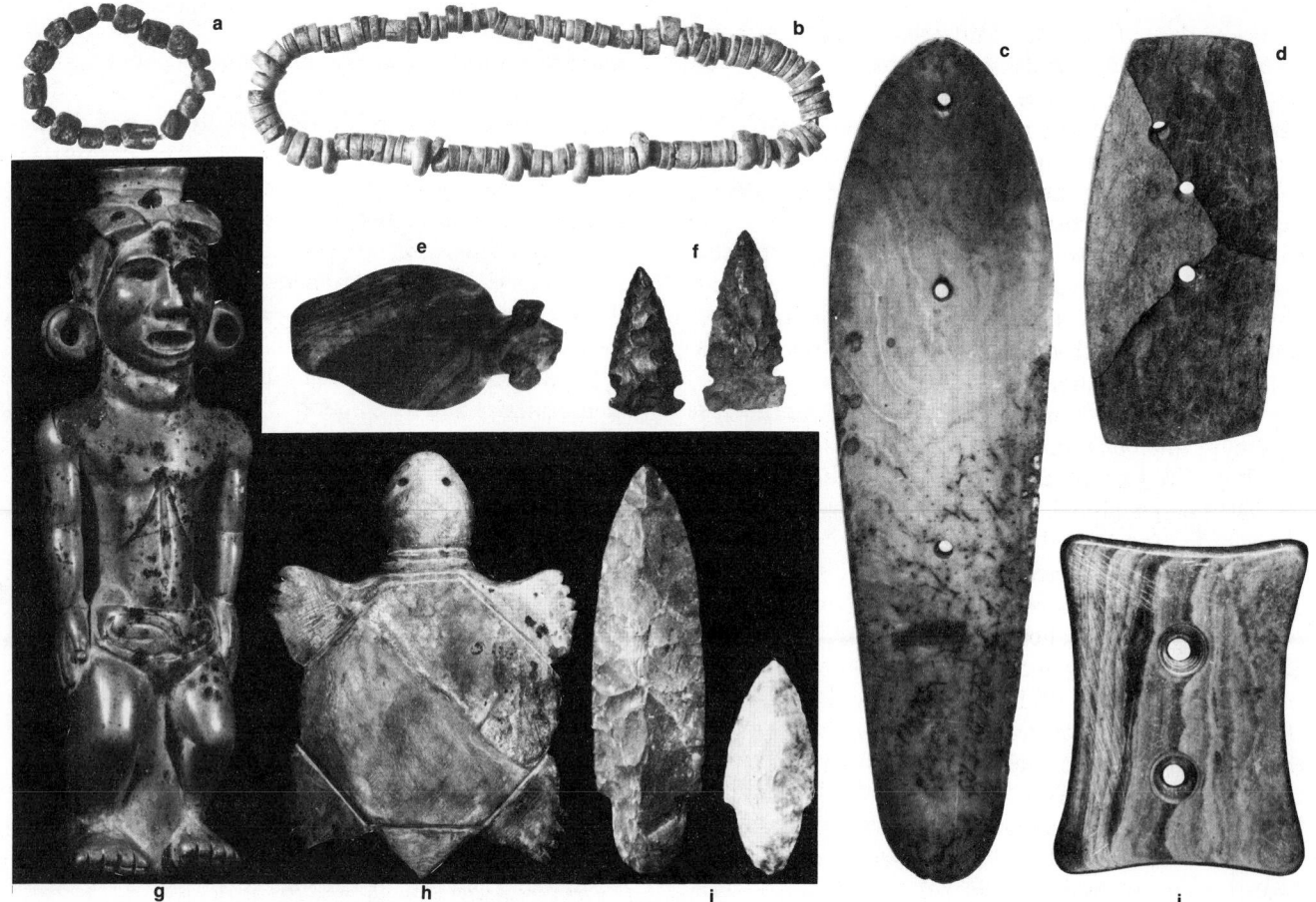

a-c, U. of Mich., Cunningham Coll.; d-f, N.Y. State Mus., Albany; g, Ohio Histl. Soc., Columbus; h-j, Carnegie Mus., Anthr. Center, Butler, Pa.

Fig. 9. Artifacts of the "Early Woodland" and Adena periods. Glacial Kame culture: a, barrel-shaped copper beads; b, shell or stone beads; c, sandal-shaped marine-shell gorget. Meadowood culture: d, stone gorget; e, birdstone of "pop-eyed" form with expanded, barred base; f, Meadowood type points (see Ritchie 1965:pl. 60). Adena culture: g, carved tubular stone pipe from Adena Mound, Ohio, with bowl between the feet and mouthpiece above the head; from Cresap mound: h, turtle effigy; i, Adena type points; j, gorget. Height of g about 20 cm, rest same scale.

aux-Buissons site near Montreal (Anonymous 1970: 7–19). The subsistence base was clearly hunting, fishing, and collecting and all indications are of economic pursuits not vastly different from their Archaic predecessors, who were probably their progenitors. Sites of the Meadowood culture are located on sizable streams and small lakes (Ritchie 1965:180) and related manifestations in the Upper Great Lakes are similarly situated in potentially rich hunting and fishing localities. It is doubtful whether there was any change at this time from the small bands that characterized the Late Archaic peoples in the same area, and evidence for year-round habitation of any single station is still lacking. A circular house made of posts driven into the ground and presumably covered with bark has been reported by Robert E. Funk (personal communication 1970) at the Scaccia site in western New York, which is to date the only evidence of house form from this culture.

Artifact complexes from these sites and those in the Upper Great Lakes include: distinctive thin triangular bifacial "blades" modified into side- or corner-notched projectile points, knives, and end scrapers and stemmed points in later phases in Michigan; conoidal-based ceramic vessels and cigar-shaped smoking pipes; bone awls, at least one bone harpoon, antler flakers; a fish net and net sinkers from the Morrow site in New York; occasional copper implements diminishing in frequency with increased distance from the Upper Great Lakes; and gorgets, "birdstones," and other exotic objects usually associated with burials (Ritchie 1965:182–189; Kochan 1961; Fitting 1970:74–75, 81–95).

While these developments from an Archaic base were taking place in the Lake Forest zone, other parts of the Midwest were feeling influences from the south and a limited amount of plant cultivation may have begun to take place, especially in connection with the Adena culture, although Adena is known primarily as a mortuary complex. Local cultigens—for instance *Chenopodium*—might have played a considerable role in this subsistence base (cf. Yarnell 1964).

Day-to-day life in the Midwest during the Early Woodland period reveals some apparent changes in settlement and subsistence. However, none suggests that there was any wholesale migration of new people to the area. Rather, new traits seem to have diffused from various areas—both north and south—which became incorporated into existing cultures in the fertile river valleys of the Midwest. The result was a somewhat more stable and productive hunting-gathering and perhaps also horticultural subsistence base, which, in turn, had something to do with the Adena ceremonial florescence during the first millennium B.C. The river valleys in which the Adena were at home are so situated geographically that many microenvironmental zones, from river bottoms to hill tops, are within easy distance. The exploitation of the fish, fowl, mammal, and vegetable resources of these zones probably resulted in a highly productive "intensified Archaic" subsistence base.

What appear to be more or less permanent villages comprised of circular houses with outsloping walls and conical roofs have been reported for Adena-period stations (fig. 10) (Potter 1971), suggesting settled villages at this early date; however, the hunting-collecting subsistence base and Adena material from rockshelters and other campsites suggest considerable mobility. Such dwellings are not presently known for temporal equivalents of Adena culture elsewhere in the Northeast. Moreover, it is doubtful whether precisely this same house form was reproduced elsewhere, although equally permanent structures may have been constructed by later Early Woodland peoples in Michigan, New York, and elsewhere. In all probability, these characteristic Adena houses were a local development.

Characteristic nonmortuary Adena artifacts include: weak-shouldered lobate-stemmed spear or dart points, possibly propelled by an atlatl weighted with bar- or keel-shaped gorgets; flat-bottomed ceramics of several varieties, often with lug handles, cordmarked on both interior and exterior surfaces (later with incised or stamped decorations); chert end and side scrapers; drills; splinter awls; cigar-shaped or blocked-end-tube smoking pipes; and a variety of ornamental and ceremonial paraphernalia (Webb and Snow 1945; Webb and Baby 1957; Dragoo 1963).

Elsewhere in the Northeast other local developments were manifesting themselves, including Ritchie's Point Peninsula culture in New York, southern Ontario, and southern Quebec, which developed from the earlier Meadowood phase (Ritchie 1944:115-121, 1965: 203-213); similar developments elsewhere in the Lake Forest zone; and at least vaguely related assemblages, still poorly known, from the Atlantic coast (cf. Ritchie 1969a:223-226). Technologically, these cultures shared many elements with Adena, with one another, and most especially with their local Archaic predecessors, from whom they were descended with a minimum of technological and economic change.

The Early Woodland period in the Northeast is marked by the invention or introduction of ceramics in several places—the Lake Forest zone, the Middle Atlantic coast, and perhaps the Midwest—albeit with little drastic change from earlier Archaic subsistence and settlement patterns, with the probable exception of some Midwestern river valleys where cultivation may have become increasingly important and set the stage for a florescence of religious belief centering around treatment of the dead, which may have persisted in the Northeast for as long as two millennia.

Mortuary Ceremonialism

From the time of the first Late Archaic occupation of the Northeast special treatment seems to have been accorded the dead, suggesting "a basic case of religious belief" persisting through several millennia and culminating in the spectacular Hopewell religion, although there were other spectacular manifestations. This burial cult achieved several climaxes in the Northeast—the "Maine Cemetery complex of the North Atlantic coast"; Transitional burials in southern New England and Long Island; Glacial Kame burials in the Great Lakes area; the early Woodland cremation burials of northern New York, Michigan, and Ontario; "Red Ocher" and related "cultures" in the western Great Lakes; and Adena culture (fig. 11) south of the lakes—each distinctive but all seeming to express a similar underlying set of beliefs, which, although they grow more complex with time, may ultimately be related to the beginnings of a burial cult

Ohio Histl. Soc., Columbus.

Fig. 10. Model of an Adena house. Paired post mold pattern based on excavation at Cowan Creek Mound. The reconstruction of the roof may be erroneous; more likely it was domed, formed by longer wall posts bent and tied together as arches across the top.

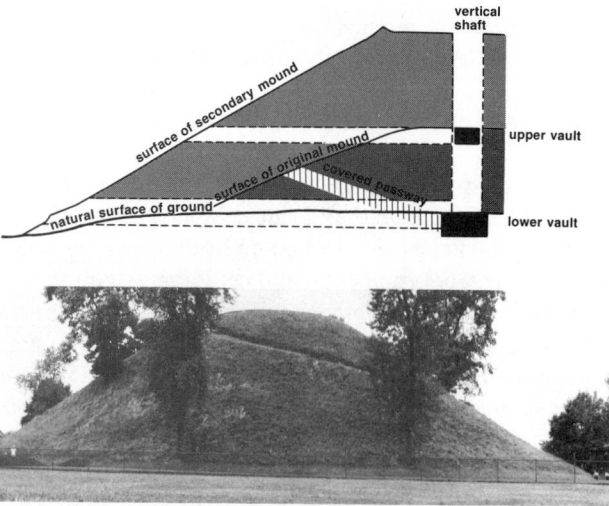

left, W. Va. Geological and Economic Survey, Morgantown, diagram after Norona 1957:18; right, Mus. of Amer. Ind., Heye Foundation, New York.
Fig. 11. Adena mounds. left, Adena attributed Grave Creek Mound, Marshall Co., W. Va., 200 ± 225 B.C. (date for upper portion of mound) and diagram based on uncertain 1838 accounts of excavations showing original mound and the secondary mound. The covered passageway is questionable. Photograph by E. Thomas Hemmings. right, Aerial photograph of the Great Serpent Mound, Adams Co., Ohio.

before 3000 B.C. This section will examine briefly these flashes of mortuary ceremonialism as they appear in the archeological record and point out their distinctive as well as similar elements.

Excepting the late Paleo-Indian cremation at the Renier site in Wisconsin (Mason and Irwin 1960) and the early burial mounds on the Labrador coast dated prior to 5000 B.C. (McGhee and Tuck 1975), it is not until the third millennium B.C. that burial ceremonialism becomes important in the Northeast. Although the more ancient dates for the Old Copper culture now seem incorrect, there are good dates from Allumette and Morrison's islands in eastern Ontario between 3290 and the middle third millennium B.C. (Kennedy 1967, personal communication 1969). These were made on materials associated with extended burials, often sprinkled with red ocher, and accompanied by various grave furnishings, mostly (but by no means entirely) utilitarian in nature. These included side-notched projectile points, scrapers, gouges, adzes, whetstones, two ground slate points, copper points and other artifacts, bone harpoons, needles, and awls (Kennedy 1967). Thousands of copper beads and several bracelets provide ample evidence for personal decoration. Although mostly utilitarian in nature and not made especially as mortuary offerings, the objects themselves and the use of red ocher foreshadow the second strong expression of this burial cult—this time in Maine and the Atlantic provinces.

Despite dates of 3400 B.C. on living sites (William Fitzhugh, personal communication 1970), the date of 2340 B.C. from a grave in Newfoundland (Tuck 1971b), and Snow's (1969) 3000 B.C. date from Maine, the first unquestionably dated "red paint" cemeteries fall between about 2000 and 1200 B.C. The strongest expression of this

ceremonialism seems coterminus with the Maritime Archaic tradition both temporally and geographically. The norm seems to be flexed or bundle burials, the latter suggesting seasonal ceremonies (perhaps for practical reasons), often located on high east-facing hills or bluffs, lavishly covered with red ocher and containing tools, weapons, ornaments, charms, amulets, and medicine bundles, all probably intended for use in some other world. The richly accoutered graves of newborn infants suggest that these were not merely personal possessions. Later Maritime Archaic burials contain ground slate spears and bayonets made exclusively as funeral offerings (cf. Sanger 1971). Finally, objects are often found deliberately broken or "killed," probably to release the spirit of the artifact, another component of the burial ritual that persists for nearly 2,000 years. Near 1000 B.C. low burial mounds were built by Maritime Archaic people on the north shore of the Gulf of Saint Lawrence (René Levesque, personal communication 1973).

To the south of the Maritime area, at least partly contemporaneous with (and probably derived from) this ceremonial complex, the indigenous peoples of southern New England, Long Island, and the Middle Atlantic coast were practicing their own version of the Northeastern burial cult. Elements of the Susquehanna tradition (broad-bladed spears, knives, and soapstone bowls) often figure prominently in this expression of ceremonialism; but the absence of elaborate burials during this time in the southeast and the presence of red ocher, specially made mortuary objects, ritually killed artifacts, and the choice of high east-facing eminences for burial (cf. Ritchie 1959; Dincauze 1968; Robbins 1968; Kraft 1970) all bespeak a northern origin for the basic elements of this mortuary ceremonialism. Cremation is an additional

42

feature, perhaps developed in New England or along the Middle Atlantic coast, which persists until well into the Christian era.

Again partly contemporaneous and clearly related are the burials in the Great Lakes area dating from 1200 to 700 B.C. Known by various names in different places and times—Old Copper, Glacial Kame, Meadowood—all are again expressions of the same basic concepts and probably similar rituals surrounding death and burial. All types of burials are known, but cremation is perhaps the most common. The bones and artifacts were burned either in place or in separate crematory basins and the residue then collected and placed in a deep grave with red ocher and occasional unburned offerings. Again, the grave was frequently on a high east-facing slope or hilltop. Grave offerings in this area include "mortuary blades" (bifaces) of various types, sometimes over 1,000 in a single deposit, "turkey tail" points or knives, the unique sandal-sole shell gorgets of the Glacial Kame period, stone two-hole gorgets in other areas, beautiful and enigmatic birdstones, copper tools and ornaments, but almost never ceramics that were in daily use by some of these people, especially those in the eastern extent of their range.

To the west and south even more spectacular developments were taking place. In the Red Ocher culture low burial mounds were being constructed containing human remains and artifacts in the same tradition as the Great Lakes. In southern Ohio are found the most spectacular Early Woodland ceremonial developments of all—the Adena complex. Much has been written and said about the Adena mounds and their builders, and theories of their origins have ranged from lost tribes or Mesoamerican migrants to much less exotic explanations. In view of the large number of Adena "traits" (and never before or since have the "traits" of a "culture" been so exhaustively enumerated) with cognates in the earlier Woodland and Late Archaic mortuary complexes of the Northeast, a simple in situ origin seems to fit the facts best. The change in geographical location of this outburst of mortuary ceremonialism is no greater than that from the Atlantic provinces to southern New England or from there to the Great Lakes, and Adena clearly overlaps in time other Early Woodland burial traditions. Very briefly, "traits" such as cremation, both in place and away from the grave, use of red ocher, intentionally killed artifacts, flint bifaces, gorgets, birdstones, and copper beads all point to Adena as a religious expression closely related to, and probably derived from, the ancient Northeastern burial cult.

By what means Adena ceremonialism was subsequently dispersed remains a subject of controversy. An actual migration of Adena people from the Middle West to the Atlantic coast has been suggested by some archeologists (Ritchie and Dragoo 1959), while others (Griffin 1961b) suggest diffusion or trade as the most reasonable explanation. Available carbon-14 dates favor the former theory, while increasing evidence of coastal-midwestern interaction throughout the Archaic period suggests that the latter theory may be correct. Neither has been satisfactorily demonstrated, and perhaps osteology will finally have to answer the question.

Consistently recurring and ever-elaborating elements of mortuary ritualism—red-ocher-covered burials accompanied by numerous artifacts, often ritually killed to ensure the well-being of the deceased in the afterlife—demonstrate perhaps the only real unifying factor among the otherwise varied cultural manifestations of the Northeast.

43

Regional Cultural Development, 300 B.C. to A.D. 1000

JAMES E. FITTING

Culture and Climate

Around 300 B.C., in some areas slightly earlier and in other places slightly later, quantitative changes took place in prehistoric northeastern North America as the relative stability achieved during the Late Archaic and Early Woodland periods gave way to the new dynamism of the Middle Woodland period. The Middle Woodland mellowed into the early portion of the Late Woodland period but new levels of energy efficiency were again achieved in the several centuries preceding A.D. 1000. Such changes can be strictly internal and brought about by small increments in the cultural inventory that eventually necessitate change in the entire culture. It would also appear that in the sensitive border areas of the northeastern biotic provinces small changes in climate could, and did, shift both biotic and cultural frontiers. Such shifts established predictable stress patterns that can be correlated with the more spectacular cultural changes in that area (Fitting 1971).

Griffin (1960, 1960a) was one of the first to note the correlation between climatic change and cultural development in this area that occurred between 300 B.C. and A.D. 1000. The sequence he proposed has been more completely developed and refined (Baerreis and Bryson 1965; Cleland 1966; Bryson and Wendland 1967). These climatic changes may have been more significant in some areas than in others and not all are convinced of their importance. They may not have served as the sole causative factors but more as triggering agents in initiating cultural change that had been building up within older societies.

Griffin (1960a, 1961) initially suggested a mild climate for the period 300 B.C. to A.D. 300, later called the Hopewell episode (Cleland 1966:28) or the Sub-Atlantic episode (Baerreis and Bryson 1965). This Sub-Atlantic was viewed as "more severe," meaning that the extent of climatic variation may have been limited to greater rainfall, or a different distribution of rainfall, rather than to actual temperature variation. A shift in spring or fall rainfall peaks or even the establishment of a more seasonal variation could have a small but significant effect on the human occupation of many areas. Apparently sea level changed dramatically along the Atlantic coast during this period and many coastal Middle Woodland sites are now submerged. This might be one reason why there

has been so much difficulty in defining the cultural components of this period along the Atlantic coast.

The Hopewell, or Sub-Atlantic, episode was followed by the Scandic episode lasting from A.D. 300 or 400 to A.D. 800 or 900. While the name has been suggested by the clear amelioration that took place in Scandinavia at this time, it too might have been marked merely by changes in the precipitation regime in the Northeast. Griffin (1961:713) suggested, however, that this was also a generally colder period. In either case, all agree that it was different from the preceding period and that this might have placed stress on the earlier Middle Woodland adaptive patterns. Perhaps it was both cooler and drier, with rains concentrated in the months of August and September rather than in the spring.

Baerreis and Bryson have called the period from A.D. 800 to A.D. 1300 the Neo-Atlantic episode, suggesting that it was similar to the earlier Sub-Atlantic. This period would have been favorable to agriculture and was the time when the first truly efficient agricultural systems developed in the Northeast (Caldwell 1958; Fowler 1969). During the Neo-Atlantic episode are first recognizable either the specific cultures or the general patterns of historically documented groups in each of the subregions recognized in this volume. After the Neo-Atlantic episode came the following climatic episodes: a cool, dry episode, at least in the Midwest, between A.D. 1300 and A.D. 1450, which Baerreis and Bryson have called the Pacific episode; then a return to conditions of the Neo-Atlantic around A.D. 1450 with another period of cooling, the "Little Ice Age," occurring between A.D. 1550 and A.D. 1880.

The remainder of this chapter will be developed against this background but will use the terminology common to the archeological literature of the region. The cultural complexes that will be described are Hopewell, Lake Forest Middle Woodland, and other possible Middle Woodland variants that were contemporary with and influenced by the more dominant cultural patterns. Adena seems to have developed as a distinctive cultural type before the beginning of the Hopewell climatic episode and continued on into it, with late Adena being contemporary with early Hopewell. Since Adena is a clear extension of the Late Archaic burial cults, and what little is known of its economic base and settlement system align it more closely with the Late Archaic, it has been thoroughly covered in the preceding chapter.

Between A.D. 300 and A.D. 500, perhaps as late as A.D. 700 in some areas, Middle Woodland culture underwent a change resulting in the transition to early Late Woodland with a number of regional variations. By A.D. 900 the Mississippian cultures of the central Midwest were beginning to take their distinctive forms, and the last several centuries discussed in this chapter deal in effect with the expansion of Mississippian influence into the Northeast and beyond the area of direct Mississippian dominance. Middle and early Late Woodland, as used here, are *horizons* throughout the Northeast—time periods of general cultural similarity over much of this large area. Within each of the subareas, it is possible to recognize cultural continuity over time. These continuities are referred to as *traditions*. A *phase* is a segment of a tradition. Some phases are long; but in areas where intensive fieldwork has been carried out, phases may be closely dated to several centuries.

Middle Woodland Horizon

Great Lakes–Riverine Hopewell

The most spectacular and still best-known cultural manifestation of the Middle Woodland time period (fig. 1) is what has been called Hopewell or Hopewellian. Like Adena, these terms have been applied in so many contexts that their meaning has become blurred. Named for a mound site near Chillecothe, Ohio, the term has come to have a meaning far beyond its original confines. Reviews of this usage are numerous (Prufer 1964; Caldwell 1964; Struever 1965, 1968a). In general, it is used to refer to similar elements within archeological assemblages found over a wide geographical area ranging from western New York to Kansas City and from the Gulf of Mexico to the shores of Lake Huron (fig. 2). Trade contacts extend from the Gulf of Mexico presumably to Lake Superior and demonstrably (Griffin, Gordus, and Wright 1969) to Wyoming.

The traits usually used to mark the presence of Hopewell (fig. 3) include mound burials and earthworks; distinctive dentate-stamped and rocker-stamped ceramic vessels, often with cross-hatched rim ornamentation and zoned decoration; platform pipes, sometimes carved with animal and bird effigies; cut animal jaws and teeth; pan pipes; and a wealth of other material. In fact this wealth of spectacular and well-crafted grave goods led early investigators to group Hopewell with Adena as Mound Builders, a group which they believed to be genetically distinct from, and culturally superior to, the American Indians present at the time of European contact. All recent work has demonstrated that Hopewell, like Adena, is part of a local developmental sequence in

each area where it is found and can be nothing other than the work of prehistoric American Indians.

Recent work has also demonstrated that in spite of widespread similarities in artifact style, each regional manifestation of Hopewell is distinctive and may be better interpreted in terms of local cultural sequences than as a part of a broad cultural horizon. Still, the horizonal element is present and implies some degree of social interaction, leading Prufer (1964a) and others to postulate a religious "cult" or at least a vague set of shared values that Caldwell (1964) has called an "Interaction Sphere."

One of the major aspects of Hopewell in the eastern United States is the evidence of widespread exchange networks. While long-distance trade is evident in the area during Archaic times, it is carried to its peak during the Middle Woodland period. Gulf coast conch shells are found in Michigan and Wisconsin. Sharks' teeth are found in Middle Woodland mounds in Illinois and an effigy alligator pipe dating to this period has been recovered from western Michigan. Copper from the Lake Superior region is traded far to the south. Obsidian and grizzly bear teeth from the far west find their way to Illinois and Ohio. Mica and special types of flint, such as that from Flint Ridge in Ohio, are also traded or carried over long distances and find their way into village and burial sites over much of eastern North America. The distribution of these goods makes it clear that some network, either social or religious, must have existed for this exchange to take place.

As is often the case with archeological complexes, the area where they were first defined is assumed to represent their climax expression. Until recently, Ohio was viewed as the source of Hopewell developments in other areas. Given the poor chronological control of the period before the development of radiocarbon dating and the forced reliance on such chronological devices as the age/area hypothesis, this was a reasonable conclusion. As of 1950, more sites had probably been excavated and formally described in Ohio than in any other area; and certainly these Ohio sites were larger and more impressive, with more and better quality grave goods than had been recovered from any other area (R.G. Morgan 1952).

As archeological fieldwork progressed after 1950 and chronology was placed on a firmer base, it became clear that many of the things that had been called Hopewellian outside of Ohio were different from those in Ohio. The ceramics in the Great Lakes–Riverine area, including the dominant Havana series, could be separated from the less elaborate Scioto series ceramics of the Ohio region. Mortuary practices varied as well. The western area was marked by numerous small mounds containing inhumations, usually in log tombs, with the occurrence of several secondary burials in many of these mounds. These mounds tend to occur in small groups, suggesting that burial areas were used for several generations. Ohio

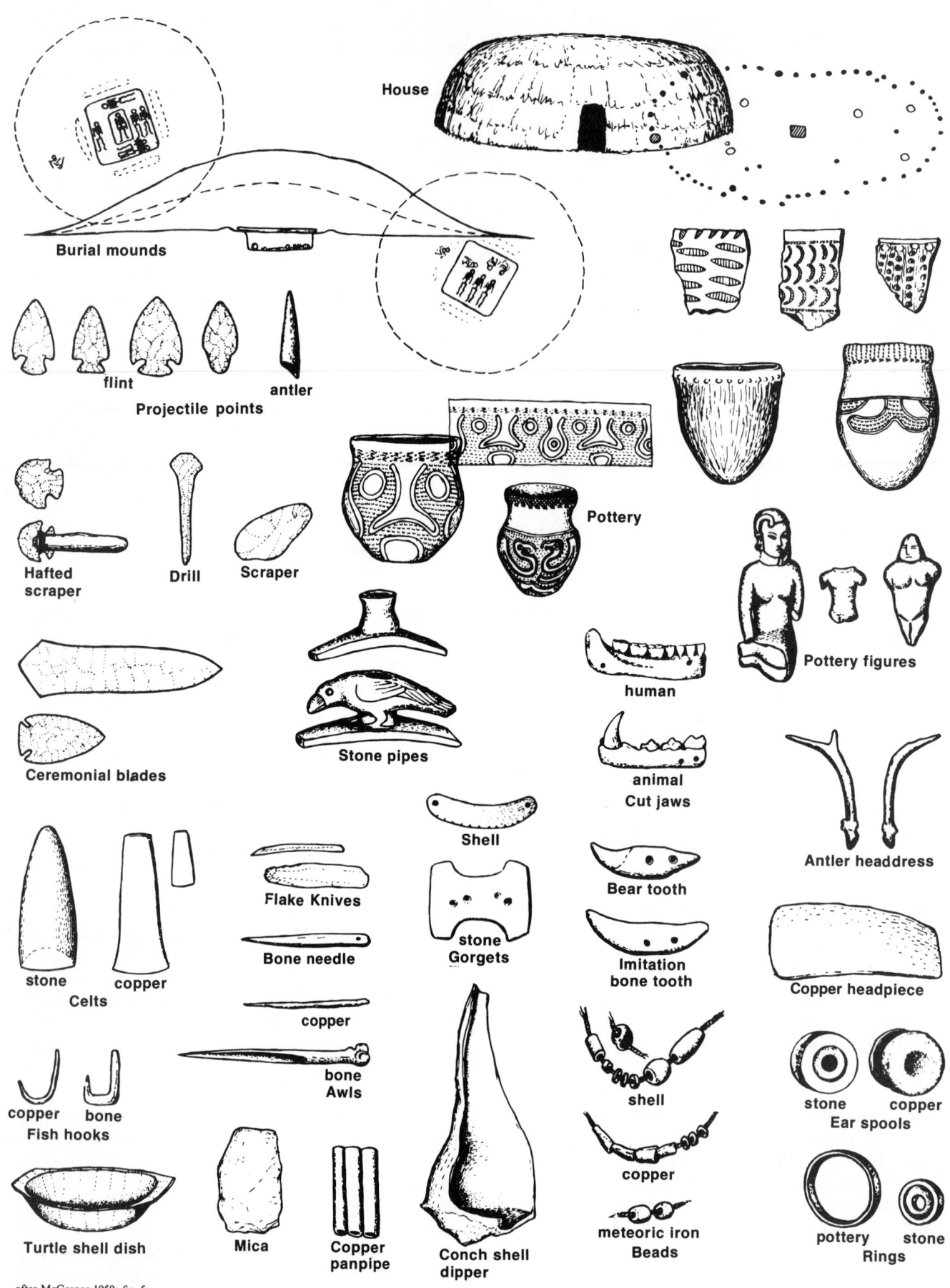

House

Burial mounds

flint   antler
Projectile points

Hafted
scraper   Drill   Scraper

Pottery

Ceremonial blades

Stone pipes

Pottery figures

human

animal
Cut jaws

Antler headdress

stone   copper
Celts

Flake Knives

Bone needle

copper

bone
Awls

Shell

stone
Gorgets

Bear tooth

Imitation
bone tooth

Copper headpiece

copper   bone
Fish hooks

shell

copper

meteoric iron
Beads

stone   copper
Ear spools

Turtle shell dish

Mica

Copper
panpipe

Conch shell
dipper

pottery   stone
Rings

after McGregor 1959: fig. 5.
Fig. 1. Artifacts from Illinois Middle Woodland assemblage.

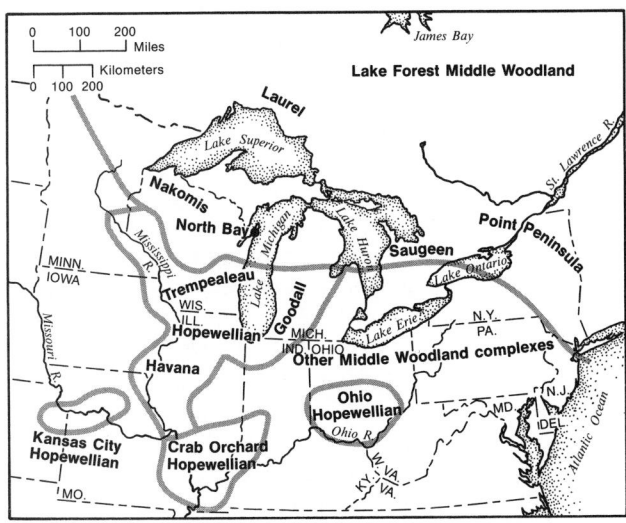

Fig. 2. Middle Woodland cultures, about A.D. 100.

Hopewell, on the other hand, was marked by larger mounds which contained elaborate cremations as well as inhumations. The burial patterns are more varied and complex in Ohio than in Illinois. The grave associations in the Ohio area are far richer, the mounds themselves are larger, and the size of some of the mound complexes and associated earthworks is so great as to suggest reuse of the main burial areas for a number of generations.

There is some variation in the chronology of the two areas as well (Griffin 1958; Struever 1964). Hopewell in Illinois, as an example, has beginnings coeval with Adena and this has led some scholars to derive Ohio Hopewell from Illinois in spite of the comparative simplicity of Middle Woodland in Illinois. The entire problem has more recently been overshadowed by the recognition of the tremendous complexity of even local developments. The division of Middle Woodland into distinctive subgroups in the Great Lakes-Riverine area is but one example of this (Struever 1965). Griffin (1967) has dealt with at least the northern expressions of Hopewell in two more or less distinctive units, Ohio Hopewell and Havana Hopewell, with the realization that there are many more actual subdivisions. Griffin's divisions are used here, with the substitution of the term Great Lakes-Riverine Hopewell for Havana Hopewell, since Havana is but one of the several regional traditions proposed for the western unit (Brown 1964). The literature on this region is rich; suggestive bibliographies are to be found in a number of surveys (Cole and Deuel 1937; Griffin et al. 1941; Wray 1952; Deuel 1952; McGregor 1959; Caldwell and Hall 1964; Struever 1965; Winters and Hammerslough 1971). The most recent review of internal Great Lakes-Riverine Hopewell, particularly for the Havana branch or tradition, has been presented by Griffin, Flanders, and Titterington (1970:1–10).

Struever (1965), on the basis of small differences in ceramics, separated Great Lakes-Riverine Hopewell into three groups: Crab Orchard, Pike, and Havana. Griffin (1967:fig. 3) has indicated separate groupings for Crab Orchard, Kansas City Hopewell, and Havana. The Havana tradition as conceived by both Griffin and Struever covers a vast area, and Griffin has further separated Tremplaleau Hopewell in Wisconsin and Goodall Hopewell in Michigan from Havana proper in Illinois. Goodall Hopewell, including the Hopewell manifestations in the Saginaw Valley of eastern Michigan, may represent an actual movement of peoples out of Illinois into Michigan (Griffin, Flanders, and Titterington 1970:188–189).

This thesis has been disputed by Brown (1964) and Struever (1965), who see distinctive stylistic elements in the Michigan and Wisconsin Hopewell materials. Fitting (1968, 1972) has demonstrated that the Havana-like groups in the Saginaw Valley of Michigan had an entirely different settlement system and economic system from those in Illinois and that even similar items of material culture function in different social and economic contexts. In spite of artifact similarities, it would appear that there are many substantive subdivisions for cultural materials even within the Havana tradition itself and that any interpretation of identity must be taken as tentative at best.

Not only has the Havana tradition geographical subdivisions, but also it has been separated into several time divisions as well (see Winters and Hammerslough 1971; Griffin, Flanders, and Titterington 1970). Quite apart from the names that are used for their phases, all writers agree on the general developmental trends. There is no clear transition from late Archaic complexes into early Middle Woodland in this region. The distinctive elements of the early Havana sequence—plain, stamped, and noded pottery—appear before the beginning of the Christian era in the Illinois River Valley, which is the heartland of Great Lakes-Riverine Hopewell. During the first several centuries of the Christian era, there is an elaboration of pottery types with rocker stamping and brushed decorations existing along with many of the older forms. This is a period of general elaboration, with greater amounts of exotic goods occurring in burial mounds. It would also appear that either Hopewell peoples, or at least their material goods and ideas of how such goods should be manufactured, spread from the Illinois River valley into surrounding areas. By A.D. 400 simple cordmarked ceramics seem to dominate the assemblages, but some of the earlier elements continue in use for several centuries marking these assemblages as Middle Woodland rather than Late Woodland.

The developmental sequence and site distribution within surrounding areas with marginal Havana or non-Havana materials is less well known. The Crab Orchard culture (Maxwell 1951) was first considered to be a local

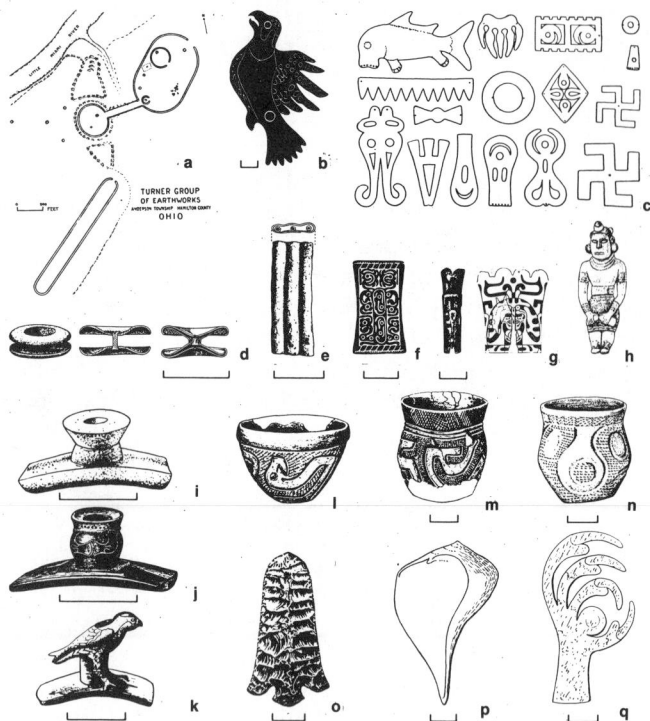

Griffin 1967: fig. 4.

Fig. 3. Hopewell earthwork pattern and Hopwellian artifacts. a, Turner Earthworks; b, flying eagle (?) embossed on copper plate; c, designs in thin copper plate; d, copper earspools; e, sheet copper over cane panpipe; f, engraved stone tablet; g, engraving on proximal half of human femur, analysis of design unrolled on right; h, painted pottery male effigy; i, platform pipe; j, pipe with engraved roseate spoonbilled duck design; k, sculptured and engraved hawk effigy pipe; l, Hopewell style vessel; m, Hopewell style vessel; n, Havana Zoned Dentate vessel; o, obsidian ceremonial spear; p, busycon cup; q, mica effigy of eagle(?). Scale indicates 5 cm length. For provenience of objects see source.

Early Woodland culture first influenced by Adena and later by Hopewell. More recent studies (Struever 1965; Winters 1967:49–52) have interpreted the paddle-edge stamped and plain ceramics that mark this culture as representative of a distinctive Middle Woodland tradition in southern Illinois that is participating marginally in the Hopewellian Interaction Sphere.

Hopewell manifestations in the Missouri River drainage are very limited in comparison to the Illinois valley. Kansas City Hopewell (Wedel 1943) includes one of the few instances of maize in Middle Woodland context, but it is late and a very limited complex (Chapman and Chapman 1964:52–54). The same seems to be true for the Wisconsin variants of Hopewell that appear on stylistic grounds to be late, although they are known primarily from excavations published before the development of radiocarbon dating.

The Goodall Hopewell materials in Michigan were initially described by Quimby (1941) and have since been discussed by Brown (1964), Flanders (1965), and Prahl (1970). Stylistically similar materials have been found in the Saginaw Valley of eastern Michigan (Fitting 1968, 1970:116–128, 1972). While distinctive in many aspects, all of these marginally related Middle Woodland manifestations can be related to the Illinois valley sequence.

It has often been assumed that an agricultural base would have been necessary to account for the elaborateness of Hopewell or that maize agriculture at least played an important part in its development. Maize has been found in a late context in a number of sites including Kansas City Hopewell and the McGraw site in Ohio (Prufer et al. 1965). Maize has been found with Havana materials dating to the first century B.C. at the Jasper Newman site in Illinois (Gardner 1969). It was reported at the Ansell site (McGregor 1958) but the associated cultural material indicates that it was found in areas of mixed deposition. While it is possible that maize agriculture played some part in the Hopewell economic base, it seems to have been a small part at best.

Struever (1964) suggested that mud-flats horticulture was important for the development of Great Lakes-Riverine Hopewell. Cleland (1966) believed they had a diffuse type of economy. There are indications that Struever has had second thoughts about the term if not the concept for in 1965 he wrote, "notwithstanding my recent speculations on early [mud-flats] horticulture, the evidence to date from the lower Illinois River Valley indicates that Middle Woodland groups here carried on primarily, if not entirely, a *collecting subsistence* and occupied nucleated communities accessible to all microhabitat zones from which their natural-food resources were drawn" (Struever 1965:214). Recent work in the Saginaw Valley of Michigan has led to a similar conclusion (Fitting 1972). The most detailed evidence for the economic and settlement system of the Havana tradition also comes from its extremes in the lower Illinois and Saginaw valleys. Within the lower Illinois, Struever (1968) recognizes four site types with a seasonal round of activities. Base settlements are located along the talus slopes, usually along the western side of the river valley where they would receive some protection from the prevailing western winter winds. These settlements are located midway between the resource zones of the bluff tops and those of the river bottom lands, both of which were exploited. The sites are fairly large with evidence of substantial occupation. There are some indications that the sites were not occupied, or not as intensively occupied, during the summer months.

During the summer agriculture, or intensive harvesting, camps were established on the higher sand ridges in the valley bottom lands. In addition to these sites, there is at least one regional exchange center, the Mound House site, which is larger than the base camps and contains more artifacts characteristic of the wider Hopewellian Interaction Sphere. Finally, there are short-term

48

camps near the mortuary centers, the mound groups on the bluffs. Maintenance activities, as well as activities related to the burial complex, were carried out at these sites.

This pattern stands in strong contrast to the settlement and economic pattern of the Middle Woodland peoples of the Saginaw Valley at the opposite end of the Havana stylistic area. Here, the base camp, where groups also gathered for ceremonial activities, was a summer population concentration center where groups were supported by fishing and collecting. Economically, it is similar to the lower Illinois summer camps but it also has characteristics of the regional exchange center. There is no environmental situation in the Saginaw Valley comparable to base camps located in the lower Illinois. In the Saginaw Valley, Middle Woodland winter camps are small and scattered hunting camps. In this sense, Saginaw Valley Middle Woodland more closely resembles the Lake Forest Middle Woodland found in areas to the north than it does the pattern of the lower Illinois area.

Ohio Hopewell

Prufer (1968:148) recognizes four time subdivisions for Ohio Hopewell: early Hopewell, represented by Tremper and certain mounds within the Mound City group; middle Hopewell, represented by Seip, Harness, Hopewell, and Rockhold; late Hopewell, represented by Turner, Marriott-1, the McGraw and Brown's Bottom sites, Ginther, Newark, and Marietta; and latest Hopewell, represented by the Hilltop enclosures in the southern part of the state. This is but a part of the regional development sequence that has been called the Scioto tradition and is centered around Chillicothe. Shane (1971) has indicated that this tradition should be divided into an Adena phase, lasting from 500 B.C. to 100 B.C.; a Hopewell phase, lasting from 100 B.C. to A.D. 500; and a Peters phase, lasting from A.D. 500 to A.D. 900, when the Fort Ancient culture makes its appearance. The greatest cultural elaboration occurs during the Hopewell phase. He has also suggested a shift from bluff-top to river-bottom settlements between Adena and Hopewell. Prufer (1964, 1968) has suggested a movement to the hilltop forts and more geographically isolated areas for the later Hopewellian occupations.

Prufer suggested that the Ohio settlement system involved small farmsteads scattered only in the valley bottoms around the major ceremonial centers. The McGraw site (Prufer et al. 1965) has been used as an example of such a site and is also notable because of the presence of maize dated A.D. 200-400. The occurrence of numerous similar settlements has been demonstrated by subsequent survey work (Shane 1971).

Not only is the material culture of Ohio Hopewellian, with its larger mound and mound groups and greater wealth of grave goods, different from that of its more western counterparts, but also the settlement pattern and, by extension, social organization seem to have differed as well. Struever (1965:212-213) has suggested that Ohio Hopewell represents a chiefdom level of sociopolitical development while that in the Great Lakes-Riverine area is at a tribal level of development (using these terms as suggested by Service 1962). The greater wealth in the chiefdom area is a reflection not of environmental difference but rather of the ability of a society to mobilize and concentrate this wealth in the hands of individuals holding high status positions. The continuity in mortuary areas suggests that these positions were hereditary. Within such a society, every individual would have a place within the social framework and there would be a tighter geographical clustering.

The tribes of the western division would have had less centralized leadership with individuals or individual families being able to amass their own wealth. This wealth was distributed among less elaborate mounds with less elaborate grave offerings. This type of society would have been more fragile and liable to segment. The rapid spread of ceramics related to those from the Illinois River valley after it began full participation in the Hopewellian Interaction Sphere might be a reflection of this type of social organization.

Lake Forest

The term Lake Forest Middle Woodland (Fitting 1970: 129-142) is used to describe a widely distributed group of cultures with general similarities in material culture and a similar ecological base. Like the other Middle Woodland cultures discussed so far, there is a certain degree of internal stylistic diversity. In general, stylistic similarities include ceramic vessels with pointed bases and a tendency toward elaborate stamped decorations. These decorations include pseudo-scallop shell stamping, dentate stamping, plain and dentate rocker stamping, banked and single bands of punctate, and some cord-wrapped-stick punctation. Occasional noding of vessels and crosshatched rims are found and serve not only to define subareas but also to indicate contemporaneity with Hopewellian groups to the south as well.

Recent reviews of the chronological placement of this material (R.J. Mason 1967; Fitting et al. 1969; Brose 1970:88-89) indicate that it is generally restricted to about A.D. 1-300, with most earlier and later dates a result of poor sample associations or radiocarbon sampling errors. The exception seems to be the Saugeen complex in southern Ontario, where a series of radiocarbon dates cluster in the sixth century B.C. and the Rock Island III site in Wisconsin, which also has a sixth-century date. This series of dates appears to be internally consistent and must be viewed at this time as a still unexplained anomaly.

These Lake Forest Middle Woodland groups are restricted, with a few exceptions, to the Lake Forest biotic zone as defined by ecologists (Weaver and Clements 1938; Potzger 1946), which stretches from Manitoba across the Great Lakes to the Atlantic coast. The more northern occurrences in the true boreal forest region seem to be in specialized situations along rivers and inland lakes where microenvironmental conditions duplicate Lake Forest conditions. There appears to be a uniform adaptive pattern within this region. It involves the concentration of population at a few major sites during the summer months. These are usually in areas where fishing furnished a rich but short-term economic base for such concentrations. These sites have concentrations of cultural debris that match, and in many instances are greater than, Hopewellian villages to the south.

Paralleling the practice of historic groups in the same region, winter camps were small and scattered. They represent the remains of mobile extended-family groups. This pattern is reported from Manitoba (MacNeish 1958), through Michigan (Fitting 1969, 1970) to New York (Ritchie 1969a:209) and presumably on to the Atlantic coast. This adaptation was most successful and, in contrast to Hopewellian groups, population density neared its maximum in the Lake Forest region in Middle Woodland times. Using the Michigan example (Fitting 1969:369), it is the Hopewellian sites that appear to be impoverished in spite of the limited numbers of exotic grave goods in Hopewellian sites. Admittedly, the Michigan Hopewellian sample is on the northern fringe of that stylistic zone.

The focal point of the western manifestations of the Lake Forest Middle Woodland is to be found in the Laurel materials first defined in Minnesota (Wilford 1941, 1950), the bulk of the data derived from the Laurel and McKinstry mounds along the Rainy River and the Pike Bay Mound along the Pike River. The materials from these mounds as well as from the Pearson village site have been restudied by Stoltman (1962, 1973). Similar materials were reported in southeastern Manitoba by MacNeish (1958) who recognized two divisions, the Anderson and Nutimk focuses with several components in the area. The information on this area has been expanded by Mayer-Oakes (1967, 1970) who used MacNeish's terminology but viewed these as phases of a local tradition rather than the focuses of the Midwestern Taxonomic system. In a recent summary of Manitoba archeology, Hlady (1970:277–278) has regrouped this material into a single Laurel phase relating it in a more unified manner to the Minnesota materials.

Laurel materials extend to the east around the Lake Superior basin in Ontario and the northern parts of the Michigan Upper Peninsula. The materials from the Ontario sites have been reported primarily by Wright (1963, 1967). Additional survey work and excavation, particularly at the McGillvary Mound and the Micipicoten

site, have been carried out by Kenneth Dawson (personal communication 1968). Bastian (1963) has reported Laurel materials from Isle Royal; they have also been found as far east as the Sault (Fitting 1970:138). One of the most extensive and richest of Laurel sites is Naomikong Point in the Whitefish Bay area of Michigan (Janzen 1968a).

The materials that have been recovered from the Lake Huron basin show many similarities to Laurel, particularly in ceramic decorative techniques; but there are also many distinctions that indicate a number of highly localized complexes in the region. The most perplexing of these is the Saugeen complex represented by Donaldson and several other sites (Wright and Anderson 1963; Wright 1967:117). The ceramics are much thicker and cruder than those from Laurel sites but this is true of a number of complexes in the Lake Huron and Lake Michigan basins. If the dates do not represent an extremely localized dating anomaly, Saugeen must be viewed as the center of origin for the Lake Forest Middle Woodland tradition. In that case the problem of defining the hiatus between Saugeen and the considerably later sites in other areas arises.

The diversity in Ontario south of the Laurel area is duplicated in Wisconsin and Michigan. In north-central Wisconsin, Salzer (1968) has excavated Middle Woodland components at a number of sites that fit into the Lake Forest Middle Woodland heading. Salzer still sees differences between this material and both Laurel and other Wisconsin Middle Woodland complexes and has referred to it as the Nokomis complex.

The most completely reported of the northern Middle Woodland groupings in Wisconsin is Mason's North Bay complex (R.J. Mason 1966, 1967, 1969). This complex is found on the Door Peninsula and nearby areas of Wisconsin. Sites on Washington Island (Richard Peske, personal communication 1968) and on Rock Island (Mason 1971) have been investigated.

A closely related Middle Woodland occupation has been reported from Summer Island, one of the chain of islands running between the Wisconsin Door Peninsula and the Michigan Garden Peninsula. Excavations (Brose 1970, 1970a) have contributed information on the economic base of Lake Forest Woodland described earlier. Brose has also been able to suggest, on the basis of artifact distribution and the association of distinctive pottery styles with different houses, that these people had a system of patrilocal postmarital residence.

Several cave sites in the Burnt Bluff area across the channel from Summer Island appear to be Middle Woodland shrine sites with either limited seasonal occupation or no occupational debris at all (Janzen 1968; Cleland and Peske 1968). Ceramics similar to those from the North Bay sites and Summer Island are found in the northern Lake Michigan area as far east as the Straits of

Mackinac. Beyond, in the Lake Huron basin, the diversity noted for the Ontario area is found in Michigan with several possible Middle Woodland components found together at the Goodwin-Gresham site (Fitting et al. 1969). Havana tradition materials, or at least cultural materials with their closest parallels to Havana, have been found in the Saginaw Bay area; however, to the south of Saginaw Bay there are a few traces of ceramics similar to those from the Goodwin-Gresham site along the Saint Clair River. Middle Woodland has proved to be most elusive in the Lake Erie basin although Fitting and Brose (1971:35) have interpreted some of the ceramics from Shane's (1967) Mixter site as a part of the Lake Forest Middle Woodland.

The eastern representatives of the Lake Forest Middle Woodland center around what has been called Point Peninsula (Ritchie 1944:115–121, 1969a:205–253) or, more specifically, Point Peninsula 2. While elements of Lake Forest Middle Woodland are present in New York sites, Ritchie has tended to interpret many of these as a result of Hopewellian influence. Interpreting this material as a part of the local Point Peninsula developmental continuum, which runs from Late Archaic or Early Woodland through Late Woodland, has somewhat obscured the northern horizonal relationships. There is a definite Hopewellian-influenced Middle Woodland in the southwestern parts of New York (Griffin 1967:fig. 3).

Many of the Point Peninsula 2 sites discussed by Ritchie are in Ontario. In addition to his own work in that area (Ritchie 1949), these include the Kant site (Emerson 1955), the Serpent Mound and other sites in the Rice Lake area (R.B. Johnston 1968, 1968a), and several sites along Montgomery Lake (Mitchell et al. 1966, Mitchell 1969).

In terms of stylistic elements, it would be difficult to state exactly where in Ontario and Quebec Point Peninsula ends and Laurel actually begins. Wright (1967: 111–112) has suggested that sites of both complexes are found near each other along the shores of Kempt Lake in Quebec. Along the Atlantic coast, Middle Woodland complexes having similarities in ceramic decoration with the interior, including dentate stamping and cord-wrapped-stick or paddle stamping, have long been known. Their position on the coast suggests that they might have had a distinctive adaptive pattern, although Ritchie (1969:226) has suggested that their adaptation is basically similar to that found on sites in the interior.

Other Complexes

While Hopewell and Lake Forest Middle Woodland form the climax Middle Woodland complexes in the Northeast, there are other contemporary groups within the area that do not fit into either classification. These groups do not form a single unit and, at present, they are poorly known and their coverage in the literature is at best sporadic. Adena, as an example, does not end with the development of Hopewell in the Ohio River Valley and there are areas where an extended Adena continues to exist with, or without, Hopewellian influence on into the Middle Woodland period. Dragoo (1964) has noted this continuation south of the Ohio River in Kentucky and McMichael (1971) has observed the same thing in his analysis of West Virginia Adena.

In the upper Ohio River Valley (Mayer-Oakes 1955: 15), New York (Ritchie 1969a:214–226), and southern Ontario (Spence 1967), there are a number of mounds with burial traits that can be related to the Hopewell complex in the middle Ohio River Valley. These traits, however, are not strongly displayed in village sites. It is felt that the village sites for these groups are so similar to generalized early Late Woodland complexes of the area that they could be recognized only by the chance occurrence of mortuary goods in a village site situation. This has been supported by the detailed survey carried out in Pennsylvania by the Pennsylvania State University Chenengo County project. Even in the Middle Ohio River valley, Middle Woodland sites may not be particularly distinctive. The majority of the ceramics from the McGraw village site (Prufer et al. 1965) were simple cordmarked forms. Prufer's review of the collections of ceramics from Ohio mounds (1968) reveals a preponderance of cordmarked forms, and cordmarked ceramics constitute the entire assemblage from the Ater Mound.

In Michigan, Fitting (1970:128–129) has dealt with the possibility of a Middle Woodland occupation in the southern part of that state that is neither Hopewellian nor Lake Forest Middle Woodland; and Struever (1965) has suggested that some type of non-Hopewellian generalized Middle Woodland exists outside of the major river valleys in Illinois. Bennett (1952:112–114) has recognized generalized Middle Woodland sites in the upper Mississippi valley although some of the material that he placed in this grouping might now be considered Lake Forest Middle Woodland. Hurley's study of the Crystal Lake village sites (1966) reveals a complex in Wisconsin that can be recognized as Middle Woodland because of a few Havana stylistic traits but is still not true Havana. Ronald Mason, in his 1968 Havana Conference paper, noted the same type of thing in southern Wisconsin.

While Hopewellian and Lake Forest Middle Woodland complexes are the most distinctive and easily recognizable of the Middle Woodland complexes, it is clear that they are not the sole Middle Woodland complexes. Other complexes are present in marginal areas and in areas that have not been subjected to intensive investigation. The nature of these complexes is quite variable and will become clear only with additional fieldwork and interpretation.

Late Woodland Horizon

Hopewell and contemporary Middle Woodland cultures possess distinctive material remains that serve as horizontal markers. Hopewell, in particular, has been viewed as a developmental peak from which the subsequent Late Woodland cultures represent a decline (Griffin 1952:361; Maxwell 1959:27) until they later participate in, or are influenced by, the Mississippian developments that constitute a second major climax; however, the nature of the change in adaptive patterns and the cultural dynamics that mark the so-called decline in the Late Woodland period are not clear. This is partially a result of the nature of the archeological materials themselves and partially a result of the way the literature on this time period developed. There are some widespread stylistic continuities that roughly parallel the division between Hopewell and Lake Forest Middle Woodland of earlier times. The transition in the southern area between Middle and Late Woodland is so gradual that it is sometimes difficult to state when it has occurred. Whereas Wray (1952), Wray and MacNeish (1961), and Morse (1963) consider the Weaver complex in the central Illinois River valley to be late Middle Woodland, Griffin, Flanders, and Titterington (1970) consider it to be post-Middle Woodland. Is the Peters phase in Ohio (Prufer and McKenzie 1966) extended Middle Woodland or a new and distinctive complex? Ritchie (1969a:228ff.) sees Middle and Late Point Peninsula as a part of a continuous cultural development; in Michigan, Fitting (1965:169) finds it difficult to classify Wayne ware as definitely late Middle Woodland or early Late Woodland. In Minnesota, Hlady (1970) carried Laurel, generally considered to be Middle Woodland, up to A.D. 1400 and Bennett (1952) even suggested that some northern Middle Woodland cultures continued on to the historic period (an impossibility using the term as a horizon rather than a tradition).

Running counter to this widespread recognition of continuity is a forced separation of similar archeological material brought about by the pattern of development of the archeological literature. Parker (1922) separated prehistoric materials in New York into Algonquian and Iroquoian. The initial formulations of the Midwestern Taxonomic system created a separation between the Woodland pattern and the Mississippian pattern that, along with Parker's classification where Algonquian became Woodland and Iroquoian became Mississippian, dichotomized much of the Northeast. The terminological division was much clearer than the division of cultural materials; a major debate occurred over whether Hopewell was Woodland or Mississippian. However, once a cultural manifestation was placed in one of these two major divisions, all suggestion of generic relationships was out of the question.

With the development of stratigraphic excavation and later of radiocarbon dating, the importance of sequential development came to the fore, but the older terminology tended to confuse the situation. Hopewell and other Middle Woodland groups could be placed on one time level while Mississippian, Fort Ancient, and Iroquoian materials could be placed on a later time level. Horizontal as well as traditional similarities were present and it became clear that the Midwestern Taxonomic system had equated similarities caused by both tradition and horizon relationships. Mississippian, as a horizon, could not be extended to many parts of the Northeast where Woodland, as a tradition, continued on to the historic period (Griffin 1952).

This presentation will survey the distribution of cultural materials, complexes, and adaptive patterns from the end of the Middle Woodland climax up to the time of the recognition of historic tribal cultures, or the prototypic representatives of later tribal cultures, roughly from A.D. 300 or 400 up to A.D. 1000 (fig. 4). Most of this material has been called Late Woodland in the literature although it is often difficult to distinguish it from earlier Middle Woodland (fig. 5). This time period also sees the emergence of Mississippian, Fort Ancient, and ancestral Iroquoian culture. They all seem to be correlated with the Neo-Atlantic climatic episode.

From an historical perspective, the Illinois area may have been the region where the problem of Late Woodland classification first came to the surface. In central Illinois, Cole and Deuel (1937) recognized Maples Mills, distinguished by cordmarked ceramics of the type that Fowler (1952) called Canton ware. They suggested that this material was post-Hopewellian, and subsequent typological analysis (Griffin 1952a) and stratigraphic excavation (Fowler 1952; Wray and MacNeish 1961) tended to support a sequence from Weaver through Maples

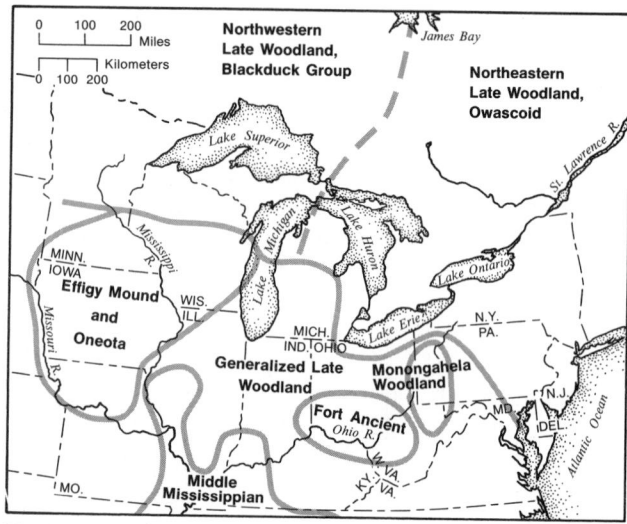

Fig. 4. Late Woodland and Mississippian cultures, A.D. 800 to A.D. 1000.

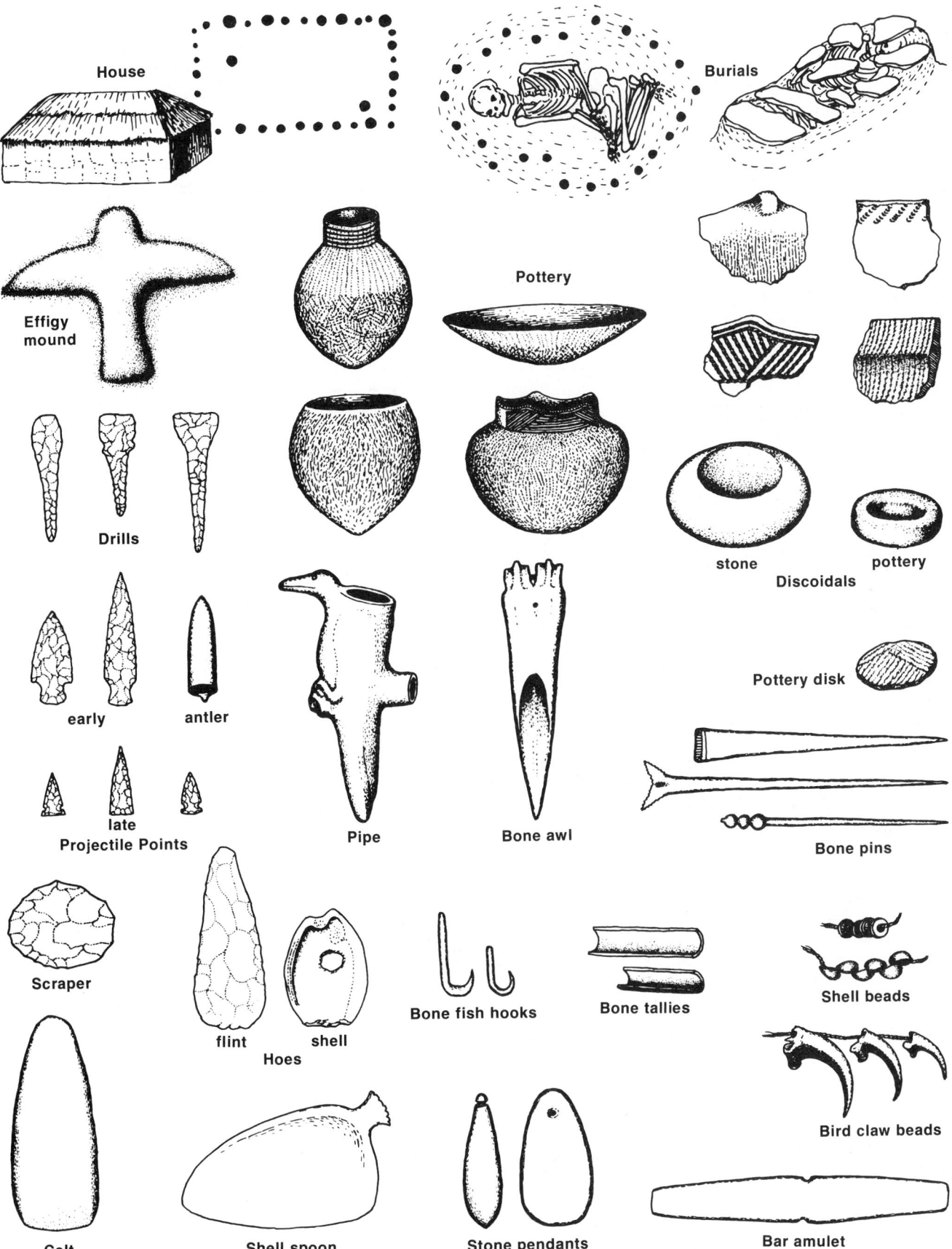

House   Burials

Effigy mound

Pottery

Drills

stone   pottery

Discoidals

early   antler

Pottery disk

late

Projectile Points   Pipe   Bone awl   Bone pins

Scraper   Bone fish hooks   Bone tallies   Shell beads

flint   shell

Hoes   Bird claw beads

Celt   Shell spoon   Stone pendants   Bar amulet

after Maxwell 1959: fig. 6.

Fig. 5. Artifacts from Late Woodland assemblage.

Mills to Spoon River, the local expression of Mississippian in the central Illinois area.

At the same time, work in southern Illinois isolated the Lewis complex (Cole 1951:165-183), the Raymond complex and the Dillinger complex (Maxwell 1951, 1952), and the Korando complex in the American Bottoms. These are marked by similar cordmarked ceramics with limited vessel variation. The sites where these peoples lived were smaller and more scattered than the Mississippian occupations within the same areas. Their economy seems to have been generalized rather than specifically agricultural. Maxwell (1952:187) comments that the Dillinger people seem to have eaten everything "from Digger wasp larvae to other humans." However, evidence of increased sedentism and reliance on agriculture seems to characterize the later parts of the internal developmental sequence in this area (Maxwell 1959). It has also been suggested that the Lewis people continued to live in southern Illinois after the arrival of Mississippian peoples with an agricultural adaptation. Harn (1971:69) has suggested that this was true in the central Illinois River valley as well.

In the area around Saint Louis and along the Mississippi, where later Mississippian cultural developments were most spectacular, the Jersey Bluff complex is the local representative of the Late Woodland occupation (Titterington 1943; Shalkop 1949). As Griffin, Flanders, and Titterington (1970:10) have since pointed out, this complex, as originally defined, covers the time period from A.D. 400 to A.D. 1100. Munson and Harn (1971:9-14) have used an early and a late division in their surface survey report on this area. They also note that work in the American Bottoms has indicated a number of subdivisions within their late category. Radiocarbon dates for their early phase range from A.D. 600 to A.D. 1000 and for their late phase from A.D. 900 to A.D. 1200. Late Jersey Bluff materials are found at a number of sites in the Bottoms themselves, sometimes at substantial sites, and would have been contemporary with the developing Mississippian culture in this area.

In the Wabash valley, Winters (1967:52-60) has recognized the La Motte culture as the principal Late Woodland occupation. La Motte is marked by simple stamped and checked stamp ceramics that seem to represent an intrusion from the Southeast. Also present is the Albee complex as well as materials similar to those from the Yankeetown complex in Indiana. The Albee complex contains cordmarked ceramics representing vessels with globular bodies and occasional rim thickening. Yankeetown ceramics are distinctive for the incising over smoothed surfaces near the rims of vessels.

In central Indiana, Dorwin (1971) has interpreted the Bowen site as a Woodland occupation with Fort Ancient influence dating to the several centuries before A.D. 1000. The Walkerton site in northern Indiana (Faulkner 1960) has been interpreted as a Middle Point Peninsula

site dating to this same time period. Faulkner looked directly to the Point Peninsula sequence in New York for correspondence to his material, but a survey of this early Late Woodland manifestation (Halsey 1968) indicates that there are closer geographical correspondences in Ohio and Michigan. Cordmarked ceramics, similar to those of the Illinois Late Woodland, are known from a number of sites in western Michigan (Flanders 1965; Fitting 1968a) where they have been placed between A.D. 400 and A.D. 1000. The late Woodland occupations in the Saginaw Valley in eastern Michigan show much wider influence in ceramic styles with elaborately decorated collared rims similar to those from southern, eastern, and northern areas. The radiocarbon dates for these Late Woodland materials in the Saginaw Valley also seem to be later, after A.D. 1000, suggesting that there may be a cultural lag in this area (Fitting 1970:163-169). Late Woodland burial complexes in Michigan are varied but there is a continuation of mound burial similar to that found with the Jersey Bluff complex in both southeastern Michigan (Halsey 1968) and southwestern Michigan (Prahl 1966). These burial mounds all demonstrate a continuity from earlier Middle Woodland mounds but the grave offerings themselves are usually less elaborate. Settlement patterns and economic systems for early Woodland peoples are not well known in any area, but in Michigan they seem to represent a continuation of the Middle Woodland pattern during at least the early part of this horizon with summer population concentration and winter dispersal. By A.D. 1000, however, a shift had taken place presumably following the introduction of agriculture. The settlement patterns by that time seem to be similar to those of the historic groups in the area (Fitting 1969, 1971; Fitting and Cleland 1969). These seem to involve seasonally or continuously occupied village sites with a variety of outlying camps and temporary sites.

Sites of the early portion of the Late Woodland period seem to be rare in northern Ohio, but this is also true of the Middle Woodland period and may reflect the failure of Middle and early Late Woodland adaptive patterns to cope with the environment found along the shores of Lake Erie. Early Late Woodland materials are known from the Mixter site (Shane 1967). One of the most extensive excavations in the area has been carried out by Prufer et al. (1965) at the large Libben site along the Portage River. A series of radiocarbon dates from Libben would place it in the later part of the first millennium but the ceramics from the site are most similar to forms which postdate A.D. 1000 elsewhere.

In southern Ohio, a post-Hopewellian complex was first recognized at the Mound City Middle Woodland site (Mills 1922), where it was designated as the Intrusive Mound culture from the practice of placing intrusive burials into earlier Middle Woodland mounds. Villages of these people have been found and excavated since then. Mounds and villages of this type have been placed in the Cole complex by Baby and Potter (1965). The Peters Cave B (Prufer and McKenzie 1966) could be considered Late Woodland and the Chesser Cave (Prufer 1967) is another, slightly later, Late Woodland site. The dates from Chesser Cave indicate that Late Woodland tradition occupations continue after the development of Fort Ancient in this area.

There appears to be a gradual development in Ohio from Late Woodland into Fort Ancient. Griffin notes (1943:308) that some of his Fort Ancient components have a much stronger Woodland cast than others and observed that his cordmarked Baum focus sherds in particular would be difficult to separate from Woodland on the basis of surface finish and temper alone. Prufer and Shane (1970:240) recognize three regional variants of Fort Ancient: the Baldwin, Baum, and Brush Creek phases, all having origins predating A.D. 1000.

McMichael (1968:26-34) has described early Late Woodland materials in West Virginia with a great deal of similarity, which he has placed in the Buck Garden, Wilhelm, Watson Farm, and Montane subdivisions. Several of these components are known exclusively from burial context. Elsewhere in the upper Ohio drainage, Mayer-Oakes (1955:220) found little evidence of an early Late Woodland occupation. Most of the Late Woodland materials in this area are a part of the Fort Ancient-influenced Monongahela complex. Recent work (Don W. Dragoo, personal communication 1966) has revealed an internal developmental sequence for Monongahela Woodland but little of it seems to predate A.D. 1000.

In contrast to other areas of the Northeast, the New York developmental sequence is well known, largely through the efforts of Ritchie and his coworkers. Ritchie places what is here called early Late Woodland in the Point Peninsula sequence (1969a:234-272) with the Kipp Island and Hunter's Home phases as its major manifestations, although other manifestations are known. Ritchie sees Point Peninsula developing into Owasco, with increased village size and elaboration of ceramic decoration, and eventually being represented in the historic Iroquois materials.

This in situ theory of Iroquoian development was proposed by Griffin (1944) and demonstrated by Ritchie and MacNeish (1949) and MacNeish (1952). It was at variance with earlier theories that suggested that Iroquoian speakers were late migrants into the area who had replaced or driven out the resident Algonquian speakers. Parker's (1922) two-fold division of New York materials into Algonquian and Iroquoian was based on this migration theory. The in situ theory did much to place an emphasis on local sequential development and adaptation, and in it are found the origins of contemporary archeological interpretive methods in the Northeast. The fact that the New York sequence became so well known at a relatively early time has had another

effect. Subsequent investigators from the Atlantic coast to the shores of Lake Huron tended to interpret their own materials in light of the New York sequence; however, most recent work has indicated that in spite of many parallels, there are major differences between New York Point Peninsula and Owasco and other local sequences.

Along the mid-Atlantic coast, Stephenson and Ferguson (1963) have emphasized the conservativeness of cultural development with little to parallel the more spectacular cultural manifestations of the interior regions of the Northeast. Although they refer to them as Middle Woodland, it would appear that the cordmarked ceramics of both the Accokeek and Mockley components at the Accokeek Creek site represent coast parallels to the early Middle Woodland materials of the interior.

Early Late Woodland is represented farther to the north along the Atlantic coast by C.S. Smith's (1950) Sebonac component within his Windsor tradition; it is contemporary with the later parts of Point Peninsula in interior New York. Coastal materials farther to the north contain cordmarked, shell-tempered pottery of early Late Woodland affiliation (MacNeish 1952a:57), which is very different from Point Peninsula. In Ritchie's sequence from Martha's Vineyard, this entire time period is not represented at all.

The early Late Woodland cultural materials from southern Ontario show many parallels with the New York Point Peninsula sequence. A developmental sequence from Point Peninsula through a Huron-type material (although probably manufactured by Algonquian peoples) was found at the Frank Bay site (Ridley 1954), and this sequence has since been much refined. The Late Woodland materials as now known in Ontario range from the early Princess Point complex into the Glen Meyer and Pickering phases of the Ontario Iroquois tradition (Wright 1966). These sites and complexes show a continuous change through time in ceramic styles and an elaboration of social organization. Village sites become larger and fewer toward the contact period.

In northern Ontario, Manitoba, and Minnesota, the local Late Woodland manifestation has been designated as the Blackduck complex although other purely local terms are also used to describe similar materials. Blackduck was a cultural classification first used by Wilford in Minnesota (1941, 1955), where he noted that the pottery was its most distinctive characteristic (see Evans 1961; McPherron 1967:97-104). In general, Blackduck ceramics are globular, cordmarked vessels with slightly outflaring rims. They are decorated by cordmarked tool impressions and punctates. Types have been distinguished on the basis of decoration. The temporal placement of this material has been variously interpreted. Some of the Minnesota sites are burial mounds and Bennett (1952) considered it to be "transitional woodland," very closely related to southern Middle Woodland. It might also be noted that Bennett (1952:117) considered Middle Woodland to be a tradition rather than a horizon and suggested that it lasted until historic times in the northern Mississippi Valley.

MacNeish (1958) took a generally similar position for his Manitoba Phase, the Canadian equivalent of Blackduck, which he felt postdated A.D. 1000 and lasted until the historic period. Hlady (1970:280) has taken a similar position with the suggestion that even Laurel lasted until A.D. 1400 in Manitoba. In Ontario, Wright (1965) has suggested that Blackduck lasted until the historic period. McPherron's (1967) review of radiocarbon dates for Blackduck suggests a range of before A.D. 900 to A.D. 1500. Blackduck materials from the Juntunen site in the Straits of Mackinac reach their greatest frequency between A.D. 800 and A.D. 1100. At Chippewa Harbor Site I on Isle Royal, the Blackduck occupation has been dated to the ninth century as well (Fitting 1970:242). Blackduck at the Juntunen site is a minority ware. The Mackinac and Bois Blanc wares represent the two local ceramic phases within the developmental sequence between A.D. 800 and A.D. 1100. While these wares have some similarities to Blackduck, McPherron feels that the closest similarities are to be found with the Heins Creek ceramics on the Door Peninsula of Wisconsin (R.J. Mason 1966), which, in turn, have stylistic similarities with the Madison wares of Wisconsin that characterize the Effigy Mound cultures or complex of that area.

Effigy Mound is a confusing cultural designation. Effigy mounds themselves are found in a variety of forms in Wisconsin (Barrett and Hawkes 1919; McKern 1928, 1930, 1963; Rowe 1956; Hurley 1970) and Iowa (McKusick 1964). The ceramic complex that accompanied these mounds was a part of McKern's Lake Michigan ware but has been more recently restricted to Madison wares, a less inclusive designation. Like much of the Late Woodland pottery in the Midwest, Madison wares have globular, cordmarked bodies and a wide range of impressed rim decorations.

McKern (1963) suggested that at least one of these sites, the Spencer Mound, represented a historic group although other investigators had suggested that the mounds themselves must be generally Middle Woodland. The Spencer Mound has since been radiocarbon dated to the prehistoric period but there are still indications that Effigy Mound, while primarily post-Middle Woodland, lasted beyond A.D. 1000. This would indicate that it was contemporary with the Upper Mississippian Oneota occupation of the same area.

There are indications (Hurley 1970) that Effigy Mound peoples had a generalized economic base similar to that of other northern early Late Woodland peoples. They can be contrasted with the Upper Mississippian peoples, variously interpreted as a migration from the south (Griffin 1960) or an acculturated local group undergoing a change in the pattern of social organization (Gibbon 1972), who did have a distinctive agricultural base.

Summary

Several clear patterns emerge from this survey of the culture history of the Northeast between 300 B.C. and A.D. 1000. First, in both the Middle Woodland portion of this time period and, to a lesser extent, in the early Late Woodland period, there is a division between northern and southern cultural manifestations. This is true for earlier time periods and the differences in adaptive strategy, economic base, and social organization, as well as of material culture, are even more evident for later groups. The stylistic zones represented in archeological materials closely follow the borders of the major biotic provinces of the Northeast. It would also appear that the cultural assemblages within the Northeast tend to evolve with these biotic zones (Fitting 1971).

Second, there is a tendency for a waning and waxing of cultural elaboration in conjunction with climatic trends throughout this time period. The Middle Woodland climax corresponds with one climatic episode and declines with the end of that episode. After a hiatus where relatively little innovation occurs, a second climax, Mississippian, occurs with a return to climatic conditions similar to those which prevailed during the Middle Woodland period. It is not now certain what these changes in climate involved, but the close correlation does suggest a cause-effect relationship. The biotic and climatic correlations warn against using an exclusively cultural model of cultural change and show the need for a middle course between environmental and cultural determinism. Mechanical trends may serve to amplify or retard existing cultural characteristics but cannot be viewed as the sole causative agents. On the other hand, many of the material traits with which the archeologist must deal are more easily handled by cultural than environmental models. Agriculture, as an example, may be best interpreted with a diffusion model. It seems to be a trait with a southern origin that spreads northward over time. Ceramic manufacture and certain stylistic elements appear to follow the same pattern. In fact, there is a distinct northern lag in innovation and an inherent conservatism in northern areas although climax developments may be simultaneous in both the northern and southern area.

Third, within a single time horizon, there is also a predictable tendency for cultural elaboration to occur along the interfaces of established cultural climaxes or along purely cultural frontiers (Fitting 1971). The development of Adena in the Ohio valley and Havana in the Illinois River valley would be expected if these were interfaces between the distinctive Great Lakes–Saint Lawrence Archaic and the Shell Mound Archaic of the middle South. Elements of this new cultural climax spread back into areas of the older climaxes where they exist in a less distinctive form but do supersede the earlier climaxes.

We can note that the new climax marking Middle Woodland spread to the north along the same channels that agriculture and ceramics had followed earlier. As has been noted, however, in spite of a lag in origin, Lake Forest Middle Woodland reached the peak of its development at approximately the same time as southern Hopewell.

The "decline" into Late Woodland, for there is still no evidence that this was more than a change in artistic emphasis, is more rapid along the southern tier as well. Even with the continuity that has been noted between late Middle Woodland and early Late Woodland in this area, no one has carried Middle Woodland traditions to A.D. 1000 or later as they have for several of the northern tier Middle Woodland complexes.

This Mississippian climax, or more traditionally Mid-dle Mississippian, is directly apparent only in the southwestern portion of the Northeast. Mississippian influence is weaker and more varied with greater distance from Cahokia as we see in early Oneota, Fort Ancient, Monongahela Woodland, and Owasco. Beyond the areas where these groups are found, there is even less Mississippian influence. This too is predictable, for the economic base in the northern areas is essentially the same for both the Middle and Late Woodland periods and the establishment of an efficient agricultural system in the southern areas has a tremendous demographic and social impact.

The cultural history of the Northeast is still poorly understood, although it is much better known now than it was before the application of radiocarbon dating to the area. With the outlines of the culture content and chronology of the area known, it is the interpretation of the observed stability and the change that furnishes the challenge for future research.

Late Prehistory of the East Coast

DEAN R. SNOW

This summary of East Coast prehistory includes those Indians living along the drainage basins of rivers that flow into the Atlantic from the Neuse River of North Carolina north to and including the basins of streams that flow into the southern part of the Gulf of Saint Lawrence, but specifically excluding the basin of the Saint Lawrence River and its tributaries (fig. 1). The island of Newfoundland is included. The area embraces territory occupied by all the Eastern Algonquian tribes, who may or may not include the Beothuk of Newfoundland. In the extreme south, the Iroquoian groups of the upper drainages of the Neuse, Tar, Roanoke, and Chowan rivers are included as well.

There is ample evidence for the localization of Eastern Algonquian tribes within major river drainages (Snow 1968). The southernmost Eastern Algonquians occupied only the tidewater portions of their drainages. Upstream from the Carolina Algonquians were the Tuscarora and other Iroquoian speakers. Upstream from the Virginia Algonquians were Siouan speakers of whom very little is known. The Iroquoian Susquehannock occupied the Susquehanna River southward all the way to its mouth about 1600.

Northward from the Delmarva peninsula the Eastern Algonquians were not confined to tidewater streams. Localization according to major drainages was modified only in certain insular and peninsular areas that are drained by many small streams. Most notably, these areas are Long Island, southeastern Massachusetts, Nova Scotia, and Newfoundland. Elsewhere, the riverine pattern was developed and often elaborated by a tendency for the people of each drainage to divide into upstream and downstream components. Figure 1 is not intended to imply a careful definition of geographic boundaries by the Indians of the Coastal Region. These are drainage basin boundaries that typically run through remote and rugged hinterlands that were usually hunting areas and not frequently visited. Nevertheless, the use of drainage boundaries here allows visual clarity and imposes some order on otherwise confusing archeological evidence.

Late Prehistoric Culture Pattern

The late prehistory of the East Coast and much of its earlier prehistory as well appear to have involved a slow economic shift from generalized hunting and gathering to more specialized exploitation of wild resources. Annual fish runs on major rivers and the exploitation of marine shellfish both became important. The shift probably began earlier in the southern drainages and took place at progressively later dates northward. The same kind of south-to-north sequence appears to have characterized the introduction of farming. By A.D. 1600 farming was diffused as far north as the Eastern Abenaki, about as far as it could be productively practiced given conditions of soil and climate.

Given the substantial ecological differences between Newfoundland at one extreme and coastal North Carolina at the other, the late prehistoric culture pattern of the Coastal Region can be summarized as three separate patterns. At the southern extreme were the Virginia and Carolina Algonquians, whose pattern was one of intensive exploitation of natural estuary resources and well-developed farming. Villages were not large, having anywhere from a few to a few dozen houses. They were permanent in the sense that they were probably occupied for most of the year, but the depletion of local soils and other resources required relocation at intervals of 5 to 20 years. Houses were elongated bark- or mat-covered structures, barrel-roofed with straight or rounded ends. The population density here was higher than in more northerly drainages, and there were strong cultural influences from the greater Southeast. Upstream on the same rivers lived various Iroquoian and Siouan tribes that had combined farming, hunting, and fishing economies.

In the middle drainages, from the Delaware to the Merrimack, farming was also important; however, it was generally more important in the lower coastal portions of the drainages, where it was supplemented by fishing and shellfish gathering. The upstream portions of these drainages were occupied by groups closely related to those downstream, but who necessarily depended more upon hunting and gathering. Within each drainage, there appears to have been regular interaction between upstream and downstream communities, probably with important implications of economic exchange. Houses were similar in size, form, and construction to those in the southern drainages. In both areas, the houses were large enough to accommodate extended family groups. None was so large as the long communal dwellings of the Iroquoians, but there is archeological evidence that they were larger than average in areas where Iroquois influ-

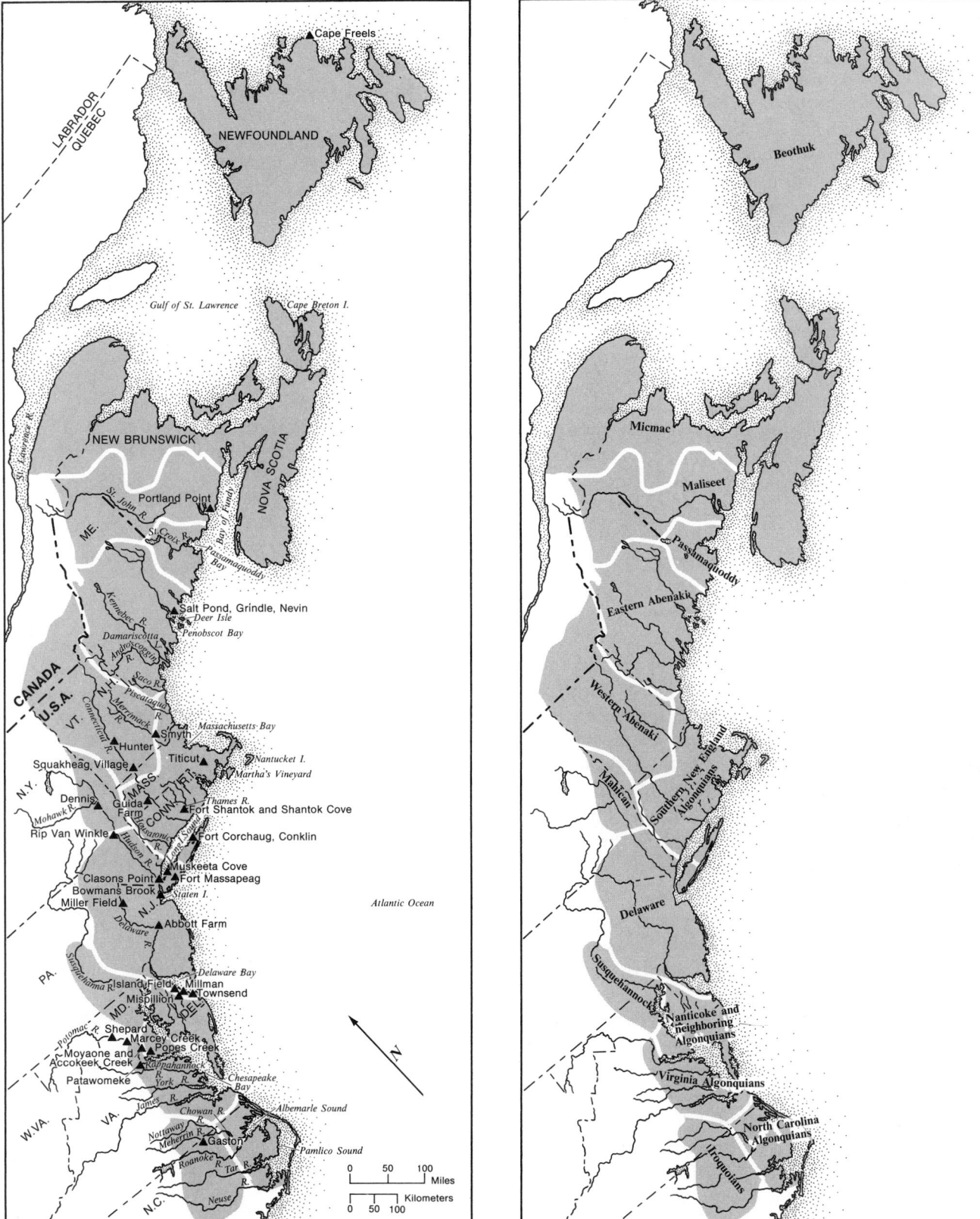

Fig. 1. Major late archeological sites of the northeast coast, with historic groups at about A.D. 1600 and the major river drainages they occupied.

59

ence was strong. As in the southern drainages, villages were sometimes palisaded. Settlements normally persisted for a decade or so in areas where agriculture was possible, but settlements in the interior uplands were less permanent, often temporary hunting camps. All the Algonquians of the middle drainages were influenced by neighboring Iroquoians in the interior.

From the Eastern Abenaki to the Beothuk of Newfoundland, farming was of little importance, and settlements were probably less permanent toward the northeast. Houses were smaller in the northern drainages, normally being square or round, bark-covered, single-family dwellings. Such settlements were probably vacated completely in seasons when the people were drawn to the coastal shellfish beds or to interior hunting grounds. Such would not have been the case farther south, where agriculture would have required that at least a few of the very young and the very old stay behind to protect crops in the summer.

The economic importance of shellfish also decreased northward. Common clams (*Mya arenaria*) are found all the way to Greenland, but oysters (*Crassostrea virginica*) are found only locally as far north as Cape Breton Island, and quahogs (*Mercenaria mercenaria*) occur only as far as Maine. Thus in the northern drainages, hunting and fishing were more important than they were farther south. As in the case of the tribes of the middle drainages, there is some evidence for the division of local groups into upstream and downstream components, probably again for economic reasons. On some rivers there appears to have been a tendency for some groups to specialize in the exploitation of marine resources in estuary environments, while other groups maintained a stronger orientation toward the resources of interior forests and streams. The split was not so strong as it appears to have been in the middle drainages. Linguistic evidence suggests dialectical contrasts in the north as opposed to the more profound contrasts found in the middle drainages. There is little or no evidence for upstream-downstream divisions east of the Saint John drainage.

Historic evidence indicates that conflicts sometimes arose between local Eastern Algonquian communities. Nevertheless there was probably some general feeling of common culture between the peoples of contiguous drainages, reinforced by contrast with the Iroquoian and Siouan communities in the interior. Diffusion of both material and nonmaterial traits along the coast was probably facilitated by frequent trade and intermarriage between contiguous tribes. Linguistically, the split between the Delaware and the Algonquians to the south appears to be relatively deep. The split between the Micmac and the other Eastern Algonquians is similarly deep.

Origins

The prehistoric cultures of the coastal plain have contrasted with those of the upland oak-chestnut-hickory forests since at least 6000 B.C. (Sears 1964:260). Archeological sequences and tribal distributions at first European contact combine to suggest that, for the most part, the coastal area was characterized by steady development without notable discontinuities. The implication is that the prehistoric traditions that lead to the historic cultures covered here extend back several thousands of years. Thus, archeology does not support the literal acceptance of origin myths that seem to say that most tribes were relatively recent arrivals from distant and unspecified lands. Instead, the picture is one of many parallel sequences, each part of a broader pattern of development, but each diverging somewhat from the main stream in response to special local conditions.

Two exceptions to this pattern may be noted. First, the cultural sequence in the southern drainages seems interrupted by a major discontinuity that appears to fall shortly after 500 B.C. (Coe 1964:121). The Savannah River complex is abruptly replaced by a fully developed intrusive technology that included ceramics and triangular points. The local expression of the intrusive technology in the upper Pee Dee drainage is somewhat different from that found in the upper Roanoke drainage, but both appear to derive from the Piedmont to the north. The discontinuity probably represents the intrusion of Iroquoian and Siouan speakers into the southern drainages. That penetration involved upper drainages from the Potomac to the Neuse and entire drainages farther south.

Intrusion also took place at the other end of the Coastal Region. The Dorset Eskimo moved into at least the coastal areas of Newfoundland beginning about A.D. 1, then gradually disappeared from the area by A.D. 600 (Tuck 1971d:28). It is not yet clear whether a local Indian population persisted through the period of Eskimo presence. The historic Beothuk may have been either survivors of the pre-Dorset Indian population or the descendents of post-Dorset Indian immigrants to Newfoundland.

Chowan, Roanoke, Tar-Pamlico, and Neuse Drainages

Coe's work in the upper Roanoke basin suggests that the historic Iroquoian residents of that area moved in after 500 B.C. The earliest ceramics from features at the Gaston site are of the Vincent series (Coe 1964:101–102). These types are analogous to those of the Stoney Creek series found in the neighboring Virginia Piedmont (C. Evans 1955:69–75). Clements series types dominated after A.D. 1000, followed by the Gaston series just before the colonial period. The Gaston series is analogous to the Clarksville series of the Virginia Piedmont (Coe 1964:102–106; C. Evans 1955:49–54); its pottery was probably made by late prehistoric Iroquoians.

Haag's (1958) survey of sites in the tidewater portions of the same drainages shows that the pottery types there contrast with those from the Piedmont and are basically similar to those of the coastal Virginia area. Cultural continuity within the area of the Carolina and Virginia Algonquians is therefore supported by archeological as well as linguistic evidence.

South of the Neuse, the post-500 B.C. intrusion penetrated all the way to the sea, terminating any Algonquian occupation of that area permanently. The Algonquians of the southern drainages of the Coastal Region therefore began their adaptive shift toward an economy that combined farming and the exploitation of estuaries by about the same time. Hunting could not have been so important as it was in the upper portions of the drainages.

No positively identified Tuscarora site has been located. The assumption that Tuscaroras were necessarily a very late intrusive culture is no longer so popular as it once was. Certainly the archeological contrasts in the Carolina-Virginia drainages suggest 2,000 years of cultural stability in the area occupied by the historic Tuscarora and their Iroquoian relatives, the Meherrin and Nottaway of the upper Chowan drainage.

Archeological and ethnohistorical evidence indicates that both the Algonquian and Iroquoian inhabitants of these southern drainages lived in dispersed settlements. Villages were small, often only 10 or 12 houses. There is some evidence that at first historic contact, some development of broader economic and political networks was going on; however, the general picture remains one of scattered independent groups. This appears to have been a very old pattern, one that will make future archeological research difficult.

James, York, Rappahannock, and Potomac Drainages and the Delmarva Peninsula

Knowledge of the late prehistory of the major Virginia drainages as derived from published sources depends largely upon ceramic analyses, most of which are structured within the Midwestern Taxonomic system and without benefit of radiocarbon dating. Discussion of archeological evidence in terms of the antecedents of historic Indians is therefore difficult at best. Nevertheless, there are a few generalizations that can be tentatively advanced.

There is a long continuum of ceramic wares for this area, each ware apparently derived from its predecessor. Early Woodland period Algonquians appear to be represented by Popes Creek ware at the Accokeek Creek and Popes Creek sites on the lower Potomac. At the Accokeek Creek site, the Middle Woodland period is represented by the Accokeek and Mockley phases, in that order. Mockley ware is ancestral to later Chickahominy and Townsend wares that are found around the Chesapeake Bay tidewater and on the Delmarva Peninsula. Similarly late Potomac Creek ware types, which define a phase of the same name, are found at Accokeek Creek, and the historically known sites of Patawomeke and Moyaone, both occupied by Virginia Algonquians (figs. 2–3). C. Evans (1955:120) suggests that tidewater Virginia and Maryland could be considered a single cultural unit in protohistoric times, despite the presumed distinctiveness of the Nanticoke-Conoy. That unit would in fact properly extend all the way to small coastal drainages of southern Delaware, on the Atlantic side of the Delmarva peninsula. There, Townsend ware types have been identified in

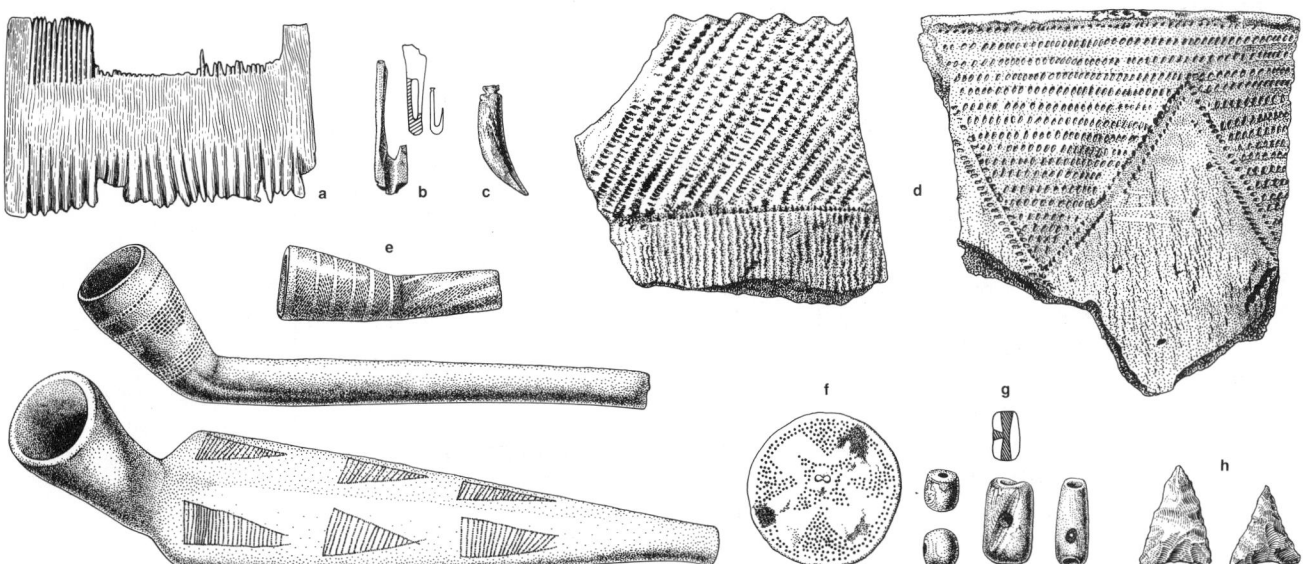

Dept. of Anthr., Smithsonian, Archeol.: a, 379023; b, 378945; c, 378842; d, 378692; e, 378819, 378914, 378892; f, 378988; g, 379019; h, 378736.

Fig. 2. Late Woodland artifacts from Patawomeke, Marlborough Point, Stafford Co., Va. a, Bone comb; b, unfinished bone fishhook; c, raccoon-tooth pendant; d, cordmarked pottery with punctate decorations; e, various clay pipe forms; f, shell gorget; g, shell beads; h, projectile points. Length of a 7.4 cm, rest same scale.

Dept. of Anthr., Smithsonian, Archeol.: 145944.
Fig. 3. Shell effigy face from the mouth of Potomac Creek, Stafford Co., Va. Diameter 10.6 cm.

Fig. 4. Part of bone concentration at Ossuary II, Nanjemoy Creek, Charles Co., Md., showing assemblage from secondary burial. Photograph by Douglas H. Ubelaker (see also Ubelaker 1974).

the Townsend and Mispillion sites (Lewis 1971:11; Thomas and Warren 1970).

The protohistoric Virginia Algonquians lived in a dispersed settlement pattern, although apparently not so dispersed as the Carolina Algonquians. The confederation of local groups was going on in 1600, and there is some evidence of rising militarism. The Accokeek Creek site and others were stockaded. Farming was well developed, as was the exploitation of the special resources of the area estuaries. Not the least important crop was tobacco (*Nicotiana rustica*).

Burial was often carried out with elaborate ceremony and interment in large ossuaries that are known to have held up to 500 individuals (fig. 4). Apparently, the skin and flesh of dead individuals were removed and the bones deposited separately. Stewart (1940) and others have excavated several such ossuaries.

Balanced against the Potomac Creek, Chickahominy, and Townsend ceramic wares of the lower drainages are the ceramics of the Gala, Montgomery, and Luray phases of the upper drainages (Schmitt 1952:62–63; Stephenson and Ferguson 1963:200–205). Distributions of the sites at which each of these wares is found leave little doubt that the latter three phases were produced by the Piedmont Siouans. MacCord, Schmitt, and Slattery (1957:28) note that Albemarle types sometimes turn up in Susquehannock sites and suggest that some Virginia communities, such as that at the Shepard site, were adopted and absorbed by the Susquehannock; however, the presence of Albemarle types on the Susquehanna might only indicate trade.

Delaware Drainage

The geographic rift defined by the Chesapeake Bay and the mouth of the Susquehanna River was apparently attended by a cultural (including linguistic) divergence of the more southerly Algonquians away from those of the Delaware drainage and northward. The Algonquians of the Delaware continued to exploit the upstream interior portions of their drainage while the Carolina-Virginia Algonquians, through either choice or necessity, confined themselves to coastal estuaries. Communication overland across the Delmarva peninsula was not difficult, and the people of Sussex County, Delaware, were tied culturally to those around Chesapeake Bay. Still, the divergence persisted, and the late prehistoric archeological evidence from the Delaware drainage is not equivalent to that found immediately to the south.

The tendency for upstream-downstream divergence that appears in the Early Woodland becomes more pronounced in the Middle Woodland. The Bushkill phase of the upper Delaware is best known at the Miller Field site (Kinsey 1971; Kraft 1970). In contrast, the Island Field site near Dover, Delaware, has yielded evidence for a separate "Webb phase" (Thomas and Warren 1970). This split parallels the historic one between the downstream Unami and the upstream Munsee.

The Late Woodland period, which dates after A.D. 1200, is not well known. The examination of ceramics, to the exclusion of other artifact classes, has led to the classification of many late components on the upper Delaware (fig. 5) with the Owasco tradition, which in upper New York State is early Iroquoian. More careful analysis of future findings will probably show that the similarities are superficial. The historic Munsee were heavily influenced by the Iroquois, and Iroquois women may have occasionally married in, but there was probably no confusion about ethnic identities at the time.

a, after W.S. Fowler 1974–1975:fig. 16; b–d, after Kraft 1975:figs. 6, 8, 13.

Fig. 5. Late Woodland pottery of Upper Delaware Valley. a, Two pots recovered from Broadhead Creek, Monroe Co., Pa.; b, Owasco Herringbone from the Pahaquarra culture (about A.D. 1000–1350), with sharply everted rim possibly to allow suspension; c, Oak Hill Corded from the Late Pahaquarra, Early Minisink culture (about A.D. 1250–1400); d–e, Munsee Incised from the Minisink culture (about A.D. 1400–1735) with stylized effigy faces at castellations; d, face formed by dowel-impressed punctates, from Harry's Farm site, Warren Co.; e, face with nostrils, from Bell-Philhower and Post sites, Sussex Co., N.J. Rim diameter of b about 25.7 cm, rest same scale.

Kraft (1970a) has already shown that similarities between Delaware longhouses and those of the Iroquois are superficial. Important differences of style and structure, reflective of parallel social differences, have been revealed by careful analysis.

The Milford Neck complex of the southern Delaware drainage is a little better known. Evidence comes primarily from the Millman site near Milford, Delaware (Thomas and Lewis 1966). Cultural connections seem to be with components of the same age upstream, although the upstream-downstream split undoubtedly persisted. Although the ceramics of the Milford Neck complex show the same shift to shell tempering seen for the Late Woodland of the southern drainages, the complex as a whole contrasts strikingly with the Townsend complex, which is found south and west of the streams flowing into Delaware Bay.

Hudson Drainage

What little Owasco tradition material appears in the upper Hudson drainage is often related to one of the early Owasco phases. Thus, despite much searching, little is known of the Woodland sequence in the Hudson drainage. Because of this, the available evidence is often assigned to phases and traditions defined for the much better-known sequences of central New York, creating the illusion of uniform cultural development over the whole area (Ritchie 1958:102, 1969a:179–324). The only well-defined indigenous Middle Woodland phase on the Upper Hudson is the Fourmile phase, which dates to about A.D. 700. There is evidence that the people responsible for this phase were specializing in the exploitation of large sea sturgeon as well as gathering nuts during at least the warm months (Funk 1976).

The Woodland sequence along the lower Hudson is somewhat less ambiguous. The Windsor tradition was established by at least Middle Woodland times with the first appearance of its North Beach phase. This tradition probably evolved from Orient culture with the introduction of pottery and new types in other artifact classes. Components of the Windsor tradition phases are found on Long Island and in the lower Connecticut drainage as well as on the lower Hudson; however, only the early Windsor North Beach and Clearview phases are known for the lower Hudson and the western end of Long Island. Here the Windsor tradition was replaced by the East River tradition beginning in about A.D. 1300. The Bowmans Brook and later Clasons Point phases define the Late Woodland locally. The East River tradition to which they belong appears to have been intrusive from the west and south, and it probably represents the arrival of the Munsee from the Delaware River drainage. The ceramics of the Bowmans Brook phase resemble Abbott ware. This ware is best known from the Abbott Farm site near Trenton, and its heaviest concentration seems to be located in the middle portion of the Delaware drainage (Cross 1941-1956, 2). Various types of Abbott ware are found throughout the Delaware drainage, Staten Island, the western end of Long Island, along the lower Hudson, and into southwestern Connecticut, the area occupied by the historic Munsee (Lopez 1961).

At least a dozen components of the Clasons Point phase have been recognized (Ritchie 1969a:270). One of these is Fort Massapeag on the western end of Long Island, a site with both late prehistoric and early historic remains. With the others, it is presumed to have been a Munsee site.

The identification of the East River tradition with the Munsee was first discussed in detail by C.S. Smith (1950). Salwen (1968) has since uncovered evidence at the Muskeeta Cove site that throws that identification into doubt. East River, Windsor, and Owasco ceramic traits appear to be blended (sometimes on the same vessels) in a way that argues against clear-cut invasion and replacement. Perhaps prehistoric intermarriage obscured ethnic boundaries here as it appears to have done on the Delaware, where some components are called Owasco. Given the apparent need to explain the arrival of the Munsee on the lower Hudson, Smith's explanation is still generally accepted.

Prior to Goddard's (1971a) linguistic investigations, there was some confusion regarding ethnic boundaries in the lower Hudson drainage. Most older sources state that there was a boundary running down the middle of the river, separating the Munsee on the west from the "Wappinger" on the east, who were supposed to occupy territory as far east as the Connecticut. Goddard has shown that the Munsee occupied all the lower Hudson drainage and that Quiripi-Unquachog was the dialect spoken in the lower Connecticut and Housatonic drainages as well as on Long Island. There appears to have been no Wappinger confederacy. These new findings fit well with the archeology and what is known of Algonquian territoriality.

In the upper Hudson drainages, the Late Woodland ancestors of the Mahican are not well known archeologically. Fortifications on Owasco and derivative Iroquois sites suggest that relations with the residents of the Hudson were at least sometimes not friendly. Ritchie (1952) has assigned the Kingston component to the Chance phase, following the general practice of extending the Owasco tradition to include scattered findings on the Hudson. The Kingston site provides the only component of the Chance phase found outside the Mohawk valley. It has strong connections with the other components, but it also has distinctive ceramic and other traits that make it unique. The Kingston component will probably ultimately be reassigned with other Hudson drainage components to a separate phase. Such a redefi-

nition will allow differentiation between prehistoric Iroquoians and Algonquians.

The Rip Van Winkle site is the only adequately reported contact site on the upper Hudson (Weinman and Weinman 1971). Dutch trade goods and items of Indian manufacture were found together on this site. The inhabitants were probably the historic Mahican. Soon after contact, these people were forced eastward out of the Hudson drainage by the Mohawk.

Connecticut and Housatonic Drainages and Long Island

The Woodland sequence of the lower Connecticut and the Housatonic rivers and Long Island closely parallels that already described for the lower Hudson; however, here the sequence of four Windsor phases is not completely truncated by the East River tradition. Strong influences radiated eastward from the intrusive tradition, but except for the western end of Long Island, the evidence does not indicate extensive invasion and replacement. Most Windsor tradition components show evidence for the expected mixed shellfish collecting, hunting, and agricultural economy (B.W. Powell 1971).

The distribution of Windsor components indicates that the lower Connecticut, most of Long Island, and much of the Housatonic drainage were culturally united during most of the Woodland period. Wappinger is not a suitable ethnic label for the historic people that descended from that tradition, and none of the several confusing labels used to identify the inhabitants of Long Island serves any better. Given the lack of any other corporate identity, the linguistic unit Connecticut-Unquachog is used here to identify this culture. Long Island Sound appears to have served as a convenient avenue of communication, rather than as a barrier. Like the other Algonquians of the middle and southern coastal drainages, these people moved about in dugout canoes.

As on the Hudson, the Woodland sequence in the upper Connecticut drainage differs from that in the lower part of the drainage. The best-known site there is the Guida Farm site in Massachusetts (Byers and Rouse 1960). Coastal influences turn up in the form of some Clearview phase ceramics; however, influences from the upper Hudson appear to be stronger here and at the Hunter site. During the Late Woodland, ceramic affiliations at the Guida Farm site are with three traditions. Windsor influences came up the Connecticut, East River influences came up the Housatonic, and Owasco influences came in via the upper Hudson. Late prehistoric remains are dominated by traits of apparently local origin. Called the Guida tradition, this development appears to lead directly to the historic Pocumtuck and related people of the Connecticut River valley between Hartford and Deerfield, Massachusetts. Little is known of the prehistory of the Western Abenaki living in the Connecticut valley north of Deerfield.

64

U. of the State of N.Y., Albany.
Fig. 6. Sebonac Stamped type vessel from Conklin site, Aquebogue, Long Island. Height about 38 cm.

On the coast, the Niantic phase follows the Sebonac phase (fig. 6). At least some of the components of this phase can be attributed to the historic Niantic Indians of the area.

Thames Drainage

The archeology of the Thames drainage is on a spatial continuum between the lower Connecticut and southeastern Massachusetts. Similarly, forms of speech within the same area formed a continuum within which variations were gradual and intergrading. Nevertheless, the historic importance of the Mohegan-Pequot, traditional confusion regarding their origin, and certain late prehistoric problems have prompted their separate treatment here.

The similarity of the name "Mohegan" to "Mahican" has led to the widespread belief that the historic Mohegan-Pequot moved to the Thames drainage in a late prehistoric migration from the upper Hudson. There are no archeological or linguistic data to support the migration hypothesis. The Mohegan-Pequot are related most closely to their coastal neighbors. Linguistic connections with the Mahican are relatively distant, just as they are with the Munsee and the Abenaki. The best conclusion is that all the southern New England peoples developed in place from a common origin (Salwen 1969).

Remains from the Shantok Cove site include Windsor tradition ceramics and some East River types as well. The site, which was first occupied around A.D. 770, is located near New London, Connecticut. These findings, uncovered by Salwen (1969), support the hypothesis of an in-place development of historic Mohegan-Pequot culture. The nearby contact period site of Fort Shantok has produced the distinctive Shantok ware, which indicates some late prehistoric individuality on the part of the Mohegan-Pequot. This is in line with linguistic evidence and other archeological evidence that suggest some local divergence characterized southern New England as a whole in the centuries just before contact. Ceramics similar to Shantok ware are known from Guida Farm and various sites in Rhode Island and southeastern Massachusetts, but there are significant differences in detail.

Shantok ware is also found at the Fort Corchaug site on eastern Long Island. This site was apparently occupied by the Montauk, who are known to have spoken the same language as the Mohegan-Pequot. It is reasonable to conclude that the eastern end of Long Island was culturally united with the Thames drainage, at least during late prehistoric times (Solecki 1950). Thus, the archeology of Long Island supports linguistic evidence for three distinct languages at contact. The indigenous Quiripi-Unquachog appears to have been supplanted first by Munsee on the western end of the island and later by Mohegan-Pequot on the eastern end. Unfortunately, ethnic identities have been obscured in much of the available literature by the application of "Montauk," "Metoac," and other inappropriate names to all the Indians of Long Island.

Southeastern New England

The small drainages of southeastern Massachusetts and Rhode Island were inhabited by the historic Massachusett-Narragansett, a division that includes the Nauset, Wampanoag, and other small local groups. The later cultures of the area emerged from the common southern New England base. Ritchie's (1969) excavations on Martha's Vineyard have shown that shellfish exploitation there developed at least 4,000 years ago. There is evidence to indicate that a similar shift toward shellfish exploitation took place 2,000 years earlier on the lower Hudson (Brennan 1962), but not until 2,000 years later on the central Maine coast (Snow 1972:215). Rising sea level has been more pronounced in the Bay of Fundy than in southern New England, and some archeologists argue that associated erosion of coastal sites accounts for the absence of early shell middens in Maine. However, evidence from the Damariscotta estuary seems to indicate the presence of large unexploited oyster beds there before A.D. 1. The distance from the mouth of the Hudson to the coast of Maine is only about 400 miles, yet the inception of shellfish exploitation along that spatial continuum appears to have moved northeastward only very slowly. The emergence of this supplement to the native economy was closely linked to a complex of slowly changing ecological factors. Rising sea level was one of these, but it appears not to have been primary.

Dincauze (1971a) has presented convincing evidence to indicate that there was a decline in the population of southeastern New England following the second millennium B.C. It appears to have ebbed for at least 1,000 years, beginning to rise once again during the millennium following A.D. 1. The initial decline was probably linked to ecological factors that also inspired the development of the shellfish industry, but precise causes are still unknown. There is no good evidence to indicate anything but gradual climatic amelioration over the last few thousand years in New England. However, the period has been marked by the steady expansion of conifers and bogs, apparently in connection with the progressive evolution of soils and drainage patterns (H.E. Wright 1971:451). Resulting changes in local fauna could explain both the population decline and the shift to shellfish collection. The later population rebound is probably best explained as a result of the introduction of agriculture. Middle Woodland period developments on Martha's Vineyard were influenced by the Point Peninsula tradition of New York. These influences have been detected primarily on the basis of ceramic evidence. Late Woodland ceramics show weaker connections with proto-Iroquoian and Iroquoian developments in New York (Ritchie 1969:226-228). The evidence from Martha's Vineyard indicates that people there were participating in the increasingly distinctive southern New England culture pattern as the colonial period approached (fig. 7). Evidence from the Titicut site in mainland southeastern Massachusetts points to the same conclusion. Shantok-like pottery and other materials typical of late prehistoric southern New England were found at this site along with some early historic remains.

The late prehistoric subsistence economy was a diversified pattern of hunting, fishing, shellfish collecting, plant collecting, and agriculture. The white-tailed deer appears to have been the most important terrestrial game animal. Some marine animals, including ducks, were also hunted. The relatively late introduction of agriculture probably led to a progressively more sedentary way of life and to the growth of settlements on the coastal plain where farming was most productive. A significant proportion of the population probably spent the summer months near the coast. Part of this time was spent gathering shellfish, but much of it would have been devoted to farming, fishing, hunting, and wild-plant gathering. The unusual bulk of shellfish remains and their tendency to preserve well have led some investigators to

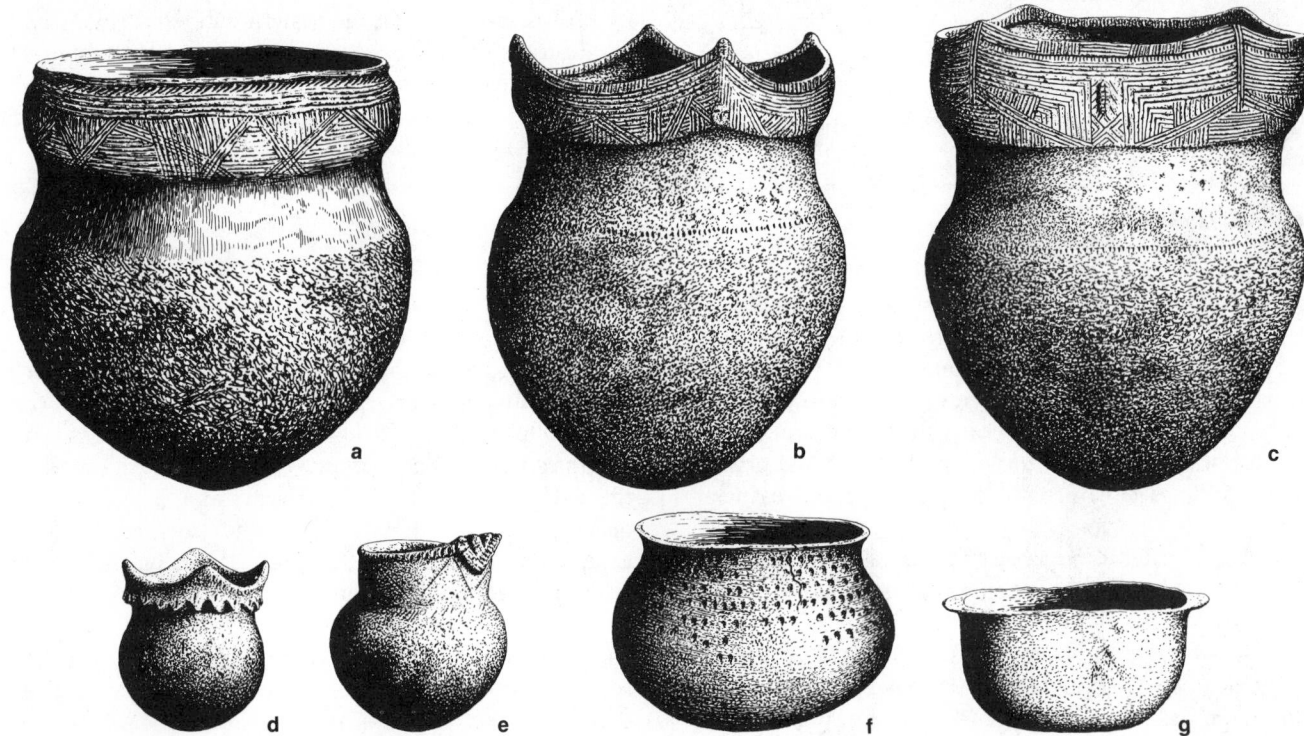

W.S. Fowler 1966:fig. 18.

Fig. 7. Late Woodland pottery from southeastern New England area. a, Early phase (around 1400) without castellations; b, with effigy face at castellation; c, with corn ear bosses between the castellations; d-e, burial pots, e with a single castellation elaborately decorated with 3 effigy faces and 2 ears of corn in a V shape; f-g, late phase (probably about 1650) showing creative decline, f may be a copy of the shape of an iron pot and g of a small copper kettle. a, c-e, g, from Narragansett Bay drainage; b, from Cape Cod; f, from Pecowsic Fort site. Rim diameter of a about 26 cm, rest same scale.

SNOW

overestimate the importance of this resource. Shellfish did not amount to a staple food and was probably a major part of the average Indian's diet for only a few days or weeks of the summer season.

Merrimack Drainage

A considerable amount of archeological investigation has been carried out along the streams of the Merrimack drainage. Unfortunately, much of it was done before the advent of radiocarbon dating and other advanced archeological techniques, and the prehistory of the drainage is still rather poorly known. The Smyth site has produced evidence of a long sequence that shows strong Point Peninsula and later Iroquoian tradition influences in its late prehistoric segment. The influences have been detected primarily by ceramic analysis. As yet, there is no well-defined chronology, nor is there clear evidence of upstream-downstream division.

The Western Abenaki, who inhabited the Merrimack drainage at the beginning of the colonial period, were closely related to the Eastern Abenaki of Maine. However, ceramic styles suggest relatively strong late prehistoric influences from southern New England Algonquians and the Iroquois. The scanty evidence available also suggests a relatively late date for the introduction of agriculture. The Hunter site has produced the charred remains of maize and beans.

There is some evidence to suggest that the territory inhabited by the Western Abenaki extended to the lower portions of the Saco drainage in A.D. 1600. Alternatively, Massachusett-related Indians may have inhabited the coastal area all the way to the Saco, living in a strip between the Western Abenaki and the sea. Champlain (1907:61) noted a sharp cultural contrast between the people of the Saco and those farther northeast in 1605. The upper portion of the Saco drainage appears to have been within the sphere of the Eastern Abenaki.

Androscoggin, Kennebec, and Penobscot Drainages

The major Maine drainages, along with the upper Saco and many smaller coastal drainages, were occupied by the Eastern Abenaki in 1600. As in the Merrimack drainage, much early work was carried out before the development of advanced techniques (Moorehead 1922; Snow 1968a), but further work led to the development of well-defined local chronology. Bourque (1971) excavated several shell midden sites on Deer Isle that are relevant to the late prehistoric sequence. Other investigations on the Damariscotta estuary and at the Grindle site on Salt Pond have provided further clarification (Snow 1972).

The emergence of the late prehistoric cultural pattern was clearly under way by A.D. 1. By that time, the accumulation of shell refuse at various midden sites had begun. It is possible but unproved that shellfish gathering was important along the Maine coast in earlier centuries. The presence of slightly earlier cultural remains not associated with shell refuse has been noted under some shell middens.

The huge oyster shell middens on the Damariscotta estuary grew slowly for perhaps 1,800 years. Elsewhere refuge colonies of oysters did not survive the slowly rising sea level, and Indian technology shifted gradually from easily collected species such as oyster and quahog to the more widely available common clam.

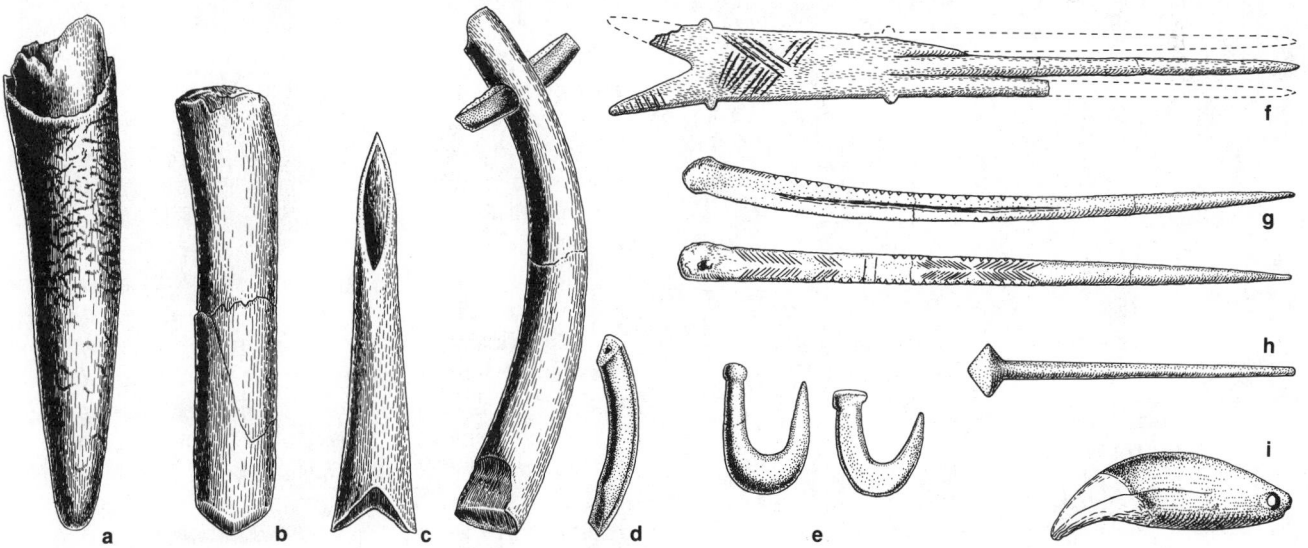

after Willoughby 1935:figs. 119, 122-124.

Fig. 8. Late Woodland bone and antler artifacts from central coastal Maine sites. a, Antler prong probably used for opening oysters, from Whaleback Shell heap, Damariscotta; b, antler implement for stone chipping, from Vinalhaven; c, bone projectile point from a Maine shell heap; d, beaver-tooth cutting tool, from Morse's I., Friendship Bay, and handle with tooth in place, from French's I., Casco Bay; e, bone fishhooks; f, antler ornamental comb from Vinalhaven; g, bone bodkin from Bremen; h, antler pin probably for fastening garment; i, bear-tooth pendant. Length of f about 19 cm, rest same scale.

Late prehistoric sea level rise appears to have been caused by crustal downwarping, which has been more pronounced in the direction of the Bay of Fundy. Thus, the effects on the Indian populations have been less noticeable in southern New England than in the Maritime Provinces of Canada. Salt Pond, on which the Grindle site is located, was probably not saline until shortly before the site was occupied in A.D. 1150. When the sea level rose high enough to enter the pond, clam beds became established there, and the site became attractive to prehistoric Indians. Many other sites from there eastward have undoubtedly been lost to erosion; however, some, like the Nevin site at the mouth of Salt Pond, have survived since the Archaic on rocky promontories (Snow 1972).

Evidence from the Deer Isle sites allows the definition of the Whitmore phase, which appears to date to about A.D. 1. The ceramics of this phase are the earliest definitely known for this area. The pottery tends to be thin, hard, and generally well made, suggesting that ceramic techniques or even the pots themselves were introduced as a developed complex from the drainages to the southwest. Ceramics of the subsequent Oak Point and Salt Pond phases are thicker and less well made. The

temporal boundary between these two phases, which is currently set at about A.D. 1000, marks the shift from grit to shell tempering in the pottery (Bourque 1971). An analogous shift took place in other subdivisions of the Eastern Algonquian region.

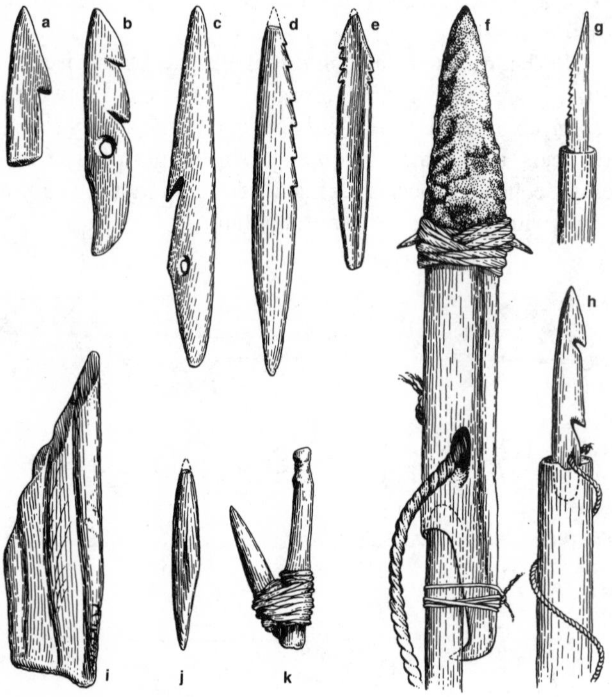

The late prehistoric subsistence pattern involved a seasonal round of summer residence on the coast and winter residence in the interior. Winter was spent in small hunting bands. Spring brought the exploitation of fish runs on the rivers, and summer afforded plenty of gathered plant and animal foods along the coast. This kind of seasonal round probably also characterized the more southerly drainages before the introduction of agriculture. In A.D. 1600 there appears to have been some agriculture on the Kennebec but little if any farther northeast. Probably owing to these factors, the evidence for upstream-downstream subdivisions within the area is relatively slight. The people from here northward made birchbark canoes and were quite mobile as compared to the other Eastern Algonquians.

Saint John and Saint Croix Drainages

The historic Maliseet and Passamaquoddy, who inhabit the Saint John and Saint Croix drainages respectively, are sometimes lumped under the name Etchemin. Their prehistory has not been extensively explored, partly because the relatively rapid rise of sea level in the Bay of Fundy over the last few thousand years has destroyed many, perhaps most, coastal sites.

Work by Sanger (1971a:17) around Passamaquoddy Bay has produced evidence of semisubterranean houses. Matthew (1892) first reported these features in 1884. They are relatively small round structures, typically depressions about 10 feet in diameter, which probably housed individual nuclear families. Sanger estimates that they were occupied about A.D. 1–1200. He concludes that winter residence was on the coast during that period, a settlement pattern probably made possible by a productive shellfish industry and an adequate local game animal population.

The pattern appears to have reverted to the kind of seasonal round practiced by the Eastern Abenaki after A.D. 1200. The reasons for the presumed abandonment of coastal residence during the cold months are not yet understood. A drop in sea-water temperature that probably accompanied the rise in sea level in the Bay of Fundy may have made shellfish beds only marginally productive. A relatively subtle temperature decline has been used to explain the decline in oyster populations along the coast over the last 2,000 years. Alternatively, or perhaps additionally, the shift in settlement pattern might have been necessitated by some progressive change in the forest ecology. There is no present evidence for a significant climatic change during this period.

a-h, W.S. Fowler 1971-1972:fig. 11; i-k, Bruce 1965:fig. 3.

Fig. 9. Late Woodland bone fishing gear from coastal Maine sites. a-e, harpoon and leister points: a, b, from Duxbury; c, from Maine; d, from Long Cove site; e, from Amsbury shellheap; f, stone point and bone foreshaft, with conjectural lashing, bone barbs, and shaft; g, conjectural hafting of bone-tipped arrow or spear, without line; h, conjectural hafting for line-connected harpoon; i, bone with partly cut out implements, from Long Cove site; j, fishhook point from Long Cove site; k, one probable method of attaching fishhook point. Length of a 4.3 cm, rest same scale.

The ancestral Maliseet-Passamaquoddy began producing pottery at about the same time as did the Eastern Abenaki. In this case too, the earliest ceramic remains appear to have been modeled after "Middle Woodland" prototypes from the west and south. Agriculture was attempted with only partial success during the early colonial period. It was apparently not practiced at all prehistorically. Excavations at Portland Point have turned up early historic Indian as well as Archaic and European remains (Harper 1956). Further work along both the Saint Croix and the Saint John will undoubtedly clarify the late prehistoric sequence.

Nova Scotia, Prince Edward Island, and Eastern New Brunswick Drainages

Relatively little archeological research has been published for the Micmac area since Smith and Wintemberg's (1929) survey of Nova Scotia shell middens. However, the Halifax Museum and other agencies have been carrying out archeological investigations that should ultimately illuminate Micmac prehistory.

The relatively deep linguistic split between the Micmac and the other Eastern Algonquians to the southwest suggests that the Micmac prehistoric sequence will show significant independence from other Eastern Algonquian sequences. The lack of any major river system in the Micmac area has undoubtedly contributed to the maritime orientation of these people, an orientation that may be quite ancient. Archeological investigation of Micmac prehistory has been made difficult by the progressive destruction of coastal sites by erosion.

Newfoundland

Tuck (1971d) has concluded that the Beothuk did not arrive on Newfoundland until after the demise of the local Dorset Eskimo population around A.D. 600. He suggested that they may have moved in from the forests of Labrador and Quebec. Later Tuck (1976:64) suggested that the Beothuk may be descended from old inhabitants of Newfoundland that survived on the island through the Dorset Eskimo occupation. Present archeological evidence does not permit an easy choice between these two hypotheses.

Tuck 1976:pl. 16.

Fig. 10. Prehistoric Beothuk artifacts from the Cape Freels site, Bonavista Bay. left, Two triangular "bifaces" probably used as knives; upper right, two scrapers probably used to dress skins or for working bone and wood; lower right, projectile points. Length of far left 8.0 cm, rest same scale.

Late prehistoric Beothuk materials have been collected by Helen Devereaux and others (fig. 10). Preliminary indications are that the Beothuk had an economy not unlike that of the Dorset Eskimo. They depended upon marine resources for much of the year and hunted caribou during their annual migrations. They lived in the interior for only a relatively short period each year. Their extermination by the early nineteenth century resulted partly from colonial genocide and partly from their confinement to unfavorable interior refuge areas (Tuck 1976:61–76).

Summary

The late prehistory of the East Coast appears in the archeological record as a smooth outgrowth from earlier periods. Each local sequence seems to reflect a long-term stability that belies the stories of recent migrations that have been popular for many years. For the most part, there are series of related in-place developments, each contained within a natural drainage unit. Innovations have tended to move from south to north through the area, moving slowly as local cultures made the appropriate adaptations in succession. Waves of change moved northward over time, as innovations such as ceramic manufacture, shellfish collecting, and agriculture were extended to their ecological limits.

Eastern Algonquian Languages

IVES GODDARD

The Eastern Algonquian languages were spoken aboriginally from the Maritimes to North Carolina along the Atlantic coast and immediately inland from it. (For their present status see table 1.) Since they share a number of innovations that the Algonquian languages farther west do not attest, it must be assumed that they descend from an ancestral Proto-Eastern Algonquian language (PEA) that had had a certain period of independent development after branching off from the common parent of the whole family, Proto-Algonquian (PA). For example, all the Eastern languages have undergone a major restructuring of the verbal paradigm that expresses action on inanimate objects, whereby, among other changes, the singular ending PA *-a·ni was replaced by PEA *-amən: Ojibwa nimikka·n 'I find it' but Unami nəmáxkamən (Goddard 1967:78-80; see also Goddard 1967a:10, 1969:97, 126, 156, 1971:139).† Consequently, the Eastern Algonquian languages do not differ among themselves as much as the languages of the entire family taken together, and the time depth of the Eastern subgroup is not so great as that of Algonquian as a whole (see fig. 1). Nevertheless the Eastern languages exhibit an extensive diversity, and (although there is no accurate method of estimation) they must have been diverging from each other for something on the order of 2,000 years. A general discussion of the prehistory of the Algonquian family is provided in the article on central Algonquian languages, in this volume.

Each Eastern Algonquian language shares features with each of its immediate neighbors, and the resulting continuum is of a sort that is likely to have resulted from the spread of linguistic innovations among forms of speech that were already differentiated but still similar enough to make partial bilingualism easy. Some subgroupings seem to be fairly clearly indicated, however, and the type of evidence available for these is discussed below. But first, it is important to review what is known of the various Eastern Algonquian languages, especially

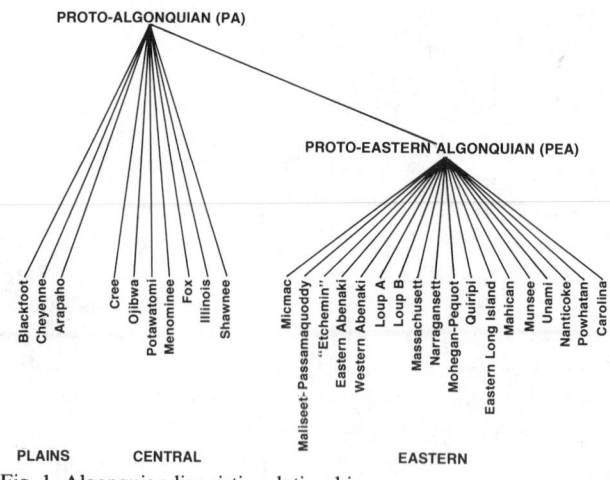

Fig. 1. Algonquian linguistic relationships.

in order to make clear the scantiness of the record that is available.

Survey of Languages

• MICMAC Micmac has been spoken in the Maritime provinces throughout the historical period. The Souriquois language recorded in the seventeenth century appears to be the direct ancestor of modern Micmac, except that the Souriquois numerals rather resemble Maliseet-Passamaquoddy (Lescarbot 1907-1914, 3:114, 117-120). There is a fair amount of dialectal diversity in the present-day language, but the only published discussion is a few remarks by Pacifique on the Restigouche dialect (1939:13-14).

• MALISEET-PASSAMAQUODDY The compound name Maliseet-Passamaquoddy is applied by linguists to the language spoken with little difference by the Maliseet, in western New Brunswick, and the Passamaquoddy, in eastern Maine. Its dialectology is little known, but although there are minor differences within each group, it is probable that the major dialectal boundary coincides with the tribal boundary.

• "ETCHEMIN" What is called the Etchemin language is known with certainty only from a list of the numbers from 'one' to 'ten' published by Lescarbot in the early seventeenth century (1907-1914, 3:114). Later writers (see Barratt 1851) have applied the name Etchemin to the Maliseet-Passamaquoddy, but their language does not match what Lescarbot recorded. The subsequent his-

† Of the forms cited in this chapter, the only ones in phonemic transcription (modern scientific orthography) are those from Maliseet, Eastern Abenaki, Munsee, Unami, and Shawnee. Forms in other languages are given in the premodern spelling systems of the available sources, which range in quality from impressionistic to highly systematic. The standard introduction to comparative Algonquian linguistics is Bloomfield (1946); some bibliographic references for the individual languages may be found in vol. 17.

tory of the speakers of what is here called Etchemin is unknown. Although the Etchemin numbers all match numbers found elsewhere among the languages of New England, as a set they do not correspond to those of any known variety of Algonquian. Lescarbot's Etchemin were said to have occupied the area between the Kennebec and the Saint John rivers (1907-1914, 2:277), but it is impossible to know precisely where these numbers came from. The vocabulary taken by James Rosier on the Saint George River in 1605 has been considered Etchemin (Hoffman 1955a:67), but it seems to be largely Eastern Abenaki, with a few Maliseet-Passamaquoddy words and a few of mysterious origin (Siebert 1943:506). If the Lescarbot and Rosier vocabularies really are of the same language, it would mean that Etchemin was rather similar to Eastern Abenaki but diverged in its lexicon in the direction of both its southern and eastern neighbors.

• EASTERN ABENAKI The Eastern Abenaki dialects were spoken in central and western Maine in the historic period and included: Penobscot, in the Penobscot River valley in two subdialects (the downriver one having a few Passamaquoddy loans; Siebert 1943:506-507); Caniba, along the Kennebec (Râle 1833); and the dialects of some of the refugees in the Canadian missions at Saint Francis (for example, Aubery 1715) and Bécancour (Speck 1928b). The aboriginal location of these dialects known only from displaced groups is uncertain but must have been in the Androscoggin and Kennebec watersheds. There is no very strong reason for taking the Bécancour dialect to be that of the Wawenocks, as in Speck (1928b).

• WESTERN ABENAKI By the beginning of the nineteenth century Western Abenaki had become the language of the Saint Francis mission village, superseding the languages of the various other displaced groups that made up the community. It is not certain which part of the Vermont-New Hampshire area the Saint Francis dialect should be traced back to, nor is it known how widely spread dialects of this language may originally have been. It is reasonable to assume, though, that the Indians of the upper Connecticut valley were Western Abenaki speakers, including the Sokoki, whose territories extended into Massachusetts. In fact the modern language may well directly continue that of the Sokokis who founded the Saint Francis band (cf. Day 1965).

• LOUP A The French applied the name Loup ('wolf') to a number of Algonquian tribes, and linguistic records have survived from two of these for which no other name is known. These two languages, attested only in word lists recorded at the northern missions from refugees, may be conveniently if arbitrarily distinguished as Loup A and Loup B. Loup A has by far the more extensive attestation, principally a manuscript of 124 pages by Claude Mathevet (Day 1975). It is clear that Loup A was originally spoken in the central New England area,

and it may well be that this was the language of one of the central Massachusetts tribes, such as the Pocumtuck or the Nipmuck (Day 1969). Beyond speculation, there is little that can be said about the details of the aboriginal dialectology of this area, such as how close the languages of the Pocumtuck and the Nipmuck might have been.

• LOUP B The language here called Loup B is attested only by a 14-page word list (Magnon de Terlaye 1755).

Table 1. Status of the Eastern Algonquian Languages, 1970

Language or Dialect (and Locality)	Number of Speakers	Date of Extinction
Micmac	ca. 6,000	
Maliseet	ca. 600	
Passamaquoddy	ca. 200	
Etchemin	Extinct	17th c.
Eastern Abenaki:		
Penobscot (Old Town)	ca. 10	
Saint Francis, P.Q.	Extinct	End of 18th c.
Bécancour, P.Q.	Extinct	Early 20th c.
Western Abenaki	22	
Loup A	Extinct	18th c.
Loup B	Extinct	18th c.
Massachusett	Extinct	End of 19th c.
Narragansett	Extinct	Early 19th c.
Mohegan-Pequot	Extinct	Early 20th c.
Montauk	Extinct	Early 19th c.
Quiripi	Extinct	18th c.
Unquachog	Extinct	Early 19th c.
Mahican	Extinct	Early 20th c.
Munsee:		
Moraviantown	ca. 30	
Muncey	3	
Six Nations Reserve	Extinct	1965
Cattaraugus	Extinct	Early 20th c.
Wisconsin	Extinct	19th c. (?)
Kansas	Extinct	Early 20th c.
Oklahoma	Extinct	Early 20th c.
Unami:		
Northern	Extinct	Early 20th c.
Southern	ca. 25	
Nanticoke	Extinct	Mid-19th c.
Powhatan	Extinct	18th c.
Carolina	Extinct	18th c.

Brief though this specimen is, it appears to exhibit forms from more than one dialect, but the scantiness of the data prevents anything very precise from being said about these variations. Typologically Loup B tends to resemble Mahican and Western Abenaki more than Loup A does, and it is a reasonable conclusion that these linguistic relationships reflect its relative geographical position.

• MASSACHUSETT On the coast and islands of southeastern New England were spoken a number of dialects that appear to have been similar enough to be considered a single language. There are published materials reflecting the speech of the North Shore (Wood 1634: following p. 98), the mission town of Natick (Eliot 1663, 1666), Martha's Vineyard (Mayhew 1709), and northern Rhode Island (Williams 1643), as well as unpublished deeds and other documents representing additional locations in the area. The number of major dialects is not known exactly, nor is there much good evidence on what area each dialect covered or on the extent to which the linguistic and political units of this region coincided. It is known, though, that the dialect of Martha's Vineyard differed enough from those of the mainland and of Nantucket to make communication difficult (MHSC ser. 6, 1:402; Trumbull 1880:476–477).

• NARRAGANSETT It is difficult to know how distinct the Narragansett language of southern Rhode Island was from its neighbors, since virtually the only source (Williams 1643) appears to contain at least some dialect mixture. Although Williams says that his book "is framed chiefly after the Narrogánsett Dialect" (1643:1. A8, r.), other information he furnishes suggests that many words may be in the Coweset dialect, which was apparently spoken at least as far south as the area of present East Greenwich, Kent County, Rhode Island (1643:106–107 [= 104–105]). There is also the possibility that Narragansett had to some extent incorporated elements originally proper to its northern neighbor.

• MOHEGAN-PEQUOT The dialects of Connecticut east of the Connecticut River are generally classed together as Mohegan-Pequot. Although this seems to be a valid grouping, the number and distinctness of the various local forms of speech are uncertain. That the problem is more complicated than simply differentiating a putative "Mohegan" dialect from a putative "Pequot" is shown, for example, by the differences between the Pequot of Stonington and that of Groton (Noyes 1690; Stiles 1973). It has been suggested that some of the remnant eighteenth-century Indians called Pequots may have actually spoken Niantic (Trumbull 1873:134); but nothing definite is known about the speech of either the Western or the Eastern Niantic, not even whether or not they were linguistically closer to each other than to the other groups nearby. It is possible that a vocabulary from the eighteenth-century Narragansetts (Stiles 1973a), which is very similar to Pequot, may actually represent the speech of the Eastern Niantic component of that group.

QUIRIPI The Quiripi language is known chiefly from a rather poorly translated mid-seventeenth-century catechism apparently based on the speech of the Indians at Branford (Pierson 1658). The evidence of dialect mixture that this work contains may correctly reflect the speech of this community. It is generally presumed that the Connecticut River coincided with the boundary between Quiripi and Mohegan-Pequot, but there is no direct evidence on the linguistic affiliations of most of the western Connecticut groups. A dialect that seems slightly different from Quiripi is attested in an eighteenth-century word list that has been called Naugatuck and may represent lower Housatonic speech (Stiles 1787). The western and northern extent of the dialects of the Quiripi type is not further known.

• EASTERN LONG ISLAND LANGUAGES At the end of the eighteenth century the Unquachog, Shinnecock, and Montauk had forms of speech that were different enough for Thomas Jefferson to be able to write that "the three tribes can barely understand each other" (Jefferson 1791). This statement appears confirmed by the many points of difference between the recorded vocabularies of Unquachog (Jefferson 1791) and Montauk (Gardiner 1798), but the materials on Shinnecock are too sparse to permit any precise statements about its dialectal affiliations (Gatschet 1889:390; Harrington 1903:39). Although diverse among themselves, the Long Island languages seem to have been rather close to those on the opposite shore of Long Island Sound. It may be that Unquachog should be considered a dialect of the western Connecticut language represented by Naugatuck and Quiripi and that Montauk should be grouped as a third dialect with Mohegan-Pequot.

• MAHICAN Mahican was the language of the Indians of that name on the upper Hudson, and judging by a few personal names (NYCD 13:119, 379, 545) it may have been spoken by the Catskills as well. In the eighteenth century, Mahican was spoken in the mission villages of Stockbridge, on the upper Housatonic, and Shecomeco, in northeastern Dutchess County, New York; but its aboriginal extent to the east and south is not known exactly. There is a fair amount of variation in the different recordings of Mahican, but no systematic study has been done to determine if this reflects major dialect differences. The language went west with the migrating Mahicans, and partial speakers were living among the Wisconsin Stockbridges as late as the 1930s.

• MUNSEE A single language appears to have been spoken, in an unknown number of dialects, from western Long Island and southeastern New York State on the east to the Delaware Water Gap and the Raritan River on the south and west (Goddard 1971a). In this area were the Canarsie, Wiechquaeskeck, Wappinger, Esopus, Tappan, Hackensack, Minisink, and many smaller groups. This language was known in the eighteenth century as Munsee, the name of the composite group, mostly of Minisinks and their neighbors, among whom it continued to be spoken on the upper Susquehanna and at locations farther west. In the nineteenth century Munsee became the exclusive language of the Delaware groups in Canada, at Munceytown, Moraviantown, and Six Nations Reserve, gaining ascendancy over the other Algonquian languages originally spoken at the last two locations; it was also spoken by small groups in Wisconsin, Kansas, Oklahoma, and among the Seneca at Cattaraugus. There was a fair amount of minor dialectal variation among the different Munsee groups.

• UNAMI   The Unami language, also called Delaware or Delaware proper, was spoken in the southern two-thirds of New Jersey and along the west side of the Delaware River and Delaware Bay, from the Water Gap to Cape Henlopen. Apparently following older Munsee usage, the Moravian missionaries applied the term "Unami" specifically to the language of the Forks region (Easton, Pennsylvania) and called the language of the northern Unami speakers in New Jersey "Unalachtigo." Unalachtigo probably differed little from the form of speech preserved in an early word list from the Sankhikans of the Trenton, New Jersey, area (De Laet 1633:75-76). But these and the dialects farther south were all merely varieties of a single language, which may be called Unami, following contemporary Munsee usage. The Forks dialect of Northern Unami, which was the one employed by the Moravian missionaries in their translations (for example Roth 1770-1772), still had speakers among the Delawares at Six Nations Reserve and Moraviantown in the late nineteenth century. The Southern Unami speech of the lower Delaware River and its tributaries survived in the 1960s among the Delawares of Oklahoma. There seems to have been a certain amount of diversity in aboriginal Southern Unami speech, but this has not been continued in the modern groups, which speak dialects that display only superficial and probably recent differences. It should be noted that most of the earliest vocabularies usually supposed to be Delaware actually record a trade jargon that was based on a variety of Southern Unami (Campanius 1696; Penn 1912; G. Thomas 1912; Nelson 1894; Prince 1912; Goddard 1971a:15).

• NANTICOKE   It has been generally assumed that a single language was spoken on both sides of Chesapeake Bay in the present state of Maryland, that is, by both the Nanticoke on the Eastern Shore and the Conoy on the west. For most of this area, there are no linguistic data at all, and what does exist is very scanty (Speck 1927). A 1792 vocabulary, collected in the Choptank village on the Choptank River of the Eastern Shore, was considered by its collector to represent the Nanticoke language (W.V. Murray 1792; Weslager 1944), although the Nanticoke proper lived on the next river south. Vocabularies

taken from refugees from the Eastern Shore and their descendants are designated Nanticoke but may reflect the speech of any of the local groups that contributed to the composite tribe known under that name in the later historical period. In sum, it is probably safe to say that dialects of the language called Nanticoke were spoken aboriginally on the Choptank and Nanticoke rivers, but the northern and southern limits of this language must be considered unknown—all the more so since early seventeenth-century writers stress the linguistic diversity of this area (Smith 1884:55). The traditional grouping of Conoy (or Piscataway) with Nanticoke appears confirmed in a general way by some previously unknown Conoy materials discovered in the early 1970s (Harrison 1633) (fig. 2). However, Conoy will remain very poorly

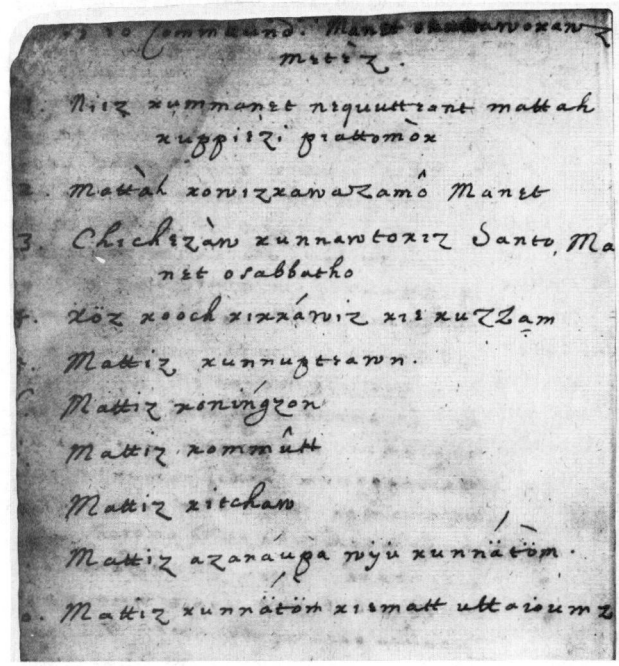

Fig. 2. The Ten Commandments in Conoy (Piscataway). Found on front endpapers of a handbook for priests belonging to Rev. Henry Harrison, S.J., who was in Maryland 1697-1700.

known unless more materials, such as Father Andrew White's lost seventeenth-century catechism (Kenny 1961:31-33), can be found. One word that seems to be found only in these two varieties of Algonquian is Conoy *tayac* 'emperor' (Anonymous 1910b:136) and Nanticoke *tall!ak* (Speck 1927:49).

• POWHATAN   The Virginia Indian language known as Powhatan seems to have been spoken at the least by the local groups that formed the nucleus of the Powhatan confederacy, those on the James and York river systems below the fall line. The same language is specifically said to have been spoken by the Accomacs and Acohanocks, on the southern end of the Delmarva peninsula (Smith

1884:55), but how far north toward the Potomac it may have extended is a matter of conjecture. The early seventeenth-century vocabularies show some internal diversity, though this could reflect the differential hearing of unfamiliar sounds just as well as a multiplicity of dialects (Geary 1953:209–210). Inevitably, however, there would have been dialectal variation within an area of the size in question. If, as seems likely, the Algonquian numerals in the otherwise Siouan Fort Christanna vocabulary of 1716 reflect in some way those used by a band then or formerly in the area, there must have been another Algonquian language distinct from Powhatan in southeastern Virginia (Alexander 1971; Goddard 1972a). Curiously, the handful of words collected in the nineteenth and twentieth centuries from the remnants of the supposedly Algonquian Pamunkey and Nansemond bear no resemblance to any Algonquian language (or for that matter to any other language), except, in each case, for the word for 'one': Pamunkey *nikkut*, Nansemond *nĭkătwĭn*. Compare Powhatan *nekut* (Dalrymple 1858; Pollard 1894:12; Mooney 1907:146). The Pamunkey vocabulary may well represent the language of one of the poorly known inland Virginia groups that have generally been lumped together as Siouan, though often on slender or no evidence (Mooney 1894).

• CAROLINA ALGONQUIAN   The southernmost Eastern Algonquian language, spoken in northeastern North Carolina, may be conveniently called Carolina Algonquian. It is known only from two short collections of words: some miscellaneous natural history terms, and a few others, recorded at the Roanoke Colony in the 1580s (Geary 1955; Swanton 1934) and a 37-word general vocabulary obtained from the Pamlico remnant in the early eighteenth century (Lawson 1709:225–230). The words in the two sources are for different things, but there is no reason to presume that they do not represent the same dialect, or dialects of the same language.

Dialectology

It should be clear from the preceding review of the attestation of the Eastern Algonquian languages that a fundamental problem is encountered in any attempt to describe the aboriginal dialect pattern of this area. In principle the goal is to determine if any languages are more closely related to some of their neighbors than to others, and to see what the patterns of overlapping relationship may be; but it is evident that in many cases some or all of the linguistic neighbors of a given language may be unknown. Thus, where there appears to be a fairly sharp break between two languages it may be that there once was an intermediate form of speech making a transition between the two, but that it became extinct without being attested. (Of course, extinctions of some intermediate dialects in the precontact period are quite possible and would have had the same net effect.)

If any sharp linguistic breaks could be established as not having arisen in this way they would be of great importance in any attempt to reconstruct the prehistory of the Eastern Algonquian speakers, as they would be a sure indication of recent contact resulting from population movement. But even though definite conclusions of this sort cannot be reached on the basis of the available evidence, the relationships of these languages can be sketched in enough detail for certain trends to be observed. It will be sufficient for the present purpose to base the discussion for the most part on some diagnostic phonological innovations and a few supplementary observations.

The phonological innovations shared by various combinations of languages permit the blocking out of the major dialect areas (table 2). The languages of New England and the Maritimes are clearly set off from those farther south; within this area the languages of southern New England and the more northerly languages form two distinct subgroups, though Western Abenaki shows some southern features. Munsee and Unami make up a Delaware subgroup, with Mahican sharing innovations both with these languages and with those of New England. Too little is known of the southernmost languages to permit much to be said in detail about their linguistic relationships, though Nanticoke seems to have diverged considerably by undergoing a number of independent changes.

Phonological Innovations

The various innovations charted in table 2 are discussed below. Although only a few representative features are treated here, these have been chosen so as to reflect the general picture that a more complete survey would provide.

1. In Micmac and Maliseet-Passamaquoddy PEA *hl* (which is from PA *ʔl* or *nl*) became *h*, which mostly drops, just like original PA and PEA *h*: Maliseet *liwəya* 'he is named', *eliwihímək* 'what I am called', with stem *wəy-~wih-* from PEA *wi·hl-*, from PA *wi·nl-*.

2. The four northernmost languages attest a particular pattern of vowel loss that may be called Abenaki syncope. Original short vowels—of which there were only PEA *a* and *ə*, from PA *a* and *e*—are dropped before any original consonant cluster that remains a cluster (all but those eliminated by innovation no. 4), that is, before pre-Abenaki *h* or *s* followed by a consonant, except under certain specific conditions: Maliseet-Passamaquoddy and Penobscot *kči* 'big', from PEA *kəhči*, from PA *keʔči*.

3. All the New England and Maritime languages lose the original contrast between PEA and PA *s* and *š*: Western Abenaki *sisikwa* 'rattlesnake', Narragansett *sések*, from PA *ši·ʔši·kwe·wa*.

4. All these same languages plus Mahican lose nasals

Table 2. Selected Diagnostic Phonological Innovations in Eastern Algonquian Languages

	1	2	3	4	5	6	7	8	9	10
	PA *ʔl > PEA *hl > h	Abenaki Syncope	*š, *s > s	*nC > C	*a· > ą	*e· > a·	some *k > kʸ	*hk > h	PEA *hl > hs	Reflexes of PEA *l
Micmac	√	√	√	√						r > l
Maliseot-Passamaquoddy	√	√	√	√						r > l
Eastern Abenaki		√	√	√	√					r > l
Western Abenaki		√	√	√	√	√				l
Loup A			√	√	√	√	√			l
Massachusett			√	√	√	√	√			n
Narragansett			√	√	√	√	√			n, y
Mohegan-Pequot-Montauk			√	√	√	√	√			y
Quiripi-Unquachog			√	√	√	√	√			r, y
Mahican				√	√	√		√		n
Munsee								√		r > l
Unami								√		r > l
Nanticoke									√	l, y
Powhatan									√	r, t

NOTE: Some languages for which only scanty data are available are omitted.

before true consonants (those other than w or y) in original PEA clusters (these continue all the PA nasal-plus-consonant clusters except *nl and *nθ, which give PEA *hl): Maliseet ə́kwítən 'it floats; canoe', Eastern Abenaki ákwitən 'canoe', Massachusett ogquidnash 'islands', from PA *akwintenwi 'it floats'.

5. The nasalization of PA and PEA *a· to [ą] occurs with a distribution that suggests that this innovation arose first in the southern New England languages and Mahican and later spread to Western Abenaki and the western dialects of Eastern Abenaki (it is not found in the Penobscot dialect; Goddard 1965, 1971): Western Abenaki wôbi, Massachusett wómpi, from PA *wa·pi 'white' (ô and óm are spellings of the nasalized vowel).

6. Clearly to be linked with innovation no. 5 is the change of original PA and PEA *e· to a low vowel a· (the exact quality is generally uncertain) in all the same languages except Eastern Abenaki. (All the languages that shift *e· to a· keep this new entity distinct from original *a· by nasalizing the latter.) Example: Western Abenaki pazekw, Narragansett pâwsuck, from PEA *pe·šəkw, PA *pe·šekwi 'one'.

7. The southern New England languages (but not Abenaki or Mahican) palatalize PA and PEA *k to [kʸ] (variously spelled) before front vowels (PEA *i· and *e·). This sound was usually not specially noted before retained i·, but it must have been quite striking before *e· (which became a· by innovation no. 6) and was generally

indicated in this position: Massachusett sontim, Montauk saunchem, from PEA *sa·ki·ma·w 'chief', from PA *sa·kima·wa; Narragansett teaug 'money', from PEA *ke·kw 'wampum'.

8. Mahican, Munsee, and Unami share the change of PA *hk to h: Mahican ôhmân, Munsee ó·hmal, Unami úhəma, from PA *o·hkwemali 'his grandmother'. This must have been an old change as it predates widespread shifts in the inherited cluster system. For example, PA *xk gave hk throughout Eastern Algonquian, falling together with original *hk in all languages but the three that underwent innovation no. 8. Thus, these three languages may descend from an intermediate protolanguage that did not split up until sometime after the Proto-Eastern Algonquian period. But the futility of explaining the linguistic history of Eastern Algonquian solely in terms of such sharp family-tree branchings is well demonstrated by the case of Mahican, which shares innovations with the languages to the east (nos. 4, 5, 6) as well as having affinities to its neighbors on the west.

9. Nanticoke and Powhatan seem to share a change of PA *ʔl to hs: Nanticoke ah!sappaneques, Powhatan (with ss written for hs) aiossapaniik 'flying squirrel' (cf. aussab 'net'), from PA *aʔlapy- 'net' and *anyikwa 'squirrel'.

The Delaware subgroup, consisting of Munsee and Unami, is delimited by innovations on the south (like no. 9) and on the north and east (like nos. 4, 5, 6). It is difficult, however, to find innovations that these languages and no others underwent, principally because Munsee is phonologically very conservative and there are thus few changes available for comparison. (Since modern Munsee phonology is little changed from Proto-Eastern Algonquian, clearly the phonology of the Common Delaware ancestor of Munsee and Unami must have been even less changed.) A significant grammatical innovation in Delaware is the loss of the distinction of number in the obviative (a second third-person category required in certain constructions) by generalization of the obviative singular ending (PEA *-al, from PA *-ali) at the expense of the plural (PEA *-ah, from PA *-ahi): Munsee wíhčəwal 'his calf (of leg), his calves', Unami hwíčuwa (-a from -al, still attested in the nineteenth century; Goddard 1969:154, 162). The situation in the languages south of Delaware is unknown, but Mahican maintains the distinction of number while Western Abenaki and the southern New England languages generalize the plural ending.

10. The various reflexes of PEA *l (from PA *θ and *l) have sometimes been considered diagnostic of the major dialect areas of Eastern Algonquian (notably in Speck 1928a:213–216), but it is clear from table 2 that this is, for the most part, not the case. (The reflexes in the languages not given there are: Etchemin r, Loup B n and r [and l; same dialect?], Naugatuck r, Conoy z and y, Christanna r, Carolina r.) In particular the diagnostic value of these changes is diminished by the fact that a number of languages show multiple reflexes, even if it is assumed that the sources or communities in question were dialectally mixed.

From the structural point of view there are basically two ways of treating PEA *l. When *l was continued as either l or r there was no loss of any phonological opposition, as there was no l or r of other origin in these languages. Accordingly the shift of r to l within the historical period in a number of languages (indicated r>l in table 2) was not a major change but merely a shift in pronunciation, probably reflecting the replacement of some sort of lateral flap by a more European l copied from English or French. On the other hand, when PEA *l became n, y, or t, it fell together with sounds that already existed, eliminating the previous opposition with these sounds; these changes are thus structurally significant. However, similar changes have occurred in all the Algonquian languages, none of which preserves both PA *θ and *l, and the common reflexes elsewhere are t, l, r, n, and y, just as in Eastern Algonquian. Even among these languages two changes occurred independently in two areas: PEA *l>n both in Mahican and Loup B and in Massachusett and Narragansett; PEA *l>y both in languages of southern New England and Long Island and in Nanticoke. Thus the treatment of PEA *l cannot be considered diagnostic of major subgroups, though it

may in some cases reflect linguistic contact and diffusion.

Evidence from Other Innovations

Numerous and complex patterns of innovation and diffusion in Eastern Algonquian can be seen in the lexical distributions these languages exhibit, but these are difficult to summarize with any precision, for several reasons. For one thing, each word must be considered in isolation and almost every conceivable distributional pattern could be found; for another, words are more susceptible to borrowing than phonological and grammatical features and hence overlapping distributions are common if not the rule; and perhaps most important in the present instance, the poor attestation of most of the Eastern Algonquian languages makes it impossible in many cases to guarantee the nonexistence of a word in a given language for which it may not have been recorded. Nevertheless, some general patterns emerge that tend to confirm the outlines of the picture afforded by the phonological innovations examined above.

Micmac and Maliseet-Passamaquoddy form an innovating nucleus on the north. (However, although a number of lexical and phonological features are shared by these two languages, Micmac has undergone an extensive grammatical evolution that differentiates it from Maliseet-Passamaquoddy and the Abenaki languages.) In the area from the Hudson to the Penobscot a rather consistent division emerges between a northern and western perimeter (the Abenaki languages, Loup B, and Mahican) and a southeastern nucleus (Loup A, Massachusett, Narragansett, Mohegan-Pequot-Montauk, and Quiripi). Of a transitional type are Unquachog, which shares words with both these groups, and Etchemin, which falls between the southeastern nucleus and Maliseet-Passamaquoddy. Some words have a coastal distribution, cutting across otherwise distinct boundaries, and may be an index of a pattern of intergroup communication. In some cases a word would occur in a continuum if an intervening language that does not attest it were assumed to have intruded among the members of the group that do. But different words and other features have different patterns of discontinuous distribution, which would lead to contradictory hypotheses of migration. And in general, even if the approach were deemed viable, the data available for Eastern Algonquian would be too fragmentary to serve as the basis for sound hypotheses about prehistoric population movements.

Contacts With Other Languages

The diffusion of words or other linguistic features into Eastern Algonquian has been little examined, though it could be very useful to the study of cultural contact. It seems, however, that there is little evidence for borrowing into these languages in precontact times. Rare examples are the Iroquoian numerals for 'two' and 'six' in the southernmost languages, and the possibility that innovation no. 5 may be the result of diffusion from Iroquoian (Goddard 1971:140, 1972a). There is essentially nothing that concretely suggests that any of the words peculiar to Eastern Algonquian are residue from the previous, presumably non-Algonquian, inhabitants of the East Coast.

In the historic period there has been a fair amount of borrowing from European languages of words for introduced cultural objects, domestic animals, and the like. There are French and English words in the northernmost languages; English words in southern New England; Dutch in the Delaware languages, Mahican, and Loup A; and even one Swedish word in Unami. Relatively recent borrowings from another Algonquian lan-guage are exemplified by Unami *ká·se·m* 'pecan' and *mášku* 'Creek Indian', from Shawnee *ka·θe·mi* and *homaško*.

Beothuk

The language of the native Indians of Newfoundland became extinct in the nineteenth century and is known only from word lists of comparatively poor quality (Howley 1915). Although attempts have been made to relate this language to Algonquian (most recently Hewson 1968, 1971), it is doubtful if the crudeness of the available transcriptions will ever permit any certain conclusion to be reached about its relationships. Certainly, the language does not look Algonquian on its face, and if it is related to Algonquian it can only be on a very deep time level.

Early Indian-European Contacts

T.J. BRASSER

Aboriginal Societies

The first meetings between Europeans and native Americans took place sometime during the hazy period of protohistory, making it difficult to arrive at a satisfactory idea of the effect of these early contacts on the Indian societies. Information on the truly aboriginal nature of these societies is extremely limited and frequently distorted by early European ideas and interpretations. The long period of intermittent contacts preceding the earliest ethnographic sources raises the question how far these descriptions are informative about Indian society before the Europeans had caused important changes.

Generalizations about the aboriginal state of the coastal Indian cultures must distinguish between the Indians on the eastern margins of the boreal forest and their neighbors to the south. The former lived by hunting and fishing only and were organized in small, seminomadic bands. Leadership was only weakly developed and did not extend beyond the hunting group, consisting of a few patrirelated families.

From the Saco River southward the native economy was primarily based on horticulture, and semipermanent villages were located near the gardens in the river valleys. Both the southern horticulturists and the northern hunters used to spend the better part of the summer along the seashore, where they gathered and smoked large amounts of fish and shellfish.

The local units in New England, Virginia, and North Carolina have been united into confederacies or "tribes" since the earliest recorded European contacts. These alliances were brought about by the intermarriage of chiefly lineages as well as by conquest, and their duration depended upon the success achieved in stabilizing these relationships.

The coastal area between New England and Virginia was inhabited by people with a similar horticultural economy but with a different sociopolitical organization. Their clan system somewhat resembled that of the Iroquois though it did not generate strong supralocal political entities. During the entire span of the seventeenth century most of this area was characterized by a multitude of small autonomous units, united only by a consciousness of being the Lenni Lenape 'real people'. Most if not all the historic "tribes" acquired their more

permanent character only during and due to European contact.

Although population densities are difficult to determine for the precontact period, it is certain that they reflected ecological differences between the cultures of the northern hunters and the southern gardeners. The earliest population estimates date from the beginning of the seventeenth century, which was preceded by many years of European contact, resulting in an unknown, but certainly substantial, decline in population numbers due to epidemics of infectious diseases. Therefore all such estimates should be considered as a minimum only. Contemporary sources provide some exceptionally detailed information for coastal Maine in 1605 and for Virginia in 1607 (Purchas 1625a, 4:1873-1875; Smith 1884:347-348.)

The available data suggest a population density of about 45 persons in each 100 square kilometers for the horticultural area. The mountain regions were uninhabited and seldom visited by hunters. A local unit, consisting of about 200 individuals, utilized the drainage system of a single river as their territory.

This demographic picture stands in strong contrast to that of the more northern parts of the coast, sparsely inhabited by isolated bands of hunters. In 1611 local Indians provided the missionary Pierre Biard with population estimates for Nova Scotia and the north coast of the Gulf of Saint Lawrence, while explaining that their numbers had been rapidly decreasing since the arrival of the Whites (JR 3:110). For Nova Scotia, an original population of 4,000 appears to be an acceptable minimum, indicating a population density of about 3 persons in 100 square kilometers. The more northern parts of the coast, including Newfoundland, appear to have had an original population density of only 1 in 100 square kilometers.

European Exploration, Fishing, and Trade

The events surrounding the first contact between alien groups of people are important to the understanding of subsequent culture change; however, the first relevant contacts are difficult to determine in this area. The series of recorded early contacts was possibly preceded and certainly interrupted by a number of others that remained unrecorded, apart from indications in the behavior of the Indians noted in the recorded contacts.

The effects of Norse contacts on the natives of Newfoundland during the early part of the eleventh century must have rapidly faded away as a bad dream. Nor do such contacts appear to have been directly significant for the natives of coastal Labrador although the Norse settlers of Greenland continued to acquire timber from the Labrador coast as late as 1347 (Magnusson and Pálsson 1965:28). Relevant culture contact for the natives of Newfoundland and the adjacent coasts of Labrador and Nova Scotia probably started about A.D. 1500, and for more southern parts of the east coast some 20 years later.

European exploration of the fifteenth and sixteenth centuries was primarily motivated by economic necessity; political aspirations and scientific curiosity were secondary to this basic factor. The increasing dependence on expensive goods imported from Asia by a long overland route to Venice forced Europe to consider the possibilities of finding a shorter route, one no longer monopolized by the Venetians. Nautical knowledge was rapidly increasing, particularly in Portugal, and great merchants were able and willing to support transoceanic enterprises.

After exploring the costs of Africa, the Portuguese opened the water way to Asia in 1488; however, this route proved to be twice as long and as dangerous as the overland route. In the belief that Asia was opposite Europe, Spain and other western European nations pressed forward with maritime adventures across the Atlantic. In 1497, only five years after Christopher Columbus discovered the Bahamas, John Cabot took possession of Newfoundland in the name of England. Apparently he made no contact with the local natives, but he found their fishing nets and some other tools. One year later, it is claimed, Cabot made a second voyage and visited the coasts of Labrador and Nova Scotia.

Portuguese interests, though mainly focused on the southern route to India, also included a long-standing concern with the North Atlantic. Gaspar Côrte-Real explored coastal Newfoundland in 1500 and again in 1501. The return of his second voyage consisted of 57 kidnapped Indians. These people were found to possess a broken sword and a pair of silver earrings, apparently left in Newfoundland by John Cabot's crew. With their capture and enslavement, Côrte-Real introduced an aspect of "commerce" that never assumed the proportions of the African slave trade. More frequently, a few Indians were kidnapped, to be used as interpreters in subsequent contacts, or to be displayed in various European cities. As late as 1632, a friend in London wrote to John Winthrop, Jr., in Massachusetts, asking him "to send over some of your Indian Creatures alive when you may best, as one brought over a Squirrel . . . and one a Rattlesnake Skin with the rattle" (Winthrop 1889:58).

During the first years of the sixteenth century the European fishermen started to come: English, Bretons, Normans, Basques, Portuguese, and their numbers rapidly increased. Although their activities centered mainly on the Newfoundland Banks, by about 1530 the fisheries had expanded along the entire coastline from Labrador to southern Nova Scotia. The activities increased so rapidly that, by 1506, a tax was levied on Newfoundland codfish brought home by Portuguese fishermen (Innis 1940; Sauer 1971:12, 47). Apart from cartographic evidence, most of these fishermen left no record. By 1550 about 30 French ships came annually to Newfoundland in addition to comparable numbers of other European nationalities. In 1578, 50 English, 150 French, and 100 Spanish fishing boats were reported in the general area (Sauer 1971:240). By that time fisheries had expanded down the New England coast because of the competition for the better harbors and the increasing scarcity of timber available for staging.

Most of the early fishermen salted their catch at sea and sailed directly home. Then, during the third quarter of the sixteenth century, it was found that "dry-fishing" was more economical, particularly along the east coast of Newfoundland and "on the Labrador." Camps were established on the shore where the codfish was cured. The fishermen made no attempt to explore the interior, but contacts with the natives must have been frequent. In the absence of any records, only a few data reveal an idea of the fishermen's attitudes toward the Indians. At Natashquan, Jacques Cartier found a party of Montagnais Indians engaged in fishing for a certain Captain Thiennot, whose ship was lying in the nearby harbor. These Indians were apparently completely at ease with Europeans and they freely boarded Cartier's ship. Relationships like this one provided a basis for subsequent trade.

Contact situations were not everywhere so satisfactory. Clearing the land around the harbors of Newfoundland resulted in forest fires lasting for weeks and the native food resources on the bird islands were wasted. Owing to kidnappings and other experiences with the rough fishermen, the Beothuk appear to have retired more and more to the interior. Occasionally they were able to acquire some iron tools or fishing nets by theft, but their relationships with the Europeans never improved again. The extremely unfavorable stereotype that Europeans developed of the Beothuk reflects the fact that these Indians were considered a nuisance and of no economic value whatsoever.

Hostile resistance against the colonists may have been tried with success by the Micmac of Cape Breton Island. Portuguese fishermen tried to establish a permanent station there in the 1520s but within a year they were forced to give up. Indian hostility is suggested to have been among the causes of this failure (Morison 1971:230).

Of major importance in the economic history of North America was the development of the fur trade. The possibilities of additional profit by trading furs from the Indians were realized by the fishermen sometime before 1519. It must have been a strong incentive for the Europeans to explore the coasts before returning home. The Indians on the coast of Maine were already acquainted with the European desire for furs in 1524. Ten years later, Jacques Cartier was offered furs by the Indians in Chaleur Bay, indicating that the trade had penetrated the Gulf of Saint Lawrence by that time. Indians from the Saint Lawrence River came up the coast as far north as Natashquan to trade with the Europeans and hunt seals in the 1540s (Hoffman 1967:23).

In the meantime, the coastline between Nova Scotia and Florida had appeared on European maps as a result of French and Spanish explorations. After 1520 Spanish slave hunters conducted raids along the coast of South Carolina; on one of these trips they kidnapped about 150 Indians and shipped them to the West Indies. How far north they operated is not known, but news of these excursions doubtless spread far and wide among the coastal tribes (Lurie 1959:35; Cumming, Skelton, and Quinn 1971:63).

The account by Giovanni da Verrazano of his voyage in 1524 is the earliest known description of a continuous voyage along the eastern coast of North America. He met with Indians at several places along the coast of North Carolina, New York Bay, Narragansett Bay, and Maine. His description of these contacts does not yet reveal the feelings of contempt and superiority of later explorers. He found the natives generally friendly and as curious as he was himself. Of the Rhode Island Indians he wrote: "These people are the most beautiful and have the most civil customs we have found on this voyage" (Wroth 1970:138). However, this favorable picture changed when he met the Indians in Maine: "We found no courtesy in them, and when we had nothing more to exchange and left them, the men made all the signs of scorn and shame that any brute creature would make" (Wroth 1970:140-141). Portuguese fishermen had been in contact with Indians in Penobscot Bay in 1522, and Verrazano's description of his meeting with the Indians of Maine clearly indicated their previous contact with Europeans. After Verrazano's voyage, European visits all along the East Coast increased. The first Europeans who were supposed to be gods according to Delaware Indian tradition cannot have been Henry Hudson's men in 1609; they must have been some earlier White visitors (Heckewelder 1841).

In the latter part of the century, the fur trade appears to have changed from a subsidiary activity of fishermen to the major occupation of many sailors. The fashion of wearing beaver felt hats was spreading in Europe, stimulating people with the required knowledge of the characteristics of fur to go in search of the raw material. Starting in the 1580s, the rivalry in the Indian trade was to make the English and French in North America natural enemies for more than a century and a half. They bartered red stroud cloth, iron nails, knives, hatchets, beads, brass kettles, and liquor for furs, mainly beaver. Occasionally even the shallop was reported as an article of trade. Some idea of the way in which the early traders enforced culture change in the horticultural areas is provided by the following directives:

> You will find thee people very false and Malitious in which respect you must bee the more cautious how you deal with Them, they are plentifull in Corne and Tobacco but have not many Scinus [skins] if you cannot otherwayes Deale with them, first making Tryall of all Fayr Courses, then do yor best to Seize their Corne and provision for that will inforce them to commerce and supply [your] wants and necessityes . . . (Bushnell 1911:237).

The European stereotype of the hunting Indian emerged during these early days of the fur trade. It was the result of the traders' manipulations as well as of the distorted picture of the native society in the early descriptions, focused as these were on Indian activities of economic value to the Whites.

European Colonization

In 1525 Estévan Gomes captured a group of 58 Indians on the New England coast and took them to Spain (Cumming, Skelton, and Quinn 1971:69). A colony started by the Spanish near Cape Fear in 1526 ended in failure the year after. Previous slave raids had made the local Indians suspicious and the prospect of having the cruel strangers as permanent neighbors may have caused their hostility.

The Spanish expedition to Virginia was preceded by other Spanish activities in Chesapeake Bay. There is no record of the first exploration, but an Indian captured during that first contact served as a guide for a group of Spanish Jesuits who founded a mission there in 1570. Hardly had they settled themselves when the priests were attacked by the Indians, led by the priests' guide. Two years later Pedro Menendez de Aviles avenged the massacre by plundering the Indians and hanging eight of the murderers. Punishments of this type were frequently reported, particularly during the subsequent colonial days. They reflected not so much European attitudes toward the Indians as the cruelty of punishments that characterized European society at that time.

The next attempt at colonization was made by the English on the coast of North Carolina. In 1584 Phillip Amadas and Arthur Barlowe had found the natives there "gentle, louing, and faithfull, void of all guile, and treason" (Quinn 1955, 1:108), and the explorers returned home with furs and two Indian volunteers. These two Indians accompanied a group of 100 colonists to Roanoke Island in 1585. Trouble started when, for the theft of a silver cup, the English burned the corn and destroyed a village of the Indians. Fearing an attack by the Indians, the English killed their chief, after which they decided it better to go home. Among them was John White, the artist who made an invaluable series of watercolor sketches of the Indians (figs. 3–8, "North Carolina Algonquians," this vol.) and of the flora and fauna of the region. Another group of colonists tried it again in 1587, but new misunderstanding did not take long to develop. When supplies arrived in 1590, there was nobody left. There are indications that the colonists had joined the Croatoans, the tribe of their loyal Indian guide and interpreter.

The sixteenth century was a tryout period and all attempts at colonization turned out to be dramatic failures. An occasional whaler lingered along the west coast of Newfoundland, and about 200 Bretons and Basques plus some 300 Indians lived off and on at a summer fishery on the nearby Magdalen Islands (Morison 1971:364). Certainly the fishermen and fur traders had been more successful than the colonists so far. Although there exists more evidence of intensive fur trade activities on the Saint Lawrence River there is no reason to assume that the fur traders ignored the Atlantic seaboard during the sixteenth century; however, it is obvious that they preferred the northern parts of the coast, where the aboriginal focus on hunting and fishing as well as the larger numbers of furbearers made the trade most profitable.

Increasing English interest in North America stimulated the French to realize their claims in the New World. In 1598 colonists were landed on Sable Island; in 1601 Tadoussac was founded; and in 1604 a group of French colonists established a settlement on the Sainte Croix River in Maine, which was subsequently removed to present Annapolis-Royal in Nova Scotia. From there, Samuel de Champlain explored the New England coast as far south as Cape Cod still in search of a better location for this French colony. Some Indians along the coast already sported European clothing or reeled off a smattering of French and Basque words.

Champlain missed the English Capt. George Waymouth, who returned from the Maine coast with "five Salvages, two Canoas, with all their bowes and arrowes" (Burrage 1906:379). Most of these Indians returned as guides on later expeditions. In 1607, when the surviving French colonists temporarily gave up their coastal enterprise and returned to Europe, 120 English settlers and two of Captain Waymouth's Indians arrived on the Kennebec River and started another colony, but it too was doomed to fail. The first Indians they met spoke some French, either picked up from the French colonists or from fishermen and traders who frequented the coasts. Friction between the natives and English colonists soon appeared, the winter was very severe, and a fire consumed most of the supplies and lodgings. Attempts to trade with the Indians failed, and the colonists returned

Newberry Lib., Chicago, E.E. Ayer Coll.: Champlain 1613.
Fig. 1. Man and woman of the New England coast. The man holds a European knife; the woman has an ear of corn and a squash. These are nearly the only depictions of coastal Indians during the exploration period—other than those by John White in North Carolina—that seem at all based on reality. Yet the man's beard is wrong and details of the clothing and arrows are also dubious. Engraved by David Pelletier as a detail on Champlain's 1612 map of his explorations.

to England in 1608. In coastal Maine, rivalry over the fur trade remained as a source of friction between English and French throughout the seventeenth century.

In the meantime, something exceptional was happening on the Chesapeake Bay in Virginia. A contingent of 144 English colonists had arrived there in 1607 and another 190 joined the survivors in 1608. Despite quarrels, starvation, and Indian hostility the colony survived, mainly because of the energetic approach of its leader, Capt. John Smith, and the exploitation of the local Indians.

This first success at colonization heralded the start of a new phase in Indian-White relations along the central East coast. A rapidly increasing number of Europeans was to arrive, introducing the Indians to a range of European culture aspects far more extensive than had ever been conveyed to them before. The newcomers differed from the fur traders not only in their attitudes but, most significantly, in their interests. From now on along most of the seaboard of the United States it would be the Indians' land instead of their furs that the Whites were after.

While exploring the Chesapeake Bay, Captain Smith met a group of Susquehannock Indians who told him that their hatchets, cloth, and other European articles had come overland, presumably from French traders to the north. Even the Susquehannocks were not located at the eastern terminus of this native trade route, for they in turn used the European goods in their trade with the Indians in Maryland.

In 1609 Henry Hudson explored the New England coast, searching for a passage to China. While trading with the Indians of coastal Maine his crew found an even cheaper way of obtaining furs. "We manned our boat and scute with twelve men and muskets, and two stone pieces or murderers, and drove the savages from their houses, and took the spoyle of them" (L'Honoré Naber 1921:31). Proceeding on his voyage, Hudson sailed up the river now bearing his name. Only one month earlier the Frenchman Champlain had defeated a group of Mohawks on present Lake Champlain, just north of the Hudson River. On his trip upriver, Hudson had several contacts with Indians who wanted to trade. Some of them were killed in incidents caused by the crew's suspicion, others were made drunk for the first time in their lives, and a few parted as good friends.

From cartographic evidence it appears that Europeans had entered New York Bay already several times between the visits of Verrazano and Hudson. Some Dutch whalers, active around Newfoundland since the 1580s, were said to have used temporary stations along the New York coast shortly before the turn of the century (Stokes 1915–1928, 2:63, 64). The news that Hudson had bartered furs there with the Indians stimulated Amsterdam merchants to send ships to the Hudson River to engage in the fur trade, starting in 1610. Two sons of a local chief arrived in Holland in 1612. After their return from this involuntary voyage one of the boys appears to have been instrumental in the murder of a number of Dutch sailors in 1619. In 1614 a trading post was established near present Albany, New York, and three Dutchmen made a trip through the interior as captives of the Susquehannocks, from whom they were ransomed in 1616. Dutch traders operated as far east as Narragansett Bay, where they still maintained a trading post long after the English had tried—and failed—to wrest the local fur trade from them.

The first colonists arrived in New Netherlands in 1624, the town of New Amsterdam was laid out on Manhattan Island, and trading posts were founded on the Connecticut and Delaware rivers. The decimating effects of the early fur trade on the coastal beaver populations are indicated by the upriver establishment of most of the Dutch trading posts. The days of the coastal fur trade were passing in this area and the traders had to move deeper into the back country in order to obtain furs. Whereas the coastal Indians were considered as a nuisance from now on, the Dutch made it a point to be friendly with the tribes in the interior. Through them the Dutch hoped to divert at least part of the profitable trade from the French in the Saint Lawrence valley to the Hudson River. The coastal Indians' loss of economic importance is reflected in the unfriendly attitude of a Swedish fur trader on the lower Delaware River about

1640: "Nothing would be better than to send over here a couple of hundred soldiers to keep here until we broke the necks of all them in this river especially since we have no beaver trade whatsoever with them" (A. Johnson 1930:117).

Though fur traders had frequented the New England coast continually and a few of them had actually been living there before 1620, no proper settlement took place until December of that year, when the Pilgrims established themselves in Massachusetts. They expected to find there "salvage people, who are cruell, barbarous and most trecherous" (Bradford 1952:40).

They first landed on Cape Cod, where they plundered somebody's store of corn and opened some graves out of curiosity (Mourt 1963: 21–28). This was not the best way to start, particularly since the local Nausets still were furious about the kidnapping of seven of their people by Capt. Thomas Hunt in 1614. Besides the seven Nausets, Hunt also had captured 20 Pawtuxets, whom he had sold as slaves in Malaga, Spain. One of these Indians was Squanto (Tisquantum), who managed to escape to England. Capt. Thomas Dermer brought him back to New England in 1619, but, in the meantime, an epidemic—of European origin—had ravaged the coast and exterminated his Pawtuxet people. In 1620 the Pilgrims founded their settlement in the former Pawtuxet territory. Squanto introduced their leaders to Chief Massasoit (later known as Ousamequin), who welcomed the settlers.

This regional history is rather marginal to the events that Euro-American history usually focuses on. Yet, it is this segment of history that most closely relates to the start of an important era relevant to the North American Indians. It is the era in which Europeans were making an increasingly complex impact upon the Indian societies, forcing them through a continuous process of adjustments.

Effects of Contact on Indians

It is especially in this early phase of contact that the record is not only scanty but also one-sided. The Indians did not have writing and there are no contemporary native accounts of their reactions to their contacts with the Whites. No amount of inference based on the meager facts recorded can ever establish the full nature of these events. The history of the Indians is hidden behind that of the European traders and colonists, and only the main outline of what was happening can be discerned.

The first reaction to contact of most tribes was one of friendly curiosity. For a short period some may have even thought of the newcomers as supernaturals. Frequently this attitude turned to suspicion and hostility during the first experiences with the White visitors. The behavior of these strangers frequently appeared unpredictable to the Indians and the kidnapping of their relatives called for revenge. Explorations like those of Hernando de Soto in the Southeast and of Jacques Cartier in the Saint Lawrence valley added to widespread and alarming rumors, resulting in a general unrest in Indian-White relationships during the sixteenth century. Early contacts affected the Newfoundland Beothuk in a particularly negative way. As they were cut off from maritime food resources, their traditional economy was disrupted and thereby their whole way of life became severely deprived.

Most traumatic were the afterpains of these first contacts. Unwittingly, the Europeans introduced measles, smallpox, typhus, and a range of other diseases to which the native populations lacked immunity. Now here, then there, epidemics ravaged the coast and destroyed whole communities, while refugees carried the microbes even farther inland. Thomas Hariot, in his report on the North Carolina colony, mentioned that in every native village visited by the English "the people began to die very fast" after their departure (Quinn 1955, 1:378). There was an epidemic in 1617, which killed thousands of Indians between the Penobscot River and Cape Cod. In 1622 and again in 1631 whole communities were exterminated south of the Merrimack River. In 1633 the Narragansets of Rhode Island lost 700 persons in a smallpox epidemic. In 1634 four Dutch traders spent the winter with a group of about 1,000 Indians up the Connecticut River. An epidemic broke out and only 50 Indians were said to have survived that winter. The following summer the epidemic spread throughout Connecticut. According to a 1640 statement by Hudson River Indians, their numbers had decreased by disease to less than one-tenth of the original population since the arrival of the Dutch. Similar statements are known from the Wampanoags, Abenakis, and Micmacs. Indian skeletons found in early contact sites along the Potomac River show much evidence of syphilis. The promiscuity of the fishermen and fur traders probably caused the spread of venereal diseases.

The epidemic diseases, insofar as known in the Northeast, all date from the last decades of the sixteenth century and later. Although strong in oral tradition, the Delaware Indians remembered "but" three smallpox epidemics as late as 1677; one in their grandparents' time, a second in their parents' time, and a third one in their own days (S. Smith 1765:100). Presuming that epidemics rapidly followed contact, the lack of earlier data seems to indicate the lack of significant contact for the greater part of the East coast before the 1580s. However, this assumption does not hold for the regions north of Maine, where fishermen and fur traders were regular visitors after at least 1530. The lack of early data on diseases in those northern regions can only be explained by the lack of interest in the writing of journals on the part of these visitors.

The misuse of liquor was another cause for the decline of the native populations. The early Basques and other fishermen appear to have used primarily wine and brandy in their fur-trading activities. By the time the first French settlers arrived in Acadia, the Indians of that region were already addicted to alcohol, and drunkenness reached frightful proportions among the Montagnais in the early decades of the seventeenth century. Brandy became the only article of trade with which the French could compete with the English and Dutch, who were able to sell most other wares cheaper (Bailey 1937:44, 66; Sauer 1971:298).

The disastrous loss in population caused by European diseases had repercussions in many aspects of life. Fear affected the native attitude toward the Europeans, who were readily recognized as the originators of the virulent diseases. In the belief that a European disease required a European curing ritual, the Micmacs were anxious to receive baptism from the early French missionaries, and a greater emphasis on native curing rituals may have developed at that time.

The most important impact of the demographic change was upon intertribal relationships and the fur trade. The first Europeans to enter the continent found indications of widespread connections along a network of ancient trails and water routes. Information concerning remote areas, as indicated on maps made by early European explorers, was frequently acquired from native informants along the coast. Archeological evidence reveals that items such as pottery, shell beads, and native copper were used in this aboriginal trade; undoubtedly, more perishable goods were exchanged as well. Some groups specialized in the manufacture of trade goods, as for example, the Nanticoke beadmakers and the Iroquois, who traded their pipes far and wide along the East coast. Existing routes and concepts of aboriginal trade were utilized to distribute the commodities introduced by the Europeans.

Of all the Indians in the Northeast only the Beothuk refused to join in the fur trade with the Europeans, and White trappers were active in Newfoundland as early as 1580 (Morison 1971:477). Passive resistance to more intensive hunting and trapping was initially encountered among the Indians in the horticultural areas, but the lure of new commodities ultimately proved irresistable. In order to get more of the White man's goods the Indians had to devote more of their time and effort to the trapping of beaver and other small fur-bearing animals. Successful trappers may have been able to maintain several wives to take care of their gardens, but it is obvious that in general, the fur trade upset and changed the annual cycle of traditional activities.

Particularly in Maine, where the yield of the native gardens may never have been abundant, the increase in time spent at the trap lines appears to have led to the gradual loss of interest in horticultural activities. Farther to the south, the direct impact of the fur trade became evident only by the end of the sixteenth century. In 1607 trade goods were still reaching the natives on Chesapeake

Bay and even in coastal Maine through native middlemen overland from the French in the Saint Lawrence valley and from the Maritimes. Passive resistance to direct trade was encountered in Connecticut as late as 1614. These facts confirm the assumption that the early traders directed most of their attention upon the relatively larger amount of fur-bearing game in the north.

Although the native economy in Nova Scotia and coastal Quebec appeared to offer easy adjustments to the fur trade, the results were often far from satisfactory. Groups like the Micmac were strongly oriented toward the exploitation of maritime food resources, whereas hunting activities were restricted mainly to about three months during the winter. Reducing the annual periods spent along the seashore and relying upon the traders to bring sufficient European foodstuffs often resulted in famine.

The very activity of trapping for the fur trade instead of hunting for their own use was detrimental to the health of the Indians. It required more time to obtain a sufficient number of small furs than it took to find and kill some large mammals. Whereas the large animals provided the people with food and skins, the small furbearers had little food value and their furs were exchanged for new needs, if not pure luxuries. The preparation of the many small pelts was added to the women's normal duties and thus also upset the sexual division of labor. This was particularly true for the central part of the East coast, where women used to take care of the gardens. After the founding of colonial settlements, Indian women were able to compare their labor with that of White women, resulting in their occasional flight to the colonists.

The fur trade resulted in a greater awareness of territoriality among the Indians. Important factors in this development were the nonmigratory nature of the beaver, the continuous demand for beaver fur by the traders, and the traders' encouragement of the Indians to trade their furs as individuals instead of as a group. Increasing territoriality manifested itself in different ways, reflecting precontact regional differences in economic pursuits along the East coast.

Obviously the traditional evaluation of land in the horticultural regions was different from that of the hunters to the north. Garden plots around the riverine villages were either owned outright by families or held in usufruct by them. The latter was the case in the stratified societies of New England and Virginia, where ownership was vested in families of hereditary chiefs. Territorial boundaries were vaguely associated with the rarely visited water divides in the hinterlands. Presumably, each man used to hunt in a particular area well known to him. Due to the pressure of the fur trade, the importance of the smaller streams in those hinterlands increased and native concepts of land ownership, once restricted to the gardens downriver, were used in the development of family trapping territories. In addition, territorial boundaries of the band became more precisely recognized (Snow 1968).

In the northern forests, each band habitually hunted over the same general area, which it held in communal use. The European concept of land ownership, whether communal or private, was unknown. Instead, there existed an exclusive and reciprocal relationship between the benevolent game spirits and respectful human beings within each band territory. The band itself consisted of those people who normally assembled at a good fishing place during the summer. In view of the extremely sparse population and the abundance of game there was no motivation for the accumulation of large tracts of land; thus the knowledge of territorial boundaries was even more vague than among the horticulturists in the south.

This situation started to change radically with the advent of the fur trade. The traders' preference for a particular good harbor forced many Indians to use the same place for their summer rendezvous and led to the formation of a smaller number of larger bands than before. By favoring a particular local Indian as interpreter and spokesman for the group, the trader stimulated the emergence of a band chief with authority to divide the communal land. A mosaic of trapping territories developed, each claimed by a particular group of patrirelated families. The boundaries of family territories were defined and trespassers ran the danger of becoming the victims of increasing witchcraft activities, if not being killed outright (Leacock 1954).

Witchcraft undermined the old supernatural dimension of daily life as well as the interpersonal relationships among the native societies of the northern forests. It was perhaps not by coincidence that Membertou, the leader of the eastern Micmacs about 1600, was a shaman. In fact, the combination in one person of band chief and shaman has been reported frequently from the boreal forest.

The selection of specific bays as annual trading centers was considered a great boon by the regional Indians, but it often harbored future tragedy and warfare for them and their neighbors. The supply of European goods was limited and competition among Indian groups was likely to result in lower prices for their furs; hence it is obvious that the Indians wanted by all means to ensure themselves of a permanent and exclusive relationship with the fur trader. Captain Smith reported that Chief Powhatan requested him to abandon the Jamestown settlement among the Paspahegh Indians and resettle in Powhatan's territory. In order to maintain these exclusive contacts, the coastal Indians frequently told the Europeans gruesome stories about the hinterland. These stories contrasted strongly with those of Indians deported to Europe, who invented wonderful tales as an incentive to be returned to their homeland.

Rivalry over direct access to the trade with the Europeans became a source of intertribal wars at an early date. Friction of this type between the Saint Lawrence Iroquoians and the Montagnais may have had an early start along the east coast of Quebec. On the basis of reports of Saint Lawrence Iroquoians as far north as the Strait of Belle Isle it has been postulated that these people were used to going there every summer to hunt seals. Considering the enormous distance from their home territory and the presence of seals closer to their villages it is debatable whether these expeditions were traditional hunting parties.

Most probably these Iroquoians were coming to the fur traders in the country of the Montagnais before the Europeans had yet ventured up the Saint Lawrence River. At any rate, there is no evidence for such trips down the coast after the French traders had reached the Saint Lawrence. By the last decades of the sixteenth century, the Micmacs had forced the Iroquoians from the Gaspé Peninsula and had acquired control of the regional fur trade. By 1600 Montagnais were found to occupy the former north shore territory of the Saint Lawrence Iroquoians while their middleman activities reached east as far as the Abenaki in Maine (Hoffman 1955a, 1967; Purchas 1625a, 4:1874; Trigger 1962a).

Similar monopolistic positions were later taken by the Penobscot nucleus of the Eastern Abenaki confederacy, the Narragansett in Rhode Island, the Pequot in Connecticut, the Woronoco on the Connecticut River, the Mahican on the Hudson River, the Susquehannock in Pennsylvania, and the Weanock in the Virginia hinterlands, to mention only the most important of the native middlemen. It did not take long for the more remote groups to find out that they were being cheated by the coastal natives. If strong enough, tribes in the interior subjected the former middlemen or drove them away to start the lucrative business themselves. The histories of these groups provide many variants of intertribal wars resulting from the fur trade. The definitive abandonment of horticulture by the Indians in Maine was caused by such a war with the invading Micmac, and the decimation of the local population by an epidemic (Day 1953:331).

Both factors—wars and epidemics—probably initiated some population movements as indicated by archeological research, vague historical references, and native traditions. The stimuli for these removals appear to have had their origin in the coastal area as well as in the Saint Lawrence valley. About 1580 the Susquehannocks moved down the river named after them. As a result of Iroquois warfare, population shifts may have taken place in New England about the same time. While large sections of the New England coast were being completely depopulated by a series of epidemics about 1617, the Narragansetts were increased in numbers by refugee bands of survivors. About the same time, if not earlier, the Hudson River Wappinger appear to have established direct contact with the fur traders by forcing parts of the

coastal Munsee to remove from the lower courses of the river.

In the course of these wars, latent political alliances of an aboriginal nature were strengthened; and by conquest and voluntary incorporation, local units were merged into tribes and tribes joined to form confederacies. This process usually was initiated by a local group that had direct access to the fur trade. Desiring to profit from the trade, neighboring groups accepted the supremacy of the chief at the trade center. The conquest of more remote groups and monopolistic desires led to warfare, forcing the members of the new confederacy to leave their scattered hamlets and concentrate in fewer but larger palisaded villages. This concentration of larger population units was made possible by the unprecedented wealth derived from conquests and intertribal trade.

In view of these developments, the question arises whether the social stratification of the native societies in New England and around Chesapeake Bay was purely aboriginal or whether it developed as a result of the fur trade. In the early years of the seventeenth century long genealogies of hereditary chiefs were recorded among the Conoy on Chesapeake Bay and the Mohegan-Pequot in Connecticut (Mooney and Thomas 1907c:339; Means 1947). Reports from the early seventeenth century show all the features of a fully developed social stratification, with land ownership and political leadership restricted to a small but rigidly separated upper class if not caste (Speck 1928d:26; Stern 1952:162). Verrazano's description of his meeting, in 1524, with some native leaders in present Rhode Island fits in perfectly with this picture and tells something about its time-depth (Wroth 1970:138–139). The Rhode Island Indians preserved a tradition about a precontact chief, who "had only a *Son* and a *Daughter;* and he, esteeming none of Degree for them to marry with, *married them together*" (Stiles 1916:28). Normally, marriage partners were found within the leading families of neighboring groups. This type of class structure was not restricted to the central East coast but extended down into the Gulf region.

The early historic emergence of confederacies cannot be explained in terms of contact change only. On the other hand, there is no doubt that the makeup of these confederacies enhanced the existing social stratification. Throughout North America the rise of such confederacies would indicate the start of the commercial phase of European contact. Depending upon the length of this phase in any particular region, such associations were able to realize an intertribal sociopolitical structure but then would shrivel again to small tribes by population decline and removals during the subsequent colonial phase. This, in fact, is the background of most surviving tribes, rather than old traditional organizations.

These political developments were particularly characteristic of the central Atlantic coast, where the concept of leadership and warfare predated European contact.

Analogous developments also took place in the northern regions, though on a smaller scale and in a less complex form. Both leadership and war raids were novelties to the northern hunters; neither before nor after contact did they set out to subject and exploit their neighbors' labor. Insofar as they made wars in historic times their motivations were either to exclude others from trade or to enlarge their trapping territories. The summer concentrations of people at the trade centers were larger than at the old fishing grounds, but every fall the band had to break up and disperse in small groups into the interior in order to trap the necessary fur-bearing animals. Apart from a few temporary strong leaders, their chiefs never acquired the power of their counterparts in the horticultural regions.

During this period, the Indians became crafty and experienced traders with the Europeans. In intergroup dealings a wary sensitivity to any sign of hostility or treachery appears to have been prevalent. Due to the corporate nature of Indian custom any European might be attacked and killed for the crime of any other White man. Particularly in the north, the promiscuity of the French and Basque fishermen with the native women frequently tended to disrupt the fur trade. In more southern areas, the settlers' encroachment on native territory started early and was viewed with increasing hostility by the Indians. The fluctuations of fur prices were proof of cheating to the Indians, who did not make a secret of such feelings. They were also outspoken in their ethnocentric feelings of superiority with respect to the Whites, although arrogant bragging may sometimes have been used to cover up for actual feelings of respectful amazement. The Indians' recognition of the superiority of iron tools and firearms undoubtedly played a major role in spurring the trade with the Europeans. For the rest, only a very small segment of European culture was visible for the Indians in their contacts with fur traders and fishermen. The points on which the Europeans felt most strongly superior were nonmaterial and, if these ever crossed the language barrier, they had little meaning for the Indians. The Indians despised the Europeans for their clumsiness in woodcraft and hunting skill and their failure to survive without Indian assistance. Yet due to their common economic interests, social relationships between the fur traders and the Indians were generally amicable.

In the course of traffic between the two races a trade jargon developed "between the French and the Savages, which is neither French nor Savage; and yet when the French use it, they think they are using the Savage Tongue, and the Savages in using it, think they are speaking good French" (JR 5:113–115). Along the central east coast, a similar mixture developed of English and Indian words. These jargons were limited in content and their use was perforce restricted to commercial transactions. Indians who had learned English or French as a

Peabody Mus., Harvard U.: 88-25-10/46959.
Fig. 2. Knife with antler handle and brass blade made of sheet metal or part of a kettle, found in a grave in Winthrop, Mass. This is a postcontact variant of an earlier form (Willoughby 1935:240). Length approximately 11.5 cm.

result of visiting these countries were rare. Conversely, few traders cared to master a native language.

Whereas the language barriers served to screen out much of a nonmaterial character, the displacement of native materials and implements was to cause major changes in the native cultures by the end of the sixteenth century. Early names for the Whites, such as Iron-men, Knife-men, or Coat-men, indicate the natives' appreciation of the new trade wares. The long-time restriction of the fur trade to the north is illustrated by the general use of stone hatchets in Massachusetts as late as 1608; in 1609 Champlain noted that the occasional iron ax used by the Mohawk was acquired in warfare with the Algonquins of the Saint Lawrence valley. Sheet copper and brass reached the central East coast during the sixteenth century. The Indians used them to make arrow-points, knife blades (fig. 2), pipe stems (fig. 3), needles, tubular beads, and bird-shaped pendants (fig. 4). Wood-carvings were inlaid with pieces of brass and iron wire, creating geometric designs upon the surface (fig. 5). The tubular copper beads were woven side by side into bandoliers, foreshadowing the later development of wampum belts. Although most of this copper and brass is identifiable as having been of European origin, the variety of uses, the ingenuity of manufacturing techniques and several Indian statements forcibly suggest an aboriginal acquaintance with native copper.

Other European items were adapted to Indian usage. The occasional steel hatchet or knife replaced aboriginal stone gorgets as prestigious decorations and the first Dutch stockings were used as tobacco pouches by the

Peabody Mus., Harvard U.: 99-54-10/A4126.
Fig. 3. Pottery pipe with sheet brass stem, found in a pre-1634 grave in Winthrop, Mass. Length approximately 12.5 cm.

Peabody Mus., Harvard U.: 88-45-10/46959.

Fig. 4. Copper gorget in the form of a bird found in an Indian grave near Amoskeag Falls (Manchester, N.H.). The thickness of the copper makes it likely that it was fashioned from a copper kettle, probably in the early contact period. Length 24 cm.

left, Nationalmuseet, Copenhagen: HB 26; right, Etnografiska Museet, Stockholm: Livrust 3932.

Fig. 6. Two 17th-century tomahawks, both probably pre-1650 and from New Sweden, New Netherlands, or the Iroquois; they differ principally in the material used for the blades. The hafts are of wood, with wampum beads inlaid in gum and then ground flat, much of the original inlay now missing. The blades are attached with leather thongs and wood wedges. left, Blade of ground and polished dark green argillite, inlay of white and purple wampum, small bits of bone, 8 small black European glass beads, and 3 cylindrical red European glass beads; length of blade 29 cm, of haft 47 cm. right, European iron blade, inlay (except plain grip) of white wampum longitudinally halved, white shell fragments, and 4 split polychrome glass European beads (with green outer surfaces), tassel of red-dyed deer hair on twined vegetable fiber wrapped around end of leather thong; length of blade 32.9 cm, of haft 44.4 cm. See Birket-Smith 1920:145–155; Linné 1955, 1958 for discussions of both specimens.

Indians. Copper kettles not only replaced pottery in daily use but also were frequently placed upside down over the heads of the deceased in burial. This use of trade goods shows that they were given a traditional function in the native culture.

New materials, such as woven fabrics, were not always better than native materials, but they were considered superior. They replaced native materials, but the aboriginal forms of artifacts tended to persist (fig. 6). This was obvious in the case of tools, since their form was closely related to their use. On the other hand, European artifacts sometimes influenced the forms of native manufactures. This is noticeable in the occasional production of pottery with flat bottoms and the modification of wooden spoons.

Glass beads were valued merchandise from the earliest days of the fur trade, and from the start the Indian preference for certain colors appears to have played a role. Most commonly found in graves are white and blue beads, the colors of the aboriginal shell ones. Originally those shell beads were highly valued in the aboriginal trade and their decorative use was restricted to the chiefs. The fur trade made glass beads available for everyone,

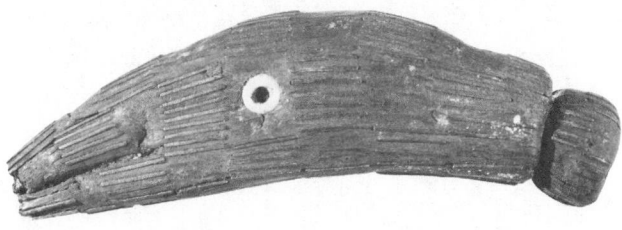

Peabody Mus., Harvard U.: 1900-6-10/55218 A.

Fig. 5. Wooden pendant in the form of a bird's head (tip of beak is broken) found in an Indian grave in Atlantic, Mass., along with a necklace of commercially made wampum. The design was formed by imbedding small pieces of brass wire into the surface of the wood; discoidal wampum beads serve as eyes. Overall length approximately 8 cm.

while imported metal tools simplified the manufacture of shell beads. The colonial use of shell beads as money and the symbolic value frequently added to archaic items in conservative societies were at the root of the ritual use of wampum beads in later times. Although pewter casting, splint basketry, and other European techniques were adopted only after intimate contact with the White colonists, a few acculturations of this type appear to date back to the coastal trade period. One of them is the occasional use of sails on Indian canoes.

Although the supply of European goods was limited, the demand for them was persistent and cumulative. Iron utensils and blankets, for instance, rapidly wore out due to the Indian way of life, and an increasing number of native groups became directly or indirectly involved in

87

the trade. For the Indians along the central East coast the real impact of European manufactures started only by the end of the sixteenth century. By 1610 the Virginia natives had abandoned their aboriginal stone industry, since "now by trucking with us, they have thowsandes of our Iron hatchetts" (Strachey 1953:109). Yet as late as 1643 the Indian women in New England, "notwithstanding our howes, doe use their naturall Howes of shells and Wood" (Williams 1936:99).

Most of the material culture traits listed by archeologists for the late prehistoric period continued in diminishing ratios, making way for the addition of artifacts of European manufacture. The time formerly used in making one's own utensils was needed for trapping and other activities related to the fur trade. The price of all the new riches was the economic dependence of the natives, resulting in the decay of the native crafts, poverty, and chronic malnutrition after the loss of the fur trade. About 1650 an old New England Indian complained that "a long time ago, they [the Indians] had wise men, which in a grave manner taught the people knowledge; but they are dead, and their wisdom is buried with them, and now men live a giddy life, in ignorance, till they are white headed, and though ripe in years, yet then they go without wisdom to their graves" (Warner 1935:185).

Sources

Although the literature of the early explorations is voluminous, the original sources on which it is based are limited. Many have been published several times. An effort has been made to list the best editions of these primary sources as well as to suggest some books to serve as further guides to the subject.

Important contributions to understanding the aboriginal cultures along the East coast are Day (1953), Feest (1966), Hoffman (1961, 1967), Leacock (1954), Mook (1944a), Mooney (1907), Snow (1968), Speck (1928), Stern (1952), and Wallace (1947). Particularly rich in ethnographic information are primary sources such as the *Jesuit Relations* (JR 1896-1901), Roger Williams's work on language (1936), John White's drawings (Hulton and Quinn 1964) and narratives of the Roanoke voyages (Quinn 1955), and Capt. John Smith's narrative (1884).

Most information concerning the early Norse explorations is provided by two Icelandic sagas; Magnusson and Pálsson (1965) contains a very useful introduction. Ingstad (1969) discovered a Norse settlement in Newfoundland.

All known sources on Cabot's activities are contained in Williamson (1962). Biggar (1911) and Hoffman (1961) are concerned with explorations from Cabot to Cartier. The best guide to the sixteenth-century explorations is Trudel (1963-1966, 1).

Detailed information on the Newfoundland cod fisheries can be found in La Morandière (1962-1966) and Innis (1940). Cartier's (1924) and other early explorations can be studied in Burrage (1906). Wroth (1970) is the most recent edition of the Cellere Codex, which is the most detailed one of the four early versions existing of Verrazano's explorations.

Lewis and Loomie (1953) is an exhaustive study of the Spanish Jesuit mission in Virginia. A new edition of Richard Hakluyt (1965) has been published by the Hakluyt Society.

Champlain (1922-1936) is the source for the explorer's voyages along the coasts of New England. Important sources for the study of Virginia are Capt. John Smith's (1884) narrative, Tyler (1907), and Strachey's history (1953). Henry Hudson's voyage and the subsequent Dutch colony are treated in Jameson's edition (1909). Detailed information on the early years of the New England colony can be found in William Bradford's narrative (1952), Heath's edition of a Pilgrim journal (Mourt 1963), and Thomas Morton's (1637) history.

The most readable monograph on the whole period of early contacts, Morison (1971), contains a detailed and annotated bibliography, although it is weak on recent studies and modern editions.

Seventeenth-Century Indian Wars

WILCOMB E. WASHBURN

The history of European contact with the Indians of the East Coast, while often compared with the establishment of a military beachhead, was in fact a slower, less abrupt process of cautious feeling out of each party by the other, mutual accommodation according to what each had to offer the other, and eventual military confrontation over issues that are often obscure in their origin. This chapter will deal solely with the full-scale wars that erupted between the Europeans and the few powerful coastal tribes with whom the seventeenth-century colonists were in direct contact. More powerful inland tribes, particularly in the Southeast and in interior New York, were not similarly involved in warfare with the English until the eighteenth century.

The early relations of the English colonies of Plymouth in New England and Jamestown in Virginia with the neighboring Indians were similar. The English relied on Indian hospitality, Indian food, and Indian advice, yet became increasingly overbearing, demanding, and insensitive to native rights (Smith 1910; Bradford 1952). Capt. Miles Standish for the Plymouth colony and Capt. John Smith for the Virginia colony moved into the hinterland browbeating native leaders, robbing Indian food caches, and obtaining food for their bickering comrades by trade or by extortion. The peaceful relations early established between the races were strained by this behavior and awaited only an excess of zeal before war erupted.

New England

Early Conflicts

Early hostilities with the natives of New England were averted by the Plymouth leaders through the sealing of a treaty of friendship between the colony and Massasoit, war chief of the Wampanoags, who visited the struggling colony in 1621. By the terms of the agreement, both sides were to keep the peace and offenses committed by one side against the other were to be punished. The peace lasted for more than a half-century (Bradford 1952: 80-81; Channing 1932-1938, 1:314-315; Burke 1967: 42-44).

Plymouth did not hesitate to use force against the natives, often with questionable justification, as in Captain Standish's assault on the Indians of Massachusetts Bay in the winter of 1622-1623, when a colony under Thomas Weston fell into disorder and was "rescued" by Standish (Bradford 1952:116-119; Channing 1932-1938, 1:316). Gov. William Bradford justified the preemptive strike on the basis of a reported conspiracy of the Bay Indians against Weston's men, and—because of the Indians' expectation that Plymouth would go to the rescue of Weston's men—against the Pilgrim colony also. Bradford cheerfully conceded that Weston's men were guilty of abusing the Indians through thievery and the like but accepted the necessity of cutting off the "conspirators" before they could strike. Although the source of the colony's information about the alleged conspiracy was their ally Massasoit, the twentieth-century historian is forced to question the accuracy of the information, particularly in the face of the invariable perception of Indian conspiracies prior to most of New England's Indian wars (Bradford 1952:116-119).

The willingness to use force against those who offended their purpose was also demonstrated by the Pilgrim assault on the colony of Thomas Morton who had, in 1625, set up a maypole on Merrymount near the present town of Quincy, where he lived in intimate contact with the natives, exchanging European goods for furs and Puritan values for native license. The little colony was destroyed and Morton sent packing. Morton's settlement was an affront to Pilgrim and Puritan morality and, in one interpretation, a threat to the very psyche of the colonists (R. Slotkin 1973; Bradford 1952:204-210). The colonial authorities had no more compunction about destroying Morton's scandalous colony than about destroying any Indian group that seemed to threaten their values.

New England's first great Indian war was with the Pequot Indians in 1637. The extermination of the Pequot tribe, feelingly evoked by the name of the doomed whaling vessel in Herman Melville's *Moby Dick,* is the subject of conflicting interpretations by both contemporary participants and later historians. The evidence is frequently clouded or missing. While it is dangerous to reason from assumed motives of the participants, it is fair to assert that both the established colony of Massachusetts and the newer colony of Connecticut sought to profit from the destruction of this powerful tribe. The causes of the war given by the English seem strained and arbitrary. The killing in 1634 of an English rogue, Capt. John Stone, by Western Niantics allied with the Pequots was the occasion for excessive and unreasonable demands by the Massachusetts Bay colony authorities on the Pequots. A treaty, signed November 1, 1634, temporarily averted war. When, in 1636, another ship captain, John Oldham, was killed on Block Island by some Narragansett Indians, the Massachusetts Bay authorities sent an expedition of 90 volunteers under John Endecott with orders to put to death the men of Block Island, capture the women and children, and take possession of the island. The expedition was then to go to the Pequot country to demand the murderers of Captain Stone and other English, 1,000 fathom of wampum for damages, and some children as hostages. If the Pequots refused they were to obtain satisfaction by force (Winthrop 1908, 1:186). Gov. John Winthrop later asserted that the original intention had been to send Endecott's force only to Block Island, "and our sending them thence to the Pequods was with hope to draw them to parley, and so to some quiet end" (Winthrop 1908, 1:214).

The expedition succeeded in little except to destroy the peace that had existed between the Pequots and the English and to put in grave peril the fort at Saybrook, at the mouth of the Connecticut River, commanded by Lt. Lion Gardiner, who was outraged at Endecott's hasty and ineffective search and destroy mission against the Pequots (Bradford 1952:292). Indian raids on outlying settlements after the departure of Endecott were costly to the Connecticut settlers. When they found both the Connecticut and Massachusetts men unyielding and threatening to destroy their women and children, the Pequots sought to heal their former breach with the Narragansetts and to unite in a struggle against the English. By a fortunate stroke of luck for the English, Roger Williams was able to interrupt the council at which Pequots and Narragansetts sought to resolve their differences with an offer from the English to the Narragansetts of an alliance against their old enemies, the Pequots. The Narragansetts succumbed to the suggestion, thus playing into the hands of the English and leading not only to the Pequots' destruction but also eventually to their own (Vaughan 1965:131-132). On May 1, 1637, the General Court of the colony of Connecticut declared "offensive warr" on the Pequots. Both Connecticut and Massachusetts then sent expeditions against the Pequots, each seeming to anticipate the advantages to be gained by destroying this nation before the other did. Capt. John Mason of Connecticut, with 90 Englishmen and hundreds of Indian allies, marched to one of the Pequot villages on the Mystic River, which he put to the torch, slaughtering all the inhabitants, most of whom were women and children, to the number of 300 to 700 (fig. 1) (J. Mason 1736). The Narragansett allies of the English were appalled by the ruthless nature of the English assault and by their killing and enslaving of all surviving Pequots, even some who had surrendered voluntarily to the Narragansetts and whom the latter wished to inte-

grate into their tribe. As Capt. John Underhill wrote, while the Narragansetts rejoiced at the victory, they "cried mach it, mach it; that is, it is naught, it is naught, because it is too furious, and slaies too many men" (Underhill 1638:42-43).

While the principal wars of New England were direct confrontations between the English colonies and the Indians, intertribal conflicts pre-existed English settlement and were fostered by the English under the expedient imperialist principle of divide and rule. The Indians, as Sylvester (1910, 1:343) put it, "like so many dogs, were to be set at the throats each of the other, as occasion offered. . . ." English encouragement of such intertribal conflict is most evident in the dealings between the Mohegan sachem Uncas and the Narragansetts, leading to the English attack on the Narragansetts in 1643. English perfidy at this time may have been one of the reasons that caused King Philip later in the century to question the integrity of his English neighbors (Sylvester 1910, 1:346-347; Metcalf 1974).

The origins of the English-Narragansett conflict are intimately related to the creation, by Articles of Confederation in 1643, of a league uniting the Puritan colonies of Massachusetts, Connecticut, New Haven, and Plymouth (Winthrop 1908, 2:100-105; Ward 1961; Andrews 1934-1938, 2:23-24). Excluded, or rather rejected, from this confederation was Roger Williams's Providence Plantations. The confederation was a threat both to Williams's colony and to the Narragansetts, and both eventually sought protection from England against the threat. The outbreak of war between the United Colonies and the Narragansetts is obscured by contradictory assertions of guilt and innocence. It is also marked by the traditional assertion of a threatened "general conspiracy" against the English (Bradford 1952:330). The pretext for war arose out of an intertribal squabble between Uncas and Sequasson, a sachem living along the Connecticut River. In the fighting that ensued, Sequasson lost seven or eight of his men and some booty to Uncas's men. When the Narragansett sachem Miantonomi (allied to Sequasson) asked the English if they would be offended if he made war upon Uncas, he was told that if Uncas had done him or his friends wrong and would not give satisfaction, the English would leave him to take his own course (Winthrop 1908, 2:131-132; Vaughan 1965: 155-173). In the war that followed, Miantonomi was captured; his tribe sought to ransom him with a £40 gift. Uncas allegedly accepted the wampum but brought him captive to the commissioners of the United Colonies (Bradford 1952:336). The commissioners, in what Andrews (1934-1938, 2:94) called a "cold-blooded murder . . . for which the colony must always bear the blame," after seeking the advice of five of the "most judicious elders" decided that Miantonomi should be put to death but that it should be done discreetly, by Uncas, after he had left the jurisdiction of the English (Winthrop 1908,

Fig. 1. Diagram of the English attack on the Pequot fort at Mystic in 1637. The two entrances to the stockade are labeled, as are "The Indians houses" and "Their Streets" (Underhill 1638). As Jennings (1975:224) points out, the illustration agrees with contemporary descriptions in showing no Indians with firearms, Englishmen shooting unarmed Indians as well as those with bows and arrows, and Englishmen shooting Pequots attempting to escape through their line to the surrounding Narragansett allies of the English.

2:134–136). The murder enraged the Narragansetts, who sought revenge on Uncas's followers for their violation of the ransom custom (Bradford 1952:334–338).

The Narragansett chiefs also, in the spring of 1644, sought to safeguard their lands against their increasingly hostile English allies by submitting themselves and their lands directly to Charles I "upon condition of His Majesties royal protection," explaining that they had "just cause of jealousy and suspicion of some of His Majesty's pretended subjects" to whom they would not submit "having ourselves been the chief Sachems, or Princes successively, of the country, time out of mind" (Records of R.I., 1:134–136). The Narragansett sachems Pessicus and Canonicus refused summons to come to Boston, explaining that "neither yourselves nor we are to

be judges; and both of us are to have recourse, and repair unto that [the King's] honorable and just Government" (Records of R.I., 1:136–138).

The Narragansetts' hoped-for protector could not protect himself, however, against those rebelling against his authority in England. Nor did the New England authorities accept the Narragansetts' constitutional argument. The daring appeal was thus frustrated and the confederated colonies declared war on the Narragansetts. While numerous causes were alleged to justify the declaration, the principal cause would seem to have been the Narragansetts' insistence on maintaining control of their own affairs in the matter of making agreements with the Rhode Island settlers and in making war on Uncas, whether the English liked it or not. The Narragansetts were always careful to avoid acts of violence against the English and to meet all their reasonable demands, but they could not be expected to agree to their own destruction as an autonomous nation. Nevertheless, under the threat of an English invasion, the sachems capitulated to a "treaty" on August 28, 1645, that made them acknowledge culpability for various misdeeds, pay 2,000 fathoms of wampum plus an annual tribute for each Pequot living amongst them, cede the whole Pequot country to the English colonies, and give hostages to the English as pledges of good behavior (Vaughan 1965:167–172). The Narragansetts continued to survive, though with diminished authority, in part protected by the support Roger Williams and others received under Oliver Cromwell in their pleas for protection against the encroachments of the Puritans of New England. Williams (1874, 2:270), for example, noted in 1654 that: "At my last departure for England, I was importuned by the Narragansett Sachems, and especially by Ninigret, to present their petition to the high Sachems of England, that they might not be forced from their religion, and, for not changing their religion, be invaded by war; for they said they were daily visited with threatenings by Indians that came from about the Massachusetts, that if they would not pray, they should be destroyed by war."

Relations between the Narragansetts and the neighboring Puritan colonies continued to be marked by periodic crises, rumors of conspiracies, and occasional overawing or punitive expeditions, as in 1654. Most historians have seen the Narragansetts as unjustly put upon by the colonists, but Vaughan (1965:166–168) has insisted that the Puritans in general acted circumspectly and justly.

King Philip's War

The origins of King Philip's War, the next great New England Indian war, are shrouded, as are all of New England's wars, in bitter controversy and deep confusion. The war grew out of the peculiar relationship between the Plymouth colony and the Wampanoag Indians. The friendship that had been firmly established between the two peoples from the earliest time began to deteriorate in the 1660s, a period coincidental with the questioning, by the newly restored Charles II, of the peculiar forms of government of the New England colonies. Each colony sought to make a proper accommodation with the monarch, some (those established during the interregnum) by obtaining appropriate royal charters from the restored Charles. The uncertainty of the Plymouth title, in the face of the aggressive designs of her other English neighbors, made her relationship with the Wampanoags, with whom she was bound by treaty, doubly important. Massasoit, though he had subjected himself to a kind of protectorate status, still assumed the right to sell land to others, as he did his claim (overlapping the Narragansett claim to the same land) to Roger Williams of the Rhode Island

colony. Massasoit's successor, Wamsutta, similarly assumed the right to sell land to outsiders, a practice that the Plymouth colony attempted to stop (Records of Plymouth 4:8). When Wamsutta continued to sell land to the Rhode Island colonists after Plymouth attempted to prevent it, Maj. Josiah Winslow, with a party of armed men, in 1664 surprised Wamsutta and carried him to Plymouth. Wamsutta sickened and was released but died before reaching home (Hubbard 1677:9–10). Wamsutta's brother, called King Philip by the English, succeeded him and was ordered to come to Plymouth where accusations of a possible conspiracy against the English were raised and where Plymouth insisted that Philip agree never to convey lands to any person by any means without the consent of the Plymouth government (Records of Plymouth 4:25–26). Philip, on the other hand, protested the continued granting of lands in and near his territory by the Pilgrim colony (Langdon 1966:162). Moreover, his treaty pledged subjection to the King of England, not to Plymouth. As Jennings (1975) has pointed out, this distinction became of particular interest when Rhode Island received its royal charter in 1663, putting King Philip's home of Mount Hope (now Bristol), within Rhode Island's boundaries. Plymouth, reluctant to lose its special relationship with King Philip, challenged Rhode Island's charter and kept the question open for many years. By 1670 Massachusetts, Rhode Island, and Plymouth were contesting for hegemony in the area where their boundaries came to a point, which included a portion of the Nipmuck country. In the meantime, Plymouth had established in 1667 the town of Swansea, which was situated at the edge of the Plymouth colony, overlapping the claims of both Rhode Island and King Philip (Records of Plymouth 4:176). The Wampanoags expressed bitterness and in 1671 made threatening moves near Swansea. Plymouth's response was to levy a fine on King Philip and to order him to surrender all his people's arms (Langdon 1966:157–159; Burke 1967:68–71). At the same time the colony authorized further expansion of the town of Swansea (Records of Plymouth 5:24). In 1671 Plymouth demands on Philip, stemming from alleged violations of his agreements with the colony, became so intolerable that instead of going to Plymouth when summoned by the governor, Philip went to the Massachusetts Bay colony pleading for help and understanding against Plymouth. The Bay authorities wrote the Plymouth authorities challenging a main tenet of the Pilgrim position by doubting whether the covenants and engagements that Philip and his predecessors had agreed to "subjected himselfe and people and country to vs any further then as in a neighborly and friendly correspondency" (Records of Plymouth 5:77). Nevertheless, representatives of Massachusetts Bay and of Connecticut came to Plymouth and on September 24 participated in a comprehensive examination of Philip's various misdeeds, which included charges such as Philip's behaving "insolently and proudly towards us on seureall occasions, in refusing to come down to our Court, when sent for to haue speech with him" (Records of Plymouth 5:78; Burke 1967:75-76). On September 29 Philip was prevailed upon to sign a document making the Wampanoags subject to the laws and government of New Plymouth as well as subject to the King of England. In addition, Philip agreed to pay a fine and pledged never to sell lands without Plymouth's approval (Records of Plymouth 5:76-79).

In January 1675 occurred the incident that set in motion the chain of events that led immediately to King Philip's War. A praying Indian named John Sassamon reported to Gov. Josiah Winslow that Philip was preparing for war. On his return from Winslow's house at Marshfield, Sassamon was murdered by persons unknown (Langdon 1966:162). Philip denied complicity in the murder. Three Indians were later tried by a Plymouth court upon which sat six praying Indians (Records of Plymouth 5:167; Leach 1958:33; Burke 1967:82-87). Condemned to death, one of the Indians on trial asserted Philip's guilt. Plymouth resolved on war and, despite the efforts of a party of Rhode Island Quakers to prevent it, the war came. First blood was drawn by the English who shot Indians pilfering a house that the English had abandoned (Easton 1913; Church 1860:30-32; Leach 1958:42; Burke 1967:88-100).

While the conventional view of the war has seen it as a conspiracy of all New England Indians against the English, there is little hard evidence to suggest that this is so (Washburn 1958). The evidence usually used to support the conspiracy theory depends upon the expressed and recorded "fears" of English colonists and officials in Plymouth, Massachusetts Bay, and Connecticut. Those fears were buttressed by the special interest each colony had in obtaining control over the lands of the Wampanoags and Narragansetts, portions of which were included in the Rhode Island boundaries that each of the other colonies, in its way, sought to violate. Still another factor was the colony of New York, which, under its governor, Edmund Andros, sought to assert its claim to all the territory formerly claimed by the Dutch, which claims included half the territory of Connecticut. When reports of fighting at Swansea in the Plymouth colony were received by the other colonies, each colony proceeded to act in its own interest. Connecticut, following the lead of Massachusetts, sent troops to its border with Rhode Island where they might pursue their claim to the Narragansett country previously ordered by royal decision to constitute a direct appendage of the Crown (Records of Conn. 2:331-332; Easton 1913:16-17). Andros took a force to Fort Saybrook in Connecticut where his demand for surrender of the Connecticut fort was rejected by the Connecticut forces assembled there (Records of Conn. 2:334, Append. xix:578-586; Craven 1968:120). Rhode Island officials protested against the movement of Connecticut and Massachusetts troops into their territory and their coercion of the Narragansetts who had given no cause for war. John Winthrop conceded that the Narragansetts had always lived in amity with the English and had voluntarily helped in the war against the Pequots, and he urged that they not be made "open, professed enemies because we may have suspicion of them or cannot be so confident or certaine of their continued fidelity." He even urged that not too strict an inquiry be made about Wampanoags who had fled from Philip, particularly women and children, to the Narragansetts for refuge. Nevertheless, the invading forces required four subordinate councilors of the Narragansetts to sign a treaty obligating the tribe to regard all Wampanoags as enemies and to give no sanctuary to any. Bounties were promised for Wampanoag heads and a number delivered by the Narragansetts. The treaty also confirmed all previous grants of land to the English (Jennings 1975; treaty text in Hubbard 1677:21-23).

Warfare quickly broke out in the Connecticut Valley and with the Eastern Indians of the present area of Maine. These outbreaks are often cited as proof of the validity of the theory of a vast Indian conspiracy against the English at this time. However, such outbreaks can more often than not be attributed to acts of brutality or aggression on the part of the English. A characteristic incident is incorporated in Capt. Benjamin Church's (1860:309-310) account of King Philip's War. He recounts the action of certain sailors who, having heard that young Indians could swim naturally like animals, to test the theory overset the canoe of the wife of Squando, a chief sachem on the river Saco, whom, with her infant son, they happened upon. The mother dove under the water and rescued the child who, however, died shortly afterward. The death was attributed to the English and the chief vowed to avenge the insult. How many such incidents, probably mostly unreported, have stained the relations between Whites and Reds in the New World? But even if such incidents themselves may not have set off war, the peremptory demand of the English that the Eastern Indians lay down their arms, for fear they might be used against the English, was met with outraged refusal. Church (1860:310), in recounting the incident, compares the Indians favorably to the Spartans who rejected the demands of Xerxes at Thermopylae that they lay down their arms: "But the English were not so generous as the Persian monarch, for he promised the Spartans a far better country than theirs, if they would comply."

The commissioners of the United Colonies, meeting in Boston in October, obtained the signatures of several minor Narragansett chiefs on a confirmation of the agreement of July by which the Narragansetts pledged to turn over all Wampanoag refugees seeking refuge in their midst. When no such Wampanoags were turned over to the English, the commissioners, in November, resolved to send a force of 1,000 men to force the Narragansetts to observe their treaty obligations. The combined colonial army was to strike only if it could not otherwise enforce its demands. The force assembled in December under the command of Governor Winslow of Plymouth. As the army advanced toward the Narragansett stronghold, the English burned a number of villages and inflicted casualties upon the Narragansetts. There is no evidence that Winslow attempted to negotiate with the Narragansetts before engaging in such acts of hostility. Indeed, as one authority has put it, "the stated purpose of the expedition seems to have dissolved in the general urge to smash the potential foe as quickly as possible" (Leach 1958:126). On December 19, the force reached and assaulted the principal fort of the Narragansetts in the Great Swamp near the present town of West Kingston, Rhode Island, killing, by one estimate, 300 warriors and more than 300 women and children (Leach 1958:112–113; Burke 1967:144–145). Whether the Narragansetts would have joined Philip's "conspiracy" was now an academic question. The "preventive war" launched by the colonies answered the question and resolved the fears of the colonists. Although Leach (1958:144) asserts that the Narragansetts "probably" would have joined Philip's uprising in the spring, it can just as reasonably be argued that they would not have.

Philip's forces, meanwhile, waged a successful guerrilla war against outlying settlements and farms. By December 1675, he had journeyed with some of his forces to the Mahican Indians north of Albany where he sought allies and support. Governor Andros of New York, at the request of the Puritan colonies, reluctantly pressured the fierce Mohawk Indians to attack Philip and his men, which they did, killing some and putting the rest to flight. The Mohawks continued to do service against their and the colonies' enemies in the backcountry of New England. Philip and his forces returned to their home territories, having suffered a serious setback by their failure to obtain support and by the losses they suffered at the hands of the powerful Mohawks. Meanwhile English forces located groups of Indians—often women and children and old men seeking safety—and dispatched them without mercy (Records of Conn. 2:444, 447–448, 458–459).

The inability of a later generation to see Philip in human terms is evident in the account of the New England historian Palfrey (1858–1890, 3:233):

And the title of *King*, which it has been customary to attach to his name, disguises and transfigures to the view the form of a squalid savage, whose palace was a sty; whose royal robe was a bearskin or a coarse blanket, alive with vermin; who hardly knew the luxury of an ablution; who was often glad to appease appetite with food such as men who are not starving loathe; and whose nature possessed just the capacity for

reflection and the degree of refinement, which might be expected to be developed from the mental constitution of his race by such a condition and such habits of life.

As the tide began to turn, Philip returned to Mount Hope to die, seemingly driven, as Leach (1958:234) has put it, "by some great compelling sense of tragic drama." There, in August 1676 in a swamp, he and his remaining followers were trapped and Philip killed by one of the Indian allies of the English. Captain Church (1860:45), the English commander on the scene, described the dead Philip as looking like "a doleful, great, naked, dirty beast." Church ordered the body decapitated and quartered, and the victorious party returned in triumph with Philip's head (Leach 1958:236).

What was the cost of the war? Edmund Randolph, in October 1676, estimated English losses at 600 men and £150,000, a bill that included 1,200 houses burned, 8,000 head of cattle killed, and, on the Indian side, 3,000 men, women, and children destroyed, "who if well managed would have been very serviceable to the English: which makes all manner of labour dear" (NYCD 3:243–244). The United Colonies claimed that their expenses totalled £100,000 (Leach 1958:244).

Further Conflicts

Severe as the devastating wars of 1637 and 1676 were (and a higher percentage of the English population suffered death or wounds in the 1676 conflict than in any subsequent American war), they were not the principal causes of the decline of the Indian population. Vaughan (1965:320, 329) estimates that the casualties of the two great New England Indian wars account for at most 15 or 20 percent of that decline. Disease took a much greater toll.

The Indian-White conflicts during the periods of King William's War (1689–1697) and Queen Anne's War (1702–1711) were part of a larger international struggle between Great Britain and France in which the Indians played an auxiliary role to the principals. In New England, the enemy were the "French and Indians," "Half Indianized French, and Half Frenchified Indians," as Cotton Mather stigmatized them (Mather 1913:206), who moved in joint bands to assault the outlying English settlements, as in the famous assault on Deerfield, Massachusetts, the last day of February 1703/4 (Leach 1966:119; Penhallow 1971). Authorities like Leach treat Indian-White conflict in these periods as merely aspects of the overall struggle between Great Britain and France, yet it is important to remember that the Indians fought in what they judged to be their own interest and for reasons that may have borne little relation to the interests of two European protagonists (Leach 1973:75–164). These reasons were carefully spelled out by Cotton Mather in his account of the "sorrowful decade," 1688–1698, when New England felt the full brunt of Indian resentment

(Mather 1913). Among the grievances cited by the Eastern Indians for their assaults on the English in 1688 were the invasion of their fisheries in Saco River, the invasion of some of their fields by English cattle, abuses in trading, and, above all, the granting or patenting of their lands to some English (Mather 1913:186-187). While Mather presumed (without demonstrating) that the Indian allegations could be answered by many English vindications, some later historians have been less confident. S.A. Drake (1897:9) in explaining why New England had an Indian war on its hands a year before the outbreak of the War of the League of Augsburg (King William's War, as it was known in the colonies), asserted boldly that "the renewal of hostilities with the Abenakis, after ten years of peace, was distinctly the result of English aggressions." While Drake believed the underlying cause to be the steady growth of English settlements in Indian territory, the spark that set off the conflict was the plundering of the trading post of Jean-Vincent d'Abbadie de Saint-Castin at Penobscot in the disputed Acadian boundary area in the spring of 1688 by Governor Andros. Under his commission from James II, Andros's government included the New England colonies as well as New York and New Jersey. The outrage of the Penobscots at the despoiling of their well-liked trader set them on edge. Another incident soon followed. Sixteen Indians were seized at Saco, Maine, by Benjamin Blackman, a justice of the peace, in retaliation for the killing of some cattle at North Yarmouth. Reprisals followed. Efforts by Andros to calm the situation proved unavailing and on June 27, 1689, the town of Dover, New Hampshire, was sacked by a band of Penacook Indians; two dozen inhabitants were killed and 29 taken into captivity. The attack on Dover was particularly satisfying to the Eastern Indians who had long nursed a desire to avenge the deception practiced upon them at the conclusion of King Philip's War by Richard Walderne, the great man of the village. Walderne had disarmed them through a stratagem and seized many of the southern Indians who had fled to them for protection after the failure of King Philip's War.

Although the Indians thus had their own reasons for fighting, their efforts were increasingly coordinated by, and used to support the larger purposes of, the French (see Parkman 1865-1892, 5, 6).

Virginia

The experience of the Virginia colonists matched closely that of the New Englanders. The Indians of both regions had cause for suspicion of the newcomers based on their close identity with the explorers, fishermen, slave catchers, freebooters, and others who occasionally had wrought violence upon them prior to the establishment of permanent colonies. Nevertheless, the reception accorded the permanent settlers was for the most part friendly and hospitable. The necessities of the colonists at Jamestown in the fall of 1607, for example, were relieved by Indian generosity and hospitality. There was enough room for all, and each side was able to profit from association with the other (Lurie 1959; Washburn 1959:20; R.L. Morton 1960, 1:14). Virginia's total Algonquian population at the beginning of English contact has been estimated at 14,300 to 22,300, a higher but better estimate than all previous estimates (Feest 1973:74). Needless to say the population declined precipitously throughout the seventeenth century.

Early Conflicts

The early relations of peaceful trade and intercourse were eroded by the increasingly peremptory and demanding tone of the English colonists. Capt. John Smith, in his forays through the Chesapeake Bay region, thought nothing of seizing stores of corn when he could not trade for them. In 1607, for example, when Smith found the Indians of Kecoughtan unwilling to turn over their stores of corn, "though contrary to his Commission: [he] Let fly his muskets, ran his boat on shore" and assaulted the startled natives (Smith 1910, 2:393). In 1609 an English detachment sent by Smith to Nansemond, frustrated in its attempt to purchase an island adjacent to the Nansemond territory and suspecting foul play to their messengers dispatched to the Nansemond king, "Beate the Salvages outt of the Island burned their howses Ransaked their Temples" and desecrated their tombs (Percy 1922:262-263; Smith 1910, 1:163; Barbour 1964:274). They were soon afterwards beaten off the island in turn by the Indians (Percy 1922:264-265). In 1610, after some English had been killed in the vicinity of Kecoughtan, the English destroyed the town, attacked two Warraskoyack towns, destroyed the Paspahegh town killing the queen, women, and children (after their capture and in a particularly reprehensible and cruel manner) and burned to the ground the town of the Queen of Appamatuck. The bitter Indian reaction to what one writer has termed "the genocidal intentions" of the English (and which the Indians undoubtedly perceived at the very least as false dealing and treachery) was evident in their response. In one case they stuffed the mouths of several slain English with bread "beinge donn as it seamethe in Contempte and skorne thatt others mighte expecte the Lyke when they shold come to seeke for breade and reliefe amongste them." In another case the Paspahegh Indians chanted the name of their unjustly slain leader after cutting off an English detachment and defying another unit sent to its relief (Percy 1922:265, 270-273; Strachey 1906, 1953: 65-66; Barbour 1969a:77-87). The colonists also resorted to ruses such as the capture of Pocahontas in order to enforce their policy upon her reluctant father (Barbour 1969a:98-111). Eventually, the comity—such as it was—that had been built up on the basis of mutual advantage was dissolved. It became apparent to the natives that the

English demands were increasing in extent and in arbitrariness and that English respect for Indian sovereignty was decreasing.

The policy of accommodation with the English on the part of Powhatan's "confederacy" was thereupon changed, and, under the leadership of Opechancanough, the Indians fell upon the English settlements on March 22, 1622, in a coordinated attack, killing 350 colonists (Feest 1973; R.L. Morton 1960, 1:72-85; Vaughan 1974). Feest, the leading scholar of the Indians of seventeenth-century Virginia, has suggested the nativistic origins of this attack ("Virginia Algonquians," this vol.).

Terrible as the blow was (and it might have been worse had not an Indian friend of the colonists warned some of the English of the impending stroke), the colony survived and struck back at the "perfidious" enemy. The "bloody shirt" provided by the attack stimulated and unified the often bickering and complaining colonists. In addition, the attack provided a ready-made justification for waging perpetual war (as Christian legal theory allowed against infidels) against any and all Indians. Too often the rules of honor were abandoned in the process. Indians were invited to treaties in order to lull them into a sense of security and thereby enable the English to attack them with a greater element of surprise. The English stooped even to administering poison in the "healths" drunk by the Indian treaty negotiators (R.L. Morton 1960,1:82). The colonists defended such actions against criticism from home by asserting (illogically and ambiguously) that "we hold nothing injuste, that may tend to theire ruine, (except breach of faith). Stratagems were ever allowed against all enemies, but with these neither fayre Warr nor good quarter is ever to be held, nor is there any other hope of theire subversione, who ever may informe you to the Contrarie" (Kingsbury 1906-1935, 4:99, 102, 221-222, 269-270, 451; quoted in Washburn 1959: 21-22; also in R.L. Morton 1960, 1:84). The colonists continued to harass the neighboring Indians, destroying crops and stores of food (when they could not destroy the Indians themselves) for about 10 years. A relationship of trust never returned even after overt hostilities declined. A law of 1632 provided severe punishments for any settler voluntarily speaking with any Indian and not immediately bringing him to the English commanders (Hening 1809-1823, 1:167, Act XXIX of February 1631/2, 1, 192, Act XXVI of September 1632). Another law, noting that *wee hold the neighbouringe Indians our irreconcileable enemyes,"* ordered that if any Indians "doe molest or offend any plantations in theire cattle, hoggs, or any thinge else, or that they bee found lurkinge about any plantation, then the commander shall have power by virtue of this act to rayse a sufficient partie and fall out uppon them, and persecute them as he shall finde occasion" (Hening 1809-1823, 1:193, Act XXVII of September 1632).

Full-scale warfare broke forth once more when, on April 18, 1644, Opechancanough launched another concerted attack on the colonists. In this attack, nearly 500 were killed (R.L. Morton 1960, 1:153; Craven 1971:55). Although the colony's population exceeded 8,000 at the time of the massacre, it was a blow nearly matching in seriousness the massacre of 1622 when the colony's population was under 2,000. After two years of indecisive warfare, the war was brought to a successful conclusion by the daring capture of Opechancanough by Gov. William Berkeley. Terms were dictated in a treaty of October 1646 by which the lands of the Indians were carefully delimited and their movement restricted. The war ended in a characteristic fashion: the captured "emperor," Opechancanough, upbraided Berkeley on being allowed to be a show to the common people, asserting that, had their roles been reversed, he would not have exposed the governor to such an indignity. Berkeley recognized the justice of the complaint and ordered him treated with the dignity befitting his station. But such recognition lasted only for a brief moment. One of Opechancanough's English guards basely shot the emperor in the back while assigned to guard him.

English expansion proceeded rapidly in the years following the defeat of Opechancanough. The English civil wars in the 1640s added to the turmoil in Virginia; and when, in 1652, royal control was lost over the colony, rapid population growth combined with looser governmental controls allowed undisciplined expansion up Virginia's many tidewater estuaries in violation of the treaty of 1646. Inevitably conflict with the natives resulted, particularly since the cleared "Indian fields" along Virginia's rivers were often the areas most eagerly patented by the colonists searching for new tobacco land having access to English ships (Washburn 1957a:39-42, 47-54).

The local tribes became more subject to English control and soon came to be denominated "tributary Indians" as opposed to the "foreign Indians"—like the Susquehannocks, Oraneechis, and others beyond the rim of settlement—with whom the English came increasingly in contact through trade and exploration. Offensive operations against both "neighboring" and "foreign" Indians were undertaken periodically in the period from 1646 to 1676. Although poorly documented in the records, there is evidence of attacks on the Pocomoke Indians in 1651 (Anonymous 1897-1898, 5:33-34); on the Rappahannocks in 1654 (Hening 1809-1823,1: 389-390); on various groups, presumably both Siouan and Iroquoian and including the "Rickohockans" in 1655-1656 (Hening 1809-1823,1:402-403; Hoffman 1964:211-220); and on the Doegs, Portobagos, and Northern Nansemonds in 1666 (Anonymous 1897-1898, 5:113-114, 1899-1900, 8:165; R.L. Morton 1960, 1:177-178; Washburn 1957a:51-52, 54-55). The attempt to remove a group of foreign Indians who settled near the falls of the James River in 1656 resulted in a crushing and

Va. Histl. Soc., Richmond.
Fig. 2. Silver passport or safe-conduct badge issued to the "King" of the Potomac Indians by the colony of Virginia in 1661.

embarrassing defeat for the English and their Indian allies (R.L. Morton 1960, 1:177-178). Throughout this period provisions were made to establish reservations for the friendly subject Indians and to regulate trade and intercourse with them (fig. 2) (R.L. Morton 1960, 1:177, 228-230).

Bacon's Rebellion

No major war, comparable to the outbreaks of 1622 and 1644, erupted within the colony until the period of Bacon's Rebellion in 1675-1676. While earlier views of the rebellion emphasized the political aspects of the conflict, the most recent interpretation has attempted to relate the clash of arms among the English to a basic difference of policy on how to deal with the Indians of the area (Washburn 1957).

The origins of the war have the same frustrating absurdity that mark the origins of the wars of New England in this period. Certain hogs were taken from a Virginian living along the Potomac in June 1675 by Doeg Indians from Maryland who claimed that the owner had never paid them for certain goods earlier obtained from them. The owner organized a party to pursue the Indians, killed some, and recovered the hogs. The survivors then, in revenge, killed the herdsman of the owner in a raid on an outer plantation he owned. At this point the local Virginia militia set out to look for the murderers of the Englishman. In the process they killed several Doegs and 14 Susquehannocks they found sleeping in certain cabins they surrounded. The killing of the Susquehannocks was an admitted mistake for which the colony began to pay in terms of raids on outlying plantations. In August Governor Berkeley commissioned two militia officers to investigate the violence and determine responsibility for the various actions. The officers called upon Maryland for a force to assist them and, with the local Virginia militia, the force—consisting of 1,000 men—marched to the fort of the Susquehannock Indians. Five Susquehannock chiefs came out to parley, demanding to know the reason

for the appearance of the English. Accused of the recent depredations in Virginia, they denied the accusations, pointing the finger instead at the Senecas, who frequently raided in the area. The English were adamant and, in a violation of the code of war, led the chiefs away and murdered them. Governor Berkeley was outraged by the breach of faith, and exclaimed, "If they had killed my Grandfather and Grandmother, my father and Mother and all my friends, yet if they had come to treat of Peace, they ought to have gone in Peace" (Washburn 1957:23). But it was too late to stem the flow of blood. The Susquehannocks withstood the ensuing siege of the fort and then slipped away one night, killing 10 English in the process. They thereupon proceeded to raid the outlying Virginia settlements, killing 36 persons in January 1676 near the falls of the Rappahannock and Potomac rivers. Following the raid they sent Governor Berkeley a remonstrance complaining of the unjustified attack upon them and the barbarous killing of their chiefs, and asserting that, lacking other means of obtaining satisfaction, they had killed 10 of the common English for every one of their chiefs, a ratio they justified because of the disproportion in rank.

Governor Berkeley now organized the defenses of the colony as best he could in an attempt to stop the raiders. He was moved also by news of the Indian war in New England and concluded that the possibility of a combination of Indians all the way from New England to Virginia was a real one (Washburn 1957b). Should the tributary Indians be induced to defect to the colony's enemies, the very existence of the colony would be threatened. Hence Berkeley worked diligently to carry on the Indian war against the professed enemies of the colony and to preserve the friendly tributary Indians as spies and auxiliaries. In this hope Berkeley was to be disappointed by the antics of a young planter, Nathaniel Bacon, Jr., who had recently come to the colony. Bacon insisted on raising a group of volunteers who, illegally and unjustifiedly, attacked many of the colony's tributary Indians (such as the Pamunkeys) and foreign tribes still friendly to the colony (such as the Ocaneechis), thus raising the specter of a general combination, which the governor sought to avoid. Bacon killed not a single enemy Indian, only Indians denominated friends by the governor. The efforts of the governor to put down the unauthorized expeditions of Bacon and his plunder-seeking volunteers led to civil war, the burning of Jamestown, the withdrawal of Berkeley to the Eastern Shore, and, finally, to the death of Bacon, the reoccupation of Jamestown, and the arrival of 1,000 royal troops from England to suppress a rebellion that was over by the time they arrived. The Indian war ceased as soon as the English stopped attacking the Indians. A treaty of peace was signed in 1677 on behalf of King Charles II with the neighboring Indians, many of whom (for example, the Queen of

SEVENTEENTH-CENTURY INDIAN WARS

Assoc. for the Preservation of Va. Antiquities, Richmond (Thomas L. Williams photo).
Fig. 3. Silver medal issued to the "Queen" of the Pamunkey Indians in the name of Charles II, in commemoration of the peace treaty of 1677.

Pamunkey) he rewarded with marks of his affection for their constancy in the face of Bacon's unauthorized attacks (fig. 3).

Although rumors of French and Indian combinations (sometimes allegedly allied to the Catholics of Maryland) provided a continuing element of uncertainty and fear in the 1680s and 1690s, Virginia was to be largely free of the fear of further wars with the Indian nations surrounding her until well into the eighteenth century when her wars would involve the more powerful Indian nations of the interior.

New York

The melancholy story of Indian-White wars in the English colonies in New England and in the South was, unfortunately, repeated by the Dutch during their administration of the New York colony from 1624 to 1664 when the colony was taken by the Duke of York. Early relations with the Indians were cautious and formal. A Dutch colony of about 30 persons, established in 1631 at Swanendael near the present town of Lewes, Delaware, was wiped out a year later (Trelease 1960:57). However, large-scale warfare did not break out until the arrival of Gov. Willem Kieft in 1638. Kieft's "hard line policy"

with the local Indians stimulated conflicts that, between 1640 and 1645, caused the death of 1,000 Indians (Trelease 1960:83). Too often Kieft's policy repaid theft with murder. In February 1643 the Dutch killed in cold blood approximately 100 Wiechquaeskeck Indians who believed themselves safely under the protection of the Europeans at Corlaer's Hook on Manhattan Island and at Pavonia in the territory of the Hackensack Indians. The massacre brought on a violent response from the aggrieved Indians who burned, looted, and murdered Dutch settlers wherever they lay exposed on the frontier. Kieft, who was charged with responsibility for starting the war, was recalled in the spring of 1645 and replaced by Peter Stuyvesant (Trelease 1960:70-73, 81-82).

In September 1655, 50 Indians attacked New Amsterdam while Stuyvesant was attempting to conquer New Sweden. The cause of the war, even in the estimation of Governor Stuyvesant, could be laid more at the feet of the Dutch than of the Indians. The Esopus Wars, as the ensuing conflict was called because of the prominent role played by the Esopus Indians, lasted until 1664, when the weakened colony fell to an invading English force. In the process the Algonquian bands of the lower Hudson were deprived of their independent status and subjected to Dutch control, but at a high and unnecessary cost, both to Dutch honor and to Dutch wealth (Trelease 1960:138-168).

Conclusion

In considering the process by which wars developed between Indians and Whites in New England, one can take the position that such wars were inevitable given the aggressiveness and expansiveness of White settlement and the declining population and power of the Indians, or one can take the position that they were historical accidents precipitated by the passions and misunderstandings of particular individuals at particular times. One can debate the inevitability of the Indian wars in much the same way that one can debate the inevitability of the American Civil War or of World War I. Equally arguable are the general and specific causes of the wars that did erupt. Certainly one precipitating factor was the uncertain legal status of the colonists and of the Indians in their relationship with each other. On the English side opinion ranged from the belief that the king and his subjects had no rights in the land independent of the Indians' willingness to convey such rights (a thesis for which Roger Williams was severely disciplined and his 1633 treatise on the subject destroyed) to the contrary thesis (best exemplified by Nathaniel Bacon in 1676 in Virginia) that the Indians had no rights that needed to be respected by Christians. On the Indian side, confusion and outrage stemmed from the frequent belief that permission granted to the colonists to settle among them did not convey authority to exclude the sellers from continuing to fish and hunt in the lands conveyed. As White power grew and English physical presence and legal authority began to encroach more and more upon the neighboring Indians, the natives felt their generosity had been abused and their independence unjustly restricted (Jennings 1971).

The Puritans went to great length to justify and sanctify their wars with the native inhabitants. In part this effort derived from a fundamental fear of, and hatred for, a society that flouted the principles upon which Puritan society was built (R. Slotkin 1973). Traditional Indian tribal culture thus became a natural enemy that must be destroyed not for faults that its members may have committed but for existing as an example of a society contradicting the assumptions of Puritan society. Yet this fear was only dimly perceived and could only with difficulty be formally justified. Hence, New England writers provided customary justifications for war—usually charging the Indians with being the aggressors or with violating their word—but their nearly hysterical and vindictive condemnation of Indian society and traits is more indicative of their true attitude. "Hellhounds," "fiends," "serpents," "dogs," "perfidious heathens" were only a few of the words with which writers like Cotton Mather denigrated foes whose virtues would only be recognized by the non-Puritanical descendants of the original writers.

None of the Indian wars of New England was inevitable—even in the psychological sense suggested by Slotkin—and certainly not in an economic sense. The Indians could and did live in a symbiotic relationship with the Whites, both as servants and subjects within the Puritan Commonwealth and also as independent hunters and husbandmen in independent nations outside the English orbit. Even in wars against other nations of Indians, Indians allied with, or subject to, the English participated fully and effectively, however blind English observers at the time were to the fact. The success of English arms was in direct proportion to the willingness of the English to use large numbers of Indian auxiliaries. Usually recourse to Indian support came late, as in King Philip's War, and yet was decisive, as it was in that war, which ended with the finding and killing of King Philip by one of the Indian allies of the English. Peaceful coexistence between Indian and White was, therefore, theoretically possible. Although it did not occur, it was not because of underlying imperatives but because both sides—particularly the English—blundered into confrontations that exploded into full-scale war. The fact that the English of New England perceived general conspiracies all about them when in fact the evidence provides little support for conspiracy theories finds its parallel in the Indian fear of English treachery as a logical consequence of the peremptory and unjust highhandedness of Puritan officials.

In Virginia also peaceful coexistence was possible but did not occur. The surprise attacks of 1622 and 1644, while traditionally labeled "conspiracies" or "massacres" by White historians, can less ethnocentrically be equated to the surprise attacks launched on the Indians by the English in the early years of the settlement. Virginia's relations with her neighboring Indians were less close than similar relations between the New England colonies and the Indians of the north; hence, outbreaks in Virginia tended to be more sudden and less documented than similar outbreaks in New England. However, in neither area is the conspiracy theory valid. The case of Virginia's Indian war in the period of Bacon's Rebellion is similar in its tragic origin to that of King Philip's War in New England at the same time. In neither case does the evidence suggest that the Indians acted otherwise than from fear or revenge. Yet both outbreaks were perceived by Whites as aggressive conspiratorial threats by the Indians to destroy the White settlements. Responsibility for inciting the Indians to war, or for providing a motive or justification for war, was often acknowledged in the legislation enacted by the general assembly of Virginia, for instance, December 1656 and March 1661/2 (Hening 1809–1823, 1:415, 2:149–155). The desire to avoid provoking war with the Indians was even more frequently cited as the reason for enacting legislation dealing with the natives, as in March 1657/8, March 1659/60, March 1661/2, and September 1671 (Hening 1809–1823, 1:467, 481–482, 541, 2:138–139, 141, 289). All the wars of Virginia could have been avoided and the conspiracies made unnecessary if English conduct toward the Indians had equaled the standards of honorable dealing that the Virginia Company and the royal government sought to uphold. But, in fact, English attitudes toward, and pressure on, the Indians of Virginia were such that war became an inevitable response on the part of her Indian neighbors. Virginia's Indian policies were thus more akin to later United States federal Indian policies (exceeding those policies in cruelty if not duplicity) than to Puritan New England's religiously motivated "holy wars" against the depraved heathen.

The impact of the early wars on both Indian and European military techniques was considerable. Indians quickly obtained European firearms despite sporadic efforts to deny such weapons to them. Colonial authorities feared that the Indians might acquire the skills to maintain and repair weapons and even to manufacture powder, but this fear proved, for the most part, unfounded, Indians remaining dependent upon Whites for such services. The Indians did learn to create European-style fortifications, the most notable examples being the wooden fort destroyed in the Great Swamp Fight in December 1675 and a stone fort west of Wickford, Rhode Island, built for Queen Quaiapen's Narragansett band. Both were probably constructed by Stonewall John, a Narragansett trained as a mason (Malone 1973).

The Indian wars strongly influenced European military techniques. Capt. Benjamin Church of the Plymouth

Colony, who commanded the assault troops in the Great Swamp Fight, was particularly effective in recruiting and utilizing Indian scouts and auxiliaries. At the same time he modified standard European formations in accordance with Indian advice. On the march he spread his formation in the looser, more widely separated Indian fashion, thus avoiding the easily set forest ambushes that plagued less perceptive European commanders throughout the colonial period. Church, and other imaginative commanders, learned how to move quickly and lightly through the forest and to utilize encirclement and surprise to a greater degree than was traditional in Europe (Leach 1973:64-67).

The experience gained by the colonists in fighting the Indians was passed down from one generation to another and proved a significant element in the ability of the colonists later successfully to oppose European-trained troops in battle.

100

Beothuk

BARRIE REYNOLDS

Language and Territory

The Beothuk (ˌbēˈyäthək or ˈbēəthuk), the people to whom the term Red Indians was first applied, formerly lived in Newfoundland (fig. 1). Knowledge of their language is based on four short vocabularies collected from captive Beothuks. These together provide more than 400 lexical items.* Gatschet (1886), from his analysis of both the linguistic and the ethnological evidence, argued that Beothuk belongs to a separate linguistic family. Others, notably Latham (1862) and Hewson (1968, 1971), have argued that it is related to Algonquian. The problem is well summarized by Hewson (1968), but the available data appear inadequate for firm conclusions.

Although the Beothuk appear to have been widely distributed throughout Newfoundland and to have maintained contact with Labrador, most knowledge of them relates to one particular group that, during the eighteenth and early nineteenth centuries, focused on the Exploits River. These people lived together as a group for the late fall and early winter at the eastern end of Red Indian Lake and scattered along the nearby east coast for the rest of the year. From the lake it was possible to move easily by various routes to the east coast and also to travel to the south or west coasts.

External Relations

In precontact times the Beothuks are reputed to have kept control of their territory without difficulty. A traditional enmity existed between the Beothuks and the Labrador Eskimos, the Beothuks having a particular dislike for Eskimos and deriding them as "the fourpaws." Fighting is reported to have occurred between the two, particularly along the east coast (Cartwright 1826).

By the Indian immigrants from the mainland—the Abenakis and Micmacs from the west and the Montagnais from the north—the Beothuks were respected for their fighting abilities. Their relationship with the Montagnais, with whom they traded for stone axes and other implements, was particularly friendly. The groups visited each other, and it is thought that the last few surviving

* The quality and quantity of these records is such that no standard orthography can be suggested for Beothuk words.

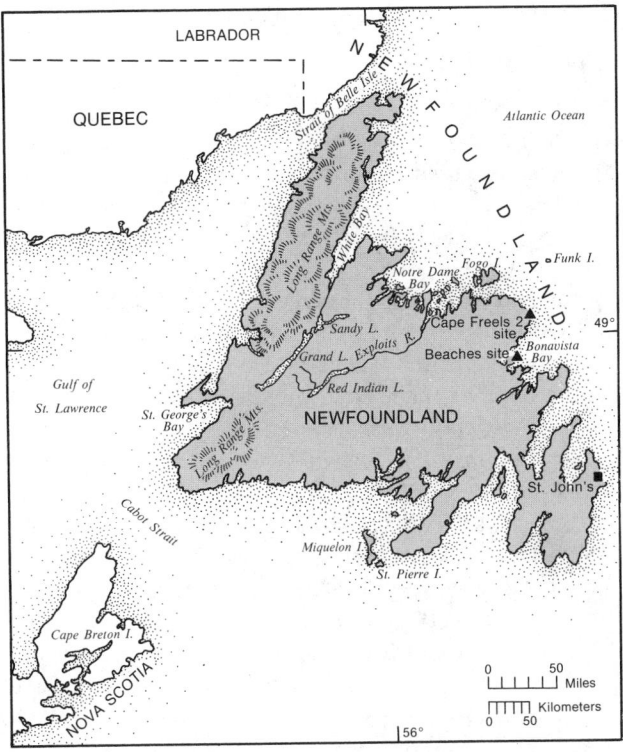

Fig. 1. Tribal area.

Beothuks may have joined the Montagnais in Labrador (Jukes 1842, 2:129).

With the arrival of Whites and the supplying of firearms to the Micmacs intertribal relations were badly disturbed. The Micmacs came from Cape Breton mainly to obtain furs for trade. The two peoples intermingled along the western shore, even sharing feasts, and perhaps intermarried. Then, in the late seventeenth century, the French, irritated by Beothuk thefts, offered the Micmacs a reward for the heads of Beothuks. The Beothuks discovered a group of Micmacs near Saint George's Bay in possession of two heads and carried out a revenge massacre at a feast to which they had invited the Micmacs. From this developed a war in which the Micmacs, by reason of their firearms, proved victorious and the Beothuks were forced to withdraw to the interior (Jukes 1842, 2:129). By the late eighteenth century the Beothuks had been pushed back from the northern and western parts of the island while, to the east and south, conflict with British settlers and fishermen was depriving the Beothuks of access to essential coastal supplies of food; life for them along these shores had become extremely hazardous.

By the early nineteenth century, even the interior was no longer a secure haven as White expeditions ascended the Exploits River to surprise the encampments on Red Indian Lake. This last surviving group of Beothuks withdrew and later dispersed, leaving the island to the Whites and the Micmacs.

Culture

Subsistence

Contemporary accounts (Howley 1915) indicate that for much of the year the Beothuks fished, gathered, and hunted from their camps on the coast. Birds and small animals were snared or hunted with bow and arrow, larger game was speared, and seals and occasional small whales were harpooned. Shellfish, edible roots and inner barks, and birds' eggs formed part of the diet. Reserves of such foods were built up for the winter. Expeditions were even made to Funk Island, beyond the horizon 40 miles to the east, the canoes returning deep-laden with eggs to be hard-boiled for later use.

Winter subsistence activities were concentrated on the mass spearing of migrating caribou herds trapped within extensive deer fences built along the Exploits River. The butchering and storage of the hundreds of carcasses were major activities. The meat was either frozen or smoked and stored in bark packs in snowbanks or pits, or kept in large storehouses. It was eaten boiled or roasted on spits.

Wild animals were not tamed though one observer noted the presence of a bitch and puppies in 1819 (Howley 1915:100).

Exclusion from coastal food resources combined with declining manpower for the winter caribou hunt must have been important factors in the final breakdown of Beothuk society.

Structures

Dwellings were conical wigwams, often set in groups of two or three. The walls were of spread poles covered with overlapping sheets of birchbark, held in place by other poles leaned against the outer side. Smoke from the central fireplace escaped through a chimney hole at the apex. The interiors were neatly arranged. Dried foods might be stored on high platforms. The entrances were closed with caribou skins. A feature peculiar to Beothuk wigwams was the practice of setting beds in hollows dug in the floor (Cormack 1829).

David Buchan in 1811 examined more elaborate winter wigwams and described one as octagonal with a floor diameter of 22 feet and a conical roof supported on walls four feet in height (fig. 2). Coverings were again sheets of birchbark but earth was banked to the top of the walls to give additional protection. Such wigwams housed 12 to 15 occupants (Howley 1915:85).

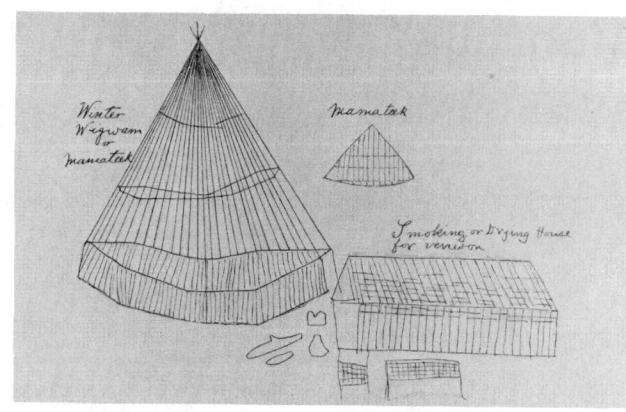

Newfoundland Mus., St. John's.

Fig. 2. Winter wigwam or mamateek showing octagonal base of upright walls and conical roof of poles meeting at top; summer wigwam, smaller and without upright walls; and ridge-roofed smoking or drying house for venison. Copy of drawing by Shanawdithit in winter 1829 for William Epps Cormack. The handwriting on the drawing is after Cormack's notes (Howley 1915: sketch VI).

Storehouses were either conical or ridge-roofed, the wall poles being covered with caribou skins, and the fireplace being set in the center of the floor with a chimney hole in the roof above. Storage pits were dug in the ground and lined with bark. Frames for drying salmon or for storing caribou legbones containing edible marrow (fig. 3) were built, as were racks for canoes.

Steam baths were taken in special shelters constructed of hemispherical frames covered with skins. Water poured on large hot stones within provided the steam (Cormack 1829).

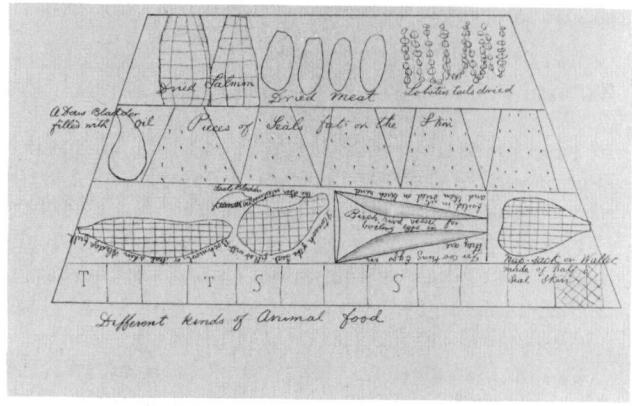

Newfoundland Mus., St. John's.

Fig. 3. A drying rack with food. top row: "Dried Salmon; Dried Meat; Lobsters tails dried;" middle row: "A Deers Bladder filled with oil; Pieces of Seals fat on the Skin;" bottom row: "Bochmoot, or Seal skin Sledge full; Seals bladder filled with oil; Stomach of the Seal filled with the other intestines; Birch rind vessel for boiling eggs in/For cooking Eggs in they are boiled in it and then dried in birch rind; Nap-sack or Wallet made of half a Seal Skin." Copy of drawing by Shanawdithit, 1829; labels by W.E. Cormack (Howley 1915:sketch VII).

Burial structures consisted of a wooden box or coffin set on the ground, of a low scaffold on which the body was laid, or of a well-constructed hut wherein the body was extended on the floor. The dead might also be buried in caves, in rock crevices, in the open ground or under a heap of stones. The corpse was buried in extended, flexed, or even sitting position (Oswalt 1966:77).

Buchan in 1820 discovered what he thought to be an observation post consisting of a temporary wigwam and a tree, 40 feet in height, stripped of all its bark except for a tuft at the peak and painted in alternate red and white bands (Howley 1915:125).

Clothing and Adornment

In contemporary accounts, from that of Cartier in 1534 onward, the immediately obvious and distinctive feature of Beothuk culture was their liberal use of red ocher (Cartier 1867). Powdered and mixed with oil or grease, this was smeared over the hair and body and also over clothing and equipment, though it is not clear whether the last two were always intentional. For Whites this practice served to distinguish Beothuks from other Indians.

The main item of dress for both sexes was a rectangular cloak, consisting of two caribou skins sewed together (Howley 1915:86, 212). This was sometimes fringed and a deep collar added (fig. 4). These might be of otter, beaver, or similar skins. Women carried infants in hoods added at the back while men would free the right shoulder when using hunting bows. Belts were sometimes worn, as also were laced moccasins, leggings, mittens, sleeves, and hats. All were of skin, many of the garments being worn with the fur inside and with the outer surface oiled and ochered to give added protection from the weather. Feathers were sometimes worn in the hair.

Some hundreds of carved and engraved bone objects from archeological burial excavations appear, in the light of historical accounts, to have been worn as pendants, probably as fringes on garments (fig. 5) (Marshall 1973).

Captive Beothuk women showed a liking for bright colors and fine materials but remained strongly attached to their cloaks, some wearing them over their European dresses (Howley 1915:172).

Transport

Travel was normally on foot. Buchan observed that in winter snowshoes were worn and sleds employed to transport heavy loads, notably venison, and perhaps people. The venison was stored and carried in large birchbark packs, 150 to 200 pounds in weight. For moving these and caribou carcasses simple three-log rafts, 30 feet long, were kept at storehouses on the Exploits River (Howley 1915:87, 123–124).

Most water travel, however, was by birchbark canoes. These were employed mainly along the coast but also on the inland lakes and rivers. At difficult points they were portaged, though on well-frequented rivers separate canoes were for convenience stationed on separate stretches. Canoes played an important part in Beothuk life, particularly in subsistence activities and even in caribou killing at the deer fences (Howley 1915:69–70).

Beothuk canoes were distinctive; in addition to the careful descriptions of Cartwright (1826) and others, models from graves indicate their main features (fig. 6). They were up to 20 feet or more in length with a broad beam. Both prow and stern were sharply pointed, and each gunwhale rose to a peak amidships. If, as Cartwright described, they were keeled and ballasted with heavy stones, they would have been particularly suitable for use on open waters. Cartwright also noted that a sail was sometimes set, though normally paddles were employed. Whether Beothuk canoes were indeed keeled and ballasted is not confirmed by other writers. One would

left, Newfoundland Mus., St. John's; right, British Mus.: 2583.

Fig. 4. left, "Dancing woman, Thub-wed-gie," wearing fringed garments. Copy of drawing by Shanawdithit, 1829; label by W.E. Cormack (Howley 1915:sketch VIII). right, Brown leather band with fringe. Length of band 47 cm, fringe 8–13 cm deep.

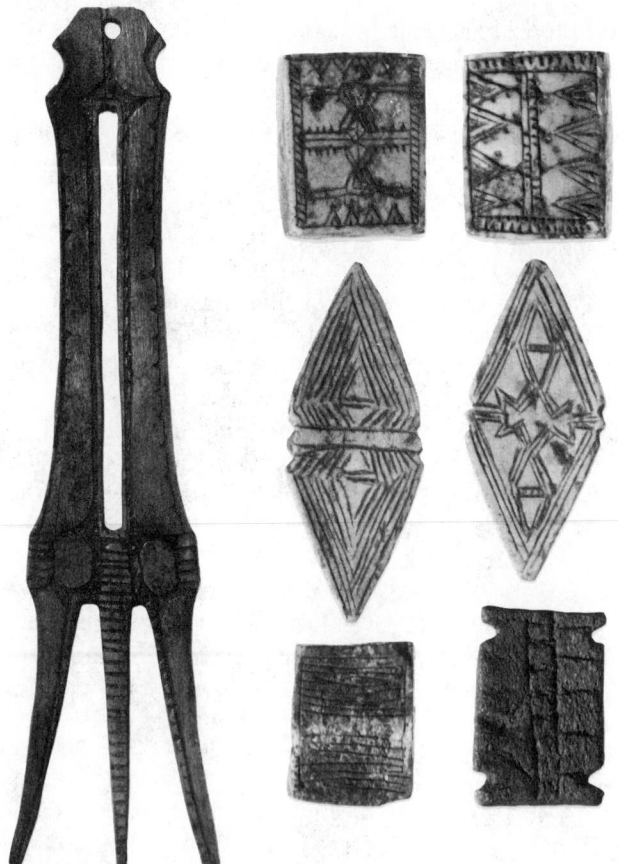

left, British Mus.: L1. 3; right, Newfoundland Mus., St. John's: clockwise from upper right, NF 3041, NF 3044, NF 3047, NF3037, NF 3042, NF 3039.

Fig. 5. Bone objects. left, Pendant, length 11.8 cm, collected before 1876; right, engraved objects possibly worn as pendants on clothing. Upper right 3.1 cm, others same scale.

surmise that the use of a sail reported by Cormack (1829) was probably borrowed from Whites.

Beothuks were confident seamen, traveling to Funk Island beyond their horizon and also crossing the Strait of Belle Isle (Howley 1915:48). On inland waters temporary canoes were perhaps used. On these, stretched caribou skins would take the place of the bark covering (Cormack 1829:69; see also Howley 1915:213).

Technology

For information on general precontact material culture one must look mainly to archeological evidence. Many of the sites already dug are from early contact times and these, like the early historical accounts, indicate the presence of European goods. Throughout subsequent centuries, Beothuks showed keen interest in White equipment, notably sails, iron and steel axes and knives, and metal utensils. They did not acquire firearms.

Contemporary accounts (Howley 1915) confirm that the traditional weapons, for both hunting and warfare, were spears, axes, knives, clubs, and bows and arrows. Blades and heads were of stone (usually chert) or bone, though wooden bird arrows were also used. Bows were of ash or fir and measured five feet or more in length; arrows were of pine, three feet long and fletched, and were carried in quivers. Bone awls too were used. For seal hunting, harpoons, 12 feet long with a bone (later iron) head, were employed (fig. 7).

Birch and spruce barks formed the basic materials not only for house and canoe walls, venison packs, and burials but also domestically for dishes, sewed boxes and

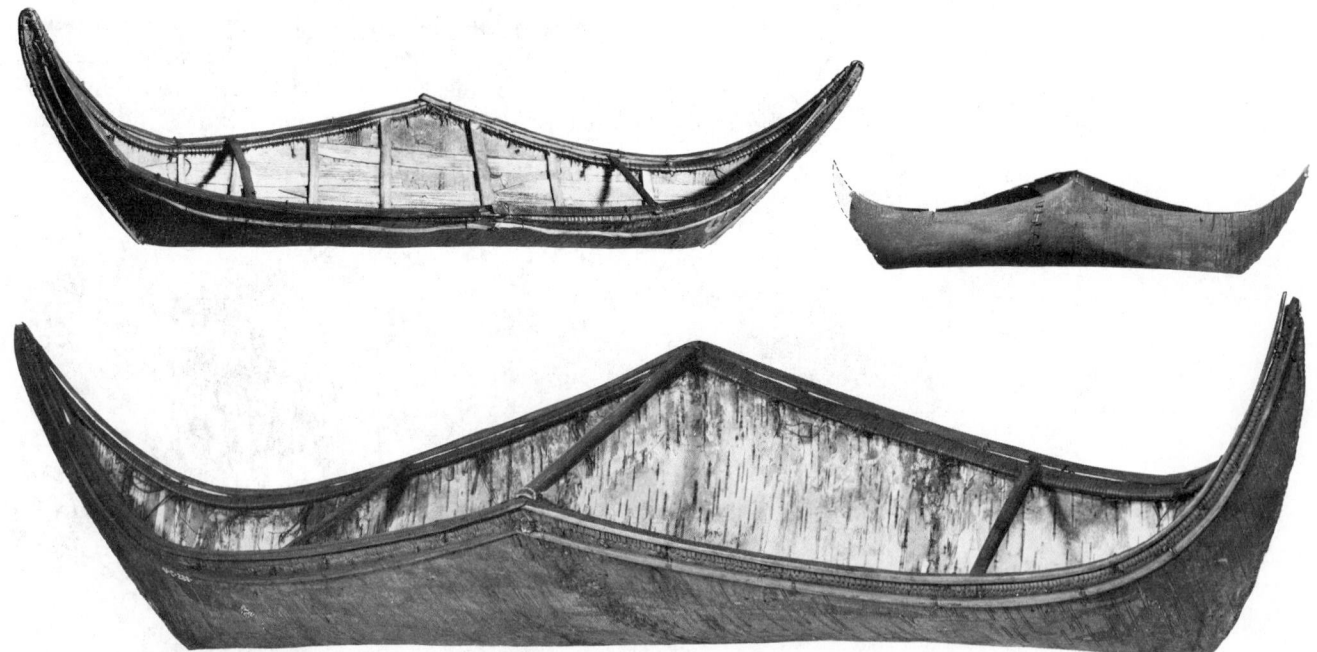

top left, Natl. Maritime Mus., London: NC (98); top right, Newfoundland Mus., St. John's: NF 3278; bottom, Royal Scottish Mus., Edinburgh: UC288.

Fig. 6. Model birchbark canoes. top left, Made by Shanawdithit 1823-1827; top right, found in 1886 in the grave of a male child; bottom, found in 1827 by W.E. Cormack. top left 54 cm, others same scale.

104

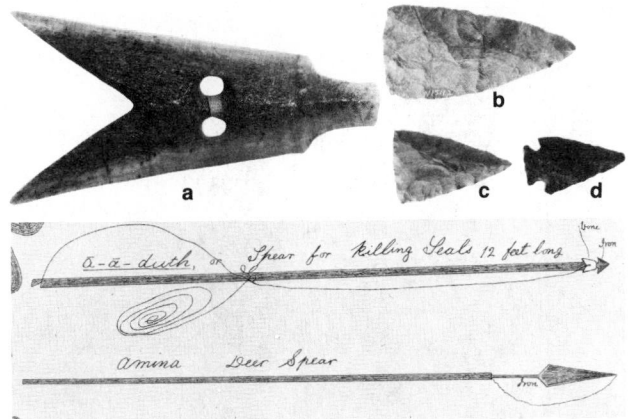

top, British Mus.: a, L1. 2; b-d, Newfoundland Mus., St. John's: DhAi-2-62, DhAi-2-20, DeAk-1-1412; bottom, Newfoundland Mus., St. John's.

Fig. 7. Hunting implements. top: a, Bone harpoon head with two holes in blade and slots at either end for point and foreshaft, length 10 cm, taken from wigwam at Red Indian Lake, Newfoundland, 1819. Complete rhyolite projectile points: b, triangular with slightly convex base, Cape Freels 2 site; c, triangular with straight base, Cape Freels 2 site; d, corner-notched, Beaches site; length of b, 5.44 cm; c-d same scale. Bottom: spears labeled "*ā-ā-duth,* or Spear for killing Seals 12 feet long" with bone harpoon head and iron point and "*Amina* [or] Deer Spear" with large lanceolate iron point. Copy of drawings by Shanawdithit, 1829; labels by W.E. Cormack (Howley 1915:sketch VIII).

buckets, and cooking vessels (fig. 8). Animal sinew and pliable roots provided materials for thread, lashings, and snares.

Blankets and clothing were of skins. Combs were carved from caribou antler and pendant ornaments from bone.

Fire was made by striking pieces of iron pyrites together.

In addition to personal effects, grave goods consisted of models of canoes and carved small human figures (fig. 9). Other wooden figures, probably of ritual importance, were also observed. Howley (1915) includes various drawings by a captive Beothuk woman, Shanawdithit. These illustrate a number of long, carved, and decorated wooden staves thought by Howley to be badges of office or of mythological symbolic significance (fig. 10). Cormack makes brief reference to carved wooden houseposts (Howley 1915:211).

Bone pendants were skillfully carved and incised with geometric designs. Shanawdithit demonstrated this skill on horn combs and in addition, using her teeth, engraved animal, figure, and flower designs in birchbark. It is not clear whether Shanawdithit was specially gifted but she had a talent for drawing and communicated easily with Cormack and others in this way both historical and cultural information on her people.

Social Organization

The society was apparently male-oriented though great respect was shown toward women. Female traits were modesty and courtesy. Neatness in behavior and in the organization of wigwam interiors is noted in various contemporary accounts. Beothuks were industrious in their subsistence activities with no apparent division of labor other than in hunting, a male pursuit (Howley 1915).

Marriages were celebrated with wedding feasts, 24 hours or more in length. They were monogamous and probably virilocal. According to Shanawdithit, as reported by one White informant, adulterers were publicly burned and most moral offenses harshly punished. A returning captive might expect to be killed because of prolonged contact with Whites (Howley 1915:181).

Each Beothuk group appeared to recognize a leader. The Exploits River group of 1811 was organized in three separate camps that in a crisis quickly joined together for concerted flight. Camps consisted of up to three or more wigwams, each of which housed up to three couples and their children, together with other males, females, and children (Howley 1915:226). The indication is that a wigwam was led by one man who was in fact considered the owner of the structure. This might form his burial house at death.

Among themselves Beothuks recognized the individual ownership of equipment, particularly weapons, and of food reserves, such as marrow bones. Although they stole frequently from White settlements they were aware that this was strongly disliked (Howley 1915:96).

In warfare Beothuks were brave and respected, defeated only by the firearms of their opponents. In encounters during the historic period they showed bravery, timidity to the level of panic, magnanimity toward enemies, and ruthlessness in vengeance killings. Lures and outright duplicity were employed to trap and murder their opponents. Heads of victims were taken and displayed on poles, the group dancing round them. Signs of truce were a fur skin or a spruce branch held in the hand.

The Beothuk camps were particularly vulnerable to surprise attack for they did not seem to have set night guards. Their losses were great and the final surprises of the early nineteenth century caused the abandonment of their winter camps on Red Indian Lake.

Cormack (1829) noted that the Beothuks showed respect for the dead, who were carefully wrapped in birchbark and buried, the bodies often being brought to special burial places on the coast. Men were accompanied by their personal weapons and other equipment; women were merely dressed in their own clothes. Carved wooden figurines, thought to depict the deceased, formed part of the grave goods. Shanawdithit considered it possible to communicate with her dead kin. At the death of a spouse the survivor underwent a ritual bathing.

Sickeness was treated with medicinal steam baths accompanied by prayers.

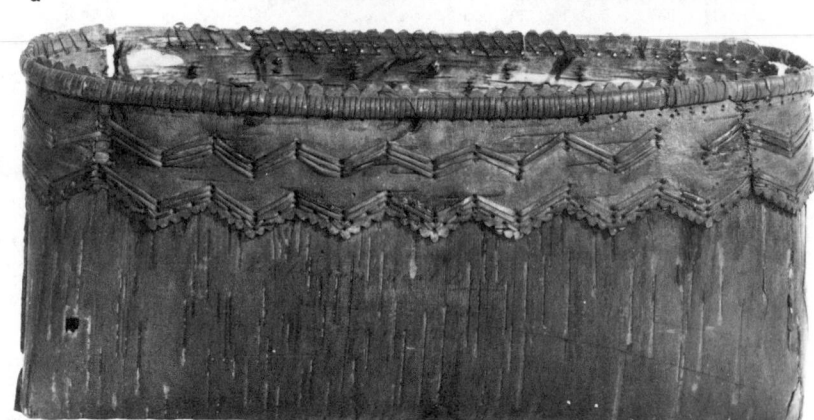

Newfoundland Mus., St. John's: a, NF 3144, b, NF 3303; British Mus.: c, 6976, d, 6975.
Fig. 8. Birchbark baskets. left: top, "Drinking cups or *Shoe-wan-yeesh*" and "*Shoe-wan*," bottom, "Water Bucket or *Guin-ya-butt*" and "Water Bucket or *Sun-ong-guin-ya-butt.*" Copy of drawing by Shanawdithit, 1829; labels by W.E. Cormack (Howley 1915:sketch VIII). right: a-b, Found 1886 in grave of a male child; c, sewed with root, probably collected with d; d, strengthened with wood rim bound with root, decorated with stitched chevrons and second layer of bark cut in chevrons, once covered with red ocher, inscribed on front "Red Indian meat dish for deer's flesh, found in the chiefs tomb at Red Indian Lake, 1827, by W.E.C[ormack]." Length of a, 12.2 cm; b-d, same scale.

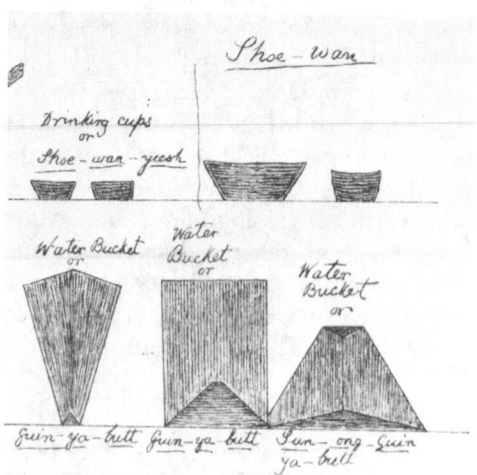

Religion

Beothuks believed in the existence of a 'Great Spirit', in the supernatural, and in life after death. Carved wooden figurines and staves are thought to have been symbolic of spiritual beings and mythological concepts (Cormack 1829; Howley 1915:100, 230).

History

According to legend the Beothuks sprang from an arrow or arrows stuck in the ground. Their traditions indicate close Labrador ties and perhaps an origin there (Tuck 1971e).

The earliest reliable historical encounter with Beothuks was that of Jacques Cartier in 1534. Although references to aboriginal peoples had occurred in European accounts of the Newfoundland and neighboring coasts from 1497 (John Cabot) and 1500 (Gaspar de Côrte-Real) onward, they did not distinguish Beothuks from other Indians, with whom Eskimos were also often confused. They did not mention the use of red ocher, the feature distinctive of the Beothuks (Howley 1915:1–13).

Early contacts with the Whites, for example John Guy in 1612 (Howley 1915:15–18), were usually amicable. However, as British and French began to settle, misunderstandings, conflicting interests over coastal fishing and

hunting resources, and Beothuk thefts from boats, stages, and settlements led to mutual hostility. Particularly lethal was the encouragement given the Micmacs by the French to attack them and the attitude of furriers (the local name for hunters and trappers) and fishermen who saw the killing of Beothuks as necessary for the protection of their own property or, all too often, as a sport (Howley 1915:183–184, 204).

During the seventeenth and eighteenth centuries contacts with Whites were usually in the form of increasingly frequent conflicts that were disastrous for the Beothuks. They were pushed back from the coasts and confined to the southeastern interior. Whereas Beothuk raids on Whites were primarily for tools and equipment they could not otherwise obtain, White raids were essentially for killing, and various eighteenth-century reports boasted of murders of tens and even hundreds of Beothuks (Howley 1915).

A few individual Beothuk women and children were captured during the late eighteenth and early nineteenth centuries. The most famous of these were Demasduit (Mary March) and Shanawdithit (Nancy April), taken in 1819 and 1823 respectively. The Beothuks also took captives; Buchan encountered one, a young mother, in 1811 at the Red Indian Lake camp (Howley 1915).

Despite rapid and sympathetic changes in public attitudes toward them, the Beothuks, by 1823, had been

Newfoundland Mus., St. John's: NF 3279.
Fig. 9. Wooden male figure. Length 19.4 cm. Found 1886 in grave of a male child.

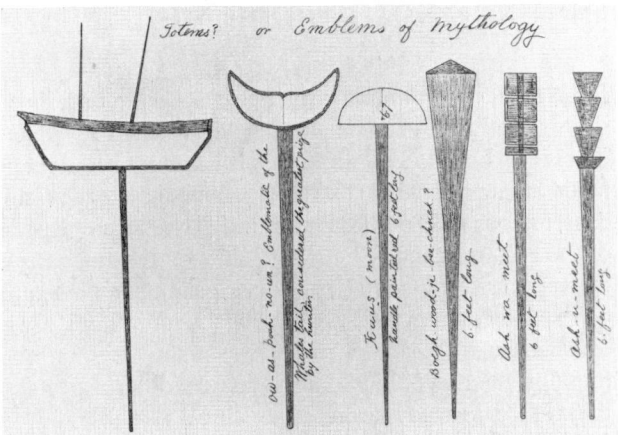

Newfoundland Mus., St. John's.
Fig. 10. Copy of Shanawdithit's 1829 drawing of "Totems? or Emblems of Mythology." left to right: unlabeled, resembles two-masted coastal fishing boat; "Ow-as-posh-no-un? Emblematic of the Whales tail, considered the greatest prize by the hunter," "Kuus (moon) handle painted red 6 feet long;" "Boegh-wood-je-bee-chnek? 6 feet long;" "Ash-wa-meet 6 feet long;" and "Ash-u-meet 6 feet long." Labels by W.E. Cormack (Howley 1915:sketch X).

reduced to a handful through White attacks, malnutrition, and diseases of White origin. Successful communication had not been established with this remnant, which then abandoned the Exploits River. The last Beothuks may have moved north to join their Indian allies in Labrador. The Boeothick Institution, formed in 1827, failed to locate any traces of surviving Beothuks. Shanawdithit died in 1829, and it is most probable that by that year no Beothuks were left in Newfoundland.

In 1911 Speck (1922) announced the discovery of an old Beothuk woman, Santu, believed to have been born at Red Indian Lake. Whether she was in fact of Beothuk ancestry was much debated.

Population

Their avoidance of direct contact with Whites together with their annual patterns of shifting settlement make it difficult to establish firm population figures for the Beothuk. In chance encounters their numbers were often overestimated and, as Cartwright (1826) realized, a correlation of population with the number of wigwams was not possible. For the Exploits River region he estimated in 1768 a total of 400 to 500 people though he notes that others estimated 200 to 300. Informants in the late eighteenth and early nineteenth centuries boasted of personal kills of 60 and 99 Beothuks, and even of one massacre of 500 (Howley 1915).

Firm figures are available for the Exploits River only after 1811. Shanawdithit stated that in that year the group consisted of 20 men, 22 women, and 30 children. These lived in seven wigwams set in three neighboring camps. By 1823 only 14 of these 72 survived: three married couples, three single men, two single women, and two boys, in addition to Shanawdithit (Howley 1915:226-229).

Synonymy

The name Beothuk does not appear until the end of the eighteenth century when vocabularies were gathered from captives. Until and even after that time the Beothuks were known as Red Indians, from their liberal use of red ocher.

Spellings were various and included Bethuk, Beothuk, Beothuc, Beothuck, Beothick, Boeothuck, Boeothick, Boethick, Behathook, and Beathook.

Modern usage is Beothuk or Beothuck. Howley preferred the latter; linguists, including Speck and Gatschet, the former.

Pronunciation varies but Cormack, perhaps the best source, stated it to be Boeóthuck (Howley 1915).

Beothuk was the name applied to the Beothuks by themselves. Gatschet (1885-1890) linked it to hadda-bothic 'body, belly'.

Sources

Face to face encounters with Beothuks were usually of short duration. For example, Buchan's in 1811 was less than four hours. The absence of a common language made communication extremely difficult. As a result contemporary accounts concentrated on visible aspects of the culture: canoes, buildings, deer fences and subsistence techniques, material culture generally, physique, conflicts, behavior, and relationships with Whites. Captive Beothuks provided vocabularies of the language and (notably Shanawdithit) limited data on other aspects of the culture. Micmac traditions are also a valuable source.

From the different contemporary accounts, many of which are conflicting and repetitive, it is possible to draw a composite though most incomplete picture of the Beothuks. Among the more valuable contemporary sources are those of: John Guy, 1612, dress, canoes, general behavior; John Cartwright, 1768, buildings, deer fences, canoes, subsistence; David Buchan, 1811 and 1820, buildings, subsistence, dress, snowshoes; William Epps Cormack, 1822 and after, Boeothick Institution, many aspects of language, history, and culture, mostly drawn from Shanawdithit, sometimes unreliable. All these accounts are reproduced in Howley (1915), which is the most complete source book for the Beothuks, though Howley failed to record the location of many of the original contemporary accounts. Some of them were also published elsewhere. Howley also reproduces various other historical accounts and local traditions together with linguistic, ethnological, and archeological reports by Gatschet (1885–1890), Lloyd (1874), and others. Speck and Howley were not in agreement regarding Santu and her possible Beothuk origin. Speck's (1922) account is the only one available.

Hewson (1968) gives a clear summary of the linguistic situation. Much archeological research was undertaken in the 1960s and 1970s, notably by Helen Devereux at Red Indian Lake. A useful general summary is Tuck (1971e) while Marshall (1973) examines the bone pendants.

Ethnological and ethnohistorical research since Speck has been negligible until Reynolds began compiling materials in the 1970s, though various researchers in related disciplines have gathered archival and museum data. A good ethnological summary is Oswalt (1966).

Ethnological artifact collections are few and scattered. Cormack deposited a few baskets, model canoes, and carved figurines in the Museum of Mankind (British Museum), London, and the Royal Scottish Museum, Edinburgh. There is also a collection in the Newfoundland Museum, Saint John's, including Shanawdithit's original drawings and the quite accurate copies of them that Howley (1915) published. Unfortunately most of the Edinburgh artifacts have been lost. It is also very doubtful that the painted dress ascribed to Shanawdithit in the Saint John's collection is of Beothuk origin. Little effective research has been undertaken on these collections. The lack of documentation is a drawback.

A very readable historical novel by Such (1973) presents a sensitive view of the Beothuks.

Micmac

PHILIP K. BOCK

Language and Territory

Micmac (ˈmĭkˌmăk) is the northernmost Eastern Algonquian language.* It is still spoken in parts of the region over which the Micmacs once roamed, although today they are limited to about 15 major reserves and another dozen tiny ones. During the sixteenth century, they occupied the region south and west of the Gulf of Saint Lawrence: the Maritime Provinces plus the Gaspé Peninsula (fig. 1). This region was heavily forested, rolling country, with numerous lakes, and many rivers running into excellent harbors along the long, indented coastline. The winters were severe, and the short growing season made risky the cultivation of grains or even root crops. But by making swift transportation by canoe possible, the extensive river system aided in the maintenance of an ethnic identity among the 4,000 or so aboriginal inhabitants. The people called themselves *ɘlnu* (now meaning 'Indian') and defended their territory against several other tribes. They disputed the Gaspé first with the Saint Lawrence Iroquoians and later with the Mohawk, while on their southern boundary they fought with the Maliseet and Penobscot, especially around the Saint John valley of New Brunswick. Micmac hunters occasionally visited Anticosti Island, and they even reached the shores of Labrador, where they raided the Eskimo. But their occupation of Newfoundland had to

await the postcontact extermination of the Beothuk, in which they played a major role.

Ethnic boundaries were maintained by emphasizing the marginal differences among the coastal tribes, but Micmac language and culture were really quite similar to that of the Maliseet, Penobscot, and Passamaquoddy (with whom they later joined in the Wabanaki Confederacy).

Most differences among northerly Algonquian groups in material culture and social organization can be understood as the results of slight variations in their ecological adaptations. But some differences, especially in ritual or folklore, seem to indicate other kinds of culture-historical processes at work. For example, the guardian-spirit complex and the shaking-tent rite, which are important among northern Algonquian groups, both appear to be absent on the coast. The name of the Micmac trickster-transformer is Gluskap (*kɘluˑskap*), whereas Chikapis or Wísakedjak performs these functions among the Cree. On the other hand, the Micmac did have a cannibal giant (*čenu*) with many attributes of the Windigo monster of the Cree (H.F. McGee 1972).

Relations with the Iroquois were predominantly hostile, but this did not prevent the seventeenth-century Micmac from adopting parts of the Iroquois "war complex," including the torture of prisoners by women. During their participation in the Wabanaki Confederacy, other Iroquoian elements were adopted, such as the ritual use of wampum.

The precontact Micmac were hunters and fishers; they cultivated no crop other than tobacco. During the fall they dispersed into small local groups to hunt moose and caribou. At appropriate times during the annual cycle they also hunted or snared partridge, waterfowl, seal, beaver, rabbit, otter, and porcupine, for food and for their feathers, skins, or quills. In the spring, when abundant shellfish and the spawning smelt, herring, and salmon made possible the easy accumulation of these resources, they again gathered in groups of 200 or more, each with its own traditional camping place on the coast or along the rivers. These large gatherings may be called bands; however, political unification on the tribal level apparently was never attained. The Micmac "tribe" was, as it still is, an "ethnic group" in the sense Barth (1969:38) uses this term, and its boundaries were maintained by a "limited set of cultural features" that in-

*A kind of "hieroglyphs" as a mnemonic device for memorizing prayers and doctrine was developed by the 17th-century Roman Catholic missionary Chrétien Le Clercq and was perpetuated by Abbé Antoine Maillard; it is no longer in use. The Micmacs themselves secretly developed a nearly phonemic orthography using the Latin alphabet, probably in the late 18th or early 19th century. Finding this in wide use, Father Pacifique modified it somewhat and used it in translating the Scriptures, in encouraging literacy, and in publishing for 17 years the newspaper *The Micmac Messenger* in the native language. The traditional orthography, Pacifique's version of it, and combinations of the two were still in use among some older Micmacs into the 1970s. In 1974 a more systematic, phonemic version of the same orthography, prepared by Paul Proulx, was introduced in March in *Agenutemagan*, the newspaper of the Union of New Brunswick Indians. This orthography can be converted to Handbook standards by making the following substitutions: *p* for Proulx's b; *t* for his d; *k* for his g; *č* for his j; *s* for his z; *x* for his h; · for his doubling of a letter; *ɘ* for his ' before *l, n,* or *m*; · for his ' in other locations. Italicized Micmac words in this chapter have been rewritten into this modification of Proulx's orthography following his advice. Instances of which he was uncertain are marked (?).

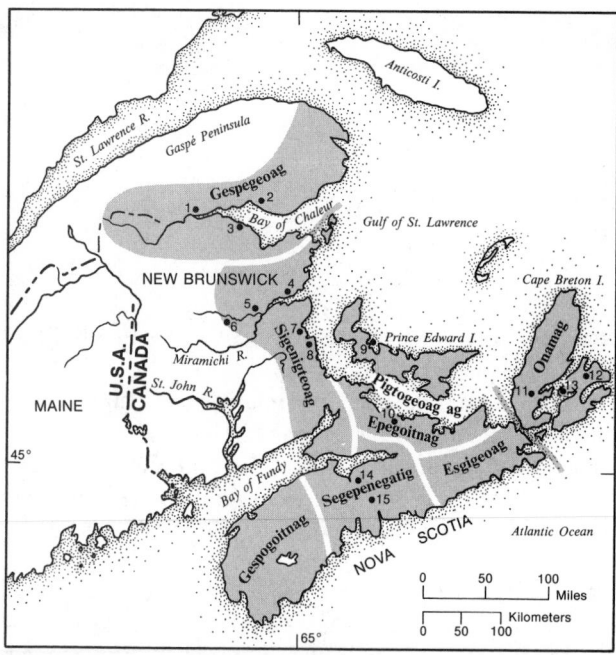

Fig. 1. Traditional tribal districts with the principal 1970 reserves: 1, Restigouche; 2, Maria; 3, Eel River, Dalhousie; 4, Burnt Church; 5, Eel Ground; 6, Red Bank; 7, Richibucto; 8, Big Cove; 9, Lennox Island; 10, Pictou Landing; 11, Whycocomagh, Nyanza; 12, Membertou (Sydney); 13, Eskasoni; 14, Truro; 15, Shubenacadie.

Onamag, or Cape Breton Island, was considered the "head district." It was, and still is, the residence of the Grand Chief. This official once played an important role in tribal decisions about warfare, but since the mid-nineteenth century his functions have been entirely ceremonial. The adjacent districts of Pictou and Esgigeoag were subordinate to Onamag, at times even lacking chiefs of their own, but apparently they preferred this arrangement to absorption by their powerful neighboring districts. At the "outer ends," kespe·k(?), of Micmac country were the Gaspé and the land of the Souriquois. These two were bound together, at least conceptually, by their similar names. The Cape Breton district was conceived as standing alone and above the others. Districts 1 through 3 were grouped together as Sigenigt (a term referring to Cape Chinectou, a notable point in district 2), and districts 5 to 7 were grouped as Gespogoitg (referring to Cape Sable, the southernmost point in Nova Scotia). According to Father Pacifique, these structures were explicitly depicted on nineteenth-century wampum belts.

Culture

Subsistence

The Micmac annual cycle had two main phases, marked by diffuse and compact settlement (Bock 1966a). The changes from one phase to another were governed by ecological factors, and each phase had several subdivisions. According to Pierre Biard, each of the "moons" was characterized by the principal kind of fish or game available. Thus, at least in southern Nova Scotia,

in January they have the seal hunting . . . . in the month of February and until the middle of March, is the great hunt for Beavers, otters, moose, bears . . . caribou . . . . In the middle of March, fish begin to spawn . . . often so abundantly that everything swarms with them. After the smelt comes the herring at the end of April; and at the same time bustards [Canada geese] . . . sturgeon, and salmon, and the great search through the Islets for [waterfowl] eggs . . . . From the month of May up to the middle of September, they are free from all anxiety about their food; for the cod are upon the coast, and all kinds of fish and shellfish . . . . [In September] the eels spawn . . . In October and November comes the second hunt for elks and beavers; and then in December . . . comes a fish called by them ponamo, [tomcod] which spawns under the ice (JR 3:79–83).

cludes language but does not include a common political allegiance.

According to the traditional account, there were seven named districts within Micmac territory (fig. 1), and the bands were composed of those individuals who habitually hunted within a given district and who camped together during the spring and summer. At least some of these groups had distinctive symbols—for example, a salmon represented the Restigouche band, and a figure of a man holding a bow and arrow (interpreted as a "cross-bearer" by the Jesuits) represented the Miramichi. But the interpretation of these as clan symbols is surely in error; despite some patrilineal tendency in succession to chieftainship, there is no evidence of any unilineal groups. Individuals and families seem to have shifted among bands with ease, and several bands often inhabited a single district. The organization of the seven districts is shown in table 1.

Table 1. The Seven Traditional Districts of Micmac Country

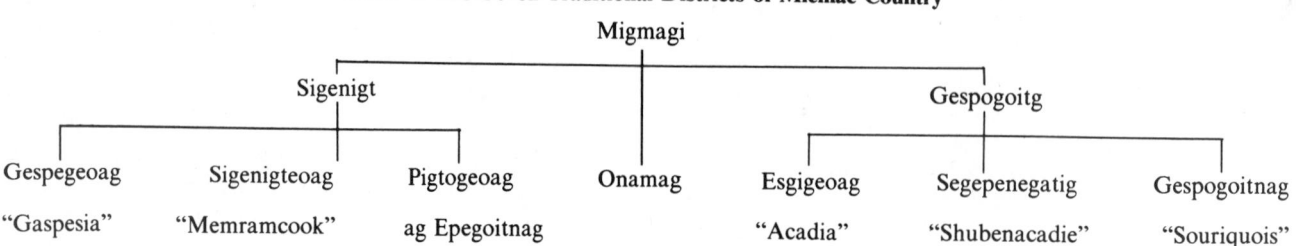

Three centuries later, the following names of months were recorded (Wallis and Wallis 1955:104):

January	Frost-fish or tomcod
February	Snow-blinding or sore eyes
March	Spring
April	Egg-laying
May	Young seals or get herring
June	Summer or leaf-opening
July	Sea-fowl shed feathers
August	Young birds are full-fledged
September	Moose-calling
October	Fat, tame animals
November	All Saints' Day moon
December	The chief moon (Christmas)

There is no reference to trapping in this set of terms; however, the name of district 5, Esgigeoag, means 'skin dressers' territory', which perhaps indicates the relative importance of trapping in that area. The traditional cycle began with the freezing of the rivers, and winter (*kesik*[?]) was marked by cold, snow, and the bears' retirement to hollow trees (Le Clercq 1910:137-139). This was the "diffuse" period, when the population was spread thinly over its territory and social relations were at a minimum.

The domestic groups that worked as economic units during the diffuse period were often larger than nuclear families. The advent of trapping encouraged territorial subdivision and exploitation by nuclear families (Leacock 1954), but folktales frequently mention winter hunting groups including two or more adult males who are either friends or cognatic relatives. In addition, some complex households were created by polygyny and by the custom of bride service (whereby a man lived with and worked for his future father-in-law for two or more years before his marriage). Few of the Micmac hunting or fishing techniques required cooperation among men. Women were expected to carry game into camp from wherever it was slain and could also be called on to paddle fishing canoes. But for stalking large game on snowshoes with stone-tipped lances or arrows, one or more hunting companions were desirable, and for harpooning seals or flushing beavers from their lodges, cooperation among adult males was necessary.

The Micmac canoe (fig. 2), says Biard, was "made of birch-bark, narrow and closed at both ends, like the crest of a morion; the body is like a large hollow cradle; they are eight or ten feet long; moreover so capacious that a single one of them will hold an entire household of five or six persons, with all their dogs, sacks, skins, kettles, and other heavy baggage" (JR 3:83). A morion—an open helmet with a semicircular crest—is a very good descriptive image for the Micmac canoe. These canoes, at least in recent centuries, often had raised gunwales on their midsections (see photographs in Adney and Chapelle 1964:58-70). The dogs mentioned

Natl. Gallery of Canada, Ottawa.
Fig. 2. Micmacs in a humped canoe, detail from an imaginative painting of the early 19th century. The woman paddler is wearing a "traditional" peaked cap.

by Biard were used for hunting big game and, on occasion, were themselves served as the pièce de résistance of a feast (Maillard 1758:5-7).

Although many aspects of postcontact Micmac culture retained the aboriginal configuration, most were affected, more or less strongly, by European influences exerted through missionaries, the fur trade, and the French-English armed conflict. The account of Micmac culture that follows is based primarily on sources from the period 1610 to 1760 and thus refers to a time when French influences were quite strong. In describing technology, social structure, and ideology, an attempt will be made to distinguish aboriginal forms from those produced by the contact situation, though this cannot always be done with certainty.

The Micmacs were hunters and fishers. They ate several kinds of wild roots, nuts, and a variety of berries (which were pounded and dried into disk-shaped cakes), and they used various plants for medicines. But the greatest part of their diet was animal flesh, fresh or smoked. The grease was carefully skimmed from a broth or extracted by heating fat on a grooved stone and then was stored in birchbark boxes or animal bladders. Fish and eels were roasted on sticks. Meat was prepared by roasting or by stone-boiling in large wooden troughs hol-

111

lowed from the trunks of fallen trees (later in copper kettles, a much-desired trade item). Moose meat and dog meat were boiled and served on bark plates. A novel device for cooking was to hang some meat from a twisted cord that rotated the roast over a fire.

Much to the surprise of the French, the Micmac at first showed no desire for bread; when they did adopt it, they preferred to cook it in the hot sand beneath a hearth. They gladly exchanged their pelts for metal tools and for dried peas, beans, and prunes, which probably were cooked in the aboriginal fashion; indeed, the method of cooking bread may relate to an earlier way of processing acorns.

Hunters made use of various snares and deadfalls as well as the spear or the simple bow. Poisoned arrows were used only in warfare. Dogs helped locate big game and beaver houses. Disguises were sometimes used in stalking moose; the great animals were attracted by the use of birchbark callers and another novel technique: on dark, calm nights during the mating season, after imitating the call of the female moose, "the Indians with a dish of bark would take up some water and let it fall into the water from a height. The noise brought the male, who thought it was a female making water" (Wallis and Wallis 1955:37).

Torches were used to hunt waterfowl and also to attract salmon, which were then speared with barbed wooden fish spears (fig. 3). Bone fishhooks and nets were

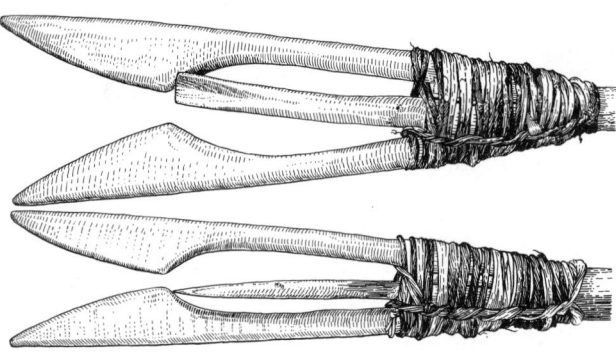

after Wallis and Wallis 1955:27.
Fig. 3. Wooden fish spears for salmon (top) and eel (bottom). The two barbs lashed to the shaft with twigs hold the fish when speared with the sharp point. The spear was most effectively used at night with light from a birchbark torch. Approximate length 37 cm.

employed to catch cod, trout, salmon, and smelt, and weirs were used in cooperative fishing ventures, the catch being shared equally among those who had constructed the weir. In some areas, sea mammals were hunted by using decoys and disguises; they were killed with clubs or harpoons. The hunting of porpoises during the nineteenth and early twentieth centuries was primarily a commercial venture; their fine oil was extracted and sold to traders (Leighton 1937).

Before the seventeenth century, many kinds of tools were made of wood, stone, bone, and shell; but metal quickly replaced stone and bone in cutting tools, and the musket soon became the standard weapon. Containers were of skin or birchbark (fig. 4), the latter being skill-

Mus. of the Amer. Ind., Heye Foundation, New York: 18/2180.
Fig. 4. Quilled birchbark box. The making of such decorated boxes was probably learned indirectly from the Ursuline nuns of Quebec. Collected in 1900, length about 18 cm.

fully sewed and decorated with porcupine quills or embroidered with moose hair. Coiled baskets of spruce root (and possibly pottery for cooking) were made in precontact times, but the fancy splint basketry found at many reserves as a tourist item and the tools associated with its manufacture are definitely European in origin.

Structures

The standard dwelling was a conical wigwam (fig. 5) of circular or elliptical floor plan, covered with birchbark, skins, woven mats, or occasionally with just evergreen boughs. It generally housed a single extended family, and the enclosed space was divided into several functional areas. In the center was a hearth, and belongings were stored around the edges. The floor was covered with boughs, and for sleeping, furs were placed on top of these. One early source mentions a summer dwelling that was long and open, housing several families, but there is no record of how the families were related or whether any special ceremonial activities were carried out in these dwellings. There are also two early references to palisaded settlements, one on Cape Breton Island and the other at Richibuctou. As late as 1850, most Nova Scotia Micmacs were still living in bark wigwams (Wallis and Wallis 1955:226ff.).

The aboriginal summer settlements do not seem to have had any distinctive form, though very likely each was strung out along a section of the coast or river bank.

Fig. 5. Conical wigwams (left) of traditional overlapped sheets of birchbark photographed at Dartmouth, Nova Scotia, 1860; and (right) of tar paper, cloth, and bark, photographed by Frank Speck, N. Sydney, Cape Breton Is., Nova Scotia, 1916.

French missionaries encouraged the Micmac to build chapels and to establish year-round settlements; nevertheless, the nomadic way of life persisted well into the nineteenth century, even after trapping had ceased to be profitable in most areas. Winter camps consisted of one or more wigwams set up in their owners' hunting or trapping territory, near a dependable source of water. In an emergency, an inverted canoe with a small fire beneath it would serve as shelter for a few hunters.

Clothing and Ornament

Both sexes wore their hair long. They dressed similarly, in animal skins; however, the men wore a carefully tanned loincloth beneath their heavy robes, and the women fastened their outer garments with two belts rather than one. Leggings and moccasins were made of moose- or deerskin with thongs of skin or sinew. Moccasins were sewed at both ends, giving much the same shape beneath at heel and toe, although the top at the front was doubled back and finely gathered. Two varieties of snowshoes were used: both had square toes, but one was large, for use on light, fluffy snow, and the lighter type was for snow with a frozen crust. At the time of contact, both sexes went bareheaded, but soon afterward they adopted caps of skin and bark, which marked both sex and rank. The "traditional" high-peaked woman's cap (fig. 2) of dark-blue cloth, beaded and embroidered, was a much later development.

Life Cycle

Birth traditionally took place outside the wigwam with the mother kneeling, assisted only by older women. Immediately afterward she resumed whatever activity she had been engaged in before the onset of labor. The newborn was washed in a cold stream, made to swallow bear or seal grease, and bound to an ornamented cradleboard, which left only its head free. Children were nursed for two or three years; the mother avoided (or terminated) other pregnancies until weaning was completed. The first solid foods were premasticated by either parent.

Children learned sex-linked tasks and etiquette by imitation and from admonition. They treated old people and parents with respect; on the other hand, children were greatly desired and received great tenderness and affection. There were ceremonies for a male child when he cut his first tooth, took his first step, and killed his first game, however small. Manhood, however, came only when he showed his ability to kill large game, such as moose. Brothers and sisters were taught to avoid one

Fig. 6. Christopher Morris with eels split and hung on stick drying in the sun. He holds two splint baskets. Photograph by Frederick Johnson, Eskasoni, Cape Breton Is., Nova Scotia, 1930.

another from an early age. Young girls would help their mothers with domestic tasks: setting up the wigwam (after the father had selected a location and marked off the floor plan); gathering firewood and carrying water; cooking; processing skins, making clothing, and fashioning bark containers (men made the wooden implements); and fetching game into camp from the woods. Those who showed ability in these tasks would surely be betrothed by puberty. For a first marriage, the groom, who was usually in his twenties, was required to perform bride service in the wigwam of his prospective father-in-law. For two or more years he worked and hunted under the older man's direction, proving his ability as a provider. During this period, sexual relations with the girl were strictly prohibited.

When the husband's period of probation had ended, he spent several days in hunting, accumulating game for the wedding feast. On the appointed day, the shaman, parents, and older relatives all made long speeches to the young couple, and all shared in the feast, which ended in dancing. Sources disagree on the amount of choice exercised by the partners. A girl would seldom be forced into a really distasteful marriage, but "arranged marriages" were still common in the nineteenth century. The early missionary accounts emphasize the former virtue of Micmac women and bitterly decry both their corruption by the brandy trade and the Indians' rather casual attitude toward divorce. (Even after the Catholic beliefs about

indissoluble marriage were adopted by the Micmac, separations and casual liaisons remained frequent.) Since men did not acquire control over their wives' property, and since grandparents were usually willing to care for the children, the common impediments to easy separation were not present. Bearing illegitimate children was considered a sign of fertility rather than a stigma; however, the children would often be raised in the household of their mother's parents. The local group took responsibility for orphans; according to Le Clercq, the chief would see that they were brought up in the household of a good hunter.

Sources also disagree on the way in which old people were treated. It is generally agreed that elders were respected and listened to in meetings and that old women spoke out freely on community matters; but whereas some sources tell of tender care given to aged parents, others speak of the neglect or deliberate abandonment of those who could not keep up with the migrations of a household. Certainly, when a person seemed near death, little effort was made to help him cling to life: some old men apparently took pleasure in arranging their own funeral feasts. If a shaman diagnosed an illness as terminal, the sick person would no longer be fed, and cold water might be poured "on his navel" to hasten his demise.

Mourners blackened their faces and wailed for three days; messengers were sent out and friends came from other settlements; on the third day, a feast was given and burial took place with each guest adding to the grave goods. Several different modes of disposal are reported, which range from cremation to exposure, but the most frequent is burial with various types of sacrifices and grave goods. In the Gaspé and New Brunswick, the body was buried on an uninhabited island, wrapped in bark, seated in a deep grave, together with the person's tools, dogs, and personal effects. The practice of exposure on scaffolds may have been limited to Cape Breton Island. Mourning continued for a year, during which time mourners wore their hair short and widows were forbidden to marry; but once the allotted time had passed, mourners were encouraged to put aside their sorrow.

The second marriage of a man or woman (whether polygynous or not) would seldom be celebrated with public festivities. The levirate was not obligatory, but if the widow were childless it might be practiced to produce offspring "of the same blood" as the deceased. Wallis and Wallis (1955:236) say that marriage with the father's or mother's sister was permitted. The cross-cousin marriage that Hockett (1964) postulates for the Central Algonquians on the basis of reconstructed Proto-Central Algonquian terminology has not been confirmed for the Micmac by any attested cases; nevertheless, the term used in 1960 for '(my) mother-in-law' (әnčukwi-čič) is clearly a diminutive of the (then) general

Fig. 7. Men playing an aboriginal gambling game with six bone dice tossed in a hardwood bowl and 38 scoring sticks. The player at the left donned his chief's coat especially for the photograph. Photograph by Wilson Wallis, Nova Scotia, 1911-1912.

term for '(my) aunt' (*ənsukwis*). This latter term, according to Rand's dictionary, formerly referred only to the father's sister (cf. Bock 1966:72-74).

Sociopolitical Organization

Micmac kinship terminology is cognatic and generational. Lineal ancestors and descendants can be named for four generations from ego; but in the third and fourth ascending generations, only the sex and generation of the relative is distinguished, and in all descending generations except that of ego's children, even the sexes are merged. Stepchildren are classed with grandchildren, the term *nuči·č* meaning only 'my little one'. Ego's generation is the only one in which fine distinctions are made: here there are different terms for the sets of male siblings, of female siblings, and of married siblings (regardless of sex), as well as specific terms for younger and older siblings of each sex. The sister terms are further marked for married or unmarried status. The general term for cousin *no·kəmaw* means simply 'my relative'.

Micmac social organization seems to have been quite flexible. Within the tribe, the only organized units were the household, the local group, and the band. The band came together only for the summer encampment and in time of war. Biard, in the earliest full account of Micmac society (which also refers at times to the Maliseet), speaks of quite sizable local groups, each dependent on a dominant male, called a sagamore, *saxamaw*, who is "the eldest son of some powerful family, and consequently also its chief and leader. All the young people of the family are at his table and in his retinue; it is also his duty to provide dogs for the chase, canoes for transportation, provisions and reserves for bad weather and expeditions" (JR 3:87). Until they were married, the young men had little control of their own affairs: they were not allowed to keep dogs and they had to turn over all that they hunted to the sagamore. After marriage, they gave him only part, but if they left his group for a period, they would bring him gifts on rejoining it. Individuals or whole households could easily shift from one local group to another to improve their situation, though this often left bad feelings. Each sagamore had territory that he effectively controlled, usually centered on a small bay or river. He extended hospitality to any visitors and exchanged gifts with other sagamores.

According to Biard, "it is principally in Summer that they pay visits and hold their State Councils; I mean that several Sagamores come together and consult among themselves about peace and war, treaties of friendship and treaties for the common good . . . . if there is some news of importance, as that their neighbors wish to make war upon them or that they have killed some one . . . then messengers fly from all parts to make up the more general assembly [where] they resolve upon peace, truce, war, or nothing at all, as often happens in the councils where there are several chiefs, without order and subordination . . ." (JR 3:89–91). The bow and arrow was the proper weapon for intertribal or even interband disputes, though pitched battles were avoided. For intraband disputes, minor problems were cause for wrestling and hair pulling, with the sagamore and common friends acting as mediators. More serious offenses (murder or wife stealing) would be avenged by the offended person or his nearest relatives, though they could also be settled by giving suitable gifts.

The sagamores, or chiefs, derived such authority as they had from their own wives and children and from the consent of their other dependents. The coming of the French and especially the fur trade may have increased this authority, for by the late seventeenth century, Le Clercq reports that the chiefs on the Gaspé allocated trapping territories to each family and took charge of the exchange of furs for goods. Knowledge of French gave some of these chiefs a strong advantage in establishing themselves as mediators, and this pattern persisted into the twentieth century. But Micmac society is basically egalitarian, and though the sons of chiefs doubtless had some advantage in the pursuit of political power, there were checks and balances built into the native system that even European intervention could not quite destroy. If a man were a powerful chief and a shaman as well, as was Grand Chief Membertou (who converted to Christianity in 1610), he might, in Biard's words, be "greatly dreaded."

Ideology

Micmac beliefs and values were similar to those of other northern hunters. There were no general food taboos, but they avoided certain foods by choice: these include snakes, amphibians, and skunks. Elaborate menstrual taboos were formerly observed, that is, monthly seclusion and prohibition of women's stepping over the legs or weapons of hunters. Menstruants were also expected to observe with special care the rules for showing respect for animals—for example, bones and even sticks used in cooking meat were treated with care and not simply thrown away. Beaver bones were never given to dogs or thrown into the river. The bear was treated with special respect. There was a belief that animals could become transformed into other species, for example, that old moose would enter the ocean and turn into whales (Wallis and Wallis 1955:106ff.). In addition to altering the landscape in significant ways during his travels, Gluskap transformed some animals into their present forms, giving the beaver his tail and the frog his voice.

Gluskap was a mighty warrior who taught the Micmac essential arts and prophesied the future. He has gone away, but he will return to help the Micmacs in their hour of need. Though his main role in legends is as trickster-transformer, he also appears in many tales with European (or at least Christian) story elements. Since his time, there have been many strong men, *kinap* (?), some of whom had supernatural powers, and all of whom (in tales) performed miraculous feats of strength to the great surprise of non-Micmacs who had mocked them.

The *kinap* uses his powers for good or, at worst, for pranks. More threatening is the *puwo·win,* a male or female witch who is able to work his will through magical spells or potions. The *puwo·win* of recent decades is the legendary descendant of the seventeenth-century shaman called "Bohinne" by Le Clercq. Like his prototype, the modern *puwo·win* may be able to predict the future, to walk under or upon the water, or to protect individuals and settlements from evil influences (perhaps emanating from other *puwo·win*). They no longer predict the location of game or engage in elaborate curing ceremonies, wrestling with spirits and sucking illness from the body; but there persists a variety of beliefs in the *puwo·win*'s ability to cause harm at a distance through an "evil wish," resulting in sickness, an apparent accident, or even a major disaster. European elements can be found in most of the *puwo·win* tales, but these are always adapted to the Indian point of view. For example, the Campbellton fire of 1910 is interpreted by some as a punishment sent by a *puwo·win* (perhaps aided by Gluskap) to those who had mocked and cheated the Indians; the houses of those residents who had behaved well were allegedly spared.

The *skəte·kəmuč* is a frightening, ghostlike spirit who often signifies approaching death. Supernatural races include the *mi·kəmuwesu* and the *pukələtəmuč*(?). The latter are dwarflike creatures who are believed to dress and live like "old time Indians," eating only wild meat and helping or harming men according to their whim. (Of late they have acquired some characteristics of the French-Canadian *lutins,* playing tricks around the house or barn such as riding horses at night and leaving their manes or tails tightly braided. In this manifestation, they may be exorcised with holy water or fronds from Palm Sunday.)

Underlying all these fragments is a coherent belief and value system that can be inferred only with difficulty. The aboriginal Micmacs apparently believed in a Great Spirit, a creator analogous to the Central Algonquian manitou. But the Jesuit missionaries applied his Micmac name, *mən·tu,* to the Devil and selected for the Christian God the name *niskam* 'great one, Lord' (compare *niskamič* 'grandfather'). The Micmacs differed from other Algonquians, however, in their identification of this creator with the sun. Several sources confirm this twice-daily "sun worship," and Maillard cites a long invocation of the sun as part of the ceremonial preparations for a raid against the Maliseets. One passage reads: "We are thy children; for we can know no origin but that which thy rays have given us, when first marrying efficaciously, with the earth we inhabit, they impregnated its womb, and caused us to grow out of it like the herbs of the field, and the trees of the forest, of which thou are equally the common father . . . . Sun! Be thou favorable to us in this point, as thou art in that of our hunting, when we beseech thee to guide us in quest of our daily support" (1758:25-26). After this invocation, a great pile of pelts gathered in Maliseet country was set on fire as a sacrifice to the sun; vows were made and weapons completed. Then the women entered to dance about the fire and urge the warriors on.

It is not possible to reconstruct the total worldview from historical sources or contemporary investigations, but a few general concepts that have apparent continuity in Micmac thought can be traced. The most general ideas are the following:

(1) *Life is everywhere—visible and invisible, beneath the ground and under the sea.* Various forms of life may change into one another. Some kinds of animals and some people are not what they seem to be.

(2) *The ancestors were great hunters—strong, dignified, and healthy.* They were just, generous, and brave. Their behavior should be a guide for their descendants.

(3) *Indians have powers which are different from those of non-Indians.* They may have supernatural helpers who bring them messages or special gifts. Some possess "Indian luck" or *keskamizit,* which enables them to do, find, or make things with great speed or reliability.

(4) *Men are equal—or should be.* No one should put himself above others, though chiefs who have exceptional abilities and who follow the traditional patterns of generosity, courage, and fairness may be allowed to lead.

(5) *Moderation is usually better than excess.* Too much of anything can be harmful; but everyone needs, on occasion, to break out of constraints and to act in extreme ways.

These principles are certainly not unique to the Micmac, but they summarize an outlook on man and his place in the world that continues to play a part in the people's adaptation to the changing conditions of the present.

History

Many changes in Micmac culture occurred during the French period (1600-1760). The most important of these were direct and indirect consequences of the fur trade and of the Micmacs' involvement in the conflict between the French and the English (cf. Bailey 1937). But even earlier, during the years when there were only sporadic contacts with European fishing vessels, the Micmac began to develop a desire for certain kinds of trade goods (especially metal knives, axes, and kettles) and to be infected by diseases contracted from the fishermen. In 1616 Biard estimated the Micmac population at over 3,000 (JR 2:73); but he noted elsewhere that there had been a great decline during the preceding century, partly due to "pleurisy, quinsy and dysentery, which kill them off" (JR 1:177). Smallpox, alcoholism, and warfare all contributed to further reductions in the Indian population, which probably reached its low point in the middle of the seventeenth century. A slight recovery followed, and the population seems to have remained fairly stable through the nineteenth century; a notable increase has occurred during the twentieth century (fig. 8). The aver-

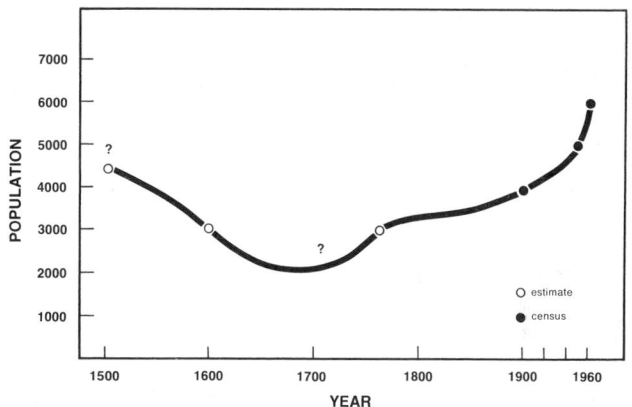

Fig. 8. Population estimates and reserve censuses, 1500-1960.

age increase in the years 1965 to 1970 was around 2.5 % a year.

Following the cessation of hostilites in 1760, the Micmac had only a short breathing period before British colonists began to arrive. After 1780, some American Loyalists were also granted lands in the Maritimes. The increasing non-Indian population quickly encroached on Indian lands; this, together with new economic opportunities furnished by colonial society, led to major changes in the Micmac way of life (table 2).

Indian reserves were established by the British governors under a variety of treaty arrangements. Chiefs were still selected by consensus and served for life, but the selections became influenced by the priests and "confirmed" by non-Indian officials. In many cases, the lands

Table 2. Culture Change, 1500–1970

Date	Historical Situation	Economic and Military Events	Primary Sources
1970	Band management by Indians Founding of Indian unions	Community development projects Micmac work in "high steel"	
1960	Increasing crime rate Pan-Indianism	Provincial relief Scholarships become available	Bock 1966 Wallis and Wallis 1955
1950	New Indian Act	Serious unemployment House-building programs	Sayres 1956
1940	World War II	Centralization program 1944 Federal relief increased	
1930	Depression	 Baseball the Micmac sport	
1920	 World War I	Population growth begins Some Micmac in Canadian army	Speck 1922
1910	Improved medical services	Schools on some reserves	Wallis and Wallis 1955
1900	 First Indian Act Colonies assume treaty obligations 1860 Miramichi fire 1825	Potato and blueberry harvesting Increased sedentarism Trapping ends in most areas Porpoise hunting Mills and railroads built Micmac in lumbering and guiding Some reserves surveyed	Pacifique 1934 Rand 1850
1800	Micmac in Newfoundland Wabanaki Confederacy begins End of French period Battle of Restigouche 1760 French Acadians deported Louisburg falls British in Nova Scotia	Population stable Limited relief by colonies Colonization by British begins	Maillard 1758
1700	Fortress of Louisburg built Religious communities at Sillery, Tadoussac, Quebec Missions closed by Jesuits (due to "drunkenness") Baptism of Membertou 1610	Micmac allied with the French against British and their Iroquois allies Trapping continues Raids against Montagnais Wars against Maliseet Brandy and fur trade	Dièreville 1933 Le Clercq 1910 Denys 1908 Biard (JR: 1-3)
1600	Founding of Port Royal Infectious diseases	 Population decrease begins	Lescarbot 1907–1914
1500	Sporadic European contacts	Some trade with fishing vessels	Cartier 1867

"reserved for the use and benefit of a band of Indians" were later whittled down in favor of non-Indians who wanted resources and water rights for commercial purposes. A great deal of work remains to be done in the colonial and provincial archives of this period, but the general outline of events is clear (cf. Hutton 1963). The colonists directed their efforts to gaining control over the fur trade, which the French had monopolized for so long. As the Indians' lands were restricted and the number of fur-bearing animals diminished, in area after area they became semisedentary; the women and children would remain in settlements while the men alternated between periods of "working out" and living on the reserves, where they made baskets and wooden craft items and received limited relief from the colonial governments.

Some men continued to tend trap lines, but more were drawn into lumbering, guiding, and commercial fishing, where at least some of their traditional knowledge and skills could be used. The mid-nineteenth century was a time of considerable economic activity in the Maritimes; sailing ships, railroads, and lumber mills were being built. Micmac men worked at all of these, though they often found themselves excluded from permanent jobs with the mills or railroads. Attempts by various government officials to interest them in agriculture repeatedly failed. The Micmacs were being gradually converted into a rural proletariat—unskilled or semiskilled laborers, available for seasonal or periodic jobs that no one else could do at wages no one else would accept. The porpoise hunting practiced for several generations in the Strait of Canso and parts of the Bay of Fundy is a good example of this. That industry ended when petroleum products were developed to replace porpoise oil in industrial applications; but while it lasted, it enabled the Micmacs to carry on a semblance of their hunting culture. When commercial potato farming began in northern Maine and New Brunswick, the Indians participated in the harvesting as migrant laborers. Some stayed on in New England as workers in lumber camps, construction, or industry, but most were periodically drawn back to the reserves by unemployment or the desire to be with family and friends (cf. Bock 1966a).

By the early years of the twentieth century, most of the Micmacs were settled on 60 reserves, some with several hundred inhabitants and others with a mere handful of Indians (fig. 1). At some of the larger reserves there were Catholic churches with full-time missionary-priests, who were often the government agents as well. The largest reserve was Restigouche with a population of 506 Indians, according to the census of 1910. This reserve also contained a Capuchin monastery, where Father Pacifique lived and worked, and a convent of Sisters of the Holy Rosary, who operated a four-grade school that they taught in the native language.

At the same time, political, educational, and economic changes were occurring at many of the reserves, inaugurating the "modern period" of culture change. The improved medical services that were gradually made available to the Micmacs contributed to the rapid growth that nearly doubled the population in 70 years. (At Restigouche, from the end of World War I until 1942, the Indian agent was also a medical doctor.) Under the provisions of the Federal Indian Act, chiefs and councilors were elected for two- or three-year terms, but their powers were extremely limited, with most of the responsibility for administration of the reserves resting with the Indian agent and the Department of Indian Affairs.

Schools were opened on or near many reserves. Attendance was irregular. Girls still married young, but gradually both sexes acquired the elements of reading and arithmetic. During World War I, Micmacs from many reserves served in the Canadian army, thus coming into contact for the first time with Canadian Indians and ethnic groups from other parts of the country. The war economy provided jobs in the Maritimes, and some Indians traveled widely in search of work and adventure. Others hoped for careers in athletics: hockey was popular, and baseball became the Micmac "national sport"—a book of baseball rules in Micmac was published by the Big Cove Reserve. But the Depression put an end to many hopes. During the 1930s there was severe unemployment throughout the Maritimes, and the Indians were hit particularly hard. Extension workers encouraged them to plant potatoes and vegetable gardens, but federal relief was necessary to prevent outright starvation.

The population continued to increase, and World War II brought renewed, if short-lived, prosperity. Returning Micmac veterans were offered assistance in building or renovating houses, and other federal programs followed that modernized the appearance of the reserves. Electrification came next and with it, radios and television. Educational programs were also important: besides new schools, transportation and scholarships were provided to enable children and young adults to acquire academic and vocational training. Courses in leadership and band management were offered, and educated young Indians were encouraged to enter the Department of Indian Affairs. But unemployment was once more on the rise, and many Micmacs could find work only in government programs or in the cities of New England. They learned that discrimination operated against educated as well as uneducated Indians.

Under these circumstances, it is hardly surprising that the Indian crime rate began to rise. The mass media presented a picture of life very different from what most Micmacs could afford. Many veterans, having seen the world, found the reserves too confining; they turned their newly built houses over to relatives and left to seek opportunities elsewhere. During the late 1940s, the Department of Indian Affairs carried out a centralization program in Nova Scotia in which Indians who had been living on dozens of tiny reserves were brought into larger settlements, principally Shubenacadie in central Nova Scotia and Eskasoni on Cape Breton Island. They were promised new houses and better educational and economic opportunities; but the only employment on these reserves turned out to be a federal house-building and public works programs, which paid little more than did relief.

The most important effect of the revised Indian Act of 1951 was on the political structure of the reserves. Band councils were enlarged and given broader powers over community affairs, though the veto was retained by the Department. This was part of a general policy to prepare the reserves for "self-determination" (parallel to the "termination" policy then being followed in the United

States). But the Micmacs were suspicious of the federal policy. They feared that their exemption from property taxes was threatened and that the proposal to transfer them from the federal program to various provincial administrations for relief would work to their disadvantage.

The centralization program tended to produce factions on the newly enlarged reserves, and some families drifted back to their old homes or into the cities. Many band councils were frustrated at finding themselves given responsibilities without real powers. Some leaders worked hard for programs to benefit their reserves; but others, finding themselves caught between the demands of the people and the sluggish bureaucracy, settled for getting what benefits they could for themselves and their relatives (Bock 1966:65-71).

The 1960s

During the 1960s, many of the economic, political, and educational changes initiated earlier in the century began to show real effects. Unemployment continued at a high rate, but Micmac men discovered an occupation that paid well and in which they were wanted: like the Mohawk before them, they went to work in "high steel." By 1970 at least one out of every three men in the labor force at Restigouche had spent some time—usually in Boston—working in construction on high-rise buildings. Scholarships to vocational schools had enabled some of these men to learn needed skills, such as welding or plumbing. But the main factor behind this adaptation was the availability of a kind of work that, though dangerous, paid well and that was compatible with Micmac values and concepts of social time (Bock 1966a). As work in high steel became popular, interest in lumbering and in the potato harvest fell off. Micmac women were also acquiring new skills. Women from reserves near non-Indian settlements had always worked as domestics; but the vocational training programs now made it possible for some to qualify as nurses, teachers, secretaries, or social workers. Some of these women were also becoming active in band politics.

None of the reserves could be said to present a prosperous appearance, but in this they are not very different from non-Indian communities of comparable size in the rural Maritimes. The Indian houses appear more standardized due to the series of federal building programs, but their interiors are finished in a variety of styles; with a few exceptions, the yard areas are untended beyond an occasional cutting back of weeds. Many ancient shacks have been left standing and, with the constant rotation of population between the reserves and urban areas, there is no shortage of living places. Newly married couples who once would have moved in with the parents of either now can rent an inexpensive place of their own while waiting for a government house to be built for

them. Electricity is available on all the major reserves (though some Indians cling to the kerosene lamp) and telephones, still a luxury, can also be had in most areas. Roads are poor; provincial governments will not maintain them on reserves and the federal bureaucracy is slow to respond. But when the people of Restigouche blocked off the entrances to their reserve in 1969 they quickly got attention (cf. Adrien 1956).

The varying appearances of the reserves are due to differences in population (table 3), proximity to cities,

Table 3. Population of Micmac Reserves, 1972

QUEBEC		NOVA SCOTIA	
Restigouche	1,385	Eskasoni	1,289
Maria	360	Whycocomagh	278
Gaspé	95	Chapel Island	199
Viger	103	Sydney (Membertou)	354
		Middle River	287
Total Quebec	1,943	Shubenacadie	896
		Truro	335
NEW BRUNSWICK		Pictou Landind	282
Big Cove	1,119	Annapolis Valley	174
Buctouche	16	Bear River	131
Burnt Church	612	Afton	216
Eel Ground	329	Acadia (Halifax)	328
Fort Folly	30		
Indian Island	72	Total Nova Scotia	4,769
Pabineau	49		
Red Bank	207	PRINCE EDWARD ISLAND	
Eel River	211	Lennox Island	305
Total		Abegweit	143
New Brunswick	2,645	Total P.E.I.	448

Total Enrolled Micmac 9,805

NOTE: Not more than 70% of the enrolled members are actually in residence on a reserve at a given time.
SOURCE: Band Lists.

and the presence or absence of certain institutions and community development programs. Thus, a given reserve may have any combination of the following: a church, a school, a community center, an agency building or band government office, a veterans' hall, grocery stores, water or sewage systems, and so on. Some reserves carry out highly specialized economic activities. At Red Bank (and other Miramichi reserves) many men cut Christmas trees; lobster trapping is still profitable at Burnt Church; at Maria (in Quebec), splint basketry is still made in quantity; Big Cove and Restigouche are developing recreational facilities in hopes of attracting tourists; and at Eskasoni a program is testing the feasibility of cultivating oysters (using Japanese techniques). Elsewhere, however, once-valuable resources have been exhausted (as by overcutting of lumber) or ruined (as at Pictou Landing where industrial pollution has made fishing and bathing unsafe).

Many of these programs reflect a new vitality on the part of band governments and a new willingness of the Canadian government to allow the people to learn by making their own mistakes. Serious problems still remain, but as trained and experienced Indian personnel become available, the bands are gaining power and independence. Indian band managers were employed at several reserves and plans were made for band councils to take overall agency functions. Pan-Indianism was important during the 1960s, as Micmac youth and adult leaders became aware of problems and programs in other parts of Canada and in the United States. National and regional organizations were formed during this decade, with Micmacs participating in the Quebec Indian Association, the Union of New Brunswick Indians, and the Union of Nova Scotia Indians (which published a monthly newspaper, *Micmac News*). The first efforts of these groups—conferences, workshops, and policy statements—may lead to action programs and effective lobbying. One international experiment, known as Teaching and Research in Bicultural Education (T.R.I.B.E.), attempts to deal with the drop-out problem among Indian students by means of an innovative program for both the Maritimes and the state of Maine (see Canada. Parliament. Standing Committee on Indian Affairs and Northern Development 1969–1970).

There is also significant variation among reserves regarding language, education, and religious practices, though here it is harder to point to the causative factors. Until the twentieth century, the Micmac language was an obligatory marker of ethnic identity. But there are few if any remaining monolingual speakers, whereas the proportion of nonspeakers has increased. On some reserves, for example, Membertou, near Sydney, C.B.I., all persons under 20 have English as a first language. Elsewhere, for instance, at Restigouche, P.Q., Micmac is still the first language for the vast majority of young persons; but even there, television and English-language schools may soon reduce the speaking ability of the younger generation to a passive, understanding one, as has already happened at Shubenacadie, Nova Scotia.

The school situation also varies greatly among reserves. At the start of the 1960s, federal day schools were being built on reserves; indeed, at Restigouche, the on-reserve school (operated by Catholic sisters and lay teachers) also had classes for non-Indian children from the surrounding communities, some of whom spoke only French. But by the end of the decade, the tendency was to have Indian children attend "integrated" schools off the reserve, and the assignment of contracts for busing reserve children had become a major political issue. (At Restigouche in 1970, Indian children were being taken out of Quebec to the English-language schools in Campbellton, New Brunswick.) Opinions of Micmac leaders are strongly divided about the desirability of various types of schooling. It is indicative of the types of change

taking place that a part-time teacher was employed at the Big Cove (Deep Cove) Reserve in 1968–1969 to instruct primary school children in Micmac language and culture. Most Micmacs are still nominally Roman Catholic, and the major holidays are observed with some ceremony—especially the day of the patron, Saint Anne, on July 26. But secularization and tourism have affected even this "Micmac national holiday," and many young people are outspokenly critical of the Church. Protestantism has made very limited gains and has usually aroused great opposition; however, a non-Catholic has been repeatedly elected as chief (again, at Restigouche, from 1962 through 1970), and Protestants have served on band councils. As in earlier times, the priests attempt to influence their Indian flock, to "excite them to the practice of acts of religion, and . . . render them tractable, sociable, and loyal . . . [and] to make them live in good understanding with the French" (Maillard 1758:2). But clerical influence is definitely on the wane, and even the "Indian wake" with its Micmac hymns and aboriginal overtones can no longer be performed at many reserves, for lack of singers (Bock 1964).

The five general points concerning basic Micmac values were still relevant in the 1960s, though they did not influence behavior in a mechanical manner. Rather, one finds a persistent fascination with life in all its forms, a tendency to fall back on traditional means and goals, a deeply ambivalent attitude toward Indian identity and "power," an explicit egalitarianism, and an implicit orientation to "least effort" strategies. Each of these general points can be contradicted by specific observations, but they provide the normative background against which degrees of deviation and change must be judged.

Synonymy

The derivation of the tribal name, *mi·kəmaw* 'Micmac', is uncertain, though many sources say that it means 'allies'. It may have some geographical significance. The present spelling is well standardized, but earlier variants include Migmagi (Pacifique), Mickmakis (Maillard, Rand) and Mikmakiques (cf. Mooney and Thomas 1907a). Subgroups were often given distinctive names; thus, the Gaspesians of Le Clercq (1910), and the Acadians and Souriquois of the *Jesuit Relations* are really different groups of Micmac who lived, respectively, in eastern Quebec and central and southern Nova Scotia. A seventeenth-century English name for the Micmac is Tarrantine (Siebert 1973).

Sources

It is probable that Cartier encountered Micmac Indians during the summer of 1534 when he visited and named the Bay of Chaleur (cf. Sauer 1971). References are fragmentary for the remainder of the century. French colonization (as opposed to fishing and trading) did not get under way in this region until the seventeenth century. The basic written sources for an understanding of Micmac ethnology begin with the *Jesuit Relations*, especially those of Father Biard, 1611-1616. Lescarbot (1907-1914) is also useful, though he does not always distinguish among the different tribes of New France. The works of Le Clercq (1910) and of Nicolas Denys (1908) deal largely with the Micmac of the middle and late seventeenth century, especially in the northern districts.

Bailey (1937) has brought together a great deal of material on European-Algonquian relations during the French period. His excellent discussion of the effects of the fur and brandy trades is highly pertinent to the Micmac experience. Hoffman (1955) is particularly good on the material culture of this period.

The principal source for the eighteenth century is Maillard (1758), though the text may be suspect since it was published in London by men who obviously wished to discredit the French. From the nineteenth century there are the works of the Protestant missionary, S.T. Rand, including an ethnography (1850), the valuable *Dictionary* (1902), and the *Legends* (1894). The twentieth-century researches of Pacifique (1934) and of Speck (1922) are mainly attempts to reconstruct the culture of earlier periods.

Wilson D. Wallis carried out fieldwork during 1911-1912, and again during 1950 and 1953 with Ruth S. Wallis. Wallis and Wallis (1955) is the basic source for Micmac ethnography. Unfortunately, it is sometimes difficult to be sure to what periods or areas the generalizations refer. For the middle twentieth century, published materials include a life history of a young Nova Scotia Micmac by Sayres (1956) and Bock's (1966) description of a large modern reserve in Quebec.

The Micmac collections of Speck and Wallis are housed in the Museum of the American Indian (Heye Foundation) in New York City. Small collections may also be found in the Peabody Museum of Salem and Peabody Museum of Archaeology and Ethnology at Cambridge, Massachusetts; the Nova Scotia College of Art Museum in Halifax, Nova Scotia; the New Brunswick Museum at Saint John, New Brunswick; the Royal Ontario Museum in Toronto; the McCord Museum of McGill University in Montreal; and the National Museum of Canada in Ottawa.

Maliseet-Passamaquoddy

VINCENT O. ERICKSON

Language, Territory, and Environment

The Maliseet (ˈmălə͵sēt) and Passamaquoddy (͵păsəməˈkwädē) speak mutually intelligible dialects of the same language.*

Recorded contact between the Maliseet-Passamaquoddy and Europeans began early in the seventeenth century. Samuel de Champlain took note of the visit of some warriors to the French trading station at Tadoussac in 1603, and the following year Pierre Du Gua de Monts founded an ephemeral colony on Île Sainte Croix in the heart of their territory. However, Basque, Breton, Norman, and Portuguese fishermen may have had contact with the Maliseet-Passamaquoddy as much as a century earlier. Champlain named the group he encountered at Tadoussac the "Etechemins" (Etchemin). A year later he applied the same name to the inhabitants of the mouths of the Saint John and Saint Croix rivers and said that the Etchemin extended from the Saint John to the Kennebec rivers inclusively (Champlain 1922-1936, 1:269, 3:362; see also Lescarbot 1907-1914, 2:277).†

National boundaries have since complicated the issue of a Maliseet-Passamaquoddy identity. These virtually identical people differed primarily in their economic adaptation. The Maliseet were inland hunters, living along the Saint John River drainage in New Brunswick and Maine; the Passamaquoddy were sea mammal hunters, living along the coasts of New Brunswick and Maine. Since 1842 a national boundary has severed the territory of both groups (fig. 1). The status of the Passamaquoddies east of the Saint Croix was long in question, too. The Passamaquoddies favored the United States government, and when Massachusetts allotted reservations for them west of the Saint Croix in 1794 (Maine Historical Society 1902:98-102), gradually all Passamaquoddies moved to these reservations. Differing national allegiances and separate governmental agencies to deal with Indian matters have tended to muddy the similarities of the two groups. Intermarriage, however, still takes place between the Maliseet and the Passamaquoddy.

The topography of the original Maliseet-Passamaquoddy territories consists largely of forested rolling hills. The climate of the coastal territories occupied by the Passamaquoddy is modified by the Bay of Fundy. The interior regions occupied by the Maliseet do not have this leveling influence and are more continental in character. Fish and game were sometimes not abundant enough to meet the needs of the rather sparsely populated territory. Gyles (1851:81), referring to the Maliseet in the last decade of the seventeenth century, writes of genuine want during the winter among the hunting band to which he was attached.

History

Settlement Patterns

Settlement patterns reflect Maliseet-Passamaquoddy acculturation during 350 years. This can be seen by examining changes within three time periods: (1) the traditional period, 1603-1785, (2) the Loyalist period, 1785-1900, and (3) the twentieth century.

Although considerable acculturation, especially in material culture, took place in the first period, it can still be called the traditional period. Large summer villages and dispersed winter settlements are typical. During the seventeenth century some summer villages were stockaded. In 1604 Champlain described the village of Ouigodi at the mouth of the Saint John River. Numerous lodges, both large and small, were present, some housing a single family, others several families. A lodge serving as council chamber could accommodate 80 to 100 persons. Lodges may refer to both conical wigwams and the rectangular lodges that housed several families and the feast house. Harper (1954:27) suggests that these rectangular buildings were possibly larger versions of the rectangular houses sometimes constructed by the Penobscots, who "built a wall of four or five tiers of logs as in a log cabin, and erected on this a roof of birch bark supported by poles. Long poles from each of the top corners were bound together in the centre with spruce roots or cedar bark cords."

At the end of the seventeenth century a palisaded village was located at the mouth of the Nerepis River on

---

*Maliseet-Passamaquoddy words here are written in the orthography of Teeter (1971) except that č is used for his c and the stressed syllable of each word is marked with an accent, with ´ for a pitch that is higher and ` for one that is lower than that of surrounding syllables. The spelling of all italicized words has been checked and corrected by Teeter and Ives Goddard with the assistance of Wayne Newell, except that they were unable to confirm the spelling of *keskamsit* 'mana'.

† For the problems involved in classifying the small "Etchemin" vocabulary recorded by Lescarbot, see "Eastern Algonquian Languages," this volume.

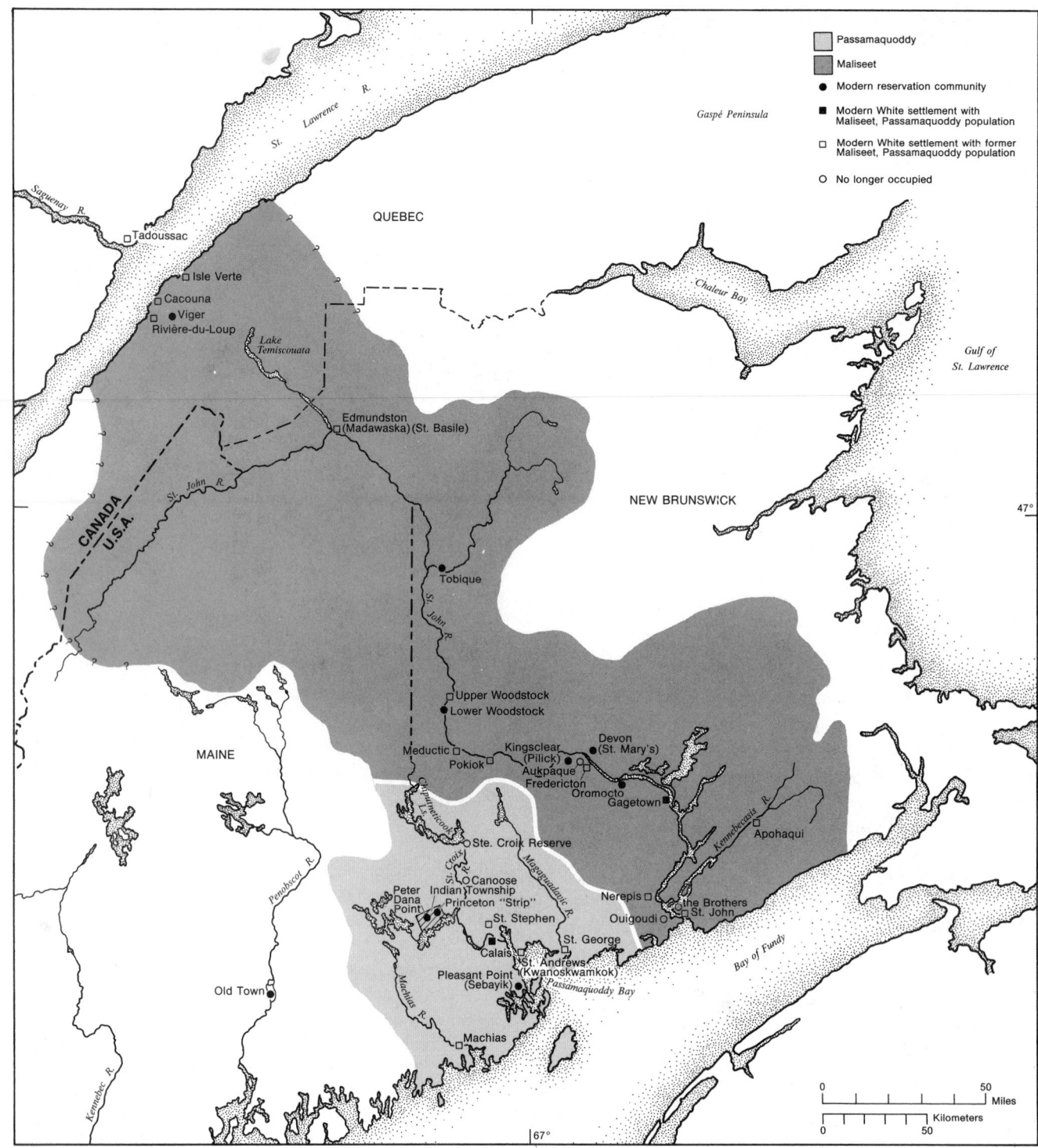

Fig. 1. Tribal territory about 1890.

the lower Saint John, but the major Maliseet village was at Meductic as it was strategically located at the end of the inland riverine and lacustrine route from Passamaquoddy and Penobscot country. By 1767 Meductic had been abandoned, most of the inhabitants having gone to Aukpaque, first mentioned in 1733 and located at Springhill, near Fredericton. Aukpaque included in addition two large and important islands, Harts Island and Savage Island. Here, on Savage Island, at least by 1765, disputes were settled and winter hunting grounds were allotted to each family. Aukpaque was the primary Maliseet settlement until the Indians lost it to a Loyalist in 1794. In the eighteenth century the major Passamaquoddy settlement was *kwənáskwamkok*, at Saint Andrews. After 1784, because of Loyalist incursions, most Passamaquoddies moved first to Indian Island in

Passamaquoddy Bay and, when this island was assigned to the British, to Pleasant Point (Sebayik, i.e., *sípayik*), in undisputed American territory. The Passamaquoddy had long occupied and used the territory on the south and east shores of Passamaquoddy Bay for maple sugaring (Eckstorm 1941:226), marine hunting, and fishing (Sabine 1852:100) and used Lewis (Lewey's) Island near Princeton for inland hunting and fishing (Ganong 1899:223). Although archeological excavations must determine how long the ancestors of the Passamaquoddy occupied the bay and Saint Croix drainage and when the ancestors of the Maliseet first moved into the Saint John drainage, clearly the Maliseet and Passamaquoddy have been separate landholding groups since at least the mid-eighteenth century.

In the first period most contact was with the French, and relations were generally friendly.

In 1794 approximately 23,000 acres of land in Washington County was set aside for the Passamaquoddy by the Commonwealth of Massachusetts (Sabine 1852:98–99). Since that time 7,960.27 acres of original grants have been occupied by non-Indians (Farnham 1902:98–102).

The second period was one of extensive settlement of English-speaking people in the area, greater acculturation, the establishment of reservations, and an attempt to encourage the Indians to become farmers on the lands set aside for them. For some families it was possible to live as hunters and trappers in dispersed seasonal residences until the beginning of the twentieth century.

After the loss of Aukpaque many families moved to Kingsclear (*pìlìčk*), which became a reservation. With 16,000 acres originally, Tobique, the largest of the Maliseet reservations in New Brunswick, was set aside to encourage Indians from all parts of the Saint John drainage to become farmers. But most Maliseets preferred a nomadic existence, as long as a livelihood could be obtained from hunting and trapping, and camped at a number of upper Saint John River localities. One, Edmonston (Saint Basile), soon became a reservation. The Woodstock reserve was purchased by the New Brunswick government in 1851 to compensate for injustices resulting from the loss of Meductic. "Today many Maliseets contend that they, as a nation, never sold or gave up by treaty any land to the Crown except for the early Loyalist settlements on the lower river . . ." (Gordon M. Day, personal communication 1972).

In the Fredericton area two additional reservations were established in the second half of the nineteenth century. With increased acculturation Maliseets were attracted to the greater opportunities for employment driving log booms, loading boats, and selling handicrafts; and a 2.25-acre area was purchased for them in 1867 at Devon. In 1928 an additional 328.5 acres (Saint Mary's) were added nearby to accommodate the increased population. Both reservations were purchased by the Canadian government. The Oromocto reserve was established in 1895 on lands on which the Maliseets were camping. A reservation of two small islands, The Brothers, near the mouth of the Saint John, was a grant from 1838.

Reservations were not established everywhere the Maliseets camped. Indian Affairs records indicate that several bands of Maliseets were camping at various places on the lower Saint John—near the city of Saint John, at Gagetown, and at Apohaqui on the Kennebecasis River. On the Upper Saint John, Indian families were living at Pokiok, at Upper Woodstock, and in Aroostock County, Maine. On the Saint Croix drainage near the outlet of Lake Chiputneticook, a Maliseet reservation was established in 1881. Farther downstream the Canoose reservation was set aside for families that later moved on to Passamaquoddy reservations in Maine. Other Passamaquoddies lived at Saint Stephen and along the coast at Saint Andrews and Saint George. In the second half of the nineteenth century some Passamaquoddies from Sebayik and elsewhere moved to their larger holdings at Indian Township near Princeton, while others lived off reservation at Calais, Maine.

In the early nineteenth century there was a migration of several Maliseet families from Tobique to Isle Verte and Cacouna townships in Quebec. A reservation was established for them at Viger.

The third period, the twentieth century, was marked by movement to the more central reservations, the abandoning of the more isolated ones, and the movement off the reservations into economically more feasible areas with or without assimilation into the White community. The Passamaquoddies in Charlotte County moved to one of the Maine reservations, the Maliseets from the Saint Croix into one of the Saint John River reservations. Apohaqui, Saint John, The Brothers, Pokiok, and Upper Woodstock settlements were abandoned by Indian families, as was Calais. Other movements were of Upper Saint John River Maliseets into Aroostook County, Maine, because of better employment possibilities in the potato industry. Other Maliseets and Passamaquoddies, encouraged by new industries, moved to the Penobscot reservation at Old Town, Maine. There is still considerable movement from the Passamaquoddy reservations to Old Town, and the Indian language heard on the Penobscot reservation is now Passamaquoddy. Many Maliseets and Passamaquoddies have moved into industrial areas in Connecticut and Massachusetts, while the Maliseets in Quebec have intermarried extensively with the French Canadians and have largely assimilated into French Canadian society.

Population

In 1612 Pierre Biard (JR 2:73) estimated the Etchemin to number less than 1,000. The coastal Maliseet and Pas-

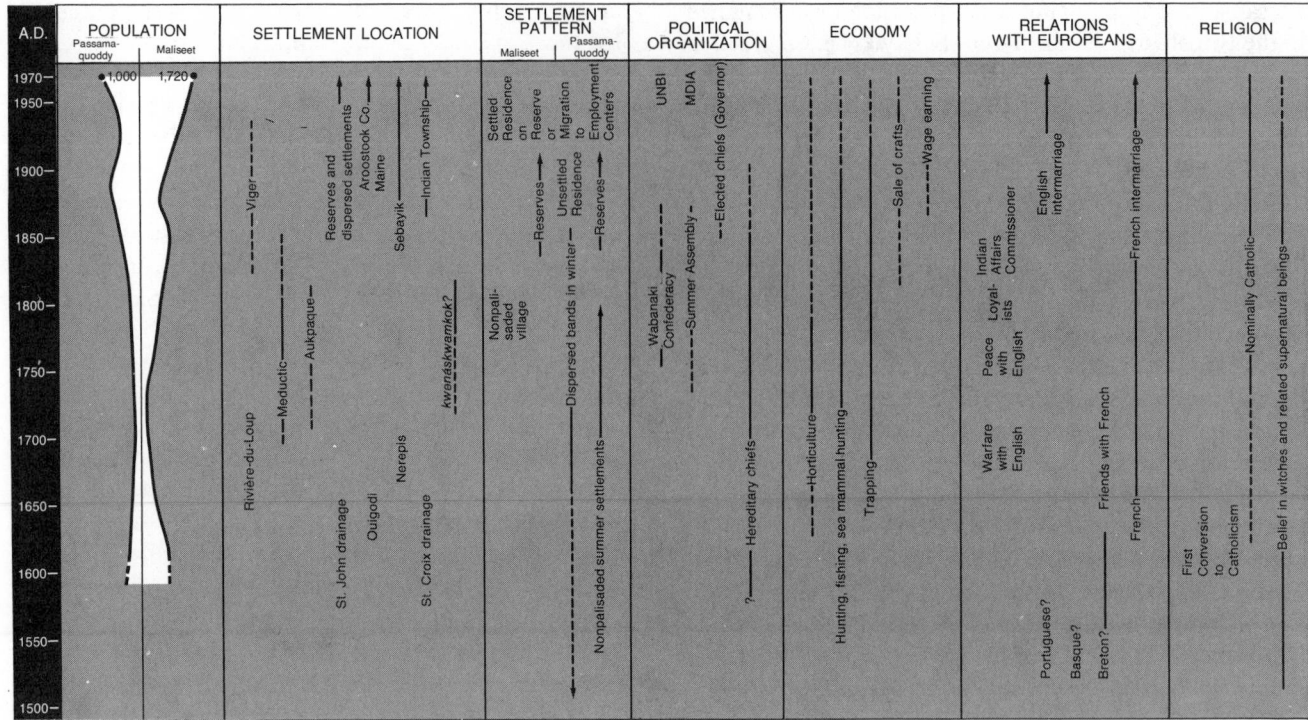

Fig. 2. Sociocultural change.

samaquoddy had experienced a decline because of European diseases, overdependence on French provisions, alcohol, and perhaps deliberate poisoning. Further declines were noted into the eighteenth century, but by 1820 the Maliseet-Passamaquoddy population may have regained the 1612 figure. With the exception of the declines shown on figure 2, the Maliseet-Passamaquoddy population has been on an upward trend since 1820. Information on census figures is given by Chauvignerie (NYCD 9), Maine Historical Society (MeHSC 3), and West (1827). The complete 1910 census gave 848 Maliseet, 386 Passamaquoddy, and 266 Penobscot (U.S. Bureau of the Census 1915). Since 1910, both groups have more than doubled (Canada. Department of Indian Affairs and Northern Development. Indian Affairs Branch 1970, 1971; Maine. Department of Indian Affairs 1970, 1971):

Maliseet

(Oct. 26, 1971)	Band	Total	On Reserve	Off Reserve
	Edmundston	67	47	20
	Kingsclear	274	216	58
	Oromocto	117	95	22
	Saint Mary's	386	312	74
	Tobique	617	437	180
	Woodstock	258	123	135
(Jan. 1, 1970)	Viger	93		
		1,812	1,230	489

Passamaquoddy

(Jan. 1, 1970)	Band	Total	On Reserve	Off Reserve
	Peter Dana Point	213		
(Jan. 1, 1971)	Pleasant Point	793	330	463
		1,006		

There are no living full-blooded Maliseet-Passamaquoddies, as intermarriage with Caucasians has occurred since the seventeenth century. Most Maliseets and Passamaquoddies growing up on the reservations speak some of their native language but few are bilingual. The oldest are Maliseet-Passamaquoddy dominant, but children tend to speak little of the language. The Pleasant Point, Woodstock, and Tobique reservations have undergone the most acculturation; Oromocto, Kingsclear, and Peter Dana Point the least.

Culture

Subsistence

The early historical period was characterized by little or no competition for resources on the winter hunting grounds, at cultivated areas, along the rivers near warm-weather villages, or at successful fishing spots. Subsistence activities and the annual cycle were scheduled according to whatever food resources were available and could be obtained most easily during a particular season. Gyles's (1851:83) account of his Maliseet family is typical of the traditional period. On returning from their

126

winter hunting territories to the central village in spring, corn was planted. In June the Maliseets went to one of the islands in the Saint John to camp, first to spear bass and later sturgeon. Several trips were made back and forth from garden plots to fishing sites in the summer. After corn was hilled the Maliseets went out to spear fish including salmon by torchlight at night (fig. 3). Fish, wild grapes, and roots provided the summer diet. In fall corn was harvested, and the portion that was dried was either stored in subterranean pits lined with bark or taken along on the migratory winter hunt. This hunt for moose or bear was done by groups of 8 to 10 people, two of whom were adult men. Until spring, the group continually traveled over a large area of Maine, New Brunswick, and the Gaspé Peninsula in search of game. A similar yearly round likely characterized other Maliseet bands until the expansion of the Loyalists at the end of the eighteenth century.

The Loyalist expansion began a period of increased acculturation and competition for lands formerly used for hunting and trapping. Both Indian groups depended

Coll. of Vincent Erickson.
Fig. 3. Joe Pielpole, Passamaquoddy, spearing whitefish by torch light. The wooden spear is three-pronged. The torch is burning birchbark held in the split end of a stick. Photographed at Peter Dana Point Reservation about 1910.

more on the fur trade; otter, beaver, and muskrat were the main pelts, but moose hides were also marketed. In late spring the Indians came to the trading posts or in later periods assembled at given points on the river, which were visited by the fur trader who purchased their catch.

Some planting of gardens, potatoes, and grain was also done, although the commissioners to the Indians were frustrated by their lack of success in encouraging farming. Other income was available for the men as agricultural laborers, log-boom drivers, guides for hunters and fishermen, and as stevedores on the river boats. Summer was a time for basketmaking and other wood industries. Migratory habits continued; often families, sometimes two together, camped near White settlements and, going from house to house, traded their wares. Ferry and steamer landings proved popular trading spots. Guiding, of course, made unimpeded traditional fall and winter hunting and trapping impossible: the good guide guaranteed his employer that he would make his kill or catch; White ownership restricted the Indians' passing over his former hunting and trapping grounds. Some Maliseets remained on the reservations or near the White settlements the entire winter, making baskets for sale or relying upon the kindness of White neighbors.

Since approximately 1920 the Maliseets have made only marginal use of nonreservation land (McFeat 1962a:238–239). Activities are still predicated on the changing of the seasons. Spring finds fiddlehead gathering; the young fern fronds, exposed by the lowering freshets, find a ready market. On the northern reservations, cutting seed potatoes provides income for many. Blueberry raking occurs in late summer, and September and October bring the busy period of potato harvesting. Indians from all of New Brunswick and Maine go to northern Maine and adjacent New Brunswick to work on the harvest. During the official hunting season most men go out to get their deer or moose, but winter is generally a quiet time, although some make baskets the entire year.

Passamaquoddy subsistence activities and annual cycle resembled the Maliseet in most details for the three periods outlined. Spring found the same fishing and planting sequences, but June precipitated a movement to the seashore. Men, two to a canoe, paddled into the open seas of the Bay of Fundy to shoot porpoise and seal (Verrill 1954:96). While it is not universally agreed that porpoise and seal hunting was aboriginal among the Passamaquoddy, Eckstorm (1932:15) suggests that seal and porpoise oil were used by Maine Indians during the ceramic period. Whales were enticed by men in canoes to swim into shallow areas where they became stranded and were more easily killed. Excursions were made to neighboring islands to fish, to gather clams and lobsters, or to collect the eggs of sea birds. Winter hunting and trapping follow most details of the Maliseet.

127

Production and consumption units varied with the yearly round. In the traditional period ownership and territorial rights appear weakly developed. No details of distribution of garden plots at Meductic are given. Obligations of sharing with those in need overrode whatever ownership attitudes existed in the traditional and Loyalist periods.

Private ownership of hunting and trapping territory appears important during the late traditional period and the Loyalist period. Yearly, the area drained by the Saint John was divided among the component families. This usage seems to parallel Aukpaque's replacing Meductic as the major Maliseet settlement. Memory of the family hunting territories enabled Speck and Hadlock (1946) to outline them in some detail. As fewer families went on the winter hunt, territory available to each group became larger. The growing scarcity of game, because of encroachment and competition from the Whites, was in part compensated by the larger territories over which each family hunting group had access. By 1870, competition from Whites for furs and moose hides led to widespread overkill on the part of the Maliseets, and the old attitudes toward conservation were abandoned.

Technology

For the Maliseet, who "were at home with wood and its products in an extremely effective way" (McFeat 1962:46), the birchbark canoe was an efficient adaptation to the riverine, lacustrine, and coastal environment. It was light and easy to carry over portages connecting the inland waterways. Adney and Chapelle (1964) give a full account of the construction of the birchbark canoe (figs. 4-5). In Gyles's time moose-hide canoes and spruce bark canoes were also made.

Fig. 4. Maliseets constructing birchbark canoe. Left to right, Frank Sappier, "Oromocto Pete" Polchies, Charles Sappier, ———Paul, ———Francis. Photograph by George T. Taylor at St. Mary's Reserve about 1900.

ERICKSON

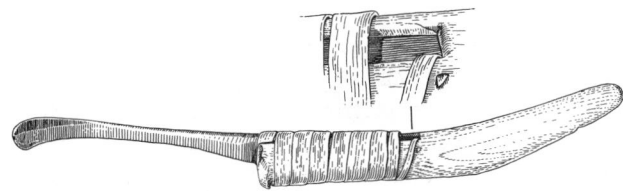

Dept. of Anthr., Smithsonian: 54338.
Fig. 5. Passamaquoddy crooked knife. The blade is in the form of a farrier's knife, held in place on the handle by a seizing of wood splint. The most important shaping tool for woodworking, the knife is drawn toward the user. The man second from right in fig. 4 whittles with a crooked knife. Length 26.7 cm; collected before 1897.

Birchbark was used for making containers such as the box, basket, tray, and dish, indeed the wigwam itself. The birchbark moose call was an indispensable part of the hunter's equipment. Birchbark served as a temporary raincoat, and messages and directions drawn on birchbark guided the traveler (N.N. Smith 1957:12).

Splint ash baskets made of the black ash were woven both for the tourist trade and for practical service in a rural economy (fig. 6). The utilitarian storage basket

Fig. 6. Passamaquoddy man using a draw knife to make ash splints for weaving baskets. He is using a wooden shaving horse with foot lever. Photographed by Harrison Howell Walker on the Passamaquoddy Reservation near Eastport, Me., Aug. 1937.

with the square bottom may have been made as early as the beginning of the nineteenth century, but the fancy basket, constructed of dyed ash splints, interwoven frequently with braided sweet grass, and with the rounded bottom, is more recent (Eckstorm 1932). Making fancy baskets is women's work, as the men weave the simpler potato basket. Porcupine-quill embroidery was lost about the time the splint basket replaced the birchbark container. Formerly ax handles, churns, and other household items were carved from white ash. These wood items provided considerable cash income, especially around the end of the nineteenth century (S.K. Squires 1930). The construction of the snowshoe with its white ash frame and mesh of caribou hide should not be overlooked. This, with toboggan construction, was formerly an important home industry. Constructing and repairing potato barrels and making potato and fancy baskets continues to provide a specialized outlet for woodworking skills among a few Maliseet-Passamaquoddy.

Life Cycle

• BIRTH AND SOCIALIZATION The following data refer to the traditional and Loyalist periods. Information on traditional parturition and associated taboos is not available. Babies were swaddled in the skins of the martin and beaver and strapped on a cradleboard (fig. 7). The genitals of the male infant were frequently exposed to allow for urination, even in winter, causing Denys (1908:403) to comment on high male infant mortality. The child was breast fed for two to three years (Mechling 1958–1959:27). The freedom that was permitted the child amazed the early French writers. Gyles commented that small children were well cared for, a trait persisting in the twentieth century.

Twins were considered a bad omen. It was believed that they would bring bad luck to the mother and that one of the twins would become a problem in later years (Mechling 1958–1959:26).

Education was informal and learning was by example. At an early age, children were encouraged to aid their parents (Mechling 1958–1959:28). Fathers made small paddles for their sons and daughters, who became skilled at maneuvering a canoe by the age of 10. Skill in using a toy bow and arrow was acquired early; as late as 1835 small children were remarkably good shots, even though adults no longer used this equipment (Levinge 1846, 1:115).

Girls, too, learned tasks relevant to the roles they would later play. They helped their mothers by getting wood and water and aided in carrying loads, for moving camp was largely the women's responsibility.

As the boy grew older he accompanied his father on the hunt and was given a full-sized bow. Although no puberty rites of passage are mentioned, the boy, upon killing his first moose, was permitted to sit in council

NAA, Smithsonian.

Fig. 7. Denny Sockabasin, daughter of Francis Joseph Neptune, Passamaquoddy chief. She wears a conical cap, overdress and leggings, two circular silver brooches, earrings, and a pendant cross on a bead necklace. A doll swaddled and laced onto a miniature cradleboard rests against a table leg. Watercolor painted in Eastport, Me., Sept. 18, 1817.

with the older men and to participate in public feasts (Mechling 1958-1959:29; Le Clercq 1910:239). Mechling writes that the young warrior taking his first scalp in warfare obtained higher rank (1958-1959:31).

• MARRIAGE In the traditional period betrothal lasted at least a year. The young man wishing to marry was required to serve his future father-in-law and to prove himself capable of supporting a wife and family by demonstrating his skill as a hunter. He made bows and arrows, a canoe, and snowshoes, all of which went to his future father-in-law. His betrothed made his clothes and footgear and corded his snowshoes. Strict sexual abstinence was observed during this time. During the wedding feast, which was marked by speeches and counterspeeches exalting the groom's genealogy, the young man promised to excel his ancestors.

Gyles omitted to mention bride service but added to the account of the ceremony interesting variants, which are still known. When the youth expressed interest in marriage he asked his relatives and, in historic times, the Jesuit, for their advice about a suitable girl. Learning of their choice, he went to her wigwam. "If he likes her appearance he tosses a chip or stick into her lap, which she takes, and with a reserved, side look, views the person who sent it; yet handles the chip with admiration, as though she wondered from whence it came" (Gyles 1851:97). If she liked the boy she tossed the chip to him with a modest smile, and arrangements were made for the Jesuit to marry them. If the girl disliked the boy, making a face she tossed the chip aside, and he came no more. Mechling's informants gave a similar account (1958-1959:37), and the marriage dance performed by a group of young Maliseets in 1967 portrayed the same custom.

The rigid moral code expected of the betrothed girl continued after marriage with fidelity of the married woman and infrequency of divorce. Mechling's informants expressed the view that adultery was very uncommon and formerly severely punished (1958-1959:49). These values were frequently expressed in the mythology, too (Mechling 1914:83).

• DEATH Specific references to Maliseet-Passamaquoddy funeral practices are rare in the early literature and the following may be based on observations of the Micmac. Shamans were summoned when a man grew seriously ill, but they attempted no cure if they thought he could not be helped. The dying person resigned himself to his fate, and from that time on was considered dead. Cold water might be poured on him to hasten his passing, or he might be buried while still alive.

Among twentieth-century Maliseets, attempts are made for the funeral to take place from the home of the deceased. If this is not done, it is felt that a death will occur in the dwelling that housed the funeral (Mechling 1958-1959:67). Referring to 1953, Wallis and Wallis (1957:24) emphasize the importance of the wake. Most Maliseets and Passamaquoddies are devout Catholics, and their prefuneral rites last for two or three nights, during which the house of the deceased is filled with guests who sing and recite rosaries.

Kinship and Social Organization

The bilaterally extended family was the basis of Maliseet-Passamaquoddy social organization. Three hundred fifty years of European contact make traditional kinship terminology and marriage practices conjectural. Mother-aunt terms follow the bifurcate collateral pattern, while cousin terms follow the Iroquois system, as female parallel cousins were grouped with sister and female cross-cousins were given another term. This may mean earlier cross-cousin marriage, but such a practice is explicitly denied by the Maliseet-Passamaquoddy. Perhaps the earlier practice was replaced in the traditional period by the one now carried out—prohibition against first- and second-cousin marriage—which is compatible with Catholic beliefs and practices. On small reservations this means that marriage tends to be exogamous, because all persons on the reservation are too

130

closely related to be eligible spouses. With exogamy postnuptial residence tends to be in the wife's community.

Cousin and brother-sister terms were differentiated both in terms of the speaker and in terms of the sex of the person being referred or spoken to. In addition there were separate terms for older sister, older brother, and younger sibling without reference to sex of speaker. These terms have been kept by some Maliseets, but the former distinctions for types of cousins and for aunt and uncle have been lost; terms of English origin have been substituted. The respect terms grandmother and grandfather, either in English or in Maliseet, are still used when speaking to anyone much older than oneself and do not necessarily reflect genealogical connections.

Chieftainship in the early traditional period was weakly developed but became more important in the late traditional period with the formation of the Wabanaki Confederacy. Formerly chiefs (sakə́mak) were good hunters, senior but not necessarily old, controlling more through manipulation of supernatural powers than through government and legislation. Later, the Wabanaki Confederacy provided a formal structure for selecting new chiefs and legislating disputes, although shamanism continued and possibly increased in importance as a technique for guarding one's hunting or trapping territory from others.

Chieftainship was hereditary in the male line. If the chief had no son, or if his son was unsuited for office, a nephew was usually selected (Mechling 1958–1959:141). In the traditional period the Maliseet appear to have had one supreme chief who resided at the dominant village. Under Indian Affairs encouragement the election of Maliseet chiefs for three-year periods first took place in 1896 (CDIA 1899). A Passamaquoddy treaty of 1852 stipulated that the chief, called governor, was to be elected every four years. The first evidence of this taking place was at Pleasant Point in 1875 or 1876, when the last hereditary sàkəm died (Reports of the Agent to the Passamaquoddy Indians 1876:6).

In 1778, under Mohawk and possibly White influences, the Maliseet tribe had one supreme sàkəm, "a second chief, and four captains and eight principal Indians" (Mechling 1958–1959:141). Mechling suggests that the second chief was merely an assistant of the chief, appointed by him, while the captains were officers who owed their authority to the Whites.

Besides these six peace chiefs there were war chiefs or war leaders called kinapíyək. The kinap was a person who had demonstrated his ability and bravery in warfare and was able to command a following on a raid. Such a man may have been a shaman (mətéwələn) as well, but he largely performed feats of strength and endurance which were impossible for ordinary individuals (not necessarily the curing of the sick or the practicing of sorcery). The status of kinap was achieved; it could be neither inherited nor bestowed by election. There was no

New Brunswick Provincial Arch., Fredericton.

Fig. 8. Maliseet gathering at Kingsclear, New Brunswick, on Corpus Christi Day. Photograph by George T. Taylor, 1887.

fixed number of *kinapíyək* within any village but the chief was usually one, too.

Evidence of a medicine society or a voluntary association of shamans is sketchy. The myth text (Erickson 1966–1974) that described a number of shamans assembled at a winter camp to divine conditions of wives and families in a distant area cannot be compared to shamans' cults among the Central Algonquians.

Other types of political organization reflect changes associated with the formation of the Wabanaki Confederacy. Essentially an alliance established in the mid-eighteenth century among the Micmac, Maliseet, Passamaquoddy, Penobscot, and Abenaki, it embraced other tribes allied to the French and had its "great fire" or principal meeting place at Caughnawaga, Quebec.

Delegates from each of the component groups attended triannual meetings and participated in ceremonies at Caughnawaga. Mnemonic use of wampum was introduced to the Algonquians at this time as was the election of chiefs, both customs due to Iroquois inspiration. The Wabanaki Confederacy ceased to meet sometime in the second half of the nineteenth century. The Wampum Records obtained in 1887 from Louis Mitchell, a Passamaquoddy, refer to ceremonies pertaining to mourning and burial following the death of a chief, the installation of a new chief, and marriage (Prince 1897). In 1847 Gesner (1847:115–116) wrote: "The chiefs and delegates of the Penobscots, Micmacs and Melicetes hold a Council annually at Pleasant Point . . . where they renew their friendship and establish regulations for the public weal. Each tribe has laws peculiar to itself, and the measures adopted by the Grand Council prevent collision in hunting and fishing." In 1841 Perley (1842) learned that the Grand Council in Caughnawaga had advised the Maliseets at Tobique not to give up any more territory to the Whites, indicating that delegations moved between the two groups periodically. The Passamaquoddy maintained close relations with the Mohawk until about 1870 (Speck 1915c:498).

Myths

Myths of the Maliseet-Passamaquoddy are well known from rich collections obtained around the end of the nineteenth century. In addition, Mechling (1913) has published an interesting collection of European fairy tales in the Maliseet genre. Telling tales began in the fall, and the Kuloskap cycle was not completed until the following spring. Taboos against tale telling in summer prevailed (Ives 1964:6–7). The tradition of myth telling survives in attenuated form with the stories involving "witches" and supernatural power among traditional Maliseet-Passamaquoddy families. At Tobique the Kuloskap cycle was told as late as the early 1940s.

Kuloskap (*kəlòskap*), the culture hero and transformer, was responsible for the creation of natural phenomena along the Saint John River and the transformation of animals into their forms.

Maliseet-Passamaquoddy myths depicted only too clearly the follies of human existence. Mythological characters represented certain qualities: Malsum, Kuloskap's younger twin brother, represented evil (perhaps an element borrowed from Iroquois mythology); Turtle was both buffoon and the ridiculed; Snowshoe hare, *máhtəkwehs,* was both trickster and the tricked. Each was a shaman.

Other tales refer to Maliseet deception of raiding Mohawks and the movement of the cannibal giants, the *kiwáhkwəyək,* into Maliseet-Passamaquoddy territory from the frozen north.

Shamanism

Mythological and ethnographic accounts verify the finding that "the greater part of Wabanaki mythology is shamanistic in character" (Speck 1919:258). Curing practices are adequately related by the early French sources, although these do not refer specifically to the Maliseet-Passamaquoddy (Denys 1908:417; JR 3:117–125; Le Clercq 1910:217 ff.). Accompanied by chants the shaman blew over the affected part, if not the entire body. If blowing brought no results the spot was sucked or incised. Gyles gives no description of the shaman's curing ceremony but mentions the sweat lodge and its use in divining success in hunting.

Traditional belief in spirits and supernatural powers persists despite more than 350 years of White contact. Both Speck (1919) and Mechling (1958–1959) give full accounts, and the survey of Wallis and Wallis (1957) and N.N. Smith's (1954, 1964) publications, as well as present-day ethnographic enquiries, show that native beliefs, if abridged, are far from extinct.

A person having a spirit helper is *mətéwələn*; contemporary Maliseets refer to him or her as "witch." These wonder workers attempted to outdo their rivals and demonstrate superior power. The spirit helper, or *pohíkən,* which took an animal form, was sent by the shaman usually in a dream to acquire the necessary information or to follow the shaman's bidding.

How a *mətéwələn* acquired his power is shrouded in confusion. He might be born with the power, especially if he was the younger of twins, was born with a cowl, or was the seventh son. Although this belief may be of European origin and a modern phenomenon, the seventh son of a seventh son is thought to be especially powerful (S.K. Squires 1930:12). Leland (1884:340) in reference to the Passamaquoddy writes that capricious infants show they were born *mətéwələn.* Prince writes that others were formally trained from boyhood on by experienced practitioners. Others acquired their powers, unexpectedly, through dreams.

Any injury to the *pohíkən* was transferred simultaneously to the *mətéwələn*. Most accounts indicate that only the person injuring the *pohíkən* could cure the *mətéwələn*. Finally, taboo relationships existed between the *mətéwələn* and his *pohíkən*. The *mətéwələn* could neither kill nor refer to his *pohíkən*.

The body of one *mətéwələn* killed by another one was said not to rot; it was capable of eating another if someone should pass too closely. When the corpse had eaten three people it became a *kìwahkw,* or cannibal ice giant. Strength of the *kìwahkw* was determined by the size of the ice heart within its body. Female ice giants had more power than their male counterparts (Leland 1884: 246–247).

The Maliseet believed that certain objects contained mana, or *keskamsit.* Such objects, chosen because of their strange appearance, were thought to bring good luck. A person did not have unlimited *keskamsit;* rather, one might have *keskamsit* for hunting or fishing, another for paddling a canoe, and a third for lovemaking. Rarely did a person have more than one *keskamsit.* A person acquired bad luck in much the same way he did *keskamsit*: with the same emotional thrill, but without an amulet. Wasteful slaughter of game was a cause of bad luck (Mechling 1958–1959:198–199).

Supernatural Beings

Supernatural beings of various kinds are part of the Maliseet-Passamaquoddy pantheon. In terms of function they are (1) agents of social control, (2) forerunners, or (3) sources of special power. The boogeyman *apotámkin* is a good example of the first; he keeps small children off freshly formed ice in fall or off unguarded beaches in summer (O'Dowd 1889). Forerunners are numerous and are given a variety of names. The older word for ghost is *nisekəpísit* (Passamaquoddy) or *kisekəpísit* (Maliseet). This creature might serve as a premonition of death (N.N. Smith 1957:31). A creature all head and limbs, who warns of impending calamities, is *(k)čipélahkw,* while *kéhtakws* is the new term for ghost. A Maliseet from Woodstock became *kéhtakws,* and his whooping could be heard whenever there was a storm. His mournful laugh forewarned every death on the reservation (N.N. Smith 1954:52, 1957:30). The ball of fire, *eskwətéwit,* was the more common and mobile forerunner of death and tragedy. It was also the portion of a person that left the body in dreams and was capable of traveling great distances (N.N. Smith 1954:53; Teeter 1967). The Maliseet as well as the Passamaquoddy believed in the little people. To the Maliseet the *kiwələtəmohsísək* made concretions of sand and clay along the stream banks. Through the objects they leave behind one can divine the future. A small coffin-shaped object forewarned death.

Scrapings taken from the horns of *wiwíləmekw,* a sea monster, now often described as an alligator, were thought to be especially powerful and could confer benefits to the individual who showed courage in the face of the monster (Leland 1884:324ff.). *wiwíləmekw* could also serve as one's *pohíkən.*

Music and Dance

The Maliseet used both a board to beat time on and a drum to accompany their dances. Rattles made from a stag's horn and filled with shot set the time for the dance. Other musical instruments were the flageolet and the flute.

Dances were for religious power. Gyles describes a dance associated with a feast of dog heads preparatory to going into battle. Both Gyles (1851) and Pote (1896) recount dances at Meductic, when war captives were tortured. In the twentieth century exhibition dances were performed by adult Maliseet males for White spectators until at least 1920. In the 1970s the Passamaquoddy from Pleasant Point had an adult dance group, but only children's groups or mixed groups from Tobique and Kingsclear performed for Whites and other Indian groups.

Games

The gambling game, *altestákən,* using round bone disks as dice and a wooden bowl, was a favorite pastime in Gyles's time and was still played in the 1970s in Kingsclear. Both Mechling (1958–1959:205–214) and Mrs. W. W. Brown (1889) give full accounts. Two ring and pin games were also performed. In addition to lacrosse (fig. 9), two other kinds of ball games were known, one similar to baseball, a second to football. Baseball was formerly played when the tribe reassembled in spring after the winter hunt. Since the 1920s regulation baseball has been a favorite game for Maliseet men and children (fig. 10). Other games of skill, snow snakes, shooting bows and arrows with betting on the results, and foot races were popular activities during the spring assembly. At the end of the nineteenth century these were replaced by rifle shooting.

The trading dance was winter entertainment. Goods were distributed from person to person, the aim being to pass off an almost worthless or novelty item to an unsuspecting host. Burlin (1907:16) contains the song that accompanied this dance.

Folk Medicine

There is discrepancy in the data as to whether a person skilled in the knowledge and uses of roots and herbs was *mətéwələn* or not. Biard (JR 3:117) says he was, Speck (1919:260) says he was not. Contemporary middle-aged Maliseet do not distinguish the witch and the herb doctor, implying that anyone who has herbal knowledge has supernatural powers, too. The herb doctor was as often a man as a woman. Some remedies were owned or known only by certain people, and the individual wishing the

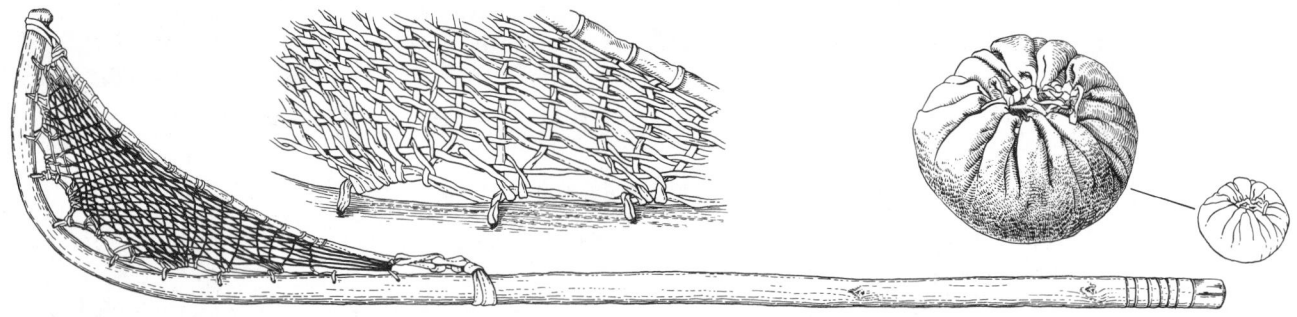

Dept. of Anthr., Smithsonian: 11425, 11426.

Fig. 9. Passamaquoddy racket and ball for lacrosse. Inset shows closely woven thong netting. The ball is made of a single piece of hide with a thong drawstring, diameter 8.0 cm; collected 1872.

preparation would have to pay for it. Three or four persons in a community had the reputation of being herbalists.

Information about herbal remedies was passed on by the aged to younger persons who showed special aptitude. Herbalists were reluctant to tell others of their medicines because with each telling the preparation lost some of its efficacy. Extensive lists of Maliseet herbal remedies are available (Mechling 1958-1959:241, 243-259; Van Wart 1948; N.N. Smith 1964). A few remedies were still used in the 1970s.

© Natl. Geographic Soc., Washington, D.C.

Fig. 10. Chief Joe Nicholas (left), Passamaquoddy, and Chief William Saulis (right), Maliseet, at an intertribal baseball game on the Passamaquoddy reservation near Eastport, Me. Photograph by Harrison Howell Walker, July-Aug. 1937.

The 1960s

Writers around 1900, including at least one Maliseet (in Squires 1968:52), commented on culture loss among the Maliseet-Passamaquoddy and predicted that within 50 years there would be neither a native language spoken nor an Indian identity felt. Persistence of, or a rejuvenation of, Indian traditions and values since 1965 shows how unmerited the pessimistic views were (fig. 11).

The Maine Department of Indian Affairs was established in 1965 with the goals of "initiating programs aimed at human and community development . . . based on expressed needs of the Indian people" (Maine. Department of Indian Affairs 1971a:13) as well as administering more routine immediate responsibilities, such as general assistance and reservation facilities. Among the Passamaquoddy, this department appears to have promoted a stronger feeling of Indian identity. In 1973 the

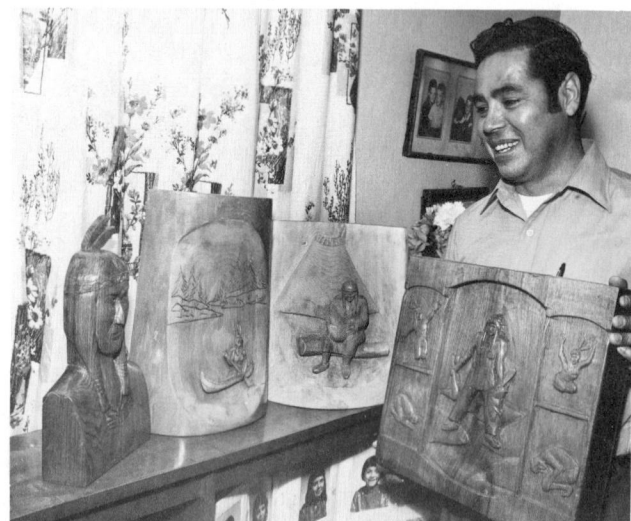

The Daily Gleaner, Fredericton, N.B.

Fig. 11. George Paul, Maliseet sculptor from St. Mary's, showing some of the work he exhibited at the Canadian National Exhibition in Toronto. Photograph by Ian Brown, August 17, 1971.

134

commissioner of Indian affairs for the state of Maine was a Passamaquoddy.

The Association of Aroostook Indians was established in 1970 (Anonymous 1972:2) through the cooperation of local Micmacs and Maliseets and Ricker College in Houlton, Maine. Among the goals stated in the charter is the initiation of programs in community development and social services. As the Maine Department of Indian Affairs is concerned only with programs for reservation Indians, the AAI, in part, tries to parallel social projects carried out by the state department and to initiate others.

Indian identity in New Brunswick was strengthened through the founding of the Union of New Brunswick Indians in 1967 (Erickson and Hunsley 1970:4). Maliseet-Micmac cooperation has been fostered through capable, articulate, and verbal executives of the organization. Definite progress in intertribal cooperation has occurred with the reduction of factionalism and autonomy of the component Maliseet-Micmac bands.

Maliseet-Passamaquoddy cooperation occurred through joint interests in the nonprofit corporation T.R.I.B.E., Teaching and Research in Bicultural Education, founded in 1969. With the Micmac and Penobscot, the groups helped improve the status of Indian education in eastern Canada and Maine (Sockabasin and Stone 1971:23-24). After T.R.I.B.E. became defunct, a similar project, the Passamaquoddy Bilingualism and Biculturalism Program, directed by Wayne Newell, a Passamaquoddy educator, introduced instruction in Passamaquoddy language and culture at Peter Dana Point School.

In practice these organizations represent the Maliseet-Passamaquoddy as well as encourage them to regain a pride in their past—their language and their culture—and to provide them with the opportunities to participate more equitably in the larger North American society. The first citizens of the Saint Croix and the Saint John through a developing body of Maliseet-Passamaquoddy leaders have a voice that, if not yet equipped to direct the destiny of their culture, is in the process of capably shaping it.

Synonymy

The term Etchemin, recorded at Tadoussac, is of unknown origin; it may have been Algonquin or Montagnais but is not a rendering of *skičin* 'Indian' in modern Maliseet-Passamaquoddy. All Etchemin groups are thought to have spoken mutually intelligible dialects in the seventeenth century and were regarded by the early explorers as one people.

A term related to Maliseet appears to have been first used in 1692 by Cadillac (1930) when he referred to the Marisiz. Amalecites was used by Chauvignerie (NYCD 9:1052) in 1736 and continued to be the term used by the French in reference to the Maliseets in Quebec into the twentieth century. In New Brunswick, Milicite and Melicite were common spellings in the nineteenth century. Early twentieth-century ethnographers selected Malecite, but the contemporary Indians prefer Maliseet. The word is from Micmac where it probably means 'lazy speakers'. The Maliseets of New Brunswick call themselves *wəlastəkwíyək* 'St. John's River people' or simply, the Saint John River Indians (*wəlàstəkw* 'St. John's River' is explained as 'beautiful river' by folk etymology). Some Micmacs refer to the Maliseets as Muskrat Indians or muskrat eaters.

Cadillac (1930:93) referred to the region around the Saint Croix River as Pesmocady in 1692, and the Indians living there were named after the area. They are the Passamaquoddy, who call themselves *pestəmohkatíyək* (singular *pestəmohkat*). This seems to have originally meant literally 'those of the place where pollock are plentiful' (with the Micmac word for 'pollock' *pestəm*), although at present there is no name used for Passamaquoddy Bay from which the form could be derived. Other imputed synonyms for the Passamaquoddy are listed by Mooney (1910:207-208).

Sources

Among seventeenth-century sources the descriptions of Lescarbot, Champlain, and Biard, who were in both Etchemin and Micmac territory, do not always separate the two groups. A valuable account from the end of the century is given by John Gyles (1851), who lived among the Maliseet as a captive. The most accessible edition (Trueman 1966) is not a verbatim account of the original Gyles, and the serious student should not use it exclusively.

Maillard (1758) describes the Maliseet and the Micmac as practically identical cultures. Pote (1896) and Campbell (1937) give accounts of Maliseet country in the eighteenth century.

Perley (1842), an influential Indian commissioner and champion of the Indian, and Levinge (1846) are the best sources on the Maliseet from the nineteenth century. Gesner (1847, 1849), Hamilton-Gordon (1864), Vetromile (1866), Kilby (1888), Shove (1866), and Baird (1890) provide valuable information.

On the Passamaquoddy, W.D. Williamson (1832) provides a good summary of early sources. Vroom (1892-1894) contains a fine summary of the Passamaquoddy role in New Brunswick and Maine history.

Twentieth-century contributions include Raymond (1910) on the pre-Loyalist period, Bailey (1969) on sixteenth- and seventeenth-century acculturation, Hoffman (1955a) on early tribal groupings and names, and Leger (1929) on Catholic missions before 1820. G. F. Clarke (1968) has written a general historical-archeological study of the Maliseet.

Anthropological materials are fuller for the Maliseet than for the Passamaquoddy. Mechling (1914, 1958-1959) is the result of fieldwork during 1910-1912. Speck (1919) contains frequent comparative notes on the Maliseet. The other major study is Wallis and Wallis (1957). N.N. Smith has published specialized short papers on medicine (1964, 1966), religious beliefs (1954), tobacco (1957a), and dances (1955, 1962), in addition to a general study (1957). Most of Smith's informants were Maliseet or Passamaquoddy. McFeat (1962, 1962a) has published studies on contemporary Maliseet crafts; his other manuscripts and reports are on deposit at the National Museum of Canada in Ottawa. Speck's shorter studies, while usually not restricted to one Wabanaki group, contain excellent data on the Maliseet. Valuable are his works on the Wabanaki Confederacy (1915c), game totems (1917), reptile lore (1923), and plants and animals (Speck and Dexter 1952), as well as his theoretical studies on Algonquian social organization (Speck 1915d, 1917a, 1918, 1920, 1926, 1935). Speck and Hadlock (1946) give data on Maliseet hunting territories. Although Adney's published accounts on the Maliseet are not extensive (1944; Adney and Chapelle 1964), his unpublished manuscripts and notes (1887-1950) on deposit at Peabody Museum of Salem, Salem, Massachusetts, provide the largest corpus of unpublished Maliseet materials. Jack (1881, 1893), D.R. Jack (1901), and M. Chamberlain (1898, 1902, 1904), although not trained anthropologists, spent years with the Maliseet and had firsthand knowledge of the culture.

Ethnographic accounts of the Passamaquoddy are restricted to games and chief-making by Mrs. W. W. Brown (1889, 1892). Leland (1884), Leland and Prince (1902), and Alger (1897) provide full accounts of the folklore, largely of the Passamaquoddy and Micmac, but the Maliseet are sometimes incorrectly listed as Micmac. Ives (1964) presented a surprisingly full study from the 1950s. Shorter papers on folklore have been written by Fewkes (1890), Jack (1895), Mechling (1913), O'Dowd (1889), Stamp (1915), and Watson (1907). Stevens (1977) has prepared a thoughtful and insightful account of the Passamaquoddy that is especially valuable for the mid-twentieth century.

Linguistic materials include a vocabulary by M. Chamberlain (1899) and numerous studies by Prince (1897, 1898, 1899, 1901, 1909, 1914, 1917) culminating in his *Passamaquoddy Texts* (1921). Teeter (1967, 1971) has published analyses of Maliseet-Passamaquoddy grammar. Szabo (1971) has worked on Maliseet linguistics for several years and has deposited a massive manuscript of native texts at the National Museum of Canada.

For the Maliseet, undergraduate and graduate students and staff at the University of New Brunswick are preparing studies on native medicines, education, recent political movements, settlement patterns, literacy programs, and a collection of life histories. Willard Walker and his students at Wesleyan University have made studies on the Passamaquoddy for a number of years.

Eastern Abenaki

DEAN R. SNOW

Language

As with many of the Eastern Algonquian speakers of New England and the Maritime provinces, the name of the Eastern Abenaki derives from *wɑpánahki*, their own name for themselves, meaning 'dawn land people' or 'easterners'. In English it is usually pronounced ˌäbə'näkē or ˌăbə'näkē. The former is preferred. Wabanaki (ˌwäbə'näkē) is sometimes used, but usually in a broader sense, such that it includes the Western Abenaki, Maliseet-Passamaquoddy, and Micmac as well. Abnaki, which appears in the literature, is inappropriate because of the loss of a syllable. Many other variations of both spelling and pronunciation also occur. Members of the only enclave of Eastern Abenaki to survive within their traditional homeland are known as the Penobscot (pə'näbˌskät) Indians.

Linguistically, Eastern Abenaki belongs to the continuum of Eastern Algonquian languages that in A.D. 1600 were spoken by tribes living in the coastal river drainages from northeastern North Carolina to Nova Scotia. The Eastern Abenaki spoke a single language having certain internal dialectal variants.* There was a strong tendency for dialects to separate according to major river drainage basins. This linguistic subdivision paralleled political subdivision within the Eastern Abenaki. Primary linguistic and political units were composed of people that interacted with one another on a regular basis, and these units were usually confined to specific river or major tributary drainages. Additionally, there was a tendency for the inhabitants of a major drainage system to bifurcate linguistically and politically into upstream and downstream (tidewater) components. Figure 1 shows the probable linguistic subdivisions of the language at the time of initial European colonization. Of these, the Penobscot dialect is best known, followed by the Kennebec, Arosaguntacook, and Pigwacket dialects in that order. Other dialectal units that are given for the

*The appropriate orthography for Eastern Abenaki is that of Frank T. Siebert, which writes the consonants *p, t, č, k, kʷ, l, s, h, w, y, m, n,* short vowel *ə,* and length-indifferent vowels *a, ɑ, e, i, o.* These symbols have values consistent with the standard transcriptional system of the *Handbook;* ɑ represents a tense, low back slightly centralized vowel. The stressed syllable of each word is marked with an accent, with ´ for a pitch that is higher than that of surrounding syllables and ` for stress without pitch rise. Italicized words have been spelled in this orthography by Frank T. Siebert (personal communication 1974).

Eastern Abenaki in other sources are for the most part either synonymous with or subsumed under the four defined here.

Territory

Precise geographical boundaries are possible only because the Eastern Abenaki defined their homeland in terms of river drainages. The boundaries shown in figure 1 run along heights of land that separated drainage basins, and their precision should not be construed as evidence that linguistic and political divisions were as neatly drawn. These people saw themselves as inhabitants of rivers and smaller streams. At first contact, they had no concept of territoriality that could be regarded as in any way equivalent to European concepts. The domain of the Penobscot, for example, simply faded away in the hinterlands away from the river, as the domain of another body of Indians was approached. Within each drainage, smaller subdivisions were made on the basis of tributary drainage basins, down to the level of the local family band. This has led to the confusing array of place names used to identify the Eastern Abenaki and their various subdivisions, especially in the early sources.

An anonymous description published by Samuel Purchas in 1625 indicates that in the early part of that century, the Eastern Abenaki were confederated under the leadership of a man called Bashabes. The name appears elsewhere in various early sources and in several forms, including Bessabez (Champlain 1907:46) and Betsabes (JR 3:297). He was one of 23 "sagamores" named for 21 villages on 11 rivers. He appears to have been first among equals, the acknowledged leader of all the Eastern Abenaki.

The "countrey of Mawooshen," as it is described by Purchas, was composed of villages on Mount Desert Island, and the Penobscot, Orland, Bagaduce, Muscongus, Damariscotta, Sheepscot, Kennebec, Androscoggin, Presumpscot, and upper Saco rivers. On figure 1, "Arosaguntacook" identifies the inhabitants of the Androscoggin drainage, and "Pigwacket" identifies those of the Presumpscot and upper Saco. Other rivers, such as the Orland, are minor coastal streams that are included in the Kennebec and Penobscot drainages. The number of houses and adult men in each village is provided in the description, but several of the villages and sagamores cannot be identified in other early writings. Neverthe-

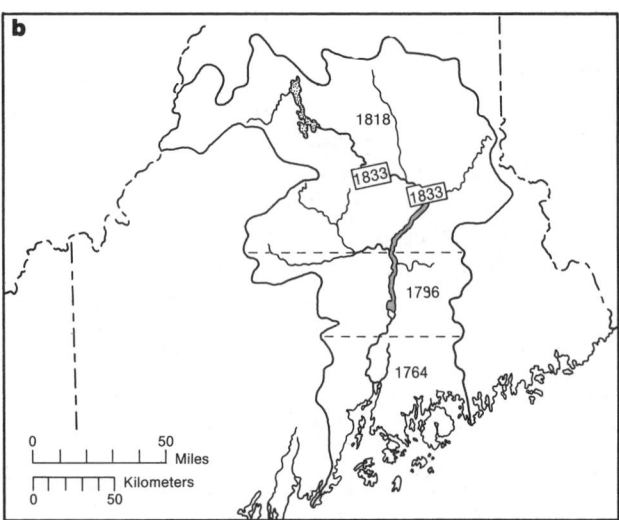

Fig. 1. Tribal territory. a, linguistic subdivisions; b, Penobscot land cessions. Darker shaded area indicates islands still owned by Penobscots in 1975.

less, the description suggests a total of about 1,250 houses and 3,000 adult men, or a total population of about 10,000 in A.D. 1600. Other estimates are possible. This one indicates that there were about eight persons in each household.

The Western Abenaki lived to the westward, mostly in New Hampshire. Champlain (1907:61) noted important cultural differences between them and the Eastern Abe-

naki; accordingly, he called them and the people he encountered farther south Armouchiquois. However, he did not carefully differentiate the Maliseet-Passamaquoddy from the Eastern Abenaki. He encountered the former first, correctly identified them as "Etchemin," but then extended the convenient term to cover the Eastern Abenaki as well. Later writers perpetuated the slip, and some modern writers have incorrectly concluded that the area defined in figure 1 was occupied by the ancestors of the Maliseet-Passamaquoddy in 1605.

The Eastern Abenaki were only sporadically allied to neighboring groups around A.D. 1600. Relations with the Micmac were particularly hostile, although European colonization later caused the disappearance of these and other antagonisms. The Micmac were called "Tarrantine" by many early writers (see Gorges 1890), but later use of this term was imprecise, and some more recent writers have incorrectly applied it to the Eastern Abenaki.

Culture in 1610

There are enough sources to allow the reconstruction of Eastern Abenaki culture for the period just before the epidemics of the early seventeenth century. Samuel de Champlain and John Smith saw horticulture along the coast only as far northeast as the Saco River, the lower portions of which were not occupied by the Eastern Abenaki. There is some evidence that horticulture was practiced upstream along the Kennebec, but it would have been a marginal effort at best. The territory of the Eastern Abenaki was covered by a mixed white pine, hemlock, and hardwood forest in coastal areas, changing to a spruce and fir forest in the interior. Neither the soil nor the climate was adequate for the available domesticates. A real economic commitment to horticulture was not possible until the fur trade made winter residence in large villages possible and provided the option of purchasing food in years of crop failure.

Subsistence was based primarily upon an annual round of hunting and gathering. Spring was spent on the coast exploiting runs of alewives, salmon, shad, eel, smelt, and other fish with hooks, leisters, pursenets, and weirs. Eels and salmon could be taken in quantity a second time, when they returned to the sea. Some fish were taken with harpoons, particularly sturgeons, which were attracted to the surface by torches at night. Lobsters and crabs were speared from canoes in shallow water.

Shellfish, particularly clams (*Mya arenaria*), were practically a staple for some groups at certain times of the year. Both clams and eels could be taken from tidal flats even in the winter as emergency rations. The spring and summer diet was supplemented by various berries, cherries, grapes, and other wild fruits. Perhaps the most important gathered plant was the ground nut (*Apios americana*), a starchy tuber prepared and eaten like potatoes. Springtime also made available the sap of the sugar maple, although this may not have been boiled down to syrup or sugar until the introduction of metal pots.

Harbor seals, porpoise, and various waterfowl were taken in the warm months. Before the adoption of horticulture and life in larger villages, fall required the dispersal of family bands into the interior. The cold months were spent hunting moose, deer, caribou, and bear. Beaver, muskrat, otter, and other fur-bearing animals were trapped. Winter subsistence usually required frequent movement on snowshoes (fig. 2) and toboggan. However, for each family band, this movement appears to have been confined to the drainage basin of a particular tributary stream. Exploitation rights within those areas apparently became more rigidly defined with the development of the fur trade.

The hunter usually carried a bow and arrows (fig. 2), a long lance, and a knife. Other necessary equipment usually included a game bag and a smaller bag made of a woodchuck skin to carry a fire-making kit of iron pyrite and chert nodules. Canoes (fig. 3), made of the bark of the white birch, were usually big enough to hold a family of five or six, plus their dogs and all their belongings. Folded bark containers were also made, and like canoes, were sewed with split spruce or cedar roots (fig. 4). Small containers could also be made from bark fibers (fig. 5), rush, sweetgrass, or leather, and the best examples were decorated with white or dyed porcupine quills. Baskets were also made of ash splints in later years, the tech-

nique having been introduced by Europeans. Dishes, spoons, and trays were carved from burls. Widemouthed pottery vessels were manufactured; these were typically thick-walled, tempered with bits of shell, decorated with cord impressions, and provided with round to conical bases. Smoking pipes were made from both clay and stone. Most of these small items were quickly replaced by European trade goods.

Like most other Algonquians in northern areas, they carried "crooked" knives. This implement may have originally developed as a hafted beaver incisor, or it may have been introduced by Europeans. In either case, it had a metal blade in 1610, a curved one not unlike that of a farrier's knife. European contacts also led to the introduction of metal-toothed gauges for evenly cutting strips of ash used in basketmaking.

Dogs were not used to pull or carry loads. They were kept for pets and for tracking game. Meat taken was distributed to other members of the band according to well-defined custom. The first kill of the season was given away completely, as was the first kill of every boy, even if it were only a small squirrel.

Houses were either hemispherical with a circular floor plan, or pyramidal, in which case the floor plan could be square. Houses were shingled with sheets of bark. There

U. Mus., U. of Penn.

Fig. 3. Penobscots building a moosehide canoe. The wet dehaired hide is being stretched and sewed over the elm-pole gunwales. Split cedar in the foreground will be used for the canoe's ribs and lining strips. Usually made after a hunt to carry home game, the canoe would later be taken apart and the hides used for other purposes (Speck 1940). Photograph by Frank Speck, Old Town, Me., 1911.

U. Mus., U. of Penn.

Fig. 2. Penobscots hunting at Lincoln, Me. The father's equipment consists of a bow and arrows and a basswood carrying bag, while his son's includes a gun and ash-splint pack basket. They wear "pollywog" style snowshoes (Speck 1940). Photograph by Frank Speck, 1911.

was a center post and a slab of rock to protect it from the adjacent fire. There were normally two doors, each covered by a deerskin. One was usually left open to provide an adequate draft for smoke exiting through a smokehole at the apex of the house. Houses were modified to meet varying needs. They could be sealed tight to hold heat in the winter or used as sweatlodges in the summer. In warm months, they were ventilated without difficulty.

Marriage was usually accompanied by the transfer of goods to the woman's family from that of her new husband. The amount of the bride price depended upon the attractiveness of the woman and the status of her father. There was occasional polygyny, confined by custom to the leading men. A sagamore often had two or more wives, primarily so that he could have more children and so that he had adequate assistance in carrying out the social obligations that went with his status. A man with several wives was able to organize more and bigger feasts than other men.

The pattern of menstrual seclusion and unassisted childbirth was like similar patterns that were widespread in North America. The severity of life in the winter

months contributed to infant mortality. Children born in the wrong season often could not survive.

Leadership was normally vested in assertive men who acquired the necessary qualifications through the force of their own personalities. Leadership was not hereditary in a strict sense, but there was a tendency for it to be transferred patrilineally. There are several popular English variants of the Eastern Algonquian words for strong man available. Sagamore comes closest to the Eastern Abenaki form *sàkəmα* and is used here to refer to local leaders. A sagamore was usually the head of a large kindred. He increased his family and gathered relatives by marrying as many wives as he could reasonably support. He established patron-client relationships with both these and nonrelatives to extend his power further. He was sometimes also a shaman, an attribute that further increased his charisma and coercive power. Bashabes was an extraordinary example of such a man. His authority extended over all the Eastern Abenaki. After his death, local sagamores usually operated as free agents; the Eastern Abenaki were politically disunited for nearly 100 years. The complete succession of chief sagamores is known only for the Penobscot. Lifetime appointments were superseded by annual elections in 1866.

Fig. 4. Penobscot birchbark container with rectangular bottom decorated with incised double-curve motif. The design on the other side is shown in the drawing (after Lowie 1910). The side seams and maple hoop rim are stitched with spruce root. Collected in 1909; height 20 cm.

Fig. 5. Penobscot woman weaving basswood carrying bag. Strips of the inner bark of the basswood tree are boiled with wood ashes to soften the fiber and shaved down to the desired width to be used in weaving. Photograph by Frank Speck, probably 1911.

Penobscot Chief Sagamores

Bashabes	?	–	1616(?)
Asticou	1615	–	?
Madockawando	?	–	1698
Wenongonet	1698	–	1724
Wenemouet (name changed to Wenongonet 1726)	1724	–	1730
Egeremet	1730	–	ca.1750
Wabemando (Louis)	ca.1750	–	ca.1760
Orson	ca.1760	–	ca.1777
Joseph Orono	ca.1777	–	1801
Attean Elmut	1806	–	1809
Joe Lola	1810	–	ca.1812
John Attean	1816	–	1858
Joseph Attean	1858	–	1870

Aboriginal dress consisted almost entirely of animal skins. A single covering tied over one shoulder and under the opposite arm was common. Beaver pelts were popular for both robes and smaller garments such as breechcloths. Moose hides were dressed on both sides and decorated with painted designs. Sleeves and leggings were separate accessories that were added when weather conditions required. Both sexes wore hide moccasins, and both usually went bareheaded. Sagamores sometimes wore coronets of red deer bristles or white feathered bird skins. Facial and body painting was frequent.

Sickness was often treated by sweating. Shamans also cured using various laxatives, teas, and salves for visible injuries. Internal illness required magical remedies as well. The shaman attempted to blow or dance the illness away, sometimes placing the patient on a surface covered with magical totemic signs, such as those still visible on a rock near Solon, Maine. Predicted death was often hastened by the patient and his relatives by neglect and starvation. A dying man distributed some of his belongings to relatives; the rest were buried with him.

History

Early Colonial Period

Various explorers, most notably Giovanni da Verrazano, contacted the Eastern Abenaki during the sixteenth century, but it was not until the beginning of the seventeenth century that prolonged colonial contacts began. Verrazano labeled the Penobscot River "Norumbega," and David Ingram concocted an elaborate fantasy about the place 60 years later (Wroth 1970; Hakluyt 1965:557–562). Ingram's imaginary fairyland never existed, but it helped stimulate interest in English colonization. Martin Pring looked the coast over in 1603, and Pierre DuGua de Monts and Champlain explored the

Mus. of the Amer. Ind., Heye Foundation, New York.

Fig. 6. Wearing a mooseskin coat and mask of deer scalp, this Penobscot is dressed to participate in the Clown or Trading Dance, a popular gaming ceremony performed at night, at which the spectators bartered with the clown. Photograph by Frank Speck, 1912.

same area a few months later. Champlain visited Kenduskeag in 1604 and the Kennebec River in 1605. The Eastern Abenaki showed a strong interest in fur trade with the French.

George Waymouth brought an English expedition to the area in 1605, but he failed to make a favorable impression. He kidnapped five men and took them back to England. Ferdinando Gorges obtained permission to colonize the area, and two years later sent out George Popham and Raleigh Gilbert with one of Waymouth's captives to establish a colony. Relations with the Indians were strained, and the winter severe. The attempt was abandoned in 1608.

French Jesuit missionaries were in Port Royal (Nova Scotia) converting Indians by 1611. The attempt by Pierre Biard and others to establish a mission in Eastern Abenaki country was quickly crushed by the English two years later. John Smith's is the last description of the area before the devastating effects of war and disease drastically altered Eastern Abenaki culture. The Micmac (Tarrantine) had been raiding in the area since at

Table 1. Eastern Abenaki Wars

Wars	Durations	English Treaties	American Treaties
Tarrantine War	1607–1615		
King Philip's War	1675–1678	1676	
		1678	
		1685	
King William's War	1688–1699	1690	
		1693	
		1699	
		1701	
Queen Anne's War	1702–1713	1703	
		1713	
		1714	
		1717	
Dummer's War	1721–1725	1725	
		1726	
		1727	
King George's War	1745–1748	1749	
		1752	
French and Indian War	1755–1759	1762	
Revolutionary War	1775–1782		1786
			1796
			1818
			1820
			1833

Mus of the Amer. Ind., Heye Foundation, New York.

Fig. 7. Costumed for a dress occasion, this Penobscot man wears a beaded cloth coat, leggings, and hood. Undecorated hoods horned like this one to represent an owl, were used as a disguise by hunters approaching deer. On the man's left is a decorated birchbark container. Photograph by Frank Speck, 1917.

least 1607. By 1615, they penetrated as far as Kenduskeag and killed Bashabes. That was the end of the Tarrantine War (see table 1), but it was soon followed by a resurgence of European diseases. The population was reduced by as much as half, villages were abandoned, and the resumption of many old social and political institutions was made virtually impossible.

Eastern Abenaki material culture was changing rapidly by 1620, as first French and later English goods became available. Utilitarian items such as iron axes, needles, guns, knives, glass beads, and broadcloth were obtained in trade for furs. The aboriginal analogues of these items were disappearing rapidly. Generally, the French and English traders were still dependent upon the Indians for emergency rations. Nevertheless, their economic influence was strong, and the old reciprocal exchange and redistribution patterns between band members began to change as exchange shifted gradually to Indians trading individually with European traders.

By 1626 the English colonists at Plymouth were trading regularly with the Eastern Abenaki. The English had access to supplies of corn and wampum in southern New England and could trade them for furs. Wampum, made extensively after the introduction of metal drills, became an important medium of economic exchange as well as an important medium of political and social symbolism.

Within a few years, settlers were following traders into the tidewater area of Maine west of the Penobscot. Quitclaims, which were later treated as deeds, were obtained from Indians who seem not to have intended the transferred rights to be either exclusive or permanent. Still, English settlement was not yet very provocative.

The Indians took advantage of the reliable trade to concentrate on the fur industry. There were now fewer villages, as surviving members of older communities congregated. The old pattern of winter dispersal of the whole population into the interior was undergoing modification; the purpose was now to obtain furs for the trade economy, rather than to hunt for subsistence and survival until spring. Those not directly engaged in trapping and hunting for furs could remain in the main villages, assured of survival on food obtained from storage or trade with the English. The availability of southern New England corn through English middlemen and the year-round occupation of main villages by at least part of the population allowed an increased commitment to local horticulture that the Eastern Abenaki could not have risked previously. Seventeenth-century accounts indicate simultaneous increases in local horticulture and late-winter dependency on bartered staple foods. Subsistence no longer required intensive coastal exploitation, so summer residence there gradually became optional. The people of the Penobscot drainage continued coastal hunting and gathering into the nineteenth century, but the English took over the southern Maine coast without significant opposition.

Eventually, rapid English colonization began to threaten the Eastern Abenaki. French settlements were not similarly swelled by immigration, but Capuchin and Jesuit missionaries became active again. The Jesuits provided a particularly important ideological counter to English domination. English incursions and Mohawk raids punctuated the years leading up to King Philip's War. The trading post at Pentagoet, originally established by the French, began to change hands as Europeans fought for trade advantages. In 1670 the French adventurer Jean-Vincent D'Abbadie de Saint-Castin settled there, married the daughter of the Penobscot Sagamore Madockawando, and thereby helped secure the Eastern Abenaki in the French interest.

King Philip's War broke out in southern New England in 1675. War spread to northern New England largely because of the murder of an infant child of Squando, sagamore on the Saco. The Eastern Abenaki held out for peace, but the English were suspicious and made the outrageous demand that the Indians turn in their guns. Guns were by now essential to the economic survival of the Indians, and the English attitude made war virtually inevitable.

The first of 17 treaties between the English and the Eastern Abenaki was drawn up in 1676. Mog, a leader from the Kennebec region, was forced to sign it, and it was therefore largely ignored by the Indians. The war was ended by a second treaty in 1678. The Indians were victorious. They gave up nothing, and their coast was virtually abandoned by English settlers. There were five more colonial wars with the English and three times as many treaties, but the Indians were not so successful in later years. French influences at the same time were directed primarily through the Jesuit missionaries. There were no peace treaties as such with the French, only aid agreements. The Eastern Abenaki never fought the French, yet never lost sight of their own interests.

Late Colonial Period

Between 1675 and 1759 the Eastern Abenaki were involved in a series of five wars that were primarily manifestations of the contest for colonial power between England and France. The Indians were supplied and sometimes led by the French, but prolonged hostility with the English was economically devastating. Regular trade with the English had become essential. English settlement was repeatedly arrested, but treaties usually reestablished the status quo as well as critical trade contacts. Tied ideologically to the French and economically to the English, the Eastern Abenaki leaders seem to have perceived that their survival depended upon holding the middle ground between the two colonial powers. While other tribes became landless mercenaries of one or the other, the Eastern Abenaki remained an important third force between New England and New France. A measure of that importance is provided by the large scalp bounties offered by both the English and the French during the colonial wars.

The Jesuit Sébastien Râle established his mission at Norridgewock in 1694. His considerable influence on the Kennebec ended with his death in an English attack on the village near the end of Dummer's War in 1724. The English had destroyed the village at Old Town the previous year. The war is sometimes called Râle's War, or even less appropriately, Lovewell's War. The last is derived from a minor battle involving Capt. John Lovewell, about which more falsehood than truth has been preserved (Eckstorm 1936). Dummer's War was an unusual colonial war in that it was not paralleled by a simultaneous European conflict.

Conference etiquette in the long series of treaties reveals the basic political structure of the four major divisions of the Eastern Abenaki. The treaty of 1713 is particularly informative. In most cases, preliminary negotiations were carried out by delegates, usually four from each major river drainage. After the groundwork was laid, the chief sagamore and the second sagamore of each area took over. Theirs were formal duties, the probable outcome of the meeting already known. What was lost in spontaneity was made up for in elaborate oratory. Sometimes the delegates, rather than the sagamores, performed the mundane task of signing the agreement.

Until 1759 the French concentrated on establishing a buffer zone of friendly Indian tribes between New France and the English. Gov. Pierre de Rigaud, marquis de Vaudreuil and others urged the tribes to confederate toward that end. The Eastern Abenaki were not willing to become mercenaries for the French, but English encroachments forced them in that direction. Internal tensions resulted in the formation of one party favorable to accommodation with the English and another that was pro-French. By the end of Dummer's War, there was some resolution of the split. Many of the Pigwacket and Arosaguntacook as well as some of the Kennebec had left to take up residence in the refugee villages of Bécancour and Saint Francis, Quebec. The Penobscot remained, however, and even took in refugees. Western Maine seemed lost to the English, but the Penobscot drainage was still in Indian hands. Although the Penobscot could not claim victory in the war, they had man-

Gagnon Coll., City of Montreal Lib.

Fig. 8. Costumes of man and woman from Bécancour. Watercolor, eighteenth century.

The Huntington Lib., San Marino, Calif.

Fig. 9. Signatures of "Representatives of Noronjawoke [Norridgewock] of the Fronteers of Massachusets Bay," on a letter to Joseph Dudley, governor of the colony, thanking him for their successful visit to Boston. Letter written and signed by the interpreter John Gyles, Jan. 18, 1713.

aged to establish their own navy with captured vessels in 1724, and the English recognized them as still powerful. At the third of three treaties that ended the war, the Penobscot spoke for all the Eastern Abenaki and for the Maliseet-Passamaquoddy and Micmac as well. From this time on, the Penobscot were preeminent spokesmen for all the surviving "Wabanaki" people in New England and the Maritimes. Eventually, this confederacy was drawn into a larger confederacy that included pro-French tribes such as the Huron and Ottawa as well.

Land, especially in western Maine, was bought up piecemeal by individuals and various groups of English, largely from Indians who had little understanding of English law or no right to sell. Conflicts over land sales and treaty violations were often settled by John Gyles. Captured as a child in King William's War, Gyles returned to act as interpreter for many years. He was one of only a few English colonists who understood the Indians.

By the early eighteenth century, the Eastern Abenaki were living in relatively large villages composed of houses that had bark roofs and log cabin walls. There were only a few such villages in 1755, and most of them were quite vulnerable. When the French and Indian War broke out, the Penobscot remained formally neutral and urged the others to do so as well; however, the other Eastern Abenaki were operating out of Quebec for the most part and had little to lose. They joined the Indians of the Maritimes in attacks on the English. The English

eventually forced the war upon the Penobscot as well, and huge scalp bounties were set as they had been in the previous wars. The war ended with the expulsion of the French from North America in 1759 and the loss of most territorial rights outside the Penobscot drainage to the English. In 1764 the English formally assumed ownership of the lower Penobscot drainage (see fig. 1). The Penobscot could no longer balance themselves between two contending powers. The treaty of 1762 was essentially a capitulation to the English.

Revolution and the Nineteenth Century

To counteract domination by the English, the Penobscot strengthened their ties with the Maliseet-Passamaquoddy, Micmac, Ottawa, Huron, and other former French allies. The center of the confederacy became the "great fire" at Caughnawaga, Quebec. In 1775 the Penobscot sided with the rebelling colonists, partly because it was politically advantageous and partly because the colonists also had the support of the French. Massachusetts, of which Maine was a province, seemed to recognize Penobscot territorial rights north of Bangor, but later there was a dispute over this. The Penobscot fought in local engagements and some more distant expeditions, such as Benedict Arnold's attack on Quebec. They were in a favorable position at the end of the war, but Massachusetts used a misunderstanding of the 1775 pledges as a device to acquire most of the middle Penobscot River drainage. The northern limit of this middle parcel was set in 1786 and clarified in 1796. Within it, the Penobscot retained only the islands in the river from their main village at Old Town northward. Elsewhere they retained two coastal islands.

The search for a new chief sagamore was more impor-

144

tant even than the British presence on the Penobscot River during the War of 1812. An uneasy consensus eventually formed in favor of John Attean and John Neptune as chief sagamore and second sagamore respectively (later styled governor and lieutenant governor). Attean belonged to a moiety composed of families with forest animals as their totems, as had the previous Attean and Joseph Orono. Resistance to him eventually came from members of the moiety of Salt Water' families. The families were the patrilineal descendents of ancient family bands where social and territorial functions had grown with the rise of the fur trade and village nucleation to the point that they assumed many of the features of clans (Snow 1968; Speck 1940: 205–216).

In 1818 Attean attempted to counter an economic decline by selling timber from northern Penobscot lands. Massachusetts claimed that the Indians had no right to sell the timber, and instead pressed for a new treaty. The Penobscot were convinced to give up all but the river islands and four townships around Mattawamkeag and Millinocket. In exchange they received a payment of goods and supplies and a promise of future annual payments. Two years later Maine became a state and assumed both the Penobscot obligation and $30,000 from Massachusetts to carry it out. The four townships were sold to Maine in 1833.

Opposition to the long rule of Attean became strong by 1838. The tribe was split, primarily along moiety lines, with most of what was called the New Party made up of Salt Water families. Designation of these factions as parties has confused later historians who have thought them to be primarily political.

The split within the tribe continued with occasional outbursts until state intervention in 1866. The state ruled that elections for governor and lieutenant governor would be held every year, with the candidates coming from one party (moiety) one year, and from the other the next. It was undemocratic, but a solution well suited to the problem. Elections were later held only every two years, but the alternating system persisted until 1931. The Penobscot dropped out of the confederacy meetings at Caughnawaga in 1862, as attention turned more toward internal matters. Joseph Attean was the last of the chief sagamores selected for life. After 1866 he also served as elected governor for the Old Party until his death in 1870.

In addition to political conflicts, the Penobscot were plagued by outbreaks of cholera during this period. Deaths during epidemics account for some of the minor fluctuations in the population curve, but major declines after 1818 and 1865 appear to have been the result of emigration.

The 1970s

There has been a growing amount of intermarriage over the last century. Young Penobscots have frequently taken Maliseet and Passamaquoddy spouses. Members of other tribes are also represented, and there has been increasing intermarriage with non-Indians. Nevertheless, Old Town remains an important and rapidly growing home base. Figure 10 shows the population curve for the Penobscot since 1720. Figures since 1810 are considered most accurate. The population, including nonresidents, was 815 in January 1970. The tribe now elects a governor and a representative to the state legislature every two years. John M. Mitchell and John Nelson held those offices in 1970. State obligations to the Penobscot are administered by an agent whose office is on the island at Old Town and by a state commissioner of Indian affairs in Augusta. Along with the Passamaquoddy, the Penobscot benefit from treaty agreements with the state alone. They are not covered directly by the federal Bureau of Indian Affairs, an unusual case in the United States. They are nevertheless eligible to benefit from federal programs and are covered by federal legislation regarding Indian citizenship and other general legislation affecting Indians.

The loss of upstream territory in the nineteenth century meant the end of heavy dependence upon the fur trade. Cash income had to be sought elsewhere, and many men became lumberjacks on the big river drives. Some also earned extra money as guides. Most were gradually drawn into the local cash economy, often the lumber mills or shoe factories. Small-scale farming persisted for a few decades because of state subsidies and other artificial incentives; however, marginal farming by either Indians or Whites in the area has been largely abandoned since 1900.

Some communities on upstream islands persisted for many years, but the village on Indian Island at Old Town has gradually become the only viable remaining community. Completion of the bridge to the mainland from Indian Island in 1951 ended the old ferry system and the isolation of the Indian community that it en-

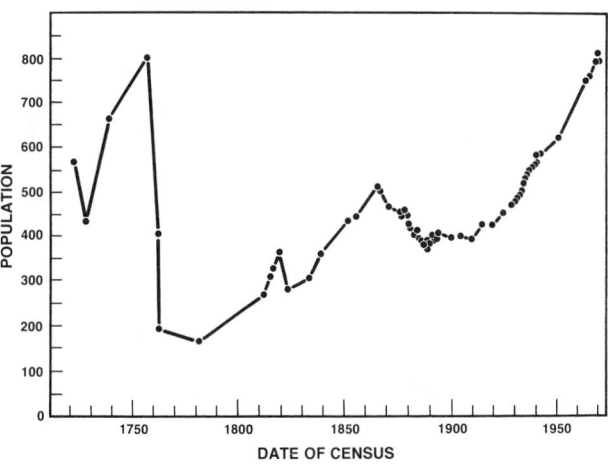

Fig. 10. Population of the Penobscot.

tailed. Most working Penobscots now commute daily from their homes on the island to their work.

Penobscot children still attend their own elementary school but attend secondary schools off the island. A small Catholic mission serves some of the religious and educational needs of the tribe. A minority of the Penobscots attend a Baptist church on the island.

Some crafts, most notably basket and moccasin manufacture, are still carried on. In contrast, the Penobscot dialect is virtually extinct.

Synonymy

Table 2 lists the major synonyms for the Eastern Abenaki and their four major divisions. The table is necessarily simplified. There are many more spelling variants; it is not unusual for an early document to contain four or five spellings of the same term. In addition, many more meanings have been attached to the synonyms than the five clear-cut definitions used here. Researchers are cautioned to proceed carefully through primary sources and to distrust all secondary sources.

The earliest use of the term Abenaki in its various spellings appears to be French. Champlain, the *Jesuit Relations,* and other sources use the term after about 1630, abandoning the earlier extension of Etchemin (Maliseet-Passamaquoddy) to include them. Many later writers lumped them with the Western Abenaki under the heading Openango (spelled variously). English writers of the seventeenth century usually called the Eastern Abenaki simply Eastern Indians. In the nineteenth century the term Tarrantine, a seventeenth-century English name for the Micmac, was revived (as Tarratine) and erroneously applied to the Penobscot (Siebert 1973). Various other obscure and confusing identifications also exist, usually as single instances.

Pigwacket is preferred to Pequawket, the other major form, because it more closely approximates the original pronunciation. As used here, the term includes the Ossipee and the Presumpscot River Indians, but probably excludes the people of the lower Saco River and the Sokoki. The Pigwacket may be the inhabitants of the "Shawakotoc" on the list published by Purchas. The Pigwacket are not clearly isolated in English documents until the treaty of 1690. French sources make specific references to them shortly thereafter (JR 67:31). Pigwacket derives from the Eastern Abenaki word *apík^{w}ahki* 'land of hollows' (F. T. Siebert, personal communication 1974), not from a term meaning 'punched-up-through hill' (Eckstorm 1936:378-379).

Arosaguntacook and Arossagunticook represent Eastern Abenaki *aləssíkɑntək^w* 'river of the cliff dwellings or rock shelters'; the form Androscoggin (River) probably is a corruption or analogical contamination with the name of Massachusetts governor Edmund Andros. The modern Penobscot name for the Saint Francis Abenaki is *aləssikɑ́ntək^{w}əyak*, the Arossaguntacook being one ancestral element in the Saint Francis population. The meanings 'river abounding in shellfish' (Speck 1940:18) and 'fish-curing place' (Eckstorm 1941:147) are erroneous (F. T. Siebert, personal communication 1974).

Kennebec appears in the Purchas publication as Kenebeke, a village name, as well as in the earliest French sources (Champlain 1907; Lescarbot 1928). It represents Eastern Abenaki *kínipek^w* 'large body of still water, large bay', probably primarily referring to Merrymeeting Bay (F. T. Siebert, personal communication 1974). It has since been broadened as a name for the entire river and its inhabitants. The Kennebec of the eighteenth century were usually called Norridgewock after their last surviving village. The Amaseconti were a subdivision from the Sandy River, most of whom migrated to Bécancour, Quebec, in 1704. The Wawenock were the people of Bécancour, called *wáwinak* in Penobscot, evidently meaning 'round or oval island' (perhaps from a nearby island in the Saint Lawrence River); it is a village name, not a tribal or dialectal division (F. T. Siebert, personal communication 1974).

Penobscot appears first to identify, apparently correctly, a village near modern Orland (Purchas 1625, 4:1873-1875). The French form Pentagoet (Champlain 1907:46) was applied to the river generally and to the site of modern Castine specifically, beginning in 1604. Later usage by both the French and English applied the term to the river and virtually any location on it. Many contemporary students believe (incorrectly) that Penobscot has always identified the village at Old Town. The Penobscot River was called Pemaquid by some early English explorers. That term was soon shifted to Pemaquid Point, to the confusion of later historians. Penobscot derives from *pənáwɑhpskek* 'where the rocks widen, open out, spread apart' (F. T. Siebert, personal communication 1974).

Most of the forms discussed above appear frequently as plurals. The number of published variants of these, their subdivisions, and village names runs to at least 1,000.

Sources

Readily available source material for the early historic Eastern Abenaki includes Thwaites, *Jesuit Relations and Allied Documents* (JR 1896-1901), especially volumes 1, 2, 3, and 36. The letters of Râle in the same set are considered frauds by some (Eckstorm 1934) and should be used with caution. There are various editions of narratives of the voyages of Champlain, Marc Lescarbot, John Smith, George Waymouth, and John Josselyn, as well as the writings of William Bradford and Ferdinando Gorges. Very important, but not so available, is the 24-volume *Documentary History of the State of Maine*

Table 2. Major synonyms for the Eastern Abenaki and their principal divisions. There are several hundred additional variants of these and smaller units.

Abenaki	Pigwacket	Arosaguntacook	Kennebec	Penobscot
Abenaque	Pagwaki	Alsigantegwi	Camba	Pamnaouamske
Abenaquois	Peckwalket	Amarascoggin	Canaba	Panagamsde
Abenaqui	Peqouaki	Amasagunticook	Caniba	Panahamsequit
Abnasque	Pegwacket	Amereangan	Carriba	Panamske
Abenkai	Pegwackuk	Amircankanne	Kaniba	Panaomske
Abonnekee	Pehgwoket	Amireaneau	Kanibat	Panaonke
Albenaqui	Pequaket	Ammascoggen	Kanibesinnoak	Panaouanbskek
Anagonge	Pequawket	Amonoscoggan	Kenabeca	Panawamske
Mawooshen	Pequawett	Amresscoggin	Kenebecka	Panawanscot
Moasham	Pickpocket	Anasaguntacook	Kenabe	Pannawanbskek
Obenaki	Pickwacket	Androscoggin	Kinibeki	Pemetegoit
Onagunga	Picwocket	Anmoughcawgen	Aridgevoak	Pemtegoit
Onnogonge	Piggwacket	Annirkakan	Aridgewoak	Penaubsket
Openago	Piguachet	Arouseguntecook	Arransoak	Penaske
Openango	Pigwachet	Arunseguntekook	Nalatchwaniak	Penobskeag
Ouabenaquis	Pigwolket	Arreguntenock	Namgauck	Pentagoet
Oubenaki	Piquachet	Arreraguntecook	Nanrantsoak	Pentagonett
Owenagunge		Assagunticook	Nantansouak	Pentagouetch
Wabanaki		Ersegontegog	Naragooe	Pintagone
Wabnaki			Naranchouak	Ponobscot
Wappeno			Narangawock	Ponobscut
Wobanaki			Narautsouak	
			Narauwing	
			Naridgewalk	
			Naurantsouak	
			Neridgewok	
			Norridgewock	

(Maine Historical Society 1869–1916). The *Collections* (MeHSC 1831–1887) of the Maine Historical society (1st series) contain some of the treaties as well as several articles. Those by Eugene Vetromile and John Godfrey are particularly inept and along with their other publications on the Penobscot should be avoided. W.D. Williamson (1832) is comprehensive, but full of errors, the most notable of which is his persistent identification of the Penobscot as "Tarratines."

There are several descriptions of the colonial wars, some of them difficult to obtain and most of them strongly biased. Most notable of these are Penhallow (1859), Hubbard (1865), and Church (1867). Charlevoix (1866–1872) provides a French perspective on the same period. Various books by Francis Parkman provide a general but somewhat biased overview of the same period. Leger (1929) provides a relatively unbiased summary of Catholic missions in Maine. Swanton (1952) provides brief summaries under the headings "Abnaki" and "Penobscot."

Eckstorm (1904, 1945) and Speck (1940) provide good descriptions of the Penobscot since 1800. Speck (1940) also contains bibliographic references to his other monographs and articles. Intensive historical analyses of specific topics are Eckstorm's (1934, 1936, 1939) strong point. Biographical sketches of famous Eastern Abenakis appear in the *Dictionary of Canadian Biography* (DCB 2:25–26). These are generally accurate, although a few, such as that for Asticou, are full of errors. Siebert (1968–1973) has worked extensively on Penobscot linguistics and history. Current data on the Penobscot can be obtained directly from the Office of Indian Affairs in Augusta, or the resident agent in Old Town.

This article is a brief summary of Snow (1971–1973).

Western Abenaki

GORDON M. DAY

Language

The Western Abenaki are usually called Abenaki in English ($_{|}$ăbə$^{|}$năkē) from their own name *wǫbanakii* and sometimes Benaki ($^{|}$benəkē) from French *abénaquis*.*

The existence of a group distinguishable as the Western Abenaki is known from a language that was documented at Odanak, Quebec, in the early nineteenth century (Wzôkhilain 1830, 1830a) and in Vermont and New Hampshire place-names of the seventeenth and eighteenth centuries. This language, which was still spoken in 1973 by the Indians at Odanak on the Saint-François River in Quebec, is distinguished from the Eastern Abenaki language of Maine by differences in phonology, grammar, and lexicon. It is not an evolutionary development from the Kennebec dialect after 1679 as Prince (1902) supposed. The geographical boundary between the Eastern and Western Abenaki languages is not clear, since data from the boundary zone between the Merrimack and Kennebec rivers are inadequate. Eastern Abenaki is documented as far west as the Kennebec River, and it is probable that Western Abenaki was spoken by the Indians of the upper Merrimack River, the upper and middle Connecticut River, and Lake Champlain (fig. 1). The intermediate dialect of Bécancour may have stemmed from the Androscoggin River. The dialect of the Pigwacket on the upper Saco is unknown, and the speech of the Almouchiquois on the lower Saco, wrongly called Sokoki by nineteenth-century writers, may have belonged with the dialects of coastal Massachusetts.

Component Groups

The geographically central tribe of the Western Abenaki region, the one that formed the beginnings of the village of Saint Francis (Odaṅak), was the Sokoki of the upper Connecticut River. The name Sokoki was wrongly shifted to the Saco River Indians by nineteenth-century historians, and writers came to regard Squakheag, the southernmost Sokoki village at Northfield, Massachusetts, as an isolated and independent group. Seventeenth-century

* The orthography used for the Western Abenaki language in the *Handbook* follows the phonemicization of Day (1964), with the omission of the largely predictable accent and the substitution, to accord with standard Handbook usage, of ə for Day's e and ǫ for ô (a slightly centralized, optionally rounded, low back nasalized vowel).

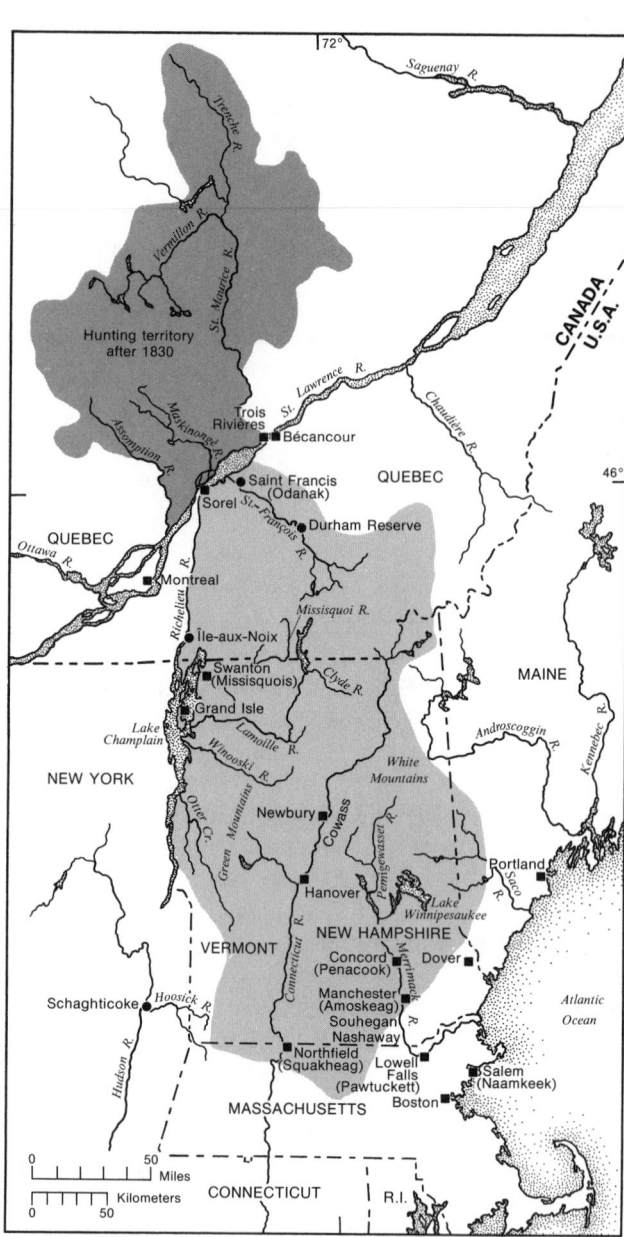

Fig. 1. Tribal territory with darker tone indicating hunting territory after 1830.

documents treat the Sokoki as the inhabitants of the entire upper Connecticut River, which would extend the name Sokoki to the Cowasucks at Newbury, Vermont. The tribes of the upper Merrimack River, the Winnipesaukees and the Penacooks at Concord, New Hampshire, were Western Abenakis. Downriver were other bands at Amoskeag (Manchester, New Hampshire), Souhegan, Nashaway, Pawtuckett (Lowell, Massachusetts), and Naamkeek (Salem, Massachusetts). It is uncertain whether any of these were Abenakis, and all were probably under the overlordship of Passaconaway, whose chief residences were at Amoskeag and Pawtuckett. Wood's (1634) map shows Penacook as a fortified village under the chief Mattacomen, which may indicate that he was coordinate with Passaconaway and independent at this time. The Vermont shore of Lake Champlain was probably occupied by Western Abenakis from prehistoric time (Day 1971). Villages at the mouths of the Winooski, the Lamoille, and the Missisquoi rivers, on Grand Isle, and elsewhere are known; but in the eighteenth century, their population gradually concentrated at Missisquoi, and the Missisquoi tribe came to stand, in most writings, for all the Champlain Valley Abenakis. The tribes of Lake Champlain and the Connecticut and Merrimack valleys appear to have been always friendly during the historic period. They were frequently allies; they settled in the same refugee or mission villages, and they gave other evidence of being essentially one people.

It appears that all the inhabitants of the country from the Merrimack River to Lake Champlain, that is, the Western Abenakis, found their way eventually to the Saint-François River. Some Eastern Abenakis from the Chaudière mission and some southern New England Indians, probably mostly Pocumtucks and Nipmucks, were incorporated in the village at one time. For convenience, therefore, the Saint Francis village and all its contributory groups will be considered together here. This means consideration of some peoples who, before their removal, were part of the southern New England culture area and who may have contributed some southern traits to the culture observed at Saint Francis in the nineteenth and twentieth centuries.

Territory and Environment

The territory of the Western Abenaki lay within the New England-Acadian physiographic province. The principal subdivisions of the territory are, from west to east, the Champlain Valley, the Green Mountains, the Connecticut River valley, and the White Mountains, whose bordering uplands to the south contain Lake Winnipesaukee and the Merrimack River valley. This territory has abundant precipitation fairly evenly distributed throughout the year. Summers are warm, and winters are cold with four or five months of snow cover. Most of the known Abenaki villages were situated where the growing season was 140 days or more.

The original forest of the lowlands was a mixture of central and northern hardwoods and hemlock with white pine occurring as occasional large individuals or dominating stands on light soils and old fields. The hills and lower mountain slopes were dominated by northern hardwoods and hemlock and the upper slopes by red spruce and northern hardwoods. Swamps were characterized by balsam fir and swamp hardwoods and bogs by black spruce, tamarack, and white cedar. The upper-slope types were found at lower elevations in the northern part of the region (Westveld 1956; Braun 1950:422-440). The large game animals were moose, deer, and black bear, and there were many furbearers—beaver, muskrat, otter, mink, marten, fisher, raccoon, foxes, and skunk. Wolf and bobcat were numerous, lynx and mountain lion less so. Wolverine were rare. Hare, rabbit, weasel, squirrels and many species of birds occurred. The northern part of the region was differentiated by the occurrence of more moose and fewer deer, by sporadic occurrences of woodland caribou, and by more beaver. The Western Abenaki territory had an abundant flora and fauna as a consequence of its latitudinal position and the environmental variety created by its mountain and valley topography.

Those southern New England Indians who removed to Saint Francis probably came mostly from the Connecticut Valley in Massachusetts and the lakes of the highland in eastern Massachusetts and northeastern Connecticut. This region has a somewhat milder climate, that is, a longer average growing season and a shorter period of snow cover. Sharing the forest cover of the lowlands farther north, it constituted a kind of transition from the characteristic northern to more southerly fauna.

History

The Western Abenaki have always been something of an unknown quantity to historians and ethnographers. Their interior location prevented encounters with the earliest explorers. The few traders and other travelers who were among them in the seventeenth century left either very scanty accounts or none at all. Their withdrawals from the southern periphery of their country and the long colonial wars restricted the opportunities of the English to know the Western Abenaki, and English testimony concerning them features battles, treaties, and captivities. The Dutch knew them through the Iroquois. The best early information on them comes from the French, who knew them as converts and allies, but French preoccupations with conversion and defense seem to have prevented even those missionaries who knew the Abenaki best from leaving a reasonably comprehensive account of their culture. Moreover, French practice of referring to both Penacooks and Sokokis as Loups, originally their name for the Mahicans, tends to confound their record. As a result, the Western Abenaki have moved through the pages of New England history under the names of their villages, regarded as tribal names, and through the pages of Canadian history under group names of vague denotation. They stand in works of secondary history characterized largely by stereotypes growing out of the errors of

149

certain influential nineteenth-century historians.

Their prehistory likewise largely remains to be unraveled. Considerable material has been collected from sites such as Missisquoi, Cowasuck, Squakheag, Winnipesaukee, Namaskik, and Massabesic, and smaller amounts from other sites, generally without documenting even relative age. The Fort Hill Squakheag site is the only systematically excavated site that can be connected with a historic Western Abenaki group (P.A. Thomas 1971).

Only glimpses of the Western Abenaki can be gained from the writers of the early seventeenth century. About 1617 Ferdinando Gorges's men at the mouth of the Saco learned of the Sockhigones to the west and southwest, who were probably the Sokokis on the Connecticut River. They also learned of a country between the Sockhigones and the Eastern Abenaki called Apistama, possibly Winnipesaukee, one of whose early names, Winnipistogue, bears some resemblance to Apistama. John Smith was told that there were 30 habitations on the Merrimack River, but those on the lower river under Passaconaway were probably Massachusett rather then Abenaki in speech and culture. The English on Massachusetts Bay had contact with Passaconaway as early as 1632. Massachusetts Bay surveyors penetrated to Penacook and perhaps up the Pemigewasset River in 1638 and to Lake Winnepesaukee in 1652. Richard Walderne knew the details of the Merrimack River from the Indians at Dover as early as 1635, and Peter Weare may have seen it in the company of Indians in 1637 (Kimball 1878). A party of Gorges's men visited a Pigwacket village in 1642 (Winthrop 1853, 2:67).

The Dutch traded with the Indians of the lower Connecticut River soon after Adriaen Block's discovery in 1614, established a post at Hartford in 1633, and in 1634-1635 made contact with the Agawams at Springfield. After 1636 William Pynchon at Springfield, Massachusetts, and his traders became well acquainted with the Connecticut River Indians in Massachusetts—the Agawams, Woronocos, Nonotucks, and Pocumtucks—but achieved only slight acquaintance with the Sokokis above Deerfield (NYCD 13:308). The "Northern Indians" at King Philip's Hoosick River rendezvous in 1676 were probably Western Abenakis from Lake Champlain (N.S. 1913:87-88), and it is not unlikely that the Dutch had some trading connections with the Indians in the Champlain Valley.

The French first encountered the Western Abenaki in 1642 when the upper Algonquins, returning from war against the Iroquois, brought to Trois Rivières a Sokoki whom they had mistaken for an Iroquois. The French released him, and, the next spring, the grateful Sokokis tried to buy the freedom of Father Isaac Jogues from the Iroquois. The Iroquois kept their presents without releasing Jogues, and this grave breach of protocol may mark the beginning of the new Sokoki-Iroquois enmity, but there were no open hostilities for several years. About this time, two Sokokis were killed by the Montagnais near the Iroquois country, and in the fall of 1645, they evened the score by killing three Montagnais from Sillery. They used their scalps to try to arouse the Mohawks against the Canadian Indians, but the Iroquois had hostages among the French at the time and were angling for a peace with the Algonquins that would allow them to hunt safely in the north (JR 55:183, 193, 31:35ff.).

In 1651 Father Gabriel Druillettes induced the Penacooks, Sokokis, Pocumtucks, and Mahicans to form a solid front with the French against the Iroquois. They do not appear to have attacked the Iroquois at this time, but Druillettes's visit was probably responsible for the Sokokis' renewing their former friendship with the Algonquins. There seems to have been an uneasy peace while the Iroquois were turning their attention to the Eries and harassing the Ottawa River fur traffic, but in 1651 the Iroquois attacked the Sokokis (NYCD 9:5). In 1663 the Iroquois launched an attack on the Sokokis that proved to be disastrous for both sides. The Dutch tried to patch up a peace the next spring, but when the English took over New Netherlands from the Dutch in 1664 and held their first council with the Iroquois at Albany, the Iroquois regarded themselves still at war, not only with the Sokokis but also with the Pocumtucks and Penacooks (NYCD 13:297-298, 308-309, 355-356). The 1663 war may have been the beginning of the major exodus from Squakheag, but Sokokis were still in place to participate in the unsuccessful joint attack by the southern New England Indians on the Mohawks in 1669, and some were still close enough to Squakheag to participate in King Philip's War in 1675 and to sell land in 1686 and 1687. The Iroquois also attacked Penacook sometime before 1668; and probably as a consequence, before 1670 many Penacooks moved to Pentucket above Lowell Falls on the Merrimack.

Some Sokokis moved to the Saint Lawrence River, and Sokoki names began appearing in Canadian church registers in 1662. Others arrived during King Philip's War. At the end of the war in 1676, the River Indians of Massachusetts fled to the Hudson River, and the next year Gov. Edmund Andros started a settlement for them at Schaghticoke (spelled Scaghticoke in "Mahican," this vol.) near the mouth of the Hoosick River. There were perhaps some Sokokis among the early settlers of this village, and a number were found there in 1735 to deed land (JR 60:135; Livingston 1956:40; H.A. Wright 1905).

In 1644 Passaconaway made a treaty of peace with Massachusetts, and the Merrimack River Indians remained at peace until Capt. Samuel Moseley's unprovoked assault on Penacook in 1675. Most of the Penacooks went to Canada, and in 1677 they persuaded Wannalancet to follow, but he returned later to the Merrimack. By 1670 there were Sokokis settled near Montreal and near Trois Rivières, and the Sokoki and

Penacook removals caused by Philip's War certainly augmented the village at Missisquoi, which had probably already received Sokokis after the Iroquois attacks. Together they brought a vigorous fur trade to Chambly for a few years. A short-lived mission was established among them by the French, and in 1680 they were again attacked by the Iroquois. From this time on, the Western Abenakis in Canada were allies of the French, particularly in the colonial wars that commenced in 1689. At the same time they maintained communication and friendly ties with the Schaghticokes, who were nominal English allies; with those Penacooks who had fled to the Androscoggin River in Maine; and with the Indians on the Merrimack River. Their relations with the French were not always perfect. In 1688 one group suddenly quit the Saint Lawrence and moved south, leaving their standing crops and even pillaging and burning French communities on the way (NYCD 9:194, 195).

About 1695 a village of Western Abenakis on one of the forks of the Saint-François River moved downriver after an Iroquois attack to swell the population at Saint Francis (Paquin 1833:220). Father Jacques Bigot established a mission at Saint Francis in 1700 to which came in that year Sokokis and Penacooks who had been sharing the mission on the Chaudière River with Eastern Abenakis (Bacqueville de la Potherie 1753, 1).

Western Abenakis figured prominently in the early history of New France. Some Penacook men intermarried with mission Algonquin and Nipissing women and followed the fur trade to Lake Huron where they were seen by Father Henri Nouvel in 1675 (JR 60:214-218). One group of Sokokis and Penacooks accompanied René-Robert Cavelier de La Salle down the Mississippi in 1682. Some Sokokis accompanied Joseph-Antoine Le Febvre de LaBarre against the Senecas in 1684, and Sokokis made up most of Joseph-François Hertel de la Fresnière's war party against Salmon Falls, Maine, in 1690. They participated in the attack on Schenectady in 1690 and the destruction of the Mohawk villages in 1693, and they accompanied Louis de Buade de Frontenac against the Onondagas in 1696.

By 1698 many Schaghticokes had become dissatisfied with their situation, and by degrees they began to move into the French zone, first to Missisquoi, later to Saint Francis.

The Cowasuck territory on the upper Connecticut River was abandoned briefly in 1704 after an attack by men from Northampton, Massachusetts, but was probably reoccupied after the Treaty of Utrecht in 1713, and Joseph Aubery's map of 1715 called it a former mission. The Pigwackets, who had been attracted to Saint Francis about 1706, likewise returned to Pigwacket in 1714 (JR 67:30-32).

Relations between the Western Abenaki and the English began to deteriorate again in 1717, and in 1723 a war

broke out between them that did not include the French. One of the most celebrated incidents of this war was John Lovewell's battle in the Pigwacket country, but the principal action took the form of repeated raids by Gray Lock of Missisquoi on the Massachusetts towns in the Connecticut River valley. Massachusetts, through the Penobscots, finally persuaded the Saint Francis Indians to peace, and the Saint Francis Indians compelled Gray Lock to desist (Temple and Sheldon 1875:191-215). A treaty was signed in Montreal with the Saint Francis Indians, but Gray Lock was absent. English settlements had crept up the Connecticut and Merrimack valleys during the peace and were struck by Abenaki raids during King George's War (1745-1748). After this war, the Indians were disturbed by rumors that the then-vacant Cowass Intervales were going to be fortified by the English; and at a conference at Montreal in 1752, the Abenakis reasserted their claim to the land and threatened war if it were occupied (NYCD 10:252-254).

The last colonial war, 1754-1763, occasioned still another withdrawal of the Western Abenakis from locations that were too exposed to English attacks. The last remaining families at Schaghticoke took advantage of a raid into the Albany region by Bécancour Abenakis to return to Canada with them. The Missisquoi withdrew for the duration of the war to François-Charles de Bourlamaque's army at Île-aux-Noix in the upper Richelieu River and to Saint Francis and Bécancour. One group on the upper Connecticut River who favored the English cause withdrew to the Clyde River in northern Vermont where they remained until 1763. The Abenakis fought with the French at the battles of Monongahela, Oswego, Lake George, William Henry, Quebec, and elsewhere and conducted their own raids against the New England and New York frontiers. After the Treaty of Paris, they returned as usual to reoccupy their lands, but this time they encountered the first wave of English settlers pushing northward to settle the lands of the Indian allies of the French; and, for the next decade or so, returning Indians and advancing English mingled in frontier regions from Lake Champlain to the upper Androscoggin River (Hemenway 1868-1891).

The American Revolution was a source of confusion to the Western Abenakis, accustomed for generations to wars between the French and the English. During the early years of the war, some took the part of the Crown while some assisted the Americans. The Missisquoi tribe withdrew from the scene of the conflict again, and later the Saint Francis Indians lapsed into a species of neutrality that the British authorities thought was a cloak for American intelligence activities. After this war, the Western Abenakis did not return to any of their former locations in force but rather united or reunited with their brethren at Saint Francis. When they deeded northern New Hampshire in 1798, they did it in the name of the chiefs at Saint Francis, and a competing land company could find only one man and two women still resident on the upper Connecticut River to give an opposing deed. Missisquoi families returned and collected rent on their land, which they gradually abandoned, but they never relinquished claim to it (New Hampshire Historical Society 1795-1810; Hemenway 1868-1891, 4:998-1000).

In 1805 the English Crown granted new lands at Durham, Quebec, on the Saint-François River to accommodate the population increase brought about by the influx of new arrivals (PAC-Q 94:9). The Durham reserve was settled not only by new arrivals but also by families that had been long at Saint Francis. By 1850 most of this band was absorbed into the Saint Francis village. The tribe at Saint Francis continued to be known in official documents as the Sokokis and Abenakis of Saint Francis until at least 1880, but by 1900, the practice of referring to the whole group as Abenakis (which may be noted as early as 1736) became general. It has been adopted by the Indians themselves, who in the 1970s think of themselves as Abenakis, which is linguistically correct.

In the War of 1812, the Abenakis of Saint Francis and Bécancour furnished two companies for the British forces, and they now refer to their participation as "the last time the Abenakis went to war," although many saw service in the two world wars. After the War of 1812, parts of the Eastern Townships were granted to White veterans and settled, and their value to the Abenakis as hunting and trapping grounds was diminished. Most of the tribe turned to new hunting grounds north of the Saint Lawrence, to a territory belonging to the Algonquins of Trois Rivières but abandoned by them in the 1830s. However, certain Abenaki families returned to ancestral locations in the United States to hunt, fish, and guide surveyors and sportsmen.

In 1774 Levi Frisbie had journeyed to Saint Francis and brought back from there four Indian students for Eleazar Wheelock's Indian Charity School, which had recently moved from Connecticut to Hanover, New Hampshire. This was the beginning of a long-lived relationship between Dartmouth College and the Saint Francis Indians, who supplied most of Dartmouth's Indian students for the next 80 years. One of the first students, Francis Annance, established a Protestant school on the Durham reserve, and several young women were sent to Burlington, Vermont, and to Boston for training (Wheelock 1775:44-54). Between 1829 and 1858 another Dartmouth graduate, Pial Wzôkhilain, conducted a Protestant church and an English-language school at Saint Francis. An Anglican mission was founded in 1866, and an Adventist congregation existed between 1884 and 1915. Father Joseph DeGonzague, son of one of the last life chiefs, served as Catholic missionary from 1895 to 1937. From about 1865 to about 1950, the

ash-splint basket industry (fig. 2) brought a considerable number of Abenakis back to the resort areas of northeastern United States. By the end of the nineteenth century, some Abenakis were combining their hunting and trapping with the guiding of sportsmen. Guiding gradually replaced hunting and trapping, and the last parties abandoned their hunting territories about 1922. Guiding at sportsmen's clubs continued until about 1970. Beginning with World War I, the lure of industrial employment started small Abenaki communities in several northeastern United States cities, and in the 1970s these far outnumbered the parent community.

Population

Data are lacking for a reliable estimate of early Western Abenaki populations. Epidemics of European diseases, which reduced native populations to one-tenth or one-twentieth, struck at the mouth of the Saco in 1617 and progressed down the coast and up the Connecticut River by 1635. Gov. Thomas Dudley estimated the Merrimack River Indians at 400 or 500 men in 1631 (Bouton 1856:18), and Druillettes reported 10 towns on the Connecticut River in 1650, of which probably only a few were Abenaki (Shea 1857:322). The Iroquois wars were responsible for undetermined mortality between 1650 and 1680, as were the almost continuous hostilities between the Western Abenakis and the Massachusetts colony after 1675, and there were repeated losses by epidemics after settling in Canada. A reasonable guess for the preplague population of the Western Abenakis

Philbrook Art Center, Tulsa, Okla.: F-BA 448.

Fig. 2. Penacook (according to Frank G. Speck) checkerwork splint basket, made from ash splints dyed (swabbed on one side only) with native dyes. Basket is lined with a *Boston Daily Courier* dated 1835, but the basket may considerably predate the newspaper lining. Height 37 cm, diameter 51 cm.

may be 5,000 persons on the upper Merrimack River, the upper Connecticut River, and Lake Champlain.

There is a reasonably good sequence of statistics only for the mission village of Saint Francis, but it must be remembered that this village never included all the Western Abenakis. Until about 1790 there were sizable bands at Missisquoi and the upper Connecticut and Androscoggin rivers, and between 1807 and about 1850 there were numerous families at Durham, Quebec. By the middle of the nineteenth century a number of families had left the reserve more or less permanently. It was estimated that 200 persons were absent in 1904, and many families left during World War I. Charland (1964:341) has assembled the census data for the Saint Francis village:

1783	342
1810	418
1828	380
1848	306
1874	266
1888	330
1904	370

An Indian Affairs census in 1965 of band members, not village residents, gives 576. "Band members" under Indian Affairs rulings comprise only descendants in the male line and do not include persons of predominantly Abenaki blood from the mother's side or individuals living away who have not made an effort to be kept on the band rolls. In 1973, out of a probable 900 to 1,000 persons with a significant amount of Abenaki blood, only about 220 lived at Odanak.

Culture

The Western Abenaki culture area lay north of a line running roughly from Portland, Maine, through Manchester, New Hampshire, and Northfield, Massachusetts, to the tops of the Green Mountains, thence northward to Otter Creek, which it followed to Lake Champlain. North of this line were Abenaki-speaking moose hunters with an important agriculture, patrilineal tendencies, and relatively weak chiefs. South of this line were non-Abenaki-speaking agriculturists whose principal game animal was deer, with some matrilineal tendencies, and strong hereditary chiefs.

Since the Saint Francis village at Odanak, Quebec, appears to be a village of immigrants and not older than 1660, reconstructing the earlier cultures of these immigrants would require identifying and characterizing the several components of the village and tracing them back to their earlier locations and habitats. It is probably too late to do this thoroughly and with confidence, so for the purposes of this sketch, the assumption has been made that the Western Abenaki were essentially homogeneous culturally. The main elements of Western Abenaki culture have been reconstructed from the data of history and from the language, oral traditions, and memory ethnography at Saint Francis. Most of the following is taken from Day's (1956–1973) field notes. The majority of the family names at Odanak in the earliest census, in 1829, came from or were associated with Missisquoi. In other words, Saint Francis cultural traits identifiable as Indian in the nineteenth and twentieth centuries are essentially Missisquoi cultural traits of the eighteenth century. This pushes back the question of their ultimate provenience but does not settle it, since Missisquoi had received increments from the same tribes that contributed to Saint Francis directly.

The earliest known Western Abenaki villages—Penacook, Squakheag, Missisquoi—were palisaded for defense as was Saint Francis. Villages were typically located on the edge of a bluff close to (1) a sizable alluvial meadow suitable for corn culture and (2) a supply of water. All villages were close to a river or lake that served both as a source of fish and as a travel route. Their houses were rectangular structures of bark with arched roofs, a smoke hole for each fire, and room enough for several families. Sweat lodges were round and dome-shaped.

Subsistence

Although local diversity in the annual round was imposed by the differences in local resources, a common round can be reconstructed. The first activity in the spring was tapping maple trees and making syrup and possibly sugar, both for immediate eating and storage. Maple and birch trees were tapped by making a slanting gash in the bark, then inserting an elderberry twig with the pith bored out in the lower end of the gash. The sap was collected in a birchbark container and was boiled into syrup consistency in either a birchbark pail or a clay pot. In later times iron trade kettles were substituted, and this may have been the beginning of maple-sugar making. Then followed the catching of spring runs of fish in large quantities for immediate eating and for smoking. Fish were taken by weirs and fish traps, by spearing from shore or from canoe by day or by torchlight, by hooks on night lines or hand lines, and by nets. Spring greens and especially groundnuts or wild potatoes were gathered. Spring flights of passenger pigeons were shot and netted. In May, fields were planted with corn, beans, and squashes, and tobacco was planted in small separate gardens. Summer subsistence activities consisted of weeding the corn fields, fishing, and picking berries as each species became ripe. Blueberries were especially prized. A lengthy sojourn on one of the larger lakes for the fishing and to escape forest insect pests was broken by return trips to the village to weed the fields. The Sokokis even traveled to the seashore in summer. In late summer, medicinal plants were collected, dried, and stored. Nuts were collected also, butternuts and the now-extinct chestnut being the most important. In the fall they shot and netted the abundant waterfowl and killed quantities of passenger pigeons as they gathered for their southward migration. Eels were caught and smoked for winter. Deer were hunted by stalking rather than by snaring and driving as in southern New England. Bears were killed after they had denned up for the winter. Moose were hunted by calling during the rutting season in the fall and by running them down on snowshoes or shooting them in yards in the winter. Muskrat, beaver, otter, and other furbearers were taken in the fall and winter, both for food and pelts. All furbearers were trapped; beavers and muskrats were taken in their lake houses, and muskrats were additionally dug or driven out of their riverbank dens. Spruce grouse and porcupine could be taken when other game was scarce. The mainstays of their subsistence were probably moose, fish, corn, and beaver in that order.

Clothing and Adornment

The basic male costume was a breechclout and belt, both of tanned skin. The belt was wrapped around the waist two or three times and knotted at the hip with the fringed ends hanging at the side or in front. Moosehide moccasins were worn in winter and often in summer. Two patterns are known, the beavertail and the rabbit nose (fig. 3) (Hatt 1916:171–178, 167–169). In winter, foot wrappers of tanned skin or of rabbit fur were worn under the moccasins and an outer pair of moccasins with higher tops was added. The moose-hock moccasin boot, which was nearly waterproof and was considered especially good for snowshoeing, was sometimes worn. Leggings, with feet, reaching to the thigh and tied to the belt were worn gartered below the knee. A long sleeveless coat of two panels of moosehide, front and back, was worn by both sexes in cold weather. It was probably painted like the Penobscot coat, but no museum specimens are known. The sleeves were separable. The young male wore

his hair long and loose, sometimes secured by a head-band, and the married man's hairdo was a coil or knot on the crown of the head held by a thong. The female wore the hair long and loose or secured by a band or, characteristically, in two braids with a flat coil on the crown of the head tied by a thong with pendant ends. Hair ornaments might be attached to this coil. Both sexes might go bareheaded or with the head covered with a blanket in cold weather, but a variety of caps was made for both warmth and dress. A man's pointed hoodlike cap falling to the shoulders was documented in the eighteenth century but may not have been aboriginal. The woman's cap was conical, and both might bear feathers at the point. Males sometimes wore a fur cap made from the skin of a young buck deer with the antlers left on. Another cap was made from the shoulder skin of a moose, the long white hairs of the moose hump forming a natural crest, which might be left white or dyed. This cap had an opening in the back for the hair knot and feathers if feathers were worn. It may be that this was the prototype of the widely distributed deer-hair roach. There is an Abenaki tradition that no more than two feathers were worn by the men.

Robes were of fur with beaver preferred. It is possible that kilts were also worn by the Western Abenakis, since they were worn by the Iroquois and the Eastern Abenakis, but there is no evidence for them. A knife was customarily worn in a sheath on the breast suspended about the neck; a wooden cup (fig. 4) and a small skin bag containing the fire-making kit, pipe, tobacco, and guardian spirit keepsake were tucked under the belt. The basic female costume was moccasins, leggings, a knee-length skirt, and a blouse reaching to mid-thigh.

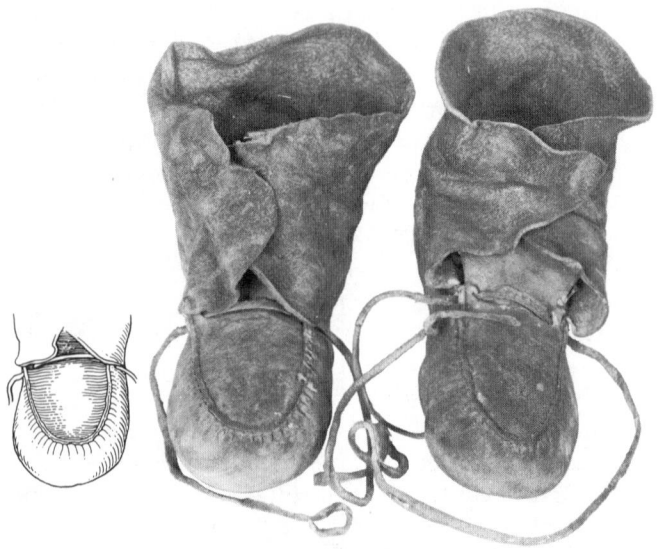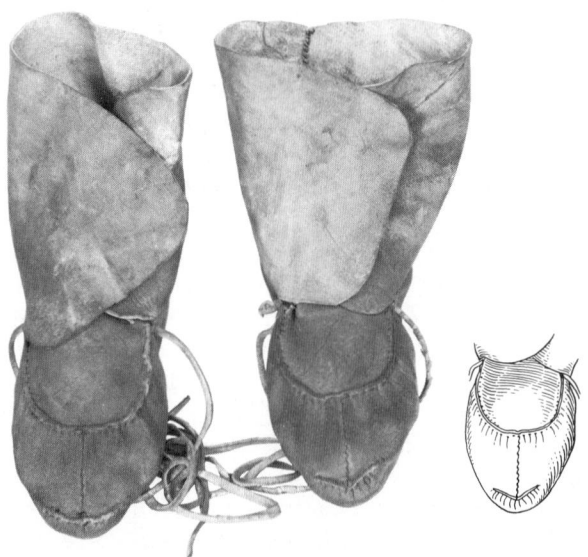

Natl. Mus. of Canada, Ottawa: left, III-J-53ab; right, III-J-6ab.

Fig. 3. Winter moccasins of beavertail (left) and rabbit nose (right) design. Both pairs were collected in 1908 from Western Abenakis living at Lake George, N.Y. Traditionally these would have been manufactured of moosehide, but these may be deerhide. Height about 25 cm.

154

Fig. 4. Abenaki carrying cup, carved of hardwood burl. The cup is attached to a wooden toggle with a leather thong that is tucked under the belt. Collected at Odanak in 1914. Diameter of cup (excluding handle), approximately 6 cm.

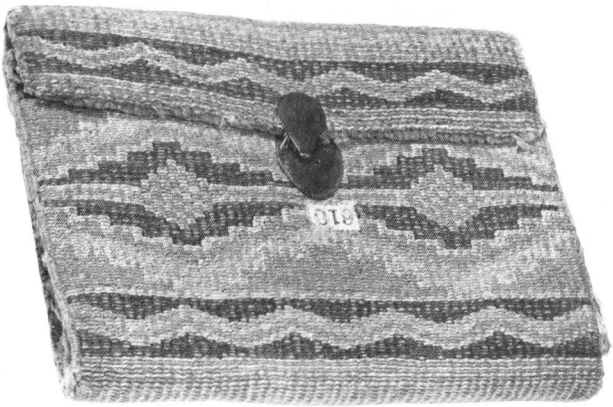

Fig. 5. European-style wallet in native design by Mollocket (Mali Agat, d.1816), an Abenaki woman, about 1785. Exterior is completely covered with false embroidery using natural and dyed moosehair over twined bast foundation. Length (unfolded) 15 cm.

Abenaki costume began to be modified early by European example and trade goods, but even after 1850 some older people wore a traditional costume consisting for men of moccasins; leggings; breechclout with the addition of a pocket for pipe, tobacco, and fire-making kit; belt; a cloth shirt worn outside the belt, hanging to mid-thigh; and long hair. Women wore moccasins, leggings, skirt, blouse, long hair, and often a blanket.

Technology

Hunting weapons were bow, arrow, knife, and spear. War weapons included these items plus a characteristic war club with a ball head made from the root crown of a hardwood with projecting sharpened root bases. Fishing equipment included hooks and lines, nets, and fish spear. The man's tool kit included crooked knife, awl, hand ax, gouge, and adz; and his chief materials were wood, bone, rawhide, moose sinew, birchbark, spruce root, and the inner bark of basswood and leatherwood. The woman's tool kit included awl, needles, wooden skin scraper, stone scrapers, stone grinders, and corn pounder; and her chief materials were tanned hides, furs, birchbark, spruce root, paints, porcupine quills, and moosehair.

Moccasin tops, garters, belts, pouches, belt cups, pipes, canoes, and containers were decorated; but the data of decoration are scattered, a study of motifs has never been made, and pottery design of sure Western Abenaki provenience is practically unknown. Geometric designs were rendered on woven surfaces by weaving and false embroidery; geometrical and curvilinear designs were rendered by paint, porcupine quill, and moosehair (fig. 5).

The Western Abenaki were dependent on the snowshoe for winter travel and on the birchbark canoe for summer travel. The wooden dugout canoe was also known. Loads were transported in winter on toboggans and on the back by blanket pack and tumpline. Splint pack baskets, which were very common in the nineteenth century, are probably postcontact, but the woven basswood-bark pack basket with chest strap may be aboriginal. Summer overland foot travel occurred, and the locations of some of the historic foot trails are known. Babies were carried in a cradle board, but a blanket hammock was used in camp.

Life Cycle

Abenakis were affectionate parents, and children were not struck. In general, education and discipline consisted of traditional stories often repeated, grave admonitions, and the pressure of group disapproval. Punishment often took the form of blackening the child's face and putting him or her outside the wigwam for a time. Disobeying an order affecting survival might receive prompt, fitting punishment. Through necessity or convenience, children were often reared by grandparents or paternal uncles, and the paternal uncle was often the boy's tutor and the paternal aunt the girl's tutor. The instruction of girls in household skills commenced early. The evidence for first rites is inadequate, but a boy was given a small bow and arrow at age five or six, and at 10 or 12 he began to go hunting with his father or uncle. At puberty, boys might seek a guiding vision, and there was menstrual seclusion for girls.

Marriage was proposed by a young man through an intermediary, the proposal being accompanied by a present or token and, in the eighteenth century at least, by a wampum string. The girl could reject the suitor by returning the gift. Some cases of child betrothal are remembered. There is an eighteenth-century record of the proposal being made by the parents of the boy placing a blanket on the shoulders of the girl's mother. A courtship dance around the secluded hut of a marriageable girl is also remembered. The variety of remembered proposal

155

procedures may be survivals from the several components of the Saint Francis tribe. If the young man's proposal was accepted—one writer has the girl reciprocating by placing an ear of corn in the young man's wigwam—he made the girl's mother the present of his first game and then departed on a hunt and did not return until he had a suitable bride present. There was then a period of trial cohabitation during which the couple slept head-to-foot; if the trial was unsuccessful, the couple separated and the man lost his presents. Marriage was celebrated in the presence of the chiefs and parents and normally was followed by feasting and dancing.

The dead were always buried when possible, since spirits of unburied dead remained around the corpse as the dreaded Ghost Fire. Those who died in winter were placed on a scaffold until it was possible to bury them. The coffin was a full-length roll of bark tied with a cord, and the grave was covered with a tent-shaped structure of wood with an upright board at one end bearing the identification of the deceased. Weapons and utensils necessary for their support in the other world were buried with them as well as food sufficient for the journey over the Ghost Trail. Graves were oriented facing the east, and the graves of chiefs were anciently planted around with an oval of tree seedlings. Children were especially mourned, the mother cutting her hair and painting her face black. Presents were customarily offered to mourning parents who responded with a feast. A widow wore a hood for one year during which time she could not participate in festivities or remarry.

Social Organization

Hunting, fishing, warfare, and the fabrication of houses, canoes, and the implements of war and hunting were the responsibilities of the Abenaki men. Child care, cooking, preparation of skins and clothing, cultivation of agricultural crops excepting tobacco, and the gathering of food plants were the responsibilities of the women and children.

Western Abenaki society was patrilineal. The basic unit was the household, one to several nuclear families of the same patrilineage living together in one long bark house. The formal unit was a patrilineal totemic descent group regarded as the descendants of a remote male ancestor, not of the totem animal, together with their wives and children. The tribe was denoted 'all the households together'. In 1736 turtle, bear, beaver, otter, and partridge totems were reported at Saint Francis (Chauvinerie 1928). Family names in the early nineteenth-century censuses suggest the presence of turtle, bear, beaver, partridge, raccoon, humming bird, and muskrat totems with fisher, eagle, and partridge totems represented by Eastern Abenaki residents. Morgan's (1877:179) list of Abenaki gens, which Speck (1935) rejected as Penobscot, is not from Saint Francis and may possibly have been from Bécancour. The winter hunting

group was a convenient nonpermanent grouping selected from the sons and brothers of one mature hunter and their families, and sometimes a daughter and her husband. The nature and degree of exogamy prior to Christian influence is difficult to determine, but there is evidence for cross-cousin marriage in the kinship nomenclature as well as special relations with paternal grandparents and uncles. Turtle and Bear moieties, representing Sokoki and Abenaki proper respectively, functioned in the council and on the ballfield. The totem animals may have been those of the most prominent clans. A constant and characteristic feature of the society was the special life-long relationship of two male partners formed in early youth.

Patrilocal residence was the norm, but when practical considerations favored it, a daughter's husband might live for a time with his father-in-law. Removal of discrete groups to Saint Francis caused some adjustments in their territorial claims and use, but families remembered their places of origin in the nineteenth century (for example, Kendall 1809). After about 1830, the Western Abenaki took over the hunting territory north of the Saint Lawrence River abandoned by the Algonquins of Point-du-Lac (Trois Rivières) extending from the Assomption River on the west, north to the Vermillon River and the vicinity of Coucoucache, and east to include the Saint Maurice drainage (fig. 1). This territory they organized into family hunting territories (Hallowell 1932), and there are indications that a family-hunting-territory system was in effect in their New England homeland. Rights to these territories seem to have been transmitted within the family of a male, but it is noteworthy that deeds and leases for agricultural land at Squakheag and Missisquoi bear the names of both men and women.

Political Organization

Each Western Abenaki nation had a civil chief and a war chief. A chief was selected for outstanding ability and installed in a chief-making ceremony in which he received a new name. His influence was considerable because of his prestige and personal powers, but the extent of his absolute authority is uncertain. Chiefs held office for life unless they were deposed for bad behavior. The civil chief usually presided at the Great Council of the Nation, which was composed of the war chief and the elders of the several families. At Saint Francis the council consisted, by the eighteenth century, of a grand chief and several chiefs, probably as an accommodation to the diverse elements that had come together there. The wampum complex probably reached the Western Abenakis in the early seventeenth century about the time it reached the Iroquois and the upriver Mahicans, and belts and strings were used to commemorate treaties and the decisions of councils. The bag of wampum records at Saint Francis was entrusted to a group of six men and seven women in 1771 (Maurault 1866:571). The best orator, at Saint Francis usually chosen from among the chiefs, held the office of "The Advisor" whose duty it was to recall to the attention of the Council the needs of the nation. The Great Council sat as a court and decreed all punishments, even to banishment or death.

The Great Council settled all national and international affairs except the question of war, which was decided at a General Council attended by men, women, and young people and at which both men and women addressed the Council. When the General Council decided for war, the war chief rose with the ceremonial red war club in his hand and asked who would volunteer. A war leader would rise and urge the young men to follow him, and when a party was raised, there would be a feast followed by a war dance. A group or groups of 10 men, each under a leader, comprised a party capable of independent action. Ten parties required a grand leader, but control was exercised by example, persuasion, and the loyalty he could inspire through his reputation and ability rather than by military discipline. Warriors painted their faces red and their body with their totem and with marks showing their war record. During the historic period, both prisoners and scalps were taken, and young warriors were given new titles in recognition of outstanding exploits. Maurault (1866) attributed the full range of the torture complex to the Western Abenakis, but the historical record, including the captivity narratives, provides no support for this idea. Prisoners were escorted by their captors between two rows of warriors who placed their hand on each passing prisoner's shoulder to indicate his captive status. During the colonial wars prisoners from New England were held for ransom or were occasionally adopted.

The only Indian enemies of the Western Abenakis during the historic period were the Iroquois, and this enmity predated European contact. The Western Abenakis appear to have been on friendly terms with the Algonquian-speaking tribes in New England and had anciently a treaty of friendship with the Algonquins. The position of the Western Abenakis in precontact trade has not been worked out.

Games

The ability to run was much esteemed. Among the boys games requiring much running were played at an early age, and races were frequent. Archery practice and contests likewise commenced at an early age and continued throughout life. The hand ball game, recorded among them by Lafitau (1724, 2:76) is probably the one recorded in detail on the lower Merrimack by Wood (1634:86), and lacrosse, played at Saint Francis in the nineteenth century, was probably aboriginal among them. Specimens of the ring-and-pin game have been collected from them, but the game is no longer remembered. In the nineteenth and early twentieth centuries, boys played a kind of snow snake and slid downhill on a

Fig. 6. Joseph Paul Denis (b.1832, d.1928), Western Abenaki, making birchbark canoe models. Photograph was taken at Odanak by an unknown local photographer in 1923 and was printed as a postcard.

single upturned stave, but by 1900 all these pastimes had been largely replaced by baseball and card playing.

Cosmogony

The Western Abenaki physical world was not created. It always existed under the supervision of *tabaldak,* the Owner, who created the living beings. Only one, *odziozo,* was so powerful that he created himself from some dust that the Owner had touched. *odziozo* became the Transformer who reshaped the surface of the earth to his liking, finally changing himself into a rock in Lake Champlain to watch over his handiwork. Man was created by *tabaldak* in two efforts. First he created a man and a woman out of stone, but, not liking the result, he destroyed them. Then he created a couple from living wood who pleased him and who became the ancestors of the Indian race. This exemplifies the concept of stone as the substance of primeval power and of wood as the substance appropriate to man. In ancient times, a man of great power was born, *pədəgwadzo,* who became the lesser Transformer whose deeds tamed the elements in favor of mankind. In the world of the Western Abenaki, many things are alive that White people commonly regard as inanimate, and every living thing has its own peculiar power, more or less specific in kind and limited in quantity. Man seeks to increase his power and to acquire other powers through the dream vision quest and the acquisition of a guardian spirit, tokens of whom were formerly preserved. A few individuals are born with unusual spiritual powers. Such a one is a *mədawlinno.* The most common acts of northern shamanism are found among the powers of different

Abenaki *mədawlinno*s—divination to locate game, far seeing and seeing into the future, sinking their footsteps into rock, and curing by mental power. For the solution of difficult oracles, the *mədawlinno* retired into a small dome-shaped hut, but the shaking tent was not used. The drum is the *mədawlinno*'s instrument, and missionary disapproval may have been the reason it fell into disuse until it was revived as a dance accompaniment in the mid-twentieth century. The basic organizing principles of the Western Abenaki world view are the animate world; the concept of personal power; the earth, Our Grandmother, which is the tangible source of the life force; the Owner's concern for the game animals and the medicinal plants, out of which grow the rituals of harvesting and recycling by tobacco burning, prayer, conservative harvesting, respectful treatment of bones, the grease incense offering before eating, and the interdiction against food waste.

Myth

Western Abenaki myth and cosmology clearly belong to the genre of the Wabanaki region rather than to that north of the Saint Lawrence River. In it, the Trickster is *azəban,* the Raccoon, and the Trickster cycle is completely divorced from the Transformer cycle. It shares with Eastern Abenaki mythology the dread flying creature *bmola;* the Wind Bird; the benevolent Thunders, who are a group of brothers, seven in number as with the Iroquois; malevolent underwater creatures; and curious little underwater people, the *manǫgəmasak.* Besides myth, their corpus of oral narrative comprises many stories that were repeated to teach and preserve the values of the culture. Sacred stories could be repeated only in winter when man's natural enemies, the underwater monsters, could not hear them. Secular and teaching stories, as well as oral historical traditions, of which the Abenaki are very tenacious, can be told at any time.

Ceremonies

Certain occasions were marked by public ceremonies, each with its own dance and ritual. The principal occasions were weddings, greeting visitors from another village or tribe, chief making, first corn harvest, declaration of war, and funerals. Numerous social dances were performed at most of these ceremonies and are still performed for pleasure in an impromptu gathering. A number of borrowed dances are now performed—the Eagle Dance and the women's Blanket Dance from the Iroquois, the Knife Dance from the Hurons of Lorette, and the Pipe Dance that descends from the Calumet Dance introduced by the Fox in 1719 (LeSueur 1952). The music for dancing is supplied by a singer who accompanies himself on a rattle.

Curing

158   Although a *mədawlinno* might be called on to treat a mysterious or stubborn illness, the use of plant medicines was highly developed and persisted in the 1970s. Certain common remedies were widely known, but a few individuals, both men and women, were highly skilled and knowledgeable and were recognized as professionals. The reputation of Abenaki doctors spread to surrounding White communities in colonial times, and their influence can be traced in colonial herbalism. The men of one family have simultaneously practiced plant medicine and collected medicinal plants for pharmacies for at least the last hundred years.

Sociocultural Situation in 1970

The Western Abenaki band at Odanak is governed under the rules of the Canadian Department of Indian Affairs by an elected chief and three elected councilors and managed by an Indian band manager. The majority of the population belongs to the Roman Catholic mission of Saint François-de-Sales, which has a resident missionary, and a smaller number belongs to the Anglican mission conducted from Sorel. There is very little subsistence agriculture, no trapping, and guiding has disappeared. Most men are employed off the reserve. Some native artifacts are produced for tourists, but ash splint-sweetgrass basketmaking has ceased being an important industry. All school children are transported to White schools off the reserve, and there is a fair proportion continuing to secondary and university levels.

In 1974 the language survived with 21 elderly, fully

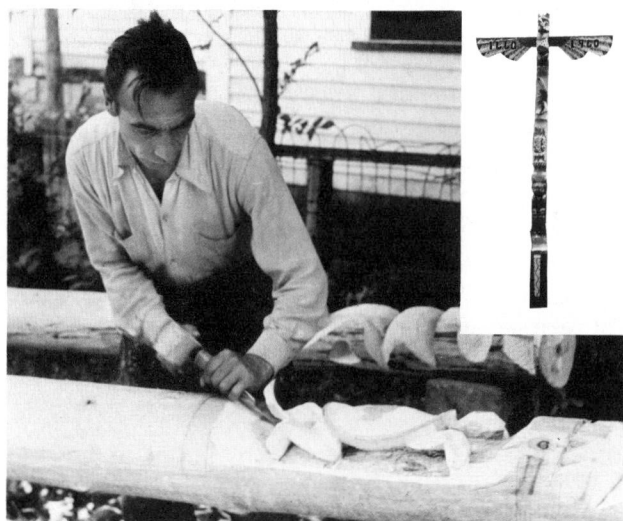

Dartmouth College Mus. and Galleries, Anthr. and Hist. Coll., Photo Archive, Hanover, N.H.

Fig. 7. Adrian Panadis, an Abenaki, carving a ceremonial pole for one of the annual celebrations at Odanak. The inset at right shows the first such pole, made for the 1960 celebration. Modern poles probably derive in part from Northwest Coast totem poles, adapted so as to continue the tradition of the medicine pole (*mədawakwam*), which stood on the same spot by the river's edge. They feature the turtle (being carved) and bear, symbols of the moieties of the St. Francis Abenaki. Photographs by William Bryant and Alfred Whiting (inset), July 1960.

competent speakers and an undetermined number of young and middle-aged persons with varying amounts of knowledge of the language, mostly passive. Young people were being raised speaking French as a first language. Odanak is superficially like the surrounding Canadian villages, and practically nothing can be observed of the traditional or contact-traditional culture in the areas of subsistence, political organization, social organization, or ceremony excepting the occasional performance of social and ceremonial dances for audiences. In spite of this, there existed in the 1960s in the minds of the older people a nearly full recollection of the elements of the traditional way of life, either from youthful participation or from tradition. Many Abenaki attitudes persist in the areas of child rearing, social relationships, and world view.

Synonymy

Abenaki: probably from Montagnais 8abanäki8ek 'dawn land people' (Fabvre 1970:208–209) through Champlain's French as Abenaquioicts. It has an Abenaki cognate wǫbanakiiak, which seems to have been adopted by the missionaries at Sillery and brought by them to Saint Francis. The supremacy of this name over those of the more numerous Sokoki and of the other tribes at Saint Francis is probably a historical accident assisted by the fact that most spoke Abenaki dialects. See "Eastern Abenaki," this volume, for full synonymy.

Sokoki: from their own name ozokwaki, plural ozokwakiak 'the ones who broke up, broke way'. Some variants encountered are French Assok8ekik, Sokokiois, Sokoquiois, Sokoquis; English Sowquachick, Squakeys, Suckquakege, Zooquagese; Dutch Soquackicks. The Mohawk Onojake appears to be a translation of the Abenaki name.

Penacook: from pǝnǫkok 'at the falling bank', the name of the village site at Concord, New Hampshire. The people were pǝnǫkoi, plural pǝnǫkoiak 'falling bank people'. They appear in French sources as penneng8s, Oupeneng8s (JR 60:214–218), Oppenago (Margry 1876–1886, 5:304), and similar forms (Day 1973).

Cowasuck: from goasǝk 'white pine place', the name of the Lower Coos Intervales at Newbury, Vermont. The people were goasi, plural goasiak 'the ones from the white pines'. Variant forms for the place are French Koés and English Cohass, Cohoss, Coos, and for the people Cohassiac (Kendall 1809, 3:191).

Missisquoi: from mazipskoik 'at the flint', referring to the chert quarry near Swanton, Vermont. The people were mazipskoi, plural mazipskoiak 'flint people'. Some of the variants are Michiskoui, Misiskuoi, Missiscoui, Masiassuck, Missisque, and Missisco.

The name Arsigantegok (variously Arrasaguntacook, Ersegontegog, Assagunticook, Anasaguntacook) was applied to the Saint-François River and Arsigantegwiak to the Saint Francis Indians in the eighteenth century. Some writers have mistakenly thought that this was the original name of the Androscoggin River tribes and that they were therefore the first to settle Saint Francis. Saint Francis was actually settled by Sokokis, and Arsigantegok seems to have its origin in Eastern Abenaki arsikañntekw 'empty cabin river', perhaps so called (Aubery 1715a) because upon the arrival of the Abenakis from Sillery, many houses had been emptied by the smallpox (Gill 1886:13). This name was adopted by the Western Abenakis as alsigǫntǝgok and several folk etymologies developed to account for it. The Mahican called the people of Saint Francis Wtanshekaunhtukko (Hopkins 1753:77).

Sources

There is no comprehensive historical or anthropological treatment of the Western Abenaki. Maurault (1866) was an attempt at a comprehensive history, but, except for three chapters and some of the footnotes, it relies on secondary sources. Charland (1964) is a painstaking work from primary documents, but it is focused on the Saint Francis village. Some information about the Saint Francis band is contained in two histories of the French parish Saint-François-du-Lac (Sulte 1886; Charland 1942) and in the several captivity narratives. The most readily accessible local sources on the Western Abenakis in New England are, for the Penacooks, Bouton (1856); for the Squakheags, Temple and Sheldon (1875); for the Cowasuck, Z. Thompson (1842); and for the Missisquoi, Crockett (1921). These works are all mixtures of primary and secondary materials and contain some dated assumptions. Hemenway (1868–1891) preserves numerous testimonies of first settlers concerning the local Abenakis. Two little-known sources are the biography of Henry Tufts (1807), who was among the bands between Lakes Memphremagog and Umbagog in 1772–1775, and the papers of Henri Vassal (1811–1889), who was agent for the Abenakis at Saint Francis in the late nineteenth century.

The only extensive ethnographic data are contained in the field notes of Hallowell (1918–1932) and Day (1956–1973) and in Hallowell's (1928, 2) study of kinship. This classic study should be considered in the light of knowledge that Western Abenaki nomenclature has an independent history and is not derived from the Eastern Abenaki terms. A fairly complete collection of Western Abenaki material culture specimens could be assembled from the combined collections of the Museum of Man, National Museums of Canada, Ottawa; La Société Historique d'Odanak; the McCord Museum, McGill University, Montreal; the Museum of the American Indian, Heye Foundation, New York; Dartmouth College Museum, Hanover, New Hampshire; University Museum, University of Pennsylvania, Philadelphia. The language has been documented by three native writers, Pial Pol Wzôkhilain, Sozap Lolô, and Henry L. Masta (Day 1961).

159

Indians of Southern New England and Long Island: Early Period

BERT SALWEN

At the time of earliest European contacts with Indians in the sixteenth and early seventeenth centuries, the region stretching southwest along the Atlantic coast from Saco Bay, Maine, to the vicinity of the Housatonic River, in Connecticut, and from Long Island inland to southern New Hampshire and Vermont was occupied by groups of Indians who shared, with minor exceptions, a single cultural pattern (fig. 1). All spoke closely related Algonquian languages, obtained their food by combining maize-beans-squash horticulture with the collecting of land and sea fauna and wild plants, and engaged in very similar social, political, and religious practices centered on the village as the basic social unit.

Southern New England, as a cultural region, could be easily distinguished from surrounding regions. Its northeast boundary, while it may have shifted somewhat over time, was particularly clear, marked by a sharp decrease in the importance of horticulture, with other accompanying differences in subsistence pattern, and by the relatively abrupt linguistic break between the Southern New England and Western Abenaki languages ("Eastern Algonquian Languages," this vol.). As early as 1524, Giovanni da Verrazano noted the contrast between the horticultural people of "Refugio" (Narragansett Bay?) and the people of coastal Maine, who were without any signs of cultivation (Wroth 1970:138-140). Traveling from north to south in 1605, Samuel de Champlain noted significant horticulture for the first time at the mouth of the Saco River, and it was at this point that his Micmac Indian guides "could understand only certain words" of the local language (Champlain 1922-1936, 1:325-327).

The southwest border of the region is not quite so obvious, since there was no sharp change in subsistence pattern, but here again, somewhere between the Housatonic River and the present Connecticut-New York border, there was a marked linguistic break—from the southern New England language group to Munsee Delaware (Goddard 1971a:20).

Language

All the people in the region spoke one of five Eastern Algonquian languages—Loup, Massachusett, Narragansett, Mohegan-Pequot-Montauk, and Quiripi-Unqua-chog.* Table 2 in "Eastern Algonquian Languages," this volume, indicates the phonological similarity of these speech varieties, but they differed in other ways. For example, they frequently used different words, even for common entities and concepts (Ives Goddard, personal communication 1972). Nevertheless, several seventeenth-century writers claim that all the languages were easily understood by speakers of any of the others (Gookin 1972:13; Williams 1936:A3; Wood 1865:103). This may have been particularly true along the coast and among speakers with some previous exposure to other languages. Other early reports emphasize linguistic differences, such as difficulties experienced by speakers of the Martha's Vineyard dialect in communicating with residents of Nantucket and the nearby Massachusetts mainland (see "Eastern Algonquian Languages," this vol.).

Culture

Subsistence

Until more archeological work has been completed at late prehistoric and early contact period sites, it is impossible to quantify the relative importance of each of the enormous number of plant and animal products that contributed to the survival of the southern New England Indians. Resources of inland forests, lakes, and rivers as well as those of the sea and tidal marshlands were exploited through a complex series of changes of residence keyed to the yearly productive cycles of the particular environments. Hoe cultivation also contributed importantly to the food supply.

Both archeological and ethnohistorical sources testify to the wide range of land mammals, ranging in size from black bear to gray squirrel, that were hunted for food (for example, Waters 1965; Morton 1838:50-56; Wood 1865:98-100), but this picture of diversity is probably somewhat misleading. Archeological evidence from a Mohegan site in Connecticut suggests that deer provided close to 90 percent of the edible mammal meat in early contact times (Salwen 1970:6; L.E. Williams 1972:203). Deer hunting appears to have been the major male activity in fall and early winter.

* There is no available phonemic analysis of the Southern New England languages, all of which are extinct. Words and names from these languages have been cited in the attested English spellings.

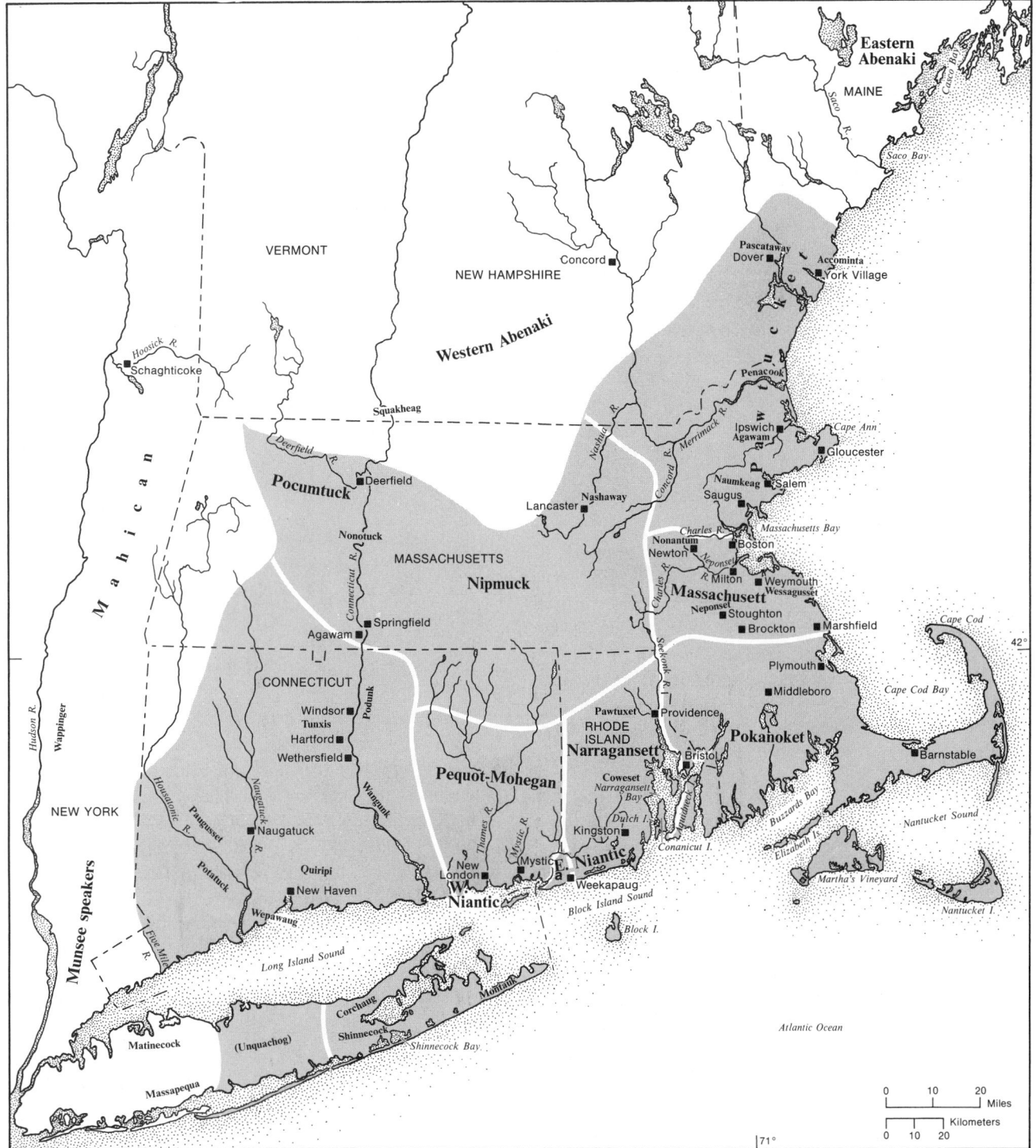

Fig. 1. Tribal territories about 1630. a, Part of Pequot territory before 1617; Pequot territory extended west to the Connecticut River after 1620. The location of the Unquachog in the 17th century is uncertain; if they belonged to the same linguistic subgroup as the Matinecock and Massapequa the boundaries would be different from those shown here. Most of the modern towns were established after 1630.

Deer were stalked or caught in traps and snares (Morton 1838:51-52; Williams 1936:163-164; Wood 1865:98-100). The communal drive has been reported for eastern Connecticut (Anonymous n.d.) and for the Narragansett territory, sometimes involving as many as "two or three hundred in a company" in the latter area (Williams 1936:163), but it is not described for Massachusetts. Its absence there may be a postcontact phenomenon, caused by the catastrophic decline in population after the epidemics of 1615-1619. V-shaped hedges a mile or two long to lead deer to hunters or traps at the funnel's mouth are reported in northeastern Massachusetts

161

(Wood 1865:99). These may have been used in conjunction with communal deer drives when populations were larger. At the northern edge of the region, moose were frequently hunted (Morton 1838:51), possibly at least partially supplanting deer in importance. In southwestern Maine moose were run down in winter by men on snowshoes (MHSC ser. 3, 3:302).

Whales do not appear to have been systematically hunted in southern New England in precontact times, but they were washed ashore fairly frequently, and stranded individuals were butchered by large parties from nearby villages (Mourt 1963:33; Williams 1936:113). In the early postcontact period, the Indians of eastern Long Island were widely known as skillful whalers. In eastern Massachusetts, Indians stalked seals sleeping on rocks along the coast in warm weather. Seal oil was highly prized (Wood 1865:101).

Waterfowl were shot with bow and arrow or netted. Cormorants were taken at night from their roosts on the offshore rocks (Williams 1936:91; Wood 1865:33). Of the larger birds, swan, Canada goose, ruffed grouse, and turkey were found in refuse pits at the seventeenth-century Fort Shantok site (Salwen 1970:5). Turtles are reported as food only by Wood (1865:36), but turtle remains were fairly common at Fort Shantok. There is both archeological and ethnohistorical evidence for many kinds of fish, both freshwater and saltwater species (Salwen 1970:5; Morton 1838:58-62; Williams 1936: 112-117; Wood 1865:100-101). These were caught on lines fitted with bone hooks (fig. 2) (Wood 1865:100), in

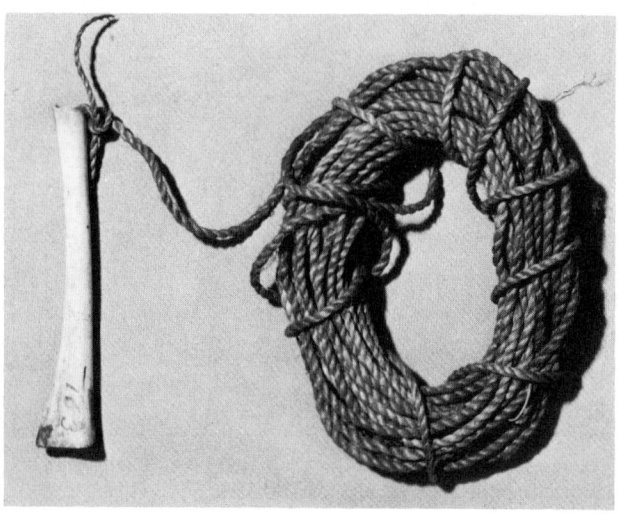

British Mus.: Sloane Coll. 1730.

Fig. 2. A fish line made of 2 strands of spun vegetable fiber (perhaps *Apocynum*), twisted together, with a gorge made of the shank bone of a fawn attached. The bone is unworked except for the cut ends. (See "Late Prehistory of the East Coast," figs. 8-9, this vol., for examples of late prehistoric bone fishhooks.) These specimens were received from "Mr. Winthorpe from N[ew] England"—probably John Winthrop (b.1681, d.1747), who was a Fellow of the Royal Society, London—and may have been collected by him or by his grandfather. Cord is approximately 13.0 m long; bone is 11.8 cm in length.

162

nets, at weirs built across streams (Mourt 1963:63), and by lance from canoes. Sturgeon seem to have been particularly important. According to Wood (1865:101), there was a sharp seasonal shift in fishing activities in eastern Massachusetts: summer fishing in the ocean and winter fishing in freshwater rivers and ponds, sometimes through holes cut in the ice. However, in Rhode Island shorefishing seems to have continued through the winter (Williams 1936:116). Spring runs of spawning fish provided opportunities for large catches with minimum effort, and locations along rivers where these fish could be most easily taken were important spring and summer campsites, particularly for the more inland Indian groups. Fish caught in times of abundance were dried on scaffolds placed in the sun or over smoky fires for use in other seasons (Williams 1936:113; Wood 1865:107).

In eastern Massachusetts, lobsters collected by women in summer were used for bait by male fishermen or dried and smoked as food for winter (Wood 1865:39, 107). Shellfish—particularly oysters, hard- and soft-shell clams, and scallops—were an important food resource that apparently served two functions. Parties of inland people made summer visits to the shore, where they collected and dried shellfish to be carried home for winter consumption (Mourt 1963:65). Shellfish also served as emergency winter fare for coastal inhabitants (Wood 1865:77).

Wild plant resources varied with season and locality. Roots were primarily winter food, according to Wood (1865:75). Through the summer strawberries, raspberries, blackberries, blueberries, and finally, grapes were available (Morton 1838:45; Williams 1936:97). In the fall, walnuts, chestnuts, and acorns were gathered, husked, dried, and stored for time of need. All of these could be powdered for use in soups and stews (Gookin 1972:15), and acorns could be turned, by thorough boiling, into a palatable dish (Williams 1936:95). The accounts of seventeenth-century observers do not stress wild vegetable foods; and, because of poor preservation, they tend to be underrepresented at archeological sites. These resources were probably much more important in the total Indian procurement system than this brief paragraph suggests.

Indian hemp was gathered to make nets, lines (fig. 2) ropes, and twined baskets (fig. 3).

From Verrazano onward, there are relatively full descriptions of Indian horticulture. Martin Pring in 1603, Champlain in 1605 and 1606, and John Smith in 1614 were all impressed by the extent of the cultivated fields that lined the shore in many places between the Saco and Cape Cod. At Cape Ann in 1606 Champlain (1922-1936, 1:401) noted that the Indians were constantly clearing new fields, possibly an indication of the growing importance of maize horticulture near the northern limit of its range.

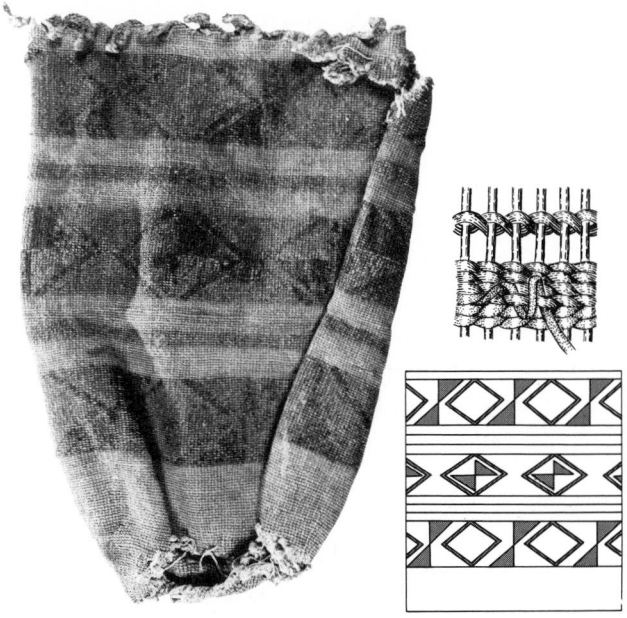

Conn. Histl. Soc., Hartford: A-56.

Fig. 3. Mohegan twined basket made of Indian hemp *(Apocynum cannabinum)*, probably dating from the mid-17th century. This basket was identified as a "Yohicake basket" (used for carrying or storing powdered parched corn) by Cynthia Tecunwass or Tocumwas (b.1775), from whom it was obtained. (See Butler 1947:42 for Tocumwas family history.) The design is of false embroidery (see detail) using natural and purplish-black dyed porcupine quills. Reconstruction is after Willoughby (1935:253). Height about 32 cm.

Crops were maize, kidney bean, squash, Jerusalem artichoke, and tobacco (Champlain 1922-1936, 1:328; Pring 1906:347; Smith 1912:667). Parties of 50 or more men and women cleared the land for planting (Williams 1936:99). Trees were cut about three feet above the ground, the branches and trunks burned, and seeds planted among the stumps, which were eventually removed (Champlain 1922-1936, 1:401). Champlain (1922-1936, 1:327-328) watched the planting of a field on the banks of the Saco in July 1605: after the soil was broken up with spade-shaped implements of hardwood, horseshoe crab shells were used to heap up corn hills, each containing three or four kernels of maize and an equal number of beans, and spaced about three feet apart. Small fish were sometimes placed in each cornhill as fertilizer (Mourt 1963:82), a practice that may be of European origin (Ceci 1975, 1975a). Fields might be allowed to lie fallow to recover fertility, being burned over when they were ready to be replanted (Champlain 1922-1936, 1:352). Clamshell hoes were used for weeding in Massachusetts (Wood 1865:106).

Planting, cultivating, and harvesting were usually done by women, though old men or a young man out of affection for his wife might help out. The exception was tobacco, which, at least among the Narragansett, was grown by men (Williams 1936:99, 14).

There are no quantitative data available concerning the amount of produce raised per person or the relative importance of horticulture in comparison to the collection of wild foods. Williams (1936:102) provides one hint: among the Narragansett of the early contact period, each woman would commonly raise enough maize to form, while drying, two or three heaps, each containing between 12 and 20 bushels of grain.

The dried maize was placed in woven sacks or baskets and buried in large holes or trenches (Champlain 1922-1936, 1:410-411; Morton 1838:30; Wood 1865: 106) to be used as needed during the fall and winter. The first Pilgrim explorers on Cape Cod found such caches and appropriated their contents (Mourt 1963:22, 26, 34).

Technology

The combination of a subsistence pattern that required frequent shifts of habitation and the lack of easy methods of land transport did not permit the accumulation of numerous or cumbersome material possessions. The emphasis was on easily fabricated multipurpose tools that could be made on the spot and discarded after use. Objects that embodied more labor time had to be as light as possible. Exceptions to this rule, such as large ceramic jars and heavy wooden mortars, were usually left behind at the camp or village site, to be used again during the next cycle of movement.

The basic weapons, in both hunting and warfare, were bows and arrows. According to Pring (1906:347-348), the bows in use in the Cape Cod area in 1603 were made of witch hazel, between five and six feet long, painted black and yellow, with strings formed of three twisted sinews. The wooden arrows, which were over a yard long and bore three long black feathers, were kept in rush quivers decorated with diamond designs in red and other colors. In eastern Massachusetts Wood (1865:101) saw arrows of elder, fitted with foreshafts set loosely into the main shafts, so that the main shaft could be recovered while the point continued to trouble the wounded beast.

Arrowheads were made of stone, deer antler, eagle claws (Mourt 1963:37), bone, and horseshoe crab tails; or arrows were simply sharpened to a point (Champlain 1922-1936, 1:326-327). Very early in the contact period, Indians began to replace these native materials with iron, copper, and brass. Metal projectile points are mentioned frequently in the contemporary literature (MHSC ser. 1, 1:123; Wood 1865:101), and such points—both European-made and fashioned by Indians from worn kettles and other metal objects—are found frequently at contact-period archeological sites (Salwen 1966; Simmons 1970:45-46; Solecki 1950:30; P.A. Thomas 1973:33).

The distributional ranges of two kinds of watercraft overlapped in southern New England (fig. 4). Dugout canoes were the basic southern type of boat, but they are reported from as far north as Massachusetts Bay, and possibly even from the mouth of the Saco River, if a

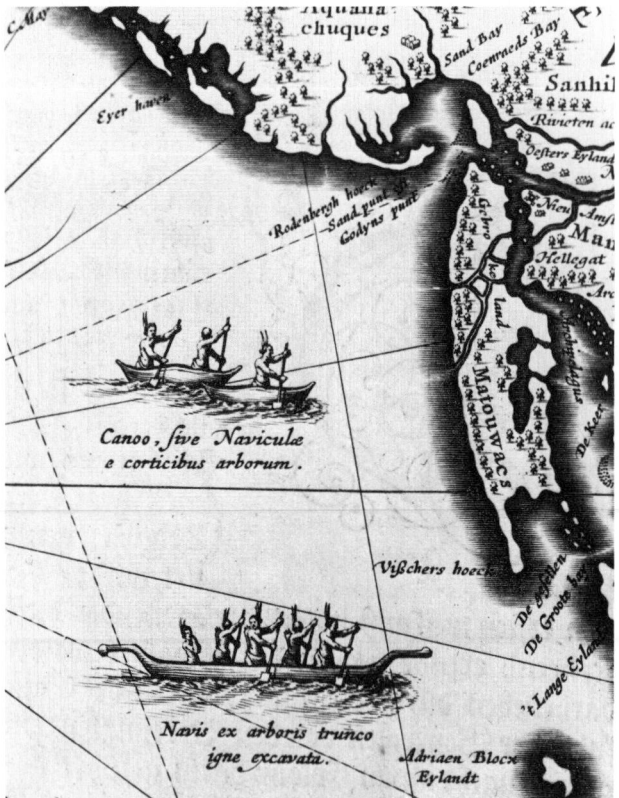

Lib. of Congress: Blaeu 1635:map 204.

Fig. 4. Detail of canoes from Willem and Johannes Blaeu's 1635 map of "Nova Belgica et Anglia Nova," depicting and identifying bark canoes (top) and a dugout canoe (below). The placement of the canoes south of New Amsterdam (east is at page bottom) was probably somewhat arbitrary, as the bark canoes are likely the more northern form, but there is evidence for dugouts of similar shape near New York. This map was the model for similar depictions of canoes and palisaded villages ("Mahican," fig. 2, this vol.) on subsequent maps of New England.

secondhand account of a 1606 encounter can be accepted (Lescarbot 1928:101). Made of pine, oak, or chestnut, a dugout could be shaped by one man, using stone tools, in 10–12 days. The largest were 40 or 50 feet long and could carry 40 men (Wood 1865:102; Gookin 1972:18; Williams 1936:107). Birch or elm bark canoes, the standard boats of the boreal forest zone, were frequently used in the Massachusetts Bay area, but there are only infrequent references to their use south of that point (see Wolley 1902:56 and Danckaerts 1913:162 for coastal New York and New Jersey examples).

Overland transportation depended primarily upon the strong backs of the women. "It is almost incredible what burthens the poore women carry of *Corne*, of *Fish*, of *Beanes*, of *Mats*, and a childe besides" (Williams 1936:38).

Structures

Houses varied somewhat in shape, and considerably in size, depending on function and time of year, but all were built on the same basic structural plan (fig. 5). Long flexible poles were driven into the ground at intervals around the perimeter of the space to be occupied, bent over until they met members from the opposite side, and lashed in place. Smaller horizontal poles were then lashed to the uprights, to stiffen the framework and provide support for the slabs of bark or woven mats that covered the structure (Champlain 1922–1936, 1:352, 413; Morton 1838:19; Mourt 1963:28–29; MHSC ser. 3, 6:39).

Smaller houses in which two (nuclear?) families could live comfortably were usually round, about 14 to 16 feet in diameter (Williams 1936:33), mat-covered, with a central fire pit, a square hole in the roof above the fire, and low mat-covered doorways. When habitation was shifted, the framework was left behind, but the mats could be rolled up and carried to the new site (Wroth 1970:139). Larger structures were also built, apparently in winter when populations were more concentrated. These were said to be up to 100 feet long and 30 feet broad, containing a row of two to four fires, and housing 40 to 50 people (Gookin 1972:14; Wood 1865:106). These "long houses" were apparently bark-covered.

Furnishings were simple. Beds were mats and skins, laid directly on the ground (Mourt 1963:29) or on low wooden platforms about 12 to 18 inches high (Champlain 1922–1936, 1:413; Morton 1838:20; Gookin 1972:15). Forked sticks driven into the ground on each side of the fire supported poles from which hung the cooking pots (Mourt 1963:28). In rainy weather, when the smoke holes had to be at least partly covered, residents sometimes had to lie down to avoid the worst of the smoke (Wood 1865:106).

Settlement Pattern

The basic face-to-face unit of population appears to have been the "village," defined here as a social unit utilizing the resources of a limited territory, usually part of a drainage system or a section of the coastal plain. There was a residential village consisting of a cluster of houses, but there were also various other locales—fishing stations, wild-plant collecting areas, marshes frequented by migratory waterfowl, shellfish collecting and processing sites, deer hunting territories—to which village members had use-rights, in some cases sharing these with people from other villages.

Summer was the time of maximum mobility, when families were dispersed (Wood 1865:106). During his summer travels along the Massachusetts coast in 1605 and 1606, Champlain (1922–1936, 1:350) saw many individual houses, each surrounded by as much land as the occupants needed for horticultural purposes (fig. 5). In Rhode Island Indians sometimes used fields a mile or more apart, and when the work at one was over, they moved their dwelling to another (Williams 1936:46). Summer was also a time for short trips to special resource sites. The people of Nemasket in southeastern Massachu-

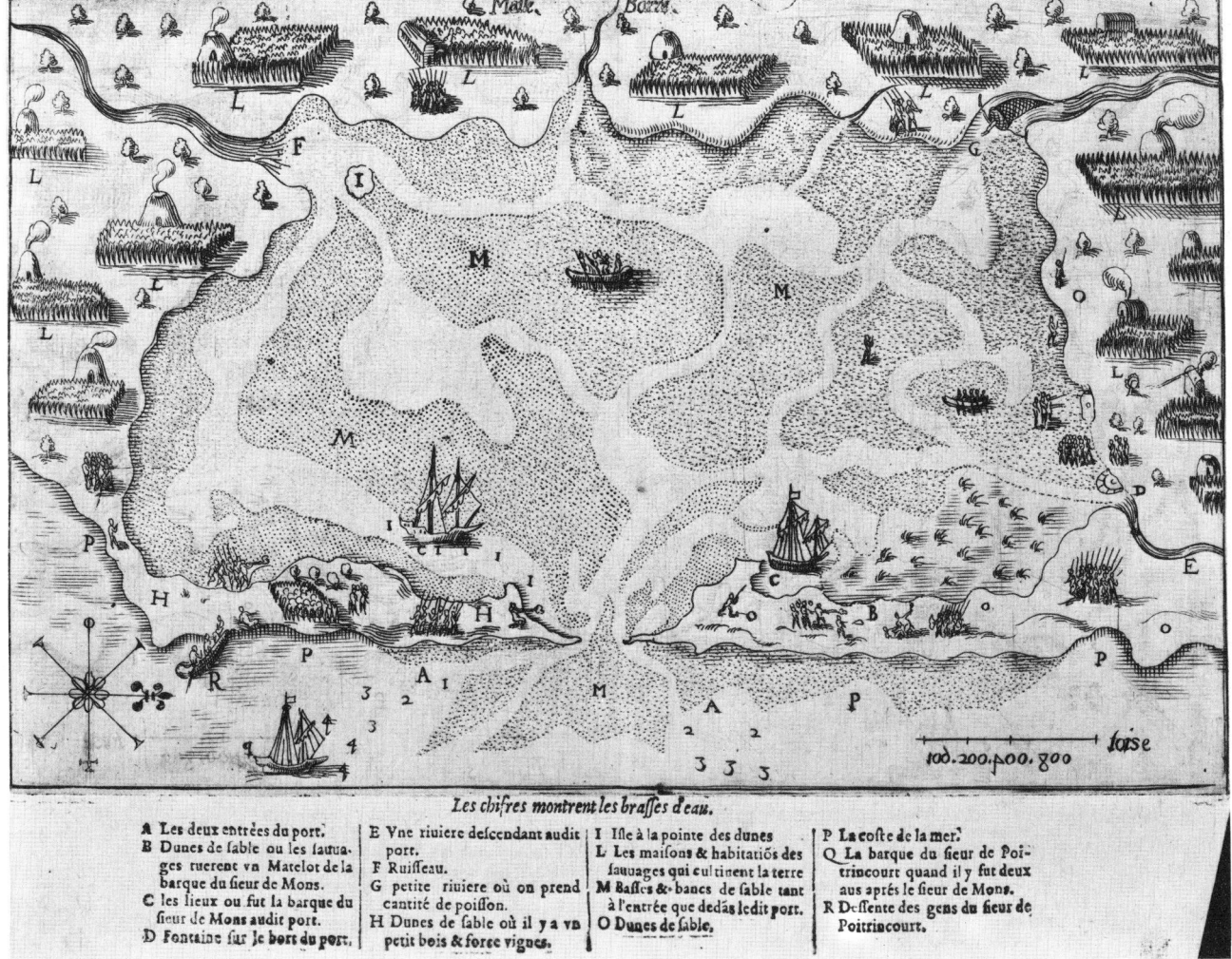

Fig. 5. Champlain's 1605 map of Malle Barre (Nauset Harbor, Mass.) showing (L) domed and barrel-vaulted wigwams with smoke holes adjacent to cornfields as well as (G) a fish trap. (See Champlain 1922–1936, 1:opp. 358 for specific geographic identifications.) The skirmish at bottom right (B) depicts the killing of a sailor by the Indians. The numbers indicate soundings.

setts traveled about 15 miles to the seacoast at Plymouth at every spring tide to harvest lobsters; they also spent much time at a fishweir site on a nearby river, sleeping in the open (Mourt 1963:62–63).

After the harvest, the Indians made their major annual move—from the summer fields to the deep forests where they spent the winter (Williams 1936:46). In October 1606, on southern Cape Cod, the French explorers observed the natives taking down their houses and sending women and children, with all their provisions, into the woods (Champlain 1922–1936, 1:416). Unfortunately, this regular seasonal activity was misinterpreted as preparation for warfare, and a series of skirmishes followed.

Populations appear to have been more concentrated in winter, but even in early winter, families were often away from the village in hunting camps, which were occupied until the deep snows came (Williams 1936:46; Wood 1865:98). Spring fish runs provided the opportunity for multivillage gatherings, which were occasions for games

and celebration (Morton 1838:20). In Rhode Island, at least, the move from the winter village to the summer fields seems to have been accomplished in two leisurely stages (Williams 1936:46–47).

The pattern of seasonal movement on Long Island may have been slightly different from that on the mainland. Denton (1845) reports that the "principal quarters" were at the cornfields; there were also hunting sites and fishing sites. Travel across Long Island Sound was quite common, but if this followed a regular seasonal pattern, it has not yet been discovered.

Houses were abandoned after the death of the occupant (Williams 1936:46). One reason for relocation of an entire village seems to have been the depletion of the local firewood supply (Williams 1936:60).

Village sizes and arrangements are difficult to determine from the seventeenth-century written sources, and archeology is just beginning to supply some of the missing information. The earliest accounts do not make specific reference to stockades surrounding entire villages, though

165

Champlain (1922–1936, 1:329) saw a large house surrounded by palisades made of rather large trees at the mouth of the Saco, and a 1621 account describes two "forts" belonging to Nanapeshamet, a northeastern Massachusetts sachem, which contained single houses surrounded by palisade rings of 40 or 50 feet diameter and breast-high trenches (Mourt 1963:78). These three examples were all located near the northeastern border of the region and may have been local responses to raids by Maine Indians. Writing about Massachusetts in the 1629–1633 period, Wood (1865) describes a fort about 40 or 50 feet square that was used as a place of refuge in time of war, and archeological excavations suggest that the Corchaug fort in eastern Long Island was a somewhat larger example of this kind of structure (Solecki 1950:15; L. E. Williams 1972:84).

The Pequot fort at Mystic, Connecticut, destroyed by the colonists in 1637, was a true palisaded village, covering at least two acres and housing a minimum of 300 to 400 people (MHSC ser. 3, 6:38–39). Fort Shantok, in eastern Connecticut (L.E. Williams 1972), and the Squakheag village in southwestern New Hampshire (P.A. Thomas 1973) are archeological examples of large seventeenth-century palisaded villages ("Late Prehistory of the East Coast," fig. 1, this vol."). It is possible, though by no means certain, that this village plan was a very early postcontact development, the result of the growing danger of enemy attack and increasing economic pressures toward sedentism.

Trade

In addition to the resources of their own local environments, southern New England groups obtained valued nonlocal materials through participation in trade networks that linked different localities within the region with one another and with groups in adjacent regions. There is evidence that these networks were established long before European contact (for example, the presence of exotic lithic materials in precontact archeological sites), but they were undoubtedly quickly and substantially modified by the introduction of European trade goods.

European-Indian trade began quite early in the sixteenth century. Most of the earliest explorers of southeastern New England noted the presence of copper earrings, bracelets, pendants, and breastplates (Wroth 1970:138; Archer 1906:305–306; Brereton 1906:337–338; Pring 1906:348). The copper may have been obtained from early, unrecorded, European visitors to southern New England, but it seems more likely that it was first obtained by Maine and Nova Scotia Indians from European fishermen and fur traders and then traveled southward down a well-established aboriginal coastal trade route.

Champlain (1922–1936, 1:395–396) witnessed an exchange of "presents" at the mouth of the Saco in 1606. A Micmac chief from Nova Scotia brought European kettles, hatchets, and knives and received in return maize, squash, and kidney beans from the other Indians. The commercial nature of this transaction was quite clear to both Champlain and the Indians involved. If furs had been traded instead of European manufactured goods, this encounter would probably closely resemble those that took place at the northern border of the southern New England region in precontact times. The movement of goods within New England did not normally involve long journeys; rather, each group traded with its immediate neighbors, who in turn passed items on to neighbors farther from the source of supply (Smith 1912:676). Among the objects traded were animal skins, earthenware pots, maple bowls, and chestnuts (Morton 1838:30).

A prime example of aboriginal trade goods was wampum, cylindrical beads fashioned from the central column of whelk (*Busycon*) shells, for the white variety, and from the violet area of quahog (*Mercenaria*) shells for the "black" variety. Wampum was produced by the Indians of Long Island, coastal Connecticut, and Rhode Island (Shinnecock, Pequot, and Narragansett are specifically mentioned), as whelk shells were not found in quantity north of Cape Cod (Van Wassenaer 1909:87; De Rasieres 1909:103; Williams 1936:153–158; Wood 1865:69). These beads moved northeastward along the trade network as far as Nova Scotia, growing more valuable as the distance from the source increased.

The wampum trade appears to have existed in precontact times, and both the manufacture and distribution of the beads are well described by Lescarbot (1928:211–212) as observed in about 1606. Before metal tools were available, the shells were ground into shape on stone slabs and drilled with stone drills. Soon after contact, Indians, using iron drills (Williams 1936:156–157), began to produce larger amounts of this commodity for trade to the Dutch and English, who, in turn, traded it to inland and northern Indians for furs (De Rasieres 1909:110; Bradford 1908:234–236). Tools, manufacturing waste, and unfinished beads have been found in quantity at seventeenth-century Corchaug, Mohegan, and Narragansett sites (L.E. Williams 1972:130–133, 141–142; Simmons 1970:74, 88–89, 138). Wampum became a true medium of exchange and was probably an important agent in drawing southern New England Indians into the European money economy.

Social Organization

The early accounts, which are so informative about the more concrete aspects of culture, are of relatively little help in elucidating precontact social structure. When they are not completely ignored, these patterns tend to be described in terms of simplistic, and often misleading, analogies to European ones.

The village was the basic sociopolitical unit, just as it was the basic subsistence unit. Day-to-day leadership was provided by the village chief, or sachem. Early European observers often characterize the Indian political system as "monarchical" (Williams 1936:140), but descriptions of specific events clearly indicate that sachems had very limited coercive power and maintained their influence largely through persuasion and generosity. Important decisions were always arrived at in consultation with the "great men" of the village (Gookin 1972:20), who may have comprised a more or less formal sachem's council (Winslow 1910:345).

There is good evidence for some degree of true hereditary social stratification, village leaders generally coming from recognized "chiefly" lineages. A number of seventeenth-century sources give the impression that the authority of Narragansett sachems over both land and subjects was patrilineally inherited ("Narragansett," this vol.). Wood (1865:89) is quite specific about rules of "royal" succession:

> It is the custome for their Kings to inherite, the sonne always taking the Kingdome after his fathers death. If there be no sonne, then the Queene rules; if no Queene, the next to the blood-royall; who comes in otherwise, is but counted an usurping intruder, and if his faire carriage beare him not out the better, they will soone unscepter him.

But this is probably an oversimplified interpretation of a much more complex situation. The evidence for patterns of inheritance is not absolutely clear for all southern New England groups.

For example, there were "squaw sachems" in the seventeenth-century in both Massachusetts (Winthrop 1908, 2:160) and Rhode Island (Church 1829:20-27), and these do not seem to have been simply the widows of sachems, but rather women who were entitled to leading roles by virtue of descent. Women inherited rights to land, and their names appear on deeds transferring these lands to the English colonists (for example, Lechford 1885:238-239; MHSC ser. 1, 1:241; H.A. Wright 1905:11).

Uncas's genealogy, a unique 1679 document through which the Mohegan sachem attempted to strengthen his claim to eastern Connecticut lands, traces his descent both matrilineally and patrilineally from sachems of the Pequot, Narragansett, and Long Island Indians and can be cited to support arguments for either line of inheritance. In discussing this document, L. E. Williams (1972:23-27) has suggested that a basically matrilineal precontact system was gradually modified to conform to the patrilineal bias of the English colonial authorities, but Burton and Lowenthal (1974:595) concluded that various relationships could be the basis of a claim to sachemship and that "the lineal mode is of little consequence in determining qualifications for chieftaincy." Morgan (1959:135) was told by a part-Narragansett woman interviewed in Kansas in 1862 that descent among both Narragansett and Pequot had originally been "in the female line."

Marriages appear to have been arranged along class lines. Among leading families, at least, they were sometimes polygynous (Wood 1865:91; Williams 1936: 146-147; Gookin 1972:13), possibly reflecting the leaders' need for the products of their wives' labors for use in entertaining visitors and fulfilling other chiefly obligations as well as their desire to cement ties with neighboring chiefly lineages through marriage. Bride price was paid, sometimes im wampum (Wood 1865:91; Williams 1936:148). This practice seems in keeping with the general tendency toward patrilocal residence evidence in references to specific chiefly marriages in the early postcontact period (see, for example, Morton 1838:28). Postmarital residence rules for ordinary village members are not known, but the ease with which individuals could change village affiliation suggests an ambilocal pattern.

Political Organization

Above the village level, multivillage alliances undoubtedly played an important role, but it is not really clear if these were enduring or highly structured enough to be classed as true "tribes." Pre-1620 descriptions of eastern Massachusetts social units generally speak only of individual villages or loose groupings of villages. For example, Champlain, after visits in 1605 and 1606, refers to all Indians from the Saco to Cape Cod as "Almouchiquois." He names individual local leaders—Marchin at Casco Bay, Onemechin at the mouth of the Saco, Quiouhamenec at Gloucester harbor, Honabetha in the Massachusetts Bay area—but never mentions broader regional subgroups (Champlain 1922-1936).

Smith traveled along the same stretch of coast in 1614, mapping the locations of over 20 villages (Smith 1912:661-662). His description indicates that these were divided into three areal political units. First, the villages from Casco Bay to Cape Ann were "alied in confederacy" with the peoples of southwestern Maine. These groups differed little in language and culture, and "though most of them be Lords to themselves, yet they hold the Bashabes of Penobscot, the chiefe and greatest amongst them" (Smith 1912:661). Second, there were three Cape Cod villages "of the language and aliance of Chawum," the present Barnstable. Third, all the remaining eastern Massachusetts villages from just south of Cape Ann to Bristol, Rhode Island, "are called Massachusets and differ somewhat in language, custome, and condition" from those of Chawum (Smith 1912:662). The Massachusetts sometimes warred with the Bashabes of Penobscot and were not always friendly with the Chawum alliance, "but now they are all friends, and have each trade with other . . ." (Smith 1912:676). This tripartite division differs from later "tribal" classifications for the area in a number of respects.

The earliest information about the Long Island Sound *167*

area (except for Verrazano's very brief 1524 account) comes from Dutch sources. The "figurative map" of 1614 (Stokes 1915–1928, 2:C, pl. 23) and the 1625 (De Laet 1909:39–43) account, both based on the trading and exploring voyages of Adriaen Block and others between 1612 and 1614, provide data about many Indian groups between Narragansett Bay and western Long Island. Most of these seem to have been limited to relatively small geographic territories—the Wapenocks (or Wapanoos) on the "lower part" of Narragansett Bay and the Nahicans on the west shore of the same bay, the Pequatoos on "the River of Siccanamos" (the Mystic River?), the Morhicans on the next stream to the west (the Thames?), and so forth (De Laet 1909:42–43).

All later and fuller descriptions date from after the terrible epidemics of 1616–1619, which all but wiped out the native populations from southwestern Maine to Cape Cod, and hence reflect a greatly changed situation. These sources describe much more rigid, hierarchically structured political units, covering much larger geographic areas. Gookin (1972:7–12), for example, assigns all southern New England Indians, from the Connecticut River to southwestern Maine, to five great sachemdoms whose chief sachems "held dominion" over many "petty governours." The more westerly groups, whose populations were less devastated by the plague, appear to have been particularly highly organized. The Pequot sachem, Sassacus, was said to have had jurisdiction over 26 undersachems in the early 1630s (Winthrop 1908, 1:227) and to control all the territory between the Connecticut River and the Rhode Island border as well as most of eastern Long Island. The two Narragansett chiefs, Canonicus and Miantonomi, are described as wielding considerable authority over a large number of "subjects."

The data can be interpreted in a number of ways. Precontact political units may have been more tightly structured in the southern part of the region than they were to the north, possibly reflecting a somewhat more sedentary, horticulture-oriented way of life. It is just as possible, on the basis of the available evidence, that precontact political units were similar throughout the region and that the subregional variation indicated by the later sources simply reflects the effect of differential depopulation after the epidemic years. Nevertheless, Brasser (1971:65–70) is probably correct in suggesting that precontact sociopolitical units were quite small, each consisting of a number of extended families exploiting the lands around individual river systems, and that the larger, more formal "tribes" of the seventeenth century developed in response to new needs that arose with the fur trade and European settlement.

It must also be remembered that it was to the advantage of each European colonial administration to emphasize, and even to enhance if possible, the power and territorial limits of the particular Indian leaders from whom it obtained treaty rights and deeds to land, in

relation to other Indian leaders. In fact, the resolution of intercolonial disputes over boundaries often pivoted on conflicting interpretations of the original rights of the Indian sellers to the lands involved. The Dutch-English conflict over the Hartford, Connecticut, region and the disputes between the Massachusetts Bay colony and the Gortonist settlers over lands at Narragansett Bay are cases in point (Winthrop 1908, 2:33, 122–126).

Political Subdivisions

Any attempt to define "tribal" units must face these ethnographic and historical realities. Hence, though many nineteenth-century local and regional historians and some twentieth-century ethnologists (Speck 1928a, 1928d, and Swanton 1952 are the most extreme examples) have attempted to define sharply bounded geographic territories and to assign long lists of villages and individuals to each, this account will utilize a less precise, but probably more realistic, framework, based in part on linguistic evidence and in part on the sometimes conflicting seventeenth-century documentation.

Of the documentary sources, that of Gookin (1972:7), who was superintendent of the Indians of Massachusetts Bay colony almost without interruption from 1656 to 1687, seems most knowledgeable: "The principal nations of the Indians, that did, and do, inhabit the confines of New England, are five: 1. Pequots; 2. Narragansitts; 3. Pawkunnawkuts; 4. Massachusetts; 5. Pawtucketts." Gookin also makes reference to the "Nipmuck country" and to the Indians of the Connecticut River, of Quinapeake (Quinnipiac), and of Long Island, on the western and southern fringes of the New England colonial area.

Goddard ("Eastern Algonquian Languages," this vol.) recognizes five closely related languages in this same region. His Mohegan-Pequot-Montauk and Narragansett languages appear to correspond closely in geographic distribution with Gookin's Pequot and Narragansett political units. The Massachusett language appears to have been spoken by three of Gookin's "nations," the Pokanoket, the Massachusett, and the Pawtucket. The Loup language would appear to be that of the Nipmuck as well as that of the little-known peoples of the Connecticut River valley of central Massachusetts and southern Vermont and New Hampshire. Finally, Goddard's Quiripi-Unquachog would seem to cover the groups that inhabited southern Connecticut between the mouths of the Connecticut and Housatonic rivers—the Quiripi (Quinnipiac), Naugatuck, and possibly some of the people of central Long Island as well.

If Gookin's political units are thought of as relatively flexible multivillage alliances, as suggested above, they provide a reasonably satisfactory framework around which to organize the discussion of the history and demography of the early contact period. For population estimates, see table 1.

Table 1. Indian Populations of Southern New England, 17th Century

	Before 1617–1619 Epidemics			1620–1643	1674
	Gookin 1970:7–12	*Mooney 1928:4*			
Pawtucket	ca. 3,000 men	Penacook	2,000	1630—ca. 2,500 "Pennacook" (Mooney and Thomas 1910:225–226)	not above 250 men, besides women and children (Gookin 1972:12)
Massachusett	could arm for war ca. 3,000 men	probably including some Pawtucket	3,000	1631—sachem has 50–60 subjects (Dudley 1838:6) 1631—ca. 500 (Mooney and Thomas 1907i: 816–817)	not . . . above 300 men, besides women and children (Gookin 1972:12) 1,100 "souls yielding obedience to the gospel" within the jurisdiction of Massachusetts (Gookin 1972: 8); may include some Pawtucket
Pokanoket	ca. 3,000 men	Wampanoag, etc. Martha's Vineyard Nantucket Nauset	2,400 1,500 1,500 1,200	1621—ca. 500 "Nauset" (Mooney and Thomas 1910a:40–41)	300 families on Martha's Vineyard 300 families on Nantucket (Gookin 1972:102)
Narragansett	could arm for war more than 5,000 men	Including Eastern Niantic	4,000	1634—700 deaths from smallpox (Winthrop 1908, 1:118)	at most 1,000 able men (Gookin 1972:8) 2,000 fighting men (Hubbard 1677:ii,viii)
Pequot-Mohegan	ca. 4,000 men	Pequot Mohegan	2,200 600	1643—2,500 "Mohegan," including Pequot and others (Mooney 1907f:926–927)	not above 300 men (Gookin 1972:8), may be Pequot only
Other groups		Nipmuck Pocumtuck	500 1,200	1634—450 of 1,000 Indians at fort "up above in the River Conigtecut" died in epidemic (Bradford 1908:312)	
		Tunxis Podunk Wangunk Western Niantic	400 300 400 250	1633—3,000–4,000 "warlike Indians" near Hartford (Winthrop 1908, 1:103) 1638—ca. 100 "Niantic" (Mooney 1910i:69)	
		Quiripi Paugusset and Wepawaug	250 400	1638—47 Quiripi "men or youth growne to stature fit for service" (New Haven (Colony) 1857:3)	

Pawtucket (often called Penacook)

•TERRITORY   In the early 1630s the Pawtucket and related groups inhabited the coast from the north side of Massachusetts Bay at least as far as York Village, Maine, as well as a poorly defined interior hinterland. Local groups included, according to Gookin (1972:10), the Penacook (lower Merrimack drainage?—the upriver Penacook at Concord, New Hampshire, were actually Western Abenakis), Agawam (Ipswich, Massachusetts), Naumkeag (Salem, Massachusetts), Pascataway (Piscataqua—Dover, New Hampshire), and Accominta (York Village, Maine). Swanton (1952:17–18) lists many other local groups.

•HISTORY   If there were no major shifts in boundaries between the early and mid 1600s, Pawtucket-related people occupied the northernmost Almouchiquois villages described by Champlain in the area between the Saco River and Cape Ann in 1605 and 1606. At that time, open warfare, or at best uneasy truce, characterized the relationship between these people and their hunter-gatherer neighbors to the northeast. In the summer of 1607, Onemechin of the Saco River and Marchin of Casco Bay were killed by a raiding party of Micmac and other Nova Scotia and Maine Indians (Champlain 1922–1936, 1:457), and by 1608 Asticou had become the new regional chief and a new truce had been arranged (Lescarbot 1928:143). In view of these events, it is surprising that Smith (1912:661) after his 1614 visit, described the people from the Saco to Cape Ann as "alied in confederacy" with the people of the Kennebec and Penobscot drainages. There is better reason to believe that the Pawtucket were on friendlier terms with the Massachusett to the south, with whom they shared both language and a horticultural way of life (Gookin 1972:10).

European fishermen and fur traders were regular visitors to this part of the coast by 1616, when Richard Vine wintered there, probably at the mouth of the Saco. He reported that intensified warfare and a great epidemic had so sharply reduced the population "that the country was in a manner left void of inhabitants" (MeHSC ser. 1, 2:24). In 1619 Nanapeshamet, the major sachem of northeastern Massachusetts, was killed by raiding Maine Indians (Mourt 1963:78). Under these conditions, it is quite possible that his widow, the "Squaw Sachem" and the remnants of her people saw the English colonists as potential protectors. In any case, she and her three sons, Wonohaquaham (Sagamore John) of the Mystic River drainage, Montowampate (Sagamore James) of Saugus, and Wenepoykin (Sagamore George) of Salem, were consistently friendly to the English and transferred great tracts of land to the colonists (Lewis and Newhall 1865:34–38). John and James both died in the smallpox epidemic of 1633, which killed many of the remaining Pawtuckets (Winthrop 1908, 1:14–15).

Passaconaway, sachem of the Penacook on the lower Merrimack River, formally swore allegiance to the colonial government in 1644 (Winthrop 1908, 2:169), and at the time of King Philip's War, his son Wannalancet carried on his father's policy and withdrew his people northward up the river in an attempt to avoid involvement in the war. This group remained neutral even after a colonial raiding party marched deep into its territory and set fire to an Indian village (Gookin 1836:462–463).

Massachusett

• TERRITORY At the time of European settlement, the Massachusett population appears to have centered around the Neponset estuary, on the south side of Massachusetts Bay. On the south, the Massachusett territory met that of the Pokanoket along a shifting boundary roughly following the line between modern Marshfield and Brockton, Massachusetts. The boundary with the Pawtucket to the north was in the neighborhood of the Charles River. Local groups, according to Gookin, included those of Wessagusset (Weymouth), Neponset, Punkapaog (a "praying town" near Stoughton), and Nonantum (Newton). The Massachusett sachem also "held dominion over . . . some of the Nipmuck people, as

far as Pokomtakuke" (Pocumtuck, near Deerfield on the Connecticut River), and the Indians of Nashaway (Lancaster), though separately listed as under Massachusett authority, were apparently also ethnically Nipmuck (Gookin 1972:9–10). Swanton (1952:19–20) lists many other local groups and, following Speck (1928d), includes among them the Pawtucket "Band of Nanepashemet." All "tribal" distinctions in this region must, of necessity, be somewhat arbitrary. The Pawtucket and Massachusett were undoubtedly closely related in many respects, but most seventeenth-century colonists considered them to be separate entities.

• HISTORY The Massachusett were certainly among the Almouchiquois groups encountered by Champlain during the 1605 French explorations of the southern New England coast (Champlain 1922–1936, 1:336–342). French traders soon followed, and there were apparently visits by Dutch ships as well (De Laet 1909:39). In 1614 Smith (1912:675) visited "the country of the Massachusits, which is the paradice of all those parts." He seems to have considered the Pokanoket (excluding the people of Cape Cod) and the most southerly of the Pawtucket groups to be part of the Massachusett political unit. The epidemics of 1617–1619 hit the Massachusett as severely as the people to the north. Many villages were wholly abandoned (Dermer 1906:129–130), and the resulting depopulation and disorganization undoubtedly prevented any serious resistance to the initial European colonizing efforts.

In 1621, after the settlement of the English at Plymouth, a group of southeastern New England sachems came to the colony and made their marks on a document pledging loyalty to King James (N. Morton 1910:45). Among them was Obbatinewat, who lived "in the bottom of the Massachusetts Bay, yet he is under Massasoit" of Pokanoket. A Plymouth exploring party that visited this sachem a short while later found him in fear of attack by both the Tarrantines, whom Siebert (1973) has identified as Micmacs, and the Squaw Sachem's people (Mourt 1963:78). Another signer was Chicataubut, sachem at Neponset.

Late in 1622 another English settlement was begun, at Wessagusset, but by midwinter the colonists were hungry and disorganized and friction grew between English and Indians. The local sachem, Obtakiest, purportedly organized a plot to drive all the English out of southeastern New England, but the plan was revealed to the Plymouth colonists, who sent a small party to Wessagusset where they killed some of the leaders and wounded others, including Obtakiest (Winslow 1910:318–331; MHSC ser. 4, 4:474–487). This was the first and only armed clash between the Massachusett and the colonists.

In 1633 Chicataubut and many of his people died in the great smallpox epidemic (Winthrop 1908, 1:111). His successor, Cutchamakin, was an active ally of the Bay colony, serving often as messenger and interpreter (Winthrop 1908, 1:186). By the 1650s many of the remnant

Massachusett has been gathered into "praying towns" and at least superficially christianized (Gookin 1972). They took little part in King Philip's War, but they often suffered, nonetheless, from the anti-Indian hysteria of the period (Gookin 1836).

Pokanoket (or Wampanoag)

• TERRITORY   About 1620, the Pokanoket comprised a group of allied villages in eastern Rhode Island and in southeastern Massachusetts, south of Marshfield and Brockton. Gookin (1972:8–9) includes all of Cape Cod, Martha's Vineyard, and Nantucket within the borders of this group. Swanton (1952:21–27), following Speck (1928d), assigns the Cape Cod subgroups a separate "Nauset" tribal identity, which may, in reality, reflect only the postcolonization situation. He lists many subdivisions and villages for each tribe.

The Pokanoket were traditional friends and allies of the Massachusett and enemies of the Narragansett (Gookin 1972:9).

HISTORY   The "two kings" who entertained Verrazano during his 1524 visit to Narragansett Bay (Wroth 1970:138) may have been Pokanoket, but it is equally possible that they were Narragansett. The more easterly segments of the group were visited for varying lengths of time by Gosnold in 1602 (Brereton 1906:333–339), Pring (1906:347–351) in 1603, Champlain (1922–1936, 1: 343–358, 402–432) in 1605 and 1606, and Hudson in 1609 (Juet 1910:324–325). These encounters almost always started amicably, but crosscultural misunderstandings often resulted in conflict before the European explorers departed.

In 1611 a Capawake (Martha's Vineyard) sachem named Epinow was captured by Capt. Edward Harlow and Capt. Nicholas Hobson and brought to England where he learned something of the language and culture of his captors (MeHSC ser. 1, 2:26; Smith 1912:651). In 1614 he was brought home to act as guide and interpreter for the same seamen but promptly escaped from the English ship (MHSC ser. 2, 9:6; Smith 1912:656). In that same year, both Smith and a Dutch party independently mapped the area and the names Pakanokick and Wapa-

noo appeared in European usage for the first time (Smith 1912:675–677; Stokes 1915–1928, 2:C, pl. 23).

The epidemic of 1617–1619 struck the Pokanoket territory unevenly. While Cape Cod, the offshore islands, and the extreme western villages were hit relatively lightly, the area around Patuxet (Plymouth) was almost completely depopulated. When Thomas Dermer traveled inland in 1619, he found no inhabitants at all until he reached Namasket (Middleboro), some 15 miles from the coast. There, he met "two kings" and 50 warriors, who had come from Rhode Island to see him (Dermer 1906:130). One of these was probably the chief sachem, Massasoit.

Following the epidemic, the weakened Pokanoket were unable to withstand attacks from the Narrangansett, their traditional enemies to the west, and were driven from one or more islands in Narragansett Bay. They welcomed the Plymouth settlers as potential allies, and in 1621 Massasoit and his brother Quadequina came to Plymouth and entered into a formal treaty of friendship with the colonists (Mourt 1963:55–58). Massasoit appears to have had considerable personal authority, and, in spite of occasional threats from individual village sachems, the peace was maintained until after his death in 1662.

Massasoit was succeeded by his elder son, Wamsutta, who died very soon after taking leadership, and then by his younger son, called King Philip. By this time many of

top, Slater Memorial Mus., Norwich, Conn.: 10.81; bottom, Peabody Mus., Harvard U.: A5919.
Fig. 7. 17th-century wooden bowls, of typical single- and double-handle design. top, Mohegan pepperidge(?) burl bowl, possibly owned or used by Uncas. bottom, Elmwood bowl of Wampanoag (Pokanoket) origin known as King Philip's samp bowl but not adequately documented as such (Willoughby 1935:261–262); perforations on handle were probably made so vessel could be hung. Length of bottom 36 cm, other same scale.

Fruitlands Mus., Harvard, Mass.: FM-I-Ol.
Fig. 6. Ball-headed war club said to have belonged to King Philip. It is of maple wood, inlaid on both sides with white and purple wampum beads. The wampum allegedly represents White and Indian enemies killed. Club was stolen from Fruitlands in June 1970. Length about 56 cm.

the more easterly villagers, particularly those on Cape Cod and Martha's Vineyard, had been christianized (Gookin 1972; "Thomas Mayhew," vol. 4), and the main body of Pokanoket in the present Bristol, Rhode Island, area were suffering the pressures and indignities that accompanied advancing European settlement. In 1675–1676 Philip led the uprising called King Philip's War that briefly united Indians from Rhode Island to Vermont and New Hampshire in a final desperate resistance to the New England colonists and that ended in his own death and the virtual extinction of a large portion of the Pokanoket. The Indians of Cape Cod and the offshore islands did not join Philip and were able to maintain their towns intact.

Narragansett

• TERRITORY   Simmons ("Narragansett," this vol.) distinguishes among the Narragansett sachemdom itself, the adjoining and allied sachemdoms of the Niantics, Cowesets, Pawtuxets, and Manisseans (Block Island Indians), and the parts of more distant groups, such as the Nipmuck and Montauk, which were subject to the Narragansett. This agrees substantially with Gookin's (1972:8) statement that the Narragansett sachem held dominion over "part of Long Island, Block Island, Cawesitt, Niantick, and others; and had tribute from some of the Nipmuck Indians, that lived remote from the sea." In the early 1600s, the Narragansett and their allies occupied almost all of Rhode Island between Narragansett Bay and Weekapaug, as well as Conanicut and Dutch Islands within the bay. After the epidemics of 1617–1619, which do not seem to have affected them, they expanded to both east and west, taking land west of the Seekonk River and the remaining bay islands from the Pokanoket and the land between Weekapaug and the present Rhode Island–Connecticut border from the Pequot.

• HISTORY   Verrazano may have visited the Narragansett in 1524. Dutch explorers had certainly visited them by 1614. De Laet (1909:42) reported that "Adriaen Block calls the people who inhabit the west side of this [Narragansett] bay Nahicans, and their sagamore Nathattou; another chief was named Cachaquant." The first recorded English-Narragansett contact occurred in 1622, when the chief sachem Canonicus sent a messenger to Plymouth carrying what was interpreted as a challenge. In spite of this inauspicious beginning, the English as well as the Dutch were trading with the Narragansett by 1623 (Bradford 1908:164; Van Wassenaer 1909:87).

Roger Williams settled in the Narragansett country in 1636 and rapidly gained respect and influence among the natives. They aided the colonists in their attack on the Pequot fort at Mystic, Connecticut, in 1637 (J. Mason 1736). After the elimination of the Pequot as a force in the Long Island Sound area, the Narragansett entered into

hostilities with the Mohegan, their neighbors to the west, which culminated in 1643, when the younger Narragansett sachem, Miantonomi, led an attack on the home village of Uncas, chief Mohegan sachem. Miantonomi was captured, and after consultation with leaders of the United Colonies, secretly executed by the Mohegan (Winthrop 1908, 2:134–136).

Relations with both the Mohegan and the United Colonies continued to be strained, but although they were probably the strongest single Indian group in southern New England in 1675, the Narragansett did not openly enter King Philip's War until the fall of that year, when an army was sent against them. In the battle at their palisaded fort in the Great Swamp, southwest of Kingston, they lost over 200 warriors in addition to the women and children who died in the burning settlement (Church 1829). Their chief sachem, Canonchet, was executed in 1676, and the power of the Narragansett was effectively broken. Many of the survivors fled New England. Others found refuge with the Niantic, who, under the sachem Ninigret, had refused to take part in the war.

Pequot-Mohegan

• TERRITORY   The Pequot first appear in the documentary record in 1614 as the "Pequatoos . . . enemies of the Wapanoos," whom the Dutch encountered on "the River of Siccanamos after the name of the Sagimos" (the Mystic?). The "Morhicans" lived just to the west between the Frisian (Thames?) River and the Fresh (Connecticut) River (Stokes 1915–1928, 2:C, pl. 23; De Laet 1909:42–43). Other early seventeenth-century documents make it clear that Uncas, the Mohegan sachem, was subordinate to Sassacus, the chief sachem of the Pequot. In the early 1630s Sassacus "held dominion . . . over part of Long Island, over the Mohegans, over the sagamores of Quinapeake [New Haven], yea over all the people that dwelt upon Connecticut River, and over some of the most southerly inhabitants of the Nipmuck country, about Quinabaag" (Gookin 1972:7). The Montauk "confederacy" of Long Island, which included the Shinnecock and Corchaug, was very close to, if not identical with, the Mohegan-Pequot in language ("Eastern Algonquian Languages," this vol.) and aboriginal material culture (L.E. Williams 1972). While the Narragansett later claimed control over them, these groups paid tribute to the Pequot before the Pequot were defeated in 1637 (De Rasieres 1909:103; Gardiner 1859:22). Swanton (1952: 29–32) lists many villages of the Pequot, Mohegan, and Montauk.

• HISTORY   Despite frequent assertions that the Mohegan-Pequot were a Hudson valley group that had recently invaded eastern Connecticut (De Forest 1851:59–60; Swanton 1952:32), there is good linguistic and archeological evidence that suggests a long period of in situ development (Salwen 1969).

The Dutch quickly developed a regular trade with both Mohegan and Pequot (De Laet 1909:43). After a 1622 incident, when a Dutch trader held the Pequot sachem hostage until ransomed with 140 fathoms of wampum, this group would deal only with Pieter Barentssz, who spoke their language and had their confidence (Van Wassenaer 1909:86). Since the trade with interior New England involved access via the Connecticut River, the struggle for control of that waterway soon involved both Indians and Europeans. The apparent Pequot effort to expand authority westward into the Connecticut valley may have been motivated, at least in part, by this consideration. The Dutch found it convenient to accept the Pequot claim to the area and in 1633 purchased land from them on the east side of the river at the site of modern East Hartford, where they built a small fort and trading house (NYCD 1:52; Winthrop 1908, 2:33).

The English, on the other hand, supported the claims of the local Indians, who had invited them to trade and settle in the same area (Bradford 1908:300-301; Winthrop 1908, 2:33), and relations between the English and Pequot deteriorated rapidly. In 1637, after raids and killings by both sides, the English, aided by the Narragansett, and by the Mohegan, who saw an opportunity to escape their subordinate status, sent a large armed force into the Pequot home territory and attacked and burned a Pequot village at Mystic. At least 300 men, women, and children were killed (Gardiner 1859:21; J. Mason 1736; Underhill 1638; MHSC ser. 3, 6:29-49). The remaining Pequot fled to the west, but many were killed or captured. Sassacus was reportedly beheaded by the Mohawk, with whom he had sought refuge (Bradford 1908:343). Some 200 prisoners were divided among the Indian allies, given as servants to English families, or sold as slaves (Bradford 1908:342-343; J. Mason 1736:15).

The void left by the destruction of the Pequot was quickly filled by the Mohegan, who, led by Uncas, became an important force in eastern Connecticut. Though often at odds with neighboring Indian groups, they were consistently friendly to the English colonists and fought as their allies in King Philip's War.

Other Groupings

Although some of the sociopolitical groups discussed above were quite loosely structured, all had some measure of functional reality, at least after the beginning of European settlement. There were other units, in the interior and on the western Connecticut coast, that seem to have normally functioned as almost completely independent local communities, without lasting political ties to any of their neighbors. Names like Nipmuck, Pocumtuck, and Mattabesec sometimes appear in the literature as designations for large "tribes" or "confederacies" (Speck 1928a:pl. 20; Swanton 1952), but this usage does not seem to fit the seventeenth-century situation. At best, some of these names may reflect linguistic or cultural homogeneity, but the scarcity of evidence makes even linguistic identification difficult in most cases (Day 1962, 1969).

According to Goddard (1971a, "Eastern Algonquian Languages," this vol.) some of the small local groups in southwestern Connecticut between the Connecticut and Housatonic valleys (Quiripi, Naugatuck, Schaghticoke) and possibly the people opposite them on Long Island spoke Quiripi-Unquachog, a southern New England language. This conclusion and the lack of any positive evidence effectively destroy the idea of a great Delaware-speaking Wappinger-Mattabesec confederacy stretching from the Hudson to the Connecticut. The boundary between Munsee Delaware and Quiripi-Unquachog was probably somewhere between the Housatonic and the present Connecticut-New York border.

By 1614 the Dutch had explored Long Island Sound and the lower reaches of the Connecticut River. They found few inhabitants near the mouth of the river, but about 45 miles upstream (near Hartford?) they met people called Sequins. Some 30 miles beyond they reached a village "resembling a fort for protection against the attacks of their enemies. They are called Nawaas and their sagamore was then named Morahieck" (De Laet 1909:43). Shortly after, a regular trade in furs had begun (Van Wassenaer 1909:87). Both the Dutch and the Plymouth colonists built small trading posts on the same stretch of the river in 1633, the Dutch purchasing land from the Pequot and the English from Natawanute, "the right Sachem of the place" (Bradford 1908:301). As so frequently happened, sickness quickly followed the arrival of the Europeans. In the spring of 1634 a smallpox epidemic killed the chief sachem and almost all his people (Bradford 1908:312-313).

Full-scale English settlement of Connecticut began in 1636, with the establishment of colonists from Massachusetts Bay at Matianuck (Windsor), Saukiog (Hartford), and Wethersfield. In 1638 settlement was begun at Quinnipiac (New Haven). In each case the land was formally purchased from the local Indian sachems. European immigration and land acquisition accelerated in the years that followed. By the time of King Philip's War, the Indian populations had been peacefully but effectively displaced from most of coastal and central Connecticut.

The native groups that lived west of the fringes of European settlement, in northern Connecticut and Rhode Island, central Massachusetts, and southern Vermont and New Hampshire, are the least known of any of the southern New England Indian societies. The local groups of the Connecticut River valley in Massachusetts and the so-called Nipmuck people of Massachusetts and northern Connecticut and Rhode Island appear to have spoken a southern New England language that the French called Loup (Day 1967, 1969:77; "Eastern Algonquian Languages," this vol.). This classification   *173* would probably cover most of the local groups listed as Nipmuck and Pocumtuck by Swanton (1952:22-24).

As early as 1614, the Dutch had contacted Indians on the lower Connecticut who lived "within the land . . . who are called Horikans; they descend the river in canoes made of bark" (De Laet 1909:43). The name does not appear in the later documents, but it was undoubtedly the people grouped under the Loup heading who came downstream to supply most of the furs, first to the Dutch and the Plymouth colony traders near Hartford, and after 1636 to William Pynchon and his partners at Agawam (Springfield, Massachusetts).

Gookin (1972:7-10) says that some of the coastal societies—Massachusett, Pokanoket, Narragansett, and Pequot—controlled and exacted tribute from the interior Nipmuck people on their borders, but both the age and the true nature of this relationship are difficult to determine. It is tempting, without any evidence at all, to suggest that the "tribute" was actually a form of payment for access to coastal resources.

European settlement of the interior moved slowly northward and westward. Agawam was settled in 1636, but Pocumtuck (Deerfield), less than 40 miles upstream, was not established until 1669, and at that time there were still large unsettled areas between the western outposts of the Bay colony and the Connecticut valley. Therefore, the Indians of the interior had a more gradual exposure to European culture than had their coastal neighbors. Conditions of contact were also quite different. Unfortunately, there is very little documentary material upon which to base comparisons of the results in each case.

On the eve of King Philip's War, some of the central Massachusetts Indians seem to have shown an interest in Christianity, and seven new "praying towns" were established in the "Nipmuck country" (Gookin 1972:79-87). This experiment in directed acculturation ended abruptly with the beginning of the war. The towns were abandoned and the inhabitants scattered. Most contemporary colonial writers believed that the majority of the praying Indians joined Philip against the English, but the truth is difficult to determine. Most may have simply withdrawn to a safe distance from colonial wrath against all Indians. In 1677, after Philip's defeat, refugees from many Indian groups settled at the missionary town of Schaghticoke, near the confluence of the Hoosick and Hudson rivers in New York.

Synonymy†

Most of the names of Southern New England Indian groups are based on names of places and mean 'people of

† This synonymy incorporates some material prepared by Ives Goddard and William S. Simmons.

such-and-such'. This synonymy, which treats only the major group names, makes no attempt to survey the historical variants of the place-names as such or to discuss etymologies that are not clear and relevant to identification.

Massachusett (₁măsə'cho͞osĭt): Massachuset, apparently first used in print by John Smith (1912:662, 675) in 1616, appears to mean 'at the great hill', presumably in reference to the Blue Hills in Milton southwest of Massachusetts Bay. The English plural Massachusetts has been consistently used since the seventeenth century, with only minor variation in spelling, to designate the Indians who occupied the lands surrounding the bay and the islands within it. The Narragansett name was Massachusêuck (Williams 1936:[A3v.]).

Montauk ('măn₁tôk): In origin the name is that of the southeastern tip of Long Island; a fuller spelling is Meantaukett (NYCD 14:648). It is also attested as Mirrachtauhacky (NYCD 14:60; W.W. Tooker 1911:137), a Dutch form derived from lower Hudson Munsee, and as Munnawtawkit (Williams 1963, 6:24), presumably the Narragansett form. Spelling variants are given by Mooney (1907e:935).

Narragansett (₁nărə'gănsĭt): This name, in the form Nahicans, first appears on Adriaen Block's map of 1614, erroneously placed on the south fork of Long Island (Stokes 1915-1928, 2:C, pl. 23). De Laet's (1909:43) 1625 edition, based on the same data that produced the map, correctly locates Nahicans on the west side of Narragansett Bay. English colonial writers from 1622 onward usually use minor variations of the modern spelling to designate this political group. Williams wrote Nanhigganêuck (1936:A3), Narragansetts (1874:24, 27), Nahigonsicks (1881:26), Nahiggonike (1881:26), Nahigonsets (1971:[2]), Nahigonsiks (1971:[3]), and Narrigansets (1945:[2]). W. Harris (1902:167), also at Providence, wrote Narragansets. Winthrop (1825-1826, 2:198, 1908, 1:79) of Boston wrote Narragansetts and Anagansetts, and Winslow (1910:280, 344) of Plymouth, Nanohigganeucks and Nanohiggansets.

Williams (1874:407) said in 1682 that "Narragansett was so named from a little island between Puttiquomscut and Musquomacuk . . . I went on purpose to see it . . . but could not learn why it was called Narragansett." Stiles (1916:141) learned in 1761 that Nayohygunsic signified a rock partly in and partly out of the water off Boston Neck.

Niantic (nī'ăntĭk): In origin this name was applied to two places (Trumbull 1881:36-37), which Williams (1963, 6:82, 119) distinguished as Pequot Nayantick (west of New London) and Nayantaquit the hither (in southwestern Rhode Island). The Indians were called in Narragansett Nayantakoog (Williams 1963, 6:46) and were later known as the Western Niantic and Eastern Niantic, respectively. De Forest (1851) used the spelling Nehantic; other forms are in Mooney (1910h, 1910i).

Nipmuck ('nĭp₁muk) (Eliot 1666:2): Also appears as Neepmuck (Williams 1936:105), Neepnet (Williams 1963, 6:7), and other spellings listed by Mooney (1910j).

Pawtucket (pə'tukĭt): Pawtuckett seems to have been first used by Gookin (1972:7, 10-12) to designate the group of related villages in northeastern Massachusetts and adjacent Maine and New Hampshire. Earlier writers refer frequently to individual villages in this region but use no collective name. Gookin sometimes uses the name interchangeably with Wamesit, a "praying town" at the confluence of the Concord and Merrimack rivers. Some modern writers, notably Swanton (1952:17-18), have incorrectly extended the name Penacook to embrace both the Pawtucket and the Penacook and Winnipesaukee of the Upper Merrimack River, who were in reality part of the Western Abenaki group.

Pequot ('pē₁kwät) and Mohegan (₁mō'hēgən): These names first appear as Pequats and Morhicans on Block's map of 1614 (Stokes 1915-1928, 2:C, pl. 23) and as Pequatoos and Morhicans in De Laet's 1625 volume (1909:42-43). Variant spellings by seventeenth-century writers include, for the first, Pyquans (De Rasieres 1909:103), Pequins and Pekoath (Winthrop 1908, 1:61, 76), and Pequants (Wood 1865:62), and for the second, Monhigg (Bradford 1908:388) and Monahegan (Winthrop 1908, 1:271). The Narragansett plural forms were Pequttôog and Monahiganeuck (Williams 1936:188, 1963, 6:84).

Pokanoket (₁päkə'näkĭt): Pakanokick, as first published in 1616 by John Smith (1912:662), refers, narrowly, to the village of the chief sachem Massasoit, near Bristol, Rhode Island. Other early seventeenth-century writers use it similarly: "Puckanokick, the chief place of Massassowat's residence" (Winslow 1910:283), Pacanawkite (Bradford 1908:113), Packanocott (Winthrop 1908, 1:76). In this context, it is sometimes used interchangeably with Sowaams (Winslow 1910:313), though this term refers, more precisely, to Massasoit's home district on the east side of Narragansett Bay. However, by the last half of the seventeenth century, English writers had expanded the meaning of the name to include all the territory allied under the leadership of Massasoit and his successors, and this is the way in which Pawkunnawkutt is used by Gookin (1972:8-9).

The name Wampanoag (₁wämpə'nōəg), which is frequently used by modern writers to refer to the same political unit (Swanton 1952:24-27, for example), does not appear in any of the early documents originating in New England. The word Wapanoos appears above Narragansett Bay on Block's 1614 map (Stokes 1915-1928, 2:C, pl. 23), and De Laet (1909:42) reports that "in the lower part of the Bay dwell the Wapenocks, a nation of savages like the rest." Goddard (1971a:20) translates Wapanoo as 'easterner' in Munsee Delaware, the language spoken at the mouth of the Hudson, the base from which the Dutch explored the southern New

England coast. It may have been the Munsee term for any non-Delaware people to their east.

Poosepatuck (₁poōs'pătək): This is a place-name, first recorded in a deed of 1700 as pospatou, according to W.W. Tooker (1911:193-194), who gives a few slightly varying spellings. The same document refers to the Indians of the area as "Indian natives of Unquachock, etc.," and they have also been referred to by variants of this name, such as Vnchechange (for Unchechauge; NYCD 14:717), Unchachage (W.W. Tooker 1911:265; cf. Hodge 1907-1910, 2:209), Unckachohok, Unquachack, Unkechage (W.W. Tooker 1911:264, 266), and Unquachog (Jefferson 1791). U.S. Department of Commerce (1974:410) uses Poospatuck.

Quiripi ('kwĭrĭ₁pē): This spelling was introduced by Trumbull (1873:9) on the basis of early Dutch forms such as Quiripeys (De Laet 1909:44). De Forest (1851) used Quinnipiac, a form also appearing in the first English recordings, in 1637 and 1638, as Quillipeage, Quillypieck, Quinopiocke, and Quinnypiock, the name of the land on New Haven harbor (Trumbull 1873:9-10, 1881:61). The Narragansett name was Qunnipiêuck (pl.; Williams 1936:[A3v.]). Other spellings are in Mooney (1910k).

Shinnecock ('shĭnə₁käk): This name generally appears with only slight variations in spelling (Hodge 1907-1910, 2:551). A variant Skinnacock (NYCD 14:600) may be compared with the Dutch Mochgonnekonck (NYCD 14:60; W.W. Tooker 1911:136-138), which appears to be from the lower Hudson Munsee name.

Sources

Because so much of the enormous body of secondary writings on early New England history presents an inseparable mixture of fact and romantic fiction when dealing with the Indians, this paper has drawn only on sixteenth- and seventeenth-century sources and, with very few exceptions, only on the reports of participants and firsthand observers rather than on even the earliest general histories. Even with this restriction, the volume of documentation is extremely large.

It is impossible to determine when the first meeting between Europeans and Indians occurred in southern New England, but the first clearly documented contacts are those made by Verrazano in 1524, and his report is the essential starting point for ethnohistorical research (Wroth 1970). Other early voyages that produced useful written accounts include those of Gosnold in 1602 (Brereton 1906; Archer 1906) and Pring (1906) in 1603. Champlain (1922-1936, 1) traveled along the New England coast from Maine to Cape Cod in both 1605 and 1606, and his accounts are extremely full and informative. The contemporary but secondhand history of Lescarbot provides useful supplementary information about these journeys: the first, 1609, edition (Lescarbot 1928) seems most accurate in regard to southern New England.

Hudson stopped briefly at Cape Cod in 1609 (Juet 1910), but the next important new information comes from two explorations in the year 1614. John Smith (1912) traveled from Maine to Cape Cod and published a description of the country that contained the names of over 20 Indian villages and a map that showed the locations of most of them. In the same year, Adriaen Block and his Dutch associates explored the mouth of the Hudson and the Long Island Sound area. The map that was presented to the Estates General in Holland in 1614 (Stokes 1915-1928, 2:C, pl. 23) and De Laet's (1909) brief characterizations of local Indian groups are based on these explorations. Dermer's brief accounts of his 1619 and 1620 voyages (Dermer 1906; Bradford 1908:111-14) provide the final bits of information about Indians in southeastern Massachusetts before the start of European settlement.

Shortly after the landing of the Pilgrims at Cape Cod in late 1620, much fuller descriptions of the Indians and their way of life began to appear, but the societies described had, by this time, been affected by over a century of European contact and by the great epidemics of 1617-1619. Mourt's (1963) 1622 account and Winslow's (1910) 1624 account are very important sources of information about the earliest years of settlement. Bradford's (1908) history, written 1630-1648, provides data about later events. The 1637 narrative of Morton (1838), who lived on the south side of Massachusetts Bay for two intervals before the wave of Puritan immigration began in 1629-1630, is valuable for its relatively early vantage point as well as for its unconventional antiseparatist attitude toward the Indians.

The Massachusetts Bay settlers produced a number of works designed specifically to tell the people at home about the New World. Wood's (1865) 1634 relation is the best source by far for information about Indians. The descriptions of Higginson in 1630 (MHSC ser. 1, 1:117-124), Lechford (1642), and E. Johnson (1910) are less reliable. Josselyn's (1833) 1674 account contains useful information but probably refers, in the main, to an area slightly to the northeast of that discussed in this paper. Roger Williams's (1936) *A Key Into the Language of America* is invaluable for information about southern New England Indians in general and is one of the few sources dealing in depth with the Long Island Sound region.

Winthrop's (1908) 1630-1649 journal does for the Bay area what Bradford's history does for Plymouth. Both provide important information about Indian-colonial relations, as do the letters and other papers of Bradford (MHSC ser. 1, 3:27-36), Winthrop (1929-1947), and Williams (1874).

The Pequot War and the events that led up to it are reported by four of the participants. Gardiner's (1859) 1660 manuscript provides the fullest account of the skirmishes that preceded full-scale hostilities. J. Mason (1736), Underhill (1638), and Vincent in 1638 (MHSC ser. 3, 6:29-49) describe the attack on the Indian fort at Mystic.

The missionary activities of the mid-seventeenth century are summarized in Gookin's (1972) 1674 manuscript, which also provides information about Indian political units and their populations. There are three contemporary histories of King Philip's War, Church's (1829) in 1716, Hubbard's (1677), and Increase Mather's (1677), as well as a collection of shorter contemporary accounts (Lincoln 1913). The closest approach to a description of the struggle from the Indian point of view is to be found in Gookin's (1836) 1677 historical account.

Seventeenth-century local and colonial government records, records of land transfers, and similar public documents contain varying amounts of information about Indian culture and history. Some of these are available in published form.

Among anthropologists, Frank G. Speck has made outstanding contributions to the study of southern New England Indians as they lived in the nineteenth and early twentieth centuries. However, Speck's efforts to reconstruct precontact social structure and territorial boundaries (1928) were strongly influenced by his conviction that precontact political units were quite rigidly organized "feudal tribes" (Speck 1928:17) and by his belief that Indian land "ownership" as expressed in early colonial land deeds truly reflects the aboriginal pattern; both views are no longer universally accepted. Swanton's (1952) work is an extremely helpful state-by-state digest of information about tribal geography, history, and demography; however, because it was compiled from a great many sources of varying dependability, detailed statements about boundaries, subdivisions, and villages of New England groups should be used with caution. Rainey's (1936) compilation provides a summary of ethnohistorical source materials, arranged by subject. The best survey (somewhat out of date) of the widely scattered surviving artifacts is by Willoughby (1935:228-275).

Indians of Southern New England and Long Island: Late Period

LAURA E. CONKEY, ETHEL BOISSEVAIN, AND IVES GODDARD*

King Philip's War, 1675–1676, caused extensive disruption and relocation of the southern New England Indians, in addition to the severe loss of life suffered by those groups directly involved in the conflict. The missionized inhabitants of the 14 "praying towns" in the Massachusetts Bay colony came under suspicion from both sides. For example, those in the praying towns of Natick, Marlboro, and Punkapog (Canton) were forced by the colonists to relocate to Deer Isle in Boston Harbor, while many of the Christian Indians at Magunkaquog (Ashland), Hassanamesitt (Grafton), and Chabanakongkomun (Webster) were at one point coerced into joining a group of Indian combatants (Gookin 1836). There was less disruption of the largely Christian Indians of Plymouth colony and the offshore islands, of the Niantics of southern Rhode Island, and of many small groups in Connecticut, who did not take part in the fighting. In fact, many Indian communities survived the war, and Indian groups have continued to exist in certain parts of southern New England until the present (fig. 1). However, the war had terminated the Indians' military and political power, and afterward dealings with Indians were no longer important matters of public policy. The Indians found themselves relegated to the lower economic levels of the colonial society at large, sometimes in the status of indentured servants (Towner 1955:131–140; "Indian Servitude in the Northeast," vol. 4; Lauber 1913; Channing 1886). As such they largely passed into obscurity and are only infrequently mentioned in contemporary descriptions. They were sometimes treated as charity cases or, at the other extreme, actively discriminated against or cheated, but generally they were simply ignored.

In 1684, eight years after King Philip's War, there were only four praying towns left in Massachusetts Bay of the original 14—Natick, Punkapog, Wamesit (Lowell), and Chabanakongkomun—but the Indians also held church services at the scattered seasonal camps where they fished, hunted, or gathered chestnuts. There were 10 communities of Christian Indians in Plymouth colony (in present Plymouth and Barnstable counties), 10 on Martha's Vineyard, and 5 on Nantucket (MHSC ser. 1, 3:185). Fourteen years later Rawson and Danforth (1698)

found about 17 Christian Indian communities in Plymouth, including some previously unreported ones in the western parts, 10 on Martha's Vineyard and the Elizabeth Islands, and 5 on Nantucket. Many of these had Indian teachers or schoolmasters (including one "schooldame"), and there were 27 Indian preachers. Several places had one, two, or four Indian "rulers." At Nukkehkummees in southern Bristol County, Massachusetts, for example, the four rulers were chosen annually, but among the generally less acculturated Indians of Chappaquiddick Island one man was "by birth their ruler or sachem." The Indian communities had a moderate amount of local self-government, including Indian magistrates or justices of the peace, who were empowered to prosecute minor infractions on the part of Indians. A booklet of laws in the Massachusett language was printed in 1705 (fig. 2). However, the precise roles of the different Indian officials are not known. Two of the three magistrates who compiled a census of the Indians near Sandwich in 1693 were among the four "Indian rulers" listed for the community in 1698 (W. Winthrop 1693; Speck 1928:92; Rawson and Danforth 1698:95), but a distinction between these two offices is shown by a 1713 warrant signed by an Indian ruler (Massachusett *negonshaenin*) directing that the culprit be arrested and brought before the magistrates (*nannauwunnuacheg*) at Nukkehkummees to answer for his crime (fig. 3).

Farther west Christian influence and acculturation was less strong. There had been no missions in Rhode Island or the western two-thirds of Massachusetts before the war, and only those at Branford and Norwich in Connecticut. Correspondingly, information on the Indians in these areas is hard to come by until the eighteenth century. It is known, though, that the war had caused extensive dislocations. Many from the defeated Indian groups fled westward to Schaghticoke (Rensselaer County, New York) in Mahican territory, whence they eventually went to join the Western Abenaki (Stiles 1916:136, 157; "Western Abenaki," this vol.). Others joined other tribes, some in New England but others as far west as the Great Lakes. The Eastern Niantic absorbed many Narragansetts and eventually the name Narragansett itself. Other Narragansetts, Pawtuckets, and Massachusetts settled on Martha's Vineyard. Within

* Most of this chapter was written by Conkey, incorporating materials drafted by Boissevain. The introductory paragraphs, the synonymy, and certain other passages were written by Goddard.

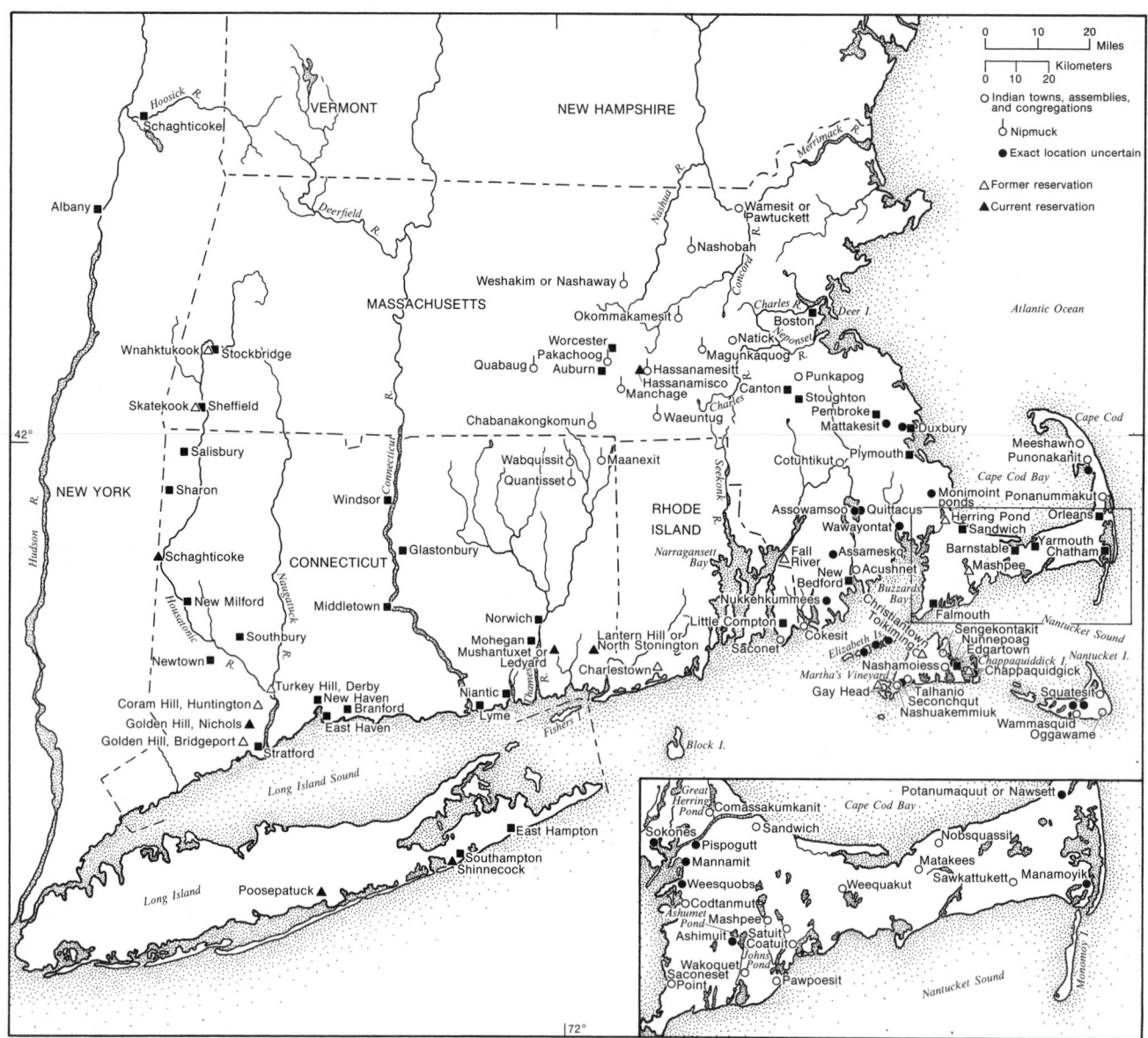

Fig. 1. Southern New England Indian settlements and reservations after 1674. Additional lands that were not official reservations or are of uncertain status are omitted.

the southern New England area the Indians tended to consolidate into a relatively small number of local groups. Intermarriage with Blacks and Whites was common, though the resulting racially mixed communities retained a strong sense of their Indian heritage and were generally regarded as Indians by others. Tribal groupings and names, controversial enough before the war, were even less clear afterward, and most Indian groups were simply referred to by the names of the places where they lived. Formalized supralocal confederacies did not exist and the tribal associations of the seventeenth century became only a memory, exemplified most strongly, perhaps, by the traditional mutual animosity that the Mohegans and the Pequots maintained into the twentieth century (Stiles 1916:156; Speck 1928a:247).

Local Groups

In many localities in southern New England, starting even before the war, White officials assigned lands to local Indian groups, but dwindling Indian population and encroachment by White settlers resulted in the alienation of much of this reserved land over time. Some reservations were founded and supported by the colonies, and later the states; some were organized by missionary societies; and some, technically not reservations, consisted of land retained and owned by Indian groups, though sometimes and to varying degrees officially recognized. The respective governments provided few services, other than some support for missions, and generally contented themselves with occasionally preventing or alleviating disputes with local Whites, usually over land

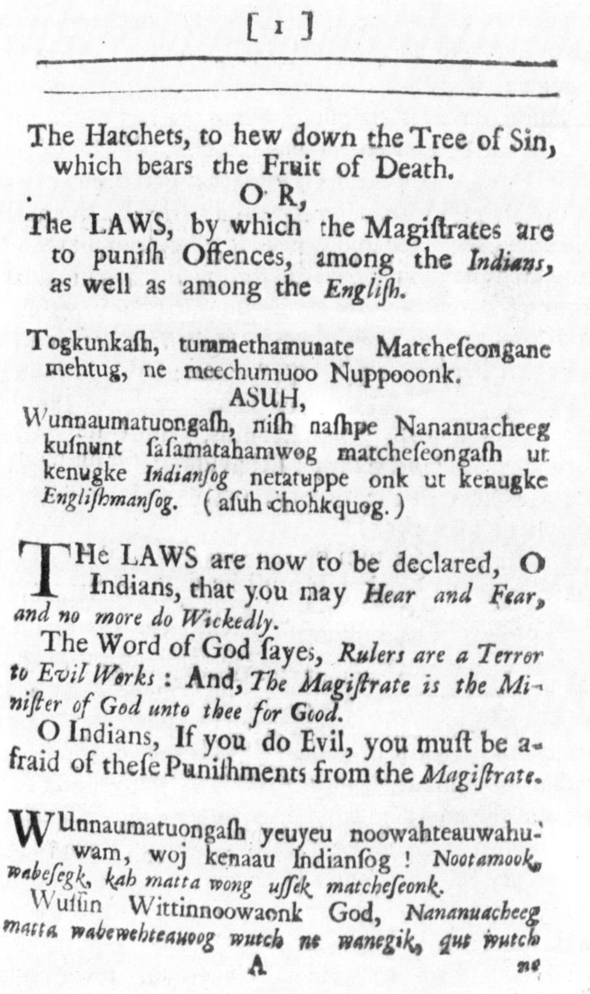

[I]

The Hatchets, to hew down the Tree of Sin,
which bears the Fruit of Death.

OR,

The LAWS, by which the Magiſtrates are
to puniſh Offences, among the *Indians*,
as well as among the *Engliſh*.

Togkunkaſh, tummethamunate Matcheſeongane
mehtug, ne meechumuoo Nuppooonk.

ASUH,

Wunnaumatuongaſh, niſh naſhpe Nananuacheeg
kuſnunt ſaſamatahamwog matcheſeongaſh ut
kenugke *Indianſog* netatuppe onk ut kenugke
Engliſhmanſog. (aſuh chohkquog.)

THE LAWS are now to be declared, O
Indians, that you may *Hear and Fear,*
and no more do Wickedly.

The Word of God ſayes, *Rulers are a Terror*
to Evil Works : And, *The Magiſtrate is the Mi-*
niſter of God unto thee for Good.

O Indians, If you do Evil, you muſt be a-
fraid of theſe Puniſhments from the *Magiſtrate.*

WUnnaumatuongaſh yeuyeu noowahteauwahu-
wam, woj kenau Indianſog ! *Nootamook,*
wabeſegk, kah matta wong uſſek matcheſeonk.
Wuſſin Wittinnoowaonk God, *Nananuacheeg*
matta wabewehteauoog wutch ne wanegik, qut wutch
A ne

Fig. 2. First page of a 15-page booklet containing 20 laws in English and Massachusett, printed in Boston in 1705 (Pilling 1891:223).

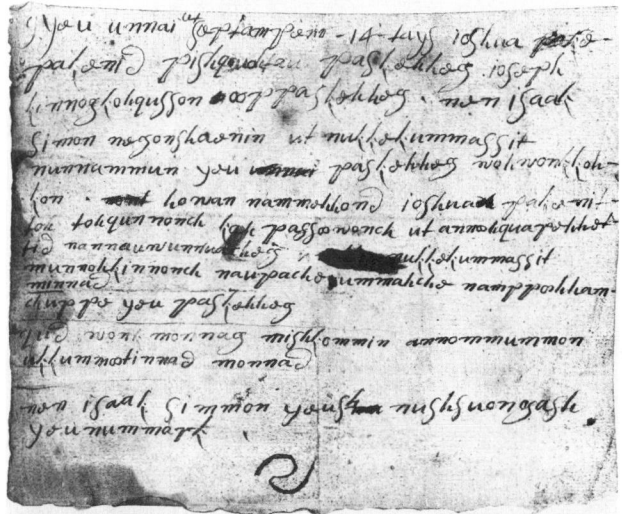

Fig. 3. Warrant in the Massachusett language issued by Isaac Simmon, an Indian ruler, ordering the arrest of Joshua Pakenid for committing some offense (the exact meaning is uncertain) against a gun belonging to Joseph Kinnogkohqusson. The text reads in part: "If anyone finds Joshua Pakenid, let him seize him and bring him before the magistrats at Nukkekummassit [Nukkehkummees]. Let him hold him until he has answered about this gun." Associated documents show the date to be 1713.

or land-use rights. The Indians tended to keep to themselves and, as long as possible, to resist assimilation, though their "reservation cultures" (Brasser 1971) combined aspects of the older way of life with an increasing proportion of elements and practices taken over from the Whites.

Massachusetts

In Massachusetts the largest of the reservations was Mashpee, on Cape Cod. The Indians there were assigned 50 square miles in 1660, and they governed themselves with courts, trials, and judgments from 1665. The area was incorporated into the District of Mashpee in 1763, but in 1788 the state repealed self-government, considering it a failure, and instituted a five-member all-White board of overseers. A measure of self-government was returned in 1834, and although the Indians were far from managing their own affairs, this time the experiment was judged more successful. Their lands were divided in 1842 with all but 2,000 of their 13,000 acres being distributed in lots of 60 acres for each family. Many laws testify to the constant problems of Whites' trespassing and taking wood from the reservation lands; and conflicts often arose over religious education and the maintenance of a church (Apes 1829, 1835). It was a large area, at one time rich in wood, fish, and game, and therefore desirable to the Whites. It was hard to ignore this continually growing community of non-Whites, and Mashpee Indians had therefore more conflicts with their White neighbors than did most other Indian settlements in the state (Massachusetts. Commissioners 1849, 1861).

The Herring Pond reservation was not far from Mashpee, in the eastern part of Plymouth. The 2,500 acres there were only divided as needed, unlike Mashpee, until 1850 when 1,800 acres were individually allotted. There was no town organization, and the community often shared Mashpee's guardians and ministers.

The Yarmouth Indians by the mid-nineteenth century had no lands left, and no tribal organization. Most had merged into the surrounding White population, working and living in nearby towns, while others had joined the Herring Pond Indians.

The Fall River reservation near the Rhode Island border was set aside in 1701 and divided into lots in 1707. Reservation status came in 1709, as a 160-acre area. A guardianship was instituted in 1818. The Indians there were said to be descendants of Wampanoags who had sided with the English in King Philip's War. Indian-White relations deteriorated greatly by the mid-nine-

Fig. 4. Mashpee woman carrying a checkerwork woven pack basket. Photograph by Frank Speck, 1914.

teenth century, and reports to the state senate suggested that "the benefits of the system of guardianship have not been commensurate with its expenses" (Massachusetts. Commissioners 1849:42; see also Dubuque 1907).

The Dartmouth Indians lived south of Fall River but like the Yarmouth Indians escaped the negative effects of being under White overseers as they had neither lands nor funds for the state to manage. Of Wampanoag descent, by 1861 they numbered 111 in and around New Bedford, and most were full citizens.

The Namatakeeset (or Manattakeesett) Indians were originally located on the northern edge of New Plymouth colony in the town of Pembroke but in 1675 were moved to Clark's Island in the war panic. They had no property remaining in either area by the mid-nineteenth century.

The Punkapog's last lands were sold around 1840 by their guardian, the proceeds going to the poorest tribal members. At that time many moved to Boston, Canton, and Stoughton but were still considered wards of the state, receiving occasional state aid.

The Natick Indians, once the successful experiment in attempted acculturation, were "practically extinct" by the time of the 1848 senate report. They had been under a guardian since 1810, who supervised the sale of the last of their lands in 1828 and still held the proceeds.

The Dudley Indians, near Webster, sold all but 26 acres of their land by 1797, hoping to live on the interest, but the sum was merged into the general state funds, so that like other Massachusetts Indians they became de-pendent on state pauper funds. In 1857 they were moved to a one-acre lot closer to town, where a five-floor tenement was built for them in an effort to end their isolation and ease assimilation into the rest of the town.

The Hassanamisco Indians prior to 1728 had owned 8,000 acres of land near Grafton that had been set aside in 1693 for the remaining praying Indians there. The Massachusetts Bay colony negotiated the purchase of the land, and the money received for it was placed in a bank for the Indians. Some of it was put into poor investments and lost, and the rest was "borrowed" by one of the tribe's trustees and never replaced. Therefore, in 1848 the state set aside 11.9 acres for the remainder of the tribe (Speck 1943a; U.S. Department of Commerce 1974:225; for all eastern and central Massachusetts Indian groups see Massachusetts. Commissioners 1849, 1861; Massachusetts (Colony) 1853–1854).

On Martha's Vineyard there were three reservations in the eighteenth and nineteenth centuries—Chappaquiddick, Christiantown, and Gay Head. The Chappaquiddick reservation was part of a small island of the same name on the eastern extremity of the Vineyard. By a land transaction in 1789 the Indians had lost valuable acres, and what remained was in 1810 divided among the Indian inhabitants. In 1823 the laws were modified to prevent the guardian from dispossessing the Indians and to establish some outward manifestation of town organization. By 1849 they owned 692 acres of barren land, and many inhabitants moved to nearby Edgartown for jobs and rights as citizens.

Christiantown was originally a praying town on the northwest side of the Vineyard, to the northwest of Tisbury. In 1849, 390 acres of the reservation remained, and all but 10 acres was divided among the inhabitants. The land held in common yielded very little in crops or rents, and there too, the tribal members were leaving for more lucrative jobs in the cities. Oral history has it that Christiantown was deserted due to a smallpox epidemic in 1888, in much the same way as the majority of the Nantucket population had disappeared after 1763.

The third reservation on the Vineyard was started in 1711 by the New England Company, which was founded in 1649 to spread Christianity among the Indians. They purchased land for the use of the Gay Head Indians, who had been living there since before 1642. Unfortunately there was a great deal of dispute about how to manage the land, with some of the better acres leased to Whites at low rates, which brought in little income for the Indians. The original purpose of providing an undisturbed area for missionary work was soon forgotten (Kellaway 1961). The state did eventually establish a reservation there, on the peninsula of land on the extreme western point of the Vineyard called Gay Head. This area, connected to the main island by an isthmus, offered the isolation the Indian group wished to maintain. In 1849 there were 2,400 acres, 500 of which were divided among the tribal members, with the rest held in common. The tribe, unlike most other Massachusetts reservation groups, had no guardian or overseer after 1820; they asked legal advice when they needed it from the Chappaquiddick guardian but otherwise managed their own affairs. They had no land titles, leaving members free to use what land they wished, cultivating and fencing to indicate ownership. They did not allow Whites to gain a foothold on their land, and tribal membership laws were strict. Thus they were able to maintain group cohesion and a strong tribal identity long after other groups were dispersed (Massachusetts. Commissioners 1849, 1861; for all of Martha's Vineyard, see also MHSC ser. 2, 3:34–37, 89-94; Mayhew 1727; Hough 1856; Tantaquidgeon 1930; Travers 1960).

In western Massachusetts and northwestern Connecticut lived the Housatonic Indians, a group greatly expanded after King Philip's War by refugees from the east and Mahicans from the Hudson River valley to the west. By 1720 the tribe had sold most of their land to the Massachusetts General Assembly for the use of White settlers, keeping two tracts for themselves, one called Skatekook in Sheffield, the other Wnahktukook 8 to 10 miles upstream in Stockbridge. In 1734, with the tribe's permission, the missionary John Sergeant began work there. Wishing to unite their two tracts, the Housatonic traded the Skatekook land for acreage near Wnahktukook, an area then called Stockbridge. This was funded by the state and the mission, and an experiment in Indian-White town living was started: the lands were held in common until 1740, when they were divided. After the Revolution the conflicts between the experiment's White and Indian members began to force a change, and the White settlers crowded the Indians first out of the town government and then out of Stockbridge itself. By 1789 "all" the Indians of Stockbridge had moved to a town in central New York named New Stockbridge. This group of Stockbridges then moved on to Wisconsin in the early nineteenth century (Hopkins 1753; R.H. Brown 1958; Brasser 1971; see "Mahican" and "Oneida," this vol.)

The Massachusetts legislature ended reservation status statewide in 1869, although individual reservations continued on state aid for a while afterward. Fall River Reservation was finally disbanded in 1907. Hassanamisco was still under state jurisdiction in 1975. The "dereservationizing" of 1869 meant citizenship for the reservation Indians, and, theoretically, the rights and responsibilities that come with it (Speck 1928d).

Rhode Island

The state of Rhode Island allotted some 64 square miles near Charlestown to the Narragansett as a reservation in 1709. White settlers were pressing on this land, leasing and purchasing lots, so that in 1713 the General Assembly declared all such purchases void. In 1717 three overseers were appointed to regulate land leasing and deal with trespassers. Around 1745 the sachem George Ninigret began to sell land to pay off debts, and a great deal of valuable Narragansett land had to be sold to pay off his son Thomas Ninigret's debts as sachem. In 1759 all land-sale restrictions were removed briefly, although a strong Indian council tried to curtail sales by individuals. The last Narragansett "king," also named George Ninigret, died in the American Revolution, after which the Indian council, chosen by annual tribal elections, directed the internal affairs of the tribe. An effort was made in 1792 to reorganize their affairs on a more permanent basis, and the tribe was then represented by a treasurer until 1818 when they petitioned for his removal. Many Narragansetts were moving to Brothertown, New York, at this time, and the Rhode Island Indian population was dwindling. With no overseer the number of trespasses and encroachments grew, so a commissioner of the tribe was appointed in 1839. A tribal constitution was adopted in 1849. An investigation in 1867 found the tribe indifferent to citizenship, wishing to remain exempt from taxes, draft, and the liability to be sued; but by 1879 the tribe wanted to change their dependent relationship. An 1880 quitclaim turned their remaining 1,500 acres of land over to the state, a tribal census was taken, and each of the 324 members was given an equal portion of the $5,000 payment. The tribe kept the lands they held in severalty, as well as their meetinghouse land. They were full state citizens, most still living in and around Charlestown (Rhode Island. General Assembly. Committee on Indian Tribes 1852; Rhode Island. General Assembly. House of Representatives 1880; Rhode Island. Commission on the Affairs of Narragansett Indians 1881-1884; Boissevain 1956; see also Z. Allen 1876; Stiles 1916; Livermore 1877; Hicks 1975; E.R. Potter 1835; "Narragansett," this vol.).

Connecticut

In Connecticut the Mohegan Indians' land was never officially a reservation, although they made up one of the more cohesive groups in New England for many years. In 1721 they had 4,000 to 5,000 acres along the Thames River, and, as in other areas, the Indian leaders attempted through legal means to control the transactions that, through fraud and misunderstanding, continually reduced their lands. In 1725 as a consequence of inter-Indian disputes all Connecticut Indians were placed under the jurisdiction of the governor and council, requiring submission to and dependence on the colony. An intricate succession problem pitted the colonial government against George II in England. By 1769 when Ben Uncas II, the last sachem, died, land conflicts were worsening. Samson Occom (fig. 5) and Joseph Johnson, both Mohegans, gathered various groups together to discuss the land problems; and in 1775 Occom led the first Connecticut and Long Island Indians to Brother-

Fig. 5. Samson Occom (b.1723, d.1792), Mohegan Presbyterian minister and missionary to other tribes, notably the Montauk. On the wall behind him, symbolizing his Indian identity, are a bow and 3 arrows. Engraving by J. Spilsbury, 1768, after a lost oil portrait by Mason Chamberlin, painted when Occom was in England in 1766.

Fig. 6. A Mohegan woman using a traditional Mohegan wooden mortar (with tapered sides, handles, and scalloped bottom edge) and stone pestle to grind parched corn into nocake. Photograph by Harrison Howell Walker at Mohegan, Conn., 1937.

town, New York, at the invitation of the Oneida Indians in hopes of settling in a new land far from White encroachment (see Love 1899). Further White expansion led to more New England Indian removals west and to the eventual move in the 1820s of the Brothertown and New Stockbridge Indian groups from New York to Wisconsin.

Lands of the Mohegan were divided in 1783, although a new and fairer division was petitioned for in 1789. The 2,700 remaining acres were then divided among 140 Mohegans in 1790. However, in 1850, they had claim to only 2,300 acres of land, 460 of which they were using and 600 of which were wooded. The rest was rented out to Whites at one dollar an acre. An act was passed in 1860 to redistribute the Mohegan lands, as many of the landowning families had moved away or died out, their lands reverting to state or tribal ownership. The population was under 100 (63 on the tribal lands), and the state was supporting a school and church in the town of Mohegan. The 1860 action provided for an overseer to lease land, collect rents to distribute to the landowners, and generally manage the land and financial affairs of the tribe.

The Pequot Indians were on two reservations, the 280-acre Stonington reservation at Lantern Hill, granted in 1683, and the roughly 2,000-acre Mushantuxet reservation of Robin Cassasinamon's followers, set up in 1667 in part of New London, in the town of Groton from 1705 to 1836, and since then in Ledyard. However, most of their land was eventually leased to and cultivated by White colonists and, in consequence, tended to slip out of the Indians' control. The smaller Stonington group had experienced such a drop in population by 1749 that they were on the verge of losing their reservation, but they petitioned and won back the rights to the land. They requested specific overseers to manage their affairs in 1788. By the early nineteenth century two-thirds of the tribe were living on the reservation with the rest working as servants in White homes or on whaling expeditions. Those at home tried to earn money with their crafts, especially basketry. They had lost 40 acres of their original grant by 1848, and the remaining acres were worn down or rented out; none of the land was cultivated by the Indians.

The western half of the Mushantuxet Pequot reservation, which then amounted to 1,737 acres, was leased to White farmers in 1732 under an act of the colonial assembly that was intended to benefit the Indians, but the problem of fake claims by the tenants became so severe that the act was repealed in 1752 after complaints from the Indians. Even so they lost much of their acreage to these claims, and after a decision by the assembly in 1761 they controlled only a fraction more than 989 acres of their original reservation. By 1776 this land was in poor shape, although the Pequot cultivated it in the English manner. Land surveys were often "lost"; attempted encroachments continued. In 1848 the Mushantuxet Pequot still held 989 acres, most of which was wooded. The cleared land was rented to Whites, and the Pequot had only one acre under cultivation.

The so-called Western Niantics, whose relationship to the Eastern Niantics of Rhode Island is uncertain, had lands at Niantic, which they continually struggled to defend from White encroachment (De Forest 1851: 381-387). In 1761 there were 85 of them, living in 6 wigwams (fig. 7) and 11 houses. The remnants of this group were absorbed by the Mohegans after 1850 (Speck 1928a:207).

The rest of Connecticut was populated by many small tribes and groups. These were constantly changing in makeup as displaced coastal and eastern Connecticut refugees moved west, many moving into established communities such as Stockbridge (Massachusetts), New Stockbridge and Brothertown (New York), and Schaghticoke (Connecticut).

According to nineteenth-century historians, the first Indian settlement at Schaghticoke, Connecticut, a few miles south of present Kent on the upper Housatonic, was established in 1730 by a Paugusset, Gideon Mauwehu (De Forest 1851:407-409; Orcutt 1882). However, the tradition among local Indians in the 1970s was that seasonally migrating Potatucks had previously had win-

Mus. of the Amer. Ind., Heye Foundation, New York: 3/5668.

Fig. 8. Western Niantic splint storage basket. Checkerwork weave with painted design, collected by Frank Speck. Documented as having been made by Mercy Nonsuch in 1839, but this date seems improbable given her 1912 photograph (fig. 12). Detail (after Speck 1951e:27) shows painted design that was also used on a similar basket made by Nonsuch in 1840. Height approximately 28 cm.

ter hunting camps in the area (Trudie Lamb, personal communication 1975). After 1730 Indians from various Connecticut groups, especially from the lower Housatonic, gradually increased the population in the upper Housatonic area. In 1742 a Moravian mission was begun at Schaghticoke, but conflicts between the White colonists and the missionaries became intense, finally forcing the Moravians to return to Bethlehem, Pennsylvania. Some of their new converts accompanied them, but most returned to Schaghticoke within a short time, demoralized.

After 1744 there were two reservations in the area, one on the west bank of the Housatonic, the other a 2,000-acre tract in the mountains. White encroachment was becoming more frequent, so that by 1767 many wanted to leave for Stockbridge, Massachusetts. The Connecticut colony would not give them funds to compensate for land they would be leaving behind, so few actually left. Over the next 100 years, the population on the reservations decreased steadily, and the reservation acreage grew smaller (Stiles 1916:59, 112, 172; Rainey 1936; Reichel 1860:74-76).

The Paugusset, on the lower Housatonic River, splintered in 1731 at the death of the sachem Konckapotanauh, many joining other groups (Stiles 1916:132, 158). Those who stayed lived on three reservations—Turkey

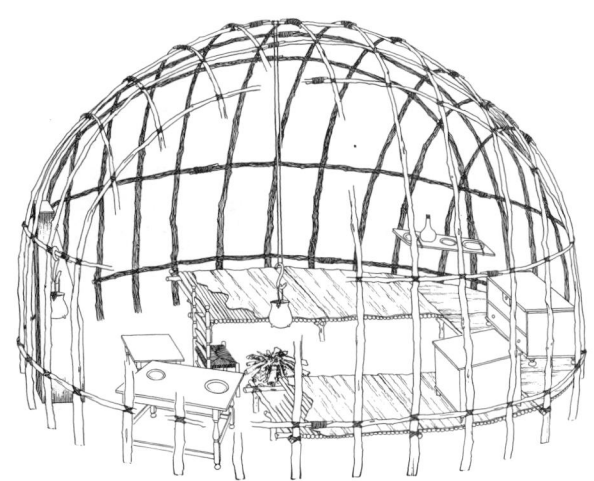

Sturtevant 1975:fig. 2c.

Fig. 7. An 18th-century Western Niantic wigwam in a cutaway view without the mat covering, showing bent and lashed pole framework, central location of fire (with cooking pot hanging over it), European furniture, and traditional sleeping platforms. Reconstruction based on 1761 notes and measured sketches by Ezra Stiles. Drawing by Edward G. Schumacher, under the direction of William C. Sturtevant. Floor dimensions 17 ft. 4 in. by 12 ft.

Hill in Derby, Coram Hill in Huntington, and Golden Hill in Bridgeport (the first Connecticut reservation, begun in 1659). There was an attempted eviction of the Paugusset from all but six acres in 1760. The Indians won their suit, but the Whites settled with a payment, and the Indians lost their reservation rights to most of the land. They sold the rest of their land in 1842 but resettled on a reservation in 1886 in the Nichols section of Trumbull, again called Golden Hill (Connecticut State Department of Environmental Protection. Indian Affairs Council 1975).

Other Indian groups in Connecticut (Quiripi, River Indians, Podunk, Wangunk, Mattabesec, Tunxis, New Milford, Salisbury, Sharon) gradually moved north and west. The numerous reservations were small, and life on them was poor and degrading. Most of the reservation Indians moved into English communities after a while, giving the impression that the Connecticut Indian population was greatly decreasing. (For Connecticut Indians see De Forest 1851; Orcutt 1882; Love 1899; McCallum 1932; Wheelock 1763; Rainey 1936; Speck 1918a, 1928a; Townshend 1900; B. Trumbull 1818; Butler 1947, 1948, 1953; Connecticut (Colony) Laws, Statutes, etc. 1850–1890; Connecticut. Commissioners on Distribution of Lands of the Mohegan Indians 1861; Connecticut. State Library 1929, 1962; J.T. Hamilton 1900; Heckewelder 1819, 1820 about the Moravian mission; MHSC ser. 1, 9:75–99; and papers from the Indian and Colonial Research Center, Old Mystic, Connecticut).

Long Island

The Indians on eastern Long Island continued to live relatively undisturbed lives after King Philip's War. The Poosepatuck reservation, between Brookhaven and Mastic, was set aside in 1666 and was still recognized by the state of New York more than 300 years later. In 1700 several individuals identified as "Indian natives of Unquachock [Unquachog], etc." were assigned a total of 210 acres at four different locations in the same area (W.W. Tooker 1911:194), but these additional lands have not been retained. The Shinnecock had land west of Southampton, and there was a settlement of Montauks in East Hampton. There was extensive dispersal from these groups in the eighteenth century, especially as the result of the large exodus after 1775 to join Samson Occom, who had been a preacher to them, in the new Christian Indian town of Brothertown. Jefferson (1791) found only three old women who spoke Unquachog, and in 1798 there were only "about seven persons" who could speak Montauk (W.W. Tooker 1890). There were only 30 Montauks left in 1829, and the last hereditary chief, David Pharaoh, died in 1875 (Mooney 1907e). At the end of the nineteenth century there were said to be about 150 Shinnecocks and 10 families of Poosepatucks, whose last sachem, Elizabeth Joe, had died in 1832 (Hodge 1907–1910, 2:550; Speck 1910).

Whaling was a major occupation on Long Island, having begun there commercially around 1650 (Brasser 1971). The whalers were mainly local Indian men, although by 1672 as more people were needed, Indian recruits were taken from southern New England as well. It was an important part of the Long Island Indian economy, and most men of working age were involved in this or other seagoing activities. The Shinnecock lifeboat crews were well known in the nineteenth century, especially as a result of an incident in which most of the Shinnecock male population was wiped out trying to rescue victims of the winter storm that wrecked the ship *Circassian* on December 31, 1876 (Harrington 1903:37).

Acculturation

The years 1700 to 1900 were ones of slow and painful acculturation, bringing changes in the economic, cultural, and religious life of the New England Indians. Farming in the settled English manner was long resisted by the Indians. Instead, much of the reservation land was rented out to White farmers, and the Indians lived on the rents thus obtained. The Indians also found revenue from the sale of wood from their lands, although occasional clear-cutting lowered the land's value and ability to maintain productive forests. Hunting on a large scale was no longer feasible, although many groups still fished and sugared for their food. Whaling was important, both as a chosen occupation and as a means of repaying debts and fines. The manufacture and sale of craft items—scrub brushes (fig. 9), baskets with and without block-stamp designs, and brooms—was an added source of income for many reservation Indians (L.A. Johnson 1957; Speck 1947; Westez 1958; Butler 1947). Otherwise, jobs were difficult to get and often only unskilled labor at low wages was available to Indians and Blacks. However, Rhode Island Indians became noted as stone-wall builders, a craft for which they were still famed in the twentieth century (MHSC ser. 1, 1:210, 9:201), and some raised sheep for the local wool industry. Indian participation in the Revolution (Stiles 1916; Love 1899:237–238) and the Civil War was widely noted, but although their bravery

Mus. of the Amer. Ind., Heye Foundation, New York: 8/1353.
Fig. 9. Shinnecock brush or small broom, made by splintering the end of a piece of wood. Length 28 cm, collected before 1919.

and good service were acknowledged, their generally low civilian status remained unchanged.

Changes in material culture were more noticeable. Wigwams gave way to English-style houses. English clothes and household goods were easily available, and the changeover to English material culture that had begun in the seventeenth century was virtually completed by the nineteenth. The intervening two centuries also saw the near disappearance of the native languages. English was learned in schools and on jobs, and by the early twentieth century a mere handful of Indian words was recalled by a few elderly individuals (Prince 1907; Prince and Speck 1903, 1903a, 1904; Speck 1904, 1928a).

One factor in the acculturation and, in some cases, loss of identity of the Indian groups of southern New England was the decline in population. Disease was the major cause of mortality, and contemporary accounts often stress the devastating effects of drunkenness. Yet the death of many of the men who served in colonial regiments against the French and later in the Revolution was also significant, since it inevitably accelerated intermarriage with non-Indians. For example, between 1755 and 1761, 7 men died of the 18 who went to war from the tiny Western Niantic community, leaving a population of 10 married couples and 9 widows, plus unmarried children (Stiles 1755-1794:397; MHSC ser. 1, 10:103-104). The catastrophic effects of disease on the Indian communities were exemplified on Nantucket. Here there were 358 Indians in 1763, but in six months 222 of them died of "an uncommon mortal distemper." Of the rest, 8 lived by themselves on the west end of the island, 40 lived among the English, and 18 men were at sea; in 1792 only 20 Indians were counted on the whole island (MHSC ser. 1, 3:158-159). There were also devastating epidemics in the 1750s among the Indians of Little Compton, Rhode Island, and Natick; the disease was said to have been brought back to Natick by men who had served in the war against the French (MHSC ser. 1, 1:195, 9:204).

The missions that had begun in the seventeenth century were hard hit in King Philip's War, and the motivation and work slackened for many years (see Stoddard 1917). The religious fervor of the Great Awakening among New Englanders in the 1740s rekindled interest in missions and brought about deep religious changes among the Indians. Even the Mohegan, who had long held out against the new religion, were turned to Christianity at this time (Brasser 1971). New communities, such as Stockbridge and Brothertown, were essentially religious as well as social experiments, and there were strong efforts at integrating Christianity into the Indian life-style. Schools were established on most reservations, although many of these were finally abandoned due to lack of state funds and Indian interest. Eleazar Wheelock's eighteenth-century Indian Charity School in Lebanon, Connecticut, designed for Indian and White children, was religious in orientation. It produced a few

successes before it moved to Hanover, New Hampshire, where it was eventually abandoned in favor of the essentially White college (Dartmouth) that grew out of it (Wheelock 1763; McCallum 1932). Churches were built on many of the reservations, often becoming focal points for community solidarity (Rhode Island. Commission on Affairs of Narragansett Indians 1881-1884; Apes 1829, 1835). The strong missionary drive of the seventeenth and early eighteenth centuries died down as the religious fervor slackened, but most of the New England Indians were by then members of Christian churches, retaining only a few aspects of their former ceremonialism and religious beliefs.

1900-1975

By the mid-nineteenth century the whaling industry had declined while at the same time suburbs burgeoned around the cities and summer tourist resorts became popular. Land thus became more valuable and real-estate speculators constantly tried to oust Indians from the last of their land. The speculators pointed out the triracial character of the Indian groups as evidence that the Indians were extinct or at least had not obeyed earlier strict antimiscegenation laws. Indian groups, like the Montauk of Long Island, that had obeyed these laws had become so small and inbred that they too were proclaimed extinct. Because of these White attitudes, friction developed between a relatively "pure" Indian core and a marginal mestizo group in Indian communities. The resultant status struggles as well as tourist expectations to see "real Indians" led to the development of a neo-Indian culture characterized by borrowings from other Indian groups and vague memories of former days romanticized by Whites. Indian first names were adopted, men grew their hair long, and Indian dress styles were borrowed from Brothertown, Wisconsin, and Saint Regis Mohawk Indians (figs. 10-11). In 1907 William F. Cody (Buffalo Bill) made a spectacular visit to the grave of Uncas, the seventeenth-century Mohegan sachem, on horseback and accompanied by Plains Indians in "full regalia" (A.L. Peale 1930). The display of early pan-Indian dress on this occasion as well as at subsequent performances in the area greatly impressed local Indians and probably helped inspire them to adopt "Indian dress" for meetings and ceremonial occasions (Narragansett Chief Clearwater, personal communication 1974). Ethnologists' inquiries helped stimulate the organization of "pow wows" and other Indian pageants (see "Narragansett," fig. 6, this vol.), which took over social functions once served by Christian religious gatherings. The emphasis on Indianism did much to reestablish a self-respect and group pride long subdued by the racial attitudes of local Whites (Brasser 1971). The Indian Reorganization Act of 1934 stimulated renewed interest in tribal incorporation. Intertribal organizations also developed, such as the Algon-

185

Fig. 10. Lester Skeesuks, a Narragansett-Mohegan from
Brothertown, Wis., who died at Mohegan, Conn., "some years"
before 1909 (Speck 1909:192). He stands before a brush wigwam
wearing a costume of traditional inspiration that includes an erect-
feather headdress (ostrich plumes on a beaded headband), collar,
bead necklaces, crossbelt and pouch, belt, armbands, wristbands,
knee garters, and a cloth kilt. The beaded decorations represent
leaves, flowers, birds, stars, and American flags.

Fig. 11. Lemuel M. Fielding at the Mohegan "wigwam festival" in
Aug. 1920. He is wearing parts of Lester Skeesucks's costume (fig.
10) with the knee garters safety-pinned to his sleeves as armbands,
but other photographs (Speck 1928a:pls. 23a, 32) show that each
man used both possible arrangements. Fielding was chief of the
Mohegan Indian Association when it was founded in 1920 (Speck
1928a:213). Photograph by Frank G. Speck.

quin Council of Indian Tribes in 1926 (Brasser 1971;
Boissevain 1956).

There were still some state reservations in southern
New England and eastern Long Island in 1975. The
Poosepatuck and Shinnecock reservations, of 60 and 400
acres respectively, were supported by New York State.
However, this support was minimal because of their small
size relative to the larger upstate reservations. Both
groups were represented by three land trustees, a president, secretary, and treasurer, elected every two years.
The Poosepatuck population in 1973 was estimated at
160, the Shinnecock 200.

In 1975 Connecticut had only four of the formerly
numerous small reservations remaining. The Lantern Hill
or North Stonington (Eastern Pequot) reservation was
surveyed at 224.6 acres in 1963 (Connecticut. State
Department of Environmental Protection. Indian Affairs
Council 1975:8). The population in 1973 was 19 (U.S.
Department of Commerce 1974:173), but a 1975 update

records 8 full-time and 18 part-time residents (Connecticut. State Department of Environmental Protection.
Indian Affairs Council 1975:9). Mushantuxet, in 1975
called Western Pequot or Ledyard, contained 175 acres
populated by nine full-time residents. This Pequot tribe
was reorganized and incorporated in August 1974, and
preliminary tribal membership rolls listed 55 on- and off-
reservation members. The Golden Hill reservation in
Trumbull was very small, with only one-third of an acre
in 1975 and four full-time residents. The tribe was
incorporated and had tribal lists of 50 persons (Connecticut. State Department of Environmental Protection.
Indian Affairs Council 1975:12). Schaghticoke reservation in Kent was approximately 400 acres, with a part-
time population of two in 1975.

Rhode Island's only reservation was sold in 1880, and
the Narragansetts were in 1975 scattered among other
Rhode Island residents, although many were still concentrated in the southwestern part of the state and retained
a sense of corporate identity.

Massachusetts had only one reservation remaining in
1974, the Hassanamisco reservation in Grafton. It was, at
that point, 11.9 acres, with only one resident. Since 1962

NAA, Smithsonian.
Fig. 12. Mercy Nonsuch Matthews, Western Niantic, with an appliquéd and beaded pouch that she made, probably based on an old model (Speck 1909:209, 1928a:pl. 18). Photograph by M.R. Harrington, 1912.

there has been a tribal organization providing for a chairman and board of directors elected from a tribal membership of everyone of Hassanamisco Nipmuck descent (U.S. Department of Commerce 1974:225).

Dept. of Anthr., Smithsonian: left to right, 203187a, 203188a, 203189a.
Fig. 13. Pottery made for sale by the Indians at Gay Head, Martha's Vineyard, from the colored clays (red, ocher, gray, white) of the cliffs that give Gay Head its name. Each color of clay is added separately, and the pottery is either formed on a wheel (as were these examples) or shaped by hand. The outer surface is then scraped away to reveal the variegated pattern. The pots are not fired, since heat destroys the colors. These vases, collected in the 1890s, are probably among the earliest such pieces made. Similar ware was still made for sale at Gay Head in 1976. Heights, left to right, 12.5 cm, 10.5 cm, 8.5 cm.

Although not many were to be found on the reservations, New England descendants of the Algonquian Indians were far from extinct in 1975. Brasser (1971) gives a population estimate of the coastal Algonquian descendants as 4,165 in 1960, and a Connecticut publication records 2,322 from that state alone in 1970 (Connecticut. State Department of Environmental Protection. Indian Affairs Council 1975).

Several legal cases in the mid-1970s promised to result in redefinition of the status of some New England Indian lands, in payments for previous land losses, and in increased recognition of these groups by the federal government, by their neighbors, and by Indian individuals and organizations elsewhere. Southern New England Indians, though very different from their ancestors of 1675, were still very much a part of New England life in 1975.

Synonymy

Since King Philip's War most of the Indian groups in southern New England have been referred to by the names of the localities in which they lived. A history of these names would in effect be a history of many local place-names, and the research for such a study has not yet been done. Instead, in this section lists of Indian groups from various sources are given, with some modern equivalents and variant forms in parentheses. Many of the names of the larger groupings of the earlier period (see the synonymy in "Indians of Southern New England and Long Island: Early Period," this vol.) have continued in use but often with varying applications.

Praying towns in the Massachusetts Bay colony in 1674 (MHSC ser. 1, 1:180–194): Natick, Punkapoag or Pakemitt (Punkapog, in Canton—Speck 1928d; also Ponkapog), Hassanamesitt (Hassanamisco, in Grafton), Okommakamesit (earlier Ogkoontiquokames—Weis 1959:170; now Marlboro), Wamesit or Pawtuckett (Lowell), Nashobah (Littleton), Magunkaquog (Magunkook, in Ashland). Praying towns established in the Nipmuck country, 1671–1674: Manchage (Manchaug, in Sutton), Chabanakongkomun (Webster), Maanexit (Thompson, Connecticut), Quantisset (Pomfret, Connecticut), Wabquissit (Woodstock, Connecticut), Pakachoog or Packachoog (Pakachoag Hill, Auburn-Worcester), Waeuntug (Uxbridge); Nipmuck towns "coming on to receive the gospel" in 1674: Weshakim or Nashaway (Sterling), Quabaug (Brookfield).

Praying Indian congregations in the colony of New Plymouth in 1674 (Richard Bourne, in MHSC ser. 1, 1:196–199): (1) Meeshawn (Truro) and Punonakanit (Wellfleet); (2) Potanumaquut or Nawsett (Orleans); (3) Manamoyik (Chatham); (4) Sawkattukett (Harwich), Nobsquassit (Dennis), Matakees (Yarmouth), and Weequakut (Chequaquet, in Barnstable); (5) Satuit (Santuit, in Mashpee), Pawpoesit (Poponesset, in Mashpee), Coatuit (Cotuit, in Barnstable), Mashpee (also Marsh-paug—MHSC ser. 1, 1:204), and Wakoquet (Waquoit, in Falmouth); (6) Codtanmut (Cataumet, in Bourne), Ashimuit (later also Shumuit; in the Ashumet Pond area, Falmouth-Mashpee), and Weesquobs (near Pocasset, in Bourne); (7) Pispogutt (north part of Bourne ?), Wawayontat (on the Weweantic River, in Wareham), and Sokones (perhaps Onset in Wareham rather than Saconesset in Falmouth); (8) Cotuhtikut (Titicut, in Middleborough) and Assowamsoo (on Assawompset Pond, in Lakeville). Other Indian locations mentioned by Bourne are Comassakumkanit (on Herring Pond, in Plymouth) and Mannamit (Monument Beach, in Bourne).

Praying towns on Martha's Vineyard in 1674 (John Cotton, in MHSC ser. 1, 1:204, 206): Chappaquidgick (on Chappaquiddick Island), Nashamoiess (in Edgartown), Sengekontakit (later also Sanchecantacket, in Oak Bluffs), Toikiming (also Taacame, Takemmy, and Ohkonkemme, later Christiantown; in West Tisbury), Nashuakemmiuk (later Nashouohkamuck, in Chilmark), and Talhanio (in Chilmark).

Praying towns on Nantucket in 1674 (MHSC ser. 1, 1:206–207): Oggawame (also Occawan), Wammasquid, and Squatesit.

Indian plantations, assemblies, and congregations in the province of Massachusetts Bay (Rawson and Danforth 1698). Little Compton: Saconet (Sakonnet, Rhode Island) and Cokesit (Acoaxet, now in Westport); Dartmouth: Nukkehkummees and Acushnet; Assameeskq (near Nukkehkummees?); Elizabeth Islands (three locations) and Saconeset Point (Saconesset, in Falmouth); Martha's Vineyard: Nashanekammuck (the earlier Nashuakemmiuck, in Chilmark), Ohkonkemme (in West Tisbury), Seconchqut (in Chilmark), Gayhead (Gay Head), Sahnchecontuckquet (on Sengekontacket Pond, in Oak Bluffs), Nunnepoag (in Edgartown), and Chaubaqueduck (on Chappaquiddick Island); Nantucket (five congregations); Sandwich; Mashpah (Mashpee); Ponanummakut (Eastham, in Wellfleet); Eastharbor and Billingsgate (in Wellfleet); Monimoy (Monomoy, in Chatham); Sahquatucket (in Harwich); Kitteaumut or Monimoint ponds (Manomet area in Plymouth); "near Duxbury saw-mills"; Mattakesit (probably Namatakeeset, in Pembroke—Hodge 1907–1910, 1:822); Kehtehticut (Titicut); Assawampset (and misprinted Assawanupset; on Assawompset Pond, in Lakeville) and Quittacus (on Quittacas Pond, in Lakeville; miscopied as Quittaub, MHSC ser. 1, 10:134); Natick; Hassinnamisco (Hassanamisco, in Grafton).

Indian groups in Connecticut, then or recently existing, according to surveys about 1761 (Stiles 1916; MHSC ser. 1, 10:101–112): Pequot (two branches); Mohege (Mohegan); Nyhantic, Nehantic, or Nihantic (Western Niantic, near Lyme); on Connecticut River: Podunk (Windsor); Hoccanum (Glastonbury), Sukíaugk (West Hartford; most went to Farmington in 1730), Tunxis Sepōs or Sēpoús (Farmington), Mattabéeset (at Wongunck, opposite Middletown); East Haven; on Housatonic River: Oronoake or Oronoque (Stratford), Paugusset (Derby), Turkey Hill (southern Derby), Pequaunnuck or Pauquanuck (Golden Hill), Pootatook or Pudaduc (Potatuck, later also Pootatuck and Poodatook; Southbury, opposite Newtown), Wyantonnucken or Youwántonnoc (also Weantinock, now New Milford; called Wyachtonok in "Mahican," this vol.); Kent (De Forest's 1851 Scatacook; now Schaghticoke); other scattered individuals and families.

For the names of the Eastern Long Island Indian groups, see the synonymy in "Indians of Southern New England and Long Island: Early Period," this volume.

Sources

Although there is a vast amount of primary documentation on these Indians in local archives and in published accounts, there has been no synthesis of these materials. The ethnographic literature is also scattered, very uneven, and mostly old, despite the continued presence of Indian communities in the area. Thus this chapter cannot claim to be complete or definitive: many opportunities remain for important studies of the history, changing cultures, and modern conditions of the Indian peoples of southern New England.

Important early documentation is outlined in "Indians of Southern New England and Long Island: Early Period," this volume. The various state and colonial documents have generally reliable data, although the early writers did not always understand the Indians' side of the issues.

For Massachusetts, the state documents are important for the statistics presented (Massachusetts. Commissioners 1849, 1861; Massachusetts (Colony) 1853–1854) and can be supplemented with firsthand accounts from Mather (1702), Sewall (MHSC ser. 6, 1:400–403), and Mayhew (1727) about Martha's Vineyard and from Stoddard (1917); all concern missions and religious topics. Other good firsthand accounts are Stiles (1916) on all of New England, Hopkins (1753) and Belknap and Morse (1955) on the Stockbridge Indians, MHSC ser. 2, 3:1–12, and Apes (1829, 1835) on Mashpee. The material from the Massachusetts Historical Society Collections is varied but extensive. Some of the modern accounts are also informative (particularly Warner 1935; W.F. Gookin 1958; Butler 1947; R.H. Brown 1958; Brasser 1971; Speck 1928, 1928a; Tantaquidgeon 1930, 1930a).

Rhode Island is well documented by its state reporting, especially around the 1880s when the reservation in Charlestown was being sold (Rhode Island. General Assembly. Committee on Indian Tribes 1852; Rhode Island. General Assembly. House of Representatives 1880; Rhode Island. Commission on Affairs of Narragansett Indians 1881–1884). Other good discussions include those by Stiles (1916), Z. Allen (1876), and Boissevain (1952, 1956, 1959).

Connecticut's main sources have long been De Forest (1851) and Orcutt (1882). General histories of Connecticut are also useful (B. Trumbull 1818; Barber 1838). More modern materials are by Speck (1909, 1928a, 1943a), Tantaquidgeon (1928, 1935, 1972), Burton and Lowenthal (1974), and Brasser (1971). For the Branford Indians see Townshend (1900). The Indian and Colonial Research Center in Old Mystic, Connecticut, houses the Eva L. Butler Library, which includes field notes on many ancient and modern aspects of Connecticut Indian life. See also Butler (1947, 1948, 1953).

Hicks (1975) and Hicks and Kertzer (1972) describe a pseudonymous southern New England group.

Material on Long Island is sketchy, but a few sources are Samson Occom's brief account (MHSC ser. 1, 10:106–111), New York colonial records (NYCD), P. Bailey (1954, 1962), and a detailed account of modern-day observations by Brasser (1966). Other articles of interest on recent times are by Westez (1944, 1945, 1958), Carr and Westez (1945), and Harrington (1903). Coles (1954) is useful in regard to the names of tribes that used to inhabit the island.

Sources on the mission work are plentiful, but care must be taken in extracting data on Indians. Beaver (1962, 1962a, 1966, 1966a, 1968, 1969) deals with the early missions. Kellaway (1961) gives a detailed, interesting account of the New England Company. Weis (1959) has a complete list of seventeenth- and eighteenth-century missions. Others to note are Love's (1899) biography of Samson Occom, Hare's (1931) of Thomas Mayhew, J.T. Hamilton (1900) and Heckewelder (1820) on the Moravian missions, and Wheelock's (1763) account of his Indian Charity School.

Some hundreds of artifacts from this region and period survive in museums and historical societies, including many local ones in New England (in addition to some archeological materials). The most important collections are probably those in the Peabody Museum of Harvard University and the Museum of the American Indian, Heye Foundation, New York. However, most of these items have dubious, interrupted, or unknown pedigrees connecting them to identified groups and dates. Frank G. Speck collected both heirlooms and recent artifacts from several of these groups in the early twentieth century and distributed them to many museums (and several private collectors), including some in Europe.

Narragansett

WILLIAM S. SIMMONS

Language

The Narragansett (ˌnărəˈgănsĭt) spoke an Eastern Algonquian language that is known chiefly from the early study by Williams (1936). Williams noted that although the dialects differed north and south of Narragansett country, one could, with the aid of his compilation, converse with speakers of these dialects. The 51-item vocabulary collected by Ezra Stiles in 1769 derived from a mixed Narragansett and Niantic community (Cowan 1973). Thomas Commuck, a Brothertown (Wisconsin) resident of Narragansett descent, published a list of six words taught to him by his grandmother who died in 1825 and who learned the words from her mother when she was a little girl (WHC 1906:297). Parsons (1861) wrote that Narragansett "has ceased to be a spoken language in the tribe for nearly half a century." Morgan's (1959:135) 1862 Narragansett informant did not speak the language. Gatschet (1973) collected 25 words and phrases from elderly Narragansetts near Point Judith, Rhode Island, in 1879.*

Territory and Environment

As an ethnic label the name Narragansett is used in both a broad and a narrow sense. The broadest social and territorial unit of seventeenth-century Narragansett culture was what might be termed the extended sachemdom, which included the Narragansett proper and all other sachemdoms where the Narragansett sachems (chiefs) exercised authority. The sachemdom was the hereditary bounded territory of a named group, such as Narragansett, Coweset, or Niantic, which was ruled by members of a dominant patrilineage and divided internally into lesser sachemdoms and a hierarchy of lesser sachems. The Narragansett sachemdom included southern portions of Kent County, Dutch and Conanicut Islands, and most of Washington County (fig. 1), except an area somewhat greater than Charlestown, which was Eastern Niantic country, and the area between Weekapaug and the Pawcatuck River, which was fought for and won from the Pequots (E.R. Potter 1835:1-2; Williams 1945).

The Narragansett sachems dominated in varying ways and degrees the Coweset (Williams 1874:21-23), Manissean (Livermore 1877:10-11; E.R. Potter 1835:1-2), Massachusett (Morton 1637:31-33; Williams 1874:407; Winthrop 1825-1826, 1:72, 149), Montauk (Fernow 1881:58, 1883:480; Gookin 1972:8), Niantic (Gookin 1972:8), Nipmuck (Gookin 1972:8; Williams 1874:326), Pawtuxet (Winthrop 1825-1826, 2:120), Pokanoket (Williams 1874:316-317), and Shawomet (Winthrop 1825-1826, 2:120) sachemdoms around their frontiers. They considered some of the closest subject sachemdoms to be theirs by ancestral right. In a genealogical fragment written before 1703, Tashtasick, the earliest remembered Narragansett sachem and grandfather of Canonicus, (sachem at the time of English arrival) was said to have ruled the "Countries of *Narraganset, Niantic, Coweesit & parts adjacent*" (Stiles 1916:27-28). Ties of kinship and marriage were particularly close between the Narragansetts and Niantics (Winthrop 1825-1826, 2:82). The Cowesets lived north of Narragansett between East Greenwich and Apponaug, and the Shawomets lived north of them in areas of Warwick, West Warwick, and Coventry. The Pawtuxets lived north of Shawomet around the village known today as Pawtuxet. The Narragansett sachems sold land in Rhode Island that belonged to weaker neighboring sachemdoms to the English (Gorton 1835:92-95; W. Harris 1902:57-58; E.R. Potter 1835:5-6). The Pokanoket frontier had extended west of the Seekonk River, for the sachem Massasoit claimed to own the site of Providence, which the Narragansett sachems conveyed to Roger Williams (1874:316-317, 406-407).

The Narragansetts utilized four distinct natural environments—coast, forest, river, and pond. The west shore of Narragansett Bay and the adjoining coast of Block Island Sound abounded with tidal inlets, marshes, and shallow beaches, where crabs, lobster, clams, oysters, fish, and waterfowl could be gathered. The mixed chestnut, oak, hickory, maple, birch, and pine forests were characterized by brooks, cedar swamps, rock outcroppings (useful for shelter), clear springs, and low hills. Here they hunted and trapped deer, moose, bear, wolves, foxes, and squirrels. They caught fish and beaver in the Pawtuxet, Blackstone, Queen's, Pawcatuck, and Pocasset rivers and built stone weirs for shad and alewives several miles up the Pawcatuck (Denison 1878:184) and Pawtuxet rivers

---

* Narragansett words are cited in the original early spellings, since no systematic orthography is now possible.

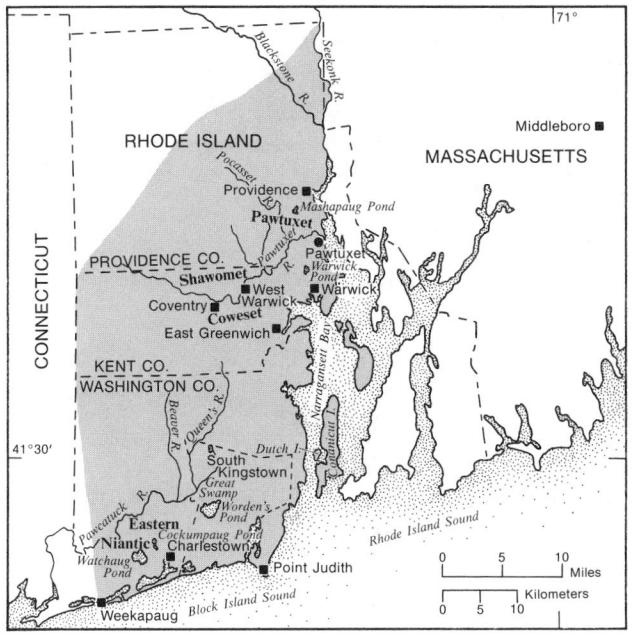
Fig. 1. Tribal territory.

(Anonymous 1937:cover photo). They settled near, among others, freshwater Mashapaug (Chapin 1927:15; Staples 1843:26, 30), Warwick (Chapin 1926:117–118, 122), Watchaug (Connecticut (Colony) Laws, Statutes, etc. 1850–1890, 2:289; Tucker 1877:47–49), and Worden's ponds (W. Miller 1936:8; Carlton 1940:504), which provided fish and waterfowl.

Culture

European writers distinguished the Narragansetts from other groups by their industry in trade and by their manufacture of items such as shell pendants and currency (wampum) and later, finely cast metal pipes (Gookin 1972:17–18; Wood 1865:69–70). In comparison with their enemies the Pequots they sought "to grow rich by industrie, [rather] than famous by deeds of Chevalry" (Wood 1865:70). The Narragansetts are reported to have differed from neighbors by more generally having one wife (Williams 1936:147) and by performance of a (winter?) ritual at which the participants burned their material possessions (Winslow 1910:344–345). According to Hubbard (1865, 1:47), the Narragansetts "were always more civil and courteous to the English than any of the other Indians." Until their destruction in 1675–1676 they were the most powerful and populous New England tribe.

Subsistence

Narragansett settlement patterns reflected recurrent seasonal shifts in the importance of forest, agricultural, and marine resources. In warm spring or seed time they pitched their dwellings by open fields, which often were near the sea, where they planted corn, beans, and squash and picked wild strawberries (W. Harris 1963:37; Williams 1936:46, 95–102, 124–125). When the corn began to sprout they erected watch houses in the middle of their fields where adults or children camped to prevent early morning birds from devouring the plants. In midsummer they moved their house sites both to get away from fleas and to begin work in distant fields. The summer house was a variant of the circular wigwam built of poles fixed in the ground and bent and laced inwardly over a fire, open at the apex to let out smoke, and covered with birch and chestnut bark. These could be dismantled and moved in a few hours (Williams 1936:32–33, 38–39, 46–47, 89). In August they harvested corn and dried it on mats in the sun to be stored in underground caches (W. Harris 1963:23; Underhill 1902:8; Williams 1936:100). "The woman of the family will commonly raise two or three heaps of twelve, fifteene, or twentie bushells a heap, which they drie in round broad heaps; and if she have helpe of her children or friends, much more" (Williams 1936:100). Harvest coincided with the start of the hunting season, which extended into winter. They built small temporary hunting houses of bark and rushes in the forest where deer and other game had been observed during the preceding months. The hunters camped with their wives and children if the hunting range was not too far away (Williams 1936:46–47, 171–172, 1874:125, 152–153, 156). Narragansetts hunted the territories of Massachuset sachems against their will (Morton 1637:31–33) and were observed hunting in Nipmuck territory as late as 1755 (Crane 1898:116). Williams (1936:46–47) noted that the most important seasonal move was from summer fields to winter quarters in wooded valleys. The winter wigwam was apparently covered with mats (ibid:31–33). Availability of firewood determined the selection of the winter site (W. Harris 1963:37; Williams 1936:60).

Division of Labor

Although men helped their wives clear and plant fields, and cultivated their own tobacco, women performed most agricultural tasks such as planting, hoeing, and preparation of the harvest (Williams 1936:14, 37, 44–45, 98–100). Men cut and arranged house poles and made dugout canoes. Some specialized in the manufacture of bows, arrows, or shell currency; and old men made turkey feather mantles (Williams 1936:46–47, 106–107, 160). Hunting, fishing, and fighting were male pursuits (ibid.:72–73, 147–148, 160). Women's tasks included setting up the house, carrying burdens, shellfishing, mortaring, and the manufacture of basketry (fig. 2), mats, and earthen pots (Chapin 1925:23–25; Williams 1936:32, 37, 47, 149, 160).

Religion

The principal religious practitioner in Narragansett culture was the powwow or shaman who in all known cases was a male who probably was called to this role in dream

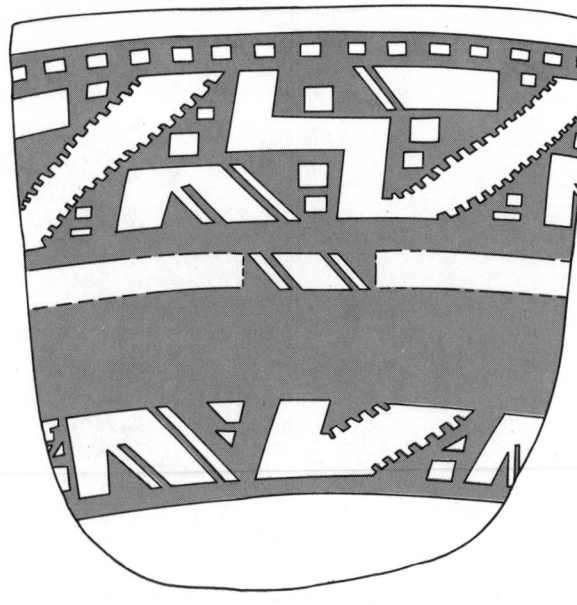

Fig. 2. Narragansett twined basket, dating from around 1675. Design formed by 2-strand twined weft of cornhusk or other fiber and red wool around a basswood warp. The red wool, now largely disintegrated, may have filled most of the open areas. Reconstructed design at right. Height about 10–12 cm.

or vision experience, which may have been induced by herbal infusions (Kittredge 1913:151). He presided over public calendrical rituals performed at harvest and midwinter and over critical rites performed in event of drought, famine, sickness, and war (Williams 1936: 125–130, 180). A distinctive longhouse near the sachem's residence was used for the harvest ritual, which attracted numerous participants and involved several days of feasting, dancing, and giving away by individuals of wealth accumulated for this purpose (Williams 1936:180). The evidence indicates that they addressed the public calendrical rituals to the creator, *Cautántowwit,* and the critical rituals to *Chepi,* an appearing spirit, perhaps the disembodied spirit of dead persons, with which the powwow had direct rapport (Stiles 1901:386, 1916:142–143; Williams 1936:203–204; Winslow 1910: 344–345). The Narragansetts referred to what Williams identified as the soul by two terms, one of which was derived from the word for sleep because "it workes and operates when the body sleepes" and the other of which was "of affinity, with a word signifying a looking glasse, or cleere resemblance" (Williams 1936:130). At least one of these returned after death to *Cautántowwit*'s house in the southwest where it continued in an afterlife similar to life on earth (Williams 1936:130, 137). According to Williams (1936:130), the souls of "great and good men and Women" entered *Cautántowwit*'s house and the souls of murderers, thieves, and liars "wander restlesse abroad." Although his perception of an afterworld based upon moral reward and punishment may have been influenced by Puritan expectations, the evidence cited here indicates a belief in two kinds of soul and different destinations for the soul after death.

The powwow was not observed to preside at individual identity and social status changes in the life of a person, which often involved changing one's name (W. Harris 1963:59; Hubbard 1865, 2:57; Kittredge 1913:154; Williams 1936:146–147) nor at death and burial ritual, when one's name went out of use (Williams 1936:202). Some of a vast range of deities associated with natural phenomena such as the sun, moon, sea, and fire, and social categories such as men, women, and children were reported to communicate with individuals through dreams and visions (Williams 1936:20–21, 124–127). Williams (1936:A5) heard stories of a mythical person named *Wetucks* who performed miracles and walked on water and was thought by him to bear "some kind of broken Resemblance to the *Sonne of God.*" *Cautántowwit* created the first man and woman of stone and disliking these broke them in pieces and made a second couple of a tree, which became the ancestors of all mankind (Williams 1936:135). All deities, gifted persons, and strange and inexplicable phenomena they described as *manitóo* 'it is a god' (Williams 1936:126). Enough evidence appears in Williams to suggest the existence of a cosmology in which the winds, directions, seasons, celestial bodies, animal species, and human social categories participated in an ordered system in which numerous dualisms—such as the two souls, two dominant deities, and two creations—are apparent.

Kinship

A Narragansett woman in Kansas in 1862 told Morgan (1871:219, 1877:174, 1959:135) that descent among her people was through the female line and because her great-grandmother on the mother's side was Narragansett, she too was Narragansett. Although other late sources support her assertion (Rhode Island Census Board 1887:409; Rhode Island. General Assembly. House of Representatives 1880:19), no seventeenth- or early eighteenth-century writer indicated awareness of or gave clear evidence for the existence of matrilineal institutions among the Narragansett. However, some fragmentary evidence can be interpreted as indicating the presence of exogamous matrilineal clans that were important for the regulation of marriage (Simmons and Aubin 1975). The authority of the sachem over his land and followers was inherited along patrilineal lines but not necessarily from father to son (in the Euro-American sense of these terms). Sachem's daughters married and moved to the residence of other sachems thus confirming or creating alliances between leading families of different sachemdoms. Instances are recorded of two or more families residing together in one dwelling (Williams 1936:33) and the wives of a polygynous male residing separately (Rowlandson 1931:150). The Narragansetts attributed the practice of polygamy to a longer than one year postpartum sex taboo (Williams 1936:147).

Political Organization

The Narragansetts were ruled by a pair of sachems, one older and one younger, who were patrilineally related (De Laet 1841:294; Hazard 1792-1794, 2:12; Williams 1936:140; Wroth 1970:138). Canonicus, the elder sachem in 1636, governed at home while Miantonomi, his brother's son, dealt directly with subjects, enemies, and the English. On early deeds Canonicus represented himself by a bow, and Miantonomi by an arrow (Chapin 1931:32). A council composed of greater and lesser sachems, other men of family and ability, and probably powwows, participated in important decisions concerning peace, war, religion, "and all things" (Williams 1936:128; E. Johnson 1910:161-164). Quaiapen (alias Magnus, Matantuck, the Old Queen, Squaw Sachem, Saunk Squaw), the sister of Ninigret who married Canonicus's son Mexanno, also participated in political decisions and assumed leadership responsibilities in King Philip's War until she was slain by John Talcott's troops in Nipsachuck Swamp in North Smithfield (Leach 1958:41; Talcott 1934:11; Williams 1874:366-367). The sachems protected their followers from internal and external dangers, allocated land, provided for the poor, and administered punishment to wrongdoers. Their followers in turn provided them with praise, deference, and tribute.

War

The Narragansetts went to war with the Pokanoket (Winthrop 1825-1826, 1:72) to prevent them from escaping subjection by alliance with Plymouth, with the Pequots over land between their frontiers (E.R. Potter 1835:248), and with the Montauk and Mohegan to avenge deaths caused by feuding (Fernow 1881:58, 1883:480; Hazard 1792-1794, 2:292, 295, 318-319, 337, 359-361; Hubbard 1865, 1:40-43; Williams 1874:145, 275). A sachem could provoke his enemies to fight by mentioning and abusing the names of their dead sachems (Hazard 1792-1794, 2:349; Williams 1936:202). When hostilities between Philip and the English began, the Narragansett sachems were unable to prevent their followers from joining the fight (Williams 1874:371). When on the offensive they sought to surprise their enemies, and they were known to attempt pitched battles; however, they relied primarily on dispersed and concealed forays rather than upon massed assaults. They maintained a number of defensive fortifications within their domain and, as a last resort, withdrew into inaccessible swamps (Chapin 1931a).

Trade

With the English they exchanged, both directly and by using shell currency as a medium, land, furs, and food for brass pots, bells, thimbles, and fishhooks; iron axes, knives, awls, and hoes; latten spoons; glass bottles and beads; and English cloth and clothing. Sometimes these goods were retraded to more remote tribes (Simmons 1970; Williams 1936:152-156, 160; Wood 1865:69-70). They traded guns, some reportedly acquired from the French, to the English. Carved stone and wooden pipes reached Narragansett country from the Mohawk (Williams 1936:185, 44-45).

History

The earliest known probable description of the Narragansetts by a European is that by Giovanni da Verrazano, who visited Narragansett Bay in the spring of 1524: "These people are the most beautiful and have the most civil customs that we have found on this voyage. They are taller than we are . . . the face is clear-cut . . . the eyes are black and alert, and their manner is sweet and gentle, very like the manner of the ancients" (Wroth 1970:138). The next recorded encounter occurred in 1614 with the Dutch navigator Adriaen Block, for whom Block Island is named (De Laet 1841:294). The "two kings, attended with a guard of fifty men" who visited the Englishman Thomas Dermer at Middleboro, Massachusetts, in 1619 may have been Narragansett (Chapin 1931:9; Dermer 1841:350). In January 1622 the Narragansett sachems sent a bundle of arrows tied together with a snake skin to the Pilgrims at Plymouth who perceived this to be a challenge and returned the skin to Narragansett with bullets in it, thereby beginning the fear, which lasted until King Philip's War, that the Narragansetts would attempt to overthrow English settlement (Bradford 1952:96). In the late spring of 1636, Roger Williams and five other English who had been banished from Massachusetts Bay crossed the Seekonk River into Narragansett territory, where tradition records they were greeted with the words, "What cheer, *nétop*" (*nétop* being a Narragansett word for 'my friend'). They acquired tracts from Canonicus and Miantonomi upon which they established Providence (Arnold 1859–1860, 1:40; Williams 1874:406–408). Largely due to Williams's diplomatic efforts the Narragansett sachems supported the Connecticut and Massachusetts Puritan army and their Mohegan auxiliaries in the campaign against the Pequots in the spring of 1637 (J. Mason 1736; Williams 1874:338). Following the destruction of the Pequots, the Narragansett and Mohegan sachems agreed at Hartford in 1638 to forget former enmity between them and to appeal to the English rather than to seek revenge if one group wronged the other (fig. 3) (E.R. Potter 1835:177–178). In 1643, Uncas's Mohegans captured Miantonomi during an abortive attack into Mohegan territory and delivered him to the English magistrates at Hartford. The commissioners of the United Colonies at Boston determined that he should be put to death secretly and returned him to Uncas for that purpose (Winthrop 1825–1826, 2:130–134). By Samuel Gorton's persuasion and by the need to protect themselves from further treachery by Massachusetts Bay, the Narragansett sachems submitted voluntarily to King Charles I of England on April 19, 1644, and confirmed their submission again in 1662 (Chapin 1931:72; Gorton 1835:158–160). Relationships between the United Colonies and the Narragansetts continued to deteriorate and at one point they were forced to mortgage their entire sachemdom for damages done in an expedition against Uncas (Chapin 1931:70–74; Leach 1958:16–17). Pokanoket refugees from the skirmishes that grew into King Philip's War entered Narragansett country in the spring

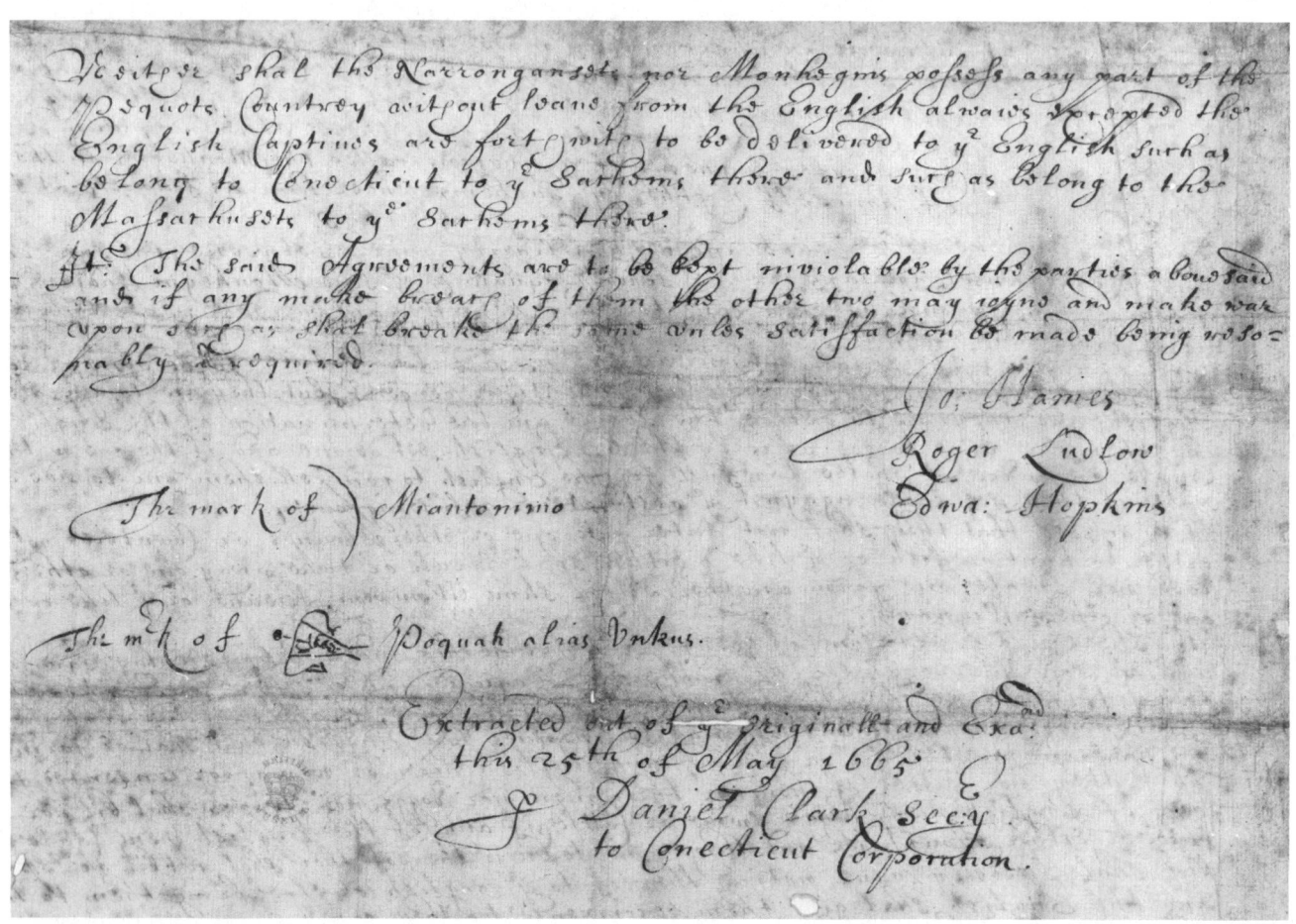

British Mus.: Lansd 1052 folio 7v.

Fig. 3. 1665 copy of part of the 1638 agreement between Miantonomi (representing the Narragansett), Uncas (representing the Mohegan), and three representatives of the Connecticut English (Chapin 1931:35–36). Text reads: "Neither shal the Narrongansets nor Monhegins possess any part of the Pequots Countrey without leave from the English alwaies excepted the English Captives are forthwith to be delivered to the English such as belong to Conecticut to the Sachems there and such as belong to the Massachusets to the Sachems there.13 That: The said Agreements are to be kept inviolable by the parties abovesaid and if any make breach of them the other two may joyne and make war upon such as shal breake the same unles satisfaction be made being resonably required."

of 1675; and when ordered by the United Colonies to surrender these, the sachem Canonchet, son of Miantonomi, replied, "No, not a Wampanoag, nor the paring of a Wampanoag's nail" (Chapin 1931:78). On November 2, 1675, the United Colonies declared war on the Narragansetts and on Sunday, December 19, 1675, their army marched across ice and destroyed the Narragansett refuge in the Great Swamp in South Kingstown, inflicted massive casualties, and drove those yet alive into guerrilla exile. When hostilities ended in 1676 the English moved into the vacated lands and the Narragansett survivors submitted to long periods of indentureship to colonial families (Easton 1858:175; Gookin 1854; E.R. Potter 1835:100-105; Society of Colonial Wars. Rhode Island 1926:40-45). Ninigret (fig. 4), the paramount Niantic sachem, maintained a nominal pro-English position during the war, and his people survived intact and mingled with the Narragansett survivors who transferred their name to the combined but mainly Niantic population. In 1709 Ninigret II, son of the deceased Niantic sachem, quitclaimed all title to vacant Narragansett (Niantic)

Mus. of Art, R.I. School of Design, Providence, gift of Robert Winthrop.
Fig. 4. Eastern Niantic sachem Ninigret, thought to have been painted for Gov. John Winthrop either in 1637 or in 1647 when Ninigret visited Boston. His black and white checkerboard headband, earrings, and necklace (probably with shell gorget) are credible early depictions of wampum. He also wears a red cloth breechclout, a robe, pucker-toe mocassins (consistent with later Northeastern types), and brown leggings. Artist unknown.

lands to the colony of Rhode Island, except for a tract of some 64 square miles in Charlestown for him and his people to inhabit, which could not be sold (E.R. Potter 1835:111-112; Rhode Island. Commission on Affairs of Narragansett Indians 1881-1884, 1:147-148). Although the Rhode Island legislature exercised control over the tribe from without, the sachem and an appointed five-man council governed within.

Few Narragansetts converted to Christianity in the decades following King Philip's War (Mather 1966:157; Matthews 1913; Mayhew 1896:110). The majority continued in shamanism until the New Light enthusiasm when they converted under the ministry of Joseph Park of the New England Society for the Propagation of the Gospel, who had been a missionary and teacher among them since 1733 (Love 1899:190-191; T. Prince 1744-1745:201-210, 1745:21-28). About 1745 the Indians separated from Park's Westerly congregation under Samuel Niles, one of a succession of Indian ministers, to establish a distinct sect that was not without factions (Backus 1871:511; Denison 1878:79-85; Goen 1962:91; Love 1899:192-194; Stiles 1901:232-233). The wooden church, built in 1750, with its nearby burial grounds and August meeting grounds, formed the center of the reservation community, which supported itself by farming, wood cutting, sheep raising, fresh- and saltwater fishing, and outside employment as servants, hired hands, fishermen, and stone masons (Boissevain 1969:4; Tucker 1877:65). Schooling on the reservation between the time of the separating from Park's congregation and the construction of the reservation school building in 1766 was intermittent and is sketchily known (Rhode Island. Commission on Affairs of Narragansett Indians 1881-1884, 4:11; Love 1899:192, 195; Park 1757:1). In 1764 The Society for the Propagation of the Gospel sent a teacher to the Narragansetts, and another in 1765, who began construction of a schoolhouse on Cockumpaug Pond, about one-half mile from the Narragansett Indian Church (Love 1899:195; Ninegrett 1765:1; Rhode Island. General Assembly. House of Representatives 1880:17).

After the death of George (Ninigret) Sachem, the last hereditary sachem of the Narragansett-Niantics, the tribe was governed by a governor, or president, and a council who were elected annually in March. "An Act for Regulating the Affairs of the Narragansett tribe of

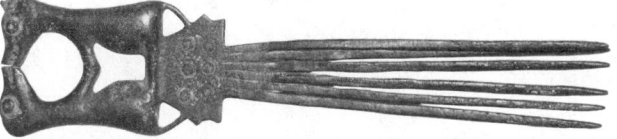

R.I. Histl. Soc., Providence.
Fig. 5. Cast brass comb excavated from an Indian grave in Charlestown, R.I., quite possibly that of Weunquesh (d.1690), daughter of Ninigret (Chapin 1931:106-108). Possibly cast from a carved antler comb (Willoughby 1935:244). Length about 15 cm.

Indians" was passed in Rhode Island in 1792, which defined voting rights for the council and established an office of treasurer who acted as "overseer" of the tribe for the state (Rhode Island. General Assembly. House of Representatives 1880:19). Financed by a grant from the SPG, the Narragansetts built or rebuilt the school structure in 1812 and resumed instruction, which had apparently lapsed during the Revolution (J. Kendall 1812:36–38; Love 1899:196). In 1849 the tribe adopted a constitution, "whereby all our town affairs may be managed for our own benefit" (Rhode Island. Commission on Affairs of Narragansett Indians 1881–1884, 4:20–21). Narragansett masons constructed a stone church on the site of the earlier wooden structure in 1859, where members of the tribe and guests continued to hold their annual meeting on the second Sunday of August (Tucker 1877:65). In 1879 the council agreed to quitclaim to the state all common, tribal, or vacant lands; and in the following year the state legislature passed "An act to abolish the tribal authority and tribal relations of the Narragansett Tribe or Indians" by which act tribal members acquired the status of citizenship and the tribe as a legal body was dissolved.

Tribal identity did not lapse after detribalization; it continues into the present around the institutional core of the corporately owned church, the August meeting (referred to locally as the Pow Wow—fig. 6), and an elected tribal council that has met since around 1948 in a "Long House" (Boissevain 1963:500). The Narragansetts incorporated following the Indian Reorganization Act of 1934

Fig. 7. Narragansett Indian Church in Charlestown, R.I., built in 1859 to replace the original wooden church. Photograph by David B. Heath, 1973.

and returned to the title of sachem for their chief elected official (Boissevain 1969:7). In 1973 the Historic Village of the Narragansett Indians in Charlestown, which includes the Indian Cedar Swamp, two ponds, the church (fig. 7), and the ruins of over two centuries of house sites, was added to the National Register of Historic Places (Anonymous 1973). Despite the convulsions of conquest in King Philip's War, revivalistic conversion in the Great Awakening, and over two subsequent centuries of accommodation to Euro-American society, Narragansett identity persists, most strongly in those areas of Rhode Island closest to the centers of the Narragansett and Niantic sachemdoms.

Population

Mooney (1928:2–4) estimated the combined Narragansett and Eastern Niantic population to have been 4,000 in 1600. Because groups within the Narragansett extended sachemdom were often identified as Narragansett, early population estimates vary greatly (Brinley 1900:74; J. Callender 1838:128–130; De Forest 1851:62–64; Drake 1841:53). A contemporary observer wrote that the Narragansetts and their subjects could, at their zenith, field a force of 5,000 fighting men; by 1674, with few subjects left, they could field 1,000 fighting men (Gookin 1972:8). Thomas and Richard Stanton, who lived among the Narragansetts, estimated their warrior population to have been 2,000 at the outbreak of war in 1675. By the end of King Philip's War, fewer than 100 Narragansetts survived who chose to live in Rhode Island (Hubbard 1865, 2:55); others had been killed, driven out of the area, or sold into West Indian slavery. Some remaining Narragansetts merged with the Niantics, and both became known as Narragansett. In 1730, 985 persons identified as Indian lived in Narragansett country (J. Callender 1838:93–94). In 1765, 73 Indian families lived within the reservation, and in the following year the reservation population was said to have been 315 persons (Love

Fig. 6. Opening procession of the 1969 Narragansett Pow Wow, in Charlestown, R.I. The participants include dignitaries from Northeastern groups other than Narragansett, and the costumes incorporate aspects of still wider Indian influences. Photograph by George Hicks.

196

1899:196; Parsons 1861:iii-iv). Of the 199 persons identified as Indian who lived in Charlestown in 1833, all but seven aged women possessed some White and/or Negro ancestry (Commissioner on the Narragansett Tribe of Indians 1858:3-4). The decline in population between 1766 and 1833 is partly due to the emigration of some Narragansetts to Oneida lands in New York after the Revolution. In 1858, 132 persons of Narragansett ancestry lived in Charlestown; and in 1861, 122 persons of that town claimed descent from the tribe (Parsons 1861:iii-iv; Commissioner on the Narragansett Tribe of Indians 1858:4). By 1870 that number had reduced to "about a hundred" (Anonymous 1870). The detribalization commission determined that 302 men, women, and children, most of whom lived in southern Rhode Island and in Providence, were entitled to a share of the purchase money for the reservation (Rhode Island. Commission on Affairs of Narragansett Indians 1881-1884, 1:11, 133-141). Although the Rhode Island census for 1885 indicated 199 Indians throughout the state, the Narragansett population of Charlestown was not included because the town clerk of Charlestown did not consider them to be Indian (Rhode Island Census Board 1887:408-409). Tribal membership in 1972 was said to be 424 (Taylor 1972:230).

Synonymy

For the synonymy of the name Narragansett, see "Indians of Southern New England and Long Island: Early Period," this volume.

Sources

The most important source on seventeenth-century Narragansett culture is Roger Williams's *A Key Into the Language of America* (1936), which was first published in London in 1643. The fourth (1866) edition is distinguished by voluminous linguistic and ethnographic notes. The Rhode Island and Providence Plantations Tercentenary Committee sponsored a fifth edition (1936), which most faithfully follows the first. The *Key* is the first English-language ethnography of an American Indian people.

The second most important source is the letters of Roger Williams (1874). Other material by Williams about Indians can be found in Thorowgood (1650:6) and Williams (1881:23-62, 1900:154-155, 1945, 1971). Seventeenth-century primary sources other than Williams include Brinley (1900:69-96), W. Harris (1902:165-177, 1963), and E. Johnson (1910:161-164). Of the many accounts of Narragansetts in King Philip's War, Church's (1829:57-63) description of the Great Swamp Fight is the most vivid.

The earliest important secondary source is E.R. Potter (1835), which provides an accurate, amply documented, year-by-year account of Narragansett history from the early seventeenth to the mid-eighteenth centuries. Dorr (1885) depends heavily on Williams for ethnographic information. Rider (1904) collected data and opinion on Narragansett culture, history, land transactions, and place-names. Chapin (1931) provides a brief outline of Narragansett history throughout the seventeenth century and accurate genealogical information on the Narragansett and Niantic ruling families; these genealogies have been analyzed by Simmons and Aubin (1975). Of the many secondary sources on King Philip's War, Leach's (1958) is the most thorough (see also Washburn 1958; Jennings 1975). Boissevain has contributed important papers and articles on Narragansett ethnohistory (1952, 1963, 1968, 1969, 1973).

The earliest known published work by a Narragansett author is an anonymous autobiography that contains no ethnographic information (Peirce 1832). The handwritten minutes and ledgers of the Narragansett tribe from 1850 to 1865 were excerpted and published with comments by Boissevain and Roberts (1974). Other works by Narragansett authors include Thomas Commuck's article on the Brothertown, Wisconsin, Indians (WHC 1906: 291-298); the journal *Narragansett Dawn*, a mixture of folkloric and historic material published in 1935 and 1936; and Ella Brown's (1971) collection of poetry.

Collections of Narragansett material culture, ethnographic and archeological, may be seen at the Rhode Island Historical Society, Providence; the Haffenreffer Museum of Anthropology, Bristol, Rhode Island; the Museum of Primitive Culture in Peace Dale, Rhode Island; the Sydney L. Wright Museum in the Jamestown, Rhode Island, Philomenian Library; and the Museum of the American Indian, Heye Foundation, in New York City.

Mahican

T.J. BRASSER

Language, Territory, and Environment

The Mahican (ˈmäˌhēkən or ˌmuˈhēkən) spoke an Eastern Algonquian language, which was probably most closely related to Wappinger and other Munsee dialects and to the Algonquian languages of New England.* Linguistic data originating from Stockbridge, Massachusetts, betray the heterogeneous makeup of the local "Mahican" population, which had incorporated many remnant groups from New England.

The homeland of the Mahican Indians extended from Lake Champlain southward into the western part of Dutchess County, New York, and from the valley of the Schoharie Creek in the west to south-central Vermont in the east (fig. 1). With increasing unity among the Iroquois tribes in the sixteenth century, relations with the Mohawk appeared to have become markedly hostile, making it impossible for the Mahican to use their domains west of the Hudson River for purposes other than hunting. On the other hand, the Mohawk did not dare to establish villages east of Schoharie Creek.

Mahican country is part of the coastal uplands through which several rivers have cut north-south valleys. Of these, the valley of the Hudson River forms a lowland passage from Lake Champlain and the Saint Lawrence to the Atlantic coast. North of the Hudson River highlands the valley is rimmed on the west by the glaciated Allegheny plateau, and on the east by the rugged area of the Taconic and Green mountains. Most of the land was forested with a mixture of conifers and broad-leaved hardwoods. The diversified environment offered a habitat for black bears, deer, moose, beaver, otter, bobcat, mink, rabbit, raccoon, turkey and many other birds, while the rivers teemed with fish. In general, animal life as well as the Indian population concentrated in the valleys of the rivers and creeks.

Culture about 1600

To a large extent, the Mahican way of life was similar to that of their direct neighbors—Mohawk, Esopus, Wappinger, Housatonic, and Sokoki. Particularly in their social organization and intertribal relations, the Mahican were most closely related to the Wappinger, Esopus, and

*The language became extinct before it could be studied by modern methods. No suitable systematic orthography for writing the language has yet been proposed; thus Mahican words are written here as they appear in the historical sources.

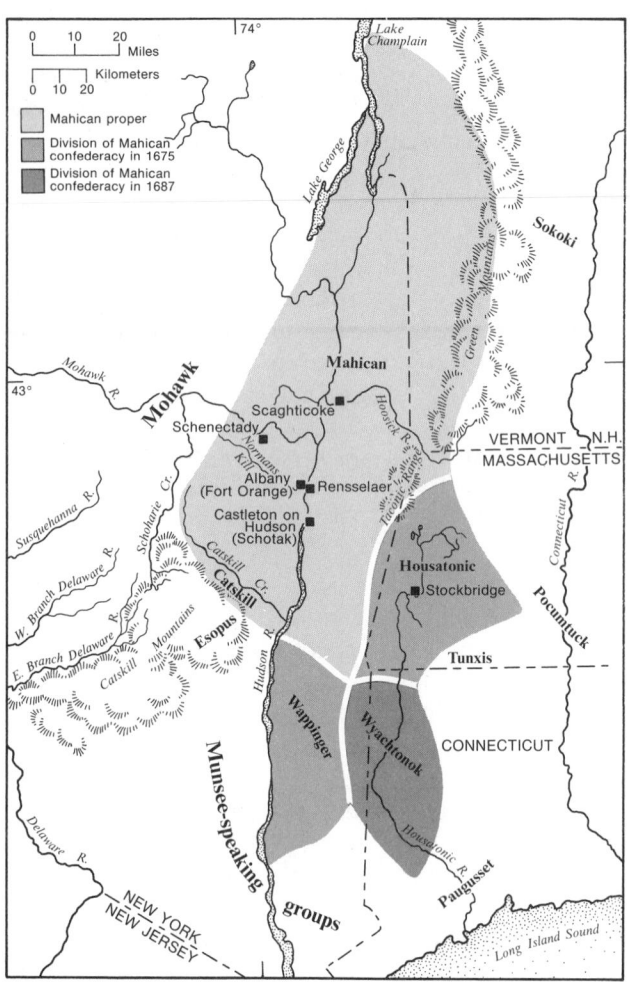

Fig. 1. Territory of Mahican and Mahican confederacy.

other Munsee-speaking groups along the upper course of the Delaware River.

Usually the Mahican Indians selected hilltops near the rivers for their palisaded villages (fig. 2), consisting of about 3 to 16 bark-covered longhouses each. The average longhouse was provided with 3 fireplaces, implying room for at least three nuclear families. Houses of chiefs tended to be larger and appear to have been decorated with paintings and carvings; these houses also served as ceremonial meeting places. The available data suggest an average of about 200 individuals in each village. Every 8 to 12 years the village had to be moved due to the exhaustion of the nearby garden plots, a shortage

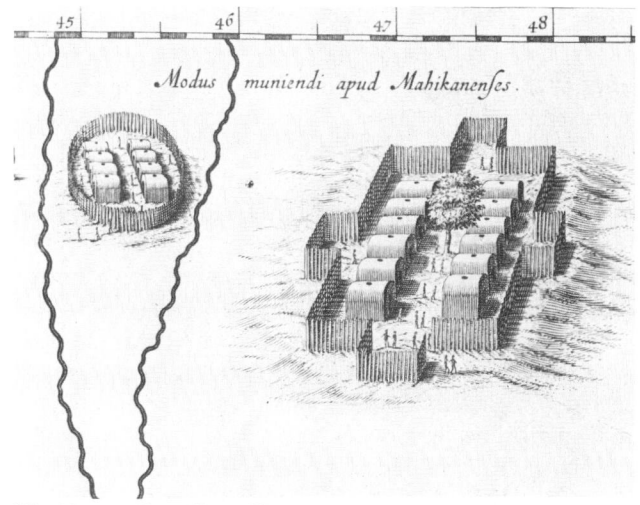

Fig. 2. Two palisaded villages, somewhat idealized, as shown on an engraved map of New England issued in 1635.

of firewood, and the increasing filthiness in and around the village.

Around these villages the people burned the woods and layed out their gardens among the charred tree stumps. The gardens were usually rather small, but by means of intercropping they appear to have produced relatively large quantities of food, primarily maize, beans, squash, and probably sunflowers. Horticulture definitely was of paramount importance; it was primarily the occupation of the women.

In the spring, immense schools of herring and shad ran up the Hudson and its tributaries, keeping the men busy along the rivers while the women planted corn in the gardens. Paddling their dugouts and bark canoes or working at the fishweirs in the smaller streams, the men spent the greater part of the summer fishing and gathering great quantities of freshwater mussels. A large part of the haul was dried and smoked on the spot for winter consumption. Meantime, the women worked in the gardens or went out to gather groundnuts, berries, and other products of the forest. In late August, most men returned to their villages to take part in the Green Corn ceremonials and to assist the women in the harvest. Ceremonies, initiating the seasonal exploitation of different foods, included first-fruits observances as well as first-game rituals.

After the harvest was stored in grass- or bark-lined pits, small groups of men might set out on the warpath. Collective hunting drives were organized in the fall, followed by a Deer Sacrifice ritual. Feasts were given in honor of particular sacred dolls, owned by some families, who believed they derived special protection from them.

In November the people scattered through the hunting territories, each family presumably to its usual area, and remained there until midwinter. Apparently they returned then to the villages, perhaps to attend a Bear

Sacrifice ritual. There are several references to the belief in guardian spirits of the game, comparable to similar ideas alive until recently among the northern Algonquian groups. In March the men went out again for the moose hunt. Bows and arrows, spears, and a variety of traps were used in hunting, which provided the Indians with food as well as skins for clothing. The hunting territories were located in the spurs of the mountain ranges, along the upper reaches of the rivers and creeks. The mountains themselves were rarely visited as those areas were poor in game and believed to be inhabited by potentially evil spirits.

The old folks, who remained at home during the winter, used to spend their time in the practice of a variety of crafts. Older men carved wooden bowls, mortars, and spoons (fig. 3), while the older women specialized in

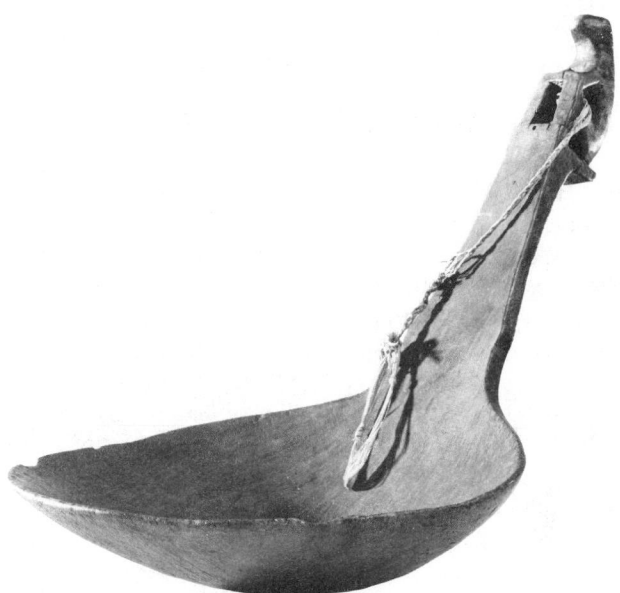

Fig. 3. Carved wooden feast ladle, 18th century. Width of bowl about 23.5 cm.

making pottery, weaving bags, baskets, and mats, or decorating skin clothing with paintings and porcupine quillwork.

The hunting groups returned to the village before the thaw made travel on snowshoes difficult. When the food supply ran out, late winter could be a lean period, until the maple trees started to produce sap. However, there is no evidence that maple sugar was of great importance before the introduction of metal kettles by the Europeans. Life became agreeable again when clouds of passenger pigeons arrived, which were netted on the hillsides, while the squabs were poked out of their nests with long poles. The Mahican appear to have been middlemen in the trade of native shell beads from the coast to the Saint Lawrence valley, and an occasional iron nail or knife from the French may have reached their villages in early trade with their Algonquian acquaintances (Trigger 1971: 278; JR 28:275).

A detailed reconstruction of other aspects of early Mahican culture is out of the question. Factual information is very limited and predominantly related to the visual aspects of Mahican society.

The longhouse was occupied by a number of closely related nuclear families, who constituted a lineage or one of its segments. The matrilineal and perhaps matrilocal character of these lineages is implied by information stating that kinship among the Hudson River Indians was traced through the female line and, in the case of divorce, that the children remained with the mother (Van der Donck 1656:61; Wassenaer 1622–1635, 8:84; Dankers and Sluyter 1867:125).

Matrilocal indications also show up in a number of Mahican land deeds. Marriages were exogamous, as "they reckon consanguinity to the eighth degree," and "they must not have (sexual) intercourse with those of their own family within the third degree" (De Rasieres in Jameson 1909:108, 109).

The matrilineages possessed the hereditary right of usufruct of specific well-defined and named tracts of garden land along the rivers. This was understood as ownership by the Europeans, who usually approached lineage leaders for land purchase. Off-river boundaries of these lineage tracts were vague; no one would consider laying out a garden in the rocky hinterlands, and there exist no indications of separate ownership of hunting territories.

A system of three matriclans, similar to that of the Mohawk, existed among the Mahican and Munsee in the eighteenth century, and at least the Munsee clans originally inhabited separate villages. This localized character may have been an early feature of the Mahican clans as well, for the early Dutch reported that the Hudson River Indians "dwell together in tribes, mostly of one consanguinity" (Jameson 1909:271). The location of Mahican villages in the early contact period and subsequent land transactions strongly suggest the existence of three local groups: (1) around the confluence of the Mohawk and Hudson rivers, whose main village was Monnemin's Castle; (2) around Fort Orange, present-day Albany, with Unawat's Castle as their main village; (3) in southern Rensselaer County and northern Columbia County, whose village was Schotak.

Although an explicit report of Mahican clans in the early contact period is lacking, their well-developed nature in the eighteenth century betrays considerable age. The available evidence suggests that the Mahican villages in the early seventeenth century tended to be autonomous communities, linked together primarily by marriage ties. The three original Mahican divisions together constituted a tribe in the sense that the people were aware of their unity in culture and language. The presumably localized character of the clans did not long survive the expulsion of the Mahican from the western parts of their territory by the Mohawks and the subsequent political integration of the Mahican tribe. According to the tribal traditions, recorded by Chief Hendrick Aupaumut about 1790, the three Mahican clan eponyms were the Bear, the Wolf, and the Turtle (fig. 4) (in E.F. Jones 1854:22). The native names are respectively Muchquauh, Mechchaooh, and Toonpaooh (Mooney and Thomas 1907b:788).

Several references in the early Dutch records indicate the existence of a graded system of leadership. Every lineage recognized an older man as their representative, and each of the three clans had a chief, who originally may have been village chief as well (Van der Donck 1656:67; NYCD 13:505). These leaders inherited their positions in the female line, that is, a brother or a sister's son succeeding a deceased chief. The prestige of the clan chief's lineage was interpreted in terms of nobility in the early colonial sources (Van der Donck 1656:71; Aupaumut in E.F. Jones 1854:20). There are, indeed, other indications of an "aristocracy" among the Mahican and their neighbors, although their social organizations did not feature the rigidly stratified class system of the native groups in coastal New England and Virginia. In the seventeenth century, these hereditary chiefs had limited authority; their decisions had to reflect the popular opinion in order to be obeyed. Their power was restricted to religious and civic affairs, whereas a renowned warrior was elected as war chief (Van der Donck 1656:71; Wassenaer 1622–1635, 9:44).

According to the early Dutch records, the Mahican counted more than 1,600 "warriors," that is, adult males, about 1610 (Van Laer 1908:307), which implies a total population of 4,000 to 4,500. Mooney's estimate of 3,000 Mahican is certainly too low, related as it is to his estimate of only 5,500 for the total population of the five Iroquois tribes (Kroeber 1939:140).

History

The Fur-trade Period

In September 1609 Henry Hudson and his Dutch crew sailed up the Hudson River. Arriving near the Mahican village of Schotak, he met an Indian chief "who carried him to his house and made him good cheere." The Indians brought the Dutch "beaver skinnes and otter skinnes, which we bought for beads, knives, and hatchets." After the chief had slept off his liquor aboard *The Half Moon*, the Mahican presented Hudson with strings

Public Arch. of Canada, Ottawa.

Fig. 4. Etow Oh Koam, or Nicholas, who went to London with 3 Mohawks in 1710. He holds a ball-headed club and wears a scarlet cloak given him in London. The turtle at his feet indicates his clan. Near his left foot is a metal trade tomahawk. Oil painting by John Verelst, 1710.

MAHICAN

of shell beads, traditionally used as a ceremonial expression of respect for chiefs (L'Honoré Naber 1921:66–71).

Although Hudson had not found the desired northern passage to China, the news that he had bartered furs with the Indians stimulated Amsterdam merchants to send ships to the Hudson River to engage in the fur trade, starting in 1610. Documentation of the early Mahican-Dutch relations is extremely sparse and lends itself to different interpretations. Both Wassenaer, in 1624, and De Laet, in 1625, mention hostility between the Mahican and the Mohawk (Jameson 1909:67, 47). The subsequent developments in their relationship constitute a variant of the trade wars common throughout the Northeast at that time.

In April 1613 Capt. Hendrick Christiaensen and Jacob Eelckens came up the Hudson River in order to establish a permanent trading post for the Van Tweenhuysen Company. They may have been already aware of the unpleasantness between their future Mahican and Mohawk customers, and the two traders appear to have made an effort to conciliate the two parties during a meeting on Tawasgunshi Hill near Normans Kill, Albany County. The memory of this treaty lived on in the oral traditions of the Mohawk, Delaware, and Mahican up to the 1740s (NYCD 3:775, 4:902–903, 6:446; Heckewelder 1819:xxvii–xxix, 60–61). These traditions have received considerable support with the publication of the original document of the treaty, acquired from the Iroquois on the Grand River Reserve in Canada (Van Loon 1968).

In this first treaty between North American Indians and Europeans, the Mahican Indians gave their approval of the founding of a trading post, which was es-

Fig. 6. Fish-shaped wooden club with iron blade. Collected from Stockbridge before 1800; length about 56.0 cm.

tablished on nearby Castle Island, opposite a Mahican village, in 1614. The peace treaty did not restrain the Mahican from exploiting their monopolistic trade position, and they forced the Mohawk to pay tribute in return for the privilege of access to the trading post. Continuous skirmishes were the result, and the traders abandoned Fort Nassau in 1617 (Jameson 1909:47–48, 67; Trelease 1960:32–34). For the time being, the Dutch confined their trading upriver to occasional visits only.

Notwithstanding all troubles, the returns of the fur trade in New Netherlands were substantial and worthy of more systematic exploitation. Moreover, Mahican relations with the Algonquin to the north promised a future access to the rich fur-bearing lands of the Great Lakes. In 1621 the Dutch government granted a trade monopoly to the West India Company and gave it political jurisdiction over the territories that it might acquire. In 1624 Dutch colonists constructed Fort Orange on the west bank of the Hudson River. Most of the colonists were employed in the trade with the Indians, the company's purpose being commercial rather than colonial. Thus, conflicts stemming from land disputes were absent in Mahican territory for a long time. The Mahican Indians were reported to be friendly, and they relocated their village from old Fort Nassau to the river shore opposite Fort Orange.

From this village the Mahican were able to control the Indians trading at the fort, while traveling throughout the hinterlands as middlemen in the fur trade (Jameson 1909:70, 84). The Mahican invited their Algonquin acquaintances from the Saint Lawrence River to trade their furs at Fort Orange instead of to the French (De Laet 1625:106; Trigger 1971:278). The Dutch colonists started to use shell beads or wampum as currency in their trade with the Indians as well as among themselves.

The Mohawk had been observing these developments with growing alarm. Subjected to Mahican taxation on trade profits, they now saw their northern enemies receiving privileges from the Dutch. In order to boycott the Mahican, the Mohawk signed a peace treaty with the French and their Algonquin allies and attacked the Mahican in 1624 (Trigger 1971:279). In the ensuing conflict the Mahican were defeated and forced to vacate

Fig. 5. Detail of portrait in fig. 4 showing facial tattoos (retouched).

their territories west of the Hudson River in 1628. The Mahican maintained their villages, gardens, and all other territorial rights east of the Hudson River, but the loss of western hunting territory resulted in the evacuation of part of the Mahican population from their Hudson River villages to new hunting grounds.

These Mahicans moved "towards the north" where they established a new village and laid out their gardens. "Towards the north" a Mahican village was discovered in later years, called Scaghticoke, situated on the Hoosick River. In 1700 and 1703 the Scaghticoke Indians recalled their early relations with the Dutch at Fort Orange and their use of the country west of the Hudson River in those days (NYCD 4:743-744, 902; Livingston 1956:188-190). With the defeat of the Mahican, the Mohawk acquired free trade at Fort Orange; however, the new relationship between the two tribes is not clear. It is generally assumed that the Mahican were reduced to being tributaries of the Mohawk by this defeat, but the sources do not bear this out.

For many years both the Mohawk and the Mahican appear to have been absorbed in trapping, in order to obtain the highly valued trade goods. With the establishment of English trading posts on the Connecticut River and the increasing numbers of Dutch traders undermining and ultimately abolishing the monopoly of the West India Company, competition resulted in lower prices, stimulating the Indians to get hold of as many furs as possible. However, by 1640 the Mohawk and Mahican were no longer able to get sufficient amounts of fur from their own territories.

The traders too appreciated the situation and their increasing though illegal trade in firearms seems to imply a cynical advice, which the Indians did not take long to understand (Trigger 1971:286). Both the Mohawk and the Mahican started their conquests of neighboring groups. The existing evidence suggests that the Mahican forced all Indian groups along the east side of the Hudson River to acknowledge Mahican rule. Early in 1643 the Mahican, armed with guns, attacked the Wiechquaeskecks and other groups on the lower Hudson River in order to obtain their tribute (De Vries 1911:262; Schulte Nordholt 1966:64, 87). This attack preceded the Indian massacre by the Dutch of New Amsterdam, resulting in their first colonial war. Peace was made between the various parties at Fort Orange in August 1645. Significantly, the Mahican chief sachem, Eskuyas alias Aepjen, represented the Wappinger, Wiechquaeskecks, Sinsink, and Kichtawank—all tribes along the east side of the Hudson—in this peace treaty (NYCD 13:18). In 1649 the Wiechquaeskecks were willing to sell part of Manhattan Island, but they appeared no longer to be masters in their own home, for they "promise to induce their Rulers on the North River to take the matter over" (Bolton 1909:100).

The Mahican were now in control of some of the best wampum sources, and their export of well-polished wampum beads led to the slow depreciation of the imperfect and broken shell currency in circulation (Nelson 1894:37). The paying of tribute by the Mahican to the Mohawk after 1640 may perhaps be explained as a sharing by the Mohawk in the wampum harvest of their Mahican allies. Mahican joined Mohawk war parties as early as 1642; Mahican and Mohawk joined in an attempt to subjugate the Indians of western Long Island in 1655; during a 1658 conference at Quebec, the Iroquois declared that they were allied to the Dutch and the Mahican; and in 1659 the Iroquois referred to the Mahican as their "brothers," a term which they never used for their tributaries (JR 26:37, 44:123; NYCD 12:99, 13:13, 122). Notwithstanding their alliance with the Iroquois, by 1660 the Mahican had restored their middleman position in a secret trade with Canadian Indians (NYCD 13:185).

Colonization by the Dutch and land sale by the Mahican slowly started after 1630, receiving impetus only in the last decades of the seventeenth century. The colonists along the Hudson River appear to have preferred the Indian garden lands for their farms. Together with the quest for furbearers in more distant areas, this resulted in the slow removal of the Mahican away from the Hudson River to more remote corners of their territory. Part of the population moved to the Catskill Valley about 1650 (NYCD 13:308, 545); however, the three main villages of the Mahican remained in or near their old locations near Fort Orange throughout the seventeenth century. Even as late as the middle of the nineteenth century, Mahican Indians were living near present Castleton on Hudson, the old site of Schotak. Several references seem to indicate that this village was the residence of the chief sachem during the fur-trade period.

In their political maneuvers the Mahican formally maintained their alliance with the Iroquois in order to share in the Iroquois privileges from the authorities at Fort Orange. At the same time, the Mahican appear to have been continually plotting with other tribes against Iroquois supremacy. In 1650 the Mahican and their Hudson River allies joined the Pocumtuck, Penacook, and Sokoki in a French-inspired projected conspiracy against the Iroquois, but for some unknown reason this plan was given up (JR 36:101-103; Day 1965:242). During the Dutch wars with the Esopus-Munsee, Mahican chiefs were acknowledged by the Dutch, Esopus, and Iroquois as the preferred mediators (NYCD 12:99, 13:119, 122, 162, 168, 179).

The growing power of the Mahican in intertribal politics had become clear to the Mohawk and their Iroquois allies by 1660. In order to break up this growing network, the Mohawk "invited" the Indian tributaries of the Mahican to remove from their coastal homelands to

Mohawk territory. The coastal Munsee tribes appear to have ignored the Mohawk order, preferring Mahican rule.

In 1662 war broke out with a Mohawk attack against the Mahican. The Mohawk suffered heavy losses and they hardly dared to come to Fort Orange, because Mahican war parties were feared everywhere (JR 47:107, 49:139, 141). During the summer of 1663 the Mahican, their Hudson River allies, and the Housatonic planned a massive offensive against the Mohawk. Although the records are far from clear, this offensive seems to have been directed against a large force of Iroquois, who were on their way to attack the Sokoki on the Connecticut River, from which the Iroquois returned with heavy losses. Mahican aggression was also feared by the Dutch, who had plundered the Mahican cornfields during the Indians' absence. The next year, Mahicans raided the Dutch farms and attacked the Mohawk again (NYCD 2:371-372; Livingston 1956:35).

In September 1664 the Dutch surrendered to the English, and the balance of power definitely shifted from the Indian to the colonial authorities. The Mohawk requested the new rulers at Albany (former Fort Orange) to make peace for them with the Hudson River Indians and to abstain from support of the New England tribes. The English agreed to this, and a peace treaty was ratified with all tribes except the Mahican (Trelease 1960:228; NYCD 3:68). The cause of this stubborn refusal of the Mahican appears to have been related to the refusal of the Iroquois to let the Mahican have a share in the western fur trade.

The recent peace treaty as well as the renewed war of the Mohawk against the New England tribes left the Mahican without any support. By 1666, when the English and the Mohawk found themselves at war with France, increasing pressure was put upon the Mahican by the colonial authorities of New York and New England to make peace with the Mohawk. After consultation with their New England Indian allies and Gov. John Winthrop of Connecticut, the Mahican were willing to give in, and a treaty was signed by the Mohawk and Mahican in August 1666, but it was broken almost immediately. Mahican war parties invaded the territory of the Mohawk, keeping them on the defensive within their villages (JR 51:83, 197).

In August 1669 a party of about 300 Mahican and other Hudson River Indians as well as Pocumtuc and other New England Indians, led by the Massachusett chief Chickataubut, invaded Mohawk territory and attacked their principal village, Caughnawaga. Relief arrived from other Iroquois tribes, and they managed to repulse the enemy, driving them back to Kinaquariones, present Taureuma Mountain near Schenectady. In the ensuing battle the Mahican and their allies were defeated and put to flight. The combined Iroquois invaded the Hudson River valley in an effort to conquer the re-

gional Mahican allies. Many River Indians were driven off and fled to the "Utawawas" Indians, in the area of the western Great Lakes. The Mahican considered moving to the Saint Lawrence River and joining the French, and some families actually moved across the eastern New York border into Housatonic territory (Trelease 1960:229, 252; NYCD 13: 460, 545; Colden 1958: 19). However, as late as 1734 the chief sachem still resided in the Hudson River valley.

A final peace was made between the two tribes in 1675. The Iroquois dropped their objections to Mahican explorations in the west and the governor at Albany promised that the Mahican would no longer be hindered by the settlers in the use of their gardens. During this peace council, the Mahican gave explicit evidence of the existence of a confederacy, stating that "we Mahicanders, the Highland Indians, and the Western Corner Indians are now one" (Livingston 1956: 36-38). Thus, the Wappinger and Housatonic had become divisions of a confederacy. Subsequent data reveal the supremacy of the Mahican chief sachem. In 1687 the Wyachtonok professed to have joined this confederacy; however, the events during the past wars suggest wider liaisons, which appear to find corroboration in the oral traditions of the Mahican, Munsee, and other coastal tribes (Brinton 1885:20; Thomson, in Jefferson 1964:189-190; Aupaumut, in E.F. Jones 1854:95-96).

Although the Mahican had ceased to be a major power factor, they maintained a respectable status among the eastern and midwestern tribes. Ravaged probably three times by epidemic diseases, the Mahican population had decreased considerably. In 1689 about 800 "River Indians" were still living in their old homeland, excluding those mixed with other Indians at Scaghticoke. Probably another 200 were living on the Housatonic River, in Canada, and in the Midwest by that time (NYCD 4:337; Trelease 1960: 326). Despite their continuing loss of territory and population, the Mahican continued to participate in negotiations between the British and the Iroquois throughout the colonial period.

The peace between the Mahican and the Mohawk coincided with the outbreak of King Philip's War in New England, named after the Indian leader in this final struggle between the coastal Algonquian tribes and the colonists. In 1676 large groups of defeated New England Indians fled to the French on the Saint Lawrence and to the Mahican on the Hudson River. Most of the refugees were settled at Scaghticoke, and they soon began to share the names River Indians and Loups with the Mahican, to the confusion of later historians.

In order to gain access to new trapping grounds, the Mahican and Munsee joined the Iroquois in their raids into the Virginia and Carolina Piedmont areas. In 1681 they returned with furs from as far away as the Spanish frontier. The next year, colonial delegates from Virginia and Maryland protested against these incursions, whereupon the River Indians promised to go farther west in search of beaver (Livingston 1956:65-67; NYCD 13:551). Mahican and other "Loups" had actually been exploring the Midwest since about 1669. From colonial records and Mahican traditions it appears that, in the 1670s, the Mahican and Esopus gained permission from the Ottawa and Miami to exploit Miami game resources. By 1680 there were two bands of New England and River Indians living among the Miami. Some of them joined René Robert Cavelier, sieur de La Salle on his expedition down the Mississippi River in 1681-1682. Mahican prestige in the Midwest was acknowledged by the Iroquois, who requested them to arbitrate for peace with the Miami and Ottawa in 1687. Insofar as they did not return to the East during the English and French colonial wars, these Indians merged with the Miami in the 1750s.

In the meantime, Catskill Mahican and Munsee were active in the southern Alleghenies and the Ohio Valley, where they competed with Cherokee and Iroquois in their fur business. According to Mahican traditions, peace was made ultimately with the Cherokee and Creek Indians, allowing the Mahican to hunt in the Southeast. When the local Shawnee were threatened with extermination by the Iroquois, the Shawnee were allowed to settle in Munsee territory on the upper Delaware River in 1694. The traditions of the various tribes involved reveal the far-reaching power of the Mahican in these intertribal politics.

According to these traditions, the Mahican invited and led the Shawnee to the land of the Munsee. Historical sources indeed mention a Catskill Mahican chief as the guide of the first Shawnee delegates in 1692. Their relocation in Munsee territory is additional evidence of a River Indian confederacy, in which the Mahican played an important role.

The Iroquois were annoyed about the Mahican interference in their war with the Shawnee. Peace was made between the two enemies under pressure from the colonial officials at Albany, who were delighted by these developments. King William's War had broken out, the first of a series in the colonial contest between the English and the French. The French lost one of their tribal allies when the Shawnee settled on the frontiers of the English colonies and the traders at Albany received the furs from the Ohio Valley.

The colonial wars interfered with the western explorations of the Mahican, who were requested by the authorities at Albany to join the Iroquois in the protection of the northern frontiers. Advised by the Iroquois, the English tried to persuade the Wyachtonok and Hudson River Indians to settle themselves closer around Albany in 1689-1690. Part of the Scaghticoke Indians, as "children" of the Iroquois, obediently settled at Half Moon, but there is no evidence that the Mahican abandoned

their old locations below Albany. Additional evidence of the Mahican ignoring Iroquois politics is manifest in the Iroquois complaint about the Mahicans who went to Canada to trade while they were supposed to assist the Iroquois in their war against the French.

Due to the ravages of a smallpox epidemic in 1690, the Mahican played only a subsidiary role in King William's War. For the first half of Queen Anne's War (the War of the Spanish Succession, 1702-1713), New York remained neutral, mainly because the Albany merchants preferred to continue their illegal trade with Montreal, and neither the Iroquois nor the Mahican could be induced to fight it out for the British. A large-scale expedition was organized against Canada in 1711. The River Indians volunteered with 54 New York Mahican, 38 Scaghticoke, 21 Wappinger, and 19 coastal Munsee warriors. Due to the failure of the English fleet to enter the Saint Lawrence River, the overland expedition returned when they were halfway (NYCD 5:265-270, 6:371).

The widespread Mahican relationships built up over the years were maintained and used in intertribal alliances, which largely escaped the attention of colonial recorders. About 1720 the Calumet ritual was introduced among the Mahican by Huron and other Indians from the western Great Lakes. At the same time, the Fox in Wisconsin sought the support of the Abenaki and Mahican in a war against the French. In 1721 part of the Mahican and Abenaki wanted to remove to the Midwest, but the French prohibited the Abenaki from going, fearing their alliance with the Fox. The Mahican found their way to Indiana, where they settled on the Kankakee River among the Miami. The Mahican Nation referred to by the Indians in the early eighteenth century was a far cry from the aggregate of independent Mahican villages of a century before.

In contrast to most other inland groups, European contact with the Mahican had started abruptly: the Hudson River brought the fur traders directly into the center of Mahican territory. The subsequent development of centralized tribal leadership appears to be related to this direct and immediate contact. Whereas the Mohawk invested each of their clan chiefs with more political power, only one chief emerged among the Mahican as their chief sachem. It is not by accident that this was the chief of a local group near the trading post. Fur traders, used to centralized government, preferred to deal with the natives through a local chief, whose aspirations were supported in return. He may have been the chief of the Bear clan, since tribal leadership was vested in the hereditary chief of that clan in the eighteenth century. The tribal integration of the Mahican villages, the expansion of Mahican power, and their role in intertribal politics necessitated the appointment of a number of official assistants of the chief sachem. These were the war chief or "Hero," a speaker or "Owl," a messenger or "Runner," and a group of elected councilors called "chiefs." Wampum belts (fig. 7) became in vogue to confirm official messages; clan ties and related kinship behavior were extended so as to realize intertribal structures (Aupaumut, in E.F. Jones 1854:20-23). The development of these political mechanisms was clearly motivated by economic factors related to the fur trade.

Trapping and increasing warfare related to this trade impinged upon the traditional activities of the men and upset the annual economic cycle. The desire to prevent the longer absence of men may have started the partial dispersal of the villages and their breakup into small hamlets; subsequent land loss and a dramatic decrease in population numbers provided extra stimuli. Clans and even lineages lost their localized nature in this process. Single-family dwellings were on the increase, and the longhouse was maintained only as the residence of chiefs and as a meeting place in religious and other communal affairs.

There is little evidence that the emphasis on private gain resulted in family-owned trapping grounds. In this respect, the Mahican seem to have resembled the Iroquois, in contrast to other neighbors. On the other hand, the fur trade and subsequent European colonization added a new value to the possession of land, and the Indians became more conscious of the exact boundaries of their tribal territory.

The tribal population decreased from an estimated aboriginal figure of 4,000 to about 500 by 1700. In addition, the incorporation of other Hudson River and New England Indians started to change its makeup. The Dutch colonists, being more wordly in outlook than the New Englanders, made little effort to convert or otherwise acculturate the natives. Less prejudiced than the English, the Hollanders were frequently involved in sexual relationships with Indian women. Although the traders cheated the Indians as frequently as they cheated one another, interracial relations were generally relaxed and friendly. A residue of Dutch words in the Mahican language testified to this communication.

Vast changes were obviously visible in the material culture of the Indians. Pottery and stone implements excepted, most of the traditional crafts continued, but their necessity diminished due to the increasing use of European manufactures. The price of all these riches was economic dependence upon the traders and new landowners.

The Mission Community

By 1700 Mahican society was being undermined by all the negative aspects of the colonial frontier. Whereas the northern parts of their territory became increasingly dangerous because of the continuous wars between the English and the French, colonists were crowding the Indians away from the fertile river bottoms in the south. Small Mahican settlements were still reported in the Hudson River valley, but the Indians complained "that many of our people are obliged to hire land of the Christians at a very dear rate, and to give half the corn for rent, and the other half they are tempted by rum to sell" (NYCD 5:661-663). Demoralization is indicated by increasing drunkenness and periods of famine among the Mahicans. The only solution left to them was removal, either to unspoiled trapping grounds in the west, or to remote corners of their old territory, where a mixed traditional economy might still be maintained. Many Mahican families removed to the territory of the related Housatonic Indians, after that group was nearly exterminated by smallpox. In 1698 only 90 Mahican warriors were left on the Hudson, implying a total population in New York of about 300 people, excluding the mixed group of about 350 Scaghticoke Indians. The White population in the area of Albany alone numbered 1,549 at that time (NYCD 4:337).

Stimulated by the French and antagonized by unfair dealings of Albany traders, increasing numbers of Scaghticoke Indians accepted the invitations of their relatives in the Saint Lawrence valley during these years. An unknown number of Mahican and Wappinger joined these Indians, who ultimately merged with the Saint Francis Abenaki at Odanak, Quebec. About 1700 the Catskill Mahican moved higher up into the Catskill Mountains, eventually merging with the Munsee on the upper Susquehanna River. In 1703 part of the Scaghticokes, including incorporated Mahican Indians, settled under Mohawk protection in two villages on the Mohawk River. The subsequent arrival of large numbers of German settlers forced these Indians to remove to Oquaga on the Susquehanna River in the 1720s. The Indians remaining at Scaghticoke complained about the increasing pressure of settlers around their village, and many Indians removed to Wyoming, Pennsylvania, in 1730.

The colonial authorities observed these developments with growing concern about their frontier protection,

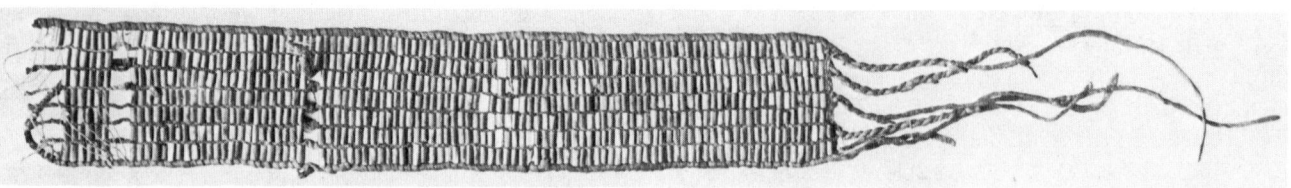

Milwaukee Public Mus.: 30127.

Fig. 7. Fragment of purple wampum belt with white wampum open diamond. Wampum beads are strung on hemp between buckskin thongs. Owned by Chief Austin E. Quinney, collected 1849; length about 28.5 cm without fringe.

but they were not even able to provide the Indians with a sufficient number of missionaries, requested by several tribes. The Indian desire for instruction in the Christian religion appears to have resulted from the noticeable difference in social conditions between those in the old villages and those of their relatives in the French Jesuit mission locations. Besides, the chiefs feared that the desertion of their people to the French would leave them powerless in their home territory.

In 1734 the first missionary arrived among the Indians on the upper Housatonic River. About 50 Housatonic and Mahican Indians were living there in four small settlements, under the leadership of two chiefs, Pophnehonuwot alias Konkapot, and Umpachenee. Colonial authorities considered Konkapot to be the most important chief, bestowing the title of captain on him, and that of lieutenant on Umpachenee. Tribal authorities seem to have felt unhappy at the White favoring of Konkapot over Umpachenee as the local representative of the nation and Dutch liquor traders stimulated the resentment of the tribal council against the missionaries.

In January 1735 a tribal meeting in Umpachenee's village, Skatekook,† was attended by nearly 200 Indians, including Corlair or Corslar, the Mahican chief sachem. A favorable agreement was reached enabling Rev. John Sergeant to establish a mission village, called Stockbridge. By 1738 all the Indians of the region had moved to this village, where the missionary opened a school, preached in the Mahican language, and translated several devotional works. His assistant in these translations was perhaps John Quinney (fl. 1735–1749), the founder of an important family in the history of the Stockbridge Indians. Among Sergeant's first converts were the local chiefs and their families. Some English families were attracted to act as examples of civilized behavior, and they instructed the Indians in agriculture and other crafts. An essentially English type of church committee and town council was introduced in which exemplary Indians (by the missionary's standards) filled most of the positions. At the request of the Indians the township had been surveyed and each family given an allotment of reasonable size.

Yet the Indians were still very attached to their old way of life. Hunting groups were frequently gone for a long time, and most of the men went off to help the Dutch farmers in the harvest. Persuaded by the missionary, the Indians left their children in his boarding school, where their time was "divided between study and labour as to make one the Diversion of the other" (Sergeant 1743:4).

The establishment of Stockbridge as a separate mission village was motivated by the missionary's desire to protect his people from the influences of both the non-

† The villages of Schaghticoke, N.Y. (in this chapter spelled Scaghticoke), Schaghticoke, Conn. (in this chapter Scaticook), and Skatekook, Mass. should be distinguished.

NCFA, Smithsonian.
Fig. 8. John W. Quinney (The Dish) (1797–1855), a Mahican Baptist preacher. Oil sketch by George Catlin, 1830.

Christian Indians and the not-too-Christian Whites. Although his acculturative influence was noticeable in many ways, the missionary focused primarily on the religious aspect, leaving the Indians to adjust or maintain their traditional lifeways to a large extent. The matrilineage survived for the regulation of descent and inheritance, but it lost its visual residential character; single families now inhabited neolocal log cabins and frame houses. The communal function of the chief's longhouse was taken over by the church. The chiefs accepted the new religion and its value system but maintained hereditary leadership within a small group of mutually related families, in which the old matrilineages are recognizable.

Although a substantial part of the population was of non-Mahican origin, the Mahican language was used in the church, the core group was Mahican, and so was the social and political organization. The missionary suppressed all visual expressions of the native religion and introduced his rather emotional type of "experimental" Christianity. Prestigious positions were created through the church committee and the township government, giving elite people the opportunity to maintain and strengthen their positions. Several references to sorcery, poison use, and suicide indicate the survival of certain traditional attitudes.

Hudson River Mahican and other Indians frequently visited the mission village and increasing numbers of them moved in permanently. In 1740 the population had increased to 120 people, consisting of Mahican, Housatonic, Wappinger, Wyachtonok, and a sprinkling of other Connecticut tribes. A variety of splinter groups merged at Stockbridge, although the major element remained of Mahican origin. The Mahican chief sachem died about 1740 and the "fireplace of the Nation" moved from the Hudson River valley to Stockbridge. Government and mission failed in their endeavors to have Konkapot recognized as the most important chief. Tribal leadership was passed on according to traditional usage, and Umpachenee, married to a former chief sachem's daughter, became the Nation's leader.

After 1740 missionaries became active among New York Mahican groups too. In 1743 David Brainerd settled at Kaunaumeek, in present Columbia County. After his departure in 1744, the Kaunaumeek Mahican removed to Stockbridge. In 1740 Moravian missionaries contacted the Mahican and Wyachtonok living in Dutchess County, New York, and in neighboring Connecticut. Here again, the most influential chiefs were among the first converts. The Moravian Brethren rapidly won the confidence of the regional natives, attracting Indians even from Stockbridge. The Indians' abstinence from liquor and the prospects of Indian communities holding on to valuable land rapidly led to growing hostility among the local Whites. False accusations were spread about the Moravians, ultimately resulting in a governmental order to stop Moravian activities among the New York Indians. In 1746 the Indians started their exodus to the Moravian headquarters at Bethlehem, Pennsylvania, where they combined with Munsee Indian converts. Part of the Mahican and Wyachtonok returned again and merged with the Indians at Scaticook, Connecticut.

A series of mission villages marked the dramatic removal of the Moravian Indians through Pennsylvania to the Ohio during the French and Indian War (the Seven Years' War) and its aftermath of Pontiac's War. When the American Revolution broke out, they found themselves in the midst of frontier fighting, culminating in the massacre of 90 Moravian Mahican by American militia, at Gnadenhütten, Ohio, March 8, 1782. Another decade of wandering followed for the survivors, until they were allowed to settle on the Thames River, in Ontario, Canada. Their descendants live there at Moraviantown.

During the eighteenth century, acculturation in material culture was no longer confined to the acceptance of finished European products but included the acquisition of a range of new technological skills (figs. 9-10), some of which provided the Indians with extra income. Indian women roamed the countryside, selling splint baskets, brooms, wooden bowls, and moccasins, while men assisted the colonists in the annual harvest. Agriculture, however, was no success, as the preferred occupations of the men were hunting and war service. The deterioration

Mus. of the Amer. Ind., Heye Foundation, New York: 10/1330.
Fig. 9. European-style cup carved from applewood knot by Chief Siacus on the lower Housatonic River. Collected in 1740; height about 8.2 cm.

N.Y. State Mus., Albany: 39594.
Fig. 10. Basswood splint basket with stamped decorations, 19th century. Height about 24.1 cm.

of the traditional cycle of seasonal activities is indicated by the reported periods of famine in the late 1760s.

The Stockbridge Indians rendered loyal and continuous assistance to the colonies in their wars, first against the French, then against Pontiac's Indians, and finally against the British in the Revolution. In 1756 the Wappinger tribe enlisted in the army, after having removed their families to Stockbridge, 227 persons in total. During their absence their land was taken by New York landlords, and the greater part of the tribe merged with the Stockbridge Indians.

The wars proved disastrous for the Indians. Nearly half the men lost their lives along the northern borders, at Lexington, Bunker Hill, White Plains, Barren Hill, and several other skirmishes. Life at Stockbridge lost much of its original religious fervor during these turbulent years. Despite the incorporation of Wappinger and other Indians, the total population numbered only 300 in 1774. Perhaps another 100 Mahican Indians were still living in pauperized conditions at various places in the

Hudson River valley, and an unknown but certainly large number was living in Pennsylvania, Ohio, and Indiana. In 1756-1757, another large body of Mahican and Wappinger had removed from the Hudson River to the Susquehanna River. These removed groups maintained continuous contacts with the Mahican Nation's political center at Stockbridge.

The Indians gathering on the Pennsylvania frontiers were far less willing to oblige the colonial officials at Albany and Philadelphia. Many of these Indians sided first with the French and later with Pontiac. During the American Revolution, 60 western Mahicans joined the English-oriented Iroquois and invaded the Mohawk River valley. As a result of Gen. John Sullivan's campaign in 1779, the Indian villages on the Susquehanna River were abandoned, and about 100 Mahican joined the perhaps 5,000 refugee Indians gathering under English protection at Fort Niagara. In 1783 a mixed group of Munsee and Mahican moved on to Canada; their descendants live at Ohsweken, Brant County, Ontario.

By the end of the American Revolution, the Stockbridge Indians found themselves depleted in numbers, enticed to sell their lands, and unwanted in their village, where Whites had taken over the local government and endeavored to oust the Indians. Accepting an invitation from the Oneida, the dispirited remnants of the Mahican Nation, 420 in all, removed to a tract on Oneida Creek in New York. The removal started in 1783, and the population numbers suggest the involvement of other Mahican remnants from the Hudson River area. Scattered throughout their old territory, a number of families stayed behind, generating several mestizo groups, such as the Van Guilders, Bushwackers, and Jukes.

On the Move

By 1786 most of the Indians had settled at New Stockbridge in Oneida country. Prospects seemed bright to many of them, who appear to have felt that complete adjustment to White lifeways would prepare them to survive the future incorporation by the advancing American society. They set out to establish farms. The women spun the wool of their sheep, wove cloth, and made splint baskets for sale. Through the treaty of Canandaigua (1794), the Stockbridges obtained $4,500 annually, which they spent in the purchase of clothing, cattle, farm tools, and the building of a sawmill. These progressive Indians were able to speak and write English, and most Stockbridges were devoted adherents of the mission church. Chief sachem Joseph Quinney and his three councilors were mission-trained, and some of them had received an education at Dartmouth College. By 1800 the Stockbridge Indians had effected a stable community, modeled after a White rural American village.

The past experiences, however, had left their traces in the opposing attitudes of many Stockbridges, producing several instances of factionalism throughout the nineteenth century. One portion of the tribe favored the leasing of lands to White farmers, with the Indian owners living off the rentals. The White-oriented faction preferred to do the farming themselves, indicating their rejection of the old division of labor by sex. The White-oriented faction, supported by missionary and government, held the power, and the excessive use of liquor among the traditional or Indian-oriented people indicates their frustrated aspirations. As usual, some White profiteers exploited this social maladjustment. In general, the Indian-oriented Stockbridges maintained their Indian dress and used only their own language. Since hunting was no longer profitable, they depended mainly upon the gardens and craftwork of the women for a living.

Reportedly the neighboring Oneida ridiculed the Stockbridge men who had taken up farming. When the Oneida introduced Handsome Lake, the Iroquois prophet, to the Stockbridges, they rejected his teachings (E.F. Jones 1854:91-94).

The speaker for the Stockbridge tribe in this affair was its new chief sachem, Hendrick Aupaumut, who played an important role in intertribal politics. As early as 1791, he felt the need of another removal, because of the undesirable influences of the Oneida and frontier Whites. Remembering the old covenant with the Miami Indians, who had permanently reserved a part of their territory for the members of the former River Indian Confederacy, Aupaumut started his explorations in the Midwest, where the Munsee and Delaware Indians had settled already. The Stockbridge removal was postponed because of the efforts of the Shawnee chief Tecumseh to organize the midwestern Indian tribes in an anti-White confederacy. During these turbulent years, the prestige of the Mahican enabled their chief sachem to play the role of broker between the American government and the midwestern tribes.

Tecumseh's fight for Indian freedom came to a bitter end during the War of 1812, after which the Stockbridges prepared to move once more. In 1818 about 75 Stockbridges, led by John Metoxen, departed for Indiana. Upon their arrival on the White River, they learned that the Delawares and Miamis had been forced to sell their land. Commissioned by the War Department, some missionaries now purchased land from the Menominee and Winnebago in Wisconsin for the New York Indians. In 1828 a band of Indians from New Stockbridge, led by John W. Quinney, moved to this tract and settled on the Fox River. Metoxen and his wandering Stockbridges soon joined them and other bands followed, the last Indians leaving New Stockbridge in 1829. Old Hendrick Aupaumut died in 1830, after all his people had arrived in their new home. With about 100 Delaware Indians, 225 Stockbridges were living on the Fox River in 1831; their chief sachem was John Metoxen.

The purchase of this location was later disavowed by the Wisconsin Indians, and a series of new treaties caused the breakup of the Stockbridge community and their removal to Calumet County, east of Lake Winnebago, between 1832 and 1834. In 1837 the population was increased by the arrival of a number of Moravian Munsee from Canada.

In 1837 John W. Quinney drafted a constitution for the tribe, which included the abandonment of hereditary leadership in favor of the election of tribal officers. Dissension among the Stockbridges was reinforced when the government made new efforts to extinguish Indian land claims east of the Mississippi. Many of the Indian-oriented Stockbridges and most of the Munsee were in favor of removal. In order to solve the problem once and for all, the Stockbridges agreed to cede the best half of their land to the U.S. government in return for money to finance the removal of those who desired so. About 70 conservative Stockbridges and about 100 Munsee departed for the Missouri River in 1839. Many of them did not survive the hardships and disease encountered in their new location, others joined the Delawares in Kansas, and a few families appear to have found their way back to Wisconsin.

The respite was of short duration, for in 1843, an act of Congress granted citizenship and individual landholdings to the Stockbridges. The issue split the Stockbridge tribe into a new Indian Party and a Citizen Party. A substantial part of their lands was lost to White purchasers before John W. Quinney (fig. 8) succeeded in having the act repealed in 1846. The Citizen Party refused to cooperate in the tribal enrollment and the partition of tribal land, required by the new act of Congress, foiling a satisfactory settlement for all people involved.

Untiring in his efforts to solve the problems of his tribe, John W. Quinney was elected as grand sachem in 1852. Negotiations with the government resulted in a new treaty with the Menominee in February 1856, by which the Stockbridges and incorporated Munsee were granted the townships of Bartelme and Red Springs, Shawano County, Wisconsin. With the exception of those who had become citizens, about 150 Indians removed to this reservation between 1856 and 1859. They were joined by a number of Brothertown Indians and New York Iroquois.

The socioeconomic conditions during this period of removals were extremely difficult. Removals and factionalism disrupted the community time and again.

Throughout this period there are references to the orthodox Christian character of the Stockbridge Indians. Particularly the White-oriented faction accepted the additional values of the contemporary White society as well. The hereditary leaders were respected by both factions. Their influence reached the people both through the traditional channels of lineage and clan and through the church and its related organizations. The matri-lineage, weakened already by the earlier disappearance of longhouses, lost its function in relation to land inheritance with the removals of the tribe; however, leadership remained largely confined to men who were related to one another through their sisters, wives, or mothers, and there is ample evidence of the strong position of the "principal" women.

The dying out of this core of Mahican lineages became evident in the 1830s. The introduction of elective leadership forestalled the total disintegration of the community, but the old chiefs were gone, and there was little left of the old esprit de corps and zest for progress among those who moved to the reservation after 1856.

The Reservation Period

The new reservation was described by a government inspector as a "poor country for white settlers but pretty good for Indians" (Schafer 1937:74). It is a sandy and swampy area, but it was covered with a valuable pine forest. Farming was started in a few locations of better quality, but logging operations were more promising. In order to strengthen tribal leadership and restore community organization, the tribe drafted and approved a new constitution in 1857; however, due to internal difficulties tribal government was allowed to lapse, and the agent of the Bureau of Indian Affairs increasingly usurped control over the community.

The General Allotment Act of 1887 allowed tribal Indians to exercise individual ownership and the right of sale of designated parcels of land, resulting in a substantial loss of land to the Stockbridge-Munsee Indians.

In 1895, 503 individuals were listed on the tribal rolls, 300 of whom were living on the reservation. The remainder lived in various places along the historical trek routes taken by the tribe after their departure from Massachusetts, as well as in several western locations. The logging industry was of economic importance to the community, which marketed 17 million feet of logs in 1895. Assuming that the tribe no longer needed government protection, the commissioner of Indian affairs advocated the termination of federal relations. This was authorized by two acts of Congress in 1904 and 1906 and put into effect in 1910. A form of township government was maintained through a Business Committee.

The Depression of the 1930s severely affected the Stockbridge-Munsee. Many Indians lost their lands when they were unable to pay the taxes. Conditions worsened when the lumber companies closed their operations, leaving behind a ravaged forest and an unemployed community. The Indian Reorganization Act of 1934 enabled the Indians to secure government aid again. In 1938, the tribal constitution and bylaws of the Stockbridge-Munsee Community were approved by the Bureau of Indian Affairs, which granted 2,250 acres of land in Bartelme Township to the Indians. A reforestation program was started to increase the economic value of the cut-over lands. Community government was put in the hands of an elected tribal council, composed of a president, a vice president, a treasurer, and four councilors.

Of a total of 750 listed on the tribal rolls, 380 Indians were living on the Stockbridge-Munsee reservation in 1966.

Only very few indications of an Indian culture survived the nineteenth century. The last indication of clan knowledge dates back to 1859. Some prestige, associated with certain old families, survived the abolishment of hereditary leadership. Indian dress, already restricted to a conservative minority, completely disappeared in the 1870s. The last speakers of the native language died during the first decades of the twentieth century. Some knowledge and use of medicinal herbs is still retained by the older people.

Since the close of the Indian reservation school in 1952, the children go to schools in Bowler and Gresham. The high degree of Euro-American acculturation among the Indians has beneficially affected their relations with the local White population, resulting in an increasing intermarriage between the two groups. Children of these interracial marriages, if they are of at least one-quarter Stockbridge-Munsee blood, may obtain tribal membership, through which they are able to benefit from the educational and training program of the Bureau of Indian Affairs.

There is no extreme wealth in the Stockbridge-Munsee community, and extreme poverty is a thing of the past. A forest management plan provides for limited logging employment. Craftwork produced in the tribal craft shop provides supplementary income in part-time work for some craftworkers. A few men farm on the reservation, and there are a few jobs available in Shawano County businesses; however, most people have to find employment elsewhere. Many younger people have found skilled vocational employment in Milwaukee and other cities, spending only the weekends on the reservation. Many women work in the potato harvest in Antigo County, after which they go to Door County for employment as cherry pickers.

Effective leadership has been able to restore community organization, although the possibilities for community action are largely determined by the policies of the Bureau of Indian Affairs.

Synonymy

According to the origin traditions of the tribe and the testimonies of its prominent leaders, the tribe's name was derived from Muhheakunnuk, which was the name of a locality. It referred to the tidal water of the Hudson River, which indeed is subject to ebb and flow as far upriver as Albany. Similar words in the related Munsee language corroborate these native testimonies. From this name were derived the terms Muhheakunneuw and Muhhekunneyuk, referring to respectively 'a Mahican Indian' and 'the Mahican Indians' (Kokhkewenaunaut, 1763, in H.A. Wright 1905:184; MHSC ser. 1, 9:99–102; Aupaumut, ca. 1791, in E.F. Jones 1854:15, in Skinner 1925:102).

Adriaen Block in 1614 and later colonial authorities usually referred to the tribe as Mahicans, Mahikanders, Maikens, and similar names. It is possible that these names resulted from the early Dutch use of Delaware or Munsee Indian interpreters, who pronounced the tribe's name as mà·hí·kan, mà·hí·kani·w, Mahi'kanɑk (Ives Goddard, personal communication 1973; Speck and Moses 1945:14). Related terms were used by the Shawnee: Mhíkana, Nhíkana, Hikanagi (Gatschet 1877). The Algonquins decided to call the Mahican 'wolves' because of the resemblance of the Algonquin word for wolf to the Mahican's own tribal name. Following the practice of their Algonquin allies, the early French too referred to the Mahican as 'wolves', either in French—Loups—or in Algonquin—Maingan, Mahingan (Champlain 1922-1936, 5:208, 214). Related to the Algonquin term is Montagnais Mahiganiouetch (mistakenly written Nahiganiouetch, in JR 18:260). By 1662 the name Loups began to lose its specificity and was used by the French to refer to several tribes in New England and New York State (Mooney and Thomas 1907b:786, 788). The Algonquin folk etymology gave rise to the common misconception that the Mahican referred to themselves as 'wolves'.

The Mahican tribe is not to be confused with the Mohegan of coastal Connecticut. These tribes were not related to each other, and their tribal names have been subject to the same mistake in translation. Starting in the early 1660s, English colonial authorities used the name River Indians for the Mahican and other Algonquian-speaking Indians residing on the Hudson River (NYCD 13:229).

The Iroquois tribes referred to the Mahican as Akochakaneñ' (Mohawk), Ranatshaganha (Onondaga), perhaps meaning 'stutterers' or 'those who speak a strange language' (Mooney and Thomas 1907b:788; Beauchamp 1907:183). According to a Mahican tradition, the Oneida used to call them Sturgeons, but this eponym of a fish was used by the Iroquois to refer to the whole population of New England (Michelson 1914; Colden 1958:97, 153). During the nineteenth century, the Munsee used the term škéhtko·w or wšəkéhtko·w, and the Unami Delaware used the term ské·tku 'person from Scaghticoke' to denote the Mahican in Ontario, Canada (Speck and Moses 1945:8, 14; Trowbridge 1824:5; Ives Goddard, personal communication 1973).

In Wisconsin, the Stockbridge Mahican referred to themselves as Wâmpʌna'kiʌkᵉ, meaning 'Easterners'. The neighboring Menominee Indians adopted this name, as wa'panahki·w, to refer to the Stockbridges (Michelson 1914; Bloomfield 1962:245).

Sources

The study of Mahican culture and history depends upon a large number of sources in which the Mahican are referred to incidentally, while the focus is upon other subjects; sources dealing primarily with the Mahican are rare and relate mainly to their more recent history.

For the seventeenth century a large number of contemporary documents were brought together and edited by O'Callaghan and Fernow (NYCD 1853-1887), Van Laer (1908), Thwaites (JR 1896-1901), Livingston (1956), Jameson (1909), and Winthrop (1908). The earliest observations of Mahican Indians are to be found in Robert Juet's account (in Jameson 1909) of Henry Hudson's voyage. Extracts from the lost journal of Hudson himself are quoted in De Laet (1625), which add valuable information from eyewitnesses. De Vries (1911) is valuable insofar as he relates his own experiences; however, numerous casual quotations from other sources, particularly on aboriginal culture, are less reliable. Van der Donck's (1656) brief description is important since he spent several years at Fort Orange in Mahican country. The major source for early River Indian activities in the Midwest is Margry (1876-1886, 2). Some of the oral traditions written down by Aupaumut (partly in E.F. Jones 1854 and Skinner 1925) and by Heckewelder (1819) may well refer to the early contact period.

The best monograph for this period is Trelease (1960), superseding Ruttenber (1872), which is full of mistakes and outdated interpretations.

Eighteenth-century sources mainly relate to the missionary activities of their authors, such as Sergeant (1743), Hopkins (1753), and Loskiel (1789). Important documents concerning the sale of tribal territory in this period were edited by H.A. Wright (1905), Handlin and Mark (1964), Allen (1870), and Wraxall (1915). Of interest to the role played by the Stockbridge Indians in the French and Indian Wars are the journals of Maj. Robert Rogers (1961). The subsequent removals are documented by Belknap and Morse (1955), Aupaumut (1827), Marsh (1859), and De Loss Love (1899). Valuable information is to be found in the journals of Rev. John Sergeant, Jr., available in the Dartmouth College Library, Hanover, New Hampshire. Starting in the nineteenth century, the Annual Reports of the Commissioner of Indian Affairs contain important data for the study of the recent history of the Stockbridges. Morgan (1959, 1964) found Stockbridge Indians in Kansas. Skinner (1925) and Mochon (1968) are the only other ethnographic sources on the Stockbridges. In addition to a survey of modern conditions of the tribe, Mochon gives a useful summary of its history. Important data on the native religion were acquired from Mahican descendants among the Ontario Iroquois by Speck (1928a, 1940; Speck and Moses 1945).

Murdock (1960) should be consulted for the more important publications of a secondary nature.

Delaware

IVES GODDARD

Delaware (ˈdeləˌwār) is the name applied to the descendants of the linguistically and culturally similar bands that occupied the valley of the Delaware River and certain adjacent areas at the beginning of the seventeenth century (fig. 1). The Delaware spoke dialects of two closely related Eastern Algonquian languages, Munsee and Unami.* Munsee is sharply distinct from its eastern neighbors, Mahican and the languages of southern New England and eastern Long Island; and the linguistic break is similarly abrupt between Unami and Nanticoke, to the southwest (see "Eastern Algonquian Languages," this vol.). In each of these cases, however, as generally among the Eastern Algonquian languages, adjacent forms of speech share many words and other linguistic features.

The groups here treated together never formed a single political unit, and the name Delaware, which was first applied only to the Indians of the middle Delaware Valley, was extended to cover all of these groups only after they had migrated away from their eastern homelands. This piecemeal westward migration, in the face of White settlement and its attendant pressures during the eighteenth and nineteenth centuries, left the Delaware in a number of widely scattered places in southern Ontario, western New York, Wisconsin, Kansas, and Oklahoma. Their history involves the repeated divisions and consolidations of many villages and of local, political, and linguistic groups that overlapped in complicated and incompletely known ways. In addition, individuals, families, and small groups were constantly moving from place to place. Hence this account can give only an outline of the major movements.

* The Delaware words cited in this paper are in the Unami language (20th-century Oklahoma Delaware) unless otherwise specified. They are written in the phonemic system described by Voegelin (1946:130–137), except that: long voiceless consonants and long vowels are indicated with a raised dot (*t·, a·*), long voiced consonants are written as geminates (*nn*), the low back rounded vowels are written ɔ and ɔ· (Voegelin o and o·), and the long mid back rounded vowel is written o· (Voegelin u·). The Munsee forms are written in the standard transcriptional system of the *Handbook,* with the following special usages: ŏ and ă are extrashort vowels of varying phonetic realization; a consonant is voiced after a homorganic nasal, except if an apostrophe intervenes; and the acute (´) and grave (`) accents indicate primary and secondary stress, respectively.

The names of ceremonies and rituals are verbs, given here in the form for indefinite actor, and may be translated 'people perform such-and-such' or 'such-and-such is performed'.

The Seventeenth Century

Language, Territory, and Intergroup Relations

In the seventeenth century the Delaware lived in village bands of a few hundred members each. The usual conjecture of the original number of such groups is about 40, corresponding to a total population of 8,000–12,000. However, imperfect knowledge of which groups were actually distinct from one another may have inflated such estimates. On the other hand, it is certain that warfare and the exposure of the Indians to smallpox and other European diseases caused the population at the end of the century to be much smaller (by an unknown percentage) than it had been in 1600 (table 1). Here, only local groups whose existence is most firmly established will be mentioned, with no attempt at a comprehensive reconstruction of the aboriginal situation in all its detail (fig. 2).

In the northern part of the Delaware area—northern New Jersey and southeastern New York—were the Munsee-speaking groups (Goddard 1971a). Of these, the Esopus occupied the Hudson watershed area west of the river, between the Catskills and the highlands at West Point. Their local subgroups included the Waoranecks, Warranawankongs, and others (Ruttenber 1875:5–10). The Catskill Indians to the north, although sometimes associated with the Esopus, were apparently linguistically Mahican. Inland, on the headwaters of the Delaware above the Delaware Water Gap were the Minisinks. South of the highlands to the west of the Hudson were the Haverstraw (beside Haverstraw Bay), Tappan (beside Tappan Zee), and Hackensack (in the Hackensack and Passaic valleys, south to the Kill Van Kull). The Raritans lived on the lower Raritan River until the 1640s, when they migrated inland because of the attacks of the Delaware River Indians and the Dutch, and because spring floods had destroyed their pit-stored corn. The so-called Raritans in this area after about 1649 were immigrant Wiechquaeskecks from east of the Hudson (NYCD 1:366–367, 13:25). The Navasinks lived in the highlands just south of Sandy Hook Bay. All the groups from the Haverstraw through the Navasink were closely associated politically. Additional names are sometimes given for groups farther inland from these, such as the Aquackanonks of the middle Passaic valley (Paterson), but the indications are that these are geographical labels

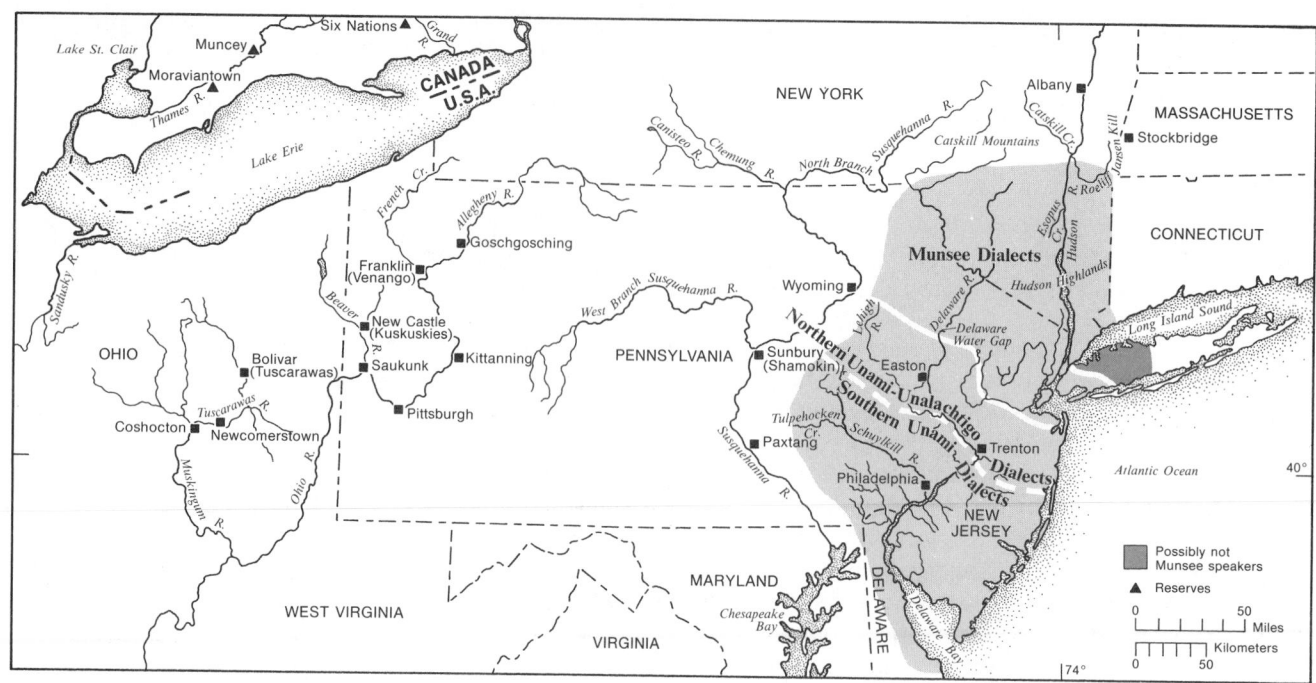

Fig. 1. 17th-century tribal territory and western relocations in the Susquehanna Valley (before 1709–1772), Ohio Valley (1724–1795), and Ontario (1785–present).

and do not indicate separate political units (Ruttenber 1872:91; Nelson 1904:12).

Another cluster of Munsee-speaking groups was east of the Hudson, though their internal and external boundaries are less than certain. The northernmost of these were the Wappinger, whose territory extended south from Roeliff Jansen Kill to the highlands, covering most of Dutchess and Putnam counties. Early records imply that a separate group of Highland Indians occupied the highland areas of Putnam County; perhaps these were the same as the seldom mentioned Nochpeems. Early on, in any case, "Highland Indians" became a synonym for Wappingers, and either term covered essentially all the Indians of Dutchess and Putnam counties (NYCD 13: 17, 104, 288). South of these were the Kichtawanks (northern Westchester County), Sinsinks (about Ossining), Wiechquaeskecks (Tarrytown-Dobbs Ferry area), and Rechgawawanks (Yonkers, the Bronx, Manhattan). The relation between the Wiechquaeskecks and Rechgawawanks on the Hudson and the Indians to the east along the shore of Long Island Sound is unclear. Some early deeds suggest that the Sound-shore residents were not organized in political groups distinct from their western neighbors, but evidence has been claimed nevertheless for a Siwanoy group extending east from the Bronx River and for locating the Tankitekes in southwestern Fairfield County, Connecticut. However, the name Siwanois is found only among early information of a general nature, not linked to specific individuals, and the Tankiteke, though their existence under this name seems clear, cannot be definitely localized. The political groupings

and proper designations for the Sound-shore Indians of Westchester and Fairfield counties thus remain obscure. (De Laet 1909:44; Ruttenber 1872:77–85; Bolton 1920:246–269). It can be conjectured that speech of the Munsee type extended as far east as the Five Mile River (Darien-New Canaan), beyond which were the Norwalk Indians, who seem to go with the Quiripi-speaking lower Housatonic groups. This supposition is supported by archeological evidence showing a cultural boundary at this same point (C.S. Smith 1950:102).

The Indians of western Long Island were closely linked politically, culturally, and linguistically to those already mentioned in the circum-Manhattan area. These included the Nayack, Marechkawieck, and Canarsee in Brooklyn (sometimes all grouped together as the Canarsee), the Rockaway (from Newtown to part of Hempstead), and perhaps the Massapequa (Flushing, North

Table 1. Delaware Population Estimates

Date	Munsee-speaking groups (excluding Long Island)	Unami-speaking groups	Total
1600	4,500	6,500	11,000
1779	1,200	2,000	3,200
1820	650	1,900	2,550
1845	500	1,300	1,800
1867	550	1,175	1,725
1900	625	850	1,475
1950	525	1,400	1,925

SOURCES: Jefferson 1801:198; Lefroy 1853:195–196; Mooney 1911, 1928; Tax and Stanley 1960.

Hempstead, as well as southern Oyster Bay and Huntington) and the Matinecock, north of the Massapequa. On Long Island it is especially difficult to distinguish between village names and those of larger local groups. The listing given is by no means well established and omits several minor groups of ambiguous status. A sharp linguistic and political division between the western and eastern Long Island Indians is clear and archeological sites seem to cluster at the opposite ends of the island (W. W. Tooker 1911:136–138; C.S. Smith 1950:102), but the eastward drift of the population in the seventeenth century has made it difficult to say exactly where the aboriginal ethnic boundary lay. It may be, for example, that the Massapequa and Matinecock were not Munsee speakers at all, but the linguistic ancestors of the eighteenth-century Unquachog. Although there were permanent inhabitants of Staten Island, Indians of the surrounding areas also seem to have had usufructuary rights there. Some of the Nayacks across the Narrows moved there in 1652 after selling their own lands, and this may indicate a close relationship with the aboriginal Staten Islanders (Bolton 1920:285–297).

South of the Delaware Water Gap and the Raritan Valley were the Delawares that spoke Unami. There is evidence for at least three major dialects of Unami, which can in part be localized, but the interpretation of the information on early political groupings presents the same problems as in the case of the Munsee speakers. The earliest detailed information on the Indian groups along the Delaware River, which dates from the 1620s, provides a series of names for those on the east bank only. The best established of these, with their presumed locations, are Sewapois (Cohansey River), Little Siconese (Salem River), Naraticonck (Raccoon Creek), Mantaes (Mantua Creek), Armewamex (Big and Little Timber Creeks), Remkokes (Rancocas Creek), Atsayonck (Crosswicks Creek), and Sankhikans (near the falls at Trenton). On the west bank the only group named in the same early sources was the Big Siconese at Lewes in southeastern Delaware, and there is evidence that the only major settlements between this and the falls at Trenton were Minguannan on White Clay Creek (London Britain Township, Chester County) and Quineomessinque at the Big Bend of Brandywine Creek (Delaware County), both just over the state line in Pennsylvania. Apparently the hostile incursions of the Susquehannocks from the Susquehanna River contributed to the depopulation of eastern Pennsylvania during this period. Later in the century other west-bank settlements are noted, such as that of the Okehocking group on Ridley and Crum creeks (Chester County) and the town of Playwicky (upper Neshaminy Creek, Bucks County). Somewhat puzzling is a 1654 account that names only six village bands for both banks, all of them within or very near to the present city limits of Philadelphia (Weslager 1954, 1972:31–49; Dunlap and Weslager 1958; Witthoft 1955; Becker 1976;

Fig. 2. 17th-century bands and dialects, interior areas poorly known.

Lindeström 1925:170–171). There were Indians in the Forks area of the upper Delaware, but these became known only in the later colonial period after some population movements had already taken place.

The Delawares below the falls of the Delaware River had particularly close relations with one another. Connections between groups across the river from each other are frequently shown by the fact that some chiefs signed deeds for areas on both banks (Myers 1937:60–96; Thomson 1759:34; Nelson 1904:23, 43, 55, 58; De Valinger 1940–1941, 3(4):32). The northern bounds of these downriver Indians were at Tohickon Creek (above the falls) on the west bank, and between Trenton and Burlington (below the falls) on the east bank. These Indians spoke what may be called Southern Unami, the dialect of Unami that survived in the 1970s among the Oklahoma Delaware. The Indians of the Forks spoke Northern Unami, the dialect used by the Moravian missionaries but now extinct. The New Jersey Indians between the Southern Unamis and the Munsee speakers to the north and east spoke Unalachtigo, a dialect of Unami attested by a seventeenth-century vocabulary from the Sankhikan band (De Laet 1909:58–60). The Unami speakers on the Delaware, specifically the Sankhikans, were constant enemies of the circum-Manhattan Munsee speakers in the early period (De Rasieres 1909:103–104; De Laet 1909:45; NYCD 1:367), and it is likely that the major linguistic and political demarcation line within the Delaware area followed at least roughly

215

the one recognized at the treaty of Easton in 1758 as separating the claims of the Munsees and Unamis: from the Delaware Water Gap to the falls of the Lamington River and thence downriver to the sea via the North Branch of the Raritan and the Raritan (but presumably dipping south of the Navasinks on the east) (S. Smith 1765:473; Goddard 1971a, 1975; Hunter 1975).

Culture

The Delaware way of life changed considerably between the seventeenth and twentieth centuries, and the information available on it is of uneven coverage in the different periods. However, a fairly complete description of Delaware culture in the seventeenth century can be pieced together, and this survey may be taken as very nearly a description of the precontact situation and a baseline for the understanding of the cultural changes in later centuries.

• POLITICAL ORGANIZATION   The political organization and interrelationships of the various named local groups are difficult to assess. These smallest units could at times act independently, for example by disassociating themselves from the hostile acts of their neighbors and making peace on their own. On the other hand, the cooperation of a number of local groups is evident in connection with hunting drives, mutual defense, and diplomatic relations with the Iroquois and the Europeans. There were also joint resource-use arrangements that governed fishing and oystering, and intermarriage and mutual visiting seem frequent. These agglomerations of interacting local groups were in effect nascent tribes, though they lacked stable centralized leadership and the structure of their political organization is unknown. Their size is suggested by, first, the fact that when the Wiechquaeskecks were attacked in 1643, "eleven tribes" (apparently most of the Munsee speakers on the Hudson) attacked the Dutch in retaliation; and second, the 1671 report from the Delaware River that if the authorities executed two Indian murderers from a group that consisted of 50 or 60 people (including seven warriors), they would risk war with the allies of this group, who numbered "about a thousand persons besides Women and Children" (De Vries 1909:230; NYCD 1:151, 12:484–487, 13:18, 303, 495, 14:56; Thurman 1975).

Within each named local group, one particular lineage appears to have supplied the chief, who was simply the first-among-equals of all the village or lineage headmen (De Laet 1909:57–58; Van der Donck 1841:205, 210; De Vries 1909:216). Chiefs acted as mediators and performed ceremonial functions, but they lacked coercive prerogatives. At times they seem to exercise little power beyond that of persuasion, unable to control the warriors and merely acting as spokesmen for their particular people in dealings with the Europeans (NYCD 13:151, 171–172). However, in the course of the seventeenth century a few chiefs, such as Oratamin of the Hackensack

and Tappan, emerged as leaders of the consolidated local groups in certain areas, a circumstance that must reflect their political effectiveness (Nelson 1894:104–109; Bolton 1920:355; Wolley 1902:65). Chiefs directed hunting when large groups engaged in fire-aided surrounds (Lindeström 1925:213–214), and they oversaw the hunting down of murderers (Denton 1845:12), though murder was ordinarily expiated by the payment of a wergild of wampum. Important decisions were made in a general council described as consisting of "all the Old and Wise men of [the] Nation, which perhaps is two hundred People" (Penn 1912:235) or of "all chiefs and persons of any distinction" (Van der Donck 1841:203). Since Penn says the young men were also present, these councils were in effect plenary meetings of the adult males. In contrast to this, the Esopus chiefs determined policy by consulting separately with the grown men (warriors), the women, and the youths (NYCD 13:171–192, 504–506). It may be that lineages had discrete hunting territories in some cases, but the consent of the whole local group seems to have been necessary to sell land (De Valinger 1940–1941; Penn 1912; NYCD 12:16–17). A chief designated his successor, but this expression of preference appears not to have been binding after his resignation or death. Succession seems to have been matrilineal; however, there are incontrovertible cases of patrilineal succession (actual and proposed), and one can only conjecture that these may reflect adoption into the father's lineage (Nelson 1894:108–109; Penn 1912:234–235; NYCD 13:58, 361; Pa. Arch. 1(1):124; Penney 1912). An office of priest is described for the easternmost groups, like the powwow of eastern Long Island and southern New England, but in other Delaware groups the chief apparently acted as a religious leader (Wolley 1902:45; Denton 1845:8). War chiefs attained their positions of influence by demonstrating their martial abilities in the field. As noted already, it seems that in the last decades of the seventeenth century stable leadership over new and larger tribal groupings emerged as a way of dealing more effectively with the Europeans, but this perhaps involved only a slight adjustment in the structure of the loose, precontact regional alliances.

• SUBSISTENCE   After the leaves had fallen each year, open areas and the undergrowth in the woods were burned over, partly in connection with the fire-surrounds that were used to trap and drive game, but also to make tracking and hunting generally easier by keeping the woods open and to prevent abandoned fields from growing over (Lindeström 1925:213–244; De Vries 1912:15, 18; Day 1953:334). Though hunting was a year-round occupation, late fall was the principal season. Winter was spent scattered in small dwellings in the woods or, in time of war, in hilltop strongholds consisting of longhouses surrounded by stockades. In April, areas were burned over that had been missed the preceding fall, and, if necessary, woodland was cleared for new cornfields near the villages. After the crops were planted most of the year's visiting and trading with Europeans was done, and some families would go to the nesting areas of the passenger pigeon to gather squabs. Spring and early summer was also the time when ocean fish and shellfish were taken, and gardens were sometimes planted at the fishing stations. Summer was a time for hunting second in importance only to the fall. After the crops were harvested the principal ceremonies of the year took place, with the greatest concentration of population in the villages being at this time (Van der Donck 1841:149–150, 173, 183, 197–198, 209; Acrelius 1912:73; Penn 1912: 234; De Vries 1909:222).

Hunting was with bows and arrows, guns (as soon as they became available), and traps (not well described), which for beaver were baited with beaver castors. At times the hunt was aided by driving animals into pounds and natural impasses (as toward a river) or by means of fire-surrounds, techniques that required the organization of hunting parties of an estimated 100 to 200 people. Deer were the most important game, but bears were also taken, along with wolves, raccoons, fishers, weasels, otters, and other small animals, as well as turkeys, passenger pigeons, and other birds. Moose were hunted inland (Van der Donck 1841:150, 168, 172, 183, 209; Lindeström 1925:213–217; De Vries 1909:220; Wolley 1902:37, 49).

Fish taken included shad, striped bass, sturgeon, eels, and many others. The means used were large stone-weighted seines, smaller nets set on poles, fish traps, weirs, hooks, and bows and arrows. Fish and shellfish were commonly sun-dried on racks and preserved, the shells of the latter being discarded to form huge shell heaps (Van der Donck 1841:209; De Vries 1912:22–23; Lindeström 1925:219–220).

The staple crop was corn, which was planted in hills with several grains to each. Alongside this beans of several podded varieties were planted to grow up the cornstalks, and squash was also grown. Native tobacco was grown, to which beaver castors were sometimes added for smoking. Wild foods are little described, but berries and nuts were gathered in season, as well as groundnuts and other wild roots and greens (Van der Donck 1841:151–152, 186–187, 189, 208, 227; Lindeström 1925:179–181; De Rasieres 1909:107; Wolley 1902:43; Danckaerts 1913:54–56; Acrelius 1912:73).

Meals were not at fixed times, but there was a tendency to eat in the morning and the evening. Cornmeal mush was eaten daily, often with meat or fish that had been preserved by drying and crushed in a mortar. Beans were added to mush or boiled separately. Fresh meat and fish (which were generally not cleaned) were boiled or else roasted on sticks set in the ground next to the fire. Ground cornmeal was wrapped in husks and baked in the ashes to make bread. Special treats were beaver tails, striped bass heads, fat meat with chestnuts, and parched corn ground fine. This last was also carried in bags as the standard warrior's and hunter's ration, since a quarter of a pound, mixed with water, provided food for a day. Berries were used as sweeteners, but maple sugar is not mentioned. Cornstalks were sucked as sweets (Van der Donck 1841:192–194; Danckaerts 1913:55, 159; Penn 1912:233; Lindeström 1925:254; De Vries 1909:219; De Rasieres 1909:107).

• TECHNOLOGY Round- or conical-bottomed clay pots were set in the fire for cooking. Bowls, dishes, and ladles were made from gourds or carved from wood, and gourds were also used for water bottles. Eating off leaves with shells is also mentioned. The ends of tree sections were hollowed out for mortars, pestles being of wood or stone. Cordage was made by rolling on the thigh the fibers obtained from Indian hemp, nettle plants, or the inner bark of certain trees; and from this tumplines, bags, and nets were woven. Baskets and mats were made of rushes and cornhusks, and all woven or plaited items could be decorated by working in painted spruce roots or porcupine quills. Paints were plant or mineral coloring in an animal grease base. After corn was dried (in narrow corncribs made of reeds, according to one source), it was shelled, put in large hempen bags, and stored in mat-lined pits. Pipes were of clay, stone, horn, or copper, and often decorated. Edged tools of stone included axes, hoes, and knives of various kinds. Triangular stone arrowheads were affixed with resin or fish glue to feathered one- or two-piece shafts. Documentary sources identify the stone used for the objects mentioned here only as "flint," but archeologically a number of varieties of stone are attested. Other convenient materials were used as alternatives to stone for most items; arrowheads, for example, were also made of bone, horn, or fish or animal teeth. Bows, some standing taller than a man, were strung with braided sinew. In war a wooden helmet was worn, a wooden war club was hung on the arm with a thong, and a large rectangular wooden or moosehide shield was carried that covered the body up to the shoulders; decorations were painted on the clubs and shields. Quivers are depicted but not well described. Among other manufactured small objects were needles, made of fish or animal bones or of "nut-wood," pine candles, and reed flutes. Wampum beads, used ceremonially and for decoration as well as in trade, were fashioned by breaking up and grinding seashells. The purple area of quahog shells (*Mercenaria mercenaria*) furnished the "black" beads and the columella of knobbed and channeled whelks (*Busycon carica* and *B. canaliculatum*) furnished the white, which was reckoned at half the value. Dugout canoes were the trunks of "whitewood" (probably *Liriodendron tulipifera*), cedar, and other trees, hollowed out by burning and scraping; smaller easily carried canoes were made of elm and other bark. Paddles were wood (Van der Donck 1841:152, 160, 163–164, 187, 206–207, 211; Anonymous 1909a:301; C.S. Smith 1950:117–119; De Laet 1909:49, 57; Juet 1909:18; G. Thomas 1912:341;

Pastorius 1912:384; Lindeström 1925:206, 221–222, 229–232, 237, 353–355; Wolley 1902:41, 43, 55, 62–63; De Rasieres 1909:107–108; De Vries 1909:218–219; Campanius Holm 1834:129–130, 137; De Vries 1912:19; Danckaerts 1913:55–56, 159; Burggraf 1938:53–55).

• CLOTHING AND ADORNMENT The Delawares went lightly clad, even in winter, the minimum clothing being a skin breechclout for men and a lapped but unsewed skirt for women. Belts were ordinarily leather and decorated with wampum, but snakeskin belts and decorations of "whalefins" and "whalebones" are also mentioned. For the aboriginal untailored deerskin upper garment the Indians soon substituted large blankets, about 10 feet long, called matchcoats or duffels. When not drawn around the shoulders or used for bedclothes these were worn over the right shoulder with the ends loosely knotted at the left side to hang below the knees, or with one end hanging loose from one shoulder and the other tucked into the belt in front, or tucked under the belt all the way around. The corresponding garment in cold weather was of bear, raccoon, beaver, or other skins sewed or skewered together, worn fur side in (fur side out in warmer temperatures). Cloaks of turkey feathers, painted or not and tied into hemp backing, are frequently mentioned. Moccasins were generally of deer or moose skin, apparently with ankle flaps and thongs for tying them on; temporary footwear of cornhusks was also made. In winter skin leggings and snowshoes were used. Skin clothing was decorated by painting and by sewing on wampum beads and tassels and fringes of wampum. For dress, wampum was worn in string necklaces and in patterned headbands, waistbands, and crossbelts (fig. 3). Copper ornaments and long tassels of red-dyed hair were strung to hang from the neck. Metal rings and short strings of wampum were used as earrings and as bracelets, and porcupine quills might be worn through the nose. Men wore on their heads bands of snakeskin, feathers or feather-crown headdresses (large feathers erect in a circle), and roaches of dyed deer hair tied to a hemp base. Hanging from around their necks they would have tobacco pouches, made of the whole skin of a small animal, in which to carry pipes and other small objects. Some men (perhaps warriors) shaved the head except for a long scalplock at the crown; otherwise the hair hung loose, with wampum braided or tied in for decoration. Chin hairs were plucked out. The women braided their hair behind (one source says in four braids), the braids sometimes being tied in a club and covered with a square pouch decorated with wampum. Face painting and the tattooing and painting of the body were often elaborate. Animal grease (especially of bears and raccoons) was applied liberally to the body, against the cold, the sun, and mosquitoes, and also to the hair (Van der Donck 1841:164, 185, 190, 194–196; Anonymous 1909a:301; Juet 1909:18; Wolley 1902:34–36, 57; De Rasieres 1909:106; Hesselius 1735, 1735a; Lindeström 1925:

Riksarkivet, Stockholm.

Fig. 3. Delaware family, dressed up in belts, bands, strings, and medallions made of black and white wampum beads. Drawn by Peter Mårtensson Lindeström, 1653. The representation is stylized, the man's skirt and the woman's crossbelt being inconsistent with Lindeström's (1925:195–200) description.

195–200, 221–222, 224–226; De Vries 1909:217; Danckaerts 1913:35; Penn 1912:230–231; Campanius Holm 1834:119, 129).

• STRUCTURES Delaware houses differed in size and type according to the time of year (which in turn tended to govern settlement size) and other factors, but the specifics of this variation and how it functioned are not known. Best described are the multiple-family longhouses, which were about 20 feet wide and could be over 100 feet long. One of 60 feet is described that housed 20 or 22 people in seven or eight families. The frames were hickory saplings, which were set in the ground in pairs opposite each other, then tied together in arches and linked up by horizontal poles. The covering was of sheets of bark—six-foot tall sections of chestnut bark are mentioned—with a smoke hole a foot wide running the length of the roof at the crown and a small doorway at either end. The fires were in the middle of the floor, one for each family, and apparently each family occupied a partially partitioned section. Kettles were hung from poles running lengthwise in the house on forked posts. These longhouses were built in semipermanent winter settlements, sometimes clustered on hilltops behind

218

stockades of logs and trees. When not stockaded, "villages" were apt to consist of a scattering of houses spread over a considerable area. The population was especially mobile in summer, but settlements were established near the cornfields and small houses are mentioned for the temporary hunting and fishing camps. Houses were furnished with woven reed mats spread on the ground and hung on the walls, and the mats and railwork had painted decorations. Carved "faces and images" are mentioned as being "generally in the houses of the chiefs"; this suggests that the chief's house was used for the religious ceremonies of his group. Sweathouses, big enough for three or four men to lie in, were built near running water and had a covering of small branches sealed with clay (Van der Donck 1841:196-197, 207-208; Anonymous 1909a:302; Lindeström 1925:211-213, 222, 255, 257; Danckaerts 1913:55, 159; De Vries 1909:217, 230).

• LIFE CYCLE   The birth of a child took place in a hut built for the purpose away from dwelling houses. The mother washed the newborn infant in cold water (but only if male, according to one source) and tied it to a board, where it was kept until the age of about one year except for periodic cleaning. Apparently the Delaware cradleboard had no protective hoop at the top, though one observer said that when the board was laid on the ground a separate deerskin covering on a hoop was fixed around it. Women carried their cradleboards on their backs with a tumpline around the forehead; a child too old for the cradleboard hung around its mother's neck supported by the skin or blanket she drew around her shoulders. Children were nursed for one or two years. As soon as they were capable, they were given tasks to perform appropriate to their sex. Boys were sent to fish, to shoot small animals and birds with a bow, and, when older, to hunt. Girls helped around the house and in the gardens. These activities prepared children for their duties as adults, which were generally distinct for the two sexes. Men did the hunting, fishing, and trading and especially in their old age made the tools and utensils of wood, stone, and the like, including nets and bags. They were the warriors, chiefs, and curers. Women handled all aspects of gardening, cooking, and housekeeping, as well as the preparing of skins and the tending of small children; they also carried the household articles when their families moved.

When girls menstruated for the first time they retired to a separate hut until after the second occurrence. While there they kept a blanket over their heads and avoided touching their hair or any food or utensils, eating instead with a stick and drinking from their hands. Similar practices accompanied subsequent menstruations.

After this first seclusion a girl indicated her marriageability by going decked with wampum and wearing a special headdress that permitted partial covering of the face. A suitor is variously said to have approached the girl herself, or her friends, or her parents with a gift of wampum, but there is one explicit statement that this was only after the marriage had been arranged by relatives of the prospective couple. A betrothal period followed lasting a year, during which the girl continued to wear her special attire. The end of this period may have been marked by a feast, but there was no other marriage ceremony. Divorce was by mutual consent and frequent, and remarriage was not formally marked. Premarital chastity was not valued, but adultery was proscribed except when consent was given. For example, a polygynous man, who would typically be a chief, might lend a visitor one of his wives for the night. One source mentions formal procedures for accusing an adulterous husband or wife before the chief and publicly shaming those found guilty. Sexual continence was practiced during menstruation, pregnancy, and lactation.

Pastimes included "football," a gambling game using reeds, and, when rum or other spirits became available, drinking bouts. Mutual delousing was also a social activity, the lice being eaten in the process (Van der Donck 1841:198-201, 207; Anonymous 1909a:302; Lindeström 1925:193-194, 201-202; Penn 1912:231-232; Wolley 1902:32, 37, 59-60; Danckaerts 1913:56; De Rasieres 1909:105-107; De Vries 1909:218; Wassenaer 1909:85; S. Smith 1765:138; Denton 1845:7).

A few days after death, the corpse was buried in a pit-grave in a sitting position. Some graves were in cemeteries, others were isolated. A few tools and utensils were placed in the grave along with food and wampum, and wood or boughs were put around the body to keep the dirt away. The grave was then filled and covered with a pile of earth and stones enclosed by a fence. At some point in the funeral there was a feast. Afterward the grave was visited annually by mourners and carefully tended to keep it free of grass. Over a man's grave was erected a post with a pictorial representation of his abilities or accomplishments. The relatives of the dead painted their faces black, and widowed persons mourned for a year. Women especially engaged in acts of mourning such as crawling daily about the grave of a husband while weeping, or burning their hair on the graves of young people or those killed in a war. The names of the dead were not mentioned. A widower offered a payment to his wife's relatives in order to be released to marry again. One source describes a form of secondary burial like that of the Nanticoke, which may represent diffusion from that group to the southernmost Delawares (Van der Donck 1841:201-203; Penn 1912:233-234; De Vries 1909:223; Wolley 1902:58-60; Lindeström 1925: 249-251; Denton 1845:9-10; Campanius Holm 1834:143; Danckaerts 1913:159).

• RELIGION   Delaware religion in the earliest period is poorly known because the Europeans who described it knew little about the system of beliefs as a whole and often misunderstood the significance of the rituals they witnessed. A tutelary being was acquired at about the age of 15 (the available account does not say how this happened or whether everyone did so). Typically this was an animal or bird, a claw, tooth, or bill of which was kept on the person. Dreaming of this being was connected with future success in hunting (it is probably not significant that this is the only area of achievement mentioned) and it was imitated vocally in connection with a certain sweathouse ceremony (Lindeström 1925:207–208, 257–259). The principal ceremony was described as a dance performed by a number of people proceeding in a circle. The verbal accompaniment alternated between words and songs, punctuated by shouts. Two men sat in the middle drumming on a "board" (actually a stiff hide, to judge by later evidence) and leading the singing. The dancers were very active jumping and making various movements, but always keeping time. Others sat on the sidelines singing and beating the ground with short sticks. This ceremony was held once or twice a year, but generally in October after the corn harvest. Apparently it was performed on several evenings, since it accompanied feasts of venison and corn that were given in a series, presumably by the different chiefs in a given area. Those attending were expected to make a contribution of wampum, some of which was thrown on the ground for "the poor and fatherless" to pick up. First-fruits ceremonies included burning "the first and fattest buck" in the fire (or simply burning the fat) and perhaps a green-corn ceremony, though the sources do not clearly distinguish this from the harvest ceremony. In addition war dances and the performance of shamanistic tricks with firebrands and coals are mentioned. There were also curing ceremonies conducted by shamans, other treatments of disease being fasting, sweating, and the drinking of herbal decoctions. Some Europeans were satisfied that the Delawares believed in creation by an omnipotent god, but a creation myth involving a pregnant woman falling from the sky was also recorded. The souls of the dead were thought to go to the west or south, where they would have an abundance of game for hunting and live easy lives (Penn 1912:234; Denton 1845:8, 11–12; Wolley 1902:45, 54, 50; Witthoft 1949a:11–17; Danckaerts 1913:174; Van der Donck 1841:207–208, 217–218).

• WARFARE When defending against enemies, the men would seclude the women and children on an island or in a swamp and attempt to ambush the attackers. On the offense, night attacks and deceptions were preferred. Fighting was on a small scale, and rarely were as many as seven or eight killed at a time. Warriors painted their faces in particular ways and wore snakeskins or other special headbands. Their attire might also include red turkey feathers or animal fetishes such as fox or wolf tails tied upright on the head. On the warpath a special jargon was used, with substitutions made for many ordinary words. Captives were either adopted to take the place of slain relatives or else tortured and executed. In the latter

event, they would sing defiantly until dead. Scalps were taken as trophies, both on the field and from slain prisoners (Denton 1845:9; Anonymous 1909a:300–301; Van der Donck 1841:211, 213; Wolley 1902:65; Campanius Holm 1834:137–138; Lindeström 1925:203–204).

Early Contacts, History, Migrations

The earliest contact between Delawares and Europeans is unrecorded. The welcoming gestures of the Indians along the shore when Giovanni da Verrazano entered New York harbor in 1524 show that they must have previously engaged in trade with passing ships (Wroth 1970:85–86). In the following century the Delaware recalled the Spanish or Portuguese as the first Europeans to have come to their country (Danckaerts 1913:179), and contacts with the Spanish especially had probably occurred occasionally before the 1580s. However, substantial information is not available until the 1609 voyage of Henry Hudson, an Englishman working for the Dutch East India Company. He traded with Indians in Sandy Hook Bay (south of Staten Island), but his explorations were curtailed when two canoes of warriors attacked the ship's boat, leaving one man dead and two wounded, and he proceeded up the Hudson River to a friendlier encounter with the Mahican. When, on the ship's return, the downriver Indians attacked again, the Dutch killed several with muskets and ordnance (Juet 1909:18–27). In the course of further exploration in 1614 a Dutch trading post was established where Albany now is, and in 1624 the first Dutch colonists settled there and on Burlington Island in the Delaware River. By the end of 1626, these colonists had been brought together with others to found Fort Amsterdam on Manhattan Island, which had been purchased from the Indians that spring for 60 guilders' worth of trade goods (Weslager 1961a:43–81).

The fur trade was the motivating factor for the Dutch colonization, and it soon had a major impact on the economy and material culture of the Delaware. The beaver in coastal areas became depleted by overhunting, and as early as mid-century they were being sought far inland on long hunts (Van der Donck 1841:209). In exchange for furs the Delaware obtained many items of European manufacture that soon became standard additions to their culture, often replacing completely their aboriginal counterparts. Readily adopted in this way were metal kettles and edged and pointed tools, household implements, bottles and jugs, and items such as glass beads, bells, and jew's-harps. By the 1650s muskets, powder, and bullet-making materials were standard items used in trade and land purchases. Liquor was also an important commodity. Cloth became a common substitute for skins in the making of breechclouts, skirts, and leggings, as well as matchcoats. One popular item of adopted European clothing was the shirt, which men wore loose and hanging to the knees. Also, the Delaware were soon growing introduced domesticates such as pumpkins (from the Spanish New World), mushmelons, and watermelons, and took up the raising of pigs and chickens (Bolton 1920:299–300; Myers 1937:60, 68–69, 80–81, 91; Van der Donck 1841:186–187, 211; De Rasieres 1909:107; Danckaerts 1913:56, 159; Lindeström 1925:198–199, 225, 255). In the context of the fur trade, a jargon came into use between the Delawares and the Europeans consisting mostly of uninflected Unami words with simple, paratactic syntax (Prince 1912; Goddard 1971a:14–16).

Friction between the Delaware and the Dutch grew more serious as the population of the colonists increased, and as intertribal rivalries were exacerbated by competition for access to the fur trade. A series of killings and retaliations, coupled with mismanagement by Gov. Willem Kieft, brought matters to a head in the early 1640s. In February 1643, several hundred Wiechquaeskecks, fleeing from Mahican attacks, took refuge on Manhattan and at Pavonia (Jersey City). The Dutch saw an opportunity to get revenge and to set an example and massacred the refugees, thus touching off two years of bitter conflict. The lower Hudson Indians united to attack outlying Dutch farms and settlements, and in February and March 1644 joint Dutch-English expeditions destroyed villages at Hempstead, Fort Neck (South Oyster Bay, Long Island), and Pound Ridge (eastern Westchester County). By the time peace was concluded in the summer of 1645, perhaps 1,000 Indians had lost their lives (De Vries 1909:225–229; NYCD 1:151; Anonymous 1909:282–284; B. Schultz 1937:39–41; Trelease 1960:72–80). A relatively minor outburst was the so-called Peach War of 1655, said to have been set off when a Dutchman killed an Indian who was stealing his peaches (Trelease 1960:138–147; Jordan 1913, 2:165). A series of incidents kept matters on edge, and land cessions continued. In June 1663 the Esopus Indians attacked a new Dutch settlement in their area, setting off a conflict that lasted until the next year, when the English took over the colony. During this conflict the Esopus Indians took refuge with the Minisink on the upper Delaware, and though a number of them subsequently remained for some years near the Hudson, their gradual consolidation with the more westerly group began at this time (Trelease 1960:147–168; NYCD 12:438–439, 13:363–364). In fact, by the end of the Dutch period the displacement of the Delaware was already well under way. Some western Long Island Indians removed to Staten Island, but the main body gathered at successively more easterly locations. The mainland groups east of the Hudson withdrew inland while continuing to plant and fish in parts of their old territories. West of the Hudson the local groups began to come together in fewer and more out-of-the-way places. Along the Delaware relations with the Swedes and later the English were more peaceable than along the Hudson, but with the continual sale of lands (fig. 4) the

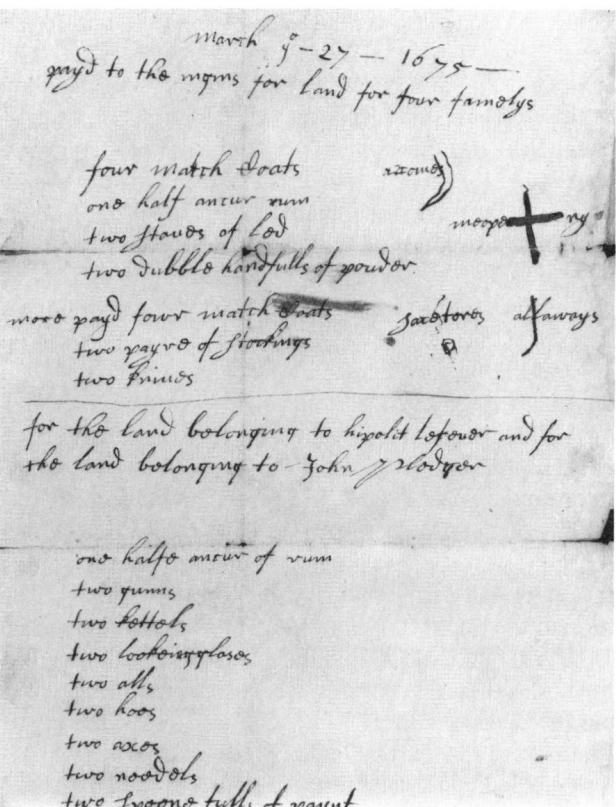

Histl. Soc. of Pa., Philadelphia.

Fig. 4. A receipt from Sacetores, Accomes, Meopeny, and Allaways, Delaware Indian chiefs, for sale of land in present Salem Co., N.J., to Hipolit Lefever and John Pledger, March 27, 1676 (erroneously dated 1675). Full text transcribed in Myers (1937:60).

same pattern emerged of consolidation into a reduced number of village groups.

In the eighteenth century these trends continued during the French and Indian Wars. The Minisinks went northwest to various places on the North Branch of the Susquehanna and its tributary the Canisteo-Chemung, and many of the Munsee-speaking emigrants from the Hudson Valley, including some Wappingers, became incorporated with them. In time Munsee replaced Minisink as the name of this new grouping and its eventual fragmented descendants. The New Jersey Indians from above the falls at Trenton generally joined the upriver Unami speakers in the Forks area (Lehigh Valley). This consolidated Northern Unami group was forced to remove by a fraudulent claim to their lands, the so-called Walking Purchase of 1737. This claim, made by the Pennsylvania government, was abetted and enforced by the Six Nations, who claimed the Delawares as tributaries. After 1742 these Northern Unamis were on the North Branch of the Susquehanna, at Shamokin (Sunbury) and Wyoming (fig. 1) (Hunter 1954; NYHSC 54:94–96; Weslager 1972:187–193).

Meanwhile the Southern Unamis lower down along the Delaware retreated from their ceded lands to the

Tulpehocken Valley, on the upper Schuylkill, and to the upper Brandywine (Weslager 1972:174-178). The Schuylkill Indians began settling on the Susquehanna before 1709, first at Paxtang (Harrisburg), and subsequent White encroachment on their territory at Tulpehocken led to its being ceded in 1732. At about the same time the Brandywine Indians were crowded off their lands and also removed to Paxtang, where they lost their separate identity. Settlement at Paxtang was first made about 1697 by Shawnees, who had fled by a circuitous route from their Ohio homelands. Other Shawnees settled in Minisink territory on the upper Delaware in 1694, and the histories of the Delaware and Shawnee have been intertwined ever since (Hanna 1911, 1:119-160; Witthoft and Hunter 1955). In the 1720s the Southern Unamis went up the Susquehanna to Shamokin, and some began settling on the Allegheny (first at Kittanning about 1724). After 1750 most of the original Southern Unamis were in the lower Allegheny and upper Ohio valleys, where they formed the nucleus of the emergent Delaware tribe (fig. 1) (Hunter 1951, 1954a; Hanna 1911, 1:183). From this time on, these Delawares were organized into three phratries, each with a chief living in a separate village. These were the Turtle, Turkey, and Wolf groups sometimes called clans. One of the three chiefs acted as first-among-equals and spokesman for the whole tribe. Additional Northern and Southern Unamis from the upper Susquehanna joined their western relatives in the 1760s. Most of the Munsees and Northern Unamis had remained on the North Branch of the Susquehanna until the end of the French and Indian War, but some went to the West Branch and in 1765 most of the Munsees moved to Goschgosching on the middle Allegheny (Forest County). The Northern Unamis that did not join the Delawares in the west became one of the tribal satellites of the Six Nations, and those that retained their identity ended up after the American Revolution with the Iroquois on Grand River (now Six Nations Reserve, Ontario) (Hunter 1954; Deardorff 1946; Johnston 1964:38, 52).

A few groups of Delawares remained behind in the East. The Dutchess County Wappingers lost their lands in a dispute and mostly joined the Mahicans at Stockbridge, Massachusetts, losing their identity. There were scattered remnants in Ulster and Orange counties, New York, who provided the Indian heritage among the triracial groups later found in the area (NYCD 8:451, 458; Handlin and Mark 1964). In New Jersey there were settlements at Crosswicks, Coaxen (also called Weekpink, west of Vincentown), and elsewhere, and in 1746 the mission town of Cranbury was founded (fig. 2). In 1758 all Indian claims to New Jersey lands were relinquished at conferences held at Crosswicks and Easton, and those wishing to remain in the colony were given a reservation, named Brotherton, on Edgepillock Creek (Indian Mills). The Delawares here, who were acculturated Christians,

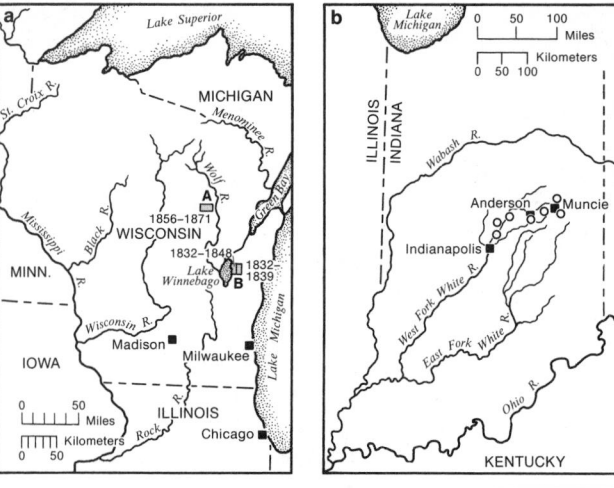

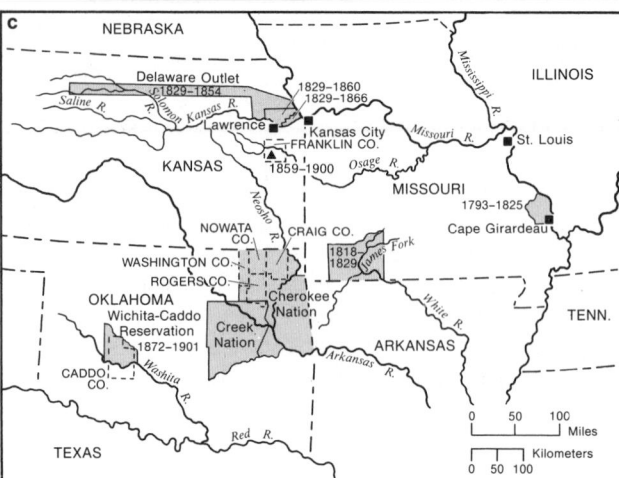

Fig. 5. Western relocations of the Delaware. Official reservation dates are given, but occupation preceded and followed dates in some instances. a, A, Canadian Munsees after 1837 with Stockbridges; B, Munsees with Stockbridges. b, Main villages, 1795 to 1818. c, Munsees with Chippewas, of Swan Creek and Black River in Franklin Co., Kan.; counties in Cherokee Nation show where main body of Delawares had allotments after 1866; Wichita-Caddo Reservation location of most Western Delawares prior to 1901 and allotments after 1901. Many additional Delaware settlements in Oklahoma and Texas in the period before allotment are not shown.

eventually went west with the Stockbridge Mahicans and a similarly named Brothertown mission group from southern New England. These all ended up in Wisconsin, where they were joined by some Munsees who had gone to Canada, and where their assimilated descendants are today (fig. 5a). The few Delawares that stayed behind contributed genetic material and some cultural memories to mixed racial groups in New Jersey (De Cou 1949:191-193, 242-250; Brainerd 1880; J. Edwards 1822:303; S. Smith 1765:440-484; Weslager 1972: 261-281, 1973:123-127; Larrabee 1976).

The relationship between the Delaware and the Iroquois in this period is complex. The Delawares' own statements indicate that the Iroquois had achieved mili-

222

tary dominance over them in the mid-seventeenth century, and chiefs from both the Southern Unamis and the Minisinks are known to have made regular trips to Onondaga to deliver tributes of wampum belts. Presumably this arrangement was a peripheral component of the Iroquois control over the fur trade from the interior, which they had consolidated during the third quarter of the seventeenth century by gaining through conquest total domination of the Susquehanna and upper Allegheny-Ohio valleys. In spite of this tributary relationship the majority of the Delaware remained politically independent, but the situation changed in the 1740s, when they were forced by land cessions to remove to the Six Nations' conquered territories. The Iroquois then asserted (first explicitly in 1742 though there are earlier allusions) that the Delaware were "women" who had no right to sell land or engage in war, and subsequently, in fact, though Delaware warriors were not notably inactive, Iroquois representatives always oversaw Delaware diplomatic dealings with Whites. That the metaphorical status of the Delaware as women reflected their dwelling on Iroquois lands seems confirmed by the fact that as soon as they reached the nominally Wyandot territory west of Big Beaver Creek (Beaver River, Pennsylvania; see "History of the Ohio Valley," fig. 1, this vol.) they reasserted their independence and their status as males (notably in a speech by White Eyes in 1775). The metaphor was, of course, rhetorically useful, and many attempts have been made to read into it other, deeper meanings (NYCD 4:98–99; Pa. Col. Recs. 2:471, 546, 4:579–580; Zeisberger and Jungmann 1769–1772, entry for 1/13/1772; Heckewelder 1820:140–141; Downes 1940:185; Weslager 1944a, 1947, 1972:181, 286; J. Miller 1974).

In Ohio the Delawares consolidated as a tribe and became a significant political and military power, having at last emerged from the domination of the Six Nations. The succession of the chiefs and their places of residence during the early period in Ohio may serve as an illustration of the complexities of the new political structures, many facets of which are not accurately known. The Wolf chief Custaloga (or Pakanke) had his village at Venango (Franklin, Pennsylvania) and later at Kuskuskies (New Castle, Pennsylvania); he was succeeded by his nephew Captain Pipe in 1773. The seat of the Turkey chief was successively at a village just below Pittsburgh, at Kittanning, at Kuskuskies, and at Tuscarawas (near Bolivar, Ohio). Shingas became chief of this division in 1752 and was succeeded while still alive by his brother Beaver in 1761; these brothers were nephews of Sassoonan (Alumapees), who had been chief of the Schuylkill Delawares until his death in 1747. Beaver died in 1769 and was succeeded by Captain Johnny. The Turtle chief Netawatwees (Newcomer) lived at Saukunk (Beaver, Pennsylvania) and later at Newcomerstown (Tuscarawas County, Ohio); he seems to have eclipsed Shingas

as head chief by 1757, but in 1773 he was replaced as tribal spokesman by White Eyes, who was the head war chief. Netawatwees died in 1776 and was succeeded as Turtle chief by his son's son Gelelemend (Killbuck). There were many other scattered Delaware settlements during this period, including towns of Christianized Indians founded by Moravian missionaries. The earliest of these had been in the Lehigh Valley, removing to the North Branch of the Susquehanna. A mission village was set up near the Munsee town of Goschgosching in 1768, and the missionaries and converts there and on the Susquehanna were invited to settle among the Ohio Delawares after 1770 (Hunter 1951, 1954, 1954a; W. Johnson 1921–1965, 12:1044–1048; Hanna 1911, 1:111, 241; Jordan 1913; Gray 1956:37–54; Zeisberger and Jungmann 1769–1772; Weslager 1972:221–260, 282–328).

The American Revolution led to additional dislocations and exacerbated factionalism in the tribe. The Continental Congress strove to influence the Delaware not to side with the British, whose agents operated widely on the frontier with the support of Loyalist settlers, and a treaty was signed at Pittsburgh in the fall of 1775, in which the Delaware gave assurances of neutrality in return for the Americans' pledge that the Ohio River would be the permanent western boundary of White settlement. At the urging of the Americans the Delawares began to gather at and near Coshocton (at the upper forks of the Muskingum), a new town that succeeded Newcomerstown as the seat of the tribal council but was planned with regular streets, in imitation of the mission villages. In spite of these consolidating moves, however, American influence was too weak to cope with the rivalries among the Indians, some of whom were intent on using the power vacuum to settle old scores against the Whites. Eventually, amid much conflict, the pro-English Delawares removed to northwestern Ohio, the pro-Americans to the Pittsburgh area, and still others to lands on the White River of Indiana to which the tribe had been invited by the Miamis sometime earlier. At the end of the Revolution none of these Delawares lived east of the northwest corner of the present state of Ohio, and after the Treaty of Greenville in 1795 most went to the upper West Fork of the White River of Indiana (fig. 5b). Some Delawares had already, in 1789, taken up lands near Cape Girardeau, Missouri, at the invitation of the Spanish governor. The border warfare had led to the massacre of 90 Christian Indians at Gnadenhütten, Ohio, in 1782. One Moravian mission band, with memories of this, withdrew to southeastern Michigan and in 1792 established the town of Fairfield on the Thames River in Ontario, the successor to which is the present Moraviantown, east of Thamesville (fig. 1). Some Munsees had gone up the Allegheny and in 1791 settled among the Senecas, where they retained their cultural identity through the nineteenth century. Of the Munsees that had gone to northwestern Ohio, one group went to the White River, where their village was at present Muncie, and another had settled at Munceytown on the Thames (now Muncey, south of Melbourne) even before the mission town was established downstream (USTP 15:105–107; Downes 1940; Gray 1956:68–92; Kent and Deardorff 1960, 3:282; Weslager 1972:282–358; Zeisberger 1972:15).

The main body of Delawares remained on the White River of Indiana, in several villages strung out over about 40 miles, for a quarter of a century, but they were on the move again after the cessions of the Treaty of Saint Marys in 1818. They settled on the James Fork of the White River in southern Missouri, where the Delawares at Cape Girardeau and nearby areas were also officially relocated at the same time (fig. 5c). As had been the case with the western Delawares, the new arrivals now went on extended buffalo hunts far to the south and west and concomitantly became involved in conflicts with the Osage, Pawnee, and other unacculturated tribes. In fact the hostilities with the Osage were already under way in 1805, and Delawares had begun settling on the Red River in southwestern Arkansas by 1817. A decade later some were in east Texas among the followers of Dutch, a Cherokee chief, being subsequently reported on the Sabine and the Neches (C.N. Thompson 1937:196–205; Weslager 1972:329–363; TPUS 13:245–247, 15:302–303, 454–455, 19:96, 134, 20:318–319, 358; Gipson 1938:385; W. Armstrong 1836; Menard 1836).

The Delawares were dissatisfied with the hostilities and the poor natural resources in Missouri, and a new treaty signed in 1829 granted them lands in northeastern Kansas and a guaranteed route of access to the buffalo-hunting grounds, called the Delaware Outlet. By the end of 1831 the main body had moved to the new reservation, on the north bank of the Kansas River east of Lawrence and south of Leavenworth (fig. 5c). They were joined by a small number of Delawares who had remained on the Sandusky in Ohio. However, another small group split off under the leadership of Black Beaver and settled in present south-central Oklahoma, where other Delawares, pressured out of Texas in 1839 and 1853, also ended up. Some Canadian Munsee speakers from Moraviantown and Munceytown moved to Kansas in 1837, and a part of these remained distinct from the other Delawares and eventually settled with some Chippewas in Franklin County (fig. 5c). In contrast, the other emigrant Canadian Munsees and the descendants of the tribal minorities that had come west with the Delawares (non-Christian Munsees, Mahicans, Nanticokes, and Conoys) generally assimilated to the Delaware majority. The Delawares who remained in Texas and their allies were given a reservation below Clear Fork on the Brazos River in 1854 to replace lands earlier reserved to them on the Sabine, but in the face of continuing pressure from White Texans they were removed to the Washita to join most of the other Delawares of Indian Territory in 1859 (Weslager 1972:363–398; S.H. Mitchell 1895:94; C. T. Foreman 1946; Foreman 1933:232, 270, 1946:160–162; Chickasaw and Delaware Chiefs 1853; Luckenbach 1917:179; Romig 1910; Weslager 1974; Adams 1901).

After the Civil War, the main body of Delawares exchanged their Kansas holdings for lands allotted in severalty in the Cherokee Nation (northeastern Oklahoma) and removed there beginning in late 1867 (fig. 5c). The more acculturated and Christianized Delawares settled in present Nowata, Rogers, and Craig counties, but the cultural conservatives balked at first and stayed for a few years on Peoria lands east of the Neosho. These so-called Neosho Delawares took their allotments in 1873, mostly in Washington County, and formed a traditionalist nucleus that maintained some aspects of Delaware culture, particularly religious practices, well into the twentieth century. The Indian Territory Delawares spent the Civil War in Kansas and afterward mostly went back to the Washita, but there was some exchange of population with those from the Kansas reservation. Eventually the reservation they shared with the Wichita and Caddo (roughly, Caddo County north of the Washita) was allotted in severalty, with the remainder being opened to White settlement in 1901 (Weslager 1972:399–439; M. H. Wright 1951:145–155; Foreman 1946:182–190; Delaware Annuity Rolls). The continuum of contacts between the western Delawares and the main body since 1789 reflects the fact that the tribe was always a single unit. The present division into Registered (or Cherokee) Delawares in northeastern Oklahoma and Western (or Absentee) Delawares in Caddo County is one of administrative convenience and cannot be projected all the way back to the Spanish period.

After the Seventeenth Century

Culture

During their migration westward, the Delaware maintained a way of life in many ways transitional between that of the Whites and that of the less acculturated Indians farther toward the interior. There was considerable diversity among the various groups, but there was an overall trend of increasing assimilation to White cultural practices, a process that has become virtually complete during the twentieth century. There was also some borrowing from other tribes, not to mention the important complicating factor of the occasional adoption of Indian cultural practices by frontier Whites. Here only the principal aspects of evolving Delaware culture in this later period can be mentioned, and it will not always be possible to sort out truly new practices from older practices that happened not to be recorded for the earlier period. The focus will be on the Unami speakers who formed the Delaware tribe in Ohio and went to Kansas and Oklahoma, rather than on the less well documented Munsees.

• SOCIAL ORGANIZATION The Delaware emerged after 1750 as a tribe organized into three phratries: Turtle (*puk·uwánku*), Turkey (*pəlé·*), and Wolf (*túkwsi·t*). The history of these groups before their first listing in 1764 (W. Smith 1765:53, 68) is uncertain, though they clearly continued many aspects of earlier corporate groupings. However, Heckewelder's (1876:51–52) connection of the three phratries with the three major political and dialectal groups distinguished by the Munsee in the eighteenth century (table 2) has been denied by all other investigators (Trowbridge 1972:480–481; Harrington 1913:209; Wallace 1949:10–11; Newcomb 1956:51). Phratry membership and eligibility for chieftainship passed matrilineally, and phratry chiefs seem to have succeeded to office in much the same way as that described for the chiefs of local groups in the earlier period. Chiefly duties and the decision-making process also show little change, except that the chiefs' role in law enforcement seems diminished. In this area, individual retaliation in kind and wergild payments for murder were the only mechanisms other than community disfavor. The chief's own house sometimes served as the council house for his phratry. A chief (*sa·k·í·ma*) had for assistants a messenger (*púčəl*), a speaker (unless he was himself an orator), a designated successor, and perhaps others. The council was a select group of men, but nothing specific is known about how the councilors or the other officers attained their positions. The war chief of each phratry (*í·la*, also meaning 'warrior') was appointed on his merits and governed during war, but he was often influential in peacetime and could be selected as a phratry chief. The chief kept wampum belts and paper documents in a special bag as records of past treaties and agreements with other tribes and with Europeans. The rituals and practices of intertribal diplomacy were essentially those of the Iroquois (Goddard 1965–1970, 1974; Zeisberger 1910:77, 91–102,

111–113, 122–123; Trowbridge 1972:476–482; Harrington 1913:211, 217; Beatty 1962:60–61; Morgan 1959:54).

The three phratries were made up of named matrilineal lineages, 12 in each according to Morgan's 1859 information. (See table 3 for the rather confused English terminology and the Delaware equivalents.) There are early statements suggesting that the phratries were exogamous, but these may be erroneous inferences based on the exogamous nature of the lineages. Certainly, marriage within the phratry was not proscribed in the early nineteenth century and later. In addition to regulating marriage, the lineages had ceremonial obligations—the so-called family feasts—and determined the inheritance of ritual property. In addition to being a member of his mother's phratry, an individual had a formalized relationship to his father's phratry. For instance, a person with a Turkey mother and a Wolf father would be referred to as *pəlé· tukwsi·t·amí·mə·ns* 'Turkey (and) Wolf-child'. He would engage in conventionalized joking with Wolf members but might also offer them ritual assistance at ceremonies. The last Delawares who knew the detailed functions of the phratry and lineage systems were dead by the middle of the twentieth century, but in the 1960s two lineages were still recognized—*ɔlamaní·yɔk* 'Red-Ocher people' and *wi·sa·whitkó·wak* 'Yellow-Tree people', both of the Wolf phratry (Goddard 1965–1970, 1968; Zeisberger 1910:81, 98; Trowbridge 1972:476–482; Morgan 1959:51–55, 1964:152; Harrington 1913:210).

The Munsee are said to have had three phratries (probably Turkey, Wolf, and Turtle, though one source has Bear for Turtle), but without subdivisions into lineages. In the nineteenth century the Munsees among the western Delawares were represented in the Delaware council by a chief, but their internal political organization is unknown. There was a tradition among the Munsee-speaking Delawares at Six Nations Reserve that villages formerly had a chief (*kíhkay* 'elder'; also *wayáwe·w*), whose lodge was in the middle, a chief's messenger (*hà·há·sɔw*, literally 'crow'), who lodged on the west side, and a war chief (*làxksəwí·lnəw*), who lodged on the east. Iroquois traits adopted by these Delawares include the recognition of one woman in the chiefly lineage as a chief-maker, and the ceremonial division into moieties, called *wə̆nà·mí·wak* and *wà·panàhkí·wak* (conventionally 'Westerners' and 'Easterners'), terms that were originally the names of dialectal or tribal divisions (Speck 1931–1946; Speck and Moses 1945:3–5, 13, 20–23; Morgan 1964: 153; Brinton 1888:42; Michelson 1922; Hewitt 1936).

At least since the early nineteenth century the Delaware kinship system (both Unami and Munsee) has had semibifurcate terminology in the first ascending generation and Hawaiian cousin terminology. That is, mother's brother is distinguished from father's brother, aunts are not differentiated, and cousins are all classed as brothers and sisters. There is evidence for some differences at an

Table 2. Synonymy for the Four Major Delaware Groups

Type of Label	Groups			
Languages	Unami			Munsee
Dialects	Southern Unami	Northern Unami	Unalachtigo	unnamed
Munsee terms, 18th century	not distinguished	Unami	Unalachtigo	Munsee
Munsee terms, 19th–20th centuries	Unami		Unalachtigo	Munsee, Lenape
Unalachtigo terms (Tatemy)	Unami	Unalimi	not named	Munsee
Unalachtigo terms (Teedyuscung)	Unami	Lenape		Munsee
Unami terms, 20th century	Lenape	not distinguished		Munsee
English terms in 1742	Delaware	Forks Indians		Munsee
English terms in 1758	Delaware			Munsee
English term, 20th century	Delaware			

225

earlier period (Trowbridge 1824a; Morgan 1871; Goddard 1973a).

• SUBSISTENCE The October-December deer hunt continued to be important until intensive settlement and overhunting caused the depletion of game in areas accessible to the Delaware. As late as the 1890s some Bartlesville-area families would go by wagon to the Creek Nation for hunting. In the Ohio Valley, deerskins were the most important commodity for trade, though wapiti and buffalo might also be taken. Zeisberger estimated that each hunter shot 50 to 150 deer each fall and reported that well over 2,000 were killed by Munsees from Goschgosching in 1768. In the early winter hunt small furbearers and bears were taken. March was the time for sugaring, maple sugar being an important trade item. The population was concentrated in the villages in April, when the cornfields were prepared in the bottomlands and one of the major ceremonies was held. After the May planting, men went on the summer deer hunt. The corn was harvested in September, after which the other major ceremony of the year took place (Zeisberger 1910:13-14; Zeisberger and Senseman 1912:103; De Schweinitz 1870:350; J. Edwards 1822:178; Gipson 1938:190, 348-350).

The subsistence activities of the Delawares changed considerably as they moved west and as the character of the frontier evolved. Away from the coasts, fishing came to be of minor importance. Besides maple sugar and syrup, occasional sources of income included corn, ginseng roots (used in the China trade), and natural petroleum. West of the Mississippi buffalo hunting increased greatly in importance, and fur trapping was done in the Rocky Mountains. With their vast knowledge of the West thus acquired, many men took jobs as scouts for the U.S. Army, and some were interpreters. In fact, Delawares could be found in a wide range of frontier occupations, from preachers to scalp-hunters. Some families became increasingly dependent on agriculture and stock raising and would in all essentials fit the popular image of the pioneers (Zeisberger 1910:52-53, 163; Zeisberger and Jungmann 1769-1772; Zeisberger 1885, 2:48, 54-55; Farley 1955; Brandes 1962; Adams 1906:53-54).

A number of soft and hard varieties of corn were grown, each with its particular preferred uses. Pumpkins, several kinds of squash, beans, and melons continued to be raised, supplemented by more recently introduced crops, such as potatoes, cabbage, and turnips. Tobacco was grown by old women, according to one source, and was commonly smoked in a mixture with dried sumac leaves. All sorts of nuts, berries, and fruit were gathered, including some types of acorns, and in later years some Delawares planted apple and peach trees. Among the numerous wild roots that were dug were the water chinquapin or yonkapin (*Nelumbo lutea*), the nuts of which were also eaten, and the Indian potato. Other sources of food included many wild greens (Goddard

1965-1970; Biörck 1731:29; Zeisberger 1910:13, 45-47, 1885, 2:109-110; Harrington 1913:221; Tantaquidgeon 1942:45-50, 74-81; Newcomb 1956:13-14, 17; G. A. Hill 1971).

Corn, the staple food, was prepared in a large variety of ways. Ears of new corn were scraped (aboriginally on a deer or buffalo jawbone) and baked into roasting-ear bread (*məlinkwé·mahpɔ·n*); crumbled and sun-dried this became *ká·hahpɔ·n*, which was stored in sacks for the winter. Roasting the green ears over open coals, then shelling and drying the kernels, produced *tɔs·əməná·na*. Dried corn could be (1) parched and ground fine to make parched corn (*kɔhəmɔ́·k·an*), (2) boiled with ashes and washed thoroughly, producing scalded corn (*pxi·skté·yɔ*), an intermediate cooking stage, or (3) in the case of flint corn, hulled by being pounded with water and winnowed, and cooked into *še·xkani·mahsá·p·a·n* ('sleet mush'). The fine grains sifted out of parched corn were eaten with sugar, honey, or grease; as in the earlier period, this was the hunter's and warrior's ration. The residue of larger grains was boiled into parched-corn mush (*kɔhəmɔ·k·anəs·á·p·a·n*). Scalded corn was cooked whole to make hominy (*sət·é·yɔ*), broken up and cooked into ordinary mush (*sáp·a·n*), or ground into flour to make squaw bread (*pxi·skté·yahpɔ·n*), to which beans, potatoes, pumpkin, cracklings, or berries might be added. Other corn products were dumplings (*čo·skənap·ɔ́·na*)—cakes boiled in water—and fried bread (*saláp·ɔ·n*), sometimes confusingly called squaw bread.

Table 3. Terminologies for the Social Groupings of the Unami-speaking Delaware

	Phratry	*Lineage*
Delaware term	*náni təlhaké·i·n* 'that's his tribe, phratry'	*náni tɔli-wihəlá·i·n* 'that's his lineage'
English, 18th century	tribe	——
English of 20th-century Delawares	clan	family
Morgan 1959:51-52	tribe	tribe, band, subdivision
Morgan 1964:171-172	gens (gentes, pl.), phratry	subgens (subgentes, pl.)
Harrington 1913:210-211	phratry or totemic group	clan
Speck 1931:75-76	zoonymic sept	so-called clans
Wallace 1949:8-10	sib	lineage
Newcomb 1956:48-51	phratry	clan

Other traditional foods recalled by the Delaware in the 1960s were dumplings of grape juice and flour (*šuwas·á·p·a·n*), a preserve made by baking persimmons into loaves (*xi·mí·nahpɔ·n*), and sectioned and dried pumpkins (*ka·x·é·yɔ*). Also eaten was fried meat with gravy (*salas·í·k·an*), jerked meat (*pxaš·í·k·an*), which was either pounded and eaten as is or thrown in the corn kettle, and meat or fowl roasted on sticks set at an angle next to the fire. Vegetables were generally boiled with corn and other food. Drying was the only aboriginal method of preserving perishables (Goddard 1965-1970; Newcomb 1956:18-20; Zeisberger 1910:14, 22, 116; Harrington 1913:221; Weslager 1972:57-58).

• TECHNOLOGY   Many objects known from the seventeenth century continued to be manufactured until the complete material acculturation of the Delawares in the twentieth century. These included most items made of wood or from gourds, and many types of weaving. In contrast, stone- and bone-working went quickly out of practice, and by the mid-eighteenth century shell-tempered pottery was only a memory. Quill-working declined, leaving paints and dyes as the means of decorating manufactured objects. With the universal adoption of European-made guns and hatchets in warfare, armor and shields became obsolete. Wampum continued to be of great importance in diplomatic and religious symbolism and ceremony, but after moving away from the coast the Delawares could obtain it only as a trade item that came ultimately from White wampum makers on the East Coast (see "League of the Iroquois: Its History, Politics, and Ritual," fig. 4). Small bows and blunt or sharpened, unheaded arrows were used for birds and small game (e.g., U.S. National Museum of Natural History, no. 6,962). Dugout and bark canoes were used in Ohio, but west of the Mississippi the only watercraft seem to have been makeshift rafts.

Some details about traditional material culture that are known only from the later period are probably true for earlier times as well. When mortars were hollowed out by burning and scraping, the fire was encouraged by blowing through elderberry stalks and retarded with mud. For travel, miniature mortars were made (fig. 6), or ordinary mortars were lightened by carving in the sides to make a narrow base. Both single-ended and double-ended pestles were used. Hides were generally tanned dry rather than fresh, by a process of soaking with brains, scraping, stretching on a frame, and smoking. Miscellaneous items included soap obtained from soapweed, locust-thorn needles, animal stomachs used for storing lard, and fishbone combs (Goddard 1965-1970; Zeisberger 1910:17, 22-24, 31-32, 86, 94, 152; Barber and Howe 1846:72-73; E.A. Smith 1885).

In the early years of contact, the Delawares learned from European craftsmen the making of splint baskets and silver and German-silver jewelry. Splint basketry was introduced by the Swedish and Finnish settlers on the

Dept. of Anthr., Smithsonian: 6900.

Fig. 6. Delaware mortar and pestle. Buckskin thong used when packing on horseback. Mortar height 38.2 cm, depth of tapered hole 28 cm; collected before 1858.

lower Delaware River and diffused to many Eastern Indian groups, among whom it was an important source of cash income (Brasser 1975; Speck 1947; Weslager 1972:277). The Delaware silver and German-silver industry, which produced buckles, pins, ornamental combs, and the like, was similar to that of the Iroquois, and it, too, appears to have been of North European origin (Barbeau 1940).

In 1907 a large number of items of traditional Munsee material culture was collected from the Delawares of Canada, who for the most part retained them only as heirlooms and curiosities (Harrington 1908). However, some woodworking and basket weaving was still done, as well as a little beadwork and the sewing of cornhusk mats. Specimens were still in existence illustrating two archaic basket types that predated splint basketry—a bag-shaped corn sieve of twisted root fibers and a coiled-grass basket. However, with a few exceptions, the objects encountered were quite similar to those known from the western groups of Delawares.

Trade goods from the Whites became increasingly important, though the same types of items were obtained as formerly. In the nineteenth century the material culture of the Delawares came to largely resemble that of frontier Whites, including many items of iron cooking equipment such as the universal Dutch oven, wagons and tack, beds, chairs, and other furniture, and so forth. Trade with other Indians brought the Delawares buffalo robes while still in the Susquehanna Valley, stone pipes from the Cherokees, and red (catlinite) pipes from the upper Mississippi (J. Edwards 1822:379; Zeisberger 1910:54). The buffalo-skin saddlebag (parfleche) was adopted from the Plains Indians, and there were surely other intertribal borrowings and trade in material items that cannot now be easily documented.

• CLOTHING AND ADORNMENT Though cloth was increasingly used instead of skins, Delaware dress remained conservative until gradually replaced by citizens' clothing in the nineteenth century. Cotton or linen shirts became standard—long hunting shirts for men and shorter types, sometimes dyed red, for women. Otherwise, a man's costume consisted of a breechcloth, ankle-to-hip leggings, and a matchcoat or stroud, while a woman wore knee-length leggings and a stroud skirt, folded lengthwise and wrapped around the hips. One-piece deerskin moccasins with a single seam in front were worn. Clothing was decorated with trade beads and ribbon-appliqué, the

latter being a technique for which Delaware women were particularly noted (fig. 7). Women wore on their shirts circular yoke collars covered with small round silver or German-silver pins (fig. 8) (*ani·xkamá·na* 'brooches'). For dress, a man would wear a richly beaded bandolier pouch, which combined features of European military uniforms and the traditional manner of wearing wampum in crossbelts. Wampum belts were also worn or carried draped around the neck. Silver or German-silver jewelry included single and double crosses, rings, hairbands, and women's large semicircular combs. Men also wore shell gorgets, and women favored circular metal medallions with cut-out designs and shell or bead necklaces.

Grease was applied to the hair, or, at times, marrow or sap. The men's shaved head and scalplock gave way to a hairstyle with two braids, though a small pigtail was kept hanging from the crown to attach feathers or a dyed deerhair roach to (fig. 9). Women parted their hair in the center and wrapped it in a club behind, to which was tied, for dress, an hourglass-shaped ornament called *a·nsi·p·əlá·ɔn,* a flat piece of stiff material covered with cloth and affixed with long ribbons (fig. 10). Men used headbands when wearing the hair loose and seem to have readily adopted the headgear of other tribes, such as

NAA, Smithsonian.

Fig. 7. Jennie Bobb (*tuk·wi·mə́·nši* 'Black Walnut Tree') and her daughter Nellie Longhat of the Western Delawares in full fancy dress, typified by the profusion of brooches and necklaces and the narrow-pattern ribbon-appliqué blanket. Photographed about 1915.

NAA, Smithsonian.

Fig. 8. Sarah Beaver (center) shortly before her death in 1914, with foster granddaughters Bessie Hunter, later Snake (left), and Jane Wilson, later Thomas, Western Delawares, in neat everyday dress as for a trip to town. The girls are wearing home-stitched print dresses and high-button shoes.

GODDARD

NAA, Smithsonian.

Fig. 9. George T. Anderson (*kwəčkipahkí·kamən*) and J.C. Webber (*wi·t·a·p·anó·x·we*), Registered Delawares, in fancy dress that combines old and new elements. They have acculturated hairstyles and hence must tie on deer-hair roaches with leather strings under the chin, rather than to the traditional pigtail. Both gave ethnographic information about Delaware culture to Frank G. Speck. Photographed in Philadelphia Oct. 1932 at a pageant celebrating the 250th anniversary of the landing of William Penn.

buffalo-horn headdresses (known from the Ohio period and later), turbans (in Kansas and Texas) (fig. 11), and later, otterskin caps. Tall hats with ostrich plumes, silver bands, and ribbons were worn by women in ceremonies in Kansas and Oklahoma.

Tattooing, especially of men, continued into the nineteenth century, animal figures being favored. Paint was also used for such designs, as well as for rather elaborate geometric patterns on the face. Women painted more circumspectly, such as with a single red circle on each cheek, and both sexes reddened the central part along the crown of the head. Of the common colors, black paint was made from charcoal and red paint from red ocher (*ɔláman*) or bloodroot (*pé·kɔ·n, Sanguinaria canadensis*).

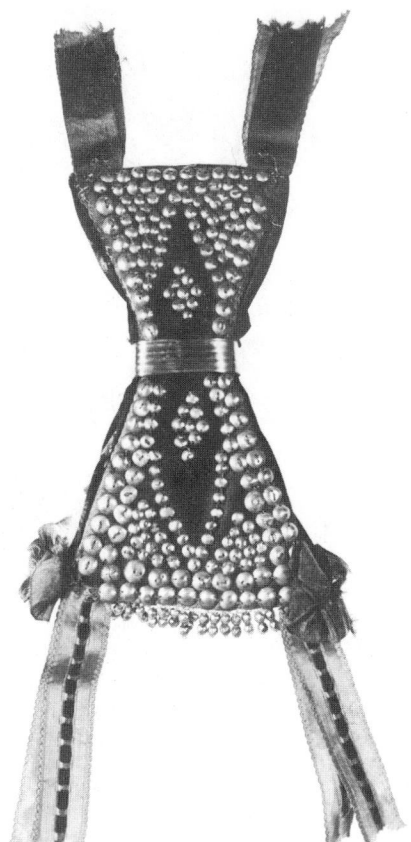

Mus. of the Amer. Ind., Heye Foundation, New York: 2/1654.

Fig. 10. Delaware woman's hair ornament decorated with German-silver buttons. Length 21 cm; collected by M.R. Harrington in Okla. before 1909.

Men often had the helix of the ear cut and sometimes hung beads or jewelry from the resulting loop of flesh. This loop sometimes got torn, and in the nineteenth century men, like women, generally wore simple earrings in pierced ears (fig. 12), or, in the case of acculturated men, gave up ear decorations entirely. As late as 1859 Delaware men with nose ornaments were still to be seen, though uncommon (Goddard 1965-1970; Harrington 1908:412-414, 1913:219-221; Newcomb 1956:108; Zeisberger 1910:12-15, 76, 86-87, 115-116; Zeisberger and Jungmann 1769-1772, 7/26/1771 entry; Jordan 1913, 1:13-14; Gowing 1912:188; Catlin 1831-1832, 1831-1832a; Berlandier 1969:52, 160; Morgan 1959:50; Whipple et al. 1855:26-27; Gipson 1938:108; Feder 1959; T. Stewart 1973; Speck 1931-1946; U.S. National Museum of National History collections, no. 6,939).

• STRUCTURES   In the eighteenth century the Delawares typically lived in one-family peaked-roof bark houses in unplanned, unstockaded villages. The new settlements after the French and Indian War contained increasing numbers of log cabins, which the Delawares hired Whites to build and later learned to build themselves. In 1766 Newcomerstown was described as a village of bark houses, but in 1771 a majority of its 100

Fig. 11. *Non-on-dá-gon, a Chief.* Nonondagumun was assistant chief of one of the three Delaware phratries from about 1826 until his death in 1842. Painted on the Kansas River reservation in the winter of 1831–1832 by George Catlin.

Fig. 12. Jack Harry (*we·ma·khwíkamən*, b.1853, d.1900), Western Delaware leader, in everyday dress with earrings. Photographed in Kay Co., Okla.; negative copy by W.M. Sawyer, Washington, D.C., 1898.

houses were said to be log cabins, that of Chief Netawatwees having a shingle roof, board floors, a staircase, and a stone chimney. There was a significant decline in the number of bark houses and a rise in the number of frame houses during the 1850s in Kansas. Small dome-shaped sweathouses and temporary or auxiliary structures were built, even into the twentieth century; these were made of arched poles covered with available materials. Dugouts are known to have been used in the nineteenth century. When the Delawares captured a number of military tents after Arthur St. Clair's defeat in 1791, some families used these in preference to log cabins. Acculturation in household furnishings was not directly related to changes in house types. The earliest log cabins had traditional raised platforms around the sides for sleeping and sitting, while twentieth-century bark houses were typically furnished with iron bedframes and other movable furniture (Goddard 1965–1970; Zeisberger and Jungmann 1769–1772, 3/23/1771 entry; Beatty 1962:60–61; Zeisberger 1910:17–18, 87; Morgan 1959:55; Brickell 1842; Harrington 1913:217–218; Newcomb 1956:25, 107).

• LIFE CYCLE Birth, child-raising, division of labor, menstruation customs, sexual practices, and marriage and divorce showed enough continuity from the seventeenth through nineteenth centuries so that only a few additional details and changes need here be mentioned.

In addition to the usual washing at birth, infants born in the hot months of summer were rolled in the first subsequent snowfall. The umbilical cord was buried. The cradleboard was on its way out of use in the eighteenth century and was not used in Oklahoma, but two specimens, with protective bows, were collected from the Canadian Delawares in 1907. Babies were put to sleep in baby hammocks, which consisted of a folded blanket suspended on two ropes. In the twentieth century babies were named soon after birth by an older person of the same sex, who was given a small gift in return. Names referred to the hour or season of birth or reflected the puberty vision of the namer. Boys' and girls' names had generally the same range of meanings but differed in derivational and grammatical endings. Nicknames were common, sometimes supplanting the real name in actual use, and in earlier times men especially could change their names. However, many details of names and their use are unclear, and the sources give much conflicting information. White, Black, and Mexican children were often captured or bought, then raised with no social stigma as Delawares. Older individuals might also be adopted and a few prosperous individuals owned slaves. In the 1820s in Indiana, Chief Anderson had a Black man as his interpreter.

Girls were dressed with a small skirt as soon as they walked, but boys went naked except for a belt until given a breechcloth when they began to practice hunting at the age of six or so. From the start they were encouraged to make and feather their own arrows. For a few mornings in the early winter, when the first ice had formed at the edge of the water, children were made to take a dip in a frigid stream; this was thought to provide lifelong protection against colds. At or before puberty, boys were made to feel unwanted and driven out of the house, in hopes that some supernatural being would take pity on them when alone in the woods and give them power, with which to perform some useful occupation in life. Such beings could also appear spontaneously to lost or troubled children and adults, and hence an individual could have power from several visions. In the early twentieth century, conservative Munsees still isolated a girl at her first menses, though in a darkened room rather than a hut. Partial menstrual isolation was also practiced by some Oklahoma Delaware women, in particular by cooking over a separate fire and eating alone. There is a tradition that when the Delaware lived in villages a single large house was built at a distance for all the menstruating women of the community to use together. Zeisberger mentions the special face-concealing headdress of newly marriageable girls but says it was worn for only two months. Traditional marriage involved a series of formalized gift exchanges between the two families, but unformalized marriages and divorces were common. There are indications of the presence of berdaches, but no information on their social role.

In time, mourning practices came to involve fewer formal obligations and conventionalized expressions of grief. In the nineteenth century, perhaps under the influence of European custom, friends and relatives of the deceased spent the night before the burial at a wake, at which the moccasin game (hide-the-bullet) came to be the central activity. At dawn all were awakened, shots were fired to the east, and the coffin was interred. The Oklahoma Delawares extended the body with the head to the east, both at the wake and in the grave, while those in Canada placed the head toward the west. The bereaved spouse was led around the open grave and then off to the east, throwing 12 small sticks alternately to one side and then the other on the way. The spouse was consoled while the grave was being filled, and a funeral meal followed. A post was erected at the head of a man's grave and a cross at the head of a woman's; these were of standard design and carried no iconic messages, though they did—for men only—as recently as the 1820s. Four days after the burial, and annually for four years thereafter, a special meal (wi·hó·mwi·n) is served to someone of the same sex as the deceased, but slightly younger. In contrast, Oklahoma families of Munsee origin hold a funeral feast (tahkwi·phóti·n) at the grave 11 days after the burial. When the Delawares were in Kansas, the Nanticokes,

another submerged group, were still holding their Skeleton Dance, a continuation of their earlier practice of secondary burial. A surviving spouse could not remarry for a year and in some cases was formally released by the relatives of the deceased or (in earlier times) provided with a new mate (Goddard 1965-1970; Zeisberger 1910:88-90, 140, 150; Trowbridge 1972:486-488; Adams 1905:47-48; Harrington 1913:215-216; Speck 1937: 117-134, 142-149; Kinietz 1946:50-53, 111-120; Newcomb 1956:39-43; Weslager 1972:74, 441-442).

● ACTIVITIES Conversation and, in the evenings, social dancing were the favorite pastimes. Story telling was done in turn around the circle of those gathered, or else a single elderly person would tell stories all night, with each member of the audience, young and old, promising the raconteur in advance to perform specific helpful tasks. Games included dice (painted plum pits), jackstraws, and ring-and-pin (kɔ·k·ɔlaškw)—a winter game that was taboo to those born in the summer, and from the Whites, cards and ninepins. Townball (later baseball) replaced lacrosse, and in the nineteenth century a secularized version of the Shawnee men-against-women ball game was taken over. Contests engaged in were shooting at marks, stone lifting, stone throwing, wrestling, and in later years horse racing (Goddard 1965-1970; Zeisberger 1910:17-20, 75-86, 116-119, 125; Newcomb 1956:31-39; Adams 1905:17-19; Kinietz 1946:133; Harrington 1908:409; Weslager 1971, 1972:354).

● RITUAL Ceremonies were of two types, vision recitals and family feasts. By the beginning of the nineteenth century at the latest, the major tribal ceremony, held at corn-planting and at the harvest, was the occasion for the stylized recitation of puberty visions by older men. This evolved into the annual fall Big House ceremony (nkámwi·n) of the late nineteenth and early twentieth centuries. Comparison of the fragmentary descriptions available suggests that this ceremony directly continued the seventeenth-century harvest ceremony, but the dearth of precise information from the eighteenth century makes it impossible to trace its history with completeness. In the more recent ritual, each reciter in turn proceeded counterclockwise around the two central fires of the Big House (xinkwi·k·á·ɔn), a longhouse built in log-cabin style (fig. 13). Pausing at intervals he would describe in a monotone his meeting with his supernatural tutelary and sing the song acquired on that occasion. He and those accompanying behind would then proceed in a shuffling dance until he stopped with a shout of kwi! and continued his recitation. Two singers (tale·k·á·ɔk 'cranes'), drumming on a dried deerskin bound with wooden slats (fig. 14a-c), provided rhythmic and vocal accompaniment. The sequence of recitations was preceded by prayers and exhortations from the chief of the phratry sponsoring the ceremony and was followed by a ritual meal. On the last night of the ceremony the women and younger men recited in a somewhat different format called

Fig. 13. A vision-recital in the Oklahoma Big House ceremony. The reciter, with a rattle in his hand (fig. 14e), and 2 official followers (*nenxkwte·ka·s·i·č·i·k*) have been joined in the procession around the 2 fires by 5 volunteer participants. The 2 singers sit by their drum in the middle of the south wall, and 4 attendants (*ašká·s·ak*) stand with brooms at the doorposts. Delawares who had attended the ceremony considered this a very accurate portrayal, except that, no doubt by artist's license, the spectators, who should be standing during the recital, are shown seated; some also commented that turkey-wing brushes were preferable as brooms (Goddard 1965–1970). Watercolor by Earnest Spybuck, a Shawnee, Dec. 23, 1912.

a·te·hó·mwi·n. Twelve nights was the usual duration in later years, but six- and eight-night ceremonies are also known. Presumably the ceremony grew longer as the originally separate rituals of each village gradually consolidated into a single, tribal ceremony. As recently as 1805 the vigorous, leaping dance of the seventeenth-century ceremony was still performed by the reciter; but by 1824 this had been eliminated and a number of other changes had been instituted, all of them cosmetic rather than fundamental, which suggest some influence from Christian church services. It became customary, for example, for all in attendance to rise while the recitation and singing were in progress. Concomitantly the sticks earlier used as noisemakers could no longer be struck against anything, and so they were merely waved in the air as "prayer sticks" (*mahte·hí·k·anak*) (fig. 14d). Virtually every action in the Big House was ritualized, and a number of distinct subrituals were performed that may originally have been independent ceremonies. An important focus of attention was the 12 carved faces (*masínkɔk*) on the central post and the wall-posts, which represented the Supreme Being (*ki·š·e·ləmúk·ɔnkw* 'Our Creator') (fig. 15). The last Big House ceremony was held in 1924 (Goddard 1965–1970; Gipson 1938:350, 611–614; Trowbridge 1972:494–497; Harrington 1921:81–126; Speck 1931; Voegelin 1942).

The family feasts are not clearly described by early writers, who generally lumped them together as "sacrifices," and hence they are mostly known from the Oklahoma period. Their ritual paraphernalia belonged to individual lineages, each of which conducted its ceremony every year or two in fulfillment of an obligation incurred by an ancestor. Typical were the Grease-Drinking ceremonies (*pəpahsuk·wíhəla·n* or *ahki·wənúma·n*), in which a bear—or in later years a hog—was devoured, grease was drunk and thrown in the fire, and there was some vision recitation. In the Otter-rite Grease-Drinking ceremony, held to appease an otter that had once made a girl sick, the leader wore an inherited otter skin (*kwənúmxkwxe·s*). Also important were the Doll Dances (*lɔ́nk·a·n* 'ordinary dance' or *énta kuhəmə́na kɔ́ntka·t* 'when our grandmother dances'), at which a doll dressed

232

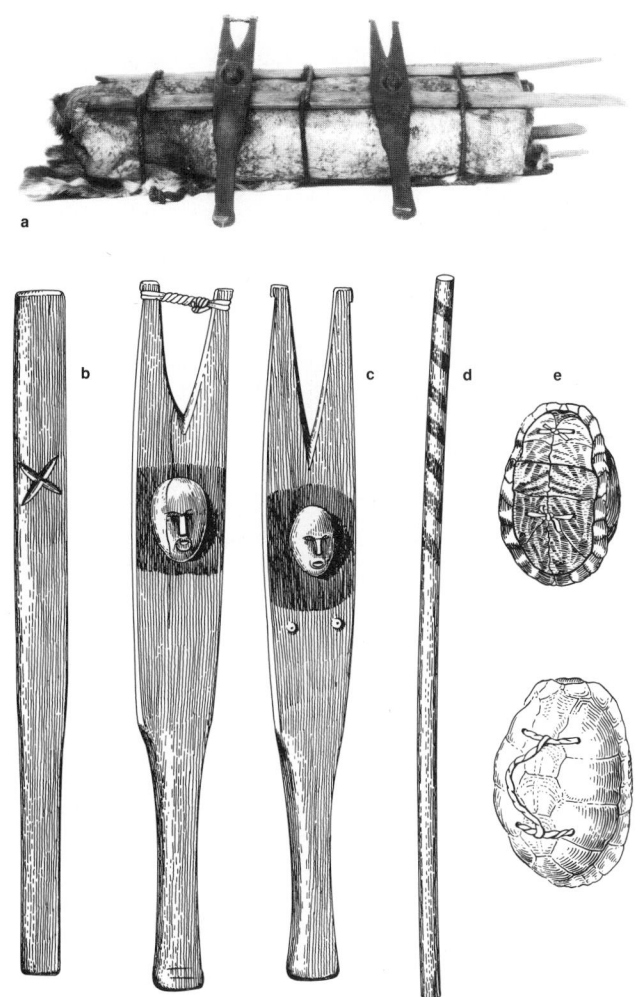

Mus. of the Amer. Ind., Heye Foundation, New York: a, 2/1087; b, 2/1035; c, 2/1042, 2/1043; d, 2/1041.

Fig. 14. Ritual paraphernalia used in the Oklahoma Big House ceremony. a, Deerskin drum with fancy drumsticks, length of drum about 97.1 cm; b, plain drumstick (1 of 2) used on first 8 nights; c, fancy drumsticks used on last 4 nights; d, prayer stick (1 of 12); e, types of box-turtle rattles used by reciter (top) and first follower (bottom). Length of b, about 45.7 cm; c-e same scale. Collected before 1909.

in accurate detail as a woman (or sometimes as a man) was carried on a stick by the men and then the women, alternately, as they danced around the fire in separate rows to the accompaniment of special songs. Other minor ceremonies are mentioned in the sources. There were two kinds of curers, the herb doctor (*məte·ínnu*, archaic *məté·*), who prescribed herbal medicines, and the sweat doctor (*nenpí·ke·s*), who performed shamanistic curing rituals in a small sweathouse (Goddard 1965-1970; Zeisberger 1910:84, 136-140; Jordan 1913, 2:196-197; Harrington 1921:162-183; Speck 1937; Newcomb 1956:65-69, 112-113).

Some individuals had medicine bundles or charms that required private rituals and conferred personal power, sometimes malevolent. Others had equipment for conducting rainmaking rituals. Witches (*no·č·íhuwe* sg.), of

NAA, Smithsonian; insert, Philbrook Art Center: Tulsa. Okla. MI-2911A.

Fig. 15. Interior of Big House, west of Copan, Okla., looking east. The carved face (*masínkw*) on the center post, with smoke hole visible behind, is about 51 cm high, and the incised face (see insert and arrow) on the doorpost (to right of boarded-up door) is 22.4 cm high. Both faces are painted red on right half and black on left and were in 1976 in Philbrook Art Center, Tulsa. Photograph by Frank Speck, Jan. 1932.

both sexes, traveled at night in the form of animal familiars.

When storms approached, tobacco was burned to the Thunderers (*pe·thakhuwé·yɔk*), winged men who protected the world from their enemy, the Great Horned Serpent (*maxáxko·k*) (fig. 16). For the Munsee, the Thunderers (*pə̆lé·sə̆wak*) appear to have been birdlike creatures. In the woods lived the benevolent but capricious Little People (*we·mahte·k·əní·s·ak*), and tales were told of the fearsome, Windigo-like Cannibal Monster (*mhúwe;* Munsee *má·le·w*). The Mask Being (*məsinkhɔ·lí·k·an*), the guardian of all wild animals, was impersonated at the Big House ceremony by a man

Lib. of Congress.

Fig. 16. "A manitou of the Indians" carved over the door of a Delaware house before 1731. Perhaps a representation of the Great Horned Serpent. Woodcut after a sketch by Andrew Hesselius (Biörck 1731:27).

wearing a bearskin costume and a large oval wooden mask, who, thus imbued with power, served as disciplinarian and insured success for the hunters (fig. 17). The manitous associated with the various aspects and forces of nature were addressed and referred to by conventional kinship terms, such as "Our Mother the Earth" and "Our Older Brother the Sun." Delaware mythology is very fragmentarily known (Goddard 1965–1970; Harrington 1921; Speck 1937:70–72, 90–92; Newcomb 1956:59–63, 69–76, 112).

Munsee ceremonies, where known, appear to have been generally similar to those of the Unami, although those of the Six Nations Delaware showed some assimilation to Iroquois Longhouse rituals (Hunter 1954:74–75,

Mus. of the Amer. Ind., Heye Foundation, New York: a, 2/814; b, 2/878; c, 2/879.
Fig. 17. Outfit of the *masinkhɔ·lí·k·an* impersonator. a, bearskin suit consisting of coat, leggings, wooden mask painted like faces in fig. 15 with attached head covering, and bearskin bag worn around the neck; b, rattle made from snapping-turtle shell on wooden handle; c, wooden staff. Length of b, 42.3 cm; a, c, same scale. Collected by M.R. Harrington in Okla. before 1909.

78; P. Jones 1860:43–44 [whence Waubuno, in Harrington 1921:144–145]; Müller 1956:340–344; Harrington 1921:127–143; Speck and Moses 1945).

The Peyote cult came to the Oklahoma Delaware toward the end of the nineteenth century in two varieties. The Big Moon version (fig. 18) was founded by John Wilson of Anadarko and spread by his sister's son George T. Anderson of Dewey, while the later but in some ways less Christianized Little Moon version was introduced into Washington County by Charlie Elkhair (Harrington 1921:185–190; Speck 1933; Petrullo 1934; Newcomb 1956:113–115, 1956a).

WARFARE   Except for the steady improvement in weaponry, the practice of warfare changed little. In the later eighteenth century a warrior's standard equipment included a blanket, extra moccasins, a tumpline for use as a prisoner tie, and a rifle, powder horn, and bullet bag. The conduct of war was highly ritualized, and Delaware scouts in the U.S. Army are even said to have administered warrior medicine (*i·la·ɔpahsí·kan*) to White soldiers to insure success. In the fighting with the Western tribes, the coup stick was adopted. Warriors recounted their deeds publicly in a ritual that involved striking a post (*pahkántama·n*) (Goddard 1965–1970; H.H. Brackenridge 1867:27).

Situation in 1970

By 1970 the Delawares had become almost totally assimilated culturally to the way of life of their White neighbors. Traditional occupations had disappeared, and the Delawares had become integrated into the local and national economies. In Oklahoma they lived scattered among the general population, with concentrations in Washington and Caddo counties. A very few older people spoke Delaware and kept up some old crafts and practices, such as traditional funeral ceremonies, and some families were Peyotists. Since the mid-1960s a powwow had been held annually on the first weekend in June a few miles northeast of Copan in Washington County. The Caddo County Delawares generally attended Caddo and Wichita powwows. An event that was particularly influential in strengthening Delaware identity in Oklahoma was the Indian Claims Commission's award of more than 12 million dollars to Delaware descendants in decisions of 1963, 1969, and 1971 (Weslager 1972:460–462). Much litigation followed, but a Supreme Court decision of February 23, 1977, freed these funds, by then increased by interest to some 15 million dollars, to be paid to the Oklahoma Delawares.

In Canada the Delawares lived in 1970 mostly on three Ontario reserves—at Moraviantown and Muncey on the Thames River and at Six Nations Reserve on the Grand River (fig. 1). Virtually no distinctive cultural practices survived, except at Moraviantown, where the language was still spoken in a few families and there were periodic attempts to organize classes in it for children.

234

Fig. 18. Big Moon peyote meeting among the Registered Delaware, in canvas tepee, about 1912. Fire guard brushes evil influences away from entering man with eagle-feather fan, while road-man (or speaker) shows him to seat. At left, shown as happening at same time by artist's license, man holding long cross (or "arrow") and eagle-feather fan in left hand and gourd rattle in right is singing peyote songs to accompaniment of water drum being played at his right. The crescent-shaped mound to the west of the central fire is the "moon." In inset, right, all have filed out carrying sacred paraphernalia to greet the rising sun. Watercolor by Earnest Spybuck.

Among all groups intermarriage with other Indians and Whites had been so extensive that population figures were no longer very meaningful, but some figures for earlier periods are given in table 1.

Synonymy

In this synonymy no attempt has been made to list the variants of names used merely as place-names, but it should be noted that most bands took their names from places in their territory. Also, the earliest use of each spelling variant has not been searched out in most cases. The various terms for the four major Delaware groups are tabulated in table 2.

Tribal Names

The Delaware take their English name from the Delaware River, which derives its name from Sir Thomas West, Lord de la Warr, the first governor of Virginia. The English in Maryland used the terms Delaware Bay Indians, 1661 (Maryland (Colony) Council 1885–1912, 1:414) and Delaware Indians, 1684 (Hall 1910:440),

though the latter expression came into use in Pennsylvania only later on, for groups that had already moved inland away from the Delaware River, 1709 (Pa. Col. Recs. 2:469). Delawares dates from 1721 (NYCD 5:623). The dialect variant Deleways, 1760 (MHSC, ser. 4, 9:248) or Dillaways, 1805 (W. Clark 1942) sometimes appears. The term Delaware was at first applied only to the Indians living on or emigrant from the lower Delaware— the Schuylkill Indians, and those that amalgamated with them—as opposed to the Forks Indians, 1744 (Boyd 1938:34). Later the term was used to include the Forks Indians, 1758 (W. Johnson 1921–1965, 2:825); and eventually it was extended to cover all the groups treated in this article, all of whom use it as a self-designation.

The Unami self-designation is ləná·p·e (etymologically lən- 'ordinary, real, original' plus -a·p·e 'person'), found as Renappi in Swedish, 1655 (Rising 1912:156); Lenappys or Delaware Indians, 1728 (Pa. Arch. 1:230); Ellenopey, 1785 (Denny 1860:479); and eventually Lenape, 1818 (Heckewelder 1876:xxiv). The tendency has been to restrict this term to one's own subgroup, as apparently in Teedyuscung's distinction between the

235

"Lenopi" and the Unami (Pa. Col. Recs. 7:665; Thomson 1759:91), and as is done by the Oklahoma Delaware. The resulting ambiguity seems to have given rise to *ləni-ləná·p·e* 'real Lenape', which appears as Lennilenape (Zeisberger 1776), Lenni-Lenape, 1779-1780 (Zeisberger 1910:114), and Linnelinopies, 1785 (Jefferson 1801:198). This term is rejected as redundant by twentieth-century speakers. Shawnee *lena·pe* 'Delaware' (Voegelin 1938-1940, 9:352) is borrowed from Unami. The Munsee cognate *ləná·pe·w* is sometimes used for 'Indian'.

Another self-designation is attested as Woapanachke, 1779-1780 (Zeisberger 1910:114), O-puh-nár-ke (Morgan 1871:289), and *ɔ·p·anáhki* (A. Pike 1861, phonemicized). This would mean literally 'person of the eastern country'. It was once said to be the Unami name for the Unalachtigo (Woapannachkis in 1804—William A. Hunter, personal communication 1972, correcting Gipson 1938:516), but phonologically it cannot originally have been a Unami word. Munsee *wà·panáhki·w* (Hewitt 1936 and Speck and Moses 1945:20, phonemicized), which may be the ultimate source of all these forms, was in the twentieth century the name of one of the moieties among the Six Nations Delawares. In any case this word was the source of the name of the Delaware in several languages (Trowbridge 1972:473), such as Kickapoo *waapanahkiiha, aapanahkiiha* (Voorhis 1967:295), Osage *wábaniki* (La Flesche 1932:183), Caddo *hapanahkih, hapanahkiyah* (Wallace L. Chafe, personal communication 1973), and Cherokee *akwa·hnki* (Floyd G. Lounsbury, personal communication 1977; cf. Mooney 1900:508).

Other names for the Delaware are Seneca *shakaną̌ʔka·ʔ* (sg. Chafe 1967:79), Wyandot *haⁿdashayá·ną̌ʔ* (Hewitt 1889; Barbeau 1960:98), and Wichita Nar-wah-ro, 1854 (Mooney 1907b:387). The Iroquoian names are variants of a general name for Algonquians, for example, Oneida *akotsha·káną̌ʔ* (Floyd G. Lounsbury, personal communication 1975) and other forms in Mooney (1907b:387). Some French sources extended the name Loup to the Delaware, 1684 (NYCD 9:261-262).

The sign for the Delaware in the Plains sign language was a downward stroking motion made at the back of the head with the flat hand, fingers together. This is said to refer to the ribbons of the women's hair ornament (Goddard 1965-1970).

Major Subgroup Names

Forks Indians: Fork-Indians, Fork Indians, 1742 (Boyd 1938:34), Delawares, from the Forks, 1742 (Pa. Col. Recs. 4:585). In the first half of the eighteenth century, a group at the Forks of the Delaware (Lehigh River, Pennsylvania), amalgamating natives of the area and emigrants from the Trenton area of New Jersey. Apparently equivalent to Unalimi.

Manhattan: a linguistic term, 1655 (Van der Donck 1841:206) for the variety of Delaware later called Munsee; from the name of the island. Also used generally for the Indians in the area, as Manhates, 1624 (Wassenaer 1909:68).

Munsee: Monseys, 1756 (NYCD 7:178); Munsey, 1757 (NYCD 7:285); Munsy, 1765 (W. Smith 1765:89); Minsi or Monsees (Barton 1798:xxvii); Munsees, 1808 (J. Morse 1822:111); Amentis in French, 1758 (Stevens and Kent 1941:135, 136). The Delaware terms are Unami *mwə́ns·i, mɔ́ns·i* and Munsee *mə́n'si·w*, meaning 'person from Minisink'. Borrowed forms are Mahican Wemintheew, 1792 (Aupaumut 1827:77) and Shawnee *homenʔθi* (Voegelin 1938-1940, 10:455). This name replaced Minisink to designate the consolidated group of emigrant Munsee speakers of whom the Minisinks were the major component. As a linguistic term Munsee includes all groups of any period that spoke dialects of the language spoken by the Munsee group, even though not all such groups were or are Munsees in the political sense.

Northern Unami: A linguistic term for the variety of Unami spoken by the Forks Indians and used by the Moravian missionaries (Goddard 1971a:14).

Savanoos: 1655 (Van der Donck 1841:206); Sauwanew from Hendricks, 1616 (Stokes 1915-1928, 2: C. pl. 24); Sauwanoos, 1625 (De Laet 1909:53); in translation 'the Southern Indians' in Dutch, 1650, 1658 (NYCD 1:367, 13:95) and the South Indians in English, 1669 (NYCD 13:423). Presumably Munsee *šá·wano·w* 'southerner' (in later years only 'Shawnee'). A general term used on the Hudson for all the Unami speakers along the Delaware, including the Unalachtigo. Also used specifically as a linguistic label (Van der Donck 1841).

Southern Unami: A linguistic term for the variety of Unami spoken by the Delawares of Pennsylvania and New Jersey below the falls at Trenton and by their descendants in Oklahoma (Goddard 1971a:14).

Unalachtigo: Wunalachtico, 1779-1780 (Zeisberger 1910:141); Unalàchtigo or Wunalàchtigo (Barton 1798:xxvii); Unalâchtgo, 1818 (Heckewelder 1876:51). The Munsee name for the Unami speakers of west-central New Jersey. Probably to be phonemicized *wə̌nàláhtko·w* (cf. Harrington 1913:208); the translation is unknown, but that of Brinton (1885:36) cannot be correct. The Unami pronunciation is reflected in Wonalatoko (Brinton 1885:88). This group was the major part of the "Jersey Indian" component of the Forks Indians.

Unalimi: "Unalimi or up River Indians" from Tatemy, 1757 (Weslager 1972:47). Would be phonemically *wənáləmi·w* 'person from upstream'. Appears once, as the Unalachtigo name for the Forks Indians. Probably the same as what Teedyuscung called the "Lenopi" (Pa. Col. Recs. 7:665).

Unami: Wename, Unamies from Teedyuscung, 1757 (Pa. Col. Recs. 7:665, 726); Wanami (Thomson 1759:84); Unami, 1779-1780 (Zeisberger 1910:141); Unàmis or

Wanàmi (Barton 1798:xxvii). This term was used both in Munsee (*wŏná·mi·w*) and in Unalachtigo (presumably *wŏná·mi·w*) and means 'person from downriver'. Having different points of reference, the speakers of the two languages used it in significantly different ways. In Munsee it referred to the Indians downstream from the Delaware Water Gap on the west side, those on the east side being called Unalachtigos (Zeisberger 1910;141); twentieth-century Munsee speakers apply it to speakers both of Northern Unami and of Southern Unami. In Unalachtigo "Unami" referred to the Indians west of the river below Tohickon Creek, as opposed to the Unalimi above the creek, according to Tatemy and Teedyuscung. Mahican used the borrowed form Wenaumeeu (Aupaumut 1827:76) to refer to the Unami-speaking Delaware. As a linguistic term Unami is used as the name of the language that comprised the Northern Unami, Southern Unami, and Unalachtigo dialects.

Munsee-speaking Bands

Canarsee: a village name used by historians (Ruttenber 1872:72-73; Bolton 1920:358-361) for "the tribe of Marechhawieck, Nayeck and their neighbors," 1645 (NYCD 13:18). Variants are: Canarise, 1647 (NYCD 14:66); Cannarse, 1650 (NYCD 1:449), Canaresse, 1660 (NYCD 13:184); Marychkenwikingh, 1637 (NYCD 14:5); Marechkawieck, 1644 (NYCD 14:56); Neyick, 1649 (NYCD 13:25); Nayack, 1657 (NYCD 14:394); Najack, 1660 (NYCD 13:167). This last was on the west end of Long Island, not at present Nyack in Rockland County.

Christian Indians (Zeisberger 1776:title; Schoolcraft 1851-1857, 5:495): the self-designation preferred by some of the Delawares at Moraviantown, Ontario, equivalent to Munsee *ké·ntŏwe·s* 'one who prays, Moravian convert'.

Esopus: Hendricks, 1616 (Stokes 1915-1928, 2: C. pl. 24); Æsopus, showing attraction in spelling to the name of the Greek fabulist, 1660 (NYCD 13:165); Soopus, 1658 (NYCD 13:96); Sopus Indyans, 1675 (NYCD 12:250). The Munsee form was apparently *só·psi·w* or *wsó·psi·w* 'person from *só·pŏs*' (cf. Kinietz 1946:120 and the nickname *šó·pši·w* in Speck and Moses 1945:2, 17).

Hackensack: Achkinkehacky, 1645 (NYCD 13:18); Hackinkesacky, 1660 (NYCD 13:167); and Hackingsack, 1663 (NYCD 13:350).

Haverstraw: Dutch spelling was Haverstroo (NYCD 13:167). Also called Remahenoc, 1649 (NYCD 13:25); Rumachenanck, 1660 (NYCD 13:148); and Reweghnongh, 1664 (NYCD 13:375).

Highland Indians: 1665 (NYCD 13:52). Perhaps originally a separate group in the highlands east of the Hudson, but the designation was later generalized to include the Wappinger ("the Wappings or Highland savages," 1659, NYCD 13:104), and still later it was

defined as "the *Wappingoes & Wickersheck* &c," 1669 (NYCD 13:440). Translates the Dutch *Hogelander*.

Kichtawank: Kichtawanck, 1644 (NYCD 13:17); Kichtawanghs, 1645 (NYCD 13:18); Kechtawangh, 1663 (NYCD 13:300); Kightenwangh, 1664 (NYCD 13:375). Ruttenber's (1872:79) Kitchawong is an error.

Matinecock: Matinnekonck, Dutch, 1644 (NYCD 14:56); Mattinnicock, English, 1666 (NYCD 14:587). Perhaps not a Munsee-speaking band.

Massapequa: Dutch spellings are Marossepinck, 1639 (NYCD 14:15); Marospinc, 1644 (NYCD 14:56); Marsepain, 1655 (NYCD 13:58); Marsepingh, 1660 (NYCD 13:147). English spellings include Masepeage, 1643 (NYCD 14:530) and Marsapege, 1657 (NYCD 14:416). Perhaps not a Munsee-speaking band.

Minisink: Manissings, 1663 (NYCD 13:324); Menissinck, 1663 (NYCD 13:289); Minnissingh, 1660 (NYCD 12:306); Minnissinke, English, 1681 (NYCD 13:551). Later called Munsee, after absorbing other groups; note "Munsey or Minisink Indians" (Thomson 1759:71). The Munsee form would have been *mŏnásŏnk*, probably an archaic word for 'on the island' (cf. Barton 1798:2 and Gatschet cited in Mooney 1907c), and the name Munsee is derived from the same stem. There is no possible connection with any word for 'stone' or 'mountain', as in Brinton (1885:36).

Navasink: Newesink, 1658 (NYCD 13:84); Neuwesink, 1660 (NYCD 13:163); Nevesinck, 1661 (NYCD 13: 204, 239); Navecinx, 1671 (NYCD 12:493); Na-ussin or Neversinks, 1701 (Wolley 1902:65).

Nochpeem: 1644 (NYCD 13:17). Perhaps these were the original Highland Indians, but data on them are scanty.

Raritan: 1660 (NYCD 13:163). The group referred to as "the Indians, living in the Raretangh," 1643 (NYCD 13:7) were apparently not the same as "the tribe called *Raritanoos,* formerly living at Wiquaeskeck [Westchester County]," 1649 (NYCD 13:25).

Rechgawawank: found as Rechgawawanc, 1643 (NYCD 13:14) and as Rechgawawanck, 1645 (NYCD 13:18).

Rockaway: English, 1643 (NYCD 14:530); Rechouwhacky, 1639 (NYCD 14:15); Reckonhacky, 1644 (NYCD 14:56); Rechkewick, 1647 (NYCD 14:68); Rechqua Akie, 1655 (De Vries 1909:230); Rechkawyck, 1660 (NYCD 13:147); Reckowacky, 1660 (NYCD 13:184); Reckomacki, 1660 (NYCD 14:474); Rechowacky, 1663 (NYCD 13:322).

Sinsink: Sintsinck, 1643 (NYCD 13:14); Sintsings, 1645 (NYCD 13:18); Sinsincks, 1663 (NYCD 13:302); Sinsincqs, 1663 (NYCD 13:303).

Siwanoy: attested as Siwanois, 1625 (De Laet 1909:44), but the Sywanois on Block's 1614 map (Stokes 1915-1928, 2: C. pl. 23) are located in northeastern Massachusetts.

Staten Island Indians: 1669 (NYCD 13:428).

Tankitekes: 1655 (De Vries 1909:211). Location and synonyms uncertain.

Tappan: 1669 (NYCD 13:428); Tappaens, 1645 (NYCD 13:18); Tappaen, 1663 (NYCD 13:300); Toppaun, 1701 (Wolley 1902:65).

Waoranecks: 1625 (De Laet 1909:46); Warenecker, 1624 (Wassenaer 1909:68).

Wappinger: seventeenth-century variants include Wappinck, 1644 (NYCD 13:17); Wappings, 1663 (NYCD 13:302); Wappingers, 1664 (NYCD 13:365); Wappingoes, English, 1669 (NYCD 13:440). The group west of the Hudson in the eighteenth century is referred to as Wawpings or Pomptons, Wapings, Opings or Pomptons (S. Smith 1765:456, 470, 480); Wapingers, and Opines or Wapings (Thomson 1759:172, 179). The name would be Munsee *wá·pi·nkw* 'opossum', 1824 (Captain Chipps in Kinietz 1946:120; Heckewelder in Goddard 1971a:20); it has no connection with any word for 'easterner'. There is no evidence that a "Wappinger Confederacy" (Ruttenber 1872:77–85; Mooney 1910f; Speck 1928a:map facing p. 212) under this or any other name extended from the Hudson to the Connecticut (Goddard 1971a:20–21).

Warranawankongs: (cf. de Laet 1909:46); Waronawanka, 1616 (Stokes 1915–1928, 2: C. pl. 24); Warrawannankonckx, 1624 (Wassenaer 1909:68); Waerinnewangh, 1655 (NYCD 13:47); Warynawoncks, 1663 (NYCD 13:259).

Wiechquaeskeck: 1664 (NYCD 13:299, 364, 376); Wiquaeskecks, 1645 (NYCD 13:18); Wiequaskeck, 1655 (NYCD 13:52); Wickerscreek Indyans, 1671, 1676 (NYCD 13:460, 495); "*Wee-quoss-cah-chau i.e. Westchester* Indians," 1701 (Wolley 1902:65).

Unami-speaking Subgroups

Armewamex: 1629 (Dunlap and Weslager 1958); Armeomecks, 1625 (De Laet 1909:53); Ermomex, 1630 (De Laet 1909:52); Armewamus, 1663 (NYCD 12:430).

Atsayonck: 1629 (Dunlap and Weslager 1958); Axion, 1641 (Weslager 1954).

Big Siconese: Groote Siconese in Dutch, 1629 (Dunlap and Weslager 1958); Sickoneysincks, 1659 (NYCD 2:71).

Brandywine Indians: this group is discussed by Weslager (1972:178).

Little Siconese: called Kleyne Siconese in Dutch, 1629 (Dunlap and Weslager 1958).

Mantaes: 1629 (Dunlap and Weslager 1958), 1662 (NYCD 12:370); Manteses, 1641 (Weslager 1954); Mantas, 1656 (NYCD 1:598).

Naraticonck: 1629 (Dunlap and Weslager 1958).

Okehocking: referred to in 1701 as "the Okehockings . . . on the banks of Ridley and Crumb creeks" (Weslager 1972:171).

Remkokes: 1629 (Dunlap and Weslager 1958); Ramcock, 1641 (Weslager 1954).

Sankhikan: Sangicans, Stankekans, 1616 (Stokes 1915–1928, 2: C. pl. 24); Sanhicans, 1625 (De Laet 1909:53); Sancicans, 1628 (De Rasieres 1909:103); Sankikans, 1629 (Dunlap and Weslager 1958), 1633 (De Laet 1909:57–58).

Schuylkill Indians: as the nucleus of the nascent Delaware tribe among the emigrants on the Susquehanna this was the first group to be called Delawares, 1742 (Boyd 1938:34). They were also referred to as Delawares, of Shamokin, 1742 (Pa. Col. Recs. 4:585).

Sewapois: 1629 (Dunlap and Weslager 1958).

New Jersey Groups in 1758

Ancocus (for Rancocus) Indians, Crosswick Indians, Indians from Cranbury, Mountain Indians, Rariton Indians, Southern Indians (S. Smith 1765:442).

Sources

Information on the Delaware is scattered in a vast number of sources that have been written over a period of 350 years and are of extremely uneven quality. The most dependable single-volume ethnography (Newcomb 1956) and history (Weslager 1972) are good places to start. For the seventeenth century Van der Donck (1841) is the most complete, but since he lived at different times both near Albany and on the lower Hudson, some details may refer only to the Mahican. Similarly, Zeisberger (1910), the best source for the eighteenth century in spite of his inadequate treatment of religion, rarely indicates tribal appurtenance. Less satisfactory, though anecdotally useful, is Heckewelder (1876). A detailed but less complete ethnography from the nineteenth century is Trowbridge (1972). For the twentieth century much useful information is in Harrington (1908, 1913, 1921), Speck (1931, 1937), and Kinietz (1946). Extensive published documentation of Delaware history is in New York colonial documents (NYCD), New York Historical Society collections (NYHSC), Pennsylvania colonial records (Pa. Col. Recs.), Pennsylvania archives (Pa. Arch.), W. Johnson (1921–1965), and the mission diaries: Zeisberger (1885, 1972), Zeisberger and Senseman (1912), and Gipson (1938). For the mission Delawares the modern study is Gray (1956). Other special historical studies are, for the Dutch period, Trelease (1960); for the Indiana period, C. N. Thompson (1937); for Kansas, Morgan (1959) and Farley (1955, which lacks documentation); for Indian Territory and Oklahoma, M. H. Wright (1951:145–155). Much information on the Delawares in Ohio is in the Government Dockets before the Indian Claims Commission (E. W. Voegelin 1974, 1974a). Manuscript collections relating to the Delaware are in the American Philosophical Society, Philadelphia; the National Archives and the National Anthropological Archives, Smithsonian Institution, Washington; the Kansas State

Historical Society, Topeka; and the Bartlesville Public Library, Oklahoma. Important collections of ethnographic specimens are in the Museum of the American Indian, Heye Foundation, and the American Museum of Natural History, New York; the Museum of Natural History, Smithsonian; and the Philbrook Art Center, Tulsa, Oklahoma. Some of the poorly documented seventeenth- and early eighteenth-century Indian objects in the Nationalmuseum, Copenhagen; the Statens Etnografiska Museum, Stockholm; and the Skokloster Slott (administered by the Kunglig Livrustkammaren), Stockholm, are probably Delaware.

Nanticoke and Neighboring Tribes

CHRISTIAN F. FEEST

Language and Territory

When first visited by European explorers and colonists, the region of southern Maryland between the lower Potomac River and Chesapeake Bay and most of the Delmarva peninsula—including two counties in Virginia, nine in Maryland, and adjacent parts of Delaware—was inhabited by a number of Algonquian-speaking tribes* some of whom were joined together to form a smaller number of larger political entities (fig. 1). Their territory bordered upon that of the related Delawares to the northeast, various Iroquoian-speaking and other groups to the northwest, and the Algonquian tribes of Virginia to the south.

Most of the Virginia Eastern Shore was inhabited by a group of tribes often collectively referred to as Accomac; however, some bands near the Maryland line were more closely allied to the Pocomokes on the bay side to the north of them. The tribes on the Atlantic side of eastern Maryland, although perhaps not fully united politically, may be subsumed under the name of the major group of this region, the Assateagues. The Nanticokes and Choptanks inhabited the drainage systems of the rivers that bear their names, while the little-known Wicomisses and Tockwoghs were first encountered on the Chester and Sassafras rivers respectively. All tribes in southern Maryland, with the possible exception of the Patuxents, were part of the Conoy group, so called by their Iroquoian name to differentiate between the larger political unit and its leading tribe, the Piscataway. Some Conoy bands lived on both sides of the Potomac, and groups like the Doeg moved back and forth throughout the seventeenth century.

Evidence for the linguistic affiliation of these groups comes from the reports of early observers and from a very small number of linguistic records, which include a Choptank word list recorded in 1792; Nanticoke word lists taken in 1785, around 1800, and in 1914 (Speck 1927:35-76); Piscataway materials dating to the time of the Jesuit mission (Harrison 1633); and a few Piscataway phrases (Md. Arch. 49:483) and Assateague (Kickotank) words (Norwood 1844). John Smith, exploring the

*The languages of the Nanticokes and neighboring Algonquian tribes are extinct. Lacking adequate early recordings, the spelling of native terms and proper names follows their historical orthography.

Chesapeake Bay in 1608, found the Accomac language the same as the tribes of tidewater Virginia, while that of the groups to the north of them was different (Barbour 1969:344, 407).

According to Nanticoke traditions recorded by Heckewelder (1819:74), the Nanticokes at an early date detached themselves from the Delawares and settled on the Eastern Shore of Maryland where they increased and subsequently split up into several separate groups; one of them, the Conoy, removed to the western shore between the Potomac and Susquehanna rivers. In a speech delivered in 1660 to the governor of Maryland, the Conoy dated their arrival in southern Maryland from the east to a time 13 generations of chiefs before 1636 (Md. Arch. 3:403). Archeology so far provides no conclusive evidence to confirm these traditions, which are supported by the close linguistic relationship. The Accokeek Creek site on the Potomac River below Washington, which was last inhabited by the Conoy, shows no significant break in cultural development throughout Woodland times.

Seventeenth Century

Throughout the early history of Maryland, there is some confusion about tribal identities and alliances. In the case of identities this is explained by the fact that groups frequently were known by the name of their village, which resulted in the use of a different name every time a new village was established. This situation applies, for example, to the designations Moyaons and Accokeek and may hold for rarely mentioned groups such as the Mikikiwomans, Manesquesend, Lamasconsons, and Kighahnixons (all of southern Maryland). Although some Maryland groups shared their names with Virginia Algonquian groups (Pamunkey, Potapaco, Mattapanient), this implies neither identity nor any especially close relationship between the namesakes. Even within the area under discussion separate groups bore the same name (Kickotank, Nasswatex or Nuswattocks).

The question of alliances is related to the political organization of the groups. The Conoy, Assateague, and Accomac (fig. 2) consisted of several bands each led by a chief, while a varying degree of central authority was vested in a paramount leader referred to as "emperor" by the English. At least in the case of the Accomac, the

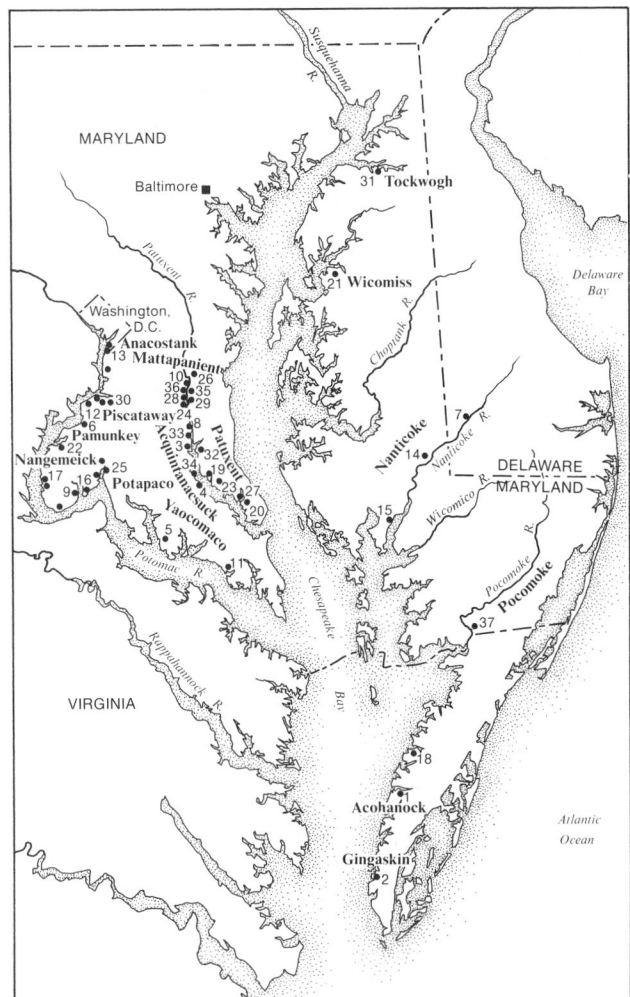

Fig. 1. Tribes and villages, 1608. Based on John Smith's map with additions from the John White map of 1585/6. Tribal names according to later usage, village names according to the source. Locations of some villages are tentative. 1, Accohanock; 2, Accowmack (Combec); 3, Acquaskack; 4, Acquintanacsuck; 5, Cecomocomoco; 6, Cinquaoteck; 7, Kuskarawaok; 8, Macocanaco; 9, Mataughquamend; 10, Mattapanient; 11, Monanauk; 12, Moyaons; 13, Nacotchtank; 14, Nantaquack; 15, Nause; 16, Nushemouck; 17, Nussameck; 18, Nuswattocks (Mashawatoc); 19, Onuatuck; 20, Opanient; 21, Ozinies; 22, Pamacocack; 23, Pawtuxunt; 24, Pocatamough; 25, Potapaco; 26, Quactataugh; 27, Quomocack; 28, Quotough; 29, Tauskus; 30, Tessamatuck; 31, Tockwogh; 32, Wascocup; 33, Wasapokent; 34, Wasinacus; 35, Wepanawomen; 36, Wesamcus; 37, Wighcocomoco. The following villages are mentioned by Smith (1884: 414, 567-568) but cannot be localized: Assacomoco or Attoughcomoco and Paccamaganaut (both Patuxent villages) and Arsek or Arseek and Soraphanigh or Sarapinagh (both Nanticoke villages).

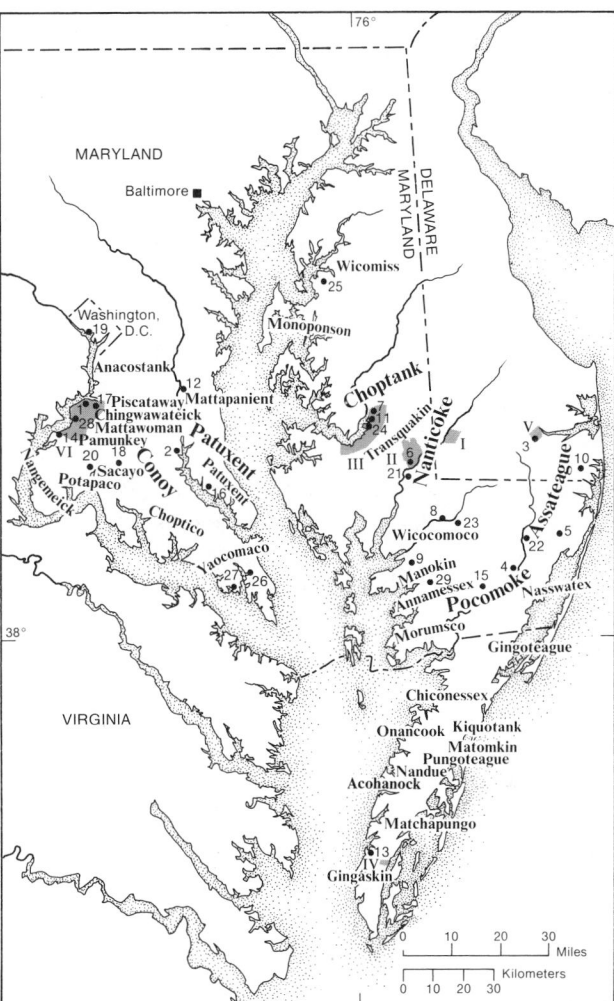

Fig. 2. Tribes and villages, 1620-1837. Locations of some villages tentative. Not all synonyms for villages are given. Dates give period of documented or inferred occupation. 1, Accokeek; 2, Acquaskac, 1640; 3, Askequeson, 1705-1742; 4, Askiminikansen, 1670-1686; 5, "Buckingham," ?-1686; 6, Chicacoan, 1668-1723; 7, Choptank Fort, 1683-ca. 1700; 8, Great Monie, 1662-1680; 9, Kickotank (Assawoman), 1650, 1685-1688; 10, Locust Neck, 1665-1837; 11, Mattapanient, 1634; 12, Pamunkey, 1670, 1700; 13, Patuxent, 1634; 14, Piscataway (Kittamaquund), 1632-1680; 15, Piscataway Fort (Sacayo), 1680-1692; 16, Piscataway Fort (Rock Creek), 1692-1697; 17, Potapaco, 1632-1663; 18, Puckamee, 1678; 19, Queponca, 1678-1686; 20, Trasquakin, 1659-1678; 21, Wicomiss, 1634; 22, Yaocomaco, 1634; 23, Yaocomaco, 1642; 24, ?, 1670; 25, ?, 1620. Reservations: I, Broad Creek, 1711-1768; II, Chicacoan, 1684-1768; III, Choptank 1669-1799 (reduced in size); IV, Gingaskin, 1641-1813; V, Indian River, 1711-1744 (reduced in size); VI, Piscataway, 1668-1700. These Nanticoke villages are mentioned for 1707 but cannot be localized (Pa. Col. Recs. 2:387): Matcheattochousie, Matchcouchtin, Witichquao, Natahquois, Teahquois, Byengeahtein, Pohecommoati. Places on the Eastern Shore mentioned in 1678 that cannot be localized (Md. Arch. 15:236): Parrahockon, Tundotanake, Cottingham Creek.

subordinate chiefs were tributary to the head chief (Anonymous 1671-1673:143, 150). Among the Conoy, members of the head chief's family could rule over dependent villages (Hall 1910:158). The Nanticokes also had an "emperor" (who during the late seventeenth century was replaced by two coequal leaders), but neither subdivisions (except for towns) nor subchiefs are ever mentioned. The Pocomokes, on the other hand, consisted of several bands, but their head chief was only known as a "king," perhaps due to some kind of loose and/or late dependent relationship with the Assateagues. The Choptanks had several chiefs (perhaps repre-

241

senting villages), but central authority was weakly developed and "emperors" are therefore only infrequently referred to; while there is strong evidence for Choptank independence, they are at various times mentioned as if part of the Nanticokes or Assateagues, reflecting temporary shifts of location between 1684 and 1694 (Feest 1975). Similarly, the tribes along Patuxent River were apparently lacking a strong central leadership while largely independent of the Conoy. Not enough is known about the groups on the Eastern Shore north of the Choptanks to allow any statement on their organizational form and their alliances.

Demography

Data on the population of the Nanticokes and their neighbors at contact time and throughout the colonial period are incomplete and unreliable. John Smith's figures (table 1) are the only ones relating to the whole area at a given time; but his estimates for Accomac cover only two tribes out of many more, and from later figures and evidence on depopulation it can be seen that the total he gives is at least four times too low. The same applies to his other Eastern Shore estimates. For southern Maryland, Smith is not so far off, primarily because he did not miss so many groups. However, in view of Fleet's estimate (Neill 1876:26, 35) of 5,000 persons on both sides of the Potomac River (excluding the Patuxents) and other evidence, even these figures could conservatively be doubled (Feest 1973). An informed guess for the population of the tribes here described during early contact times would be upward of 12,000 persons.

By 1700 Accomac population was said to have decreased by 90 percent, even though there were few armed conflicts in this subarea. Although only one epidemic has been recorded for Accomac during that century, smallpox and other diseases introduced by Europeans were primarily responsible for population decline in the whole area (Feest 1973; Md. Arch. 23:247, 25:256). The use of poisons by the Nanticokes has been likewise blamed for depopulation, but ruthless wars of extermination as waged by the English colonists against the Wicomisses, as well as early quarrels with Iroquoian groups, probably had a greater impact (Marye 1938–1939; Neill 1876:26).

Contact and Dislocation

The earliest evidence for European contacts with Indians of this area dates to the 1580s when the English Roanoke colonists located three Indian villages on Accomac and Spanish explorers left records of their activities in the Potomac area and on the Eastern Shore (Quinn 1955, 1:map 7, 2:807–809). Interaction increased with the establishment of the Jamestown colony in 1607.

Table 1. Population estimates, 17th century

	1608[a]	1621	1632	1634	1648	1697[i]
Accomac	400[b]	2,000[e]				335[j]
Assateague						——[k]
Choptank						——[k]
Conoy	1,000[c]		2,500[f]	1,665[g]		265–300[l]
Nanticoke	665					10 towns[m]
Patuxent	665[d]					
Pocomoke	335					——[k]
Tockwogh	335					
Wicocomoco						
Wicomiss	200				235[h]	

[a] These estimates, by John Smith (Barbour 1969:341–344), are given in terms of warriors. Smith's own ratio of 3:10 is used throughout the table for computation of total population.

[b] Including the Accomac (Gingaskin) and Acohanock.

[c] Including the Yaocomaco, Potapaco, Pamunkey, Piscataway, Anacostank.

[d] Including the Acquintanacsuck, Patuxent, Mattapanient.

[e] John Pory's estimate (Smith 1884:570) of Eastern Shore total population probably refers to Accomac population only.

[f] Henry Fleet (Neill 1876:26, 35) estimates a total population of 5,000 persons along both sides of the Potomac River. The distribution of villages on the Smith map suggests about equal distribution of population on both sides.

[g] Father White (Hall 1910:41) says that 500 bowmen greeted the colonists at Piscataway. While this may be too high for village population, it certainly does not represent total Conoy fighting strength.

[h] The Wicomiss is mentioned as one of two tribes, tributary to the Susquehannock, who had together 140 warriors (Marye 1938–1939: 150).

[i] The Accomac estimate is by Gov. Edmund Andros (Sainsbury 1860–1912, 15:456); the other estimates, by Sir Thomas Lawrence (Md. Arch. 25:256). Both were replying to queries from the Board of Trade.

[j] 100 bowmen living in 9 unnamed towns. Nicholson (1699) lists 5 towns and another report to the Board of Trade in 1702 lists 8 towns, both without population figures, while Beverley (1705:232) names 10 towns with notes on population that imply a total slightly higher than 100 bowmen.

[k] The existence of Eastern Shore Indians besides the Nanticokes is acknowledged but "tis almost impossible to have the Exact number of men or Towns."

[l] 80 or 90 bowmen including the Piscataway, Choptico, and Mattawoman. The Pamunkey are mentioned but not included in this figure. Two years later, the refugee Conoy at Harrison Island were also estimated at 80 or 90 bowmen (Palmer et al. 1875–1893, 1:64–65).

[m] The Nanticokes themselves claimed to have 7 towns in 1696 and again in 1707, so 10 perhaps includes towns of neighboring groups as well (Md. Arch. 20:434; Pa. Col. Recs. 2:387).

The peacefulness of the Accomac tribes induced many English to settle there, even though the bay separated them from the center of colonization. The bad state of Indian-White relations near Jamestown diverted the beaver trade to the Potomac region and the Eastern Shore, where early flares of hostility (such as Conoy participation in the 1622 massacre) subsided in the face of profitable trade (Barbour 1969:403; Smith 1884:586,

592, 596; Kingsbury 1906-1935, 4:9, 61, 450; Torrence 1935:7, 485; Neill 1876:20-25). The Algonquian groups of Maryland were also glad to ally themselves with the English against the "Massawomeck" and Susquehannock who raided them, but to some extent also traded with them. After the "Massawomeck" had severely attacked the Conoys in the late 1620s, the Anacostank placed themselves under their protection and acted as their middlemen in the fur trade. The foundation of Maryland and the establishment of a Jesuit mission were welcomed by the Yaocomaco, who needed help against the Susquehannock (Neill 1876:25-26; Hall 1910:42, 74; Barbour 1969:361, 401, 407, 409). With the depletion of local resources and increasing direct contacts of the colonists with the Iroquoian groups, the tribes in southern Maryland lost most of their share in the fur trade but peacefully remained under the protection of the colony. On the Eastern Shore of Maryland, where intensive colonization began only during the 1650s and the Iroquoian threat was less severe, some hostilities between the Indians and the Whites developed. In 1642 both the Wicomiss and Nanticoke were declared enemies of the colony, but while the Nanticokes came to terms with the English, the Wicomiss were first subjected by the Susquehannock, who pushed them and other groups north of the Choptank River southward, and finally almost obliterated in the Wicomiss War of 1669, when their remnants were deported to Barbados (Md. Arch. 3:106, 116; Marye 1938-1939). Expeditions against the Assateagues and Pocomokes were planned and executed by the Virginian colonists of Accomac (Anonymous 1651-1654:40, 1666-1670:55; Md. Arch. 2:379-380).

The policy of colonial Maryland toward its Algonquian-speaking Indians was to enter into formal treaty relations with them. By placing themselves under the protection of the colonial government, the tribes received guarantees for reserved lands (see fig. 2) and hunting and fishing rights, for which they were to (1) pay an annual tribute, usually consisting of bows and arrows, (2) return fugitive servants and slaves, and (3) have their chiefs confirmed by the governor. The treaties further regulated Indian-White contacts and determined judicial procedures in cases involving Indians and Whites. The Nanticokes signed such treaties in 1668, 1678 (renewed in 1687), 1693, 1705, and 1742; the Conoys, in 1666 (renewed in 1670), 1692, and 1700; the Assateagues, in 1668, 1678, 1705, 1722, and 1742; the Pocomokes, in 1678, 1692, 1722, and 1742; the Choptanks and various other groups of the Eastern Shore, in 1659; the Choptanks alone, in 1705. The Patuxents were granted protection in 1640, while separate treaties were signed by the Choptico and Mattawoman in 1692 and the Pamunkey in 1700. Treaties with the Nanticokes were also made by the governor in 1642 and by a group of settlers in 1662, but their texts have not been preserved (Md. Arch. 2:25-27, 3:87-88, 129, 362-364, 5:558-560, 29-30, 65-66, 8:317-323, 533-538, 15:173-174, 213-215, 25:87-90, 393, 26:442-444, 27:40-44, 28:582-589). The Indians of Accomac never signed any treaty with Virginia, but they were regarded as tributary Indians by virtue of the treaties of 1646 and 1677 made with the Algonquian tribes on the Western Shore. Even the Pocomoke of Maryland were considered tributaries of Virginia by 1663 (Anonymous 1663-1666:44).

These treaties did not adequately protect the Indians from encroachments on their lands by White settlers. Typical complaints referred to the destruction of fences around the Indians' corn fields by the English and their livestock, and—on the other side—to the killing of English hogs by the Indians. White pressure on the Indians' lands and increasing inroads by the Five Nations, particularly after 1676, led to a further consolidation of the scattered groups in southern Maryland. Some Patuxents, for whom a joint reservation with the Chopticos and Yaocomacos had been planned in 1651 but who by 1674 were still living on their own lands, joined the Chopticos in 1692 (Md. Arch. 1:329-330, 2:354, 369-370, 10:272). An attempt to induce the Conoys to remove to the Eastern Shore failed in 1680. The Piscataways instead fled to Zachiah Swamp where after being besieged by the Iroquois, a peace was made (Md. Arch. 15:284-285, 17:365-367; NYCD 3:321-328). At about the same time, the Nanticokes and with them probably other neighboring tribes had become tributary to the Five Nations (Pa. Col. Recs. 2:387).

Consolidation on reservations also took place on the Eastern Shore, but nevertheless most of the Pocomokes and Assateagues were continually pushed northward by the advancing White settlements, while the Choptank lands were drastically reduced in size by repeated land sales (Marye 1936-1938, 5:1-15, 1940). In 1742 an attempt by the Eastern Shore tribes to jointly rebel against the English was detected in time by the colonists. The resulting treaties aimed at preventing a repetition of the "conspiracy" of 1742, but were basically similar in content to the former treaties and were the last to be concluded between Maryland and its Algonquian Indians (Md. Arch. 28:257-270).

Culture

The meagerness of the available source materials on the Indians of seventeenth-century Maryland makes it difficult to provide an adequate summary of their culture and in particular to deal with regional variations within the area. Such differences are to be expected in economy where environmental variations probably influenced patterns of exploitation. Scarcity of deer in the Accomac region, for example, caused a greater reliance on fishing and fowling in this area. Horticulture was apparently of greater importance among the Piscataways and in the territory of the Accomacs than among neighboring Virginia Algonquians. The Jamestown colonists regarded the Indians of Accomac as the best cultivators, producing a surplus of corn that was traded to both Indians and Whites on the Western Shore; similarly, the colonists found it easier to trade for corn on the Maryland side of the Potomac than south of the river (Smith 1884:568, 570, 592, 596; Kingsbury 1906-1935, 3:705).

The crops, planted by the women on patches cleared by the men, included corn, beans, and pumpkins. The men hunted deer, bears, squirrels, turkeys, partridges, and other game and fowl with bows and arrows, whose shafts of wood or reed were armed with glued-on points of flint, antler, or bone and fletched with turkey feathers. Bows and arrows were soon replaced by guns, as were wooden clubs by trade tomahawks. Trapping increased in importance with the developing beaver trade. Spring-pole snares for catching deer are reported from Kickotank in Maryland, while the Nanticokes are said to have been notable for their custom of felling trees across rivers on which to set their traps (Hall 1910:43, 82, 86; Anonymous 1907:333-334; Norwood 1844:39, 42; Heckewelder 1819:76).

Fishing and shellfishing along the sea coast, in the bay, and in the rivers were of considerable economic importance. Among fishing methods, only the use of bone-tipped spears among the Accomac and the shooting of fish with bow and arrows in Maryland are reported, but others were undoubtedly present. The gathering of wild plant foods, such as various kinds of nuts, contributed also to the diet (Anonymous 1907:333; Barbour 1969:359, 400).

Corn was pounded to meal in a mortar and baked into bread, or boiled to make hominy, which was eaten with vegetables, meat or fish. Meat was also roasted on spits, stewed, or eaten with oysters that were also roasted. Food was served in wooden bowls, with shells serving as spoons (Norwood 1844:35, 37-38, 42; Hall 1910:44, 82, 85, 87; Anonymous 1907:333). Other household utensils, all made by the women, included baskets of yucca or rushes and pottery vessels for cooking, some of which were traded to the Whites from the 1650s onward.

Boats were usually of the dugout type, but bark canoes were also made by both the Nanticokes and Piscataways, probably for use in expeditions beyond the fall line. During the second half of the seventeenth century, Indians were frequently employed to make dugouts for Whites (Hall 1910:42; Neill 1876:26; Norwood 1844:31; Md. Arch. 8:10-11, 15:364-369, 416).

Clothing was made of skin and consisted for men and women at least of a breechclout or apron reaching to the knees, fastened by a belt. Untailored cloaks were worn in winter with the fur inside, in summer without fur. Subadults sometimes wore no clothes at all. European dress was introduced early and was accepted particularly by Indians of high status. The chiefs of Piscataway,

Patuxent, and Potapaco had English clothes before 1640 (Hall 1910:43-44, 87-88, 127; Norwood 1844:36). At least among the Conoy, chiefs and their great men wore distinctive types of dress and ornaments, such as cloaks ornamented with circular rows of shell beads and fish-shaped copper ornaments on their foreheads (Hall 1910:43, 125).

Both men and women used vegetal and mineral pigments to paint their bodies and faces and anointed themselves with bear grease. Considerable variation prevailed in men's hairstyles: while some part of the hair was usually cropped, locks were left growing at one or both ears, on the forehead, or on the crown of the head. Women wore their hair long and loose. Bird wings and claws were worn as ornaments, as were animal teeth, copper beads, and shell beads of tubular and discoidal types worked into necklaces, bracelets, or headbands. Shell beads were also used as a substitute for money, to compensate crimes, and (in the tubular form) woven into belts used in connection with treaty making. Kuskarawaoke, in the country of the Nanticokes, was famous for its production of shell beads (Hall 1910:43, 86-88, 79, 90; Norwood 1844:45; Anonymous 1907:333; Smith 1884:418; Md. Arch. 2:15, 26, 5:167).

A mnemonic device used by the Indians of the Virginia Eastern Shore consisted of little sticks, by which they kept "their promises, as a tally" (Smith 1884:570). Similarly, Conoy delegates in 1666 asked the Maryland Assembly to furnish them with sticks painted with black or red characters to signify English laws (Md. Arch. 2:72).

Villages usually were situated near the banks of rivers. In areas bordering on Iroquoian groups, they were frequently rather compact and enclosed by palisades fortified with brush or bark (Barbour 1969:407; Stephenson and Ferguson 1963:49-55). The rectangular, barrel-roofed houses of the Piscataway area were covered with bark or mats, furnished with a smoke hole to let out the smoke arising from the central fire and with low, mat-covered scaffolds along the sides for beds. About 10 feet high, their length ranged from 20 feet upward. The chief's house at Kickotank was partitioned with mats to form several compartments along both sides, each with its own platform and apparently also its own fireplace. The chief's compartment within this house was twice the size of the other divisions, and his bed was made particularly comfortable with skins and furs. Mats were generally laid on the ground to sit on. At Piscataway, the chief soon after the founding of Maryland asked the colonial authorities to build him an English-style house (Hall 1910:43-44, 73, 85-86, 88; Norwood 1844:35-36).

Little is known about the size and composition of the household. In 1699 the average household size of the Conoy village on Harrison Island was around 10 persons (Feest 1973). Polygyny was common, at least among the Conoy, depending on the wealth and economic capacity

244

of the husband. Monogamy was obviously encouraged by the Jesuit missionaries. After marriage, the wife would move to her husband's house. Marriages are described as stable; in case of divorce, the children remained with their mother. Marriage restrictions in the Accomac region excluded a large number of consanguineal and affinal relatives as possible spouses (Hall 1910:44, 85–86, 127; Smith 1884:570).

Hereditary chiefs ruled over the tribes and the greater political entities with considerable authority. Tribal chiefs, some of which were women, were called wizoes by the Conoys, while the term for paramount chief or "emperor" was tayac among the Conoys and tallak among the Choptank or Nanticoke. The Conoy paramount chiefs were assisted by their council, consisting of the wizoes and perhaps others. War captains are mentioned for both the Conoy and Nanticoke. A special position was that of "speaker" for the tribe. The term crotemen, reported as the word for councilor among the Kickotank (Assateague), may be a corruption of Dutch *groot man* 'big man' or *groote* 'nobleman'. The chiefs and their advisers (fig. 3) together formed an upper stratum of society distinguished from the common people by their wealth, distinction in attire, and respect accorded them (Hall 1910:43, 84, 87, 71, 73, 124–125; Norwood 1844:36; Md. Arch. 3:453, 5:65, 555, 15:291, 25:85; Beverley 1705:212; Speck 1927:49).

Chieftainship was inherited matrilineally among the

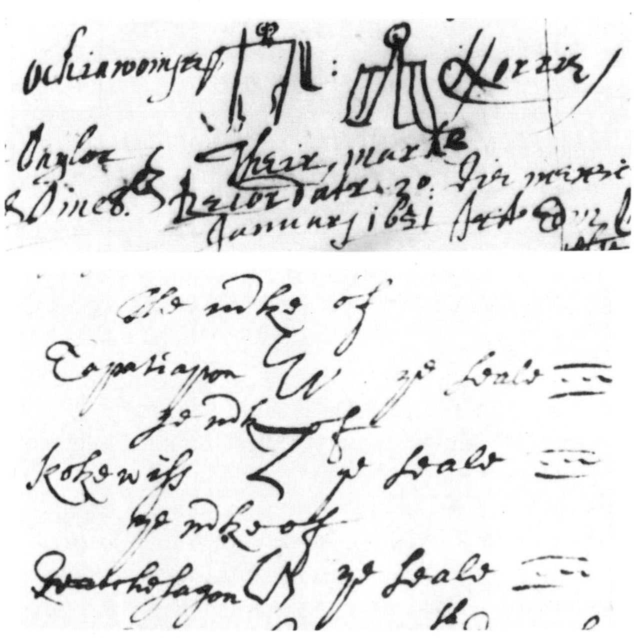

Va. State Lib., Richmond.
Fig. 3. Top, signatures of Ochiawompe (Okiawampe), "great Kinge of the Eastern Shore" or Accomac paramount chief, and Norris, one of his "great men" on copy of a deed dated October 10, 1650. These are rare examples of clearly figural signatures by Algonquian Indians of this area. Bottom, signatures of Tapatiapon (Debedeavon), Okiawampe's successor, and two of his "great men" (Kokewiss and Watchesagon) on a deed dated November 9, 1663. These signatures are typical of nonfigural marks by Algonquians of Virginia.

Conoy, but during the second half of the seventeenth century a strong patrilineal tendency appeared. Evidence for succession to office among the Nanticoke, Accomac, and the Conoy subtribes, all dating from after 1650, invariably indicates patrilineality (MacLeod 1926; Md. Arch. 2:15, 8:53, 533; Weslager 1961:27).

The huskenaw ceremony, a puberty rite better known from Virginia and North Carolina Algonquians and in early records referred to as the "making of black boys," was practiced in southern Maryland; but it was absent from the Eastern Shore of Virginia. The expression "black boys" has its origin in a confusion between "black" and "blake" (northern English for white) and refers to the white body paint of the participants in the rite (Hall 1910:85; Smith 1884:570).

Various plants were used by the Indians for their medicinal qualities (Hall 1910:79). Particularly the Nanticokes were famous for their proficiency in preparing a poison of unknown composition, which was used for poisoning arrows and wells in fighting their enemies and also to clear the way for changes in political leadership. This reputation as poisoners was frequently combined with accusations of the practice of witchcraft. It was claimed that the Nanticokes introduced this complex to both the Delawares and the Six Nations (Weslager 1948:108–110; Speck 1937:135–142; Gipson 1938:195; Anonymous 1663–1666:44; Anonymous 1645–1651: 217).

The Conoys believed in a benevolent, remote god but made offerings mainly to appease a punishing deity whose image was kept in temples. Priests were present, but their functions are not precisely known. The first fruits of horticulture, hunting, and fishing were offered to the friendly god by old men (perhaps the priests) and subsequently feasted upon by the people. Another ceremony involved the blowing of the smoke of tobacco on all parts of the body. The widely distributed flood myth was also known to the Conoy (Hall 1910:45, 88, 130).

For both the Potomac region and the Nanticoke territory there is ample archeological evidence for ossuary burials (of up to 600 individuals, but usually less than 300) as the prevalent mode of burial in early historic times. These secondary interments were preceded by primary inhumation among the Nanticokes and apparently by scaffold burials among the Conoy. Chiefs' corpses were treated differently, at least among the Assateagues, Choptanks, and Nanticokes, by preserving their bones in the temples. This conforms to a general southeastern Algonquian practice (Ubelaker 1974; Feest 1973a; Thomas 1973).

Migrations

In 1697 about 300 Conoys left southern Maryland in the face of increasing pressure on their lands and their physical security. They first retired to a hideout in the Bull

Run Mountains. Two years later they moved to Harrison Island in the Potomac River, just above the mouth of Goose Creek. They were repeatedly visited by emissaries from the governor of Maryland to induce them to return, which at least some of them (including most of the chiefs) did in 1700, when another treaty was signed and the village of Pamunkey was accepted as their new residence. But since the majority of the tribal population apparently was unwilling to come to Pamunkey, even those who had returned decided not to stay. Shortly thereafter, the refugee Conoy moved higher up the Potomac River and settled on Conoy (now Heater's) Island where an epidemic drastically reduced their population in 1704 (Palmer et al. 1875-1893, 1; Md. Arch. 22-26, 19). In the following year, the Conoy petitioned the governor of Pennsylvania for permission to settle at Tulpenhocken, but nothing seems to have happened, because by 1712 they were still living on Heater's Island. While the exact year of their removal from that island is unknown, they had already lived at Conejoholo and later at Conoy Town, both on the Susquehanna River, when in 1743 they decided to follow the advice of the Six Nations to settle at Shamokin. By 1749 some Conoys were living with a Nanticoke group at the mouth of the Juniata River, in 1755 they are found in the same company at Otsiningo on Chenango River near Birmingham, New York, and by 1758 the two refugee groups were considered to be one nation. Sharing their history of migrations with the Nanticokes, the Conoy nevertheless retained their identity up to their removal to the Maumee River (Pa. Col. Recs. 2:191, 4:657, 5:390, 8:176; Weslager 1948:86; Todd 1920:247, 383, 391; Kemper 1921; Aupaumut 1827:97-98).

Dissatisfied with their condition in Maryland, the Nanticokes of Broad Creek in 1743 applied to the Six Nations for permission to remove to Pennsylvania, and in the following year they were permitted to leave Maryland (Md. Arch. 28:338-33; Weslager 1948:10-11). In 1744 the emigrants had established themselves at the mouth of the Juniata River where they were joined by the Conoy, while others were living between 1747 and 1753 at Wyoming on the Susquehanna River. By 1755 the Nanticokes had moved to settlements at Otsiningo and Chemung (the latter on Chemung River near present-day Chemung), which they shared with other tribes (Weslager 1948:57-68). In 1753 the Nanticokes were admitted as nonvoting members to the League of the Iroquois under the wing of the Cayugas, where they were regarded as "one family" forming the "Wolf Clan" (Weslager 1948:65; Speck 1927:22-26). During the 1750s and 1760s, Nanticokes from Chicacoan and probably neighboring groups as well joined their tribesmen in Pennsylvania and New York. Except for the Conoy, no group is ever mentioned by a separate name in contemporary records.

246 Remaining neutral during the French and Indian

Wars, the Nanticokes and Conoys then sided with the British during the American Revolution and consequently removed to Niagara. In 1781 at least 166 Nanticokes lived together with others at Buffalo Creek, having removed from Aughquagy near Colesville, New York, which they had shared with some Cayugas and Tutelos. After the Revolution, part of the Nanticokes took up residence with the Six Nations at Grand River in Canada, although by 1785 only 11 and by 1811 only 10 were found there, while in 1789, 28 of the "Wolf Tribe" dwelled at Buffalo Creek. About 50 Nanticokes were living there in 1843 and 1845, forming two groups known as "Old Families" and "New Families," these names probably referring to their arrival at Grand River at different dates. During the early twentieth century the number of Nanticoke descendants at Grand River was given as around 300. A few words of the old language were still remembered, but no specific Nanticoke customs apparently survived. Before 1870 they delegated four, and afterward two chiefs to the council of the League (Weslager 1948:67-90; Speck 1927:17-19; Johnston 1964:52, 281, 307; Schaeffer 1942:xv).

A faction of the Nanticokes and Conoys, rather than going north to the Six Nations, went west with the Delawares. By 1769 some Nanticokes had come from Otsiningo to the predominantly Munsee village of Goshgoshink on the western side of the Allegheny River. In 1785 a Nanticoke party "not amounting to 50 men" moved probably from the Buffalo Creek settlement to a village on the Maumee River, close to both the Shawnees and Delawares, after having visited their old chief Robert White (Wolahocremy) at the Clinton River mission in southeastern Michigan. They apparently had their own village on the Maumee in 1792, while the Conoy in the same year are mentioned as living at Big Cat's Town. Sometime after Anthony Wayne's Treaty of 1795 (Greenville) they settled on the White River, Indiana, where in 1805 they were living 20 miles downstream of the Moravian mission. By 1818 they had crossed the Mississippi, in the course of time to live with the Delawares in Kansas and, after 1867, in Oklahoma. During the early twentieth century, a few Indians still knew about their Nanticoke ancestry, although they had been absorbed by the Delawares for some time. A ceremony known as the Skeleton Dance, which was associated with the custom of secondary burials, was according to tradition performed up to 1860 by Nanticokes who were also referred to as "Wolf Clan." Here as well as among the Iroquois the term "Wolf Clan" was apparently used to integrate the newcomers into the existing framework of the clan structure of the tribes that incorporated them, rather than implying such a structure for the Nanticokes themselves (Speck 1937:135-149; Weslager 1948:90; Heckewelder 1819:76, 1820:360; Gipson 1938:359; Aupaumut 1827:97-98).

Remnants

When the majority of the Conoy left Maryland, an unknown number of them remained near their old homes, some of whom worked as indentured servants on White plantations. Since their tribe was no longer officially present in the colony, and the remnants apparently did not reorganize, they lost their official status as Indians and were classified as "free Negroes." Little is known about their history until the 1880s, when they started to identify themselves as "Wesorts" in an attempt to be recognized as a separate, non-Black group. They succeeded to the extent of having this term used for their racial identification on birth certificates, marriage licenses, and church records; but they never had schools of their own. There has been a strong tendency to marry within the group or with Whites. Although unions with Blacks were ostracized, some probably took place particularly on White plantations and may have been tolerated in their early history. The prevalence of endogamy is illustrated by the small number of surnames.

Some of these remnants identify themselves specifically as descendants of the Piscataway, Mattawoman, Nangemaick, or Sacayo tribes and prefer these names to the term Wesorts, while others have adopted the designation "Brandywine People." Around 1970 there were an estimated 7,000 of them living in several neighborhoods in Charles County and adjacent parts of Prince Georges and Saint Mary counties. In 1974 a group incorporated under state law as the Piscataway tribe. While many of them are still farmers or farm laborers, an increasing number live in or commute to Washington, Baltimore, and other cities in the Middle Atlantic area. Practically all are and have been for a long time Roman Catholics. Small groups of Conoy descendants have also been reported from near Point of Rocks, Frederick County, and other locations in Maryland along the emigration route to the north (Gilbert 1945).

Of the 10 small groups still present on Virginia's Eastern Shore around 1700, only one kept its identity into the nineteenth century. On their reservation of about 650 acres, laid out in 1641 and confirmed to them in 1680, the Gingaskin Indians continued to decrease in numbers. Trustees were appointed for them in 1769 to aid and protect them in legal and land matters. The Gingaskins carried on their traditional economy of fishing, hunting, and horticulture. They paid an annual tribute of three arrows for their lands to the colony and later to the state of Virginia, which was their only safeguard against White encroachments. From at least the 1780s onward, their White neighbors pressed for allotment of the reservation, on the grounds that it had become "an Asylum for free Negroes," and in the hope of subsequently being able to buy out the individual landowners. Allotment of the reservation in fee simple was finally carried out in 1813 upon the petition of the Indians themselves, who in turn sold most of their land to their neighbors until 1832. The last three of 26 plots remaining in Indian ownership were sold between 1832 and 1860. While some of the Gingaskins left Virginia after selling their lands, others merged with the local Black community. By the 1970s, there was no group or individual claiming Indian identity on the Eastern Shore of Virginia (Rountree 1973; W. Hall 1952:376).

After the Nanticokes had left Maryland following the treaty of 1742, several small bands remained on the Eastern Shore. Some Nanticokes continued to live on the Chicacoan reservation until part of them joined the Choptanks of Locust Neck, while the rest removed out of the colony. Chicacoan and Broad Creek reservations were sold in 1768. Payment was apparently made only to some of the former inhabitants. Chicacoan was fraudulently claimed in 1801 by a man who had obtained a forged deed allegedly signed by Nanticokes among the Six Nations. In 1852 a group of Canadian Nanticokes claimed compensation for this reservation, which was denied them by the Maryland Assembly (Weslager 1948:81–83; Anonymous 1910; Anonymous 1852).

The village at Locust Neck was inhabited by nine persons living in six households in 1792. Seven years later, the reservation was reduced to 100 acres, to be divided among the four Indians still living on their lands. The Indians were also to receive annuities from the proceeds of the sale of the remaining part of the reservation. By 1837 two or three descendants were occupying this land, who were regarded as "intermixed with negro blood" by their White neighbors (Marye 1936–1938, 5:13–14; Bozman 1837, 1:115; Speck 1927:41).

While nothing is known about the fate of the Pocomokes living off-reservation in 1742, the Assateague reservation on Indian River decreased in size through sales to a White neighbor, and in 1744 it was completely in White ownership. Although some of the Indians probably continued in the vicinity, others ended up with the Nanticokes on Nanticoke River where they were competing for leadership in the tribe (Marye 1940:13–16). A strong group of Indian descendants who identify themselves as Nanticokes survived off-reservation as a separate part of the "free colored" population. The majority of this band was located near the old Indian River reservation, Sussex County, Delaware, incorporated in 1881 under state laws, and reorganized in 1922 as Nanticoke Indian Association (inactive since 1955). During the 1920s and 1930s they were active in the newly formed "Powhatan Confederacy" consisting mainly of off-reservation groups in coastal Virginia. A smaller number of Nanticokes was living in Worcester and Dorchester counties, Maryland. The only eighteenth-century Indian name in use among the modern Nanticokes is Mulberry, an old Choptank name. The name Street occurred among both the Canadian and Indian River Nanticokes. The location of the groups may also indicate some Assateague ancestry.

Mus. of the Amer. Ind., Heye Foundation, New York.

Fig. 4. Corn cribs of the Nanticoke. Photograph by Frank Speck, southern Delaware, 1911-1914.

The last speaker of the native tongue died in 1856, but several survivals in the realm of material culture were recorded in the twentieth century. These include spring-pole snares and gravity box traps for catching small game, various implements of the corn-farming complex (figs. 4, 5) (digging sticks, corn-husking pegs, log mortars), wooden netting needles, and splint basketry (figs. 6, 7, 8) (Speck 1915b). As with the groups in southern Maryland and in Virginia, endogamy has been the rule. Marriages with Whites have occurred, but those with Blacks have been avoided for a long time for fear of further discrimination. Close association with Blacks, however, certainly occurred among the Nanticokes at an early date, since a word list recorded among them in the 1740s in Pennsylvania has been identified as Mandingo, a West African language. This Black element may account for early reports about the dark complexion of the Nanticokes (Brinton 1887; Weslager 1948:116).

The modern Nanticokes are predominately Methodists. Until the time of integration they had their own schools; some of the children were sent to Indian schools in Oklahoma to receive higher education.

Synonymy

Since the languages of the Nanticokes and their Algonquian neighbors are no longer being spoken, no attempt has here been made to supply either etymologies or pronunciations of tribal names.

Accomac: Accawmack, 1612 (Barbour 1969:359); Easterlings, 1621 (Smith 1884:569); Eastern Shore Indians, 1672 (Anonymous 1671-1673:143).

Accomac subtribes: Acohanock, 1612 (Barbour 1969:344); Occahannock (Anonymous 1657-1664:117). Chiconessex (Beverley 1705:232); Chicconessick, 1663 (Anonymous 1663-1666:22). Gingaskin, 1660 (Anony-

mous 1657-1664:73); Gingaskoyne, 1650 (Anonymous 1645-1651:217); Gangascoe (Beverley 1705:232); also known first after their village, later after the region as Accomack, 1612 (Barbour 1969:344); Accomack, 1784 (W. Hall 1952:376); Combec, 1586 (Quinn 1955, 1: map 7, village name). Kiquotank, 1702 (Anonymous 1894:362); Kikotanke, 1650 (Anonymous 1645-1651:217); Qiuotanck, 1675 (Anonymous 1673-1676:285); Kickatanck, 1675 (Anonymous 1673-1676:314); Kiequotank (Beverley 1705:232). Matchapungo, 1702 (Anonymous 1894:362); Machepungo, 1653 (Anonymous 1651-1654:217); Matsiapungo (Nicholson 1699); Matchopungo (Beverley 1705:232). Machateege, 1650 (Anonymous 1645-1651:217). Matomkin (Beverley 1705-232); Motomkin, 1651 (Wise 1897:34); Matompkin, 1702 (Anonymous 1894:362). Nandue, 1648 (Anonymous 1645-1651:135a); Nandewy (Nicholson 1699); Nanduye (Beverley 1705:232); also known after the name of a subvillage as Nuswattocks, 1653 (Anonymous 1651-1654:174); Mashawatoc, 1586 (Quinn 1955, 1:map 7, village name). Onancock, 1663 (Anonymous 1663-1666:39); Anancock, 1661 (Anonymous 1657-1664: 117); Oanancocke, 1654 (Anonymous 1651-1654:225). Pungotege, 1702 (Anonymous 1894:362); Pungoteque (Beverley 1705:232).

Assateague: Assatege, 1659 (Md. Arch. 3:379); Assateagues, 1684 (Md. Arch. 5:480); Asouthteague, 1684 (Md. Arch. 17:193); Assetegue, 1722 (Md. Arch. 25:392). At least part of the Assateague later became known as Indian River Indians, 1705 (Md. Arch. 26:442).

Assateague subtribes: Manasksons, Maraughquaick, Moteawaughkin, Quequashkecasquick, Wachetak, 1684 (Md. Arch. 5:480, where also the Choptank subtribes are mentioned as dependent on the Assateague); probably also the Kickotank, 1650 (Norwood 1844:46).

Choptank: Choptank, 1682 (Md. Arch. 7:291); Chapticoe, 1697 (Md. Arch. 19:574), not to be confused with the Conoy subtribe.

Choptank subtribes: Trasquakin, 1659 (Md. Arch. 3:363); Traskokin, 1661 (Anonymous 1657-1664:117); Transquakines, 1686 (Marye 1936-1938, 5: appendix 8); while this was a village name, they were also known after their chief: Ababcos Indians, 1669 (Md. Arch. 2:195); Abapco's Indians, 1702 (Marye 1936-1938, 5: appendix 6); Babcos, 1705 (Md. Arch. 26:442); Babco, 1759 (Md. Arch. 31:356). Quowaughkutt, 1659 (Md. Arch. 3:363) band or village of chief Tequassino, 1669 (Md. Arch. 2:196); probably identical with the Choptico mentioned as an Assateague subtribe, 1686 (Md. Arch. 5:480). Taquasons, 1726 (Marye 1936-1938, 5: appendix 10). Hatsawap, 1686 (Md. Arch. 5:480) after the name of their chief, 1669 (Md. Arch. 2:196). Hatswampt, 1704 (Marye 1936-1938, 5: appendix 15); Hatchswamp, 1726 (Marye 1936-1938, 5: appendix 18); Heard Swamp,

Fig. 5. Nanticoke man demonstrating shelling mortar for removing corn kernels from the ears. The hollow log has wooden bars as a grating across the cavity. When the ears are beaten with a pestle the loosened kernels fall through the grating. The woman is pounding the kernels into flour. Photograph by Frank Speck, southern Delaware, 1911-1914.

1759 (Md. Arch. 31:355); Ahatchwoops, 1705 (Md. Arch. 26:442); they were probably identical with one of the following bands signing the treaty of 1659 with the other two Choptank bands: Amusteack, Maquamticough, Monoponson, Rasoughteick, Sequawaughteick, Tetuckough (Md. Arch. 3:363). Of these tribes, the Monoponson were the former inhabitants of Kent Island, and the Tetuckough may possibly be identical with the Tockwogh; the others are in all likelihood similar to the Monoponson and Tockwogh inhabitants of the region north of the Choptank River, which was ceded in 1652

by the Susquehannocks to Maryland. They may have been living with the Choptanks in 1659.

Conoy: Conoys, 1759 (NYCD 7:380); Connays, 1757 (NYCD 7:268); Cachnawayes, 1682 (NYCD 3:323). Ganawense, 1705 (Pa. Col. Recs. 2:191); Gonoois, 1685 (Md. Arch. 17:366); Canai (Heckewelder 1819:74); Ganàwagohóno (Speck 1927:30, Cayuga name for Nanticokes); Kuhnauwautheew (Aupaumut 1827:77); Piscataway, 1682 (NYCD 3:322).

Conoy subtribes: Anacostank, 1666 (Md. Arch. 2:25); Anacostin, 1694 (Md. Arch. 20:68); Anacostans, 1640

Mus. of the Amer. Ind., Heye Foundation, New York.

Fig. 6. Old Nanticoke splint baskets. Photograph by Frank Speck, southern Delaware, 1911-1914.

Mus. of the Amer. Ind., Heye Foundation, New York.

Fig. 8. Nanticoke splint baskets used for catching eel. These eel-pots are about 45 to 65 cm in length. They were sunk with stones in the water along the shore. Photograph by Frank Speck, southern Delaware, 1911-1914.

Mus. of the Amer. Ind., Heye Foundation. New York.

Fig. 7. Nanticoke man with large flat splint basket. Photograph by Frank Speck, southern Delaware, 1911-1914.

(Hall 1910:132); Necosts, 1624 (Smith 1884:596); Necochincos, 1623 (Kingsbury 1906-1935, 4:9); Nacotchtanke, 1612 (Barbour 1969:341); Nacostines, 1632 (Neill 1876:25); Annacostin, 1679 (Md. Arch. 15:252). Chingwawateick, 1666 (Md. Arch. 2:25); Chingwoatyke, 1663 (Md. Arch. 3:482); Cinquaoteck, 1612 (Barbour 1969:map facing 374, village name). Choptico, 1666 (Md. Arch. 2:25); Chapticoe, 1676 (Md. Arch. 2:489); Chopticons, 1651 (Md. Arch. 1:329). Doegs, 1666 (Nugent 1934:558); Doags, 1666 (Md. Arch. 2:25); see also "Virginia Algonquians" under Tauxenent. Manesquesend, 1666 (Md. Arch. 2:25). Mattawoman, 1670 (Md. Arch. 15:291); Mattawomans, 1666 (Md. Arch. 2:25).

Mikikiwoman, 1666 (Md. Arch. 2:25). Nangemaick, 1666 (Md. Arch. 2:131); Nangemy, 1676 (Md. Arch. 2:489); Nushemouck, 1612 (Barbour 1969: map facing 374, village name); Nanjemy, 1679 (Md. Arch. 15:252). Pamunkey, 1700 (Md. Arch. 25:85); Pamunkie, 1676 (Md. Arch. 2:489); Pamunckye, 1676 (Md. Arch. 15:91); Pamacacack, 1612 (Barbour 1969:341); Pomonky, 1689 (Md. Arch. 8:85); Pomunkey, 1698 (Md. Arch. 25:256). Pangayo, 1666 (Md. Arch. 2:131). Piscataway, 1682 (Md. Arch. 17:214); Pascatowies, 1632 (Neill 1876:26); Paschatoway, 1634 (Hall 1910:88); Pazaticans, 1624 (Smith 1884:586); Pascoticons, 1624 (Kingsbury 1906-1935, 4:450); Paskattaway, 1638 (Hall 1910:158); Pascatacon, 1634 (Md. Arch. 5:165); Piscattaway, 1698 (Md. Arch. 25:256); Puscattaway, 1676 (Md. Arch. 2:489); also known by the name of their villages Moyaoncer, 1608 (Barbour 1969:186); Moyowances, 1612 (Barbour 1969:341) or Accocick, 1699 (Md. Arch. 25:72); Accokicke, 1697 (Md. Arch. 19:574). Potapaco, 1612 (Barbour 1969:341); Portoback, 1634 (Hall 1910:88); Portaback, 1663 (Md. Arch. 3:489). Sacayo, 1666 (Md. Arch. 2:25); Sachia, 1689 (Md. Arch. 8:85); Zakiah, 1690 (Md. Arch. 8:224); perhaps identical with Secowocomoco or Cecomocomoco, 1612 (Barbour 1969:341, map facing 374). Yaocomaco, 1634 (Hall 1910:73); Youcomako, 1676 (Md. Arch. 15:91); Wicomocons, 1651 (Md. Arch. 1:329).

Nanticoke: Nanticoke, 1655 (Anonymous 1654-1655:135); Nantaquack, 1612 (Barbour 1969: map facing 374, village name); Nanticoque, 1642 (Md. Arch. 3:106); Nantecoke, 1693 (Md. Arch. 8:533); Nentégo (Heckewelder 1819:76); Kuskarawaokes, 1612 (Barbour 1969:344, after a village); Trappers (Heckewelder 1819:76). They were called by the Munsee wənéhtkoˑw (Ives Goddard, personal communication 1973), earlier written Wəneˑtˊko (Speck 1931:16), Unéchtgo (Heckewelder 1819:76); by the Unami wənéˑtku (Ives Goddard, personal communication 1973); by the Mahican Wenuhtukowuk, 1792 (Aupaumut 1827:77) and Otayáchgo (Heckewelder 1819:76), Tiawco, 1757 (NYCD 7:294); by the Iroquois Sganiateratieh-rohne (Heckewelder 1819:76), *skanyataratihá·ka⁷* (Mohawk), *skanyata·tihó·nǫ⁷* (Cayuga; Speck 1927:30; Wallace L. Chafe, personal communication 1974).

Patuxent: Pautuxuntes, 1612 (Barbour 1969:361); Pawtuxunt, 1621 (Smith 1884:567).

Patuxent subtribes: Acquintanacksuck, 1612 (Barbour 1969:342). Mattapanient, 1612 (Barbour 1969:342); Mattapanians, 1651 (Md. Arch. 1:329); Mattapany, 1674 (Md. Arch. 2:354). Patuxent, 1639 (Hall 1910:124); Pawtuxunt, 1612 (Barbour 1969:342); Patuxants, 1651 (Md. Arch. 1:329); Patuxon, 1674 (Md. Arch. 2:354); Pattuxunt, 1634 (Hall 1910:57). Perhaps also Lamasconsons and Kighahnixons, 1651 (Md. Arch. 1:329).

Pocomoke: Pocomoke, 1651 (Wise 1897:33-34); Pokomoke, 1663 (Anonymous 1663-1666:44); Wighcocomoco, 1612 (Barbour 1969: map facing 374); from confusion between Wicomico and Pocomoke rivers).

Pocomoke subtribes: Acquintica, 1678 (Md. Arch. 15:213); Aquinteca, 1686 (Md. Arch. 5:520); Aquintankee, 1668 (Anonymous 1666-1670:55). Annamessex, 1678 (Md. Arch. 15:213); Annamessick, 1661 (Anonymous 1657-1664: 117). Gingoteque (Beverley 1705:232); Gingateege, 1650 (Anonymous 1645-1651:217); Gingo Teague, 1650 (Norwood 1844:46); Yingoteague, 1678 (Md. Arch. 15:213); Chingoteague, 1678 (Md. Arch. 15:215). Manokin, Mannanokin, 1661 (Anonymous 1657-1664:117); Monoakin, 1686 (Md. Arch. 5:479). Morumsco, 1678 (Md. Arch. 15:213). Nasswatex, 1686 (Md. Arch. 5:479); Nuswattax, 1678 (Md. Arch. 15:215). Quandanquan, 1686 (Md. Arch. 5:520).

Tockwogh: Tockwogh, 1612 (Barbour 1969:344).

Wicocomoco: Wichocomocos, 1638 (Md. Arch. 3:74); Wiccacomoco, 1661 (Anonymous 1657-1664:117); Wicocomico, 1682 (Md. Arch. 17:95).

Wicomiss: Ozinies, 1612 (Barbour 1969:344); Wiccimisses, 1669 (Md. Arch. 2:195); Wiccomeese, 1677 (Md. Arch. 15:146); Wicomeses, 1648 (Marye 1938-1939, 4:150); Wicomesses, 1634 (Hall 1910:88).

Sources

Ethnographic sources are not plentiful for the Nanticokes and their Algonquian neighbors. No prephotographic pictures have survived, and no collections of material culture were made before the twentieth century. Archeological evidence is therefore of even greater importance than elsewhere, even though many of the published reports on excavations of historic and late prehistoric sites have been mainly concerned with mortuary practices and the Potomac River area (Graham 1935; Stewart and Wedel 1937; Ferguson 1940; Stephenson and Ferguson 1963; Ubelaker 1974).

John White's map and the Spanish report on the expedition of 1588 are the earliest European sources on the southern margin of this area (Quinn 1955). John Smith explored the Chesapeake Bay in 1608 and particularly his map, but also his brief notes, on the Indians of the Eastern Shore and southern Maryland are of considerable interest (Barbour 1969). His *Generall Historie of Virginia* has material on Indian-White relations in the Potomac area up to 1623 and also contains John Pory's account of Accomac and Patuxent of 1621 (Smith 1884:245-784). The fur traders on the Potomac River left few records, with the major exception of Henry Fleet's journal of 1631-1632 (Neill 1876:19-37). The most detailed information on southern Maryland is contained in *A Relation of Maryland* (Anonymous 1910a; see also Hall 1910:70-112), which draws on Smith and White but adds much original material, including a map. White's *Briefe Relation* written in 1634 and excerpts from the annual letters of the Jesuit missionaries have been published in both Latin (Hughes 1907-1917, 1) and English (Hall 1910:29-45, 118-144). The only narrative dealing with Eastern Shore Indians is Norwood's (1844) account of his brief sojourn with the Kickotank near Assawoman Bay in 1650.

During the late seventeenth century, George Fox at least mentions the Algonquians of Maryland in his journal (Hall 1910:393-406), while Heermans' map (1673) gives clues to the location of villages. Hugh Jones (1700) and an anonymous writer (Anonymous 1907) give some ethnographic details, while in 1792 Murray deals with the Choptank remnants in Maryland (Speck 1927: 39-42). After leaving Maryland, the Nanticokes were contacted by Moravian missionaries, who recorded additional specific information (Heckewelder 1819, 1820; Zeisberger 1910). Beverley (1705) supplies little more than population data for the Accomac region.

The majority of data derive from administrative records. The *Archives of Maryland* in particular is a mine of information on Indian-White relations and is also a rich source for ethnography. For the Accomac region, an unbroken set of court records is available, the earliest of which have been published (S.M. Ames 1954, 1973; see also Anonymous 1645-1651, 1651-1654, 1657-1664, 1663-1666, 1671-1673, 1673-1676). Kingsbury (1906-1935) and Palmer et al. (1875-1893, 1) relate to both the Eastern Shore and the Potomac area, while the colonial records of Pennsylvania (Pa. Col. Recs.) and New York (NYCD) deal with the emigrant groups. The remnant bands in Delaware were briefly described by Babcock (1899) and subsequently studied by Speck (1915b, 1942, 1943, 1946, 1949), who in addition assembled a collection for the Museum of the American Indian, New York, and by Weslager (1943, 1955). The Indian descendants in southern Maryland received attention from Gilbert (1945). Speck (1927) also supplies valuable material on the Canadian Nanticokes.

The secondary literature on the history of the Nanticoke and neighboring Algonquians includes the writings of Semmes (1929, 1937), who made extensive use of the *Archives of Maryland*; Marye (1936–1938, 1938–1939, 1940), who in addition drew on unpublished land records; and Weslager (1943a, 1944, 1948, 1961).

Virginia Algonquians

CHRISTIAN F. FEEST

Territory and Environment

Algonquian-speaking tribes* living in tidewater Virginia are best grouped under the common label "Virginia Algonquians." Too little is known about the southeastern Algonquian tribes to permit well-defined distinctions among major groups on the basis of political, cultural, and dialectic affinities. Classification, therefore, will be made on geographical and historical grounds.

The western border of Virginia Algonquian territory is well marked by the fall line; beyond it in the Piedmont region lived Siouan tribes, traditional enemies of the coastal people. To the south, the Dismal Swamp and the presence of Iroquoian groups around the tributaries of the Chowan almost separated the Virginia Algonquians from their linguistic relatives in North Carolina. Although there were possibly significant cultural and political differences across the Rappahannock River, few sources are specific about these variations, while most early written records refer to Algonquian tribes within the limits of Virginia in general. The Potomac River, therefore, makes a sensible northern boundary. There were some connections across Chesapeake Bay between Virginia Algonquians and the groups of the southern Delmarva peninsula, but differences probably outweighed existing links.

The Virginia Algonquian tribes lived on the alluvial coastal plain, which rises to 300 feet in elevation and is characterized by its indented coastline and extended marshes and swamps. Four tidal rivers draining into Chesapeake Bay (Potomac, Rappahannock, York, James) divide the tidewater region into four main peninsulas: Northern Neck, Middle Peninsula, Virginia Peninsula, and Southside Virginia. Further peninsulas are formed by the forking of the James into the James and Chickahominy rivers, and of the York into the Pamunkey and Mattaponi rivers.

A zone of humid subtropical climate extends to the northern border of this region. Annual precipitation is normally abundant, excepting occasional severe droughts. The annual growing season reaches 200 days in southeastern Virginia. North of James River, vegetation is dominated by dry southeastern oak-pine forests.

*The language of the Virginia Algonquians is extinct. Lacking adequate early recordings, the spelling of native terms and proper names follows their historical orthography.

To the south, humid pine forests appear. Marsh vegetation is typical for the coastal region.

Numerous species of fish live in the coastal and inland waters, clams are common in lower Chesapeake Bay, and oyster beds are found in many of the estuaries. Besides local species of birds, several migrant waterfowl winter in Virginia. Among the more important mammals were deer, bear, fox, raccoon, opossum, beaver, otter, squirrel, and puma.

Prehistory and Language

During protohistoric times, shell-tempered Chickahominy ware was general throughout most of tidewater Virginia. Only north of the Rappahannock River was crushed quartz-tempered or coarse sand-tempered Potomac Creek ware replacing shell-tempered pottery during Late Woodland times. The fact that shell tempering did not occur west of the fall line is partly due to ecological reasons (limited availability of shells) but at the same time serves to distinguish Algonquians from Siouan and Iroquoian populations in Virginia (Holland 1966). While there is a marked continuity of prehistoric developments south of Rappahannock River since at least Early Woodland times, some late external influences are discernible, as in the occurrence of Roanoke simple stamped sherds in southern Virginia, particularly in Kecoughtan.

A fragment of traditional history, collected around 1610, relates that the Indians of tidewater Virginia had moved into this region only 300 years previously (Strachey 1953). Archeological evidence shows this situation may apply only to the tribes north of the Rappahannock River, among whom this story was possibly collected. The Piscataway Indians of Maryland shared similar traditions. John Smith's word list (Barbour 1972) and Strachey's (1953) vocabulary are the main sources for knowledge of the Virginia Algonquian language. Place and personal names have been unduly neglected (Barbour 1971). Available evidence suffices to place Virginia Algonquian in the Eastern Algonquian subgroup of languages. At least two dialects can apparently be distinguished on a phonological basis, but they cannot now be associated with particular areas.

Fig. 1. Coastal Virginia 1570-1606. Based on the maps of White (1585-1586 a,b) and contemporary accounts. 1, Apasus; 2, Chesepiuc; 3, [Kecoughtan]; 4, Skicóak.

Sixteenth Century

Cartographic evidence for some Spanish knowledge of Chesapeake Bay after 1525 hints at contacts of Virginia Algonquians with European explorers during the first half of the sixteenth century. It is unknown what consequence these contacts had for the Indian population, though some slave raiding and incipient trade is likely.

Around 1560 a Spanish ship picked up an Indian who turned out to be a member of a chief's family on York River. He was baptized Don Luis and educated in Cuba and Spain. In 1570 Don Luis led a small group of Spanish Jesuits to his tribe to establish a mission there, but he

turned against his former teachers and joined his tribesmen in the murder of the missionaries early in 1571. A Spanish boy survived among friendly Indians (probably Kecoughtan) and was rescued by the punitive expedition of 1572, during which at least 40 Indians were killed (Lewis and Loomie 1953).

The English Roanoke colonists made first and hostile contact with Virginia Algonquians in 1584 (Quinn 1961). The following year, a group of settlers went by land to southern Virginia and lived for a while with the Chesapeakes. They only heard about a few other tribes. The Spanish entered Chesapeake Bay again in 1588 in search of the English colony. No further bloodshed occurred, but one Indian was taken prisoner (Quinn 1955). Virginia Algonquian traditions recorded in the early 1600s refer to experiences with Whites, mostly of a hostile nature (Barbour 1969, 1). Spanish and English reports before 1600 and native historical recollections recorded after 1607 provide the basis for the following summary of sixteenth-century Virginia Algonquian ethnography (see also fig. 1).

The Chesapeake tribe of northeastern Southside Virginia and its western neighbors lived in peace and possibly alliance with North Carolina Algonquian groups. By 1584 the Chesapeakes apparently had strained relations with the tribes of the Virginia Peninsula; according to native reports, they were wiped out by the Powhatan group shortly before 1607 but their territory was soon repopulated (Quinn 1955, 1961; Strachey 1953).

Don Luis's family ruled over the tribes along lower York River in 1570. Powhatan, who may have been Don Luis's sister's son or otherwise related, between 1572 and 1597 inherited this territory (Pamunkey, Youghtanund, Mattaponi, Kiskiack, Werowocomoco) and the region on James River below the falls, where he was born (Powhatan, Arrohateck, Appamatuck I, Orapaks). In 1597 he conquered Kecoughtan after the death of its powerful chief, and before 1607 he had added almost all other tribes on James and York rivers to his tribal empire. A chief ruling over several tribes headed by subchiefs is also reported from upper Chesapeake Bay by Spanish documents. It is likely that European contacts encouraged this rise of larger political entities (Feest 1966).

Indian population was greater near the fall lines than on the coast. While ecological reasons may have been partly responsible, Powhatan's conquests must also have contributed to this difference. Additional population decrease was possibly caused by infectious diseases originating from White visitors (Mook 1944).

Spanish sources report the cultivation of corn, which was planted from March to early May and stored on raised platforms after harvest. Hunting, fishing, and gathering of wild plant and animal foods are mentioned.

These activities were particularly important after corn stores had been depleted in winter (Lewis and Loomie 1953).

Aboriginal trade included raw materials, such as copper, and manufactured goods, such as Mississippian shell pendants found in Patawomeke (Schmitt 1965). European trade materials entered the region both directly and through Iroquoian middlemen on northern Chesapeake Bay (Barbour 1969). Copper ear ornaments, necklaces, bracelets, and headbands are described for the Potomac region and the Virginia Peninsula. Copper headbands served as marks of distinction for chiefs. Spanish golden chalices and plates were likewise used as ornaments after the death of the Jesuit missionaries (Lewis and Loomie 1953).

Seventeenth Century

Demography

Figures 2 and 3 show the location of Virginia Algonquian tribes and villages throughout the seventeenth century. Several tribes were annihilated during that period; others joined their neighbors and became known under new names.

Upon English arrival in 1607, all tribes on James, York, and (by 1608) Payankatank rivers and their tributaries (except the Chickahominy) were part of a centralized state governed by Powhatan as paramount chief. Some of its more recent acquisitions, such as the Chesapeake and other tribes in Southside Virginia, were never fully integrated into this empire. The independent

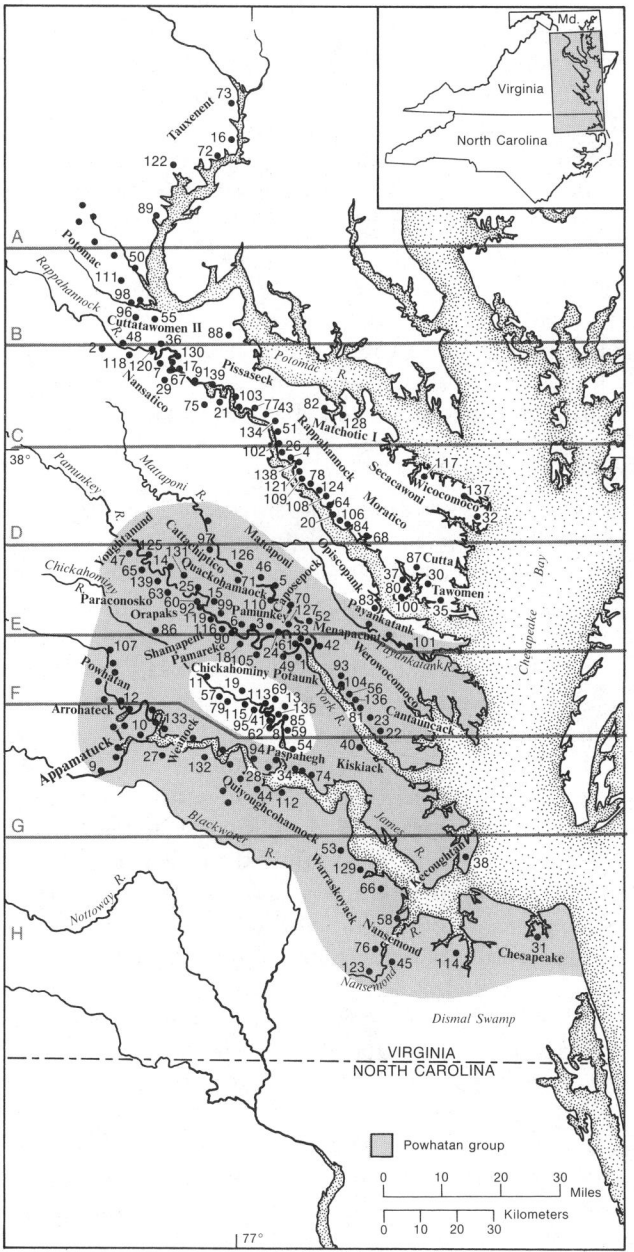

Fig. 2. Location of tribes and villages ca. 1610. Compiled from Smith and Zúñiga maps, with additions from other sources. Locations of villages are in some cases tentative. F1, Acconoc; C2, Accoqueck; E3, Accossumwinck; D4, Acquack; E5, Amacouncock; E6, Amkateck; C7, Anaskenoans; F8, Apanaock; G9, Appamatuck, King of; G10, Appamatuck, Queen of; F11, Appocant; F12, Arrohateck; E13, Askakep; E14, Askocack; E15, Askococack; A16, Assaomeck; C17, Assuweska; F18, Attamtuck/Weanock; F19, Attamuspinck; D20, Auhomesk; C21, Aurenapeugh; F22, Cantauncack; F23, Capahowasick; E24, Caposepock; E25, Cattachiptico; D26, Cawwontoll; G27, Cecocomake; G28, Chawopo; C29, Checopissowo; E30, Chesakawon; H31, Chesapeake; D32, Cinquack; F33, Cinquaoteck I; G34, Cinquaoteck II, E35, Cuttatawomen I; B36, Cuttatawomen II: E37, Kapawnich; H38, Kecoughtan; C39, Kerahocack; G40, Kiskiack; F41, Mamanahunt; F42, Mamanassy; C43, Mangoraca; G44, Mantapoyac; H45, Mantoughquemend; E46, Martoughquaunk; E47, Maskunt; B48, Massawoteck; F49, Matchamins; B50, Matchipongo; C51, Matchopick; E52, Matchutt; H53, Mathomauk; G54, Matinoack; B55, Matacunt; F56, Mattacock; F57, Mattahunt; H58, Mattanock; F59, Mattaponi; E60, Matunsk; F61, Menapacunt; F62, Menascosick; E63, Menaskunt I; D64, Menaskunt II; E65, Menoughtass; H66, Mokete; C67, Monanask; D68, Moratico; F69, Moysonec; E70, Muttamussinsack; E71, Myghtuckpassun; A72, Namassingakent; A73, Namoraughquend; G74, Namqosick; C75, Nansatico; H76, Nansemond; C77, Nawacaten; D78, Nawnautough; F79, Nechanicock; E80, Nepawtacum; F81, Nighsacan; C82, Onawmanient; E83, Opiscopank; D84, Oquomock; F85, Oraniock; E86, Orapaks; E87, Ottachugh; B88, Ozaiawomen; A89, Pamacocack; E90, Pamuncoroy; C91, Papiscone; E92, Paroconosko; F93, Pasaughtacock; G94, Paspahegh; F95, Paspanegh; B96, Pasptanzie; E97, Passauncack; B98, Patawomeck; E99, Pauncack; E100, Pawcocomocac; E101, Payankatank; C102, Pissacocack; C103, Pissaseck; F104, Poruptanck; F105, Potauncac; D106, Powcomonet; F107, Powhatan; D108, Poyektank; D109, Poykemkack; E110, Quackohamaock; B111, Quiyough; G112, Quiyoughcohannock; F113, Qosaugh; H114, Rickahake; F115, Righkahauk I; E116, Righkahauk II; D117, Secacawoni; C118, Secobeck; E119, Shamapent; C120, Sockobeck; D121, Tantucquask; A122, Tauxenent; H123, Teracosick; D124, Toppahannock; E125, Unekent; E126, Utcustank; E127, Uttamussak; C128, Uttamussamacoma; H129, Warraskoyack; C130, Waconiask; E131, Washasatiack; G132, Weanock, Great; G133, Weanock, Tanx; C134, Wecuppom; F135, Werawahon; F136, Werowocomoco; D137, Wicocomoco; D138, Winsack; E139, Youghtanund.

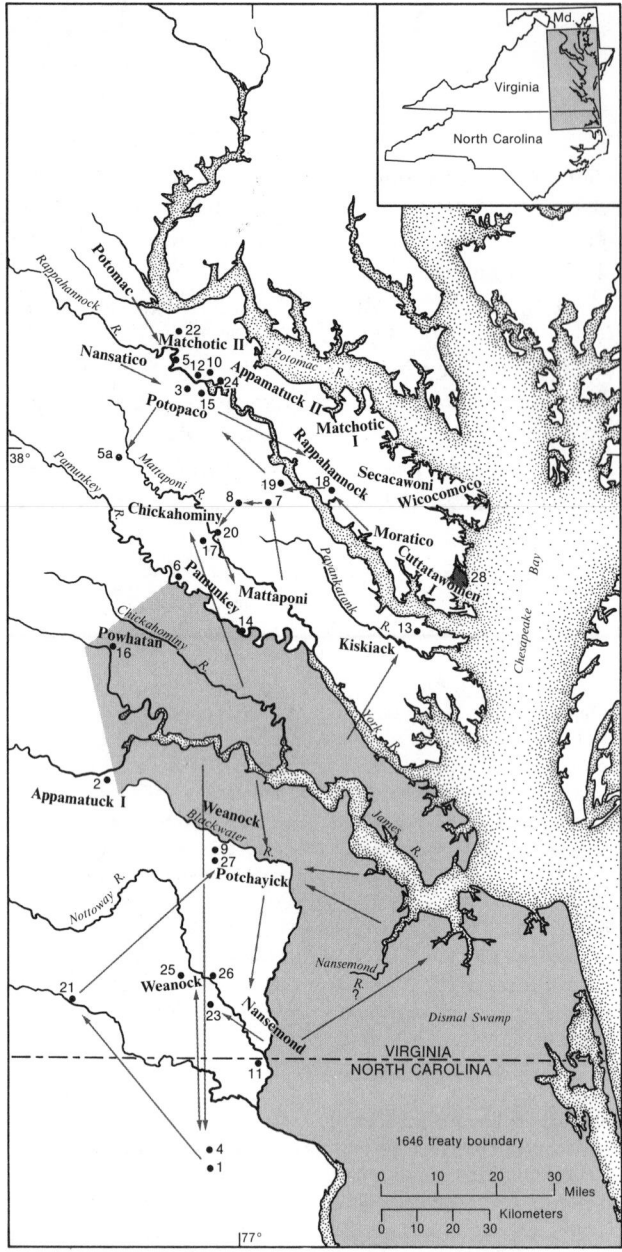

Fig. 3. Tribes and villages 1646–1750. Dates in parentheses indicate documented periods of occupation of villages. Arrows mark tribal dislocations. 1, Ahotsky (1646–1653, 1664–1667); 2, Appamatuck (1692); 3, Camden Site (ca. 1670); 4, Cotchawesco (1646–1653, 1664–1667); 5, Doeg (1664–1673); 5a, Doeg (1714–1720); 6, Manskin (1664–1670); 7, Mattaponi village (1653–1660); 8, Mattaponi village (1662–1667); 9, Musketank (1668–1676); 10, Nansateqond (1655–1666); 11, Nansemond I (1711–1733); 12, Nansemond II (1654–1666); 13, Nimcock (1649); 14, Pamaomeck (1653–present); 15, Port-Tobago (1666); 16, Powite (1663–1670); 17, Quaynohomock (1660–1689, 1702–?); 18, Rappahannock (1649–1676); 19, Rappahannock (1676–1684); 20, Rickahock, (Mattaponi 1667–1670, Chickahominy 1689–1702); 21, Unote (1667); 22, Upper Matchotic Town (1657); 23, Warekeck (1653–1662, 1663–1664); 24, Warisquock (1655); 25, Weanock village (1653–1662); 26, Weanock village (1653–1662); 27, Weanock village (1678–1693); 28, Wicocomoco Reservation (1656–1713). Tone indicates English area in 1646.

Chickahominy tribe alternately allied itself with its Powhatan neighbors and the English to preserve its independence. Little is known about groups along Rappahannock River, except that they sometimes were at war with one another. The same applies to the groups on the Virginia side of the Potomac, where small states like the Powhatan group possibly existed. The Powhatan group broke apart after the war of 1644–1646. Particularly the tribes on James River could no longer be controlled by the hitherto dominant Pamunkeys, who had absorbed most other tribes on the York and Pamunkey rivers. The Weanock were at war with the Nansemonds, Potchayicks, and Powhatans (Binford 1967). Although the colonial government backed their attempt (Stern 1952), the Pamunkey were unsuccessful in trying to retain control over the Chickahominies. Growing isolation of Indians in White areas contributed to the disintegration of the former state.

Seventeenth-century population figures supplied by contemporary sources (table 1) illustrate the numerical decline of tribal membership, but (with the partial exception of Strachey) they are all too low. Computations made with documented control cases place Virginia Algonquian population in the range of 14,000 to 21,000 people or, roughly, two persons per square mile (Feest 1973). Taking into account early depopulation through imported infectious diseases and warfare, total aboriginal population was probably even greater. Waning tribal cohesion possibly accounted for different estimates of individual tribes in the period around 1700.

Interethnic Relations

With the establishment of a permanent English colony in Virginia in 1607, nearly all groups immediately felt the presence of the settlers, tribes in Southside Virginia and the Virginia Peninsula being most affected. Fear caused by previous traumatic experiences with Whites and hope of deriving benefit from relations with a technologically superior group are responsible for the mixed feelings with which the colonists were met. Indian groups frequently changed their minds on whether to trade and ally themselves with, or to destroy the strangers. This vacillation allowed the English to survive the first years and even to learn from the Indians corn cultivation, fishing methods, and the construction of bark-covered huts (Smith 1884; A. Brown 1890).

Until 1622 each side tried to gain control over the other one: treaties were concluded, but no agreement was reached on their interpretation. Small-scale war resulted in the depopulation of large parts of the Virginia Peninsula where the English had gained a foothold (Percy 1922; Hamor 1615; Smith 1884). When the Indians saw that time worked against them, nativistic feelings were easily aroused by their priests. On March 22, 1622, the Powhatan group, assisted by the Chickahominies and some tribes on Potomac River (Wicocomoco,

Table 1. Virginia Algonquian Population Estimates, 17th Century

	1608 Smith (1612: 339–341)	*1608 Smith (1624: 347–348)*	*1610/1611 Strachey (1953: 45–46, 64–69)[a]*	*1669 (Hening 1809–1823, 2:274–275)*	*1703 Beverley (1705: 232–233)*	*First/last mentioned*
Powhatan group						
Appamatuck I	200	200	400	165	30	1607/1705
Arrohateck	100	100	200	-	-	1607/1611
Cantauncack	-	-	335	-	-	1608/1629
Caposepock	-[b]	-[b]	1,335	-	-	1608/1611
Cattachiptico	-	-	1,000	-	-	1608/1611
Chesapeake	335	335	335	-	-	1585/1627
Kecoughtan	65	65	100	-	-	1607/1610
Kiskiack	135–165	135–165	165	50	-	1607/1677
Mattaponi	100	100	465	65	-	1607/present
Menapacunt	-[b]	-[b]	335	-	-	1608/1611
Nansemond	665	665	665	150	100[e]	1585/present
Orapaks	-[b]	-[b]	165	-	-	1608/1611
Pamareke	-	-	1,335	-	-	1608/1611
Pamunkey	1,000	1,000	1,000	165	135[f]	1607/present
Paraconosko	-	-	35	-	-	1608/1611
Paspahegh	135	135	135	-	-	1607/1610
Potaunk	-	-	335	-	-	1608/1611
Payankatank	135	165–200	135–165	-	-	1608/1611
Potchayick	-	-	-	100	-	1661/1669
Powhatan	135	135	165	35	-	1607/1670[k]
Quacohamaock	-	-	135	-	-	1608/1611
Quiyoughcohannock	85	85	200	-	-	1607/1627
Shamapent	-	-	335	-	-	1608/1611
Warraskoyack	135	135	200	-	-	1585/1627
Weanock	335	335	500	50	almost wasted	1607/1707
Werowocomoco	135	135	135	-	-	1607/1611[k]
Youghtanund	200	200	235	-	-	1607/1611
Total	3,895–3,925	3,925–3,990	10,380–10,410			

Piscataway, Nacotchtank), launched the first coordinated attack against the colonists. Since other tribes on Potomac and Rappahannock rivers were neutral or friendly toward the English, the death of 350 English brought no advantage for the Indians; rather, it led to a decade of intermittent warfare (Kingsbury 1906–1935, 3 and 4).

Personal contacts were now severely restricted, and, except along the Potomac, the Indians were largely isolated. When for a second time the Indians tried to expel the English on April 18, 1644, they faced 15,000 colonists and their Indian allies from Accomac and the Rappahannock country. After two years of war, a peace was concluded that reduced the Indians to a tributary status and cost them all lands between York and Blackwater rivers. Though the English were nominally prohibited from entering Indian territories, they soon occupied large areas of land there (Hening 1809–1823, 1). In the 1650s, Pamunkey and Chickahominy troops fought for the English against intruding foreign Indians. Yet during Bacon's Rebellion, latent anti-Indian feelings were mobilized and the innocent Appamatuck I, Chickahominy, and Pamunkey tribes were attacked. In 1677 another treaty was made, by which the Indians ceded their remaining lands and were confined to small reservations for which an annual tribute had to be paid to the colony (Washburn 1957).

In spite of lip service paid by the English toward the education and Christianization of the Indians, nothing was done throughout the seventeenth century. Few Indians spoke English even by 1700, because administrative business was ordinarily transacted through interpreters, and there was little further need to learn the language. It was mainly the Indians who worked as hunters, scouts, or servants for the English who came into closer touch with European civilization. Some stayed among the Whites, while others formed the core of pro-English factions on the reservations.

Beginning in 1627, Negro slaves sometimes escaped to the Indians (McIlwaine 1924), but the effect of this contact on the Virginia Algonquians is as difficult to establish as the importance of intermarriages with Whites (starting with the Pocahontas-Rolfe marriage). Relations between Algonquian groups and their traditional Siouan and Iroquoian enemies remained hostile but lost their original importance under White dominance. In 1685 a

Table 1. Virginia Algonquian Population Estimates, 17th Century

	1608 Smith (1612: 339–341)	1608 Smith (1624: 347–348)	1610/1611 Strachey (1953: 45–46, 64–69)[a]	1669 (Hening 1809–1823, 2:274–275)	1703 Beverley (1705: 232–233)	First/last mentioned
Other tribes						
Chickahominy	665	835[c]	1,000	200	55[g]	1607/present
Appamatuck II	-	-	-	35	-	1608/1669
Cuttatawomen I	100	100	100	-	-	1608/1656
Cuttatawomen II	65	65	65	-	-	1608/1611
Matchotic I	335	335	335	-	-	1608/1659
Matchotic II	-	-	-	-[d]	-	1652/1669
Moratico	265	265	265	135	-	1608/1669
Nansatico	500	500	500	165[d]	-[h]	1608/1705
Opiscopank	-[b]	-[b]	-	-	-	1608/1611
Pissasec	-[b]	-[b]	-	-	-	1608/1611
Potomac	535	665	535	-	-	1608/1666[k]
Potopaco	-	-	-	200	17[h]	1669/1703
Rappahannock	335	335	335	100	a few families	1608/present
Secacawoni	100	100	100	-	-	1608/1660
Tauxenent	135	135	135	-	-	1608/1675?
Wicocomoco	435	435	435	235	10[i]	1608/1719[k]
Total	9,365-9,395	9,695-9,760	14,185-14,215	1,850	347+[j]	

NOTE: All data were originally given in terms of "warriors" or "bow-men." A 3:10 ratio (Smith 1612:354) has been used throughout to compute total population.

[a] Figures for tribes on Rappahannock and Potomac rivers copied from Smith (1612). Some tribal identifications of groups on Pamunkey and Mattaponi rivers are not established beyond doubt.

[b] Shown on Smith's map (1612) as a tribe ("King's house"), but no figures are given in the text.

[c] Hamor (1615:13, 55) gives 1,665; Smith (1624:525) edits this to 1,000.

[d] Nansatico and Matchotic II.

[e] Census of 1702: 35 including some Weanock (Anonymous 1894:362). Gov. Edmund Andros in 1697 substantiates Beverley's figure (Sainsbury 1860-1912, 15:456).

[f] Probably including the Mattaponi. 1702 census: 165 (including Mattaponi ?); Andros in 1697 gave 165 (including Mattaponi, Chickahominy).

[g] 1702 census: 100. Andros includes them with Pamunkey. Their village had 11 houses in 1699.

[h] Andros gives a total of 135 for two tribes on Rappahannock in 1697; this is reduced to 100 in the 1702 census. There were at least 70 Rappahannock in 1684 and around 50 Nansatico in 1704.

[i] Andros: 40. Only mentioned by 1702 census.

[j] Andros: 330; 1702 census: 300 +.

[k] Identity with 20th-century groups doubtful.

treaty was concluded with the Five Nations to end their inroads into Virginia (McIllwaine and Hall 1925-1945, 1). In Southside Virginia, relations with neighboring Iroquoians became even cordial: part of the Weanock tribe joined the Nottoways before 1700 (Binford 1967).

Subsistence

Hunting, fishing, and gathering wild plants provided the economic basis, while horticulture contributed about 25 percent of the diet. The annual cycle started in winter when the tribes moved upriver to their hunting grounds; here up to 300 people participated in organized communal hunts. Fires were set up to drive large numbers of deer into the shooting range of the hunters, or game was scared across rivers to be killed from boats. Stalking in disguise was common in individual hunting, and trapping was practiced to some degree (Strachey 1953; Clayton 1965; Ewan and Ewan 1970; Beverley 1705).

The men cleared from 20 to 200 acres of land around the village by the slash-and-burn method. Corn was planted from April to June with digging sticks by the women and children, who also did the weeding. The men were obliged to work on the chief's fields. Besides corn, two sorts of beans, gourds, pumpkins, passionflower, and tobacco were cultivated (Pargellis 1959). A few tribes had orchards after 1660 (Binford 1967; Stern 1952). Until harvest (August to October) the tribes split into small parties that lived by individual hunting, fishing, shellfishing, and gathering. While the gathering of roots, nuts, and acorns was women's work (assisted by old men and children), the men did their fishing with weirs of reed, hook and line, nets, and bows to which the arrow was tied. Fire-fishing was done at night with fires maintained in a boat to lure the fish (Glover 1676).

In aboriginal times dogs were kept and sometimes used in hunting, and some fowl may have been tamed as pets (Barbour 1969, 1). English efforts to "civilize" the Indians included unsuccessful attempts to introduce cattle breeding after 1650. Some Indians were known to have raised pigs by 1673, but most groups preferred to hunt the hogs of their English neighbors. Horses were rare among Virginia Algonquians even late in the seventeenth century (Clayton 1965).

The English colony greatly affected native economic patterns. In the early days huge quantities of corn were traded and stolen by the settlers from the Indians who in turn had at times to import corn from Southside Virginia and Accomac. After the 1622 massacre, English policy was to punish the Indians every summer by burning their fields (Smith 1884; Kingsbury 1906-1935, 3 and 4; McIlwaine 1924). Later on, reservations frequently proved too small to allow for the effect of soil exhaustion through corn cultivation, but hunting, fishing, and gathering rights outside the reservation had to be granted by the colonial administration. Communal hunts lost their importance with fragmented and diminishing tribal populations (Hening 1809-1823, 3; McIlwaine and Hall 1925-1945, 2).

Ecological differences between coastal and interior regions stimulated trade, which was rigidly controlled by the hereditary ruling families. Exotic raw materials, such as copper, were imported from far away (Smith 1884; Strachey 1953). Copper and shell beads served as money and wealth objects; shell beads lined on strings and measured by the arm's length were even accepted as ordinary currency in Virginia around 1650. Tubular beads, at least by the colonists called wampumpeak, and dark colored beads had greater value than disk-shaped roanoke and white beads (Feest 1967a). While trade for corn was important during the early years of the colony, only the tribes on Rappahannock and Potomac rivers derived some benefit from the more profitable fur trade; however, gradually even these groups lost their monopoly on trade with other tribes and their position as middlemen (Kingsbury 1906-1935, 3 and 4).

Meat, fish, and shellfish were roasted or boiled in a broth. Dough made of corn meal ground in wooden mortars could be either boiled or baked in the shape of balls or flat cakes; otherwise it was used to cook a thick mush known as hominy. Green corn was used with several dishes, and even burned and powdered corncobs were eaten. Bread and broths were also made from acorns, chinquapin nuts, chestnuts, and grass seeds. Poisonous food plants, such as the fungus known as tuckahoe, had to be leached before consumption. In the absence of salt, ashes of hickory or other plants served as substitutes. Water was the only drink before the introduction of alcohol (Hamor 1615; Pargellis 1959; Ewan and Ewan 1970; Beverley 1705).

To a limited extent food was preserved and stored on scaffolds or in pits. The chiefs alone were able to put away greater quantities of corn, beans, dried meat, fish,

and oysters in their "treasure houses" (Smith 1884; Strachey 1953).

Material Culture

Men did all work in stone, bone, shell, wood, and metal. Stones were flaked with bone pressers or ground and polished. Tree felling was accomplished with fire or by peeling off the bark. Wood was worked with stone and shell tools. Animal brains were used in the oil tanning of skins and hides. Coiled pottery of clay, tempered with crushed shells or quartz and frequently decorated with fabric impressions, was made by the women. The women also made baskets of yucca fiber and Indian hemp, mats of reeds and rushes, and cords of yucca, the inner bark of trees, and sinews. The simple fire drill served for fire making, with moss, dry leaves, or rotten wood being used for tinder (Barbour 1969; Strachey 1953; Beverley 1705; Southwell 1691; Pargellis 1959).

Knives of reed splinters, stone and shell scrapers, burins of hafted beaver teeth, bone awls and needles, wooden hoes, and stone celts fastened to wooden handles—all were soon replaced by iron implements of European origin. Iron axes (tomahawks) were also used as weapons, thus replacing wooden ball-headed and saber-shaped clubs, which could be armed with stone or metal points. Simple bows of maple, locust, or witch hazel were braced with strings of twisted leather or guts. Arrows had a shaft of wood or reed fletched with two radial feathers, and headed with a point of stone, bone, turkey claws, bird beak, shell, or a blunt wooden end. Points and feathers were fastened with deer sinews and a glue made of boiled antlers (Beverley 1705). In spite of prohibitions, the Indians soon learned the use of firearms, which they held like a bow with the extended left hand grasping the barrel (McIlwaine 1924; Michel 1916). Shields were made of bark and sometimes painted (Smith 1884; Feest 1967a).

Villages consisted of several neighboring hamlets lined up along the rivers; there may have been up to 100 houses in some settlements, but smaller numbers were the rule. Only few villages (particularly in northern Virginia) were more compact and fortified with palisades. Increasing depopulation and pressure from Iroquoian tribes led to the fortification of other settlements during the seventeenth century. Houses with a rectangular floor plan were made of a framework of arched poles and lashed-on cross bars and a covering of bark or reed mats. Two doors of removable mats, the smoke hole, and a central open fire lighted the room, which was from 25 to 50 feet long. Mat-covered, raised platforms along the walls served as beds. Other permanent structures in the village included storage facilities, sweat lodges, temples, and chief's or council houses (machacomocko), which were like ordinary dwellings but larger, and perhaps contained more than one room. During the hunting season small temporary huts, covered with mats, were erected by the women (Strachey 1953; Schmitt 1965; Durand 1932; Glover 1676; Berkeley and Berkeley 1968). A few chiefs of the seventeenth century lived in English-style houses (Kingsbury 1906-1935, 3; Hening 1809-1823, 1; Binford 1967). Windows without frames and panes were introduced in Indian houses before 1700 (Beverley 1705).

Except for children who went naked or wore wads of moss to cover their genitals, all Indians wore some sort of breechclout consisting of a belt and an apron of leather or vegetable material. Deerskin moccasins of a simple pattern and leggings fastened to the belt were used chiefly in winter. Upper garments of deerskin or raccoonskin were tied over one shoulder (fig. 4) or wrapped around the body. Both types were frequently fringed, painted, or adorned with shell (fig. 5) and copper beads; and both were originally worn only by members of the upper class, and later only by men. The same applies to feather coats of turkey feathers knotted in a net. European trade cloth, preferably red, gradually replaced skin dresses. Most types of headdresses (fig. 6)—colored deer hair roaches, single feathers, feather caps, copper ornaments, woven bands of shell beads, or antler headdresses—distinguished rank and class. Priests wore other distinctive costumes and ornaments (Michel 1916; Feest 1967).

Hair style differed according to sex and status. Girls shaved the front and sides of their heads and wore the remaining strands in long braids. Married women cut off their hair below the ears, while men usually shaved the right side of their heads to keep the bowstring from getting tangled, and tied the hair of the left side in a knot at the neck, or let a roach of hair stand on the crest of the head. Beards were rare; facial hair was usually plucked out with two shells. The Indians greased and painted their bodies regularly with bear grease, oil made from acorns and walnuts, and mineral or vegetable paints. Tattooing was apparently limited to women. Chains of shell, bone, copper beads, later also glass beads, preferably blue, were worn as necklaces, bracelets, and ear ornaments as was almost any suitable material.

Besides pottery and woven bags and baskets, gourds, wooden and stone bowls, and leather pouches served as containers. Babies were carried in cradleboards according to Beverley (1705). Dugout canoes up to 50 feet in length were paddled or poled on waterways; bridges of forked wooden poles and rails spanned creeks and swamps; well-marked paths traversed the woods.

260   Fig. 4. Eiakintomino in St. James's Park, London, about 1614. Watercolor copy of lost original. See Feest 1972:3-5.

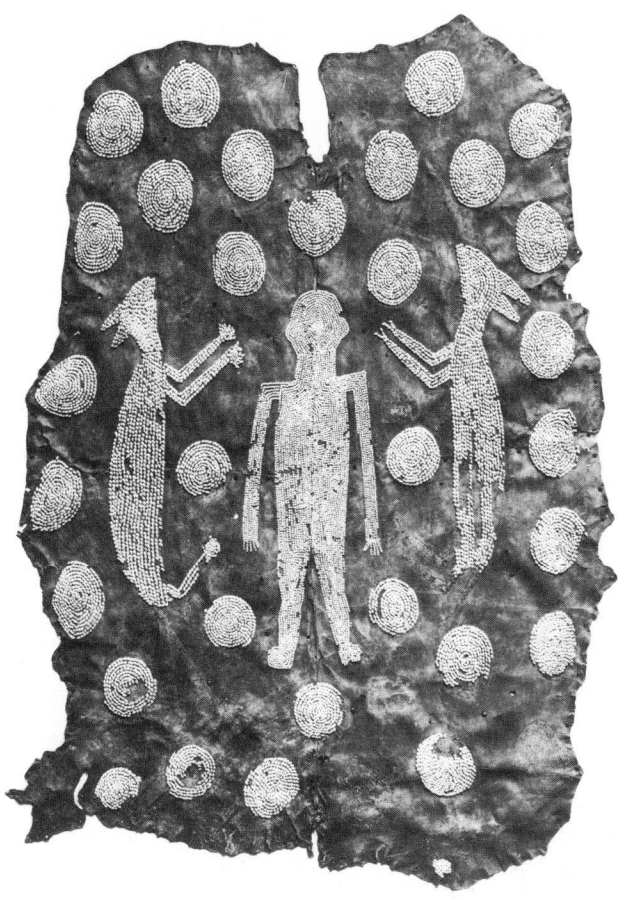

Fig. 5. Skin garment embroidered with shells, possibly marginella shell. Known as "Powhatan's Mantle." Collected before 1656.

Fig. 6. Virginia Algonquian, 23 years of age. Engraving by Wencelaus Hollar, 1645.

Obtuse angle pipes were made of clay and decorated with punctured designs or copper inlays. Stone pipes were rare (Schmitt 1965; McCary 1950).

Social Organization

The smallest unit of Virginia Algonquian society was the household (probably some sort of extended family) with 6 to 20 members. Nothing is known about larger kin groups. Every tribe consisted of one or more villages and was headed by a chief (werowance). Some dependent villages had their own subchief. Chieftainship was inherited in the female line.

Virginia Algonquian society was characterized by social stratification based on the accumulation of wealth. Status and wealth could be acquired by everyone through war deeds and individual economic capacities, but several restrictive practices enforced by the chiefs and their advisers favored social stability: tributes amounting to great parts of the economic yields had to be paid to the chiefs for the support of their families and the priests; the chief's fields were worked by the common people; trading monopolies reserved profits for the ruling class. Social mobility was regulated by the upper class. Good warriors or other persons were rewarded by the werowance with material goods or names. Besides the werowance, his advisers (cockarouses, cronoccoes) and the priests (quiyoughcosucks) belonged to the upper class. While women could be chiefs, all advisers and priests were men. The Chickahominies were ruled by eight great men (munguys), probably including the priests, and did not acknowledge werowances (Stern 1952). Powhatan's state misleadingly has been called a "confederacy." It is better classified as a small-scale monarchy. Membership of tribes within the group was not voluntary but through inheritance or conquest by the paramount chief. Political and economic coercion held the state together. Too little is known about groups outside the Powhatan group to allow statements on their political organization (Feest 1966).

During the first years, European contacts tended to strengthen Powhatan's position as paramount chief of his state and the position of the tribal werowances. The chiefs gained from developing trade relations and their prestige increased as the colonists acknowledged their leadership in intratribal affairs. While the role of werowance continued to be important (among the Chickahominies the rank of "great munguy" developed), the position of paramount chief disappeared as fragmentation of tribal territories continued (Hening 1809-1823, 1; McIlwaine and Kennedy 1905-1915, 2; McIlwaine 1924). War was waged for women and for revenge and by Powhatan's group also for territorial expansion. Priests had the ultimate decision on war in the council; the werowance or someone appointed by him led the war party. Ordinary men were killed in action or tortured to death in captivity; werowances, women, and children were kept prisoner. War customs included the taking of scalps and head-trophies. Powhatan's bodyguard of at least 50 men was a kind of standing army in times of peace (Percy 1922; Bland 1651; Berkeley and Berkeley 1968).

Life Cycle

Shortly after the birth of a child it received a name. In the course of a lifetime a person might acquire additional names according to special merits or abilities, or change it upon the death of a near relative. Infants were regularly bathed in cold water early in the morning. Economic activities were learned informally. Puberty was marked for part of the youths by the huskenaw rite: boys aged from 10 to 15 were selected by the werowances and priests, ritually separated from their parents who believed they were put to death, and secluded in the woods for nine months, where they were trained to become priests and advisers. Returning to their villages they were said to have been reborn and had to relearn everything, including the language (Barbour 1969; Spelman 1872).

A bride price had to be paid by the groom to the bride's family before marriage. A man could marry as many women as he was able to support, but generally only upper-class members were rich enough to marry more than one. After marriage the wife moved to her husband's house. Powhatan bestowed his wives after he had kept them for some time upon his friends to strengthen alliances. For the same reason intermarriages between ruling class families took place (Hamor 1615; Durand 1932).

After death, property was passed on in the male line. Mourning fell to the women, who blackened their faces and cried for 24 hours. Methods of corpse disposal included primary inhumation of the dead wrapped in mats or furs and scaffold burials with subsequent removal of the decayed flesh from the bones and secondary inhumation, partly in ossuaries. Werowances' bodies were preserved by cleaning the bones and sewing the original skin over them again; then they were laid on a scaffold in the western part of their temple of which there was at least one in every tribal territory. Special rites were associated with the manipulation of the corpses (Feest 1972).

Religion

Quiyoughcosuck was the designation not only for priests but also for a variety of lesser, benevolent deities served by their namesakes. These and their malevolent counterparts (tagkanysough) were probably more important north of the Powhatan group where religion was dominated by the belief in oke or okewis, a frightful and punishing god whose images were kept in the temple and carried into battle, and who could appear to the Indians in the shape of a man. Dead werowances and priests were believed to continue in the shape of oke. Another deity was ahone, a peaceful god to whom no offerings were made. Manitous were also acknowledged. According to upper-class ideology, only chiefs and priests could expect any sort of life after death, but throughout the region people believed in reincarnation and afterlife for all. Offerings of beads, copper, tobacco, or red paint were made to the oke, the water, and at altarstones in the woods by the priests and by commoners (Barbour 1969; Spelman 1872; Purchas 1617; Strachey 1953; Clayton 1965; Pargellis 1959; Beverley 1705).

The priests, of which there were at least two classes, lived in the temples where they tended a perpetual fire and kept picture-writing records of the past. They organized ceremonies (chiefly from September to mid-November), managed the treasuries of the werowances, and acted as conjurors (as in detecting crimes) and as doctors in curing the sick by magical procedures and the application of medical herbs. In their rituals the priests used language not understood by the common people (Smith 1884; Glover 1676; Berkeley and Berkeley 1968; Lederer 1958).

Activities

Nonlinguistic forms of communication included smoke signals and sign language. Strings of shell beads were used by orators in delivering speeches (later belts were used in concluding treaties). Stone heaps served to remind passersby of previous battles. Notched sticks and knotted cords helped counting and computing and pictographs carved on sticks or painted on hides told of past events (McIlwaine and Hall 1925-1945, 2).

Music was frequently connected with dance and ritual. Instruments included a flute or reed, wooden kettle drums and water drums of pottery, gourd rattles, and a folded piece of rawhide that was beaten with the hand. Dances were mostly circular.

A game of chance played with sticks provided a major opportunity for gambling. Ball games were football, shinny, and distance kicking. Boxing, wrestling, and running races were other popular sports.

Eighteenth and Nineteenth Centuries

Tribal Indian population continued to decline after 1700; however, many Indians were living among their White neighbors without receiving much attention. The Weanock, Appamatuck I, Potopaco, and Rappahannock tribes were reported to be extinct by 1722 (Beverley 1722), though the Rappahannocks continued to the twentieth century in their late seventeenth-century territory. The same applies to the Chickahominies, who faded from public view before 1760, and to the Nansemonds, who shared their fate after selling their reservation in 1786 (see table 2). The history of the Nansatico ends abruptly in 1705 when after a murder committed by some of their tribe they (and possibly the Potopaco) were deported to Antigua (Stern 1952; Hening 1809-1823, 13; McIlwaine and Hall 1925-1945, 2 and 3). Only the Pamunkey and Mattaponi tribes retained their tribal status on reservations whose size was constantly shrinking. Trustees were appointed for the Nansemonds in 1744 and for the Pamunkeys in 1759, who were to prevent the Indians' being cheated in land sales. Tribal locations remained stable except for that of the Chickahominies, part of whom drifted southward to Chickahominy River during the eighteenth century, and possibly the territory of the Nansemonds.

Increasing acculturation led to conflicts within the groups between traditionalists and English-oriented factions. Both sides met the same fate: largely conforming to White standards, they were not, however, accepted as Whites.

Intermarriages with Whites and, among off-reservation groups, Negroes were encouraged by the isolation and small size of Indian groups, even though endogamy was definitely the rule. Escaped Negro slaves and Whites discontented with life in their own society occasionally took abode with the Indians and were soon linked to them by marital ties. On the other hand, Indians living among Whites were frequently forced to mix with Negroes, either for lack of other opportunities or—as many Indians later claimed—under White pressure aimed at claiming their children in slavery. Real but more often alleged racial intermixture opened the way for racial discrimination after the Indians were legally put into the non-White category in 1705. Discrimination

was further facilitated by large-scale deculturation of the tribal societies and simultaneous replacement of the Indian dialects by English (Stern 1952).

Marriages with Whites were regarded as prestigious and some later became an important part of tribal histories. Eighteenth-century White ancestors are claimed, for example, by the Bradby family (fig. 7) of the Pamunkeys, the Bradbys and Winns of the Chickahominies, the Nelson family of the Rappahannocks, and the Newtons of the Potomac group (Speck 1925, 1928; Stern 1952).

Although a treaty with the Five Nations concluded in 1722 marks the last appearance of Virginia Algonquians on the stage of Indian politics, contacts with other Indian groups remained important. Between the Algonquian and Iroquoian remnants of Virginia, relations were good and helped to retain a feeling for Indianness. At least part of the Nansemonds joined the Nottoway in 1744. The tribes on the Chickahominy, Pamunkey, and Mattaponi rivers remained particularly close and intermarried frequently. After the Revolution, several Catawba families lived on the Pamunkey reservation. A few Pamunkeys returned with their guests to South Carolina and later moved with them to Utah. There was at least one intermarriage with the Chippewa Indians of Ontario at the time of the Civil War (Hening 1809-1823, 8).

Culture

Economic patterns changed slowly. A mixed economy made up of corn cultivation and hunting and fishing activities remained basic. Cotton was added to the crops grown by the women. Men began to engage in agriculture only around 1850. Fish were used as fertilizer. Bows and arrows or guns were used in individual and collective hunts; a wide variety of traps—some probably of non-Indian origin—was in use. Livestock finally became part of Indian economy: chickens and cows were kept around the houses, while cattle and hogs ranged freely to

Table 2. Virginia Algonquian Population Estimates, 18th Century

	1722 Beverley (1722:199-200)	ca. 1735 Gooch (1896:120)	1755 Gov. Dinwiddie	1769 Gov. Fauquier (Robinson 1959:63)	1787 Jefferson (1787:96)
Wicocomoco	few men	——	——	——	——
Chickahominy	16 families	——	——[b]	——	——
Mattaponi	——	——	——	——	3-4 men
Pamunkey	40 bowmen	10 families	——[b]	"remains"	10-12 men
Nansemond	30 bowmen	} 50 fighting men	——[b]	——	——[c]
Nottoway[a]					
Total			60 warriors		

[a] The Nottoway, although Iroquoian, are included because of joint mention by Gooch.

[b] Included in the total figure.

[c] Records of 1786 and 1791 give them 5 persons living in Southampton Co. (Hening 1809-1823, 12:386, 13:288).

Fig. 7. Pamunkey Indians in costumes made of turkey feathers and fringes of late 19th-century derivation. The costumes may have been used in their representation of the story of Pocahontas and John Smith. Left to right: William Bradby, J.T. Dennis, Howard Lee Allmond (girl), former chief William Terrill Bradby holding tomahawk and bow, Chief T.T. Dennis, George Cook, Captola Ulalah Cook, and Rev. Alex E.R. Allmond. Photograph by DeLancey Gill, October 1899.

be hunted or penned for fattening. Pottery making was commercially important for the Pamunkeys until the 1880s when competition from mass-produced wares seriously hurt the native industry.

Log or plank houses gradually replaced bark or mat-covered huts. Likewise, most groups started to use plank boats instead of dugouts. Clothing was chiefly made of woven goods either purchased or homespun. Technology and material culture remained traditional with the exception of innovations introduced by intermarried outsiders or Indians returning from life and work in White communities. Men frequently wore their hair long to be easily distinguished from Negroes. Except on the two reservations, formal tribal organization faded away.

Awareness of tribal identity was maintained in the face of outside pressures. Group solidarity was further strengthened by marriages within the community; among the reservation groups, tribal laws prohibited marriages with Negroes, a restriction later also adopted by the nonreservation groups. Polygyny was practiced as late as 1712 but must have disappeared shortly thereafter together with stratification of society based on the tribute system. Similar reasons led to the disappearance of native religion. After formal religious organization had broken down, the way was opened for Christianization. Most groups accepted the Baptist faith before 1800. Herbal lore, formerly a domain of the priests, persisted as common knowledge.

Twentieth Century

By 1900 only the Pamunkey and Mattaponi tribes still living on their reservations could claim unbroken continuity as tribes since the seventeenth century. Other groups, whose ultimate historical origin was not known, lived in various rural locations. Like the reservation tribes, they were not universally accepted as Indians by their neighbors. Fieldwork by Mooney and Speck supplied some groups with names and stimulated the reorganization of several tribes, but others retained their informal status. A new Powhatan Confederacy founded in the 1920s was short-lived, lacking the prestigious support of the reservation tribes. Another attempt at intertribal organization was made in 1970.

Different procedures in defining Indian status account for variations in population estimates made since 1900 (table 3). An increase of overall Indian population in eastern Virginia is accomplished by a decrease of the number of residents on the reservations, which do not offer sufficient economic opportunities for younger people. Since 1960 Indians living in rural districts have been outnumbered by those residing in metropolitan areas (see fig. 8). Some urban and suburban Indians are still affiliated with their tribes, while others may not even be descendants of tidewater Virginia groups. A main difference between reservation and nonreservation groups is that the former are still in possession of treaty rights dating back to 1646 and 1677. These include tax exemption on their reservation, local self-government, hunting and fishing rights, and the right to their reservation land, which is owned in common and held in trust by the Commonwealth of Virginia. In fulfillment of their treaty obligations they pay an annual tribute of fish, fowl (fig. 9) or venison to the governor, who personally must handle Indian affairs. In view of their special rights and their tribal continuity, reservation Indians feel somewhat superior to "citizen" Indians.

Approximately 550 acres out of a total of 900 acres of which the Pamunkey reservation consists is forested swamp not suitable for farming. While the arable land is allotted to the residents, the remainder is subdivided into six tracts or hunting territories, which are leased annually for the highest rent offered. Some of them were leased or sublet to non-Indian sportsmen by 1970. The Mattaponi reservation contains only 125 acres with consequently small allotments to residents. Land is owned individually among the other Virginia Algonquian tribes.

Farming remained an important economic activity for the Indian groups until after World War II. Oak husking pegs and gumwood mortars were still being used until truck farming became the rule. Another survival was the custom not to plant gourd seeds but simply to sow them on rich ground. While summer gardening was done by most of the tribes, only the Chickahominy and Rappa-

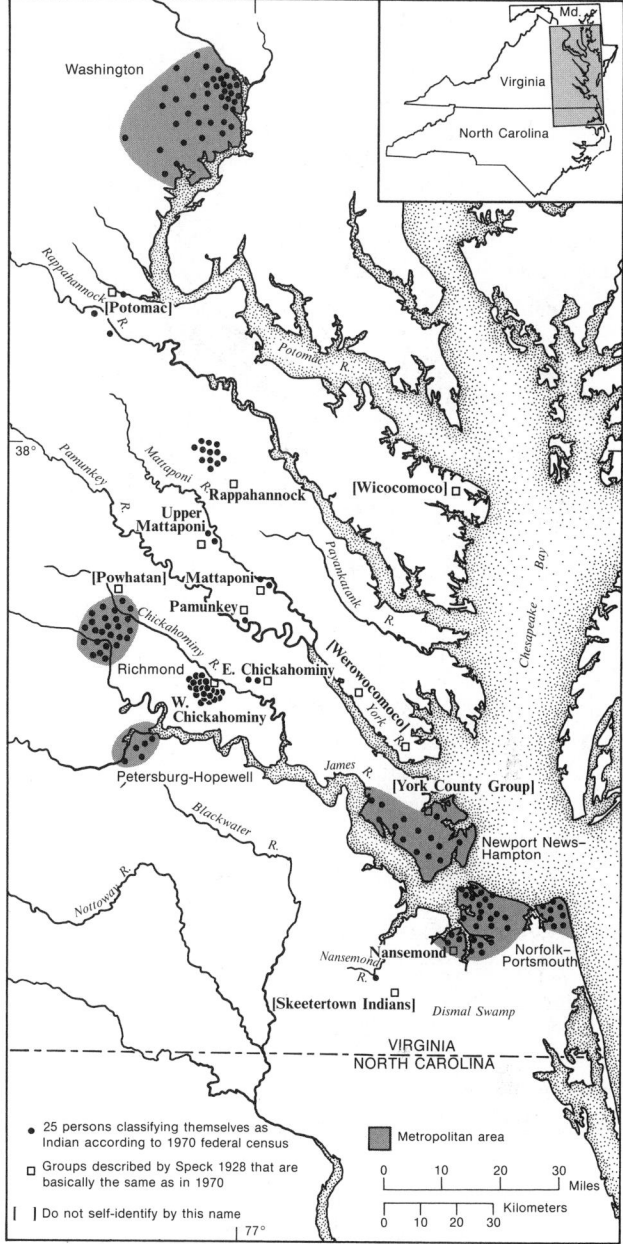

Fig. 8. 20th-century tribes and groups and 1970 population.

hannock remained largely farmers (Speck 1928; Rountree 1972a).

Individual and group hunting, trapping, and fishing with gill nets, trotlines, and rod and reel is widely practiced, although several devices and methods formerly used were prohibited by state game laws. During the shad season catches of fish are sold daily to a Richmond corporation by the Pamunkeys and Mattaponis. On both reservations shad hatcheries funded by the state are run by the Indians. Several Indians act as hunting guides for non-Indians. Others work as pulpwood procurers for a paper mill. Many men commute to jobs in the cities, like Richmond, Fredericksburg, or Washington, working in a great variety of occupations.

265

Fig. 9. Chickahominy Indians paying annual tribute to the governor of Virginia. Photographed in 1919.

Some native industries survived among the Indians of eastern Virginia into the twentieth century. Baskets made of splints of white oak had a wide distribution; rim constructions of these baskets differed among the Rappahannocks and Potomacs from that of the southern groups. The Rappahannocks also made baskets from rushes, while the Mattaponis used honeysuckle stems. Most adults at Mattaponi could make baskets in 1970, having learned the skill in their old reservation school. Neither was it a dead art among the Rappahannocks. Featherwork made by knitting and inserting feathers at the loops or by insertion into cloth was discontinued between 1920 and 1970 (Speck 1925, 1928; Rountree 1972a). Pottery was revived at Pamunkey in 1932 when a "pottery school" was built by the state. Molding is more common than coiling in making bowls, vases, and miniature canoes, which are afterwards fired in an electric kiln, painted in bright colors, and glazed (Stern 1951). These and other products are sold in a trading post on the reservation. Here as at another post on the Mattaponi reservation, crafts originating from non-Virginia tribes were sold.

The tribes of tidewater Virginia are each governed by a chief and council of four to eight members. Elections usually take place every four years; reelection is allowed indefinitely. The reservation groups practice only male suffrage. The council enforces the written laws of the tribe, which are kept secret from outsiders by both reservation groups. At Pamunkey these laws are known to exist at least since 1887 (Pollard 1894). On the reservations, the council also handles business relating to reservation lands and selects the trustees for the tribe from among local White men sympathetic to the Indians, to assist the council when called upon. The chief represents

his tribe to the outside world and is always selected for his personal qualifications, even though he may be the son of the former chief (as was the case among the Pamunkey, Western Chickahominy, and Rappahannock). Long tenure of office is therefore quite common. Tribal organization is more easily maintained on the reservation than among the "citizen" Indian groups (Rountree 1972a).

Descent is reckoned bilaterally. While marriages with Whites have become more frequent, marriage with other Indians is still preferred. Intermarriage with Blacks results generally in expulsion from the tribe. Nevertheless, the Indians were as frequently discriminated against as Negroes, particularly by application of Virginia's Racial Integrity Law of 1924. A high frequency of paired-sibling marriage has been reported from the Western Chickahominy (Stern 1952).

Fig. 10. Mattaponi Chief Curtis Custalow and family in Plains-inspired ceremonial dress. Photograph by Helen C. Rountree, 1970.

Schooling has always been a matter of great concern for all Virginia Algonquian tribes. Most Indians were barred from White schools and refused to go to "colored" schools. The small private schools of the Chickahominies and Upper Mattaponis as well as the state reservation school for the Pamunkey and Mattaponi offered education only through the seventh grade; higher grades were added in some of them after 1950. The Rappahannocks and Nansemonds never had any schools of their own, but the Nansemonds were admitted to White schools. Despite all shortcomings, Indian schools were important for the groups who had them as a focus of tribal identity. Teachers were mainly Indians, and Indian arts and crafts could be learned there.

Integration has changed the picture considerably. Sharon Indian school (Upper Mattaponi) was closed in 1965, the Mattaponi school in 1966. The Western Chickahominies' Samaria Indian school became part of the Charles City County school system, but after reapportionment in 1968 only a few Indian children could continue to attend it. The closing of the schools and resulting busing was strongly resented by the tribes.

All Indians of eastern Virginia are Baptists, except for the Nansemonds who are partly Methodists. The Nansemonds also have churches in common with their non-Indian neighbors, while the other groups have churches of their own, which after the closing of their schools won added importance for retaining visibly Indian identity (Rountree 1972a). The oldest of these is Pamunkey In-

dian Baptist Church, founded in 1865; Samaria Indian Baptist Church has served the Western Chickahominies since 1901; the Eastern Chickahominies have Tsen Commocko Indian Baptist Church since they split from the rest of the tribe in 1921; the Mattaponi Indian Baptist Church has existed since 1931. The Rappahannocks have two churches near Beazly and Helmet. The Upper Mattaponis' church is known as Indianview Baptist Church. These churches form part of the Dover Baptist Association within the Southern Baptist Convention. Most communities are served by White ministers, al-

Table 3. Virginia Algonquian Population Estimates, 20th Century

Tribe or area [a]	Date of organization	Mooney 1899[b]	Census 1910[c]	Speck 1923[d]	Census 1950[e]	Beale 1950[f]	Blume 1951[g]	Census 1960[h]	Census 1970[i]	Rountree 1971[j]	McCary 1972[k]
Nansemond	1923[l]	220(150)		200 (58)						(40?)	
Eastern Chickahominy	1921				61	100[m]	86 (69)	64	45	60	60
Western Chickahominy	1908	220(200)	225	400(264)	272	690	392(351)	426	510	700(600)	800(650)
Pamunkey	tribal	150(130)		300(125)	50		114 (55)	48		140 (40)	333 (33)
Mattaponi	tribal	40 (30)	180	75 (75)	60		173 (60)	55	113	140 (40)	394 (44)
Upper Mattaponi	1923	40		78 (78)	118	130	195(175)	110		200(100)	100
Rappahannock	1919			500(376)	54	430	225(160)	165	231	450(350)	
Potomac	——			150		230		1	17		
Wicocomoco	——			300				1	4		
Werowocomoco	——			100					5		
Powhatan	——			15	10			23	——[n]		
Washington Metropolitan Area					94			215	1,027		
Richmond Metropolitan Area					30			141	635		
Norfolk-Portsmouth Metropolitan Area					89			340	851		
Newport News-Hampton Metropolitan Area					25			102	346		
Other groups or areas		80	46		19	30[m]		82	203		
Total		750(630)	451	2,118(976)	882	1,610	1,185(870)	1,783	3,987	1,730(1,230)	1,687(887)

[a] Federal census publications report Indian population by area rather than tribe. See fig. 8 for the equation of tribes and areas.

[b] Based on census figures collected by Mooney (1907:147–151). Resident population is given in parentheses.

[c] Racial status as adjudged by community (U.S. Bureau of the Census 1922).

[d] Estimates by Speck (1925:vii, 1928:286). Enrolled tribal membership by 1923 in parentheses.

[e] All full-bloods, Indian-White issues if enrolled tribal members, mixed bloods if one-quarter or more of Indian blood, or if regarded as Indians within the community (U.S. Bureau of the Census 1952).

[f] Based on 1950 federal census data but including individuals classified there as Whites or Negroes (Beale 1957:195–196).

[g] Figures supplied by chiefs of the bands to Blume (1951). Resident population in parentheses.

[h] Racial status according to self-identification (U.S. Bureau of the Census 1963).

[i] Racial status according to self-identification (U.S. Bureau of the Census 1971).

[j] Figures supplied by chiefs of the bands or estimated by Rountree (1972a).

[k] Figures supplied by chiefs of the bands or estimated by Ben C. McCary (personal communication 1972).

[l] Organization defunct since at least 1960.

[m] 30 Eastern Chickahominy in James City Co.

[n] Hanover Co. figures included in Richmond Metropolitan Area.

though a Mattaponi pastor serves the Western Chicka-hominies.

Many Western Chickahominy men are members of the Woodmen of the World, a fraternal organization. There is also a strong and active Parent-Teacher Association in this group. Since about 1950 the Chickahominy Fall Festival is held each year on the fourth Saturday in September. Organized by the Western Chickahominy, who also actively take part in pan-Indian politics, this event features speeches, Indian dances, and other activities designed to strengthen contacts among the Virginia Indian groups and Indians from out of state.

Synonymy

In spite of frequent attempts, no satisfactory etymologies of tribal names have been established. Similarly, no records exist that would permit phonetic transcription of most of these names. Pronunciations (in English) will therefore be supplied only for groups still using these designations in modern times.

Appamatuck I: Apamatecoh (Archer 1607:97); Apamatica, 1607 (Percy 1625:137); Apaomateke, 1612 (Percy 1922:273); Apomatick, 1687 (Clayton 1965:24); Appamatuck (Smith 1612:map).

Appamatuck II: Appamatuck (Smith 1608:185); Appomatux, 1669 (Hening 1809–1823, 2:275).

Arrohateck: Arrahatecoh (Archer 1607:84); Arahatteak (Tindall 1607); Arrohateck (Smith 1612:map); Arsahattocke (Hamor 1615:27); Arssateck (Zúñiga 1608); Irrohatock (Smith 1612:340).

Cantauncack: Candaungack, 1639 (McIlwaine 1924:482); Cantauncack (Smith 1612:map); Cantaunkack, 1611 (Strachey 1953:69).

Cattachiptico: Cakkiptaco (Zúñiga 1608); Cattachipico (Velasco 1611); Cattachiptico (Smith 1612:map); Chepeco, 1611 (Strachey 1953:69).

Chesapeake: Cassapecock, identity doubtful, 1611 (Strachey 1953:69); Checepiock (Velasco 1611); Chesapeack (Smith 1612:map); Chesapeiacks, 1627 (McIlwaine 1924:151); Chesepians, tribe (Lane 1589:257); Chesepiuc, village (Lane 1589:257); Chissapiack (Zúñiga 1608); Cissapeack (Smith 1624:570).

Caposepock: Caposepock, 1612 (Strachey 1953:69); Kupkipcock, identity doubtful (Smith 1612:map).

Chickahominy (ˌchĭkəˈhämənē): Chechohomynaies, 1608 (Barbour 1969:226); Checka Hamania (Smith 1608:178); Chekohomini, 1619 (Kingsbury 1906–1935, 3:147); Chickahomini, 1661 (Hening 1809–1823, 2:34); Chickcahomaniacke, before 1620 (Barbour 1969:176); Chicohominies (Hamor 1615:11); Chiconamians, 1612 (Percy 1922:271); Chikahominy (Hamor 1615:57).

Cuttatawomen I: Corotomen, 1656 (Nugent 1934:343); Cuttatawomen (Smith 1608:184).

Cuttatawomen II: Cuttatawomen (Smith 1612:map).

Kecoughtan: Cecoughtans (Purchas 1625, 4:1692), Chechotanke (Tindall 1607); Kecotan (Velasco 1611); Kecoughtan, 1607 (Percy 1625:135); Keequotancke, before 1620 (Barbour 1969: 174); Kekowhatan, 1612 (Percy 1922:268); Kequoughtan (Smith 1608:185).

Kiskiack: Cheescake, 1677 (Hening 1809–1823, 2:411); Chescaik (Archer 1607:98); Chescheak (Purchas 1625, 4:1772); Cheskyake, 1675 (McIlwaine 1924:401); Chesquiack, 1662 (Hening 1809–1823, 2:153); Kiskiack (Smith 1612:map); Kiskieck (Zúñiga 1608).

Matchotic I: Machoatick, 1650 (Fowke 1899:24); Machotics (Jefferson 1787:95); Onawmanient, identity doubtful (Smith 1612:341).

Matchotic II: Machotick, 1662 (MacCord 1969:55); Matchoatick, 1652 (Browne 1885:281); Mattehatique, 1669 (Hening 1809–1823, 2:275); Upper Matchotix, 1657 (Nugent 1934:490).

Mattaponi (ˌmătəpōˈnī): Matapoll (Archer 1607:97); Mattapanient (Zúñiga 1608); Mattapanies, 1669 (Hening 1809–1823, 2:275); Mattapony (Mooney 1907: 147); Mattaponi (Speck 1925:vii); Mattaponies (Jefferson 1787:96).

Menapacunt: Manapacumter (Smith 1608:187); Menapacunt (Zúñiga 1608); Menapacute (Smith 1608:184); Mummapacun, 1611 (Strachey 1953:69).

Moratico: Maraticund, 1662 (McCary 1950:4); Marraugh tacum (Smith 1608:184); Moraughtacund (Smith 1612:map); Totas Chees, 1669 (Hening 1809–1823, 2:275); Totuskeys (Jefferson 1787:95).

Nansatico: Nandtanghtacund (Smith 1612:map); Nansiatico, 1704 (McIlwaine and Hall 1925–1945, 2:359); Nantaughs tacum (Smith 1608:185); Nantiatico, 1700 (McIlwaine and Hall 1925–1945, 2:44); Nantsattaqunt, before 1620 (Barbour 1969:185); Nanzaticoe, 1674 (McIlwaine 1924:500); Nazatica (Smith 1624:596); Noncottecoe, 1662 (McIlwaine 1924:493); Nonsowhaticond (Hamor 1615:54).

Nansemond (ˈnănsəmänd): Nancemondies, 1612 (Percy 1922:277); Nandsamund (Smith 1612:map); Nansamund (Zúñiga 1608); Nansimum, 1646 (Hening 1809–1823, 1:315); Nattamonge (Tindall 1607); Nawsamond (Smith 1608:201); Tripanicks, possible North Carolina Algonquian name (Lane 1589:257).

Opiscopank: Opiscopank (Smith 1612:map).

Orapaks: Orapakes (Purchas 1625, 4:1692); Orapaks (Smith 1612:map); Orohpikes (Spelman 1872:civ).

Pamareke: Pamakeroy (Zúñiga 1608); Pamareke, 1611 (Strachey 1953:69); Pamuncoroy (Smith 1612: map).

Pamunkey (pəˈmuŋkē): Pamaunck (Smith 1608:181); Pamonke (Tindall 1607); Pamunky, 1611 (Strachey 1953:57); Pameunkok, 1623 (Kingsbury 1906–1935, 4:37); Pomucke, 1622 (Kingsbury 1906–1935, 3:584); Pomunkeye (Spelman 1872:cxi); Powmunkey, 1613 (Spelman 1872:civ).

Paraconosko: Baraconos, 1611 (Strachey 1953:69); Parokonosko (Zúñiga 1608).

Paspahegh: Paspahe, 1612 (Percy 1922:274); Paspahegh (Smith 1612:map); Paspaheyans (Smith 1608:207); Paspeiouk (Archer 1607:97); Paspihae, 1607 (Percy 1625:139).

Payankatank: Payankatank (Zúñiga 1608; Smith 1612:map).

Pissaseck: Pissaseck (Smith 1612:map); Pissassac (Smith 1624:429).

Potaunk: Pataunck, 1611 (Strachey 1953:69); Potaūcac (Smith 1612:map); Potavncak (Smith 1624:462); Potawunkack (Zúñiga 1608).

Potchayick: Poackyacks, 1707 (Saunders 1886-1890, 1:660); Pochaicks, 1707 (Binford 1967:158); Pohics (Jefferson 1787:95); Potchiacks, 1707 (Binford 1967:158); Powchay-icks, 1669 (Hening 1809-1823, 2:274).

Potomac (pə'tōmək): Pataomecke (Hamor 1615:4); Pataromerke (Smith 1608:186); Patawomeck (Smith 1612:map); Patomeck, 1613 (Spelman 1872:ciii); Potomack, 1662 (Hening 1809-1823, 2:149).

Potopaco: Port-Tabago (Beverley 1705:233); Portobaccoes, 1669 (Hening 1809-1823, 2:275).

Powhatan (päwə₁tăn): Poetan (Tindall 1607); Powáhtan, 1613 (Spelman 1872:cii); Powaith, 1672 (Lederer 1958:map); Powhatan (Smith 1608:171); Powhites, 1669 (Hening 1809-1823, 2:275); Powite, 1663 (Bushnell 1919:37); Tanx Powhatans, 1623 (Kingsbury 1906-1935, 4:9).

Quackohamaock: Ochahannauke, identity doubtful, 1611 (Strachey 1953:69); Quackohowaon (Smith 1612:map); Quacohamaock (Zúñiga 1608).

Quiyoughcohannock: Coiacohhanauke, 1611 (Strachey 1953:64); Quayoughcohanek (Velasco 1611); Quiocqahannock, before 1620 (Barbour 1969:172); Rapahanna, 1607 (Percy 1625:136); Tapahanna (Tindall 1607); Tappahanocke (Smith 1608:172).

Rappahannock (₁răpə'hănək): Rapahanocks (Smith 1624:424); Rappahannocke, before 1620 (Barbour 1969:184); Tapohanock (Smith 1608:185); Toppahanock (Smith 1612:map).

Secacawoni: Cecocawonee (Smith 1624:417); Cekakawwon (Smith 1612:map); Chickakone, 1659 (Hiden and Dargan 1966:11); Sekacawone (Smith 1612:341); Yaocomoco, 1652 (Browne 1885:281).

Shamapent: Shamapa, 1611 (Strachey 1953:69); Shamapent (Zúñiga 1608).

Tauxenent: Tauxenent (Smith 1612:map); Tauxent (Velasco 1611). The following entries are possibly synonymous: Doeggs, 1663 (Hening 1809-1823, 2:193); Doegs, 1666 (Nugent 1934:558); Taux (Smith 1612:113); Toags (Smith 1624:417).

Upper Mattaponi (upər ₁mătəpō'nī): Adamstown Indians (Speck 1928:265); Upper Mattaponi (Speck 1925:vii).

Warraskoyack: Waresquokes, 1623 (Kingsbury 1906-1935, 4:222); Wariscoyans, 1612 (Percy 1922:273); Waroskoyack (Smith 1608:175); Warraskoyack (Smith 1608:190); Weraskoyks (Smith 1612:386); Weroscoick (Purchas 1625, 4:1756); Oriskayek (Tindall 1607); Opossians, possibly North Carolina Algonquian name (Lane 1589:257).

Weanock: Wainoake (Bland 1651:9); Weanock (Smith 1608:172); Weianoacks, 1627 (McIlwaine 1924:151); Weyonaques, 1623 (Kingsbury 1906-1935, 4:251); Winauk (Archer 1607:93); Wyanokes, 1623 (Kingsbury 1906-1935, 4:9); Wynagh (Tindall 1607).

Werowocomoco: Warowocomo (Zúñiga 1608); Weramocomoco (Smith 1608:18); Werowocomoco (Smith 1612:map); Worowocomoco, 1611 (A. Brown 1890:504); Poetan (Tindall 1607).

Wicocomoco: Wiccocomico, 1660 (Hening 1809-1823, 2:14); Wickacomio, 1669 (Hening 1809-1823, 2:275); Wickicomoco, 1659 (Hiden and Dargan 1966:11); Wicomico, 1656 (McIlwaine 1924:505); Wighcocomoco (Smith 1612:map).

Youghtanund: Yaughtawnoon, 1613 (Spelman 1872:cv); Yawtanoone, 1613 (Spelman 1872:ciii); Yoghtanunt, before 1620 (Barbour 1969:183); Youghtamong (Archer 1607:97); Youghtanund (Smith 1612:map).

Sources

Knowledge of Virginia Algonquian tribes before 1607 is chiefly based on archeological evidence. Excavated sites of historic villages, such as Patawomeck (Schmitt 1965), Cuttatawomen II (MacCord 1965), or Qosaugh (McCary 1953) provide important links with the prehistoric past. The Spanish sources on the abortive Jesuit mission are assembled in Lewis and Loomie (1953), while Quinn (1955, 1961) includes all the information the English Roanoke colonists noted on the Indians of their northern neighborhood.

The seventeenth century is the period for which remain the fullest data before modern times. John Smith's writings (1884) frequently betray his anti-Indian sentiments, but they include the first ethnographic description of the Virginia Algonquians. Reports written by other colonists are often used and edited in his works. Archer (1607) and Percy (1625) deal with the exploration of James River in 1607; Barbour (1969) includes these and all other pertinent documents up to 1609. Further early sources are in Purchas (1617, 1625), Force (1836-1846), A. Brown (1890), Sainsbury et al. (1860-1912), and Kingsbury (1906-1935).

Strachey (1953) depends partly on Smith and Percy but adds much new information; his linguistic interests and systematic work with informants make up for Smith's better knowledge of the whole country. Spelman's *Relation* (1872), an interesting but almost illiterate account, written when the author was only 18 years old, is based on personal experiences among the Powhatan and Potomac tribes. Hamor (1615) adds to knowledge of the Chickahominy and Powhatan groups.

After the 1622 massacre and the dissolution of the Virginia Company in 1624, interest in Indian topics declined; only the 1644 massacre and its aftermath aroused fresh curiosity. Virginia Algonquian groups continued to play their part in colonial history until Bacon's Rebellion, but few sources are worth noting; Bland (1651), Lederer (in Lederer 1958), and Glover (1676) deal partly with these tribes. For printed and manuscript sources on the rebellion itself and the role played in it by Virginia Algonquians, see Washburn (1957). During the last quarter of the seventeenth century, the Indians attracted the attention of several interested observers, among them Sir Robert Southwell (1691), a clergyman (Clayton 1965), a naturalist (Ewan and Ewan 1970), an anonymous author (Pargellis 1959), a French emigrant (Durand 1932), a Swiss traveler (Michel 1916), and a Quaker (Story 1747). Although Beverley (1705) copied and quoted from earlier authors, he adds some good new information, particularly on religion. Updated population figures are supplied by the second edition (Beverley 1722).

Early collections by Strachey, Newport, Whitaker, Stioring, Byrd I, and five Virginia items in the British Museum (Bushnell 1906) are now lost. Only two Virginia pieces from the Tradescant collection survived in the Ashmolean Museum, Oxford (Tradescant 1656; Tylor 1888; Bushnell 1907). More details about some aspects of material culture are supplied by archeology, particularly by material from seventeenth-century villages, such as Warekeck (Binford 1965) or the Camden site (MacCord 1969).

For a discussion of early pictures of the Virginia Algonquians see Feest (1967). The maps of Smith, Tindall, Zúñiga, and Velasco (Barbour 1969) are of great importance in locating early seventeenth-century villages. Later maps of interest are Heermans (1673) and Lederer (1958).

Indian-White relations during the seventeenth and eighteenth centuries figure prominently in official records (Hening 1809-1823; McIlwaine 1918-1919, 1924; McIlwaine and Hall 1925-1945; McIlwaine and Kennedy 1905-1915; Palmer et al. 1875-1893; Nugent 1934). Other reports on Virginia Algonquians are rare between 1705 and 1900; Fontaine (1972), Burnaby (1775), Jefferson (1787), Dalrymple (1858), Aylett (in U.S. Census Office 1894), and Pollard (1894) are among the exceptions, but are generally of doubtful quality. Nineteenth-century documents used and printed by J.H. Johnston (1970) reflect the bias of their time in regard to Indian-Negro relations.

Investigations by anthropologists among twentieth-century groups have yielded a considerable amount of tradition relating to the eighteenth and nineteenth centuries. Fieldwork was mainly conducted among the reservation groups, the Upper Mattaponi, Western Chickahominy, and Rappahannock. Published information is contained in the works of Mooney (1890, 1907), and especially in the writings of Speck (1925, 1928) and his pupils (Speck, Hassrick, and Carpenter 1942, 1946; Speck and Schaeffer 1950; Stern 1951, 1952; Hassrick and Carpenter 1944; Rowell 1943). Unpublished field data are available in the National Anthropological Archives, Smithsonian Institution, Washington (Gatschet 1890-1893) and in the Library of the American Philosophical Society, Philadelphia (Speck 1919-1946; Kremens 1940; Solenberger 1940; Stern and Mook 1941). More recent data were published by Blume (1951) and Rountree (1972, 1972a).

Notable modern museum collections from Virginia Algonquian tribes may be found in the National Museum of Natural History, Washington; the Denver Art Museum, Denver; the American Museum of Natural History, New York, and the Museum of the American Indian, New York.

Several scholars have combined their fieldwork with historical research on the Virginia Algonquians. Among the studies relating mainly to the seventeenth century, the following merit particular attention: Barbour (1967, 1971, 1972), Binford (1967), Feest (1966, 1966a, 1967a, 1969, 1972, 1973), Garrow (1968), Gerard (1907), Lurie (1959), McCary (1950, 1957), Mook (1943, 1943a, 1943b, 1944), Robinson (1959), and Willoughby (1907). An analysis of data in comparison with other coastal Algonquians is Flannery (1939). The best bibliography available on the subject of the Virginia Indians is by Pierce and McCary (1969).

North Carolina Algonquians

CHRISTIAN F. FEEST

Language, Territory, and Environment

The Algonquian-speaking tribes who once lived in coastal North Carolina represent the southernmost extension of Algonquian groups along the Atlantic seaboard.* Like their Virginia relatives to the north they combined a southeastern habitat with a northeastern heritage and are grouped together with them as "southeastern Algonquians." Differences in cultural as well as natural environment brought about variations of the same basic pattern, which justify separate treatment.

To the north, the tribes of eastern North Carolina were bordered by Virginia Algonquian groups and by the Dismal Swamp. Unlike the situation in Virginia, there was no natural western boundary to Algonquian territory; and the coastal plain extending farther to the west and south of it was inhabited by Iroquoian tribes. It is in fact very hard to define this boundary clearly all along its course. The Tuscaroras, for example, were claiming all the region west of Chowan River and south of Cuttawhiskie Swamp during the seventeenth century; but in 1585 several villages, presumably or even certainly belonging to Algonquian tribes, had been located in this region (Hoffman 1967).

Evidence for the linguistic relationship of coastal groups with the Algonquian family of languages is small. Less than 100 words, besides place, tribal, and personal names, were recorded by the English colonists of the Roanoke voyages. In all likelihood these were mainly from the Roanoke, Croatoan, and Secotan dialects (Quinn 1955, 2). Another 37 words, this time of the Pamlico language, were published by Lawson (1709). Both word lists are sufficient to prove an Algonquian affiliation of those groups. Other tribes can be classed as Algonquians only on nonlinguistic grounds. The Weapemeoc and Chawanoke tribes may be considered as certainly belonging to this family. The evidence for the Moratuc (Mook 1943c) and Neusiok is far from convincing; both may have been Iroquoian tribes. Algonquian affiliation of the Pomouik rests on their suggested identity with the Pamlico.

*The language of the North Carolina Algonquians is no longer spoken. In the absence of adequate early recordings, the spelling of native terms and proper names follows their historical orthography.

The North Carolina coastal plain has an almost flat surface with many lakes, extensive swamps, and sand dunes. The coastline is deeply indented by sounds (Currituck, Albemarle, Pamlico) and tidal rivers. A chain of narrow islands and sand bars closes the sounds against the Atlantic Ocean. Predominately sandy soils are covered by coarse grasses, marsh vegetation, and evergreen forests. Climate is of the humid subtropical variety, with an annual growing season of about 250 days. Both freshwater and saltwater fish, oysters, and clams are abundant in the coastal region, which is also much frequented by local and migrant water birds and by game birds. Mammals include deer, fox, squirrel, opossum, rabbit, and in former days also bear and puma.

Archeology

Very little is known about the archeology of coastal North Carolina. On the basis of a survey made by Haag (1958), a few sites in this region may be tentatively identified with historic Indian villages. For the area occupied by the Roanoke and Croatoan Indians, shell-tempered pottery appears to be typical, which indicates similarities with tidewater Virginia. Clay-grit tempered wares predominate along the Chowan River; sand-tempered pottery characterizes the Secotan area. Thus, a greater differentiation of protohistoric manifestations than in coastal Virginia becomes apparent. Late cultural influences from the south can be traced in an increase of simple stamped sherds.

Late Sixteenth Century

The history of early European contacts along the North Carolina coast is similarly clouded. Several explorers, including Giovanni da Verrazano in 1524, are credited with reaching that region and even contacting the Indians; however, evidence is in no case conclusive. Native traditions recorded at the time of the English colony on Roanoke Island refer to only one previous contact with Whites: in 1558 shipwrecked people, probably Spanish, were saved by the people of Secotan and after a short time tried to make their way home on an improvised ship. Other ships wrecked on the Carolina coast first provided the Indians with iron implements (Barlowe

271

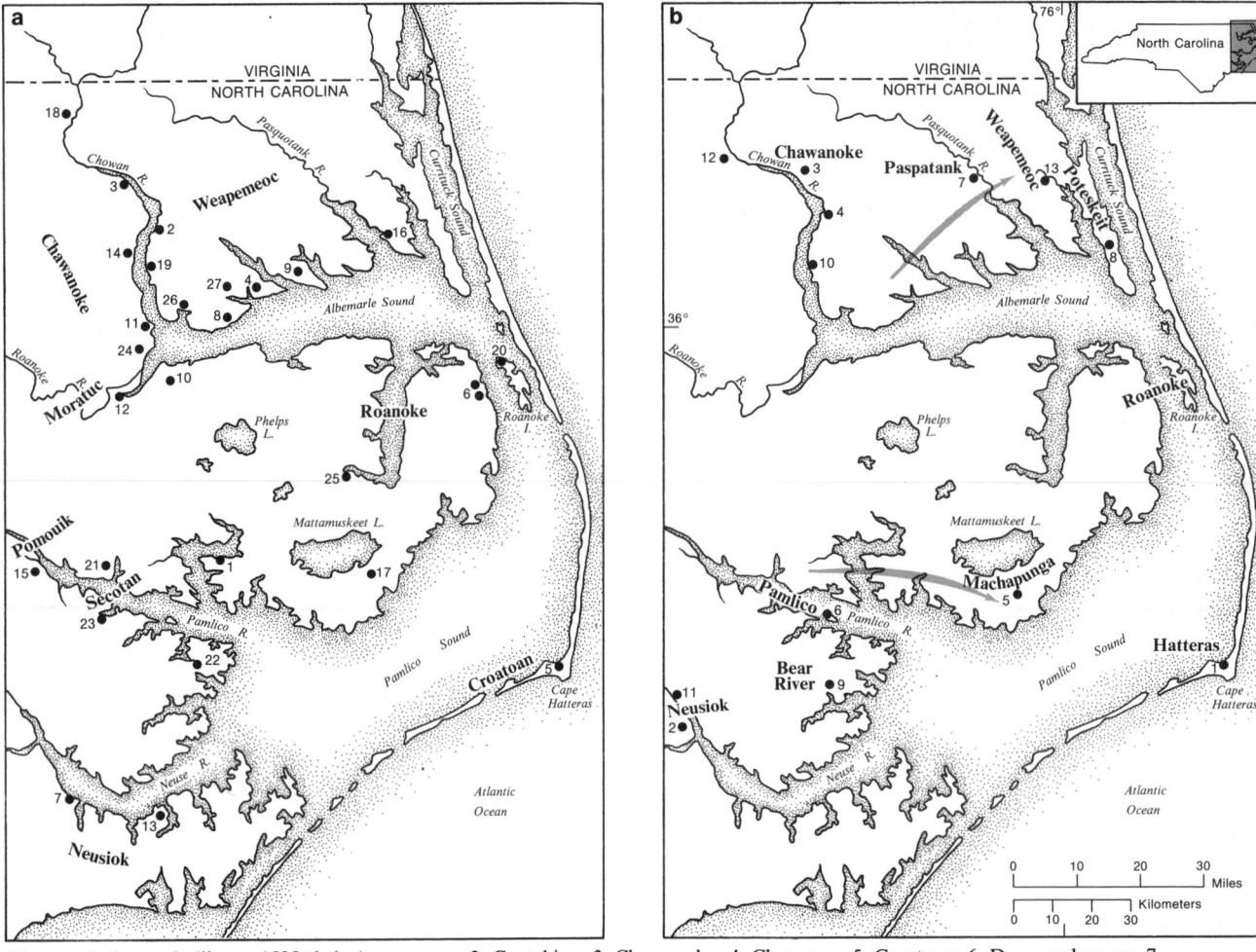

Fig. 1a. Tribes and villages, 1585/6. 1, Aquascogoc; 2, Cautaking; 3, Chawanoke; 4, Chepanoc; 5, Croatoan; 6, Dasemunkapeuc; 7, Marasanico; 8, Mascomenge; 9, Masequetuc; 10, Mequopen; 11, Metacquem; 12, Moratuc; 13, Newasiwoc; 14, Ohanoak; 15, Panauuaiok; 16, Pasquenoke; 17, Pomeiooc; 18, Ramushonnouk; 19, Ricahokene; 20, Roanoke; 21, Seco (Cotan); 22, Secotaóc; 23, Secoton; 24, Tandaquomuc; 25, Tramaskecooc; 26, Warawtani; 27, Weapemeoc.

Fig. 1b. Tribes and villages, 1657-1795. Some locations are tentative. Arrows mark tribal dislocations. Dates in parentheses indicate documented periods of occupation of villages. 1, Cape Hatteras Indian Town (1708-1788); 2, Chatooka (1708-1712); 3, Chowan Indian Town (1708-1795); 4, Katoking (1657); 5, Mattamuskeet (1733); 6, Pamlico (1708); 7, Paspatank (1708); 8, Poteskeet (1708-1733); 9, Raudauquaquank (1708); 10, Rickahock (1657); 11, Rouconk (1708-1712); 12, Wohanock (1657); 13, Yeopim (1696-1733).

1589). For most Indian groups in coastal North Carolina, the history of European contacts therefore began only with the first arrival of the English ships in 1584 and the establishment of a colony one year later.

Demography

Very little is known about late sixteenth-century demography. Figure 1a provides information on the distribution of tribes and villages reported by the sources. The total number of tribes and villages was probably somewhat greater than these. Thus, there is evidence that the largest tribe encountered by the English (possibly the Chawanoke) had 18 villages and a population of around 2,500. The total North Carolina Algonquian population must have been 7,000 or more by 1585. Estimates of individual tribal strengths made by modern authors are nothing but informed guesses (Mooney 1928; Mook

1944a); most of them appear much too low (Feest 1972). Density of population was certainly greater along the rivers than near the sounds or on the outer banks.

Tribal boundaries cannot be established beyond doubt. Allied but independent groups were sometimes regarded as single tribes by the European observers. Thus, the Roanoke, Croatoan, and Secotan tribes are frequently referred to as one tribe (Mook 1944a). Uncertainty about locations of villages makes assignments to tribes difficult. This applies particularly to the Weapemeoc, Chawanoke, and Moratuc, and to the Algonquian boundary with their Iroquoian neighbors.

Early depopulation was mainly the result of imported European diseases. During the presence of the early English colonists in coastal North Carolina, measles, smallpox, and colds must have pushed the death rate to 25 percent or more in some villages (Hariot 1588).

Losses suffered through warfare with the English were only slight, although intertribal warfare was held responsible for the fact that "the people are marvelously wasted, and in some places, the Countrey left desolate" (Barlowe 1589).

Interethnic Relations

Soon after the English established their colony on Roanoke Island in 1585, differences among Algonquian tribes in their relations with the Whites became apparent. The Roanoke Indians, who most clearly felt the presence of the English, became increasingly disenchanted with the colonists whom at first they believed to possess supernatural powers. On the other hand, a pro-English faction was formed by those Indians who hoped to profit from trade and alliance with the colonists. This in turn led to a weakening of old alliances between Indian groups: the Croatoans sided with the English against the Roanoke; part of the Weapemeoc followed the Chawanokes' advice to stay neutral; while the rest of that tribe joined the Roanokes. There is evidence for precontact hostilities between the Secotans and their allies, and the Neusioks and Pomouiks. The Chawanokes were generally on good terms with Virginia Algonquians as far away as the Kecoughtan, who at that time were not yet part of what later became Powhatan's state; but they—probably like most Algonquian groups of the region—were frequently at war with the Tuscaroras (Mangoaks) though the Roanokes believed they could count on the Tuscaroras in their fight against the English (Lane 1589; Barlowe 1589).

The final fate of the "lost colonists" of 1586 and 1587 remains unknown. The first group was driven by the Roanoke Indians from Roanoke Island, removed to a location near the Croatoan tribe, and disappeared before the 1587 supply arrived from England. Those left behind in 1587 apparently also first left Roanoke Island for Croatoan, but reports gathered by the Virginia colonists after 1607 suggest that they made their way to the west and/or north (Quinn 1955). What lasting effect their prolonged presence in coastal North Carolina may have had on the Indians can only be guessed.

Indian-English contacts took place mostly on a personal level and were in all probability limited to members of the Indian upper class. Reasons for contacts included trade, political maneuvering, search for geographical knowledge by the English, and exchange of information on the respective cultures, particularly on religion. These contacts were restricted in consequence of the small number of bilinguals on both sides, which included on the Indian side two Indians who had been taken back to England in 1584 (Quinn 1955).

Subsistence

Early English reports on native economy give no clues on the relative importance of hunting, gathering, fishing, and horticulture. It can only be assumed that fishing was of even greater importance here than among the coastal tribes of Virginia.

Corn cultivation (fig. 2) was the basis for the sedentary life of the Indians. Three varieties of corn (among them, Northern Flint) were planted from late March to early July. After the fields had been cleared of weeds by both men and women with wooden hoes, holes about one yard distant from one another were made with digging sticks. Four grains of corn were put in each hole, which was then covered with earth. As in Virginia, no fertilizers were used. In separate, sometimes fenced patches or in the corn fields were planted two varieties of beans, at least two kinds of gourds and pumpkins, sunflowers, and chenopodium or amaranthus. Tobacco was always grown in separate fields. Harvesting of corn was done from July to September; long growing seasons allowed two crops to be harvested from the same field in one year, but this was not the rule (Hariot 1588, 1590; Hulton and Quinn 1964; Sturtevant 1965; Bland 1651; Smith 1624).

Weirs and fish traps made of reeds were set up in rivers and estuaries (fig. 3). Another method was to spear the fish either from the canoe or while wading through shallow water. The use of fire to lure fish by night to the boat's side was also known and practiced by the Indians. Dip nets were needed to take the catch out of the water. Fishing and shellfishing were of prime importance in the spring, before corn could be harvested (Hariot 1588, 1590; Hulton and Quinn 1964; Lane 1589).

Little is known about hunting methods, although hunting must have contributed substantially to the diet. Birds and mammals were hunted with bow and arrow, and bears were chased up into trees to be shot down easily. Different roots, nuts, and berries were gathered by the North Carolina Algonquians during the fall of the year; small animals, such as turtles or snakes, were similarly gathered for use as food. Dogs were kept as pets; it is not known whether they were used in hunting, but they were possibly sometimes eaten by the Indians (Hariot 1588; Lane 1589).

Trade with the interior furnished the coastal tribes with stones and copper, and probably with other items not otherwise available to them. Incipient European trade greatly diversified the supply of such items and consequently tended to lessen the importance of intertribal exchange.

Fish, meat, and corn were roasted or boiled separately or in a single pot. Corn, beans, seeds of the sunflower, and chestnuts were also used to make broths or were ground for flour of which bread was made. Bread was likewise made of acorns, chinquapin nuts, and hazelnuts. Pumpkins were eaten either raw or boiled, as were groundnuts and other roots. The roots and berries of the arrow arum had to be leached before being eaten. Wal-

Their rype corne

Their greene corne

Corne newly sprong.

Their sitting at meate

The place of solemne prayer.

The house wherein the Tombe of their Herounds standeth.

SECOTON.

A Ceremony in their prayers wth strange iestures and songes dansing abowt posts carued on the topps lyke mens faces.

Fig. 2. Secoton. Watercolor drawing by John White, 1585.

Fig. 3. "The manner of their fishing." Watercolor drawing by John White, 1585.

nuts were pounded in mortars and mixed with water, and wild rice was boiled. Seeds of chenopodium or amaranthus were used to make pottages, while the stalks of these plants were burned to serve as a substitute for salt. As a drink, water was used either pure or seasoned with various herbs. Preservation of food obviously took place to some extent, but nothing is known about methods of storage (Hariot 1588, 1590).

Material Culture

Due to the lack of suitable raw materials, stone was rarely used by the coastal tribes, being largely replaced by shell, bone, or wood. Trees were felled by well-controlled burning of their base; then they were further worked with fire and scraping tools of shell or stone axes. Wood was hardened probably also by the use of

Fig. 4. Shell-tempered clay pot with overlapping stamped impressions. It was excavated near the campfire at Ft. Raleigh, Roanoke Is. Diameter at rim about 25.0 cm.

fire. Skins were oil tanned, with or without the fur left standing. The women made globular pots with hemispherical to conical bases of coils of clay tempered with crushed shell, sand, or clay-grit. Pots were placed on heaps of earth to keep them in an upright position in spite of their pointed bottoms (fig. 4). Fabric impressions or simple stampings were among the common forms of decoration. Baskets and mats were made of rushes and probably also of other vegetable fibrous material (Hariot 1588, 1590; Hulton and Quinn 1964; Haag 1958).

Tools included shell scrapers and knives, wooden hoes and pickaxes, and hafted stone celts. Saber-shaped clubs of wood were about a yard long and sometimes further armed with antler points. Simple curved bows (fig. 5) of maple or witch hazel were used with arrows of reed, perhaps with a wooden foreshaft, headed with points of shell, the "tooth of a fish," or possibly stone, and were fletched with two radial feathers. Arrowpoints could also be poisoned. Spears used for fishing consisted of reed or wooden shafts with a sharpened fore-end or a hafted king crab tail for a point. There is only insufficient evidence for the use of multipronged fish spears among the Algonquians of coastal North Carolina and Virginia. Fish weirs were made of reeds that were kept parallel by twining; they were frequently combined with fish traps (Barlowe 1589; Hariot 1588, 1590; Hulton and Quinn 1964).

Household utensils documented for the sixteenth century include hammerstones for cracking nuts, mortars of unknown shape, wooden and shell spoons, wooden barbecue frames, fish-broiling sticks, and perhaps forks, and a variety of plates and vessels. Liquids were kept or carried in pottery or gourd (fig. 6) containers, and food was eaten from round wooden platters (fig. 7) (Hariot 1588, 1590; Hulton and Quinn 1964).

Villages were made up of about 10 to 30 houses, which were either grouped around a central plaza and surrounded by wooden palisades (fig. 8) or scattered among the corn fields (fig. 2). Usually they were located near the waterside, although sometimes ponds had to be dug to serve as a source of water. The houses were rectangular (some possibly oval) with barrel roofs of bent poles lashed together at the top, connected by horizontal crossbars, and covered with bark, rush mats, or boughs of trees. This cover could be partly removed to let in light; smoke holes are not recorded. Most houses were between 36 and 48 feet long and had only one room, but some houses were up to 72 feet in length, and at least the house of the Roanoke chief's brother was partitioned into five rooms (Barlowe 1589). Raised platforms along the walls were used for sleeping. Chiefs' houses and temples generally resembled ordinary houses in shape and construction, though they were usually bigger and the temple of Pomeiooc (fig. 8) is shown with an exceptional type of roof. The field watcher's hut (fig. 2) in summer served to shelter a man whose duty it was to chase birds and other beasts away from the fields. This structure, as were the large platforms within the temples, was built on piles (Hariot 1590; Hulton and Quinn 1964).

As among the Virginia Algonquians, dress styles and ornaments differed according to social rank rather than sex. While occasionally no clothing was worn at all, usually at least a belted breechclout or a single or double apron skirt of deerskin was used. Another garment shared by men and women was a deerskin or rabbitskin cloak fastened over one or both shoulders (fig. 7) and sometimes belted, the fur being worn next to the body. Moccasins of a simple pattern were likewise made of deerskin. Dresses were frequently fringed and with upper-class Indians also beaded or painted. Little girls had their genitals covered with a pad of moss or milkweed bark (fig. 6). Priests wore distinctive capes of twined rabbitskin strips. Specialized forms of dress included the bowman's bracer (also present in Virginia), wicker armor, and wooden breastplates for the warrior, who also used bark shields (Hariot 1590; Hulton and Quinn 1964).

The women wore their hair fringed in front and either knotted at the nape or hanging loose at shoulder length; headbands were sometimes used. Men's hairstyles were mostly roached, either with a knot at the nape or with a forehead crest (priests only). While men frequently painted themselves (fig. 5), women usually tattooed their

Fig. 5. Man with body paint. Watercolor drawing by John White, 1585.

Fig. 6. Woman and girl of Pomeiooc. The doll is English. Watercolor drawing by John White, 1585.

bodies and faces (fig. 6). Necklaces and ear pendants of bone or shell were used by both sexes; feathers and copper or shell head ornaments that served to distinguish rank are documented only for men. Young men removed facial hair, but older persons occasionally grew thin beards (Hariot 1590; Barlowe 1589; Hulton and Quinn 1964).

Dugout canoes (fig. 3) could transport up to 20 people and were propelled either by shouldered paddles or by poles. There were special pack baskets with tumplines across the chest and quivers made of rushes (fig. 5). Children were carried by the hip-straddling method.

Clay tobacco pipes of the obtuse-angle type (fig. 9) frequently exhibited punctured or incised designs (Hulton and Quinn 1964).

Social Organization

No data have been preserved on kinship, form of family, marriage, descent, residence, and kin groups among sixteenth-century North Carolina Algonquians. Household size must have ranged around a mean of 10 persons. There was possibly a kind of group (whose exact nature is not clearly understood) below or independent of the level of village and tribal organization. Its outward sign consisted of painted or tattooed markings on the backs of men. Another possible interpretation is to consider these marks as indications of individual rank (Hariot 1590; Hulton and Quinn 1964). Every tribe consisted of from one to 18 villages. No formal organization extended beyond the tribal level, although confederacies

Fig. 7. "Theire sitting at meate." Watercolor drawing by John White, 1585.

Fig. 8. "The towne of Pomeiock." Watercolor drawing by John White, 1585.

Fig. 9. Tubular tobacco pipe of reddish-brown clay. Excavated at Ft. Raleigh, Roanoke Is. Length 9.1 cm.

ple. They were visibly distinguished by wearing special ornaments. Political decision-making was reserved to the council composed of upper-class members, who also administrated the law and were generally feared and obeyed by their tribesmen. The term werowance was understood by the English colonists to refer either to the tribal chief or other persons of high social ranking. No other term applied to the members of the upper class has been recorded (Barlowe 1589; Lane 1589; Hariot 1588).

War was waged for revenge; fighting generally took place at dawn or in moonlight, with ambushing as a main tactical precaution. Formal military organization was probably only weakly developed. As a rule, women and children were spared, while men were killed (Hariot 1588; Barlowe 1589).

Religion

North Carolina Algonquians believed in a plurality of gods and spirits (montoac); the principal one may be classified as a supreme being who first created minor gods to create the world. These gods were thought to be of human shape, and idols representing them (known as kewas) were made by the Indians to be set up in the temples (machicomuck) or to be carried into battle. While the temples, which also served as ossuaries for the dead werowances, were attended by the priests, another group of persons whom the English called "conjurors" acted as seers and probably also as medicine men (Hariot 1588, 1590; Hulton and Quinn 1964). Belief in an afterlife for everyone, with different treatment according to moral conduct in this world, was general. Evil persons were thought to go to a fire pit (popogusso) in the west. Reincarnation was assumed throughout the whole area (Hariot 1588).

Ceremonials included rites connected with burials of werowances and probably a green-corn festival. Individuals made offerings of tobacco by throwing it into the air, into the water, or into the fire, accompanying these deeds with certain gestures and utterances (Hariot 1588; Hulton and Quinn 1964; Feest 1972). If a disease was thought to derive from some sort of pathogenic substance existing in the body of the patient, the curer would try to suck it out. Other treatments were based on

appear to have been common (Hariot 1588; Lane 1589).

As among Virginia Algonquian tribes, social stratification was pronounced in coastal North Carolina. The upper class included the chief, his family and relatives, his advisers, and possibly also the priests, all of whom enjoyed certain privileges (such as trade monopolies) and consequently greater wealth than the common peo-

278

the knowledge about the virtues of medical plants and clays (Hariot 1588).

Simple interment in graves about three feet deep was the ordinary method of disposing of the dead; however, members of the upper class were treated differently. Their bodies were skinned, the bones cleaned of the flesh, again covered with the original skin, and stuffed to resemble a corpse. Afterward they were placed on a scaffold within the temple together with the dried flesh wrapped up in mats (Hariot 1588, 1590).

Circular dances (fig. 2) (in which both sexes participated) and songs were accompanied by the shaking of gourd rattles filled with pebbles or fruit stones and fastened to a wooden stick. European toy rattles made their appearance among the Indians shortly after the establishment of the Roanoke colony. Circles of posts with carved faces and the kewas idols testify to the development of woodcarving among the North Carolina Algonquians (Hulton and Quinn 1964).

Seventeenth to Nineteenth Centuries

As there is little continuity in the sources on North Carolina Algonquians there is not much evidence for continuity in tribal histories. Figure 1b shows many new names when compared with figure 1a. It is not always possible to establish these designations as synonyms for names used before.

Population continued to decline through disease and warfare (table 1). "A great Mortality" that fell upon the Pamlico Indians and their neighbors is reported for 1696 (Salley 1911). During the Tuscarora war, 1711–1713, more Algonquian allies of the Tuscarora were killed than Tuscaroras themselves (Saunders 1886–1890, 1). By 1709 North Carolina Algonquian population was down to some 600, and by the end of the century only a handful were still being regarded as Indians. Decrease in numbers was accompanied by loss of tribal lands. Thus, the Weapemeoc Indians sold their lands on Albemarle Sound in 1660 and 1662 and started to move into the interior, but by 1697 they had to complain against the encroachments of White settlers in their new location (McPherson 1966; M.E. Parker 1971). The reservation on Bennet Creek assigned to the Chawanokes before 1700 was reduced from 12 to 6 square miles by 1707; further land was sold by that tribe in 1713. After the Tuscarora war, the Machapungas were similarly confined to a reservation, while the other groups of Pamlico Sound joined either the Machapungas or the Tuscaroras (Saunders 1886–1890, 1–3).

During the seventeenth century, the Chawanokes were in frequent—partly hostile—contact with their Virginia Algonquian neighbors (Bland 1651). Their traditional hostilities with the Iroquoian Tuscaroras continued during that tribe's war with the Whites, when they were actively engaged in expeditions against the hostiles. The Machapungas and other tribes of Pamlico Sound, however, changed their alliances: before 1700 they were still at war with the Tuscaroras and Corees, but in 1711 they sided with them against the English (Salley 1911). The Hatteras, Weapemeoc, Paspatank, and Poteskeit Indians were at that time the most acculturated groups and remained on the side of the English. The friendly attitude of the Hatteras may be explained by their tradition of having White men among their ancestors (Lawson 1709).

Except for the Tuscarora war, there was little open fighting between North Carolina Algonquians and Whites. Due to small numbers, trade was of little importance. Sale of strong liquors to the Indians was probably the greatest problem created by White traders around 1700. Alcohol was banned from Indian towns in 1703, but the prohibition was never strictly enforced. Little was done for Indian education, even though native languages were being replaced by English during the eighteenth century. A small number of Indians was baptized by Anglican ministers throughout the late seventeenth and the eighteenth centuries (Yeardley 1911; Hawks 1857–1858, 2). English names made their appearance shortly after 1700. In the absence of adequate medical care by White physicians, Indian conjurors could earn money by curing White settlers. Indian servitude and slavery were present, but their extent is not fully known (Lawson 1709; M.E. Parker 1971).

Besides hunting and agriculture, the coastal groups still relied much on fishing and shellfish gathering, drying the products for preservation on reed hurdles over an open fire or in the sun. Sturgeon was not used as a food by the Indians along the coast. Cattle raising is documented for the Paspatanks around 1700 (Lawson 1709). The Tuscarora war disturbed the economic balance of many of the Algonquian groups: the fields of the Machapungas and their allies were destroyed by the English, while the Hatteras were prevented from planting by their enemies and in 1714–1715 had to be supplied with food by the colonial authorities (Saunders 1886–1890, 2 and 3).

With growing White presence in eastern Carolina, more products of European origin were introduced to the Indians. Guns were regularly used instead of bows and arrows during the eighteenth century. Iron hatchets had likewise replaced wooden clubs. English clothes were also widely used by the Indians. The Roanoke chief even had an English-style house built for himself in 1654. Yet baskets were still being made by the coastal Indians of rushes and silk grass and decorated with woven-in life motifs (Lawson 1709; Yeardley 1911).

Marriage restrictions that prohibited marrying first cousins made it difficult to find mates within rapidly shrinking communities. Resulting marriages into other tribes certainly strengthened intertribal bonds. The huskenaw rite appears to have been used as an initiation for both boys and girls. It was held around Christmas and lasted for five or six weeks during which the adolescents were separated in a special building outside the village (Lawson 1709). Circumcision was practiced by only two out of 50 families among the Machapungas, but unfortunately no more details are known (Lawson 1709; Klingberg 1956).

Political organization with hereditary chieftainship was obviously still functioning around 1700. Chiefs' corpses were deposited in the temples as before, but the right to be buried there now could also be bought by everyone. Shell beads served as money, for example, in compensating crimes (Lawson 1709).

Twentieth Century

Around 1915, about 100 persons of suspected Indian descent were found living on Roanoke Island, some of the adjacent sand islands, and on the mainland in Dare and Hyde counties. They were identified as remnants of the Machapunga Indians by Speck (1916, 1924). Physically, they exhibited definite signs of Negro and White admixture, with the former obviously increasing. Important economic pursuits included hunting and fishing, with agriculture as a supplementary activity. Leaves of the yaupon bush were gathered, dried, and used for a tea. Large-scale use of White products had replaced almost all native industrial arts. Hickory and oak-splint basketry was only a memory, but nets of different-sized meshes for different species of fish were still being made of the fibers of *Asclepias syriaca*. In excursions to the outer banks, temporary shelters of palmetto leaves supported by cross poles were used. As twice before in their history, these Indians disappeared from view after Speck's visit. Dunbar (1960:414) suggests that the mixed-bloods seen by Speck "must have joined the Roanoke Island Negro community of 'California', just outside the incorporated limits of the town of Manteo."

Gilbert (1948) also refers to the Laster Tribe, another mixed-blood group living near Hertford in Perquimans County; its relation to former Algonquian tribes is in doubt. Beale (1957) reports no triracial isolates from the coastal region.

Synonymy

Since none of the groups mentioned below has survived and no adequate records exist to settle the question of the etymology and correct pronunciation of tribal names, neither etymologies nor pronunciations will be supplied.

Bay River Indians, 1713 (Saunders 1886–1890, 1:946) or Bear River Indians (Lawson 1709:211), so called from their location on Bay or Bear River.

Chawanoke: Chaonists (Lane 1589:265); Chawan (Bland 1651:13); Chawons (Smith 1612:map); Chawwonoke (Smith 1608:186); Choanoke (Lane 1589:259); Chowan, 1686 (Hawks 1857–1858, 2:379); Chowanoake (Barlowe 1589:110); Chuwon (Lawson 1709:242).

Croatoan: Croatoan (J. White 1585–1586, 1585–1586a). Probably identical with the eighteenth-century

Table 1. North Carolina Algonquian Population Estimates, 18th Century

	1709 Lawson (1709:242)[a]	1731 Gov. Burrington (Saunders 1886–1890, 3:153)	1733 Moseley (Cumming 1966:pl. 6)	1755 Gov. Dobbs (Saunders 1886–1890, 5:xli)	Last noted
Poteskeit	100 (75)[b]		[d]		1733
Paspatank	35 (25)				1709
Weapemeoc	20 (15)		[d]		1733
Chawanoke	50 (38)	[c]	[d]	7	1796
Roanoke					1763
Hatteras	53 (40)	[c]	6-8	8-10	1788
Machapunga	100 (75)	[c]	[d]	8-10	1915
Pamlico	50 (38)				1709
Bear River	165(125)				1712
Neusiok	50 (38)				1712
Total	621(469)				

[a] Lawson gives population estimates by number of fighting men. Total populations have been computed both on a 3:10 ratio and, in parentheses, on the 2:5 ratio preferred by Lawson (1709:243).

[b] James Adams speaks of 70 or 80 Indians in Currituck Precinct by 1710 (Hawks 1857–1858, 2:314).

[c] Mentioned as consisting of less than 20 families.

[d] Villages shown on map; no population figures given.

Hatteras (Lawson 1709:201); Hatteress, 1714 (Saunders 1886–1890, 2:129).

Machapunga: Machapunga (Lawson 1709:209); Matchepungoes, 1686 (Hawks 1857–1858, 2:379). Also known after the name of their village: Matamusket, 1712 (Saunders 1886–1890, 1:875); Marmusckits, 1713 (Saunders 1886–1890, 1:933); Maramoskees, 1716 (Klingberg 1956:176); Altamuskeet, 1761 (Saunders 1886–1890, 6:563).

Moratuc: Moratiks (Lane 1589:265); Moratuc (J. White 1585–1586, 1585–1586a); Morotico (Lane 1589:264).

Neusiok: Neiosioke (Barlowe 1589:264); Nesioke (Anonymous 1585); Neus (Lawson 1709:242); Newasiwac (J. White 1585–1586a).

Pamlico: Pampticough (Lawson 1709:226); Pemlicoe, 1707 (Salley 1911:286). Possibly identical with the sixteenth-century Ponouike (Barlowe 1589:113); Panauuaioc, 1590 (Quinn 1955:facing 462); Panawiock (Zúñiga 1608).

Paspatank: Paspatank (Lawson 1709:242); Paspitank (Lawson 1709:200).

Poteskeit: Poteskeit (Lawson 1709:242); Potoskite, 1733 (Cumming 1966:pl. 6).

Roanoke: Rhoanoke (Yeardley 1911:27); Roanoke, 1761 (Saunders 1886–1890, 6:563); Roanoak (Barlowe 1589:106); Rowanoke (Yeardley 1911:28).

Secotan: Secoton (J. White 1585–1586, 1585–1586a); Sequotan (Barlowe 1589:113).

Weapemeoc: Jaupin (Lawson 1709:242); Weapemeoc, 1590 (Quinn 1955:facing 462); Weopomiock (Lane 1589:258); Yausapin, 1660 (McPherson 1966:80); Yawpim, 1696 (M.E. Parker 1971:80); Yeopim, 1662 (Saunders 1886–1890, 1:17).

Sources

The North Carolina Algonquian tribes were the first group of American Indians to have prolonged contact with English colonists. In a rather short period of time a large amount and variety of information was collected by the members of the first English colony in America. Barlowe's report (1589) on the 1584 voyage is the earliest document to describe North Carolina Algonquians in some detail. Manteo and Wanchese, two Indians brought back to England, served as linguistic informants and interpreters for the 1585–1586 colonists, who were therefore able to gain a better understanding of the native culture. Thomas Hariot's "Briefe and true report" (1588) contains a most valuable section on the ethnography of coastal North Carolina, which he supplemented in his commentaries on John White's drawings (1590). Unfortunately, Hariot published only a fragment of the ethnographic data he collected. Lane's letters and his discourse on the first colony (1589) add to knowledge of Indian-White relations. All these documents together with other pertinent material relating to the Roanoke voyages may be found in Quinn (1955). Together with Hariot's work, the watercolor drawings by John White and their derivatives provide the best source on North Carolina Algonquian culture. Considering the absence of ethnographic collections and the paucity of archeological finds in the coastal region, these pictures supply the basic information on material culture (Hulton and Quinn 1964). Three manuscript maps (Anonymous 1585; J. White 1585–1586, 1585–1586a) are the earliest sources on the location of tribes and villages. From a corrected version of White's map, now lost, derives the information contained in de Bry's and Velasco's maps and in the Molyneux globe (Quinn 1955).

The seventeenth century is much less well documented. Virginia colonists exploring northern North Carolina and the early settlers of Carolina under the 1663 charter left few records of their dealings with the Indians, let alone ethnographic accounts. Smith (1624) relates briefly some early visits to the southern neighborhood of the Jamestown colony. Bland (1651) only heard about North Carolina Algonquians. Yeardley (1911) paid them a short visit. Comberford's map of 1657 and later important maps are reproduced by Cumming (1966). Surveyor-general John Lawson (1709) was the last author to give vivid details from the life of North Carolina coastal Indians. He explicitly refers several times to Algonquian tribes, and much of other Indian matters related by him may also apply to them rather than to the Tuscaroras or any of the Siouan tribes. Lawson's book was plagiarized by Brickell (1737), who adds little on Algonquian groups. Missionaries sent to America by the Society for the Propagation of the Gospel (Adams, Rainsford, Newman, Stewart) mention the Indians all too briefly. Their notes and other records relating to the colonial period may be found in Saunders (1886–1890), Hawks (1857–1858, 2), Salley (1911), and M.E. Parker (1968, 1971).

With decreasing numbers interest in the Indians was lost completely during the eighteenth and nineteenth centuries. Speck (1916) tried to locate remnants of North Carolina Algonquians, and his researches provided the last published record on them. His small collection of Machapunga material is in the American Museum of Natural History, New York.

Frequently, data on North Carolina Algonquians have been used to illustrate Virginia Algonquian culture, but very little research has been done on the North Carolina Algonquian tribes themselves. Mook (1943c, 1944a), Quinn (1955, 1970), Dunbar (1960), Dillard (1906), Sturtevant (1965), Hoffman (1967), and Feest (1967a, 1972) are among the exceptions. Summarized information is also available in the writings of Swanton (1928, 1946) and Rights (1947).

Iroquoian Tribes of the Virginia-North Carolina Coastal Plain

DOUGLAS W. BOYCE

Language, Territory, and Environment

Several distinct ethnic groups speaking languages of the Iroquoian family lived on the Virginia-North Carolina coastal plain during the early historic period. The Tuscarora (ˌtuskəˈrôrə) was the largest and best known of these groups (fig. 1). They are easily identified linguistically through a number of word lists beginning with John Lawson's of 1709 and others recorded in the nineteenth century (Lawson 1967:233-239; Gallatin 1836:307-367; Catlin 1926:299-302; Schoolcraft 1846:251-258). Likewise, the Nottoway (ˈnätəˌwä) language is known through an occasional term in the historical record and two word lists recorded between 1820 and 1836 from survivors living on the Southampton County, Virginia, reservation (Binford 1967:106; Gallatin 1836:82). The Iroquoian identity of the Meherrin (məˈherən) is based on indirect evidence, primarily their political association with the Nottoway and Tuscarora. In the absence of other evidence, this can be only tentatively accepted.

Two other ethnic groups mentioned in historical accounts may have spoken languages of the Iroquoian family. The Coree and Neusiok (ˈno͞osēˌäk), who during their later history were called the Neuse River Indians, lived southeast of the Tuscarora settlement area. Lawson (1967:174, 242) reported in 1709 that an Indian slave woman from "beyond the Mountains" spoke the same language as the "Coranine," which he identified as a village of the Coree. Swanton (1952:78, 82) thought this may refer to the Erie who formerly had lived across the Appalachian range to the northwest (Hoffman 1964). Geary (1955a) has suggested, on the basis of their ethnic or tribal names, that the Neusiok and Coree were possibly Iroquoian. However, concrete evidence for such a conclusion is lacking.*

The ethnic and territorial boundaries of these Iroquoian peoples are confusing but significant factors of their identities. The territory occupied by these groups includes an eastern fringe of the Piedmont and portions of the coastal plain of Virginia and North Carolina. The area is cut by major rivers such as the Nottoway, Meherrin, Roanoke, Tar, and Neuse. The soils of the coastal plain are sandy, light textured, easily worked, and well drained. Therefore, the soils warm up quickly in the spring and are less sensitive to early frosts, permitting long growing seasons (Binford 1967:112). Most Tuscarora, and all Meherrin, Nottoway, Coree, and Neusiok villages were located east of the fall line on the fluvial terraces of these rivers.

The areas occupied by these Iroquoian-speaking peoples contained a variety of plant communities. Southern pine forest, broad-leaf deciduous forest, freshwater marsh, hydrophytic deciduous forest, and black gum–juniper swamp characterized the coastal plain and pro-

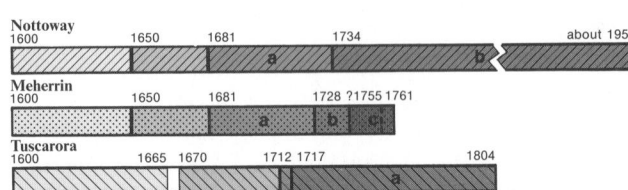

Fig. 1. Territory of the Tuscarora, Meherrin, and Nottoway in Va. and N.C.

* Lack of information precludes the development of a systematic orthography for any of these languages except Tuscarora, for which the orthography is described in "Tuscarora Among the Iroquois," this vol.

vided different wild plant foods on a nearly year-round basis (Binford 1967:113–114).

Settlement Pattern

Within this primarily coastal-plain territory the people lived in villages having a dispersed settlement pattern. This seems clear for the Meherrin and probably the Nottoway from Bland's 1650 account (1911:12; see also Binford 1967:138). Col. John Barnwell stormed through Tuscarora settlements early in 1712 and wrote: "Tho' this be called a town, it is only a plantation here and there scattered about the Country, no where 5 houses together, and then ¼ a mile such another and so on for several miles" (Barnwell 1908:32). As he continued through Tuscarora territory with his troops, Barnwell found one "plantation" followed by another. The fortifications he encountered had all been recently constructed and such structures were apparently lacking in early historic Meherrin and Nottoway villages (Binford 1967:137–138). Christoph von Graffenried, based on observations during his late 1711 capture by the Tuscarora ("Tuscarora Among the Iroquois," fig. 1, this vol.) describes one Tuscarora village as being palisaded (Todd 1920:270), but it was the exception rather than the rule.

Sociopolitical Organization

The sociopolitical boundaries of these ethnic groups are unclear. The similar languages, annual cycles, and material cultures of the Meherrin, Nottoway, and Tuscarora do not necessarily imply they were consistently political allies. It cannot be assumed that each group possessed a cohesive tribal political organization simply because of their shared ethnicity. Hewitt suggested, based solely on oral traditions collected in the nineteenth century, that a Tuscarora Confederacy of three tribes existed prior to 1711 in North Carolina. According to tradition, these tribal groups were the *kahtehnoʔáˑkaˑʔ*, literally 'people of the submerged pine-tree', the *akawǫtsáˑkaˑʔ* (meaning unknown), and the *skaròˑrǫʔ*, this last name being the one used in later years as a self-designation by the Tuscarora in the North (Hewitt 1910c:842, forms phonemicized; synonymy in "Tuscarora Among the Iroquois," this vol.). However, Boyce's (1975) examination of the written historical literature for the 1711 period concludes that no confederacy of tribes existed, but rather that each village was governmentally autonomous. A century of participation as the sixth member of the Iroquois Confederacy in the north led to an interpretation of past history in terms of more recent political identity. The traditional *kahtehnoʔáˑkaˑʔ* tribal group is probably the village variously referred to in the historical record as Catechna (Todd 1920:264–265), Caughteghnah (McIlwaine 1925–1945, 3:294), or Contah-nah (Lawson 1967:242). The traditional *akawǫtsáˑkaˑʔ* tribe was a recognized non-Tuscarora element living on the New York Tuscarora reservation, apparently without equal political rights (Hewitt 1907; Gatschet 1883–1885:92). They may have been political allies from North Carolina, as Wallace (1952:21) has suggested, or they may have been an element adopted by the Tuscarora who were settled during the eighteenth century in New York.

Whatever the precise nature of Tuscarora political organization, their common ethnic identity provided much of the cohesive mechanism that led colonists to speak of them as a "nation." The most effectively organized governmental units were the villages, which allied with other Tuscaroras and non-Tuscarora settlements during years before the 1711–1713 war. Southern Tuscarora villages had in their alliance the villages of the Coree, Neusiok, Matchapunga, Pamlico, Woccon, and Bear River. The Northern Tuscarora villages, seven or eight in number, had as their allies the Shakori, Sissipahaw (Chickahaws, McIlwaine 1925–1945, 3:295), and probably the Nottoway and Meherrin. These alliances, which crossed ethnic lines, were brittle organizations whose members remained associated only as long as the alliance represented the goals of individual villages. This emphasis on village autonomy has also been expressed with regard to the Nottoway and Meherrin, which "were societies politically organized into territorial units not exceeding the local community. There were no customary mechanisms for the ultimate settlement of disputes which transcended the organization at the community level. Leadership was at the community level and status was weakly developed with respect to high status differential access to goods and services" (Binford 1967:140). Men who were called "kings" among the Virginia–North Carolina Iroquoians were most often village chiefs. Lawson (1967:236) writes they were referred to as "teethha" among the Tuscarora, and the colonial records of Virginia show that the Nottoway counterpart was called "teerheer" (McIlwaine 1925–1945, 3:366, 368). These Native American statuses were not equivalent to European monarchs. Although the precise nature of their roles is unclear, they probably maintained their effectiveness through personal ability; instead of directing and determining village policy, they coordinated what village councils decided.

Culture

The Tuscarora, Nottoway, and Meherrin were agriculturalists, but they, along with their neighbors, relied heavily on hunting and gathering as well. The annual cycle of the Tuscarora was marked by the movement of entire villages to hunting quarters in the late fall. They remained in these until late winter or early spring using fire-drives and other cooperative community methods to secure deer (Lawson 1967:65). An October 17, 1706, letter written by Thomas Garrett (1901) about the Meherrin confirms the pattern for them. Although the deerskin trade probably encouraged an increase in mass-kill techniques, the general pattern seems to have been an old one since Yeardley (1911:27-28) mentions it for the Tuscarora as early as the winter of 1653-1654.

Lawson reported in 1709 that the Tuscaroras' house construction and settlement pattern were different while in their hunting quarter. Normally their dwelling structures had a circular or oval floor plan made with saplings that were pulled to the center to form a semispherical shape. Inside they had "Benches all round . . . [covered by] Beast-Skins, and Mats made of Rushes" (Lawson 1967:182). In their hunting-quarter they built rectangular, ridged roofed houses that were situated close together, contrary to their regular settlement pattern of scattered hamlets interspersed with agricultural fields (Lawson 1967:65). William Byrd, during a visit to the Nottoway village in 1729, described houses built in a fashion similar to those of the Tuscarora. "These cabins are no other but close arbors made of saplings, arched at the top and covered so well with bark as to be proof against all weather. The fire is made in the middle. . . . The Indians have no standing furniture in their cabins but hurdles to repose their persons upon which they cover with mats or deerskins" (Byrd 1966:217).

The environmental diversity of their territory and the reliance of these Iroquoian coastal-plain people on fishing, hunting, gathering, and agriculture made their subsistence adaptation successful. In addition to winter communal hunting, men pursued deer, bear, beaver, raccoon, opossum, rabbit, squirrel, turkey, and other creatures as important protein sources (Lawson 1967:182; Barnwell 1908:43). Coastal Algonquians would not touch freshwater sturgeon according to Lawson, but these fish and herring were caught and used inland, especially during their spawning runs up the rivers in the spring. Fish weirs, nets, and simple clubs were all used to catch them (Lawson 1967:162, 218; Bland 1911:15). Alewives were reportedly caught in swamps and freshwater streams and then dried before transporting them to villages. Crayfish were used a great deal by the Tuscarora. They baited sharpened reeds with roasted venison cut into strips. The baited ends of several of these reeds were placed in a stream and watched by an attendant who occasionally pulled in the crayfish and added new bait. Trout and other desirable freshwater fish were most often caught with fish weirs. Saltwater fish were apparently obtained through trade with coastal people who dried them for that purpose (Lawson 1967:163, 165, 218).

Men and women gathered materials used for ceremonies, for the production of household and personal items, for trade goods, and for food. Allegheny chinquapin nuts were gathered communally in the late summer (Anonymous 1897:35, 39). Hickory nuts, wild parsnips, and wild turnips were used by the Tuscarora (Barnwell 1908:37,

39). A general statement concerning the food of Carolina Indians probably applies to the coastal-plain people as well. They ate "wild Fruits that are palatable, some of which they dry and keep against Winter, as all sort of Fruits, and Peaches, which they dry, and make Quiddonies, and Cakes, that are very pleasant, and a little tartish; young Wasps, when they are white in the Combs, before they can fly, this is esteemed a Dainty . . .; Ground-Nuts, or wild Potato's; Acorns and Acorn Oil" (Lawson 1967:182).

Fiber sources included silk grass, wild hemp, rushes, and cattails. Baskets and mats were made from these for their own use and traded to Euro-American and indigenous neighbors (Byrd 1966:222; Lawson 1967:195-196). Wooden bowls and ladles were likewise made and traded for furs with the people of the Piedmont by the Tuscarora during the year prior to the 1711-1713 war. Many plants and other desired raw materials were gathered close to settlement areas for utilitarian and ceremonial purposes, but some required travel to distant areas or trade with neighbors. Bloodroot (*Sanguinaria canadensis*) was highly desired by the Tuscarora as a dye for the hair even though they had to go to the Piedmont or foothills of the mountains to find it, risking encounters with Five Nations war parties and other enemies (Lawson 1967: 174-175). The Tuscarora were well known for the use of copper for body ornamentation and made frequent western trips for it and also for salt (Quinn 1955, 2:102, 209, 268-270, 332-333, 388; Lederer 1958:33; Bland 1911:17; Yeardley 1911:27-28). Yaupon (*Ilex vomitoria*), which grows only on the coast, was desired by inland people for its curative powers and for ceremonially important beverages and was therefore a valuable trade commodity (Lawson 1967:97-98, 229-230). These few examples illustrate the resourcefulness and the priorities for the gathering activities of coastal-plain Iroquoian people.

Corn was the single most important crop. It was parched and ground into meal, used in soups, made into bread, eaten from the ear, and dried for winter use. When Barnwell (1908:34) went through the territories of five Tuscarora villages in late January and early February 1712 he found more than "2000 bushells of corn" in the 374 houses that were destroyed. Early in March he passed through the Coree village and observed that they had "hid their corn, which is in abundance, in a great Swamp" and found hundreds of bushels stored by hostile Tuscaroras late in the same month (Barnwell 1908:47, 49). All of this is a good indication of their productivity considering they were under siege and still had these resources available at the end of the winter. Bland (1911:12) wrote in 1650 that the Meherrin grew two crops of corn per field in a given year. The scattered settlement pattern ideally complemented this high productivity by distributing population where arable land was available. Concentrated land use without crop rotation meant soils were rapidly depleted, and travelers often referred to grass-choked Indian old fields. In addition to corn, Carolina-Virginia Iroquoians grew gourds, squash, and beans of several varieties (Lawson 1967:182).

In addition to an abundance of corn, in 1712 Barnwell (1908:34) found fruit trees bearing an abundance of apples, peaches, and quinces in the Tuscarora settlements. Some varieties were probably adopted from the Euro-Americans but Lawson (1967:115) is careful to state that others were cultivated before colonists arrived.

Glimpses of the traditional division of labor, age-sex categories, and life cycle are provided by several early observers. In a general statement that probably referred in part to the Tuscarora Lawson (1967:195) explained that the "women's Work is to cook the Victuals for the whole Family, and to make Mats, Baskets, Girdles of Possum-Hair and suchlike. They never plant the Corn amongst us, as they do amongst the *Iroquois*" or Five Nations in New York. Young Tuscarora men apparently worked in the fields during the agricultural season (Lawson 1967:177, 184), but their work as well as everyone else's varied somewhat throughout the year. During their move to winter hunting quarters women carried grain and other provisions. After arriving most of their time was spent in getting firewood, cooking, and making craft items. Men who were poor hunters (possibly berdaches) procured bark for the cabins, ran errands back to the town where the old people were left, made wooden bowls and dishes, and clay tobacco pipes. Those men who were good hunters were expected to concentrate on that activity (Lawson 1967:65, 215-217). Young girls, commonly several together, beat the corn to be used in bread or soup with a large wooden mortar and pestles. During the appropriate seasons they helped the women gather nuts, wild fruit, and tubers (Todd 1920:271; Lawson 1967:216).

William Byrd's description of the Nottoway, written 20 years later in 1729, differs on one significant point. He claimed that the only work done by Nottoway men was hunting and fishing (Byrd 1966:219). It may have been that Tuscarora men did work in the fields and Nottoway men did not, but the truth is probably that some agricultural work was done regularly by males of all these groups during periods of maximum labor requirements, for example clearing new fields, planting, and harvesting. Given the Tuscarora males' later reputation for doing such work in New York it is probably true that they did help more in the fields than their Five Nations counterparts (Boyce 1973:129-130).

Besides fishing, hunting, trading, and to some extent farming, Tuscarora men were involved in warfare, which sometimes took them far from home. Lawson (1967:213-214) was impressed by their ability to organize distant expeditions, which often split into several groups yet managed to meet at the heads of previously unknown rivers 500-700 miles away. Planning, organization, and

cooperation were all important for such endeavors. In the case of war parties, advice was sought from the "ancient Men of Conduct and Reason, that belong to their Nation; such as superannuated War-Captains, and those that have been Counsellors for many Years, and whose Advice has commonly succeeded very well" (Lawson 1967:208). Then final plans of strategy were worked out by what may have been war chiefs.

The old men of the village were important sources of time-tested reason and caution. Lawson (1967:177, 184, 188-189, 204) repeatedly refers to their important place in decision making or ceremony. Virginia Gov. Alexander Spotswood wrote of the Tuscarora in July 1711 that "their old men . . . have the greatest sway in their counsels" (Brock 1882-1885, 1:96).

Information concerning several aspects of Nottoway and Tuscarora life cycle has been preserved, specifically, on adolescence rites and disposal of the dead. General accounts of the indigenous people of eastern Virginia and North Carolina mention a ritual called the huskanaw that marked the transition of boys and perhaps girls to adult status (Beverley 1947:208-212; Lawson 1967:106, 241-242). In brief outline, these young people were taken to an isolated cabin where they were deprived of food and given what may have been hallucinogenic plants or beverages. They were kept in isolation for periods of two or three weeks to a few months. Upon returning to the village they did not speak for several weeks. That this kind of rite was important to the Tuscarora is affirmed in a relatively late—1755—reference. The North Carolina Tuscaroras were going to supply warriors to assist the English against the French at the request of the Tuscaroras who had joined the Five Nations. North Carolina Gov. Arthur Dobbs wrote that they were "Sasquehanning [huskanawing] them to have them ready" (Pa. Arch. 2:537). Hewitt's (1895:1-4) research on the New York reservation revealed this kind of ritual complex was still remembered although no longer practiced.

Lawson recorded a brief account of the burial of a Tuscarora man who had been struck by lightning while attending a festival at the Neusiok village of Chattooka. Burial took place the next day. The body was wrapped in mats made with reeds. Before interment took place, food was served and a shaman spoke to the people concerning the origin and nature of lightning. On such occasions the good qualities and achievement of the deceased were discussed. Village chiefs, renowned elders, and other people of importance were treated differently at death by the Nottoway and probably by the Meherrin and Tuscarora as well. The remains of such individuals were kept in a quiocosin or mortuary house (McIlwaine 1925-1945, 3:98; Lawson 1967:188-189, 219), a practice they shared with coastal Algonquian groups. While burial customs differed greatly, all groups shared two features: formal mourning continued in the evening for an indefinite period after burial and women were normally buried with a less elaborate ceremony than that accompanying the death of a man (Lawson 1967:189).

History

Nottoway and Meherrin

The Nottoway and Meherrin remained relatively undisturbed by the English colony expanding from Jamestown during the first half of the seventeenth century. They were familiar with English-Indian policies and may have occasionally visited Fort Henry on the Appomattox River. Their unfamiliarity with guns and their apprehension at the visit of Edward Bland's party in 1650 suggest that their contacts with the English were not frequent. Trade activity began to increase after this time. The settlements of the Nottoway (Rowantee, Tonnatorah, and Cohanahanhaka) and Meherrin (Cowinchahawkon) were apparently on the main trading path called Weecacana that paralleled the fall line to the south toward the Tuscarora. Indians could not go into colonial settlements without a pass, but Whites were also prohibited from going to Nottoway and Meherrin villages unless licensed as traders. At the end of Bacon's Rebellion in 1677 a treaty was signed by Virginia colonists and nearby Virginia Indians including the Nottoway and Meherrin. The Indians became tributary groups who were to serve as military buffers protecting the White settlements from raids by the Five Nations and other distant Indians. By this time, colonial fur-trading operations began to bypass the Nottoway and Meherrin for more numerous and productive peoples to the west and south—Ocaneechi, Tuscarora, Catawba, and Cherokee. Colonists also began to move out from the James River into the territory of these tributaries and by the early eighteenth century had surrounded them. The Meherrin and Nottoway responded as early as 1681 by moving southeast along the rivers bearing their names and establishing new settlements (fig. 1). Throughout this period they acquired elements of Euro-American culture. By 1692 the Nottoway were raising hogs for sale, and when Byrd (1966) visited their village in 1729 he found a fort built in part

after the English manner. A treaty with the northern Indians in 1718 put an end to even the fiction of the Nottoway and Meherrin serving as buffer groups. Although reservations had been set aside for them, land encroachment by Whites continued to be a problem. Population (tables 1, 2) continued to decline in spite of the incorporation of several ethnic remnants (Weanocks and Nansemonds) by the Nottoway (Binford 1967). Little research has been done on the late history of the Meherrin, but in 1761 they were said to have been still living in Northampton County, North Carolina, near the Roanoke River. They may have been absorbed shortly thereafter by the Tuscarora (Saunders, Clark, and Weeks 1886–1914, 6:616).

Throughout the final two-thirds of the eighteenth century reservation lands (originally two plots, one six miles square and the other circular with a diameter of six miles, located south and north, respectively, of the Nottoway River in the area of the twentieth-century towns of Courtland, Capron, and Sebrell, Southampton County, Virginia) were slowly sold. Assimilation of material culture progressed rapidly. In 1824 the Virginia Assembly voted to allow individual Nottoways to apply for private tracts of reservation land, and in succeeding years the legal breaking-up of the Nottoway reservation took place. According to Rountree (1973a) this was the second officially legislated "termination" in United States history. All state government services were stopped, and their legal status as a tribe ended. Nottoway intermarriage with free Blacks, their reported love of alcohol, and their alleged disdain for work made them unpopular with their White neighbors, who coveted tribal lands. The allotment of land to individual Nottoways was not completed until 1878 due to a continuing resistance of some who did not want to lose their Indian status (Rountree 1973a).

In 1883 a New York Tuscarora informant told Gatschet (1883–1885:4, 36) there were Nottoways living in Canada on the Grand River reservation who spoke Tuscarora and were "darker than others, perhaps by negro intermixture." It is not known for certain when

Table 1. Meherrin Population

Year	Location	Fighting Men	Villages	Total	Sources
1669	Va.	50	2		Neill 1886:325–326; Binford 1967:153–155
1709	Va.	50	1		Lawson 1967:242
1731	East of Chowan R., N.C.			less than 20 families	Saunders, Clark, and Weeks 1886–1914, 3:153
1755	Northampton Co., N.C.	8			Saunders, Clark, and Weeks 1886–1914, 5:321
1761	Northampton Co., N.C.	20			Saunders, Clark, and Weeks 1886–1914, 6:616

Table 2. Nottoway Population

Year	Fighting Men	Villages	Total	Sources
1669	90	3		Neill 1886:325–326; Binford 1967:151–152
1709	30	1		Lawson 1967:242
1729			200	Byrd 1966:219
1730	50			Saunders, Clark, and Weeks 1886–1914, 3:89
1774			35	Rountree 1973a:9
1818			26	Rountree 1973a:21
1820			27	J. Morse 1822:31
1821			30	Rountree 1973a:21
1822			28	Rountree 1973a:24
1837			25[a]	Rountree 1973a:34
1852			12[a]	Rountree 1973a:36
1854			9[a]	Schoolcraft 1851–1857, 3:36
1963			1	Painter 1961; Rountree 1973a:41

[a] Does not include those who were allotted a tract of reservation land and thereby terminated their Indian legal status.

these Nottoways went north. One source states that they emigrated to the New York Tuscarora in 1776 (Mead 1832:127), but since that was the peak of the Revolutionary War, it is doubtful. A large number of Tuscaroras left North Carolina in 1766, and the remainder abandoned their reservation in 1804. It is likely that a few Nottoways joined them at one or both of these times.

The Nottoways who remained in Virginia after termination was completed can be traced in part through Southampton County records. The last person claiming Nottoway identity, William Lamb, was born in 1875 (Painter 1961:34) and died in 1963. Other Nottoways can be traced into the early years of the twentieth century, and Rountree (1973a) found people of apparently Indian-Black-White ancestry living in the area of the old Southampton County reservation in the early 1970s. However, intermarriage with Whites and Blacks as well as geographical fragmentation resulting from individuals and families leaving the area had resulted in the disappearance of the Nottoway as a group.

Tuscarora

Initial colonial settlement of North Carolina came in the late 1650s and early 1660s on the north side of Albemarle Sound. By the late 1660s colonists and the Tuscarora were engaged in brief reciprocal raids against each other (Anonymous 1900:346, 348). An undated peace treaty that was probably drawn up at that time has been discovered among records in the courthouse at Edenton, North Carolina. It specified that no Tuscarora settlements were to be north or west of the Roanoke River and no Tuscaroras were allowed to live within a half-day's travel from the English (Anonymous 1901:219). Relations were fragile between Tuscaroras and North Carolinians. The Tuscarora saw their land taken without proper compensation and their people captured for slaves, cheated by traders, and plied with liquor.

Since they remained peripheral to the slow English expansion, the Tuscarora maintained their autonomy. Except for superficial material additions like trade goods and weapons they had changed very little culturally up to the outbreak of large-scale warfare in 1711 (see "Tuscarora Among the Iroquois," this vol.). One article of the treaty made between Barnwell and the southern Tuscarora villages that were involved in the war relinquished Tuscarora land rights for settlement or hunting use south of the Neuse River. After about 1,500 Tuscaroras fled north to New York in 1713–1714 the consolidation of those who remained took several years. As many as 1,000 to 1,500 Tuscaroras had fled to Virginia, some of these even accepting tributary status under that colony, but most returned to North Carolina. In 1715 a force of 70 Tuscaroras went to South Carolina to help that colony against the Yamasee. This band later asked permission to have other Tuscaroras, including their wives and children, join them in the area of Port Royal.

Because of harassment from the Catawba and other enemies, the Tuscaroras remaining in North Carolina under the leadership of Tom Blount asked that a reservation be established for them on the north side of the Roanoke River in what is now Bertie County. This request was granted, and they moved to the villages of Ooneroy and Resootskeh. Blount, who was only a village chief prior to the 1711–1713 war, assisted the English during the war by rallying the support of both his own and other northern Tuscarora villages that wanted an end to the war and reestablishment of peaceful trade with Virginia. The motivation for Blount's support of the English is not clear. He may have felt that this avenue of helping the English was the best for his people. Or he may have been motivated by personal ambitions for leadership aroused through extensive Euro-American contact, as is suggested by his use of an English name. Whatever factors were involved, Blount was set up as the "king" of the Tuscarora by Virginia and North Carolina. These colonial governments agreed to look upon as friends only those Indians who accepted Blount's leadership. As their reservation became surrounded by White settlements they bore the brunt of increasing prejudice. No longer able significantly to protect colonial settlements, they were overcharged for or denied the use of ferries, restricted in hunting, and cheated in trade. Their land was encroached on by herders and squatters, and their timber lands illegally logged.

Internally there were problems for the Tuscarora as well. Many individuals were dissatisfied with Tom Blount's leadership. Some of these left the reservation, but others stayed and created enough trouble so that Blount several times asked the North Carolina government for assistance in maintaining his position. Blount died between 1733 and 1739. He was succeeded by a series of popularly elected chiefs who seemed more responsive to the Tuscarora people. Reservation life was not a good one for the Tuscarora, as population (table 3) and economic productivity continued to decline. In fall 1752 Bishop August Spangenberg and other Moravians visited the reservation. They wrote that many had grown dissatisfied and had gone north to live "on the Susquehanna; . . . others are scattered as the wind scatters the smoke." Spangenberg wrote that they were living "in great poverty, and are oppressed by the whites." They had continued traditional agricultural practices, planting "until the grass grows so freely that they cannot till their corn,—for they have neither plough nor harrow,—and then they clear and plant a new piece" (Fries 1922, 1:41–53).

Other bands moved north to Tuscarora settlements in Pennsylvania and New York in 1763 and 1766. Some individuals and families may have merely moved off the reservation southwest to the sandhills or a few counties northwest to contribute in part to the marginal populations that developed in those areas, such as the Lumbee and Haliwa Indians. Finally in 1804 what was left of the original reservation was sold (in some cases preexisting long-term leases complicated matters). The proceeds were used to expand the New York reservation through purchases from the Holland Land Company, and the last band of North Carolina Tuscaroras moved north.

Synonymy

The English adventurers who arrived at Roanoke Island in 1584 and Jamestown in 1607 were told of an inland people called the Mangoaks whose language differed from that of the coastal Algonquian-speaking people (Hoffman 1967). Swanton (1946:218), Mooney (1910a), who gives variant spellings, and Mook (1944a:185, 195) claimed the Mangoaks were the Nottoway. Speck (1928:map) believed they were the Meherrin, and Paschal (1953:16–21) identified them as the Tuscarora. Binford (1967:124) suggested that all the Iroquoian peoples of the Virginia-North Carolina coastal plain were called Mangoak by their Algonquian-speaking neighbors. The name continues the Proto-Eastern Algonquian tribal name *me·nkwe·w;* see the synonymy in "Northern Iroquoian Culture Patterns," this volume.

Table 3. Tuscarora Population in Virginia and the Carolinas

Year	Location	Fighting Men	Villages	Total	Sources
1709	N.C.	1,200	15		Lawson 1967:242
1712	N.C.	1,200 to 1,400			Barnwell 1908:34
1712	N.C.	2,000			Brock 1882–1885, 1:167
1713	Refugees from N.C. in Va.		5	1,500	Anonymous 1911:272–273; Brock 1882–1885, 2:42
1715	Port Royal, S.C.	70			Hassell 1715:2
1722	Bertie Co., N.C.	300	2		Newnam 1722:2
1731	Bertie Co., N.C.	200	2		Saunders, Clark, and Weeks 1886–1914, 3:153
1755	Bertie Co., N.C.	100	2	301	Saunders, Clark, and Weeks 1886–1914, 5:321
1761	Bertie Co., N.C.	100			Saunders, Clark, and Weeks 1886–1914, 6:616
1766	Bertie Co., N.C.			230	Saunders, Clark, and Weeks 1886–1914, 7:219
1767	Bertie Co., N.C.			104[a]	Saunders, Clark, and Weeks 1886–1914, 7:431
1804	Bertie Co., N.C.			10 to 20 "old families"	Gatschet 1883–1885:83

[a] 130–160 Tuscaroras emigrated in 1766.

The name Nottoway had a similar application, for a tribal name reconstructible as Proto-Algonquian *na·towe·wa* is reflected in many Algonquian languages as the name of various Iroquoian and Siouan groups. The extension of the term as the name of a species of snake seems to be found only in certain Central Algonquian languages and is best regarded as an innovation (Ives Goddard, personal communication 1974). The earliest recognizable appearance of Nottoway (and also Tuscarora and Meherrin) is in an account of a trading expedition written in 1650 (Bland 1911:5–19). Subsequent variant spellings are similar: Nottawayes, Notowegee. Only after 1800 was it learned that the Nottoways' name for themselves was Cheroenhaka, which possibly meant 'fork of a stream' (Mooney 1910a).

There are several versions of the name Meherrin: Maherin, 1705 (Saunders, Clark, and Weeks 1886–1914, 1:615); Maherring, 1709 (Lawson 1967:242); Meherries (Schoolcraft 1851–1857, 5:36); Meherron, 1711 (Saunders, Clark, and Weeks 1886–1914, 1:751); Menchaerink, 1670 (Lederer 1958); Menherring, 1722 (Saunders, Clark, and Weeks 1886–1914, 2:475).

For the synonymy of Tuscarora see "Tuscarora Among the Iroquois," this volume.

Sources

The historical summary in this chapter is taken largely from Boyce (1971, 1973, 1975). An additional useful source is Paschal (1953). Very few published secondary sources exist. F.R. Johnson's books (1967–1968) contain a great deal of useful information; but editing is poor, statements are made without sufficient evidence, and reliable as well as unreliable data are presented. J.N.B. Hewitt's (1910c) early published account is basically reliable, and Milling's work (1940:113–134) offers some useful elaborations, especially with regard to the Port Royal band of Tuscaroras.

For additional information concerning the Nottoway and Meherrin during the colonial period, Binford (1967) should be consulted. There is a definite need for additional research on the late history of the Meherrin, since Binford thought they were being absorbed by the Tuscarora in 1730 yet they are known to have been living in Northampton County, North Carolina, separate from the Tuscarora, in the early 1760s. Rountree's (1973a) research on the Nottoway takes up where Binford left off and follows the reservation population and its dissolution in the twentieth century.

Marginal Groups

BREWTON BERRY

Throughout the eastern United States there are communities that are not fully accepted as Whites, Blacks, or Indians. Many of these groups have emphasized an Indian ancestry while others have identified with either the Black or White segments of the American population. In the race-conscious atmosphere characteristic of contemporary America, these groups frequently are confronted by challenges to their expressed ethnic identifications and have sought historical documentation of their claims. Although the historical evidence in many cases has not yet been located (and, in fact, has not yet been properly searched for), there are good reasons to believe that most of these groups are descended in part from aboriginal American Indian populations.

There has been some difficulty in establishing a generic term for these groups. Many members of these communities find the names that have been applied to them extremely objectionable, and some goups have been described according to derogatory folk definitions of race as "colored," "half-breeds," or "mongrels." Scholars, not wishing to offend but compelled to be precise, have proposed a number of generic terms, including "triracial isolates," "metis," "racial islands," "Aframerindians," "marginal peoples," and "quasi-Indians," but none has met with general acceptance. The term *mestizo*, widely used for ethnically or biologically intermediate peoples in Latin America and the Philippines, has also been applied to the racially mixed people in the United States. It, too, is offensive to those who are firmly committed to a uniquely Indian identity (Dane and Griessman 1972; Dunlap and Weslager 1947).

The origin of the mestizo groups has always been something of an enigma, and, in the absence of historical data, myths and legends have flourished. Among the reputed ancestors of the mestizos have been Turks, Portuguese, Moors, Italians, Mexicans, Greeks, Cubans, Blacks, and of course, American Indians. The myths are replete with stories of shipwrecked sailors, pirates, Sir Walter Raleigh's colonists, English noblemen, romantic ladies, Hessian soldiers, runaway slaves, adventurers, and explorers. That Negro-White hybrids, with probably some Indian admixture, were the ancestors of mestizo groups has been proved for the Ramapo Mountain People (Cohen 1974), the Brandywine People (Harte 1963), the "Guineas" (Burnell 1952), and the Coes (Montell 1970, 1972). Price (1953) lends support to this thesis by analyzing the distribution of characteristic mestizo surnames; and Pollitzer (1972), on the basis of genetic evidence, reaches a similar conclusion. The research of Porter (1971), Aptheker (1939), and Woodson (1918) demonstrates the extent to which Negro slaves ran away, were sheltered by Indians, and intermarried with them. Furthermore, Indians themselves were often enslaved and held in bondage along with Blacks, with whom they mixed. Free Black ancestors are also demonstrable for some groups. However, the history of only a few mestizo communities has been the subject of scholarly research, and the origin and development of most of them remain undocumented.

These are communities that hold no reservation land, speak no Indian language, and observe no distinctive Indian customs. Although it is difficult to establish a firm historical Indian ancestry for many of them, their members often display physical features that are decidedly Indian. Because they bear no other historic tribal names, they often emphasize a Cherokee ancestry (Beale 1957, 1958, 1972; Berry 1963, 1972; Gilbert 1946, 1948; Price 1950).

Most facets of mestizo existence are touched by outsiders'—and sometimes their own—uncertainties about how to fit them into the American folk classification of "races." Personality studies have never been conducted, but observers have reported a high incidence of hypersensitivity, alienation, and hostility. Mestizos are sensitive regarding derogatory epithets such as "Guinea" and "Jackson White"; and they are often infuriated by those that impute Negro ancestry, such as "Guinea Niggers," "Black Coes," and "Nigger Hill." When speaking of themselves they will usually say, "our people," but resent it when outsiders say to them, "your people." The term "colored" is acceptable to the Ramapo Mountain People (Cohen 1974), to some of the "Guineas" (Burnell 1952), to the Brandywine People (Gilbert 1945), and to many of the Ohio groups, for in those communities it means no more than non-White. In the South, on the other hand, "colored" is resented by mestizo peoples, for it is equivalent to Negro or Black (Dane and Griessman 1972). Often the group names by which specific communities prefer to be known are not available. Without scholarly research, only the popular, often derogatory, labels by which their neighbors refer to them are familiar.

Most mestizos deny that they have any Negro ancestry. In conversation they will describe themselves as "mostly White," "part Indian," or "Indian-White." Exceptions are the Gouldtowners, the Darke County group, and the Coe Clan; and Cohen (1974) reports that some of the younger Ramapo Mountain People, impressed by the Black pride movement, have begun to identify with Negroes, much to the distress of their elders.

Middle Atlantic States

Some 30 miles northwest of New York City, in the New Jersey counties of Bergen and Passaic and the New York counties of Orange and Rockland is a group known as the Ramapo Mountain People, or, derogatively, as "Jackson Whites" or "Jacks." Their history goes back to the seventeenth century, when free mulattoes of Dutch-Negro origin, with perhaps some Indian ancestry also, began buying farms in the Hackensack River valley. A century later, harassed by their White neighbors, they sold their farms and sought refuge in the Ramapo Mountains. There, and in the nearby towns, their descendants have remained (fig. 1).

The Ramapo Mountain People maintain that they are descended from Hessian mercenaries, who defected from the British during the Revolutionary War, fled to the mountains, and there intermarried with Tuscarora Indians. A variation of this history, long accepted by the local Whites, includes prostitutes and runaway slaves among the progenitors of the Ramapo Mountain People (Cohen 1974).

In central New Jersey live the Sand Hill Indians, who regard themselves as descendants of the Tuscarora, the Cherokee, or the Delaware. This group has lived for generations in Monmouth County, where they have preserved certain Indian traditions and practiced crafts such as basketry and beadwork. Eventually they settled at a spot near Asbury Park called Sand Hill. They are now widely scattered, though a few remain. Another group, called the Pineys or more derogatively "Pine Rats," lives in a sparsely populated region known as the Pine Barrens, in Burlington County, New Jersey. Most of them have always been accepted as Whites, but some are thought to be triracial. They manifest little interest in maintaining an Indian identity (Gilbert 1948).

Early in the eighteenth century a free Negro named Gould and his White wife, Elizabeth Adams, found refuge in southern New Jersey near the present town of Bridgeton. They were joined by other people of diverse ancestry. There were the Murrays, who claimed to be descended from Delaware Indians and Swedes, and the Pierce brothers, mulattoes from the West Indies, and their Dutch wives. The members of the community intermarried, prospered, and multiplied. The Gouldtowners, as they came to be called, have emphasized neither their Black nor their Indian heritage. Many have

gone forth from the community and achieved prominence as Negroes and many more have assimilated into the White population (Steward and Steward 1913; Frazier 1939).

In isolated rural settlements in central Pennsylvania live a group of people of possible Indian ancestry. These people prefer keeping to themselves and avoiding their White neighbors, who refer to them as the "Nigger-Hill people" (in western Clinton County) and the "Karthus half-breeds" (in Clearfield County). They are not especially visible, though they tend to have dark complexions, and some of them display Negroid characteristics. There are only faint rumors of Indian ancestry, affirmed by certain of the group members themselves. The neighboring Whites maintain that these people are the offspring of fugitive Negro slaves who mixed with the backwoods families that gave them shelter in the decades prior to the Civil War.

In the northeast corner of Pennsylvania, near Towanda, lives the so-called Pool Tribe or Pooles, so named because of the prevalence of the surname Vanderpool among them. As a group, they are stigmatized by the local White community. The tradition is that they are descended from Sir William Johnson, eighteenth-century superintendent of Indian affairs for the northern colonies, and numerous Indian women by whom he had children. One of his daughters, Elizabeth, married Anthony Vanderpool, of a prominent New York Dutch family. He was promptly disowned by his family and, with his wife and a few followers, fled to Pennsylvania.

There are several mestizo groups in Maryland. A few "Guineas" have moved from West Virginia into Garrett County, while "Melungeons" from Tennessee have established themselves in Ellicott City. The Brandywine People, or "Wesorts" ("We-Sort"), numbering perhaps 5,000, have long resided in Charles and Prince George's counties, where the Whites have always regarded them as

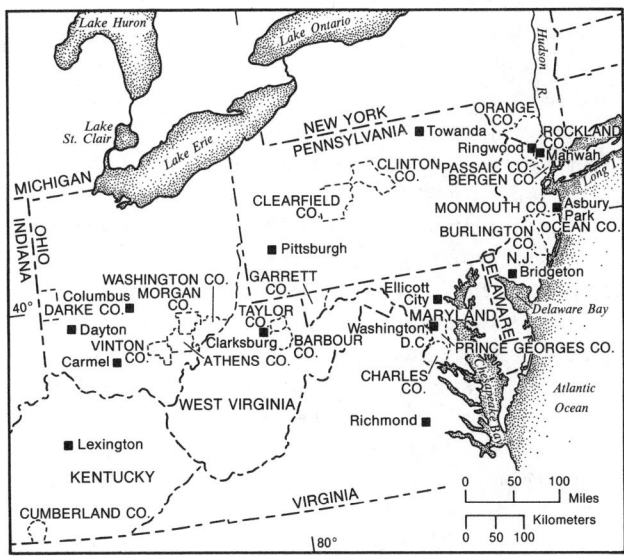

Fig. 1. Distribution of marginal groups.

mulattoes, have counted them as Negroes in the census, and, until recently, forced them to attend the Negro schools. The Brandywine People deny that they have Negro blood and insist that they are Indian-White hybrids. Their origin is something of a mystery, but it appears that the Brandywine People arose from unions as early as the seventeenth century between Whites, Blacks, and Indians, especially Nanticokes, Conoys, and Piscataways (see "Nanticoke and Neighboring Tribes," this vol.).

Ohio Valley States

In West Virginia, the so-called Guineas live principally in Barbour and Taylor counties whence they have spread, not only to many other counties of the state, but also to Ohio, Maryland, and Michigan. They are accustomed to hearing themselves referred to as "colored," which they interpret as meaning simply "non-White"; but they loathe the sobriquet "Guinea." They maintain that their ancestors included Dutch settlers, English colonists, veterans of the American Revolution, and a beautiful young Delaware Indian woman named Pretty Hair. The Whites reject this as pure myth, though they themselves have invented a number of mythical explanations for the origin of the "Guineas." Some Whites say that the "Guineas" are the progeny of Italian laborers who came into the region after the Civil War, and, shunned by the local Whites, sought the company of Negro women. Others maintain that an English nobleman visited the Guinea coast of Africa, married a Black woman, and fathered a large family who, in some unaccountable manner, found their way to West Virginia. Still others say they are the offspring of migratory Mexican laborers, or that they are mulattoes whose ancestors came from a section of Virginia known as Guinea's Neck (Burnell 1952; Gilbert 1946a; Price 1950a).

In 13 counties of southeastern Kentucky there are many clusters of a people known to local Whites as "Melungeons." For the most part they are undistinguishable economically, culturally, and physically from their White neighbors, although some of them do have brown complexions and straight black hair. Their forebears came from Virginia and the Carolinas in the 1790s, first to Tennessee and from there to Kentucky. In the earliest records they are listed as "free persons of color," but for many years they have been designated in public records as either White or Indian. There has been much intermarriage with Whites, so that there are no longer sharp social distinctions, and the "Melungeons" are identifiable chiefly by the surnames they bear, among the most common being Gibson, Mullins, Collins, and Goins (Beale 1957, 1972; Gilbert 1946, 1948; Price 1950, 1950a, 1951).

Kentucky has also been the home of a people known to Whites as the "Pea Ridge group," the "Coe Clan," or the "Black Coes." The origin of this community goes back to the first decade of the nineteenth century, when a certain John Coe, with his aggregate of slaves, moved from North Carolina to Cumberland County, Kentucky. Among his slaves were the part-Black offspring of a Cherokee Indian slaveholder known as "Master Stove." After the Civil War the slaves adopted their former owner's name, purchased a plot of raw land on Pea Ridge, and undertook to sustain themselves in relative isolation in the midst of an unfriendly White population. They succeeded reasonably well for a time, until the erosion of their economic base forced them to migrate. Most of them crossed the Ohio River, finding employment in Indianapolis, Chicago, Dayton, Gary, and Fort Wayne, until by 1958 none remained on Pea Ridge. Although the Coes have always proudly proclaimed their Cherokee ancestry, they freely acknowledge their Black and White ancestry as well (Montell 1970, 1972).

In Ohio no county in the state is without its coterie of those who profess to be Indian or at least to have Indian ancestors. "Melungeons" have been moving in from Kentucky for more than a century, and one group has resided near the village of Carmel since 1870. These people consider themselves to be Cherokee and are affronted by the local Whites who refer to them as "half-breeds," "Carmel Indians," or "Carmelites." From Carmel they have gone forth to establish communities elsewhere in the state (Price 1950, 1950a). A large number of "Guineas" have migrated from West Virginia and are found in all the cities of Ohio, and a sizable community has long flourished in the rural areas of Morgan, Washington, and Athens counties. Those around Cutler, Ohio, are known as the "Cutler Indians." Between 1830 and 1850 numbers of "free persons of color" migrated from Virginia and settled in Vinton County. Their progeny, while still a submerged group, have intermarried with Whites so extensively that they are now regarded as White people.

Darke County, Ohio, is the home of a group of people who regard themselves as "colored," but, they add, "not like other colored folk." Here on the wild, uninhabited frontier free Black people began to find refuge early in the nineteenth century. First to settle was a man of Indian-White-Negro ancestry from Virginia. He was joined by others of similar racial stock from North Carolina and Tennessee. These people purchased land, built comfortable homes, established schools and churches, and became well-to-do by frontier standards. They take considerable pride in their Indian ancestry and have steadfastly held themselves apart from their Negro neighbors (Frazier 1939).

Occupations

The vast majority of the mixed-bloods are impoverished rural folk. They have been disposed or forced to follow the generally unprofitable occupation of small farming, and, what is more, they have done so with primitive equipment on plots of ground that are rocky, hilly, and eroded. The Darke County mestizos are an exception, for they own sizable farms in the rich corn belt of western Ohio and eastern Indiana; and the Gouldtowners have prospered by raising vegetables that they market in the nearby towns. The Ramapo Mountain People, on the other hand, were driven from their rich farmlands in the valley into the less desirable Ramapo Mountains. The "Guineas" possess little of the fertile bottom land of West Virginia, subsisting instead on their bleak hillside farms. The same is true of the "Melungeons," the Pennsylvania groups, the Carmelites, the Cutler Indians, and others. Many do not own the land but work as tenants or seasonal farm laborers for their more affluent White neighbors. Most of them supplement their meager earnings by hunting and fishing and by digging for ginseng, yellowroot, and sassafras, which they sell to local dealers. Some of them capitalize on their reputation as Indians and earn a little money by weaving baskets and making pottery or by hiring out as guides for hunters and fishermen.

Not all mestizos, of course, are farmers. For many years the Coes supported themselves comfortably by lumbering and rafting, and the "Pineys" have always made their living from the cranberry bogs. As early as 1826 some of the Ramapo Mountain People found employment in the iron mines, while others had jobs as gardeners, coachmen, blacksmiths, machinists, oilers, stone masons, and teamsters (Cohen 1974). When the mines shut down, the majority of them became craftsmen, operatives, and laborers. "Guineas" and "Melungeons" have long been employed as coal miners in Appalachia, with all the uncertainties of that occupation. The Brandywine People have been farmers for generations, but in the 1970s scarcely 15 percent of them continued to work the land, most of them having moved into clerical and unskilled jobs. Almost everywhere mestizo women are frequently engaged as domestic servants.

The mestizos have always been a mobile people. They were in the vanguard of the movement to the frontier. In the mid-twentieth century there was a prodigious exodus from their rural enclaves to the cities, impelled doubtless by high birth rates as well as by the decline in the coal-mining, lumbering, and other industries that have supported them in the past. In the cities they find jobs as construction workers, factory operatives, mechanics, carpenters, truck drivers, painters, and day laborers. Very few rise to the professions, though increasing numbers are becoming teachers and social workers.

Schools

The public school has been a battleground for the mestizos, for it was there that the question of their racial identity was explicitly raised. Typically, in those areas where the mestizos were numerous, they were excluded from the White schools and only under duress would they attend the Negro schools. In some places they constructed and financed their own schools; elsewhere missionaries provided education for them; or special schools were established by the state; or they simply did not attend school at all. Invariably the facilities provided for them were inferior to those of the Whites.

At Hillburn, New York, where many Ramapo Mountain People settled, the school district was established in 1880, and it was segregated from the outset. Non-Whites attended the Brook School, which was initially organized and maintained by private subscription. Eight years later, it was taken into the regular school system but was never properly supported. The Ramapo Mountain People resigned themselves to this inequity until, in 1943, they decided to do something about it. They sought to enroll their children in the White school but were rebuffed. They called upon the National Association for the Advancement of Colored People, which sent a lawyer—Thurgood Marshall—to direct their litigation. The resulting decision, favorable to the Ramapo Mountain People, foreshadowed the 1954 Supreme Court integration ruling in *Brown* v. *Board of Education*. There were boycotts, more litigation, protests, gerrymandering, establishment of private schools for Whites, and eventual integration (Cohen 1974).

Prior to 1954 Barbour County, West Virginia, provided eight small special schools for its "Guinea" population. The "Guineas" were displeased that their schools were classified as "colored," and they protested that the teachers assigned to them were Negroes. On numerous occasions they took their grievances to court, but invariably the decisions ran against them. Periodically they resorted to boycotts and demonstrations, and in two instances schools were burned to the ground. Finally, convinced of the futility of all their efforts, the "Guineas" unwillingly accepted a segregated system.

The situation was somewhat different in adjoining Taylor County. While the "Guineas" were barred from the White schools, their own special schools were not classified as "colored" in the school directory, and the teachers chosen for them were either members of their own group or Whites. Yet in neither county were there provisions for the secondary education of non-Whites. Transportation was made available, accordingly, for those who would go to the Negro high school in Clarksburg, 25 miles away. Few "Guineas" chose to do so. Instead, if they desired education beyond the elementary grades, they would go to live with relatives in Ohio or in other West Virginia counties, where they found no obstacles to attending White high schools.

Even with the integration of schools in West Virginia, subtle forms of discrimination continued to be practiced, so that achievement scores for "Guinea" pupils are low and dropout rates high. Some parents say that "it was better when we had our own schools."

Religion

The influence of the church appears to be less pervasive in most mestizo communities than in other rural American communities. Although the church in a few mestizo communities does serve as a focus for group loyalty, elsewhere it has made for divisiveness. The problem of their identity is uppermost in the minds of the mestizos and, in fact, affects and takes precedence over doctrinal and denominational issues.

The religious affiliation of most mestizos follows that of the larger community of which they are part. The Brandywine People are Roman Catholics, as are many Whites and Blacks of southern Maryland. Elsewhere the mestizos belong to one of the various Protestant bodies, if indeed they belong at all.

The unsettled nature of the mestizos' religious affiliations is revealed by the Ramapo Mountain People. Those in Mahwah, New Jersey, were discouraged by the Whites from joining the local Methodist Church; therefore, in 1857 they formed their own organization and reluctantly affiliated with the African Methodists, a Negro denomination. When Blacks began joining their church, most of the Ramapo Mountain People withdrew and joined the Pentecostal sect. In nearby Hillburn, New York, another group established their own chapel, which became loosely associated with the Presbyterians. An effort was made in the mid-1960s to merge the several Presbyterian congregations in the vicinity; but the Ramapo Mountain People, made skeptical by a long history of racial prejudice there, decided against the merger, much to the relief of the Presbyterians (Cohen 1974).

The African Methodist is also the oldest denomination among the "Guineas"; but most of them, growing uneasy at holding membership in a Negro institution, withdrew and joined the Wesleyan Methodists. Still others went with the Baptists, Church of God, Saints of Christ, United Brethren, and the Pentecostals (Burnell 1952). Those who remained with the African Methodists represent the most conservative element of the "Guinea" population.

Family and Community Life

The typical mestizo family is large, nuclear, and patriarchal. Children are appreciated and are indulged, the objects of much parental concern. They, in turn, display respect and loyalty to parents, grandparents, and other relatives. Traditionally the authority of the father has been recognized, but certain economic changes have served to enlarge the role of the mother. To find employment many men have had to commute to nearby cities, returning home only on weekends; and increasing numbers of families have been forced to depend upon welfare.

Kinship is reckoned bilaterally, and the terminology is the same as that employed elsewhere in the United States. The ties of kinship are very strong, forming the basis for family and community organization, for mutual aid and support, and for the resolution of conflicts. Mestizos keep and treasure family records, display great interest in genealogy, and find it a favorite topic of conversation.

From the earliest times mestizo communities have been geographically isolated—in swamps, on ridges, or in mountain hollows; further, they were socially isolated by bitter racial prejudices. Under these circumstances local endogamy prevailed to such an extent that a limited number of patronyms became associated with each community (Gilbert 1945), and even Christian names were applied repeatedly. The resulting confusion is resolved by the extensive use of nicknames; among the more imaginative are Pizen John, Whistlin' George, Screech, Squeeky, One Nose, and Tonto. Cousin marriages are common, and in some instances have come to be preferred. The Brandywine People, who are Roman Catholics, frequently have had to seek ecclesiastical dispensation for such unions (Harte 1959).

The practice of local endogamy is less common in the 1970s than formerly. There has always been a degree of exogamy, especially by those who chose to sever their ties with family and native community. Marriage to Whites and Indians has always been favored; but rarely does one who makes such a union bring his nonmestizo spouse back to the community. Marriage to Blacks is strongly discouraged and usually results in ostracism. Even so, it appears that increasing numbers of mestizos are choosing Black spouses. In the 1930s approximately 10 to 15 percent of recorded marriages of Brandywine People were to Negroes, while in the 1960s the number had increased to 20 percent. Cohen (1974) reports a similar trend among the Ramapo Mountain People. Exogamy was considerably accelerated during World War II, when service in the military increased contacts with outsiders; and urbanization and improved means of transportation and communication have served to continue the trend.

Mestizo communities are loose, flexible social entities. Ethnocentrism is present in very limited degree, although the Gouldtowners and the Darke County mixed-bloods do manifest some pride in their achievements as a group. Mestizo groups have been able to survive primarily because of their geographic isolation and the antipathy of the larger society.

Factionalism is evident in all communities. Those with money disdain the poor. Ramapo Mountain People who live in Hillburn and have well-paying blue-collar jobs deride the indigents of Mahwah and Ringwood (Cohen 1974). Stratification and friction arising from differences in color are everywhere in evidence. A high premium is placed upon White physical traits, and even within a family the darker children may be a source of embarrassment. In certain "Melungeon" communities the Morris families, who tend to be lighter, are reputed to be of "better stock." The Gibsons feel superior to the Gipsons, for the latter are suspected of having some Negro ancestry. In southern Ohio the Mayles are said to aspire to marry Crostons, who are supposed to be "more Indian." Dissension emerges as a result of different racial orientations. Those who see Indianness as the solution of their problem despair of those who remain indifferent. "Guineas" who are willing to accept the designation "colored" are scorned by those who are determined to be White.

Despite high birth rates, mestizo communities are not increasing in size. As a result of emigration some have disappeared altogether; however, they are not expected to vanish entirely for many years if ever. The most viable, and most likely to endure, are those that are large enough to support a community life, that have an adequate economic base, and that have a body of tradition to provide cohesion and a name of which they can feel proud.

Sources

The literature on these communities is extensive but very widely scattered, often unreliable, and generally of poor quality, in many instances limited to journalistic materials, frequently by authors exhibiting prejudice against the people they describe. Berry (1963) presents a general survey, with an extensive annotated bibliography. A good conceptual treatment is by E.T. Thompson (1972). Gilbert (1948) provides a useful summary, state by state, of group names, locations, typical surnames, and bibliography. An important listing of all groups known in 1957 based on federal census records (especially from the 1950 census) is by Beale (1957). Perhaps the most useful general treatment, although somewhat out of date, is by Price (1950; see also Price 1953). On group names see Dunlap and Weslager (1947). Pollitzer (1972) summarized available physical anthropological data. Among the very few intensive studies of individual communities by trained scholars are those by Cohen (1974; see also Collins 1972) and Montell (1970, 1972).

Northern Iroquoian Culture Patterns

WILLIAM N. FENTON

The term Iroquois (ˈērəˌkwoy; Canadian English ˈērəˌkwä) refers to the old Five Nations of New York—Mohawk, Oneida, Onondaga, Cayuga, and Seneca—whose confederacy extended from Schoharie Creek west of Schenectady to the Genesee at Rochester, and to the Six Nations after 1722 or 1723 when the Tuscarora who had come north from Carolina a decade earlier formally joined the League ("The League of the Iroquois: Its History, Politics, and Ritual," this vol.). The term Iroquoian includes all the languages of the family, one branch of which is Northern Iroquoian ("Iroquoian Languages," this vol.); but the northern Iroquoians whose culture patterns are treated here are a smaller grouping, geographically definable as the Iroquoian-speaking peoples of the Lower Great Lakes region. Although the Five Nations are the only northern Iroquoian group extant in their original homeland, their way of life was not unique but was comprised of cultural patterns that were shared by the others, including the Huron and their congeners. At the start of the seventeenth century, these northern Iroquoians encircled Lake Ontario, flanked Lake Erie, and held parts of the adjacent Saint Lawrence and Susquehanna valleys. The Iroquois way of life is much better known than that of the Susquehannock, to their south, but for the seventeenth century less well known than that of the Huron, north of them, who were rather fully described by French writers in a period when Indian customs fascinated readers in France. After midcentury, when the Hurons, Neutrals, Petuns, and Eries were dispersed, destroyed, or incorporated among the Five Nations, the lifeways of New World peoples were losing their fascination for literate Europeans. As a result, except for vignettes of dream rites, warfare, and some other details, scholars are dependent on the ethnography of Huronia for early Iroquoia as well, the assumption being that the Iroquois and the Huron were generally similar. Conversely, many of the major patterns so well understood for the nineteenth-century Iroquois can be assumed to have been present among all the northern Iroquoians during earlier times. An attempt at delineating the northern Iroquoian culture patterns is thus at best a reconstruction, based both on the early French sources and on the later ethnographic research on the Iroquois, which, beginning with the work of Morgan (1851) and continuing well after 1900, has been largely retrospective.

The time perspective in this reconstruction is essentially a continuum running from twentieth-century observations and those of ethnologists in the nineteenth-century backward to the contact period. To cite the legacy of Bloch (1953:28), the French philosopher of history, the great problems of historical inquiry derive from the antithesis of continuity and perpetual change. Patterns are the stuff of continuity; their isolation and synthesis is a synchronic act of the scholar; viewed over time, the substitutions within their framework afford a diachronic perspective—the stuff of change. Those patterns that persisted for the observation of ethnologists and are not demonstrably European but can be identified in the early sources represent the Iroquois cultural heritage. Some of these may well be pre-Columbian. Wherever possible, their earliest manifestation is indicated. Elements and patterns that represent a response to European contact are so denominated. The process is ongoing and regenerative. For the Hurons, the time perspective is largely the seventeenth century. For the Iroquois proper, the drama opened in the century before Samuel de Champlain and Henry Hudson arrived for the second act, and it is still going on (Fenton 1971).

For one who arrives at the end of a time span of three centuries to observe the contemporary Iroquois scene, the logical progression of research is to proceed from what is known best to what is most obscure (Bloch 1953:45). This approach, sometimes called "upstreaming" or reading history backwards, is often beneficial before restoring time to its true direction.

Environment and Territory

Iroquoia, the territory covered by the Longhouse of the Five Nations, south of Lake Ontario, is one physiographic and vegetational unit with the country just north of Lake Ontario and Lake Erie and southeast of Lake Huron. The south lakeshores are dissected by northward-flowing streams, which drain glaciated valleys that were gouged out of sedimentary formations. Where impounded, they form the Finger Lakes. High hills rise to the south to the height of land near the Pennsylvania line where the streams flow south into the Allegheny, Susquehanna, and Delaware drainage systems. The uplifted sedimentary formations that form the Niagara Escarpment reach from western New York into southwestern

Ontario, where the land is less broken and the climate moderated by the lakes. To the east, the Trent waterway connects Iroquoia via the Thousand Islands with Huronia. Southeast of Lake Ontario, between the uplifted plateau and the higher Adirondack mountains to the north, the Mohawk River and its broad valley cuts through these formations and affords the only water route through the Appalachian chain. These were the communication routes of the Iroquois and of ,their neighbors. They were the Indians' corridors of trade, war, and peace and for Europeans became the avenues of exploration and western expansion. The Iroquois were strategically located to exploit the geopolitics of the region.

Throughout Iroquoia deciduous birch-beech-maple-elm forests with coniferous admixture of pine and hemlock give way in the north to fir and spruce (Kroeber 1939:17, 91-92). The Appalachian deciduous forest of oak-chestnut-yellow poplar (ibid.:18) reaches eastern Iroquoia through valleys tributary to the Hudson; and the hunting range of the Seneca in southwestern New York, northwest Pennsylvania, and eastern Ohio affords deciduous trees and herbaceous plants typical of the Ohio drainage. Sycamores, walnuts, and butternuts of prodigious girth are reported from islands and bottoms; hickories, a source of food, oil, and staves, occur throughout; and the Genesee country features oak openings and savannas. But the sugar maple, the American elm, and the white pine were the climax forms important to Iroquois technology; they were venerated and appealed to in political metaphors. Elm bark was crucial for shelter, containers, and vessels; indeed, the culture could not function without it because birch of sufficient girth for covering canoes, shingling lodges, and making vessels does not grow south of a line encompassing the Adirondacks. This was not true for the Huron whose country transcends this line to the north. Birch products were obtained by the Huron in trade from Algonquian neighbors from whom they probably learned how to use the bark itself. The forest and vegetation of Huronia differed little from Iroquoia except that certain species, wild plum (*Prunus nigra*) and bitternut hickory (*Carya cordiformis*), there reached their northern range (Heidenreich 1971:59-63).

The Iroquois traveler to Huronia, or the Huron in Iroquoia, could easily find basswood bark or slippery elm bast for making rope, oak or basswood to staunch his wounds, and any of several hundred herbaceous plants for medicines. These usages were widely shared, with cognate plant names from the Seneca country to the Mohawk valley, and presumably Huronia (Fenton 1942a).

Deer, bear, and small mammals abounded in the forests a day's travel from Iroquois settlements until hunted out. Hunting parties ranged south into Pennsylvania, north into the Champlain and Black River valleys,

and into Ontario. The Adirondacks were a Mohawk beaver preserve, but after the mid-seventeenth century, when beaver were largely depleted in Iroquoia, the demands of the trade drove hunters much farther afield.

Although turkeys were rare in Huronia, they were once fairly common in the uplands adjacent to the Mohawk and Hudson valleys and in the Allegheny plateau near the Senecas. The partridge, as now, was cyclical. These same regions witnessed spectacular flights of migratory game birds—both waterfowl and passenger pigeons (*Ectopistes migratorius*)—which summoned the Iroquois to their roostings and nestings with bow, spear, net, and snare (Fenton and Deardorff 1943).

The availability of and ready access to an enormous variety of freshwater fishes in the lakes and streams of both regions constituted a resource in the Iroquoian subsistence pattern that is difficult to comprehend. Tackle and tactics covered the range of hook, line, nets, traps, drags, and spearing techniques. Family groups repaired to fishing stations during the spring runs, and the catches, fresh or dried, were packed back to the villages (Heidenreich 1971:208 ff.; Trigger 1969:30; Fenton 1942).

Although the Iroquois dislike snakes (especially the rattlesnake), people their mythology with horned and feathered serpents, and associate newts and salamanders with witchcraft, they venerate the snapping turtle, accord him a role in the cosmology as "Father Turtle," and use his carapace for rattles.

The spectacular raids of Iroquois war parties, which during the seventeenth and eighteenth centuries reached from Tadoussac to Michilimackinac and from James Bay to the cane brakes of Georgia, have misled historical writers to overlook the fact that their effective occupancy was confined to their principal towns and surrounding forests and streams within the range of their subsistence activities. Territories were defined by heights of land and water courses. That of the League of the Iroquois, which comprised its confederated village bands, greeted the sunrise on the Schoharie and saw the sunset west of the Genesee River; the Adirondacks and Lake Ontario were its northern flank, the headwaters of the Delaware, Susquehanna, and Allegheny invited expansion to the south (Fenton 1940). By contrast, Huronia, north of Lake Ontario, was a compacting entity, which concentrated some 22,000 people near Georgian Bay (Heidenreich 1971:map 19).

Subsistence

Of the eastern woodland Indians the Iroquois are best known as horticulturists, for the slash and burn agriculture that was practiced by the women near the villages. The men, in season, cleared the forest, hunted deer, bear, and small mammals, and at other seasons carried on extensive fisheries. Meanwhile, women collected roots, berries, greens, nuts, and other edibles. The balance among these activities is difficult to judge from the sources: the only full account of hunting practices is of eighteenth-century Mohawks in Ohio (James Smith in Drake 1851). Traditional patterns of Iroquois food habits persisted among the conservative reservation folk to the twentieth century (Parker 1910; Waugh 1916) even after new species were introduced and the culture was radically transformed.

While Heidenreich (1971:158) demonstrates that the growing of corn and catching of fish predominated in Huron subsistence activities, hunting was more important to the Iroquois. A recurring theme in Iroquois folklore is: "They went to the woods to hunt for meat." After the harvest, hunting parties of men and a few women abandoned the villages, leaving the old people, some pregnant women, and children, and walked several days into the forest where they set up camp to hunt deer and bear, dry the meat, and pack it home at midwinter. Next to warfare and attending council, hunting enjoyed great prestige. Going into the forest meant risking one's life and perhaps having a supernatural encounter (Fenton 1941a:419). Snares were important early, but the essential gear for hunting comprised bow and arrow (soon replaced by the gun), knife of stone (or Sheffield steel), ax (later a tomahawk), and the pack frame and tumpline. The few statistics on the annual deer harvest by village bands are unreliable and widely separated in time so as to be useless in estimating the amount of meat in the Iroquois diet, but close to 2,000 deer for each tribe in a season is not an exaggeration. Both the Mohawks and the Cayugas are reported to have been great hunters. The previous figure would mean that each of the 2,200 Iroquois warriors (an average figure, Snyderman 1948) took five deer, or 11,000 total. Their hunters brought in 100 deer in a day after the first snow while attending the Canandaigua treaty of November, 1794 (Fenton 1965:317). These figures seem small when compared with the annual deer harvest in New York State in the 1970s, about 80,000 deer.

The Iroquois knew two types of traps—deadfalls for small and large mammals, and the twitch-up snare (Cooper 1938). The latter in its early history was used for deer, later for partridge and turkey.

The Iroquois diet included all parts of nearly everything that walked, crawled, swam, or flew. Food taboos are conspicuously absent, even in the eponymous clan animals and birds, such as the snapping turtle (fig. 1, top left), so prominent in the creation myths. Some minor taboos may be later refinements: woodchucks because they dig in cemeteries, bats and porcupines for having special powers, moles for causing nosebleed, and turtles for prolonging death (Waugh 1916:131–132; Fenton 1933–1934). Snakes would probably fall into this category.

At the height of the fur trade there was a surfeit of beaver meat in the Iroquois diet, and during the spring nestings of the passenger pigeons there was a glut of squab and oil. Although such hunts are best documented from the Seneca in the nineteenth century, there are also records for the Mohawk and Oneida (Fenton and Deardorff 1943).

While in theory the Iroquois were conservationists, showing respect for the animals they hunted by not throwing their bones to the dogs (JR 44:301, 303), by placing skinned carcasses in the crotch of a tree rather than throwing them to the ground (Waugh 1916:131), and by sacrificing the first deer to birds of prey (Fenton 1953:92), in practice they often contributed to the decline of species. This was true of the beaver and to an extent the deer toward the end of the eighteenth century.

Although fishery resources, tackle, and tactics were important, little is known of the extent of the catch except for that of the Hurons, which is amply documented (Heidenreich 1971:208). Fish drives among the Seneca cannot be projected back beyond the eighteenth century (Fenton 1942).

Judging by later activity the contribution to the Iroquois diet of women's collecting activities was substantial. The maple sap harvest dates at least from the eighteenth century and may well be older. The sap, which was collected, boiled, and evaporated, was used for sweetening mush, for flavoring the staple corn meal that hunters and warriors carried, and for a variety of other purposes. The maple industry was taken over, like maize culture, by the colonists of New York and New France, who enhanced it by improved utensils and techniques. New York and Ontario farmers used many of the same implements and utensils that are featured by Parker (1910:103) and Waugh (1916:140–143, pls. 10, 24–25).

The question whether the Indians or the Whites first discovered how to reduce maple sap to sugar is an old controversy. Henshaw (1890) and Chamberlain (1891a) supported aboriginality, but Flannery's (1939:22) exhaustive search of the sources yielded "not one of the very early observers in any section [noting] that the Indians made maple sugar." In 1973 J.F. Pendergast uncovered an article in the London *Philosophical Magazine* quoting a letter of 1684 from Canada that "the Indians have practised it time out of mind" (Thornton 1798:322).

Although there are rich Silurian deposits of natural salt in central New York the Iroquois seem not to have made much use of salt before Europeans began to exploit this natural resource. After being introduced to it, the Onondagas demanded salt annuities in one of their treaties and the Senecas became heavy users. The Caughnawaga Mohawks are reported not to be (Gunther Michelson, personal communication 1974).

Berry picking—of strawberries (the first fruit to ripen), huckleberries, blackberries, and raspberries—which was

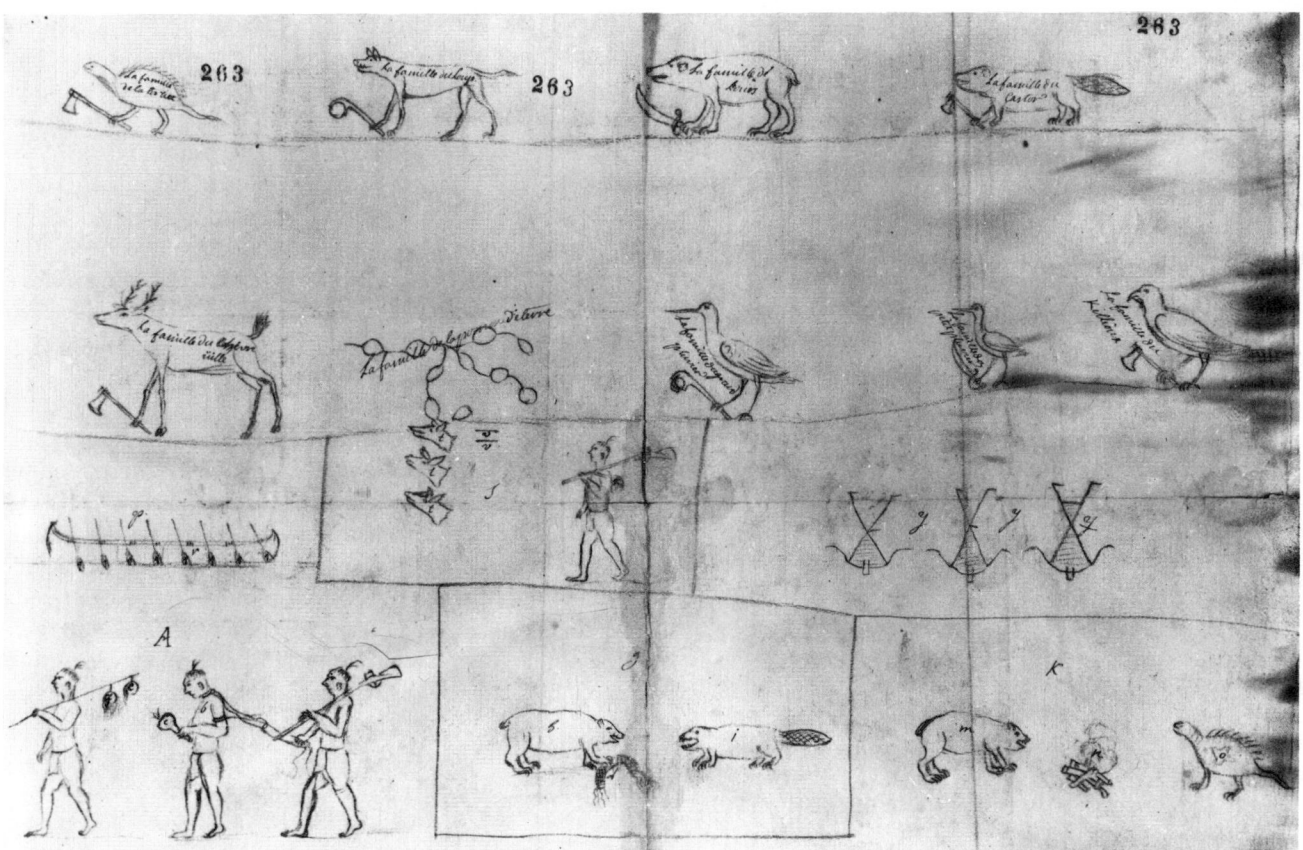

Archives Nationales, Paris: Colonies C11A^2 f. 263 = Musée de l'Histoire de France AE II No. 1745 (Giraudon photo).

Fig. 1. French copies of Iroquois (probably Seneca) pictographs, in a document assigned to 1666. A composite to show the type of drawings made on a tree by a passing war party. Each member of the party drew the totem animal of his clan holding a weapon (ball-headed club, tomahawk, sword); here are shown 9, arranged according to the 2 moieties. top row, left to right, Turtle, Wolf, Bear, Beaver; second row, Deer, Wild Potato *(Apios americana)*, Large Snipe, Small Snipe, Hawk; third row, left, canoe, with the number of paddles indicating the size of the party (the clan animal of each would be shown above); right (marked y) is the manner of indicating enemies killed (a woman with a skirt, 2 men without). In the bottom row, center, is represented a war council between the Bear and Beaver clans, the Bear holding a wampum belt representing vengeance; at right is a council, with council fire, between Bear and Turtle clan spokesmen; bottom row, left, marked A, is a nonpictographic French depiction of returning warriors (the Iroquois form substituted clan animals for human figures); the leading figure carries a male scalp (indicated by its scalplock) and a female scalp below; the prisoner holds a gourd rattle and is described as tied at his neck, belt, and arms. The area labeled S represents a returning hunter with backpack, with pictographs indicating his absence for 2 days (bars marked v) having killed 3 does (heads marked t, bucks were shown with antlers). See NYCD 9:47–50.

still a part of reservation life in the 1930s, is reported back to the earliest times. Berries were spread in bark trays, dried in the sun, and sacked for winter storage, to be later baked into bread. After the harvest, women and children gathered a variety of nuts of the hickory, walnut, beech, and chestnut families (Waugh 1916:123), as well as acorns and others for food and for oil.

"Indian tobacco" *(Nicotiana rustica)* was grown to some extent by all the northern Iroquoian peoples for ceremonial and social smoking, and still is. The Petun have their name from the French word for tobacco, and prodigious quantities of tobacco were still raised in the 1970s in the former Neutral country of southwestern Ontario. It seems to have received little care, but the leaves were plucked and strung to dry.

The twentieth-century Senecas celebrate "wild onion week" in honor of spring leeks at Allegany. A host of other succulents—skunk cabbage, poke, milkweed— were picked and eaten within the day as greens by other Iroquois (Waugh 1916:117–118). Another important survival food, often mentioned in the captivity literature, was groundnut or wild potato *(Apios americana)*.

The triad of maize, beans, and squash, the "three sisters" of Iroquois ceremonial, was cultivated by all northern Iroquoians up to the territorial margins of 120 frost-free days. These crops provided the foundation of subsistence and afforded the leisure to develop institutions of sedentary life. They yielded a surplus in good years and could be dried and stored for winter use, even held over into lean years. Settlements of up to 1,500 persons were possible. Growing crops was the principal occupation of women in the village (Lafitau 1724, 2:70 ff.); the village and its surrounding fields comprised their domain (figs. 2–3). Since they planted, cultivated, and

299

Fig. 2. Julia Scrogg using typical Iroquois dumbbell-shaped pestle and vertical log mortar to pound corn. Photographed in 1910 on the Tonawanda Seneca Reservation, probably by Arthur C. Parker.

harvested in work parties that, directed by a senior matron, operated on the principle of mutual aid, it was natural that women's activities became ritualized and celebrated in song and drama at the Green Corn and Harvest festivals (Fenton 1936, 1941a, 1942b, 1963; Parker 1910; Tooker 1970a). Sibling terms were extended from the women to the crops they cultivated. "The women and the life sustainers are as sisters" is the recurrent theme. The same organization of women gathered and packed in the firewood that stoked the long-

Fig. 3. Josephine Snow leaching hominy corn. Photograph by William N. Fenton, July 30, 1933, on Allegany Seneca Reservation.

house fires. At home they prepared the meals, largely corn soup flavored with meat brought in by the menfolk, and they retrieved and apportioned the shares to their household. Their economic importance contributed to their position in the society. Not for nothing were "the three sisters," and the women, household, lineage, and continuity of society deemed one and the same.

The details of Iroquois subsistence have been presented (Parker 1910; Waugh 1916), and the importance of maize in the subsistence economy of Huronia has been thoroughly treated (Heidenreich 1971).

Ecological Time

Iroquois life was marked by a diurnal round, a yearly round, a duodecennial village movement, and a lifetime of activity. Their sense of time, geared to these cycles, was essentially ecological. The day varied with the season, but in general people retired early. They put a block of wood, a stone, or a bundle of precious objects under their heads and slept on mats, on raised platforms at home, with their feet to the fire. Coverings were of pelts. They were up to greet the dawn with thanks that they were alive before going about their activities. Meals were when one was hungry, when a traveler arrived at the lodge, or when a hunter returned. They shared whatever there was and no one went hungry, or all did. In the 1970s food is still apportioned at ceremonies by the "appointed ones" equally to all, ladle by ladle in everyone's dish. "Come now, set down your kettles," still is heard at longhouse feasts, followed by "so now, pick them up," whereupon people gather their pails and carry them home, "scattering like birds after a feast," while "the steam of the cooking settles down." These are old themes in the culture. The tendency to "eat all," be it feast or famine, while it may have originated when food could not be preserved, has its modern counterpart in the rule that everything must be distributed.

Ecological time is most apparent in the yearly round of activities that synchronized a hunting and gathering cycle with a maize cycle. "These activities were keyed to a lunar calendar divided into four seasons and marked by a calendric cycle of ceremonies, with the great ceremonial mark at midwinter and a lesser climax at late summer for the ingathering of crops" (Fenton 1971:135). It would seem that the Iroquoians were once primarily hunters and gatherers, but from protohistoric times forward they were more or less freed of dependency on meat (indeed the Hurons had little of it), greens, berries, roots, and nuts by the surplus of maize, beans, and squash grown by the women with increasing productivity into the historic period. Having taken to the woods to hunt for meat after the ingathering of the crops, hunters remained in camp until the Pleiades were observed to have reached the zenith at dusk, at the winter solstice, when they commenced the return home to their villages, packing the meat that had been smoked and dried. On the fifth night of the next new moon occurred the great midwinter festival held to reveal new dreams and to renew old dreams and fulfill ceremonial obligations so revealed. From this time on they subsisted on stored maize and vegetables, supplemented with nuts, fish, and the odd mammal. Toward spring, as the days grew longer, they were apt to be hungry, sometimes driven to borrow grain from other villages. Two moons from the moon of midwinter, they repaired to the maple groves to tap trees, to gather sap, and to boil it down to syrup and sugar. Back at the village they returned thanks to the forest, especially to the maple. Next came the spring flights of millions of passenger pigeons to roost in the beechwoods, where they were netted on the hillsides, and the squabs were poked out of the nests with long poles, to be tried into oil and the meat packed in bark tuns. These forays were interspersed with removals to fishing stations, where weirs of converging stones directed the fish under the spears of waiting men or into basket traps. Prodigious runs of fish ascended the Mohawk from the Hudson, the outlets of Oneida Lake from Lake Ontario, the Oswego River, and the outlets of the Finger Lakes. The quantity of bone harpoon and spear points found on sites there attests to the importance of fisheries to the subsistence economy. Early travelers confirmed this. Meanwhile, women were busy gathering spring greens (Waugh 1916:117–118).

When the white oak leaves are the size of a red squirrel's foot, the old people said, it is time to plant, and they blessed the seed of the "three sisters," having soaked the seed for several days in medicine to ward off crows, and returned them to the earth. Men assisted in the heavy work of clearing fields, but the stirring of the corn hills with wooden spades and the planting was done by a work party of women.

The Berry Moon (June) is still remembered fondly for the strawberry, and in the 1970s the strawberry festival in the Seneca longhouses calls for the preaching of Handsome Lake's message in commemoration of his vision. The Little Water Medicine Society still meets on the fifth night of the new moon to sing over the bundles that the holders bring to the meeting and to renew the strength of the "great good medicine." This is also the season when bark peels readily and men working in gangs were formerly busy building houses, repairing stockades, and working elm bark into bark utensils (fig. 4) and canoes. It is the season of the long days.

The Thunder rite addresses the most important hazard of the growing season. The invocation asks the sun, the elder brother and patron of war, not to scorch the earth. Men dance the war dance in his honor and play the hoop and pole game—the rolling sun being snared by the spear. The prayer pleads for the thunders, "our grandfathers of the rumbling voices who come from toward the sunset," to water the "three sisters." A second and third

Dept. of Anthr., Smithsonian: 18839.
Fig. 4. Bucket of elm bark, St. Regis Mohawk. Height 26 cm, collected in 1875 or earlier.

hoeing of the corn again was carried out by a work party of primarily women and a few old men.

When the corn is adjudged ready, even in the 1970s the officials gather the community to celebrate the ingathering of the crops in honor of the "three sisters" coming to maturity. At the next moon they dance in honor of the bread, returning thanks that the cycle is complete and that they have lived to see it, that the maize is husked, strung, shelled, and put away in the barns. On that day the women's song says, "The 'three sisters' are happy because they are home again from their summer in the fields." Formerly husking bees were the main autumn activity (Fenton 1963).

The leaves then turn red and fall, marking the season when, as the old saying runs, the hunter with his dogs (Ursa Minor) rounds Polaris, overtakes the bear (Ursa Major), and slays him. It is then that families separated from the communal longhouses and went hunting in the deep woods for venison. Deer was thus the paramount item of subsistence then and also the symbol of men's labor and the emblem of the chiefs. Hard cold is followed by the short days. Men were still hunting and dressing meat in shanty camps, jerking it over the fire, to be packed home, when the deer yarded up and hunting became difficult in deep snow, save on snowshoes. So the cycle ends.

Autumn was the great season for councils. It was also a time when men were free to go on the warpath.

Of the preceding reconstructed annual cycle, only the agricultural festivals were observed in the 1970s, even though the Iroquois have largely abandoned farming their reservation lands. And these festivals owe their perpetuation, together with the supporting music and dance, to the Handsome Lake religion. That this cycle is not atypical of the pattern prevailing for centuries among the northern Iroquoians may be seen by comparing it with Heidenreich's (1971:216-218) reconstruction of the Huron seasonal cycle. It is both a spatial and a sequential pattern. The primary ecological difference is the greater dependence of the Hurons on fish, of the Iroquois on game, and of the symbiotic relationship of the Huron to the neighboring Algonquians who wintered near them.

In the process of raising on the order of 189,000 bushels of corn per year, the 21,000 Hurons had cleared and cultivated close to 7,000 acres of land (Trigger 1969:28; Heidenreich 1971:193-197). The Iroquois who were half as numerous (at least after 1650) moved rather easily in their environment and did little to alter it. They too cleared, burned, and planted crops between stumps; but Iroquoia was a much larger area than Huronia, and with the population less dense, the apparent effect on the landscape was minimal (Ritchie 1955-1956). By the late seventeenth century Seneca fields were extensive, and high maize yields were reported by the expedition of Jacques René de Brisay, marquis de Denonville. The large plantations reported destroyed by John Sullivan's army in 1779 near the Cayuga and Seneca towns included orchards of introduced peach, pear, and apple trees. Admittedly, the British at Fort Niagara stimulated this horticultural activity to make the Iroquois self-sufficient during the American Revolution.

In general, when the soil was exhausted and firewood became scarce, about twice in a generation, the town was moved. Removal was a gradual process, one town going up while the other was decaying, as commemorated in the place-name theme: "New Town" and "Old Town." The final removal was marked by the Feast of the Dead (Fenton and Kurath 1951), which among the Hurons meant committing the collected bones in an ossuary. In the 1970s, in the Iroquois ritual of condolence the eulogy to the founders recalls "the places where they stopped to smoke [hold council] were soon overgrown with brush" and how indeed "abandoned fields overlie the places where your bones rest!" (Fenton 1950:50). These village removals, recurring approximately every 12 years, constituted a cycle in the lives of the Huron-Iroquois into which each person's life was segmented.

Material Culture

Technology

Iroquois technology, although its mastery does not lead to great art, demonstrated great facility in utilizing whatever comes to hand. It neither attains the refinement of the birchbark industry of the northeastern Algonquians nor approaches the woodworking of the Northwest Coast. The grotesque wooden masks worn by the members of the Society of Faces, known commonly as false faces (Fenton 1941a, 1972b), which are displayed in the major ethnographical museums of the world and are prominently featured in contemporary shows of American Indian art (fig. 5), represent a living tradition of wood carving that has evolved considerably since the introduction of steel tools (fig. 6). As art objects they include several local styles, and they related to a whole genre of carving in the round and supporting techniques of woodworking.

The practitioners of these arts understand the properties of woods and fibers, and individuals may know upward of 200 medicinal plants (Fenton 1942a). Such knowledge survived into the twentieth century, although recently aptitudes have been transferred to other skills and media.

In early summer the men stripped the inner bast of hickory, basswood, and slippery elm for binding and rope making. The women leached the fibers of nettle, milkweed, and Indian hemp; spun the fibers between palm and thigh; and braided cord into burden straps, prisoner ties (fig. 7), and rope. Many items from the nineteenth century seen in museum collections are embroidered with dyed moose hair or deer hair and porcupine quill. The Iroquois knew how to bend and shape wood when green or after steaming—for house frames, pack frames (fig. 8), snowshoes, toboggans, basket rims and handles (fig. 9), and lacrosse sticks (fig. 10). They recognized the principle of the spring in the bow and twitch-up snare, the principle of gravity in the deadfall and corn pounder (fig. 2), centrifugal force in the war club (fig. 11) and pump drill, and the lever in moving and erecting timbers. Old motor habits persist. Javelin, fish spear, and snowsnake are alike propelled with the right index finger from the proximal end (fig. 12), which has been the motive principle of the spear thrower since paleolithic times. Finally, the blow gun and dart for small game and birds (a device that they undoubtedly acquired from the Southeast in historic times) utilizes the principle of the piston (Morgan 1851; Fenton 1971:137).

The wide variety of splint baskets that Iroquois women wove from ash and maple splints (fig. 9) are thought to be of European derivation (Brasser 1975:87). Formerly they did finer weaving of bags, belts, garters, and sashes in several media (figs. 7, 13). Impressive is the list of utensils made and used for food preparation—kettle, washing baskets, sieves, bread bowls, nested bark eating dishes, spoons decorated with clan crests, and stirring paddles. These items are seldom present in Iroquois homes in the 1970s but may be seen in museum collections (for example, Rochester Museum and Science Center, New York; New York State Museum, Albany; National Museum of Man, Ottawa) and are illustrated in publications (Beauchamp 1905a; Parker 1910; Waugh 1916; Speck 1945a).

Iroquois food habits, nevertheless, persist in new forms. Iroquois women still make hulled corn soup, corn bread, and other traditional food recipes under the most modern conditions. The kettle, be it aluminum, is still a symbol of hospitality, and to have a kettle set down for one is the ultimate gesture. The traditional feast foods are still prepared for the medicine societies, for example, mush for the False Faces and hulled corn soup for Eagle and Little Water Societies. Occasionally ceremonies are "passed" at Six Nations "bare pole," that is, without putting up a feast or hanging a kettle (Shimony 1961).

Another area in which technology has survived is games. The making of lacrosse sticks (fig. 10) has developed into a cottage industry in Canada, with its own tools that have evolved with the product. Snowsnakes are still made only for local use, for as yet this characteristic Iroquois winter sport has attracted fewer adherents among Whites (fig. 12).

Structures

No sketch of Iroquois material culture would be complete without mention of the longhouse (fig. 14). Typically, it had from three to five fires, each of which was shared by two nuclear families of five or six persons. Houses were on the average 25 feet wide; the length depended on the number of families to be sheltered. Houses of 200 feet were not uncommon on Mohawk sites, although 80 feet is a better average (Ritchie and Funk 1973:299, 318–319). Each fire added a two-apartment module of about 25 feet to the length of the longhouse. Each of these apartments consisted of a low, wide platform, walled by a section of outer house wall and a partition at either end, and was open toward the central aisle, where there was a fire shared with the apartment opposite. The platforms, built about a foot off the ground to avoid the damp and fleas, were covered with reed mats or pelts and served as seats by day and as beds by night. Above was a long shelf or rack where gear and food were stored. Between apartments were large bark storage bins for corn and dried food, and firewood was stacked in the vestibules near the end doors (Lafitau 1724, 2:5–16; Bartram 1751; Morgan 1851). The longhouse was the most conspicuous feature of Iroquois settlements. It was synonymous with a residential unit, the household or maternal lineage; it was their own symbol of identity, and, together, the Iroquois were "The People of the Longhouse," as they called their confederacy.

For Huronia, the longhouse was described by Sagard-Théodat (1939:93–95), Champlain (1922–1936, 3: 122–123) and the Jesuits (JR 8:105–109, 17:203–205); longhouses in Ontario have been excavated, measured, and described by archeologists (Wright 1974). Summaries are found in Heidenreich (1971) and Trigger (1969). Because of differences in the resources of the two environments, cedar-bark sheathing was favored in Huronia and elm bark in Iroquoia. Roofs were vaulted at first; pitched roof, eaves, and straight walls reflect European influence.

Transport

Great travelers, the Iroquois were essentially landsmen, and their messengers and war parties covered remarkable distances over forested trails in fast time. This tradition was carried on by Deerfoot, a Seneca runner, and Tom Longboat of Six Nations at the turn of the century. In contrast, the Hurons were great traders and canoemen. Living within the range of the paper birch, the Hurons probably acquired the birchbark canoe, the knowledge of its manufacture, and the techniques of paddling, running rapids, poling, and portage from Algonquian neighbors who came to them for maize. Mohawk war parties raiding down the Saint Lawrence acquired these same goods and skills. However, the typical Iroquois canoe, which Lafitau (1724, 2:216) mentioned at Caughnawaga in 1712 and Peter Kalm (1966, 1:363) described in the Champlain valley in 1749, was of elm bark, a clumsy craft unsuited to long voyages, dangerous for crossing lakes, and suicide in white water (fig. 17) (Fenton and Dodge 1949). A similar comparison of Iroquois and Huron and Algonquian snowshoes has been made (Davidson 1937). These are matters partly of tradition, partly of geography.

Clothing and Adornment

Important as clothing styles undoubtedly were, the want of museum collections of early Huron and Iroquois costumes makes any meaningful comparison impossible. Both seem to have favored black-dyed buckskin. The Huron and some Mohawks affected the bull-nose moccasin, but the seamless moccasin was the usual Iroquois footwear. The Iroquois are the only northeastern people known to have worn twined corn-husk slippers in summer; the same technique carried over into weaving husk faces, tobacco trays, and salt bottles to the twentieth century. A parallel technique of coiled braided corn-husk masks and door mats persists (fig. 18); and corn-husk dolls are made without faces and dressed in the nineteenth-century costumes of Morgan's (1850, 1851, 1852) plates, now considered traditional.

Iroquois warriors are said by modern informants to have painted three stripes on each cheek, one for each of the Six Nations (which means since the eighteenth century), but only the single red spot on each cheek worn in recent years by the followers of Handsome Lake at longhouse festivals continues the enormous variety of face painting mentioned in the literature. In general, black meant war or mourning. When first encountered, as evidenced in the first known portraits, Northern Iroquoian men, and specifically Mohawks, were walking galleries of the tattooist's art. They sported geometric designs, the double-curve motif, and clan crests, which were pricked with bone awl and rubbed with charcoal on chest, shoulders, and face (Bruyas 1863:82). Witness the John Verelst and John Faber portraits of the Four Indian Kings in London in 1710 (figs. 19–20) (R.P. Bond 1952),

Dept. of Anthr., Smithsonian: 1, 381410; 2, 381416; 9, 381417; 26, 248705; 38, 221152; 41, 248706; Mus. of the Amer. Ind., Heye Foundation, New York: 3, 13/6605; 5, 1/1878A; 7, 6/1104; 8, 22/4283; 10, 8380; 14, 13/6609; 15, 2/6354; 16, 20/3423; 18, 18/6098; 20, 20/7168; 22, 20/6746; 23, 22/4256; 24, 1/1878B; 27, 22/2541; 28, 9150; 30, 20/3424; 31, 16/9214; 32, 2/9605; 34, 20/6763; 35, 6/334; 36, 21/450; 37, 2/9606; U. Mus., U. of Pa., Philadelphia: 4, 38526; 12, 38530; 33, 38527; N.Y. State Mus., Albany: 6, 36909; Nationalmuseet, Copenhagen: 11, Hc369a; 13, Hc369b; Milwaukee Public Mus.: 17, 3241; 29, 24213; 39, 24196; 40, 24216; Rochester Mus. and Science Center, N.Y.: 19, AE 10; 21, AE 578; 25, AE 309.

Fig. 5. Wooden masks, commonly called False Faces in English, are worn and used by the Society of Faces in the prevention and cure of illness; they also appear during the Midwinter ceremony both in curing and worn by small boys who go from house to house begging for tobacco and cookies (see "Iroquois Since 1820," figs. 13-15, this vol.). Most have hair of horsehair, are painted, and have tin eyeplates. Some have small bags of Indian tobacco attached to the top, indicating that they have been compensated for particular cures or periodically appeased by their owners. This series gives an incomplete indication of the range of forms found in different times (the dates are dates of collecting or receipt in museums) and different communities (A: Allegany Seneca; C: Cattaraugus Seneca; GR: Six Nations Reserve; NY: one of the Seneca communities in New York; O: Onondaga, New York; T: Tonawanda Seneca). Length (excluding hair) of 1 about 30 cm, rest same scale. 1, GR 1916, red; 2, GR 1916, black, lips red; 3, A 1925, red; 4, GR 1901, red; 5, GR 1906, black, no eyeplates; 6, GR 1850, collected by L.H. Morgan, dark brown stain, lips and tongue red; 7, GR 1917 (said to have belonged to the Mohawk Joseph Brant before 1800), black; 8, A 1954, purple; 9, GR 1916, black, lower lip dark brown; 10, GR Onondaga 1906 (made about 1870 by John Buck), black, wrinkles red; 11, Seneca, probably NY 1860, red, tin mouthplate, once had hair; 12, GR 1901, black, lips red, paper hair; 13, Seneca, probably NY 1860, black, lips, nostrils, and circles around eyes red, no eyeplates; 14, A 1925 (said to date from before 1825), brown, eyeplates brass; 15, T, 1910, black, mouth red, eyeglasses tin; 16, C 1940, black, with cowhorns and fur (said to represent a buffalo); 17, GR Mohawk 1906, red, eyeplates and teeth brass, movable lower jaw (said to represent a wolf); 18, GR Cayuga 1933, unpainted, nose, eyes, and lips red, eyebrows and outline of nose black, hair white sheep wool (represents a pig); 19, C 1926, brown and yellow, beak interior red, forehead unpainted, eyeplates copper; 20, C 1945, red; 21, NY 1925, black; 22, C 1945, red; 23, T 1954, red; 24, GR 1906, black; 25, C 1925, red, teeth unpainted; 26, C 1908, red, teeth unpainted, hair fur; 27, C 1953, black; 28, GR 1906, black, lips red, teeth white; 29, NY 1918, orange, ears leather (probably represents the Devil); 30, C 1940, red and black (said to represent a White man); 31, Okla. Seneca-Cayuga 1930, red, teeth unpainted; 32, C 1910, brown (with suspended miniature False Face unpainted); 33, GR 1901, red, lips and eyebrows black; 34, O 1945, black, wrinkles red, no eyeplates; 35, C 1917, brown, lips black, tin teeth, with cowhorns and leather cap; 36, GR Cayuga 1947, red and black; 37, GR 1910, red; 38, NY 1903 (said to have belonged to Cornplanter, 1836), red; 39, NY 1918, unpainted, cheeks and nose red, around mouth black; 40, O 1918, orange; 41, O 1908, red, eyebrows black, teeth tin.

NORTHERN IROQUOIAN CULTURE PATTERNS

Fig. 6. In traditional False Face carving it is said that the preliminary carving was done on a living basswood tree, while tobacco was burned to transfer the healing power of the living tree to the mask. This ancient ritual was staged for Arthur C. Parker, who photographed it in June 1909 on the Cattaraugus Seneca Reservation. However, most carvers prefer seasoned wood since a green mask checks.

the John Trumbull portraits at Yale University (fig. 21), the description of the technique by Lafitau (1724, 2:38); see also "The League of the Iroquois: Its History, Politics, and Ritual," figure 7, this volume. These designs recall the boastful cartoons of war parties painted on trees stripped of bark at river crossings (fig. 1).

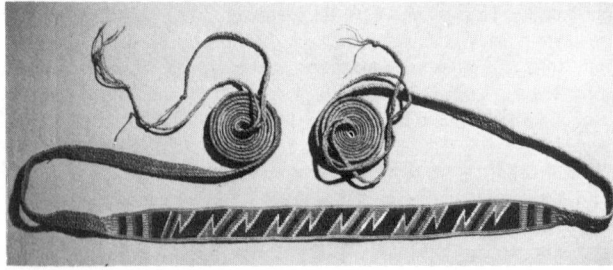

Fig. 7. Cord made of vegetable fiber (perhaps *Apocynum*), the center section twined and the ends braided, decorated with moosehair dyed orange, black, and white in false embroidery. Similar straps were used as tumplines, prisoner ties, and (on the evidence of figs. 19-20) as belts. This one, collected from the Mohawks who visited London in 1710 (see figs. 19-20), was described by Sir Hans Sloane who preserved it as "for tying their prisoners." Overall length 496 cm, decorated center section about 4 by 54 cm.

Fig. 8. Chauncey Johnny John lashing a meat-packing frame with hickory bark. Photograph by William N. Fenton, July-Aug. 1938, at Coldspring, Allegany Seneca Reservation.

Settlements

The typical large northern Iroquoian settlement was a cluster of 30 to 150 longhouses, surrounded by a palisade, and situated on a height of land accessible to drinking water and not too far removed from a navigable waterway ("Onondaga," fig. 2, this vol.). Mohawk towns were rather smaller and Huron towns rather larger, as were the Seneca towns. From a hamlet of 50 people to a large village of 1,000 or more was the range. The longhouse as a residential group of kin and those married-in was a microcosm of the larger community.

The localized character of much of Iroquois culture is as true today of the reservation communities as it was when the League was formed out of autonomous village bands. The lineage is a core of mothers, sisters, and daughters who in native theory are a longhouse family, or residential group, together with a fringe of spouses of other lineages. Together they comprise what the Mohawk call the *ohwatsirayé·tǫ'* 'families exist plurally *or* distributively', i.e. the ongoing family. The group identifies with an eponymous animal—bird, mammal, or reptile—that becomes its crest, was anciently displayed on the gable ends of lodges, and might become the name of the community. It was in this sense that the Mohawks had three clan towns. With the passage of generations, persons whose families identified with the same crest became fictive siblings, were welcomed at clan lodges,

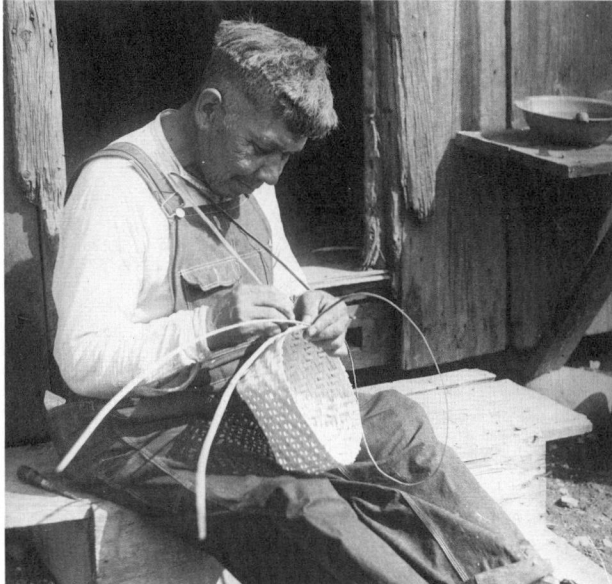

Fig. 9. Making splint baskets. top, Dan Denny preparing rims with draw knife on shaving horse; his wife with partly completed basket; photograph by Huron H. Smith Oct. 18, 1929, at Oneida, Wis. bottom, Chauncey Johnny John attaching rim to basket; photograph by William N. Fenton, 1938, at Coldspring, Allegany Seneca Reservation, N.Y.

granted hospitality, and accepted as if they were members of the same blood line. Even today in traveling to other reserves to attend Handsome Lake conventions, one is asked: "What is your clan?" and one is assigned to an appropriate household. Moreover, each community has its local ways that are zealously maintained and defended. In the 1970s this has mainly to do with the way traditional ceremonies are conducted. The relevance of this contemporary diversity for history is that something of the same character obtained between settlements or village bands and between nations composed of several such settlements or village bands; these differences had to be composed and unified in the formation of the League.

Fig. 10. The Caughnawaga Indian Lacrosse Club in 1867, the year in which they played against the Montreal Lacrosse Club on the first Dominion Day, celebrating the adoption of lacrosse as Canada's national game. The lacrosse sticks are of the old type without guard strings (see Eyman 1964). Photograph probably by William Notman.

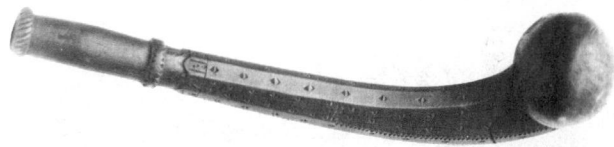

Fig. 11. Seneca ball-headed war club, collected at Allegany Reservation, said to have been used in the War of 1812 and to have belonged to Red Jacket. Maple wood, decorated with chip carving, once rubbed with red ocher, length about 47 cm. See Skinner 1926.

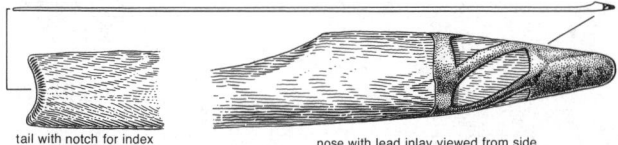

tail with notch for index finger, viewed from top   nose with lead inlay viewed from side

Fig. 12. Snowsnake game. top, 2 men at the left applying wax, while another man launches the wooden snowsnake into the end of a trough in the snow. The game is a contest for distance. Drawn by the Cattaraugus Seneca artist Jesse J. Cornplanter in 1905. bottom, Snowsnake, with typical lead inlay in nose; length 230.5 cm, collected in 1903, Tuscarora, N.Y.

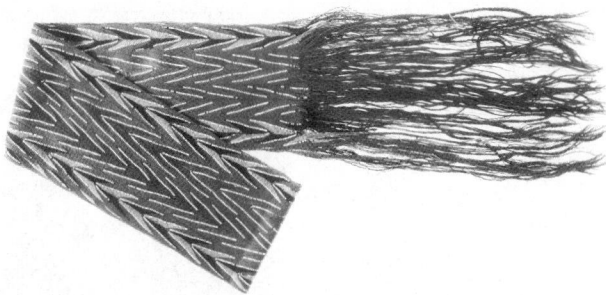

Dept. of Anthr., Smithsonian: 72703.

Fig. 13. Mohawk finger-woven belt *(ceinture aux flèches)* from Caughnawaga. Wool, red ground, center arrows khaki, outer arrows gray and dark blue, outlined with white seed beads. Width about 19 cm, collected in 1837.

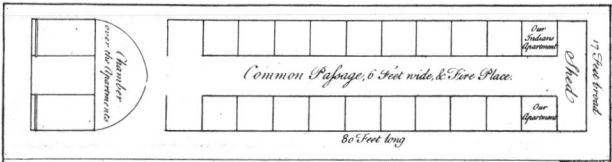

Lib. of Congress: Bartram 1751: frontispiece (detail).

Fig. 14. Plan and cross-section of the bark-covered council house of the main Onondaga town, as drawn by John Bartram in July 1743.

Southwest Mus., Los Angeles.

Fig. 15. Caroline G. Parker, sister of Ely S. Parker, wearing then-traditional Seneca clothing made by herself, decorated with beadwork and with silver brooches around the collar and down the front of the overdress. Photograph copy of a lost hand-tinted daguerreotype, probably with the image laterally reversed, taken slightly before 1850.

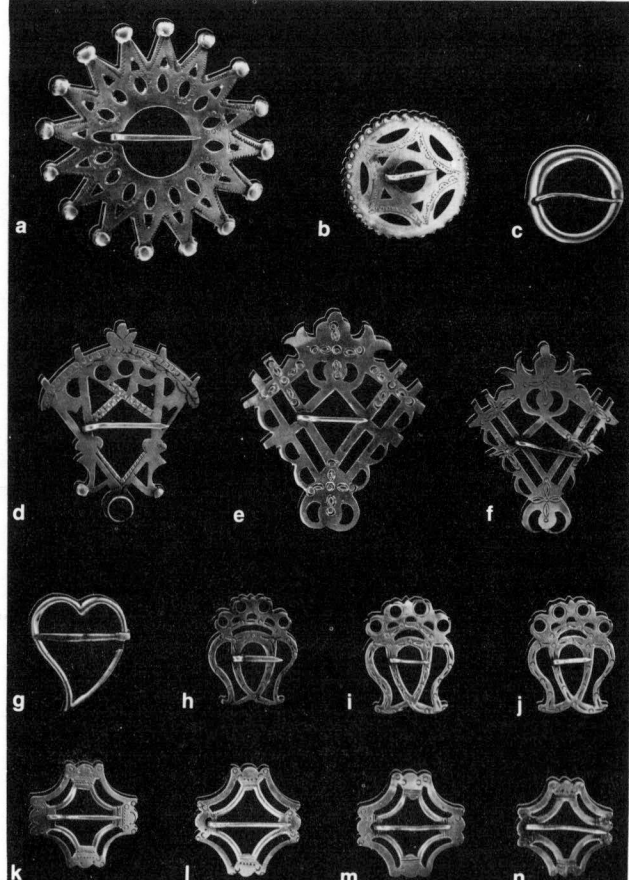

Dept. of Anthr., Smithsonian: a, 361992, b, 248728, c, 248729, d-e, 361992, f, 248727, g, 248732, h, 387068, i, 248730, j, 387068, k, 248731, l-n, 387068.

Fig. 16. Iroquois silver brooches in typical patterns, reinterpretations of European (especially Scottish) models. a-b, sometimes called 'sunshine'; c, sometimes 'eye'; d-f, derived from Masonic emblem and inverted, 'council fire' or 'crucifix'; g, 'heart'; h-j, 'owl' or 'two jaws interlocked', formerly worn as a sort of Iroquois national badge; k-n, 'council square' or 'two parallel lines'. a, d-e, Iroquois before 1931; b-c, g, i, k, Cattaraugus Seneca before 1908; f, Cattaraugus Seneca before 1904; h, j, l-n, Six Nations Reserve, about 1880–1890. Diameter of a 5.6 cm, rest same scale.

The settlement and its chief, who took his name from the place or gave his name to the settlement, is a recurrent theme in Iroquois political literature from the Degana-wida epic to the present. The fact that the Five Nations were comprised of a disparate number of such settle-ments accounts in part for the unequal distribution of federal chiefs among them. On arriving in a foreign town the ambassador sought the lodge of the chief who then assembled the community to hear the message. His lodge was built in proportion to accommodate such gatherings, it had extra apartments for guests, and it became in fact the council house. In the 1970s the council house or longhouse was no longer a residential building.

Equally important, and proof that chiefs were chosen from smaller residential segments, even a single house-hold, is the fact that multiple chiefships are associated

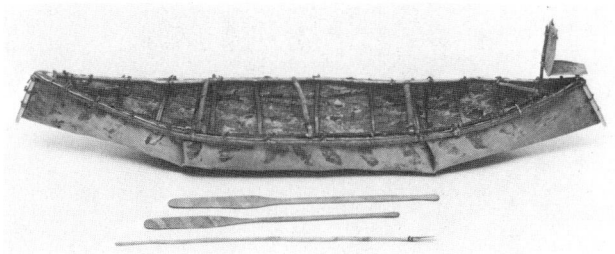

Fig. 17. Model of an Iroquois elm-bark canoe, made of a single piece of bark, the outer surface of the bark on the inside of the canoe. Decorated with diagonal stripes of red paint, with a torch and reflector for night fish spearing mounted on the bow. The accompanying paddles and fish spear, also with red stripes, are out of scale (full size bow paddles were about 5 feet long, stern paddles 6 feet, fish spears 10-12 feet, while a full-size canoe of this sort may have been some 25 feet long). Model about 122 cm long, collected 1823-1825, probably from the Iroquois in Ohio or perhaps at Buffalo Creek.

with a single town. The Mohawks had three towns, each identified with a clan, but each of these clans had three chiefships, each belonging to a segment, lineage, or household. Moreover, with but a single town, Oneida had precisely the same distribution of chiefships among the same three clans resident within the same palisade. Onondaga, one main town and one satellite, had 14 chiefships. The 10 Cayuga chiefs were distributed among three villages, the eight Seneca chiefs in two great towns and two small ones. Factors other than locality were obviously at work.

Fig. 18. Cornhusk masks, called Husk Faces or sometimes Bushy Heads, appear prominently at the Midwinter ceremony. Although they frequently also appear as messengers for the False Faces, they form a separate society, appear alone, and perform cures on their own in response to dreams or as prescribed by a clairvoyant. right, Twined, from Allegany Seneca Reservation, about 20 cm long excluding fringes, collected about 1924; left, coiled braids (the more common technique), same scale, collected from Isaac Roundsky, Six Nations Reserve, before 1910.

Social Organization

The basic patterns of Iroquois social structure have been known for more than a century. There is first the division of labor between the sexes, which has both a functional and spatial aspect. Although Iroquois towns were built and governed by men, and to all appearances the women were drudges, men owed their offices to female succession, and the village and its environs of cleared fields up to the wood's edge were the domain of women. Save the council, men's roles were carried out in the forest—hunting, the war path, and embassies of peace and trade.

As Goldenweiser (1914:473) noted, each tribe as well as being divided into villages and longhouse families was divided into two moieties. Each moiety comprised two or more clans, and the clans were again segmented into one or more maternal families or lineages. Every maternal family traced its home to some longhouse of which it once formed the household, and so the terms for the two are synonymous. These lineages, which later formed the segments of clans and with which they share their functions, are the building blocks of the social system.

Viewed from within, as Hewitt (Hewitt and Fenton 1944:82) thought, tribal society rested on certain fundamental organic analogies, most important of which was a fundamental dualism that consisted in the symbolic recognition of the sexes. This started with the fireside family of husband and wife; it extended to the clans, to the moieties, to the nation, and to the confederacy. In operation it was the principle of reciprocity, which still governs the function of the moieties, both tribal and confederate. Hewitt attributed this to the extension of the rules of incest, through the classificatory system of kinship; but another explanation lies in the historical distribution of these same phenomena among neighboring peoples of the Southeast and the Upper Great Lakes. The simplest unit of Iroquois society, then, is the "fireside," the primary or nuclear family of husband and wife and their children. The Iroquois recognize this family, and it continues to be the residential unit. Stemming from the fireside family, it includes the siblings of the wife's mother, the wife's siblings, the wife's children and her daughter's children, and the descendants of the preceding women in the female line. The senior living woman is the matriarch and presides over the household of fact and legal fiction, *ohwatsirayę́·tǫʔ* (in Mohawk). It is composed of a lineage of persons tracing direct descent from a common mother, and it forms an exogamic incest group. It is what Hewitt and Fenton (1944:82) termed the "uterine family" and Goldenweiser (1914:467) the "maternal" family. It is the primary unit of Iroquois government. In time it might occupy several longhouses in several villages, giving rise to segments of a clan.

An Iroquois clan is composed of two or more maternal families who behave as if the members of each generation are indeed siblings, or as if they constitute a single

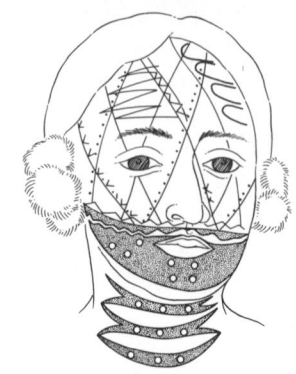

left, Public Arch. of Canada, Ottawa; upper right, Newberry Lib., Chicago: E.E. Ayer Coll.

Fig. 19. Sa Ga Yeath Qua Pieth Tow (Brant, grandfather of Joseph Brant), Mohawk. He wears a scarlet cloak (given him in London), white cloth shirt, belt or burden strap decorated with black, red, and white dyed moosehair or porcupine quills, brown pouch with red double-curve design and red (deer hair?) tassels in (copper?) cones, moccasins decorated with red and tan quills and tied with red ribbons, downy white feathers by each ear and red ribbons hung from his right ear, and a powderhorn on a red cord. Behind him is a bear, representing his clan. His face, chest, and left arm bear complex blue tattoos. Painted from life, in London, by John Verelst in 1710. upper right, Mezzotint by John Faber after a lost portrait by him also done in London in 1710. lower right, Tattoo designs reconstructed from these two independent portraits.

maternal family. Actually the two maternal families or segments may be derived from a single lineage, but long since the links connecting the collateral lines have been forgotten; or there has been a village removal and a separation; or possibly an adoption of a woman and her female descendants. The Iroquois clan, therefore, is as Goldenweiser pointed out a legal fiction, but the maternal family is a physical reality. The Iroquois constantly confuse the two, and so do anthropologists. As time passes family lines are forgotten, but clan identity is remembered so that in a given generation individual behavior is strongly colored by membership in a clan (table 1).

One or more clans constituted a moiety and acted together as if their memberships were indeed siblings. In an Iroquoian community and tribe there are usually two

such moieties. Their functions are mainly ceremonial, since they act reciprocally to condole and bury each other's dead and to perform games and other ritual acts. If the moieties were ever exogamous, as some informants say and Morgan (1877) thought, they are not now. Frequently, as among the Seneca, there are clans named for birds and the deer grouped on one side, and other mammals and the turtle on the other (fig. 1). The Longhouse Iroquois today refer to them as the "sides." At the level of the League two similar moieties of tribes carry out symbolic functions derived from a lower level of integration. Here the Mohawk, Onondaga, and Seneca tribes comprise the "Three Brothers," or symbolically the Male principle or the Father side; and the second moiety comprised originally of the Oneida and Cayuga (but later including Tuscarora and Delaware and other adopted

310

I.Faber Fecit & Excud.1710.

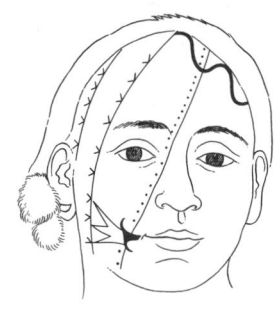

left, Public Arch. of Canada, Ottawa; upper right, Newberry Lib., Chicago: E.E. Ayer Coll.

Fig. 20. Ho Nee Yeath Taw No Row (John of Canajoharie), Mohawk. He wears a scarlet cloak (given him in London), white cloth shirt, belt or burden strap decorated with black, red, and white dyed moosehair or porcupine quills, moccasins decorated with red and tan quills and tied with red ribbons, a downy white feather behind his ear, and red ribbons pendant from each ear. Behind him is a wolf, representing his clan. Painted from life, in London, by John Verelst in 1710. upper right, Mezzotint by John Faber after a lost portrait by him also done in London in 1710. lower right, Facial tattoos reconstructed from these two independent portraits.

entities) and now known as the "Four Brothers" represent the Female principle in nature, or the 'offspring' of the preceding. The two moieties of the League are sometimes referred to as Elder Brothers and Younger Brothers respectively, or 'uncles, sires' (Mohawk *akatǫ·ni*, Seneca *akatǫ·ni·*) and 'nephews' (Seneca *kheyá⁷tawęh*). The two sides condole each other's dead chiefs and install their successors in the Condolence Council (see "The League of the Iroquois: Its History, Politics, and Ritual," this vol.).

Returning to the fireside family for the derivation of these terms and procedures reveals that ramifications of the fireside family were two-fold. As a bilateral kin group united by ties of the classificatory type, the fireside family functioned in marriage by setting the parameters of exogamy; it censured conduct of its members; it afforded two avenues of appeal for the individual in assuming a

second name, in joining a society, anciently in forming a war party, and still in any undertaking. These expectations and obligations between members of the same generation, and between those persons a generation apart, were reciprocal and binding. One owed special obligations to his mother's brother who may be the clan chief. It is here on balance that the *akatǫ·ni·/ kheyá⁷tawęh* principle—'my father's kinsmen–my offspring'—is at work. As Lafitau (1724, 1:552) discovered among the Mohawk, one's father's sister could demand of her brother's son that he organize a war party to return prisoners for adoption or torture, and only she could stop a war party once organized and underway. In the 1970s this bilateral group functions in mutual aid activities such as wood cutting and housebuilding. A joking relationship still obtains between men and women whose fathers are

311

Yale U. Art Gallery, New Haven.

Fig. 21. Good Peter, Oneida, aged 75, showing fine tattooed pattern in gray on neck and chest. His earlobe is pierced and stretched to hold an ornament, and his head is shaved except for a scalplock. Miniature in oils painted by John Trumbull in Philadelphia in 1792.

siblings, real or classificatory, or members of the same clan. Women chose as partners men so related in one social dance, a symbolic reminder that their exogamous relationship is limited.

Of greater significance than the father's line, as Goldenweiser (1914, 1914a) discovered, is the maternal family or lineage, which is comprised primarily of the male and female descendants of one woman and her female descendants through females. This group was once synonymous with a household and was identified with a particular longhouse. It was headed by a matron, the eldest female. As a group it held certain religious, ceremonial, and political prerogatives. It passed on to its members obligations to the medicine societies, which might come secondarily from the father's side. It exercised a moral influence in controlling the appointment and conduct of sachems, succession following the lineage with brothers over first cousins, and first cousins over third (Goldenweiser 1912-1914a). A kind of social status adhered to the lineages that held League chiefships. The word for Confederacy chief, Mohawk *royá·ner* (cf. Lafitau's Roïander Gôa 'great noble'), is the masculine singular form corresponding to gaïander 'nobility; eminent person' and agoïander (collective), applied to the members of the chiefly lineages, the community leaders

312

referred to by the French as nobles, *gens d'affaires,* and *hommes et femmes considérables* (Lafitau 1724, 1: 469-475; Bruyas 1863:58; JR 58:184, 64:80). The maternal family exercised the right to rear the children of its female members, and it extended control over the children of its sons. It was and continues to be the functional unit in adoptions, and it controls a stock of first names for its children, which were originally derived from the first thing seen by the midwife after the birth. Shimony (1961) found that the lineage had merged its functions with the clan, a tendency that Goldenweiser noted, but M.G. Myers (1962) restores its importance as a useful concept.

Descent, inheritance, and succession passed in the female line. Morgan (1851:84) spoke of the perpetual disinheritance of the son. Chiefships are identified with clans, but Goldenweiser's (1912-1914a) genealogies show that actual succession follows the maternal family. And this was the nub of the issue in the famous Tonawanda Gypsum case (Fenton 1951:45). There has been much controversy, both at Tonawanda and at Six Nations Reserve in the twentieth century, as to which clans properly possess certain titles that are associated by ritual with the formation of the League, but these arguments only document the fact that when a lineage runs out of candidates, the title may be loaned to another lineage of the same clan, which afterward claims it, or to another clan of the same moiety. As one compares lists of the 50 federal chiefs and their clan identities, there is a good deal of variation (Beauchamp 1886).

Kinship

The Iroquois relationship system, made famous by Morgan (1877) but first discovered by Lafitau (1724, 1:552), groups blood relatives into five generations, the classificatory principle being evident in each. In one's own generation and the first ascending and first descending generations, parallel relatives (for instance, father's brother and mother's sister) are classed with one's lineal relatives (father and mother, respectively, in this case), cross relatives (such as father's sister and mother's brother) being labeled differently. Cross-uncle and aunt are distinguished and cross-nephew and niece show some further differentiation, but cross-cousins are all called by a single term. Elder and younger siblings (and classificatory siblings) are distinguished, with separate terms for brother and sister. An important effect of the classificatory principle is that the lineal bias of the society is not reflected in the female descendants of the father's sister, as in Crow and certain Southeastern societies. Indeed it is the same system found among the Ojibwa and Dakota where sibs are unimportant. It seems unlikely that the Iroquois system reflects once prevalent cross-cousin marriage as Eggan (1966:104-105) suggests.

It would seem that in the Northeastern woodlands the wide extension of a comprehensive network of kinship

Table 1. Iroquois Names for Clans of the Six Nations

	Mohawk	Oneida	Onondaga	Cayuga	Seneca	Tuscarora
Turtle	*ratinyáhtę* cf. *aʔnó·waraʔ* 'turtle'	*latinyáhtę* cf. *aʔno·wál* 'turtle'	*hatíenyàhtę* cf. *hanyáhtę* 'turtle'	1. *kanyáhtę·ʔ, kʔanó·waʔ* 'mud turtle' 2. *kanyahtęʔkó·waʔ* 'snapping turtle' 3. *kʔanowaká·hea* (?) 'swamp turtle'	*hatinyáhtę·h* cf. *kanyáhtę·h* 'snapping turtle'; *haʔno·wa·h* 'turtle'	1. *raʔkwihs* 'turtle' 2. *kaθriʔkwe·s* 'sandturtle'
Bear	*rotihskeré·wakeʔ* cf. *ohkwá·ri* 'bear'	*lotiskle·wákeʔ* cf. *ohkwálí* 'bear'	*honáhkwà·i* cf. *ohkwá·i* 'bear'	1. *(o)hnyákwai·ʔ* '(baby) bear' 2. *(o)hnyakwaihkó·waʔ* 'big bear' 3. *otáʔthraʔ* 'suckling bear'	*hotitsǫníʔka·ʔ* cf. *nyakwaiʔ* 'bear'	1. *ohtsíhrǫʔ* 'bear' 2. *tihréhtsyaks* 'white bear'
Wolf	*rotikwáho* cf. *okwáho* 'wolf'	*lotikwáhoʔ* cf. *othahyǫ́ní* 'wolf'	*honatháhyò̧·ni* cf. *tháhyò̧·ni* 'wolf'	*(o)thahyǫ́·ni·* 'wolf'	*honǫ́tha·yǫ·nih, thá·yǫ·nih* cf. *(o)thá·yǫ·nih* 'wolf'	1. *θkwari·nǫ* 'wolf' 2. *onǫʔtakǫ̧hwʔa* (other wolf)
Snipe	*(rotinehsí·yo)* (cf. *tawístawis* 'snipe')		*tahwístawis*	1. *towístawi·ʔ* 'snipe, etc.' 2. *hotiʔnEsí·yoʔ* 'small snipe'	*hotíʔnehsi·yoʔ*	*tawístawis* 'snipe'
Beaver	*(tsyaní·to)*		*hatíyę̧taks, na·ká·yàʔki*	*nyaʔkanyáʔkǫh* 'beaver'	*hotíkęʔke·ka·* cf. *nǫkanyáʔkǫh* 'beaver'	*tsyóʔnakę̧·* 'beaver'
Ball	*(ahthę́·no)*		*tewęʔnhé·kaʔ*	*tewęʔnhé·ka·ʔ* 'ball, rock deer, small deer'		
Hawk	*(rotihswaʔkarí·yo)*		*hotishwéʔkàiyǫʔ* (?)	*hotiswęʔkáiyoʔ* 'hawk'	*hotíswęʔkaiyoʔ* cf. *oswęʔæ·taʔké·a·ʔ* 'red-tailed hawk'	
Deer	*(rotihskenǫ́·to;* also *rotinęyothró·nǫ* 'rock people')*		*skęnętǫ́hè·nǫʔ*	*tewáhǫhte·s* 'deer'	1. *hotí·nyǫkawiyoʔ* 'deer' 2. *hotinǫ́ʔteoka·ʔ* (?) 'doe' cf. *neokęʔ* 'deer'	
Eel	*(rotinyáhto)*		*akǫ·te·náʔ nahóʔsè·ʔtę*	*kǫ́·te*		*kę̧·ʔneh*
Heron				*skayaʔtí·kaʔ* (?) 'heron'	*honǫtáęʔǫ·ka·ʔ, hotitáęʔǫ·ka·ʔ* cf. *tsóæshæʔ* 'heron'	

Calumet *(rotihsęnakéhte)*
Pigeon *(rotirî·teʔ)*

Note: Some ordinary names for the clan animals were not available. Parenthesized Mohawk clan names refer to clans that were not originally Mohawk. The plural prefixes appear in the forms *rati-, roti-, lati-, loti-, hati-, hoti-,* and *hon-.*

Sources: Chafe 1963:27, 1967; G. Michelson 1973; Cuoq 1882:154; and personal communications from Marianne Mithun (Mohawk, Cayuga, Tuscarora); Clifford Abbott (Oneida); Floyd G. Lounsbury (Oneida, Onondaga); Hanni J. Woodbury (Onondaga); Michael K. Foster (Cayuga). Reconciliation of conflicting data has been necessary in some places.

terms was not sufficient. Not only was the use of these terms elaborated and projected from the fireside to the League level, but also their symbolic usage was extended to neighboring tribes. The terms Brother, Nephew, Father, and Uncle were used in this way in treaties of the colonial period, where their significance has sometimes been a source of confusion.

The widespread American Indian custom of ceremonial friendships extended throughout Huronia and Iroquoia. It was one of the incentives for the diffusion of the Calumet Dance at the close of the seventeenth century, and it survives in the obligation between "friends" to put up particular rites of the medicine societies (Tooker 1964:89; Fenton 1953; Shimony 1961).

Another sort of lumping that has received little attention in the literature on Iroquois social organization, although it is prominent in the literature on the Plains tribes, is the matter of age-grading. The Iroquois revere the dead and include them as the highest grade; the next grade is the Elders, "the Old Men" and the "Old Ladies"; they next speak of "Young people"; they always include children, "those still on the boards" or "crawling on the ground"; and the Unborn "whose faces are turned this way from beneath the ground" complete the cycle. Indeed, babies are barely separated from the spirit world: the saying runs, "an infant's life is as the thinness of a maple leaf." Parents cut a hole in the moccasins of children on the cradleboard lest they be enticed back to the spirit world by unseen spirits following the mother on the forest path.

Political Organization

Iroquois political structure extends the basic patterns of social structure and local organization to a wider context. As one moves from the lineage to the clan, to the moiety, to the tribe or nation, to the League, the projected use of kinship terms becomes more fictional and the expected behavior more symbolic. Duality or reciprocity is the principle that operates throughout. The League "contained the germ of the state" but it was not a true state based on territorial arrangements (Morgan 1877:119 ff.). The same could be said of the Huron and Neutral confederacies. This organizational pattern is also relevant to understanding the Iroquois of the late twentieth century.

> "Four principles have been at work in the expansion and retention of Iroquois culture. First, the projection of spatial and structural principles from the local to the confederate level has facilitated institution building. Second, the endowment of institutions with symbols derived from a lower level of social integration has enabled the least individual to understand the more complex institution. Third, as the culture has declined in power and effectiveness, new functions have been found for institutions by the transfer of functions from lower to higher levels of social integration, or vice versa. Fourth, the system has continued to function because of the imperative of reciprocity over structure" (Fenton 1965a:258).

The village, its headman, and the council of elders is a theme that recurs throughout Iroquois culture history. The clans had their separate councils; but an ad hoc village council of ranking clan chiefs, elders, and wise men made local policy. In a sense, the same thing happened at the national and League levels. Clan chiefs had their offices and titles ascribed in specific maternal families or households, which were segments of clans, and the ranking matrons of that lineage presided over the caucuses that nominated, censured, or recalled them. The holders of these titles were tribal chiefs and they represented their village and nation in the General Council of the League. They enjoyed great prestige but had little power. In the village the operating counterpart of the council was the mutual aid party, which involved relatives bilaterally, but its service functions were apolitical.

The best statement of political procedures comes from Asher Wright, who spent a lifetime among the Senecas (Wright in Fenton 1957a). Officers were known by the name of the office, and each clan had its own names and titles that descended matrilineally. These offices were graded. A vacancy, whether created by death, resignation, or deposition "was filled by raising all below a degree higher . . . ." The process of review was hierarchical and clear. "Hence, at every occasion of filling vacancies, the character and merits of all the officers in the series and of all candidates, were liable to be passed upon first, in the discussion of the families interested; secondly, in the convocation of the clans to which they belong; thirdly, in the meeting of the four clans, which occupied respectively the two ends of the council house; fourthly, by the assembled council of the particular nation; and fifthly [by the] council at the Longhouse of the Six Nations" (Fenton 1957a:310).

Similarly, there was a regular way to communicate concerns from the least fire to the great council fire, and for the great chiefs to enlist public opinion.

> If any individual desired to bring any proposition before the general council, he must first gain the assent of his family, then his clan, next of the four related clans in his end of the council house, then of his nation, and thus in due course . . . the business would be brought up before the representatives of the confederacy. In the reverse order, the measures of the general council were sent down to the people for their approval. It was a standing rule that all action should be unanimous. Hence, the discussions were . . . continued till all opposition was reasoned down, or the proposed measure abandoned.

This is what Wright thought contributed to the power of the confederacy, and so it went "until their councils were divided by bribery and Whiskey of the Whites." (Fenton 1957a:310–311).

Civil Chiefs

Throughout the Northeast to Huronia, and perhaps a weak echo of the Southeast, a distinction was made between civil chiefs—the sachems (from an Algonquian term), the agoianders of Lafitau, or the *hotiyanéshǫʔ* of the Seneca, whose offices were ascribed in clan segments—and other chiefs whose statuses were achieved on the war path, for instance, or for council oratory, and whose titles died with them and were not hereditary. The former and their families apparently constituted a class apart; the latter included the so-called Pine Tree Chiefs, honorary titles that carried no voting power, as well as the Speaker for the Women, and for the Warriors. Even the sachems employed a speaker to announce decisions reached in committee. He was chosen for his ability to grasp principle and fact, for his rhetorical gifts, and for an enormous memory in a society in which all men and women were walking archives. His presence had a powerful effect on history, since the speaker is often identified by colonial recorders when the decision makers are not. This greatly affects the writing of history. To this day Iroquois councils prefer to reach consensus quietly in committee, they reluctantly vote openly in public, and the gifted speaker still exerts influence. Quiet men and women in the background are the real decision makers.

Chiefs of lineages were the entrepreneurs in the Huron trade (Heidenreich 1971:220 ff.), which entailed elaborate arrangement of external affairs, which was a function of civil chiefs also in Iroquoia. This lends credence to the aphorism: "Trade and Peace we take to be one thing..." (Wraxall 1915:195).

Iroquois society, in their terms, may be summarized as a body of relatives, "my people," who are residents of a place—a village or settlement. The public includes everyone (so that any stranger must be adopted). They see themselves as a "nation," literally "a native land," a concept that is at once kindred and territorial; and the several bands, tribes, or nations are confederated on a model of the longhouse that implies both kin and territory.

Vertically, society is ranked into "grandfathers of old," the founders; chiefs (sachems or lords) who take the metaphor "Trees"; Warriors or "Matbearers," sometimes "Big Tobacco Pouches," otherwise "Tree Watchers" or "Props" to the chiefs; Women, our Mothers, who really count; as well as the age-grades.

Warfare

Despite the great message of peace inherent in the Longhouse, Iroquois men revered war above all else, and with the fur trade it became a shattering force in their culture that threatened the very structure of their society. Enormous amounts of energy were expended on the warpath—in training, preparations, and travel—and heavy losses of manpower were only partly compensated by adopting captives. The native population of the Iroquois towns steadily declined during the seventeenth century, and from the mid-century on there were more outlanders than natives in Iroquoia.

War could be the result of policy that the old men debated and decided in council (Lafitau 1724, 2:171) or of vendetta by which ambitious young men achieved glory, going on the warpath without council sanction. In either case, the activities of raising a war party, setting out, conducting the campaign, taking scalps and prisoners (fig. 1), and the return fulfilled ritual patterns in a sequence that made a ceremony, if not a game, of warfare and locked its participants in a career from which the exits were capture, torture, and death or graduation to the status of ancients. Even the old sages, having adopted

a policy of peace or neutrality, could only persuade but not enforce the young men to keep the peace. This conflict between the old men and the young only worsened during the contact period, until the power of the hereditary chiefs waned and the war chiefs took over at the American Revolution.

Descriptions of the raising and departure of an Iroquois war party (Lafitau 1724, 2:161 ff.; Colden 1747:5ff.) were written after the gun had revolutionized strategy and tactics. Small guerrilla bands under rising leaders replaced large expeditions led by distinguished chiefs and shamans. Individual initiative supplanted policy and group action. Men loved hunting and fishing second only to warfare because the same capabilities were involved. Indeed warfare was a necessary exercise in their culture because "it fulfilled a very law of their being" (Lafitau 1724, 2:161 ff.). Since manpower was their only asset, the loss of a single person created the demand for his replacement, which was the obligation, not of his household (lineage), but of the akatǫ·ni·, an obligation that extended to their offspring who were thus duty bound to their father's lodge to which otherwise they were strangers. The matron of a lodge could force these persons to go to war to make up the loss or she could keep them at home to prevent further losses. It is evident that the power of the matrons increased in relation to these losses at the close of the seventeenth century.

If the matron decided "to raise up the tree" (replace the loss), or if she put on the mat the name of some dead person she mourned, she spoke through a wampum belt to a war leader related to her household as akatǫ·ni·, asking him to form a war party. Accepting the belt was his commission (Lafitau 1724, 2:164).

Or some warrior bent on glory might initiate the action by circulating a belt without revealing his purpose (fig. 1). This kind of engagement is known in the literature as "private" or "little war," as opposed to "general" or "public war," which was sanctioned by the council and done in the name of the nation (Lafitau 1724, 2:167). Either the Old Men or the initiating matron could recall a war party, but this had to be done with deference to the pride of those engaged.

A "little war" is comparable to a blood feud, and the means of composing both were similar. Relations with neighboring tribes were from remote times a delicate balance of suspended blood feud tempered by fragile alliances. Deganawida brought a message of peace—that all men are brothers, that killing, scalping, and cannibalism should cease, and that the "great immutable law" should restore civil society. He devised the means of lifting up men's minds with the condolence ritual, which provided for paying presents to the aggrieved. The same ceremony on a broader scale took former enemies into a network of alliances.

From the "hanging of the kettle" to the return of the war party with prisoners and scalps the whole procedure of warfare was hedged in with ritual. To "sing for war" was at once a social and a ceremonial occasion. "Upsetting or breaking the kettle" and thereby quenching the fire symbolized the act of stopping a war party. The war leader through his speaker appealed to the war god (Mohawk Agreskoué or Agriskoué, Huron Aireskoui, and variants) to sanction the enterprise and to the sun, their elder brother, to guide them to victory (Lafitau 1724, 1:126, 132, 205-206, 2:189-190; JR 33:225, 39:207-209, 53:224, 57:96; Cuoq 1882:223, 225). To Agreskoué they dedicated the feast of dogs, the captives they hoped to take, and of him they begged their safe conduct and return (Lafitau 1724, 2:189-190). Killing and eating captives was considered a sacrifice to him, and he might also be appeased with a feast of bear (Megapolensis in Jameson 1909:177). The torture ritual was both a necessary preparation for war and its aftermath.

War feasts were far from acts of piety. Seeing the kettle and the steaming platters of dog meat, which symbolized the broth and flesh of captives that they would later drink and eat, transported the beholders into fits of rage and fury as they mentioned their enemies in songs and compared them to dogs. "In fact they give no other names to their captives," remarked Lafitau (1724, 2:189). The most distinguished warriors present received the heads of dogs boiled in the kettle; the head was the symbol of the feast, as it has remained for two centuries (Fenton 1953). The Personal Chant, marked by striking a post with a club, has a similar history of transformations to a thanksgiving rite at present.

The ceremony of departure ended at the wood's edge with guns fired in rotation and finery exchanged for hunting gear and moccasins brought out with provisions by the warriors' wives. After 1640 the gun rendered obsolete the traditional weapons—bow and arrow, *casse-tête* (ball-headed war club) (fig. 11; "The League of the Iroquois: Its History, Politics, and Ritual," fig. 8, this vol.), shield, and twined rod armor—although several of these items persisted as ceremonial objects into the eighteenth century.

The northern Iroquoians and their Algonquian neighbors were headhunters from the earliest times. The dead and scalped invariably appear in pictographs as headless (fig. 1). Widespread in the Southeast from contact times, scalping may have reached the Iroquois through the Susquehannock well before the sixteenth century, since Jacques Cartier and Champlain witnessed the results in the Saint Lawrence valley. Scalping was indeed a New World custom, although it was later much encouraged by the payment of bounties by the English and the French (Biggar 1924; Champlain 1922-1936, 1:101-103, 178-180; Friederici 1906:8-20, 21-37).

Killing and scalping were secondary alternatives to taking prisoners and returning them for adoption. Warriors carried a prisoner tie (fig. 7) and new moccasins for victims who were driven ahead loaded with booty. Few prisoners were brought back unscathed by preliminary torture in camp.

At home people anticipated the return of the war party. Special cries announced their luck, losses, and gains. Their reception at the wood's edge, the prisoners' running the gauntlet at each town, the council that settled the adoption or torture of the prisoners, the elaborate drama of torture, the joy of reclothing a victim in the name of the dead—all followed a series of prescribed acts that everyone understood and expected. They have been abundantly described by participants and observers (JR 1896-1901; Lafitau 1724, 2:278 ff.) and summarized by Knowles (1940).

Models of Continuity

The society perpetually maintains itself by a number of models, or continuators. First, the fireside family generates the ongoing human family, which is bilateral, arbitrarily identifying the matrilineage with the household, and recognizing a collateral responsibility to the father's kinsmen (*akatǫ·ni·*) and of them to their offspring. Together these agnatic and matri-kinsmen constitute an entity that performs economic and social functions. Their reciprocal actions afford the model for the larger confederate body—both the tribe and the League. The clans, metaphorically fireplaces or hearths, fictionally extend the lineage, sharing its crests, names, offices, rights, and obligations. The longhouse, as a model for society, is divided into sides or moieties, composed of clans grouped as siblings ('Brothers'), own and collateral, over and against 'Cousins' and their siblings, the two halves reciprocating in games, performing ceremonies in honor of a third party, the Creator, and condoling and burying each other's dead. Together the two moieties form the community and occupy a "native land" (the nation), which is grouped into the Three Brothers and the Four Brothers, the *akatǫ·ni·* and the *kheyáʔtawęh*, to form the League. The League or the "Whole House" is symbolically a "household of one family, with one mind, one body, and one heart"; politically it is a confederation of autonomous tribal territories. A policy of adoption, which commences with the lineage taking in individuals, extends to the League, which is symbolically a great pine with roots reaching in the cardinal directions, "the Great White Roots of Peace," which are followed by wandering nations to the central fire.

Metaphors of union, increase, and continuity of life in contrast to death comprise a series of continuative models that apply equally to local society and to its extensions; they unite society with its religious system. There is first the earth and its products left by the Creator for human use and enjoyment. Clearings and native lands contrast with wilderness. Growing things, especially the life supporters, flourish in summer and perish if not stored for winter, the season of death. The ever-growing tree of the long leaves is a metaphor for the commonwealth, and it should not be permitted to topple.

Individual chiefs are trees that do topple and have to be raised up again, just as the "Tree of Peace" is planted. Four White Roots of Peace extend cardinally; they should be followed to the fire; but if chopped, they bleed. The deer is the food of hunters, man's contribution to the larder, the fulfillment of his marriage contract; because antlers are the marks of identity for chiefs, a rack is installed with his office; but as deer shed their racks, they are removed from the head of a chief in illness or at death, or for malfeasance in office. Just as the deer rub antlers on brush during rutting season, so the great social dance after the installation of a new chief is called "rubbing antlers," when they socialize and diffuse their power. In time they may lose power.

Second, there is a proper way: life and society are governed by certain procedures and rituals. Life follows a set path, and one who strays from it is likely to get lost in the woods. This is true even of chiefs. A path runs through the longhouse, which the ceremonies follow, and to obstruct it, locally or politically, is to throw a log in the path. So the path of peace contrasts with the warpath. At death the clear-minded moiety takes up the path to the lodge of the mourners, whose house is disordered. "Death the faceless," who stalks men on the trail, has kicked the logs apart and stomped on the hearth. To rekindle the fire is to restore life, and so the column of smoke rising to pierce the sky symbolizes an ongoing society.

Third, Iroquois culture redounds with predictions of gloom and sets measures for meeting such contingencies. Sentient minds contrast with rolling skulls, which enemies may kick contemptuously out of their way. The depression of mourning is relieved by the Requickening ritual (Hewitt and Fenton 1944), which lifts up the minds and restores the sun that they once more may see the light of day. It is interesting that the Senecas named their newspaper, the first published (1841) in Buffalo from the mission press of Asher Wright, the *Mental Elevator* (Ne jaguhnigoagesgwathah) (Pilling 1888:175; Fenton 1956a:575). Foretelling the day when the Longhouse would break open at both ends, the prophet urged the League tribes to seek a giant rock elm with great lateral and cavernous radial roots and there to deposit the heads and minds of the League in refuge. Some say they found it at Six Nations Reserve on Grand River in Canada.

Finally, the very heritage of the League manifests principles of continuity that maintain society. Its cardinal principles of "Good Word, Peace, and Power," which comprise the "Great Law," have their humbler counterparts in truth (justice, right behavior), health, and physical strength. A note of humility toward the past runs through Iroquois culture: "in later days we have grown destitute," in contrast with the wisdom and knowledge of the "Founders who sleep in their graves on the pillow of the law." With it runs a respect for elders who "know a lot," and one hears the constant admonition to "listen." And that is how the heritage passes.

Life Cycle

Iroquois life-cycle patterns are imperfectly known. Neither childbirth in kneeling posture nor puberty fast or seclusion at first menses distinguishes the northern Iroquoians from their neighbors. Arrangement of marriages by the Old Ladies and the ritual exchange of marriage bread for venison is perhaps unique. No rites marked passage to adulthood, save name changes that go with offices conferred. Separate patterns of suicide for males and females—men for losing prestige, women for being deserted, and children for being scolded—are reported in both Huronia and Iroquoia, *Cicuta maculata* being the favorite agent (Fenton 1941a). Sickness, shamanism, dreams, and death were major preoccupations in both areas.

The Iroquois are preoccupied with good luck and health (Shimony 1961). Personal health and social welfare depend on fulfilling obligations to the tutelaries revealed in dreams and participating in particular rites.

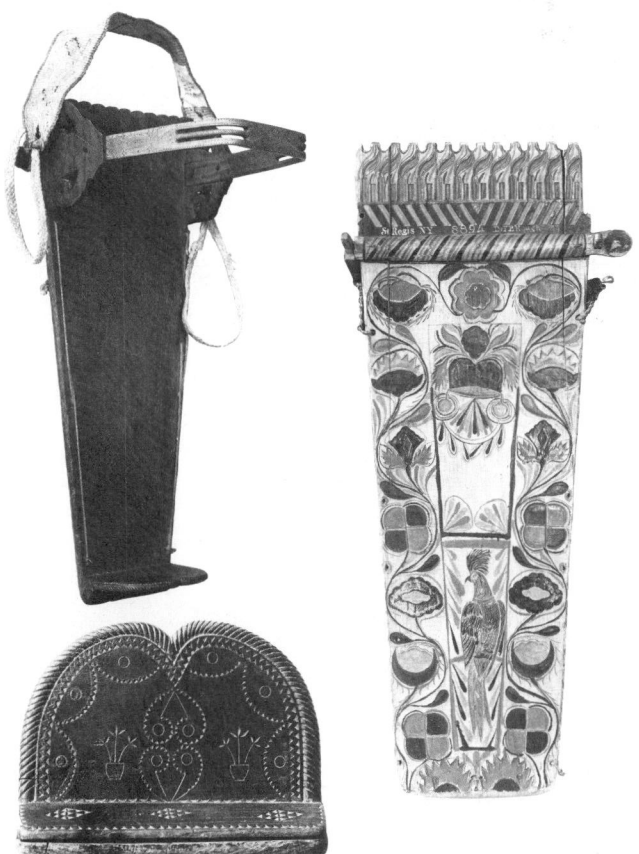

Dept. of Anthr., Smithsonian: left, 381021, right, 8894.

Fig. 22. Cradleboards. left, Cayuga, Six Nations Reserve, probably made before 1850, with tumpline for suspension; detail shows carving on footrest (back is undecorated). right, Back of Mohawk example collected at St. Regis in 1875, with elaborate carved and painted decoration. Left 62 cm long, right same scale.

Neglect brings sickness, death, and doom to society. To sing, dance, and go through ceremonies increases one's power or control, and the word for the power that is inherent in things, processes, and supernaturals—Orenda (Hewitt 1902; i.e., an assumed Huron *oręˑⁿdaʔ,* cognate with Mohawk *oręˑnaʔ,* Onondaga *oęˑnaʔ,* and Seneca *oęnǫʔ,* which also means 'song with power')—is related to the word for song (Mohawk *karęˑnaʔ,* Seneca *kaęnǫʔ*). Comparing the celebration of medicine society rites or the Midwinter festival among the Longhouse Iroquois in the 1970s with the seventeenth-century descriptions of the Hurons (Tooker 1964:72–117) confirms that Iroquois ceremonialism is of one piece and one tradition constantly evolving. Recordings of the music (Fenton 1942b, 1947) and analysis of it (Kurath 1951, 1964) demonstrate that shamanistic music in both places conforms to a narrow melodic line and is quite ancient (fig. 23). Iroquois music reveals considerable embroidery on ancient patterns, particularly in Fish Dance and Women's Dance (fig. 24) songs and the stomp dances the Iroquois share with Southeastern tribes whose descendants still practice them in Oklahoma. Perhaps the most Iroquoian form is the Personal Chant, now a thanksgiving form, which goes back to the death songs of individual warriors in the torture ritual (Knowles 1940).

Condolence

Just as the medicine societies have encapsulated in ritual form shamanistic behavior once free and innovative, as described in the Huron literature (Tooker 1964:97–100),

Dept. of Anthr., Smithsonian: a, 253672; c, 380929; d, 380933; e, 248715; f, 381396; i, 380913; Peabody Mus., Yale U.: b, 145157; Nationalmuseet, Copenhagen: g, Hc365; Mus. of the Amer. Ind., Heye Foundation, New York: h, 15/4747.

Fig. 23. Some typical Iroquois musical instruments. a, Rattle made from snapping turtle (back and underside shown), used for Feather Dance and by False Faces, Seneca, Six Nations Reserve, collected before 1909; b, hickory-bark rattle, used as a substitute for snapping turtle rattle, made about 1951 by Avery Jimmerson, Allegany Seneca; c–d, cowhorn rattles with wood handles, used to accompany most dances, usually with water drum but alone for dances of the stomp dance pattern, Allegany Seneca Reservation, before 1940, c, made by Chauncey Johnny John, distal end painted red, d, made by Jonas Snow; e, water drum and beater, used by lead singer for most dances, drum made from cut-down commercial paint keg with iron hoop and added bung, head from commercially tanned leather, Onondaga Reservation, N.Y., collected before 1908; f, gourd rattle, used in planting and harvest ceremonies, Six Nations Reserve, collected before 1916; g, one of pair of deer dewclaw leg rattles worn by male dancers, mounted on commercial leather bands, Iroquois, probably New York, collected before 1860, this type succeeded by leg rattles of brass pellet bells (one such bell was included here); h, rasp used in Chipmunk Dance, form similar to those used at wakes by Tonawanda Seneca, Cayuga, Six Nations Reserve, collected before 1933; i, box turtle rattle, used by lead singer of women's *thǫwiˑsas* ceremony, from Bertha Redeye, Seneca, Allegany Reservation, collected 1940. Length of a 39.5 cm, rest same scale.

318

Fig. 24. Herbert Dowdy (with horn rattle) and Johnson Jimerson (with water drum), Senecas, singing Women's Dance song during a singing party and recording session in Edward Curry's house at Quaker Bridge, Allegany Reservation, May 28, 1957. Photograph by William C. Sturtevant.

so the Condolence ceremony for mourning and installing new chiefs has become a great ritual drama (see "The League of the Iroquois: Its History, Politics, and Ritual," this vol.). It is compounded of the ancient Huron Feast of the Dead, the litany of the ancients, the wood's edge protocol for receiving returned war parties with prisoners, the greeting of foreign embassies, compensation for murder by payment of presents (which evolved into the elaborate wampum ritual), and finally, requickening the living in the name of the dead and conferring a new name (the ancient title), which is the heart of the adoption rite. Otherwise there is a taboo on naming the dead, or "raising up the tree too soon."

The modern Iroquois Feast of the Dead (Mohawk *ohkí·we*, Seneca *ohki·we·*) is but a weak echo of the ancient Huron rite described by Brébeuf (JR 10:265–305; Fenton and Kurath 1951; Kinietz 1940:99–120). The great ossuaries of Huronia are not found in Iroquoia, save on the margins at Niagara.

Cosmology

The Iroquois still believe that the soul commences its long journey westward to where the sky lifts and admits entrance, through a series of ordeals, to the land of the dead in the sky world. In this they differ little from the ancient Huron beliefs (Hewitt 1895a). Dreams are interpreted as the wishes of the soul (Wallace 1958a); and the Iroquois folk literature contains some beautiful examples of other-world journeying, of which Handsome Lake's vision is an example (Wallace 1969). Otherwise, with the exception of the three great set pieces of Iroquois mythology—the cosmology, Deganawida's epic of the League, and Handsome Lake's code—by which the Iroquois periodize their history, their folk literature runs to cannibal tales, vampires, and devouring monsters in addition to animal tales. This is a tradition that places an enormous premium on ability to internalize long verbal

streams; the myth-teller, the singer of the chant cycle, the ritualist, and the prophet are the heroes honored in this country.

Huron and Iroquois cosmology is of one piece. The cosmological legend recounting how the Sky Woman fell from the world above, how the animals below made a place for her to land by diving into the waters for earth to put on Turtle's back, how she gave birth to a daughter, how this daughter gave birth to the Twin Brothers, and the subsequent exploits of the Good Twin Tharonhiawagon (Mohawk *tharǫhyawâ·kǫ*, Oneida *t(e)halǫhyawâ·kǫ*, Onondaga *thaęhyawá·ʔki* or *tehaęhyawáʔkhǫʔ*, all meaning 'He Who Grasps the Sky') or Sapling and his evil brother exists in many variants since first recorded by the Recollect Gabriel Sagard-Théodat in 1623 (Fenton 1962). The content of this myth is a mirror of Iroquois culture, but its principal motifs are known the breadth of the continent. Much of later Iroquois religious culture is projected back into it. Thus the rationale for the False Face Society is provided in an encounter between the culture hero and the mask spirit who is more or less patron of winds and disease besides being gamekeeper and protector of mankind, who remember to honor him with tobacco and mush. In the epoch of human society of the "first times" occurs the division into moieties, with people living on opposite river banks. The second coming of the Creator is occasioned by the need of people to learn the Four Sacred Ceremonies. The prayer to the spirit-forces that comprise the pantheon, which is the most important pattern of sequence in Iroquois ritual because it must be done first before any other ritual act, is ascribed to these times. The present cycle of longhouse festivals, in all their diversity, respresents commitment to the Longhouse faith of the Handsome Lake religion and incorporates much that is old with innovations. It is through the fulfilment of these ceremonies that the 'Real Indian People' (Seneca *ǫkwéʔǫwe·kha·ʔ*) manifest their identity and renew their faith. The ceremonies provide a regular way to give order to their lives. Through the ceremonies they strengthen one another by reciprocal and cooperative acts, which serve to keep the culture alive.

Synonymy*

In this synonymy are discussed the names for the Iroquois confederacy.

The name Iroquois was learned by Champlain (1922–1936, 1:96 and passim) as early as 1603 from speakers of an unidentified but probably Algonquian language spoken on the Saint Lawrence River; he spelled it Irocois and Yrocois, probably pronounced [irokwe]. Other spell-

* This synonymy was written by Ives Goddard. The uncredited Iroquois forms were furnished by Marianne Mithun (Mohawk, Cayuga, and Tuscarora), Floyd G. Lounsbury (Oneida and Tuscarora), Hanni J. Woodbury (Onondaga), and Michael K. Foster (Cayuga).

ings in the primary sources vary only slightly, showing that the name became standardized and universally known very early; among those listed by Hewitt (1907f) are: Erocoise, Hiroquois, Hyroquoise, Irecoies, Iriquois, Iroquaes, Irroquois, Yroquois. No such form is attested in any Indian language as a name for any Iroquoian group, and the ultimate origin and meaning of the name are unknown. The problem is discussed by Day (1968).

The term Upper Iroquois (French Iroquois supérieurs, Iroquois d'en haut) was sometimes used in the seventeenth century for the Seneca, Cayuga, Onondaga, and Oneida, as opposed to the Lower Iroquois (Iroquois inférieurs, Iroquois d'en bas), who were the Mohawk (JR 42:256, 43:186). Less frequently the Oneidas were included with the Mohawks (JR 51:118).

The Iroquois confederacy was referred to as the Five Indian Cantons, the Five Canton Nations, the Canton Indians, and especially the Five Nations, or in French *les cinq Nations Iroquoises* (Hewitt 1907f; JR 41:86). After the official adoption of the Tuscarora was announced to New York officials on May 21, 1723 (Wraxall 1915:144; Livingston 1956:236), the name Six Nations came into widespread use, though it did not completely replace Five Nations (see NYCD 6:588 for a 1750 example). Equivalent terms in Iroquois languages are Seneca *ye·iʔ níonǫetsake·h* (Chafe 1967:77), Onondaga *áhyaʔk niyakáǫhwetsyaʔkè*, Oneida *yâ·yaʔk niyonǫhwetsyáké*, Mohawk *yâ·yaʔk nihonǫhwetsyá·ke*, and Tuscarora *ó·hyaʔk tiwoʔwná·ke·*. Unami Delaware used *palé·naxk entxi·skwtáye·k*, literally '(house of) five fires' (Zeisberger 1887:220; Heckewelder 1876:98, corrected and phonemicized); and Shawnee had Nekoatewāūthwee skoatawāātskee, literally 'six fires' (Trowbridge 1939:66). However, the common designation of the Iroquois League in their own languages was by a series of names conveying the idea of 'the people of the longhouse', in reference to the usual metaphor for the League. One set of forms has *-nǫhs-* 'house' and *-yǫni-* 'be extended, finished, whole, real': Seneca *hotinǫhsyóniʔ* 'they (who) are of the extended lodge' (Hewitt 1907f:617, 620, normalized), Onondaga *hotinǫhsyǫ̀·ni* 'their real house', Mohawk *hotinǫhsyǫ́·ni* (a borrowing from Seneca) or *rotinǫhsyǫ́·ni* (with substitution of Mohawk prefix), Tuscarora *yǫkwanǫhsyǫ́·niʔ* 'our extended house' (also a borrowing), Huron Hotinnonchiendi 'the completed lodge', 1654 (JR 41:86) and hotinnonchiondi (Potier 1920:154). A second set of forms has the same nominal root followed by *-ǫni-* 'make': Seneca *hotínǫhsǫ·ni·h* 'house builders' (Chafe 1963:56, 1967:71, 77), Cayuga *hotinǫsǫ́·nih*, Onondaga *hotinǫhsǫ̀·ni*, Mohawk *rotinǫhsǫ́·ni* (G. Michelson 1973:83). The various pronominal prefixes attested with these forms are *hoti-* (*roti-*) 'they, their', *ǫkwa-* (*yǫkwa-*) 'we, our', *akwa-* 'we', and *ka-* 'it'. In early recordings *-yǫni-* 'extended' seems more common than *-ǫni-* 'make', and the form with *ka-*, which would be, for example, Mohawk *kanǫhsyǫ́·ni* 'the

extended house', is especially frequent (from Hewitt 1907f:619-620, except as noted): Kanosoni, 1635 (Van den Bogaert, in Jameson 1909:152, as corrected from the original manuscript by Charles Gehring, personal communication 1976), akwanoschioni, Aquanuschioni (Zeisberger 1887a), Cannassoone, Canossoone, Ho-dé-no-sau-nee (Morgan 1851:51), Hotinnonsionni (Bruyas 1863:18), Ke-nunctioni, Konossioni, Rodinunchsiouni.

In other languages the Iroquois are often often called by a name that is said to refer especially to one of the individual tribes, typically the Seneca or the Mohawk. Such names have been included in the following lists where warranted by the available evidence. In the South the Iroquois were referred to as Senecas, Nottawagees, and Northern Indians (NYCD 6:588). Variant spellings include Sannagers, Sennagars, Sennecca, Sinagars, and Sinnagers (Hewitt 1910b:507-508).

The Algonquian languages attest two widespread names applied to various Iroquoian tribes or to the Iroquois as a group. Reflexes or derivatives of one of these, Proto-Algonquian **na·towe·wa,* are found as tribal names throughout the Algonquian family. Those used for the Iroquois are the following: Cree *na·towe·w* (Lacombe 1874:176, 486; Faries 1938:103, 353), Menominee *na·tawew* 'Iroquoian', especially applied to the nearby Oneida (Bloomfield 1975:149), Algonquin *na·towe·* 'Iroquoian' and *mači-na·towe·k* 'bad Iroquoians', the old name for the hostile Iroquois later applied to those at Six Nations Reserve (Cuoq 1886:263-264; Lemoine 1911), Ojibwa *na·towe·* (Baraga 1878-1880, 2:264), Ottawa Nautowaig (Tanner 1956:316), Shawnee *na·towe,* glossed 'Seneca' (Trowbridge 1939:66; Voegelin 1938-1940, 9:377; synonymy in "Wyandot," this vol.). Miami natawia is glossed 'Seneca' (Voegelin 1938-1940, 9:377) but probably should be 'Wyandot' (synonymy in "Wyandot," this vol.). In Fox, Menominee, Ojibwa, Potawatomi, and perhaps Illinois this word is also used to refer to an unidentified species of snake, but this is probably an extension in the use of the ethnic name rather than its source. Proto-Algonquian **na·towe·wa* should instead be compared to the verbal element **-a·towe·-* 'speak a foreign language', to which it can be related by regular grammatical processes. As an English borrowing, presumably from Ojibwa, this name is attested as Nautoway, Naudoways (Tanner 1956:88, 310, 316), and Nahdoways (P. Jones 1861:32, 111), among other variants. For reflexes applied to other Iroquoian groups, see synonymies in "Wyandot" and "Iroquoian Tribes of the Virginia-North Carolina Coastal Plain," this volume.

A second set of names, found only in the Eastern Algonquian languages, reflects Proto-Eastern Algonquian **me·nkwe·w,* an unanalyzable form with no known etymology. Reflexes that refer to the Iroquois are Western Abenaki magua (Laurent 1884:52); Munsee Delaware *mé·nkwe·w,* in Canada especially applied to the Oneidas; and Unami Delaware *ménkwe,* used in Oklahoma especially for the Seneca-Cayuga. From Delaware came the name Mingo, applied to the non-League Senecas, Cayugas, and other Iroquoians in the Ohio Valley in the eighteenth century, whose descendants are the Seneca-Cayuga of Oklahoma. For reflexes applied to the Mohawk, see the synonymy in "Mohawk," this volume. For reflexes referring to other Iroquoians, see the synonymies in "Iroquoian Tribes of the Virginia-North Carolina Coastal Plain" and "Susquehannock" this volume.

Some Central Algonquian languages have a distinctive set of names for the Iroquois, sometimes glossed 'Seneca', of unknown origin and meaning: Illinois psicania, psigania (Le Boullenger, in Belting 1958; Gravier 1700:487), Miami psikania, if 'Seneca' is the correct gloss (see the synonymy in "Wyandot," this vol.; Dunn, in Voegelin 1938-1940, 1:90), Fox *osikane·ha, asikane·ha*, glossed 'Seneca' and 'the Six Nations' (Gatschet 1882-1889:3; Michelson 1931, phonemicized), Potawatomi síkne (Gatschet 1878-1893:30). The Ojibwa form of this name must be the source of Schoolcraft's (1851-1857, 1:191, 307)

Assigunaigs, the name of a supposedly extinct group "spoken of by the western and Lake tribes."

Early Montagnais had Kouetakiou, 1634 (JR 8:23), and Fabvre's (1970:126) 1696 dictionary has the derivaive K8etatchi8in 'to be Huron (or) Iroquois'. From this comes the Micmac loan goetètjg 'Iroquois' (pl.; Pacifique 1939:106), given by Rand (1888:172) as Kwĕdĕch' 'Mohawk', which Hoffman (1955a) suggests may originally have referred to the Saint Lawrence Iroquoians.

Other names for the Iroquois are Illinois atchiss8e8a (Le Boullenger, in Belting 1958; Gravier 1700:79), Cherokee nądawegi, also 'Seneca' (Mooney, in Hewitt 1910b:507), and Creek natuági (Gatschet, in Hewitt 1907f:620.

Six Nations Reserve, Ontario, has the following names: Seneca *swe·kę?*, Cayuga *ohswé·kę?*, Tuscarora *swé?kǫ*. Munsee has borrowed this as *šǒwé·ka* and calls the people there *wšǒwè·kí·wak*. It is referred to in English as Six Nations, Grand River, Ohsweken (äsh¹wēgən), and Brantford.

Northern Iroquoian Prehistory

JAMES A. TUCK

Theories of Iroquoian origins have been many and varied, but the hypothesis of a local origin for Iroquoian groups, probably well prior to the beginning of the Christian era, and subsequent in-place development is the most likely. On the other hand, long-distance migrations were the keystones of most earlier theories, which have been summarized by Ritchie (1961a:27–31), Wright (1966:3–9), and Tuck (1971:10–18), among others. This chapter will discuss what is known of the archeological manifestations of historically defined Iroquoian groups and some important changing facets of Iroquoian culture—settlement patterns, social correlates, and subsistence patterns that resulted in the general Iroquoian culture pattern observed at the time of European contact (fig. 1).

Regional Sequences

The prehistory of the Five Nations (the Iroquois confederacy made up of the Seneca, Cayuga, Onondaga, Oneida, and Mohawk) is fairly well known and seems characterized by the in-place development of all five tribal groups. The Owasco-period (Ritchie 1944) people were almost certainly Iroquoian speakers and the Owasco-Iroquois cultural continuum has been divided into a number of phases, each of approximately 100 years duration and each grading almost imperceptibly into the next. These phases (after Ritchie 1965, 1969a) and their approximate dates are: Hunter's Home A.D. 800 or 900 to 1000; Carpenter Brook Owasco, A.D. 1000 to 1100; Canandaigua Owasco, A.D. 1100 to 1200; Castle Creek Owasco, A.D. 1200 to 1300; Oak Hill Iroquois, A.D. 1300 to 1400; Chance phase Iroquois, A.D. 1400 to 1500; Garoga (Late Prehistoric) Iroquois, 1500 to 1550 or 1575; and protohistoric and historic Iroquois 1550 to the present. The dates are determined by carbon 14 in the earlier cases and from historic records or datable European artifacts in the later cases. The correspondence to centuries in the Gregorian calendar is fortuitous but real; recent determinations have clarified and reinforced these earlier hypotheses (cf. Tuck 1971:197).

Regional sequences have been established for all five tribal areas. The Seneca sequence, especially in the protohistoric and historic periods, was investigated and reported on by Wray and Schoff (1953) and subsequent work by the Rochester Museum of Arts and Sciences has begun to elucidate the prehistoric sequence. The general picture is one of a progressive northward drift of two large towns with varying numbers of small outlying hamlets. The contact components (Adams and Tram sites) begin north of Lakes Conesus, Hemlock, and Honeoye and trend northeastward toward the present town of Victor, New York, where a large Seneca village, Gannagaro (now called the Boughton Hill site) was destroyed in 1687 by Jacques-René de Brisay, marquis de Denonville (see Graham and Wray 1966). The earlier components are generally south of these historic towns. The Farrel Farm site (Charles F. Hayes, personal communication 1972) seems to fall into the Oak Hill phase, and Robert Ricklis (personal communication 1967) reports a series of villages culminating in the Richmond Mills site (Parker 1918), which may be a late prehistoric Seneca component.

The Cayuga are perhaps the least known archeologically of any of the Five Nations, but several historic towns have been explored (mostly by relic collectors) on the northeast side of Cayuga Lake. Excavations by Pratt, White, and Tuck (personal communication 1975) have identified prehistoric villages of the Garoga and Chance phases that seem to indicate a south to north series of village removals along the east side of Cayuga Lake. Marian E. White (personal communication 1972) has also discovered what appears to be a parallel development on the west side of the lake, which is in keeping with a more dispersed settlement pattern prior to about A.D. 1500 but which confuses the picture as the relation of this series of villages to historic Cayuga remains to be explained.

The Onondaga sequence begins about A.D. 1100 at the Maxon Derby site (Ritchie 1965:281–284) and progresses through all the above-mentioned phases to the present Onondaga reservation, settled in the late eighteenth century, and located south of Syracuse, New York. Investigations have shown an unbroken chain of village removals and resettlements from prior to A.D. 1200 to the present (Tuck 1971), positively indicating an in situ development. Also, these researches show no evidence whatsoever of a migration of the Onondaga from Jefferson County or the Saint Lawrence Valley (Tuck 1971:205–207), a migration frequently postulated (Morgan 1901:5–6; Hale 1883a:10–11; Parker 1916; MacNeish 1952).

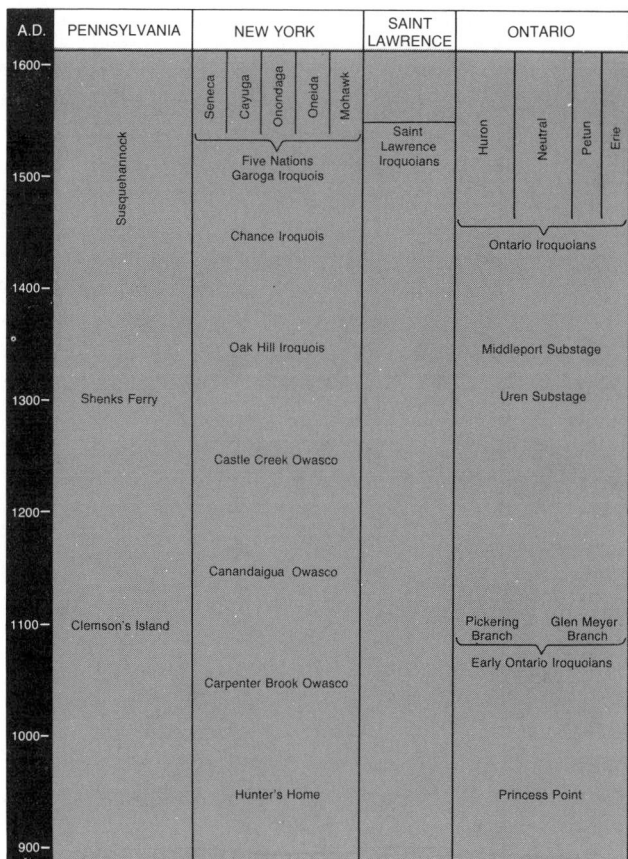

Fig. 1. Suggested correlations of northern Iroquoian archeological complexes.

General Oneida prehistory and history (Pratt 1966) and their ceramics (Engelbrecht 1971) and smoking pipes (Weber 1970) have been described. The consensus seems to be that the postcontact Oneida followed a pattern of village removals of two to three miles, analogous to that of the Seneca or Onondaga, but the question of Oneida population origins is still in debate. Pratt and Engelbrecht see a migration to Oneida, Engelbrecht postulating a split with Onondaga, although Onondaga data do not indicate such an event. The Oneida do not seem descended from the Saint Lawrence Iroquoians, and a search much closer to home might be profitable. Four important early proto-Onondaga sites west of Syracuse remained undiscovered until the 1960s despite years of cultivation, and some surprises may yet be in store in Oneida country.

Mohawk prehistory can be much better documented, largely because of the efforts of Lenig (1965), Ritchie (1952), and Funk (1967), who have revealed a series of clearly related villages ranging from late Owasco hamlets of the thirteenth century to large historic walled towns such as Garoga (Funk 1967). All are located in the Mohawk valley or on its surrounding hills, and the pattern of short village removals conforms to that found elsewhere among the Five Nations.

In Ontario a similar series of broad chronological phases has been outlined (cf. Wright 1966). The earliest

of these is the Princess Point complex, an Ontario equivalent of Ritchie's early Owasco Hunter's Home phase, with stations along the Grand River, near the present city of Hamilton, Ontario, and on the west bank of the Niagara River (Stothers 1971). It is now dated prior to A.D. 1000 (David M. Stothers, personal communication 1972). Following this, Wright's "Early Ontario Iroquois" stage existed from about 1000 to 1300. It comprised two branches: a southern or Glen Meyer branch along the north shore of Lake Erie and possibly on the Niagara Peninsula and a northern or Pickering branch stretching from the north shore of Lake Ontario to Georgian Bay. These may represent an early expression of the Neutral-Erie versus Huron-Petun ethnic-linguistic separation, although subsequent developments seem to make this hypothesis somewhat unlikely. At about 1300 Wright (1966:53) believes that the Pickering Branch people conquered the Glen Meyer people resulting in a more homogeneous "Middle Iroquois" stage divided into an earlier (1300-1350) Uren substage and a later (1350-1400) Middleport substage. Wright's stages and substages seem valid, but the conquest hypothesis has been questioned by several researchers (cf. White 1971a).

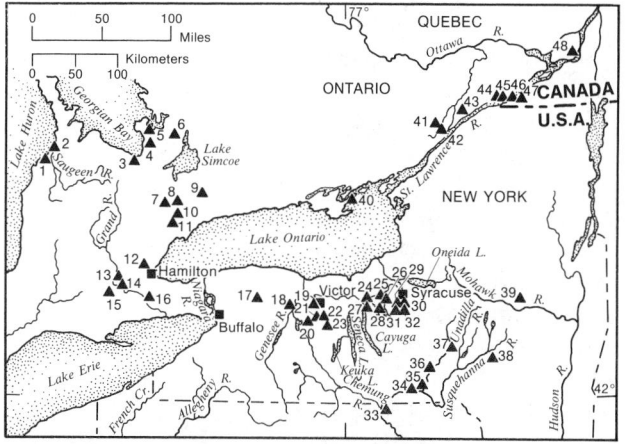

Fig. 2. Archeological sites. 1, Nodwell; 2, Donaldson; 3, Sidey-Mackay; 4, Orr Lake; 5, Train; 6, Warminster; 7, Seed; 8, Aurora; 9, Miller; 10, Black Creek; 11, Woodbridge; 12, Princess Point; 13, Cleveland; 14, Porteus; 15, Moyer; 16, Grand Banks; 17, Oakfield; 18, Farrel Farm; 19, Boughton Hill; 20, Adams; 21, Tram; 22, Sackett; 23, Richmond Mills; 24, Hunter's Home; 25, Chamberlin; 26, Maxon-Derby; 27, Kipp Island; 28, Lakeside Park; 29, Howlett Hill; 30, Furnace Brook; 31, Schoff; 32, Onondaga Reservation; 33, Clemson's Island; 34, Roundtop; 35, Castle Creek; 36, Bates; 37, White; 38, Hilltop; 39, Garoga; 40, Waupoos; 41, Roebuck; 42, Crystal Rock; 43, Beckstead; 44, Grays Creek; 45, Salem; 46, Gogo; 47, Berry; 48, Dawson.

After 1400 the Middleport substage evolves directly into the "Late Ontario Iroquois" stage during which time the two cultural and geographical variants—the Huron-Petun to the north and the Neutral-Erie to the south—become identifiable. Because individual communities have not yet been traced in Ontario as they have in New York State, scholars must still talk in terms of units greater than the tribe or nation, units more nearly equatable with the Five Nations confederacy as a whole. The Huron-Petun branch first becomes distinguishable from Neutral-Erie during part of a more general trend toward consolidation of villages. This resulted in a gradual northward shift of some Huron-Petun villages toward Simcoe County (joining an existing population in that area) and the south shore of Nottawasaga Bay. These areas correspond with the historic Huron and Petun countries, respectively. The Neutral-Erie situation seems analogous, with the Neutrals concentrating in the vicinity of the Niagara Peninsula where local series of village removals are being investigated (Ian Kenyon, personal communication 1972) and the Erie in what is now southwestern New York (White 1971).

Another group of Iroquoians occupied several groups of villages on the north shore of the Saint Lawrence and in New York at the eastern end of Lake Ontario. They are known collectively as the Saint Lawrence Iroquoians. Former speculation made these people ancestral to various of the Iroquoian peoples of the Northeast, and a persistent form of this tradition attributed the origin of the Onondaga and/or Oneida to these people; however, later studies both in Canada and in New York have shown this to be patently untrue. Pendergast (1964, 1966, "Saint Lawrence Iroquoians," this vol.) has shown that these people developed in place from a resident Middle Woodland population subject to influences from both New York and Ontario (especially from the Pickering Branch). A series of local and sometimes culturally distinguishable developments seems to have taken place from Middle Woodland times until the early to mid-sixteenth century when the entire sequence was truncated. The reasons are not demonstrable but perhaps include disease, conflict with the Five Nations, or some other decimation related to the coming of the Europeans, whose presence was being increasingly felt in the Saint Lawrence Valley (cf. Trigger 1968a). Occasional traces of their material cultures show up in Onondaga about 1550 but the main destination of refugees seems most likely to have been Huronia.

On the southern extreme of the northern Iroquoian area the cultural development and history of the Susquehannocks remain somewhat unclear. Following earlier migration hypotheses (Cadzow 1936) the currently accepted reconstruction (Witthoft and Kinsey 1959; Kinsey and Graybill 1971:39) argues a late prehistoric arrival of the Susquehannock in the lower Susquehanna River valley (now Lancaster County, Pennsylvania) where they conquered and absorbed a resident Algonquian population. Some sort of north-to-south shift of population down the Susquehanna River is suggested since there is a good developmental sequence near the New York–Pennsylvania border (cf. Lucy 1959). This sequence begins

prior to A.D. 1000 and is apparently truncated sometime in the mid-sixteenth century. To the south the Shenk's Ferry culture parallels at least the later stages of the more northern sequence. Some aspects of Shenk's Ferry culture resemble contemporaneous manifestations farther down the Susquehanna and along the Atlantic coast. Comparable attributes—collared ceramics decorated with incised chevrons, elbow pipes, triangular arrow points, longhouses regularly arranged within a palisaded village (Kinsey and Graybill 1971; Heisey 1971)—indicate prolonged contact with Iroquoians and other people to the northeast. Both combined to give Shenk's Ferry a distinctive cast but probably no more so than the Saint Lawrence Iroquoians. The evidence for a mid-sixteenth-century conquest is not entirely convincing, and a simple population concentration centering in the lower Susquehanna may have taken place some time after the formation of the Iroquois league. Such a shift away from the Five Nations, a mirror image of the shifts of certain elements of the Ontario Iroquoians away from one another, would have resulted in the historic clustering of Susquehannock villages and would account for the persistence of both Susquehannock and Shenk's Ferry attributes into the historic period without having to invoke the earlier conquest hypotheses.

In every case village and tribal movements A.D. 1000–1500 are devoid of drastic population shifts, conquests, and the annihilation of whole prehistoric populations. Regardless of the lack of dramatic conquests these centuries were a time of interesting and important changes in subsistence and in demographic, social and political, religious, and other cultural subsystems.

Subsistence

Middle Woodland (before the Late Woodland cultures discussed herein) tradition subsistence patterns are suggested by a number of important sites. For the most part these stations are located in the Lake Forest zone and subsistence remains indicate intensive hunting, collecting, and fishing in this biome, with an emphasis on the fishing. The largest summer camps seem to have been located along or near waterways with a high fishing potential. The Donaldson site, on the Saugeen River two miles from Lake Huron, produced only a few mammal remains; but fish, notably sturgeon, sucker, drum, and walleyed pike, provided considerable food refuse (Wright and Anderson 1963:42–43). At the Kipp Island site in central New York State, fish (bullheads, channel cat, walleyed pike, northern pike) accounted for an estimated 694 pounds of meat in a total of about 4,000 pounds, which Guilday and Tanner (1965:242) remark "is extremely high and indicate[s] extensive utilization of fish."

Sometime prior to 1000 B.C. horticultural products and their cultivation were introduced into the Northeast from the south or west. Neither the time nor the route of the dispersion of cultigens into the Northeast is as yet clear but there are some educated guesses. Corn, beans, and squash may have entered the Northeast as a complex from the south or west. For instance, at the Roundtop site in southern New York State, dated A.D. 1070, all three products were found in abundance (Ritchie 1969a: xxv–xxvi). These crops were grown in the warmer reaches of the Northeast considerably earlier. Dispersion within and throughout the northern Iroquoian area, where growing seasons vary considerably and are generally shorter than in the south, depends upon the existence or development of varieties that will mature in these less favorable areas.

In the case of corn this appears to equate with Northern Flint corn or closely related Flour or Sweet varieties. All are eight-rowed corns, subsumed under Eastern complex maize, and are distinguishable by a number of criteria from other varieties, notably the 12-to-14-row Chapalote complex corns (Mangelsdorf and Smith 1949; Mangelsdorf, MacNeish, and Galinat 1956; Nickerson 1953:81–83; Yarnell 1964:108–109). These may have originated in the Guatemala highlands, hence were preadapted for entry into the relatively cool and moist Northeast. Regardless of origin, they soon spread as far as Huronia, north of which the average growing season of less than 120 frost-free days seems to have bounded the northern spread of corn agriculture (cf. Yarnell 1964:126ff.).

Beans, on the other hand, and perhaps squash, present a different situation. There is only one variety of beans that diffused to the Northeast from areas having a considerably longer growing season. Changes in appearance between southern and northeastern beans do not approach the magnitude of the differences between, for instance, Chapalote and Eastern complex corns. Therefore, while corn was preadapted or took a "quantum jump" that allowed a rapid spread of corn into the Northeast, the gradual selection of bean varieties (or subvarieties) suitable to cooler climates may have taken a much longer time. Squash and sunflowers may have experienced a similar slow spread throughout Iroquoia.

This hypothesis explains the seemingly anomalous distribution of cultigens in the Northeast, where corn spread rapidly among Iroquoians and other groups. It has been recovered from the Princess Point, Porteous, and Grand Banks sites in southern Ontario, all dated prior to A.D. 900 (Stothers 1971). Beans, on the other hand, while known from New York shortly after A.D. 1000, did not reach Huronia until the "Late Iroquois" stage, some time after 1400 (Wright 1966:98). Squash also seems retarded in its northward spread, perhaps for similar biological reasons. The routes or even times of the spread of horticulture among Iroquoian peoples cannot be precisely outlined. All the major products—corn, beans, squash, sunflowers, and tobacco—were utilized to some extent by all the Iroquoian peoples by the beginning

of the historic period; however, all products were not grown to the same extent by all peoples. The prime example of this is the Iroquoians on the lower Saint Lawrence encountered by Jacques Cartier in the sixteenth century, among whom fishing seems to have been the principal subsistence activity. Moreover, in no area did agriculture completely supplant older subsistence activities. All Iroquoians continued to hunt, fish, and gather wild foods as their Middle Woodland predecessors had done.

The diffusion of agriculture into the Northeast around A.D. 1000 has been interpreted as a "historical accident" based upon the development of strains of crops suitable to the area. Perhaps of equal importance, but the subject of much less investigation, are possible social factors in the spread of agriculture. It has been questioned whether people come to live in permanent villages *because* of the introduction of cultivation; in the case of the Iroquoians it might well be profitable to look for evidence of some commitment to settled life *prior* to the introduction of agriculture. This commitment might have served as a sort of "preadaption" to the type of existence necessary to cultivate vegetable products successfully.

Settlement Patterns and their Social Correlates

During the late Middle Woodland period, roughly A.D. 500, there is evidence for an emerging settlement system that was somewhat more localized than the seasonally mobile bands of the Late Archaic and Early Woodland periods in the Northeast. Initially these seem to have been located at favored fishing stations, although subsistence activities were by no means confined to pescatorial pursuits. At Summer Island in Lake Michigan (Brose 1970a:28–30) and Kipp Island, New York (Ritchie 1965:240–247), both mammal and bird bones, some wild vegetal remains, and storage pits were found. Such relatively permanent settlements, where people may have dwelt continuously during the spring, summer, and early fall months (precisely the growing season) may have been a sort of "preadaption" that facilitated the rapid dispersion of suitable species, initially corn, through the Iroquoian area. Without this commitment to semipermanent settlement such rapid diffusion might not have taken place. There is some evidence for this speculation in the fact that the earliest known horticultural villages in the Iroquoian area are located on land easily accessible to the water and near good fishing stations. Princess Point complex sites in Ontario that have produced good evidence of corn agriculture are located as follows: nine on river flats, four on a stream near a river, three on low peninsulas, two on islands, and two on low hills near a river or stream (Stothers 1971). A similar situation obtains for the Roundtop site in southern New York (Ritchie 1969a:xxiv–xxvi) and for related Clemson's Island sites in both New York and Pennsylvania.

It is significant that the latest site in Stothers's Princess Point sequence "seems to have been a small permanent village located on the summit of a low hill overlooking the Grand River" (Stothers 1971). Moreover, excavations of William Noble (personal communication 1972) have produced evidence of a permanent occupation with incipient longhouse forms clearly foreshadowing later Iroquoian settlements.

A parallel development seems to have taken place in New York State where, during the Hunter's Home phase (a terminal Middle Woodland phase), there are found occupations on low-lying land (for example, the Hunter's Home site) analogous to the early Princess Point stations, and later proto-Owasco sites on high lands far removed from any major waterway (for example, the White site). Radiocarbon dates for this phase are A.D. 905 ± 250 and A.D. 955 ± 250 (Ritchie 1965:257, 269–270), close enough in time to the Roundtop site (A.D. 1070) to suggest that the current absence of evidence of cultigens in the Hunter's Home phase may be an accident of preservation or discovery rather than a reflection of the actual situation.

In both Ontario and New York, villages of this period seem to have consisted of unwalled clusters of round and/or oblong houses, implying some permanence of settlement.

This relocation of villages from river flats or other poorly defended sites to hilltop situations sets the tone for the next 800 years of Iroquoian settlement types. In Ontario both the Pickering and Glen Meyer branches of Wright's "Early Ontario Iroquois" stage are characterized by large villages located "inland on naturally defensible sites [that] appear to have been palisaded" (Wright 1966:22). In the northern Pickering branch there are, in addition, numerous small camp sites usually located at fishing stations, which are lacking in the Glen Meyer area. Wright suggests that this may indicate a greater reliance upon agriculture in that somewhat warmer portion of Ontario.

In New York this same 300-year span (A.D. 1000–1300) encompasses the fluorescence of the Owasco culture's three phases—Carpenter Brook, Canandaigua, and Castle Creek. During this time the shift from riverine villages to permanent towns located on hilltops, or at least away from major waterways, became complete. Ritchie (1965:274) has postulated a Pickering-like set of farming and fishing villages for the earlier half of the Owasco period; but by the Castle Creek phase, villages were situated on defensible knolls or hilltops and some were palisaded, for instance, the Bates site (Ritchie 1965:285) and the Sackett site (Ritchie 1936). The reasons for this retreat to less accessible village locations are unclear, but the suggestion of Wright (1966:22) and others that the well-documented pattern of Iroquoian internecine warfare and blood revenge was already established at this time is probably the most reasonable. However, factors such as local soil distributions may have had a limited effect.

Following the year 1300—during the "Middle Ontario Iroquois" stage or the Oak Hill phase in New York State—this basic pattern of permanent stockaded villages located away from major rivers and lakes, usually in defensible locations, continued into the historic period. At this time the pattern of short (two- to three-mile) village removals and resettlements every 25 to 50 years (and probably more often as villages grew larger) became established, although some significant demographic trends, sometimes resulting in village relocations over some considerable distance, were also becoming apparent.

From excavations in the Onondaga subarea of New York State (Tuck 1969, 1971, 1971c) emerges a model of village fusion and convergence, probably for reasons of defense in an atmosphere of endemic warfare, which can be demonstrated archeologically at this time (palisaded villages, human bone in refuse deposits) and which Iroquois legend also confirms. The reasons for this internecine warfare are unclear and probably will remain so although a possible population increase related to the introduction of a horticultural subsistence base and resulting competition for land, local game supplies, and other resources has been suggested. Factors less directly related to the natural environment are probably more basic to this seemingly disruptive institution. Witthoft's (Witthoft and Kinsey 1959:33) hypothesis that the obsolescence of the male's role as hunter as women became dominant food producers led to an increase in hunting *of* men and an inevitable increase in blood revenge has considerable merit.

It seems that among the Onondaga there was an amalgamation of small villages into large concentrated palisaded towns (presumably internally peaceful), which would both reduce the number of potential enemies and provide some measure of security in numbers. Uren and Middleport substage villages in Ontario are sizable (Wright 1966), and the Oakfield site in western New York State is surrounded by an earth ring that encompasses five acres (White 1961:53). Although numerous small fishing stations are still apparent (Wright 1966:64), it seems probable that a similar situation of amalgamation of small villages may have obtained in Ontario.

At the beginning of the Chance phase in Onondaga there was an unusual village resettlement of some 10 miles, which located a large Iroquois settlement within two miles of a smaller one. This would seem to have been a disastrous move for one, if not both, towns had there not been some mutual nonaggression agreement between the two communities. Surely this movement of two villages close to each other was an outgrowth of earlier observed patterns of actual population amalgamations (Tuck 1971:212ff.). This shift marks the founding of the Onondaga Nation or tribe and in this local-level alliance is the seed of further alliances between nations that ultimately resulted in the Five Nations confederacy. This two-village pattern persisted among the Onondaga from the mid-fifteenth century until nearly 1800 when the present reservation was established. It is interesting that there is mention of Deganawida blotting out the sun as part of the traditional account of the founding of the Iroquois league. A solar eclipse was visible in central New York State in the year 1451.

Such specific evidence is currently lacking from other Iroquois and Huron areas, but the locations of settlements seem to indicate that the trend of village convergence was not peculiar to the Onondaga. The scattered fourteenth-century and earlier settlements in the Seneca, Cayuga, and Mohawk areas became concentrated into two or three major villages and remained so until well into the historic period. There is a similar situation among the Saint Lawrence Iroquoians where small riverine villages moved inland and later (about 1425) became concentrated in clusters of sequentially occupied and contemporaneous large inland villages. Moreover, there is not one but at least two such village clusters in the Saint Lawrence valley and probably several others in Jefferson County, New York, around the eastern end of Lake Ontario.

In the Huron and Petun area, villages are again large (up to 10 acres), clearly the result of fusion and not natural population increase. The villages are much less widely scattered than in earlier times with the historic Huron clustered in Simcoe County and the Petun to the west. Finally there are at least some instances of contemporaneous villages located within a very short distance of one another, far less even than the one to two miles typical of the Five Nations (Noble 1968).

Neutral archeology is only beginning to be investigated with an eye to looking at settlement distributions, but there is beginning to emerge a picture of clusters of contemporaneous palisaded villages relocating from time to time along various water courses or other topographical features (William Noble, personal communication 1972; Ian Kenyon, personal communication 1972).

In western New York White (1961) has developed similar sequences of village movements and population clustering, and the evidence from the Susquehannock area indicates large preplanned villages derived from earlier dispersed settlements during the Shenk's Ferry period (Kinsey and Graybill 1971).

The net effect of these populations was the crystallization of the various historically recognized ethnic units, each centered a respectable (and safe) distance from one another in contrast to an earlier much more homogeneous population distribution. The outstanding social correlate of this entire demographic shift was almost certainly the establishment of a series of tribal alliances that in every case prevented blood revenge from being practiced between allied peoples and in at least three cases—the Hurons, Neutrals, and Five Nations—provided the political means for some internal and external regulation of confederacy affairs.

These were not, of course, the only changes in settlement and social systems that occurred among the Iroquoians between A.D. 500 and 1700. Relations among villages are indicated by the settlement and demographic trends outlined above but there were also important changes within villages.

The traditional Iroquoian dwelling was the multifamily bark longhouse. Its existence can be traced back to a period well before the year 1000 and a pattern of communal living probably still earlier. The confusing patterns of post molds and the plethora of overlapping hearths at the Lamoka Lake site, dated to the third millennium B.C. (Ritchie 1969a:72-73), do not make it clear whether the small rectanguloid houses measuring up to 18 to 12 feet were occupied by a single family or by several families. Somewhat later, and in the Lake Michigan area, may be the prototype for a longhouse in the oval structure with two hearths from the Middle Woodland Summer Island site (Brose 1970a:14-22). That similar developments were taking place in the Iroquoian area is suggested by: the discovery in a Princess Point context of a 36-by-22-feet "incipient longhouse" at the Porteous site dated A.D. 825 (Stothers 1971); both round and ovate houses at the Kipp Island No. 4 site identified with the Kipp Island phase and approximately contemporaneous with Princess Point (Ritchie 1969a:234ff.); "oblong communal houses" at the Hunter's Home phase White site (ibid.:259); and similar ovate houses at the Roundtop site, on the upper Susquehanna, dated A.D. 1070 (ibid.:xxiv-xxvi).

By the twelfth century the multifamily longhouse pattern was clearly established throughout the Iroquoian area. The Miller site, a palisaded Pickering Branch village in Ontario, contained at least six longhouses ranging in length from 45 to 60 feet and with up to five hearths in each, arranged down the center in typical Iroquoian fashion (Kenyon 1968:17-21). The Maxon-Derby site, in central New York, contained similar longhouse outlines although in this case the hearths were not centrally located but were arranged along one wall in a fashion not characteristic of recorded Five Nations dwellings (Ritchie 1969a:281-285). Additional similar structures are known from other northeastern sites but the Sackett site in New York presents an anomalous pattern of small circular houses within a large village surrounded by a ditch and presumably an earth ring and wooden stockade (Ritchie 1936). The reasons for this unusual house plan are not clear but the Maxon-Derby date of A.D. 1100 (Ritchie 1969a:282) may be suspect on the grounds of variation in the production or distribution rates of carbon 14. The more probable age of the later-appearing Maxon-Derby house forms is something like 740 years (Stuiver and Suess 1966:538), which would place them in the thirteenth century and therefore much closer in time to the nearby Chamberlin site (Tuck 1971:23-24) dated at A.D. 1290, where the transition to Iroquois house forms has progressed another step.

Throughout the thirteenth and fourteenth centuries there seems to have been a trend toward increasingly larger houses associated with the increase in village size. The Nodwell site overlooking Lake Huron in Ontario dated at A.D. 1340 (Wright 1971:3) produced evidence of 12 longhouses up to 139 feet in length; at the Furnace Brook and Howlett Hill sites in New York, houses of 210 and 334 feet, respectively, were found (fig. 3); and at the succeeding Chance phase village now called the Schoff site (A.D. 1410) a house almost exactly 400 feet long was revealed (Tuck 1971:59-60, 79, 85, 96-97). The early fifteenth century seems to have seen the apogee of longhouse construction elsewhere besides New York, for a 307-feet longhouse has been discovered at the Moyer site in southern Ontario (Wagner 1972). Similar structures may well be revealed as settlement excavations proceed in other areas.

These large houses are almost certainly equatable with some large social group. The most commonly proposed group is a large, likely matrilocal, extended family, perhaps a whole clan segment. It may be that prior to the formation of tribal groupings village intercommunication was restricted by warfare. This might maintain or even result in a situation where a single extended family would predominate in a single village. Movement of marriage partners between villages was of course necessary, at least to a certain extent, but might have been both relatively limited and restricted primarily to males (as suggested by some studies of ceramic attributes), resulting in the

presumed Iroquoian pattern of matrilocal residence. It is not unlikely, therefore, that the large houses that dominate certain Iroquoian villages represent the dwellings of a "headman" and his kinsmen.

Concurrent with what the evidence from the Onondaga indicates is the consummation of some alliance regulating internecine warfare (ca. A.D. 1400), there seems to be a decrease in the size of the largest houses and an increase in the size and number of smaller houses to form a village of more nearly homogeneous house size. This trend, indicated by Onondaga data and suggested by settlement excavations at other Iroquoian villages, seems to indicate the breakdown of the single large residence groups occupying the large houses at a number of fourteenth-century villages. It may be, of course, that it was simply more convenient to live in a number of small adjacent houses than in a single structure. On the other hand, it may be that there was less emphasis on village endogamy in this atmosphere of relaxed tensions and/or a breakdown of earlier matrilocal residence patterns as persons of both sexes began to travel among confederated villages. Evidence pertaining to the latter possibility is conflicting, it must be pointed out, and it may be that such hypotheses can never be demonstrated. Nevertheless, it seems very likely that some changes in residence patterns were occurring at the time of confederation, as evidenced by the changes in house types and dimensions. Changes in residence patterns may even account for the relatively homogeneous distributions of clans among villages in the historic period.

Iroquois settlement data, then, provide evidence for at least two major trends during the centuries between about A.D. 800 and the first European contact in the 1500s or 1600s. The first, and clearly the better documented, is a population shift from a more or less homogeneous distribution of small fishing villages or farming hamlets to a population distribution centering at first in larger villages and later also in certain geographical areas generally far removed from other centers of population. This shift may be interpreted as evidence for the crystallization of the several confederacies known in historic times from the previous state of autonomous local villages. The second trend, presently only hinted at by the archeological evidence and perhaps not universal among northern Iroquoians, seems to have involved a shift from small villages dominated by a single large house (and by extension a single large social group) to larger villages with a greater number of smaller structures (and, again by extension, a larger number of clans or lineages of roughly similar size).

Other Cultural Institutions

Concomitant with these major cultural changes, which produced the characteristic northern Iroquoian cultural

James A. Tuck.
Fig. 3. Outline of Oak Hill phase longhouses (stakes inserted in post molds) at Howlett Hill site, Onondaga Co., N.Y. Structure at left is 335 feet long.

configuration, there were other, perhaps less significant, changes in other cultural systems.

Ceramics usually comprise over 90 percent of the artifacts recovered from an Iroquoian site. Throughout the area several trends are apparent over the last six or seven centuries before European contact. Prior to A.D. 1000 ceramic vessels seem to have consisted of elongate globular-bodied pots, usually with a cord-roughened surface. Vessel necks were constricted and rims flaring, but the characteristic Late Woodland collared pots had not yet appeared. Cord-wrapped paddle edge impressions and occasional incised lines, punctates (especially in Ontario), or dentate stamping forming a variety of geometric motifs—vertical or oblique lines, herringbone or zigzag patterns, or occasionally crossed lines—decorated vessel lips, rims, and necks (fig. 4) (Stothers 1971; Wright 1966).

Between A.D 1000 and 1300 ceramics underwent gradual evolution, which resulted in globular, round-bottomed vessels. An increasing percentage of vessels display a pronounced collar, often castellated, which seems to have evolved in the Northeast from thickened and/or everted lips of an earlier stage. Decoration is again confined to neck, collar, and lip areas with geometric motifs predominating, executed with linear stamping (especially in Ontario), cord-wrapped paddle impressions, and a variety of minor techniques including incising, which was later to become the predominant decorative technique throughout the northern Iroquoian area. Significantly, too, the horizontal, chevron, and oblique

William C. Noble, McMaster U., Hamilton, Ont.
Fig. 4. Artifacts from Princess Point site: rim fragments from typical pottery vessels, projectile points, and (lower left) pottery fish effigy. Length of right point about 5.8 cm, rest same scale.

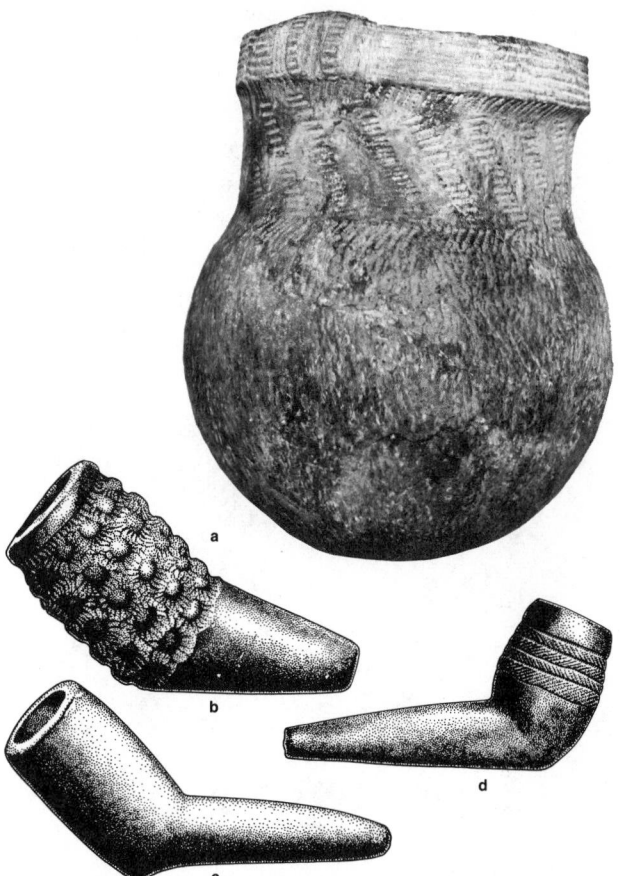

a, Rochester Mus. of Arts and Science; b-d, after Ritchie 1965:pl. 100.
Fig. 5. Owasco phase artifacts. a, Castle Creek Owasco restored pot with cordmarked collar, from Castle Creek site; b, Carpenter Brook Owasco pipe decorated with mammillary bosses, from Hilltop site; c, Canandaigua Owasco pipe, from Lakeside Park site; d, Canandaigua Owasco pipe decorated with pointillé work, from Lakeside Park site. Height of a, about 14.6 cm; rest same scale.

collar motifs so common on later Iroquoian vessels were also well established by the year 1300 (figs. 5-7).

From A.D. 1300 to the demise of Iroquoian ceramics through the introduction of copper and brass kettles, the course of Iroquoian (and much of Northeastern Late Woodland) ceramic evolution followed the patterns set in the preceding centuries. Round-bodied, collared ceramics predominated, but with varying percentages of uncollared, everted lip types in all areas. Decoration was heavily concentrated on the collars although neck and shoulder decoration is often found. Incising is the dominant technique and various combinations of oblique, horizontal, and opposed lines comprise the dominant motifs (figs. 8-12).

Iroquoian smoking pipes have been the subject of numerous studies (Weber 1970). The basis for all Iroquoian smoking pipes seems to have been the Middle Woodland elbow or obtuse angle pipe, which by A.D. 1000 had been developed to the "barrel bowl" form (figs. 5-7). By about 1400 various elaborations had developed, including the "puff sleeve" and vasiform pipes in New York and various conical forms in Ontario. These in turn were

Natl. Mus. of Canada, Ottawa.

Fig. 6. Pickering branch artifacts. a, Rim fragments from typical pottery vessels; b, pottery gaming disk; c, small pottery pipes; d, modified deer toe bone, typical but of unknown use; e, chipped stone scraper; f, stone arrow points. Length of d about 3 cm, rest same scale. See Wright (1972:pl. 16).

Natl. Mus. of Canada, Ottawa.

Fig. 7. Glen Meyer branch artifacts. a, Rim fragments from typical pottery vessels; b, pendant made from a slate pebble; c, bead of native copper; d, woodworking adz of polished stone; e, small pottery pipe; f, stone drill; g, stone arrow points. Length of d about 7.4 cm, rest same scale. See Wright (1972:pl. 15).

supplanted by related trumpet pipe forms with either a round or square flaring bowl, or by "acorn" or ring bowl varieties, and occasionally by elaborately modeled or carved effigy pipes depicting birds, snakes, lizards, and occasionally human faces (figs. 8, 11–12). The last deserve special mention as they seem to have a separate evolution that may date to the Owasco period in New York (Ritchie, Lenig, and Miller 1953) and that may reflect the developing masking complex among the Iroquois.

Iroquoian lithics include a range of more or less equatable triangular projectile points, occasionally corner- or side-notched on early sites but generally progressing from broad, concave-based examples to longer and narrower specimens (figs. 4, 6–12), which were finally copied in brass or copper, as the first European kettles to reach the Iroquoians were quickly broken up into more usable objects. Perhaps of more importance, although far less well documented, are the developments of other "nonmaterial" aspects of Iroquoian culture and their relation to the major social changes discussed above.

The warfare-torture-sacrifice-cannibalism complex seems intimately bound up with the development of Northeastern horticultural peoples. Although its origins are obscure, its presence is well attested to before the fourteenth century; and the fear of reprisals in this never-ending pattern of blood revenge was probably a major factor in the formation of large villages, tribal units, and ultimately the several historic confederacies. It is interesting to note that the formation of alliances to regulate aggression succeeded only in suppressing blood revenge within a league and as a result made even more intensive the raiding among the various confederacies. The blood revenge patterns of a single lineage segment or village of the thirteenth century were transferred to tribal units and finally to allied tribes. For instance, when the Iroquois or Hurons ceased to acquire their victims from among their own respective peoples they were even more likely to conduct long-distance raids on each other or some other neighboring tribe. The demise of the Saint Lawrence Iroquoians in the sixteenth century may be in some way related to their position between the Iroquois and the

Natl. Mus. of Canada, Ottawa.

Fig. 8. Middle Ontario Iroquois phase artifacts. a, Rim fragments from typical pottery vessels; b, pottery pipe of a form introduced from N.Y.; c, pottery pipe in form of a corncob; d, pottery pipe in form of lizard with stripes of black paint across its back; e, bone comb or hair ornament with only one tooth remaining; f, bone awl; g, bone netting needle; h, bone whistle or flute; i, antler tool for flaking stone; j, perforated bear canine, perhaps from a necklace; k, stone arrow points. Length of a about 17.3 cm, rest same scale. See Wright (1972:pl. 17).

James A. Tuck.

Fig. 9. Oak Hill phase artifacts from the Furnace Brook site. a, Bone awl; b, rim fragments from vessels decorated with cord-wrapped paddle impressions; c, small celt or chisel; d, stone arrow points. Length of a about 17.3 cm, rest same scale.

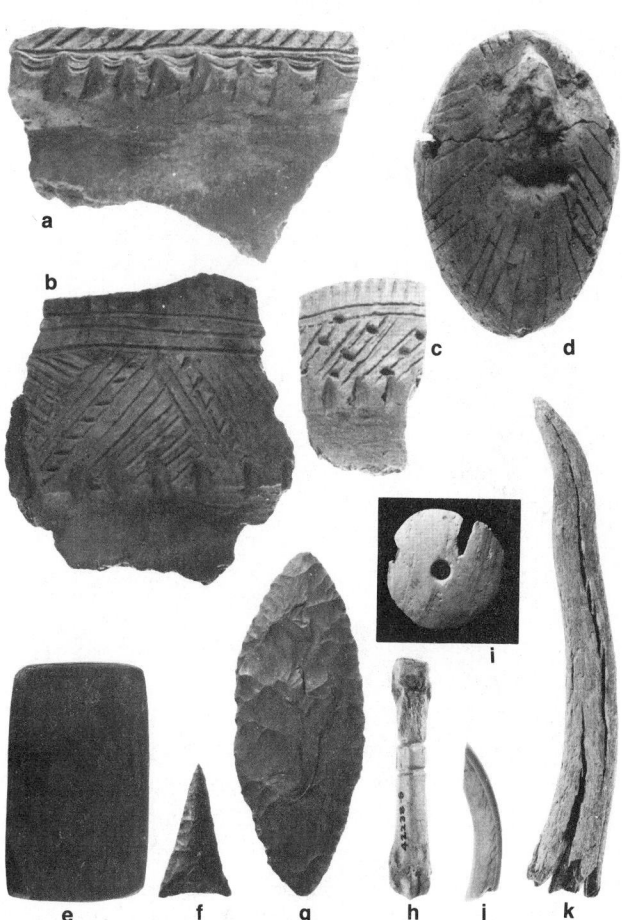

N.Y. State Mus., Albany.

Fig. 10. Artifacts from the Garoga site. a, Rim fragment of Rice Diagonal type vessel; b, rim fragment of Cayadutta Incised vessel; c, rim fragment of punctated variant Cayadutta Incised vessel; d, pottery maskette; e, stone net spacer; f, Madison type arrow point; g, ovate knife; h, bead in process of manufacture on bear metatarsal; i, shell disk bead; j, beaver incisor tool with ground edge; k, antler tine flaking tool. Length of k about 13.6 cm, rest same scale. See Ritchie and Funk (1973:pls. 191–192).

Huron confederacies; and the Five Nations Iroquois's slaughters of the Neutral and Erie, while influenced heavily by White presence, may also have had their roots in prehistoric patterns of intertribal blood revenge. Although there is not adequate evidence, this situation may be reflected in the ceramic and perhaps other artifact traditions that developed in the various confederacy areas. It seems that from the probable time of league formation (perhaps the mid-fifteenth century) until the

Natl. Mus. of Canada, Ottawa.

Fig. 11. Late prehistoric Huron-Petun artifacts. a, Rim fragments from typical pottery vessels; b, stone pipe bowl with hole at base for string to attach bowl to wooden stem; c, pottery pipes; d, stone turtle amulet; e, vessel believed made by a girl learning potting; f, dagger made from human ulna bone; g, antler harpoon head; h, stone and bone arrow points. Length of g about 16.4 cm, rest same scale. See Wright (1972:pl. 21).

European domination of the area ceramics *within* the Huron, Five Nations, and Neutral areas became increasingly more similar to one another while a comparison of ceramics *between* areas shows a concomitant dissimilarity. This suggests that warfare was only one factor in a much larger pattern of increased communication within a political unit and decreased communication among political units.

Whether the seasonal cycle now characteristic of Iroquian ceremonialism is an aboriginal or postcontact phenomenon is uncertain, but evidence seemingly favors a hypothesis of later origins. Nonetheless, many of the elements of the seasonal round were undoubtedly present before the European presence was felt. The mixed farming, collecting, and hunting economy was aboriginal and some of the individual ceremonials or elements thereof may also have been aboriginal.

If the calendrical cycle was not typically Iroquoian, the many shamanistic curing societies clearly were. They were probably the dominant religious form during the precontact Iroquoian period. These societies were many in number and their rise may be intimately associated with village fusions and political unions. They acted as socially integrative institutions by cutting across tradi-

tional kin lines that might have formed barriers to integration in the newly formed communities (Tuck 1971:213).

Burial patterns also underwent considerable change during the centuries following A.D. 1000. In the Five Nations area little is known of mortuary practices between 1000 and 1550 or 1600; the rule seems to have been simple burials, usually single flexed interments, in or near the village area, not infrequently in abandoned cache pits. An exception seems to have been the middle Owasco Sackett site near Canandaigua where at least two large cemeteries have been found suggesting the later Iroquois pattern of burial in family or clan cemeteries. Grave offerings are usually few during these years, consisting of articles once attached to the clothing or occasionally a pipe or ceramic jar.

In the contact and historic periods burials were concentrated in clan cemeteries outside (and often some distance from) villages, and within these there have occasionally been indications of "family plots." Simple flexed disposal burials are replaced by extended inhumations, usually lavishly accompanied by grave offerings—kettles, axes, beads, firearms, smoking pipes, and almost every imaginable object of native and European manu-

332

William C. Noble, McMaster U., Hamilton, Ont.

Fig. 12. Neutral artifacts from the protohistoric (A.D. 1540) Cleveland site. a, Rim fragment with handle; b, rim fragment from Huron Incised type vessel, showing finger painting; c, fragments of pottery pipes; d, stone pipe in form of owl; e, antler thong preparer; f, antler percussion drift; g, worked deer toe bone; h, bone awl; i, antler spoon; j, chert arrow point; k, chert scrapers. Length of i 9 cm, rest same scale.

facture. This change is presently unexplained but may be related to the increased wealth of the Five Nations as a result of commerce with the Europeans.

In Ontario a very different and perhaps socially more significant form of burial characterizes the Huron, Petun, and Neutral. This is the ossuary type of secondary burial, a festival held every decade or so during which the bones of persons who had died since the previous Feast of the Dead were ceremonially interred in a common grave. Indications are of a long history for this practice, dating perhaps to the Middle Woodland period. Moreover, this festival may have integrative functions akin to medicine and curing societies, for village and tribal burial ceremonies would involve members of all kin groups in the participating sociopolitical unit, thereby providing the basis for still another form of peaceful interaction.

Northern Iroquoian cultural development during the Late Woodland period was comparable to the cultural development of many non-Iroquoian-speaking horticulturalists in the warmer portions of the Northeast whose cultural form at the time of European contact included such "typically Iroquoian" features as palisaded villages composed of bark longhouses; a mixed horticultural, hunting, fishing, and collecting economy; warfare, torture, and cannibalism; and even tribal and confederacy organizations. In all cases the pattern was one of progressive population increase and centralization, probably influenced respectively by a stable subsistence base and intergroup warfare, which resulted in population centers that were also political units with varying elaboration of political organization. Other integrative institutions, such as medicine societies, helped to weld these groups of disparate origins into the more or less cohesive units encountered by European explorers in the sixteenth century and later.

Iroquoian Languages

FLOYD G. LOUNSBURY

There are 16 different Iroquoian peoples to whom sufficiently frequent reference is made in historical sources to warrant the assumption that these were, to at least some extent, linguistically as well as politically separate groups. Whether it is legitimate to speak of that many different languages is questionable. In some cases the linguistic differences may have amounted to no more than that between dialects such as are for the most part mutually intelligible; in other cases, the differences are of such a magnitude, and must go back to such an antiquity, that the languages are totally lacking in mutual intelligibility and have only a very distant relationship to one another. Such is the relationship of Cherokee to the other languages of this family.

The Iroquoian groups from which linguistic materials are available are the Saint Lawrence Iroquoians (of the sixteenth century), the Huron and the descendant or closely related Wyandot, the Five Nations (Seneca, Cayuga, Onondaga, Oneida, and Mohawk), the Susquehannock, the Nottoway, the Tuscarora, and the Cherokee. Known to be Iroquoian speakers on the basis of historical testimony but without linguistic documentation are the Neutrals, the Wenro, and the Erie. There is also no direct record of the speech of the Petun, but it may be virtually documented by the materials from the Wyandot, who descended from a group of refugees that appear to have been predominantly Petun in origin. Also, the Jesuits described the speech of the Petun and that of the Attignawantan Huron as being the same (JR 20:43), while indicating greater differences between those of the Huron and the Neutral (JR 21:193). The last two appear to have been quite similar themselves from the fact that their speakers called each other Attiwendaronk (*atiwęⁿdahrǫk*), meaning 'they (who) understand the language'. For the Wenro and the Erie, on the other hand, nothing can be said about their linguistic relationships except that they certainly spoke Northern Iroquoian languages.

The Iroquoian languages share the same underlying patterns of an elaborate verb morphology, of phonemic inventory, and, to varying extents, of underlying word roots, which show them to be related to one another and set them apart from the languages of other families. One must assume that the languages of a family such as this are descended from a single ancestral language. The ancestral language cannot have been the same as any one of the descendant languages, for each of these has had its own history of innovations and development—partly shared and partly unique. It is possible to infer what the ancestral language was like in many of its details by comparing the descendant languages with one another and reconstructing prototypic forms from which the various descendant forms are derivable. It is also possible to make some judgments of the relative degrees of relatedness among the descendant languages as well as rough estimates of the time depths between them.

Subgroupings

The deepest cleavage within the family is that between Cherokee and all the other languages. One can get a rough impression of the magnitude and of the time depth of this cleavage by comparing it, either impressionistically or quantitatively, to the divisions found among the familiar European languages. The differences between Cherokee and the other languages of the Iroquoian family are of a magnitude that is appreciably greater than that of the differences among the various languages of the Germanic family or among the languages of the Romance family. On the other hand, the differences between Cherokee and the rest of Iroquoian do not appear to be of quite so great a magnitude as those among the various major branches of the Indo-European stock, such as between the Romance branch and the Germanic branch, or between Germanic and Slavic. If this rough comparison is translated into one of time, which can be done only by assuming that there is some comparability between rates of development of different languages, it would appear reasonable to suppose that the division between Cherokee and the rest of Iroquoian is of an age somewhat greater than two millennia but somewhat less than five. The lexicostatistic method known as glottochronology predicts a time depth on the order of 3,500 to 4,000 years for the division. While not all linguists are in agreement about the degree of trust that can be placed in this method, the results cited appear to be within reason. There was, then, at a time that may be placed, speculatively, at about 3,500 to 4,000 years ago, a division of this family into a Southern branch, from which Cherokee has descended, and a Northern branch, from which all the other Iroquoian languages have descended.

There is no evidence of further subdivision of the Southern or Cherokee branch of Iroquoian until relatively recent times, with the development of several local dialects of that language. All these local dialects of Cherokee are mutually intelligible; therefore, their differentiation cannot be more than a few hundred years old. However, some of the dialects were already distinct by earliest colonial times. In the mid-twentieth century the major distinction was between Eastern and Western Cherokee, in North Carolina and Oklahoma, respectively. If there were any earlier and deeper linguistic cleavages within Southern Iroquoian, no offshoot other than Cherokee has survived to give witness of it.

The problem of classifying the languages of the Northern branch of the family on the basis of apparent degrees of similarity is complicated by the fact that for some the record is very deficient or even nonexistent, while for others the records that do exist have not yet been adequately studied. Beyond this it is complicated also by the fact that where the data are most abundant and where the nature of the relationships can be seen and understood best, they are not of a sort that permit clear subgroupings. However, there does seem to be at least one supportable subdivision of the Northern branch, possibly a second, and speculatively a third, of antiquity greater than that of the differentiation of the Five Nations languages.

There is evidence—morphological, lexical, and phonological—to support the hypothesis that the second oldest division in the Iroquoian family, or the oldest within the Northern branch, was one that produced Nottoway and Tuscarora as a separate branch. Lexicostatistical and other considerations have yielded estimates on the order of two millennia, or a bit more, for the probable time depth of this linguistic division. Within this branch, Nottoway is the more conservative in phonology, and Tuscarora the more deviant. The Nottoway language survived until the early nineteenth century in southeastern Virginia. The Tuscarora language was still spoken in the 1970s by a few of the Tuscaroras living near Lewiston, New York, and near Ohsweken, Ontario.

Less certain are the remaining intermediate divisions and subgroupings. To the extent that the evidence from Huron and Wyandot has been studied for historical purposes, it is possible to see them (as well as, presumably, the languages of the Petun and the Neutrals) as constituting a subgroup that should be distinguished from that of the Five Nations languages and Susquehannock and may be called Huronian. The time depth to be attributed to this division must be intermediate between that of the Nottoway-Tuscarora offshoot and that of the internal branching within the Five Nations and Susquehannock. Two closely related varieties of Huron-Wyandot were spoken until the nineteenth century at Lorette, Quebec, and until the third quarter of the twentieth century near Miami, Oklahoma.

The Cartier Vocabularies

Most problematic is the position of Laurentian. This is the sparsely documented language of Stadacona, the Iroquoian settlement at the site of the present-day city of Quebec, at the time of Jacques Cartier's visits (see "Saint Lawrence Iroquoians," this vol.). It is documented in the vocabularies, totaling some 200 items, that were appended to the accounts of Cartier's voyages of 1534 and 1535-1536. These were written down in France by someone more lettered than Cartier. The main sources of the information were Indians, of whom there were 10, who were taken back to France on the return voyages. Not all these were natives of Stadacona and some of the vocabulary may record the language of Hochelaga, the site of present-day Montreal.

There has been much controversy concerning the identity of the language of Stadacona (Cuoq 1869: 198-204; Hale 1894:3-4; P.J. Robinson 1948; Hoffman 1959; Barbeau 1961). Lounsbury (1961) recognized in these vocabularies a separate Iroquoian language that he called Laurentian. However, it is apparent that the words in the Cartier vocabularies must have been derived from speakers of more than one Iroquoian language. Some of them show phonetic developments that clearly align them with Onondaga, Cayuga, or Seneca; others could be Mohawk, with a phonetic development shared by the Caughnawaga and Saint Regis dialects; and yet others appear to be of a phonetically conservative or archaic dialect of Huron, closer in crucial respects to that documented by Gabriel Sagard-Théodat for 1623-1624 than to that of Pierre Joseph Marie Chaumonot about 1670 or Pierre Potier, 1745-1751. These three sets of words, Onondaga-like, Mohawk-like, and Huron-like, are mutually exclusive and require the positing of at least three languages as spoken by the persons whom Cartier took to France. If Laurentian or Stadaconan be identified with one of these three languages, then it was but a local dialect of that language, and the other two varieties represented in the vocabularies must have been from visitors, migrants, or captives resident in Stadacona at the time. But there is a residue of items in the vocabularies that do not fit into any of these three categories. It is not yet clear whether these constitute sufficient evidence for positing a fourth language at Stadacona. Thus, the question of whether there was a separate Laurentian language, distinct from the other well-known languages, is not yet answerable.

The Five Nations Languages

The remaining group of languages within the Northern branch is that of the Five Nations and Susquehannock. Within this group, different criteria yield different subgroupings. The only one that can be asserted with confidence is that of an especially close relationship between Mohawk and Oneida. These might be regarded as divergent dialects of a single language, since there is a considerable degree of mutual intelligibility between them. Yet their differences are substantial, and it would not be wrong to treat them, for linguistic as well as political reasons, as separate languages. Politically, the two peoples were clearly separate entities at the time of the formation of the League of the Iroquois; and their separation, and the beginnings of their linguistic differentiation, must have antedated that by a few centuries. The other divisions, between these and Onondaga, Cayuga, and Seneca, appear to be slightly older. Lexicostatistic estimates assign to them probable ages ranging from 1,000 to 1,500 years. But further subgrouping is impractical, at least for the present. Each language has more in common with its next-door neighbor, in the east-west distribution of the languages, than it does with the geographically more distant languages of the group. Susquehannock, which became extinct in the mid-eighteenth century, appears to have had more in common with Onondaga than with the others. But the data are sparse (Campanius 1696; Holm 1834), and the inferences are correspondingly insecure.

The relationships within the Iroquoian linguistic family, insofar as they can be discerned, are diagrammed in figure 1. The diagram has the form of a branching taxonomic tree. Although a diagram of this form cannot adequately portray the complexity of the relationships among the languages of the family, it shows the major divisions and gives an approximate view of the cumulative effects of a very great many linguistic changes in the several languages. It does not show the groups or pairs of languages that have shared different particular innovations or how such innovations have spread from language to language. Nor does it show how incipient divisions were superseded by others that attained greater magnitudes. The linguistic history of the family cannot have been one of a series of simple and permanent bifurcations but must have been one of recurrent separations and fusions. The frequent adoptions of groups of refugees or captives from other tribes, both Iroquoian and non-

Iroquoian, would have contributed to the complexity of the relationships among the languages.

Implications for Original Homeland

In the geographic distribution of the Iroquoian-speaking tribes, the "center of gravity" may be seen as an area comprising much of New York State, central and northwestern Pennsylvania, and perhaps northeastern Ohio. Comparative study of the languages shows that those that have undergone the most severe phonetic changes in their histories, away from the required ancestral prototypes, are in the first instance Cherokee, and after that, the southern and more western members of the family. For example, where cognation of form can be demonstrated between Cherokee and Northern Iroquoian words, it is the Cherokee that can be derived by the application of a series of rules of change from a prototype that is more similar to the Northern forms, rather than vice versa. Similarly, though to a lesser extent, Tuscarora bears this kind of a relationship to the remaining Northern languages; and so also do Seneca and Cayuga to Onondaga, Mohawk, and Oneida. It would be difficult to interpret the linguistic evidence as favoring a hypothesis of a southern or more westerly origin of the Iroquoian linguistic family within the last 4,000 or 5,000 years. More probably it should be seen as favoring a long occupation of the area of central New York State and north-central Pennsylvania, extending back in time for perhaps as much as four millennia, with expansions or migrations first to the south and then to the north and immediate west.

Characteristic Features

An examination of some of the shared features that characterize the Iroquoian family as a whole provides a basis for understanding the nature and extent of the similarities and differences among the individual languages.*

In morphology, the Iroquoian languages are of a polysynthetic, fusional, and incorporating type. That is to say, words may be made up of a great many component parts, whose relative order is strictly determined; these parts are variable in their phonetic forms (adjusting to variable contexts) and are unintelligible and without meaning if taken out of proper context; and verb forms

* The sources of the Iroquoian forms cited in this article are Lounsbury (1939–1973), Barbeau (1915a, 1961), Campanius (1696:157–160, 1938:48–52), Holm (1834:158–159), Chafe (1967, "Comparative Sketch of the Northern Iroquoian Languages," vol. 17), Gallatin (1836:307–367, line 32, 1848:cii–ciii, 115), Goddard (1967b), Hewitt (1889), Hoffman (1961:217–227), G. Michelson (1973), Pilling (1880), Potier (1920, 1920a), Rudes (1976), and personal communications (1977) from Michael K. Foster, Marianne Mithun, and Hanni J. Woodbury. Phonemic transcriptions appear in italic.

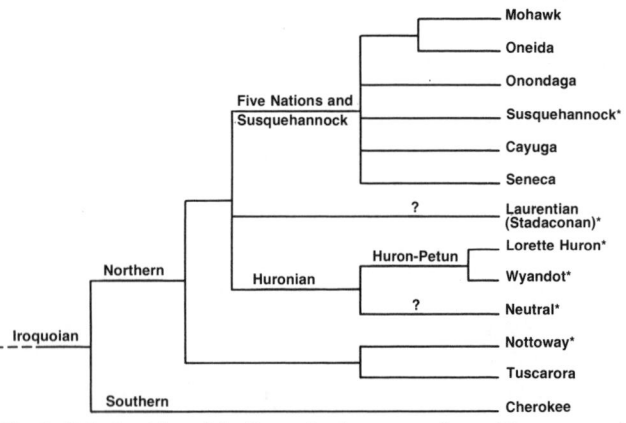

Fig. 1. Relationships of the Iroquoian languages. Starred languages were extinct in 1977.

may incorporate noun roots—as direct objects with transitive verb roots, and as subjects with intransitive verb roots—as well as incorporating subject and object pronominal reference. Some of the component parts are radical (noun roots and verb roots), some are derivational, and some are inflectional. Briefly, the sequential pattern of parts in a verb is as follows: (1) several inflectional elements, and combinations of these, that precede the prefixed pronominal elements; (2) the pronominal elements—subjective, objective, or transitive—inflected for person, number, and gender; (3) reflexive element; (4) incorporated noun root; (5) verb root; (6) various derivational affixes to the verb root; (7) an inflectional suffix for verbal aspect. Of these, a pronominal, a verb root, and an aspect inflection are necessary in all verbs. The other types of elements are present or absent as the meanings or the contexts may require. The verb root, the preceding noun root and reflexive element if either or both are present, and whatever following derivational affixes are present, go together to make the verb stem. The other parts, prefixed and suffixed, constitute the inflection of the stem ("Comparative Sketch of the Northern Iroquoian Languages," vol. 17).

Though the phonetic forms of cognate lexical and inflectional elements have undergone many changes—in some of the branches of the family apparently more so than in others—the phonemic inventories of the languages have remained similar. They are comprised of the following: two oral stop consonants (apico-alveolar and dorso-velar, usually written *t* and *k*), a sibilant (*s*), from three to five resonant continuants (*y, w, r* or *l*, and *n* being the basic set), two laryngeals (spirant *h* and glottal stop ʔ), from five to seven vowels, of which one or two are nasalized, and one or two prosodic or accentual phonemes. Notable are three characteristics of these systems: their small number of unit consonant phonemes, the nondistinctiveness of voicing, and the lack of labials. The smallness in number of consonant phonemes is balanced by their combinability into complex clusters. As for voicing, the stop and resonant consonants may be either voiced or voiceless, not distinctively, but depending on contexts; and the same is true for vowels in two of the languages. (It is thus immaterial whether the stop consonants be represented with the letters *t* and *k*, or with *d* and *g*. The former two have been traditional in Mohawk spelling, as well as in Huron, for over two centuries.) The absence of labials is also characteristic. There are no *b* or *p* sounds; and *m, f,* and *v* are lacking also in most of the languages, with the exceptions being borderline cases. Cherokee has *m* in about a score of nouns, at least some of which have been shown to be borrowings from non-Iroquoian languages. It is probable that all are borrowings. Wyandot had an *m*-sound also, not as a phoneme in its own right, but as a manner of pronouncing *w* adjacent

to a nasalized vowel. Mohawk and Oneida occasionally have an *f*-like sound as the pronunciation of *w* in a few contexts, as between ʔ and *h*. Even *w* is not properly classifiable as a labial in these languages, since the lip musculature is neutral in its articulation, being neither rounded nor spread. The *b* and *p* of words and names borrowed from other languages are usually replaced by *k* or *kw,* and, except in Cherokee, *m* is replaced by *w*. Thus, for example, Peter became *kwíˑter* in Mohawk, and Mary or Marie became *wáˑri.*

Noun Incorporation

Against the background of common characteristics may be set a few examples of differences. In morphology, one of the noteworthy differences between Cherokee and the remainder of the languages is in the employment of noun-root incorporation. In Cherokee it is restricted to noun roots that designate body parts or items of personal clothing, and to a few relic noun roots that serve as noun classifiers: *tsíˑkwaˑʔsteˑhi* 'I cut its head off' (-*kwaˑʔs-* 'head'), *tsiˑníˑteˑhi* 'I cut its tail off' (-*níˑ-* 'tail'), and *teˑtsiˑlíˑsteˑhi* 'I cut its ears off' (-*líˑs-* 'ear(s)'); *toˑtikaláˑʔsuˑleˑs* 'I am going to take my shoes off' (-*ʔsuˑl-* 'shoe(s)') and *toˑtikalayéˑʔsuˑleˑs* 'I am going to take my gloves off' (-*yeˑʔsuˑl-* 'glove(s)'); *tsiʔyeˑha* 'I am carrying it' (-*ʔy-,* classifier for a round object, such as *nəˑya* 'rock', also used as a general classifier); *tsineˑha* 'I am carrying it' (-*n-,* classifier for long rigid object, such as *ata* 'stick of wood'), *tsiʔneˑha* 'I am carrying it' (-*ʔn-,* classifier for flexible object, such as *ahnawa* 'piece of cloth'), and *tsinəˑʔtseˑha* 'I am carrying it' (-*nəˑʔts-* classifier for liquid, such as *ama* 'water'). In the remaining Iroquoian languages noun incorporation is not thus restricted. Most noun roots, as well as derived noun stems, the latter often of considerable length and internal complexity, can be incorporated. In Oneida, for example, the verb root -*yętho-* 'to plant', as in *layéthos* 'he plants', may occur with the incorporated stems of the nouns *oˑnésteʔ* 'corn' and *ohnęnâˑtaʔ* 'potatoes': *lanęstayéthos* 'he plants corn'; *lahnęnaʔtayéthos* 'he plants potatoes'. Similarly *kalǫtóˑtsliʔ* 'box' and *ohǫˑwâˑ* 'boat' are incorporated in *wahaklǫtóˑtslónyęʔ* 'he made a box for me' and *wahakhǫyǫnyęʔ* 'he made a boat for me', with the stem -*ǫnyę-* of *wahakǫ́nyęʔ* 'he made it for me'. An example of the incorporation of a complex noun is in *waʔthatekhwahlakslatokęhtiʔtslataˑsêˑ* 'he went around to the other side of the altar', in which the third through ninth syllables are the noun stem for 'altar', literally meaning 'holy table', the noun for table being itself a complex derivative with four constituent parts meaning 'what is used to place food on'. Rules of syntax, emphasis, and style, as well as lexical conventions, govern the choice between the alternative possibilities of incorporating noun roots into the verbs or expressing them separately in any given sentence.

337

Phonetic Changes

Phonetic changes, as well as morphological changes, have taken place in the several languages, with the consequence that cognate words may appear in varying forms. The differences are slight or great, depending on the number of sound changes that have been involved in the differentiation of any two languages; and this again tends to vary with the time depth of their separation. These sound changes are many. Only a few will be illustrated here. The most convenient approach is to consider what has happened to certain of the Proto-Iroquoian phonemes during the course of development of the different branches of the family. Phonemes of the ancestral Proto-Iroquoian language are marked with prefixed asterisks as is customary in linguistic usage to draw attention to their status as hypothetic constructs of an ancestral language without direct historical documentation.

*n. In the Huronian branch of the Iroquoian family the nasal continuant *n was replaced in most phonetic environments by a prenasalized and fully voiced stop that was written as nd (ⁿd) in the French sources on that language (Sagard-Théodat and Chaumonot in the seventeenth century, Potier in the eighteenth). In some varieties of Huron and in Wyandot this ⁿd became ⁿg before y. Only before a nasalized vowel, and before k, did *n remain a simple n. In Wyandot of later times the change went further, with loss of the prenasalization being general, at least as the prevailing option (Barbeau 1915a, 1960). This resulted in a t/d contrast, unusual for the language family as a whole.

The Nottoway-Tuscarora branch appears to have undergone a similar development but to have taken it one step further, in its loss of the full voicing of the stop. Thus Proto-Iroquoian *n appears simply as t in both Nottoway and Tuscarora, except before a nasalized vowel, where it remains n. In Nottoway, *n and *t appear to have undergone phonemic merger in most environments, both appearing as t, except before nasalized vowels (Rudes 1976). In Tuscarora this merger took place only in a restricted class of phonetic environments, because in the more general class of environments *t had become ʔn.

In the remaining branches of the Iroquoian family, both Southern (Cherokee) and Northern (the Five Nations and Susquehannock) *n remains n, except in *nk clusters and in *nh clusters in Seneca, which lose the *n. In the Cartier vocabularies there are no words that exhibit changes of *n to ⁿd, d, or t. In all instances where pertinent words in these vocabularies can be identified, Proto-Iroquoian *n appears as n. Thus, if any portion of these vocabularies is to be considered as "Huron" (and some items are indeed Huron-like in other respects), then it must represent a Huron dialect that—perhaps because of either its remoteness or its earlier date—had not been affected by the otherwise general change of *n to ⁿd.

The developments of Proto-Iroquoian *n in the Iroquoian languages are seen in the items 'two' and 'four' in table 1 and 'bread', 'tongue', and 'town' in table 2.

*nk. This consonant cluster was preserved as nk in Huron and Wyandot; it was divided by means of an epenthetic vowel e in Mohawk, and by epenthetic i in Oneida, yielding nek and nik in these languages; and it was replaced by the cluster tk in Onondaga, Cayuga, Seneca, Susquehannock, Nottoway, and Tuscarora. In the one pertinent example recorded in the Cartier vocabularies, *nk appears as nek, as in Mohawk. No sure examples have yet been found in Cherokee to show the outcome of *nk in that language, although 'belly' in table 2 is a possible case. The words 'belly', 'blood', 'knee', and 'wampum' (table 2) illustrate the developments of *nk.

*t. In Tuscarora *t was replaced by ʔn in all phonetic environments that permitted this; in some special environments it became ʔ, in others n, and in still others it remained t. This results in a systematic alternation among all four of these, and a single linguistic element (or morpheme) may appear, in different contexts, in four correspondingly different forms. These changes, taken together with the change of *n to t, result in what appears to speakers of other Iroquoian languages as a scrambling of t's and n's. Compare for example the related words for 'Northern Lights': Tuscarora newaʔrǫ̨hyaʔnyerę̨·nyǫ̨·, Oneida tewatlǫhyatyelǫ́nyǫhe ʔ, Onondaga tewatę̨hyátyeȩ̀·nyǫk, Seneca oʔtwátyǫ·yatyȩǫnyǫ·ʔ. Further examples may be seen in the words 'two', 'seven', 'eight', and 'nine' in table 1, and 'bread' and 'town' in table 2.

In all the other languages of the family the original *t remains as t in most phonetic environments and has suffered changes only in quite limited special environments. For example, in Cherokee it has been lost before n and in Seneca it has been replaced by h before n. In some varieties of Huron and in Wyandot it was replaced by k before y, paralleling the change of ⁿd to ⁿg; the same replacement is found in Lower Cayuga, for most speakers (Foster 1974:265–266), and in Saint Regis Mohawk. In Caughnawaga and Oka Mohawk ty and ky have fallen together to ty, pronounced [ʒ], thus leaving the variety spoken at Six Nations as the only surviving Mohawk dialect that keeps ty and ky separate.

*k. In Huron and Wyandot *k became y in most contexts, was lost before w (if in the same morphological element), but remained k before h, after *t, s, or h, or in word-final position; *tk became hk. The exact pronunciation of Huron y is open to question, since it is no longer possible to consult speakers of the language, but Potier (1920:1) described it as a "semi-letter" equivalent to i, and he and other French writers wrote it as a subscript iota. All writers on Wyandot have written it as y. While *k became y in these languages, original *y was lost before vowels though retained after consonants. These

Table 1. Numbers 1-10 in the 12 Attested Iroquoian Languages

	'one'	'two'	'three'	'four'	'five'
St. Lawrence	segada	tigneny	asche	hannacon	ouyscon
Huron	skat	tendi	achienk	ndak	8ich
Wyandot	skat	teⁿdí	(ah)šę́hk	(ę)ⁿdáhk	wiš(·), owiš
Nottoway	unte	dekanee	arsa	hentag	whisk
Tuscarora	ę́·tsi	né·kti·	áhsę	hę̨́ʔtahk	wihsk, wisk
Cherokee	so·kwu·hi, sa·kwu·hi	thá ʔli	tso ʔi	nę̨hki	hihski
Susquehannock	onskat	tíggene	áxe	rajéne (misprint for kajére)	wisck
Seneca	ska·t	tekhni·	sęh	ke·ih	wis
Cayuga	ska·t	tekhní·	ahsę́h, Asę́h	ké·ih	Wis
Onondaga	ská·ta	tékni	áhsę	kayé·i	hwiks
Oneida	ǫskah	tékni	áhsę	kayé	wisk
Mohawk	ę́skah, ę́skat	tékeni	áhsę	kayé·ri	wihsk, wisk

	'six'	'seven'	'eight'	'nine'	'ten'
St. Lawrence	aiaga 'seven'	judaié 'six'	addegué	wadellon	assem
Huron	8ahia	ts8tare	a 'tere	entron	a 'sen
Wyandot	wa·žáʔ	tsətà·reʔ, detsuta·réʔ	aʔtèyreʔ	ę́ʔtrǫ́ʔ	(ah)sęh
Nottoway	oyag	chatag	dekra	deheerunk	washa
Tuscarora	(w)ó·hyaʔk	tsá·ʔnahk	né·khrę̨ʔ	níhrę̨	wáhθhę̨·
Cherokee	su·tali	kahlkwo·ki	tshane·la, tsahne·la	sohne·la	skohi
Susquehannock	jajáck	tzadack	tickerom	wáderom	wásha
Seneca	ye·iʔ	tsa·tak	tekyǫʔ	tyohtǫ·	washę·
Cayuga	hyé·iʔ	tsya·tahk	tekrǫ́ʔ	tYOtǫ́·, kYOtǫ́·	WAshę́·
Onondaga	áhyaʔk	tsyá·tak	té·kę·ʔ	wáʔtę·ʔ	washę́
Oneida	yâ·yaʔk	tsya·ták	téklǫʔ	wâ·tlǫʔ	oye·lî·
Mohawk	yâ·yaʔk	tsyá·tah	shaʔté·kǫ	tyóhtǫ, kyóhtǫ	oyé·riʔ

NOTE: Comparison with the other Northern Iroquoian languages suggests that 'six' and 'seven' were accidentally reversed in the vocabularies of Saint Lawrence Iroquoian, but the word given for 'six' appears to be cognate with Cherokee 'six'. The symbol here transcribed 8 was used by French missionaries to write the equivalent of French *ou*.

changes are among the salient distinguishing features of the Huronian branch of Iroquoian. In the Cartier vocabularies *k was recorded variously with the letters *g*, *c*, and *qu*, and there are no words showing the characteristic Huron change to *y*, not even in those examples that have cognates only in Huron and Wyandot. Thus, if some portion of these vocabularies is to be regarded as Huron, it must represent a remote or an early dialect of the Huronian branch in which this second typical Huron feature had not yet developed.

In the other Northern Iroquoian languages *k remains mostly *k*. The only major exception is in the Caughnawaga and Oka dialects of Mohawk, in which *ky and *ty fell together, both having become *ty* (pronounced [ǯ]). This new segment could be written *tsy*, since earlier *tsy* (from *sy) has become *ts* (pronounced [ǯ]) in these dialects.

In Cherokee, before any vowel or before *w*, *k remained *k*, but in clusters with *n or *l a short epenthetic vowel *i* was added, so *kn and *kl became *kin* and *kil*. Before *h* it was replaced by *ts*, with subsequent

Table 2. Comparative Vocabulary Illustrating Similarities and Differences among Iroquoian Languages

	'belly'	'blood'	'bread'	'knee'	'log, wood'
St. Lawrence	eschehenda [ehšehę́ʔtaʔ]	—	carraconny [karahkǫ́·ni]	agochinegodascon [akohšinekoʔtáhkǫ]	conda [kaǫtaʔ] or [kǫǫtaʔ]
Huron	ˌask8a [yáskwaʔ]	ˌang8eñia, ˌangon	ˌandatara, andatarondi	ochingoda [ohšinkóʔtaʔ]	ondhata
Wyandot	osé·mę́ʔtaʔ or ohšé·mę́ʔtaʔ	yúñgoⁿ, yagóⁿ [yankǫ́, yaⁿgǫ́]	oⁿdáʔtaraʔ	yúciñguta [yohšinkóʔtaʔ]	yarǫ́·taʔ 'trunk'
Nottoway	—	gatkum	gotatera [katáʔtara(ʔ)]	—	—
Tuscarora	ótkweh	ótkwareh	otáʔnareh	awątkwéhθeh	oʔskwéhseh (o·rą́ʔeh 'tree')
Cherokee	u·skwo·li	ki·ka	ka·tu·ʔi	khani·ke·ni	ata
Susquehannock	—	—	canadra	—	—
Seneca	otkwístaʔ	otkwę́hsaʔ	óæhkwaʔ	kosháʔke '(on) my knee'	kæǫtaʔ
Cayuga	okséʔtaʔ	otkwę́hsaʔ	onáʔta(·)ʔ	ǫtshaʔ, áǫtshaʔ	káǫtaʔ
Onondaga	otkwę́ʔtaʔ	otkwę́hsaʔ	ohǽ·hkwaʔ	okíhiʔnaʔ	káętaʔ
Oneida	onikwę̂·taʔ	onikwę́hsaʔ	kanâ·talok	ohsinikô·taʔ	kalǫ·tâ·
Mohawk	onekwę̂·taʔ, ohsyęhǫ́·taʔ	onekwę́hsaʔ	kanaʔtarǫ́·ni	okwítshaʔ (ohsinekô·taʔ 'ankle')	karǫ́·taʔ

	'sky, heaven'	'sun'	'tongue'	'town'	'wampum'
St. Lawrence	quenhya, cainet [kaęhyaʔ] or [-at]	ysnay, isnez [íhneʔ]	osnache [oʔnáhše]	canada [kaná·taʔ]	esnoguy
Huron	ˌaronhia [yarǫ́hyaʔ]	ˌarak8i [yaráhkwi]	ˌandachia [yaʔⁿdáhšaʔ]	ˌandata [yaⁿdá·taʔ]	onnonk8ar8ta
Wyandot	yarǫ́hyaʔ	yaⁿdísraʔ	ę́ʔⁿdáhšaʔ	yaⁿda·taʔ, yaⁿdata·ęʔ	—
Nottoway	quahorwntika	aheeta [ahíhteʔ]	dachsunke [tahsą́ʔke]	—	—
Tuscarora	o·rą́hyeh	híhteʔ	awą́ʔtáhseh	katá·ʔnaʔ, katá·ʔnayą̈ʔ	tsyotí·tshe·θ
Cherokee	kalą·lati	nę·ta	ka·hnkoʔi, ka·nę̈hkoʔi	katu·hę·ʔi	—
Susquehannock	—	—	—	—	ottchoorha [otkóʔrhaʔ]
Seneca	kæǫyaʔ	kǽæhkwa·ʔ	óǽʔnǫhsaʔ	kanǫtayęʔ	otkóʔæʔ
Cayuga	káǫhyaʔ, káǫhyateʔ	káahkwaaʔ	awę́ʔnAsaʔ	kanátaęʔ	otkóʔaʔ
Onondaga	kaęhyaʔ, kaęhyá·teʔ	káæhkwa·ʔ	oʔnáhsaʔ	kaná·taʔ, kaná·tà·yęʔ	otkóʔæʔ
Oneida	kalǫ̂·yaʔ, kalǫhya·tê·	kaláhkwaʔ	oʔnáhsaʔ	kana·tâ·, kana·táyęʔ	onikô·lhaʔ
Mohawk	karǫ̂·yaʔ	karáhkwaʔ	awę́ʔnáhsǫʔ, oʔnáhsǫʔ	kaná·taʔ	onekô·rhaʔ

NOTE: Forms in brackets are phonetic interpretations of early recordings of languages that became extinct before they could be studied by modern linguistic methods; for many of these the details are uncertain.

loss of the *h*, so that **kh* is now represented by *ts*. However, before *hn*, further changes resulted in the transformation of the Proto-Iroquoian cluster **khn* into Cherokee *st*, as in the first-person dual subjective prefix *st(i)-*, from **khni-* (table 3, fourth Cherokee form). The series of steps appears to have been **khn > *tsn > *sn > st*. Before stop consonants, **k* was also replaced by *ts*, with two different further outcomes. One was its reduction to *s*. The other, which took place only at the morphological juncture between pronominal prefix (first-person singular **k-*) and verb stem, was the division of the resulting cluster by epenthetic short *i*. In verb inflection the resulting form, *tsi*, was generalized then to other consonant stems as well. A result of these various changes is one of the striking features of Cherokee morphology, namely the variability in the form of the first-person pronominal morpheme in verb inflections (table 3). It is *k-* before verb stems beginning with vowels, *tsi-* before those beginning with consonants, *ts-* before the plural morpheme, *s-* before the dual morpheme; and in objective forms, reflecting a variation that goes all the way back to Proto-Iroquoian and that has analogs in all the languages of the family, it is *kw-* before vowels and *ki-* before consonants.

Examples of the various outcomes of Proto-Iroquoian **k* may be seen in items 'one', 'two', 'four', and 'eight' in table 1, and 'log', 'sky', 'sun', and 'town' in table 2.

*r. In the languages that still retain this phoneme from Proto-Iroquoian, it appears either as *r* or as *l*. Cherokee has *l*, but there was formerly also a Cherokee *r* dialect. In Northern Iroquoian it appears as *r* in Huron, Wyandot, Mohawk, Susquehannock, Cayuga, Nottoway, and Tuscarora. In Caughnawaga and Saint Regis Mohawk its pronunciation often has both *r* and *l* qualities (phonetically it is in this pronunciation a retroflex lateral flap); it is always written as *r* in Caughnawaga, but for Saint Regis it has also been written as *l* (Bonvillain 1973).

Seneca and Onondaga have lost this phoneme, though not without its having left certain traces of its presence. These involve changes in adjacent vowel phonemes. Cayuga has also lost *r* in most contexts but retains it after *t*, *k*, and *s*. In Cayuga and Seneca it was replaced by *n* before *y*.

In the Cartier vocabularies there are three words written with *l* and three with *r*, but there are 16 that show loss of this phoneme. Since the phonetic contexts of retention and those of loss are not complementary, these examples constitute part of the evidence for regarding the Cartier vocabularies as representing an assemblage of words from more than one language. The words showing loss of *r/l* share this feature with Onondaga, Seneca, and Cayuga. Some of these are similar in other respects to one or another of these languages, but others are in words that have cognates, with *r*, only in Huron and Wyandot, and with *l*, in Cherokee. The developments of **r* are illustrated by the words 'four', 'eight', and 'nine' in table 1, and 'bread', 'log', 'sky', 'sun', and 'wampum' in table 2.

Vocabulary

Analogous vocabulary items in any pair of related languages may be cognate or noncognate; that is, they may have been separately inherited from the same vocabulary item in the ancestral language and may show some degree of inherited similarity to each other, or they may have been derived from different and unrelated items, with semantic changes, or borrowed from other languages, and thus show no such similarity to each other, or at most accidental and unsystematic similarity. Of course, words borrowed between related languages show nonaccidental similarities, but such loanwords are not cognates in the technical sense of the term.

Generally speaking, the greater the time depth between two related languages, the fewer are the cognate items

Table 3. First-person Prefix in Cherokee and Oneida

	Cherokee	Oneida
Subjective prefixes		
before vowel	*ka·ʔi* 'I am walking'	*i·kê·* 'I am walking'
before consonant	*tsikiʔa* 'I am eating it'	*íkkęheʔ* 'I see it'
before plural affix	*o·tsa·ʔi* 'we (plural, exclusive) are walking, they and I are walking'	*yákweʔ* 'we (plural, exclusive) are walking'
before dual affix	*o·sta·ʔi* 'we (dual, exclusive) are walking, he (or she) and I are walking'	*yákneʔ* 'we (dual, exclusive) are walking'
Objective prefixes		
before vowel	*a·kwatu·li·ha* 'I want it'	*waʔǫkwatkáthoʔ* 'she or they saw me'
before consonant	*a·kíkə·ʔi* 'I ate (or have eaten) it'	*waʔǫ́kkęʔ* 'she or they saw me' (synonym of preceding)

NOTE: Underlining indicates the first-person prefix.

that survive with a given meaning. Thus, between Cherokee and any other language of the Iroquoian family, the noncognate items far outnumber the cognate. Examples of noncognate vocabulary, comparing Cherokee with Oneida for purposes of illustration, are Cherokee *yoꞏna* and Oneida *ohkwálí,* both meaning 'bear' (the animal), and Cherokee *seꞏlu* and Oneida *oꞏnę́steʔ,* both meaning 'corn'. Other examples may be found under most headings on tables 1 and 2.

With greater time depth and linguistic distance, cognate vocabulary items not only become fewer but also become more difficult to recognize. This is due, in part, to the accumulation of phonetic changes, and in part to accretions of noncognate elements joined to the cognate ones. The Oneida word *wahâꞏsęhteʔ* and the Cherokee word *koꞏhoꞏhnta,* both meaning 'he dropped it', have cognate verb roots. One would not know this from simple inspection of the two forms, for both of the reasons just mentioned. Both words are causative forms based on verb roots for 'to fall'. ('To drop it' is expressed as 'to cause it to fall'.) The root is *-ę-* in Oneida, *-oꞏ-* in Cherokee. That these are cognate roots is known from the regularity of the *-ę-/-oꞏ-* phonetic correspondence in these languages. That is, there are other pairs showing the same correspondence (e.g., Oneida *-atawę-* and Cherokee *-atawoꞏ-,* verb stems for 'to swim or bathe'; Oneida *-atawęhlat-* and Cherokee *-atawoꞏhilat-,* verb stems for 'to cross over a fence'). Such regularities greatly decrease the probability of chance as the explanation of any particular instance of such a correspondence. They permit the assumption that a particular vowel of the ancestral language regularly became *ę* in Oneida and *oꞏ* in Cherokee. The Oneida and Cherokee roots for 'to fall' thus satisfy the phonological condition for recognition as cognates, even though they are phonetically different. But the fact that the two stems for 'to drop' contain these roots for 'to fall' is not at all obvious from inspection, for both have accretions of other linguistic elements that are not cognate in these two languages. These can be isolated by analysis, based on extensive paradigmatic comparisons, in each of the languages separately, as in the following Cherokee words: *koꞏhoꞏhnta* 'he dropped it', *aꞏnoꞏhoꞏhnta* 'they dropped it', *koꞏhoꞏhntiꞏha* 'he drops, is dropping, it', *aꞏnoꞏhoꞏhntiꞏha* 'they drop, are dropping, it', *aꞏkwoꞏhoꞏhnthanęꞏʔi* 'I have dropped it'. Comparison of these words allows isolation of the constant part, *-oꞏhoꞏhnt-,* as the stem of which these full words are inflections. But these words are appropriate only where it is some rigid object that is being dropped, and where the dropping is intentional rather than accidental. In the case of a flexible object the corresponding words are: *aꞏtoꞏhnta* 'he dropped it', *aꞏnatoꞏhnta* 'they dropped it', *aꞏtoꞏhntiꞏha* 'he drops, is dropping, it', *aꞏnatoꞏhntiꞏha* 'they drop, are dropping, it', *aꞏkwatoꞏhnthanęꞏʔi* 'I have dropped it'. These have a constant part *-atoꞏhnt-* as the stem of verbs for dropping flexible objects, intentionally. Similarly, if it

were an animate object, an analogous process permits isolation of a constant part *-loꞏhnt-* as the stem of verbs for dropping animate objects, intentionally. The three verb stems thus isolated may in turn be compared: *-oꞏhoꞏhnt-* 'to drop it (rigid object, intentionally)', *-atoꞏhnt-* 'to drop it (flexible object, intentionally)', *-loꞏhnt-* 'to drop it (animate object, intentionally)'. These permit the further isolation of variable incorporated-noun object classifiers (*-oꞏh-, -at-,* and *-l-*) and the constant underlying verb stem *-oꞏhnt-.* In agreement with the typical Cherokee pattern the classifiers are specialized for use with this verb stem and differ entirely from those already exemplified with the verb 'to carry'. However, if the dropping is accidental in all of these cases, rather than intentional, the underlying verb stem used is *-oꞏh(i)s-.* Comparison of these two underlying stems, together with knowledge about the behavior of *h* in Cherokee (the stem *-oꞏhnt-* derives from an underlying form *-oꞏnVht-* by loss of the vowel and metathesis of *h*), permits yet a further isolation of the variable causative elements (*-nVht-* and *-his-*) and a constant root for 'fall', *-oꞏ-.* Further sets of words describing various kinds of objects falling verify each of the incorporated classifiers as isolated above and confirm the root for 'fall'.

The Oneida word also can be subjected to comparisons such as are appropriate to the inflectional categories of that language. Consider, for example, the following words: *wahâꞏsęhteʔ* 'he dropped it', *loʔséhtǫ* 'he has dropped it'; *wahathwístęhteʔ* 'he dropped his money', *lothwistéhtǫ* 'he has dropped his money'; *wahayâꞏtęneʔ* 'he fell', *loyaʔtêꞏǫ* 'he has fallen'; *tǫ̂ꞏsęneʔ* 'it fell', *tyoʔsê̌ꞏǫ* 'it has fallen'. Comparison of these forms allows isolation of their various component parts. Among these are a stem for 'drop', which is *-ęht-,* and one for fall, which is *-ęʔ-* (with *-ęꞏ-* and *-ę-* as predictable variants), both of which may be preceded by incorporated noun roots and various prefixes and followed by inflectional suffixes for verbal aspect. Comparison of the two stems thus isolated, *-ęht-* and *-ęʔ-,* allows isolation of a constant root *-ę-* for 'fall', and variable derivational affixes (causative *-ht-* and inchoative *-ʔ-*).

It is clear, then, that even when two languages are already known to be related, extensive analysis may still be required to demonstrate cognation of analogous elements. It can be shown, for example, that the following pairs of words are also cognate, though the resemblance is not obvious before analysis: Cherokee *atsaʔti* and Oneida *kétsyǫʔ* 'fish'; Cherokee *uꞏlahsteꞏni* (from a more explicit *uꞏlaꞏsihteꞏni*) and Oneida *ohsîꞏtaʔ* (from **ohsíʔtaʔ*) 'foot'. Even among the Northern Iroquoian languages, which are generally more similar, the sound changes that have occurred and the differences in derivational and inflectional affixes may sometimes result in cognates being difficult to recognize. Compare, for example, Tuscarora *yerihǝhtyáʔthaʔ* and Oneida *yǫtatlihǫnyęnî̌ꞏthaʔ* 'school' or Tuscarora *néꞏktiꞏ* and Mohawk *tékeni* 'two'. Nevertheless, it is sometimes possible to find related words in which several morphemes in a row are cognate. In the forms in table 4, for example,

Table 4. Cognate Inflected Verb Forms

Cherokee	*tsi·koʔi*	'I see her (or him)'
Tuscarora	*khé·kə̨*	'I see her (or him)'
Oneida	*khe·kę́heʔ*	'I see her (or them)'

there is exact correspondence in the Cherokee, Tuscarora, and Oneida words of the pronominal prefixes (indicating subject and object) and of the following verb stems (reconstructible as *-kę̨*). The pronominal prefixes go back to something like *khe-*, in which *k-* marks the first-person subject and *-he* the object. The development of special masculine forms in Five Nations Iroquoian and of different ways of indicating plural objects in the different languages accounts for why the meaning of the Oneida form is not exactly the same.

Early Iroquoian Contacts with Europeans

BRUCE G. TRIGGER

Late Prehistory

By A.D. 1500, the Iroquoian-speaking peoples of the Northeast had evolved a cultural pattern that contained most of the elements that characterized them in the historic period. Subsistence was based primarily on horticulture and fishing. Extended (presumably matrilocal) families were living in longhouses. Clan segments had joined together in villages that had 1,000 or more inhabitants, and neighboring villages were linked together to form tribes. It is uncertain whether any political entities had developed beyond the tribal level as yet. The Hurons later claimed that the Attignawantan and the Attigneenongnahac had founded the nucleus of their confederacy about A.D. 1400, but the only evidence for this is a vague oral tradition (JR 16:227–229). The age of the Iroquois confederacy is equally uncertain. Individual tribes may have formed alliances earlier, but it does not appear likely that all five tribes were joined together until late in the sixteenth century (Fenton 1961:271). There is also no evidence that, at this time, membership in the Iroquois confederacy involved anything more than an agreement among tribes to suppress blood feuds and to cease raiding one another.

In the late prehistoric period, the Iroquoian-speaking peoples were distributed in a series of tribal clusters, each of which contained several thousand people living in one or more nearby villages. These clusters were separated from one another by extensive tracts of hunting and fishing territory and were spread out over a large area, roughly centered on Lake Ontario (fig. 1a). Between Lake Ontario and the shores of Georgian Bay lived the four Huron tribes and the Petun. West of Lake Ontario and in the Niagara Peninsula were the various Neùtral tribes, while the Erie, Wenro, and possibly other groups lived to the southeast of Lake Erie. Beyond the Niagara River, the five Iroquois tribes stretched across upper New York State as far as the Mohawk River valley. Farther south, along the Susquehanna River were one or more Iroquoian tribes, while the Saint Lawrence lowlands were occupied by still more groups now referred to collectively as the Saint Lawrence Iroquoians. Villages were generally confined to low-lying areas, to be close to fishing grounds and to have over 130 frost-free days for growing corn. Higher inland regions remained uninhabited but were used as hunting territories.

The archeological record indicates that the late prehistoric period remained one of local self-sufficiency. Intertribal warfare was common and long-distance trade was limited in volume and restricted to luxury items, such as native copper and marine shells. The notable exception to this pattern was the Hurons who were living in Simcoe County, Ontario, just south of the Canadian Shield. From the beginnings of horticulture in this area, they appear to have traded corn, tobacco, fishing nets, and other products of southern Ontario for the skins and dried fish and meat that were produced by the hunting and gathering peoples who lived to the north. This symbiotic exchange was beneficial to both groups and probably supported a denser population on both sides of this ecological boundary than would have been possible otherwise (Trigger 1962, 1963). There is some evidence that a similar trade may have gone on between the Iroquoian tribes in the upper Saint Lawrence Valley and the Algonquins and Montagnais who lived north of them (Trigger 1972:80–81).

It is entirely speculative what might have happened had the northern Iroquoian peoples continued to develop solely within an Amerindian context. In fact, this separate development came to an end in the first half of the sixteenth century, when Iroquoians first encountered Europeans. Henceforth, the history and cultural development of the northern Iroquoians were inseparably linked with that of the newcomers.

The Sixteenth Century

The first recorded contact between Europeans and Iroquoians took place in the Baie de Gaspé on July 16, 1534. Earlier that year, the French explorer Jacques Cartier had traded for furs with the already experienced Micmacs in Chaleur Bay, but when sailing north he was forced by inclement weather to take shelter in this smaller bay. Here the French met about 300 men, women, and children who had no furs to trade but who had come down the Saint Lawrence River from their village in the Quebec City area to fish for mackerel. These Indians slept underneath their overturned canoes and wore only breechcloths and a few skins over their shoulders; the men had their heads shaved except for a long tuft on top. They welcomed the French with songs and dances and were eager to get hold of the knives, combs, and other small articles that the French had with

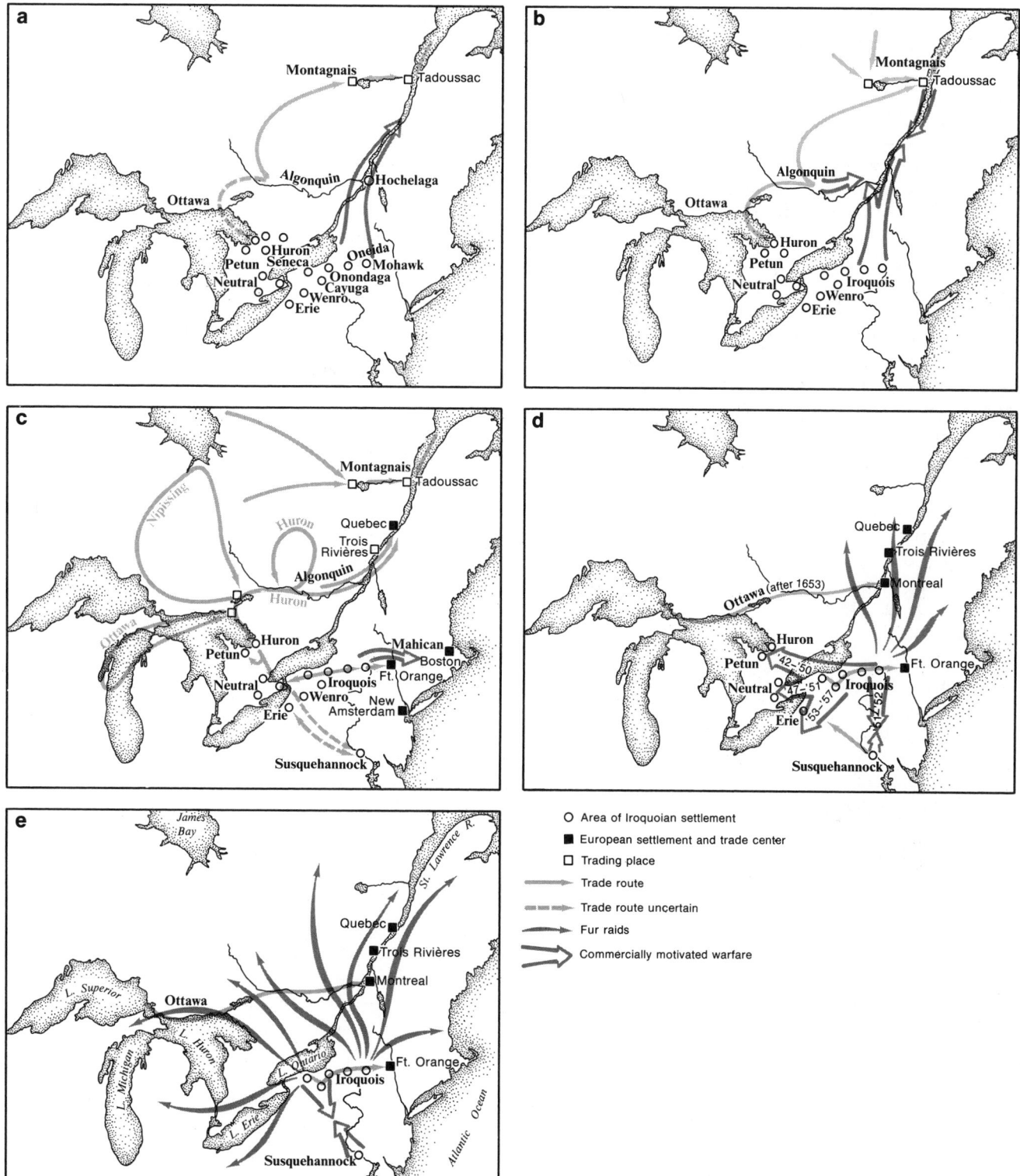

Fig. 1. Area of settlement, warfare, and trade. a, late 16th c.; b, by 1603; c, 1615–1640; d, 1642–1657; e, 1659–1663.

them—so eager, that the French described them as marvelous thieves. True to the traditions of the time, however, the French showed themselves to be the greater thieves by kidnapping the two sons of the leader of this fishing party—Donnacona, the principal headman of the Saint Lawrence Iroquoian village of Stadacona. These boys were taken back to France in the hope that on future voyages they might serve as guides and interpreters (Biggar 1924:60–67).

Cartier returned to France without discovering the mouth of the Saint Lawrence River, but the following year he went back to Canada. Directed by Donnacona's two sons, he sailed up the Saint Lawrence to visit the Iroquoian villages in the vicinity of Quebec and then pushed upriver for a brief visit to the palisaded Iroquoian village of Hochelaga, on Montreal Island. Cartier spent the winter at Quebec, in the course of which accounts of the native copper found around Lake Superior were exaggerated into rumors of a wealthy kingdom called Saguenay, which was supposed to be located in the interior of the continent. In order that King Francis I might hear these stories firsthand, Cartier kidnapped Donnacona and took him and nine other Indians back to France. None of these Indians ever saw the New World again, although Donnacona's interviews with Francis I eventually helped to lead to the establishment of two successive and short-lived colonies a few miles upriver from Quebec City. These lasted only from 1541 to 1542 and 1542 to 1543, under the command of Cartier and Jean-François de La Rocque, sieur de Roberval, respectively. Both were abandoned in part because of the hostility of the Saint Lawrence Iroquoians towards the French on account of their kidnappings and unwarranted intrusion into their territory. For many years the opposition of the Stadaconans seems to have ruled out any further attempts by Europeans to travel upriver from Tadoussac (Trudel 1963-1966, 1:65-175; Morison 1971:339-463).

Far more important in its impact on the Iroquoian-speaking peoples of the Northeast than these early attempts at exploration and colonization was the slow development of the fur trade. Already by 1534, European fishermen were earning extra money by trading for furs with the Indians in the Gulf of Saint Lawrence, and by the middle of the century, Basque whale hunters seem to have penetrated as far up the Saint Lawrence as Tadoussac. In the latter half of the sixteenth century, the demand for beaver pelts increased as beaver hats came into fashion. By 1580 the fur trade on the Saint Lawrence had become the object of commercial speculation and a few shipowners once again began to hazard their way as far up the Saint Lawrence as Lachine (Innis 1956:9-15; Biggar 1901). The principal center of trade remained, however, the port of Tadoussac.

Very little archeological or historical evidence is available concerning what happened in the Saint Lawrence Valley between 1534 and 1603. It is certain, however, that sometime during this period, the Saint Lawrence Iroquoians disappeared and that in the early part of the following century, the Montagnais and Algonquins were attempting to break the power of the Mohawks, who seem to have overrun much of the area, although they had not settled there. Many reconstructions of the history of the intervening period have been attempted, but most of these have been vitiated by what now appear to be erroneous assumptions that the Saint Lawrence Iroquoians were the ancestors of one or more of the tribes of either the Huron or Iroquois confederacies. The majority of these theories maintain that the Saint Lawrence Iroquoians were the victims of Algonquian aggressiveness. At the present time, it appears likely that the Iroquoians in the vicinity of Quebec may have opposed the movement of Europeans upriver not only because they disliked the French but also because they wished to maintain for themselves a middleman position in any trade with tribes who lived farther inland. By 1580 their restrictions may have generated enough hostility to induce the Hochelagans, or some other group, to attack and disperse them, thus reopening the upper Saint Lawrence to European traders (Trigger 1962a, 1972:71-93).

The growing trade at Tadoussac must, however, have given both the northern Algonquian peoples and the remaining Saint Lawrence Iroquoians, whom there is no reason to believe were ill disposed to one another, a great advantage over the Iroquois tribes who lived to the south. None of these inland tribes had any means of securing goods from Europe except from the people who were living in the Saint Lawrence Valley. The valley dwellers, however, seem not to have been on good terms with the Iroquois and were probably unwilling to supply them with iron knives, hatchets, sword blades, or any other items that would have made them more powerful than they were. It is not surprising, therefore, that the Mohawk appear to have started launching raids on the Saint Lawrence Valley in order to obtain trade goods by plundering them from the Saint Lawrence Iroquoians and the Algonquians. It is even possible that they intended to drive these groups from the valley so that they might visit Tadoussac or gain control of this nearest dependable source of trade goods. The Mohawks may have solicited the assistance of the other Iroquois tribes in this endeavor or at least sought to ensure their goodwill. It has been suggested that the need to obtain European goods and to resist the northern tribes at this time may have greatly strengthened, if it did not lead to the formation of, the Iroquois confederacy (Tooker 1964:4). It seems likely that Iroquois attacks led to the dispersal of the Saint Lawrence Iroquoians late in the sixteenth century. Some of the survivors may have been incorporated by the Iroquois, while others are reported to have found refuge among the Huron, Algonquin, Abenaki, and other neighboring peoples, who eventually absorbed them. Iroquois war parties penetrated down the Saint Lawrence as far as Quebec City, and for a time even the Algonquins and Montagnais feared to approach the river in order to fish, as they had done prior to this time.

While the Mohawk invasion of the Saint Lawrence Valley may have netted the tribe considerable booty in the form of European goods, it did not result in their gaining access to Tadoussac. The French traders already knew that far greater quantities of furs could be obtained north of the Saint Lawrence than south of it, and, moreover, that these furs were of superior quality. By 1603 the traders who were carrying on business at Tadoussac under Pierre Chauvin's trading monopoly were authorized to promise their Montagnais trading partners that the king of France would help them in their struggle against the Iroquois. For some time, however, this aid appears to have been limited to supplying them with weapons, which at this period did not include guns. Possibly because of the superior numbers of Iroquois, this limited French intervention did not lead to a Montagnais victory. It did, however, permit the Montagnais to defend Tadoussac and produced a stalemate in the struggle with the Iroquois farther up the Saint Lawrence. This failure to gain access to trading ports compelled the Mohawks to remain dependent on warfare for obtaining their supply of iron tools, which is precisely the situation in which Champlain found them in 1609 (1922-1936, 2:96). In spite of this stalemate, a small amount of European goods appears to have been available as far west as the Seneca country well before the turn of the century (Wray and Schoff 1953).

The Seventeenth Century

The Northern Alliance

At the beginning of the seventeenth century, trade between the Saint Lawrence and the interior followed the same route along which copper from Lake Superior had been reaching the Saint Lawrence in the sixteenth century (see fig. 1b). This route ran up the Saguenay River to Lake Saint John and then by a network of lakes and rivers across northern Quebec to the upper Great Lakes. The Montagnais at Tadoussac were anxious to retain for themselves the very profitable role of middlemen in any trade between the French and the Indians living farther inland (Champlain 1922-1936, 1:121-124). For many decades they did not permit tribes living in the interior to visit Tadoussac, nor did they permit any Frenchman to travel up the Saguenay River. In so doing, they were taking advantage of intertribal etiquette, which made it an offense for one group to travel across the territory of another without permission. The Montagnais of Tadoussac were sufficiently anxious to protect their trading monopoly that, on occasion, they killed Indians who blatantly threatened it.

In order to oppose the Iroquois, however, the Montagnais needed allies, and to win the support of the Algonquins, who lived to the west of them, they appear to have made an exception for them by agreeing that they could come to Tadoussac and trade with the French. Tessouat, a headman of the Kichesipirini Algonquins, was a welcome guest at Tadoussac when the French traders conferred with the Montagnais in 1603 (Champlain 1922-1936, 1:107-109). It therefore seems likely that the alliance of peoples living north of the Saint Lawrence against the Iroquois, which was to play such an important role in the historic period, began to develop about this time. One effect of this alliance seems to

have been to increase the amount of European trade goods that was reaching the interior. Some appears to have begun reaching the Huron by about 1580 but in very small quantities (Noble 1971). A desire for Huron corn probably led the Algonquins to increase their trade with the Hurons as soon as more European goods were available to them.

The impact of the trade goods that were reaching the Huron at this time appears to have greatly exceeded their utilitarian significance; many times in the Indian history of the Northeast, trading in exotic goods has played precisely this role. The desire to be in a favorable location to receive trade goods by way of Lake Nipissing and Georgian Bay appears to have led the Arendaronon, in 1590, and the Tahontaenrat, in about 1610, to join the confederacy and to move into Simcoe County. Hereafter, the four Huron tribes continued to live as close as their horticultural economy would permit to the one source of European trade goods that was known to them. At this time, the Hurons probably also began to supply trade goods, in limited quantities and at high prices, to the other Iroquoian tribes of southwestern Ontario. This trade seems to have stimulated a growing demand for luxury goods from the south, including gourds and marine shells, and may explain the Hurons' contacts with the Susquehannocks, which were of some importance at this time. The possession of trade goods, even in limited amounts, provided a further stimulus for the Seneca and neighboring Iroquois tribes to attack the Huron, thus initiating the first step in the transformation of the largely ritual warfare of prehistoric times into economic warfare. Thus, the initial impact of this trade appears to have been to stimulate more intensive and wide-ranging contacts of both a friendly and hostile nature throughout the region. Both processes helped to break down the isolation of earlier times.

In order to obtain trade goods in larger quantities and at cheaper prices, Hurons soon became interested in establishing their own trading relationship with the French. This action was contrary to the self-interest of the Algonquins, who, like the Montagnais, wished to preserve a role for themselves as middlemen. As Iroquois raiders began to attack the Algonquins more fiercely, in an effort to steal trade goods from them, the Algonquins were compelled to look for military allies; they found these among their Huron trading partners. By 1609 at the latest, Huron warriors were visiting the Saint Lawrence Valley in order to fight with the Algonquins against the Mohawks.

The French traders soon realized the potential that this expanding coalition of northern tribes had for greatly increasing the volume of furs that was reaching them from the interior. They hoped to encourage this development by establishing new trading posts upriver from Tadoussac and by freeing the Saint Lawrence River to become a major artery of trade. In 1608 Samuel de Champlain was commissioned to build a fortified trading post at Quebec, and the following summer he began to intervene directly in the struggle to control the Saint Lawrence by joining the Montagnais and Algonquins in an expedition against the Iroquois. He and two other musketeers (fig. 2) played a major role in the defeat of a Mohawk war party near the southern end of Lake Champlain, and in 1610 he helped his allies to wipe out about 100 Mohawk warriors near the mouth of the Richelieu River. Although the Mohawks quickly learned to drop to the ground when they saw guns about to be fired to avoid being hit, this battle was the last occasion on which the Mohawks were to be active in the Saint Lawrence Valley until 1633. While the Iroquois continued their attacks on the Ottawa Valley, these too came to an end as soon as armed Frenchmen began traveling in that area (Trudel 1963-1966, 2:151-181; Desrosiers 1947:47).

The growing power of the Northern Alliance and Champlain's intervention on behalf of his trading partners had been making the Mohawks' attacks on the Saint Lawrence Valley increasingly dangerous and costly for them. Yet, it is doubtful that the Mohawks would have been able to risk abandoning even such costly warfare had another source of trade goods not become available to them. Soon after 1609, when Henry Hudson sailed up the Hudson River under the flag of the Dutch East India Company, the fur trade began to develop in the Hudson valley as well as along the Saint Lawrence. This development made a new, and far safer, source of trade goods available to the Mohawks, who were soon crossing Mahican territory to trade with the Dutch at Fort Nassau. Very little is known about relations between the Mohawks and Mahicans prior to 1624, and what is known seems to be contradictory; nevertheless, there is no evidence that the Mohawks were unable to travel through Mahican territory to trade with the Dutch. Dutch traders visited both peoples, and around 1615 some of them appear to have helped the Mohawks to fight the Susquehannocks. Unlike Champlain, these Dutch were captured by the enemy and had to be ransomed by their compatriots (Trigger 1971).

Throughout this early period, the Dutch were anxious to establish good relations with the Algonquins and the Montagnais, in the hope that their rich fur catches might be diverted from the French trading centers to their own. The Dutch had strong hopes of succeeding in this venture, since they controlled the sources of wampum in the vicinity of Long Island and thus were able to offer the Indians this highly valued commodity as well as Eu-

British Mus.: Champlain 1613:pl. between pp. 232-233.

Fig. 2. Imaginative engraving depicting encounter of Champlain and the Mohawk, July 29, 1609. The hammocks and palm trees prove that this was not drawn by an eyewitness, but rather by a cartographic illustrator who was familiar with South American Indians.

ropean trade goods. The Mohawks knew that they had less to offer the Dutch than did their northern rivals and feared that once again they might find that their enemies were preventing them from trading with Europeans. The Mohawks therefore decided to forestall such a move by seizing control of the area around the Dutch trading post, which was then called Fort Orange. Their struggle with the Mahicans lasted four years but finally resulted in a Mohawk victory. The local Mahicans fled eastward to the Connecticut River valley, giving the Mohawks effective control of the path to Fort Orange. Because of their own military weakness, the Dutch, who at one stage in the war had aided the Mahicans, now had no alternative but to comply with the Mohawks' wishes. This was a crippling blow to Dutch trading ambitions, because it became the Mohawks' policy never to permit the Algonquins, Montagnais, or any other northern people to trade with the Dutch, except with themselves as intermediaries. This arrangement was in the long run in the interests of both the Mohawks and the French (Trigger 1971:278–282).

The French-Huron Alliance

The first Hurons known to have contacted the French were the Arendaronon warriors who accompanied Champlain's expedition against the Mohawks in 1609. The leader of this group was a headman named Ochasteguin. He was traveling with Iroquet, an Algonquin headman who seems to have been in the habit of wintering near the Arendaronon village of Cahiague. Two years later, the council chiefs of the Huron confederacy secretly sent a valuable present to Champlain and stated that they wished to conclude an alliance with the French that was independent of the Huron trading alliance with the Algonquins. Their envoys promised to help Champlain to visit their country in the near future so that he could ratify such a treaty. Champlain was prevented, however, from visiting the Hurons for several years mainly because of the objections of the Algonquins, who were anxious to remain middlemen in any trade between these two groups. In 1615 Champlain was enabled to reach the Huron country by promising to help the Hurons and Algonquins in a joint raid they were planning against one of the central tribes of the Iroquois confederacy (fig. 3). Although this campaign turned out to be merely a traditional skirmish (viewed by Champlain as a total failure), it provided him with an opportunity to meet the Huron headmen and conclude an alliance with them (Trigger 1971a:87–93). According to the terms of this alliance, Atironta, the principal headman of the Arendaronon, was recognized as a special friend and ally of the French; but, in return, he agreed to share his right to trade with the French with the headmen of other tribes and clan segments of the Huron confederacy (JR 20:19). The resulting distribution of authority to control this trade seems to have reinforced, rather than altered,

the traditional political and social organization of the Huron. Moreover, while the Arendaronon were honored for being the first members of the confederacy to develop a trading relationship with the French, the effective control of this trade seems soon to have fallen into the hands of the Attignawantan, who dominated the confederacy in many other ways. While the Algonquins were too few in number and too dependent on the Hurons for corn and military assistance to prevent them from trading with the French, certain groups, particularly the Kichesipirini, continued to collect what amounted to tolls for allowing them to pass through their tribal territory. The Hurons sometimes objected to the amount of these tolls, but at no time did they deny the Algonquins' right to them.

From 1615 to 1629 the Iroquois remained under control and the Hurons were able to trade with the French in relative peace and security (see fig. 1c). Each year, groups of Huron traders traveled by way of Lake Nipissing and the Ottawa River to the Saint Lawrence. There, they met the French traders, either at the mouth of the Richelieu or Saint Maurice rivers or at Quebec. Once trade was established on a regular basis, they appear to have supplied the French with about 10,000 to 12,000 skins each year. A large number of these were obtained by exchanging corn, tobacco, nets, and European goods with the Nipissings, who traveled as far north as Hudson Bay each year, and with the Ottawas, who traded westward into the Lake Michigan area. Huron traders visited the interior of Quebec and penetrated some of the areas visited by the Nipissings and Ottawas. They also traded corn for furs with the Algonquins in the Ottawa Valley. By preventing either the Petuns or the Neutrals from concluding trading alliances with the French, the Hurons and Ottawas were able to secure a position as middlemen in trade with the French, while the Hurons and the Senecas must have shared a similar role in relationship to the Neutral. The origin of the famous aloofness from war of the Neutral Confederacy may, in fact, have resulted from the dual nature of their trade with these rival Iroquoian confederacies. While both the Neutrals and the Petuns supplied the Huron with tobacco and other luxury goods from the south in return for European produce, it would appear that no small part of their purchases was paid for with beaver skins.

The expanding trade of the Hurons must have required extra effort to produce the corn needed to supply their customers. Some time was saved in clearing the forests by the use of iron axes, although the utility of the axes that were supplied at this time may be somewhat exaggerated. In any case, the fur trade brought much additional wealth into Huron society. Instead of breaking down the traditional redistributive system, this new wealth enhanced it. Old ceremonies, such as the Feast of the Dead, grew increasingly elaborate, as more wealth was consumed as offerings or given away to validate the

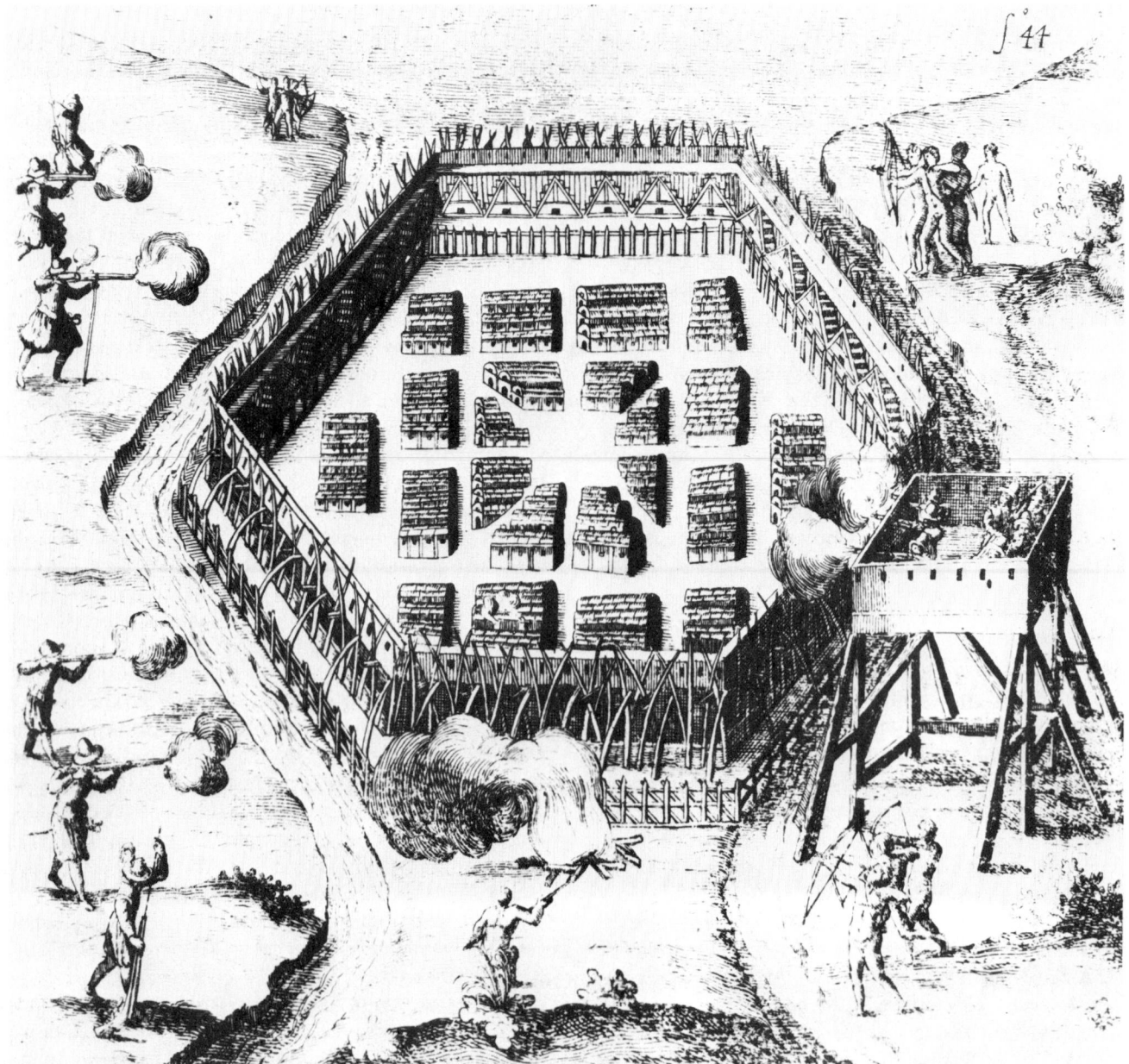

Lib. of Congress: Champlain 1619:opp. fol. 44[r].
Fig. 3. Imaginative engraving portraying the siege of an Iroquois village by Champlain and his Huron and Algonquin allies in 1615.

status of the participants. While such activities may have enhanced the prestige of the Huron headmen and emphasized existing differences in Huron society, there is no evidence that these changes were undermining traditional Huron social organization, let alone leading to any sort of social crisis. In particular, there is no basis for recent claims (W.M. Smith 1970) that the matrilineal organization of Huron society was being undermined by these changes.

Because of the remoteness of the Hurons from areas of European settlement, the number of Europeans who visited their country was small. Most of them were men who were employed by the trading company to live among the Hurons and encourage them to bring their

furs to the Saint Lawrence each year. The best known of these was the interpreter Étienne Brûlé. He appears to have been sent to the Huron country in 1610 and was absent only for short periods between then and 1633, when he was murdered by some Hurons who suspected him of having secret dealings with the Senecas (Trigger 1971:282–283). Many of these early *coureurs de bois* learned to speak Huron and adapted themselves to the Huron way of life. Prior to 1629 a few Roman Catholic missionaries, most of whom were members of the Recollect order, also visited the Huron. They made an effort to record the Huron language, but their insistence that an Indian could be converted only if he agreed to leave his people and live as a Frenchman at Quebec led to their mission work's having no practical results. A Recollect named Joseph de la Roche Daillon infuriated the Hurons when they learned that in the course of a visit to the Neutrals he had attempted to undermine the Hurons' monopoly by concluding a trading alliance between Neutrals and the French. The Recollects did, however, persuade a Huron trader named Soranhes to allow his son Amantacha to travel to France, where he remained for two years and was trained by the Jesuits to speak, read, and write French. After his return to the Huron country in 1629, Amantacha played an important role as an intermediary between his own people and the French. Another young Huron, Savignon, had visited France in 1610, but aside from the stories he was able to tell about his adventures, his trip seems to have made little impact on him (Trigger 1960:24-28, 1968:115-123).

Quebec was occupied by a group of English traders from 1629 until 1633, when it was restored to the French. The Society of Jesus exercised great influence over the trading company that now controlled New France, and the Jesuit fathers were able to ensure themselves a monopoly of mission work in the colony. They also made certain that they would encounter no opposition to their plans for mission work among the Huron, by having the traders who had formerly lived among the Indians withdrawn. In return, they promised that the duties of these men would henceforth be discharged, wherever possible, by laymen who were employed by themselves and hence subject to their own discipline and control. The opposition of the Algonquins to the return of any Frenchmen to the Huron country had to be overcome before it was possible for the Jesuits to begin a new mission there in 1634.

The Jesuits, unlike the Recollects, attempted from the beginning to devise strategies for converting whole communities and eventually the entire confederacy. The Jesuits also saw no advantage in attempting to assimilate the Huron; on the contrary, they feared that contact with any or all Frenchmen other than themselves might help to corrupt their converts. They therefore did not wish to alter Huron culture more than was necessary to ensure that their converts' behavior conformed to the rules of the church. The period 1634 to 1640 was largely one of experimentation for the Jesuits. During this time, life was made difficult for them by a series of epidemics which led the Hurons to accuse them of practicing sorcery. After 1640 the Jesuits established a fortified, agriculturally self-sufficient mission center on the banks of the Wye River. Pigs, calves, and even a cannon were imported from Quebec to equip this establishment, which soon became a sizable, all-male, European settlement in the heart of the Huron country (Jury and Jury 1954).

After 1640 the Jesuits succeeded in converting over 100 Hurons every year, and by 1646 there were about 500 practicing Huron Christians. To accomplish this, the Jesuits used a variety of different approaches. They consciously strove to impress the Hurons with their technological superiority and greater knowledge, including the ability to predict eclipses. The Hurons, it was hoped, would interpret this prescience as evidence of their supernatural power. They also offered material assistance to those who lacked kinsmen, or suffered from other misfortunes, in the hope that succor would win their affection. Although a small number of Hurons became Christians in the hope of acquiring the Jesuits' shamanistic power, relatively few appear to have been converted by these techniques alone. On the other hand, many men decided to convert for other highly practical reasons. Christians were treated better than were non-Christians when they traded with the French, and they were also paid higher prices for their furs. Moreover, after 1641, when muskets were sold to the Hurons for the first time, they could be obtained only by reliable converts. These regulations led to the baptism of many traders and warriors. Because the Huron already believed that those who died in different ways went to different places after death, it was easy for them to accept the claim that Christians went to the separate heaven that the Jesuits spoke about. While a desire to live with non-Christian relatives after death inhibited many conversions, once a man or woman became a Christian, many friends and relatives would ask to be baptized so that they would not be separated from them after death. This eventually led to a rapid increase in the number of converts, particularly in the large villages of Ossossane and Teanostaiae.

The Jesuits insisted that converts could not attend any function where traditional rituals were practiced, which made it impossible for them to participate in most of the public activities in their villages. So strong did this feeling of Christian separateness become that warriors who were Christians and non-Christians often refused to go to war together, even though both were fighting a common enemy. By the winter of 1648-1649, the Christians were in a majority in the single village of Ossossane. While the Christians in this village had been free to behave as they wished when they had been in a minority, the Jesuits now directed them to forbid non-Christians the right to practice their traditional religion if they wished to remain in the village. Even before this happened, a growing number of Hurons had begun to fear that their culture was being undermined by the spread of Christianity. There was also a tendency to blame the military weakness of the Hurons, and all their other misfortunes, on the abandonment by the Christians of the ways of their forefathers. The result of these strains was the development of a traditionalist faction, which opposed the spread of Christianity and whose more radical supporters argued that the Jesuits should be expelled from the country and, along with them, all Indians who refused to renounce their teachings. Some Hurons were sufficiently angry that they were prepared to break their 33-year-old trading alliance with the French. As an alternative, they proposed to make peace with the Iroquois and to trade their furs with them. These people found enough support to begin negotiating a peace treaty with the Onondaga; but when a group of headmen precipitated a crisis by killing one of the lay assistants of the Jesuits and then demanding that the Jesuits and their converts be expelled from the country, they found themselves outnumbered by an alliance of Christians and traditionalists who were afraid to make peace with the Iroquois. This event marked the triumph of Jesuit policy in the Huron country and indicates that, under different circumstances, the Jesuits might have succeeded in making the Huron confederacy at least nominally Christian. What was more serious, however, was that the Jesuits had created new factions among the Hurons that involved various feelings for and against the French and for and against Christianity. These factions were the more dangerous because some of them corresponded, roughly, with tribal divisions. For example, it seems to be no accident that the Attignawantans, who were the tribe that was best disposed toward Christianity, were also the most hostile to the Iroquois, while the Arendaronons, who were the least disposed to accept Christianity, were also the most disposed toward making peace with the Iroquois. The growing division and uncertainty among the Hurons was a very dangerous development at a time when the Huron confederacy was fighting for its survival (Trigger 1960:28–43, 1968:133–141; on factions see also Fenton 1955).

Epidemics

The Iroquoian-speaking peoples were no more immune to a wide variety of European diseases than were other North American Indians. Fenton (1940:175) has reasonably suggested that epidemics in the sixteenth century may have played a role in the dispersal of the Saint Lawrence Iroquoians, although there are no clear references to such epidemics in the Iroquoian area prior to 1634–1635, when Harmen van den Bogaert reported that many Mohawks had died of smallpox (Jameson 1909:140). The best-recorded epidemics are those which took place among the Hurons between 1635 and 1640. These were a series of maladies, culminating in a violent outbreak of smallpox over the winter of 1639–1640. As a result of these epidemics, the population of the Huron confederacy was reduced from about 20,000 to 10,000 people. During the same period the Petun, Wenro, and Neutral were also stricken; and in the winter of 1640–1641, a severe ailment—probably smallpox—was reported to be raging among the Senecas.

In 1646 and 1647 the Iroquois were again visited by contagious diseases, although these maladies did not reach the Hurons. The Iroquois continued to be afflicted by epidemics after 1650, the worst of which was an outbreak of smallpox that killed over 1,000 people in 1662, after decimating the Susquehannock the year before (Jennings 1968:18). These epidemics were particularly fatal to children and elderly people. Since political skill, as well as ritual information, tended to be a prerogative of older men, the Iroquoians must have found themselves deprived of much of their most experienced leadership at a time when such leadership was much needed. The ratio of population to political offices also declined, altering the meaning of these offices and making their validation in terms of clan productivity far more difficult. The Iroquois, in particular, attempted to maintain their fighting strength by incorporating prisoners of war into their tribal structure on an unprecedented scale. Yet, in spite of their evident success in naturalizing these prisoners, the combined effects of disease and spiraling warfare were such that the Iroquois failed to maintain the population of their confederacy much above half of its estimated level prior to European contact.

The Iroquois Wars

Throughout the first half of the seventeenth century, all the Iroquoian-speaking peoples of the Northeast grew increasingly dependent on European trade goods. The Mohawks and the Susquehannocks were probably in the vanguard of this development, which is not surprising since they lived closer than any of the other tribes to European trading posts. However, by the late 1630s even the Hurons were sufficiently dependent on the fur trade that they believed they would be ruined if two years should elapse without their traders visiting the Saint Lawrence. The growing demand for beaver skins soon began to exert pressure on the beaver population in the more thickly inhabited areas south of the Canadian Shield. It appears, for example, that the Huron had killed off the beaver in their own hunting territories by 1630 (Sagard-Théodat 1866:585), although this matter was of relatively little concern to them since they were more than able to make up for it by expanding their trade with the north. Even after 1640, a much reduced Huron population was able to sell as many furs to the French as the Hurons had done previously. George T. Hunt (1940:33–35) has argued that a sudden decline in the number of beaver pelts reaching Fort Orange in 1640 is evidence for the exhaustion of beaver in the Iroquois country. The evidence he cites, however, makes it far more likely that Iroquois furs were being diverted that year by traders from New England who had captured the Mohawk market by offering to sell them guns. French sources a few decades later speak of the exhaustion of beaver among the Iroquois, but Allen W. Trelease (1960:120) does not agree that this evidence is sufficient to prove Hunt's contention.

It is, nevertheless, clear that this was a period of growing militancy among the Iroquois (see fig. 1d). In the 1630s the Mohawks began once again to raid the Algonquins in the Ottawa Valley. In 1633 they even attempted unsuccessfully to ambush a party of Frenchmen on the upper Saint Lawrence. By the early 1640s Mohawks and Oneidas were attacking the French and raiding their Algonquin and Montagnais allies throughout the Saint Lawrence Valley. Soon they were also attacking the Abenaki and were joining with the other tribes of the Iroquois confederacy, in an unprecedented manner, to attack and destroy Huron villages. After 1650 the area that was being raided by the Iroquois increased dramatically in size (see fig. 1e). In the east, the Iroquois attacked the Mahicans, Sokokis, Abenaki, and even the Maliseets, while in Quebec they raided as far east as Tadoussac and northward beyond Lake Mistassini. At the same time, war parties were penetrating into the upper Great Lakes area and southwestward into the Ohio Valley. C.H. McIlwain (in Wraxall 1915:xlii–xlv) has argued that the aim of the Iroquois in these wars was to coerce the major entrepreneurial tribes, first the Huron and then the Ottawa, into trading with them rather than with the French. The idea that the Iroquois, and in particular the Mohawks, wished to become middlemen between these tribes and the Dutch has been adopted by many historians and serves as the central theme of Hunt (1940). Hunt interprets the raids that were carried out against the Algonquins and Montagnais as an effort to disrupt the fur trade in the Saint Lawrence Valley. He also views the peace that was arranged in 1645 between the Mohawks and the French as a "commercial treaty," which the Mohawks wrongly hoped would oblige the Hurons and Algonquins to sell them some of the furs that they had previously traded with the French (Hunt 1940:77–82). Hunt's arguments are, however, based entirely on circumstantial evidence; and as Trelease (1960:120) has shown, they do not explain adequately what was happening. Nor do they explain Pierre Boucher's (1664) blunt, and apparently accurate, observation that the Iroquois at this time had no ability as traders (Fenton 1971:142).

There are numerous references in contemporary accounts to the Iroquois's robbing other Indians of beaver skins or European trade goods. Algonquin or Huron convoys were attacked with equal enthusiasm whether they were going to, or coming from, the French trading posts; in the winters, the Mohawk warriors roamed the northern forests in search of Algonquian hunting bands in order to despoil them of the furs they had collected. Conquered villages were likewise carefully plundered before they were put to the torch. There is also evidence that the Iroquois hunted in enemy territory at the same time they were raiding it and that territory that was abandoned by tribes who could no longer resist the Iroquois was annexed by them as hunting grounds. If left alone, a beaver population recovers quickly; hence it is not surprising that not long after it was abandoned by its native inhabitants, southern Ontario had become the main "beaver ground" for the Iroquois confederacy (NYCD 4:908). In 1669 Father Fremin reported that half the Iroquois young men spent the winter waging war, while the other half went out in bands to hunt beaver (JR 54:117).

There is, in fact, no convincing evidence that prior to 1673 the Iroquois were interested in exploiting their central location in relationship to other tribes in order to play the role of middlemen. In 1667 the Iroquois had been forced by a series of defeats to conclude a general peace with the French and their allies. Afterward, they took advantage of this peace to send gifts to the Indians at Sault Sainte Marie and cautiously began to cultivate a trading relationship with them. This, however, was a new departure. It is significant that when, in 1647, the Hurons in a last desperate effort to save themselves seem to have offered to trade with the Onondaga and the other Iroquois tribes, their offer was violently rejected by the Mohawks and the Senecas. It was, moreover, received with favor by the Onondagas mainly because that tribe was jealous of the growing power of the Mohawks, which threatened their own role as the leading tribe in the confederacy. Hunt (1940:90) attributes the Mohawks' reaction to their lack of faith in Huron promises, but this seems to be a weak explanation for turning down an offer that promised everything that Hunt claims they wanted. Hunt's theory also does not explain why, once the Iroquois had acquired hegemony over the Huron, they did not have them remain as traders in their own country, or at least consider having some of their own people settle in Ontario where they could have taken over the Hurons' role as traders. Hunt also cannot explain why, the same year that they defeated the Hurons, the Iroquois carried war and destruction to the Nipissings and all of the other Algonquian-speaking tribes around the shores of Georgian Bay—those with whom they might have been expected to seek trading alliances.

The answer seems to be that the Iroquois, being surrounded by tribes that had horticultural economies like their own and with whom they were competing for resources, had become experienced warriors but never had an opportunity to cultivate the entrepreneurial skills that were such an important aspect of Huron culture. Already in the sixteenth century, the Mohawks had been compelled to wage war to obtain European goods; hence, as their need for these goods increased, they tended to rely on ways of getting them that were familiar to them. It was only when these methods ceased to be profitable that the Iroquois painfully began to explore alternative ways.

Given the nature of the wars that were being waged by the Iroquois against neighboring tribes after 1640, it is reasonable to attribute their origin to a scarcity of furs among the Iroquois. What is not clear, and perhaps not particularly important, is whether these wars began because beaver had become exhausted in the Iroquois's own territory or because their desire for trade goods had grown to the point where not enough furs could be trapped in this area to satisfy them. Between 1625 and 1640 about 5,000 to 6,000 skins were traded each year at Fort Orange, not all of which came from the Iroquois (Van Laer 1908:483-484). By 1656 the number had risen to 46,000 a year, although the trade soon fell off again as Iroquois raiding became less effective (Trelease 1960:131).

It is impossible to explain the success of the Iroquois solely in terms of their need for furs. While this need seems to have driven the Mohawks to renew their attacks on the Saint Lawrence, at first these raids tended to be very circumspect. By 1642 the French seemed to be well on their way to halting them by building a chain of forts and settlements that extended as far upriver as Montreal. These plans were frustrated, however, when the Mohawk suddenly acquired several hundred muskets and began to use these to wage a very effective guerilla warfare against both the French and their allies. Prior to 1640 the Indians living around Quebec had been able to obtain a small number of guns, but the French, who feared these guns might be used against them, kept the Indians' supplies of ammunition very low. The Dutch trading company similarly disapproved of the sale of guns to the Indians, and before 1640 the Iroquois do not appear to have been able to get hold of any. By contrast, after 1640 they were able to obtain large quantities of guns. The Dutch traders at Albany claimed that the supplying of arms to the Mohawk was necessary at this time to counteract attempts by New Englanders to lure off their trade, but it appears more likely that once the trade in New Netherland was thrown open to everyone, the settlers threw caution to the winds in the hope of greater commercial gain. Even most Dutch officials seem to have approved of this action since it was impossible to persuade the Mohawk to let Indians from the north and west trade at Albany. Enabling the Iroquois to rob these Indians more effectively seemed to be the most likely means by which the fur trade of the colony might be dramatically increased (Trelease 1960:99-102).

The French attempted to counter this development by making muskets available to their Huron and Algonquian allies. These guns were, however, inferior to those supplied by the Dutch, and the fear that they might be used against either French colonists or the Jesuits who were working in the Huron country led French officials to restrict their sale to reliable Christian converts. The fact that the Hurons, unlike the Iroquois, had no alternative source of European trade goods also meant that these regulations could be enforced. As a result, the Iroquois were able to achieve a numerical superiority in muskets, which gave them a considerable psychological advantage over their enemies. It is likely that it was this psychological advantage, rather than any intrinsic supe-

riority of guns over bows and arrows, that explains the success of the Iroquois. The Iroquois also enjoyed the advantage of having a far shorter trade route than any of the other Iroquoian tribes except the Susquehannock, and one which did not require traders who were on their way to Fort Orange to go outside the limits of the Iroquois confederacy.

The Great Dispersions

The Mohawks began the beaver wars with their attacks on the Algonquins in the 1630s. One of their principal aims, then and later, was to secure French neutrality, which would leave them free to raid at will north of the Saint Lawrence River. This goal, and not a desire to force the French to share their trade with them, explains the numerous negotiations and treaties that they and the other Iroquois tribes, either individually or collectively, entered into with the French. The Mohawks also diversified their sources of furs by attacking the Abenakis in the 1640s. By this time, the western tribes of the confederacy were also experiencing a growing need for furs. They, however, were not in a convenient location to raid hunting bands, such as the Algonquins, since all of their neighbors were Iroquoian-speaking horticulturalists like themselves. All of these tribes were involved in one way or another in the fur trade and hence their villages had become collection points for furs; however, because of their size and fortifications, these villages were much more difficult to attack than were Algonquin hunting camps. It is possible that the dispersal of the Wenro in 1638 was an effort by the Senecas to expand their hunting territory, although the evidence to confirm or deny this suggestion is insufficient. The earliest certain evidence of warfare over beavers is the attacks that the Neutrals are reported to have been making against the Algonquian-speaking peoples in southeastern Michigan in the early 1640s. The aim of these attacks was apparently to gain control of the marshy areas around Lake Saint Clair, which were rich in beaver. These attacks may have been responsible for the dispersal of some of the Michigan tribes who seem to have fled to Wisconsin prior to 1650 (Wilson 1956).

By 1642 the western tribes of the Iroquois confederacy were beginning to attack Huron villages to obtain furs. At first, their aim seems to have been to raid and plunder individual Huron villages, but within a few years the Seneca and their neighbors made it their policy to disperse the Hurons, so that they would be free to raid the hunting peoples who lived to the north of the Hurons, as the Mohawks and Oneidas were raiding the Algonquins. To accomplish this task, the Senecas enlisted the help of the Mohawks, who still had more guns than did the other members of the confederacy and who were anxious to join in a war that promised to deliver larger quantities of Huron furs into their hands than ever before.

The Iroquois plan of attack was a very practical one:

to whittle away the Huron confederacy village by village, beginning with the more isolated communities on the eastern borders. In 1642 an Arendaronon village was burned and by 1647 the Arendaronon were forced to seek refuge among neighboring tribes. Peace talks were undertaken between the Huron and Onondaga but were soon brought to an end when the Mohawks ambushed the Huron envoys. In 1648 two Attigneenongnahac villages were destroyed, and the following spring a war party of over 1,000 Senecas and Mohawks destroyed two more villages. At this point, the Hurons lost their nerve and the remaining villages dispersed. Some Hurons attempted to hold out on a nearby island, but after a year of starvation and sickness the survivors were forced to disband. A small number of these went with the Jesuits to Quebec, where some of the survivors were to become the Hurons of Lorette. One whole tribe, the Tahontaenrat, moved south to join the Neutral confederacy; other groups of Hurons found refuge in the north, or affiliated themselves with the Petun, Neutral, or even the various Iroquois tribes, among whom many of them had relatives living as prisoners. In the winter of 1649-1650, the Iroquois took advantage of their victory to penetrate into central Ontario where they attacked the Nipissings and other allies of the Hurons. This was the first of many fur raids that they were to carry out in the upper Great Lakes region. To prevent the Petun from forming the nucleus around which the Huron might attempt to stage a revival, the Iroquois descended on them in the winter of 1649-1650, no doubt capturing many furs when they attacked the village of Etharita. The Petun also dispersed. Many of them fled to the northwest in the company of Huron refugees, and these together became the Wyandots of later times (Tooker 1963).

With the Huron and Petun out of the way, the Senecas were free to deal with the Neutrals. Their villages, like those of the Huron, offered the prospect of rich booty, while their dispersal opened up a new route along which it was possible to raid the upper Great Lakes. Most important, their disappearance would give the Seneca free access to the rich beaver grounds around Lake Saint Clair, for control of which the Neutrals themselves had recently been fighting. Already in 1647, the Seneca had pillaged one Neutral village on the pretext that the Neutrals had allowed an Iroquois to be killed by Huron warriors within sight of their village. In spite of talk of an alliance between the Neutrals and the French, and the reported storming of a Seneca village by the Neutrals, the Neutrals were decisively defeated by the Iroquois in 1651. The Tahontaenrat surrendered as a group and were allowed to settle among the Seneca in a town of their own, which was called Gandougarae. Here they were joined by Arendaronons, Neutrals, and other refugee groups. The inhabitants of Gandougarae retained their separate identity within the Seneca tribe for a considerable period. Other Neutrals joined the Seneca

or fled west; 800 of them gathered on the western shore of Lake Michigan in 1652-1653. If the Nicolas Sanson map of 1656 is to be trusted, still more fled south into Ohio. None of these groups retained their ethnic identity for long (Trelease 1960:120-121).

The main rivals of the Iroquois in the west were now the Eries, who had strengthened themselves by adopting many Huron and Neutral refugees. To the Iroquois, the problem that was posed by the Erie was similar to that which had been posed by the Huron, except that it was in a different geographical area. The location of the Erie inhibited the Iroquois from raiding and hunting in the Ohio Valley, where beaver were plentiful. Moreover, by trading with the Susquehannocks, the Eries were diverting the furs from this area into the hands of the Iroquois's rivals. In 1651-1652, the Mohawks attacked the Susquehannocks, hoping to disperse them as they had dispersed the Hurons; however, the Susquehannocks were sufficiently well equipped by their Swedish trading partners to withstand this attack in good order (Jennings 1968:23-26). The combined threat of the Erie and the Susquehannock was more than the Iroquois wished to face in their present condition. Thus, in 1653, the Seneca led the other tribes of the Iroquois confederacy into the first general peace between themselves and the beleaguered French. This peace lasted until 1658 and its high point was the establishment of a short-lived Jesuit mission center among the Onondagas, similar to their former establishment among the Hurons. Freed from the fear of an attack by the French, the Iroquois now concentrated on the capture and dispersal of the Eries. The war with the Erie continued until 1657, after which time a considerable number of Eries appear to have drifted to the southeast toward Chesapeake Bay. These were compelled to merge with the Iroquois about 1680 (JR 62:71). Following their victory, the Iroquois began to raid into the Ohio Valley, where they are said to have encountered tribes that had still no knowledge of European goods (JR 44:49).

After 1650 the Mohawks became increasingly arrogant in their dealings with the other tribes of the Iroquois confederacy, who needed their permission to pass through the Mohawk River valley to trade with the Dutch. This difficulty encouraged the western tribes to seek a separate trading alliance with the French. These activities so aroused the jealousy of the Mohawks that they threatened to destroy the confederacy. In particular, the Mohawks feared that the close ties between the Onondagas and the French would undermine the power that they derived from their special relationship with the Dutch. The seizure of New Sweden by the Dutch in 1655 forced the Susquehannocks to make peace with the Mohawks, who were thus freed to resume their attacks on the French and their allies. In spite of dissensions among the Iroquois, this conflict soon led to a general resumption of hostilities between the Iroquois and the French.

The dispersal of the Eries solved few problems for the western tribes of the Iroquois confederacy. The Susquehannocks continued to need furs and to secure these they hunted in the Ohio watershed and began attacking Seneca trading parties as they carried their furs to Fort Orange. In 1659–1660, war broke out between the Senecas and the Susquehannocks, and the Cayugas and the Onondagas were soon drawn into it. The war did not go well for the Iroquois, who were once again engaged in hostilities on too many fronts. Aid sent from the English colony of Maryland permitted the Susquehannocks to withstand a major Iroquois attack in 1663. As the war continued, many Cayugas fled from their tribal territory and settled along the north shore of Lake Ontario. In the meanwhile, the Mohawks, who were having increasing difficulty with the Sokokis and the Mahicans, continued their friendship with the Susquehannocks.

At this low ebb in the fortunes of all the Iroquois tribes, they were induced once more to seek peace with the French and their allies, even though this meant freeing the French to develop a flourishing trade in the upper Great Lakes region. The three western tribes were ready for peace in 1663, but a treaty embracing the whole confederacy was not arranged until 1667, after the Carignan-Salières Regiment had burned the Mohawk villages and food supply (fig. 4). Even after this peace, the western Iroquois had little luck in curbing the Sus-

quehannocks and soon were asking for French assistance to deal with them, although such help was not forthcoming. The final breaking of the power of the Susquehannocks in 1675 did not come about as the result of an Iroquois victory, but because of an attack by European backwoodsmen from Maryland and Virginia. After much intrigue between the colonial governments of New York and Maryland, many of the Susquehannocks were brought under the protection of a reinvigorated Iroquois confederacy (Jennings 1968).

The crushing of Susquehannock independence extinguished the last of the Iroquoian groups that, in earlier times, had surrounded the Five Nations Iroquois on every side. Each of these groups, except the Susquehannock, appears to have been broken by the Iroquois as a result of rivalry over the possession of furs or hunting territory. The Iroquois victories did not, however, bring them the prosperity and security that they were seeking. The peace of 1667 made it easier for the French not only to trade in the north but also to extend their trade routes through the lower Great Lakes into the Illinois country. Hence, when the Iroquois were driven to launch a full-scale war against the Illinois in 1680, this war did not bring them into conflict merely with Indian traders but with Frenchmen who were competing with them for furs. Having dispersed the Indian nations that had surrounded them, the Iroquois were now forced to enter an era of more direct involvement with the European powers that were establishing themselves in North America.

Social Effects

Although very little is known about the development of Iroquois society in these early years, it is apparent that, whatever Iroquoian society was like in late prehistoric times, dramatic changes came about as a result of European contact and the ensuing struggle for beaver pelts. The mortality rate from disease was abnormally high at this time and a large number of capable leaders must have perished. A growing emphasis on warfare also resulted in a sharp increase in the mortality rate among young men. The Iroquois attempted to compensate for these losses by adopting large numbers of prisoners, who were gradually naturalized by means of a subtle mixture of rewards and punishments. Sometimes whole groups were adopted by the Iroquois, but more often families or individuals became members of existing clan segments.

As warfare increased in intensity and was conducted farther afield, men spent less time in their own villages than they had previously. This absence, combined with a higher male mortality rate, must have led women to play an even more important role in the management of their villages and in the political activities of their tribes generally. While there is no reason to doubt that the matrilineal institutions of Iroquoian society antedate European contact, it appears likely that much of the political importance of women dates from this period.

Bibliothèque Nationale, Paris: Baluze 196, fol. 79.

Fig. 4. Signatures on a treaty between 10 Seneca ambassadors and the French at Quebec, May 25, 1666. This was one of the treaties leading to the General Peace of 1667. For the French the signers are Alexandre de Prouville de Tracy, lieutenant-general of troops of New France; Daniel de Rémy de Courcelle, governor of New France; and Jean Talon, administrative officer of Justice, Police, and Finances of New France. Francois-Joseph Le Mercier, superior-general of the Jesuit missions in New France, and Pierre-Joseph-Marie Chaumonot, Jesuit missionary, signed as witnesses and interpreters. The Senecas drew their clan totems: turtle, bear, and three birds, possibly hawk and snipes.

356

Saint Lawrence Iroquoians

BRUCE G. TRIGGER AND JAMES F. PENDERGAST

Saint Lawrence Iroquoians is one of the names used to denote the Iroquoian-speaking Indians who were encountered in the vicinity of what are now Quebec City and Montreal by the French explorers who first visited the Saint Lawrence valley between 1535 and 1543. These Indians are described in the accounts of Jacques Cartier's voyages to Canada in 1534, 1535–1536, and 1541–1542 and of Jean-François de La Roque, sieur de Roberval's attempted colonization in 1542–1543 (Cartier 1924). By the time the next records concerning the indigenous inhabitants of this region become available, in 1603, the Saint Lawrence Iroquoians had vanished. Their identity and historical relationship to Iroquoian-speaking groups who were encountered farther south and west in the seventeenth century have been a matter of considerable controversy. There is no evidence that these Indians constituted a single tribe or people; indeed, their far-flung distribution makes this highly unlikely. The older name that was given to them, Laurentian Iroquois, is doubly misleading. It implies that they were members of one or more tribes of the Five Nations Iroquois, an idea that now appears to be doubtful. Second, the term Laurentian, which there refers to the Saint Lawrence valley, can all too easily be confused with the much earlier and unrelated Laurentian tradition. Hence a more neutral and less misleading designation for these Indians seems required (Trigger 1972:45).

On the basis of Cartier's description, it is possible to distinguish between the Saint Lawrence Iroquoians who lived in the vicinity of Quebec City and those who lived on Montreal Island (fig. 1). These two groups differed strikingly in their patterns of subsistence and settlement (Bailey 1933:100; Beaugrand-Champagne 1936:189; Fenton 1940:171). They also appear to have been rivals for control of trade on the Saint Lawrence and to have had differing relationships with the Ottawa valley Algonquins and other tribes living to the west. This makes it highly likely that there were at least two tribal or ethnic divisions, which may be called Stadaconans and Hochelagans, after the names of their principal and best-known villages (Trigger 1972:45). The so-called Cartier vocabularies imply that a common language was spoken by both groups, but it is not certain that the French who visited the Saint Lawrence valley knew enough Iroquoian to determine whether the language of Hochelaga was identical or merely similar to that spoken at Stada-

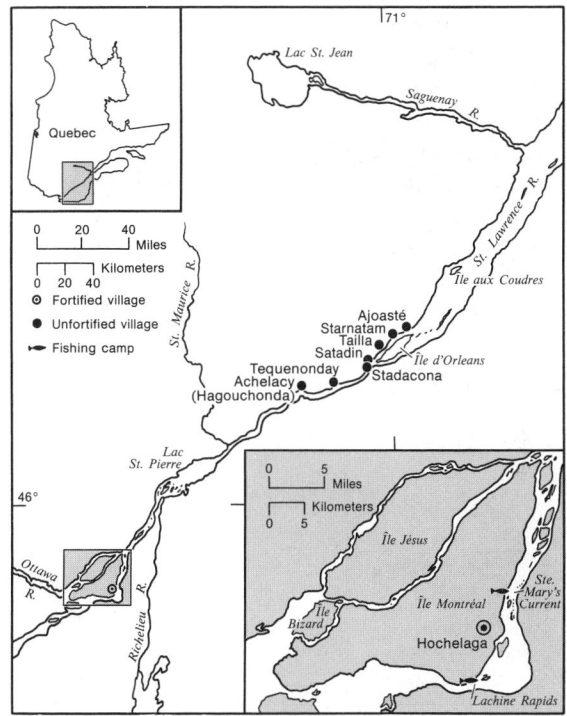

Fig. 1. Approximate locations of Iroquoian villages mentioned by name in accounts of Cartier's voyages.

cona. The vocabularies were drawn up either in Canada or in France, but in either case using only Stadaconan informants.

Culture

The territory of the Stadaconans stretched along the Saint Lawrence River from the Ile aux Coudres at least as far inland as the Richelieu Rapids near Portneuf, Quebec. Cartier recorded the names of 7 to 10 Iroquoian villages that stretched upriver, beginning near the Ile d'Orléans. All these villages were located on the north side of the river. It has been suggested that the south bank of the Saint Lawrence remained uninhabited because of attacks by a hostile people known as the Toudaman, who were probably the Micmac or Maliseet (Hoffman 1961:204). The Stadaconans grew corn but seem to have depended for most of their food supply upon fishing and catching eels in summer and hunting in winter. Each summer, large groups of men, women, and chil-

357

dren went down the Saint Lawrence River to the Gaspé Peninsula where they fished for mackerel; it was one of these groups that Cartier encountered in the Baie de Gaspé in 1534. Other groups appear to have traveled eastward along the north shore of the Saint Lawrence to hunt for sea mammals (Hoffman 1961:208). During the middle of the winter, hunting parties made up of men were absent from the villages for long periods. The largest Stadaconan villages seem to have had a population of about 500 people and the account of Cartier's second voyage states that all of them were unfortified. Although the French took special notice of the longhouses at Hochelaga, they nowhere describe the houses of the Stadaconans. This omission leaves unresolved whether or not the Stadaconans lived in longhouses.

It is unclear from the French accounts whether the Stadaconan villages belonged to a single tribe or whether each was politically autonomous. There is evidence that, in their dealings with the French, the headmen of different villages acted independently of one another. On the other hand, when faced by external threats the warriors from the different villages came to one another's aid. Donnacona, the headman of Stadacona, seems to have wielded considerable influence over the region as a whole. It is possible that, given the less sedentary life of the Stadaconans, the traditions of tribal organization characteristic of other northern Iroquoian-speaking peoples were less strongly developed among them. Each community may have constituted a separate unilineal band, as seems to have been the case amongst the marginally agricultural, Algonquian-speaking groups who lived in the Ottawa valley and around the shores of Georgian Bay.

Farther upriver, near the center of Montreal Island, Cartier visited the Iroquoian settlement of Hochelaga (fig. 2). This town contained an estimated 50 longhouses

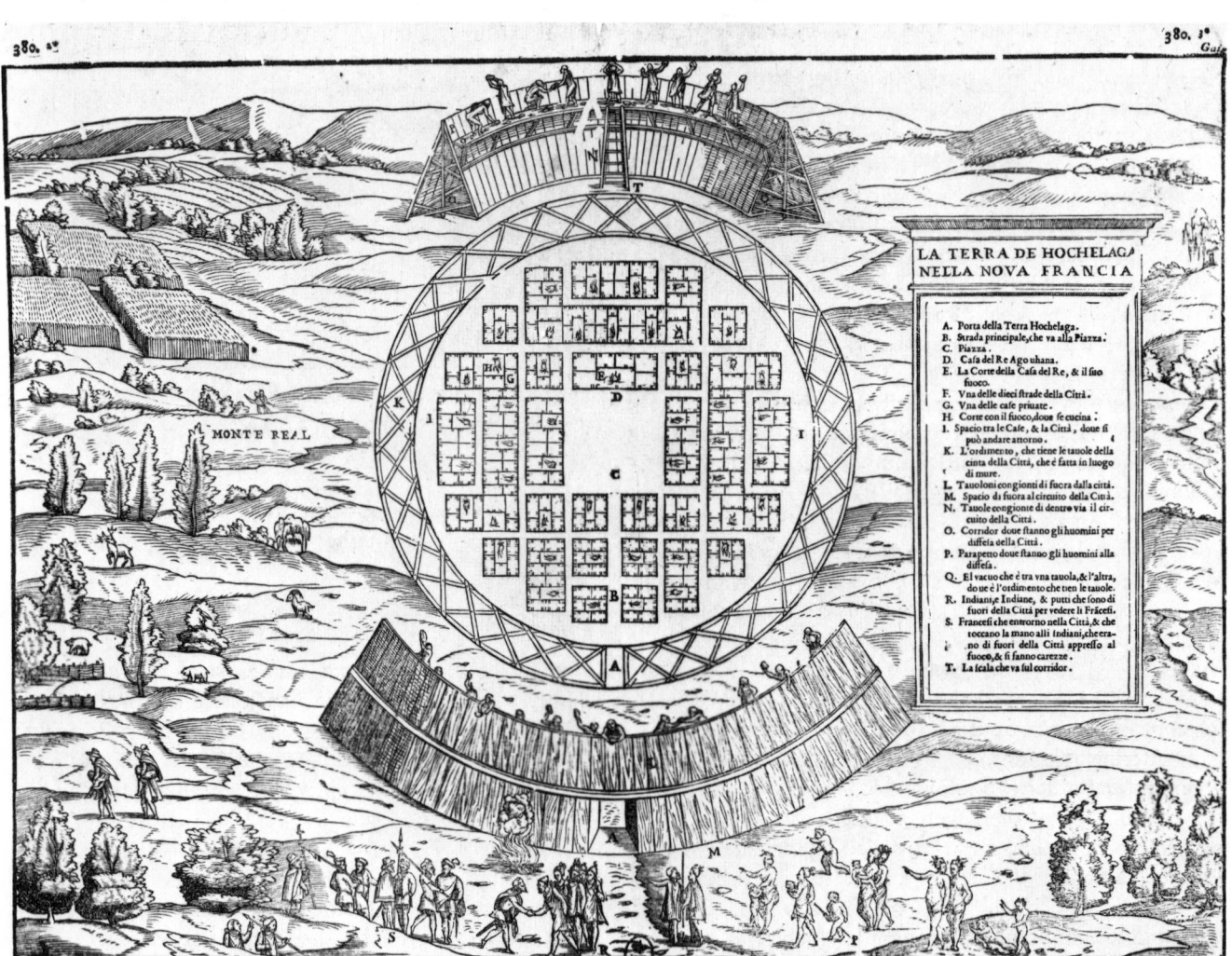

Bibliothèque Nationale, Paris: Vd. 20b, tome II, fol. p. 6.

Fig. 2. Plan of the village of Hochelaga that illustrated the Italian translation of the account of Cartier's second voyage (Ramusio 1556, 3). Although long accepted as from an original drawing approved by Cartier himself, W.D. Lighthall (1932) has shown that it was merely an engraver's attempt to give visual form to the text. It should not be considered ethnographically accurate. Woodcut, about 1556.

and was surrounded by a triple palisade and extensive cornfields. The population of Hochelaga has been estimated at about 1,500 people, which would make it similar to large Huron and Iroquois villages visited by Europeans in the next century (Trigger 1972:14–16). Along the shores of Montreal Island Cartier found two smaller settlements, which were apparently camps used by the inhabitants of Hochelaga during the fishing season. The greater dependence on agriculture and the sedentary habits of the Hochelagans contrasted sharply with those of the Stadaconans. In general, the subsistence patterns of the Stadaconans appear to resemble those of the semi-horticultural Ottawa and Algonquin more than they do those of any of the Iroquoian tribes known in the seventeenth century. This may reflect the marginal location of the group, in an area where corn could not be depended on to ripen every year (Fenton 1940:75; Barbeau 1949:228–229; Martijn 1969). Hitherto, the Stadaconans have been interpreted as a group whose agricultural economy deteriorated as they moved northward down the Saint Lawrence; however, the in-situ theory of the origin of Iroquoian culture makes it equally probable that the Stadaconans were an Iroquoian group that, because of their location, had failed to develop the agricultural economy and many of the associated social and political characteristics of their Iroquoian neighbors. If archeology supports this theory, the Stadaconans may eventually provide an interesting historical example of the survival of an early stage in the development of the standard Iroquoian cultural pattern.

It is uncertain whether or not the entire Saint Lawrence valley between Quebec City and Montreal was inhabited by Iroquoian-speaking peoples. Cartier encountered numerous groups of fishermen upriver from Portneuf, but the account of his voyages mentions no villages between there and Hochelaga. It is also uncertain whether these fishermen were Iroquoian- or Algonquian-speaking; some, if not all, of them may have been northern Algonquians who came to the river each summer as part of their seasonal cycle. The situation upriver from Hochelaga is also unclear. Pendergast's (1972) study of Iroquoian sites in that area has revealed clusters of sites that seem to represent local groups who lived there in prehistoric times. However, no historic sites have been found as yet in that area or in the apparently culturally related sites in Jefferson County, New York. There is therefore no evidence of an Iroquoian occupation of the Saint Lawrence valley upriver from Hochelaga later than the time of Cartier's visit.

Identity

Speculation concerning the ethnic identity of the Saint Lawrence Iroquoians has gone on for over a century. During that time, they have been identified as the ancestors of almost every Iroquoian tribe, including unlikely ones such as the Tuscarora (Beaugrand-Champagne 1937). The two theories that were most popular in the nineteenth century were that they had retreated south to become the Mohawk or westward to become one or more of the historic Huron tribes. All the theories advanced at that time were based on seventeenth-century accounts of doubtful significance, eked out with fragmentary archeological and linguistic evidence. All too often, evidence supporting a favorite theory was accepted uncritically, while negative evidence was discounted or simply suppressed. Unfortunately, the results of this early speculation continue to be accepted as fact, particularly by historians who are unaware of more recent work or of the slender factual basis for these early reconstructions.

Following his study of pottery from the Dawson, Lanoraie, and Roebuck sites, Wintemberg (1936:121–124) concluded that all three of these sites closely resembled ones from Jefferson County, which W.M. Beauchamp had identified as early Onondaga. Wintemberg proposed that, sometime after Cartier's visit, the Saint Lawrence Iroquoians had moved south to become the ancestors of the historic eastern Iroquois. MacNeish (1952:57, 84) proposed more specifically that the Saint Lawrence Iroquoians were the ancestors of the historic Oneida and Onondaga. According to MacNeish, the Onondaga-Oneida developed as a single people in the vicinity of Watertown, and after A.D. 1100 spread down the Saint Lawrence as far as Quebec City. After 1535, they withdrew into central New York, where they were found living in the seventeenth century. By 1966, this theory was so well accepted by most archeologists that it could be argued that the term Laurentian Iroquois was redundant and confusing and should be replaced by Onondaga or Onondaga-Oneida (Wright 1966:4).

In 1948 Pendergast began a study of Iroquoian sites in the upper Saint Lawrence valley that has produced a local Iroquoian sequence dating from approximately A.D. 1200 when the Pickering Branch of the Ontario Iroquoian tradition and the later Middleport substage extended their influence eastward into the Saint Lawrence valley, in which an indigenous Middle Woodland Point Peninsula culture was still flourishing. The introduction of agriculture led to this riverine-oriented economy giving way to food production and the rise of inland palisaded villages of which Hochelaga is typical (Pendergast 1964:195, 1966:79, 1967:32, 1972). Work that has been carried out simultaneously in New York indicates that the Mohawk, Oneida, and Onondaga developed in their own tribal territories (Tuck 1971). While these three tribes and the Saint Lawrence Iroquoians shared many traits of material culture, it seems clear from the archeological evidence that each group developed separately. Thus, while some of the Saint Lawrence Iroquoians eventually may have found refuge among the Iroquois or the Huron and Petun, they can in no sense be said to have given rise to any one of the Iroquoian tribes that is known from the seventeenth century.

The theory that the Saint Lawrence Iroquoians were the ancestors of the Mohawk received strong support in the nineteenth century from Cuoq's (1869) suggestion that the language recorded in Cartier's vocabularies was Mohawk. Alternatively, historians and archeologists have identified the language of Cartier's vocabularies as being Oneida or Huron, and Barbeau (1961) has advanced the claim that both Huron and Mohawk are recorded in these lists. As Hoffman (1959) has pointed out, most of these theories have been based on the comparison of statistically insignificant amounts of vocabulary and offend modern linguistic practice. The Iroquoian language, or languages, recorded in these vocabularies must be studied in greater detail before its linguistic affinities are entirely clear. Twentieth-century work does not support the theory that all of the Saint Lawrence Iroquoians spoke one or more languages closely related to those of the Five Nations Iroquois. Both P.J. Robinson (1948) and Hoffman (1959) have found a closer resemblance to Huron than to the Iroquois languages, and Lounsbury (1961) has shown that the vocabularies differ significantly from Iroquois and cannot be ancestral to any of the languages of the Five Nations. On the other hand, Lounsbury's (1961) studies have led him to conclude that important elements of these vocabularies are also significantly different from Huron and apparently not ancestral to any Iroquois language that was spoken in the seventeenth century. Lounsbury has proposed that this separate Iroquoian language be called Laurentian, while Hoffman (1959) has more romantically called it Kwedech, the name that the Micmacs use in their legends to refer to their ancient enemies in the Saint Lawrence valley (see also "Iroquoian Languages," this vol.).

The independent status of the language of the Saint Lawrence Iroquoians would mean that, on linguistic grounds at least, some of the Iroquoian-speaking inhabitants of the Saint Lawrence valley cannot be considered the same as, or ancestral to, any Iroquoian tribe known from later times. Since the Cartier vocabularies were collected from Stadaconan informants, it is possible that sixteenth-century sources err when they state that the same language was spoken at Hochelaga and that, in reality, the Hochelagans spoke Onondaga or Oneida, or some closely related dialect. However, taking the archeological and linguistic evidence together, it appears more likely that the Saint Lawrence Iroquoians as a whole represent a distinct branch of northern Iroquoians who lived in the Saint Lawrence valley at the same time that the Iroquoian groups who survived into the seventeenth century were living in Ontario and New York.

Disappearance

The question remains: what happened to the Saint Lawrence Iroquoians? Various Indian traditions rather hap-

hazardly recorded by the French in the seventeenth century suggest alternatively that they were attacked and annihilated or dispersed by the Huron, Algonquians, or Iroquois (Trigger 1972:72–82). These stories are mutually contradictory and most are of questionable authenticity and accuracy. They can therefore be evaluated only in relationship to other bodies of data, such as archeological evidence, but at the present time these remain very limited. Excessive speculation based on these stories alone has resulted in a web of unverifiable explanations that have obscured rather than explained the fate of the Saint Lawrence Iroquoians. Moreover, these explanations almost invariably assume that the disappearance of these Indians was part of the "slow flux of native population that . . . is an inevitable characteristic of aboriginal life on a large and thinly populated continent" (Hunt 1940:13). Beaugrand-Champagne (1948: 39–51) was one of the few exegetes of this sort to connect the disappearance of the Saint Lawrence Iroquoians with the Europeans. He argued that they fled the region once they despaired of defending it against repeated French attempts at colonization.

In the mid-twentieth century, it became more fashionable to view the disappearance of the Saint Lawrence Iroquoians as part of the general disruption that befell Indian groups who inhabited the eastern seaboard of North America as a result of early contact and trade with Europeans. It is significant that the Saint Lawrence Iroquoians lived just west of, and were in contact with, the Gulf of Saint Lawrence. This was one of the areas where European fishermen first began to trade intensively with the Indians for furs. Hoffman (1961:202–214) has suggested that, as the fur trade spread up the Saint Lawrence, the Indians of this region, like those living in the Maritimes, spent more time hunting in the interior and as furs became depleted near the river they moved inland and northward in search of game. The resulting curtailment of their riverine subsistence economy led to social disorganization and made these Indians fall easy prey to the Iroquois when the Iroquois attacked them around A.D. 1600. Among other weaknesses, Hoffman does not explain why the Saint Lawrence Iroquoians were attacked by the Iroquois or why they disappeared as a people, as opposed to being forced from their tribal territories. He also overlooks the general tendency of Indians living along the Saint Lawrence to become middlemen in the fur trade rather than to move inland themselves.

Alternatively, Innis (1956:12–15) has suggested that, as the fur trade spread onto the Canadian Shield by way of Tadoussac and the Saguenay valley, the Montagnais and Algonquins were able to acquire iron axes and hence gained a significant military advantage over the Saint Lawrence Iroquoians. Innis assumed, as did most anthropologists at that time, that the Saint Lawrence Iroquoians had invaded the Saint Lawrence not long before and had driven out its original Algonquian-speaking inhabitants, who were, therefore, trying to regain control of their ancestral homeland. This argument now appears highly unlikely. Iroquoian-speaking peoples lived in the Saint Lawrence valley not for a few decades, but for centuries, prior to their disappearance. It also seems more likely that friendly, rather than hostile, relations existed, at least between the Hochelagans and the northern Algonquians, since the Algonquians would likely have sought to trade meat and skins for the corn produced by their southern neighbors.

It is clear that as early as 1535 the Stadaconans attempted to prevent Cartier from traveling upriver, in the hope of preserving a monopoly of trade between the French and themselves. There is some evidence that they may have continued to do this as late as 1580 (Hakluyt 1589:723). The military and economic advantage that this gave the Stadaconans may have led tribes living farther west to take desperate measures either to eliminate such middlemen or to redress the military balance by attempting to secure iron weapons for themselves through war. This could have led either the Hochelagans or the Algonquins to take advantage of superior numbers to destroy the Stadaconans around 1580. Champlain states that as late as 1609 the Mohawks were obtaining their iron axes by waging war on the inhabitants of the Saint Lawrence valley (Champlain 1922-1936, 2:96). This suggests that the Mohawks, being the Iroquois who lived nearest to the Saint Lawrence valley and who were most affected by these events, may have attacked the Hochelagans and other inhabitants of this region toward the end of the sixteenth century and either annihilated or dispersed them in an effort to secure iron tools and possibly access to European traders at Tadoussac. Their power in the Saint Lawrence valley appears to have been at its height around 1600, when the valley was uninhabited as far downriver as Quebec City, and the Algonquians living to the north feared even to fish along the river because of them (Trigger 1972:90-92). A victory by the Five Nations Iroquois may have been easier if, as Fenton (1940:175) suggests, European diseases had decimated the population of the valley prior to their final victory.

Using later Iroquois victories as analogies, it appears highly likely that some of the defeated Saint Lawrence Iroquoians were absorbed by the Mohawks, or by other Iroquois tribes, although archeological confirmation of this is so far lacking. Concentrations of Saint Lawrence Iroquoian-type pottery are known to occur on a contact site in Huronia and on a contact and a late prehistoric site on the Trent River waterway (Emerson 1954:205; Wintemberg 1946:154; P. Pratt, personal communication 1971). This suggests that other refugees may have fled westward. On the basis of historical evidence, it has been argued that still others found refuge among the Ottawa valley Algonquins, particularly among the Onontchataronons, who seem to have been a division of the Petite Nation and whose headmen in the 1640s claimed that their ancestors had inhabited Montreal Island (Trigger 1972:77-80). Still others may have joined the Abenaki. Considering their greater proximity to the East Coast and earlier contact with Europeans, the disappearance of the Hochelagans and Stadaconans as a result of early "trade wars" is no more remarkable than the disappearance of Neutral, Erie, and most of the Huron as a result of similar wars only a little more than a half-century later.

Synonymy

No name or names are known by which groups of Saint Lawrence Iroquoians called themselves. The name Canada, which Cartier used to designate the region of Stadaconan settlement, appears to be derived from a Saint Lawrence Iroquoian word meaning 'village'; however, there is no evidence of its aboriginal status as a toponym (Ganong 1964:308-309). The most recent speculation concerning the meaning of Hochelaga (P. J. Robinson 1942) and a similar study of the Stadaconan toponyms (P. J. Robinson 1945) are available.

Sources

For a summary and evaluation of the literature dealing with the Saint Lawrence Iroquoians, see Fenton (1940) and Trigger (1972). For a summary of the archeological material relevant to these same groups, see Pendergast (1972).

Susquehannock

FRANCIS JENNINGS

From the archeological record, the Susquehannock (ˌsus-kwəˈhǎnək) are first identifiable as a culturally distinct Iroquoian people at about A.D. 1550 when they were living in scattered hamlets along the North Branch of the Susquehanna River between the Wyoming Valley and present-day Binghamton, New York.* Witthoft (1959: 26–29, 35, 39) postulates that they abandoned this region before 1570 and had settled by 1580 in one large community in Lancaster County, Pennsylvania (fig. 1), a possible cause being prssure from the Five Nations Iroquois. However, Hunter (1959:13) asks whether the Susquehannocks may have been "drawn, not driven" to their new home by superior trade opportunities. In 1615 they were numerous enough to send 500 warriors to aid Samuel de Champlain and his Indian allies in an attack upon the Iroquois, but their party returned home when they arrived two days after Champlain had withdrawn.

Identification

Looking southward from New France, Champlain identified the people on the Susquehanna River on his map of 1632 as Carantouannais. This name has been taken to be a French rendition of Iroquoian Skahentawaneh 'big, grassy flat' (Fenton 1940:233), the name for Wyoming Valley; Floyd G. Lounsbury (personal communication 1972) compares Mohawk *skahętóˑwanę* and Oneida *skahętowáńę*, both meaning 'great field'. The proposition has been advanced that the Carantouan were probably the same as the Atrakwaeronnon, whom the Iroquois defeated in 1652 (Hanna 1911, 1:34; JR 37:97, 38:191). Gen. John S. Clark located the chief fortified town of this hypothesized tribe on Spanish Hill at Athens, Pennsylvania (L.W. Murray 1931:20–32); however, systematic digging at this site has produced no archeological evidence of a seventeenth-century town (Griffin 1931; Barry C. Kent, personal communication 1972). It seems more likely, therefore, that the 1652 battle took place between the Iroquois and the Susquehannock proper or their allies who lived farther south on the main stream. This supposition gains strength from what little can be gleaned of population figures. In 1647 a Canadian Jesuit recorded that "a single village" of the

---

* Since the Susquehannock language has long been extinct, words from it are cited in the *Handbook* in the orthographies used by the original sources.

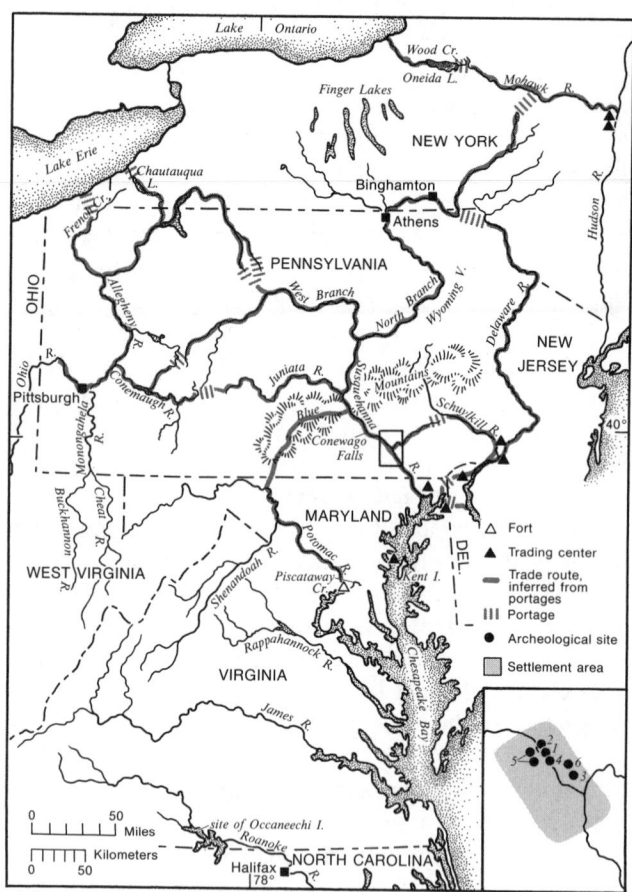

Fig. 1. Tribal territory and archeological sites. 1, Schultz, 1575–1600; 2, Washington Boro including Eshelman and Keller, 1600–1625; 3, Roberts, 1630–1650; 4, Strickler, 1650–1666; 5, Oscar and Bert Liebhart, 1666–1675; 6, Conestoga, 1697–1736. Sites located and dated by Barry C. Kent, Pennsylvania State Archeologist.

Susquehannock had 1,300 warriors, implying a total population in that village of 5,200 to 6,500. In the battle of 1652 the beaten side suffered an unknown number of casualties besides the loss of 500 to 600 prisoners, mostly male, carried off by the Iroquois; and a very thorough archeological examination of the village site occupied by the Susquehannock after that date indicates a remaining population of 2,000 to 3,000 (Barry C. Kent, personal communication 1972).

The French knew the Susquehannock by their Iroquoian name, either in its Five Nations form Gandastogué or in its Huron form Andaste, both with

Pa. Histl. and Mus. Commission, Harrisburg: B115, 888, 1/162, 1/260.

Fig. 2. Washington Boro Incised pottery from the Keller site, Lancaster Co., Pa. Height of right 20 cm, others same scale.

variants. Clark thought this meant 'people who build houses with curved roofs', Hewitt rendered it 'at the place of the immersed pole' (L.W. Murray 1931:122; Hewitt 1907g:335), and Floyd G. Lounsbury (personal communication 1972) accepts Beauchamp's (1907:260) 'people of the cabin poles' as most probable.

More vaguely than the French, the Dutch and Swedish colonists projected their vision westward from bases on the lower Hudson and Delaware rivers, where they lived in the midst of Algonquian tribes who gave the name Minquas or Minquaes (or other variants) to Iroquoians living along the Susquehanna and beyond (Van Laer 1924:211). This term has been applied to various Iroquoian groups; see synonymy in "Northern Iroquoian Culture Patterns," this volume. A distinction was made between the White Minquas—apparently the historic Susquehannock—and the Black Minquas, who have been tentatively identified as the Erie of the Great Lakes region (Weslager and Dunlap 1961:120). However, an English writer in 1648 described the Black and White Minquas as "enemies to the Susquehannocks" (Plantagenet 1648:25). The Swedes distinguished—but how is unknown—between the "true" Minquas and their "united nations," identifying among the latter the Tehaque, Skonedidehaga, and Serosquacke (A. Johnson 1911, 2:569–570). The remark hints at confederacy on the order of the Huron or Five Nations type. A Maryland treaty of 1661 identified five distinct "nations" explicitly distinct from "families." They were the Ohongeoguena, Unquehiett, Kaiquariegehaga, Usququhaga, and Sconondihago, the last one apparently the same as the Swedish-named Skonedidehaga. English-rendered Usququhaga would also seem to be the same as Swedish Serosquacke (Md. Arch. 3:420–421). An Englishman wrote in 1648 of the Ihon-a-does (Juniata? Sconondihago?) and Wicomeses as "forced Auxiliaries" (Plantagenet 1648:24).

The term Sasquesahanough (Susquehannock) was first recited to Capt. John Smith by his Algonquian-speaking interpreter when he was visited by 60 Susquehannocks in 1608 (Smith 1612:407–409). It has been translated as 'people at the falls' or 'roily water people' and attributed

to the location of the village below Conewago falls. Smith's map named five villages along the Susquehanna and its branches, but all the evidence unearthed at Susquehannock sites indicates that only one village was occupied by the Susquehannock at any one time (Smith 1612:374–375: Barry C. Kent, personal communication 1972).

Deeds given by the Susquehannock attest that the tribe claimed possession of the entire Susquehanna valley as well as large territories on both shores of Chesapeake Bay, the latter claims apparently deriving from rights of conquest over the indigenous tribes. These deed claims have to be read with skepticism, because the colonial recipients who wrote them were always eager to magnify the extent of their own claims thus acquired.

Characteristics

Susquehannock population was large compared to nearby European colonies in the early seventeenth century, but smallpox, war, and migration reduced it swiftly and catastrophically. By 1698 only "about fifty men"—some 200 to 250 people all told—were left (Md. Arch. 23:444). An unguessable additional number may have assimilated by that time into the Iroquois Five Nations.

Physically the Susquehannock were a "giant-like people" according to John Smith, but anthropometric reconstruction of a few skeletal remains computes to an average male height of 5 feet 3.7 inches (Witthoft, Kinsey, and Holzinger 1959:111; Witthoft 1959a:41; Barry C. Kent, personal communication 1972). There are no extensive ethnographic reports in the source documents. Data are fragmentary and oriented toward concerns of commerce or diplomacy. An approach to a cultural description in the 10 pages of Alsop is marred by sensationalism and obvious fabrication so that the only safe use of it is with confirmation from other sources; however, John Gilmary Shea's notes on Alsop were a valiant early effort in Susquehannock studies (Alsop 1666:71–81, 117–121). Archeological data and the official records of colonial governments combine to portray a culture very similar to that of other Iroquoian tribes, with heavy reliance on maize horticulture and a familiar

363

Pa. Histl. and Mus. Commission, Harrisburg: Yo 170/75, 1/722, 1/867, La 3/118, 125, 2/451.
Fig. 3. Antler combs. Site sources from left to right: Leibhart, York Co., Pa.; Schultz; Schultz; Strickler; Shenks Ferry; and Washington Boro Village, Lancaster Co., Pa. Length of right 10.8 cm, others same scale.

sexual division of labor consigning cultivation to the women and hunting, trading, diplomacy, and war to the men (Witthoft 1959:33; JR 18:233-234). An apparently authentic Swedish source briefly describes a religion of two gods, good and evil, with worship and sacrifice devoted exclusively to the evil god because of fear. The rituals of sacrifice and dancing combined elements of both Iroquois and Delaware practices (Weslager 1946). A clan system of some sort existed, including Turtle, Wolf, and Fox clans and possibly more (Md. Arch. 3:420-421, 549-550).

History

Importance in Trade

Despite the enigmas and brevity of the tribe's known existence, it became historically important because of its strategic location and the role it played in trade (Hunter 1959). The Susquehanna River carried canoe traffic north and south from Chesapeake Bay to the Finger Lakes and Mohawk River of upper New York State, and east and west from the Delaware Valley to the Great Lakes and tributaries of the Ohio River (fig. 1). The river thus provided means for transporting freight between the western sources of the best peltry and the eastern sources of the best trade goods. Simultaneously it served as a "warriors' path" in all directions. From their homeland, the Susquehannock commanded the river's crossroads, the chief of which was at the forks of its West and North branches. The headwaters of the Potomac and James rivers permitted movement into the back country of Virginia, and other streams could have been used. A network of foot trails also existed. The tribe dominated and controlled trade, and it was an effective barrier until 1675 to southward forays of the Iroquois Five Nations.

The Susquehanna River had been an artery of aboriginal trade long before European colonization transformed intertribal to Indian-White exchange. Archeological evidence suggests the Juniata and Susquehanna West Branch routes had been used in trade since about 500 B.C., and perhaps earlier (Kent, Smith, and McCann 1971:197-198). When Capt. John Smith first met the river's people, they already possessed trade goods, and the Virginians lost little time in opening their own trade. Virginian William Claiborne began to trade at Kent Island (opposite present Baltimore) in 1630-1631 and extended his operations soon afterward to Palmer's Island at the head of Chesapeake Bay. The founding of Maryland destroyed his arrangements. Cecilius Calvert, second Lord Baltimore, asserted charter rights and sent his brother Leonard to seize Claiborne's posts, whereupon—according to Maryland sources—Claiborne instigated the Susquehannocks to hostility (Anonymous 1897a:401; Md. Arch. 3:64, 66). Maryland declared war against the tribe in 1642 but was unable to organize a campaign until April 1643 (Md. Arch. 3:116-117, 130-132). Two expeditions were then launched successively. The Indians fled from the first as soon as gunfire began; however, the second expedition came to grief. A Susquehannock defending force routed it, capturing two field pieces and 15 prisoners (Lindeström 1925:241-244; Md. Arch. 3:149). The inference seems to be that in the interim between the two expeditions the Indians had enlarged their supply of firearms from their Swedish allies. They tortured their prisoners to death, and Maryland remained in a state of formal but quiescent war until 1652.

To the eastward, the Susquehannock had attempted to open trade with Dutch New Amsterdam as early as 1626. It appears that the Algonquian tribes of the Delaware Valley interdicted this effort and attempted to control access to the traders on both the Hudson and Delaware rivers. Intertribal war broke out, during which European observers reported Susquehannock raids on Delaware villages (Van Laer 1924:192, 211; De Vries 1911:22-24; Plantagenet 1648:22). These reports have been interpreted as signifying that the Susquehannocks conquered the Delawares and made them subjects (Hanna 1911, 1:106; Weslager 1972:98-99), but this seems unlikely for four reasons. First, although the last reported hostilities between Delaware and Susquehannock are dated 1641, the Delawares were not listed among the "forced auxiliaries" in 1648 (Plantagenet 1648:24). Second, although the Susquehannock sold land of their tributary Indians on the Chesapeake Bay, they never sold Delaware lands (Jennings 1968:19, 50-53). Third, in 1655 the Swedes were unable to persuade their Susquehannock allies to relieve Delaware pressures on the Swedish settlements, which might have been accomplished easily if the Delaware had been a conquered people (Rising 1912: 156-159). And fourth, in 1661 the Susquehannock rejected their Maryland ally's request to "destroy" the Delaware (NYCD 12:344-345). Rather than a conqueror-subject relationship, the modus vivendi between the Susquehannock and the Delaware seems to have been an agreement concerning movement and relationships in trade.

Beaver Wars

Northward, the Susquehannock may have been visited in the winter of 1615-1616 by Champlain's emissary Étienne Brûlé, but Brûlé's account was vague and far from inspiring confidence in its reliability (DCB 1:131-132). Data are scanty for several decades during which the Iroquois blocked access to the Dutch trade at Fort Orange-Rensselaerswyck while trying to gain independent access for themselves to the peltry of the Great Lakes and Ohio Valley regions. They were pitted against the Huron confederacy, which monopolized fur gathering through an intertribal trading network. To break through the barrier of surrounding tribes, the Iroquois obtained unprecedented quantities of firearms from the English and the Dutch, with which they made the lightning conquests of the Beaver Wars between 1649 and 1656 (Hunt 1940:53-65; Jennings 1968:24). To meet this new situation the Susquehannock made peace with Maryland in 1652, subscribed by "Sawahegeh, Treasurer [?]," Auroghtaregh, Soarhuhadigh, Ruthchogah, and Wathetdiandeh (Wastahandow). In return for arms and the safety of their southern flank they ceded Maryland large territories on both shores of Chesapeake Bay. The peace was broadened to full alliance in 1661, but it was an uneasy alliance in which the Maryland government tried unsuccessfully to use the Susquehannock as cat's-paws in jurisdictional quarrels with successive governments on Delaware Bay. The 1661 treaty was signed by seven chiefs, among them Dahadaghesa of the Terrapin "family" and Sarangararo of the Wolf "family" (Md. Arch. 3:276-278, 420-421). In 1666 the alliance was renewed over the names of Wastahunda (Wastahandow) Harignera, "Terrapin," and Gosweinquerackqua, "Fox," identified as war captains (Md. Arch. 3:549-550). The names suggest a leading role for the Terrapin or Turtle clan.

In the struggle with the Iroquois the Susquehannock held their own after 1652. In 1663 Chief General Counselor Wastahandow appeared before the Maryland Council to tell how his warriors had turned back a great Iroquois attack, and a Dutch source states that 100 Delaware braves had assisted (Md. Arch. 1:471-472; NYCD 12:430). In later years Susquehannocks carried the war into Iroquoia to the terror of the Five Nations. Casualties were great, and a series of smallpox epidemics probably took an even greater toll, but the Iroquois declined at the same time from the same causes (JR 49:147-149).

Properly speaking, the fighting was between the Maryland-backed Susquehannock and all the Iroquois tribes except the Mohawk, for, after the Dutch conquest of New Sweden in 1655, the Susquehannock and Mohawk had no quarrel. Each then had its own vested interest in a Dutch trading center—the Susquehannock at Delaware Bay, the Mohawk at Fort Orange—and each attempted to control access of other tribes to its center, but neither had any interest in intruding on the other's domain. Susquehannocks also traded heavily at the store of one Jacob Claeson (anglicized to Jacob Young) who often appeared in the records as Jacob, My Friend. This Dutchman traded at the head of Chesapeake Bay and made his home on Delaware Bay. As no one in Maryland understood the Susquehannock language, he was often employed by that province to do diplomatic errands (Jennings 1968:25-26, 37, 48-49).

During New Netherlands's second incarnation, the Maryland government feared Dutch instigation of Iroquois hostilities. To forestall this, Maryland proposed to make formal peace overtures to the Iroquois, but the enduring Susquehannock-Iroquois feud stood as an obstacle. Gov. Charles Calvert, soon to become third Lord Baltimore, therefore "invited" the Susquehannock to evacuate their valley and take up residence in an abandoned Piscataway fort at the junction of Piscataway Creek with the Potomac River, just below modern Washington (Talbot 1910:440-441; Md. Arch. 2:429-430). Scholars unaware of Maryland's initiative have mistakenly interpreted the Susquehannock removal as a consequence of heavy defeats inflicted by the Iroquois, but no evidence of such defeats has ever appeared (Hanna 1911, 1:48). Despite the arrangement, Maryland's Iroquois negotiations did not materialize.

English Attacks

The Susquehannock change of location proved disastrous. Backwoods troubles in Virginia caused mobilization of the militia with instructions to pursue into Maryland, if need be, the Indians blamed for the troubles. Under protest, Maryland mobilized also. In confusion about their enemy's identity, the joint forces ended by besieging the Susquehannock fort. Five chiefs who emerged for parleys were seized and put to death by the colonial commanders in violation of their safe-conduct pledge. Though Marylanders and Virginians debated the responsibility for this act, the Susquehannocks blamed both. Escaping by night through the ranks of the sleeping English troops, the Indians killed 10 men silently as they went, then launched vengeance raids on exposed back settlers in Virginia (Washburn 1957:19–24).

They settled briefly in two forts near Ocaneechi Island in the Roanoke River, where they unwittingly precipitated the chain of events called Bacon's Rebellion. Nathaniel Bacon mobilized a troop of backwoodsmen and marched in pursuit. He arranged with the Ocaneechi chief to attack and conquer the smaller of the Susquehannock forts, containing 30 to 40 persons, and ordered seven Susquehannock prisoners to be tortured to death. During a subsequent quarrel between Bacon and Ocaneechi chief Persicles, which developed into a massacre by Bacon, the bulk of the Susquehannocks escaped (Washburn 1957:40–46).

The Covenant Chain

These events coincided in time with King Philip's War in New England. In the middle of the turmoils, the governor of New York, Edmund Andros, worried over the possiblity of a general Indian uprising. He launched the Mohawks against the New England Indians, smashing their rebellion, and then offered the defeated Indians sanctuary in New York from the vengeance of the northern colonies. Similarly he offered refuge to the Susquehannocks, some of whom returned to the Susquehanna River while others came to Andros's jurisdiction at Delaware Bay to live among their Delaware allies (Jennings 1968:36).

With Andros's sanction, the Iroquois persuaded most of the Susquehannocks to journey farther to settle in Iroquoia, but a few remained with the Delaware. In the general peacemaking at Albany in 1677, an extensive Indian-White confederation called the Covenant Chain was created under New York auspices. It linked a number of English colonies, with New York as their mediator, to an alliance of Indian tribes, with the Iroquois in a preeminent position among the Indians. In the peacemaking process the dispersed Susquehannocks lost their tribal identity, being submerged politically among the Iroquois and Delaware. A few recalcitrants still wandering in the backwoods of Virginia and Maryland were pursued and subdued by the Iroquois (Jennings 1968:39–44).

In their new circumstances, Susquehannock warriors persuaded Iroquois friends to join in vengeance raids against the tribes who had aided Virginia and Maryland, and the raids continued until these tribes accepted tributary membership under Iroquois suzerainty in the Covenant Chain. Susquehannocks also participated in the Iroquois wars against Canada, in which they took calamitous losses.

Revival at Conestoga

About 1690 some of the Susquehannocks abandoned the wars to return to their river as a separate polity again. By 1697 they had settled in the Conestoga village of historic record near the confluence of Conestoga Creek and the Susquehanna. They provided hospitality in 1692 for a wandering band of Shawnees, and both groups subscribed to a treaty of alliance with William Penn in 1701 (Md. Arch. 8:517–518; Pa. Col. Recs. 2:9–12). At this time the "king" of the Susquehannock was Connoodaghtoh and a chief counselor was Andaggy Junkquagh. Penn purchased the cession of the Susquehanna Valley in 1700, an act not recognized later by the Iroquois who asserted rights of conquest over the valley, and Penn's heirs found it expedient in 1736 to repurchase the valley, south of Blue Mountain, from the Iroquois (Pa. Arch. 1:133; P.A.W. Wallace 1945:65–71).

In the early eighteenth century the Susquehanna Valley was resettled by an ethnic mixture. Iroquois, Shawnees, Conoys, Nanticokes, Delawares, Tuscaroras, and Tutelos apparently intermingled and intermarried with the Susquehannock-Conestoga, although bands settled in separate villages and treated separately with Pennsylvania's government. The most prominent chief at Conestoga during the early decades of the century was named Civility, an echo of a Susquehannock name of the seventeenth century.

Once more, trade became the dominant force in the valley. An extensive trading organization created by Pennsylvania Secretary James Logan became a means for gradual introduction into the region of great numbers of European colonists. To repress consequent Indian unrest, Logan allied Pennsylvania to the Iroquois in a new policy that put Pennsylvania's power behind Iroquois authority over the Susquehanna and Delaware tribes (Jennings 1967, 1965; P.A.W. Wallace 1945:39–49).

Disturbance over these developments caused mass migration to the Ohio region. In 1755, when hostilities between England and France began the Seven Years' War, only a handful of Indians were left in the vicinity of Conestoga. Pennsylvania backwoodsmen suspected them of complicity with hostile Indians, and in 1763 a lynch mob called the Paxton Boys massacred the unresisting small remainder—seven men, five women, and eight children—of what had once been the powerful Susquehannock tribe. One of these was old Shehaes who had been present at the 1701 treaty with William Penn. The atrocity called forth an outraged denunciation from Benjamin Franklin (Franklin 1764).

Synonymy

Susquehannock was the English name in use in the seventeenth century; its earliest appearance was in the form of Sasquesahanough on John Smith's (1612:374) map. The English term used in the eighteenth century was Conestoga (NYCD 4:579), from the Iroquois name for the tribe. The Huron form corresponding to Conestoga was Andaste, which was the most commonly used French name, first appearing as Andastoerrhonon (JR 8:116). The Dutch and Swedish term, Minquas, appeared first in the form of Minquaas on the *Carte Figurative* of New Netherlands in 1614 (NYCD 1:13; Hart 1959:33). A rarer name of uncertain significance is Akhrakuaeronon. Identified variously as an alternate term for the Susquehannock, a constituent of the Susquehannock, and a "nation" distinct from the Susquehannock, they are first distinguished in the 1640 *Jesuit Relation* (JR 18:232). The *Jesuit Relation* for 1652 is ambiguous: it may mean that an attack had been made either upon the Atrakwaeronnons or upon the Andastoeronnons or that they were the same people (JR 37:104). The Kaiquariegehaga, a possible variant of Atrakwaeronnon, are mentioned in a Maryland treaty of 1661 as part of the "united nations" of the Susquehannock (Md. Arch. 3:420–421).

Most of the documentary references to this people are variants of the foregoing terms. Two deviations appear solitarily. Huskchanoes was a form given by a newcomer Englishman with an inexperienced ear and erratic spelling (NYCD 3:74). Machoéretini appears in a Dutch geographer's listing of tribes in the phrase "Minquosy or Machoéretini" (De Laet 1841:315). A full synonymy is in Hewitt (1907a:113, 1907g:336–337).

Sources

Susquehannock sources exist in the records of New France, New Netherlands, New Sweden, New York, Maryland, and Virginia, but they are fragmentary and tangential to other concerns. Two compilations of extracts useful as guides are Eshleman (1908) and Hanna (1911,1). The most recently published archeological work is in Witthoft and Kinsey (1959). Information on the considerable work done since its publication is available at the Pennsylvania Historical and Museum Commission, Harrisburg. Hunt (1940) pioneered in recognition of the importance of trade in Indian history, but his work is factually flawed in regard to the Susquehannock. Fenton (1940) established intertribal positions and relationships. Washburn (1957) best reports the hostilities of 1675–1676 in Maryland and Virginia. Jennings (1968) reinterprets the sources. Jennings (1967) centers on the years 1700–1720. L.W. Murray (1931) has to be taken into account because of her sheer quantity of data, but the work is useful only to the specialist who can screen out its substantial material from much guesswork and error.

The Susquehannock are still largely unknown as compared with their neighbors the Iroquois Five Nations or the Delaware. What is known is the by-product of research by scholars primarily interested in other subjects. The potential sources have not been examined exhaustively for Susquehannock materials. Excepting the *Jesuit Relations,* the French sources have been little used. The Swedish translations made by Amandus Johnson show such strong indications of his ethnocentric bias as to raise questions of their completeness and accuracy. No one has systematically culled the British Library or the Public Record Office in London, not to speak of the volumes of the Historical Manuscripts Commission. Such efforts might indeed prove futile; however, until they are made, judgment must be withheld.

Huron

CONRAD E. HEIDENREICH

Collectively the Huron ('hyōōr¡än) called themselves Ouendat (Wendat).* Late in the 1630s, the Jesuits listed five tribes as constituting the Huron confederacy: Attignawantan, Attigneenongnahac, Arendaronon, Tahontaenrat, and Ataronchronon.

Language

The Huron spoke a Northern Iroquoian language. The Attignawantan and Petun are described by the Jesuits as speaking the same language (JR 20:43) but there is evidence of dialect variation between the Attignawantan and Tahontaenrat (JR 10:11). Numerous manuscript grammars and word lists of Huron survive from the seventeenth century, some of which have been published (for a detailed discussion see Hanzeli 1969:19-23). For the later Wyandots there are Pierre Potier's grammar and glossary from the eighteenth century (Potier 1920, 1920a) and the largely unpublished records of Marius Barbeau's fieldwork in Oklahoma in the early part of the twentieth century, just before the Wyandot language became extinct. There has been no systematic linguistic study of these materials and the position of Huron among the Northern Iroquoian languages remains uncertain; however, it is likely that Huron and Five Nations Iroquois were differentiated prior to the separation of the Iroquois languages, although the separation of Huron and Iroquois does not appear to be so great as that between Iroquois and Tuscarora.

Territory and Environment

The southern frontier of Huronia was defined by the Jesuits in terms of these regional strongholds and principal villages: Ossossane (La Conception), Scanonaenrat (Saint Michel), Teanaustaye (Saint Joseph II), and Contarea (Saint Jean Baptiste) (fig. 1). To the northeast, vast swamps stretched along the contact line separating the rock-knob area of the Canadian Shield from the arable uplands of Huronia. The southwest was sharply defined by the tangled cedar and alder swamps of the Nottawasaga lowlands. Only along the southeastern frontier

* Because of the lack of linguistic studies or native speakers there is no scientific orthography for the Huron language; hence the spellings used here are those of the early 17th-century French sources. There is no assurance of internal consistency in these spellings.

between Orr Lake and Lake Couchiching were the swamps more discontinuous. Huronia was in fact an upland area of arable soils surrounded by water and swamp.

The climate in the sixteenth century seems to have been similar to that of the twentieth. Winters may have been slightly longer with a somewhat shorter frost-free season, but not short enough to hinder agricultural activities except perhaps tobacco growing. The mid-twentieth-century growing season in Huronia is about 140 days, while Huron corn matured in 90 to 120 days. Summer droughts, which were carefully recorded by the missionaries because they sometimes got blamed for them, occurred with about the same frequency as recorded in the twentieth century, about twice every 10 years.

Although the extent of the forest cover has changed greatly since the Huron occupance, the dominant species are the same. All the major tree species present in the area as well as many common flowers and shrubs were mentioned by the early explorers. The dominant association throughout the area is maple (*Acer saccharum*), beech (*Fagus grandifolia*), and basswood (*Tilia americana*). White pine (*Pinus strobus*) is common, as well as hemlock (*Tsuga canadensis*) and elm (*Ulmus americana*), particularly on the moister soils. There is no doubt that the cedar and alder swamps found in the area in the 1970s were at one time more extensive as was the abundance of surface water. Many archeological sites in Huronia are beside dry spring and creek beds or shallow swampy depressions that held water in the seventeenth century (Heidenreich 1971).

The occupied portion of Huronia consisted of four major upland areas separated from one another by small rivers with floodplains of swamp or poorly drained heavy soils. These upland areas are generally bounded by steep, boulder-strewn, recessional shorelines. Most of the surface area of the uplands is covered by a sandy till that forms the parent material of sandy loam soils, well drained and of fair to moderate fertility (Heidenreich 1971). Judging from the distribution and tribal affiliation of Huron villages and Jesuit missions, the tribal areas coincided with the major physiographic divisions of Huronia. Only one physiographic area was shared by two tribes.

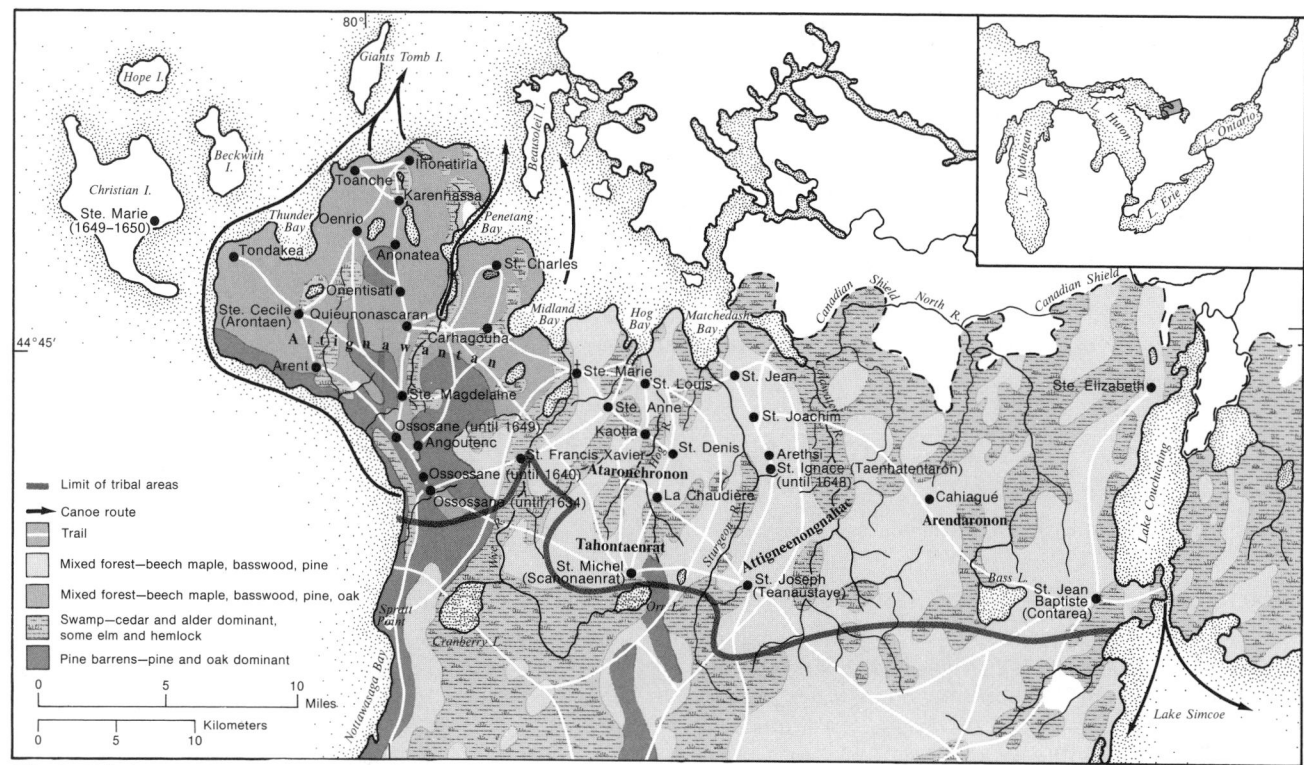

Fig. 1. Tribal areas of Huronia, 1615–1650.

Population

Samuel de Champlain and other French writers claimed that Huronia was for the most part cleared. Huronia was described as a country "full of fine hills, open fields, very beautiful broad meadows bearing much excellent hay..." (Sagard-Théodat 1939:90). The numerous statements regarding grass-covered fields (*prairies*) are probably references to abandoned corn fields. Statements such as these convey the impression that the occupied upland areas were a patchwork of cleared fields and abandoned fields in grasses and various stages of successional forest interspersed with mature stands on the heavier soils. The low-lying swampy areas were virtually untouched.

Population

From Champlain's visit to the Huron to well after the destruction of the Huron confederacy, the early writers and compilers seem to have been in agreement that the Huron population prior to the smallpox epidemics of the mid to late 1630s stood somewhere at about 30,000 (table 1). Similarly, postepidemic population figures are fairly consistent at about 10,000, or about one-third of the original population.

The most important of these early estimates is the one cited by Jerome Lalemant in 1640 because it was based on a village-by-village census taken by the Jesuits in the autumn and winter of 1639. Apparently some effort was made to conduct an accurate census because the deploy-

ment of missionaries was partly dependent on it. This estimate includes the Khionontateronon (Petun) for whom there are no separate population estimates. If the nine Petun villages were roughly proportional in size to the Huron villages, postepidemic population figures would be about 9,000 for the Huron and 3,000 for the Petun.

Champlain's preepidemic figure of 30,000, which was a Huron estimate, was not seriously questioned until Trigger (1969:11–13) and Heidenreich (1971) attempted to derive independent estimates. Both authors accept the postepidemic estimate of 9,000 and, using smallpox death rates compiled by Dobyns (1966) and others, arrive at estimates ranging from Trigger's 18,000 to Heidenreich's 22,000. Two other estimates by Heidenreich (1971) are 18,000 Huron using warrior totals and an average family size of six, and 20,000 taking what is known about the number and size of Huron villages into account. Although only estimates, in the light of present knowledge, a preepidemic Huron population of 18,000 to 22,000 seems reasonable.

Using a population estimate of 20,000 and a settled area of 340 square miles, Huronia had an average population density of about 60 people to a square mile (2,400 to 100 sq. km.) with densities in the central part of the area perhaps twice that number. In view of the efficiency of Huron agriculture and past migration movements high population densities should be expected.

369

Table 1. Huron Population Estimates, 17th Century

Date of Observation	Date of Publication	Compiler or Observer	Population Estimate	Number of Warriors	Number of Villages	Sources
1615–1616	1619	Champlain	32,000	2,000+	18	Champlain 1922–1936, 3:122
1615–1616	1632	Champlain	22,000	2,000+	18	Champlain 1922–1936, 4:302
1623	1632	Sagard-Théodat	30,000–40,000	2,000–3,000	25	Sagard-Théodat 1939:91
pre-1630	1633	LeJeune[a]	30,000	—	—	JR 6:59
1634–1635	1634–1635	Brébeuf	30,000	—	20	JR 7:225, 8:115, 10:313
pre-1630	1640	Lalemant	30,000	—	—	JR 17:223
pre-1630	1653	LeMercier[a]	30,000–35,000	—	—	JR 42:221
pre-1630	1658	Druillettes[a]	30,000–35,000	—	—	JR 44:249
pre-1630	1691	LeClercq[a]	10,000	—	18	LeClercq 1881:96–97
1639	1640	Lalemant[a]	10,000	—	—	JR 17:223
1639	1640	Lalemant[a]	12,000[b]	—	32[b]	JR 19:127
post-1639	1645	Lalemant[a]	10,000–20,000	—	—	JR 28:67

[a] Compiler.

[b] Includes the Khionontateronon (Petun), who had 9 villages.

Social Organization

Soon after reaching puberty the Huron engaged in premarital sex, which could be initiated by either partner. All sexual activity whether by youth or adults was performed outside public view, either at night or in a private place. These relationships could result in marriage or a more informal companionship in which two people would simply live together as long as it suited them. In the latter case both could have sexual relations with others (Sagard-Théodat 1939:121).

The steps leading to formal marriage involved the consent of the couple and their parents. The parents tried to encourage their children to marry into prominent families, and the girl's parents in particular made sure that the prospective groom could prove himself as a warrior and provider (Sagard-Théodat 1939:123–124). In spite of the role of the parents, neither the girl nor the boy could be coerced into an unwanted marriage.

It would appear that a Huron could not marry or have sexual relations with any person of his mother's clan or anyone on his father's side up to and including first cousins (JR 8:119, 10:213; Sagard-Théodat 1939:123). Marriages with a brother's widow or a deceased wife's sister were strongly encouraged.

All Huron marriages were monogamous (JR 8:119). Divorce could be initiated by either party. A woman would simply ask her husband to remove himself from her house, which he would have to do, taking only his clothes. In the same way a man could leave his wife after informing her and her parents with whom he lived. Divorce was most frequent among young married couples, stemming from childlessness or inability of one to supply the needs and wants of another (JR 2₁:135, 28:51–53). Divorce was rare once a couple had children (Sagard-Théodat 1939:124–125; Boucher 1881:56–57). If a divorce seemed imminent, relatives tried to intercede to bring the couple back together. It is not clear who kept the children. Sagard-Théodat (1939:125) wrote that the father took the boys and the mother the girls, while Boucher (1881:57) stated that all the children remained with the mother. In view of the residence, descent, and inheritance systems the latter seems more likely.

According to Boucher (1881:56–57) residence was matrilocal, and the same can be inferred from Sagard-Théodat (1939:121–125). However, other evidence shows that this may have been an ideal that was not always followed in practice (Richards 1967; Trigger 1969:56).

Descent and inheritance were matrilineal (Champlain 1922–1936, 3:140; Sagard-Théodat 1939:130). Children did not succeed to their father's property, but to that of their mother's brother. This practice was also followed in the inheritance of the chieftainship, which usually went to a man's nephew on his sister's side (JR 10:233, 20:215). Furthermore, in old age a man could count more on his nephews and nieces for support than on his own children (JR 26:297), and it was these who publicly exhibited the greatest sorrow at his death (JR 17:123).

Although the Huron were monogamous and formed nuclear families, the matrilineal extended family appears to have been the fundamental social and economic unit. Each nuclear family had its own place within the longhouse, but the members of the longhouse worked together as a closely cooperating unit. The daily running of the longhouse was done by the women, probably under the direction of the senior matron who exercised considerable authority over her daughters even when these were married (Trigger 1969:55). Major decisions were made by the male head of the household, probably in consultation with his wife and family members.

It can be inferred from the ethnohistoric sources that every Huron was a member of one of eight clans. The best evidence for the Huron clan system comes from the historic Wyandot (Trigger 1969:54–57). These were fictive, apparently exogamous kinship groupings tracing descent to a common female ancestor. The historic

Wyandot had eight clans: Turtle, Wolf, Bear, Beaver, Deer, Hawk, Porcupine, and Snake. Since the Huron confederacy was composed of four or five territorial tribes with a defined political hierarchy, the clan system with its chiefs must have been a social organization that cut across tribal divisions. Judging from the way the Huron political system operated, the manner in which chiefs were appointed and councils operated, the clan system must have had mainly a ceremonial function rather than a political one. There is no contemporary direct evidence that Huron clans were grouped into moieties or phratries.

Localized clan segments were fundamental to political organization (Trigger 1969:55). The ethnohistoric sources make references to "large families" and "important families," each of which had a "distinct armorial bearing" (JR 15:181). Large villages were made up of a number of clan segments each having its own civil and war chief who represented them in their respective councils; relatives of the chiefs acted as their councilors (JR 10:231, 233). Succession to a chieftainship was partly inherited in that the men who could be considered for the chieftainship were "nephews" or "grandsons" of an existing chief and partly elected in that the other family members had to approve the succession. Some lineages within each clan segment seem to have been more important than others. These furnished the chiefs who represented the larger clan segment within the village council and at higher levels.

Political Organization

In theory every clan segment had a civil and a war chief. Villages therefore had as many chiefs as there were clan segments (JR 10:229-231). The civil chief, chosen from among the best-qualified candidates of a particular lineage by the members of his clan segment, had to have shown wisdom in decision making, skill in oratory, and liberality. If upon appointment he failed to meet these qualifications he could be removed. The new chief assumed the title, duties, regalia, and name of the old chief at a special ceremony (JR 23:165-169). The rules of succession regarding a war chief are not explicit but appear to have been the same rules as those of the civil chief. A war chief had to have demonstrated bravery and leadership qualities. Neither chieftainship was lost at old age, but only upon death, unless a chief lost popular support through misconduct.

Village affairs were run by two councils with separate membership and duties (fig. 2). The war chiefs and senior warriors met in the house of the most recognized war chief or the initiator of a campaign to make their plans (JR 13:59). If the meeting demanded great secrecy it would be held in a secluded spot outside the village (JR 10:251). Civil affairs were discussed in the longhouse of the most recognized civil chief, who also acted as the head of the council and was chief of the most important clan segment of the village. The council could be attended by all the old men of the village, most likely those over 30 years (Sagard-Théodat 1939:150), as well as the civil chiefs of the various clan segments. Women had no part in the councils. The clan-segment chiefs acted as spokesmen for their relatives and initiated most discussions. Everyone who wanted to speak was given the opportunity. Although matters were decided by consensus, the Jesuits felt that it was the chiefs and old men who really decided things because the others solicited their advice and were easily swayed by their arguments (JR 10:251).

Fig. 2. Council, and three women showing tumpline used for loads, two methods of carrying babies, and snowshoes. Detail from the map "Novæ Franciæ Accurata Delineatio," attributed to F.J. Bressani, engraved by G.F. Pesca in 1657.

After a decision was made the council chief would announce it to the village. Decisions were not binding on individuals but affirmed the majority opinion on a matter.

The chiefs had no coercive powers; however, village members knew that going against majority opinion would lay them open to criticism. Serious crimes, such as witchcraft with intent to kill or treason, were punished by death simply by placing the accused outside the law whereupon anyone could kill them without fear of reprisal (JR 8:123). Murder was probably settled by the clan segments involved, but if these could not come to a decision the village council would attempt to settle the matter (JR 10:215–223).

Tribal councils could be called by any chief of a clan segment whenever matters arose that involved more than the interests of his village. The meeting was announced by messenger to the villages of the tribe or the villages involved in a particular matter. The seating at the council was in terms of villages so that the chiefs and their advisers could consult with one another. Prior to the meeting the most important chiefs might be given presents, which the Jesuits believed to be a form of bribery. The meeting would begin by making certain that the main chiefs were present; if any were absent without explanation the council was dissolved. After an exchange of greetings the chief who had called the council would outline in detail the matter to be discussed, phrasing it in the form of a request for advice. The language used in the discussions was highly ritualized, full of metaphors and circumlocutions. Every new speaker would summarize previous arguments, which would be repeated by the head of the council. In the end a majority opinion would be given that, as in village matters, was not binding on the members of the council (JR 10:251, 255).

As at the village level, some chiefs were considered more important than others. These men were invested with particular responsibilities and were sought out for advice on special matters. The most highly regarded chief was considered the embodiment of the tribe. In his name treaties were made and in formal councils his name was a synonym for the tribe (JR 10:231).

Confederacy councils were held at least once a year (Sagard-Théodat 1939:150). The main functions of these councils were to renew and strengthen ties of friendship among the tribes and to plan the ruination of their common enemies. The second function suggests that the confederacy was primarily a defensive alliance, although in most cases each tribe followed its own interests. Confederacy councils were usually held once a year. Representation and seating on the council were by tribe and village (JR 15:39). Each village sent its clan-segment chiefs of whom one became the spokesman, the rest his advisors. As in the other councils no women were present. The meetings proceeded in the same manner as at the

tribal level. Again, no decisions were binding on individual members.

At the confederacy level policy depended on all tribes agreeing, which was not always easy and often resulted in indecision. This merely repeated the decision-making process at lower levels where clan segments or villages had to come to a common agreement but often could not due to conflicting interests. Prior to the Iroquois onslaughts of the 1640s this disunity probably did not matter. When the Huron were faced with forces that threatened their existence the weaknesses of these councils became apparent. They were simply not equipped to make rapid or binding decisions that would force members of the tribe or confederacy to act in concert.

Religion and Ceremony

Religion, mythology, feasts, dances, and other customs formed integrative institutions that were an important part of Huron life. It was what they called their *onderha,* or the 'foundation, prop, or maintenance' of the country (Trigger 1969:90). Huron ceremonial life was in the hands of the old men and transmitted by them (JR 10:147). The best accounts of Huron ceremonial life and beliefs can be found in Sagard-Théodat (1939), the *Jesuit Relations* (JR 8:117–131, 10:125–317), Tooker (1964), and Trigger (1969).

Spirits

To the Huron all things whether animate or inanimate had a soul or spirit. The more powerful of these spirits, those that exerted control over the daily affairs of men, were called *oki.* Unusual men such as shamans, powerful warriors, or madmen were also called *oki,* as were proved charms (Sagard-Théodat 1939:170; JR 10:49). The most powerful *oki* was the sky because it controlled the seasons, the winds, waves on the sea, and all other natural phenomena (JR 10:159–161). The sky was invoked at special occasions such as the conclusion of a treaty, the healing of the sick, or the giving of a promise. Feasts were given in its honor, and tobacco and on occasion the body of a dead man was burned as a sacrifice (JR 10:163–165).

Since animals also had spirits the Huron were careful not to offend them. Animal and fish bones were not burned (Sagard-Théodat 1939:186–187) nor were they fed to the dogs. Fishing nets were never displayed before the dead and to ensure a good catch the nets were married at the beginning of the fishing season to two virgins (JR 10:167). While fishing, prayers were offered to the fish and tobacco offered as a sacrifice to the spirit of the waters (Sagard-Théodat 1939:188–189).

Some of the more important spirits could appear in human or semihuman form. *ondoutaehte,* for example, was the god of war and appeared as a dwarf or old woman (JR 10:183), while *onditachiaé,* part human and part turkey cock, was the spirit of thunder, lightning, and rain (JR 10:45, 195). After the sky, the two most important spirits were *ataensic,* a woman identified with the moon, and her grandson *iouskeha,* who was identified with the sun (Sagard-Théodat 1939:169; JR 8:117–119, 10:127–139). *iouskeha* made the lakes and rivers, freed all the animals from a great cave, made the corn grow, provided good weather, and passed on the secret of fire making to mankind. All living things were in his care. *ataensic* had fallen from the sky to become the mother of mankind. It was she also who made men die, was in charge of their souls, and continuously tried to undo the good works of *iouskeha.* Both these spirits lived very much like mankind but could rejuvenate themselves once they got old.

Illness and Dreams

The Huron classified illnesses into three broad categories: illness due to natural causes such as an arrow wound, illness caused by witchcraft, and desires of the soul. In order to cure any of these, specialists were needed. Illness due to natural causes was the sphere of the medicine man whose cures involved a combination of herbal medicine and good sense (Sagard-Théodat 1939:192–204). Curing those afflicted by witchcraft was in the hands of a shaman (*ontetsans*). The cures involved magic, feasts, dances, counterspells, and if possible, determination of the person responsible. If a witch was identified and could or would not remove the spell, he or she might be executed on orders of the chief and council. The shaman helped in removing the spell and finding the witch. Witchcraft was considered the most serious of crimes and a clever chief could use accusations of witchcraft to rid himself and the community of antisocial elements (Trigger 1969:86–89).

The Huron believed that unfulfilled personal desires could lead to illness and madness (Wallace 1958a). The curing of such an illness demanded that the desired object be identified and given to the person no matter who owned it. In some cases the desire had to be acted out by the sick person or others. In order to identify the desire a shaman was required, and the most important means of identifying the desire was dream interpretation. Dreams were believed to be a subconscious revelation of the spirits or desire of a person's own soul. Dreams foretold future events; prescribed feasts, dances, games; and told people how to conduct their daily lives (JR 10:169–175). No Huron would act counter to the dictates of his dreams. The shaman helped to interpret the dream and helped in its fulfillment.

Each winter a large part of the population of a community would participate in a three-day festival called *ononharoia* 'the upsetting of the brain' (Sagard-Théodat 1939:201–204; JR 10:175–177). Bands of people would stream through the village feigning madness and demanding objects they claimed they had seen in their dreams. Most often *ononharoia* was precipitated by the illness of a well-known person. At the end of the "festival" those that had participated retired to the woods outside the village to "cast out their madness," hoping that the sick person would recover. *ononharoia* probably served as a means for giving vent to pent-up emotions. It also resulted in a redistribution of wealth because many objects taken during these days were not returned.

Feasts, Dances, and Games

Feasts were an important means of maintaining friendships and gaining status. A feast giver was an honored and respected man because he shared his good fortune with others (JR 17:153). Usually a great deal of food was consumed, and the majority of the feasts were probably prompted by abundance and a desire to share it. There

Public Arch. of Canada, Ottawa: Map Division (H-12-900-1657); Lib. of Congress.
Fig. 3. Dance as depicted on the Bressani map (fig. 2) and girl dressed for a dance as shown in Champlain 1619:87.

were four main types of feasts: *enditeuhwa,* to express thanksgiving and gratitude (JR 10:177); *awataerohi,* to cure someone of a disease; *athataion,* a farewell feast from a dying man to an assembly of friends (JR 10:61, 267); and *atouront aochien,* a singing feast given prior to going to war, when a man wished to become renowned, or when a person received the name of a deceased chief (JR 10:181). The feasts were accompanied by singing, dancing, and eating. At some feasts, called *anondahoin,* only tobacco was smoked (Sagard-Théodat 1939:112). At all feasts it was customary that the giver of the feast ate nothing or very little and spent his time entertaining his guests with song and talk.

Formal dances were performed for four main reasons: to propitiate spirits so that they might confer benefits, to welcome someone important, to rejoice at a victory, and to cure illness (Sagard-Théodat 1939:115-120). The last two were probably associated with the *enditeuhwa* and *awataerohi* feasts. Women participated in the dances (fig. 3).

Games were played for pleasure, in response to dreams, and to cure illnesses. The most popular games were lacrosse, played by village teams or between entire villages, and a number of gambling games played by large or small numbers of individuals with heavy betting by players as well as bystanders (Tooker 1964:114-117; Trigger 1969:100-101). Like feasts and dances, games were important integrative institutions that brought people from different social segments and villages together. The gambling games in particular were also a mechanism for redistributing food surplus and other goods.

Death

The Huron did not fear death, believing that they went to an afterlife that was not too different from that of the living. A person who was dying was often prepared for death prior to the actual event. The dead person was placed on a mat in a flexed position and a chief announced the death to the village and friends in neighboring villages. While lying in state the body was attended by members of a clan or clan segment other than the dead person's own. If the deceased had been an important person, the chiefs from other villages would attend. Lamentations would begin as soon as a person died. At the same time various people who had known the deceased would give speeches extolling his virtues. On the third day after death, the chief in charge of the ceremonies would announce a feast at which the soul of the deceased took part. During the feast gifts were exchanged and heaped upon the deceased. Most of the gifts were given to the bereaved and to the persons who directed the funeral. The body was placed on a scaffold 8 to 10 feet above the ground accompanied by some grave goods. No one spared himself in giving gifts; Brébeuf claimed that some funerals were so expensive that it seemed as if people worked and traded only to acquire grave goods (JR 10:265-271).

Those killed in war or by drowning were buried below the ground (JR 10:273). A shrine was built over the grave and encircled by a fence (Sagard-Théodat 1939: 207-208). Children less than one month of age were buried on a path or some other frequented place so that their spirit could rise and reenter the womb of a woman who passed that way (JR 10:273).

General mourning for the deceased lasted for about 10 days, but the wife or husband of the deceased was expected to mourn for one year. During that time they would not participate in any feasts or festivals, nor would they remarry (JR 10:273-275).

The burials described above were only temporary. About every 8 to 12 years the Huron would disinter all single burials and prepare them for the most important ceremony of all, the great Feast of the Dead (Champlain 1922-1936, 3:161; Sagard-Théodat 1939:211-214; JR 10:279-317). On the whole, the Feast seems to have been a tribal affair in which the villages got together and buried their dead in a common grave. This was not only a religious ceremony but also an occasion to symbolize tribal union through common burial and to renew friendship with the living and the dead. The Feast also acted as a general catharsis of personal grief.

When time grew near to hold the Feast, the old men and chiefs would meet in a tribal council to determine the exact date and place. Once the coming of the Feast was announced, each family would get the bodies of their deceased relatives from the keepers of the graves. All except those who had died recently were cleansed of all flesh, which was burned. The whole bodies were arranged on litters while the bones of the others were wrapped in beaver robes. All were carried into the village where feasts were given in their honor. Then each village set out for the place where the Feast of the Dead was to be held. Some journeys took several days to complete.

At the place designated for the Feast a pit had been dug large enough to hold all the dead. In the case of an ossuary excavated at Ossossane, which had been described by Brébeuf in 1636, the pit was 20 feet in diameter and 5 feet deep (Kidd 1953:365). Once the processions arrived at the pit each bundle was opened for a final farewell. The inside of the pit was lined with beaver robes and the whole bodies placed on the bottom. Next, the assembled people were placed into village groups, each subdivided by clan and lineage. On a signal by the master of the Feast, each chief led his delegation to the platform that surrounded the pit and suspended from it the bags of bones and grave goods. Formal announcements were made as to the nature and quantity of the grave goods. Grave goods such as kettles were placed at the bottom of the pit. Upon a signal each family threw the bones of their deceased plus grave goods into the pit. Finally the grave was covered with mats, bark, and a mound of sand. Logs were placed into and on top of the mound; the whole was surrounded by upright wooden posts. Only a fraction of the grave goods was placed into the grave. Some were given to the master in charge of the Feast, others went to relatives of the deceased. The greater part of the beaver robes was given to the assembled crowd. Presents were also given to foreigners who had sent gifts or attended the ceremonies and to the young people of the villages. Some goods placed into the grave were broken in order to release their souls so that they could accompany the dead on their long journey to the afterlife (Sagard-Théodat 1939:172).

The Huron believed that each person had two souls. One hovered near the corpse until the Feast of the Dead, after which it was released and could be reborn. Some of these souls were resurrected in name-giving ceremonies. The other soul departed after the Feast for the village of the dead. Each Huron tribe, as well as the Algonquians and others, had a village of the dead that lay in the direction of the setting sun (JR 10:143). After the Feast the souls would assemble covered in their robes and grave goods and depart on a path along the Milky Way (Sagard-Théodat 1939:172). The souls of dogs would go to the same place by a slightly different route. Children and the very old or infirm who were not strong enough to undertake the journey would stay behind in a special village. Here they would use the corn fields abandoned by the living (JR 10:143–145). The souls of those killed in war as well as suicides went to places of their own. Along the path to the village of the dead, the souls had to go past the rock *ecaregniondi* in the Petun country. Near this rock lived *oscotarach* 'head-piercer' who drew out their brains. Next, the souls had to pass over a log that lay across a raging river guarded by a fierce dog. Many who were frightened by the dog fell off the log and drowned. After many months the souls would finally get to the village of the dead, which was very much like that of the living. There they would continue as they had in life, their occupations and status unchanged (JR 10:147).

Settlement

The Huron took considerable care in choosing a site for their village. Each site had to have a combination of specific requirements among which proximity to a source of water, arable soils, available firewood, a young secondary forest, and a defendable position seem to have been paramount.

There is no doubt that a permanent water supply in proximity to the village was of major importance. Every known Huron site is immediately adjacent to a spring or some other water supply. Water was carried to the village in fragile earthenware or bark vessels. This must have been a frequent chore because Sagard-Théodat (1939:

109) relates that Huron pottery disintegrated when water was stored in it for any length of time.

Similar to many slash-and-burn agriculturalists, the Huron had a marked preference for certain soil types (Cruickshank and Heidenreich 1969:36). Of 139 known village sites 94.5% occur on well-drained soils ranging from gravels to silt loams. Together these soils comprise 75 percent of Huronia. The preferred soils were well-drained sandy loams, which covered 40 percent of Huronia but contained 68.5% of the sites. These were among the more fertile soils within the capabilities of the Huron digging-stick technology; but on the whole these sandy loams tend to have a low moisture-holding capacity and are deficient in phosphorus, potassium, and nitrogen, all necessary elements for corn growing (Hoffman, Wiklund, and Richards 1962). Once depleted through overuse, their recovery rate is slow. A young forest growth may become established again in 30 to 60 years depending on the size of the clearing and drainage conditions. Avoidance of the more fertile silt and clay loams was probably prompted by a heavier forest growth, lack of drainage techniques, and difficulty in working the soil with a digging stick once it got too dry.

Certain species of trees were preferred as building material and firewood—cedar, birch, elm, and pine. All four are widely distributed in Huronia. Cedar and elm bark were major roofing materials for the longhouses; birchbark was used in small quantities for utensils and canoes; pine was a source of resin, firewood, and palisade posts. Oaks were sought in times of famine for their acorns.

Far more important than any single species or association was the size composition of a timber stand. The Huron with their technology could not cope with heavy timber, nor did they have any use for it. The nature of the construction of their villages demanded an enormous number of logs under 10 or 12 inches in diameter. A minimum of 20,000 poles and 162,000 square feet of bark roofing were needed for a large single-palisaded village of 6 acres housing 1,000 people in 36 longhouses; moreover, these estimates are conservative since most villages of this size or larger had double or triple palisades (Heidenreich 1971). It is evident that these materials are not readily available in a mature forest. Therefore, by necessity the Huron located their villages in or near areas of secondary forest that were a natural consequence of the normal cycle of shifting cultivation. Archeological surveys have confirmed that precontact village sites are often found in proximity to sites that were in existence during the French period; the precontact sites often predate the historic ones by 50 to 80 years.

A defensive position is often cited as a site requirement. Since Iroquoian warfare depended on surprise attacks rather than sieges, a mere break in slope would not be sufficient for defensive purposes. The village would have to be palisaded along the break in slope for any defensive position to be effective. Since not all villages were palisaded, probably many stood at the edge of a break in slope simply because a spring issued there. In general, only the largest villages seem to have been deliberately placed on a defendable site with steep slopes on three sides.

The Longhouse

The Huron longhouse varied in size according to the size of the extended family that inhabited it (JR 16:243, 35:87; Sagard-Théodat 1939:94; Lafitau 1724, 2:9–16). Champlain (1922–1936, 3:123) and Sagard-Théodat (1939:93) both describe the longhouse as being about 30 by 125 to 160 feet, while Brébeuf and Bressani give dimensions of 12 to 220 feet with a width of 20 to 24 feet (JR 8:107, 35:247). From the archeological evidence, an average Huron longhouse appears to have been 25 by about 100 feet. The fairly constant widths seem to reflect limitations in building materials and construction methods. Heights were about the same as widths (fig. 4).

According to the ethnohistoric accounts the hearths were set in a passageway some 10 to 12 feet in width running down the center of the longhouse. Storage areas or vestibules were placed at either or both ends of the longhouse for corn casks and firewood, with additional storage facilities under long sleeping platforms that ran along both sides of the lodge (Champlain 1922–1936, 3:123; Sagard-Théodat 1939:94–95; JR 8:107–109). Food and clothing were stored by being suspended on poles and in storage pits dug into house floors. The large central hearths were spaced about five to eight feet apart (JR 17:177) and usually varied between 7 and 10 feet in length and three to four feet in width. Most excavated longhouses reveal the presence of smaller fire pits, which may have been cooking fires, while the larger hearths were also used for heating in the winter. Since there were two nuclear families to a fireplace, each family would have about 12 to 20 linear feet, which would give them 120 to 200 square feet of living space assuming a depth of 10 feet from the hearth to the walls. With an average family size of six, each individual would have 20 to 30 square feet of living space, which seems adequate in view of the fact that the villages were mainly occupied in the winter.

Sleeping platforms along the sides of longhouses (Champlain 1922–1936, 3:123; Sagard-Théodat 1939:93; JR 17:203) were used in the summer, while in the winter the family slept on the floor near the fire. The space beneath the platforms was used to store firewood (JR 8:109). There is no evidence that the interiors of the houses were subdivided into family cubicles although such cubicles were described in later ethnohistoric accounts (Lafitau 1724, 2:9–16; Morgan 1851:315) and have been archeologically confirmed in New York State (Ritchie 1965:308; Hayes 1967:93). In some cases sweatbaths may also have been located within the longhouse along the central aisle (Lafitau 1724,1:371–372; Tyyska 1972).

Public Arch. of Canada, Ottawa: Map Division (H-12-900-1657).

Fig. 4. Longhouse (shown much too short), woman pounding corn, women carrying firewood and (probably) water, and the torture of a war captive. Detail from the Bressani map (fig. 2).

376

In appearance the Huron longhouses reminded European visitors of "arcades, bowers," or "garden arbors." They were long structures with a vaulted roof and slightly rounded ends. The outer walls were composed of a double row of staggered posts some two to four inches in diameter drawn together in an arch to form the roof. Sheets of elm, cedar, or ash bark were woven between the posts. Openings were left in the roof for the smoke to escape. Doors were placed at either end or on the sides near the ends. Roof and door openings could be closed with sheets of bark or skins. The best time for building these structures was in the spring, when the sap was rising and bark and wood were pliable (Champlain 1922-1936, 3:122-124; Sagard-Théodat 1939:95; JR 8:105-107; Lafitau 1724, 2:9-16). Construction of a house was a communal affair.

In a large village only two longhouses served other than residential functions. These were the houses of the principal civil and war chiefs. Both structures were considerably larger than the rest, some according to Brébeuf reaching lengths up to 180 feet (JR 10:1). The house of the civil chief, besides being a dwelling, served as a meeting place for village and other councils and some feasts and dances (Sagard-Théodat 1939:115, 149; JR 10:33, 13:59). The house of the war chief had similar communal functions.

Lalemant described life in the longhouse as "a miniature picture of hell," in which dust and smoke blind the eyes, children and dogs give themselves free rein, and fleas and mice get at one's person and belongings (JR 17:13-15). The Huron of course saw things quite differently. To them the longhouse represented the physical manifestation of their social and economic system. It was at this level and in these surroundings that the Huron values of family solidarity, economic cooperation, and rule by the mutual agreement of adults found their basic expression. The values of the longhouse were projected to the village through kinship ties and ultimately to the tribal level.

The Village

Just as the longhouse was the physical expression of the extended family, so was the village the physical expression of a number of closely cooperating lineages. Structurally the Huron village can be defined as a cluster of closely spaced longhouses, interspersed with small open areas and sometimes surrounded by a palisade.

As a rule only the larger villages and those on the frontier were strongly fortified. In the case of an attack the people from the smaller villages fled to the regional strongholds or hid in the forest (Sagard-Théodat 1939:92, 155; JR 10:51). Where palisades have been excavated they have usually been composed of a single, double, or triple row of staggered upright posts, but palisades up to four and five rows have been found (Emerson and Russell 1965). The individual posts were spaced 6 to 12 inches apart. When more than two rows were present, the central row was usually composed of logs up to 12 inches in diameter while the rest were in the range of three to six inches. According to early observations the palisade varied in height from 15 to 35 feet (Champlain 1922-1936, 3:48; JR 34:123-125). The rows were interlaced with branches and bark with logs rolled between them. If the palisade was wide enough, galleries would be built on top of them and watchtowers at strategic corners (Champlain 1922-1936, 3:122; Sagard-Théodat 1939: 91-92). Part of the defensive equipment of the galleries were stones for throwing and water for extinguishing fires. One or two gates were built into the palisade in such a way that it was difficult to see them from a distance. These gates could easily be blocked and one could not enter them "striding straight in," but was "forced to pass turning sideways" (Sagard-Théodat 1939:92).

Surprisingly little is known about the internal layout of Huron villages. Beyond stating that houses were usually placed three to four yards apart "for fear of fire which they greatly dread" (Champlain 1922-1936, 3:125) and that villages had "streets" and "public places" (carrefours), the ethnohistoric sources are mute on the point (Sagard-Théodat 1939:203; JR 15:157, 16:247). The orientation of most of the excavated houses has been north by northwest, the direction of the coldest prevailing winter winds in Huronia (Norcliffe and Heidenreich 1974:27).

Garbage was disposed by dumping it against and over the palisade, or if the village was large, at convenient places within the village, probably near the entrances of the houses. Both the garbage dumps (middens) and soil within the longhouse areas are rich in calcium, phosphorus, magnesium, and other elements. The magnesium stems from the large quantities of wood ash, and the others from decomposed organic garbage as well as human excrement and urine (Hurley and Heidenreich 1971:181-212).

Huron villages varied in size up to 100 longhouses (JR 10:210), although Champlain (1922-1936, 3:49) estimated 200 "fairly large lodges" at Cahiagué. Since Champlain's estimates were never very accurate this may be an exaggeration. The largest village during the Jesuit period was Teanaustaye (Saint Joseph II) with 80 longhouses and 400 families (JR 15:153, 34:87), while Ossossane, one of the largest villages, had 40 houses (JR 15:153). Assuming that these were average-sized longhouses with three fireplaces, six families, and six members a family, Teanaustaye had a population of about 2,800 and Ossossane 1,400. The estimate of 400 families (2,400 people) at Teanaustaye would seem to indicate that the above reasoning is fairly accurate. On the basis of the little that is known about Huron sites, a density of five to eight houses an acre seems to be reasonable (Heidenreich 1971). This ratio would put village densities at about 180 to 280 people an acre.

Based on data from 46 sites in Huronia, an average village size seems to have been about four to five acres (Heidenreich 1971). Only 9 villages were over 6 acres and 13 over 5 acres. In terms of population, it would seem then that few villages grew over 1,000 or 1,600. The vast majority must have been 800 people or less. The large villages coincide with a large hinterland of fertile arable soils, but this access does not seem to be the major reason for their size or existence. From what is known of the large villages during the Jesuit period they were regional strongholds, the seats of tribal authority and residence of chiefs with unusual ability. In a society that depended on rule by mutual agreement rather than coercion it would not be unusual for villages to fission once they reached a certain size, which among the Huron seems to have been about 800 to 1,600 people. Clan segments could simply move off and establish their own village if there was no compelling reason for them to stay together. In the case of the largest villages the powerful chiefs may have been able to hold larger numbers of people together through their governing abilities as well as embryo coercive institutions such as a group of loyal followers or the threat of witchcraft (Heidenreich 1971). Cross-cultural studies by Naroll (1956) suggest that coercive institutions are necessary once settlements grow much over 1,000 to 1,600 people. It would seem that there were some social limitations to Huron settlement size, since the Huron subsistence economy permitted larger settlements.

Some of the largest settlements were multiple villages. The Warminster site (Cahiagué) for example was composed of six- and nine-acre segments, Quieunonascaran was a triple village (JR 13:125), and Saint Ignace (Taenhatentaron) and Arethsi were so close together they sometimes went by the same name. Other large villages such as Ossossane (JR 10:291, 14:15-17), Toanche (JR 14:23), and Cahiagué (Sagard-Théodat 1939:92) split into segments during the process of village movement. It would be interesting to find out how many of the large sites in Huronia were indeed multiple villages. In view of Huron social and political institutions as well as Iroquoian methods of warfare, multiple villages offered obvious advantages over single large villages. They are easier to defend, minimize social friction, and have the advantages of large villages such as a labor pool and talented leaders.

Except for the regional strongholds, the function of all Huron villages was the same: They were economically self-sufficient agricultural units. None appears to have had special economic functions such as regional markets or specialized manufacturing. Contact with neighboring villages was purely on a social, and perhaps semipolitical, basis. The spacing of villages was therefore a matter of physical site requirements such as the presence of water and the area of available agricultural soils. Dependence on environmental factors is reflected by the near random distribution of villages during the Jesuit period, which would be more patterned if economic factors, such as marketing principles, had played a role in village distribution (Heidenreich 1971).

Communication between settlements was by an extensive trail network; water transport was not used within Huronia. The trail network (fig. 1) can be approximated from the ethnohistoric sources and the trails present in the early nineteenth century (A.F. Hunter 1889, 1899, 1900, 1902, 1903, 1904, 1907; Heidenreich 1971). Whenever possible trails followed high ground, crossing swamps only at their narrowest extent. These trails were difficult to negotiate and a newcomer frequently got lost on them (Sagard-Théodat 1939:69; JR 13:181, 17:17, 20:99), especially in the winter, when snow made them almost invisible (JR 20:45). In general, winter travel was avoided except for some socializing with neighboring villages and ice fishing. Even in the summer, most travel seems to have been to the fields and points outside Huronia. Travel between villages was primarily in the fall, after the harvest, for social and political activities, and then mainly with neighboring villages. This pattern is reflected by the trail network, which shows that every village was connected to its neighbor but that a wider regional trail network integrating distant parts of Huronia was absent. In view of the self-sufficient economic, social, and political nature of Huron villages this is to be expected.

Subsistence

Diet and Health

It was the unanimous opinion of all the early writers that corn formed the overwhelming staple throughout the year (Champlain 1922-1936, 3:125; Sagard-Théodat 1939:80, 105-106; JR 10:93, 101, 11:7, 15:153, 159). All other foods, with rare exceptions, were mixed into the ubiquitous corn soup (sagamité) or baked into little corn cakes. Beans were of lesser importance, and pumpkins or squash only in the late summer and fall when they were available. Various fruits formed the bulk of the gathered produce, and acorns in times of famine. On the whole, gathered vegetable foods were of little importance except as a source of vitamin C.

Numerous references demonstrate that meat was a rarity (Champlain 1922-1936, 3:126; Sagard-Théodat 1939:82, 106-107; JR 7:223, 13:109, 17:17, 143). Bressani, for example, was of the opinion that the Huron "hunted only for pleasure or on extraordinary occasions . . ." (JR 38:245). Meat was more plentiful in the late winter and fall, the principal periods for deer hunting. Although butchering practices may be partially responsible, the rarity of meat in the Huron diet is reflected by the paucity of bone material on Huron sites.

Fish, and to a lesser extent other aquatic animals such as turtles and clams, seem to have been of considerably more importance than meat. Fish is usually mentioned as a major component of the usual corn gruel (Champlain 1922–1936, 3:127; Sagard-Théodat 1939:71, 106–107; JR 10:93, 101, 15:159). Fish could be dried and stored longer than meat; they were more predictable in their habits, easier to catch, and more plentiful in Huronia than any meat source. Pound for pound, fish brought a higher return for effort expended than any meat brought in by hunting.

Apart from the occasional feasts during special occasions or times of abundance, the Huron ate twice a day, in the morning and early evening (Champlain 1922–1936, 3:130; JR 8:113, 15:183). From the numerous references in the ethnohistoric sources a reasonable estimate would put the total corn intake at about 65 percent of the diet, and beans, squash, and pumpkins at about 15 percent (Trigger 1969:26–27; Heidenreich 1971). Fish may have amounted to 10 or 15 percent while meat made up about 5 percent, the rest being gathered produce. If a Huron consumed an average of 3,000 calories per day, the amount of corn in the diet would be about 1,900 calories or 1.3 pounds (Heidenreich 1971).

A detailed breakdown of Huron diet in terms of its nutrient content seems to show no obvious deficiencies (Heidenreich 1971). The calcium and vitamin C intake may have been a bit low in the winter, but not low enough to affect bone growth. Moreover there is no record of scurvy, pellagra, or rickets among the Huron. Scurvy could be cured if it occurred, while pellagra, a vitamin deficiency common to a high corn diet, was prevented by the high fish intake. Judging from the Cahiagué skeletal material, the most common Huron ailments that left their mark on the skeleton were osteoarthritis of the lower spine and squatting facets, an ankle deformity, both brought about from squatting habitually cross legged on the ground (Harris 1949). Champlain (1922–1936, 3:135–136), Sagard-Théodat (1939:192–204), and the Jesuits (JR 33:199–209, 15:155) all agreed that the Huron were unusually healthy, on the whole "more healthy than we" (JR 38:257).

Annual Round

The early observers recognized that the Huron followed a definite seasonal pattern (JR 15:157). The cycle of activities began in early March when some men went hunting to places where deer had "yarded" to escape the deep ice-encrusted snow of late winter. After returning from the hunt the men went fishing until mid-May to take advantage of the spring spawning runs of walleye, sucker, pike, and sturgeon (fig. 5). About this time the women gathered firewood and began preparing the fields by burning them over, a task men helped with if new fields had to be cleared. Toward the end of May the women put the seed in the ground while the men departed on trading or war expeditions. A predetermined number of men would stay at home in case of enemy raids. These would help at odd jobs or go fishing and hunting near the village.

Throughout the summer the villages were virtually deserted as the women and children stayed in the fields hoeing the corn and chasing away pests. During the late summer most of the gathering took place, particularly wild fruits and Indian hemp. In this task the women were helped by the children. A constant threat during the summer were Iroquois raiding parties who tended to pick on small parties working away from the village. Similar attacks were carried out by the Huron among the Iroquois tribes.

By the end of August and early September the corn was harvested, dried, and stored away. It was about this time that the men returned from trading and warfare and began to get ready for the large autumn deer hunts. Deer hunting was carried out a few days' journey to the south of Huronia in the oak (mast-producing) areas of Ontario. Here deer congregated for the rutting season, the last half of October. On returning from deer hunting the village populations concentrated on the fall spawning runs of whitefish, lake trout, and cisco, which lasted from early November to the beginning of December. Most of the fish would be dried and stored away for the winter.

During the late fall a number of Algonquian bands settled near the Huron villages to spend the winter. The Nipissing usually settled among the Attignawantan in the west and various Ottawa Valley groups among the Arendaronon in eastern Huronia. On their way to Huronia the Algonquians would obtain fish, meat, and furs

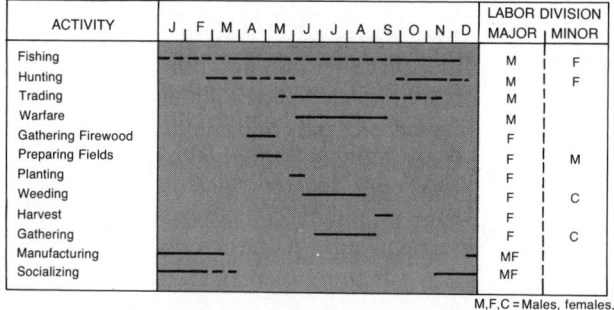

Fig. 5. Seasonal cultural and natural cycles.

to trade for corn and other items. As soon as the ice broke in May, these groups would depart to the north.

By early December everyone was back in the villages marking the beginning of a variety of social activities to celebrate successful harvesting, hunting, fishing, and trading. These feasts were accompanied by gambling and gift giving. If captives had been taken, some were tortured at this time. Among the few activities performed during the winter were ice fishing and trade with Algonquian neighbors. The women would weave mats, manufacture fish nets, and prepare corn for the next season's trade.

Roughly every 8 to 12 years this cycle would be interrupted through village relocation and the great Feast of the Dead. Sometimes only one village would be involved, but most commonly several villages with strong social ties and a common past would undergo these burial activities together. It was a period of social reaffirmations and realignments.

Agriculture

Among the Huron all unused land was common property. Farm plots seem to have been owned and operated by individuals or nuclear families, although the task of land clearance as well as a large part of the produce were shared by the extended family. Every family took as much land as it could cultivate, whereupon that land became theirs. When land was abandoned it reverted back to the community and was free to be taken up by someone else (Sagard-Théodat 1939:109). Since land could not be sold or inherited, it could not be accumulated as wealth. Status was not derived from the ownership of land but, in part at least, from the judicious disposal of produce through gift giving, feasts, or other institutionalized means of redistributing wealth.

Huron agricultural methods were fairly typical of slash-and-burn farming. In a new clearing trees and brushwood were chopped down, piled against stumps, and burned. Old fields were simply burned over. Large trees were girdled and removed at a later time. Most of the clearing took place at the beginning of May, at the same time that firewood was gathered (Champlain 1922-1936, 3:156; Sagard-Théodat 1939:103-104). The next step was planting the seed, which had been carefully selected and sometimes germinated in a bed of moist bark within a longhouse (Lafitau 1724, 2:76-78; Kalm 1935:107). Up to 10 grains were placed into clusters of holes a few inches deep, made with a digging stick. These seed clusters were spaced about a pace apart. As the corn grew, earth was hoed up against the stalks forming mounds up to a foot and a half high and two to three feet across. Judging from archeological finds, hoes were made from moose antlers and deer scapulae. Fields up to 60 acres of irregularly spaced mounds were reported in Huronia in the nineteenth century (Heidenreich 1971).

From these observations an average of 2,500 corn hills an acre seems reasonable (Heidenreich 1974).

Once the corn was a few inches high, kidney beans were planted in the same hills. In view of the relative importance of corn to beans in the Huron diet it is not likely that beans were planted in every corn hill. Squash and pumpkins were probably planted separately from the corn fields.

The women and children spent the greater part of the summer pulling weeds and chasing a host of predators from the corn fields. Particularly troublesome were blackbirds, grackles, jays, raccoons, and the sandhill crane (Sagard-Théodat 1939:220). Crane remains form the largest part of the avian bone material recovered at the Robitaille site (Savage 1971:168). Grasshoppers and caterpillars were also considered pests (JR 10:195, 14:105, 18:85).

Harvest commenced in late August and continued well into September (JR 13:85). Like most agricultural work, harvesting was the responsibility of the women (Sagard-Théodat 1939:101, 104). The ripe corn cobs were picked and brought to the longhouse where some were shelled, dried, and stored in communal bins or underground pits. The rest of the corn was hung in bunches from the ceiling and sides of the longhouse after the husks had been pulled back. Even in the longhouse the corn was not safe from pests. Huron villages were overrun by mice who were there "in thousands . . . without number" (Sagard-Théodat 1939:227).

Judging from descriptions and archeological remains, the Huron grew mainly flour and flint corn, the latter outnumbering the former by about three to one on archeological sites (Heidenreich 1971). The average cob seems to have been about four to six inches long, eight rowed (though occasionally reaching 10 and 12 rows), and holding anywhere from 100 to 400 kernels. Each stalk produced two to three cobs and each corn hill about three stalks (Sagard-Théodat 1939:104; Kalm 1935:109). The preponderance of flint over flour corn probably reflects the frost-free period in Huronia of 130 to 140 days: flint corn matures in three months and flour corn in four.

Farmers in Huronia in the 1970s estimated that they would not get a crop from the sandy loams preferred by the Huron after four to six years of continuous cultivation if they did not use fertilizer. The Huron did not use fertilizer, but they doubled the time a plot could be used through burning, weeding, interplanting with beans, and planting their crops in irregularly spaced hills. The immediate effect of burning is a rise in soil fertility because wood ash is rich in magnesium, calcium, potassium, and phosphorus, all necessary for corn growth. Nitrogen, another element critical to corn growth, was added to the soil, first, through the interplanting of a leguminous crop such as beans and second, through burning, which reduces soil acidity thus stimulating bacterial activity and therefore nitrogen formation (Ahlgren and Ahlgren 1960:498). In the long run, continuous burning is detrimental because it decreases soil organic matter. Weeding, a common practice among the Huron (Sagard-Théodat 1939:104), not only reduced competition for corn plants but also helped to delay the establishment of a sod that would be difficult to remove with the crude Huron hoes. The irregularly spaced corn hills were an effective measure to prevent serious erosion, as was the fact that the Huron disturbed the soil surface only at the places where the corn hills were located. Although erosion studies have been conducted at and near Huron sites, the only evidence for serious erosion is from areas immediately adjacent to a village, and not near the former corn fields (Heidenreich 1971a:213–228). In view of these considerations and evidence from other slash-and-burn agriculturalists in a temperate forest environment, it is likely that the Huron cropped their fields for about six years on sands and gravels and as much as 12 years on a sandy loam (Heidenreich 1971).

Once the fields ceased to be productive, they were abandoned. This point was reached when returns amounted to about 7 to 10 bushels an acre. The fields were then left to recover, a process that took over 30 years, far longer than the existence of a village. The Jesuits claimed that the villages were shifted when the fields gave out, or about every 8 to 12 years (JR 15:153, 19:133). Champlain (1922–1936, 3:124) and Sagard-Théodat (1939:92) wrote that abandonment took place after 10 to 30 years, but neither lived in Huronia long enough to observe the process. One other reason given for village abandonment was exhaustion of firewood near the village (Sagard-Théodat 1939:92–93; JR 11:7).

From a number of descriptions a likely sequence leading to village relocation can be formulated. In the first year of settlement, or more likely the previous year, land was cleared in patches near the village on suitable soils. As yields began to decline the fields were added to through further clearing or opening of new patches. After 8 to 12 years the original fields gave out and the village

was moved. To start fresh clearings beyond the original fields would mean a long walk; more important, those tending the fields would be too far from the village and scattered over too large an area for protection from enemy raids (fig. 6) (Heidenreich 1971). Summer raids were invariably concentrated on the women working in the fields, and due to other activities there were never enough men available to protect them adequately. A village move was never very far from the old site, in most cases only two to nine miles (Champlain 1922–1936, 3:124–125), just far enough for new land and firewood.

Huron yields are difficult to estimate. The Jesuits estimated an average yield of about 27 bushels an acre (JR 15:157), a figure with which Heidenreich (1971) concurs. Early nineteenth-century settlers in the area who also practiced slash-and-burn agriculture and planted their Indian corn in mounds got yields of about 20 to 30 bushels an acre. Both Trigger (1969:28) and Heidenreich (1971) calculated that yearly Huron corn requirements could be grown on about 7,000 acres. In view of Huron agricultural practices, the care and labor expended in the fields, and the importance of corn to their diet, such high yields should be expected.

References to tobacco growing among the Huron are virtually absent (JR 11:7). Most of their tobacco was imported from the Petun, Neutral, and later also the French, the climate of Huronia being too marginal to grow the crop in the quantities demanded by the Huron. Some tobacco was grown in proximity of the longhouse, probably because microclimatic conditions within the shelter of the palisade and near the houses permitted it (JR 15:79). Tobacco growing, the manufacture of pipes, and smoking were apparently male activities (Boucher 1881:55).

Gathering

Gathering was not an important activity except in times of famine. Sagard-Théodat (1939:239) specifically mentioned that many wild greens were available in Huronia but that they were taken little notice of. The main

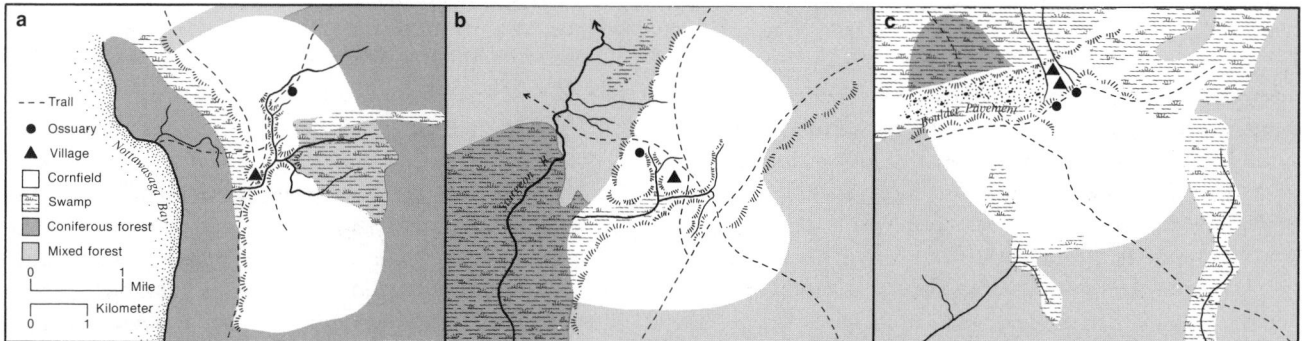

Fig. 6. Three major Huron villages, showing the probable extent of cornfields in sandy loam after 7–10 years' continuous occupation. Ossossane (a) had about 40 longhouses occupied by some 1,500 people; Teanaustaye (b) about 80 occupied by about 2,400; and Cahiagué (c) about 100 occupied by about 3,200.

gathered products were fruits, such as raspberries, strawberries, cranberries, blueberries, and wild cherries. With their clearing of the woodland and field abandonment the Huron were constantly creating a favorable habitat for most of these plants. Another important gathered product was hemp, probably *Apocynum cannabinum* and *A. androsaemifolium,* which grew on "the untilled fields" (JR 23:55). Hemp was collected in the late summer and manufactured into twine and ultimately fish nets and other products (Sagard-Théodat 1939:98; JR 23:241). The same articles were also manufactured out of bark fibers from a tree called *atti,* most likely basswood.

Other commonly gathered foods were clams, crabs, and turtles. There is no clear evidence that snakes and frogs were eaten, although mice were (Sagard-Théodat 1939:227).

Hunting

Hunting was of relatively little importance. The most frequently mentioned food animals were dog, deer, and bear. The dog was the only domesticated animal and a major source of meat (JR 7:223; Sagard-Théodat 1939:226). Most references state that dogs were mainly eaten at feasts and ceremonies (Champlain 1922–1936, 3:129; Sagard-Théodat 1939:220, 226; JR 9:111, 21:161, 23:173). Dog bones frequently turn up on archeological sites, and along with beaver, constitute the major bone material at the latest sites (Savage 1971:168).

Due to their solitary nature, bear were hunted by small groups of men with the use of dogs (JR 14:33–35, 15:99). Since their density and reproductive rate are low they were not a major food source. Some bears were raised in captivity for special feasts, but the practice does not seem to have been widespread (Champlain 1922–1936, 3:130; Sagard-Théodat 1939:220).

The primary source of meat was deer. Deer were hunted in snares (JR 23:157), traps (JR 30:53), with the bow (JR 26:313), but most commonly in large, well-organized communal drives (JR 15:183, 33:83). Two types of communal drives are described; in both, a line of people is formed in the woods and the animals are driven ahead of them. In one case the animals are driven into a body of water and killed from canoes (Champlain 1922–1936, 3:60–61; JR 22:273), while in the other, the animals are driven into a large triangular enclosure with a compound at its apex where they are speared (Champlain 1922–1936, 3:81–85). In one communal hunt using the enclosure method, Champlain witnessed the capture of 120 deer by 25 men in 38 days. Women sometimes accompanied these hunts to help drive the animals, butcher them, and take the meat back to the village (JR 33:89).

Other animals that were hunted when the opportunity arose were moose, muskrat, woodchuck, fox, hare, turkey, ducks, and other kinds of fowl. All of these were hunted with the bow, spear, or snare. None was a major food source for a population as large as the Huron. There is no mention of any food taboos except the crow (Sagard-Théodat 1939:221).

Fishing

Fishing was carried on virtually throughout the year. Since this activity was closely attuned to the seasonal habits of the various fish species, the spring and late fall spawning runs were the peak periods in the fishing season.

Most of the species that spawned in the spring such as the sturgeon, pike, maskinonge, catfish, sucker, and walleye, did so in shallow, weedy bays and creeks. The larger of these fish were speared, while the smaller, particularly those that moved in large schools, were caught in dip nets and weirs. According to Champlain (1922–1936, 3:56–57), the entire "Narrows" between Lake Couchiching and Lake Simcoe was blocked off by rows of stakes except for a few openings behind which weirs were placed to take advantage of spawning runs. There is little doubt that similar structures were placed at the mouths of creeks and small streams.

Fall fishing concentrated mainly on lake trout, cisco, and whitefish, all of which spawned in well-known shallow areas of Lake Simcoe and Georgian Bay. Fishing was done with seine nets set into the water in the evening and drawn together in the morning (Sagard-Théodat 1939:186). The same technique was used in the winter for fishing under ice (Champlain 1922–1936, 3:167–168; JR 35:175). During the fall fishing season, which could last up to a month, the fishermen lived in camps away from the village.

Some fishing was carried out by hook and line, but apparently not very successfully because the lines were not strong enough (Sagard-Théodat 1939:189).

Fish were eaten fresh, smoked, or dried. Some of the larger whitefish were boiled, and in the process the oil was skimmed off and stored in gourds imported from somewhere south of the Great Lakes. In most cases the fish were prepared directly at the site where they were caught. In the case of one species, the *einchataon* (probably the catfish), the fish were not gutted, but simply hung in bunches within the longhouse (Sagard-Théodat 1939:95, 185–186, 230–231).

Division of Labor

Male and female tasks were fairly clearly defined. Although there was apparently no full-time specialization in manufacturing or economic pursuits, it is obvious that some individuals were more adept at making pottery, pipes, or flint items than others. Each extended family, comprising a household, looked after its own requirements.

The women were responsible for all aspects of agriculture except the arduous task of clearing new fields (Champlain 1922-1936, 3:136-137; Sagard-Théodat 1939:101-102). In the spring the women gathered firewood (fig. 4), which was stored in and about the houses (Sagard-Théodat 1939:94). Only dry wood of certain species was chosen. The women prepared skins and made clothing, which was often brightly decorated (fig. 7) (Champlain 1922-1936, 3:131-135; Sagard-Théodat 1939:143-147). The men especially took great pride in adorning themselves with paint, tattoos, and elaborate hairdos (Sagard-Théodat 1939:145). The women also made most household utensils such as pottery; baskets and mats of reeds, bark, or corn husks; leather bags; tobacco pouches; and string of hemp and bark fibers (Sagard-Théodat 1939:101-102). Bags, pouches, and baskets were decorated with paint and colored porcupine quills.

The men were generally in charge of heavier construction such as the palisade, houses, and canoes (Sagard-Théodat 1939:101). They did all the hunting and most of the fishing. The men manufactured wooden spoons and bowls, fish nets, wooden armor and shields, and clay or stone tobacco pipes (Boucher 1881:55). It is likely that the men also made the stone axes, adzes, arrow points, scrapers, and other stone work. Large tools such as adzes and axes were pecked and ground out of a fine-grained granite and hornblende schist, while the smaller tools such as scrapers, points, and drills were usually chipped out of chert.

Other manufactured items included a variety of bone tools such as awls, needles, combs, and hide fleshers; beads made of bird bones, red slate, shell, stone, and turtleshell; and domestic tools such as stone and wooden mortars and grinders.

Children were socialized into the roles they had to assume in later life. The boys learned to fish and become

proficient with the bow and arrow; they did not perform female work such as getting water (Sagard-Théodat 1939:132). The girls were taught to perform household duties, to make pots, and to grind corn and shell it (Sagard-Théodat 1939:104, 133). In the summer the children would help to weed the fields and chase the birds away (JR 10:53, 145).

Internal Economy

While a barter economy existed between Huron and non-Huron there is no evidence of any kind of barter system among the Huron themselves. There is no evidence that goods and services were redistributed in Huronia through commercial transactions or any kind of marketing system. Within the kin sphere, goods and services were largely shared (JR 10:223-225). Beyond the kin, goods were diffused through ceremonial exchanges such as name-giving ceremonies (Sagard-Théodat 1939:209-210; JR 23:167-169) and burial ceremonies (Champlain 1922-1936, 3:161-163; Sagard-Théodat 1939:172-173; JR 8:121, 10:265-271) and through gift giving such as at a marriage (Sagard-Théodat 1939:122-123; JR 14:19) and a visit (Sagard-Théodat 1939:140). Curing ceremonies were another major form in which goods were spread through the community. Games of chance, the preparation of feasts, and sponsoring of festivals were other occasions on which goods were redistributed.

Hoarding of goods and stinginess met with strong village disapproval and could lead to accusations of witchcraft and expulsion, while liberality was highly valued and received strong social approval (Trigger 1969:40-41).

External Relations

Trade

As a rule the Huron did not trade with groups with whom they were at war or with strangers with whom they had no formal peace treaties. The conclusion of a "treaty" involved not only trade between groups but also mutual aid in warfare. It is for this reason that the Huron sought a military alliance with Champlain and a demonstration of French goodwill through their participation in raids on the Iroquois before they would trade any furs. Such alliances were initiated and renewed through reciprocal gift giving, feasts, long speeches, and eventually a limited exchange of people. Although they were an expression of mutual goodwill, the people who were exchanged acted in effect as hostages and spies.

In order to keep good relations between allies and trading partners, every effort was made to suppress murder, the most common cause of intergroup warfare. *383*

Public Arch. of Canada, Ottawa: Map Division (H-12-900-1657).
Fig. 7. Man, woman, and children in traditional dress but depicted as Christianized. Detail from the Bressani map (fig. 2).

Murder was a matter that affected not only the family of the deceased but also the entire tribe (JR 10:225). In order to prevent wars arising out of murder, heavy payments were made to the family of the deceased. Such payments could not possibly be made by an individual and for this reason each clan segment and village established a "public treasury" to which everyone would contribute (JR 10:217-221, 33:229-249). This accumulation of capital was administered by a chief and used not only to pay off a murder but also to arrange treaties and exchange prisoners (Sagard-Théodat 1939:163-164; JR 28:87). The size of the payment seems to have been directly related to the value the Huron placed on the trade contacts with a particular group (JR 38:283-285).

The rights to particular trade routes lay in the hands of the person who had discovered and pioneered the route (JR 10:223-225). Only the members of his lineage or clan segment ('those who bear the same name') could share in the trade automatically. Non-family members could buy their way into a trade route through payments to the owner of the route. The owners, or "masters," of a trade route regulated trade over that route because anyone who traded on it had to give them presents and ask for permission. Since the accumulation of wealth and its judicious disposal was one of the surest ways of acquiring social and political status, some of these "masters" became important chiefs (Sagard-Théodat 1939:99). There was no reason why some of the successful traders could not also become lineage chiefs, since such a chief was elected from among the qualified members of a lineage who could trace descent through their mother's family to an existing chief (JR 10:233). It is also possible that some important chiefs assumed control of newly found trade routes in name of their clan segment. Permission to leave the village for trading had to be obtained from the village chiefs and council, because these had to ensure that enough men stayed at home as protection against enemy raids (Champlain 1922-1936, 3:166).

Poaching on the trade route of another family was severely punished if the offending member got caught in the act; however, if he made it back to his village he would not be touched (JR 10:225). In protecting their trade from members outside their confederacy the Huron were quite ruthless. They would permit neither the Petun nor the Neutral to cross Huron territory or routes under Huron control to trade on the Saint Lawrence with the French (JR 21:177, 203-205). Similarly, they did everything in their power to discourage the French from making permanent contacts with these tribes. In this practice the Huron were simply following trade conventions set up in eastern Canada. To cross the territory of another group, permission had to be sought. Such permission was often refused if it was deemed to be against the interest of the group. Disregard for these conventions would cause a war. The Huron traders ran into these

problems themselves when they proceeded down the Ottawa, particularly from the Kichesipirini (Allumette) and Weskarini (Petite Nation). Due to French intervention, the Kichesipirini could not stop the Huron, but they made them pay heavy transit fees (Sagard-Théodat 1939:87-99; JR 10:77). The Huron complained continuously but never attempted to force their way in spite of their numerical superiority. To do so would have meant warfare with the Kichesipirini and others and would have given other groups the excuse to do the same thing to the Huron (JR 9:275). Significantly, these rules did not apply to war parties on their way across allied territory to the Iroquois.

Trading was carried on for a number of reasons. To some men it was a form of adventure, similar to warfare, through which they could prove their manhood and gain prestige. Others undertook the journeys in order to acquire goods for gambling, as games of chance were a favorite pastime (JR 5:241, 10:81, 187, 17:205). Unquestionably, the major reason for trading was the acquisition of desirable goods and the conversion of these into social status through reciprocal and other forms of institutionalized gift giving. A Huron was expected to give gifts on a variety of occasions; he had to participate in ceremonies where gifts were given and he took part in gambling; he shared his goods directly with his extended family, and through social pressure, with the needy and lazy (Sagard-Théodat 1939:88-89; JR 8:95). He therefore had to acquire goods in order to fulfill his social obligations; the more successfully he fulfilled these obligations through liberality, the more prestige he acquired. Trade brought desired goods to the community and status to the trader.

The extent of Huron trade with neighboring groups prior to their contact with the French in 1609 is difficult to estimate. The only durable foreign articles that turn up with any regularity are shell objects and chert. To these can be added the occasional piece of red slate and native copper.

The shell objects, mainly wampum beads manufactured from the columellae of conch shells, came from the sea coast of the southeastern United States through a string of middlemen. Prime suppliers seem to have been the Neutral (JR 21:201) and the Andaste (Susquehannock). With the latter, the Huron had a loose military alliance against the Iroquois (Champlain 1922-1936, 3:53-55; JR 30:53, 33:73, 131-133). Chert was probably obtained from the Petun and Neutral, in whose areas the best deposits can be found. Native copper is common on the south and east shores of Lake Superior and could have been obtained by the Huron themselves (Champlain 1922-1936, 1:164).

The best indicators of Huron trade before it became strongly influenced by the fur trade are the early observations of Champlain and Gabriel Sagard-Théodat. Essentially these observations convey the impression that Huron trade with the Petun and Neutral was less developed than with the Algonquian groups. Both the Neutral and Petun were known as growers and exporters of tobacco, a product the Huron could never get enough of and later traded from the French (Champlain 1922–1936, 3:99, 6:248). Some of the tobacco would be traded further to the Algonquians (JR 6:273). The Neutral also traded black squirrel and *tiron* (raccoon) skins to the Huron who would work them into cloaks to trade to the Algonquians. Extensive trade of Algonquian products by the Huron to the Petun and Neutral seems unlikely in view of the fact that the Ottawa were regular visitors among the Petun and military allies of the Neutral against the Assistaeronnon. Moreover it was the Ottawa who tried to dissuade Champlain from visiting the Neutral (Champlain 1922–1936, 3:100). Few other products seem to have been exchanged among these three groups as they had similar subsistence economies. At the time of French contact the Huron lived at peace with the Neutral and Petun, although past wars were still fresh in their minds (Sagard-Théodat 1939:151, 157; JR 20:43).

Precontact Huron trade was strongest with some of the Algonquian groups, notably the Ottawa, Nipissing, and Ottawa Valley Algonquins. The Ottawa were considered great traders with extensive relations for 400 to 500 leagues (about 800 to 1,500 miles) into Lakes Superior and Michigan (Champlain 1922–1936, 6:248–249; Sagard-Théodat 1939:67). Their main products were dried berries, reed mats, fish, furs, and other products for which the Huron exchanged wampum, nets, and pigments. No Ottawas were ever seen on the Saint Lawrence prior to the destruction of the Huron in 1649, probably because they were not permitted to cross Huron and Nipissing trade routes. Huron trade with the Nipissing was of long standing, as Ridley's (1954) excavations on Lake Nipissing show. The Nipissing in turn traded northward to the Cree (Champlain 1922–1936, 3:39–40; Sagard-Théodat 1939:86–87). Although the Huron had close relations with the Ottawa Valley Algonquins, notably the Kichesipirini and Weskarini who sometimes wintered in eastern Huronia, it is doubtful whether the Huron did much traveling on the Ottawa River prior to the development of the fur trade. In their first meeting with Champlain the Huron were guided to the Saint Lawrence by the Weskarini and complained that in previous years the Kichesipirini would not let them pass (Champlain 1922–1936, 2:71). Moreover, the French did not see any Huron on the Saint Lawrence before 1609 (Champlain 1922–1936, 2:68, 109) and mentioned that prior to that date the Huron got French trade goods through Algonquian middlemen (Champlain 1922–1936, 1:164).

Huron pottery has been found as far north as the mouth of the Michipicoten River on the east shore of Lake Superior, showing that the Huron had precontact connections with various Ojibwa groups (Ridley 1961a; Wright 1969). In the main, however, Huron trade con-

tacts prior to the fur trade seem to have concentrated on Algonquian groups within about a 200-mile arc from the Ottawa in the west to Ojibwa groups and the Nipissing in the north to the Kichesipirini and Iroquets in the east. Trade was not only in luxury items such as wampum and squirrel skins but also in corn, fish, and nets. The number of traders who participated in these ventures is impossible to estimate, but it must have been considerably less than the number who were later engaged in the fur trade. During the height of the fur trade 700 Huron once made it to the Saint Lawrence, the usual number being less than 300 (Heidenreich 1971). Pre-European trade among the Huron should be seen in terms of its social and political importance rather than as an important occupational or economic activity.

Warfare

At the time of French contact early in the seventeenth century, the Huron were embroiled in a long-standing war with the five Iroquois tribes but especially with the Seneca. Within their memory, the Huron had also been at war with the Petun (JR 20:43) and possibly the Neutral (Sagard-Théodat 1939:151, 157). A peace had been concluded with the Petun shortly before Champlain's arrival in Huronia, while the Neutral tried to be on peaceful terms with both the Iroquois and Huron-Petun. The Neutral in turn were allied with the Ottawa and probably the Petun against the Assistaeronnon of Michigan (Champlain 1922–1936, 3:97–100). Peaceful relations existed between the Huron and the Algonquian groups of Ontario and Quebec with whom they were in contact. The Huron also had an alliance with the Andaste (Susquehannock) who lived south of the Iroquois (Champlain 1922–1936, 3:53–55; JR 30:253, 33:63, 73, 129).

Prior to the late 1630s when both the motives and methods of Iroquoian warfare changed as a result of the fur trade, warfare was largely motivated by blood revenge, the gaining of personal prestige, and to some extent religious ideals (Trigger 1969:52). Wars for hunting rights or territorial gain were not fought prior to the 1640s. While it was easy to start a war, usually through murder and subsequent refusal to pay restitution, it was exceedingly difficult to arrange a peace. On several occasions when attempts were made to conclude a peace between members of the Huron confederacy and one or all the Iroquois tribes, either some groups on one side refused to join in the negotiations or the negotiations or peace collapsed because of a few murders (JR 26:31, 69–71, 27:229–303, 28:277, 291, 33:119–127). Murder had to be avenged (JR 10:225–227), and the glory of a warrior depended on the perpetuation of the annual raids (JR 26:65).

Theoretically any man could plan and organize a war party if he got enough support, but in most cases this task was assumed by the experienced war chiefs (Champlain 1922–1936, 3:159; Sagard-Théodat 1939:151). Plans were made in secret for fear of enemy spies that both sides had within their villages (JR 10:229, 22:309). After the plans were set a war feast was given. The usual number of men that took part in the annual spring and summer raids was 500 to 600, although war parties got larger during the later years of Huronia's existence. These men would scatter in groups of five or six once they got into enemy country. The usual aim was to capture or kill isolated groups of people working in the fields or fishing. Some of the more daring would try to sneak into a village at night to kill and terrorize. As proof of their prowess the warriors would try to bring back the heads of those they had killed, or if this was not possible, the scalps, which would be dried and hung from the palisade walls in time of war (Sagard-Théodat 1939:151-153, 164). The ultimate aim was to return with captives.

The frequency of large-scale raids, bent on the destruction of a village, in precontact times is difficult to determine. According to Champlain (1922-1936, 3: 66-75) the Huron were completely inept in such an undertaking. Men fought as individuals or in small groups rather than in organized formations with a common purpose. In contrast to their offensive capabilities Champlain (1922-1936, 3:78-79) was favorably impressed by the way the Huron would conduct their retreats.

Public Arch. of Canada, Ottawa: Map Division (H-12-900-1657).

Fig. 8. Warrior wearing rod armor and carrying a gun. Detail from the Bressani map (fig. 2).

A Huron warrior was equipped with a cuirass made of tightly laced sticks (fig. 8), a wooden shield that could cover his entire body or a small shield made of boiled leather, clubs, bow and arrows. A standard with the symbol of the village was carried with the warriors. While on the warpath each man had a bag of roasted corn meal, which would last him for up to two months (Sagard-Théodat 1939:98, 153-154).

The fate of prisoners was variable. If too many were captured, or the retreat had to be conducted in a hurry, the prisoners were killed, usually preceded by the women and children. If taken back to Huronia, the alternatives were torture and death, or particularly for the women and children, formal adoption by families who had lost someone through warfare (Sagard-Théodat 1939:159; JR 15:171, 17:73, 101, 23:39).

While individuals received recognition for the prisoners they had taken, it was the chiefs who had led the expedition that decided how to dispose of the prisoners (Champlain 1922-1936, 3:159; Sagard-Théodat 1939: 151). A council was called and the prisoners were distributed among the families, villages, or tribes who had participated in the raid.

The torture and death of a prisoner was a highly ritualized affair in which all members of a village participated (fig. 4). Torture was often preceded by adoption into a family who would then address the prisoners as "brother" and "nephew" throughout the ceremony (JR 13:53-79). During the ceremony, which could last several days, the prisoner sang songs and generally tried to project an image of bravery that would reflect favorably on himself and his tribe. At the same time the torturers would increase the ferocity of their activities culminating in the eating of the heart and other parts of the body (JR 10:227-229, 15:173, 17:75, 99, 18:31-33). Archeological proof of this activity is sometimes found in middens in the form of bits of human bone (Wright 1966:99).

Descriptions of torture and cannibalism among the Huron indicate that this ritual involved the transformation of normal group behavior into a universal outpouring of pent-up emotions. The person who was tortured became in fact a symbol of the tribe he represented, a hate object on whom the frustrations of life and past wrongs could be expended. It is significant that much as the Jesuits abhorred the practice of torture and ritual cannibalism they were never able to put a stop to it.

History

The annals of a tribe during the historic period are probably better known for the Huron than for any other aboriginal group in Canada (Trigger 1960, 1968, 1969; Heidenreich 1971). The 1609 meeting of a group of Huron warriors, composed largely of Arendaronon with Champlain on the Saint Lawrence marked the beginning of increasingly close relations between Hurons and

French. In order to establish friendly relations with the Huron and promote the fur trade Champlain felt he had to commit the French to the Huron-Algonquin-Montagnais alliance against the Iroquois. Although subsequent events proved that French involvement in intertribal warfare was disastrous to all concerned it was necessary if the fur trade was to penetrate inland. Champlain definitely felt that without a strong French commitment he would not have peace on the Saint Lawrence or a broadening of the fur trade (Heidenreich 1971).

In 1615 the Huron were visited by Champlain, a contingent of 14 soldiers, and a Recollect priest, Joseph Le Caron. These had probably been preceded by Champlain's interpreter Étienne Brûlé. From that year on some Frenchmen were always present among the Huron. The first Jesuits entered Huronia in 1626 accompanied by the Recollects. Two years after the English occupation of the Saint Lawrence, 1629 to 1632, the Jesuits entered Huronia permanently, first among the Attignawantan and after 1638 among the other tribes. In 1639 the central mission Sainte Marie was built on the Wye River.

The disintegration of traditional Huron society began with a series of epidemics that lasted from 1634 to 1640 and culminated in the smallpox epidemic of 1639. Before that time the Huron had acquired trade goods and expanded their trade network, but attempts at religious conversions had been unsuccessful. Even Champlain's and the Jesuits' proposals of Huron-French intermarriage were rejected (JR 5:211, 14:17-21).

The result of the epidemics was the loss of approximately half the population in a span of about five years, and with them most of the older people who were the traditional leaders. After this period religious conversions became more frequent, which created traditional and Christian factions in the community. Other factions developed between those who wanted to sever all ties with the French and those who wanted to maintain them. Political disunity arose as young men increasingly tried to assume roles previously held by elders and their councils. By the late 1640s it became apparent that Iroquois methods of waging warfare had changed as well as their aims. The Seneca, Onondaga, Cayuga, and at times the Oneida began to raid Huronia in large, well-organized armies bent on destroying entire villages. The Mohawk and Oneida concentrated on blockading the route to the Saint Lawrence. To the original aims of warfare, which had been revenge and blood feuds, was added the dispersion of the Huron confederacy. The driving motives apparently became the acquisition of the fur-bearing areas of the Canadian Shield.

The Huron never seemed to realize what was happening until the disasters of 1648. Even as late as 1647 their councils could not come to any agreement on how to meet the Iroquois threat. The Arendaronon were dispersed by the end of 1647. Some fled to Huron villages farther west; others were adopted into the Iroquois. In 1648 the large village of Teanaustaye and a neighboring one were destroyed and Saint Ignace abandoned. By mid-1649 all villages east of Sainte Marie were abandoned or sacked. In a grand council with the Jesuits the Huron then made the decision to abandon Huronia. Some eventually found refuge at Lorette near Quebec; others fled to the Petun and ultimately to the Neutral and Erie. Some Huron dispersed to, and intermarried with, the Ottawa. A large part of the Huron were adopted by the Iroquois.

Synonymy

Lalemant explained in 1639 (JR 16:229-233) that the name Huron was first used by some French soldiers or sailors as a nickname for a group of Indians whose haircut reminded them of the ridge of erect bristles on the head of a boar (*hure* 'boar's head, bristly head'). A second explanation is that the name may be from an Old French word meaning 'ruffian, knave, lout' or simply 'unkempt person'. The name is first found in a passage written by Champlain (1922-1936, 5:100) in July 1623 and published in 1632; it seems to have come into common usage between 1619 and 1623.

The following names were used for the Huron collectively: "the good Iroquois," 1603 (Champlain 1922-1936, 1:164); Ochateguins, 1609 (Champlain 1922-1936, 2: 57-293); Charioquois, 1611 (Champlain 1922-1936, 2: 186); Attigouantan, 1615 (Champlain 1922-1936, 3:42-46); Houandate, 1623 (Sagard-Théodat 1866, 4); Ouendat, 1638 (JR 16:227); and 8endat, meaning the eighteenth-century Huron and Wyandot (Potier 1920:154).

The following variants were used by Champlain (1922-1936), Sagard-Théodat (1866, 1939), or the Jesuits (JR) in the years noted.

Attignawantan, 1639: Attigouautan, 1615; Atignouaatitan, 1615; Attigouantan, 1632; Atingyahointan, 1623; Attignaouentan, 1640; Atinniawentan, 1643; Attinniaoenten, 1649.

Attigneenongnahac, 1639: Atigagnongueha, 1623; Attiguenongha, 1635; Atignenonghac, 1636; Atignenongach, 1637; Attigueenongnahac, 1638; Attinguenongnahac, 1640; Attinguenennonniahak, 1640; Attingueenongnahak, 1641.

Arendaronon, 1640: Henarhonon, 1623; Arendarhonon, 1635; Renarhonon, 1636; Arendoronnon, 1636; Arendarrhonon, 1637; Arendahronnon, 1638; Ahrendaronon, 1640; Arendaeronon, 1641; Arendaenhronon, 1642; Arendaenronnon, 1647; Arendae'ronnon, 1651; Arendageronnon, 1657.

Tahontaenrat, 1643: Tohontaenras, 1637; Tohontaenrat, 1639; Atahonta enrat, 1651.

Ataronchronon, 1640: Ataconchronon, 1637.

Sources

The major primary source material on the Huron stems from the writings of the explorer, trader, and colonizer Samuel de Champlain (1922-1936), the Recollect friar Gabriel Sagard-Théodat (1866, 1939), and the Jesuit priests who labored among the Huron (JR 1896-1901). Champlain's observations originate from his visit to the Huron in 1615 and are generally reliable on Huron material culture. Sagard-Théodat lived among the Huron from 1623 to 1624. His writings range from Huron social and political institutions to agricultural methods and aspects of the animal and plant life of the area. Unlike Champlain, Sagard-Théodat could speak some Huron and compiled the earliest phrase book of their language (Sagard-Théodat 1866). Jesuit missionary work began in 1626 but did not become permanent until 1634. From that date on yearly reports were compiled on the Huron mission. Unlike Champlain and Sagard-Théodat, the Jesuits made few attempts to write a concise account of the Huron. The *Jesuit Relations* (JR 1896-1901) contain the most complete information on Huron religion, mythology, government, and law.

Primary sources of lesser importance are Boucher (1881), Gendron (1868), Du Creux (1951-1952), and Le Clercq (1881). Works of minor interest that make some reference to the Huron prior to their dispersal are by Charlevoix (1761), Hennepin (1903), Lafitau (1724), Jouve (1915), and Radisson (1967). One of the most complete studies of the Huron language was written by Potier (1920). Contemporary maps of Huronia and adjacent areas have been discussed by Heidenreich (1966, 1968, 1971).

Archeological work in Huronia has been reviewed by Kidd (1952) while a preliminary bibliography has been published by Kenyon (1966). Work in the area began with the site surveys of A.F. Hunter (1889, 1899, 1900, 1902, 1903, 1904, 1907). Recently these have been put on a systematic basis by Ridley (1947, 1966-1968). The results of Hunter's site surveys formed the archeological basis of A.E. Jones's (1909) massive study on the identification of Jesuit missions in the area. Work on mission sites continued in the 1930s and 1940s with Wintemberg's (1938) and later Jury's (W.S. Fox 1941; Jury and Fox 1947) work at the supposed site of Saint Ignace, Kidd's (1953) work at the Ossossane ossuary, Jury and Jury's (1955) work at Saint Louis, and the beginning of the excavations at the Warminster site (Cahiagué) (McIlwraith 1947; Harris 1949). The most ambitious project in the area has been the excavation and rather problematical reconstruction of the Jesuit mission Sainte Marie (Kidd 1949; Jury and Jury 1954).

Huron migrations and artifact typologies have been treated by MacNeish (1952), Emerson (1954, 1959, 1961, 1968), Ridley (1952, 1954, 1958, 1963), Wright (1966) and Noble (1968, 1969). Further discussions of prehistory can be found in Emerson and Popham (1952), Ridley (1952a), and Trigger (1969, 1970).

Unfortunately most of the archeological work in Huronia has not been problem oriented, nor has much of it been published. The most comprehensive statements are Wright (1966), Noble (1968), and Trigger (1970). Tooker (1964) and to some extent Kinietz (1940) are careful paraphrasings of the ethnohistoric sources and as such excellent source books. Trigger (1969) gives anthropological and historical (1976) analyses of the Huron, and Heidenreich (1971), a historical geography of Huronia.

Huron of Lorette

CHRISTIAN MORISSONNEAU

The first and largest group of Hurons who sought refuge from their Iroquois conquerors at Quebec arrived from Georgian Bay under Jesuit leadership on July 28, 1650. After spending the winter at Quebec, they took up residence on the Île d'Orléans, where they continued to be attacked by their enemies. They returned to Quebec until 1668, when they moved to Beauport and then Notre-Dame-de-Foye (Sainte-Foy) and again, in 1673, to Ancienne-Lorette. The Jesuits established them in 1697 at their present location, near the fall of the Saint Charles River, eight miles from Quebec (fig. 1). A chapel was constructed to honor Our Lady of Lorette, which was modeled on the Casa Sancta of Loreto, in Italy. The name of this mission has been extended to the neighboring community of Jeune-Lorette (Loretteville), which surrounds the reserve. The official name of the Indian settlement according to the Commission de géographie du Québec is the Village-des-Hurons and not Lorette (fig. 2).

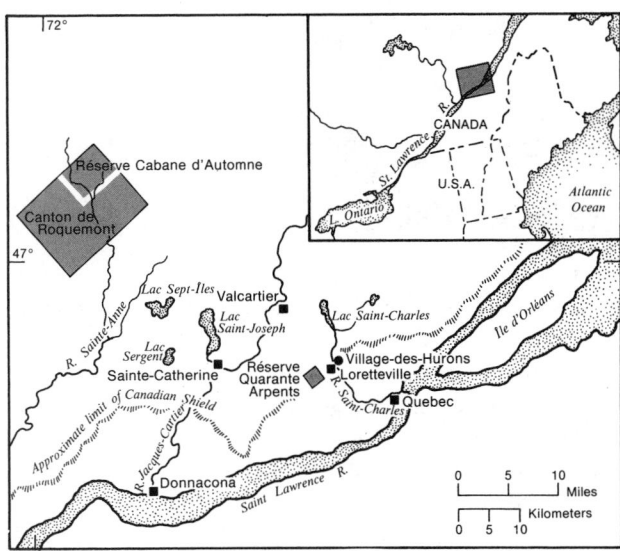

Fig. 1. Huron reserves.

Fig. 2. The Huron village of Lorette in 1838. Watercolor by Henry William Bernard.

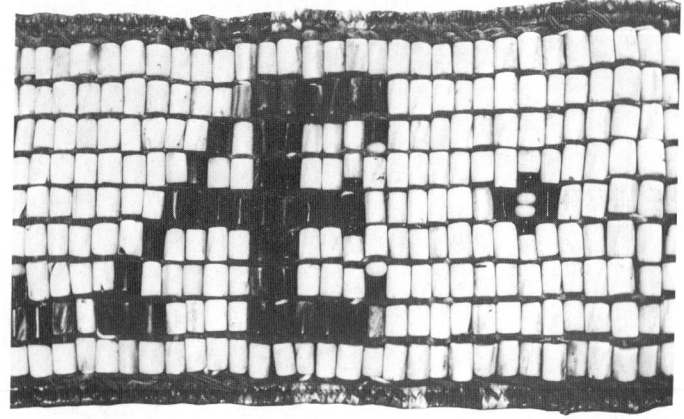

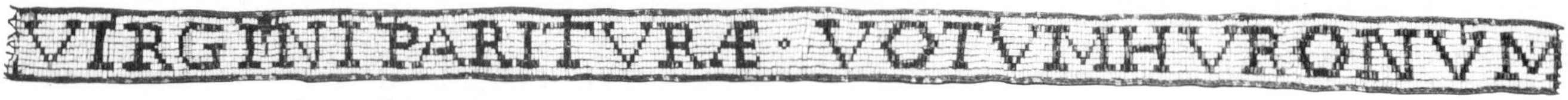
VIRGINI PARITVRÆ · VOTVMHVRONVM

© Natl. Geographic Soc., Washington, D.C.

Fig. 3. Wampum belt sent to Chartres Cathedral in 1678 by the Hurons of Lorette. Although constructed mainly of wampum, it contains a few white and black glass beads and has red-dyed porcupine quill edging. The words 'Offering of the Hurons to the virgin with child' are in Latin. Length 144.5 cm.

In the early years, the Hurons continued to live in longhouses and the women practiced slash-and-burn agriculture, while the men contributed to the defense of New France by continuing to fight the Iroquois. Kalm (1935) reported that, by the eighteenth century, the Indians were imitating the French in many ways and particularly in their agriculture: men now took part. Every family grew maize and some also grew wheat and rye. They also planted sunflowers (*Helianthus annuus*) in their cornfields since they liked to add the oil of this plant to their corn soup. Some families owned a cow or two. The soil that was suitable for agriculture was neither extensive nor particularly fertile; however, the Huron did not complain during the early years at Jeune-Lorette, largely because of the proximity of the Laurentide forests and the ready market for furs that existed in Quebec City. These conditions encouraged the Huron men, who were little interested in agriculture, to become more deeply involved in hunting, fishing, and trapping.

By the end of the eighteenth century, hunting was becoming less productive in the hinterland of the Huron village. In response to this, the Huron sought to derive the maximum profit from their skins and other forest products by using them to manufacture various items that they sold either at the Quebec market or at the entrance to the village. These included "mocassins, snow-shoes, sashes, Indian sleighs, fur caps and mittens, collars of porcupine quills, purses, bows, arrows and paddles" (Bouchette 1832). These items were not only sold but also often bartered for European goods. Handicrafts very soon began to make up for the relative scarceness of game. Nevertheless, until the end of the nineteenth century, many Hurons left the village each autumn for a season of hunting and trapping. They were encouraged to do this when, in 1851, they obtained the hunting reserve called the "Cabane d'Automne" (9,600 acres) in the canton de Roquemont, which supplemented their reserve of Quarante Arpents (1,352 acres) obtained nearer to Quebec in 1772. A declining interest in hunting corresponded with the sale of the former in 1903 and the latter in 1904.

By the end of the nineteenth century, agriculture had practically disappeared in favor of handicrafts and work in factories. The poor soils at Nouvelle-Lorette explain, at least in part, why agriculture was abandoned. However, projects that had sought to correct this situation in the middle of the nineteenth century had come to nothing. For example, in 1830 Gov. James Kempt proposed to cede to the Hurons arable land around Lorette instead of having them clear forested land in the hilly regions farther inland. Trapping was also partially abandoned by the turn of the century.

The proximity of European settlement has led to much interbreeding and French slowly replaced Huron as a spoken language; the last Indian who spoke Huron died in 1912. While all the Hurons in the 1970s speak French, some speak English as a second language. From the beginning, the mission was exclusively Roman Catholic (fig. 3).

The reserve dwindled in size until 1968, when it was increased from 26 acres to 167.5 acres to cover projected needs for the next 20 years. Most of the reserve (73.6%) consists of vacant land; the remainder is covered with buildings (65 percent residential; 34 percent commercial and industrial). The residential sector consists of single-family dwellings (81 percent, 140 units), two-family

Gagnon Coll., City of Montreal Lib.; McCord Mus., Montreal; Royal Ont. Mus., Toronto; Chateau de Ramezay Mus., Montreal; Public Arch. of Canada, Ottawa; Glenbow-Alberta Inst., Calgary, Alb.

Fig. 4. Clothing styles of the Lorette Hurons. left to right, top to bottom: Woman and man, mid-18th century (anonymous watercolor); man, 1808 (watercolor by Sir James Archibald Hope); Zity and child, 1838 (lithograph by Coke Smyth); self-portrait in oils of Zacharie Vincent Telariolin (b.1793, d.1886), chief; three chiefs, 1825 (lithograph after a painting by E. Chatfield); Maurice Bastien, head chief (left) and Phillipe Vincent, chief, probably 1880s (photographs by J.E. Livernois).

HURON OF LORETTE

dwellings (17 percent, 30 units) and multifamily dwellings (2 percent, 3 units). The population density varies from 11 to 60 persons an acre. The Canadian National Railway cuts across the reserve.

The population had gradually increased as a result of the general lowering of the death rate and especially because of the decline in infant mortality from 331 per 1,000 between 1905 and 1909 to none for the 1960s (parish register). The population had also grown as a result of the return of Indians who had formerly gone to live elsewhere in Quebec or even in the United States. This in-migration has reversed a trend that from 1900 into the 1930s had resulted in a decrease in population. As of 1971 only 616 of the 841 who lived on the reserve had legal status as Indians, but 471 Indians lived off the reserve out of a total of 979 inscribed on the band list in 1966.

The average number of children in a Huron family is 2.2, compared with an average of 1.9 in non-Indian families on the reserve. The population is an aging one; for example, 36 heads of family out of 206 (18 percent) are widows, widowers, or otherwise single. A program aiding construction has resulted in almost all Indians becoming property owners; the tenants are mainly non-Indians. Two hundred out of 319 children are of school age, and of these 64 have passed the ninth grade. A small school on the reserve handles the first four grades, while higher grades are taught in schools at Loretteville or in Quebec.

Handicrafts continue to flourish and provide an important source of employment. In 1964, 11 small workshops, employing 2 to 8 men each, manufactured 37,000 pairs of snowshoes, which were sold throughout Canada and the United States. Three workshops manufactured 3,000 canvas canoes. Of workers employed on the reserve, 3% are guides, 14% are artisans, 32.3% are unskilled workers, 18.5% are skilled workers, 10.1% are in service industries, 2% are professionals, and 19.5% are proprietors. The annual duration of employment is extremely variable for male laborers. For example, in 1967, 5.7% worked two months a year; 5.7% worked six months; 94.3% worked nine months. The opportunities for work on the reserve are limited: in 1971, 60 worked in the manufacturing and 26 in the commercial sector. Of 206 heads of families, about 25 percent are 65 years of age or over and draw pensions. The annual salary on the reserve in 1967 was $3,529 and the income per capita $630.

The location of the Village-des-Hurons near the flourishing provincial capital of Quebec is an important factor in explaining the acculturation of these Indians and the unique features of the community (fig. 4). Hurons are playing an increasingly active role in the administrative and economic life of their community, which, while having the legal status of a reserve, closely resembles neighboring Quebec towns.

Bibliothèque Historique de la Marine, Paris: Album 66, carte 12.

Fig. 5. Detail from cartouche of a 1699 manuscript map of North America by Jean Baptiste Louis Franquelin showing an unidentified group of Indians, perhaps local Hurons near Quebec, cooking in a large metal trade pot suspended from a tripod. A trade ax is shown (at bottom edge of engraving), along with aboriginal birchbark containers, wooden spoons, and a twined bag (at far left). Some of the women wear checkered (wampum) headbands. Some of the men wear roach haircuts and decorated breechclouts; others wear very European-looking garb (figure at far left).

Synonymy

A late seventeenth-century letter in Huron calls the Huron of Lorette 8endat Loretronon, literally 'Lorette-people Huron' (8 = ou; Hurons 1678), whereas Potier (1920:154) recorded two eighteenth-century Wyandot or Huron names for 'the Indians of Lorette', hatindia8ointen (with a dialect variant hatingia8ointen) and ekeenteeronnon. Their Eastern Abenaki name is abémadenaĩak (Râle 1833:477).

Sources

The best source for the seventeenth century is the *Jesuit Relations* (JR 1896-1901). For a detailed description of the community in 1899, see Gérin (1900) and also Lindsay (1900). Hunting practices are discussed by Speck (1927b) and material culture by Speck (1911, 1911a). A modern chief of Lorette has published his autobiography (Gros-Louis 1971).

Khionontateronon (Petun)

CHARLES GARRAD AND CONRAD E. HEIDENREICH

Territory and Environment

The Petun ('pā₁toon) were located about 26 miles south-west of the western end of Huronia, a journey that usually took the Jesuits a little more than a day to accomplish (JR 35:147). According to ethnohistoric sources and the distribution of archeological sites, the occupied portion of the Petun area lay below the Niagara Escarpment and generally above the major recessional shoreline of glacial Lake Algonquin in what are now Nottawasaga and Collingwood townships, Ontario. The area between these two breaks-in-slope consists of undulating moraines, interlaced with outwash deposits and recessional shore-lines (Chapman and Putnam 1966). The soils are pre-dominantly well-drained loams, ideally suited for dig-ging-stick agriculture. Surface waters are ample, as the area is heavily dissected by creeks issuing from the base of the Niagara Escarpment. Reportedly, portions of the area possess a somewhat longer frost-free growing season than the lands above the escarpment and in neighboring Huronia. During the nineteenth-century European settle-ment of the area, semiannually migrating deer herds were reported. The land between the recessional shoreline and Nottawasaga Bay is a rough, boulder-strewn, swampy area, unsuitable for Indian settlement. No major sites have been reported in this area.

During the historic period a northward movement within the area is suggested by the remains. Within the area there is a pattern of large villages located in a line running northwest by southeast, with nearby small de-pendent villages and more remote campsites (fig. 1).

Villages

In 1616 Samuel de Champlain (1922–1936, 3:95–101, 4:278–284) found eight occupied villages and mentioned that two more were under construction. Near one of the Petun villages he visited the Ottawa who were wintering in the area. In 1639 the Jesuits listed nine "villages," and some "little villages" or "hamlets" (JR 20:43–45). It is fairly certain that these villages were listed from south to north, enabling one to match them up with contact sites in the area to produce a map of the distribution of Petun missions. The double names seem to refer to double villages or villages with nearby dependent "little vil-lages."

In organizing the Mission of the Apostles to the Petun,

the Jesuits divided the territory to recognize the existence of "two different nations," one called the Nation of the Wolves (Mission of Saint Jean) and the other the Nation of the Deer (Mission of Saint Mathias) (JR 33:143). Unfortunately the Petun names for these two groups are not given. The Jesuits took up residence in the principal village of each "nation."

The principal village of the Deer was Ekarenniondi 'the place at the rocky point' or 'the standing rock',* which the Jesuits called Saint Mathias (JR 33:143; A.E. Jones 1909:230–231). The village evidently took its name from the part of the Niagara Escarpment that forms a

* For the orthography of Petun words the same usage is followed as for Huron.

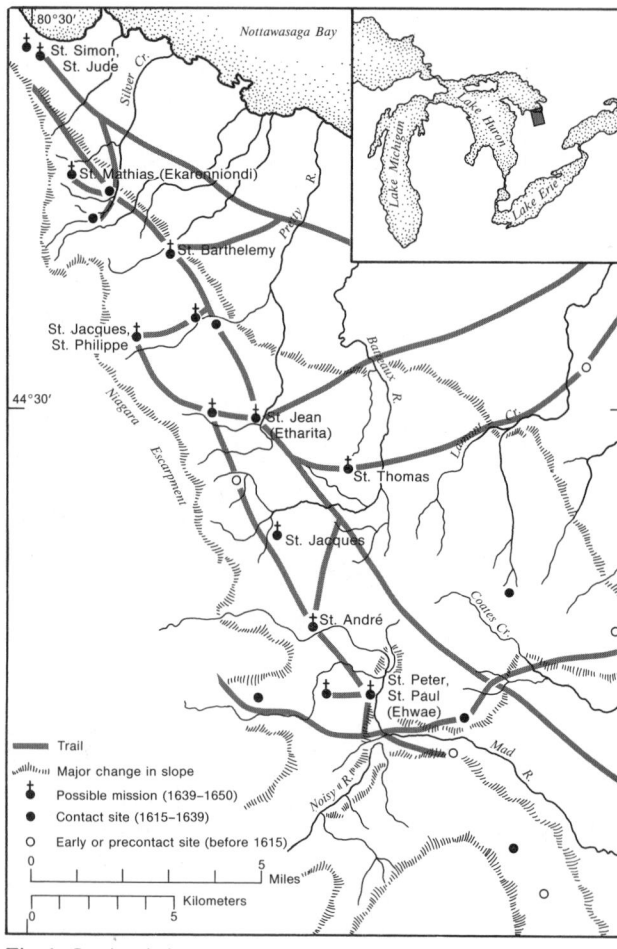

Fig. 1. Jesuit missions and archeological sites in tribal area.

394

massive rocky point at Nottawasaga Bay; at least the escarpment is so named on a Jesuit map drawn about 1631–1651 (Heidenreich 1966:113). It was this point that the souls of the Huron dead had to pass on their way to the life hereafter (JR 10:145).

Until 1641 the principal village of the Wolves was Ehwae, which the Jesuits called Saint Peter and Saint Paul. It was a large village of "forty-five or fifty cabins" on the southern frontier of the area. In 1640 Ehwae contained a substantial number of Neutrals who had been driven to the Petun by famine. The same year, the village was raided and partly destroyed by a force of Iroquois or Assistaeronnon (JR 20:45–47, 21:181). After Ehwae was abandoned, Etharita, called Saint Jean by the Jesuits, became the principal village and seat of the mission to the Petun (JR 35:107). Etharita was the village on the southern frontier. It was a large village of 500 to 600 families, no doubt composed mainly of refugee groups from the abandoned villages to the south (JR 35:107).

Some Petun, together with Huron refugees, coalesced west of Lake Huron in the second half of the seventeenth century into the tribe later known as the Wyandot.

Population

Virtually no information is given concerning the size of the Petun population. According to a Jesuit census of 1640, taken after the smallpox epidemic, the Huron and Petun together numbered about 12,000 in 32 villages (JR 19:127). If Petun and Huron villages were proportional in size, the postepidemic population of the Hurons must have been about 9,000 and that of the Petun 3,000. With a preepidemic Huron population of 18,000–22,000, the Petun population could have been on the order of 8,000 (Heidenreich 1971; Trigger 1969:11–13). With an average of six families or 36 members in each longhouse, the 45 or 50 dwellings listed for Ehwae in 1639 would give it a population of about 1,600 to 1,800. However, by this time, due to the epidemics, family size had dropped to about three or four persons, giving Ehwae a population more on the order of 1,000 to 1,200.

Sociopolitical Organization

The French sources provide only a sketchy glimpse of Petun society. Like other aspects of the Petun, their social and political structure seems to have been similar to that of the Huron.

In 1647 the Jesuits, aware that the Petun were made up of two major groups, the Wolves and the Deer, organized their mission accordingly. In view of the fact that the Wolves and Deer are Iroquoian clan names (Trigger 1969:57), occurring among the Seneca, Cayuga, and Onondaga, as well as the Hurons of Quebec, the Wyandot (Connelley 1900a), and the eighteenth-century Hu-

ron-Petun of the Windsor-Detroit area (Potier 1920:152), some authors have speculated that the Wolves and the Deer were dominant clan segments, clans, or phratries (Hodge 1913:456; Tooker 1964:12). The weakness of these speculations is that the Jesuits, who were familiar with Huron tribes, seem to have regarded the Wolves and the Deer as similar. Furthermore, if the Petun, like the Huron, practiced clan exogamy (Trigger 1969:55), territorial clans would make little sense. The least problematical explanation is that the Wolves and Deer were tribes with their own territories, who, like the Attignawantan (Bear) among the Huron, had tribal names that were also clan names or were taken perhaps from the principal clans in the area.

Culture

Unless it be the degree of specialization in growing and trading tobacco, the Petun do not appear to have possessed a single trait not shared completely or in some degree with the Huron. They spoke the same language as the Attignawantan (JR 8:115, 41:77; Sagard-Théodat 1939:9), were sedentary, cultivated the land (JR 18:233–235), and raised corn and tobacco. Several authors specifically pointed out that Petun customs were similar to those of the Attignawantan even down to the way the women dressed their hair (Champlain 1922–1936, 3:94–96, 4:279–280, 6:248; JR 20:43, 38:235). The men were reported to have tatooed their bodies more than the Huron, a practice they may have picked up from close relations with the Neutral (Sagard-Théodat 1939:143–145; JR 1:279–281). The Petun shared with the Huron the same beliefs in sorcery, spirits, curing feasts, and other "diabolical ceremonies" (JR 10:195, 20:51–53, 65; Sagard-Théodat 1939:194). Their "reverence for the dead" was well developed as was the practice of ossuary burial. They also adopted prisoners, sheltered wintering Algonquian groups, and took in refugee Neutrals (Champlain 1922–1936, 3:94–96, 4:278–279; JR 20:47, 49, 61, 21:125, 185).

The association of the Petun with tobacco must have predated Champlain's visit to the group in 1616. From the first mention of the Petun until Sagard-Théodat's visit they were always called by this name. On the legend of his map of 1632, Champlain specifically mentioned that "the Tobacco People is a tribe which cultivates this herb, in which they have a great trade with other tribes" (Champlain 1922–1936, 6:248). This observation was later reinforced by Sagard-Théodat (1939:158), Lalemant (JR 20:43), and Bressani (JR 38:235). Considering that the Huron had a great demand for tobacco, and that the relations between the Petun and Neutral were particularly close, it is possible that the Petun may also have imported tobacco from the Neutral for Huron consumption (Champlain 1922–1936, 3:99, 4:282).

External Relations

At the time of Champlain's arrival, the Petun and Huron were at peace; however, they had recently "waged cruel wars against one another" (JR 20:43). In 1640 the Jesuits reported the renewal of an alliance between the two groups. This alliance included friendship, trade, and mutual help against common enemies. Petun relations were particularly close with the Huron Attignawantan (Bear) tribe, a large part of whom sought refuge among the Petun in 1649 (JR 34:203, 223, 35:79-81, 39:251, 40:45).

In spite of their friendly relations with the Petun, the Huron tried to prevent any long-term contacts between the Petun and the French. Over the 1620s and 1630s the Hurons had developed a strong position as middlemen between the Petun and French traders. When the Jesuits attempted to establish a mission to the Petun they were met by extraordinary hostility, which was instigated and fanned by the Hurons (JR 20:51, 21:177). The Jesuits were convinced that the Hurons were playing on Petun fears of European diseases, for which the Jesuits were blamed, to keep the French and Petuns apart. So complete was the Huron trade monopoly with the Petun that no Petun was ever reported to have crossed Huron territory or to have made a trading journey to the Saint Lawrence.

The ethnohistoric accounts suggest strong relations between the Petun and Neutral but provide no extensive explanation. Both groups were allied with the Ottawa against the Assistaeronon, Algonquian speakers of the Michigan Lower Peninsula (Champlain 1922-1936, 3:97, 99; JR 20:61, 21:125). In 1626 it was a Petun chief who guided the Recollect priest Joseph Daillon to the Neutrals and provided baggage bearers after the Hurons had refused (Le Clercq 1881, 1:263-272). In 1640 a large group of starving Neutrals was taken into the Petun country and fed until their hosts' supplies were almost gone (JR 20:47-51), and in 1642 Neutral chiefs were observed among the Petun (JR 23:183).

The strong relations between the Petun and the Ottawa suggest an exchange of Algonquian products between the Ottawa and Neutral with the Petun as middlemen. The Neutral were known as traders of tobacco, seashells that were made into wampum, black squirrel skins, and raccoon skins, all of which were desired trade items with the Algonquians.

The most intimate relations the Petun had with any other group were with the Ottawa. Ottawa bands wintered regularly near the northern Petun villages and in areas farther west along the shore of Nottawasaga Bay and the Bruce Peninsula (Champlain 1922-1936, 3:96-101, 4:280-284). By 1647 there were so many Algonquians wintering in Ekarenniondi, for example, that an Algonquian-speaking missionary was sent there (A.E. Jones 1909:230). Judging from Champlain's state-ment that the Ottawa persuaded him not to visit the Neutral while he was among the Petun, the Ottawa must have had considerable influence among their hosts and neighbors (Champlain 1922-1936, 3:100, 4:283).

The Assistaeronnon were regarded as hostile and had been for some time. In 1639-1641 a captive from that group was living among the Petun (JR 20:61, 21:125). Petun hostilities with the Assistaeronnon probably came from their close relations with the Neutral and Ottawa, who were the chief protagonists in the war.

Petun relations with the Iroquois are not clear until the destruction of Etharita in December 1649 (JR 35: 107-117, 40:15-19). Ehwae had been partly destroyed in 1640 by an unidentified enemy (JR 21:181). Because it was on the southern frontier of the Petun country, "nearest to the enemy," one might infer the Iroquois were responsible. The renewal of the Huron-Petun alliance against "their common enemies" came just before the attack on Ehwae (JR 20:43). It is likely that the Petun were gradually drawn into the Iroquois-Huron conflict through their growing relations with the Huron.

Petun-French relations fluctuated over time. Champlain was well received, as were traders and missionaries in the 1620s (Le Clercq 1881, 1:263-272; Sagard-Théodat 1939:194). During the 1630s, with the outbreak of European diseases and growing Huron trade protectionism, the Jesuits were extremely unwelcome (JR 15:21, 20:47-49, 21:177-183). In the early 1640s, resistance to the Jesuits lessened, leading to the establishment of two permanent missions in the area. French influence on the Petun was confined to the trade goods they received through the Huron traders and the few Jesuits who lived among them.

Synonymy

The Khionontateronon were called the Petun or Nation of the Tobacco by the French. The name Petun, a term of Brazilian origin, was first used by Champlain in 1632 in observing that this tribe cultivated and traded tobacco (Champlain 1922-1936, 6:248, map of 1632). Later writers stated that this is why they were given the name (JR 20:43, 38:235). Sagard-Théodat (1939:71) was the first writer, in 1623, to call the Petun by an Indian name, Quieunontatéronon. It is not clear whether this, or any of the later synonyms, was the Huron name for the Petun or their own. A.E. Jones (1909:216-219) proposed slightly different translations for the major spelling variants Khionontatehronon, Tionnontatehronnon, and Etion-nontatehronnon, but all seem to be equivalent to *tyonqtatehró·nqʔ* (in phonemic interpretation) 'people of the place where the hills are', a reference to the hilly nature of their territory. The forms spelled with Khi- have undergone a dialectal sound shift of *t* to *k* before *y*, and those with E- have an added particle *eh* 'there'

(Wallace L. Chafe, personal communication 1974; Floyd G. Lounsbury, personal communication 1976).

The following variants in spelling occur in the *Jesuit Relations* (JR 1896-1901): Khionontaterrhonon, 1635; Khionontateron, 1639; Khionontatehronon, 1640; Khionontateronon, 1640; Kionontatehronon, 1642; Tionontatehronnon, 1654. For forms of this name later applied to the Wyandot, see the synonymy in "Wyandot," this volume.

Sources

The principal sources for the Petun are the writings of Champlain (1922-1936), Sagard-Théodat (1866, 1939), and the *Jesuit Relations* (JR 1896-1901). Maps showing the location of the Petun and some of their villages have been listed, and to some extent discussed, by Heidenreich (1966) and Garrad (1970a).

Archeology in the Petun area began with the site surveys of Boyle (1889) and Lawrence, Gaviller, and Morris (1909). Several attempts have been made to identify the Jesuit missions in the area, notably by E.H. Thomas (1959), A.E. Jones (1909), and Lawrence, Gaviller, and Morris (1909). Of these, the last-named has stood the test of time remarkably well.

Detailed excavations have been conducted at only two sites: the early contact MacMurchy site (Bell 1953) and the precontact Sidey-Mackay site (Wintemberg 1946). Other archeological work has been done on iron trade knives (Garrad 1969) and on an unusual tool made from modified bear jaws, which seems to be associated with some Petun sites (Garrad 1969a). The only osteological report from the Petun is a single burial of a woman who suffered from dislocation of the hips and severe osteoarthritis (Garrad 1970).

Due to the meager ethnohistoric record, future knowledge of the Petun must come from archeology. Recent archeological work, all unpublished, has included: a thorough site survey of the area, examination of public and private collections, placing of all remains into a temporal framework, and the determination of historic village sites as far as possible.

Wyandot

ELISABETH TOOKER

The Indians known to the English as Wyandot ('wīyən₁dät) were known to the French after 1650 as Tionontati (Khionontateronon or Petun), Tionontati Hurons, or simply Hurons. They were a group of Tionontati and Hurons, probably more Tionontati than Hurons who, after being defeated by the Iroquois in the middle of the seventeenth century, fled west into the Upper Great Lakes area. There they continued to rely on a combination of agriculture, hunting, fishing, and gathering, and on the fur trade. Each location the Wyandots chose as a village site was one at which all these activities could be successfully pursued. Their several removes in the seven-

teenth and eighteenth centuries were motivated primarily by their desire to maintain their advantage in the fur trade, that is, to continue their position as suppliers of furs to the French, albeit on a smaller scale than before their defeat by the Iroquois in 1649–1650 (fig. 1).

The Wyandots were never to be the military power that the Hurons had been before 1650 (eighteenth-century estimates of the number of Wyandot warriors usually range between 150 and 250), and partly in consequence they entered into a complex series of alliances with other Indians, often emerging as the most influential member of such confederations (cf. Charlevoix 1923, 1:303; Kel-

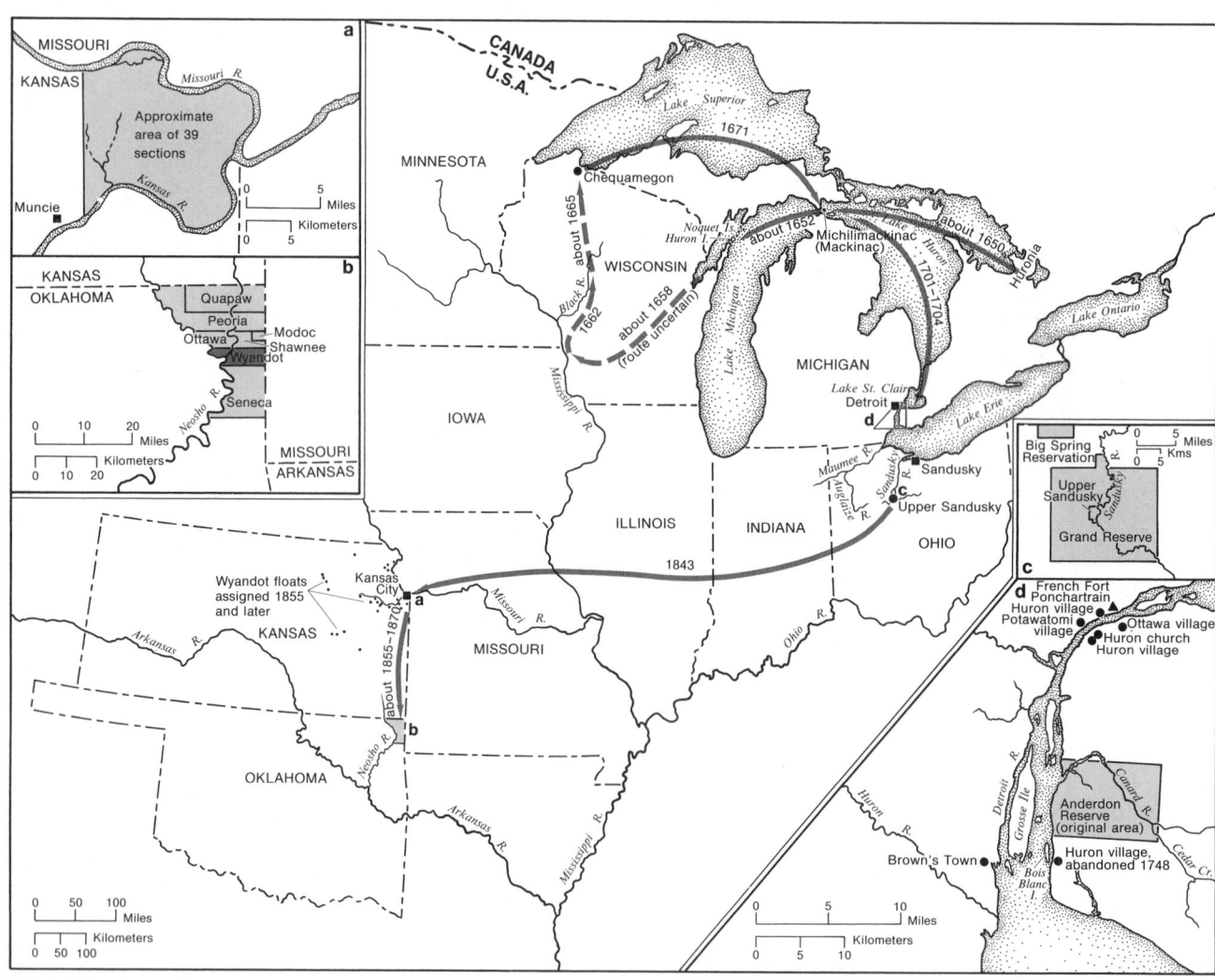

Fig. 1. Wyandot settlements and movements.

logg 1916:311). Although these alliances of the Wyandots and other Indians of the old Northwest embraced peoples speaking different languages and having different cultures and therefore had a somewhat different organization from that of the League of the Iroquois, Wyandot sociopolitical organization remained basically Iroquoian in character (Powell 1881; Connelley 1899b:25–36, 1900a; Barbeau 1912; Tooker 1970) as did other aspects of their culture.

The history of the Wyandots, then, is the history of a Northern Iroquoian group who, although lacking the numbers and the particularly advantageous geographic position of the Iroquois, were often to play a crucial role in the complex interrelationships between various Europeans and Indians on the North American continent.

Seventeenth-Century Trade

The history of the Wyandots begins in the early 1650s when they fled from the Petun country to Michilimackinac (JR 56:115), apparently there joining the Ottawa who were to remain their allies for a century. After a relatively short stay at Michilimackinac, they moved to Huron Island (later called Potawatomi Island, then Washington Island, now Rock Island, R.J. Mason 1974:149) at the entrance of Green Bay. Resuming their trade with the French and so to the extent possible their old position in the fur trade, they sent a fleet of canoes to the Saint Lawrence in 1654 (JR 41:77–79). This event was of major importance to the French as the Iroquois war had previously caused such trade to stop and left the beavers "in peace" (JR 40:211). However, the Wyandots were not to remain long in the Green Bay area. Attacked by the Iroquois, they moved farther west, living briefly on the Mississippi, and then on the Black River (Blair 1911–1912, 1:165). In the mid-1660s, they moved still farther north and settled at Chequamegon—a center of the region in part because fish were abundant there (JR 50:297, 54:149–151, 167, 55:97). At Chequamegon, the Wyandots built a village near that of the Ottawa and resumed their trade with the French. On their part, the Jesuits resumed their missionary work among them, establishing the mission of Saint Esprit. At that time, the Wyandots numbered about 500 (JR 54:169, 283).

In 1671, a general peace had been established with the Iroquois, and Wyandots, under attack from the Sioux (also known at the time as "the Iroquois of the West"), moved back to Michilimackinac, a location that not only afforded both excellent fishing and land suitable for horticulture, but also permitted them to continue to trade with the French on the Saint Lawrence. As it had in Huronia and at Chequamegon, this trade led to the establishment of a Jesuit mission; it was called Saint Ignace (JR 55:157–161, 57:203, 59:71, 217).

The move to Michilimackinac brought the Wyandots not only closer to the French trading posts on the Saint Lawrence, but also closer to the English on the Hudson River and their Iroquois allies. As a result, the Wyandots were drawn more fully into the complicated game being played in the Northeast for control of the fur trade. In order to keep their control of the northern part of this trade, the French wanted to maintain their alliance with the Huron and Ottawa middlemen at Michilimackinac, center of the western Great Lakes trade. At the same time, the French attempted by various means to get the Iroquois to trade with them rather than with Albany. The English wished to keep up their alliance with the Iroquois. On their part, the Iroquois were attempting to play off the English and French, often lending a sympathetic ear to French overtures while keeping up their old alliance with the English to their east and trying to extend their influence over the lands to the west that produced the beaver and the Indians who hunted them. For their part, the Wyandots attempted to play off the French and the Iroquois, sometimes seeming to enter into a trading alliance with the Iroquois, sometimes maintaining their old trading relationship with the French, and sometimes (often not all Wyandots agreed on the proper course of action) both at the same time.

Opportunities for intrigue were many, and they increased after the Iroquois, no longer menaced by the Susquehannock in 1676, turned more of their attention to the western tribes. In 1680 the Iroquois attacked the Illinois and Miami, and the French feared that the Iroquois were planning to defeat one by one the various other western tribes as they had earlier the Hurons and other Iroquoian tribes of the region. In this and succeeding years, some Wyandots believed that the Iroquois planned to destroy them, and they sought the aid of the French, while other Wyandots sought an alliance with the Iroquois. In 1686 Gov. Thomas Dongan and his Iroquois allies further increased their efforts to gain the Wyandot trade, and an expedition led by Johannes Rooseboom and Maj. Patrick McGregory successfully traded English goods for Indian furs at Michilimackinac itself. Jacques René de Brisay, marquis de Denonville, governor general of Canada, decided he could no longer delay action, and in 1687 he led an expedition against the Seneca, ruining the villages the Senecas had abandoned. But the seeming success of Denonville's expedition did not deter the Iroquois, and by various means, including attacks on the Saint Lawrence and negotiations with the Hurons, they continued to attempt to gain control of the French trade. Finally, in 1696, Louis de Buade de Frontenac led an expedition against the Onondaga, and in 1701 at a grand council of Indian tribes at Montreal peace was concluded (Parkman 1883; Eccles 1964; Broshar 1920; Buffinton 1922; Wallace 1957).

Eighteenth-Century Settlements

In 1701 Antoine Laumet de Lamothe Cadillac realized his dream of founding a settlement at Detroit—a plan now made more attractive by both this peace and increasing English influence among the Indians. Cadillac realized as did others that Detroit was the key to the Upper Great Lakes. French control of Detroit and so the passage from Lake Erie to Lake Huron would serve to shut the English out of the northwest, as well as put a barrier between the Iroquois and the western tribes. But to the extent Detroit prospered, Michilimackinac (which had grown into the principal center of the fur trade in the Upper Great Lakes during the Wyandots' sojourn there) was doomed to decline—a fact the Wyandots apparently recognized. Despite the urgings of Father Étienne de Carheil, the Jesuit missionary at Michilimackinac, to remain (entreaties in part occasioned by the antipathy between Cadillac and the Jesuits), the Wyandots began to move to Detroit. After the last left in 1704, the Jesuits burned their house at Michilimackinac and returned to Quebec (Charlevoix 1866–1872, 4:182).

At Detroit, the Wyandots built their village near Fort Pontchartrain (fig. 2). The Potawatomi village was located a short distance away and the Ottawa village on the opposite side of the Detroit River. Although in the early years Detroit did not prosper as greatly as Cadillac hoped it would, it remained the important trading center of the Great Lakes region, and in 1728 Father Armand de La Richardie came to Detroit to reestablish the Jesuit mission among the Wyandots; this was the first such permanent Jesuit mission since the Wyandots had left Michilimackinac a quarter of a century before. Various troubles led to the abandonment of the Wyandot village on the north side of the Detroit River. (Some authorities, such as Elliott 1898:529, say Richardie located the Wyandots on the south side of the Detroit River.) In 1742 the Jesuits transferred their mission to Bois Blanc Island

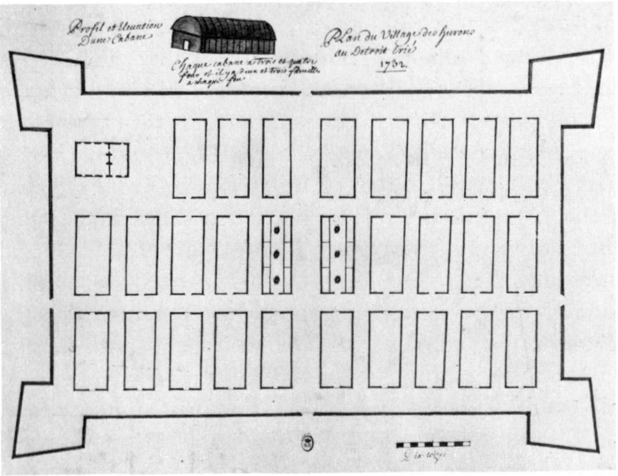

Bibliothèque Nationale, Cabinet des Estampes, Paris: Vd. 20b, t.1, fol.
Fig. 2. Plan of the Wyandot village at Detroit in 1732, with a fortification surrounding the longhouses. Two of the longhouses are shown with 3 central fires and adjacent compartments; a label indicates that each house had 3 or 4 fires with 2 or 3 families per fire. A perspective view of one longhouse is at the top. The bar represents 10 *toises*, or 19.49m.

(now Bob-lo Island) at the mouth of the Detroit River opposite the present town of Amherstburg, Ontario, where many Wyandots then lived (Lajeunesse 1960:37).

The English continued to court the trade with the Wyandot, first at Detroit and later in their Ohio hunting territories. After the Wyandots settled at Detroit, they began to hunt south of Lake Erie in the territory that included the Sandusky River and the lower Maumee. Not long after, the colonies south of New York became increasingly interested in the possibilities of trade west of the Alleghenies, and traders began crossing the mountains and entering the Ohio country. Among the various tribes they met were the Wyandots, and in 1745 traders from Pennsylvania built a block house at Sandusky where Nicolas, a Wyandot chief, and his band had settled apparently following a quarrel with the Ottawas at Detroit in 1738. The first fort to be built by Whites in the present state of Ohio, Sandusky probably encouraged Nicolas in his attempts to rally (perhaps at the instigation of the English) the various Indian tribes of the area to his cause—to drive the French out of the Upper Great Lakes area. The date set for the attack was late August 1747, but the plans were revealed to the French, and finding they had been detected, the Wyandots who were to attack Detroit withdrew. Finally, when 150 soldiers arrived at Detroit from Montreal on September 22, Nicolas abandoned his plans. That winter Pennsylvania traders continued to deal with the Sandusky Wyandots, but in early spring of 1748, his influence greatly weakened, Nicolas destroyed the villages and fort and the following day left Sandusky for the White River with about 120 warriors and their families (Trent 1871:15–22; Randall and Ryan 1912, 1:200–204; Hanna 1911, 1:320–332, 2:163–167).

To check English activity such as that among the Sandusky Wyandots, the French attempted to strengthen their military position in the region, first by sending an expedition led by Pierre Joseph Céloron de Blainville down the Ohio in 1749 and in 1753 by building a series of forts protecting the route from the eastern end of Lake Erie to the Ohio. On their part, the Indians of the area, including the Wyandots, were to range themselves on the side of France in the conflicts that were to follow. The Wyandots were among the Indians who helped defeat Gen. Edward Braddock's expedition near Fort Duquesne in 1755, and having themselves been defeated in the French and Indian War, rallied around Pontiac in his attempt to drive the English from the region in 1763. In the Pontiac conflict, the Wyandots took part in the siege of Detroit and the attack on Fort Pitt and destroyed the fort at Sandusky.

The Proclamation of 1763 prohibiting settlement of the colonists west of the Alleghenies deterred a number of Whites from settling in the area, but traders from the colonies continued their activities among the Indians of this region. The peace that followed Pontiac's defeat did not last long. When the American Revolution began, the

Indians of the area, including the Wyandots, sided with the British. In an attempt to stop the increasing Wyandot attacks on them, the Americans sent an expedition against the Sandusky Wyandots and in June 1782 attacked the principal Wyandot settlement at Upper Sandusky. Col. William Crawford, leader of this expedition against the Wyandots, was captured during the retreat and burned at the stake.

Land Cessions

For the Wyandots and other Indians in the area, the conclusion of the Revolutionary War did not end the controversy. They did not wholeheartedly support the treaties of Fort McIntosh (1785) and Fort Finney (1786) with their extensive land cessions and became increasingly disturbed as Americans settled in the Ohio country (Bond 1941-1944, 1:312). Further, the British still intrigued with the Indians for control of the fur trade. Another treaty was concluded with the Wyandots and other Indians at Fort Harmar in 1789, but that did not settle matters. Finally, after Arthur St. Clair's defeat, Gen. Anthony Wayne led a successful expedition into the area in 1794. His victory in the Battle of Fallen Timbers

opened the way for the Treaty of Greenville negotiated the following year.

By the Treaty of Greenville, the Indians of Ohio, including the Wyandots, ceded the territory south and east of the Greenville treaty line, almost two-thirds of the state. Ten years later, in 1805, they signed another treaty at Fort Industry (Toledo) ceding the eastern portion of the land they still held, almost one-third of what remained, and two years later signed a treaty at Detroit relinquishing except for some small reservations their title to the land north of the Maumee River as far west as the mouth of the Auglaize River (Shetrone 1918:453; D.L. Smith 1949:308).

About the same time, comparable land cessions were being made on the Canadian side. After Nicolas's uprising against them, the French were anxious to have the Detroit Wyandots closer to the fort, and a tract of land on the south side of the Detroit River at La Pointe de Montreal was given to the Jesuits. They built a church and house there. The Wyandot village opposite Bois Blanc Island was abandoned in 1748, and the Wyandots built a village near the mission. In the years that followed, increasing numbers of Whites settled on the south side of the Detroit River and the number of Wyandots living near the mission dwindled, some settling along the Canard River (La Rivière aux Canards). In 1781 Father Pierre Potier, who had been a missionary to the Wyandots since 1744 and later (since 1767 when the parish of the Assumption was established) pastor also to the French settlers, died. With his death, the long Jesuit mission to the Wyandots ended (Lajeunesse 1960:xlvii-xlviii, liv, xcii-xciii, xcvii). After the Revolutionary War, the Loyalist immigration to the Detroit River region increased the population of the area. Deputy Superintendent of Indian Affairs Alexander McKee began negotiations to purchase the Wyandot lands on the Canadian side of the Detroit River, and in 1790 portions of the southwest part of the present province of Ontario were ceded by the Indians. By this treaty, the Wyandots retained two reserves: one at the old Huron Mission site opposite Detroit and a larger tract on the Canard River (the Huron or Anderdon Reserve). In 1800, four years after the British evacuated Detroit, the Huron Mission Reserve opposite Detroit was ceded to the Crown. Later (in 1836), the Huron Reserve (now the township of Anderdon in Essex County, Ontario) was surrendered to the Crown, the land surveyed, and the farm lots not conveyed to the Wyandots sold. Under this cession, the Wyandots sold two-thirds of their reserve and retained one-third, a block of 7,770 acres. Subsequently, portions of this land were sold, and in 1876, the band applied for enfranchisement under the terms of the Indian Act. The application was approved, and in 1880-1881, all 41 heads of families received enfranchisement, the reserve having been divided in severalty (C.C. James 1906:332-333, 344; Hale 1888:177).

British Lib.: Jefferys 1757-1772, 4:pl. 198.

Fig. 3. Wyandot woman before 1772, according to an English engraving after a drawing by an unknown artist.

In the first decade of the nineteenth century, the tensions between the British and Americans in the northwest continued as did those between the Indians and Americans. They finally erupted into the War of 1812, a conflict in which the Wyandots were not united. The Wyandots living near Detroit sided with Tecumseh and the British, while the Sandusky Wyandots under the leadership of Tarhe (the Crane, whose name appears first in the list of Indians signing the Treaty of Greenville) sided with the Americans.

In 1817, by the Treaty of the Rapids of the Maumee, the Ohio Indians ceded all their remaining lands in the state. However, the Wyandots by this treaty retained two reservations, the largest being a tract of land 12 miles square at Upper Sandusky called the Grand Reserve. The Grand Reserve was enlarged the following year by a treaty signed at Saint Marys; and two other reservations were established, one at Big Spring four miles northeast of the Grand Reserve and another on the west side of the Sandusky River (Shetrone 1918:453; D.L. Smith 1949:308-309). By another treaty signed a few days later at Saint Marys, the Wyandots ceded two tracts in Michigan including the villages of Brownstown and Maguagua, which had been reserved for them in 1809. In consideration for this cession, they received a reservation of almost 5,000 acres on the Huron River in Michigan Territory (Kappler 1904-1941, 2:164).

The Nineteenth Century

Culture Change

The fur trade, which had been important in the economy of the Wyandots in earlier centuries, ceased to be so in the nineteenth. As more Whites settled in the area, the game became scarce and the Wyandots increasingly began to turn to White farming methods—adopting plow agriculture, fencing their fields, and raising sheep and hogs in addition to horses and cattle. They began replacing their old bark houses with ones made of logs and dressing in the White manner (Finley 1840:188, 256, 365-366; H. Jackson 1830:106). They also increasingly began to turn to White religion. In earlier centuries, the Jesuits had successfully introduced Roman Catholicism and maintained a mission among them, but when the last Jesuit missionary died in 1781, the Wyandots ceased to participate in its rites. In the first decade of the nineteenth century, the Presbyterians sent missionaries to the Wyandot, but their efforts met with little success. It was not until John Stewart, a free Negro, began preaching among them in 1816 that a number of Wyandots became converts to Protestantism. Not long after a Methodist mission was established at Upper Sandusky.

Some continued to believe in the old Wyandot religion and accounts of this religion published at the end of the nineteenth and beginning of the twentieth century indi-

cate it was still basically Iroquoian in character. As did the Iroquois, the Wyandot believed the supernatural powers of the world above included the sun, moon, wind, and thunderers. The Milky Way was regarded as the path of the souls, and the earth as an island resting on the Turtle's back. Races of giants and the "Little People" (pygmies or dwarfs) figured in myths and belief as they did among the Iroquois, and the distinctive cosmological myth with its account of the woman who fell from the sky, the animals diving for earth, and the birth and exploits of the Twin Brothers continued to be recalled. Ceremonies similar to those of the Iroquois were held: the Green Corn ceremony, sun or "war" dance, Blackberry feast in honor of the moon, and annual feasts for the dead (Barbeau 1914, 1915; Connelley 1899, 1899b, 1923; Hale 1888).

Removal to Kansas

In the 1830s, after the passage of the Removal Act of 1830, efforts to induce all the Indians including the Wyandots to move west of the Mississippi increased. However, the Wyandots were reluctant even to discuss the matter, although they did agree to send a party to examine the country designated for them in the West in 1831. On their return, this delegation reported unfavorably on the land (Oliphant 1947). Efforts to get the Wyandots living on Big Spring Reservation to sell their land were more successful, and in 1832 this band of Wyandots sold their 16,000-acre reservation and removed to the Grand Reserve and the Huron River. Aware that the so-called Christian Party was opposed to removal and the Pagan Party favorable to it, the government continued its efforts to conclude further treaties to remove the Wyandots west of the Mississippi. Another party of Wyandots was sent west in 1834; and as the earlier group had, they reported unfavorably on relocating there. In 1836 the Wyandots sold a strip of land five miles wide on the eastern end of the Grand Reserve and the two small tracts they held under the treaties of Maumee Rapids and Saint Marys (Klopfenstein 1957:121-124; D.L. Smith 1949:309-310).

Finally, in 1842, the Wyandots ceded the Grand Reserve—all their remaining lands in Ohio (now Wyandot County), almost 110,000 acres—and the Wyandot Reserve located on both sides of the Huron River, which was all their remaining lands in Michigan (Kappler 1904-1941, 2:534-537). They then began preparations to leave Ohio for Indian Territory. By March 1843 many of the Huron River Wyandots had moved to Upper Sandusky (Klopfenstein 1957:131), and in July of that year all left for what is now Kansas. There were about 700 (the official count was 674) in the caravan. They were the last Indians to leave Ohio (Foreman 1946:94-97).

By the treaty of 1842, the United States had agreed to give the Wyandots a tract of 148,000 acres west of the Mississippi. But when the Wyandots were unable to find an unoccupied area of such size that was suitable to their needs, they purchased from the Delawares a 36-section tract of land immediately in the fork of the Missouri and Kansas rivers; and the Delawares gave them an additional three sections. This agreement signed by the Wyandots and Delawares on December 14, 1843, was finally approved by the United States Senate on July 25, 1848.

Although to some White observers, this choice of location was unfortunate as it brought the Wyandots close to the "evil" influences of "civilization" (for example, close to the whiskey sellers in Missouri), at least some Wyandots clearly saw its advantages (it was later to become Kansas City). Further, for many years, the Wyandots had refused the lands offered farther west on the grounds that they were unsuitable areas, being too far from civilization and ill adapted to the economy they then practiced. This same concern for finding suitable land is also to be noted in the so-called Wyandot floats. By the treaty of 1842, the United States agreed to grant a section of land (640 acres) in fee simple to each of 35 Wyandots. These "floating" grants could be taken up on any land still unoccupied west of the Missouri River.

If at one time the land west of the Mississippi was of little value to the Whites (its lack of economic worth in the White economy was one of the reasons for removing the eastern Indians there), it did not remain so. In 1842 "Oregon fever" struck the frontier, and later in the decade the rush to California was on. The next decade witnessed the opening of the prairie to farming and the rapid building of railroads to carry the wheat from the prairie farms to the port cities. When this westward movement began, the Indians were living athwart the central route to the Pacific, and beginning about 1848, a new policy respecting the Indians developed: the Indians were to be removed from the Platte and Kansas valleys and grouped to the north and the south in such a manner as they would not interfere with western expansion (Malin 1921:81-90).

About the same time, the slavery question intensified. In 1845, shortly after the Wyandots had arrived in Kansas, the Methodist Episcopal church split on the slavery issue, the Indian missions of Kansas coming under the jurisdiction of the proslavery Methodist Episcopal Church South. Having recently arrived from a free state and not having lived long enough in Kansas to be much affected by the proslavery sentiments there, a number of Wyandots objected to this arrangement and sought a missionary from Ohio. Some other Wyandots, however, were sympathetic to the Church South, and a few were slaveholders. The issue split both the Wyandot church and the tribe as a whole (Lutz 1906:213-225).

In 1849 "gold fever" struck the Wyandots as it did so many others in the country, and at least 24 went to California during 1849 and 1850 (Foreman 1946:194). Shortly after, the Wyandots remaining in Indian country became involved in the efforts to make Nebraska a territory. In the 1840s, some efforts had been made in Congress (notably by Stephen A. Douglas) to establish a Nebraska territory. These proved unsuccessful, but the issue remained. In 1851-1852, the Wyandots themselves petitioned Congress to establish a territorial government and, being unsuccessful, sent a delegate to Congress in 1852-1853 to the same end. In part motivated by the possibility that the transcontinental railroad might be built by the central route, they were instrumental in organizing a provisional territorial government in the summer of 1853. But the movement failed when a proslavery delegate to Congress was elected that fall (Connelley 1899a, 1900, 1928, 1:273-288).

Removal to Oklahoma

On March 3, 1853, Congress authorized the Indian Office to negotiate with the emigrant Indians then in a solid array along the Kansas-Missouri border for the cession of their lands; later that year, George Manypenny, commissioner of Indian affairs, went there to negotiate new treaties. In 1854 he renewed negotiations with them and a series of treaties was signed. But, before any of these treaties was ratified (the treaty negotiations with the Wyandot had not even been completed), Congress passed the Kansas-Nebraska Act, opening Kansas Territory to settlement (Gates 1954:15-19).

The treaty with the Wyandots was signed and ratified early in 1855. This treaty provided for the allotment of the Wyandot lands at the fork of the Kansas and Missouri rivers and gave citizenship to the Wyandots. The tribe was to be dissolved as those receiving allotments became citizens. However, those who so wished or were so deemed were to be exempt from citizenship for a limited time. As a result of this exemption, there developed two classes of Wyandots: a "citizen" or "competent" and an "Indian" or "incompetent" class and party.

Two years after the signing of this treaty, the lands had been divided, each individual receiving about 40 acres (ARCIA 1858:169), and the way was open for the selling of these allotments. The 1855 treaty had also made the Wyandot floats more easily assignable. In the Kansas land craze, title to these floats was in great demand as they were a means of securing town sites, and within two years almost all these warrants had been laid on land somewhere in Kansas (Gates 1954:44; Socolofsky 1970:247).

During this same period, a number of Wyandots moved to the Seneca reservation in the northeast part of the present state of Oklahoma. In 1857 an estimated 200 Wyandots had settled there at the invitation of the Seneca (ARCIA 1858:205). In 1858 the Senecas conveyed to the Wyandots a strip of land four miles wide across the northern end of their reservation from the Missouri line west to the Grand or Neosho River.

After the Civil War ended, there was on the part of the United States a general reevaluation of the situation of the Indians, including the Wyandots. Those Wyandots who had gone to Oklahoma before the war and who had fled (as had other Indians living in that area) north to Kansas during the war returned to Oklahoma. A number of Wyandots who had remained in Kansas after the treaty of 1855 wished to join them. A considerable portion of their land in Kansas had been sold to Whites for taxes and debts. Whites were also encroaching on the land they still held and were stealing their stock and other property. Many Wyandots including some who had become citizens wished to be relieved of the heavy state taxes, and a number of both the "citizen" and "incompetent" classes wanted to make some arrangement by which they could sell their lands in Kansas and move to those given to the Wyandots by the Seneca in Indian Territory (ARCIA 1866:52, 253–255). In the Omnibus Treaty of 1867, the United States confirmed the 1858 agreement by which the Seneca conveyed part (about 20,000 acres) of their reservation to the Wyandots. The treaty also provided for a register of those who wished to remain members of the tribe, that is, those who did not wish to become citizens. Those who were citizens could not become members of the tribe except by consent of the tribe and the agent (Kappler 1904–1941, 2:963).

During the next several years Wyandots of both the "citizen" and "incompetent" classes moved to Oklahoma, and in 1872 the "citizen" class was adopted into the tribe. At that time, the Wyandots on the Oklahoma reservation numbered about 220 (ARCIA 1868:263, 273, 1870:360, 376, 258, 268, 1872:38–39, 244) (fig. 4). In the 1870s, all these Wyandots were engaged in farming, and a portion of the reservation was rented to White farmers. In 1879 over 130 Whites were living on the reservation renting a total of 890 acres of the 1,250 acres under cultivation (ARCIA 1878:66, 1879:232, 250). In 1888–1890, this reservation too was allotted (ARCIA 1888:109, 1890:84). Most Wyandots in the 1970s continued to live in Oklahoma. The Wyandot language is extinct, though there were two elderly speakers alive in 1961.

Synonymy*

In the second half of the seventeenth century the Wyandots were often known to both the French and the English by variants of the name of their largest constituent group, the Tionontati (Petun), and the English continued this usage into the middle of the eighteenth century. Examples from French sources are: Tionnonta-tehronnons, 1654 (JR 41:76); Tionnontateheronnons, 1667 (JR 50:306, 51:20); Tionnontaté, 1672 (JR 56:114); Tionnontateronnons, 1673 (JR 57:248, 254); Étionnon-tatés, 1675 (JR 60:52); Tionontateronons and Thiononta-toronons, 1681 (Margry 1876–1886, 2:267, 272–273; cf. NYCD 9:161–164); Tionontatés, 1682 (NYCD 9:173,

* The synonymy section was prepared by Ives Goddard, incorporating material and references supplied by the author.

Fig. 4. Wyandot delegates to Washington from Indian Territory (Okla.) in 1875. left, Mathew Mudeater, head chief, born in 1813 in Canada; right, Nicholas Cotter, councilor, born in 1822 in Canada. Photographed in Washington by unknown photographer (W.H. Jackson 1877:93–94).

186); Tionontaté, 1703 (NYCD 9:752); Theonontateronons (Lahontan 1703, 1:94). English sources have: Dionondade, 1687 (NYCD 3:478); Tionondade, 1687 (NYCD 3:443); Dionondadoes, 1691 (NYCD 3:781); Donondades, 1695 (NYCD 4:121); "Dionondades or Jenondades," 1700 (NYCD 4:768); Jenondathese, 1700 (NYCD 4:799); Innondadese, 1700 (NYCD 4:805); Dienondades, 1701 (NYCD 4:834); Deonondade, 1702 (NYCD 4:979); Tienondaideaga, 1723 (NYCD 5:693); Kenondadie, 1724 (Wraxall 1915:152); Janondadies, 1725 (Wraxall 1915:152); Chenondadees, 1747 (NYCD 6:359); Chonondedeys, 1747 (NYCD 6:387); Younondadys, 1747 (NYCD 6:391); Chanundadies, 1751 (NYCD 6:706); Jenundadees, 1756 (NYCD 7:86); Chenundady, 1756 (NYCD 7:93); Tynondady and Tsyenundady, 1757 (W. Johnson 1921-1965, 9:650, 652, 653); Chenundaddey, 1761 (W. Johnson 1921-1965, 13:230-246). Equivalent to this is the Onondaga name tyonontateʔkāʔ (Hewitt in Mooney 1910b:756).

The French in the second half of the seventeenth century also used the name Huron for this group, at first usually with qualification but eventually by itself. The close linguistic affinity that the French recognized between the Huron and the Petun (JR 41:77) probably accounts for this usage. Examples include references to them as the Hurons of the Tobacco Nation (in French, *les Hurons de la Nation du Petun*) in 1660 and 1667 (JR 45:235, 50:306); explicit designations such as "The Hurons of the Tobacco Nation, called Tionnontaté," 1672 (JR 56:114; cf. JR 57:249); and expressions such as "[l]es Hurons Etionnontatehronnons," 1670 (JR 54:166); les Hurons de Tionnontaté, 1671 (JR 55:96, 166; cf. NYCD 9:202); the Hurons called Etiennontatehronnons, 1671 (JR 55:159); les Hurons d'Etionnontaté, 1675 (JR 59:216); la mission huronne de tionontate, 1679 (JR 61:102); "Hurons, or Tionnontatez," 1682 (NYCD 9:178); "the Hurons at lemikariagi" (for l'Ennikariagi, a place near Michilimackinac), 1686 (contemporary English translation in NYCD 3:489); "Tionnontatez or Hurons of Missilimakinac," 1691 (NYCD 9:524). Sometimes they were called simply "Hurons" (see, for example, JR 48:127, 50:297, 309, 54:151, 167, 169, 55:171, 59:71; NYCD 9:753).

The French continued to use the name Hurons in the eighteenth century. In English sources Huron appears as a name for the Wyandot only in direct translations from French, until England gained possession of Canada in the French and Indian War, when the English began to adopt French usage. Examples are: Hurons, 1761 (W. Johnson 1921-1965, 13:248, 258, 260); 'the Hurons of this place [Detroit]', 1765 (NYCD 7:782); 'Hurons, from Sanduskey', 1767 (W. Johnson 1921-1965, 13:406); 'Hurons' in Ohio, 1774 (W. Johnson 1921-1965, 13:666). This usage continued in the nineteenth century, and those living on the Canadian side of the Detroit River usually were called Hurons rather than Wyandots. However,

except where the Huron of Lorette are being referred to, the names Huron and Wyandot are synonymous in documents from the eighteenth, nineteenth, and twentieth centuries.

Starting at the time of the first contacts between traders from Pennsylvania and the Wyandots in Ohio, the standard English name, especially for those in the United States, comes to be Wyandot. This was an adaptation of the Huron and Wyandot self-designation *węˑⁿdat*,[†] written 8endat by Potier (1920:154; 8 = ou), which is probably an elliptical shortening of some longer form corresponding to Mohawk *skawę́·nat* 'one language' or *tshaʔtekawę́·nat* 'the same language (word, speech)' (Floyd G. Lounsbury, personal communication 1975). Some early attestations are: "the Wondats, otherways called Ionontady Hagas," Owandaets, Owendaets, Wandots, 1748 (Thwaites 1904-1907, 1:28, 30, 35); Wayandotts, 1749 (NYCD 6:531); Wayundotts, Wayundatts, 1749 (NYCD 6:533); Wyendotts, 1750 (Gist 1893:37); Owendats, 1750 (NYCD 6:593); Wiandotts, 1756 (NYCD 7:236); Wyandots, 1761 (W. Johnson 1921-1965, 13:231); "the Wyondatts or Huron," 1765 (NYCD 7:782); "Weyondotts or Hurons," 1767 (W. Johnson 1921-1965, 13:437). The Seneca name, borrowed from Wyandot, is *węˑtat* (Wallace L. Chafe, personal communication 1974).

Among the Northern Iroquoians, a tribe was sometimes referred to by the name of its principal chief. Until the latter part of the eighteenth century the name of the principal Wyandot chief was Sastaretsi (variously spelled Sataretsy, Sasteratsy, Sastharhetsi, Sastaghretsy), a name-title held by the Deer clan, and the Wyandots were sometimes known by that name (NYCD 9:672; Connelley 1899b; Hale 1894:12).

The name Quatoges, 1726 (NYCD 5:791), Quatoghies (Colden 1747, passim), is used as an equivalent of the French name Huron in just these two sources and a late secondary work (Schoolcraft 1847:113). Its origin and meaning are unknown, but it may be the same as the unidentified place name Quadoge, said by the sachems of the Five Nations in 1701 to mark the western boundary of the conquered "seven nations of Indians called the Aragaritkas," of whom the "Tionondade" were a remnant of one nation (NYCD 4:908-909).

The Unami Delaware name for the Wyandot is *te·ləmátˑənu,* meaning 'person of the range of hills', a translation of the self-designation of the Khionontateronon; see the synonymy in "Khionontateronon," this volume. This name has occasionally been used as an English word: Delamattenos (Heckewelder 1876:80). The Mahican name Paumtonnauweew (Aupaumut

[†] There is no modern study of the phonology of the Wyandot language, and Wyandot words cited in italics in the Handbook are tentative phonemicizations using the standard Handbook phonetic symbols. The one special symbol is ⁿd, a voiced, prenasalized dental stop that is the regular reflex of Proto-Iroquoian *ⁿ.

1827:77) has the same meaning; this also appears as Paumittunnawseu, a place "near Detroit" in 1748 which appears to be the Wyandot settlement at Sandusky (NYHSC 53:12).

Attested names for the Wyandot in the Central Algonquian languages are based on the Proto-Algonquian tribal name *na·towe·wa, applied especially to Northern Iroquoians. In some languages this word also refers to a species of snake (see synonymy in "Northern Iroquoian Culture Patterns," this vol.). Ojibwa dialects have na·towe· 'Wyandot; Six-Nations Iroquois'; from this comes Nahdooways or Nahdoways, used as an English word (P. Jones 1861:32, 111). The two meanings are differentiated in Algonquin as ni·ʔina-na·towe· 'our Iroquoian; Huron-Wyandot' and mači-na·towe· 'hostile Iroquoian; Iroquois' (phonemicized from Cuoq 1886:263–264). Shawnee na·towe·θaki 'Wyandots' and na·towe·ki 'Senecas' were kept distinct in 1824, spelled Nautoawaathakēē and Nautoawāākee (Trowbridge 1939:66), and in 1879 (Gatschet 1878–1893:77), but were both used in both meanings in the 1930s (Voegelin 1938–1940, 9:377). Fox na·towe·wa (from Gatschet 1882–1889:5), Potawatomi natwe (from Gatschet 1878–1893:30), and Illinois nad8eia (Le Boullenger in Belting 1958:288) refer only to the Wyandot; the situation was probably the same in Miami but early twentieth-century speakers appear to have reversed the names for the Wyandot and the Seneca (Voegelin 1938–1940, 3:90, 9:377).

Two seventeenth-century Mohawk names for the Huron or Huron-Wyandot are found in Bruyas (1863:22, 55, 69): Hati8endogerha (and miscopied Hah8endagerha) and garennajenhaga. The former of these was used "because they used to live on an island" (Mohawk kawehnô·ke 'on the island'; G. Michelson 1973:118).

Sources

Unfortunately, no good history of the Wyandots exists. Of the various brief summaries that have been published, Merwin (1906) is the most comprehensive. Shea (1861) summarizes the Jesuit period of Wyandot history. Clarke (1870) is also of some interest as Clarke was a Wyandot.

Some discussion of the Wyandot language is to be found in Barbeau (1915a) and some texts in Wyandot in Barbeau (1960). A comparison of nineteenth-century Wyandot culture to Huron culture before 1650 and to nineteenth- and twentieth-century Iroquois culture is to be found in the footnotes of Tooker (1964).

Neutral and Wenro

MARIAN E. WHITE

Territory

Neutral ('nōotrəl) was the name the French applied to a number of allied groups of Northern Iroquoian speakers* who lived between the Huron and Five Nations Iroquois and who remained neutral in the hostilities between them. Their villages were mostly in Ontario between the Grand and Niagara rivers until their dispersal in 1652 (fig. 1).

Wenro ('wen₁rō) was a tribe located on the eastern margin of the Neutral adjacent to the Seneca and at one time associated with the Neutral. They were the first of the Western New York-Ontario groups to abandon their aboriginal territory, which was in the northern portion of the Niagara Frontier in the path of both their expanding and more powerful neighbors. In 1638 the survivors moved to Huronia.

The Neutral country was shown first on Samuel de Champlain's map of 1632 (Champlain 1922-1936, 3:pl.

* This identification as Northern Iroquoian depends on early French statements, for no direct information that could be used for comparisons has survived on the speech of either the Neutral or the Wenro. Proper names are best written in one of the spellings used by contemporary French writers.

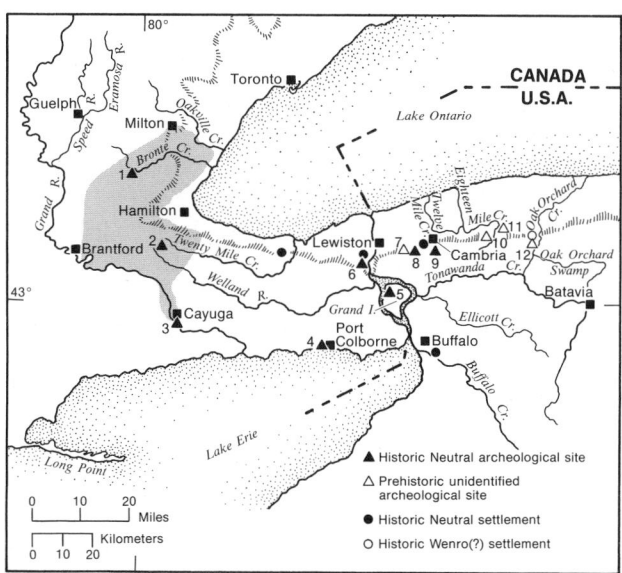

Fig. 1. Tribal territory and archeological sites. 1, Hamilton (after Noble 1974); 2, Donovan; 3, Cayuga; 4, Port Colborne; 5, Van Son; 6, Saint Davids; 7, Kienuka; 8, Kienuka; 9, Cambria; 10, Orangeport; 11, Fort Peace; 12, Shelby.

10) in a position difficult to locate because Lake Erie is missing, but the placement is still consistent with Champlain's 1615 statement that they were south of Huronia and west of Lake Ontario. The first precise location came from the visit of Fathers Jean de Brébeuf and Pierre Joseph Marie Chaumonot to the Neutral in 1640. They reported villages extending south and southeast from the entrance to Neutral country, which lay 40 leagues directly south from Sainte Marie. "On this [the west] side of that River [Niagara] and not beyond it . . . are the greater part of the villages of the Neutral Nation. There are three or four beyond, ranging from East to West . . ." (JR 21:191). The fathers visited 18 villages and located these on a map of Neutral country that has not survived.

Only one contemporary map, "Novæ Franciæ Accurata Delineatio 1657" believed to be the work of Father François-Joseph Bressani (Heidenreich 1966) shows the Neutral in a position corresponding to the textual descriptions. The legend "Gens neutra" stretches between the Grand and Niagara rivers.

The 1650 map by Nicolas Sanson shows the Neutral stretching across the Ontario Peninsula to the Saint Clair River (see "Erie," fig. 2, this vol.). This location provided the information for later maps, but there is no evidence, either textual or archeological, for extending the Neutral that far west. The distribution of early historic village sites agrees well with the location on the Bressani map.

A later map of uncertain date and source shows the location of four groups in Neutral territory north of Lake Erie (fig. 2). The map is probably the work of Abbé Claude Bernou who might have used information supplied by René-Robert Cavelier de La Salle around 1680 (Delanglez 1938:115). It shows the Attiragenrega, Niagarega, Antouaronons, and Kakouagoga confined to the eastern portion from just above Long Point east. The Attiragenrega are shown just south of the western tip of Lake Ontario with two village markers. On the west side of the Niagara River halfway between the two lakes is a single village marker labeled "Niagagarega." West of the Grand River just inland from Long Point is Antouaronons with two village markers. Kakouagoga is shown as a village just inland near Buffalo, New York. A fifth group identified with the Neutral is the Ahondihronon, shown on François Du Creux's map of 1660, "Tabula Novæ Franciæ," east of the Niagara River near the south shore of Lake Ontario where there are two village

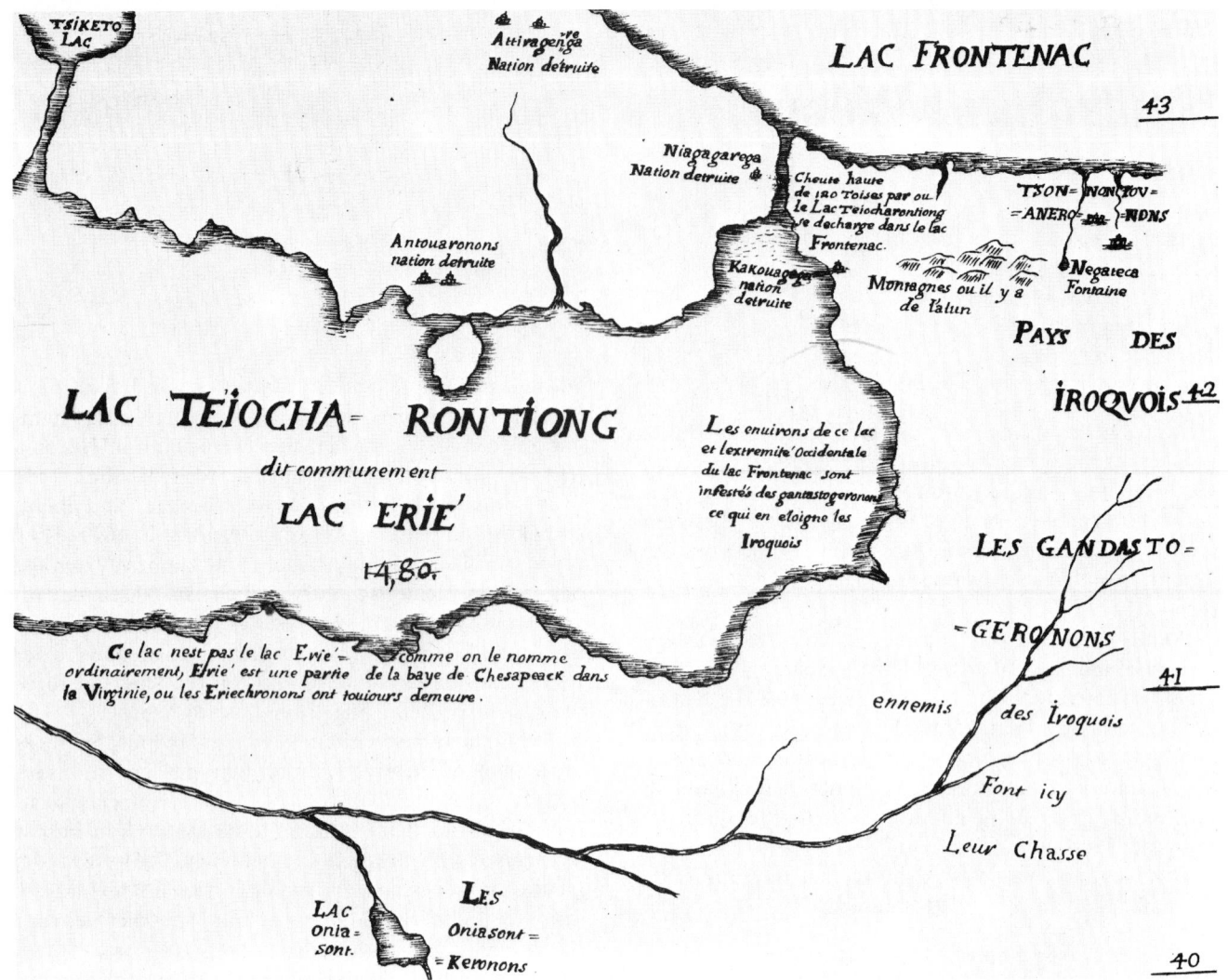

Les enuirons de ce lac et l'extremite Occidentale du lac Frontenac sont infestés des gantastogeronon ce qui en eloigne les Iroquois

Ce lac nest pas le lac Erie comme on le nomme ordinairement, Erie est une partie de la baye de Chesapeack dans la Virginie, ou les Eriechronons ont touiours demeure.

Fig. 2. Northeastern segment of a manuscript map of about 1680, attributed to Claude Bernou, showing the Antouaronons, Attiragenrega, Niagagarega, and Kakouagoga, all labeled 'destroyed'. At least the first 3 of these appear to be Neutral tribes.

markers. This map location differs from a textual note that has been interpreted as placing them adjacent to the Huron (White 1972:69).

The documentary and cartographical information is too vague to allow the definite identification of any archeological site as a known Neutral village. The distribution of early historic sites corresponds well to the locations of the names on the Bernou and Du Creux maps. The largest concentration is around Hamilton where the sites form a broad U-shaped distribution parallel to the west end of Lake Ontario with the center near Brantford. Here are both prehistoric and early historic sites in the same position as the Attiragenrega.

Archeological work around Hamilton by McMaster University shows several clusters of historic sites attributable to at least three tribes. If Attiragenrega was the name of a tribe, it may not have applied to this whole group of sites, which seems much more numerous than the other Neutral tribes. For example, William C. Noble (personal communication 1973) has located 43 historic Neutral villages within a 20-mile radius of Hamilton. One of these, the Donovan site, is a good candidate for Father Joseph Daillon's village of Ounonisaton. Since Father Daillon used no name other than Neutral, it remains unclear whether Attiragenrega referred to a tribe or to the main body of Neutral villages around Hamilton, which seems to have been more than a single tribe.

The Niagageraga may well have occupied the Van Son site, which has been identified as a Niagara Neutral cemetery of 1635–1645 (White 1968), on the north end of Grand Island in the Niagara River. The closest reported early historic site north of Long Point where the two Antouaronon villages are shown is near Cayuga, Ontario.

East of the Niagara River the name Kakouagoga is located in such a position that the Fenton-Barnard Streets site in Buffalo is a likely but undemonstrable candidate. The Kienuka (historic component) and Gould sites on the edge of the Niagara Escarpment east of

Lewiston at Kienuka and Cambria are in the proper location for the Ahondihronons if a location east of the Niagara is accepted.

The Wenro are not shown on any map. They were said to be one day's journey from the Iroquois. When they left their home territory to join the Huron, they were said to have made a journey of over 80 leagues or about 275 miles. By this estimate of trail distance the Wenro could be 30 miles or more to the east of the Niagara River. Such a location could be in the vicinity of Oak Orchard Swamp to which the translation 'people of the place of the floating scum' might apply (Hewitt 1910a:932). Hewitt thought this referred to the Oil Spring near Cuba but that region has no early historic sites reported and the terrain is not that usually associated with Iroquois sites. Nor would such a location place the Wenro between the Seneca and Neutral as would the vicinity of Oak Orchard Swamp. The only candidate for a Wenro village near the swamp is the Shelby site, which dates earlier than 1638 on the basis of only two reported finds of trade goods. A descendant settlement, if one could be located nearby, would strengthen the suggested identification.

In summary, the term Neutral might apply in its particular usage to any or all of the groups (tribes) known as Attiragenrega, Ahondihronon, Antouaronon, Onguiaronon (Niagara Neutral), Kakouagoga, and Wenro, located in the eastern Niagara Peninsula of Ontario and in the northern Niagara Frontier of western New York.

History

There are two recorded visits of French missionaries to the Neutral villages, but no permanent mission was ever established contrary to their original hopes. Therefore, the history of the Neutral was recorded mainly from accounts told to the French in Huronia. Étienne Brûlé and other French traders who were familiar with the Neutral left no account of their adventures. Brûlé was influential in Father Daillon's decision to visit the Neutral in October 1626 and to try to conclude a trading alliance with them. Daillon (Sagard-Théodat 1866, 3:809) spent three months among the Neutral and visited six villages, all close to one another and probably part of the Attiragenrega. The village of Ounonisaton was his abode and he was under the personal protection of Tsohahissen whom Daillon identified as the principal leader of the Neutral and who still held a prominent position in 1640. It was here that at least 10 men from Ouaroronon, probably Wenro, came to trade and invited Daillon to their village, one day's journey from the Iroquois. Then they became violent and took with them the father's writing desk, blanket, breviary, compass, and bag of trade goods; everything except the trade goods they later returned. Daillon's efforts to conclude a trading alliance were defeated by Huron opposition.

There is little more information until late 1638 when the Wenro began to arrive in Huronia. The 600 refugees, mostly women and children, suggest one or two villages before their flight. The circumstances of their joining the Huron impressed Father Jérôme Lalemant who had just arrived at the Huron settlement of Ossossane (JR 17:29). This is one of the few as well as the earliest recorded cases of a migration resulting in movement into another group's territory because of pressure to leave their own territory. It also gives some clues to the Neutral confederacy and interconfederacy relationships in the Niagara Frontier. The Neutral were a confederacy or shifting alliance of tribes and represented a level of sociopolitical organization equivalent to the Huron and Five Nations confederacies.

The Wenro had been the farthest east of the "associate Nations" of the Neutral and closest to the Seneca. "As long as this Nation of Wenrôhronons was on good terms with the people of the Neutral Nation, it was sufficiently strong to withstand its Enemies, to continue its existence, and maintain itself against their raids and invasions; but the people of the Neutral Nation having, through I know not what dissatisfaction, withdrawn and severed their relations with them, these have remained a prey to their Enemies . . ." (JR 17:25, 27).

An epidemic was also causing depletion of their numbers. Some died along the way and others continued to die for two months after their arrival in Huronia.

The Wenro had planned for their migration and had sent ambassadors to Huronia asking to move there. In contrast to later defeats like those of the Huron, Neutral, and Erie, where the survivors were described as fleeing wildly after their villages were burned, the Wenro either anticipated a final defeat or else Iroquois war tactics were still closer to their aboriginal feuding ones and there was no final decisive victory. Their request to move into Huronia suggests that there was no place else to go without encroaching on some group's territory. Their breach with the Neutral may have prevented them from requesting to move into Neutral territory. They must have passed through Neutral lands and some individuals were living in one Neutral village in 1640. Nevertheless, the remnants of the tribe formally chose to ally themselves with the Huron and were no longer members of the Neutral confederacy.

The Wenros' removal from their territory left a void west of the Seneca, perhaps extending all the way to the Niagara River. Historic villages of other Neutral tribes were not on or adjacent to the Niagara River until about this same time according to archeological studies. It may well have been their establishment on or intended shift to the Niagara that caused the withdrawal of confederacy support from the Wenro. The establishment of Neutral villages on the Niagara probably was related to the Erie shift to the southwest in the early 1640s.

The Wenro move apparently allowed the rest of the Neutral confederacy to maintain its position of neutrality between the Huron and Five Nations (particularly the Seneca) for a while longer. At least when the second recorded visit to the Neutral took place in 1640, Fathers Brébeuf and Chaumonot mention no war preparations against the Seneca. Instead they were actively fighting their traditional enemies, the Assistaeronons, first noted by Champlain (1922-1936, 3:99) in 1615. By the early 1640s these attacks involved large numbers of warriors: 2,000 Neutral took 800 Assistaeronons cáptive (JR 21:195, 27:25-27). In the meantime, the Five Nations accelerated their hostilities against the Huron until Huron dispersal in 1649. Then many Huron settled among the Neutral.

In 1647 the Seneca interrupted their campaign against the Huron to attack the Ahondihronon Neutral. The Seneca were apparently passing through the territories of the Neutral tribes to reach Huronia and certain conditions of neutrality were adhered to. Some Seneca went inside an Ahondihronon village under these conditions and then attacked the inhabitants and destroyed the village. This act was said to be in revenge for the capture of a Seneca by a Petun in Neutral territory and the Neutral failure to intervene.

No retaliation by the Neutral was reported and after the defeat of the Huron, the French information was greatly decreased. A report without detail said that there was open war between the Neutral and Iroquois in 1649. In 1650 they received help from the Susquehannock, and the Mohawk were helping the Seneca.

A major attack in the fall of that year by 1,500 Iroquois destroyed the Neutral village Teoto'ndiaton, but a loss of 200 Iroquois was incurred. In spring 1651 a second village was taken, and Neutral will to stand their ground was destroyed. The inhabitants of the villages farther west are reported to have taken flight also (JR 36: 117-119). Still this last may have been overstated since sometime before March 1652, it was reported that the Neutral and Susquehannock had defeated the Seneca so close to home that the Seneca women had taken refuge with the Cayuga.

Remnants of the Neutral were shown south of Lake Erie on the Sanson map of 1656. Some spent the winter of 1652 in Michigan with other defeated groups. Large numbers were captives among the Seneca (G.K. Wright 1963:57). No remnants are identified at a later date.

Culture

The Neutral were said to be similar to the Hurons in most respects and so the French commented on differences at the expense of general description. The following comes mainly from the descriptions of the visits by Daillon in 1626 and Brébeuf and Chaumonot in 1640. Brébeuf himself reported "almost 40" villages (JR 20:103-105). His use of the term Neutral included the allied tribes since he mentions Onguiaahra or the Niagara Neutral,

but not the Wenro who were destroyed. This number differs from Daillon's estimate of 28 plus several little hamlets. Iroquois villages were known to fission and consolidate so that a change in village total would not necessarily mean an increase in population. In fact Neutral population was said to have been reduced through wars, famine, and epidemic. Brébeuf and Chaumonot estimated 3,000 people and 500 fires in the 10 villages where they spent some time. This is the basis for the total estimate of 12,000 for the 1640 reduced population, of which 4,000 were warriors. These estimates suggest that most of these villages contained several hundred people, unlike the larger villages of the Huron and Seneca. The Hamilton site, estimated to be a terminal Neutral site, covered about eight acres (Noble 1972).

Their villages were palisaded and contained longhouses (Noble 1970). There were extensive fields of corn, beans, and squash outside. Their exceptional skill in hunting and the abundance of game impressed the French as a contrast to Huronia. They also grew very good tobacco, which they traded. Excavations on Neutral sites reveal abundant European trade goods. The Wenro in particular were said to have traded with the Europeans to the east and south directly while French and Huron traders were active in Ontario.

Other differences noted were the extensive use of body paint and tattooing and a lack of embarassment about nudity. Their ceremonies were more exaggerated than those in Huronia, which frightened the Jesuit fathers because they thought the participants were "mad." Witchcraft and the importance of dreams were noted. The Wenro were said to be especially skillful at withdrawing an arrow and healing the wound. There were also differences in their treatment of the dead. The Neutral were reluctant to move the bodies of the dead from their longhouses and kept the bones around in the houses or on nearby scaffolds. At intervals, the bones were gathered together for group reburial in an ossuary. Differences between Huron and Neutral ossuaries indicate that the Neutral ceremony at the time of reburial was not identical to the Huron Feast of the Dead.

Synonymy

A variety of names and variant forms have been applied to the Neutral and to the Wenro. These can best be understood through Tooker's statement (1970:90) that the French had no term other than "nation" to apply to several levels of sociopolitical organization that are now distinguished as confederacy, tribe, and clan. Neutral, or in French *la Nation neutre,* was first used by Champlain (1922-1936, 3:99) in 1615. Later, as the French themselves recognized, different French writers used the name Neutral to apply to different groups at different times. The groups included in the designation that referred to a confederacy varied also with new alliances or defeats.

The Wenro were first mentioned under this name in Paul LeJeune's tribal list of 1635 (JR 8:116) as Ahouen-rochrhonons. After their defeat and arrival in Huronia in 1638, they were referred to as follows: 8eanohronons (8 = ou; JR 16:252), 8enroronons (JR 17:212), Oneronon (JR 18:234), A8enrehronon (JR 21:230), Oenronronnons (JR 39:138). Ouaroronon (Sagard-Théodat 1866, 3:804), the last Neutral village and one day's journey from the Iroquois, may be still another variant. The name Wenro, according to the Tuscarora Hewitt (1910a:932), comes from the Huron word awĕñ′rǎ′ meaning 'scum, moss, or lather', plus the verb stem -o′ 'to float, to be immersed or contained in liquid or in the earth'—thus *awę̆·ro?* (Floyd G. Lounsbury, personal communication 1975). The Wenro were 'the people of the place of floating scum'.

The Huron name for the Neutral first appears in 1632 as Attiuoindaron, French plural Attiuoïndarons (Sagard-Théodat 1939:169, 151), and Attihouandaron (Sagard-Théodat 1632, s.v. Nations). However, more correct are the spellings with added -k: Atiouandaronks, 1635 (-s is the French plural; JR 8:116); and Attiouendaronk and Attiouendarankhronon, 1640 (-hronon is 'people'; JR 18:234). These forms indicate that the name is probably to be interpreted as *atiwę́ⁿdahrǫk* 'they (who) understand the language' (Floyd G. Lounsbury, personal communication 1975). Other spellings are Atti8andarons and the equivalent Attiouandarons (JR 17:164, 20:50). After 1655 this name was replaced by Attiragenrega (fig. 2), which is said to be what the Iroquois called them (Hewitt 1910i:60); a variant is Atiraguenrek (JR 42:146).

Two Neutral groups or villages are first named in 1640 (JR 18:232): Aondironon (later variants: Ahondihron-nons and the Latinized Ondieronii) and Onguiarahronon (misprinted Ongmarahronon), assumed to be the same as Niagagarega on the Bernou map (fig. 2). Antouaronons appears in Neutral country on the Bernou map and on Jean-Baptiste Louis Franquelin's map of 1684 south of Lake Erie, where they are indicated as destroyed (White 1972). This name is not found in the written accounts but probably refers to a Neutral tribe. Kakouagoga (Rakoua-gega) or Kahkwas also appears only on the seventeenth-century maps and these seem to be the source for a controversy in the literature concerning the identity of the Kahkwas as Neutral or Eries. The first appearance of the name is on the Bernou map at the eastern end of Lake Erie where it is shown as *nation detruite*. Vincenzo Maria Coronelli's globe of 1688 shows it without the notation. The Franquelin 1684 map shows it as Rakouagega. The word Kakouagoga is probably Iroquois and perhaps Seneca rather than Huron, for the Seneca use a similar word to refer to the people who formerly lived west of them (Fenton 1940:194): *kahkwa?ké·onǫ?* 'people at the *ká·hkwa?* place' (Wallace L. Chafe, personal communication 1976).

Sources

Most of the contemporary information on the Neutral is found in the *Jesuit Relations* (JR 1896-1901). Other scattered references are in Champlain (1922-1936), Du Creux (1951-1952), Radisson (1967), and Sagard-Théodat (1866, 1939). For a list of maps on which the Neutral appear, see G.K. Wright (1963:83-86).

The Neutral have been a favorite subject of historical research (W.R. Harris 1896; A.E. Jones 1909; Ridley 1961; White 1972; G.K. Wright 1963). Their archeology has been under intensive investigation (Fox 1972; I.T. Kenyon 1972; Noble 1970, 1972).

Erie

MARIAN E. WHITE

Erie ('ēr₁ē) was the name for several tribes culturally and linguistically related to the Huron, Neutral, Five Nations, and other northern Iroquoian peoples; however, their identification as a Northern Iroquoian-speaking group is based solely on seventeenth-century French statements since no Erie words are recorded. They lived south of Lake Erie until their dispersal in the mid-seventeenth century. Because of their early disappearance as a group and lack of recorded contact with Europeans, knowledge of them is fragmentary.

The Erie were known to have sedentary villages and were regarded by the Huron as being similar to them. Since no European visit to an Erie village was ever recorded, documentary information about their culture is limited to obscure comments noted by the French, probably from other Iroquoian sources. It was said that the Erie lacked guns, although a later statement attributes their loss of the decisive battle of 1654 to depletion of their ammunition. No guns have been reported among archeological finds from any Erie site.

The Erie were said to have used poisoned arrows in fighting (JR 41:83). This characteristic would make them unique among Indian groups in the United States and Canada and therefore must be regarded with some caution. Their flint projectile points recovered archeologically are similar in form to those of other Iroquois groups in New York.

Other archeological evidence also bears out the Huron's observation of similarity to themselves and indicates that Erie material culture and settlement patterns are part of that widespread pattern referred to as Iroquoian.

It is possible to infer the sociopolitical structure of the Erie from that of the Huron and in more detail from that of the Five Nations Iroquois (Tooker 1970:90). The Huron and Five Nations were confederacies or alliances composed of more than a single tribe. Each tribe consisted of villages. For example, each tribe of the Five Nations consisted of one to three main villages in the first half of the seventeenth century, the number varying from time to time as villages divided or consolidated. It is likely that the Erie had similar units. Erie probably referred to a group of tribes, possibly an alliance. Each tribe may have had one or more villages.

The name of a village was often applied to a tribe by the French and presumably by the Huron as well. The village name might refer to a geographical feature and was not applied to the new community when a village moved to a new location. The names of two Erie villages have been recorded and each has been applied in a different form to what is probably a tribe.

Rigué was an Erie village in 1655–1656 (JR 42:186) and the Rigueronnons or Riquehronnons were frequently mentioned. The interval between the earliest and latest reference is about 25 years and does not exceed the length of time during which a village might remain at one location. Therefore, it is possible that Rigué and the Riquehronnons, a village and a tribe respectively, were for a time the only names known to the French in addition to the names Erie and Cat, which applied to the entire group of tribes.

Gentaienton was named as a village of the Erie in a reference of 1679 (JR 61:195) long after their dispersal. The names Gentaguetehronnons and Gentagega are used in constructions where they refer to a tribe. This tribe was not mentioned before 1655–1656 and may have been known only because of its destruction. This date would place it contemporary with Rigué. It seems likely that two tribes of the Erie have been identified, the Riquehronnons and the Gentaguehronons.

The designations Kakouagoga and Kahkwas have been identified as names of a village and group of Erie by some nineteenth-century writers (see JR 21:313 for a summary). These terms are discussed in the chapter on Neutral, with whom the terms may be associated.

Territory

The Erie have been located south of Lake Erie across an area varying in extent and in definition from Buffalo, New York, to Toledo, Ohio, and from the southern lakeshore to below Pittsburgh, Pennsylvania, in the Allegheny drainage. Hoffman (1964) extends their aboriginal territory into Virginia by equating Erie, on the basis of similar cartographic locations, with the Pocaughtawonauck, Massawomeck, Massomack, Black Minqua, Arrigahaga, Richahecrian, and Rickohockan. The assignment of such a vast area on the basis of weak and disputed evidence seems unacceptable and at odds with the size of territories identified with the Huron confederacy, the Iroquois league, or the Neutral.

The area generally associated with Erie settlement

includes two physiographic provinces, the Central Lowland and the Appalachian Plateau. In western New York, the Portage Escarpment is selected as the boundary between the two (fig. 1). North and west of the Portage Escarpment are the lake plains, widest at the east end of Lake Erie and running as a narrow strip paralleling the southern shoreline. Drainage here is from streams that take their start on the northern slopes of the Appalachians and flow generally north into Lake Ontario. The soils are lacustrine deposits with good productivity. Alluvial soils occur in wide stream valleys and have high productivity.

The Appalachian Plateau is composed of the glaciated and unglaciated sections of the Allegheny Plateau. The altitude rises to 2,200 feet in Warren County, Pennsylvania. The streams are part of the Allegheny drainage system, which is part of the Ohio and Mississippi rivers. The temperatures are significantly lower and the growing season shorter on the plateau. The soils have low productivity. Exceptions occur in some of the stream valleys, particularly the Conewango and Allegheny. Portions of the Allegheny had a wide floodplain north of Kinzua, Pennsylvania, and conditions on the bottomlands were more favorable for agriculture than on the adjacent uplands. Still the general terrain and soils are distinctly different from those where Iroquois villages were located in New York and Pennsylvania.

The general location of the Erie was first published in 1647-1648 (JR 33:63). A similarly worded reference that is said to have been written in 1644-1645 is, in transla-

tion: 'This lake called Erie was formerly inhabited in its southern shores . . . by certain people whom we call the Nation of the Cat, . . . this nation has been obliged to withdraw very far into the country to escape from their enemies who are toward the west' (Gendron 1868:8-9). They are shown south of lake Erie on Nicolas Sanson's map of 1650, and the legend *N. du Chat* stretches from the east end of Lake Erie south to an unnamed stream and lake that are probably Chautauqua Creek and Chautauqua Lake. The headwaters of the Allegheny are shown without any occupants indicated. The Neutral are not represented as destroyed, suggesting that the information preceded 1647, the time when they were being defeated.

A comparison of Sanson's 1650 map (fig. 2) with his 1656 map (fig. 3) makes it clear that the legend locating the Erie is farther south on the later map. There they are shown extending south from an unnamed creek that may be Rush or Eighteenmile to the stream connecting to Chautauqua Lake. Again the headwaters of the Allegheny are not included under the legend. The change in location plus the addition of several creeks along Lake Erie's southern shoreline suggest that the 1656 map was depicting new information, probably dating after 1647. The shift in location shown by a comparison of the two Sanson maps may well be the one described by Gendron in 1644-1645 as a withdrawal farther inland.

François Du Creux's map of 1660 (JR 1:map end of vol.) shows the Erie west of Chautauqua Creek. They are the only group shown under the southwestern portion of Lake Erie in the position occupied by the Ontarraronon (Kickapoo) on the Sanson 1656 map. It is probably the Du Creux map that influenced certain later cartographers to locate the Erie generally south of Lake Erie rather than in a more restricted position adjacent to the southeastern portion.

The earliest map that suggests a location for the Erie in the upper Ohio-Allegheny valley is the famous Jean-Baptiste Louis Franquelin map of 1685, "Carte de la Louisiane," of questionable reliability where Indian locations are concerned (Delanglez 1943).

In brief, most useful of the cartographic evidence showing the location of the Erie are the contemporary Sanson maps, mainly because Sanson was noted for his honesty and accuracy. No known contemporary map of the Erie, including the Du Creux map of 1660, shows any group in the Allegheny drainage. Later maps such as those of Franquelin and Lewis Evans (1755) may be portraying locations after the dispersal. Contemporary maps show the Erie along the lakeshore of the eastern end of Lake Erie, with the Ontarraronon or Kickapoo beneath the western portion.

Clearly no village of the Erie can be documented from either the literature or maps. The limited evidence allows a choice across a wide area of western New York and Pennsylvania and northern Ohio. Various archeologists have identified Late Woodland sites as Erie across this

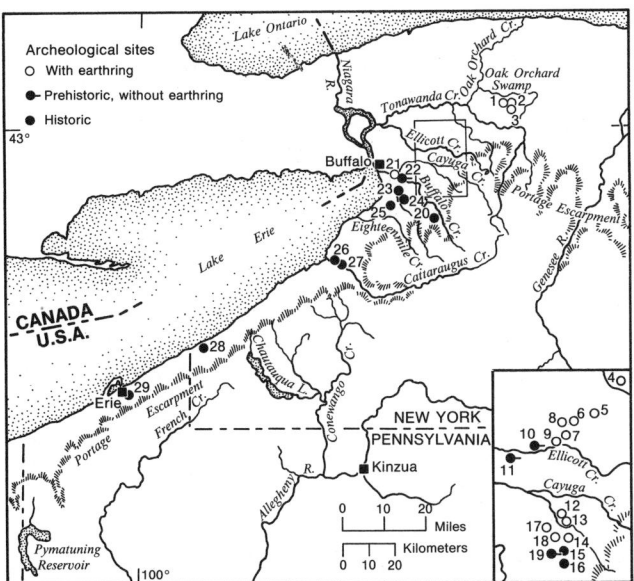

Fig. 1. Archeological sites. 1, Ganshaw; 2, MDA-8-4; 3, Oakfield Fort; 4, Akron; 5, Vanderventer; 6, Henry Long; 7, Clarence Hollow; 8, Clarence Hollow; 9, Clarence Hollow; 10, Nursery; 11, Harris Hill; 12, Lancaster; 13, Webster; 14, Turner, Holland Purchase; 15, Goodyear; 16, Simmons; 17, Big Buffalo; 18, Little Buffalo; 19, Newton-Hopper; 20, Bead Hill; 21, Buffam Street; 22, Eaton; 23, Ellis; 24, Green Lake; 25, Kleis; 26, High Banks; 27, Silverheels; 28, Ripley; 29, 28th Street Erie.

Fig. 2. Detail from Nicolas Sanson's map of 1650 showing location of the Erie as "N[ation] du Chat."

whole area and even into western Ontario; see Fitting (1964:167) and Potter (1968:63) for summaries and general conclusions. Most of these identifications are based on assumptions about the location of the Erie that cannot be supported. The best evidence that can be anticipated will be from sites producing artifacts clearly attributable to European trade of the first half of the seventeenth-century, located in this area, and linked to earlier prehistoric sites so that the aboriginal position can be determined.

A group of sites meeting these conditions has been found in the Niagara Frontier region of western New York. Here a series of sites has been identified as the communities of two contemporary villages. The movement of this pair of villages has been traced from about 1550 to 1635. Sites stretching northeast from the eastern village are probably antecedent and if so carry the sequence back to A.D. 1175-1200. The latest communities living at Bead Hill and Kleis had moved out of the area by 1640. The location of these seventeenth-century sites and the disruption in their regular pattern of village movement that signals their removal from the Niagara Frontier corresponds well with the contemporary ethno-

historical information. Therefore, these two communities may be identified as Erie and the prehistoric settlements as ancestral Erie. They probably represent a single tribe.

A large number of other prehistoric Late Woodland sites are located throughout the area. They tend to concentrate in linear distributions that represent unstudied village movements. In no case has European trade material of the first half of the seventeenth century been reported. The majority of sites have earth rings or earth banks, a precontact custom that elsewhere persists no later than 1530-1550. Moreover, estimates would place most of them prior to 1450 (Dragoo 1972; W. Johnson 1972; Schock 1972). None of these sites has been linked to an early historic site and questions of ethnic identity are unsettled. Nevertheless, there are no candidates for historic Erie sites in the Upper Allegheny and few elsewhere. West of the New York-Pennsylvania line on the lake plain are Late Woodland sites of the Whittlesey tradition. Brose (1972) has indicated that Whittlesey probably does not last into historic times and is probably not Erie.

In contrast to numerous prehistoric sites is the small number of early historic sites. None outside the Niagara

Fig. 3. Detail from Nicolas Sanson's map of 1656 showing location of the Erie as "Eriechronons ou N[ation] du Chat" (arrow).

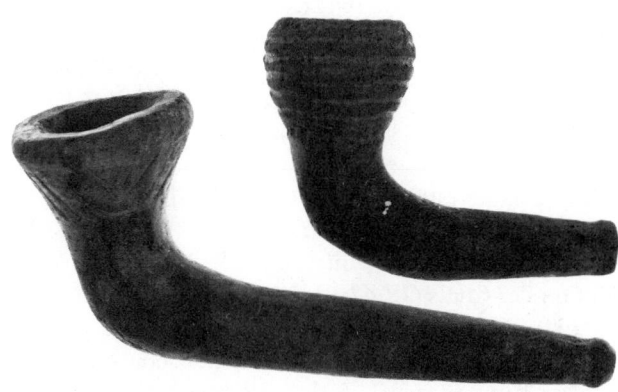

Fig. 4. Pottery pipes from the Green Lake site. top, Acorn ring bowl type, about 10.3 cm long; bottom, decorated rimless trumpet type, same scale.

Frontier has been connected firmly to prehistoric sites and so they may represent either an in situ village movement or an abrupt move from a greater distance. These sites, whose relationship to each other may be either contemporary or successive, are: High Banks-Silverheels, here regarded as the village and cemetery of a single site; Ripley; and 28th Street in Erie, Pennsylvania. The last site has been linked by local tradition to Rigué but is not the only historic site in the vicinity of Erie. There may be a village movement here, probably along the lake plain.

In conclusion, historic Erie communities have been noted as follows: two in the Niagara Frontier, one in the Cattaraugus Creek valley, one at Ripley, and one or more around Erie. The distances separating these sites are excessive for a village movement shift, which averages about two miles. It is closer to the distance separating different tribes in New York and may represent three tribes at least. This is still in contrast to the large populations that many have claimed for the Erie. It seems likely that the Erie villages were all located on the lake plains or the adjacent edge of the Allegheny Plateau. Their hunting territory may have extended into the nearby uplands.

History

The history of the Erie begins with their move inland prior to 1644–1645, by which time they were already enmeshed in complex events arising from European contact and the fur trade. The easternmost Erie communities at the Bead Hill and Kleis sites probably included in their territory to the north the Buffalo River and its rich beaver grounds and the east shore of the Niagara River, perhaps to Tonawanda Creek. The Oak Orchard Swamp, also beaver country, could have been in the territory of the eastern Erie, the Wenro, or divided between them. Ancestral Erie lands had been close to the swamp but their village movement had taken them to the southwest with the result that they were moving away from the swamp while the Wenro were moving toward it.

In 1638 the Wenro abandoned their territory, leaving a temporary void between the Neutral territory that extended to the Niagara River from the west and the Seneca territory that includ ' an unknown extent west of the Genesee. Nearly simultaneously some Neutral villages were located east of the Niagara for the first time. These Neutral villages were probably the enemy to the west that is referred to in the Erie shift from the Niagara Frontier to a position farther south and west. This shift may have removed the Erie from the hot spot between the Seneca and the Neutral. There is no further mention of conflict with the Erie until 1654.

After the dispersal of the Huron and Neutral, the French and Five Nations, tribe by tribe, began peace negotiations. The Jesuit accounts of these negotiations at Quebec and Montreal occasionally mention the Erie in the context of their relationships with the tribes of the Iroquois league. There is no notice of the Erie in the accounts of 1653 but some 1654 statements may refer to a time in 1653. In June 1654 the Onondaga told the French (JR 41:75) that they were planning to lead an army against the Erie that summer. In summarizing the events leading to this intention, the Onondaga indicated that recently the Erie had in separate incidents burned a Seneca village, decimated an Onondaga war party returning from the direction of Lake Huron, and captured the Onondaga chief Anenraes. Hostilities were occurring at this time because Huron individuals living with the Erie were inciting them to attack.

The Onondaga did not mention certain other events that probably also took place before June 1654. These events are described in 1656 by Father Claude Dablon from Onondaga without specific earlier dates but seem logically to have followed the burning of the Seneca village and to have preceded the capture of Anenraes, which drew the Onondaga into the struggle (JR 42:31, 57–59, 85–203).

The Erie sent 30 ambassadors to the Seneca to confirm peace. A Seneca was killed by an Erie—time, place, and circumstances unstated. In retaliation, the Seneca killed 25 of the ambassadors and five escaped. Then two Onondaga were captured and one was taken to the Erie village from which one of the ambassadors had come. This has usually been identified as Anenraes, although Father Dablon does not give the name of the captive. The prisoner was given to the sister of the dead ambassador with the expectation that he would be adopted. Instead she chose to have him killed in revenge. Thereafter feuding was intensified and the Onondaga became involved. In the June 1654 statement it was said that the Seneca, Cayuga, Onondaga, and Oneida were uniting to fight the Erie.

In late August or September 1654, a large Iroquois expedition entered the Erie territory; it was composed of 1,200 Onondaga who went to avenge the death of Anenraes. Seven hundred Mohawks were probably part of the same expedition (JR 45:209). The Onondaga burned villages and pursued the fleeing Erie. Finally the Erie took a stand in a fort built for the occasion out of wood. The Onondaga used canoes to storm and climb the palisade. They finally subdued the Erie inhabitants, who ran out of ammunition. The Mohawk may have participated in this attack or may have conquered still another village. The victorious Five Nations spent the next two months in Erie country burying their dead and getting back home with loot and captives before winter.

The Onondaga talked of hostilities and preparation for spring attacks on the Erie during the winter of 1654–1655. No reports of these having taken place reached the French, although the missing *Jesuit Relation* of 1655 might have contained information. The Onondaga were still concerned about the Erie in the fall of 1655 when they asked for French soldiers and weapons, and a war feast was held at Onondaga with Seneca, Cayuga, and Oneida present. The French interpreted this as directed against the Erie and anticipated further war activity in 1656. At least there is every indication that the Erie during the winter of 1655–1656 were still a formidable foe. The situation must have changed during 1656

leaving the Iroquois finally victorious. But there is not a single mention of the fighting as a contemporary occurrence.

Later information places the remnants of the Erie in widely separated places. Six hundred men, women, and children who remained as a group surrendered to the Iroquois near Virginia (JR 62:71) about 1680, which at that time was to the French an uncharted region down the Ohio across the mountains and below Pennsylvania. At least one Erie was at the mission at La Prairie, Quebec (JR 63:151). Large numbers were taken captive by the Five Nations and many of the later Seneca frontier settlements west of the Genesee had a large proportion of Erie (Parker 1926:48).

The Black Minqua may have been, at least in part, the descendants of the Erie after their defeat. After the mid-seventeenth century the Black Minqua probably embraced many remnant groups living in the Allegheny River valley.

Synonymy*

The Erie are commonly referred to in French sources by the full form of their Huron name, in various spellings: Rhiierrhonons, 1635 (JR 8:116), Eriehronon, 1640 (JR 18:234), Erieehronons, 1641 (JR 21:190), Ehriehronnons, 1654 (JR 41:74); an early misprint is Ekriehronoms (Radisson 1967:159). This name means ' "Erie" people', and Erie or Erié is sometimes used alone: 1641 (JR 21:190), 1642 (JR 21:230), 1648 (JR 33:62).

The Erie were also known to the French as *la nation de Chat,* a name published in 1632 from data obtained in 1623–1624 (Sagard-Théodat 1939:224, 382–383; also JR 42:96, 112), la Nation du Chat (JR 21:190; 42:74), la Nation des Chats (JR 42:52, 56), or simply les Chats (JR 43:260). Though often translated misleadingly as 'the Cat Nation', these names in fact mean 'Raccoon Nation', as is clear from Sagard-Théodat's description of the "wild cats" (*chats sauvages*), called in Huron *tiron*, that abounded in the country of this nation, from the handsome fur of which they made distinctive blankets with the tails left attached around the edge (cf. JR 41:80). Canadian French *chat sauvage* and Mohawk *atì`rǫ* both mean 'raccoon', and it is quite unlikely that the reference is to the mountain lion (Hewitt 1907d:430) or to the short-tailed lynx or bobcat. Schoolcraft's (1847) information from the Seneca Ely Parker, repeated by Morgan (1851), that the Cats were the Neutral has no support in the seventeenth-century historical sources.

The Iroquois form of the name is spelled Riquehronnons, 1660 (JR 45:206), and Rigueronnons, 1661 and

* The synonymy was prepared by Ives Goddard, incorporating some information supplied by Marian E. White.

1666 (JR 47:58, 50:116), meaning 'people of the village Rigué' (JR 42:186). Rhiierrhonons, without the k ("qu") or g, would be the expected Huron form of an Iroquois name Riquehronnons (ignoring the nondistinctive variations in the French spelling), but the meaning of Erié and its variants is a matter of controversy among specialists.

Sources

The basic ethnohistorical source for the Erie is the *Jesuit Relations* (JR 1896–1901). Scattered references were also made by Charlevoix (1866–1872), Du Creux (1951–1952), Gendron (1868), and Sagard-Théodat (1939). Archeological information is found in White (1961, 1971).

ERIE

The League of the Iroquois: Its History, Politics, and Ritual

ELISABETH TOOKER

Of all Indians in the Northeast, the Iroquois of the League—the famed confederacy of the Mohawk, Oneida, Onondaga, Cayuga, and Seneca tribes—most profoundly influenced history in the seventeenth and eighteenth centuries. Although the Iroquois were not especially numerous and were reduced in numbers by the epidemics of the early seventeenth century (see table 1), other individuals, both Indian and White, often found their fate rested on an Iroquois decision, and whole peoples also were to learn that their destinies were similarly determined. No nation was exempt. As both France and England knew, their contest for control of the North American continent ultimately would be decided by the choice the Iroquois made between them. Aware of this, the Iroquois occasionally courted the French but usually found their interests best served by an alliance with the British, and England prevailed.

At the opening of the seventeenth century, the Iroquois found themselves living in a peculiarly strategic region in respect to the fur trade that came to dominate all affairs in the Northeast. As they themselves said, their country "possessed many advantages superior to any other part of America" (Morgan 1901, 1:38). They held the Mohawk Valley, one of the two gateways through the "Endless Mountains" and so an important access route to the furs in the west. Their villages stretching westward across what is now upstate New York were protected by mountains to the south. In these mountains rose the Susquehanna, Delaware, and Ohio rivers, which afforded convenient routes to the beaver grounds of the south and west. To their north lay Lake Ontario, once often termed the Lake of the Iroquois—the source of the Saint Lawrence River and the other major route between the Atlantic and the west. Iroquois control of this lake usually forced their competitors traveling from the western Great Lakes to the French trading posts on the Saint Lawrence to take a more northerly route. But even these French posts were ill-protected by geography. Another gap in the mountains provided an easily traveled highway by way of Lake Champlain and the Richelieu River (once called the River of the Iroquois) to the Saint Lawrence and so a road to the French settlements there and the route from the west to the principal settlement at Quebec (fig. 1).

However, advantage unused avails nothing, and without the strength afforded by their League, it is doubtful

that the Iroquois would have played such a crucial role in the history of the Northeast. Other tribes, including other northern Iroquoian tribes, formed confederacies; therefore, that fact alone cannot account for Iroquois superiority. But combined with skillful use of geographic advantage, it earned the Iroquois a reputation for political genius. Gov. Clinton (1812:9) termed them the Romans of the West, and Morgan (1901, 1:3) stated that the Iroquois had achieved for themselves the most remarkable civil organization in the New World excepting only Mexico and Peru. The League organization still serves the Iroquois on some reservations as a basis of governance.

Establishment of the League

According to Iroquois tradition, there was once a time when the tribes of the region were at war with one another. To prevent a continuation of the conflict, the Great Peace, the Confederacy of the Iroquois was established. Thereafter the Iroquois styled themselves the People of the Longhouse; the Iroquois terms used and their precise translations are discussed in the synonymy in "Northern Iroquoian Culture Patterns," this volume. In this Longhouse, the Senecas, the most western of the Iroquois, were designated the Keepers of the Western Door and the Mohawks, the most eastern, the Keepers of the Eastern Door. The other three tribes were arranged in a line between them, the whole resembling the arrangement of families and their fires in the ordinary longhouse. Thus, by analogy, the Iroquois called it a confederacy of five fires as later they termed the United States "the 13 fires."

There has been much scholarly debate regarding when the League was established. It is certain that it was in existence by the 1630s when Europeans were beginning to acquire more than casual acquaintance with Iroquoians. The French living among the Hurons in the 1630s and 1640s were told of the five Iroquois nations, statements that indicate the League existed then (JR 8:115-117, 17:77, 21:21, 201, 33:65, 71), while Champlain (1922-1936, 6:250) seems to have implied its existence even earlier.

The traditions of the Iroquois themselves state that the League was founded before Whites first visited their country, but how many years before remains a question.

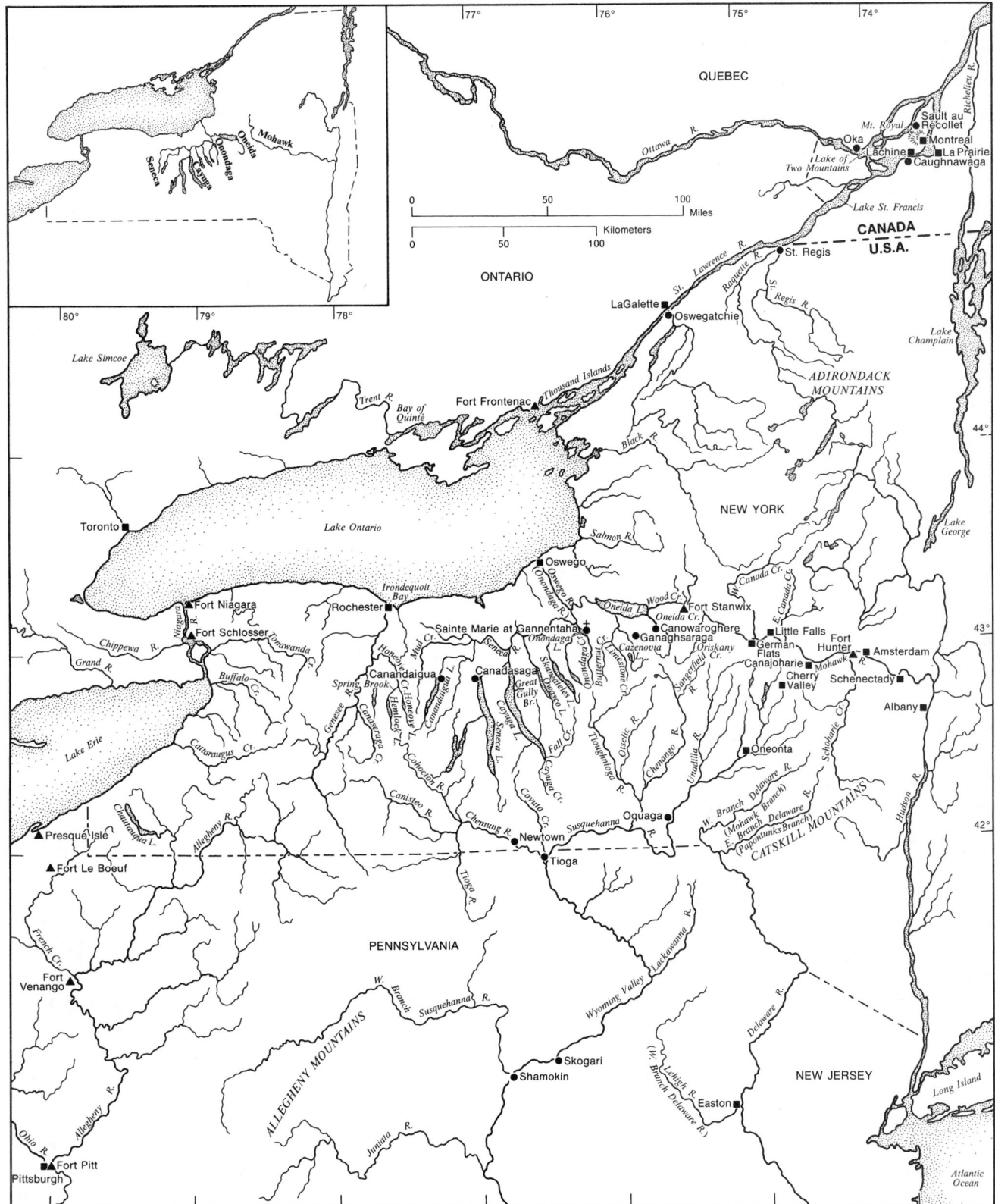

base map after Cappon 1976:4.

Fig. 1. Iroquois territory in the 17th and 18th centuries. Core areas for each tribe in the 17th century are indicated by the placement of the tribal names in inset. Where river names have changed, earlier names are in parentheses.

419

THE LEAGUE OF THE IROQUOIS: ITS HISTORY, POLITICS, AND RITUAL

The various Iroquois traditions give different estimates of the length of time the League had been in existence before Whites arrived. Nevertheless, although there is disagreement, virtually all suggested dates for the founding of the League fall in the period from A.D. 1400 or slightly before to 1600 or slightly before.

A relatively late date is indicated in some early written accounts. The earliest of these known was recorded by the Moravian minister Christopher Pyrlaeus (Heckewelder 1819:38) in the 1740s: "The alliance or confederacy of the Five Nations was established, as near as can be conjectured, one age (or the length of a man's life) before the white people (the Dutch) came into the country." Similar traditions were recorded a century later. Ephraim Webster, a noted trader and interpreter among the Onondaga, was told the League was founded about two generations before White people came to trade with the Indians (Clark 1849, 1:20) or about the length of a man's life before White man appeared (Schoolcraft 1847:120). Schoolcraft (1847:262) also learned of a Seneca tradition affirming the League was founded four years before Henry Hudson sailed up the river that bears his name. Similar traditions persist. Old people on the Six Nations Reserve say that the Confederacy was formed three lifetimes before the coming of the White people (William N. Fenton, personal communication 1974), statements comparable to that given by the chiefs of the Reserve suggesting the League was founded about 1390 (Parker 1916a:61).

A still later date is indicated in other traditions. Pyrlaeus suggested that the Tuscaroras joined the Confederacy probably 100 years after it had been founded (Heckewelder 1819:30)—a statement that can be interpreted as meaning that the Confederacy was established in the second decade of the seventeenth century or even later. Beauchamp (1905:148-149, 1921:29) reported that the New York Onondagas told him that the League was founded about 1600.

Other traditions indicate a greater antiquity (Morgan 1901, 1:7). However, the earliest date—some thousand years before Columbus—suggested by Cusick (Beauchamp 1892:16) has generally been rejected as much too early; Cusick's chronology in this as well as other matters is extravagant.

The question of when the League was founded has not been resolved in the published discussions of these traditions. Rather, different writers, offering conflicting interpretations of the same data, have suggested various dates. One of the first such dates was proposed by Schoolcraft (1847:118) on the basis of Pyrlaeus's statement. Schoolcraft took 1609 as the era of Dutch discovery and by estimating "the length of a man's life" by "the patriarchal and scriptural rule," arrived at a date of founding for the League no more remote than 1539.

Morgan (1901, 1:7) suggested a somewhat earlier date, a century or a century and one-half before the era of

Dutch discovery. Although he noted that the principal Iroquois traditions indicated a date far more remote, he felt there were some circumstances (which he did not specify) connected with the first intercourse of the Europeans with Indians that indicated the League had been founded at the date he suggested. Later, Morgan said that he based his opinion that the League had been established a century and one-half or two centuries before the Iroquois met Europeans on the traditions of the Iroquois themselves (Morgan 1877:128, 1881:26; Hale 1883a: 177).

Hale (1883a:177-180) concurred. He had been told by New York Onondaga chiefs that the League had been formed "about six generations before white people came to these parts," which suggested to Hale a date of 1459—assuming that Hudson's 1609 expedition was being referred to in the tradition and that a generation is equal to 25 years. He also received some confirmation for this date, one that Morgan (1871:151) had earlier suggested, from John Buck (Skanawati), wampum keeper at the Six Nations Reserve, who told Hale in 1882 he thought the League was founded about 400 years before. This date was somewhat earlier than that indicated in Pyrlaeus's account, and Hale attempted to reconcile it with his own conclusions by suggesting that Heckewelder had added the gloss "the Dutch" to Pyrlaeus's statement and that this gloss was incorrect. Hale proposed that the tradition recorded by Pyrlaeus referred not to Hudson's 1609 expedition, but to Jacques Cartier's exploration of the Saint Lawrence in 1535. Taking "the length of a man's life" as 75 years, he found confirmation that the League was established about 1460. In reaching his conclusions, Hale did not consider the traditions published by Schoolcraft and Clark indicating a later date.

Although not part of the long versions of the epic recounting the founding of the League, one Iroquois tradition suggests a mid-fifteenth-century date. One version of this tradition states that at the time the Senecas were considering whether or not to join the League, there was a total eclipse of the sun ("the sun went out and for a little while it was complete darkness") and that this eclipse took place when the grass was knee high or when the corn was getting ripe (P.A.W. Wallace 1948:399). Another version states that a total eclipse occurred when the Mohawks, angered at the Senecas for having taken some Mohawks captive, were about to attack a Seneca village. This eclipse, which took place when the corn was receiving its last tilling, was taken as a sign that the war should end and the Seneca should join the Confederacy (Canfield 1902:23-40, 197-198). Some examination of the dates on which total eclipses occurred in this region suggests that the one referred to in these accounts occurred June 28, 1451 (Julian calendar) (Canfield 1902:199; P.A.W. Wallace 1948:400).

The difficulties involved in reconciling the various Iroquois traditions regarding the date of the founding of the League led some students of the matter to turn to other kinds of data. One to do so was W.M. Beauchamp, who suggested on the basis of various data that the League had been founded between 1570 and 1600, perhaps in 1590, but most likely in 1600. He noted that Iroquois tradition states the Mohawks were living in what is now New York State when the League was formed; hence, it could not have been founded before the Mohawks moved into the valley that now bears their name. Beauchamp thought this must have occurred after 1535 since Cartier found them living on the Saint Lawrence and since archeology revealed no earlier Mohawk settlements in the Mohawk Valley (assertions that have been discredited; see "Saint Lawrence Iroquoians," this vol.). Allowing a suitable interval of time after Cartier left in 1542 for the war between the Algonquians and the Mohawks, which some interpretations of tradition state drove the Mohawks from the Saint Lawrence Valley, Beauchamp suggested the Mohawks had moved to the Mohawk Valley perhaps by 1550, although more probably later. Beauchamp thought it likely some years

would then have lapsed before the League was established. Thus, he noted the date of 1539 for the founding of the League indicated by the Pyrlaeus account was too early and offered some alternative interpretations of Pyrlaeus's statement. If instead of a "lifetime" of 70 years, a generation of 30 years is subtracted from 1609 (the date of both Hudson's and Samuel de Champlain's explorations), a date of 1579 is obtained, which to Beauchamp was a more probable date; further, if the tradition refers to the settlement of the Dutch rather than to Hudson's or Champlain's expedition, neither of whom reached the settlements of the Iroquois in 1609, an even later date is indicated. Moreover, the lack of wampum in prehistoric sites and the statement in the traditional accounts that wampum was not used before the League was founded seemed to suggest an approximate date of 1600 (Beauchamp 1886:363-366, 1892:138, 1891:295-296, 1905:147-154, 1921:33-35).

Hewitt (1894) stressed the unreliability of tradition and turned to other evidence in the documents. Noting that "no league or confederation of peoples was perhaps ever

Table 1. Iroquois Population Estimates by Fighting Men, 1660-1779

	Seneca	Cayuga	Onondaga	Oneida	Mohawk[g]	Sources
1660	1,000	300	300	100	500	JR 45:207
1665	1,200	300	300	140	300-400	JR 49:257-259, cf. JR 52:193, 56:51; Galinée 1903:25
1677	1,000	300	350	200	300	O'Callaghan 1849-1851, 1:12-14; NYCD 3:250-252; Clinton 1812:30; cf. JR 57:27
1679?	300[b]	300	300	about 150	at most 400	Hennepin 1903, 2:511
1685	1,200	200	300	150	200	O'Callaghan 1849-1851, 1:196; NYCD 9:282
1689[a]	1,300	300 320	500	180	270	O'Callaghan 1849-1851, 1:690; NYCD 4:337
1698	600[c]	200	250	70[e]	110[h]	O'Callaghan 1849-1851, 1:690; NYCD 4:337
1736	350[d]	120	200	100	80	O'Callaghan 1849-1851, 1:22-23; NYCD 9:1056; cf. NYCD 9:1058; Schoolcraft 1851-1857, 3:555
1763	1,050	200	150	250	160[i]	O'Callaghan 1849-1851, 1:26-27; NYCD 7:582
1768	1,000	200	260	300	160	Jefferson 1964:100; cf. O'Callaghan 1849-1851, 4:427; NYCD 8:458
1779	650	220	230	400[f]	100	Jefferson 1964:100; cf. Schoolcraft 1851-1857, 3:561

[a] These figures, given in a 1698 report on the losses suffered in King William's War, seem inflated.

[b] Probably an error, especially as Hennepin (1903, 2:511) says the Senecas "are the greatest and most considerable of all the Iroquois."

[c] Seems too low. In 1696 the Senecas were said to number not more than 1,000 (NYCD 4:181).

[d] An error. In 1720 the Senecas were reported to number over 1,000 men (NYCD 5:571).

[e] Too low. In 1709 the Indians reported 105 Oneida men would join an intended British expedition (Wraxall 1915:69), and the number of Oneida men who came to Albany in 1711 to march against Canada is given as 93 (Wraxall 1915:91).

[f] Including Tuscaroras.

[g] Not including those settled on the Saint Lawrence.

[h] Probably too low. In 1709 the Indians reported 150 Mohawk men would join an intended expedition (Wraxall 1915:69), and the number of Mohawk men who came to Albany in 1711 to march against Canada is given as 155 (Wraxall 1915:91). In 1713 there were reported to be about 580 Mohawk men, women, and children in the Mohawk villages (Lydekker 1938:40).

[i] In 1750 there were reported to be 204 Mohawks living at the Lower Castle at Fort Hunter and 214 at the Upper Castle, a decrease in population size from a few years previously and one that was attributed chiefly to the number of Mohawks who had gone over to the French and settled in their territory (Lydekker 1938:68). These figures are approximately those reported in 1773: 185 at the Lower Castle and 221 at the Upper Castle (NYCD 8:458).

formed without a sufficient motive in the nature of outside pressure" and that Cartier had found the Iroquoians of the Saint Lawrence at war with the Iroquois, a war that Champlain noted in 1622 had lasted for more than 50 years, Hewitt suggested the League was formed in response to this aggression from the north about 1560 or 1570. Rejecting Hale's interpretation of the Pyrlaeus account and assuming 60 years to be the length of "one age," Hewitt found confirmation in this account for a date of about 1559 for the founding of the League. Nevertheless, this conjecture, like others regarding the precise date of the founding of the League, is open to question.

Although the Iroquois accounts of the founding of the League differ, reflecting varying degrees of individual Indians' knowledge and the vagaries of translation, all these traditions tell of the efforts Deganawida (generally regarded as the founder) or Hiawatha or both made to establish the Confederacy.* According to them, Deganawida, Hiawatha, and on occasion their embassies went to the various tribes proclaiming the Great Peace, finally gaining acceptance for the plan in each and even from Thadodaho (Atotarho, Adario), the powerful Onondaga chief. Then a great council of all the chiefs of the five Iroquois tribes was called and the laws of the Confederacy, the customs that were to be maintained, were stated and agreed to.

When the Confederacy was established, it was decided that the Onondagas should become the "firekeepers" of the League, that is, that the great councils of the

* That the name Hiawatha is better known to Whites in connection with H.W. Longfellow's poem about Algonquians rather than as a founder of the League is a result of several errors of interpretation. In 1845 Clark (1849, 1:21–31) obtained an account of the founding of the League from the two leading New York Onondaga chiefs. As published, this account confounded Hiawatha *(hayéhwàtha?)* with a quite different personage, the culture hero Tharonhiawagon (Onondaga *thaęhyawá?ki*), perhaps (Hale 1883a:35–36) because of the similarity of the two names in the language of the Onondaga. Schoolcraft (1847:270–283) published this version, not acknowledging Clark as his source (Clark 1849, 1:30; Beauchamp 1921:11), later publishing a shorter version of it (Schoolcraft 1851–1857, 3:314–317) stating he had obtained it from one of the Onondaga chiefs acknowledged by Clark. Perusing these volumes in 1854 for material for his poem modeled on the Finnish epic *Kalevala*, Longfellow identified Hiawatha with the Algonquian mythic hero Nanabozho and shortly after beginning work on it decided to call his poem Hiawatha, not Nanabozho as he first had (Longfellow 1886, 2:248). Published in 1855, *The Song of Hiawatha* was an immediate success. Probably seeking to take advantage of the poem's popularity (Schoolcraft 1956:xxi, 300), Schoolcraft (1856) republished a number of legends that had appeared before (1839). The Nanabozho legend, now titled "Hiawatha; or, Nanabozho" and its similarities to the Iroquois legend noted (Schoolcraft 1856:51) became the first in this collection, giving credence to Longfellow's misidentification. As Hale (1883a:36) noted, "If a Chinese traveler, during the middle ages, inquiring into the history and religion of the western nations, had confounded King Alfred with King Arthur, and both with Odin, he would not have made a more preposterous confusion of names and characters" than this.

Confederacy would be held at Onondaga, the most centrally located of the five Iroquois tribes who had confirmed the Great Peace. Thus, it became the responsibility of the Onondagas to call such councils. And so it was that each year, the Five Nations of the Confederacy were drawn from their respective council fires to the great council fire at Onondaga to rehearse their ancient system and compose their differences.

Thadodaho, the principal chief of the Onondagas who initially had been so forcefully opposed to the establishment of the Iroquois League, became its leading chief; however, his position was that of "first among equals." Before any action could be taken, all the chiefs who constituted the council of the League had to agree, had to be of "one heart, one mind, one law." If the chiefs were unable to "roll their words into one bundle," that is, unable to reach unanimous agreement, the issue could only be set aside and the council fire "covered with ashes." This requirement of unanimity meant that any chief had a virtual veto on any proposal before the council.

Wampum

The Onondaga also became the "wampum keepers" of the League, that is, keepers of its archives, and one of their chiefs became "the Keeper of the Wampum." By Iroquoian custom, all important statements should be accompanied by a gift or gifts, the gift indicating both that the statement is one of serious moment and that it is a true one. In time, wampum came to be regarded as the most appropriate and customary gift and so, as Beauchamp (1901:347) noted, served as a letter of introduction and a certificate of authority. Consequently, treaties between the Iroquois and other Indian nations and between the Iroquois and European nations customarily were accompanied by an exchange of wampum, the wampum serving to acknowledge the sincerity of the parties agreeing to the treaty (figs. 2-3).

Although wampum came to be regarded as most valuable by the Iroquois, and hence the customary gift, its use has no great antiquity. It is found only in archeological Iroquois sites of the historic period, and then only rarely in those dating to the sixteenth century. It is more commonly found in the seventeenth- and eighteenth-century sites, that is, in the period of extensive fur trade; and the frequency of its occurrence in these sites reflects the increasing importance of the fur trade (Fenton 1971a:440). In part, this is the case because Europeans quickly learned the value wampum had to the Iroquois and other Indians and thus learned that the beaver skins they so greatly desired could be bought with wampum. As Weeden (1884:15) aptly stated it, Europeans found that "Wampum was the magnet which drew the beaver out of the interior forests." To produce

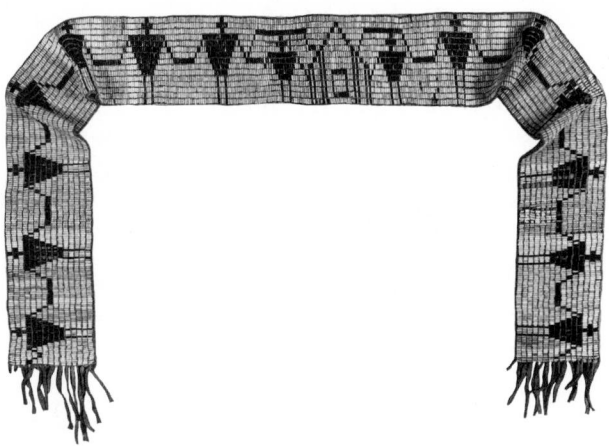

N.Y. State Mus., Albany: 37210.
Fig. 2. The Washington Covenant Belt, the longest Iroquois wampum belt extant in the U.S., containing some 10,000 purple and white beads. This testifies to friendship between the 13 colonies (represented by 13 of the figures, one of whom has a repair replacing his head) and the Six Nations (represented by 2 figures grasping a Longhouse). It was given to the Iroquois either at a conference with colonial representatives at Albany in 1775 or at the treaty between the Iroquois and the U.S. signed Jan. 9, 1789, at Fort Harmar. Length about 190 cm, width about 13 cm.

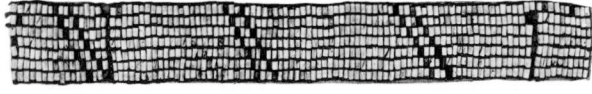

N.Y. State Mus., Albany: 37415.
Fig. 3. Wampum belt given by the Iroquois to the American negotiators in 1784 to document the Treaty of Fort Stanwix, which reestablished relations after the Revolution. Length about 39 cm.

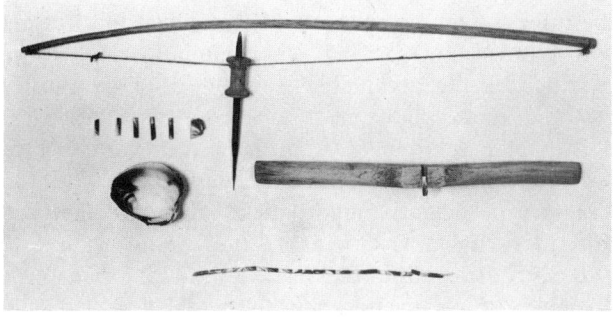

Mus. of the Amer. Ind., Heye Foundation, New York: top, 13/2890; lower right, 13/2893.
Fig. 4. Materials from the Campbell wampum factory at Pascack (now Park Ridge), N.J., in operation 1770-1899. Shell of *Mercenaria mercenaria* with blanks from purple area of such shells; hickory vice about 35.6 cm long used to hold blank for shaping against a grindstone; bow drill with bit made from a saw file, used to drill holes in blanks held in another vice similar to the one shown; string of finished wampum. For details see Orchard 1929:70-74.

wampum in sufficient quantity to satisfy the demand, the Europeans established wampum "factories" on Long Island and in New Jersey (fig. 4). White wampum could be made of a number of species of marine shells, but it was often made from the central column of the whelk *(Buccinum undatum)*. However, the only source of purple (sometimes called black) wampum was the hard-shell, or quahog clam *(Mercenaria mercenaria)*. Its value to Indians meant that wampum also came to have value to Whites; and in colonial times Whites used it as a form of currency much as they used Spanish, Portuguese, French, and Dutch coins in addition to English ones. It was not regarded as money by the Indians, except that being something valuable it could be used for economic exchange and for gifts.

As wampum confirmed that any statement it accompanied was deemed important by those who sent it, wampum was used not only in treaty agreements but also in connection with other statements. In the seventeenth and eighteenth centuries when wampum was plentiful, it was often woven into belts, and it was in this form that it was usually given to confirm treaties, its design of purple and white beads serving as a mnemonic device to recall the particular treaty it accompanied. Sometimes it was merely strung, and this usage persists. Wampum in the late twentieth century is scarce, and there is not a sufficient quantity in use to make belts. For example, a string of wampum attached to a notched stick is still used to call certain councils; the notches on the stick indicate the number of days before the meeting is to take place, and the wampum certifies that the meeting is important.

Wampum also was given to condole a death. By old Iroquois custom, if a man killed another, he forfeited his life, and the family of the murdered man could kill him or another of his family or his clan. If the man murdered belonged to another nation, war could ensue. However, gifts in a quantity deemed sufficient to atone for the murder could be given to prevent such retaliation. In cases of a man being murdered by another of the same tribe, it was the responsibility of the clan of the murderer to provide these gifts; but in cases of murder of a member of another tribe, the matter became one of more national importance.

One of the practical measures instituted by the founders of the League was to set the amount of these gifts, thus preventing war between the tribes when a man of one tribe killed another. The amount established was 10 strings of wampum for the life of a man and 20 strings for the life of a woman. Thus, if a man killed a woman, 30 strings were given—20 for the life of the murdered woman and 10 for the life of the murderer that had been forfeited by his act. Similarly, if a man murdered another man, 20 strings of wampum were so given (Hewitt 1917:323, 1920:541). (At least Iroquois tradition has it so; it seems likely that the League was founded before wampum was widely used. Nevertheless, it may be that the price for murder was established when the League was founded, and in later years wampum came to be regarded as the acceptable substitute and the earlier custom forgotten.)

Although wampum was and is used in a number of different contexts, to the Iroquois its association with the League is particularly important. In fact, it is sometimes said that Hiawatha originated the use of wampum, although other traditions differently account for its introduction; and in some traditions, Hiawatha is said to have used quills rather than wampum, perhaps indicating that after wampum became abundant, it replaced beads made of quills. The name Hiawatha is sometimes translated as 'seeker after wampum'. However, like many other names of League chiefs, the etymology is uncertain, and several different meanings have been suggested including 'he who combs', a reference to the tradition that Hiawatha combed snakes from the hair of Thadodaho (Hale 1883a:154; Beauchamp 1891:296; Fenton 1950:59).

Selection of Chiefs

As did other Indians, the Iroquois discussed and decided issues of importance in council. According to tradition, the organization of the League itself was established in a council composed of chiefs of the tribes, and this council of chiefs continued to be the deliberative body for matters of concern to the Confederacy. Successors to the founding chiefs of the League were chosen in accordance with Iroquois custom, the new chief assuming the name of his predecessor and hence his place on the council of the League. Since no successor was ever appointed to Deganawida's position, his name does not appear on the list of the 50 chiefs of the League, the so-called Roll Call of Chiefs. The second name on this list is Hiawatha, but it remains a position unfilled (table 2).

Among the Iroquois, the perpetuation of personal names was and is a responsibility and right of the clans. By Iroquois custom, each clan owns a number of personal names. When a child is born, he or she is given a name not in use. As Iroquois clans are matrilineal, the child receives a name belonging to his mother's clan. This name is usually later changed for another, "adult" name, also a personal name belonging to the clan. Commonly in the past, when an important man died, another of his clan would assume his name, announcing that change at a feast. Thus, certain personal names came to be associated with certain positions (in effect, roles) in the society, and as the right to use a particular name belonged to a clan, the rights and obligations associated with that name belonged to the clan. In earlier centuries, some of these names may well have had special associations with activities of trade and war. Some (the Faithkeeper names) still designate individuals with special religious obliga-

424   tions.

Table 2. Confederacy Chiefs' Titles in Iroquois Languages

Mohawk

1. Dekarihokenh	M *tekarihó·kẹ*, Oi *tekalihóké*, Oo *tekaíhò·kẹ*, C *tekaihó·kẹh*
2. Ayonhwathah (Hiawatha)	M *ayọhwátha?*, Oi *ayọhwátha?*, Oo *hayẹhwàtha?*, C *hayẹhwáhtha?*, S *hayǫ́·wẹ·tha?*
3. Shadekariwadeh	M *sha?tekarî·wate?*, Oi *tsha?tekalî·wate?*, Oo *tsha?tekaíhwà·te?*, C *sha?tekáihwate?*
4. Sharenhowaneh	M *sharẹhó·wane*, Oi *shalẹhowáné*, C *sho?ẹhó·wa·?*
5. Deyoenhegwenh	M *teyọnhéhkwẹ*, Oo *teyǫ́nhèhkwi*, C *tyǫnhéhkwẹh*
6. Orenregowah	M *orẹhre?kó·wa*, Oo *awẹhe?kó·na*, C *awẹhe?kó·wah*
7. Dehennakarineh	M *tehana?karí·ne?* or *tehẹna?karí·ne?*, C *tEẹn?aká·ine?*
8. Rastawenseronthah	M *rastawẹhserǫ́·tha?* or *hastawẹ?serǫ́htha?*, C *hastawẹ?trǫ́·tha?*
9. Shoskoarowaneh 'great branch'	M *shoskoharó·wane*, Oo *shoskoháewanẹ*, C *shoskohá·ina·?*

Oneida

10. Odatshedeh	M *rotatshéhte?*, Oi *otatshéhta?* or *o?tatshéhte?*, C *hotátshehte?*
11. Kanongweniyah 'standing corncobs'	M *kanọhkwẹ?yó·tọ?*, Oi *kanọhkwẹ?nyo·tǫ̂*, Oo *kanọhkwé?yò·tọ?*, C *kanọhkw?ẹyó·tọ?*
12. Dayohagwendeh	M *teyohakwę́·te*, Oi *teyonhakwéhte?* or *thoha?kwẹ·tê·*, Oo *tyohá?kwẹ·te?*, C *teyoha?kwę́·te?*
13. Shononses 'his house is long'	M *shonǫ́hses*, Oi *shonǫ́hsese?* or *shonǫ́hses*, Oo *shonǫ́hses*, C *shonǫ́hse·s*
14. Dehonareken	Oi *thonaokẹ́ha?*, Oo *twẹ·naikhǫ́?*, C *hatwẹná·ikẹ?*
15. Adyadonneatha	Oi *atya?tonẹ́tha?*, Oo *ha(t)yá?tonèntha?* (?), C *hatya?tonẹ́htha?*
16. Adahondeayenh	Oi *tehatahọhtẹ·yệ·*, Oo *thahǫ́htè·nyọk*, C *tewatAọhtẹ́·yọh*
17. Ronyadashayouh	M *rọya?tashá·yọ*, Oi *anyẹtáshat*, C *honya?tashá·yẹh*
18. Ronwatshadonhonh	M *rọwatshatǫ́họ*, Oi *watshatẹ́ha?*, C *họwatshatẹ́họh*

Onondaga

19. Adodarhonh (Thadodaho)	M *atotárho*, Oi *atotálho?*, Oo *thatótà·ho?*, C *thatotá·ho?*

Table 2. Confederacy Chiefs' Titles in Iroquois Languages *(Continued)*

Onondaga *(Continued)*

20. Awennisera — M *oneʔseráhę* (?), Oo *kaneʔsǽ·hę·ʔ* or *oneʔsǽ·hę·ʔ*, C *onéʔtrAę*

21. Dehatkadons 'he looks both ways' — M *tehatkáhtǫs*, Oo *thatkáhtǫs*, C *tEátkAtǫhs*

22. Yadajiwakenh 'his body or throat is bitter' — Oo *hoyáʔtatsì·wak* or *honyáʔtatsì·wak*, C *nyàʔtatsí·wak*

23. Awekenyat — M *awakę̂·yat* or *aweʔkę̂·yat*, Oo *(h)awéʔkę̀hyat*, C *awéʔkEya·t*

24. Dehayatgwareh — M *tehayaʔtkwá·ri*, Oo *thayatkwá·eʔ* or *tehayaʔtkwá·eʔ*, C *tEayʔatkwái*

25. Ononwireh(tonh) — M *honǫwiréhtǫ* or *ronǫwiréhtha*, Oo *honǫwíyèhti*, C *honǫwiyéhtǫh*

26. Oewenniseronni — Oo *kawęnęʔsę́·tǫk* or *kowanęʔsę́·tǫ*, C *kowanʔęsę́·tǫk*

27. Arirhonh — M *ahrírhǫ*, Oo *hahíhǫk* or *hahí·hǫʔ*, C *hahíhǫ*

28. Oewayonhnyeanih — Oo *hǫwayǫ́·nyę·ni* or *hoyǫnyę́·ni*, C *hoyǫnyá·nih*

29. (Tho)Sadegwaseh — M *shotekwá·shę*, Oo *shotekwá·skǫ* or *shotekwá·tsi*, C *shotekwá·shę*

30. Sakokeaeh — M *shakó·kę*, Oo *shakókęhe·*, C *shakókEe*

31. Seawi — Oo *hoʔsæ·há·hwi*, C *hoʔtrahá·hǫh*

32. Skanaawadi 'across the swamp' — M *skaná·wati*, Oi *skana·wáti*, Oo *skanáwà·ti*, C *skanáwati*

Cayuga

33. Dekaeayough — M *hakaʔę́·yǫ*, Oo *hakáʔę̀·yǫk*, C *hakaʔę́·yǫk*

34. Tsinondawerhon — Oo *katsiʔnǫtawéheʔ*, C *katsiʔnǫtáwEoʔ*

35. Kadagwarasonh — M *kataʔkwará·sǫ*, Oo *kataʔkwá·tsi*, C *kataʔkwá·shę*

36. Soyouwes — M *shohyǫ́·wes* or *shoyǫ́·wesheʔ*, Oo *shoyǫ́·wes*, C *shoyǫ́·we·s*

37. Watyaseronneh — M *hatyaʔseróhne*, Oo *hatiyaʔsé·hneʔ*, C *hatyáʔtrQneʔ*

38. Dayohronyonkah 'it reaches or pierces the sky' — M *teyorǫhyǫ́·ko*, Oo *teyowęhyǫ́·koʔ*, C *teyoǫhyǫ́·koh*

39. Deyothorehgwen 'it's cold on both sides' — M *teyothoréhkǫ*, Oo *teyothó·wèhkwi*, C *teyothowéhkǫh*

40. Dawenhethon — Oo *teyohǫwéhthǫ*, C *teyohǫwê·thǫ·*

Cayuga *(Continued)*

41. Wadondaherha — M *watǫtahéhrhaʔ*, Oo *thatǫta·hé·haʔ*, C *(t)hatǫtá·heha*

42. Deskae (Deskahe) — M *teskárheʔ*, Oo *teskáheʔ*, C *teskáhe·ʔ*

Seneca

43. Skanyadariyoh 'handsome lake' — M *skanyatarí·yo*, Oi *skanyatali·yôʔ·*, Oo *kanyá·tàiyo*, C *(s)kanyatá·iyoʔ*, S *(s)kanyotaiyoʔ*

44. Shadekaronyes 'skies equal in length' — M *shaʔtekarǫ̂·yes*, Oi *tshaʔtekalǫ̂·yes*, Oo *tshaʔteką́ęhyès*, C *tshaʔteką́ǫhye·s*, S *shaʔtekę́ǫye·s*

45. Shakenjohwaneh 'large forehead' — M *shakę́ʔtsyó·wane*, Oo *hakęʔtsyó·wà·nę*, C *shokęʔtsyó·wanęh* or *shokęʔtsyó·waʔ*, S *shokę́ʔtso·wa··ʔ*

46. Kanokareh — M *kaʔnó·kariʔ*, Oo *kaʔnó·kaiʔ*, C *kʔanókaiʔ*, S *kaʔnokaeh*

47. Deshayenah — M *nishayé·nęʔ*, Oo *nishayené·nhaʔ*, C *nishayénęnhaʔ*, S *níshanye·nęʔt*

48. Shodyenawat — M *shatyé·nawaht(eʔ)*, Oo *shatyé·nawat*, C *shatyená·waht*, S *shatyenǫwǫs*

49. Karonkerihdawih — Oo *kanǫhkíʔtawiʔ*, C *kanǫhkʔitá·wiʔ*, S *kanǫhkí·ʔtawiʔ*

50. Deyohninhohhakarawenh 'the door is open' — M *teyoninhokarâ·wę*, Oo *teyoninhó·ka·ʔwę*, C *teyoninhoká·ʔwęh*, S *to·nihokæ·ʔwęh*

NOTE: The nontechnical spellings are those of Seth Newhouse, a Mohawk (Fenton 1950:fig. 3); they are used for convenience only and have no particular claim to be taken as standard. Otherwise only forms available in phonemic transcription are given here; there are other renderings (Hale 1883a:154–163; Fenton 1950:59–67; Shimony 1961:104–117). Most of these names are unanalyzable or have been given different, often widely divergent translations by equally knowledgeable native speakers; many have clearly been reshaped in one or more of the languages. Even where the analysis is clear, the intended meaning may not be. For these reasons, and since the etymological meanings of the names have no relation to the function of the chiefs' offices, translations are given only where they seem particularly unproblematical. Abbreviations: M, Mohawk; Oi, Oneida; Oo, Onondaga; C, Cayuga; S, Seneca.

SOURCES: Chafe 1963:29, 1967; G. Michelson 1973; Lounsbury 1960:53; Foster 1974:34, 39, 81; and personal communications from Michael K. Foster (Mohawk, Onondaga, Cayuga); Wallace L. Chafe and Hanni J. Woodbury (Onondaga); Marianne Mithun (Mohawk); Clifford Abbott and Floyd G. Lounsbury (Oneida).

The names of the original founders of the League were similarly perpetuated in the clans. When one of these "federal" chiefs died, the clan mother (senior woman of the clan, that is, the "aged sensible" woman recognized as   *425* such) in consultation with other women belonging to that clan in the same tribe chose the man who would assume that name and hence become successor to the deceased chief. Often she chose a man of her lineage (and of the lineage of the deceased chief), but if there was not a suitable man of this lineage, a man of another lineage in the clan might be chosen. If the clan did not have a suitable candidate, the name might be "loaned" to another clan, that is, the name given to a man belonging to another clan with the understanding that at his death the name would return to the clan that had loaned it. In the twentieth century, some names have been loaned to another clan as the clan in which they belonged became so small it had no suitable candidate for the chieftainship. Such temporary arrangements can easily become permanent ones, and it is probably such a process that accounts for some of the discrepancies noted in the lists of clan affiliations of the chiefs. Further, if the person who had been given the chief's name proved unsatisfactory, his name could be taken away from him by the clan mother, a process called by the Iroquois "dehorning" of the chief, that is, taking away the metaphorical deer antlers that symbolized his office.

Roll Call of Chiefs

Although the manner by which names and hence positions within the clan were transferred and the manner in which the clan system itself operated was much the same in all five Iroquois tribes, there were and are differences among them, such as differences in the number of clans in each tribe and their relationship to each other. In turn, these differences are reflected in the relationship of the various chiefs of a tribe to each other. These are undoubtedly old differences and Morgan (1901, 1:75) is correct in observing that "the founders of the Iroquois Confederacy did not seek to suspend the [clan] divisions of the people, to introduce a different social organization; but on the contrary, they rested the League itself upon the [clans], and through them, sought to interweave the race into one political family." In fact, so interwoven is the League and the clan organization some Iroquois traditions state that the clans were named by Deganawida (Shimony 1961:55–56) or by Hiawatha (Beauchamp 1891:303; Henning 1898:477–478). The names of most Iroquois clans are not the common Iroquois words of the animals and birds as they are translated into English but usually denote some feature or characteristic of them. ("Northern Iroquoian Culture Patterns," table 1, this vol.).

The relationships among the chiefs, phrased in kinship terms, are delineated in the Roll Call of the Chiefs, the litany of the names of the 50 League chiefs that comprises one of the rites of the Condolence ceremony. In the Roll Call, the chiefs are grouped into classes, each class usually consisting of two or three members, the grouping indicating the committee structure by which decisions were reached in the councils of the League. In these councils, the chiefs of each class were expected to reach an opinion first. Then these opinions were discussed within the tribe. The tribes then discussed their opinions in the full council of the League, where again consensus was sought (Morgan 1901, 1:106–107). When unanimity was reached, the Onondagas as firekeepers reported the judgment of the council to Thadodaho who pronounced it in the name of the Five Nations.

The Mohawk and Oneida had only three clans: Turtle, Bear, and Wolf. They also resembled each other in the number of chieftainships each held and their distribution among the clans. Both had nine League chiefs, each clan holding three titles. Among both also two clans constituted one moiety, addressing each other as "siblings" and standing in the relationship of "cousins" to the single clan of the opposite moiety. In council, the arrangement was a tripartite rather than a bipartite one. One of the clans acted as "firekeepers" ("judges"). The two other clans discussed the question before the council; first one clan considered the issue and then passed it "across the fire" to the other clan for discussion. When they reached agreement, they referred the matter to the firekeepers for confirmation. If they disagreed, they might refer the matter back with suggestions as to how the two differences of opinion might be reconciled (Hewitt and Fenton 1944:84).

Among both Mohawks and Oneidas, the Turtle and Wolf clans composed one moiety and the Bear clan alone the other moiety. However, they differed in regard to the clan designated as firekeepers. Among the Mohawks the Turtle chiefs served as firekeepers, but among the Oneidas the Wolf chiefs were the firekeepers of the tribal council.

This difference is also expressed in the Roll Call of the Chiefs (fig. 5). In the litany of names in the Roll Call, the names of the three Mohawk Turtle chiefs, the firekeepers, are enumerated first; then the three Wolf chiefs, "siblings" of the Turtle clan as they are in the same moiety; and finally the three Bear chiefs, "cousins" to the Turtle and Wolf chiefs of the opposite moiety. Next are listed the chiefs of the Oneidas again beginning with the firekeepers, in this instance the chiefs of the Wolf clan. Next are enumerated the three chiefs of the Turtle clan, "siblings" of the Wolf chiefs as they are members of the same moiety. Finally, the three chiefs of the Bear clan, "cousins" of the chiefs of the Wolf and Turtle clans of the opposite moiety.

The other three Iroquois tribes have a greater number of clans and a different arrangement of the chiefs. The best evidence suggests that the Onondaga had nine clans (the published lists vary slightly): Wolf, Turtle, Snipe, Beaver, and Ball clans constituting one moiety and Bear,

Hawk, Deer, and Eel clans the other.† The Cayugas and Senecas had approximately the same number of clans and a comparable, but not identical, moiety system.

Of all the tribes in the League, the Onondaga have the greatest number of chiefs, 14 in all, including the most important chieftainship, Thadodaho, whose name is the first Onondaga name in the Roll Call of the Chiefs. This name belonged to the Bear clan but is now held by the Deer clan at the Six Nations Reserve and by the Eel clan among the New York Onondaga. The next title belonged to the Beaver clan. In the language of the Roll Call, this chief is "cousin" to Thadodaho, that is, of the opposite moiety, as are the next four titles. At Six Nations, these first six titles are regarded as one class and as the firekeepers of the Confederacy. Among the New York Onondaga the first three titles apparently comprised one class (the second and third names being regarded as councilors to Thadodaho) and the second set of three names, another class (Morgan 1901, 1:61, 1845; Hale 1883a:157).

The next Onondaga title belonged to the Wolf clan and is the name of the keeper of the wampum records of the League. In this capacity, he was often called on to mediate disputes within the council. His name is the only one in this class, and it is the only class on the Roll Call having only one member, which is indicative of the special status of the wampum keeper in the councils of the Confederacy.

The next five Onondaga names belong to the opposite moiety; the Deer clan holds the first two of these, constituting one class, and the Eel clan the next three, constituting another class. The final class consists of two names, but there is some dispute as to whether these two names belonged to two different chiefs of the Turtle clan or are two different names for one chief—an issue that leads to some disagreement as to whether the Onondagas have 13 or 14 chiefs, and the League 49 or 50. The last seven Onondaga titles have a somewhat different ar-

† The published lists of New York Onondaga clans are of two types. One lists the Wolf, Turtle, Snipe, Beaver, and Ball clans as belonging to one moiety and the Deer, Eel, and Bear clans to the other moiety (Morgan 1877:91; Hale 1883a:53; Lounsbury in Shimony 1961:119; Brown 1950:38-39). Both Lounsbury and Brown state that some Wolves sit on one side and some on the other. The other type lists Wolf, Turtle, Snipe, and Beaver clans in one moiety and the Deer, Eel, Bear, and Hawk clans in the other (E.A. Smith 1883:113; Beauchamp 1905:145; Fenton 1953:71). Clark's (1849, 1:32) list is similar; it includes an Eagle (Hawk) clan and a Heron clan, perhaps an error for Snipe. A list in a report published in 1889 (New York (State) Legislature. Assembly 1889:42) is also similar; it includes a Falcon (Hawk) clan and both Plover and Crane clans but not Eel.

Lists of Onondaga clans on the Six Nations Reserve in Canada give 9 clans, including both Pigeon Hawk (Hawk) and Ball as well as Wolf, Turtle, Snipe, Beaver, Deer, Eel, and Bear clans (Hewitt 1910g:129-130, 1903-1928, 2:459; Parker 1916a:95).

It has also been suggested that the Ball clan is really a subdivision of the Turtle clan known as Small Turtle (Beauchamp 1905:145; Chadwick 1897:84) or as Sharp-shinned Hawk (Hewitt 1928:459).

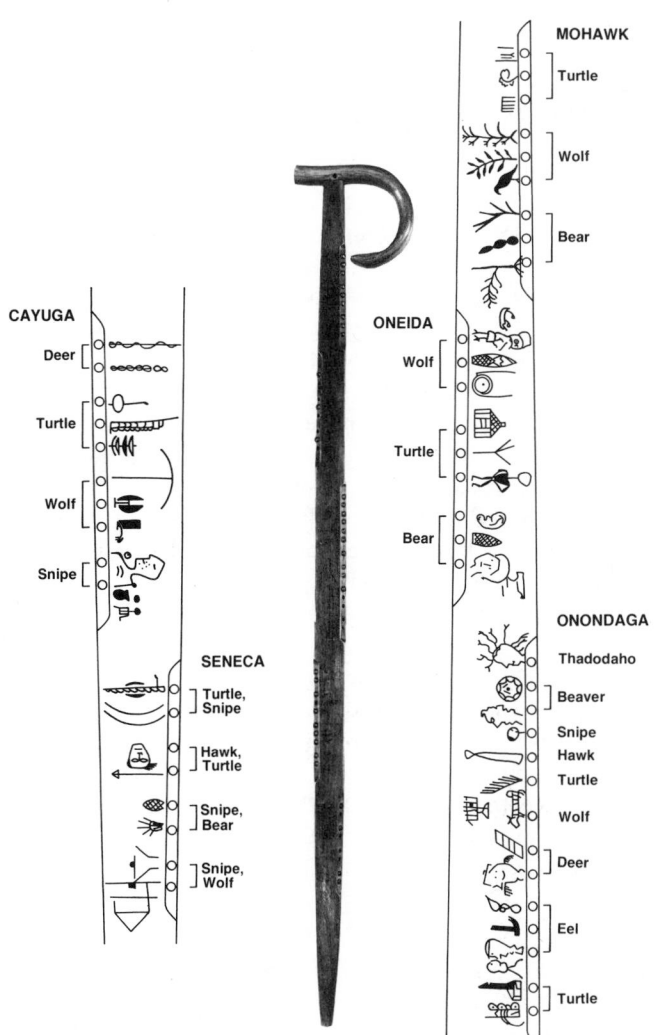

Cranbrook Institute of Science, Bloomfield Hills, Mich.: 1914.

Fig. 5. Cane of sugar-maple, 89 cm long, used by the Younger Brothers moiety in the Condolence council as a mnemonic representation of the 50 chiefs' titles. The pegs and pictographs are grouped by tribe and moiety (Older Brothers on the right, Younger Brothers on the left): 9 Mohawk titles according to clan, 9 Oneida titles by clan, the 14 Onondaga titles, 10 Cayuga titles, and 8 Seneca titles. For the titles themselves, arranged in this order, see table 2. The arrangement of the pegs is a much older feature than the 19th-century pictographs. This cane, used by the Cayuga ritualist Andrew Spragg (b.ca. 1865–d.ca. 1921), was collected about 1920 on the Six Nations Reserve. Canes of this type made and used by the Iroquois since then derive from blueprints of this cane that were distributed in 1945. On the other side is incised "A SPRAG" and pictographs that comprise a mnemonic for the preface to the eulogy chant of the Condolence ceremony. Photograph by Jack Kausch. See Fenton 1950, 1966:78-81; Shimony 1961:101-103.

rangement on the nineteenth-century New York lists from that used at Six Nations, which is followed here.

The Cayugas hold 10 League chieftainships, but their grouping into classes as well as the names and number of Cayuga clans and their grouping into moieties before the Cayuga dispersal in the late eighteenth century remains a question. The data collected by Morgan (1901, 1:61,

1877:91) in New York State is at variance with practice of the Cayugas living on the Six Nations Reserve in Canada. In Canada, the Cayuga Deer, Ball, Bear, and Turtle clans comprise the Turtle moiety and the Heron, Wolf, and Snipe clans, the Wolf moiety. There is more than one kind of Bear clan as there is also more than one kind of Turtle and Snipe. Hence, the Cayuga clans number more than nine (Shimony 1961:57).

The 10 Cayuga chieftainships at the Six Nations Reserve are grouped into four classes. The first two chiefs, the firekeepers of the Cayugas, stand in the relationship of father and son, and both names were once held by the Deer clan. The next three titles belong to the Turtle moiety and the following three to the Wolf moiety. The last two names, the "doorkeepers" of the Cayugas, once belonged to the Snipe clan, although more recently the last name has been held by the Bear clan. They have variously been said to be related to each other as "brothers" and as "cousins."

In the councils of the Cayuga, the doorkeepers (the last two Cayuga chiefs on the Roll Call) decide what matters should be discussed and announce these topics. The matter is then discussed by the three chiefs of the Turtle moiety and the three chiefs of the Wolf moiety. They announce their decision to the firekeepers, who either concur or refer it back for further discussion. The decision becomes final when the firekeepers announce it (Shimony 1961:122).

The Senecas, largest of the Iroquois tribes, have the fewest chiefs. Their eight chiefs are equally divided between the moieties and each is paired with a chief of the opposite moiety. This practice is unique to the Senecas and may have had its origin in the old division of the Seneca into a western and an eastern group—a division also unlike any found among other Iroquois tribes (Fenton 1940:226-227; "Seneca," this vol.).

Among the Seneca, the Turtle, Bear, Wolf, and Beaver clans constitute one moiety; the Snipe, Hawk, Heron, and Deer clans, the other. Although there are eight clans and eight chieftainships, the chieftainships are not equally distributed among the clans. Among the Tonawanda Senecas (the only Senecas in 1976 with a full set of chiefs; the other New York Senecas had an elected council and the Senecas on the Six Nations Reserve were so few in number some positions remained unfilled), three names are held by the Snipe clan, two by the Turtle clan, and one each by the Hawk, Bear, and Wolf clans. This distribution of names among the clans seems to be of some antiquity, as Morgan (1901, 1:61) recorded it before all the titles went to Tonawanda.

In the Roll Call of the Chiefs, the first Seneca name belongs to the Turtle clan, a name usually translated 'Handsome Lake' (the name once held by the noted Seneca prophet). The next name belongs to the Snipe clan and is the chief of the opposite moiety who is paired with Handsome Lake. The remaining six Seneca chief-

tainships are also paired, but various lists differently order the third, fourth, fifth, and sixth names. Nevertheless, these names are always paired in the same fashion. Of the final two names, the seventh belongs to the Snipe clan and the eighth to the Wolf clan. In former times, the two chiefs in each of these pairs consulted each other first, and after reaching an opinion, the opinions of the four pairs were discussed.

In the organization of the League, each chief (or at least some chiefs; the accounts differ) had a subchief who served as his assistant or deputy. These chiefs were and are also raised up at a Condolence ceremony, but there are no special personal names associated with these positions.

In addition, the Senecas have two war chiefs (sometimes called "runners") selected in the same manner as the League chiefs. They are also raised up and the name associated with each of these positions transferred at the Condolence ceremony.

Councils of the League

Within the League, the tribes were also divided into two sides or moieties. The Mohawk, Onondaga, and Seneca constituted one side, the 'Older (or Elder) Brothers', also referred to by the opposite side as 'father's kinsmen.' The Oneida and Cayuga (and the Tuscarora after they joined the League) comprised the other, the 'Younger Brothers', also referred to by the opposite side as 'offspring' ('fraternal offspring', 'nephews'). At the Six Nations Reserve, the Mohawk, Onondaga, and Seneca are also termed the 'Three Brothers'; and the Oneida, Cayuga, Tuscarora, and Tutelo, the 'Four Brothers'. Another remnant group, the Nanticoke, is also included on the Four Brothers side.

One of the most important reciprocal obligations between these two sides was also an important reciprocal obligation of the moiety division based on clans. By Iroquois custom, when an individual died, it was the responsibility of the opposite moiety to conduct the mourning and burial rites, condoling the mourners of the deceased's moiety (Fenton 1936:19; Shimony 1961:236). After the League was established, mourning for a deceased chief became also a League matter. When a chief died, it was the responsibility of the tribes of the opposite moiety to mourn the deceased chief. Thus, if the deceased chief had belonged to the Older Brothers, it fell to the Younger Brothers to conduct the Condolence ceremony, which was the first order of business in the councils of the League, and which concluded with the rite of raising up the new chief selected by the clan mother to assume the name of the deceased chief. The Condolence council should be held in the autumn or winter months. This custom is in part a practical measure as the winter months were times of relative leisure, but it is also justified by the Iroquois belief that the ritual would be destructive of growing seeds and plants as it was concerned with the effects of death (Hewitt 1916:165-166, 1917:323).

When the council of the chiefs of the League met to decide an issue the arrangement of the tribes was not a bipartite division, as in the Condolence ceremony, but a tripartite one resembling to a degree the arrangement of clans in the Mohawk and Oneida tribal councils. In the councils of the League, the Onondaga were the firekeepers (fig. 6). The Mohawk and Seneca sat on one side of the fire and the Oneida and Cayuga on the other side. As firekeepers, the Onondaga gave the topics for discussion to the Mohawk and the Seneca. The Mohawk discussed the matter first among themselves, then referred it to the Seneca, who after discussion returned it to the Mohawk. The Mohawk then announced this opinion "across the fire" to the Younger Brothers, where it was discussed first by the Oneida and then by the Cayuga. The Oneida then referred the matter back across the fire to the Mohawk, who announced the combined opinion to the Onondaga. If the Onondaga disagreed, they referred it back for further discussion; but in so doing they had to show that the opinion of the other tribes was in conflict with

established custom or with public policy. Or, if the opinions of the other tribes differed, the Onondaga might suggest a resolution. If the Onondaga agreed, Thadodaho announced the decision, so confirming and proclaiming it as the decision of the council (Hewitt 1910g:130, 1903-1928, 2:459-460; Shimony 1961:121-122; Hewitt and Fenton 1945:305-307).

Although it was the responsibility of the chiefs of the League to decide matters that affected its members, the chiefs themselves were not necessarily those men whose names became most familiar to Whites. In fact, such men were apt not to be League chiefs. For example, Joseph Brant and Red Jacket, the most famous Iroquois chiefs of the end of the eighteenth and beginning of the nineteenth centuries, were not League chiefs but chiefs of another class, often called "Pine Tree chiefs" or "merit chiefs," who held positions that were not hereditary. Even the most famous of the League chiefs of this period, Handsome Lake, gained greater renown as a religious prophet than as a League chief. As Morgan (1901, 1:98) noted of Red Jacket, "the Senecas themselves aver, that it would have been unwise to raise up a man of his intellectual power and extended influence to the office of sachem; as it would have concentrated in his hands too much authority." In the Iroquois form of government, then, the system of checks and balances rested in part on not making all the ablest men chiefs of the Confederacy. Further, it stipulated that war chiefs should not be League chiefs, and that if a League chief went on a war expedition he set aside his "horns of office."

But the League and its councils were not considered by the Iroquois to be ordinary affairs, and this is evident in the symbolism of the League. One set of such symbols concerns the Longhouse with its five fires, its eastern door facing the sunrise and its western door, the sunset, and the pillar of smoke that pierces the sky above Onondaga. Another concerns the circle of chiefs, who with joined hands surround the people. Should any chief depart, his horns of office would catch on the circle, and so his title remain with them. Yet as Fenton (1975:142-143) has noted:

> the most majestic image of the League is the Great White Pine with its four white roots extending to the cardinal directions. The tree has long needles ("the tree of the great long leaves") which grow as the confederacy prospers. Tribes attracted by the smoke spy the tree and follow its roots to the trunk. If they accept the principles of the Great Law, they enter the Longhouse as props to strengthen it. At the foot of the tree is the main council bench. An eagle is perched atop the pine to watch out for the safety of the peace.

A tree is also the symbol of chieftainship to be raised-up, uprooted by death, and a new one replanted in its place. Similarly a tree is uprooted to bury the hatchet, to cast the weapons of war into the underground stream that carries off pollution of war, and then the tree of peace is replanted. **429**

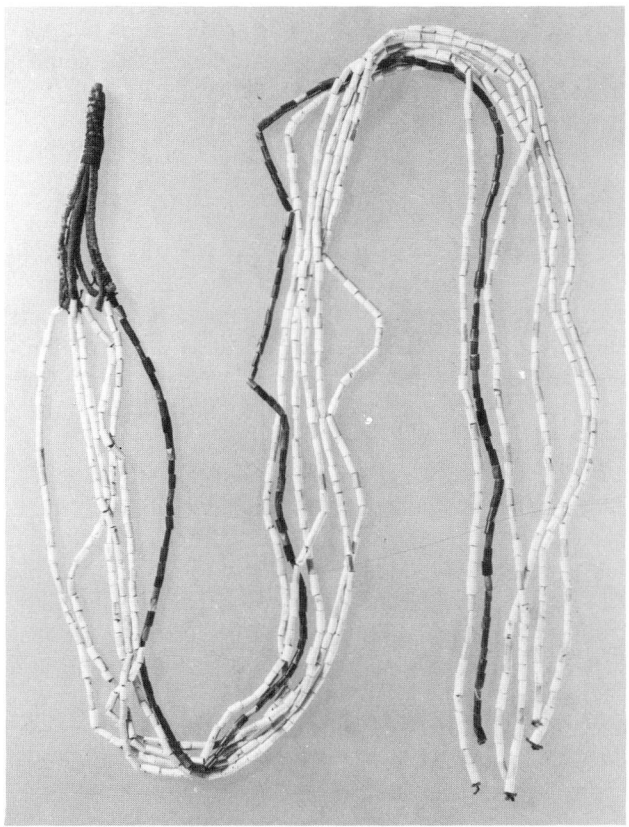

Dept. of Anthr., Smithsonian: 391948.
Fig. 6. Wampum strings representing the authority of the League and its council, held by the speaker or firekeeper to open and close meetings of the council of chiefs of the League on the Six Nations Reserve. The five white strings represent the original five tribes of the League, while the purple string represents other tribes subsequently adopted. Length 104 cm; collected in 1928.

The Seventeenth Century

The establishment of the Confederacy did not mean that each tribe ceased to pursue its own national interests as some have supposed. Each tribe continued to seek a policy that would give it an advantage in the fur trade—the activity that dominated affairs in the Northeast in the seventeenth and eighteenth centuries—establishing new or renewing old trade relationships if that course of action seemed profitable and, as the Great Peace established by the League extended only to its members, going to war if success there promised some advantage. Neither did any member tribe of the League wish any other tribe in the Confederacy to dictate policy, for what one tribe wanted often could be gained only at the expense of another.

It was in the interest of the Mohawk to turn their location as the easternmost member of the League and hence the one nearest to the European settlements to their advantage by attempting to serve as middlemen between the more western Iroquois tribes and the traders at Albany. It was also to their advantage to use the relatively easily traveled Lake Champlain-Richelieu River route to the Saint Lawrence to make their influence felt there with the French. But, although it was to the interests of the other Iroquois to have the Mohawks bear some of the brunt of dealing with Europeans, it was not in their interest to become vassals of the Mohawk. In their turn, the Mohawks did not have the military strength to subjugate the Upper Iroquois (as the more western Iroquois were once called), and as they were dependent on the Upper Iroquois for access to the furs found in the west, they were forced to reach some accommodation with them.

Of all the tribes of the League, the Seneca, the most western as well as the most populous tribe, had the easiest access to the furs to be found in the western territories, a factor of some importance after the beaver had been hunted out of Iroquois lands. Seneca activities in this western region brought them into an area where the French had considerable influence. But it was not to Seneca advantage to ally themselves solely with the French and thus become merely one of a number of Indian groups allied and trading with the French. They could profit more by using the trading alliance of the Mohawk, and of the League generally, with Albany—playing off the French and first the Dutch and later the English at Albany.

In their turn the Onondaga, unwilling to be a pawn of either the Mohawk with their Albany connections or the Seneca with their access to the western furs, intrigued with both, using when possible their geographic advantage of easy access to eastern Lake Ontario and hence the direct Saint Lawrence route to the French settlements at Montreal and Quebec. Somewhat similarly the Younger Brothers of the League, the Oneida and Cayuga, asserted their independence. The Oneida living as they did between the Mohawk and the Onondaga lent their support sometimes to the Mohawk and sometimes to the Onondaga, and the Cayuga on occasion had close relations with the Seneca to the west and sometimes with the Onondaga to their east. But whatever maneuvering for position each tribe might do within the League, its ultimate best interests lay with the League itself and in the united action of all five tribes.

It was in the interest of the League to play off the European rivals in order to obtain the best price for their furs, and the Iroquois excelled in the complex diplomacy necessary to keep this position. Not only did the League sometimes court the French while at the same time strengthening their relations with Albany, but also on occasion one tribe or one part of a tribe would seek favor with the French while another sought similar favor with the English. However, in the long range, Iroquois interests lay with the English, and consequently the Iroquois alliance with them was stronger than any of those negotiated from time to time with the French.

It was considerations such as these rather than merely the memory of Champlain's expeditions against the Iroquois between 1609 and 1615, as some have suggested, that most influenced the course of Iroquois-French relationships. In fact, Champlain was drawn into a conflict that already existed among the Indians of the region. The development of French trade on the Saint Lawrence in the late sixteenth century had led to a series of Indian trading alliances by which French trade goods were exchanged for furs. However, this network of trading alliances excluded the Iroquois and in order to obtain European goods they were forced to resort to war—warfare that ceased for a time when French soldiers armed with guns joined their Indian allies to fight against the Iroquois. Fortunately for the Iroquois, about the same time the Dutch began to trade on the Hudson River. The Mohawks seized this opportunity and established themselves as preeminent traders with the Dutch at Albany and as middlemen between the other Iroquois and the Dutch. As this trade developed, so also did French trade with the more northerly Indians, one of the more important being the Huron. This brought the Iroquois and the Huron into sharper conflict, the war between them ending in 1649 with the defeat and dispersal of the Huron. Shortly afterward, the Iroquois defeated and dispersed the Petun, allies of the Huron, and then the Neutral, so named as they had maintained neutrality between the Huron and Iroquois (see "Early Iroquoian Contacts with Europeans," this vol.).

The Iroquois did not rest with these victories but continued their attacks in an effort to gain greater control over the fur trade. For a few years they succeeded in preventing furs from the west from reaching the French posts on the Saint Lawrence, but in 1653 they sent a delegation to make peace with the French. The four

Upper Iroquois tribes wished to pursue war with the Eries unencumbered by another war with the French and their Indian allies (JR 41:51, 81). However, the Mohawk were less inclined to enter into a peace with the French, in part because they were not involved in the Erie war and in part because they knew that such a treaty would permit the Upper Iroquois to carry their furs across Lake Ontario and down the Saint Lawrence to the French as well as through Mohawk country to Albany (JR 41:201). Consequently, the Mohawk complained that the French by going directly to Onondaga wanted to enter the Longhouse (the League of the Iroquois) by the chimney (JR 41:87).

Nevertheless, the Jesuit priest Simon Le Moyne went to Onondaga in the summer of 1654 to explore the possibilities of a closer alliance of the French with the Iroquois and in 1655 visited the Mohawks on a similar mission. That year also a delegation of Onondagas representing the Upper Iroquois came to the Saint Lawrence to confirm peace with the French; and two more Jesuits, Pierre Joseph Marie Chaumonot and Claude Dablon, went to Onondaga where they spent the winter. Dablon returned to Quebec in early spring 1656 and shortly after went back to Onondaga with three other Jesuits, some soldiers, and a number of other Frenchmen where they built the mission of Sainte Marie near Onondaga Lake (Gannentaha). The mission was five short leagues from the principal village of the Onondaga, which the Jesuits visited as well as the other Upper Iroquois tribes. But the peace proved to be an uneasy one and in 1658, not long after the Iroquois had defeated the Eries, the mission was abandoned.

Nevertheless, there remained a pro-French faction among the Iroquois led by the Onondaga orator, Garacontié, who attempted to reestablish peace with the French. For almost a decade after the Onondaga mission closed these attempts had only limited success, and during this period the Iroquois continued to trade with Albany. The transfer of New York to England in 1664 had little effect on this relationship. Albany remained a Dutch town in population and the Iroquois continued to deal with Dutch traders living there (fig. 7). As earlier, the Mohawks, who were anxious to maintain their position as intermediaries between the Albany traders and the Upper Iroquois, were most hostile toward the French, while the Upper Iroquois, who were now engaged in an inconclusive war with the Susquehannocks, were less hostile to them.

Faced with these circumstances, the French decided to humble the Mohawks. In the winter of 1665–1666 Daniel de Rémy de Courcelle, governor of Canada, led an expedition against them, but near Schenectady the French were led into an ambush by the Mohawks and retreated to Canada. Another and more successful attempt was made in the fall of 1666 when Alexandre de Prouville de Tracy led an expedition against the Mo-

N.-Y. Histl. Soc., New York.

Fig. 7. An entry from the 1695–1726 account book of Evert Wendell, a Dutch trader to the Indians living at Albany. This entry, dated Aug. 13, 1706, reads in Dutch: 'A young Seneca, living in Canosedaken, his name Tan na Eedsies, used to come to Niklaas Bleskers, 2 pairs of blue duffel stockings for 1 fisher or otter. 1708, the fisher paid. July 24, to his wife again one duffel blanket for 1 fisher; Ditto, 1 shirt for 1 beaver; Ditto, 1 pair of stockings for 1 fisher, [for] himself' (transcript and translation by T.J. Brasser, personal communication 1966). The pictographs were evidently for the benefit of the nonliterate customer, one identifying him by the tattooed patterns on his face, neck, and chest, and the others showing the skins owed (with one fisher struck out when paid).

hawks and burned their villages. Peace between the French and all the Iroquois tribes was concluded in 1667, and that same year the Jesuits returned to reestablish missions among the Iroquois. By the end of 1668 they had established missions among all five Iroquois tribes. At the same time, the Sulpicians established a mission among some Cayugas who had settled at the Bay of Quinté to escape the Susquehannock.

The peace established in 1667 also led to increased French exploration in the west and establishment of Jesuit missions in the Upper Great Lakes region; the defeat of the Hurons had induced the French to go farther west to obtain furs. Further, for the dual purpose of controlling Iroquois travel down the Saint Lawrence and drawing off trade of the western Indians with Albany, Fort Frontenac was established at Cataraqui (now Kingston, Ontario) in 1673. A few years later, a fort and trading post was built at Niagara to control the route between Lakes Erie and Ontario. In the same period, a number of Iroquois, including a number of Mohawks, settled on the Saint Lawrence near Montreal (see "Mohawk," this vol.). For many years, these Iroquois not only remained allies of the French and participants in the French fur trade but also were involved in the important contraband trade between Montreal and Albany, a trade that also involved some French coureurs de bois.

After the conclusion of the war with the Susquehannock, Iroquois relations with the French, including the Jesuits in the Iroquois missions, became less friendly. At the same time, the elimination of the Susquehannock as a power in the region led the Oneidas, Onondagas, and Cayugas to attack the borders of Maryland and Virginia to the south and the Senecas and Cayugas to extend their attacks west, notably against the Illinois, a move that brought the Iroquois into conflict with the French who had intensified their efforts in this area. As the relations between the Iroquois and the French became increasingly strained, the Jesuits closed their missions among the Iroquois except that at Onondaga; and Joseph-Antoine Le Febvre de La Barre, governor of Canada, fearful that the Iroquois would not only control the Illinois country but also extend their war to Michilimackinac, the most important French trading center in the Upper Great Lakes region, planned an expedition against the Iroquois in 1684. But La Barre's expedition got only as far as La Famine at the mouth of the Salmon River where a council was held with the Iroquois that changed little.

As French influence among the Iroquois decreased, English influence increased. At a council held in 1684 at Albany for the purpose of inducing the Iroquois to cease attacking Virginia and Maryland, England claimed the Iroquois as her subjects, although it is doubtful that the Iroquois understood what the English intended by this assertion of sovereignty. Nonetheless, the alliance between the Iroquois and the English was strengthened and in 1686 a trading expedition was sent from Albany to Michilimackinac. By that time, the Iroquois also had begun their attempts to induce the Indians at Michilimackinac to trade with them. What both the Albany traders and the Iroquois could offer were better goods at cheaper prices than the French, a circumstance that only further troubled the French.

The continued efforts of the Iroquois, particularly the Seneca, to gain control of the western trade induced Jacques René de Brisay, marquis de Denonville, successor to La Barre as governor of Canada, to lead an expedition against the Senecas in 1687. After destroying the corn and the burned and abandoned villages of the Senecas, Denonville went on to Niagara where a new fort was built. The fort was abandoned the following year after a number there had died of disease, and the Iroquois continued their harassments on the Saint Lawrence. Nevertheless, in 1689 the Iroquois appeared to be ready to conclude a peace with the French. The establishment of such a peace was prevented by the outbreak of King William's War (War of the League of Augsburg); that same year, the Iroquois attacked Lachine and killed a number living there in what came to be known as the Lachine massacre. For the next several years, the Iroquois continued their raids along the Saint Lawrence, successfully preventing for a few years any furs from reaching the French at Montreal and Quebec. Consequently, the French sent an expedition against the Mohawks early in 1693 that burned the Mohawk villages, and that spring the furs from the west again reached the Saint Lawrence. The Iroquois, however, continued to threaten the French and three years later, in 1696, Louis de Buade de Frontenac, successor to Denonville as governor of Canada, led an expedition against the Onondagas and Oneidas and burned their villages ("Onondaga," fig. 2, this vol.). The following year (1697), the Peace of Ryswick was signed ending King William's War, but peace with the Iroquois was not made until 1701 at a council held at Montreal. Simultaneously, Iroquois delegates at Albany affirmed their alliance with England. These treaties served to set Iroquois policy for succeeding decades of the eighteenth century: a neutrality with the French protected by the English that left the Iroquois free to pursue their role in the fur trade by holding the balance of power between the French and the English.

The Eighteenth Century

True to this policy the Iroquois remained neutral when Queen Anne's War (War of the Spanish Succession) broke out in 1702. For the most part, the French and English also desired that they remain so in order that the fur trade, including the contraband trade between Albany and Montreal in which the Caughnawaga Mohawks played an important role, continue. No such consideration obtained in New England, and consequently war was waged there between the French aided by their Indian allies and the English. These Indian allies of the French included the Caughnawaga Mohawks who took part in some of the raids including the attack on Deerfield in 1704. As these attacks on New England continued, the English made more concerted efforts to draw the Iroquois into the war. In 1709 the Jesuits who had earlier returned to Onondaga left, and the Onondagas burned the Jesuit mission house and chapel. The following year the so-called Four Indian Kings (whose number included three Mohawks) were taken to London both to impress them with English power and so strengthen the Iroquois alliance with England and to help the colonies gain additional aid for the war (see "Northern Iroquoian Culture Patterns," figs. 19-20; "Mohawk," fig. 4; "Mahican," fig. 4—all this vol.). Later that year and in part a consequence of the visit, plans were drawn up for building Fort Hunter at the junction of Schoharie Creek and the Mohawk River. The fort and its Indian chapel were completed in 1712.

Although by the Treaty of Utrecht that ended the war in 1713 the Iroquois were acknowledged to be British subjects and although Fort Hunter secured the Mohawk Valley and thus opened the way for White settlement there, the war had little effect on the Iroquois and they continued to pursue the same course as they had before: to extend their position as middlemen between the Indians to the west and Albany. New York continued to rely on the cheapness and quality of English goods as compared to French ones as well as on the Iroquois traders and warriors to maintain this trade with the western Indians while the French continued their policy of sending traders and soldiers into the west to maintain trading posts there. The situation changed somewhat in the 1720s. The French built a fort at Niagara in order to control and attract the trade passing between Lakes Erie and Ontario. Shortly after, the English built a fortified trading post at Oswego to attract this trade to Albany. The French then built a trading post at Toronto in an effort to gain the trade of the Indians who had been traveling by this more northern route rather than by Niagara to trade at Oswego. Nevertheless, trade at Oswego prospered and it rather than Albany became the center of English trade with the Indians. Of all the Iroquois tribes, the Mohawks remained most strongly pro-British, the Senecas (particularly the western Senecas), most strongly pro-French, and the Onondagas the center of intrigue.

About the same time these trading centers were being built in Iroquois country, traders from Pennsylvania, whose population had greatly increased after the Peace of Utrecht, began to extend their activities across the Appalachians and into Ohio. Such trade was possible as the Pennsylvania Indians were under the protection of the Iroquois, who after the defeat of the Susquehannocks had extended their activities to the south as well as to the west and in the process brought the Pennsylvania Indians under their control. These Indians included the Tuscaroras, who had begun leaving North Carolina in 1712 to move to Pennsylvania and who about 1722 were adopted into the League of the Iroquois as the sixth nation of the Confederacy. The Tuscaroras were admitted only as a "junior" member of the League and the number of League chiefs was not expanded to include any Tuscarora chiefs (see "Tuscarora Among the Iroquois," this vol.).

The Pennsylvania traders extended their trade in the west during King George's War (War of the Austrian Succession) when England imposed a naval blockade on New France and so reduced French fur trade. This war had broken out in 1744 after years of uneasy peace between France and England. As they had in Queen Anne's War some 40 years earlier, the Iroquois initially endeavored to remain neutral. Later, some, notably the Mohawk, were induced to take up arms against the French; and the Iroquois on the Saint Lawrence participated in French attacks on the English colonies. Nevertheless, the Iroquois, lacking enthusiasm for the war, participated little in it.

After the Treaty of Aix-la-Chapelle brought King George's War to an end in 1748, France renewed her efforts to gain influence in the west, an influence that had waned during the war and was further threatened by increasing activity of traders from Virginia as well as those from Pennsylvania and by interest of settlers in these western lands. In 1749 Abbé François Picquet began a settlement on the Saint Lawrence at Oswegatchie composed principally of pro-French Onondagas (see "Onondaga," this vol.). It as well as the settlement of

Saint Regis by some Indians from Caughnawaga about the same time (see "Mohawk," this vol.) served to strengthen French control of the Upper Saint Lawrence. In 1749, also, Pierre Joseph Céloron de Blainville led a military expedition through the upper Ohio Valley to reassert French claims in this region and so attempt to keep the English east of the Alleghenies and to forestall English attempts to break French control of the route between their settlements in Canada and on the Mississippi. In succeeding years French influence increased, and in 1752 a party of Chippewa and Ottawa Indians under the leadership of a French trader destroyed Pickawillany, a trading post of the Pennsylvania traders on the Miami River. The following year, the French began building a chain of forts connecting Lake Erie with the Forks of the Ohio. They built forts at Presque Isle (now Erie, Pennsylvania), at Lake Le Boeuf at the head of French Creek, and at Venango (Fort Machault) where French Creek enters the Allegheny River in 1753 and Fort Duquesne at the Forks the following year, driving out some Virginians who had begun to build a fort of their own there. An expedition led by Gen. Edward Braddock to take Fort Duquesne in 1755 ended in defeat and left the region in French control (fig. 8).

In 1756 England declared war on France and the French and Indian War in America was merged with the Seven Years' War in Europe. Oswego was taken that same year by the French, and Lake Ontario became a French lake. But in 1758 Fort Stanwix (now Rome, New York) was built at the Great Carrying Place, where the portage between the Mohawk River and Wood Creek began, and an expedition from there passing through ruined Oswego took Fort Frontenac, regaining English control of Lake Ontario. That same year the English took Fort Duquesne and renamed it Pittsburgh. The following year the fort at Niagara was taken by the English, the forts at Presque Isle and Venango abandoned by the French, and Quebec taken by the English (fig. 9). In 1760 an expedition went up the Saint Lawrence, the largest of three English forces then converging on Montreal, and took it. With the fall of Montreal, all of Canada was surrendered to the British and the war was effectively over in America although it continued elsewhere and did not formally end until the Treaty of Paris was signed in

Denver Art Mus.: QIro-9.
Fig. 8. Fine ball-headed club of maple, found at the site of Braddock's 1755 defeat by the French and Indians. Almost certainly Iroquois. Length about 49 cm.

Natl. Gallery of Canada, Ottawa, gift of the Duke of Westminster.
Fig. 9. *The Death of General Wolfe.* This rendering of Brig. Gen. James Wolfe's demise at the British capture of Quebec in 1759 was painted in 1770 by Benjamin West. It is without value as a historical document on the battle, but the prominently placed Indian is symbolic of Iroquois participation. The figure (detail), which is probably based on West's knowledge of Mohawks, has a scalp lock ornamented with red and quill-wrapped feathers, silver earrings, a red and green wool pouch and sash, a pipe tomahawk, a musket with red painted design, and a painted or tattooed body and face. Behind him is a figure wearing the uniform of Rogers' Rangers, incorporating leggings, moccasins, and other Indian items.

1763. That same year the western Indians, dismayed that they now had to deal with the English rather than the French as they previously had, united under the leadership of Pontiac and attempted to drive out the English, an attempt that failed and left the region in English hands.

As they had in previous conflicts between France and England in the eighteenth century, the Iroquois initially tried to remain neutral during the French and Indian War but were drawn into the conflict as it progressed. Some, notably the Mohawks, were drawn to the English side at various times during the war and others, notably the Senecas, remained pro-French, while those who had settled on the Saint Lawrence maintained their close association with the French there. Nevertheless, the victory of the English spelled defeat for the policy their Iroquois allies had pursued for many decades—to maintain ascendancy in the region and in the fur trade by an alliance with Albany that allowed them to deal with Indians more closely identified with the French. Both the Iroquois and the French had wanted some hostility between the Iroquois and the Indians allied to the French. The French knew that if peace was established between their Indian allies and the Iroquois, the furs they had been receiving would go to Albany, as the English could offer better prices and in general better-quality goods for them. On their part, the Iroquois knew that if there was general peace in the area, their position as middlemen between Albany and the western tribes would be undermined, for these western Indians could trade directly with the English. With the success of the English in the French and Indian War, this fear became a reality. The trade in the west that had belonged to the French now belonged to the English, and the Iroquois no longer controlled the balance of power in the Northeast.

The elimination of France as a rival of England in North America had another important consequence that was to weaken Iroquois power further: the colonies, no longer needing protection and aid from England that they had when France and her Indian allies were threatening their existence, could more easily break with her. When they did take this course of action in the next decade, the Iroquois lost even more advantage.

However, the more immediate consequence of English victory in the French and Indian War was an increased interest of the colonists in the western lands, an interest that if pursued would only lead to increased conflict between Whites and Indians in this area. The Crown attempted to prevent this by the Proclamation of 1763, which forbade White settlement west of a line drawn along the crest of the Appalachians, thus leaving the western lands as an Indian domain. But the continued interest of the colonists in these lands led the Indians, particularly the Iroquois, to surrender their claim to the lands south of the Susquehanna and Ohio rivers in 1768 by the Treaty of Fort Stanwix. The Iroquois retained only those lands north and west of the line agreed to in that treaty (fig. 1).

When the Revolution did break out, neither the tribes that comprised the League nor the members of the separate tribes could agree on the course of action they should take, that is, whether to side with the English, to side with the Revolutionaries, or to remain neutral. Many of the Mohawks decided to espouse the British cause, but many of the Oneidas were sympathetic to the Americans, while the Onondagas, Cayugas, and Senecas were more inclined to the English. Being unable to agree, they covered the council fire of the League in 1777, leaving each tribe to pursue its own course of action during the war. Later that same year, the Mohawk settlements were attacked and many of those Mohawks who were living there fled the valley. Two years later in the face of the expedition led by John Sullivan and James Clinton the Onondagas, Cayugas, and Senecas abandoned their villages and a number fled to Niagara where some Mohawks had earlier gone. They remained in this area until the Treaty of Paris was signed in 1784.

The Treaty of Paris made no provision for the Indians; consequently, the Iroquois had to treat with each government separately. This meant that as individuals the Iroquois had to decide where they should go to live and with which country they wished to enter into a treaty agreement. The Lower Mohawks, who had gone to live near Montreal during the war, decided to settle on land given them at the Bay of Quinté; and the Upper Mohawks, who had gone to live at Niagara, decided to settle on land along the Grand River in Ontario. With the Upper Mohawks went a number of Cayugas, some Onondagas, and a few Senecas. Other Cayugas and Onondagas chose to stay with the Senecas settled at Buffalo Creek in western New York State, while still others decided to live in their own homelands: the Cayugas at Cayuga Lake and the Onondagas at Onondaga Creek. Some Senecas determined that they would continue to live in the Genesee Valley where they had lived before the war, but others decided to move to or remain in the more westerly parts of New York State. There were four such large settlements that by the Treaty of Big Tree in 1797 became reservations. All of them took their names from the streams along which they were located: Buffalo Creek, Cattaraugus, Allegany, and Tonawanda (fig. 1). The Oneida, who had fought on the side of the Americans, had not been dislocated during the war and they remained in their old homeland. Those Iroquois who had moved to Oswegatchie in the 1750s abandoned that settlement in the two decades following the end of the American Revolution and moved to other reservations, but the Caughnawaga, Saint Regis, and Lake of Two Mountain Iroquois remained on the lands they had occupied before the war.

Nineteenth and Twentieth Centuries

In the latter years of the eighteenth century, the fire of the League was rekindled in the two places where the largest numbers of Iroquois had settled after the Revolution: at the Six Nations Reserve in Canada and at the Buffalo Creek Reservation in the United States. Each had its own council of hereditary chiefs holding a parallel set of names and each held a portion of the wampum that

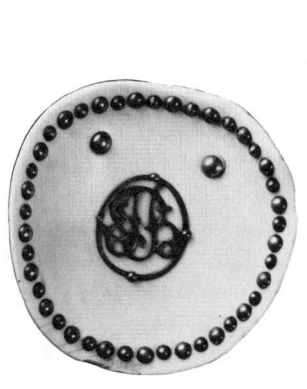

left, Royal Ont. Mus., Toronto: HD6627; center and right, Buffalo and Erie Co. Histl. Soc., Buffalo, N.Y.

Fig. 10. left, Shell gorget belonging to the Mohawk Joseph Brant, leader of the pro-British Iroquois after the American Revolution. Silver monogram and silver studs, the form and materials partly of aboriginal origin and partly derived from British military officers' insignia. Diameter 9 cm. center and right, Engraved silver medal given to the Seneca Red Jacket by President George Washington at a conference in Philadelphia in 1792, to represent peace and friendship between the United States and the Six Nations. It was inherited by Red Jacket's nephew Jimmy Johnson and then by Ely S. Parker. Length about 17 cm.

435

before the Revolution had been kept at Onondaga. However, in the nineteenth century as the reservation became important as a social and political unit and the tribe and confederacy less so, the old Iroquois tribe and confederacy organization was adapted to serve as the system of governance on some reservations.

In New York State, the fire that had burned at Onondaga was rekindled after the Revolution on the large Buffalo Creek Reservation where a number of Onondagas as well as some Cayugas and a greater number of Senecas had settled. The council fire there was kept by Captain Cold (fig. 11), and the Senecas gave a square mile of land to honor the chief who kept it (Clark 1849, 1:124).

In the 1840s as a consequence of the sale of the Buffalo Creek and Tonawanda Reservations by the Compromise Treaty of 1842, this system of governance was further modified. The council fire that had burned at Buffalo Creek was rekindled at Onondaga and the wampum of the Confederacy returned to Onondaga after Captain Cold died at Tonawanda in 1847 (Clark 1849, 1:109, 124). The Onondaga Reservation continued to be governed by a council of 27 chiefs—the 14 League chiefs and

13 assistants to these chiefs (Thadodaho does not have a deputy). Efforts to change this system to a council composed of elected officials failed, and it remained a council composed of chiefs belonging to the "pagan" party, that is, followers of the Iroquois Longhouse religion. The New York Onondaga continue to be governed by a council of chiefs, all of whom must be adherents of the Longhouse religion.

The Onondagas continued to hold the wampum that had been brought back from Buffalo Creek, but in 1878 it was reported that only 12 belts remained. Four of these were sold in 1891 by Thomas Webster, who then held them. Concern that the rest would be lost or sold led to efforts to preserve them that resulted in the Onondagas agreeing to make the University of the State of New York wampum keeper, and the remaining five belts were transferred to the New York State Museum, Albany, in 1898. In 1927 the four belts sold in 1891 were bequeathed to the New York State Museum (fig. 2 among them). In the late 1960s efforts were made to revise the laws pertaining to this wampum, with the result that a bill was passed by the New York State legislature to amend the earlier bill and return the five belts transferred by the Onondaga in 1898 after an appropriate facility has been built at Onondaga for them (Fenton 1971a).

Although by the terms of the Compromise Treaty of 1842 the Senecas retained the Allegany and Cattaraugus reservations, which had been sold four years earlier under the terms of the treaty of 1838, Seneca faith in their system of hereditary tribal chiefs had been undermined by the chiefs' actions in 1838. At that time, although sentiment among the Senecas was generally against sale of their New York reservations (as it was among almost all of the eight federal Seneca chiefs) and removal west, some of their chiefs out of conviction and some others after having been bribed or otherwise induced signed the treaty of 1838, which provided for the sale of these reservations and removal of the Senecas to Kansas. Protests of the Senecas, aided by Whites sympathetic to their cause, restored some of their land, but the fear that the chiefs might again sell what land remained was one of the factors that led to the adoption of the constitution in 1848. It provided for an elected council to replace the council of chiefs.

The Tonawanda Senecas did not join those at Allegany and Cattaraugus in this change of governance. At the time, they were engaged in an effort to retain their reservation, which had been sold under the terms of the Compromise Treaty of 1842. They argued that not only were all of the Senecas then living on the Tonawanda Reservation opposed to removal to Kansas, but also none of their chiefs had signed the treaty of 1842 and therefore it was not binding on them. They were not dissatisfied, then, with the actions of their chiefs. Further, to deprive the chiefs of their position would seriously weaken their argument that the treaty was not binding on them as their

Fig. 11. Captain Cold, Ut-ha-wah, Onondaga keeper of the League council fire at Buffalo Creek. He wears a turban of red, white, and blue calico with split white feathers. The red yarn sash has green edges and white beads. The portrait is signed by William John Wilgus and dated Buffalo, Oct. 1838.

436

chiefs had not signed it. Consequently, they did not join the revolution of 1848 that established the elected council at Cattaraugus and Allegany. Their efforts to retain their reservation were finally successful; by a treaty signed in 1857 the Tonawanda Senecas bought back their reservation. A few years later, they adopted a form of government that retained the chiefs' council although it provided for the election of some officers. In time, this council come to be composed of 16 chiefs, the eight Seneca federal chiefs and eight subchiefs. When one of these chiefs dies, his replacement is still selected by the clan mother and raised up at a Condolence ceremony. At Tonawanda there is no requirement that the chiefs be followers of the Longhouse religion and a number are not.

In Canada, despite some pressure to change the form of governance on the Six Nations Reserve, the council of Confederacy chiefs remained in power throughout the nineteenth century; however, by the end of the century, these pressures for change led to various attempts to codify the traditions of the League. In 1880 Seth Newhouse (Dayodakane) began to write down the traditional history and constitution of the Iroquois Confederacy. But his attempts to get his version accepted by the chiefs' council failed and the Council appointed a committee of chiefs to produce an authoritative version. Their report was approved by the chiefs in 1900. A number of factors (see "Six Nations of the Grand River, Ontario," this vol.) led to replacement of the chiefs' council by an elected council in 1924. Nevertheless, the chiefs have continued to hold meetings, at various times attempts have been made to reinstate the chiefs' council, and chiefs continue to be raised up at Condolence ceremonies.

In 1840 a group of Oneidas, having sold their land in New York State, moved to a tract of land they had purchased near London, Ontario; and during the next few years, others joined them. There were few League chiefs in this group, but shortly after they had settled in Canada, they established a hereditary chiefs' council patterned after that in New York State, and the chiefs from the Six Nations Reserve came to raise up the new chiefs. The council was composed of 18 chiefs—the nine federal chiefs (as in New York State, the Wolf, Bear, and Turtle clans each held three titles) and their subchiefs—and their successors were chosen and raised up in accordance with old custom. In the early years of the twentieth century, some Oneidas became followers of the Handsome Lake religion and built a Longhouse on the reserve (previously there had been no adherents of the Longhouse religion on that reserve), and in 1915 they established their own chiefs' council duplicating the structure of the already existing chiefs' council but separate from it. The Christian hereditary chiefs' council, however, continued in power. In 1921, as a consequence of Oneida involvement in a land claims case the Onondaga had brought against the state of New York, the

Christian hereditary chiefs' council shifted its affiliation from the Canadian Six Nations council to that in New York. They attended the councils of the League held at Onondaga rather than those at Six Nations, and the New York Onondaga participated in their Condolence ceremonies. In 1934 this council was replaced by an elected council, but the Longhouse hereditary chiefs' council continued. Its chiefs continue to be raised up in Condolence ceremonies joined by the Six Nations Reserve Iroquois (A.F. Ricciardelli 1961; Ricciardelli 1966; Shimony 1961:105-106).

The Condolence Council

The Condolence council, or ceremony—the great convocation for condoling deceased chiefs of the League and raising up their successors—is still held on various Iroquois reservations in the 1970s as the occasion demands. In New York State the Onondaga and the Tonawanda Seneca, the two Iroquois groups in the United States still governed by councils of hereditary chiefs, join in the Condolence ceremony to raise up chiefs. They also join the Tuscarora to raise up members of the Tuscarora chiefs' council, the governing body of the New York Tuscarora; although not League chiefs, Tuscarora chiefs are customarily raised up at a Condolence council held for that purpose. In Canada, League chiefs residing on the Six Nations and Oneida reserves are raised up at Condolence councils held in the Longhouses there.

Although the Condolence ceremony as given on any particular occasion varies according to circumstances and the participants' knowledge of the component rites, and although practice as maintained among the New York Iroquois differs slightly from that in Canada, the same general form is followed on all occasions and the same basic rites included. It is a long ceremony, often beginning in the early afternoon and ending in the early evening, and one that requires considerable knowledge by those who carry out the rites.

It is customary in Iroquois councils and ceremonies to include some statement regarding the nature and purpose of the occasion. Usually in such a statement mention is made that somebody ordained something, that this responsibility is still being kept up, and that a particular responsibility so ordained is being kept up on this occasion. In the Condolence ceremony, the rite known as "Over the Forest" and as the "Laws of the Confederacy" makes this kind of statement. It takes note that the forefathers established the League, that it has now become old, and what its founders ordained should happen when a loss occurred (a chief died), for by raising up chiefs at the Condolence ceremony the League itself is perpetuated.

The names of the founders themselves are mentioned in the Eulogy or Roll Call of the Chiefs, also called "Journeying on the Trail" and sometimes "Hai Hai," the general name for the Condolence ceremony (Fenton 1950:47). As the "Over the Forest" serves to remind those present of the "Laws of the Confederacy," so also does the litany of the Roll Call serve to remind them of the founders and, as the names are grouped into "committees," how the League chiefs, the present holders of these names, may counsel among themselves. In the Roll Call, the names of the Mohawk chiefs are mentioned first, then the Oneida, Onondaga, and Cayuga chiefs, and finally the Seneca ones (fig. 5). The statement 'Continue to listen, you who were a ruler' follows the mention of each name, and the statement

> This was the roll of you,
> You that joined in the work,
> You who completed the work,
> The Great League

is repeated after each group (committee), the whole interspersed with the refrain, *hai, hai* (Hale 1883a:33, 80, 129–139; Beauchamp 1907a:352, 365–377). *hai, hai* is said to be the cry of the souls, and if it should be omitted the departed spirits would be displeased and send disease. Its repetition in the Condolence ceremony consoles the spirits of the dead (Hewitt 1917:325, 1920:543–544).

Two other rites of the ceremony are more specifically concerned with mourning. One is the Condoling Song, the great hymn of farewell to the deceased chief. It consists of a half-dozen or so verses (sometimes called "songs"), each of which greets or otherwise recognizes one of several classes of people, including the League, the warriors (the men), the women, and the forefathers.

The other, the Requickening Address, so named for its symbolic power to restore life as well as for its power to lift up the minds of those depressed by grief, consists of a number of "words" or messages, each of which is accompanied by a string of wampum. As is usually the case in Iroquois ritualism, not all speakers list exactly the same items or matters in exactly the same order, nor does each speaker deliver precisely the same address each time he speaks it. Nevertheless, the same general form is evident in all such addresses.

With one or two exceptions, each "word" or section of the Requickening Address describes first a particular hurt that has arisen as a result of the grief occasioned by the loss through death. Next mention is made that this hurt is affecting those present, and then that this hurt is now either removed or healed and the person or situation restored to its former condition. (Hewitt 1927:241). Then, giving a wampum string (some such strings are two or three strings tied together) to those addressed, the speaker says that the "word" (the attesting wampum) is on its way to them.

In the Requickening Address as customarily delivered on the Six Nations Reserve, 15 such "matters" or "words" are so discussed. With the exception of the last three sections, the order is generally the same. This order phrased in terms of intent of each word and a name commonly given to the accompanying wampum string (fig. 12) is:

1. To wipe away the tears (wampum string called "the Tears" or "the Eyes").
2. To remove obstructions from the ears ("the Ears").
3. To remove obstructions from the throat ("the Throat").
4. To restore the disarranged organs of the body and remove the yellow spots from inside it ("Within his Breast").
5. To wipe the bloodstains from the mat ("the Bloody Husk Mat Bed").
6. To dispel the darkness and cause it to be day ("the Darkness of Grief").
7. To cause the sky to be beautiful ("the Loss of the Sky").
8. To replace the sun in the sky ("the Loss of the Sun").
9. To level the earth over the grave ("the Grave Cover").
10. To bind the bones together by the 20 strings of wampum given for murder ("the Twenty Matters" or "Twenty is the Penalty for Homicide"). Sometimes this is called the "inserted matter"; it is omitted in the address when given at the Tenth-day feast for a deceased chief. In the Condolence ceremony (at least ideally), the wampum string that accompanies this message is not returned by the bereaved side but is kept by them until the next Condolence ceremony. If, however, in the next Condolence ceremony the same side is the bereaved moiety, it is returned to the clear-minded so it can be handed to the mourners, who again keep the string (Fenton 1946a:120–122; Shimony 1961:120–122).
11. To gather together the scattered firebrands and rekindle the fire ("the Council Fire").
12. To raise up the minds of women and warriors and cheer them ("the Creator's Assistants—Matron and Warrior").
13. To dispel the insanity caused by grief ("Anything can Happen on Earth, Even Insanity").
14. To restore to its place the torch that has been carried through the Longhouse of the Confederacy by the person notifying them of the death ("the Torch").
15. To restore the chief by raising him up and again name him ("the Federal Chief").

The traditional Requickening Address of the New York Onondaga is slightly different and consists of seven sections, each of which is accompanied by a bunch of wampum, that is, three strings of wampum attached at one end. Nevertheless, the topics mentioned are much the same as those in the Six Nations version.

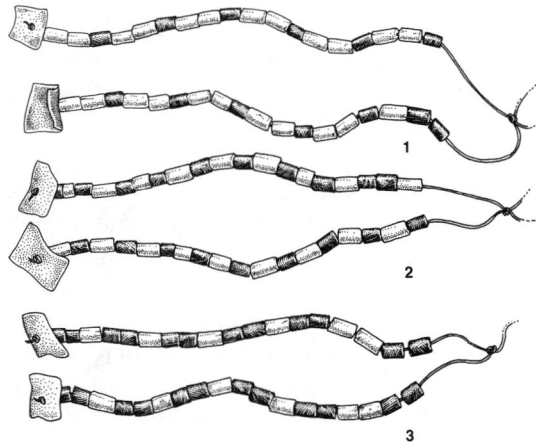

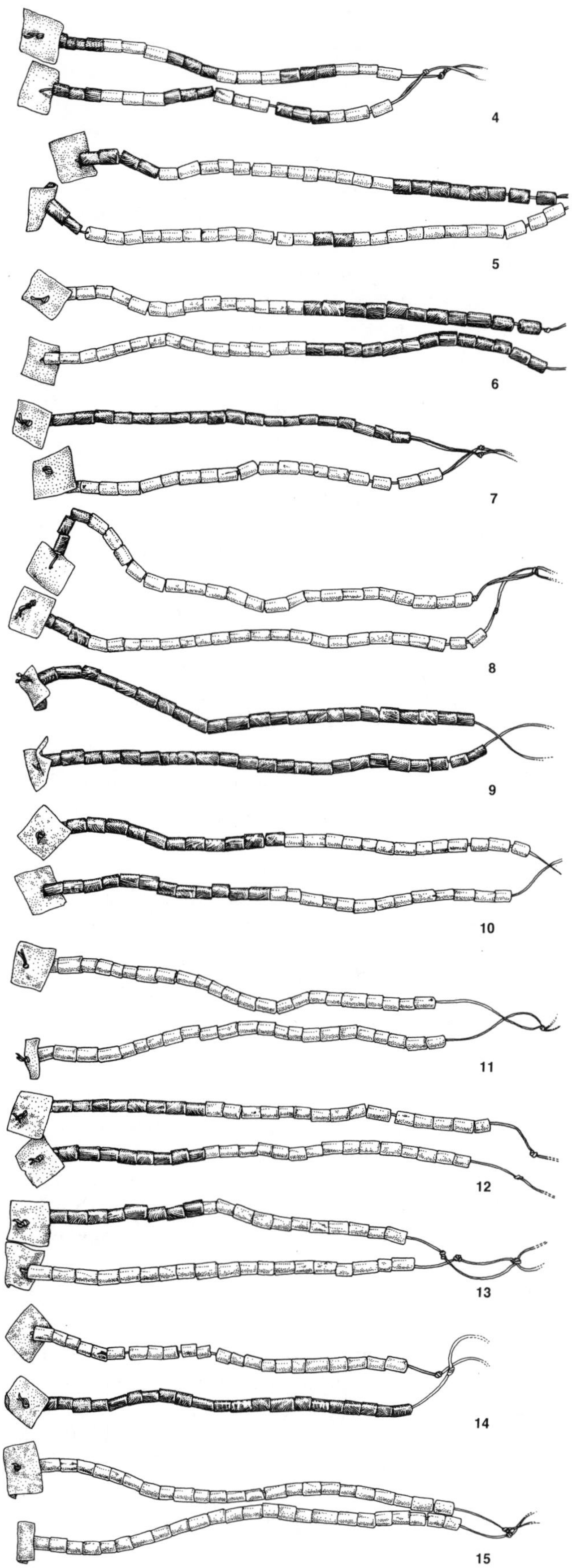

Dept. of Anthr., Smithsonian: 391949.

Fig. 12. Wampum strings representing the 15 matters of the Requickening Address at the Condolence ceremony used for installing chiefs at the Six Nations Reserve. In this set, numbers 13 and 15 are interchanged from the normal order. These strings are models restrung by J.N.B. Hewitt with beads and information he collected about 1926–1929 (see Hewitt and Fenton 1944; Shimony 1961:256–260). Length of 4 from leather square to knot 12.5 cm, rest same scale.

It is the responsibility of the Older Brothers (Mohawks, Onondagas, and Senecas) to condole the Younger Brothers (Oneidas, Cayugas, and Tuscaroras) on the loss of one of their chiefs and conversely for the Younger Brothers to condole the Older Brothers for the loss of one of theirs. Thus, in the Condolence ceremony the tribes are grouped into two sides, the bereaved side and the clear-minded side. It is the obligation of the clear-minded tribes to condole the mourners, the bereaved side, and this obligation is evident throughout the Condolence ceremony. The ceremony itself is held in the Longhouse of the mourning nation or one lent to it for the occasion. For example, the New York Onondagas may lend the use of their Longhouse to the New York Oneidas and the Tonawanda Senecas theirs to the Tuscaroras who have none of their own. Somewhat similarly a man who knows the ritual may be lent to the other side to perform it for them if no man can be found on that side to do it.

Although the major part of the Condolence ceremony takes place in the Longhouse, it begins with a preliminary rite of greeting called "At the Woods' Edge" at a fire kindled a short distance away. The clear-minded tribes meet a little distance beyond and send notice of their approach to the bereaved tribes gathered at the fire. They then march toward the fire, one of the men at the head of the line chanting the Roll Call of the Chiefs, punctuated with the responses of *hai, hai*. When they reach the small fire, they stop and a speaker for the bereaved side gathered there greets them in the ancient fashion (similar greetings addressed to visiting tribes are recorded in the early documents), giving thanks that they have arrived safely and that none has perished on the way. At Six Nations, there follows a brief rite of condolence: mention is made that the forefathers made the rule that on such occasions they were to kindle a fire at the edge of the woods and condole each other in a few words, and the first three words of the Requickening Address, "the Three Bare Words of Requickening" are recited, each accompanied by wampum. (It is reported that at Onondaga the invitation wampum is returned.) Then the mourning side, as they are the hosts, leads the way to the Longhouse. The visitors, the clear-minded side, follow, and the Roll Call of the Chiefs is picked up again and chanted on the way. Inside the Longhouse, each party takes its proper end.

When the man who has been chanting the Roll Call reaches the door of the Longhouse, he stops. The ceremony in the Longhouse begins with a recitation of the Roll Call by another man who begins at the beginning and, walking to and fro in the middle in the Longhouse, continues through the 50 names of the founders of the League. After this rite has been concluded, the blankets that have been hung on a rope or wire are pulled across the middle of the Longhouse separating the two sides, and the clear-minded side sings the mournful verses of the Condoling song, the last verse of which may be sung in conjunction with the Laws of the League, the next rite to be performed. If so, if the curtain has been drawn back, it is drawn again to separate the two sides while they sing the last verse.

After the "Laws of the Confederacy" have been recounted, a speaker for the clear-minded side delivers the Requickening Address (at Six Nations, the remaining 12 matters of the address). At the conclusion of each section, a string of wampum (the strings of condolence wampum have been hung over a stick or cane) is passed to the mourning side. After all the matters of the address have been so delivered, the curtains are drawn across the Longhouse again and the bereaved side sings all the verses of the Condoling Song. Then the curtains are drawn back for the last time and a speaker for the bereaved side reciting the Requickening Address returns at the end of each section the wampum that earlier had been passed to his side. He concludes with the statement, "Show me the man," that is, show us the man who is to take the name of the deceased chief. This is done, and any other men who are to take the place of deceased chiefs are similarly presented. (The expense of the Condolence ceremony is great, and it is often postponed for several years and several vacant positions filled at one ceremony.) After all the new chiefs have been named, they are addressed on their responsibilities. This done, the feast is served to all present. By Iroquois custom, each ceremony has its appropriate feast food, that for the condolence ceremony being meat and bread and usually also a corn soup. After all have eaten, the remainder of the evening is devoted to social dances.

Thus is the founding council of the League kept up, and the principles established by these chiefs perpetuated and kept before the people. In the four centuries or more since the founders of the League met to establish the Great Peace and agree to the form of governance for the Confederacy, the Iroquois successfully contested for a place in the fur trade that came to dominate affairs in the Northeast, became a military power all in the region—White and Indian—feared and courted, were scattered by forces over which they had little control, and yet continue to live "a nation within a nation" in the region where they achieved success, suffered defeat, and sometimes merely groped to find the least painful course through the troubles that confronted them. In this long history, the Confederacy, built on foundations of familiar custom and constructed along a plan agreeable to them, served the Iroquois as well as it poorly served the hopes of others, who, frustrated by its actions, often found its organization and those governed by it incomprehensible. Yet the League of the Iroquois still exists, a reminder of how diverse are the solutions people have found for human problems.

Sources

Morgan's (1901) classic work remains the best single description of the structure of the League. Subsequent work, including that done by Hale, Beauchamp, Hewitt, and Fenton, has described in greater detail particular aspects of the organization of the League but has not provided a better general description than Morgan's.

A number of English translations of the Iroquois traditions that recount the founding of the League and summaries of these traditions have been published. One of the first of these to appear was Dunlap's (1839–1840, 1:29–30) summary of the traditional account as Ephraim Webster had told it to him in 1815. In 1845 Clark obtained a version, or at least some incidents of the epic (Hale 1883a:180–183), from Captain Frost and Abram La Fort, the two most learned New York Onondaga chiefs of the time. Clark published this version first in the *New York Commercial Advertiser* and later in 1849 (1849, 1:21–30). Schoolcraft (1847:271–283) also published this version and a summary of it (1851–1857, 3:314–317).

Hale (1882:327–341, 1883a:19–38) summarized the information on the founding of the League he had obtained from the New York Onondaga and from Iroquois living on the Six Nations Reserve. Hewitt (1892) published the English translation of an Onondaga text given to him in 1888 by John Buck, record keeper of the Six Nations Reserve, and Henning (1898) published an account he had heard from Daniel La Fort, son of Abram La Fort and one of Hale's (1883a:22) sources. Parker (1916a:114–118) published a fragment of the epic as told by the New York Onondaga, Baptist Thomas, as he had heard it from Thomas Commissary. Brant-Sero (1901:166–167), a Mohawk Indian, published an incident relating to Deganawida (the Mohawk versions are apt to describe the activities of Deganawida; the Onondaga

440

TOOKER

versions, the activities of Hiawatha). Two early nineteenth-century summary accounts of the founding of the League, one probably Mohawk (Boyce 1973a:288-289) and the other Onondaga (J. Norton 1970:98-105), have been published.

In the 1880s Seth Newhouse, an Onondaga living on the Six Nations Reserve who spoke Mohawk fluently, prepared a manuscript on the origin of the League (Parker 1916a:14-60). Newhouse attempted to get the Council of Chiefs at Six Nations to accept his draft, but they rejected it and appointed a comittee of chiefs to draw up another document. This was ready in 1900 (Scott 1912; Parker 1916a:61-113). Later, John A. Gibson, the most learned member of the chiefs' committee, dictated a long version in Onondaga. These three versions of the epic of the founding of the League have been more fully discussed by Fenton (1949a, 1975:134-135, in Parker 1968:38-46).

The Roll Call of the Chiefs (Morgan 1901, 1:60-61; Hale 1883a; Chadwick 1897:86-95; Scott 1912:241-245; Parker 1916a:92-97; Hewitt and Fenton 1945; Shimony 1961:58, 101-117) is given the best introduction by Fenton (1950). The rites of "At the Woods' Edge" and "Laws of the Confederacy" have been translated (Hale 1883a:117-129; Scott 1912:239-241), as has the Condoling Song (Hale 1883a:62-64, 123, 149-150; Scott 1912:239). The Six Nations form of the Requickening Address is given in a number of sources (Hewitt 1916, 1927; Hewitt and Fenton 1944, 1945:314-315; Shimony 1961:257-259; Scott 1912:234-236; Parker 1916a: 110-113). A New York Onondaga version, originally written down in Onondaga by Abram La Fort and subsequently copied by Daniel La Fort, was later translated by Daniel La Fort and Albert Cusick; both the Onondaga text and English translation appear under the somewhat misleading title, "The Book of the Younger Nations" (Hale 1883a:45-47, 140-145). The use of wampum in this address has been described by Beauchamp (1901:452-454).

Published accounts of particular Condolence ceremonies include Fenton's (1946a) description of the Condolence ceremony held in November 1945 at the Lower Cayuga Longhouse on the Six Nations Reserve and Hale's (1895) description of that held in the Onondaga Longhouse on that reserve, Beauchamp's (1895) of a Condolence ceremony held at the Onondaga Longhouse in New York State, and that (Beauchamp 1891a:39-40; cf. Beauchamp 1892:145-146) at Tuscarora in 1889.

Beauchamp (1905) has reviewed various events in Iroquois history. A readable and still useful account of the seventeenth- and eighteenth-century history of the Northeast, including that of particular Iroquois tribes, is contained in the various volumes of Parkman's (1851, 1865, 1867, 1869, 1874, 1883, 1884, 1892) classic work. Other general histories of the period include those by Leach (1966) and by Eccles (1969, 1972), who has also discussed in more detail events in the latter part of the seventeenth century (Eccles 1959, 1964). The history of the Iroquois-European relations in the seventeenth century has been described by Trelease (1960) and the various Iroquois alliances by Wallace (1957). Shea (1855) has provided a summary of Catholic missionary work in the region including that among the Iroquois. McIlwain's introduction to Wraxall (1915) is still a useful perspective on the fur trade although Trelease (1962) has offered some corrective to McIlwain's interpretation. Hunt's (1940) somewhat overwritten description discusses the influence of the fur trade on Iroquois policy to 1684, and Norton (1974) examines the Iroquois fur trade from 1686 to 1776. Iroquois relationships with the Pennsylvania traders and the Indians of Pennsylvania and Ohio in the eighteenth century are discussed in Buck and Buck (1939), Downes (1940), and Hanna (1911). Peckham (1964) has described the wars between France and England for the period 1689-1762 as has Hamilton (1962). The role of the Iroquois in the American Revolution is described in Graymont (1972).

Origins of the Longhouse Religion

ANTHONY F.C. WALLACE

The Longhouse religion began in 1799 as an episode of religious enthusiasm among the several hundred Seneca Indians living on and near the Allegany Reservation in southwestern New York State. It was based on the revelations of the prophet Handsome Lake. Before the prophet's death in 1815 his gospel had spread to several other Iroquois reserves in the United States and Canada (see Deardorff 1951; Wallace 1969). By at least 1850, and perhaps as early as the mid-1820s, his message had been codified and a religious organization formed to promulgate it as a religion. The "church," and the system of religious belief and ritual associated with it, have survived among the Iroquois into the latter half of the twentieth century as a non-Christian alternative to the several Protestant and Catholic denominations that have established themselves on the reservations and as a forum for the continued assertion of the integrity of an Iroquois ethnic identity.

The circumstances that led to the founding of this religion and account for its particular character go back into the middle of the eighteenth century. Before the ending of the French and Indian War (Seven Years' War) in 1763, the Iroquois tribes had enjoyed two generations of relative peace and tranquillity. During this time, their political institutions, their material comforts, and their self-esteem were constantly augmented by the advantages accruing from their strategic location between the centers of British and French colonial power. They were able to play off these two imperial contenders against each other, maintaining a balance of power by threatening each side that if they were dissatisfied, they would join the other. Iroquois neutrality, and the threat of its abandonment, thus became a lever by which Iroquois diplomats at the endless round of treaties were able to extort courteous treatment, promises of territorial integrity, large quantities of "presents" (which included guns, powder, lead, traps, cloth, kettles, knives, axes, awls, food and drink, and body ornaments), and favorable credit for Indian fur-trade hunters. They were also able to use their alliance with the imperial powers as an argument to induce Indian tribes on their periphery to come under the shelter of their own confederacy; and this, too, the Europeans paid the Iroquois to do, for it simplified their own Indian diplomacy to have to deal only with the Iroquois.

The Iroquois thus between about 1701 and 1763 did not suffer directly from imperial domination. Rather, they profited temporarily. During this period many of their villages grew to be substantial towns, containing two-story log houses with stairs, paneled doors, and glass-paned windows; defended by cannon and by warriors wielding not muskets but rifles; and surrounded by vast and well-kept orchards and cornfields. Iroquois hunters could range in relative safety throughout the Ohio Valley and along the Great Lakes in search of peltries. Iroquois diplomats were received with respect at the capitals of a half-dozen colonies and provinces.

The traditional religious system also was well calculated to provide both cognitive assurance and emotional support. An annual round of communal ceremonies, basically expressing thanks to the pantheon, was performed on the occasion of various significant events in the seasonal food cycle (see particularly Fenton 1936; Tooker 1970a; Chafe 1961). Another system of rituals, directed at the individual rather than the group, sought to anticipate or cure disease by the satisfaction of dream wishes and by the ministrations of the "secret" medicine societies like the Society of Faces (Fenton 1941a). Shamans diagnosed the sources of illness, whether from the neglect of dream wishes, or from the malevolence of witchcraft (Wallace 1969). The rituals of mourning—and particularly the Condolence ceremony performed whenever a confederate chief died—sought to assuage the disabling effects of grief and to preclude the blood feud, born of the deep-seated resentments and witchcraft suspicions of bereavement (Fenton 1946). In general, these therapeutic rituals tended to elicit the acting out, or conscious fantasizing, of repressed desires of a passive or dependent nature, but in such a cautious fashion and in such ritually insulated circumstances as to disturb only minimally the smooth and harmonious course of ordinary social life.

Iroquois Catastrophe, 1763–1797

The equilibrium of this cultural system was destroyed by a series of military, political, and economic disasters that befell the Iroquois after 1763. With the victory of the British in the war with France, the Iroquois found themselves outflanked, no longer able to play off the British and the French against each other, and surrounded by a circle of British forts. Their abortive effort to break this ring of steel by instigating and participating in the so-called conspiracy of Pontiac was followed by a radical decline in their fortunes. The credit extended to their hunters was reduced. Fewer presents were given. They were persuaded at Fort Stanwix in 1768 to sell their interest in the lands west of the Allegheny Mountains and south of the Ohio, an act that virtually destroyed their influence over the western Indians, including the Shawnee, Delaware, and Wyandot peoples living in the Ohio Valley. This left them unable to exert a strong enough influence to stop frontier struggles such as Lord Dunmore's War. But probably the daily round of activity in the villages was not greatly changed by all this, except for a somewhat lowered material affluence and for the more prolonged visits with their families of disgruntled hunters and diplomats.

With the outbreak of the American Revolution in 1775, it appeared for a time as if the old play-off system could be reestablished. The neutral Iroquois could deal between the British in Canada and the Americans in the lower colonies as they had earlier between the French in Canada and the British to the south. But the early efforts at neutrality foundered in a succession of outrageous incidents between various Iroquois groups and the relatively inexperienced and undisciplined Americans, and by 1777 the bulk of the Iroquois warriors had committed themselves to the side of their old allies the British. Although their war parties brought devastation to the American frontiers, from the Mohawk River south to Pittsburgh, their own heartland was devastated by the John Sullivan expedition in 1778, which in a three-pronged offensive managed to burn the houses and the crops in almost every major Iroquois town. Many of the women and children, and the surviving warriors, took refuge at Fort Niagara with the British, who housed them in a refugee camp, inadequately clothed, inadequately fed, inadequately sheltered, and swept by disease. By the end of the war, despite their military successes, the Iroquois population had been cut approximately in half (see Graymont 1972).

The aftermath of war, from 1783 to 1797, saw the Iroquois deprived of their land and of their diplomatic and military power, brought under the effective sovereignty of the United States, and confined to a few small reservations in the United States and Canada. This decade and one-half of abrupt decline began with the second treaty of Fort Stanwix in 1784, where Iroquois delegates were subjected to insult and physical abuse and were forced to sign treaties by which they alienated the rest of their lands in western Pennsylvania and Ohio and to make peace with the United States as individual tribes rather than as a confederacy. Thereafter various Iroquois representatives proceeded to sell, in a series of major land cessions immediately after the war, their remaining territories in the state of New York, leaving themselves only a series of relatively small reservations lying about the sites of existing villages. At the last of these major transactions, the Treaty of Big Tree in 1797, the Seneca alienated the bulk of their holdings in western New York. Everything west of the Genesee River was sold for $100,000; this sum was to be invested at 6 percent interest to pay an annuity to each of the Seneca tribal members individually. The Seneca retained 11 reservations, ranging in size from the 129 square miles of Buffalo Creek, down to a string of two-square-mile reserves along the Genesee, and one square mile at Cuba Lake (see Royce 1899).

The group with which the future prophet Handsome Lake was affiliated, the so-called Allegany band, retained a ribbon of land, 42 square miles in all, along both sides of the Allegheny River up from the New York State–Pennsylvania line (much of which is now under the waters behind Kinzua Dam). Just below lay the privately owned "Cornplanter grant," also occupied by members of the Allegany band, which the local chief named Cornplanter (a half-brother of Handsome Lake) had been given by the Commonwealth of Pennsylvania as a reward for his exertions on behalf of the state during earlier treaties.

In the meantime, while the land in New York State was being lost, the erstwhile allies and dependents of the Iroquois confederacy living in the Ohio Valley were under severe pressure. A series of land-cession treaties was extorted from the Shawnee, Delaware, Mingo (displaced Iroquoians), and other western Indians, culminating in the treaty of Fort Harmar in 1789 (where Cornplanter earned his grant). Like the Iroquois, the western Indians denied the legality of these treaties and repudiated them, claiming that they were made by unauthorized persons. Unlike the Iroquois, however, the western Indians were in a mood to fight, and when Whites attempted to settle the purchased lands in Ohio they were met with force. A protracted and bloody Indian war followed, in the course of which the small remaining army of the United States was badly mauled. During the fighting, the Iroquois stood uncomfortably to one side. Some of them attempted to act as mediators and peacemakers and thereby earned the vociferous contempt of the western Indians. Some issued loud promises of military aid to their allies and loud threats against the Americans; but all they did was talk. Nor did the British move out from their forts to aid the Indians whom they were instigating to fight. Eventually the western Indians were crushed by forces under Gen. Anthony Wayne at the Battle of Fallen Timbers in 1794. There followed the Treaty of Canandaigua, which regularized the relationship between the United States and the Iroquois. Next year the Treaty of Greenville established peace between the United States and the warring Indians, drew boundary lines (including substantial cessions of Ohio land), and established the legal charter of the reservation system, by placing the Indians in a fiduciary relationship with the United States.

The effect of these transactions on Iroquois morale was extremely destructive. The sequence of land cessions in which Iroquois chiefs and representatives were involved, from Fort Stanwix in 1784 to Big Tree in 1797, established a pattern of popular distrust of the political institutions of Iroquois society. Chiefs by one means or another, including the use of alcohol, threats of bodily harm, and prolonged verbal harassment, were persuaded to sign away the tribal lands for pittances in return to the tribe. In the process many of these same chiefs acquired grants of land as personal property, private annuities hundreds of times as large as the common Indians secured, and other personal advantages.

It is too easy to interpret all this as mere corruption on both sides. The White officials and entrepreneurs were at least recognizing the principle of aboriginal title and were probably treating Indians no worse than they treated one another. The Indians who drank too heavily and took bribes were dealing with Whites who drank heavily and who took bribes themselves. Furthermore, accepting a handsome payoff for being publicly cooperative in a losing situation was almost the only way in which a political leader could secure enough cash and land to maintain his own people. Cornplanter, at least (when sane and sober), made his land available to his fellow members of the Allegany band and used his own cash income for purposes such as paying fines and bail for jailed Indians in Pittsburgh. In a community that had no system of cash taxation (even after cash annuities were given), the private cash income of political leaders was the only reliable source of money for certain indispensable transactions with the Whites. Nonetheless, the common tribal members were apt to feel jealousy and betrayal.

A further consequence of the land transactions, and of the miserable posture of the Iroquois during the war for the Northwest Territory, was an exacerbation of factionalism. The Mohawks, most of the Cayuga, and some from the other tribes refused to live in the United States. Led by Joseph Brant, many of them removed to a reservation at Grand River set aside for them in Ontario by the Crown; their descendants have remained there. This act split the confederacy in half. Among those remaining in New York, further factional divisions arose over issues such as the war in the west and relationships with White Americans generally.

The deep disunity revealed by the emergence of these factions was a source of anxiety for many, for no effective leadership existed beyond the individual village that could assert and carry through a policy on behalf of a whole tribe or of the League of the Iroquois itself. Beset by assaults on every side, there was no one chief nor any council of chiefs to whom an Iroquois individual could look with confidence to unite the nation or devise more than local, opportunistic responses to general problems.

Reservation Beginnings, 1797–1799

For the Seneca, the reservation period began in 1797 with the sale of their lands at the Treaty of Big Tree. For them, unlike many other Indian groups, the reservations were what the term literally implied—lands reserved by the Indians from a cession of land and intended for their own use and occupancy. Generally such reservations included an already existing settlement and some surrounding area deemed minimally adequate to supply the subsistence needs of the local population living by traditional custom.

The reservations thus, for them, were not intended to be legal ghettoes from which Indians could not step foot. The intention was more the reverse: to provide a minimal base of land to which the Indians had unquestioned title, which could not be alienated except by sale, and from which the Indian occupants could exclude any Whites whom they considered to be unacceptable, whether they were whiskey sellers, overardent missionaries, or local ne'er-do-wells. At this period, when the nearby White settlements were small and few, Indians felt free to hunt as before over nearby grounds, to make sugar at favorite maple groves off the reserve, and to travel freely to Warren, Pittsburgh, and other market towns to sell peltries and purchase goods. They moved back and forth among the reservations without hindrance. Whites were not prevented from traveling through the reservations by water or trail on their way to other locations. White men or women married to Indian spouses were welcome and various Whites were hired (for instance, by Cornplanter at Allegany) to operate locally useful enterprises on the reserves such as blacksmith shops and grist and saw mills; others were allowed to use reservation land for farming, on a rental or crop-sharing basis. Indians in turn were able to secure some employment among White settlers as occasional laborers and no doubt some peddled the products of Indian woodcraft, such as bowls, brooms, butter spoons, and splint baskets.

The legal status of the reservations remained, therefore, somewhat vague as to matters such as local taxation or the extension of the civil or criminal jurisdiction of state and local courts over matters internal to the reserve. The system was essentially a federally sanctioned one. Federal Indian agents at various locations were available to the Indians for the registry of complaints and requests for aid. These men also handled the payment of annuities. They served as a communications link between the reservation group and the secretary of war, in whose department their affairs were handled. Each reserve functioned as an independent community, as before, with its own chief's council. Such tribal cohesion as might be required was developed at occasional ad hoc meetings of the chiefs from the various local councils, and the federal establishment made no effort to prevent this.

The federal policy was a vaguely benevolent one that grew out of the prevailing optimistic philosophy of the

Federalist government. In this official view, the Indians were as capable of civilization as any other people and could be expected to scale the ladder of progress just as the ancestors of the Whites had. It was something of a moral duty to aid the Indians along the path to civilization by educating them. But coercive methods were not to be applied. Thus, there was no effort to force conversion to Christianity, there was no intrusion of local law with respect to the formalities of marriage or the legitimacy of offspring, there was no garrison placed on the reserves to detect or punish crime as defined by Whites. Congress merely passed legislation establishing a small fund to support efforts to civilize the Indian natives.

For the Allegany Seneca and other New York State Iroquois, the actual effort to introduce civilization was made by Quakers from the Philadelphia area. They were motivated in part by their own benevolent tradition toward the Indians, which then was over 100 years old, as well as by the public intent as expressed in federal statutes and administration. In 1798 a Quaker mission was established among the Allegany band that commenced a century-long effort to help the Indians civilize themselves. The aim was not evangelical, for the Society of Friends was quite willing to accept the theological validity of non-Christian religious experience. Rather, they concentrated on very practical goals: to teach at least some of the youngsters to read and write in English and to do arithmetic; to teach men and women the arts and crafts of the successful up-to-date farm family; to make available, by gift or purchase, the necessary tools and equipment. They also laced their practical instruction with moral advice, attempting to persuade them to be sober, clean, punctual, industrious, and so on—in a word, to take up the Protestant ethic without, necessarily, becoming Protestants.

This official policy of benevolent laissez-faire, with educational opportunity available to a few of the reserves and relatively innocuous, if irritating, evangelistic missionaries on others, such as Buffalo Creek and Cattaraugus, sounds admirable in comparison with the barbaric acculturation policies of other times and places. But the reservations were not healthy communities by either White or Indian standards. They suffered from a combination of disadvantages that led to a rapid deterioration of morale and even of material welfare. Within a few years they were slums in the wilderness, displaying unacceptably high levels of drunkenness, of fighting and brawling, of instability of households, and of witchcraft accusation.

The disadvantages arose, in part, out of a fundamental incompatibility between Iroquois social structure and reservation life. Iroquois social structure was adapted to a situation in which males ranged widely on hunting, war, and diplomatic missions and females managed the villages and agriculture. While Indians could and did hunt off the reserve, the old days of grand-scale hunting and trading across half a continent were gone. No more war parties could go out except as auxiliaries of the U.S. Army. And diplomacy was reduced to annual conferences with the local Indian agent. The men, in effect, had been rendered politically powerless and now were jammed in what was for them—but not for many Whites—an intolerably crowded situation, where antipathies between men silently grew into deadly feuds and where sexual jealousies easily forced couples to separate. Although there was enough land for the women to farm as before by traditional methods, the men were left virtually unemployed much of the year.

To reduce the added pain and anxiety produced by these circumstances, the traditional religious rituals by themselves were inadequate. They were designed to provide cathartic relief to the stoic and self-deprived good hunter and to the bereaved kinsman, all expressed in a posture of thankfulness to and solidarity with the pantheon. But the ritual indulgence of dependency wishes, of aggressive fantasies, and of alcoholic cravings was not helpful in a situation where there was already, because of the constraints of the reservation system, too much dependency, too much hostility, too much drunkenness.

The New Religion, 1799–1815

In the spring of 1799, most of the members of the Allegany band were living in the old village on the Cornplanter grant. Three young Quaker missionaries were also in residence. Cornplanter's half-brother, a League chief named Handsome Lake, lived in Cornplanter's house. The spring had been a difficult one, marred by drunken brawls, accusations of witchcraft, and finally the public execution of a witch who was believed to be responsible for the death of a niece of Cornplanter and Handsome Lake. Handsome Lake himself was bedridden, reputedly at least as a consequence of prolonged alcoholic excess.

One morning in June, Handsome Lake collapsed at the door of the cabin, in the presence of his daughter; she summoned aid from his nephew, Blacksnake (who later dictated an account of the event). He appeared to have died, but actually he was in a trance state and was experiencing the first of a series of visions in which messengers of the Creator instructed him in his own and his people's religious obligations. In this first vision, three "angels" appeared, dressed in old-time Indian garb, and told him that he must give up alcohol, on pain of death, and so also must all the Indians (fig. 1). They warned that witches were corrupting the tribe and must be stopped; guilty persons must repent and confess. Handsome Lake was instructed to tell these things to the people and to make sure that the traditional Strawberry festival was held, that year and always (see Parker 1913, 1968).

Handsome Lake described his vision in council; it was also translated for the benefit of the Quaker schoolmas-

Fig. 1. *From the Story of Handsome Lake,* pastel drawing by Andrew W. Lewis, Iroquois, perhaps about 1920. Depiction of Handsome Lake and the three messengers from the Creator who appeared in his first vision (at right), and Handsome Lake emerging after the vision (at left)—based on descriptions of these events recited in the Code of the Longhouse religion. Original in the possession of a family affiliated with the Seneca Longhouse, Six Nations Reserve, Ont. Photograph by William C. Sturtevant, Oct. 19, 1962.

ter, who wrote it down. A few weeks later, Handsome Lake had another vision in which he was taken on a journey through heaven and hell. On this journey he met George Washington, who got half-way to heaven, and a disillusioned Jesus, who complained that he had no followers. Through vignettes showing social types (like the drinker, the wife-beater) and their punishment or reward in the next world, a moral code was defined, outlawing drunkenness, witchcraft, sexual promiscuity, wife-beating, quarreling, and gambling. In a third vision in February of the following year, the prophet was instructed to advise his people that they must keep their traditional religious rituals, and particularly the Midwinter ceremony. All this advice was presented with an accompanying apocalyptic threat that if the Indians did not obey, the world would be destroyed by fire.

Handsome Lake's health improved noticeably and he began, in effect, to assume religious leadership of the community (fig. 2). He traveled to Washington to call

Fig. 2. Handsome Lake preaching, holding a short wampum belt. Drawn in 1905 by the Seneca artist Jesse J. Cornplanter, on the basis of tradition and the seating and behavior he had observed in longhouses.

446

upon President Thomas Jefferson to support and comply with his code and did in fact receive a benevolent response. He continued to receive revelations, whether by vision or through meditation; until his death in 1815 (fig. 3) he advised the people of their religious and moral duties. His later communications tended to focus more and more on social and cultural issues, such as problems of family structure, the relative importance of specific religious rituals, the proper policy toward acculturation, and whether Indians should participate in the War of 1812.

The early gospel of Handsome Lake thus can be seen as primarily directed to an apocalyptic theme: the imminent death of the prophet himself and the fiery destruction of the whole world, if the Indians did not give up alcohol, cease the practice of witchcraft (including love magic and abortion medicine), and return to the practice of the traditional ceremonies of the annual calendar. It was evidently a response to anxiety produced by the social disorganization in the village that centered around marital discord and brawling. The prophet blamed this on witches, who through use of their black arts turned husbands and wives away from each other and made women sterile and who through their role as purveyors of

Fig. 3. Handsome Lake's grave, beneath the floor of the Longhouse until the Longhouse was moved a few feet away, Onondaga Reservation, N.Y. (see also "Onondaga," fig. 3, this vol.). The marker was erected between 1901 and 1912; it reads "Ga-nyah-di-yoh, author of the present Indian religion, born at Ca-noh-wa-gus, Genesee Co. N.Y. 1735, died Aug. 10, 1815 at Onondaga Reservation." Photograph by William C. Sturtevant, Oct. 15, 1962.

whiskey turned men into brawling, destructive animals incapable of maintaining the ancient ideal of stoicism and solidarity.

For a time, the prophet was preoccupied with witch hunting. He demanded confessions of persons he suspected of witchcraft and some, at least, of those who refused to confess were killed (including some from other reserves). On one occasion he nearly precipitated a war with the Indians on a nearby reservation by denouncing one of their principal young men as a witch and demanding that he be punished. But gradually popular sentiment congealed against him on the witchcraft issue. He was accused of using it to remove political rivals, like Red Jacket, and in general of assuming a dictatorial stance not congenial to Iroquois taste. He himself came finally to the opinion that he had gone too far and virtually dropped the persecutory mode of handling suspected witches.

The formulation of a social gospel was a somewhat more gradual process because it involved the gradual realization of the consequences of taking certain initial positions. The prophet endorsed the Quaker mission and advised the Indians to follow its example by sending some children to school and by learning to plow and farm in the White man's manner. This simple position raised two salient cultural problems: the role of men in agriculture and the relative importance of the nuclear family household vis-à-vis the maternal lineage. Handsome Lake forthrightly recognized that Iroquois men and women alike had for a century or more resisted suggestions that the men take up the plow and become farmers, by arguing that horticulture was woman's work and for a man to farm would be effeminate. He also realized that the old system of easy and frequent divorce, often facilitated by the primacy of the maternal lineage, was functionally incompatible with the ideal model of the family farm. He went to some lengths to condemn behavior that was destructive to the family, such as philandering, gossip, and (specifically) the interference of the wife's mother in her daughter's domestic affairs.

The prophet also actively opposed any further alienation of Indian land. He sought to gain support of the president of the United States for his reform movement. But he bitterly resisted efforts by the War Department to recruit Iroquois warriors for service in the War of 1812 and thereby earned the sobriquet "The Peace Prophet" (in contradistinction to Tecumseh's brother who was known to some as "The War Prophet"). In general he took a position of favoring material acculturation and friendly accommodation with the Whites but of resisting any further encroachment on Indian lands, involvement of Indians in White men's wars, or loss of identity-preserving institutions such as the traditional system of religion.

In assessing the cultural origins of Handsome Lake's code, as he expressed it during his lifetime, it is apparent that it was a blend of several streams of cultural tradition amalgamated in a unique formula by his visionary experience. Explicit recognition of Christian theology is made in the code in his encounter with Jesus Christ, whom the prophet regarded as his counterpart among the Whites. The images of heaven and, most particularly, hell seem clearly to have been based on a Christian model. Inasmuch as the Seneca had been in contact with Christians, both Catholic and Protestant, for about 200 years by the time Handsome Lake had his visions, it is likely that the concept of a hell filled with the damned being tortured was widespread. It is not necessary to find some specific contact, such as the presence of the Quakers, to account for its presence in Handsome Lake's thinking. Nor need the Quakers be seen as the source of his concern about whiskey, for the Iroquois and their neighbors had been pleading with the colonial authorities for years—and in vain—to put an end to traffic that brought so much misery to their villages. And even his insistence on confession need not be seen as copied from Catholic or other Christian models, for the traditional means of ending a witch's power (and this was his chief preoccupation in the confession ritual) was to extort a confession from him. Thus in some ways one can see Christian influence as simply having reinforced analogous Indian custom.

Handsome Lake's emphasis on a high god, the Creator, differently named from the traditional Tharonhiawagon (whose statue was tumbled into the river soon after his mission began), may also have reflected a Christian model. But this is uncertain, for the Iroquois traditionally admitted into their system of ritual and belief new items revealed in dreams or visions. Thus Handsome Lake's high god may not have been intended to replace but merely to complement the earlier deity.

For the most part, Handsome Lake's religious views were regarded by his contemporaries as conservative. He was, in his own eyes, essentially attempting to restore and revitalize an existing system of beliefs and ceremonies that had been falling into disuse. He was calling people back to an ancient faith, with only so much innovative scaffolding as was necessary to justify his authority. He was not challenging the old pantheon, the old annual calendar, the old myths, the old dream rites; he was firmly endorsing them (except insofar as they had been contaminated by alcoholic practices or perverted to witchcraft). And he was thus claiming that the traditional religion was basically compatible with the practical social and technological reforms dictated by the new reservation-bound existence.

Nor were the Iroquois unaccustomed to receiving the impetus for religious and cultural change from divinely inspired prophets. The *Jesuit Relations* (JR) record the close attention the Iroquois paid to prophetic dreams; and there is reason to believe that even the Deganawida myth, telling of the founding of the great League of the Iroquois itself (which probably occurred only 380 years before) was based on the visions of a prophet named Hiawatha (Wallace 1958).

On a somewhat deeper level, perhaps, there was a subtle shift of emphasis, from a religion that relied on the therapeutic value of cathartic acting out of dream wishes to a religion that relied on the social value of confession and the repression of disruptive desires. But this shift—probably also functionally demanded by the reservation way of life—was more a matter of style and emphasis than of formal doctrine. And it probably lay beyond the prophet's own level of conscious awareness.

With respect to Handsome Lake's social gospel also, it would appear that he was at least as much an acute social critic of his own society as he was an imitator of White models (Wallace 1971). In traditional Iroquois social structure, the mother-daughter tie was in a formal sense the axial relationship around which other features of organization revolved, for it to a large extent determined genealogical reckoning, clan membership, nominations to League titles, agricultural schedules, and matters related to the blood feud (and thus to war and peace). This matrilineal nexus Handsome Lake directly attacked on the grounds that the special sympathy between mother and daughter rendered the nuclear family unstable; although he did not criticize the institution of the matrilineal clan, nor the privilege of clan matrons to nominate chiefs for consideration by the council, he undercut the moral authority of matriliny by condemning the interfering mother-in-law as the sinful, damnation-destined wrecker of many an Iroquois man's marriage. Inasmuch as the family farm, run by a stable cooperating married couple, with the man plowing and the woman doing other chores, was the backbone of the new economic system he and the Quakers advocated, mothers-in-law who poked fun at their daughters' husbands for working in the fields and who accused them of extramarital affairs were an obvious danger.

Conclusion

The rise of the Handsome Lake religion is in many ways typical of a large number of important Indian social and religious movements that sprang up, both before and

Fig. 4. Idealized portrait of Handsome Lake done by an unknown Seneca artist about 1920 and prominently displayed in the Newtown Longhouse, Cattaraugus Reservation. Shallow relief carving on thin wood, diameter about 60 cm. Photograph by William C. Sturtevant, June 27, 1957.

during the reservation period, in response to the pressures of alien political powers, of acculturation, and finally of the reservation system itself (see Wallace 1956, 1966). His was perhaps more successful than most because it was realistic in stressing accommodation with White society and the need for selective acculturation. At the very least, it can be said to have provided effective moral sanction for certain moral, technological, and social adaptations that the Iroquois had to make if they were to survive at all. More generally, it can be seen as having not only made possible the adoption of survival techniques but also enabled Iroquois people to do this in a time of crisis without losing contact with their past and without sacrificing their identity and self-respect as Indians. And to the present time, it has played an important part in the preservation of the Iroquois cultural heritage.

Iroquois Since 1820

ELISABETH TOOKER

By 1820, the various social, economic, and political consequences of the Iroquois defeat by the Americans in the Revolution were apparent. A number of Iroquois, including many of those who had been allies of the British during that war were living on reserves in Canada; others remained in their old homeland, which became part of the United States of America. The War of 1812 had confirmed the territory held by both the British Crown in Canada and the United States. In so doing, it confirmed that each government would continue to deal separately with the Iroquois living within its borders. The once powerful and independent Iroquois confederacy had become "nations within nations."

In the first two decades of the nineteenth century, the basic policies that were to guide the relations between the Iroquois and the governments of the United States and Canada were developed. There were two separate councils of Iroquois federal chiefs—one in the United States and one on the Six Nations Reserve in Canada. Each held a portion of the wampum of the League, and each had a parallel complement of chiefs. Each council usually acted independently of the other and was concerned not only with purely internal matters on the reservations but also with matters involving the respective governments of both countries.

By this time also, it had become even more apparent to the Iroquois than it had been that they would have to deal with Whites as neighbors and that they would have to change their economic base. Although such had been foreseen by a number of Iroquois including leaders such as Cornplanter and Handsome Lake in the first years of the nineteenth century, at that time there were few Whites in the area, and a number of Iroquois continued to follow their old way of life. The Iroquois in the United States had sold a considerable portion of the lands they once owned, but they had reserved for their own use some of the best land in the area. In western New York State, they still owned fertile lands along portions of the Allegheny and Genesee rivers and the Cattaraugus, Buffalo, and Tonawanda creeks. In Canada, the Iroquois had been given a large tract of land along the Grand River (fig. 1). In these places, the Iroquois could continue to raise their ancient crops—corn, beans, and squash. They could also continue to hunt in the surrounding forests. But as Whites came in increasing numbers to settle in the area and as they cleared more land for fields,

the game declined. The result was a decrease in Iroquois reliance on hunting in the first two decades of the nineteenth century. At the same time, the once-fertile soil probably had become less productive. In the preceding centuries, the Iroquois had moved their villages every 8, 10, or 25 years or so as the fields cleared near the villages became exhausted and as the firewood easily collected in the surrounding forests was depleted. Once the reservations had been established, such movement of village settlements was not possible. One result was the adoption of White agricultural techniques by increasing numbers of Iroquois, a process that had begun at the turn of the century. Although requiring more work than the older Indian methods, these methods (which included use of the plow) could produce more on the available land, and some Iroquois learned the rudiments of these techniques in the first decades of the nineteenth century.

In New York State, the annuities the Iroquois received for the sale of their land eased the transition from an economy based partly on hunting and partly on horticulture to one of intensive agriculture. The annuities paid not only for the work of gunsmiths and blacksmiths (essential services in the economy of both Whites and Indians at the time) and for provisions such as pork, beef, flour, salt, and rum, but also for the manufactured items the Iroquois previously had obtained through trade in furs. These included blankets and the various kinds of cloth, guns, powder, lead and flints, axes, hoes, shovels, knives, chisels, nails, needles, scissors, kettles, and sheet iron. In addition, the annuities bought the sundries—ribbons, vermillion, beads, thread, yarn, mirrors, spoons, plates, tobacco, paper, shawls, and silk handkerchiefs—that stores of the period customarily stocked. The annuities also provided the animals and implements needed to practice the plow agriculture being introduced on the reservations. This required an investment in draught animals, especially oxen (the animals most adapted to the work), to clear the fields and to pull plows and wagons, and an investment in plows and wagons themselves as well as other implements of farming. White farmers settling in the area customarily brought such equipment with them, but the Iroquois had no source of capital with which to buy it other than the annuities and gifts from Whites such as the Society of Friends.

As White settlers came in increasing numbers, so also did White missionaries. In the seventeenth century, the

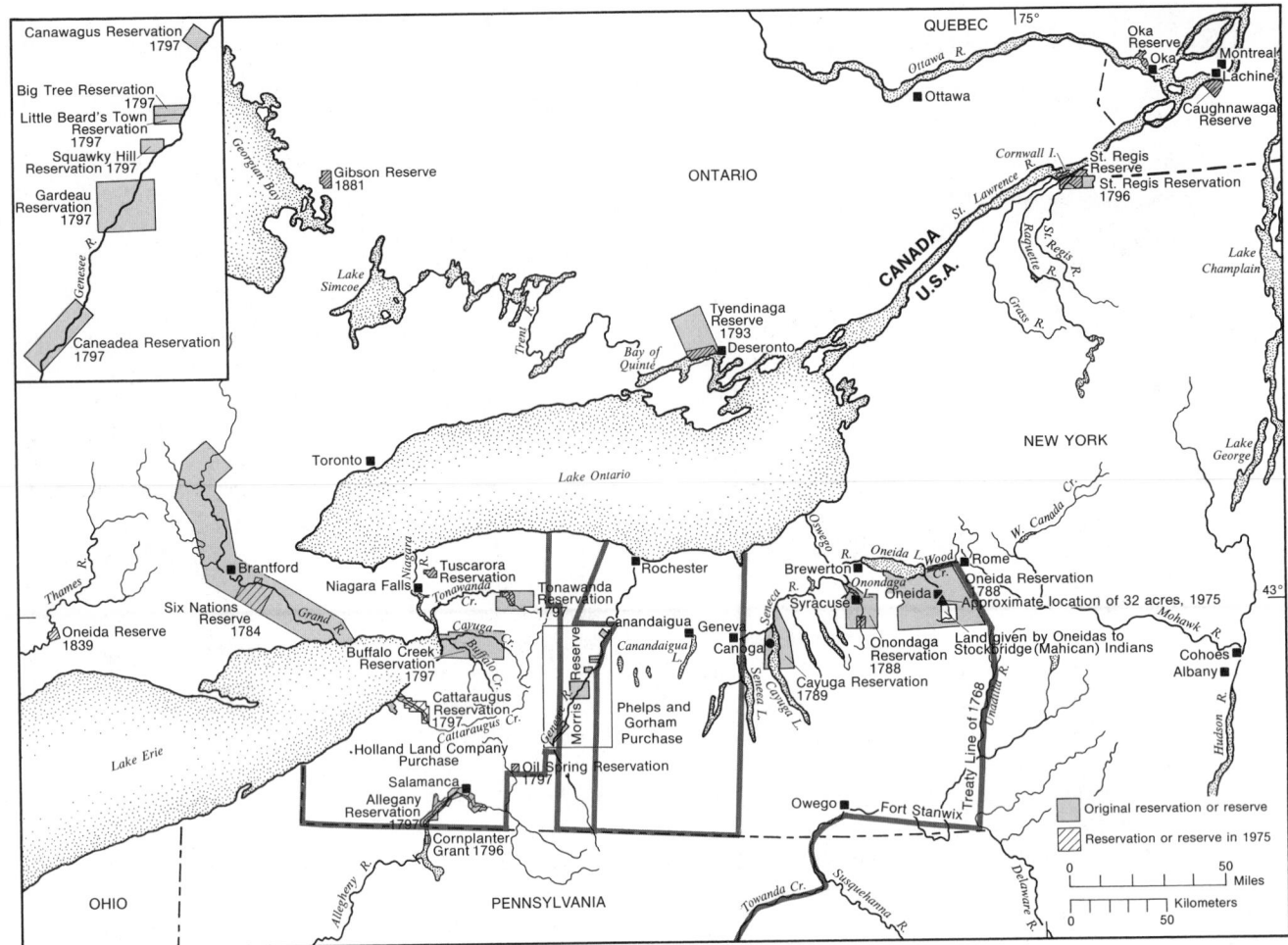

Fig. 1. Iroquois reservations and reserves (except those in Wis. and Okla.). Dates are given for those established after the American Revolution. Tyendinaga Reserve was established in 1783; tone shows it as it was enlarged in 1793. Tuscarora Reservation was established in 1797; tone shows area as enlarged in 1804.

French had made some converts to Christianity, especially among the Mohawk, and a number of these Iroquois had settled along the Saint Lawrence at Caughnawaga and Oka and later at Saint Regis. In the eighteenth century, a number of converts to Protestant forms of Christianity had been made among the Mohawks and Oneidas, but the more westerly Iroquois had proved less favorably disposed to such proselytizing. In the early years of the nineteenth century when the Iroquois were living peacefully on the reservations, missionary work increased and new mission stations, which often included a school (fig. 2), were established with the intent of converting the Indians to both Christianity and the White way of life. Still other Whites, notably the Society of Friends, continued to see an opportunity to be of service by pursuing a course of teaching White customs and technology without emphasizing White religious beliefs.

At the same time, the Iroquois also faced the threat of further loss of land. As the number of White settlers in the area grew, the encroachment of these settlers on reservation land increased, adding to the tension already existing between the Iroquois and Whites. In New York State, an act passed by the legislature prohibited Whites from living on the reservations, a ban that was at least partly successful (Houghton 1920:148). Similar encroachment occurred on the Grand River Reserve, and steps were taken to curtail it. However, there the matter was complicated by the policy advocated by Joseph Brant, the Mohawk leader of the reserve, to sell Indian land to White settlers in order that the Iroquois might learn White ways by their example (Johnston 1964:xlii-lxix).

Although the situations that the various, scattered groups of Iroquois faced in the nineteenth century were similar in many respects, each group had had somewhat different experiences. Important among these was previous contact with Whites. Those who had lived near the

Hirschl and Adler Galleries, New York.
Fig. 2. The Seneca Mission School House on the Buffalo Creek Reservation, as depicted in 1821 by Dennis Cusick, son of Nicholas Cusick the Tuscarora chief and interpreter. top, Pupils approach at the left while a boy shoots squirrels at the right; center, James Young's class with examples of the writing he taught; bottom, Mrs. James Young teaching carding, spinning, and knitting.

450

Seneca Mission School House

eastern door of the confederacy had had more intimate contact with Whites than those of the western end. One result was a difference in the issues espoused by the "conservative" and "progressive" factions on each reservation, a difference that persisted in the 1970s. Thus, on the Seneca and Onondaga reservations in New York and on the Six Nations Reserve in Canada, those who are labeled "traditionalists" or "conservatives" tend to be followers of the old Iroquois religion. On some other reservations—the Ontario Oneida Reserve and the Mohawk Caughnawaga and Saint Regis reserves—the religion of the Longhouse did not figure in political discussions until the twentieth century when the then-current form was introduced to them. On yet other reserves it has been unimportant.

The Code of Handsome Lake

As Protestant missionary activity increased in the years immediately following the death of Handsome Lake in 1815, the question of what religion the Iroquois should follow became a matter of some concern, particularly among the western Iroquois who had had relatively little previous acquaintance with Christianity. In 1818, it became a major issue. A number of Iroquois attending the regular spring council meeting (which at that time was customarily held on the Buffalo Creek Reservation, then the largest and most important of the New York State reservations) decided to hold another council a month later at Tonawanda to discuss the matter of religion. Representatives of the Iroquois living in Canada as well as representatives from the various reservations in the United States came to this council, which lasted 12 days. At its conclusion, the decision was made to hold yet another council about two months later for further discussion.

Although the published accounts of these meetings (Hyde 1903:257-268; Alden 1827:50-62) are somewhat sketchy, it is evident from them that Christian doctrine was discussed, the teachings of Handsome Lake recalled, and other opinions as to the state of religion among the Iroquois presented and discussed. It is also evident that extended discussions took place on the separate reservations before and after these councils and that there was no general agreement. Although greatly outnumbered by the Pagan Party, the Christian Party made its opposition felt. The depth of this division between "Christian" and "Pagan" was apparent again in the spring council of 1819 where "the warriors reported that the council fire was in confusion; some were pulling the brands one way and some another." In the discussions that followed, the two parties faced each other across the council fire, each presenting its arguments. Then, when commissioners of the United States arrived at the council to discuss further sale of Indian lands, the religious issue was set aside; both parties were opposed to allotment of land to individuals

and to removal west. However, the division between the Christian and Pagan parties remained, and in the council of 1820 they still sat across the fire from each other. It was to continue to be a major division in Iroquois society, although not one based on strictly religious grounds. As one missionary put it, "when I say Christian [party], you will not understand me to mean anything more than a respect for the gospel, and a disposition to become civilized" (Tuttle 1834:83).

In 1826 the Iroquois sold all the remaining small reservations along the Genesee River and substantial portions of the Buffalo Creek, Tonawanda, and Cattaraugus reservations. About the same time, the teachings of Handsome Lake were codified and their recitation came to be a yearly event. The women Faithkeepers at Tonawanda felt that the people were going back to the immoral ways prevalent before Handsome Lake's preaching. They met and decided to ask Jimmy Johnson (*shosheowa·ʔ* 'great burden strap') (fig. 3), Handsome Lake's grandson, to recall the teachings of his grandfather. He first refused to do so and was asked a second time. He then set about the task of recalling to mind what he could of these teachings. The first meeting at which he preached the teachings proved so successful that the Iroquois decided to hold a similar meeting each year at Tonawanda (Shimony 1961:200-201; Fenton 1972;

Rochester Mus. and Science Center, N.Y.
Fig. 3. Jimmy Johnson, aged about 75, of Tonawanda, wearing the Red Jacket medal ("League of the Iroquois: Its History, Politics, and Ritual," fig. 10, this vol.). Daguerreotype taken at Rochester June 1, 1849.

TOOKER

Tooker 1972). These teachings of Handsome Lake as Jimmy Johnson annually recalled them were recorded by Ely S. Parker in 1845 (Parker 1919:251–261) and again in 1848 (Morgan 1901, 1:223–248). They have come to be known as the Code of Handsome Lake and are called by the Iroquois 'the good message': Seneca *káiwi·yo·h,* Cayuga *kaihwí·yoh,* Onondaga *kaihwí·yo,* Mohawk *karihwí·yo.*

It is no accident that the Tonawanda Senecas became the "firekeepers" of the Handsome Lake religion. The reservation was centrally located in respect to the other Iroquois reservations where his influence had been felt: the Onondaga Reservation in central New York State; the Allegany, Cattaraugus, and Buffalo Creek reservations in western New York State; and the Six Nations Reserve in Ontario. In the early years of his mission, Handsome Lake had collected around him a group of followers at Coldspring on the Allegany Reservation, but a few years before his death he was forced to leave Allegany. He chose to move to Tonawanda, where his mother had been buried in the winter of 1779–1780 and where a number of his followers were already living. After Handsome Lake's death, the Tonawanda Reservation gained the reputation among Whites as being the most "conservative" reservation, the most resistant to Christian proselytizing, although the farming practiced there was equal to that on other reservations.

During the years that Jimmy Johnson preached the Code of Handsome Lake efforts to buy what land the Iroquois still held in New York State and to remove them west of the Mississippi continued. These negotiations eventually resulted in the sale of the large Buffalo Creek Reservation and the removal of those who lived there to the remaining Seneca reservations: Cattaraugus, Allegany, and Tonawanda. (The claims of the Tonawanda Seneca respecting their rights to retain their reservation were not finally settled until 1857.) Jimmy Johnson was one of the leaders in the effort to prevent the sale of the Tonawanda Reservation; he apparently died within the year preceding the final settlement.

During this period of negotiation, the Senecas were becoming increasingly dissatisfied with the method of distributing the annuities. In the first decades of the nineteenth century, the annuities were given to the chiefs and headmen, who in turn distributed them to the people by giving to each woman the shares due her, her children, husband, and relatives without family. When the annuities were to be paid by the United States government, the chiefs and headmen, with numbers of others from the reservations in western New York (the Oneidas and Onondagas living in central New York State were represented by a delegation of chiefs and headmen) met at Buffalo Creek. At this council the accounts due, including those for work done by blacksmiths and gunsmiths, were paid, other monies were divided per capita, and the dry goods and implements were apportioned. The chiefs and

headmen kept a record of the people who were to receive annuities, and these were totaled so that the amount of the per capita distribution could be determined. The merchants with whom the Indians had accounts also came to the council grounds, and after the annuities had been distributed, they collected the money owed them. The task of dividing the annuities, involving as it did the review of accounts and claims in council, took some days, which afforded an opportunity for those assembled to engage in games and other social activities (O. Allen 1903).

Although this method of distributing the annuities was satisfactory to most Iroquois during the early decades of the nineteenth century, it became less so, and increasing numbers wanted the annuities to be given directly to the heads of households rather than to the chiefs. In part, it was the desire for this change that led to the removal of the hereditary chiefs from power on the Allegany and Cattaraugus reservations and the establishment of the Seneca Nation in 1848 (Abler 1967). The Seneca Nation (that is, the Allegany and Cattaraugus reservations) was still governed in the 1970s by an elected council of 16 members.

The Tonawanda Seneca did not change their system of government. By the treaties negotiated during this period, the Tonawanda Reservation had been sold; but the Tonawanda Senecas objected to the sale, arguing that the treaty was not binding on them because their chiefs had not signed it. To abandon their system of governance by hereditary chiefs would have undermined their best argument that the treaty was invalid. Thus, they retained them in office, although in time the Tonawanda Seneca also came to distribute the annuities to heads of households rather than to the chiefs.

At the time of Jimmy Johnson's death (ca. 1856), the Buffalo Creek Reservation no longer existed and the Allegany and Cattaraugus reservations were no longer governed by hereditary chiefs. Moreover, although the Onondaga, Tonawanda, and Six Nations reserves still maintained a system of government by hereditary chiefs, the Onondaga and Tonawanda chiefs were part of a League council separate from the parallel League council established in Canada after the American Revolution. On the other Iroquois reservations in the United States and Canada neither the old Iroquois religion nor the teachings of Handsome Lake were kept up. It may be that the practices used in the 1970s for keeping up the teachings of Handsome Lake were originated in the years following Jimmy Johnson's death.

The teachings of Handsome Lake are still recalled in a series of meetings termed the "Six Nations meetings" by the Iroquois. Early each fall, the Tonawanda Longhouse sends invitations (tally sticks to which wampum is attached) to the other Longhouses to meet at Tonawanda on a particular day in September to begin the Six Nations meetings. When all the representatives of the various

Longhouses have assembled, the wampum is returned, reports made, and arrangements for the meetings that follow announced. The next three or four mornings are devoted to the recitation of the Code of Handsome Lake. Social dances are held in the Longhouse in the evenings. In the weeks that follow, the Code is recited in the various other Longhouses following a biennial circuit that includes the Tonawanda, Caughnawaga, Saint Regis, New York Onondaga, Allegany (at Steamburg, formerly at Coldspring), Canadian Onondaga, and sometimes Sour Springs (Upper Cayuga) Longhouses one year and the Tonawanda, Cattaraugus (Newtown), Oneidatown (Muncey), Canadian Seneca, Lower Cayuga, and sometimes Sour Springs Longhouses the following year.

The preaching of the Code in the various Longhouses is done by those who know it, and in the instance of the Six Nations meetings, by those who have preached before a committee of chiefs and preachers at a Tonawanda Six Nations meeting and whose preaching has been found acceptable by that committee. Not all preachers of the Code learned its content from the same individuals, and there is some variation in the versions of the various speakers. Some of these differences may go back to the first decades of the nineteenth century, when Handsome Lake's followers on the various reservations on occasion remembered and emphasized slightly different aspects of his teaching (Parker 1913:19; Deardorff 1951:99; Shimony 1961:192).

Although they vary in details, preachers of the Code customarily begin with an account of Handsome Lake's first vision and other incidents in the prophet's life. The preacher then mentions the various messages given by the Creator to the Four Beings to communicate to Handsome Lake. These include the admonitions that people should not drink, witches should confess and cease their activity, witchcraft charms should not be used, women should not practice abortion, husbands and wives should not desert each other or their children, people should help each other, and the Thanksgiving ceremonies should be kept up. The preacher then describes the punishments in the afterlife through a recounting of the journey on which Handsome Lake guided by the messengers saw people being tormented for their misdeeds in life.

Portions of the Code may be repeated on other occasions as interest dictates. But the Six Nations meetings insure that the entire Code of Handsome Lake is heard in each Longhouse at least once every two years.

The Longhouse Religion

The "Thanksgiving ceremonies" of the Iroquois religion are kept up in the Longhouses, the council houses of the faithful. There are 11 such Longhouses: the Coldspring Longhouse on the Allegany Reservation; the Newtown Longhouse on the Cattaraugus Reservation; the Tonawanda Longhouse on the Tonawanda Reservation; the Onondaga Longhouse on the Onondaga Reservation; the Onondaga, Seneca, Lower Cayuga, and Sour Springs (Upper Cayuga) Longhouses on the Six Nations Reserve; the Oneida Longhouse on the Oneida Reserve; the Saint Regis Longhouse on the Saint Regis Reserve; and the Caughnawaga Longhouse on the Caughnawaga Reserve (fig. 4).

The central concern of this religion is to return thanks to and to express gratitude for the existence of various beings in this world. Some of these, like the sun and moon, are to be seen about every day; some, like the thunderers, are to be seen or heard less frequently; still others are occasionally to be seen in the forests or while on the lakes or rivers when away from the village. Some are known from having appeared in dreams and visions of individuals, and some are known and talked about in the traditional narratives, or "myths."

Like human beings, these beings, or "spirit-forces," appreciate being listened to, paid attention to, and honored. In Iroquois society, recognition of friendship and concern for others is appropriately expressed by the giving of food or by a feast. In Iroquois religion, respect for and recognition of supernatural beings is also expressed through a feast or at least the giving of food to those attending the ceremonial. Thus, an essential part of most Iroquois gatherings called "religious ceremonies" was and is a distribution of food to those participating.

In the past, and to some extent still, the goodwill of these supernatural beings was deemed necessary in order that an individual have good fortune, and so be favored with success in hunting and war, with abundant crops, and with good luck generally. To maintain this goodwill, it was appropriate to acknowledge the aid of these beings in a ceremonial. It was also of some necessity to pay attention to dreams for the beings on occasion indicate what they desire in dreams.

The dream could also indicate what an individual should do in order to gain or restore his good health and his good fortune. Certain dreams indicated "the desires of the soul" (as the Jesuits recorded it in the seventeenth century), what dances and other ceremonies, feasts, and material objects the soul wished to have given. If an ill person's dreams had not indicated the necessary cure, one who had special talents frequently was asked to determine what the desires of the sick person's soul were, and so what had to be done for the cure.

In earlier centuries, the proper course of action to be taken in respect to community affairs also might be indicated in a dream. A person having such a dream reported it—if need be, to a council—so that appropriate action could be taken. With the conversion of a number of Iroquois to Christianity, the dream lost its importance in political affairs, although the ritual of the Longhouse ceremonies may still be changed if someone's dream indicates that it should be.

454

Mad Dog Graphics, Salamanca (for new Coldspring); Mus. of Ind. Archeol., U. of Western Ont., London (for Oneida).

Fig. 4. The modern Longhouses of the Iroquois: 11 in the east (and 1 replaced in 1965) where the standard forms of the rituals of the Longhouse religion are performed and one in Oklahoma where a divergent variety is practiced. left to right, top row first: Tonawanda Longhouse, kitchen-dining hall, cookhouse, photographed facing southwest Oct. 20, 1962; Newtown Longhouse (Cattaraugus) and cookhouse, photographed facing southeast, May 21, 1957; old Coldspring Longhouse (Allegany) replaced in 1965, with cookhouse at left, photographed facing northwest, Apr. 1953; new Coldspring Longhouse near Steamburg, built 1965, photographed facing northeast, Jan. 6, 1977; Onondaga Longhouse (near Syracuse), photographed facing southeast, Oct. 15, 1962; Sour Springs Longhouse (Six Nations), dining hall, cookhouse, photographed facing southwest, Oct. 19, 1962; Lower Cayuga Longhouse (Six Nations), cookhouse, dining hall, photographed facing southwest, Oct. 19, 1962; Onondaga Longhouse (Six Nations), dining hall, cookhouse, photographed facing southwest, Oct. 19, 1962; Seneca Longhouse (Six Nations), dining hall, cookhouse, photographed facing southwest, Oct. 19, 1962; Oneida Longhouse (Thames R., Ont.), photographed facing northwest, June 1977 (new Longhouse under construction in 1977); Caughnawaga Longhouse, photographed facing northwest, Mar. 11, 1977; St. Regis Longhouse, photographed facing south, July 18, 1939; Seneca-Cayuga Longhouse (near Turkey Ford, Okla.), built about 1935, photographed facing northwest, Aug. 23, 1961. New Coldspring photograph by Jeff Snow; Oneida by Victor Killing; Caughnawaga by Frank Natawe; St. Regis by William N. Fenton; rest by William C. Sturtevant.

Economic and social changes in Iroquois life in the nineteenth and twentieth centuries have not changed the basic principles of Iroquois religion but rather have changed the importance of certain rites. Hunting is no longer important, and virtually all the rituals for success in hunting have lapsed, including the reliance on hunting fetishes. As war has become unimportant in Iroquois life, ceremonies for success in war have been given up. Various ceremonies to cure the sick are still held. So also are the ceremonies for the foods that were particularly important to the Iroquois in the nineteenth century: corn and the other cultivated crops, strawberries, and maple sap. These were the foods that provided the major subsistence and whose reappearance each year afforded the promise of continued life to individuals in the community and so the community as a whole.

These foods are mentioned in the Thanksgiving Speech, the ubiquitous speech that opens and closes almost every Iroquois ceremony and that mentions the beings that the Iroquois recognize as important. The Thanksgiving Speech is called *kanǫ́·nyǫk* (Seneca) and *kanǫ́hǫnyǫk* (Cayuga), words which literally mean 'let it be used for expressing gratitude'. It affords a concise statement of the Iroquois view of the world around them. In this view, certain natural objects and phenomena— sun, moon, winds, and thunder—that White Americans regard as inanimate are regarded as animate. They are treated as human beings and, for example, may be addressed by kinship terms. Thus, the sun is "our elder brother"; the moon, "our grandmother"; the Thunderers, "our grandfathers"; the earth, "our mother"; the food crops—corn, beans, and squash—"our sisters."

In customary Iroquois practice, council meetings begin with a speech acknowledging the safe arrival of those present and expressing gratitude that all have come. In a similar fashion, the Thanksgiving Speech acknowledges the supernatural beings. Even if given in abbreviated form as it often is, the speech alludes to these various beings and returns thanks to and expresses happiness for the existence of each.

Although different speakers list the items that comprise the Thanksgiving Speech in a slightly different sequence, the general order is the same. First are mentioned the things on the earth (the terrestrial items) and then the things and beings above (the celestial items). Within these two parts, the order is also from the things nearest the earth upward to the things above. After an opening section on the people, the Thanksgiving Speech mentions first the earth "on which the people move about." Next or at virtually any place in the half of the speech devoted to terrestrial items is mention of the water—the springs, streams, rivers, and lakes. Next are mentioned the plants (grasses, berries, weeds, and medicinal herbs) and the bushes and saplings. This is followed by mention of the larger trees and the forest, then the animals who live in the forests, and next the birds. In the later part of this portion devoted to terrestrial things, mention also may be made of the cultivated foods—corn, beans, and squash.

The portion of the Thanksgiving Speech devoted to celestial beings usually begins with a section on the wind and one on the Thunderers. This is followed by sections on the sun, moon, and stars. Next are mentioned the Four Beings, the four messengers from the Creator to the prophet Handsome Lake; then Handsome Lake himself; and finally the Creator (Chafe 1961; Foster 1974).

Although not all the beings mentioned in the Thanksgiving Speech are still honored in a special ceremony in the Longhouse, a number are, and it is possible that all once were.

The ritual of these ceremonials follows the same basic form as other Iroquois ceremonials. Typically, Iroquois ceremonies begin with the Thanksgiving Speech. In some ceremonies, there follows next a tobacco invocation, that is, a speech during which loose tobacco is thrown on the fire. Next are given the rituals appropriate to the occasion. At their conclusion, the Thanksgiving Speech is repeated in abbreviated form. The ceremony ends with a feast, often distributed to those present to be taken home to eat (fig. 5).

What distinguishes one ceremony from another is not the basic sequence of the ritual, but the particular rituals that are performed between the beginning and final Thanksgiving Speech and the particular foods that comprise the feast at the conclusion of the ceremony. Often the particular rituals performed as part of each ceremony may also be given as part of other ceremonies. There is, then, a repertoire of Iroquois songs, dances, and games from which the rites of each ceremonial have been selected and that over time have come to be considered the appropriate rites to be performed.

N.Y. State Lib., Albany: 13801-4.

Fig. 5. Cooking for a Longhouse feast: husking corn, removing the kernels, and stirring corn mush or soup with a paddle. Drawing by the Cattaraugus Seneca artist Jesse J. Cornplanter, about 1905.

456

Table 1. Main Calendrical Ceremonies of New York and Six Nations Reserve Longhouses

1. Midwinter (New Year's): S *kaiwanoǫskwá[?]ko·wa·h; hotíną[?]yas* 'they are having the Midwinter ceremony'. C *kaihwanǫ·ska[?]kó·wa·h*, literally 'very precious matter'; *tsha[?]tekOsráhę[?]* 'midwinter'; *kanaháowi·* (perhaps part of the ceremony). Oo *hotinǫ́hwaiyàha[?]*. M *kanǫhwaró·ri; kohséhra*. The first Mohawk term and the related terms in Cayuga and Onondaga may be compared to the one used for the ceremony by the 17th-century French missionaries among the Huron and at least some of the Iroquois: ononharoia, onon8aroia, ononhoüaroia, honnonouaroria, and other variants, sometimes explained as meaning 'giddiness' (JR 10:174, 17:166, 23:52, 42:154, 44:30); early dictionaries give Mohawk gannonh8arori (Bruyas 1863:81) and Huron ąnnonh8arori (Potier 1920a:432) as 'to sing a death song or other song to which there is no response'.

1.A. The Four Sacred Rituals: S *ke·i niyóiwa·ke·h*.
   a. Feather Dance: S *ostówæ[?]ko·wa·h*. C *ohstow[?]akó·wah* or *staos*. Oo *ostoæ[?]kò·na*. M *ostowa[?]kó·wa*.
   b. Thanksgiving Dance (Skin Dance): S *konéoǫ[?]*. C *konéhǫ·[?]*. Oo *koné·yǫk* (?). M *tehǫtenehwará·tǫs*.
   c. Personal Chant: S *atǫ·węˀ*. C *atǫ́·waˀ*. M *atǫ́·waˀ*. The modern Mohawk term is a recent borrowing, the earlier word being, as in Huron, atonront 'sing a war song having the response henh henh' (Bruyas 1863:40; Potier 1920a:200; Lafitau 1724, 1:521, 2:190), the cognate of the Seneca verb *-atǫǫt-*, as in *hotǫ·t* 'he is singing a personal chant'.
   d. Bowl Game: S *katsę[?]keha·ˀ*, literally 'characterized by a bowl'; *kayętowa·nęh*, literally 'big game'. C *kayętowá·nęh*. M *kayęta[?]kó·wa* (also *tehǫtęnéhaye*).

1.B. Our Life Supporter Dances: S *tyǫhéhkǫh*, literally 'what we use to be alive' (i.e., corn, beans, and squash); C *tyǫnhéhkǫh*.
2. Bush Dance (at Six Nations): C *otehatǫ́·nih*.
3. Maple: S *ta·tinǫ́·nyǫ wahta[?]* 'they are thankful for the maple'; *ta·tinǫ́·nyǫ kahatayę[?]* 'they are thankful for the forest'; *hęnǫtsiskóa[?]* 'they boil mush'. C *hatitsyestǫ́·tas* 'they are putting sap in'.
4. Sun: S *ta·tinǫ́·nyǫ kǽ·hkwa[?]* 'they are thankful for the sun'; other languages have similar expressions, in some cases naming the moon as well in a combined ceremony for both.
5. Thunder: S *tǫ·wǫtínǫ·ǫnyǫ hatiwęnotatye[?]s* 'they thank the Thunderers'; *hǫwǫtiyęnǫkóhtani hatiwęnotatye[?]s* 'they put in a song for the Thunderers'; *wasa·se[?]* 'war dance' (a component of the Thunder ceremony but also used to refer to the whole). C *ethíhso·t hatiwęnótatye[?]s*, literally 'our grandfathers are speaking'.
6. Seed Planting: S *hęnǫhnęǫkwa[?]syóa[?]*, literally 'they put seed corn in water'. C *ękaǫthǫ́·wis*. M *ká·nę[?] tehǫtenǫhwerá·tǫ* 'they lay down thanks for the seed'.
7. Strawberry: S *hęnǫta·yé·es*, literally 'they gather berries'; *hęnǫta·yo·s* or *hęnǫta·yóa[?]*, literally 'they put berries in water'. C *tsIsǫ́·tahk hęnatAyáohe·s*, literally 'they gather strawberries'. Oo *hǫtáhyos*. M *yohǫtésha[?]*.
8. Bean: S *hęnǫtetkǫwǫ́séoa[?]*, literally 'they put string beans in water'. C *hęnatesahe[?]táohe·s* 'they gather beans'. Oo *tehǫtétkwę̨[?]tya[?]ks* 'they break the bean'.
9. Little Corn (Corn Testing): C *hęnatekhwáohé·s nika·khwá·[?]ah*, literally 'they gather the small food'.
10. Green Corn: S *hęnǫtekhwé·es*, literally 'they gather food'. C *hęnatekhwáohé·s kakhówanę*, literally 'they gather the big food'.
11. Harvest: S *hęnǫthæhkwé·es*, literally 'they gather bread'. C *kothętIs[?]ánhǫ[?]*, literally 'the harvest is completed'.

NOTE: Names that are simply the ordinary words for the entities being celebrated, as is the case in much of the available Mohawk data, are omitted.
Abbreviations: S, Seneca; C, Cayuga; Oo, Onondaga; Oi, Oneida; M, Mohawk.
SOURCES: Chafe 1963:29-31, 1967; G. Michelson 1973; Foster 1974; and personal communications 1976 from Marianne Mithun (Mohawk, Cayuga); Michael K. Foster (Cayuga); Hanni J. Woodbury (Onondaga). Compiled by Ives Goddard.

The longest of the Iroquois ceremonials is Midwinter, also called the New Year's ceremony (table 1). It is held in January or February, beginning on a date set with reference to the new moon of midwinter and lasting at least a week; practice in the various Longhouses differs. Formerly, one or two pure white dogs were ritually strangled at the beginning of the ceremony and burned a few days later. Although the dogs are no longer burned, the tobacco invocation to the Creator that was a part of this rite still is given. At the beginning of the Midwinter ceremony, special messengers (fig. 6) go through the houses, stirring ashes (fig. 7) and announcing the beginning of the ceremony. These messengers are called Big Heads or Our Uncles, in Seneca *yaté·yęǫ[?]* (masculine dual form). There follow several days devoted, in part, to the fulfillment and renewal of dreams, and so of dances, including those of various medicine societies (fig. 8) and games sponsored by individuals. In the New York Onondaga Longhouse, whose practice differs in a number of respects from that in the New York Seneca and Six Nations Reserve Longhouses, these days are devoted to dream guessing, a rite that is infrequently performed in the other Longhouses. The concluding days of the Midwinter ceremony are devoted to the performance of the Four Sacred Rituals given by the Creator and confirmed by Handsome Lake—Feather Dance, Thanksgiving Dance, Personal Chant, and Bowl Game (fig. 9)—and the Our Life Supporter Dances—a series of dances (differing in the various Longhouses) honoring corn, beans, and squash.

The Four Sacred Rituals and the Our Life Supporter Dances are also performed as the principal rites of the Green Corn ceremony in the New York Seneca and Six Nations Reserve Longhouses and of the Planting, Green

Fig. 6. The messengers known as "our uncles the Big Heads," wearing buffalo robes tied at top with cornhusk ropes and a cornhusk braid around each ankle and carrying pestles marked in red, approach a house on the first day of the Midwinter ceremony. Watercolor done in 1900 or 1901 by Jesse J. Cornplanter, Seneca, then resident on the Cattaraugus Reservation.

Fig. 7. Wooden paddles used in the Stirring Ashes rite during the Midwinter ceremony. The burnt designs represent clans, Heron (Deer on other side) on the top, Turtle (Wolf on other side) on the bottom, corresponding to the 2 moieties. Cayuga, Six Nations Reserve, length about 125 cm, collected before 1933.

Fig. 8. Buffalo Society dance during the Midwinter ceremony. The singer uses a water drum; the dancers take cornmeal mush from the bucket. Postures, activities, and bench are accurate as of 1906, the approximate date of the drawing, but the clothing is partially reconstructed and the walls and roof are also not contemporary. Drawing by the Seneca artist Jesse J. Cornplanter.

Fig. 9. The Bowl Game in the Longhouse during the Midwinter ceremony. Peach-stone dice are tossed by thumping a wooden bowl on the floor, the 2 moieties playing against each other. Some of the clothing here is slightly antique for 1903 (the date of the drawing), but the postures and activity as well as the interior of the Newtown Longhouse are accurately shown (compare fig. 10 and Brush 1901:521). Drawn by Jesse J. Cornplanter, Seneca.

Corn, and Harvest ceremonies of the New York Onondaga Longhouse, all ceremonies that continue for three days or longer. Customarily, other Longhouse ceremonies are shorter, lasting only a few hours. These include Planting, Bean, and Harvest, the ceremonies honoring cultivated foods at which the Our Life Supporter Dances are given; the Strawberry ceremony at which the Feather Dance is danced and berry juice drunk; the Maple ceremony, which often includes a tobacco invocation to the maple and the playing of the bowl game; the Thunder ceremony, which includes a tobacco invocation to the Thunderers and performance of the War Dance; and the Moon ceremony, a tobacco invocation to the moon and the playing of the bowl game. (These ceremonial patterns are discussed in greater detail in Tooker 1970a.)

As there is variation in other aspects of Iroquois ritual, so also there is some variation in the particular ceremonies that constitute the ceremonial calendar of each Longhouse. The typical calendar includes the Midwinter ceremonial (the New Year's ceremony, the ceremonial that both closes the old year and begins the new one), and the Maple (Sap Dance), Planting, Strawberry, Bean, Green Corn, and Harvest (Bread Dance) festivals. Not always included in the 1970s but once more frequently given are the Sun, Moon, and Thunder ceremonies. Other ceremonials are also included in the calendar at some Longhouses (see "Seneca," "Onondaga," and "Six Nations of the Grand River, Ontario," this vol.).

A number of these ceremonies recognize the appearance of the item mentioned in the Thanksgiving Speech and are so timed. For example, the Maple ceremony is held when the sap begins to flow in the maple trees; the

Strawberry ceremony, "when the berries hang on the bushes"; the Thunder ceremony when the Thunderers are first heard in the west in the spring or when it is wished that thunder will be heard and rain fall; the Sun ceremony when the sun begins to feel warm in the spring; the Bean ceremony when the green beans are mature; the Green Corn ceremony, when the first corn is ripe.

The Longhouse in which these ceremonies are held is rectangular, with fireplaces or stoves located at or near each end. The Longhouse is furnished with two rows of benches along both long walls with additional benches along the short walls (fig. 10). This arrangement provides seating while leaving most of the floor space available for the dancing that is such an important part of the ritual. Most commonly, seating is by age and sex, the women and young children sitting on the benches on both sides at one end of the Longhouse and the men on those at the other end (fig. 11). If the musicians for a dance are to be seated, benches are placed in the middle of the Longhouse for them. The dances are for all, and all who wish to dance (including old people and young ones) do so.

The food that is to be distributed at the end of the ceremony is customarily brought into the Longhouse before or during the rites and placed near the stove at the women's end of the Longhouse. For each ceremonial, there is an appropriate type of soup to be served and it is brought into the Longhouse in large caldrons. Those attending bring pails in which to carry the soup home to eat, as they also take home any other food distributed at the end of the ceremony.

The responsibility for setting the date for the ceremonial, for making all arrangements, and in general for overseeing Longhouse affairs is vested in the Faithkeepers, or "Deacons" of the Longhouse. These men and women have been (1) appointed to the position and in consequence have been given a name or (2) given a Faithkeeper name and therefore should assume the duties of a Faithkeeper. If the name associated with such

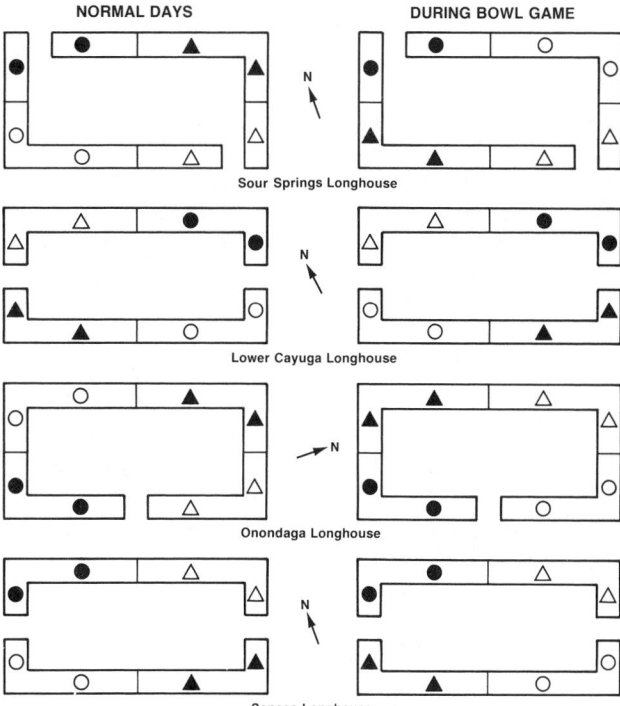

after Shimony 1961:61-67.

Fig. 11. Seating during the Midwinter ceremony at the four Longhouses on the Six Nations Reserve, according to moiety affiliation and sex (similar rules apply in the other Longhouses). Triangles indicate males, circles females, solid for the moiety that includes the Wolf clan, open for the moiety that includes the Deer clan. There are some differences even among these 4 Longhouses in the assignment of clans to moieties and in the customary labels for the moieties. See Shimony 1961:56-60.

a hereditary position has been forgotten, the individual selected fills the position without receiving a new name.

Medicine Societies

Many dances and games performed in the ceremonials held in the Longhouse may also be given separately in order to cure an individual. Which particular rite or rites will so cure either are indicated in a dream of the sick individual or a "fortuneteller" or else are ascertained by use of some method of divination such as looking into a bowl of water or reading tea leaves. Herbs were and still are to some extent important in restoring and maintaining health, and a few Iroquois possessed extensive knowledge of such plants.

The rituals of the so-called medicine societies also are used to cure the sick. Each of these societies (whose membership consists of those who have been cured by having the rituals of the society performed for them) owns a distinct set of songs and other rituals that are addressed to a particular set of beings associated with that society. Each also has a myth or legend that recounts the origin of its most important rites. These societies meet as the occasion demands, usually in private homes rather than in the Longhouse as the rituals of a medicine society

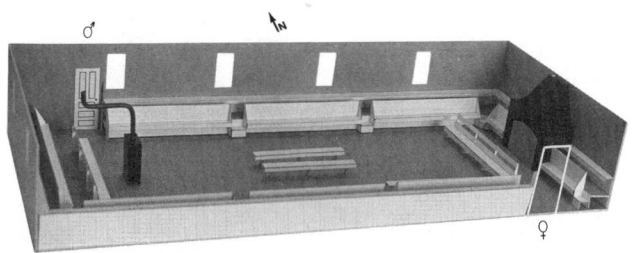

Fig. 10. Internal arrangement of Newtown Longhouse, Cattaraugus Reservation. This organization, with 2-tiered built-in benches around the walls, 2 stoves (or fireplaces), movable backless benches for singers, movable benches with backs, and open central area for dances and other ritual activity, is typical of all modern Longhouses (except the one in Okla.). Most longhouses have 2 doors, one for each sex (on most occasions), but some have only 1, centrally placed. After Sturtevant 1957.

belong to that society and not to the people generally. Those invited to attend the ceremony include members of the society, musicians and singers (some of whom may not be members of the society although they know the songs), and others. Customarily, the ceremony begins with a short recitation of the Thanksgiving Speech and a tobacco invocation to the tutelaries of the society and ends with another recitation of the Thanksgiving Speech and a feast (for description of these societies see Parker 1909; Fenton 1941a, 1953; Speck 1949a:64–114; Shimony 1961:281–285).

One of the most important of these societies is the Society of Medicine Men (also called Shake the Pumpkin), and in a sense the other medicine societies are orders of this society, since members of the other societies are members also of this society (table 2). Included in its ritual is the singing of individual songs by its members. The society also owns several masks that are not False Face Society masks.

Another important society is the Little Water Society. It holds a powerful medicine made of parts of various animals. A small amount of this medicine mixed with water is given to cure a sick person. The principal ceremonies of the Little Water Society are the meetings held three or four times a year to renew the strength of the medicine.

The Pygmy or Little People Society is concerned with the Little People, beings who although small in size are very powerful. The society is also called the Dark Dance after its practice of singing the songs that belong to the society in darkness.

The Bear, Buffalo (fig. 8), Eagle, and Otter Societies constitute the "company of mystic animals." Each of these societies has not only distinctive songs but also distinctive rites in which its tutelary beings are imitated. In their dances, members of the Bear Society may imitate bears by eating nuts, berries, honey, corn mush, or corn pudding (foods that bears like); and members of the Buffalo Society may butt each other and stomp like buffalo. Somewhat similarly, in the distinctive Eagle Society dance, pairs of men each holding a rattle in the right hand and a feather fan in the left (fig. 12) pick up objects in the mouths in imitation of feeding birds. Unlike the other medicine societies, the Otter Society, a society of women, has no set of songs; but it does have a distinctive water-sprinkling rite.

Masks figure prominently in the rituals of two societies: the False Face Society and the Husk Face Society. The False Face Society is a particularly popular one; more Iroquois belong to it than to any other society. The masks of the society are carved of wood and depict beings seen in the forest or in dreams. When wearing these masks, members of the society have special powers and can handle hot coals without being burned. The masks themselves have power and should be specially treated. They should, for example, have tobacco burned for them periodically and they should not be closed up in boxes. The society holds a special meeting for all its members and masks each year in conjunction with the Midwinter ceremonial (fig. 13), and once or twice a year members of the society go through the houses in a body performing a ritual to clear them of disease (figs. 14–15).

The tutelaries of the Husk Face Society are agricultural spirits, not those of the forest as are the False Face, although on occasion members of both societies appear together. Its masks are made of braided and formerly woven corn husks. Like the False Faces, the Husk Faces may handle hot coals and blow ashes on patients in order

Table 2. Main Noncalendrical Ceremonies

Medicine Society Ceremonies
1. Society of Medicine Men (Shake the Pumpkin): S *yéi ʔto·s* (*hatí· ʔto·s*, with plural prefix); *kái ʔtowa·nęh*; *kái ʔo·ǫ ʔ*. C *hi ʔtos*. Oo *ehí ʔtos* (*hatíhi ʔtos*, pl.).
2. Little Water Society: S *nika·neká ʔa·h*. M *nikahneká· ʔa*. Both are basically names for the Little Water Medicine. Seneca also has the expressions *hatiyę ʔkwayę·nih* 'they are putting down tobacco for it' and *hatinotayę·nih* 'they are putting down a flute for it', both referring to the performance of this ceremony.
3. Little People Society (Dark Dance): S *teyótahsǫtaikǫh*, literally 'it is dark'. C *teyotAsǫtaikǫh*.
4. Company of Mystic Animals.
    a. Bear Society: S *nyakwai ʔ oęnǫ ʔ*, literally 'bear song'; C *hnyakwáikEa ʔ*, literally 'bear dance'.
    b. Buffalo Society: S *tekiyá ʔkǫh oęnǫ ʔ*.
    c. Eagle Society: S *kané ʔkwæ· ʔe· ʔ*; *kane ʔǫta· ʔtǫh*, literally 'shaking the Eagle Dance fan (*kané ʔæ ʔ*)'. C *kanre ʔkwá· ʔe· ʔ*.
    d. Otter Society: S *tawę́·ętǫ ʔ oęnǫ ʔ*.
5. False Face Society: S, C *kakǫ́hsa ʔ*, literally 'face, false-face'. Oo *hǫtó ʔi*. M *okǫ́hsa ʔ; ato ʔwíhtshera ʔ* is the society.
6. Husk Face Society: S, C *katsíhsa ʔ*. Oo *hatsíhsa ʔ*. M *katíhsǫ*.

Other Ceremonies
7. Tenth-day Feast: S *atyæ·khǫ·shæ ʔ*. Oo *atye·hǽkhǫshæ· ʔ*. M *atyera ʔkǫ́hsera ʔ*.
8. Feast of the Dead: S *ohki·we·h*. C *ohki·weh*. Oo *ohki·wé*. M *ohki·we*.

NOTE: S, Seneca; C, Cayuga; Oo, Onondaga; Oi, Oneida; M, Mohawk.
SOURCES: Chafe 1963:29–31, 1967; G. Michelson 1973; Foster 1974; and personal communications 1976 from Marianne Mithun (Mohawk, Cayuga); Michael K. Foster (Cayuga); Hanni J. Woodbury (Onondaga). Compiled by Ives Goddard.

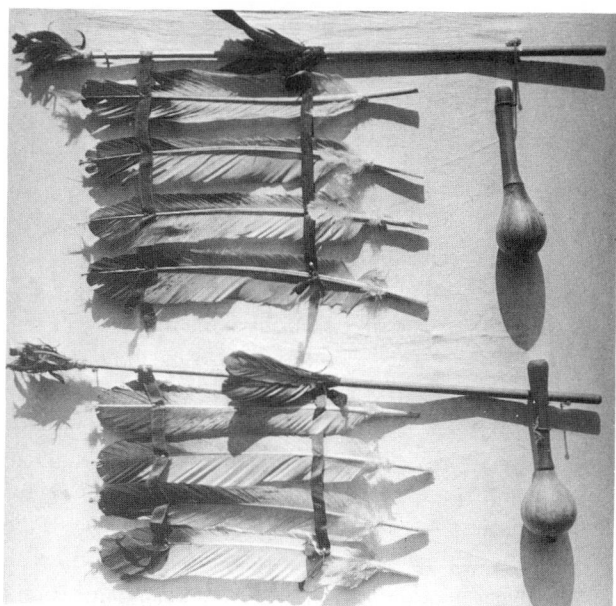

Fig. 12. Eagle feather fans and miniature rattles used in Seneca Eagle Dance. The rattles may be of gourds as here, or of cow horn, and are usually about 20 cm long. Photograph by William N. Fenton, Aug. 4, 1933, at Quaker Bridge, Allegany Reservation, N.Y.

to cure. The society also holds an annual ceremony for its members in conjunction with the Midwinter ceremonial.

Rites of Community Status

Many of the rites and legends of the medicine societies have associations with the forest, while many of the thanksgiving ceremonies held in the Longhouse have agricultural connotations—a difference that reflects the two worlds of Iroquois culture: the world of the forest and that of the clearing. In prereservation Iroquois society, the forest was the domain of the men. They cut the clearing out of the forest and constructed the village in it using materials from the forest. But once this was done, the clearing and the village became the domain of the women. Women did virtually all the agricultural work—planting, weeding, and harvesting. When not in the fields, women were often in the village preparing food for storage, making the baskets and pots in which these provisions were kept, cooking the food, taking care of the children, and making the clothing. Men were often away from the village on hunting, trading, and war expeditions. Life in the village was dominated by women.

At their establishment, the reservations became the focal point around which life revolved, providing the continuity of Iroquois existence. And as the women earlier had provided the continuity of the Iroquois village, they also were to do so for the reservation. Community children of women who were members of the group (sometimes called the "band") that owned the reservation were also members. Thus, rights such as to own land on the reservation and to receive a share of the

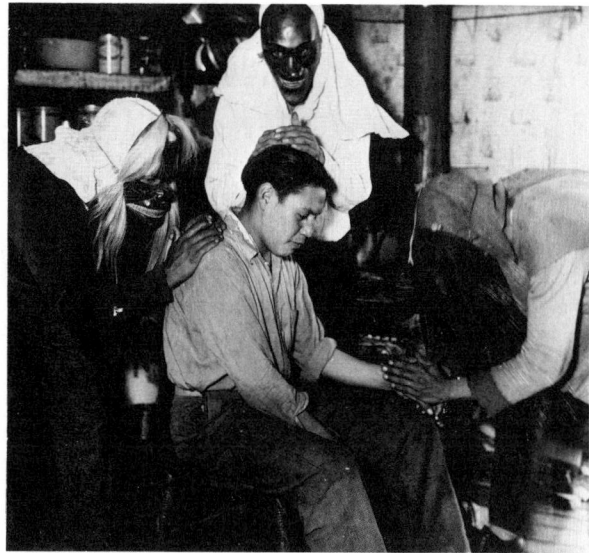

bottom, N.Y. State Mus., Albany: 13801-2.

Fig. 13. False Face Society curing. top, Members of the Society cure a patient in his house by blowing through hands dipped in hot ashes and rubbing them on the patient; photographed in Indian house at Coldspring, Allegany Reservation, in 1940 by William N. Fenton; bottom, the Society renews a cure in the Longhouse at Newtown during the Midwinter ceremony, drawing by the Seneca artist Jesse J. Cornplanter, probably in 1903.

annuities were inherited through the matrilineage. This still obtains in the United States. For example, only those whose mothers are members of the Tonawanda band can own land on the Tonawanda Reservation or receive a share of the annuities due the band; only those belonging to the Seneca Nation can own land on the Cattaraugus and Allegany reservations or receive a share of the annuities and other monies due the Seneca Nation. However, within the band, land and other real property is inherited bilaterally, that is, property may be inherited from both father and mother and may be given equally to both sons and daughters. In Canada, the situation is different; the Canadian government has insisted on a patrilineal system of band enrollment (Shimony 1961:22).

461

Fig. 14. False Face wearers approach a house on the Cattaraugus Reservation during the spring or fall circuit of the community to prevent illness and renew the powers of the False Faces. Each masker carries a rattle (turtle rattles and one bark rattle); 2 Husk Faces accompany them; one person wearing a pig mask crawls in the foreground; 2 leaders carry hickory canes, striped with hematite and with miniature False Faces, Husk Faces, and tobacco bags attached. Drawn by the Seneca artist Jesse J. Cornplanter in 1903.

In both the United States and Canada, the hereditary chieftainships are still held by the clans, and succession is in the matrilineage. The clan mother in consultation with the women of the clan still selects the man who is to be "raised up" and given the name of the deceased chief who belonged to that clan. Similarly, Iroquois children still belong to the clan of their mother; they are still given Indian names selected from those names belonging to the clan that are not in use. The announcement of the name as well as the changes in name (as the change of a baby name to an adult name or the change of an adult name for a Faithkeeper name) are customarily made at either the Green Corn or Midwinter ceremonials, the two most important Longhouse ceremonies.

Fig. 15. Sherman Red Eye driving a Packard preparatory to a feast for the False Face Society at the Allegany Seneca community. Photograph by William N. Fenton, Aug. 1, 1934.

As the ceremonies for other beings assume that they are present, the traditional ceremonies following the death of an individual presume that the spirit, or "ghost," of the deceased is still present and will not leave until the Tenth-day feast (so called as it is held 10 days after the death). At that time the soul leaves and travels along the Milky Way, the Path of the Souls.

After a person has died, the body is dressed in the "dead clothes," that is, clothes of old Indian design. The house is cleaned, and preparations made for the wake and funeral. Mirrors and all other large reflecting surfaces (like glass-framed pictures) are covered with cloth in order that no one, especially no child, may accidently be frightened by seeing the ghost in them. They remain so covered until after the Tenth-day feast. Food is set out for the deceased, and at least two individuals stay with the body until the funeral. A wake is held on one or on both nights preceding the funeral. At the wake, a game (often a version of the widespread North American Indian moccasin game or a special dice game) is played (fig. 16).

After the funeral and interment, preparations are begun for the Tenth-day feast. These include plans for the distribution of the personal property of the deceased, all of which, especially clothing and other articles made of cloth, should be distributed at the Tenth-day feast; otherwise, the ghost will return and bother the living. Plans are also made for the feast itself, and particular attention may be paid to the kind of food the deceased liked; food is ever a concern in Iroquois ceremonies. The ritual of the Tenth-day feast consists of a speech and the distribution of the personal effects of the deceased as well as the distribution of the feast.

A year later, on the anniversary of the death, another feast is given for the deceased. It marks the end of a year of mourning.

A special ceremony, called *ohki·we·h* in Seneca (Feast of the Dead, Chanters for the Dead), for all the dead of the community is held annually or semiannually. The all-night ceremony begins with a customary speech and tobacco invocation to the dead. There follow the special *ohki·we·h* songs and dance and then various social dances. The dancing is often clockwise rather than the customary counterclockwise, for these dances are for the dead, and the dead are believed to dance also. After midnight, food is served to all present and sometime later goods (many of which are of cloth) are distributed to those present.

On occasion, particularly if someone is being disturbed by a ghost, the *ohki·we·h* songs may be sung at a ceremonial in a private house. Such gatherings resemble those of the medicine societies, and for this reason *ohki·we·h* is occasionally called a medicine society and listed as such.

462

TOOKER

Dept. of Anthr., Smithsonian: 384288.

Fig. 16. Cane of white hickory used as a pointer in the moccasin game held at wakes of chiefs on the Six Nations Reserve. The significance of the incised designs near the handle is somewhat uncertain; the band at top (from right side of cane) represents wampum belts; in center (from front of cane), top to bottom, evil (sickness, death), man (top circle), wampum belt, black wampum (dentate design), lodge or house, all are notified, assembly hall, and people; at bottom (from left side of cane), top to bottom, evil (circles probably 2 people), loss of view of sky and sun (caused by death), face of the dead, house of the dead, assembly hall (crossed lines indicating death-caused alteration), all are notified, curved paths of the world, winding path of the dead. The bear head carved on the end may represent the owner's clan. Length 90.0 cm. Collected in 1916. See Fenton 1950:35–37.

Religious Affiliation

By the middle of the nineteenth century, Iroquois reservations in the United States and Canada had become rural ethnic enclaves surrounded by English-speaking White farmers. Such ethnic enclaves were not uncommon at the time, and in some ways these Iroquois communities resembled those of European origin. Iroquois languages continued to be the languages of everyday discourse on the reservations, and this tended to set the Iroquois apart from the surrounding communities as did Iroquois ownership of the reservations themselves. Schooling on the reservations also was that typical of rural communities. Small one-room district schools with either Indian or White teachers were common. Those who did not attend these went to Indian boarding schools, like the famous Carlisle school in Pennsylvania and the Thomas Indian School on the Cattaraugus Reservation.

Religious participation also was primarily a local affair and served to set the Iroquois apart from their neighbors. Those who had become Christians attended churches on the reservations. Sermons often were translated into "Indian" and Indian hymnals used, as those who attended the ceremonies in the Longhouse still heard the speeches of that religion delivered in "Indian" and danced to Indian songs.

These religions themselves also reflected the concerns of the reservation community. The teachings of Handsome Lake emphasizing as they did restraint and harmony provided a set of values consistent with the agricultural practices being adopted by the Iroquois. However, some aspects of life on the reservations still resembled Iroquois life in the eighteenth century and earlier, and to the extent that they did, the old Iroquois religion was practiced. For many, the necessities of life were obtained by some combination of a variety of occupations much as they had been in earlier times. Many had kitchen gardens, and the women still helped grow a significant amount of the food eaten by the family. Hunting pigeons during their annual roosting and fishing in season were important, particularly in the earlier part of the nineteenth century. Berrying (especially for strawberries), nutting, and maple-sugar collecting provided food both for home use and for sale. Although hunting came to have little importance in the economy, temporary jobs on larger farms on and off the reservation were still "hunted." Cottage industry, particularly the manufacture and sale of baskets and brooms, provided some income. For those who followed this way of life, the Longhouse religion with its attention to the change of seasons and its emphasis on thankfulness for what had been provided in the course of the seasonal changes was meaningful.

Not all Iroquois continued this partially traditional way of life. Some were more disposed to adopt White ways, and those who adopted White economic practices were apt to adopt White religious ones also. As a result, the lay leaders of the Christian churches on the reservations often were the most successful farmers in the community. During the nineteenth century, increasing numbers of Iroquois adopted White life-styles. As they did, the proportion who followed the Longhouse religion declined and the proportion of Christians to the total reservation population increased. This change was accompanied by an increase in the number of Christian churches and a decrease in the number of Longhouses. Each of the New York Seneca reservations once had at least two Longhouses; in 1973 each had only one.

As the Iroquois have adopted White agricultural practices, they have bound their economy to that of the Whites, and so are subject to the same economic vicissitudes as the White farmer. An agricultural depression such as that in the 1880s affected both Whites and Indians, and Iroquois interest in farming decreased to the extent that the once-popular agricultural fairs on the reservations ceased to be held (Carrington 1892:49). This trend has continued in the twentieth century. With new farming methods fewer farmers have been needed, and among both Whites and Indians small farms have declined in number. Very few Iroquois in the 1970s made a livelihood from farming, and much of the land still under cultivation on the reservations was land leased to White farmers who had made the capital investment necessary to engage in modern farming. Most Indians lack such capital, and like most Whites, have turned to other occupations. Economic opportunities on the reservations are few, and consequently many Iroquois work off the reservations (fig. 17). Some commute from the reservation to these jobs, others have moved to cities and towns near the reservations, and others have sought work in more distant locations such as California. This movement

off-reservation was reversed during the Depression of the 1930s when a number of Iroquois returned to the reservations, where small gardens could be cultivated and some money (especially relief money and from Works Progress Administration projects) could be obtained. But, with the advent of World War II, off-reservation movement resumed with increased vigor.

These changes have also meant that the ability to speak and to read and write English has become increasingly important, and many children in the 1970s do not know any Iroquois language. Formal education has become more important, and Iroquois children spend more years in school than their parents did. Although to some extent the daily affairs of the reservation are still those of a rural community, the reservations also bear some resemblance to White suburban communities, the children leaving on the bus in the morning to go to school and the parents leaving to go to work in the nearby towns and cities.

But as was true in the past, affairs on the reservations are not identical to those in other parts of the country, and the issues of the past remain in the present. One is the land itself. In the 1950s a portion of the Tuscarora Reservation was taken to provide land for a dam for a New York Power Authority project and in the 1960s a larger portion of the Allegany Reservation for the Kinzua Dam, the perceived need of Whites for electric power and flood control at the middle of the twentieth century being equivalent to the perceived need to "improve" the land in the nineteenth century.

Whites, particularly those living near the reservations, are conscious that Indians are not like them in some respects, and discrimination is practiced. The result—as is apt to be the case when relations between two different peoples are involved—is a complex one, and one that is not made simpler by the ambivalent attitudes of both the Iroquois and the Whites. As Whites are apt to view Indians as both "noble" and "savage," so Indians are apt to both envy and disparage Whites. In this situation, things Iroquois have symbolic importance and may be espoused. For example, classes have been formed from time to time to teach children "the Indian language." Significance is still attached to the payment of annuities although the amount each individual receives is very small. Because the practice of the Longhouse religion is distinctively Iroquois, it also serves as an outward sign of Iroquois identity. Yet there are diverse attitudes on the question of religious loyalty. Some Iroquois Christians will have nothing to do with the rituals of the Longhouse religion, while others attend them from time to time to "see how we used to do it." Some attend activities in both the Longhouse and a Christian church; some avoid both. In some Longhouses, Whites are welcome at the "doings"; in others, Whites and even Christian Iroquois are forbidden to attend.

Further, as the Iroquois have increasingly been drawn into the society about them, so also have they become

Thomas Y. Crowell Company: Farber and Dorris 1975.
Fig. 17. Roger Littlehorn, a Mohawk high steel construction worker on the site of Gimbels at 86th St., Manhattan, N.Y. The high steel occupation became an Iroquois (especially Mohawk) specialty during the late 19th century. Photograph by Joseph C. Farber, 1970.

464

interested not only in things Iroquois but also in things Indian. In the twentieth century, opportunities for Iroquois to meet other Indians have increased—in part, a result of the inclination of Whites to treat Indians as "Indians" rather than as members of particular tribes. In the earlier part of the twentieth century Indian boarding schools provided one such important opportunity, and this experience was to give rise to pan-Indian movements (Hertzberg 1971). In the mid-twentieth century, improved transportation and communication media have given Indians of different tribes increased opportunities to further their common cause, and Iroquois participation in various pan-Indian movements, including pan-Indian religious movements, has increased.

Mohawk

WILLIAM N. FENTON AND ELISABETH TOOKER

The Mohawk (ˈmōˌhôk) were the keepers of the eastern door of the Iroquois Confederacy. In the second half of the seventeenth century they were reported to have had about 400 warriors, one-third to one-half as many as the Senecas and perhaps 100 more than the other Iroquois tribes (" The League of the Iroquois: Its History, Politics, and Ritual," table 1, this vol.). Nevertheless, their position in the League (according to some traditions their chief Deganawida was instrumental in establishing it) and their location as the Iroquois tribe closest to Albany and the fur traders there gave them considerable influence among the other Iroquois tribes.

Seventeenth Century: Territory

The homeland of the Mohawks, the region where their principal villages were located, was a section of the middle Mohawk Valley extending from Schoharie Creek a little west of Amsterdam upriver to East Canada Creek, a few miles east of Little Falls ("The League of the Iroquois: Its History, Politics, and Ritual," fig. 1, this vol.) (Lenig 1965:1; Grassman 1952:98). Much of this land is now part of Montgomery County. Their hunting territories extended north into the Adirondack Mountains and south down the East Branch of the Susquehanna nearly to Oneonta.

Thus, the lands of the Mohawks lay athwart the principal route between the Hudson River and the Upper Iroquois. This trail went west from Albany across the pine barrens to Schenectady (*skahnéhtati* 'beyond the pines',* the name now given to Albany—Lounsbury 1960:26), so avoiding the unnavigable section of the lower Mohawk River that falls precipitously into the Hudson at Cohoes. From Schenectady, the route went up

---

* The italicized Mohawk words in the *Handbook* are spelled in the phonemic system described by Chafe ("Comparative Sketch of the Northern Iroquoian Languages," vol. 17). The nasalized vowels are central ę (the ʌ, v, or eñ of other sources) and high back ǫ (the u or oñ of others). The circumflex over a vowel indicates the falling accent resulting from the loss of a following laryngeal. Other letters are used in their standard *Handbook* values. Phonemicizations of Mohawk forms have been provided by Marianne Mithun and the cited published sources. Since the available materials reflect different local varieties of Mohawk there is some dialect mixture in the cited forms. In particular it has not always been possible to determine whether or not final glottal stop (ʔ) should be written, as this sound is not pronounced by many speakers.

the Mohawk to Rome (Fort Stanwix). There a portage ("The Great Carrying Place") led to Wood Creek, a stream that empties into Oneida Lake. The Oneida lived southeast of this lake near Oneida Creek. The route to the other Iroquois tribes went across Oneida Lake to its outlet at Brewerton, long an Indian fishing station, and down the Oneida River to the Oswego River. Downstream from this junction was Oswego, a fort and trading post built by the English in the eighteenth century in order to attract Indian trade from the French posts on the Saint Lawrence. Upstream lay Onondaga Lake and beyond that the principal Onondaga village, a village that could also be reached by taking an overland trail that went south of Oneida Lake through the Oneida village (Morgan 1851:map).

In the seventeenth-century accounts, the Mohawks are said to have had anywhere from three to eight villages. Although some of these differences may reflect a population decline through war, disease, and migration (Hewitt 1907b:924; Fenton 1940:208), they do not reflect any sudden and radical change in the number of Mohawk villages in this period. Rather, the available data indicate that throughout the seventeenth century, the Mohawks had three principal villages (often termed "castles") and several smaller ones. These smaller villages were apt to be noted by those traveling through Mohawk country, such as the Dutch journalist who recorded seeing eight in 1634 (Jameson 1909:140-155), the Jesuit missionaries who mentioned six in 1667 and 1670 and seven in 1669 (JR 51:205, 52:123, 53:153), and Wentworth Greenhalgh who mentioned five in 1677 (O'Callaghan 1849-1851, 1:11-12). Those with more intimate knowledge, such as Johannes Megapolensis writing in 1644 (Jameson 1909:178-179; and cf. NYCD 13:15, 72, 112), Isaac Jogues in the 1640s (JR 24:283, 29:23, 31:39, 45-47, 83, 32:25; Shea 1857a:180-187; Grassman 1969:623), and the Jesuits in some accounts of their mission (JR 51:187, 201, 57:83, 89), most often mention three villages or castles. In so doing, they undoubtedly refer to the principal villages. From the time of the first recorded visits of Whites until 1666 when they were burned by the French, these Mohawk villages were located on the south side of the Mohawk River.

Of the three castles, the name of the most eastern (also called the Lower or the First Castle) is the most variable, perhaps indicating that this village moved several times in the 1630s and 1640s. The Iroquois often changed the name of the village when they rebuilt it in a new location, although in the latter half of the seventeenth century a new Mohawk village was usually given the name of the older one. The Dutch journalist (probably Harmen Meyndertsz van den Bogaert) who visited the First Castle in 1634 recorded its name as Onekagoncka (Jameson 1909:142). In 1644 Megapolensis said the First Castle was called Asserué (Jameson 1909:178–179), a name Jogues writing a year earlier recorded as Ossernenon (Shea 1857a:186; Grassman 1969:623). This village was located one-quarter mile south of the Mohawk River, southeast of present Auriesville (Fenton 1940:206; Martin 1885:259–263; Ewing 1953) and was subsequently moved west. In 1646 Jogues said that Osserrion (i.e., Ossernenon) was called Oneugiouré (JR 29:51), perhaps indicating it had moved since he had been there four years earlier. In any case, it undoubtedly had moved by 1659 for that year the name of the village is given as Kaghnuwage (NYCD 13:112), a spelling of Caughnawaga (*kahnawâ·ke* 'at the rapids'). After this village was destroyed by Alexandre de Prouville de Tracy's expedition in 1666, it was rebuilt north of the river on the west side of Cayadutta Creek and west of present Fonda (JR 51:295; Grassman 1952a). Nevertheless, it retained the name Caughnawaga, a name also given to the settlement which was established on the Saint Lawrence in 1676 by Mohawks, many of whom came from the Mohawk Valley Caughnawaga. In 1668 two-thirds of its population was said to be Huron and Algonquian captives (JR 51:187).

In this period, the name of the second Mohawk castle, Kanagaro, although variously spelled, remained the same (Jameson 1909:142, 179; Shea 1857a:186; Grassman 1969:623; JR 53:139, 57:111; NYCD 2:712, 13:479; O'Callaghan 1849–1851, 1:11). The name *kaná·karoⁿ* has been translated as 'a pole in the water' (Hewitt 1907c:649). It was located two leagues from the first castle (JR 51:201); and after it had been burned by the French in 1666, it also moved north of the river (Fenton 1940:207).

Occasionally another large village between Kanagaro and the upper castle is mentioned (Jameson 1909:144; O'Callaghan 1849–1851, 1:11). Apparently the Mohawks had a relatively large village in addition to the three principal castles with the result that sometimes the Mohawks are reported to have had four castles (NYCD 13:122, 464, 499, 500).

The name of the upper castle, the largest Mohawk village and the "capital" of the country, remained the same during this period. It was known as Tionnontoguen, variously spelled (Jameson 1909:145, 179; Shea 1857a:186; Grassman 1969:623; JR 51:201–205, 53:137; O'Callaghan 1849–1851, 1:12, 2:87; NYCD 3:565), which has been interpreted as *teyonǫtó·kę* 'valley; between two mountains' (Lounsbury 1960:26; compare

Cuoq 1882:49). After it had been burned in 1666, it was rebuilt one-quarter of a league from its old location (JR 51:201–203).

In 1644 Megapolensis, noting that the Mohawks were divided into three tribes (that is, clans), implied that the Tortoise (Turtle) lived in the first castle, the Bear in the second, and the Wolf in the third (Jameson 1909:178–179), a statement that often has been interpreted as meaning that the Mohawks had clan villages. If the Iroquois custom of clan exogamy was in existence in the seventeenth century (as seems certain), Megapolensis's statement cannot be literally correct. If all the women in a village belonged to the same clan, their husbands would belong to at least one different clan (more probably to both of the other two clans). If all the men in a village belonged to one clan, their wives would belong to one or probably the two other clans. Furthermore, assuming as is likely that the Iroquois preference for matrilocal residence also then prevailed, all or most of the married men in a village would have come from other villages. The married men holding chiefly titles would not be living in the same village as would the women who selected them or the other women and the unmarried men of their clan to whom they had the obligations associated with clan affiliation. Thus it seems likely that villages were endogamous, multiclan units. Some confirmation of this conclusion is found in the 1646 report that Jogues gave a present of wampum "to one of the great families [probably clans] of the Annierronnon [Mohawk] scattered through their three villages" (JR 29:53, 293). Most probably Megapolensis's statement, if true, refers to the principal or dominant clan in each village, and chiefs holding names belonging to that clan also lived in the village associated with it. If this was the case, it would mean that with the possible exception of the Turtle clan (the position associated with the name Hiawatha is not now filled), three chiefs of the Iroquois Confederacy lived in each principal Mohawk village. The Mohawk hold nine chieftainships in the League, each clan holding three such names (see "The League of the Iroquois: Its History, Politics, and Ritual," this vol.).

History to 1670

Because they were the easternmost of the Iroquois tribes, the Mohawk were the first to feel the impact of European activities along the eastern seaboard. At the end of the sixteenth century the Mohawk were at war with the Algonquin and Montagnais who were trading with the French at Tadoussac. At least one aim of the Mohawk was to acquire as booty some of the iron axes, knives, and sword blades that were making their northern neighbors more formidable (Champlain 1922–1936, 2:96). Still earlier, the desire to circumvent groups who lived nearer these sources of European goods may have led the

Mohawk to attack the Saint Lawrence Iroquoians. It has been speculated that the need to protect their western flank while engaging in these conflicts led the Mohawk to become the prime movers in founding the Iroquois confederacy (Tooker 1964:3–4).

Additional French support for their Algonquin trading partners after the founding of Quebec in 1608 and in particular the loss of 100 Mohawk warriors near the mouth of the Richelieu River in 1610 made raids along the Saint Lawrence increasingly costly to the Mohawk. Moreover, the previous year Samuel de Champlain had assisted an Algonquian expedition to defeat a Mohawk war party along the southwestern shore of Lake Champlain, killing several headmen ("Early Iroquoian Contacts with Europeans," fig. 2, this vol.). The Mohawk were therefore willing to abandon their attacks in favor of trading with the Dutch after fur traders of that nationality began to frequent the Hudson River soon after Henry Hudson's exploration of it in 1609 (Desrosiers 1947:47). There is a tradition that a treaty of friendship between the Dutch, the Mohawk, and the Mahican was concluded about 1618, and what was presented as the document of that treaty, dated 1613, has been published (Van Loon 1968). However, it has been argued that a treaty of this date is unlikely (Hunt 1940:26–27; Trelease 1960:34), and although some scholars accept the validity of the document ("Mahican," this vol.) others do not. In any event the Mohawk seem to have been able to cross Mahican territory to trade with the Dutch, and Dutchmen accompanied the Mohawk on a raid against the Susquehannock in 1615. Dutch efforts to use Mahican contacts to forge trading links between Fort Orange and the Montagnais and Algonquins led the Mohawk to forestall such an alliance. Following the conclusion of a shaky truce with the French and their Algonquin allies, the Mohawk attacked the Mahican and in a hard-fought war that lasted 1624–1628 extended their influence eastward to seize control of the territory around the Dutch trading post at Fort Orange. As a result of this war, the Mohawk acquired rights of passage over trade and other forms of contact between the Dutch and the tribes living to the north. The Mohawk determined not to allow groups who were or even potentially were their enemies to have dealings with the Dutch and insisted on being friendly intermediaries between the Iroquois tribes to the west and the Dutch to the east. The Dutch resented Mohawk control but were too weak to do anything about it. Moreover, the Mohawk used periodic rapprochements with the French to persuade the Dutch to lower the price of their trade goods (Trigger 1971).

Throughout the early seventeenth century the Mohawk became increasingly dependent on a wide range of European goods. To secure greater numbers of furs to trade with the Dutch, the Mohawk abandoned whatever conservation they had formerly practiced within their own territory and began once again to raid the Algonquian peoples to the north. While they continued to seize European goods as booty, the primary objectives of these raids came to be to seize beaver pelts from the Algonquians and to hunt beaver within Algonquian territory. At various times the Mohawk sought to persuade the French to adopt a policy of neutrality with respect to Indian quarrels and to confine their activities to trading with whatever Indians reached their posts. When this policy proved unsuccessful, they waged war on the French, seeking to confine them to their settlements and if possible to force them to withdraw from Montreal and Trois Rivières (Trelease 1960; Trigger 1976:603–664).

In the early 1640s the Mohawk obtained guns, first from the English and then in large numbers from the Dutch. Firearms put an end to the traditional combat of large parties meeting face to face, exchanging taunts, and after a few volleys of arrows closing to slug it out with spear and club before retiring carrying their dead and wounded to some prearranged enclosure. Hereafter the Mohawk excelled at fighting in the woods and particularly from tree to tree. Father Jerome Lalemant marveled how so few people could wreak such havoc and admired the military skill of the Mohawk (JR 45:207–211). Taking advantage of their new firepower, the Mohawk increasingly harassed the French, their Algonquian allies, and the Huron who came to the Saint Lawrence valley to trade. Although the Mohawk concluded a brief truce with these groups in 1645, in order to recover some Mohawks who had been taken prisoner, this truce came to an end the following year after the inhabitants of Ossernenon slew the French envoy, Father Isaac Jogues, on a charge of practicing sorcery (JR 30:227–229). Father Jogues had been adopted by a Mohawk family after he had been captured by them in 1642 but had escaped and returned to France soon after. After 1646 the Mohawk aided the western Iroquois to disperse the Huron, Petun, Neutral, and Erie. This netted them a rich booty in furs and captives. The captives were valued as replacements for a population that since at least 1634 had been repeatedly decimated by smallpox and other epidemics of European origin. During this period a brief alliance with the Mahican secured the Mohawk's eastern flank, but a Mohawk attack on the well-armed Susquehannock in 1651–1652 did not eliminate these trading rivals to the south. However, after the Dutch seized New Sweden in 1655 the Susquehannock were forced to make peace with the Mohawk (JR 37:97).

Maintaining public policy became more difficult as mounting dependence on European goods, an unprecedented mortality rate, and the need to naturalize growing numbers of aliens into Mohawk society produced increasing dependence on warfare. Leadership diffused, figures of authority multiplied, and traditional chiefs lost power to military leaders. Being a segmented society with multiple chiefs, the Mohawk were poorly structured to cope with such contingencies. Also, drinking rum brought by Dutch traders set off brawls making the towns unpleasant to live in.

After 1651, Mohawk efforts to supervise relations between the other Iroquois tribes and European traders led the western tribes of the confederacy to seek their own trading alliances with the French, thereby challenging the Mohawk's role as keepers of the eastern door of the confederacy. To avoid isolation and in an effort to receive their share of the Hurons at Quebec (whom the Jesuits were helping to persuade to join the missions they hoped to establish among the Iroquois), the Mohawk followed the other Iroquois tribes into making peace with the French in 1653. This peace, agreed to by the French out of weakness, allowed the Mohawk to continue to wage war on the Indian allies of the French. Despite four visits to their country by the Jesuit missionary Simon Le Moyne between 1655 and 1659, many Mohawks continued to oppose this peace. In 1658, after increasingly violent confrontations, they persuaded the Onondaga to terminate the Jesuit mission of Sainte Marie at Gannentaha that had been established in their midst (JR 44:149–153). After 1659 the Mohawk held aloof from the prolonged war between the western Iroquois and the Susquehannock.

New York became an English colony in 1664, but the change little affected the Mohawks. They continued to trade with Albany, dealing with the Dutch who remained there to carry on trade under the English flag. English goods were generally of better quality and sold at lower prices than French goods—a circumstance that helped the Mohawks maintain their position in the fur trade and their close ties with Albany. The other Iroquois tribes made peace with the French in 1665. They did this in part because they were engaged in a war with the Susquehannock to the south that was of little interest to the Mohawks and did not wish to continue war on other fronts, particularly as the French threatened to attack the Iroquois. They also did it because some wished to open trade relationships with the French and thereby not remain so dependent on the Mohawk-Albany trade. The Mohawk did not make peace, and that winter an expedition led by Daniel de Rémy de Courcelle went to attack them. By mistake the expedition arrived near Schenectady rather than the Mohawk villages; led into an ambush there by some Mohawks, they retreated. The failure of Courcelle's expedition induced de Tracy to lead another expedition against the Mohawks in the fall of 1666. This expedition succeeded in burning the Mohawk villages and their supplies of corn, and in 1667 the Mohawks along with the other Iroquois tribes concluded a peace with the French at Quebec. That same year the Jesuit Fathers Jacques Frémin and Jean Pierron went to the Mohawk country to begin a new mission there.

Seventeenth and Eighteenth Centuries: Saint Lawrence Settlements

In the decade following the conclusion of peace with the French, a number of Iroquois, particularly Mohawks, left their homeland and settled on the Saint Lawrence in the vicinity of Montreal. Two such settlements were established in the 1670s—one on the south side of the Saint Lawrence and the other on the north side on the Island of Montreal. There, although they adopted Catholicism, the Iroquois continued to practice an economy similar to that of their homeland. Their alliance was with the French, and they often joined the French on expeditions against various Indians, including the Iroquois who had remained in their old homeland, and against the English. In the eighteenth century, they played a prominent role in the illicit trade between Montreal and Albany and also became voyageurs for the fur companies.

In the middle of the eighteenth century, two other Iroquois settlements were established on the Saint Lawrence. One composed principally of Onondagas was established at Oswegatchie (now Ogdensburg, New York) in the late 1740s (see "Onondaga," this vol.). Another was established about the same time at Saint Regis by some Iroquois from Caughnawaga. Both these settlements were situated so as to afford protection against possible English invasion of the upper Saint Lawrence, although they proved inadequate when that invasion finally came.

Caughnawaga

In 1667 some French families, no longer fearing Iroquois attacks, took up residence on the south side of the Saint Lawrence opposite Montreal at La Prairie (also known as La Prairie de la Madeleine) on land that had been given to the Jesuits 20 years before (JR 25:289, 48:295; Devine 1922:13). That same year Father Pierre Raffeix, who was encouraging the French to settle at La Prairie, also persuaded a half-dozen Oneidas who had come to Montreal to spend the winter there. One of this group was Catherine Gandeaktena, an Erie woman held captive by the Oneidas. Having been converted by Father Jacques Bruyas at Oneida, she had resolved to live with the French and had persuaded a few others including her husband to join her. In early spring 1668 a few other Oneidas who had been hunting that winter in the surrounding country joined their relatives at La Prairie, and toward the end of the summer the group went to Quebec where they were further instructed and baptized. They returned to La Prairie in the fall and spent the winter hunting in the vicinity, coming back to the house that had been built for them at La Prairie for important feast days, a practice continued in later years. In spring 1669 François-Xavier (Pierre) Tonsahoten, husband of Catherine Gandeaktena, built a house at La Prairie. Others followed his example, and in 1670 there were five houses and about 20 families at the new mission (JR 55:35, 61:195-199, 63:149-161).

They were joined by yet others who also had decided to live there permanently, and during the 1670s the settlement grew rapidly. Some who settled were Iroquois who had come to the Saint Lawrence to hunt and trade. La Prairie's location attracted a number of visitors, some of whom stayed. Also, residents of La Prairie persuaded some of the Iroquois they met when hunting in the region to visit their village, and some of these Indians decided to settle there. Still others decided to move to La Prairie after they had been converted by the Jesuits living in the Iroquois villages south of Lake Ontario or had been influenced by their countrymen to migrate to the Saint Lawrence (JR 63:159, 167-181, 195-197, 58:81-85, 249-251). Of these, some went to the La Prairie settlement and others to Notre Dame de Foy, where the small group of Hurons who had fled to Quebec after the destruction of their country in 1649 had moved their village in 1669. This village was moved again at the end of 1673 to Lorette, a league and one-half farther from Quebec. In the mid-1670s about 300 Hurons and Iroquois lived there (JR 57:53, 71, 58:131, 147, 171, 60:27, 69-85, 145, 309, 61:169; see "Huron of Lorette," this vol.). But during the 1680s the population at Lorette declined (JR 62:169).

The Iroquois who had settled at La Prairie found the soil unsuitable for growing Indian corn—it was too damp—and in 1676 they moved a league and one-quarter upriver to the Sault Saint Louis (Lachine Rapids) (JR 60:275, 61:241, 63:191). In consequence, the name of the mission was changed from that of Saint François Xavier des Près to Saint François Xavier du Sault, and the Indians living there came to be known as the Indians of the Sault. The Indian name for the place was Caughnawaga, the same name as given to the Lower Mohawk castle in the Mohawk Valley from which a number of

Mohawks at the Saint Lawrence settlement had come.

Although the first settlement at La Prairie had been composed principally of Oneidas, it soon attracted large numbers from other tribes, particularly Mohawks. In fact, so many Mohawks came to La Prairie that it was said that in 1673 there were more Mohawk warriors living there than in their own country (JR 63:179). Particularly notable among those Mohawks who decided to migrate was a chief known to the people of Albany as Kryn and to the French as Joseph Togouiroui and as the Great Mohawk. In 1673 he led some 40 Mohawks from the Caughnawaga village in the Mohawk Valley to the Saint Lawrence (JR 57:105-109, 58:83-85, 61:169, 63:177-179). Another was the pious Catherine Tekakwitha *(katerí tekahkwí·tha?)* the first Indian to be declared venerable by the Roman Catholic Church. Some Onondagas and Hurons also took up residence at La Prairie and were numerous enough so that both of these groups had their own chiefs as did the Mohawks. Among the various Indians who came were a number of captives; consequently, it was said that some 20 tribes were represented there (JR 55:35, 56:19, 57:75, 58:75, 207, 60:277, 287, 61:241, 63:153, 169, 181).

Although they initially tried to remain neutral as relations between the French and the Confederacy became increasingly strained in the 1680s, the Caughnawagas were drawn into the conflict on the French side. After the massacre of Lachine in 1689, the Caughnawagas moved to Montreal (NYCD 9:438, 441) where they remained for a year. Previous to this, they had lived for 13 years at the Sault village and consequently the soil nearby was becoming exhausted. Therefore, it was decided to move the village a few miles upriver onto land granted by the king in 1680. The village was moved again a couple of miles upriver in 1696, the year before King William's War formally ended. In this war the Caughnawagas had been subject to Iroquois raids on the Saint

Fig. 1. Caughnawaga in the mid-18th century. At right the church (A) and the missionary's house (B), at left the Mohawk bark-covered longhouses (3 at left with raised smoke hole covers). Fields are in the background; nearer are a few horses and people carrying guns, fishing with poles, and canoeing. Contemporary sketch in ink and watercolors.

Lawrence and also had taken part in French expeditions against the Iroquois including Louis de Buade de Frontenac's expedition against the Onondagas in 1696, the last French expedition of the war against the Iroquois (Devine 1922:89–129).

In Queen Anne's War, 1702–1713, they participated in many raids on New England including those on Deerfield in 1704 and on Groton, Massachusetts, in 1707. At the same time, they were the key participants in the contraband trade between Montreal and Albany, a role they continued to play after the conclusion of the war in 1713. Later in the century as the fur trade moved west, they

became voyageurs and trappers for the fur companies in western Canada where some of them remained (see "Iroquois in the West," this vol.).

By 1714 the soil at Caughnawaga was exhausted as was the wood that could be gathered nearby, and the Indians decided to move their village two leagues farther up the Saint Lawrence. In 1716, they began the process of moving to the new village, which retained the name of the old (fig. 1) (JR 67:25; Charlevoix 1761, 1:218; Devine 1922:173–181). Caughnawaga remained a seigniory of the Jesuits until 1762 when the new English governor of Montreal refused to recognize the claims of the Jesuits and the lands were retained by the Crown for the use of the Indians (fig. 2) (Devine 1922:282–284).

In 1716 there were estimated to be about 200 warriors at Caughnawaga (JR 67:25), although there had been only 100 there in 1687 (Lahontan 1940:49). In 1736 there were reported to be 300 warriors (O'Callaghan 1849–1851, 1:17; NYCD 9:1053), the same number reported to be living at Caughnawaga and Saint Regis in 1763 (O'Callaghan 1849–1851, 1:27; NYCD 7:582).

Fig. 2. Modern Mohawk reserves and reservation. a, Gibson Reserve; b, Oka Reserve; c, Caughnawaga Reserve; d, St. Regis Reservation and Reserve; e, Tyendinaga Reserve; f, Six Nations Reserve, see also "Six Nations of the Grand River, Ontario," fig. 1, this vol.

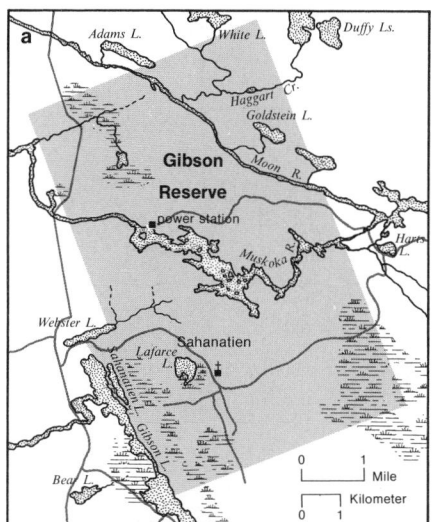

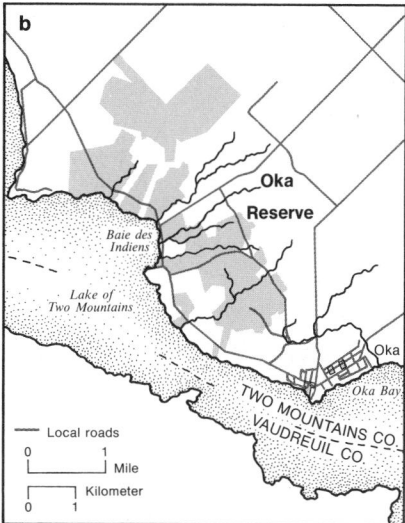

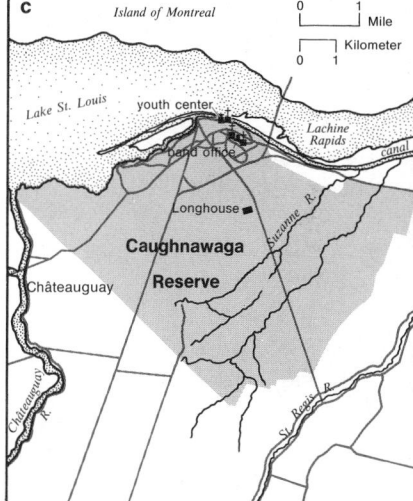

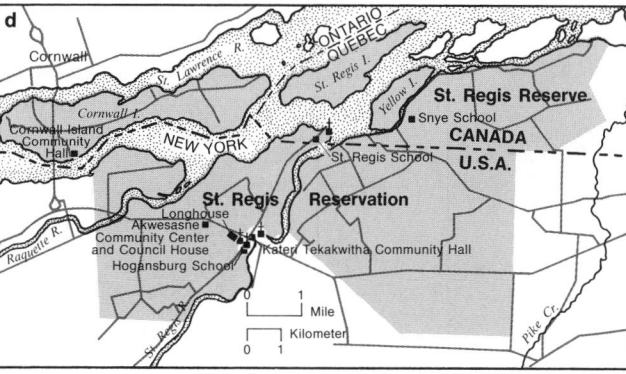

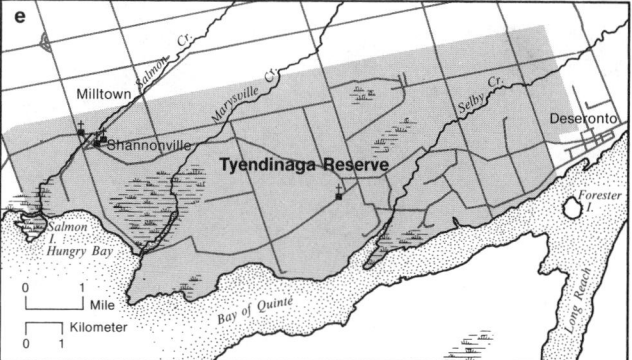

471

Iroquois of the Mountain

About the time the Iroquois settlement at La Prairie moved upriver to the Sault Saint Louis, some Iroquois asked to settle on the Island of Montreal. This request was granted, and in 1676 the Sulpicians, seigneurs of Montreal, established a mission at Mount Royal. The Indians who settled there, including some from the Sault, came to be known as the Iroquois of the Mountain, after the location of the mission. Like the Iroquois of the Sault, the Iroquois of the Mountain became increasingly attached to the French, participating in the French expeditions against the Iroquois and in turn being attacked by those Iroquois who continued to reside in their old homeland (Shea 1855:309-311, 317-323).

In 1687 there were reported to be 80 warriors in this Iroquois group (Lahontan 1940:49). In 1694, this settle-ment at Mount Royal consisting of 50 houses, 15 French houses, a church, and palisade burned after a drunken Indian had set fire to one of the houses. After the destruction, a stone fort—completed in 1698—was built. In 1696 many of the Indians had moved from this village to a new one on the Rivière des Prairies near Sault au Recollet called Nouvelle Lorette, but some Indians remained at the old mission at the Mountain until 1704 when it was abandoned. In 1721 the village at the Sault au Recollect was moved to the Lake of Two Mountains on land that had been granted to the Sulpicians as a seigniory. Not long after, they were joined by Nipissings from Île aux Tourtes and Algonquins from Sainte-Anne-de-Bout-de-l'Île (Shea 1855:327-329, 333-334; O.Maurault 1930:122-123). In 1736 there were estimated to be 50 Nipissing and 20 Algonquin fighting men living at the Lake of Two Mountains as well as 60 Iroquois warriors

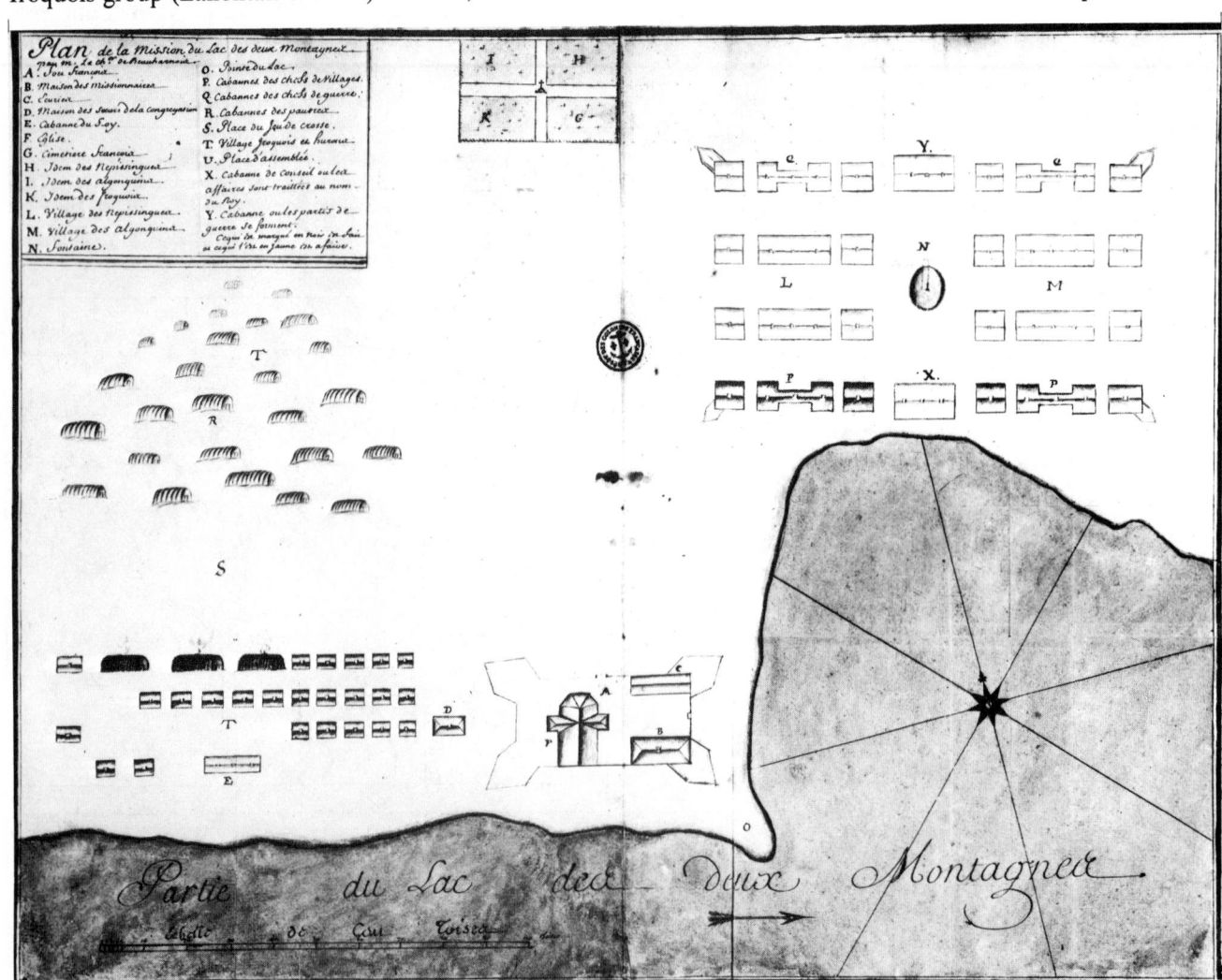

Archives de la Ministère de la France d'Outre-Mer, Paris: Plans et Fortifications, Amér. Sept., 490B.

Fig. 3. Map of the Lake of Two Mountains settlement in 1743. The letters are explained as follows: A, French fort; B, missionaries' house; *C, stables; D, nuns' quarters; *E, royal lodge; F, church; G, French cemetery; H, Nipissing cemetery; I, Algonquin cemetery; K, Iroquois cemetery; *L, Nipissing village; *M, Algonquin village; N, cistern; P, lodges of village chiefs; *Q (above L and M), lodges of war chiefs; R, lodges of the poor; S, lacrosse field; T, Iroquois and Huron village; *X, council house; *Y, lodge for organizing war parties. * = "to be built." The squares in the structures shown in plan seem to represent smoke holes. Contemporary drawing in ink and watercolors probably by Claude Chevalier de Beauharnois, nephew of the governor-general of New France.

(O'Callaghan 1849-1851, 1:16-17; NYCD 9:1053); in 1763, 150 Indian warriors were reported living there (fig. 3) (O'Callaghan 1849-1851, 1:27; NYCD 7:582).

First at Montreal and later at Lake of Two Mountains the settlement attracted Indians of various tribes, but Mohawks apparently predominated as the language that came to be spoken there by all groups was Mohawk. Like those at Caughnawaga, they often participated in raids against the English in the eighteenth century. However, although throughout their history the Iroquois of the Mountain have maintained a close relationship to those of the Sault and have often engaged in the same kind of activity, there are differences. For example, Oka contained an Algonquin community, from which the Oka Iroquois learned Algonquin hunting techniques, sharing with them the hunting grounds north of the Ottawa between the Matawin on the north and the Black River on the east. Nevertheless, they continued to practice agriculture in the traditional Iroquois fashion (Speck 1923a).

Saint Regis

In the middle of the eighteenth century, for various reasons—including exhaustion of land at Caughnawaga, a factional dispute there, and the desire of the French to establish an additional post on the Upper Saint Lawrence—a group from Caughnawaga moved to the head of Lake Saint Francis and built a village where an elevated point juts into the Saint Lawrence between the Saint Regis and Racquette rivers. It was named Saint Regis in memory of Jean François Régis, a French ecclesiastic canonized in 1737 who before his death in 1640 at the age of 43 had wanted to become a missionary to the Iroquois (Hough 1853:113-114).

The exact date of the first settlement at Saint Regis is uncertain. In 1747 it was reported that some Indians from the Sault had recently settled at the mouth of the River Louis at the head of Lake Saint Francis (NYCD 10:105), and it may be that this account refers to those Caughnawagas who by Saint Regis tradition first settled at Saint Regis. One such tradition states that the first settlers were two brothers (another tradition states only one brother came), John and Zachariah Tarbell, who had been taken captive by Caughnawagas during a raid on Groton, Massachusetts, on June 20, 1707. The brothers were subsequently adopted and later married daughters of Caughnawaga chiefs, but they quarreled with others at Caughnawaga and the missionary advised them to leave. The two brothers, their wives, and their wives' parents settled at what is now Saint Regis (Hough 1853:112-113; cf. DCB 3:615).

It has also been suggested that Saint Regis was founded in 1755 (Devine 1922:255; Frisch 1970a:208). In 1754 it was reported that more than 30 families living at Caughnawaga planned to settle at Lake Saint Francis as the lands at the Sault were exhausted, and by July of the following year the new mission had been established at Saint Regis. The French felt that it along with the other Iroquois settlements along the Saint Lawrence at La Presentation, Lake of Two Mountains, and Caughnawaga would form a barrier between them and the pro-British Iroquois living in their old homeland, and they also hoped to attract to Saint Regis other Iroquois who wanted to leave that area but who did not want to settle at Caughnawaga (NYCD 10:266-267, 301).

About this time the French and Indian War broke out; presumably in this war the Saint Regis Indians sided with the French, although a few joined Jeffrey Amherst and the British when they came up the Saint Lawrence in 1760. The year before, the Abenaki settlement on the Saint François River some 60 miles below Montreal had been destroyed by the British, and some of the surviving remnants were given refuge at Saint Regis. Their village was rebuilt in 1767, but the Abenakis remained at Saint Regis for at least another seven years before returning to it (Frisch 1970a:209).

During the American Revolution, a considerable portion of the Saint Regis Indians joined the British while the sympathies of others were with the Americans (Hough 1853:122). After the war, some Oswegatchies (see "Onondaga," this vol.) and perhaps also Indians from other Iroquois communities moved to Saint Regis (Frisch 1970:70).

History from 1670

Mohawk Valley 1670-1770

The migration of Mohawks from the Mohawk Valley to the Saint Lawrence continued into the early years of the 1680s. In 1683 it was reported that as many as 200 had come to settle at the Sault within the last two years (JR 62:237). And, in the early 1680s, the Iroquois were deterred from attacking the French as the Mohawks said that they would not agree to such a war so long as their countrymen lived among them (JR 62:255). Nevertheless, they were drawn into the conflict, and in 1693 the French sent an expedition that included Iroquois from the Sault and Mountain against the Mohawks in the Mohawk Valley and burned their villages. The success of this expedition as well as that three years later against the Onondaga led the Mohawks and other Iroquois eventually to conclude a peace with the French in 1701. But even before the peace was formally concluded, some Mohawks left the Mohawk Valley for the Saint Lawrence and in 1700 it was reported not only that the Mohawks had lost men in the war but also that with these new immigrants almost two-thirds of the Mohawks were living in Canada (NYCD 4:648).

The peace established with the French at Quebec in 1701 and the renewal of the Iroquois alliance with the English that same year continued when war broke out the following year between France and England. This policy of neutrality permitted the contraband trade involving the Iroquois on the Saint Lawrence, a trade by which English goods were exchanged for French furs. In the seventeenth and eighteenth centuries, the Iroquois used war and skillful diplomacy to maintain their advantage in the fur trade, playing off French against English when necessary. The important illicit trade (usually tacitly consented to by both French and English) in the eighteenth century was only one facet of the complex strategy the Iroquois used to achieve this end.

Although for the most part the Iroquois pursued a policy of neutrality during Queen Anne's War—a policy desired by the French—the English from time to time attempted to draw the Iroquois into it. The most famous of such efforts to keep the Iroquois in the English interest was the visit of the "Four Indian Kings" to London in 1710. Three of the four "Kings" were Mohawks (one was Hendrick—fig. 4—and another the grandfather of Joseph Brant) and the other a River Indian (possibly a Mahican). The four toured London, were feted, had an audience with the queen, of whom they requested missionaries, had their portraits painted ("Northern Iroquoian Culture Patterns," figs. 19-20, "Mahican," fig. 4, both this vol.),

Public Arch. of Canada, Ottawa.

Fig. 4. Tee Yee Neen Ho Ga Row, or Hendrick (b. ca. 1680, d. 1755), Mohawk, painted from life during his visit to London in 1710, by John Verelst. He wears European clothing, including a scarlet cloak given him in London, except for a belt or burden strap decorated with dyed moosehair or porcupine quills in black, red, and white. He holds a wampum belt, while behind him is a wolf, indicating his clan.

and were the subject of a number of literary pieces (R.P. Bond 1952).

One result of the visit was the building, 1710–1712, of Fort Hunter where the Schoharie empties into the Mohawk. A wooden chapel was built within the fort and Queen Anne gave to it a set of communion plate, each piece bearing the inscription "The gift of her Majesty Ann, by the grace of God, of Great Britain, France and Ireland, and of her Plantations in America. Queen, to her Indian Chappel of the Mohawks" (Frey 1898:32).

The building of the chapel at Fort Hunter represented an intensification of Protestant missionary activity begun in the previous century and conducted by Dutchmen out of Albany and Schenectady. Notable early missionary work was carried out by Johannes Megapolensis, pastor at Fort Orange from 1642 to 1649, who admitted about 30 to church membership. After Megapolensis left, little such work was done until Godfreidus Dellius became pastor at Albany and Schenectady in 1683. Dellius translated a few portions of the Bible into Mohawk, preached among the Indians, and organized an Indian church. He was suspended from his office by civil authorities in 1699, and the following year Johannes Lydius who had just settled in Albany received an appointment to teach the Mohawks. That same year Bernardus Freeman was appointed minister at Schenectady, where he continued the work of translation and conversion. After he left in 1705 and Lydius died in 1709, Dutch missionary efforts declined, although a few pastors did do some missionary work in addition to their other duties (Corwin 1925).

English missionary work among the Mohawks began in 1704 when the Society for the Propagation of the Gospel in Foreign Parts (organized in 1701) sent Thoroughgood Moor (Moore) as missionary. Discouraged by the lack of Indian interest in his efforts, Moor left after spending nearly a year in Albany. Subsequent missionary activity met with little greater success. William Andrews, sent as missionary to the Indians at Fort Hunter in 1712, left in 1719 also discouraged by the lack of Indian interest in the church and school established there (Humphreys 1730:284–311; Lydekker 1938:13–51).

At this time there were two principal Mohawk settlements in the Mohawk Valley: the Lower Mohawk Castle near Fort Hunter, also called Tiononderoge (*teyǫtaró·kę* 'junction of two waterways', a name variously spelled — Hewitt 1910h— and not to be confused with the name of the seventeenth-century upper castle), and the Upper Mohawk Castle, or Canajoharie (*kanaʔtsyóhare* 'washed kettle' after a kettlelike basin worn in the rocks of a creek), 20 or more miles upriver (Lounsbury 1960:25). In 1713 the lower castle was a palisaded village of 40 or 50 houses and had a population of 360, and the upper castle, a village of between 20 and 30 houses. In addition, there were several small villages of approximately seven or eight houses (Lydekker 1938:37, 40). The village at Fort

Hunter may have been established when the fort was built: in 1705, it had been reported that one of the Mohawk castles was located on a high hill and the other about 12 miles distant (Humphreys 1730:289; Lydekker 1938:19)—half the distance later reported to separate the two villages. Be that as it may, the Mohawks continued to have only two principal settlements during the first three-quarters of the eighteenth century.

The Mohawk settlements were not the only ones in the region. Throughout the seventeenth century, the westernmost White settlement was at Schenectady. But after Fort Hunter was built the Mohawk country became relatively safe from attack, and White settlers began buying land from the Indians and moving into the area. As early as 1713, some may have settled as far west as Palatine. In 1712 Palatines (German Protestant refugees from the Palatinate) began to settle on the Schoharie Creek, but the great influx of Palatines into the Mohawk Valley began in 1723 after several large patents had been granted. Their numbers so increased that by 1735 the Mohawk between Fort Hunter and Frankfort had become a German river. At the same time, traders established themselves in the region as well as at Oswego, attracting the Indian trade in furs away from Albany and Schenectady. By 1730 flatboats and bateaux were transporting traders' merchandise as well as the farmers' grain and potash and pearlash along the river (Frey 1898; Hislop 1948:114).

About the same time, interest in reestablishing missionary work among the Mohawks revived. In 1727 the mission at Fort Hunter was reopened, and John Miln, who had been appointed to serve both the Indian mission and Albany, visited Fort Hunter four times a year. He returned to England four years later, and in 1735 Henry Barclay was appointed catechist. Two years later Barclay was ordained, and in 1741 he rebuilt the chapel at Fort Hunter. The following year, schools were opened at both the upper and lower castles, and in 1743 most of the Mohawks were reported to be at least nominal Christians. Barclay left in 1746, and the Mohawks were without a minister until 1750 when John Ogilvie took up the work. He was followed by several others, one of whom dedicated the church built at the upper castle by William Johnson (Lydekker 1938:52-64, 111-150).

Although a number of Whites had settled in the Mohawk and Schoharie valleys on land sold by the Mohawks, the Mohawks continued their active participation in the fur trade. Of the traders who established posts in their territory, the most notable was William Johnson, who had come to the Mohawk Valley in 1738 to manage lands his uncle had purchased there. The following year he himself began to buy land in the valley. At the same time, he began trading at Oquaga, a village on the Susquehanna River where some Mohawks as well as other Indians had settled, and on the Mohawk River, the latter activity successfully drawing away trade from

Albany. As his trade grew, so also did his influence with the Indians, particularly the Mohawks, whom he endeavored to keep in the English interest. In their turn, these activities led Johnson into military command, first in King George's War and later to a more important role in the French and Indian War. He was made a baronet for his role in the Battle of Lake George in 1755, an engagement in which Hendrick, the influential chief of the Upper Mohawks, was killed. After the French and Indian War, he continued to exercise his influence among the Indians of the Northeast and until his death in 1774 was the leading figure at a number of councils including that at Fort Stanwix in 1768, which established a new boundary line between the Indian and White territories (Pound 1930; Flexner 1959).

Final Exodus from the Mohawk Valley

Those Mohawks who had remained in the Mohawk Valley had prospered, so much so that at the time of the American Revolution it was said that they lived considerably better than most White farmers in the valley (Stone 1838, 2:38; Graymont 1972:146-147, 219). They still had two principal settlements, one at Canajoharie and the other at Fort Hunter. In 1773 the Upper Mohawks at Canajoharie were reported to number 221 and the Lower Mohawks at Fort Hunter, 185 (NYCD 8:458); but by the end of the war, virtually none remained. Both the Upper and Lower Mohawks had permanently settled in Canada.

As the Mohawks of the Mohawk Valley had long been allied with the English more strongly than the other Iroquois tribes, when the war began between the disaffected colonists and the Crown, many Mohawks joined the British cause. But not all concurred, and some of the Mohawk chiefs wished to remain neutral. Most notable of these was Little Abraham (Tigoransera) of the Fort Hunter Mohawks, who on various occasions, including the council at Albany with the Six Nations in August 1775, averred Mohawk neutrality (Stone 1838, 1:71-72, 100-101, 121-132, 135-137, 147-148). Nevertheless, those who remained in their villages did not escape the war's destruction. In 1777, to avenge the defeat at Oriskany, some Oneidas and Americans attacked and plundered the Canajoharie and Fort Hunter Mohawk settlements. In consequence, 100 Lower Mohawks fled to Gen. John Burgoyne's army then invading New York and eventually went to Montreal (NYCD 8:725-726; Graymont 1972:146-148; Lydekker 1938:164). A few remained at Fort Hunter, and in October 1779 Gen. John Sullivan, believing that they were supplying intelligence to the enemy, sent Col. Peter Gansevoort with 100 men to imprison the Lower Mohawks. At the time there were six or seven families left, and Gansevoort found only four houses still occupied. Gansevoort took all the Indian inhabitants of the settlement prisoner, but they were later ordered released by Gen. George Washington on Gen.

Philip Schuyler's advice that they had remained peaceful (Stone 1838, 2:37-40; Graymont 1972:218-220). Early the next year, Little Abraham and three other Iroquois volunteered to deliver a message to the British at Niagara. The four envoys were subsequently imprisoned at Niagara, and Little Abraham died as a result of the harsh confinement there (Graymont 1972:225-228, 279).

The Fort Hunter Mohawks who fled to Montreal in 1777 established a settlement near Lachine (Cruikshank 1930:391; Lydekker 1938:163). Their leader was Capt. John Deserontyon. At about the same time, the Upper Mohawks from Canajoharie under Capt. Joseph Brant (brother of Sir William Johnson's mistress, Molly Brant) gathered at Fort Niagara. In the course of the war, parties from both settlements attacked what was then the northwest frontier of New York, Captain Brant's incursions achieving particular notoriety in the region.

Once the war had ended, resettlement of these Mohawks in their old valley was an obvious impossibility. Further, not only was the Treaty of Paris silent regarding the future of the Indians, but also the Americans held the territory guaranteed to the Iroquois in 1768 by the Treaty of Fort Stanwix. The Loyalist Mohawks were understandably reluctant to settle on these lands still held by the Iroquois (Stone 1838, 2:238). Accordingly Gov. Frederick Haldimand in fulfillment of an old promise obtained some land at the Bay of Quinté for them in the fall of 1783 from the Mississauga Indians. But Brant and others at Niagara wanted to remain closer to the Senecas and other Iroquois living in what was to become a part of western New York State a few years later. Consequently, Haldimand purchased from the Mississauga in 1784 a large tract of land along the Grand River and granted it to the Iroquois. Attempting to unite the Mohawks, Haldimand and others urged the Lower Mohawks then at Lachine to settle at Grand River, but Deserontyon refused. He felt that the location was too close to the Americans, and in 1784 he and most of the Lachine Mohawks moved to the Bay of Quinté. They arrived on May 22, the same day the Mississauga announced at a council at Niagara their decision to transfer the Grand River land to the Iroquois. In the winter and spring of 1784-1785, Brant and the Mohawks at Niagara and a number of other Indians moved to the Grand River Reserve. In addition, about 25 out of the total of 125 who were living at Lachine early in 1784 went to Grand River instead of the Bay of Quinté, but they rejoined the Mohawks at Quinté four years later after some disputes with Brant (Herrington 1921:1-11; Johnston 1964:xxxiii-xl; Torok 1965:76).

Thus, a year after the Treaty of Paris was signed, the Mohawks who were living in the Mohawk Valley when the American Revolution began were settled on two reserves in Canada. Their descendants still live there. One is the Tyendinaga Indian Reserve (sometimes referred to as Deseronto). The original grant of this reserve was increased in 1793 to include the whole of Tyendinaga Township (in Hastings County, Ontario) ("Iroquois Since 1820," fig. 1, this vol.), but a series of land surrenders has reduced the reserve to 17,000 acres (27 square miles) (fig. 2) (Torok 1966:39). The original grant of the other reserve, the Six Nations Reserve on the Grand River, has also been reduced in size.

With the establishment of these reserves, village autonomy reasserted itself (Torok 1965). After 1784 the Mohawks who had moved from Fort Hunter by way of Lachine to the Bay of Quinté developed and maintained a political organization separate from those who had migrated from Canajoharie to the Grand River by way of Niagara (see "Six Nations of the Grand River, Ontario," this vol., for the subsequent history of the Mohawks who settled there). The separation is symbolized by the disposition of the silver communion service given by Queen Anne to the Mohawks. In 1783 Captain Deserontyon returned to the Mohawk Valley and brought back the silver, which was later divided between the two Mohawk groups (Herrington 1921:8).

Nineteenth and Twentieth Centuries

When those Mohawks who had been allies of the British for over a century left the Mohawk Valley and settled permanently in Canada after the American Revolution, they came to live in the country where their compatriots—allies of the French in the long struggle between France and England for control of the continent—had resided for almost 100 years. To these five settlements, a sixth was added when some Mohawks left Oka in 1881 and settled at Gibson (Watha) on the Moon and Muskoka rivers near Bala east of Georgian Bay (fig. 2) (Mooney and Hewitt 1910a:113). As can be seen from table 1, Oka and Gibson remained the smallest of these Mohawk settlements and of the total Mohawk population, about one-third were descendants of those who had moved to Canada after the American Revolution.

Some of these Mohawks, however, rather inadvertently found themselves living in the United States. By the terms

Table 1. Mohawk Population in 1890

Grand River	1,344	19.2%
Tyendinaga	1,056	15.1%
Caughnawaga	1,722	24.7%
St. Regis (Canada)	1,190	33.6%
St. Regis (United States)	1,157	
Oka	375	5.4%
Gibson	137	2.0%
Total	6,981	100.0%

SOURCE: U.S. Census Office. 11th Census 1892:5.

NOTE: Not included in these figures are the few Mohawks living in the west ("Iroquois in the West," this vol.).

of the Treaty of Paris, the boundary line between Canada and the United States was drawn at 45° north latitude, which placed part of the Saint Regis lands in Canada and part in the United States. By an agreement signed in 1791, Alexander Macomb bought from New York State a considerable tract of land in the northern part of the state. Excepted from this purchase was a tract of land six miles square near the Saint Regis village and two islands, which were reserved for the use of the Indians. But the following year, the first of a series of delegations was sent to Albany to assert the claims of the Saint Regis Indians to various lands in the state. The dispute was finally resolved in 1796 when a treaty was signed with the Seven Indian Nations of Canada ceding all the Saint Regis lands on the American side to New York State except a tract six miles square near Saint Regis village, a square mile on the Salmon River (now Fort Covington), and a square mile on the Grass River and the meadows on both sides of this river. In a series of treaties between 1816 and 1845, various of these lands were sold except for about 14,000 acres (Hough 1853:126-151, 159-172, 245; Fletcher 1888:562; New York (State) Legislature. Assembly 1889:11-12; Kappler 1904-1941, 2:45-46). In addition to this tract in Franklin County, New York, the Saint Regis Indians in 1976 owned 7,384 acres in the Province of Quebec and the 2,050-acre Cornwall Island in the Province of Ontario (fig. 2).

The international boundary bisecting the Saint Regis lands was largely ignored by both governments in administering these lands and by the Indians themselves until the War of 1812 when as a consequence of their location they were drawn into the conflict despite some attempts to remain neutral. After the war, the American government paid annuities only to the "American Indians"; the British government similarly ordered that annuities and presents be given only to the British party at Saint Regis and refused to permit members of the "American" party to live on lands on the Canadian side. As a result, a schism developed that has remained to the present day (Frisch 1970:75-83).

With the exception of the Saint Regis Mohawks on the American side who adopted an system of governance by three elected trustees (now called "chiefs") in 1802 (Frisch 1970:76-77, 92), the old system of governance by hereditary chiefs was retained on the various Mohawk reserves throughout much of the nineteenth century (fig. 5), although on some reserves modifications of the system were introduced. At Saint Regis, the council consisted of 12 chiefs—three chiefs from each of the four major clans, Wolf, Turtle, Bear, and Snipe (the Snipe clan apparently introduced by migrants from Oswegatchie)—rather than the nine chiefs of traditional Mohawk practice. At Tyendinaga, the tribal council consisted of 11 life chiefs, each selected by a "family mother" and said to represent one of the 11 lineages of Mohawks who originally settled

McCord Mus., Montreal: Notman Photographic Arch.
Fig. 5. Chief at Oka with wampum belts and wearing crucifix. Photograph by William Notman, 1870.

at the Bay of Quinté. However, at the insistence of the Canadian government the system of governance on all the Mohawk reserves was changed to that of an elected council, and the chieftainship systems of these reserves lapsed (Hough 1853:173, 177; Frisch 1970:78, 81-82, 91, 102-108; Voget 1951:225, 230; Speck 1923a:225; Torok 1966:132-135, 1967).

As it had been in the eighteenth century, Catholicism continued to be important at Caughnawaga, Saint Regis, and Oka in the nineteenth century, but Methodist (United) churches also were established on all three reserves. The Methodist church established at Saint Regis in the 1840s had communicants on both sides of the border although the church was located on the American side, much as the Catholic church on the Canadian side also served residents on both sides (Frisch 1970:89-91). A number of Oka Iroquois became Methodists in the 1870s after a missionary was sent there. The Algonquins remained Catholic and subsequently many of them moved to Maniwaki (Speck 1923a:226; Parent 1887; D.B. Smith 1974:130). As it had been earlier when the Lower Mohawks were living in the Mohawk Valley, the Anglican church continued to be important at Tyendinaga. A Pentecostal church was established at Tyendinaga in the early 1930s, but residents of this reserve remain predominantly Anglican (Torok 1966:118, 1967:31).

As a consequence of the conversion of the Mohawks to Christianity in the seventeenth and eighteenth centuries, old Mohawk religious practice had largely lapsed and the teachings of Handsome Lake, grounded as they were in old Iroquois religious practice and belief (see "Origins of the Longhouse Religion" and "Iroquois Since 1820," this vol.) had no adherents among the Mohawks of the six eastern reserves in the nineteenth century. The Long-house religion was introduced at Caughnawaga in the 1920s (Postal 1965:272) and at Saint Regis in the 1930s (Frisch 1970:113-115). Subsequently, the Saint Regis and Caughnawaga Longhouses ("Iroquois Since 1820," fig. 4, this vol.) were included in the biennial circuit of Six Nations meetings at which the Code of Handsome Lake is preached, although they do not always elect to host such a meeting. The ceremonials of the Longhouse were also introduced, and although practice is not identical to that of the older Longhouses, many of the same ritual patterns are followed.

At both Caughnawaga and Saint Regis, the Longhouse followers constitute a political as well as religious move-ment and have reinstituted the hereditary chieftainship system in opposition to the elected council. The Saint Regis chiefs are affiliated with the Confederacy in New York State (Frisch 1970:113-117, 181-182); at Caughna-waga, two sets of hereditary chiefs have been raised up, one affiliated with the New York Confederacy and the other with the Six Nations Confederacy in Canada (Voget 1951:222-225; Postal 1965:272; see "The League of the Iroquois: Its History, Politics, and Ritual," this vol. for a description of the Condolence council at which chiefs are raised up).

The economic changes on the Mohawk reserves have followed much the same course as those on other Iroquois reservations in Canada and the United States: in the nineteenth century, reliance on hunting declined and reliance on agriculture increased, and in the twentieth century, Mohawks have become increasingly engaged in wage work. In the eighteenth century, some Mohawks from Caughnawaga and Saint Regis became raftsmen and lumberjacks (Fenton 1940:212). Craft work includ-ing basketry and bead work also was an important source of income on these two reserves (Fletcher 1888:565; U.S. Census Office. 11th Census 1892:40; Carse 1949:41). More recently, Mohawks from Caughnawaga and Saint Regis have become renowned as high steel workers. They first learned of this type of work in 1886 when the Victoria Tubular Bridge was being built across the Saint Lawrence River near the Caughnawaga Reserve. They have become so interested and adept at it that numbers have continued to be employed as high steel workers ("Iroquois Since 1820," fig. 17, this vol.)—an occupation that values certain attitudes of mind not unlike those valued by Mohawk warriors in earlier centuries (Freilich 1958; J. Mitchell 1960).

Synonymy†

The name Mohawk, in general use in this spelling since Colden (1747), continues that originally used by the seventeenth-century English settlers in southern New England. It appears in many forms (from Hewitt 1907b, except where indicated), for example Mahwukes, 1666; Mawhawkes, 1648; Mohacks, 1673; Mohaggs, 1691; Mohaukes, 1666; Mohoggs, 1702 (Livingston 1956:185); Mowacks, 1644; Mowhakes, 1650. The most etymolog-ically correct early spelling is Mohowawogs, 1638 (Roger Williams), which has the English plural -s added to a Narragansett or Massachusett word for 'man-eaters', cognate with Unami mhuwé·yɔk 'cannibal monsters'.

A second set of Algonquian names for the Mohawk derives from Proto-Eastern Algonquian *me·nkwe·w 'Iroquoian' (see the synonymy in "Northern Iroquoian Culture Patterns," this vol.). These include the alternate Narragansett name Mauquàuog (pl.; Williams 1936:16), Eastern Abenaki mèkwe (pl. mékwak), and the Mahican source of the Dutch and early New York English name, recorded as follows: Maquaas, 1614 (Block in Stokes 1915-1928, 2: C. Plate 23); Maques, 1633; Maquas, 1714 (Livingston 1956:221); Moquas, 1678. Only one source has variants of the apparently blended form Mahakuaas (Megapolensis 1909:172).

The Mohawks' name for themselves is kanyę̃ʔkehá·kaʔ or kanyę̃ʔkehró·nǫʔ (Cuoq 1882:164), meaning 'people of kanyę̂·keʔ'; the earliest recordings are Dutch Kajinga-haga, 1644 (Megapolensis 1909:172); and French gannie-gehronnons, 1668 (JR 51:118). kanyę̂·ke, originally refer-ring to the Mohawk country on the Mohawk River and now used for any Mohawk reservation, has long been interpreted as 'the place of the flint, or gun-flint' (Hale 1883a:72; Cuoq 1882:164). The stem -nyę̃- does not match that of modern Mohawk kánhyaʔ 'flint' (Oneida kánhyę̃ʔ) but can be compared with seventeenth-century kannien 'firesteel' (Bruyas 1863:76). A 1736 source says "the Mohawks . . . have for device of the village a steel and a flint" (NYCD 9:1056), and Sir William Johnson (O'Callaghan 1849-1851, 4:432) wrote in 1771 that the symbol of the Mohawk nation was "a steel, such as is used to strike fire out of Flint." But Johnson, although he suggested that Canniah 'firesteel' was the basis of their self-designation Canniungae(s), observed that the impli-cations of this were uncertain since firemaking with flint and steel was of European origin. A similar semantic notion is reflected by Unami Delaware Sankhícani 'peo-ple of the gunlock' (Heckewelder 1876:99). The other Iroquoian languages mostly have related or borrowed names: Oneida latinyę̃ʔkeha·kâ· (pl.), Cayuga

† This synonymy was prepared by Ives Goddard, incorporating some references from Elisabeth Tooker. Iroquois forms were furnished by Marianne Mithun (Mohawk, Cayuga, and Tuscarora), Michael K. Foster (Cayuga), Hanni J. Woodbury (Onondaga), and Clifford Abbott and Floyd G. Lounsbury (Oneida).

kanyę?kEó·nǫ? or kayę?kEó·nǫ?, and Council name kanyę?ké·ka·?, Seneca kanyę?ke·onǫ? (Chafe 1967:74), Tuscarora kani?ke·há·ka·?. Different is Onondaga kohsáshè·nǫ?, though kanyę?kè·ka? refers to any Mohawk reservation in Canada and Zeisberger (1887a) has Gamingehága (mi for nie?).

The Huron name corresponding to the Mohawk self-designation was recorded as Annieñęr'onon (JR 38:188) and añnieneeronnon (Potier 1920:154), probably for (γ)anyę?ʸehró·nǫ?; compare Wyandot yaniéyerûnû (Gatschet 1881:5). This was borrowed as the French name, appearing as Ignierhonons and Aguierhonon, with u misprinted for n (Sagard-Théodat 1865:41, 1865a); Agnierrhonons, 1635 (JR 8:116); Agnierhonon, 1639 (JR 17:76); Agneehrono[n], 1640 (JR 18:232); Agneronons, 1647 (JR 30:226); Annieronnons, 1648 (JR 33:64); Agnieronnons, 1655 (JR 41:216); Agniehronnons, 1671 (JR 55:158); Anniehronnons, 1653 (JR 40:160); Annienhronnons, 1657 (JR 43:272). Occasional spellings with ng show contamination with the Mohawk form: Annienge'ronnons, Agniengeronons (JR 45:92, 42:254). The Huron name for the Mohawk country was Annieñę, appearing as Agné, Agnée, Agnié, Anié (JR 38:198, 47:148, 23:154, 53:152, 40:160), and they are sometimes referred to as les Iroquois d'Agnié or la Nation d'Agnié (JR 51:208, 236). From this comes the shortened French name appearing as Agnez, 1669 (JR 52:116); Agnies, 1670 (JR 53:54); Agniés, 1691 (JR 64:58); Aniez (Perrot in Blair 1911–1912, 1:199); Aniers (Bacqueville de la Potherie 1753, 1:319); and the eventually standardized Agniers, 1691 (JR 64:58; DCB 1:14).

Other names for the Mohawk include Munsee čkáha·w (Michelson 1922:41; Goddard 1965–1970) and Micmac kwědéch' (Rand 1888:172). For the use of Lower Iroquois for Mohawk, see the synonymy in "Northern Iroquoian Culture Patterns," this volume.

The Mohawk and Seneca are referred to in Mohawk council language as ronathnáwerote? (G. Michelson 1973:51). Another council name, equivalent to the first Mohawk chief's title tekarihó·kę (G. Michelson 1973:91), is attested as Tgarihóge, about 1750 (Pyrlaeus in Gatschet 1881–1882); Teakawreahogeh (Hewitt 1907b:926); and Seneca Da-gä-e-ó-gä (Morgan 1851:97).

Villages and Reservations

Caughnawaga (ˌkäknəˈwägu), Quebec, has its name from Mohawk kahnawâ·ke 'at the rapids'; the people there are called kahnawa?kehró·nǫ?. The Oneida place-name is the same, but the people are kahnawa?keha·kâ·. Cayuga has kAnáw?akeh, and the Onondaga forms are kahná·wà?ke and kahnawa?kéhè·nǫ?, the latter also being a general name for 'Mohawks'. Algonquin has borrowed the Mohawk words as kanawage 'la mission du Sault-St.-Louis' and kanawagenâno 'Iroquois du Sault' (Cuoq 1886:144; Lemoine 1911). From this also comes Shawnee

ka?nawa·ki 'Mohawk' (sg.; Voegelin 1938–1940, 8:305). The numerous spellings in the historical sources, such as Cagnawagees, Coghnawagees, and Conewagas (Trowbridge 1939:66), are listed by Hewitt (1907b).

The Gibson settlement has also been referred to as Watha.

Oka Reserve has its name from Algonquin oka· 'walleyed pike'. The Mohawk name is kanęhsatâ·ke or kanehsatâ·ke 'place of reeds' (Mary McDonald, personal communication 1976), or kanehsahtâ·ke 'there is plenty of sand' (G. Michelson 1973:78), or 'at the foot of the hillside' (Cuoq 1882:10). This last interpretation is taken to refer to the high hills behind the Oka village, but the name was first used for the predecessor settlement at Montreal (Charlevoix 1761, 1:217–219; Speck 1923a:220; Boyce 1973a:292). Algonquin has the borrowings kanactage 'Lac des Deux-Montagnes' and kanactagenâno 'Iroquois du Lac' (c = š; Cuoq 1886:144; Lemoine 1911). These Mohawks are referred to in historical sources as Iroquois of the Mountain (French Iroquois de la Montagne), a reference to their earlier settlement at Montreal, and by variants of the place-name, such as Canaghsadagaes and Conasadagahs, or of a name appearing, for example, as Scawendadeys, Scenondidies, and Shouwendadies; for these and other forms see Mooney and Hewitt (1910a).

Saint Regis Reserve is called in Mohawk ahkwesáhsne 'where the partridge (Bonasa umbellus) drums', and the people there are ahkwesahshró·nǫ?. An explanation of this name is in Fletcher (1888:563). It appears in English and French contexts in the traditional missionary spelling Akwesasne, and in other Iroquois languages as Oneida ahkwesásne, Onondaga shakósàske, Cayuga kwésAsne?, and Seneca wakui-saskeóno 'Saint Regis tribe' (Gatschet, in Mooney 1910l). Algonquin has wejacininano 'Iroquois de St.-Régis' (Cuoq 1886:431). By synecdoche residents often refer to the reservation by the name of one of the towns on it or nearby, Rooseveltown and Ogdensburg (Mohawk showé·katsi; Swekatsi in Cuoq 1882:155; Oswegatchie and other early forms in Hewitt 1910h; see "Onondaga," this vol.).

Tyendinaga, probably from the name of Joseph Brant (thayętané·kę?), and Deseronto, from the name of John Deserontyon, are used as names for the reserve of the Mohawks of the Bay of Quinté.

Sources

The history of the Mohawks has been summarized by Carse (1949) and incidentally in T.W. Clarke's (1940) military history of the Mohawk Valley. Seventeenth-century Mohawk history is extensively detailed by Grassman (1969). French missionary activity in the seventeenth century has been described by a number of authors including Shea (1855), and Dutch missionary work, by Corwin (1925).

Various aspects of the visit of the "Four Indian Kings" to London in 1710 are treated in R.P. Bond (1952). The history of Anglican missionary work in the Mohawk Valley is discussed in Humphreys (1730) and more fully in Lydekker (1938). Sir William Johnson's life has attracted a number of biographers, two of the most important being Pound (1930) and Flexner (1959). Joseph Brant's role in the American Revolution and in the subsequent establishment of the Six Nations Reserve is considered in Stone's (1838) biography. John Deserontyon's comparable role in the Revolution and the establishment of the Tyendinaga Reserve has been discussed by Cruikshank (1930), Herrington (1921), and Torok (1965). The history of the Saint Regis Reserve is discussed in Hough (1853:110-203) and Frisch (1970, 1970a). A general history of Oka is given by O. Maurault (1930, 1937); for additional sources on Oka see D.B. Smith (1974:129-131).

Oneida

JACK CAMPISI

Territory

The historic homeland of the Oneida (ōˈnīdu)—the area in which their villages were located—was the region around Oneida Creek, a stream that flows into Oneida Lake where the Oneidas had fishing stations. The Oneidas also controlled the Wood Creek and upper Mohawk valleys. Their hunting territories extended north of this region to the Saint Lawrence and south to the Susquehanna ("The League of the Iroquois: Its History, Politics, and Ritual," fig. 1, this vol.) (Morgan 1901, 1:40-41, map; Beauchamp 1900:13-15; Fenton 1940:213).

At the time they were first visited by Europeans in the seventeenth century the Oneidas had a single principal village, the tribe and the village being nearly synonymous. The first authenticated description of this village (which like other Iroquois villages was relocated as the need arose) was given by a Dutch journalist, probably Harmen Meyndertsz van den Bogaert, who visited the Oneidas in 1634. He said this village, which was probably located near Munnsville in Madison County (Beauchamp 1900:90; Pratt 1976:37, 134), was strongly palisaded, 767 paces in circumference, and had 66 houses (Jameson 1909:148-149). Some three decades later, the French Jesuit missionary Jacques Bruyas, who had established the mission of Saint François Xavier there in 1667, described the Oneida village as being located five leagues from Oneida Lake (JR 51:121, 221). The next recorded description of the village is by Wentworth Greenhalgh who visited it in 1677. He reported that the stockaded village had about 100 houses and was located 20 miles (perhaps an error for two miles) east of a small river that flowed into Oneida Lake. At that time, the village was newly settled and because of this, the inhabitants were forced to buy corn from the Onondagas (O'Callaghan 1849-1851, 1:12; Beauchamp 1900:90). It was apparently this village that was burned by the French in 1696 (O'Callaghan 1849-1851, 1:334-336).

In the eighteenth century the principal Oneida village continued to be located near Oneida Creek. In 1757 it was located about two leagues from Oneida Lake and a smaller village on the bank of the lake (O'Callaghan 1849-1851, 1:526). Five years later a new village called Canowaroghere (or Ganowarohere, Hewitt 1907e), in Oneida *tkanęʔalóhaleʔ* 'where there is a skull impaled'

(Lounsbury 1953:50),* was reported to have been built (NYCD 7:512). At this time some Oneida families resided at Oquaga (now Windsor, New York) on the Susquehanna River along with some Mohawks and other Indians.

During the eighteenth century, the Oneidas became host to a number of immigrant Indian tribes. Shortly after the Tuscarora Wars, 1711-1713, had ended, a number of Tuscaroras moved north and settled on Oneida land where subsequently other Tuscaroras joined them (see "Tuscarora Among the Iroquois," this vol.). In 1785 the Stockbridge Indians, accepting an invitation of the Oneidas to come live near them, began to move there, building a village called New Stockbridge (Mooney 1910g). Finally, in 1788, a band of Mahican, Mohegan, Pequot, Narragansett, Montauk, and other Algonquians joined the Oneidas and established a community near New Stockbridge called Brothertown (Mooney 1907d).

Along with the changes in town location there were changes in residence patterns. The Dutch journalist of 1634 described a longhouse or multiple-family pattern, but by the middle of the eighteenth century the palisaded village had disappeared and the household pattern had shifted to nuclear-family cabins.

The Seventeenth Century: Contact

The seventeenth-century contacts with the Dutch, French, and, later, English led to modifications in Oneida life-style. European fabrics were adopted to replace furs and skins, but the style of dress and ornamental designs continued in use throughout the eighteenth century. Earthen pots and bark vessels gave way to copper and iron vessels and ash-splint baskets. In all likelihood, the Indians learned the technique of splint basketry from the Dutch or Swedes. For hunting, guns, hatchets, and iron traps came into general use, supplanting the bow and arrow, lithic tools, deadfall, and snare.

Contacts with White society had equally important effects on the social and political systems of the Oneida.

* The italicized Oneida words in the *Handbook* are in the phonemic system described by Chafe ("Comparative Sketch of the Northern Iroquoian Languages," vol. 17); see also Lounsbury (1953:27-34). They are cited in utterance-medial form. The nasalized vowels are transcribed ę (Lounsbury's ʌ) and ǫ (Lounsbury's u); other letters are used in their standard *Handbook* values. Phonemicizations of Oneida forms have been provided by Floyd G. Lounsbury and Clifford Abbott.

The Oneidas were soon enmeshed in the fur trade, which engaged men in an endless round of councils, trade, diplomacy, and war. As warriors they were to range from the Saint Lawrence valley to the Carolinas and west to the Mississippi River. By the 1640s the fur supplies of the eastern Iroquois were insufficient to meet the rising demand for trade goods and the Oneidas faced a crisis. Corn, meat, and fish were available but increasingly the beaver trade provided the material means to secure European goods. The Oneidas, like their Iroquois brethren, had already made the technological shift to the use of European goods and the old lithic skills were falling into disuse.

By 1640 two competing trade networks had developed, one consisting of the Algonquin, Huron, and French and the other made up of the Iroquois and Dutch (later the English). Each vied with the other for control of the same western fur supplies giving the impetus to a 60-year period of nearly continuous warfare. Oneida war parties made repeated raids against the Hurons and eastern Algonquians. They ranged into Virginia and Maryland taking booty and prisoners, much to the consternation of the governors of these colonies (NYCD 4:386). They and their Iroquois brethren dispersed, annihilated, or conquered the tribes that surrounded them, including the Hurons, Neutrals, Petuns, Potawatomi, Ottawa, and Susquehannock. Their influence extended west to Green Bay and Illinois, while to the south they held control through Pennsylvania. It is no wonder that the Jesuit Jerome Lalemant believed it "a marvel that so few people work such havoc and render themselves so redoubtable to so great a number of tribes who, on all sides, bow before this conqueror" (JR 45:207).

Because they were few in number, the Oneidas were particularly sensitive to losses in war, but these losses were offset by the adoption of enemy captives and the "borrowing" of men from other tribes (see "The League of the Iroquois: Its History, Politics, and Ritual," table 1, this vol.). The *Jesuit Relations* of 1645 and 1646 mention the repeopling of the Oneidas by Mohawk men, following a great defeat that the Oneidas suffered at the hands of the Algonquin and Huron (JR 27:297, 28:281). Bruyas, living among the Oneidas, reports that in 1668 two-thirds of the Oneida population was made up of Algonquins and Hurons "who have become Iroquois in temper and inclination" (JR 51:123). This remarkable conversion of the enemy was possible because individuals were not just adopted into the tribe but were brought into a specific lineage to fill a position vacated by the death of some family member; and under the watchful eyes of the leading women, they learned the roles attendant to the new position. Failure to satisfy the clan mothers resulted in death.

The influence of these wars extended beyond changes in material culture and the constituency of the tribe. Warfare, diplomacy, and the wealth derived from trade offered the means for individuals to gain prestige. The demands for revenge provided overt reasons for raiding while the tangible rewards of captured booty bore testimony to the skill and valor of the leaders. Even the final cessation of war in 1698 and a declared neutrality by England and France toward the Iroquois did not eliminate the raiding, which had become an important aspect of the prestige system. Men found they could gain power and prestige and achieve the status of Pine Tree chiefs through war. Young men followed proven leaders, and individuals with large followings were in a position to convert prestige into power. Oneida leaders like the adopted Susquehannock warrior Shenandoah and Daniel Bread achieved prominence in this way. The result was an increase in the number of Pine Tree chiefs. This placed an increasing strain upon the political structure of Oneida society as sachems and other tribal leaders found it difficult to control the actions of young men. As a result two factions emerged: a chief's faction that derived power from the clan mothers on the basis of the traditional complex of beliefs and a warrior faction asserting power based on their military prowess. While the warriors could not assert their will in village affairs neither could the village councilors or sachems command the warrior's obedience. The sachems, recognized as the legitimate agents of the tribe by the French and British, relied in turn upon the warriors to implement any military action. While the warriors had sufficient power to ignore the dictates of their elders, they lacked a system of beliefs that would validate their demands for power.

The Eighteenth Century: Faction

In 1767 a Presbyterian minister named Samuel Kirkland came to establish a church among the Oneida. A product of the Great Awakening of the 1740s, Kirkland adhered to the fundamentalist teachings of Jonathan Edwards with their emphasis on determinism, stern self-discipline, repentance, regeneration, and baptism. In exhorting a rejection of traditional Oneida beliefs, he exalted the individual, who was required to repent and accept Jesus and the "New Light" if he was to be saved.

Kirkland challenged the traditional beliefs of the Oneidas, and it is no coincidence that his followers came mainly from the ranks of the warriors. However, he did not cause factionalism; what he did was to introduce a doctrine that gave religious validation to the political reality that was already extant. As he pointed out in his journal in 1770, "the Warriors for ye most part are uncontrowled by the Sachems or Lords" (Kirkland 1764-1804). Kirkland capitalized on this division and challenged the efficacy of the political structure by his insistence upon the rejection of Iroquois religious beliefs. In so doing, he attacked the symbolic basis of the political structure, thus weakening the position of the hereditary chiefs. Needless to say, they opposed Kirkland's religion and, by extrapolation, his politics. However, Kirkland's influence did not depend upon the support of the sachems but of the warriors who, by converting to the new religion, found a means of challenging the strictures and limitations of the Iroquois political system. The sachems were in the unenviable position of not being able to act without risking the loss of what influence they had in the tribe as the result of a test of strength (Kirkland 1764–1804).

It must have seemed to the Oneidas in the 1760s that they were a forsaken people. In spite of their proclaimed neutrality, they had been drawn into another corrosive war—the French and Indian—with all its attendant dislocation. After considerable pressure from both sides the Oneidas reluctantly supported the British cause. In addition, pressure from Whites for land was mounting, and to make matters worse the decade of the 1760s was marked by repeated famines. Internally there was an increase in alcoholism, factional disputes, and crime. From Kirkland's point of view, his arrival could not have been better timed.

As the Revolutionary War approached, the Oneidas were pulled in opposite directions by the American influence of Kirkland and the pro-British advocacy of Sir William Johnson, commissioner of Indian affairs (see "Mohawk," this vol.). Johnson was, by far, the most influential White in Iroquoia. He was quick to see that the interests and attitudes of the New England ministers could have a significant impact on Iroquois policy and so he sought to have them withdrawn. Failing this, he attempted to neutralize their influence by challenging their religious doctrines. It became a struggle of Calvinism against Anglicanism as well as revolutionary against Loyalist.

The Oneidas rejected all attempts to have their minister Kirkland removed, but at the price of increased disharmony between themselves and their Iroquois brethren, as well as internally. Although their sachems tended to be pro-British, the group of pro-American Oneida warriors, led by the venerable Shenandoah, close friend and confidant of Kirkland, prevented resolute action on the part of the Oneidas and the League. Finally, after several years of indecision, the League covered the council fire at Onondaga, leaving each tribe to act on its own. The pro-American element of the Oneidas and their allies, the Tuscaroras, did not remain neutral. They urged that the council fire at Albany be rekindled and that Fort Stanwix (Rome, New York) be refurbished to prevent attacks in the Mohawk Valley. They steadfastly refused to join the other pro-British members of the League, often boycotting meetings. When they did attend, they defended colonial interests. Finally, in 1779 Gen. George Washington ordered James Clinton and John Sullivan to attack the Onondaga, Cayuga, and Seneca villages in order to eliminate their military potential. Oneidas participated in this campaign with several of them receiving officers' ranks (New York (State) Commissioners of Indian Affairs 1861:1).

The Oneida contribution to the American cause extended beyond diplomacy and participation in a single raid. When the British forces attempted in 1777 to divide the rebellious colonies by capturing the New York colony, Oneidas fought valiantly at the Battle of Oriskany to blunt Col. Barry St. Leger's and Joseph Brant's invasion. In 1779 they reputedly drew from their meager resources to provision Washington's army.

Like their colonial allies, the Oneidas suffered the privations of war. The following year their fortunes changed, and in June 1780 about 30 Oneidas were persuaded to move to Niagara. The next month the Oneida villages were burned. Some Oneidas went to Niagara, but a number fled to Schenectady, where they lived in squalor and misery, with little food or clothing, and dependent upon handouts (Graymont 1972:233–235, 242).

The end of the Revolution saw the Oneidas scattered from Niagara to Schenectady, their villages destroyed, their fields laid waste, their social system disrupted, and their brothers in the League alienated from them. With famine a yearly occurrence, the seasons to follow were particularly trying. The Oneidas had paid a high price for their loyalty to the "Bostonians."

Evidence of social disorganization pervades the literature of the time (Belknap and Morse 1955; New York (State) Commissioners of Indian Affairs 1861; Kirkland 1764–1804). Alcoholism, murder, suicide, and factionalism all attest to the patterns of disintegration in the postwar period. In addition, the problems of adjustment for the Oneidas were intensified by internal divisions and external pressures. The Oneidas returning to their former territories around Lake Oneida at the end of the Revolutionary War included those with both pro-British and pro-American sympathies, for whom the war had served to intensify their mutual enmity. To make matters worse, the returning Oneidas settled in five adjacent villages, each with its own council. Kirkland wrote in September 1790 that "yesterday mourning the Oneidas and Oriskes again met in council on the subject of the disputes and difficulties subsisting betwixt them" (Kirkland Papers Sept. 28, 1790). Meetings of this kind were continuous during the period from 1783 through 1800 without a resolution of the differences.

The problems of the Oneidas worsened under the influence of neighboring Whites. Kirkland complained on November 2, 1793 that "the unprincipled white men, who reside in the village, are a nuisance and clog every good work" (Kirkland 1764–1804). It took little urging to persuade the members of a faction to sell or lease portions of tribal holdings. In 1788 a land company headed by John Livingston convinced the Oneidas to lease the bulk of their lands for 999 years, in contravention of the New York State constitution. The agreement was held void by the state legislature (New York (State) Commissioners of Indian Affairs 1861:120). In another instance a French entrepreneur, Peter Penet, said that he had dreamed of a land gift covering 100 square miles and that he was an ambassador of France to the Oneidas and, because of this, all negotiations were to be carried on through his office. In addition, he instituted a Catholic mission among the Oneidas. This was too much for the governor of New York who quickly took steps to expose Penet, thus forcing the withdrawal of the French priests and preventing the development of the Penet tract. Eventually Penet left the community but not before he had renewed the nucleus of opposition to Kirkland. After his departure the Penet, or French, Party became the Pagan Party.

The interest in Oneida land was not limited to private speculators. New York State desired to purchase and open it for settlement. At the end of the Revolutionary War, both New York State and the national government recognized the sacrifice and contribution made by the Oneidas, and in 1784 the Continental Congress guaranteed their territorial integrity by the Treaty of Fort Stanwix. This guarantee, covering nearly six million acres, was repeated in the treaties of Fort Harmar, 1789; Canandaigua, 1794; and Oneida, 1794. In addition, the United States Congress passed the Indian Non-Intercourse Act in 1790, reserving to the national government the exclusive right to negotiate with Indian tribes. The state of New York appeared to be similarly concerned with the protection of Indian lands in that its constitution prohibited the purchase of Indian land by individuals and invalidated all such purchases made without legislative approval after 1775.

These guarantees so magnanimously given were soon forgotten as the interests of federal and state governments diverged. For its part, the national government settled its obligations to the Oneidas for their losses in the Revolution by an award of $5,000 and a promise to build a gristmill, sawmill, and church. The Oneidas were to share with the other five Iroquois nations in an annuity of $4,500 (Treaty with the Oneidas, Dec. 2, 1794).

The Oneidas were not unmindful of the effects of land sales on their survival when approached in 1785 to sell their lands along the Susquehanna River. Their spokesman Petrus noted that such a sale would adversely affect their survival (New York (State) Commissioners of Indian Affairs 1861:91). Yet the land commissioners were persistent and, in the end, gained the land they sought. Although New York repeatedly professed the best interests of the Oneidas and paid lip service to concern for the preservation of their land and way of life, it nevertheless entered into a series of treaties with the Oneidas to sell their lands. In 1785 the Oneidas sold to the state of New York the present counties of Broome and Chenango for $15,500. In 1788 the Oneidas reserved for themselves some 300,000 acres in Madison and Oneida counties

("Iroquois Since 1820," fig. 1, this vol.). Most of the subsequent treaties relate to this land. In all, over 30 treaties of purchase were made with segments of the Oneida tribe. Typical of these treaties was one written in 1809 by which the state of New York purchased 7,200 acres near the inlet of Oneida Lake for $1,600 and a perpetual annuity of $120. Later, the state removed the annuities by a single payment.

The divisions in existence before the Revolution reappeared, and two factions fought for political control. On the one side were the warriors, pro-American in the Revolution, Christian, and favorably inclined toward White society. They were led by Chief Shenandoah. On the other side were the followers of Chief Cornelius, who supported the traditional hereditary political and religious systems, opposed White contacts, and were pro-British in the Revolution. By 1805 the cleavage between the factions was so intense that they signed articles dividing their territories around Oneida Lake into two separate reservations.

The Nineteenth Century: Division and Movement

Factional conflict was but one dimension of the social change occurring among the Oneidas. The reduction of the land base seriously compromised the hunting-fishing components of their economic system. White settlement in the first decades of the nineteenth century increased contacts and further disrupted elements of the traditional culture such as religious beliefs, clan system, and political structure. Whites encouraged Oneida men to become farmers, to seek education in White schools, and to practice religion in White-controlled churches. The male-dominated nuclear family was held up as the model in opposition to the matrilineal extended family. Those who sought to maintain the old traditions were treated as backward savages, in need of salvation.

Thus, at the turn of the nineteenth century, the Oneidas were divided on the degree to which they would adjust to the values of the dominant society. Most Oneidas were Christians in a nominal sense, subject always to the appeal of an itinerant preacher or passing revival. However, in the last decade of the eighteenth century the followers of the traditional Iroquois beliefs grew steadily in numbers and influence, stimulated by the threats to their land, the exhortation of a few stalwart leaders, and the appearance of a new prophet. In 1798 a Mohawk at Grand River, Ontario, had a vision in which he was visited by the culture hero Tharonhiawagon (Oneida *thalǫhyawâ·kǫ* 'he who grasps the sky') and was told that the troubles of the Iroquois were due to their failure to hold the White Dog ceremony. The news of this revelation reached Oneida in 1799, and by 1800 the Oneidas had reinstituted the ceremony, which they had not held for more than 30 years (Tooker 1965:132–134).

By the time the teachings of Handsome Lake reached Oneida, the revitalized Iroquois beliefs were well established, and the reservation had been divided along religious lines. Some disagreement occurred between the followers of Handsome Lake and those who "plead for the traditions of their fathers as the only proper religion for Indians" (Kirkland Papers Nov. 27, 1806). In the end, the latter group won out and the practice of the ceremonial cycle and belief in traditional Iroquois cosmology continued, along with the rejection of the changes proposed by the Seneca prophet. No Handsome Lake movement survived among the Oneidas.

Kirkland died in 1808 and his good friend Shenandoah died eight years later. Christian church membership declined sharply until 1816 when Eleazar Williams, an Episcopal lay reader and catechist, moved to the Oneida reservation. He possessed a command of Oneida, good oratory style, religious fervor, and considerable political acumen. He quickly won the support of the few Christians among the Oneida who were known as the First Christian Party (Shenandoah Party). Next he concentrated upon the so-called Pagan Party (Cornelius Party) converting them by 1818 and receiving an assignment of land for the support of a church (Bloomfield 1907: 145–148). This group became known as the Second Christian Party.

With the tribe at least nominally Christian, Williams proposed that they sell their remaining lands in New York and move to a new location near Green Bay, Wisconsin. This idea met with almost universal opposition, but Williams persisted, and with the support of a few young warriors, influential congressmen, and the Ogden Land Company, which held preemptive rights to the Iroquois lands, negotiations were entered into with the Menominee and Winnebago. Once again the tribe split into two factions with some members of the First and Second Christian Parties willing to follow their leaders to Wisconsin and others, now calling themselves the Orchard Party, opposed to any move.

Without waiting for tribal approval, Williams and a delegation of Oneidas made several trips to Wisconsin. By 1823 they had secured from the Menominee joint and undivided occupation of more than 4,000,000 acres of land for approximately $3,000. President James Monroe, concerned over the size of the grant, reduced it to 500,000 acres. In 1838 it was reduced again, this time to 65,426 acres. Oneidas began emigrating in 1823, and by 1838 there were 654 relocated in Wisconsin.

For some, such as Jedidiah Morse, noted geographer and Congregational minister, the move suggested a way of protecting the Oneidas from the worst effects of White acculturation, by permitting time for adjustment. For the Ogden Land Company, it was a way to clear title by securing alternate lands for the New York Indians. For Williams the move meant the establishment of an Iroquois ecclesiastical empire with himself as its leader, an empire that would include the bulk of the six Iroquois nations, resettled in the vastness of Wisconsin. Although the motives of the three parties differed, each was aware of, and gave support to, the objectives of the other. It is no wonder that the rejection by the Oneidas of the plan to resettle them in the west had no effect on the outcome.

Separate Oneida Communities

The Treaty of Buffalo Creek in 1838 provided for the removal of all Iroquois in New York State including the Oneidas to the Kansas territory, but the Oneidas refused to go. They divided into three groups: those intending to move to Ontario, those desirous of moving but uncertain where, and a few who wished to remain in New York. In 1839, 242 Oneidas sold their land in New York and, pooling their money, purchased a tract of 5,200 acres near London, Ontario. Between 1840 and 1845, 410 moved to Ontario, and by 1848 only 200 Oneidas resided in New York on the remnants of their land or at the Onondaga Reservation near Syracuse, New York. In 1843 New York State passed legislation permitting the division of the remaining lands in severalty. In 1976 only 32 acres remained of the communally owned tribal lands.

Wisconsin

The two communities—near London, Ontario, and at Green Bay, Wisconsin—provide some interesting contrasts in subsequent development. The Oneidas of Wisconsin settled in two general areas according to religion, with Anglicans occupying the northern portions of the reservation and the Methodists the southern part. Within these two spheres there developed eight small centers or neighborhoods (fig. 1). Much of the social and economic life of the Oneidas revolved around these neighborhoods. Neighbors aided each other in clearing fields, planting, harvesting, constructing and repairing buildings and roads, as well as with other activities common to farming communities. Social gatherings and Sunday visits were neighborhood ones and each neighborhood tended to view itself as superior to the others.

Kinship provided a second important network of relations for the Oneidas of Wisconsin. The nuclear family was the primary economic unit, and the ties between husband and wife were emphasized. Descent was bilateral with third and often fourth cousins considered as close kin. Between these kin, reciprocal gift giving and assistance in various communal activities such as building bees were expected. These obligations applied equally to both sides of the family and reflected the adjustment of the older kinship system to a newer emphasis on the nuclear family unit.

Marriage was arranged by parents who gave serious consideration to the rules of clan exogamy as well as to the social prestige and economic conditions of the fam-

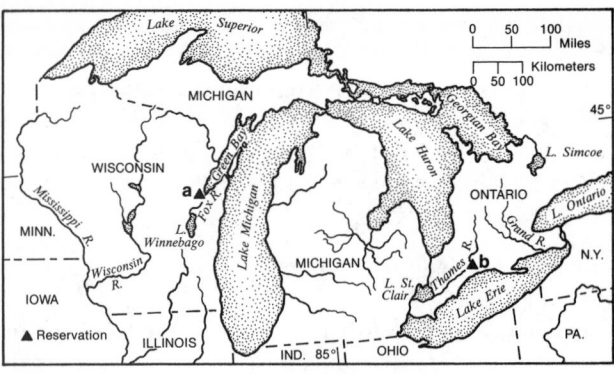

Fig. 1. Location of some Oneida lands. a, Wis. reservation with neighborhoods: 1, *latihǫlahelaˀa·kâ·* 'gun-laid-on people'; 2, *tekahsokęha·kâ·* 'between-the-lips people'; 3, *talǫˀkowanha·kâ·* 'Duck Creek people'; 4, *tiksęha·kâ·* 'Dixon people'; 5, *latinatakǫha·kâ·* 'in-the-village people'; 6, *tatsmęnha·kâ·* 'Dutchman people'; 7, *kętsyohaleˀkeha·kâ·* 'fish-on-a-pole people'; 8, *simoha·kâ·* 'Seymour people'. b, Ont. reserve. For Oneida lands in N.Y. see "Iroquois Since 1820," fig. 1, this vol.

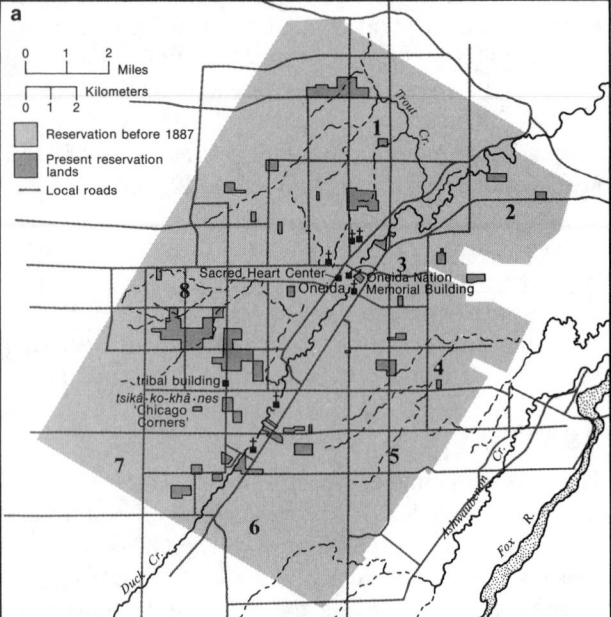

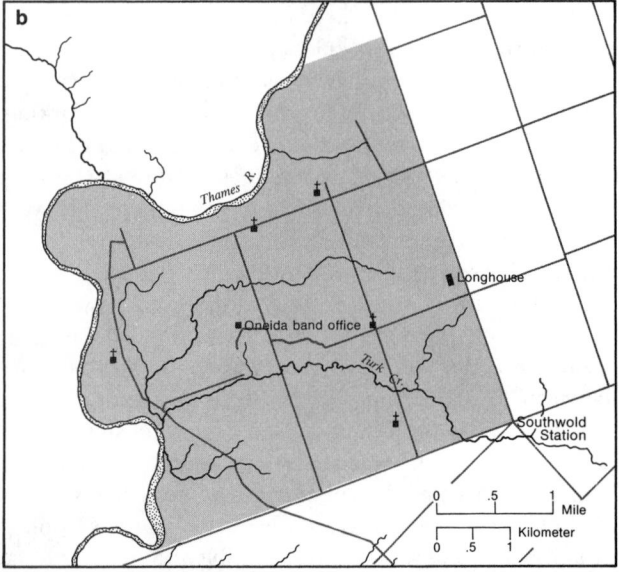

Most Oneidas being either Anglican or Methodist, there was no Longhouse or religion of Handsome Lake at Oneida, Wisconsin. White missionaries served both congregations, but church control resided with the local congregation. Certain Iroquois practices were fitted into the Christian religious system. These include the particular manner of collecting holy water (*kahnekano·lǫ́*) on Easter morning, which appears to be a survival from a ceremonial practice of the Little Water Society, and various practices at the wake and Tenth-day feast that are derived from traditional Iroquois funeral customs. Other practices continued in spite of the opposition of church leaders. There was a strong belief in the presence of malevolent witches and spells, in the efficacy of herbal medicine, and in rituals of the curing societies. These beliefs were still held in the 1970s, although the last acknowledged cure by a medicine society occurred in 1949.

The Oneidas who immigrated to Wisconsin brought with them little of their traditional political structure. As the members of the various factions arrived, their leaders took a place in the political structure basing their legitimacy on claimed chiefly prerogatives attained in New York. The result was a political system consisting of a number of chiefs some of whom claimed hereditary rights. However, of more importance than clan affiliation in the selection of a chief was the size of his kindred and his neighborhood, religious affiliation, and personal prestige. In addition, there was a variable number of Pine Tree chiefs (*yohnehtako·kǫ́* or *yohnehtahnyô·ǫ*) who achieved recognition on the basis of their leadership abilities.

The council came to consist of one head chief (*thǫwakwánę*) and 12 "big men" or chiefs (*latikwa·nę̂·seˀ*) appointed by the senior women of the lineages (*kǫtinaˀtsyanǫ̂·ne*). The status of senior woman of the lineage (comparable to clan mother among other Iroquoians) was more honorific than politically effective since it descended along the male line to the eldest daughter, who was required to appoint her oldest brother as chief upon the death or resignation of their father.

The hereditary council exercised considerable control over the affairs of the tribe. It allocated land, determined eligibility for its use, made rules to govern the reserve, and enforced these with sentences of banishment and execution. The council represented the tribe in its dealings with the federal government. It secured laws prohib-

ilies concerned. Married couples were expected to stay together for life; divorce and infidelity, being serious offenses against the church, led to expulsion and social ostracism.

iting the sale of alcohol on the reservation, made contracts for the sale of lumber, and negotiated for the payment of annuities due under federal and state agreements.

When the Oneidas moved to Wisconsin in the 1820s it was a wilderness, with the nearest White settlement 15 miles to the east at Green Bay. By 1860 this situation had changed. First the lumber barons came to strip the pine forests, and following them were settlers anxious to farm the rich lands. Speculators pressured the Oneidas to sell their lumber and land, and efforts were made to have Congress terminate the reservation and move the Oneidas west. It became increasingly more difficult for the hereditary tribal council to resist these pressures. Additionally, some Oneidas opposed the hereditary structure and demanded the institution of an elective system. They were supported by the federal agents, and finally in 1871 an elective system was introduced. However, it had little chance to function. There were difficulties in organizing the new council as adherents of the older system refused their support, while many Oneidas simply ignored its rules concerning land and timber use.

The passage of the General Allotment Act in 1887 was by far the most important event since the Oneidas had moved to Wisconsin. Oneidas began receiving patents in fee simple in 1892, and by 1908 almost all the land had been allotted. Under the law, individuals over 18 years of age were given 40 acres while those under 18 received 26 acres each. Often the allotments members of a family received were not contiguous, making farming difficult. After 1908 most land became subject to town and county taxation, and tax sales and foreclosures were so common that by the mid 1920s only a few hundred acres remained in the hands of Oneidas. Formal tribal government ceased to function after the implementation of the General Allotment Act and was replaced by town and county governments.

The loss of their land forced a number of Oneidas to seek employment in the factories and farms in the surrounding White communities. Many moved from the area to large metropolitan centers like Green Bay, Milwaukee, and Chicago. However, these individuals did not completely sever their ties with Oneida. Often men went to work in seasonal industries leaving their families behind. Except for employment, little interaction with Whites occurred. The Oneidas centered their social fabric around kin, church, medicine societies, and voluntary associations such as Oneida singers (groups that sing hymns in Oneida) and a number of welfare and burial associations.

The passage of the Indian Reorganization Act in 1934 brought significant changes to tribal structure. The Oneidas incorporated and wrote a constitution providing for a town meeting type of government with an executive committee to administer tribal affairs. This committee consists of nine members elected at large, four of whom

are the tribal chairman, vice-chairman, secretary, and treasurer. There are two general meetings a year as well as monthly meetings of the executive committee. The constitution limits tribal membership to those persons who have at least one-fourth Oneida blood quantum and who can trace descent from at least one consanguineal kin who was on the 1934 tribal roll.

In 1972 the Oneidas of Wisconsin occupied a checkerboard reservation of 2,200 acres interspersed among private White-owned property (fig. 1). This is land repurchased for tribal use by the federal government under provisions of the Indian Reorganization Act. According to tribal records there were 6,684 on the rolls with approximately 2,000 residents on or near tribal lands. Only a few hundred elderly people continued to use the Oneida language, the voluntary burial associations had declined, and medicine societies had disappeared except in the memories of the old. Religion, in particular Methodism and Anglicanism, was still an important aspect of the social order, and the singing societies continued to perform at church functions. Although many Oneidas have married out, kin ties remained the most important unifying factor. Tribal land use has changed from agricultural to residential, and the Oneidas have constructed two large housing projects. In addition, tribal funds were available for the construction of private dwellings on reservation land.

Ontario

Under the leadership of Moses Schuyler and William Taylor Doxtator the Oneidas desirous of leaving New York after 1839 moved to Ontario. The land was purchased and held in common (fig. 1). Upon arriving in Ontario the immigrating Oneidas held a council at which they decided that for settlement purposes an individual could claim the use of all the land he could clear and had the right to sell, transfer, or will the property to others within the tribe who had contributed to the purchase of the reservation land or to their descendants. Soon a number of settlements sprang up in different parts of the reserve, each composed of a number of interrelated families.

Shortly after their arrival, the Oneidas reinstituted a tribal council along traditional lines, each of the three matrilineages of the three Oneida clans (Wolf, Bear, and Turtle) appointing a sachem and a deputy to the council. These chiefs were raised up at a council with Iroquois from the Six Nations Reserve, which both legitimated the position of the Oneida chiefs and brought them into the Six Nations Confederacy in Canada. It also served to ameliorate the enmity that had grown up between the Oneidas in the United States and the Iroquois in Canada as a result of the American Revolution and the War of 1812.

This alliance with the Six Nations Confederacy was motivated chiefly by political factors. First, the Oneidas *487* were attempting to demonstrate their loyalty to the Crown by gaining acceptance from their pro-British brethren. This was an important issue in view of the pro-American actions of the Oneida Nation during the Revolutionary War. Second, the Oneidas were fearful that their lands would be subject to taxation by the province and they sought the support of the League in preventing this. However, their contacts with the Iroquois at Six Nations did not lead to the introduction of the Code of Handsome Lake at Oneida. The Oneidas continued to practice either the more dominant Methodist teachings or the Anglican religion.

The council of sachems exercised little power on the reservation, its primary function being to mediate disputes. Issues of general concern were handled in open meetings at which all band members were eligible to participate. Issues were discussed until the band members arrived at a general agreement or consensus. Failing this, the issue was simply set aside. After Canadian confederation in 1867 the Canadian Department of Indian Affairs exerted increased influence in the affairs of the Oneidas. When the general council of the Oneidas was unable to resolve an issue it was passed on by the agent, with his description of the facts and sometimes a recommendation, to the department, which usually decided the question by applying the appropriate section of the Indian Act (A. Ricciardelli 1961:44–90).

In addition to the hereditary chiefs (lotiyanélę?), there existed a variable number of Pine Tree chiefs (latilǫtanǫ̂·ne) selected by the sachems and the clan mothers because of their prominence, community respect, and oratorical skill. These acted as advisors to the hereditary chiefs by serving on committees to determine facts and make recommendations regarding individual disputes or community concerns.

Much of the traditional Oneida kinship system remained in operation in Canada during the nineteenth century. The strongest ties existed between a mother and her daughter; of next importance were those with grandparents, particularly those on the mother's side. While band membership was traced bilaterally to an ancestor who had contributed to the purchase of land, membership in clans was determined through the mother's side. Marriages were arranged by the parents, usually the father of the bridegroom. Intraclan marriages were common, and although subject to criticism, no sanctions were brought to bear on the couples. It was commonly believed that intraclan marriages resulted in weak, deformed, or mentally deficient offspring. However, the tendency for intraclan marriage was a natural outgrowth of the community attitude against marrying out and the relatively small Oneida population from which to select mates (Ricciardelli 1966:186–189).

The principal medicine societies were the False Face and Little Water. In order to belong to a society, an individual had to be cured by it or have dreamed of membership. Dreaming was an instrumental part of curing with individuals being noted for their ability to divine the future from their dreams. Often dreamers were consulted in order to determine the kind of cure suitable for their specific ailments. Along with belief in the efficacy of cures were beliefs in witchcraft and magic potions that continue in the 1970s.

During the nineteenth century subsistence farming was the principal economic pursuit for most Oneidas, supplemented by lumbering during winter months. The individual's right to claim all the land he could clear gave advantage to large and ambitious family units, but sufficient land was available to all settlers. A variety of crops was grown and stored for winter use in barns, nearby grain elevators, or ground pits. Meats were salted or dried and stored in barrels. Cash income came from the sale of surplus crops and the supplemental home industries of basketry and cornhusk mats. In addition, individuals hired out to work in the flax and tobacco fields in the vicinity. Much of the work of clearing, planting, and harvesting was done by work bees.

Toward the end of the nineteenth century major changes occurred in the socioeconomic system of the reserve. There was a decline in the number of farmers as families shifted to wage labor in the neighboring White communities. The increased contact led to strains within the society and eventually to the development of factionalism. There were serious challenges to the traditional form of government, which involved conflict over the degree of acceptance of White value systems. Out of this conflict, in 1915, came the organization of a second hereditary council supported by the newly organized Longhouse religion. This council refused to accept the legitimacy of the older council that, by 1920, was called the Six Nations Confederacy. Both the Canadian government and the leadership from Six Nations gave support to the Confederacy faction causing the Longhouse faction to look to the Onondagas of New York for support.

Another factor involved was the settlement of the Kansas claims lawsuit in 1900. In 1892 the United States Supreme Court awarded the Oneidas the sum of $1,998,-744.46 for land in Kansas illegally opened to White settlement. The Oneidas of both Wisconsin and Ontario shared in the award, but in order to receive payment, it was necessary for each to provide membership lists. At this time there were a number of persons living on the reserve who had not contributed to the purchase of the land but had married into families that had rights. Serious disputes divided clans and families and became another basis for the division between the factions. The Confederacy faction supported the inclusion of the "squatters" but the dispute has continued to the 1970s.

The Six Nations Confederacy faction was recognized by the Canadian government as the legitimate government of the reserve. The Confederacy people were led by a Pine Tree chief, W.K. Cornelius, who became involved

488

in an attempt by the New York Onondaga to initiate a series of claims against the United States government and the state of New York. The efforts were part of a pan-reservation movement called the Kellogg Party, a movement that originated in Oneida, Wisconsin, in the wake of the effects of the General Allotment Act. Individuals were encouraged to contribute monthly to the support of the group with the result that many Oneidas were bankrupted. Dissatisfaction developed and by the mid-1920s a third faction called the Oneida Welfare Association, complete with its set of hereditary chiefs, arose to challenge the Confederacy. Finally, in 1934, on the application of the Oneida Welfare Association and contrary to the wishes of a majority of Oneidas, the Canadian government instituted an elective council system (A. Ricciardelli 1961).

In 1972 the Oneida of the Thames band included 1,964 members, of which approximately 1,200 resided on reserve lands. Most earned their livelihood working in nearby communities such as London and Saint Thomas or on the many farms that surround the reserve. Few Oneidas farm their own land; most of the cleared land is leased to Whites.

Kin-based relationships continued to play a dominant role in the social and political relations on the reserve although in recent years there has been an increase in marriages to non-Oneidas. Under Canadian law band membership is determined through the patriline; women who marry out lose their tribal status along with their rights to reside on the settlement or own property. Except for the Longhouse minority, clan identification has lost most of its political significance, although it is still necessary to know one's clan in order to benefit from medicine and curing ceremonies.

The majority of Oneidas are members of one of several Christian sects, the principal ones being the Methodist, Baptist, and Anglican. The Longhouse religion continues although its adherents are largely from three or four intermarried families. The Longhouse ("Iroquois Since 1820," fig. 4, this vol.) is responsible for the perpetuation of the Iroquois calendrical ceremonial cycle—the Midwinter, Strawberry, Green Corn, and Harvest festivals—and is the center for the activities of the False Face and Little Water curing societies. Members of all religions take part in these activities, and the belief in medicine society cures remains strong. Membership in the societies includes both Christians and Longhouse people.

Politically the band is governed by a chief and 12 councilors elected, at large, for two-year terms. With funds provided by the Canadian government, the council controls various settlement activities such as education, welfare, housing, road construction and maintenance. Most Oneidas accept the elected council, with the exception of the Longhouse group, which maintains its own hereditary council.

New York

A few hundred New York Oneidas remained in New York after the two major migrations. Gradually their land base was reduced through sales until few acres remained in Oneida ownership. Many moved to the Onondaga reserve near Syracuse, while others dispersed into neighboring White communities. They continue to exist as a tribe although their legal status is anomalous at best. They determine membership through the matriline, and many speak Oneida. They neither merged with the Onondagas nor disappeared into White society.

The New York Oneidas are under the jurisdiction of the state of New York but the basis for their continued recognition lies with the provisions of the treaty of 1794, which grants a small annuity. This annuity necessitates the maintenance of a tribal list. In 1972 there were an estimated 600 Oneidas living on the Onondaga Reserve and in the vicinity of Oneida, New York.

Synonymy†

The Oneida have generally been known by variants or cognates of their own name *oneyote ʔa·kâ·* 'people of the erected stone (*oneˑyóteʔ*)'; an Oneida village name that refers to the large syenite boulder (Hewitt 1910j) that, according to legend, always appeared near the main Oneida settlement. What is reputedly the stone in question was returned to the New York Oneida in 1974 and installed on their reservation near Oneida. The earliest recordings are Onneyatte and Onneyuttehage, 1635 (Van den Bogaert, in Jameson 1909:150). The Huron name, recorded as onneï8 ʻtr8nnon (8 = ou; Potier 1920:154), was borrowed into French: Onoiochrhonons, 1635 (JR 8:116), Oneiochronon, 1640 (JR 18:232), Onnejohron-nons, 1653 (JR 40:160), Onneïotchronnons, 1658 (JR 44:194), Onnei8theronnons, 1660 (JR 46:52). Later the village name recorded as Ononjoté, Ononïoté, and Onne-ïout (JR 27:296, 30:258, 47:216) was used as the tribal name: onnei8t, 1658 (JR 44:122), Onei8tes (JR 45:80), Onneiouts (JR 53:54; DCB 1:15), Onneyouts (Bacqueville de la Potherie 1753, 1:321). Colden's (1747) spelling Oneida was in general use by the mid-eighteenth century; other variants, among those listed by Hewitt (1910j:125–126), include Anayints, Onayiuts, Oneides, Oneidoes, Oneiyutas, Oneydas, Oneydes, Oniadas, and Onyades.

The general term for any Oneida settlement is *okwehowê·ne*. This is used especially for Oneida, Wisconsin, which is called in Cayuga *(o)nrahtʔaéʔkeh*. The

† This synonymy was prepared by Ives Goddard incorporating material from Jack Campisi and Bruce G. Trigger. The uncredited Iroquoian forms were furnished by Clifford Abbott (Oneida), Marianne Mithun (Mohawk, Cayuga, and Tuscarora), Michael K. Foster (Cayuga), and Hanni J. Woodbury (Onondaga).

reserve in Ontario is usually referred to in English as Southwold, Munceytown, or Muncey.

The names for the Oneida in the other Iroquoian languages are: Mohawk *oneyote?á·ka?* (onenhiotehaka, Cuoq 1882:164); Onondaga *niyótka?* 'different-way people' (older Anajotròhne, Zeisberger 1887a); Cayuga *(o)náyotka·?*, *onáiyotka·?*, and *onéyotka·?*; Seneca *néyotka·?* (Chafe 1967:69); and Tuscarora *twahrò·nęh*. Other forms are Oklahoma Wyandot yumérunu, literally 'Indian, or person, people' (Gatschet 1881:4), Canadian Wyandot wažesa?yerónǫ? (Hewitt 1889, normalized), Munsee *wtásəni·w*, literally 'people of the stone' (sg.; Michelson 1922:41 and Hewitt 1936, phonemicized), Fox *ki·waho·haki* (pl.; Michelson 1930a), Winnebago *wa·bánoxgé* (Kenneth L. Miner, personal communication 1974), a borrowing from Menominee *wa·panahki·w* 'eastern Indian'. See also the synonymy in "Northern Iroquoian Culture Patterns," this volume.

Van den Bogaert (Jameson 1909:139-162) called the Oneidas Sinnekens, a name later used for the Senecas (see synonymy in "Seneca," this vol.). Champlain (1922-1936, 3:54, 5:283, 6:map) probably used the otherwise unattested Huron name Entouhonorons, or Antouhonorons, to designate the Oneida; however, it is unclear whether this term was applied solely to the Oneida or to other Iroquois tribes as well.

Within the context of the League of the Iroquois the Council names of the Oneidas are Oneida *nihatilǫta?kó* 'they of the big tree', Mohawk *ratirǫta?kó·wa* (G. Michelson 1973:100), Cayuga *satyǫta?kó·wa*, and Seneca niundakówa and ne-ar-de-on-dar-go-war (Hewitt 1910j: 125). One explanation of this name is that Hiawatha found a party of Oneidas resting near a big tree that they had cut down during the journey on which he and Deganawida were bringing the Great Law to the Iroquois (Hale 1883a:78-79; Beauchamp 1900). Present-day Oneidas say the name refers to the central position of the Oneidas in the maintenance of the League—that is, as the trunk supporting the Great Tree of Peace.

Sources

Several excellent sources exist for the seventeenth and early eighteenth centuries. There are the *Jesuit Relations* (JR 1896-1901), which describe not only the aspects of the Iroquois social system but also related interaction between the colonial powers and the Iroquois nations. Of particular value are the writings of the Jesuit Fathers Milet (JR 58) and Bruyas (JR 51, 56), who lived for extended periods among the Oneidas. In addition, the New York colonial documents (NYCD 1853-1887) and the Livingston Indian records (Livingston 1956) provide

more documentation, particularly on political aspects of White-Iroquois relations.

The copious journals of Samuel Kirkland, missionary to the Oneidas for 43 years, document tribal affairs during the second half of the eighteenth century. Kirkland's interests were primarily religious and political so that he reports only in an incidental manner on the social system of the Oneida.

Indian-White relations are described in a number of sources, the most important of which is the Hough Report of 1861. This legislative document reprints, with annotation, the commissioners of Indian affairs reports for the crucial period from 1784 through 1791. Displayed here is the complex array of White-Indian relations: the ambitions, artifices, and aims of the various participants to the treaties ceding Oneida lands to New York State. The legislative report of 1889 (New York (State) Legislature. Assembly 1889) provides a record of the subsequent treaties entered into by the Oneidas as well as testimony concerning tribal affairs and organization. The report, although biased, offers valuable data, particularly on White attitudes toward Indians.

Two documents provide some valuable description of Oneida life around 1800. Belknap and Morse (1955) visited Oneida and reported on aspects of the economic, social, and religious life of the society. In 1810 Gov. DeWitt Clinton (1849) visited the Oneida and wrote a short, but valuable, description of the community.

Several journals are of value for the Wisconsin Oneidas. First, there are the Eleazar Williams (1832-1840) papers, which document the motives behind immigration, problems of land negotiation, and the organization of the community during its early days. During the period from 1850 to 1870 two Oneidas, John Archiquette and Joseph Powliss, kept diaries that were later translated. Finally, a missionary's wife, Ellen Goodenough, wrote a journal that described Oneida life around 1860 (Bloomfield 1907). Ritzenthaler (1950) has contributed a short anthropological account of the Wisconsin group. No comparable body of material is available on the Ontario or New York Oneidas.

Basehart (1953) traced changes in the kinship system among the Wisconsin Oneida from the 1820s to the 1940s and compared this with a reconstruction of Iroquois kinship at the time of contact. Ricciardelli (1966) studied the kinship and family structure of the Ontario Oneidas. Both studies provide excellent historical and ethnographic data. A. Ricciardelli (1961) concentrates on the problems of factionalism among the Ontario Oneidas. Campisi (1974) traced the tribal history from 1600 to 1973 comparing aspects of the social, political, and belief systems of the three Oneida communities. Lounsbury (1953) has studied the Oneida language.

Onondaga

HAROLD BLAU, JACK CAMPISI, AND ELISABETH TOOKEʀ

Of the five tribes that comprised the Iroquois Confederacy, the most centrally located were the Onondaga (ˌänənˈdägu, ˌōnənˈdägu). To the east of them lived the Oneidas, and beyond the Oneidas, the Mohawks, "guardians of the eastern door." To their west lay the Cayugas and beyond them the Senecas keeping watch on the western door of the League ("The League of the Iroquois: Its History, Politics, and Ritual," fig. 1, this vol.). Thus relatively safe from invasion from the east and west, Onondaga warriors—reported to number 300 in the seventeenth century ("The League of the Iroquois: Its History, Politics, and Ritual," table 1, this vol.)—were more concerned with defense against attack by Hurons and French from the north and from the Susquehannocks to the south.

When the Confederacy was established, the Onondaga were designated "firekeepers" of the League and so charged with the responsibility of convening its councils and keeping its wampum records. As a consequence, their political position in the League and that of their 14 League chiefs became as central as their geographic one.

Territory

During the seventeenth century, the Onondaga continued to build their villages in the same area as they had in the two preceding centuries—near Limestone and Butternut creeks in the region between Cazenovia Lake and Onondaga Creek. Their principal hunting territory included all of Onondaga County, that is, from the region around Cazenovia Lake to that around Skaneateles Lake. It extended north to Lake Ontario and south to the Chenango Forks (fig. 1) (Fenton 1940:219-220). In this area, also, were located the streams and lakes where the Onondagas took fish and eels and where they had temporary camps (Beauchamp 1900:112-125; Beauchamp in JR 51:293-294; Fenton 1940:221). However, the famous Salt Springs near Syracuse apparently were not used by the Onondagas in earlier times, although later salt from these springs became important to the economy of Whites living there and to the Onondagas themselves.

As did other Northern Iroquoians, the Onondagas relocated their villages after the land that could be cleared nearby became exhausted and the firewood that could be collected in the vicinity became scarce. Although they moved their villages every decade or two, the Onondagas usually had only two villages at any one time: a large village that also served as the capital of the League, as the meetings of its chiefs were held there, and a much smaller village (Tuck 1971). The Jesuits did not establish a mission in this smaller village, a circumstance that probably accounts for their failure to mention it. However, it was noted in a 1677 report that the large Onondaga village contained about 140 houses and the small village then located about two miles away had about 24 houses (O'Callaghan 1849-1851, 1:12). A few years later, the large Onondaga village was moved and rebuilt, and when Father Jean de Lamberville arrived at Onondaga in 1681, he found its inhabitants in the process of transporting their crops and other belongings from the old village where they had lived for 19 years to the new one two leagues away (JR 62:55-57) on the east side of Butternut Creek one mile south of the present village of Jamesville (fig. 2) (Tuck 1971:188-189).

During the wars with the French, the Onondagas moved south into the hills of Butternut Creek. Then they moved west and settled along Onondaga Creek, a move perhaps made about 1720 (Beauchamp 1916: 115, 175; Hewitt 1910g:129; Fenton 1940:221; Tuck 1971:189). The eighteenth century was a period during which the Onondagas were relatively free from military attack and consequently their settlements along Onondaga Creek did not need to be either concentrated or palisaded. As a result, the houses, often occupied by only one or two families, were spread out along the creek. In 1743 when John Bartram visited the principal Onondaga village, he found fewer than 40 houses, many of them occupied by two families, scattered for two or three miles along both sides of Onondaga Creek, rarely more than four or five of them clustered near each other. The Onondaga council house was constructed in the manner of the old longhouse. It was a bark-covered building 80 feet long and 17 feet wide with a six-foot-wide passage down the middle. Benches one foot high with shelves above five feet from the ground ran along both long walls and were divided into apartments five feet wide ("Northern Iroquoian

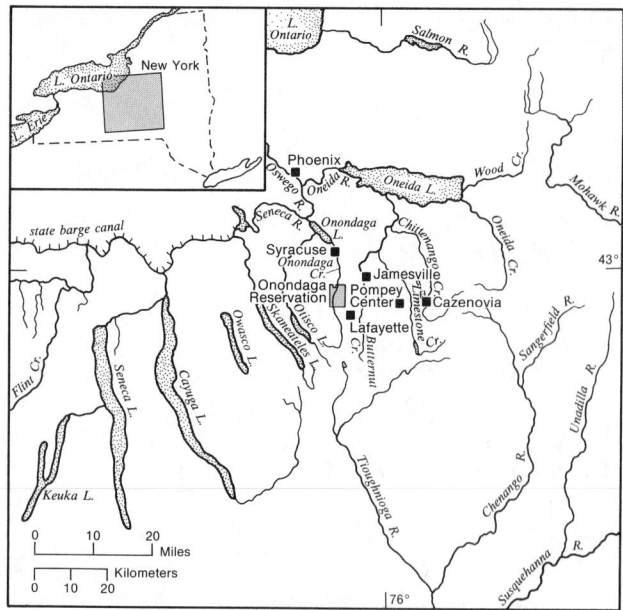

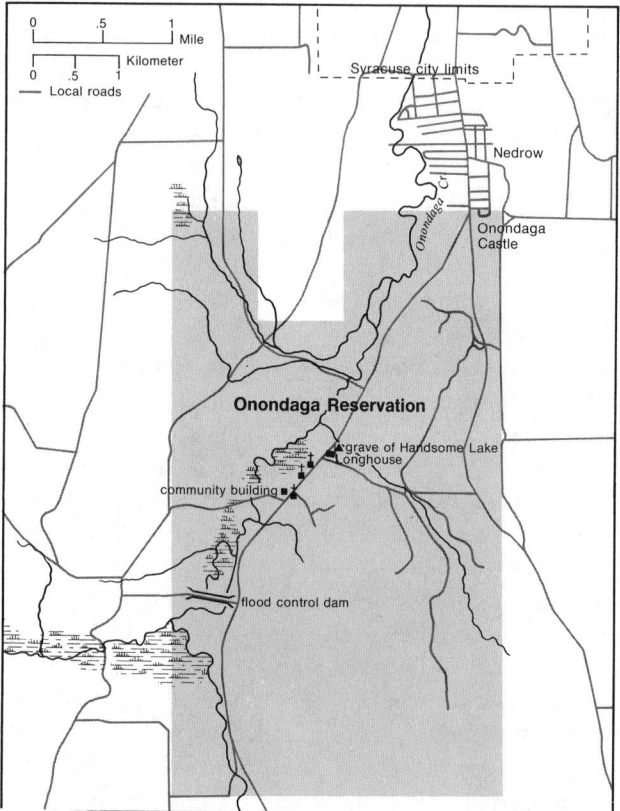

Fig. 1. Onondaga region and modern reservation.

Culture Patterns," fig. 14, this vol.) (Bartram 1751:40-42). Within the next few years, most of those living on the east side of the creek moved to the west side; in 1750 Conrad Weiser found only one house still remaining on the east side (Pa. Col. Recs. 5:475; Beauchamp 1892:107). The same year the Moravians Frederick Cammerhoff and David Zeisberger reported finding five small towns in addition to single scattered houses

(Beauchamp 1916:60). At the time, the Onondagas also occupied a smaller village a few miles south of their larger one (Beauchamp 1916:14, 23, 50, 127; O'Callaghan 1849-1851, 1:27; NYCD 7:582).

History

1650-1755

Both because they were "keepers of the fire" at the capital of the Confederacy and because of their central location between the Dutch and later the English at Albany and the French and their Indian allies to the west and north, the Onondaga became the center of intrigue in the play-off system that characterized Iroquois policy in the seventeenth and eighteenth centuries (see "Early Iroquoian Contacts with Europeans," "The League of the Iroquois: Its History, Politics, and Ritual," and "Origins of the Longhouse Religion," this vol.). This intrigue intensified after the Iroquois had defeated the Hurons (who had dominated Indian trade with the French to the northwest), the Petuns (allies of the Hurons), and the Neutrals and so eliminated except for the Eries and Susquehannocks the other Iroquoians competing for trade with the Europeans. To replace those lost in war, the Onondagas as did the other Iroquois adopted Indians from those tribes they had defeated, including the Hurons.

After the war with the Eries began the Upper Iroquois, preferring not to wage war on two fronts, decided to make peace with the French. By establishing peace with the French the Upper Iroquois also hoped to free themselves from the regulations the Mohawks had imposed on their trading with Albany and so their dependence on them (JR 44:151). Consequently in 1653, an Onondaga delegation went to Montreal for that purpose (JR 41:51, 81-83), and the following year Father Simon Le Moyne visited Onondaga (JR 41:91-129). Disturbed by this threat to their control of the trade between Iroquois and Europeans, the Mohawks attacked the party taking Le Moyne back to Montreal. They captured Le Moyne, letting him go only after the Onondagas convinced them to do so (JR 41:199-201). The following year, although Le Moyne went on an embassy to the Mohawks, the Onondagas sent a delegation representing the Upper Iroquois to confirm peace with the French (JR 42:49); and two Jesuits, Pierre Joseph Marie Chaumonot and Claude Dablon, went to Onondaga to establish a mission there. For the permanent mission, they chose a site that was near Onondaga Lake and between four and five leagues from the principal Onondaga village (JR 42:61-97, 43:161). In 1656 a number of Frenchmen including other Jesuits came to construct this mission, called Sainte Marie at Gannentaha (Onondaga Lake) JR 42:215, 43:133-135, 44:185-187). The Onondaga name is *kanę̀ntà·ha·ʔ* 'place on the hill'.* The intention of the Jesuits was to build a mission establishment similar to the one they had earlier had among the Hurons, also called Sainte Marie, which had been abandoned in 1649 when, faced with defeat at the hands of the Iroquois, the Hurons and French had fled the country (JR 42:53). But after the Eries had been defeated by the Senecas, antagonism to the French grew, and on the night of March 20, 1658, the French abandoned the mission having learned the Onondagas were planning to destroy it (JR 44:153–183, 213–217).

There continued to be a pro-French faction at Onondaga, and in 1661 the Jesuits were invited to return there. Consequently, Le Moyne went to Onondaga where he spent the winter (JR 46:225–245, 47:67–115, 174–199). The following year the western Iroquois, still engaged in a war with the Susquehannocks and ravaged by a smallpox epidemic, planned to enlist the aid of the French, but a false report of thousands of soldiers being sent from France for the purpose of destroying the Iroquois thwarted the effort (JR 48:77–83). In spring 1664 Onondagas still divided into a pro- and an anti-French faction led an Iroquois embassy to seek peace with the French, but the embassy was attacked by the Algonquins, and those not killed or taken prisoner took flight (JR 49:137–147). The efforts of those Onondagas attempting to restore friendly relations with the French in the years following the abandonment of the mission to the Onondagas at Gannentaha in 1658 were also thwarted by other Iroquois, particularly the Mohawks, who were opposed to such an alliance. However, after Alexandre de Prouville de Tracy's expedition had succeeded in burning the Mohawk villages in 1666, the Mohawks and other Iroquois concluded a peace with the French, and not long after the mission of Saint Jean Baptiste was established at Onondaga (JR 51:237–239).

The peace concluded with the French did not mean that the Onondaga ceased to trade with the Dutch traders at Albany, now British territory. Rather they continued to go to Albany for that purpose (JR 53:229), the peace permitting them to trade there as well as with the French and leaving them free to pursue their war with the Susquehannocks—a war that was proving to be both long and costly. In 1669 the Jesuits reported that nearly all the Onondaga warriors had been killed in this war (JR 54:111), perhaps an exaggeration but nevertheless a report that suggests the Onondaga war with the Susquehannocks was taking a heavy toll.

After the war with the Susquehannocks ended in 1675 the Iroquois, particularly the Seneca and Cayuga, became more hostile to the French, but the Mohawks initially opposed an open conflict with the French as a number of Mohawks had settled on the Saint Lawrence (see "Mohawk," this vol.). Those who had remained in the Mohawk Valley were reluctant to engage in a war with their relatives (JR 62:255). But the growing antagonism of the Iroquois toward the French led the Jesuits to withdraw most of their missionaries in the early 1680s. However, they remained at Onondaga until 1687, when Jacques René de Brisay, marquis de Denonville led an expedition down the Saint Lawrence to attack the Seneca, making impossible continued friendship between the Jesuits and the Onondagas.

The war between the French and the Iroquois, which in 1689 merged with King William's War, continued until 1696 when Louis de Buade de Frontenac, in an effort to bring the Iroquois to a peace that proved successful, led a large expedition of French and Indians against the Onondagas and Oneidas. After learning of the strength of the army that had invaded their country, the Onondagas burned their heavily palisaded village (fig. 2) and fled. The French completed the ruin by destroying the extensive cornfields around the village (O'Callaghan 1849–1851, 1:323–355; NYCD 4:180–181, 242, 9:649–656).

After the war had ended and the Iroquois had established peace with both the French and English, the Onondagas remained as they had been earlier, about equally divided into pro-English and pro-French factions (NYCD 4:689, 998). After the establishment of peace with the French in 1701, the French Jesuits returned to Onondaga, but they were forced to leave in 1709 and their mission house and chapel were burned (NYCD 4:917–920, 9:829, 836, 838). In 1710 the English were asked to come and build a fort at Onondaga (Wraxall 1915:69, 76; NYCD 5:218). Subsequently, tensions between the French and the Onondagas apparently eased, for in 1711 the French built a blockhouse at Onondaga. However, the English arrived and pulled it down (NYCD 5:243–244, 248–249; Wraxall 1915:81–87). The French again attempted in 1715 to build a fort at Onondaga (Wraxall 1915:104–105) but were unsuccessful in doing so. The English were equally unsuccessful (Lydekker 1938:43), and the set of communion plate Queen Anne had made for "her Indian Chappel of the Onondawgus" similar to that she had had made for the Mohawks in 1712 remained in Albany at Saint Peter's Church (Clark 1849, 1:214–215). Instead, the English built a trading post at Oswego in 1725 to attract the fur trade from the west. It became one of the most important trading centers in the Northeast.

In the following decades as the Pennsylvania trade expanded west the Iroquois found themselves treating

---

* The italicized Onondaga words in the *Handbook* are transcribed in the phonemic system used by Chafe ("Comparative Sketch of the Northern Iroquoian Languages," vol. 17); see also Chafe (1970:4, 6, 72–80). The words are cited as pronounced in isolation, but without the predictable initial ʔ and final *h*. The acute accent (´) marks the highest-pitch vowel in the word; in words where this is the only accent this vowel also bears the primary stress. The grave accent (`) indicates primary stress on a vowel of lower pitch than that marked with the acute, but higher than unmarked vowels. Phonemicizations have been supplied by Wallace L. Chafe and Hanni J. Woodbury.

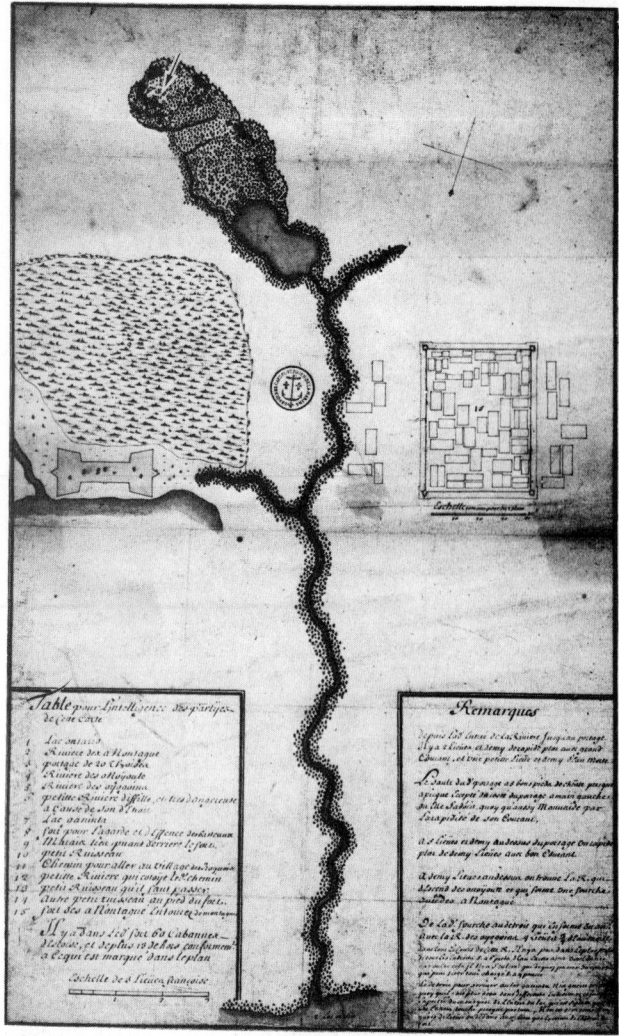

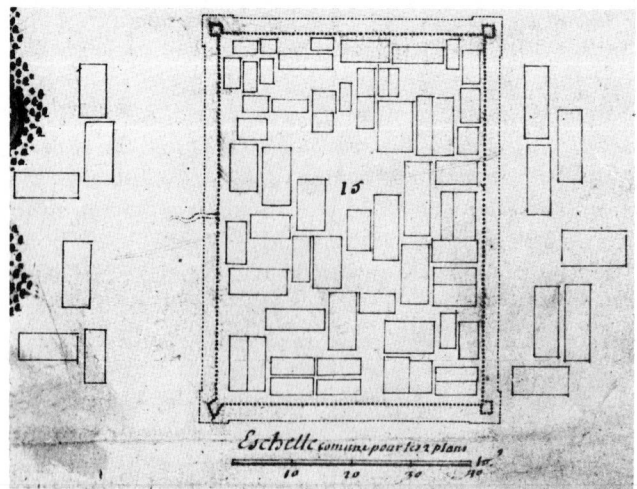

Bibliothèque Historique de la Marine, Paris: Album 67, No. 91 (Sirco France photo).
Fig. 2. Anonymous undated manuscript map, probably drawn to illustrate Frontenac's 1696 attack on the Onondaga. A bit of Lake Ontario is at the bottom (north), while the Onondaga River (present Oswego R.) runs through the center to Lake Ganinta (present Onondaga L.). To the southeast, surrounded by hills, is marked (arrow added) the site of a fortified Onondaga town, apparently the present Jamesville Pen archeological site. The applicable scale bar at bottom left represents 3 French leagues (12 km). At the left is an inset showing a temporary French fort at the southwestern corner of Onondaga Lake (with a marsh behind it). At the right is an inset (see also detail above) showing the Onondaga town, which according to the map legend contained 60 bark lodges (as shown) with 13 more outside the fort. The scale bar beneath the town is for the 2 insets; it represents 40 *toises* (about 78 m).

not only with the French to their north and west and the English at Albany and Oswego but also with the English in Pennsylvania as well as with various Indian groups in the region. This involved the Iroquois, who wished to maintain their position in the fur trade, in complex diplomatic relations. In the course of these negotiations, various French and English delegations were sent to Onondaga, the "capital of the Iroquois." The recorded history of the Onondagas during this period becomes an account of these missions.

It was not only traders in Pennsylvania who were interested in the Iroquois. Moravian missionaries, particularly David Zeisberger, visited Onondaga during the period 1750-1755. The outbreak of the French and Indian War put an end to this work (Loskiel 1794, 2:120-123, 140-141, 155-156; Beauchamp 1916), in the course of which Zeisberger had compiled a dictionary (1887) and grammar (1887-1888).

Oswegatchie

In the 1750s a number of Onondagas and some Iroquois from other tribes especially Oneidas and Cayugas

(NYCD 7:90, 278, 6:856) but no Mohawks (Hough 1853:87) went to live at La Presentation, a fort and mission established for them on the Upper Saint Lawrence at what is now Ogdensburg, New York, by Abbé François Picquet, a Sulpician missionary from the Lake of Two Mountains. The site, chosen by Piquet in 1748, the year King George's War ended, had obvious advantages. Located at the junction of the Oswegatchie River and the Saint Lawrence where the Saint Lawrence channel is narrow ("The League of the Iroquois: Its History, Politics, and Ritual," fig. 1, this vol.), the fort could protect Fort Frontenac and the Upper Saint Lawrence from British control as well as regulate trade on the river. In the seventeenth century after Fort Frontenac had been established, a trading post was established at La Galette, a few miles downriver from La Presentation (Hough 1853:41-42; NYCD 9:384). After La Presentation had been established, it was occasionally referred to as La Galette (NYCD 7:136, 573). However, more often it was called Oswegatchie (variously spelled including Swegachie and Wegatchi), and the Indians living there came to be known as Oswegatchies.

Picquet began the settlement at La Presentation in 1749. Later that year it was attacked and largely destroyed by some Indians presumed to be Mohawks. Nevertheless, Picquet remained, a fort was built, and the

Indian settlement grew. Six heads of families settled there in 1749, a number that increased to 87 the following year and to 396 in 1751. Shortly after there were over 500 families living in several villages there (O'Callaghan 1849–1851, 1:426, 431–433; Hough 1853:71). By 1753 so many Onondagas had moved to Oswegatchie that the Mohawk chief Hendrick observed that the fire at Onondaga had almost expired (NYCD 6:810; Hough 1853:56–57), and the following year Sir William Johnson said that half the Onondagas had gone to Oswegatchie (NYCD 6:887), a figure he had mentioned to Conrad Weiser in 1750. Weiser was also told that year by the Onondagas that Picquet had made about 100 converts among the Onondagas at Oswegatchie (Pa. Col. Recs. 5:475).

By moving to La Presentation, the Oswegatchies had allied themselves with the French, and when war broke out in 1754 they fought on the side of the French. On their part, the Onondagas who had remained in the Onondaga valley attempted to remain neutral but of necessity were drawn into the war although apparently to a limited degree.

After the defeat and death of Louis-Joseph de Montcalm at Quebec in 1759 Picquet saw the war was lost; and in May 1760, three months before Sir Jeffrey Amherst led his army up the Saint Lawrence, he left La Presentation in order not to fall into the hands of the British. Traveling by way of Michilimackinac, Picquet went to New Orleans where he spent almost two years before returning to France (O'Callaghan 1849–1851, 1:438–439; Hough 1853:79–80).

The Indians continued to live at Oswegatchie after the French and Indian War. Eighty warriors were reported dwelling there in 1763 (O'Callaghan 1849–1851, 1:27; NYCD 7:582) and 100 in 1768 (Jefferson 1964:99). During the American Revolution, the Oswegatchies apparently sided with the British (Hough 1853:107). In April 1779 the garrison the British maintained at Oswegatchie was unsuccessfully attacked by a body of Indians under two American officers from Fort Schuyler, as Fort Stanwix was named during the Revolution (Hough 1853:100–101; Stone 1838, 1:410–411).

After the Revolutionary War, the Oswegatchies who had been living at Johnstown on the Canadian side were moved by the British to a village on Indian Point in the town of Lisbon. But Americans did not begin to settle in the area until 1796, when by the provisions of Jay's Treaty, the British gave up their Northwest posts. At that time the village had 23 houses. The houses, uniformly built, had been constructed on both sides of a street running parallel to the river. Each house had been built for two families; it had two front doors, a double fireplace with one chimney, and glass windows. The village was occupied mostly in the winter, the Indians spending much of the summer at Black Lake hunting and fishing. About 1806, after the settlers had complained, the Oswegatchies were removed by order of New York State and dispersed. Some went to Saint Regis and others to Onondaga and elsewhere (Hough 1853:108).

Dispersal

When the American Revolution broke out, the Onondagas who had remained in their homeland—said in 1771 to number 800 (O'Callaghan 1849–1851, 4:1093)—were divided, as was the League itself, into at least three factions: pro-British, pro-American, and neutral (Graymont 1972:192). However, the British faction was sufficiently strong and active that the plans for the campaign led by John Sullivan and James Clinton against the Iroquois included an attack on the Onondagas. This 1779 campaign consisted of four parts, the first of which was an expedition from the upper Mohawk River and Fort Schuyler to Onondaga designed to prevent attacks of the eastern Iroquois tribes when the main drive against the Senecas and Cayugas began. Led by Col. Goose Van Schaick, this expedition destroyed the Onondaga villages said to consist of from 30 to 50 houses extending for 8 or 10 miles along the creek with other scattered houses in the vicinity (New York State Historical Association 1933–1937, 4:191–193; Stone 1838, 1:404–409; New York (State) Secretary of State 1887:16–17, 192–193; Clark 1849, 1:329–332). Many Onondagas fled to Niagara.

After the Revolution, about 225 Onondagas chose to follow Joseph Brant, the Mohawk chief, to Canada and to settle on the Six Nations Reserve (Johnston 1964:52). Approximately the same number of Onondagas were reported living on the Six Nations Reserve in 1810–1811 (Johnston 1964:281), suggesting that all those Onondagas who moved to Canada did so as a group in 1784. There, they and those belonging to the other Iroquois tribes who had also settled on the Six Nations Reserve rekindled the council fire of the Confederacy (see "Six Nations of the Grand River, Ontario," this vol.). Another council fire of the Confederacy was rekindled at Buffalo Creek where a number of Senecas and some Cayugas and Onondagas were then living. Thus, after the Revolution, two separate League councils were established, one in the United States and the other in Canada, each with its own complement of hereditary chieftainships. Each also had its own wampum for the wampum of the League held by the Onondagas had been divided, half being given to the Onondagas at the Six Nations Reserve and half remaining in New York State (see "The League of the Iroquois: Its History, Politics, and Ritual," this vol.).

Of those Onondagas who elected to remain in the United States, about 300 were living at Buffalo Creek, and over 100 in their old homeland at Onondaga in the early 1790s. The precise numbers at this time are uncertain (see Kirkland 1764–1804; Deardorff 1944).

In 1806 it was reported that 143 Onondagas were living at Onondaga and that there were 21 houses on the reservation (Sergeant 1807). However, in succeeding years, a number of other Onondagas apparently returned. In 1821, 272 were reported living there (J. Morse 1822:323). In the mid-1820s approximately 260 Onondagas were said to live at Onondaga, 115 at Buffalo Creek, and almost 70 at Allegany (National Archives Microcopy 234, Roll 832, Frames 34 and 172–173). In 1830 and 1833 the Onondagas at Onondaga were reported to number 310, at Buffalo Creek 94, and at Allegany almost 80 (National Archives Microcopy 234, Roll 832, Frames 415 and 669–670). In 1837 there were 300 living at Onondaga and 194 on the Seneca Reservations (Kappler 1904–1941, 2:508).

When the council fire of the Confederacy was rekindled at Buffalo Creek, more Onondagas as well as other Iroquois were living there than at any other location. The Onondaga village at Buffalo Creek, which in 1791 was said to consist of 28 good houses (Proctor 1864–1865, 2:307), was located near the ford on Cazenovia Creek (near the present junction of Potter Road and Seneca Street, a mile west of Ebenezer). The Onondaga council house stood on the east bank of the creek near the ford and the cemetery on a terrace on the opposite side (Houghton 1920:11, 115–116).

Despite the efforts of the Onondagas at Onondaga to have them returned to Onondaga, the council fire of the Confederacy and its wampum records remained at Buffalo Creek until after that reservation had been sold and Captain Cold ("The League of the Iroquois: Its History, Politics, and Ritual," fig. 11, this vol.), keeper of the council fire and the wampum, had died. In 1847 both were moved back to Onondaga (Clark 1849, 1:109, 124). However, a number of Onondagas (approximately 150) continued to live on the Seneca and Tuscarora Reservations in western New York State, the largest number on the Allegany Reservation (New York (State) Secretary of State 1857:507; Fletcher 1888:551; New York (State) Legislature. Assembly 1889:59; U.S. Census Office. 11th Census 1892:6).

The Onondaga Reservation

In 1788 by a treaty signed at Fort Schuyler the Onondagas ceded to the state all their lands in New York except a 100-square-mile tract of land in Onondaga County. This tract of land extended along Onondaga Creek from a point three miles above the Onondaga village to Onondaga Lake where the city of Syracuse now stands ("Iroquois Since 1820," fig. 1, this vol.). By a treaty signed in 1793 the Onondagas sold in two tracts about three-fourths of this reservation, and in 1795 by a treaty signed at Cayuga Ferry they sold their rights to the Salt Lake (Onondaga Lake) and the lands one mile around it reserved to them by the 1788 treaty and some land along the creek and adjoining the lake reserved to them by the 1793 treaty. In 1817 they sold to the state a 4,320-acre tract east of the reservation known as the "Onondaga Residence Reservation" and in 1822, 800 acres from the south end of the reservation. For these sales, the Onondagas received $33,380 in cash, $1,000 in clothing, and an annuity of $2,430 and 150 bushels of salt. Of the original reservation of 100 square miles, they retained 6,100 acres (fig. 1) (New York (State) Legislature. Assembly 1889:9; Clark 1849, 1:320–321, 348–356; Fletcher 1888:521, 550–551).

Subsequently, efforts were made to induce the Onondagas to sell their remaining lands in New York State and remove west. These efforts culminated with a treaty signed in 1838 by which the Iroquois sold all their remaining lands, but this treaty was widely regarded as fraudulent, and the subsequent treaty signed in 1842 made no provision for the sale of the Onondaga Reservation (Kappler 1904–1941, 2:502–516, 537–542). However, in this period the Oneidas did sell their lands, and a number moved to Canada to live on lands they had purchased there. But some elected to remain in New York State and some of these lived on the Onondaga Reservation (see "Oneida," this vol.). In 1845 there were reported to be 23 Oneidas at Onondaga (Schoolcraft 1847:37), and in 1890 they numbered 86 of the 212 Oneidas living in New York State (U.S. Census Office. 11th Census 1892:6).

Like the other Iroquois living on reservations in New York State, those on the Onondaga Reservation initially depended to a significant degree on hunting and fishing. But as their land base was reduced and White farmers moved into the region, the game declined and of necessity they turned to White farming practices and day labor.

At the same time, the Onondagas turned to new religions, most important, to the new religion of Handsome Lake. Within a year or two of Handsome Lake's first vision in 1799, some Onondagas who had gone to Buffalo Creek to attend a council (the Onondagas customarily sent a delegation of chiefs and headmen to Buffalo Creek to collect their annuities) heard the prophet speak. They were so impressed by what they heard that they and a number of others on the Onondaga Reservation decided to abstain from the use of alcohol. Handsome Lake subsequently visited the Onondagas where he continued to have much influence, and it was while he was on such a trip in 1815 that he died. He was buried beneath the floor of the council house, which at that time was a bark-covered longhouse 25 feet wide and 40 feet long (fig. 3). A stone monument marks the grave (see "Origins of the Longhouse Religion," fig. 3, this vol.) (Clark 1849, 1:105–108; O. Allen 1903:541; Cram 1803:68; Sergeant 1807; Friends, Society of. London Yearly Meeting 1844:162–164; Parker 1913:12–13).

In the early decades of the nineteenth century, various ministers visited the Onondaga and other efforts were made to convert them, with only limited success. In 1816 Eleazar Williams, an adopted Mohawk catechist and lay reader (see "Oneida," this vol.), visited the Onondagas. In that and the following year, a few Onondagas were

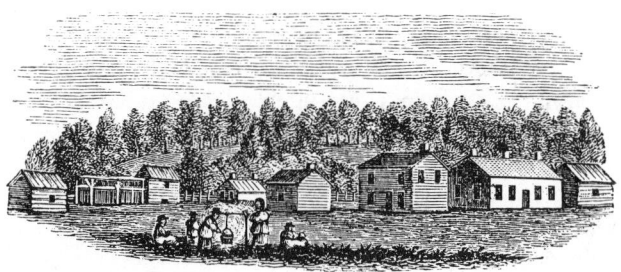

Barber and Howe 1841:389.
Fig. 3. Part of the settlement on the Onondaga Reservation about 1840. At the left is the framework of the former council house, which was replaced by the building at the right with 3 chimneys.

baptized by Episcopalian clergymen, and subsequently some attended the church at Onondaga Hill (Clark 1849, 1:238–240). About the same time, a local Presbyterian minister also proselytized among the Onondagas, and in 1821 there were said to be 34 who professed Christianity in the Presbyterian form of worship. In 1820 a school taught by a Stockbridge woman opened, but the teacher died a few years later (J. Morse 1822:323–324, 394; Clark 1849, 1:240–241). About 1828 a Quaker opened an industrial school and stayed for six or seven years (Fletcher 1888:551). Nevertheless, there remained considerable opposition to Christian missionaries, and after a Methodist church was established at Oneida in 1829, Indian exhorters rather than ministers were appointed to visit Onondaga as the Onondagas remained hostile to Christianity (Clark 1849, 1:241).

In the 1840s there was some lessening of opposition to both church and schools. In 1842 a building that had once been a house was fixed up for use as a Methodist church, and in 1848 a new church was built. A school was opened in 1845, and the following year the state of New York appropriated money for a schoolhouse and for the salary of a teacher (Clark 1849, 1:242–245; Fletcher 1888:570), support the state has continued to provide.

Nevertheless, Christianity attracted few Onondagas. In 1890 there were reported to be 23 Methodists, 21 Wesleyans, and 24 Episcopalians among the 494 living on the Onondaga Reservation (U.S. Census Office. 11th Census 1892:6, 9). The Longhouse continued to attract the largest number of followers, and the Onondaga chiefs, who constituted the governing council of the reservation, continued to be adherents of the Longhouse religion although the Christian faction wanted this hereditary system abolished and replaced with an elected one. The Onondagas also continued to be the firekeepers of the League of the Iroquois in New York State and continued to hold the wampum of the League until 1898 when the few remaining belts were tranferred to the New York State Museum, Albany.

Of all the long-established Longhouses (the New York Onondaga Longhouse and those on the New York Seneca reservations and the Six Nations Reserve in Canada), the ceremonial practice of the Onondaga Long-house ("Iroquois Since 1820," fig. 4, this vol.) differs most from the others. For example, the major Iroquois calendrical ceremonials—Midwinter, Seed Planting, Strawberry, Bean, Green Corn, and Harvest ceremonies—are given at the Onondaga Longhouse, but four of them are considerably longer. At the Onondaga Longhouse, the Seed Planting and Harvest ceremonies last from 6 to 8 days, the Green Corn ceremony for 8 days, and the Midwinter ceremony for 15 days. Also, at the Onondaga Longhouse, all Four Sacred Rituals (Feather Dance, Thanksgiving Dance, Personal Chant, and Bowl Game) in addition to the Our Life Supporter dances are performed as part of these four ceremonies, not just at the Green Corn and Midwinter ceremonies as at the other Longhouses. At other Iroquois Longhouses, the dream-guessing rite is given during the Midwinter ceremonial only if someone requests it, but at the New York Onondaga Longhouse it is a major rite lasting three days (it is the Onondaga rite of dream fulfillment). For the Onondaga dream-guessing rite, again unlike practice in other Longhouses, the moieties separate. Members of the

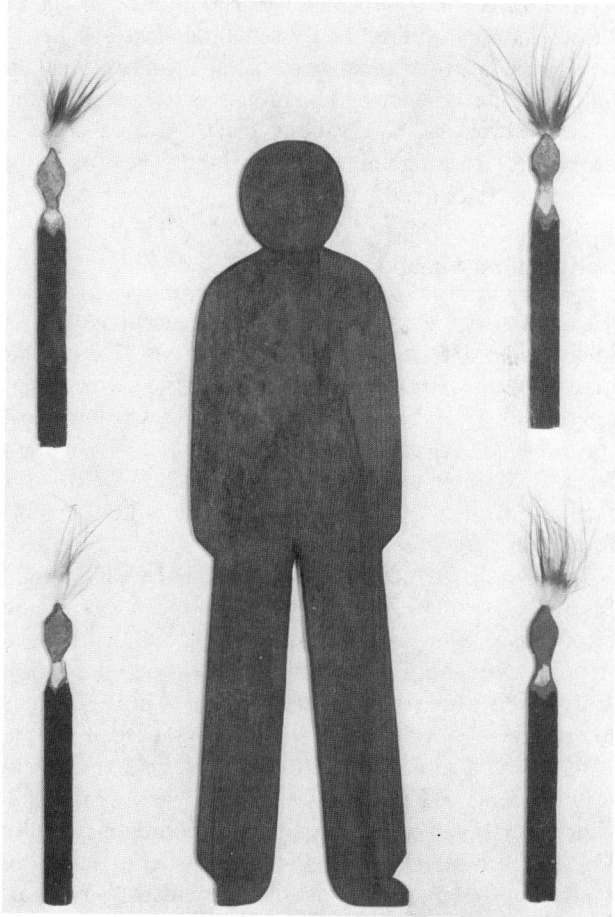

Mus. of the Amer. Ind., Heye Foundation, New York: 24/993.
Fig. 4. Figure and counters used in the Bowl Game at the Onondaga Midwinter ceremony, and usually destroyed immediately thereafter. Made about 1949, collected in 1964. Length of figure 23.5 cm, rest same scale.

Longhouse moiety (*kayé·i hotinǫ̀skè* 'at the four houses') consisting of the Wolf, Turtle, Snipe, Beaver, and Ball clans go to the Longhouse, and members of the Mudhouse moiety (*tehotí'ʔtàike* 'two chimneys') consisting of the Hawk, Deer, Eel, and (formerly) Bear clans go to the Mudhouse, a smaller building near the Longhouse that is also used as a cook house. So separated, those of one moiety guess the dreams of the other, each dream phrased as a riddle. Moieties also figure in other rites of the Onondaga Midwinter ceremony: a Bowl Game is played between the moieties for three days before the dream-guessing rite begins (fig. 4) and two baskets of ribbons and two baskets of tobacco—a basket of ribbons and a basket of tobacco for each moiety—are burned on the day following the conclusion of the dream-guessing rite in place of the two dogs that were formerly burned.

As at the other Iroquois Longhouses, the False Face Society participates in the Onondaga Midwinter ceremony; it holds special rituals on the seventh, eighth (after the dream-guessing rite has been concluded), and last nights of that ceremonial. At other times of the year, members of the False Face Society may be asked to cure a sick individual. Other Onondaga ceremonials similar to those of the New York and Six Nations Reserve Longhouses include the annual Feast of the Dead (*ohki·wé*). In addition, the Onondaga Longhouse participates in the biennial cycle of Six Nations meetings held for the purpose of reciting the Code of Handsome Lake (see "Iroquois Since 1820," this vol.).

Sociocultural Situation in the 1970s

The Onondaga continue to hold that portion of their ancestral land (6,100 acres) south of Syracuse, New York, lands that moved Morgan (1851:30-31) to remark that "perhaps . . . the Onondagas have been the most fortunate nation of the League. They still retain their beautiful and secluded valley of Onondaga." Within this territory live nearly 1,000 Onondagas and other Iroquois for whom they have provided land.

In general, the Indians at Onondaga live in one-family residences that are strung out along the roads of the reservation. The houses tend to be small; many are without central plumbing, a few are without electricity, and wood stoves are a common source of heat. There is one village about five miles south of Syracuse on Route 11A. Located in this village are the reservation elementary school; Methodist, Wesleyan, and Episcopal churches; the Onondaga Longhouse; community building and fire station. Except for a few craft shops or trading posts no other services are provided. Individuals customarily shop in nearby Syracuse.

Most individuals work as semiskilled or skilled laborers or in factories in the surrounding urban areas. Except for garden plots no farming is practiced. There has been an increase in the number of professional occupations, but the majority still rely on construction and the factory for their livelihood. Similarly, there has been a revival of interest in craftwork, particularly among the young. Traditional styles and techniques are utilized to produce items with an authentic flavor, which young and old alike appear to enjoy. Costumes, jewelry, sculpture in wood and stone, and painting give expression to traditional themes in Iroquois life.

The majority of residents are Christian and attend one of the churches on the reservation or commute to Syracuse. Each church has the usual ancillary social groups such as choirs, altar society, and Sunday school. These provide services to members of the community as well as regular social contact with neighboring White society. It is estimated that about one-fourth of the population identifies with the teachings of Handsome Lake, referring to themselves as belonging to the "Council House." It is this group that performs the more traditional Iroquois ceremonies connected with the calendrical cycle and the Feast of the Dead. It is not unusual for Christian Indians to attend "Council House" activities, particularly the Feast of the Dead.

In addition to church-related activities, a number of informal mutual-aid groups perform varied duties such as house repair, new home construction, aid in planting and harvesting, corn husking and shelling, gathering of wood for the old or needy, and a variety of community services. Older residents have been known to find firewood cut and stacked, or deer meat placed outside their doors in the middle of winter. Such items arrive anonymously during the night and recipients accept these gifts without embarrassment. Individuals suffering from physical ailments may receive help from one of the societies, most commonly the False Face. The Onondaga Volunteer Fire Department is a more formal example of the mutual-aid society. In addition to fire protection it sponsors a fair every August to raise funds to support its activities. The fair is open to all and features traditional foods such as Indian bread, corn soup, and parched corn; Indian crafts; dancing; and games such as box lacrosse, at which the Onondaga excel.

The Onondaga Reservation is governed by a council of hereditary chiefs chosen by the appropriate clan mothers. The council conducts the social, political, religious, and economic affairs of the tribe. It determines eligibility to reside on the reservation, gives help to the needy, and negotiates agreements with local contractors for the sale of gravel from the reservation's quarry. It is continually involved in discussions with New York State and federal representatives over proposed legislation. In the period from 1970 to 1974 it prevented the state of New York from taking reservation land to widen a major arterial highway and negotiated the return of several wampum belts in the possession of the state.

The Onondaga council represents more than the government of a single reservation. All hereditary chiefs must be followers of the teachings of Handsome Lake, the so-called Longhouse or Council House religion. In this way they are tied to the Longhouses on other Iroquois reservations in the United States and Canada. The Onondaga chiefs represent the interest of the tribe at grand councils of the League of the Iroquois where they are the keepers of the fire and fierce protectors of the faith, the traditional Iroquois ·beliefs, ceremonies, and practices embodied in the Longhouse religion.

Synonymy†

The Onondaga have generally been known by variants of their own name for themselves onǫtáˀkeˑkàˀ 'people of onǫ́ˑtàˀke', this being the name of the chief Onondaga town, literally 'on the hill'. The other Iroquoian languages use very similar forms: Mohawk onǫtaˀkehróˑnǫˀ; Oneida onǫtaˀkehaˑkâˑ; Cayuga tˀakéˑkaˑˀ or taˀkéˑkaˑˀ, shortened from onǫtˀakéˑkaˑˀ and archaic hǫtinǫtaˀkéˑkaˑˀ; Seneca onǫtaˀkeˑkaˑˀ (Chafe 1963:56); Tuscarora onǫtaˀkeháˑkaˑˀ; Huron onnontaeeronnon (Potier 1920:154). These forms are so similar that is it often not possible to say from which language a particular French or English name comes; variants used include Onontagueronon, 1632 (Sagard-Théodat 1865a); Onontaer(r)honons, 1635 (JR 8:116); Onontaehronon, 1640 (JR 18:232); Onnontae'ronnon, 1653 (JR 38:176); Onontageronon(s), 1647 (JR 30:226); Onontagheronons, 1657 (JR 44:68); and Onontaguehronnons, 1660 (JR 46:52). Later, shorter forms corresponding to the name of the town were used for the tribe: Onnontaé, 1668 (JR 51:208); Onnontagué, 1670 (JR 53:246); Onontaguez (Bacqueville de la Potherie 1753, 1:360), Onontagués (DCB 1:15); Onondagoes and Onondages, 1677 (Livingston 1956:43, 45); Onondagas (Colden 1747:66); and other more divergent forms listed by Hewitt (1910g:133).

† This synonymy was prepared by Ives Goddard. The uncredited Iroquoian forms were furnished by Wallace L. Chafe and Hanni J. Woodbury (Onondaga), Marianne Mithun (Mohawk, Cayuga, and Tuscarora), Clifford Abbott (Oneida), and Michael K. Foster (Cayuga).

The Munsee name for the Onondaga is mùxòˑtéˑnayiˑw 'people of the big town' (sg.; Michelson 1922:41 and Hewitt 1936, phonemicized).

There are two sets of Council names in use for the Onondaga. Meaning 'name bearers' are Cayuga hotihsẹnákEteˀ and a number of forms in earlier sources such as Seuh-no-keh'te, Sagosanagechteron, and Yagochsanogéchti (Hewitt 1910g:133). Meaning 'fire keepers' are Mohawk ronatsístayẹ (G. Michelson 1973:36), Cayuga hatitsIstáˑnǫh, and Seneca hutchístanet (Gatschet, in Hewitt 1910g:133).

The name used for the Onondaga reservation is onǫ́ˑtàˀke, continuing the name of the principal town in earlier times; equivalent are Mohawk and Oneida onǫtâˑke, Seneca onǫtaˀkeh (Chafe 1967:72), and Tuscarora onǝˀnáˀkyeh. Other Seneca names are katsístayẹˀ 'council fire' (Chafe 1967:62) and kanǫktiyóˀkeh 'at the good place' (Chafe 1963:57). In English the reservation is sometimes referred to as Nedrow or Syracuse, names of nearby places.

Sources

Onondaga settlements in the seventeenth and eighteenth centuries have been discussed by Beauchamp (in JR 51:293-294 and more fully in Beauchamp 1900:112-125), Tuck (1971:171-225), and Bradley (1976). Parker's (1922:637-650) account is based on Beauchamp.

The history of the Oswegatchie settlement is given in Hough (1853:49-109, 367-383). The early history of the Onondaga Reservation is described in Clark's (1849) history of Onondaga County.

Various Onondaga religious rites have been discussed in a number of articles including those by Beauchamp (1885a, 1888, 1891a, 1893, 1895a), Blau (1963, 1964, 1966, 1967), Kurath (1954), E.A. Smith (1883), and D.C. Smith (1888, 1889, 1889a) as well as in Beauchamp (1892:86-87) and Clark (1849, 1:53-67; see also Tooker 1970a:107-108, 161-169).

Cayuga

MARIAN E. WHITE, WILLIAM E. ENGELBRECHT, AND ELISABETH TOOKER

The Cayuga (₁kä¹yōogu), one of the Younger Brothers of the League of the Iroquois, occupied the land between the Onondagas, the firekeepers of the Confederacy, and the Senecas, Keepers of the Western Door—two of the three Older Brothers of the League. In the seventeenth century, their warriors apparently numbered 300, approximately twice that of the Oneida, the other Younger Brother of the League and the tribe with whom the Cayugas sat in the councils of the League. Their population was roughly equal to that of the Mohawk and that of the Onondaga and one-fourth to one-third that of the Senecas (see "The League of the Iroquois: Its History, Politics, and Ritual," table 1, this vol.).

Territory

The homeland of the Cayugas, the area in which they had their villages, was the region between Cayuga and Owasco Lakes, now part of Cayuga County in New York State. Their hunting territory—a considerably larger area— probably included the territory around both these lakes and extended north to Lake Ontario and south an indeterminate distance toward the Susquehanna River ("The League of the Iroquois: Its History, Politics, and Ritual," fig. 1, this vol.). Nevertheless, the region around their principal villages abounded in deer and consequently the Cayugas relied more on hunting than did the other Iroquois tribes. Also plentiful in the area were various kinds of fish, including eels, and pigeons and other kinds of birds (JR 56:49-51).

In the seventeenth century, the Cayugas had three principal villages; at least the few reports of this period so indicate. The earliest of these reports is contained in Pierre Esprit Radisson's account of his captivity. In the spring of 1653 Radisson (1967:28) visited three Cayuga villages located near one another; he apparently confused the order in which he visited the Cayugas and Senecas. Fifteen years later after the Jesuits had established a permanent mission to the Cayugas, they also reported that the Cayugas had three principal villages: Oiogouen (Goioguen), Thiohero (Tiohero), and Onontaré. Oiogouen, where the Jesuits established their mission of Saint Joseph, was probably located a few miles south of Union Springs near Great Gully Brook. The two other villages were located on the Seneca River. Thiohero, which took

its name from the great quantity of rushes in this river and where the Jesuits established the mission of Saint Estienne, was located four leagues from Oiogouen and probably near the outlet of Cayuga Lake. Onontaré where the Jesuits had their mission of Saint René was almost six leagues from Oiogouen, that is, almost two leagues downriver from Thiohero (JR 51:293, 52:179, 262, 54:53; Hawley 1879:21, 40, 48; Skinner 1921a:56). Apparently sometime during the next 10 years (perhaps after the defeat of the Susquehannock in 1675) the Cayugas moved their villages, for in 1677 Wentworth Greenhalgh reported that the three Cayuga villages were about a mile from one another and within two or three miles of Cayuga Lake. They were not palisaded (O'Callaghan 1849-1851, 1:12-13; Fenton 1940:223).

History

During the first half of the seventeenth century as they became increasingly dependent on the fur trade and as the beaver that could be found in their own territory declined, the Iroquois intensified their attacks on neighboring tribes. Finally, in 1649, the Senecas and Mohawks defeated the Hurons and, shortly after, the Petuns and Neutrals. Of the Northern Iroquoians living to their west only the Eries remained.

After the defeat of the Hurons, the Iroquois intensified their attacks to the north. But in 1653, after their war with the Erie had intensified, the Upper Iroquois tribes (including the Cayugas) established a peace with the French; and three years later, in the fall of 1656, after the central mission of Sainte Marie had been established among the Onondagas, Father René Ménard went to Cayuga to establish a mission there. However, this peace with the French was an uneasy one, and after two months Ménard was forced to return to the mission station on Onondaga Lake. He was visited there by an influential Cayuga and asked to return, which he did (JR 43:185, 307-317). This missionary effort was short-lived for in 1658 the Jesuits were forced to abandon Sainte Marie and leave Iroquois country.

In the following years the Susquehannock war with the three westernmost Iroquois tribes intensified, and in 1661 a Cayuga chief led a delegation of Cayugas and Onondagas to Montreal seeking peace with the French (JR

46:181, 225-233). On their invitation, Simon Le Moyne visited the Cayugas for a few weeks in the winter of 1661-1662 while he was staying at Onondaga (JR 47:185-189). In 1664 a delegation of Cayugas went to Quebec and asked for missionaries (JR 48:237-239, 49:149-151). Two years later, in 1666, the Jesuits planned to go to Cayuga but were prevented from doing so when Alexandre de Prouville de Tracy decided to attack the Mohawks (JR 50:197-199).

In part, the Cayuga desire to establish peace with the French was a consequence of the war they were then waging with the Susquehannock, which had intensified in the 1660s (JR 47:71, 48:77-79). Fear of the Susquehannocks also had induced some Cayugas to move to the Bay of Quinté, and in 1668 the Sulpicians established a mission at this new Cayuga settlement (JR 50:326, 51:177, 257, 290; Charlevoix 1866-1872, 6:110; Hawley 1879:83-99). That same year, the Jesuits reestablished their mission to the Cayugas, which they called the mission of Saint Joseph (JR 51:251, 255-257, 52:173). At that time, a number of Huron and Susquehannock captives as well as some Neutrals were living among the Cayugas (JR 43:307, 47:187, 51:257, 52:179, 56:51). Nevertheless, there was opposition to the Jesuits among the Cayugas (JR 52:177-193, 54:53-55, 57:177-185), which increased after the Susquehannocks had been defeated (JR 59:245, 251, 60:173-175, 61:159), and in 1682 the Jesuit missionary was forced to leave (JR 62:99-107, 229-231).

In succeeding years, Iroquois relations with the French worsened, and in 1687 a French expedition against the Senecas burned their villages. In 1693 another French expedition burned the Mohawk villages, and in 1696 Louis de Buade de Frontenac led a final expedition against the Onondagas and Oneidas, resulting in the destruction of their villages. Frontenac had originally planned to attack the Cayuga also but later decided against it (Charlevoix 1866-1872, 5:20; JR 65:25-27). Thus, the Cayugas were the only tribe in the League to escape attack by the French in the series of expeditions that was intended to humble the Iroquois and that finally led in 1701 to the establishment of peace between the Iroquois and French as well as between the Iroquois and English.

This peace allowed the Iroquois to pursue a policy of neutrality in the following decades, although the English on occasion convinced them to provide warriors in their wars against the French as they did during Queen Anne's War (Wraxall 1915:69, 91). But by usually remaining neutral in respect to the conflicts between France and England and by continuing to trade with both, the Iroquois could continue their dominant position in the fur trade, trading and warring with the Indians to their south and west—activities that engaged the Cayugas as well as the other Iroquois tribes.

The success of this policy during the eighteenth century meant that the Cayuga villages did not need to be palisaded and that the houses comprising the village did not have to be so concentrated. Consequently, the settlements of the Cayugas became more dispersed. During this period also, the Cayuga had villages on the west side of Cayuga Lake and to the south toward the Susquehanna River. But they also continued to have a village on the Seneca River, and their principal village continued to be located on the east side of the lake. In 1750, when the Moravians visited it, this village where the Cayuga chiefs lived had about 20 houses, many with three or four fireplaces and each capable of housing four or five families (Beauchamp 1916:32, 41-44, 65-66, 108; O'Callaghan 1849-1851, 1:27; NYCD 7:582; New York (State) Secretary of State 1887:76-77, 113, 142-144, 236-237).

In 1753, the year before the French and Indian War began, the Tutelo and Saponi—two tribes speaking Siouan languages—joined the Cayuga. Seventy years earlier, the defeat of the Susquehannocks had led the Iroquois, particularly the Senecas and Cayugas, to attack groups farther south. These assaults led the Tutelo and Saponi to abandon their villages in Virginia and move into Carolina. About 1710, persuaded by Gov. Alexander Spotswood, they returned to Virginia and settled at Fort Christanna. The Iroquois continued their attacks on them there until 1722 when a treaty was made between the Iroquois and their allies and the Indians of Virginia and Carolina. Increasing White settlement in the area induced them to move north about 1740 and settle at Shamokin, a village just south of the Forks of the Susquehanna where a number of other Indian immigrants lived and at Skogari farther up the northern branch of the Susquehanna. After their adoption by the Cayuga and thus by the Iroquois League about 1753, they continued to move north; and by 1771, their principal village was located three miles south of Cayuga Lake (Mooney 1894:37-51; Hale 1883b:1-8; Schaeffer 1942; New York (State) Secretary of State 1887:77-78; NYCD 6:811).

Dispersal

When the American Revolution began, the Cayugas, said in 1771 to number 1,040 (O'Callaghan 1849-1851, 4:1093), attempted to remain neutral as did the other Iroquois tribes. However, they were drawn into the war on the side of the British, and Cayuga warriors including their famous chief, Fish Carrier, fought on that side. In 1779 an American expedition was sent to humble the pro-British western Iroquois and in September of that year, after the main force of this expedition under Gen. John Sullivan and Gen. James Clinton had destroyed the Seneca villages, two detachments were sent to destroy the villages of the Cayugas. One group under Col. William

Butler destroyed the villages on the east side of Cayuga Lake, and a smaller group under Col. Henry Dearborn destroyed those on the west side (New York (State) Secretary of State 1887:76-77, 113, 142-144, 236-237, 303; D.W. Adams 1889:176-180).

After the American Revolution, a considerable number of Cayugas moved to Canada establishing two villages on the Six Nations Reserve (see "Six Nations of the Grand River, Ontario," this vol.). In 1785, the year after this grant had been given to the Iroquois, 382 Cayugas were reported living there. With the Cayugas went a number of Tutelos. In 1785 there were said to be 74 Tutelos living on the Grand River Reserve (Johnston 1964:52). The greatest number of them settled on the heights near Brantford where they built a council house. Two epidemics, one in 1832 and another in 1848, killed most of the Tutelos; the few that remained were absorbed by intermarriage with the Cayugas (Hale 1883b:8-9). However, the Saponi apparently did not go to the Grand River Reserve (Hale 1883b:10), and their fate is unknown. It seems likely that they remained with the Cayugas in New York State and were absorbed by them. At least some Saponi were living with the Cayuga in 1789 on their reservation on the Seneca River (Mooney 1894:51-53).

A number of Cayugas and Tutelos decided to remain with the Senecas at Buffalo Creek. There they established a straggling village along Cayuga Creek at the northern edge of the reservation (Houghton 1920:116). In 1789, 38 Cayuga families totaling about 350 individuals and 55 Tutelos were reported living at Buffalo Creek (Schaeffer 1942:xiv-xv; Kirkland 1764-1804). But in 1824 and 1827, only 90 Cayugas were said to be living there (National Archives Microcopy 234, Roll 832, Frames 34 and 172).

Still other Cayugas continued to live in their old homeland. In 1790 130 were reported living there on the east and west sides of Cayuga Lake (Kirkland 1764-1804). Shortly after, these lands were sold, and a number of them including Fish Carrier settled on the Grand River Reserve (O. Allen 1903:540).

By a treaty signed at Albany in 1789 and confirmed at Fort Stanwix the following year, the Cayugas sold to the state all their New York lands except a 100-square mile tract of land around the northern end of Cayuga Lake ("Iroquois Since 1820," fig. 1, this vol.). In 1795, by the Treaty of Cayuga Ferry, they sold this reservation to the state retaining only two tracts, one of two square miles and the other of one square mile, on the east side of Cayuga Lake. In addition, by this treaty, one square mile of land at Canoga on the west side of the lake was given to Fish Carrier. The two small tracts on the east side of the lake were sold to the state in 1807 as was Fish Carrier's grant in 1841 (New York (State) Legislature. Assembly 1889:216-230; Taft 1914:96).

Sometime after the sale of their lands in New York State, a number of Cayugas and some other Iroquois moved to Ohio and settled on the Lower Sandusky River. They subsequently came to be known as the Sandusky Senecas. These Iroquois fought on the side of the Americans in the War of 1812, and in 1817 by a treaty signed at the Foot of the Rapids of the Miami they were given a 30,000-acre tract of land on the Sandusky River (Kappler 1904-1941, 2:145-155). In 1818 by the Treaty of Saint Mary's this reservation was enlarged by 10,000 acres (Kappler 1904-1941, 2:162-163).

A census taken in 1829 reported that there were 322 Iroquois living on the Seneca Sandusky reservation, of whom 157 were Cayugas (National Archives Microcopy 234, Roll 669, Frame 650). At that time, an approximately equal number of Cayugas were living on Seneca reservations in New York State: in 1830, it was reported that 133 Cayugas were living there—94 on Buffalo Creek, 25 on Cattaraugus, and 16 on Tonawanda—about the same figures reported in 1833 (National Archives Microcopy 234, Roll 832, Frames 415, 669-670).

The Sandusky Senecas sold their reservation in 1831 (Kappler 1904-1941, 2:325-327) and that same year left Ohio for land west of the Mississippi. In the party were about 340 including a few individuals from other tribes (Foreman 1946:86). They settled on a reservation in what is now northeastern Oklahoma (see "Oklahoma Seneca-Cayuga," this vol.). At the same time, before the Sandusky Senecas left Ohio, the Cayugas divided their annuity agreeing that the Sandusky Senecas receive $1,700 and the New York Cayugas $600 of the $2,300 payment to the Cayugas (New York (State) 1849:5). When the War of 1812 broke out, the Cayugas living in Canada ceased receiving any share of this annuity (New York (State) 1849:3). The Canadian Cayugas subsequently repeatedly asked that they be given their share of these annuities, a claim that was not finally settled until the 1930s.

In 1838 the Iroquois sold all their land in New York State. However, there was considerable opposition to this treaty, as most of the Indians living on these reservations were opposed to selling the land and to removal west (see "Seneca," this vol.). A census taken at this time reported that 130 Cayugas were living on the Seneca reservations in 1837 (Kappler 1904-1941, 2:508). Of the approximately 153 Cayugas living on the Cattaraugus and Buffalo Creek reservations two years later, about 47 percent were opposed to emigration; of the approximately 82 Cayugas at Cattaraugus, 18 were opposed to emigration; and of the 71 living at Buffalo Creek, 54 were opposed (Society of Friends 1840:161-164).

The opposition to the 1838 treaty led to negotiation of a new treaty signed in 1842. By this treaty, only the Buffalo Creek and Tonawanda reservations were sold, the Senecas retaining the Cattaraugus and Allegany reservations. Those who lived on the two reservations that had been sold were to remove to those that had not, and in the next few years many of those living at Buffalo Creek including the Cayugas moved to Cattaraugus. A census taken in 1845 reported 114 Cayugas living at Cattaraugus (Schoolcraft 1846:32, 95). At the same time, those Iroquois living in New York State who wished to were encouraged to emigrate west, and in 1846, a party of 215 Indians including 44 Cayugas left for lands assigned them on the Marmaton River near Fort Scott in the Osage Agency. A number died there, and the following year 73 emigrants including 25 Cayugas returned to New York State. Of those Cayugas who emigrated in 1846 only three elected to remain in Oklahoma. At the time, the Sandusky Senecas numbered about 30 Cayugas and 44 of other tribes (New York (State) 1849:7-16). The number of Cayugas living in Oklahoma had become so reduced that in 1850 provision was made for a periodic census to be taken of those Cayugas living in the United States for annuity purposes. The first such census taken in 1855 reported that 143 Cayugas were then living in New York State and 58 west of the Mississippi (New York (State) Secretary of State 1857:503).

The Cayugas who remained in New York State continued to live on the three Seneca and the Onondaga reservations, principally at Cattaraugus. In 1890, of a total of 183 Cayugas reported to be living in New York State, 153 lived at Cattaraugus (U.S. Census Office. 11th Census 1892:6, 25).

Synonymy*

The Cayuga name for themselves is *kayohkhó·nǫ*ʔ, less commonly *kayokwęhó·nǫ*ʔ.† This means 'people of Oiogouen', but the etymology of this town name is unknown; the translations 'where the boats were taken out' (Fenton 1940:222; Beauchamp 1892:17), 'where the locusts were

* This synonymy was written by Ives Goddard incorporating some materials from Marian White. The uncredited Iroquoian forms were supplied by Michael K. Foster (Cayuga), Marianne Mithun (Mohawk, Cayuga, and Tuscarora), and Hanni J. Woodbury (Onondaga).

† Cayuga words appearing in italics in the *Handbook* are written in the phonemic system used by Chafe ("Comparative Sketch of the Northern Iroquoian Languages," vol. 17); see also Foster (1974:258-266). Vowels written with capital letters are voiceless; they reflect sequences of vowel plus *h* (Foster's vowel plus H) under certain accentual conditions. Under the same accentual conditions sequences of vowel plus ʔ are metathesized to ʔ plus vowel (Foster's vowel plus ?); these are here written in metathesized order. Phonemicizations of Cayuga words have been furnished by Michael K. Foster and Marianne Mithun.

taken out' (Mooney and Hewitt 1907), and 'mucky land' (Morgan 1851:51) appear to be folk-etymological guesses. The name in other Iroquois languages is similar but shows many unexplained variations: Mohawk *koyohkwęhró·nǫ*ʔ (Cuoq 1882:164; Roy Wright, personal communication 1976) and *kayǫ*ʔ*kwęhá·ka*ʔ; Onondaga *kayokwę́·ka*ʔ, Seneca *kayókwe·onǫ*ʔ (Chafe 1963:56), Tuscarora *kwǝyokwǝhá·ka·*ʔ. Seventeenth-century Huron was the source of French forms such as Oüioenrhonons, 1635 (JR 8:110), but eighteenth-century Huron shows a reborrowed goïögoinronnon (Potier 1920:154); compare Wyandot Cayóga (Gatschet 1881:5). Other forms in early French records include several from Huron but with on misprinted for ou—Oniouenhronon, Ouionenronnons, Onioenhronnon (JR 18:232, 33:64, 40:100)—and later spellings reflecting Five Nations languages: Oïogoenhronnons (JR 42:168), Oïogouanronnon (JR 43:166), Oiogeronon (JR 44:86), Oïogueronnon (JR 44:194), Oiochronons (JR 45:160), Oiogoenheronnons (JR 46:116), Oïogouenronnons (JR 47:70), 8iog8er[onons] (JR 48:236), Oiog8ehronnons (JR 51:118). Eventually the French adopted a shortened name based on the name of the town Oiogouen (also spelled Oiogoën, Oïogouan, Goiogoüen): oiog8en, 1656 (JR 44:122), Ojogoüens (JR 52:160), Oïogoüens (JR 52:178), Goyogouins (JR 54:263; DCB 1:13), Goiogouen (JR 54:53, 263, 267), Goiog8ens (JR 64:143), Goiogoen (JR 64:75), and Goyogouans (Perrot, in Blair 1911-1912, 1:199). Radisson (1967:28) has Oiongoiconon. English sources have Caijougas, Caiougos, Cayouges, Cajougoes, Cajuges, Cayogas, Cojages, Coujougas, and others listed by Mooney and Hewitt (1907). The spelling Cayuga appears as early as 1676 (NYCD 13:500) and has been common since Colden (1747).

The Munsee name for the Cayuga is *kwayó·kwe·w* (phonemicized from Michelson 1922:41; Hewitt 1936; and Speck and Moses 1945:12).

The Council names of the Cayuga refer to them as 'those of the great pipe' (cf. Johnson in O'Callaghan 1849-1851, 4:432): Mohawk *shotinǫnawęʔtó·wane* (*kanǫ́·nawę* 'pipe'), Onondaga *shotinanawęʔtó·na*ʔ (Michael K. Foster, personal communication 1976), Cayuga *honatshokwahtowá·nęh* (*otshókwAta*ʔ 'pipe') or *nawęʔtó·wa·* (Floyd G. Lounsbury, personal communication 1977), Seneca *honosuguaxtuwáne* (Gatschet, in Mooney and Hewitt 1907:224). Another formal term in Mohawk is *kwęnetáhkwęh* (Michael K. Foster, personal communication 1976).

Sources

The possible locations of the Jesuit missions in 1668 have been suggested by Clark (in Hawley 1879:21, 40, 48) and Beauchamp (in JR 51:293-295). An archeological survey—not without error—of Cayuga County is given in Beauchamp (1900:35-41) and repeated with a few additions in Parker (1922:500–506). Skinner (1921a:37–117) has reported on the excavation of some Cayuga sites. The principal sources for the location of eighteenth-century Cayuga settlements are the Moravian journals (Beauchamp 1916) and the journals of members of the Sullivan-Clinton expedition (New York (State) Secretary of State 1887).

Material on Cayuga history since the American Revolution contained in the nineteenth-century reports of the New York State senate and assembly is partly summarized in a series of papers by Taft (1912, 1912a, 1912b, 1913, 1914). The removal of the Sandusky Senecas from Ohio to Oklahoma is described by Foreman (1946:65–71).

Seneca

THOMAS S. ABLER AND ELISABETH TOOKER

The Seneca (ˈsenəku, locally also ˈsenəkē), westernmost of the Iroquois tribes, were the largest in the Confederacy. Their numbers were often reported to be almost equal to or to exceed those of the other four Iroquois tribes combined ("The League of the Iroquois: Its History, Politics, and Ritual," table 1, this vol.). Nevertheless, of all the Iroquois tribes they had the fewest number of chiefs on the League council; they held eight such chieftainships.

Territory

The historic homeland of the Seneca lay between the Genesee River and Canandaigua Lake. It was in this area, now part of Livingston and Ontario counties and the southern portion of Monroe County, that the Senecas built the various villages they occupied from at least the early sixteenth century until the American Revolution. Their hunting territory was considerably larger. It extended north to Lake Ontario, south to the headwaters of the lesser Finger Lakes, and east to the highlands between Seneca and Cayuga lakes ("The League of the Iroquois: Its History, Politics, and Ritual," fig. 1, this vol.) (Fenton 1940:225). After the Iroquois had defeated the other Iroquoian speakers who lived in the area—Eries, Neutrals, and Hurons—the Senecas extended their hunting territories to the west, ranging into Ohio and southern Ontario, and established some small settlements in these regions notably at Niagara.

Both the archeological data and accounts in the historical documents indicate that in the seventeenth century there were two Seneca groups, an eastern and a western one, each of which had a large village. According to Iroquois tradition, these two groups existed when the League was founded, the chief of the eastern group becoming the first name on the Roll Call of the Chiefs and the chief of the western group, the second name (Parker 1916a:86-87).

The archeological evidence also suggests that sometime during the first half of the sixteenth century the scattered Seneca villages consolidated into two large villages and one or two smaller ones, all built near one another a few miles north of Hemlock Lake. In the successive removes and rebuilding of these villages during the next century and one-half (the Senecas as other Northern Iroquoians moved their villages every decade

or two as the land that could be cleared for fields and the firewood that could be collected nearby became exhausted), these villages slowly moved north. The western Seneca in their various removes followed the course of Spring Brook north to its junction with Honeoye Creek. During the same period, the eastern Seneca moved northeast to the valley of Honeoye Creek and then east to the valleys of Mud Creek, Fish Creek, and Great Brook, that is, to the tributaries of Ganargua Creek (Wray 1973:1-8; Wray and Schoff 1953; Houghton 1922:47-59; 1927: 244-246).

They were living in these more northerly locations in the second half of the seventeenth century when the Jesuits visited their villages and established missions in some of them. The first such recorded visit was by Father Pierre Joseph Marie Chaumonot in 1656. He reported that the Senecas had two large villages in addition to a number of smaller ones and that Gandagan (Gandagaro, the large eastern village) was the principal Seneca village (that is, the Seneca "capital"). He also found one village composed largely of Hurons, which he called Saint Michel because most of these Hurons came from the village of Scanonaenrat (the village of the Tahontaenrat tribe of the Huron League) where the Jesuits once had a mission called Saint Michel (JR 44:20, 52:53-55). It was said that there were adopted captives from as many as 11 nations living among the Seneca at this time (JR 43:265).

The Jesuits returned in 1668 to establish a permanent mission among the Seneca, and from their accounts as well as those by Galinée in 1669 (1903:23-25, 81), Greenhalgh in 1677 (O'Callaghan 1849-1851, 1:13-14), and Denonville in 1687 (NYCD 9:365-367), it is evident that in the period 1668-1687 the Senecas still had two large villages, each with 100 or more houses and two smaller ones of from 20 to 30 houses each. The Jesuits established missions in three of these villages—a mission they called La Conception in the large village of the western Seneca, one they called Saint Jacques in the large village of the eastern Seneca, and a third at Saint Michel, located a few miles south of Saint Jacques (JR 54:79-85, 115, 55:79, 56:59, 57:27, 191-195, 58:229, 223, 237). They did not establish a mission in the smaller village of the western Seneca.

There is some evidence that in the early part of the 1670s these villages were moved. The village known to the Jesuits as Saint Michel or Gandougaraé burned in

1670 and consequently had to be rebuilt (JR 55:79, 57:190-191). The large western village was named Gandachioragon in the early years of the 1670s (JR 54:81, 115, 121, 55:79, 56:59), but its name was given as Tiotohattan in 1677 (O'Callaghan 1849-1851, 1:13) and as Totiakton in 1687 (NYCD 9:366)—an apparent change of the name of this village that might indicate a change in its location. The large village of the eastern Seneca may have also moved as Galinée reported it was palisaded in 1669, but Greenhalgh said it was not in 1677 (Galinée 1903:23; O'Callaghan 1849-1851, 1:13). The lack of a palisade suggests that it had been moved after the defeat of the Susquehannocks, which made fortifications less necessary.

Seventeenth-Century History

Like the other Iroquois tribes, the Seneca became increasingly involved in the fur trade during the seventeenth century, their growing use of European trade goods being confirmed by the archeological evidence (Wray and Schoff 1953). As the westernmost of the five tribes of the Iroquois League, the Seneca were farthest from the Dutch traders at Albany and the French on the Saint Lawrence and nearest the rich beaver grounds to the west. These beaver grounds became more attractive to the Senecas as their own reliance on European trade goods increased and the beaver available in their own country decreased, leading to the attempts by the Seneca to expand their hunting territories. When the Senecas began such efforts is not known, but it is possible that the decision of the Wenro to leave their country near the Iroquois about 1638 and to join the Hurons and Neutrals (JR 16:253, 17:25-29, 21:231-33) was in response to Seneca efforts to gain new hunting territory.

In the 1630s the Hurons, supported by their trading alliance with the French, had shielded the northern hunting peoples against Iroquois raiders. In the 1640s the Senecas and other Iroquois made a number of attacks on Huron villages. Finally, in 1649, a party of Senecas and Mohawks estimated to number about 1,000 attacked and destroyed the Huron villages of Saint Ignace and Saint Louis (JR 34:123). This blow was sufficient to disperse the Hurons. The Iroquois next turned to the Petun, allies of the Huron, attacking them during the winter of 1649-1650 and dispersing them. The following year, the Neutrals were attacked by the Seneca and also dispersed.

In 1653 the Upper Iroquois, engaged in a war with the Erie, decided to make peace with the French and sent a delegation to Montreal for that purpose (JR 41:51, 81-83). Although the Senecas did not accompany this delegation, they had earlier planned to try to get the Cayugas, who did go, to join with them in such an endeavor (JR 40:163). The following year at a council with Father Simon Le Moyne at Onondaga, they again expressed approval of this peace (JR 41:101). Conse-

quently, in 1656, after the Jesuits had established their mission of Sainte Marie in Onondaga country, Father Chaumonot visited the Senecas (JR 43:307, 44:21-27). But both the peace and the Jesuit mission lasted only a short time. In 1658 the Jesuits were forced to abandon Sainte Marie, and it was not until 1668 that the Jesuits returned to begin again their mission to the Senecas (JR 52:53).

Growing Iroquois antagonism toward the French was the result of Iroquois victories, particularly those of the Senecas (JR 44:153) in their war with the Eries. However, these victories did not bring peace in the region, but rather an intensification of the war between the Iroquois and Susquehannock—a conflict that forced the Senecas when taking their furs to Albany to travel together in large groups for fear of Susquehannock ambush along the route (JR 47:111). It also led the Senecas to seek peace with the French. They hoped that by making such a peace the French would come and settle among them to protect them and furnish guns (JR 49:141). But the Mohawks, who wished to maintain their control of the fur trade by permitting trade only with Albany, thwarted the efforts of the Upper Iroquois to establish peace with the French until the French destroyed their villages in 1666 ("Early Iroquoian Contacts with Europeans," fig. 4, this vol.).

In 1668, in response to a request of the Senecas, Father Jacques Frémin was sent to establish a mission among them (JR 52:53, 195) and the following year was joined by Father Julien Garnier (JR 54:79-81). That same year, in the hope of finding guides to take them to the Ohio River, René-Robert Cavelier de La Salle with a small party of his men visited the Seneca. Peace with the Iroquois allowed the French to explore the western lands and to establish trading posts in the upper Great Lakes area. But after the long war between the Iroquois and the Susquehannock ended with the defeat of the Susquehannock in 1675, the maintenance of peace with the French seemed less attractive, and the Seneca began to talk of waging war against Indian allies of the French and even against the French themselves (JR 59:251, 60:173).

Although the Senecas remained the most hostile of all the Iroquois tribes to Jesuit missionaries (JR 60:173, 61:21, 159), they allowed La Salle to build a fortified trading post at Niagara in 1679. Although the fort accidentally burned down that year, La Salle had correctly recognized the importance of Niagara to the developing western fur trade. Control of Niagara would mean control of the route between Lake Ontario and Lake Erie, an important gateway to the West.

Yet continued peace, or at least uneasy neutrality, between the French and the Seneca became increasingly difficult to maintain. In 1680 the Seneca, desirous of limiting French trade in the west, including La Salle's efforts there, attacked the Illinois; and in the next few years this war between the Iroquois and the French and their Indian allies intensified. Joseph-Antoine Le Febvre de La Barre planned an expedition against the Seneca in 1684, but his army was much weakened by sickness after it had reached Fort Frontenac, and he agreed at the council held with the Iroquois at La Famine at the mouth of the Salmon River not to attack the Seneca. It fell to Jacques René de Brisay, marquis de Denonville, La Barre's successor as governor of Canada, to lead another expedition against the Seneca in 1687. The Seneca ambushed the invading force on July 13 before Denonville's army had reached the large eastern Seneca village; but realizing that they were badly outnumbered, the Senecas abandoned the field. They had already burned the village, leaving to Denonville only the task of destroying the corn and leveling it and the other Seneca villages. However, fearing further ambush, Denonville did not pursue the Seneca; he went to Niagara where he built a fort, which had to be abandoned the following year. But as Parkman (1883:156, 168) noted, the destruction of the Seneca crops and villages only overturned the wasps' nest. Denonville had left the wasps alive and the wasps he had failed to kill continued their raids on the Saint Lawrence. It was not until the French had sent two other expeditions, one against the Mohawks in 1693 and one against the Onondagas and Oneidas in 1696, that the conflict ended and the Iroquois formally made peace with the French in 1701.

Eighteenth-Century History

The peace the Iroquois established with both France and England in 1701 lasted a half-century. It permitted the Iroquois to extend their wars and trading to the south and west and thus exert some control over the beaver trade in these areas. At the same time, they played off French against English in the contest between these two European powers for control of this trade and hence control of the continent.

After Denonville's expedition, the Senecas apparently did not resettle their destroyed villages. The eastern Seneca drifted east, finally establishing one village at the foot of Canandaigua Lake and another, their principal village, at the foot of Seneca Lake. From there, they also established settlements on both sides of Seneca Lake and down the Chemung River. The western Seneca drifted westward, settling along the fertile flats of the middle Genesee. From there, they also moved up the Genesee, across to the Allegheny and down that river into Ohio. No longer threatened by attack, the eighteenth-century Senecas built unpalisaded villages in which the houses were dispersed.

After peace had been established, the Jesuits returned to continue their endeavors among the Senecas, but their effort was short-lived. Of more importance were the activities of the interpreter and trader, Louis-Thomas Chabert de Joncaire, who had as a youth been a captive among the Senecas, and his son, Daniel. During King William's War Joncaire worked to keep the Senecas in the French interest, and after the war ended he developed the fur trade at Niagara, building a trading post there. The French later built a fort at Niagara to control this important passage between Lakes Erie and Ontario and so the western fur trade. Thus, in the second quarter of the eighteenth century, while the English were developing their trade at Oswego, the French were developing theirs at Niagara and increasing their influence among the western Seneca.

The influence of the French was particularly strong among the western Seneca, also called the Chenussios. During the French and Indian War (the Seven Years' War), they remained pro-French, although the eastern Seneca were pro-English and permitted Sir William Johnson to build a fort at Canadasaga, their village at the foot of Seneca Lake, in 1756. After this war ended, the western Seneca continued to be opposed to the English and so joined Pontiac's uprising against the English in 1763. They attacked and took Fort Venango, moved north and took Fort Le Boeuf, and then joining with other Indians took Fort Presque Isle (Peckham 1947:167–170). Later they ambushed the British at Devil's Hole on the trail between Fort Schlosser at the top of the falls and Fort Niagara, administering what Peckham (1947:226) called "the worst drubbing of the war to British arms." The rebellion failed and the price that Johnson extracted from the Seneca for peace was the cession of a tract of land along the Niagara River.

American Revolution

When the American Revolution broke out the Seneca—said in 1771 to number 4,000 (O'Callaghan 1849–1851, 4:1093)—attempted to maintain neutrality as did the other Iroquois. Reluctance to enter the fray disappeared in 1777 when a large part of the Seneca attended councils with the British and were persuaded to join the British cause. Although at the time the Senecas had not realized these councils were being held to enlist warriors for Col. Barry St. Leger's attack on Fort Stanwix, they were drawn into this campaign.

The Senecas' first battle was one of the bloodiest of the war. Fort Stanwix did not fall, and a relief column under Gen. Nicholas Herkimer marched to lift the siege. A force largely composed of Indians caught the column in a ravine near Oriskany Creek and casualties were high on both sides. The rebels retreated, but the British attempt to capture Fort Stanwix failed.

The next year, 1778, the Seneca participated in the famous Wyoming and Cherry Valley attacks. In addition, there were other small engagements, part of the British strategy to cripple the frontier economically and to deprive the colonies of one of their richest granaries.

In an attempt to halt the depredations of the Seneca and other Iroquois allies of the British, Gen. George Washington sent an expedition into Iroquois country. After a preliminary attack led by Col. Goose Van Schaick on the Onondaga villages, an expedition under Gen. James Clinton went from Canajoharie down the Susquehanna to Tioga. There the expedition joined Gen. John Sullivan and the main force that had moved from Easton to Wyoming and up the Susquehanna. From Tioga, the large army advanced up the Chemung River. At Newtown they met a force of Rangers and Indians, and in the engagement that followed the Rangers and Indians were forced to flee. From Newtown, the army moved north and up the east side of Seneca Lake to Canadasaga. They destroyed this village of about 50 houses and other settlements in the region and then marched through and destroyed Canandaigua and Honeoye, finally reaching the Genesee. After destroying villages there, including Genesee castle, a village of approximately 130 houses, they returned by the same route to Tioga. On the return, two detachments were sent to destroy the Cayuga villages and another to the Mohawk valley to destroy the Lower Mohawk village.

At the same time the army under Gen. Sullivan's command was marching toward the Genesee, another force under Col. Daniel Brodhead marched from Fort Pitt up the Allegheny River. There he also destroyed the Seneca villages he found.

After the battle of Newtown, the Indians offered no resistance to Sullivan's advance but rather abandoned their villages, leaving the expedition to burn them and destroy the crops. As Graymont (1972:213) has noted, "the business of this campaign would prove a strange task indeed for men at arms—a warfare against vegetables." Sullivan's army destroyed beans, squash, potatoes, watermelons, cucumbers, and other produce as well as an enormous quantity of corn. Apple, peach, and other fruit trees were cut down as well as corn standing in the fields.

But as did Denonville over 90 years earlier, Sullivan had only overturned the wasps' nest leaving the wasps alive. Many Iroquois fled to Niagara where a number spent the winter of 1779-1780, one of the worst recorded. That spring they renewed their raids and took part in an expedition against the Mohawk valley settlements. It so devastated this region that Schenectady was regarded by Americans as the westernmost limit of their frontier. The Iroquois continued to harass the Americans until the end of the war.

Establishment of the Reservations

In the Treaty of Paris signed in 1783 that ended the war between England and her American colonies, no provision was made for the Indians. Consequently, they had to reach their own agreements with both countries and decide where they would live. Some elected to move to Canada. Among these were 78 Senecas (including 31 Senecas from the west) who went with a number of other Iroquois in 1784 to the Grand River Reserve in Ontario (Johnston 1964:52) where their descendants still live ("Six Nations of the Grand River, Ontario," this vol.).

That same year, 1784, the Six Nations met American officials at Fort Stanwix to make peace and discuss land. There they signed a treaty ceding their claim to lands west of New York and Pennsylvania (Kappler 1904-1941, 2:5-6). There was opposition to this treaty: a number of Indians had not attended because of illness, and those who did had little choice but to accept the conditions of the United States commissioners. It was subsequently confirmed by some Senecas at Fort Harmar in 1789 (Kappler 1904-1941, 2:23-25). But Iroquois dissatisfaction with the treaty continued, and they attempted through a series of conferences and other means to reach some better accommodation. In these negotiations the Iroquois were not entirely powerless. Western Indians were waging an effective campaign against the Whites and the United States was most anxious to prevent veteran Seneca warriors from joining these Indians. Finally, in 1794 a council was held at Canandaigua with Timothy Pickering representing the United States and a large number of Iroquois attending. Much influenced by the news of Gen. Anthony Wayne's victory at Fallen Timbers, a treaty was signed that confirmed the lands reserved to the Oneidas, Onondagas, and Cayugas by their treaties with the state of New York and defined the boundaries of the Seneca lands (Kappler 1904-1941, 2:34-37).

Although by the Treaty of Paris the lands of the Seneca had become part of the United States, the question remained as to which state they belonged. Both New York and Massachusetts claimed them, a dispute that was finally resolved by an agreement signed at Hartford in 1786. This agreement gave to the state of New York sovereignty and jurisdiction to the land then held by the Iroquois under treaty agreement (that is, the land then claimed by the Iroquois was to become part of New York State), and the Commonwealth of Massachusetts was granted the preemption right (sometimes termed the preemptive right) to this land (that is, the right to purchase it from the Iroquois). In 1788 Massachusetts sold these preemption rights to a land company formed by Oliver Phelps and Nathaniel Gorham for one million dollars payable in three years in Massachusetts scrip. That year at a council held at Buffalo Creek the Senecas sold to this company for $5,000 and an annuity of $500 all their lands east of the Genesee River and a line drawn from the confluence of the Canaseraga and Genesee south to the Pennsylvania line in addition to a tract of land west of the Genesee. This came to be called the Phelps and Gorham Purchase (see "Iroquois Since 1820," fig. 1, this vol.).

By the time the payment to Massachusetts came due, the value of Massachusetts scrip had appreciated so much that Phelps and Gorham were unable to meet it. This led to an agreement by which Phelps and Gorham retained the lands they had purchased and the remaining portion was reconveyed to Massachusetts, who in 1791 sold the preemption rights to the Philadelphia financier Robert Morris for $225,000. In 1792 and 1793 Morris sold much of this land to individuals acting as trustees for the Dutch banking houses that organized as a stock company in 1796 and came to be called the Holland Land Company. Morris reserved for himself a tract of land west of the Phelps and Gorham Purchase that came to be called the Morris Reserve.

Morris's agreement with the Dutch investors stipulated that the Indian title be extinguished before the Holland Land Company paid for the land. By the Canandaigua Treaty (also sometimes called the Pickering Treaty) of 1794, this land had been recognized as belonging to the Seneca; consequently, Morris had to deal with the Seneca rather than all the Iroquois. By the Treaty of Big Tree (near Geneseo), signed September 15, 1797, the Senecas sold to Morris most of their lands for $100,000, this money to be invested and the interest distributed as an annuity. They reserved for their own use lands totaling 310 square miles where their settlements were then located. Ten tracts of land were so reserved: four large reservations in western New York and six small ones along the Genesee River (Kappler 1904–1941, 2:1027–1030). By the provisions of the treaty, land totaling 200 square miles was to be divided between two reservations—one along Buffalo Creek where some Onondagas and Cayugas as well as Senecas had settled and the other along Tonawanda Creek. The survey of these lands later alloted 130 square miles to the Buffalo Creek Reservation and 71 square miles to the Tonawanda Reservation. In addition, two other tracts each of 42 square miles, one along the Cattaraugus Creek and the other along the Allegheny River, were reserved for the use of the Senecas. As did the Buffalo Creek and Tonawanda reservations, these two reservations came to be called by the name of the streams along which they were located: the Cattaraugus and Allegany reservations. Of the 26 square miles reserved along the Genesee River, 16 square miles were located at Caneadea and two square miles each at Canawaugus, Big Tree, Little Beard's Village, Squawky Hill, and Gardeau. Additionally, the Oil Spring reservation of one square mile near Cuba, New York, was also reserved (fig. 1) (see Fletcher 1888:515–517; New York (State) Legislature. Assembly 1889:20–21).

In 1796, over a year before the Treaty of Big Tree was signed, the Commonwealth of Pennsylvania gave to the noted Seneca chief Cornplanter a tract of land two miles long and one-half mile wide on both sides of the Allegheny River a few miles south of the Allegany Reservation (fig. 1). This grant was in consideration of the services Cornplanter had rendered the Whites, especially that of preventing the Iroquois from joining the confederacy of western Indians in 1790–1791. After Cornplanter's death, the grant passed to his heirs. In 1871 it was allotted to 23 heirs of Cornplanter, by commissioners appointed by the Commonwealth of Pennsylvania, with the right to sell only to the descendants of Cornplanter and to other Seneca Indians. Because the Cornplanter Senecas did not regard themselves as separate from the Senecas living on other reservations and because they were recognized by the Allegany and Cattaraugus Senecas as owning equal rights with them on their reservations, the Cornplanter Senecas shared with the other Senecas annuities payable to them under treaties made with the United States (Fletcher 1888:518, 561; U.S. Census Office. 11th Census 1892:29).

In the first half of the 1790s and presumably also at the time the Treaty of Big Tree was signed, there were between 1,700 and 1,800 Senecas living in New York State. Of these, approximately one-third lived in the Genesee valley, another third at Buffalo Creek, and the remainder at Allegany, Cattaraugus, and Tonawanda. The smallest number—about 100—lived at Tonawanda (Kirkland 1764–1804; I. Chapin 1792; MHSC ser. 1, 5:23).

Nineteenth-Century History

Christian Missions and Schools

Efforts to convert the Senecas to Christianity in the seventeenth and eighteenth centuries had proved unsuccessful. The Jesuit mission had left no Christian community among the Seneca, and the Protestant missionary Samuel Kirkland, who visited them in 1764–1765, found the Senecas so unreceptive that he gave up the effort and devoted his life instead to a mission among the Oneidas.

A more successful effort was begun by the Society of Friends at the end of the eighteenth century. Quakers had been present as observers at the Canandaigua Treaty in 1794, and four years later they began to teach the "arts of civilization" to the Senecas, first at Genesinguhta and from 1803 at Tunessassa located just off the Allegany Reservation, where a few years later they began a school that operated for over a century (Wallace 1969:273–274, 315). They also had a station at Cattaraugus for a time.

Other Protestant efforts began shortly after that of the Friends. In the first few years of the nineteenth century, the New York Missionary Society attempted to establish a school and mission at Buffalo Creek, but this effort was unsuccessful. Renewing its interest in establishing a mission there, the Society sent a missionary and teacher to Buffalo Creek in 1811. Although the missionary was not permitted to stay, the teacher was and he conducted a school there, on a somewhat irregular basis, for six or eight years. By the end of the decade, ministers of various denominations were occasionally holding services on the reservation. The Western Missionary Society of Pittsburgh conducted a school on the Cornplanter Grant from 1814 to 1818.

Missionary efforts to establish schools and churches on the Seneca reservations were more successful in the next decade. A permanent school was established at Buffalo Creek in 1820 by the New York Missionary Society (see "Iroquois Since 1820," fig. 2, this vol.). Shortly after, this society joined the United Foreign Missionary Society, which in 1821 sent a missionary to Buffalo Creek. He organized a church there in 1823, and although for a year (in 1824–1825) neither he nor the teachers were permitted to live on the reservation, the mission church and school were continued at Buffalo Creek until 1846, when the reservation having been sold, the members of the mission moved to Cattaraugus.

By the end of 1821 both the Society of Friends and the United Foreign Missionary Society had expressed an interest in establishing a school on the Tonawanda Reservation, but shortly thereafter the Tonawanda Senecas decided the Baptists should conduct it. Some Tonawandas were opposed to the school and in June 1822 threw the schoolteacher and his wife off the reservation. Nevertheless, the school was reestablished, and in 1829 a Baptist church was organized at Tonawanda.

In 1822 the United Foreign Missionary Society sent the teacher who had been designated to go to Tonawanda to Cattaraugus, where he began a school. A church was organized by this mission at Cattaraugus in 1827 and at Allegany in 1830. In 1826 the United Foreign Missionary Society joined the American Board of Commissioners for Foreign Missions, and subsequently the work of both the Cattaraugus and Buffalo Creek mission stations was done under the auspices of the American Board until 1870, when these missions were transferred to the Presbyterian Board of Missions (Fletcher 1888:578).

It was the intent of these mission societies not only to provide instruction in the Christian religion and to convert the Indians to Christianity but also to teach them the "arts of civilization." To them, Christianity and "civilization" were virtually interchangeable words. They regarded "Christianity" as not just belief in a particular religious doctrine but also acceptance of the White way of life as the proper one. Consequently, in their schools they taught those subjects they felt necessary to achieve this end—agricultural arts to the boys and homemaking arts to the girls as well as English, reading, writing, and arithmetic. The first schools opened were often taught by a single teacher, but as soon as possible these became boarding schools run by the "mission family"—the missionary in charge of the station, his wife, and several female teachers. However, day schools often proved more successful than the boarding schools.

Nevertheless, the Presbyterian and Baptist missionaries at Buffalo Creek, Cattaraugus, and Tonawanda reservations did not ignore more purely religious matters, and as soon as they felt they had a sufficient number of converts organized them into a church. Membership in these churches included the mission family and some school children as well as adult Indians.

The Quakers did not organize such churches. Their beliefs led them to emphasize instruction in the arts of civilization, and as they did not seek converts, they gave little Bible instruction and taught little in the way of Christian doctrine (Wallace 1969:275–277; "Origins of the Longhouse Religion," this vol.).

At the time, those Whites having business with Indians needed interpreters, and the missionaries and teachers in the mission schools were no exception. Nevertheless, with the help of interpreters, a few of them did translate hymns and parts of the Bible into Seneca. This work of translation was greatly expanded by the most noted missionary to the Senecas, Asher Wright. His translations included those of the four Gospels into Seneca. He also established a press to publish materials such as a newspaper, *The Mental Elevator,* in both Seneca and English (Pilling 1888:175–178). Wright went to the Buffalo Creek reservation as a missionary in 1831 and spent the next 15 years there. When this reservation was sold, he and his wife moved to Cattaraugus where Wright died.

Handsome Lake

About the time Christian missions were being established among the Senecas, there was developing among them what later came to be called the "new religion of Handsome Lake." In June 1799 the Seneca chief known by the chiefly name of Handsome Lake, who had been born at Canawaugas on the Genesee River 64 years before but was then living at the settlement of his half-brother, Cornplanter on the Allegheny River, had the first of a series of visions. In this and subsequent visions, the messengers from the Creator (there were four such messengers) appeared to Handsome Lake. They told him what the Creator wished the Iroquois to do, and these messages Handsome Lake duly communicated to his people.

Handsome Lake preached on Cornplanter's Grant until a quarrel with his half-brother led him and his followers to move to Coldspring on the Allegany Reservation in 1803. A worsening political position at Coldspring induced Handsome Lake to move to Tonawanda where he continued to preach. He died in 1815 on a visit to Onondaga.

510

The Code of Handsome Lake, called *káiwi·yo·h* 'the good message',* touched on many aspects of life and included the admonitions that the Iroquois should not drink, that witchcraft should stop, that abortion and adultery should cease, that children and old people should be treated kindly and taken care of, and that the Four Sacred Rituals (the Four Sacred Ceremonies)—Feather Dance, Thanksgiving Dance, Personal Chant, and Bowl Game—should continue to be given (see also "Origins of the Longhouse Religion," this vol.).

After his death, the various teachings of Handsome Lake were codified and the preaching of them became an annual event. The Tonawanda Seneca were designated as the "firekeepers" of the new religion, and each year the Tonawanda Longhouse still sends out invitations to the other Longhouses requesting them to come to Tonawanda to hear the Code of Handsome Lake preached there. It is subsequently preached in a biennial circuit that includes the Coldspring Longhouse on the Allegany Reservation one year and the Newtown Longhouse on the Cattaraugus Reservation the other (see "Iroquois Since 1820," this vol.).

Final Land Sales

During the first decades of the nineteenth century, the pressure exerted on the Seneca to sell the land they still held and remove west steadily increased. Little Beard's Village on the Genesee was sold in 1803, and in 1810 the Holland Land Company sold to David A. Ogden the right to purchase the remaining Seneca reservations. Odgen sold shares to various individuals and thereafter the Senecas dealt with the Odgen Land Company. Finally, in 1826, in a treaty signed at Buffalo Creek, the Senecas sold their remaining lands on the Genesee including that portion of the Gardeau Reservation Mary Jemison, the "White woman of the Genesee," had not sold in 1823. Of the Buffalo Creek Reservation, then 83, 557 acres in size, all but 49,920 acres was sold; of the Tonawanda Reservation then containing an estimated 46,209 acres, all but 12,800 acres was sold. Eight square miles (5,120 acres) of the Cattaraugus Reservation was also sold by this treaty (Fletcher 1888:542-543; New York (State) Legislature. Assembly 1889:23-24).

At the time this treaty was signed there were approximately 550 Senecas living at Buffalo Creek, 350 at Cattaraugus, 500 at Allegany, 325 at Tonawanda, and 450 on the Genesee. Within a few years after the sale of the Genesee lands, the Senecas who had lived there had moved to the other Seneca reservations (National Ar-

---

* The italicized Seneca words in the *Handbook* are written in the orthography used by Chafe ("Comparative Sketch of the Northern Iroquoian Languages," vol. 17). This differs from the earlier orthography of Chafe (1963, 1967) in that the nasalized vowels are written ǫ (for earlier ɛ) and ǫ (for ɔ), æ is used for ä, and the automatic glottal stop before initial vowels is not indicated.

chives Microcopy 234, Roll 832, Frames 34, 172, 415, 669-670, Roll 808, Frame 70).

These sales were not the last. In 1838 the Seneca sold to the Ogden Land Company the four remaining Seneca reservations (Allegany, Cattaraugus, Tonawanda, and Buffalo Creek). The proceedings were blatantly corrupt; land appraised at $2,000,000 was purchased for $202,000 (Society of Friends 1840; Manley 1947). The Seneca had 81 to 91 chiefs at this time, but only 43 chiefs signed the treaty. Of these at least 16 were bribed, while others testified that their signatures were obtained through threat or were forged. The Seneca were to remove to lands in Kansas.

While a faction of chiefs was pro-Treaty, most Senecas unequivocally opposed it. With aid from the Society of Friends and other Whites, a compromise treaty signed in 1842 negated the 1838 agreement. It relinquished the Buffalo Creek and Tonawanda reservations and provided for their residents to remove to the two Seneca reservations in New York State that had not been sold—Cattaraugus and Allegany (figs. 1-2).

Although the 1842 compromise treaty by restoring to the Seneca a portion of lands that had been sold four years before allowed them to remain in New York State, a few Senecas encouraged by some Whites decided to move west and in 1846 joined the party of Iroquois going to Kansas. A number of this group became ill and died, and the following year almost all the survivors returned. A census taken after their return reported that of the 66 Senecas who had emigrated west, 26 had died, 2 remained in the West, and 38 had come back to New York State (National Archives Microcopy 234, Roll 587, Frames 414-417).

In 1845, the year before these Iroquois emigrated west, approximately 2,280 Senecas were reported living on the New York reservations: 400 at Buffalo Creek, 710 at Cattaraugus, 670 at Allegany, and 500 at Tonawanda (Schoolcraft 1847:32, 37).

The Seneca Nation Revolution of 1848

In 1848 Senecas living on the Cattaraugus and Allegany reservations petitioned the federal government to change the method of distributing their annuities. In the past they had been distributed through the chiefs who took a portion for government purposes; by the new method they were to be distributed directly to heads of families. The chiefs opposed this move, and the dispute opened old wounds.

On December 4, 1848, a convention held on Cattaraugus abolished government by chiefs on Allegany and Cattaraugus. The convention adopted a written constitution that instituted an annually elected council of 18 members and an executive consisting of president, clerk, and treasurer. It retained the judicial offices of peacemakers, which had been established under the chief's government (Society of Friends 1857).

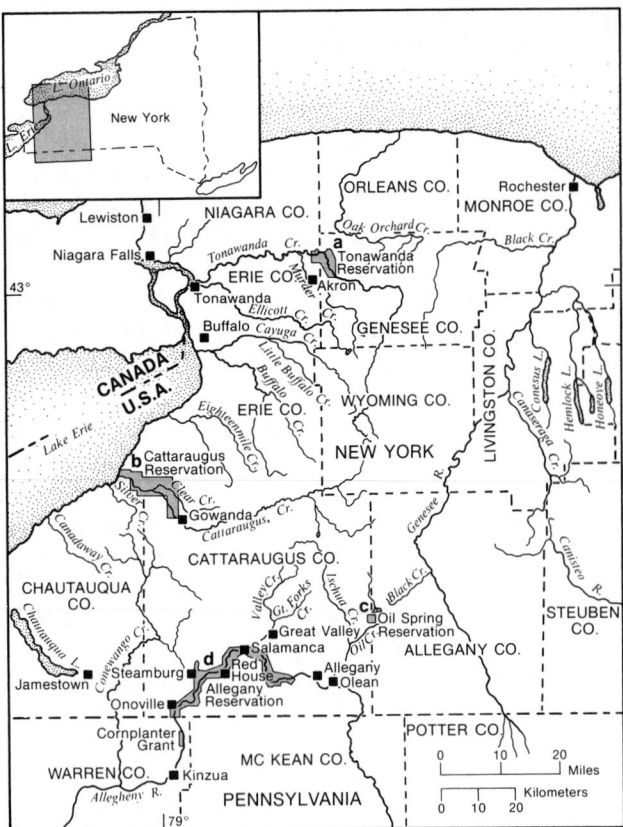

Fig. 1. Modern Seneca reservations. a, Tonawanda; b, Cattaraugus; c, Oil Spring (not inhabited by Senecas); d, Allegany (and Cornplanter Grant). See fig. 2 for detail.

This "revolution" severed the few tenuous threads that bound Tonawanda to Allegany and Cattaraugus with the result that the "Tonawanda Band of Seneca Indians" (the Tonawanda Senecas) and the "Seneca Nation" (the Allegany and Cattaraugus Senecas) became separate political entities. It also split the Allegany and Cattaraugus Seneca into two new factions unrelated to previous factionalism (Berkhofer 1965; Abler 1969). Those favoring the elected council, called the New Government Party, were led by the Cayuga physician Peter Wilson and enlisted the aid of influential Hicksite Quakers in their cause. The Old Chiefs utilized the talents of young and educated members of their faction such as Maris B. Pierce and Nathaniel T. Strong. Like their opponents, they petitioned Washington and Albany for recognition as the legitimate government of the Seneca.

Although Washington recognized the "revolutionary" government, the Old Chiefs Party continued to fight. Perceiving an opening when the opposing faction itself split in 1851, they entered and won the election under the new constitution in May. Adroit political maneuvers on the part of the New Government faction prevented recognition of the chiefs' form of government even though the Old Chiefs Party carried the elections of 1852 and 1854 (Abler 1969:133–145). Having observed the futility of their fight, the Old Chiefs ceased their efforts to

destroy the new constitution but instead acted as a political party in elections under that charter.

Buying Back Tonawanda Reservation

During the 1840s and 1850s the Tonawanda Senecas were engaged in a fight to retain their reservation, which by the 1842 compromise treaty had been sold along with the large Buffalo Creek Reservation. The Tonawanda Senecas argued that they were not a party to this treaty and that as none of their chiefs had signed it, it was not binding on them. Under the leadership of John Blacksmith, who had become a sachem chief in 1839 (Parker 1916a:133, 140), and Jimmy Johnson, grandson of Handsome Lake and codifier of the teachings of the prophet ("Iroquois Since 1820," fig. 3, this vol.) (Morgan 1851:230), they began what was to be a 15-year effort to retain their reservation. They successfully kept the assessors appointed under the provisions of the 1842 compromise treaty off the reservation, thus preventing the appraisal of their improvements, which under the provisions of the treaty was necessary before payment for these improvements could be made and the Tonawandas moved. Thereby, they provided a case by which the provisions of the treaty as it applied to them could be tested in the courts. Meanwhile, they took their case to Albany and to Washington, over the years sending a number of delegations to these two capitals. Ely S. Parker, Lewis H. Morgan's interpreter and collaborator in his ethnographic studies of the Iroquois, served first as interpreter and then as principal spokesman on these trips. After Blacksmith died in 1851, Parker was raised up as sachem chief in his place.

Finally the case reached the United States Supreme Court, and the Court's decison forced the United States Senate to resolve the matter. The result was a treaty signed in 1857 by which 7,549 acres of the Tonawanda Reservation were to be bought back with money that had been set aside for their removal to Kansas (fig. 1) (Kappler 1904–1941, 2:767–771).

The Tonawanda Senecas had refused to participate in the Revolution of 1848 that changed the form of government on the Cattaraugus and Allegany reservations from governance by hereditary chiefs to an elected council as that would have weakened their argument that the 1842 compromise treaty was not binding on them because their chiefs had not signed it. Thus they retained their council of hereditary chiefs. After their fight to retain their reservation had been won, they changed their form of governance to provide for the election of three peacemakers (from the chiefs), a clerk, a treasurer, and a marshall by the adult men at an annual election. But they retained the council of chiefs as their governing body. In the 1970s this council was composed of 16 hereditary chiefs (eight chiefs each of whom holds one of the chiefly names of the Confederacy and eight subchiefs) selected in accordance with old custom, that is, by the clan mother

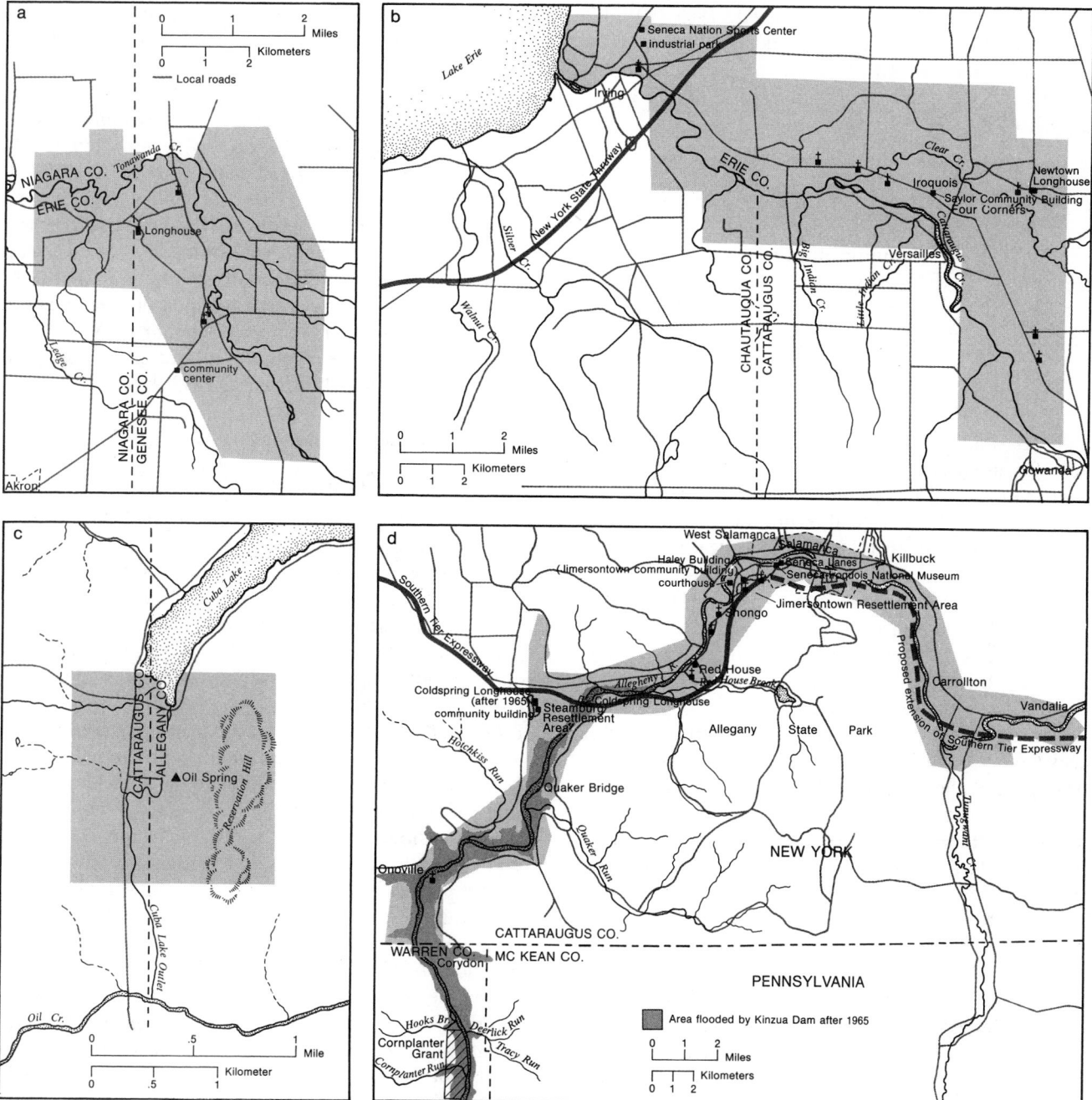

Fig. 2. Modern Seneca reservations. See fig. 1 for names and locations.

in consultation with other women of the clan and raised up at a Condolence ceremony.

Allegany Reservation Leases

Although no Seneca land in New York State has been sold to Whites since the 1842 compromise treaty, land has been leased to them since that time. As early as the 1830s, railroads were built through the Allegany Reservation on leased land. There grew up beside these railroads several villages, on lands leased from individual Senecas or from the Seneca Nation Council. These leases were illegal, not

being confirmed by Congress. An act of Congress in 1875 (Kappler 1904–1941, 1:155–156) authorized six villages, almost 10,000 acres, on the Allegany Reservation to be leased to Whites for five years. (Of these six "Congressional villages," the largest is Salamanca. The others are Carrollton, West Salamanca, Vandalia, Great Valley, and Red House.) In 1880 these leases were renewed for a 12-year period, and in 1892 they were extended for 99 years (Kappler 1904–1941, 1:368).

The lease issue caused considerable disruption in the Seneca Nation community. Strife within the political system increased significantly (Abler 1969:192–240). There were charges that the councils of those years allowed substantial reductions in the yearly rentals in return for bribes (New York (State) Legislature. Assembly 1889:785–786, 1110–1111).

Status in 1890

In the first several decades of the nineteenth century, the economy of the Senecas changed from one relying on hunting, fishing, and horticulture to one based on plow agriculture and wage work. But by the end of the century, the Senecas like their White neighbors farmed less. In 1890 many of their barns were reported to be old and in poor repair. Stock raising, particularly of sheep, had declined as had the old orchards. Nevertheless, farming was reported to be the chief employment of the Senecas, although much of this farming produced crops sufficient only for home use. In part, lack of capital prevented greater reliance on agriculture, and consequently the Senecas leased a considerable portion of their arable lands to White farmers (U.S. Census Office. 11th Census 1892:49–50). This trend has continued in the twentieth century. The Senecas have increasingly relied on wage work and less on agriculture with the result that the acreage under cultivation, both that worked by Indians and that leased to White farmers, has continued to decline in the twentieth century.

Concomitantly, an increasing proportion of the Senecas have learned English and attended schools. At the beginning of the nineteenth century, few Senecas knew English, and in their dealings with Whites they relied heavily on the assistance of two interpreters, Horatio Jones and Jasper Parrish, both of whom had once been captives of the Senecas. The mission schools established in the early decades of the century were in large part replaced by district schools supported by the state beginning in 1846 at Cattaraugus and Allegany and 1853 at Tonawanda (Fletcher 1888:570). In 1890 there were 10 such district schools on the Cattaraugus Reservation, six at Allegany, and three at Tonawanda. Each was taught by a single teacher, who was sometimes a Seneca with normal-school training (U.S. Census Office. 11th Census 1892:63–66). By the end of the century, some children were attending boarding schools off the reservation, such as Hampton Institute and Carlisle Indian School. A number attended the Thomas Indian School (Thomas Orphan Asylum), a boarding school established in 1855 on the Cattaraugus Reservation with help from various sources, including the state and the Senecas themselves, and transferred to control of the state in 1875 (Fletcher 1888:554–557; U.S. Census Office. 11th Census 1892:67).

Of the approximately 3,000 Indians living on the three New York Seneca reservations in 1890, about two-thirds could speak English and more than 930 of those over 20 years of age were reported to be able to write English also (U.S. Census Office. 11th Census 1892:9). The three

reservations reported 2,664 Seneca residents: 1,355 at Cattaraugus, 792 at Allegany, and 517 at Tonawanda. In addition, 87 Senecas were living on the Cornplanter Grant in Pennsylvania, 183 on the Six Nations Reserve in Canada, and a few on other Iroquois reservations in New York State (U.S. Census Office. 11th Census 1892:5–6).

In the second half of the nineteenth century, more churches were established on all three New York Seneca reservations. By 1890 there were Presbyterian, Baptist, and Methodist churches on the Cattaraugus and Tonawanda reservations, Presbyterian and Baptist churches at Allegany, and a Presbyterian church on the Cornplanter Grant. Fewer than 400 Indians on the three reservations were reported to be communicants of these churches (U.S. Census Office. 11th Census 1892:9, 43–44).

Twentieth-Century History

The Longhouse Religion

Although the proportion of Longhouse believers has declined since 1890, and with it, the number of Longhouses, three Longhouses continue to serve as places where the old Iroquois ceremonies are kept up among the New York State Seneca: the Tonawanda Longhouse on the Tonawanda Reservation, the Newtown Longhouse on the Cattaraugus Reservation, and the Coldspring Longhouse (forced by the rising water of the Allegheny River Reservoir to move from Coldspring to Steamburg in 1965) on the Allegany Reservation (see "Iroquois Since 1820," fig. 4, this vol.). In addition to the preaching of the Code of Handsome Lake, the yearly ceremonial cycle in these Longhouses includes the long Midwinter ceremony that begins the fourth night after the January new moon, the Maple ceremony (no longer given at Allegany) and the Planting, Strawberry, Green Bean (at the Tonawanda Longhouse), Green Corn, and Harvest ceremonies. Only occasionally given are the Sun, Moon, and Thunder ceremonies, except at the Newtown Longhouse where the Thunder ceremony is customarily performed each spring.

Although the ritual that constitutes each of these ceremonies is basically the same in all three Seneca Longhouses, there are local differences. For example, in all three, a series of dances known as the Our Life Supporter dances are given as the principal ritual of the Planting, Green Bean, and Harvest ceremonies and as part of the Midwinter and Green Corn ceremonies. However, the particular dances that comprise the series and the order in which they are performed is somewhat different in each. Similarly, in all three Longhouses, the Four Sacred Rituals are given as part of the Green Corn and Midwinter ceremonies, but practice differs slightly respecting the particular day of the ceremony each of these four rituals is customarily given. Comparable similarities and differences are also evident in the performance of those rituals distinctive of Midwinter. There are also some differences between the New York Seneca practice and that at the Six Nations Reserve. For example, in the New York Longhouses, the "Uncles" (also termed by the New York Senecas the Bigheads) who go through the houses at the beginning of the Midwinter ceremony to stir the ashes and announce that the ceremonial is beginning, wear distinctive dress (see "Iroquois Since 1820," fig. 6, this vol.); they are not so dressed in the other Longhouses (Tooker 1970a).

In addition to these ceremonies, the medicine societies also conduct their own rituals. Some of these are performed as part of the Midwinter ceremony, but a number are given to cure individuals, a method of curing that supplements the herbal and other curing procedures known to the Seneca (Fenton 1940a, 1940b, 2, 1942a). These societies include the Society of Medicine Men (Shake the Pumpkin); Little Water Society; Pygmy Society; and the Bear, Buffalo, Eagle, Otter, False Face, and Husk Face societies (see "Iroquois Since 1820," this vol.).

Kinzua Dam

The 1950s and 1960s were an era of political reform in the Seneca Nation. The old practice of each party printing a distinctly colored ballot, which eased the purchase of votes, was discontinued. The vote was extended to women in 1964, and in 1966 women attained the right to hold office.

This political reform took place against a background of unprecedented disaster. The United States government determined that a dam at Kinzua in Pennsylvania was necessary for flood control on the Allegheny River. A reservoir behind this dam was to flood one-third of the Allegany Reservation. The plan, initially authorized by Congress in 1941, was taken up again in 1956 (E. Wilson 1960:191). An attempt to fight the dam in the courts failed. Former Tennessee Valley Authority head Arthur E. Morgan, author of an alternate plan for Allegheny flood control, called the plan of the Corps of Engineers an example of "extreme incompetence and inadequacy" (A.E. Morgan 1971:326). Incompetent or not, the Corps of Engineers could not be stopped and the Kinzua Dam became a reality.

The Seneca Nation, with assistance from Quakers, campaigned for compensation. The long and frustrating fight led to $15,000,573 in direct damages and rehabilitation funds for the lands and homes lost to the Allegheny waters.

The initial project with these funds was relocation of roughly 100 families who owned homes in the reservoir "take area" to two new settlements, Jimersontown and Steamburg (fig. 1). These suburbanlike developments constituted a "housing revolution" (Fenton 1967:12) for Allegany residents. On June 12, 1965, the Longhouse fire was moved from Coldspring to Steamburg in a nine-hour ceremony (Abrams 1967). Also constructed with rehabili-

tation funds were community buildings for both Cattaraugus and Allegany complete with gymnasiums and stainless-steel kitchens. An educational fund for postsecondary education was created. An industrial park was established on Cattaraugus. Much of the rehabilitation fund remains, with plans evolving toward exploiting the recreational potential opened up by the reservoir.

The Southern Tier Expressway cuts through Allegany, while the New York State Thruway passes through the northwestern corner of Cattaraugus. Television stations in Buffalo, Toronto, and lesser centers disseminate White American culture to the three reservations. Unemployment is a problem but is not nearly so severe as in other North American reservation communities. Approximately one-third of the enrolled Senecas reside off-reservation, and the Seneca Nation mailing list sends materials to members in all 50 states.

Yet when the Little Water medicine is renewed (E. Wilson 1960:298) it is covered by unbleached muslin, still distributed annually by a United States government partially honoring treaty obligations made nearly two centuries ago with Seneca warriors and diplomats.

Synonymy†

In its earliest attestations in New York records of the seventeenth century the name now applied to the Senecas was used for the Oneidas as opposed to the nearer and more familiar Mohawks: Sinnekens, 1635 (Van den Bogaert, in Jameson 1909:135-162); Sineques, 1678 (Andros, in NYCD 3:271). Some maps have an unspecified Sennecas, 1614 (Block, in Stokes 1915-1928, 2:C. Plate 23), or Sennecaas, 1630 (De Laet, in JR 28: opp. p. 122), to the west of the Mohawks. One interpretation of this use of the name is that it was originally applicable to all four of the Upper Iroquois tribes, as contrasted with the Lower Iroquois or Mohawks, and that as knowledge of the Iroquois improved in the course of the seventeenth century the name was gradually restricted until it applied only to the westernmost group, the Seneca (Hewitt 1910b:503-504). Hewitt assumed that the name Seneca was originally the Mahican name for the Oneidas specifically and meant 'people of the place of the stone', with the same allusion as their own name (see synonymy, "Oneida," this vol.), but it is not attested in Mahican and Hewitt's analysis is linguistically impossible. The etymology of the name thus remains obscure. Among the many variant spellings in the early sources listed by Hewitt (1910b:507-508) are: Cinnikos, Cynikers, Senacas, Senakees, Senekies, Sennecks, Sennekas, Shinikes, Sinakees,

† This synonymy was written by Ives Goddard. The uncredited transcriptions of Iroquois words were provided by Marianne Mithun (Cayuga and Tuscarora), Clifford Abbott and Floyd G. Lounsbury (Oneida), Hanni J. Woodbury (Onondaga), and Michael K. Foster (Cayuga).

Sinecas, Sinicker, Sinnequaas, Sinnicars, Synekees, Synneks. Colden (1747, 1:66, 2:14) used Senekas and Sennekas.

The Seneca name for themselves is *onǫtowá'ka·'* (or *nǫtowá'ka·'*), literally 'people of the big hill' (Chafe 1963:56). Names of similar formation are Mohawk *shotinǫtowane'á·ka'* (pl.: G. Michelson 1973:85), Cayuga *onǫtéw'aka·'*, Huron tsonnont8oinronnon (8 = ou; Potier 1920:154), and Wyandot sonotuárono, used specifically for the "mountain Senecas" of Pennsylvania (Gatschet 1881:32). Shortened forms are Cayuga *tewá'ka·'*, or *towá·'ka·'* (Floyd G. Lounsbury, personal communication 1977), and Tuscarora *to'á·ka·'*.

The French borrowed the Huron name, which appears in French sources in variants such as the following: Chouontouaroüon, 1615 (read on for first ou and oü; Champlain 1922-1936, 3:55); Sontouhoironon, 1632 (Sagard-Théodat 1865a); Sonontoerrhonons, 1635 (JR 8:116); Sonontouehronon, 1640 (JR 18:232); Sonont8ehronons, 1641 (JR 21:208); Sant8eronons, 1643 (JR 24:270); S8nt8aronons, 1647 (JR 30:226); Sonont8oen'-r[onon], 1653 (JR 38:188); Sonnontouaheronnons, 1653 (JR 40:162); Sonnontoehronnon, 1654 (JR 41:42); Sonont8aehronon, 1660 (JR 45:206); Sonnontoüehronnons, 1664 (JR 49:150). The village and district name Sonnontouan (also Sonontoen, Sonnonthouan, Tsonnontoüan, Tsonnontoüen—JR 8:116, 41:110, 40:162, 53:40, 296, 54:46) eventually came to be used as a shorter name for the tribe: Sonnontoüan, 1668 (JR 51:248); Tsonnontoüans, 1669 (JR 52:194; also Bacqueville de la Potherie 1753, 1:332); Tsonnontoüens, 1670 (JR 53:54); Tsonnontouans (DCB 1:16). This name also appears in Dutch and English documents from New York, sometimes as a name for the whole tribe and sometimes with a narrower reference: Sinnedowane, 1673 (NYCD 2:598); Sinnondowannes, 1677 (Livingston 1956:47); Sinnondowanne, a town "in the Sinnekes Land," 1679 (Livingston 1956:57); Sinondowans (Colden 1747:42). For names of the Seneca used to refer to all the Iroquois, see the synonymy in "Northern Iroquoian Culture Patterns," this volume.

Other names for the Seneca are Oneida *otsi'tena'a·kâ·*, literally 'bird people', Munsee *màxkaláne·w*, literally 'red-tailed hawk' (Hewitt 1936, phonemicized), and Wyandot hutinuxšiniúndi 'Senecas of New York' (Gatschet 1881:32). Unami Delaware had Mæchachtínni (Heckewelder 1876:99), presumably *mexahtə́ni* 'people of the big hill', a translation of their own name. Modern Onondaga uses separate names for the residents of the different Seneca reservations, and eighteenth-century Onondaga has only the apparent loanword Senecashága (Zeisberger 1887a).

The Council name of the Senecas is Ho-nan-ne-hó-ont 'the doorkeeper' (Morgan 1851:122), or in Mohawk Ronaninhohonti (Hale 1883a:79).

Reservations

Allegany Reservation has its name in Seneca, as in English, from that of the river, *ohi·yo'*, literally 'beautiful river', the name for the Allegheny-Ohio (Chafe 1963:56, 1967:59). Cognate are Cayuga *(o)hí·yo'* and Onondaga *ohí·yo'*, and the Onondaga call the people living there *ohiyóhè·nǫ'*. In English the reservation is sometimes referred to by the name of the town of Salamanca.

Cornplanter Grant is named after the Seneca chief Cornplanter, *kayéthwahkeh* (Chafe 1963:57). In Seneca it is called *tyonǫ́hsate·kęh* 'burnt house' (Chafe 1963:56).

Cattaraugus Reservation has a name derived from that in general use in the Six Nations languages, meaning 'where the mud (or clay) stank' or the like: Seneca *ka'tæ·késkę·ǫ'* (Chafe 1963:56), Cayuga *katá·krahs*, Onondaga *taækæ·skèhæ·'* (the people from there being *taækǽshè·nǫ'*), Oneida *kę'taláklahse'*, Tuscarora *kahtarákraθ* (Hewitt in Hodge 1907-1910, 1:219, phonemicized).

Tonawanda Reservation has its name from Seneca *tha·nǫwǫte'* 'his rapids are there' (Chafe 1963:56); similarly Onondaga *thahnáwà·te'*. The people living there are called (Cayuga) *tahnowatEó·nǫ'* or (Onondaga) *tahnawatéhè·nǫ'*. The reservation is sometimes referred to by the name of the town of Akron.

Sources

Although authorities have generally agreed that in the 1670s and 1680s the eastern Seneca village of Gandagaro was located at the Boughton Hill site south of Victor and that the western Seneca village of Totiakton was located near Rochester Junction, they have offered somewhat differing interpretations of the location of other Seneca villages in the years 1657-1687. These include those by John S. Clark (in Hawley 1884:25-26 and map), Beauchamp (in JR 51:293, 295), Houghton (1912:368-380, 1922:50-59), Parker (1922:650-652), and Hamell (1975). The translation of Seneca village names of this period has been discussed by Fenton (1940:228-229). The location of eastern Seneca villages in the period 1687-1779 is discussed in Conover (1889). Archeological surveys covering both prehistoric and historic Seneca settlements are to be found in Beauchamp (1900), Houghton (1912: 407-444, 1922), and Parker (1922).

Houghton (1912:380-407) has also surveyed Seneca history to 1687 and Parker (1926) has provided a history of the Seneca, but the definitive scholarly history has yet to be written.

Seneca participation in the American Revolution has been described by Wallace (1969:125-148) and more fully by Graymont (1972). New York State Historical Association (1933-1937, 4:185-216) has provided a useful overview of the Sullivan-Clinton expedition and New

York (State) Secretary of State (1887) has compiled journals of members of this expedition that detail the destruction of Iroquois villages.

The sale of Seneca lands after the American Revolution is summarized by Fletcher (1888) and New York (State) Legislature. Assembly (1889). A history of the Buffalo Creek reservation is to be found in Houghton (1920) and of political events on the Allegany and Cattaraugus reservations in the second half of the nineteenth century in Abler (1969).

The most extensive published version of the Code of Handsome Lake is to be found in Parker (1913) and an earlier, although briefer, version in Morgan (1851: 233-259). The most thorough discussion of Handsome Lake's life is by Wallace (1969) who also gives some account of the history of the Seneca in the late eighteenth century and early nineteenth century including Quaker activities. Protestant missionary activities at Buffalo Creek and Cattaraugus are described in Howland (1903), Severance (1903), Alden (1827), and Fenton (1956).

The best single description of Seneca culture and society remains Morgan's (1851) classic study of the League of the Iroquois. Morgan's interpreter and collaborator for this study was the young Tonawanda Seneca Ely S. Parker, and much of the data in this work relate most specifically to the Tonawanda Seneca.

More recent descriptions of the ceremonials of the New York Seneca Longhouses are those by Fenton (1936, 1941), Chafe (1961), and Tooker (1970a). The Seneca medicine societies are discussed by Parker (1909; reprinted in Parker 1913:113-130). Particular description of the myth and ritual of the Little Water Society is given by Converse (1908:149-183) and E. Wilson (1960: 290-310), the Dark Dance by E. Wilson (1960:203-215), the Eagle Dance by Fenton (1953), and the False Face Society by Fenton (1937, 1941a).

Tuscarora Among the Iroquois

DAVID LANDY

Defeat and Betrayal in North Carolina

The northward migration of the Tuscarora (ˌtuskəˈrôrə) resulted not simply from final defeat in the Tuscarora Wars, 1711–1713, but also from the conditions that led to those conflicts, which had already made Indian life nearly unbearable in North Carolina. Governance of the White settlers was chaotic and unsure. Central authority existed more in name than in fact, and critical decisions were made not in North Carolina but in England by the Lords Proprietors (Ashe 1908–1925, 1; Hawks 1857–1858; Moore 1880). Whites were continually staking out plantation boundaries with little regard for the presence or title rights of Indians, who were viewed as less-than-human savages to be dominated or ignored. Agreements and treaties were casually forgotten or based from the beginning on subterfuge. The hunting territories of Tuscaroras and other Indians shrank, and they were killed or driven off if they attempted to use these traditionally owned lands. Within this anomic state it became impossible to trust any White, even government officials. Several Indian groups were easily induced to harass the Tuscarora. They and the Whites kidnapped or captured Tuscarora children, women, and men and sold them into slavery in the northern colonies or in the Caribbean. While controlling a major part of the rum trade with other Carolina Indians, the Tuscarora were themselves debauched and demoralized by drink (Lefler and Powell 1973:55–80).

The Tuscarora selected a propitious moment to strike against the Whites, since many Quakers (who went there after persecution in New England and were in profound dispute with the Carolina English) refused to take up arms against them, and even among non-Quakers there was widespread resistance to military draft or enlistment. In 1711 Christoph von Graffenried, leader of large numbers of Swiss and Palatine settlers, and John Lawson, provincial surveyor-general and, though a professed friend (Lawson 1952) of Indians, a hated symbol of official and unofficial usurpation of their lands, made an unannounced expedition through Tuscarora territory. They were captured by men loyal to the Tuscarora leader, Hancock (or Hencock), taken to the principal town of Catechna, and tried before a council of chiefs (fig. 1). Graffenried persuaded their captors to free him by

forming a mutual nonaggression pact with them, but he was unable to save Lawson, who was condemned to death and executed. Soon after, the Tuscarora, in concert with several allied Indian tribes—Coree, Pamlico, Mattamuskeet, Bear River, and Machapunga—(Hewitt 1910c:843), struck successfully at settlers along the Trent and Pamlico rivers. Later, despite their earlier agreement, they also attacked Graffenried's settlers because Lawson had sold to them Tuscarora land for which he did not have title (Hewitt 1910c:844). These sudden unexpected massacres sent shock waves of terror throughout the colony. Lacking the men or resources to mobilize sufficiently, Gov. Edward Hyde of North Carolina sought aid from Virginia. Virginia, involved in border disputes with North Carolina, sent little assistance, and that reluctantly. Hyde also appealed to South Carolina, which sent Col. John Barnwell with a small number of Whites and about 500 Yamassees and other tributaries. Barnwell defeated the Tuscarora and exacted a peace agreement in 1711. Soon afterward, angered at not receiving pay, supplies, or adulation from the North Carolinians, Barnwell violated the treaty by killing hundreds of Tuscaroras and selling many into slavery. The outraged Tuscarora in 1712 struck back at several settlements along the Neuse, Pamlico, and Trent rivers but after nearly two years of fighting were put down by Col. James Moore of South Carolina with about 1,000 Indians and 33 Whites in 1713. The Tuscarora suffered the extreme loss through death and capture of more than 950 men, women, and children (Lefler and Powell 1973:78) having been capable of mustering not more than 1,200 fighting men (Swanton 1946:199, 1952:87).

The final betrayal of the Tuscarora offensive was by the powerful leader of the northern Carolina and Virginia Tuscaroras, Tom Blount (or Blunt), who maintained a "neutral" position for most of the conflict. Subsequently, feigning friendship, he captured Hancock, principal leader of the Tuscarora revolt, by trickery. He handed Hancock over to the Whites, who promptly executed him. Blount also helped to mop up the remaining pockets of Tuscarora and allied resistance. The main body of the rebellious Tuscarora then began their flight northward that continued at intervals for 90 years, while Blount was recognized by the North Carolina and Virginia governments as the only Tuscarora leader.

Burgerbibliothek, Bern, Switzerland: Mül. 466(1).

Fig. 1. The Tuscarora trial of Christoph von Graffenried and John Lawson, after their capture in 1711. Sketch from memory by von Graffenried.

Flight to the Northeast and Adoption by the Iroquois

In 1712, after the war had broken out, the Iroquois seemed ready to aid the Tuscarora—a circumstance that particularly worried Albany. Gov. Robert Hunter of New York thought the French had instigated this idea (if the Iroquois had gone to the aid of the Tuscaroras in their war with the English, Iroquois relations with Albany would have been seriously strained and in fact such an action might have involved the Confederacy in a war with Great Britain), and he sent an embassy to try to dissuade them, for as he wrote "the war betwixt the people of North Carolina and the Tuscarora Indians is like to embroil us all" (NYCD 5:343, 346, 371; Gallatin 1836:82). The Iroquois, however, had decided, as they often did, to steer a middle course, offering on one occasion to mediate between the Tuscaroras and the English. In September 1713 the Iroquois informed a delegation from Albany that the Tuscaroras had abandoned their villages and were dispersed, and in September of the following year told Governor Hunter that some of the Tuscaroras had come and taken shelter among them (NYCD 5:343, 376, 387; Wraxall 1915:94, 96, 101). Apparently some 500 Tuscarora families went to live among the Iroquois at this time (Lydekker 1938:49).

However, it was not until 1722 or 1723 that the Tuscarora refugees were formally adopted into the League as the sixth nation of the Confederacy.* Thereafter, they participated in the councils of the League, but their chiefs were not made sachem chiefs of the League, and consequently the roll of League chiefs was not expanded beyond the original number (see "The League of the Iroquois: Its History, Politics, and Ritual," this vol.). Nevertheless, as Morgan (1901, 1:93) noted, they "enjoyed a nominal equality in the councils of the League, by the courtesy of the other five, and their sachems were 'raised up' with the same ceremonies. They were not dependent, but were admitted to as full equality

* A number of early writers (Morgan 1901, 1:23, 93; Schoolcraft 1847:112; E. Johnson 1881:69, 73; Hale 1883a:79) say that the Tuscaroras joined the League about 1714 or 1715. A number of later writers (e.g., Fletcher 1888:520) set the date as 1722 or about 1722. These later dates are apparently based on an account written on June 25, 1723 (NYCD 5:684), stating that the Iroquois "had before [this date] admitted the Tuskaroras to make a sixth nation." This information was not available to Morgan and Schoolcraft, and they apparently assumed that the Tuscaroras formally joined the League as the sixth nation shortly after their arrival in New York. The later date is confirmed by a report (Wraxall 1915:144) stating that the interpreter Laurence Claasse told the Commissioners at Albany on May 21, 1723, "that the Tuscarores are received to be a Sixth Nation, so that from this time the Six Nations take their Date." As these records (Wraxall 1915:142-143) still speak of the Five Nations in September 1722, the adoption of the Tuscaroras into the League must have taken place sometime after the middle of September 1722 and before the end of May 1723.

as could be granted them, without enlarging the framework of the Confederacy."

Landy (1958) concluded that their secondary rank within the League affected the Tuscarora outlook. The Five Nations were warmly receptive and generous in allotting land and other amenities, but the Tuscaroras, defeated and humiliated remnants of a once proud Indian power in the tidewater country of North Carolina and Virginia, were profoundly dependent upon that largesse. Yet the Tuscarora were conscious of a need to maintain their national identity, and though scattered in a new land, they succeeded in doing so. They participated fully in the affairs of the League, including many conferences with the governors and other officials of New York, Pennsylvania, Virginia, and North Carolina; were signatories to both the League's and their own treaties and agreements with the United States and various separate states; and have maintained a viable tribal council through the 1970s.

At the time they were formally admitted into the Confederacy as the sixth nation and presumably since they had first arrived to live among the Iroquois, the Tuscaroras had a village located between the Oneida and Onondaga villages (NYCD 5:672, 7:573; Wraxall 1915:143; cf. Colden 1958, 2:16) and were also settled on the Susquehanna (NYCD 5:674). In the eighteenth century, some Tuscaroras also resided on the Juniata and the Susquehanna in Pennsylvania and in scattered bands elsewhere in Pennsylvania and New York (Hewitt 1910c:852; Wallace 1952:15).

In 1736 a reported 250 warriors lived in the Tuscarora village west of the Oneidas (O'Callaghan 1849–1851, 1:23; NYCD 9:1056). By the 1750s they had several villages in this area (Beauchamp 1916:114, 120–121, 150, 177). At the same time, a number were also living in a Tuscarora village on the Susquehanna a few miles south of Oquaga (Beauchamp 1916:162; F.W. Halsey 1906:67–68; Boyce 1973:55–64), where some Oneidas lived, and presumably had a few other settlements in this area. In 1763 there were reported to be 140 warriors in their village six miles from Oneida and in several villages near the Susquehanna (O'Callaghan 1849–1851, 1:27; NYCD 7:582), and in 1768, an estimated 200 warriors (Jefferson 1964:100)—an increase perhaps to be attributed to the arrival of a group of 160 Tuscaroras in 1766 (NYCD 7:883).

Fortunes and Misfortunes of War

When the Tuscaroras joined the Iroquois, they became involved in the complex diplomacy the Iroquois engaged in to maintain their position in the fur trade. At the time, the Iroquois attempted to maintain a policy of neutrality toward both the French and the English. This allowed them to seek French favor when it suited their purposes and English favor when that seemed to their advantage.

Nevertheless, their interests ultimately were best served by maintaining good relations with the English (see "The League of the Iroquois: Its History, Politics, and Ritual," this vol.). But although the political position of the Tuscaroras changed considerably after their arrival in New York, their economy did not. They continued to be heavily involved in hunting and the fur trade as they had been earlier in North Carolina while also following their old agricultural practices.

Within the League, the Tuscaroras apparently had close relations with the Onondagas, but their closest association was with the Oneidas. They had settlements near the Oneidas both in the Oneida Lake region and on the Susquehanna River and were subject to the same influences in both places. These included missionary visits, which began in the period between King George's War and the French and Indian War and were resumed after the French and Indian War ended (Beauchamp 1916:162; F.W. Halsey 1901:52–84; Graymont 1972: 33–40). Apparently, the influence of these missionaries, especially that of Samuel Kirkland, led the Tuscaroras and Oneidas to side with the Americans in the American Revolution.

As did the other tribes of the Iroquois League, the Tuscaroras—said in 1771 to number 1,000 (O'Callaghan 1849–1851, 4:1093)—attempted to remain neutral when the Revolutionary War began. But in the spring of 1776, they found that neutrality was no longer possible (Graymont 1972:100–101). Subsequently, although a few Tuscaroras under the leadership of Sagwarithra joined the British and their Iroquois allies established at Niagara and fought with them (Graymont 1972:127, 168, 184, 209, 225, 236–237), most were sympathetic to the Americans and fought on that side in the first years of the war (Graymont 1972:16 ff.). In August 1779, Gen. James Clinton's expedition burned three Tuscarora villages on the Susquehanna below Oquaga (Beauchamp 1905:364). In June 1780 some Iroquois with Sir John Johnson's expedition persuaded the Tuscaroras living at Ganaghsaraga and the Onondagas who had fled there after the destruction of their village to move to Niagara (Graymont 1972:233–235; Beauchamp 1905:368). Avowing allegiance to the British, they along with some other Onondagas and Oneidas arrived at Niagara July 2. Later that month a party led by the Mohawk captain Joseph Brant burned the remaining Tuscarora and Oneida settlements. Some who had been living in these villages went to Niagara, but a number fled to Schenectady where they spent a particularly miserable winter (Graymont 1972:233, 242–244). Thus, by 1780 the Tuscaroras had been dispersed from the regions they had lived in just prior to the Revolution.

After the Revolution, about 130 Tuscaroras (Johnston 1964:52) moved to Canada with a number of other Iroquois who had sided with the British to live on lands granted by the Crown along the Grand River (see "Six

Nations of the Grand River, Ontario," this vol.). For a time, a number of other Tuscaroras lived in a village near Big Tree's village on the Genesee. In 1790 over 200 Tuscaroras were reported residing in this village of 26 houses (Kirkland 1764-1804);† however, shortly after, they seem to have moved to the Niagara River area.

In 1789 some 110 Tuscaroras were reported living near Niagara Landing and over 170 on the Genesee; but in 1792 over 260 were living near Niagara Landing (another set of figures says 300 Tuscaroras were living west of the Genesee), while none are mentioned as living on the Genesee. At the time, also, some 50 or 60 were reported living near the Oneida in central New York State (O'Rielly Papers). A total of 400 Tuscaroras were said to reside in the United States in 1796 (MHSC ser. 1, 5:23).

When at the Treaty of Big Tree in 1797 the Senecas had sold much of their land to Robert Morris, who sold his interest in it to the Holland Land Company, they reserved for the Tuscaroras one square mile to be located near the present Lewiston where they had built a village after leaving Niagara Landing. However, this provision was not written into the treaty (Kappler 1904-1941, 2:1027-1030). Shortly after, the Tuscaroras took up the matter with Thomas Morris, who, in behalf of Robert Morris, granted the square mile and this grant was confirmed by the Holland Land Company. In 1798 the Indians requested and received another square mile, and in 1799 this two-square mile reservation was laid out so that it included the Tuscarora village (Ellicott 1937-1941, 1:23, 54-55, 87, 92). The Senecas also rectified their oversight and in 1808 executed a deed giving a square mile to the Tuscaroras, stating that this tract had been reserved from the sale of Seneca lands in 1797 (Houghton 1920:106; E. Johnson 1881:76). Thus, the original Tuscarora reservation consisted of three square miles.

In 1801 a delegation was sent to North Carolina to try to obtain payment for their lands there, and in the following year the North Carolina legislature passed an act authorizing the lease of these lands. For these leases, the Tuscarora received $13,722, which they used to purchase 4,249 acres from the Holland Land Company in 1804 (E. Johnson 1881:77; Hewitt 1910c:848; F.R. Johnson 1967-1968, 2:218; Chazanof 1970:74-75). Thus, their total reservation came to comprise 6,249 acres or just under 10 square miles (fig. 2).

At the time the delegation was in North Carolina arranging for this payment some Tuscaroras living there decided to move north and join their brethren in New York State (Hewitt 1910c:848-849). About 10 years later,

† When the Tuscaroras settled on the Genesee is not known. Although some writers say that the Tuscarora village of Ohagi was destroyed by the John Sullivan expedition, this seems not to have been the case and Sullivan was told there were no villages in this area (New York (State) Secretary of State 1887:133). Ohagi was located on the flats two or three miles below Cuylerville (Morgan 1901:434).

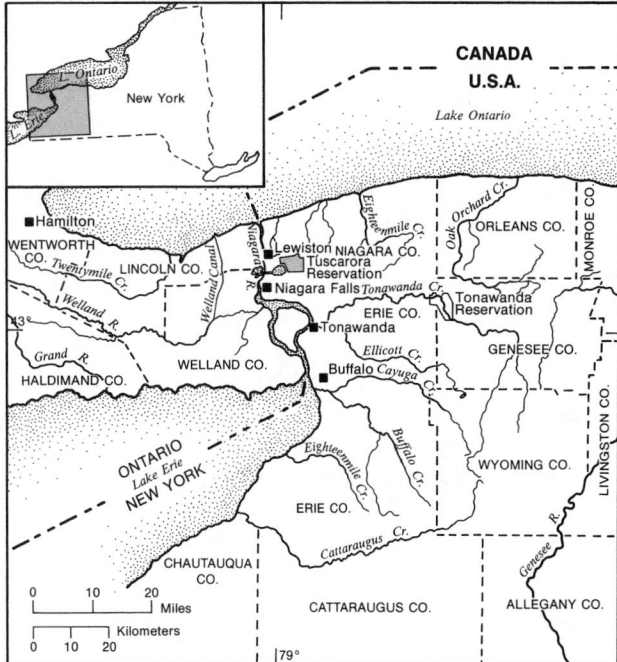

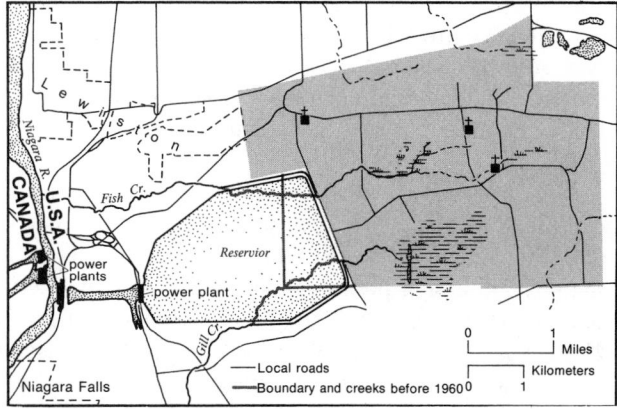

Fig. 2. Tuscarora Reservation and adjacent area.

after the War of 1812 embroiled the Niagara region, the Tuscarora village was burned by the British (F.R. Johnson 1967-1968, 2:220-221).

The matter of the land in North Carolina continued to be one of concern to the New York Tuscaroras, and in 1828 the North Carolina legislature authorized the sale of these lands. The transaction was completed in 1831; the Tuscaroras received $3,250 for the deed for these lands. The land issue came up again after the leases expired in 1916, but in 1956 all claims were determined to have been settled (F.R. Johnson 1967-1968, 2:227; Severance 1918:330-331).

Nineteenth-Century Life and Culture

During the first half of the nineteenth century, the Tuscarora men abandoned hunting as their major economic activity and the majority became farmers, engag-

521

ing, in Wallace's (1952:16) words, in "a cultural revolution which tended in some respects to make the Indians live like white people." Reports of missionaries and other observers during this period indicate that the Tuscaroras were becoming among the most economically successful and self-sufficient of all the Six Nations.

Missionary work on the Tuscarora Reservation began in 1800, and in 1806 a church was organized, 8 of its 11 members having been communicants of the church while living in central New York. Missionaries continued their activities until interrupted by the War of 1812. However, this work, which was resumed in 1817, and which also included maintenance of a school, resulted in few conversions. In 1820 the church had only 16 members. That same year, following a dispute apparently similar to that between the Seneca "Christian" and "pagan" parties (see "Iroquois Since 1820," this vol.), about 70 Tuscaroras emigrated to Canada (E. Holmes 1903; Graymont 1969:148-149; Hyde 1903:248-250), a migration that seems to be reflected in the census figures of the time. In 1818 the Tuscaroras were reported to number 314, but in 1824, only 253, and three years later, 220 (J. Morse 1822:46, 77; Letters Received by OIA, 1824-1880 in National Archives Microcopy 234, Rolls 832 and 808). Nevertheless, the conflict between the two factions continued, finally ending after the Christians burned down the Longhouse. It was not rebuilt (Graymont 1969: 152-153).

It is not known what ceremonials the Tuscaroras continued to practice after they arrived in New York or after they settled on the reservation in the western part of the state, although the Longhouse burned by the Christian faction was probably used for ceremonial purposes. Neither is the influence of the teachings of Handsome Lake among the Tuscaroras known. Handsome Lake himself is not known to have gone to Tuscarora to preach, but the Tuscaroras undoubtedly had heard of his teachings and also heard him speak at the councils of the Six Nations at Buffalo Creek.

Although the Iroquois had sold much of their land in the last decade of the eighteenth century, efforts continued in the nineteenth century to induce them to sell the remainder and move west of the Mississippi. Finally, in 1838, the Iroquois signed a treaty selling all the land they then held in New York State including the Tuscarora Reservation (Kappler 1904-1941, 1:502-516). This treaty came to be so widely regarded as having been signed under suspect circumstances that a new treaty was negotiated. Signed in 1842, it provided for the sale of the Seneca Buffalo Creek and Tonawanda Reservations, but not the Tuscarora and other Iroquois reservations in the state. Nevertheless, some Iroquois decided to move west, and in 1846 about 200 left for Kansas territory. Among these emigrants were about 40 Tuscaroras, many of whom were members of the Baptist church that had been organized in 1836. About one-third died in Kansas, and most of the survivors returned the following year (E. Johnson 1881:120; F.R. Johnson 1967-1968, 2:225; Graymont 1969:150).

In 1845, the year before these Tuscaroras emigrated to Kansas, their population was 312, a slight increase over the figures of approximately 275 reported in the 1830s (Schoolcraft 1847:32; Letters Received by OIA, 1824-1880 in National Archives Microcopy 234, Rolls 832 and 834; Kappler 1904-1941, 1:508). Membership in two churches on the reservation totaled 63. There were two schools, but many Tuscaroras did not speak English and five interpreters were then living on the reservation. A few Tuscarora men still derived part of their livelihood by hunting, but most were farmers. Approximately 2,080 acres of the reservation were improved (Schoolcraft 1847:33, 37-38).

During the second half of the nineteenth century, the life of the Tuscaroras continued to become more like that of the Whites around them. In 1890 there were 400 Tuscaroras living on the reservation, almost 60 other Indians (including 41 Onondagas), and 23 Whites. The number of churches had increased to three and the number of church members to 238. Those who spoke no English numbered just under 100, while 343 spoke English, and 292 could also read it. Farming had also increased and 4,200 acres were cultivated (U.S. Census Office. 11th Census 1892:6, 9, 12). As Henry Carrington described the reservation at the time:

It would be difficult to better balance, settle, and utilize a tract of this size than has been done in its development. Nearly the entire land not reserved for timber has been put to use. . . . The whole reservation is under fence, the chiefs enforcing a rule that every land owner shall maintain a fence at least 4 feet high. . . . The migration of young men and the death of energetic heads of families have left widows who are land rich but purse poor. They have not the means to hire labor, and are thus compelled to lease their farms to white men and live on the rental income. Even the most successful farmers are unable to find Indian laborers sufficient for the demand, and they also rent portions at a cash rental or on shares. Following the example of the white people, who have utilized the rich valley north of the mountain for fruit, the Tuscaroras have also developed fine orchards of peach and apple trees to the extent of 269 acres. These have been carefully trimmed and kept in good bearing condition. There is not a ragged, untrimmed orchard on the reservation (U.S. Census Office. 11th Census 1892:31).

By the middle of the twentieth century, the number of Tuscaroras engaged in farming had declined, as it had among Whites, and only about a dozen Tuscarora men were full-time farmers. Most men and some women worked for Whites off-reservation. Beyond the first four grades, children also commuted off-reservation to attend school (Wallace 1952:29, 39). All Tuscaroras spoke English, but so few children knew Tuscarora that from time to time attempts were made to organize classes to teach the language (Graymont 1967).

Social Organization

In the early years of the nineteenth century, the Tuscaroras probably had eight clans: (Great or Large) Turtle (*ráʔkwihs*),‡ Small (Land or Sand) Turtle (*kaθríʔkweˑs*), Wolf (*θkwariˋnə̨*), Bear (*ohtsíhrə̨ʔ*), Beaver (*tsyóʔnakə̨ˑ*), Snipe *(tawístawis),* Eel (*kə̨ˊˑʔneh*), and Deer. Some sources suggest the existence of two Wolf clans and two Bear clans, in addition to the two Turtle clans that are generally recognized. Morgan (1877:93) and one of Hewitt's (1910c:849) native authorities list Grey Wolf and Yellow Wolf, and Lounsbury (1947) recorded a second Wolf clan *onə̨ʔtakə̨ˊhwʔa* 'under the pine'; Lounsbury was also told of a White Bear clan (*tihréhtsyaks*), said to be descended from two White women adopted into the tribe in Pennsylvania. The Deer clan of the New York Tuscaroras had died out by the middle of the century (Schoolcraft 1846:219; Morgan 1877:93; U.S. Census Office. 11th Census 1892:39; Hewitt 1910c:849; Wallace 1952:21; Landy 1955), but it should be noted that some Tuscaroras now say that the Sand Turtle clan is really Deer. The Eel clan died out in the 1960s (F.R. Johnson 1967-1968, 2:239; Rickard 1973:xxi). The moiety grouping of clans noted by Morgan (1877:93) has also lapsed perhaps because old Tuscarora religious practice has lapsed; moiety organization is more prominent in Iroquois ritual than in political organization (Wallace 1952:23). However, burial of the dead in special areas according to clan affiliation—perhaps once a common Iroquois custom—has long been Tuscarora practice, although this too is now often neglected (Morgan 1877:83-84; Rickard 1973:166). The rule of clan exogamy is still usually followed, and clan mothers still choose those men who are to be chiefs and subchiefs (council and warrior chiefs) (Wallace 1952:18-19). The aboriginal names of these chiefs also are still retained and the chiefs raised up at a Condolence ceremony held either at Tuscarora (see Beauchamp 1891a:39-41 for a description of such a Condolence held in 1889) or at the Tonawanda Longhouse.

The chiefs' council putatively governs the political affairs of the community, but its resolutions carry only moral force, and at times they are ignored (Landy 1958). In theory the council may adjudicate in both civil and criminal cases, but it has no powers of enforcement. In 1948 Congress gave criminal jurisdiction to the state of New York, to the resentment of the Tuscarora who placed greater trust in the federal government. The state of New York also provides schools, medical care (a clinic

‡ The italicized Tuscarora words in the *Handbook* are transcribed in the orthography used by Chafe ("Comparative Sketch of the Northern Iroquoian Languages," vol. 17). Stressed vowels have a rising tone, marked with the acute accent (´), or, before resonants, a low tone, marked with the grave accent (ˋ). Other symbols have their standard *Handbook* values. Phonemicizations of Tuscarora words have been provided by Marianne Mithun and Floyd G. Lounsbury.

on the reservation), and welfare assistance (Wallace 1952:30-34). In the 1950s the Tuscarora chiefs' council consisted of 15 members, two representatives of each of the seven clans plus one additional chief. Since at times the clan mothers had felt that a vacancy for a particular clan could not be filled with an eligible or promising candidate, they could and occasionally did go outside the clan to select a representative. Thus, the apparent paradox that confronted other observers is explained: each clan is *represented* by a chief and subchief, but the representatives may come from another clan. In the 1950s the clan affiliation of the members of the chiefs' council was as follows: five clans sent two members, one clan sent four, and one sent one. All seven clans were represented among the chiefs, but disproportionately; still each clan retained equal representation (a chief and subchief) in the council (Landy 1955; Wallace 1952:32).

Among contemporary Tuscarora Wallace (1951) found not only the retention of the earlier social structural elements but also several major personality characteristics noted by sixteenth- and seventeenth-century observers (Adair 1775; Buchanan 1824; Lawson 1952; Lederer 1958) of this tribe in the Southeast. Understandably, the Tuscaroras also appear to resist acquiring those character traits (compulsive concern about time, property, money, and orderliness) usually associated with the Euro-American "Protestant ethic." Landy (1955a, 1958) confirmed at least partially Wallace's findings, and in addition certain seeming continuities in methods and techniques of socialization of children. In spite of two and one-half centuries in the Northeast, devastating demographic loss and cultural trauma in the Southeast and in many instances thereafter, a subordinate social position in relation to both White society and other Iroquois nations, and the adoption of many Euro-American cultural traits and most material culture, the Tuscarora have preserved a significant core of traditional culture, social structure, and personality structure.

In 1957 social cohesion of the Tuscarora underwent a severe test. The New York Power Authority had decided to take over 1,383 acres, more than one-fifth of the reservation, in order to flood it as a storage reservoir (E. Wilson 1960:138-139). Several younger leaders and some older ones including some chiefs exhorted the tribe to resistance. The Tuscaroras fought back legally through attorneys, taking their case to the Federal Power Commission and the federal courts. The United States District Court of Appeals sent the issue back to the Federal Power Commission, which in 1959 ordered the New York Power Authority to desist. Prior to this time barricades had been thrown up to prevent state surveyors from proceeding, and bulldozing crews were halted when 30 Tuscarora operators were called out by the resisters (Rickard 1973:134-168). The Power Authority appealed to the United States Supreme Court, which in 1960 reversed the Federal Power Commission ruling. Though losing the case and having a substantial portion of their reservation flooded (fig. 2), the example of the Tuscarora fired the emerging movements of American Indians everywhere (Steiner 1968). The struggle of the Tuscarora to preserve their land has been attacked as self-defeating by some (Manners 1962) and defended by others (Collier 1962), but out of it has come a new strengthening, as after so many trials in the long, difficult past of Tuscarora national identity.

Synonymy§

The Tuscarora self-designation *skarò·ręʔ* is traditionally interpreted as 'those of the Indian hemp, *Apocynum cannabinum*' (Hewitt 1910c:842), but the exact meaning of the term is not completely certain since the longer forms used in the other Iroquoian languages cannot be analyzed in the same way: Mohawk akothaskaróręʔ (Hewitt 1910c:852, normalized), Oneida *taskalô·lę,* Onondaga *taskáiyęʔ,* Cayuga *taskáowęʔ,* Seneca *táske·owęʔ* (Chafe 1967:82), and Wyandot taskáho (Gatschet 1881:5). Among the numerous spellings of the name listed by Hewitt (1910c) are the following: Caskarorins, Kaskarorens, Tachekaroreins, Tascororins, Taskarorens, Taskiroras, Tasks, Tescarorins, Toscororas, Tuscarara, Tuscarorens, Tuscarories, Tuscaroroes, Tuscararo, Tuscorure, Tuskarorers, Tuskarorins, Tuskoraries, Tusquarores.

§ This synonymy was prepared by Ives Goddard. The uncredited transcriptions of Iroquois forms were furnished by Marianne Mithun (Tuscarora), Clifford Abbott (Oneida), Hanni J. Woodbury (Onondaga), and Michael K. Foster (Cayuga).

Borrowed forms of the name appear in Munsee *táskalo·w* (Michelson 1922 and Hewitt 1936, phonemicized), Shawnee taskalónu (Gatschet 1878-1893:77), and Cherokee aniskalá·li (pl.; Mooney in Hewitt 1910c:852, normalized). The Saponi name is recorded as Keewahomomy, perhaps the same as Tewohomomy (Hewitt 1910c).

The Tuscarora Reservation, also referred to by the name of the town of Lewiston, is called in Seneca *taskéowęʔkeh* (Chafe 1963:56) and in Onondaga *taskáiyęʔke.*

Sources

The most comprehensive history of the Tuscaroras is to be found in F.R. Johnson's (1967-1968) study, which although marred by occasional errors and omissions is a useful reference work. Mid-twentieth-century reservation life has been surveyed by Wallace (1952). Some account of the Tuscarora fight with the New York State Power Authority is given in E. Wilson (1960:126-168). The effect of the Tuscaroras' secondary rank within the Iroquois Confederacy on Tuscarora national identity has been discussed by Landy (1958). The Tuscarora New Year festival has been described by Graymont (1969) in an article that also contains some useful data on the history of Christian missionary effort on the Tuscarora reservation. Two autobiographical accounts (T.C. Williams 1976; Rickard 1973) provide both useful information on and insights into twentieth-century reservation life.

Six Nations of the Grand River, Ontario

SALLY M. WEAVER

Prereservation Settlement

In 1784 following the American Revolution Joseph Brant, the prominent Mohawk war chief and British ally (Stone 1838), led some 1843 Iroquois Loyalists from New York State to the land granted them in Ontario by Sir Frederick Haldimand as restitution for their losses in the war (Johnston 1964). The original tract, an estimated 675,000 acres, lay six miles deep on each side of the Grand River from its mouth to its source.

After temporarily gathering at Lewiston in 1784 during American-British peace negotiations, members of all six tribes (though primarily Mohawks and Cayugas) emigrated to the valley in the winter and spring of 1784–1785. They were accompanied by a few Delaware, Nanticoke, Tutelo, Creek, and Cherokee who had been taken into Iroquois villages before the Revolutionary War. The migrants settled in small tribal villages along the river. The Delaware and Cayuga (later known as the Lower Cayuga because of their location on the lower part of the river) settled near the mouth on the northeast side. The Seneca originally settled near the mouth on the opposite bank, but by the 1820s they had moved upstream and across the river to locate near the Onondaga. The Mohawk, Upper Cayuga, Oneida, Tutelo, and Tuscarora settled in villages near the present site of Brantford, but by the 1820s the Upper Cayuga had moved across the river (fig. 1). The remaining tribes stayed in the areas where they had originally settled until the late 1840s when they moved to the reserve. Land above Brantford was not occupied by the tribes.

Initial controversy surrounding the nature of Iroquois title set forth in the Haldimand Proclamation of October 25, 1784, remains unsettled. The Proclamation was an instrument conveying to the Mohawks "and such others of the Six Nation Indians as wish to settle in that quarter" the Grand River tract of land as compensation for the loss of their settlements in New York State (Canada 1905, 1:251–252). Brant claimed that the title was an estate in fee simple, giving the Iroquois not only national recognition but also the right to sell the land at their option. The Crown held that the land was not alienable by the Indians and that the Proclamation did not recognize political sovereignty of the League. In 1793, determined to reinforce the Crown's trusteeship interpretation of the title, John Graves Simcoe, lieutenant governor of Upper Canada, drafted the Simcoe Patent (Canada 1905, 1:9–10), which stipulated that all land transactions of the Six Nations had to be approved by the Crown. But Brant and the chiefs rejected Simcoe's Patent (Johnston 1963) and over the next few years leased or sold over 350,000 acres of the tract in six large blocks to Whites (Johnston 1964:129). Most of them had been invited by Brant to live on these lands. Brant felt that White farmers and merchants would be useful models from which the Iroquois could more rapidly adopt agricultural skills replacing the hunting economy that could not be sustained in the valley. The squatters' presence was opposed by the Crown, but the fledgling Indian administration was not equipped to prevent Brant's influencing their movement onto the land. By 1834 an investigation of Indian land was held, but it was felt by the Crown to be too late and too costly to remove the many White settlements, and the Brant leases were legally confirmed (Johnston 1962).

The lands draining into the headwaters of the Grand River above Nichol Township were never explicitly recognized by the Crown as belonging to the Iroquois despite the clear wording of the Haldimand Proclamation and repeated Indian protests. The Crown argued that the original tract purchased by Haldimand from the Mississaugas in 1784 did not extend beyond the Nichol "block" and therefore Haldimand did not, in fact, have the land to transfer to the Iroquois (Canada. House of Commons 1887). The earliest completed survey of 1791 and subsequent ones did not extend beyond the Nichol block. The issue of the land at the headwaters of the Grand continues to be a major grievance, and many Iroquois still contend that Brant, despite the power of attorney given him by the chiefs in 1796, had no right to alienate any land and that his leases should not have been validated.

By the late 1830s less than a quarter of the population of 2,223 lived in the two remaining villages. Of the 397 log houses, only 30 existed in the Tuscarora village and 24 in the Mohawk village (Canada (Province) 1844–1845). Most of the population had dispersed along the tract on small farms cultivating an average plot of 20 acres. Farming practices were generally similar to those of the surrounding Whites with the exceptions that the Iroquois tended to spend less time preparing seed grain to prevent smut and sowed less seed. On the small farms women cultivated primarily Indian corn and potatoes with a hoe, but on the larger farms (50–200 acres) men grew wheat, oats, timothy, and peas and prepared the land with plows pulled by oxen. Hogs, cows, and oxen were the common livestock, but only one out of eight families had built barns to house the animals and to store the grain and hay.

Many of the Mohawks and Oneidas had adopted Christianity before migrating to the valley. In 1786 the Mohawk Chapel (Anglican) had been built by Brant and his friends in the Mohawk village, and it housed the prized Queen Anne Silver Communion Plate and Bible. By the 1840s many Tuscaroras became Baptists. These three tribes became collectively known as the Upper Tribes because of their location upriver, and they became associated with Christianity and "progress" by the Indian administration. When the tribes moved to the reserve in the late 1840s these three settled at the upper end of the reserve (northwest), and the designation has been retained. The Cayugas, Onondagas, and Senecas were collectively referred to as the Lower Tribes, because of their original location downriver, and their subsequent location "down below" (northeast) on the reserve. They had retained their traditional religious beliefs and gradually adopted the beliefs of the rapidly spreading Handsome Lake movement. As the decades passed the Upper Tribes became more readily influenced by missionary activity, and their children became educated in the missionary-operated schools.

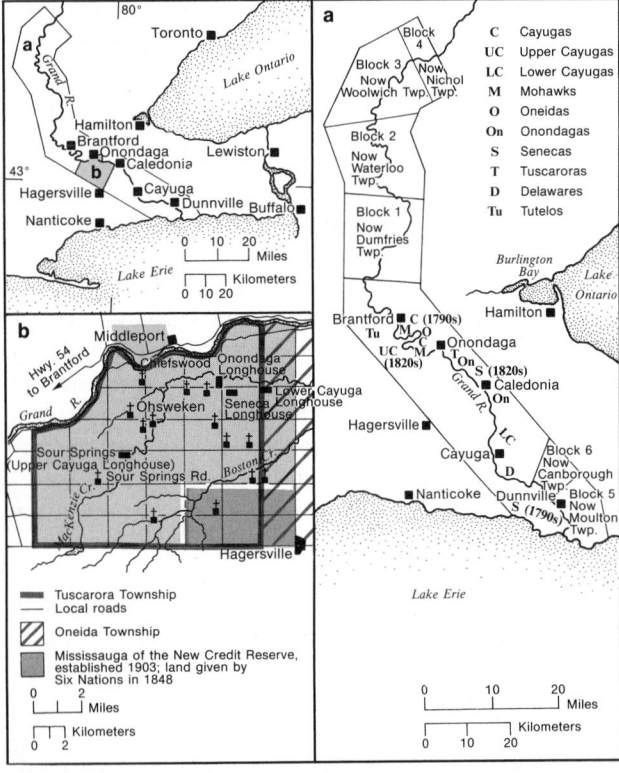

Fig. 1. Area of Six Nations Reserve. a, Tribal locations along the Grand River in the 1820s, with blocks 1–6 surrendered to Whites in 1790s (after Johnston 1964:figs. 2–3; A. Jones 1791); b, Six Nations Reserve in 1970.

The Anglican Church, then organized as the New England Company, was the earliest and most powerful mission in the valley (Johnston 1964). Until the first resident clergyman (Anglican) settled in the valley in 1827, itinerant missionaries had served the Iroquois. By the 1830s itinerant Methodists and Baptist clergy became active, but with fewer financial resources than the New England Company. The Company had built the Mohawk Institute, a day school, in Brantford in 1831 where it offered free formal education and domestic and farming skills to boys and girls. By the 1840s it had become a residential school and remained in operation until 1970. In the early 1840s five day schools operated in addition to the Mohawk Institute, four of them run by the Anglican church and one by the Methodists. All schools suffered sporadic attendance with many parents viewing education as a major threat to their traditional way of life (Canada (Province) 1847).

In 1830 Indian administration was transferred from military to civil control. With the threat of American invasion no longer present, military control of Indians was unnecessary. Although the Iroquois contributed to the British cause in 1812–1814, particularly at the Battle of Beaver Dam (Stanley 1963), they were no longer treated as "allies" though they claimed this status politically. Under civil control an active assimilationist policy developed according to which Indians were to be educated, converted to Christianity, and taught farming skills in keeping with the expanding frontier culture (Canada (Province) 1847).

But the growing frontier town of Brantford and other villages persistently encroached on Iroquois lands (Johnston 1967). With pressures to sell scattered parts of their land in piecemeal fashion, the Crown became concerned that no single contiguous tract would remain to the Iroquois. Consequently in 1841, at government suggestion, the chiefs formally surrendered to the Crown their remaining lands of some 220,000 acres in return for a reserve of some 20,000 acres in addition to the lands then under cultivation by the Iroquois along the river (Canada 1905, 1:119–123). The Crown's efforts to consolidate the tribes into a smaller area, where the White squatters could be evicted more easily and where schools and churches could be economically built, had succeeded.

Removing the squatters from the reserve proved costly and frustrating, primarily because of the lack of sufficient administrative personnel to supervise the task. Often after being paid for their improvements (houses, barns, fences) squatters returned to the land, and sometimes new ones arrived after eviction notices had been posted. By 1853 most had been removed (Canada (Province) 1853) and paid from the Six Nations band funds, funds created from land sales. These funds had originally been managed by three White trustees appointed initially (in 1798) by the Iroquois, and later (in 1830) by the Crown. But their management proved satisfactory to neither the

Indians nor the government. By 1840 the Crown took direct control of the funds, but not before these monies were severely depleted by the trustees' ill-fated investment in the Grand River Navigation Company, beginning in 1834 (B.E. Hill 1964). Designed to make the river more navigable by building a system of locks, canals, and barges, the company's efforts failed due to the advance of railway and road transportation (Reville 1920). When bankruptcy came in 1861 the Six Nations, the largest stock holders, lost their entire investment. This loss remained a major grievance and in the 1920s became the subject of an unsuccessful claims action against the Canadian government.

In the spring of 1847 the chiefs were asked by the Crown to assign land on the reserve to the male head of each household. By then the reserve contained some 55,000 acres. The chiefs had argued that the original size of 20,000 acres was too small for their needs and they had convinced the Crown to let them retain from their original tract an additional 35,000 acres. But subsequent surrenders reduced this main block of 55,000 acres* to 44,900 acres. Additional dispersed pockets of land, totaling 278.09 acres retained from the original tract, remain to the band within the southeast limits of the city of Brantford. The reserve is mostly clay and clay loam soils. It is located on the southwest bank of the river between Brantford and Caledonia, with an additional two-square-mile block of land on the northeast side near Middleport (fig. 1). It occupies all of Tuscarora township and the southern part of Onondaga township, both in Brant County, and the western portion of Oneida township in Haldimand County (Weaver 1963–1974).

* Among other surrenders at this time, the Six Nations chiefs, in 1848, gave the Mississauga of the New Credit band 6,000 acres in the southeast corner of the reserve. The New Credit band has retained this land as their own reserve.

Each male head of a nuclear family was allotted a 100-acre parcel of land with the intent that it be farmed. By early 1848, 325 nuclear families (1,271 individuals) had taken up land and assignments were complete. The 100-acre parcels were laid out in the typical concession system of the province. The concessions were blocks of land surveyed in an east-west direction through the reserve. The grid system of roads enclosed blocks of land containing 1,200 acres, or 6 parcels of 200 acres. In allotting land, each 200-acre parcel was divided into north and south halves, each family receiving a 100-acre "lot," which abutted on a road called a "line."

The nuclear family had become both the residential and the economic unit. While lineage and clan affiliations continued to function in other spheres, the distinction between the two units became blurred by the end of the century (Goldenweiser 1914, 1914a). The clan and lineage have been retained in Longhouse social organization, but Christians have rarely kept a knowledge of the traditional kinship units. The patrilineal basis of legal Indian status and tribal affiliation established in 1869 by federal statute (Canada. Laws, Statutes, etc. 1869) for Indian administration further confused tribal affiliations, which had traditionally been matrilineal.

By the 1840s the tribal census showed the Mohawks and Cayugas the most populous tribes, with the Tuscarora third largest, and this pattern has remained stable (table 1). The Onondagas outnumbered the Oneidas until the turn of the century when this became reversed. The Nanticokes and Tutelos lost most of their cultural distinctiveness through acculturative pressures from and extensive intermarriage with their Six Nations neighbors (Speck 1927; Hale 1883a). By the mid-1800s the Nanticokes and Tutelos ceased to be officially recognized as separate tribes in the census, although both retained chiefs in council until 1924 when all chiefs were removed

Table 1. Population by Tribe

	1785	1810	1843	1857	1875	1900	1910	1920	1930	1949	1970	1973
Mohawk	464	451	793	933	1,020	1,615	1,827	1,893	1,866	2,400	3,783	3,974
Cayuga	381	408	421	470	801	991	1,041	1,127	1,165	1,344	2,354	2,525
Onondaga	245	196	283	267	339	343	364	371	322	346	542	560
Tuscarora	129	289	192	209	266	382	416	444	431	487	780	789
Oneida	162	141	199	172	217	330	367	378	396	551	786	802
Seneca	78	212	107	105	190	214	217	235	237	228	333	345
Delaware	231	41	127	87	113	164	170	167	171	179	255	256
Nanticoke	11	82	47	76	25	–	–	–	–	–	–	–
Tutelo	74	9	40	–	–	–	–	–	–	–	–	–
Other	68	27	–	–	4	–	–	–	–	–	–	–
Total	1,843	1,856	2,209[a]	2,319	2,975	4,039	4,402	4,615[b]	4,588	5,535	8,833	9,251

SOURCES: Figures for 1785 come from Johnston (1964:52); for 1810 from Johnston (1964:281); for 1843 from Johnston (1964:307); for 1857 from Six Nations Agency, Council Minutes, Feb. 1857, p. 141; for 1875, 1900, 1910, 1920, 1930, 1949, from Six Nations Agency Archives, Extracts from Paylists, in Dec. of each year; and for 1970 and 1973 from the Six Nations Agency, Official Band Lists, Dec. 31 of each year.

[a] Census total reads 2,223.

[b] "Less 4 included twice = 4611" appears after the total.

from power. The Senecas since the 1840s have been the smallest of the six tribes and the Delawares the least numerous of all registered groupings.

Establishing the Reserve Community

With the creation of the reserve in 1847 the first Iroquoian community containing populations of all six tribes came into existence. It remains the most populous reserve in Canada, and the largest Iroquois reserve in Canada and the United States. It was the most wealthy Indian community in Canada during the nineteenth century, with band funds totaling over $800,000.

After migration to the Grand River the chiefs established a League that duplicated the American League in New York State. But unlike its American counterpart, the Canadian League held domain over a single reserve, a fact that led to its unique adaptation as a municipal government. The chiefs continued to assert the claim of sovereign status despite a classic report in 1839 by Justice Macaulay (1839) that disclaimed such unique treatment.

The Confederacy councils of the 1840s and 1850s were preoccupied with the corporate interests of the band: road construction and maintenance, ownership and use of natural resources, land surrenders, census taking, band membership, and the semiannual disbursements of interest money to the band members. The major issue of the two decades was the problem of Indians paying individual debts to the White merchants in surrounding villages (Weaver 1975). By legislation Indians were not responsible for their personal debts to Whites (Canada. Laws, Statutes, etc. 1850), but this did not prevent merchants from advancing credit. When these debts accumulated, the merchants collectively petitioned the Crown to repeal the Indian Protection Act (Canada. Laws, Statutes, etc. 1850). Although they did not succeed in revoking the act, their threat did intimidate the chiefs and Indian administration; and on three occasions in these decades the chiefs agreed to apply the band's annuity against existing debts of individual members of the band. After the third payment, the council decided that the band should not be held collectively responsible for individual debts, and the Indian administration enforced this decision.

Gradually and sometimes reluctantly the council assumed many of the powers of the tribe, clan, and lineage, thus contributing to the attrition of these units. For example, the council began to settle property and land disputes, to allocate land to families, and to provide relief to the aged and infirm. Tribal councils, infrequent in the 1840s and 1850s, were condemned by leading chiefs as damaging to the unity of the Confederacy council and they soon ceased to figure significantly in reserve politics.

The council continued to be composed of hereditary chiefs, who together with the "war chiefs" from 1812 and the Pine Tree chiefs numbered over 50. The Crown made no attempt to interfere with the appointment or dismissal

of chiefs (Weaver 1975). The chiefs met in the Onondaga council house, a log structure near Middleport, two or three times a year to deliberate in traditional fashion matters of community interest (Weaver 1963-1974). The Onondagas, known collectively as the firekeepers, acted as mediators in the proceedings according to traditional custom. However, the tribal seating plan differed from the traditional one in that the Mohawks and Senecas occupied the positions east of the council fire, while the Oneidas and Cayugas sat on the west, together with the dependent nations: Tuscaroras, Nanticokes, Delawares, and Tutelos. Although the dependent nations were to speak through "their voice," the Cayugas, in fact they often directly addressed the assembly of chiefs, and operated quite independently, though not equaling the original five nations in power or status.

Council meetings were usually attended by the visiting superintendent, who was David Thorburn from 1847 to 1862, who traveled from Queenston, 60 miles southeast of the reserve. Both he and his successors depended upon the interpreter to present their directives and information to the council and to receive the chiefs' decisions. The interpreter, usually a chief, was a government employee appointed by the Indian administration and paid a salary from band funds. He was required to do all interpreting for the superintendent in council proceedings and in court cases. In 1858 the first permanent speaker of the council, Chief John Smoke Johnson (Mohawk) was appointed, and this office became institutionalized as did that of deputy speaker in the 1870s. The deputy speaker's office was usually filled by a chief from the opposite side of council. In 1880 the council appointed its first secretary, Chief Josiah Hill (Nanticoke), who until his death in 1915 assumed the tasks of recording the official council minutes in English and executing council decisions (fig. 2). Previously the superintendent's clerk had performed these duties with the interpreter's aid (Weaver 1963-1974).

In addition to the interpreter and secretary, the council employed only two additional officers in these years: the medical officer and forest warden, both of whom were White, and who, like the superintendent, were paid from band funds but not appointed by the council. The warden's task was to enforce the unpopular timber conservation regulations that proved so contentious during the midcentury.

With the transfer of Indian administration from the imperial to the provincial government in 1860, which allowed for more rapid communication between headquarters and field offices, and the appointment of Jasper T. Gilkison as superintendent in 1862, Indian Department supervision of local affairs increased. Gilkison, who served 1862-1891, was the first superintendent to assume residence in Brantford where the Agency office has remained. He came into office determined to effect many changes and shortly pressed the chiefs to create a village

Rochester Mus. and Science Center, N.Y.: RM 1355.
Fig. 2. Confederacy chiefs in Council House, about 1910. Note flags with clan symbols, Onondaga chief holding wampum strings (see "The League of the Iroquois: Its History, Politics, and Ritual," fig. 6, this vol.). left to right, Peter M. Jamieson, Jim Skye, Jacob S. Johnson (Deputy Speaker, 1910), Richard Hill, Jesse Johnathan, David Skye (with cane), J.C. Martin (Speaker, 1910), David John, Sr. (with wampum), William Smith (interpreter), Joseph Jacob(?), Josiah Hill (arm outstretched; Secretary), Dan Bomberry, A.G. Smith, John W.M. Elliot, Harry Martin, Abram Lewis, Thomas J. Thomas, George Gibson. Photograph probably by Arthur C. Parker.

in the center of the reserve and to build a new council house there. Despite the Onondaga chiefs' protests that they, not the council, determined the seat of government, the village of Ohsweken soon developed around the new council building completed in 1865 (Weaver 1963-1974).

"Progress" and the Protestant ethic became the driving force behind many changes and attempted innovations at midcentury. Some educated Mohawks had become influenced by recent municipal legislation in the province (Weaver 1963-1974); and attempting to gain more local self-determination, they collected a petition in 1861 urging the government to apply the legislation to the reserve, thereby instituting an elected government. At that time there were no provisions in Indian legislation for elected local governments on reserves. The Indian Department did not support the petition; and efforts to change the form of local government, although still in the background (Montgomery 1965), were to subside until 1890.

Education and agriculture, the means of "civilizing" the Indians, were pursued vigorously by Gilkison. The adoption of White agricultural practices was gradual

during midcentury and there was still heavy reliance on seed grants from the Indian Department by farmers who found it difficult to set aside enough seed for spring planting. But the Upper Tribes were adopting farming methods more rapidly, and in 1867 several wealthy Mohawk farmers founded the Six Nations Agricultural Society. By 1883 it held its annual fall exhibition in a newly built hall in Ohsweken, and it remained in the 1970s one of the most prestigious organizations in the community. This association, and the council-sponsored Union Temperance Society, with its several branches on the reserve and affiliations in Muncey and Lewiston, were the major voluntary associations until the 1890s when the Orangemen's Lodge was founded in Ohsweken (Weaver 1963-1974).

Education continued to be viewed by the Lower Tribes as a threat to their way of life. But in 1877 the Mohawks persuaded the chiefs to vote their first education grant from band revenue. This became an annual appropriation equaling that of the New England Company, the unchallenged missionary and educational establishment on the reserve. The school board, established in 1877, was

529

composed of three chiefs elected annually, the Anglican clergy in charge of the Mohawk Institute, and the superintendent. It set the local educational policy and built and staffed the eight schools under its charge. In addition, the Wesleyan Methodists independently operated two schools, and the chiefs maintained one school independently. Many Six Nations people, themselves educated at the Mohawk Institute, were employed as teachers. By 1880 the 13 schools were attended by one-third of the school-age children. Increasing the educational standards was proceeding at too slow a pace for the Upper Tribes and too rapid a pace for the traditional Longhouse adherents (Weaver 1963–1974).

The major religious alignments in the community were apparent when the reserve was settled in the 1840s. Longhouse adherents had outnumbered the Christians until midcentury (Canada (Province) 1847) when the reverse trend became evident. Despite relentless proselytizing by missionaries and equally strong, but often unrecognized, pressures from Christian Iroquois, the Longhouse community persisted. By 1865 it comprised approximately 23 percent of the band's population. This proportion has remained stable, fluctuating between 24 percent and 19 percent over the years (Weaver 1963–1974). Until 1883 the Longhouse community centered on three longhouses; the Upper Cayuga or Sour Springs, southwest of Ohsweken, and the Lower Cayuga and the Onondaga "down below." These buildings had been built in the 1840s and 1850s. In 1884 the Seneca Longhouse was created from a splinter group of Onondaga Longhouse adherents after a dispute developed in the singing society (Goldenweiser 1912–1914). Unlike the Christian churches, the Longhouses have not suffered subsequent splintering. Together these centers provided the basic social fabric for the traditionalists who have remained conservative in religion, politics, and life-style.

The Christians supported several denominations and within each at least two if not more churches. By 1890 the Anglicans comprised 40 percent of the Christian population and had built four churches. The Baptists comprised 24 percent of the Christians and operated three churches. The Methodists with two churches and other small sects such as Brethren, Mormons, and Salvation Army attracted the remaining third of the Christians (CDIA 1890). During the next half-century, the pattern of Christian affiliation stabilized with the Anglicans and Baptists each attracting a third of the Christian adherents.

Both religious traditions fostered their own sets of social activities, networks of friendship, and kinship. Social interaction between the two was infrequent, sometimes forbidden by orthodox parents of both faiths, and intermarriage was condoned by neither. Christian knowledge of the Longhouse faith and rituals has remained minimal and bireligious adherents have always been few in number. Although symbolized as religious divisions, the fundamental division in the community remains one of differential acculturation. The two most populous tribes, Mohawks and Cayugas, held polar positions on the continuum of culture change. The Longhouse community has historically opposed acculturative influences although it has been affected by them. The Christian community slowly began to adopt White middle-class values and beliefs and by the late nineteenth century cautiously but actively sought to educate their children, practice agriculture on an expanded basis of large farms rather than subsistence level, and secure material possessions far beyond those aspired to by the nonmaterialistic ethic of the Longhouse. The Protestant ethic was accepted as a legitimate and desirable life-style by the Upper Tribes, who not only continued to dominate the social activities of the reserve but also soon gained economic ascendency and later political domination (Weaver 1963–1974).

The Established Community Flourishes

The major economic and political patterns established in the 1880s continued to develop until World War I. In the mid-1880s the first brick houses were built, and by the turn of the century, frame and brick structures were more common than log ones. Farming reached its peak in the 1890s with half the reserve land being prepared for pasturage and of this, some 10,000 acres cultivated with the major crops of wheat, oats, corn, and barley. The practice of turning cattle free in the spring to roam the pastures and rounding them up in the fall declined with the increase of fencing and the building of larger barns. Both types of improvements were made possible through the loan fund established by the council in 1895. More cattle were being raised with some farmers specializing in prize stock. A smaller number attempted to raise sheep despite the lack of dog controls to protect the flocks (Weaver 1963–1974). Hogs were the most common livestock, contributing substantially to the common diet of pork, hot biscuits, and corn bread. Gardens provided vegetables and fruits, some of which were canned; and chickens and cows supplied families with eggs, milk, butter, and meat. By the turn of the century the average farm was about 60 acres (Sample 1968). The largest was over 300 acres and worked by hired hands. Surplus produce was marketed in Brantford and Hamilton, providing cash for farm improvements and to a smaller extent clothing and furniture (Voget 1969). Spring annuities provided cash used primarily for seed purchases, and the Indian Department granted seed loans when widespread crop failures occurred. The Farmers' Institute held its first meeting on the reserve in 1895 and began to disseminate the latest agricultural skills and knowledge to large audiences of farmers. Beginning in 1905 the wives' counterpart, the Women's Institute, began to establish branches, teaching farming, domestic skills, health care, and sanitation procedures to the women of the Upper Tribes. Both these organizations provided social entertainment and the opportunity to exchange local news.

With the expansion of farming came more wage labor and craft division of labor. In the 1880s small numbers of men worked as farm labor and women as domestic help off the reserve (Weaver 1963-1974). By the 1890s flax pulling and peas and hops picking north of the reserve near Galt as well as berry picking in the Niagara peninsula attracted several hundred seasonal workers away from the reserve; this pattern held until the Depression of the 1930s. On the reserve specialized trades began to develop with more men trained in carpentry, stone masonry, blacksmithing, and brick laying. A few others established small businesses, general stores, post offices, and grist and saw mills. A few men purchased threshing machines and gained wages from threshing grain on farms both on and off the reserve (Weaver 1963-1974).

Political pressures intensified on the chiefs in the 1880s with the passage of many amendments to the Indian Act, designed to expand the duties of local band councils and to encourage elected governments on reserves. These years witnessed the council struggling to clarify its domain of power and traditional procedures of decision making. The old ideal of consensus proved impossible to achieve in some of the heated issues of the day, the major one being whether the council would agree to abide by the Indian Act in making its decisions (Weaver 1963-1974). Discussions repeatedly occurred in council over whether the Confederacy was an autonomous local government or whether it should operate within the constraints of the Indian Act. Many chiefs argued that the act did not apply to the Six Nations because they were a sovereign nation with their own political constitution in the teachings of Deganawida. Although many council decisions were made in accordance with its provisions, the council's ideological posture would remain one of denying the validity of the act. The government has consistently maintained that the act applies with no exceptions to the Grand River Iroquois.

Faced with an expanding administrative bureaucracy and frequent legislative amendments, the council became apprehensive about its freedom to govern and repeatedly reaffirmed its position of local self-determination in council speeches and memorials to the government (Weaver 1975). One example of this reaffirmation was Seth Newhouse's preparation of his classic version of the constitution of the League (Newhouse 1885; Fenton 1949a). As self-appointed codifier of the laws of the Confederacy, he recorded his own views of the proper composition and functioning of the Confederacy, hoping to correct what he saw as the erring ways of the Grand River Council (Fenton 1968; Weaver 1975). Reexamination of chieftainship titles resulted from Newhouse's efforts, but no major changes were made in council procedures. Newhouse's request to the chiefs to sanction

his version of the constitution in 1899 was denied, and the council appointed its own committee, which produced the "official version" in 1900. Largely the work of Chief John Arthur Gibson (Seneca), it was ratified by the council and subsequently published (Scott 1912).

While holding to traditional deliberation procedures, the council continued to expand its domain into the community. It provided welfare to the sick, aged, and infirm; compensation for fire losses; assistance for funerals; annual contributions to education, the Agricultural Society, and the Temperance Society; and small grants to churches and longhouses. It also offered the use of the council house for teas and suppers organized for fundraising purposes (Weaver 1975). Because of the high cost of using external legal counsel in settling disputes, the Indian Department had encouraged the chiefs to establish a disputes committee within council, and by the 1870s the disputes committee had become a permanent feature of council. At each council meeting a chief from each tribe would be appointed to the committee to handle the disputes of the day (Noon 1949). Its recommendations were passed on to the general council for further debate and ratification. Because the chiefs sometimes rejected evidence thought by the superintendent to be important, he shortly established an "appeals court" at the Agency. Despite the council's protest, the appeals procedure continued to operate until the 1930s. Criminal cases involving homicide, theft, and rape were historically processed in the provincial court system, an arrangement to which the chiefs had agreed shortly after the reserve was formed.

In its offices, committees, bylaws, and policies the council by the 1890s resembled more a municipal government than a tribal federation. Although its powers in judicial matters exceeded those of regular municipalities (J.B. Mackenzie 1882, 1896), its fiscal powers were far less, because it did not control its band funds. Its enforcement of decisions was unsystematic, because the chiefs were reluctant at times to enforce bylaws even when powers to do so were available (Noon 1949). The duties of inspector of public works to oversee road and school construction were made a full-time job in 1897 because they became too time consuming for the secretary of council, who had performed these duties since 1884. The job of a constable to enforce the bylaws also became a full-time position in the late 1890s. Both were Six Nations men, paid as other officers from band funds. Under the strong direction of the chiefs of the Upper Tribes, who dominated council through their ability to read and write English, council established a set of bylaws in the early 1890s controlling fence construction, weed control, statute (compulsory) labor for road maintenance, cattle impounding, sanitation, and public order and decorum (Six Nations 1910). By 1901 the Board of Health was created as a standing committee, with its own set of bylaws (Six Nations 1900), which it used that year to control a smallpox epidemic (Weaver 1971). Educational facilities expanded as the chiefs built new schools and refurbished old ones, expanded the school board to include lay members, and appointed a truant officer in 1907. Schools were regularly visited by the county inspector who passed his recommendations to the chiefs. School attendance became compulsory in 1920 (Weaver 1963-1974).

While the 1880s and 1890s saw expanded services being rendered the community by the council, it also witnessed additional political pressures both from within and without the reserve. The Conservative Party under Sir John A. Macdonald gave Indians the right to vote in federal elections in 1885. Although council officially urged residents not to exercise their franchise, individual chiefs of the Upper Tribes became heavily involved in local campaigning (Montgomery 1965). In 1898 when the Liberals withdrew the franchise, because the Indians had supported the Conservative Party, the council unsuccessfully petitioned to have it returned (Weaver 1975).

Despite council's proved ability to adapt to the local demands of a farming community, the pace of change was found to be too slow by a growing number of Upper Tribes members who wanted more extensive bylaws protecting the farmer, more consistent enforcement of the laws, and a higher standard of education. This newly emerging reform group, known then as the Progressive Warriors, claimed that the conservative bent of council—a view not shared by Longhouse adherents—was due to the ascriptive and closed basis for council office. The reform movement of 1890 was organized by young men from the Upper Tribes, who were educated at the Mohawk Institute, spoke and wrote English, operated large farms or specialized in certain trades, were leaders in their churches, and were members of the Six Nations Agricultural Society or the Orangemen's Lodge. Few could claim hereditary chieftainship titles and most felt that education should be a requisite for council office (Weaver 1975). In 1890 they drafted a petition signed by some 20 percent of the male adults in the community, urging the government to apply the elected system to the reserve, but their activities in subsequent years went unheeded by the federal government. By the spring of 1906 these men formed the Indian Rights Association, also called the Dehorners, and they began a determined campaign to remove the chiefs from power.

Until this time neither the council nor the community considered the Dehorners a serious threat, and many Dehorners acknowledged the improbability of change. In 1907 and again in 1910 they unsuccessfully petitioned the federal government to establish an elected council, but they could muster no more than 25 percent of the adult male support in each memorial (Weaver 1975). Nevertheless, opposition began to crystallize against the movement as the chiefs feared that the federal government was encouraging the Dehorners, as its official policy would

dictate. The federal government was now becoming concerned with the possibility of local unrest if even a minority opposed reform. It consequently held to its noninterference policy until after World War I, but the chiefs' official position on participation in the war effort did not bring administrative sympathy to their cause.

When war broke out in 1914 the council took the position that it was a sovereign nation and that it would not participate in the war effort unless asked to do so by the king himself. Without conscription legislation, all participation was voluntary. As the council began to reassert its ideology of sovereignty, political tensions intensified. The chiefs did contribute small sums to the Women's Patriotic League, organized by the Six Nations women during the fall of 1914 to provide soldiers with socks, cigarettes, and other small items. Despite official council policy, 292 men voluntarily enlisted, most of them being assigned to the 114th Battalion of the Haldimand Rifles. Many suffered the first horrors of gas warfare in the trenches in France and received commendation for bravery and leadership (Scott 1919). Of those enlisted, 29 were killed in combat, 55 were wounded, 5 died from illness, 1 was taken prisoner, and 1 was missing in action. While abroad the soldiers had unsuccessfully petitioned the federal government in 1917 to establish an elected system of local government on the reserve. Their disagreement with the council's official stand on the war continued when they returned home, and this attitude contributed to the increasing tension as politics became a preoccupation of the community.

Ottawa's noninterference policy began to erode as the council grew more determined to assert its sovereignty claim in the face of the Indian Department's denial of that claim (Weaver 1963-1974). The chiefs were angered at the department's increased scrutiny of council procedures and decisions and no longer cooperated with the local superintendent in handling administrative matters. The application of the Soldiers' Settlement Act to the reserve only heightened the tension. Designed to encourage veterans to take up farming, capital loans were advanced at low interest rates, and land was assigned the men. Council saw this act as a major encroachment on its domain and feared that lands subject to foreclosures would be lost to the reserve. Repeated statements from Ottawa that "citizenship" should be the ultimate goal of the Six Nations furthered the council's uneasiness.

Also, by this time, the council's composition had radically changed with the death and retirement of the "progressive" Upper Tribes chiefs who led the reforms of council in the 1890s. Replacing these moderate chiefs were young, more militant chiefs who, aided by the "Mohawk Workers Club" formed of Mohawk supporters in 1922, began to formulate strategy that they hoped would save the hereditary system. Since the 1890s the majority of chiefs (over 80 percent) had been Christian, a fact that dulled the traditionalist impact of the Lower

Tribes in council. By the war years the new leadership of council fell to Levi General, who held the Cayuga title Deskahe and was a member of the Sour Springs Longhouse. Through his powerful oratorical skills and strategy he formed a strong following, which lasted until his death in 1925. Although his visits to England and Geneva in 1920 and 1923 and his support from American colleagues did not produce the international recognition he sought for the Confederacy, it did prove embarrassing to the Canadian government (Weaver 1975).

By 1923 the federal government was becoming impatient with the militancy of Deskahe and his vocal Mohawk supporters. Col. Andrew Thompson was appointed special commissioner to investigate the political and social state of the reserve. A.T. Thompson's (1924) recommendation to establish an elected council was effected by an Order in Council, September 17, 1924. No referendum was held to determine if the people would support the change. The first election was held on October 21, 1924, and was closely watched by the newly arrived Royal Canadian Mounted Police officers, brought into the reserve in the winter months of 1923 without prior knowledge of the chiefs. The termination of Confederacy rule, the establishment of an RCMP detach-

ment, and the broken promises that Confederacy rule would not be interfered with remain a source of deep bitterness to many Six Nations people. Many consider this the major moral injustice brought upon the community, and some in the 1970s continued activities designed to reinstate the Confederacy (Weaver 1975).

After 1924 the Confederacy council did not disband. Instead the chiefs continued to hold regular monthly meetings in the Onondaga longhouse where they sought recognition and privilege, though divested of administrative powers (Shimony 1961).

Between 1924 and the early Depression years, activities to reinstate the Confederacy heightened; and support was sought from other reserves, White sympathizers, and legal counsel. But the Depression slowed the tempo of protest and overshadowed the activities of the newly organized elected council.

The new council established in 1924 was elected annually from an all-male electorate and was presided over by one of the 12 councilors selected from among themselves as the chief councilor (fig. 3). In 1951 the chief councilor became elected at large, and the term of office for the councilors was extended to two years by a second Order in Council. The reserve is divided into six electoral

Public Arch. of Canada, Ottawa: C33652.

Fig. 3. Session of first elected Council, 1924. At back (behind rail), left to right, unknown, Col. C.E. Morgan (Superintendent), Hilton M. Hill (Chief Councilor); at Secretary's desk, left, Frank W. Montour, William F. Powless (Secretary, holding pen); at tables, left to right, Pat Sero, David General, William Smith II, George Garlow, John Anderson, Archie Russell, William Staats, Wilbur Monture, Joseph F. Hill, Jim Davis, Frank Miller.

districts, each providing two councilors. The council's early years were devoted to increasing the standard of education, hospital care, and roads. Despite Confederacy supporters denying legitimacy to the council, it has drawn its mandate since 1924 from 20 to 41 percent of the electorate (Weaver 1970).

The Depression of 1929-1939 hit hard at the economy of the reserve. With the difficulty of procuring capital for farm investment even at the best of times, many turned to seasonal employment when they could obtain it off the reserve. Some families who had left the reserve years ago returned so that they could at least produce their own food. The Temperance Society branches and the newly established Benevolent Society and Christian Aid Society offered death benefits and mutual aid through these difficult years to both Christian and Longhouse adherents. Increased prosperity, war-time factory work, and many voluntary enlistments during World War II attracted many away from the reserve. Those who returned faced a rapidly changing community that, economically, was becoming a suburb to the cities of Brantford, Hamilton, and Buffalo where employment was sought.

Changes After 1945

Despite postwar economic expansion and increased pressures on the community to change, the fundamental cleavages on the reserve remained those of religion and politics. Proselytizing by missionaries had ceased, but pressures of mass media, education, and encroaching urbanization continued to challenge the continuity of the modified traditional culture carried by the Longhouse adherents. The reserve contains two "communities" derived from the Christian and Longhouse ethics, each with its own heterogeneous social and cultural patterns. Although interaction between the two occurs of necessity, and some intermarriage exists, the two remain distinct socially. Generally the traditionalists are Longhouse in faith, speak one or more of the Indian languages, tend to live "down below," retain the matrilineal descent system, support the Confederacy, and uphold the retention of the "Indian way" as decreed in the Code of Handsome Lake (Shimony 1961). By choice the traditionalists can live a relatively isolated existence from the Christians by participating only in religious and social activities that pivot on the longhouse. Excepting organized sports, few Longhouse people participate in the extensive range of voluntary associations operated by the Christians.

There were in 1977 still four Longhouses on the Six Nations Reserve: Onondaga, Seneca, Lower Cayuga, and Sour Springs (Upper Cayuga) ("Iroquois Since 1820," fig. 4, this vol.). The yearly round of ceremonies held in these Longhouses includes those customarily given in the New York Longhouses: Midwinter, Maple (no longer given at Sour Springs), Planting, Strawberry, Bean, Green Corn,

and Harvest ceremonies. The ritual of these ceremonies is also much like that of the New York Seneca Longhouses, although the Our Life Supporter ceremony, which forms an integral part of the Midwinter and Green Corn ceremonies of the New York Seneca, is considered a separate ceremony at Six Nations and is held immediately after the longer ceremony or within 10 days. Additionally, the Six Nations Longhouses have four ceremonies not in the New York ceremonial calendar: Bush Dance (held after Midwinter and reckoned as the first ceremony of the cycle at Six Nations), Corn Spouting (no longer given at Sour Springs), Raspberry (held after Strawberry, when the raspberries ripen), and Corn Testing (when the corn is not quite ripe). The three Longhouses down below (Onondaga, Seneca, and Lower Cayuga) hold a Thunder ceremony and a Sun and Moon ceremony at the Onondaga Longhouse each year—ceremonies more infrequently given at the New York Longhouses (Shimony 1961:140-191).

Other important ceremonies include the Six Nations Convention held each October or November in at least one of the Longhouses for the purpose of hearing the Code of Handsome Lake and the ceremonies of the medicine societies. There are eight medicine societies: Bear, Otter, Eagle, Buffalo, Husk Face, False Face, Pygmy, and Shake the Pumpkin. Each has its own set of officials, origin myth, rituals, and healing practices, and (with the exception of the False Face and Husk Face societies who also hold rituals in the Longhouse) holds its ceremonies in private homes (Shimony 1961:191-205, 281-284).

As an institution the Longhouse functions to perpetuate certain aspects of the kinship system, medicinal complex, languages, and since 1924, the Confederacy. The majority of chiefs in 1976 were Longhouse adherents, and it was claimed that a Christian cannot become a "real chief" because he lacks the cultural background from which the ideology and social structure of the League is derived. The Longhouse institution also provides a substantive cultural basis for identity as Iroquois and Indian, which the Christian can not claim. Among many Christians acculturation has proceeded to the degree that although they identify as Indian, they are in behavior and belief indistinguishable from Whites. The longhouse also exemplifies what remains of the traditional culture of the League, which held such prominence in colonial times. Great pride is taken in being Iroquois and being historically treated by Britain as a unique nation among Indians. Finally, the Longhouse serves to moderate the pace of change in the reserve community, not only by constraining its members through doctrine and sanction (Shimony 1970) but also by impeding, through political influence, innovation by the band council.

Although there is a small number of apathetic residents, the reserve community sustains a preoccupation with local politics. Cross-cutting the Longhouse-Christian alignment is a divided allegiance to either the Confederacy or the elected band council (Rioux 1952; Nicholas 1965). Whether Confederacy supporters are Christians or Longhouse adherents, together they constitute a nonvoting opposition to the band council, carefully monitoring the council's decisions. In 1959 (E. Wilson 1960; Montgomery 1963) and again in 1970 (Putt 1971) factional dispute reached maximum expression in abortive attempts by Confederacy supporters to take possession of the council house and reinstate the chiefs. The factions have learned to coexist since 1924, and their sharing of norms of nonviolence prevents aggression. They are all constrained by the fact that no faction wants the social or physical dissolution of the community, local taxation, or the loss of Indian rights and land (Weaver 1963-1974).

The band council since the 1950s has dramatically expanded its administration and domain over community affairs (Weaver 1963-1974). In 1951 legislation gave women the franchise, and in 1963 the first women were elected to office. The council meets in public assembly twice a month, and with its many committees it makes decisions within the constraints of the Indian Act. Its total budget of $251,000 in 1975 derived from the annual interest on its capital fund ($127,200) and annual accountable government grants ($123,800). The only additional income the band receives is royalties from gypsum deposits, which are placed in the capital fund. Band council decisions are carried out by the councilors, its administrative staff of four employees, and the roads and maintenance employees.

The 1950s and 1960s witnessed many changes in community services (Weaver 1963-1974). The postwar welfare state brought income benefits to the disabled, aged, blind, and unmarried mothers. Although Confederacy supporters state these payments should not be accepted as this would imply Canadian domain over the reserve, they in fact comprise an important contribution to the household economy of both Longhouse (Myers 1962) and Christian adherents. In the 1950s medical and hospital insurance plans of the province of Ontario extended to the reserve at a time when the hospital was closed down, against the unsuccessful protests of the community (Weaver 1972). Medical and hospital services are sought off the reserve with the exception of a public health unit and a one-doctor clinic remaining in Ohsweken. The RCMP detachment was replaced by the provincial police in 1968, and legal aid has been extended, as has police protection from the surrounding towns. With band council control many improvements have been effected. The council-renovated home of Pauline Johnson, the Mohawk poet, is a major tourist attraction. Telephones and electricity, initially brought onto the reserve in the 1910s and 1920s, extend to most houses, and incentive programs have increased indoor sanitation.

The federal government's capital housing program has resulted in many large houses being constructed since 1967. In the mid-1960s a local newspaper was established, reporting council business and the many sports and social activities. A new senior public school was built in Ohsweken in the early 1950s to which all grade seven and eight pupils are bussed. This school brought children from all parts of the reserve together for the first time, and an increasing number continued on to high school and postsecondary education in technical colleges, teachers colleges, and universities throughout the province. With the exception of teachers and nurses, professionals seek employment off the reserve. The resident employment is limited to a few council employees, teachers, nurses, store owners, the few craft producers, and less than a dozen full-time farmers. The decline in the farming economy, from the 271 farms in 1951 to 47 in 1961 (Sample 1968), continued, with the majority of landholders who have certificates of possessory title to their land holding less than 25 acres. Residence has become neolocal, and from this base the majority of the skilled and unskilled labor force commuted daily to Brantford, Hamilton, Hagersville, Nanticoke, and Caledonia for employment. Many women sought clerical and unskilled labor jobs in these towns, and some continued seasonal work in tobacco and berry picking. Very few families depended upon permanent welfare payments, administered by council.

As education, transportation, the mass media and the diversified urban-based economy have pressed in on the community, the proportion of the resident population began to decrease. From 1959 to 1973 the resident population rose from 4,350 to 5,007, but this represents a proportion from 60 percent to only 54 percent of the total band population (Weaver 1963-1974). The above factors also influence the high degree of intermarriage with Whites. During the late 1960s and early 1970s, 40 to 47 percent of the annually recorded marriages were to Whites.

A resurgence of federal political concern over Indian affairs and proposed reorganization of the administrative structure posed the major threat of termination of federal service. To counteract this threat the band council developed external contacts with other Iroquoian and a few Algonquian band councils in Ontario in 1969, founding the Association of Iroquois and Allied Indians (AIAI). Their position paper in response to Minister of Indian Affairs Jean Chrétien's 1969 policy spelled out a need for educational and economic development programs while retaining the physical land base of the reserve and a modified version of the Indian Act (Association of Iroquois and Allied Indians 1971). Despite external ties to band councils with similar problems and pressures, the band council continues to be seen, as was the Confederacy during its rule, as too conservative by some and too reformist by others. It and the Confederacy continue to guard the community against pressures that neither political tradition has the power to deflect completely. Pressures from the surrounding urban communities and regional governments will continue to challenge the community's social and physical integrity.

Sources

The most extensive bibliographies on the rich archival sources and published documents for the prereserve period have been prepared by Johnston (1964:315-325, 1967:154-163). Of particular interest to Grand River history are the Public Archives of Canada, Record Group 10, records of the Six Nations Council meetings from 1763 to 1845 (vols. 716-717 and vol. 15, ser. 2); the census materials for 1814, 1830-1836, and 1840-1852 (vols. 708, 715, 747); the "Six Nations Funds Investment and Grand River Navigation Company, 1834-1862" (vols. 624, 796-798, 1025); and the "Report of the Executive Council on the Grand River Lands, 1843" (vol. 714). The "J.B. Macaulay Report, 1839" (vols. 718-719) contains the seminal judgment denying political sovereignty to the Six Nations. The Province of Ontario Archives contains the papers of Joseph Brant, Jasper T. Gilkison, John Norton, and John G. Simcoe. The Toronto Public Library holds the papers of William Jarvis and Peter Russell. The Haldimand papers are deposited in the British Library.

The Province of Canada's special reports of 1844-1845, 1847, and 1858 contain valuable narratives of Grand River conditions, including census materials. Extensive archival materials from the 1840s to the 1950s exist in the Six Nations Agency Archives in Brantford. This collection has been microfilmed by the Mohawk Institute Woodland Indian Cultural Education Centre of Brantford. Council minutes are available there with permission of the band council.

Special government reports on Grand River response to Indian legislation of 1869 and timber regulations (Canada. House of Commons 1874), lands claimed at the headwaters of the River (Canada. House of Commons 1887), and a special investigation of health conditions (CDIA 1900) are published.

A popular book on Grand River history is Dunham's (1945) work but the major references for Brant County history remain Johnston (1967), Reville (1920), and *The History of the County of Brant* (Anonymous 1883). An illustrated historical atlas of Brant County (Page and Smith 1972) provides extensive sketches and maps, and old photos are reproduced by the Brant County Historical Society (R. Clark 1966). All contain valuable census, biographical, and historical information on the Six Nations. Early missionary activities are described by A.J. Clark (1932), French (1962), A.H. Young (1922), Pryse (1963-1964), and Talman (1929). C. Lee's (1944) descrip-

tion of historic land-use patterns remains the most reliable. Stanley (1963), Johnston (1965), and Cruikshank (1902) provide accounts of the Six Nations participation in the War of 1812, and Scott (1919) gives a more extensive description of World War I.

A full history of the Grand River reserve remains to be written, but popular accounts by Cork (1962), Reaman (1967), and Beattie (1960) claim to have done so from "the Indian" viewpoint. Useful historical biographies exist of Joseph Brant (Stone 1838), Chief George Martin (E.H.C. Johnson 1913), Chief George H.M. Johnson (Hale 1885), Chief John Smoke Johnson (E.H.C. Johnson 1914, 1928), and Pauline Johnson (Van Steen 1965). A few obituaries on outstanding Iroquois informants exist: John Arthur Gibson (Goldenweiser 1912a), Simeon Gibson (Fenton 1944), and Howard Sky (Fenton 1972a; Foster 1972). Six Nations people themselves have authored several articles and books: John Brant-Sero (1899, 1899a, 1901), A.R. Hill (1922), Elmer Jamieson and Peter Sandiford (1928), Julia Jamieson (1969), Alam Greene (1971), and Ethel B. Monture (Chalmers and Monture 1955).

Victorian authors such as J.B. Mackenzie (1882, 1896), Boyle (1898, 1900, 1900a, 1900b, 1906), and Chadwick (1897), the last the most able among them, provide the few glimpses of the Grand River community in the late nineteenth century. Hatzan's (1925) popular work provides similar coverage of the early twentieth century.

Anthropological interest has focused on the Longhouse institution and the League, and within the League, on the ideology and the Condolence ceremony. The classic works remain the constitution recorded by Parker (1916a) using Seth Newhouse's (1885) manuscript, Fenton's (1946a, 1949a, 1950) many contributions on Condolence, Scott's (1912) publication of the Grand River chiefs' official version of the constitution, Hale's rendition of the Condolence (1883a, 1895) and the founding legend (1882), Hewitt's short articles (1892, 1917a, 1920, 1930, 1933) and his extensive treatment of myths (1903-1928), Goldenweiser's (1916) review of Parker's (1916a) work, and Rioux's (1952) analysis of the relationship between religion and politics. Noon (1949) produced the major analysis of the Confederacy's adaptation to local government. Waugh (1916) has written on food, Randle (1951) on the changing role of women, Goldenweiser (1914, 1914a, 1915) on kinship, and Shimony (1970) on witchcraft. Medicine has been treated in traditional aspects by Rioux (1951), and Shimony (1961a, 1970), and in modern political context by Weaver (1972). Shimony's (1961) work on the Longhouse community remains the most definitive account of Longhouse culture, together with Kurath's (1953, 1961, 1962, 1968) work on the accompanying song and dance patterns, and Speck's (1949a) on the Midwinter ceremony.

Oklahoma Seneca-Cayuga

WILLIAM C. STURTEVANT

The Seneca-Cayuga of northeastern Oklahoma are the descendants of Iroquois from several tribes who moved into Ohio during the eighteenth century and of subsequent Iroquois emigrants from Ontario and New York.

Origins and History

By about 1660 the aboriginal inhabitants of the country just south of Lake Erie had been driven out by the Iroquois, who may have begun moving into the region soon thereafter. However, there is no evidence that the nearby Seneca or any other Iroquois occupied this Ohio country or even used it for hunting until about 1740. The region was traversed by war parties of Susquehannocks (until 1675) and of Ottawas, Chippewas, Illinois, Miamis, and Wyandots supplied with French guns, until peace was established between them and the Iroquois in 1701. Then Shawnees and Wyandots began using it for hunting, and Miamis and Weas allied to the French established some settlements in the region. But the first reference to Iroquois in the area dates from 1743, when a rapidly increasing settlement of perhaps 2,000-2,400 emigrants from all the Five Nations (and Delawares, Mahicans, Ottawas, Saint Francis Abenakis, and Chippewas, but probably mostly Iroquois) was reported to have been on the lower Cuyahoga River for some years. In 1745-1747 Senecas and Mohawks were living in a fortified Wyandot village near Castalia. This Iroquois movement into the Ohio country may have been related to famine conditions among the Seneca. For the remainder of the eighteenth century there are scattered records of Iroquois from all the Six Nations—but primarily Senecas and Caughnawaga Mohawks—hunting in Ohio and occupying many different farming settlements there (fig. 1). Most of these towns seem to have been small, forced by frontier warfare to move every few years, and very often of mixed tribal composition. Iroquois associations with the Wyandot, Shawnee, and Delaware were especially close, and some intermarriage is recorded. However, the degrees and effects of the social amalgamation are not known, and by the time the picture becomes clearer in the early nineteenth century, the Ohio settlers are identified by the traditional tribal and language names of the Five Nations (Wheeler-Voegelin 1963:1-14, 1963a:3-40, 1965:6-133).

Although in 1750 the Confederacy council at Onondaga denied the independence of the Ohio Indians, the Pennsylvania colonial authorities often dealt with them separately, and it is clear that in the 1760s and 1770s the Iroquois in New York had very little influence or control over those in Ohio (Wheeler-Voegelin 1963:93, 1963a:136, 1965:167, 413-421). During the Revolution the Ohio Iroquois mostly supported the British, but in the War of 1812 many fought on the American side.

From about 1807 to 1817 Cayugas are known to have emigrated from the Buffalo Creek Reservation to join the "Senecas" in the Sandusky area—perhaps at the invitation of those Senecas, or of the Wyandots whose land the Indians considered this to be (Wheeler-Voegelin 1959:7-17). Treaties signed in 1817 and 1818 and put into effect in 1819 ceded to the United States most of northwestern Ohio and established two reservations for the Ohio Iroquois: one of about 61.9 square miles for the Senecas of Sandusky (plus a tract of 1,000 acres at Honey Creek just to the south for some Mohawks who had settled there between 1815 and 1817) and one of 62

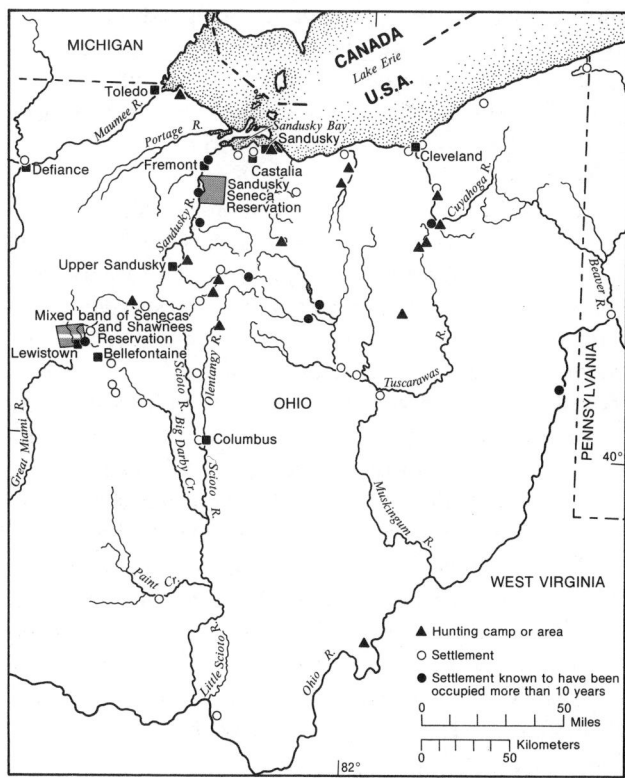

Fig. 1. Approximate locations of Iroquois settlements and hunting areas in the Ohio country, 1742-1831.

square miles for the Mixed band of Senecas and Shawnees around Lewistown (fig. 1). The north half of the latter was assigned to the Senecas of this "mixed band" and the south half to the Shawnees. On the Sandusky reservation the Cayugas and Senecas, who were non-Christians, were settled in the north, and the mostly Anglican Mohawks and Oneidas, to the south (Wheeler-Voegelin 1959:26–27, 29). There were also a few Onondagas at Sandusky, while some of the "Senecas" on the Lewistown reservation were in fact Cayuga, and one person later recognized as Tutelo was evidently descended from these Ohio communities (McElvain 1829; Winney 1880; Anonymous 1880).

With rapidly expanding White settlement of Ohio and the passage of President Andrew Jackson's Removal Bill in 1830, both groups of Ohio Iroquois signed treaties in 1831 providing for their removal west of the Mississippi, exchanging their Ohio lands for land in northeastern Indian Territory and for annuity payments. Three men from Sandusky had already searched for new lands in the west on a three-year expedition beginning in 1825 (Wheeler-Voegelin 1959:29). The Sandusky people traveled west by steamboat and overland between November 1831 and July 1832, while the Mixed band of Senecas and Shawnees was removed between September and December 1832. Between 25 and 30 percent died on the way, due to much illness and to bad planning for the winter movements under harsh circumstances. In December 1832 these two emigrant groups agreed to amalgamate and slightly rearrange the lands assigned in Indian Territory that then became the Neosho Reservation, the northern half occupied by the Mixed band and the southern by the Senecas from Sandusky (fig. 2) (Wheeler-Voegelin 1959:44–49; Foreman 1946:67–82; Kappler 1904–1941, 2:383–385).

Among the ancestors of the Oklahoma Seneca-Cayuga are also Iroquois who moved in 1846–1852 from New York to a tract in Kansas set aside by the 1838 treaty with the New York Iroquois. Most of those who survived soon returned to New York, but some remained (evidently mainly Cayugas and probably fewer than 50). Some moved to the Neosho Reservation in 1849 for about five years and then most rejoined those who had remained near Fort Scott, Kansas (about 65 miles north of the Neosho Reservation). In 1860, 32 had taken allotments in Kansas. Many enlisted in the Union Army during the Civil War. When the Kansas allotments were sold to Whites in 1873 about one-third of the holders were identified as living on the Neosho Reservation; most of the rest had returned to New York, while a few stayed in Kansas (Wheeler-Voegelin 1959:55–68, 86; Foreman 1946:332–335; E.P. Smith 1874; H.W. Jones 1874; Dyer 1880).

In 1862 most of the Seneca and Shawnee on the 538 Neosho Reservation moved to the Ottawa Reservation in

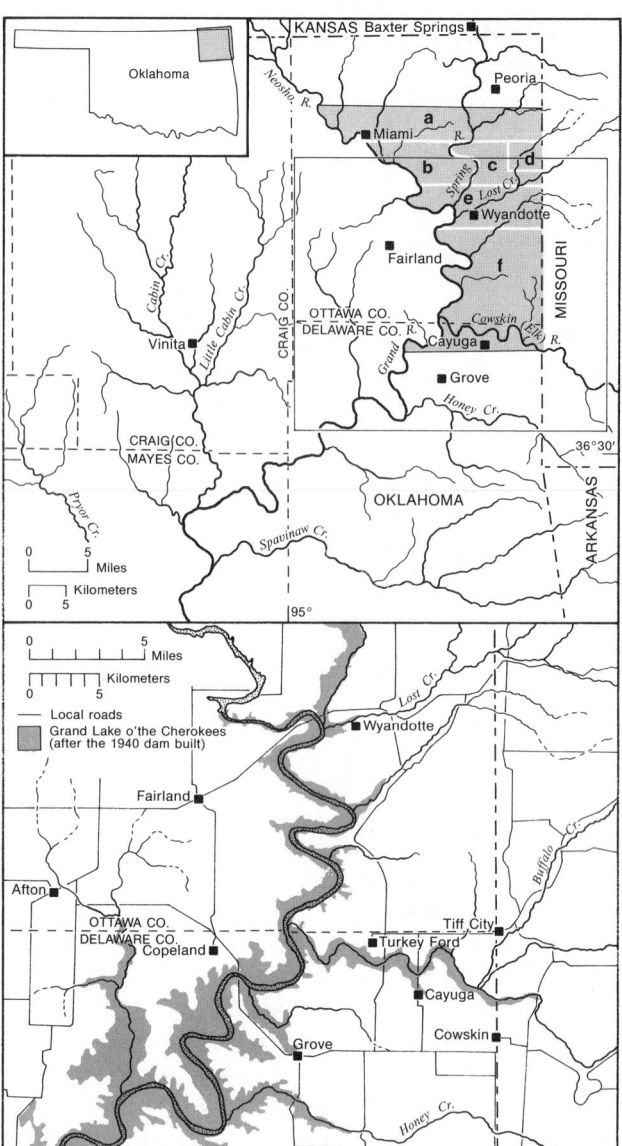

Fig. 2. top, Neosho Reservation as assigned in 1832. Subdivisions show reassignments of 1869: a, to Peoria, Kaskaskia, Piankashaw, Wea; b, to Ottawa; c, to Eastern Shawnee; d, to Eastern Shawnee and then in 1875 to Modoc; e, to Wyandot; f, retained by Seneca-Cayuga until allotment. bottom, 20th-century Seneca-Cayuga region.

Kansas as refugees from Civil War depredations. In the spring of 1865 they moved back to the Neosho Reservation, where agreements between the Indians were made the following year and confirmed by a treaty signed with the United States in 1867 that went into effect upon ratification in 1869. In addition to transferring some of their lands for the use of the Ottawas, Wyandots, and others (fig. 2), this treaty provided for the dissolution of the Mixed band. The Shawnees received part of the reservation and became known as the Eastern Shawnee, while the Senecas of the Mixed band joined the Senecas from Sandusky on a reservation retained in the southern part of the old Neosho Reservation. From this date all former distinctions between the Sandusky and Lewis-

Table 1. Seneca-Cayuga Population Estimates

Date	Total	Components	
1748	1,230	650 Seneca, 300 Mohawk, 140 Onondaga, 80 Cayuga, 60 Oneida[b]	Wheeler-Voegelin 1965:164
1777	320[a]		Wheeler-Voegelin 1963:93
1819	608	348 Sandusky, 57 Honey Creek Mohawk, 203 Lewistown[c]	J. Johnston 1820:270
1829	502	157 Sandusky Cayuga, 64 Seneca, 48 Oneida, 7 Onondaga, 46 (Honey Creek?) Mohawk, 198 Lewistown Seneca[c]	McElvain 1829
1832	368–394	251 Sandusky, 117–143 Lewistown[d]	Wheeler-Voegelin 1959:45
1845	287	153 Sandusky, 134 Lewistown[d]	ARCIA 1845:460, 527
1865	247	130 Sandusky, 117 Lewistown[d]	ARCIA 1866:347
1868	216	101 Sandusky, 115 Lewistown[d]	ARCIA 1868:354
1872	214		ARCIA 1872:243
1881	243		ARCIA 1881:278
1890	255		ARCIA 1890:452
1903	358		ARCIA 1903:510
1924	525		ARCIA 1924:34
1944	861	In Ottawa Co., 476	Wright 1951:238
1959	1,230	"per capita roll"	Quapaw Agency, personal communication 1961
1960		In Ottawa Co., about 495	Lamb 1960
1974		In or near Ottawa Co., 540	U.S. Dept. of Commerce 1974:476

[a] Four times an estimate of Seneca or Mingo men of the Ohio valley; too low.

[b] Four times an Indian count of warriors "settled on the Waters of Ohio"; probably too high.

[c] Census by local Indian agent.

[d] Senecas and Shawnees of the Mixed band not separately counted; Lewistown Senecas here estimated from ratios reported in 1829 and, after separation, in 1872.

town "Senecas" ceased (table 1) (Wheeler-Voegelin 1959a:70–81; M.H. Wright 1951:240; Royce 1899:842–845).

About 1870 and again in 1879 and 1881, invited immigrants arrived from the Six Nations Reserve and a few from Cattaraugus and perhaps elsewhere in New York. Some returned, but 20 or more stayed, were adopted, and eventually received allotments. Most were Cayugas, but Senecas, Mohawks, Onondagas, and Oneidas were also represented. These emigrations established family connections with the East, especially with the Six Nations Reserve, and resulted in significant cultural influences (Sturtevant 1961–1962; Barbeau 1912a; Dyer et al. 1881–1882; Foreman 1946:335–336; Gilkison 1881, 1882).

After the passage of the Dawes Severalty Act in 1887 about half the Seneca Reservation was allotted in 40- to 160-acre tracts during 1888–1891. In 1902–1903 the remaining land was allotted, with 120 acres assigned to each person born since the first allotment, 80 acres set aside for the ceremonial grounds and cemetery and 40 acres for the Friends (Quaker) Meetinghouse, and the rest, about 10,000 acres, declared "surplus" and sold. At the same time annuities due from treaties made in Ohio ceased with a final per capita payment; however, the older Cayuga annuities from New York State continued (ARCIA 1888:109, 1890:83, 1891:234, 1892:243, 1901:218, 1902:188–189, 1903:161, 1904:181–182; U.S. Census Office 1894:247). Some of the allotted lands and

half the ceremonial area were subsequently lost under the Grand Lake formed by the completion of the Pensacola dam in 1940 (fig. 2). About 1940 the federal government began purchasing land for the Seneca-Cayuga, some of which was also soon flooded; in 1974 about 1,000 acres remained as tribally owned (Sturtevant 1961–1962; U.S. Department of Commerce 1974:475).

Culture

Subsistence

Until about 1820 the Ohio Iroquois lived in farming villages during the spring and summer. In the fall hunting parties left by canoe, caching furs and hides until December, when base camps were established. There the women and children lived for three or four months while the men hunted in the surrounding area, the women making maple sugar in February. At the end of March these smaller groups returned to the home villages (Wheeler-Voegelin 1963a:93–94). Plow agriculture was borrowed from nearby Whites by the Sandusky Iroquois after 1821 (W. Lang 1880:96). After the removal to Indian Territory some hunting continued (mainly for deer and turkey in the Cherokee Nation to the south), and seining in the Cowskin River provided fish, but the economy was principally based on agriculture (Sturtevant 1961–1962). By 1873, 460 acres were under plow, for corn, wheat, oats, and potatoes—103 plows of four types were owned, as well as one reaper—while there were 500 fruit trees (apples, pears, plums, grapes), 245 head of cattle, 350 hogs, and 110 horses (General Council of the Indian Territory 1873:30, 1875:26, 104). Indian Bureau annual reports for subsequent years consistently report productive agriculture, and by 1890 some 6,000–7,000 acres were in cultivation (U.S. Census Office 1894:111, 246). By 1960 farming was still more important than in the New York and Canadian Iroquois communities, although it supported only a small minority of the population. Others worked in neighboring towns in a wide variety of occupations: as truck drivers, mechanics, restaurant cooks, factory workers, teachers, and nurses, for example (Sturtevant 1961–1962).

Political and Social Organization

The form of political organization is unknown for the eighteenth century and most of the nineteenth century, although it seems that the hereditary chiefs' titles of the Confederacy were not represented among these Western Iroquois. That some political relations with the Confederacy were maintained up to removal is hinted at by the delivery of a wampum belt to the New York Iroquois by a delegation in 1831 (Foreman 1946:67); another purpose of the visit was to negotiate a more convenient manner of payment of the annuities owed the Cayugas by the state of New York, as the Ohio Iroquois were about to move to Indian Territory. There are some indications that around the 1830s the western Iroquois had no overall organization corresponding to the parallel Confederacies in New York and Canada (New York (State) Legislature. Senate 1890:265, 431–435).

By the early 1870s annual elections were held in Indian Territory for a first, second, and third chief and three councilmen. This elected Seneca council was described in 1881 as functional, not "purely honorary" as among other groups under the Quapaw Agency (ARCIA 1881:95). There seems to have been a parallel organization of three Cayuga chiefs (perhaps more or less hereditary, probably patrilineally, but often including at least one of the elected "Seneca" chiefs), largely, evidently, for the purpose of signing for the annuities from New York State that were due only to the Cayugas among this by now thoroughly intermarried group.

In 1937 the Seneca-Cayuga Tribe of Oklahoma was organized under the Oklahoma Indian Welfare Act. Offices of chief, second chief, secretary-treasurer, interpreter, and three councilmen were established, to be filled by elections at yearly general councils of the adult tribal members residing in Oklahoma (the officers necessarily residents of Delaware and Ottawa counties) (Seneca-Cayuga Tribe of Oklahoma 1937). The Cayuga annuities were still being paid in 1977; by 1961 they came to $858.43 a year and were not divided per capita; $400 of the amount was allotted each year to the upkeep of the tribal ceremonial grounds.

For some purposes the Seneca-Cayuga community is defined by the official tribal rolls, which include all those on the rolls in 1937 plus all children born since who had both parents on these rolls; children of out-marrying members are admitted to membership at their request if the non-Seneca-Cayuga parent is Indian, or subject to the approval of the Council if that parent is not Indian (Seneca-Cayuga Tribe of Oklahoma 1937). As early as 1875 strict matrilineal rules for tribal affiliation had been dropped, at least for identification as Cayuga (H.W. Jones 1875). By 1960 most if not all the enrolled tribal members were known to have some non–Seneca-Cayuga ancestry (although the 1937 rolls identified most members only as "Seneca," not recording other ancestry). Some known White ancestry is very common; the most frequent non-Iroquois Indian ancestry is Wyandot, Cherokee, and Shawnee. A significant number of Seneca-Cayuga have Osage, Winnebago, Creek, and Peoria ancestors, while at least 12 other tribes were mentioned.

By 1962 the majority of enrolled members lived outside Delaware and Ottawa counties. Many lived elsewhere in Oklahoma and in nearby Missouri, but there were also large numbers in California and Oregon and many scattered elsewhere in the United States. Neither residence nor enrollment were perfect indicators of community participation. Many living elsewhere returned regularly for visits, especially during the Green Corn ceremony in August. Some who lived in the community did not participate in the rituals, while some who were not enrolled did participate in the rituals and in other community affairs, especially individuals married to Seneca-Cayugas who were on other tribal rolls or were White (Sturtevant 1961–1962).

For ceremonial purposes only, the Seneca-Cayuga are organized in clans. These are remembered as formerly matrilineal but by the mid-twentieth century a child often took the clan of the parent of the same sex (Sturtevant 1961–1962). Clan exogamy, also traditional, had been dropped by 1912 (Barbeau 1912a). There are moieties named (in English) according to their positions in the Longhouse at the Green Corn ceremony during which they provide the opposing sides for the Bowl Game. The North moiety includes the Wolf, Bear, Turtle, Porcupine, and Beaver clans, while the South moiety consists of the Snake, Snipe, and Deer clans. Of these the Beaver has died out since 1912 (Barbeau 1912a), while the Porcupine is Wyandot in origin and the Snake is also of foreign origin, probably Wyandot or Shawnee (Sturtevant 1961–1962).

Religion

In earlier locations the "stomp grounds" included a brush arbor, but on the present site at Turkey Ford ceremonies were conducted in an open area surrounded by benches (a pattern common at the "stomp grounds" of other eastern Oklahoma tribes) (fig. 3) from 1902 until the

Natl. Mus. of Canada, Ottawa.
Fig. 3. Jim Kingfisher burning Indian tobacco during the principal prayer at the Sun dance of Sept. 29, 1911. The costumed Sun dancers ("war dancers") sit on the bench at right, with the leader holding the Sun symbol (arrow). Photograph by C. Marius Barbeau.

open-sided longhouse measuring 58 feet 5 inches by 30 feet was erected about 1935 (see "Iroquois Since 1820," fig. 4, this vol.). Those attending the major ceremonies held there camp on the grounds, where a few concessions are also rented for sales, in the regular eastern Oklahoma manner (Sturtevant 1961–1962; Howard 1961; Speck 1940a; Finkelstein and Marriott 1940). The calendrical ceremonies in the longhouse are organized and supervised by Faithkeepers, colloquially called "pothangers," of whom there are 12, three women and three men from

Natl. Mus. of Canada, Ottawa: III.I.459.
Fig. 4. Representation of the Sun carried by the chief dancer in the Sun dance. Wooden disk, painted with blue-green center, then orange, then red circles (the colors differ somewhat on the other side and on later examples), with goose down glued around the edge and pendant split eagle feathers (replacing scalps used anciently), mounted on a staff with red spiral stripe. Disk diameter 9.5 cm. Collected in 1912, the staff then new but the disk said to have been brought from N.Y.

each moiety, headed by one woman from the South moiety. The women pothangers take the leading roles, holding the offices for life. A replacement is chosen—usually a daughter of the previous incumbent—by the other female pothangers, who also appoint the male pothangers who assist them (normally a man is followed in the position by his son).

The calendrical ceremonies are similar to those of other modern Iroquois communities, although they diverge from those at the eastern longhouses more than the latter differ among themselves. The most striking difference is the absence of the Midwinter or New Year's ceremony. Usually called the "dog dance" since it involved the sacrifice of a pair of white dogs, it was held for several days in January or February and is described among the Seneca-Cayuga in Ohio as well as in Indian Territory (W. Lang 1880:97–99, 124; Crowell 1944; ARCIA 1852:104), but it was given up by a formal decision of the council in 1877 (H.W. Jones 1877; date confirmed by Sturtevant 1961–1962). The major ceremony in the 1970s was the Green Corn ceremony, held in mid-August when the corn reaches the roasting ear stage and other crops are ripe, to give thanks to the Creator for the crops and for his other gifts of the previous year, and to ensure their continuation for the following year. The "Sun dance" or "Rain dance" is held twice a year, in April or May at the time of first planting ("when the tree leaves are the size of squirrels' ears") and again formerly in September, to end the year, but since about 1935 a day or two after the end of the Green Corn ceremony. This ceremony combines elements of the Planting, Thunder, and Sun ceremonies of the eastern Iroquois, giving thanks to the Sun and the Thunderers for light and water for the crops and providing protection against lightning and windstorms (figs. 3-4). In late May when the strawberries ripen there is a one-day Strawberry ceremony to give thanks for the first fruits of the year. During a full moon night in July a Blackberry ceremony is held, to give thanks to the Moon (Sturtevant 1961-1962; Howard 1961, 1970; Barbeau 1912a; Finkelstein and Marriott 1940; Nieberding 1956; C.B. Wilson 1956; Splitlog 1941).

Several Medicine Societies are known to the Seneca-Cayuga, membership in which tends to be inherited although at least some could be joined for curative purposes. As in the east, the primary curative rituals are private, although preventative repetitions may occur at the stomp grounds at the time of the Green Corn ceremony. Among these the curative football games and the Otter Society (usually called "sprinkle" in English) are still active, the Dark Dance ("hoghead dance") is perhaps moribund, "doll dinners" were last held about 1940, and the Society of Medicine Men has long been extinct. The False Face Society still has a few members (see "Northern Iroquoian Culture Patterns," fig. 5, no. 31, this vol.) and may occasionally perform cures, but the spring and fall prophylactic circuits of the community by 12 False Face doctors accompanied by six Husk Faces were abandoned about 1880 (Sturtevant 1961-1962; Barbeau 1912a; Howard 1970).

Another series of rituals is connected with death. Wakes are still held, but since about 1910 without moccasin games. There are three sorts of "dead feasts": the Tenth-day Feast, the feast repeated by the family on the anniversary of the death for 4 to 10 years, and a "community supper" for all the dead held one or two days after the Green Corn ceremony. A "ribbon dance," long extinct, may have been equivalent to the eastern Feast of the Dead (since its name is recalled as *ki·weh*). Once important was an "adoption dance" at which someone was adopted to replace a deceased relative. This had become extinct before 1912; annual feasts to commemorate the adoptions were then still held although they are no longer (Barbeau 1912a; Sturtevant 1961-1962).

The Ohio Iroquois were influenced by the prophet Handsome Lake during his lifetime. Delegates were sent from Sandusky to New York to hear him preach on several occasions between 1804 and 1807, and in 1806 and 1808 Handsome Lake himself attended councils at Sandusky (Wallace 1969:297-298, 302). His teachings were remembered in Ohio in 1823 (Finley 1840:175-177) and among Sandusky emigrants in Indian Territory about 1850 (Winney 1975; cf. New York (State) Legislature. Senate 1890:210-214). Later visitors from the Six Nations Reserve carried his message: very likely William Jacobs did so in 1881 and 1882 (Winney 1881-1882), and certainly the preacher John Isaac from Sour Springs Longhouse did when he visited perhaps about 1910 (on his return he reported that the Catholics had jailed him

for it), while his son Chancey Isaac spoke of Handsome Lake during ceremonies he attended in Oklahoma in 1936-1937 (Chancey Isaac and Enos Williams of Six Nations Reserve, personal communications 1962). But the Seneca-Cayuga were beyond the reach of the institutionalization of Handsome Lake's "New Religion." They never developed their own preachers of his Code, and by the 1960s many of them were entirely ignorant of him, although a few recognized his name and one or two remembered something of his message as it had been taught by visiting Canadians.

The Peyote religion, of the Big Moon type, was introduced in 1907 by the Delawares George T. Anderson, his brothers John and Sam, and Reed Wilson. A Seneca-Cayuga Peyote meeting with about 20 members was maintained for 25 or 30 years, and a few Seneca-Cayugas in the 1960s occasionally attended Shawnee and Quapaw Peyote meetings. Peyotists continued to participate in the calendrical ceremonies, although at least some severed their memberships in Medicine Societies (Sturtevant 1961-1962; Speck 1933; Howard 1970).

Among the Iroquois who moved into Ohio in the eighteenth century were Catholic Mohawks from Caughnawaga, and many Anglican Mohawks were reported at Sandusky in 1801 (J. Smith 1851:206, 255; Wheeler-Voegelin 1963:218; Wallace 1969:302). In 1821 one of the Mohawk and Oneida Anglicans at Sandusky was a minister, holding regular services, and in 1833, just after the removal, it was reported that an Episcopal church had 50 members, used the Book of Common Prayer and the gospel of Mark translated into Mohawk by Joseph Brant, and was led by a Mohawk minister who also spoke Seneca (W. Lang 1880:97; Foreman 1946:166, 180). But most Seneca-Cayugas remained non-Christian, and Catholic and Anglican adherents evidently decreased. A Quaker school was built in 1872, Quaker and Methodist conversions increased in the early 1880s, and a Friends Meetinghouse was built in 1884; still, by 1890 only 58 church members were counted in a total population of 255. Quaker missionaries have been in continuous residence since 1893 (H.W. Jones 1872; Hubbard 1975:31-34, 38; Winney 1883; Dyer 1884; U.S. Census Office 1894:100, 247; Simms 1962). Catholic missionizing evidently began in 1892 (ARCIA 1892:245). The stone Cayuga Church (Splitlog Mission) was built by the Catholics in 1896 but was later taken over by the Baptists (Nieberding 1954). By 1962 religious divisions in the community were not very prominent. There were many members of the Quaker meeting, some Catholics (although they had little contact with priests), and some Methodists. Many prominent participants in the Longhouse ceremonies were also active members of Christian churches, while others, though certainly not anti-Christian and not considering themselves to be non-Christian, nevertheless felt some conflict between Longhouse and formal church membership.

Languages

As early as 1833 most Seneca-Cayugas were said to know English. In 1890, 198 of the total population of 255 were reported to speak English and some young men knew no other language, but English was not allowed to be spoken in council meetings (Foreman 1946:166; U.S. Census Office 1894:98, 246, 247). It is not clear which Iroquois languages were spoken in the community until 1912, when Barbeau (1912a) found only Cayuga spoken except for one family of Seneca speakers. By 1962 only Cayuga was known, and that was hardly used except in ritual contexts and had only 11 fluent speakers and 12 others with some competence, the youngest speaker having been born in 1918. Oklahoma Cayuga is a distinct dialect, differing from the Canadian variety in details of pronunciation and vocabulary (Sturtevant 1961–1962).

Synonymy

In the eighteenth century the Ohio Iroquois, of whatever tribal origin, were usually known either as Mingo or as Seneca, the name Mingoes being used for Iroquois of western Pennsylvania at least as early as 1731 (Pa. Arch., 1st ser., 1:299–301). Wheeler-Voegelin (1965:329) cites an equation of 1766: "the Mingos or Senecas" of Ohio; there is a similar instance in 1818 (Wheeler-Voegelin 1959a:72). By 1829 the general term was Seneca: after listing all Five Nations as represented at Sandusky McElvain (1829) commented, "all go under the name of Senecas." After the removal the terms Sandusky Seneca and Mixed band Seneca or Lewistown Seneca continued in use for a time; an alternate name for the Sandusky

group, from their new location, was Cowskin Senecas (Whitetree 1873; Wheeler-Voegelin 1959:101). After 1869 the usual term was simply Seneca, despite occasional objections that this obscured the existence of other elements, especially Cayuga (Winney 1880). Barbeau (1914a) used (Oklahoma) Cayuga-Senecas. Seneca alone continued to be ordinary English usage in Oklahoma in 1976, although Seneca-Cayuga was adopted in 1937 as the official designation.

In Oklahoma Cayuga the usual self-designation is *hotinQsǫ́·nih* 'Iroquois'; *kayohkhó·nǫʔ* 'Cayuga' is used occasionally (Sturtevant 1961–1962). See also the synonymies in "Northern Iroquoian Culture Patterns" and "Cayuga," this volume.

Sources

No thorough historical or ethnographic research has been conducted on the Seneca-Cayuga. Documentary sources are voluminous but scattered, major repositories being the National Archives (in Washington and at the Federal Records Center in Fort Worth, Texas) and the Oklahoma Historical Society, Oklahoma City. An unpublished brief study by Wheeler-Voegelin (1959) is the best historical summary. Ethnographic research is largely unpublished except for that by Howard (1961, 1970); other work is by Barbeau (1912a, 1914a) and Sturtevant (1961–1962). Large, well-rounded collections of Seneca-Cayuga artifacts, mostly from 1908–1912 and the 1920s, are in the Museum of the American Indian, Heye Foundation, New York, and the National Museum of Man, Ottawa.

Iroquois in the West

JACK A. FRISCH

The rapid expansion of the western fur trade lured many of the Caughnawaga, Oka, and Saint Regis Mohawks to seek employment with the North West Company as voyageurs and trappers. By 1794 these Iroquois had made their way into western Canada. An entry in the journal of a "bourgeois," or partner, of the North West Company records the presence of "3 Iroquois . . . now employed in the Company's service" at Sturgeon River near Prince Albert, Saskatchewan (M'Gillivray 1929:48). Not to be outdone by their rival, the Hudson's Bay Company began to explore the same western regions of North America. This drive for furs involved the migration of many Indians to act as suppliers to the British companies. "The Nepissings, the Algonquins and Iroquois Indians having exhausted their own countries, now spread themselves over these countries [the Swan River area of Manitoba and Saskatchewan], and as they destroyed the Beaver, moved forwards to the northward and westward . . ." (Thompson 1916:205).

By 1798 the Iroquois had advanced as far west as Fort Augustus near Edmonton, Alberta (fig. 1). According to Thompson (1916:312) about 250 Iroquois men and women accompanied the North West Company's canoes to Fort Augustus, while some of them went up the Red Deer River. Once at Fort Augustus, the Iroquois did not pay heed to the advice given to them on the perils of life on the Plains. It appears that the local Indians were not too awed by the behavior of the Iroquois. When a party of some 75 Iroquois entered a Gros Ventre (Atsina) camp and invited the natives to gamble with them, a quarrel soon ensued that ended with the death of 25 Iroquois. The surviving Iroquois returned to Fort Augustus where they formed a force of 120 men to avenge the deaths of their comrades; however, the Cree, natives of the area, persuaded the Iroquois to call off their retaliatory expedition against the Gros Ventre. The next day, the Iroquois and Cree took part in a large feast. The Iroquois danced their "grand Calumet" dance; then, a Cree danced his tribe's war dance, which had a humbling effect upon the Iroquois (Thompson 1916:314–316).

There is little doubt that these Iroquois came from Caughnawaga, Oka, and Saint Regis. Alexander Mackenzie (1801:400) noted that "a small colony of Iroquois emigrated to the banks of the Saskatchewine, in 1799, who had been brought up from their infancy under the Romish missionaries, and instructed by them at a village within nine miles of Montreal."

Very few women came with this Iroquois party. "For their whole number had only about six women with them, each had a husband" (Thompson 1916:317). Some of these Iroquois men married Cree women and remained in Alberta, near Edmonton, where they became known as Michel's band. Among the members of Michel's band were the descendants of two brothers, Michel and Baptiste Callihoo, who were the two surviving sons of the original Callihoo who came to Fort Augustus around 1800, probably from Caughnawaga (Callihoo 1959; Chamberlain 1904:461). Masson (1889–1890, 1:398) lists a Louis Calihue as a voyageur in the Fort Des Prairies (Edmonton) department of the North West Company. The name Callihoo is derived from *karhí·yoʔ* 'beautiful forest'. Thus, Louis Calihue could very well be a progenitor of Michel's band. The band was alloted a 25,600-acre reserve west of Saint Albert, Alberta; however, land surrenders reduced the reserve lands to 15,485 acres (Canada. Department of Indian Affairs. Surveys Branch 1928:67). On March 31, 1958, the members of Michel's band became enfranchised under section III of the Indian

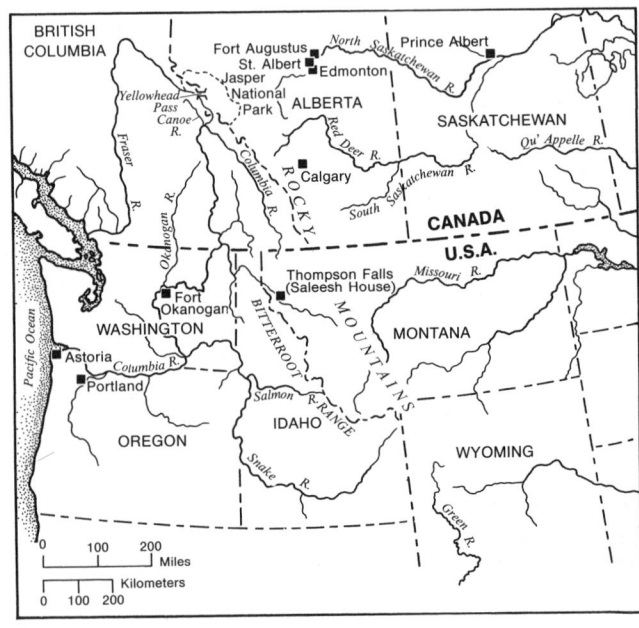

Fig. 1. Range of Iroquois in the West.

Fig. 2. An Iroquois "mountain man" in Plains dress, including a red roach, painted buffalo robe, and beaded shirt, leggings, and moccasins, holding a metal pipe tomahawk. Painted in 1837 by Alfred Jacob Miller, probably at the Green River trappers' rendezvous, Wyo.

Act of Canada. These Iroquois still lived near Edmonton in the 1970s.

Another group of Iroquois settled in the Alberta-British Columbia border region, near Jasper National Park. This group, sometimes called the Rocky Mountain People, are descendants of Iroquois trappers and voyageurs who were employed by the Hudson's Bay Company (Callihoo 1959:18). Havard (1880:318) refers to them as a "settlement of a band of Iroquois in the Rocky Mountains"; Teit (1909) also refers to them as living "in the neighborhood of Yellow Head Pass and east of there," but he notes that they are mixed with Shuswaps and Crees. While Teit (1909:468) estimates that contact between the Shuswap and Iroquois occurred around 1816, MacGregor (1969) places the date around 1819. The Yellowhead Pass across the Rocky Mountains on the Alberta-British Columbia border is named for Pierre Hatsination (sometimes spelled Hathawiton), an Iroquois known as Tête Jaune or Yellow Head after his blond hair (MacGregor 1969).

These Iroquois trappers, canoemen, and freemen also made their way into the western regions of the United States; and according to Ewers (1963:4), "the first Iroquois west of the continental divide may have been free trappers rather than company men."

David Thompson had engaged the services of six Iroquois to help him find bark for making canoes while at Saleesh House near Thompson Falls, Montana, during February 1810 (Thompson 1916:418-419). Journeying down the Columbia River in 1811, Thompson met a party of Nipissings and Iroquois on their way to the Canoe River in British Columbia to hunt moose and trap

Fig. 3. Mohawks among the Flathead of the Bitterroot Valley, Mont., in 1854. left to right, Pierre Kar-so-wa-ta (probably *kahsowâ·ta?* 'lime, chalk'), wearing a cap of gray blanket cloth and a buckskin shirt, who farmed and raised cattle and spoke "the mountain french, and english, besides several Indian languages" (according to the artist's caption)—probably Pierre Gaucher, who went to St. Louis in 1839; Young Ignace, also a member of this 1839 expedition; Charles Lamoose, son of Ignace Lamoose and a Flathead or Pend d'Oreille mother. Drawn from life, May 16 and June 1854, by Gustavus Sohon. See Ewers 1948:54-62.

beaver. On May 4, 1811, he "engaged Charles a fine, steady Iroquois" to be his bowsman; and on May 19, 1811, he hired another Iroquois named Ignace to be his steersman (Thompson 1916:457–460). On July 11, 1811, this party reached the Pacific Ocean where the Pacific Fur Company had established Astoria only a short time before. Later that same year, Ignace Shonowane, an Iroquois, and his family arrived at Astoria from Fort Okanogon, in Washington, along with several other hunters (Franchère 1969:92; Irving 1964:120).

When Astoria changed hands during the War of 1812, many of its employees remained and joined the North West Company. In 1816 the North West Company sent brigades of trappers and traders into the interior of the Oregon country. Many Iroquois, along with Abenakis, Algonquins, and Hawaiians were employed in these brigades (Ewers 1963:6; Quimby 1972). When the Hudson's Bay Company absorbed the North West Company in 1821, the brigade system was continued for the fur trade in the Columbia River valley.

It was during this period that a group of Iroquois under the direction of Ignace Lamoose, or Old Ignace, settled among the Flatheads of Montana (Ewers 1963:8; Kelly 1954). Old Ignace told the Flathead about the Catholic faith, and in 1835 he set out for Saint Louis where his sons were baptized. In 1837 Old Ignace, three Flatheads, and a Nez Perce set out again for Saint Louis, but on the journey they were killed by a band of Sioux. In 1839 Pierre Gaucher and Young Ignace (fig. 3) reached Saint Louis where they met with Bishop Joseph Rosati and persuaded him to send a priest to the Flathead; Father Pierre Jean De Smet (1905, 1:28–30) was chosen for this mission.

Other Iroquois went west in search of a new life. A New York Oneida named Milo Skeeter married the daughter of a Crow chief in 1868 and was adopted into the Crow tribe. In 1874 he applied to the local Indian agent for seed for his farm (Ewers 1963:9). One of the more notable Saint Regis Mohawks to travel west was Thomas Williams, *tehorahkwané·kę* 'two suns side by side', who journeyed to the Rocky Mountains in 1801; upon his return, he became a chief at Saint Regis (Hough 1853:202). All that remains in the twentieth century of the Iroquois bands that went west are the legends of their contact with the western tribes and the small numbers of individuals who, although intermarried with the local tribes, preserve their Iroquois heritage through personal family histories.

Sources

The only comprehensive sources on the Iroquois in the West are Chamberlain (1904), Ewers (1963), and Frisch (1976).

Late Prehistory of the Ohio Valley

JAMES B. GRIFFIN

In late prehistoric times, approximately A.D. 1000 to 1700, the Ohio Valley from the mouth of the Wabash to southwestern Pennsylvania (fig. 1) was occupied by many different Indian societies, all of which became increasingly dependent upon agriculture, following the pattern of most Indian groups during this time period in the eastern United States. Over time, the cultural behavior of the Ohio Valley societies increasingly came to resemble that of Mississippian societies in the Southeast and in the lower Mississippi Valley. This general trend was accentuated by the probable intrusion of populations with a Mississippian cultural complex into the lower Ohio Valley, the possible movement of some societies into the Fort Ancient area of southwestern Ohio, and by cultural exchange with southeastern groups, which appears to have increased through time. Communication into and within the Ohio Valley was both by water and by a series of well-established trails, some of which are discussed and

illustrated for the Southeast by Myer (1928) and for Ohio by Mills (1914).

Other waterways and trails in Illinois and Indiana led north to the Great Lakes area; still others in West Virginia and Pennsylvania assisted movement of people into the Appalachians and to the east coast. These routes of contact are reflected in the finds of Fort Ancient ceramic attributes in western Virginia, Pennsylvania, the Lake Erie basin, central and northern Indiana, and Tennessee. Ideas and items representative of areas surrounding Fort Ancient reached the central Ohio Valley by the same routes. The actual amount of material carried either into or out of the Fort Ancient area is not very large and consists primarily of small art objects or items of religious significance. The same observations can be made for the Middle Mississippi occupations of southwestern Indiana where there is little evidence of prehistoric trade either into or out of the area and for the Monongahela complexes in the upper Ohio Valley.

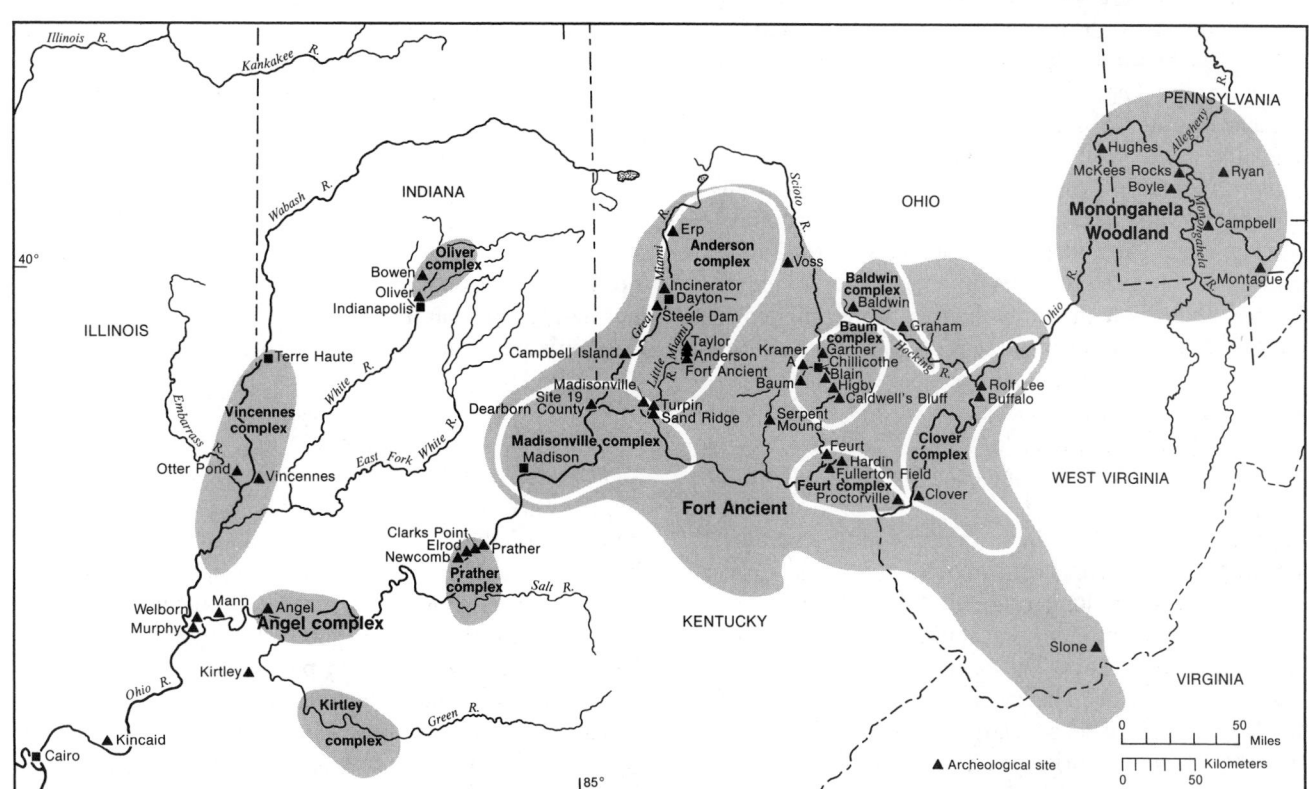

Fig. 1. Relationships of archeological sites and complexes in the Ohio Valley.

547

Mississippian Occupations

The Mississippian occupations in southwestern Indiana are dominated by the Angel site in Vanderburgh County; the Murphy, Welborn, and Bone Bank sites in Posey County; and the Merom site in Sullivan County. On the Illinois side of the Wabash the Vincennes complex, to which the Merom site belongs, has been given a preliminary description by Winters (1967), who also recognizes a somewhat different Mississippian occupation as the Etchison complex.

Angel Complex

The Angel site is a classic example of a major Middle Mississippi fortified town with three platform mounds plus three to eight other mounds, a town square or plaza, house remains with evidence of much rebuilding and relocation of successive structures, burials in a wide variety of position and location, and evidence of agriculture and extensive exploitation of the rich floral and faunal food resources. Located on the second terrace of a wide Ohio River floodplain and only a short distance from the river, the Angel site was in the environmental setting preferred by the Mississippian populations.

While this site was intensively excavated for many years (Black 1967), only about one-eighth of the total area delimited by the stockade was uncovered. The major stockade line was about a mile long and included 51 bastions placed at regular intervals. Approximately 4,500 stockade posts were set in a trench four feet and more deep and the stockade was plastered with daub. Between 90 and 100 habitation areas were enclosed within the fortified area. The rectangular houses of the village averaged about 25 feet square and were placed in excavated shallow pits, with wall trenches prepared to receive the upright posts for the wattle-and-daub walls. Some of the walls were painted with red, black, and blue-gray pigments. The houses were oriented with the corners pointing to the cardinal points of the compass. While it is possible that contemporary houses were aligned in "streets" and in groups representing social units within the village, such an alignment was not recognized by the excavators. It is estimated that about 200 houses were occupied at the same time. Assuming five individuals to a house, an estimated population of 1,000 would be reasonable.

Mound A is an excellent example of a multilevel platform structure with a conical offset near the southeast corner. It is 644 feet long, originally about 350 feet wide, and 28 feet high, with the conical offset projecting 14 feet above the upper terrace. This terrace is 248 feet long and about 120 feet wide. The magnetic bearing of the long axis is N 22°E. The second largest mound is Mound F, which has a similar orientation and runs 235 feet in a north-south direction, 239 feet east-west, and is 13 feet high. Mound E is also 13 feet high, but only 160 feet in an east-west line and 140 feet from north to south. The flat top of this structure measures about 45 by 40 feet. The upper part, or secondary mantle, covers a primary mound some five feet high, which formed the substructure for a rectangular building 90 feet long and 44 feet wide with double wall trenches and an orientation 20-22° east of north. Along the interior of the four walls was a clay banquette that served as a bench and was worn glossy from use. A small earth ramp on the southern half of the east mound flank leads to the structure that Black (1967) regarded as the town "temple." The town square or plaza is believed to be an area 420 feet long, east to west, and 160 wide, north to south located between Mound A on the east, Mound C on the north, and Mound F on the west.

Burials at the Angel site were flesh inhumations in an extended position or in varieties of flexed positions. Some were carefully buried while others were interred in an apparently haphazard manner. Some infants were buried in the floors of houses. Some bundle burials and cremations were uncovered. Imperishable grave goods were rarely placed with the dead. None of the 300 or so burials contained grave goods of the Southeastern Ceremonial complex. Burial orientation was not consistent but there was some preference for a northwest to southeast alignment.

The site was occupied for between 200 and 400 years in the period from about A.D. 1200 to 1600. It is difficult to be more precise. There is now no evidence of the gradual development of the Angel society in the immediate area and it is presumed that the group moved into the area from western Kentucky. All the material remains and the settlement patterns support the view that the closest cultural connections of the Angel site are to the Kincaid site in southern Illinois and to related sites in the western Kentucky area.

The ceramic industry is best known for the large amount of the distinctive Angel negative painted style on bottles and particularly on plates (fig. 2). Cooking jars normally have strap handles although there is a smaller, and perhaps earlier, series of jars with loop handles (fig. 3). A small proportion of the bowls is decorated with bird or human effigy heads. Although some of the bottles have a carafe neck, more commonly they have necks of the short wide mouth form. Salt pan vessels bear fabric impressions of at least 14 different patterns. The most common of these techniques are plaiting and twining, both plain and twilled. In addition to pottery, there are pottery trowels, disks and discoidals, earplugs and ear pins, beads, rattles, ladles, pendants, and elbow pipes of baked clay. A few clay effigy pipes have been recovered, including one human effigy of the "captive" type.

The lithic industry produced triangular arrow points (fig. 4), drills and perforators, chisels, adzes, spades and hoes (fig. 5), a few stone mortars, hammerstones and anvils, abraders and saws, stone earplugs, a few beads

after Black 1967, 2:figs. 532, 540.

Fig. 2. Bottle and rim sherds of broad rimmed plates with negative painted designs from Angel site, Vanderburgh Co., Ind. Height of bottle about 19.5 cm, sherds not to same scale.

Black 1967, 2:figs. 544-545.

Fig. 3. Pottery vessels from Angel site. Rim diameter of bottom about 20.7 cm, rest same scale.

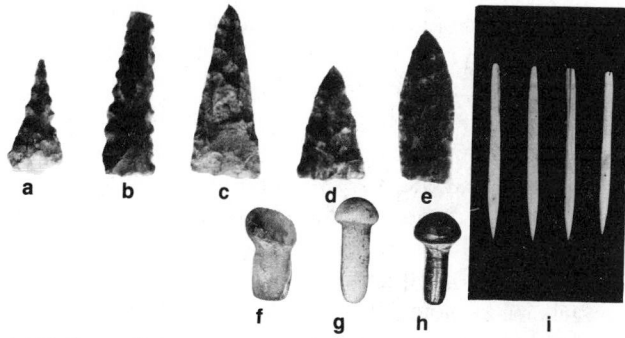

Ind. U., Glenn A. Black Laboratory of Archeol.

Fig. 4. Angel site artifacts. a-e, Triangular points; f-h, ear pins; i, bone pins possibly bound together into a comb used for weaving or as a "scratcher." Length of a about 2.9 cm, rest same scale. See also Black 1967, 1-2: figs. 102, 164, 483.

Ind. U., Glenn A. Black Laboratory of Archeol.

Fig. 5. Angel site artifacts. a-b, stone pipes; c, stone discoidal; d, perforated clay discoidal; e, adz; f-g, ground-stone celts; h, chert spade. Length of h 22.1 cm, rest same scale. See also Black 1967, 1: figs. 490, 493-494, 497, 502.

and pendants, discoidals, a few elbow pipes, and one catlinite disk pipe, which was probably an import. The most unusual specimen is a small fluorspar kneeling male human effigy figure found in the secondary mantle of

Mound F without association with other indications of human activity. The style is similar to other larger human effigy forms from the mid-South.

Deer antler tips were made into projectile points; and animal and bird bones were used for a variety of awl forms, pins, flakers, tubes, beads, rings, gaming pieces, and fishhooks. Only one flute and three beaming tools were recovered. Canine teeth were made into pendants. Relatively few shell hoes, spoons, beads, pendants, and gorgets were found. There was very little native copper, although some scrap copper fragments appeared in the village excavations.

Animal remains from the site reflect exploitation of a number of environments. Incomplete studies have identified 26 different species of mammals, 5 species of reptiles, 9 of fish, 32 of birds, 22 of mussels, and 15 of plants. The birds particularly reflect the location along the Ohio River. Habitat preferences of the animals reflect hunting activities in the deciduous forest, forest-edge prairie, and aquatic environments. The Angel site is an excellent example of a focal agricultural economy in Cleland's (1966:94-97) terms.

Black (1967, 2:546) reports that "the existence of many small Middle Mississippi sites within a radius of several miles of Angel is known." These are without platform mounds or known stockades, but they have a very similar material-culture complex. Subsidiary villages of this type have been identified approximately 25 miles east of Angel in Spencer County. One of these covers 8 to 10 acres and was apparently intensively occupied (Kellar 1967, 2:485).

It is not possible to connect these prehistoric people directly with a historic tribal group. A reasonable hypothesis is that the Angel society spoke a Muskogean language. It was the dominant and the most highly developed group in southwestern Indiana. Its social, political, and economic structure was similar to that of the tribes described by the Hernando de Soto expedition in the mid-South in the 1540s. For its size and temporal span there is very little concrete evidence of trade and exchange outside of its sustaining area.

Murphy Complex

The Murphy site (Moorehead 1906; Lilly 1937; W.R. Adams 1949) presents a marked contrast to the Angel complex. Located near the mouth of the Wabash River, it represents a late Mississippi complex that is normally found from the Cairo Lowland to the northeast Arkansas area and that existed for a short time in extreme southwestern Indiana. The pottery strongly suggests this relationship, the disk pipes are of a late prehistoric to early historic style in the Mississippi Valley, and the copper ornaments also apparently include forms believed to be late prehistoric. Pottery vessels were placed above or to the left of the head or at the shoulder of burials. Many of the bowls were accompanied by mussel-shell spoons.

Some of the infant and child burials contained clay rattles and small jars, bowls, and bottles. Although some bundle and skull interments were uncovered, most of the adult burials were extended. Of 163 burials, the heads of 39 were pointed south, 39 north, 18 east, and 26 west. Burials with copper ornaments contained no pottery; the heads of these burials lay primarily to the south. Burial goods probably indicated sex and status differentiation, but the excavation record is not adequate for any further elaboration on this point.

Collections from the village include a large number of flint end scrapers, presumably for working animal hides. Scrapers outnumber triangular arrow points and are unusual in southwestern Indiana. Ovate flint projectile points at the Murphy site are also unusual in the area. Three small mounds were located at the north end of the occupied area of the site.

Other Mississippian sites in Posey County, Indiana, have not yet been sufficiently described to ascertain their more precise affiliations, although they would probably be most closely associated with the Angel-Tolu complex in Kentucky and the Kincaid complex in southern Illinois. Prominent among these known sites are the Mann site and the Welborn Mound at Murphy's Landing (Lilly 1937:30-31, 48), which was 16½ feet high, 290 feet long and 180 feet wide at the base. Pottery from this village includes plain and fabric-impressed salt pans, plates, bowls, and jars. A few sherds with broad, shallow, incised lines on the shoulder are suggestive of Oneota vessels, but the primary affiliation of the site is with neighboring Ohio Valley Mississippian sites.

Vincennes Culture

A Mississippian complex that differs significantly from that of Angel or Murphy is located in the Wabash River valley from about 35 miles north of the Ohio River in the area of Terre Haute. The term Vincennes culture has been given to this distinctive assemblage by Winters (1963:84-99), who also identifies a possible early variant as the Etchison culture. A major center of the Vincennes culture is at the Otter Pond site on the T-1 terrace of the Embarrass River in Lawrence County, Illinois. It covers more than 60 acres and has 12 platform mounds on four sides of a central plaza. Smaller subsidiary villages and hamlets of five acres or less probably were associated with the major center. All phases of the activities of this complex are less elaborate than those found along the Ohio River to the south. The ceramic and lithic industries appear to have evidenced far less variety and elaboration.

Other Complexes

A variant of the lower Ohio Valley Mississippian occupations has been briefly described by Rolingson (1961) and may be referred to as the Kirtley phase or complex. It is

550

located in the Green River valley of Kentucky north of Wattern County. Excavations at the Kirtley site were not extensive enough to uncover the complete village. All 15 houses excavated were rectangular, most of them of wall-trench construction with a north-south orientation. The materials recovered were representative of Mississippian complexes but did not include nearly the variety or quality obtained from large Mississippi culture towns in the lower Ohio Valley. A number of sites in the Kirtley phase with Mississippian pottery may represent farming or fishing locations of people connected to the Kirtley site. This appears to be a regional variant of a small "tribal" group that would be an offshoot of the Kincaid-Tolu-Angel complex.

The Prather site excavated by Guernsey (1939) in Clark County, Indiana, has a single radiocarbon date of A.D. 1045 ± 70 (U Ga-308). This is an early Mississippian site with rectangular houses, central fireplaces, and other indications of settled village life. An extended male burial in a mound was accompanied by a small jar and a straight-neck bottle at the right foot, a circular shell gorget with large central opening at the neck, and a copper eagle(?) effigy on the skull. Other sites in the Jeffersonville area include Elrod, Newcomb, and Clark's Point, also excavated by Guernsey. Floyd County to the west, bordering the Ohio River, is reported to have had many sites with Mississippian materials (Lilly 1937: 100-101).

The Louisville area seems to have been the eastern border of Mississippian sites but no significant analysis of any of the material—which apparently represents important settlements—has been published.

Surveys and test excavations in Spencer County, Kentucky, along the Salt River have identified a number of small Mississippian sites (J. Granger, personal communications 1973, 1975) that probably belong to the complexes recovered by Guernsey in Indiana.

Oliver Complex

There are seven sites in the White River valley near Indianapolis, dating from A.D. 950 to 1250, that belong to the Oliver complex. Materials from these sites indicate ceramic connections to Fort Ancient, Fisher, Maples Mills, and Late Woodland groups from the upper Mississippi Valley to the Atlantic.

The one site completely excavated, the Bowen site, has a circular habitation area some 200 feet in diameter with pits and fireplaces around the periphery (Dorwin 1971). The central area is devoid of occupational debris and contains no features. Features are concentrated particularly in the north-central, northeast, and northwest activity areas of housing units. No structure outlines were identified.

The material culture remains include many tools, implements, and ornaments similar to the Fort Ancient

and Oneota cultures, although the variety of the several items is not so great as in Fort Ancient; and very little use was made of shell for ornaments and implements. Subsistence was based on a wide variety of animal, fish, mollusk, and bird remains supplemented by corn, hickory, and walnut. Twenty species of mammals were found, deer being by far the most common; turkey was the dominant bird of the 10 species recovered.

The physical type of the burials is identified by Robbins and Neumann (1972) as Ilinid. The 39 burials were primarily flexed. Twenty-six adult burials were recognized, of which 10 were males and 16 were females. The Oliver phase population was physically as well as culturally related to the populations of the northern Fort Ancient sites in Ohio and to the contemporary populations in the upper Illinois and Kankakee River valleys of northern Illinois. Their sites were occupied on a seasonal basis by groups of approximately 100 people.

Fort Ancient Complex

The late archeological complexes of the central Ohio Valley, known collectively as Fort Ancient, cover a time span from before A.D. 1000 to about A.D. 1700. The area covered is from western West Virginia to southeastern Indiana and from south-central Ohio to north-central and northeastern Kentucky (fig. 1). This is, of course, precisely the area occupied by the earlier Adena and Hopewell populations from about 500 B.C. to A.D. 400. While the intervening period between late Hopewell and early Fort Ancient is not well known, it is assumed that there was a significant continuity of populations and also gradual change of cultural behavior. The Fort Ancient complexes are regional groups that reflected the increasing importance of agricultural activities in much of the eastern United States and evidenced to an increasing degree the cultural changes that accompanied the growth of the more complex Mississippian societies in the southeast and the Mississippi Valley.

The term Fort Ancient was coined by Mills (1904:134-136) to distinguish a few sites in the Scioto and Miami drainages from the more advanced Hopewell culture sites. It has been known since the late 1930s that the Fort Ancient earthwork in Warren County, Ohio, was built by Hopewell people and that there were later occupations by Fort Ancient culture societies both within the Fort Ancient site and in the Anderson village site below it (Griffin 1943:216-222). Griffin identified four focuses or distinctive areas: one in the lower reaches of the Miami and Little Miami valleys called the Anderson focus, one primarily in the central Scioto Valley called the Baum focus, one in the area of the mouth of the Scioto called the Feurt focus, and one in southwestern Ohio and north-central Kentucky called the Madisonville focus.

Since that formulation was made the number of known sites that can be called Fort Ancient has greatly increased and the known time depth has doubled or tripled. This development requires that at some time in the future intensive regional studies be undertaken to ascertain the historical development within the several major river valleys flowing into the Ohio River and in the several segments of the Ohio Valley from Marietta on the east to about Madison, Indiana, on the west. It is clear that the use of the term Fort Ancient for the societies represented is an archeological construct and does not give a real unity to these societies. The same may also be said for the several divisions of Fort Ancient identified here as "phases."

Illustrations of Fort Ancient sites, burials, and materials are available (for example, Griffin 1943; Hanson 1966; Hooton 1920; Mayer-Oakes 1955; Mills 1904, 1906, 1907–1926, 3; H.I. Smith 1910).

Fort Ancient burial patterns had considerable diversity. Burial mounds are found in all phases and were located in the village sites. They are not present on all sites. Burials were placed in close proximity to individual houses as well as within houses. The bodies were most often placed in an extended position, but cremations and flexed and bundle burials are not uncommon. While single interments were the normal pattern, double burials and group burials were found at one or more sites in all the phases. Burials were made with stone slabs over the bodies, and in the Anderson and Madisonville phases stone-box graves were fairly common. At the Madisonville component a large area was essentially a cemetery. At the Buffalo site in West Virginia many burials were located around the edges of the central plaza. Other burials were scattered throughout and outside the village.

Few comprehensive studies of the association of grave goods exist for Fort Ancient sites. Hanson (1966) found that burials of subadults contained twice as many grave goods as those of adults. Most of the artifacts with burials were primarily decorative. Projectile points, bone needles, celts, and pipes were usually found with adult burials. There is no clear indication of status differentiation on the basis of burial position, location, or associated grave goods. Many burials were without recoverable grave goods. Mound burials may have included one distinct social group, for all ages and sexes are represented. Another social group may be represented in the village. The types of burial goods in mounds and in the villages are similar.

The number of burials varies according to the size of the village, its length of occupation, and the amount of excavation. At the Baum village site, 127 burials were recovered from 2 of the 10 site acres. At Madisonville the number of burials recorded by various excavators is 1,236 and the total number of burials was certainly more than 1,350 (Hooton 1920:20). While this is by far the largest number of burials from a Fort Ancient site, others, such as the Buffalo site in West Virginia, produced 560 burials (McMichael 1966).

Hooton estimated the population at Madisonville to have been from 450 to 500 over a period of 100 years. Since Madisonville was almost certainly occupied longer than that period of time, the resident population at any one time was probably significantly smaller.

One of the most important discoveries in Fort Ancient studies is that some of the major sites along the Ohio River, or close to it, were fortified. Another discovery is that many Fort Ancient sites had a central courtyard or plaza area. The Hardin Village in Greenup County, Kentucky, is believed to have had a stockade, and the Buffalo site in West Virginia had an oval palisade surrounding the site that measured 650 feet in length by 450 feet in width. The central courtyard, about 250 feet in diameter at Buffalo, had larger house structures—50 by 25 feet—around it and together they formed the public square. The Slone site on the southeastern periphery of Fort Ancient in Pike County, Kentucky, had three circular stockade lines, two of which had overlapping gateways (Dunnell, Hanson, and Hardesty 1972). The largest stockade was about 250 feet in diameter. The stockades enclosed a group of 12 houses, each rectangular with rounded corners, that surrounded a central courtyard. The Slone village pattern has close analogies to the Monongahela culture, whereas the Buffalo Village settlement is reminiscent of Middle Mississippi. It is reasonable to suggest that many Fort Ancient sites had a stockade.

The basic food supply was the well-known pattern of corn, beans, and squash plus the substantial addition of a wide variety of native nuts, seeds, berries, and other vegetal products. There was strong dependence upon deer (80% at some sites), elk, bear, and raccoon, and lesser emphasis on beaver, bobcat, mountain lion, and smaller animals. At some sites large numbers of mollusks were consumed. Turkey furnished most of the bird meat; at some sites the passenger pigeon was second in importance. The box turtle was the most common turtle. The most common fish were a number of varieties of suckers, freshwater drum, bass, and catfish.

One of the distinctive features of most of the Fort Ancient sites is a large and diverse bone industry (fig. 6). This is not true of the earlier Hopewellian and early Late Woodland sites in the Ohio Valley; however, this emphasis on the utilization of bone and antler for tools and ornaments is also found in cultural complexes contemporary with Fort Ancient. Antler tips were made into arrow and spear points, awls, knives, perforated phalanges for the cup-and-pin game, and pins and gorges. Turkey and other bird bones were shaped into awls, beads, fishhooks,

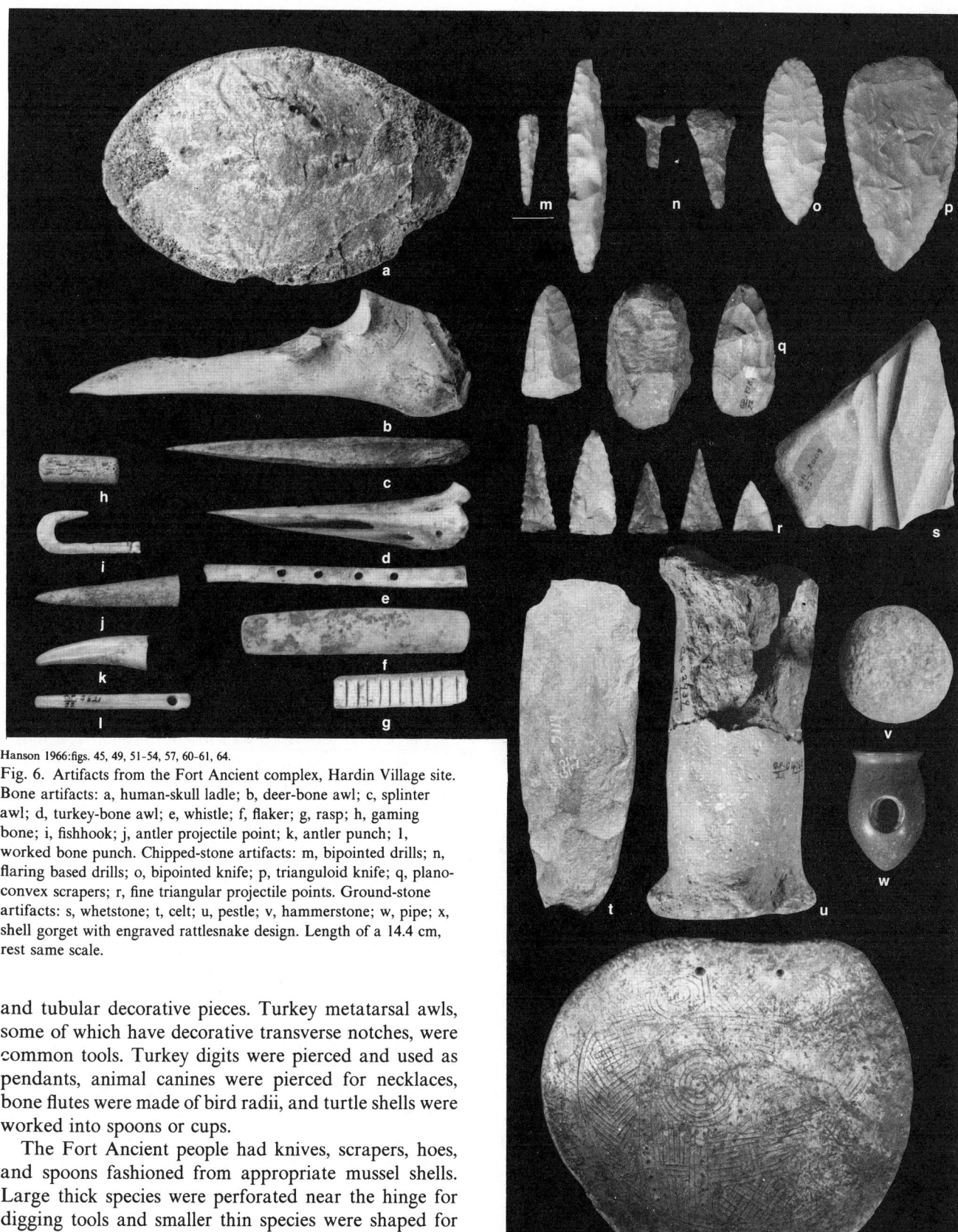

Hanson 1966:figs. 45, 49, 51-54, 57, 60-61, 64.
Fig. 6. Artifacts from the Fort Ancient complex, Hardin Village site. Bone artifacts: a, human-skull ladle; b, deer-bone awl; c, splinter awl; d, turkey-bone awl; e, whistle; f, flaker; g, rasp; h, gaming bone; i, fishhook; j, antler projectile point; k, antler punch; l, worked bone punch. Chipped-stone artifacts: m, bipointed drills; n, flaring based drills; o, bipointed knife; p, trianguloid knife; q, plano-convex scrapers; r, fine triangular projectile points. Ground-stone artifacts: s, whetstone; t, celt; u, pestle; v, hammerstone; w, pipe; x, shell gorget with engraved rattlesnake design. Length of a 14.4 cm, rest same scale.

and tubular decorative pieces. Turkey metatarsal awls, some of which have decorative transverse notches, were common tools. Turkey digits were pierced and used as pendants, animal canines were pierced for necklaces, bone flutes were made of bird radii, and turtle shells were worked into spoons or cups.

The Fort Ancient people had knives, scrapers, hoes, and spoons fashioned from appropriate mussel shells. Large thick species were perforated near the hinge for digging tools and smaller thin species were shaped for spoons, sometimes with a section cut to form a handle. Some shell disk and tubular beads were manufactured, and pendants and gorgets were also shaped. The gorgets

553

are primarily made from marine shells. The small circular and triangular forms and small whole-shell pendants and "hairpin" form were probably manufactured locally. A number of larger specialized gorgets—for instance, engraved rattlesnake and mask gorgets—may well have been traded from eastern Tennessee.

Chipped flint items include triangular arrow points and knives, a few stemmed and notched points, ovate and large ovate knives, celts, a variety of scrapers and choppers, and core scrapers. The primary heavy wood-working tool is an almost straight-sided, blunt poll celt. Some celts are made of slate. There are stone mortars or grinding slabs and biscuit-shaped mullers. Hammer-stones are round or disk-shaped with edges showing hammer marks. Whetstones are usually of sandstone including a few arrowshaft smoothers and some sandstone saws. Discoidals of the southeastern, chunky-stone style are found along the Ohio River from the Madisonville to the Clover phases.

Stone pipe forms are normally without a stem and are vase- or jar-shaped, ovoid, conoidal or rectanguloid. The next most common form is a short-stemmed stone pipe. Equal-armed pipes of stone or clay are most common in the southern phases of Fort Ancient.

Robbins and Neumann (1972) give a valuable assessment of the physical relationships among the inhabitants of the several phases and their relationships to non–Fort Ancient populations. They believe that a distinctive physical type called Ilinid is found in the two northern phases of Baum and Anderson and in the Feurt phase near the mouth of the Scioto River. Some Ilinid individuals are also found either at early sites within the Madisonville phase or in early levels of long-occupied sites of the Madisonville phases in southwestern Ohio. The Fort Ancient Ilinid populations are related to those in central Indiana at the Bowen site (Dorwin 1971:294-296) and to at least some of the population of the Fisher phase in the Chicago area. The second major physical group in Fort Ancient sites is identified by Robbins and Neumann under the term Muskogid; this type is by far the dominant one in sites of the Madisonville phase, although significant subtypes will eventually be recognized. Such subtypes may well conform to archeological units within what is now called the Madisonville phase. The Muskogid type is associated primarily with Middle Mississippi populations from Spoon River in central Illinois into the Southeast. The manner in which the apparent physical diversity within Fort Ancient took place is not now fully understood and is still being studied.

Baum Phase

The Baum phase, located near Chillicothe, Ohio, is known from excavations at the Baum, Gartner, Graham, Blain, Higby, Kramer A, and Caldwell's Bluff sites (Prufer and Shane 1970:240-243). It is possible that the

Voss site, in Franklin County to the north, should also be included in this phase (Baby, Potter, and Mays 1966). An early related complex in the Hocking Valley to the east has been named the Baldwin phase by Prufer and Shane, who also have proposed a Brush Creek phase at Serpent Mound in Adams County, Ohio. Sites of the Baum phase may have been in existence as early as A.D. 1000 and may have lasted until the sixteenth century, although the number of sites and the evidence of occupation does not seem to indicate such a long span of time. The artifacts that were manufactured or obtained by the people of this phase do not include items suggestive of a date in the sixteenth and certainly not into the seventeenth century.

The villages covered between 3 and 10 acres and none of them has been sufficiently excavated to obtain a precise idea of the internal structure. The Baum site is the only one in the phase to have a pyramidal mound with two successive floors on which structures were placed. The upper structure was circular and measured 26 feet in diameter. The lower structure was circular and 36 feet in diameter. All the 17 burials in the mound were within these two structures. There is evidence for an open central courtyard at the Blain Village site, which was associated with a burial mound on one side. The Gartner site may have had a similar arrangement. The "ceremonial" structure in the village at Baum is an ovoid one, 21 feet long and 12 feet wide. The usual village structure is circular and between 10 and 12 feet in diameter. Mills (1906) uncovered 40 such small, single-family houses in the two acres he excavated and reports that the village covered 10 acres. This could mean a population as large as 1,000, but all of the area was not available for houses because of the mound and presumed courtyard and there is evidence of some rebuilding. The 234 refuse pits also suggest continuing occupation over a period of time.

A population estimate for the larger Baum phase village would be from about 200 to 400 people and for the smaller sites less than half that number. The villages were probably occupied most of the year and there is no available evidence suggesting seasonal sites or loci of specialized procurement activities.

The Baum phase ceramic complex is clearly derived from Late Woodland. The vessel forms are almost always a simple jar with almost vertical to slightly flaring rim and subconoidal to rounded bases (fig. 7) (Griffin 1943:pls. I-XII; D.H. McKenzie 1967:pls. 1-6A). The percentage of shell for tempering material ranges from 2 percent of the vessels at some components to almost 25 percent at late Baum phase sites. Most of the vessels are grit-tempered and cordmarked. A variety of lugs ranging from rim strips and nodes to semicircular forms decorates the upper rim and rim-lip area. A somewhat thickened ovoid strap handle was also used that differs markedly from the normal Madisonville phase handles. The most common decoration is a two- or three-line curvilinear guilloche made with an incising tool similar in shape to

554

a, Dept. of Anthr., Smithsonian; b, U. of Mich., C.C. Anderson Coll., negative 3995; c, Amer. Mus. of Nat. Hist., New York; d, Peabody Mus., Harvard U.

Fig. 7. Pottery vessels from the Fort Ancient complex. a, Cordmarked vessel from Baum phase; b, incised jar from Anderson phase; c, plain vessel from Madisonville phase; d, Fox Farm site cordmarked bowl from Madisonville phase. Lip diameter of a 24.2 cm, rest same scale. See also Griffin 1943:pls. V, XLIX, LXII, LXVIII.

an antler tip. There are a few line-filled triangle designs on the rim. Many of these decorative attempts are of poor quality. There are very few bowls, no salt pans or plates, and no bottles.

Anderson Phase

For years no information was available on the house forms of the Anderson phase or even on the settlement patterns of the villages or the societies of which the villages were a part; then, in 1969, the Incinerator site at Dayton, Ohio (Allman 1968), produced a house pattern (John C. Allman, personal communication 1969). This structure is very nearly square, 26 feet on each side. The posts are small and closely spaced. No burnt daub was found. The entrance is on the south side. It is possible the house was rebuilt once and the same burnt clay fireplace, just east of the center, seems to have been used for both houses. Three burials were found in the house: two burials, one extended and one flexed, were under limestone slabs; the third burial was covered by one log and had three charred logs alongside it. It is possible that the house form of early Anderson phase villages was circular, like those of the Baum phase, and that a shift took place to rectangular structures. Uncovered at the Incinerator site was an oval stockade 400 feet long on a north-south line. There is a central courtyard surrounded by a burial zone, then a larger ring of trash pits, and finally a ring of houses (J.M. Heilman, personal communications 1973, 1975).

In terms of the vessel shape the Anderson phase pottery is somewhat similar to the Baum phase: the normal vessel is a simple jar with straight to slightly flaring rim and a subconoidal to rounded base (fig. 7). Most of the pottery is grit-tempered and cordmarked, but

shell tempering becomes more common from typologically early sites such as Erp (Allman 1960) to later sites within the phase. The rim decoration consists primarily of line-filled triangles. Two- to four-line guilloche patterns are the second most common design. A distinctive feature is a thickened rim strip that has short oblique gashes. There are relatively few lug handles compared to Baum and more strap handles, which are usually ovoid in cross-section and trianguloid in shape (Griffin 1943:pls. XXXVI-XLIII). The pottery of this phase in basic vessel form, temper, added rim strips, and lack of variation in shape is clearly a regional variant of the Late Woodland period and of contemporary ceramic practices from the Atlantic to the Midwest.

A number of unusual artifacts were found in the Anderson phase. The large bipointed flint ceremonial knife and the small excised equal-armed cross shell gorget from the Taylor site are both similar to Mississippian forms in Tennessee. The large clay elbow pipe from the Taylor site with fine punctate decoration was probably made in a Monongahela site in southwestern Pennsylvania. At the Stokes component two pottery fragments said to be from the site are from vessels almost certainly made in eastern Tennessee (Griffin 1943:pl. LIX).

Feurt Phase

The Feurt phase, located near the mouth of the Scioto River in Ohio and adjacent Kentucky, is perhaps the least known of the Fort Ancient phases. Most of the more than 400 Feurt site burials were flexed and not a single pottery vessel was with a burial. Burials were placed either in three mounds or in the village, which covered about five acres. While Mills (1907-1926, 3) refers to "tepee" sites, he does not describe their shape or size. The Feurt site is unusual because of the number of triangular arrows with serrated edges, large decorated bone awls, stone conoidal pipes sculptured into human effigy heads, a black slate tablet with an engraved design of a horned serpent, and extensive use of cannel coal for ornaments and implements.

The pottery complex at Feurt is unusual. It has a strong element of Baum phase ceramics; other vessels are Madisonville phase types; there is a distinctive incised complex called Feurt Incised and there are other unusual features (Griffin 1943:pls. XX–XXIV). The Fullerton Field site also has a mixture of Baum phase, Fox Farm, and Madisonville. The depth of the village occupation at Feurt suggests that the site was occupied over a considerable time period, and there is some probability that the early part of the Feurt phase was very similar to the Baum phase.

Madisonville and Clover Phases

It is assumed that sufficient differences between sites in the western and eastern ends of the continuum along the Ohio River will eventually be recognized, and these will establish a Madisonville phase on the west and a Clover phase on the east. Certainly, the old Madisonville focus of Griffin (1943) is too encompassing.

House structures have not been identified at the majority of sites of the Madisonville phase. This is probably more because of the nature of the excavations than because the inhabitants did not live in houses. At Turpin at least one subrectangular house, 20 by 18 feet, is on record (Griffin 1943:120), and Oehler (1950:2) reported daub fragments from the site. In marked contrast to this house form are the eight known rectangular structures from Hardin, which ranged in length from 51 to 70 feet and were 18 to 30 feet wide. They were oriented more or less east and west with a door about four feet wide on the east end. There was no daub present so that the walls are believed to have been bark or thatch.

The Buffalo site produced large rectangular houses 25 by 50 feet, with three 15-inch diameter center poles and a large rectangular fireplace between two of these. These houses were around the central plaza. Two outer rows of rectangular houses about 18 by 25 feet were placed end to end three to four feet apart and the rows were 15 to 20 feet apart. These houses had circular fire basins and two center posts. The Buffalo houses were not of wattle-and-daub construction (McMichael 1963, 1964, 1966).

The pottery complex associated with the Madisonville phase and the Clover phase, particularly in its late period, is similar to the ceramics of Middle Mississippi. It is shell-tempered, many of the jars have handles, and bowls and salt pans are common. In contrast is the absence of the bottle form, plates, and either red filming or negative painting. In early Madisonville times—for instance, at the Sand Ridge site in Hamilton County, Ohio, and in Indiana University excavations in the 1970s at Site 19 in Dearborn County, Indiana (Black 1934:192–194)—there are indications in the vessel shape, added and decorated rim strip, and relative lack of incised decoration of a closer ceramic connection to the Anderson phase. There also are vessels at Madisonville that suggest this association with the Anderson phase. The "typical" Madisonville jar has a slightly flaring rim, four thin strap handles, smooth rim, and a cordmarked or plain body (fig. 7). It does not have an added rim strip. Many Madisonville bowls are cordmarked and there are very few effigy-head bowls. This helps to distinguish the phase from the normal Middle Mississippi assemblage. At many Madisonville phase sites there are a small number of grooved-paddle and check-stamp vessels. A distinctive ceramic form is the pestle, which is either cordmarked or plain (Mayer-Oakes 1955:pl. 108). Pottery disks, both plain and perforated, are a common feature of Madisonville and Clover phase sites.

A striking feature of cultural connections of late Madisonville-Clover sites is the appearance of shell gorgets of the circular engraved and spider types and the mask gorget form. The shell gorgets probably date around A.D. 1400–1500, while the mask seems to be later and is found on sites that are late prehistoric or early historic. They were probably made in eastern Tennessee. Sites along the Ohio River also had tablets of slate or cannel coal or pebbles with engraved designs. Some of these are suggestive of Middle Mississippi art forms. At Madisonville, an antler comb had an engraved rattlesnake design.

Pipe forms in the Madisonville phase also have an association with Middle Mississippi, for frog and human effigy pipes have been recovered from some of the sites (Oehler 1950:pls. 21, 28–29).

A few Madisonville phase sites—Madisonville and Hardin—have European trade goods and items made from European metal. Clover phase sites with historic material include Buffalo and Rolf Lee (Youse 1965). Representative trade items include glass beads. Brass was made into tubular beads, flattened beads, coils, bracelets, and a cross. Copper, which may or may not be European, was made into tubes, tubular beads, coils, a cross, and a bell. Madisonville had an iron adz deep in a cache pit, an iron bead, and an iron sword guard from a woman's grave.

Relationship to Historic Tribal Groups

In spite of the presence of European trade goods at certain sites, there are no precise identifications of specific villages at an identifiable geographic location occupied by an identifiable Indian group. While a very few Fort Ancient sites do come up into the early historic period from about A.D. 1650 to 1700, the Indian tribe that occupied those sites cannot be certainly named. There are no sites having Fort Ancient material for which it can be proved that that material was made and utilized after A.D.

1700 or slightly earlier. Most students trying to identify the tribal affiliations of Fort Ancient have concluded that the Shawnee are the most likely tribe known in the early historic period to have occupied the area. This association has not been, and may never be, firmly established. It is possible, perhaps even probable, that some Fort Ancient sites were occupied by Shawnee. Other sites may not have been and the farther back in time that a specific site existed, the more dubious a specific tribal identification becomes. Some early Shawnee bands may not have participated in the Fort Ancient complex.

While it is reasonable to think of the total Fort Ancient complex in terms of recognition of temporal differences such as the classic Early, Middle, and Late three-fold division, it is most difficult to make them. The end of the Late period is relatively secure since it can be defined as the association of European goods of the latter half of the seventeenth century with a Fort Ancient complex, usually in burial or house-floor association. The beginning of a "late" period cannot be established, nor can any other beginning or ending date of an "early" or "middle" period. An indefinite and highly arbitrary "beginning" is when some of the characteristic ceramic designs and other attributes of later Fort Ancient pottery first begin to appear. This would seem to be, on the basis of radiocarbon dates, from one site about A.D. 900–1000 (Prufer and Shane 1970); but most of the occupation is probably closer to A.D. 1200. The Voss site has a wide range of dates from the A.D. 970 cited by Prufer and Shane to A.D. 1500 (Crane and Griffin 1972:202). Actually the 12 dates given by Crane and Griffin range from A.D. 920 to A.D. 1500, a range not unexpected from such a site. One or two dates from a fair-sized prehistoric site can give a very misleading temporal estimate. The pitifully few dates from Fort Ancient sites and the almost complete lack of stratigraphic data or carefully compared site or site segment complexes make significant temporal subdivisions of Fort Ancient an interesting game, but the results cannot be definitive.

Monongahela Woodland Complex

Monongahela Woodland is used to refer to the prehistoric sequence in the contiguous area of northern West Virginia, southwestern Pennsylvania, and eastern Ohio (Dragoo 1955). The time span is estimated to be about 600 years—from A.D. 1000 into the seventeenth century. The drainage area of the Monongahela and the Youghiogheny rivers is the heart area of Monongahela Woodland (fig. 1). The initial recognition and description took place just before and after the 1930s with the work of Robert M. Engberg (1930, 1931), George S. Fisher (1931), Mary Butler (1939), and Francis M. Cresson (1942). Archeologists of that time regarded Monongahela as of rather short duration close to the early historic period. A summary of the area by Karl Schmitt (1952)

pointed out the possibility of developing a comparative chronology and stated that there was no evidence that Monongahela extended into the historic period. Attempts have been made to connect this archeological complex with historic tribes such as the Shawnee or Erie but these have not been successful (Weslager 1948a; Hoffman 1964) because no known Indian sites of the appropriate time can be shown to have been Monongahela.

Monongahela sites are located on high bottomland near major streams, on saddles between hills, and on hill tops, sometimes a considerable distance from water sources. The majority of the excavated sites have had an oval to circular stockade pattern surrounding a series of usually circular house patterns placed near the stockade and leaving a central courtyard. Village size varied from less than an acre to about five acres. Representative stockade diameters vary from 190 feet by 194 feet to 480 feet by 360 feet, and one circular pattern was 450 feet in diameter. Stockades are present irrespective of the location on hills or on terraces, depending primarily on a level area large enough for the village. The circular houses are normally about 20 feet in diameter with a central fireplace. Saplings were placed in the ground from one to two feet apart and bent into the center where they were tied. They were almost certainly bark-covered with a roof hole to let out smoke and provide a draft. Small post-hole patterns within the house may represent low sleeping platforms placed near the inner wall. Some refuse pits are within houses. Other pits were close to the outer wall, were enclosed within a small structure, and had access from the house. Many refuse pits were in the village area between houses. At some sites, where an interior ditch had been dug along the stockade, presumably to provide dirt for its support, the ditch was filled with refuse. Some refuse pits were first used for food storage of corn and nuts and had a bark-and-grass floor.

Some sites were occupied only a short time, as there is no evidence of rebuilding and a relatively small amount of village refuse. Others show much reconstruction and areas of village debris from one to two feet deep. At the Ryan site in Westmoreland County, Pennsylvania, Richard George (personal communication 1973) found a structure 30 feet in diameter on the east side of the village. The doorway of this "Big House" faced east. Within it was the post-hole pattern of a small structure that may have been a sweathouse, as in the Delaware Big House. There was one rectangular structure at the Ryan site. At the Montague site M. Butler (1939) reported that most of the houses were rectangular. These varied in size from 16 feet by 8 feet to 30 feet by 20 feet. This site was dug under the Works Progress Administration in the 1930s. The large number of rectangular houses is still unusual for a Monongahela site.

The village size averaged about 25 single-family houses, which would accommodate from 75 to 150 people. Burials of adults were most commonly flexed in pits, and burial goods with adults are usually ornamental, perhaps associated with clothing rather than utilitarian. Infant and child burials were both flexed and extended, and juvenile burials at one group of sites represented 50 percent of the total burials. Consistent burial orientation toward the east has been reported for at least one site, but this is not common. There is no indication of significant status recognition in terms of burial goods.

The subsistence pattern of the Monongahela people is one of agriculture and mixed hunting and gathering. Some villages, such as the Campbell site in Fayette County, Pennsylvania, located about two miles from the Monongahela River, had very little deer remains but a large number of fish scales and bones and some corn remains (William Johnson, personal communication 1973). Most sites have a diversified hunting pattern as represented at the atypical McKees Rocks Village in the excellent interpretation of Lang (1968).

The corn from McKees Rock Village has been described by V.H. Jones (1968) as the eight-rowed Eastern complex corn, which is the predominant type in the late prehistoric period in the eastern United States. There are very few references to other vegetal materials. Beans were tentatively identified at the Boyle site, in Washington County, Pennsylvania, by Nale (1963:187) and squash or a similar plant at the Hughes site in Ohio County, West Virginia, by Dunnell (1962:6). It is likely that more careful attention to refuse-pit contents will produce evidence of additional plant materials exploited by Monongahela people.

A considerable variety of stone and bone tools are recovered from the villages (fig. 8). Most common are splintered bone awls from animal and bird leg and wing bone. There are also bone or antler tubes, gouges, spatulas, fishhooks, chisels, hoes, projectile points, drifts, whistles, pendants, beads, scrapers, turtle carapace cups, beaver incisor chisels, perforated canine teeth, and others. Many of these are described in site reports by Buker (1968, 1970).

The predominant projectile point is triangular, with a number of variations in length and width at different sites. Some small-stemmed and corner-notched points may be associated with early phases of Monongahela. Knife forms are large triangular or leaf-shaped. Flint scrapers were made from various flakes without a consistent pattern. Slender straight drills, expanded base drills, and perforators and gravers are a part of the flint tool complex. Flint was obtainable in the river gravels near most of the sites, but chert sources such as the Chartiers outcrop were also exploited (Nale 1963:172).

Ground-stone tools include adzes and celts of a rectanguloid form with battered poll ends, hammerstones, whetstones, and hematite sections. Discoidals and cannel coal pendants are found in sites in or close to the Ohio Valley and perhaps from the later sites in that area. Very few tools or ornaments were made from mussel shell.

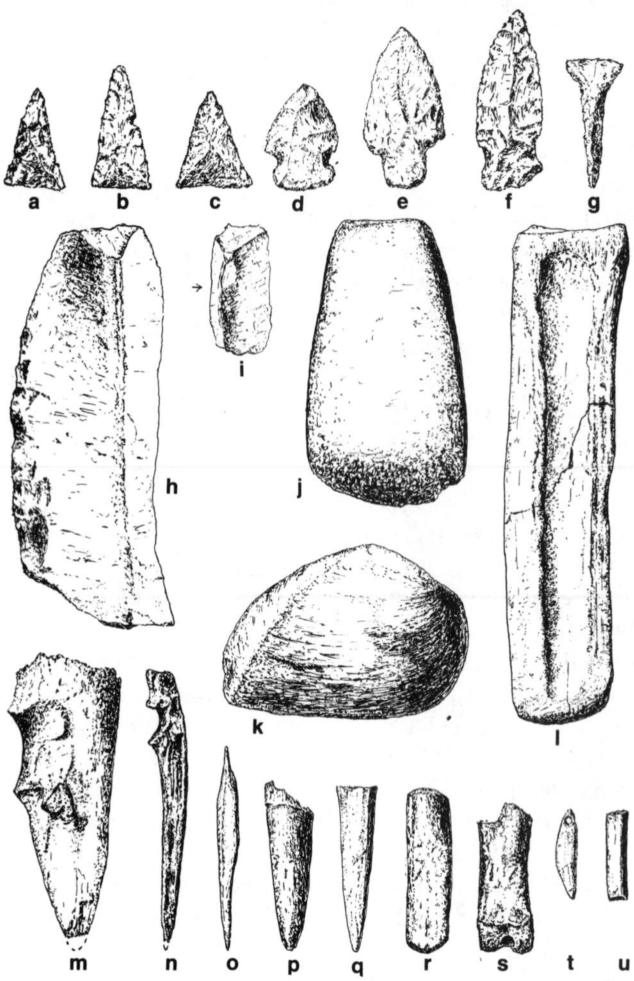

drawings by William E. Buker.

Fig. 8. Artifacts from Kelso site, Washington Co., Pa., a hilltop "L-shaped" village in the Drew phase of Monongahela culture, about A.D. 1300–1400. Lithics: a–c, triangular points; d, notched point; e–f, stemmed point and knife; g, expanded base drill; h, limestone knife; i, scraper; j, celt. Shell: k, mussel shell scraper. Bone and antler: l, gouge; m, deer ulna awl; n, awl; o, double-pointed awl; p, scored antler; q, antler projectile point; r, antler draft; s, drilled deer phalanx; t, drilled canine; u, bird-bone tube. Length of j 7.7 cm, rest same scale.

Shell hoes, scrapers, and pendants also seem to be found primarily in western Monongahela sites in or near the Ohio Valley although some from *Busycon* shells from the east coast are also known. Beads from *Marginella apicina* were most often found with children.

One of the most common and distinctive characteristics of Monongahela is the pipe forms, which range from vasiform stone examples to elbow clay pipes. The normal pipe of the Montague and related sites in the Somerset County, Pennsylvania, area is an obtuse-angle clay form that sometimes had an incised design but more commonly was impressed with fine cord or left plain without decoration. A rigorous analysis of pipe forms and decoration would surely indicate regional and temporal variations within what has been called the Monongahela Woodland complex.

The ceramic complex from Monongahela sites offers perhaps the best opportunity for eventual recognition of regional enclaves, their gradual change through time, and the interregional relationships. By far the most common vessel form is a simple jar with a rounded base and a gradually in-sloping shoulder area. The rim area may be vertical to slightly flaring (fig. 9), or markedly flaring, or collared. The vessel surface is plain or cordmarked. The lip of the vessel may be plain or notched and is often raised above the location of rim lugs. There are a few loop handles. The most common decorative technique is incising on a plain or cordmarked rim in line-filled triangles or in groups of oblique lines. Cordwrapped stick impressions and punctates were also used. Added outer horizontal rim strips or otherwise thickened rims were notched or punched on the lower edge of the strip. Some sites in northern West Virginia have a grooved-paddle surface but such treatment is not common at most Monongahela sites. One wide-mouth, short-neck bottle form is attributed to a Washington County, Pennsylvania, site (Mayer-Oakes 1955:120) but this is so unusual

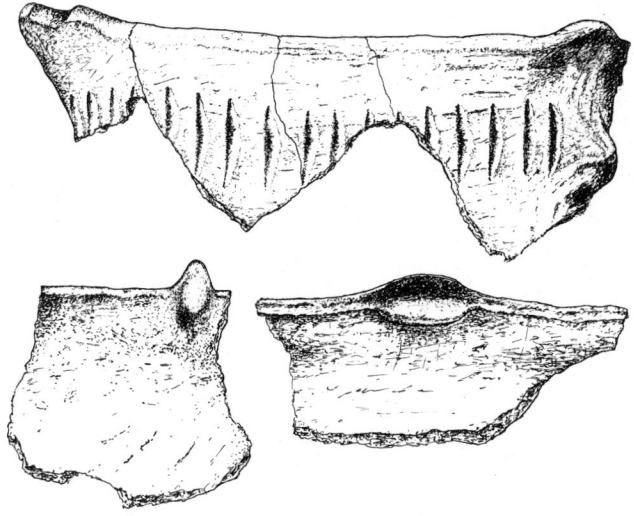

drawings by William E. Buker.

Fig. 9. Shell-tempered pottery rims from Kelso site. Diameter of top 21 cm, rest same scale.

that it must be regarded as a trade vessel of some kind, as would be the case with rare examples of the Fort Ancient curvilinear guilloche design in the upper Ohio Valley.

It is estimated that there are at least 500 components of Monongahela Woodland, only very few of which have a small amount of European trade goods. There are indications in the ceramics and lithic materials of a development from earlier Late Woodland populations in the Monongahela area. Through time there is evidence of the participation by Monongahela people in the increasing dependence on agriculture that was common to many of the resident groups in the eastern United States. Their fortified village pattern resembles that of other societies from New York and New England into Virginia and the Carolinas. They also acquired the bow and arrow, a weapon that may have been as much an impetus to the construction of fortified villages as was the increased interest in defending their villages and agricultural fields.

While the few published reports on Monongahela are from villages, these people also occupied rockshelters and there is some evidence of small farmsteads with storage structures. Functional differences among these several locations have not been documented but should exist. Population size of the village would be from less than 100 to between 100 to 150. If the estimated number of villages is evenly spread over some 500 to 600 years it is certain that population density was not at all comparable to the Fort Ancient occupation of the Ohio Valley, or the Mississippi populations of the Southeast, or the Iroquois in New York, or the coastal and Piedmont tribes of the Middle Atlantic states.

Some of the archeologists studying Monongahela Woodland are so impressed with the variation among regions and through time that they are questioning the validity of Monongahela as a meaningful cultural name; however, most of the archeological features described above are not found together in other areas, nor is there found in areas surrouding the Monongahela concentration cultural material that could be confused with it. Such a recognition of some unity within Monongahela does not imply political control for the area or even social or linguistic unity.

559

Late Prehistory of the Illinois Area

MELVIN L. FOWLER AND ROBERT L. HALL

The overwhelming fact of the prehistory of the Illinois area after A.D. 1000 is the dominance of the Cahokia site. No other site in the eastern United States influenced such a wide area as did Cahokia between the eleventh and fourteenth centuries. No other prehistoric peoples in the present area of the United States achieved such a complex social-political organization or developed such a large community as their center. To understand this development one must look back into the prehistory of the Midwest to the period a few centuries before A.D. 1000.

Late Woodland

The period of about A.D. 400 to 900 in this area is one of a shift away from the dominance of the Hopewellian integration to the reassertion, emergence, or arrival of regionally distinct cultural entities. These groups undoubtedly interacted with one another, but the material expression of this interaction and of the social organization of the groups individually was not of a conspicuous or dramatic nature. The phrase "post-Hopewellian decline" so often used to describe this period masks its importance in prehistory. The bow and arrow was introduced into Illinois by A.D. 700 and replaced the atlatl and throwing spear as a principal weapon. Maize agriculture, present but of unknown importance during Hopewellian times, emerged by A.D. 900 to be a staple in the economic base of the Mississippian period. There is the unproved but likely possibility that the era of A.D. 400 to 900 figures importantly in the emergence of effective maize agriculture in Illinois. There are also no real grounds for saying that population totals declined following the Hopewellian episode in Illinois. The post-Hopewellian era will probably be shown to have been a period of societal reorganization and redistribution. There was certainly no complete replacement of the Hopewellian populations in Illinois because there are many examples of continuity from Hopewellian into post-Hopewellian times. One of the academic problems of prehistory in Illinois is where to draw the boundary separating Middle Woodland from Late Woodland and Late Woodland from Mississippian.

In the lower Illinois Valley Struever (1968a) sees a break at about A.D. 400, which he uses to divide the Pike-Hopewellian phase of the Middle Woodland period from the succeeding White Hall phase, which initiates the Late Woodland period in that part of Illinois. Struever compares White Hall in time and cultural position to what is known as Weaver to the north in the central Illinois Valley. However, in its own area Weaver was created as a Late Middle Woodland (Griffin 1952a) or Late Hopewell (Wray 1952; Wray and MacNeish 1961) cultural unit. Dates of A.D. 450 ± 120 (M-1685) for the Scovill site in Fulton County and A.D. 625 ± 200 (M-440) and A.D. 675 ± 200 (M-441) for the Weaver levels at the Steuben site help to place Weaver in the central Illinois Valley sequence (fig. 1) (Crane and Griffin 1964:6; Morse 1963;

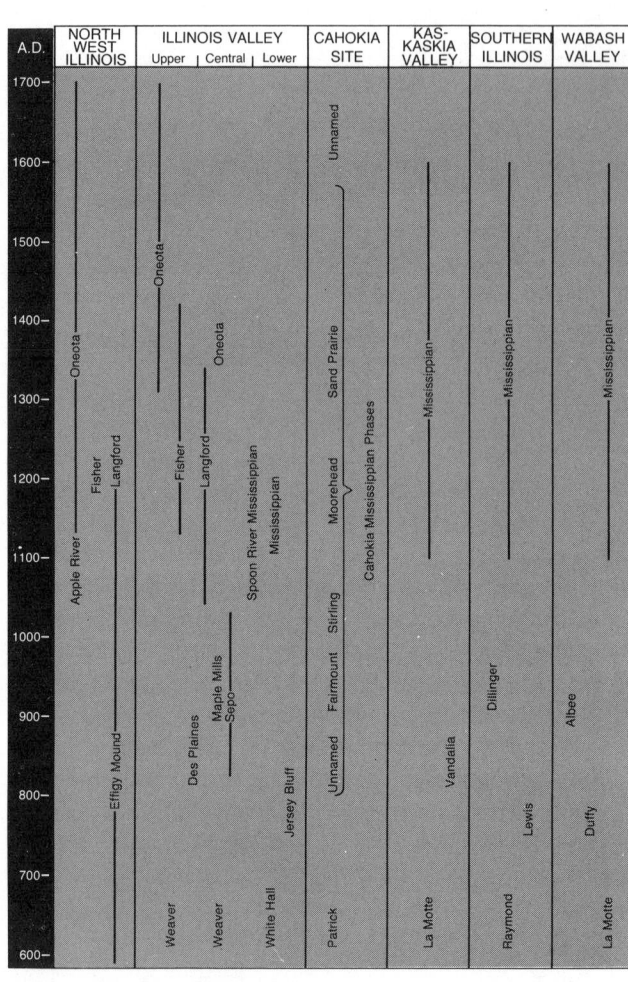

Fig. 1. Suggested relationships of archeological complexes in the Illinois area, A.D. 600–1700.

Munson, Parmalee, and Yarnell 1971). In the Wabash Valley Winters (1967) continues Middle Woodland through the period of the La Motte culture or until about A.D. 900 to 1000, in part because of an apparent continuity of development from the antecedent Allison culture of A.D. 1 to 400. This is obviously a problem of archeological systematics. White Hall, Weaver, and La Motte probably equate in their relationship to the Hopewellian climax, as does early Effigy Mound at the extreme opposite, northern end of Illinois. By and large no culture or phase with the bow and arrow as a principal weapon is considered Middle Woodland; no culture or phase with evidence of participation in the Hopewellian interaction is considered Late Woodland. This leaves a span of several centuries from A.D. 400 to 800 (the date varying with locality) that are in this sense in limbo, considered Middle Woodland or Late Woodland, sometimes for arbitrary reasons of the investigator.

The earliest radiocarbon evidence in Illinois for the bow and arrow comes from Klunk Mound 8 in Calhoun County with a date of A.D. 600 ± 110 (M-1355; Crane and Griffin 1964:6) and from the Scovill site with its date of A.D. 450 ± 120. "The use of the bow and arrow may have made available new sources of food and new methods of warfare which helped to break up the old [Hopewellian] order" (Wray and MacNeish 1961:68).

For more southerly Illinois a somewhat similar effect may have been produced by effective corn agriculture alone or in conjunction with new weapons technology. The first broadly represented and defined unit of Late Woodland archeology in southern Illinois is the Bluff Aspect (Mac-Neish 1944; Maxwell 1951) embracing the Lewis, Raymond, and Jersey Bluff focuses (fig. 2). The easily worked, well-drained loessial bluff-top soils of the Illinois and Mississippi rivers and many lesser streams, thinly sodded beneath a hardwood forest cover that could be eliminated by girdling, may have contributed considerably to the effectiveness of corn agriculture and the apparent dispersal of Woodland populations in the post-Hopewellian era. Population pressures in societies well adapted to a "broad spectrum" (K.V. Flannery 1968) resource exploitation system in the riverine lowlands areas may have forced groups into these upland and minor tributary areas (see Farnsworth 1973:25ff.).

In the central Illinois Valley this Middle to Late Woodland transition is represented by the Weaver phase of the Havana tradition in the period around A.D. 500 and by the Sepo phase A.D. 900. Weaver is represented by primarily conoidal, grit-tempered pottery vessels. The surface is often smoothed over cordmarked, and varieties of lip notching as decorative techniques are present. The trend suggested by the Sepo phase is that globular bodies

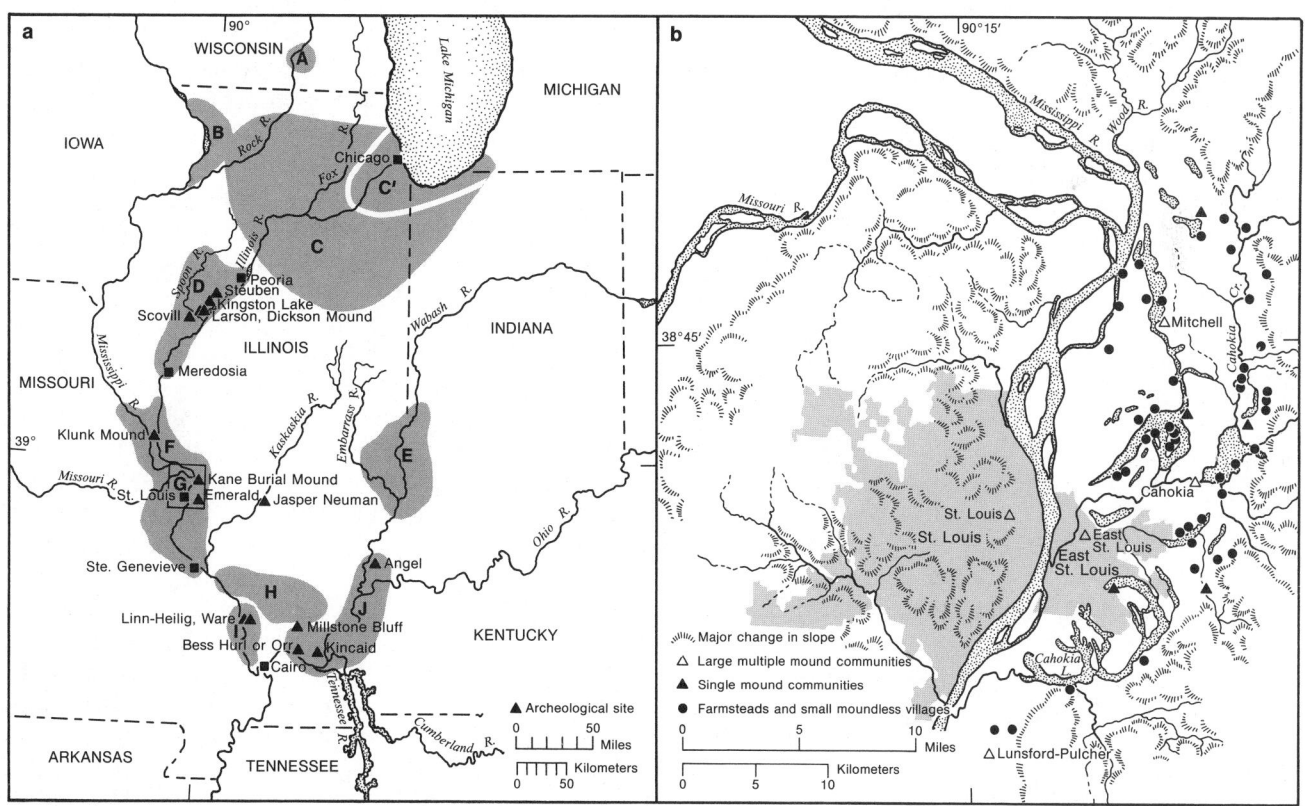

after Gregg 1975:fig. 74.

Fig. 2. Archeological sites. a, Areas of main cultural units: A, Aztalan; B, Apple River; C, Fisher, Langford; C′, Huber–Blue Island; D, Weaver, Sepo, Larson, Dickson Mounds; E, La Motte and Vincennes cultures; F, G, Jersey Bluff culture; G, Cahokia; H, Raymond and Dillenger; I, Ware, Linn-Heilig; J, Kincaid and Lewis. b, American Bottom region, sites dated approximately A.D. 1200.

of vessels become more common. Little can be said at the present time of the house types and other artifacts that accompany these ceramic trends.

In the lower Illinois River valley the White Hall phase (Struever 1968a) is contemporary with and similar to the Weaver phase in the central Illinois Valley. This is followed by the Jersey Bluff phase (Titterington 1935, 1943; Shalkop 1949), which is characterized by conical based vessels with cordmarked surfaces, smoothed above the shoulder in later years.

In the East Saint Louis region of the Mississippi River valley the Patrick phase (Fowler and Hall 1972) is probably contemporary with Late White Hall and Early Jersey Bluff. It is characterized by cordmarked ceramic vessels that are both conoidal and subconoidal in form, and many have interior rim notching as a decorative feature. These Patrick phase vessels are associated with rectangular pit houses with upright posts set in individual post holes.

In southwestern Illinois the period from A.D. 500 to 1000 is represented by two cultural units. In the Jackson County area, particularly along the Mississippi Valley, are two such cultural manifestations that may be sequential. The Raymond (Maxwell 1951) ceramics are similar in form and finish to the Patrick phase. The later Dillinger phase is characterized by globular-bodied jars often with folded rims. Another common Dillinger form is a hemispherical bowl. Dillinger was probably contemporary with the early Mississippian developments and therefore may represent a Woodland culture in the process of Mississippianization. A Dillinger phase pit at the Linn-Heilig site in Union County, Illinois, dates to A.D. 1000 ± 150 (M-890). Some of the Dillinger vessel forms are similar to Mississippian.

In the Ohio Valley region of the Illinois area the Lewis phase (MacNeish 1944; Maxwell 1951; Cole 1951) is present and is very similar to Raymond, Patrick, and Jersey Bluff.

In the northern and eastern parts of the Illinois area different manifestations are present in this time period. These are characterized by large globular jars with squared and peaked orifices and cord-impressed decorations. One type of this pottery has been called Canton ware (Fowler 1955) and another in Wisconsin without angular orifices, Madison Cord Impressed (Wittry 1959b). This general type of ceramics has a northern distribution reaching as far south as the central Illinois River valley.

The trend suggested by this wide variety of what has been called Late Woodland in the Illinois area is toward regionalism. There is a general similarity in all this pottery in that it is all thin walled, grit or grog tempered, tending toward globular forms, with interior rim stamping or notching as a main decorative touch. Three units may be slightly later than and derivative from the others; these are the Sepo, Dillinger, and cord-impressed deco-

rated ceramics of the north. The settlements associated with these ceramic variations are generally indicative of small, sedentary villages predominantly engaged in farming.

It was on this Bluff base that the Mississippian cultural pattern developed in Illinois. This is best exemplified by the development of Cahokia, which is not only the largest but probably the earliest Mississippian community in the Illinois area.

Early Mississippian Development

The Cahokia site is located near the present town of East Saint Louis, Illinois, in an expansion of the alluvial valley of the Mississippi River known as the American Bottom (Fowler 1969a). The location of the site within the American Bottom is at the confluence of two creeks, Cahokia and Canteen (fig. 2). The site includes an area of nearly six square miles, and within that area there were more than 100 man-made mounds of various shapes and sizes (fig. 3). The largest of these, Monks Mound (Reed, Bennett, and Porter 1968; Reed 1969), covers nearly 16 acres and rises in four terraces to a height of 100 feet above the surrounding valley floor (fig. 4).

The earliest late prehistoric occupation of the site area was during the Patrick phase when there were apparently several small farming village communities along the banks of Cahokia Creek. There were several other such communities in the American Bottom, which were mostly concentrated along the bluff edge terraces on the east. These sites apparently represent the intrusion of agricultural peoples into the bottomland area.

Fairmount Phase

The following phases, beginning about A.D. 800 to 900, saw the expansion of people throughout the American Bottom so that there are sites in all areas except the very low oxbows and slough areas of the western one-third of the Bottom. There seems to be no distinct differentiation of sites in this phase, but there is no doubt about a population increase within the American Bottom. During this period the ceramics were changing, with limestone tempering being more common and red-slipped and polished surfaces appearing (fig. 5). Between A.D. 900 and 1050, in the Fairmount phase, the Cahokia site became the major center of the area. In this phase Monks Mound was begun, as well as many other mounds, and there is evidence that the site was planned, there apparently having been a north-south axis or centerline. Social stratification is apparent in the burials as well as in the site organization. External contacts with areas as far away as the Caddo region, northern Wisconsin, and others are manifest in the burial goods in Mound 72 (Fowler 1969a) as well as artifacts from various other excavations. A wider variety of vessel forms is present, including seed jars, everted rim jars, wide-mouth water

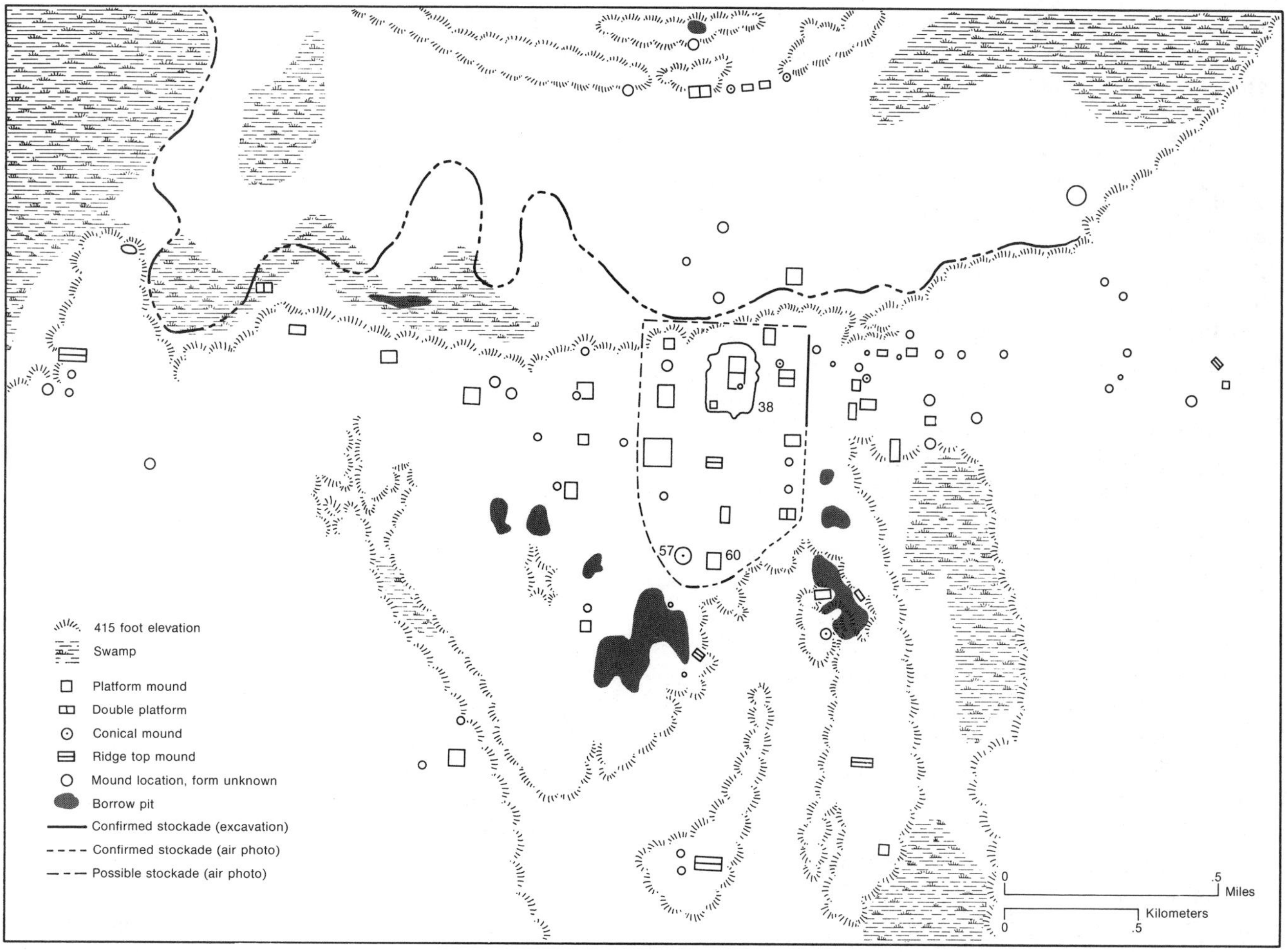

415 foot elevation
Swamp
☐ Platform mound
⊞ Double platform
⊙ Conical mound
⊟ Ridge top mound
○ Mound location, form unknown
⬤ Borrow pit
── Confirmed stockade (excavation)
----- Confirmed stockade (air photo)
-- - Possible stockade (air photo)

| Miles |
| 0 .5 1 |
| Kilometers |
| 0 .5 |

after Fowler and Hall 1975:fig. 4.
Fig. 3. Cahokia site mound locations.

bottles, and large conical footed objects. Shell tempering is present although much of the pottery is limestone tempered. Both polished red and polished black slipped surfaces on the vessels are noted. Throughout the American Bottom are Fairmount phase sites. Some of these are sites with single mounds and may represent support communities for Cahokia. There are also small sites without mounds that appear to be farmsteads and small villages.

One large site at the southern end of the American Bottom may have been equal to Cahokia during the Fairmount phase. This is the Lunsford-Pulcher site. It covers over 300 acres and has several large mounds within its area. Although ceramics of other phases are found at Pulcher, the predominant material seems to relate to the Fairmount phase.

Stirling and Moorehead Phases

Following A.D. 1050 the Cahokia site reached its maximum extent. From A.D. 1050 to 1250, during the Stirling and Moorehead phases, Monks Mound apparently was finished in essentially the form that it remains today. During the early half of this period Monks Mound had a large structure on the top terrace. This was undoubtedly a public-function building but whether a temple, chief's residence, or council house is not known. The fourth terrace was apparently enclosed with a wall. Some

Fig. 4. Monks Mound (#38 at the Cahokia site) viewed from the southeast. One of the largest earthworks in North America, it is a terraced truncated pyramid about 1,080 ft. long, 710 ft. wide, and 100 ft. tall at the highest point. Photograph by Melvin Fowler.

smaller buildings were also inside this wall. The western one-third of the first terrace was also the location of a group of public buildings during this phase. The "wood-henges" (Wittry 1969) probably date to this phase.

In the latter half of this period, during the Moorehead phase, the fourth terrace was no longer occupied by a public building but was covered over with a layer of sterile fill. The southwest corner of the first terrace was the location of the construction of a pyramidal mound with a public building on its surface. This platform was rebuilt seven times. A small mound on the southeast corner of the third terrace may have been built at this time and had a similar function.

Many other mounds were contemporary with Monks Mound but as yet it is not known how many. During the Moorehead phase, A.D. 1150 to 1250, a large wall or palisade (Anderson 1969) was built around the central portion of the Cahokia site. This encompassed an area of probably 300 acres and included within this were Monks and 16 other mounds. Most of these mounds appear to have been platforms. These may have served as residences for important persons in the community. At the south end of the palisaded area is a pair of mounds, one a conical and the other a platform mound. These may have been a charnel house mound and a burial mound serving the higher status people living within the walled area (fig. 6).

Outside this walled area were other mound groupings that may represent the residences and burial complexes of personages of lesser status. Together, the groups inside and outside the wall occupied the entire Cahokia site area with their platform mounds, plazas, gardens, burial precincts, and residences. Population estimates for the site during this period suggest a figure of 10,000 or more. Surveys of the American Bottom (Munson and Harn 1971) have suggested that the smaller sites in the area were not occupied at this time, indicating that the population was nucleated in the larger communities.

To the north of Cahokia is another large site covering over 200 acres and containing eight mounds. This site, Mitchell (J.W. Porter 1969), was occupied for a period of around 100 years. The mounds are arranged around a central plaza. One of these mounds appears to have been built in a single stage rather than the customary multiple sequence of construction. In the center of the plaza was a large cypress log column 30 inches in diameter. Outside the mound-plaza area was the residential section. There is some indication from aerial photographs that the Mitchell site may have been palisaded. It is located near the mouth of the Missouri River and may have been a community for the control of resources coming into the Cahokia area from the north.

In the present city of East Saint Louis was another large Mississippian site that was probably occupied during the Stirling and Moorehead phases. It was composed of a large group or groups of mounds that were apparently laid out in lines. One of these mounds appears to have been a burial mound (Snyder 1962). The function of the others is unknown since they were destroyed in the nineteenth century. Connecting the Cahokia site and the East Saint Louis site was a row of mounds along the south bank of Cahokia Creek. One of these is the Sam

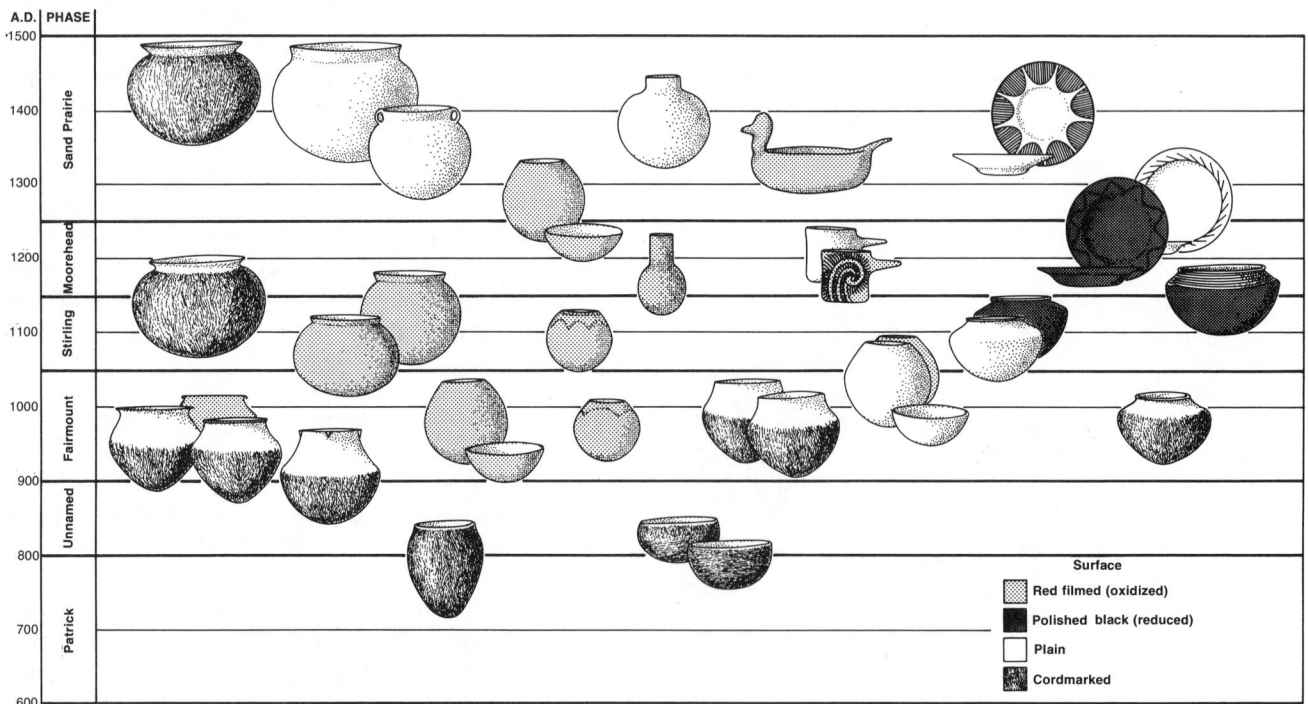

adapted from J.O. Vogel 1975:fig. 32 and Fowler and Hall 1975.

Fig. 5. Some trends in form and finish characteristics of ceramics in the Cahokia area.

U. of Wis., Milwaukee.

Fig. 6. A conical mound (#57) on left and platform mound (#60) at the Cahokia site, viewed from the southwest. These may represent a charnel house mound (the platform) and associated burial (conical) mound.

Chucallo Mound partially excavated by Moorehead (1929:53–54) in 1922. Burials were found in the fill of the mound. These burials were apparently covered by a primary mound with a later addition of soil to cap this interior mound. No data are available to suggest the function of the other mounds in this series.

Across the Mississippi River in what is now downtown Saint Louis was another large site composed of at least 27 mounds. Although these mounds were destroyed in the middle of the nineteenth century (see Williams and Goggin 1956) they were recorded by the Long expedition of 1819 (E. James 1905; Peale 1862). These mounds formed a group around a plaza area (see maps in Peale 1862:287; Bushnell 1904:fig. 4) with large rectangular mounds at both the north and south sides of this plaza area. The Saint Louis mounds were of a variety of sizes and shapes. One of these was a rectangular mound with three terraces or platforms and was recorded by E. James (1905:113) as the "Falling Garden." It was 114 feet long. The largest of the mounds was an oval mound over 1,400 feet to the north of the northernmost mound of the main group. It was 319 feet by 158 feet in dimension and 34 feet high with a "large step on the east side" (E. James 1905:116). The extent of habitation areas surrounding this site is unknown.

On the bluffs to the east of the American Bottom are mounds of many different sizes and shapes that relate to the Mississippian occupation of the Bottom. Some are called sugar-loaf mounds. Some of these were excavated by early archeologists who encountered charcoal and floor layers (Snyder 1894; C. Thomas 1894). Because of what appeared to be their strategic location and the remains of fires, Snyder called them signal mounds. One mound on the bluff edge has been excavated under controlled conditions (Melbye 1963). This is the Kane Burial Mound directly east of the Mitchell site on the bluff's edge. It contained nearly 90 burials, some with accompanying grave goods. The pottery vessels associated with some of these burials and radiocarbon dates of

A.D. 1220 ± 95 (GX-440) and A.D. 1250 ± 85 (GX-441) suggest the contemporaneity of this burial mound with the peak of the Cahokia occupation, that is, the Stirling-Moorehead phases, and with the Mitchell site. Some of the burials in the mound were clearly oriented (head) toward the Mitchell site and others directly toward Monks Mound, suggesting that persons buried in this mound were of different social affiliations in life.

Outside of the American Bottom, about 15 miles to the southeast, in the prairie upland, is the Emerald site. This site is composed of one large multiple-terraced mound with a small mound on one corner of the upper terrace and several still smaller mounds. Only preliminary testing has been done at this site but it seems to have had an early, perhaps Fairmount phase-related occupation, and a later, perhaps Sand Prairie phase-related occupation. According to Snyder (1894) there was an ancient trail that led from this site into the Bottom and to the Cahokia site. It must be considered as one of the major satellite communities to Cahokia.

Mississippian Interactions

Cahokia's relationship to areas outside the American Bottom region extends to the Caddo area, the lower Mississippi Valley area, and the Upper Great Lakes. A major site in Wisconsin is Aztalan, which had definite ties to Cahokia at this time. Aztalan was palisaded, with over 20 acres inside the fortification, which included three large mounds, one of which was double terraced. Rectangular wall trench houses were also found inside the palisade (see "Late Prehistory of the Upper Great Lakes Area," this vol.).

Various explanations have been put forward to explain the presence of Aztalan. One of the longest-lived ideas is that Aztalan was a colony of Cahokia and that this colonization was a response to population pressure at the Cahokia site. More recently it has been suggested that Aztalan was an outpost established by Cahokians for purposes of economic exploitation of resources to the north of Cahokia. On the opposite end of the range of possibilities is the explanation that Aztalan was not established from Cahokia directly but from the Cahokia hinterland in Illinois where Indians with a Woodland culture similar to that found at Aztalan had been acculturating toward the Mississippian pattern for several centuries. Aztalan was established at a point in time when, for example, Indians of this mixed background disappear from the archeological record in east-central Illinois and are replaced by the carriers of the Fisher and Langford traditions. What all explanations of Aztalan have in common is the recognition that the influence of Cahokia extended directly far into Illinois and ultimately into Wisconsin, Minnesota, and other states for reasons that remain to be discovered.

565

An Aztalan-like situation exists also with the Apple River phase in northwestern Illinois where shell-tempered Mississippian ceramics, platform mounds, and other Mississippian characteristics have been noted (Bennett 1945). Apple River is an outlier or extension of culture with obvious Cahokia relationships but what more it represents cannot yet be specifically said. Here, as at Carcajou Point in Wisconsin (R.L. Hall 1962) and at sites of the Silvernale phase in eastern Minnesota, the mixture of traits points partly toward Woodland-Mississippian interaction but, more important, toward the apparent interaction of Mississippian culture of a Cahokia cast with the parallel, emerging, Upper Mississippi tradition that comes to be known as Oneota. By A.D. 1300 Indians bearing cultures of the Oneota tradition appeared in Minnesota, Wisconsin, Iowa, Missouri, Kansas, Nebraska, and Illinois. In most of this area Oneota would seem to be the archeological expression of Siouan-speaking peoples, in particular the Iowa, Oto, Missouri, Winnebago, and Kansa. In Illinois the picture is not so clear because Oneota sites such as those of the Huber phase in the Chicago area may be Miami, an Algonquian tribe, and the Huber phase itself may not have appeared by intrusion from the northern Mississippi Valley but by evolution from a base in the Fisher tradition under Oneota influence. Decoration on ceramics of the Spoon River tradition comes to have an Oneota appearance in the period of about A.D. 1350 to 1400 in response to this same kind of interaction, which was extending some of the most archeologically visible and distinctive aspects of Oneota culture beyond the peoples with whom they were originally identified.

A common artifact at Cahokia and throughout much of the Mississippian network was the flint hoe made of material from the Mill Creek quarries in Union County, Illinois. At this time these quarries seem to have been controlled by Mississippian peoples. Also in Union County, in the Mississippi River Bottoms, are two fairly large Mississippian sites, the Ware site and the Linn Heilig site (C. Thomas 1894:155–159; Perrin 1873; B.W. Merwin 1935). These sites may represent a part of the Cahokia network and the Mississippian control of local resources such as the Mill Creek chert; however, it is probable that the major occupation of these sites was slightly later in time.

In the Kaskaskia River valley are Mississippian communities from the fourteenth century (Crane and Griffin 1968), but these appear to be small farmsteads and villages. No platform mounds are known for the lower Kaskaskia valley. Some of the Mississippian pottery from the Kaskaskia sites pertains to the period of the Stirling-Moorehead phase at Cahokia, but much of it is later. A probable platform mound is known from the central Kaskaskia valley at Jasper Neuman site (Gardner 1973).

There are Mississippian communities with temple mounds in the Wabash Valley area. These probably relate to the Cahokia area but do not seem to be directly involved with the Kaskaskia valley.

Late Mississippian

The next phase at Cahokia, the Sand Prairie phase between A.D. 1250 and 1500, saw major changes in the nature of the Cahokia site. No further public structures appear to have been built on the fourth or the first terraces of Monks Mound. During the Sand Prairie phase a ridge connected the small platform mound on the southwest corner of the first terrace with the mass of the main mound. Further, two ramps appear to have been constructed on the east side of Monks Mound apparently to give access to the top terrace. The palisade seems to have been abandoned at this time. Sand Prairie phase materials are found in most areas where excavation has taken place so that this occupation appears to have extended over much of the site area. It does not appear to have been so elaborate an occupation as that proposed for the Stirling-Moorehead occupation. There is a suggestion of Sand Prairie phase-related sites back into the tributary valleys of the American Bottom. The Mitchell site was abandoned by this time as perhaps were the East Saint Louis and Saint Louis sites.

The major ceramics of this phase are cordmarked shell-tempered jars with large outflaring rims. Also present are high-rimmed plates with incised decoration. Beaker forms are common. Art motifs present at Cahokia, such as the winged, hooked-nose dancer (fig. 7); weeping eye; and cross designs, are similar to those found in Alabama, Tennessee, Georgia, and Oklahoma and called the Southeastern Ceremonial cult. The weeping eye appeared in the earlier phases as well. At the Saint Louis site long-

Fig. 7. Carved tablet with winged hooked-nose figure on obverse side and cross-hatched lines on reverse side. From the east lobes of Monks Mound. Height 9.2 cm.

nosed god masks were found (Williams and Goggin 1956).

Outside of the American Bottom this period saw the establishment of Mississippian manifestations on a regional basis and the development of cultures more or less independent of one another, each with its own hinterland and territory. They may have been tied together in an exchange network, but Cahokia no longer seemed to be the focal point of that exchange system.

In the central Illinois River valley there appeared a series of Mississippian towns with temple mounds, plazas, and fortifications. These were apparently rather evenly spaced up the valley from Meredosia on the south to Peoria on the north (Harn 1970, 1973; Conrad and Harn 1972). One of these sites was the Kingston Lake site, which was destroyed in the 1930s by a gravel quarry. Another is the Larson site on the bluff overlooking the Illinois River valley and associated with the Dickson Mound site. The Larson site was a fortified town with mounds, plaza, and residences inside the palisade. Dickson Mound was an accretional mound cemetery. Other Mississippian sites scattered throughout the Spoon River valley were smaller and apparently related to this town center.

To the south of Cahokia similar settlement systems developed in the Mississippi River valley. One such Mississippian nucleus was the Ware and Linn Heilig sites. South of this area and south of the Thebes gap was another such grouping. One Mississippian site of this period is at Dog Tooth Bend in Alexander County. This practically unknown site is composed of one double-terraced mound and other smaller mounds around a plaza. The extent of the habitation area and whether this site was palisaded or not is at present not known. This site may be one of the sites of the Cairo Lowlands phase defined by S. Williams (1954) for the Mississippian manifestations in Missouri, Illinois, and Kentucky centering around Cairo, Illinois.

Along the Ohio River in Illinois were other Mississippian sites. One of these is the Bass Hurl or Orr site, which has a platform mound on it. A large amount of fluorspar in the form of artifacts has been found at this site. The exploitation of this resource, which does not seem to be widely spread in Mississippian sites, may have been the reason that this Mississippian community was established there.

Situated on the Pope and Massac county line in the bottomlands of the Ohio River is the Kincaid site (Cole 1951). It was occupied largely during this period. This is supported by the interpretation of the ceramics but also by dendrochronological analysis of wood specimens from the site. These suggest that the earlier occupation started before A.D. 1523 and that the site was occupied as late as A.D. 1612 (R.E. Bell 1951).

The main part of the Kincaid site is composed of a group of five mounds around a plaza area. All these mounds were platforms that were rebuilt several times and served as bases upon which important structures were placed. The largest of these mounds is at the north end of the plaza area. It is a long rectangular platform, 485 feet long, 195 feet wide, and 30 feet high. On the southwest corner of this platform was an additional mound structure. The main mound was built up in five stages, and there were four construction stages to the additional mound. There were steps leading to the elevated surface of the added mound and a structure had been built on it as well as on the top of the main mound. The top of the main mound had been palisaded.

To the east of the main Kincaid group was another group consisting of five mounds. One of these, at least, was a burial mound that included log tomb burials in the earlier stage and slab stone cists in the later stage. This burial mound bears an interesting relationship to a platform mound about 150 feet to the southwest of it. These two mounds are connected by a ridge or platform of earth. This same type of relationship of a conical and platform mound has been noted at Cahokia. It is possible that this represents a charnal house mound and an accompanying burial mound. Other mounds in this smaller Kincaid group show this same feature. It is possible that this small group to the west of the main group is the charnel house and burial area of the Kincaid site.

The ceramics at the Kincaid site suggest that it was first occupied by Lewis phase people. The Mississippian occupation may have been an intrusion into the area. The Mississippian influence or invasion seems to take place about the time of the beginning of the Sand Prairie phase or earlier at Cahokia. The dendrochronological dating of the Kincaid site comes largely from one small mound in the northeast corner of the main plaza; however, this probably does not date the range of occupation of the total site, which must have extended back a few centuries earlier. This earlier Mississippian occupation at Kincaid may have been as early as A.D. 1200, as a small amount of what appear to be Stirling-Moorehead ceramic types was found there (Orr 1951).

Farther up the Ohio River but on the Indiana side is the Angel site (see "Late Prehistory of the Ohio Valley," this vol.), which is very similar to the Kincaid site in form. On the basis of artifact similarities it was probably occupied about the same time. In Kentucky, particularly in the Tennessee and Cumberland river drainages, are related Mississippian sites. Together with Kincaid, Angel, and related sites these form the Tennessee and Cumberland variant of Mississippian culture.

North in the Illinois area along the Wabash and Embarrass rivers is another Mississippian concentration referred to by Winters (1967) as the Vincennes culture.

In general the picture of Mississippian settlement in the period of the Sand Prairie phase at Cahokia is one of Mississippian towns each with its own base territory.

Mississippian culture is more uniformly spread over larger areas but without the single dominating center that had previously prevailed. The interaction of these communities was perhaps through a trade network distributing throughout the system the specialized resources exploited by each of these communities. Such specialized resources might be the salt in the Sainte Genevieve, Missouri, and Saline County, Illinois areas; the Mill Creek chert of the Union County, Illinois, area; and the fluorspar of the Hardin County, Illinois, area.

Little is known of the prehistory of the later (after A.D. 1500) period in the Illinois area except for the northern regions. In the south this is probably the period of the stone-box grave phenomena. Stone-lined graves are found along the lower Ohio and Mississippi river valleys, usually along the bluff edges. Most such graves have been looted long ago. One location of extensive stone-box graves and what appears to have been an associated village is the Mill Stone Bluff site in Illinois. Other concentrations of these graves are on the bluffs near Prairie du Rocher, in Randolph County, Illinois. These stone box graves extend as far north as the Cahokia area.

Contact Period

At the time of actual French contact the Illinois area presented a picture quite different from the complexity of the late prehistoric period. The contours of culture were not so sharply drawn. The sites of Cahokia, Kincaid, and other Mississippian temple towns were not occupied at the time of French exploration. The first European contacts in the southeastern United States had taken place over 150 years earlier. Perhaps the breakdown of cultural integration and depopulation due to the disruption of this European intrusion and the consequent epidemics of introduced diseases had reached as far north as the Ohio and central Mississippi valleys by the time of the first French contact in the late seventeenth century.

Until just before the arrival of the French the Illinois area had apparently been largely controlled by groups of the Algonquian-speaking Illinois Confederacy and perhaps the closely related Miami. The actual picture is confused by the tribal dislocation and movements caused by fear of the Iroquois who had shortly before destroyed the Erie and decimated or driven before them many tribes of the Great Lakes and Ohio Valley. When history becomes clearly written the Illinois country contains not only the Miami, and tribes constituting the Illinois—the Kaskaskia, Peoria, Tamaroa, Michigamea, Cahokia, and others—but also bands of the Fox, Kickapoo, Mascouten, Shawnee, and other recently displaced tribes (see "History of the Illinois Area," this vol.).

Late Prehistory of the Upper Great Lakes Area

DAVID S. BROSE

Regional Development and Mississippian Influences

The period from A.D. 1000 to A.D. 1400 is poorly understood due to inability to conceptualize clearly the nature of "Mississippian." The continued interactions and regional developments of local populations and their relationships with these Mississippian developments is the focus of much research in this area (figs. 1–2).

The Western Area

In Wisconsin the Effigy Mound tradition maintained considerable vitality after A.D. 1000 (Rowe 1956; Hurley 1966, 1970). Although at the Bigelow site mound interments ceased by A.D. 1120, domestic activity continued

until A.D. 1370 ± 55 (WIS-187). Large complex mound construction dated to this period suggests an increase in mound and open-site utilization with a reduction of shelter occupation. Population size cannot be shown to have increased, however, and there is no evidence to suggest any change in subsistence-settlement system (Gibbon 1972) although maize has been recovered from the twelfth-century Dietz site. There is an increase in small triangular points, while ceramics display a clear tendency for motif restriction and elaboration and an increase of thickened lips and collared rims. Some relatively high collared and castellated ceramics with complex design are associated with this period (McKern 1930; Barrett 1933; Baerreis and Freeman 1958).

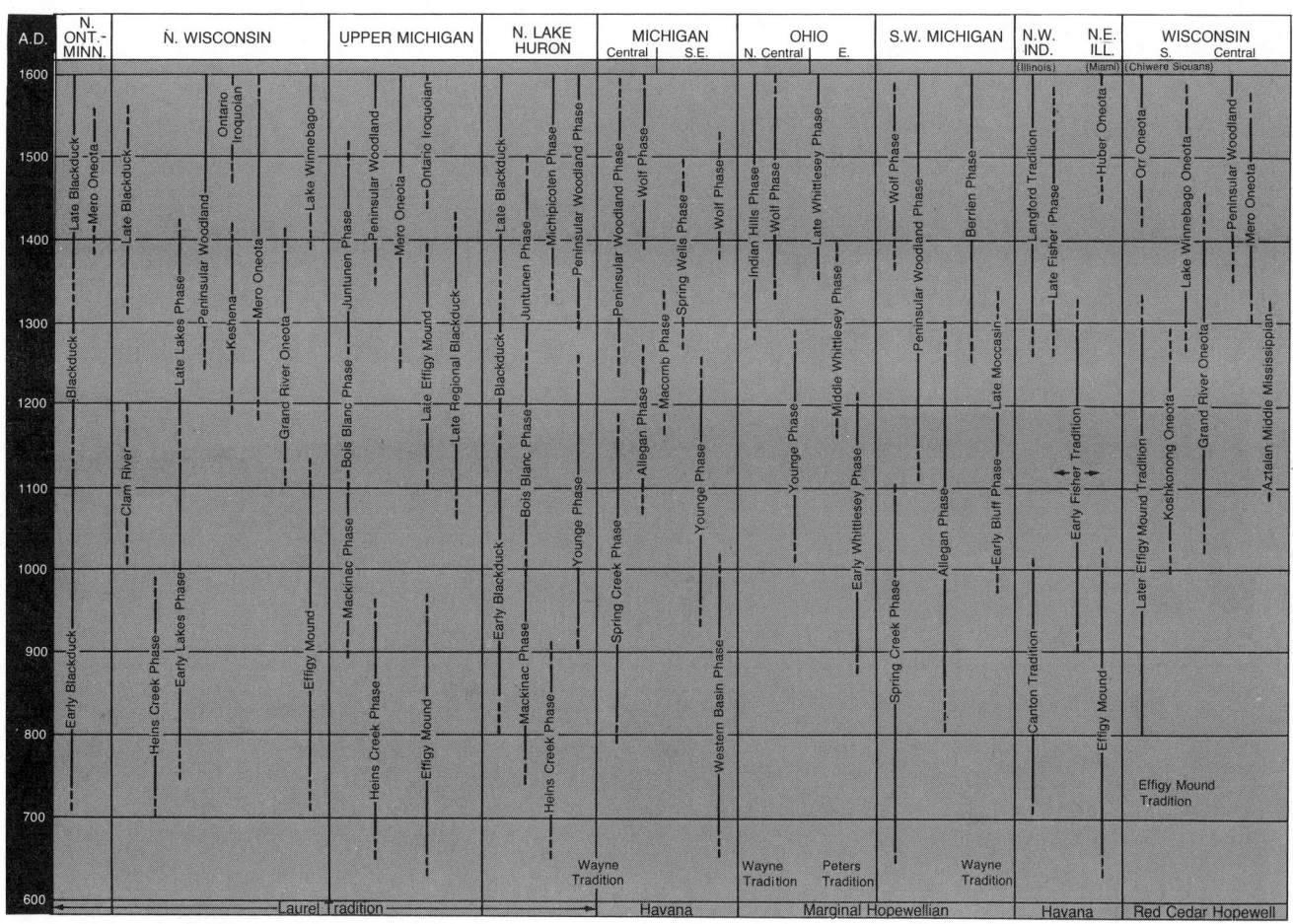

Fig. 1. Suggested relationships of archeological complexes.

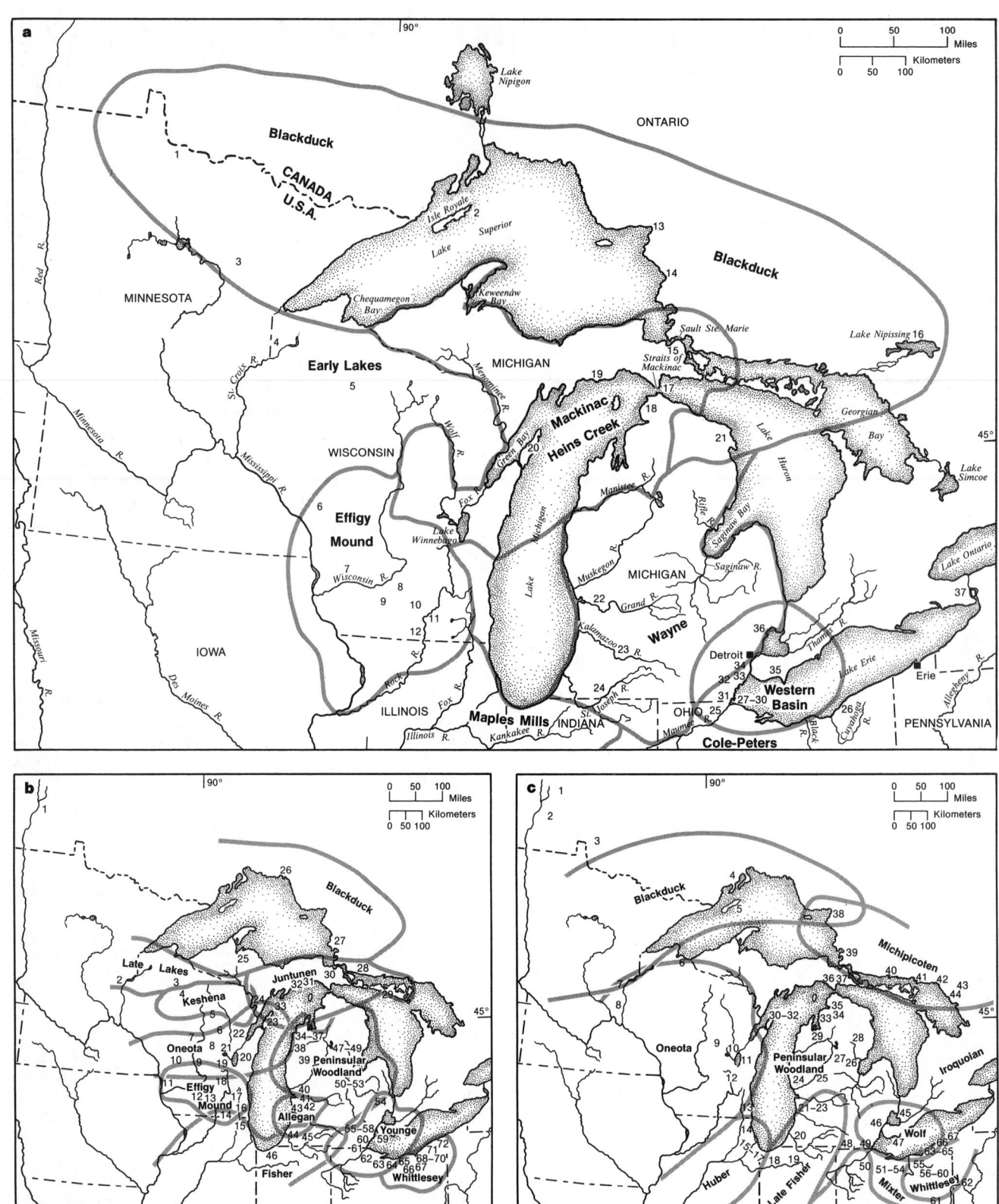

Coeval with these are regionally distinctive Upper Mississippian (McKern 1945) or Oneota (R.L. Hall 1962) sites characterized by: larger, more intensive occupation, often at fortified planned villages; small narrow-based triangular points; unifacial end scrapers; and predominantly squat, globular, plain-surfaced, everted-rim bowls with a strong tendency for shell tempering (Jeske 1927). This complex has been variously considered an actual intrusion of Mississippian peoples (Griffin 1937, 1943, 1960; McKern 1945; Wilford 1941, 1955; Bennett 1952;

Fig. 2. Upper Great Lakes Area showing archeological traditions and sites. a, Period before A.D. 1000: 1, Rainy River; 2, Indian Point, Chippewa Harbor; 3, Scott; 4, Clam River; 5, Robinson, Squirrel Dam; 6, Sanders; 7, Bigelow; 8, Durst; 9, Knoop; 10, Blackhawk; 11, Horicon; 12, Beloit College; 13, Heron Bay; 14, Pic River; 15, Sault Ste. Marie; 16, Frank Bay; 17, Juntunen; 18, Fisher Lake; 19, Ekdahl-Goudreau; 20, Heins Creek, Mero, Porte Des Mortes; 21, Goodwin-Gresham; 22, Spring Creek; 23, Spoonville; 24, Moccasin Bluff; 25, Sissung; 26, Ahlstrom; 27, Squaw Island; 28, Point Place; 29, Point Mouillee; 30, Erie Islands; 31, Cufr, Campernall; 32, Gibralter; 33, Morrin; 34, Springwells; 35, Point Pelee; 36, Rivière Au Vase; 37, Princess Point. b, Period A.D. 1000 to 1400: 1, Hungry Hall; 2, Cooper, Petaga Point; 3, Cookstove, Robinson, Badger; 4, Burnt-Rollways, Strawberry Island, Shannon; 5, Big Eddy, Kakwatch, Watasa Lake Swamp, Makimatas; 6, McClaughry; 7, Grand River; 8, Kleitzen, Nitzschke; 9, Picknic Point, Frost Woods; 10, Wakanda Park; 11, Diamond Bluff; 12, Dietz; 13, Hahn; 14, Hamilton-Brooks; 15, Blue Island; 16, Aztalan; 17, Carcajou Point, Crescent Bay; 18, Raisbeck; 19, Karow; 20, Big Lake Butte Des Morts; 21, Walker-Hooper; 22, Point Sauble, Beaumier Farm; 23, Mero, Heins Creek; 24, Backlund; 25, Sand Point; 26, Nyman; 27, Pic River; 28, Michipicoten; 29, Manitoulin; 30, Naomikong Point; 31, Point Scott; 32, Ekdahl-Goudreau; 33, Summer Island; 34, Fife Lake; 35, Headquarters; 36, Bear Creek; 37, Stoney Lake; 38, Boven; 39, Crystal Lake, South Flats; 40, De Boer; 41, Fauver; 42, 46th Street, Nordhoff; 43, Allegan Dam; 44, Moccasin Bluff; 45, Whorley; 46, Fifield, Griesmer, Yahl, Rader; 47, Butterfield, Birch Creek; 48, West Twin Lakes; 49, Rifle River, Walters-Linsenman Earthworks; 50, Schultz, Bussinger; 51, Kantzler; 52, Hodges, Mahoney, Foster, Stadelmeyer; 53, Valley Sweets; 54, Younge; 55, Verchave I and II; 56, Farmington, Bates; 57, St. Mary's Vineyard; 58, Turkey Creek; 59, Tessmer; 60, Indian Trails; 61, Albin, Harwick School; 62, Harris Yard; 63, Libben; 64, Mixter; 65, Eiden; 66, Dupler; 67, South Park; 68, Cleveland Zoo; 69, Euclid; 70, Greenwood; 71, Fairport Harbor; 72, Ashtabula Gulf # 1. c, Period A.D. 1400 to contact: 1, Swan Lake; 2, Pelican Falls; 3, Hungry Hall; 4, McCluskey, Cressman; 5, Lookout; 6, Madeline Island, Cadotte; 7, Cooper; 8, Rice Lake; 9, Big Eddy, Five Island; 10, Furman, Doty Island; 11, Bell; 12, Pipe, McCauley, Lasleys Point; 13, Carcajou Point; 14, Blue Island; 15, Anker, Huber; 16, Oak Forest, Hoxie, Bowmanville; 17, Palos-Au Sagaunaske; 18, Fifield, Griesmer; 19, Brems; 20, Moccasin Bluff; 21, Ada; 22, Fauver; 23, Nordhoff; 24, Dumaw Creek; 25, Arnold Lake; 26, Rifle River # 3; 27, Porter site 8; 28, Mikado; 29, Reider; 30, Summer Island; 31, Detroit Island; 32, Rock Island II; 33, Ponshewang Point; 34, Skegemog; 35, Ft. Michilimackinac; 36, Richardson; 37, Gros Cap; 38, Pic River; 39, Michipicoten; 40, Shebishakong; 41, Montreal River; 42, Ellsmer-Morrison; 43, Frank Bay; 44, Missisauga; 45, Parker; 46, Wolf, Furton; 47, Kelley's Island; 48, Keeney; 49, Bay Creek; 50, Biggers, Williams, Ft. Meigs; 51, Libben; 52, Mixter; 53, Heckleman; 54, Eiden; 55, South Park; 56, Ft. Island; 57, Windsor Ft.; 58, Greenhouse; 59, Eastwall; 60, Tuttle Hill; 61, Riker; 62, McKee's Rock Village; 63, Reeves; 64, Offut; 65, County Fairgrounds; 66, Ahlstrom; 67, Kaiser.

Quimby 1960; Hurley 1970) or local populations modified toward a Mississippian pattern (Ford and Willey 1941; R.L. Hall 1962, 1967; Cleland 1966; Brose 1970; Gibbon 1969, 1972).

Aztalan on the Rock River seems to represent Mississippian intrusion into the region at A.D. 1100. That site is marked by a square-bastioned stockade with walkways, enclosing over 900,000 square feet with interior plazas and platform mounds. Circular semisubterranean and rectangular structures with puddled clay hearths were scattered within and beyond the palisades along with refuse pits filled with maize, squash, and charred and fragmented human bones. The platform mounds supported large rectangular wattle-and-daub-covered "temples" with bark roofs (Barrett 1933; McKern 1946; McKern and Ritzenthaler 1945; Bennett 1952). Multiple notched and unmodified small triangular points are common. Flint hoes, chunky stones, steatite ear spools, sandstone abraders, Gulf Coast shell pendants, copper-covered ear spools and long-nosed god masks reinforced the idea that Aztalan represented a colony. Ceramics included shell- and limestone-tempered vessels indistinguishable from types associated with the Stirling-Moorehead phases at Cahokia (Griffin 1964). However, most ceramics were grit-tempered, cord-decorated and collared cordmarked vessels (Barrett 1933; Bleed 1970), many with castellated collared rims having pentagonal perimeters (fig. 3) (Baerreis and Freeman 1958; R.L. Hall 1962).

Upper Mississippi Area (Oneota)

Wisconsin indicates differential adoption of pre-Aztalan Mississippian influences in ecologically distinctive subregions at different times, by differing routes, and to markedly different degrees. Distinctive ceramic complexes characterize the Orr, Grand River, Koshkonong, Lake Winnebago, and Mero focuses (McKern 1945; R.J. Mason 1966). Although it is probable that Orr and Mero postdate the rest, radiocarbon dating does not provide strong support for the priority of any one of the other focuses, all of which date from A.D. 1000 (Hall 1962; Baerreis and Bryson 1965; R.J. Mason 1966; Brose 1968, 1970; Gibbon 1969, 1972).

The Koshkonong focus in the Rock River drainage is characterized by plain pottery with pinched lips and occasional loop handles. Rare decoration consists of trailed scroll and/or linear motifs on rim-shoulder areas. Sites represent fortified villages with rectangular wall-trench houses as well as oval single-post mat-covered wigwam structures. Primary extended burials in cemeteries and bundle burials in refuse pits are known (McKern 1945; R.L. Hall 1962; Gibbon 1969).

Along the Fox River, especially about Lake Winnebago, are components of both the Grand River and Lake Winnebago focuses, although the former has wider distribution. Distinctions between these focuses are primarily ceramic, Grand River vessels being predominantly plain bowls with unmodified lips and Lake Winnebago vessels having more rim eversion with wide strap handles and being decorated with broad vertical and horizontal trailing (R.L. Hall 1962). Settlement data for Lake Winnebago components are unclear; but small, fortified, intensively occupied villages of single-post oval houses are reported. Mortuary practices are confined to primary extended burials as at the Karow Cemetery site (McKern 1945). Grand River components represent large sites

Milwaukee Public Mus.: top, 25964; bottom, 35734.

Fig. 3. Aztalan cordmarked pottery, late Woodland. top, Aztalan site, Jefferson Co., Wis.; bottom, Schultz site, Green Lake Co., Wis. Maximum diameter of top 29 cm, other same scale (see also Barrett 1933:pl. 78, fig. 2; Hall 1962, 2:pl.51, fig. 2).

with, perhaps, seasonal reutilization by loosely organized matrilineage segments (Jeske 1927; Gibbon 1969). Houses were oval bark-covered wigwams or rectangular gabled bark-covered "summerhouses" (McKusick 1973; Bennett 1952). Maize was grown although its importance is uncertain (Peske 1966; Cleland 1966). Flexed burial within mounds is characteristic of the Grand River focus (Gibbon 1972) although primary extended burials outside mounds are known (R.L. Hall 1962).

The Mero focus, centered around Green Bay, extends northeast to the Ontonagon River in Upper Michigan (R.J. Mason 1966, 1967; Freeman 1956; Brose 1968, 1970; Quimby 1960; Prahl and Brose 1970). Ceramics are predominantly Grand River-like although many display cordmarking and are grit-tempered. Sites are small unfortified seasonal campsites (Cleland 1966). Oval bark- or mat-covered wigwams appear associated. Flexed and bundle submound interments have been reported from Upper Michigan (Binford and Quimby 1963; W. Moore 1971). The Orr focus, primarily within the Mississippi River drainage, falls beyond the scope of this section.

It seems the intrusive Middle Mississippian occupation at Aztalan contributed relatively little to succeeding cultural developments in the Upper Great Lakes, although sherds of Ramey Incised have been noted from Isle Royale (Bastian 1963) and Juntunen (McPherron 1967). A developmental interpretation of Effigy Mound–Oneota (Gibbon 1969) seems strengthened by the fact that Effigy mounds dated after A.D. 1000 contain significant proportions of local Upper Mississippian ceramics (Jeske 1927; McKern 1928; Maxwell 1950; Wittry 1959; R.L. Hall 1962; Brose 1968, 1970; Hurley 1970; Gibbon 1972).

Northwestern Ontario

Northwest of these Mississippian developments there is relatively little change in the cultural adaptation to the northern Lake Forest. Within the Blackduck complex there may be a tendency for more rounded-based pottery reflecting Mississippian influences (Wilford 1955; Evans 1961). There is some suggestion of population increase dependent upon intensive utilization of wild rice (E. Johnson 1969). In northeastern Minnesota ricing villages display Blackduck and Mero ceramics associated with defensive palisades and semisquared, semisubterranean houses. Squash seeds were also recovered (L.R. Cooper 1965; Bleed 1969). In northern Ontario several components represent small Blackduck fishing camps occupied during the eleventh or twelfth century (Wright 1967a). The Michipicoten site on the east shore of Lake Superior (Wright 1969) has produced a stratum dated at A.D. 1100 ± 60 (S-170) with ceramics indicating southern influences. Most of southern Ontario represents developing Iroquoian traditions at this time.

Late Lakes Phase

In northern Wisconsin components indicate seasonal mobility with a diffuse economic adaptation utilizing wild rice, fish, and small mammals (Cleland 1966; Salzer 1969). No cultigens are known. Both campsites and large seasonal villages are represented. Defensive fortifications are absent. At the Badger site a small oval "wigwam" was partially excavated; other structures are unknown. Burials are bundle, flexed, and cremations in linear, conical, simple effigy mounds. Both intrusive and submound pit burials are found. Associated ceramics consist of Blackduck and Effigy Mound types intermixed with Grand River and Mero Oneota pottery. Mississippian ceramics similar to Aztalan were also recovered from the Robinson Village site. Lithic assemblages are dominated by small narrow triangular points made of local quartz. Native copper tools were also common. An early component of this complex is dated A.D. 1100 ± 120 (M-1811) and A.D. 1210 ± 100 (M-1810) at the Shannon site (Salzer 1969).

The Lakes phase is similar to the Keshena culture in the upper Wolf River valley (McKern 1945; Bennett

1952). Riparian village sites suggest a similar settlement pattern (Salzer 1969) and a mixture of Grand River and Mero Oneota, and corded castellated Woodland ceramics have been recovered (Barrett and Skinner 1932). The mortuary complex includes intrusive and submound burials although no Mississippian ceramics were associated, suggesting multicomponent sites. Along the Menominee River the Backlund mound group dated A.D. 1340 ± 110 (M-1891) included a mixture of Oneota and late Effigy Mound ceramics with minimal Blackduck material (Brose 1968). Similar mixed ceramics occurred at the Sand Point site near Keewanaw Bay in an accretional platform mound (W. Moore 1971).

The Green Bay-Northern Lake Michigan area is characterized by small lacustrine campsites with mixed Grand River-Mero Oneota, and collared, occasionally castellated, cord-decorated Woodland ceramics. This assemblage has been dated to the late thirteenth century at Summer Island (Brose 1970b), at Ekdahl-Goudreau (Prahl and Brose 1970), and at Point Scott (Fitting 1970), although the last two sites reflect developments in the Mackinac Straits region. The large fortified village sites of Point Sauble and Beaumier Farm at the bottom of Green Bay also contain some proportion of Grand River-like ceramics (Freeman 1956; Baerreis and Freeman 1958). There is some suggestion of horticulture at these sites (Brose 1970) and their subsistence-settlement system relates more toward the mixed economic adaptation than to the lacustrine orientation of the Lake Michigan sites (Cleland 1966).

Northern Developments

At Juntunen subsistence-settlement systems show little change. The Bois Blanc phase, dated at A.D. 900 ± 75 (M-1141), A.D. 1060 ± 75 (M-1140), and A.D. 1130 ± 120 (M-1817), displays Blackduck traits on collared, occa-sionally castellated vessels, although definite Blackduck ceramics are rare. In the succeeding Juntunen phase, dated at A.D. 1320 ± 75 (M-1188) and A.D. 1330 ± 100 (M-1391), ceramics are characterized by castellated collars and rim and lip decoration of linear punctations and push-pull techniques (fig. 4). Horizontal bands and nested chevrons below castellations are common motifs and extend from the collar to shoulder (McPherron 1967). While fishing appears to have been the primary subsistence activity, deer, elk, and small mammals were hunted (Cleland 1966). Gathering of local flora occurred and maize is also present (Yarnell 1964). Local stone was used for small, narrow-based triangular points (fig. 5), unifacial end scrapers, and small core tools. Awls, rolled beads, and knives of copper as well as awls, needles, and barbed harpoon heads of bone are common. Large numbers of postmolds were encountered but patterns were difficult to follow. The site appears never to have been fortified, and a single "longhouse" at least 25 feet by 100 feet was located. Multiple-bundle burials in five shallow pits covered with a single low mound were found. Considerable disarticulated bone occurred and many skulls exhibited postmortem removal of large disks. Some red ocher was present within these ossuaries along with "medicine bags" and a miniature grit-tempered cord-impressed vessel inverted over a shell-tempered punc-tated Oneota vessel. Associated with the Juntunen phase deposits were Mero complex ceramics as well as Ontario Iroquoian pottery. Several Middle Mississippian sherds were also present (McPherron 1967).

This Juntunen tradition is represented at numerous sites along the Lake Michigan shore north of Grand Traverse Bay. At Skegemog Point a Juntunen component with Blackduck and Mero ceramics represents a late summer fishing and horticultural village dated at A.D. 1210 ± 120 (M-1836) and A.D. 1310 ± 120 (M-1864)

U. of Mich., Mus. of Anthr.: negatives 16440, 16443, 16441.

Fig. 4. Juntunen site pottery. left, Bois Blanc rim sherd, Bois Blanc I., Mich.; middle and right, Juntunen pottery. Left rim diameter about 20 cm, rest same scale. (See also Fitting 1975:figs. 109–111.)

U. of Mich., Mus. of Anthr.: negative 16445.
Fig. 5. Juntunen chipped stone from Juntunen site, Bois Blanc I., Mich. Length of far right about 3.5 cm, rest same scale. (See also Fitting 1975:fig. 112.)

U. of Mich., Mus. of Anthr.: negative 16422.
Fig. 6. Younge tradition pipes. Stem length of left about 9.7 cm. (See also Fitting 1975:fig. 89.)

(Fitting 1970). Juntunen ceramics mixed with Iroquoian ceramics have also been recovered from Isle Royale (Bastian 1963) and from sites along Superior's south shore east of Keewanaw Bay (L.M. Stone 1967; Janzen 1968; Bigony 1968; Fitting 1970). Juntunen influences are noted in northern Georgian Bay (Lee 1959; Wright 1969). Farther south, occasional components in Bruce County, Ontario, suggest Juntunen-like affinities (Wright 1967, 1971). The western Huron shore displays a mixture of Juntunen and Younge tradition influences (Fitting 1968a).

Southern Michigan

The Younge tradition (Fitting 1965, 1970), originally described for southwestern Lake Huron, is now seen to extend east to the Black River in Ohio (Prahl, Brose, and Stothers 1976; Prufer and Shane 1976; McKenzie and Blank 1976; Brose 1976). Recent data suggest the in situ development of Younge tradition ceramics from the Western Basin complex (Prahl, Brose, and Stothers 1976). The earliest Younge phase is characterized by grit-tempered cordmarked pottery with collars and rarely castellated rims with bands of diagonal tool impressions. Plats of vertical and oblique motifs occur as do triangular zones of shoulder incision (Fitting 1965; Shane 1967). Several types of drills occur along with small scrapers. Broad-based triangular points predominate. Bone and shell artifacts include ulnar awls and barbed harpoons. Copper is rare. Plain and cord-decorated elbow pipes are known (fig. 6). Habitation sites are located behind the lake shore on sand knolls or fossil beach ridges along small creeks or estuaries (Fitting 1965). While maize is present at some large sites (Prahl 1969; Shane 1967; Prufer and Shane 1976) the economy seems characteristic of a diffuse hunting-gathering fishing orientation (Brose 1976). Large cemeteries with varied multiple burials were common. Postmortem alteration included the removal of skull plaques and perforation of crania and long bones (Hinsdale and Greenman 1936; Fitting 1970; Brose 1976). Several extreme longhouses have been reported at the Younge site although these are probably charnel houses (Greenman 1937a). Oval to circular wigwamlike structures within large palisaded villages are dated at A.D.

955 ± 110 (GX-1365) at Libben and between A.D. 890 ± 130 (M-2044) and A.D. 1110 ± 100 (M-2045) at Indian Hills. Small unfortified campsites have been dated at A.D. 1085 ± 100 (M-1431) at Verchave II and A.D. 1070 ± 100 (M-2087) at the Morrin site.

The Springwells phase of the Younge tradition shows similarities with Juntunen ceramics and is characterized by significant increase in collared, castellated ceramics with linear and push-pull tool impressions in horizontal or triangular motifs. Neck-shoulder incised and tool-impressed decoration is continued, as is the trend toward narrow triangular points. Multiple bundle reburials in ossuaries are present at sites near Detroit (Greenman 1958) and have been dated at A.D. 1185 ± 75 (CWRU-1) at the Indian Trails site (Brose 1973a) and A.D. 1159 ± 75 (M-741) at Springwells (Fitting 1970), and in Ontario at the Turkey Creek Ossuary. Village sites such as the Saint Mary's Vineyard with coeval Iroquoian linear ceramics produce maize but still suggest a diffuse economic adaptation (Brose 1976). Springwells phase materials are minimally represented south and east of the Maumee River, and two distinct regional developments can be isolated. The western region is characterized by a continuation and elaboration of cordmarked, dentate, and tool-impressed pottery with chevron motifs below the shoulder occasionally accompanied by added clay strips. At Mixter these ceramics have been dated at A.D. 1280 ± 85 (GX-1317) and A.D. 1310 ± 105 (GX-1740); A.D. 1110 ± 100 (M-2045) is the date at Indian Hills (Brose 1976). Some shell-tempered vessels with rare strap handles, resembling materials from central Indiana (Griffin 1943; Dorwin 1971), have also been recovered.

Southeastern Area

From the Black River to Erie, Pennsylvania, the early phases of the Whittlesey focus (Greenman 1935, 1937, 1939) date between A.D. 900 and A.D. 1300 (Brose 1976a). Small summer agricultural villages are located along the lake shore and on the floodplain at secondary stream junctions. Smaller campsites suggest autumn and spring fishing stations. Winter hunting and gathering camps are represented by interfluvial upland or beach ridge stations. Preliminary analyses suggest that agriculture was of minimal importance and the economic adaptation was rather diffuse. Sites are unfortified and single-post oval structures are represented at the lower levels at South Park (Brose 1973a) dated at A.D. 1000 ± 65 (WIS-576) and at the Dupler site (Baby 1971). Ceramics are grit-tempered and cordmarked to the rim (fig. 7). Decoration, where present, is predominantly oblique tool impressions although circular punctations in triangular plats occur; corded decoration is absent. Thickened rimstrips occasionally occur as do small teatlike lug handles. These ceramics resemble several early Fort Ancient types (Griffin 1943; Prufer and Shane 1970) as well as Younge phase materials farther west. Lithic materials are characterized by broad-based triangular points although most artifacts consist of retouched flakes. Unifacial scrapers and bifacial drills were infrequent. Bone beads, fishhooks, antler drifts or gaming pieces were common, while split or ulnar awls were rare.

Western Michigan

With the exception of the Prairie Peninsula (a phytogeographic zone of continuous grasslands) in southwestern Michigan most of the lower peninsula is characterized by a late phase of the Wayne tradition from A.D. 1000 to at least 1400. Within the Saginaw valley levels at the Schultz site dated to A.D. 1180 ± 100 (M-1648) indicate a small seasonal hunting village characterized by ceramics identical to Wayne Cordmarked although one castellated vessel was also recovered (Fitting 1972). The lithic assemblage is dominated by expanding-stemmed projectile points. Shell beads, beaver-tooth chisels, and bone projectile points were present. Maize may be associated with this component (Yarnell 1964; Fitting 1970) but the major economic focus was hunting (Cleland 1966). Additional smaller sites yielded similar materials between A.D.

1000 and 1400 (Bigony 1970). The few features recovered were circular, straight-sided, flat-bottomed, and nearly sterile pits. Narrow expanding-stemmed and triangular points were associated with plain cordmarked ceramics with occasional lip notching. Most sites represent short-term hunting and fishing camps. Agricultural villages are unknown. The mortuary complex is represented by refuse pit cremations as in the Valley Sweets site (Brose 1966) or by isolated flexed burials with Wayne ware ceramics, dated to A.D. 1220 ± 100 (M-1796) and A.D. 1290 ± 100 (M-1755) at the Bussinger site.

Similar ceramics characterize most of central and western Michigan during this period at Crystal Lake Village and the South Flats club earthwork (Quimby 1965); late lip-notched variants are assigned to the eleventh century. In the upper Muskegon River valley the Boven earthwork represents a small fortified agricultural village dated A.D. 1200 ± 75 (M-790), with pottery transitional between the material just described and what Quimby (1960, 1966a) has called Peninsular Woodland: cordmarked ceramics with moderately everted rims with most decoration consisting of lip-notching only (Greenman 1927; Quimby 1952; Prahl 1968). Farther north in the Manistee River drainage small fishing and hunting camps are associated with multiple bundle burials in low conical mounds at A.D. 1200 (Quimby 1964; Fitting 1968a, 1970). Small scrapers and triangular points are common. Bone tools include awls, antler points, and barbed harpoons. Copper celts, awls, and rolled beads occur as grave goods. Ceramics represent a blend of plain and cordmarked globular vessels with outflared rims decorated by lip modification, although some vessels display collars, castellations, and motifs reminiscent of the late Younge or Juntunen phase. The subsistence-

Cleveland Mus. of Nat. Hist.

Fig. 7. Whittlesey pottery from South Park site, Cuyahoga Co., Ohio. Rim diameter of bottom sherd about 18 cm, rest same scale.

575

settlement system indicates seasonal mobility and diffuse economic orientation, not unlike the historic Ottawa (Fitting and Cleland 1969).

A similar pattern occurs in the eastern part of Michigan at this period although population density seems to have been lower (Fitting 1970). Small, unfortified villages with mixed economic orientation are associated with mounds containing flexed and multiple bundle burials with late Wayne Cordmarked and Bois Blanc-like ceramics (Hinsdale 1929). Somewhat later are a number of large earthwork enclosures with relatively little artifact content. Along the Rifle River, high wall-and-ditch oval earthworks enclose areas of about 50,000 square feet. Internal features are not apparent and the ceramics represent the Younge tradition (Dustin 1932; Fitting 1970). At the Walters-Linsennan site (Cornelius and Moll 1959), dated at A.D. 1350 ± 75 (M-779), the earthen embankments were stockaded and within the enclosure were at least 19 single-post, subrectangular structures with storage pits. Post-mold patterns suggest seasonal reoccupation as an agricultural village. Materials recovered and the economic patterns suggested are similar to those farther west within the state.

In southwestern Michigan, the period from A.D. 1000 to A.D. 1400 is marked by the introduction of considerable Mississippian influence (Faulkner 1970; Bettarel 1970). The component at Moccasin Bluff dated at A.D. 1060 ± 110 (M-1937) and A.D. 1090 ± 110 (M-1938) represents a large permanent village with maize and squash agriculture (Yarnell 1964; Cleland 1966). Chipped-stone and bone tools are not common although small narrow triangular points and flake scrapers are noted, and deer-jaw "sickles" and bone fishhooks occurred. The cordmarked and plain grit-tempered ceramics are infrequently collared, semiglobular pots with moderately everted notched rims. These Peninsular Woodland ceramics of the Moccasin Bluff phase are associated with cordmarked shell-tempered globular bowls with everted rims and occasional trailed designs (Bettarel 1970) and with ceramics closely related to the early Fisher-like occupation at the Fifield site in Indiana and indirectly to Fisher and Early Langford materials in northern Illinois. Later occupation at Moccasin Bluff, dated A.D. 1150 ± 110 (M-1490) and A.D. 1210 ± 110 (M-1939), indicates some population increase, possibly as the result of the introduction of beans to the agricultural complex (Yarnell 1964; Fowler 1969). It is marked by a decrease in shell-tempered cordmarked pottery and an increase in grit-tempered cordmarked and plain ceramics. Collars and corded decoration disappear with the exception of several high-collared castellated vessels decorated with horizontal push-pull motifs analogous to late Younge phase materials farther east.

Farther north within the Prairie Peninsula the 46th Street site, dated at A.D. 1040 ± 100 (M-2233) and A.D. 1140 ± 100 (M-2232), and the lower levels of the Nordhoff site on the Kalamazoo River, dated at A.D. 1040 ± 100 (M-2234) represent, respectively, an extensive winter hunting camp and a large, probably agricultural, village. Ceramics, classified as Allegan wares, resemble early Moccasin Bluff material and differ from Wayne-Spring Creek wares (Fitting 1965, 1968a) in their greater frequency of lip decoration (M.B. Rogers 1972). These were associated with small stemmed and triangular points (Baldwin 1972). Similar ceramics were noted at the Whorley earthwork (Speth 1966), dated at A.D. 1080 ± 100 (M-1758), a small palisaded village on the upper Saint Joseph River.

Around A.D. 1200 there is a northward expansion of Mississippian elements. The Allegan Dam site at the mouth of the Kalamazoo River, dated at A.D. 1210 ± 100 (M-2230) and A.D. 1310 ± 100 (M-2231), represents a rather large winter camp. One partial post-mold pattern, probably a circular to oval wigwamlike structure, was discovered. Ceramics include grit-tempered straight rim vessels with cordmarked and plain surfaces as well as plain and cordmarked shell-tempered bowls with flaring rims. Low, rounded castellations and lip notching occur on both types. Small side-notched and triangular points are present. Baldwin (1972) has noted the Illinoian affinities of this component. Similar grit-tempered ceramics were found at De Boer, a small campsite on the Little Rabbit River to the east, associated with small triangular points and tool-impressed collared ceramics analogous to Macomb-Springwells material farther east, or Juntunen-like ceramics from the Traverse Bay region.

Lower Lake Michigan

In northern Illinois and northwestern Indiana the nature of Mississippian-Woodland interaction is unclear (Brown 1965). In the central Illinois River valley the twelfth century is marked both by intrusive Middle Mississippian sites and by the adoption of Mississippian ceramic attributes by local groups. This manifestation has been designated Fisher A (J.W. Griffin 1946). By the mid-thirteenth century similar grit-tempered cordmarked Upper Mississippian assemblages are components of the related Langford culture (Brown et al. 1967; Faulkner 1970) in the Illinois River valley. Fisher components continue in northern Illinois where Langford Trailed ceramics also occur. By the mid-fourteenth century Langford components are noted in the prairie areas of the middle to upper Illinois River valley while Fisher components are found on the glacial lake plains of the Chicago area and northwestern Indiana coeval with Koshkonong and early Lake Winnebago components in Wisconsin (R.L. Hall 1962). The Yahl site in the middle Kankakee River valley represents an early Fisher component at A.D. 1000–1200; sites in the upper Kankakee represent Fisher occupation by A.D. 1300–1400 (Faulkner 1970; Bettarel 1970). In addition to ceramics, Fisher components are characterized by small triangular points, humpbacked end scrapers, rectangular sandstone abraders, sherd disks and elk-scapula hoes. Floral and faunal analyses of large semipermanent villages and smaller extractive camps (Faulkner 1970) suggest a seasonal cycle involving winter hunting on the wooded uplands, spring exploitation of local marsh resources, and summer agriculture in river-bluff villages. Intrasite settlement or burial data are unavailable, although at the Fisher site rectangular wall-trench and semisubterranean houses were suggested; and extended burials below and intrusive into low mounds occurred (J.W. Griffin 1946).

The Late Prehistoric Period: A.D. 1400 to Contact

If the prehistoric period appears confused, the protohistoric period must appear chaotic, having been described as a period of widespread population movements, tribal decimation, and the near-total abandonment of large portions of the Upper Great Lakes area (Griffin 1960; Brown 1965). This period is also one of cooler and wetter summers (Baerreis and Bryson 1965), the importance of which is debatable.

Late Oneota

Gibbon (1969, 1972) has suggested that by A.D. 1400 most large Oneota settlements in Wisconsin had fragmented into smaller dispersed communities with population relocations. An exception is the increase in size and number of plains-adapted Orr focus sites in eastern Wisconsin after A.D. 1400 (McKern 1945; McKusick 1973).

Few Grand River sites postdate A.D. 1450, and no European contact has been documented for those that seem latest. The Koshkonong focus is not recognizable after A.D. 1350 (Gibbon 1969); and the latest prehistoric material from the Carcajou Point site, dated at A.D. 1528 ± 250 (M-748), represented everted rim, boldly finger-trailed, and punctated Lake Winnebago types. These are the latest ceramics throughout the Rock River drainage and appear associated with simple stamped, Fisher-like, and/or Peninsular Woodland ceramics in southeastern Wisconsin (R.L. Hall 1962). Within the Wolf River-Fox River drainage Lake Winnebago ceramics are the latest prehistoric materials, dated to the late fifteenth century. This manifestation includes small narrow triangular points, numerous humpbacked end scrapers, and bison-

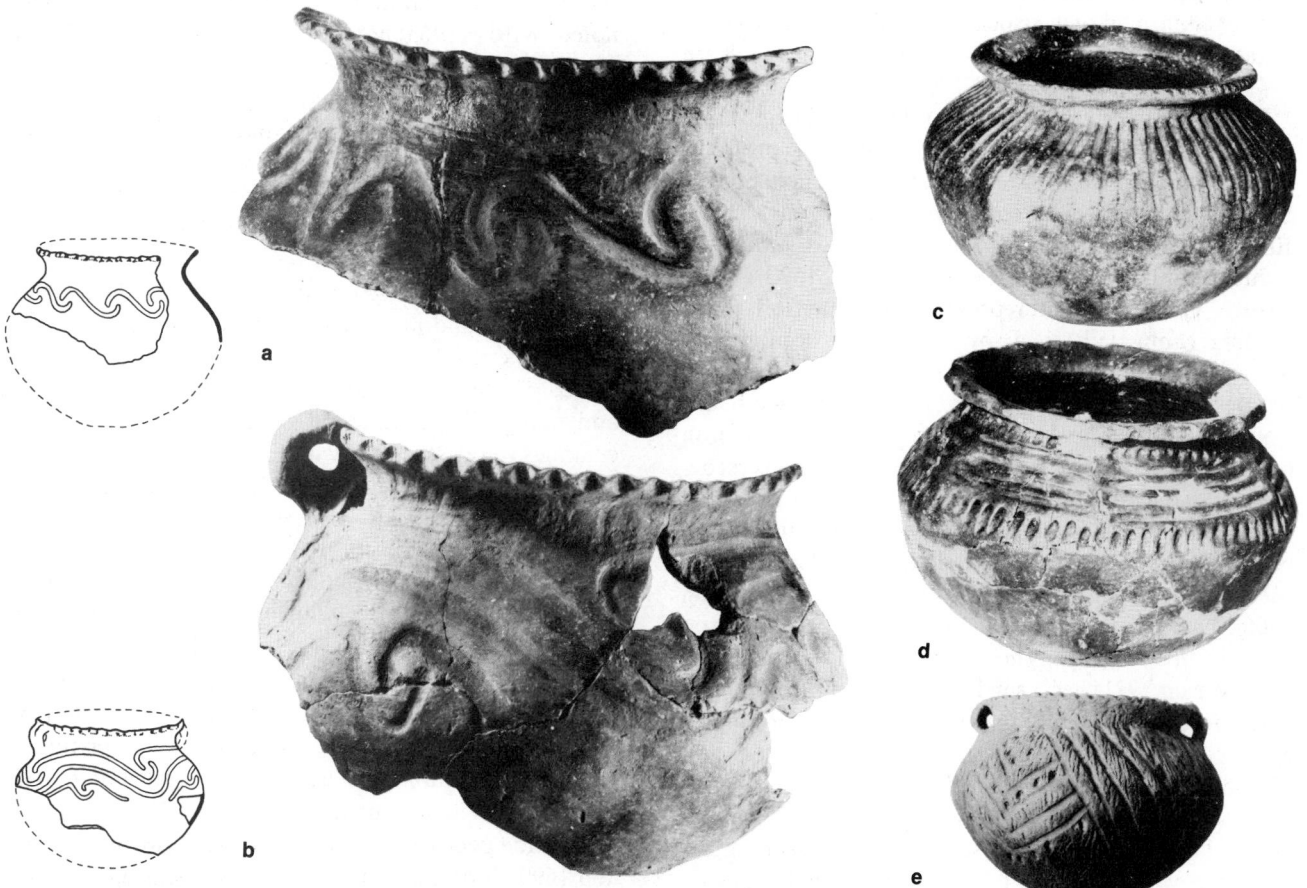

Fig. 8. Oneota pottery. a-b, Rim sherds of Carcajou Curvilinear type from Carcajou site, Jefferson Co, Wis., with reconstruction of whole pot to left; c-d, vessels of Lake Winnebago Trailed type from Karow site, Winnebago Co., Wis.; e, vessel from Fisher Mounds, Will Co., Ill. Shoulder diameter of c, 21 cm, rest same scale. (See also R.L. Hall 1962, 2:pls. 22-23, 74; Langford 1927:pl. 12.)

scapula hoes. The hoes are late and may represent trade with western Orr focus groups whose characteristic ceramics occur on most late Lake Winnebago sites (Peske 1971). Bone or antler shaft-wrenches and grooved sandstone abraders are found, as are cut copper shell pendants and effigy serpents representing "Southern cult" influences (McKern 1945; R.L. Hall 1962; Gibbon 1969; Peske 1971). Sites are small, fortified, semipermanent villages or small seasonal villages and cemeteries. Ridge and furrow "garden beds" or agricultural fields appear associated (Fox 1959; Peske 1966). The economy reflects seasonal reliance on maize; however, sites are located in aquatic situations, and analyses (Yarnell 1964; Cleland 1966) suggest exploitation of local resources. Structures include multifamily wigwams. Projectile points are characteristically small narrow triangles. The presence of catlinite disk pipes and pendants represents the major addition to earlier assemblages (see McKern 1945; Quimby 1966a). Evidence for large communal bison hunting is limited (Gibbon 1969; Faulkner 1970; Peske 1971). Lake Winnebago focus has been associated with the historic Winnebago by relating respective geographical distributions and associating historically known Winnebago villages with late Lake Winnebago sites. Isotopic dating has not confirmed such association, and early trade goods in late Lake Winnebago context are lacking (McKern 1945; Griffin 1960; R.L. Hall 1962).

Farther north, Lake Winnebago-influenced Mero complex (R.J. Mason 1966) is a minor element on protohistoric sites associated with early French trade material. At Summer Island the final component, dated A.D. 1620 ± 100 (M-2014), contained French materials indicating occupation between A.D. 1650 and A.D. 1690 (Brose 1970b). This component represents a summer to late fall hunting camp with small oval wigwams occupied by several extended patrilocal families. Triangular points, scrapers, and core tools dominate the lithic assemblage. Bone and copper tools are rare, replaced by their iron counterparts, although a copper effigy serpent was recovered. Ceramics represent two variants of grit-tempered Peninsular Woodland ceramics associated with vessels bearing Lake Winnebago-like design but derived from Mero ceramics in morphology and paste (R.J. Mason 1966). Lake Winnebago Trailed and postcontact Huron ceramics were present. The stratified Rock Island II site (R.J. Mason 1971) has a small summer camp component with Mero and Lake Winnebago ceramics intermingled and a later component with French trade beads and Huron-Petun ceramics assigned to the immediate postcontact period. Overlying these a palisaded village enclosed large oval wigwam structures and rectangular structures with chimneys, fireplaces, split plank walls set in trenches with stone footings, and large amounts of French trade goods and personal property attributable to the mid-seventeenth century. This site probably represents the Potawatomi village in which René-Robert Cavelier de La Salle's agents spent the winter of 1678–1679. Ceramics include some Mero and Lake Winnebago types but predominantly two variants of Peninsular Woodland ceramics similar to Summer Island (R.J. Mason 1971).

The Bell site at Big Lake Butte des Morts represents a Fox village of the A.D. 1680–1730 period (Wittry 1963). Within the small palisaded village were at least one small bark-covered wigwam and at least two rectangular wall-trench houses. The population was strongly acculturated to the European fur trade and much native material had been replaced by French goods. Bone tools were rather frequent, and notched and triangular projectile points occurred. Ceramics represented the same variants of Peninsular Woodland ceramics found in the earlier Green Bay area sites, Type I being smoothed globular vessels with a punctated flattened lip, everted rim, and narrow incised line neck and shoulder decoration and occasional strap handles. Type II pottery, less common, represents straight-rimmed cordmarked vessels with piecrust lips. Several Lake Winnebago vessels were recovered as were vessels representing Ramey Incised, Allegan Incised, and a late Fort Ancient-Whittlesey type. Flexed refuse pit interment and extended cemetery burials were noted. Wittry (1963) noted some duration for the site and suggested temporal priority for Type I pottery. Bell site Type I pottery was recovered from sites on the upper Wolf River along with Late Madison wares, projectile points representing a 10,000-year time span, and nineteenth-century Menominee materials (Barrett and Skinner 1932). Farther northwest, Salzer (1969) has indicated an occupational hiatus between the Late Lakes phase materials at A.D. 1400 and the John Badger phase, representing mid-nineteenth-century Chippewa.

In western Wisconsin, excavations at Rice Lake revealed a late seventeenth-century burial mound group and ricing village. Late Effigy Mound and Blackduck ceramics were associated with historic artifacts in graves. L.R. Cooper (1959) suggested a Dakota ethnic identification. Oneota ceramics were not present at Rice Lake although Mero-like pottery appears farther west at the Cooper site (L.R. Cooper 1965; E. Johnson 1969, 1969a), a palisaded historic ricing village with rectangular wall-post structures inhabited by both Mdewakanton Sioux and Chippewa in the eighteenth century.

At Chequamegon Bay a historic component from southeastern Madeline Island represents a mixture of Huron-Petun ceramic styles, with vessels attributed to the Lake Winnebago focus and Peninsular Woodland vessels. Trade goods indicate occupation between A.D. 1668 and 1690, during which time the region was inhabited by Huron, Petun, Ottawa, Sauk, Fox, Potawatomi, and Illinois, but *not* Winnebago. A nearby site represents a Huron-Petun village occupied from A.D. 1650 to A.D. 1670 (Quimby 1966a).

The Northern Area

North of Lake Superior sites display variable proportions of late Blackduck, Late Juntunen-Younge, and Peninsular Woodland ceramics similar to the Bell site. A considerable degree of ethnic continuity is suggested throughout the protohistoric and historic period (Kidd 1969). Many sites represent nearly pure late Blackduck summer fishing villages (Wright 1965). Associated seventeenth- and eighteenth-century trade goods are present at the Swan Lake site (Kenyon 1961). These sites were occupied by Cree and/or Chippewa in the seventeenth century. Along the northern Superior shore, stratified small seasonal fishing villages show historic seventeenth-century and late prehistoric components estimated between the eleventh and fourteenth centuries (Wright 1963, 1965, 1969; Dawson 1971). Most are late Blackduck. At Pic River a component dated to the early eighteenth century has, in addition to a late Blackduck complex, collared castellated vessels with chevron motifs below the peaks, with the collars and rim interiors bearing horizontal rows of push-pull decoration derived from the late Juntunen-Younge materials in Michigan (Quimby 1961; Wright 1967a). The Michipicoten site (Wright 1969) yielded seven distinct levels. Stratum II, dated by French trade goods to A.D. 1700, the underlying Stratum III dated to A.D. 1460 ± 75 (S-169), and underlying components represent small fishing villages with: Huron-Petun ceramics; Peninsular Woodland ceramics; a third ceramic group with push-pull techniques analogous to the Juntunen tradition; and one last ceramic group represented by folded, rarely castellated collars, decorated with a single row of tool impressions, similar to Younge phase and earlier Ontario Iroquoian tradition materials. Coeval analogs do not exist. Dawson (1971) has reported a number of nearby stratified sites that display similar ceramic sequences although the Nyman site represents a predominantly Blackduck manifestation. At the Montreal River mouth a small protohistoric fishing camp, dated to A.D. 1700, yielded Michipicoten-like and Blackduck ceramics (Wright 1965). A similar mixture has been reported from the Lookout site on Isle Royale, dated at A.D. 1625 ± 100 (Bastian 1963). From initial European contact this area has been inhabited by groups subsequently assigned to the Chippewa. From the Sault Sainte Marie area little aboriginal material exists for the period following A.D. 1400, due to canal construction since 1846.

The northern Huron shore at this period suggests greater Huron-Petun influence. At Shebishakong (Wright 1969) the protohistoric and the overlying stratum assigned by trade goods to the seventeenth century yield Huron-Petun, Blackduck, and collared ceramics with linear push-pull decoration (Wright 1965). The mid-seventeenth century stratum at the Frank Bay site (Ridley 1954) displays Huron-Petun ceramics associated with linear stamped ceramics. The contemporary Mississauga site (Quimby 1966a) and the Ellsmer-Morrison site (Wright 1965) are similar.

These northern Lake Huron sites may generally be assigned to the Ottawa who were encountered in this region. In the Mackinac region similar Huron-Petun, Peninsular Woodland, and linear stamped ceramic styles cooccur on village sites at Fort Michilimackinac (Maxwell 1964) and in the Gros Cap and Richardson ossuaries (Quimby 1963, 1966a; Greenman 1958), attributable, in part, to historic Ottawa (Quimby 1966a). Fort Ancient-Whittlesey ceramics also occur at these sites.

Similar mixed styles have been recovered from small seasonal fishing campsites and villages along northern Lake Michigan (Fitting 1970) in post-1400 components. Juntunen-like push-pull and linear stamped ceramics are rare on the north shore where ceramics are predominantly grit-tempered Peninsular Woodland vessels with Upper Mississippian influences. Late variants of linear stamped Juntunen wares, Mero, and Peninsular Woodland ceramics were common on the surface and in post-1350 strata at Juntunen (McPherron 1967).

Southeastern Area

Eastern Michigan yields little post-1400 occupation, leading Fitting (1965, 1969, 1970) to postulate an abandonment of the region except as a hunting preserve seasonally utilized by numerous ethnic groups. These data do not correspond with historical and ethnographic data that suggest that groups such as the Sauk and Fox lived in this general area prior to their flight into Wisconsin in the mid-seventeenth century.

In southeastern Michigan the final (Wolf) phase of the Younge tradition is characterized by small agricultural and fishing villages often associated with circular earthworks (Brose and Essenpreis 1973). Intrasite settlement patterns are unknown although individual flexed and bundle burials have been reported. Narrow triangular points dominate a lithic assemblage containing ovate bifacial knives and hafted end scrapers (Greenman 1939). Late varieties of collared, castellated, linear-stamped, and push-pull ceramic types occur with castellated ceramics with notched and filleted strips, accompanied by incised and/or punctate borders, forming elaborate lines and festoons on vessel shoulders (Lee 1958; Fitting 1965, 1970; Brose 1976; Prahl, Brose, and Stothers 1976). Grit temper predominates although shell-tempered varieties are frequent from village sites along the lower Detroit River (Fitting 1976). In this area strong Upper Mississippian influences appear after A.D. 1300 in small sites yielding plain globular shell-tempered ceramics with everted rims (Greenman 1958). Acculturated Woodland groups are located along the floodplain and bluffs of the Maumee River or its tributaries in stockaded villages with wigwamlike houses grouped around the interior of the stockade (Prahl 1969). Economic adaptation involved maize-beans-squash agriculture with intensive utilization of local riparian resources. Small, seasonal, special-purpose campsites are also known. Primary extended burials occur within village areas while flexed refuse-pit interments and multiple reburials in ossuaries are known. Material culture displays little change from earlier periods. Uncollared ceramics with everted rims show grit and shell tempering as free variation. Peninsular Woodland and Fisher or Fort Ancient–Whittlesey vessels are present; but most ceramics have high thickened rims incised in vertical, oblique, or opposed triangular plats with adornos and effigy faces at their apex. A number of stamped, punctate, and cord-impressed rims might be classified as proto–Parker Festooned; other Younge tradition ceramics are absent. While this complex postdates A.D. 1350 the only indications of European contact are mid-seventeenth-century Huron ceramics associated with Parker Festooned at the Bay Creek site, and early glass beads from a pit at Indian Hills dated to A.D. 1610 ± 100 (M-2268) (Brose 1976; Prahl 1969; Prahl, Brose, and Stothers 1976).

Northern Ohio

Farther east small agricultural villages with similar shell- and grit-tempered ceramics, narrow triangular points, bone beamers, and scapulae hoes have been dated to A.D. 1495 ± 95 (GX-1745) (Prufer and Shane 1976). A palisaded fishing village on the Black River contained wigwam structures and is associated with a large cemetery containing Southern cult imports dated at A.D. 1490 ± 55 (WIS-535) (McKenzie and Blank 1976; Brose 1976).

In northeastern Ohio middle and late phases of the Whittlesey focus postdate A.D. 1400 (Brose 1973a). The middle phase represents increased maize-beans-squash agriculture and reduction in seasonal movement. Summer agricultural villages are surrounded by small hunting-collecting camps. Fall through spring occupation clusters at lacustrine villages such as the Ahlstrom site, dated at A.D. 1450 ± 55 (WIS-534), are associated with small short-duration hunting campsites in interfluvial uplands. Small triangular points dominate a lithic assemblage characterized by utilized waste flakes. Scrapers or drills are rare. Bone tools, similar to earlier components, include combs, beamers, turkey metatarsal awls, and an elk-antler effigy phallus. Shell hoes are common at summer villages. Engraved shale gorgets and celts with Southern cult motifs have been reported (Greenman 1937; Brose 1973a). Subrectangular houses with evidence for wall-trench and wattle-and-daub construction are dated to A.D. 1440 ± 55 (WIS-539) and A.D. 1470 ± 55 (WIS-538) at South Park II. Ceramics of this phase have folded rims with strap handles and notched added rim strips with lug handles. Decoration forms parallel triangular and horizontal motifs of trailed, punctated, or punctate-bordered incised line. Shell tempering is present

in about 20 percent of the ceramics. About 15 percent of all vessels are simple-stamped, with plain and cord-marked surfaces equally represented on the rest. Parker Festooned is ubiquitous but never frequent. Relationships of the Whittlesey types are found in late Fort Ancient types (Griffin 1943). This phase was geographically expansive, and locally anomalous sites such as Riker near Zanesville or McKees Rock Village at Pittsburgh represent intrusive Whittlesey sites of this period.

The final Whittlesey phase sees large fortified permanent villages practicing floodplain maize-beans-squash agriculture, located on isolated promontories along the major river valleys (Brose 1976a). Sites such as Tuttle Hill, Boice Fort, and South Park III are dated at A.D. 1625 ± 55 (WIS-537), A.D. 1645 ± 55 (CWRU-2B), and A.D. 1650 ± 100 (M-2271). These villages are associated with numerous small elk-hunting and butchering stations along river bluffs and in interfluvial regions, many of which have associated earthworks. No major sites are known on the coast; lacustrine occupations are small autumn and/or spring fishing-fowling stations. Structures, known only from large villages, indicate "longhouses" about 60 feet by 20 feet, with artifact distributions suggesting matrilocal residence (Brose 1973a). The southern influences of the middle phase are replaced by eastern ceramic influences. Shell tempering increases as do smoothed surfaces. Low castellations are associated with vertical appliqués. Incising in punctate-bordered horizontal bands, triangular plats of opposed parallel lines, and chevrons bordered by appliqué strips shows intergradation with Parker Festooned. Classic Whittlesey types (Fitting 1964; J. Murphy 1971) comprise 70 percent while varieties of Parker Festooned and late Iroquoian types account for 30 percent of the ceramics. Lithic materials show reduction in utilized debitage, and points are narrow triangles. Drills and scrapers are quite rare. Bone and shell artifacts are similar to those noted earlier. Burials are characteristically flexed refuse-pit interments without grave goods as at Tuttle Hill (Greenman 1937). Evidence for cannibalism has been noted (Brose 1973a). No European material is associated with any Whittlesey site; by the time of initial exploration northern Ohio was unoccupied (Brose 1971a).

Lower Michigan

Throughout lower Michigan few post-1400 sites exist. In the Saginaw valley Quimby (1952) and Wittry (1963) have noted shell-tempered Parker Festooned and Peninsular Woodland ceramics similar to the Bell site, in addition to late Younge tradition materials. A similar assemblage was recovered at the Porter site 8, a seasonally reoccupied fall-spring hunting village consisting of seven wigwam structures possibly occupied by a number of male-related extended families (A.R. Pilling 1966; Cornelius and Moll 1959). In mid-state, small winter hunting-gathering stations yield Whittlesey ceramics associated with a late Iroquoian pipe (Cushman 1968). North of Saginaw, Peninsular Woodland-Younge ceramics are found at small campsites and earthworks (Greenman 1927; G.A. Wright 1966). Along the Rifle River small earthworks yield Bell site Type I ceramics (Dustin 1932; Fitting 1970). The Mikado Earthwork, postdating A.D. 1450 ± 100 (M-777), encloses 96,000 square feet within a palisade-topped bank-and-ditch earthwork. Post molds indicate multifamily wigwamlike structures. Charred maize and beans were recovered from refuse-filled storage pits (Yarnell 1964). Associated with narrow triangular points were ceramics analogous to the Tuttle Hill Notched vessel from the Gros Cap Cemetery (Quimby 1963), Bell site Type I, and late Juntunen-like linear-stamped collared vessels with coarse grit temper (Carruthers 1969).

West-central Michigan yields small seasonal campsites and a few larger fortified villages (Fitting 1966, 1970). The Reider Earthwork, dated to A.D. 1470 ± 100 (M-1768), produced Peninsular Woodland ceramics similar to those from the Dumaw Creek site, dated A.D. 1680 ± 75 (M-1070). Primary flexed burials were wrapped in robes of beaver, bison, and raccoon. Grave goods include zoomorphic stone pipes, beads of copper and Gulf Coast shell, copper hair pipes, tinkling cones, an effigy snake, and a Southern cult gorget of marine shell. Small triangular points, leaf-shaped bifacial knives, bone and antler awls and points were rare. Settlement data were not recovered, and the economic adaptation is not clear although charred pumpkin seeds were found. Ceramics represent a Peninsular Woodland assemblage of globular cord- and fabric-marked grit-tempered vessels with everted pie-crust rims (Quimby 1966a). Little additional information is available for northwestern Michigan, although there is no indication of Peninsular Woodland influence in the Juntunen-like ceramics at the Fauver site dated to A.D. 1600 ± 100 (M-1866).

Lower Lake Michigan

In the Grand River valley a late prehistoric agricultural village (Herrick 1957) shows Juntunen, Younge, Peninsular Woodland, and Mississippian decoration and morphology intermingled on the same vessels. Globular, shell-tempered, strap-handled, trailed ceramics attributable to the Moccasin Bluff site were also found (Bettarel 1970). On the Kalamazoo River a village dated to A.D. 1540 ± 100 (M-2235) yielded grit- and shell-tempered Peninsular Woodland ceramics (Baldwin 1972). Strong Mississippian influences in southwestern Michigan seem confined to the Saint Joseph River system after A.D. 1400. The latest occupation at Moccasin Bluff, dated A.D. 1590 ± 100 (M-1936) and A.D. 1640 ± 100 (M-1935), represents a permanent agricultural village. Deer, elk, and beaver were common food animals; bison was absent

(Cleland 1966). There may have been a population decrease from the earlier component. Small triangular points and ovate knives occurred as did bone rasps, elk beamers, and scapulae hoes. A Southern cult motif occurred on a Gulf Coast shell dipper. This occupation was characterized by: grit-tempered cordmarked ceramics analogous to Dumaw Creek; shell- and grit-tempered plain and cordmarked pottery with notched rim strips identical to Whittlesey-Fort Ancient types; and, most frequent, shell-tempered plain globular vessels with flaring rims, handles, and finger-trailed and punctated shoulders similar to Huber-Blue Island occupations in the Kankakee valley (Faulkner 1970) and the Chicago area (Griffin 1943; Bluhm and Fenner 1961; Bluhm and Liss 1961; Munson and Munson 1969; Slaymaker and Slaymaker 1971). Parker Festooned and Middle Mississippian ceramics also were noted (Bettarel 1970) but no European artifacts. A similar ceramic complex was dated to A.D. 1455 ± 250 (M-48B) at the Brems site a slight distance south (Faulkner 1970; Bettarel 1970).

In northwest Indiana late sites contain shell- and grit-tempered cordmarked ceramics associated with plain-surfaced finger-trailed and punctated ceramics with handles, analogous to protohistoric Huber material. Small triangular points and humpbacked endscrapers were common. Bent copper snake effigies, grooved rectangular stone abraders, weeping-eye gorgets of sherds and Gulf Coast shell, bone beamers, and scapulae hoes of elk and bison—all suggest an occupation between A.D. 1550 and A.D. 1700 although trade goods are absent. Faulkner (1970) suggests a seasonal cycle of spring marsh exploitation at small camps, large semipermanent fortified summer agricultural villages, and fall-winter elk and possibly bison hunting on the dry prairie.

The Huber sites of the Chicago area are distinguished from local Fisher components by the presence of smoothed, globular, shell-tempered, everted-rim jars with strap handles and trailed and punctate rectilinear shoulder design. These ceramics and the presence of antler shaft-wrenches and catlinite disk pipes show considerable late Oneota influences (R.L. Hall 1962; Brown 1965; Quimby 1966a; Gibbon 1969). Subsistence-settlement patterns do not differ markedly from Fisher adaptations with palisaded semipermanent summer agricultural villages of multifamily bark-covered subrectangular "longhouses" and larger "ceremonial" structures. Corn, beans, and squash were all cultivated (Quimby 1952; Bluhm and Fenner 1961; Bluhm and Liss 1961; Slaymaker and Slaymaker 1971). Smaller seasonal special-purpose camps are characterized by single- or two-family oval (probably bark-covered) domed wigwams. Indirect evidence suggests winter bison hunting on the prairies. Occasional refuse-pit or flexed burials occur, but more common are extended cemetery burials, as at the Anker site. Grave offerings include medicine bags with animal skulls, disk pipes, and copper and local and Gulf Coast shell gorgets. Copper snake effigies, weeping-eye masks, effigy and painted water bottles indicated southern contacts. Temporal change is represented in the ceramic complex; sites yielding French trade materials of the mid-seventeenth century have relatively pure Huber ceramics, while nearby, slightly earlier sites yield significant amounts of late Fisher material as well (Fenner 1961; Faulkner 1970). This pattern suggests gradually increasing contact with western Oneota groups, with a gradual adaptation of local populations to winter bison hunting following the arrival of bison east of the Mississippi, an event referable to a period of increasedly dry summers after A.D. 1550 (Griffin and Wray 1946; Griffin 1961a; Baerreis and Bryson 1965; Cleland 1966; Faulkner 1970). At the time of initial European contact, about A.D. 1680, this region of the Prairie Peninsula was primarily occupied by various groups of Miami, although transient Illinois groups were also noted.

Ethnic Identity

Specific ethnic identification for any of the late archeological manifestations described above is, unfortunately, speculative. Radical population displacements are suggested by European accounts of the seventeenth century particularly as these appear to involve the movement of aboriginal populations westward from Michigan and southern Ontario into Wisconsin. Thus, there is little assurance within the Upper Great Lakes that the ethnohistorically reported groups of the mid- to late seventeenth century are necessarily related to those responsible for proximal archeological components of the early seventeenth century (Brose 1971). From the archeological point of view, however, it is reasonably safe to accept Quimby's (1960:107) statement that "the tribes found by European explorers in the Upper Great Lakes region after A.D. 1600 were all descended from various . . . cultures that had occupied the region previously."

Central Algonquian Languages

IVES GODDARD

The Central Algonquian languages are those members of the Algonquian linguistic family that were spoken aboriginally in the area of the Upper Great Lakes and the Canadian North, to the east of the Great Plains. They are distinguished from the Plains Algonquian languages and the Eastern Algonquian languages. Of these three groups, only Eastern Algonquian is a genetic unit that underwent a period of separate development as a whole after splitting off from the Proto-Algonquian parent language (PA). Plains Algonquian and Central Algonquian are merely convenient geographic groupings, and the use of these labels does not imply that the languages so grouped share innovations that set them apart from the rest of the family. In this chapter only those Central Algonquian languages spoken in the area covered by this volume will be discussed. Cree-Montagnais-Naskapi and the northernmost varieties of Ojibwa and Algonquin are treated in volume 6, except that the speech of the Plains Cree and Plains Ojibwa is covered in volume 12. A general account of each language will first be given, including a survey of dialects and recent history. The relationships between the languages will then be treated, and finally the possible implications of the history of the Algonquian languages for the prehistory of the groups speaking them will be reviewed.

Survey of Languages

Ojibwa and Its Congeners

A single language with numerous dialects is spoken by the Indian groups known as Ojibwa, Chippewa, Saulteaux, Ottawa, Mississauga, Nipissing, and Algonquin. For convenience this language will be referred to as Ojibwa in the present discussion. Little or nothing specific is known of the type of speech used in most of the local settlements speaking this language, so statements about the dialectology of these groups are necessarily tentative and incomplete; however, it is clear that the conventional group labels just listed do not correspond well to the linguistic divisions.

Linguistically there is a major break between what may be called Southern Ojibwa and the varieties of Ojibwa to the north and west. Southern Ojibwa is most strikingly characterized by the weakening or complete loss of odd-numbered short vowels (except in final sylla-

bles), so that what elsewhere is *inini* 'man' and *anim* 'dog' comes out as *ənini* and *ənim*, or even *nini* and *nim*, with the initial vowels either falling together to ə or dropping completely. Dialects of this subtype are spoken by the Ottawas and Chippewas of the Lower Peninsula of Michigan, the Ottawas (or Odawas) of Manitoulin Island, and, as far as is known, by all the Indians in southern Ontario called Chippewas, Ojibwas, and Mississaugas at least as far north as Parry Island (Parry Sound) on the west and Curve Lake (Peterborough) on the east. A representative description is Bloomfield (1957).

Other dialects of Ojibwa seem less well defined. The Algonquin of Oka Mission at the mouth of the Ottawa River (Cuoq 1886) and now at Maniwaki, Quebec, is taken to reflect the speech of the Nipissing segment of the mission population, originally from Lake Nipissing. This, the Algonquin originally spoken on the Saint Lawrence, and the Algonquin now spoken by other local groups north of the Southern Ojibwa area are all presumed to constitute an Algonquin subtype, but knowledge of its dialectal details is incomplete. Detailed information is also scarce for the Ojibwa-speaking groups in the Upper Peninsula of Michigan and northern Wisconsin, but it appears that there is a dialectal break between the speech of the south shore of Lake Superior (specifically that of L'Anse, Michigan, La Pointe, Wisconsin, and Fond du Lac, Minnesota, represented by Baraga 1850) and that of the Ojibwa of central and northern Minnesota. In the latter area a Mississippi dialect (at Mille Lacs) can be distinguished, and the large northern reservations differ somewhat among themselves; in particular the speech of Red Lake seems to go with that of the Saulteaux to the north. This distribution of dialects may indicate that the Ojibwa speakers now in Minnesota came there at various times or from various previous locations.

There is a large body of material on Ojibwa dating back to the mid-seventeenth century (see Hanzeli 1969), and although almost none of the early manuscripts have been published or even systematically studied, enough information is available to permit the description of some significant aspects of the recent history of these dialects. The seventeenth-century missionaries distinguished between Algonquin and Ottawa (they were ig-

583

norant of the western varieties of Ojibwa), but these were much more similar to each other than the modern dialects that are their descendants. In particular the early records of Ottawa do not show the vowel-weakening characteristic of modern Ottawa and the rest of Southern Ojibwa, giving, for example, *ilini* 'man' and *alim* 'dog'; and the full-sounding vowels were still being written in nineteenth-century religious materials prepared for the Ottawas of the Lower Peninsula (Baraga 1832). Whatever the details, it is clear that this vowel-weakening was an innovation that spread over a rather large area among dialects that were already somewhat differentiated, a circumstance that must reflect continuing intense contact between the groups around Lake Huron and Georgian Bay. It is reasonable to assume, however, that the dialects that adopted this change were quite similar even beforehand, as they are spoken by groups that spread out within the historical period from the same small area at the north of Lake Huron.

Another striking feature of the seventeenth-century forms cited above, in which they differ from all modern types of Ojibwa, is the presence of *l* (reflecting Proto-Algonquian *θ and *l*); the corresponding Algonquin forms have *r* (*irini* and *arim*), but all modern dialects have *n*. By the beginning of the eighteenth century Algonquin had replaced *r* by *l* (Lahontan 1703, 2: 195–214); and *l* is still found, for example, in the Ottawa man's name *Macátepilesis* (presumably 'Black Bird'), recorded in 1761 (W. Johnson 1921–1965, 3:487). During this period, however, the replacement of *l/r* by *n* was spreading. The *n* variant is mentioned in the seventeenth century, but seems to be attested only for word-initial position, as in the tribal name *Noukek* in 1658 for the 1640 *Roquai* (Hanzeli 1969:71; JR 44:246, 18:230). By Alexander Henry's time (1760–1776), though *l* remained in Algonquin, it had become *n* in all positions in what he called "Chipeway" (Henry 1901:105); and *n* seems to have become universal in all varieties of Ojibwa by the early part of the nineteenth century. A network of linguistic contacts is revealed by the spread of this innovation, and when more is known about the details, this and other similar evidence will clearly provide valuable insight into the dynamics of recent culture contact and acculturation among Ojibwa speakers.

Potawatomi

The number and degree of difference of the dialects spoken by the various Potawatomi groups cannot be determined from the presently available information. There are said to be some variations in vocabulary, but the only definitely known feature of dialectal difference is the retention of *w* between *k* and a following consonant in the so-called Forest Potawatomi of Wisconsin, contrasting with its loss in Oklahoma Potawatomi (Hockett 1948:216). The speech of the Potawatomis of Kansas and Michigan has not been studied, and there is no in-

formation on the language of the Potawatomis who settled at various places in Ontario.

From the time of the first published recordings of Potawatomi in the nineteenth century (Simerwell 1834), vowel weakening of a type even more extensive than that of Southern Ojibwa is in evidence: basically (as described in the twentieth century) short vowels become *ə*, which drops in nonfinal odd-numbered syllables. It is very likely that this vowel weakening is related to that of Southern Ojibwa, but the direction of the presumed diffusion is not clear. In any case it must reflect the closeness of the contact between these linguistic communities in the nineteenth century.

Menominee

The Menominee language has been spoken in the same area by a single homogeneous tribe since the time of the earliest records in the seventeenth century, but the language itself is not attested before the early nineteenth century. There have always been many Menominees who also spoke Ojibwa and used it in their contacts with outsiders (a 1721 reference is Charlevoix 1744, 5:430), and as a result there are many Ojibwa loanwords in the language. Areal differences seem to be confined to minor vocabulary variations at certain locations, notably among the Menominee at Marinette (see Bloomfield 1962:34). Some fairly significant age-dialect differences were noted in the early 1920s, when the language was already going out of use (Bloomfield 1962:3–5, 93); and an appreciable range of variation among speakers in linguistic competence and stylistic ability was also described (Bloomfield 1927). By the 1970s the language was still spoken only by a rapidly dwindling minority of the tribe.

Fox and Its Congeners

The Sauk, Fox, and Kickapoo speak three dialects of a single language, for which there is no name in use either in English or in the language itself; it is usually referred to simply by hyphenating the names of the three tribes: Sauk-Fox-Kickapoo. Each dialect has archaisms and innovations that set it off from each of the other two, but in general Sauk and Fox seem to be more similar to each other than either is to Kickapoo. Kickapoo and Fox differ in a number of inflectional endings and other grammatical details.

Of the three dialects, Sauk is the least known, but some of its features are mentioned by Michelson (1912:258, 1925a:628). Sauk is spoken by the so-called Sac and Fox of Oklahoma and by the remnant of the Nemaha Sauks of Kansas, and Fox is still the language of the Mesquakie settlement near Tama, Iowa. It is assumed that these two dialects respectively continue the speech of the Sauk and the Fox of the earlier period, but there has been so much exchange of population between the two tribes since the eighteenth century that certainty

584

GODDARD

on this point is impossible. Kickapoo is spoken with no essential differences in Kansas, Oklahoma, and Coahuila (Voorhis 1974); the most conspicuous divergence is the tendency of the speakers in Mexico to borrow Spanish words, while the others borrow English words for the same items. There is good reason to believe that the Mascouten (a tribe absorbed by the Kickapoo at the beginning of the nineteenth century) spoke a fourth dialect of this language. A missionary of the seventeenth century who had learned Sauk wrote in different places that the Kickapoo had the same language as the Mascouten and that the Mascouten and Fox had the same language as the Sauk; these and other confirmatory statements outweigh some vaguely contradictory evidence (JR 54:222, 232, 60:206; WHC 16:372; cf. JR 66:236).

There is evidence from personal names recorded in the eighteenth century that Fox (and, undoubtedly, the other two dialects) had an *l* (from PA *θ and *l), which has become *n* in the modern form of the language: Kiala (d. ca. 1734; WHC 17:210) must have borne the name that is now *kya·na·wa* ('Hidden One', from PA *$kya\cdot\theta a\cdot wa$*). By the early nineteenth century *l* and *n* are found indiscriminately for original *θ, *l, and *n; that is, the earlier *l* and *n* had fallen together to a single structural unit, the pronunciation of which varied freely between the two sounds (see the vocabulary of 1827 in Forsyth 1912:239-244). It is very likely that this shift of *l* to *n* is connected with the identical change that spread through the Ojibwa dialects about the same time, and it thus furnishes evidence for continuing extensive contacts among the Central Algonquian peoples at a time when they were becoming increasingly scattered geographically.

Between the 1920s and the 1960s a number of changes occurred in Fox, most notably a general dropping of semivowels (*w* and *y*) between vowels (with some exceptions: Voorhis 1971:74-75). This innovation has tended to make Fox resemble more closely Kickapoo, in which a similar semivowel loss is older (in Jones 1915:119-123, but not in the vocabulary of ca. 1825 in Trowbridge 1939:67-70). It seems quite likely that the modern Fox have borrowed this feature from the Kickapoo, whom they admire for being culturally conservative (and thus fit models for imitation).

Miami-Illinois

Miami-Illinois is the name given for convenience to the language that was spoken in two clusters of dialects by the Miami and Illinois tribal groupings. Although there were at least partial speakers living as late as the 1960s, no systematic scientific study was made of this language before it became extinct. There is a large amount of material from seventeenth- and eighteenth-century missionaries and early modern recorders, but this has not been analyzed. The number and degree of relationship of the dialects is very uncertain, all the more so since the dialect identification of much of the available material is in doubt. Accordingly much in the present discussion must be regarded as tentative.

It is assumed that the major dialect cleavage coincided with the political boundary between the Miami (Miami proper, Wea, Piankashaw, and others) and the Illinois (Peoria, Kaskaskia, Cahokia, and others); but this seems to be contradicted by kinship terminologies obtained in 1860 on the three Kansas reservations, where the refugees were grouped as (1) Peorias and Kaskaskias, (2) Piankashaws and Weas, and (3) Miamis. These sets of terms, in effect the most extensive comparative vocabularies of Miami-Illinois that there are, show Miami to be rather divergent, though sharing some features with Wea and Kaskaskia, and these two are opposed as a pair to Peoria and Piankashaw, which are virtually identical (Morgan 1871). All of these differ in several respects from supposedly Illinois kinship terms recorded a century and a half earlier (Le Boullenger 1725). Acculturative changes in social organization might explain the discrepancy, and perhaps the historically unexpected subgrouping attested by the 1860 data reflects confusion of tribal boundaries among the refugee survivors. Nevertheless, the result is an unclear picture as far as the dialectology of Miami-Illinois at any period is concerned, although at least some differences between Miami and Illinois can be concretely established (not to mention a modicum of lexical discrepancies). For example, where Illinois has *sk*, Miami has *hk* (usually written simply *k* in our sources), and where Illinois has *r* (replaced in the historical period by *l*) from PA *θ and *l in all positions, Miami has *n* word-initially and *l* medially.

Shawnee

The three groups of Shawnee in Oklahoma (Absentee Shawnee, Eastern Shawnee, and Cherokee Shawnee) are said to speak three distinct dialects which "show some lexical differences, very few phonetic, and no phonemic differences" (Voegelin 1935:23). There may also be some differences in morphological detail, but specific information about Shawnee dialectology, or about possible changes since the first recordings in the late eighteenth century, is unavailable. Nothing is known about dialect differences among the five traditional Shawnee divisions (*čalaka, θawikila, mekoče, kišpoko,* and *pekowi*), except to the extent that these divisions may be partially continued by the present Oklahoma groupings.

Relationships Among the Languages

The seven Central Algonquian languages (the six discussed above plus Cree and its congeners) appear to be seven independent branches descending from the Proto-Algonquian parent language. The only languages that

Speakers of Central Algonquian Languages, 1965

Language	Number of Speakers
Ojibwa (includes all Ottawa, Chippewa, Algonquin, and Saulteaux)	41,000 to 52,000
Potawatomi	100 to 1,000
Menominee	300 to 500
Sauk-Fox-Kickapoo	2,000
Miami-Illinois	Extinct ca. 1965
Shawnee	300 to 400

SOURCE: Chafe 1962, 1965.

may be more closely related to each other than to any of the rest are Ojibwa and Potawatomi, which have undergone many identical phonological and grammatical developments since Proto-Algonquian. However, Potawatomi also shares with Sauk-Fox-Kickapoo a number of features not found in Ojibwa, both innovations (such as the loss of nasals before other consonants) and retentions (such as postconsonantal *y*, which is lost in Ojibwa). The net impression left is that Potawatomi shared its earlier history with Ojibwa and its more recent history with the Fox group, a situation that would be consistent with the Potawatomis' having at some point in prehistory moved away from the former and settled near the latter. The aboriginal location of the Potawatomi on the Lower Peninsula of Michigan with the Sauk, Fox, and Kickapoo would be in agreement with such a conclusion.

Similarly, most other cases of shared developments in the Central languages reflect aboriginal contiguity rather than a common genetic source. Some of the changes that spread across already established dialect and language boundaries in the historical period were discussed above; those to be mentioned here are presumably prehistoric. There are some lexical and phonological parallels between Shawnee and Sauk-Fox-Kickapoo, such as the culturally important word *mi·ša·mi* 'sacred bundle', which must go back to the time when the Shawnee were southeast of the Michigan homelands of the Fox group. Sauk-Fox-Kickapoo and Miami-Illinois, which were aboriginally contiguous, shared the change (not found elsewhere) of PA *nl* and *nθ* to *nt*; the fact that this innovation necessarily preceded the loss of nasals before other consonants in the Fox group (whereby *nt* became *t*) proves that this later change (shared with Potawatomi and Shawnee) spread among languages that were already distinct (Goddard 1973). In other cases similar innovations in two languages are likely to have been parallel independent developments. For example, in the evolution of the independent indicative verbal paradigm (Goddard 1967) the possibilities were structurally limited, so the fact that one resultant pattern is shared by Miami-Illinois and the Fox group (as well as Arapaho among the Plains languages) and another by Ojibwa,

Potawatomi, and Shawnee (as well as the northernmost of the Eastern languages) does not mean that these patterns must necessarily have emerged only once and diffused among the languages in question. Of the Central languages considered here, Menominee appears to have the largest number of unique and independent developments, a fact that clearly must reflect the long isolation of that language west of Lake Michigan until the mid-seventeenth century. The one attempt that has been made to estimate the relative amounts of lexical similarity among the Central languages is inconclusive because of the unequal sizes of the available lexicons (Hockett 1957:249-251).

Prehistory of the Algonquian Family

The lack of any separate genetic unity among the Central Algonquian languages means that the time depth they reflect is equivalent to that of the Algonquian family as a whole. Hence, it is necessary to discuss their deeper prehistory in the context of that of the entire family. There are no accurate means of estimating how long ago the Proto-Algonquian parent language was spoken, but a reasonable guess would be about 2,500 to 3,000 years ago. A careful study of the natural history terms that can be reconstructed for Proto-Algonquian has shown the likelihood that the ranges of the flora and fauna familiar to the speakers of the protolanguage overlapped only in the area between Georgian Bay and Lake Ontario; accordingly this would be the most probable original homeland of the Proto-Algonquian language (Siebert 1967). The fact that cultural terms such as 'snowshoe' and 'ice-chisel' can also be reconstructed supports this conclusion. The comparative linguistic evidence suggests that when the original Proto-Algonquian-speaking nucleus expanded it became fragmented rather early into 10 or so increasingly distinct and decreasingly interacting speech communities: the forerunners of the three Plains languages, six Central languages (assuming Ojibwa and Potawatomi were not yet distinct at this early stage), and Proto-Eastern Algonquian. The linguistic break between the last-named and the other languages is abrupt enough to suggest that Eastern Algonquian has been separated from the rest of the family by intervening Iroquoian languages since the very earliest period of its development; the distinctness and internal cohesion of the Eastern Algonquian languages as a group rule out any possibility that the continuum of Central and Eastern languages could have been split by a northward movement of Iroquoian speakers after the Eastern languages had become differentiated. Under such a circumstance a pattern of innovations common to both Central and Eastern languages (like the pattern within each of these groups) would be expected, but the special relationships between some Eastern languages and Central Algonquian that were formerly postulated (see Michelson 1912, 1933; Bloomfield 1925, 1946) are now known not to exist. The picture of Algonquian prehistory that emerges leaves the impression that the Eastern Algonquians must have spread east and south from the area of upper Saint Lawrence valley. For the most part, the prehistoric migrations of the Algonquians are a matter of speculation, at least on the basis of present linguistic knowledge.

Words borrowed into Algonquian languages provide some indication of contact with speakers of other languages, but they have received little systematic study. Borrowing between Algonquian languages seems to have been not uncommon, as, for example, the Ojibwa loanwords in Menominee already mentioned. Also, there is evidence for extensive mutual borrowing between Cree and Ojibwa. A number of words for postcontact items spread among some of the Central languages by borrowing or loan translation, such as those for 'whiskey' (Cree *iskote·wa·poy*, Menominee *esko·te·wa·poh*, Ojibwa *iškote·wa·po·*, all meaning literally 'fire liquid'), 'gun', 'trading-post', and 'Frenchman'. Words diffused from French include the names of the playing card suits, 'Montreal', 'pig', religious terms, proper names, and others. More recently, English borrowings have become common, and whereas the older, French loans generally were assimilated to Algonquian phonology, the more recent words from English tend to retain their foreign sounds. Thus Menominee has *tanɛ·s* from both French *trèfle* 'club (suit)' and *Thérèse* (girl's name), with elimination of the non-Menominee sounds *r, l,* and *f,* but it has *telɛfo·newɛw* 'he telephones' and *ri·tewɛw* 'he reads' from English, with retention of these sounds. Such a situation must reflect the widespread ability to speak English among these groups.

Borrowings from non-Algonquian Indian languages are sparsely attested. It has been argued that there is evidence for very early prehistoric mutual borrowing between Algonquian and Siouan, but most of the proposed word comparisons are unpersuasive (Siebert 1967a: 52–53). Algonquian languages do, however, attest a number of tribal names borrowed from Siouan, Muskogean, and Iroquoian languages. Two rather isolated borrowings from Siouan of words with cultural significance are the Fox moiety name *to·hka·na,* for older *oškaša,* from the Iowa society-name *túkala* (Michelson 1925: 548), and the word for 'warrior' in the western dialects of Ojibwa (*okiččita·*), and in Plains Cree and Menominee, which is from Dakota *akičita.*

Non-Algonquian Languages

There is reason to believe that there may originally have been some non-Algonquian languages immediately south of the Central Algonquian groups. Some early accounts suggest that the Michigamea spoke a separate language before ascending the Mississippi to join the Illinois confederacy toward the end of the seventeenth century (JR 59:150–152). Before the incursions of the Iroquois in the third quarter of the seventeenth century several tribes are known to have lived in the Ohio River valley region, but except for the Shawnee virtually nothing was recorded about them beyond their names. Among the prominent groups for which no linguistic data are known are the Mosopelea, Caskinampo (or Kakinonba), Cisca, Tomahitans, Monetons, Mohetans (assumed to be the same as one of the two preceding), Massomacks, Arrigahagas, and others; there are many hypotheses about the identities of most of these, but none that has been universally accepted (general discussions are Griffin 1943; Bauxar 1957; Hoffman 1964). The chances are good that one or more of these groups spoke a Siouan language, but the evidence falls short of being conclusive.

History of The Ohio Valley

WILLIAM A. HUNTER

At the beginning of historic times the Ohio valley was inhabited by a number of little-known, apparently sedentary groups, who were almost completely disrupted and evicted by about 1680 in the so-called Beaver Wars (Hunt 1940). Thereafter the area served for a time as hunting land; but it underwent a further and more gradual change as the fur trade altered and the region was repopulated by Indian groups whose original homes lay beyond its borders (fig. 1).

Even before the period of devastation European contacts had affected some Ohio groups. Tramontane Indians identified as Black Minqua or Arrigahaga (A. Johnson 1930:132, 140, 188; Van der Donck 1841:209; NYCD 1:588; Heermans 1673) as well as the Susquehannock (or White Minqua) traded with the Dutch and the Swedes on Delaware Bay; and the Shawnee in the southern part of the area appear to have had early commerce with the Spaniards. It must be assumed that these Indians also were affected by European diseases that, spreading along the routes of native communication, far outran the Europeans themselves; and epidemics may have played a part in depopulating the region.

The violent dispersal of the early Ohio valley residents and the reduction of their lands to hunting territory is generally attributed to the Iroquois, who were indeed the chief benefiters, though there is evidence that the Susquehannock, prior to their defeat in 1675, also had a hand in this, and perhaps other groups as well (A. Johnson 1930:188; Heermans 1673).

The Ohio was explored by Europeans at a relatively late date. A mountain barrier on the east delayed entry from the coastal colonies, and the Ottawa River and the Great Lakes, farther north, provided easier access from Canada to the interior of the country and even to the Mississippi. It was in fact by this route that French explorers first reached the mouth of the Ohio River. Contemporary accounts of the early inhabitants of the Ohio country are therefore unavoidably vague and confusing, since they deal with a country of which the reporters had no accurate and direct knowledge. A supposed exploration of the Ohio by René-Robert Cavelier de La Salle in 1669–1670 is fictional, and Charles Le Moyne de Longueuil's 1739 descent of the Ohio from Lake Chautauqua to the Mississippi provided the earliest firsthand information available to map makers. The resultant Mandeville-de Léry map (Mandeville 1740) is

588

of very uneven accuracy; but the 1749 Bonnecamps map, a product of the descent by Pierre Joseph Céloron de Blainville by the same route to the mouth of the Miami, shows the courses of the Ohio with remarkable accuracy (Bonnecamps 1749).

Specific information on Ohio peoples begins with the Erie, mentioned as early as 1635 as one of a number of "nations" speaking Iroquoian languages (JR 8:115). Their country lay inland from Lake Erie according to the *Jesuit Relations* of 1647–1648; they had been compelled to retire far inland to escape their enemies, who were farther to the west (JR 33:63). The enemies here referred to obviously are not the Iroquois, who defeated and dispersed the Erie in 1654. The names Erie and Black Minqua (the latter used by the Swedes and the Dutch) appear to be synonymous, but whether their meanings coincide or merely overlap is uncertain; nor is it clear whether either name applies to a specific tribe or to a wider grouping. Jesuit records name Rigué and Gentaienton as towns of the Erie but do not locate them (JR 42:186, 61:195); if Gentaienton is to be identified with the Kentaientonga of later mention, the name Erie must have been more inclusive than commonly supposed. Coincidences of name and date suggest that the Richahecrian, strange Indians who appeared in Virginia in 1656, were a fugitive group of Erie (Hoffman 1964:221 ff.); and a band of Erie near Virginia reportedly joined the Seneca voluntarily as late as 1681 (Md. Arch. 17:5; JR 62:73). Others who were not killed were adopted into Iroquois tribes, the Seneca especially.

The French began to learn of the Ohio River itself about 1670. In 1668 La Salle, then at Montreal, understood from some visiting Iroquois that "this river took its rise three days' journey from Seneca, that after a month's travel one came upon the Honniasontkeronons and the Chiouanons, and that, after passing the latter, and a great cataract or waterfall [at present Louisville], one found the Outagame and the Iskousogos . . ." (trans. from Margry 1876–1886, 1:116). In the following year La Salle visited the Seneca, where he heard of "the tribes called by them the Touguenhas, living on the River Ohio," and saw a Touguenha prisoner, whose "language differed from Algonquin even more than that of the Ottawas" (trans. from Margry 1876–1886, 1:130, 134). In descending the river, he was warned, he would be in danger from both the Touguenha and the Antastoez (Susquehannock)

(Margry 1876-1886, 1:137-138). In 1673 Louis Jolliet and Jacques Marquette made their descent of the Mississippi, in the course of which they passed the mouth of "a river called Ouaboukigou" (or Wabash, actually the Ohio): "This river flows from the lands of the East, where dwell the people called Chaouanons [Shawnee] in so great numbers that in one district there are as many as 23 villages, and 15 in another, quite near one another. They are not at all warlike, and are the nations whom the Iroquois go so far to seek, and war against without any reason . . ." (JR 59:145).

The special interest of the quoted passages lies in the fact that they date from a time before the final destruction and dislocation of the old Ohio population. Later records preserve some additional data, and Franquelin's (1684) map of Louisiana, based on information that La Salle had obtained from Indian refugees at his colony in Illinois, provides a summary (Hanna 1911, 2:92). Because La Salle had not himself explored the country, the streams and other features are vaguely and inaccurately presented; however, a river with the threefold identification "Ohio alias Mosopeleacipi alias Olighin" undoubtedly represents the Allegheny and the Ohio above the falls, and the tribal names and the numbers of destroyed villages are valid data, even though their sites cannot be identified on the modern map. On the north side of the Ohio, from east to west, the peoples and destroyed villages are: Kentaientonga, 19; Oniassontke, 2; Casa, 1; and Mosapelea, 8. The Shawnee are not located as such; but southeast (south) of the Ohio, between it and a stream identified as Skipakicipi (Shawnee 'blue or green river';

the Kentucky River?) are placed Chaskepe and Meguatchaiki, from which goes a "road by which the Casquinampo and the Chaouenons go to trade with the Spaniards." The Meguatchaiki are readily identifiable as the *mekoče* division of the Shawnee, and the Chaskpé were associated with the Shawnee who took refuge in Illinois.

For the most part these names disappear from history. The possible connection of Kentaientonga with the Erie has been noted. The Oniassontke are the Honniasontkeronons of earlier report; their name had appeared on the Bernou (1680) map and reappears without explanation on De l'Isle's (1702) map and some later maps. Casa is not otherwise known. In 1682 La Salle found a chief and five lodges of fugitive Mosopelea living on the lower Mississippi (Margry 1876-1886, 1:610). The name Shawnee ('southerner') is unquestionably Algonquian and may refer to a group of peoples rather than to a single tribe. Some of the Shawnee appear to have retreated toward Carolina; but a number of fugitives, identified as Chaouesnons and Chaskpé, took refuge at the French post in Illinois (Margry 1876-1886, 2:142-143, 314). The Shawnee who entered Maryland in 1692 appear to have derived from this latter group. Touguenha, an Iroquoian term that may sometimes refer to the Shawnee, had a much broader meaning, explained in the *Jesuit Relation* of 1661-1662: "Ontoagannha, signifying 'the place where people cannot speak' " (JR 47:145). The term appears also in early New York records as Dowagenhaws, Wagenhaes, and other variants (Wraxall 1915:169ff.); it is simply the general Iroquois designation for the Algonquians to their west: Mohawk *tewaʔkę́nhaʔ* and related

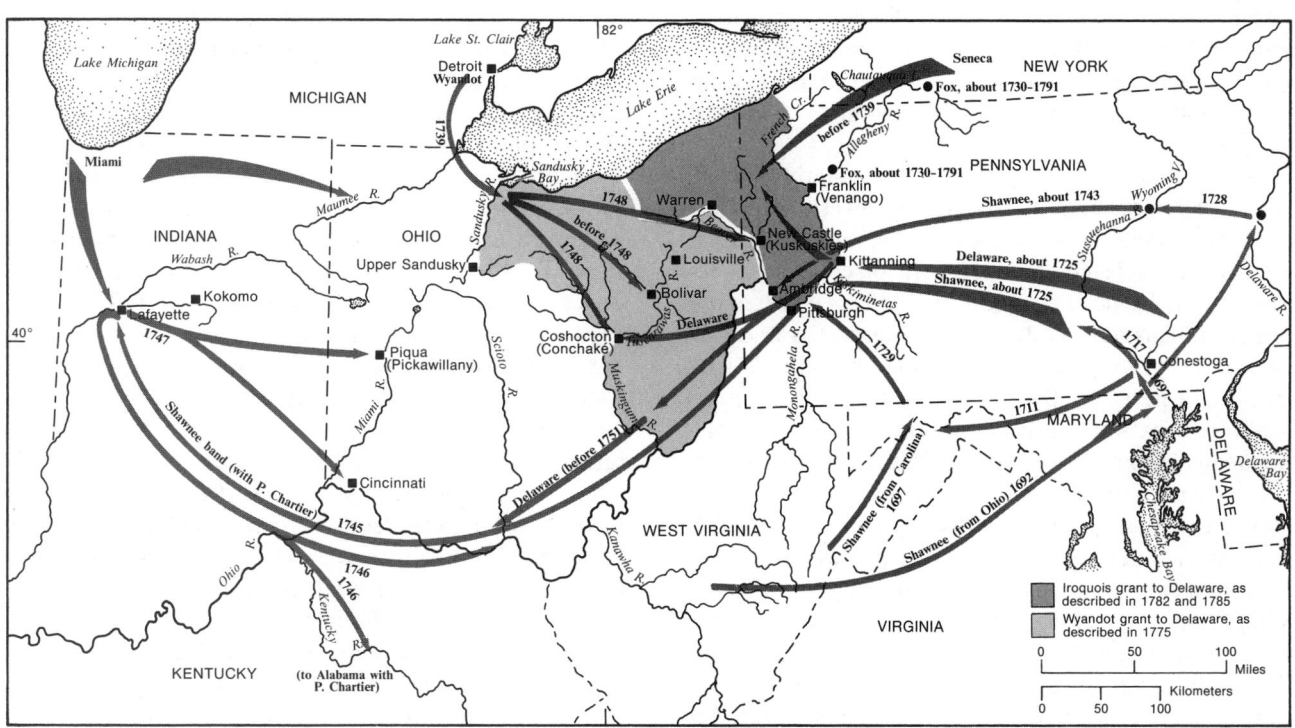

Fig. 1. Ohio Valley area after 1700. Broad arrows indicate general tribal migration, single-line arrows show specific movement.

HISTORY OF THE OHIO VALLEY

forms (Floyd G. Lounsbury, personal communication 1975). It is one of several terms—Far Indians, Naked Indians, Lakes Indians, Mingoes—inclusive in nature rather than designating specific tribes.

It is evident from the recorded names that Indian informants from the Ohio spoke languages of the same Algonquian and Iroquoian families represented there in later times. Other, unrelated, languages may also have been spoken in the region, but the hypothesis of a Siouan-speaking population in the central Ohio area at this time remains unproved. The Moneton who settled on the Kanawha presumably had recently left the Siouan-populated Piedmont, and Swanton's (1952:231–232) identification of the Mosopelea with the Ofo, a Siouan-speaking group, is questionable. At the same time, there is some archeological and traditional evidence for the presence of Dhegiha Siouans on the lower Ohio in southern Illinois (Bauxar 1957:295–300).

Westward, Iroquois devastation reached its farthest extent with attacks on the Illinois beginning in 1680 and was slowed thereafter by distance and the beginnings of French-supported opposition. Southward, after the dispersal of the Shawnee, hostilities settled into an inconclusive exchange of raids and retaliations with the Cherokee. These Beaver Wars provided the basis for both the English and the French official claims to the area. In the English version the Iroquois, after their conquest of the Ohio country, submitted their lands to the British crown in 1701 and were by the Treaty of Utrecht in 1713 acknowledged as under British dominion (NYCD 10:244). The French at the same time claimed the country on the ground that "La Salle took possession of it when it was inhabited by the Cha8oinons [Shawnee], against whom the Iroquois made war incessantly, and who have always been our friends . . ." (trans. from Grenier 1952:57). Both claims were mixtures of historic fact and fiction.

The Iroquois had craved the Ohio country not for habitation but for hunting, and having devastated it they had little interest in resettling it. Their only claim to it rested on forcible possession, which of course was rejected by the French and might be challenged or ignored by any Indians able to do so. Hunting parties and war bands of various origin traversed the country. In 1681 La Salle met a party of 40 Algonquians from the Hudson-Delaware area hunting near the southern end of Lake Michigan (Margry 1876–1886, 1:525ff., 2:148ff.); in 1686 a Miami war party was seen near present Rochester, New York (Seneca Sachems 1687). Seeking furs for the European trade, Indians entered this hunting area from two major directions: from the north, where the French were establishing posts along the lakes; and from the east, where the British had settled or acquired coastal colonies. This set the stage for the Anglo-French struggle for the area, beginning as a competition for trade and for preference among the Indians and culminating in British military victory over the French in 1760 and in the Indian repercussion of Pontiac's War.

The first and most important new settlers of the Ohio country from the north were the Wyandot (Huron) and the Miami; detachments of the Fox tribe crossed the area to take refuge with the Seneca; warriors of the Illinois, Ottawa, and others operated in the area as French auxiliaries in the colonial wars; and portions of the Kickapoo and the Potawatomi moved into the area at later dates. From the east the chief settlers were the Iroquois, the Seneca especially, the Delaware (including some Munsee and detached remnants of the Mahican and other related groups), and the Shawnee. A few others came in from the south; some Shawnee bands reentered from this direction (others may never have left the area). A plausible interpretation of one contemporary account would place a Siouan group, the Moneton, on the Kanawha River in 1673 (Alvord and Bidgood 1912: 221–222). Southern warriors—Cherokee, Catawba, and others—acted as British auxiliaries on the upper Ohio in 1757–1758.

The Wyandot and the Ottawa were the two chief groups settled at Detroit by the French, who established a post there in 1701. Under French protection the Wyandot hunted toward the Ohio, but they also had some contact with New York officials seeking to extend the trade of that colony. In 1732, when the French undertook to draw the Shawnee to the upper Ohio, the Wyandot objected that any settlement north of that river would injure their hunting (NYCD 9:1035). Because of trouble with the Ottawa, the Wyandot chiefs asked in the late 1730s to be moved elsewhere; and on the failure of a plan to do this, part of the tribe moved to Sandusky Bay, where it came under the influence of English traders and English-affiliated Indians (WHC 17:287). About this time the Wyandot also had a post or small village "at Ohio," probably near present Bolivar, Ohio, on the Tuscarawas River (Potier 1748:200; Gist 1893:36). Tuscarawas is a Wyandot name, written and translated by Moravian missionaries as Tuscarabi 'open mouth (of a stream)'. A popular association of the name with the Tuscarora Indians is erroneous (Mortimer 1798).

In 1747, with England and France at war, the Wyandot chief Orontony (Nicolas) broke with the French. In 1748 he burned the village at Sandusky Bay and then withdrew to the Ohio country. About 100 of his warriors settled at Conchaké (Coshocton, Ohio); Orontony and 30 others went to Kuskuskies on the Beaver River (below present New Castle, Pennsylvania). The Wyandots probably abandoned Kuskuskies after Orontony's death in 1750 (WHC 18:74–75), while those at Conchaké seem to have returned to Sandusky Bay on the outbreak of the French and Indian War (Pa. Col. Recs. 6:567–568).

The Miami were first encountered by the French in Wisconsin before 1670, but part of the tribe was at the southern end of Lake Michigan in 1680 and may have been there earlier. In the ensuing two decades their war and hunting parties ranged well into New York, Pennsylvania, and Maryland (Pa. Col. Recs. 1:448, 2:121; Md. Arch. 23:84). The party seen near present Rochester, New York, in 1686 probably was engaged in a retaliatory raid against the Iroquois, but those who made peaceful overtures in Virginia in 1700 probably were more interested in trade (McIlwaine 1925-1945, 2:41). By 1721 the Miami resided in three localities: at the southern end of Lake Michigan, on the Maumee River, and on the upper Wabash. The Wabash group, more particularly known as the Wea (Ouiatanon), had had their chief town near present Lafayette since at least 1718. Part of the tribe joined Orontony in 1747 and destroyed the French trading post at Ouiatanon (NYCD, 10:140); and on July 23, 1748, three of their chiefs, sponsored by the Iroquois on the Ohio, signed a treaty of alliance with Pennsylvania (Pa. Col. Recs. 5:316-318). In the following year Céloron found a small Miami village near present Cincinnati and a larger one at Pickawillany (present Piqua, Ohio) (Margry 1876-1886, 6:714-722). The latter place, headed by a chief known as Memeskia, La Demoiselle, or Old Britain, was an important resort of English traders until 1752, when the place was taken and the chief killed by a French-Indian party from Detroit (Pa. Col. Recs. 5:599-600). Two divisions of the Miami, the Wea and the Piankashaw, came to be regarded as distinct tribes.

The Fox (Mesquakie) refugees played a marginal and minor part in the Ohio region. Two bands joined the Iroquois in 1712 after a defeat by the Wyandot and the Ottawa, and others joined the Seneca after trouble with the French in 1730. Most of them were settled on the borders of the Seneca country in New York, but one group lived farther down the Allegheny River near present Tionesta. Céloron reported a 10-cabin Delaware and Fox village here in 1749; David Zeisberger found "several families of the Misquachki Nation" living here with the Delaware in 1768; and Col. Daniel Brodhead listed "Mahusquechikoken, about 20 miles above Venango" (present Franklin, Pennsylvania), among the towns destroyed by his troops in 1779 (Hunter 1956).

Reentry into the Ohio country from the east, as contrasted with that from the north, had two distinguishing features: it was made under Iroquois supervision, and it involved groups with an early interest not merely in hunting but also in residence. Officially the Iroquois League regarded those of its people who went to the Ohio as having the status of hunters, unqualified to sit in council or to negotiate with their neighbors. On the other hand, the Iroquois had evolved a practice of settling dependent groups on their borders in a kind of buffer zone, and they extended this practice to the Ohio, where refugee Fox and landless Shawnee and Delaware Indians were settled on and near the Allegheny River.

Iroquois success on the Ohio was of special advantage to the Seneca, who had readiest access to the new hunting territory and the best opportunity to increase their manpower by adopting captives and refugees. However, the Seneca were badly situated for trade, being the Iroquois group farthest from Albany and excluded by the hostile Susquehannock from markets on Delaware and Chesapeake bays. In the 1690s, after the defeat of the Susquehannock, the Seneca established a town, Conestoga, inhabited partly by Susquehannock captives, in the Susquehanna Valley, presumably for trade to the south. Establishment of a French post at Niagara in 1720 and extension of English traders' activities to the Ohio later deprived this town of most of its Seneca population and its original importance (Hunter 1959:16-17).

Excepting some Seneca colonization of the upper Allegheny, where villages near present Warren, Pennsylvania, are first documented in 1740 (Mandeville 1740), Iroquois residence in the Ohio country seems to have been characterized by family-size settlements and by Iroquois families scattered among other populations. Thus Aliquippa's Town, near present Pittsburgh, was described in 1731 as consisting of "4 settled families but a great Resort of those People" (Pa. Arch., 1st. ser., 1:301). Aliquippa was a Seneca woman (though her popular name was Delaware) who may have lived previously at Conestoga.

Refugee Shawnee groups appeared in eastern Maryland in 1692. One band, escorted from the Ohio by a Mahican-Munsee hunting party, obtained, with New York colony assistance, Iroquois permission to settle on the upper Delaware. The episode established the long respected relationship between the Delaware and the Shawnee figuratively described as that of elder and younger brother (Witthoft and Hunter 1955:50-52). Another group, accompanied to Maryland by Martin Chartier, a French deserter, received Iroquois and Pennsylvania permission in 1701 to live on the lower Susquehanna (Md. Arch. 8:458-470, 517; Pa. Col. Recs. 3:471-472). However, the Iroquois kept strict watch over their former enemies and after a minor disturbance in 1728 ordered them "back toward ohioh The place from whence you Came" (Pa. Arch. 1:329). By 1731 the Shawnee had three towns (200 men in all) on the Kiskiminetas River and they made subsequent settlements on the lower Allegheny and the upper Ohio (Pa. Arch., 1st ser., 1:302). Relations with the Iroquois were not improved when in 1734 the θawikila, a Shawnee division from the south, killed a Seneca chief who had come to counsel with them (Pa. Col. Recs. 3:660). From their arrival on the Ohio the Shawnee were sought after by the French, trying to offset the work of English traders (NYCD 9:1013ff.); but the French worked at a disadvantage and had little success until 1745, when Martin Chartier's half-breed son Peter persuaded part of the tribe to plunder some Pennsylvania traders and decamp down the Ohio (Anonymous 1745; Pa. Arch., 8th ser., 4:3041). Instead of remaining on the Wabash where the French resettled them, these Shawnee then divided: part followed Chartier to Alabama; the rest settled at the mouth of the Scioto River (WHC 18:19–20) and, with other Shawnee on the Ohio, enlisted Iroquois support in 1748 for renewed friendship with Pennsylvania (Pa. Col. Recs. 5:311–315).

Referring to this reversal, the French minister in charge of the colonies wrote that the Shawnee and others had formed "a sort of republic dominated by some Iroquois of the Five Nations who form part of it" (WHC 18:11–13). In fact the British colonies whose traders were busy in the Ohio country and the resident Indians with whom they dealt were finding it inconvenient to have to negotiate through the Iroquois Council at Onondaga, and over the protests of that council they were entering into direct negotiations with one another. A trading center, Logstown (present Ambridge, Pennsylvania), became the site for treaties between the Indians and Pennsylvania and Virginia officials, who recognized a resident Seneca, Tanaghrisson, as the Indians' "half-king" or spokesman, to whom the colonies furnished the wampum and gifts necessary for his diplomatic dealings (Pa. Col. Recs. 5:358). The two colonies concurred with him in designating Shingas, a Delaware, as "king" of the pertinent portion of this people (Anonymous 1905:167). Scarroyady, an Oneida, oversaw the Shawnee (and so was often called Monacatootha, a Shawnee version of his name) (Pa. Col. Recs. 5:615). This trade "republic" was augmented by the Wyandot and Miami who defected from the French in 1747, but it suffered a setback in the destruction of Pickawillany in 1752, and it was completely disrupted by French occupation of the Forks of the Ohio (Pittsburgh) in 1754. Scarroyady then burned Logstown (Grenier 1952:180), and Tanaghrisson's pro-British followers retired first to eastern Pennsylvania and then to the Iroquois country in New York. The Shawnee defected to the French, who built them a new village at Logstown. Ohio Iroquois who accepted the French occupation lost their status with the British victory in 1758; and some of those who remained formed detached and roving bands, reminiscent of the Shawnee, that for lack of a better name were identified as Mingo, a term loosely applied to Iroquoian peoples. The Iroquois League itself retained a considerable degree of prestige and influence, but the British had no further need to support its claims to the Ohio country and the Iroquois were not in a position to repeat their warlike exploits of the previous century.

The Delaware migration to the Ohio was a piecemeal operation. From an early date they and other coastal Algonquians went there on long hunting trips; later, when White traders extended their operations to the Ohio and the hunters no longer had to carry their peltry to the eastern markets, it became possible for these Indians to remain on the Ohio permanently. The French knew these Algonquians as Loups, possibly from a mistranslation of the name Mahican; however, the largest and most important group were Delaware and their name is used here to include such Munsee, Mahican, and other groups as became associated with the more southern Delaware in this westward movement. By 1737 the Delaware had sold all their land in Pennsylvania and with few exceptions were living and hunting on lands assigned them by the Iroquois. By about 1725 some of them were settled at Kittanning, on the Allegheny River (Pa. Arch., 1st ser., 1:299–300, 2:131). According to later information, the Iroquois designated this as a council place for the Delaware but later moved the council fire to Venango, present Franklin, Pennsylvania (Council Door 1785). The intention presumably was to draw them nearer the Iroquois country, and some Delaware did in fact settle as far up the river as present Warren; however, others moved down the river to and below the Forks of the Ohio, and by 1751 their farthest town was on the Scioto a few miles above its mouth (Gist 1893:43). These Delaware were included in the Logstown-centered trade complex. With no refuge to which they could retreat, the Delaware, lacking a unifying tribal organization, accommodated themselves to the French military occupation of 1753–1759 in various ways, ranging from pacific retirement to vigorous attack on English settlers.

This war and its consequences of British military occupation and threatened civilian settlement accelerated the Indians' westward movement, with the Delaware converging on the Muskingum, where they strengthened earlier contacts with the Wyandot. This association is reflected in the fact that although the Delaware acknowledged that the Iroquois had granted them the land between French Creek and the Beaver River, they later asserted that they had settled the country between the Beaver and the Muskingum and north to Lake Erie by permission of the Wyandot (Thwaites and Kellogg 1908:86–88).

The congregation of scattered Delaware groups, together with a coincident nativist revival, contributed in the 1760s to a renascence of the "Delaware nation" under the leadership of "King" Netawatwees, or Newcomer (Jordan 1913:157), whose influence, though he did not unite all the Delaware, long survived his death in 1776. An approximately contemporary reassociation of Shawnee bands about the Scioto River was less effective. The fugitive band in Alabama, returning from the South, moved to Illinois but may have rejoined those on the Scioto sometime after the French defeat in 1760. The Shawnee were involved in hostilities with Virginia in 1774, and the American Revolution proved a difficult time for the Delaware. Accommodations with their western neighbors, the Miami and others, enabled both groups to shift their settlements westward, and small parties broke away to cross the Mississippi.

The second and final dispersal of Indians from the Ohio valley had now begun, and this time the expulsion would be final. Pontiac's War in 1763-1764, an uprising that was partly planned and partly spontaneous, involved most Indian groups of the area but failed in its attempt to end British military occupation and to halt English settlement (Peckham 1947). At the first Treaty of Fort Stanwix, in 1768, the Iroquois surrendered their claim to land south of the Ohio, as far up as Kittanning. The eastern part of this area, where they had the only recognized claim, was the first part of the Ohio valley lost by the Indians for White settlement.

Following the American Revolution, the new nation dealt with the Indians' Ohio claims in two treaties, one with the Iroquois at Fort Stanwix in 1784 and one with the western Indians at Fort McIntosh in 1785. At Fort Stanwix the Iroquois surrendered to the United States all their claim to lands west of New York and Pennsylvania and, in separate negotiations, released to Pennsylvania all claims to land within that state. The United States's settlement at Fort McIntosh was repudiated by the Indians, but Pennsylvania obtained there a Delaware and Wyandot counterpart of the previous Iroquois release. At the Treaty of Greenville, in 1795, after a period of hostilities in the Northwest Territory, the Indians lost land that included almost all the part of the Ohio valley lying within the present state of that name. Other tribal cessions, individual and collective, followed; and by 1818 the Indians had released almost all of Ohio and most of Indiana south of the Wabash. In that year the government, to expedite White settlement, began to remove the tribes to reserved lands beyond the Mississippi; however, the final cessions of Ohio valley lands were delayed until 1840, when the Miami surrendered a tract about Kokomo, Indiana, and 1842, when the Wyandot released land at Upper Sandusky, Ohio (Royce 1899).

History of The Illinois Area

J JOSEPH BAUXAR

The Illinois Country

The Illinois region was occupied by a group of 12 related villages or tribes identified historically as Kaskaskia, Maroa, Cahokia, Tamaroa, Peoria, Tapouaro, Coiracoentanon, Moingwena, Espeminkia, Chinkoa, Michigamea, and Chepoussa. Referred to in the more recent records as the Illinois Confederacy, they were never politically organized like the Iroquois Confederacy, with whom they generally have been equated (Bauxar 1954).

When Europeans first intruded into the region, in 1673 or perhaps earlier, the Illinois occupied a roughly triangular region the base of which extended from the Chicago River westward into western Iowa. Its eastern boundary extended southward through eastern Illinois along the Missisippi-Wabash watershed, and its apex was situated in northeastern Arkansas (fig. 1). This region came to be referred to by the French as "the Illinois country." It was under the authority of the governor of New France until 1717, when that portion south of a line drawn eastward from the mouth of the Illinois River became a part of Louisiana.

Immediately to the east of the Illinois during the late prehistoric period lived the Miami, including the Wea and Piankashaw, who were later regarded as distinct groups. Farther to the east were the Shawnee. On the lower Michigan peninsula were the Sauk, Fox, Kickapoo, and Mascouten; and to the north of these were the Potawatomi. All were linguistically related to the Illinois; but traditional distrust and inherent differences prevented close, lasting alliances. All were to take up residence in the Illinois country at different times during the historic period.

To the north and northwest of the Illinois lay the domain of the hostile Chiwere Sioux and their linguistic kin the Winnebago. To the south of the Ohio River and southwestward were the unfriendly Dhegiha Sioux (Bauxar 1957:295-300). Beyond the undefined western limits of the Illinois country and the Mississippi River resided the Caddoan-speaking Pawnee and Arikara, traditional enemies of the Illinois.

The thrust westward, first by the Neutral and then by the Iroquois, during the middle decades of the seventeenth century exerted extreme pressure on the tribes to the east and northeast of the Illinois and on the Illinois as well. By midcentury the Miami and their associates had moved westward to settle in northwestern Illinois and adjacent areas in Wisconsin and Iowa, filling the void that had been created by the somewhat earlier withdrawal of the Chiwere Sioux around to the west of the Illinois. The tribes in lower Michigan had withdrawn around the head of Lake Michigan into northern Illinois and southeastern Wisconsin, and from the region of the Straits of Mackinac the Potawatomi had moved westward to Washington Island and the Door County peninsula of Wisconsin.

At about the same time, but for reasons as yet not known, the Dhegiha Sioux abandoned the lower Ohio River, leaving southern Illinois open to use by the Illinois (Bauxar 1957:295-300).

Illinois

The Illinois were first attacked by the Iroquois about the year 1655 (Blair 1911-1912, 1:152). Periodic Iroquois forays as far west as the Chicago River and the upper Illinois River were to plague the Illinois throughout the ensuing half-century. However, when the Illinois were not being directly threatened by the Iroquois or by hostile neighbors, Illinois warriors were often out on forays against the Quapaw, the Osage, and the northern Sioux— or against the Iroquois.

The firm attachment of the Illinois to the French probably dates from the establishment of the mission of Saint Esprit and nearby trading post near La Pointe on Chequamegon Bay, which Illinois parties began visiting at least as early as 1667. Small groups of Illinois were frequent visitors to the post and mission. The Illinois frequented in even greater numbers the trading center established by the French at the Miami-Mascouten village on the Fox River of Wisconsin about 1670 (JR 50:289, 51:47, 58:23).

When visited by Louis Jolliet and Father Jacques Marquette in 1673, three villages of Peoria and Tapouaro on the Iowa River had a total population of 8,000; and the village of the Kaskaskia on the Illinois River consisted of 74 lodges, representing about 1,200 persons (JR 58:97, 59:61; Tucker 1942:pl. V). Perhaps motivated by the promises of Jolliet and Marquette to return and establish a trading post and mission, and almost certainly after learning that two traders had in fact appeared on the Illinois River the following year, bands and even whole villages of Illinois (including especially the Peoria and Tapouaro) flocked to the Kaskaskia village in such numbers that an estimated 1,500 warriors alone were in attendance at Marquette's Easter Mass when he returned in 1675 (JR 59:189). It was at this time that the Mission of the Immaculate Conception of the Blessed Virgin was established among the Kaskaskia. René-Robert Cavelier de La Salle in 1680 found all or part of 11 Illinois tribes living at the "Grand Kaskaskia Village," then grown to 460 lodges (Hennepin 1880:153). There were also 200 families (about 3,000 individuals) of Tamaroa on the Mississippi (Margry 1876-1886, 1:505, 479).

Threatened in September 1680 by a large Iroquois war party while most of their warriors were absent, the Illinois abandoned the Grand Kaskaskia Village and withdrew to the Mississippi. The Iroquois followed after destroying the village. The Tapouaro, Maroa, and Espeminkia, electing to remain at the mouth of the Illinois when the others dispersed, were attacked by the Iroquois. All three tribes suffered heavy losses in dead and captives—the Espeminkia so much so that they are not mentioned again in the records (NYCD 9:162; Margry 1876-1886, 1:506 ff.; Shea 1903:166).

Heartened by Henri Tonti's construction of Fort Saint Louis atop Starved Rock in 1682, the Illinois reassembled on the Illinois River. They were further reassured by the presence of several bands of Shawnee, Miami, Wea, and Piankashaw, as well as a stray band of 18 Eastern Algonquian warriors and their families, who had been enticed by Tonti and La Salle to settle near the fort for mutual defense against the Iroquois. The Kaskaskia and their erstwhile neighbors established a new village across the river from the fort and just below their previous village site (Tonty 1898:59 ff.; N. La Salle 1898:67; La Salle 1901:249 ff.). This assemblage of tribes boasted some 4,000 warriors (Illinois and Miami 1,500 each and Shawnee 500) representing a population of nearly 18,000 individuals (LHC 1:37; Franquelin 1684). But the community was plagued by intertribal jealousies and distrust, as a result of which the Miami and their associates abandoned the area in 1688 and the Shawnee withdrew the following year (IHC 1:149 ff., 23:307, 392).

The Kaskaskia Village site was abandoned in the fall of 1691 and a new village, commonly called Pimitéoui, was established lower down the Illinois River (Kellogg 1917:305). Tonti relocated the fort and trading post nearby. The mission, again administered by a priest after having been unattended during the lifetime of the anti-Jesuitical La Salle, also was moved. The community, 260-300 lodges comprising a population of over 3,500 inhabitants, was composed of six groups, whose numerical strength was balanced in the intratribal lacrosse games by the numerically superior Peoria being joined by the Coiracoentanon against the Kaskaskia, Moingwena, Maroa, and Tapouaro (IHC 23:324 ff.).

The relationship between the Kaskaskia and the Peoria became increasingly strained as the Kaskaskia became more thoroughly Christianized. Dissolution of the community was precipitated by two external developments: Louis XIV's restriction of trade to the Illinois River to two canoe loads of goods a year and Pierre Le Moyne d'Iberville's arrival at the mouth of the Mississippi. Under the leadership of Rouensa, the Kaskaskia, joined by the Coiracoentanon, in 1700 departed Pimitéoui in anticipation of d'Iberville's plan to relocate the upper Mississippi River tribes below the mouth of the Ohio. Belatedly influenced by Father Jacques Gravier's evaluation of the plan, the Kaskaskia went only as far as the Des Peres River, across the Mississippi from the Tamaroa, who by this time were settled in the vicinity of Cahokia (JR 65:101 ff.; Shea 1861a:116 ff.). Joined the following year by the Tamaroa, the Kaskaskia community doubled in size to about 60 lodges (Garraghan 1928:119-120). In 1703 the village moved to the mouth of the Kaskaskia River. An epidemic in 1714 reduced the population of the community by as much as one-fourth (Palm 1933:36 ff.).

The Mission of the Immaculate Conception, ministered at the time of the move by Father Gabriel Marest, went with the Kaskaskia to the Kaskaskia River and its missionaries continued to influence the Kaskaskia and their neighbors until the Jesuits were banished from the Mississippi in 1763 (JR 66:39 ff., 69:149 ff.; Charlevoix 1923, 2:236).

Meanwhile, there had been movement elsewhere in the Illinois country. Soon after La Salle appeared in the area the Tamaroa moved over to the east side of the Mississippi and established their main village near the present village of Cahokia. In 1682 this community consisted of 180 or more lodges; in the course of the next 18 years it was reduced to some 30 lodges (Habig 1934:228). Near this village the Seminary of Foreign Missions in 1699 established the Mission to the Tamaroas, the only non-Jesuit mission permitted in the interior of New France (Kellogg 1917:346). Very soon thereafter the Cahokia moved down the river and settled near the Tamaroa. In 1700 the two villages were composed of about 90 lodges (Garraghan 1928:109).

Although some Coiracoentanon and Moingwena were living on the Des Moines River as late as 1700, hostilities with the Osage and Missouri during the preceding decade had caused the greater portion to join the community at Pimitéoui. The Moingwena elected to remain with the Peoria when the Coiracoentanon moved out with the Kaskaskia. Each was absorbed by the host group and their individual identity lost.

Far to the south the Chepoussa and Michigamea were forced to withdraw up the Mississippi in the face of increased Quapaw hostility. By 1693 they were settled on both sides of that river in the vicinity of the mouth of the

Kaskaskia River (IHC 23:277). The joined the Kaskaskia when that tribe arrived at the Kaskaskia River mouth. Here the Chepoussa were absorbed by the Michigamea.

During the ensuing six and one-half decades were three Illinois population centers. Warrior components were distributed as follows in 1736: 250 Michigameas and 100 Kaskaskias on and near the Kaskaskia River, 200 Cahokias and some Peorias at Cahokia, and 50 Peorias on the Illinois River (NYCD 9:1055). These figures imply a total population of over 2,500 individuals. Estimates in 1763 and 1765 place the total number of warriors at between 460 and 480, representing approximately 2,000 individuals (IHC 11:126).

The arrival and rapid development of a French agriculturally based society in the Illinois country soon after 1710 created a situation that contrasted radically with the earlier symbiotic trade-mission-garrison relationship that existed between the natives and the French. Serious contentions arose over land ownership and social discrimination. In 1719 the commandant at Kaskaskia, in a move to alleviate the tension, requested the Indian community to remove itself from the French settlement. The Kaskaskia and Tamaroa moved a few miles up the Kaskaskia River; the Michigamea settled near the first of the three forts, all called Fort de Chartres, that the French were to build about 15 miles to the north of their settlement. At Cahokia the Indian community moved of its own volition in 1734, resettling about three miles below the mission. Nine years later they moved six miles farther to the south (Palm 1933:50; Mereness 1916:67 ff.; Schlarman 1929:279 ff.; IHS 3:322; McDermott 1949:18).

Despite sometimes harsh treatment by the French settlers the Illinois remained constant in their loyalty. They continued to deal with the French when the traders withdrew to the west side of the Mississippi following the French loss of Canada to the British and reestablished their trading posts at Pain Court (Saint Louis) and Misere (Sainte Genevieve). Illinois also harassed the British during their 10-year occupation of Fort de Chartres (Mereness 1916:472 ff.; H.R. Stiles 1864:10b; Waller 1928:208). In addition, they supported the colonies during the American Revolution and through subsequent confrontations with the British, honoring their signature to the Treaty of Greenville in 1795 (Kappler 1904–1941, 2:39).

Because of their loyalty to the French the Illinois were repeatedly attacked by the Fox and other pro-British neighbors to the north and occasionally by the Shawnee and Chickasaw from the south. A heavy loss of life was inflicted upon the Cahokia when their village was attacked and destroyed in 1752. The survivors resettled near the Michigamea, who had been attacked in the same raid (ISHS 29:24; IHC 29:654; W. Johnson 1921–1965, 7:525).

The Peoria were forced on several occasions to withdraw from the Illinois River valley, the last time in 1769. After a Peoria killed the Ottawa leader Pontiac they were attacked by a combined force of Potawatomi, Ottawa, Chippewa, Fox, Winnebago, and others. After a last stand atop Starved Rock, starvation forced the Peoria to withdraw. They settled on the west side of the Mississippi, abandoning forever their traditional homeland (Matson 1882:149 ff.; TPUS 15:305).

The interior of the Illinois country was then exposed on the north, and the Kickapoo quickly moved down to the Illinois River and beyond to the Sangamon. The Potawatomi also moved in to occupy the headwaters of the Illinois River.

During the last three decades of the century the Illinois were confined to the waters of the Kaskaskia and Big Muddy rivers. In 1751 the Kaskaskia had turned back the Piankashaws' attempt to occupy these rivers (Waller 1928:209). After 1770 they were engaged in a desperate struggle to resist the attempted encroachments of the Kickapoo and Potawatomi from the north and the Shawnee from the south (W.H. Smith 1882, 2:138). A pitched battle with the Potawatomi about 1790 was fought to a draw with heavy loss of life on both sides

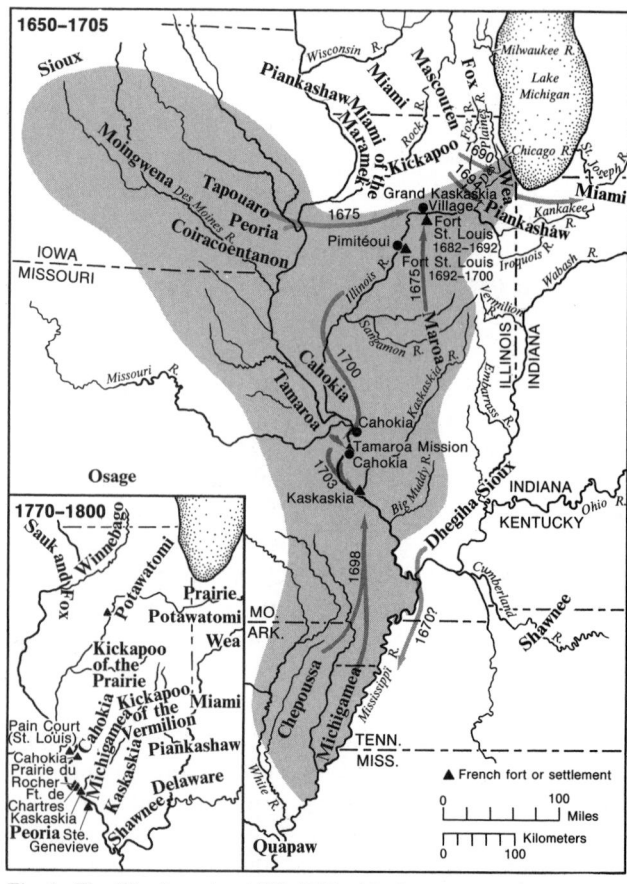

Fig. 1. The Illinois region 1650–1700 with the area of the Illinois Confederacy and the Illinois region 1770–1800. For additional information on movements of the tribes shown here, see the maps in tribal articles.

(Matson 1874:259). In 1802 a large Kaskaskia hunting camp was taken by surprise by a Shawnee war party and they again suffered heavy casualties (Anonymous 1887:337).

Completely demoralized, the Kaskaskia ceded to the government the following year the Illinois land lying south of a line drawn eastward from the mouth of the Illinois River, reserving two small tracts on the Big Muddy and hunting privileges on the land ceded (Kappler 1904-1941, 2:67; TPUS 2:547). On one of the tracts the remnants of the Illinois in the state of Illinois established their last village in their traditional homeland—60 lodges sheltering fewer than 300 individuals (J.W. Allen 1945:20b).

In 1832 the Peoria joined the Kaskaskia (including specifically the Tamaroa, Michigamea, and Cahokia) in acknowledging their previous cession and ceded the land they claimed north of the line. The Kaskaskia ceded also their two small tracts and the last of the Illinois withdrew permanently from the Illinois country (Kappler 1904-1941, 2:165; Royce 1899:pl. CXXIV).

Miami, Wea, and Piankashaw

Miami was the name commonly used to refer both individually and collectively to the closely related Atchatchakangouen, Kilatika, Mengakonkia, and Pepikokia (JR 58:41); it sometimes included the Wea and Piankashaw, though these two groups maintained individual political independence into the nineteenth century.

Withdrawing from the Wabash-Saint Joseph region in the mid-seventeenth century, the main body of the Miami settled in central and southwestern Wisconsin; other Miamis settled in northwestern Illinois, where they were sometimes referred to as the Miamis of the Maramek (NYCD 9:619-621); and the Wea and Piankashaw settled in western Wisconsin along the Mississippi, some crossing over into northern Iowa. Together with the Mascouten, the Atchatchakangouen in 1670 or perhaps a year earlier established a large village on the Fox River, which quickly attracted French traders and a Jesuit mission. Within five years there was a schism among the Miami over the acceptance of Christianity (JR 58:63).

At the instigation of the traders at Green Bay a body of Atchatchakangouen, Mascouten, and Wea settled on the Saint Joseph River in 1679 with intentions of preventing La Salle from gaining access to the Illinois on the Illinois River. Finding their scheme thwarted and themselves exposed to attacks by the Iroquois, they were amenable to La Salle's invitation in 1682 to make peace with the Illinois and remove to the vicinity of the fort La Salle was building on the Illinois River. Joined by others from the north, the Atchatchakangouen settled along the Iroquois River while the Mengakonkia, Kilatika, Pepikokia, Wea, and Piankashaw settled within short dis-

tances of Fort Saint Louis. The combined population of these villages totaled about 7,500 individuals (Margry 1876-1886, 2:204; Franquelin 1684:map).

Unable to overcome their traditional distrust of the Illinois (which became even more intense as a result of their close contact) the Miami and their associates in 1688 abandoned the Illinois and Henri Tonti on the presumption that the campaigns against the Iroquois the previous year had eliminated that threat and absolved them from their commitment to Tonti. Some returned to the Mississippi and settled opposite the Miamis of the Maramek. Another group, hoping to gain the patronage of the British, returned to the Saint Joseph River; a few years later they moved down to the Wabash River, where other kinsmen already had settled. The Wea occupied the Chicago area until French trade to the Illinois River was restricted in 1698. They moved to the Saint Joseph and about 1717 moved down to the Wabash, where they established the village of Ouiatanon (IHC 23:392). A French post was soon established nearby (WHC 16:332).

The Miamis of the Maramek and those on the west side of the Mississippi were never free from harassment by the Sioux to the north despite the efforts of the trader and agent Nicolas Perrot. In desperation, the Piankashaw abandoned the region for the forks of the Illinois in 1692 (Kellogg 1917:349). By 1717 they had moved on to the Wabash and occupied the tributaries from the Vermilion to the Ohio (Esarey 1922, 2:77). The French installed Vincennes Post in their midst in 1731. They were compressed into the southern part of their territory when the Kickapoo, after the loss of their villages near Ouiatanon in 1791, moved down the Wabash into the Vermilion valley and beyond.

Shortly after 1700 the Miamis of the Maramek and the Miamis in Wisconsin moved to the east side of the Wabash between the Wea and the Piankashaw. In time they extended their range eastward into Ohio.

Despite the presence of the French at Ouiatanon and Vincennes the Miami established a firm attachment to the British, and the Wea and Piankashaw also turned against the French (MPHC 33:138). Their attachment to the British apparently prompted the Piankashaw in 1751 to attempt, unsuccessfully, the destruction of the Kaskaskia. During the Revolution the three tribes attempted to observe a conscientious neutrality, but the Miami and the Wea turned against the Americans after suffering repeated breaches of the peace by the White settlers and the militia.

As early as 1800 small bands of Miamis, Weas, and Piankashaws were moving to the west side of the Mississippi. Treaties ceding their land to the government began in 1803. In 1828 the last of the Piankashaw left Illinois, the Wea left Indiana in 1832, and the Miami made their last Indiana land cession in 1840 (Kappler 1904-1941, 2:64 ff.; Royce 1899:pls. CXXIV, CXXVI, CXXVIII). *597*

Sauk and Fox

After moving out of Michigan the Sauk settled on the lower Fox River of Wisconsin while the Fox ranged from the upper Fox River southeastward to the Chicago River.

The Sauk were dependable allies of the French until 1733, when they gave asylum to the Fox and incurred the temporary enmity of the French; thereafter their loyalty vacillated. The Fox had constantly defied the French and harassed their native allies. Their hostile acts eventually led to retaliatory actions that almost destroyed the tribe. The first came in 1712, at Fort Pontchartrain (Detroit), where a Fox settlement made there two years earlier was destroyed by other tribes attached to the fort who felt they had been given every reason to wipe out the troublesome community (WHC 16:268 ff.). The incident precipitated the retaliatory "Fox War," in which the Fox were joined by Mascouten and Kickapoo.

Their position in Wisconsin in 1730 having become untenable, some 300 Fox warriors and their families set out for New York to join a band of Fox that had settled there with the Seneca 20 years earlier. Taking a route that led to the friendly Wea and injudiciously attacking the Peoria on the way, they were intercepted in central Illinois and heavy casualties were inflicted upon them. Those who escaped and the captives who were later released returned to Wisconsin and settled on the Wisconsin River. Here suffering repeated attacks by hostile tribes on all sides, they returned to the Fox River (WHC 17:100 ff.; Tucker 1942:pls. XX, XXI).

In 1733 the French decided that the only way to resolve the Fox problem was to exterminate the Fox. Because of the "vile" nature of the Fox they and the Sauk had frequently been at odds with each other, but when the Fox sought sanctuary in the fortified Sauk village it was granted with full recognition of the jeopardy involved. Forced to abandon the beleaguered fort, the Sauk and Fox fled to the banks of the Mississippi. Settlements were made as far down that river as the mouth of the Rock River, where a Sauk settlement was to be continuously occupied for almost a century. In 1743 the French persuaded the Sauk (except the settlement on the Rock River) and the Fox to return to the Fox River (WHC 17:182 ff.).

By 1766 the two tribes again had withdrawn from the Fox River, the Sauk to the Wisconsin River, where their "Great Town" was composed of about 90 houses, with about 300 warriors; and the Fox to the Mississippi, where their village (above the mouth of the Wisconsin) was composed of 50 lodges, but their population had been reduced by half that year by an epidemic (Carver 1778:46 ff.). Defeated in their conflict with the Chippewa in 1783, they withdrew farther down the Mississippi and established villages on both sides progressively lower down the river as far as the Des Moines River.

During the French and British conflict the Sauk and Fox vacillated in their support and very often were at odds among themselves, but in any case the Fox persisted in their harassment of the Illinois. At the conclusion of the war they promised to keep the peace with the British, which they did; but they continued to keep close contact with the French traders who had moved across the Mississippi into Spanish territory (Houck 1909, 1:44).

At the outbreak of the American Revolution the Sauk and Fox again were split in their loyalty. However, when it was reported that Sauk and Fox had participated in the British attack on Saint Louis and Cahokia in 1780 the American militia retaliated by burning the Rock River villages; and as these were predominantly pro-American villages, all the Sauk and Fox turned against the Americans (WHC 11:156 ff., 12:51-52, 18:404-405). Neither tribe signed a treaty of peace with the Americans at the conclusion of that conflict and many supported the British through the War of 1812. American attempts at amelioration were unsuccessful: a farm agent proved of little value as the Sauk and Fox already were producing a surplus of corn—enough to supply the needs of less skillful neighbors, and a poorly conceived factory system was short lived. Until 1823 Sauk and Fox traveled to the British post at Michilimackinac for the distribution of arms and goods.

It was reported in 1805 that the Sauk numbered 700 warriors, 750 women, and 1,400 children in three villages; the Fox numbered 400 warriors, 500 women, and 850 children, also in three villages (Pike 1811:134-135; Tucker 1942:pl. XXXII). A census taken 14 years later showed the Sauk figure somewhat larger and the Fox figure almost double (WHC 20:238).

In 1804 Gov. William H. Harrison of Indiana Territory negotiated with the leaders of a small band of Sauk living on the Missouri a treaty that relinquished the claim of the Sauk and Fox to all land lying east of the Mississippi (Kappler 1904-1941, 2:74; Royce 1899: pl. CXXIV). The treaty was denounced by the main body of the Sauk and by the Fox; however, it was ratified by both tribes in the peace negotiations subsequent to the close of the War of 1812 (Kappler 1904-1941, 2:121, 126).

Seeing the steady influx of White settlers into the area about the mouth of the Rock River and the lead mines in the vicinity of Galena as a portent of their eventual loss of the whole area, by 1829 most of the Sauk and Fox leaders had capitulated to the urging of the territorial governor and had moved with their followers to the west side of the Mississippi (Blair 1911-1912, 2:147 ff.). Black Hawk eventually also acceded to the treaty of 1804 and moved over into Iowa, but he refused to abandon completely the ancestral burial ground on the Rock River, and he continued to visit the area annually. In 1832 he again crossed over to the Rock River. An apparent defiance of an agreement made the year before, the act was construed by Gen. Henry Atkinson as an invasion of the United States. The subsequent military campaign culminated in the defeat of Black Hawk and his followers at Bad Axe Creek and the final expulsion of the Sauk and Fox from Illinois.

Kickapoo and Mascouten

The Kickapoo and Mascouten moved out of Michigan with the Sauk and Fox. The early associations of the Mascouten in the west were with the Miami. They established with the Atchatchakangouen the large village on Fox River of Wisconsin. Their hunting range extended southeastward to the Milwaukee River.

In 1679 a band of the Mascouten joined the Atchatchakangouen and the Wea in the move to the Saint Joseph River to cut off La Salle's approach to the Illinois country. When the interception failed the Mascouten withdrew to the Fox River of Illinois. Attacked there by an Iroquois war party, in 1685 they moved with the Kickapoo to the Mississippi, where they remained but a short time before reoccupying their old village on the Fox River of Wisconsin.

Internal friction caused some Mascouten families to join the Miami while others attached themselves to the Fox. The main body, in 1691, settled with the Kickapoo.

In 1702 a band of Mascouten accompanied Charles Juchereau to the mouth of the Ohio to establish a tannery. The following year smallpox decimated the community. It apparently was the surviving Mascouten who settled at about this time on both sides of the Wabash River above the Piankashaw. This community was joined by other Mascouten groups in subsequent years. They retained their tribal identity into the second half of the century; but eventually they were absorbed by their neighbors, particularly the Kickapoo.

When the Kickapoo rounded the southern end of Lake Michigan they moved northwestward as far as the Mississippi. By 1680 they were entrenched on the middle Rock River.

The Kickapoo were the most conservative tribe in the Illinois region, a fact that is reflected in the exceedingly high percentage of full-bloods as late as 1950 (M.H. Wright 1951:168). Their conservatism was perhaps basic to their general anti-European posture, which was so firm that few Europeans were visitors to their villages under any circumstances. They were divided in their general attitude toward the French, but they maintained close relationships with the strongly French-oriented Illinois, and their relationships with other native neighbors were influenced by that factor.

The Kickapoo became strongly attached to the Indian agent and trader Nicolas Perrot, who established a trading post near East Dubuque in 1685 to serve both the Kickapoo and the Sioux to the north. It was Perrot's counsel that largely guided their actions until his recall in 1699 (Blair 1911–1914, 1:364).

The Kickapoo were a relatively small tribe even at that early period. Census information for 1684 shows one village of 300 warriors. In 1702 the Kickapoo and Mascouten together could muster about 450 warriors, indicating a population of about 2,250 individuals. In 1710 a body of 40 Kickapoo and Mascouten families was attracted to the French at Fort Pontchartrain, settling briefly at the mouth of the Maumee and then moving on to the Wabash. They settled with the Wea and resumed contact with the Mascouten who earlier had settled lower down the river (WHC 16:285). In 1750 their combined numbers were estimated at about 1,500 individuals. These Kickapoo supported the French and Illinois during the French and Indian War despite the hostility of the neighboring pro-British Miami.

Meanwhile, the Kickapoo who had remained on the Rock River joined the Fox and turned on the Illinois. However, as allies of the Fox they inherited numerous enemies and by 1717 their numbers had been reduced to about 200 warriors. Peace with the French and Illinois was restored in 1729 (WHC 16:341 ff.).

In 1769 the Kickapoo joined the Three Fires (Potawatomi, Ottawa, Chippewa) in driving the Peoria from the Illinois River. The Kickapoo then moved from the Rock River to the middle Illinois River and beyond to the valley of the Sangamon, where they came to be known as "Kickapoo of the Prairie." They subsequently attempted to occupy the headwaters of the Kaskaskia River, but they were repulsed by the Illinois, the several encounters taking a heavy toll of lives on both sides.

Although the Kickapoo on the Sangamon and those on the Wabash now were near neighbors, antagonisms of long standing could not be resolved and contacts between the two groups were few and not amicable. However, both groups turned against the Americans, who were moving into the Wabash valley. The Wabash Kickapoo joined with the Miami in the uprising of 1791. Some of their villages having been destroyed by the militia, the Kickapoo moved down the west side of the Wabash, impinging upon the territory occupied by the Piankashaw and establishing themselves on and below the Vermilion River. Here they came to be known as the "Kickapoo of the Vermilion." Having made common cause with Tecumseh, the Kickapoo suffered in the defeat at Tippecanoe in 1811 and in the destruction the following year of some of their towns on the Sangamon and the one at Peoria on the Illinois.

Small bands of Kickapoo began moving to the west of the Mississippi soon after 1800. There was an acceleration of emigration after the destruction of the Prairie towns. In 1819 the two Kickapoo groups, in separate treaties, ceded to the government their lands in Illinois and Indiana with the proviso that they could continue to live and hunt upon the land (Royce 1899:pl. CXXV; Kappler 1904–1941, 2:182 ff.). Relations with the White settlers were amicable, but in 1832 their removal to Kansas was ordered by the government.

Potawatomi, Ottawa, and Chippewa

The Potawatomi began to move into the Green Bay region from the Straits of Mackinac about 1641. Their relations with the local tribes were harmonious and they became reliable allies of the French. The restricted trade policy imposed in 1699 caused a deterioration in relations with the French and several bands moved to the Saint Joseph River in hopes of establishing contacts with the English in the Atlantic colonies. However, unable to establish entente with the Iroquois, in 1712 they resumed friendly contacts with the French at Fort Pontchartrain (WHC 16:168).

Joined from time to time by small bands of Ottawa and Chippewa, the Potawatomi on the Saint Joseph extended their occupation eastward (forcing the Miami from the Saint Joseph region) and around the head of Lake Michigan to the Milwaukee River (Edwards 1870:39). The Potawatomi there and in the Green Bay region during this period numbered about 3,400 individuals.

As relations among the Three Fires and the Peoria were traditionally good, the Ottawa leader Pontiac settled his band on the Kankakee River with the consent of the Peoria in 1767. In 1769 the Three Fires, joined by more traditional enemies of the Illinois, attacked the Peoria and drove them from the Illinois valley. The Potawatomi subsequently occupied the whole of the upper Illinois River valley. Those who occupied the waters of the Kankakee and eastward became known as "Prairie Potawatomi."

The Potawatomi remained loyal to the French through the French and Indian War, and after the cessation of that conflict they continued to trade with the French traders who had reestablished at Saint Louis. When the American colonies rebelled the Potawatomi made common cause with the tribes on the Wabash and supported the British. After peace was established there were very few Potawatomi leaders who declared allegiance to the new federal government. Loyalty to the British continued through the War of 1812, expressing itself most sanguinely in the massacre of the Fort Dearborn garrison. As late as Black Hawk's resistance the majority of the Potawatomi leaders supported any native anti-American movement; yet friendship toward the American settlers on the part of other Potawatomi leaders, notably Shabonee, was amply demonstrated (Matson 1878).

The combined forces of Potawatomi, Ottawa, and Chippewa in Illinois in 1812 were estimated at about 620 warriors distributed in seven bands ranging in size from 30 to 200 warriors.

The Potawatomi economy based on the trade of hides and furs lasted well into the first quarter of the nineteenth century, but buffalo had long since vanished from the northern Illinois prairie and wapiti had so diminished in numbers that they were no longer a major item (Matson 1878:34). The increasing density of White settlers was denying the Potawatomi access to the beaver ponds, which in turn were becoming depleted. Small groups had begun moving west of the Mississippi before the turn of the century. Land cessions were initiated in 1816; others followed in 1829, 1832, and 1833, the Prairie Potawatomi and the Three Fires acting independently (Kappler 1904–1941, 2:132 ff.). After each cession there were the usual population displacements and emigration to the west of the Mississippi. By 1834 there were few Potawatomis remaining in Illinois and Indiana.

Shawnee and Delaware

As speakers of an Algonquian language and victims of Iroquois attacks, the Shawnee in the upper Ohio River valley sought security as allies of the French. Thus, the Shawnee first appeared in appreciable numbers in Illinois in 1683 when several bands composed of some 500 warriors and their families attached themselves to the Fort Saint Louis community at the invitation of La Salle (Margry 1876–1886, 1:612–613, 2:313). One band settled adjacent to the Kaskaskia village; the Chaskpé established an independent village a few miles down the river (Franquelin 1684: map). Despite traditional friendships, rapport with the Illinois became so strained that when the Miami withdrew from the Fort Saint Louis community in 1688 the Shawnee found it expedient to withdraw the following year. They joined kinsmen on the Cumberland River in Tennessee (Margry 1876–1886, 2:313). It was perhaps as much due to this experience as to their attachment to the British that the Shawnee, joined occasionally by their pro-British Chickasaw and Koasati neighbors on the Tennessee River, subsequently staged frequent raids against the Illinois.

About 200 Shawnee warriors from Pennsylvania augmented the French garrison on the Ohio River near the present Shawneetown in 1745 as a barrier to threatened British attempts to reach the Mississippi. The garrison was withdrawn two years later and the Shawnee returned to the east. In 1759, 40 lodges of Shawnee from the Scioto River were brought to Fort Ascension on the Ohio established by the French two years earlier. Dissatisfied with the situation, the Shawnee returned to the Scioto about a year later.

The Delaware in the headwaters of the Ohio, also subjected to Iroquois depredations, withdrew down the Ohio and settled among the Shawnee on the Scioto and westward into Indiana.

A large body of Shawnee and Delaware having settled in Missouri in 1787, southern Illinois became a regularly frequented thoroughfare between the Scioto and the Mississippi. The Shawnee again occupied the Shawneetown site, and Delaware settled nearby along the west bank of the Wabash and on Saline Creek.

The Delaware established amicable relations with the neighboring Kaskaskia. The Shawnee, although they did not attempt to establish villages in the area, encroached upon the Illinois hunting grounds on the easterly side-streams of the Big Muddy River. The vigorous resistance of the Kaskaskia culminated in a final confrontation in 1802 when a group of Shawnee warriors fell upon the Kaskaskia village out on a hunt and took a heavy toll of lives. The Shawnee continued to pass back and forth through southern Illinois until well into the nineteenth century, but they did not at any time lay claim to the region (Anonymous 1887:250, 337).

Winnebago

The Winnebago were the traditional occupants of the Lake Winnebago–Green Bay region. Abandoned by their kin and neighbors, the Chiwere Sioux, early in the seventeenth century and reduced in numbers by warfare and disease, they became dependent upon their new neighbors, particularly the Potawatomi, Sauk, and Fox, with whom there was considerable intermarriage.

Although otherwise reliable allies of the French, the Winnebago were uncomprising enemies of the Illinois. Never deviating from their avowed intent to destroy the Illinois, they eventually participated in the expulsion of the Peoria from the Illinois River valley.

Prior to 1770 the Winnebago had begun moving onto the headwaters of the Rock River. After the Kickapoo abandoned the middle Rock valley the Winnebago moved slowly into the vacated region and made direct contact with their friends the Sauk and Fox on the Mississippi. By 1804 the Winnebago Prophet, who was half-Sauk and uncle to Black Hawk, had established his village 40 miles up from the mouth of the Rock River.

Some of the Winnebago were actively engaged against the Americans during the War of 1812, but most of the tribe declared themselves at peace with the government in 1816. In 1829 they ceded the region in Illinois that the government previously had designated as Winnebago land, but they were granted permission to continue to reside and hunt upon it (Royce 1899:pl. CXXV; Kappler 1904–1941, 2:252). Thus, when Black Hawk defied the government in 1832 the Winnebago Prophet was still living at Prophetstown. The Prophet at first surreptitiously aided his nephew and later joined Black Hawk in his retreat up the Rock River. Later in the same year the Winnebago ceded their remaining bit of land in Illinois and quit the area.

Menominee

The Menominee intermarried with their later-day neighbors; and small groups frequently attached themselves to the Potawatomi, Miami, Sauk, Fox, and Winnebago, for various reasons and generally only temporarily. These relationships account for the presence of Menominee families in northern Illinois (particularly on the Fox and Rock rivers) and the occasional identification of mixed villages in the area as Menominee villages.

History of the Upper Great Lakes Area

LYLE M. STONE AND DONALD CHAPUT

European Establishment, 1600–1690s

Samuel de Champlain first saw Lake Huron in 1615, while traveling in the Nipissing-Huron region. His reports and those of Gabriel Sagard-Théodat in the 1620s contain many scattered comments about Indians to the west and north of Georgian Bay. From these accounts (for example, Champlain 1922–1936, 3:40–41, 119–120; Sagard-Théodat 1939:86–87) and those in the *Jesuit Relations* (JR 1896–1901), certain generalizations can be drawn about the Great Lakes Indians during the early part of the seventeenth century.

Small bands were frequently mentioned, many of which would appear in the later decades as part of the Ottawa and Chippewa tribes. Some names that appear first as designating bands or clans subsequently are used for larger groupings, as for example Saulteur (later Saulteaux) and Outchibouec (later Ojibwa), and some, like Ouinibigou and its variants, were applied to groups living in several different areas (JR 30:130, 33:151, 59:97).

European reports usually stressed Indian proclivity for warfare, but occasionally economic conditions and habitation patterns are mentioned. For example, a definite system of exchange existed between the Nipissings and Hurons; the Nipissings would fish and trap their waters, then visit the Huron villages to the south, where they would stay for some time and exchange the fish and furs for corn (JR 13:191, 14:7). These interband and intertribal relationships, then and later, were not determined by cultural or linguistic affinity. An Algonquian band went to war with another group of Indians for a variety of reasons, but they fought against other Algonquians as easily as against Siouan or Iroquoian groups.

In the early part of the century the Algonquians dominated the Upper Great Lakes area numerically, carrying on a seminomadic hunting-fishing way of life. The Siouan groups (the Dakota proper and the Assiniboin) controlled the western edge of Lake Superior, and other Siouans (Winnebago) were along the west side of Lake Michigan (Sanson 1692:31–32). After 1650, scattered bands of several Iroquoian groups found refuge on the Michigan side of the present Michigan-Ontario border (JR 20:43).

European contact had little obvious direct impact in the Upper Great Lakes area prior to the Huron-Iroquois "war" of the late 1640s, although Upper Great Lakes groups, and particularly the Ottawa, were familiar with French trade goods being introduced by the Huron in exchange for furs. The notable journeys of Étienne Brûlé about 1622, Jean Nicollet in 1634, and the Jesuits Charles Raymbault and Isaac Jogues in 1641 were French exploratory probes to the region of Sault Sainte Marie and into Lake Michigan. Some knowledge was gained of the peoples and geography and of the areas' resources and potential economic value, but no immediate military, missionary, or trade activity resulted. The Hurons were the important middlemen in the French fur trade in the 1630s and 1640s. Although tribes from the Upper Great Lakes participated in the trade, there is no evidence that their culture or material possessions were significantly affected by this participation (Tooker 1964:4–14).

However, by the middle of the seventeenth century the Neutral and later the Iroquois had begun to attack the indigenous tribes of southern Michigan in an effort to seize furs and expand their hunting grounds. This caused the Sauk, Fox, Kickapoo, Mascouten, Miami, and some Potawatomi to retreat west into the prairie and wild-rice districts of Illinois and Wisconsin where the Menominee and various Siouan groups were encountered. These contacts between tribes led to major cultural changes and created economic and political difficulties that led all the groups involved to become engaged in the fur trade. However, before this process was complete, the Hurons and other Ontario Iroquoian groups (Petun and Neutral) had paid dearly for their trading with the French. In one of the continent's major Indian wars, the Iroquois invaded Huronia between 1648 and 1650, burned five Huron villages, and caused other villages to be abandoned. The blow was so devastating that the Hurons were scattered, the survivors being largely absorbed by the Petun, Neutral, and other groups. The Huron and Petun who sought refuge in the Upper Great Lakes area were eventually called the Wyandot in English.

After the Huron dispersal and through the 1690s a further economic and social upheaval took place among the Indians as the French founded missions, forts, and trading posts and began to promote France's economic and religious interests. By the late 1660s, small French groups had penetrated from Quebec to Hudson Bay, western Lake Superior, and Green Bay; Pierre Esprit Radisson and Médard Chouart des Groseilliers had

602

verified the rumors of rich furs, and the Jesuits went in pursuit of Indian souls. Before 1670, key Jesuit missions had been established at Chequamegon Bay in western Lake Superior, Sault Sainte Marie, and Green Bay. In 1671 the important mission of Saint Ignace was founded by the Jesuit Father Jacques Marquette, at present-day Saint Ignace, Michigan (fig. 1).

One of the major developments during this era was the linking of Huron and Ottawa interests. Before 1649 the Ottawas had played a subsidiary role while the Hurons were the key middlemen. After the Huron-Petun (Wyandot) dispersion, many joined friendly Ottawa groups, and the Ottawa assumed a dominant role in trade with the French. For the next century Ottawa and Wyandot villages were frequently established side by side, notably in Chequamegon Bay, Mackinac, and Detroit. The Wyandot, an Iroquoian agricultural people from the south, were thus part of an uneasy but fairly compatible arrangement with the Algonquian Ottawa, a semisedentary northern forest people who engaged in substantial hunting and fishing as well as agriculture.

The impact of the European presence on the Indians had become staggering. Beaver areas determined trade routes and tribal locations, which in turn led to the eventual establishment of Jesuit missions. These missions soon became economic and social centers, as bands and tribes gravitated there on the urging of traders and missionaries. Soon these military posts and mission centers attracted other bands, so that in addition to the Ottawa and Wyandot, groups such as Nipissing, Sauk, Fox, Potawatomi, and Chippewa began to gather and interact. This alteration of native settlement patterns was clearly advantageous to the interdependent religious and economic interests of the French. The geographic and cultural bases for distinct tribal or band identities were being undermined as the central feature of native life became the influence of the French military, political, economic, and religious interests. Thus, it is usually deceptive to call any mission "Ottawa," "Chippewa," and so forth, as many groups either lived at a specific mission or frequently went there to trade (JR 61:69-73). Sault Sainte Marie was a traditional Chippewa stronghold, but bands of Cree, Potawatomi, and Sioux visited periodically.

A Jesuit report for Mission Saint Esprit (Chequamegon Bay) for 1670 provides an interesting ethnological comment. Ottawas and Wyandots were at the mission, working in the fur trade. These Indians fished and hunted on the nearby Apostle Islands of Lake Superior, where they also cultivated corn. They also made several joint expeditions against the Sioux, near the western edge of Lake Superior. In other words, native systems of economy, religion, and warfare had changed to such a degree that French interests were becoming a major determinant of Indian activities. However, although native social systems were changing in response to the pressure of European economic and political interests, the Indians were becoming increasingly aware of their role in the development of these interests between competing European powers. As such, the Indians often held their cooperation in question, seeking the most advantageous alliance in view of changing political considerations. In part because of this implied threat of Indian neutrality, lack of cooperation, or realliance, European powers attempted to ensure favorable support through the distribution of presents such as trade goods and supplies. This "play-off" system is well documented by relationships that existed among the Iroquois, French, and British until the 1740s (Wallace 1969:111-114). Similar but less effective play-off systems were undoubtedly practiced by the Upper Great Lakes groups, each attempting to maximize the benefits of their relationships with Europeans.

Further French developments at this time included major exploration efforts by René-Robert Cavelier de La Salle, Henri Tonti, Father Jacques Marquette, and Daniel Greysolon Dulhut. It became clear that a major French center at the Straits of Mackinac was essential, not only to support French (and Indian) needs but also to prevent English incursions. In 1683 Olivier Morel de La Durantaye established Fort de Buade at modern Saint Ignace, giving this location a military and political prominence that it would keep for most of the next 70 years (Anonymous 1924). Two other important military posts were established, subordinate to Fort de Buade: Fort Saint Joseph at modern Port Huron, Michigan, in 1686 and Fort Saint Joseph at Niles, Michigan, in 1691. To the north of Lake Superior the French built a fort on Lake Nipigon as well as Fort La Tourette in 1684 and Fort de Français in 1685 in order to threaten British interests on Hudson Bay (Innis 1956:49-50).

The military history of the 1680s shows how closely the Indians of the Great Lakes had become tied to the French orbit. The newly appointed governor-general of New France, Joseph-Antoine Le Febvre de La Barre, decided to deal a crushing blow against the Iroquois, who were again raiding French outposts along the Saint Lawrence River. In 1684 Durantaye organized Indian and French military groups from Fort de Buade, Green Bay, and Fort Saint Joseph to go between 500 and 1,000 miles to fight for the glory of the French king. A roster of the Indian groups from the Upper Lakes who participated reads as though every band had thrown in with the French: Chippewa, Huron, Ottawa, Menominee, Potawatomi, Illinois, Fox, Kickapoo, Mascouten (Perrot 1864:138-143). This of course meant that Durantaye had to supply provisions and some arms for the warriors. The entire episode was a dismal failure for the French, but it does show how their plans influenced the lives of the Upper Lakes Indians. Fox, Kickapoos, and Ottawas from the Green Bay vicinity, who a few decades earlier were involved in local hunting, fishing, and warfare, were now traveling 1,000 miles in a large war party to pursue the goals of European powers.

Fort de Buade continued to be the key French post in the west until the mid-1690s. However, under the command of Antoine Laumet de Lamothe Cadillac, affairs at this post became chaotic (Eccles 1956). Cadillac was involved in a series of intrigues against the settlement's Jesuits, who claimed that the Indians were being corrupted by the French army and traders. Liquor was everywhere, and problems involving Indian women were numerous. Perhaps these charges were Jesuit exaggeration, but there is no doubt that the Indians were heavily dependent upon the French and that furs, women, and liquor were common ingredients of the French frontier in North America. By the 1690s the French impact on the Indians was overwhelming. Mackinac had become a key center: houses of worship, a place to secure brandy and trade goods, the site to peddle furs, a gathering place for war parties, and a meeting place for tribes and bands.

Expansion and Consolidation, 1690s–1760

The abandonment and razing of posts in the Upper Great Lakes that was ordered by the French government in 1697 was the result of both religious and economic pressures. Montreal was glutted with furs, and merchants requested the governor to close the western posts. The theory was that only those furs personally delivered by the Indians to Montreal would enter the market, thus keeping supply low and prices high. At the same time the Jesuits were blaming the army and traders for degrading the Indians in the outlying posts. Furs, of course, meant brandy and women. No controls had worked, so the Jesuits also recommended the closing of the posts.

The post at the Straits of Mackinac, Fort de Buade, was abandoned in the late 1690s. Only Cadillac was able to alter empire plans, as he convinced the French government that a post at Detroit not only would prevent English penetration but also would provide a fine setting for a thriving Indian-French settlement. He won his argument over the bitter protests of Montreal merchants and established Fort Pontchartrain at Detroit in 1701. For the next decade Cadillac continually encouraged the Great Lakes Indians to settle there, and many of them did (MPHC 33:424–452, 384). There were villages of Chippewa, Potawatomi, Huron, Fox, Sauk, and Miami. From time to time bands of Shawnee, Mississauga, and other tribes would trade there. Detroit had become the major entrepot, although a few Huron and Ottawa bands remained at the Straits of Mackinac.

French attitudes toward the western country changed after the Treaty of Utrecht in 1713, which ended Queen Anne's War. The treaty declared that the Iroquois were British subjects, and the French feared that this combination would immediately expand into the Upper Great Lakes. The treaty also permitted both the English and the French to trade with the western Indians. This was potential disaster, as all the Indians, especially the many Algonquian tribes, knew that English trade goods were better and less expensive than those of the French.

The French response to the treaty was to establish a string of military and trading posts through the Upper Lakes. Some of the more notable were Michilimackinac, reestablished about 1715; Fort Saint Joseph at Niles, 1715; and Fort Beauharnois in Minnesota, 1728. Other Lake Superior posts were soon established: Michipicoten, Nepigon, and Kaministiqua. As a result of this renewed activity, Indian dependence on French goods and economic interests became more pronounced. Indian clothing, tools, arms, and occupations changed to meet new French demands.

This new French empire in the Upper Lakes stretched into northern Ontario and west into modern Wisconsin, Minnesota, and Manitoba, primarily over land populated by Chippewa, Ottawa, Sioux, Cree, and Menominee. In addition to the established posts, the French had many traders who lived in Indian villages as part of the trade network. Thus, direct cultural influences from Paris and Montreal could be found during this era as far west as the wilds of Lake Winnipeg. In 1730 the Upper Great Lakes center for most French activity was Michilimackinac, where "voyageurs from all these places come to sell their furs and to buy corn and canoes" (Anonymous 1730). To a lesser extent Detroit served as a trading and social center for the Chippewas, Ottawas, Miamis, Potawatomis, and Shawnees of the Lower Lakes.

Missionaries were at most of the posts, but Catholicism was often only a veneer over Indian religion, a condition that prevailed for generations. Jesuit accounts of mission

Fig. 1. Upper Great Lakes area.

STONE AND CHAPUT

success must be cautiously interpreted. The Jesuits were enthusiastic, and the number of persons baptized was often seen as the measure of a mission's success. For example, Father Pierson, missionary to the Hurons at Michilimackinac, reported 45 children and 47 adults as new Christians in 1676 because he had just baptized them (JR 60:209-211). The rate of baptisms did not decrease, but there is no evidence that Christianity made much of a spiritual impact on Huron or Ottawa life. The missions did exert a strong social and political influence, however, as the missionaries' role in allying various Indian groups with French interests was very important.

Alcohol was a problem from earliest European contact with the Indians of this area. The ramifications go far beyond the commonplace statement that the French got the natives drunk and then stole their furs. Brandy was foremost a gift, a means of opening negotiations. Furthermore, brandy was a political weapon. In 1716 Philippe de Rigaud, marquis de Vaudreuil, governor of New France, explained why brandy was essential for the posts of Forts Frontenac, Detroit, and Michilimackinac: "Tis certain that the Indians, finding French brandy at home, will not go in search of any rum to the English." Vaudreuil felt that disorders in the native villages could be controlled by rationing the amount of brandy given to the Indians (NYCD 9:871).

All was not harmonious in the widespread French empire. In 1712 the acting commandant of Detroit, Jacques Renaud Dubuisson, made a decision involving an intertribal dispute that would cost the French dearly in coming decades. A group of Fox and Mascouten, intending a retaliatory attack on the Ottawa at Detroit, were instead set upon by the French and their Indian allies. After being besieged for 19 days the Fox broke out, were pursued, and lost about 1,000 men, women, and children in the ensuing battles (MPHC 33:537-571). Some of these Indians escaped to harass the French for decades. In 1716 and again in the late 1720s and 1730s, major French-Indian expeditions were sent into Wisconsin from Michilimackinac to exterminate the Fox and their Sauk protectors without success. These Indians were the only Algonquians in the Upper Lakes who did not cooperate in French imperial plans. Their prolonged resistance slowed the rate of French recovery in this area, while the possible threat that they might combine with the Iroquois against the French was a constant worry in Montreal and Detroit (Kellogg 1908).

In 1739 the French sent a major expedition from Montreal and Michilimackinac down the Mississippi Valley in a campaign against the Chickasaw. Michilimackinac was a staging area, and groups of Potawatomi, Sioux, Sauk, Fox, Chippewa, Ottawa, and Nipissing were outfitted there. Obviously, the necessary food, canoes, and arms were provided to the warriors. The all-pervasive French paternalism even cared for those not going on the expedition. For example, the French provided corn, tobacco, and powder and ball to Nipissing families whose men were away with the war party.

A series of minor revolts in the Great Lakes in the late 1740s caused the French to increase amounts of gifts and supplies, and for the next few years a procession of Nipissing, Ottawa, Huron, Sauk, Fox, Potawatomi, Winnebago, and Illinois chiefs was entertained by officials in Montreal. They returned with arms, wampum, beef, brandy, tobacco, bread, and clothing. Most of these trips originated from Michilimackinac, some from Lake Superior, and a few from Detroit. Hence, prestige and success for the Indians of the Great Lakes was, to a certain extent, related to French aims during this era. The zenith in the career of an Ottawa chief from Michilimackinac was to return from a conference in Montreal with the governor with rich provisions, plus a medal or a belt.

By the mid-1700s Indian tribal and band names were less frequently used, as settlement patterns had radically shifted and as significant cultural differences among most Indian groups were decreasing. Important warriors in each village now had flintlock muskets, iron hatchets, beads, tobacco, knives, and clothing provided by the French. Previously, these differences had been important enough so that the French referred to specific groups by tribal or band name, either for religious purposes or for treaties of understanding. In the mid-1600s the French would not refer merely to the Ottawa but would specify Kiskakon Ottawa or Sinago Ottawa, for example. Originally the Indians who had settled near Saginaw Bay, on the Michigan side of Lake Huron, were Ottawas. By the early 1700s large numbers of Chippewas had settled there also. In the following decades these Indians were sometimes referred to as the Ottawas of Saginaw, or more frequently as the Indians of Saginaw, a general term applying to all the Algonquians living there. For the French, and for the Indians, once-important cultural differences were subordinate to political and economic considerations.

Of importance to an understanding of native culture change during this period was the development and spread of the Midewiwin. The Midewiwin developed during the early eighteenth century as a response to European influence and is particularly well documented among the Chippewa and other Central Algonquian groups (Hickerson 1963:75-82, 1970:51-63). Hickerson (1970:52) describes the Midewiwin as "a set of ceremonials conducted—by an organized priesthood—who had occult knowledge of 'killing' and 'curing' by use of herbs, missiles, medicine bundles, and other objects which had medicinal properties. Members of the Mide society were repositories of tribal traditions, origins, and migrations integrated in systems of myth and legend. . . . A feature common to these [nativistic] movements is the transmutation of ancient ritual practices and beliefs to new ideological and ritual contexts that also tend to incorporate material from outside cultures, especially if these cultures exert a dominating socioeconomic influence."

A major change in Indian life resulted from the French and Indian War, 1756-1760. This event, another extension of hostilities in Europe, meant that the Indians again had to align themselves with traditional White allies. Most of the fighting took place in the eastern part of the continent, but major expeditions of warriors from Sault Sainte Marie, Mackinac, Green Bay, and Detroit joined French forays against the English in modern Pennsylvania and New York. The English won the war, seized control of the Saint Lawrence valley, and terminated French military activity in North America. This meant a major adjustment for the Algonquian tribes of the Upper Great Lakes. The French army, missionaries, and traders had been present in scattered numbers since the 1660s. But after 1763, the major political and economic policies affecting the Indians and French would be English, enforced by the British army.

British Regime, 1760-1796

Major hostilities of the French and Indian War ended in September 1760 with the capitulation of Montreal and the French colony of Canada to British forces under Gen. Jeffrey Amherst (Beers 1964:95). All the French military posts in the Upper Great Lakes area were transferred to British control. Several of the articles of capitulation ending this war (Nish 1965:153-155), particularly those guaranteeing religious freedom and continued property ownership, were to have important effects on the status of European-Indian relationships by assuring that French culture would continue in the future course of these relationships. The ending of this conflict, then, although not producing dramatic changes in the existing pattern of relationships, due in part to the continuing presence of the French civilian population, did initiate a new political system whose differing philosophy, objectives, and methods of administration would ultimately be felt (I.A. Johnson 1919:64-77; Kellogg 1935:23-32). The earlier French regime had been interested both in maintaining control of the fur trade by promoting friendly relations with the Indians and in converting heathen Indians to Christianity. The British were interested not only in pursuing the fur trade but also in expanding the colonization and settlement of new areas of North America and in acquiring and developing other types of resources and products, such as mining interests and forest and agricultural products. The British interest in native religious practices was relatively limited.

In order to consider the effects of this change in political control during the next 30 to 35 years, it is useful to characterize certain aspects of Upper Great Lakes area Indian society during the early 1760s. First, native settlements had become more centralized near the major

forts and trading posts. This trend, noted as early as the late 1600s, led to increased intertribal and European-Indian interaction and presumably to the additional sharing or combination of specific cultural traits, as well as to an increased dissemination and utilization of European goods and provisions among native peoples. This increasing interaction was a response: to intertribal alliances that had been established as a result of the Indians' participation in the French and Indian War, to the greater frequency of intertribal conferences held by both the French and the British in attempting to promote and maintain friendly Indian relations, and to the pervasive need that the native population had developed for European goods and provisions. The native population was, by this time, inextricably dependent on European goods for their existence, since they had largely abandoned their traditional tools in favor of more efficient and durable European goods. Also the Indians' ability to provide for themselves had declined with the increasing elimination of important game animals, previously basic to their subsistence. Thus, it was essential for the Indians to participate in the fur trade; this was the only way in which they could hope to enjoy continued access to European trade goods and staple supplies. It can be readily understood that such a close native adaptation to European objectives made the native culture increasingly susceptible to even relatively minor changes in the structure of European occupation.

Because of this susceptibility, an acceleration and diversification of native culture change is noted during the 30 to 35 years after 1760, stimulated by a developing British policy of Indian trade. Such policy changes were rapidly introduced by the British after 1760 (I.A. Johnson 1919:64-77). Trade goods and provisions were no longer freely dispensed to the Indians as a traditional means of securing their alliance and cooperation as had been the French regime's policy (W.F. Dunbar 1965:166-177, 122). These goods and provisions were now distributed only in exchange for valued commodities such as furs. The hardships created by this policy, by the growing frequency of fraudulent trade practices, by the Indians' growing concern that their lands were being seized by the British, and by the denial of guns and ammunition to the Indians, precipitated an Indian rebellion against the British, led by the Ottawa Chief Pontiac during the early summer of 1763 (Peckham 1947). Fort Michilimackinac and other western posts were taken at this time. Neither Green Bay nor Detroit was captured, although Detroit was besieged through the summer of 1763, and Green Bay was abandoned.

This conflict hastened the British government's adoption of major changes in Indian policy of seeming benefit to the Indians. Several of the new measures included the reservation of all lands west of the Alleghenies for the Indians and the prohibition of Indian land purchases except by royal agents. European traders now had to have licenses to conduct trade, and trade could only be conducted at major military posts such as Detroit and Michilimackinac, where it was regulated by the officer in charge (Kellogg 1935:30). This license system appeared to allow more freedom than had the earlier French monopoly system since anyone, French or British, could presumably secure a license. Unfortunately, the increased number of traders and fur-trade interests led to new competition for a diminishing resource and to a consequent increase in fraudulent fur-trade practices. Although the proposed new land policies had some initial positive effects, after 1776 these benefits were lost as a result of the pressure of colonial land interests and the Revolutionary War.

During the Revolution, Indian support and alliances were once again promoted as they were called on by the British to put down the colonial rebellion. The majority of Upper Great Lakes area Indians, except for the Sauk and Fox, aligned themselves with the British, viewing them as less of a threat to their land than the expansion-oriented colonists. The Sauk and Fox were later compelled to support the British cause. The opposing side consisted of the American revolutionaries allied with the French and ultimately the Spanish. Again, the majority of Indians had allied with the losing side in a major conflict between European powers.

The war, although physically distant from the Upper Great Lakes area, did have major effects: British forts were strengthened; the Indians were again called from their home areas to participate in a European war; trade in the area was made more difficult because traders needed both a trading license and a pass to enter the Great Lakes area; also, trade was curtailed by restrictions placed on ship passage into the area (I.A. Johnson 1919:83). This decrease in trading activity placed severe hardships on the area's native peoples, who were largely dependent on a regular supply of trade goods.

After 1783, the official beginning of the American period of control, more critical problems arose for the Indians within the territory of the United States, particularly in relation to land policy. Western lands were viewed by the American public as "conquered" and, therefore, available for settlement and development. Although the "conquered" Indians were allocated reservations and American settler encroachment was prohibited, much of their land was ceded to the American government as recompense for their part in the Revolutionary conflict. Much of this ceded land was eventually sold to American settlers. Attempts to resume the orderly settlement of Western land were largely unsuccessful and despite repeated government efforts, land that had been reserved for Indians was ultimately claimed by Americans. This encroachment again precipitated Indian rebellions that were put down by American forces. Indian lands thus continued to be absorbed by the expanding American settlements; most of these properties were ceded by treaty or purchase.

Although the British had lost title to most of the Upper Great Lakes area at the close of the Revolution in 1783, they remained at the western posts and continued to control the fur trade and manipulate their Indian allies until the posts were turned over to the Americans in 1796. Trading during these intervening years had become more regularly established with the founding of the North West Company and the Mackinaw Company during the 1780s. The trade patterns produced by these companies created a new era of Indian relations in the Upper Great Lakes.

The location of specific Indian tribes and bands during this period was fairly stable, although these had measurably changed from areas occupied at the beginning of the eighteenth century. It is nearly impossible at this time to speak of correlations between environmental areas and settlement patterns, since the location of tribal units had become largely determined by the location of European settlements. Thus, Ottawa, Chippewa, and Huron bands are noted in southeastern Michigan and adjacent Ontario. Smaller groups of Chippewa were also at Mackinac, Chequamegon, Sault Sainte Marie, along the western shore of Lake Superior, and in the Saginaw, Michigan, area. The Ottawa also had an important settlement at L'Arbre Croche on the northeastern shore of Lake Michigan, below Mackinac. The Potawatomi were centered in southwestern Michigan near Fort Saint Joseph. The Sauk and Fox remained in Wisconsin but had moved farther to the north and west along the Mississippi.

American Regime, 1796–1800s

The fur trade reached its peak in the region during the American regime especially after the formation of the American Fur Company in 1808, centered at Mackinac. A system of subagents who were scattered throughout the area lessened the need for Indians to come to central points; instead, they would deliver their furs to European settlements such as Green Bay, Milwaukee, and Grand Haven, where they would in turn receive trade goods (I.A. Johnson 1919:102–126). Thus the Indians' annual cycle until the decline of the trade during the 1830s and 1840s was to spend the winter months trapping, deliver the furs in the spring, and then gear up the following winter's trapping. The subagents, and the center at Mackinac, were usually supplied with provisions by the Indians.

By this time the half-breeds (Métis) had become a formidable force in the fur trade and in Indian village life. Thousands of Métis were in villages around the Upper Great Lakes, and to the west of Lake Superior their numbers were so great that they had settlements of their own. In most cases the Métis were French and Indian, *607* although there was also a considerable number of Métis of part Scottish or Irish ancestry. In terms of the economic status of the fur trade, the Métis normally held a higher position than the Indian; in social-cultural measurements they were more European than Indian. The majority of the Métis were to be found in the Chippewa and Cree country to the north and west of Lake Superior (Giraud 1945).

Many of the Métis played key roles in the history of the Upper Great Lakes. Families such as the Johnsons, Bottineaus, Boileaus, and LaFramboises contributed many agents or subagents, interpreters, and assistants to surveyors, explorers, and missionaries. They were invaluable both to the Indians and to the U.S. federal government during the period of 1820 to 1860.

European problems continued to have an impact on the American frontier, and in the War of 1812 the Indians were again to choose between two foreign nations. In general, the Indians sided with the British, on the assumption that if the Americans won the war, the country would soon be swarming with settlers. Large contingents of Indians helped the British, especially in the successful attacks at Fort Mackinac and Detroit. The most notable Indian tribe in the war was the Shawnee, led by Tecumseh. The problem for the Indians, of course, came after the war, as once again they had backed the losing side. In a series of treaties from 1814 through 1825, usually encouraged or controlled by Michigan territorial governor Lewis Cass, the Indians were reminded of their participation on the wrong side during the war.

After the Indian Removal Act of 1830, some of the Indians from the Upper Great Lakes joined other tribes in finding new homes west of the Mississippi. The Potawatomis from southwestern Michigan and some Ottawas and Wyandots from southeastern Michigan and northwestern Ohio were removed to Kansas and Indian Territory, although some fled to Canada. Through the 1850s there was periodic pressure to remove the large bands of Chippewa and Ottawa, but no substantial removal took place (Bauman 1952). In one semisuccessful attempt, some Winnebagos were removed from Wisconsin to Minnesota (Fadner 1966).

Typical of the pressure for removal was the comment from the *Minnesota Pioneer* (Dec. 29, 1853:2, col. 3), in which desire for Indian lands and an alleged interest in Indian welfare were expressed: "It is a fact, well established by experience, that the Indian and the white man cannot 'dwell together in unity,' and in nothing has the philanthropic justice of our Government been more apparent than in the removal of Indians from land to which the Indian title has been extinguished, before they become contaminated by intercourse with the whites on the ceded lands."

The United States government dealt with the Indian problem by treaties. From the late 1790s to 1870, dozens of tribes sold their lands in Michigan, Wisconsin, and Minnesota and were assigned reservations that were increasingly diminished by later treaties. The Americans knew of the copper, lead, and iron in the region; and good timber lands were everywhere. Before exploitation, though, the land question had to be settled. Of the many treaties, that of La Pointe in 1842 stands out, as it opened up the copper and iron lands. In fact, the year the treaty was ratified, 1843, land surveys were in progress and the federal Mineral Land Agency was opened on the shores of Lake Superior. The following year Fort Wilkins was erected at Copper Harbor, Michigan.

As part of the treaty system, the federal government made token efforts to "civilize" the Indians, placing an occasional blacksmith, farmer, and carpenter at selected reservations. Interestingly, the government also provided funds for both Protestant and Catholic missions for reservation schools. A typical example of this system and its bitter Catholic-Methodist feuds was the L'Anse-Baraga Chippewa reservation on the Michigan shores of Lake Superior. In addition to those protagonists, there was also the nearby garrison at Fort Wilkins. Also, the American Fur Company was everywhere usually favoring the Protestants. In the jockeying for position, the Indians were harmed, as they were constantly compelled to take sides with powers and influences they did not understand (*New York Herald*, Jan. 8, 1848:4).

Throughout most of the nineteenth century, government relations with the Indians were handled by superintendencies and agencies. Superintendents had general responsibility for a specific geographic area, while agents were usually responsible for the affairs of one tribe or reservation. In Michigan, for example, the superintendent was usually stationed in Detroit, with key agents at Sault Sainte Marie, Mackinac Island, L'Anse, Traverse Bay, and Saginaw Bay. Agencies changed in significance as White settlements increased. The Grand Rapids Ottawa Agency diminished in significance after the treaty of 1836, which extinguished Indian title to most of the land in northwestern lower Michigan.

Other key agencies in the Upper Great Lakes were the Saint Peters Agency, Minnesota, established in 1819 (Sioux and some Chippewa); Winnebago Agency, Minnesota and Wisconsin, 1848 (Winnebago and some Chippewa); Green Bay Agency, Wisconsin, 1824 (Menominee, Winnebago, Chippewa, Ottawa, Potawatomi, and others); and La Pointe Agency, Wisconsin, 1831 (Chippewa).

By the mid-1800s the cultures of the tribes in this region had developed many similarities. Bands were shifted from place to place, either at a federal whim, because of a new Indian betterment program, or because of forced removal from traditional locations. The results were often tragic, such as expecting the forest-dwelling Winnebago to adjust to the Dakota plains. The Green Bay Agency is a good example of multicultural activity, as Ottawas, Menominees, Chippewas, Potawatomis, and

Winnebagos lived there; these were Algonquian groups, except for the Siouan Winnebago. By mid-century the Oneida, Stockbridge, Munsee, and Brothertown Indians from New York State had been resettled near Green Bay; these were eastern Algonquian and Iroquoian bands.

This mélange of Indians of different linguistic and cultural backgrounds accelerated the process of changing life-styles. There came to be in the Green Bay vicinity a new Indian way of life, far removed from the hunter-trapper-canoe traditions of the 1600s. To be an Indian had come to mean now that one lived in an inadequate wooden shelter, hoped that annuities or handouts were available, worked occasionally in the woods for White lumber barons, and exposed one's children to a conglomeration of wandering Methodist, Baptist, and Catholic clergymen.

Missionaries, government agents, and the army tried to end the "old ways" of the Indians, but their efforts throughout the century were not successful. For example, nothing could diminish the traditional hatred that the Chippewa and Sioux held for each other. From La Pointe down into central Minnesota, sometimes near settled White communities, Chippewa-Sioux combats took place (*Minnesota Pioneer,* May 23:2, May 30, 1850:2). The ability of the Minnesota Sioux was undercut after the famous 1862 uprising, when many were killed and hundreds imprisoned or exiled. Missionaries were com-

plaining until after 1900 that the Mide society was still powerful among the Chippewa, which hampered the introduction of religious and medical changes.

By the late nineteenth century the Indians had sold their best lands, some of them were removed from the region, and others were placed on small reserves. They were surrounded by usually hostile White communities, while missionaries, Indian agents, soldiers, and teachers sought to regulate most aspects of Indian life.

British policies had proved more favorable to the Great Lakes Indians. In the 1830s and 1840s, when removal was a major United States policy, many Ottawas, and some Ojibwa, left the Midwest and settled on Manitoulin Island, Parry Island, and in other parts of Ontario under British control. On these islands and on Walpole Island, the composite villages usually included Ottawas, Ojibwas, and Potawatomis.

Because land pressures were not so severe in Ontario and Manitoba, the Indians retained traditional practices longer than did Indians remaining in the United States. Landes (1937) mentions that as late as the 1930s, the "medicine man" was the most important person in Ojibwa villages on the Canadian side of the Manitoba-Minnesota border. This cultural retention was more difficult in the United States, where mining, farming, lumbering, and manufacturing had forced the scattering of Great Lakes bands.

Great Lakes–Riverine Sociopolitical Organization

CHARLES CALLENDER

The societies that at the time of European contact were established in the upper Great Lakes area and the valleys of the Ohio and upper Mississippi were mostly Algonquian but included the Siouan-speaking Winnebago (fig. 1). The sociopolitical organizations of these groups fell into two sharply contrasted configurations.

The dominant configuration included the Shawnee, the Illinois and Miami tribes, the Sauk, Fox, Kickapoo, Potawatomi, and Menominee and may by inference be extended to the Mascouten. Overall similarities that justify the provisional inclusion of the Winnebago also reflect strong postcontact Algonquian influence (Lurie 1960). The earlier nature of Winnebago society and its relations with those of trans-Mississippi Siouans are dimensions that cannot be treated here.

While important differences separated these societies, they shared a cluster of significant features. These included an economic base that combined maize agriculture with seasonal hunting and gathering activities, which acquired greater importance after European contact introduced the fur trade. The settlement pattern alternated between concentration into semipermanent riverine villages in summer and large camps in winter, with dispersal among scattered camps in spring and fall. Kinship systems were of Omaha type. Their behavioral patterns were generally consistent with strong patrilineal lineages yet showed marked bilateral tendencies. Lineages had corporate functions that regulated marriage and other aspects of social structure but concentrated most heavily in the area of ritual and were largely divorced from the ownership or control of productive property. Each tribe also had a system of patrilineal exogamous clans that similarly emphasized ritual but extended into the political organization and helped integrate outsiders into the society. Moiety systems or dual divisions were common, while ritual societies and warrior associations provided institutions that crosscut the descent groups. All these groups were organized as tribes with a dual political structure consisting of parallel organizations for peace and for war, with different sets of officials attached to each.

The second configuration comprised the Ottawa and Chippewa living along the northern fringe of the region. Here agriculture was absent or at best marginal. The settlement pattern included summer concentration at fishing sites (later, at trade centers) and dispersal the rest of the year. Settlements were generally small. The kinship system was of Iroquois type. Cross-cousin marriage, probably bilateral, may have been practiced at contact and certainly existed at an earlier time. Patrilineal clans were present but their corporate features and functions were at best very weak, and corporate lineages were absent. Political organization was generally of the band type, with sporadic tendencies toward wider integration.

The position of the Potawatomi involves special problems. Some northern Potawatomi apparently fall into the second configuration (Skinner 1924–1927, 1:9–16). Most of this tribe clearly belongs to the first (Jenness 1935:7–8; Landes 1970). Several features suggest that the Potawatomi shifted from a sociopolitical organization of Chippewa-Ottawa type into one characteristic of Configuration 1 at a relatively late date, during protocontact or early postcontact times. Perhaps Skinner's "Forest" Potawatomi never made this shift, but more likely they reflect later Chippewa-Ottawa influence (see "Potawatomi," this vol.).

A full account and analysis of both configurations is difficult. Extensive gaps impair the data for all these

Fig. 1. Tribal locations about 1670.

societies and for long segments of time. The rapid and sometimes drastic changes affecting these systems after contact further complicate a delineation of their features. The following account thus relies heavily on inferences and extrapolates knowledge from the more completely described groups to those that are less well known.

Configuration 1

The kinship systems characterizing the larger configuration, consistently Omaha in terminological structure, belonged to the variety that Lounsbury (1964a) calls Type I. Their basic pattern is illustrated here (fig. 2) by Fox terminology, the best preserved and most completely described (Tax 1955). The Father term, *no·sa,* is applied to ego's father and to all the men whom the latter calls 'Brother', to the husbands of almost all women of the mother's lineage, and to the sons of women belonging to the father's mother's lineage. Mother, *nekya,* is restricted to ego's own mother. Its diminutive *neki·ha* is used for all her 'Sisters' and for most other women of her lineage, for the daughters of women belonging to her mother's lineage, and for the wives of all men in the 'Father' class. The term for Paternal Aunt, *nesekwisa,* is used for women whom ego's father calls 'Sister', for the wives of all 'Maternal Uncles', and for the daughters of all women of the father's mother's lineage. Maternal Uncle, *nešise·ha,* designates all men of ego's mother's lineage below the second ascending generation and the sons of women of the mother's mother's lineage. All consanguineal relatives in the second ascending generation are Grandfather, *nemešo·ha,* or Grandmother, *no·hkomesa,* as are all members of the lineages of the father's and mother's mothers.

The sibling class includes ego's siblings and parallel cousins, as well as the children of all persons called 'Father' or 'Mother' and of all women of the mother's lineage. A variety of terms distinguishes these relatives by such features as sex and relative age: *nesese·ha* 'Older Brother', *nemise·ha* 'Older Sister', *nesi·ma* 'Younger Sibling', *neto·te·ma* 'Sibling of the same sex', *netawe·ma·wa* 'Brother, female speaking', and *netehkwe·ma* 'Sister, male speaking'.

Male ego uses the terms *nekwisa* 'Son' and *neta·nesa* 'Daughter' for the offspring of all men he classes as 'Brothers' and of all women he calls 'Sister-in-law' and for the children of his wife's paternal aunt. He applies the terms for Niece, *nešemi·ha,* and Nephew, *nenekwa·ha,* to the children of all women whom he calls "sister" and of all women of his own lineage except those in the "daughter" category. Female ego reverses these patterns.

Grandchild, *no·šisema,* is used for the offspring of every person called 'Son', 'Daughter', 'Nephew', or 'Niece'.

Affinal terms are similarly extended widely in a nongenerational pattern. Father-in-law, *nemešo·ma,* and Mother-in-law, *no·hkoma,* designate one's spouse's parents and their siblings, and all members of the mother-in-law's lineage. Terms for siblings-in-law include *ni·hta·wa* 'Brother-in-law, male speaking', *neta·kwa* 'Sister-in-law, female speaking', and *ni·nemwa* 'Sibling-in-law of opposite sex'. They are used for the spouses of all persons in the 'Sibling' class, for all members of the 'Sibling' class of one's spouse, and for men married to women of the first and second ascending generations in one's own lineage. Male ego also uses them for members of the second and third descending generations in his wife's lineage, and both sexes apply them to offspring of women of the spouse's mother's lineage. The spouses of all 'Children' and of all persons called 'Niece' and 'Nephew' are *nenekwana* 'Son-in-law' or *nesemya* 'Daughter-in-law'.

As far as other terminological structures are known or can be reconstructed, their most important deviations from the Fox system involve bifurcation or fairly recent changes. In the Algonquian systems the terms themselves are usually cognate with the Fox forms, although those for affines and the auxiliary sibling terms show variability. The Sauk and Kickapoo systems seem structurally identical with Fox (Callender 1962:113-121; Jones 1913; Morgan 1871:291-382). One can extend this identity to the Illinois and Miami tribes as well as the Shawnee, although their systems did not differentiate within the 'Mother' class by using a diminutive form of the regular term (Morgan 1871:291-382). The Menominee system tends to be bifurcate collateral, distinguishing lineal from collateral relatives in the first ascending and descending generations (Bloomfield 1962). The Potawatomi system recorded in 1859 by Morgan (1871:291-382) was similarly bifurcate collateral, but a general shift toward bifurcate merging was evident by 1936 (Landes 1970:325-333) and by 1955 was almost complete (Callender 1962:56, 113-121).

The systems of the Winnebago and the Potawatomi living in Michigan and Wisconsin show the greatest divergence. The traditional Winnebago system agreed with Fox in restricting the Mother term (*hiųní*) to ego's mother and using a diminutive (*hiųnínik*) for other members of this class (Mathews 1959; Morgan 1871: 291-382). Unlike Fox, grandchildren, cross-nieces, and cross-nephews formed a single class, although diminutives apparently defined subclasses within this. The terms later collected by Radin (1923:80-85) show extensive changes. Ego's father was now distinguished from the rest of this class by using a former Stepfather term for its other members. Even more significant, Omaha features were breaking down. Although the maternal uncle's son was still called by a diminutive form of the Maternal Uncle term, his children were classed as niece and nephew. The maternal uncle's daughter was called Paternal Aunt and her children were also placed in the Niece-Nephew class. Landes's (1970:333-337) Michigan Potawatomi material shows rather similar features while the terms Tax collected among Potawatomi in Wisconsin

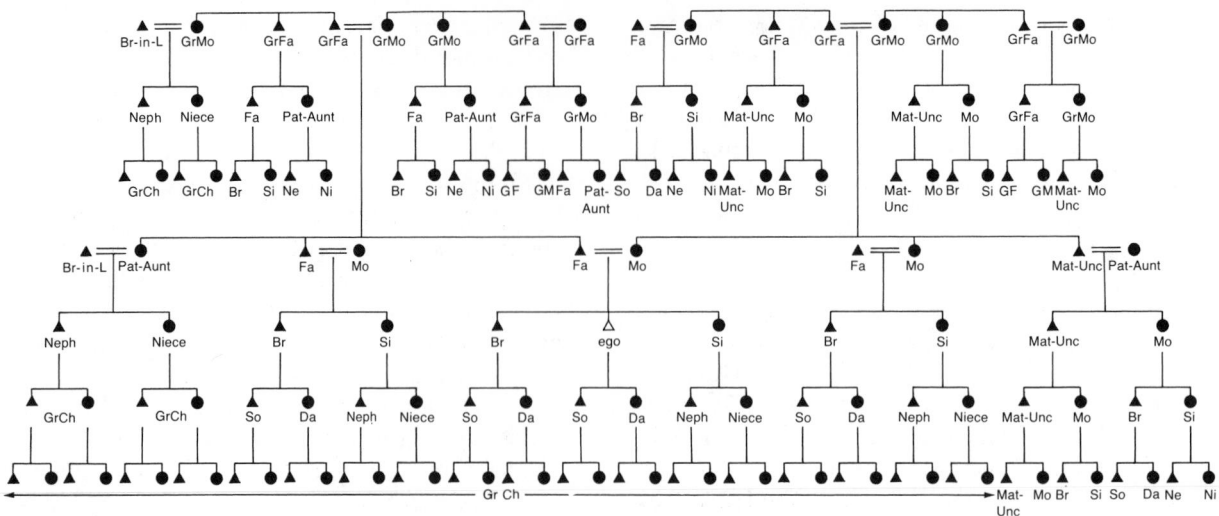

Fig. 2. Fox kinship terminology for male ego (after Tax 1955). Each abbreviation represents a single term, except that Br and Si each cover 3 terms (see text).

represent a system of Iroquois type (Callender 1962: 55–56).

The behavioral component of these kinship systems has also been most completely described for the Fox (Tax 1955), although considerable data are available for the Sauk (Callender 1962; Skinner 1923–1925), Potawatomi (Landes 1970), Menominee (Bloomfield 1928; Skinner 1913), and Winnebago (Radin 1923). Behavioral patterns showed an overall distinction between respect and joking categories that parallel those described for Plains tribes (see Eggan 1955), but were rather less intense. Respect was given to those relatives whose positions within the system carried some measure of authority, even potential, and in a weaker form to classificatory relatives in these categories. These included parents, older siblings of the same sex and all siblings of opposite sex, and parents-in-law. Even in its most intense form, involving parents-in-law of the opposite sex, respect fell short of real avoidance among the Algonquian tribes. Certain topics were prohibited and the tenor of speech was restricted, but speech itself was not forbidden. Behavior toward grandparents was intermediate between joking and respect, including mutual affection and indulgence. Relatives belonging to the joking category included maternal uncles and paternal aunts as well as siblings-in-law. Mutual teasing characterized relations with these uncles and aunts. The siblings-in-law were required to engage in constant joking, often sexually oriented and frequently suggestive, but entirely verbal when this style of interaction crossed sex lines.

The forms of prescribed behavior involving maternal uncles and paternal aunts require detailed discussion. These were unusually complex, shifting with the ages of those involved, and were partly inconsistent with the classic formulations for patrilineal societies. Among the Sauk, Fox, and Kickapoo, these relatives were objects of fear used by parents to frighten small children into good behavior. While adults found this practice a source of amusement, and thus a form of joking, the children were genuinely terrified. As they grew older, they began to retaliate, surreptitiously at first but by adolescence initiating open teasing with the encouragement of other relatives. At this point the relationship evolved into a close and friendly one characterized by mutual teasing that was obligatory only in public and, unlike sibling-in-law joking, could be ignored if others were not present. This teasing further differed from sibling-in-law behavior by its exclusion of sexual references, although the relationship explicitly permitted discussion of marital problems and other topics verging on sex that were prohibited in respect relationships.

The exchange of gifts between nepotic relatives has been described as a right of the junior member to demand property of the senior, but an equivalent return in property or services was expected. Lurie (1961:xi–xiii) gives a Winnebago example. The relationship also involved important obligations in warfare and sometimes in ritual. Young men often accompanied their maternal uncles on raids, particularly when it was their first venture. The Menominee forbade uncle and nephew to desert each other in warfare and required them to avenge each other's death. Among the Sauk and Potawatomi, the man leading a raid and carrying the expedition's sacred pack was attended by his nephews. Sauk women held races to assist their maternal uncles in obtaining war honors. Fox warriors shared such honors with their nieces and perhaps with their paternal aunts, and often gave them prizes, equivalent to war honors, won in lacrosse games. The Winnebago preferred sister's sons as attendants in clan rituals as well as in raids.

"Privileged familiarity" toward the maternal uncle, who lacks authority, is a common feature of many patrilineal systems; however, in those described here, this kind of behavior is reciprocal rather than one-sided. It is also only one facet of a complex relation that includes some obligations that seem inconsistent with a system of patrilineal lineages. Moreover, while indulgence is expected from the maternal uncle in classic patrilineal complexes, the paternal aunt typically receives considerable respect as an older member of one's own lineage. In these groups both relatives are treated as essentially equivalent. This same equivalence extends to their spouses. The Fox class the paternal aunt's husband as a brother-in-law and treat him as such. The maternal uncle's wife is similarly treated as a sister-in-law with whom one jokes, using sexual allusions. Although called 'Paternal Aunt', she may be terminologically distinguished from other relatives of that class as *nekaka·činesekwisa* 'joking paternal aunt' (Tax 1955:253–254; Voorhis 1971:66). Like her husband, she can have a quasi-disciplining function (Tax 1955:258).

The forms of marriage described in the literature varied widely from formal negotiations between families to relatively informal unions agreed upon by couples without apparent guidance from their relatives. The second type has come to predominate. In the past the degree of formality involved in marriage probably varied with status. Early French accounts, for instance, give some basis for inferring that intertribal unions were particularly common among the families of chiefs. Traditional practice generally permitted some courtship, but marriage was usually preceded by a formal proposal, most often made by the parents of the man. Marriage was validated by an exchange of gifts, ranging from valuable property such as horses and guns to a symbolic exchange of food in which the husband's family presented meat and the wife's family responded with maize and other vegetables. Such exchanges were always reciprocal and usually equivalent, but among the Winnebago the husband's family gave more (Lurie 1961:122).

Information about preferential forms of marriage is limited to unions between persons already linked as affinal relatives. Sororate and levirate marriages were favored but not actually compulsory, although the family of a deceased spouse could insist on the survivor's serving out the full mourning period before releasing him or her, while marriage to another member of their lineage often abbreviated this period. Such remarriages, like sororal polygyny, were not limited to actual siblings of the spouse, but involved any person belonging to the proper sibling-in-law classes.

Household composition is particularly difficult to reconstruct. The evidence indicates a shift through time from large extended-family units toward nuclear families that often include one or more odd relatives. The nature of the former extended families is unclear. Most tribes prescribed initial matrilocal residence lasting a year or more after marriage. While the Fox data may suggest an emphasis on matrilocality (Callender 1962:25), the Winnebago favored patrilocal residence (Lurie 1961:122).

Another point that remains unclear is whether an extended family remained together throughout the year or reshuffled its members seasonally.

Clan Systems

A system of patrilineal clans characterized every tribe in the series. Few adequate accounts of these systems were produced before the 1930s. By that time extensive restructuring of clans and attrition of their functions precluded a definitive reconstruction of their aboriginal features. Information is most abundant for the Fox, Potawatomi, and Winnebago and almost nonexistent for the Miami and Illinois tribes, with other groups falling between these extremes. Illinois clans had disappeared before 1750 (Morgan 1959:80). Those of the Miami disintegrated in the nineteenth century. In other societies they have persisted, often as very significant units, yet their importance is ritual rather than social.

This analysis of Fox clans is based primarily on Tax (1932–1934, 1955) with some additions from Callender (1955a). It supersedes and corrects the earlier accounts of Jones (1939), Fisher (in Jones 1939), and Michelson (1925:541, 1937:2, 1938). Tax (1955) described Fox clans in 1932 as name groups—classifications of personal names by their totemic reference to an eponym or a group of linked eponyms—that were also loosely organized as cult groups centering on periodic ceremonies. They tended toward patrilineality, but with many exceptions, and were no longer exogamous. The members of a clan shared common ritual links but were not regarded as relatives. Among other Algonquian tribes, such as the Sauk (Callender 1962:91–92), Shawnee (Voegelin and Voegelin 1935), Prairie Potawatomi (Landes 1970), and apparently the Kickapoo (Callender 1962:99; Jones 1913; Ritzenthaler and Peterson 1956), clans have diverged even further from patrilineal descent groups while retaining at least some important ritual functions. Even in the past, the ritual aspects of clans in the Upper Great Lakes-Riverine area probably outweighed their secular functions. It may also be argued (Callender 1962:102–103) that attrition of secular functions resulted from measures taken to preserve the naming complex and, among the Fox, clan ritual.

Clan names showed a certain overall patterning. Animals or mythical beings were the most frequent eponyms. The most widespread animal names were Wolf, Bear, Elk, Fox, and Deer, which were recognized by most tribes. Among mythical beings, Thunder was very common, as well as an underwater being known variously as Water-Spirit or Panther and often equated with aquatic mammals such as beaver and otter. Eagles apart, bird eponyms were less common and more likely to be specific to a particular tribe. The same was true of fish. Plant eponyms, very rare, included the Bear Potato (*Apios americana*) clan of the Sauk, the Berry clan of the Kickapoo, and the Shawnee and Kickapoo Tree clans.

Movement away from totemic names was rare. The Winnebago had replaced Hawk as a clan name with War People, while the Sauk and the Fox preferred the name War Chief for their Fox clans.

The relation between clan and lineage is a particularly difficult problem. These units may once have been equivalent, at least in certain tribes. Such an explanation seems necessary for the Menominee, a small tribe with 19 clans, and probably for the Potawatomi, who had 24 clans. Both these tribes had a formal phratry system. In general, however, any equivalence between clan and lineage was long ago disrupted. Every tribe freely incorporated outsiders who, if male, sometimes introduced new clans but were often assigned membership in existing clans according to their personal names. The Fox retain traces of a complex division of their large clans into subclans named after particular colors or other traits of the eponyms (Callender 1962:27-28). These units, which almost certainly represented lineages, probably characterized the Sauk and Kickapoo as well. Landes (1970:222-223) describes a similar practice among the Prairie Potawatomi. Even if other tribes did not distinguish the component lineages of a clan by name, they recognized their differential rights in the inheritance of political and ritual office.

Postcontact changes eroded the functions of lineages even more deeply than those of clans, yet even in the past these were relatively limited. Throughout the series, the lineage was the vehicle for the transmission of political office and ceremonial leadership. Among the Fox, Sauk, Kickapoo, and Potawatomi it was often a corporate group for ritual action, tending to have its own cult. Its role of providing spouses for secondary marriages seems clear, and apparently its members could punish infringements of its rights in this area by destruction of the offender's property. Lineages had no discernable functions connected with landholding and the ownership of nonritual property. Evidence that lineage affiliation determined residence is at best ambiguous and strongest for the Menominee and Winnebago.

In spite of extensive gaps in the data, clan systems may be divided into several rather well-defined types. One type includes the Sauk, Fox, Kickapoo, and Potawatomi. Their clans lacked characteristics of corporate descent groups like control over land or productive property and probably did not determine residence. They were primarily name groups and cult groups. Contact with the supernatural, sought by individuals through the vision quest, could also be achieved by groups through rituals centering on the sacred packs that were concrete embodiments of visions. Each clan was conceptually founded through a vision in which the clan ancestor was blessed by a spirit in the form of the eponym. This original vision, perhaps supplemented by later recurrences of the same event, conventionally included instructions for semiannual ceremonies centering on the pack that the person who experienced it was directed to assemble, as well as names referring to the eponym. The pack was used in naming ceremonies and was the object of periodic rituals for which all members of the clan shared responsibility. It is not clear whether each lineage was similarly a cult group in its own right or whether, as among the Omaha (Fletcher and La Flesche 1911:137), only some lineages owned packs. In any case, the pack of the dominant lineage functioned as the clan pack. Ritual societies whose members consisted of persons blessed by the same spirit had functions very similar to those of clan cults, and sometimes assumed certain clan traits, such as inheritance of membership. In ritual contexts the Buffalo societies of the Fox were considered equivalent to clans and they also developed a few Buffalo names, although these remained under the control of clans. Each clan owned a stock of personal names, one of which was given to each member shortly after birth, reverting to the clan stock at its holder's death. These names carried with them a share of the power derived from the vision in which the clan was founded. Clan names also existed for horses and dogs.

The Prairie Potawatomi, and probably other bands of this tribe, were grouped into five phratries, each combining clans whose eponyms shared similar features or a common habitat. Thus, all hoofed eponyms were classed into the Buffalo phratry, while aquatic mammals and birds were combined with fish in the Water phratry. Other tribes of this group, who had fewer clans, apparently lacked phratries. The Fish "clan" of the Fox in the 1970s resembles such a structure, consisting of several small clans with aquatic eponyms, but this is a recent amalgamation.

The Winnebago system (Radin 1923:133-205) showed some striking differences that emerge most clearly in the existence of moieties and in the "friend" relationship postulated between specific paired clans; however, the clans themselves differed only in minor respects from those just described. Common features included rituals centering on sacred packs, which apparently belonged to lineages but involved participation by the entire clan, and a similar stock of clan names. The differences included a concept of descent from the eponym and a much stronger association of specific political functions with particular clans.

The drastic and apparently rapid restructuring of Shawnee clans during the nineteenth century leaves many features of their earlier shape uncertain. Some of the changes may be traced by comparing the accounts written in 1824-1825 by Trowbridge (1939:16-17) and in 1859 by Morgan (1959:44-47) with the description of Voegelin and Voegelin (1935). Both Trowbridge and Morgan reported a system of 12 functioning clans, although more were said to have existed in the past. One could propose, as an unconfirmed hypothesis, that each Shawnee community once consisted of 12 clans, since this was also the number of male and female officials selected to organize major ceremonies. Trowbridge described the clans as exogamous patrilineal descent groups. By 1859 Morgan found that clan exogamy was no longer practiced and that patrilineal affiliation was being replaced by a system that assigned children to the clan of either parent or, rarely, into a still different one. He reported that this practice ensured that all clans would remain approximately equal in size. By the 1930s the Shawnee clans had evolved into a system of six name-groups that lacked any connection with descent. While the classification of personal names resembled a phratry structure, the names themselves were given to individuals without regard for the affiliation of either parent. As far as the corporate functions of Shawnee clans may be deduced from the literature, their nature was ritual but diverged somewhat from the patterns described above for other tribes. Instead of name stocks owned by clans, the Shawnee obtained personal names from the dreams of name-givers who were called upon for this service shortly after a child's birth. In the past a name had to refer to the eponym of its holder's clan. Rather than carrying power obtained from a vision in which the clan was founded, it carried vision power derived from the name-giver's dream. Important power also derived from the eponymous relation. Positions in warfare, ritual, and government were assigned to individuals or clans on the basis of qualities that were considered particularly appropriate for the type of action required. These qualities were shared with, and in a sense derived from, the eponym. Shawnee clans were not cult groups. The major ritual units were the divisions or communities, each owning a sacred pack and presenting annual ceremonies in which positions were assigned by clan affiliation. Clans also provided the structure for organized joking in which individuals were expected to extol their own eponyms while teasing members of other clans on this same basis.

Information about clans among the Miami and Illinois tribes is particularly scanty. Assuming that these groups shared essentially similar institutions, one can infer from Trowbridge's (1938:18-19, 20, 38) report on the Miami that their clans controlled names through a system resembling that of the Shawnee and that they may have had a similar role in organizing ritual and the ritual aspects of warfare. However, any assumption of further resemblances to the Shawnee system is unwarranted, if only because the Miami had moieties.

The clan system of the Menominee, like other features of their precontact society, broke down so early that its form is very hard to reconstruct (Keesing 1939:38; Skinner 1913:15-16). As described by Skinner (1920: 47-48), it included some 19 clans, divided among seven phratries. Phratry organization was based on the mythological association of eponyms as well as on their resemblances. In spite of a moiety organization very similar to that of the Winnebago, Menominee clans contrasted sharply with those of all the preceding tribes in important respects. The phratry principle was applied more consistently. An elaborate origin legend described the formation of the clan system. Each clan owned a few eponymous names, but these were primarily titles given to certain adults while ordinary names were derived from the dreams of parents or shamans without reference to clan affiliation. Sacred packs were the objects of ceremonies very similar in form to those of neighboring tribes, but neither the packs nor ceremonies were associated with clans (Skinner 1913:20-21, 1921:48-49). Individuals could obtain supernatural power through their eponyms or with their aid. This required effort and was not engaged in by groups. Some association of clans with political organization has been postulated.

Moieties

In respect to moieties these tribes fell into three distinct groups. True moieties, consisting of a grouping of clans according to their eponyms into divisions associated with Earth and Sky, characterized the Winnebago, Menominee, and Miami and may be inferred for the Illinois. The Sauk, Fox, and Prairie Potawatomi, on the other hand, shared a system of dual divisions that were not descent groups and cut across clans rather than combining these units. Similar divisions were apparently being transformed into a moiety system by the Kickapoo. The third pattern is limited to the Shawnee, who lacked either moieties or dual divisions.

Only the Winnebago moieties have been described in detail (Radin 1923:133-142). The four clans with bird eponyms constituted the Sky moiety while the other clans made up its Earth counterpart. Lacking the complex and pervasive symbolism of Omaha moieties (Fletcher and La Flesche 1911:134-141), the Winnebago units served functions that were similar if much less extensive. They were exogamous. Radin (1923:140) was told that they determined the residential structure of villages, with Earth clans inhabiting the northeast half of each settlement and those of the Sky moiety the southwest. This arrangement, denied by some informants, resembled the organization of the Omaha camp circle. It also provided the structure for the camps of war parties but was not used on journeys for other purposes or on occasions when an entire community moved. Besides segregating clans spatially and linking them through reciprocal obligations in activities such as burial, the moieties structured opposition through providing the organization for lacrosse games. The pronounced tendency for members of the Earth moiety to deny statements made by those of the opposite group might also reflect such opposition. Perhaps the moieties were also associated with a division of political functions, although these seem to have adhered to specific clans within them, with the Thunder clan of the Sky moiety providing the tribal chief and the Bear clan charged with police functions.

Menominee moieties were very similar in structure, even to the extent that the Bear clan headed the Earth moiety and the Thunder clan the Sky, although their political functions apparently reversed the Winnebago pattern. Most of their functions disappeared very early, but Keesing (1939:36-37) discerned a tendency for conservative Menominee to divide into Bear and Thunder settlements corresponding to moiety affiliation. He also reported traditions that clans of the Sky moiety once provided war leadership and occupied the west side in tribal councils while those of the Earth moiety furnished the peace chief and took the east side. Moiety affiliation determined sides in lacrosse games, a practice that according to myth began when the culture hero founded these (W.J. Hoffman 1896:131-135). Trowbridge (1938: 18) describes Earth and Sky moieties for the Miami but says nothing of their functions.

The dual divisions of the Sauk are called *ki·ško·ha* and *aškaša,* corresponding to Kickapoo *kiiskooha* and *oskasa* and the cognate Potawatomi terms. Those of the Fox are *ki·ško·ha* and *to·hka·na.* This last term may be derived from the Tukala warrior society of the Iowa tribe (Michelson 1925:548). Among the Fox, the first child born to a couple belongs to the division opposite that of its father. The next child is assigned to the father's division, and so on in alternating sequence. The Prairie Potawatomi also alternate membership by relative age but without regard for the father's affiliation, assigning the first child to the *aškaša* and the second to the *ki·ško·ha.* Both rules have been reported for the Sauk, who have probably shifted from an earlier practice identical with the Fox to substitute that followed by the Potawatomi (Harrington 1914:131; Skinner 1923-1925: 12; Callender 1962:165). The difference is in any case negligible, since either rule produces similar nonhereditary dual divisions that are not descent groups, have no reference to clan affiliation, and cut across all other social units including sibling groups. Such divisions also remain numerically equal regardless of demographic fluctuations. The Kickapoo have apparently diverged from this pattern by classing all members of clans with hoofed or clawed eponyms as *oskasa* (a term meaning 'hoof, claw, nail'), and all other persons as *kiiskooha.* This practice would convert their dual divisions into true moieties, although its effect may possibly be counterbalanced by alternately naming siblings into different clans and thus into different divisions. In any event, the Kickapoo system represents an approach to a moiety structure perhaps acquired from Miami or Illinois sources. This practice also suggests that dual divisions were equated with the moieties of other tribes. So does the custom, found among two very small Fox lineages of Winnebago origin, of assigning all their members to the *ki·ško·ha* division.

The functions of dual divisions were much more restricted than those of moieties, although broader than Forsyth's (1912:192-194) and Marston's (1912: 156-157) descriptions of them as warrior societies. Including both sexes, they provided a system of organizing people for various purposes, including games, dances, and ritual, as well as warfare. They also organized opposition. Besides the usual lacrosse games, this included competition among warriors for war honors. Persons were also required to joke with all members of the opposite division who did not fall into respect relationships.

Goddard (1975a) presents an alternative analysis of the dual divisions, which he suggests originated as warrior societies and acquired their present characteristics during the nineteenth century as a system of clan-based moieties broke down.

Alford (1936:50) describes a kind of dual organization among the Shawnee based on their five divisions. One grouping consisted of the *čalaka* and *mekoče* divisions; the other of the *kišpoko, pekowi,* and *θawikila* divisions. Such a system, although perhaps once characteristic of this tribe, has disappeared without any other record. The functions of moieties or dual divisions in organizing opposition were in recent years carried out by name groups, whose members teased each other about their eponymous relations. In the past this was probably based on clan affiliation. While some pairing of name groups occurs, this practice does not form a complete system. Another basis for opposition, appearing in major rituals, was sex, with males and females pitted against each other in football games.

Political Organization

Knowledge of political organization is generally slight and very unsatisfactory. Continuous change affected all these systems throughout their adjustment to the fur trade and on into the period of removal in the nineteenth century, while outside agencies increasingly interfered with their modes of government. By 1900, if not earlier, few traces of traditional political organization remained. Other aspects of social structure have persisted longer and changed less. Older ethnographies usually handled this topic by presenting a traditional account of political organization that, if not a projection back to a time before the extensive dislocations that followed contact, has been greatly idealized. Its institutional framework can be reconstructed, although with important gaps. Many details of its actual operation remain unknown. While much information has been irretrievably lost, detailed studies of reports by local agents and military commanders who had direct contact with these tribes might fill in some gaps.

A major problem involves the articulation of tribal government and the separate residential or territorial units that composed each tribe. The community or village was a unit in summer, dispersing in autumn, perhaps reconstituting itself in a different location in winter, and often breaking up again in spring. Probably the tribal political institutions were unnecessary during the seasonal periods of dispersal. The more critical aspect of this problem centers on the division of tribes into distinct bands that often maintained separate summer villages. Among the Shawnee these bands, called "divisions," were highly organized units rather similar to the "towns" of southeastern tribes. Each constituted an autonomous political and ritual organization. They were linked together at the tribal level by an overall organization, including a council composed of the divisional officials as well as a tribal chief, and were further integrated by specific political or ritual functions for which each division was responsible when tribal action occurred. However, even among the relatively well-described Shawnee, the standard accounts of political organization assume a tribal unity that this group never entirely attained after their precontact dispersal. No other tribe in the series had such a formal system of political subdivisions unless one assumes that the historical Miami and Illinois tribes represented the remnants of similar systems whose breakdown at the tribal level resulted in their divisions becoming completely independent tribes. The usual form of subdivision involved two or more bands, sometimes approximately equal but often of very disparate sizes and apparently quite fluid in their composition.

Decentralization apparently increased after contact. Keesing (1939:76-77, 118-119) sees the Menominee shifting away from a single village that embraced the entire tribe to develop an initial split into two bands during the early contact period and ultimately breaking up into a series of nine independent bands, each with its own summer village. Lurie (1960) says the Winnebago maintained a large central village until the fur trade disrupted their settlement pattern. Even as late as the early nineteenth century almost the entire Sauk tribe concentrated in a single town. A statement by their agent, Forsyth (1822), contrasting them with the Fox suggests that their greater centralization fostered a much more effective political organization. Yet even the Fox, who in 1723 inhabited three adjacent villages (Kellogg 1925: 314), were by 1822 living in settlements that were still close enough for frequent contact through canoe transportation and retained their tribal organization intact until the late nineteenth century. Setting aside such exceptions as the widely dispersed Shawnee, most tribes in the series probably retained enough centralization to facilitate tribal action until the late eighteenth or early nineteenth centuries. By the time that they began breaking up into independent units, traditional political organization was also disintegrating. Although the Fox were an exception, their success in averting or postponing these last two developments was facilitated by a reduction in population to less than 300 persons. At earlier periods village-band organization may have replicated tribal structure on a smaller scale, but this remains unclear.

The formal political institutions operating at the tribal level were quite uniform in general outline, although differing in details. An overall dichotomy separated the institutions centering on peace from those concerned with war. The peace organization consisted of the tribal chief and, apparently, lesser chiefs of similar type who perhaps were clan heads. To these officials were attached assistants, called criers, ceremonial runners, or speakers. The war organization included a paramount war chief as well as war leaders of lesser rank and a group of warriors, variously selected, who in certain contexts carried out police functions and could enforce tribal regulations. War chiefs, like the peace counterparts, had assistants and speakers. Another institution, the tribal council, almost certainly included both peace and war officials, although its composition is very unclear. All aspects of political organization were highly ritualized.

Formal political offices were usually held by men. While occasional references to female chiefs occur, it is often unclear whether these women actually held public office or simply dominated their communities through their abilities. The Potawatomi were apparently an exception, since women were among those who signed several treaties with the United States. Unfortunately, this practice has attracted little attention and is not covered in the literature. Otherwise, the strongest evidence that women held recognized offices in political organization is presented by Trowbridge in his reports on the Miami (1938) and Shawnee (1939). For both tribes he describes female chiefs, divided like their male counterparts according to membership in the peace or war organization. His description of these officials' functions among the Shawnee resembles later accounts of the committees of 12 women appointed to help organize major ceremonies, yet their roles in earlier years could well have included duties whose nature was more obviously political. E.W. Voegelin (1944:403) reports that the widow of a divisional chief among the Shawnee customarily took over his functions until his successor was appointed. French accounts of events among the eighteenth-century Miami suggest that the widow of a chief had a very important political role, particularly if his successor was relatively young. On the whole, the political role of women, although important, was not public enough to be noted in contemporary accounts or was misunderstood. An example of misunderstanding is the contrast between Black Hawk's (1955:112) account of the speech addressed to Gen. Edmund P. Gaines by a chief's daughter and Gaines's description of this incident (Hagan 1958:130).

Tribal chieftainship was hereditary. The right to hold this office usually belonged to a specific lineage although it was often described as the right of a clan or, among the

Shawnee, either the čalaka or θawikila divisions. Its transmission required the approval of the tribal council or a similar body that could pass over the closest heir and, in exceptional circumstances, shift the position to a different lineage. As head of the peace organization and its main symbol, a chief was supposed to show behavior appropriate to this role, avoiding any display of anger or aggression (Forsyth 1822; Radin 1923:272-273). A Fox myth (Jones 1907:9) suggests that appointment to a peace office could be used as a technique to control the behavior of excessively aggressive men. In war and other tribal emergencies the chief and his organization usually went into temporary retirement. His participation in warfare was generally forbidden (Trowbridge 1938:14) or strictly limited (Radin 1923:161). The symbolism pervading the position emerges in other practices. The lodge of a Winnebago chief was a sanctuary in which any person who took refuge was spared (Radin 1923:161). This right of asylum extended even to dogs designated for sacrifice. Miami and Shawnee female peace officials could prevent the deaths of war captives. The chief or his organization sometimes exercised limited control over warfare. The techniques included appeals to the war chief by female officials among the Miami and Shawnee (Trowbridge 1938:29, 1939:12-13, 53) as well as the Sauk practice of restraining a war leader by giving him valuables (Forsyth 1827) and the right of a Winnebago chief to place his pipe across the path of a war party and thus withdraw tribal sanction from the enterprise, making its leader personally responsible for any deaths (Radin 1923:161). All such actions probably depended for their success or even their initiation on the backing of tribal opinion and the consent of the war officials. Many of the chief's duties were ritual. This aspect emerges clearly in Marquette's (JR 59: 117-123) account of his reception among the Peoria and Bacqueville de la Potherie's (1911-1912, 1:332) description of Nicolas Perrot's reception by the Miami chief. The Winnebago chief led the annual rituals of his clan as well as ceremonies he was asked to hold to avert epidemics and similar emergencies (Radin 1923:271-272). With the help of others he was expected to mediate in intratribal murders to prevent feuds. His actions were limited to pleading for a settlement or assembling goods to be offered as compensation, and in the last analysis he could not forbid vengeance. Trowbridge (1939:13-14) reported that Shawnee chiefs took such action only when the life of important persons was endangered, but their society had other checks that inhibited feuds. Generosity was another virtue required of tribal chiefs. Their property was available to anyone needing it. In return, gifts were regularly presented to them. The importance of this practice, which parallels certain aspects of the role of traders, is uncertain. It could be interpreted as a form of redistribution except that its scale is unknown.

The roles of lesser chiefs and the bases of their appointments are very unclear, as is the distinction, if any, between these officials and members of the tribal council. Some evidence suggests that each Shawnee clan had a chief, whose functions were primarily ritual. This may have been a general pattern. Another kind of official whose position was apparently important but is not well known was that called aška·pe·wa by the Fox and kapia by the Miami. Among the Fox these men made public announcements and served as messengers and sometimes as speakers for the chiefs (Michelson 1927). Their Miami counterparts inherited their office and seem rather more important; they were able to act as deputies for the chief or even in certain circumstances to succeed him.

The nature of the political organization centering on war is similarly clouded by ambiguity and contradictions. Most men engaged in warfare at least at some period in their lives and thus belonged to the war organization. An implicit hierarchy of status among warriors may be inferred from the practice of publicly reciting one's war honors. As Fletcher (1910:914) pointed out, these recitals stated one's credentials for public office. Black Hawk (1955:72) noted that a Sauk warrior could not take part in tribal councils until he had killed an enemy. Those men holding the title of war chief had highest rank within the war organization and acted as its leaders; however, this title seems to have been used loosely and was usually held simultaneously by several men, of whom one was recognized as paramount. The constituency or public that a war chief served is unclear, as is the basis of his appointment. Besides their tribal war chief, each division of the Shawnee had such an official (Trowbridge 1939). Among the Miami one was apparently attached to each clan (Trowbridge 1938:19). Each band among other tribes probably had its own war chief, but this is uncertain.

The office is often said to have been achieved through consistently successful leadership of war parties. Thus, the Shawnee required four such actions (Trowbridge 1939:11-12). Several well-known war chiefs, such as Keokuk and Little Turtle, illustrate this process, although it may be significant that these men first became prominent by leading action when American armies threatened their tribes. Yet Trowbridge (1938) explicitly describes Miami war chiefs as inheriting their offices, and ethnographies often state or imply that the position was attached to specific clans. The paramount Shawnee war chief, for instance, was supposed to belong to the Panther clan and to the kišpoko division. Fox tradition associates the office with the Fox, or War Chief, clan, even though those men known to have been war chiefs during the nineteenth century belonged to other clans. Certain assumptions could resolve some of these contradictions. Warfare was heavily ritualized. Among the Fox, the leader of a raid made his main contribution through the effects of his religious power and did not necessarily fight. Perhaps this was also true of war chiefs, at least in earlier times when their primary concern may have been the ritual aspects of war. Similarly, war ritual could have been the main responsibility of a specific clan. A related possibility is that the personal names associated with warfare, although owned or controlled by a particular clan, could be assumed by any successful warriors. Another alternative is that the hereditary form of war chieftainship involved control of the tribal police, rather than actual leadership in warfare. By the late eighteenth century, if not earlier, these traditional characteristics of war chieftainship were beginning to disappear as the nature of the office changed. Becoming the main intermediaries between their tribes and agents of United States society, paramount war chiefs greatly expanded their power. At an early stage they took over the treaty-making functions properly belonging to tribal chiefs. Eventually they became tribal chiefs in effect and sometimes in name, while the ritual aspects of both kinds of chieftainship disappeared.

All the tribes had warrior organizations charged with enforcing regulations on specific occasions. Except among the Winnebago, whose Bear clan undertook all policing functions, the men charged with these duties were apparently chosen by the war chiefs. Their functions were very similar to those of camp police among tribes west of the Mississippi. They acted as guards and prevented straggling when large groups—tribe or community—were in movement, supervised and controlled buffalo hunts and wild rice harvests, guarded council meetings, and enforced decisions of the tribal council. The standard punishment they were authorized to use was destruction of the offender's property, which was restored or replaced upon his admitting that his behavior had been wrong. Resistance to them drew whipping or, if necessary, death.

Tribal councils were convened by the chief, who presided. Apparently classed as an activity belonging to the peace organization, they nevertheless included war officials and discussed issues such as war. The widespread traditions that their members were in some sense representatives of clans are hard to confirm but may draw some support from the council maintained by the Fox faction supporting the hereditary tribal chief, which as late as the mid-twentieth century was composed mostly of the ritual leaders of clans. Council meetings are consistently described as characterized by extended discussion until consensus was reached.

The factionalism that characterizes recent political systems among the Upper Great Lakes-Riverine tribes has obvious historical antecedents. Accounts such as Bacqueville de la Potherie's (1911–1912, 1:359–360) description of Fox "lineages" suggest its presence in the early contact period. Factional division may be inevitable in a political system that requires consensus for tribal action to occur. Yet one may reasonably assume that whatever precontact forms existed changed in nature after Europeans were present. Lurie's (1968:38) sugges-

tion that factionalism may have been an important strategy for dealing with outside powers is a useful hypothesis for interpreting some of the postcontact developments. A further shift in the character of factions becomes evident during the late eighteenth century, when increasing pressure from outside forces often split tribes into independent groups that formed along factional lines.

Configuration 2

The problems of insufficient data for the preceding group of tribes expand tremendously when one turns to the Ottawa and Chippewa-Ojibwa. The accounts dating from early contact times, very incomplete and often hard to interpret, are followed by a long period of even scantier information lasting until the early nineteenth century. The extensive accounts by Warren (1885) and Schoolcraft (1851–1857) are often unreliable. While excellent ethnographic accounts were published in the twentieth century (Dunning 1959; Hallowell 1955; Landes 1937, 1938), these concentrate on the Northern Ojibwa. Comparable information about those south of Lake Superior or about the Ottawa is not available.

The Chippewa-Ojibwa and Ottawa of the contact period almost certainly used kinship terminology like that recorded by Morgan (1871) among their nineteenth-century descendants. This system was of Iroquois type (fig. 3), bifurcate collateral in the first ascending and descending generations but merging parallel cousins with siblings. Its most notable feature is the presence of terminological equations that imply a system of cross-cousin marriage. Thus *nisikosiss* 'Mother-in-law' is a diminutive of *nisikoss* 'Paternal Aunt'; *nišiššeˑnˀ* 'Maternal Uncle' is related to *nisiniss* 'Father-in-law'; *niˑttaˑwiss* 'Male Cross-cousin', male speaking, is a diminutive of *niˑttaˑ* 'Brother-in-law', male speaking. This same relationship holds for *niˑnimoššeˑnˀ*, 'Cross-cousin of the opposite sex', and *niˑnim* 'Sibling-in-law of the opposite sex', as it does for *nintaˑnkoššeˑnˀ* 'Female Cross-cousin', female speaking, and *nintaˑnkweˑnˀ* 'Sister-in-law', female speaking, *nininkwaniss* 'Cross Nephew', is similarly a diminutive of *nininkwan* 'Son-in-law', as *niššimiss* 'Cross Niece', is of *nissim* 'Daughter-in-law'.

The Chippewa-Ojibwa and Ottawa had abandoned and prohibited cross-cousin marriage before contact. Its form is thus uncertain, but it probably resembled the bilateral variety practiced by the Northern Ojibwa; however, their kinship terminology shows exact equations for every cross-affinal pair, rather than one term's being a diminutive form of the other (Callender 1962: 53–55). This difference is minor and probably reflects a more consistent practice of cousin-marriage. While an assumption that the Ottawa and southern Chippewa were characterized by matrilateral cross-cousin marriage has *619*

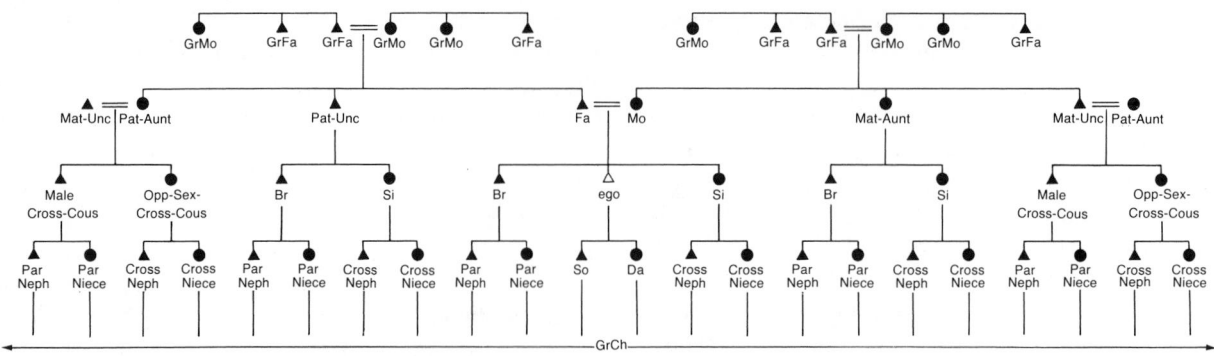

Fig. 3. Chippewa kinship terminology for male ego (after Morgan 1871). Each abbreviation represents a single term, except that Br and Si each cover 3 terms.

interesting theoretical possibilities (cf. Eyde and Postal 1961; Hockett 1964:256), the weight of the evidence strongly indicates bilateral cross-cousin marriage (Eggan 1966:78–111).

Without information about kinship behavior, one is tempted to assume patterns similar to those described for the Northern Ojibwa, which prescribe joking between cross-cousins and siblings-in-law and enjoin respect between other relatives. However, some very slight evidence (Callender 1962:62) suggests that maternal uncles and paternal aunts may have been classed as joking relatives among the southern groups. Such a pattern would conflict with any form of cross-cousin marriage.

Hickerson (1960, 1962, 1963, 1966) reconstructs the ancestral Chippewa-Ojibwa and Ottawa as divided among a number of small, localized, totemically named patrilineal descent groups that represented the earlier form of their present clans. During the second half of the seventeenth century, while the Ottawa concentrated at the Mackinac straits, the fur trade drew some of the proto-Chippewa westward along the northern shore of Lake Superior and others gathered into large multiclan settlements at Chequamegon and Keweenau. In the eighteenth century these large communities broke up as their residents scattered. The local bands that succeeded them included members of several clans, and the earlier pattern never reconstituted itself.

Ottawa and Chippewa-Ojibwa clans in the 1970s are nonlocalized exogamous patrilineal descent groups. Clan names resemble those of the southern tribes, but the clan system seems relatively unstructured. Even though phratries are sometimes present, these groupings are loose and very weak. Clan functions are generally confined to establishing kinship ties between nonrelatives, with the attendant obligations of hospitality and exogamy. The corporate functions that characterized clans among the tribes of Configuration 1 are present only in abortive, relatively undeveloped forms; or, as in naming practices, they exist as well-developed systems that lack any connection with clans. The most detailed descriptions involve the Northern Ojibwa. Those by Landes (1937),

Dunning (1959), and Rogers (1962) indicate an increasing attrition of clan functions correlated with northern location and ultimately the complete disappearance of these units. Yet Ottawa and southern Chippewa clans seem equally lacking in corporate features (Kinietz 1947:77).

Chippewa-Ojibwa and Ottawa political organization tended to be loose and informal, contrasting with the tribal organization characterizing most other groups within the area. The broader integration that temporarily characterized the large postcontact communities was, in Hickerson's (1963) view, achieved primarily through the Midewiwin. This use of ritual for integrative purposes strongly parallels its similar functions in the sociopolitical systems of Configuration 1.

Conclusion

The sociocultural systems of the Algonquian-speaking tribes belonging to Configuration 1 almost certainly developed out of a background that resembled the precontact features of Configuration 2. Evidence for such antecedents is mostly linguistic in nature, including details of kinship terminology and clan nomenclature.

The kinship systems of these tribes formerly included terminological equations between pairs of cross and affinal relatives similar to those characterizing Chippewa-Ottawa terminology. Only traces of these remain. The restructuring of terminology into Omaha form destroyed the equations of cross-cousins and siblings-in-law by obliterating the former class of relatives as well as the terms denoting them, while generally leaving sibling-in-law terms intact. The destruction of other equations related to cross-cousin marriage accompanied the abandonment and prohibition of this practice. Its form took the adoption of new terms for certain affinal relatives. The Fox, for instance, replaced the former parent-in-law terms, related to those for maternal uncle and paternal aunt, with new forms derived from those for grandparents. Yet they retained the older sets of terms equating cross-niece with daughter-in-law and cross-nephew with son-in-law. The same shifts occurred among the Sauk and, in most respects, the Kickapoo. The Prairie Potawatomi reversed this pattern, retaining cross-affinal equations in the first ascending generation but substituting other terms for son-in-law and daughter-in-law. In every tribe involved, substitutions have been partial, leaving enough evidence of a terminology consistent with the practice of cross-cousin marriage to make such a background probable.

The Chippewa-Ottawa term *ninto·te·m,* used to specify a clan, literally means 'my fellow clan-member', hence 'my clan totemic animal', and derives from a Proto-Algonquian verb stem **o·te·-* 'to dwell together as a group/village' (Goddard 1973b; Bloomfield 1962:260–261). This form also underlies the Menominee and Potawatomi terms for clans, even though the nature of these units in both tribes has changed greatly from their Chippewa and Ottawa counterparts. The Miami and Illinois terms are unknown. Among the Shawnee, 'clan' is *mʔšo·ma.* The term used by the Fox, Sauk, and Kickapoo is *mi·so·ni* 'name'. Yet *neto·te·ma,* the Fox term denoting 'sibling of the same sex', formerly had a range much broader than its present meaning (Goddard 1973b). It was used, at least in ritual contexts, in the sense of sibling,

regardless of sex, and was reciprocally used between individuals and their clan eponyms. Moreover, it may once have designated fellow members of the same clan, corresponding to contemporary practice among the northern groups.

If the remote antecedents of these systems probably resembled the societies of Configuration 2, their more immediate archeological background seems to have been Upper Mississippian. While an exact equation of the Shawnee with Fort Ancient has not been established, some correspondence between these entities is probable. Illinois and Miami cultures also seem derived from Upper Mississippian antecedents, perhaps Langford and Huber, respectively, in the areas they historically occupied. As a very tentative working hypothesis, one could postulate an association of the Sauk, Fox, and Kickapoo with the Younge tradition in southeast Michigan and northwest Ohio or, even more tenuously, with the Whittlesey focus in northeast Ohio (cf. "Late Prehistory of the Upper Great Lakes Area," this vol.). Such a background could also account for their resemblances to historical Siouan societies that were descended from Upper Mississippian cultures.

621

Shawnee

CHARLES CALLENDER

Language, Territory, and Environment

The Shawnee (ˌshôˈnē) speak an Algonquian language having some slight but poorly known internal differentiation.*

An exceptionally fragmented people, the Shawnee during their recorded history were never united into a single society. Their fragmentation, combined with the extent and frequency of their movements, make it difficult to assign them to a specific area. As far as they can be associated with a particular region this was southern Ohio, where most of the tribe lived during the second half of the eighteenth century, and which was probably their precontact home. In the seventeenth century the Shawnee were scattered widely. At the time of contact various groups were reported in Illinois, on the Ohio, in Maryland, and along the Savannah River. During the late seventeenth and early eighteenth centuries most of the Shawnee assembled in eastern Pennsylvania and gradually worked westward into the upper Ohio drainage, although some remained with the Creek in Alabama. After a second dispersal on a much smaller scale shortly before 1750, the tribe coalesced again in southern Ohio. A third period of dispersal occurred during the Revolution and the years of warfare that followed, when bands began moving westward across the Mississippi. Ultimately all the Shawnee settled in Oklahoma, forming three separate groups (fig. 1).

During these movements the Shawnee occupied a variety of habitats, and it seems impossible to associate them with any one type of environment.

External Relations

Traditional Shawnee culture, while distinctive in important respects, showed extensive resemblances to several other groups. A complex of very old traits, including general linguistic relationship, specific terms for significant institutions such as sacred packs, and also certain ritual concepts (Voegelin 1936:7-8), reflects prehistoric relationships with the Sauk, Fox, and Kickapoo. Another

set of traits, consisting of a town organization with extensive political and ritual functions and a council house whose uses were similarly varied, seems Southeastern at first sight, but it probably represents the Upper Mississippian background of Shawnee culture rather than borrowing from Southeastern tribes during the historical period. Shawnee town organization may also be interpreted as a more evolved form of a pattern that characterized the Illinois and Miami tribes, with whom the Shawnee shared other features as well (Callender 1962:36-42). The Shawnee resembled the Delaware in their use of a system of opposition in ceremonies based on sex and in their lack of moieties or dual divisions. On the whole, their culture lacked the Prairie traits acquired or developed by other Central Algonquians of the Ohio and upper Mississippi valleys and showed rather strong similarities to Eastern and Southeastern cultures.

The dispersal of the Shawnee brought them into association with a variety of other tribes. The closest and most consistent associations involved the Delaware, Iroquois, and Creek. The Delaware relationship began late in the seventeenth century when Shawnees settled in eastern Pennsylvania, where the two tribes were neighbors and sometimes shared the same settlements (Hanna 1911, 1:139, 358, 362). Both later moved into the Ohio valley. In the early nineteenth century trans-Mississippi bands often combined members of both tribes (Foreman 1936:72, 185, 1946:34, 159).

Relations with the Iroquois were very complex and shifted through several different phases. The Iroquois League drove the Shawnee out of the Ohio valley before European penetration of the area (Witthoft and Hunter 1955:53) and long remained hostile toward them. The Shawnee movement into Pennsylvania did not reach large dimensions until they were assured that the Iroquois were willing to accept the war between them as closed (Hanna 1911, 1:136-141). For some time afterward the League classed the Shawnee as a subordinate group whose status was much like that of the Delaware, although as the Shawnee moved west League control inevitably became weaker and ultimately lapsed (Downes 1940:20-21, 27-30). In western Pennsylvania and Ohio the Shawnee were closely associated with that section of the Iroquois called the Mingo, later known as the Seneca of Sandusky (Hewitt 1910b; Mooney 1907a; E.W. Voegelin 1944:305). The so-called Eastern Shawnee

---

* Italicized Shawnee words are in the orthography of Voegelin (1938-1940, which has an analysis slightly revised from Voegelin 1935), but with long vowels marked by a raised dot instead of by gemination (e.g., Voegelin's aa is equivalent to the a· of the *Handbook*).

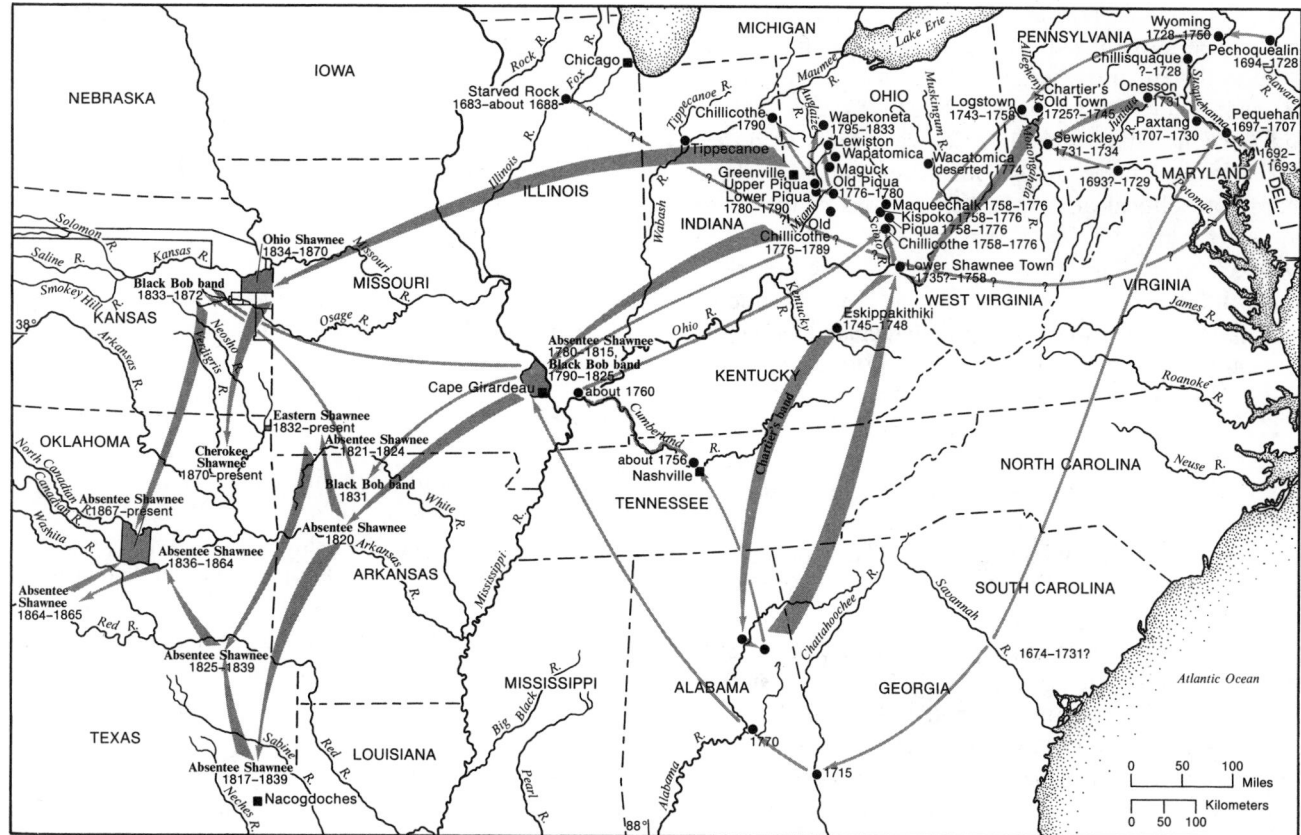

Fig. 1. Shawnee locations and movements.

eventually split away from the rest of their tribe to accompany these Seneca to Oklahoma (Voegelin and Voegelin 1935:632–633).

The Shawnee connection with the Creek, far from adequately known, was apparently old and rather close, although limited in its extent (Swanton 1922:277–279; Witthoft and Hunter 1955:52–53). From the early post-contact period until the late eighteenth century the Creek confederacy usually included at least one Shawnee town (Swanton 1922:318–320). There was also an ancient association with the Yuchi (cf. JR 65:144), but its nature is unknown. The Shawnee were often at war with other Southeastern tribes, particularly the Catawba and Chickasaw. In the nineteenth century, Shawnee association with the Cherokee was often close, and a large group ultimately joined the Cherokee Nation.

While living in eastern Pennsylvania the Shawnee were closely tied to the English, who provided their main market for trade and encouraged their settlement in that area. Yet they began negotiating with the French even before their movement to the Ohio valley (Downes 1940:46, 76, 82). During the years of English-French rivalry the Shawnee tried to secure their own independence by playing the colonial powers against each other and shifting their alliances. Their consistent opposition to trans-Appalachian settlement led them to join Pontiac's uprising and fight Lord Dunmore's War largely without

allies. They were probably the main force in the Indian coalition that resisted American expansion during and after the Revolution. Nevertheless, contact with Americans during this period considerably changed certain aspects of Shawnee culture. Kroeber's (1939:90) characterization of the resulting product as "a partly new, assimilated, hybrid-Caucasian culture" is an overstatement but emphasizes an important aspect of this process. Continual warfare ultimately split the Shawnee and apparently exhausted them. Although resistance to American expansion continued under Shawnee leadership in the persons of Tecumseh and Tenskwatawa (The Prophet), most of the tribe did not follow them.

Component Groups

The Shawnee tribe included two types of subgroups. The first and more formal type consisted of the five units that are usually called divisions. These were the čalaka, kišpoko, mekoče, pekowi, and θawikila. Each was a descent group whose members patrilineally inherited their affiliation. A division was conceived as a distinct territorial unit centering on a town that bore its name (Alford in Galloway 1934:21; Hanna 1911, 1:148; Mooney 1910c:536; E.W. Voegelin 1944:256, 269). It also constituted a political and ritual unit in a pattern that resembled a Creek or Cherokee town (Voegelin 1936:10;

E.W. Voegelin in Trowbridge 1939:xiii). The divisions were linked into a tribal system through specific responsibilities toward tribal welfare assigned to each (Alford 1936:44; Alford in Galloway 1934:21, 181). The *čalaka* and *θawikila,* whose sacred packs were equal in power and surpassed those of the other three divisions, had charge of political affairs. Either one was supposed to provide the tribal chief (E.W. Voegelin in Trowbridge 1939:xvii–xviii). The *pekowi* were responsible for tribal ritual, the *kišpoko* for war, and the *mekoče* for medicine and health. The Shawnee origin myth included sequences accounting for each division (Trowbridge 1939:4–6, 61–62; Voegelin 1936:10–11).

This divisional system developed during the precontact period of tribal unity. The details of its operation in historical times are far from clear. In later years Shawnee towns often included residents belonging to different divisions. The divisional identity of a mixed town seems to have been determined by the affiliation of its chief, who was apparently drawn from the division that dominated the community numerically. Moreover, the name of a town occasionally changed, probably reflecting a shift in its leadership or population, or both (Alford in Galloway 1934:40–41; Galloway 1934:16–17; Hanna 1911, 1:146).

The second kind of subgroup consisted of the geographically defined groups into which the Shawnee were split. These varied in number and size, often merging and then breaking up again. They tended to function with almost complete autonomy and were often separated by great distances. This system was eventually frozen in the late nineteenth century into three permanent independent groups known as the Eastern Shawnee, Cherokee Shawnee, and Absentee Shawnee.

The extent to which the two kinds of subgroups coincided is unclear (E.W. Voegelin in Trowbridge 1939:xiii). Franquelin's 1684 map (Griffin 1943:map 8) shows the Meguatchaiki—the *mekoče* division—as a separate group. Some obsure names that occur briefly in early records, such as Chaskpé and Cisca (LaSalle in Margry 1876–1886, 2:196, 314), may be badly garbled divisional names. E.W.Voegelin (1944:276) suggests that the Shawnee who went to Starved Rock in 1683 were *mekoče.* Those who first settled in eastern Pennsylvania are sometimes identified as *pekowi* (Alford in Galloway 1934:25; Swanton 1922:317–318). The earliest definite evidence for members of one division moving as a group is provided by the *θawikila,* who apparently constituted the Shawnees living among the Creek in the eighteenth century (Alford in Galloway 1934:22, 40; Swanton 1922:317–320). The Assiwikales, described in 1731 as a group that recently arrived in Pennsylvania from the south (Hanna 1911, 1:150–151), were part of the *θawikila.* Alford (Galloway 1934:40) says that in the late eighteenth century the *θawikila* of Ohio joined the rest of their division among the Creek (cf. McKenney and Hall 1849–1854, 2:130). Divisional action and movement also

seem evident in the dissension that disrupted the Shawnee during the Revolution. The peace party that followed the *θawikila* example in breaking away from the tribe consisted mostly of the *kišpoko* and *pekowi* divisions, while the *čalaka* and *mekoče* remained in Ohio (Alford in Galloway 1934:40–41; Trowbridge 1939:8; E.W. Voegelin in Trowbridge 1939:xiv). Later developments perpetuated this split. The Absentee Shawnee are apparently *kišpoko, pekowi,* and *θawikila;* the Eastern Shawnee, *mekoče;* and the Cherokee Shawnee, *mekoče* and *čalaka* (Alford in Galloway 1934:41; E.W. Voegelin 1944:422).

Culture

The following outline combines the account that Trowbridge (1939) wrote in 1824–1825 with discussions by Voegelin (1936), E.W. Voegelin (1941, 1944), and Voegelin and Voegelin (1935, 1944), based on fieldwork in Oklahoma during the 1930s. This procedure carries a danger of confusing time periods, but material for an adequate presentation of Shawnee culture at a single clearly defined level of time is not available.

Subsistence

Shawnee economy, combining hunting with agriculture and some food gathering, had been strongly oriented toward the fur trade since the early eighteenth century. In Pennsylvania and the Ohio valley this activity centered on deerskins rather than beaver pelts (Hanna 1911, 1:3, 2:314). The annual cycle (Harvey 1855:146–151; E.W. Voegelin 1941:514–515) began around the end of September when the Shawnee left their towns to establish winter camps in sheltered valleys. Older persons, small children, and others who found travel difficult stayed in camp throughout the winter while parties of active men and women undertook long hunting trips lasting two or three months. The most important game animals were deer, buffalo, bears, mountain lions, and turkeys. These hunts usually ended in December. During January and February men trapped smaller fur-bearing animals. In March the Shawnee returned to their towns. After the fields were prepared, planting began in April. During the summer women tended crops and gathered wild plant foods while men fished in the vicinity or set out on deer hunts. After the final maize harvest in August the community again prepared to move to its winter quarters.

Although fields were owned by individual households they were grouped together into a single area, apparently lying south of the town (E.W. Voegelin 1941:518–519). Women seem to have planted collectively, but each individual owned her own crops. Men sometimes helped, but the extent of their participation is unclear. Planting was associated with important rituals sponsored and carried out by the town and was organized by female officials belonging to the town government (Trowbridge

1939:13; E.W. Voegelin 1941:516). Town ritual also preceded the fall hunt.

Settlement Pattern

Traditional Shawnee towns, semipermanent settlements inhabited in summer, consisted of bark-covered lodges resembling Iroquois longhouses or the similar buildings used by the Sauk, Fox, and Kickapoo (Alford in Galloway 1934:174-175). By the later eighteenth century, house types also included one-room log huts roofed with bark and buildings made of boards or shingles (Galloway 1934:13, 44). Bushnell (1919:47-48) quotes a contemporary description of Old Chillicothe that represents this town as similar to the American forts in Kentucky, but an account cited by Galloway (1934:13) does not bear out this characterization.

Each town had as its nucleus a large wooden structure used for council meetings and for ritual as well as secular celebrations, besides serving for the seclusion of warriors after a raid (Gist 1893:44; Trowbridge 1939:19). Alford (in Galloway 1934:54) calls these buildings temples, although their functions were not confined to ritual. The council house at Old Chillicothe was about 60 feet square

(Galloway 1934:13; Alford in Galloway 1934:62). The one Gist (1893:44) saw at Lower Shawnee Town in 1751 was about 90 feet long. The Shawnee town in Alabama that Hawkins visited in 1796 also had a square council house, differing in form from those built by the Creeks, and roofed and covered with pine bark (Swanton 1922:320). During their war with the United States in the late eighteenth century the Shawnee used council houses as forts when attacks caught them by surprise or when the residents of a town decided to fight rather than withdraw. In 1779 the Shawnee of Old Chillicothe who took refuge in this structure successfully stood off an American army of 265 men, although their own fighting force included only 25 warriors and 15 boys, not all of whom had rifles (Alford in Galloway 1934:60-65).

From Gist's (1893:44) statement that Lower Shawnee Town contained about 300 men in 1751, one can assume a total population of about 1,200. At that time it included some 140 lodges, on both sides of the Ohio at the mouth of the Scioto. In 1779 Old Chillicothe had a resident population of 300 (Galloway 1934:13), but this represented a recent drastic reduction from an earlier size that may have totaled 1,200. Both these towns were unusually large

Tulane U. Lib., New Orleans: La. Coll.

Fig. 2. Temporary camp on the Mississippi River. The numbers label: 1, pole shelter covered with bark, with leaf or brush flooring; 2, infant's cradle—a hammock of blue cloth over two cords; 3, hole in a log for a temporary mortar for grinding corn with a pestle; 4, deerskin stretched for drying. Unlabeled are a drying or storage rack at the right, a slanting post (near the shelter) probably for scraping hides, and a man with blue cloth headband, black breechclout(?), powderhorn, and gun. Watercolor by Fleury Generelly dated March 6, 1820.

625

SHAWNEE

settlements that apparently functioned as capitals of the Shawnee tribe.

Life Cycle

Birth occurred in a small hut built at some distance from the family's lodge. A newly delivered woman and her infant remained in this building until the naming ceremony, held 10 days after birth (Voegelin and Voegelin 1935:622). In the early nineteenth century a child was named by an elderly man who was required to belong to a different clan (Trowbridge 1939:26), although the name pertained to the eponym of the child's clan. It was publicly announced at a feast to which the parents invited their friends and relatives. This event included prayers for the child and its parents and exhortations urging the parents to raise it properly. If a name duplicated that held by another member of the clan, a different one was substituted (Trowbridge 1939:26-27). Adults who were frequently ill or often wounded in battle could change their names to obtain better luck; this required a ceremony similar to that at which the original name was given.

By the late nineteenth century, after clans had developed into name-groups, two middle-aged or elderly men or women whose own affiliations were irrelevant offered a child names that had occurred to them after praying. The parents chose one of these. After holding the child while addressing a long prayer to the Creator, the name-giver announced the name four times (Voegelin and Voegelin 1935:622-627).

Unlike other Central Algonquians, who undertook vision quests about the time of puberty, the Shawnee prescribed this action for younger children, who began it some time after the age of seven (Alford in Galloway 1934:309-310; Voegelin 1936:18-19). Prepubescent girls also fasted for visions (Voegelin 1953:11-13).

According to Trowbridge (1939:30-31), marriages had formerly been arranged by parents, or at least required their consent. The proposal, made by the man's mother to that of the woman, was accompanied by a gift of skins and other items. Acceptance of these signified assent. The woman's female relatives divided the gifts and prepared a feast of vegetable foods as a countergift. Accompanied by the bride, they carried this to the groom's house. However, by 1824, marriage apparently consisted of open cohabitation without preliminary negotiations or gift exchange (Trowbridge 1939:33). Divorce had become equally casual and could be initiated by either party. The Shawnee practiced polygyny (Trowbridge 1939:31), but Alford (in Galloway 1934:197) describes it as very rare. Although the sororate was practiced (Trowbridge 1939:31), refusal to follow it seems to have incurred no punishment.

Corpses were dressed and painted by friends, who also prepared the grave and carried the body to the cemetery. These attendants, belonging to clans other than that of the deceased, were compensated for their services by receiving some of the deceased's possessions, the bulk of which were divided among the surviving relatives. While men handled funerals of males, funeral attendants for females included both sexes, evenly divided. The corpse was dressed in new clothing, but no grave goods were used. Burial occurred in extended position with the head toward the west. Before the grave was filled, friends and relatives circled it, sprinkling small amounts of tobacco over the body and asking the soul not to look back or think about those remaining behind. Later, at a feast held in the lodge, an elderly man advised the mourners about their behavior. Twelve days of prescribed mourning ended with another feast, after which the relatives could resume their usual work and amusements. Surviving spouses were required to mourn for a year, without changing their clothing or wearing paint and jewelry. Relatives of the deceased spouse dressed the survivor in new clothing and ornaments and prepared a feast to mark the end of restrictions (Trowbridge 1939:24-25, 48). The death of a distinguished person was commemorated a year later by a town ceremony called the "turning dance" (Trowbridge 1939:57). This event, lasting four days, included a feast and dances, followed by the distribution of goods that the relatives had accumulated for this purpose.

Social Organization

Kinship terminology was of Omaha type (Morgan 1871:291-382, 1959:77-78). Information about kinship behavior outside the nuclear family is very slight. One of Trowbridge's (1939:47) statements implies restraint between siblings of opposite sex, who formerly had important roles in arranging each other's marriages (Trowbridge 1939:31). By 1824 the household seems to have been a nuclear family; its earlier form is not known.

Trowbridge (1939:16-17) described a system of 12 patrilineal clans—Snake, Turtle, Raccoon, Turkey, Hawk, Deer, Bear, Wolf, Great Lynx, Elk, Buffalo, and Tree. He reported that 34 clans had once existed. In 1859 Morgan (1877:173, 1959:44-47) obtained a list of 13 clans—Snake, Turtle, Raccoon, Turkey, Deer, Bear, Wolf, Great Lynx, Horse (originally Elk), Turkey Buzzard, Owl, Rabbit, and Loon. He noted that the Loon clan no longer existed. Both Trowbridge and Morgan thus describe a system of 12 functioning clans, which would be particularly convenient if the committees of 12 persons responsible for important rituals (Alford in Galloway 1934:190-193; Voegelin 1936:13) represented these units. The differences in the clans they list could indicate variation among divisions. Morgan's (1959:47) data show that significant changes in clan structure had occurred between 1824 and 1859. Clans were no longer exogamous, nor were they patrilineal. A child's name could belong to the clan of either parent, or even still a different clan, although this was uncommon. Morgan suggested that the Shawnee used this technique to maintain approximate equality in clan size. After 1859 Shawnee clans evolved into a system of six name-groups: Turkey, Turtle, Rounded Feet, Horse, Raccoon, and Rabbit (Voegelin and Voegelin 1935). Names referring to similar eponyms were grouped together in phratrylike structures; but since children were named without regard for the affiliation of their fathers (or mothers), name-groups were not in any sense descent units.

The corporate functions of Shawnee clans apparently centered on their control of personal names and on the qualities and characteristics that individuals were believed to share with their eponyms. Trowbridge (1939:17, 19) reported that the paramount tribal war chief belonged to the Great Lynx clan and that a returning war party was led by warriors belonging to the Wolf clan while those of the Great Lynx clan served as the rear guard. Important ritual, political, and other positions were assigned to persons on the basis of their clan affiliations and the traits that conceptually accompanied these (Voegelin and Voegelin 1935:629-631). Although clans were involved in the organization of important ceremonies, the formal ritual unit in Shawnee society was the division (Voegelin 1936:18). An ambiguous statement by Trowbridge (1939:11) that could imply that each clan had a chief seems confirmed by Morgan (1959:47). Except that this office involved peace-chief functions, its nature is not described and it may have been ritual rather than political. Prescribed behavior required Shawnees to boast about their eponyms and on the same basis to tease or joke with members of other name-groups (Voegelin and Voegelin 1935:628-629, 631). This behavior can probably be projected back to the period when these units were clans. Alford (1936:52) says that the "comradeship or partisanship existing between those of the same branch [name-group] was outstanding, and it meant a delightful feeling of kinship or intimacy, a kind of fellowship which afforded much merriment and innocent fun among both old and young."

No moiety organization has been reported for the Shawnee. In the joking that characterizes the present name-groups, the Turtle and Turkey units are considered "friends" and are opposed to the Horse and Rounded Feet groups (Voegelin and Voegelin 1935:631). However, this pairing does not extend to the other name-groups. Alford (in Galloway 1934:181, 1936:50) suggests that the five divisions were grouped into two units, one consisting of the čalaka and mekoče and the other combining the kišpoko, pekowi, and θawikila, but does not specify any moietylike functions for these groups. The Bread Dance ceremonies included opposition between formal categories in ball games and song contests, but these pitted men against women.

Political Organization

Political functions were divided between peace and war organizations (Trowbridge 1939:11, 12-13, 17). The peace organization was apparently based on the five divisions, each having its own chief (Alford in Galloway 1934:21, 181). This official was autonomous as far as action was limited to his own town, but in national or tribal contexts he acknowledged the authority of the tribal chief, who belonged to either the θawikila or čalaka division. The specific tribal duties, political or ritual, assigned to each division were carried out through its chief. Unfortunately, information about the actual functioning of this system is very slight. Chieftainship was normally hereditary but by 1824 apparently no longer belonged to a specific lineage. Trowbridge (1939:11) reports that when one of these officials died the other chiefs and leading men chose his successor, usually selecting one of his sons; if he lacked sons they did not necessarily limit their choice to his relatives.

Information about war chiefs is similarly insufficient. The tribal war chief apparently belonged to the kišpoko division, which had charge of war (Alford in Galloway 1934:181) and to the Great Lynx clan (Trowbridge 1939:17), whose eponym had the appropriate qualities. Probably each division had such an official as the counterpart of its peace chief. Trowbridge (1939:11-12) says that a war chief acquired his position by leading four raids, returning each time with at least one scalp and without losing any men. After 12 expeditions he was allowed to resign if he wished, although whether he gave up his political office or simply his active leadership of raids is unclear.

Tribal councils apparently consisted of chiefs belonging to both organizations. Elderly men also attended these to give advice and assistance, besides providing information about earlier events and the decisions reached by past councils. Only chiefs could vote. If war was decided upon, the tribal war chief made the public announcement of this decision (Trowbridge 1939:11, 13, 17). Besides the tribal council, whose deliberations probably centered on national policy, one has to assume the existence of a council for each town.

Trowbridge (1939:12-13) describes a system of women chiefs, who he says were usually the mothers or other close relatives of male chiefs. Their level of operation seems to have been the town, rather than the tribe. Some of the functions ascribed to these officials suggest that they were an earlier form of the committee of 12 women appointed to supervise the Bread Dance feasts among the Shawnee in more recent years (Alford in Galloway 1934:190-193; cf. Morgan 1959:47). Like male chiefs, they were divided between peace and war organizations. The most important political role of a female chief of the peace variety was her right to ask a war chief to abandon a raid that he had planned. Peace chiefs opposing the venture could ask her to make such a plea, which was usually successful (Trowbridge 1939:13). She could also grant captives their lives (Trowbridge 1939:53), even, in some cases, those who had already been marked for death. Women chiefs directed the planting of crops. They supervised feasts, where the female war chief handled the cooking of meat while her peace counterpart had charge of white corn and the finer vegetables.

When murder occurred within the tribe, the victim's family could retaliate in kind or accept as compensation a quantity of wampum defined as 60 fathoms for a male and 150 for a female. Chiefs normally refused to intervene unless the murderer had high status or was important in other ways to the town or nation. In such cases the chiefs themselves began accumulating the necessary amount of wampum. If a relative of the victim killed the murderer the issue was regarded as settled, but vengeance taken by a nonrelative was defined as another murder. Theft was a serious crime requiring a trial by the town council, which prescribed a public beating as punishment (Trowbridge 1939:13–15). It could proscribe an incorrigible thief, whom a victim could then kill without fear of retaliation.

Warfare

After the tribal council voted for war and the paramount war chief had announced this decision, a tomahawk painted red was circulated through the Shawnee towns as an invitation to join the first war party. Prospective members met at the war chief's town to discuss their plans. After this initial action, raids could apparently set out from any town, each led by the war chief who planned it. The members usually included a shaman whose functions included divination as well as treating the wounded. A war dance preceded the raiders' departure. As they approached the enemy, the young men went hunting to obtain 12 deer. These were served as a feast, during which the leader made an exhortatory speech. While returning, he sent a messenger ahead to notify the town chief. He in turn informed his female counterpart, who began preparing a feast. Approaching the town, the raiders gave the war cry. Boys and young men who came out to meet them were allowed to beat any prisoners until they reached the council house. There the female war chief examined them and thanked the warriors for this gift. Prisoners who had been painted black were destined for death unless the female peace chief claimed them before they entered the town. Other captives were distributed among the residents according to economic needs or their desire to adopt replacements for dead relatives. A peace chief then began the war song in the council house, where the warriors danced until dawn, stripping themselves naked during this event (Trowbridge 1939:17–22). Each warrior struck a post while reciting his honors. The raiders remained in the council house for four days, drinking herbal infusions and eating as little as possible.

Religion

The Shawnee recognized a large number of deities. Most of these were in some sense controlled, or at least influenced, by the supreme being, a woman usually called Our Grandmother or the Creator, rather than by her personal name *pa·po·θkwe* 'Cloud' (Voegelin 1936:3–4; Alford in Galloway 1934:17). Closely associated with her were her grandson, called Rounded Side or Cloudy Boy, and a small dog. She was also associated with a variety of "witnesses" she had created as intermediaries between herself and the Shawnee. The most important of these were tobacco, fire, water, and eagles. Other figures and objects such as the Thunderbirds, the four winds, and the divisional sacred packs were less significant as witnesses but had other very important functions. Our Grandmother created the earth and the turtle that supports it and recreated earth after her grandson unloosed a flood that destroyed it (Voegelin 1936:6–11). She also created the Shawnee, although some divisions were originated by her grandson instead. She taught people "how to take care of themselves, how to live, to conduct ceremonial dances, how to raise corn and hunt, what kind of houses to build, and their laws" (Voegelin 1936:11). After imparting this knowlege she left earth and went to her present location in the sky, which is also the home of the dead.

The Shawnee laws, a very important part of the knowledge and instruction received from the Creator, number 12 (Voegelin, Yegerlehner, and Robinett 1954; Yegerlehner 1954). The first law sets forth their origin and purpose, describing their benefits and the consequences of failing to observe them. It also outlines modes of sexual conduct involving intercourse and states such as menstruation and pregnancy. The second law is also general in scope. Each of the remaining 10 laws centers on a particular animal—deer, bear, dog, birds, wolf, buffalo, raccoon, turtle, turkey, and crow—describing the service it performs for humans and the manner in which it should be treated.

The influence of Our Grandmother penetrated almost every aspect of Shawnee religion but was strongest in the communal forms of worship and weakest in individual activities such as the vision quest and the practice of witchcraft (Voegelin 1936:3).

The main medium for communal worship was the annual ceremonial dances (Voegelin 1936:13–14). The most important of these were the Spring Bread Dance, held to ask for an abundant harvest, and the Fall Bread Dance that expressed thanksgiving and requested that game be plentiful. Each dance included a feast for which 12 men undertook a special hunt to obtain meat that 12 women cooked. Alford (in Galloway 1934:190) says these officials were appointed for life, although they could be removed for misconduct. They were called into session before a Bread Dance by the divisional chief, who opened a ball game played by women against men (fig. 3) (Alford in Galloway 1934:191). The losing team had to provide wood for cooking the feast and for the bonfires that lighted the night dancing. The entire town assembled to receive the 12 hunters at dawn on the third morning after they set out. While the women officials cooked the game, the hunters danced. An elderly man skilled in oratory delivered a prayer to the Creator. Voegelin (1936:13–14) gives an example. Sequences of dancing followed until late afternoon, when the feast was served, followed by more dancing at night (Alford in Galloway 1934:191–193). The Creator herself, in the past, returned to earth to attend these events (Voegelin 1936:15–16).

The Bread Dances opened and closed a ceremonial season that included dances of a purely social nature as well as other important rituals, one of which was the Green Corn Dance in August, marking the first maize harvest (Alford in Galloway 1934:193–194; J. Johnston 1820:285–286; Morgan 1959:47; Voegelin 1936:13). On this occasion persons were absolved of misconduct, and all injuries except murder were forgiven. Johnston, whose brief account is the most detailed description of this event, reports that the entire town gathered around the council house, bringing quantities of food for the feast. This ritual lasted 4 to 12 days and included an address that expressed thanksgiving as well as provided moral instruction. The Men's Dance or War Dance, held in August under the auspices of the *kišpoko* division (Alford in Galloway 1934:194; Voegelin 1936:13) may have been a relatively late introduction observed by only part of the

Shawnee. Another annual ritual, long abandoned, was a false-face festival called the Doll Dance, formerly held by each division (Voegelin 1936:13).

Prayers were also offered Our Grandmother at first-fruits ceremonies, funerals, and naming rituals, and at annual events such as ghost feasts and the end of the lacrosse season (Voegelin 1936:14–15).

Another major ritual focus was the sacred packs, one of which belonged to each division (Alford in Galloway 1934:21, 181, 304–305; Voegelin 1936:18). These were also created by Our Grandmother and remained under her control, although somewhat overshadowing her. The sacred packs were one of the most esoteric features of Shawnee culture and were seldom discussed even within their society. Knowledge of them is thus very slight.

The gift of prophecy was also bestowed by the Creator. Although given to individuals, this capacity was regarded as benefiting the tribe and thus communal in its effects. The vision quest, on the other hand, was exclusively an individual undertaking, and the blessing received from an encounter with a spirit was not public knowledge. Persons who experienced very potent visions could become sweat-lodge doctors. Their ability to heal the sick was defined as more or less communal in nature, and this occupation consequently involved prayers to the Creator (Voegelin 1936:16, 19).

Earlier descriptions of Shawnee religion, particularly those included in Trowbridge's (1939:1–6, 40–42) account, describe the Creator as the Great Spirit or Finisher, a male. Although Trowbridge (1939:40) mentions Our Grandmother and describes her as sharing with her grandson the function of watching over Indians, her role is decidedly subordinate to the Great Spirit, to whom most of her functions and deeds are ascribed. Examining this discrepancy, Voegelin and Voegelin (1944) concluded that the concept of a female creator was a rather late innovation that the Shawnee had borrowed from an Iroquois source. They interpreted the 1824 accounts, particularly the warning that no being except the Great Spirit was to be credited with the creation (Trowbridge 1939:2), as indicating that the shift was occurring then. Certain counterarguments should be noted. By 1824 the Shawnee had been irrevocably split for some years and never again reunited; yet Voegelin (1936:3) described belief in Our Grandmother as characteristic of all three separate Shawnee groups in Oklahoma. The time involved seems insufficient for so consistent a shift and one of such importance. This issue of time is sharpened by Morgan's (1959:47) statement that the god "anciently worshipped" by the Shawnee was a female creator called Our Grandmother. Finally, Trowbridge's main informant was Tenskwatawa, who had recently preached a religious reformation of intertribal scope and may have had reason to minimize the status of a uniquely Shawnee deity.

Mus. of the Amer. Ind., Heye Foundation, N.Y.: 2/9244.

Fig. 3. Beaded leather football used in the Bread Dance. Diameter about 6 cm; collected in Okla. before 1912.

History

The precontact location of the Shawnee has provoked much discussion (Griffin 1943:11-13; Hanna 1911, 1:119-160, 2:87-124; Mooney 1910c:530-532; Royce 1881; C. Thomas 1891; E.W. Voegelin 1939; Witthoft and Hunter 1955). A basic problem is that in their earliest recorded contacts with Europeans the Shawnee were encountered either as captives or other isolated individuals or else as refugee groups. Surveys of the evidence by Griffin (1943:34-35) and Witthoft and Hunter (1955) place the Shawnee homeland in the upper Ohio valley. Most of the early documentary sources bearing on the problem seem to point to this conclusion.

The Ontouagannha, whom Garnier (JR 56:62-63) explicitly identified with the Shawnee, were described by Jerome Lalemant in 1662 (JR 47:144-149) as living along a beautiful river southwest of the Iroquois. In 1669 Galinée's Seneca informants placed the Shawnee above the Falls of the Ohio (Margry 1876-1886, 1:116). Hanna (1911, 1:120-121) interprets a 1670 statement by Jacques Marquette (JR 54:188) as placing the Shawnee east-southeast of the Illinois (presumably the Peoria or another northern tribe of this group). In 1673 Marquette described the Ohio as flowing "from the lands of the East, where dwell the people called Chaouanons in so great numbers that in one district there are as many as 23 villages, and fifteen in another, quite near one another" (JR 59:144-145). A similar interpretation may be drawn from Marquette's map (reproduced in Griffin 1943:14), as well as from the 1684 Franquelin map (Griffin 1943:map 8). This last, however, has been subject to widely varying interpretations (cf. Bauxar 1957; Griffin 1943:19-20; Hanna 1911, 2:91-95). The salt-making group beyond the Appalachians that was described to Thomas Batts and Robert Fallam in 1671 has been identified as Shawnee, as have the people living on the Ohio who captured Gabriel Arthur from the Tomahittans in 1674 (Alvord and Bidgood 1912:87-88, 199, 222-223); however, the evidence for these conclusions is very slight (Griffin 1943:32-33). Of much more value are Hanna's (1911, 1:137-142, 155, 189-190) quotations from seventeenth- and eighteenth-century documents indicating that some of the Pennsylvania Shawnee came directly from the Ohio valley during the years from 1692 on.

As far as any archeological culture can be associated with the precontact Shawnee, the most likely possibility seems to be Fort Ancient (Griffin 1943). While many archeologists seem inclined to assume some correlation, if not complete identity, between the Fort Ancient culture and the Shawnee people, clear evidence of such a link has not been demonstrated (cf. "Late Prehistory of the Ohio Valley," this vol.).

An alternative precontact location often given for the Shawnee is the Cumberland valley. This hypothesis, proposed by C. Thomas (1891), has been accepted by many authorities. It rests primarily on Thomas's assumption, based on very tenuous evidence and never proved, that the precontact Shawnee built stone-lined graves. Documentary evidence that might support it is scanty and generally later than the evidence pointing toward the upper Ohio valley. This includes Franquelin's 1684 map, Gravier's 1700 statement that the Shawnee lived on a southern tributary of the Ohio (JR 65:106), an undated detached sheet attributed to René-Robert Cavelier de La Salle (Margry 1876-1886, 2:196) describing such a tributary as "la riviere des Chaouesnon," and DeLisle's 1718 map (Hanna 1911, 1:122) denoting the Cumberland as "riviere des anciens Chaouanons." A group of Shawnees from Pennsylvania briefly settled on the Cumberland in the middle of the eighteenth century, while others probably passed through that general area in late precontact times. But the evidence does not support an early or consistent Shawnee occupation of the Cumberland valley.

Accounts during the years between 1662 and 1673 (Galinée in Margry 1876-1886, 1:133, 137; Lalemant in JR 47:144-149; Marquette in JR 59:144-145; Perrot 1911:226; Bacqueville de la Potherie 1911-1912, 1:348) document a pattern of Iroquois attacks, gaining in intensity and ultimately driving the Shawnee out of the Ohio valley. Their movements during the rest of the seventeenth century are, with a few exceptions, very obscure. Apparently they split up into a number of fragments that moved off in different directions. In 1683 several hundred Shawnees went to La Salle's post at Starved Rock in Illinois, remaining there until 1688 or 1689 (Deliette 1934:306-307; La Salle in Margry 1876-1886, 2:314, 318). Other Shawnee groups moved into the Southeast, reaching the Savannah River about 1674 (Swanton 1922:307, 317). In 1692 a band numbering about 172 appeared in Maryland, settling near the mouth of the Susquehanna River (Hanna 1911, 1:126-135, 158). This group probably came from Starved Rock, since they were accompanied by Martin Chartier, who described himself as a deserter from that post. Another Shawnee band, apparently coming directly from the Ohio valley, was brought into eastern Pennsylvania in 1694 by Aernout Viele (Hanna 1911, 1:137-142, 158).

Shawnee distribution becomes much clearer in the early eighteenth century. Chartier's band had moved up the Susquehanna into Pennsylvania (Hanna 1911, 1:149-151), which became the major center for the Shawnee, who settled among the Delaware and Susquehannock. A second center along the Savannah River in South Carolina was shrinking as small groups migrated to Pennsylvania. After 1715 part of these southern Shawnee moved to the Chattahoochee and then settled among the Upper Creek, while the rest went to Pennsylvania (Swanton 1922:317-318).

By 1720 the Pennsylvania Shawnee were moving westward, impelled by depletion of game and sales of land by the Delaware and Iroquois (Downes 1940:19–20; Hanna 1911, 1:182–191). Other factors were friction with the Iroquois and a favorable response to overtures the Shawnee had made to the French. In 1731 about 1,200 Shawnees lived on the headwaters of the Ohio, with others on the Juniata and Susquehanna and some in the Wyoming valley (Hanna 1911, 1:154, 187, 296). The Wyoming group moved west about 1743, founding Logstown on the Ohio (Hanna 1911, 1:154, 187, 354–356). The settlement later called Lower Shawnee Town was established at the mouth of the Scioto sometime before 1739, perhaps by the θawikila who fled down the Ohio in 1735 after killing an Iroquois chief (Hanna 1911, 1:302–303, 2:129).

The flight of the θawikila foreshadowed a new period of dispersal. Its ultimate causes were abuses in the fur trade, particularly the activities of unlicensed traders who used rum to obtain furs cheaply, leaving the Shawnees impoverished and in debt to the licensed traders who had provided goods on credit (Downes 1940:20–25, 30–41). Their chiefs asked the Pennsylvania government to regulate trade and enforce the antirum laws. When these requests were ignored, most of the tribe joined in a minor uprising in 1745, pillaging several unlicensed traders and leaving Pennsylvania with Peter Chartier, a half-Shawnee trader. Their subsequent movements were very complex. Apparently they went to Lower Shawnee Town. Some remained there, while others returned to Logstown, and the main body founded a new settlement in northern Kentucky (Hanna 1911, 1:311–312, 2:134, 138, 240). They later abandoned this town and moved south where, after a clash with the Chickasaw, they settled among the Creek. By 1752 a large group had returned to Lower Shawnee Town, which was the tribal center. Another section moved to the Cumberland, settling near the site of Nashville. When the Chickasaw drove them out in 1756 they moved to the lower Ohio (Adair 1775:2, 409; Draper in Hanna 1911, 2:240–242; Pease and Jenison 1940:29, 64, 242, 369–372, 584–585; Swanton 1922:416).

English traders temporarily regained the allegiance of the Ohio Shawnee but could not furnish protection against attacks by the French and their allies (Downes 1940:57–62). In self-defense the Shawnee joined the French and after Gen. Edward Braddock's defeat in 1755 attacked the frontier settlements in Pennsylvania and Virginia. This phase ended in 1758 when the fall of Fort Duquesne restored the English presence. The Shawnees of Logstown then joined the rest of their tribe in the Scioto valley (Darlington in Gist 1893:121). With the accession of those from the lower Ohio a few years later (Draper in Hanna 1911, 2:241), the Shawnee were again united except for the Alabama group.

As far as the Shawnee took part in the final years of the French wars they fought as English allies (Downes 1940:101–102), but dissatisfaction with postwar English policies combined with apprehension about their land led them to embrace Pontiac's movement. They made peace in 1765.

By the Treaty of Fort Stanwix in 1768 the Iroquois opened Kentucky to settlement, depriving the Shawnee of their main hunting lands. Friction over this issue came to a head in 1774, when frontiersmen killed 13 Shawnees and Mingos in a particularly brutal series of unprovoked murders (Downes 1940:161–178). Unable to secure allies, the Shawnee chiefs decided against war, but relatives of the victims joined a group of Mingos to kill 13 settlers. Their retaliation precipitated Lord Dunmore's War. A Virginian army destroyed a Shawnee town in the Muskingum valley. After unsuccessfully trying to block an invasion of the Scioto valley, the Shawnee made peace and accepted the Ohio as their southern boundary (Downes 1940:184).

External events involving the Shawnee during the Revolution are fairly well documented. They first adopted a policy of neutrality and moved from the Scioto to the headwaters of the Miami and its tributaries. In 1777 part of the tribe entered the war and joined the Mingo in attacking American settlements. Later the murder of the chief Cornstalk by Americans while he was a hostage at Fort Randolph brought the peace party as well into the war (Downes 1940:189–190, 194, 197–200, 204–210). The Shawnee devastated Kentucky and other frontier areas, but their own towns were repeatedly destroyed by American armies (Downes 1940:278–279, 298; Galloway 1934:43–44), and they were forced north to the Auglaize River. In 1795 they and their allies concluded peace with the United States at the Treaty of Greenville.

Information about the internal developments that disrupted the tribe and produced a third period of dispersal is slight. The peace party left Ohio, moving across the Mississippi to Spanish territory. According to Alford (in Galloway 1934:40–41), the vanguard left after 1774 and the main movement occurred in March 1779. E.W. Voegelin (in Trowbridge 1939:xiv) places the migration in 1780, after the first American invasion of Shawnee territory. Most of the Shawnee remaining in Ohio eventually settled at Wapakoneta on the Auglaize and Hog Creek on the Ottawa (Harvey 1855:164–165). Others joined the Ohio Seneca at Lewiston. Still another group, apparently a faction that opposed the 1795 treaty, withdrew to the Wabash drainage.

In 1805 this last group moved to Greenville, Ohio, but returned to the Wabash area in 1808 and established a village at Tippecanoe (B. Drake 1841:86, 105). Its leader, Tecumseh, fashioned an intertribal movement to resist American expansion. Encouraged by the English, he tried to weld the Indian tribes into an alliance whose members would sell no more land to the United States,

Bibliothèque Nationale, Dépt. des Cartes et Plans, Paris: Ge A664, detail.
Fig. 4. Shawnee man with roach haircut, red face paint, distended ear rims, silver ear and septum ornaments, blue bead necklace, blue cloth shirt and breechclout, white blanket robe with blue stripe, silver armband with red and yellow feather pendants, red cloth leggings, red garters with blue zigzag, bow and three fletched arrows with triangular metal(?) points. Drawn from life by Joseph Wabin in 1796 in the Illinois country.

while his brother, Tenskwatawa, preached a nativistic movement supporting this aim. Although Tecumseh's clan and divisional affiliation qualified him for the position of tribal war chief, the Ohio Shawnee refused to join him (B. Drake 1841:91, 96). Most of his followers were drawn from other tribes, particularly the Kickapoo and Potawatomi and, in the early stages, the Delaware. The Miami also remained aloof, but tribes farther west, such as the Sauk and Winnebago, were strongly attracted. Recognizing the threat as serious, William Henry Harrison, the governor of Indiana Territory, led an army to Tippecanoe in 1811 while Tecumseh was on a mission to the southeastern tribes. Although the battle that followed was actually a draw (Dillon 1859:471–472; Hill 1957:55–56), it destroyed Tenskwatawa's credibility and the movement dissolved. Those Shawnee who had followed Tecumseh withdrew to Ontario with him and later moved to Kansas.

The later movements of the Shawnee were as complex as those in their earlier dispersals and ultimately split them into three independent tribes, the Absentee Shawnee, Cherokee Shawnee, and Eastern Shawnee.

The Absentee Shawnee originated as the peace faction that left Ohio during the Revolution and settled in southeast Missouri near Cape Girardeau, where they were granted land in 1793 by the Spanish administration (Foreman 1946:34). Sometime after 1797 the Shawnee of the Creek confederacy joined them (Alford in Galloway 1934:40–41; Swanton 1922:320), as did other migrants from Ohio (Foreman 1946:52–53; Mooney 1910c:536). The intrusion of newcomers belonging to the war faction apparently revived internal dissension. In the early nineteenth century most of the peace party moved away. Some drifted into Arkansas and Oklahoma, often in association with Delawares and Cherokees (Foreman 1936:69, 188–191, 1946:34, 159). Others were encouraged by the Spanish authorities in Texas to establish settlements near Nacogdoches and on the Red River (Berlandier 1969:142; Gibson 1963:143–144). After their expulsion in 1839 the Texas Shawnees eventually moved to the Canadian River in central Oklahoma, where part of the tribe had been living since at least 1836. In 1854 they were formally designated the Absentee Shawnee, that is, those who were not residents of the Shawnee reservation in Kansas when it was allotted (Foreman 1946:160, 162–163, 169–170, 172). They received official recognition as a separate body in 1872, when their land titles in Oklahoma were also confirmed.

The Cherokee Shawnee are descended from the part of the tribe that remained in Ohio. In 1825 the United States liquidated the Shawnee grant in Missouri and established a reservation in Kansas for the tribe. The Ohio Shawnee moved there between 1832 and 1835 (Foreman 1946: 74–85, 168). Those currently in Missouri, the Black Bob band, wanted to settle in Oklahoma and went to Kansas under duress (Foreman 1946:60–61). The Kansas settlement was torn by continuous conflict between these two groups until American pressure forced them to Oklahoma, where they separated (Foreman 1946:168–178). The Ohio Shawnee formally joined the Cherokee Nation in 1869 and settled in its territory under the name Cherokee Shawnee (fig. 5), while the Black Bob band merged with the Absentee Shawnee.

In 1831 the so-called Mixed band of Shawnee and Seneca moved directly to a reservation in northeast Oklahoma. When its Shawnee component separated from the Seneca in 1867 it took the name Eastern Shawnee.

By 1950 the Shawnee numbered 2,252, of whom the 1,100 Cherokee Shawnee were the largest group, followed by 712 Absentee Shawnee and 440 Eastern Shawnee (Tax and Stanley 1960). The Eastern Shawnee were attached to the Quapaw Agency in northeast Oklahoma (fig. 6),

NAA, Smithsonian: Eva M. Horner Coll.

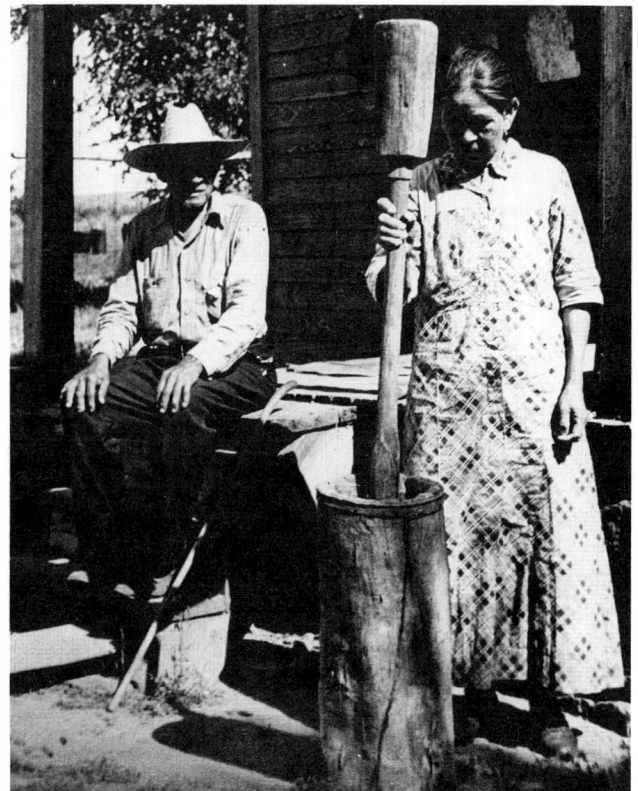

Fig. 5. Ely and Eliza Ellis, Cherokee Shawnees, with mortar and pestle for grinding corn. Photograph by Jim Lynch or John Day at Sperry, Okla., June 13, 1936.

where traditional tribal cultures disappeared very early (Foreman 1946:345-348). Although they and the Seneca were the most conservative groups in this area, they have given up more of Shawnee culture than other groups. In 1940 they organized as the Eastern Shawnee Tribe, with a business committee (M.H. Wright 1951:244-245). The Cherokee Shawnee, living in Craig and Rogers counties in northeast Oklahoma, have also abandoned much of traditional Shawnee culture. Those belonging to the *mekoče* division, which adopted a policy of acculturation while still living in Ohio (Alford in Galloway 1934:41; E.W. Voegelin 1944:255, 422), reversed this position in the late nineteenth century and began borrowing customs from more conservative groups, particularly the Black Bob band. The Cherokee Shawnee gave up their tribal organization on joining the Cherokee Nation, and since the dissolution of the latter they have had no formal political organization. The Absentee Shawnee, living in central Oklahoma in Cleveland and Pottawatomie counties, historically included the most culturally conservative section of the tribe and retain this characteristic (fig. 7). They still maintain the most important traditional Shawnee rituals, including the War Dance as well as the Spring and Fall Bread Dances (M.H. Wright 1951:245). They are organized as the Absentee Shawnee Tribe of Indians of Oklahoma, with a business committee.

Mus. of the Amer. Ind., Heye Foundation, N.Y.: 1/9833.

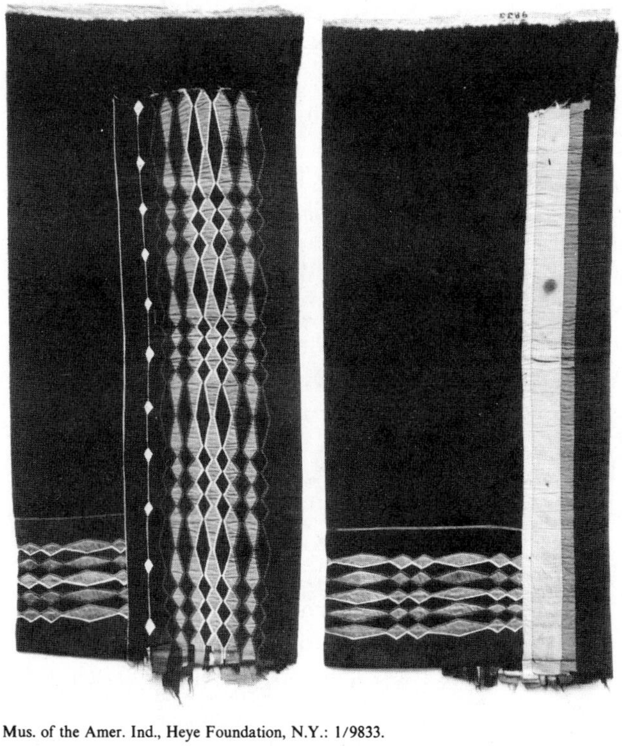

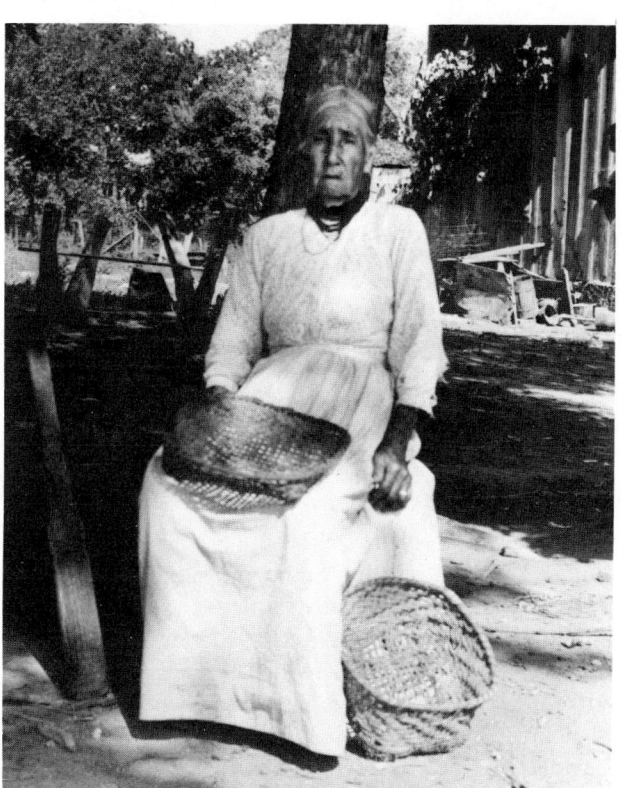

Fig. 6. Pair of red stroud leggings with ribbon appliqué decoration. Length about 64 cm; collected at Quapaw Agency, Okla., before 1908.

Fig. 7. Jennie Segar, Absentee Shawnee, aged about 80, with 2 baskets used in corn preparation. Photographed in 1934 by Erminie Wheeler Voegelin between Tecumseh and Shawnee, Okla.

Population

Shawnee dispersal precludes any reliable population estimates until very late times. A population of 1,440 can be projected for the Shawnee of western Pennsylvania in 1731 (Hanna 1911, 1:296), but this figure does not include those living on the Susquehanna River or in the Southeast. The South Carolina center included 233 persons in 1715 (Swanton 1922:317). In 1760 about 400 lived among the Creek, but a year later only 120 (Swanton 1922:319). Mooney's (1910c:536) estimate of 1,500 for various years from 1759 to 1812 is almost certainly far too low, hardly more than their central town in 1751 (Gist 1893:44). In 1824, 1,383 Shawnee were reported in Missouri (Foreman 1946:52). Two years later 500 left Ohio to join them, and in 1831, 600 remained in Ohio (Foreman 1946:53, 65-66). These figures give, for 1824-1831, a total of 2,483. Adding an estimated 2,400 living in Texas in 1827 (Berlandier 1969:142) gives 4,883, probably far too high. By 1909 they numbered 1,388 and in 1944, 2,139 (M.H. Wright 1951:241).

Synonymy

The earliest reference to the Shawnee seems to be Ouchaouanag, in 1648 (JR 33:151). Though probably borrowed by the French from the Ottawa (Mooney 1910c:537) this form is a variant of the Shawnee self-designation *ša·wanwa*, which literally means 'person of the south' (Voegelin 1938-1940, 8:318). The standard French form was Chaouanons (JR 59:144-145; cf. B. Drake 1841:9), with variants such as Chaoenons, 1683 (Pease and Werner 1934:37); Cha8anons, 1750 (Pease and Jenison 1940:156); Chaoesnon (Margry 1876-1886, 2:196); Chavouanons, 1752 (Pease and Jenison 1940:680); Chiaouenons, 1721 (Deliette 1934:307); and Shounaus, 1830 (Berlandier 1969:142).

In the early years of contact the English used various forms, sometimes borrowed from other Indians: Chaovonon, 1698 (Hanna 1911, 1:134); Satanas and Sattanas, 1692 (Hanna 1911, 1:137); Savana, 1674 (Swanton 1922:307); Shallna-rooners, 1693 (Hanna 1911, 1:135); Shanwans, 1694 (NYCD 4:98); Shawanah, 1704 (MPCP 2:148); Shawaneles, 1698 (Hanna 1911, 1:130); Shawhena, 1709 (Hanna 1911, 1:144); Shevanor, 1697 (Hanna 1911, 1:130); and Stabbernowles, 1693 (Hanna 1911, 1:139). Earlier English forms such as Shawano's, 1756; Shawnoes, 1777; and (reshaped with English -ese) Shawanese, 1701; Shawnese, 1750 (Mooney 1910c:537-538) were eventually superseded by Shawnee, which arose from Shawnese being interpreted as a plural Shawnees.

The seventeenth-century Dutch terms Sauwanew (Carte Figurative, NYCD 1) and Sawanoos (Brinton 1885:31) are borrowed from Munsee and designate 'southerners' rather than the Shawnee tribe (cf. Mooney 1910c:531, 537).

Algonquian forms include Delaware *šá·ɔnu* (Ives Goddard, personal communication 1975), Miami *šawanwa* (Voegelin 1938-1940, 8:318), and Menominee *osa·wanow* and *sa·wanow* (Bloomfield 1962:67, 249). Other forms are Creek *sa·wanó·ki* (Mary R. Haas, personal communication 1974), Cherokee Aní-Sawănúgĭ and Sawanúka (Mooney 1910c:536-537), Dakota Sawala (Riggs 1852:441), Osage Zhoⁿni (La Flesche 1932:327) or Šawana (Mooney 1910c:536), and Caddo *šawanuh* (Wallace L. Chafe, personal communication 1973).

The earliest recorded Iroquois name for the Shawnee, Ontouagannha, is loosely translated 'one utters unintelligible speech' by Hewitt (1910e:136), who says it denoted a variety of Algonquian tribes; this is a variant of Mohawk *tewaʔkę́nhaʔ* 'western Algonquian' (Floyd G. Lousbury, personal communication 1975). Yet Lalemant's Ontôagannha (JR 47:145) and Garnier's Ontoüagannha (JR 56:62) clearly designate the Shawnee, while Lalemant's earlier reference to the Ont8agannha, or Fire Nation (JR 45:206-207) echoes the 1648 citation of the Ouchaouanag as part of the Nation of Fire (JR 33:151). The forms most closely resembling Ontouagannha generally come from early French sources and probably refer to the Shawnee. Forms similar to Dowaganha (NYCD 3:434) and Wagenhanes (NYCD 4:61) apparently designate the Ottawas and other northern Algonquians (Colden 1958:xv). Colden (1958:xv) gives Satanas as the Iroquois name for the Shawnee, and Mooney (1910c:537) cites a Tuscarora form Sawanuháka, which is *sawà·noh* plus *-há·ka·* 'people' (Marianne Mithun, personal communication 1975).

The *čalaka* division is usually referred to as Chillicothe, an anglicization of *čalaka·θa* 'member of the *čalaka* division' (Voegelin 1938-1940, 5:149). *kišpoko* has minor variants such as Kiscopokes (B. Drake 1841:69) and Kiskapocoke (J. Johnston 1820:271). Names for the *mekoče* show greater differences. The earliest reference is Meguatchaiki, on Franquelin's 1684 map (Griffin 1943:map 8). Other forms are Machachee (B. Drake 1841:50), Maguck (Hanna 1911, 1:148), Makostrake (McKenney and Hall 1849-1854, 3:111), and Mequachake (J. Johnston 1820:271). *pekowi* appears in forms such as Peckawee and Pecowick (Hanna 1911, 1:145, 148), Pickaway (Hanna 1911, 2:261), Picks (Hanna 1911, 1:145), and Piqua (J. Johnston 1820:275).

Some of the forms used for the *θawikila* division are Asswekalaes and Asswikales (Hanna 1911, 1:295, 296), Hathawekela (Mooney 1910c:536-537), Sawakola (Adair 1775:256), Sewickleys (Evans map, in Hanna 1911, 2), perhaps Shaircula (Swanton 1922:319), and Shaweygira (Hanna 1911, 1:302).

Sources

The earliest full-scale treatment of Shawnee culture is Trowbridge's (1939) 1824-1825 account. Alford's (1936) autobiography and his contributions to Galloway's (1934) history have particular interest as statements by a Shawnee. The articles and monographs by Voegelin (1936), Voegelin and Voegelin (1935, 1944), and E.W. Voegelin (1941, 1944) provide unusually rich coverage of religious and mortuary practices and, in some respects, social organization, although this remains an important gap in knowledge of the Shawnee. The basic treatments of Shawnee as a language are contained in several publications by Voegelin, particularly his phonemic analysis (1935) and dictionary (1938-1940). Downes (1940) and Hanna (1911) treat certain periods in Shawnee history. Unlike many historians, Downes is very successful in presenting an Indian viewpoint, and his study, dealing with the period 1729-1795, is excellent. Hanna, whose primary concern is the period of the early fur trade, brings together an invaluable collection of material.

Fox

CHARLES CALLENDER

Language, Territory, and Environment

The Fox ('fäks) call themselves *meškwahki·haki* 'Red Earths'. Although known to the French at least by 1683 (Bacqueville de la Potherie 1911–1912,1:360), this name has remained uncommon as a designation for them.

Throughout their postcontact history the Fox have been a single clearly defined tribe, but the United States government has blurred their identity by bracketing them with the Sauk. Their relationship with the Sauk after 1733 was a close alliance rather than a union or even a confederacy. These two tribes sometimes acted jointly but remained politically and territorially distinct. Nevertheless, the government classed them as a single unit under the name Sac-and-Fox. After a Sauk band split away in the early nineteenth century and acquired official recognition as the Sac-and-Fox of the Missouri, the Fox and the rest of the Sauk were designated Sac-and-Fox of the Mississippi. During the 1850s the Fox ended their Sauk alliance and returned to Iowa from Kansas. This event introduced a further distinction into official terminology, and the Fox are now called the Sac-and-Fox of the Mississippi in Iowa. The Fox, together with the Sauk and Kickapoo, speak dialects of a single Algonquian language conventionally called Sauk-Fox-Kickapoo.*

The linguistic and cultural similarities linking the Sauk, Fox, and Kickapoo indicate that these tribes, and perhaps the Mascouten, lived close together not long before European contact. More diffuse resemblances suggest that this grouping was once combined with the Shawnee. Vague traditions (see Marston 1912:146) and early cartographic data place the precontact Fox in southern Michigan. Northwest Ohio is another possible location. Some time before contact they were driven into Wisconsin by Iroquois or Iroquoian raids. At contact they were centered on the Wolf River in northeastern Wisconsin, ranging over an area that extended from Lake Superior to the Chicago River and from Lake Michigan to the Mississippi (fig. 1). About 1677 they moved south to the upper Fox River. In spite of extreme dislocations during their early eighteenth-century wars with the

French, the general direction of their movements was southwest, to the lower Wisconsin River and ultimately to Iowa where they settled along the western bank of the Mississippi. They remained there until the early nineteenth century. Since contact their total range has always included a prairie component, which dominated their habitat after they moved to Iowa.

External Relations

In overall cultural pattern the Fox and their cognate tribes had apparently moved away from a Shawnee-like Woodland culture and through adaptation to a prairie habitat were developing toward a configuration with strong Prairie Siouan affinities. Fox resemblances to the Iowa were particularly strong. An argument has sometimes been advanced (see Jones 1939:1–2, 7) that the strategies the Fox used to recoup their losses during the French wars introduced so much alien cultural material that continuity with their past is debatable. The evidence available does not support this view.

Relations with colonial powers varied. Almost from the beginning the French had difficulty controlling the Fox, who eagerly accepted trade relations but refused to settle near posts or missions. When some Foxes broke with this policy and moved to Detroit in 1712, the constant suspicion and mutual friction characterizing their relations with the French broke out into open warfare that continued for years, with brief intervals of relative peace. The courage of the Fox, the prohibitive cost of expeditions against them, and surreptitious aid from other tribes forced the French authorities to shift toward a strategy of accommodation and peace. Even then the Fox remained distrustful. The years of British rule were generally quiet. By the time the United States established its control in the Midwest, the Fox had given up warfare with colonial powers.

Component Groups

The Fox tribe was divided into loosely defined units that may be called bands or villages (Marston 1912:148). Such a group formed a summer village but broke up for part of the year and might join the rest of the tribe for the spring buffalo hunt before returning to its own settlement. Bands were apparently named after their leaders. Their

* The best orthography for Fox is that of Voorhis (1971), which cites earlier sources and is used in italicized words here, with the substitution of a raised dot for a colon as the mark of long vowels; the spellings have been checked by Ives Goddard.

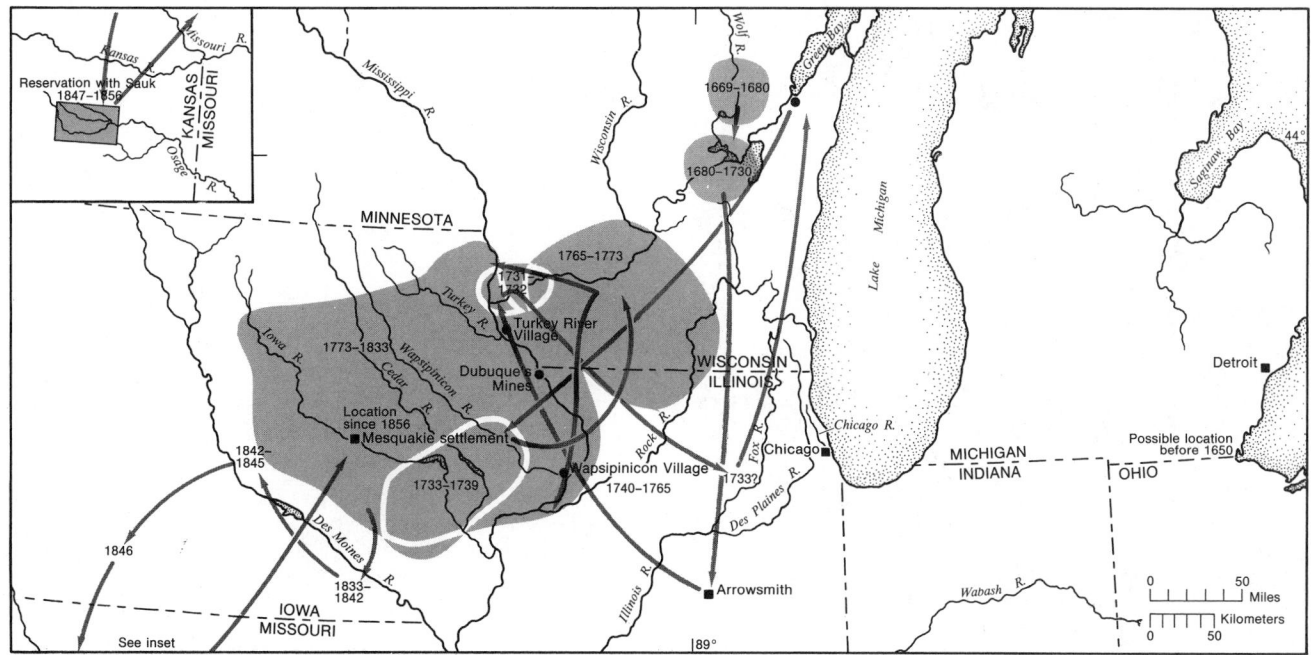

Fig. 1. Fox locations and movements, generalized. Some minor temporary settlements outside the areas indicated are not shown.

composition was fluid and evidence that they maintained their identities over long periods of time is lacking.

Culture

French reports about the Fox were abundant but say little about their culture. Detailed accounts were first produced in the early nineteenth century, particularly the decade 1820-1830. This outline is set in that period but supplements the contemporary accounts by projecting back data gathered in later years by anthropologists.

Subsistence

Fox economy combined hunting and agriculture. Annual tribal buffalo hunts ended in 1821 when these animals disappeared from Fox territory (Forsyth 1912:234). Subsistence hunting centered on deer, whose hides and tallow were also important trade articles (Marston 1912:150). Hunting and trapping were also undertaken for the fur trade. Fishing was negligible unless meat animals were scarce (Forsyth 1912:229). Women gathered nuts, berries, milkweed, honey, beeswax, and several tubers, but collecting had minor significance. In river-bottom fields near their villages women grew maize, beans, squash, pumpkins, and melons. Surface mining of lead ore for trade was also an important activity. These occupations were organized in a marked seasonal cycle (Forsyth 1912:233-234; Marston 1912:148-153; Tax 1955:243-244). In fall, after the harvest had been gathered and supplies obtained on credit from traders, the Fox left their villages and traveled by horse or canoe to their hunting grounds east of the Iowa-Missouri watershed.

There they broke up into small scattered groups for about two months of hunting. When winter set in they gathered into larger camps in sheltered river valleys. Traders visited the winter camps to collect for the goods they had provided in fall and to exchange cloth and ammunition for furs. Small parties of men went hunting again in early spring while their families remained in camp. When these hunters returned in April each band gathered to return as a group to its village. Crops were planted in May and June. Many men took part in summer hunts, while the rest of the tribe tended the fields or worked the lead mines. The hunters returned in August for the harvest.

Settlement Pattern

The Fox summer dwelling consisted of a pole scaffolding 40 to 60 feet long by 20 wide, covered with slabs of elm bark (Forsyth 1912:227). It housed an extended family (Marston 1912:176). These lodges were aligned east and west and arranged in two parallel rows separated by an open area used for dances, horse races, lacrosse games, and similar activities. Always built in river bottoms, with gardens nearby, and not too distant from higher ground where the graveyards were located, the summer villages were permanent settlements occupied until firewood became scarce or external causes forced their residents to move. The two largest villages in 1820 contained 35 and 20 lodges (Marston 1912:148).

Winter camps varied in size from one or two families through larger clusters up to an entire band. Their component dwellings were dome-shaped round or oval structures whose pole frameworks were covered with layers of cattail mats (figs. 2-3) (Forsyth 1912:227-228).

Fig. 2. Women engaged in domestic chores on a shaded work platform in front of a winter lodge covered with rush mats. Photographed at Tama, Iowa, probably about 1900.

Fig. 3. Mrs. Charles Keostak using a bone needle (see "Sauk," fig. 6) to make a cattail mat. Cloths decorated with ribbon appliqué hang on clothesline in background. Photograph by Huron H. Smith at Tama, Iowa, 1923.

Life Cycle

Births took place in small lodges set up for the occasion, where the mother and child were attended by other women and entirely isolated from contact with men (Jones 1939:62). After 10 days the mother returned to the family lodge at night but still ate in the birth lodge and observed many restrictions until after her first postparturital menstrual period. During this time she gave a small feast for elderly relatives of her infant, one of whom gave the child a name taken from the stock belonging to its father's clan and not held by any living person (Forsyth 1912:210). This name was apparently permanent. Men could take new names after going to war and women could do so after dreams, but these supplemented those given in infancy. They had no direct relationship to clan affiliation.

Physical punishment of children was rare (Marston 1912:165). The technique usually applied to correct misbehavior was fasting, a practice that was beneficial as well as corrective (Tax 1955:256). Boys of six or seven began hunting birds with a bow and otherwise imitating the activities of men (Marston 1912:165), while girls worked with their mothers. The physiological aspects of puberty were strongly emphasized for girls, who during their first menstruation retired for 10 days to a separate lodge where they were secluded from males and placed under restrictions that prevented their endangering themselves and other persons (Jones 1939:63-64; Tax 1955:275). Later menstrual periods required similar isolation (Marston 1912:170-172) but for briefer periods and entailing fewer restrictions. Puberty among boys was marked by the vision quest (Tax 1955:275-276). Girls also sought visions, but at home rather than in isolation;

and their search apparently had no connection with menstrual seclusion. Both sexes painted their faces with vermilion to indicate that they were adults (Forsyth 1912:236).

Courtship usually began before the age of 20 (Forsyth 1912:216; Marston 1912:165). After speaking to the girl in whom he was interested, a young man entered her family's lodge at night holding a piece of burning bark as a light (Jones 1939:55-56; Tax 1955:271-272). The couple held whispered conversations at her bedside. If they agreed to marry, the suitor stayed until morning, allowing her family to see him. A man could also use the girl's brother as a go-between (Marston 1912:166) or leave negotiations to his family (Forsyth 1912:214). Others forms of courtship, such as calling a young woman out by playing the lover's flute, were respectable only if she had been previously married. Marriage was validated by an exchange of gifts of equivalent value between the families (Jones 1939:56-57). Similar exchanges on a smaller scale continued as long as the union lasted. A married couple lived with the wife's parents for a period that usually ended after a year or the birth of their first child (Forsyth 1912:212). During this time their position was subordinate. When this phase ended they could remain on more equal terms, live with the husband's parents, or move to their own lodge. The Fox practiced

638

polygyny, usually in its sororal form (Marston 1912:166) but including most women of the wife's lineage in this definition (Tax 1955:274). Its frequency is uncertain.

Death was the most ritualized event in the life cycle, drawing the greatest public attention. A crier announced each death. Members of the deceased's clan came to the lodge for an all-night mourning ceremony. Burial was carried out by men whom a funeral director selected through a system of clan reciprocity (Jones 1939:69, 65). Scaffold burial was rare and perhaps confined to outsiders to avoid giving their tribes potential claims to land. Graves were grouped by clan and lineage, and oriented east and west with the corpse's feet toward the west. Extended burial was usual, although a seated position could be used for noted warriors. The corpse, dressed in its finest clothing (Marston 1912:172–173) and wrapped in bark or mats, was accompanied by a few grave goods, including food and water (Forsyth 1912:209). The director addressed it, advised it not to look back or envy those still alive, and sprinkled tobacco in the grave (Jones 1939:67). More tobacco was offered by the mourners as they filed past. Sometimes a warrior listed the enemies he had killed and offered their spirits to accompany the deceased. The grave was then filled and later covered with a small wooden shed. A post set at its head was painted to indicate the person's clan affiliation and any war honors. The burial attendants and surviving relatives divided the personal property of the deceased (Forsyth 1912:206–207, 212; Marston 1912:173; Jones 1939:65).

Mourning lasted from six months to a year or longer. It was most rigorous for surviving spouses and the parents of small children, especially those dying at birth. These persons had to show sorrow by an unkempt appearance, shabby clothing, abstention from dances and other amusements, and avoidance of laughter (Forsyth 1912:207–208; Jones 1939:69; Marston 1912:173). They observed many precautions to avoid endangering others. Thus, because the touch of their bare feet on the earth would cause drought, they wore moccasins at all times. Women in this condition refrained from agriculture and men from hunting. Neither sex attended clan rituals. Release from mourning behavior was probably effected by ceremonial adoption (Jones 1939:69). Although early nineteenth-century writers mention only the adoption of war captives (Forsyth 1912:197), ceremonial adoption within the tribe was almost certainly practiced. In the form consistently reported since the late nineteenth century (Jones 1939:65–66, 70; Tax 1955:260, 276–277) the Fox replaced each death by adopting another person, usually a friend of the deceased chosen by the surviving relatives. This person retained his or her own identity and did not change households. The adoption ceremony, held within four years of the death, included a feast, games and dances that were believed to be particularly enjoyed by the person it commemorated, and an exchange of gifts between the adoptee and the new relatives. This event

marked the formal end of mourning and also ensured that the deceased's ghost would not become a malevolent spirit.

Relatives held informal ghost feasts irregularly to commemorate individuals or groups (Jones 1939:66, 71–72). They served food and water and named all the persons for whom the event was held.

Social Organization

The Fox household was usually an extended family ranging in size from 5 to 30 persons, with 10 residents the average (Marston 1912:176). While the data suggest an emphasis on matrilocal residence and matrilocal extended families, at least in the summer villages, this was no more than a preference (Callender 1962:25). Like the Omaha, the Fox may have shifted their forms of residence seasonally, although the evidence for such a practice is not sufficient. Each household was an economic unit whose men hunted together while its women worked about the house (figs. 2, 4) or in the fields (Marston 1912:176). Lodges and their furnishings belonged to women, who were in charge of ordinary household activities (Forsyth 1912:218).

The kinship system, described by Tax (1955:247–258), was of Omaha type. The Fox also had a system of exogamous patrilineal clans. Forsyth's list (1912:192), which may be incomplete, names eight such units: Bear, Fox, Wolf, Swan, Partridge, Thunder, Elk, and Black Bass. This differs from later lists only in its omission of the Eagle and Kenwamewok clans, the last of which may not be of Fox origin (Callender 1962:27). Clans were conceptually kin groups, although apparently rather weak in this respect and less important than the lineages they included. They lacked control over land or other forms of productive property. Their corporate features were primarily ritual and centered on two related aspects (Tax 1955:262–266). First, each clan was a name group with exclusive rights to a stock of names referring to its eponym. This feature was explicitly recognized in Fox nomenclature: the term *mi·so·ni* means 'name' as well as 'clan' (Michelson 1927:122). Second, the Fox clan was a cult group whose members were organized around a sacred pack for which they presented semiannual ceremonies (Callender 1962:30–31). Each clan was descended in theory from a person who, seeking a vision, had been blessed by a spirit in the form of the eponym. This original vision included instructions for assembling the pack and directions for its ceremonies as well as its names. Through the names and the pack, the powers of the ancestral vision extended to all members of the clan and could be invoked through pack ritual.

The component lineages of a clan were named after varieties of the eponym. Thus, the Bear clan included Brown Bear and Black Bear lineages. Lineages were the primary vehicle for transmission of hereditary ritual positions and political offices (Callender 1962:26–28).

Fig. 4. Woman wearing silver brooches on cloth dress, making finger-woven yarn sash in doorway of a rush-covered winter lodge. Photograph by F.A. Rinehart at Tama, Iowa, about 1899.

They regulated secondary marriages. Widows and widowers were expected to replace their deceased spouses with members of the same lineages, unless specifically released from this obligation (Tax 1955:273-274, 280-281). Violations of this rule were collectively punished by women of the offended lineage, who destroyed the offender's property. A lineage was often a cult group centering on a sacred pack, with the clan pack being that of its dominant lineage.

The Fox tribe was split into two divisions, called ki·ško·ha and to·hka·na, symbolized by the colors white and black (Marston 1912:156; Tax 1955:268-269). Although these units functioned like moieties they were not descent groups, since siblings were assigned to alternate divisions according to their order of birth. The first child born to a couple belonged to the division of which its father was not a member, while the next child belonged to the father's division, and so on alternately. This method of assigning membership had the great advantage of producing units that remained approximately equal under any circumstances and cross-cut all other social groupings. The divisions organized people for games, ceremonies, dances, and warfare and provided the framework for the camp police (Jones 1939:81). Members of each division were expected to joke with those belonging to the other group. By structuring group competition within the tribe along lines that divided bands, clans, lineages, and families, the divisions probably inhibited tendencies toward cleavage.

Another type of social unit was the society, a loosely defined voluntary association formed for diverse purposes ranging from warfare to ritual (Callender 1962:31).

Societies could be temporary, dissolving when their ends had been achieved. Raiding parties are an example of this type. Those whose main purpose was ritual activity tended to be permanent. One example is the Midewiwin (Forsyth 1912:223-225). Another is associations formed by persons who had been blessed by the same spirits. The associations closely resembled the clan cults and sometimes acquired rudimentary traits of clans (Tax 1955:266).

Political Organization

The political structure of Fox society involved a division of functions between peace and war organizations (Callender 1962:13, 18; W.B. Miller 1955). Their membership tended to include the same persons, while their leaders differed. Each organization had its own paramount chief, lesser chiefs, and criers. The peace chief had nominal authority within the tribe under ordinary circumstances, but the mild nonaggressive behavior required by his office inevitably weakened his leadership. His role within the tribe was primarily a moderating and conciliatory one. He called meetings of the tribal council, presided at gatherings, and was very active in ritual. His property was customarily available to anyone in need. In return, he received furs and other gifts from members of the tribe. This process was too informal to be called redistribution. His assistant or crier made announcements, carried messages, and could serve as a speaker (Michelson 1927:1-50). In time of war or other conditions endangering the tribe or requiring strict control of its members, authority was transferred to the war organization, which had considerable power within a limited context. The war chief commanded the camp police, an organization of warriors that regulated tribal movements, patrolled camp grounds during buffalo hunts, and enforced decisions made by the tribal council (Marston 1912:163-164). Their right to destroy, without fear of retaliation, the property of anyone who disobeyed their orders let the camp police function effectively within the spheres where their role was acknowledged.

The office of peace chief was vested within a specific lineage, from which the tribal council selected a man to fill the position when it became vacant. Fox tradition holds that the peace chief historically came from the Bear clan (Jones 1939:82-83). The office has shifted around among lineages within this unit. When the chief was killed in 1829, a woman of the Black Bear lineage announced that a vision had given her the right to name the new chief. The council accepted her statement and she chose her brother's son. This lineage held the office until 1883, when the council transferred it to the Brown Bear lineage (fig. 5).

The process by which a war chief acquired his position involves difficult problems. A persistent Fox tradition holds that this position belonged to the Fox clan, which is almost always called War Chief, rather than Fox, and

U. of Okla. Lib., Western Hist. Coll., Norman.
Fig. 5. left, *pašito·ni·kwa* 'old man's (i.e., bear's?) eye', a member of the Brown Bear division of the Bear clan, born 1842, the last Fox chief recognized by the U.S. government, wearing a roach, bear-claw necklace, calico shirt, and blanket robe. right, Joe Tesson, an Iowa who acted as interpreter for Fox, dressed in Fox style with fur turban, bear-claw necklace, beaded bandolier bag on chest and another on right hip, beaded breechclout, leggings with beadwork garters, beaded moccasins, holding a ball-headed club. Photograph by F.A. Rinehart at Tama, Iowa, about 1899.

owns many names pertaining to war rather than to its eponym. The tradition may date from an earlier period when the functions of the war chief were primarily ritual in nature or involved supervising police duties within the tribe. In any case, by the early nineteenth century the office was achieved through consistently successful leadership of war parties and the incumbent's clan affiliation was not relevant.

The tribal council decided issues such as peace and war, the selection of winter hunting grounds, and general relations with other tribes. Very little is known about its composition. Forsyth's account (1912:186) suggests that membership in this group may also have been hereditary within specific lineages.

Within a society characterized by rather weak authority, the Fox nevertheless maintained reasonably effective social control. Forsyth (1912:187) noted that traders left their storerooms unlocked and unguarded without fear of theft. Apart from the rules enforced by the camp police, certain sanctions—especially those used against violators of the restrictions governing secondary marriages—were enforced by lineages (Jones 1939:84-85). The relatives of

a murderer's victim could accept compensation or insist on vengeance. Forsyth (1912:186-187) describes the course of vengeance as rare and says that it drew the intervention of the chiefs and council, although he does not describe their techniques. While affronts to constituted tribal authority or to a descent group usually drew collective action or the threat of this, personal wrongs were seldom avenged. Jones (1939:59-60) gives the case of a man whose divorced wife and her family refused to return a valuable horse that had been included in the gift exchange validating their marriage. Although he had the right to take it back forcibly, he instead resorted to the severest punishment he knew, having nothing more to do with them. Moreover, in spite of the severe penalties prescribed for adultery, this action seldom led to anything more extreme than divorce (Forsyth 1912:214, 218).

War

During the decade 1820-1830 only the continued interposition of the United States government prevented full-scale warfare with the Dakota (Forsyth 1912:184), whose hunting grounds the Fox were encroaching upon as they pushed up the Iowa rivers. Vengeance was another cause of hostilities. Retaliation for the killing of a Fox by members of another tribe might be averted if the offending group offered a payment of goods, but this practice of "covering the dead" canceled the offense only in theory and its effect was usually temporary. Another factor promoting warfare was the high status accorded to warriors. This was constantly instilled into boys (Forsyth 1912:194-197), who were eager to join raiding parties as soon as they reached the age of 16, or even earlier. The tribal council could try to prevent a raid of which it disapproved by giving the leader a horse or some other valuable property but had no other formal recourse if he refused the gift (Forsyth 1827). On the other hand, the leader of any war party that the council had not authorized was personally responsible for the losses it suffered in action.

A man wishing to lead a raid fasted to obtain a vision, which he related publicly (Forsyth 1912:194-196). Building a lodge outside the village, he hung up a strip of red cloth or a belt of wampum painted with vermilion. His followers enlisted by smoking with him and drawing the emblem through their hands. No particular ceremonies preceded the group's departure. The number of men it included depended on its leader's reputation and experience. Women occasionally accompanied their husbands on raids. Young men without previous experience were expected to cook, serve as sentries, and sleep on the outskirts of the group. The leader carried his sacred pack, which he kept at all times between his party and the enemy. When advancing toward the enemy, he led the group; returning, he brought up the rear. The power

Fig. 6. Nesouaquoit, a Fox chief, son of Chemakassee, visiting
Washington with a delegation including Keokuk and accompanied
by Black Hawk. The name is *ne·sawa·hkwatwa* 'he of the forked
tree', a Bear clan name (William Jones in McKenney and Hall
1933-1934, 1:315, phonemicized), so the connotation is 'bear in the
forks of a tree', which is the artist's translation. He wears a red-dyed
roach with eagle feather; a red and green finger-woven shawl around
his head; ear ornaments of red and white beads and bone hair pipes;
necklace of white, red, and black beads with a silver presidential
peace medal on a blue cord; brass arm rings with fur(?) pendant; red
wool and red, blue, and white beadwork belts with red and green
fringe; blue-edged red breechclout; red leggings with blue and green
decoration; fur garters with brass bells and triangular brown flaps
decorated with white and red beads or quills; a white furry anklet;
and plain brown moccasins. His face is painted red, yellow, and
black and his body red and yellow; he holds a metal trade tomahawk decorated with red feathers(?) and blue wrapping, and a blue-
lined red robe lies behind him. Painted by Charles Bird King in
1837.

inherent in his pack was his main contribution to the
project, and often he took no part in the actual fighting.

A defeated war party broke up, its members returning
individually. One that was successful returned in order
and stopped outside the village to send word of its
victory. Female relatives, especially their sisters' daughters, came out to strip the warriors of their ornaments and
blankets (Marston 1912:158). If the council agreed, a
dance was held in which the warriors were again joined

Fig. 7. Detail from a photograph of *ne·sawa·hkwatwa* (see fig. 6),
showing a complex headdress. Photograph probably by A. Zeno
Shindler in Washington, D.C., 1858.

by their nieces. After this celebration, members of the
party spent a brief period observing major restrictions,
such as celibacy. Less rigorous observances were required
for a year.

Prisoners whose age or infirmity would delay the trip
back were usually killed (Forsyth 1912:197). Those who
reached the village alive were safe and were usually
adopted at once. Women were incorporated through
marriage, but males were considered outsiders until they
proved their new loyalty by joining a war party.

Religion

The Fox universe was divided into Upper (sky) and
Lower (under the earth) regions, sometimes described as
good and evil respectively. Ruling the Upper region and
located at the zenith was the Great or Gentle Manitou
(Forsyth 1912:222-223). Other important manitous or
spirits were identified with the four directions. The sun
had the east. The culture hero and creator *wi·sahke·ha*
lived in the north, and his younger brother *ki·ya·pa·hte·ha*
ruled over the spirits of the dead in the west. The great
manitou of the south was *ša·wano·ha,* who controlled the
Thunderers. The earth, *mesahkamikohkwe·wa,* was also
important (Jones 1939:12-13, 20). There were lesser
spirits in infinite numbers. Most spirits personified na-

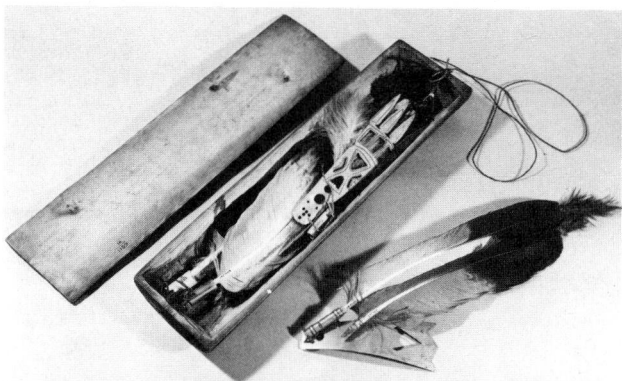

Mus. of the Amer. Ind., Heye Foundation, New York: 14/1189, 14/1201-1207.
Fig. 8. Box with parts of roach headdresses: bone and metal roach spreaders, eagle feathers with bone and metal sockets. Length of box about 40 cm; collected at Tama, Iowa, before 1925.

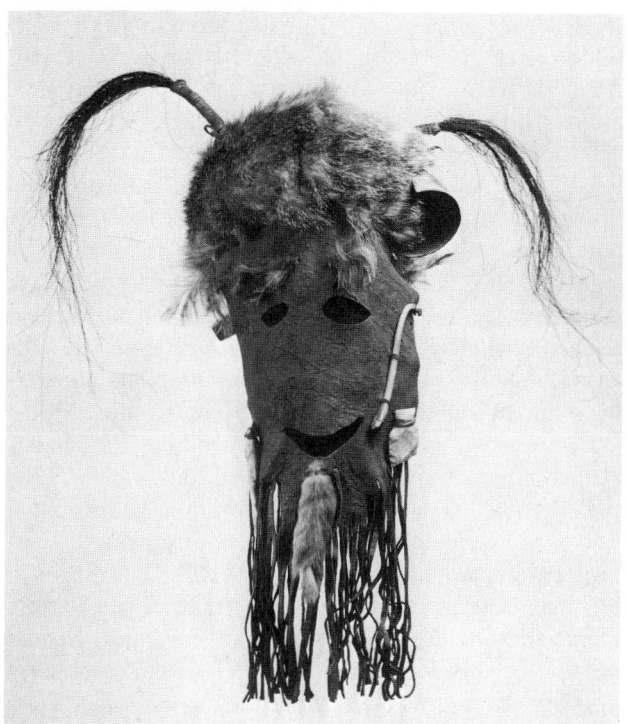

Mus. of the Amer. Ind., Heye Foundation, New York: 4/3789.
Fig. 9. Mask used in the Crawling Around Man Dance, of fur, green-painted leather, feathers, hair, bone, flaked stone point, and horn (at upper right). Length about 43.3 cm; collected by Truman Michelson at Tama, Iowa, before 1916.

ture, ordering the universe and relating it to the tribe. Thus, the Fox were the maternal aunts and uncles of the culture hero and the grandchildren of the earth and everything that grew on her.

To achieve contact with the supernatural the Fox prescribed actions that attracted the attention of manitous, placed them under obligation, and aroused their pity. Four practices were particularly important. Blackening one's face with charcoal invoked the spirit of fire, a messenger to the manitous. Fasting purified one. Wailing gained the manitous' attention and also made one pitiable. Smoking or offering tobacco was perhaps the most important. The manitous desired tobacco above anything else, could obtain this only from humans, and were thus both pleased and obligated. These observances characterized even ordinary life but had paramount importance in the individual vision quest and in organized sacred-pack ceremonies (Michelson 1925, 1925c, 1925d, 1927, 1930, 1937).

Behavior foreshadowing the vision quest began in childhood, at first limited to brief periods but eventually leading up to the crucial quest at puberty. A Fox who experienced an intense vision assembled a pack that embodied the power granted in the vision and could be drawn upon for this purpose. Certain persons received very powerful multiple blessings from several manitous, whose benefits extended beyond the original questors to their lineages and clans and in some respects to the tribe. The packs attributed to these elaborate visions belonged to descent groups whose members could draw on their powers as long as the packs were properly maintained and their rituals performed.

Two ceremonies were held annually for each major pack. The small winter ceremony lacked dancing. The larger and more elaborate summer ritual included a feast, dances, songs, and prayers, as well as exhortations and an account of the original vision and the history of the pack. This ceremony was a ratification of the original agreement, reminding the manitous of their promises and explaining their own obligations to the assembled members of the group. It also reestablished an exchange of gifts between both parties.

History

Allouez (JR 50:288-289, 51:42-45) met some Foxes during his mission at Chequamegon between 1665 and 1667. Soon after this, the new post at Green Bay drew the tribe to the Wolf River (Bacqueville de la Potherie 1911-1912, 1:317-319). Traders who visited their village found very few metal tools—only five or six hatchets in the entire tribe and no more than one knife to a lodge. The fur trade and the new goods it introduced eventually transformed Fox economy and material culture.

Several factors soon caused conflict with the French. The Fox opposed extending the fur trade to their Dakota enemies (Kellogg 1925:267, 275; Bacqueville de la Potherie 1911-1912, 2:17-20, 28-30) and disliked the French policy of repressing intertribal warfare in Wisconsin (Bacqueville de la Potherie 1911-1912, 1:357-362). They were also responding to overtures from the Iroquois, who wanted to establish trade relations with them (Bacqueville de la Potherie 1911-1912, 2:54, 104-105). Friction turned into open warfare in 1712 after a party of Foxes and Mascoutens moved to Detroit. Claiming that they planned to destroy that post, its commander incited a coalition of other tribes to attack the Foxes, who withstood a siege of 19 days, twice attempting to make peace (Dubuisson in WHC 16:267–287; Léry in WHC 16: 293–295). They escaped under cover of a storm but were pursued and fought another four days. The warriors who surrendered were burned. Those who made their way back to Wisconsin joined the rest of their tribe in disruptive attacks on traders that forced the French authorities to send an army against them in 1716 (Kellogg 1925:282, 286–288). After a three-day siege of their main village, the Fox agreed to peace on terms that seemed severe but were obviously not enforceable. Wittry's (1963) excavation of this site provides data illustrating changes in Fox material culture since contact.

Discovering that the Fox were assembling an alliance against them, the French reopened the war in 1728 (Kellogg 1925:316–318). The policy they had adopted was one of genocide, explicitly aimed at solving the Fox problem by wiping out the tribe (WHC 17:21) through inciting incessant attacks on them by other tribes. Besides their traditional Chippewa and Dakota enemies, the Fox became involved in major conflicts with the Ottawa, Potawatomi, and Wyandot while their Winnebago, Kickapoo, and Mascouten allies went over to the French. In 1730 a large group of Foxes set out to take refuge with the Seneca, among whom part of the tribe had been living since at least 1712 (Dubuisson in WHC 16:268; Hunter 1956). They were overtaken south of Lake Michigan (fig. 10). The events that followed closely paralleled those at Detroit 17 years earlier: a long siege, attempted escape during a storm at night, and discovery (WHC 17: 109–118). Although the French commanders reported the complete annihilation of the Fox, they again regrouped in Wisconsin. Weakened by extreme losses and under constant attack from Indians allied with the French, the surviving Foxes took refuge with the Sauk at Green Bay in 1733 and offered to surrender. Embarrassed by the persistence of a tribe whose destruction it had several times publicly announced, the French authorities decided that the Fox should be killed or sent as slaves to the West Indies (WHC 17:182–183). The Sauk refused to surrender the Fox, and the commander of the army sent to collect them was killed trying to force his way into the village (WHC 17:188–191). After a battle the two tribes fled to Iowa. An expedition sent against them failed ludicrously (WHC 17:200–203). In 1737 the French government ended the Fox wars by granting them and the Sauk a general pardon (WHC 17:255–260).

Skeptical, but now strengthened by their Sauk alliance, the Fox returned to Wisconsin, where they still lived when visited in 1766 by Carver (1778:48–50) and in 1773 by Pond (1933:42). Late in the eighteenth century they moved to the Iowa side of the Mississippi. Like most of the Sauk they remained neutral during the so-called Black Hawk War, but the United States forced them to cede land as reparations in 1832. After further cessions in

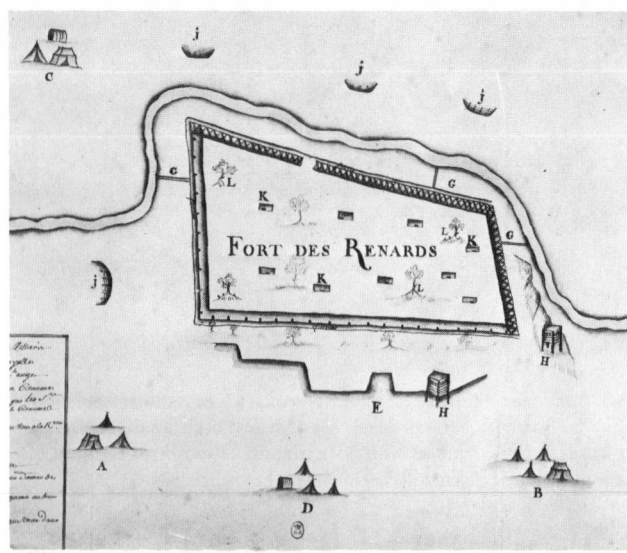

Fig. 10. Fox fort, perhaps near present Arrowsmith, Ill., attacked in Aug. and Sept. 1730 by the French and Indians under French commanders. The quadrilateral fort, covering about half a hectare, is shown with a stockade on two sides and ditches on the other two; covered paths open into the ditches and run to the river (G). Inside the fort are 9 subterranean lodges (K) and 6 trees (L) left to provide shade. Outside are the attackers' camps (A, Miamis, Potawatomis, Sauks, Kickapoos, Mascoutens; B, Miamis; C, French and Illinois; D, Weas), temporary besieging tower (H), guard posts (J), and trench (E). A contemporary French drawing.

1837 and 1842 both tribes were assigned a reservation in Kansas.

Serious friction with the Sauk was evident as early as 1843 (Fallers 1960:66–67; Hagan 1958:207–209). It involved several issues, particularly the government's alliance with Keokuk, whom it had appointed chief of the Sauk and allowed to distribute the annuity payments for both tribes. The Fox were also dissatisfied with reservation conditions such as epidemics, lack of game, and poor crops (Rebok 1901; D.Ward 1906) and feared a further move to Oklahoma. During the 1850s they returned to Iowa. In 1856 they obtained an act from the state legislature legalizing their residence there. In 1857 five members of their tribal council purchased 80 acres of land in Tama County with $1,000, raised by contributing annuity payments and by selling horses and jewelry. Many details of these events are unclear. Several sources (Ferris 1910:345, 359; Jones 1907:35–37) attribute the Fox actions to resentment over the agent's deposition of their chief, which actually occurred later, in 1859. Ferris (1910:359) and Hagan (1958:232–233) accept the Agency's argument that those who returned to Iowa were only a faction. Yet the circumstantial accounts by Rebok (1901) and D. Ward (1906) describe a tribal movement, extending over several years, planned and led by the traditional organization of the Fox tribe. Their view is corroborated by Fox genealogies indicating that the leaders in this process were descended from early nineteenth-century chiefs and councilors. Although the legal safeguards with which the Fox had surrounded themselves prevented their forcible removal from Iowa, the government tried to force them into returning to Kansas by cutting off their annuities. In 1867 it capitulated, resuming the payments and appointing an agent in Iowa.

In 1955 the Fox numbered 653, of whom about 500 lived on the Mesquakie Settlement, near Tama, or close enough to take active part in community life (fig. 12) (Callender 1955). Although urban employment had become important, it usually took the form of commuting to nearby cities. Additional purchases of land since 1857 had brought the tribal holdings up to 3,300 acres (Tax and Stanley 1960:285). Formerly the Bureau of Indian Affairs paid state taxes on the land, but after 1930 the tribe took over this responsibility, renting 500 acres to a local farmer and using this income for the purpose (Rietz 1960:105). Tribal ownership of the Fox land prevented allotment and inhibited other techniques of forcible acculturation. The Fox preserved their tribal community and retained much of their traditional culture (Callender 1962:85–89; Fallers 1960; Gearing 1970; Peattie 1960; Rietz 1960). Fox was still the language used in the home. Most of the tribe took part in clan-organized ritual

centering on sacred packs. A few Foxes were exclusively Christian or Native American Church members; and a larger number, mostly women, attended church services as well as pack ceremonies. The clan system also persisted, but a series of adaptations designed to maintain traditional ritual had turned these units into cult groups without significance apart from ritual and naming (Tax 1955:262–266). The dual division continued without significant change. The Fox maintained their traditional tribal government until 1937, when they adopted a new constitution under the Indian Reorganization Act that replaced the hereditary chief and his appointed council with an elected business council. However, one faction still recognized the hereditary chief.

Population

Most early estimates of the Fox population are untrustworthy, while later figures often fail to distinguish them from the Sauk. The best-informed estimates from the early nineteenth century fall between Forsyth's (1822) 1,600 and Marston's (1912:148) 1820 guess of 2,000. By 1867, when reliable figures became available, the Fox numbered only 264 (ARCIA 1867). Since then they have increased, slowly at first but later expanding rapidly. By 1932 there were 403 (ARCIA 1932), and in 1955, 653 (Callender 1955).

Synonymy†

The Fox name for themselves, *meškwahki·haki* (pl.) 'Red-Earths', is relatively infrequent but appears in the literature in several variants, for example, Mechecaukis (Schoolcraft 1851–1857, 3:554), Mechecouakis (W.

† The synonymy was edited by Ives Goddard, who also provided some of the material in it.

© Natl. Geographic Soc., Washington, D.C.

Fig. 11. Kenneth Blackbird, aged 3, next to seated male dancers, all in powwow costumes. Photograph by J. Baylor Roberts at Tama, Iowa, 1938.

NAA, Smithsonian: U. of Chicago Fox Project Coll.

Fig. 12. Jimmy Morgan auctioning off a box lunch at a "box social" to raise money for the All-American Legion Post, a Fox veterans' club at Tama, Iowa. Photographed in 1952 or 1953.

Tama News-Herald, Tama, Iowa.
Fig. 13. Mesquakie Day Care Center of Tama, Iowa, with the director, Alma Ward. Traditional baby hammocks are installed in two of the cribs. Photograph by Ron Slechta, Nov. 1974.

Smith 1765:69), Meskwaki (D. Ward 1906), Mesquakie (Polgar 1960), Miscouaguis (Coxe 1741a:map), Misquachki (Zeisberger and Senseman 1912:77), Muskwaki (McGee 1898), and Musquakies (Busby 1886). A set of names, ultimately based on *meškwahki·haki* but immediately derived from Seneca *haskwáhkihah* (Chafe 1967:80), included forms such as Squaghkies (Stone 1838, 2:4), Squatchegas (New York (State) Secretary of State 1887:300), and Squawkihow (Hewitt 1910f:630–631). These denoted the Foxes living among the Seneca (Hunter 1956). The Menominee name *meskwahki·y* (Bloomfield 1962:265) is a borrowing from Fox. George Croghan's Masquitamis (IHC 11:494–495) and Musquattimies (Thwaites 1904–1907, 1:139) refer to the Mascouten rather than the Fox.

The Ojibwa name *otaka·mi·k* (pl.) 'people of the other shore' (Jones 1911:741) is one of the earliest and most widespread names attached to the Fox. Its standard form, Outagami, first appeared in Claude Allouez's 1667 report (JR 51:42–45) and was used by most seventeenth-century French writers. Variants include O-dug-am-eeg (Warren 1885:33), Odugamies (Warren 1885:242), Ontagamies (Schoolcraft 1851–1857, 5:184), Ottigaumies (Carver 1778:48), Outagamie (P.V. Lawson 1900), Outigamis (Nuttall 1821:184), and Outouagamis (Hennepin 1880: 117). This also is found as a second Menominee name *ota·ka·me·w,* which Bloomfield (1962:312) calls foreign, without explanation.

The most common name for the Fox, in English, French, or other Indian languages is a word meaning 'fox'. The earliest known reference to them uses their Huron name Skenchiohronon, 1640 (JR 18:234; cf. Potier 1920:155), also attested in the locative form Sken°chioę, 1653 (JR 38:180), which Gatschet's Wyandot data show to mean 'red-fox people' (Mooney and Thomas 1907f:474). A 1673 reference to the Ouagoussac

(JR 58:41) is ambiguous, denoting either the tribe or its Fox clan (*wa·koše·haki* 'foxes'). Jones (1911:741) reports a tradition that the name originated through such a confusion. The French name Renards (*renard* 'fox') was used in addition to Outagamis by Jacques DuChesneau in 1681 (Margry 1876–1886, 2:267) and became the standard eighteenth-century French name. English borrowed the French name, sometimes as Reynards (NYCD 13:437), and this was eventually replaced by its translation 'Fox'. The Spanish name Rencor (Houck 1909, 1:146) may be a corruption of the French. Other names for the Fox with the same literal meaning are Winnebago *wašéreké* (Kenneth Miner, personal communication 1974), spelled O-sher-a-ca by Morse (1822:21), Shawnee *mškwaʔki·θilenawe,* literally 'red-fox (*mškwaʔki·θa*) person' not 'red-earth person' (Voegelin 1938–1940, 9:364), and Potawatomi *wakwšᵉe* (Gatschet 1878–1893:26, phonemicized). Related in some way to the Winnebago name, but not meaning 'fox', is the Dakota name *bešdéke* (Riggs 1852:34, normalized), also recorded as Mich-endick-er (Morse 1822:21), and Messenacks and Messenecqz (Hennepin 1903:278, 1880:117).

The three types of names are found together in a French account of events of 1683 in which the Outagami are said to be of two *extractions,* the Terre-Rouge 'Red-Earth' and the Renards 'Foxes' (Bacqueville de la Potherie 1911–1912, 1:360). These may have been two factions or, as Goddard (1975a) suggests, moieties. Eighteenth-century New York sources give the English names for these groups, adapted from Iroquoian, as Quacksis 'Renards' and Scungsicks 'Terre-Rouge' (NYCD 5:791; Colden 1747:xvi).

The Illinois name, attested as pac8kimina and pac8askimina (Le Boullenger in Belting 1958:288), is of uncertain etymology.

For variants of names for Sauk that are applied also to the Fox, see synonymy in "Sauk," this volume.

Sources

Bacqueville de la Potherie (1911–1912), who obtained valuable firsthand information from Nicolas Perrot, is the main source for the Fox during the contact period. Material from the early nineteenth century includes the excellent ethnography by Thomas Forsyth (1912), the agent for the Fox and Sauk from 1812 to 1827, and a briefer but important account by Marston (1912). Anthropological studies began in the late nineteenth century with William Jones, himself a Fox; his texts (1907) have great value, but his ethnography (1939), posthumously published, is disappointing. Michelson's (1925, 1925c, 1925d, 1927, 1930, 1937:79–118) texts about Fox religion are valuable raw data. Tax (1955) published the basic study of Fox social organization. About the same time Joffe (1940) described the Fox from the standpoint of acculturation. Results of extensive fieldwork carried out between 1948 and 1957 by students under Tax's supervision are available (Gearing 1970; Gearing, Netting, and Peattie 1960; Polgar 1960; W.B. Miller 1955). The main treatments of Fox history are Kellogg's (1908, 1925), excellent in quality but concentrating on the colonial period, and Temple's (1958:83-125). Although little is known about their culture during the eighteenth century, the Fox are by far the best known Central Algonquian tribe. On the other hand, the abundance of unusually rich material on this group has not yet been brought together into a comprehensive ethnography.

Sauk

CHARLES CALLENDER

Language, Territory, and Environment

The Sauk (sôk) call themselves *asa·ki·waki*. This name has often but erroneously been interpreted as meaning 'Yellow Earths' corresponding to 'Red Earths' for the Fox (see Forsyth 1912:183). Although the terminology established by the United States government treats the Sauk and the Fox as a single unit, these tribes, while very similar in culture and often closely associated, have been quite distinct since their recorded history began. From 1733 until about 1850 they were linked by a formal alliance that never became a union. The Sauk consist of two groups that are politically and administratively distinct. Their so-called Missouri band broke away from the rest of the tribe in the early nineteenth century and acquired official recognition by the government as a separate body known as the Sac-and-Fox of the Missouri, while the other Sauk as well as the Fox tribe were called Sac-and-Fox of the Mississippi. The Missouri band was eventually given a reservation in Kansas. Many of its members transferred their affiliation to the main tribe during the period when they also lived in Kansas, but the rest remained separate, staying behind when the Sauk proper moved on to Oklahoma. The Sauk spoke a dialect of the same Algonquian language used by the Kickapoo and Fox.*

The Sauk once lived considerably southeast of northern Wisconsin, where they were established at the time of contact, describing themselves as refugees from Iroquois attacks. An old tradition places their precontact home in the Saginaw valley (Marston 1912:146). Considerable linguistic and cultural evidence indicates that they were once united with the Fox and Kickapoo and that all three tribes had been in close contact with the Shawnee even earlier; however, unlike these southern tribes, Sauk culture exhibited certain northern traits, such as the use of the canoe. The Green Bay region remained their center from the contact period until 1733, when their protection of the Fox involved them in war with the French and both tribes moved to eastern Iowa (fig. 1). They later

---

* Little work has been done on the Sauk dialect, but what is known of it seems to indicate that the same orthography can be used for it as for Fox—Voorhis (1971), which is converted to *Handbook* standards by substituting a raised dot for a colon as the mark of long vowels. Ives Goddard has checked the spellings used here.

returned to Wisconsin, settling along the lower Wisconsin river. Before the end of the eighteenth century the Sauk had established themselves along the Mississippi in Iowa and northern Illinois, with their center at the confluence of the Rock River and the Mississippi. Like the related Fox and Kickapoo tribes, their postcontact movements thus involved a shift from a woodland to a prairie habitat.

External Relations

Sauk culture was related most closely to that of the Fox, with the Kickapoo and Potawatomi more divergent but still very similar. They were tied to the Fox by common cultural institutions and language, frequent intermarriage, and for a time, formal political alliance (Forsyth 1912:232-233). In early postcontact times they were also closely linked with the Potawatomi (JR 51:43), whom Perrot (1911:270) described as half-Sauk. Like the Fox, they were bitterly hostile to the Illinois tribes (Forsyth 1912:184, 202). After settling on the Mississippi their main enemies were the Osage and Dakota.

The Sauk maintained fairly good relations with the French until their championship of the Fox provoked a brief period of hostilities. They were on friendly terms

Fig. 1. Sauk locations and movements.

with the English. After the establishment of American rule the Sauk were consistently divided between a hostile faction and one that was either friendly or neutral.

Culture

The most complete descriptions of Sauk culture are contained in a series of accounts (Forsyth 1912; Galland 1869; Marston 1912) that generally fall into the decade 1820–1830, the period to which this outline pertains. These accounts also describe the Fox, who shared a common culture with the Sauk. The persistent cultural conservatism of the Fox and the extensive anthropological studies carried out among them combine to make their variant of this culture by far the better known. Rather than repeat material already included in the outline of Fox culture, the following sketch concentrates on aspects of Sauk culture that diverge from Fox forms and those where information about the Sauk is more abundant.

Subsistence

Subsistence activities among the Sauk and their seasonal organization into an annual cycle were practically identical with those of the Fox, combining hunting and trapping with agriculture and gathering. Apparently the surface mining of lead more directly concerned the Fox, but it also engaged Sauks who lacked horses for the summer hunt or when the harvest failed (Marston 1912:153; Forsyth 1822). Although some smelting was done, most of the ore was sold to traders. This activity centered at Dubuque's Mines in Iowa and at several sites in northwest Illinois. The animals most important to the trading sector of Sauk economy were deer, raccoons, muskrats, and beaver (Marston 1912:151). Besides furs and hides, the Sauk procured deer tallow, feathers, and beeswax and sold maize. Marston estimated that Sauk women had over 300 acres under cultivation at their main

U. of Okla. Lib., Western Hist. Coll., Norman.

Fig. 3. A Sauk summer lodge, covered with bark. Seated third from left (R.E. Cunningham 1957:62) is the chief Pashipaho (*pašipaho·ha* 'little stabber, gigger' or perhaps *pe·šipahowa* 'he touches lightly in passing', William Jones in C. Thomas 1910a, phonemicized). Photograph by William S. Prettyman in Indian Territory about 1885–1890.

village, producing 7,000–8,000 bushels of maize annually, of which over 1,000 bushels were sold to traders and others.

Settlement Pattern

The Sauk practiced the usual alternation between summer residence in river-bottom villages and fall and winter residence in hunting camps (Marston 1912:148–152). Their most outstanding difference from neighboring groups was the practice of assembling almost the entire tribe into a single summer village. Carver (1778:46–47) in 1766 described the Sauk village, which contained about 90 bark-covered longhouses, as "the largest and best built Indian town" he ever saw; he was struck by its "regular and spacious" streets. Their early nineteenth-century center, Saukenak, near the present site of Rock Island, similarly impressed observers (Hagan 1958:5–6). It contained 100 lodges, and its total population probably ranged between 2,000 and 3,000.

Social Organization

Forsyth (1912:190–191) lists 12 clans: Bald Eagle, Bear, Bear Potato, Black Bass, Deer, Great Lake, Panther, Ringed Perch, Sturgeon, Swan, Thunder, and Wolf. These units were exogamous and patrilineal. The lineages that they subsumed may have been named after varieties of the clan eponym like those of the Fox, but evidence is lacking. Conceptual kin groups that regulated important aspects of marriage, Sauk clans also governed the inheritance of those political offices that were included in the peace organization (Hewitt 1910:478). The paramount tribal chief was drawn from the Sturgeon clan, and lesser chiefs from other clans. The most important functions and corporate features of Sauk clans were ritual in nature, centering on semiannual ceremonies for the

Okla. Histl. Soc., Oklahoma City.

Fig. 2. Sauk summer lodges, covered with bark (and rush mat at right), with arbor porch. Photograph taken in 1879 in Indian Territory (now Okla.).

sacred packs attached to them and on stocks of personal names (Forsyth 1912:210; Hewitt 1910:478-479). As among the Fox, this emphasis on the ritual aspects of clans occasionally led to religious societies acquiring rudimentary clan features (Callender 1962:31).

The Sauk had a dual division consisting of units called *ki·ško·ha* and *aškaša,* symbolized by white and black. The precise rules for affiliating individuals with these groups are uncertain. Marston (1912:156-157), who described them as organizations of warriors, reported that the first son born to a couple was a *ki·ško·ha*, the second son an *aškaša,* and so on alternately. Forsyth (1912: 192-194), on the other hand, said that the oldest son belonged to the same division as his father and the next son to the opposite division. Later studies of the Sauk (Harrington 1914:131; Hewitt 1910:478; Skinner 1923-1925, 1:12) disagreed with these reports and with one another. Probably the older system followed the same rules as the Fox, which are easily misinterpreted; but by the middle of the twentieth century Sauk practice assigned the firstborn child to the *aškaša* and the second to the *ki·ško·ha*. All the systems reported for the Sauk would produce the same effect, assigning siblings to alternate divisions according to their order of birth.

Political Organization

The Sauk divided political functions between peace and war organizations. Their peace organization articulated closely with the clan system, including a paramount chief as well as others of lesser rank (Marston 1912:154-155, 157). These offices were inherited within specific clans. Criers or ceremonial runners had important roles in the political system, announcing decisions, serving as messengers for the chiefs and tribal council, and sometimes acting as speakers (Forsyth 1912:186, 234). One or more of these officials was attached to each chief.

Forsyth (1912:186) specifically denied that women could hold the office of chief or exercise its functions. Yet as individuals or collectively they could take actions that may be described as political. Thus, Black Hawk (1955:107-108) noted that the women of his band supported his policies; and on one occasion the elderly daughter of a former chief was chosen to address an

American commander about the treaty of 1804 (Black Hawk 1955:112; Hagan 1958:130).

The Sauk apparently recognized two war chiefs, one associated with the warriors belonging to the *ki·ško·ha* division and the other with those who were *aškaša* (Forsyth 1912:192-194; Marston 1912:156-157). The former had the higher status. In dealing with agencies of the United States, war chiefs usually overshadowed the peace chiefs. This could reflect the differences in their roles and in the behavior considered appropriate to each. Yet the role of war chiefs among the Sauk was changing during the early nineteenth century (Forsyth 1912:186). Men without antecedents obtained power through their own ability, first overshadowing the hereditary chiefs and eventually replacing them. The archetype of this kind of war chief was Keokuk, who by a combination of effective oratory, shrewd manipulation, and astuteness in dealing with representatives of the United States, acquired power, later increased this by obtaining control of the tribal annuity payments, and finally was vested by the United States with tribal chieftainship. Forsyth (1822), while agent for both tribes, hoped vainly that the Fox war chief would follow a similar course.

In spite of basic similarities between the two tribes, Sauk political organization was notably more complex (Forsyth 1912:226), perhaps because their settlement pattern required this. The Fox were divided into several village-bands, which often acted independently although the chief of one of these units was recognized as tribal chief. Under normal circumstances, Sauk bands emerged as important units only in winter, while in summer their identities were submerged through common residence in a single large town (Forsyth 1822). In 1821 Forsyth reported that the Sauk chiefs asked his aid in forcing the residents of a small splinter village to return to Saukenak. In discussing political organization he wrote: "It is surprising to me that there should be such a wide difference in the characters of the Two Nations. The Foxes have no kind of system in any of their arrangements as respects their Nation, and when any way embarrassed they always claim assistance of the Sauks to help them out of their difficulties" (Forsyth 1822). Yet the relatively loose tribal organization of the Fox may have had advantages, since they avoided the extreme factional disputes that repeatedly split the Sauk.

A further difference from the Fox is evident in the growing role of American authority within the Sauk political system between 1820 and 1830. Rock Island, which included a fort and garrison as well as the Agency for both tribes, was the main focus of this influence. Throughout the decade, the Agency aggrandized more authority. Beginning with the regulation of intertribal relations, it gradually took over more authority in internal affairs. This situation was facilitated by the agent's ability to make arrests, his control over the essential

Mus. of the Amer. Ind., Heye Foundation, New York: 2/5717.
Fig. 4. Wooden ladle used in the Midewiwin ceremony, with Indian-mended bowl. Length about 39 cm; collected before 1911.

Fig. 5. Sauk chief Pashipaho (standing), and council seated on rush mats in front of a winter lodge. Photograph by William S. Prettyman in Indian Territory about 1885.

services of the government blacksmith (Marston 1912: 179), and his alliance with collaborators such as Keokuk, whose position he was able to bolster.

History

Sauk visits to the Chequamegon post were reported in 1667 by Allouez (in JR 51:45), who characterized this tribe as very numerous but scattered and wandering. This last information was almost certainly faulty, since the French who went to Green Bay in 1668 found the Sauk settled there. When the Fox moved to this area they sent messengers to the Sauk, who became their intermediaries with the French during the early years of the fur trade (Bacqueville de la Potherie 1911–1912, 1:303, 317–319).

During the Fox wars the Sauk remained on good terms with the French, while often surreptitiously aiding the

Fig. 6. Bone needles used for making rush mats (see "Fox," fig. 3). Length of one at top 15.5 cm; collected in Okla. before 1910.

Fox (Dubuisson in WHC 16:281, 17:111–112). In 1733 the largest Fox remnant took refuge with the Sauk, whom they asked to intercede with the French and arrange their surrender. Nicolas-Antoine Coulon de Villiers, the elder, the newly appointed commander for Green Bay, brought an army of 60 French and 200 Indians to carry out the final destruction of the Fox (Kellogg 1925:331–332). When the Sauk chiefs refused to set a date for delivering the Fox to him, Villiers led a small party to their village and attempted to force his way in. He and several followers were killed. The Sauk and Fox fled, fought off an attack by the French army, and made their way without further interference to Iowa, where they successfully resisted a punitive expedition (Kellogg 1925:334–335). In 1737 the French government accepted face-saving pleas from other tribes and forgave the Sauk and Fox. In spite of this new policy, the Sauk refused to return to Green Bay. Some settled on the Rock River, while most of the tribe moved to the lower Wisconsin (Carver 1778:46–47; Pond 1933:40–42). Late in the eighteenth century all the Sauk established themselves along the Mississippi between the Rock and the Des Moines rivers.

In 1804 at Saint Louis a small party of Sauks was induced to sign a treaty exchanging all the Sauk and Fox lands in Illinois, Wisconsin, and Missouri for goods valued at $2,234.50 and an annuity consisting of goods worth $1,000. Later they claimed that this transaction had been misrepresented to them as involving a much smaller area (Black Hawk 1955:54). The tribal council, which alone had the authority to sell land, refused to accept the treaty as valid. Although the Sauk were eventually forced to acknowledge it, the 1804 treaty

651

Natl. Coll. of Fine Arts, Smithsonian.

Fig. 7. Nah-wee-re-coo, wife of Keokuk. With jaws, hair part, and neck painted red, she wears silver ear ornaments, black cloth blouse covered with two sizes of silver brooches, brass bracelets and finger rings, pink flowered shawl, red skirt with ribbon appliqué borders, red leggings edged with white beads, and decorated buckskin moccasins. Painted by George Catlin in fall 1835 at Keokuk's camp on the Des Moines River.

continued to disturb their relations with the United States.

Some Sauks joined Tecumseh's movement (Black Hawk 1955:58-60), but most of them held aloof. They sided with the British during the War of 1812, sending their noncombatants to join the Missouri band, now practically independent, which had chosen neutrality. Although the Sauk defeated an American attack on Saukenak, their military successes were canceled when the English concluded peace and abandoned their Indian allies. In the treaty of 1816 that followed, they confirmed the treaty of 1804; yet Black Hawk (1955:87), who signed it, insisted that he had not been told of this provision. The Fox made the same charge about a similar treaty they had signed in 1815. During the years that followed, the Sauk divided into two parties. One group, called the British band, was hostile to the United States and refused to accept the treaty of 1804. Its effective leader was the

warrior Black Hawk. The peace party was led by Keokuk, who followed a policy of accommodation.

The 1804 treaty allowed the Sauk use of all the ceded lands until their sale by the government; however, by 1828 both the secretary of war and the state governor were demanding that all Indians leave Illinois (Hagan 1958:107). American squatters occupied Saukenak during the winter hunt of 1828-1829. Some of the Sauk decided to stay in Iowa. The rest, returning to their village, met constant harassment from the squatters, who destroyed lodges, appropriated fields, sold whiskey, and filed fraudulent claims against the tribe for damage to property. In 1831 the Sauk withdrew into Iowa to avoid a confrontation with the state militia. Many remained there. However, the British band returned to Illinois in April 1832.

Black Hawk's motives in leading this movement were complex and are not entirely clear. Bitterly aware of the series of injustices suffered by the Sauk since 1804, and of the illegal basis of their expulsion from Illinois, he believed that the policy of accommodation followed by Keokuk invited aggression and felt that a militant stance would produce a different reaction. Although his followers were clearly ready to fight, if necessary, they did not constitute a war party and included the noncombatant members of the British band. In case trouble developed, Black Hawk felt assured of aid from the Winnebago and Potawatomi, as well as the British. His actions were partly guided by the advice of Wabokieshiek, a Winnebago visionary, and he may possibly have seen himself following the earlier example of Tecumseh. Economic factors may also have been involved. The preceding years had been disastrous for the Sauk, and conditions in their new location in Iowa were unsatisfactory (Black Hawk 1955:104).

Although the British band crossed the Mississippi and moved up the Rock River without incidents, the state government termed their movement an invasion and called up the militia, whose advance guard approached the Sauk camp on May 15. By this time Black Hawk realized that he was without allies and had decided to return to Iowa. He sent a small party to meet the militia and negotiate the band's withdrawal. His emissaries were attacked through a misunderstanding. Those who were not killed fled back to their camp, pursued by a disorganized rabble whom the Sauk easily routed (Black Hawk 1955:122-123; Hagan 1958:159-195). The band then moved up the headwaters of the Rock into southern Wisconsin, where they established a camp and sent out raiding parties, augmented by warriors from other tribes whom their victory had attracted. Faced with starvation and an advance by the U.S. army, Black Hawk decided to return to Iowa by way of the Wisconsin River.

The army overtook the British band at the Wisconsin. While the noncombatants crossed the river, the warriors covered them by fighting until dark, when they also the cession of more land as reparations. Another cession occurred in 1836, and in 1842 the Sauk sold all their remaining lands in Iowa.

The years between the Black Hawk War and their final removal from Iowa saw a steady erosion of Sauk society (Hagan 1958:205–224). Factionalism crystallized around the rivalry between the hereditary chief Hardfish and Keokuk, the chief installed and recognized by the United States, whose close alliance with the Agency made his position invulnerable. All annuities from land sales, which had become the major source of income for the Sauk, were paid to Keokuk and distributed by him. The deeply divided Sauk were also becoming estranged from their Fox allies, who resented Keokuk's control over their

Natl. Coll. of Fine Arts, Smithsonian.
Fig. 8. Wáh-pa-ko-lás-kuk, Bear's Track, a Sauk warrior. His face, body, and hair are painted red, and he has a roach haircut with an added roach of red-dyed deer hair. He wears brass arm and neck rings, silver ear ornaments, red breechclout, red yarn sash, buckskin leggings, red yarn and fur garters with brass bells and red and blue beaded pendants, beaded buckskin moccasins with exaggerated red flaps, and a complex feather and bird-head bustle. He holds a metal-tipped lance and a shield. Although Catlin's translation of this man's name shows his interpreter took it as a Bear clan name, his name may have been *wa·pa·kone·škaka* 'white snow tracks', a Turkey clan name (Skinner 1923–1925:24, 152, phonemicized). Painted by George Catlin in fall 1835 at Keokuk's camp on the Des Moines River.

crossed. An attempt to arrange their surrender failed (Hagan 1958:181). Part of the band descended the Wisconsin, but most of this group were killed or captured at the Mississippi. Black Hawk and the main group moved overland, closely pursued by the army. While trying to cross the Mississippi on July 20 they were intercepted by the steamboat *Warrior* whose commander misunderstood their signals of surrender and ordered an attack, inflicting heavy casualties. The next day, again attempting to cross, they were overtaken by the army and slaughtered.

Although most of the Sauk stayed in Iowa throughout the so-called Black Hawk War, the United States charged the entire tribe with unprovoked aggression and forced

Nationalmuseet, Copenhagen: Hc393–403.
Fig. 9. Sauk man's outfit, consisting of a fur turban, bear-claw necklace, beaded leather shirt, bead-decorated blanket robe, cotton breechclout, leather leggings, fur garters, and beaded moccasins. The fur turban was probably worn with the tab extended horizontally to one side. Given to the Danish national museum by the Sauk chief Moses Keokuk and received in 1860–1861.

653

annuities. Population rapidly declined. For some years the Sauk were outnumbered by the Fox, who had historically been the smaller tribe.

Settled on a Kansas reservation, the Sauk continued to decrease even though an influx from the Missouri band partly offset these losses (Hagan 1958:225-244). They also experienced a succession of agents who were usually incompetent and often corrupt. The conservatives were now led by the hereditary chief Mokohoko, while Keokuk had been replaced by his son. Under pressure from settlers the Sauk agreed in 1867 to move to Oklahoma, where most of them went in 1869. Mokohoko's band resisted until 1886, when the army forcibly removed them from Kansas. In 1890 the Sauk reservation was divided into individual allotments, with the surplus made available to American settlers.

In 1950 the Oklahoma Sauk numbered 996 while the population listed for those in Kansas, descended from the Missouri band, was 129 (Tax and Stanley 1960). The number of either group living on its former reservation was very small. Very little is known about the Kansas Sauk, who apparently moved toward acculturation quite early, with more conservative persons drawn toward pan-Indianism. The Sauk of Oklahoma retained much of their culture until the early twentieth century, but rapid acculturation followed. By 1960 conservative families still maintained pack ceremonies and other forms of traditional ritual on a small scale. The only large-scale ceremony was the annual powwow, nonsectarian but incorporating features of the defunct Drum Society's rituals. In many ways this event was the most important feature of tribal activity. Even while clan ritual declined, the Sauk maintained the naming complex attached to clans. Loss of knowledge during the period when the tribe was reduced to a few hundred persons combined with a later population increase to produce a drastic shortage of names. Although a slight preference for naming children into their fathers' clans was still evident, in practice they were given names from any clan with a surplus stock. Clans had consequently become nondescent name groups with minimal ritual functions. Organized as the Sac and Fox tribe of Indians of Oklahoma under the Oklahoma Indian Welfare Act of 1936, the Sauk had an elected chief and business committee.

Population

Estimates of Sauk population have fluctuated so extremely that their reliability is minimal. In 1736 Céloron (NYCD 9:1055) estimated 600, while Carver's (1778:47) figures give 1,200 as the population of their main town. Marston (1912:147) thought they numbered 3,000 in 1820. Two years later Forsyth (1912) placed them at 4,000. The 1838 Report of the Commissioner for Indian Affairs gave them a population of 2,100. By 1845 the Sauk and Fox together numbered only 2,200 (Foreman 1946:146). The decline apparent in this last figure contin-

ued. By 1870 the Sauk population was 627, and by 1884 it was 450 (Foreman 1946:224-227).

Synonymy†

The common French name for the Sauk was Saki, 1670 (JR 54:232), which was borrowed into English as Saukies, 1804 (MHSC ser. 1, 9:92), or Sacky, 1741 (Hewitt 1910:480), shortened to Sauk and Sac (săk). Variant spellings are Sachi(s) (JR 60:214; NYCD 4:749), Satzi, 1670 (JR 54:222), Saquis, Saugies, Saukeas (WHC 18:335), Sakes (NYCD 5:622), Sawkeys, Sacks, Saxes, and others listed by Hewitt (1910:480). The form Sac has become standard in the name of the Oklahoma Sac and Fox ('săkən₁făks), though Sauk and Fox is also used (Wright 1951:222). Saki is a borrowing of an Algonquian form of the name such as Ojibwa osaki· (Baraga 1878-1880, 2:333), perhaps in a variant without the o-prefix. In 1667 Claude Allouez (JR 50:308, 51:42, 44) referred to them as Ousaki, a form with some use by later writers, and Ousakiouek, which is their own name asa·ki·waki (pl.; a- is from earlier o-). By its etymology this must mean 'people of the outlet', although it has been interpreted to be 'they that came forth, or out into the open' (Jones 1907:34); the reference is to the mouth of the Saginaw River (Ojibwa sa·ki·na·nk '(at) the country of the Sauk', Goddard 1972:130). Related forms in other Algonquian languages are Illinois saki8o (8 = ou; Le Boullenger in Belting 1958:288), Potawatomi wsaki (Gatschet 1878-1893:26, phonemicized), Shawnee hoθa·ki (Voegelin 1938-1940, 9:451), Kickapoo oθaakia (Voorhis 1967:281), and Menominee asa·ke·w (Bloomfield 1962: 249). Fox has both asa·ki·waki and sa·ki·waki (pl.; Michelson 1930a, 1931, phonemicized). Borrowed forms are Winnebago za·gí (Kenneth Miner, personal communication 1974) and Dakota záke (Riggs 1852:275). Other borrowed names appear to be applied to both the Sac and Fox of Oklahoma and the Fox of Iowa; the following are from sources that give no separate name for the Fox: Omaha θáge (Fletcher and La Flesche 1911:102, normalized), Osage θagéwa (La Flesche 1932:271, 322, normalized), Delaware sá·kiya (Goddard 1965-1970), Creek sa·kiyá (Mary R. Haas, personal communication 1974), Caddo sá·kiyah (Wallace L. Chafe, personal communication 1973), Pawnee asá·ki·wa (Douglas R. Parks, personal communication 1975).

The Sauk were first mentioned in print under their Huron name Hvattoehronon, 1640 (JR 18:233), more accurately given as 8a'toęronnon, meaning 'people of Saginaw' (ę = ye; Potier 1920:155). Hewitt (1910:480) also cites the variants Ouatoieronon and Quatokeronon from an unidentified Potier manuscript and gives Onon-

† This synonymy was prepared by Ives Goddard incorporating material and references supplied by the author.

daga hoti?nestakǫ? (normalized). His assertion that the Scungsicks (NYCD 5:791) are the Sauk is directly contradicted in the document cited.

The Missouri band or Missouri River Sauks have also been known as the Nemaha Sauk (Callender 1962:6), from their Sauk-Fox name *ni·maha·haki* (pl.; Jones 1907:35).

Sources

The basic description of Sauk culture is still Forsyth's (1912) 1827 account which may be combined with other early nineteenth-century accounts by Marston (1912) and Galland (1869). Black Hawk's (1955) autobiography, first published in 1833 and occasionally attacked as a fabrication, now seems established as authentic. The Sauk have not fared well at the hands of anthropologists. Harrington (1914) was primarily interested in material culture, which was also Skinner's (1923-1925) basic concern. Although Skinner included information about social organization, this is not notably reliable. Unfortunately, the kind of ethnography that could have been produced in the 1920s is no longer possible. The culture of the Kansas Sauk is almost unknown. Except for several publications concerning the Black Hawk War, the main treatment of Sauk history is Hagan (1958).

Kickapoo

CHARLES CALLENDER, RICHARD K. POPE, AND SUSAN M. POPE

Language, Territory, Environment

The Kickapoo (¹kĭkəˌpōō), an Algonquian-speaking tribe, call themselves *kiikaapoa,* a name whose meaning is unknown. Although Mooney and Jones (1907:684) derive it from *ki·wika·pa·wa,* a form loosely meaning 'he stands around' or 'he moves about, standing now here, now there', this is a folk etymology and linguistically impossible.*

The movements of the Kickapoo were so frequent and extensive that this tribe cannot really be associated with a specific area. Southern Wisconsin, where they were found at the time of contact in the late seventeenth century, is often given as their location. Yet their Wisconsin period was rather brief. Not many years before contact they had lived west of Lake Erie (JR 18:233–234). Soon after contact they moved to central Illinois and the western part of the Wabash drainage, remaining there until United States expansion forced them across the Mississippi in the early nineteenth century. Later movements split the tribe. One group settled permanently in northeast Kansas. Most of the Kickapoo went through a complicated series of movements taking them west to Missouri and then south-southwest as far as Texas and Mexico, with frequent reversals of direction. Eventually they concentrated into two communities, one in central Oklahoma and the other in the northern part of the Mexican state of Coahuila (fig. 1). While the Kickapoo cannot be assigned to a particular area, their postcontact settlements were consistently associated with a prairie habitat (Wilson 1956:1063).

External Relations

In language and culture the Kickapoo were most closely related to the Sauk, Fox, and Mascouten (Dillingham 1963:161; Hockett 1964:240; Marston 1912:142; Michelson 1912:252). With a few brief exceptions their postcontact associations with the Sauk and Fox were not particularly close, but they maintained very strong bonds with the Mascouten, whom they ultimately absorbed (Wilson

1956:1063; Goddard 1972). All four tribes shared important cultural and linguistic ties with the Shawnee, from whom the Kickapoo, according to legend, separated after a quarrel over a bear's foot (Schoolcraft 1851–1857, 4:255; Trowbridge 1938:69, 1939:64; cf. Marston 1912:142–143). A close association with the Miami-speaking tribes during the contact period in Wisconsin (JR 58:22–23, 49:101–104; Bacqueville de la Potherie 1911–1912, 2:74) continued in the eighteenth century as many Kickapoos followed these groups to the Wabash. These Miami ties probably involved the Mascouten even more than the Kickapoo proper. The Kickapoo living in central Illinois had close links with the Potawatomi, which the group in Kansas has maintained.

Tribes toward whom the Kickapoo were particularly hostile shifted through time. At contact they were at war with their Dakota neighbors and with the Iroquois who had recently driven them to Wisconsin. Later they joined other Wisconsin groups in a long period of intermittent warfare with the Illinois tribes, pushing them south and taking over much of their territory. Their main long-term enemies were the Chickasaw and Osage. The Chickasaw war, promoted by French colonial officials and later by their Spanish successors, died down as the Kickapoo moved westward, but as late as 1841 their attitude was still hostile (Gibson 1963:22, 48–49, 142, 164–165). The long Osage war, first instigated by the Spanish, continued as Kickapoo movements west of the Mississippi further infringed on Osage territory (Gibson 1963:33, 49–51, 200, 255), and hostility between the two tribes persisted until fairly recent times.

For much of their postcontact history the Kickapoo were closely tied to one or another colonial power. After an early phase of generally hostile relations, the French won over the Kickapoo with such success that they did not really accept friendly relations with the English until after the Revolution, and then only as a source of aid against the United States (Gibson 1963:21–24, 30–32). Their alliance with the Spanish, replacing the French relationship, was also very close. This Spanish (and later, Mexican) association continued for many years and was an important factor attracting the Kickapoo to Missouri, Texas, and Mexico. Relations with the United States were generally hostile.

---

* Italicized Kickapoo forms are in the orthography of Voorhis (1974), which conforms to the standard transcriptional system used in the *Handbook;* sequences of two identical vowels may count as one or two syllables, according to complex accentuation rules.

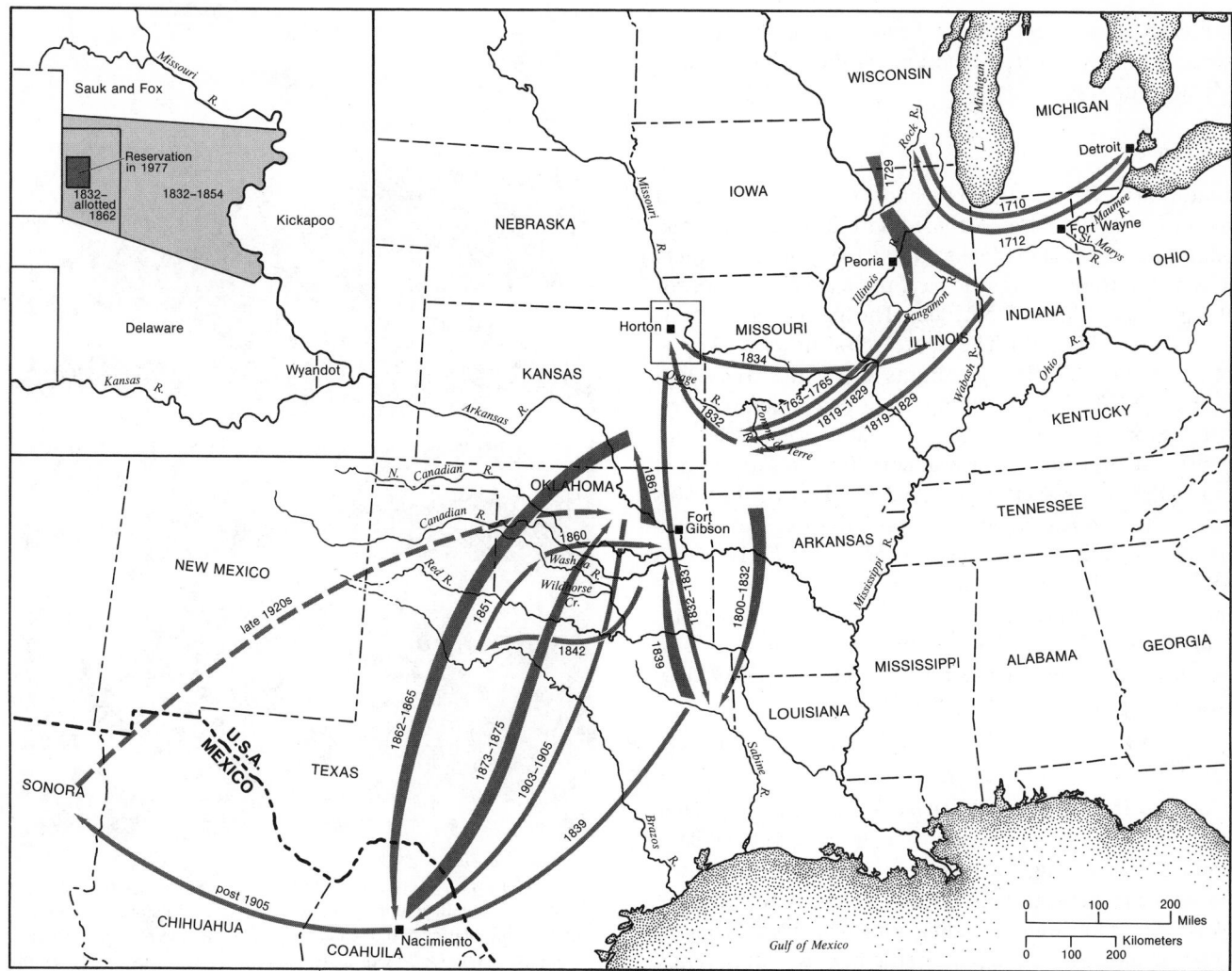

Fig. 1. Tribal movements.

Component Groups

The Kickapoo were divided into the loosely defined and rather fluid political and territorial units called bands that characterized the Central Algonquian tribes. Records from the early contact period give very little information about these. After moving from Wisconsin to Illinois the tribe divided into two autonomous and unusually permanent sections of roughly equal size. One, the Prairie band, inhabited central Illinois while the other, the Vermilion band, occupied the western fringe of the Wabash drainage. They sometimes coordinated their policies (Gibson 1963:32) but occasionally followed very different courses. Thus, the Vermilion band supported Tecumseh's movement, which the Prairie band opposed. Each negotiated a separate treaty ceding its land to the United States in 1819. The factors producing this unusually sharp division are unclear. Perhaps the incorporation of the Mascouten—who apparently merged with the Vermilion band—played a part, and their absorption

may have expanded Kickapoo population to a size too large for a single tribal government.

The movement of a Kickapoo group to the lower Missouri in 1763 or 1765 (Gibson 1963:32, 91) produced a third and smaller band. From this point on, the tribe broke up into several such units, often forming about particular leaders. One such group, whose members were followers of the prophet Kenekuk, became entirely independent and is represented by the Kickapoo now living in Kansas. Other bands, after a complex process of splitting and merging, ultimately combined, only to divide again into the two groups now settled in Oklahoma and Mexico.

Culture

Given the many gaps in information about Kickapoo culture, particularly in earlier periods (Dillingham 1963:3; Ritzenthaler and Peterson 1956:17; Silverberg 1957:61–62), this account of traditional culture is drawn   *657* primarily from descriptions based on mid-twentieth-century fieldwork carried out among the Oklahoma and Mexican groups.

Subsistence

Traditional Kickapoo subsistence followed the usual pattern of agriculture combined with hunting and food gathering. Although Jenks (1900:1038) classed them among the tribes using wild rice, there is no evidence for this practice (Wilson 1956:1062). The main game animals were deer and buffalo. The eighteenth-century Kickapoo often conducted their winter hunts west of the Mississippi (Gibson 1963:32, 91). An important component of their tribal economy after the early contact period was compensation by colonial governments for warfare carried out in their interests (Gibson 1963:91). During the 1840s and 1850s one Kickapoo band specialized as middlemen in trade with the Comanche (Gibson 1963:171–176), and raids to capture horses and other livestock were very important activities for much of the nineteenth century. Hunting and food gathering remain important parts of Mexican Kickapoo economy (Goggin 1951:319–320; Ritzenthaler and Peterson 1956:36–40).

Settlement Pattern

The Kickapoo alternated between semipermanent summer villages and temporary winter camps. A village consisted of rectangular houses ((w)iikiaapi sing.) based on a pole framework with slabs of elm bark forming the walls and roof, and including an open-sided arbor of poles at the entrance. Such a settlement was apparently associated with graveyards and a field for games and dances (Dillingham 1963:64). Winter houses, either round (Goggin 1951:321) or oval (Dillingham 1963:85), were covered with rush mats. The Mexican Kickapoo settlement is still composed of traditional structures, modified to fit the environment and their circumstances (Goggin 1951:320–321; Ritzenthaler and Peterson 1956: 30–31). A typical compound includes both winter and summer dwellings as well as a cook house and menstrual hut. The summer house retains its traditional form, although the walls consist of vertically set poles while the roof is covered with mats (figs. 2–3).

Life Cycle

• BIRTH Among the Oklahoma Kickapoo birth takes place near the family's house in a small hut that is also used for menstrual seclusion. Other women attend the delivery. The child's umbilical cord is carefully saved. A woman remains in this hut for 30 days if her child is male, for 40 days if she has given birth to a female (Dillingham 1963:202–203). Practices among the Mexican Kickapoo seem similar (Ritzenthaler and Peterson 1956:57), except that a woman undergoes delivery in the bush before

moving into the hut (fig. 4).

Milwaukee Public Mus.

Fig. 2. Houses in Nacimiento, Coahuila. top, Building a winter house covered with tule mats. bottom, Interior of a summer house, with sleeping platform and walls of sotol stems; the roof is covered during use (Mar.–Oct.) with mats from the winter house. Photographs by Robert E. Ritzenthaler, 1954.

Fig. 3. Kickapoo compound near Shawnee, Okla. Frame house, mat-covered winter house, and summer house (with mat roofing not yet in place) with attached arbor. Photograph by William C. Sturtevant, May 2, 1958.

A naming ceremony that includes prayers and a feast is held several months after birth, usually during the ceremonial season. The husband selects the person who will name the first child born to a couple, the wife chooses the namer for the second child, and so on alternately.

Fig. 4. A menstrual hut in the Mexican Kickapoo village. Photograph by Robert E. Ritzenthaler, 1954.

Usually relatives are selected. The namer chooses a personal name belonging to his or her clan, but its selection also requires a validating dream or vision. At the ceremony he or she announces the name and describes how it was chosen. The child is affiliated with the clan, or name-group, to which its namer belongs and from which its name is taken. Dillingham compares the relationship of namer and child to that of the compadre in Latin America. The naming ceremony identifies the child as a member of the Kickapoo tribe and also identifies it to the Creator, enabling it later to enter into personal relations with the supernatural. Besides the namer and parents, the ceremony requires a speaker as well as witnesses—apparently four of each sex—who pass the infant around and address it by name. It is also carried outside to touch water or a tree (Dillingham 1963:120-121, 203-204; Jones 1913:335). Ritzenthaler and Peterson (1956:58) describe a Mexican Kickapoo ceremony that differs somewhat in form but seems to have very similar functions.

Dillingham (1963:134-135) notes that parents treat children permissively only in those areas of behavior regarded as unimportant. Punishment for serious misbehavior includes fasting, switching, and immersion in water, all of which are probably assumed to benefit as well as punish the child. These practices are also discussed by Michelson (1923) and by Ritzenthaler and Peterson (1956:58).

• PUBERTY During her first menstruation a girl is isolated for 10 days in a hut built for this purpose in the woods at some distance from the family house. Contact with males is forbidden, but females may pay visits and an older woman instructs her in the behavior proper for adult women. When her ritual seclusion ends, she bathes and is switched with twigs (Dillingham 1963:206-208). Seclusion during later menstrual periods is much less rigorous. On these occasions a woman may prepare meals

for her family but may not eat with them and cannot have any contact with sacred things.

A somewhat comparable ceremony for males was a ritual feast, including songs and prayers, traditionally held after a boy killed his first game animal (Dillingham 1963:207-208). Ritzenthaler and Peterson (1956:60) mention fasting for dreams, but these apparently fell short of actual visions.

• MARRIAGE Jones (1913:332-333) describes an older form of courtship much like that formerly practiced by the Fox, involving nocturnal visits to a woman in her family's lodge. Ritzenthaler and Peterson (1956:61-62) say that the former use of the lover's flute (fig. 5) for courtship among the Mexican Kickapoo has been replaced by whistling. Use of whistle speech for communication during courtship, according to Voorhis (1971a), is confined to the Mexican group and is neither used nor understood by the Oklahoma Kickapoo.

The traditional form of marriage involved an exchange of gifts between the families of the couple (Jones 1913:333).

• DEATH When a death occurs, relatives gather at the house for an all-night ceremony (Dillingham 1963:208-216). Those charged with special duties on this occasion include a man who leads prayers and songs, two cooks, an elderly woman who dresses the corpse, and an elderly man to lead the gravediggers. These persons are chosen through a system of clan reciprocity. Besides a feast, the ceremony includes prayers and songs, alternating with periods of rest and quiet conversation. As dawn approaches, the corpse is dressed and painted and then carried to the grave by four men. Only selected attendants witness the burial, which includes an address to the corpse. Tobacco, a bowl of food, and other items are placed in the grave. The grave goods also include the wooden spoon belonging to the deceased, an item of native manufacture to which the Kickapoo attach great significance. Anyone buried without such a spoon must eat foam throughout eternity (James H. Howard, personal communication 1974). The relatives leave after the noon meal. Formerly the entire community, except the surviving spouse, left the settlement for four days. Children under 12, who are regarded as particularly susceptible to death, are taken away from the house during the wake, or else concealed. Widows and widowers are required to observe a period of formal mourning.

A ceremonial adoption follows death after an interval varying from four days to four years (Dillingham 1963:218-221; James H. Howard, personal communication 1974). The person who named the deceased, if still living, sponsors this; otherwise it is held by close surviving relatives such as parents, siblings, or children. The adoptee should be of the same sex and age as the person whom he or she replaces. The ceremony, held at night, allows the spirit of the deceased to enter the home of the dead. It includes a general feast, as well as a feast for the

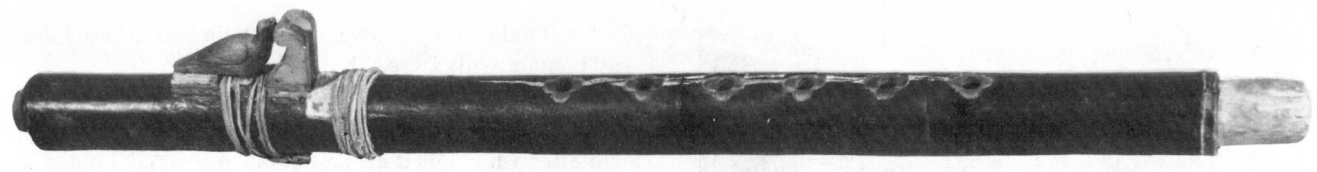

Mus. of the Amer. Ind., Heye Foundation, New York: 2/7605.

Fig. 5. End-blown courting flute, of leather-covered wood with carved bird-shaped external flue. Length 56.5 cm; collected in Okla. before 1912.

dead that is limited to invited guests who receive gifts of cloth, while the adoptee receives new clothing. Besides songs and prayers, this event features a game or dance, held just before dawn. Its nature depends on the sex and preferences of the deceased. For a man it may be a ball game, moccasin game, archery contest, or ceremonial war dance; for a woman, squaw dice, the women's dance, or a woman's ball game.

Social Organization

Traditional kinship terminology was of Omaha type (Callender 1962:113-121; Dillingham 1963:115-119; Jones 1913:333-334; Morgan 1871:291-382) and retains this overall pattern. Information about kinship behavior beyond the immediate family is slight (Dillingham 1963:115-119). In the gift exchange that formerly accompanied marriage (Jones 1913:332-333), the groom's niece (sister's daughter) brought the bride the presents from his family. Except for horses, which went to her brothers, these gifts were distributed among the bride's maternal uncles and sisters' sons. Although Jones's account thus suggests special ties with the mother's brother, other aspects of this relationship are very different from the practices of related tribes. Thus, the punishments prescribed for impudence toward the maternal uncle and paternal aunt (Michelson 1923) indicate lack of the teasing or joking elements characteristic of other Central Algonquian groups (cf. Callender 1962:23-24; Tax 1955:257). Dillingham (1963:118) reports that besides sexually oriented joking between siblings-in-law of the opposite sex, the Kickapoo also permitted mild teasing of parents-in-law.

The Kickapoo are divided into eponymous name-groups that, by analogy with similar units among the Sauk, Fox, Shawnee, and Potawatomi, were formerly patrilineal clans. Dillingham (1963:123) found nine name-groups among the Oklahoma Kickapoo: Blackberry (or Berry), Eagle, Water, Bear, War (or Man), Tree, Raccoon, Elk, and Buffalo. Similar lists obtained by Jones (1913:335; cf. also Mooney and Jones 1907:685), Michelson (1929), and Ritzenthaler and Peterson (1956:45) differ primarily by including Fox, Wolf, Turkey, and Thunder groups. These differences may reflect the extinction of the last-named groups or perhaps shifts in population between the Oklahoma and Mexican sections. The Buffalo, Universe, Heaven, and Flowering Cactus units that Ritzenthaler and Peterson (1956:45)

describe for the Mexican Kickapoo apparently are ritual societies centered on sacred packs, rather than name-groups.

Kickapoo name-groups are not unilineal. Affiliation is determined by one's personal name, which in turn depends upon the affiliation of its donor. Although these units are neither descent groups nor composed of relatives, their members use grandparental kin terms for each other (Dillingham 1963:109, 120). Exogamy had lapsed before 1900 (Jones 1913:335). The functions of the name-groups in the 1970s are primarily ritual. These center on the religious significance of names and are also linked to pack ceremonies, although the relationship of the latter to name-groups is far from clear (Dillingham 1963:120). In ritual and related contexts, including burial, name-groups are paired off in a system of reciprocal obligations (Dillingham 1963:149) resembling those of the Fox. This pairing is most evident in the reciprocity between the Raccoon and Tree groups, on the one hand, and the Berry and Eagle on the other.

Like the Sauk, Fox, and Potawatomi, the Kickapoo have a dual division. This consists of units called *oskasa* and *kiiskooha,* respectively symbolized as black and white. Since divisional affiliation follows that of one's namer, these units are not descent groups. Unlike the systems of related tribes, the Kickapoo divisions are closely tied to the name-groups, and all members of any group should belong to the same division. While Dillingham's (1963:126-127) census does not show complete correspondence between name-group and divisional affiliation, the correlation is very high and the exceptions may be informants' errors. The Bear, Buffalo, Eagle, and Man groups are *oskasa,* while the Raccoon, Water, Berry, and Tree are *kiiskooha.* Michelson (1929) gives another arrangement in which name-groups with animal eponyms—Beaver, Bear, Elk, Fox, Raccoon, and Wolf—are *oskasa,* while Eagle, Berry, Turkey, Tree, and Water are *kiiskooha.* Kickapoo divisions thus approximate a moiety form. If the same rules held in the past, when name-groups were true clans, the divisions would then have been true moieties. This system may have been borrowed from Miami-speaking tribes, although this hypothesis is very speculative.

The dual divisions provide a basis for joking and for competition in activities such as games, races, and eating contests. They also determine seating at rituals, with the *oskasa* seated on the north side and the *kiiskooha* on the south (Dillingham 1963:127, 147).

Political Organization

Information about the traditional Kickapoo political system is very sparse. For the Oklahoma Kickapoo, Dillingham (1963:137) describes a council of clan (name-group) heads, whose offices were, in concept, patrilineally inherited; however, by 1953 a head could be succeeded by a sister's or daughter's son who belonged to the same name-group. The tribal chief traditionally came from the Eagle clan, while the Raccoon clan provided a second chief who apparently functioned as a speaker. These two clans were also regarded as the leaders of their respective divisions (Dillingham 1963:124, 126, 139). By the 1950s the concerns of the tribal council were mostly social and ceremonial. Crimes such as murder and theft, once punished severely by the tribe, by then resulted in a decision to "disown" the offender or to turn him over to local United States authorities (Dillingham 1963:137, 139-140). Decisions of the council must be unanimous.

For the Mexican Kickapoo Ritzenthaler and Peterson (1956:41-43) describe a council of adult males, as well as a hereditary civil chief whose functions include calling meetings and presiding over them, judging and punishing minor crimes, and controlling to some extent assigning land. Persons guilty of serious crimes are turned over to Mexican authorities. Before 1948 the chief appointed two tribal policemen (but cf. Goggin 1951:324). During the four-month ceremonial season the regular chief is replaced by another official whose functions are religious.

Dillingham (1963:140-141) describes a female official, called a "queen" by contemporary Kickapoos. This position was first noted in 1791. The activities attached to her office were apparently religious rather than political in the strict sense and included giving the approval needed to hold certain religious dances. The last two women to hold this position, which no longer functions, were mother and daughter.

Religion

Kickapoo religion centers on techniques for dealing with the manitous, or spirits, "in order to keep life untroubled and secure" (Dillingham 1963:143). The spirits form a hierarchy, headed by the Great Manitou, or Creator. Other important figures include the four winds, the sky, the sun, moon, and stars, and the earth, regarded as grandmother. *wiiθahkeeha,* the culture hero, probably belongs in this group, or did so in the past. Jones (1915:5-19) includes stories about *wiiθahkeeha* (cf. also Mooney and Jones 1907:684), but the silence of recent anthropologists about this figure suggests that his significance may have diminished. Lesser manitous, according to Dillingham (1963:144), "include anything which is of importance to the Kickapoo way of life, including . . . such things as the animals and plants they use and

know." Tobacco and the Thunderers are particularly important messengers for communicating with supernatural beings (Dillingham 1963:145).

Dillingham (1963:147) suggests that traditional Kickapoo religion differed only in details from that of the Fox. Like the Fox, the Kickapoo have also gone through a series of changes by which the vision quest and related practices that formerly brought individuals into contact with the supernatural world have been partly replaced by personal names and partly absorbed by group ceremonies centering on sacred packs, in which older patterns survive.

The Kickapoo hold a number of important public rituals, whose scheduling is markedly seasonal. Because of a belief that the spirits sleep during winter, this time of the year is limited to small private feasts, although it is the proper season for recounting religious myths and folk tales. The ceremonial season opens in spring with a series of sacred-pack ceremonies (Dillingham 1963:165-167). The Oklahoma Kickapoo have four major packs. These, and their rituals, are closely associated with name-groups, although the details of this link are very unclear (Dillingham 1963:151-154). After the ceremonial year formally begins, families may put on smaller-scale rituals such as feasts for the dead, naming ceremonies, and adoptions. A group of tribal religious feasts including the Green Corn Dance clusters around the time of the maize harvest (Dillingham 1963:166). Another set of sacred-pack rituals closes the season. The ceremonial cycle that Ritzenthaler and Peterson (1956:45-47) describe for the Mexican Kickapoo seems broadly similar, also beginning with the opening and renewing of four major sacred packs. James H. Howard (personal communication 1974) notes that many Oklahoma Kickapoo move to Mexico in March to join in opening the ceremonial season there,

Mus. of the Amer. Ind., Heye Foundation, New York: 2/4923.
Fig. 6. Two-headed drum used in Buffalo Dance. Inset shows other side. Diameter 30 cm; collected in Okla. before 1909.

661

and the Mexican group reciprocates a month later when the season begins in Oklahoma.

History

The Kickapoo were first mentioned by the French in 1640 under the Huron name Ontarahronon (JR 18:233-234), while they still lived in the general area of southeast Michigan or northwest Ohio. In the next few years Iroquoian attacks drove them westward (Trowbridge 1938:69-70) to southern Wisconsin where the French found them after 1665 (Bacqueville de la Potherie 1911-1912, 1:316-317). Their locations and distribution in Wisconsin are uncertain (Silverberg 1957:71-85), partly because they often shared settlements with the Mascoutens and Miamis (JR 58:22-23, 59:101-103), but they tended to remain in the southern part of that state. As early as 1680 Kickapoo parties ranged south as far as the Illinois River (Tonty 1917:294). Franquelin's 1684 map locates them on the upper Rock River, which it designates the Kickapoo River (Griffin 1943:map 8).

They entered the fur trade almost at once (Bacqueville de la Potherie 1911-1912, 1:317) but like the Fox and Mascouten they resisted missionization (JR 55:182-183), opposed extending the trade to the Dakota, and were sometimes overtly hostile toward the French (Perrot 1911:245; Bacqueville de la Potherie 1911-1912, 2:17-18). About 1710 some Kickapoos joined the French-sponsored movement to the new post at Detroit, settling at the mouth of the Maumee (WHC 17:285), perhaps within their protocontact area. They returned to the upper Mississippi valley when tribes allied with the French followed their 1712 massacre of the Foxes and Mascoutens at Detroit with an attack on a Kickapoo group. During the series of wars precipitated by these events the Kickapoo were initially allied with the Fox. In 1729 they changed sides, making peace with the French and forming an alliance with them. They took a prominent part in the 1730 attack on the Foxes (WHC 17:36-55, 62-69, 100-101), but their actions during the final campaign of these wars were ambiguous (Kellogg 1925:335).

During the first half of the eighteenth century the Kickapoo expanded southward at the expense of the Illinois tribes. Centered on the lower Rock River by 1729, within a few years they had moved into central Illinois (Dillingham 1963:17) and were pushing south and east to the Wabash. During this process the tribe split into two autonomous bands. The Prairie band settled in central Illinois, ranging from the Sangamon valley to Lake Peoria. The Vermilion band lived along the western bank and tributaries of the Wabash in close association with the Mascouten whom they were absorbing.

The Kickapoo remained dependable French allies even during the years when their Miami-speaking neighbors were gravitating toward the English (Pease and Jenison 1940:196, 209-213, 660-661). Besides helping ensure the loyalty of other tribes, they aided the French by fighting the Chickasaw allies of the English. When the French withdrew, the Kickapoo transferred allegiance to their Spanish successors in Missouri and in 1763 or 1765 one band moved to the lower Missouri River (Gibson 1963:22-23, 32, 91). They enthusiastically supported Pontiac's movement (Thwaites 1904-1907, 1:144-145) and even after concluding peace sporadically attacked English settlements in Illinois as late as 1771 (Gibson 1963:31).

Spanish influence affected Kickapoo actions during the early years of the Revolution. Their initial policy was one of neutrality. Later they formed a quasi-alliance with the Americans who occupied the Illinois and lower Wabash settlements. However, after American designs on Indian land became clear, the Kickapoo finally turned to the British and joined other tribes in years of intense warfare against the United States. The Vermilion band, whose towns were destroyed during these actions, temporarily moved across the Mississippi (Gibson 1963:38, 46). Later returning to the Wabash area, they gave strong support to Tecumseh even while the Prairie band opposed his movement. After the Battle of Tippecanoe in 1811 dispersed the multitribal settlement in which Tecumseh's followers had gathered, the Vermilion Kickapoo began raiding American settlers. The Prairie band was also drawn into these hostilities, which reached a climax during the War of 1812. Although the Vermilion band defeated an army from Kentucky, the Illinois militia surprised and destroyed the main town of the Prairie band. Even after the peace treaty of 1815 the Kickapoo continued to oppose American settlement of their area (Gibson 1963:78-80). However, in 1819 both bands signed treaties exchanging their lands for an area in southwest Missouri, south of the Osage River and west of the Pomme de Terre. Their removal across the Mississippi was a slow piecemeal process that extended over 15 years. One small band remained in central Illinois until 1829, when its members briefly joined the Sauk faction led by Black Hawk before moving to Missouri. The band led by the prophet Kenakuk, consisting of adherents of his religious movement, managed to delay their departure until 1834 (Gibson 1963:83-90).

The small Kickapoo population established in Missouri during Pontiac's war received increments during each major crisis in their tribe's relations with the United States. These early migrants soon began moving south in small groups, reaching the Red River as early as 1800 (Gibson 1963:141). The flood of new arrivals from the east after 1819 rapidly exhausted the game resources of their Missouri reservation. Many of these Kickapoos also went south. By 1832, when the Kickapoo yielded to pressure from the United States government and accepted a new reservation in Kansas by the Treaty of

Castor Hill, only about 400 of them remained in Missouri (Gibson 1963:109).

The Kansas reservation combined this remnant of Missouri Kickapoo with Kenekuk's band, which came directly from Illinois. Kenekuk, called the Kickapoo Prophet, had begun preaching a nativistic movement after the War of 1812 (Forsyth 1912a:280-281; Gibson 1963:88-90; Howard 1965; Mooney 1896:692-700). His doctrine, borrowing elements from Christianity, included strict injunctions against alcohol, polygyny, and warfare and was explicitly directed toward a policy of acculturation. The rules laid down by Kenekuk were rigidly enforced within the community (figs. 7-8). Ostracized by the rest of the Kickapoo, Kenekuk and his followers were favored by government officials who approved of their attitudes. In Kansas their bent toward accommodation produced incessant conflict with the traditionalist faction from Missouri. Small groups of the latter repeatedly left to join the bulk of the Kickapoo in the south until by 1837 only 100 of them remained. (Gibson 1963:117). They were replaced by converts Kenekuk had obtained among the neighboring Potawatomi, who officially joined the Kickapoo tribe in 1851 (Gibson 1963:118). Dissension over the forcible and fraudulent allotment of the Kansas

reservation eventually drove the remaining traditionalists south in 1864, along with some of Kenekuk's followers. Those who remained are now represented by the Kansas Kickapoo.

The Kickapoo who moved south from Missouri, partly at the invitation of Spanish authorities (Gibson 1963: 143-145), ranged through Oklahoma and western Arkansas into Texas. About half of them eventually settled on the Sabine River in eastern Texas as part of the intertribal combination of Cherokee, Shawnee, Delaware, and Kickapoo communities established by the Cherokee chief called The Bowl. The stability they enjoyed under Mexican rule was threatened by the anti-Indian policy Texas adopted after it became independent. When settlers encroached on their hunting territory the Kickapoo retaliated with a series of raids. Fearing Texan reprisals, The Bowl disowned the Kickapoo, who then responded to overtures from Mexican agents and joined these new allies in guerrilla actions. Many Kickapoos moved north across the Red River after a Texan attack on their main town. Most of the remainder followed in 1839 when The Bowl's entire combination was expelled, although a few went to the Mexico where they were welcomed and incorporated into the army (Gibson 1963:152-159).

The Kickapoo in Oklahoma formed two bands that settled in the area set aside for the Chickasaw, whom they prevented from occupying this territory (Gibson 1963:159-165). When the United States army expelled them in 1841, they were invited into the Creek Nation. One band settled on Wildhorse Creek and the other on the Canadian River. In 1842 the Texan government decided that the best strategy for coping with incessant Kickapoo raids was to form an alliance with the tribe and invited the Canadian River band to return to Texas and settle on the Brazos. Part of the band did so. This divided the Kickapoo into three bands, those of Mothakuck in Texas, Papequah on Wildhorse Creek, and Pecan on the Canadian. Gibson (1963:169-178) notes that each band developed a distinctive economic specialty. Mothakuck's group hunted and trapped, trading skins and furs over a large area, while Papequah's band specialized in trade

Fig. 7. Ah-tón-we-tuck, The Cock Turkey, one of Kenekuk's followers, repeating his prayer from a prayer stick (see fig. 8). He wears red face paint, a silver gorget, calico shirt, and white fur robe. Painted by George Catlin in Illinois in 1831 or in the Fort Leavenworth area in 1830.

Fig. 8. Kickapoo prayer stick of the Kenekuk religion, with pictographs probably representing heaven at top (right) and hell at bottom, and shaft carved with three sets of the same 5 symbols as mnemonics for a prayer. Maplewood, 31.5 cm long, said to have been once painted red on one side and green on the other; the other side is blank. Said to have been collected in Indiana in 1830.

663

Fig. 9. *paapiisikita,* an Oklahoma Kickapoo, holding a beaded fan. Photograph in Washington, D.C., by Charles M. Bell, probably in 1894.

with the Comanche, and Pecan's protected the Creek from raiders.

Some Kickapoos moved to Mexico in 1850 as part of the Indian colony planned by the Seminole, Wildcat, but returned the next year (Gibson 1963:174–183) to join Mothakuck's band, which after growing friction had withdrawn from Texas to Big Beaver Creek in Oklahoma. Its members launched a new and devastating series of raids on Texas, often returning with hundreds of horses. After Texas Rangers and the United States Army attacked their Comanche neighbors and allies in 1860, this Kickapoo group joined the eastern section of their tribe (Gibson 1963:188–192).

After a proposed Confederate alliance foundered on the Kickapoo's hatred of Texas, they moved into southern Kansas during the Civil War and as Union allies raided Oklahoma tribes that joined the Confederacy. When scope for this activity dwindled, a large group left to find a new home. They ultimately reached Mexico where, joining the Kickapoos who had lived there since 1839, they settled near Nacimiento in Coahuila (Gibson 1963:201). Other sections of the tribe followed, until by 1865 only the Kansas groups remained in the United States.

The Mexican government subsidized the Kickapoo as a defense against Comanche and Apache raids. When post–Civil War actions by the United States army greatly

reduced these, the Kickapoo again turned to raiding Texas, obtaining livestock to sell locally as well as captives to hold for ransom (Gibson 1963:209–217). While the United States government was trying to negotiate a Kickapoo agreement to return from Mexico, the Fourth Cavalry raided their settlement while the warriors were absent, killing many noncombatants and taking about 40 prisoners to Fort Gibson in Oklahoma (Gibson 1963:236–252). After long negotiations, about half the tribe—mostly close relatives of the captives—agreed to come to a reservation in Oklahoma, while the rest temporarily scattered through northern Mexico. A second group returned to the United States in 1875. Those who refused gathered again at Nacimiento.

At first the Bureau of Indian Affairs treated the reservation Kickapoos gently, hoping this would encourage the rest of the tribe to return (Gibson 1963:271–290). However, after 1875 it began pressing them to accept

Fig. 10. Two Kickapoo men in Mexico. The man at the left has a long pendant of silver or German silver hair plates, and both wear moccasins decorated with ribbon appliqué. Photographed probably about 1900.

allotment, compulsory education, and similar measures designed to promote acculturation. Most Kickapoos resisted, although a "progressive" faction developed around a group from Kansas that moved to Oklahoma in 1875. In 1891 the leaders of both factions were fraudulently induced to sign a request for the allotment of their reservation and sale of surplus lands. The "progressives" eventually accepted the allotment, but the conservative faction—the so-called Kicking Kickapoos—created so much disturbance that a special agent was appointed for them. The events that followed were very complex (Gibson 1963:295–346). The conservatives, numbering about two-thirds of those in Oklahoma, were caught between conflicting exploiters whose techniques ranged from misrepresentation to outright terrorism. One of these, their former agent, persuaded them to return to Mexico and facilitated their migration (fig. 11). By 1905 only the progressive faction remained in Oklahoma. The dissidents first settled at Nacimiento but later moved to a new location in northern Sonora. Although the legal issues were finally resolved in 1914 with the restoration of Kickapoo lands (Gibson 1963:347–361), the emigrants did not finally return until the late 1920s.

The Kansas Kickapoo, numbering about 343 (Tax and Stanley 1960), have a small reservation in northeast Kansas near the town of Horton. Generally neglected by anthropologists (cf. Howard 1965), they are the least known Kickapoo group. Given an early bent toward acculturation and a long process of selection in which culturally conservative members repeatedly left the community, they expectably retain less indigenous Kickapoo culture than the rest of their tribe. They have also been strongly influenced by the neighboring Potawatomi community, to the point of occasionally being described as essentially Potawatomi rather than Kickapoo (cf. Dillingham 1963:39). Although their linguistic and cultural differences from the Potawatomi are few (Clifton 1969), they are still a distinct community and apparently maintain name-groups that show the characteristic Kickapoo association with divisions. Apart from the Kenekuk religion, ritual includes sacred-pack ceremonies as well as intertribal institutions such as the Drum cult and the Native American Church.

While the Kansas Kickapoo are sharply distinguished from the rest of the tribe, the boundary between the

Fig. 12. Pehkotah, a chief of the Mexican Kickapoo, born in Coahuila about 1851. He wears a fur turban, silver armbands, beaded breechclout, leggings, and moccasins. Photographed in Washington, D.C., by DeLancy Gill in 1907.

Fig. 11. Kickapoos moving to Mexico, 1903–1905. Photograph supplied in 1907 by Martin J. Bentley, former agent for the Kickapoos.

Oklahoma and Mexican Kickapoo is diffuse and movement between these groups is frequent. The Oklahoma Kickapoo numbered about 379 in 1953 (Dillingham 1963:67-68). They are centered along the North Canadian River in Lincoln, Potawatomie, and Oklahoma counties, generally within the boundaries of their former reservation. The Mexican group, numbering 387 in 1954 (Ritzenthaler and Peterson 1956:23), own a 7,000-hectare reservation northwest of Nacimiento (Goggin 1951:317) and live in a concentrated settlement there although hunting (fig. 14), gathering, migrant farm labor, and other economic activities take them far outside its boundaries.

The Oklahoma and especially the Mexican Kickapoo are often described as one of the most conservative Indian societies extant (for example, Jones 1939:1; Gibson 1963:361). This characterization accords with their history and particularly with their pronounced tendency to isolate themselves from American society even when, as with those Mexican Kickapoos who work as farm laborers in the United States, they live in its midst. The Mexican Kickapoo have maintained a settlement of traditional type without precedent among other groups outside the Southwest. They have preserved much of their material culture. A surprising continuity is evident

in their subsistence activities (Goggin 1951). Yet in other respects their conservatism, although undeniable, is not unique. Thus, Kickapoo social organization has apparently diverged from traditional Central Algonquian patterns much more than has that of the Fox, although the extent of change in this area may be offset by greater adherence to traditional forms of political structure. In religion the Kickapoo and Fox seem equally conservative, with the latter somewhat more receptive than the Mexican Kickapoo to new forms of ritual as adjuncts to pack ceremonies. A ceremonial season, which may not be Central Algonquian, is much more pronounced among the Kickapoo, while the Fox have maintained a greater number of pack ceremonies. Religion is probably the heart of Kickapoo conservatism. Several observers (for example, Dillingham 1963:271) have compared this tribe to a religious sect, a characterization that also holds for the Fox.

Population

Mooney (1928; cf. Kroeber 1939:140) estimated the precontact Kickapoo population at 2,000; however, this figure is based on several erroneous assumptions (see Silverberg 1957:135, 163). Reliable estimates for the early historic period are not available. Spanish figures from the late eighteenth century give a total of 2,700, including 1,200 each for the Prairie and Vermilion bands and about 300 living west of the Mississippi (Gibson 1963:32). By 1832 they numbered about 2,000. This figure includes 350 members of Kenekuk's band in Illinois, 400 on their Missouri reservation, about 900 in Oklahoma, and 300 in Texas (Gibson 1963:109). Later figures are usually limited to those Kickapoos living in Kansas or receiving annuity payments there. By 1875 the Kickapoos in the United States, both Kansas and Oklahoma, numbered 706 (Mooney and Jones 1907:685), with about 350 in Mexico (Gibson 1963:271). The figures for 1905 were 185

NAA, Smithsonian.
Fig. 13. Emma Kickapoo Williams Ellis (b.ca. 1883, d.1942), *pemiθaahkwa* 'flying past' of the Eagle clan, wearing fine blue woolen robe with ribbon appliqué and silver ornaments, standing in front of "Democrat quilt" she made for Franklin D. Roosevelt during his first presidential campaign. Photograph by Brooks Studio, Shawnee, Okla., 1931 or 1932.

666

Milwaukee Public Mus.
Fig. 14. Tanning: stretching deerskin preparatory to crutching and drying. Photographed at Nacimiento, Coahuila, by Robert E. Ritzenthaler in 1954.

in Kansas, 247 in Oklahoma, and an estimated 400 in Mexico (Mooney and Jones 1907:685).

Synonymy

The Kickapoo term *kiikaapoa* underlies the French, English, and Spanish names for this tribe, which occur in a variety of slightly different forms beginning in 1670 with Kikabou (JR 54:232–233). The terms used by other Algonquian tribes, such as Shawnee *ki·kapo* (Voegelin 1938–1940, 8:296), are also based on *kiikaapoa,* as are Siouan names such as Osage ígabu (LaFlesche 1932:77). Still other names that probably have the same source are Huron tékapu, the Apache forms shíkapo, shikapu, and sík-a-pu, and Wichita shake-kah-quah (Mooney and Jones 1907:686). The Tonkawa called the Kickapoo ʔaw-ya·ʔax, perhaps meaning 'deer-eaters' (Hoijer 1949:4).

Ontarahronon, an older Huron form meaning 'lake people' (Hewitt 1910d), is the earliest name recorded for the Kickapoo, first occurring in 1640 (JR 18:233–234). It has the variants Ontarraronon and ontaraęronnon (Potier 1920:155; Goddard 1972).

Outitchakouk, a name occurring in 1658 (JR 44:267), which Mooney and Jones (1907:684) interpret as probably referring to the Kickapoo, more likely designated the Miami-speaking Atchatchakangouen tribe.

Sources

Knowledge of Kickapoo culture is greatly handicapped by the lack of early source material (Silverberg 1957:61–62, 64) and further impaired by years of anthropological neglect. The earliest fieldwork, carried out at the beginning of the twentieth century by William Jones, resulted in a collection of folktales (1915) and a very brief article on social organization (1913). There are important discrepancies between his 1907 and his 1913 articles. Michelson occasionally worked with the Oklahoma Kickapoo over a number of years; except for a short note about the punishment of children (1923), his contributions centered on editing or translating the material gathered by Jones. By the middle of the century Goggin (1951:326) described the Kickapoo as the least-known extant Central Algonquian group. During the following years fieldwork by Dillingham (1963), Howard (1965), Pope (1957, 1958–1959), and Ritzenthaler and Peterson (1956) greatly increased knowledge of Kickapoo culture, but there are still important gaps and much of their material remains unpublished. The most comprehensive account of any Kickapoo group, and the main source for this chapter, is Dillingham's (1963) thesis, based on fieldwork done during the 1950s. The Mexican Kickapoo, whom Fabila (1945) had briefly described, were visited by Goggin, who wrote on their material culture (1951). Ritzenthaler and Peterson (1956) have published the most detailed account available (an inadequate book-length description, Latorre and Latorre 1976, appeared after this chapter was completed). Pope has worked in Oklahoma and Mexico, but his published material (1959) is primarily historical in nature. Information about the culture of the Kansas Kickapoo is limited to Howard (1965).

Several linguists have worked on the Kickapoo language (Michelson 1912; Voorhis 1971a), and a grammar for nonspecialists has been published by Voorhis (1974).

For many years the only account of Kickapoo history was the very inaccurate sketch included in Mooney and Jones (1907). Silverberg's (1957) detailed study of the early history of this tribe is complemented by Gibson's (1963) comprehensive account of its later period.

Mascouten

IVES GODDARD

The Mascouten (məsˈkōōtən, ˈmăskəˌten) were a semi-sedentary Algonquian tribe that lived in the earlier historical period mainly in southern Michigan and Wisconsin and in northern Indiana and Illinois (fig. 1). After considerable moving about and a sharp decline in population (table 1) they lost their separate identity by amalgamating with the Kickapoo after 1800. Their obscurity and relatively early disappearance have engendered a number of attempts to identify them with some other group or groups, but none of these theories is borne out by the abundant if fragmentary historical record.

The Mascouten language, although virtually unknown, was most likely a dialect of Sauk-Fox-Kickapoo.

History

In the first half of the seventeenth century the Mascouten were in the Lower Peninsula of Michigan, probably in the southwestern quadrant. A map obtained from the Huron in the 1630s apparently located them (under the name Attistaehronon) to the west of the Sauk (Huattoehronon), Fox (Skenchiohronon), and Kickapoo (Ontarahronon), the last three groups being in the area between Saginaw Bay and Lake Erie (JR 18:234; Sanson d'Abbeville 1656; Potier 1920:155; Goddard 1972). Some less precise sources for the early period appear to use the name of this group as a cover term for the various Algonquian tribes of the Lower Peninsula that were enemies of the Ottawa, Algonquin, Petun, and Neutral, then east of Lake Huron (Champlain 1922-1936, 3:96-99; JR 21:194, 27:25-27, 33:150); however, this usage disappeared as soon as the Mascouten became known to the French at first hand.

As a result of Iroquoian attacks around the middle of the seventeenth century, the Lower Peninsula Algonquians fled west of Lake Michigan. At one time the Mascouten and some of their allies, under attack by both the Iroquois and the Winnebago, went as far as the Mississippi (JR 38:180, 44:114, 249; WHC 16:7). In 1666, a year after the resumption of the fur trade from the Upper Lakes, the Mascouten, Kickapoo, Miami, and some Illinois made a large village 30 leagues (about 70 miles) from Green Bay near the Fox, perhaps on the upper Fox River of Wisconsin (WHC 16:41). From 1670 or before to 1679 the Mascouten and some Miami (mostly of the Crane band) are known to have lived in a single palisaded village on this river, apparently southeast of present-day Berlin; these tribes had been closely associated as early as 1655 in Wisconsin and no doubt before their flight west as well. At different times the Kickapoo and some smaller groups are said to have lived either nearby or in the same village (JR 44:247, 54:226-228, 55:184-200, 58:20-22, 59:98-102, 61:148; J.J. Wood 1907; A.E. Jones 1907). Winter hunting camps were probably scattered over a fairly large part of the southern Wisconsin area; one was encountered on the lower Milwaukee River in 1674 (Kellogg 1917:264).

After an unclear series of events in 1679 involving French factional struggles, a group of Miami, Mascouten, and Wea settled on the Saint Joseph River near present-day South Bend, Indiana, but a rift between the Miami and the Mascouten resulted in the main part of the Mascouten remaining on the Fox River in association with the Fox and Kickapoo (Margry 1876-1886, 1:463, 2:216-220; Blair 1911-1912, 1:353; WHC 16:99; Hennepin 1880:258). For over a half-century thereafter there appear to have been two groups of Mascouten: a more easterly one associated with the Miami (especially the Wea subtribe) and one farther west generally with the Kickapoo and the Fox; but it is often not possible to distinguish the two in the available sources.

The groups on the Saint Joseph retreated westward in 1682 in fear of the Iroquois, with the Mascouten settling eight leagues (about 19 miles) northwest of the Chicago portage, between the Des Plaines and Fox rivers. The next year 60 Mascoutens were killed there by the Iroquois, and the anxiety among them and their allies was not quieted until the La Famine peace conference of October 1684. Here the French got the Iroquois to declare their peaceful intentions toward the Miami and Mascouten and sent these tribes a message that "they could remain secure at the place where they had been before they were at war with the Iroquois" (Margry 1876-1886, 1:612-613, 2:174, 341; IHC 23:61-62; NYCD 9:238, 260). The eastern Mascoutens may have stayed near the southern end of Lake Michigan during the ensuing period, though the evidence is circumstantial, but in any case at the beginning of the eighteenth century they were reported near Chicago with the Wea (Charlevoix 1866-1872, 5:141-142). There were some Mascoutens and Foxes on the Milwaukee River in 1680 and again, together with some Potawatomis, in 1698, but since they were with the Fox they were presumably

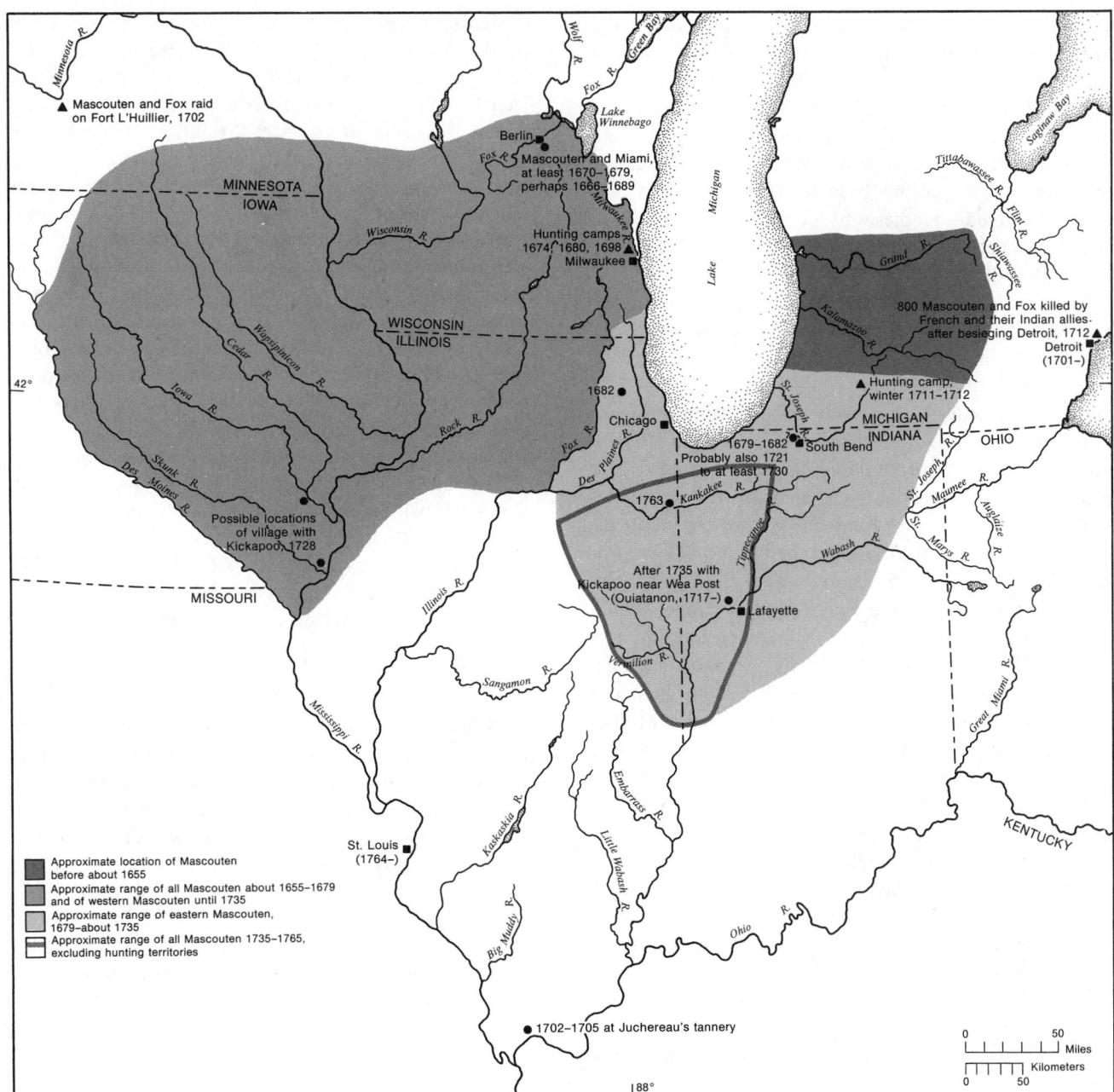

Fig. 1. Tribal locations 1640–1765. Their later range was coextensive with that of the Kickapoo.

bands detached from groups to the west and north (Shea 1852:150; Kellogg 1917:345). Eighty lodges of Mascoutens were induced to settle near a short-lived French tannery on the lower Ohio (in Pulaskie Co., Illinois) from about 1702 to 1705, but more than half were killed by an epidemic (JR 66:236–240; Fortier and Chaput 1969). Afterward the survivors may have withdrawn to the northern Indiana area, as there were Miamis and Mascoutens on the Wabash in 1711 (MPA-F 3:162). In the meantime, the main body of Mascoutens was mostly near the upper Mississippi, though there was still a village on the upper Fox River of Wisconsin in 1689. They were closely associated with the Kickapoo, and together

with the Fox they were in fairly constant conflict with the Prairie Sioux and the Iowa. Their intermittent contacts with the western Miami were somewhat strained after the murder of three Miami women, and their annoyance at the French trade with the Sioux led them to attack and plunder Frenchmen on occasion (IHC 23:276–277; NYCD 9:570, 609–611, 619–621, 724; WHC 16:200; JR 1:220; Blair 1911–1912, 2:54–114).

The antagonism between the Mascouten and the French came to a head in 1712, when some Ottawas and Potawatomis of southwestern Michigan killed or captured 50 of the tribe in an attack on a winter encampment on the upper Saint Joseph. When the Mascouten and Fox retaliated against the Ottawas at Detroit, the French rallied their allies and dealt the two tribes a crushing defeat in which over 800 were killed (WHC 16:267–295; MPHC 33:537–571). After this defeat, the Mascouten and Fox who survived in the west were joined by the Kickapoo in unrelenting warfare against the Indian allies of the French. The Mascouten and Kickapoo lived together on the Rock River and in nearby places along the Mississippi and constantly raided the Illinois (WHC 16:295–381).

Eventually, however, French military pressures on the Fox forced their two allies to try to disassociate themselves from the campaign. Some Mascoutens asked to settle near the Potawatomi on the Saint Joseph in 1720 and 1721 in order to get away from hostilities engendered by the Fox. As the French were receptive to the idea, the move was presumably made. In October 1728, when the Mascouten and Kickapoo captured and detained in their village 12 Frenchmen who were descending the Mississippi, they resisted the urgings of Fox ambassadors to execute the captives and join against the French. Instead, after the Fox, leaving in anger, killed and scalped a Kickapoo and a Mascouten hunting at a distance, the two tribes were easily persuaded to turn against the Fox and ally themselves with the French and the Illinois. Subsequently, the Mascouten aided attacks on the Fox in 1730 and 1731 (WHC 16:398–467, 17:36–57, 100–118, 149).

The main body of Mascouten and Kickapoo settled near the Wea Post (Lafayette, Indiana) on the Wabash in 1735, perhaps joining fellow tribesmen already in the area, and a final contingent of eight lodges of Mascoutens arrived in 1741. After this reunion, all the Mascoutens seem to have stayed together in the same area; a 1742 reference to "two bands" of Mascouten among other Wabash tribes probably reflects the earlier division

into eastern and western subgroups, which had come together by that time. In 1747 the Mascouten sent war parties against the Chickasaw with the support of the French, but there was increasing English influence among the tribes of the area, resulting in a tendency toward independence. From 1751 to at least 1754 they were allied with the Kickapoo, Potawatomi, and others in hostilities with the Peoria (and as late as 1788 a Mascouten chief claimed he raided the Illinois annually to avenge harm done to the French). The Mascoutens declared their loyalty to the English after the French and Indian War but refused to fight the Americans during the Revolution. In 1788 they were still a separate group, some of whom used to travel to Saint Louis to get presents from the Spanish. But by 1813 they were reported to have become incorporated with the Kickapoo, their constant associates during the preceding century, and in 1825 mention was made of the Kickapoos, "of whom one tribe was called" Mascouten (Krauskopf 1955; NYCD 10:150, 162, 220, 263; WHC 17:336, 380–387, 18:89, 385; IHC 29:240, 359, 678; W. Johnson 1921–1965, 13:406–415; Kinnaird 1946–1949, 2:244–245; Brackenridge 1819; Trowbridge 1938:69).

Culture

The Mascoutens lived in areas where they had access to both grasslands and woods. In the spring they set up or refurbished their large summer village and planted corn and other garden crops. In the summer they hunted buffalo, sometimes joining in large parties with members of allied tribes, and in the fall they scattered into small camps for the winter and hunted deer and bear. As late as 1712 they were said not to use canoes, but they had them in 1728. They were engaged in the fur trade. They had civil chiefs and war chiefs, and they are once described as having five or six "nations," which may have

Table 1. Estimated Population of Mascouten and Allied Tribes

| Date | Mascouten | | Other Tribes | Source |
	Men	Total	and Combined Figures	
1670	400	1,500		JR 55:200
1694			F + K + M: 1,400–1,500 men	NYCD 9:594
1702			M + K: 450 men, 450 families	Margry 1876–1886, 4:597, 601
1718			M + K: 200 men; F: 500 men	NYCD 9:889
1729			K + M: 200 men	WHC 17:55
1762	90		K: 180 men; P: 100 men; W: 200 men	W. Johnson 1921–1965, 10:545
1764		500		Jefferson 1801:200
1777	200		K: 300 men	Houck 1909, 1:146
1778			P + M + K: 1,000 men	Schoolcraft 1851–1857, 6:714
1779			P + M + K: 800 men	Jefferson 1801:201
1812			P + K + M + W: 1,000 men	Schoolcraft 1851–1857, 3:554

670   (F = Fox; K = Kickapoo; M = Mascouten; P = Piankashaw; W = Wea)

been a reference to an organization into clans. They believed in tutelary-animal manitous and practiced dog sacrifice. In short, the few cultural traits that can be definitely ascribed to the Mascouten confirm early statements that their way of life was virtually identical to that of the Kickapoo and Fox (JR 54:226–228, 58:34, 60:206, 66:236–240; WHC 16:372, 381, 17:38; MPHC 33:557).

Identity

Some scholars have considered the Mascouten mysterious and have sought to identify them with one or more better-known tribes. Yet the available sources seem consistently interpretable only as the record of an originally independent tribe that merged with the Kickapoo in the historical period; accordingly, a review of some of the evidence against these opposing theories may be useful. The idea that the tribe the Huron called *atsistaehronon* (in French *Nation du Feu* 'Fire Nation') was not the Mascouten but the Potawatomi (Hewitt 1910) is disproved by numerous explicit statements, including a list of tribal names in a Huron grammar (Potier 1920:155; JR 54:226, 55:102, 198, for example). This theory starts from the incorrect assertion that *Potawatomi* (in Ojibwa *po·te·wa·tami·*) means 'people of the place of the fire' (contrast Ojibwa *po·tawe·* 'he makes a fire'), and from the unwarranted assumption that names for the same tribe in different languages have to have the same literal meaning (*Mascouten* is related to, for example, Fox *maškote·wi* 'prairie' rather than *aškote·wi* 'fire'). There seems to be no merit at all to the notion (inconsistent with the preceding) that the Mascouten were a division of the Potawatomi (see Michelson 1934a, 1935; Goddard 1972). Fox has *me·ško·te·wa* 'Illinois, especially Peoria' for the name of their traditional enemies (Jones 1907:14; Blair 1911–1912, 2:202), agreeing with the Miami name for the Kaskaskia (Trowbridge 1938:68), but this usage is not reflected in the French sources. The completely distinct history of the Mascouten shows they cannot be the Shawnee (Carr 1901) or the Sauk (Wakefield 1966), and the same mass of data disproves the thesis that the name referred to no one tribe but was used by the French for any unidentified Algonquians (Brose 1971).

Synonymy

The Huron called the Mascouten by a term meaning 'People of the Place of the Fire' or 'Fire Nation', and in the earliest period the French used this or its translation: Asistagueronon,* les gens de Feu (information of 1616

*In this section the spelling of the original sources is kept; in some cases phonetic interpretations are supplied in brackets.

in Champlain 1922–1936, 4:280, 283); La Nation de Feu: Atsistarhonon (cf. Feu: Assista, Atsista; Sagard-Théodat 1632); Atsistaehronons, Nation du feu (1640: JR 20:60); la Nation du feu (1644: JR 27:26); Athistaëronon (1646: JR 30:89); ceux du Feu (1658: JR 44:114); Atsistagheronnons (1658: JR 44:248); Assista Ectaeronnons (1670: JR 54:226); ątsistaeęronnon: Mask8tins (ą = ya; ę = ye; 8 = ou; Potier 1920:155).

Later on the French used a term borrowed from an Algonquian language (presumably Algonquin or Ottawa, rather than Potawatomi as stated in Charlevoix 1744, 2:251): Makoutensak (1658: JR 44:246); Machkoutenk, Machkoutench, Machkouteng (1670: JR 54:218, 226, 232); Maskoutench (1671: JR 55:184); Mascoutens ou Nation du Feu (1671: JR 55:map); Mascoutechs, Mascouetechs (with French plural -s: Perrot in Blair 1911–1912, 1:171, 223); Maskouten (French singular, by back-formation; 1681: Margry 1876–1886, 2:217); Mascoutins (1679: JR 61:148); and other minor variants in French. English borrowed the French word, with some corruption: Máskoutins (1761: W. Johnson 1921–1965, 3:501); Musquetoons, Musquetons (1762: W. Johnson 1921–1965, 10:526, 545); Mascotain (1763: Mereness 1916:362–363); Mascoutens (1765: W. Johnson 1921–1965, 4:823); Musquattamies (1765: IHC

Thomas Gilcrease Institute of Am. Hist. and Art, Tulsa: Granville 1701.
Fig. 2. A Mascouten man drawn about 1700.

671

11:40, 57); Musketoons (1778: Schoolcraft 1851–1857, 3:561); Musquitans (1812: Schoolcraft 1851–1857, 3:554). The directly attested Algonquian forms are: Illinois masc8tenta (8 = ou; Le Boullenger 1725:s.v. *nom*); Miami Maskŏāteeau, M'skŏāteeau ([m(a)skotia]; Trowbridge 1938:69); Ottawa Muskotanje ([maskoteˑnš]; Tanner 1830:315); Ottawa and Chippewa of the Lower Peninsula mush-ko-dains ([maškoteˑns], a traditional group; Schoolcraft 1851–1857, 1:307); Ottawa Mush-co-desh (traditional group; Blackbird 1887:90). These forms appear to mean 'person (people) of the (small) prairie(s)'.

Sources

Most of the available information on the Mascoutens is in the *Jesuit Relations* (JR) and in the historical series of the states the tribe occupied (especially WHC 16, 17, 18; MPHC 33; Krauskopf 1955); also valuable is Blair (1911–1912). For a narrative historical background consult Kellogg (1925). A recent summary is Temple (1958:156–172). It should be noted that many early maps, censuses, and lists of tribal names are secondary sources, often containing outdated or erroneous information. The illustration in the *Codex Canadiensis* (fig. 2) is the only known one of any Mascouten subject.

GODDARD

Illinois

CHARLES CALLENDER

Language, Territory, and Environment

The term Illinois (ˌĭləˈnôy) denotes a group of independent tribes united by a common language and sharing a tradition of common origin. Although they are often described as a confederacy (Mooney and Thomas 1907d:597) and sometimes assembled into very large settlements that incorporated several tribes, there is no evidence of any overall intertribal organization or political institutions like those found among the Creeks or the League of the Iroquois. The Illinois language, which included several dialects, belonged to the Algonquian family. Its closest relative, Miami, most likely constituted a second group of dialects within the same language, which may be referred to as Miami-Illinois. No comprehensive description of the language exists.*

The earliest accounts of the Illinois name as many as 12 tribes (Deliette 1934:341–342; La Salle 1934:5; Margry 1876–1886, 2:134), but some of these may have been subtribal bands or simply variant forms of the same names. After 1700 the Chepoussa, Chinkoa, Coiracoentanon, Espeminkia, Maroa, Moingwena, and Tapouaro disappeared by incorporation into other Illinois groups or perhaps, in some cases, through clarification of their status ("History of the Illinois Area," this vol.). The five tribes whose identities are clearest and who persisted longest were the Cahokia, Kaskaskia, Michigamea, Peoria, and Tamaroa. However, as their populations dwindled, they were ultimately affected by the same processes of absorption and merging responsible for the earlier disappearance of the lesser-known Illinois tribes. The Kaskaskia absorbed the Tamaroa and Michigamea, while the Cahokia merged into the Peoria, whose name was eventually extended to all the surviving Illinois. In 1854 the Peoria united with the Wea and Piankashaw under the name Confederated Peoria (see "Miami," this vol.).

In 1673, when the first recorded visit by Europeans occurred (JR 59:86–163), the Illinois tribes were centered along the Mississippi River between Iowa and Arkansas, with extensions along the Illinois River to its upper reaches (fig. 1). The Peoria, Coiracoentanon, and Moingwena were in eastern Iowa. South of them were the Tamaroa in eastern Missouri and the Cahokia in western Illinois. The Michigamea lived in northeast Arkansas. The Kaskaskia were settled on the upper Illinois with their main village near Starved Rock. During the early postcontact period the Illinois retracted into a much smaller area, with one concentration on the upper Illinois and another in the American Bottom along the Mississippi between the Illinois and Kaskaskia rivers. Their habitat may be characterized as long-grass prairie, wooded along rivers and streams.

External Relations

The Illinois most closely resembled the Miami, whom the early French accounts describe as linguistically and culturally identical (Deliette 1934:392). Cultural affinities with other Central Algonquian groups were also strong. They also shared significant traits with the Prairie Siouans, particularly the Chiwere group. In many re-

---

* Miami-Illinois became extinct without a scientifically accurate orthography having been worked out for it. Hence, when words in this language are cited imprecise sources must be used and the phonetic details of the forms cannot be guaranteed.

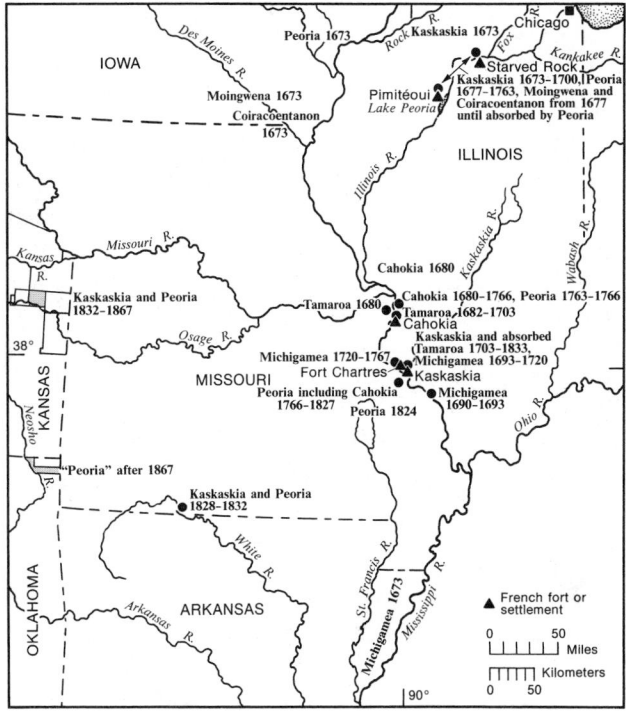

Fig. 1. Tribal locations.

spects Illinois culture was transitional between Central Algonquian and Prairie Siouan forms, with some faint and perhaps misleading Southeastern traits.

The close cultural ties between the Illinois and Miami tribes did not entail close political relations before their remnants merged in the mid-nineteenth century. These groups were seldom friendly and occasionally were actively hostile (Tonty 1917:306). The nature of Illinois relations with other Indian groups changed extensively through time. At contact and even earlier, they were under heavy pressure from the Iroquois. In this same period they were also fighting several tribes living west of the Mississippi, particularly the Missouri, Osage, Quapaw, and Pawnee, on whose territories they may have been encroaching. During the late seventeenth century the Iroquois threat diminished, and as the Illinois withdrew to areas east of the Mississippi their relations with the western tribes became much less hostile. A very different pattern emerged in the eighteenth century, when the Illinois were engaged in almost constant warfare with the tribes on their northern periphery, whose attacks eventually drove them out of northern and central Illinois. Throughout this century they were also at war with the Chickasaw.

Culture

The sources that provide detailed information about Illinois culture fall into the period beginning with the journey of Jacques Marquette and Louis Jolliet in 1673 and continuing until roughly 1700 (fig. 2). The following description pertains to that time span. It is specifically limited to the Peoria and Kaskaskia, since almost nothing is known about the culture of the Cahokia, Michigamea, and Tamaroa.

Subsistence

Illinois subsistence combined agriculture with hunting, fishing, and gathering. Agriculture, like food gathering, was primarily carried on by women, while men hunted and fished. The annual cycle began at the end of March or in early April, when people returned from their winter camps to the semipermanent summer villages (Deliette 1934:339–340). Women spent the first weeks of village residence gathering stores of firewood to free them from this task during the intensive work of planting maize, which began the first of May. After the maize was hilled up, about June 1, most residents left the villages for a communal buffalo hunt that lasted some six weeks. The first crop of maize was harvested and dried at the end of July, followed by a second harvest in late August (Deliette 1934:343–345). After this the villages were again deserted as their residents left to establish winter hunting camps.

The main crop was maize. Other plants noted by the French were beans, squash, and watermelons (Deliette

Thomas Gilcrease Inst. of Amer. Hist. and Art, Tulsa, Okla.: Granville 1701.
Fig. 2. An Illinois man with pipe and spear, drawn about 1700. He has tattooed or painted designs on his face and body, either a roach haircut or feather head ornaments, and one garter.

1934:344–345). Melons, obtained ultimately from a European source, were cultivated at least by 1673 (JR 59:129). Women also gathered a variety of tubers, nuts, berries, and fruits. Animals were usually hunted by individuals or small groups, but buffalo and occasionally deer were objects of communal hunts. On these occasions young men surrounded a herd on foot, driving the animals into an ambush formed by the rest of their party (Deliette 1934:310, 318–320). Members of the summer hunt that Deliette joined killed over 1,200 buffalo, whose flesh they preserved by drying. Other game obtained by this group included deer, bears, turkeys, lynxes, and mountain lions.

Settlement Pattern

Illinois settlements included semipermanent summer villages, summer hunting camps, and winter camps. Summer villages were strung out along the banks of rivers, sometimes for considerable distances. They could be very large. The Peoria village visited by Marquette and Jolliet

Fig. 3. Illinois ornament said to have been worn suspended from the crown of the head. Diagonally woven buffalo hair decorated with wrapped quillwork as well as hair and feather pendants. Total length 116 cm; collected before 1845.

in 1673 included 300 lodges (JR 59:123), and the Kaskaskia village had 351 lodges in 1677 (JR 58:41). Some evidence suggests that each village included a very large lodge used for ritual and perhaps for a council house (JR 59:133). Summer lodges were large rectangular structures that consisted of a pole framework covered with a double layer of rush mats. Summer camps, consisting of temporary bark-covered structures, were built on the edge of prairies at sites that provided coolness and defense against surprise attacks (Deliette 1934:308). Except that lodges were covered with rush mats, information about winter camps is not available.

Life Cycle

Birth occurred in the small lodges to which women retired during menstruation (Deliette 1934:354–355). Before a woman could move back into her own lodge after delivery, it was thoroughly cleaned. All ashes were removed from the fireplace, and her husband kindled a new fire. The only other restriction reported is that a couple should not have intercourse until their infant had been weaned.

The first game killed by a boy provided the occasion for a ritual feast. When Deliette (1934:313–314) shot a buffalo calf, two elderly men sponsored such an event on his behalf, inviting other persons to join in eating the meat to thank the Master of Life for allowing him to start killing game.

Deliette (1934:329–330) reported that boys who showed a preference for the implements used by women

Fig. 4. A Kaskaskia wooden bowl in the form of a beaver. Eyes inset with brass tacks. Length about 48 cm; collected before 1797.

were dressed as girls and became transvestites, imitating women in every respect. While agreeing that transvestism began at a very young age, Marquette (JR 59:129) emphasized its religious aspects. He noted that these persons were regarded as manitous, were present at major rituals, and were invited to council meetings where their advice was highly valued. They could join war parties and fight, but were required to use clubs rather than bows.

Males probably undertook a vision quest at adolescence, although direct evidence for this practice is limited to statements that each man had a personal manitou of which he dreamed while sleeping (Deliette 1934:365). Information about corresponding practices among females is more abundant (Deliette 1934:352–354). At the onset of her first menstruation a girl retired to a small lodge outside the village where she fasted in seclusion until she obtained a vision that ensured her well-being and gave her "the gift of great power as regards the future." During succeeding menstrual periods women secluded themselves in similar lodges, within the village, and without fasting.

Men could not marry before proving their hunting ability. An earlier requirement that they also had to accompany several war parties postponed marriage until about the age of 30, but by 1691 men married around 20 and women at 18 (Deliette 1934:330). Courtship could involve an open declaration of love, although this practice was frowned upon. A man could also open negotiations by giving presents to the brother of the woman he wanted (Deliette 1934:337). In the most formal pattern, a man first approached his father, who during his son's absence on a hunting trip or a raid assembled gifts such as kettles, guns, skins, dried meat, cloth, and perhaps a war captive (Deliette 1934:331–333). Their quantity indicated his family's wealth as well as their esteem for the woman. Women of the man's family carried these gifts to the lodge of the woman's family. The proposal, made to her father, involved imagery such as a request to warm themselves at their fire or a statement that they had come to seek moccasins. The discussion that followed included the woman and her brothers as well as their parents, who returned the presents if they rejected the offer. If they accepted it, they assembled an equivalent set of gifts and took these, with the woman, to the lodge of her new husband. Such exchanges could continue over four days.

Polygyny was apparently common. It usually involved other women of the wife's lineage. Sororate remarriages, and probably the levirate as well, were also determined by lineage affiliation.

Each sex buried its own dead, painting the face and hair of the corpse red; dressing it in fine clothing; and adding kettles, pots, calumets, bows, food, tobacco, or other items as grave goods (Deliette 1934:357–358). Forked sticks bearing a crosspiece were set at both ends of the grave. Those of distinguished war chiefs were marked by an upright tree trunk, painted to record their exploits. To this was tied a small log for each enemy killed by the person it commemorated.

Ceremonies following death were designed to ensure the spirit's entry into the land of the dead. They included a reenactment of activities he or she had particularly enjoyed, such as lacrosse games, gambling, races, the discovery dance, or other dances (Deliette 1934:356–360). Participants received gifts from the mourning relatives. Death also involved an exchange of property between the immediate family of the deceased and other relatives. A widow mourned for a year or until her husband's family released her. Release was symbolized by the dead man's sister's combing the widow's hair and giving her permission to attend dances (Deliette 1934:334). Similar restrictions were probably placed on widowers. If a man remarried too soon, choosing a woman who did not belong to the lineage of his deceased wife, women of the wife's group could destroy his property (Deliette 1934:361).

Social Organization

The Illinois household was probably an extended family, since lodges included one to four fireplaces (Deliette 1934:327), each perhaps shared by two nuclear families. Statements about kinship, while fragmentary, indicate a system of Omaha type with very strong obligations binding siblings and siblings-in-law (Deliette 1934: 355–356, 361, 363–364). Deliette also outlines a few functions of lineages. Although patrilineal clans almost certainly existed, the only possible reference to them is Céloron's (NYCD 9:1052–1058) obscure list of the crane, bear, white hind, fork, and tortoise as Illinois "devices" in 1736. In 1860 Morgan (1959:80) was told that clans had disintegrated a century before. The Illinois probably grouped clans into Earth and Sky moieties like the Miami (Trowbridge 1938:18), but no direct evidence of these units exists. Lacrosse games at the village of Pimitéoui were organized by tribal affiliation, the Peoria and Coiracoentanon constituting one team, whose opponents were drawn from the other four tribes inhabiting this settlement (Deliette 1934:342). This division was apparently based only on relative size.

Political Organization

Accounts of political structure are particularly deficient. Apparently each tribe normally maintained one village or occupied a particular section in an intertribal settlement. From the practices of neighboring tribes a division of political functions between peace and war chiefs may be assumed. Marquette's account (JR 59:117–123) of his ceremonious and highly ritualized receptions at Illinois villages illustrates one function of peace chiefs. He also notes the role of criers in making announcements and prescribing public behavior.

During the buffalo hunt young men took turns serving as camp police, destroying the property of anyone whose disobedience jeopardized the hunt's success (Deliette 1934:309–310). Women inflicted similar punishment on men who flouted their lineages' authority to control remarriage. A man could punish his wife's adultery by death, mutilation, or ordering mass rape by the warriors who were at hand (Deliette 1934:335–337). He could also attack her lover, but was liable to blood vengeance if he killed him. When murder occurred, the victim's family could accept a property settlement or insist on vengeance.

The raiding season began in February. Except for the very large groups, accompanied by women, that engaged in warfare with tribes living west of the Mississippi (Deliette 1934:386), raiding parties were fairly small. Each raid was led by a recognized war leader, who invited his followers to a dog feast before leaving the village at night. A successful raid was carried out without losses. If members of the party were killed, their leader had to compensate their relatives by gifts and undertake another raid to avenge their deaths (Deliette 1934: 381–382). Two unsuccessful forays usually ended his career. In reckoning war honors, the capture of prisoners ranked much higher than killing enemies. Men were usually burned, while women and children were distributed among the households that had lost residents through enemy raids. Some were adopted. Others apparently kept a slave or quasi-slave status (fig. 5) and could be sold, exchanged, or given away. French accounts imply the presence of institutionalized slavery even before their colonization of the American Bottom. Its functions are uncertain.

Religion

The Illinois recognized an overall being, the Master of Life, who was the ultimate source of the visions courted at puberty (JR 51:49). Descriptions of ritual practice center on warfare, shamanism, and the calumet dance. Warfare emphasized birds as the emblems of supernatural power (Deliette 1934:375–376, 379–380, 383). Each warrior kept bird skins in a colored reed mat. The departure of raiders was preceded by an all-night ritual to secure the favor of their bird spirits, whose skins were displayed together. When they set out, these were placed

676

Fig. 5. Illinois Indians taken by the French to New Orleans in 1735 (Bushnell 1927:9). The 2 men labeled "Illinois" have black and red face paint and brown and red body paint; the 'chief' wears a green necklace and red breechclout and rests his right hand on a crane; the 'dancer' has black and red face paint, brown body paint, a red breechclout, and holds squash and dewclaw(?) rattles. The woman at right wears a red skirt, while the boy has a green breechclout. All the males have roachlike haircuts. The seated woman is labeled 'Fox Indian slave'. Detail of a watercolor by Alexander de Batz.

in their leader's mat, along with medicines. In attacking, warriors gave the cries of their birds. Captives singing their death chants held long sticks containing the feathers of birds killed by the raiders.

Shamans, called "jugglers" by the French, were usually elderly men, although women also held this status and took active part in public displays of their abilities. Each shaman had his own animal spirit from whom he received knowledge of his medicines and practices. Midewiwin-like public performances, held several times each summer, involved the mock death and resurrection of patients and the exhibition of defanged rattlesnakes as the spirits causing the deaths (Deliette 1934:369-371). One shaman justified their practices to Deliette by arguing

that belief in their powers helped control the young men. Shamans apparently provided the main resistance to French missionaries (JR 66:235, 263-265).

The ritual nature of the calumet dance is clear in Marquette's account (JR 59:129-137). Later writers (such as Deliette 1934:389-391) emphasized its social aspects and connection with prestige and war honors.

History

The precontact Illinois are probably represented by an Upper Mississippian culture of the Fisher tradition, possibly Langford. However, knowledge of the southern tribes of this group is very slight, and their archeological background may have been diverse. Illinois distribution at contact perhaps reflected a recent shift westward under pressure from the Iroquois, whose earlier possession of firearms gave them a marked advantage in warfare. Yet the Kaskaskia location in northern Illinois does not support this assumption, and if the Illinois were moving westward, other factors may have been responsible. Their protohistoric war with the Winnebago (Lurie 1960: 802-804; Bacqueville de la Potherie 1911-1912, 1: 293-301) occurred within a context of Algonquian displacement, but the Illinois were not part of this particular movement.

Illinois parties began visiting the French post at Chequamegon at least as early as 1667 (JR 50:289). By 1673 Marquette (JR 59:127) found the Peoria using trade goods, including guns. Desire for closer trade relations may have stimulated his enthusiastic reception by the northern Illinois tribes and almost certainly precipitated their rapid concentration afterward at the Kaskaskia village near Starved Rock. Disrupted by an Iroquois raid in 1680, this community reformed on a larger scale two years later about René-Robert Cavelier de La Salle's fort and trading post at the same site. It was temporarily increased by Miami and Shawnee increments. In 1691 depletion of firewood in the area led its residents to establish a new settlement downstream at Pimitéoui on Lake Peoria (Deliette 1934:326-327). Meanwhile the southern Illinois tribes were forming a second area of concentration in the American Bottom, in the form of distinct tribal villages rather than a single large community. The Cahokia remained in their traditional area about the confluence of the Illinois and Mississippi, while the Tamaroa moved to the eastern bank of the Mississippi. About 1693 the Michigamea moved north to settle near the Kaskaskia river. This southern grouping became dominant after 1700, when the Kaskaskia broke away from the Pimitéoui settlement to join it, followed by most of the French traders and missionaries (JR 65:100-103). The Peoria remained alone in the north, alternating between Pimitéoui and Starved Rock. French colonization of the American Bottom began early and included an influx of settlers as well as the personnel usually attached to trading posts, missions, and forts. Illinois tribes became associated with specific French settlements: the Cahokia with Cahokia, the Michigamea with Fort de Chartres, and the Kaskaskia and Tamaroa with Kaskaskia (fig. 6).

The Illinois decline, foreshadowed in 1700 by the factionalism that disrupted Pimitéoui and perhaps by indications of decreasing population, set in at a rate that reduced the group within a century to a small remnant and destroyed their culture. One factor was continuous warfare with the Wisconsin tribes that began expanding southward as Iroquois raids ended. The Peoria, whose northern location made them particularly vulnerable, received the main thrust of these attacks and were finally

Bibliothèque Nationale, Dépt. des Cartes et Plans, Paris: Ge A664, detail.
Fig. 6. A Kaskaskia man drawn at Kaskaskia in 1796. He has a roached haircut with red feather pendant, a black and white headband with silver ornaments, red face paint, silver ornaments in his nasal septum and ears, a white and gray calico shirt, silver armband, blue cloth robe, purple leggings with blue-edged red garters, a sash and belt with knife scabbard, and a pipe tomahawk. Watercolor by Joseph Wabin, on a map.

driven south in the late eighteenth century. Parkman (1905, 2:329-330) gave wide circulation to a tradition that tribes supporting Pontiac avenged his murder by an Illinois by almost wiping out the Peoria. Alvord (1920:273) notes that contemporary accounts make no reference to such an event, and Peckham (1947:316) dismisses it as a myth.

Although the French settlements gave the southern Illinois tribes some protection, they also imposed frontier conditions on them. These conditions probably made cultural regeneration impossible and perhaps explain the relative vigor of the Peoria. Demoralized by liquor and poverty and apparently completely missionized (Alvord and Carter 1915:216, 1916:228), the Illinois grew more dependent on the French (Pease and Jenison 1940: 718-724). Like the French, they began moving across the Mississippi during the brief period of British rule. This movement was interrupted by the Revolution, when the Kaskaskia allied themselves with the Americans. It soon resumed as the Shawnee and other groups displaced by the advance of American settlements began encroaching upon Illinois hunting grounds. In the early nineteenth century the Illinois, most of whom were already living west of the Mississippi, began selling their land. They completed this process in 1832 (figs. 7–8). Reduced to a small remnant whose culture had largely disintegrated, they settled on a reservation in eastern Kansas. A regenerative movement headed by Baptiste Peoria and directed toward acculturation (Morgan 1959:40–42) ensured their survival as a group united under the name Peoria. In 1854 they merged with the remaining Wea and Piankashaw, calling themselves the Confederated Peoria. When American settlement of Kansas threatened their relatively successful adaptation, they moved to a new reservation in northeast Oklahoma.

In 1956 the Peoria numbered 439 (Tax and Stanley 1960), mostly living outside the jurisdiction of the agency. They have been incorporated as the "Peoria Indian Tribe of Oklahoma" since 1940. Little, if any, traditional culture remains (Alvord 1920:53).

Population

Early estimates of Illinois population are phrased in terms of lodges or warriors and are limited to the northern tribes. In 1673 Marquette (JR 59:123) reported 300 lodges in the Peoria village and 74 at the Kaskaskia settlement. By 1677 Kaskaskia, then including the Peoria

Natl. Coll. of Fine Arts, Smithsonian.

Fig. 8. Kee-mo-rá-nia or No English, a Peoria "dandy" with cloth turban, red and brown face paint, silver ornament in his nasal septum, bead necklaces, white cloth shirt, beaded sash, and blue cloth coat edged in pink, holding a small mirror. Painted by George Catlin in the Fort Leavenworth area, 1830–1832.

Natl. Coll. of Fine Arts, Smithsonian.

Fig. 7. Pah-me-ców-ee-tah or Man who Tracks, a Peoria chief, with red face paint, silver ear ornaments, bead necklaces, cloth turban, and red and blue yarn belt, holding a bow. Painted by George Catlin in the Fort Leavenworth area, 1830–1832.

and other tribes, contained 351 lodges (JR 58:41). Deliette in 1691 credited the Pimitéoui settlement, where the northern tribes were gathered, with 260 lodges and estimated its warriors, whom he defined as men aged 20 to 40, as numbering 800 (1934:327, 342). He estimated over 60 lodges for the Cahokia and Tamaroa. The decline that may be inferred from Deliette's figures becomes obvious in Céloron's Enumeration of 1736 (JR 9:1056), which gives a total of 600 warriors for all the Illinois tribes, or a projected population of 2,400. By 1756, assuming three persons to each warrior, this figure had shrunk to 1,720 (Stirling 1916:125). Although later figures show a continuous decline, they seldom include all the Illinois until their resettlement in Kansas. In 1840 they numbered only 200 persons (Foreman 1946:205).

Synonymy

The Illinois self-designation was inoca (Le Boullenger 1725; Belting 1958:287), a word of unknown etymology.

The widely used name Ilinioüek (Mooney and Thomas 1907d:599; JR 50:288), whence Illiniwek (Shea 1855:348) and other variants, is of uncertain etymology; it is not Illinois ireni8a 'man' and may not even be an Illinois

679

word (Ives Goddard, personal communication 1976). The common French spelling Illinois would have been pronounced [ilinwe] in the seventeenth century. The earliest known reference to the Illinois group has the singular form of this name, Eriniouai, 1640 (JR 18:231). Other variants are Liniouek (JR 42:220), Aliniouek (JR 44:246), Ilinois (JR 54:166), and Ilinoués (JR 58:22), as well as Linneway and Ninneway (Forsyth 1912:200). Ilimoüec (JR 51:46) is a misprint for Ilinioüec.

Fox me·ško·te·waki (pl.), primarily the name for the Peoria, was extended to other Illinois tribes as well (Michelson 1934a) and probably accounts for occasional statements (for example, Foreman 1946:19; Forsyth 1912:202) describing the Mascouten as Illinois. The Iroquois form appears in variants such as Chicktaghicks (Colden 1958:xiv), Geghtigeghroones (NYCD 7:384), and Kichtages (NYCD 3:325). Gatschet (in Mooney and Thomas 1907d:599) recorded the Huron name as witish-axtánu.

The Cahokia were first noted, in 1680, as Caokia (La Salle 1934:5). They are also called Cahau (Margry 1876–1886, 6:654), Caos (WHC 16:456–463), Caouaouce (Deliette 1934:342), Kaockia (Margry 1876–1886, 2:201), and Kaoukia (JR 64:161). Ooukkea (La Salle 1934:5) may be a synonym, but this seems a very remote possibility. The Illinois term was Ca8kiaki (pl.) (Le Boullenger in Belting 1958:289). From this the French derived their nickname Ca8x (Belting 1958:288).

The earliest mention of the Chepoussa, also in 1680 (La Salle 1934:5), gives them as Chepoussea. Other forms are Chepousca (Margry 1876–1886, 2:134), Chepousia (IHC 23:277), and perhaps Chépontia (Margry 1876–1886, 2:189).

The Chinkoa (Margry 1876–1886, 2:134) are also given as Chinko (La Salle 1934:5).

The Coiracoentanon (Margry 1876–1886, 2:201) are also given as Coirachietanon (Margry 1876–1886, 2:134), Coueracouitenons (Deliette 1934:360), Karakoenitanon (La Salle 1934:5), Koeracoenetanon (Margry 1876–1886, 2:42), and Kouerakouitenoux (Deliette 1934:342).

The Espeminkia (Margry 1876–1886, 2:134) are also listed as Epiminguia (Coxe 1741:11).

The first reference to the Kaskaskia is Allouez's report for 1672 (JR 58:40–41), which gives the name as Kakach-kiouek. Variants include Carcarchia (La Salle 1934:5), Cascaschia (Margry 1876–1886, 2:134), Caskakias (JR 58:264–265), Caskaskias (JR 66:37), Casquiar (IHC 10:5), Kachkachkia (JR 60:159), Kaskakias (Deliette 1934:390), Kaskascia (Margry 1876–1886, 2:121), Kaskasia (JR 59:161), Kaskaskia (JR 64:173), Kaskaskeys (IHC 11:494–495). The Illinois term was Cascakia (sg.), Cascakiaki (pl.), from which the French derived their nickname Cas (Belting 1958:288–289). The Shawnee term was ka'kaški (Voegelin 1938–1940, 8:295), and the Miami, kakkakkia (Voegelin 1938–1940, 8:298). Trow-

bridge (1938:12, 68) also gives Mekoateeaukee and Makoateeāūkee as Miami terms for the Kaskaskia.

Maroa may simply be a variant of Tamaroa, and several citations (Margry 1876–1886, 1:479, 2:134, 246; Hennepin 1880:362) explicitly list both names as alternatives for the same group. Yet Deliette (1934:342) mentions the Maroas after an earlier reference to the Tamaroa (cf. Margry 1876–1886, 2:201).

The Michigamea were first described by Marquette, who in 1673 called them Mitchigamea (JR 59:151). Other variants are Machigama (IHC 23:277), Matchagamia (Coxe 1741:11), Mechegames (IHC 8:124), Meeches (IHC 11:596), Metchigames (JR 65:105), Metchis (IHC 10:4), and Mitchagamis (IHC 11:596).

The Moingwena were variously called Moingoana (Margry 1876–1886, 2:134) and Mouingouena (JR 65:101; Deliette 1934:392). Their French nickname was les Moines (whence the name of the river and city).

Allouez in 1673 referred to the Peoria as Peoualen (JR 58:40–41). Marquette called them Peouarea (JR 59:125). Other variants include Peiorias (IHC 11:301), Peoarias (JR 66:51), Peoreanas (JR 8:124), Peouareoua (JR 64:161), Peoucaria (Margry 1876–1886, 2:134), and Pewarias (JR 5:57), and Pianria (W. Smith 1765:70). The Illinois form of their name was Pe8are8a, from which the French took their nickname les Pez or les Pe (Belting 1958:288). The Shawnee term was pe·wa·le; the Miami, pewalia and peolia (Voegelin 1938–1940, 3:97); the Delaware pe·yó·le (Ives Goddard, personal communication 1973). me·ško·te·waki was the Sauk and Fox name. The Osage called the Peoria δόδǫ (La Flesche 1932:304).

Tamaroa was cited in 1680 (IHC 23:5). Other forms are Tamaroids (WHC 17:59), Tamarois (JR 65:71), Tamaroua (Deliette 1934:342), Tamarouha (JR 65:103), and Tamarrais (JR 66:57). Maroa and its variants may also belong here.

Tapouaro and Tapouero appear in Margry (1876–1886, 2:134, 201). Deliette (1934:342) gives Raparouas.

Sources

The basic source for Illinois culture is Deliette's (1934) account based on his own observations among the Peoria and Kaskaskia in the late seventeenth century. His coverage is uneven and sometimes grossly prejudiced, but the description is invaluable. The *Jesuit Relations* (JR 1896–1901) also contain valuable material, particularly Marquette's surprisingly sympathetic report (JR 59:86–163). Good (1972) is an archeological-ethnohistorical study of the Kaskaskia. Among historians who have dealt with the Illinois, Alvord (1920) is probably the most useful, although they are not his central concern. Knowledge of the Illinois tribes is far from adequate, and except for the Peoria and Kaskaskia their cultures are practically unknown.

Miami

CHARLES CALLENDER

Language, Territory, and Environment

The term Miami (mä'yămē, mä'yămə) has been used to designate both a specific tribe and, in earliest postcontact times, a grouping of related tribes. The Miami spoke an Algonquian language most closely related to Illinois; these two dialects, or clusters of dialects, can probably be considered varieties of the same language.*

French accounts of the seventeenth and early eighteenth centuries (JR 58:41; Deliette 1934:393; Bacqueville de la Potherie 1911-1912, 2:67) described the Miami as including six groups or tribes—Atchatchakangouen, Kilatika, Mengakonkia, Pepikokia, Piankashaw, and Wea. These units were sometimes clearly distinguished but were often simply referred to collectively as Miami. After several of them disappeared early in the eighteenth century, the outlines of the group became much clearer. The Piankashaw and Wea retained their distinct status and were recognized as fully independent tribes. The term Miami was restricted to a tribe living along the upper courses of the Wabash and Maumee rivers. From the consistent use of the crane as its symbol (Trowbridge 1938:7), its core was probably the Atchatchakangouen, a name apparently based on čačakwa 'sandhill crane' (Voegelin 1938-1940, 5:148). It may also have included the Kilatika and Mengakonkia. The Pepikokia maintained their identity at least until 1742 (Thwaites 1904-1907, 1:381-382). At that time they were closely associated with the Wea, who probably absorbed them. In 1854 the Wea and Piankashaw formally merged with the remnants of the Illinois tribes under the name Confederated Peoria. The Miami joined this group in 1873, when it became the United Peoria and Miamis.

In the early contact period and probably for some time before, the Miami-speaking tribes occupied the area around the southern end of Lake Michigan from the Saint Joseph River to northern Illinois. Early in the eighteenth century they moved into the Wabash drainage, the region with which they are most closely associ-

ated historically (fig. 1). Their earlier habitat was primarily prairie interspersed with woodland, and their later range on the Wabash included a large prairie component.

External Relations

The culture of the Miami tribes closely resembled that of the Illinois but showed stronger affinities with other Central Algonquian cultures and fewer similarities to the Prairie Siouans. However, deficiencies in the data may exaggerate these differences. The most complete account of Illinois culture (Deliette 1934) dates from the late seventeenth century while the basic description of the Miami (Trowbridge 1938) was written in 1824-1825 after economic and technological changes introduced through the fur trade had promoted major cultural shifts.

Cultural similarities aside, relations with the Illinois were not particularly close. The tribes most consistently associated with the Miami group during their recorded history were the Mascouten and Kickapoo. This relationship was evident at the time of contact, when some of the Miami shared a village in Wisconsin with the Mascouten

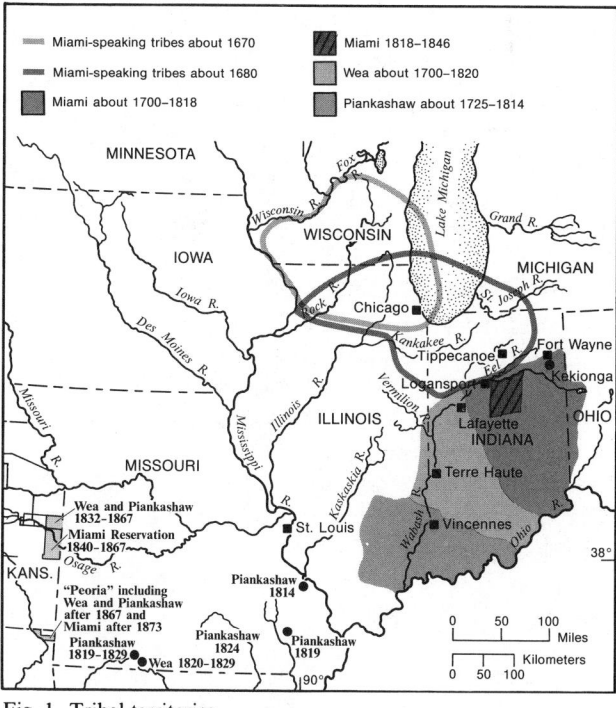

Fig. 1. Tribal territories.

---

* The Miami-Illinois language became extinct without a scientifically accurate orthography having been worked out for it. Miami-Illinois words cited here follow the available sources (notably J.P. Dunn in Voegelin 1938-1940), which are deficient in not indicating vowel length and the preaspiration of stops and in occasionally confusing vowel qualities (Ives Goddard, personal communication 1975).

and occasionally the Kickapoo. It continued in later years, when both tribes followed the Miami toward the Wabash area. A Mascouten group settled near the Piankashaw early in the eighteenth century. Somewhat later a mixed Kickapoo-Mascouten band occupied an area near the Wea. During later periods the Miami tribe was also associated with the Potawatomi, who had occupied their earlier habitat south of Lake Michigan. In the late eighteenth century they were intermingled with Shawnee, Delaware, and other refugee groups forced into their region by war with the United States during and after the Revolution.

In the early postcontact period the Miami tribes were apparently under pressure from the Iroquois, which diminished toward the end of the seventeenth century. They carried on extensive warfare with the Dakota until their shift to the Wabash ended contact with this group. Like the Illinois, they were usually at war with the Chickasaw and other southeastern tribes. While this may have represented the persistence of a precontact pattern (Trowbridge 1938:8), these hostilities were encouraged and promoted by the French.

Component Groups

Accounts from the early postcontact period imply a kind of political unity among the Miami-speaking tribes by frequent references to the "great Chief" of the Miami (Bacqueville de la Potherie 1911–1912, 1:327, 346, 2:66). While some of these statements suggest that all the tribes in their group acknowledged this official, others refer to the multitribal village in Wisconsin and may stress the paramount status of the Miami chief in that community. Perhaps the various Miami-speaking groups were subtribes within a larger unit at the time of contact, but by the eighteenth century they formed three entirely independent tribes, the Miami, Wea, and Piankashaw, with a fourth tribe, the Pepikokia, rapidly losing its identity. These tribes recognized their common origin, and the Miamis were conceptually the elder brother of the rest (Trowbridge 1938:12), yet each acted with full independence.

Each tribe was divided into bands, taking their names from their chiefs or from the location of their summer villages. Around the middle of the eighteenth century the Miami consisted of the three bands of Le Pied Froid, La Demoiselle, and Tepicon. This pattern lasted at least to the end of the century, with one band centered at Fort Miamis, another on the northern Eel River, and a third at Tippecanoe. The Wea and Piankashaw each included at least two bands.

Culture

Miami culture disintegrated before significant anthropological studies were made. The seventeenth- and eigh-

teenth-century accounts are not adequate. Even Trowbridge's (1938) extensive description written in 1824–1825 is incomplete. Information about Wea and Piankashaw culture is hopelessly fragmentary.

Subsistence

The Miami practiced the mixed hunting-farming economy typical of their region. Hunting was strongly oriented toward the fur trade, so much so that fishing had replaced the summer hunt to ensure that animals would be killed only when their hides were in best condition (Brice 1868:42). The buffalo, formerly an important game animal, disappeared long before 1800, but an echo of the communal buffalo hunt survived in the equal division of all the game killed by a hunting party (Trowbridge 1938:66). Wild tubers and roots were extensively used (Trowbridge 1938:64–65). An American army that occupied the Eel River village in 1791 found many of its residents, including the chief, engaged in gathering these (Dillon 1859:269). Extensive maize fields surrounded Miami villages (fig. 2).

Settlement Pattern

Like other tribes of the area, the Miami alternated between summer villages and winter hunting camps. Seventeenth-century villages consisted of oval lodges whose pole frames were covered with rush mats. By the late eighteenth century, if not earlier, these had been replaced by log structures, although the earlier form persisted in the winter camps, with bark or hide replacing mats. The houses comprising a village were typically scattered irregularly along a river bank; for example, the Eel River village extended for three miles (Dillon 1859:268). A large council house, used only for public purposes and distinct from the chief's lodge, was apparently a standard feature of Miami settlements (Gist 1893:50, 53).

Life Cycle

There is no specific information about the treatment of birth. Infants were sometimes named by the parents. More often an elderly woman whom the mother summoned and paid for this service gave the child a name derived from an incident in a well-omened dream whose details foreshadowed traits it would show as an adult

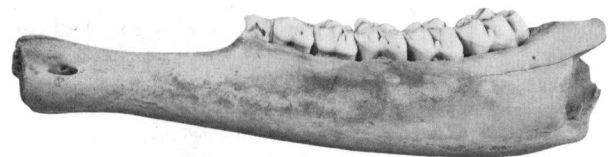

Mus. of the Amer. Ind., Heye Foundation, N.Y.: 2/7944.
Fig. 2. Piece of deer jaw used for removing kernels from corn ears—an implement type widespread among eastern North American Indians. Length 16.5 cm; collected in Indiana before 1912.

(Trowbridge 1938:37-38). This name usually designated an animal or natural phenomenon and apparently had to be one proper to the child's clan. Adults could change their names to avert illness or misfortune, asking a friend to give a new one in exchange for a gift.

Children were brought up according to the general practice of the region, with physical punishment rarely applied. A common technique was a daily lecture from both parents, who exhorted their offspring to behave properly (Trowbridge 1938:38-39). Both sexes undertook a vision quest at puberty, according to Trowbridge (1938:56, 58). He does not mention any connection between this event and the onset of menstruation, nor does he describe menstrual seclusion. Men and women indicated adult status by painting their faces with vermilion (Trowbridge 1938:18, 24). Before doing so, a male had to accompany a war party (figs. 3, 4).

The formality of marriage varied widely, and courtship ranged through several alternatives from direct action by the couple to negotiations between their families (Trowbridge 1938:41-42). In the most common form, a young man who contemplated marriage came at night to the lodge where the girl he preferred lived with her parents. Holding a piece of burning bark as a light, he shook her awake. By smiling as she asked him to leave, she

Fig. 4. Mem-són-se-ah or The Left Hand, a Piankashaw warrior, with red face paint, earrings and bracelet of silver, red robe, red yarn belt, holding a stone ax. Painted by George Catlin in the Fort Leavenworth area, 1830-1832.

Fig. 3. Go-to-ków-páh-ah or He who Stands by Himself, a Wea warrior, with red face and body paint, a painted fur robe, white cloth shirt, buckskin coat with fringes tipped with blue and white beads, silver bracelet, shell(?) gorget, and a trade pipe tomahawk. Painted by George Catlin in the Fort Leavenworth area, 1830-1832.

effectively accepted his proposal. On his next visit he stayed the night, allowing her parents to see him the next morning and leaving some piece of property as evidence of his intentions. He then went hunting and brought game to the lodge, sometimes leaving his rifle there as well. A suitor could also initiate courtship by enlisting the good will of a woman's father or brother, or he could accept a proposal made by the father (Trowbridge 1938:45). The most formal pattern, family negotiation, was apparently used when the suitor was unsure of the woman's response. His parents took a quantity of gifts to her family. The wording of their proposal—that they were bringing fire, water, and moccasins—used symbolism very like that Deliette (1934:331-332) reported much earlier for the Illinois, but reversed this. Probably Trowbridge's account involves a misunderstanding, and they described themselves as asking for these, since their provision was traditionally part of a woman's role in the division of labor within the household. When they left, the other couple discussed the offer with their daughter. If she consented, she dressed in her best clothes and accompanied her parents to the others' lodge.

Marriage included an exchange of gifts (Trowbridge 1938:42-43), which the husband initiated by giving his wife a horse, rifle, or other valuable gift for her brother. The brother reciprocated with a present of meat, which his sister brought to her mother-in-law. She divided this among women of her family, who presented a counter-gift of vegetable food. Residence after marriage was apparently patrilocal. The extent of polygyny is uncertain. Trowbridge (1938:33, 43-44) is silent about its sororal variety but cites the sororate and levirate as preferred forms of remarriage.

Death was followed by a brief wake for which the corpse, dressed in fine clothing, was laid out within the lodge where relatives and friends gathered to mourn (Trowbridge 1938:30-31). Although extended burial was usual, a person could request scaffold burial or interment in a seated position. The family selected four nonrelatives to carry the corpse to its grave. There an elderly relative addressed it, asking that it not take any living persons with it. Except for silver jewelry (fig. 5) and other valuables in which the corpse was dressed, grave goods were limited to food and water. After the burial the mourners ate at the grave before going home. For the next four evenings an elderly relative of the same sex as the deceased watched the grave to prevent a sorcerer's stealing part of the body. Women sometimes fed the dead by taking food to the grave and inviting a friend of the deceased to eat this (Trowbridge 1938:32).

The Miami sponsored a performance of the favorite dance or activity of the deceased as soon after the burial

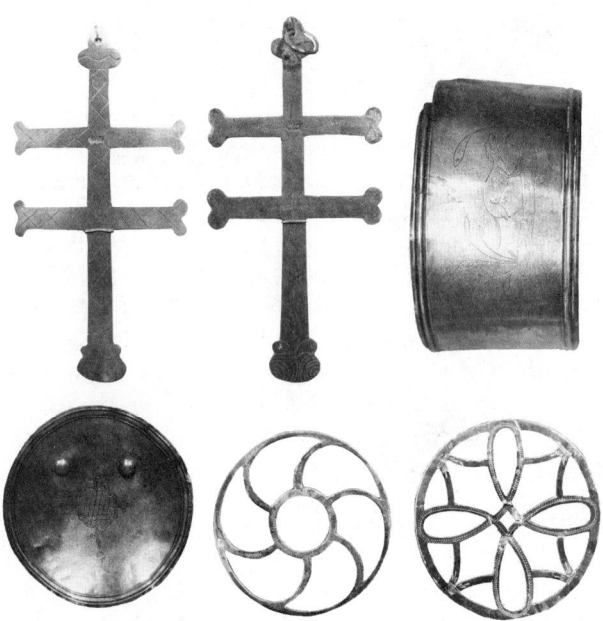

Fig. 5. Trade silver ornaments. From the grave of Little Turtle, buried in 1812: top left and center, crosses with engraved designs and mark of Robert Cruickshank of Montreal (b.1767, d.1809); right, arm band with engraved stylized wolf or dog and mark of Robert Cruickshank; lower left, gorget with two rivets and engraved 4-petaled flower. From Indian graves in Spy Run area of Fort Wayne: center, ear wheel with mark of Robert Cruickshank; right, ear wheel with mark of Narcisse Roy of Montreal (b.1765, d.1819). Diameter of bottom left about 7 cm; rest same scale.

as convenient. A year after the death of a parent, the offspring ceremonially adopted a replacement (Trowbridge 1938:34-37). The adoption ceremony included another performance of the favorite activity. Afterward the person adopted received clothing and other property belonging to the person he or she replaced. These gifts were later repaid by counter-gifts of food or fur. A war captive adopted in this manner actually took the position of the person replaced, joining the household and marrying the surviving spouse. Adoption ceremonies marked the formal end of mourning. Mourning restrictions were particularly stringent for surviving spouses, who had to avoid festivities and display carelessness in dress and appearance (Trowbridge 1938:33-34). The mourning period could be abbreviated by a formal release from the family of the deceased spouse, obtained through a request accompanied by gifts.

Social Organization

The kinship terminology that Morgan (1871:291-382) obtained in 1860 is the earliest reported for the Miami. His schedules show a system of standard Omaha type. Information about kinship behavior beyond the immediate family is lacking. Knowledge of the clan system is also scanty. Trowbridge (1938:18) described a system of five patrilineal clans—Little Turtle, Snow Thaws, Raccoon, Turkey, and Moon. Morgan (1959:80) listed 10 clans—Wolf, Loon, Golden Eagle, Turkey Buzzard, Panther, Turkey, Raccoon, Snow, Sun, and Water. Trowbridge (1938:18) gives very little direct information about the functions of clans except for reporting that they were traditionally instituted for "government," a purpose made obsolete by declining population. Statements scattered through his account (1938:19, 20, 38) indicate that clans controlled names and suggest that they may have had an extensive role in organizing ritual and the ritual aspects of warfare. The fact that the leader of a war party was not responsible for the deaths of members of his own clan suggests that clans may also have been units of collective responsibility. By 1860 the clan system was rapidly disappearing (Morgan 1959:80).

Trowbridge (1938:18) also described a system of Sky and Earth moieties similar in form to those of the Chiwere and Dhegiha Siouans. The Little Turtle and Snow Thaws clans were called mašokia, a term of uncertain meaning; the other clans were known as šonkisia 'those of the air' (spellings normalized). Morgan's silence about moieties probably indicates that these had disappeared by 1860.

Political Organization

The Miami political system involved the customary duality between village chiefs and war chiefs, whose functions were sharply divided. Village chiefs were concerned with administration and with negotiations for peace; they were forbidden to join war parties or even show ill humor (Trowbridge 1938:14). Their property was available to anyone needing it. In exchange they received game and furs each spring. This office was patrilineally inherited, although Trowbridge (1938:13) said that a chief without sons could be succeeded by his daughter's son. Succession was validated by the tribal council, whose composition is not specified. Both kinds of chiefs had speakers whose offices were also inherited (Trowbridge 1938:13, 15–16). A speaker could act as regent until a young chief came of age.

Trowbridge (1938:14–15, 29) described female chiefs, usually the daughters of chiefs and similarly separated by peace and war functions. They supervised major feasts, prepared supplies for war parties, and could demand an end to a blood feud or a war that had continued for a long time.

When murder occurred within the tribe the victim's family could accept compensation in the form of property or insist on their option to kill the murderer (Trowbridge 1938:16–18). This action could initiate a blood feud. Killing his wife for adultery was regarded as a husband's right and drew no retaliation. A woman who killed her husband in self-defense was similarly free from retaliatory action (Trowbridge 1938:44, 47).

War chiefs, according to Trowbridge (1938:14), differed from village chiefs only in function and inherited their offices in the same manner. His account of the role of the war chief for the Raccoon clan (1938:19) suggests that every clan had such an official. Perhaps hereditary war chiefs were primarily concerned with ritual aspects of war. In any case, successful leadership of a war party could also elevate a man to this office. The best-known war chief, Little Turtle, acquired the position by defeating an American expedition in 1780.

Tribal warfare (Trowbridge 1938:19–27) was decided upon by a council of war chiefs, summoned by a speaker who carried a belt of wampum, painted red, to each official. If they agreed upon war, they called a meeting of warriors to whom they explained their decision and outlined their plans, organizing a war party. The night before its departure, members brought their personal sacred packs to the council house, where these were combined in one bundle to be carried by the shaman who led the march. An all-night war dance followed. After a state of war formally existed, war chiefs could also lead smaller parties made up of their relatives or members of their clans or villages. Such groups set out secretly without public ritual preparation, but always with a pack combining the individual packs of their members. Younger men served the established warriors during a raid, cooking, bringing water and firewood, and mending their moccasins. This division by age was further emphasized at night when the two groups slept on opposite sides of the fire.

Occasionally a woman who had lost a close relative had a dream, sometimes deliberately courted, sanctioning her leadership of a war party and her right to carry its pack (Trowbridge 1938:26). If the war chiefs accepted her vision as valid, she could carry out its instructions. Her role was ritual rather than military.

A defeated war party or one that suffered losses returned to its village without ceremony or public announcement. A successful party usually announced its arrival by shouting as its members approached the village. At its outskirts they began the Buffalo Dance and moved in this fashion to the council house. Their pack was hung inside this building and its custody assumed by two elderly women who sang, thanking the supernatural for the group's safe return. As his name occurred in their song, each warrior gave them cloth, beads, or a hide. At nightfall the group disbanded. Their shaman took the pack to his own lodge. Several days later four shamans brought it back to the council house where the raiders again assembled. The four men vomited up and reswallowed bones, glass, ice, and other objects, afterward staging a Midewiwin performance. The pack was later opened. Its components were separated and returned to their owners, each of whom gave a feast for his individual pack before putting it away.

Religion

Early sources describe the Miami as believing in an overall deity called the Master of Life (Kinietz 1940: 211–212) and also indicate that the sun held a significant place in ritual (Bacqueville de la Potherie 1911–1912, 1:332). While the Master of Life remained important into the nineteenth century (Trowbridge 1938:30), the role of the sun diminished.

Children began training for the vision quest while quite young, fasting for periods of increasing length (Trowbridge 1938:56, 58, 67–68). Boys blackened their faces with paint or charcoal. Girls, described as more scrupulous in observing the fast, used earth. The full-scale fasting that began at adolescence eventually attracted the pity of a spirit, usually in animal form (Trowbridge 1938:25). A few males, called White Faces, were directed by a female spirit to assume the dress and occupations of women. These persons, who were generally respected, could engage in warfare, although they had to dress as men if they joined a raid (Trowbridge 1938:68).

The aspect of Miami ritual activity described in greatest detail and in reports covering the longest span of time was the Midewiwin. Bacqueville de la Potherie (1911–1912, 2:85–88) described a late seventeenth-century performance held at Maramek and sponsored by the "great chief" to ensure the safe return of a war party. Attendance was apparently compulsory. The director of the ceremony, accompanied by four elderly men and women, entered each lodge to announce its beginning. Bearskins whose heads were painted with green clay were placed on

Fig. 6. Wooden dolls used in Medicine ceremony. Left, height about 18 cm; collected at Crown Point, Ind., 1835.

an altar and saluted by everyone who passed these. The most active participants were the persons Potherie called "jugglers, medicine men, and sorcerers," who divided themselves into two parties for a mock combat in which they used packs, snakeskins, and otter skins to attack each other, later reviving those who feigned death. The ceremony continued for five days and nights. Many dogs were killed as sacrifices, and their bones were burned. Trowbridge (1938:77-87) described the traditional origin of the Midewiwin and gave a brief account of its organization in the nineteenth century.

Little is recorded about pack ritual other than what is associated with warfare. Bacqueville de la Potherie (1911-1912, 1:332) described a ritual feast in 1679 held to thank the sun for bringing Nicolas Perrot to a Miami settlement where he had distributed presents to stimulate interest in the fur trade. The feast took place in the chief's lodge where a sacred pack was placed on an altar set up for the occasion. Trowbridge (1938:66-67) reported that each family held ritual feasts for the Master of Life three or four times a year and oftener during periods of war. Failure to do so could lead to illness. He explicitly denied the existence of ritual feasts connected with hunting or the agricultural cycle.

History

If the Upper Mississippian antecedents of the Miami-speaking tribes are represented by the Huber culture,

their precontact location corresponded closely with their late seventeenth-century habitat embracing the southern end of Lake Michigan. Some displacement westward apparently occurred in the early contact period or just before. Its extent is uncertain. References to Miamis living on the Mississippi (Deliette 1934:392; St. Cosme 1917:349) or west of it may denote hunting camps rather than villages (Kinietz 1940:162). Contact with French traders occurred by at least 1654 (JR 44:247) but reliable accounts begin in 1670, when part of the Miami group was sharing a village in Wisconsin with the Mascouten and other tribes (JR 54:207). Although this settlement is occasionally described as containing all the Miami, it was almost certainly only an outpost, probably established for closer access to the source of trade goods. The reception its residents gave Perrot and other French visitors reinforces this interpretation (Bacqueville de la Potherie 1911-1912, 1:321-322, 327-329). By 1680 the Miami groups had apparently reoccupied their precontact territory, extending from the Saint Joseph River across Indiana and Illinois to the Mississippi. In 1682 they temporarily shifted to sites near Fort Saint Louis on the Illinois River, either for protection from the Iroquois or more probably from interest in trade. By 1688 (Deliette 1934:392) they had again returned to their traditional habitat, resisting French attempts to concentrate them at the Saint Joseph as a barrier against Iroquois raids (NYCD 9:624-627; Bacqueville de la Potherie 1911-1912, 2:112).

Although sometimes recalcitrant, the Miami-speaking tribes were closely allied with the French as long as the Iroquois were a threat, but they appreciated the terms offered by English traders. This consideration probably motivated their drastic redistribution in the early eighteenth century. Several groups, mostly from the Saint Joseph River, moved to the upper Wabash and headwaters of the Maumee, where they coalesced into the Miami tribe. Most of those who settled along the middle Wabash between Terre Haute and Logansport eventually identified themselves as Wea. The Piankashaw kept their own identity by moving on to a new location on the Vermilion and the lower Wabash rivers. After several unsuccessful attempts to reverse these movements the French accepted the situation and established a garrisoned trading post for each tribe. Fort Miamis, on the site of Fort Wayne, serviced the Miami. The Wea post, later shared with Kickapoo, was Ouiatanon near Lafayette, while the Piankashaw, the Mascouten, and one Kickapoo band centered on Vincennes. These posts became indispensable to the tribes, providing not only trade goods but also necessary services such as blacksmiths. In time they also attracted French settlers. Vincennes, in particular, which belonged to Louisiana rather than Canada, developed into a community like those in Illinois.

In 1747 English traders detached one Miami band from the French interest. Its members moved to the

Great Miami River in southwest Ohio. The rapid growth of this community, drawing Weas and Piankashaws as well as Miamis (Gist 1893:47-55), threatened the entire French establishment until an expedition from Detroit destroyed it (Pease and Jenison 1940) and reestablished French control. Dissatisfaction with English policies after 1763 brought the Miami and Wea into Pontiac's movement. Apparently they were sufficiently doubtful of the outcome to store up credit by taking excellent care of their English prisoners and made peace as soon as possible.

Knowing that loss of their lands would be the inevitable consequence of American rule (Downes 1940: 281-282), the Miami fought as English allies during the Revolution and had a leading role in the Indian coalition that continued the war for 10 years after the English made peace. The Piankashaw, who sided with the Americans after their capture of Vincennes, paid heavily for this choice when disruption of the trade network forced them to return to hunting with bows and to abandon agriculture (James 1912:445). The Wea first announced their neutrality and later joined the coalition. For some years Miami territory was distant enough from military action to serve as a refuge for more exposed tribes and a source of food supplies for the Shawnee and others whose villages were devastated. However, toward the close of the war their towns and fields were repeatedly destroyed. Under their war chief, Little Turtle, the Miami had notable military success, including their rout of American armies under Augustin Mottin de la Balme in 1780 and Josiah Harmar in 1790 and culminating in their defeat of Arthur St. Clair in 1791, an action in which 630 Americans were killed (Downes 1940:318). This period ended with the American victory at the Battle of the Fallen Timbers in 1794, followed the next year by the Treaty of Greenville (fig. 7). Miami policy then shifted to acceptance of American rule. They refused to join Tecumseh, and during the War of 1812 they remained neutral even after their villages were attacked by Americans.

All three tribes declined very rapidly during the nineteenth century. This decay was already evident by 1796 among the Piankashaw (Volney 1804:393-503), whose circumstances paralleled those of the Illinois tribes. They sold their lands in 1805 and moved to Missouri in 1814. The Wea followed suit, emigrating after 1820. Although the Miami sold land, they resisted attempts to move them. Yet their population was rapidly dwindling (Foreman 1946:126; Trowbridge 1938:18, 46) and their culture falling into decay (Trowbridge 1938:10, 33, 39, 40, 53), while movements toward acculturation failed. The causes are not clear. Perhaps the main problem was their relative wealth, based on annuities from land sales. This exposed them to gross economic exploitation by the American settlers who surrounded them, undermining their traditional economy without providing viable substitutes and increasing the demoralization resulting from traffic in

Fig. 7. Paccane, a Miami man, with roach haircut, ear wheels and other ornaments of silver, holding a trade tomahawk. Etching done between 1790 and 1796 by Elizabeth Posthuma Gwillim Simcoe, wife of the lieutenant governor of Upper Canada.

liquor (Foreman 1946:126-127; Trowbridge 1938:40, 47). In 1846 the army forcibly removed the Miami from Indiana, although about half the tribe evaded the troops. Resettled in Kansas, they continued to decline. Their catastrophic loss of population after removal may partly reflect a surreptitious movement back to Indiana, although they also received increments from that area. The Kansas group eventually moved to northeast Oklahoma, where in the 1870s they joined the confederacy that the Wea and Piankashaw had already established with the Peoria.

In 1950, 323 Miamis were attached to their agency in Oklahoma, while about 700 still lived in Indiana (Tax and Stanley 1960). The conditions and government of the Oklahoma group are the same as those of the Peoria. Very little is known about the Indiana Miami, who are usually assumed to be almost entirely acculturated. The Piankashaw and Wea no longer exist as entities, being completely merged with the Peoria.

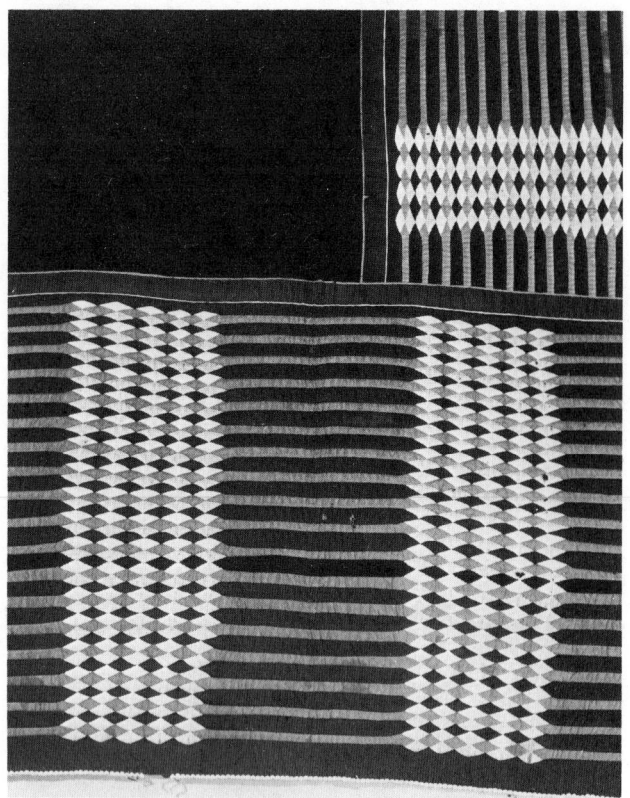

Mus. of the Amer. Ind., Heye Foundation, N.Y.: 14/5988.

Fig. 8. Fine ribbon appliqué on a pair of blue wool leggings collected about 1870 in Wabash Co., Ind. Detail shown about 29 cm wide.

Kinietz (1940:164) estimates that the Miami-speaking tribes numbered 4,000 to 5,000 at the time of contact. Sabrevois's 1718 figures (WHC 16:375-376) show a total population of at least 5,600 for the entire group, of whom 1,600 were Miamis. Those given by Céloron (NYCD 9:1057) for 1736 are 2,200 and 800, respectively, and probably too low. Croghan's (1904:168) 1765 estimates give 1,000 Miami, 1,200 Wea, and 1,200 Piankashaw. By 1839-1840 the Miami, although rapidly decreasing, still numbered 700 while the Wea and Piankashaw had been reduced to 200 and 100 (Foreman 1946:126, 205). The Miami who were transferred to Kansas fell from 500 in 1846 to 91 by 1868 (Foreman 1946:204).

Synonymy

The name Miami is of uncertain origin and meaning (Dunn 1908:280-281), but it was used in the Miami-Illinois language as the usual self-designation of this tribe. Recorded forms are miami8a in Illinois (Belting 1958:287) and meeār̄meear (=[mia·mia]) and miamia in Miami (Trowbridge 1938; Dunn in Voegelin 1938-1940, 9:374). The English form continues the French spelling. The Ojibwa equivalent oma·mi·, plural oma·mi·k, shows up as Oumamik, the first recorded use of the name, 1658 (JR 44:247), and in the spellings Omameeg (Schoolcraft

1851-1857, 5:39) and O-maum-eeg (Warren 1885:33). The early sources attest a wide range of variants of the above forms, for example, Maumees (B. Drake 1841:159), Maumies (Warren 1885:33), Meames (NYCD 9:202), Miamioüek (JR 54:184), Miamiack (JR 58:22), Miamihas (Coxe 1741:49), Miniamies (Schoolcraft 1851-1857, 3:5), Myamicks (NYCD 3:489), Myamis (Shea 1852:152), Omianicks (NYCD 3:489), Oumanies (Lahontan 1905, 1:map facing p. 156), and Oumeami (NYCD 9:238). Of the same origin is Potawatomi miamik (Mooney and Thomas 1907a:854).

A Miami tradition recounts that their original name was Twaatwāā, or Twautwāū, an imitation of the alarm call of cranes (Trowbridge 1938:6). A name of this shape was used in the Iroquois languages and became current among English speakers in forms such as Tewicktowes (B. Drake 1841:159), Tweeghtwees (NYCD 6:873), Twicktwigs (NYCD 3:565), Twightwees (NYCD 6:593), Twightwighs (NYCD 3:431), and Quitways (NYCD 6:391). Of the same source is the Unami Delaware name tuwéhtuwe (Ives Goddard, personal communication 1976). The occasional use of the term Naked Indians for the Miami may have been due to a confusion of this name with that of the Ottawa (Hanna 1911, 1:127).

Other names for the Miami are Shawnee lo·wa·ni (Voegelin 1938-1940, 9:352), Huron Attochingochronon, 1640 (JR 18:233; Goddard 1972:124-126), and Wyandot säⁿshkiá-a-rúnû (Mooney and Thomas 1907a:855).

The Atchatchakangouen, possibly the core of the later Miami tribe, were probably the Outitchakouk of 1658 (JR 44:247). In 1673 Claude Jean Allouez called them Atchatchakangouen (JR 58:41), and possibly they were his Atchaterakangouen as well. Other variants include Chacakengua (Coxe 1741:map), Chachakingoya (Deliette 1934:393), Chachakingua (Coxe 1741:12), Tchatchakigoa (Margry 1876-1886, 2:216), and Tchidüakoüingoües (Bacqueville de la Potherie 1911-1912, 2:67).

The Kilatika were first mentioned, as Kilitika, by Allouez in 1673 (JR 58:41). Other forms are Kalatekoë (Margry 1876-1886, 2:216), Kilataks (Bacqueville de la Potherie 1911-1912, 2:67), Kiratikas (Deliette 1934:393), and Kolatica (Margry 1876-1886, 2:201).

The Memilounioue, mentioned once in 1672 (JR 58:40), may have been a Miami band, or this may be the garbled form of some other name.

Allouez (JR 58:41) noted the Mengakonkia, who are also called Mangakekis (Bacqueville de la Potherie 1911-1912, 2:67), Mangakokis (Bacqueville de la Potherie 1911-1912, 2:67), Megancockia (Margry 1876-1886, 2:201), and Minghakokias (Deliette 1934:393).

The Pepikokia, cited in 1673 by Allouez as Pepikoukia (JR 58:41), are also transcribed Pegoucoquias (Margry 1876-1886, 4:592), Pepepikoia (Raudot in Kinietz 1940:383), and Petikokias (NYCD 9:1057). Tepicons, cited with reservations by Mooney (1910e:229), is apparently not a synonym.

The Piankashaw called themselves peangišia (Voegelin 1938–1940, 3:78), a name whose meaning is uncertain. Its form has remained fairly stable since its 1682 notation as Peanghichia (Margry 1876–1886, 2:201). Variants include Peahushaws (McKenney and Hall 1849–1854, 3:79), Peanguichias (NYCD 9:891), Peouanguichias (Bacqueville de la Potherie 1911–1912, 2:119), Piou-anguichias (Bacqueville de la Potherie 1911–1912, 2:128), and Pouankikias (Bacqueville de la Potherie 1911–1912, 2:67). Deliette (1934:393) called them Anghichia and noted that their former name was Marineoueia.

The Wea (waiatanwa, Voegelin 1938–1940, 10:415) were first noted in 1673 (JR 58:22–23) as Ouaouiatanou-kak. Variants are Aoiatenon (Margry 1876–1886, 2:216), Aouciatenons (Deliette 1934:393), Ochiatenens (Margry 1876–1886, 2:99), Oiatenon (Margry 1876–1886, 2:201), Oua (McKenney and Hall 1849–1854, 3:80), Ouachte-nons (W. Smith 1765:70), Ouaouiartanons (Bacqueville de la Potherie 1911–1912, 2:67), Ouatanons (NYCD 10:482), Ouias (NYCD 10:447), Ouiatanon (NYCD 9:178), Wah-we-ah-tung-ong (Dunn 1908:315), War-raghtinooks (NYCD 7:384), and Wyatanons (NYCD 10:263). Newcalenous, which McKenney and Hall (1849–1854, 3:114) describe as their "proper" name, is equivalent to the Illinois self-designation inoca plus a suffix meaning 'person'. The bizarre Selugrue (NYCD 9:178) may be a miscopying of French de la grue '(nation) of the crane'.

Sources

Accounts of Miami culture written before the nineteenth century are fragmentary. Bacqueville de la Potherie (1911–1912, 1) includes excellent detail from the contact period, mostly obtained from Perrot and based on Per-rot's experiences while establishing the fur trade. Gist's (1893:47–55) account of his visit to the settlement on the Great Miami River in 1750, while valuable, describes an atypical community and can be extended to the Miami as a whole only with much caution. Kinietz (1940) uses these and other sources to reconstruct Miami culture of the seventeenth and eighteenth centuries but obtains a comprehensive description only by incorporating mate-rial from the Illinois tribes. His study, and Trowbridge's 1824–1825 account (1938), both indispensable, are the most complete descriptions available even though they share important gaps in coverage. Brice (1868) includes descriptions of the Miami by early settlers of the Fort Wayne area, but the material is too inaccurate to have much value. Dunn (1908) is based on a series of newpaper articles but is both useful and scholarly. On the whole, the Miami cannot be described as well known. Knowledge of the Wea and Piankashaw is even slighter.

Winnebago

NANCY OESTREICH LURIE

Language and Territory

Winnebago (wĭnə¹bā₁gō) is a Siouan language, quite closely related to the Chiwere language spoken by the Iowa, Oto, and Missouri; it has sometimes been included under the label Chiwere (Chafe 1973:1178, 1181–1182).* It is more remotely related to the speech of the Dakota (Sioux proper), with whom Winnebagos readily recognize a common linguistic heritage despite the fact that the languages are by no means mutually intelligible. The traditions of the various Chiwere tribes tend to agree that the three western tribes broke away from a common stock leaving the Winnebago behind in Wisconsin.

The Winnebago origin story generally places their creation at *mó·gašúč* 'red banks', identified with a location on Green Bay. However, Radin (1923:50) believed that the tribal origin story recounted most commonly in the twentieth century was only that of the Thunder clan in its earliest version. Other, less precisely defined locations in Wisconsin were sometimes identified as *mó·gašúč*. The earliest written reports of the Winnebago indicate that they lived in a relatively restricted and intensively used area of east-central Wisconsin. They are portrayed as a populous and sedentary people, more heavily dependent on horticulture than were surrounding tribes.

The Winnebago dispersed west and south into small settlements during the eighteenth and early nineteenth centuries in adaptation to the fur trade (fig. 1). Differential White pressure on the large region finally occupied by the tribe resulted in a permanent division of the population. By the mid-nineteenth century, the *Annual Reports of the Commissioner of Indian Affairs* began to distinguish between the "Treaty Abiding Faction" of the Winnebago that agreed to leave Wisconsin and the "Disaffected Bands" that resisted removal. After 1874

*Winnebago words in italics have been respelled by Kenneth L. Miner in a systematic orthography developed from the work of several previous linguists. The consonants are those briefly described by Lipkind (1945), although a few simple substitutions are required to conform to *Handbook* standards. The vowels are *a, e, i, o, u, ą, į, ų*. Any vowel may occur long, stressed, or both. Stress is chiefly a matter of pitch, a stressed vowel having higher pitch than surrounding unstressed ones; when several stressed vowels occur in a word, separated by unstressed ones, each is somewhat lower in pitch than the last preceding one. Miner's analysis of the vowels and the interaction of stress and pitch confirms, except for a few details, Susman's (1943) insightful monograph.

the two groups were treated as separate entities for administrative purposes: the reservation enclave in northeastern Nebraska and the nonreservation but federally recognized enclave scattered throughout central Wisconsin. The two groups of Winnebago call each other by somewhat jocularly pejorative terms; *nį·šójačí* 'dwellers on the muddy' (Missouri river in Nebraska), and *wa·zíjačí* 'dwellers among the pines' in Wisconsin. Tribal enrollments of 1974 indicate about 2,500 people in each group. Populations of up to several hundred people each, drawn from both Nebraska and central Wisconsin, reside in the Albert Lea and Twin Cities areas of Minnesota, Milwaukee, and Chicago. A few Winnebagos live in urban areas from the east to west coasts, largely as a result of the government's Indian relocation program in the 1950s. Winnebagos also alternate residence, irrespective of enrollment, between Nebraska and Wisconsin. Common tribal identity between the eastern and western enclaves is promoted through ties of history, language, and culture and is maintained by visits and intermarriage. However, the fact of a federal separation of the tribe has long engendered a certain amount of mutual suspiciousness and competitiveness where tribal claims to money or land are concerned.

History

European Contact, 1620–1665

The first notice of the Winnebago reached the French shortly after 1620 through Hurons and Ottawas acting as middlemen in their attempt to extend the fur trade westward (Sagard-Théodat 1939:67). In 1634 Samuel de Champlain sent Jean Nicollet to visit the formidably warlike Winnebago and establish peace between them and the tribes to the east who were receiving French goods, probably including the Ottawa. The only extended account of Nicollet's mission was written nearly 10 years later by the Jesuit Barthélemy Vimont on the basis of conversations with Nicollet. The whole narrative raises more questions than it answers (cf. Lurie 1960). The site of Nicollet's landfall in Wisconsin remains open to conjecture, but according to Vimont it was two days' journey from the Winnebago. The Winnebago were probably living at Green Bay, called *Baye des Puans* in the earliest French maps of the region (Tucker 1942:pls.V, VI) although there is no mention of Nicollet

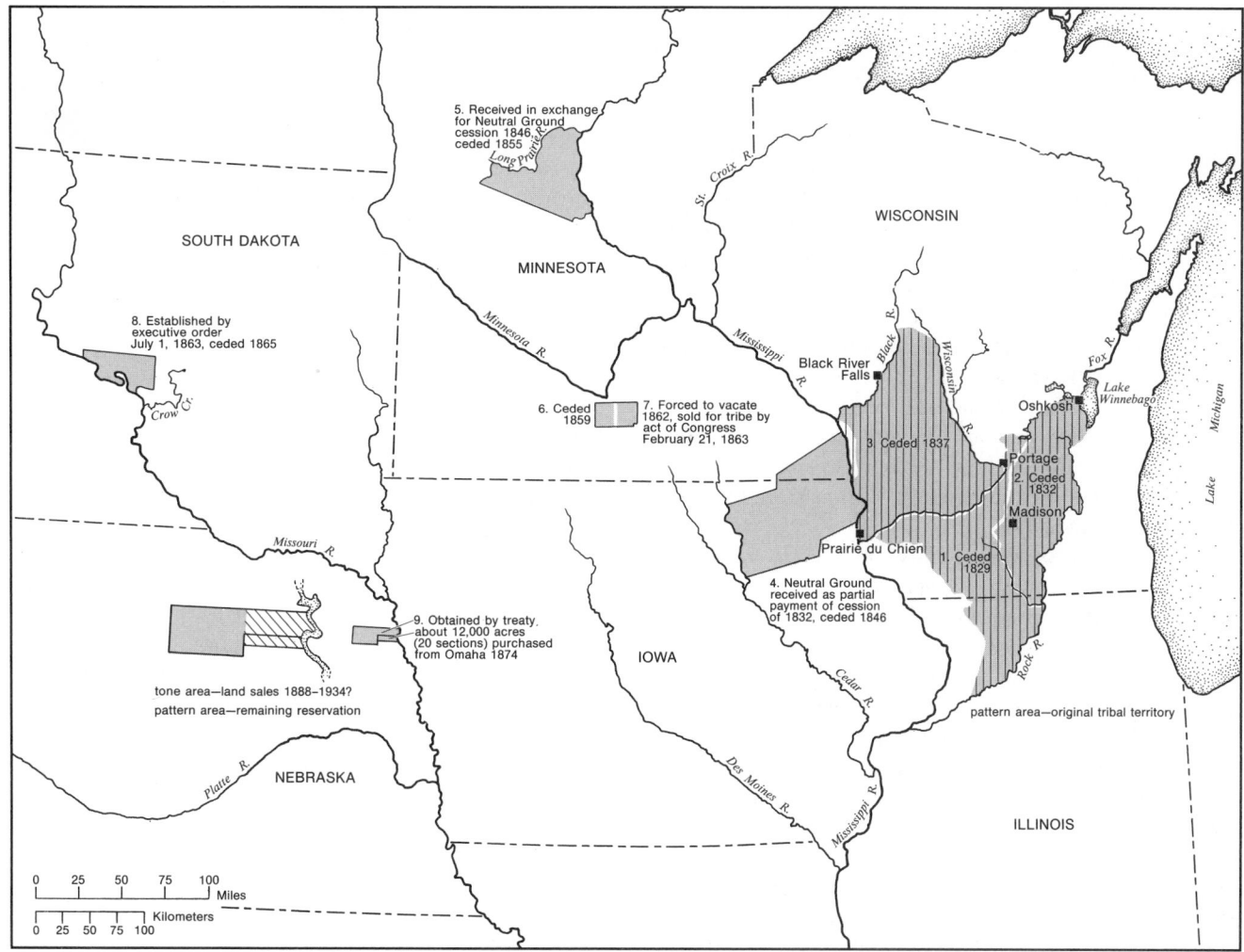

Fig. 1. Territory, land cessions, and removal 1829–1934. Detail of Nebraska lands shows most recent sales and modern reservation.

actually visiting any village. It is not until after 1665 when Nicolas Perrot was sent as interpreter and agent for the French in the western Great Lakes that Winnebago history becomes more documented. By that time the Winnebago were reduced to 150 warriors, or some 450 to 600 people in all. However, their might of 30 years before as well as the causes of their reduced condition were still fresh memories.

At first, the Winnebago had spurned the idea of trade with the French, and had eaten their Ottawa envoys. This act led to a union of the Ottawa and other tribes who made frequent attacks against the Winnebago, compelling them to gather together in a single large settlement for protection (Blair 1911–1912, 1:293).

Perrot makes no mention of Nicollet's intercessions and it may be that Nicollet had arrived when the Winnebago still held the ascendancy in the hostilities. Possibly the dramatic arrival of the first European led some of the Winnebago to reappraise their situation regarding the desirability of trade with the French. It may also be that the French unwittingly carried more than tidings of peace because when the Winnebago were clustered in

one village, epidemics broke out that are reported to have reduced them to 1,500 men (Blair 1911–1912, 1:294).

Despite their misfortunes, the Winnebago sent a party of 500 warriors against the Fox Indians who "dwelt on the other shore of the lake, [Green Bay or Lake Winnebago]; but all those men perished, while making that journey by a tempest which arose" (Blair 1911–1912, 1:294). The Fox had entered Wisconsin from Michigan between 1634 and 1650. Wherever they were located at this time, "the frequent raids of their enemies had even dispersed the game; and famine was the last scourge that attacked them" (Blair 1911–1912, 1:295).

The Illinois finally took pity on the Winnebago and brought them food but, in the midst of feasting, the Winnebago disarmed their guests by surreptitiously cutting their bowstrings and slew them all. Knowing revenge would follow, the Winnebago withdrew to an island because the Illinois allegedly did not use canoes. The reference here may well be to Doty Island on the north end of Lake Winnebago. The Illinois waited until winter to make an expedition over the ice, but the Winnebago had

691

left in a body for their winter hunt the previous day. Pursuing them overland, the Illinois killed and captured as many Winnebago as they were able (Blair 1911–1912, 1:296–300).

Winnebago tradition substantiates Perrot in regard to a period of wars, admitting it was their own treachery of spilling blood in the sanctuary of a chief's lodge that brought supernatural punishments of war, plague, famine, and near annihilation (Radin 1923:58; Lurie 1960:803–804). Perrot's account, references to these events in the *Jesuit Relations,* and the Winnebagos' own versions differ as to the precise number of people who finally survived to continue the tribe, but there is overall agreement that the Winnebago were brought to the brink of extinction. At this juncture, and perhaps even during the wars, Winnebago territory was overrun with Algonquian peoples and remnant Hurons from the East fleeing the Iroquois (JR 41:79).

The Winnebago were finally obliged to maintain peaceful relations with former enemies and strange tribes and intermarried with them, thereby recouping their population loss. In the process, they borrowed many traits from their Algonquian neighbors and in-laws, reorganizing their socioeconomic patterns and much of their material culture to engage in the pursuit of peltry animals. The Winnebago had models more or less ready-made for them by the Algonquian speakers who had already established working adaptations to the fur trade. A recurrent theme in Winnebago references to this period is that there are now few or no "pure Winnebago" because of extensive mixture with the Ojibwa, Potawatomi, Menominee, Sauk, and others—even the Fox with whom the Winnebago, in alliance with the French, were to engage in more conflicts during the eighteenth century.

Fur Trade Period, 1665–1828

By the beginning of the eighteenth century, the Winnebago had withdrawn from the Green Bay area and settled along the north and west sides of Lake Winnebago. The refugee tribes that had clustered in Wisconsin began to fan out again as the Iroquois threat abated in the western Great Lakes region and the Winnebago followed into territory vacated by these tribes. When the period of treaties and land cessions began for the Winnebago, the tribe had gained firm control of an area bounded on the east and south by Lake Winnebago and the Rock River, on the north and east by the Fox-Wisconsin portage route and the Black River, and on the west by the eastern watershed of the Mississippi River, their territory actually extending to the Mississippi River north of Prairie du Chien. Large villages gave way to much smaller, widely scattered settlements.

At the inception of the fur trade, the tribe continued to concentrate in the Lake Winnebago area in a few villages—perhaps one primary village with outlying settlements. Large gardens were planted and tended in the summer and a good part of the dried harvest of corn, beans, squash, and wild foods was stored in pits or fiber bags for winter use. Sizable parties of the able-bodied people, probably including women, then set forth in dugout canoes along the Fox-Wisconsin portage route to hunt for large game in the area bounded by the Wisconsin, Black, and Mississippi rivers. Traveling as far as feasible up some western tributary of the Wisconsin River, they buried the canoes in the earth in order to use them for the return trip. A well-known canoe cache site is located near Wyeville, Wisconsin, on the Lemonweir River. Organized hunts associated with the large Lake Winnebago villages may even have occurred when the tribe was located at Green Bay.

There are traditions of crossing the Mississippi to hunt buffalo on the prairies. During organized hunts, each day's travel and hunt plan were directed by the Bear clan men who served a similar function when large war parties went on the march. Individual hunting of both large and small game was carried on near the village when the opportunity arose, as well as extensive fishing with spear and bow. According to Wisconsin accounts collected since 1944, when hunting parties went to western Wisconsin and stayed through the winter months, runners (probably using snowshoes) returned regularly to the village with fresh meat and carried stores of dried vegetable food back to their camp. The runners also communicated news between the hunting party and the people who remained at home.

Large marshy areas along the Mississippi River and its eastern tributaries from Prairie du Chien to La Crosse, Wisconsin, were rich in muskrat, beaver, and other fur-bearing animals and were still exploited for peltry by a few Wisconsin Winnebagos in the 1970s. Hunting for the fur trade promoted greater dispersion and mobility, each generation establishing settlements farther west and south of Lake Winnebago. It was probably at this time that substantial rectangular buildings gave way completely to domed wigwams, although emphasis on village life remained strong. The Winnebago continued to take pride in their gardens to see them through lean hunting periods, looking with disdain on the Ojibwa who depended primarily on the hunt and uncertain harvests of wild rice.

Historical references bolstered by ethnographic data indicate that conventional fur-trade arrangements were made whereby traders extended credit on gear in the fall, to be repaid in the spring. Because they apparently always had large stores of corn, the Winnebago do not seem to have suffered economically from the fur trade as did more northerly tribes whose trapping for peltry was apt to be at the expense of the food quest. Nevertheless, the traps, guns, textiles, household and garden implements, and general personal finery adverted to or actually depicted in the records of the eighteenth and early nineteenth centuries attest to the Winnebagos' technological dependence on the traders.

The importance of the fur trade is clearly evident in the spread of villages of 100 to 300 people along riverbanks and lakeshores although small hunting parties apparently continued to use the rich marshes along the Mississippi as well. As settlements extended down the Rock River, the Dixon Swamp in Illinois became an important game area for the more southerly villagers. The dispersion of the tribe was facilitated by the establishment of Portage and Prairie du Chien as major trading centers, drawing the Winnebago away from exclusive dependence on Green Bay. Smaller operations run by independent traders were also set up at different times throughout their territory (P.V. Lawson 1907; Lurie 1952:fig. 1).

As the Winnebago scattered into nearly 40 settlements noted on maps and in other records of the second decade of the nineteenth century, they still retained many ideals and certain actual features of the social organization that had been appropriate to large, fairly permanent villages; but, as a matter of expedience, they appear to have depended increasingly on Algonquian-style clan and leadership arrangements in the virtually autonomous management of localized affairs. Descriptions of the role and functions of chieftainship collected by Radin (1923:194-195, 304-305) and Lurie (1960:790-808) contain an abiding theme of *the* chief underlying the fact of many village chiefs recalled from the fur-trade period by Radin's oldest informants and still remembered by name in both Nebraska and Wisconsin. The ideal of a head chief among the Winnebago was not a function of the fur-trade and treaty periods. Although the Winnebago argue on hereditary grounds as to which people were "real" village chiefs, this class is sharply separated from the "bread chiefs" the Whites appointed and dealt with.

Naw-Kaw, or Wood (fig. 2) was the head chief of the Winnebago until his death in 1833 at the supposed age of 98 years. Naw-Kaw evidently presided over much of the transition to increasing autonomy. His successor, a nephew (presumably his brother's son) who took his name, moved to Iowa with the treaty-abiding faction of the tribe after 1832, but by his time the title of chief was purely honorific. Although Naw-Kaw is described as a member of the "*Caromanie* or Walking Turtle family" (McKenney and Hall 1933-1934, 1:146-155), he is known to have belonged to the upper moiety of so-called bird clans. Caromanie is not a clan name and is believed to reflect an Algonquian ancestry (Lurie 1966:53).

Whether applying to the entire tribe or localized by village, chieftainship was dual. The civil or peace chief, such as Naw-Kaw, sought to resolve problems by peaceful and conciliatory means. He was wise and generous, receiving gifts to redistribute, even to impoverishing himself. He heeded the views of village elders and his

NAA, Smithsonian.

Fig. 2. Naw-Kaw, wearing three peace medals. Colored lithograph after original oil painting by Charles Bird King, 1828.

decisions were the voicing of community consensus. Members of the Buffalo clan acted as town criers to the chief, announcing news to the village at his direction. When a man became a civil chief, he no longer went on the war path and dissuaded all but the most justifiable war parties from leaving the village. His symbol and badge of office was the peace pipe. His lodge was a sanctuary for wrongdoers, including murderers, and he endeavored to arrange for payment of indemnities to avoid bloody and violent revenge.

Although it is agreed that the civil chief came from the upper moiety, there is disagreement whether he was necessarily from a particular lineage of the Thunder clan. It is certain that his counterpart came from a particular lineage or subdivision of the Bear clan of the lower moiety. Among the lower-moiety chief's symbols of authority was a baton resembling a war club. A Bear clan member was called *mą́·ną́·pe,* translated as 'soldier', but the Bear clan really operated as a police force regarding internal affairs. The word for 'warrior', *wągwášošé,* could be applied to any man regardless of clan. The Hawk clan, in contrast to the Bear clan, was particularly concerned with warfare; for example, it was authorized to decree life or death for captives taken in war.

The Bear clan chief and his men handled offenses against the common good, such as breaking hunt rules, and decided upon and carried out punishments such as whipping, destroying a culprit's belongings, or banishing him. In personal offenses, if the civil chief was unable to intercede, the Bear clan punished the offender or turned him over to the victim's aggrieved kinsmen for execution.

A dramatic illustration of the different approaches of the two chiefs occurred in regard to the presence of sickness in the population. If the civil chief's ceremonial feast failed to appease this threat to the community, the Bear clan chief led his followers as if on the warpath, engaging this invader of the village in mock battle (Radin 1945:51-53). There are no data on how chiefs of either moiety achieved office except that the person best suited in talent and disposition was somehow selected from a group of eligible hereditary candidates.

It would appear from treaty signatures and ethnographic data that during the last part of Naw-Kaw's civil chieftainship the primary Bear clan chief was Black Wolf, whose village was located on the west shore of Lake Winnebago. Apparently, he died within a year or two after signing the treaty of 1829. Although his son signed the treaty of 1832, Black Wolf's successor appears to have been Four Legs (fig. 3), still well remem-

Fig. 3. Four Legs, chief of the Winnebago village on Doty Island. He is wearing a long military-style coat. Colored lithograph after original painting by James O. Lewis, made during the Treaty of Green Bay, 1827.

694

bered in old stories regarding the treaty at Fort Armstrong in 1832 when he held a handful of earth as he spoke, symbolizing the authority of the Bear clan to deal with matters concerning land (Lurie 1966:57, 55, 67).

Although Radin's (1923:166-189) account of the moiety division and clanship among the Winnebago is frequently cited in comparative analyses of social organization, it is possible that it is more a logical systematization toward which the Winnebago were striving during the fur-trade period than an empirical description. Radin's fieldwork was among the Nebraska people, who were able to preserve significant quantities of only their religious practices, while the Wisconsin enclave followed traditional eighteenth-century itineraries as well up to the 1900s albeit with ponies and wagons. They remained in familiar terrain and managed their own affairs with a great deal less interference from government and missionaries than had been the case among the Nebraska people since the 1840s.

According to Radin, the Winnebago had exogamous moieties that regulated marriage, the differentiation of leadership roles and functions, and the selection of lacrosse teams. There were 12 patrilineal clans unevenly divided between the moieties. The *wą·grégi hererá* 'those who are above' included the Thunder, Eagle, Hawk, and Pigeon clans; the *mą·négi hererá* 'those who are below' included the Bear, Wolf, Water Spirit, Buffalo, Deer, Elk, Fish, and Snake clans. The origin story of each clan underlay that clan's list of personal names, obligations, prerogatives, taboos, reciprocal relationships regarding other clans, duties to the tribe as a whole, and prescribed and proscribed etiquette regarding its members to be observed by people belonging to other clans.

According to Radin (1923:181-190, 207-212) there was an inherent instability in the clan system that antedated reservation times. For example, the Thunder clan had gained ascendancy over the others after White contact, the unequal numbers of clans in the upper and lower moieties probably reflected an effort to keep population size about equal in each moiety, and the small Fish and Snake clans were of relatively late origin. Anomalies in the data Radin explained as recent exceptions due to cultural deterioration on the reservation. The occasional inheritance of war bundles in the female line was attributed to lack of qualified male heirs, and the naming and claiming of children by the mother's clan supposedly rested entirely on the mother's clan being better able to afford the cost of a naming feast. However, when a Winnebago woman married a White man, the traditional procedure used when a husband belonged to another tribe was required: the children were adopted by the mother's clan but thereafter clanship continued through her male descendants. A notable example concerns the celebrated Decora family (DeKaury, DeCora, Decorah), descendants of a French officer at Green Bay and Glory of the Morning, said to be the daughter of the head chief at the time, a member of the Thunder clan. According to most accounts of this early eighteenth-century marriage, the couple had two sons who rose to prominence and wielded great influence during the French regime; their numerous progeny held village leadership positions throughout the fur-trade and treaty periods. Some Decoras are considered Thunder clan and others are considered Eagle clan, and it has been suggested that Decora was later ascribed as a surname to others with French ancestry.

The necessity for firm clan affiliation is open to question in cases such as Dog's Head, *šų́·képagá*, who is known to have been Sioux or of Sioux ancestry. In all probability this means the Eastern Dakota, among whom there are no clans. Dog's Head was a sufficiently important person, most likely a village leader, to have signed the first three Winnebago treaties. His direct patrilineal descendants, among the most conservative and traditional of Wisconsin Winnebago families in the 1970s, are still not identified explicitly with any of the 12 Winnebago clans.

Moiety exogamy was certainly a well-defined ideal, but there were exceptions among old couples even in the early twentieth century (Lurie 1961:5, 114). What might be construed as clan exogamy seems to have been fairly rigidly observed, but so was proscription against marriage between people who were deemed close matrilineal relatives, reckoned according to a fairly conventional Omaha kinship system. Prescribed and proscribed kin behaviors included avoidance of people of the opposite sex who were classified as parents-in-law; respectful deference between brothers and sisters, which would include parallel cousins; actual male siblings and classificatory brothers arranging marriages for sisters; and joking relationships between people who stood in a terminological relationship as brothers-in-law to sisters-in-law. Uncles, that is, ego's mother's male siblings and classificatory brothers and their male descendants, were called upon as needed by the mother to be official punishers during ego's childhood. Later, such an uncle took a boy on his first war party. Ideally, in adulthood a warm bond existed wherein an uncle was obliged to give nieces and nephews whatever he had that was asked for, and the uncle in turn could exact services of nieces and nephews. The relationship was also characterized by teasing.

A distinction between the father's brothers (who would be called father) and the mother's brothers (designated in English by Winnebagos as uncle) is to be expected in an Omaha system, but the Winnebagos' avuncular emphasis seems exceptionally strong. The statement of this relationship embodies the idea that the uncle is closer to nieces and nephews than to his own children because they are of the same body, that is, share the same female line. Radin eventually concluded that

"internal evidence, myth, tradition, custom, all point to a period in Winnebago history where descent was reckoned in the female line . . ." (1948:45). Given the Winnebagos' early strong emphasis on gardening, Winnebago patriliny may be a development of the fur-trade period patterned after Algonquian models and reinforced by shifting economic emphasis from gardening to male pursuits of the hunt and trapping.

In addition to the usual listing of 12 clans making up 2 moieties, there was an alternative, four-part classification of the Winnebago clans: the Thunderbird, or invisible Thunderbird people; the air family, the visible Thunderbird people; the land or quadruped people; and the water family (Radin 1923:191). Radin includes passing but unexplained references to ranking of lineages within clans, particularly the Thunder and Bear clans, and rankings of the clans themselves. After deeper comparative analysis of social practices embedded in myths collected between 1908 and 1913, Radin (1948:45) concluded that the Winnebago derived from a society that had been stratified.

Idealized in sacred tradition, warfare was enthusiastically practiced in historic times. The Winnebago figured prominently among the tribes who fought as allies of the French against the British and, with the final defeat of the French, as allies of the British against the Americans. The old stories dwell on the journeys, personal valor, and magical powers exercised rather than on the final outcome of the battle. In 1793 Winnebagos fought against Gen. Anthony Wayne at Fallen Timbers. They traveled to the Ohio country again to fight beside Tecumseh in the War of 1812. In addition to engagements of interest to the Whites, Winnebagos went on skirmishes of their own against traditional enemies such as the Ojibwa, Sioux, and Fox, with a Wisconsin account noting an expedition against the Osage.

The stress on warfare permeates much of Winnebago religion. The vision quest provided the successful supplicant with blessings to excel in warfare, the hunt, or curing, the last being particularly desirable if blessings were bestowed by the grizzly bear who gave miraculous power to heal wounds and broken bones sustained in battle. Although the Winnebago expected men to seek war honors, which included grades of coup counting, they allowed for men who may have viewed themselves as constitutionally unfit for warfare. Great respect was accorded those individuals who were blessed by the Moon with the gift of prophesy and the requirement that they become berdaches (Lurie 1953).

Among the tribe's most sacred objects were the war bundles, the focus of important ceremonies and the property of clans. Each clan might have a number of bundles of which particular lineages were the custodians. However, war-bundle ceremonies were distinct from clan ceremonies. New bundles were created as a result of spiritual direction and new items were added to the bundles, but the bundle ceremonies always involved a series of ritual offerings to a series of supernatural beings associated with war.

Although bundles might contain scalps, bundle rites were separated from the Victory Dance or so-called Scalp Dance in which scalps passed to four successive people, each of whom held a large ceremony, after which the scalps were usually placed as offerings on graves.

At four night wakes for the dead, warriors told of their adventures and exploits, and gambling games were played for the souls of slain enemies. The winning side turned such souls over to the deceased to assist on the arduous journey to the next world.

The Night Spirit rite was the most prominent of a number of rites held by societies of people who had been blessed by the same spirit. In later times it was associated with warding off illness, but it was originally performed to assure success in warfare and opportunities to go to war. The Winnebago Medicine Lodge differs strikingly from Algonquian versions despite borrowings from Algonquian sources in the shamanistic shooting rite. It is highly esoteric, centering in the metaphor of the road of life and death, and even the shooting rite symbolizes reincarnation rather than magical resuscitation of the dead. It is characteristically Winnebago in posing a philosophical alternative of peace to war (Radin 1945, 1950).

The richness and complexity of Winnebago cosmology have been treated in detail by Radin (1915, 1923, 1945, 1948, 1950, 1956). There is belief in a layered universe, multiple souls, and reincarnation. An aloof creator, Earth Maker, was an old deity but possibly as a result of Christian influence may have usurped the central role once accorded the Sun, who in historic times remained a primary war deity. The Earth and Moon were female deities. Other supernatural beings included spirit equivalents of the creatures of the natural environment, the usual bestowers of blessings in the vision quest. Semidivine heroes could take human and animal forms and were sent by Earth Maker from time to time to help mankind in various ways. Among these are Trickster, Hare, the Twins—Flesh and Spirit, Red Horn, and Turtle. The long myth cycles and other stories contain plots and motifs found across North America; however, there is one recurrent theme in Winnebago narratives that is also reflected in the different chiefly roles, the Medicine Lodge, and in the Winnebago value system generally. This theme poses the question, "how are we to meet the two aspects of life and of reality with which we are being continually confronted, the protective, constructive and positive, and the repelling, destructive and negative?" (Radin 1945:52). An interesting embodiment of this theme is seen in the deity, Disease Giver, who deals out death from one side and life from the other. On the other hand, the opposition of the good Thunders to the evil, serpentine Water Spirit, so common in Algonquian tales, is curiously blurred among the usually dualistic Winnebago.

Although the profundities of Winnebago religion were known only to an elite, religion was intimately woven into the whole fabric of daily life with the individual observance of taboos and ritual prescriptions. These observances were related to clan membership, the nature of one's vision quest, sacred or unfamiliar places or objects, birth, death, menstruation, and the like. An equivocation regarding menstrual taboos was not unique to the Winnebago but remains to be satisfactorily explained. While menstruating women were deemed dangerous to men and surrounded with many taboos, women were courted while isolated in the menstrual lodge.

The social functions of shamanism demand closer attention. The healer, a role reserved to the elderly, relied on both herbal and shamanistic remedies. Shamanism was also tremendously important to warfare. Warrior-medicine men were not evil and were highly respected and admired. Shamanistic power was also deemed good if used in hunting, but some people who possessed such powers as well as bad medicines were evil old witches, literally "poisoners." Witches were given to jealousy, selfishness, and greed, traits that the Winnebago considered the absolute worst of human failings. Witches coveted other persons' lives and killed people to claim their unused span of allotted years. While it was good to support those who had reached old age because, ideally, they had led exemplary lives and could bestow blessings, it was also prudent to cosset and indulge old people since their advanced years might be due to witchcraft. In addition to assuring that the aged would be cared for, fear of witches and of being suspected of being a witch reinforced conformity to the positive values of sharing, generosity, and general goodness of character and encouraged modest norms in personal possessions to preclude a witch's jealousy. The persistence of belief and fear regarding witchcraft even among nontraditional Winnebago people in the 1970s suggests that the functional utility of witchcraft as a social control became increasingly important with the erosion of formal institutions for community management during the treaty and reservation periods (Kluckhohn 1944).

In ethnographic terms much of "traditional" Winnebago culture is the culture of the fur-trade period, and while the term traditional suggests a predictable, established way of life, this was an era of revitalization and renewed optimism after the Winnebagos' overwhelming defeats in the first half of the seventeenth century. If a formerly more complex sociocultural system was lost, the fur trade offered new opportunities to stimulate innovation, creative adaptation, and resourcefulness; however, this golden age depended on the prospect of continuous struggle among different White nations for sovereignty over the Winnebagos' territory. The Winne-

696

bago did not actively play off the White nations as the Iroquois did to maintain a balance of power to their own advantage (cf. Wallace 1969). They simply went over to the side of the winner in each phase of the struggle. Nevertheless, the Whites who happened to be temporarily in power were obliged to bargain for the Indians' alliance and good will lest the Indians be tempted by other Whites to upset the precarious victory achieved. With uncertain peace during the long period of intermittent hostilities from the French and Indian wars to the War of 1812, the Whites could not afford the vulnerability of extensive settlements in the hinterland west of Lake Michigan. Thus the Winnebago were able to expand their domain and flourish. The establishment of lasting peace between Britain and the United States after 1815 heralded the end of traditional Winnebago culture.

Treaties and Land Cessions, 1816–1865

The treaty period for the Winnebago (fig. 1) opened in 1816 when Naw-Kaw and Spoon Decora headed a delegation of 11 that journeyed to Saint Louis to sign a treaty of peace and friendship with the United States. Although these Winnebagos made clear that they represented only their own Wisconsin River village, the fact that Naw-Kaw made the overture indicated the official direction of tribal policy. The Winnebago had similarly shifted their allegiance from the French when the British gained sovereignty over their area. Now, the Americans were in power. The end of the War of 1812 ushered in a new era in Indian-White relationships that resulted in tribal factionalization and a permanent tribal division. By 1821 the Winnebago had an indication of what was in store for them when a group of Oneida from New York State approached the Menominee for permission to relocate themselves along the lower Fox River. The Winnebago had vacated the area but their ancient rights were still respected by the Menominee who invited them to participate in the agreement. When negotiations were continued the next year for more land for the New York Indians, including the Stockbridge, the Winnebago refused to take part. Nevertheless, the government regularized the informal, intertribal agreement and obtained further cessions in a series of treaties with the Menominee that gave no consideration to the Winnebagos' claims (Ellis 1856). In 1836 the Menominee ceded a large portion of land that included the northern end of Lake Winnebago where the Winnebago had long maintained villages.

While other tribes had encroached upon and usurped their eastern holdings, the Winnebago in turn had followed upon the heels of tribes moving west and acquired sufficient land to hunt, plant gardens, and trap for the fur trade. The real threat to their territorial needs began to loom in 1825 when the United States convened a huge intertribal conclave at Prairie du Chien to sign a treaty

Oberösterreichisches Landesmuseum, Linz, Austria.
Fig. 4. Bust of man with multiple earrings and feather hair ornament. Drawing by Johann Baptist Wengler, 1851.

establishing firm boundaries among the various tribes in the western Great Lakes region in order to expedite future land cessions. The Winnebago signed two more intertribal boundary treaties in 1827 and 1828. However, problems over land had begun to develop even before the treaty of 1825, in regard to the lead-mining country south of Prairie du Chien. A mining rush in 1821 brought thousands of miners from the East and inevitably precipitated hostile confrontations between Indians and Whites. Increasing traffic on the Mississippi River also led to critical incidents.

In 1827, as a result of a series of indignities and assaults perpetrated against Winnebagos by Whites, a warrior named Red Bird was delegated by leaders in the tribe's western villages to take revenge. Red Bird apparently had little enthusiasm for the assignment and after passing up several opportunities to attack settlers' homesteads, he and two companions finally struck a French household near Prairie du Chien, killing and wounding several people. When the government threatened a general reprisal against the tribe, Red Bird surrendered to spare his people. He and his accomplices were sentenced to be hanged, but Red Bird's nobility of bearing and the seriousness of the Winnebagos' grievances against the Whites led to the official suggestion that a delegation of chiefs go to Washington to ask for presidential clemency. The government seized on the Red Bird affair to obtain the Winnebagos' lead-mining area. In effect Red Bird was redeemed with a treaty in 1829 that ceded half

Cranbrook Institute of Science, Bloomfield Hills, Mich.: 2249.

Fig. 5. Wooden medicine bowl, carved in one piece. Used in the Medicine Lodge ceremonies. The brass-headed tacks used for the bird's eyes were trade items. Collected 1922; length about 9.0 cm.

Dept. of Anthr., Smithsonian: 233553.

Fig. 6. Twined storage bag. Typically used to store dried foods, household items, and sacred objects. a, obverse pattern partially shown, pattern repeats over rest of side; b, reverse pattern with deer designs and lower right showing pattern of twining; c, detail of zigzag twining, with the dark threads wool and light threads basswood. Collected before 1905; length 59.5 cm.

the tribe's territory south of the Wisconsin River. Meanwhile, Red Bird had died in prison (McKenney and Hall 1933–1934, 2:434–436; WHC 2:98–196; Turner 1951:73–87).

The area along the Mississippi River immediately west of the Winnebagos' cession was also ceded in 1829 by a mixed population of Ojibwas, Ottawas, and Potawatomis who had been drifting into the region for a number of years. Actually, much of the land embraced in both these 1829 cessions had already been ceded to the United States in 1804 by the Sauk and Fox who had agreed to move west of the Mississippi River. However, the so-called British Band of Sauk led by Black Hawk had never recognized any of the cessions. In the spring of 1832 this band tried to resettle in the ceded area, setting off the Black Hawk War. The war ended in early August when Black Hawk's band was massacred at Bad Axe (Victory), Wisconsin, north of Prairie du Chien. The Winnebago played a diplomatically cautious role in the Black Hawk War. One of Black Hawk's main supporters was "The Winnebago Prophet," of half-Sauk and half-Winnebago ancestry, but apparently he attracted no Winnebagos to his standard. Most Winnebagos appear to have avoided involvement but a few served as scouts for the army and with some Sioux warriors actually took part in the fighting against the Sauk at Bad Axe. Black Hawk eluded capture at Bad Axe and sought refuge among the Winnebagos on the Black River. They treated him well and gave him safe conduct to the military authorities at Prairie du Chien where he surrendered on August 27, 1832 (Jackson 1964; Turner 1951:94–109). While the Black Hawk War was still in progress, the United States was already planning to obtain the Winnebagos' remaining land south of the Fox-Wisconsin portage route. A treaty of cession was signed on September 15, 1832, at Fort Armstrong, in Illinois.

The treaties of 1829 and 1832 contain similar provisions, following a general formula employed in such negotiations at the time: White captives would be returned; half-breeds and Indian wives of Whites were given their own parcels of land and other remuneration to remain in the ceded areas when the full-bloods were expected to leave; payment of traders' debts was deducted from the amount of money stipulated as the price of the land; the land was to be paid for in annuities of cash and goods over a period of 30 years; and blacksmiths and other specialists would be available to help the tribe acquire White habits of life. The signatures of all Winnebago treaties since 1825 reveal that the Winnebagos also observed a certain formalized protocol of their own. In every case, at least one-quarter of the signers are Bear clan men and another quarter or more are from the Thunder clan, with the remaining signers from a scattering of the other 10 clans (Lurie 1966). Two features of the 1832 treaty are of special importance. First, the signers comprised three delegations but in fact signalized a two-part division of the tribe. Of the 39 signers, 18, or almost half, belonged to the Prairie du Chien group whose northern holdings were not yet ceded. There were 21 signers from the southern regions ceded in 1829 and 1832: 13 from the Rock River area and 8 from around Fort Winnebago near the present city of Portage. Second, the treaty recognized that the Winne-

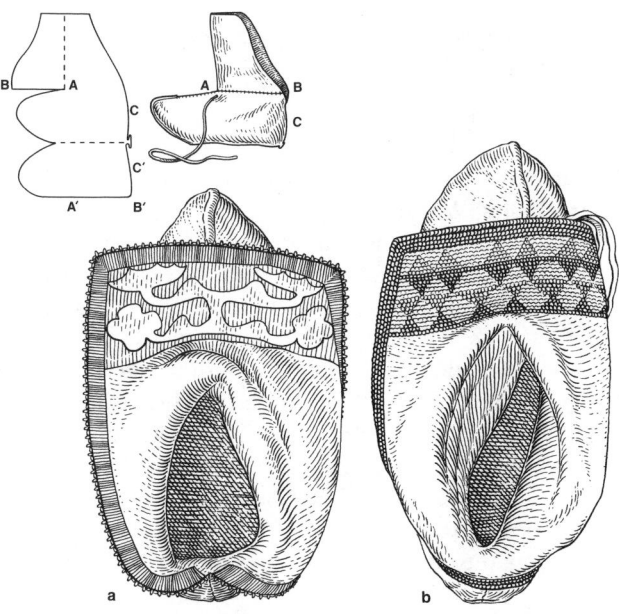

Fig. 7. Women's moccasins with unique large flap folded down over the toe and decorated on the upper surface. This style differs from the men's moccasins and also from those worn by neighboring tribes. a, silk appliqúe, length 23 cm; b, beaded. Collected 1909.

bagos' remaining land was not adequate to support all the people. In partial payment for the cession of 1832, the tribe was granted a reservation along the west bank of the Mississippi River, the Neutral Ground on the Turkey River in Iowa, actually a contested no-man's-land between the Sauk and Sioux. Winnebagos from the ceded areas who settled there soon found themselves the target of Sauk hostilities. Despite these problems, the government began pressing for cession of the tribe's remaining land in Wisconsin and removal of all the Winnebagos west of the Mississippi River.

The tribe refused to sell more land and in the summer of 1837 accepted an invitation to send a delegation to Washington to meet the President. They were only to plead their case to keep their remaining homeland. To make sure no land would be sold, the tribe sent 20 men who had no authority to sign a treaty of cession. Two respected civil chiefs—old Naw-Kaw's successor Kar-i-mo-nee and Big Boat Decora—led the delegation of generally young men who were the sons or other relatives of prominent men, including several Decoras and another member of the Kar-i-mo-nee family. Only two can be identified with the Bear Clan—Little Priest, who later gained prominence, and a man named Little Soldier. If Four Legs was still living, he was not in the delegation, nor was any other Bear clan man of comparable stature. Upon arriving in Washington, the Winnebago were immediately pressured into ceding their remaining Wisconsin land, but they held out until it became apparent they would not be allowed to return home unless they signed a treaty. With winter drawing on, they worried that they

were not able to hunt and that their families would be short of food. They finally signed, protesting they did so under duress and that since they had no authority to sell land the government could not expect the tribe to abide by the treaty. The treaty provided for the usual emoluments and promised that the Neutral Ground would be exchanged for more desirable land; however, what really persuaded them to sign was the assurance that the tribe would have "eight years" before having to leave Wisconsin. The delegation believed they were buying time for the tribe to renegotiate a better and properly authorized treaty. The treaty reads "eight months." Later, the interpreter admitted that he was directed to deceive the Indians (WHC 7:393).

Meanwhile, complaints from traders about irregularities in carrying out the provisions of the two previous treaties resulted in the appointment of a presidential commission in 1838 to settle matters and get payment of the 1837 annuities off to a satisfactory start. The commission was headed by Simon T. Cameron, later to become a member of President Lincoln's cabinet. He was completely unprincipled—favoring the American Fur Company's claims over those of other traders, bilking the half-breeds, and accepting kickbacks from attorneys representing the few private traders who won their cases. An outraged Indian agent present at the time estimated that Cameron pocketed between $60,000 to $100,000 of the $300,000 disbursed by the commission (Street 1905:115–139).

The Winnebago were not as upset about the commission scandal as they were about the requirement that they leave Wisconsin by the spring of 1838. They had no intention of joining the rest of the tribe at the dangerous Neutral Ground that, in any case, was supposed to be exchanged for other land. Although all the treaty signers insisted to their angry people that they had been misled regarding the period of "eight years," the treaty created a permanent split in the tribe. One faction led by Kar-i-mo-nee and Big Boat Decora believed it would be wise to move and make the best of a bad bargain. The other, led by Yellow Thunder, who had also signed the treaty of 1837, and Dandy, a Thunder clan nephew of Four Legs, refused to leave and were to lead a fugitive existence in Wisconsin for the next 27 years.

Meanwhile, the treaty-abiding faction negotiated a treaty in 1846 for a new reservation in central Minnesota. Located between the warring Sioux and Ojibwa, the land proved almost as dangerous as the Neutral Ground, and in 1855 it was exchanged by treaty for a smaller but fertile farming area at Blue Earth in southern Minnesota. The treaty-abiding Winnebago took to farming with enthusiasm, cooperated with their agent in laying out family acreages in anticipation of receiving titles in fee simple, cut their hair, donned "citizen's dress," and even built their own jail to handle miscreants. Their agent observed with wonder that drunkenness was no great problem in Blue Earth. In 1859 the tribe agreed to a treaty to sell half the Blue Earth land to pay for substantial improvements on the other half. When the Civil War broke out, Blue Earth men enlisted in the Union army. During their absence, the 1862 Sioux uprising in Minnesota prompted a measure to remove not only the Sioux but the peaceful Winnebago as well. Over their agent's despairing protests to the commissioner of Indian affairs, the Winnebago were forced without benefit of treaty to forfeit the Blue Earth land for a vastly inferior tract on the Crow Creek in South Dakota. Although the removal was orderly, it was carried out in cold weather and fraught with hardships. By piercing together the *Annual Reports of the Commissioner of Indian Affairs* for 1862 to 1865, it appears that of 1,934 Winnebago taken from Blue Earth, only 1,382 survived the harsh winter of 1862. Though warned that if they tried to run away they would be fired upon, 1,357 managed to escape by the summer of 1863. Many of them decamped in cottonwood dugouts. Descending the Crow Creek to the Missouri, they traveled downstream and some 1,200 finally landed among the Omaha. Others were reported as having scattered out to the Sauk and Iowa or joined the disaffected bands in Wisconsin (fig. 8). In 1865 negotiations were completed whereby the Winnebago located in Nebraska signed a treaty giving up the Crow Creek reservation and accepted a new res-

ervation comprising what had been the northern strip of the Omaha reservation.

Nebraska Reservation

For several years after their arrival in Nebraska, the treaty-abiding Winnebago made shift as best they could, putting in small gardens and hunting in the wooded area along the Missouri River that fringed the eastern edge of their reservation. The government initiated allotment on a modest scale in 1871 and, except for some 3,000 acres of wooded bottom land where the shifting river channel made allotment impossible, parceled out the entire reservation under the provisions of the Indian Allotment Act of 1887. But the Winnebagos' enthusiasm for owning farms was irrevocably diminished by the injustice of their removal from Minnesota. For the most part, the people remained in little settlements (fig. 9) "down in the

NAA, Smithsonian.
Fig. 9. Log house in Nebraska, late 1880s, when such log structures began to replace wigwams on the reservation. They were in turn replaced by frame farm houses after the reservation was allotted.

timbers," and readily availed themselves of the opportunity to lease their farm land to Whites when this was permitted after 1891. Many accumulated sizable bank accounts but the money could be spent only for useful purposes approved by their agent.

With the advent of a large White population in the area, commercial centers sprang up. The town of Winnebago near the Indian agency in the eastern end of the reservation became the hub of Indian life. Winnebago moved into substantial farmstead homes on allotments near town, merchants set up shop, and the Chicago, Burlington, and Quincy Railroad connected the reservation with Sioux City, Iowa, and a larger world in general. The towns of Emerson, Walt Hill, and Pender in the western portions of the Winnebago and Omaha reservations served mainly Whites who used Indian land. Sur-

NAA, Smithsonian.
Fig. 8. Blackhawk and Winneshiek, important leaders among the "disaffected bands" of Wisconsin in resisting removal west. Photographed before 1900.

rounded by White farmers profiting from their land, it was not long before new desires arose among the Winnebago for rubber-tired buggies, fine driving teams, and even automobiles. The Winnebago resented the federal restraints on their affairs that were designed to protect them from their own fiscal naiveté but actually prevented their learning the use of capital in a money economy. The Winnebago, like other tribes, became easy prey to unscrupulous Whites who played upon their discontent with the government supervision when a series of congressional acts between 1902 and 1910 relaxed the restrictions against the sale of Indians' allotments. Despite the best efforts of their agent to prevent it, by 1913 almost the entire western two-thirds of the Winnebago reservation passed out of Indian ownership (Kneale 1950:203-204).

After a brief period of unprecedented prosperity, the Winnebagos' land sale money was quickly dissipated and cultural disorganization and social demoralization set in. Old customs for ordering community life had been steadily eroded since 1832. At this crucial juncture at the turn of the twentieth century the Winnebago were faced with a bewildering array of alternatives in religion and education while still denied the right to participate in elective self-government like their White neighbors.

Initially the Winnebago were ministered to by the Presbyterian Omaha mission. In 1908 a Dutch Reform Church mission took over the work among the Winnebago; it was soon in serious competition not only with the tribe's traditional religion but also with the Peyote Religion as well. Introduced among the Winnebago in 1889-1890, Peyote appealed to some but not all Winnebago as offering a stable moral order combining Indian and Christian values and doctrines. Soon the tribe was rent into traditionalist, mission Christian, and Peyote factions. This factionalization was exacerbated in succeeding years when yet more denominations proselytized among the Winnebago.

Educational alternatives included a reservation day and boarding school, government and denominational boarding schools off the reservation, public schools with Indians and Whites in attendance, and a Dutch Reform boarding school on the reservation. The Dutch Reform school was closed in 1927, but by the late 1940s, the Roman Catholic church began establishing a parochial school a few grades at a time. Adults soon played one White institution against another, and their children were shuttled between the various schools. By the time of the First World War, many young Winnebagos were losing fluency in their language and their interest and skills gave them a sense of identification with the White socioeconomic system. But they were still unable to direct their affairs like the Whites, who controlled the county government and sources of employment on the reservation. Whites monopolized the jobs for which Indians also had training and the idea of education became increasingly meaningless.

What land remained in Indian hands was usually too fragmented by heirship to be farmed and Indians lacked capital to buy or lease land and work it like White farmers. Community pressures also militated against emulating White patterns of individual enterprise. Sheer physical survival and the psychic support of Indian esteem in a hostile and prejudiced White world came to depend increasingly on the old values of sharing with one's fellow tribesmen. Although living cheek by jowl on the reservation, the White and Indian communities were socially isolated.

In 1936 the Winnebago attempted to improve their situation by means of the Indian Reorganization Act of 1934. Their 12-member council enjoyed a reputation with the Indian Bureau as conscientious in its limited duties of administering loans and negotiating with the agency in the community's general economic interests. But it was unable to cope with the tremendous problems of social disorder created by ubiquitous individual poverty and powerlessness. The Indian community's pent-up frustration was turned inward in the form of delinquency, drunkenness, broken homes, school dropouts, and acts of personal violence. The federal government's Indian police system languished for lack of candidates willing to take on unpopular jobs. The old clan functions were long since lost. For lack of anything else, old, informal social controls had to be depended upon beyond the point that they could be very effective. These included ridicule, gossip, physical withdrawal from dangerous troublemakers, and fascination with witchcraft. Witches remained a major explanation for bad luck, a source of fear lest a witch's jealousy of some temporary (or alleged) affluence result in misfortune, and a subject of skeptical but cautious joking. Likewise, there was continuing knowledge on the part of a few specialists of both herbal and magical properties of native medicines. However, the formalized aspects of traditional Winnebago religion virtually disappeared from the reservation. The last Medicine Lodge ceremony was given about the time of the Second World War; only two families held medicine-bundle ceremonies through the 1950s; and there was some persistence of the four-night wake, often abbreviated to one night of warriors' stories and gambling games followed by a Christian burial ceremony. Nominally, at least, religious affiliation tended to stabilize at about an even division between the Native American Church (Peyote) and various White Christian denominations. The persisting minority of traditionalists availed themselves increasingly of opportunities to participate in the ancient ceremonies still flourishing in Wisconsin.

Despite increasing social problems on the reservation, Indian community life continued to retain some satisfactory aspects. Winnebagos looked out for one another in family crises, such as deaths or house fires. Generally, they found much to enjoy in one another's company. Spontaneous, powwow-style dances were frequently held on Saturday or Sunday afternoons and evenings, with a feast of donated food. There was often gift giving, usually small sums of money, in honor of occasions such as birthdays or departures for the armed services or to raise money for some community cause. Ideas for economic improvement began to be discussed after the Second World War as former servicemen and defense plant workers came home with knowledge of new, promising alternatives for community development. But these plans met with official coolness because of the federal policy enunciated in 1953 to terminate Indian reservations and relocate Indians in urban areas. By 1961 the errors of termination were becoming apparent in the few places it was tried; and as the threat of termination lifted, the national Indian movement to improve Indian life and assert tribal rights was felt on the Winnebago reservation as elsewhere. The old council was challenged and accused of having operated in a conciliatory and dependent manner in regard to the Indian Bureau. The 1960s was a period of new Indian programs with funding available from a variety of federal agencies. Younger activists began campaigning for tribal offices on platforms promising economic improvement, social reform, and dynamic leadership. The old guard, who had managed to hold things together under adversity, resented being supplanted when there was finally a chance to use their hard-earned experience in leading the tribe to better times. Reservation politics became lively, if at times bitterly acrimonious. However, the younger people looked beyond the reservation for strength. Utilizing techniques of protest and boycott employed by other minorities across the country, they attacked discrimination in employment, law enforcement, education, and all aspects of reservation life, even to carrying their fight to the bastions of White power in the towns at the western end of the reservation. Joining with the other Nebraska tribes around 1970, they began negotiations with the state government to establish a state Indian commissioner and forced greater responsiveness to the Indian constituency in Nebraska. The new-found sense of intertribal strength came before political unity was achieved among the Winnebago themselves. In the early 1970s the Nebraska Winnebago were endeavoring by legal and other expedients to reestablish effective tribal government.

Wisconsin Winnebago

Following the disputed treaty of 1837, defiant Winnebago managed to hide out in central Wisconsin. Periodically, the federal government rounded them up and transported them to whatever reservation the tribe was currently in possession of, but they always returned to Wisconsin. The last major removal occurred in 1874

when the government purchased additional land from the Omaha to settle 860 Wisconsin Winnebagos. By the summer of 1875 the majority had found their way back home again (Lurie 1961:1–4). During their fugitive existence, the Wisconsin Winnebago tried various expedients to legalize their residence in their homeland. Dandy got a friendly White man to write a letter appealing to the governor but received no sympathy from the state capital. Yellow Thunder (fig. 10), who appears to have

NAA, Smithsonian.

Fig. 10. Yellow Thunder, a leader of the Wisconsin "disaffected bands." Sitting in front of a mat-covered wigwam, he holds a gun stock war club. Photograph by H.H. Bennett about 1880.

taken over the traditional peace chief's role, got White help to obtain land under the Homestead Act in 1862.

Extension of the Homestead Act to Indians offered all the Winnebagos a means of remaining in Wisconsin after 1875 but many were fearful of appearing before any White authorities, suspecting a ruse to catch them for another removal. Furthermore, most were too poor to even "prove up" such claims with the type of dwelling required by law. In 1881 special legislation permitted the Winnebago to take up 40-acre homesteads, with an annual stipend of $25,000 to be distributed among these settlers for 25 years to help them establish farms. The land was also tax free and inalienable for 25 years. Over 600 Winnebago homesteads were eventually registered. Because much of the area was already settled by Whites the Indian homesteads were scattered over 10 central Wisconsin counties. A few were even located across the Mississippi River in Minnesota. A special Wisconsin enrollment signalized their administrative separation from the Winnebago in Nebraska.

Generally, only the poorest land in central Wisconsin was left for the Indians. The homesteads were used mainly as headquarters to put in small gardens and build wigwams where belongings could be kept. The tribe continued to practice a seasonal, itinerant economy that was gradually adapted to the changing market economy of the country. Although scattered into quite small enclaves after 1837 to hide while living off the land, the Wisconsin Winnebago appear to have retained many of the traditional village and even overall tribal structures of the fur-trade period. In 1857, for example, when a Winnebago murdered his sister's husband, a group of men gathered for a whole day in a long wigwam in the Baraboo area to discuss the matter. Yellow Thunder was finally able to secure the murderer's release by paying an indemnity to the dead man's family in the form of blankets, calico, and ponies (Atkinson 1913).

Even prior to the granting of homesteads, the Wisconsin Winnebago had begun to form two territorial enclaves with summer settlement scattered widely around the focal areas of Black River Falls in the western part of the state and Wittenberg in the eastern part. Recognizing the need to learn more of White ways, particularly the English language, a group of Winnebagos built a log schoolhouse seven miles east of the town of Black River falls in 1875, but they had difficulty in attracting a regular teacher. In 1878 the Evangelical and Reform Church established a mission and began holding classes at the school. An Indian parent gave the teacher a pony for his daily trip between the school and Black River Falls. Jackson County subsequently gave the mission 120 acres where a parsonage and chapel were built in connection with the school. In time the school was enlarged to take boarding students and was transferred to a large, new building at Neillsville, Wisconsin, in 1921. Since the mission insisted on total conversion, it was not

Fig. 11. Women playing game with bone dice. The photographer claimed woman on left wears blindfold; modern Winnebagos say she was avoiding being photographed. Woman on right wears multiple ball-and-cone earrings and hair pipe and bead necklaces. Photograph by Robert C. Gebhardt, Black River Falls, Wisc., about 1907.

until 1898 that the first four Black River Falls Winnebagos were baptized. One of these had been among the first students at the school in 1878 and eventually became a lay preacher in charge of the mission.

In 1884 a Norwegian Lutheran mission and boarding school were established four miles from Wittenberg to serve the Oneida, Stockbridge, and Menominee, as well as the local Winnebago. Partially supported by federal funds until this procedure was abolished in 1895, the school passed totally into federal management until 1917 when it reverted to the church and was finally closed in 1933. Meanwhile, Winnebago children throughout the state were also enrolled in county schools close to their homes or were sent to the government Indian school at Tomah, Wisconsin, until it was converted to use as an Indian hospital after the First World War. When parents enrolled their children in school, these conservative people often made a point of telling the youngsters to be obedient and diligent students but to pay no attention to any religious instruction they might receive.

The Winnebago generally planted gardens in the summer and picked wild blueberries in the summer and cranberries in the fall to sell to the local Whites. In the early fall, many families moved with ponies and wagons to campsites along the Mississippi River in the LaCrosse region to trap and hunt during the winter. They gathered together during times when they were not working in order to hold Medicine Dances and other ceremonies. In the summer they held large social gatherings to dance and play lacrosse games. A great deal of visiting occurred between the western and eastern settlers for religious and social purposes, and there was visiting between Nebraska and Wisconsin people. It was at the large Wisconsin conclaves, particularly, that the Bear clan exercised its traditional function to maintain law and order, even to tying up obstreperous drunks until they were sober.

In 1906 the majority of Winnebagos did not realize that their homesteads would be listed on county tax rolls. When they did not pay their taxes, a land company quickly bought up most of their better land. Eventually, tax-free status was restored to homesteads remaining in Indian ownership, but by then the parcels were divided by heirship like the reservation allotments. Being worthless land in general, the homesteads were not a matter of much administrative concern to the succession of Wisconsin Indian agencies and superintendencies that held nominal jurisdiction over the Winnebago and interfered little in their affairs.

In 1908 Wisconsin people who had been converted to the Peyote Religion while living in Nebraska, as well as Nebraska people, began an active campaign of proselytizing in Wisconsin (Lurie 1961:39–51). Although their first services were held at Black River Falls, their efforts were more successful at Wittenberg, where virtually the

entire community became affiliated with the Native American Church. Peyote made other converts among the Wisconsin Winnebago: there is a congregation at Black River Falls, and the Native American Church in the Wisconsin Dells region, like the congregation at Wittenberg, owns church land and buildings. However, western Wisconsin remains the center of Winnebago religious conservatism (fig. 12). The three-way religious

Milwaukee Public Mus.

Fig. 12. Big Wave, also known as A. White, making the sacred fire for a war-bundle ceremony of the Thunderbird clan. He uses a palm drill from the war bundle. Photograph by W.C. McKern at Wisconsin Rapids, Oct. 1927.

pull of traditionalism, mission Christianity, and the Native American Church created bitter schisms in Wisconsin for several generations, undercutting tribal unity and eroding traditional institutions of community organization and management. Changing economic conditions shortly before the First World War to which the Wisconsin Winnebago made effective adaptations also affected tribal organizational structures in cutting down on the general summer socializing that transcended religious differences.

Blueberries began to diminish as a result of state restrictions against burning underbrush that stimulated their growth, but the summer income they once provided was replaced by wage work in strawberry fields owned by Whites. About 1917 the wild cranberry bogs were bought up by Whites who instituted a system of dikes and dams to make the marshes more productive and extend the season, thereby creating additional employment for Winnebagos in the fall. At about this time, the Door County peninsula became an important cherry-producing region; and the Winnebago, along with people from other tribes, spent the midsummers working in the orchards. Between the cherry and cranberry seasons, Winnebagos had a choice of work harvesting corn, potatoes, peas, and other vegetables for White growers. Winnebagos had generally acquired automobiles by the time of the First World War, making it possible to move quickly from one crop to another from early spring to late fall. The automobile also stimulated White tourism, which some Winnebago families exploited with stands along the highways where they sold beadwork and splint baskets made during the winter months or bought from other Winnebagos.

In 1913 White entrepreneurs at Wisconsin Dells added Indian dances to local tourist attractions such as boat rides on the scenic Wisconsin River. By the mid-1920s Winnebagos began settling in increasing numbers in the Dells area to sell handcrafts and earn summer money as singers and dancers. A few Winnebagos had also begun to explore winter wage work in urban factories.

The Winnebago, like the country at large, suffered in the international depression of the 1930s. As the Depression lifted, the Winnebago continued to develop their seasonal itinerary with its several options and enjoyed a busy, independent existence, at least on a day-to-day basis. The years of the Second World War brought a measure of real prosperity to the Winnebago from wage work in defense factories and regular income received by families of servicemen, but this comfortable state of affairs began to change rapidly after the war. Despite the tribe's early appreciation of education, for most people this did not extend beyond the first few grades. Their seasonal economy had militated against regular schooling. As crop work became increasingly mechanized, cutting down on the labor force, the Winnebago not only were deprived of customary sources of income but also were unskilled in other kinds of employment. In the meantime, tribal organizational structures had become practically inoperative and factional cleavages along religious lines prevented the kind of overall coordinated action required to deal with the massive economic problems facing the entire tribe.

The process of tribal reorganization was already set in motion in 1949 when the Nebraska and Wisconsin Winnebago, after long discussion, agreed to bring a common claim before the United States Indian Claims Commission. The Nebraska tribal council could act for the reservation group in retaining attorneys, but the Wisconsin people had to elect a special claims committee. Several committee members were also active in the newly formed Winnebago Veterans group, a state-chartered benevolent association intended to help the Wisconsin Winnebago as a whole. The claim dragged on for more than 20 years, but the value of elective organizations to coordinate work in the tribal behalf was readily recognized. In 1961 the American Indian Chicago Conference attracted many Wisconsin Winnebagos and inspired one young, college-educated woman in particular. Building

on an existing foundation of tribal interest in community action, she was instrumental in the development of an acting business committee and in obtaining a small grant from the Social Security Administration for the tribe to study its own problems as a basis for community development—an unprecedented experiment for any tribe at the time (Miller, Lurie, and Sieber 1963–1965). Operating entirely independently of the Indian Bureau, the business committee carried out a survey to the complete satisfaction of the Social Security Administration and at the same time recycled its two grants of about $7,500 each to create an effective tribal administrative body, become recognized as an Indian Reorganization Act tribe, acquire land to be eligible for new federal housing projects, institute educational programs, reestablish tribal powwows, and cut across religious and regional factionalism in the general Wisconsin Winnebago economic interest.

This remarkably successful endeavor began to lose momentum about 1965, due in large part to the administration of various federal poverty programs directed toward Indians in the state. Many officials tended to repeat the old paternalism and distrust of Indians' financial talents that had long characterized the Indian Bureau. The attitude of White officialdom and its meddling in tribal business outraged the Winnebago who felt they had proved themselves with their recent grants. Winnebago leaders fell out among themselves, mustering their own factions in the process, in disagreements as to how much decision-making power the Wisconsin Winnebago should relinquish to outside agencies in exchange for benefits that might be available. The struggle, a new one for the Wisconsin Winnebago who never had any federally controlled tribal assets to worry about, had all the earmarks of the familiar political factionalism of reservation tribes who can only manipulate power and funds that are actually in the firm grasp of the Indian Bureau. However, by 1970 it was possible to discern the beginning of a promising trend toward reunification and political stabilization.

Conclusion

Both the Nebraska and Wisconsin branches of the Winnebago face a common problem requiring mutual agreement and, after that, the need for internal unity of each group. The claim on which the two branches agreed to cooperate in 1949 (as one astute Winnebago argued at the time, "you can't divide the peanut until you've got the peanut") has been settled to the amount of a little over $4,000,000. This represents the difference between the value of their Wisconsin-Illinois homeland and what they were paid for it in the nineteenth century, less costs of litigation and other expenses. Ironically, the tribe received no compensation for the 1837 cession obtained by chicanery, which did irreparable social damage in dividing the Winnebago as a people. The Indian Claims

Commission decided simply that the Winnebago had been paid what the land was worth in 1837, 50¢ an acre. Although there was bitterness about the settlement in both Wisconsin and Nebraska, the Winnebagos' attorneys prevailed in convincing the tribe to accept the decision rather than to spend more time in trying to appeal it. A mutually agreeable division of the total amount must be settled upon between the Nebraska and Wisconsin groups. When that can be arranged, each group will have to provide its own proposal for Congress to appropriate its portion of the money. In both Nebraska and Wisconsin, the tribal councils will each have to cope in its own way with the fact of local Winnebago opinion that ranges from demands for immediate 100 percent per capita distribution of the money to equally clamorous demands for 100 percent investment for continuing community benefit. Meanwhile, responsible leaders in both groups, though at odds with one another and within their own groups, note with satisfaction that the money is earning substantial interest and they can afford to study the alternatives carefully before taking action.

Synonymy

The English name Winnebago is derived from an Algonquian form, perhaps Potawatomi *winpyeko* (pl. *winpyekok*; from Gatschet in Dorsey and Radin 1910:961), which would mean etymologically 'people of the dirty water'.† The name refers to the muddy water of their river (the lower course of the Fox River of Wisconsin plus Lake Winnebago), described by Cadillac (WHC 16:360) as yearly becoming clogged with the rotting bodies of dead fish during the heat of the summer. Other Algonquian forms show phonological evidence of being loanwords: Menominee *wenepeko·w* (from Bloomfield 1962:257), Fox *wi·nipye·ko·haki* (from William Jones in Dorsey and Radin 1910:958), Ojibwa *wi·nipe·ko·* (with a naturalized form *wi·nipi·ko·*; both from Gatschet in Dorsey and Radin 1910:961). Other attested Algonquian forms include Ottawa *winnebagoag* (Tanner 1956:316), Miami *winipikwa* (Voegelin 1938-1940, 5:123), Shawnee *winipeeaakoakēe* (Trowbridge 1939:66). The early French name was *gents puants* or *gens puants* 'stinking people', 1638-1639 (JR 15:154); it was later abbreviated to *Puans*, 1670 (JR 55:182); *Pouans*, 1736 (NYCD 9:1055); *Puyon, Pewins*, 1783 (MHSC ser. 1, 10:123), 1766 (MHSC ser. 1, 10:122) and translated into English as Stinkards (Jefferys 1761, 1:47) or simply Stinks (Lapham, Blossom, and Dousman 1870:8). That these names derive ultimately from the same source is made explicit by LeJeune who opts for the more poetic, and to him more correct, name *nation de mer* 'nation of the sea', 1640 (JR 18:230; see also Ragueneau in JR 33:150). *Ouinipigou* appears in the *Jesuit Relation* of 1640, *Ouen-*

† The synonymy section has been prepared by Susan Golla and Ives Goddard.

bigoutz in 1670 (JR 18:230, 54:204). The English spelling Winnibagoes occurs in 1793, Winnabagoes in 1797 (Imlay 1793:259, 1797:293); note also Winebago, Winibagos, Winnebagoes (Drake 1833, 5:123), and Winnepeg (in Dorsey and Radin 1910:961 unless otherwise cited). Banabeoüik, 1671 (NYCD 9:803) stems from a misreading of the symbol 8 (used by the French for the ou sound) and appears in several minor variants. The name Nipegons has also been used (Carver 1778:415), and Mipegoes (Boudinot 1816:107) is perhaps a misrendering of the same form. Webbings or Webings (Imlay 1797:294, 1793:261) seems to be an abbreviation and a distortion of the name Winnebago.

Dorsey and Radin (1910:961) mistakenly identify Ouenebigonchelinis with Winnebago; in fact this name, while nearly identical in meaning, refers to an eighteenth-century Algonquian group (Michelson 1934; cf. Hodge 1907-1910, 2:174).

The Huron name for the Winnebago, A8eatsi8aenrrhonon (JR 10:82-83, see also 322) was used, in several forms, by the Jesuit fathers. A Wyandot form Hati'hshi′rû′nû is also attested (Gatschet in Dorsey and Radin 1910:961); the etymology is uncertain (Gatschet's etymology is clearly incorrect) but it evidently means 'dwellers at [some kind of] place' (Floyd Lounsbury, personal communication 1974).

The Siouan-speaking Winnebago call themselves *ho·čágra*, from *ho* meaning either 'fish' or 'voice' plus *čąk* meaning 'big' in the sense of elemental or genuine, which is variously translated 'people of the parent speech' (McGee 1897:162) and 'great voice' (Forsyth in Dorsey and Radin 1910:961) or 'Trout Nation' (Gallatin 1836:120). The Winnebago usually prefer the translation 'big fish' as reflecting their traditional dependence on the huge sturgeon that once abounded in their area. French and English renderings of the Winnebago include Hochungohrah, Hote-shog-garah, Otchagras, Octagros, Otchun-gu-rah, and O-chunk-o-raw (in Dorsey and Radin 1910:961).

Other Siouan names for the Winnebago are Dakota (Lakota) *hótąke* (from Riggs 1890), Osage *hótǫga* (from Dorsey in Dorsey and Radin 1910:961), and Iowa-Oto-Missouri O-chunga-raw (Fletcher in Schoolcraft 1851-1857, 4:227).

Sources

The principal ethnographic reconstruction of Winnebago culture from the time of contact through the fur-trade period is Radin (1923), supplemented by shorter studies dealing primarily with cosmology and ritual (Radin 1909, 1915, 1926a, 1926b, 1945, 1949, 1956). The earliest European notice of the Winnebago, about 1623, appears in the writings of the Recollect brother Sagard-Théodat (1939), but the richest ethnohistorical source for the seventeenth century is the combined narrative of

Nicolas Perrot and Claude Charles Le Roy Bacqueville de la Potherie (Blair 1911-1912, 1:31-372, 2:13-136). Although the *Jesuit Relations* (JR 1896-1901) contain valuable bits and pieces of information that are supplemental to and extend beyond the period covered by Perrot and Bacqueville de la Potherie, the Jesuits made less precise and thorough observations about the Siouan-speaking Winnebago in comparison to their accounts of many of the Algonquian and Iroquoian-speaking tribes of the Great Lakes area, with whose languages the Jesuits were more familiar. Eighteenth- and nineteenth-century data on the Winnebago abound in the memoirs of early settlers and important Indians contained in the *Collections* of the State Historical Society of Wisconsin; however, personalities and events are stressed rather than ethnographic information. The *Annual Reports* of the commissioner of Indian affairs (1855-1875) provide basic ethnohistoric data on the period of treaties and removals, which are augmented by autobiographical accounts (Radin 1926c; Lurie 1961). Ethnographic information since the 1940s is drawn from fieldwork by Lurie (1944-1972).

Menominee

LOUISE S. SPINDLER

Menominee (mə¹nämə₁nē) is an Algonquian language; it has been classified as a member of the Central Algonquian subgroup, but Menominee cannot be said to have a particularly close relationship to any other single language in the subgroup.* In late aboriginal times the language was spoken in an indefinitely bounded region of what is now northern Michigan and Wisconsin.

First estimates of population are late and already postdate a long decline following exposure to European disease (table 1). They vary from 500 to 2,464 people (W.J. Hoffman 1896:33). By 1820 the number of full-bloods had been decreased by extensive intermarriage (Keesing 1939:102). In 1834, according to George Catlin's observation, about one-fourth of the tribe died in a smallpox epidemic (Keesing 1939:137). In 1864, 12 years after removal to the reservation, the tribe is reported to have decreased by about 100 (Keesing 1939:166). By 1915 it was increasing, due to the declining death rate and the addition of new members admitted to the roll, including many mixed-bloods and persons married to Menominees admitted by vote of the tribal council (Keesing 1939:224).

* The orthography used here is that of Bloomfield (1962). Spellings and translations have been checked by Ives Goddard, who reports that the terms *mi·ʔs-kenu·pik*, *maska·wesen*, and *okehceta·wehsemon* are not given as such by Bloomfield.

Culture

Subsistence

The precontact Menominee had small gardens in which they grew squash, beans, and corn, but they were basically hunters and gatherers. They also made extensive use of the resources of streams, particularly sturgeon and wild rice. Hunting was done by individuals and small congenial groups, with occasional larger hunts for deer and buffalo. A variety of charms for hunting, "hunting bundles," and rituals to ensure the cooperation of special powers and guardian spirits were used. Reverence was paid to particular animals, such as the bear, from whom mankind was believed to have descended. Some of these same rituals were used by a few hunters in 1960.

Early accounts describe the importance of wild rice as a food, and the techniques for harvesting were still used in the early twentieth century (Jenks 1900). It became increasingly less important as a food after that time. It was no longer harvested in the Menominee area by 1960.

The fur trade caused substantial changes in the social and economic adaptation of the Menominee. The semisedentary seasonal village pattern declined, though the persistence of village sites into the nineteenth century suggests that the pattern was never entirely abandoned.

Table 1. Population

	Tribal Estimate	Women	Men	Children	Full-bloods	Sources
1718			100			W.J. Hoffman 1896:32
1761	750		150[c]			W.J. Hoffman 1896:32
1820	3,900	900	600	2,400		W.J. Hoffman 1896:33
1847	2,500					Keesing 1939:139
1857	1,697	425[a]		914		W.J. Hoffman 1896:33
1886	1,308				633	Keesing 1939:225
1902	under 1,300					Keesing 1939:224
1916	1,736				434	Keesing 1939:224
1929	1,939				463	Keesing 1939:224
1956	2,917	320[b]	380[b]		82	L. Spindler 1962:22, 23

[a] Including 67 with less than half blood.
[b] Individuals with 1/2 or more Menominee blood.
[c] Warriors only.

In modern times the people do not fragment into nomadic bands in the winter, yet life retains a nomadic and intermittent character. Some of the men in the tradition-oriented group† work with logging crews in the forest, and this work is dependent upon the season of the year, the depth of the snow, and the "cut" needed to keep the sawmill operating. Most men and boys in this group fish and hunt. Until about 1960, most families went to pick cherries, potatoes, and strawberries in season for farmers and orchardists in Wisconsin and Michigan. Many individuals and families pick ferns and evergreen boughs. A few people go to Minnesota to gather wild rice each year. During the summer, members of the tradition-oriented group organize themselves into a loosely defined "troupe" that performs weekly "play dances" for tourists (fig. 1), often traveling to various towns throughout the state.

Technology

The precontact Menominee had both birchbark and dugout canoes (fig. 2-3), the dugout probably more common. They had bows and arrows; clubs; stone, shell,

† "Tradition-oriented group" refers to those Menominees who self-consciously retained traditional customs and who were members of the Medicine Lodge or Dream Dance organizations. They have sometimes been called "native oriented" (Spindler and Spindler 1971:2). Some members of this group are descendants of Potawatomis who intermarried with the Menominees; very few now identify themselves as Potawatomi. All spoke Menominee, which was the language used at the ceremonies. Most of this group live near Zoar, but others are scattered elsewhere throughout the reservation. In the 1950-1960 period the membership of the group totaled about 70 adults, but in the mid-1970s there was strong evidence of a tradition-oriented revival.

Fig. 1. Tradition-oriented Menominees at a "play dance" at Bear Trap Falls. They wear deertail roaches on their heads. Aprons and vests are decorated with beadwork in traditional floral designs. from left, Maykiss Wolf, Johnson Awanohopay, Joe Notinokey, Dewey Wynos. Photograph by George Spindler in 1950.

bone, and copper knives; and stone axes with grooved heads. They prepared skins; wove bags and baskets of vegetable fiber, bark, and buffalo hair; manufactured bark and reed mats and pottery; prepared dyes; and made a variety of household utensils, firemaking apparatus, drums, and pipes. Except for the sacred artifacts and hunting and fishing equipment, the women made most of the articles (JR 3:101). Skinner (1921) provides a more detailed account. W.J. Hoffman (1896) found that reed mats were still made at the end of the nineteenth century. Skinner (1921:202) reported skin tanning and clamshell spoons still in use, while bone and antler were also still used occasionally for implements and clay for pipes. Splint basketry had been introduced by the Oneida and Stockbridge Indians (fig. 4). The bow and arrow were still in occasional use in the early twentieth century (Keesing 1939:28). By 1890, the canoe was little used. Copper working had disappeared. However, items related to the ceremonies of the Medicine Lodge, Dream Dance, and Peyote religion persisted in the 1960s.

Structures

Dwellings at the time of contact consisted of a rectangular bark cabin for summer and a dome-shaped lodge of mats or bark for winter. Temporary "sweat lodges," a women's lodge for periodic seclusions, places for dreaming and fasting, and the lodge of the "juggler" or shaman were erected. W.J. Hoffman (1896:253-256) found log or frame structures used for winter dwelling and for summer, a residence of sapling and bark, built in a conical shape. Skinner (1921) found bark houses still in existence (fig. 4) and a long ceremonial Medicine Lodge structure (fig. 5). A few bark houses were used by elderly Menominees in the 1950s. An elongated Medicine Lodge structure was built of canvas over a framework of bent saplings for the ritual in 1954.

Art

The only art forms that can be established as precontact are simple markings found on pottery fragments and designs on medicine pouches. These show a well-developed geometric art and indicate the use of highly conventionalized figures (Skinner 1921:252-276). The older art forms included work with porcupine quills and animal hair with a religious motif, such as representations of thunderers and sacred beings. The period around 1830 marks the beginning of a new phase in Menominee art characterized by extreme elaboration, with replacement of skin and quill by cloth and bead with new color pigments and elaborate floral and realistic designs in place of older geometric motifs (fig. 6). This new art development had a wide distribution through tribes of the woodland area and into the plains area (Keesing 1939:117). These forms persisted in the 1950s for special events and tourist dancing (figs. 1, 7).

Royal Ont. Mus., Toronto.

Fig. 2. Menominees spearing fish attracted by the jacklights in iron frames mounted on birchbark canoes. Painting by Paul Kane after his sketch made on the Fox River in 1845.

Clothing and Adornment

Except for general facts, little is known from which to reconstruct the precontact Menominee dress or the distinctions made between sexes or among various ranks and for different occasions. Aspects of dress reliably old were oil and grease rubbed on hair and body and a variety of colors applied to the skin with particular meanings on ceremonial occasions (Keesing 1939:25). The early fur traders and missionaries reported that garments—breechcloths, leggings, and moccasins—were made predominantly of deer skins. It was reported that a cloak of dressed skin was used on special visits (fig. 8). Most forms of upper garments worn in later times are of postcontact origin (Keesing 1939:24). During the first half of the nineteenth century Menominee women began to copy the full gathered skirt and waist worn by White women (fig. 7). By the twentieth century Menominee of

all groups used clothing bought at stores, with the exception of the moccasin, which persisted as common wear in the tradition-oriented group through 1960.

During the nineteenth century traditional Menominee in the Medicine Lodge group used beads, ribbons, earrings, combs, headdresses of fur, eaglefeather roaches, pouches, bands, garters, and ankle and arm bells. Many of these adornments were still used for tourist dancing in 1960. A pan-Indian ceremonial dress on a modern Plains model became widely adopted in the mid-twentieth century (fig. 7).

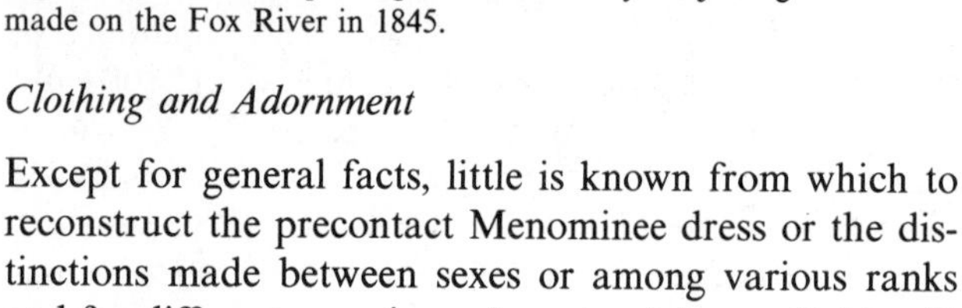

Religion

The concepts concerning the universe described by W.J. Hoffman (1896) and Skinner (1921) correspond with the accounts of fur traders and Jesuits who encountered the Menominee first in the late seventeenth century.

> The earth is believed to be an island, floating in an illimitable ocean, separating the two halves of the universe into an upper and a lower portion, regarded as the abode of the benevolent and the malevolent powers, respectively. Each portion is divided into four superimposed tiers, inhabited by supernatural beings, the power of whom increases in ratio to their remoteness from the earth. In the highest tier above the earth resides the deity to whom all others are subordinate. The testimony of the early writers is unanimous that this being was the sun . . . (Skinner 1921:29).

Dept. of Anthr., Smithsonian: 307246.

Fig. 3. Dugout canoe from Keshena, Wis. Length about 6 m; collected by W.J. Hoffman in 1893.

710

Fig. 4. Exterior and interior of the *wa·panow* Somen Jim's rectangular bark-covered summer house on the Menominee reservation. On the sleeping platform are reed mats, splint baskets, and a cradleboard. A pair of moccasins is on the box, and a wooden pothook of an ancient type hangs from a rafter next to a metal pot (with spoon) suspended by a metal pothook. Photograph by Alanson Skinner or S.A. Barrett about 1909–1920.

Beneath the highest tier, and in descending order, are (1) the Thunderbirds, gods of war, and the Morning Star, (2) the golden or war eagles and the white swan, and (3) birds of other species, headed by the bald eagles. Beneath the earth and in the lowest tier is the Great White Bear with a copper tail who is purported to be the traditional ancestor of the Menominee tribe and is the main power for evil. The Great Underground Panther comes next in ascending order. He plays an important role in the mythology of the Central Algonquian and southern Siouan tribes. Then comes the White Deer, who is important in the origin myth of the Medicine Dance. And, finally, is the Horned Hairy Serpent, *me·ʔsekenεpik* 'great serpent' (modern *mi·ʔs-kenu·pik*), who inhabits the lakes and streams and tries to capsize boats in order to drag people to the Underground Place.

The earth itself is believed to be peopled with evil spirits and hobgoblins. There are cannibal giants, *mεʔnapε·wak* (sg. *mεʔnapε·w*), who dwell in the north and eat Indians; there is a malevolent living skeleton with deadly eyes who roams the forests after nightfall. Then there is the ghostly old man, *pe·hcekona·h nε·yo·htah,* who carries a sacred bundle upon his back and is doomed to travel endlessly to atone for some sin. In addition: "a race of pygmies inhabits remote rocky fastnesses. A well-disposed elf smites people on the head with a soft warclub, causing sleep. Flying heads and skulls, of varying intentions toward the race of men, exist; and there is a mysterious man who follows and molests belated travelers. Rocks, ponds, and hills have their fancied denizens. All species of animals are ruled by supernatural chiefs" (Skinner 1921:32).

NAA, Smithsonian.

Fig. 5. Long mat-covered lodge used for the *mete·wen* ceremony on the Menominee reservation in 1892. Photograph perhaps by W.J. Hoffman.

There was also a system of complex sacred bundles. Each bundle contained "medicines," such as "thunder eggs" (rounded stones), miniature war and lacrosse sticks, roots, powders, and so forth, which were invested with powers evoked by ritual, song, and reverence, and that

Milwaukee Public Mus.

Fig. 6. Men wearing wool sash turbans, blanket robes, brightly colored cloth clothing decorated with beads and ribbons, and silver earrings. Old types are the shell gorget, feather, wampum necklace, black buckskin pouch (here decorated with ribbon appliqué and glass beads), and the buckskin moccasins (here with beaded decoration). Three white clay trade pipes are shown. standing. Na-a-nos-a-ko-sa, left, and Tik-ko; seated, left to right, Ne-kan-a-quok, Kis-kan-a-keom, Na-ke-wai-mi. Painted by S. M. Brookes, Dec. 1858.

Fig. 7. Tradition-oriented Menominees at the annual Menominee Fair and Pageant. Elizabeth Pamoska, at left, wears a Plains-inspired buckskin dress while Mary Dowd and Helen Wynos wear more traditional cloth appliquéd dresses. Photograph by George Spindler, 1960.

could do great good or harm. There were also pictographs done on birchbark or hides (fig. 9).

The Menominee belief system is dualistic, with a continuing cosmic conflict between good spirits above the earth and evil spirits below. These specific and basic beliefs about the universe and its inhabitants persist among Menominee in the tradition-oriented group (Slotkin 1957).

Social and Political Organization

Early documents and origin myths of the Menominee point to the existence of a dual organization or moiety system defined as the Thunderers and Bears, with subdivisions into patrilineal totemic descent groups (or clans). One version of the system collected from an informant born around 1827 included a system of five phratries, divided into five, six, four, three, and four subgroupings or clans. The old system began to disintegrate in the seventeenth century and great confusion existed when W.J. Hoffman (1896) attempted to reconstruct it. An exogamic principle probably existed; but how it related to moieties, phratries, and clans is uncertain (Keesing 1939:38).

Polygyny was practiced according to statements by Jesuit missionaries. The stability of marriages is obscure. Marriages were arranged between kin groups, perhaps as results of liaisons arising from previous nightly courting practices referred to in folk tales. Reciprocal presents were exchanged by relatives of the prospective bride and groom. A newly married couple usually lived with the husband's parents (Keesing 1939:43).

SPINDLER

Natl. Coll. of Fine Arts, Smithsonian.
Fig. 8. Two young men with roaches and eagle feathers in their hair, red face and body paint, quill-decorated pouch, and other clothing and ornaments in the transitional period when introduced materials were used to reproduce largely aboriginal forms: green blanket edged with ribbon appliqué, green cloth breechclout, red cloth leggings, finger-woven yarn belt and garters. Painted by George Catlin at Prairie du Chien in 1835 or at Green Bay in 1836.

after Skinner 1913:105.
Fig. 9. Portion of painted design on sacred inner skin wrapping of a war bundle. Thunderers' power is shown as lightning lines from eyes and beaks.

On the basis of somewhat fragmentary data, the kinship terminology has been classified as an Omaha-type system. One of the main features of Menominee family relationships was a classificatory system of terminology: father and father's brother were given one term and father's brother's children or mother's sister's children (parallel cousins) are given the same terms as brothers and sisters. The mother's brother–sister's son relationship was important. Rigid distinctions between parallel and cross-cousins and restraints in parents-in-law relationships existed. A prescribed "joking relationship" was maintained between certain classes of relatives (between ego and his uncles and aunts, nephews and nieces, sisters-in-law and brothers-in-law on either side); it was tabooed between cousins according to Skinner (1913:20). Skinner also claimed that sexual intercourse was permissible between these same groups of relatives.

Hereditary chiefs—heads of descent groups—with the chief of the Bear group as tribal chief were included in the formal sociopolitical structure of the precontact Menominee. The lineage chiefs constituted a village council and regulated civil affairs to a limited extent. Aside from this civil leadership there were said to be chiefs who won prestige through individual dreams or due to their special prowess. Those persons acted as keepers of the war medicines and as public spokesmen for hereditary leaders and as masters of ceremonies during public celebrations (Keesing 1939:40).

After the French fur traders arrived in 1667, the village and clan system broke down and the "band" system emerged. By 1830 there were nine bands. Since large groupings would not be feasible under these conditions, families ranged in congenial groups. As the forest areas nearby became denuded of game, the groups had to go farther, and each family claimed customary rights over a given river path and hunting territory. Because of the credit system, the fur traders sent agents along with the band. During the summer months the Menominee camped at places convenient for fishing, making gardens, and gathering maple syrup, berries, and wild rice. These groups tended to remain stable. Bands were primarily friendship groups but tended to follow clan lines. Later the distinctiveness broke down, but some of the bands retained strong clan marks up to the reservation period. The small family or household group fit into the band organization as well as it had the village type. Monogamy became more prevalent. The individual family grew in importance in the loosely knit band system, and this trend toward individualism persisted among the tradition-oriented Menominee in 1960.

Modifications occurred in the tribal leadership. New standards for leaders included success in obtaining furs, directing hunting and trading operations, obtaining credit, orating, and getting along well with Whites and other Indian tribes. The tribal council came into being and frequent tribal council and intertribal councils were held.

When the Menominee reservation was formed in 1854, a sedentary-type subsistence was required, and the band system of the fur-trading era began to disintegrate. The various band leaders, it is said, chose locations that

713

appealed to them on the reserve, and the members of their bands either grouped themselves nearby or selected other areas where they and their families might live. The band type of organization did not entirely disappear. People regrouped in congenial cooperative groups under different leaders and were still called bands. When these new bands became settled and less isolated from other groups, they in turn tended to lose their unity (Keesing 1939:150). The old dualism seemed to persist in the division of the tribe into "Christians" and "pagans." Those following the traditional religion also divided into two groups more or less based on the old division of Bear and Thunderer. When some families started to farm and others began to log, a variety of regroupings occurred to fit the environmental demands of the particular subsistence technique. Members of the contemporary tradition-oriented group in 1960 lived in and around Zoar. They are often referred to as the pagan group by others. The social organization remains similar to that found in the early reservation period.

Many older members of the tradition-oriented group have a totem or clan affiliation. It was common practice until the mid-twentieth century for each individual to have his totem painted, usually upside down, on a grave stick at his place of burial. Some marriages are still arranged by elders. The kinship terminology described by Skinner (1913) was still in use in the Menominee tongue in the 1960s (mixed with Potawatomi and Chippewa terms) and is frequently projected indirectly into the English kinship usage, for instance, referring to a parallel cousin in phrases such as "he is like a brother to me." The same term is used for father and father's brother and for mother's father and father's father, and distinctions are still made between cross-cousins and parallel cousins. All the people around Zoar are conscious of kin relationships to one another, which has created a powerful force pulling them together into a cohesive group.

Some of the old obligations and prerogatives between relatives have been retained. The old joking relationships, particularly between a man and his brother-in-law, are very much alive. Other kinship obligations survive in the distribution of meat killed in hunting and the understanding that certain relatives, when called upon, must provide economic help in time of distress, or when a candidate is being "put up" for the Medicine Lodge.

Elders are still the most respected persons in the group. This is the age set from which the leadership is drawn. The elders know the ritual of the Medicine Lodge and Dream Dance, are in direct contact with the supernatural powers, can prophesy with their dreams, can name a child appropriately, and are the authorities for questions on kin relationships.

The exercise of authority in the 1950–1960 period was much like that described by the Jesuits and fur traders in the eighteenth century. Nicolas Perrot (1911:144–145), the fur trader, wrote: "The father does not venture to exercise authority over his son, nor does the chief dare to give commands to his soldier . . .."

World View

Power Gaining

The fundamental relationships that existed between the Menominee and the supernatural can only be understood in terms of power and power gaining. The emphasis was upon securing a guardian spirit to obtain power, and the central experience of Menominee religion was the dream revelation. This was commented upon by the Jesuit missionaries in the seventeenth century (JR 56:265–267). The gaining of power was essential for survival among the Menominee. Three terms were used interchangeably for power: tata·hkesewen 'that which has energy' ('strength, power' from a verb meaning 'he is strong, powerful'); maska·wesen 'that which has strength' (from a verb meaning 'he is of sound health'); and ahpe·htesewen 'that which is valuable' ('spiritual power' from a verb meaning 'he is so powerful, costly, old') (Slotkin 1957:25, from whom the first gloss in each case is taken; the parenthetical glosses are from Bloomfield 1962).

A boy or girl undergoing the puberty fast—mesa·hkatewɛ·w 'he fasts; one who fasts'—received a dream that gave the individual power by which to live. The importance of the dream, in which a person received special power in the form of a tutelary spirit (fig. 10), was as described by early Jesuit writers for groups farther east: "They look upon their dreams as ordinances and irrevocable decrees. [The dream] prescribes their feasts, their dances, their songs, their games—in a word, the dream does everything" (JR 10:169–171).

Preparation for the fast began during early childhood with short fasts of a day or two, with instruction in the proper humble state of mind. The average fast lasted 10 days at puberty, during which time the supplicant, with blackened face, was isolated in a small wigwam without food or water. The vision came as one of the many supernatural figures, usually in animal form. It was interpreted later by a shaman who indicated what powers had been given and what obligations the receiver was under for having received them.

Power was so important and precious that it had to be guarded at all times. During menstruation and following childbirth, women were a threat to the power of the male or small child. A woman was isolated during these periods, using her own utensils, refraining from touching herself or looking up, which might offend the gods above. If a man were to eat food prepared by her at these times, he was in danger of losing his guardian spirit, which lived inside him in the form of a tiny turtle or fish. If he found out about the woman's condition in time, he could take an emetic and vomit the food before it killed the little animal. The menstruating woman was careful not to feed, touch, or even breathe upon a small child for fear of causing its death. A small child may be a powerful reincarnated elder, whose power must be protected. One's power increases as he or she grows older. It is only elders who become men and women of great power.

Skinner (1913) found the basic beliefs regarding power gaining and menstrual taboos still operative. In 1936 Hilger (1960:55) collected accounts of the fasting experience from elderly Menominee, and in the 1948–1960 period Spindler and Spindler (1970) found several elders who said they had experienced the Great Fast. After 1960 none remained.

In spite of some changes the pattern of securing a guardian spirit remained in 1960 an integral part of the culture both in spirit and in specific form. All adults in the group had fasted for short periods as children. Some received notifications from the spirits in these preparatory fasts and ritually observed the relationship thus formed. Others have inherited both the powers and obligations of ritual observance from departed relatives. For the tradition-oriented Menominees, "ordinary" dreaming was in 1960 also a very significant activity. No dream is casually dismissed. Even songs are acquired in dreams, and many personal decisions are made on the basis of them.

Ceremonial Organizations

The older Menominee ceremonial organizations consisted mainly of medicine men or persons with outstanding powers who worked more or less entirely as individ-

Mus. of the Amer. Ind., Heye Foundation, New York: 9/2013.
Fig. 10. Wooden carving representing a personal dream guardian, set up outside the rear wall of a bark lodge. Height about 117 cm; made about 1865, collected west of Neopit, Wis., about 1909–1919.

uals (Keesing 1939:50). The earlier religious groupings consisted of the Thunder cult and a Buffalo Dance cult, the *wa·panow*s and the *ce·ʔsahkow*s. An unresolved question remains as to whether the Witches' Society is a comparatively recent development or not.

Very little is known of the Thunder cult and the Buffalo Dance cult except that members of each shared the same tutelary spirit and performed certain prescribed rites. Members of the Witches' Society were said to perform special cannibalistic rites. This society was reported to have had eight members, four using the Bear as tutelary spirit and four using the Owl.

The *wa·panow*s are basically medicine men with special powers. Early reporters of Menominee culture often equated them with witches. They were said to be able to furnish hunting medicine, prescribe herbal remedies, and sell love powders and charms that would cause an indifferent person to fall in love with the owner.

The *ce·ʔsahkow*s, or jugglers (French *jongleurs*) as they were called by the early writers, were diviners and doctors of great powers who worked in a small birchbark lodge when they consulted the spirits to cure the sick. The lodge swayed from side to side (thus the term "shaking-tent rite"); wind was heard and voices spoke to the seer. The *ce·ʔsahkow* supposedly replied through the medium of the turtle, who acted as an interpreter.

It was the role of the *ce·ʔsahkow* to find out the cause of the patient's illness, which was usually witchcraft. The *ce·ʔsahkow* would then attempt to coax the soul of the patient to return and enter a small wooden cylinder where it was imprisoned and delivered to its relatives. The cylinder was then attached to the patient's breast for four days, so that the soul could return to his body (see Skinner 1921:72).

The following Menominee religious groups arose after contact and persisted in varying degrees among the tradition-oriented group in 1960.

The *metɛ·wen*, or Medicine Lodge Society, probably of Chippewa origin, is the oldest and has the most elaborate ritual connected with power. Most students agree that it is probably of early postcontact origin; however, many of the elements are of great antiquity, and the ritual and beliefs of the lodge are a fundamental aspect of the religious systems of all Central Algonquians (Spindler 1955:42). This organization still played a vital role in the lives of the tradition-oriented Menominee as late as 1960. It is still an integral part of the belief system of Menominees familiar with their old culture.

The Medicine Lodge is an exclusive organization with membership by invitation or inheritance of a medicine bag. The declared intent of the ritual is to prolong life and insure the good health of its members (*metɛ·wak,metɛ·w* sg.) including protection against the machinations of witches. All information was paid for by the candidate in installments, and it was believed that the teachings would be of no use if the payment was not appropriately large.

Each member became the possessor of a medicine bag—an otter, mink, or other whole small-animal skin filled with small packets of herbal medicine. He or she was given the power to shoot a small, magically endowed cowrie shell and a medicine for retrieving it (W.J. Hoffman 1896; Skinner 1915, 1920). All medicines and power were declared to be benevolent and protective. And yet, in the sacred origin myth of the lodge, given by the culture hero, *mɛʔnapos,* specific directions are given for members possessing both good and evil bags (Skinner 1920:61–62).

Another postcontact religious organization was the Dream Dance or Drum Dance, *ni·mihɛtwan.* Although it incorporated Christian elements with aboriginal elements, it is essentially native North American in pattern and has been invested with characteristic Menominee attitudes and values (Spindler 1955:43). This association and ceremony were extremely important in the culture of the most conservative Menominees during 1950–1960 (see Slotkin 1957).

Unlike the *metɛ·wen,* membership in the Dream Dance organization is relatively open, and the sacred knowledge is obtained at the cost of only a few ritual gifts. Further, the weekly meetings or seasonal rites are more intimate and more directly related to everyday life. The dogma and cosmology of the organization resemble traditional Menominee beliefs. It is crucial that a man obtain supernatural power necessary to enable him to carry out his activities. This is done by members petitioning the spirits through the sacred drum and the ritual related to it.

The doctrines of the Dream Dance organization are based on revelations received by a young Sioux woman from the Great Spirit, who gave her the original drum and taught her the rituals (Skinner 1915:167–176). Each drum has a number of offices, which are related to each "leg" of the drum—one for each of the four directions of the compass. There is a drum owner, a man in the older age group, who retains major responsibility for the conduct of the ceremonies in which it is used. He is the authority on proper ritual, and he is supposed to look out "like a father" for the people occupying offices connected with his drum and their families. There is also a "keeper" for each drum who maintains the drum in his home in its sacred wrappings, keeps a lighted lantern near it at night, and is responsible for its care. When a "song service" or a seasonal rite is being conducted, from four to eight men sit around the drum, singing in chorus and hitting the drum in unison (fig. 11). During the meetings, when drumming, singing, or praying is not going on, someone is speaking. One of the old men exhorts all present to do the right things, which means that one should respect the rights of others and not arouse antagonism, live quietly, observe the sacrifices required to maintain good relations with the sources of one's powers, and be modest, even-

Fig. 11. One of the Dream Dance drums surrounded by singers at an annual fall ceremony. From left, Dewey Wynos, Star Amos, Pete Wabanascum, Star Shoshey. Photograph by George Spindler, 1950.

tempered, and guard against undue pride (Skinner and Satterlee 1915; W.J. Hoffman 1896; Spindler 1955).

Another postcontact rite still in existence in 1960 among the tradition-oriented group is the Warrior's Dance, *okehceta·wehsemon.* The original War Dance has been lost, but the Chippewa, in 1925, introduced the present rite and songs to the Menominee. It is performed for men being drafted and participating in contemporary wars. In 1960 there were more War Dance drums (six active drums) among the tradition-oriented group than Dream Dance drums (fig. 12), of which there were three.

Each of the songs connected with the rites is associated with the spirits in one of the four cardinal directions. Before the singing begins, a prayer of notification is given by one of the older men to inform *ma·ma·waw ko·hnenaw* 'Father-of-All-of-Us' and the *awɛ·tokak* 'spirits' of the purpose of the dance and ask to have the men involved in wars looked out for.

Fig. 12. A War Dance song service in the Zoar community hall on the Menominee reservation. In foreground, from left, Wallace Peywasit, Dewey Wynos, Sam Boyd, Johnson Awanohopay. Photograph by George Spindler, 1949.

The Peyote religion, known as the Native American Church in its chartered form, was another adaptation to the impact of White culture, with periodic meetings held through the 1950s. It is characteristically Menominee in conception and pan-Indian in practice but uses some Christian symbols and beliefs. Slotkin (1952) and Spindler and Spindler (1971:94-140) provide detailed accounts. The cult, like the other postcontact ceremonial organizations, is for the purpose of acquiring and maintaining power. The Menominee received the ceremony in 1914 from a Potawatomi missionary. The contemporary ritual is composed of many different elements, many of Plains Indian origin and some of Christian origin.

Witchcraft Patterns

Fear of witchcraft, both during the early and later contact periods, has been intimately linked with the Menominee concept of power. Included in the reports of the people who came in contact with the Menominee earliest are statements concerning the awe and fear held by the Menominee for men and women with great powers. W.J. Hoffman (1896:138-151) attributed acts of witchcraft to certain classes of shamans, for example, the ce·ʔsahkows, who were mentioned as early as 1698 (Hennepin 1903, 2:464-465) as opponents to Christianizing the Indians.

Early writers attribute witchcraft powers to another group of shamans as well, the wa·panows. These powerful old men possessed many different kinds of powers. They claimed to have the morning star as their tutelary spirit. W.J. Hoffman (1896:151) reports that "it is positively affirmed that evil" spirits favor the shaman's desires. On the basis of reports by early observers, Hoffman attributes practices to the wa·panows that are later claimed to belong only to "witches." One might conclude from these early documents that some powerful shamans possessed both good and evil powers and that the same shaman who performed an act of witchcraft might also cure persons who had been bewitched (see L. Spindler 1970).

Three anthropologists studying the Menominee in the early twentieth century described a formalized, patterned system of witchcraft beliefs that was found in almost identical form in 1960, particularly among groups who were not completely acculturated. Skinner (1921:69-71) first described the belief in a witches' society. He describes witches as persons who have obtained the patronage of some evil power, in return for which they are obliged to slay relatives as votive offerings. They are able to transform themselves into balls of fire, owls, bears, foxes, turkeys, and other animals and can travel with great speed at night. Skinner reports the existence of a witches' society of eight members who perform cannibalistic rites, robbing the heart and lungs of their victims at the graveyard. Hilger (1960) in 1936 and Keesing (1939) found the same set of beliefs in existence.

In the period 1947-1960, a strong belief in the power of witchcraft functioned as a form of social control among the tradition-oriented Menominee. The witch could be any powerful elder and his victims deviant members of the group who failed to observe the group's prescriptions for behavior (L. Spindler 1970:200-203). Witchcraft beliefs also survive among the Peyote religion group and among members of the transitional and lower socioeconomic acculturated groups. Among the last two groups, these beliefs are expressed mainly by the women (L. Spindler 1970:205-210).

Early observers reported that a corpse was painted with red to signify happiness at the privilege of the soul in departing to the spirit land. Burial took place apparently within the day, sometimes on a scaffolding or beneath logs on the ground or, perhaps, in a mound. The ghost was believed to linger around the grave indefinitely and to have influence on the living. The soul, it was thought, passed on a four-day journey to the spirit land. The souls of four or more enemy warriors slain in battle were called upon during the funeral ceremony by persons who could claim to have killed such to accompany the dead. Weapons and utensils for the journey were placed with the body. Widows were said to observe four years of mourning. In spite of fears of the ghost of the dead, mourners visited the burial place to offer food. Games and ritual activities were performed at the grave to keep the ghost contented.

During Skinner's period of observation (1920s) the burial ceremonies of the Medicine Lodge people were essentially unchanged, except for the absence of warriors who had killed an enemy in battle and shorter periods of ceremonial mourning. In the 1950-1960 period Spindler and Spindler (1970) found the essentials of the old pattern in existence among the tradition-oriented group. One burial was observed in 1955 where the corpse was taken through the window to confuse the lingering spirit-soul. This was purported to be an old practice.

Mythology and Folklore

There were four major types of folklore: cosmogonic myths, such as those of the origin of the Menominee people and the Medicine Lodge; tales of the culture hero, meʔnapos, emphasizing his dual character as the buffoon and hero; informal talks dealing with the exploits of heroes and wizards; and "true" stories of war, hunting, love, ghosts, and experiences with witchcraft. The meʔnapos cycle is closely related to Nanabozho, the Ojibwa culture hero.

One pervasive Menominee theme is that the hero is helpless without his particular dream-bestowed power and that he may lose it by abuse, neglect, or lack of constraint. On the other hand, the hero is particularly successful only because he has acquired a certain power. Similarly, in contests between individuals, such as those

717

in a struggle between a great *meteˀw* and a *waˑpanow,* one of the central figures admits that his power is not strong enough to withstand that of the other and so gives in without further contest. It he loses a struggle or if life turns against him, it is not so much that he is weak or defective; it is because his power is insufficient.

Another important emphasis related to the *meˀnapos* tales is that this great culture hero is capable of miraculous acts, but he frequently behaves like a fool. At times he can outwit the Great Bear, chief of the underworld, but he is no match for a fox. Through all his escapades and heroic acts two aspects stand out: one is that it is not so much his own character that makes him act this way but the manifest destiny charted for him by the greater powers and the unalterable pattern of events for which he is not personally responsible; the other is that despite his fumbles and buffoonery, he manages to maintain his character as a hero.

Role Differentiation and Socialization

At contact, the division of labor called for the male to hunt and fish; conduct warfare; perform tribal, family, and individual ceremonials for ensuring the cooperation of the spirit powers; prepare sacred artifacts; manufacture canoes, weapons, tools, nets, snares, wood bowls; cut and chop wood. It was the responsibility of the woman to cook; manage the household and the children; perform all agricultural work; collect berries and wild foods; gather firewood; carry water; carry household goods when traveling, such as mats; dress skins, make clothing, weave mats and bags, and prepare household utensils (Keesing 1939:33).

Except for specifically defined male roles, a Menominee woman could participate with males and perform many male roles. If she fished well or raced or hunted or danced like a male, she was highly respected.

In early postcontact Menominee culture (and probably before), girls also fasted at puberty for a guardian spirit and women practiced witchcraft as well as men. During the early reservation period, some of the most famous witches were women. The Medicine Lodge included women on an equal basis with men. Women members of the Dream Dance had auxiliary groups as participating members. Women were at first excluded from membership in the Peyote religion but were soon admitted as members, sitting behind the men.

Among the tradition-oriented Menominee in the 1950s there was extensive sharing of economic roles (fern gathering, cherry and potato picking, house building). In the late reservation period, women from all groups filled what were previously defined as male roles (judge, advisory council member, consultant in the mill office, and political positions).

Child training is related to the description of values expressed in tales and myths told and retold by the old men for the inculcation of these values. There was formalized exhortation, when all the children would be gathered about some respected elder who would tell them how to live, illustrating his points with stories. A consistent theme in these stories was constraint and self-control.

Discipline and care of very young children was left largely to the women. The infant was usually kept in a cradleboard until the age of two or until the child could walk. The penis of the male child was pinched after birth to keep it from growing to abnormal size and so that he would be able to control his sexual passions as an adult. A child was nursed for as long as it would reach for the breast, and weaning was not sudden. The naming ceremony for the infant was an important familial event. Later, the feast for the boy's first game kill was of great importance.

Children, close to the supernatural through the event of birth, and the elders, close to it through the approaching end of life, were of more importance and received more cultural emphasis than any other age groups. Children were watched carefully for evidence of unusual behavior, such as stopping in the middle of play "to stand quietly with sad heart" (Skinner 1913:40), or appearing chronically listless and sickly, or crying more than usual. If the child was so young as to be unable to speak, and if he exhibited any of these behaviors, an old man who understood baby talk was called in to diagnose his needs. Frequently it would be found that the source of the infant's trouble was that his proper name had not been recognized and that he was actually the reincarnation of a deceased ancestor or one of the supernatural powers.

There was a distinct sanction against striking any child until he was at least eight years old. Then he might be whipped about the legs, but never struck around the head, for it was believed that to do so would make him dumb. Other punishments included throwing cold water in the children's faces "to wash away their troubles" (Skinner 1913:40-41), scolding, or immersion in water. But the favorite form of coercion has probably always taken the form of threats—not of corporal punishment or deprivation but by reference to the owl or other creatures of the night. Physical training was severe. A boy of seven or eight would be sent to the lakeshore or riverbank in the cold of the winter to break the ice and bathe in the icy waters, then roll in the snow.

As the children grew older, the mother relied more and more upon other members of the group for the transmission of cultural values. These same general beliefs and practices persisted through the 1950-1960 period among the traditional Menominee group (Spindler and Spindler 1971:18-93).

History

Early missionaries picture the Winnebago and the Menominee as inhabiting the region bounded by Green Bay,

Lake Michigan, and Lake Superior. Between 1635 and 1653, when the Iroquoians pressed into the territories of the Central Algonquians, the Potawatomi, Ottawa, and Sauk retreated to the north; and the Illinois, with the Fox, Kickapoo, and Mascouten, migrated to the south. Because of their sheltered position, the Menominee escaped from direct Iroquois attack. After peace was made with the Iroquois, other tribes, such as the Ottawa and Huron, came to Green Bay to trade and acted as intermediaries between the Whites and other tribes (Keesing 1939:16). The tribes that maintained the closest cultural relations with the Menominee until immediately prior to the reservation period were the Winnebago and the Chippewa (fig. 13). Intermarriage became so extensive with the two that close links have continued through the modern period.

Trade relations between tribes were so stimulated by the coming of Whites and new goods that records cannot be regarded with any certainty concerning pre-White conditions. The Menominee, probably in precontact times, received catlinite from the Sioux quarries in Minnesota and copper from the Lake Superior region. The Winnebago claimed to have obtained manufactures in stone and wood from the Menominee. There are early records of exchange of products of the hunt and of cultivation between Algonquian and Iroquoian peoples, with references to market gatherings occasionally held in the northern wilderness (JR 44:243). Trade in Huron corn and French trade goods with Lake Superior and Michigan areas was probably mainly through intermediary Nipissings and Ottawas, respectively.

The earliest record of contact was by the French fur trader Nicolas Perrot about 1667. The first White residents, Jesuit missionaries, came in 1671. With the coming of the French fur traders the former village pattern of the Menominee disintegrated, and the tribe divided into roving bands organized for the purpose of trapping furs. The cycle introduced by the fur trade placed the Indians in the roles of debtors. They were encouraged to charge large amounts of supplies at the French trading posts in the summer with the promise of repayment in furs during the winter. Since this arrangement destroyed the old pattern of village life, the primary extended family group became split into roving bands consisting of smaller families. As close allies of the French, the Menominee prospered and by 1736 became one of the dominant tribes in the area.

When the English came in 1761, they were not readily accepted, but eventually the paternalistic attitude of the English, coupled with extensive gift giving, won the support of the Menominee.

The Menominee came under the control of the Americans in 1815. In 1852 the tribe, consisting of 2,002 men, women, and children, entered their reservation area—an area with plentiful sturgeon and wild rice beds, numerous small lakes, streams, and creeks, and plentiful game. However, the game and fish were not sufficient for the large numbers in the limited area, and some Menominee began to turn to farming (Keesing 1939:53–101). Farming was never successful, and in the 1950s there were only a few successful farms. Farming was soon replaced by lumbering as a means of subsistence. In 1908 a large tribally owned lumber mill began operating (fig. 14).

Between 1830 and 1852 Menominee lands passed continuously into the hands of the Whites. Figure 15 depicts the loss of Menominee lands through land cessions between 1827 and 1852, when the tribe was removed from their homes at Poygan Lake and in the Fox and Wolf valleys to the upper Wolf, the site of the allocated reservation. This consisted of nearly 400 square miles of heavily timbered country on the Wolf River in northeast central Wisconsin, in the heart of the area they inhabited when first encountered by Whites. Soon after their arrival on the reservation, the members of the tribe dispersed widely across it, often following band affili-

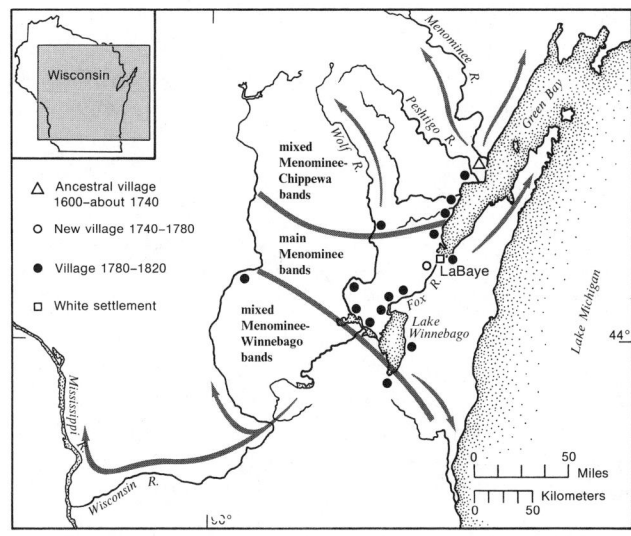

Fig. 13. Tribal area. Arrows indicate main travel routes of bands to winter hunting grounds between 1780 and 1820.

Fig. 14. The Menominee lumber mill at Neopit, Wis. Photograph by George Spindler, 1950.

ations. There has been a reverse tendency since 1900 for the population to concentrate in the village centers of Neopit and Keshena, and this process accelerated continuously through the 1950s. Keshena also served as the location for the buildings and operations of the United States Indian Service until termination in 1961.

From aboriginal times, matters of general tribal policy have always been discussed and resolved in tribal meetings open to all adults. In 1928 a tribal constitution and bylaws were adopted and the Menominee Indian Advisory Council was established, which was operating through the 1960s.

The Reservation Community 1950–1960

In 1954, 3,280 Menominee Indians resided on their reservation. The largest portion of the reservation was thickly forested. As State Highway 47 entered the reservation from Shawano (fig. 15), there was little to mark the passage, for the small farms stretched out on either side of the road, just as they did in the miles preceding. This, and the area directly to the north along State Highway 55, included practically all the approximately 1,500 acres used for raising crops, and 2,000 acres used for grazing out of the total of 233,902 acres comprising the reservation. As Highway 47 crossed the northern boundary from the village of Phlox, below Antigo (the other sizable town near the reservation) the cleared fields of White farmers contrasted with the reservation's dense forest. It is in this forested area of the northwestern section that the remnants of the old culture survived around Zoar and along the highway above Neopit. Besides sheltering this small group of Menominees who maintained an essentially tradition-oriented way of life, the forest provided a livelihood for most of the tribe and indirectly made it possible for some to attain occupational and material success in terms of Western values. The productive forest, covering an area of about 175,000 acres, consisted of the numerous varieties of softwood and hardwood characteristic of the "transitional" Great Lakes region. There was a standing timber inventory of about 850 million feet. Since the cutting was done on a selective basis (due to an act of 1908 engineered by Sen. Robert La Follette, Sr. at the Menominees' behest), and between 20 and 25 million feet were cut each year—approximately the annual growth—the forest maintained itself. This provided the economic base for the reservation community.

In contrast to the outlying farm and forest areas, the towns of Keshena and Neopit were centers for acculturation in its most dramatic aspects. Neopit was a fairly typical mill town, except for certain higher-status neighborhood areas. Keshena, by contrast, with its tree-shaded, well-kept homes, gave (and continues to give) an impression much like that of any small residential village in the surrounding countryside.

The Menominee in the 1950–1960 period were divided into approximately 550 households, sometimes including

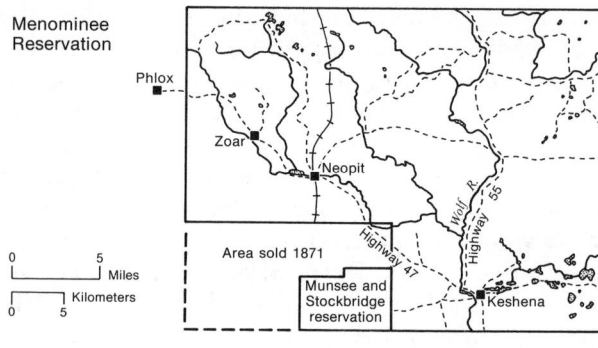

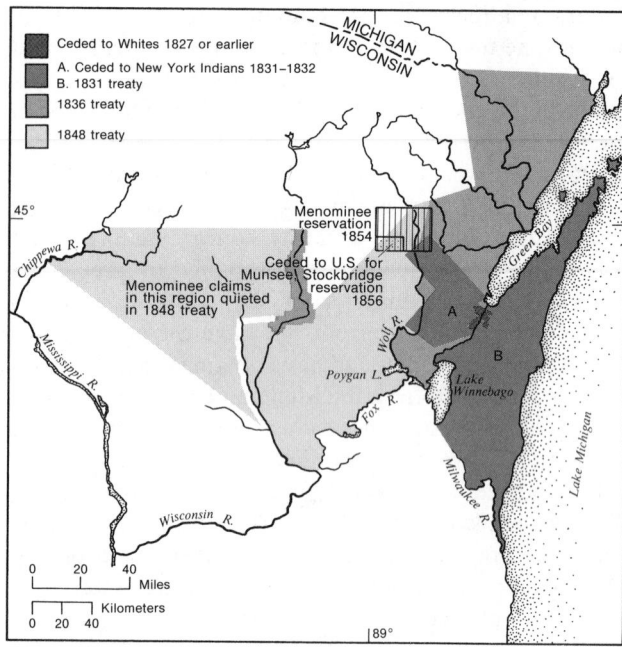

Fig. 15. Land cessions, 1827–1856, and Menominee Reservation, 1974.

several generations, but more often consisting of a nuclear family or an old couple sometimes with grandchildren or an unmarried daughter and her child. Of these 550 households, about 450 were located at or near Keshena or Neopit, with the larger number in Neopit.

Federal census figures from 1918 through 1929 show that the reservation population increased from 1,733 to 1,939; and from 1929 to 1949 it increased to 2,917. Of this total population, in 1910, 50.4% of the Menominee were reported as mixed-bloods. By 1930 the percentage of mixed-bloods was 74.8%. By 1950 the proportion was 97.3% mixed-blood, with only 82 persons recorded on the tribal rolls as full-blooded (Spindler 1955:51).

There was considerable occupational diversity, though most of it was related directly to the lumber industry. There were foresters, lumberjacks, truck drivers, stackers, saw operators, planers, electricians, mechanics, engineers, warehouse workers, accountants, clerks, stenographers, salesmen, and typists. There were supervisory positions at all levels, from foreman of a six-man logging crew to mill manager, and a range of pay from around

$1,500 a year to over $10,000. Of the approximately 500 men employed in jobs connected directly with lumbering, not more than 10 percent of the regular positions were held by "outside" Whites, but these included the highest-status and best-paid jobs. There were 55 persons engaged in administrative and service functions for the reservation as a whole. Before termination in 1961 most salaries and wages for mill and administrative or service functions were paid from Menominee monies. Civil service appointments were paid through funds held by the federal government in an operating reserve derived from tribal funds. All other salaries and wages were paid directly out of tribal funds, with federal approval. The occupational structure of the mill and the number of administrative and service positions reveal the degree to which the Menominee had available and took advantage of occupations and functions comparable to those in the American economy at large.

Besides lumbering, there were only a few relatively minor economic activities carried on within the reservation. Forty-five of the households on the reservation were sufficiently large to be considered productive farm units. Some raised a few swine, goats, or chickens. The Menominee also hunted, fished, and gathered wild fruits. Some men who held steady jobs in the mill hunted or fished several times a week. During blackberry season the entire family spent many hours in the forest picking the wild fruit. Trapping was carried on by some of the younger men, though the area is not large enough for a reliable or fruitful yield. These activities continued in the 1970s to constitute a reliable supplement to the larder in many families. Another source of income was derived annually from off-reservation cherry orchards and potato, corn, and strawberry fields during the late summer and early fall.

In the tradition-oriented group the subsistence gained by hunting and gathering was sometimes of critical importance. In this group there was also some gathering of evergreens and ferns for buyers, doing beadwork, tanning skins, and making handicraft objects for the tourist trade. In addition, dances and pageants were put on for the tourists during the summer.

Until 1961 there were a few entrepreneurs who operated gasoline pumps, a dining place that catered to tourists, a half-dozen or so soft-drink and curio stands, two grocery stores, and several places where scenic spots could be seen for a fee. Tourists brought some money into the reservation. Once a year, the "Menominee Indian Fair and Pageant" attracted fairly large numbers of tourists and residents from nearby towns.

All Menominee children attended school, and the tribe in 1960 was 95 percent literate. There were three schools on the reservation providing education through the eighth grade. One of them, at Keshena, was a day and boarding school combined; the other two at Neopit were day schools only. The Keshena school and one of the two at Neopit were run by the Roman Catholic Church under contract to the tribe; the other Neopit school was under federal control. About one-fourth of the approximately 400 children in school during the year attended the non-Catholic one.

Education beyond the eighth grade was provided by Shawano High School as well as by Indian boarding schools such as Haskell Institute and Flandreau. Approximately 80 percent of those who finished the eighth grade went on to high school or its equivalent, and of those about 75 percent finished the four years. The Menominee Committee on Education apportioned loans up to $1,500 and awarded one $1,000 scholarship each year for special or advanced training.

The political situation was unstable. Agents, advisory boards, factions, and "behind-the-scenes" leaders came and went. Issues on almost every aspect of administration, particularly those concerned with the budget, were continually being raised.

There was an advisory board of 10 Menominees, broadly equivalent to the old tribal council but no longer constituted by chiefs or sons of chiefs, made up largely of young men between 25 and 40. The 10 were elected by districts, after having been nominated by a petition carrying at least 20 signatures. The chairman was elected by the board from its own members. This board, once invested with only informal and purely advisory powers, had risen to special prominence since 1934, when the Indian Reorganization Act gave it the specific right of review over budget. Every item of expenditure over $250 was passed upon by this board, and investigations were frequently called of the records and the motives of the appointed administration.

Besides this advisory board, there was a general council consisting of all adult members of the tribe. This council had veto power over the advisory board, and all important decisions of the administration or advisory board were reviewed at the general council meetings. These meetings could be called by the superintendent, the advisory council, or by petition from other members of the tribe. It was in these large public meetings that the open fights for power took place and the most severe tensions arose.

Between 1950 and 1960 there were within the Menominee community four major cultural divisions representing different adaptations to the impact of White culture (Spindler 1955; L. Spindler 1962; Spindler and Spindler 1971). First, there was the tradition-oriented group, which maintained the Dream Dance (the niˑmihɛtwan), the Medicine Lodge (the metɛˑwen), the War or Chief's Dance (okehcetaˑwehsemon), and other rituals. In social interaction, and in the values, perceptions, and personalities of its members, recognizable though often attenuated patterns were functioning that appeared to be of traditional derivation, modified to meet present conditions. Second, there were the Peyotists, who were raised in culturally conservative households, at least through early childhood, and had substantial contact with White culture. Their rites included the eating of peyote, the bud of the cactus *Lophophora williamsii,* which has hallucinogenic properties. Though there was considerable antagonism between the tradition-oriented group and the Peyotists, members of both groups lived in the same general area, interacted with one another more than with others, and shared a common cultural fund of belief and values. Peyote meetings were held less frequently toward the end of this period, and after 1960 most meetings were held by Winnebago groups. Third, the transitionals included individuals loosely joined together in informal groupings such as drinking groups, people who were almost wholly isolated, and people who were striving toward fuller participation in the non-Menominee world. It was a heterogeneous category. The people within it had in common early experience with traditional cultural forms, but they were people who had moved away from overt identification with the old culture and who were not participants in any traditional organization. Some of the transitionals exhibited signs of social marginality in their behavior and uncertain identities, but not all did. Fourth, the acculturated were people who were overtly assimilated into Western culture and who were not members of traditional groups. Some supported themselves with jobs that, while by no means menial, were not management or professional positions. Others could be regarded as the people who had, in White terms, "made it." Included among them were entrepreneurs, men and women with supervisory positions in the lumber mill or associated enterprises, and skilled white-collar workers. There were also people who left the home community to reside in Milwaukee, Chicago, and other large cities (Spindler 1955). The Menominee may be said to have adapted to the impact of Western culture as represented by the whole gamut of personnel from French fur traders to nuns and priests and Antigo businessmen. Seen from that point of view, these adaptations do not represent a steady progression from "traditional" to "modern." They are all contemporary attempts to get along in conflicting social, cultural, political, and personal environments.

The role of religion in these adaptations was of particular significance. The tradition-oriented group maintained the Dream Dance, Medicine Lodge, Chief's Dance, and various lesser rituals as a way of defining its existence and identity. The Peyotists created a religion that resolved some of the conflicts created by the confrontation of White and Menominee cultures and served to give its members an identity. The transitionals had no firm identity and no firm religious affiliation, though individuals within this large category were moving in various directions to an identity and in some cases to a religious affiliation: a few to a tradition-oriented position, others to that of the Whites. Some of the acculturated were strongly Catholic and presented a clear identity as members of White-affiliated groups and cultural patterns (Spindler and Spindler 1971).

Termination

The Menominee were the first tribe to be terminated under the policy formalized in 1953 in House Concurrent Resolution 108, which set forth the general policy of termination.‡ On June 17, 1954, Public Law 83-399 (25 U.S.C. 891-902) provided for the termination of the federal jurisdiction over the Menominee reservation, which had been guaranteed by treaty in 1854. In 1961 the state of Wisconsin assumed jurisdiction over the reservation when it became Menominee County.

In 1934 the Menominee began a lawsuit alleging federal mismanagement of their forest resources. In 1951 the case was settled, with the Menominee awarded $7,600,000. The tribe voted that part of this money was to be distributed in per capita payments of $1,500 to enrolled Menominees. When the Menominee requested release of the per capita funds, a rider was attached to the bill by Congress. The Menominee protested the rider with the result that they did not get their money. They were still trying to get their funds released in 1953, when Sen. Arthur V. Watkins, the moving force behind the termination policy, visited the Menominee reservation. He made it very clear that whether or not the tribe wanted termination, Congress would terminate the Menominee. At this time, a confusing double-issue vote was taken. The Menominee were to give a single yes or no to release of their per capita payments *and* agreement to "the principle of termination." The vote was 169 for and 5 against the resolution. When it was understood what had happened, another meeting was held one month later, where the nearly 200 members present voted unanimously against termination, even though they expected to lose the $1,500 payment; however, this later vote was not acknowledged in Washington.

The Menominee were not prepared for termination and were not in a position to take over the responsibility. Sufficient funds were not made available by the federal government for proper studies of the needs of the people and for preparation for termination. Moreover, the Menominee were obliged to pay half the cost of legal and clerical expenses to develop a termination plan they had not wanted. By the time termination became final in 1961, the tribe's treasury was virtually wiped out. From 1958 to 1960 criticism was rapidly growing in Congress of the termination policy in general, but there was no reevaluation of the Menominee decision. This was in spite of the statement made by the secretary of the interior on September 13, 1958, that "no Indian tribe or group should end its relationship with the Federal Government unless such tribe or group had clearly demon-

‡ Section on termination was prepared from materials supplied by Nancy Oestreich Lurie and Verne Ray.

722

strated—first, that it understands the plan under which such a program would go forward, and second, that the tribe or group affected concurs in and supports the plan proposed" (Ray 1971:81).

Menominee Enterprises, Inc. (MEI) was set up to manage the Menominees' forests, mill, land, and other assets. As originally constituted, it gave non-Menominee people inordinate power over Menominee affairs. Each of the 3,280 Menominees enrolled in the tribe as of 1954 received a bond with a face value of $3,000, paying 4 percent interest and reaching maturity in the year 2000, as well as 100 shares of stock. The bonds are negotiable, with MEI having first option to buy, but the stock was nonnegotiable until 1971, nonnegotiability being later extended to the end of 1973. The block vote of minors and incompetents, involving about 45 percent of the vote at the beginning of termination, was controlled by a Milwaukee trust company (Lurie 1972:263).

The situation of the Menominee deteriorated rapidly after termination. Taxes were unrealistically high, unemployment rose, proper medical care was lacking because the tribe could no longer support their hospital, and a large proportion of the housing became substandard. Finally in 1967, under a contract between MEI and a land developer, artificial lakes were created and Menominee land was subdivided for sale to vacationers in an attempt to broaden the tax base. This caused outraged reactions from the whole range of Menominee society leading to organized resistance in late 1969 and formation of a group named DRUMS (Determination of Rights and Unity for Menominee Stockholders). DRUMS engaged in litigation against MEI, protested land sales to outsiders, and was committed to restoration of federal jurisdiction—restoring Menominee eligibility for BIA services and restructuring political and economic institutions so that the Menominee could administer their own affairs. In 1970 the group succeeded in having their candidates elected to MEI as representatives in the voting trust and by 1972 effectively controlled the board of directors. Efforts of DRUMS and other opponents of termination have met with success. In 1971 President Richard Nixon publicly repudiated HCR 108 as a mistake that created rather than solved problems for Indian people (Lurie 1972:268).

On May 2, 1973, a restoration bill (HR 7421, S 1687) was introduced to restore tribal and reservation status to the Menominee, which was finally enacted into law on December 23, 1973. The Menominee Restoration Act provided for the election, duly accomplished, of a Restoration Committee as an interim tribal government charged with the responsibilities of settling the financial affairs of MEI to permit the return of unencumbered Menominee property to full reservation status, updating the roll since it was closed in 1954, and creating a new tribal constitution to be approved by the tribe. The tribal corporation was transferred from state to federal jurisdic-

tion, enrollment procedures were completed, and a constitution that is unprecedented in Indian affairs in the great degree of tribal self-determination was prepared. Meanwhile, the Restoration Committee established many community improvement projects in regard to health, housing, education, and general welfare in the effort to overcome the problems brought about by termination. Its aftermath was still felt in 1976 in regard to severe intratribal differences as the people were faced with alternative courses of action to reorganize socioeconomic structures and to restore community stability.

Synonymy

The name Menominee, formerly pronounced məˈnōməˌnē, as shown by Trowbridge's (1823a) Munnoa′min-nee, derives from the Ojibwa mano·mini· (from Baraga 1878-1880,1), etymologically 'wild rice people' (cf. mano·min 'wild rice'). The word is the same in Algonquin (see Cuoq 1886:206) and similar in other Algonquian languages: Fox mano·miniwa (from Michelson 1927:92), Kickapoo manoomina (Voorhis 1967:262), and Ottawa Mahnomoneeg (Tanner 1956:314). A form omano·mini· also occurs, with the optional initial o found in many Algonquian tribal names. The Menominee name for themselves, omɛ·ʔnomene·w, is of obscure etymology but is clearly not derived from their word mano·mɛh 'wild rice'.

The earliest recorded name for the Menominee is Maroumine, 1640. Other early variants include Malouminek, 1658; Oumaloüminek, 1670 (JR 18:230, 44:246, 54:204); Malominis (Lahontan 1703, 1:104, cf. 231); Malhominy by Cadillac, 1718 (in Margry 1876-1886, 5:121); Mathomenis (misprint? Bacqueville de la Potherie 1753, 2:90). Malhommes (Jefferys 1761, 1:48) may be a French folk etymology. Meynomenys first appears in 1763 (NYCD 7:583) and is first spelled in the modern form in the treaty of 1825 (U.S. Commissioner of Indian Affairs 1837:376). Other old spellings include Manomines, 1809; Mennominees, 1766; Menomonees, 1788; Menonomees, 1842; Menamenies, 1846; Minomonees, 1788; Monomonees, 1855; and Mynomanies, 1778 (Mooney and Thomas 1907:843-844). Walhominis (McKenney and Hall 1849-1854, 3:79) and Ounabonims, 1671 (NYCD 9:803) are misprints according to Mooney and Thomas (1907:844). Contrary to the interpretation in Mooney and Thomas, Sagard-Théodat's Malouin (1636, 2:424) and LaSalle's Melomelinoia (in Margry 1876-1886, 2:201) probably do not refer to the Menominee.

For some time anthropologists preferred the spelling Menomini (W.J. Hoffman 1896; Keesing 1939:xi).

The French called the Menominee Nation de la folle avoine 'nation of the wild rice', literally 'crazy oats', 1671, (JR 55:102) or simply Folles Avoines, 1718 (Cadillac in Margry 1876-1886, 5:121), corrupted to Felles Avoins,

1721; Folsavoins, 1763; Falsavins, 1764 (NYCD 5:622, 7:583, 641); Fulawin, 1783 (MHSC 1st ser., 10:123) and Followens (Long 1791:146). The French nickname Les Fols 'crazies' (Badin 1830:537) is reflected in the English Addle-Heads and Moon-calves (Jefferys 1761, 1:48).

The Winnebago call the Menominee ka·γí, literally 'crow' (Kenneth L. Miner, personal communication 1975), which is probably the source for the Dakota term Kah'hray (Trowbridge 1823). Similar in meaning is the Illinois name piressi8a (8 = ou), literally 'raven' (Le Boullenger in Belting 1958:288; Gravier 1700:473).

Sources

Keesing (1939) is a detailed account of available historical documents and reports by travelers and missionaries from first contacts to 1930. It provides an excellent integration and interpretation of historical changes.

The most important documents for the earliest period are the *Jesuit Relations* (JR 1896–1901), published every year from 1632 to 1673 with various important documents thereafter. They are regarded by historians as reliable records for the most part. There is a preponderance of material on law, government, and religion, with little on subsistence and social structure. Another source for the earliest period is the memoirs of Nicolas Perrot (1911). Some of the best published collections of documents describing the Menominee before 1830 are those of the State Historical Society of Wisconsin, which has important photographs of Menominee life and individuals and records of Menominee music. The Neville Public Museum at Green Bay houses a great deal of the oldest material on the Menominee.

Although there is an extensive ethnographic and linguistic literature for the Menominee between 1890 and 1924, contradictions in informants' materials often make reliable reconstruction difficult. W.J. Hoffman (1896) gives a rather complete account of the major aspects of Menominee culture. The works of Skinner include detailed monographs on social life and ceremonial bundles (1913), associations and ceremonies (1915), the Medicine ceremony (1920), material culture (1921), and folklore

(Skinner and Satterlee 1915). Much of the material in Hoffman and Skinner on social organization is based on a few very elderly informants, who gave contradictory material. Further, the authors do not always clarify to which period in Menominee history their materials are related. For example, neither author succeeded in showing the relationship between the earlier totemic groupings and the "band" system that emerged during the fur-trade era. Jenks (1900) gives a full account of Menominee methods of gathering, preserving, and using wild rice; Barrett (1911) described the Dream Dance, which can be considered a revitalization movement; Michelson (1911) collected and interpreted Menominee tales; and Bloomfield (1928, 1962) collected Menominee texts and made an extensive study of the Menominee language.

After Keesing's (1939) study from 1928 to 1930, the Menominee were visited and studied by Hilger (1960) in 1936. Spindler and Spindler (1970) collected data on the modern Menominee with emphasis on acculturation and accompanying social and psychological adjustments of individuals (Spindler 1955; Spindler and Spindler 1971), male-female differences (Spindler and Spindler 1958), and witchcraft (L. Spindler 1952, 1971).

Slotkin (1952) provides detailed ethnographic description of the Menominee chapter of the Native American Church. Slotkin (1957) describes the Dream Dance in the process of "cultural decay," with extensive verbatim documentation. Sady (1947) discusses the "transition from trusteeship," and Ames and Fisher (1959) deal with termination. Edgerton concluded that Menominee values were related to acculturation (Goldschmidt and Edgerton 1961). Lurie (1972) collected and interpreted Menominee reactions to termination. Ray (1971) drawing on materials from Orfield (1964) made a complete report of Menominee termination, with extensive historical background, for the law firm of Wilkinson, Cragun, and Barker, representing Menominee in the U.S. Court of Claims suit under litigation for damages resulting from termination. Shames (1972) provides other documentation regarding damage done by termination, in a plea for public support of the tribe's drive for restoration of the reservation.

Potawatomi

JAMES A. CLIFTON

The Potawatomi (ˌpätəˈwätəmē) have been distinguished from kindred and neighboring tribes by their named identity, their distinctive language, their own traditional history of separation from the ancestors of the modern Chippewa and Ottawa, their claims to a territory that expanded increasingly in size up to the time of American settlement in the Great Lakes region, and particularly by a tribal political organization based upon a dispersed clan structure. They also had differences of dress, folklore, ritual, and other aspects of their culture that marked them as distinctive, although their cultural patterns were essentially similar to those of their Central Algonquian neighbors. Boundaries between the Potawatomi and other communities were quite permeable: their many villages often contained numerous representatives from other societies, particularly the Chippewa and Ottawa.

Language

Potawatomi is a separate Algonquian language, not simply a dialect of Ojibwa as was formerly believed (Hockett 1943:541). In sound and structure, it shows many parallels with Southern Ojibwa and Ottawa, although it shares much vocabulary and many phonetic features with Fox, Sauk, and Kickapoo (Hockett 1943, 1957). There has been no generally accepted orthography for Potawatomi, although various syllabic and alphabetic spelling systems employing English letters have, since the 1830s, been in limited and temporary use (Schultz 1972:155-156, 164-167; Gailland 1914-1917; Simerwell 1832; McMurtrie and Allen 1930).

A small number of western Potawatomi ritualists continued to use their own ancient mnemonic system of pictographs drawn on birchbark scrolls so as to prompt their memories in the recall of details of long and complex religious ceremonies (Howard 1960). Hockett (1948:1-10) developed a phonemic alphabet for Potawatomi, but it has received neither wide acceptance nor practical application. Nichols (1974) developed yet another spelling system and some basic teaching materials for this language in cooperation with the Forest County Potawatomi of Wisconsin.*

---

* The orthography adopted here is Hockett's (1948), except that ə is written for his u, and the cluster -sks- is marked with a raised dot, indicating that it is fortis. Italicized Potawatomi words have been rewritten in this orthography by John Nichols, with Mary Daniels, Billy Daniels, Jr., and Mabel Deverney as Potawatomi-speaking consultants.

In the 1970s the Potawatomi are characterized by extreme geographic scattering and by considerable assimilation into other communities: White American, Menominee, American and Canadian Chippewa and Ottawa, Kansas Kickapoo, for example. Moreover, a number of elderly speakers live in urban areas, isolated from other speakers, with their English-speaking children and grandchildren. By the 1970s the principal places where there were pools of Potawatomi speakers and something approximating a speech community were Kansas Potawatomi and Kickapoo reservations (perhaps 350), Oklahoma (possibly 200), northern Wisconsin and Upper Michigan (probably no more than 70), Lower Michigan (possibly 125), Wisconsin Rapids (possibly 20), the Menominee reservation (possibly 40), and several locations along the eastern shore of Lake Saint Clair and Lake Huron (perhaps 100, see fig. 1). In the absence of systematic research, and with so many elderly people and other individual speakers living away from Indian communities, it is difficult to offer more than a guess: there were something on the order of 1,000 Potawatomi speakers in 1970, as compared with an estimated peak of 9,000 in the 1820s.

Territory and Environment

Until the time of the breakup of the tribal structure and the removal of most Potawatomi villages from the Lake Michigan area in the 1840s, the Potawatomi had occupied three successive territories, the last and largest of which overlapped the previous two (fig. 1). The first of these, their "protohistoric estate," was in the lower peninsula of Michigan, which they vacated beginning about 1641. A scant archeological record and difficulties of identifying the historic Potawatomi tribe with prehistoric sites make accurate mapping of this homeland difficult. Yet the weight of archeological, linguistic, and ethnohistoric evidence places them in this area, west and north of but adjacent to their Central Algonquian neighbors, the Sauk, Fox, Mascouten, and Kickapoo (Quimby 1952; Fitting and Cleland 1969; JR 55:183; Chief Assikinak in Schoolcraft 1851-1857, 1:308).

The second territory occupied by the Potawatomi may be called their "refuge area," although it also served as a staging ground until they had successfully established themselves in a profitable political and economic alliance with the French and with neighboring tribes. The refuge area consisted of much of the Door County peninsula in

Wisconsin, with parts of the upper peninsula of Michigan and the interior forests of Wisconsin used for hunting and fishing. They also occupied the islands off the northern tip of the Door, which had earlier been called the Huron but were for many years later called the Potawatomi islands. Of these, they briefly employed Rock Island as their fishery and trading center, on the same site earlier employed by the Ottawa. This site was later (about 1652) reoccupied by refugee Ottawa and Petun (R.J. Mason 1974).

The Potawatomi did not long remain confined to the Door peninsula refuge. Before 1670 they had been enlarging the scope of their power and influence, and this, together with the development of their alliance with the French, brought their expansion into the "tribal estate," the largest territory they ever controlled (27 Indian Claims Commission 187). The tribal estate by 1820 included the earlier refuge area, the entire Lake Michigan shoreline south to Milwaukee and Chicago, and then east and north to the Saint Joseph and Grand rivers in Michigan. It included also parts of southern Michigan along the Saint Joseph River and in the Detroit area; much of the northern half of Indiana, especially along the Wabash River drainage; most of northern Illinois—along the Kankakee, Des Plaines, Chicago, and Illinois rivers; and the southern parts of Wisconsin, west to Lake Geneva and the Mississippi. By the opening of the nineteenth century the Potawatomi had established more than 100 known villages in this tribal estate, 14 in northern and central Illinois, 21 in Indiana, 11 in south-

ern Michigan, and more than 80 in Wisconsin (P.V. Lawson 1920; Swanton 1952:247-250). Not all these villages were necessarily occupied at the same time, nor were they of the same kind or size. Yet their distribution marks both the limits of a tribal territory far greater in extent than that of the protohistoric or refuge periods and the success of Potawatomi adaptations to economic opportunities and tribal dislocations occasioned by the arrival of Europeans in the upper Great Lakes.

The protohistoric estate in lower Michigan was lush Indian country, particularly suitable for a tribe that combined maize horticulture with pedestrian hunting and fishing. The setting consisted primarily of oak and hickory forests mixed with beech and maple stands, with some marsh and open prairie lands in the south, and hardwoods interspersed with Great Lakes pine forests in the north. Adjacent to the upland savannas of Indiana and Illinois, easily accessible by canoe via the Saint Joseph and Kankakee rivers, this habitat provided excellent access for hunting a wide variety of animals from muskrat to buffalo.

When the Potawatomi entered the refuge area they came into a zone with a shorter growing season and a harsher climate, although it did not seem to interfere much with their production of maize and other crops (JR 51:27, 54:207). Indeed, even as far north as the French trade and mission center at Chequamegon, which a large group of Potawatomi visited in 1668, they first planted their corn in spring and left only after the fall harvest for their home villages on the Door peninsula (JR 51:41). Although it was becoming overpopulated with the concentration of so many refugee Algonquian tribes there, the Green Bay area provided considerable quantities of natural foods, particularly wild rice, water fowl, buffalo (along the upper Fox river), and especially fish (Wilson 1956). This environment also offered social and strategic advantages: temporary security from Iroquois raids; direct access to French trade agents who had begun dealing directly with western Indians rather than through Indian middlemen; the ready availability of French technology, weapons, and goods; and a social and political climate offering many opportunities for expansion and cultural growth.

By 1820, when the Potawatomi had expanded their territory into the fullest range of the tribal estate, they had set their villages and cornfields in a wide variety of natural habitats. These included the northeastern Wisconsin refuge area and the Saint Joseph-Grand River areas. Added to these were a full 380 miles of Lake Michigan shoreline (where the cold winters were tempered by the warmth of the lake water); the maple-basswood groves between Lake Winnebago and Lake Geneva; the Illinois and Kankakee river drainages, including the bluestem prairie lands adjacent thereto; and the mixed hardwood forests, marshlands, and prairies of northern Indiana.

726   Fig. 1. Tribal territories and 1970 locations of communities.

This considerable range of environments obviously affected how the widely scattered Potawatomi villages subsisted in the different parts of the tribal estate, as well as the nature of their social life. The variety of landscapes occupied has also led some writers to conclude that there were major cultural and social differences between the "Forest" Potawatomi and the "Prairie" Potawatomi (Mooney and Hewitt 1910; Michelson 1934a). However, this division is entirely too simple and does not correspond to the facts of Potawatomi subsistence patterns or ecological adaptations in the eighteenth century. What all Potawatomi exhibited in common was a preference for a lakeshore or riverside setting for their permanent summer villages. Even the Potawatomi of the "Prairie," that is, villagers in southern Wisconsin, Illinois, and Indiana, maintained their villages in wooded river valleys, while the greatest share of those in other parts of Wisconsin and Michigan settled near the shoreline of Lake Michigan and Lake Erie, generally along the many streams that flow into their waters. This preference involved a heavy dependency on fishing for a basic food supply, especially in the early spring. Their dependency on fishing was qualified only later in their history, when the southernmost Potawatomi had acquired sufficient horses to gain reliable access to the buffalo herds on the plains west of their villages. By the mid-eighteenth century the Potawatomi were becoming more than pedestrian hunters and fishermen, transporting their heavy goods and supplies in canoes. They were rapidly adapting to horse nomadism and hence could greatly extend the range of their hunting, trapping, trading, diplomacy, and military activities over what they had been in the previous century.

Moreover, whether living on the Door peninsula or along the Tippecanoe River, their economy was a dual, seasonal one involving annual migrations of most of a village's population. Thus most of the Potawatomi, whether in northern Wisconsin or in southern Michigan, lived part of the year in the forests or woods and part on more open prairie lands, each appropriate to its season and the availability of natural food supplies. The supposed "Forest" Potawatomi living at Hannahville in the upper peninsula of Michigan and those in Forest County, Wisconsin, are not, as Skinner (1924–1927, 1) argued, the contemporary representatives of the ancient northern Potawatomi. They are instead remnant groups who fled into the area after 1850 to avoid removal to Iowa Territory. They include the descendants of some villagers from the prairie lands of the Milwaukee-Waukesha area and Lake Geneva, others from the "Prairie band" in Kansas who later returned to Wisconsin, and some migrants to Canada who returned after several decades of residence there (Ritzenthaler 1953; Tiedke 1951; C.E. Brown 1922–1932).

External Relations

Relations with other tribes consisted of maintaining a balance of alliances advantageous to the Potawatomi, particularly with those who shared a common relationship with or against the French and British, as well as periodic hostilities directed against other tribes and Euro-Americans. Very early in the historic period, and perhaps some years before (about 1648), the Potawatomi entered into a rivalry with the Ottawa for a share of the role of middlemen in the trade into the Green Bay area. As early as 1655 this rivalry required the peacemaking efforts of Médard Chouart des Groseilliers and his unknown French associate (Radisson 1967:148–151).

By 1653, the Potawatomi apparently were the numerically dominant tribe in the Green Bay area. In that year the "Journal of the Jesuit Fathers" records that, to meet the threat of Iroquois invasion, there were marshaling in the Green Bay area 400 Potawatomi warriors, 200 Ottawa, 100 from the Winnebago and "A'cha8i's tribe," 200 Ojibwa, and 100 Mississauga and Achiligouan (JR 38:181). Being able to marshal almost half the warriors available to meet threatened Iroquois invasions perhaps encouraged the Potawatomi a few years after to hazard control of the trade with the tribes farther south and west.

In the summer of 1668 the Mascouten, Miami, Kickapoo, and some Illinois came to Green Bay to avoid an Iroquois raiding party and to develop relationships with the tribes already in contact with the French (Bacqueville de la Potherie 1917:83–84). The visiting tribes, who were pedestrian hunters and not canoe Indians like the Potawatomi, sent an invitation to the French to visit, but the Potawatomi did not tell Nicolas Perrot and accepted the invitation themselves. When Perrot realized what had occurred, he planned a meeting with the tribes, which the Potawatomi attempted to block by telling him that "there were no beavers among those people—who, moreover, were very boorish—and even that they [the French] were in great danger of being plundered" (Bacqueville de la Potherie 1917:84). When Perrot met with the tribes anyway, the Potawatomi sent a "slave" (a captive who had not been adopted or killed) to the visiting tribes to undercut the reputation of the French. The Potawatomi had recently returned from their first visit to Montreal and were jealous of their prestige, new wealth, and trade relationships, hoping to maintain a position of ascendancy with other tribes in the area. But Perrot made them realize what the French expected, and the Potawatomi capitulated. Thus began a relationship mutually beneficial to both parties, which lasted until the end of the French era.

French policy at the time was to break the monopoly of the middleman tribes so as to increase profits; hence, the attempt by the Potawatomi to imitate the role of the

Ottawa and Huron was outdated before they began (Innis 1956:54-55). They quickly adopted a different posture, making "themselves arbiters for the tribes about the bay, and for all their neighbors; and they strive to preserve for themselves that reputation in every direction" (Bacqueville de la Potherie 1911-1912, 1:301-303). At Perrot's request, the Potawatomi manned 30 canoes for the next brigade to Montreal and continued their cooperation thereafter.

On this basis Potawatomi expansion into their tribal estate began, always maintaining alliances with strong tribes, but intruding themselves into the territories of weaker ones. In the early 1670s the Potawatomi joined with the Sauk, Fox, and Ottawa in a war against the Sioux in which they suffered fewer casualties than their allies "because they took to their heels at the beginning of the combat" (Perrot 1911:189). They also escorted Perrot on a visit to the Miami in Chicago in 1671. This same year they persuaded the great chief of the Miami that the long journey to Sault Sainte Marie to attend the French ceremony taking formal possession of the West might injure his health and induced the chief to allow the Potawatomi to represent the Miami at this grand celebration (Parkman 1897:59-60). Regardless of official French policy and the acquiesence of Potawatomi leaders, no one could entirely restrict the fur trade to the French posts: in 1674, for example, some Potawatomi were exchanging French goods for beaver with the Kaskaskia in Illinois (JR 55:175).

The Potawatomi assisted the French with warriors in the 1684, the 1687, and the 1696 expeditions into the Iroquois country (Deale 1958:329). The last invasion was mounted by a Potawatomi war chief from the Mackinac area. In 1695, 200 Potawatomi warriors and their families moved into the Miami territory north of the Saint Joseph River in Michigan, soon displacing the Miamis; thereby a substantial number of Potawatomis reentered the lands the tribe had abandoned hardly 53 years before (Kinietz 1940:309). In 1712 a mixed Potawatomi-Ottawa party from Mackinac destroyed the Fox and Mascouten groups near Detroit and two years later settled into this new territory (fig. 2).

By 1720 Potawatomi hunting parties from Saint Joseph in Michigan were hunting buffalo along the Mississippi. In 1740-1741 other Potawatomis joined with the Ottawa to raid the Chickasaw in west Tennessee and Mississippi; and in 1747, allied with the French, the Potawatomi were raiding the British colonies in Connecticut and New York. During the last half of the eighteenth century, the Potawatomi destroyed the waning power of the Illinois tribes and commenced moving into their prairie habitat. In 1763, allied with Pontiac, they conquered the British garrison at Saint Joseph and gave very substantial aid in the siege of Detroit. By 1769, they were trading extensively with the Spanish in Saint Louis, a relationship that

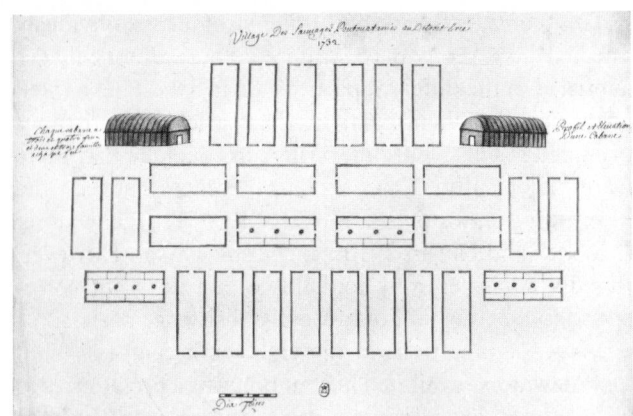

Bibliothèque Nationale, Cabinet des Estampes, Paris: Vd. 20b, t. 1, fol., p. 66.
Fig. 2. A French plan of the Potawatomi village at Detroit in 1732. Four houses have interior compartments and fireplaces indicated; according to a label, each house had 3 or 4 fires with 2 or 3 families per fire. Sketches of the houses appear at the top. The bar scale is 10 *toises*, equivalent to 19.49 m.

was particularly strong among the Illinois and the southeastern Wisconsin villages.

This pattern of centrifugal migration and expansion at the expense of other tribes continued well into the midnineteenth century. For instance, as a result of the 1833-1834 Treaties of Chicago, many of the villagers from southern Wisconsin and northern Illinois were assembled and called collectively the "United bands of Ottawa, Chippewa, and Potawatomi." The villages involved were principally Potawatomi, with a minority of Chippewa and Ottawa residents. Once moved west onto the plains of Iowa, the United bands (by 1841 more frequently called the Council Bluffs band) quickly adapted to the imperatives of equestrian warfare and buffalo hunting, and in 1840 they there began attempting to forge a coalition of other tribes against the Yankton Dakota to obtain access to a larger share of buffalo hunting grounds (Clifton 1968, 1970).

Culture in 1600

The two centuries of movement, expansion, and adaptations to new environments between 1642 and 1842 do not make for ease of cultural characterization. This is particularly true of the earliest period of Potawatomi history, before considerable social and cultural changes arising out of contacts with Europeans had occurred. Moreover, there are few direct descriptions of Potawatomi culture in this early period (1640-1660) and none for the years preceding this while the Potawatomi were yet in their Michigan homeland.

The traditional histories of the Chippewa, the Ottawa, and the Potawatomi are in concert, agreeing that they once constituted a single people, with a common culture and language. Such traditions claim a migration from the eastern seaboard and a splitting into three divisions at some unknown date (Mooney and Hewitt 1910:289–290; Skinner 1924–1927, 1:10–12). The splitting, traditionally, occurred at the Straits of Mackinac, with those who later became known as Potawatomi moving southward into Michigan (Schoolcraft 1851–1857, 1:308).

The archeological sites that can be probably identified as early Potawatomi are few. But if the Dumaw Creek culture of Michigan, dated about 1600, can be accepted as an example of Potawatomi villages immediately prior to the arrival of the French, this provides a reasonably complete sketch of protohistoric Potawatomi life (Quimby 1966). The Moccasin Bluff Village site in Berrian County is also probably a Potawatomi village, though somewhat earlier than the Dumaw Creek culture (Fitting and Cleland 1969).

In either instance, large summer villages were established on the edge of the forest, adjacent to marginal prairies and convenient to streams and the lakeside. The Potawatomi living in these villages practiced a dual, seasonal economy, involving farming, hunting, fishing, and the gathering of wild plant foods. In summer they grew squash, beans, tobacco, and maize; they collected a wide variety of plant foods; and they hunted deer, elk, and beaver nearby. In late fall, the large summer village dispersed and probably moved to convenient winter hunting grounds, where smaller, temporary winter camps were established in sheltered valleys. In the spring these camps would again combine, banding together for communal hunting, in the south, of buffalo in the more open prairie lands or communal fishing for the early spring spawning runs in the streams emptying into Lake Michigan.

In these years, the Potawatomi lived in dome-shaped wigwams, constructed of bent saplings covered with woven mats or sheets of bark. They were armed with bows and arrows and spears tipped with triangular-shaped flint points. The villages were established on small streams somewhat inland from navigable waters, which location, possibly combined with palisades, afforded limited protection from surprise attack.

The Potawatomi made a variety of fired, well-tempered pottery. Clothing was of sewed skins and of fabrics woven in a plaiting technique. They decorated their hair, bodies, clothing, and goods with paints and with ornaments, both of native copper imported from the shores of Lake Superior and of shell beads, gorgets, and pendants imported from the Atlantic coast (figs. 3–4). They smoked their tobacco in stone or fired-clay pipe bowls, some elbow shaped, others molded or carved as animal effigies, but all with wooden or reed stems. Their burials were elaborate, the corpse oriented in an east-west direction, the body interred in full finery with an array of grave goods, tools, weapons, food, and other necessaries for the journey to the spirit world (Quimby 1966:23–34). However, members of the Rabbit clan were cremated instead of buried (JR 51:33).

Royal Ont. Mus., Toronto.
Fig. 3. Coe-Coosh, i.e., *kok·oš·* 'hog', painted by Paul Kane from his sketch made in 1845 when this Potawatomi was visiting the Menominee at Fox River. The straight hair and the ornaments reflect ancient styles, although by this date the hair ornaments were of German silver.

The Potawatomi already had likely developed an Omaha-type kinship system, which strongly emphasizes patrilineal descent and a corporate clan system, with the clan being the basis of village organization (Callender 1962). The kinship system practiced by the Potawatomi also emphasized the vital functions of women in the economy, by aligning each individual secondarily with the line of his mother's father. This system was particularly well suited for a population expanding in numbers and territory, as events of the late seventeenth and of the eighteenth centuries amply demonstrated. It was also well adapted to the ecological situation of the Potawatomi, where cooperation between substantial groups of

Mus. of the Amer. Ind., Heye Foundation, New York: 23/9335.
Fig. 4. Man's choker of beadwork on buckskin with shell gorget with incised underwater panther. Length 54 cm; collected at Peshtigo River, Wis., perhaps in the 20th century.

729

men and women was imperative for agriculture, hunting, fishing, seasonal village relocations, and warfare.

The corporate property of each local clan was more supernatural than corporeal. They may by this time each have owned a sacred bundle (*pičkos·an*), the contents of which embodied the supernatural power of the clan. However, the sacred bundles might have become associated with the clans later in their history. Skinner's (1924–1927, 1:56–57) analysis of 15 clan and bundle origin myths indicates that in each case the clan preexisted the acquisition of a bundle. The clan also "owned" ancestral names and the powers associated with them, various ritual goods, and the vision powers of its members. Real property, canoes, wigwams, weapons, and so forth belonged to individuals and nuclear or extended families. Each Potawatomi summer village contained representatives of several clans, the adult males, boys, and unmarried girls who were members of the core clan, and women from other clan-villages who had married into the local group.

In this fashion, via intermarriage and the exchange of women, each local clan community was tied to others. However, there were undoubtedly other intervillage bonds as well, involving trade, mutual ritual obligations, and economic and military reciprocity. There is no suggestion of an established, hereditary office of tribal "chief" at this time, although the principal men of the major clans might occasionally have recognized or nominated a strong man from a larger village as temporary leader of the whole for war or intertribal negotiations.

Perrot provides an insight into the style of Potawatomi governance and policy formation: "The old men are prudent, sensible, and deliberate; it is seldom that they undertake any unseasonable enterprise" (Bacqueville de la Potherie 1911–1912, 1:302). Later he describes in detail the communal decision-making processes involved in the Potawatomis' decision to heed Perrot's request and accompany him to Montreal. This involved elaborate preparatory discussions of the critical issues and merits of this new kind of alliance, capped by a major feast wherein all elements of the community dramatized their commitment. The presence of a "tribal chief" rendering decisions on the basis of formal authority is not indicated or suggested in these very important, tribal-level decisions. The "chief of the feast," obviously an important personage, is simply the advocate of the alliance wanted by Perrot. The important social elements of the community involved in this decision were: the advocate, the warriors, religious specialists, and the elders. Clan representatives were very probably involved, but Perrot does not single them out. Similarly ignored is the role of women, without whose collaboration the ritual feast could not have occurred.

This was the basic structure of Potawatomi society and the nature of their culture when war parties of the Iroquoian Neutral confederacy and later of the Five Nations thrust into Michigan, disrupting and dislodging the Algonquian tribes in that region. Until they settled in northeastern Wisconsin, many aspects of their social life, ecological adaptations, relations with related tribes, and their cultural patterns were greatly altered.

Transformations in the Refuge Area

From the date on which they enter the historical scene (1640) the Potawatomi were invariably called by a single name, marking the tribe as a whole. There are no known references to separate, geographically localized autonomous clans or bands, such as those that mark the several local groups who later became collectively identified as the Chippewa and Ottawa tribes. Indeed, in the early historical records, when Potawatomi clans are mentioned, these are always clearly specified as subunits of the tribal entity. Perrot, for instance, describes a conflict between two French traders and a leader of the Red Carp clan, which soon involved the Black Carp clan and the head of the Bear clan, who was a good friend to the French (Bacqueville de la Potherie 1917:82–83). This uniformity of reference strongly suggests that the Potawatomi had formed a tribal identity and a higher degree of solidarity earlier than their Chippewa or Ottawa relatives. If this process of tribal unification had not occurred prior to their leaving lower Michigan, then it characterized their adaptation to the new setting in Wisconsin.

This use of a single, tribal name to designate any Potawatomi group is probably at the root of much historical confusion such as the old but unsubstantiated tradition that Jean Nicollet had visited "the Potawatomi" during his visit to Green Bay in 1634. He may very well have visited with *some* Potawatomi during his stay, but it is doubtful that the whole tribe was present at this time. LeJeune, who very briefly described Nicollet's visit, says only that the Potawatomi were "in the neighborhood" of the Winnebago on Green Bay; but he says the same of the Sioux, the Assiniboin, the Illinois, and the "Rasaouakoueton" (Nassauakueton, an Ottawa group), which makes it a very extensive neighborhood, indeed (JR 18:228–233).

Similarly, in 1642 when Lalement writes that he has secondhand information about a more remote "Nation," the Potawatomi, taking refuge at Sault Sainte Marie from "some other hostile Nation who persecuted them with endless wars" (JR 23:225), or when archeological findings place the Potawatomi on Rock Island about 1650 (R.J. Mason 1974), or when Ménard in 1659 writes that some few Potawatomi had been at his Keweenaw Bay station in June and that 40 others 11 days' journey away died of dysentery the previous winter (JR 46:143), there is no certain knowledge of the whereabouts of the main body of the tribe or whether all were involved in the incidents described. In 1652 the main body of the tribe was likely at the large new fortified village called by the Potawatomi Méchingan, for which the Jesuits soon commissioned the new Saint Michel mission (Kellogg 1925:95-96; JR 44:245). The exact location of this large village is unknown, but it was somewhere near the head of Green Bay or on the opposite side of the Door peninsula on Lake Michigan.

What brought so many Potawatomi together at Méchingan was the threat of Iroquois raids, which also moved them into an intertribal alliance with the remnants of the Petun and Winnebago, as well as Chippewa elements from the north. Originally fugitives, they had now arrived at a situation where they enjoyed a measure of political dominance as well as military success, for the defensive coalition against the Iroquois was successful.

The cultural and historical circumstances of this Potawatomi tribal reaction to the Iroquois threat were ideal for intensifying the degree of tribal-level morale and solidarity and for generating that high value the Potawatomi placed on themselves as a society. As Perrot noted, they regarded other tribes as inferior to themselves and set themselves up as arbiters for all the tribes in the Green Bay area (Bacqueville de la Potherie 1911-1912, 1:302). Yet neither external threat nor success in war is sufficient to meld a highly individualistic people and the economically independent producing units of clan or family into a functioning, localized tribal unit. Pan-tribal sodalities and symbols are also required. Hickerson (1963) has fully described how one such pan-tribal sodality, the Midewiwin, came into existence among the Great Lakes Algonquians in response to the altered conditions of life in this era. The first specific historic mention of the Midewiwin, about 1714, concerns the Potawatomi in the Detroit region (WHC 16:363-376), by which time it was an established institution.

However, among the Potawatomi in 1670, there were counter-currents at work of such strength that the single village tribal community soon collapsed. Undoubtedly, population expansion and economic opportunities elsewhere were involved as the threat of Iroquois invasion waned, but internal cultural pressures provided the push, and the clan structure the mechanism, for the breakup of the large village and the migration of Potawatomi clans and clan-segments (that is, patrilineages) into new territories.

Perrot, who was on the scene in 1670 and who knew the situation, ambitions, and wants of the Potawatomi intimately, carefully described the factors involved. In a passage that is often incompletely quoted, he describes how in these years the Potawatomi labored to win the respect, loyalty, esteem, and trade of the neighboring tribes. "They make presents of all their possessions, stripping themselves of even necessary articles, in their eager desire to be counted liberal." But Perrot also carefully explains the consequences, observing that "their ambition to please everybody has of course caused among them jealousy and divorce; for their families [that is, clans or patrilineages] are scattered to the right and to the left along the Mécheygan [Lake Michigan]" (Bacqueville de la Potherie 1911-1912, 1:302-303). The Potawatomi had most successfully intruded themselves into the Ottawa-Green Bay area trade by this year: in the same context Perrot comments that most of the merchandise the Ottawa obtained (from Montreal) went to the Potawatomi. But the Potawatomi were trying to be traders, not producers of furs, and they now found themselves in the classic position of middlemen traders at the lower (or retail) end of an exchange network.

To obtain a continuous supply of furs from the producers in other tribes, Potawatomi leaders had to deprive themselves, their immediate families, and their clan and village mates of even basic necessities. This precipitated the great intratribal jealousy Perrot noted. Potawatomi leaders were failing to attend to their most fundamental obligations, generosity to kinsmen within the village and clan. Divorce, or the separation and out-migration of structurally independent, economically viable social units, was the result.

Culture in 1800

In 1800 the Potawatomi still constituted a single tribal organization; but they occupied and controlled an area far more extensive than in the previous century. Although it has been a common practice for some to apply the word "band" to the various regional coalitions of Potawatomi villages, there is no evidence that the Potawatomi themselves recognized traditional, formal subdivisions such as subtribes or bands, each with autonomous control of part of the tribal estate. The permanent and most important political-geographic unit was the village, of which there were more than 100 by this period. These villages were generally named after some geographic feature, such as 'village of the old red wood creek', a large village in Indiana, although Euro-Americans generally called them by a chief's name. Thus Potawatomi society had changed in important ways from the time, in 1600, when "the snow, the rabbit, and the men" were one family living in the same village (JR 51:33-34). By 1800 the idea of clan kinship with an animal was gone, and the villages contained representatives of several or more dispersed clans, with the village organized internally as a group of clan-segments or lineages.

As Swanton (1952:247) has pointed out, the "band" divisions were distinguished only late in Potawatomi history, and they were generally names of groupings brought together for treaties with the United States or as a consequence of them. These included reservation-based groups (like the Citizens' band), treaty groups (like the United bands of Ottawa, Chippewa, and Potawatomi), or scattered groups of refugees (such as the Forest band).

Similar considerations apply to older designations for geographic clusters of villages, such as the Huron, Kankakee, Chicago, and Saint Joseph "bands."

Village and Tribe

The importance of the village political unit is well expressed in a letter John Kinzie wrote to Lewis Cass, governor of Michigan Territory, in 1818 concerning the southernmost Potawatomi. Kinzie said that they "are scattered over a large tract of country, divided into small villages, at the head of each is a chief who holds himself independent. On this account, it is impossible to get the general consent of their nations without calling a meeting of every individual composing them who are perfectly republican and will not acknowledge anything well done, which is not done by the consent of the whole or the majority of them" (TPUS 10:877).

The social ties that bound these many widely scattered villages together were several and varied. Kinship, actual and metaphorical, was one important means of maintaining solidarity, particularly on a regional basis. Potawatomi tribal expansion largely consisted of pushing out one or more clans or clan-segments into a new area, there to establish a new village, while maintaining an affiliation with a parent village and clan. There is even an occasional expression of a sense of seniority and priority, for example, the deference in council given to the leading civil chief at Saint Joseph, Topenebe. However, it is doubtful that Saint Joseph had achieved the position of a recognized seat of tribal (or subtribal) power or Topenebe the formal powers of a full-scale tribal chief. Similarly, through personal influence, wealth, and demonstrated success, a local chief might hold sway for long periods over a large number of villages. Such a man was L'Etourneau (s·əknak· 'blackbird') at Milwaukee, whose influential efforts kept many Potawatomis out of a British alliance in the Revolutionary War. Clearly, the Potawatomi tribe was not, in Sahlins's (1968) terms, a standing political entity or a sovereign governing authority.

Relations within villages were as profoundly egalitarian as they were between villages. The position of wkəma 'leader' in a village involved ceremonial deference, but little effective power. The person occupying this position was a man of proper character who was a senior member of the clan that "owned" the office (Skinner 1924–1927, 1:19–20; Keating 1824, 1:122–124). Yet the occupant was selected from several possible candidates by the village; he did not acquire the office by birthright. As Metea, the civil chief of a large village north of Fort Wayne, carefully pointed out, the powers of a wkəma were severely restricted. Metea indicated that he was obligated to repeat to his council of warriors all questions he was asked and his responses and that there were things he could not speak about without first securing their permission. Keating (1824, 1:122) then concluded that the power of the chief depended on his personal influence and that he held no formal authority. A large part of the leader's influence rested on the degree of supernatural power he controlled, that is, his own mnəto 'spirit power', as measured by his successes.

The leader was aided in the tasks of governance by a council of adult males, who would express public opinion and their own interests, validate decisions, and exercise the real authority necessary to back them up. In addition there was a specialized sodality composed of the more successful warriors, the wkəč·tak, with their own songs and dances, who exercised police functions (Wissler 1916; Skinner 1924–1927, 1:227; Keating 1824, 1:123). This was a pan-tribal sodality, with members in many villages, and consequently it also functioned to promote intratribal cohesiveness. The leader was attended by a pipe-lighter, in Metea's case his younger brother, and further by a šk·apewəs· 'speaker-herald-messenger', who carried announcements, arranged ceremonies, called council meetings, and otherwise assisted in routine administration.

The pattern of decision making within the village in the 1800s seems to have been like that described by Perrot in 1670, with very similar social roles, procedures, and values involved. There is no evidence of the degeneration of a chiefly office with vested powers and considerable authority such as has been suggested by Baerreis (1973). Indeed, in 1824 the council of warriors most carefully observed and controlled the actions of their wkəma, and they had good reason to do so. Tecumseh's pronouncements against chiefs who signed away tribal lands provided their positive model, and the allocation of new authority to the chiefs by outside powers such as England and America, their undesirable experience. They had no wish to see a new kind of satrap emerge in their midst, and their wariness and caution prevented this.

Clans

By 1800 many Potawatomi clans had become thoroughly dispersed, with constituent lineages or members found in several or more villages. Nonetheless, some clans—perhaps newer ones—seem to have had a more restricted geographic range. In 1823 Keating (1824, 1:118) learned from Metea that the Potawatomi did not have clan communities that were associated with an animal ancestor. Instead, he found that "they have a sort of family distinction, kept up by means of signs resembling those of heraldry." These signs were called by them ntotem 'my clan totem'. Keating went on to determine that the totemic group did not involve belief in kinship with an ancestral animal, that the clans were organized patrilineally and exogamously, and that they were not ranked in order of "nobility or inequality" (ibid.:119). Potawatomi clans have since been fairly well studied (Skinner 1924–1927; Callender 1962; Landes 1970). It is clear that they were grouped into six larger units, or phratries: Water, Bird, Buffalo, Wolf, Bear, and Man.

There are several separate listings of Potawatomi clans, each list representing only part of the tribal whole. These are for Kansas-Oklahoma, 1859 (Morgan 1959), 1923 (Skinner 1924-1927), and 1936 (Landes 1970); for Wisconsin, 1670 (Bacqueville de la Potherie 1917:82) and 1951 (Ritzenthaler 1953); and for southern Michigan, 1736 (Kinietz 1940). Together these certainly do not add up to a full list of all Potawatomi clans of the past 300 years. Yet the facts available do indicate some interesting features of the system.

Of the 23 clans identified by Skinner in 1923, 13 years later Landes found only 11 with living members. But she also found a new one that neither Skinner nor Morgan had noted earlier, the "Angel" clan in the Man phratry. Hence old clans die out and new ones are invented. Ten clans are found in both the Wisconsin and the Kansas-Oklahoma areas, but others are not this widely distributed. There is a tendency for the southernmost clans to be associated with large game animals—Buffalo, Grizzly Bear, and Moose—and the northern ones with smaller furbearers—Otter, Muskrat, and Martin. Thus the clans that are shared are generally named for animals that range over the whole tribal estate. The Red and Black Carp clans noted by Perrot are long gone, and the Golden Carp clan of Michigan is unknown elsewhere. The facts available thus are quite consistent with the pattern of tribal expansion by clan or clan-segment migration.

As many Potawatomi clans were dispersed, having their lineages and members in several villages and regions, the clan system also functioned to add cohesion to the tribe. The clans acted as important agents of status placement as well, helping fix each individual into a particular place in the village and tribe. As a child, each Potawatomi received one of his several names and part of his personal stock of 'spirit power' from the clan, for an inventory of names of deceased ancestors was part of the clan's property. Thus placed, the individual was bound into a system of social relations with clan mates and members of other clans. The principal clan functions were in the arrangement and conduct of important rituals, feasts, and dances, with one phratry or clan being obliged to serve as host, another to provide the waiters, and the third a speaker for a ceremony. The name a child received from his clan was a personal one appropriate to the clan eponym. Thus a Thunder clan woman might be named "Coming Noise" or a Wolf clan man "Growler" (Skinner 1924-1927, 1:24-29). Each individual also had several other names, including war names and nicknames, by which he was ordinarily called.

Ritual

Each clan had associated with it a sacred bundle, an origin myth of the bundle, and a set of songs, chants, and dances. Individual clans also had specialized rights, rules, and obligations. The Fish clan had special quarterly medicine-renewing ceremonies, for example, and the men of the Man clan were subject to special rites and prohibitions before going to war.

The Potawatomi believed that the clans and bundles had been given them by *wisk·e,* the culture hero. But the origin myth of each bundle was more specific. First setting a mythopoeic time frame, the myth went on to tell how a named individual received the bundle and its powers in a vision quest, a day dream, or in a vision during an illness. The bundle proper consisted of a skin bag of otter or mink decorated with ribbon and bead work. It contained powerful mementos, talismans, and fetishes appropriate to the clan and to the powers the clan had got from *kč·ə-mnəto* 'the great spirit', speaking through an animal familiar to the founder of the bundle.

The Potawatomi shared the common Central Algonquian dual division that aligned the whole population, women and men, young and old, on two sides, corresponding to their order of birth. The first, third, and fifth born were assigned to the 'senior side', *wšk·əš,* and the second, fourth, and sixth born to the 'junior side', *kišk·o.* This dual division, which had some parallels in beliefs about the spirit world, was of substantial importance only in the organization of teams for games (figs. 5-6) and of

Fig. 5. Pkuknokwe, a Prairie band woman, playing the kwsəkənək dice game. This is a woman's game, played by teams from the *wšk·əš* and *kišk·o* sides. Photograph by James Clifton, 1964.

Fig. 6. Dice for the kwsəkənək game used by the Prairie band. A woman dreams the right to own the bowl and dice. The dice consist of 6 or 7 disks and 2 special pieces representing totems—horse, turtle (as here), buffalo, man, for example. Photograph by James Clifton, 1964.

some rituals. Thus the dual division cut across lineage, clan, village, and family memberships and served as an organizing principle and a tension-releasing mechanism in formalized rivalries (Skinner 1924–1927; Landes 1970).

The Potawatomi had a number of other sodalities, ceremonies, and specialized religious practitioners who enlivened village life and linked members of one village to others. The Midewiwin (*mtewən* 'Medicine Society') consisted of a pan-tribal semisecret society of very influential sorcerers, who could work their powers for good or evil. The *šawnoke* 'southern person dance' was a spring ritual held on behalf of those who had lost relatives the previous winter.

In addition, there were specialized individual role performances by several types of shamans. The *čask·yet* was a diviner who used ventriloquism, juggling, and other skills to impress his audience before foretelling the future or the location of lost possessions. The *wapno* was a fire-handling sorcerer with similar functions, who mystified, amused, and provided practical advice. And there was a curer, who used his skills in the treatment of illnesses (fig. 7). The French and English classed all three roles together and called them jugglers, looking on them with scorn and skepticism (Keating 1824, 1:134–135).

Household

The villages were annually shifted from summer to winter quarters, with the latter being smaller and more dis-

persed. The summer villages varied greatly in size, from less than 50 to more than 1,500 persons. By 1800, the greater Milwaukee area contained at least nine villages, with a total population of approximately 4,000 (P.V. Lawson 1920). The summer villages contained several different kinds of structures: rectangular, peaked-roof houses covered with slabs of bark; open-sided structures roofed with bark or boughs used as cooking shelters; and secluded away from the village, the women's menstrual hut of rush mats. Winter homes were dome-shaped bark- or mat-covered structures, somewhat smaller than the summer homes (Skinner 1924–1927, 2:268–270).

Houses were occupied by nuclear and, as the family expanded, extended families. Extended family units grew with age, and might include three or more generations. They grew also by the addition of wives, for polygyny was the preferred form of marriage and was common; up to 25 percent of marriages were multiple, as estimated by Keating (1824, 1:113). Sororal polygyny was the preferred form of multiple marriage. Marriages involved formal exchanges of considerable amounts of property between the clans and the agreement of senior kinsmen that the marriage was proper. The young man lived with the wife's family for one full year, serving them by hunting and caring for the horses; thereafter, the young couple moved back to the groom's village or neighborhood (Keating 1824, 1:96, 112–113; Skinner 1924–1927, 1:34–37).

Subsistence

Potawatomi economic and social life was tied closely to the rhythms of nature. They recognized four named seasons and at least 12 months that were named after the principal resource or economic activity of the time. The suffix *kisəs·* 'month' marked the calendar division. Thus, *kč·ə-mk·o-kisəs·* 'big bear month' was January, when a hunter and his dog could most easily kill a hibernating bear. The February period had at least four names, sucker month, wolf month, snow month, and baby bear month. Others were named trapping month, hunting month, planting-time month, and so on. In the north, the year started in mid-April with maple sugar or sucker month, for this was the beginning of the time of plenty, after a cold, hungry winter.

The Potawatomi fished with trap, weir, net, hook, and harpoon. They used long cylindrical "hoop" nets in combination with dams across streams to trap fish and harpoons with deer horn or stone points for taking fish from lakes or streams. They also gathered a wide variety of natural foods: maple sugar, choke cherries, raspberries, blackberries, cranberries, roots of several kinds, plums, and grapes. The animals they hunted for food included bear, deer, elk, buffalo, squirrel, muskrat, raccoon, porcupine, wolf (a ceremonial delicacy for certain chiefs), turtles, ducks, and geese. Dogs were the only

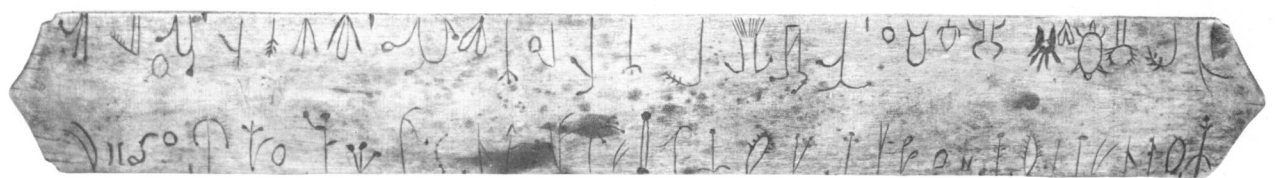

Fig. 7. Wooden stick with mnemonic symbols used as guide by a curer in preparing 10 herb remedies. Length 47.1 cm; collected in Ind. before 1862.

domestic animal eaten, and then mainly for ritual purposes.

The food collected or grown was prepared and stored against the winter's needs. Many foods were dried and stored in bark containers and pottery jars. Squash was sliced in rings and smoked or sun-dried, then stored. After parboiling, corn was scraped from the cob, then dried and made into preserves, or when fully ripe dried or parched. Cranberries were strung on strings and smoked inside the house. Most meat not consumed immediately was sliced, dried, and smoked. Ducks, geese, and turkeys, however, were pickled in brine, then smoked and stored, while fish were dried and smoked. Maple sugar was used as a condiment more often than salt.

Transportation

A Potawatomi village had considerable need for transportation other than human muscle power. The seasonal migrations of the community, long-distance trade, hunting, war, and the accumulated possessions of a sedentary village made this imperative. By 1800 the Potawatomi traveled along the waterways of the Great Lakes and their tributaries and over land. On water, they used both dugout canoes, which were the more common, and larger, built-up framed canoes, covered with sheets of birch, white elm, or linden bark. The bark-frame canoe ran up to 25 feet long and 5 feet wide. It could not be constructed or owned by just anyone, but only by some members of the Man clan, or by a man who had appropriate dream power; and they were only owned by the builders or by members of the Water phratry, being loaned to others for their use (Skinner 1924–1927, 2:294–295). But the Potawatomi had apparently no great love for long-distance water transport, and by 1800 many were losing their skills or their taste for the more arduous or risky canoe trips.

Well before 1800, many Potawatomi were substituting horse transportation for canoes, particularly in the southern reaches of the estate, and canoes were increasingly used for local transportation, for fishing and hunting near the village, rather than for long-distance travel. By 1800 the Potawatomis' freely grazing pony herds in the Milwaukee area were so large that villagers were starting to fence in their cornfields to protect them (P.V. Lawson 1920:57). The horses were ridden, using a wood framed saddle covered with rawhide, or used for burdens (figs. 8–9). Large saddlebags made of woven rush matting were employed to hold goods, meat, and vegetable foods gathered in large quantities such as wild rice. The Potawatomi also used a litter, twin poles slung between two horses in tandem, to transport goods or the ill or infirm.

Life Cycle

The pregnant woman was subject to numerous restrictions designed to protect the infant from evil influence and to ease childbirth and nursing. These restrictions included avoidance taboos and prohibitions on eating certain foods. Childbirth took place in a special bark house, where the mother delivered on her knees or extended over a stretched cord. She was assisted by women but never men (Keating 1824, 1:131; F. Clifton 1964; McElroy 1965). The mother and *pemotešək p·ənoče* 'infant' stayed in isolation for a month or more and then returned home, where the infant was feasted by clan members. A year or so later, the child would be given a name from the clan's stock, thus connecting it to the clan and fixing its primary status. The child was weaned after several years or when the mother had become pregnant again.

From the onset of walking until puberty, the child was called *wšk·ənikš·i* 'young boy' or *kikyako* 'young girl'. During this period, the children were expected to master skills appropriate to their sex, but endurance, discipline, and fortitude in the face of hunger and privation were expected of all. Boys and girls acted out in play the work of the adults: boys made tiny bows and arrows (fig. 10), manufactured small bark canoes, and played lacrosse; girls made dolls of ears of corn and played at household duties.

Adulthood came at puberty. The girl became *s·esks·i* at menarche and thereafter during her menses would have to fast in the menstrual hut away from the village (Keating 1824, 1:133; McElroy 1965:29–30). When the community was on the move, she was required to travel parallel with but at some distance from the main column. An adolescent boy was called *wšk·ənwe* and was expected to isolate himself, to fast, seeking vision power. Girls

Mus. of Fine Arts, Boston: M. and M. Karolik Coll.

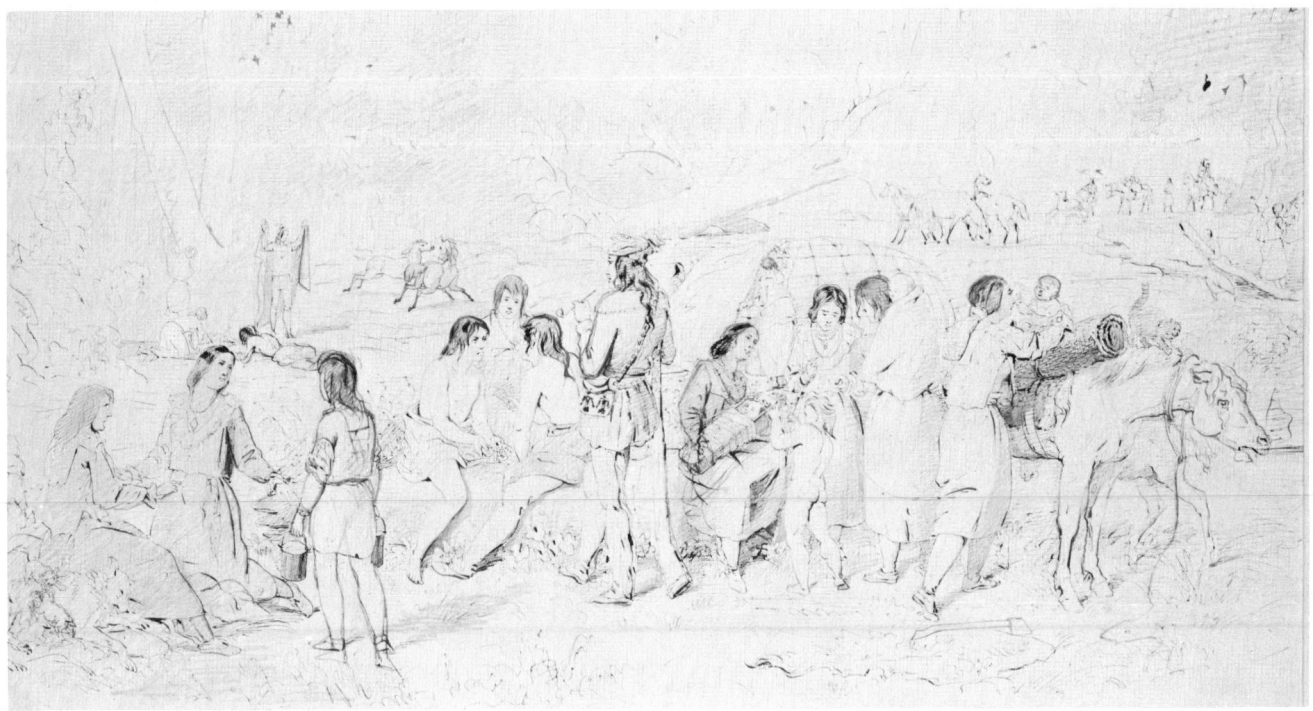

Fig. 8. Potawatomis setting up camp in northeastern Kansas. The women unload a horse, set up a domed lodge, and bring water, while the men smoke and play cards. Drawing by Rudolph Friederich Kurz, May 14, 1848.

married somewhat earlier than boys. Marriage marked full adult status; afterwards the girl was called *k·we* 'woman' and the boy *nənə* 'man'.

Potawatomi elders, wise, experienced, and powerful, were treated with great respect. With much responsible work in the village, including the moral education of children and participation in councils, they had a full life until death took them on the journey toward where the sun sets, where *čipyapos·*, twin brother of the culture hero *wisk·e* and guardian of the afterworld, waited to receive them. The death was marked with special funeral rituals by the clan members or, if the individual had been a Midewiwin (*mtewən*) member, by the members of the Grand Medicine Lodge. The body was dressed in best clothing and laid out with both necessary and precious possessions: moccasins, rifle, knife, money, silver ornaments, food, and tobacco. The style of interment followed the expressed wishes of the deceased. The body was buried erect, seated, or inclined, or else placed in the crotch of a tree. The grave was then marked with a post with painted or incised pictographs denoting the clan and perhaps some of the important deeds of the deceased (Keating 1824, 1:116). Soon thereafter, the principal mourner would adopt a replacement for the deceased. That is, a daughter or a grandson would adopt a new mother or grandfather, thus ending a period of mourning.

Mus. of the Amer. Ind., Heye Foundation, New York: 2/7810.

Fig. 9. Horse-medicine bundle. A calico outer wrapper encloses two pieces of strouding containing two small wooden horse charms and three bags of paint. Size of cloth 30.6 by 17.8 cm; collected in Kan. before 1911.

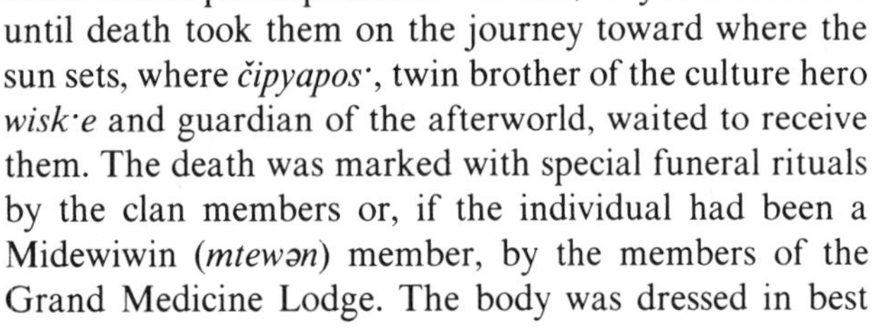

History

By 1800 the Potawatomi had already participated in two treaties with the United States, those of Fort Harmar in 1789 and Greenville in 1795. Beginning in 1803 they were to sign or participate in 52 more treaties, ending with the establishment of the Citizens' band in Oklahoma in 1867.

During the opening years of the nineteenth century more Potawatomi villages developed alliances with Britain than had been the case during the Revolutionary War. Memories of French associations and loyalties were gone, and the possibilities of trade relations with the Spanish at Saint Louis had disappeared. Thus the Potawatomi stood between two adversaries and were forced to choose sides. Soon after the end of the War of 1812, during which the majority of the Potawatomi had served the British, most village chiefs quickly indicated that they

Fig. 10. Little Smoke, grandson of Shabonee. He wears a shawl turban, shell gorget, complex ear ornaments, fringed buckskin shirt, and yarn sash. Photographer unknown; probably taken near Chicago about 1856.

recognized the power of the United States. Their conditions of life then changed rapidly as the Old Northwest Territory filled up with American settlers. Nonetheless, until 1839 many Potawatomi from all parts of the tribal estate continued in their allegiance to Britain, and visited the British posts at Amherstburg, Sarnia, Drummond Island, and Manitoulin Island annually for their presents and rations (Clifton 1975).

The Potawatomi in southern Michigan and Northern Indiana were first affected, for their villages were in areas first to be heavily settled by Americans. They were already much intermarried with French and English, and were greatly dependent on trade goods in an era when their principal source of wealth—furs—was increasingly scarce and their services for military purposes were no longer marketable.

The Potawatomi of Michigan and Indiana were quickly subject to intensive missionization and education programs (Schultz 1972). Their experience seems to have been entirely parallel to that of the Miami tribe in this period, and they demonstrated great reluctance to mi-

grate west of the Mississippi. Until 1841 they resisted removal and tried to subsist on annuity payments. But by that date they were finally forced out of their former lands to a reservation along the Osage River in Kansas.

The situation of the Illinois-Southern Wisconsin Potawatomi after 1833 was somewhat different. Most villages in this area still had access to furs, even if they were muskrat and raccoon, not beaver. They had started orienting themselves to hunting and raiding on the plains west of the Mississippi, in alliance with the Sauk and Fox. They were not so quickly overwhelmed by settlers. They were, therefore, both more independent economically and more autonomous politically, and their cultural patterns continued to provide a more satisfying and dependable life. The treaties they signed provided for an option of removal, and led by their chiefs, they elected to migrate westward. They were joined in this by some, but by no means all, of the other Wisconsin Potawatomi (Clifton 1968, 1970, 1975).

Meanwhile, in lower Michigan, a substantial number of highly acculturated Potawatomi hung on, living in small settlements on the fringes of American population centers. In Wisconsin a great many more tried to maintain themselves with traditional subsistence and farming techniques in the path of American settlement of the territory, but these were gradually forced northward into the forests.

The Illinois-Wisconsin Potawatomi relocated to a reservation near Council Bluffs in western Iowa Territory. For 15 years they adapted rapidly and successfully to high-plains equestrian hunting and warfare, enlarging on skills they had already begun to develop while east of the Mississippi. In 1847 the Potawatomi in Iowa (now called the Council Bluffs band) and the Osage River Potawatomi (called the Mission band) were brought together in a new reservation on the Kaw River in eastern Kansas. This was an experiment promoted by the Rev. Isaac McCoy aimed at developing a unified, geographically isolated Potawatomi nation, which could be properly Christianized and civilized; but it was an experiment that failed (Schultz 1972; Clifton 1970). The two major groups on this reservation were very discordant, the one staunchly traditional, resistant to change, and determined to manage their own internal affairs, the other increasingly acculturated. The conservatives, now known as the Prairie band, retained their share of the Kaw River reservation and held it in joint, common ownership until 1890, when the Dawes Allotment Act forced them to take individual parcels of land in severalty (fig. 11). The Mission band, on the other hand, earlier had taken their lands in severalty, selling the balance; within a few years they were impoverished. In 1867 the last Potawatomi treaty signed provided them with a new reservation in Oklahoma, as well as a new name, the Citizens' band (Murphy 1961). The effects of the Dawes Allotment Act on the Prairie band were such that by 1960, only 22

Fig. 11. Nashiwaskuk, called Jack Davis, a Prairie band member. The clothing style reflects the Prairie band's life on the high plains where they had become horse nomads. Photograph by DeLancey Gill, 1898.

Fig. 12. Potawatomi woman dressed for the annual powwow on the Prairie band reservation in Kansas. Photograph by James Clifton, 1964.

percent of the Kansas Reservation lands were owned by Prairie band members (Clifton and Isaac 1964).

By 1970 there were in the United States and Canada some 20 groups who identified themselves as Potawatomi or who were identifiably descended from a Potawatomi group of the nineteenth century, although they may have since altered their ethnic status (fig. 1). Obviously, the cultural and social circumstances of these groups vary considerably.

Included in the United States are four federal reservation groups—the Citizens' band reservation in Oklahoma, the Prairie band reservation in Kansas (fig. 12), the Hannahville community in the upper peninsula of Michigan, and the Forest County Potawatomi settlements in northern Wisconsin (fig. 13). The last group is divided into two communities, at Stone Lake and Wabeno, where they occupy scattered households. Of these, all adopted constitutions under the Indian Reorganization Act of 1934 except the Prairie band, who bitterly resisted this development (Clifton 1968). There are also two other identifiable groups of Potawatomi who have been assimilated into other tribes. These include some 500 Potawatomi who in 1833 joined Kenekuk, the Kickapoo prophet, and eventually settled on the Kansas Kickapoo reservation adjacent to the Prairie band (Schultz 1972:176). The second assimilated group consisted of the advocates and disciples of the Dream Dance religion, an Algonquian revitalization movement, who appeared on the Menominee reservation in 1881 attempting to infuse the Menominee with enthusiasm for this new anti-White, anti-Catholic Indian religion (ARCIA 1881:176–179). This group, approximately 200 in number, settled first at Phlox, and then at Zoar, where they have long been legally enrolled and have since become identified by some as the "native-oriented" element of the Menominee population (Wooster 1907).

In addition to these reservation groups, there are three other substantial clusters or settlements in Wisconsin and the lower peninsula of Michigan. The Wisconsin settlement used to be known as the "Skunk Hill band" but has since adopted the name "Wisconsin Rapids Potawatomi." Less than 200 in number, these people are descendants of Prairie band Potawatomi who migrated back to Wisconsin in the last part of the nineteenth century. The two lower Michigan groups represent elements who remained in Michigan, joined by some from northern Indiana. Together they total about 1,400 persons. The one is settled in Cass County (the Pokaguns) and the other in Calhoun County (the Potawatomi of the Huron, or the Potawatomi of Michigan and Indiana, Inc.). Most of the very highly acculturated people of the Michigan

Amer. Mus. of Nat. Hist., New York: left to right 50.1/7060, 50.1/7058, 50.1/7059.

Fig. 13. Ribbon appliqué decoration on blue cotton shawl (left), women's leggings, and red broadcloth skirt (right). Collected in Wis. between 1912 and 1929.

settlements, influenced by the early mission schools in this area, were recognized as citizens for many years before recently reverting to legal Indian status, although they have always been identified as Indians in the rural areas where they live (Claspy 1966).

In addition to the Potawatomi in the United States, between 1837 and 1840 approximately 2,000 Potawatomi from Wisconsin, Michigan, and Indiana moved into southwestern Ontario, mostly by way of Detroit and Port Huron to Sarnia and Walpole Island, but some across the north shore of Lake Huron (Clifton 1975). They were groups who had regularly traveled to Canada for presents, rations, and payments, either for military services rendered during the War of 1812 or for continuing to declare their loyalty to the British cause. By 1970, fairly substantial groups occupied some 12 different locations, the major ones being Walpole Island, Sarnia, Kettle Point, Orillia, Cape Croker, Saugeen, and Manitoulin Island (fig. 14) (Clifton 1973, 1975).

The situation of the Canadian Potawatomi differs from that of their relatives in the United States in that nearly all of them have since assimilated into other Indian communities, principally Chippewa and Ottawa. When they arrived in Canada they had no treaty rights, and hence no lands held under Crown grants, nor regular annuity payment for lands sold. They gradually settled in on the reserves of other Indians, where after some years of confusion and moderate conflict, they were eventually accepted and in many cases formally adopted in reserve membership. In the 1970s there are few of them who make much of their Potawatomi ancestry, since they identify their interests as being connected with the fortunes of a particular reserve or, more generally, with Canadian Indians.

The Potawatomi in the United States have had a variety of experiences and have attempted equally varied

solutions to them. By 1870 there was evidently a grave cultural crisis among those Potawatomi who remained subsisting in Wisconsin, almost constantly on the move as farms were established, towns built, or forests cut over. For it was some of these Potawatomi, along with some Chippewa, who quickly adopted and became disciples of the new religion created by the Santee Sioux prophetess Wananikwe. At first this religion preached a message of magical hope: should the believers beat the great Dream Drum four days and four nights, all the Whites and Catholic Indians would fall paralyzed on the earth, and the believers could then simply tomahawk them (ARCIA

Mus. of the Amer. Ind., Heye Foundation, New York: top, 16/2618; bottom, 16/2620.

Fig. 14. Ritual accessories from war bundle. top, Wooden war club charm; bottom, rattle, with wooden handle carved to represent a thunderer with red and blue paint in incised decoration and notched deer hoofs attached with thong. Length of top about 30.2 cm; bottom, same scale; collected at Parry Island Reserve, Ont., before 1928.

739

1881:176-179). However, magical devices do not work great changes in historical circumstances, so that in the years since, although the Dream Dance religion has persisted, its fundamental myth and message have altered drastically (Clifton 1969). This religion was carried to Kansas by 1882, where it soon adopted a very different form. By 1962, the message of the Dream Dance religion had become one of peace and brotherhood, and its promise was cultural continuity: if the rituals are practiced and the songs sung, then the Potawatomi will persist as a culturally distinct people (fig. 15). This is a promise that can and has been kept.

The prosecution of claims against the United States and other parties is another adaptive device that has occupied the time and attention of many Potawatomis for well over a century. Although the exceedingly complex Potawatomi claim that has been before the U.S. Indian Claims Commission since 1948 seems to be uniquely difficult, it is well to remember that the Potawatomi had been involved in claims against the United States for more than a century before the Commission first convened. In 1901, for example, Chief Pokagon from Michigan booked passage on a ship for Chicago for himself, 200 adults, 100 children, 40 ponies, and 1,000 pounds of baggage per family. He was going to Chicago to settle in Grant Park on a strip of land that supposedly had not been deeded in the 1833 Treaty of Chicago (Claspy 1966:26-27). This "Sand Bar" claim was initiated well

before the Civil War, and for a time it had been argued by Abraham Lincoln.

Population

Estimates of the total size of the Potawatomi population are complicated by a lack of comprehensive and comparable data and by shifting definitions of what constitutes a Potawatomi. Throughout the eighteenth and nineteenth centuries all population figures are fragmentary and incomplete. They usually consist only of estimates of the number of warriors under arms and available to serve for or against the French or British. Moreover, whole blocks of villages are often omitted, principally those in southern Wisconsin and northern Illinois and after 1800 especially those in northeastern Wisconsin. When Keating arrived in Fort Wayne in 1823, he was told by traders and government officials there that there were more than 10,000 Potawatomis in all areas at that time. Although Keating did not accept this figure, since he was looking at the Potawatomi from the perspective of one village at the extreme northeastern part of the tribal estate, it was probably an accurate estimate.

The standard figure of the number of Potawatomi in the protohistoric period, about 1600, has been 4,000 (Kroeber 1939), which number is approximately that of the earliest French counts. Mooney and Hewitt's (1910:291) statement that the Potawatomi never exceeded 3,000 is clearly wrong, by a factor of from 50 to 65 percent. This was based upon official U.S. government counts of those Potawatomis actually living on reservations, and these were always very low.

The first historic estimates of the number of Potawatomi are those of French missionaries and government agents for the period 1653-1695, which give a maximum of 700 men or a total of 3,000 (see Kinietz 1940 for a summary of sources). After 1760, the British gauged the number of Potawatomi to be about 2,250, but these estimates covered only parts of the tribal estate, the Saint Joseph and Wabash rivers and the Detroit region (Schoolcraft 1851-1857, 6:271, 275, 3:559). An American estimate for the 1820s and 1830s gives an undifferentiated total of 6,500 for all areas, but it is vague with respect to the entire Wisconsin area and hence incomplete by about 30 percent. In the 1850s, for example, there were known to be more than 600 "strolling Potawatomi" in Wisconsin; but even then, no American was concerned with counting the number of Potawatomis who had fled into Canada during the removal era, from 1837 on.

The best population estimates for the nineteenth century were drawn specifically with respect to the claims of these "strolling Potawatomi" in Wisconsin who, because they had not removed west, had not been receiving their annuity payment from earlier treaties. This study (Garfield 1908) includes a careful enumeration of the Potawatomis still living in Wisconsin, an equally careful enumeration of those Wisconsin Potawatomis who had fled

Fig. 15. Curtis Pequano, Prairie band member. He was speaker of the Mattwaoshe Drum in the Dream Dance religion; here he holds the sacred and powerful staff that symbolizes the great power placed in the drum by Jesus Christ. Photograph by James Clifton, 1964.

to Canada, an estimate of the number of Potawatomis from other areas who had fled to Canada, and an average of the number of Potawatomis enumerated elsewhere in the United States in the period 1836-1907. The estimated total from these calculations was 8,500.

In addition, a fair number of Potawatomis had gotten lost in the nineteenth century. Five hundred had joined the Kickapoo under Kenekuk, several hundred had assimilated into the Menominee reservation community, and some few had joined the Mexican Kickapoo. If these are added to the 8,500 estimated above, then the figure given Keating by his Fort Wayne contacts was surely of the right order of magnitude. This can be partially verified by the official U.S. census of Potawatomi for 1836, which gave a total of 6,694. This was of course the critical year for removal, and at least several thousand Potawatomi were out of contact with the U.S. government, moving northward into the forests of Wisconsin or migrating east toward Canada. With these qualifications in mind, a total of 9,000 to 10,000 Potawatomis in the first half of the nineteenth century is reasonable.

There are no figures for the mid-twentieth century that can be legitimately compared with the estimates of the number of village-dwelling tribal Potawatomi in the first half of the nineteenth century. Since most Canadian Potawatomis have assimilated into Canadian Chippewa and Ottawa communities, if they are counted at all, it is as Chippewa, or Walpole Island Indians, or Canadian Indians. Similarly, reservation-based membership groups such as the Citizens' band in Oklahoma, which use a descendancy roll defining membership regardless of the degree of blood or sociocultural characteristics, yield a membership figure that cannot be compared with estimates of earlier populations or with the Prairie band's total of 900. For years the conservative elders of the Prairie band were successful in excluding from membership persons with minimal hereditary claims and few or no Potawatomi linguistic, cultural, and social characteristics. In the instance of this band, the resistance of the cultural conservatives was broken when the "absentee" Potawatomi secured control of the Prairie band business committee, at which point the population quickly soared to 2,185, with another 550 applicants awaiting approval (Jack Carson, personal communication 1974). It is for reasons such as these that extreme care must be taken in using raw numbers based upon counts or estimates of undefined units. This is especially true in an era when the prestige and rewards associated with legal Indian status have risen considerably, from claims case awards, equal opportunity employment programs, college scholarships, and similar privileges associated with the status of a legally recognized Indian.

Synonymy

The name Potawatomi is from Ojibwa *po·te·wa·tami·*, which corresponds to the Potawatomi self-designation *potewatmi*. This word is an unanalyzable name with no known literal meaning, and the commonly cited translation 'people of the place of the fire' is merely a folk etymology (Goddard 1972:131). There is certainly no connection with *šk·ote* 'fire', and the vowel differences rule out derivation from Ojibwa *po·tawe·* 'makes a fire'. Nevertheless, the traditional interpretation has suggested to some commentators that they are the "chosen people" or a "leading tribe" (P.V. Lawson 1920:42), that they have established a separate sovereignty by making their own council fire (Schoolcraft 1851-1857, 1:308), or that they had a special way of starting a fire (Gatschet 1878-1893:22; McDonald 1899:6). Another self-designation, which is actually the one more commonly used by Potawatomis when speaking their own language, is *nəš·nape* 'person' (pl. *nəš·napek*, vocative pl. *nəš·napetək*), a word that may also mean 'Indian' as opposed to European American.

Many variant spellings of the name Potawatomi from English and French sources are listed by Mooney and Hewitt (1910:291-293). Most of these are easily recognizable, typically involving different spellings of the vowels or doubling of the consonants, with a few more extreme variants like Pedadumies and Pontowattimies. Typical representatives are the county names Pottawatomie (Kansas and Oklahoma) and Pottawattamie (Iowa). The vowels are more correctly rendered in the French forms Pouteouatami and Oupouteouatamik (from an Algonquian form with the tribal-name prefix *o-* and the plural suffix *-k*). The French sources also frequently use the abbreviated nickname Pouës, often with the spelling Poux of the homophonous French word for 'lice'.

Names in other languages for the Potawatomi (Mooney and Hewitt 1910, except as stated) include a number of borrowed versions of their own name, such as Adawadenys and Atowateany (Iroquois); Undatomátendi, Ndaton8atendi, or Ondatouatandy (Huron-Wyandot); Pa-tuátami (Kansa); Pú-te-wa-ta (Dakota); and perhaps the Miami nickname Pō-tŏsh'. Names of other origins include: Koasati (from Creek) Tchĕshtalálgi 'watermelon people' and Caddo *ƙunuʔ hayá·nuh* 'melon people' (Wallace L. Chafe, personal communication 1974); Fox *pehkineni·haki* 'aliens' and Kickapoo *peehkita* (pl. *peehkiciki*) 'different one(s)' (Michelson 1934a:229, 231, phonemicized). There is also a set of forms apparently diffused from a single unidentified ultimate source language: Illinois 8a8rahe (Belting 1958:288) and Miami wahonaha (Dunn in Voegelin 1938-1940, 10:420); Winnebago *wo·ráxe* (Kenneth Miner, personal communication 1974), Iowa-Oto woraxa, Omaha wáhiúðaxá, and Kansa wáhiúyaha (last three normalized). Pawnee *rá·waruhki* (Douglas R. Parks, personal communication 1975) seems to be isolated.

The only important correction to Mooney and Hewitt's listing of tribal names for the Potawatomi consists of deleting all references to the Fire Nation or Gens de Feu so far as they are supposedly derived from the Huron Asistagueronon and the several variations thereof. As Hunt (1940:108–109) pointed out and as Goddard (1972, "Mascouten," this vol.) has demonstrated with additional data, the Huron, Neutral, and Petun sometimes used Fire Nation for *all* the Algonquian tribes in the lower peninsula of Michigan collectively, but never for the Potawatomi specifically.

Sources

Although many of the early French travelers in the Upper Great Lakes encountered Potawatomi or heard of them secondhand, it is unusual to find more than a fragment of information about Potawatomi culture. For this reason, Perrot's (1911:148–151, 188–190) rich if brief comments are invaluable (see also Bacqueville de la Potherie 1911–1912,1:300–317, 332–343, 2:13–43, 83–96). Claude Allouez and Claude Dablon's commentaries on the Potawatomi at Chequamegon and Green Bay are equally valuable (JR 54:264–265, 196–237, 55:26–41, 184–189). Numerous briefer references to the Potawatomi are listed in the index to the *Jesuit Relations*. Deale (1958) provides a fair summary of primary sources for the period before 1722, except that he places too much reliance on Le Jeune's relation locating the Potawatomi "in the neighborhood of Green Bay" in 1634, which ambiguous information was from Nicollet. Kinietz (1940) provides a fair summary of some Potawatomi materials as well. Similar comments hold true of British contacts with the Potawatomi, which provide scanty source materials.

Keating (1824) is definitive for Potawatomi culture in the early 1800s, just at the point of their dispersal. However, Keating has to be supplemented with numerous letters and reports of government officials and traders such as John Kinzie.

Callender (1962) cannot easily be improved and is invaluable. However, to get straight to Potawatomi culture, there is nothing better than the ethnographic treasures collected in Skinner's mistitled work (1924–1927). Had Skinner done a little historical research or paid attention to the work of his contemporary Lawson, he might not have been led to the erroneous assumption that the Forest County Potawatomi were the true and pure representatives of ancient, northern-forest Potawatomi life. P.V. Lawson's (1920) compilations of information about the Wisconsin Potawatomi are very useful, although his conclusions are sometimes stretched and his citations frequently wrong. No similar compilations are available for Michigan, Illinois, and Indiana. The work of the Great Lakes Anthropology Research Project, done under contract with the Department of Justice to provide materials for the government's side in cases before the Indian Claims Commission, is also of great value as a compilation, although it hews to very narrow issues and is not rich in interpretation and conclusion (Horr 1974). Landes (1970) is a fine example of configurational thinking in anthropology, as is Landes (1963); she does what Skinner did not do: she deals brilliantly with Potawatomi ethos, values, and interpersonal styles. Ritzenthaler's (1953) small monograph on the Wisconsin Potawatomi remains very valuable as an introduction to this group. Clifton (1975) provides information on the Canadian Potawatomi. There are also research studies of the Potawatomi in Kansas (Bee 1964; F. Clifton 1964; Clifton 1962–1964, 1965, 1970, 1977; Gossen 1964; McElroy 1965a). Murphy (1961) details the transformation of the Indiana-Michigan Potawatomi first into the Mission band, then into U.S. citizens, and then back as Indians in the Citizens' band. Clifton has written on contemporary Potawatomi (1975a) as well as on the history of their culture change (1977).

Skinner's Wisconsin and Kansas Potawatomi collections are housed at the Milwaukee Public Museum. There are smaller collections at the Neville Public Museum, Green Bay, Wisconsin, good collections at the Field Museum of Natural History, Chicago, and odds and ends elsewhere such as the Museum of the American Indian (Heye Foundation), New York.

Southwestern Chippewa

ROBERT E. RITZENTHALER

The Chippewa ('chĭpə₁wô), or Ojibwa (ō'jĭbwə), was the largest tribe north of Mexico in 1972. Formerly they lived over an extensive area, mainly north of Lakes Superior and Huron. Since the seventeenth century they have expanded into western Saskatchewan, and south into what are now the states of Michigan, Wisconsin, Minnesota, and North Dakota, as well as into southern Ontario. An Algonquian-speaking tribe,* their closest cultural relatives are the Cree, to the north, and the Potawatomi and Ottawa, to the south. With these last two, in the nineteenth century, some of the Chippewa formed a loose confederacy known as The Three Fires.

The first historical mention of the Chippewa-Ojibwa was in a listing of the bands in the Upper Great Lakes area in 1640 (JR 18:230). This information, which had been obtained by Jean Nicollet on his 1634 voyage to the Winnebago, included no mention of any groups farther west than the Saulteaux, then at the Sault Sainte Marie, and the Noquet and Mantouek of the nearby Upper Peninsula of Michigan, though a secondhand account of 1658 associated the Mantouek with the Eastern Dakota (JR 44:248), and there may have been Chippewa fishing camps along the southern shore of Lake Superior during this period. After 1679, however, when they entered into a truce with the Dakota, the Chippewa established villages at Chequamegon and Keweenaw bays and began their gradual expansion to the west (Hickerson 1962:65–67, 96). The following groups, and there may have been others, are recorded for the mid-seventeenth century: Ousasouarini, Outchougai, Achiligouan, Amikwa, Mississauga, Saulteaux, Noquet, Mantouek (JR 18:229–230), Nikikouek (JR 33:149), Ojibwa, and Marameg (JR 54:133). Some of the less well known of these groups, which lived along the eastern and northeastern shore of Georgian Bay prior to 1650, have also been classified as Ottawa and it is possible that some of them were Nipissing. There are simply not enough data to resolve this problem.

The bulk of the Chippewa-Ojibwa population at the time of contact was in the present province of Ontario, and the same was true in 1972. Their numbers in 1650 have been estimated as 35,000 (Mooney 1928). Kroeber (1939:6–8), reviewing Mooney's work, allowed that fig-

ure to stand, but it seems low, reconstructed on the basis of 1970 numbers. The U.S. Bureau of the Census figure of 41,946 for Chippewa living in the United States in 1970 is reasonably firm. The Canadian population poses more of a problem. Canadian Indian Affairs figures for 1970 of enrolled "Treaty Indians" total nearly 64,000 (Ontario, 43,975; Manitoba, 14,187; Saskatchewan, 5,687), but perhaps only one-half of the Canadian Chippewa-Ojibwa were enrolled in 1972 and some enrollees were actually non-Indians (Edward S. Rogers, personal communication 1972). Thus, after doubling the number of Treaty Indians and reducing the figure by an arbitrary 8,000 to account for the non-Indians, a rough estimate of 120,000 is reached. Adding the U.S. Chippewa population, the total is about 160,000. Supposing this figure to be somewhere near the truth, there would have to be either a minimum of 100,000 at contact time or else a fantastic growth rate unique to the population dynamics of tribes in the Woodland area during the historic period (cf. "Southeastern Ojibwa," this vol.).

The settlement pattern in early historic times was that of numerous, widely scattered, small, autonomous bands. Thus the term "tribe" is applicable to the Chippewa-Ojibwa in terms of a common language and culture, but it does not apply in the political sense that an overall authority or unity was present. To a considerable extent this settlement pattern was dictated by their hunting-fishing-gathering type of economy, which required a large area to support few people.

History

The Fur-Trade Period, 1670–1800

The Chippewa-Ojibwa were deeply involved in the fur trade, especially during the eighteenth century, and were deeply affected by it. During the seventeenth and eighteenth centuries, the French and British established a series of trading posts in their country to engage in the lucrative business of supplying furs, particularly beaver for making hats, to the European market. The licensed trader or his staff exchanged European goods firearms, metal implements and utensils, cloth, beads, and liquor for furs collected by the Indians. There was a rapid shift in material culture, from a stone-bone-wood-pottery complex of their own manufacture to the metal replace-

---

* For the transcriptional system used in italicized Chippewa words, see the orthographic footnote in "Southeastern Ojibwa," this vol.

ments of foreign manufacture. The gun replaced the bow, thus adding an efficiency factor to the hunt and to war. The economic life of the men shifted to one concentrating on trapping, and there developed a certain dependency on the post for "necessities" such as guns and ammunition.

The fur trade also resulted in a westward movement of the Chippewa as the French extended their posts westward. There was a tendency toward concentration of population as they sometimes clustered near, or at, a trading post. An example of this was the estimated population of 1,000 Indians at the settlement of Chequamegon, on the south shore of Lake Superior in present Ashland County, Wisconsin, after the French reestablished a post there in 1692. E. Johnson (1965:398) noted that "one aspect of culture change which seems to have resulted from the close association of the Ojibwa with the trader was the strengthening of the position of the band headman and the eventual changing of this position from that of a relatively weak leader to a strong hereditary position." The trader, finding it more expedient to work through a band leader, strengthened the prestige and authority of the civil leader, who was traditionally weak in the almost apolitical system of precontact Chippewa-Ojibwa. E. Johnson (1965:398) further suggested that this, coupled with their patrilineal tendency, probably gave rise to the patrilineally inherited line of "chiefs."

Another effect of the fur trade was to make liquor available to the Indian. The excessive use of it was already a problem during the trading-post period, and by 1832 the United States government deemed it serious enough to pass the Indian Nonintercourse Act, which prohibited the further sale of alcoholic beverages to Indians. There was also a considerable amount of marriage between Indian women and the traders, factors, and *coureurs de bois,* particularly the French, as is attested by the many French surnames among modern Chippewa. The deep affection and empathy the Chippewa-Ojibwa and French held for each other was in complete contrast to the Chippewa-Ojibwa feelings toward the British. They supplied warriors in the French attempt to maintain their forts along the northern frontier at Quebec, Montreal, DuQuesne, Niagara, and Detroit, and it was with deep regret that they saw the surrender of French Canada to the British in 1760.

This period also saw the major geographical expansion of the Chippewa-Ojibwa. Hickerson (1962:2–3) has delineated a four-part division that had emerged by the onset of the nineteenth century, as a result of this expansion. First, the Northern Ojibwa, or Saulteaux, occupied the forests of the Laurentian uplands north of the Great Lakes. They were characterized by small, discrete, scattered bands with a hunting-fishing-gathering economy, which made little or no use of wild rice or maple sugar, and later with family hunting territories.

Skinner (1911:117) divided them into northern and southern groups, noting that the former were considerably influenced by the Eastern Cree. (They are discussed in vol. 6.) Second are the Plains Ojibwa, or Bungee, of southern Saskatchewan and Manitoba. They exhibited the most radical change in adopting certain political and ceremonial traits, as well as a bison-hunting economy, from the northern Plains tribes with whom they came in contact (see vol. 12). Third, the Southeastern Ojibwa, who began occupying the lower peninsula of Michigan and adjoining areas in Ontario by the eighteenth century, were hunters, fishermen, gardeners, and gatherers of maple sugar, and, only in some instances, of wild rice. They were organized in somewhat larger aggregates than were the Northern Ojibwa, with relatively large summer villages (for this division, see "Southeastern Ojibwa," this vol.). Fourth, the Southwestern Chippewa moved into Wisconsin's northern rim and the northern half of Minnesota extending up to the Lake of the Woods on the Ontario-Manitoba border. There they found a rich supply of wild rice, which became an important part of their economy. They also collected maple sugar and did some gardening, in addition to their important mainstays of hunting, trapping, and fishing. Hickerson (1962) went to some length to establish the thesis that this group showed important change toward a more elaborate sociopolitical organization. One impetus to greater (but not pronounced) organization was their involvement in war, first with the Fox, whom they encountered in northern Wisconsin (Mooney and Thomas 1907g:278) and later, more important, with the Dakota, farther west. The rest of this chapter deals exclusively with the Southwestern Chippewa.

Intertribal Wars, 1800–1854

After continuing intermittently for more than 100 years, hostilities between the Southwestern Chippewa and their hereditary enemies, the Dakota, reached their peak during the first half of the nineteenth century. The cause was mainly the use of hunting and trapping territory and the use of the wild-rice fields; it took place, primarily, in what is now Minnesota. Ordinarily, it was small-scale warfare, one village against another, while other villages on either side might be at truce; also, hunting parties often were attacked. The common pattern was for a warrior to invite a number of other warriors to join him in a war party that he would lead. Upon completion of the raid, the war party was dissolved. While only small numbers were normally involved, the loss of life was relatively high. Warren (1885:169) presented a lengthy account of the battles and methods of warfare employed in these "border wars" and noted that in one of the most successful raids by the Chippewa, the war party returned with 335 Dakota scalps. Armstrong (1892:94–97), in an eyewitness account of the Battle of the Brulé in 1842, noted that firearms and ammunition were so scarce that the gun was used for signal purposes only and that both parties waged war with a club in one hand and a scalping knife in the other. In this encounter the Chippewa lost 13 warriors and took 101 Dakota scalps. Ultimately, the Chippewa were successful in driving the Dakota across the Mississippi River. One Chippewa group established residence as far west as the Turtle Mountains in North Dakota, now a reservation. Hostilities continued into the nineteenth century. Even the Prairie du Chien Treaty of 1825, dividing up the disputed territory, did little to stem animosities. Their cessation awaited the United States government reservation program, when the various Indian tribes or bands gave up most of their claimed territory for annuities and a reservation plat. The final battle between them was not fought until May 1858.

This period was marked by land adjustments, the result of a series of treaties between the Chippewa and the U.S. government. In Wisconsin, the treaties of 1835, 1837, 1842, and 1854 resulted in a diminution of Chippewa territory, from the considerable area they claimed to their present, comparatively small, reservation holdings. The Minnesota Chippewa, too, in exchange for annuities of goods and provisions, ceded mineral rights or territory in treaties of 1826, 1847, 1854, 1855, 1863, and 1864.

The Reservation Period, 1854–1972

As a result of the treaties made during the 1850s and 1860s (C. Thomas 1910:377–378), the various Minnesota bands were allocated 11 reservations, 7 of which were Chippewa and existed in 1972: Fond du Lac (21,367 acres), Grand Portage (44,752 acres), Leech Lake (26,766 acres), Mille Lacs (3,620 acres), Nett Lake (41,784 acres), Red Lake (636,964 acres), and White Earth (56,116 acres). With the Treaty of 1854, four reservations were established in Wisconsin: Bad River (in 1972, 54,932 acres), Lac Courte Oreilles (43,719 acres), Lac du Flambeau (44,477 acres), and Red Cliff (7,267 acres). In 1934 two small reservations of 1,750 acres each were created: Mole Lake and Saint Croix (fig. 1). The effects of the reservation system on the southwestern Chippewa were considerable; it froze them into their locales with reduced lands. Besides stemming further expansion, it was a blow to the traditional economic system that required substantial territory, especially for hunting. Also, by the mid-nineteenth century, the fur trade had declined to a trickle and the reservation period began with the Chippewa in an economic plight from which they have never recovered. There was some respite toward the end of the nineteenth century, when the lumbering interests, exploiting the area, employed Indians as lumberjacks. There seems to have been a good working relationship between the lumber companies and the Indians: the employers found the Indians excellent workers, and the Indians, at home in the woods, enjoyed the relatively small, but welcome, wages.

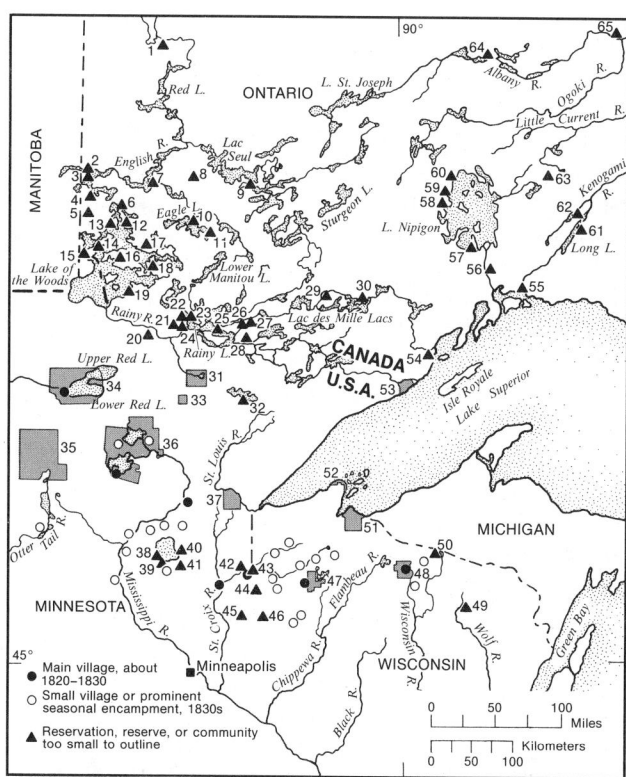

Fig. 1. Southwestern Chippewa settlements in the 19th century (after Hickerson 1962) and Chippewa reservations and communities in 1970. 1, Pikangikum; 2, One Man Lake; 3, Islington; 4–5, Shoal Lake; 6, The Dalles; 7, English River; 8, Wabauskang; 9, Lac Seul; 10, Eagle Lake; 11, Wabigoon; 12–13, Rat Portage; 14–15, Northwest Angle; 16, Big Island; 17, Whitefish Bay; 18, Sabaskong Bay; 19, Big Grassy; 20, Manitou Rapids; 21–25, Rainy Lake; 26, Seine River; 27, Sturgeon Falls; 28, Nequagon Lake; 29, Seine River; 30, Lac des Mille Lacs; 31, Nett Lake; 32, Vermilion Lake; 33, Deer Creek; 34, Red Lake; 35, White Earth; 36, Leech Lake; 37, Fond du Lac; 38–42, Mille Lacs; 43–46, St. Croix Communities; 47, Lac Courte Oreilles; 48, Lac du Flambeau; 49, Mole Lake; 50, Lac Vieux Desert Community; 51, Bad River; 52, Red Cliff; 53, Grand Portage; 54, Fort William; 55, Pays Plat; 56, Red Rock; 57, McIntyre Bay; 58, Gull River; 59, Jackfish; 60, Whitesand River; 61–62, Long Lake; 63, Aroland; 64, Fort Hope; 65, Martin Falls. For all Michigan groups, see "Southeastern Ojibwa," fig. 3, this vol.; for Ojibwa groups to the north, see "Northern Ojibwa," vol. 6; for those to the west, see "Saulteaux of Lake Winnipeg," vol. 6. The repartition of the modern Chippewa-Ojibwa groups on these maps is geographical, since the dialect affiliations of a number of the groups have not been determined.

With the Allotment Act of 1887, which parceled out reservation lands to the individual, the Indians could, and did, sell their timber rights, a source of income that left them with cut-over lands. The Allotment Act resulted in a sharp reduction of Indian-held land throughout the United States until it was reversed by the Indian Reorganization Act of 1934. In 1924 citizenship status was conferred upon Indians, allowing them to vote for the first time. While Chippewas, along with other Indians, had fought as volunteers in World War I, the citizenship act made them eligible for the draft; many served in World War II (and subsequent wars) as either selectees or volunteers. The returnees brought back a wider experience of travel and contacts and, in some instances, usable skills.

Culture

While acculturational forces were already at work in the seventeenth century, this section will be generally concerned with presenting Chippewa "traditional" culture as it still existed and was recorded in the latter half of the nineteenth century.

In Wisconsin and Minnesota the Chippewa found themselves in a mixed conifer-deciduous environment of which they made full use. This was also a well-watered region; many lakes and rivers provided abundant fish, avenues of travel and transportation, extensive wild-rice fields, and cattails and bulrushes needed for mats. The large and small game inhabiting the forests provided the primary source of food, with the hides, especially buckskin, converted into clothing.

The basis of Chippewa material culture was forest products: wood, bark, and plant fibers. Wood was used to make utensils, implements, and weapons. Birchbark served as wigwam coverings, storage containers, and the "skin" of their canoes, for which they are famous. Inner barks were used: basswood for bag weaving and twine, cedar for mat making, and willow for kinnikinnick, which was smoked with their tobacco. The sugar maple was tapped for sap that was converted into sugar. Nuts, berries, and fruits were gathered. A great variety of medicine was concocted from roots, stems, and leaves of local flora. Their knowledge of the forest and its resources was impressive and it was necessary for survival in a region of long, and often severe, winters. Considerable time and effort were invested in wresting a living from the forests.

Subsistence

The search for food involved a seasonal shifting of activities and necessitated a seminomadic way of life. The Chippewa operated out of a summer village base, staying within a radius of perhaps 50 miles. During the summer the main economic activities consisted of fishing (year-round activity); gathering wild foods, especially berries and nuts; and, in some areas, gardening small plots of corn, beans, and squash. The women were highly involved in these activities and much of the food gathering was done by women and children.

In the early fall they moved to the wild-rice fields, a number of families joining together to camp and work. After the wigwams were set up, the greater amount of time, for several weeks, was spent harvesting and preparing the rice (*Zizania aquatica,* which is not related to domestic rice). The men poled the canoe through the fields, while the women knocked the grains into the canoe with a pair of cedar sticks. After it was brought to shore, the rice was laid out to dry, then parched over a fire. The outer husks were removed by tramping in a skin-lined pit, and finally the rice was winnowed with the aid of a birchbark tray. As with other crops, they held a ceremony for the "first fruit," to thank the *manito·k* (gods); at this time, some of the first harvest of rice was cooked and eaten. When they returned to the village, the prepared rice was stored in mococks (birchbark containers) and would keep indefinitely. Wild rice has remained important to the Chippewa, both as a food, which they prize, and as a cash crop, which is sold to the Whites (fig. 2).

While hunting was done much of the year, it was intensified in winter, when the Chippewa moved to the hunting grounds where they could find deer, moose, wolf, fox, and bear. Deer, usually the most plentiful game, were

right, Thomas Y. Crowell Company: Farber and Dorris 1975.
Fig. 2. Southwestern Chippewa wild-rice harvesting in aluminum canoe and old-style parching. Photographs by Joseph C. Farber, 1972, at Nett Lake, Minn.

valued for both the food and the hide, which was used to make most of their clothing. After killing a bear, there was a special ceremony and feast.

Meat was roasted or boiled for eating. The surplus was cut into thin slices, dried, and then smoked on a rack over a slow fire, pounded on a rock to flatten it, and finally stored in birchbark containers.

During the winter the men also tended their trap lines and fished. Baited steel traps were set along the shores of lakes and streams to catch mink and muskrat. For fishing, a hole was cut in the ice and the fisherman dangled a wooden lure in the water to attract the fish, which was speared.

In late spring, usually in March, a number of families set up a wigwam camp in a sugar bush and, as in the rice camps, a festive spirit prevailed. The sugar maple tree was tapped by making a horizontal gash in the trunk, three or four feet above the ground. A cedar spile was inserted, at a downward angle, allowing the sap to drip into a birchbark bucket on the ground. The sap was collected, boiled, granulated in a wooden trough, and then stored in the mococks (fig. 3). The sugar was used on wild rice, vegetables, and even fish. Thus, it served as a seasoning (they did not use salt), as candy (fig. 4), and as a refreshing drink mixed with water.

Clothing

The basic dress of the men was a breechclout, leggings, and moccasins, all fashioned of tanned buckskin. In cold weather a buckskin robe was worn, and in later times, trade blankets. The breechclout was a buckskin strip, about four feet by a foot and a half, that was passed between the legs and over a thong, leaving a flap free in

Dept. of Anthr., Smithsonian: left to right, 278160, 278170, 278122.
Fig. 3. Maple sugaring equipment from Minnesota. left, Spoon to stir granulating sugar; center, birchbark cones containing sugar; right, mocock (from White Earth) made of sewed birchbark with etched designs, containing about 5 pounds of sugar. Height of right 18.5 cm, rest same scale; all collected before June 1913.

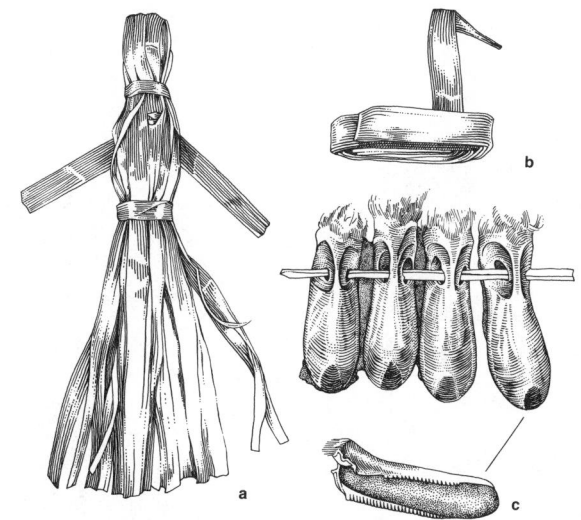

Dept. of Anthr., Smithsonian: a, 317214; b, 317213; c, 278169.
Fig. 4. Children's toys from Minnesota. a, Female doll made of cattails; b, duck made of cattails; c, strung duck bills, filled with maple sugar for a child's treat. Length of female doll 16.5 cm, rest same scale; a and b collected before 1921, c before 1913.

the front and rear. During the early twentieth century, this was replaced by a pair of square panels worn front and rear over trousers. The leggings reached from the ankle to the crotch; they were held up by a thong tied to the belt. They had an outer fringe and often were decorated with beadwork. The Chippewa had several styles of moccasins, the oldest of which was made of one piece of buckskin with a plain seam up the back and a "puckered" seam up the front. The popular style, in more recent times, had a pair of cuffs and elliptical vamp piece sewed onto the upper front in puckered fashion, with a central seam leading down to the toe. Both the cuffs and the vamp were usually beaded (fig. 5). The headdress could be a fur fillet, a yarn sash wound around the head as a turban (fig. 6), or, on special occasions, a roach. This was a brushlike crest of animal hair worn down the center of the head. It consisted of deer or moose hair, dyed red, and was combined with rows of porcupine hair. The final embellishment was a single eagle feather swiveling in a bone socket at the center of the roach (fig. 7).

The women's basic garment was a sleeveless dress made of two buckskins, one for the front and one back. These were sewed together at the shoulders and held in place by a belt. It was worn over a nettle-fiber undershirt. Moccasins and leggings, which were shorter and wider than the men's, completed the costume. With the coming of the trader, there was an ever-increasing use of broadcloth in place of buckskin for the dress and leggings; this was also true for the men's costume. In 1972, the only element of Chippewa costume in daily use was the buckskin moccasin worn by a few of the older people. Indian costumes appeared only on ceremonial occasions and at dances for the tourists.

Fig. 5. A group from Red Lake, Minn., visiting Washington. left to right, Matchis-skank 'someone traveling' (Johnson) with medicine pouch; Tabaiwatang (*te·pwe·we·ttank* ?) 'sound of eating' wearing a James Buchanan peace medal issued in 1857; Bashicta-nogueb 'high up in the sky' (Charles Sucker). Photographs by DeLancey Gill, 1901.

Structures

The most common dwelling was the dome-shaped wigwam. This consisted of a pole framework covered with birchbark and cattail matting. The butt ends of cut saplings were sharpened and set vertically into the ground about two feet apart in a circle or ellipse. One pole and its opposite were bent toward the center to form an arc, the ends tied with basswood strips. After the vertical poles were tied, other saplings were added in a horizontal position. Beginning at the doorway, a mat was unrolled along the base and tied to the first horizontal pole. Other mats were added to complete the circumference. The upper portion of the structure was covered with sheets of birchbark panels sewed together, about three by five feet in size; at each end was fastened a wooden strip to which the ties were attached. A smoke hole was left at the top center. The only other opening, the doorway, was covered with bark, hide, or a blanket (figs. 8–9). The cattail mats, prepared in summer, and the birchbark sheets, prepared in spring, were rolled up and transported to the house site. The saplings were collected from the area of the new house site at the time of building. Inside the wigwam was a central fireplace and around the sides were mats and furs for sleeping and for storage. The larger, elliptical wigwams, occupied by several families, had a fireplace at either end, opposite the door. Adults lived along the sides with the eldest near the door; the young occupied the central portion.

Another type of structure was the peaked lodge: a type of A-frame supporting a ridgepole on which poles were laid sloping to the ground. It was covered with bark and used mostly by hunters as a temporary shelter. A birchbark conical lodge, or one covered with cloth, resembling a tepee, was used to a lesser extent. The bark-covered, gabled style of dwelling, which was utilized as a summer house by adjacent tribes to the south on their semiannual shift from the wigwam, seems not to have been used by the Chippewa. However, Densmore (1929:27) reported that a bark-covered house with a rectangular floor pattern was used in the sugar camps or as a work house when weaving mats.

There were several structures for special purposes: the sweat lodge, the menstrual hut, and the Mide lodge. The first was a small, conical tent in which steam was created by throwing water on hot stones. These were used for individual therapy or at the Midewiwin rites for ceremo-

Fig. 6. Minnesota chief *pakwane·ki·šik,* Hole-in-the-Day (b. 1820s, d. 1868), the second of that name. He wears a wool sash turban. Photograph about 1859–1860, probably by Whitney's Art Gallery of St. Paul, Minn.

Fig. 7. A Leech Lake band delegation to Washington. front row, left to right, *wa·panani·* (?) 'white feather'; *ni·ka·nipine·ss* 'leading bird' (also known as Flat Mouth, his father's name); *ke·kwe·čiwe·pinank* 'trying to throw' (also known as Red Blanket); unknown (or perhaps this is *ke·kwe·čiwe·pinank*). Photograph by DeLancey Gill, 1899.

nial purification. The menstrual hut was a small wigwam, adjacent to the larger ones, used only by a woman during her period. The Mide lodge, or Medicine Lodge (*mite·wika·n*), was a long, arched, pole framework, partially covered with cedar boughs, used only during the semiannual Midewiwin ceremonies (fig. 10).

Technology

The handcrafted products of the Chippewa reflected their forest environment. Wood was the favored and most accessible material, and it was used for a host of utilitarian objects: bowls, ladles, bows and arrows, snowshoes, lacrosse racquets, canoe parts, flutes, drums, cradleboards, fish lures. A profusion of bowls and ladles was carved from burled portions of hardwoods such as maple and birch; these combined a simple beauty of form with attractive grain, which resulted in some of their finest art products. There were human, bird, and animal forms, for magical or religious uses, sculptured with varying degrees of artistry and skill.

Bark was another important medium. Birchbark was the "skin" of the graceful Chippewa birchbark canoes. It covered their wigwams. In lieu of basketry, they constructed a variety of birchbark containers for carrying, storing, and cooking. An art form unique to the Chippewa was the dental pictograph: designs bitten into a thin sheet of folded birchbark that, when opened, exposed a mirror pattern, usually floral (fig. 11). Cedarbark was used to weave mats.

Cattails were sewed into mats to cover the lower portion of the wigwam. Dyed bulrushes were twined over basswood bast to make colorful floor mats (fig. 12). Rectangular bags were woven of basswood twine, later of commercial yarn, utilizing the twining and finger-weaving techniques. Colorful sashes and garters were woven of commercial yarn (fig. 12).

Before European glass beads were introduced, quillwork was the most important decorative applicative. Porcupine quills were dyed, flattened, and sewed in floral designs on buckskin clothing and Mide bags, medicine bags presented to Midewiwin initiates. Floral designs were added to birchbark boxes by inserting the quills into holes punched with awls. Geometric designs were achieved by loom-weaving, the panels then attached to clothing, knife sheaths, and Mide bags. When glass beads arrived, they were substituted for the quills, although the traditional designs were continued. Beadwork embroidery and loomwork was characterized by a heavy emphasis on floral designs: leaf, plant, and flower motifs (figs. 5, 7).

Silk appliqué, or "ribbonwork," was introduced to the Chippewa probably toward the end of the eighteenth century, but it was used only sparingly and never developed into the rich art form found among other tribes of the Great Lakes area. It consisted of cutting a design from one color of silk, sewing it onto a panel of another color, and then attaching this to a broadcloth garment (fig. 13).

Life Cycle

Much of the infant's first year was spent on a cradleboard, a cedar board about two feet long, 10 inches wide,

Fig. 8. Southwestern Chippewa wigwam covered with cattail mats and sheets of birchbark; moccasins and birchbark containers hang outside the entrance. Photograph by Huron H. Smith at Lac du Flambeau, Wis., Dec. 18, 1933.

and three-eighths of an inch thick. A foot brace was attached near one end and a hickory hoop, to protect the head, near the other. The baby was placed on a bedding of sphagnum moss and securely bound to the board with two wrappers of buckskin or cloth. These had been beaded by the mother with great care, and some of the finest floral beaded embroidery was found on these wrappers. At intervals during the day, the baby was taken off the cradleboard for cleaning and exercise. The infant's moccasins had a number of holes cut into the soles, so that if tempted by the spirits (death) to return to their land, he could inform them that his moccasins were in no condition for the journey (Skinner 1911:121). The child was not weaned until the age of two or even later.

The child was named at a special, small gathering of relatives and friends, to which a namer had been invited.

After the traditional offering of food and tobacco to the spirits, the namer held the baby on his lap and conferred not only the name he had obtained during his own fasting dream but also the help and protection of his guardian spirit. A very close and special relationship existed between the two for the rest of their lives; they called each other *ni·yawe·nˀe·nˀ* 'my namesake'.

Children were well treated and raised in a permissive fashion. The raised voice, reprimand, or corporal punishment were rare. Education largely took the form of the father teaching his son the male roles and skills, especially those of hunting, while the mother taught her daughters the female duties and skills. Games and play with the peer group were an important part of the growing-up

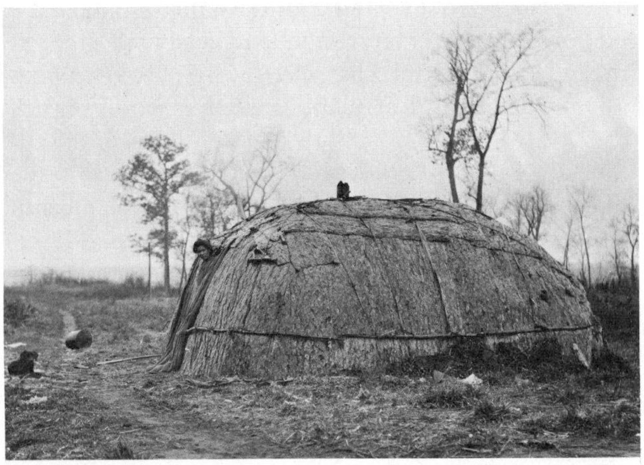

Fig. 10. Interior view of a medicine lodge for the ceremony of initiation into a high degree of the Midewiwin society. Photograph by Frances Densmore, May 1909, at Elbow Lake, White Earth reservation, Minn.

Fig. 9. Southwestern Chippewa wigwam covered with bark. Photograph by Sumner W. Matteson in Wis. before 1920.

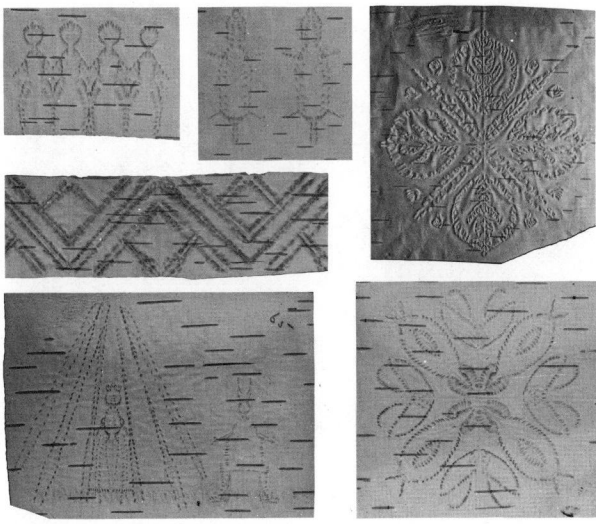

Fig. 11. Southwestern Chippewa bitten pattern transparencies, made by a woman biting soft folded birchbark as an evening pastime. Upper right 8.5 cm vertical measure, rest same scale; collected before 1928.

Fig. 13. Southwestern Chippewa man with scalp locks; red, green, and yellow face paint; brass earring; bead necklace; and blue shirt with red and white appliqué bands. Watercolor by Johann Baptist Wengler, painted in 1851 in Minn. or Wis.

process. The boy's future role as a hunter was reinforced by his early acquaintance with the bow and arrow as well as by institutions such as the Feast for the First Kill. When he had killed his first game, a feast was given by his parents who invited a small group of guests, including a person with power to speak to the spirits. This man gave thanks and asked for continued help for the boy in the hunt. The feast was unpretentious and everyone present ate a small bite of the boy's kill.

The most important phase of the boy's life occurred about the time of puberty: his vision quest for a guardian spirit. He was encouraged by his parents to go into the forest for a few days, to fast by day and dream by night.

Fig. 12. Woman seated on rush mat, weaving yarn sash. Photograph by Robert Ritzenthaler, 1941, at Lac Courte Oreilles reservation, Wis.

At the morning meal he was offered either food or charcoal; if he eschewed the food and chose the charcoal, he rubbed some on his cheeks to indicate he was on a vision quest. Then he would leave for the forest. On the first day the father might go along to help prepare a shelter or a nest in a tree; and he might return to check on the son's welfare and take him water or a bit of food, if he stayed very long. Four days was considered the ideal length of time, four being the religiously symbolic number among the Chippewa. Dreams were regarded as revelations, with the fasting dream being of paramount importance. It gave him a guardian spirit to aid and protect him the rest of his life. It provided him with a supply of names and songs and, in some cases, the power (to be used only later in life) to heal or harm. Rapport was maintained with the guardian spirit, and also with other spirits, by frequent offerings of food and, of great importance, by smoking tobacco in the spirit's honor.

At the time of her first menses, a young girl was required to isolate herself in a small wigwam to fast for four days and nights. If she had a vision, it was regarded as a special blessing, but it was not a requirement, as with the boys.

Courtship behavior of the young was strictly controlled by the adults; the mothers and grandmothers, especially, guarded the maidens. A young man could visit his girl friend within her wigwam, under the watchful eyes of her family, but they could not leave together. The youth could court her by playing his courting flute outside, but the girl was not to leave the lodge. The engagement was established with the young man bringing a deer or some other animal he had killed to the girl's parents. He would be asked to stay and share in the repast and thereafter allowed greater freedom in visiting her. There was no formal marriage ceremony; the couple simply moved out of the lodge for a few days, or they established a lodge of their own. It was most usual for them to live with her parents awhile after marriage. Marriage often was arranged by the family of the young man. Marriage within the clan was banned; cross-cousin marriage was permitted but not preferred. Cross-cousin behavior involved a special "joking relationship," and gifts from the mother's brother to the niece were common. Most marriages were monogamous, although polygyny was sanctioned. An important man might have two or, rarely, three wives. Divorce was simple. If the couple were not compatible, the wife returned to her parents.

Social life was marked by a great penchant for visiting. Besides calling on relatives and friends, there was considerable visiting and conversation before and after religious feasts and ceremonials. Also there was a variety of social dances, with the men always dancing apart from the women. However, dancing was most often a phase of religious rites.

There were athletic games, games of dexterity, and games of chance, all of which usually were accompanied by gambling. The men's major game was lacrosse, in which a team tried to fling a small ball, with the aid of a racquet, across the goal of their opponents. It was a rough game, with many injuries. There was a religious tone to it, in that a game was sponsored by an individual in honor of his guardian spirit. A similar, and less lethal, game was played by the women with a straight stick and a double-ball. There were contests of wrestling, archery, and snowsnake by the men. Their favorite gambling game was the moccasin game (fig. 14). Women gambled with bone dice shaken in a wooden bowl.

Older people were treated with respect and cared for, if necessary. For some, old age was the time when their spiritual power reached its acme; it was a common pattern that a man, in his vision quest, be told that he had the power to cure, but it must not be used until he had "white hair."

Upon death, the person's body was washed and dressed in its finest clothing and ornaments. The hair was carefully combed and braided and the face painted; Densmore (1929:73) reported that the Minnesota Chippewa put a spot of brown, with a red line through it, on each check. In its wigwam, the body lay in state on a sheet of birchbark. If the deceased had been a member of the Midewiwin society, his Mide bag was tucked under his arm. Relatives and friends assembled for the funeral ceremony, conducted by a Mide priest. After the usual

NAA, Smithsonian.
Fig. 14. Moccasin game at White Earth reservation, Minn. Photograph taken or obtained by Frances Densmore, about 1910.

offering of tobacco to the spirits, the priest talked to the dead person. He described the four-day journey the soul would take to the west to join friends and relatives in the Indian village in the sky. The soul was admonished to take the correct trail and to expect along the way to be confronted by a quaking "log," actually the dreaded Water Monster, laid across a stream. He was to address the log as "grandfather" and throw an offering of tobacco into the water. The log would then stop quaking, and the soul could cross in safety to meet his escort to heaven.

At the end of the ceremony, several men carried the body out through a hole, in the west side of the wigwam, to the grave. The doorway was never used, lest the soul return one day through that door. In recent times, with log or frame houses, the body was removed through a west window, which, in instances, had to be enlarged to accommodate the coffin. The body, in early days, was wrapped in heavy birchbark and placed in a shallow grave along with some of the dead person's prized possessions. Later, when sawed boards were obtainable, a low, gabled grave house was built over the interred body (oriented with feet to the west); at the west end an opening was cut for the release of the soul. Beneath the hole a wooden ledge was placed, where food and tobacoo were laid for the four-day journey. Although it was symbolic in nature, the food could be eaten later by any hungry adult or child. Each evening, for four days, a fire was lit at the grave, symbolizing the fire built by the soul as he rested after each day's journey. A grave marker was set into the ground in front of the grave house; this was a narrow board with a drawing of the deceased's totemic animal, inverted to indicate death.

A period of mourning was observed for one year, at the end of which time a ceremony to remove the mourning was held, and the dead person's spouse was allowed to remarry. Shortly after the death of his wife, the husband was brought a bowl of food by several women of his wife's clan. He ate the food and was required to keep the bowl with him for one year, filling it with food to give away and taking it to feasts. If a member of a Drum Society, he could not join in a Drum Dance until a special ceremony was performed. He was not to eat any "first fruits" until fed by another, or the crop would be harmed. He was not to have close contact with women. He must collect women's clothing and blankets. At the year's end he invited, by sending a tobacco invitation, members of his wife's clan to a feast held at a clan member's dwelling; he brought her dish and the bundle of clothing and blankets. After the feast a speaker reviewed his behavior during the past year. If the audience decided he had conducted himself according to the prescribed code, the husband was washed, dressed in new clothing, and his cheeks painted red. The bundle of clothing and blankets was distributed among the women and his mourning bowl given to one of them. He was now released from mourning and free to remarry.

Personality

Some of the characteristics that have been applied to the Chippewa are: self-reliance, individuality at the expense of cooperation, hospitality, patience, control of (and rare exhibition of) emotion, great fear of malevolent sorcery, a lively sense of humor, and lack of enthusiasm for war. Hallowell (1937) used the term "indirect aggression" to describe the situation where an attack on a foe was carried out by gossip or by hiring a sorcerer, in place of a face-to-face encounter.

Social Organization

The aboriginal Chippewa-Ojibwa had a classless, egalitarian society, not highly organized. However, there were people of importance and prestige who achieved positions earned as the result of outstanding abilities as warriors, civil leaders, religious leaders, or shamans. Often the shaman was the most respected and feared member of the band.

The smallest social unit was the nuclear family: parents and their unmarried offspring. A number of families living together formed a band. These bands had from 20 to 50 members and a leader whose political, religious, and economic roles were based on ties of kinship.

This pattern of small, widely scattered, discrete, autonomous bands has been characterized as "atomistic" or "particularistic." However, Hickerson (1962) has argued that this characterization does not apply to the Southwestern Chippewa, who from an early period exhibited collective, relatively large-group interaction in areas such as warfare, sociopolitical organization, and religious ceremonials.

In addition to family affiliations, every individual was a member of a totemic clan named after some animal, bird, or fish. The eponym was called *ninto·te·m* 'my totem'. Clans were exogamous and patrilineal. Thus, a man of the Bear clan must marry a woman of a different clan, but the children would belong to the Bear clan. Clan names and number varied from area to area. Morgan (1877:166) listed 23 clans for the nineteenth-century Minnesota Chippewa. Warren (1885) gave 21 for Minnesota and included five not listed by Morgan.

The dual division, or moiety system, found among other Central Algonquian tribes was not used by the Chippewa; however, there were linked clans, or phratries. Warren (1885:44-50) reported five phratries in use by some Minnesota bands, given here in his spelling and with his English labels, which are not direct translations:

PHRATRY	CLAN
Awause (Fish)	Catfish, Merman, Sturgeon, Pike, Whitefish, Sucker
Businause (Crane)	Crane, Eagle
Ahahwauk (Loon)	Loon, Goose, Cormorant
Noka (Bear)	Bear
Monsone (Marten)	Marten, Moose, Reindeer

In 1972 most people on the Wisconsin Chippewa reservations knew to which clan they belonged, and it still regulated marriage in the sense that, ideally, one should marry outside the clan. The clan animal was drawn, upside down, on the grave marker of those given a non-Christian burial. The offspring of a marriage between Indian and White were facetiously referred to as belonging to the "chicken" clan. The close feeling that existed in former times among clan members has waned, although traces of the respect once demanded in the name of the clan were still found in the 1930s at Lac Courte Oreilles in cases of totemic insult (Ritzenthaler 1945). It was the custom for someone who insulted another's clan animal to be asked to a feast attended by members of the clan insulted. A speaker related the incident of the insulting; the insulter was obliged to eat a bit of the clan animal he had insulted and to gorge himself on other food.

● KINSHIP   The Chippewa kinship system was similar to that of the Cree and differed from the Omaha type found among other Central Algonquian tribes. Kinship terms were nearly all classificatory and through three generations, in accordance with cross-cousin marriage (Landes 1937:19). Two classes were distinguished terminologically in ego's generation: one of prospective mates, the other sexually taboo.

Children were highly desired and a warm relationship existed between parents and children. Parents were responsible for the care, education, and discipline of the child, who was expected to help his parents to the extent of his own capacity. Upon puberty, brother and sister acted with shyness and considerable avoidance, which continued until one of them married.

Expected behavior between kin was expressed in general terms of kindness, and a special behavioral relationship existed between grandparents and grandchildren, with the former expected to watch over and, if necessary,

753

care for the latter. Grandchildren were expected to help their grandparents. A special relationship existed between nephew and maternal uncle, the uncle assuming the functions of teaching and gift-giving. The "joking relationship" between cross-cousins was expected to take on a ribald tone.

Chippewa society was kin-oriented and kinship ties were its chief binding force. Nearly everyone was related to another in the band, either affinally or consanguineally. For kinship schedule and analysis see Landes (1937).

Religion

The religious life of the Chippewa was rich, deep, personal, and of daily concern. Their supernatural world held a host of spirits (*manito·k*) that inhabited trees, rocks, birds, animals, and cosmic phenomena; some dwelt in the sky, some on earth, others underground or in the water. Presiding over all was a paramount spirit, *kičči-manito·*, although this concept may have been the result of Christian influence. Of major importance were the sun, moon, the four winds, thunder, lightning, and thunderbirds. Of great personal concern to the individual was his guardian spirit, acquired in his vision quest, which could be called upon for guidance, help, and protection. Dreams, in general, were regarded as revelations of utmost import, and each dream was reviewed for possible significance.

Besides the benign spirits, there were fearsome, malevolent ones: ghosts, witches, the Water Monster, and the Windigo, a cannibalistic giant who stalked the winter woods in search of people to devour.

The spirits were placated, honored, or manipulated by the individual through prayers and offerings of tobacco and food or through priests and shamans paid in kind for their services. Tobacco was of supreme significance in religious and ceremonial life; it was regarded as an almost sacred substance. A pinch of it could be placed on a rock or stump to alert the spirit to ward off a bad storm or other catastrophe. The initial rite of all religious and ceremonial occasions was the smoking of tobacco, accompanied by a prayer. The smoke ascended to the spirits for their use and comfort; it apprised them that the Indians were thinking of them and honoring them. A gift of tobacco to another carried a holy additive more than its substantive value, and even the outsider soon became aware of the effect of a gift of tobacco. Tobacco usually accompanied an invitation to a feast or ceremony. It was presented, as an overture, to a shaman who, if he accepted it, was committed to use his powers and abilities to aid the client. A warrior accepted an invitation to join a war party by smoking the proffered pipe. Tobacco was placed on the waters before harvesting wild rice, at the base of a tree from which something was to be taken or, in other instances of harvesting or gathering in which an offering was considered a necessary prelude. Food, also,

was a significant offering to the spirits, but secondary to tobacco.

While religion, ordinarily, was an individual affair, there also were small gatherings in the home, involving religious practices. Until the Drum Dance was introduced in the 1870s, and the Peyote cult (in a few places) in the early twentieth century, the Medicine Dance was the only large religious ceremonial.

• MIDEWIWIN The Midewiwin, or Medicine Dance (*mite·wiwin*), was the important ceremony of the Midewiwin society, or Medicine Lodge Society, a curative society, to which membership was obtained by preliminary instruction, payment of considerable fees, and formal initiation at one of the semiannual (in some cases, annual) meetings. The instruction and ritual were conducted by recognized priests, each of whom had an assistant, or runner (*oška·pe·wiss*). Among Wisconsin bands, the ceremony was held in late spring and early fall; it lasted from two to five days, depending on the number of candidates. At a special site, where wigwams had been erected for the closed, nightly sessions, candidates received their instructions. For the final, public ceremony, the special Mide lodge was erected.

There were some regional variations in the ceremony. The following account is based on observations of the dance and on information obtained at the Lac Courte Oreilles Reservation during the 1940s (Ritzenthaler 1953a:182–184).

If someone was sick, or had dreamed he should "go through" the Midewiwin, he sought advice from the Mide priest who gave him instructions and designated the number of blankets and pails for the initiation fees. Each degree required two galvanized water buckets, with the number of blankets being higher for each of the four degrees. Sometimes clothing was substituted. The candidate received a cowrie shell (*mi·kiss*) on a thong, to wear at all times. He was expected to give a series of feasts, to which his sponsors and the priests were invited.

When the priests had decided where the initiation ceremonies would take place, the candidates were sent a small amount of tobacco and then given secret instructions; they were taught songs, meanings, and secrets, depending on the degree each was to take. For the first degree, the origin myth was told in a sketchy version, in greater detail for the higher degrees. The first day, the candidates were led into the Mide lodge, where their blankets and pails had been hung from the ridgepole. Entering from the east, they were seated in the center, each at a decorated stake. The members brought tobacco, food, and their medicine bags; then, led by a priest, they marched around the lodge. They deposited a bit of tobacco on the rock outside the east entrance, entered, and sat along the sides. The cardinal, and dramatic, feature of the initiation was the magical "shooting" of the shell into the candidate's body; actually, the shell was dropped in front of him. This drove out the sickness and

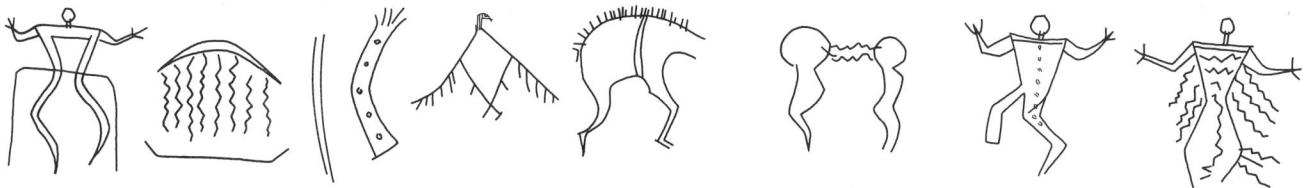

Dept. of Anthr., Smithsonian: 153136.

Fig. 15. Pictographs serving as mnemonics for a Midewiwin song, incised on a birchbark scroll. While some Chippewa pictographs used for songs and other texts have conventional meanings (the fifth and sixth from left represent a thunderbird and a bear, and the double bar in third position indicates a rest period) songs are often specific to an individual and the interpretation of their mnemonic pictographs requires esoteric knowledge derived from personal religious experience (much of the interpretation of this scroll obtained by Hoffman 1891:218-219 is dubious). Length 39 cm; collected at Red Lake, Minn., 1887-1889.

renewed life. He was given a Mide bag as follows: first degree—mink, otter, muskrat, or beaver; second degree—owl or hawk; third degree—snake and fox, or wildcat claw; fourth degree—bear paw, or cub bear.

Then the candidate distributed his blankets and pails to the priests, the runners, and his sponsors. When everyone was initiated, the members marched around the wigwam, holding their Mide bags and "shooting" each other in a general melee. Everyone exited by the west doorway; the initiates were last, taking their Mide bags and the decorated stakes where they had sat.

The question of the antiquity of the Midewiwin has been raised. Warren (1885) and W.J. Hoffman (1891) believed it to have been precontact. Landes (1968:178) stated: "Canadian Ojibwa generally were skeptical of midéwiwin. This agreed with their isolated location on the northern outskirts of the midéwiwin spread. In 1933, Ontario's Manitou Reserve Indians remembered that the Midé Society had been brought to them not much more than thirty years before by the Ponemah villagers at Red Lake reservation, Minnesota. In 1934-35, the Ponemah and neighboring Cass Lake reservation Ojibwa spoke to me of a remembered time when forebears lived without the institution. Still, that was 'long ago'."

Hickerson (1970:54) preferred to regard it as a post-contact, nativistic reaction to European contact, emphasizing "that in the Jesuit Relations covering the period 1640 to 1700 there is not one reference to anything called, or referent to, *Midewiwin* among any upper Great Lakes people. This sets one wondering, since in later times, authors, whether missionaries, traders, or officers of government frequently mentioned, and even in some cases, described, the rites of the Mide Lodge, or 'Grand Medicine,' as they often called it."

Certainly the early explorers in their often hurried visits to the tribes could have easily missed a rite patently secret even among the Indians themselves, a rite that occurred only once or twice a year, and at a special site away from settlement. It is less likely, however, that the missionaries would have missed it, although one might

logically argue that special efforts were made by the Indians to conceal a religious rite in direct conflict with the missionary message. Its antiquity is also suggested by the wide distribution over the Great Lakes region, among many tribes other than the Chippewa. In early historic times, it was being practiced by the Menominee, Winnebago, Ottawa, Potawatomi, Sauk, Fox, and Kickapoo.

Whatever the age of the Chippewa rite, it was certainly woven of Chippewa cultural cloth and without European admixture. The whole concept and ritual appear to be rooted in, and consistent with, the earliest recorded reports of their mythology, cosmology, religious and ethical concepts, preoccupation with health (Ritzenthaler 1953a:179-251), and weltanschauung. The question of its being consistent with the individualistic nature of the Chippewa was raised and answered by Landes (1968:71): "A puzzling question about the Midé Society is why it took root at all among these individualistic Ojibwa bands whose traditional ways ignored a political system and supported only loose, shortlived organizations, chiefly for summer games, dances, and war parties, which ended with each occasion. The puzzle feeds on the secrecy that curtained off knowledge of the Midéwiwin. When [my informant] lifted this secrecy for me, it became evident that the traditional rampant individualism actually operated here too."

DRUM DANCE The religious complex of the Drum Dance originated on the Plains and was brought into Wisconsin during the 1870s. It seems to have been based on the Omaha Grass Dance. The story concerned a young Dakota girl who tried to flee some Indians and White soldiers after a battle, but was trapped in a nearby lake. There she stayed for 6 to 10 days, hidden by lily pads, neither eating nor drinking. Finally, the spirit, praising her for her courage, took her up to the sky, where he told her about the Drum Dance. He explained how the ceremony was to be carried on and gave certain ethical instructions; he told her that peace would occur between all Indians and Whites if she induced her people to perform this ritual. Although she had been close to death, when she awoke, she was cured. The "drum religion," with the sacred drum as the central element, was presented by the Dakota to the Minnesota Chippewa who, in turn, taught it to their Wisconsin relatives. The tenets included peace, good moral conduct, a sense of responsibility, obedience to law, and helping one another.

The ceremony itself revolved around a number of sacred drums, wooden washtubs, each supported off the ground with four stakes. They were copiously decorated with symbolic paint, beadwork, and covered with calf hide (fig. 16). Members were spoken of as "belonging" to a certain drum, each owned by two individuals. Each member had his place around the drum and specific duties: speaker, singer, drum beater, pipe tender, and heater of the drumhead. An intrinsic part of the ritual was smoking the calumet, or peace pipe. Women belonged but had no duties; they accompanied the men's singing by humming, and they joined in the dancing.

The main ceremony, ideally, was held immediately after the Midewiwin and was a four-day event; smaller meetings occurred at other times in private homes. All the drums were assembled in a special lodge, or in an outdoor square (originally, a circle), surrounded by benches or low fencing. Dogs were not allowed, on pain of death. The speakers thanked everyone for coming, acknowledged the help of the drum spirit, and mentioned all the virtues listed above. Only those members seated around the drum sang and drummed, while the other members danced, hopping on one foot and then the other in the

NAA, Smithsonian.

Fig. 16. Drum Dance drum. Photograph by A.E. Jenks, 1899, in Minn.

same place. Each member had his own song, to which he danced when his turn came; after that, others joined him. When he finished his song, he contributed something to a fellow member of his choice; perhaps a blanket, gun, or piece of clothing. An invited representative from another settlement was given a bundle of gifts for his people. He, in turn, would have donations for his hosts. This exchange of gifts was an essential part of the ceremony.

The Drum Dance served as a social clearinghouse, at which there could take place marriage, divorce, or the removal of mourning. In recent years it became primarily social, although prayers were still sung for prosperity, good health, and brotherhood.

• CHIEF DANCE   The Chief Dance (*okiččita·-ni·mi?itiwin* meaning 'Brave Dance') originally was a ceremony held before a war party went out. It enlisted the guardian spirits of a number of people to protect an individual or an entire community and to insure success in battle. Termed the "Chief Dance" at Lac Courte Oreilles, it was called the War Dance at Lac du Flambeau and Lac Vieux Desert, and by the 1940s it had undergone a complete shift in purpose.

The ceremony, as observed at Lac Courte Oreilles Reservation, involved the usual invitation, by tobacco, sent out with a runner. At the feast the speaker, who had rapport with the spirit world, dedicated the tobacco and food. At this dance a tambourine drum was used. The participants recited their war exploits and asked help of their own guardian spirits. They might ask the spirits to ward off sickness, help cure one who was ailing, protect a young man going to the armed services, give a bountiful harvest, or avert severe weather.

• BEAR CEREMONIALISM   Like their Woodland counterparts among the Menominee, Ottawa, and Potawatomi, the Chippewa revered the bear, which played a significant part in their religion, particularly the Midewiwin. This ceremonialism was circumpolar and had come down from the northern tribes.

After the hunter had killed a bear, the head, liberally decorated with ribbons and beadwork, was laid out, with the hide, on a mat. A slice of the tongue was hung up for four days. The body was not chopped up but, to show the respect with which it was held, carefully disjointed with a knife. At the feast, though other food was provided, everyone ate some bear meat. Food bears eat, including maple sugar and berries, was laid next to the body. If it was a male, a nicely beaded man's costume was placed next to the hide; if a female, a woman's costume. The speaker talked to the bear village, calling attention to the fine treatment accorded this visitor and promising that other bears would be similarly, and respectfully, welcomed. The bones were gathered up and buried, never left lying about.

• PEYOTE   Although the Chippewa were preoccupied with health and disease concepts, they did not seem to accept readily the curative cult of Peyote. During the

1940s there was a small, but active, cult for curative purposes, primarily at the Lac du Flambeau reservation in northern Wisconsin. The Lac Courte Oreilles band was in close contact with the Potawatomi, Winnebago, and Lac du Flambeau bands, but the older people resisted efforts to introduce it; the influential Mide priests felt it would interfere with the Midewiwin religion.

• SHAMANISM AND CURING Shamanism was of great moment to the Chippewa. Shamans were both feared and respected for their superior supernatural power, which they could use for good and evil. This power was acquired through the vision quest, but one was warned not to use it until middle age or even later.

There were three classes: the conjuror, the sucking doctor, and the *wa·pano·* 'Morning Star Man'. The conjuror employed the shaking-tent technique, mainly for curing; but he could also cause sickness and death, prophesy, and locate lost persons or articles. The tent varied, as each was built according to the shaman's dream, but basically it was a small pole framework, covered except for the top. Inside, the conjuror consulted with the spirit, or spirits, which came in through the top. Their presence was indicated by the shaking of the tent. The conjuror's role was that of intermediary with the spirits; it was believed that he did not shake the tent, nor did he imitate the spirit voices by ventriloquism. Emerging from the tent, he instructed his client as to the remedy for his illness or gave the answer to his problem.

The sucking doctor's only function was curing. The object causing the disease was removed from the patient's body by sucking it out, magically, through a bone tube.

While rituals of the first two classes of shamans were witnessed in Wisconsin during the 1940s, the *wa·pano·* shaman had long disappeared from the scene. According to W.J. Hoffman (1891:156–157): "It is positively affirmed that evil man'idōs [*manito·k*] favor his desires, and apart from his general routine of furnishing 'hunting medicine,' 'love powders,' etc., he pretends also to practice medical magic." The *wa·pano·*'s ritual involved demonstrations such as his ability to handle red-hot stones or thrust his hands into boiling syrup with no apparent discomfort.

The shaman always worked for a fee. If he accepted the client's gift, he was committed to perform and the fee would be agreed upon. Shamans worked at night or in the evening, aided by an assistant, who took charge of the physical arrangements and did the drumming. Ordinarily, the shaman of the first two classes was also a Mide priest.

Music

Chippewa music was functional and individualistic. Instruments were few: tambourine (fig. 14) and water drums, a variety of rattles, and courting flutes. With the exception of the flutes, the instruments were used to accompany singing. There was a plethora of songs, most

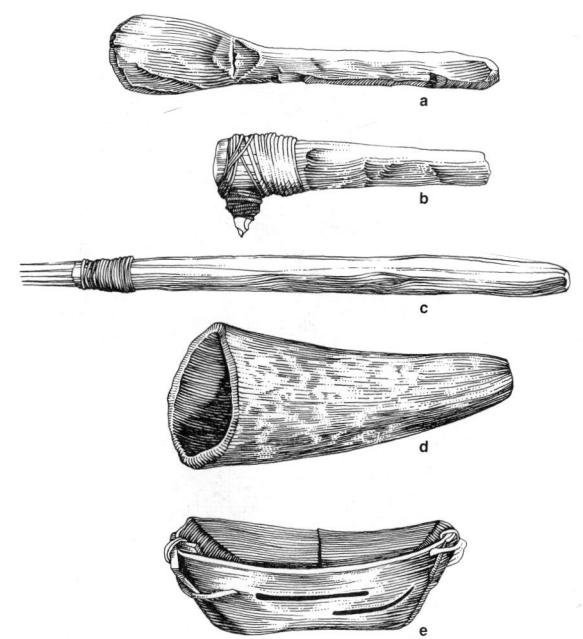

after Densmore 1928:pl. 46.

Fig. 17. Southwestern Chippewa medical appliances. a, Spatula for powdered herbal medicines; b, surgical lance; c, instrument for inserting medicine beneath skin; d, cupping horn; e, birchbark measure for liquid medicine.

of them derived from dreams. They served many purposes: to bring success on a hunt, to insure a good harvest of maple sugar and wild rice, to invoke a guardian spirit, to aid in curative and prophetic rituals. There were also songs for specific situations: before and after a war, during the Midewiwin, and for social occasions such as the Women's Dance. All dancing was accompanied by singing, with the drum for rhythm (fig. 18). The singing had a throaty quality, much vibrato, and a tendency to begin on a high note and descend to a lower. Meaningful words, usually, were interspersed with meaningless syllables.

Folklore

There was a rich store of folktales, serious and humorous, that were told in the wintertime both to entertain and to teach ethical precepts. A major portion of these tales revolved around the culture hero Nanabozho (*we·napošo*), who played a dual role: that of bringing the Indians great gifts such as tobacco, hunting, and agriculture, as well as that of being a prankish and sometimes obscene fool. There were stories of a race of dwarfs and of the Windigos as well as nature tales, such as how the skunk got his stripes. A request for a story was accompanied by the usual gift of tobacco.

Sociocultural Situation in the 1970s

The Chippewa in the 1970s still have some remnants of the traditional economy of hunting; fishing; gathering

757

Fig. 18. Drummers and dancers with large beaded pouches at a powwow at Barwick, Ont., on the Rainy River, June 23, 1899.

berries, nuts, wild rice, and maple sugar; and, to a very limited extent, gardening. Added to this subsistence base are income-producing activities such as cutting and selling pulpwood, seasonal harvesting of off-reservation crops, working for wages in nearby towns, and guiding White fishermen. That the Indians are the lowest income group in the United States is reflected by the fact that a higher number than the national average is on some form of relief.

The economic plight of the Chippewa is quite visible. Houses are mainly of frame; usually in poor repair; without insulation, plumbing, or electricity. The wigwam is rarely seen; it is used occasionally as a temporary dwelling during wild ricing or in the maple sugar camp. Chippewa dress, ordinarily, is that of the poor rural White. Some of the older folk may wear Indian moccasins, and some have Indian costumes donned for their own dances or those performed for the tourist.

Despite long contact with Whites and considerable intermarriage with them, elements of the old culture survive. In somewhat attenuated form may be found religious rites and concepts, folklore, medical practices, the use of clan names, games, arts and crafts, and the value system. The Chippewa language is in lively use,

especially among the older folk, but English is the common language. Pitted against their attempts to retain Indian ways are the impacts of modern education, Christianity, the advantages of modern medical facilities, and the need to make a living in a money economy.

After World War II, the lack of economic opportunity on the reservation resulted in a considerable movement, particularly by the young people, to large cities in search of work. This was stimulated by the Volunteer Relocation Program begun in 1954, whereby offices were set up in the cities to aid in placement of Indians, to provide federal funds for transportation, and to cover interim costs until the family was established. It is estimated that in 1972 nearly half the Chippewa were living in urban centers, particularly in Minneapolis (about 8,000), Milwaukee (about 1,500), Chicago (about 1,000), and Duluth (about 700).

While the city offers economic improvement over the reservation, the urban Indian too often finds himself at the low end of the pay scale, due to the lack of education or a skill, and living in substandard housing. He tends to be law abiding; violations are usually drink-associated. He prefers to interact with other Indians rather than with Whites (almost never with Blacks). The larger cities have

758

set up Indian Centers for social, recreational, or business purposes. Usually, close ties are maintained between urban Indians and their home reservations, and there are frequent returns for various reasons: to visit friends and relatives; to hunt and fish; to attend a wedding, funeral, or religious ceremony.

Synonymy

For a discussion of the tribal names of the Chippewa, see the section on synonymy in "Southeastern Ojibwa," this volume.

Sources

The earliest historical source for the Chippewa is the 73 volumes of the *Jesuit Relations* (JR 1896-1901) covering the period from 1610 to 1791. The descriptions and maps are particularly useful in tracing the distributions and movements of the Chippewa. Warren (1885) concentrates on the eighteenth and first half of the nineteenth centuries in the Minnesota-Wisconsin area. Based mainly on oral traditions collected by Warren, himself part Chippewa, there is a tendency to glorify the Chippewa, especially in the very ample coverage of Chippewa-Sioux wars. Armstrong (1892) presents eyewitness accounts of Chippewa-Sioux battles and Chippewa–U.S. government treaty making during the first half of the nineteenth century. There has been no single attempt to bring together the history of the reservation period, although there have

been numerous articles and monographs, and some books, on Chippewa culture and cultural dynamics for this period. Also, there is Kinietz's (1947) community study of a small band on the Wisconsin-Michigan border.

Important anthropological volumes for the reservation period include Densmore's (1929) excellent general ethnography, volumes on Chippewa music (1910, 1913), and on the use of native plants (1928); Landes's solid fieldwork on the Minnesota-Canadian border produced works on Ojibwa sociology (1937, 1938) and Ojibwa religion (1968). Also, for religion and comprehensive data on the Midewiwin there is W.J. Hoffman's (1891) classic work. Arts and crafts are competently presented by Lyford (1943). Jones (1917-1919) offers folklore in the form of texts. In the field of culture and personality there is Barnouw's (1950) monograph based on fieldwork in Wisconsin as well as the excellent series of articles by Hallowell (see Murdock 1960:212-213). For the prereservation period there are the two provocative monographs focusing on ethnohistory by Hickerson (1962, 1970), and worthy of mention is an interesting and useful account of the Chippewa in the 1850s by the perceptive German traveler Kohl (1860).

Major museum collections of Southwestern Chippewa objects are found at the American Museum of Natural History, New York; Cranbrook Institute of Science, Bloomfield Hills, Michigan; Field Museum of Natural History, Chicago; Milwaukee Public Museum; Museum of the American Indian, Heye Foundation, New York; and Science Museum of Minnesota, Saint Paul.

759

Southeastern Ojibwa

E.S. ROGERS

Within a century after European contact, Ojibwa (ōˈjĭbwā or ōˈjĭbwə) began to expand into southern Ontario and Michigan from a "homeland" that is difficult to define with any precision on the basis of cultural or linguistic data. It is reasonably certain that their homeland was somewhere within an area extending from the east shore of Georgian Bay, west along the north shore of Lake Huron, and a short distance along the northeast shore of Lake Superior and onto the Upper Peninsula of Michigan (fig. 1). Here at the time of European contact lived a number of named groups of Algonquian speakers, who it can be assumed spoke a common dialect although, no doubt, with minor regional variations.* Each group numbered no more than several hundred people, totaling probably not more than 3,000-4,000. The history of these groups is not known in detail, but they were the antecedents of the Indians known in the twentieth century as Chippewa, Ojibwa, Mississauga, and Saulteaux. The first three of these names have been applied to various of the Southeastern Ojibwa groups discussed here, depending on period and location. Their history has been closely linked with that of the Ottawa and Potawatomi and, at times, the Huron, and the present Southeastern Ojibwa population is in part descended from members of these tribes and of the Shawnee and Menominee.

A linguistic survey in the 1970s (Rhodes 1976) found evidence for two major dialects in the Southeastern Ojibwa area, although both share a characteristic pattern of vowel weakening ("Central Algonquian Languages," this vol.). One, which Rhodes calls Central Ojibwa-Odawa, can be identified with the form of speech called Ottawa in the nineteenth century (Baraga 1878-1880) but in the 1970s spoken not only by the Ottawas (or Odawas) of Manitoulin Island and Michigan but also by the Ojibwas (or Chippewas) of the Lower Peninsula of

Michigan and of that part of southwestern Ontario lying west of a north-south line drawn through the base of the Bruce peninsula. East of this line is the second major dialect, Rhodes's Eastern Ojibwa, spoken by people called Ojibwa (or Chippewa) and Mississauga and showing certain resemblances to the Ojibwa of the Upper Peninsula. There is also subdialectal variation within each major dialect, and some groups and individuals whose speech is fundamentally of one type use certain forms characteristic of the other.

Contact, 1615-1650

Ojibwa were first encountered by the French in the early 1600s. Samuel de Champlain in 1615 most likely met some along the eastern shores of Georgian Bay. As the French explored westward—Étienne Brûlé was the first about 1622 (Butterfield 1898:100-108)—they encountered other groups. The Jesuits made their way to Sault Sainte Marie in 1641 (JR 11:279) and opened the Mission of Saint Peter in 1648 for the Indians of Manitoulin Island and the northeast shore of Lake Huron (R.B. Orr 1915:7).

Extremely little is known of the way of life of the Southeastern Ojibwa until after 1650. The Jesuits reported in 1647-1648 that the Algonquian tribes north of the Hurons "live solely by hunting and fishing and . . . roam as far as the 'Northern sea' " to trade for "Furs and Beavers, which are found there in abundance" (JR 33:67), and "all of these Tribes are nomads, and have no fixed residence, except at certain seasons of the year, when fish are plentiful, and this compels them to remain on the spot" (JR 33:153).

Dispersal, 1650-1760

After the Huron had been routed in 1649-1650, the Iroquois began putting pressure on Ojibwa to the north. Temporarily some groups withdrew westward but no mass exodus appears to have taken place. In fact, some Ojibwa are thought to have retaliated (Elliott 1896:354). In spite of what may have happened, the Iroquois continued their attacks. Algonquian groups, previously politically autonomous, often became reduced in numbers through warfare, starvation, and European diseases. When this occurred, they amalgamated with other

* The orthography used to spell words in Ojibwa (including Chippewa, Saulteaux, Ottawa, and Algonquin varieties) in this *Handbook* follows the analysis of Bloomfield (1946, 1957) and uses his symbols. Vowel length is indicated by the raised dot rather than vowel doubling, and the preaspirated stops (such as *hk*) written in words from the Severn dialect correspond to the long or tense consonants of the other dialects, written as geminates (such as *kk*). Severn and Saulteaux *h* when not before a consonant corresponds to ʔ in other dialects. Short vowels are written with their maximally differentiated pan-Ojibwa qualities (*i, a, o*), Bloomfield's reduced-vowel symbols (e and u) not being used. The Ojibwa forms were phonemicized by Ives Goddard and John Nichols.

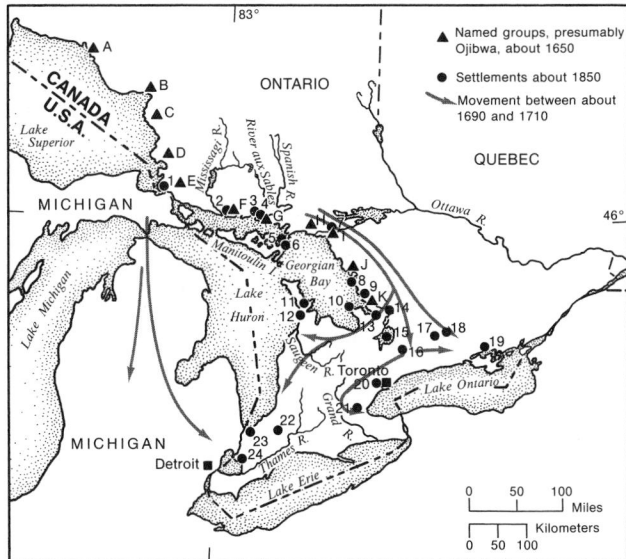

Fig. 1. Southeastern Ojibwa locations, about 1650-1850. Named groups, presumably Ojibwa, about 1650: A, Marameg; B, Ojibwa; C, Mantouek; D, Noquet; E, Saulteaux; F, Mississauga; G, Amikwa; H, Nikikouek; I, Achiligouan; J, Outchougai; K, Ouasouarini. The locations of these early groups are uncertain; at least some of A-D were probably on the Upper Peninsula of Michigan. Settlements about 1850: 1, Sault Sainte Marie; 2, Blind River; 3, Serpent River; 4, Spanish River; 5, Manitowaning; 6, Wikwemikong; 7, Pickerel; 8, Parry Island; 9, Moose Deer Point; 10, Christian Island; 11, Cape Croker; 12, Saugeen; 13, Matchedash; 14, Rama; 15, Georgina Island; 16, Scugog; 17, Alnwick; 18, Chemong; 19, Rice Lake; 20, Credit; 21, New Credit; 22, Chippewas of the Thames; 23, Sarnia; 24, Walpole Island.

living on Manitoulin Island (JR 55:153), as had about half of the Mississauga.

Until the last decade of the seventeenth century, Southeastern Ojibwa had occupied only the Precambrian Shield about the northern shores of Lake Huron. During the 1690s, some began moving south into extreme southern Ontario and soon replaced, often it appears by force, the Iroquois who had settled after 1650 along the north shores of Lakes Erie and Ontario (P.J. Robinson 1965:58-59; NYCD 4:505, 694-695, 899, 5:247; Hammond 1905:71). By 1702 a group from the mouth of the Humber River had settled near Fort Frontenac at the east end of Lake Ontario and proceeded to terrorize the Iroquois who lived there, destroying their village in 1704. Around 1707 Ojibwa arrived in the Niagara region unopposed by the Iroquois (Wraxall 1915:52; Severance 1917, 1:162). Several years earlier, some "Mississauga" who wished to join the Iroquois and transfer their trade to the English settled near a Seneca village at the mouth of the Humber River (P.J. Robinson 1965:59-60). This desire was voiced again in 1708 (Wraxall 1915:52). In 1710 these Ojibwa were joined by some Amikwa (P.J. Robinson 1965:69). About 1720, the French, to intercept the Ojibwa and secure their furs, built a post at the mouth of the Humber River and a fort at Niagara (NYCD 5:588-590). As Ojibwa moved into southern Ontario, others extended their occupation of the Lower Peninsula of Michigan (Kinietz 1940:319). Antoine Laumet de Lamothe Cadillac contributed to the southern expansion

groups. In the process, many lost their group identity. The Amikwa, Marameg, and Nikikouek, for example, as named entities had disappeared by the end of the period but not necessarily the people themselves. The Saulteaux of Sault Sainte Marie by about 1670 had become so reduced in numbers, to about 150, that they formed a union with three other groups who numbered slightly more than 550 (JR 52:133). Throughout the period, Sault Sainte Marie was a focal point for the native people who inhabited specific areas both to the east and to the northwest as well as for the Saulteaux (the French name for the people of this locality), who considered it their home (JR 54:129-131).

Starting in the mid-seventeenth century, the Ojibwa began coming to the Saint Lawrence to trade. At the same time, the Jesuits expanded their work in the interior by building more mission stations. About 1667, they established the "Mission to the Outchibouec" at Sault Sainte Marie (JR 51:61) and several years later the "Mission of St. Simon" on one of the islands on the north shore of Lake Huron. The second mission was to serve the Mississauga, Amikwa, and other groups in the area (JR 55:99-101). Some, if not all, of the Amikwa (fig. 2) had by this time moved from the mainland and were

Thomas Gilcrease Inst. of Amer. Hist. and Art, Tulsa: Granville 1701.
Fig. 2. An Amikwa man, rather imaginatively drawn about 1700.

when in 1701 he brought Ojibwas from the area of Sault Sainte Marie to Detroit (Kinietz 1940:229). Ojibwas in 1723 resided along the Saginaw River (WHC 16:430); in 1737, the River aux Sables, (MPHC 34:151); and in the 1740s expanded in the neighborhood of L'Arbre Croche (WHC 17:63; NYCD 10:34).

By the early part of the eighteenth century, Ojibwas were well established in country to the south of their former homeland. Toward the close of the second decade of the eighteenth century an estimated 300 Ojibwa or "about 60 or 80 men" were living in a village at the north end of Lake Saint Clair (NYCD 8:1058, 9:888; WHC 16:370). Others lived along the north shore of Lake Ontario, some at Quinté (Kent), others at Toronto, and at the Head of the Lake, in all consisting of about 150 able-bodied men (P.J. Robinson 1965:64), perhaps totaling 700-800 people. For 1736 the French gave the following estimates of Ojibwa in southern Ontario: 60 men at Lake Saint Clair and 150 at Quinté, the head of Lake Ontario, the Humber River, and Matchedash (NYCD 9:1054, 1056-1058), perhaps in all 1,000-1,500 people.

As the period advanced, a generalized Upper Great Lakes Indian culture emerged (Quimby 1960:147-157). Groups that formerly had distinctive styles of dress and other customs in time became intermingled, blending into one their slightly varied ways of life. Furthermore, the adoption of similar European trade goods gave a certain uniformity in the material culture of all the Indians of the area. It was reported in 1718, for example, that the Mississauga of Matchedash Bay had the same customs as the Ottawa (WHC 16:370).

The people living along the north shore of Lake Huron were migratory except for certain seasons of the year when they remained in those localities most productive of fish or when they planted and harvested their crops. The Saulteaux, Mississauga, and Amikwa undertook some gardening, but because of adverse climatic conditions their corn did not always ripen (Kinietz 1940:370-371). In any event, none was dependent upon their crops.

During the summer, Indians, some on a regular basis, others irregularly, traveled to Sault Sainte Marie. The rapids there supported an extensive fishery during September and October (Carver 1778). Dexterity and strength were needed to be successful. An individual had to stand upright in a bark canoe among the rapids and thrust a dip net deep into the water to secure the fish. The operation was repeated over and over again, six to seven large fish being taken each time, until a load was obtained (Bacqueville de la Potherie 1911-1912, 1:275-276).

The Saulteaux, Mississauga, and Nikikouek left their gathering centers in June and dispersed along the shores of Lake Huron. The Mississauga before doing so gathered at the mouth of the Mississagi River where they took sturgeon and other fish. While gone from their gathering centers, the Saulteaux collected sheets of bark from birch trees for making canoes and covering their lodges both summer and winter. The Amikwa secured trout, sturgeon, and whitefish. The Saulteaux and Amikwa during the fall gathered blueberries, which they preserved for the winter; the Saulteaux speared sturgeon. When the crops were nearly ripe, the people returned home. At the approach of winter, they again moved to the shores of Lake Huron where they killed beaver and moose. They did not return to their gathering centers until spring when they again planted their gardens (Kinietz 1940:370-371).

Those Ojibwa who had settled on an island slightly upriver from Detroit had by the early part of the eighteenth century cleared the land for cultivation and apparently lived much like their neighbors, the Ottawa and Huron (Kinietz 1940). An important summer occupation was the making of birchbark canoes for sale to the traders (WHC 16:370). The Ojibwa who inhabited the north shore of Lake Ontario and the Lower Peninsula of Michigan no doubt subsisted by hunting and fishing and, it can be surmised, by gathering wild rice and maple sap. The trapping of fur-bearing animals must have been undertaken, enabling the Southeastern Ojibwa to secure European trade goods on which by now they had come to rely. Yet life during this period was not easy, especially for those Ojibwa about the north shore of Lake Huron. The Mississauga often suffered from famine during the winter and those on Manitoulin Island sometimes faced the same conditions in September. At these times, the people were forced to eat the inner bark of trees (fir), roots, acorns, tripe-de-roche from which they made a soup, mooseskins, and moccasins (JR 55:151).

The sociopolitical organization of the Southeastern Ojibwa is difficult to discern from the accounts that have been left. Partly this is due to the paucity of information but, more important, it was a time of change. The native people were often on the move, preventing stabilized conditions. The regrouping of peoples, often of diverse origins, disrupted the sociopolitical organization, and the continued recurrence of reamalgamations throughout the period hampered the development of new structures. Moreover, attempts were often made by Europeans to gain political control over the Indians, and this had a tendency to suppress any native political organization that might have emerged. Nevertheless, these events did not prevent some formal sociopolitical system from existing.

The Ojibwa along the north shore of Lake Huron were organized in small bands, each consisting of several hundred people. Each band appears to have been headed by a chief, who was sometimes installed by means of a special ceremony. In one instance, the chief of the Amikwa had died and his eldest son three years later intended to assume his father's title. He invited various bands to attend the games and other ceremonies that he wished to hold in his father's honor. At the same time, he planned to resuscitate his deceased father by taking his name (JR 55:137).

762

It is suggested that during this period new social units, patrilineal and nonlocalized totemic associations, emerged among the Ojibwa of southern Ontario. As the small bands extant during the previous period became dispersed, often reduced in numbers and intermingled, a totemic system of identification is assumed to have developed that allowed people to maintain bonds with one another even though they had become widely scattered. It has been argued that the groups (bands) that existed during the preceding period were localized patrilineal clans (Hickerson 1966:7-9), but evidence for this is problematical (see Eggan 1955:527; Rogers 1967a). Whatever the case may have been at the time of European contact, by the middle of the eighteenth century totemic groups existed among the Southeastern Ojibwa.

Although missionaries were active during the period, the traditional religion of the Southeastern Ojibwa remained strong. The "vision quest" was of extreme importance, the elderly women being most determined in this belief. When a child reached the age of between 10 and 12, his father instructed him in the proper way of determining what his guardian spirit throughout life would be. The youth was told to fast for several days in order to receive a dream or vision in which his future guardian spirit would visit him. At the end of the fast, the father questioned his son in great secrecy as to what had occurred. If no spirit had appeared, the fast began again and continued until the individual had received the blessings of a spirit. When this finally occurred he told his father the good news (JR 51:159). An individual's guardian spirit might be a bear, a beaver, a bird, or similar creature. After having acquired his guardian spirit, the youth killed the animal or bird that had blessed him and placed a segment of it in the most conspicuous part of the lodge. He then made a feast in its honor during which he addressed it in a most respectful manner. Thereafter this particular species was recognized as his guardian spirit and the individual carried the skin of this animal or bird to war, on the hunt, or on a trip (JR 67:161).

Although each individual received spiritual "power" from the spirits, some received more than others and thereby could assume the role of medicine men. Often one of the leading old men of the group discharged this function for the whole community.

Disease and illness were frequently considered due to improper conduct exhibited toward the supernatural or inflicted upon an individual because of some social transgression. A common cause of illness was the failure to give a feast after a successful hunting trip.

The Saulteaux, perhaps others, held a ceremony that, by a description given in 1710, was the Midewiwin (*mite·wiwin*). The members of the society made known to the public by a speech that they were going to perform the Medicine Dance in the lodge of a given person and at that time the medicine men would show the effects of their knowledge and power (Kinietz 1940:372-374).

Land Cessions, 1760-1830

The Southeastern Ojibwa first began to cede the land they occupied to the British and Americans after about 1760, at which period some Ojibwas residing about the Niagara River had an alliance with the Six Nations confederacy of New York State, first initiated over 50 years previously. Here in 1764, the British made their first purchase of land in Ontario from these two peoples; however, not until 1781 did the Ojibwa and the British sign a treaty regarding this property (Morris 1943:15). Sales continued, and by 1830 the Ojibwa of southern Ontario had ceded most of their land to the British Crown and were becoming confined to less and less territory, finally being encouraged to reside upon a series of relatively small reserves set aside for "their benefit" (Surtees 1966). In the United States, Southeastern Ojibwa began signing treaties with the government in 1815 (Mooney and Thomas 1907g:278). By 1842 the Indians of Michigan had ceded all their land (Greenman 1961:26). The establishment of small villages, such as Rice Lake, Saugeen, Walpole Island, Credit, and Chemong, began during the last decade of the period. As time passed, the Ojibwa became more and more economically interrelated with the Euro-Americans. The Ojibwa kept the inhabitants of Kingston, Niagara, and other towns in southern Ontario supplied with fish and game (Wild 1799:295). The Ojibwa of the Bay of Quinté sold maple sugar to the Whites. At the same time, the Ojibwa frequently became involved with various military enterprises. After the British secured control of Canada from the French, they initiated a new policy toward the Indians: no gifts, no ammunition, no provisions. Pontiac's attempt (which nearly succeeded) to oust the British in 1763 from the Upper Great Lakes followed. Ojibwa from the Grand and Thames rivers in Ontario joined his cause (W. Johnson 1921-1965, 3:457, 4:134, 10:861, 937; Peckham 1947:149). During the War of 1812, Oshawana led the Ojibwa at the Battle of the Thames (Cumberland 1904:54, 57, 87); also involved was Shinguacouse ("Little Pine") and his men from Sault Sainte Marie (A.B. Jameson 1838, 3:233); and Okemos of Michigan was said to have been second in command to Tecumseh (Greenman 1961:28).

Little information exists about the way of life of the Southeastern Ojibwa during this period. On many of the islands on the north shore of Lake Huron from the French River to the Mississagi River, they continued to raise limited quantities of corn. Some who resided during the summer at Sault Sainte Marie went to the west during the winter to hunt. The main animals taken were deer, raccoon, beaver, and marten. Each family had its own lands with the exclusive rights to hunt upon them (Henry 1969:36, 62, 123, 141). Apparently at this time "family trapping territories" emerged in southern Ontario as a mechanism of resource allocation.

A major subsistence activity of the Southeastern Ojibwa was fishing. On the borders of Lake Ontario, the Ojibwa speared salmon and other large fish by torchlight from a canoe. Along the north shore of Lake Huron, sturgeon fisheries were exploited during the summer (Henry 1969:35-36). The Ojibwa who resided at Sault Sainte Marie and others from surrounding areas depended as formerly upon the productive whitefish fishery occurring in the Saint Mary's River. These fish, weighing between 6 and 15 pounds each, formed a large portion of the native people's winter provisions. Once caught, they were dried over a smoky fire (Henry 1969:52, 62).

Where possible the Southeastern Ojibwa gathered wild rice, maple sap, and other vegetal products. The Ojibwa of Sault Sainte Marie often relied upon maple syrup for food, and its preparation was an important activity. In the spring, after the winter search for furs and during the final muskrat hunt, the women left for the maple groves to make sugar, some of which they bartered to the traders. While the women collected the sap, boiled it, and completed the sugar, the men were busy cutting wood, making fires, and hunting and fishing, in part to supply food for the camps. Occasionally, Indians lived solely for a time upon maple sugar (Henry 1969:70).

As the period drew to a close increasing White pressure forced many of the Southeastern Ojibwa to occupy a series of villages usually located on reserves (in Canada) or reservations (in the United States) allocated to them by treaty. These villages were established roughly between 1820 and 1850 in the extreme south and later farther north (fig. 3). The government and missionary societies played a role in the establishment of some, if not all, of these villages (M. Ray 1954:10-18, A.B. Jameson 1838, 1:296; U.S. Department of Commerce 1974:227). The economic system of the Ojibwa then began to alter still further as the people started to farm (A.B. Jameson 1838, 2:271). In 1807 the Ojibwa of Saginaw, Michigan, at their own request were supplied with agricultural and iron-working equipment and a blacksmith was hired to instruct them (Greenman 1961:29).

Although missionary endeavors were intensified at this time, the medicine men remained the spiritual leaders of the people. They had the knowledge and ability to heal and to perform other functions. Their services were always paid for by a present made before they began a performance. To effect a cure, a medicine man with special training employed a rattle and "sucking tubes." Medicine men could inflict as well as remove disorders (Henry 1969:115-116).

A special sacrifice might be made to ask the blessings of the spirits to aid in hunting and to protect the family from the dangers of winter. A dog was secured, his feet tied together, and the animal then thrown into a stream. At the same time, a long prayer was addressed to the Great Spirit (Henry 1969:128-129). Burial customs are

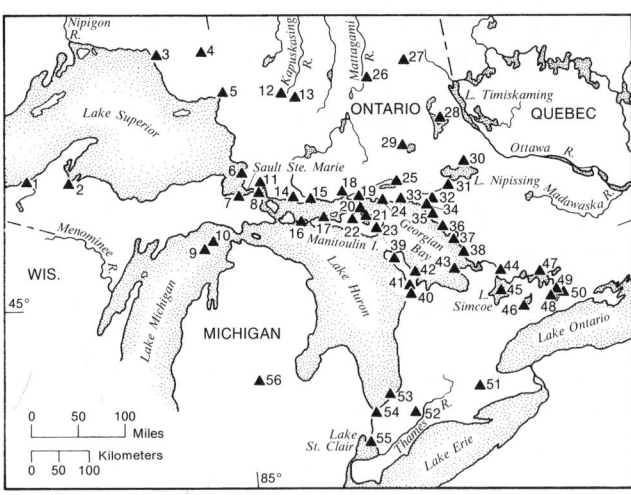

Fig. 3. Southeastern Ojibwa reservations and reserves in 1968: 1, Ontonagon; 2, L'Anse; 3, Pic River; 4, Mobert; 5, Gros Cap; 6, Goulais Bay; 7-8, Bay Mills; 9, Beaver Island; 10, Hog Island; 11, Garden River; 12, Chapleau; 13, Mountbatten; 14, Thessalon; 15, Mississagi River; 16, Cockburn Island; 17, Sheshegwaning; 18, Serpent River; 19, Spanish River; 20, Sucker Creek; 21, Sheguianda; 22, West Bay; 23, Manitoulin Island (Wikwemikong); 24, Whitefish River; 25, Whitefish Lake; 26, Mattagami; 27, Matachewan; 28, Bear Island; 29, Wahnapitae; 30, Nipissing; 31, Dokis; 32, French River; 33, Point Grondin; 34, Henvey Inlet; 35, Magnetawan; 36, Shawanaga; 37, Parry Island; 38, Moose Deer Point; 39-40, Saugeen; 41, Chief's Point; 42, Cape Croker; 43, Christian Islands; 44, Rama; 45, Georgina Islands; 46, Scugog; 47, Mud Lake; 48, Rice Lake; 49, Sugar Island; 50, Alnwick; 51, New Credit; 52, Caradoc; 53, Kettle and Stony Point; 54, Sarnia; 55, Walpole Island; 56, Isabella. The dialect affiliations of a number of the Southeastern Ojibwa and the Southwestern Chippewa groups have not been determined, and the repartition of the groups shown on the maps of reservations and reserves is geographical (see "Southwestern Chippewa," fig. 1., this vol.). For the groups that have been identified as specifically Ottawa, see "Ottawa," fig. 6, this vol.

not known with the exception of one interment of a young man attributed to this time period (Kidd 1951).

Farming, 1830-1930

As the occupation of southern Ontario and Michigan by Euro-Americans continued, the Ojibwa had to restrict their movements and utilization of the land more and more. In Michigan a series of treaties was signed during the early nineteenth century (H.H. Tanner 1974), some with the intent of removing the Indians westward; but few left. One treaty signed in 1836 was with the Swan Creek and Black River bands. Approximately 60 members of these two bands in 1839 moved to Kansas (see "Delaware," fig. 5c, this vol.). Their descendants became enfranchised in 1900 (Morgan 1959:82; Romig 1910; Weslager 1974). And by 1840 a few Ojibwas had migrated to Manitoulin Island (Neumeyer 1971:277-281). Additional treaties were signed in the 1850s (U.S. Department of Commerce 1974:227, 232). In addition to the land cessions concluded in Ontario during the preceding period many signed the Robinson-Huron Treaty in 1850 (Morris 1943:30-33). William B. Robinson on behalf of the British Crown negotiated with the Indians about the shores of Georgian Bay, Lake Huron, for the transfer of their land, considered to extend to the height of land to the north and east, to the government in return for a series of reserves (fig. 3).

The Ojibwa rapidly adopted farming in the extreme southern part of Ontario and Michigan between 1820 and 1840 and somewhat later to the north. For a time, farming appears to have been on a rather extensive scale. The people raised hay, wheat, oats, peas, Indian corn, potatoes, and other vegetables, and kept livestock; some families had small orchards. Near the end of the century, the Indians on Manitoulin Island were reported to be showing a "steady improvement" in agricultural pursuits. Some lived in log cabins, and at Birch Island the people had built wooden cottages (Burden 1895:68). Although farming continued to be practiced by the Indians throughout the century, there are indications that after the initial start, farming did not increase greatly in economic importance and in some cases soon began to decline (De Mille 1971; Rogers and Tobobondung 1975).

While farming played a crucial role in the economy, the Ojibwa also collected wild rice and maple sap, hunted, and fished (see Flannery 1940; Johnson 1929; Jenness 1935). At Rice Lake, along the western shores of Lake Ontario, and in the Bay of Quinté, wild rice was an important food, although maple sugar was probably more so. Each family at Chemong Lake had its own sugar bush, and a common occupation of the women each spring was the preparation of maple sugar (Chamberlain 1888:155-156; Radin 1928:663-664). The collecting of berries was no doubt undertaken by all the Southeastern Ojibwa whenever the opportunity occurred.

Hunting and fishing supplied the Southeastern Ojibwa with food, and trapping supplied the pelts for exchange with Whites for their merchandise and sometimes food. Undoubtedly, considerable variation existed from group to group depending upon the availability of game resources. In the 1840s the Ojibwa living along the Thames River usually left home toward the end of October and returned at the beginning of January. They were away again for a month in the spring hunting (Slight 1844). To the north at Spanish River, the Indians went fishing in the fall, during the winter took rabbits and partridge, and then in the spring planted their crops (Burden 1895:87). The Indians hunted primarily deer, occasionally bear and duck, and most other forms of wildlife (Radin 1928:661-662; P. Jones 1861:71).

The Ojibwa as late as the middle of the nineteenth century still did considerable trapping of fur-bearing animals, even marketing bearskins. Particular families possessed hereditary hunting and trapping territories (P. Jones 1861:71), a form of land allocation that had developed during the previous period. It is not clear whether or not the rights to these territories included only the fur-bearing animals or all the resources. Most likely the rights encompassed only the former. The valleys of the Credit, Thames, and Moria rivers and the series of lakes between Lake Simcoe and the Bay of Quinté were the main hunting grounds of each Ojibwa group living within each area (Chamberlain 1888:154-155; Copway 1847:14, 20). Their use for hunting probably only lasted until about 1850 if that late. To the north, the Rama and Parry Island Ojibwa hunted and trapped in the Parry Sound-Muskoka districts until at least the end of the century, each family having its own designated area (Murray 1963:36; Rogers and Tobobondung 1975). Along the north shore of Lake Huron trapping territories continued in existence well into the twentieth century (Rogers 1972-1973).

Fishing may have been more important to the Indians of southern Ontario and Michigan than hunting or trapping during the nineteenth century. The Ojibwa about Sault Sainte Marie, as in the past, lived on whitefish summer and winter (fig. 4) (R. King 1847:22). In extreme southern Ontario, the areas exploited for fish were the same as those used for hunting and, in addition, the Ojibwa visited Lakes Erie and Saint Clair and occasionally crossed over to New York State. The mouth of the Credit River was a place noted for spearing salmon (Chamberlain 1888:154).

Another form of economic activity engaged in by the Ojibwa was the sale or barter for food to non-Indians of native-made goods: ax handles, pike poles, splint baskets, brooms, wooden bowls, ladles, and scoop shovels (P. Jones 1861:73; Greenman 1961:28; Rogers and Tobobondung 1975).

Clothing styles changed gradually during the period. Initially, more traditional styles were worn. In time, the Ojibwa adopted a Victorian type of costume although they continued to wear moccasins and perhaps a few other items of traditional dress (figs. 5-8) (Slight 1844:54-55; P. Jones 1861:75-77).

Water transport consisted of several different craft: birchbark canoes (fig. 9) and, toward the end of the nineteenth century, dugouts (Rogers 1965:458), sailboats, and rowboats (fig. 4). For winter travel the Ojibwa had sleds and snowshoes. Mothers carried their infants in cradleboards made by the men, sometimes elaborately carved on the back.

Housing types changed as the period advanced. As long as the Ojibwa were mobile, traditional lodge types were used, the commonest being the conical lodge. As the people became settled, they began to build log cabins. By the end of the nineteenth century, square timber and frame houses had come into use.

Sociopolitical organization of the Southeastern Ojibwa was a mixture of the old ways of their ancestors and those

Fig. 4. Ojibwas fishing in St. Mary's Rapids at the Sault, Ont., about 1900.

that had been introduced through contact with Euro-Americans. Councils of several "tribes" or smaller social units (various villages) continued to be operative, and periodically meetings of the chiefs were called. The participants were concerned with relations between the groups attending and the government. Wampum belts were employed as records (Slight 1844:74). Such meetings became known as the "Grand Council" held by the Ojibwa and other Algonquians of Georgian Bay often at either Saugeen or on Manitoulin Island (Kane 1859:1).

Besides the general councils that encompassed several groups, a political organization existed in each community consisting of a chief, sometimes assisted by a second and third chief, and a council. The chief and council system was, in part, a government-imposed institution based on free elections. The chief had one, sometimes two, messengers who were appointed by him. In addition, there might be a secretary-interpreter for the band. Other officials were appointed as the need arose, such as school

trustees, bailiffs, truant officers, school caretakers and others to look after the community halls and churches. The chief, councilors and residents met as a rule monthly (Rogers and Tobobondung 1975).

Although missionaries had their difficulties, nominal conversions were made (Slight 1844:134–137; M. Ray 1954:10–18; A.B. Jameson 1838, 3:228–232); and a number of Ojibwas began to attend church services, to hold family prayers and bible readings, and to attend camp meetings. The meetings were a prominent feature of religious life during this period (Young 1902:46; M. Ray 1954:13). Yet there were those Ojibwa who maintained their traditional religion and even those who had been converted did not abandon the traditional belief system.

The Southeastern Ojibwa believed that almost everything had a spirit. In addition, there were many super-

Fig. 5. Belt of deerskin backed with red stroud cloth and faced with quillwork. Mississauga, about 1820. Length 82.5 cm.

Fig. 6. Pair of Ojibwa moccasins of black-dyed buckskin decorated with porcupine quills. Length 25.5 cm; collected before 1867, probably between 1820 and 1848.

Fig. 7. Southeastern Ojibwa group that visited Europe in 1845-1846, photographed in 1851 in formal or stage dress. left to right: *awassiki·šiko·kkwe·* 'beyond-the-sky-woman' (Hannah Henry), *mankotta·ss* 'courageous' (George Henry, husband of Hannah Henry), *awanwa·pe·* 'mist man' (John Tecumseh Henry), *wa·patikk* 'white caribou' (Abraham Henry), *ačiča·kk* 'crane' (George W. Henry), *no·tino·kke·* 'wind-maker' (William Henry). Individuals identified in 1903 by John Tecumseh Henry of the Chippewas of the Thames band, from whom the original daguerreotype (now in the Chicago Histl. Soc.) was obtained. Phonemic respellings and translations of the Ojibwa names by Ives Goddard, after spellings and glosses by J.T. Henry and George Henry, the latter in Catlin 1848:49-50; see also Donaldson 1887:686-698.

Fig. 8. Isaiah Assance and family. Probably photographed by D.F. Macdonald, the Indian agent for the Parry Island band, about 1890.

natural beings. The Thunder conceived of as a giant bird who attacked "serpents" for food was perhaps one of the most important. The youths always undertook a vision quest in search of a guardian spirit who would bless them with "power" and be their protector throughout life. Some received greater powers than others and became medicine men. There were four different types: the *wa·pano·*, the "Spirit Man," the "Shaking-Tent Performer," and "Healer" (Slight 1844:85-97; Chamberlain 1888:157-158; A.B. Jameson 1838, 3:231-232; Radin 1928:659-660). In addition, the Feast of the Dead continued to be held on November first (Rogers 1972-1973). Moreover, the Ojibwas often performed private sacrifices during the year.

Urbanization, 1930-1972

Since the 1930s innumerable changes have taken place in the life of the Southeastern Ojibwa. Most of the changes have occurred since the 1950s. One has been the large increase in numbers. By about 1970, there were approximately 5,000 registered Ojibwas in southern Ontario and an estimated equal number who were not enrolled on any band list in addition to about 800 officially recorded for Michigan on Isabella and Bay Mills Reservations (U.S. Department of Commerce 1974:227-232) and an indeterminate number no longer on the rolls. Probably 12,000 or

more inhabited a large area extending from the east shore of Lake Michigan to eastern Ontario, a considerable increase in numbers and extent of territory since the middle of the seventeenth century. A most fundamental change has been the migration from the reserves to the cities (see Nagler 1970). By 1970 an estimated one-half, perhaps more, had moved to urban centers. This period is difficult to describe for several reasons. For one, no uniform adaptation to Canadian or American society had taken place. Rather, varied life-styles evolved. Yet in spite of the external diversity, there was a retention by many of the people of the older belief systems to such an extent that one cannot speak of assimilation as having taken place, only integration. Finally, there was a reluctance on the part of the Southeastern Ojibwa to expose themselves to intensive scrutiny by ethnologists.

Fig. 9. Southeastern Ojibwa birchbark canoes at Brunswick House, Missinaibi Lake. Photograph by Alanson Skinner in June 1908.

767

Fig. 10. Antler drumstick and rattle of deer dewclaws. Right 30.5 cm, left same scale; collected by Rev. Peter Jones before 1844, probably from the Mississaugas of the Credit.

Economically many Ojibwa located within or near urban areas had become members of the Canadian or American work force. They were employed in a variety of jobs, such as educators, social counselors, nurses, and administrators. Those who remained in their home communities, especially those located at some distance from industrial areas, found it more difficult to find meaningful employment (see Dunning 1964). Because of this, economic development programs were implemented such as marinas, craft production, and other activities.

The sociopolitical organization changed to a certain extent toward the end of the period. On the reserves, the chief and councilor system based on free elections continued in force but with the addition of band administrators and their staffs to manage the affairs of the community. Those who left became an integral part of the Canadian system; nevertheless, they did not lose their identity and remained in contact with their home communities through a wide-ranging network of kin ties. In addition, many Ojibwa became associated with various Indian organizations—political, economic, and social in content to varying degrees (Rogers 1971; Rogers and Shawana 1974).

Throughout the period, the adults continued to socialize their children in the Indian ways. Then in the 1960s efforts were intensified as the Ojibwa saw their traditional values and beliefs being eroded by the forces of Canadian society, especially through the educational system. Great efforts were made by the various levels of government to see that the Ojibwa youth became an integral part of the Canadian school system. Mixed blessings accrued and the dropout rate continued high, few obtaining a university education.

The religious orientations of the Southeastern Ojibwa remained a mixture of their traditional belief system and that taught by the Christian churches. The former in many cases appears to have been stronger of the two. Although traditional rituals may not have been held during this period, they have been remembered and the values they sustained adhered to.

Due to the increasing pressures, first felt in the early 1600s, brought to bear by the Euro-Americans, many expected that the Southeastern Ojibwa would disappear as an entity. Yet this has not happened. By 1972, they were more numerous and more conscious of their identity and heritage than ever before.

Synonymy†

Although the Indian groups now referred to as Chippewa, Ojibwa, and Saulteaux descend from closely related bands that were living in a fairly compact area in the mid-seventeenth century, at no time has there been a single distinctive name for these groups alone. In the early period they were included under the general labels Algonquin and Ottawa (JR 54:127), which in narrow usage were proper only to these other groups. Their modern names were originally those of specific bands. Since the scope of reference of some of these names changed through time it is generally much easier to trace the history of the forms of the names than to specify the exact reference of each name at every point in time. Accordingly information of the latter sort is at a minimum in this discussion.

Most Ojibwa speakers use the self-designation *aniššina·pe·*, which often has the more general meanings 'Indian' or 'human being' (Baraga 1878–1880, 2:38; Bloomfield 1957). Some northern Ojibwa use the form *aniššinini* (Evelyn Todd, personal communication 1975). These words etymologically mean 'ordinary man, ordinary person'.

The three band names that have expanded the scope of their reference are (in their modern forms) Chippewa/Ojibwa, Mississauga, and Saulteaux.

Chippewa/Ojibwa. Chippewa (ˈchĭpəˌwu, ˈchĭpəˌwô; older ˈchĭpəˌwā) and Ojibwa (ōˈjĭbwā, ōˈjĭbwə) are variant English renderings of the self-designation *očipwe·*. The spelling Chippewa is preferred for groups in the United States and southern Ontario and Ojibwa, or especially in Canadian usage Ojibway, for those in the

† Prepared by Ives Goddard, incorporating some sections by E.S. Rogers.

rest of Canada. Ojibwa is also the linguistic cover term used for the language spoken, in numerous local varieties, by all the groups under discussion. The most consistent native explanation connects this word with a root meaning 'puckered up', the reference being to the form of Ojibwa moccasins (Keating 1824, 2:151). The folk etymology that connects the latter part of the word with *apwe·* 'he roasts' (Warren 1885:36) is linguistically impossible. The band that originally bore this name is mentioned in 1670 as the Outchibous (JR 54:132), who together with two other bands had recently united with the People of the Sault (Saulteaux). A report of 1667 implies that *les Outchibouec* and *les sauteurs* were synonymous terms even then (JR 51:60).

Variant spellings are: Achipoës and Etchipoës, 1671 (Margry 1876-1886, 1:97; NYCD 9:803); Odchipewa, 1770; Ojibaway, 1806; Ojibbeways, 1830; Ojibwas, 1838; Ogibois, 1849; Odjibwas, 1851; Ojebway, 1861; Otchipwe (Baraga 1850); Otjibwek, 1864; Odzibwe (Josselin de Jong 1913); Uchepowuck, 1743 (Isham 1949:113); Uchipweys, 1783; Ougebowy, about 1775, given as a division of the Saulteaux (Graham 1969:206). Without the initial vowel: Shepawees, 1749; Chepewas, 1759; Chippoways, 1754; Chippewas, 1754 (Washington in Rupp 1846:67); Chippawas, 1759; Chipewas, 1784; Chipaways, 1760; Gibbaways, 1797; Chippuwas, 1798; Jibewas, 1799; Chipiwa, 1820; Tschipeway, 1839 (all from Mooney and Thomas 1907g:280-281 unless otherwise credited).

This name has been borrowed into other Algonquian languages as Fox *ačipwe·waki* (pl., Jones 1907:66, line 14), Kickapoo *ocipwea* (Voorhis 1967), Menominee *oci·pi·w* (Bloomfield 1962:248), Shawnee *hočipwe·ki* (pl., Voegelin 1938-1940, 10:446) and Tshipewaathakēē in 1825 (Trowbridge 1939:66), Cree *očipwe·w* (Mandelbaum 1940:165), Mahican Wchip-pow-waw, 1790 (Aupaumut 1854), Unami *ší·p·uwe* (Goddard 1965-1970).

The Winnebago name is *re·gáči* (Kenneth L. Miner, personal communication 1974), earlier recorded as Ne-gá-tcĕ (pl. Ne-gátc-hi-ja^n; Saint Cyr in Mooney and Thomas 1907g:281) and Daygótcheerah (Trowbridge 1823:1). The Iroquois name was one used widely for non-Iroquoian groups, for example, Mohawk *tewaʔkénhaʔ* 'western Algonquians' (Floyd G. Lounsbury, personal communication 1975), Tuscarora *nwaʔka·ʔn* (Marianne Mithun, personal communication 1975); early spellings are Dowaganhas, 1687 (NYCD 3:434); and Dewoganna's, 1698 (NYCD 4:407). Blackfoot has the loan *čípowaawa* (Allan R. Taylor, personal communication 1975). Premodern recordings are Hare Bedzietcho (Mooney and Thomas 1907g:280), Canadian Wyandot kwaʔyátha (Hewitt 1889, normalized), and Assiniboin Wah-kah-towah (Tanner 1956:138). Some other languages use translations of Saulteaux. The upper Missouri tribes have the same name for both the Cree and the Ojibwa: Mandan *šahí*, Hidatsa *šahí·*, Arikara *šahíʔa*

(Robert C. Hollow and Douglas R. Parks, personal communications 1975).

Mississauga (ˌmīsəˈsôgu). This term was at first the name of a band near the Mississagi River on the northern end of Lake Huron but later came to be used for most of the Southeastern Ojibwa (P.J. Robinson 1965:64; Morris 1943:7, 9; Chamberlain 1888). Variants are: oumisagai, 1640 (JR 18:230); Michisaguek, 1648 (JR 33:148); Michesaking, 1658 (JR 44:250); Mississague, 1670 (JR 54:132); les peuples de Mississagué, 1671 (JR 55:100); Missisakis, 1683 (JR 62:202); Massesagues, 1761 (MHSC ser. 4, 5:541); Messassagas, 1746 (NYCD 6:322); Missasagas, 1749 (NYCD 6:538). The meaning of the name is 'river with several outlets' (Chamberlain 1888:150). The interpretation 'eagle totem' (P. Jones 1861:164) is not a translation but a description of uncertain significance.

A reshaped borrowing is found in Iroquoian languages. Huron-Wyandot: Aoechisaeronon, 1649 (JR 34:204); A8echisaeʻronnon, 1653 (JR 38:180); Mississaeęronnon, 1745, an Algonquianized form glossed 'Saulteaux' (Potier 1920:155); axšisʻayérunu 'Ojibwa' (Gatschet 1882-1889:19, normalized). Iroquois (Mohawk?): Assisagigroone, 1700 (NYCD 4:737); Aghsiesagichrone, 1723 (NYCD 5:695); Achsisaghecks (Colden 1747:xvi); IshisagekRoanu (Dobbs 1744:47); Tisagechroanu (Pa. Col. Recs. 5:351); Zisagechrohne (Zeisberger in Mooney and Thomas 1907h:910).

In the twentieth century the name Mississauga in its broadest sense has been widely replaced by Eastern Ojibwa (Radin 1924:491; Bloomfield 1957) and Southeastern Ojibwa (perhaps first in Dunning 1959:5).

Saulteaux (ˈsōtō). The band living at the Sault Sainte Marie in the mid-seventeenth century was referred to by Ojibwa expressions meaning 'people of the Sault' based on *pa·wittik* 'rapids' or *pa·wittink* 'Sault Sainte Marie': baouichtigouian, 1640, with -ian an error for -irin (JR 18:230); Paüoitigoüeieuhak, 1642, probably an error for Paoüitigoüirin8ak (JR 23:222); Paouitagoung, 1648 (JR 33:148); Pagouitik, 1658 (JR 44:251); Pahoüiting dach Irini, 1670 (JR 54:132; the emendations are wrong). French translations were 'les gens du Sault', 'la Nation du Sault', and eventually 'sauteurs', 'Saulteurs' (JR, as cited). The latter form was superseded by Saulteux, 1669 (Gallinée in Margry 1876-1886, 1:163), which has been borrowed as English Saulteaux. Spellings are Salteur, 1753; Sautor, 1778; Sotoos, 1824; Sautoux, 1836; Souties, 1843; Sotto, 1859 (Mooney and Thomas 1907g:280-281). In 1974 some Saulteaux had begun to use the simplified spelling Soto (John H. Steinbring, personal communication 1974).

A translation of this term is used as the name for the Chippewa/Ojibwa in several languages: Huron Eskiaeronnon, 1649 (JR 34:204), and Enskiaęʻronnon, 1653 (JR 38:180) from Skiaę̨ 'Sault Sainte Marie'. Cognate is Iroquois (Mohawk?) Estiaghes, 1726 (NYCD 5:791); Estiaghicks (Colden 1747:xvi); Ostiagaghroones, 1759

(NYCD 7:384); Stiagigroone, 1700 (NYCD 4:737); these were the "Saulteurs" as opposed to the Mississaugas. The forms with plural -s show use as English words. Another example is Dakota xaxátqwą 'dwellers at the falls' (Riggs 1890).

The contemporary Saulteaux (Northern Ojibwa) are called in Plains Cree nahkawe·wiyiniw (Lacombe 1874:475, specifically for the Red River Indians; Faries 1938:160) or nahkawiyiniw (Faries 1938:372; "Sketch of Cree, an Algonquian Language," vol. 17). This appears earlier as an English borrowing from Woods Cree: Nakawawuck, 1743 (Isham 1949:112), and Nakawewuck about 1775 (Graham 1969:206).

The names of a number of other Ojibwa bands mentioned in the early sources fell into disuse as the people became dispersed or decimated by disease. Some of these, however, are similar to the names of patrilineal clans known from the later period. The following were the more prominent of these bands in the seventeenth century.

Amikwa (cf. amikk 'beaver'). Variants: les Amikoüai, ou la nation du Castor, 1640 (JR 18:230); amikouek, 1648 (JR 33:148); Amicoüés, 1671 (JR 55:100); Amicois, 1693 (NYCD 9:566); Amikouest, 1753 (Bacqueville de la Potherie 1753, 2:58). Also referred to by the French as 'the pierced noses': des Naiz percez, ou de la Nation du Castor, 1636 (JR 10:82); Neds percés, 1656 (JR 42:74); Nez percez, 1656 (JR 42:92). Not the same as Ameko8es, the Beaver clan of the Nipissing (NYCD 9:1053). A group referred to as Ennikaragi, lemikariagi (NYCD 3:489), Denighcariages, Neghkereages (NYCD 5:693), and Necariages (Colden 1747:map) has been identified as the Amikwa (Hodge 1907–1910, 2:128, 1053, 1101) but is probably the Ottawa of Michilimackinac.

Achiligouan. Attested as: Atchiligoüan, 1640 (JR 18:230); Achirigouans, 1647 (JR 30:112); Achiligoüiane, 1670 (JR 54:132). The Huron name is recorded as Achir8achronnon in 1653 (JR 38:180).

Mantouek. Attested as: mantoue, 1640 (JR 18:230); Mantouek, 1658 (JR 44:248); Nantoüé, 1671 (JR 55:184). Perhaps the same as the Mun-dua tribe of Chippewa tradition (Warren 1885:91).

Marameg (cf. ma·name·k 'catfish'), 1670 (JR 54:132). Also Malamechs, 1671 (Margry 1876–1886, 1:97), and Malanas ou gens de la Barbue, 1697 (Margry 1876–1886, 6:6). Not to be confused with an identically named Miami band (JR 58:40).

Nikikouek (cf. nikik 'otter'), 1640 (JR 33:148). Also Nikikoüets, 1683 (JR 62:202); Mikikoüet or gens de la Loutre, about 1700 (Perrot 1864:83).

Noquet (cf. no·kke·, a name for the Chippewa Bear clan; Jones in Hodge 1907–1910, 2:82). Variants are: Roquai, 1640 (JR 18:230); Noukek, 1658 (JR 44:246); Nouquet, 1670 (JR 54:132); Noquets, 1671 (Margry 1876–1886, 1:97); Nocké, 1684 (Margry 1876–1886, 6:41).

Ouasouarini (cf. perhaps awa·ssi 'bullhead'), 1640 (JR 18:230). Also Aouasanik, 1648 (JR 33:148); Ouasaouanik, 1658 (JR 44:250).

Outchougai, 1640 (JR 18:230). Other variants: Atchougue, 1648 (JR 33:148); Atchougek, 1658 (JR 44:250). Archouguets (JR 24:266) is a misprint for Atchouguets. Not the same as Achagué, recorded as the Heron clan of the Nipissing (NYCD 9:1053).

In the later period most Ojibwa communities became known by a specific local name, frequently one assigned by government administrators. All groups, of course, that fell under federal jurisdiction were given a specific designation, "reserve" in Canada and "reservation" in the United States. Examples were the Bay Mills and Isabelle Reservations in Michigan; the Walpole Island, Rice Lake, Cape Croker, Rama, and Parry Island Reserves in Ontario; and Red Lake and Mille Lacs (mə'lăks) Reservations in Minnesota. Each could also, at the same time, be referred to as such and such a band following the reserve designation. Northern Ojibwa and Saulteaux bands are generally known after their locations, such as Trout Lake, Berens River, Osnaburg, and Whitefish Bay. Earlier groups had been referred to by band names: the Isabelle Reservation was formed by the Saginaw, Swan Creek, and Black River bands (U.S. Department of Commerce 1974:232); and the "Newash Band of Chippewa Indians" became resident on the Cape Croker Reserve after selling their reserve of Newash (Morris 1943:36–38). Often the band was referred to after the name of its chief, a practice that occurred during the nineteenth century especially for the Robinson-Huron Treaty of 1850 (Morris 1943:32–33): "Dokis and his band," "Windawtegawinini and his band."

Sources

Materials relating to the Southeastern Ojibwa are limited in content, scattered in a multiplicity of diverse publications and archival repositories, and often ambiguous as to whether the author does indeed refer to the Southeastern Ojibwa. This is especially true of earlier sources.

Source material for the period of initial contact is sparse. Champlain (1922–1936) and Sagard-Théodat (1939) most likely met Ojibwa along Georgian Bay but recorded no information that can be clearly attributed to them. The Jesuits (JR 1896–1901) give only brief accounts of Algonquians at this time with little indication of who might be considered Ojibwa.

The record improves somewhat for the period of dispersal. The Jesuits with few exceptions give the most information both historical and ethnographic. Their accounts relate primarily to the first half of the period, little attention being given the Ojibwa during the last half. Recorders who presented ethnographic data of considerable interest were Bacqueville de la Potherie

(1911–1912), Lahontan (1905), Raudot (Kinietz 1940), and Perrot (1911), although Perrot often generalized in such a way that one is not sure whether he is referring to Ojibwa or not. Galinée in 1669–1670 prepared a map (1903) locating the Southeastern Ojibwa with cryptic notes regarding each group. Two others, Sabrevois (WHC 16) and Wraxall (1915), give minimal information. The New York Colonial Documents (NYCD) and the Wisconsin Historical Collections (WHC) cannot be overlooked even though the data included on the Southeastern Ojibwa are limited.

Severance (1917) and P.J. Robinson (1965) are among the very few historians who have given any attention to the Southeastern Ojibwa. These authors consider the movements and settlements of the Ojibwa and their relations with the Iroquois but give little regarding their culture. Few ethnographers have given any attention to this period. Kinietz (1940) assembled data on the "Chippewa" and Greenman (1961) has provided a short article on the history of the Indians of Michigan. Eggan (1955:527) postulated a late development of clans, while Hickerson (1966:4) has argued for their being aboriginal. Hickerson has also dealt with the Feast of the Dead (1960) and the Midewiwin (1963) in historical perspective. Quimby (1960:122–127) has described the "Chippewa" of this period with special emphasis on the effects of their contact with Europeans.

Information on the period of land cessions is also quite meager. The papers of Sir William Johnson (1921–1965) have something to say but the best source by far is Henry (1969), the elder, who described in detail life among the Ojibwa of northern Lake Huron from their subsistence quest to their religion. A.B. Jameson's (1838) account of her trip from York (Toronto) to Sault Sainte Marie gives glimpses of Ojibwa life toward the close of the period. McLean (W.S. Wallace 1932) gives passing mention to the Southeastern Ojibwa.

Others in recent years have examined the early documents and assembled data on specific events during the period. Morris (1943) brought together a compilation devoted to the treaties for this and later periods. Surtees (1966) as a lawyer examined Canada's government policy and treaty making. Peckham (1947) and others have dealt with Pontiac's rebellion, in which Southeastern Ojibwas were involved. Cumberland (1904) noted the role played by Oshawana at the Battle of the Thames. Kidd (1951)

has reported on an Ojibwa burial estimated to date from this time period.

Somewhat more information is available for the period of farming yet in general this period in the history of the Southeastern Ojibwa has been ignored. Two Ojibwa missionaries, Copway (1847, 1850) and P. Jones (1860, 1861), published accounts of their work and the history of their people. But since these men traveled widely and had many contacts it is not often possible to know, unless they specify, whether the Southeastern Ojibwa are being referred to. Van Dusen (1867) and the Wesleyan missionary Slight (1844) described in some detail the customs of the Southeastern Ojibwa for the early part of the period. Neumeyer (1971) reviews the attempted removal of the Indians from Michigan. Others (Kane 1859; R. King 1847; Young 1902; D. Wilson 1876, 1892) have made mention of the Southeastern Ojibwa but without elaboration. The first ethnographer (and the first to be trained in North America), Chamberlain (for example, 1888) published a number of papers on the Southeastern Ojibwa based on limited field investigations among them. He was followed by Radin (1928), Johnson (1929), Jenness (1935), and Flannery (1940). Several others working with elderly informants and historical documents have made reconstructions for the period (De Mille 1971; Rogers and Tobobondung 1975). Other sources of significance are the Sessional Papers, published by the government of Canada, Band Council Records and other band documents, copies of which, in some cases, are preserved in the Provincial Archives of Ontario and the Methodist archives housed at Victoria College, Toronto.

For the mid-twentieth century, there is considerable documentary material on the Southeastern Ojibwa although the sources do not always identify them as such. Newspaper accounts, government reports, and papers prepared by various Indian organizations all contain information on a variety of topics about the Indians in the contemporary world (see Haycock 1971). Yet much remains unrecorded. Nagler (1970) has published on the urban Indians and Dunning (1964) on one reserve community. Rogers (1971) and Rogers and Shawana (1974) have reviewed the Indian involvement in various economic and political movements. The Economic Development Administration, U.S. Department of Commerce prepared a report (1974) that includes some information on the Ojibwa of Michigan as of 1969.

Ottawa

JOHANNA E. FEEST AND CHRISTIAN F. FEEST

Language, Territory, and Environment

At the time of first European contact, the Ottawa ('ätəwu, in Canada often ˌōˈdäwu), speakers of a southeastern dialect of Ojibwa,* were located on Manitoulin Island, the adjacent parts of the Bruce Peninsula, and probably the north and east shores of Georgian Bay (cf. "Southeastern Ojibwa," this vol.). Later those on Georgian Bay became more closely associated with the main group. During historic times, the Ottawas were chiefly living in various coastal and riverine regions of the Michigan Lower Peninsula and in adjacent parts of Ontario, Ohio, Indiana, Illinois, and Wisconsin, and (at a later date) also in Kansas and Oklahoma.

The Michigan Lower Peninsula, the Ottawa heartland during most of the past 300 years, is part of an old coastal plain that is covered with dark clay loams in the south and light sandy loams in the north and drained by 34 primary river systems into Lake Michigan and Lake Huron. The area was mostly wooded except for small prairies in southwestern Michigan, hardwoods dominating in the south, mixed conifers and hardwoods in the north. Fish, fowl, and mammals were found in great variety, while the temperate, humid climate with annual growing seasons of up to 180 days easily permitted the cultivation of corn and other crops.

It is sometimes difficult to separate Ottawa territory from that of their linguistically closely related neighbors. Seventeenth-century sources apply the term Ottawa not only to a local group otherwise known as Sable but also to both the total of totemic or local groups that together formed the tribe (Kiskakon, Sinago, Sable, Nassauakueton; later also others) and to all other "upper Algonquians" who came down to Montreal for trade. The affiliation of such rarely mentioned groups as the Ouacheskesouek or the Outaouakamigouk must remain in doubt. During the nineteenth and twentieth centuries, moreover, those Ottawas living near or with Chippewas and/or Potawatomis cannot be clearly distinguished except on the basis of self-identification. The facts that no

*The orthography preferred by the Odawa Language Project, University of Toronto, for transcribing the Ottawa language is that used for Eastern Ojibwa by Bloomfield (1957 in the text rather than the glossary), except that *h* stands for the glottal stop, *nh* represents nasalization of final vowels, and reduced vowels (e,u) are not written. Italicized Ottawa words have been respelled in this orthography by Jonathan Kaye. Other spellings of native terms and names are those of the historical sources.

Ottawa village before the 1660s can definitely be localized and that some of their later places of residence were multitribal population centers make the application of the direct historical approach to late prehistory difficult. The great mobility of Ottawa groups documented throughout early contact times contributes to this problem. Equations of historic tribes and prehistoric cultures must therefore largely remain guesswork (cf. Quimby 1960; Fitting 1970). Those few sites that can be associated with certainty with the Ottawas, on the other hand, all date from the period after 1760 and are of little help in establishing prehistoric ethnic identities (Herrick 1957; Quimby 1938, 1966).

The French period

History

The Ottawas enter written history with Samuel de Champlain's report on his encounter with a group of Ottawa men near the mouth of French River in 1615 (fig. 1). The following year Champlain visited one of their villages west of the Petun, in the vicinity of the Bruce Peninsula. While fighting the Mascoutens to their west, they also served as middlemen in the trade between the Hurons and tribes living in the west. By 1634 the Nassauakueton were known to the French, but at an uncertain location (Champlain 1922–1936, 3:43, 96, 6:248–249; Sagard-Théodat 1632a:77; JR 18:230, 33:150).

After the dispersal of the Hurons in 1649, part of the Ottawas reportedly had four villages around the Straits of Mackinac where, according to later tradition, they had superseded the Assegun or Bone Indians. Others (including Kiskakon and Sable groups) fled with other Algonquians and the Hurons to Green Bay and fortified themselves against the Iroquois. Some Ottawas lived at least temporarily on Thunder and Saginaw bays. In the late 1650s some pushed farther west and settled on an island in Lake Pepin, from whence they were driven by the Sioux. They ascended the Black River and crossed the country to Chequamegon Bay in 1660; another group at that time was living on Keeweenaw Bay. At Chequamegon, three Ottawa bands had a joint village in 1666, and five villages three years later, although some of these may have been of allied tribes (JR 38:180, 41:76–78, 44:344, 48:264, 51:20, 54:168, 55:158; Perrot

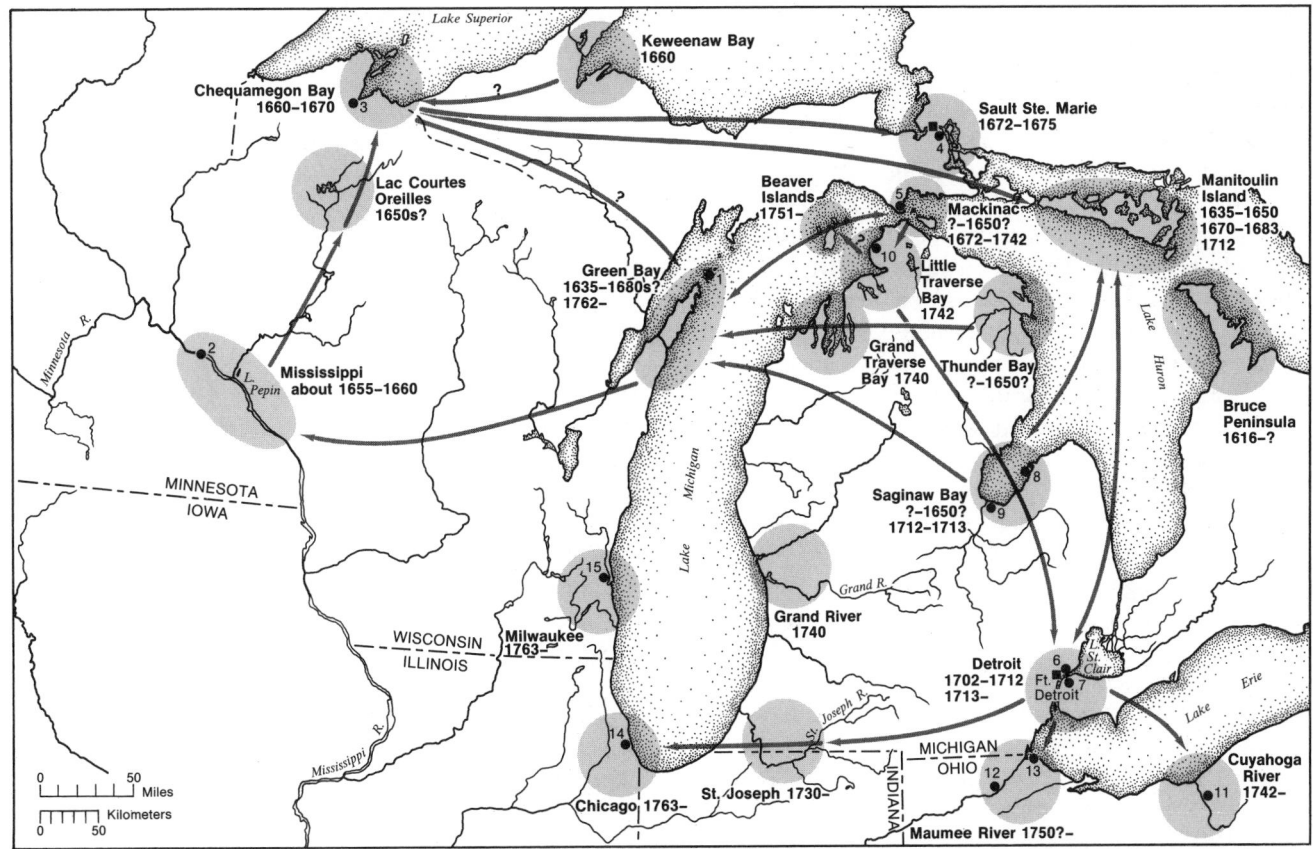

Fig. 1. Ottawa territories, villages, and migrations during the French period, based on contemporary sources. Dates given only for documented or inferred periods of occupation by Ottawas. Territorial limits are conventionalized; locations of villages tentative. Except for 10 (Waganakisi) none of the native names of villages is known. Many villages cannot be localized at all. Some of the territories were occupied by other tribes at the same time. 1, Little Detroit 1650-1653, 1762-?; 2, Bald Island ca. 1655-1660; 3, Chequamegon Bay 1663-1670; 4, Kiskakon village near Sault Ste. Marie 1672; 5, Mackinac 1676-1686; 6, Detroit 1702-1712?, 1755-1763; 7, Detroit 1713?-?; 8, Saginaw 1717-?; 9, Saginaw 1744-?; 10, (Old) Arbre Croche 1742-?; 11, Cuyahoga River 1755-1760; 12, Roche de Bout 1750?-?; 13, Maumee Bay 1760; 14, Chicago (mixed Ottawa, Potawatomi, Sauk village) 1763; 15, Milwaukee (mixed Ottawa, Potawatomi, Sauk village) 1763.

1864; Radisson 1885; Schoolcraft 1851-1857, 1: 305-308, 6:202-205).

War with the Sioux and a short period of peace with the Iroquois brought the Ottawas back east. In 1670 and 1671 groups returned to Manitoulin Island; some Sinagos moved for a few years to Green Bay; and the partially Christianized Kiskakons took their abode near Sault Sainte Marie from whence they moved in 1676 to Saint Ignace Mission near the Hurons at Mackinac. By 1695 parts of the Sinagos, Sables, and Nassauakuetons had settled there as well (JR 55:132, 170, 57:228, 248, 58:41, 228, 59:200, 61:69, 102, 122, 126, 62:192; Margry 1876-1886, 5:80). According to Lahontan (1703), it was particularly the Sables who claimed Manitoulin as their former home.

After 1700, a part of the Mackinac bands was induced to remove to the newly established Fort Detroit, where they lived with the Hurons, Potawatomis, and Chippewas until after the end of the French period, except for a brief period after 1712 when they retired to Manitoulin after defeating the Fox and their allies near Detroit and

the Mascoutens in southwestern Michigan. The traditions of their victories against the Mascouten and Assegun later became blended into one tradition, mentioning only the Mascouten (WHC 16; Margry 1876-1886, 5; Blackbird 1887; Assikinack 1858; Radin 1926). While there is no clear evidence for permanent Ottawa settlements on Grand River during the French period, there were Ottawas at Saginaw Bay since at least 1712 and near Saint Joseph's River since at least 1730. The Mackinac bands finally moved to Arbre Croche, a site north of Little Traverse Bay marked by a huge crooked tree, in 1742. The Beaver Islands were settled shortly thereafter. Some Ottawa bands preferring the English trade established villages on the Maumee and Cuyahoga rivers in the 1740s and 1750s (WHC 16:290, 17:367, 372; NYCD 9:1072, 10:163, 608; Hanna 1911, 1:333-334; Pease and Jenison 1940:168, 199, 352-353).

Except for minor quarrels, the Ottawas were on good terms with neighboring Algonquian tribes, such as the Chippewas, Potawatomis, and Menominees, while their relations with the Hurons were strained in spite of their

773

close association for more than a century. The Ottawas frequently suspected the Hurons of conspiring with the Iroquois and other enemies, while the Hurons accused the Ottawas of beating their women, children, and old men (WHC 16:251, 17:287, 334).

Early French relations were dominated by the Ottawas' role as middlemen in the fur trade between northwestern tribes and Montreal. The French also allied themselves with the Ottawas against the Iroquois and the English, who since the 1670s were rather unsuccessfully trying to secure the Ottawa trade for themselves. As the frontier advanced and the trade was opened by the French for licensed traders, the Ottawas gradually lost their monopoly. The Ottawas sided with the French in their colonial wars, but many switched alliance easily after the British gained control over Canada in 1760. Resulting factionalism is partly responsible for Pontiac's failure in forging a powerful pan-Indian coalition against the English in 1763, with notably the Arbre Croche Ottawas leaning toward the British (Peckham 1947).

French Jesuits established missions among the Ottawas after 1660 at Keeweenaw, Chequamegon, Green Bay, Sault Sainte Marie, Mackinac, and Manitoulin, but few of the Indians accepted Christianity. The Recollect priests at Detroit were even less successful (JR 67:152; WHC 19; Stuart 1926:74).

Available data on population, however fragmentary, are presented in table 1. Total population may conservatively be guessed at somewhere between 4,000 and 6,000. The spread of European contagious diseases (such as the epidemics recorded in 1637, 1752, and 1757) certainly contributed to the numerical decline of Ottawa population, which was partly offset by incorporation of related bands into the tribe (JR 14:100; NYCD 10:249; WHC 19:50–52; Assikinack 1858a; Blackbird 1887).

Culture

Fishing was of decisive importance for the Ottawas living along the lake shores. Chequamegon Bay and the Straits of Mackinac were chosen as village sites for the abundance and variety of fish available, which were caught in nets by the Ottawas. Individual or group hunting (fire drive) of deer, bear, beaver, other mammals, and fowl was likewise important, particularly during the winter when the Indians moved to their southerly hunting grounds although the Ottawas were not regarded as the most efficient hunters. After losing their position as middlemen in the fur trade, they had to augment their own hunting capacity, especially by increased trapping, which may have led to the development of a system of family hunting territories (Lahontan 1703; Margry 1876–1886, 5).

While hunting and fishing were men's work, the women planted corn, beans, and squash. The yields of horticulture diversified and stabilized the native food

Table 1. Population Estimates, 1615–1765

	1615[a]	1653[b]	1669[c]	1678[d]	1720[e]	1736[f]	1765[g]
Georgian Bay	1,200						
Manitoulin Island	?			?			
Green Bay	800	?		?			250
Chequamegon Bay			1,100				
Mackinac		?		1,300	1,500	750	
Little Traverse Bay							1,000
Beaver Islands							200
Grand River							?
St. Joseph's River						?	600
Saginaw Bay		?			250	300	400
Detroit					500	1,000	1,200
Ohio							?
West of Lake Michigan							?

NOTE: Most figures from this period are given in terms of warriors; such figures have been converted into total population figures on the basis of a 1:4 ratio. Whenever an Ottawa population for an area can be documented or inferred, but no figures are available the symbol ? is used; when no Ottawa population can be documented the space remains blank.

[a] (Champlain 1922–1936, 3:43).

[b] Refugees living with other tribes in Aotonatendia, a Potawatomi village (JR 38:100).

[c] (JR 54:166, 168, 170); 60 Sinagos of Green Bay visited St. Ignace Mission near Mackinac in 1672 (JR 57:248).

[d] Kiskakons and three other tribes (probably not including the Hurons) at St. Ignace (JR 61:102). In 1677 there were 500 Kiskakons at this place (JR 61:68).

[e] Mackinac: Population of Great Hare, Bear, and Carp bands given as 500 each by Râle in 1723; perhaps too high (JR 67:152). Saginaw and Detroit: Sabrevois, 1717 (WHC 16:370) and Vaudreuil, 1721 (MPHC 33:638).

[f] Chauvigniere (NYCD 9:1053, 1058); Kiskakons and Sinagos in all three areas. For Detroit, cf. the anonymous "State of Canada, 1730" (MPHC 34:76).

[g] Croghan (Thwaites 1904–1907, 1:168–169) partly based on Hutchins's 1762 estimate (W.L. Jenks 1926:365). For Green Bay: Ottawa village on Little Detroit (Washington Island) according to Carver (1778:26); for Beaver Island and for general comparison see Bougainville (1964; NYCD 10:608).

economy and were traded to supply the French at Mackinac and Detroit. Gathering of wild food plants (except rice) was widely practiced. Only the collecting of maple sap and not the process of sugar making is reported. Plants collected included a kind of lichen used as emergency food, blueberries, raspberries, and strawberries (Lahontan 1703; Margry 1876–1886, 5; Champlain 1922–1936, 3:43, 6:248; JR 50:256, 54:162, 56:100).

Cooking methods included the frying, roasting, boiling, and smoking of meat and fish, which was also boiled with corn into a broth. Bread made of corn meal was baked in hot sand or ashes (Margry 1876–1886, 5; J. Smith 1799). Trade with the French is responsible for the rapid changes in material culture at an early date. Thus, while scraperlike wooden digging sticks for breaking the ground remained in use and log mortars and pestles were even adopted by the French frontiersmen, bows and arrows were soon supplemented by guns in both hunting and warfare. Wooden clubs remained in use besides iron trade tomahawks, while various other iron tools and implements became part of standard equipment. Round shields of leather protected the warriors (Margry 1876–1886, 5; Champlain 1922–1936, 3:44–45; Bacqueville de la Potherie 1753; Perrot 1864).

Ottawa men characteristically wore their hair short and upright in front; they pierced both their nasal septum and their earlobes, ornamenting them with stone, copper, and shell ornaments (figs. 2–3). Feathers were worn in the hair, in ear holes, and on collars around the neck. Little dress except aprons or breechclouts and fur cloaks in winter was reportedly worn before the introduction of trade cloth. Tattooing of the body and face painting were common (Champlain 1922–1936, 3:43–44, 6:248–249; Sagard-Théodat 1632a:190–191; Radisson 1885; Margry 1876–1886, 5).

Permanent Ottawa villages were located near river banks or lake shores. Their houses were probably much like those of the Hurons, but smaller: barrelroofed rectangular structures (fig. 4) covered with sheets of fir or cedar bark. Some of the villages were fortified with palisades. On their hunting trips, the Ottawas used mat-covered conical tents (Margry 1876–1886, 5; WHC 16:369; J. Smith 1799).

Rush mats, made by the women, dyed, and woven in symmetrical designs, were traded to other Indian groups for shells, paints, and pottery. These items were later

Thomas Gilcrease Institute of Amer. Hist. and Art, Tulsa: Granville 1701.
Fig. 3. An Ottawa man drawn about 1700. The hair style, breechclout, ear and nose ornaments, and body decorations are typical for the late 17th century. The sun emblem may be an early breast plate, a forerunner of trade silver brooches and gorgets. The long-stemmed pipe has been substantiated by museum specimens; the bag is labeled as for tobacco.

Lib. of Congress: Champlain 1619:pl. 1, fig. C.
Fig. 2. The earliest known picture of an Ottawa. No ethnological specimen exists to document the shield; the bow and arrows are very stylized and European. Engraving, 1619, possibly from a verbal description.

replaced by French glass beads, vermilion, and copper kettles, which the Ottawas obtained for furs and birchbark canoes. Birchbark boxes and leather pouches were of their own manufacture (Sagard-Théodat 1632a:191; Perrot 1864; JR 59:202).

During the late seventeenth and early eighteenth century the Ottawa are usually described as consisting of four component subgroups: Kiskakon 'cut-tail', (referring to the bear); Sinago (black squirrel); Sable 'sand'; and Nassauakueton 'fork'. While the first two are generally supposed to have been totemic groups, it has been suggested that the latter two derived their names from their original homes near a sandy beach and the forks of a river respectively (Kinietz 1940:226-227, 246-248; NYCD 9:1053, 1058; Margry 1876-1886, 5:80). Fork was later also a totemic clan name and Nassauakueton was a common chiefs' name in this band (Radin 1926; NYCD 9:621, 623, 627; WHC 18:388; Blackbird 1887). Keinouché (kino·še· 'pike'), mentioned in 1669 as a group besides the Kiskakon and Sinago at Chequamegon (JR 54:170), is probably identical with Sable, in which band Kinongé (Le Brochet, Pike) was a chief's name (MPHC 33:331-335, 362, 384). In 1757 Bougainville (1964) distinguished between the Ottawa proper

and other groups living with them, such as the Kiskakons, the Big Feet, the White Fish, the people from Beaver Island, and the people of the Fork, while in his census he lists the Mignojan (probably a misspelled variant of Kinongé) instead of the Ottawa proper, just as earlier writers had used the term Ottawa when referring to the Sables (JR 33:150). The Big Feet are later identified as the Bear clan, thus adding to the confusion, while the totem of the Ottawa proper is given as "moose" or "elk" (Assikinack 1858a; Blackbird 1887; Lahontan 1703). In 1723 three apparently totemic groups were reported from Mackinac: Michabou (misša·po· or misša·po·s) or Great Hare, Namepich (name·piš) or Carp (i.e. sucker), and Machoua (makkwa) or Bear (JR 67:152, 156). These cannot readily be correlated with the more common set. According to later tradition, totemic clans originally lived in separate parts of larger villages (Assikinack 1858a), while eighteenth-century evidence confirms the existence of separate Kiskakon and Sinago villages at Detroit, and a Kiskakon village near Arbre Croche (NYCD 9:1058; WHC 18:390; MPHC 9:655). The fact that totemic signatures do not necessarily correspond to band designations is shown by the treaty of 1701, which was signed with a fork for the Nassauakueton, but with

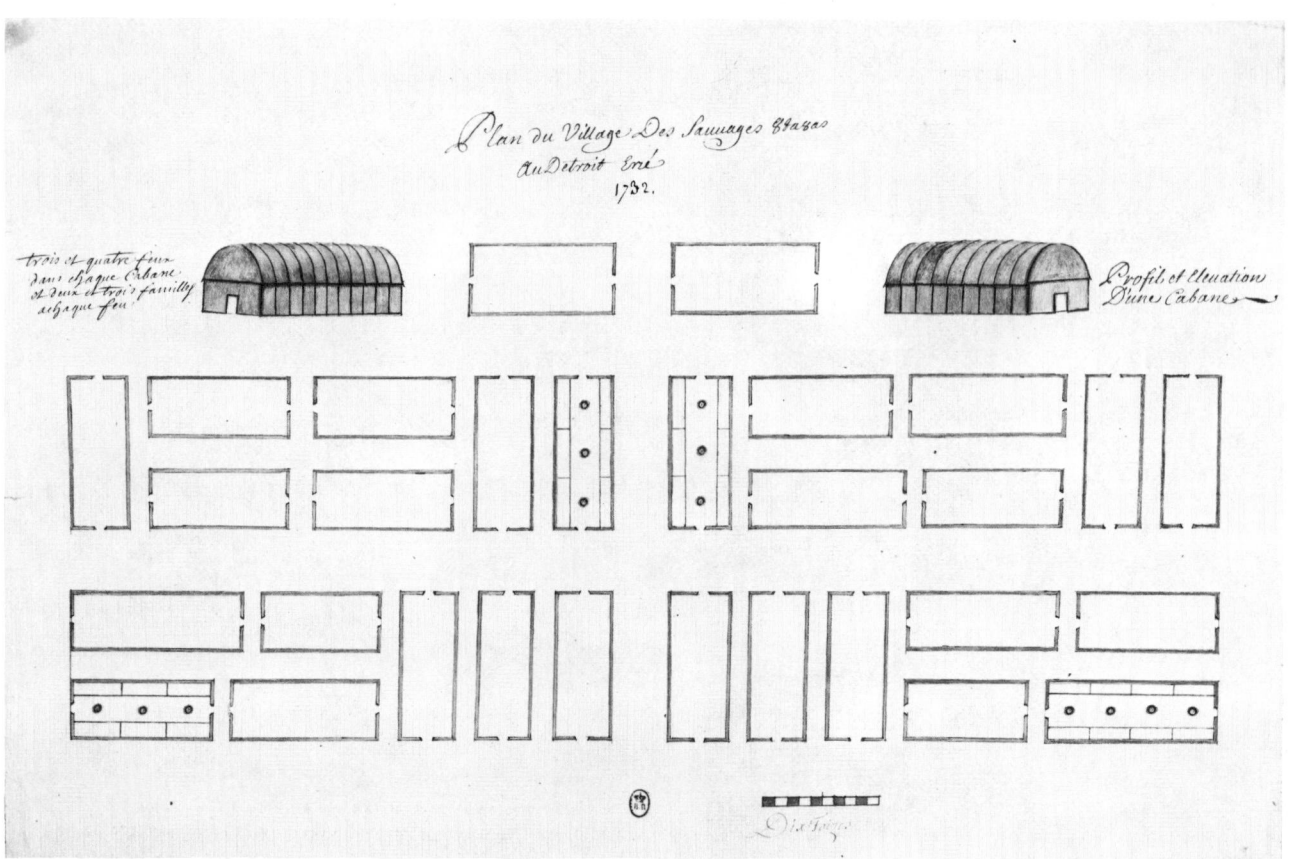

Fig. 4. Plan of the Ottawa Village at Detroit drawn in 1732. Thirty longhouses, with the inner arrangements of 4 shown, including fireplaces. At the top 2 are shown in perspective, and a label specifies that each house has 3 or 4 fires, with 2 or 3 families to a fire. The scale bar represents 10 *toises*, equal to 19.49 m.

a bear for both the Sinago and Sable, and with a fish for the Kiskakon (Margry 1876-1886, 5:frontispiece).

Each of the independent subgroups and each of the villages had its own chiefs who had apparently little coercive authority (Kinietz 1940:248).

After its birth, a child was washed and tied to a cradleboard where it remained most of the time until it was weaned around the age of three years. A name was selected for the child from those belonging to the family; this name could be changed on various occasions during later life. Training for future economic pursuits started early. During puberty, children received guardian spirits through dreams or visions obtained by fasting and prepared bundles corresponding to the vision. Marriages were markedly stable; polygyny depended on the husband's economic capabilities. Women separated from men during confinement, for a certain period after childbirth, and during their menses. Disposal of the dead was by inhumation, scaffold burial, or cremation. Except in the case of cremation, the bones were subsequently cleaned and tied up in mats or bark coffins, which were finally disposed of after a feast for the dead, which was held regularly every three or more years (Lahontan 1703; Perrot 1864; JR 48:116, 67:156-160, 59:202; Margry 1876-1886, 5; Sagard-Théodat 1632a; Raudot 1904; Hickerson 1960; NYCD 9:176).

War customs included scalping, torturing prisoners of war, and eating their flesh; however, some prisoners were adopted to replace Ottawa dead. Mock battles were performed to welcome important visitors (Margry 1876-1886, 5; Bacqueville de la Potherie 1753; N.B. Humphrey 1941; Carver 1778).

The Ottawas believed in a multitude of good and evil supernatural powers or beings (manito·, pl. manito·k) to whom offerings of tobacco were made and who were invoked as occasion demanded. Among these beings were the Underwater Panther, a manito· of the waters, another whose domain was the land animals and birds, and the Great Hare who was credited with the creation of the earth. The belief in a supreme being, called kičči-manito· or "Master of Life," was likewise present. Some persons specialized in interacting with the spirits and used their powers for curative purposes; herbal medicines were also applied (Perrot 1864; Lahontan 1703; JR 50:264-266, 284-288, 67:158-160; Kinietz 1940:286, 289).

The souls of the dead were thought to go to a pleasant country in the east or west (both directions are given by both seventeenth- and nineteenth-century sources) after being expelled from the village and having crossed a dangerous river over a feeble bridge (Margry 1876-1886, 5; Radisson 1885; Perrot 1864).

Numerous different dances were performed, usually at night, accompanied by songs, gourd rattles, and drums. Amusements consisted of various games of chance with dice or straws, footraces, and lacrosse in which different villages were pitted against one another (WHC 16:367-368; Perrot 1864; Bougainville 1964).

The Anglo-American period

History

After the pro-French Ottawa groups had failed to drive the British from Detroit, they removed—like the pro-British groups before them—to the Maumee River and toward the southern shores of Lake Michigan. Probably at the same time, the region of the Grand River valley developed into another center of Ottawa population (fig. 5).

Although formally allied with the British, many Ottawas tried to keep themselves out of conflict during the American Revolution, and some even tended toward siding with the Americans (MPHC 9, 10, 19; WHC 18). The War of 1812 saw the Ottawas similarly divided and wavering between British and American interests. Up to the 1830s Ottawa groups from the United States regularly went to Canada to receive British annuity payments. This practice was first discouraged by the U.S. government and later also by the British, who in 1843 stopped the payments to Indians from across the border (MPHC 15, 24; A.B. Jameson 1838, 3).

Scarcity of game resulted in the search for new hunting territories by the bands from Arbre Croche and Saginaw: by the late 1780s some had established themselves on the Minnesota River, but friction with Siouan groups led to a northward movement. Small bands of changing composition became engaged in fur hunting around Lake Winnipeg and even up to Lake Athapasca until the 1820s. Most Ottawas afterward returned to Arbre Croche, which had become a densely populated megalopolis of many neighboring villages, while Saginaw was left to the Chippewas. The region of Grand Traverse was ceded to the Chippewas, according to later tradition, in compensation for a murder committed by an Ottawa; nevertheless, many Ottawas continued to live there (Tanner 1830; Blackbird 1887; MPHC 11:544, 553, 12:262; Schoolcraft 1851:479).

The groups south and west of Lake Michigan united with the Potawatomis and Chippewas of that region, thereby gradually losing their political independence as a tribe. The confederated tribes, sometimes called The Three Fires, were removed after 1833 to Iowa and later to Kansas (WHC 20:237, 350; Temple 1958).

Although the Ottawas first entered into treaty relations with the United States in 1785, continued hostilities prevented actual realization of land cessions until Gen. Anthony Wayne's treaty of 1795 when the Ohio groups lost part of their land (fig. 6). Some Ottawas thereupon removed to Walpole Island and neighboring parts of Ontario. Those who planned to join the Arbre Croche bands were not permitted to settle there by their tribesmen. By 1817 the Ohio bands were confined to six

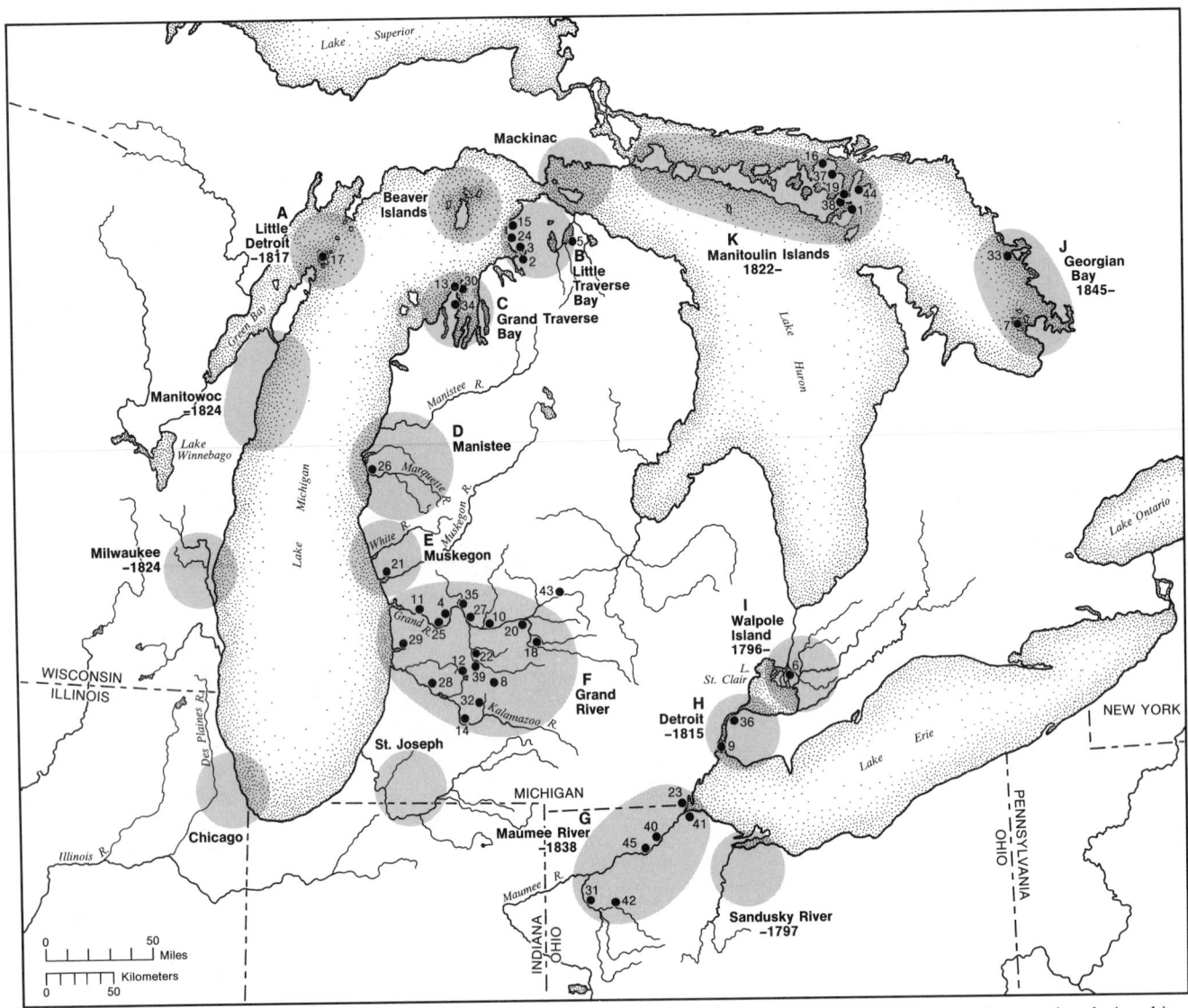

Fig. 5. Ottawa territories of the Great Lakes Region during the Anglo-American period. Only initial or terminal dates of occupation during this period are given. Village location is tentative; Agagotchiwing, Boozwah's village, Chabwasonendad, Shabawywyagun, and Wikwemikonsing cannot be located. The Ottawa hunters' village Menawshetaunang is northwest of Lake Superior. Not all synonyms for villages are given. Villages are grouped by lettered area. 1K, Achittawahnegunig; 2B, Agaming; 3B, Arbre Croche (Waganakisi); 4F, Bawqueting; 5B, Cheboygan; 6I, Chenail Ecarté; 7J, Christian Island; 8F, Clear Lake; 9H, Fighting Island; 10F, Flat River; 11F, Fort Village; 12F, Griswold Colony; 13C, Kachagensodibanig; 14F, Kekalamazoo; 15B, Lacroix (Cross Village, Anamiewatigonwink); 16K, Little Current; 17A, Little Detroit; 18F, Looking Glass River; 19K, Manitowaning; 20F, Maple River; 21E, Maskikong; 22F, Meshinmekons; 23G, Meskemau's village (Waugau's village); 24B, Middle Village; 25F, Muckatasha's village; 26D, Nindebakatunnig; 27F, Nongee's village; 28F, Old Wing Colony I; 29F, Old Wing Colony II; 30C, Old Wing Colony III; 31G, Oquanoxa's village; 32F, Ottawa Colony (Gull Prairie); 33J, Parry Island; 34C, Peshabestown (Kitchiwikwedonk); 35F, Prairie Village; 36H, Sandwich; 37K, Sheguiandah; 38K, South Bay; 39F, Thornapple River; 40G, Tontogami's village (Roche de Boeuf); 41G, Tushquegan (McCarty's village); 42G, Upper Tawa Town (Blanchard's Fork); 43F, Wabegahke's village; 44K, Wikwemikong; 45G, Wolf Rapids.

small reservations along the Maumee and Auglaize rivers, which they were forced to cede in 1831 and 1833 prior to their removal to a reservation in Franklin County, Kansas. A few individuals remained in Ohio; others migrated to Canada (MPHC 20; Baumann 1949; Schoolcraft 1851:483; Kappler 1904, 2; Foreman 1946).

In Michigan, all lands south of the Grand River were ceded in 1821 against the will of most Indians (Kappler 1904–1941, 2; McCoy 1840; Gordon 1959). A delegation

sent to Washington in 1836 to prevent removal to Kansas was finally induced to cede the remaining lands in the Michigan Lower Peninsula. Reservations established by that treaty were only partially surveyed, but the Indians were allowed to live on their lands beyond the five-year period originally stipulated. The 1836 treaty entailed large-scale emigration of Michigan Indians (particularly Catholic Ottawas) to Manitoulin Island, which was set aside for the use of the Indians in the same year.

FEEST AND FEEST

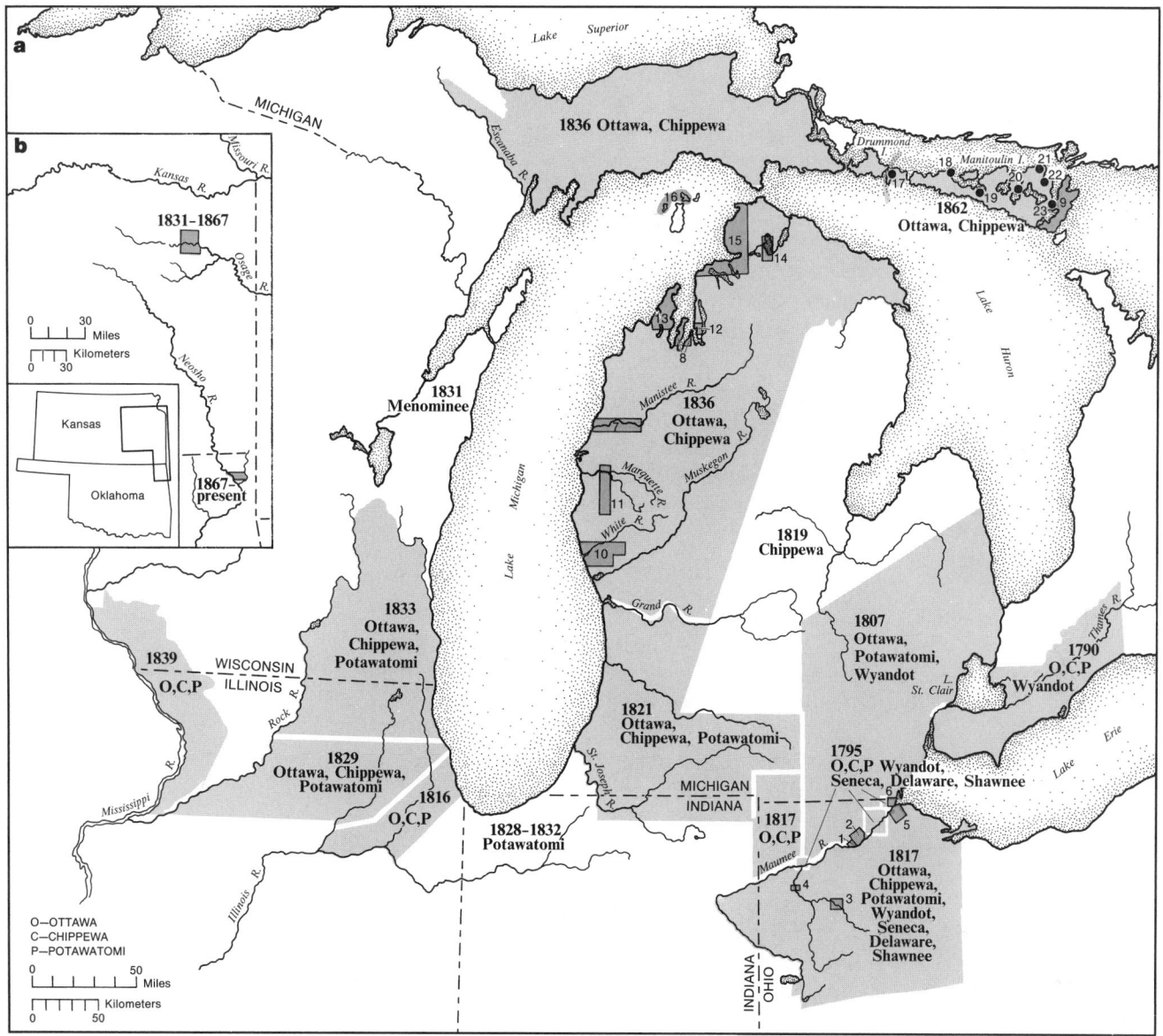

Fig. 6. Reservations and land cessions. a, the Great Lakes region (after Royce 1899): 1, Wolf Rapids, 2, Roche de Boeuf, 1807-ceded 1831; 3, Blanchard's Fork, 4, Oquanoxa's village, 1817-ceded 1831; 5, Tushquegan, 1807-ceded 1833; 6, Meskemau's village, 1817-ceded 1833; 7, Manistee, 1836-sold 1848; 8, Grand Traverse Bay, 1836-ceded 1855; 9, Manitoulin Island (eastern portion), 1833-present. Set apart in 1855 for allotment: 10, reserve in Muskegon and Newaygo counties; 11, reserve in Mason and Oceana counties; 12, Grand Traverse East; 13, Grand Traverse West; 14, Cheboygan (Burt Lake); 15, Little Traverse Bay; 16, High and Garden islands. Reservations established 1862: 17, Cockburn Island; 18, Sheshegwaning; 19, Obigewong; 20, West Bay; 21, Sucker Creek; 22, Sheguiandah; 23, Sucker Lake. b, Kansas and Oklahoma.

A similar but smaller movement to Drummond Island (still British at that time) had been occasioned by the 1821 treaty (Royce 1899; Blackbird 1887; Schoolcraft 1851–1857, 3:538; Saenderl 1833–1836:3.60). In 1855 lands were allotted in severalty to the Ottawas remaining in Michigan, and their tribal organization was formally dissolved. While most Grand River Ottawas took up lands on the reservations set aside for them in Mason and Oceana counties, others joined the Ottawas, Chippewas, and Potawatomis of Manitoulin Island or settled among the Chippewas of Georgian Bay, partly in anticipation of the consequences of the 1855 treaty, as other

bands had already done in the 1830s (Kappler 1904–1941, 2; ARCIA 1858:22–30; Murray 1963).

When in 1862 the Province of Canada approached the Manitoulin Indians regarding a cession of land, those bands living east of Manitowaning Bay and South Bay—mostly Ottawas—refused to sign the treaty, while the other bands were assigned eight small reserves and received annuities from the proceeds of the sale of their lands (Dominion of Canada 1905, 1). After their tribal organization in Kansas was dissolved in 1867, the Ottawas sold their individual allotments and moved to northeastern Indian Territory within the jurisdiction of the

779

Quapaw Agency to avoid mounting conflicts with their White neighbors (Foreman 1946).

Apart from formal relations with British and American government agencies, missionary contacts were of primary importance in Ottawa-White relations. In 1799, slightly more than 30 years after the end of a century of French Catholic missionary efforts among the Ottawas of that region, only one Catholic Indian could be found in Arbre Croche (MPHC 1). In 1825, however, Catholic missions, first served by French, later by Austrian and German priests, were reestablished in the Arbre Croche region on the initiative of the Ottawas. The mission not only succeeded in the formal conversion of a majority of the Indians there but also helped to make the villages of Arbre Croche a frequently quoted model for successful acculturation. With the emigration to Manitoulin Island, the Catholic faith gained another stronghold there, in spite of competition from Church of England missionaries, who arrived in 1838. Catholic missions on Grand River and Grand Traverse Bay were less successful (J.E. Feest 1972).

Presbyterian missions were founded in Mackinac in 1823 and on Grand Traverse Bay in 1838. The Baptists, who favored removal of the Indians to the West, established themselves in 1825 near Grand Rapids. After the removal of the Ohio bands to Kansas, the Baptists served these groups, which since the early 1820s had had a missionary affiliated with the United Foreign Missionary Society. The Baptist Ottawas of Grand Rapids after 1836 established Ottawa Colony near Gull Prairie, which was discontinued in 1852. Old Wing Colony, a Congregational mission, was started in 1838 with a group of Arbre Croche Indians near Allegan, removed to a location near Holland one year later, and finally to Grand Traverse Bay in 1848. An Episcopalian mission near Wayland, known as Griswold Colony, was also founded in 1838 after funds for education and missions became available under the treaty of 1836.

A substantial part of the activities of the various missions was concerned with the establishment of schools for the Indians. The missionaries frequently also tried to help the Indians against the encroachments of White settlers and in fighting the problem of alcoholism. Distilled liquor had been introduced by White traders at first legally, later illegally on Indian lands since early contact times. Later, Indian temperance societies and Indian antiliquor laws helped to control abuses to some degree. Although data on population become more reliable during the nineteenth century, they are still far from being satisfactory. Moreover, assignment of figures to tribal rather than polyethnic local groups becomes increasingly difficult (table 2). Epidemic diseases such as measles and smallpox continued to affect the Ottawas into the 1860s, while the frequent removals also cost a heavy toll of lives.

Table 2. Population Estimates, 1782–1863

	1782[e]	1800[f]	1820[g]	1838[h]	1845[i]	1863[j]
West and northwest of Lake Superior	?	?	?			
Mackinac, Bois Blanc and Drummond Islands[a, b]	?	?	?	50	50	?
Beaver Islands[b]	?	?	?	150	50	?
Cheboygan[b]			?	100	60	100
Little Traverse Bay	1,000	1,300	1,500	1,000	550	1,200
Grand Traverse Bay[a, b]		?	750	450	500	750
Between Grand Traverse and Grand River		?	350	400	?	1,200
Grand River	1,200	?	1,000	950	700	
Kalamazoo River		?	500	250	400	
Illinois[c]	?	?	?			
Wisconsin[c]	?	?	500			
Manitoulin Island[a]				300	1,100	1,500
Christian Island[d]				?	?	100
Walpole Island/Detroit	?	170	?	?	?	150
Ohio	?	?	380	150		
Kansas				240	200	200

[a] Includes Chippewas.
[b] Sometimes identified only as Chippewas.
[c] Includes Chippewas and Potawatomis.
[d] Includes Potawatomis.
[e] John Coates (MPHC 10:635). There were at least two villages north of Little Traverse Bay by 1778 (MPHC 9:655) one of which alone could muster 260 warriors (perhaps 1,000 total population) (MPHC 11:506).
[f] Little Traverse Bay: Gabriel Richard, 1799 (MPHC 1:485). Walpole Island and Detroit River: bands at Chenail Ecarte, Harsens Island, and near Sandwich, 1797–1799 (MPHC 20:564, 617–618, 641).
[g] Michigan: Census of Indians on east and west sides of Lake Michigan, 1819 (WHC 20:50; cf. J. Morse 1822: Appendix 23, 362). Wisconsin: Census of Wisconsin Indians, 1824 (WHC 20:350; for 1821: WHC 20:237); J. Morse 1822: Appendix 362. Ohio: J. Morse 1822: Appendix 362.
[h] Michigan: Lanman, 1837 (1839:311–312); ARCIA (1838:453), 1840 (1851–1857, 3:615–616). Manitoulin Island: O'Neill (1838–1839:4). Ohio: emigrants to Kansas 1837, 1839 (Foreman 1946:91). Kansas: McCoy (1835–1838, 4:36).
[i] Michigan, Kansas: Schoolcraft, 1847 (1851–1857, 1:458–478). Manitoulin Island: Chazelle (1845:457).
[j] Michigan: ARCIA (1864:374–380). Kansas: ARCIA (1864:244). Manitoulin Island, Christian Island, Walpole Island: Spragge (1865:22, for Walpole Island a total of 700 Chippewa, Potawatomi, and Ottawa).

Culture

New crops—such as potatoes, turnips, and wheat—and various vegetables, fruit trees, and new agricultural techniques and implements introduced by missionaries and government farmers affected traditional economic patterns in varying degrees. During the 1840s the villages of Arbre Croche and the emigrants on Manitoulin Island and in Kansas were the first groups to subsist chiefly on the produce of their fields; in both regions this was accompanied by a decline of hunting and abandonment of seasonal mobility, which before and elsewhere was still marked. In Michigan, the Ottawas annually moved to their hunting grounds and sugar camps; on Manitoulin where game was particularly scarce, they moved to their fishing stations (Schoolcraft 1851-1857, 1; McCoy 1840; Pierz 1837-1864, 17:58, 1934-1935, 26:396).

Fishing remained important for all groups except those in Kansas; autumn and spring were the main seasons. Northern groups practiced ice-hole fishing in winter. Hunting, both for food and for furs, was, of course, vital for those Ottawas roving the country northwest of Lake Superior. Until the depletion of game resources and the opening of the country for settlement, the Grand River bands also had their share in the fur trade (Jacobs 1857-1861, 2, 3; Tanner 1830; Saenderl 1833-1836:3.52).

Maple sugar was produced for trade, mainly in the northern Lower Peninsula, where in 1847 the annual production from each family was almost 20 times as great as in the Grand River area. A few groups also produced honey (Schoolcraft 1851-1857, 1).

Cattle and pigs were raised by most groups from the 1820s and 1830s. Poultry was kept by the Arbre Croche groups and the emigrants in Wikwemikong, who also owned sheep. Dogs were kept as pets and were sometimes eaten. Horses were to some degree used for transportation (Baraga 1831-1864, 7:20; Hanipaux 1846; McCoy 1840).

Changes in the economic situation are mirrored in changes in the sexual division of labor (such as male participation in agriculture), specialization of economic

pursuits (the development of professionalism), and incipient wage labor.

Except for Indian masonry in Wikwemikong, work in stone was limited to the manufacture of catlinite pipe heads, while woodworking grew in importance as many Indians (particularly of the Arbre Croche region) became carpenters: they built log and frame houses and made furniture and plank boats that gradually replaced bark canoes, while the older men still carved wooden spoons and dishes (Frémiot 1855; Pitzer 1854; Baraga 1831-1864, 30; Schoolcraft 1851-1857, 1, 3).

A few Ottawas worked as smiths in government forges established according to treaty regulations in their villages; and some became shoemakers, although most leatherwork was still done by the women. Textile techniques (with spinning, knitting, and weaving introduced through mission schools) remained as much a female domain as beadwork, porcupine-quill and moosehair embroidery and appliqué on leather (fig. 7) and birchbark, some of which was also done in the schools (Blackbird 1887; McCoy 1840; Schoolcraft 1851-1857, 1; Dejean 1831; ARCIA 1850:201-202; Pitzer 1854).

Hunting would have been impossible without guns, although traps were more important for the bands engaged in fur hunting. Bows and arrows served for fowling and as a boys' toy, and wooden ball-headed clubs likewise lost their importance. Fishing gear included fishing spears, hook and line, and nets. Nets were also used in hunting on Beaver Island. After 1825 all groups came into the possession of ploughs, hoes, spades, shovels, and other agricultural implements (Pitzer 1854; Pierz 1837-1864, 17). Before wooden houses became common around 1830, the Ottawas had given up Huron-type longhouses for dome-shaped wigwams. Roofs of bark were also used with log houses. Conical tents with bark or mat coverings (fig. 8) remained in use as tempo-

Fig. 7. Decorated beaver skin. Dorsal side natural, ventral side painted black with a vertical slit opening. Tail and legs are appliquéd with layers of cloth and beaver skin with silk and beadwork overlay; fringes are of multi-color ribbons. The bag kept arrows dry and was frequently used for traveling. Collected in 1851-1853, length 94.5 cm.

Fig. 8. Ottawa village, Mackinac Is. Conical bark-covered tepees and bark canoes in a temporary fishing village. Lithograph after original by Castelnau, 1838-1839.

rary dwellings on hunting trips or in traveling (Gordon 1959; Mrak 1851; Schoolcraft 1851a; Pierz 1934-1935, 26).

Trade cloth increasingly replaced leather in clothing (fig. 9), and Euro-American garments were worn by segments of the population. Blankets were used instead of fur robes, trousers supplanted leggings and breechclouts, and finally moccasins gave way to shoes. Various ornaments were still worn in pierced noses and earlobes, and silver jewelry found a wide distribution until missionaries banned traditional styles of attire among their flocks. Some Catholic priests insisted on cutting the hair of their converts after White fashion, while pagan Ottawas either wore theirs long and occasionally braided or let only a tuft of hair stand on the crowns of their shaved heads. Face painting likewise faded from common usage (Gordon 1959; Schoolcraft 1851-1857, 3; Dejean 1828-1831, 4; Pierz 1934-1935, 26).

Snowshoes of the bear-paw frame type facilitated traveling in winter. Wooden yokes were used to carry birchbark buckets filled with maple sap. Bark canoes were usually propelled with short oars, but on Lake Michigan some of them were equipped with sails (fig. 10) (Pitzer 1854; Schoolcraft 1851-1857, 1).

During the Anglo-American period the tribe consisted of several largely autonomous local segments made up of several villages each, which rarely took joint action. At least the Grand River and Arbre Croche bands had in addition a large number of exogamous patrilineal totemic descent groups, while the Kansas Ottawas by 1859 disclaimed any knowledge of such units. Totems included bear, pike, henhawk, sparrow hawk, forked tree, gull, wolf, eagle, beaver, panther, panther's foot, panther's track. Lists recorded during the early twentieth century name up to 50 different clans (Tanner 1830; McCoy 1840; Dejean 1828-1831, 4; Morgan 1959; Radin 1926; Michelson 1911a).

Besides the war chiefs, whose importance was diminishing, there were several village chiefs for each village. Chiefs were elected, usually from among the near relatives of the former chief. Their authority with the tribe was small, although both missionaries and government officials were interested in strengthening the power of cooperative leaders. Female chiefs are also mentioned. Most decisions were made by the council consisting of the adult males of a village or region (Baraga 1831-1864, 5; Mrak 1851; McCoy 1840; King 1915; MPHC 12:108; Assikinack 1858a).

Peabody Mus., Harvard U.

Fig. 9. "Two Ottawa Chiefs who with others lately came down from Michillimachinac Lake Huron to have a talk with their great Father, the King or his representative." They wear clothing of trade cloth and complex trade-silver ornaments. Watercolor and quoted title by Sir Joshua Jebb, 1813-1820.

Murderers were tried by a jury consisting of the relatives of both concerned parties. Speakers for both sides outlined their positions, and the defendant's group offered compensation. Finally, the pipe was passed around, and the victim's relatives had the choice of accepting it or killing the murderer. In all cases involving Whites, justice was administered by White courts (Pitzer 1854; MPHC 4:544-556; G.S. Hubbard 1911).

Formal education in mission schools supplemented and partly replaced traditional ways of learning. Besides religious instruction, the boys usually learned reading, writing, mathematics, and geography; the girls, reading, needlework, and occasionally quillwork. At first, instruction was in Ottawa (with different systems of transcription used by Catholics and Baptists); later it became bilingual with French originally preferred to English in Catholic schools, which also favored the use of native teachers. School attendance varied according to seasonal mobility connected with economic pursuits.

Polygyny (including the sororal variety), the sororate, and the levirate were practiced into the 1830s, while missionary influence favored monogamy and introduced restrictions on cousin marriage (Gordon 1959; Baraga 1831-1864, 7; Dejean 1828-1831, 4; Clicteur 1830; Assikinack 1858).

Burial was by primary inhumation. At the head of the grave a wooden post with pictographic inscriptions was set up. Food was offered at the grave a few days after the burial and also every year in a communal feast for the dead, which consisted of decorating the graves, mourning, fasting, and finally feasting. Mourning customs included blackening of the face and scratching it with sharp stones (McCoy 1840; G.S. Hubbard 1911; Gordon 1959; Clicteur 1830).

Every person was believed to have two souls, one which died with the body, while the other one traveled to the afterworld. Missionary contact gave rise to a story, frequently recorded among the Ottawas and neighboring tribes, about a Christian Indian who was refused admission to Christian heaven as an Indian and to the Indian afterworld for being a Christian (Baraga 1831-1864, 7; Clicteur 1830; Dejean 1828-1831, 4; O'Meara 1846; Radin 1926).

Before intensive Christianization, three native religious institutions are known to have existed, whose members were called Meta (*mite·*), Wabeno (*wa·pano·*), and Jossakeed (*ča·ssakki·t*). The *mite·wiwin* or Medicine Society was open to men and women who were initiated during the medicine feast (fig. 10). Its purpose, like that of the Wabeno society, was to secure the well-being of its members through the powers of the medicine. The Jossakeeds had the gifts of prophecy and divination and performed the shaking-tent rite during which the prophet was visited in his specially prepared tent by spirits who made the structure shake (Schoolcraft 1851a; Meeker 1908; McCoy 1840; Assikinack 1858a).

The Citizenship Period

In the modern period, sizable Ottawa groups remained in the lower Michigan peninsula and on Manitoulin Island. Most of the Indians on the unceded portion of Manitoulin were Catholic Ottawas, but over the years they were joined by bands from the ceded portion (such as the South Bay band) or from the coasts of Georgian Bay (such as the Tahgaiwinini band of Chippewas). Many of the Ottawas on the ceded part of the island, on the other hand, were integrated by the Chippewas there. Likewise, the Ottawas of Parry Island, Christian Island, and Walpole Island merged with the Chippewa and Potawatomi, without, however, fully losing their identity as Ottawas. A similar but still less marked amalgamation of Ottawa and Chippewa populations occurred in Michigan. Outside the main Ottawa area, groups of the tribe continued in Oklahoma and on the Lac du Flambeau Reservation in Wisconsin (see table 3).

As the Ottawas within the United States became citizens and had their lands allotted in severalty, they suddenly came into full contact with White society. The groups in Oklahoma and the northern Lower Peninsula of Michigan due to their higher level of acculturation had less difficulty in coping with resulting problems than the former Grand River bands in Mason and Oceana

Fig. 10. Top, probably participants in a Medicine Dance; middle figure holds a medicine pouch. Bottom, canoe with sail and flag showing European influence. Drawing from sketchbook of the mission school at Arbre Croche, about 1838-1848.

Table 3. Population Estimates, 1872-1970

	1872[b]	1910[c]	1970[d]
Oklahoma	150	170	500
Wisconsin	?	50	?
Ontario[a]	1,900	1,900	3,000
Michigan	?	2,500	4,500

[a] The figures for Manitoulin Island include Chippewas and Potawatomis.

[b] Oklahoma: ARCIA (1872:389). Ontario: Spragge (1874:30); 1,650 on Manitoulin Island, the rest among mixed groups in Georgian Bay and on Walpole Island.

[c] Oklahoma, Wisconsin, Michigan: U.S. Bureau of the Census (1915:19). Ontario: Canada. Department of Indian Affairs (1910:112-114); 962 on the unceded portion of Manitoulin Island, 711 on the ceded portion.

[d] Oklahoma estimate for 1950: Tax and Stanley (1960). Michigan: estimate by Robert Dominic (personal communication 1972). Ontario: Wikwemikong band list of 1968 showed 2,725 registered, of whom 1,922 were actually resident on the unceded reserve (Emöke Szathmáry, personal communication 1972).

counties. After termination of federal services to them at a time when they correctly believed the government still owed them treaty money, these groups frequently had to mortgage their lands, generally losing them in the process. With hunting and fishing rights infringed contrary to treaty stipulations, many Indians left their former reservation. Some members of the old Griswold Colony returned to Allegan County (Spooner 1931; MHPC 32:381-383; U.S. Census Office 1894).

While in the late nineteenth century many Ottawas were still monolingual, increased contact with Whites rapidly reduced the number of Ottawa speakers. By the 1960s the language was rarely remembered in Oklahoma, spoken by about one-third of the Michigan groups, and spoken by approximately two-thirds of the Indians on the Wikwemikong Unceded Reserve. Another consequence of living with Whites was the growing number of Indian-White marriages. White admixture follows the same patterns as linguistic acculturation, with Oklahoma Ottawas most and Wikwemikong Indians least mixed (Chafe 1965; U.S. Bureau of the Census 1915, 1937).

Around 1900, most Oklahoma Ottawas were engaged in farming, while the majority of the Michigan Indians (and similarly those of Manitoulin Island) had their own farms, worked as farm laborers, or worked as lumbermen. Many Ottawa women produced baskets for sale. Berry picking and gathering of roots was of seasonal importance, as was maple-sugar production on Manitoulin. Particularly since World War II, many Indians have moved from their rural locations where employment was hard to find to the cities in southern Michigan, or from Wikwemikong to Sudbury, Toronto, and other places.

Mat making was given up by the Michigan Ottawas in the early twentieth century, but splint baskets and quill-decorated birchbark boxes were produced to a limited extent throughout the 1960s. Knowledge about native herbal medicines was still widespread among traditionalists, while native religious ideas and practices were little more than remembered. Most traditionalists in the field of songs and dances had died by the 1960s; however, this was compensated for by a revival with at least pan-Indian influences (fig. 11). The tendency to preserve

Ann Arbor Publishers.
Fig. 11. Blue Cloud, wearing typical pan-Indian fringed buckskin jacket and feather warbonnet. Photograph by Gertrude Prokosch Kurath, powwow ground, Isabella Reservation, 1954.

the Ottawa language and culture was probably most pronounced among the Indians of Wikwemikong.

While tribal organization with elected chief and band council at Wikwemikong continued to function under the Canadian Indian Act of 1876, the Oklahoma Ottawas was reorganized in 1938–1939 under the Oklahoma Indian Welfare Act and were terminated by Act of Congress in 1955. The Northern Michigan Ottawa Organization, founded in 1948, having won claims judgments for the Grand River band under the treaty of 1821, became involved in further litigation. Numerous other organizations were formed in Michigan in the 1960s to derive benefit from Office of Economic Opportunity antipoverty programs.

Synonymy

The spelling Ottawa is usual in the United States and in Canadian government usage, while Odawa is preferred by Canadian Indians. The term in the Ottawa language is *otaʼwaˑ*. Other spellings include: Ahtawwah (Kane 1859:23), O-dah-wah (Schoolcraft 1851–1857, 5:192), Otawa (Pierz 1837–1864, 15:63), Oatouats (1684, WHC 16:115), Ottaways (Carver 1770:12), Ottavois (1707, MPHC 33:327), Ottowa (1831, MPHC 37:222), Ottah-wahs (O'Meara 1846:1), Outaouan (1641, JR 18:230), Outaouak (1656, JR 42:234), Outaoüax (1663, JR 48:116), Outaois (1708, MPHC 33:433), Outaouas (1703, MPHC 33:552), Outa8ois (1708, MPHC 33:680), Outavas (1717, MPHC 33:584), Outaouats (1683, WHC 16:119), Outaouacs (1703, WHC 16:221), Outavois (1694, MPHC 33:71), Outáwas (1778, MPHC 9:479), 8ta8ak (1653, JR 38:180), 8ta8as (1701, MPHC 33:113), 8ta8ats (1665, JR 49:161), Ontanaak (1648, JR 33:150), Utavois (1701, MPHC 33:113), Uttawaw (1764, Thwaites 1904–1907, 1:302), Tawa (1760, MPHC 19:44), Tawaw (1757, Stuart 1926:74), Taway (1790, MPHC 12:21). Some Huron designations are: Andatahouats (Sagard-Théodat 1632a:131), Onadata8a8ak (1653, JR 38:180), ondataüaüat (1653, JR 39:14).

Ottawas first became known to the French as cheueux releuez (Champlain 1922–1936, 3:43), Poil leué (Sagard-Théodat 1632a:77), and stairing haires (Radisson 1885:153). Sometimes they were also called Courtes Oreilles (1790, MPHC 11:607), Courtoreiller (1780, MPHC 10:435), Short-Ears (1778, MPHC 8:466), Kurzohren (Kohl 1857:370). The Iroquois called them Dewagunhas (Colden 1747, 1:cxi), Waganis (1691, NYCD 3:808), or Wagenhaes (1693, NYCD 4:61).

Sources

A partial explanation for the inadequate treatment the Ottawas have found in the ethnological literature may lie in the great number and diversity of sources on their culture and history, none of which, however, gives a full and coherent account. Champlain (1922–1936) gave the first brief description of Ottawa Indians, to which Sagard-Théodat (1632a, 1636) adds further details. Reliable data are supplied in the reports of Jesuit missionaries such as Ragueneau, Ménard, Allouez, Marquette, André, Nouvel, Dablon, and Râle, which cover mainly the period between 1660 and 1723 (JR, especially 33, 41, 50-52, 54-57, 59, 61, 67). These data are supplemented by those furnished by the French explorer Radisson (1885) writing in broken English, the trader and interpreter Perrot (1864) who had lived among various Indian tribes for more than 30 years, Bacqueville de la Potherie (1753) who used extensively Perrot's other writings now lost, and Lahontan (1703) who in 1688-1689 had lived in the old French fort near Mackinac. As in Lahontan's account, little explicit distinction between data on the Hurons and the Ottawas is made in Cadillac's report on Michilimackinac, which he commanded from 1694 to 1697 (Margry 1876-1886, 5:75-132). Further French sources are Raudot (1904), Charlevoix (1744), Bougainville (1964), the documents published by Margry (1876-1886), unpublished archival material (see W.G. Leland 1932), and records published in English translations in NYCD (9, 10), WHC (16-18), and MPHC (33, 34). Among the English reports on the Ottawas of the 1750s and 1760s are the narratives of the Indian captives J. Smith (1799), Stuart (1926), and Henry (1901), and the explorer Carver (1770, 1778). Further sources on the old Northwest, partly also covering the British period, are discussed in Beers (1964). Many of those relating to the Ottawas have been used by Peckham (1947). No documented collections of Ottawa material culture are known from the French period. For early maps see Karpinski (1931).

Records connected with the American Revolution, Indian affairs in the American-Canadian border region, and the War of 1812 supply most of the data on the Ottawas until the 1820s (MPHC 8-12, 15, 16, 19, 20, 23, 24; WHC 18-20; Alvord and Carter 1916). An exception is Tanner's (1830) captivity narrative, describing the life of northern Ottawa hunting groups around 1800. Pioneer settlers' reminiscences (not always very reliable) and related documents are printed in various volumes of MPHC and WHC.

In spite of their professional bias, missionaries' accounts are the most interesting group of nineteenth-century sources, because their authors lived and worked among the Indians. On the Arbre Croche region, there are the reports of French and Austrian Catholic priests (see Badin 1826; Dejean 1828-1831, 1831; Clicteur 1830; Baraga 1831-1864; Pierz 1835-1843, 1837-1864, 1934-1935; Mrak 1851; Saenderl 1833-1836). On Manitoulin there were both Catholic (Gaulein 1840; Chazelle 1845; Hanipaux 1846; Choné 1848; Frémiot 1855) and

Church of England missionaries (O'Meara 1846, 1846a, 1838-1857; Jacobs 1857-1861). The Grand River Ottawas are best known from Baptist sources (McCoy 1840; see also Bolt 1967) that refer also to Kansas (McCoy 1835-1838; Meeker 1850, 1908), while the sole missionary source on the Maumee bands is Van Tassel (1826-1836). On other missionary activities see MPHC 4:544-556, 30:190-212, 32:381-383 and Vogel (1967).

Some reports of travelers add appreciably to the data on the nineteenth-century Ottawas: Gordon (1959) on the Grand River, G.S. Hubbard (1911) on the Grand River and Manistee, Kane (1859) on Manitoulin, A.B. Jameson (1838) on Mackinac and Manitoulin, Castelnau (1842) on Mackinac, Pitzer (1854) on the Arbre Croche region, and Morgan (1959) on Kansas. Pitzer also assembled a well-documented collection of Ottawa material culture, which with other Ottawa pieces from before 1850 is preserved in the Museum für Völkerkunde, Vienna (Feest 1968). The Southwest Museum, Los Angeles, owns a large collection of Ottawa quill-decorated birchbark (Watkins 1935).

Several of the writings of Schoolcraft (1851, 1851a, 1851-1857), who was Indian agent in Sault Sainte Marie and Mackinac and later superintendent of Indian affairs, add valuable data on the Ottawas. The same is true for the reports of Indian agents (Schoolcraft, Stuart, Richmond, Gilbert, Fitch, Leach) and the appended school and farm reports in the annual Reports of the Commissioner of Indian Affairs since 1838 and their Canadian counterparts.

The reminiscences of the Ottawa Indian Blackbird (1887), his tribesman Assikinack (1858a), as well as the materials recorded by ethnographers (Michelson 1911a, 1932; Radin 1926) shed further light on nineteenth-century Ottawa history and ethnography. Modern data were chiefly collected by Kurath (1956, 1957, 1966), Kurath and Willets (1955), and Willets (1947, 1947a, 1948). Among the few secondary sources Baumann (1949, 1954), J.E. Feest (1972), Foreman (1946), Kinietz (1940), Shurtleff (1963), Temple (1958), and J.C. Wright (1917) merit particular mention.

Data on the Ottawa in the 1960s in this chapter were provided by Robert Dominic, president of the Northern Michigan Ottawa Association; Jonathan Kaye, Centre for Linguistic Studies, University of Toronto; H. Kirkland Osoinach, Northern Michigan University; and Emöke Szathmáry, Department of Anthropology, University of Toronto.

Nipissing

GORDON M. DAY

Language, Territory, and Environment

The Nipissing (ˈnĭpĭˌsĭŋ) were an Algonquian-speaking people whose homeland was the environs of Lake Nipissing, Ontario. Nipissing speech had an obvious relationship with Algonquin, Ottawa, and the Ojibwa dialects. The first missionaries among them discovered that their speech differed in many respects from the Algonquins (JR 21:245), but in 1752 Franquet (1889) was told that the Nipissings and Algonquins living together at the Lake of Two Mountains mission spoke the same language with slight differences. Long (1791) thought they all spoke "Chippeway" and began to learn from them the Chippeway that he used later in the Great Lakes region. McLean (1932) thought they spoke a dialect of "Sauteux." By 1847 Nipissing had become the dominant speech at Lake of Two Mountains, but Algonquin became the name of the mixed descendants and of their speech (Cuoq 1872; Pilling 1891:374). The distinguishing characteristics of the Algonquin dialects and of Nipissing remain to be worked out from fieldwork and the abundant manuscript materials.*

The precise limits of Nipissing territory are not known. They seem to have had for neighbors the Temiskaming and Temagami on the north; the Ottawa, Bonnechere, and Kipawa Algonquin bands on the east; the Hurons on the south; and the Amikwa and Achiligouan Ojibwa bands on the west.

Nipissing territory all lay within the glaciated Canadian Shield, within the mixed coniferous-deciduous forests of the Great Lakes-Saint Lawrence region (J.S. Rowe 1959:44, 48–49), and at or near the northern limit of maize cultivation. The fauna was that of Dice's (1943:13–16) Canadian Biotic Province and Rogers's (1967) Moose-Fish Subsistence Area. The earliest travelers noted the beauty of Lake Nipissing and the surrounding forests; the abundance of game, ducks, and swans; and the especial abundance of fish (Champlain 1922–1936, 3:39–41; Sagard-Théodat 1939:221). To mis-

* Words in the Nipissing dialect, which had become difficult to separate from Algonquin by the time modern scientific recordings became possible, are cited in the transcription used for Ojibwa (Bloomfield 1946, 1957). Modern recordings are generally unavailable for these dialects, but the forms have been phonemicized by Ives Goddard on the basis of information from other varieties of the Ojibwa language.

sionaries who followed the Nipissings in winter, their country was a land of lakes and treeless rocks but abounding in beaver (fig. 1) (JR 55:149).

Culture

A picture of the culture of the Nipissings at the time of White contact must be pieced together from the scattered observations of early writers whose interest in them was primarily religious or economic, which omits many details. Moreover, deducing aboriginal traits from the study

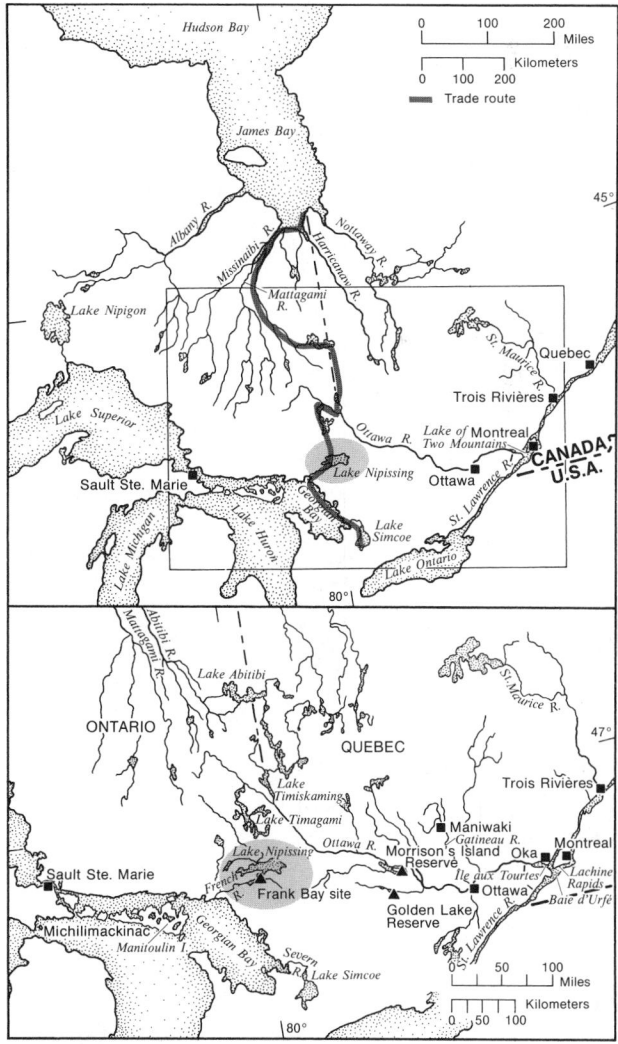

Fig. 1. Early territory and modern reserves.

of modern descendants is not possible, since apparently no ethnographic work has been done among unmixed Nipissing descendants, if indeed such exist. There is some Nipissing ancestry for the Algonquins at Maniwaki and Golden Lake and perhaps elsewhere and perhaps for the Ojibwa at Lake Nipissing, but Nipissing traits cannot be isolated from Algonquin ones, and no work has been published from Ojibwa excepting synopses of seven tales (Laidlaw 1922).

Enough was recorded by early writers to place the Nipissings basically among Flannery's (1946) Northeastern Hunters, probably in the Ojibwa subarea. Their subsistence was based on an annual round of fishing, hunting, and trading. Father Jerome Lalement recorded their annual round in detail:

> They seem to have as many abodes as the year has seasons,— in the Spring a part of them remain for fishing, where they consider it the best; a part go away with the tribes which gather on the shore of the North or icy sea, upon which they voyage ten days, after having spent thirty days upon the rivers, in order to reach it. In summer, they all gather together, on the road of the Hurons to the French, on the border of a large lake which bears their name. . . . About the middle of Autumn, they begin to approach our Hurons, upon whose lands they generally spend the winter; but, before reaching them, they catch as many fish as possible, which they dry. This is the ordinary money with which they buy their main stock of corn, although they come supplied with all other goods, as they are a rich people and live in comfort. They cultivate a little land near their Summer dwelling; but it is more for pleasure, and that they may have fresh food to eat, than for their support (JR 21:239-241).

This round was not invariable. Some winters all the Nipissings remained in the woods to hunt (JR 23:227, 30:125). Samuel de Champlain and Gabriel Sagard-Théodat had already learned of the Nipissings' northern trade with tribes who traded with a bald people who came in great wooden boats and traded axes, boots, and other things. Champlain thought the hides obtained from this northern tribe were bison. Hunt (1940:46) accepted Champlain's identification, added the word "west" to Sagard-Théodat's statement, and concluded that the Nipissings were trading with the Winnebagos; however, it is quite clear that this trade was with the Cree (JR 21:123, 44:243-245, 46:251), the "bald people" being the English explorers who visited Hudson Bay periodically beginning in 1610. Champlain had also observed that the Hurons were in part clothed by deer and beaver skins obtained from Nipissings and Algonquins in return for cornmeal, wampum, and fish nets.

It is possible to reconstruct only a sketchy outline of Nipissing cosmology and religion. Their Transformer was probably the Great Beaver (Perrot 1864:20-21), and they may have had a deluge story with the Earth Diver theme, since their neighbors both east and west had one (McLean 1932:111; Assikinack 1858:123-125). They shared shamanism—with both the properties of oracles and curing—with the boreal forest hunters generally and the Thunder Bird with many tribes (JR 5:233). They and other tribes westward to Sault Sainte Marie celebrated a Feast of the Dead that differed in many details from the Huron one. It was the occasion for transferring the names of the dead to living persons to perpetuate their memory and for electing and installing chiefs (JR 23:209-223). The presents that the Nipissings gave their guests in 1640 were estimated to be worth 40,000-50,000 francs. The sun may have been their Master of Life (JR 62:201) and the Great Panther their Master of Winds (Perrot 1864: 19-20). Father Henri Nouvel found four nations of Nipissings at Maskounagoüng on Lake Huron in 1682 or 1683, but little is known about their social organization. Maray de la Chauvinerie's statement that their totems were heron, beaver, birchbark, squirrel, and blood probably refers to the same kind of grouping, of "nations" that Nouvel made (NYCD 9:1053).

A few unsystematic observations may be gleaned from the *Jesuit Relations* as, for example, Nipissing refusal to whip children (JR 5:219) and their practice of throwing away the cradleboard of a deceased child (JR 33:159). They were much given to singing, and the missionaries thought their music harmonious (JR 21:123, 23:213).

Father Denis Jamet said the Nipissings were more slender than the Hurons but hardy and ready in traveling; wore long hair; went bareheaded; and dressed in the skins of beaver, marten, and other animals. He included them with the Montagnais and Algonquins as having no God but invoking the devil, and as being warlike, cruel, and revengeful (Jouve 1915,1:60-61). This characterization was probably obtained from a trader-interpreter, and it is possible that all Jamet's statements were second-hand, since Champlain, who was present at the Lachine Rapids at the same time as Jamet, did not mention the Nipissings' presence but proceeded up the Ottawa River to visit them. He found the Nipissings kindly and hospitable and enjoyed a two-day stay with them.

Some cultural observations were made during later periods of Nipissing history. Franquet (1889) described a joint Nipissing-Algonquin greeting dance at Lake of Two Mountains in 1752, and five years later Bougainville (1924) described a war dance. Father Pierre Roubaud left a description of a warrior's funeral after the battle of Fort William Henry in 1757 (JR 70:149-151).

History

The stratified Frank Bay site (Ridley 1954) may represent the prehistoric development of Nipissing culture. (See "Prehistory of the Canadian Shield," vol. 6).

Champlain first heard of the Nipissings at Montreal in 1613 and tried to visit them, but the Algonquins of Morrison's Island refused to help him. They said the Nipissings were malevolent sorcerers, but their reason was probably their unwillingness to put the Nipissings in direct contact with the French trade. He did visit them in 1615 and the following winter tried to get the Nipissings in Huronia to take him to the north sea where they traded, but they in turn put him off.

Between 1615 and 1629 the Recollect Fathers knew the Nipissings, but they took relatively little notice of them, preferring to focus their western activities on the Hurons. Brother Sagard-Théodat although disturbed by their shamanism, found them "very kindly and polite" and called them an "excellent people" who spoke Huron in addition to their own language. After the recall of the Recollects, the Nipissings continued to come to the French to trade, but not with total regularity. In 1636 a Huron-Nipissing band going down to trade was held up by the Algonquins, who wanted to control the traffic with the French. The Hurons and Nipissings retaliated by refusing the Algonquins' help against the Iroquois (JR 8:71-73, 9:271, 10:73-77). Already in 1634 there had been an epidemic among the Hurons and Nipissings. In the winter of 1636-1637, the Nipissings who were wintering in Huronia were afflicted by a sickness from which 70 died, which they blamed on the sorcery of an Algonquin captain retaliating for their failure to help against the Iroquois. In the spring they carried the bodies of their dead back to their own country, and in late summer they were still so beset by disease that the shamans complained that Manitou caused them to die as well as other people, thus making a mockery of their calling. This development may have made them more receptive to the teachings of the Jesuits, Claude Pijart and Charles Raymbault, who established in 1640 a mission for the Nipissings, wintered in Huronia, and followed them back to their country the next summer. Here they had considerable success due, at least in part, to the circumstance that all the sick children whom they baptized recovered. (Headman Mangouch and the chief headman Wikassoumint were converted.) Fathers René Ménard and Leonard Garreau were added to the Nipissing Mission of the Holy Ghost, and they continued their work in Huronia and even with the winter hunting parties.

In 1647, after the Iroquois had decimated the Lower Algonquins, the Nipissings joined them and the Montagnais in a defensive alliance, but little came of it (Perrot 1864:109-110). The ax was about to fall. In 1649 the Iroquois destroyed the Huron confederacy, and although this event occupied most of the attention of the Jesuit chroniclers, it is clear that the Nipissings also were attacked. Father Paul Ragueneau, on his retreat from Huronia in 1650, observed where the Iroquois had camped the previous winter to attack them. Perrot records that the Nipissings made a stand for several years, and this finds support in the record of a skirmish at Lake Nipissing in 1653 (JR 38:177). They finally fled westward, and by about 1661 both the Nipissings and the

Amikwas were at Lake Nipigon. In the summer of 1662 these Nipissings and Amikwas, having joined the Ottawas and "Saulteurs" for fishing near Sault Sainte Marie, ambushed and destroyed a sizable Mohawk and Oneida war party (Perrot 1864:81,93, 97-99; JR 48:75-77). The Nipissings continued to trade with the Cree about James Bay from their new location on Lake Nipigon and visited Trois Rivières by the northern route in 1657 and 1660. In July 1664, 60 Nipissings reached Montreal with their furs by the Ottawa River route, having been twice ambushed by the Iroquois, and Father Claude Allouez returned with them to work the western mission from Chequamegon. Not until 1667 did he visit the Nipissings at Lake Nipigon, where he found a number of Christian families who had not seen a missionary for nearly 20 years (JR 44:245-249, 46:251, 51:63-69).

Following the French-Iroquois peace of 1667, many Nipissings returned to their old country and became more prominent in the colony records. The Sulpician Father Dollier de Casson spent the winter of 1668-1669 with them, probably in their own country; there were Nipissings present at the installation of the new chief at Sillery in 1669; and in 1670 meetings between Nipissings and Iroquois were peaceable. Father Louis André spent the winter of 1670-1671 with them in Nipissing country, and Father Henri Nouvel visited them there two winters later; however, the Nipissings were still a dispersed people. A few were at the predominantly Iroquois mission of Saint François Xavier des Près near Montreal in 1671 or 1672; Nouvel encountered some in Michigan in 1675; and during the Illinois war, about 1677-1680, there were still Nipissings in the west being attacked by the Iroquois (JR 50:320, 55:147-153, 56:99, 105, 58:75, 60:219, 225-227; Perrot 1864:131). Father André Bonneault visited the eastern Nipissings in 1677, and about the same time Father Pierre Bailloquette established a mission for the Western Nipissings, serving them out of Michilimackinac. In the ensuing decade Iroquois-English and French rivalry increased, and events proved the Nipissings to be firmly on the side of the French, although they were at the same time trying to resist the brandy trade that the French urged on them (NYCD 9:196, 3:489; JR 62:201-203; Bacqueville de la Potherie 1911-1912, 2:79).

When King William's War broke out in 1689, the Nipissings seem to have participated in attacks on the English, presumably on Schenectady, Salmon Falls, and Falmouth, and they also went against the Iroquois from Michilimackinac with the Amikwas and the Kickapoos (Blair 1911-1912, 2:51, 79; NYCD 9:466). The eastern Nipissings also went out against the Iroquois and Fort Orange in 1695 and 1697 (NYCD 9:602, 669).

In the general peace that followed the Iroquois treaty of 1701, the Sulpicians gathered their Nipissing converts at Baie d'Urfé and later at Île aux Tourtes, where Gov.

Fig. 2. Portrait of a man from Lake Nipissing in 1845. Identified by the artist, Paul Kane, as Sha-nu-oh-ke-zhick or Against the Heavens. Beneath the portrait is a totem mark, possibly a heron.

Philippe Vaudreuil built a fort and missionary's house for them about 1706-1707 (Raudot 1904:213). A new Sulpician mission was founded at Oka on Lake of Two Mountains in 1721, and by 1735 all residents of Sulpician missions in the vicinity of Montreal had moved there (LaFontaine 1866-1907:87; O. Maurault 1930:3, 7). In 1742 additional Nipissings, possibly the remainder of the displaced westerners, joined the mission, but about 1748 smallpox decimated the village (O. Maurault 1930:18, 26). In 1752 Franquet found the Nipissings at the Lake living adjacent to, but separated from, the Algonquins in rectangular or square houses of wood built in the French manner. The French fur market declined after the Iroquois treaty of 1701; and after Queen Anne's War, the Nipissings and other Indians at the Lake began a trade with the English at Albany, a trade that continued in spite of French prohibition, until the outbreak of the War of the Conquest in 1755 (Faillon 1850-1865, fol. E:173). They stayed at the Lake only for the trade, departing in the late summer for hunting grounds far up the Ottawa River (Franquet 1889:45-47, 51, 121). When Bougainville (1924:270) visited the Lake of Two Mountains in July 1757 to sing the war song and recruit warriors, he observed that the different nations there had separate council houses. The Nipissings remained steady allies of the French against the English and fought at the battles of Oswego, Fort William Henry, and elsewhere. They sent warriors to Fort William Henry under Louis La Corne and were active in raiding behind the English lines.

After the fall of New France, the Canadian Indians came under the administration of Sir William Johnson, the English superintendent of Indian affairs. The Nipissings were enumerated and participated in the great council of 1,600 Indians held by Johnson at German Flats in July 1770 (NYCD 7:582, 8:299). They became allies of Great Britain and participated in the War of 1812 against the Americans (Ford and Ford 1969, 3:24). The French regime trading post at Lake of Two Mountains was succeeded by a post of the North West Company and, in 1819, by a Hudson's Bay Company post. Settlement in the Ottawa Valley caused Nipissings and Algonquins to move into hunting territories of other bands as early as 1828 with consequent friction and incidents (Ford and Ford 1969, 2:7, 3:24). Shortly after 1830 the Algonquins from Trois Rivières moved to Lake of Two Mountains, but in 1835 a cholera epidemic decimated the Lake of Two Mountains villages again, and the best hunters died or moved away. The Hudson's Bay post became unprofitable and was closed in 1847 (C.C.J. Bond 1966:15-16).

One group had moved away and settled at Golden Lake as early as 1807 (Public Archives of Canada, RG 610, 1, vol. 245, pt. 1; Lake 1966:157). In 1854 a large group moved to Maniwaki (Speck 1929:115-116). The remaining Nipissings and Algonquins kept their separate identity as long as they remained at Lake of Two Mountains (Parent 1887:121), but following disturbances and the burning of the church in 1877, all of both groups left. Some, perhaps all, removed to Maniwaki (Speck 1923a:226), but it is likely that the nominal Algonquin families and groups in the Ottawa Valley in the late nineteenth century derived at least in part from Lake of Two Mountains. These and the nominally Algonquin bands of Maniwaki and Golden Lake surely contain Nipissing descendants, but the destruction of the church records in 1877 prevents tracing Nipissing families in these groups.

Population

In 1615 Champlain (1922-1936, 3:40) estimated the Nipissing population at 700 or 800 persons. It suffered reductions in the seventeenth century from epidemics and the Iroquois wars. In 1710 those Nipissings that had gathered at Lake of Two Mountains were estimated at 50 warriors, perhaps 250 persons (Raudot 1904:213). After taking in more families and undergoing an epidemic, they sent 53 warriors to serve with Montcalm in 1757 (Bougainville 1924:278, 282). After the War of the Conquest, their warriors were estimated at 40 by Sir William Johnson (NYCD 7:582). An official census in 1827 gave them 250 persons (Ford and Ford 1969, 3:34). Population figures about 1965 for reserves that probably contain some Nipissing descendants are given as: River Desert

Algonquin (Quebec), 898; Lac Simon Algonquin (Quebec), 273; Golden Lake Algonquin (Ontario), 446; Nipissing Ojibwa (Ontario), 493 (Canada. Department of Indian Affairs and Northern Development 1967:9, 12).

Synonymy

The Nipissing were said to have taken their name from Lake Nipissing, where they lived in the seventeenth century (JR 44:242). This appears to be an archaic word meaning 'at the lake'. Variants include: Episingles (Dumont de Montigny 1753, 1:135), Epissingue (NYCD 10:485), Nepesinks (NYCD 6:281), Neperinks (NYCD 6:276), Nipistingues (JR 70:92, 100, 148, 198).

The seventeenth-century Algonquin or Nipissing form for 'Nipissing person' had substitution of -irini 'person' for the locative ending -ink; it usually appears with the French suffixes -(i)ens or -ains: Nebicerini, Nipisierinji, Pisierinij, 1613 (Champlain 1922–1936, 2:259, 3:39, 101), Nipisiriniens (JR 44:242), Nipeceriniens (Colden 1747, 1:28), Ebicerinys (Sagard-Théodat 1866, 1:172), Epicerinyens (Sagard-Théodat 1866, 3:718), Bisseriniens (JR 5:279, 8:71, 73, 10:77, 13:23, 191), Bissiriniens (JR 7:296), Pisirinins and Bissereins (Champlain 1922–1936, 3:104, 5:131).

The Nipissing's long-standing reputation for shamanism seems to have been the basis for their name in Iroquoian languages, which is translated 'nation des Sorciers' (JR 5:218) or 'sorcerers' (Mooney 1910d:74). Huron forms are Askic8aneronnons, 1639 (JR 17:164); Askik8anehronons, 1641 (JR 21:238); Kekerannon-rounons (NYCD 3:489), Skecaneronons (Sagard-Théodat 1866, 3:727), Skequaneronon, 1632 (Sagard-Théodat 1939:43); Squekaneronons (Sagard-Théodat 1866, 1:172). Mohawk Skekwanenhronon (Cuoq 1882:42) appears as Skaghquanoghronos, 1763 (NYCD 7:582); Skaghnanes, 1763 (NYCD 7:544); Skighquan, 1701 (NYCD 4:899). The resemblance of the Nipissing's name

to their word for sorcerer, nipihki·winini (from Cuoq 1886:281), may or may not be significant.

The Ojibwa and Algonquin name otiškwa·kami·k 'those at the last stretch of water' (from Cuoq 1886:314; Baraga 1878, 2:314) is reflected in Outiskoüagami, 1671 (JR 55:148); O-dish-quag-um-eeg (Schoolcraft 1851–1857, 2:139); odishquáhgummee (E.F. Wilson 1874:157); Juskwaugume (P. Jones 1861:178); and Ottawa Tuskwawgomeeg (Tanner 1830:316).

Sources

Although Étienne Brûlé and Nicolas de Vignau may have known the Nipissings, Champlain (1922–1936) was the first writer to mention them. Jamet (in Jouve 1915), Sagard-Théodat (1939), and, after 1634, the *Jesuit Relations* (JR 1896–1901) are the other principal early sources of information. The man who knew the Nipissings best was Jean Nicollet. He went to live with them about 1620 and lived with them eight or nine years. Barthélemy Vimont wrote that he "passed for one of that nation, taking part in the very frequent councils of those tribes, having his own separate cabin and household, and fishing and trading for himself." Unfortunately, his memoirs, which Father Paul LeJeune had at hand, have disappeared (JR 9:215–217, 23:275–277). Perrot (1864) is the authority for much information about the western sojourn of the Nipissings. An outline of later Nipissing activities can be gleaned from the colonial documents (NYCD), but the most abundant source after 1700 is the writings of the Sulpician Fathers, Archives de Notre-Dame de Montréal, whose manuscripts are virtually unworked for cultural data. Some information exists in the journals of fur traders, especially that of McLean (1932).

Rather abundant documentation of the language exists in the writings of Mathevet, Cuoq, and other Sulpician missionaries (see Pilling 1891).

Algonquin

GORDON M. DAY AND BRUCE G. TRIGGER

Language

The name Algonquin has been derived from the Maliseet *elakómkwik* 'they are our relatives (or allies)' (Day 1972:228). The English pronunciation is either ăl'gäŋkwĭn or ăl'gäŋkĭn (or either one with n in place of ŋ). Even the early writers extended the term to denote a wide variety of Algonquian-speaking peoples in eastern Canada, to the consequent confusion of historians. Today, the term Algonquin is used to signify a group of closely related bands that inhabited the Ottawa valley and adjacent regions to the east in the first half of the seventeenth century. Voegelin and Voegelin (1946: 181-182) have classified the Algonquin language as belonging, along with Ojibwa, Ottawa, and Saulteaux, to the "Middle Tier" of Algonquian. This Middle Tier is described as a single language, within which contiguous dialects were mutually intelligible. The linguistic definition of Algonquin in this group has not been worked out. The earliest sources testify to an *r*-dialect of Algonquin along the Saint Lawrence River (JR 24:38-42; Anonymous 1661; Nicolas 1672-1674), while later sources indicate an Ottawa and possibly an Algonquin *l*-dialect farther west (André 1688-1715; Mathevet 1750). Although the relationship between Algonquin and Ojibwa is obvious, it may not be so close as has been assumed on the basis of data from the Lake of Two Mountains mission (Bloomfield 1925:130). This mission sheltered both Algonquins and Nipissings, but by the middle of the nineteenth century Algonquin had disappeared and the well-known published writings of Cuoq, although called "Algonquin," are in fact Nipissing (Cuoq 1872:1). Study of the abundant manuscripts in the Sulpician archives would elucidate the Algonquin-Nipissing relationship. Although Lemoine (1911:3) thought his dictionary represented the speech of all nominal Algonquin bands, field checks turn up differences. Geary's data from the Abitibi region have not been published, but he has stated that this dialect lacks the Ojibwa hallmark of nasal-plus-stop sequences (Geary 1941:308).*

* Algonquin and Nipissing words are cited in the transcription used for Ojibwa (Bloomfield 1946, 1957). Modern recordings are generally unavailable for these dialects, but the forms have been phonemicized by Ives Goddard on the basis of information from other varieties of the Ojibwa language.

Territory

The Algonquins had the Montagnais as their neighbors to the east, with the Saint Maurice River apparently being the boundary between these two groups (JR 23:303-305). In earlier times, the Saint Lawrence Iroquoians had lived to the south. Culturally, as well as linguistically, the Algonquins closely resembled their nearest neighbors to the west, the Nipissings and Ottawas, more than the Montagnais to the east. It is unclear how far north the Algonquins extended, or whether, at the time of contact, the various bands living in the Lake Timiskaming and Abitibi region should be classified as Algonquin, Cree, or Montagnais.

From south to north, the bands that are clearly attested as having inhabited the Ottawa valley are the following (with the spellings of the early sources): the Weskarini (Wescarini) or Petite Nation, who lived in the vicinity of the Rouge, Petite-Nation, and Lièvre rivers (fig. 1); the Matouweskarini in the Madawaska River valley; the Keinouche (Pike), who may be the same as the Quenongebin, or Champlain's People of Nibachis in the Muskrat Lake region; the Kichesipirini (Big River People), whose main encampment was on Morrison's Island; and the Otaguottouemins (Kotakoutouemi), who lived in the upper part of the valley (Champlain 1922-1936, 2:264-277, 3:38; JR 18:229, 29:145). Another Algonquin group was the Onontchataronon, or People of Iroquet, who seem to have lived in the valley of the South Nation River in eastern Ontario, and who may or may not have been part of the Weskarini. This band, who are known only by their Iroquoian name, were reported to have incorporated some of the people of Hochelaga when the latter were dispersed from the Saint Lawrence valley (Trigger 1972:77-80). The names of other Algonquin groups have been recorded, some of whom may have lived in the Ottawa valley and along the Saint Maurice River.

The Algonquins had a special interest in Trois Rivières; and as early as the 1620s, after peace had been restored in this area, a mixed group of Algonquins and Montagnais settled there and planted crops (Sagard-Théodat 1866:846). Pierre Charlevoix recorded a tradition that the Petite Nation were so called because they were the remnant of a larger group, whose power had been broken when many of their warriors were slain in an

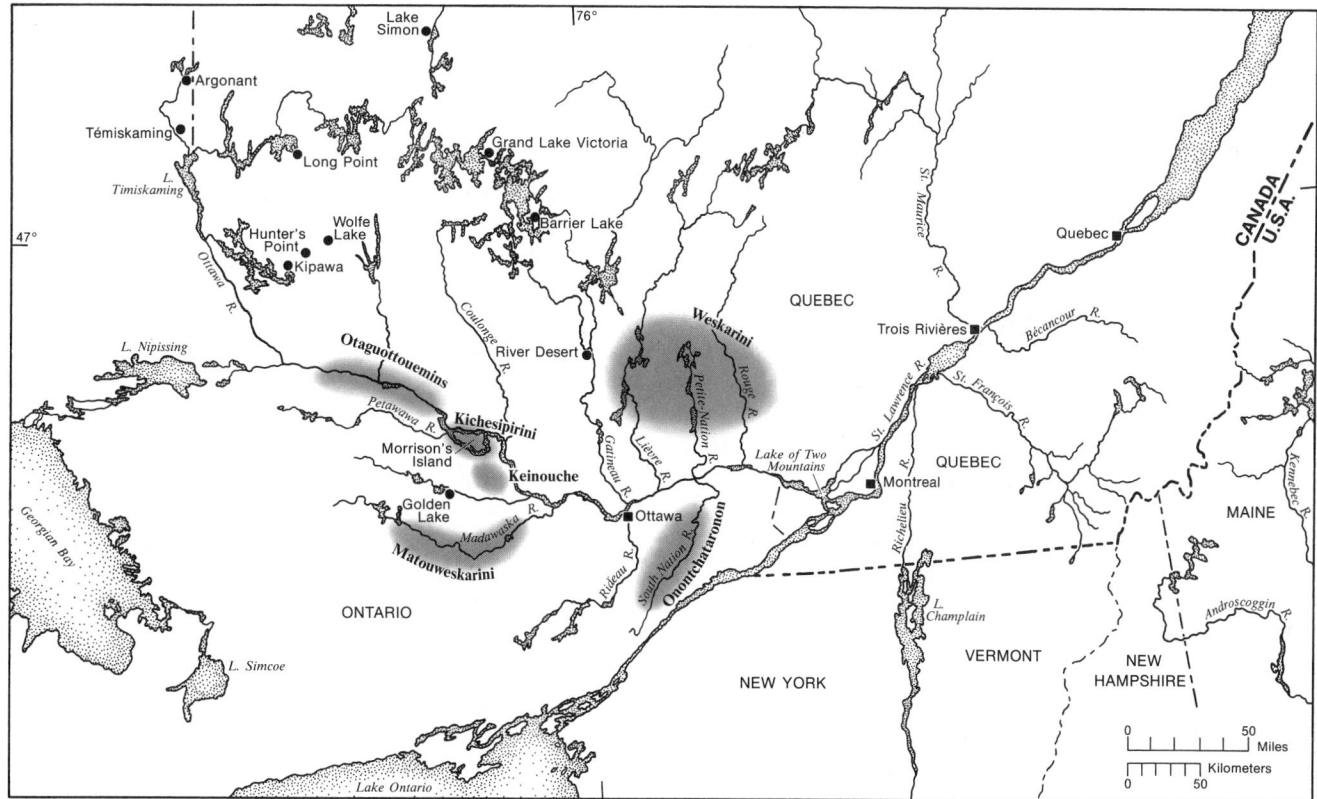

Fig. 1. Bands of the Ottawa valley in the early 17th century and Algonquin reserves in 1970.

encounter on the Bécancour River near Trois Rivières. This too suggests that the Algonquins may have had a more easterly distribution in the Saint Lawrence valley prior to European contact, as does the tradition of living by tidal waters remembered by the Algonquins of Maniwaki (Speck 1929:107–108).

History

The Algonquins first appear in history at Tadoussac in 1603 participating, with the Montagnais and Etchemins, in a celebration of victory over the Iroquois (Champlain 1922–1936, 1:96ff.). It appears that they had been at war with the Iroquois since about 1570 (ibid., 5:78), had begun to trade with the French some time before this at Tadoussac (Biggar 1965:47), and had entered into an alliance with the Montagnais to oppose the Iroquois (Champlain 1922–1936, 1:107–109). It is possible that even earlier they occupied parts of the Saint Lawrence valley and were living in a peaceful relationship with the Saint Lawrence Iroquoians. The tradition recorded by Perrot (1864:9–12) suggests such a coexistence of Algonquins and an Iroquoian group at some period in prehistory.

The hostilities between the Algonquins and the Iroquois may have arisen from the Iroquois desire to obtain trade goods directly from the French. In 1603 the Hurons and Algonquins were coming to Quebec by the northern

route rather than along the Saint Lawrence, but subsequent French assistance helped them to inflict major defeats on the Iroquois in 1609 and 1610 and to reopen the Saint Lawrence trade route. In 1613 Samuel de Champlain pushed up the Ottawa River and left an account of his visit to Tessouat's village on Morrison's Island. These Algonquins, Champlain was given to understand, had withdrawn up the Ottawa to this strong point on account of the Iroquois menace. Iroquois raiding parties, traveling north along the Rideau to attack Indians living in, or using, the lower part of the Ottawa River valley, may account for the tendency of the people living in this area to locate their summer camps along tributaries flowing into the Ottawa River rather than to have them along the Ottawa itself.

Until 1615 the Algonquins played a major role in supplying their Huron allies with European trade goods. This relationship was especially close with the Arendaronon tribe, in whose territory considerable numbers of Algonquins spent the winter, exchanging French trade goods for Huron corn. So long as the Iroquois continued to block the Saint Lawrence River, the Algonquins were living astride what was by far the easiest trade route into the interior and thus were anxious to protect their role as middlemen between the French and the tribes who lived around the shores of Lake Huron. The Kichesipirini, who were the most powerful and commercially oriented of the Algonquin bands, were particularly anxious to prevent

Champlain from traveling to the Huron country and encouraging the Huron to trade directly with the French. Although unable, in the long run, to prevent the development of this relationship or to restrain the Huron, who were more numerous and powerful than they were, the Algonquins bitterly resented what the French had done to them. They therefore took advantage of every opportunity to harass Huron traders and to stir up trouble between them and the French. This, more than anything else, made it necessary for the French to have their agents living with the Huron, to encourage them to trade and to travel with them through Algonquin territory.

In the 1620s Iroquois attacks against the Algonquins were inhibited by the armed Frenchmen traveling to and from the Huron country, and the Algonquins even enjoyed a certain amount of peace with the Iroquois until 1627. In order to bolster their own position, the Algonquins attempted repeatedly to put the French at a disadvantage by playing them off against the Dutch traders at Fort Orange, but on each occasion Mohawk jealousy prevented the Algonquins from achieving their goal. In 1634 the Algonquins concluded another peace treaty with the Mohawk that Oumasasikweie, one of the headmen of the Kichesipirini, and Tessouat, the principal headman of this band, hoped would permit their people to travel through the Mohawk country to trade with the Dutch. When Oumasasikweie and some of his companions attempted to do this, however, they were promptly slain by the Mohawks, who had no desire to permit the Dutch to establish trading relations with these fur-rich northern tribes. This incident led to a new outbreak of war between the Algonquins and Mohawks that, because of the growing Mohawk need for furs, turned into a life-and-death struggle, in which the greater number of firearms available to the Iroquois gradually gave them the upper hand. By the early 1640s the Weskarinis were being compelled to seek refuge among the Kichesipirinis, whose territory had hitherto escaped attack by the Iroquois. Soon, the Kichesipirinis themselves were seeking refuge, in times of crisis, at the French settlements along the Saint Lawrence. In spite of this, the Algonquin retained their reputation for being proud and independent.

In 1645 the French initiated peace proposals to the Iroquois and convened a council that included the Hurons, Montagnais, Attikamegues, and Algonquins and confirmed a peace that included a private deal between the French and the Iroquois abandoning the non-Christian Algonquins (JR 27:247-305, 28:149-51). Some Algonquins moved to the Jesuit mission at Sillery after its establishment in 1637, but Trois Rivières seems to have remained the focus of the more easterly Algonquin bands. The peace of 1645 allowed the Iroquois to hunt on the edges of Algonquin territory, a concession they took full advantage of, killing more than 2,000 deer the first winter (JR 28:287). But in 1646 the Mohawks broke the peace and, by treachery, succeeded in killing Simon Piskaret, the most renowned Algonquin warrior, and killing or capturing two unsuspecting hunting parties from Trois Rivières (Perrot 1864:106-109). Thus reduced in numbers, the eastern Algonquins sought assistance from the Attikamegues, the Montagnais, the Micmacs, and the Nipissings. Nothing came of this combination; Perrot blamed the failure on lack of coordination, since he regarded the Algonquins as much better warriors than the Iroquois (Perrot 1864:109-110).

Unfortunately, very little is known about the Algonquins between 1650 and 1675, which was the period of their temporary dispersal from the Ottawa valley. Some Algonquins retired to the Lake Saint John region and were still there in 1710 (Rochemonteix 1904:98, 108). The Kichesipirinis were still at Morrison's Island in 1650 and inspiring respect with their 400 warriors. When the French retreated from the Huron country that year, Tessouat is reported to have had the superior of the Jesuit mission suspended by his armpits because he refused to offer him the customary presents for being allowed to travel through Algonquin territory (Perrot 1864:95). Others joined the mission at Sillery and were mostly destroyed by an epidemic by 1676. Still others, encouraged by the French, remained at Trois Rivières (Rigaud de Vaudreuil and Bégon 1722; Lahontan 1905:50; JR 63:71); and their settlement at nearby Point-du-Lac remained until about 1830, when the last 14 families, numbering about 50 (Tuckerman 1821:42), moved to Oka. The Sulpician Mission of the Mountain was founded at Montreal in 1677, and some Algonquins settled there together with Iroquois converts. In 1704 a separate Algonquin mission was founded at Sainte-Anne-du-bout-de-l'ile under François-Saturnin Lascaris d'Urfé; and in 1721 a new mission was formed at Lake of Two Mountains, where the Algonquins were brought together with Iroquois and Nipissings (Cuoq 1894:170). Additional Algonquins joined this mission in 1742 (O. Maurault 1930:18).

The Algonquins who were apparently frequenting Trois Rivières in 1684 accompanied Joseph-Antoine Le Febvre de LaBarre to his council with the Iroquois at Fort Frontenac (Lahontan 1905:50-51, 733; JR 63:67). In the last quarter of the seventeenth century, whatever hunting territory the Algonquins may have had south of the Saint Lawrence River began to be taken over by Abenakis. Before 1670 Sokokis had settled on the Saint François River, and in 1704 Father Sébastien Râle brought eastern Abenakis from the Androscoggin River to Bécancour (Charland 1964:18, 37-38). These Abenakis asked permission of the Algonquins to settle (Speck 1928b:173). Algonquin and Abenaki relations were thenceforth good, and at some point they made a treaty agreeing to regard the Saint Lawrence River as the dividing line and asserting that the land north of the river had always been Algonquin country (Duchesnay

1829:531). Their territories extended to the Sainte-Anne-de-la-Pérade River on the east and north to the vicinity of Coucoucache.

After the great peace between the Iroquois and the French and their allies in 1701, trade, often clandestine, was carried on between the northern Indians and Albany. It had begun for the Algonquins at Montreal at least as early as 1715 (Faillon 1850-1865, fol. E:173). During the frequent conflicts with the English, the Algonquins were constant allies of the French. Their warriors were at Fort Necessity, Lake George, Monongahela, Fort Edward, Schenectady, Fort Orange, and the Plains of Abraham among other battles (O. Maurault 1930:27). In 1752 the Algonquins of Lake of Two Mountains were living with, yet distinct from, the Nipissings and Iroquois in houses of squared timbers. Together with the Nipissings they numbered 113 warriors. They were not cultivating the land, but they were making a good living from their furs, which they obtained in the winter 250 to 300 leagues from the village. Much of their trade was with Albany at this time (Franquet 1889:42-49, 121). Sometime in the mid-eighteenth century, the Algonquins of Two Mountains became members of the so-called Seven Nations of Canada, a confederacy of French mission Indians.

In the latter part of the eighteenth century, the Two Mountains Indians, continuing their hunting on the upper Ottawa River, became involved in the activities of the fur-trading companies. One group, having settled at Golden Lake in 1807, petitioned for confirmation of land title there and a reserve was established in 1870 (Lake 1966:157). Gradual removals of other families of Algonquins and Nipissings from Lake of Two Mountains to River Desert took place during the first half of the nineteenth century, and in 1854 a group removed there and a reserve was established at Maniwaki (Speck 1929:115-117). The remaining Algonquins and Nipissings left Lake of Two Mountains sometime after 1868 (Parent 1887:198, 221). Other bands existing on the upper Gatineau and Ottawa rivers in the nineteenth century were the Temiskaming, Abitibi, Grand Lake Victoria, Quinze Lake, Mattawa, Kipawa, and Lake Dumoine (Speck 1915:3). There are also bands at Lac Simon and Lac Barrière, but the history of all these bands is less well known. Algonquins still regard the region of Mazinaw Lake, Otter Lake, Baptiste Lake, and the Bonnechere and Mattawa rivers as their territory south of the Ottawa River; but this land was sold by Iroquois, Mississaugas, and Ojibwąs, not by the Algonquins (Morris 1943). Nonreservation Algonquins continued to live on the Lièvre and the Ottawa rivers into the twentieth century.

Culture

Evidence concerning the nature of Algonquin culture is extremely limited. Considerable information about Algonquin tribes is contained in Perrot (1864), Raudot (1904), and the *Jesuit Relations* (JR), but it is seldom possible to assign details to the Algonquins specifically. Moreover, data obtained by anthropologists in the twentieth century cannot be attributed with certainty to the Algonquins of the contact period. It is likely that the various seventeenth-century bands were made up of patrilineal extended families, although it is less certain whether each band constituted a single exogamous clan of the type that Hickerson (1970:42-50) has reconstructed for the precontact Ojibwa and Ottawa. The members of these bands appear to have lived in a single community during the warmer months of the year, when fishing was good, and to have either dispersed or sent out hunting parties to obtain food during the winter. Henry (1969:23) found the classic family hunting system in strict operation among the Lake of Two Mountains Algonquins in 1761, much as it was remembered by Speck's informants in 1913 at Temiskaming, Kipawa, and Lac Dumoine (1915:6-7). Historical references to group hunting by Algonquins can perhaps be explained as reactions of temporarily displaced groups exploiting a new and perhaps controversial territory (Lahontan 1905:46; Marie de l'Incarnation 1967:315).

Although the growing season was too short for corn to provide a reliable source of food in most parts of the Ottawa valley, the seventeenth-century Algonquins practiced a simple type of swidden agriculture wherever suitable soil was available. Fields were cleared by burning tracts of pine forest and were then planted with corn, beans, and squash. Shortly after A.D. 1600, peas, which had been obtained from European traders, were also being grown. In general, the subsistence economy of the Algonquins resembled that of the Nipissings and Ottawas, and together these three groups represented the northernmost penetration of a marginally agricultural economy in eastern North America.

The seventeenth-century Algonquins shared other traits with the Algonquian and Iroquoian peoples of the less rigorous environment of the Eastern Woodlands to the south and west of them, and probably more specifically with the Huron, with whom they traded. Like the Hurons, but unlike the Montagnais, the Algonquins fished through the ice by means of nets in the winter (JR 8:39). This method may have been possible because the Algonquins were able to obtain Indian hemp nets from the Hurons, who are known to have supplied them to the Nipissings and their other Algonquian-speaking neighbors who lived around the shores of Georgian Bay. Like the Hurons, the Algonquins also ate dogs, which the Montagnais regarded as a shameful practice (JR 9:111). The Algonquins entertained their guests in the same manner as the Hurons, with the host tending his guests but not eating any food himself. Councils were also conducted in the Huron manner with tobacco being smoked in silence before any important issue was discussed. Algonquin use of turtle-shell rattles in a curing

Fig. 2. Costumes of man and woman. Watercolor, mid-18th century.

Fig. 3. Wife and children of Dan Sarazin in a late type of birchbark canoe called *wa·panakki·-či·ma·n* 'Abenaki canoe'. Photograph by Edwin T. Adney, about 1927, on Bonnechere River, Golden Lake Reserve.

ceremony also suggests itself as a borrowing from the Hurons (Sagard-Théodat 1939:65). The Algonquins constructed longhouses, but this was not an exclusively Iroquoian trait and even the Montagnais erected such structures in some of their summer camps along the Saint Lawrence. The graves of prominent individuals were covered with painted wooden structures shaped like a ridged roof. These were about seven feet long and four feet wide, and at one end they had a wooden upright bearing a figure that represented the deceased. Franquet (1889:48–49) has left a detailed account of a dance he witnessed at Two Mountains in 1752. In the nineteenth century, splint basketry was probably borrowed from the Iroquois or the Abenaki.

Whatever the character of the contact-period Algonquin culture, twentieth-century fieldwork among Algonquin bands shows them sharing much of the inventory of traits characteristic of the other boreal forest peoples as outlined by Flannery (1946). Among these are: a supreme being who is owner of everything; a trickster-transformer culture hero; the Windigo; the *pa·kahk,* a disembodied starveling; the *pakwačininiwak,* a race of powerful little men; shamanism and the shaking tent; the dream vision quest; scrying and scapulimancy. Their world view is purely that of a hunting-fishing people. Material culture items included the birchbark canoe (fig. 3); snowshoes;

toboggan; rectangular bark hunting camps; birchbark containers sewed with spruce roots (fig. 4); porcupine quillwork in the south; moosehide tumplines; basswood bags, mats, and temporary tumplines; deer and moose-hide clothing; cradleboards and blanket hammocks; moccasins of beavertail and deernose types (Hatt

Fig. 4. Birchbark container sewed together with split spruce root, with thong handle. The design is formed by scraping away the dark inner bark to expose the layer of light bark beneath. Length 17.8 cm; collected at Mattawa, Ont., in 1913.

1916:171-178, 167-169); bows, preferably of hop horn-beam. Knowledge of plants and their properties was extensive. Maple sugar was made by some bands.

The Algonquin population about 1965 was in Quebec: 197 at Barriere Lake, 225 at Grand Lake Victoria, 273 at Lake Simon, 898 at River Desert, 3 at Argonaut, 11 at Hunters Point, 91 at Kipawa, 247 at Long Point, 389 at Timiskaming, and 57 at Wolfe Lake; and in Ontario: 446 at Golden Lake and an unknown percentage of the Iroquois-Algonquin band at Gibson. To the total of approximately 2,500 should be added an unknown number of persons of Algonquin descent scattered throughout the Ottawa valley but unaffiliated with any reserve. The total Algonquin population appears to be rather stable, perhaps showing a slight increase since 1900, although direct comparison with the 1900 census is not possible (Canada. Department of Indian Affairs and Northern Development 1965:9-10, 12).

Synonymy

The earliest form of the name was Algoumequin, 1603 (Champlain 1922-1936, 1:103). Algonquain appeared as early as 1632 (JR 5:70). Names in other languages are: Huron Aquannaque, 1632 (Sagard-Théodat 1939, s.v. Nations) or Ak8anake, 1641, used for any tribe of unintelligible speech (JR 21:192), perhaps an adaptation of Abenaki; Mohawk *atirǫ́·taks* literally 'tree-eaters' (G.

Michelson 1973:100; Hewitt in Hodge 1907-1910, 1:13) whence the Iroquois designation Adirondacks (Colden 1747:xv); Western Abenaki *wǝsǫgǝnak* (Day 1956-1973); Nipissing dialect *oma·mi·wininiwak* literally 'down-river people' (from Cuoq 1886:298). They called themselves *aniššina·pe·k*.

Sources

The history of the Algonquins begins with Champlain (1922-1936) and must be gleaned from the *Jesuit Relations* (JR 1896-1901) and French historical writers of the seventeenth century (Sagard-Théodat 1939; Perrot 1864). In the eighteenth century travelers like Franquet (1889) and military men like Bougainville (1924) and Mont-calm-Gozon (1895) recorded ethnological information. After about 1720 the best sources are the writings of Sulpician missionaries at Oka, most of which remain in manuscript in the Sulpician archives in Montreal. Some information may be found in the fur-trade records of the eighteenth and nineteenth centuries (Henry 1969; Long 1791; McLean 1932; Mackenzie 1801). In the late nineteenth and early twentieth centuries several ethnologists (Chamberlain 1891; Davidson 1928, 2; Speck 1914, 1915, 1915a, 1927a, 1928b, 1928c, 1929; Johnson 1928, 1930) wrote on particular expressions of Algonquin culture. A significant collection of Algonquin material culture is preserved in the National Museum of Man, Ottawa.

Cultural Unity and Diversity

BRUCE G. TRIGGER

The Indian societies that have been examined in this volume manifest a considerable degree of cultural heterogeneity. Yet it has long been recognized that any attempt to divide the early historic cultures of the Eastern Woodlands into a tidy pattern of subareas is made difficult by the absence of sharp geographical barriers that would have inhibited human interaction within this zone. Caldwell (1958:viii) has suggested that an historical approach, in which traditional boundaries can be seen changing through time, can help to overcome the inadequacies of a synchronic classification. Such an approach is adopted in this chapter. Neither the later processes of convergence that resulted from disruption, displacement, and encapsulation by White society nor the pan-Indian movements that are giving rise in the mid-twentieth century to an awareness of continent-wide Indian identity (see vol. 2) will be discussed. For the Paleo-Indian period, during which a single lithic tradition covered the Plains and the Southwest as well as Eastern North America, see volume 3. Much of this chapter is based on the work of Caldwell (1958), Eggan (1952, 1966), and Griffin (1966).

An historical approach involves a consideration not only of patterns of internal development but also of cultural relationships with other parts of the New World. In keeping with anthropology's preoccupation with ecology and evolution, most studies in the 1970s have focused on the internal development of social systems in adaptation to their natural environment. Steward (1955:182) has justified the de-emphasizing of external influences by arguing that every borrowing can be construed as an "independent recurrence of cause and effect," that is, as a new invention. Murdock (1949:200) asserts that any form of social organization can develop anywhere, if conditions are propitious. Therefore, it is legitimate for certain purposes to study the functioning and development of individual cultures as if they were closed systems. It is also true that cultures are not random collections of discrete traits and that the invocation of diffusion (which itself is merely a cover term for a collection of more specific cultural processes) is sterile unless it is demonstrated under what circumstances a culture becomes open to specific kinds of external influences. Yet, in statistical analyses of North American Indian trait distributions, Driver (1967) demonstrated that purely functional correlations account for only some of these patterns, while "accidental" borrowings must be invoked to account for the rest.

While Driver's study was mainly concerned with aspects of social organization, diffusion can be no less important in respect of technology, economic behavior, and beliefs and values. In general, borrowing probably occurs more easily than does invention; hence when a culture is open or predisposed to change, the presence of acceptable solutions in neighboring societies may exert a decisive influence in determining which of a variety of solutions is adopted. Diffusion also appears to play a more important role in complex or transitional environments than it does in homogeneous ones and on the peripheries rather than at the centers of cultural advances. On both scores, the Northeast qualifies as an area where the importance of diffusion should not be underestimated in spite of the difficulties that are involved in demonstrating that specific instances of diffusion took place.

The known cultures of the Northeast before 1650 may be examined in terms of six major patterns. The criteria used to identify these patterns are subsistence, technology, settlement, social organization, political structures, and in some cases ritual activities. These are essentially the same features that Steward (1955:94, 184) included in his concept of a cultural core.

The Eastern Collecting Pattern

The first evidence of cultures specifically adapted to the Northeast appears about 8000 B.C. At first the population of the region not now covered by risen lake levels appears to have remained extremely sparse, possibly because boreal vegetation with a very low carrying capacity (one person per 200 or 300 square miles) covered most of the area (Fitting 1968b). Comparisons with adjacent boreal forests in historic times would suggest that band structures were of two major types. Where migratory big game were hunted, the distance separating bands encouraged the development of endogamous, bilateral units held together by cross-cousin marriage, as among the Barren-Ground Naskapi of Labrador (Eggan 1966:87–88). Where the environment sustained higher population densities, marriage outside the band was more common. Cross-cousin marriage was practiced, but bands tended toward exogamy and patriliny, as exemplified by the historic Ojibwa. While it is tempting to think that all Paleo-Indian groups were of the first type, there is no reason to believe that all those who lived in the Eastern Woodlands were big-game hunters (Griffin 1966:113).

By 3000 B.C. the deciduous forests had completed their northward movement and the natural environment of the Northeast had assumed roughly its present outlines. Migratory game had disappeared except in the far north and been replaced by a varied range of edible plants and by nonmigratory animals, especially deer (and moose in the extreme north). This change facilitated a considerable increase in human population, a reduction in the size of band territories, as well as a trend toward less movement, which facilitated the acquisition of more and heavier equipment than was usual prior to this time (Caldwell 1958:14). Increasing population probably encouraged the more intensive exploitation of local resources, thereby helping to produce distinctive regional traditions. These traditions correspond in part with natural variations within the region.

The exploitation of natural resources in the Northeast required the seasonal mobility of a band within its territory. While fishing permitted the band to occupy a central base or a series of such bases throughout the summer months, it was generally necessary for members to scatter in smaller groups in order to find enough game to eat during the winter (Eggan 1966:83). Bands varied from a few dozen to a few hundred members. Where the overall population density was high, there was greater emphasis on exogamy, the clan system developed more corporate functions, and moieties or dual divisions constituted the basis of cooperation between bands. Band membership seems generally to have continued to be determined by patrilineal or bilateral descent, probably because of the economic importance attached to cooperation between brothers.

The size of bands and the length of time their members could remain together each year came to vary according to the abundance and diversity of local resources and the sophistication with which these resources were exploited. In general, base camps were larger and occupied for more of the year in riverine and maritime areas than they were inland, in the coastal region than in the interior, and in the south than in the north. More sophisticated subsistence techniques appear gradually but not necessarily continuously to have enhanced the carrying capacity of most regions by varying degrees. This pattern of intensive, centrally based collecting (Caldwell's 1958:6–18 Primary Forest Efficiency; cf. Asch, Ford, and Asch 1972:25–30) intensified throughout the Northeast during the Archaic period and over much of the area during the succeeding Woodland periods. Pottery, which marks the beginning of the Woodland sequence, appears to signify nothing more than growing sedentarization (i.e., increasing emphasis on centrally based settlements) or a more efficient substitute for soapstone cooking vessels. The

Eastern Collecting Pattern survived into historic times among northern groups such as the Ojibwa of the Upper Great Lakes, the Beothuk, Micmac, Maliseet, and Eastern Abenaki of the Coastal region, and in adjacent southern regions of the boreal forest. Although influenced by more southerly patterns based on horticulture, the Menominee, Nipissing, and Algonquin basically conformed to this pattern.

The development of this pattern of local adaptation seems to owe little to outside influences. It was formerly hypothesized that there was a circumpolar and specifically Asiatic (occasionally a transatlantic) origin for many features of the Archaic and Early and Middle Woodland periods, such as copper working, burial mounds, pottery, and specific types of stone tools (McKern 1937; Griffin 1946, 1960b; Ritchie 1946; Spaulding 1946, 1952, 1955; Lopatin 1960; Kehoe 1962, 1971; Willey 1966:20–21; Wright 1967). While some such connections are possible, none has been firmly demonstrated, and the arguments generally now seem less convincing than they did formerly. No convincing similarities have been demonstrated between Northeastern and Siberian burial mounds (Chard 1961), while the similarities between Northeastern and Siberian tool types may simply reflect a common type of adaptation to similar environments (Byers 1959). Old Copper culture tools have strong local coloration and apparently are modeled on Laurentian Archaic lithic prototypes ("Regional Cultural Development, 3000 to 300 B.C.," this vol."). Finally, Early Woodland pottery seems to occur first in the southern part of its range (Wright 1967:130; Brose 1970a:67–68). This suggests the possibility of local invention, although the possibility of some remote and unspecified relationship with the much earlier fiber-tempered pottery of the Southeast or with Mesoamerican pottery must remain open (M.D. Coe 1960). This does not, of course, rule out the possibility that some circumpolar traits that were present in the Northeast in early historic times were ultimately of Asiatic origin. These include the bear cult (Hallowell 1926), snowshoe, various shamanistic practices, and perhaps the steam bath.

The Adena-Hopewell Pattern

Between about 500 B.C. and A.D. 500, the central Mississippi, Ohio, and Illinois valleys were the heartland of a series of interrelated cultures of unprecedented complexity for eastern North America. These were characterized by a larger population, an emphasis on burial rituals, elaborate earthworks including burial mounds and other ceremonial structures, widespread trade in exotic raw materials, an art style that represented a high point in the artistic expression of the Northeast and indicates the presence of craft specialists, and marked differences in wealth and status. The small size of habitation sites, which normally do not exceed five acres, does not indicate strongly centralized authority, and Caldwell (1958:30) notes that more architecture was devoted to public than to domestic use. The frequent occurrence of multiple high-status burials in single mounds and monumental works apparently associated with important "tribal" or intertribal meeting places suggest that the Adena-Hopewell cultures may have consisted of a series of simple or group-oriented chiefdoms similar in general type to what Renfrew (1973) has proposed for late neolithic Wessex.

Intensive collecting clearly played an important role in the Adena-Hopewell subsistence base. Among the plants that were exploited were a number of highly productive seed-bearers including marsh elder (*Iva*), lamb's quarters (*Chenopodium*), pigweed (*Amaranthus*), canary grass (*Phalaris*), and smartweed (*Polygonum*). It has been suggested that these plants were perhaps grown on the floodplain along with some cultigens of Mesoamerican origin. As yet, however, the proposal that they were brought under cultivation, either independently or as a result of stimulus diffusion resulting from familiarity with Mesoamerican crops, has not won universal acceptance (Griffin 1966:116). The best evidence for cultivation is the large size of *Iva* seeds from Early Woodland sites, which has been interpreted as an indication of artificial selection (M. Black 1963; Yarnell 1976; for a summary of arguments in favor of an "eastern agricultural complex," see Struever and Vickery 1973).

Gourds, squash, and sunflower appear to have been grown in the Northeast before 700 B.C., and corn and perhaps beans are attested for Hopewell (Yarnell 1964:101–106; Watson and Yarnell 1966). Some archeologists view these exotic domesticates as essential to the development of Adena-Hopewell (Spaulding 1955:20; Willey 1966:268), but the evidence for them remains insignificant in the archeological record. Therefore either local domesticates were of unexpected importance or the Adena-Hopewell climax was based largely on intensive collecting (Caldwell 1958:30).

The cultigens of Mesoamerican origin are clear evidence of at least indirect contact between the Northeast and Mesoamerica beginning about 700 B.C. Whether this contact was made along the Gulf coast, overland across the Southeast, or by a more circuitous route through the American Southwest is uncertain. Various other Mesoamerican influences have been proposed for the Adena-Hopewell culture. Hopewell earspools seem to be inspired by Mesoamerican prototypes but attempts to attribute Olmec origins to Adena-Hopewell mounds; greenstone celts; figurines; or motifs such as serpents, raptorial birds, felines, or the hand-and-eye are based upon analogies that are too general to be persuasive. Likewise, no convincing Mesoamerican origins can be demonstrated for a common emphasis on blade production, negatively painted pottery, or similarities with the stamped, zoned, and fabric-impressed pottery of the Ocós

culture of Central America (Griffin 1966:117–125). Nor does the enigmatic Poverty Point site in northeastern Louisiana, which seems to date prior to 600 B.C., offer to clarify the relationship between Mesoamerica and the Northeast or even between itself and Adena-Hopewell at this time level.

What is clear is that nothing like the Adena-Hopewell burial complex is known in Mesoamerica (Griffin 1949:87). The intensification of trade in eastern North America and the elaboration of an indigenous ceremonial-mortuary system have been postulated as important mechanisms in the development and diffusion of Hopewell culture (Prufer 1965:128, 132; for a speculative and far-reaching assessment of Mesoamerican connections, see Tooker 1971). Hopewell cultural influences spread over large areas of the Southeast, although much remains to be learned about the specific mechanisms by which they did so. Some of these influences outlived the demise of Hopewell to become an enduring part of the Southeastern cultural tradition.

While Adena traits penetrated as far as Delaware and New Jersey, the influence of Adena-Hopewell on neighboring cultures of the Northeast appears to have been limited to individual items of material culture, such as platform pipes, and to a simplified and short-lived burial cult that made its way into southeastern Ontario; however, this cult was associated with a Middle Woodland collecting economy that does not appear to have been affected in any way by it (R.B. Johnston 1968). The Adena-Hopewell pattern did not extend north of territory that experiences an average of 170 or more frost-free days (Yarnell 1964:137). This must reflect the lack of natural resources to support such a pattern north of this line or the inability of available cultigens to grow there. Corn-based horticulture appears to have expanded north beginning soon after A.D. 500. This was made possible by the Northern Flint (also called Eastern Complex) corn, which could be grown where there were as few as 140 frost-free days by A.D. 1000 and 120 days by A.D. 1600 (Yarnell 1964:107, 137). The primary motivation for the experimentation needed to adapt corn and squash to a shorter growing season was probably a desire to find new sources of food that could be stored for winter use and used to extend the period that bands could remain at their summer base camp. Especially around the Lower Great Lakes, domestic corn was a desirable alternative to wild rice because it could be grown in a greater variety of localities and was less susceptible to serious crop damage (Hickerson 1970:106). Eventually, corn horticulture permitted the development of year-round villages in this area, which evidently had not been possible with a collecting economy.

The Hopewell culture had declined and disappeared before this northward spread of horticulture took place. Griffin suggests that this decline may be related to climatic deterioration between A.D. 200 and 700, although he also acknowledges that a broad spectrum of cultural factors must have been involved (Griffin 1960a). The view of this decline as an anomaly results from undue faith in unilineal evolution. Long periods of breakdown are a chronic feature of preindustrial civilization and the power of rehabilitation may be even less at the chiefdom level.

The Mississippian Pattern

The vigorous Mississippian tradition developed in the central Mississippi and adjacent valleys shortly before A.D. 1000. Unlike the Adena-Hopewell climax, the Mississippian one was clearly based on maize horticulture with Basketmaker corn of Southwestern origin being grown as well as Northern Flint corn (Yarnell 1964:114, 119). Unlike the Adena-Hopewell cultures, the Mississippian one exhibited a number of distinctive and important Mesoamerican features. Earth mounds, often of vast size, were erected as platforms for temples of general Mesoamerican plan and for high-status dwellings; and settlements of rectangular wattle-and-daub houses were laid out around central plazas where community rituals were performed. The engraved and negatively painted pottery are also suggestive of Mesoamerican prototypes. The greatest number of resemblances to late Mesoamerican art and religious concepts is found in the so-called Southeastern Ceremonial complex, represented by artifacts decorated with warriors, priests, and a rich and distinctive iconography. This complex, which diffused among the Mississippian and other Southeast cultures reaching a peak about A.D. 1300, is similar rather than identical to any Mesoamerican iconography and presumably represents a southeastern reworking of Mesoamerican religious ideas. It does not seem to have been introduced as a complex and no single center is found to account for its origin and spread (Griffin 1966:127). It has been suggested that these traits were transmitted to the Gulf coast of the United States from the Haustec area of Mexico (MacNeish 1947; Kelley 1952, 1955). So far, the only evidence of direct contact that has been seriously considered are human teeth mutilations from Illinois sites, which are of types that occur in Mesoamerica after A.D. 1000. Griffin (1966:129) assumes that these are from individuals who had dental work done in Mexico.

Mississippian settlements were frequently fortified and the largest are estimated to have had over 10,000 inhabitants. Social control within such communities and the regulation of their hinterlands could not have been based solely on public opinion but must have required a certain measure of coercion (Naroll 1956:690); hence it seems proper to view Mississippian political organization as consisting of a series of rudimentary states, each with a major town as its center. An analogy can perhaps be drawn with Renfrew's (1973) more advanced or individualizing chiefdoms. These are characterized as material-istic, acquisitive, and aggrandizing societies in which personal display became the means by which leaders communicated their power to their followers.

The Mississippian pattern expanded, at least in part by migration, northward into Wisconsin and into the lower Ohio Valley. The expansion may have been prompted by a rapidly growing population's need for easily worked bottomland, although control of other natural resources may also have been involved. In many cases the Mississippians appear to have by-passed established populations before they settled down in areas that were only sparsely settled; hence their expansion may not have displaced or even submerged the former cultures of these areas (Caldwell 1958:65). Archeological evidence indicates that, beyond the areas they occupied, Mississippian influence was limited in the north, much as Hopewell had been, to isolated traits. These include a few Southern Cult elements that appear on Fort Ancient pottery or on engraved shell gorgets. Corn had spread to the north and east prior to Mississippian times and did not include the Basketmaker type that occurs in Mississippian sites (Yarnell 1964:119). Many social and religious attributes of historic northern and eastern cultures that appear to be of Mesoamerican origin may have been derived from the Mississippian tradition, but they also may have diffused northward along the Atlantic coast or the western flanks of the Appalachians.

The influence of Mississippian culture was far greater in the Southeast than in the north. As a result of migration and local growth, the Mississippian pattern spread into eastern Tennessee, central and southwestern Georgia, and northwestern Florida while more general Mississippian influences radiated over a much wider area. Together with Mesoamerican traits transmitted directly through the Gulf tradition and the Southern Cult, these influences played a major role in shaping the historic cultural pattern of the Southeast (Caldwell 1958:60-70). This pattern was characterized by towns laid out around central squares; rectangular houses of pole and thatch construction; both matrilocal residence and descent; various kinds of dual divisions; Crow kinship terminology; marked class divisions: social classes based on chiefs, honored men, warriors, and commoners; parallel peace chiefs and war chiefs; some rulers having the power of life and death over their subjects; retainer sacrifice; a war cult involving prisoner sacrifice; a priest-temple-idol cult; ossuary and perpetual fire temples; rituals in the town square culminating in a Green Corn ceremony; platform beds; litters for carrying chiefs; and an emphasis on incised and plastic pottery decoration (Kroeber 1939:62; Eggan 1966:17-19; Caldwell 1958:61). Most specialists correlate Crow kinship terminology with a "mature" matrilineal system, kin terms being organized so that certain classes of relatives are grouped with reference to lineage and clan regardless of generation.

801

The Central Algonquian Pattern

It has been suggested that the collapse of the Mississippian pattern can be attributed to depopulation resulting from the introduction of European diseases in the sixteenth century; however, its decline may have been underway well before the arrival of Europeans in the New World. Whatever the reason, this pattern had vanished from the central Mississippi Valley by early historic times. Nowhere has it been possible to trace the historic cultures of that area irrefutably back to Mississippian antecedents. The Central Algonquian cultures of the Potawatomi, Sauk, Fox, Kickapoo, Mascouten, Shawnee, Miami, and Illinois were variants of a common and very different pattern, which archeologically seems to have its roots in the local cultures of the upper Mississippi Valley ("Great Lakes-Riverine Sociopolitical Organization," this vol.). The best period of the development of these cultures appears to be about 1400-1600, which suggests that the Central Algonquians may also have been adversely affected by European diseases in the sixteenth century (James B. Griffin, personal communication 1974).

These groups inhabited forest and prairie parkland, which encouraged the development of a number of different ecotypes (Fitting and Cleland 1969). In spite of this, they all subsisted primarily by horticulture and secondarily, but importantly, by hunting game including deer and buffalo. The main villages were occupied seasonally in the summer and were composed of rectangular multifamily houses with peaked roofs and bark-covered frames; winter huts, by contrast, were dome-shaped and covered with mats of cattail reeds. All these groups seem to have been organized in patrilineal clans that had the right to perform specific rituals centered on clan bundles, although the details are not known for the Illinois and Miami, and Shawnee organization was somewhat different. They also had dual divisions (often not related to clans) and a strongly patrilineal Omaha type of kinship system (Eggan 1966:95-97). The distinction between civil chiefs, war leaders, and ceremonial leaders tenuously may suggest Mississippian or Southeastern influences, but effective action depended on unanimous decisions by the village council and little effective organization is reported at the tribal level. Lowie (1954:94) explained the similarities between the Central Algonquian social systems and those of the Central Siouan groups in terms of diffusion, but Callender (1962:106) has postulated that the Algonquian ones evolved from a simpler proto-Algonquian system in response to expanding population and the development of semipermanent villages as a result of warfare and ritual activity.

The Menominee shared many aspects of Central Algonquian social organization, although their dependence on collecting resulted in an attenuation of these features and an economy and life-style more like those of the Ojibwa. The strongest Mississippian influences appear to have survived among the Siouan-speaking Winnebago, with their elaborate cosmology and hints of formerly matrilineal institutions; however, even the Winnebago appear to have been strongly Algonquianized prior to the earliest descriptions of their culture. The displacement of Central Algonquian tribes, such as the Sauk and Potawatomi, from southern Michigan westward into the wild-rice district of Wisconsin in the middle of the seventeenth century resulted in certain changes in the subsistence patterns of these groups (Wilson 1956). This displacement as well as the expansion of the Chippewa accounts for the anomalous concentration of population in the wild-rice district, which Kroeber (1939:88-89) saw as a feature of indigenous life. Other Michigan tribes (Fox, Kickapoo, and Mascouten) were forced into eastern Wisconsin, but they continued to spend much of their time buffalo hunting on the prairies to the south. The shift westward involved these peoples in new and more competitive relations with other tribes, all of whom had become deeply involved in the fur trade.

The Northern Iroquoian Pattern

The cultures of the northern Iroquoians have long been recognized to have many Southeastern affinities and formerly were believed to be intrusive from that direction (Parker 1916). However, archeological evidence has established the development in situ of these cultures from local Middle Woodland collecting groups. After A.D. 500, an economy based on fishing and hunting was transformed into one in which horticulture provided up to three-quarters of the food that was eaten, exceeding in importance the role that it played among the Central Algonquians. While hunting was the second most important source of food for the Central Algonquians, among the Iroquoians this role was played by fishing. In historic times, the largest Iroquoian villages had 1,500 or more inhabitants and were fortified; however, they lacked the plazas, platform mounds, and priest cults of Mississippian and Southeastern settlements. Women, children, and the aged remained in these villages throughout the year, while men frequently were absent fishing, hunting, trading, waging war, and visiting other tribes. This encouraged the development of matrilocal residence and thereby of matrilineal institutions. In spite of this, Iroquoian kinship relations retained many bilateral features; and kin terms were of the Iroquois type, which shows no special development in a matrilineal direction (Eggan 1952, 1966:104-105; Lounsbury 1964:1079). Longhouses, which were inhabited by matrilineal extended families, evolved from smaller Middle Woodland prototypes found in the Upper Great Lakes area (Brose 1970a:53-59) or shared a common origin with the houses found among the agricultural societies along the Middle Atlantic seaboard. Clan chieftainships tended to be hereditary in particular lineages, but there was little development of classes or evidence of a tendency toward high-status endogamy. Government was founded on complex cross-cutting ties of clanship and village and tribal membership, but the enforcement of decisions depended entirely on public opinion and no individual could be bound by a decision with which he did not personally agree. Blood feuds were effectively suppressed within confederacies embracing several tribes and numbering as many as 20,000 people.

No Southern Cult elements are noted among the northern Iroquoians, and their material culture was less complex than that of the Southeast. The pattern of civil chiefs and war chiefs appears to be of southern origin and there may also be some connection between the 50 sachems of the Iroquois (and probably of the Huron confederacy council) and the 50 chiefs of the Creeks (Driver 1961:345). Although prisoner sacrifice was linked to age-old patterns of blood feud and to requirements of achieving male prestige that were structurally inherent in northern Iroquoian society, it shared many crucial features with prisoner sacrifice in the Southeast and Meso-america. These include killing the prisoner on an elevated platform and in view of the sun, the removal of the heart, and the cooking and eating of all or part of the body. These similarities seem to constitute a core of ideas, probably of Mesoamerican origin, that were elaborated differently in other parts of the New World depending on levels of sociocultural complexity and local cultural patterns (Knowles 1940; Rands and Riley 1958). The religious significance accorded to games (and especially to ball games) may also have been of Mesoamerican origin while a general similarity is apparent between lacrosse and the stickball played in the Southeast (Swanton 1946:674). The calendrical ceremonies of the Iroquois seem to have been inspired by those of the Southeast. They appear to overlay shamanistic curing ceremonies (Tooker 1960; Chafe 1964) and may not have reached the Iroquois until the early historic period. The shamanistic curing rituals that were attested in the early seventeenth century are of a distinctly northern type. Some of these were elaborated to form medicine societies that cross-cut and helped to integrate the lineages and clan segments of Iroquoian society.

Although the Algonquian-speaking peoples who lived farther north also grew corn, they were less dependent on it than were the Iroquoians and had kept a patrilineal band structure. The Ottawa made considerable use of their base camps in the winter as well as in the summer and their modes of settlement and subsistence probably resemble an early stage in the development of the Northern Iroquoian pattern. Their social organization appears to have been similar to that of the Ojibwa. The Nipissing and Algonquin were essentially Ojibwa-like collectors who practiced a little horticulture, traded for horticultural produce with Iroquoians, and had adopted various aspects of Iroquoian culture without these adding up to a new pattern. While the Ottawa are a transitional type, all three can be treated as part of the Eastern Collecting Pattern.

The horticultural Algonquian-speaking groups who lived along the eastern flank of the Iroquoians, the Mahican and the Delaware, appear to have participated to some degree in the development of "Iroquoian" material culture and in the historic period their cultures had many "Iroquoian" features, such as matrilocality and matrilineal descent. This is not to assume that these particular influences necessarily traveled in only one direction or that they necessarily originated among Iroquoian-speaking peoples. Conspicuously lacking, however, were the political structures that characterized the Iroquoian-speaking groups. The apparent uniformity of the basic structures that were shared by the northern Iroquoian groups and the failure of any neighboring Algonquian groups to take up this pattern in its entirety suggest that related languages were to some degree important in assuring the diffusion and sharing of a common life-style.

The Northeastern Coastal Pattern

The coastal peoples from the Western Abenaki south had horticultural economies in the late prehistoric and historic periods. This region supported a population that was as dense or denser than that of the northern Iroquoians; nevertheless, because of the diverse and abundant coastal and riverine resources of this area, these groups tended to retain a pattern of seasonal movement that facilitated the exploitation of these resources. The result was the general absence of large fortified villages. They also did not undertake the large communal construction works that are associated with the Adena-Hopewell and Mississippian patterns. The largest houses were shorter versions of the Iroquoian longhouse rather than the rectangular ones of the Southeast. Evidence concerning kinship organization is poor for the New England and Virginia–North Carolina areas, but patrilineal and bilateral tendencies seem to have been stronger than they were in the Iroquoian area. This appears to be in keeping with the retention of many features of an earlier collecting economy in this naturally rich area.

Current studies of political organization raise serious difficulties. In the seventeenth century the coast from southern Maine to North Carolina was described as an area that had chiefdoms or sachemships of varying degrees of complexity with a tendency toward endogamy among the higher status groups. Some scholars have suggested that these units developed as a result of European intrusion and see a simpler village or centrally based band organization as prevailing at an earlier period; other anthropologists regard the more complex units as aboriginal. If the first hypothesis is correct, the tribal-wide organization and head chief reported for the Micmac in historic times may be an analogous development among coastal collecting populations farther north. The most complex political development occurred with the Powhatan polity in Virginia and certain neighboring groups. These were chiefdoms with coercive statelike institutions, whose rulers had the power of life and death over their subjects. Relatives of paramount rulers were established as leaders of subject towns and districts. It is unclear whether these chiefdoms were a northern extension of the indigenous states that flourished farther south or were a local reaction to European incursions. Whichever, they indicate the developmental potential of an Eastern Collecting Pattern that had been enriched rather than transformed by horticulture. While these coastal societies were not spectacular in terms of their material achievements, they provide some idea of the economic and cultural base from which societies of the Adena-Hopewell Pattern might arise.

Other Factors

The concept of patterns accounts for only part of the cultural similarities and diversity of the Northeast. In the past, archeologists invoked population movements to account for the physical and cultural differences they observed among the people of this area. On the basis of cultural affinities, it was suggested that the Archaic Lamoka culture (see Ritchie 1965:78) and the Northern Iroquoian pattern were intrusive into the Lower Great Lakes area from the Southeast, while the Adena culture was derived through the migration of a brachycephalic people from Mesoamerica (Webb and Snow 1945:328-335). Most archeologists now regard all these cultures as essentially local developments. It was also once popular to seek correlations between specific culture types and subracial physical types. In many cases, however, changes in skeletal characteristics that were believed to be sudden and to represent the incursions of new populations with distinctive cultures have been shown to have been gradual and unconnected with the appearance of new cultures (Wright and Anderson 1963:109). Efforts to line up cultural traditions, physical types, and language families in the Northeast appear to be increasingly unproductive and the focus of cultural historical interest has moved elsewhere.

This does not, however, rule out the likelihood that movements of population have significantly influenced the cultural profile of the Northeast. The expansion of the Mississippian pattern seems to be one example where migration may have been of considerable importance. In the past several thousand years, the Algonquian languages are believed to have spread from a point of origin possibly to be pinpointed in Central Ontario (Siebert 1967) along the East Coast and into the Great Lakes-Riverine region. Expansion must also be postulated to account for the distribution of the Iroquoian languages; however, the split between Northern Iroquoian and Cherokee is on the order of several thousand years, and it is unclear whether this family spread from south to north or in the reverse direction. Finally, it is likely that the Siouan languages were formerly more widely distributed in the Northeast than they were in early historic times, when the expansion of Algonquian at the expense of Siouan occurred in the Midwest. Some rough correlations between language and cultural groupings have been observed for the historic period, and these tentatively have been attributed to easier communication facilitating the spread of innovations; however, such correlations are not sufficiently precise so that similar ones can be projected into prehistoric times with any confidence.

Contributors

This list gives the academic affiliations of authors at the time this volume went to press. The dates following the entries indicate when each manuscript was (1) first received; (2) accepted after all revisions had been made; and (3) sent to the author for final approval of editorial work.

ABLER, THOMAS S., Department of Anthropology, University of Waterloo, Waterloo, Ontario. Seneca: 6/14/73; 7/8/76; 4/4/77.

BAUXAR, J JOSEPH, University Archives, Northern Illinois University, DeKalb. History of the Illinois Area: 5/3/74; 7/9/74; 11/4/76.

BERRY, BREWTON, Department of Sociology, Ohio State University, Columbus. Marginal Groups: 8/24/72; 3/4/76; 9/13/76.

BLAU, HAROLD, Social Science Department, New York City Community College, City University of New York, New York. Onondaga: 4/27/72; 7/8/76; 3/2/77.

BOCK, PHILIP K., Department of Anthropology, University of New Mexico, Albuquerque. Micmac: 3/15/72; 4/11/72; 10/11/74.

BOISSEVAIN, ETHEL, Department of Anthropology, Hebert H. Lehman College, City University of New York, Bronx. Indians of Southern New England and Long Island: Late Period: 7/31/72; 2/77; 2/11/77.

BOYCE, DOUGLAS W., Department of Sociology/Anthropology, Emory and Henry University, Emory, Virginia. Iroquoian Tribes of the Virginia-North Carolina Coastal Plain: 2/5/74; 2/3/75; 3/8/77.

BRASSER, T.J., Canadian Ethnology Service, National Museum of Man, Ottawa. Early Indian-European Contacts: 11/2/72; 12/13/73; 2/14/77. Mahican: 1/15/73; 12/10/73; 10/11/74.

BROSE, DAVID S., Cleveland Museum of Natural History/Department of Anthropology, Case Western Reserve University, Cleveland. Late Prehistory of the Upper Great Lakes Area: 8/25/72; 4/11/74; 12/23/76.

CALLENDER, CHARLES, Department of Anthropology, Case Western Reserve University, Cleveland. Great Lakes-Riverine Sociopolitical Organization: 3/22/73; 5/16/74; 10/26/76. Shawnee: 8/14/72; 7/21/75; 11/2/76. Fox: 8/5/72; 9/12/73; 11/30/76. Sauk: 8/5/72; 7/10/74; 11/30/76. Kickapoo: 11/16/72; 3/4/75; 11/30/76. Illinois: 8/5/72; 9/13/73; 10/27/76. Miami: 8/5/72; 9/10/73; 10/27/76.

CAMPISI, JACK, Departments of Anthropology and Secondary Education, State University College, New Paltz, New York. Oneida: 5/22/73; 6/15/76; 3/18/77. Onondaga: 4/27/72; 7/8/76; 3/2/77.

CHAPUT, DONALD, Department of History, Los Angeles County Museum of Natural History, Los Angeles. History of the Upper Great Lakes Area: 4/20/73; 12/73; 10/29/76.

CLIFTON, JAMES A., Department of Humanism and Cultural Change, University of Wisconsin, Green Bay. Potawatomi: 11/21/73; 10/30/74; 9/24/76.

CONKEY, LAURA E., Laboratory of Tree-Ring Research, University of Arizona, Tucson. Indians of Southern New England and Long Island: Late Period: 7/31/72; 2/77; 2/11/77.

DAY, GORDON M., Canadian Ethnology Service, National Museum of Man, Ottawa. Western Abenaki: 8/20/73; 2/1/74; 2/14/77. Nipissing: 11/26/73; 1/18/74; 9/13/76. Algonquin: 8/2/72; 4/16/74; 10/5/76.

ENGELBRECHT, WILLIAM E., Department of Anthropology, State University College, Buffalo. Cayuga: 8/31/74; 6/2/76; 4/15/77.

ERICKSON, VINCENT O., Department of Anthropology, University of New Brunswick, Fredericton. Maliseet-Passamaquoddy: 1/22/73; 9/24/74; 10/11/74.

FEEST, CHRISTIAN F., Museum für Völkerkunde, Vienna. Nanticoke and Neighboring Tribes: 8/3/73; 12/3/73; 8/27/74. Virginia Algonquians: 2/6/73; 5/73; 8/27/74. North Carolina Algonquians: 1/15/73; 5/73; 8/27/74. Ottawa: 1/8/73; 9/10/73; 10/11/74.

FEEST, JOHANNA E., Vienna, Austria. Ottawa: 1/8/73; 9/10/73; 10/11/74.

FENTON, WILLIAM N., Department of Anthropology, State University of New York, Albany. Northern Iroquoian Culture Patterns: 9/18/74; 12/9/74; 2/16/77. Mohawk: 9/21/73; 4/28/76; 3/23/77.

FITTING, JAMES E., Jackson, Michigan. Prehistory: Introduction: 2/7/73; 12/15/76; 12/23/76. Regional Cultural Development, 300 B.C. to A.D. 1000: 7/26/72; 7/26/72; 4/8/77.

FOWLER, MELVIN L., Department of Anthropology, University of Wisconsin, Milwaukee. Late Prehistory of the Illinois Area: 9/6/73; 10/2/75; 12/23/76.

FRISCH, JACK A., Gould-Hough Cultural and Educational Center, Lyons Falls, New York. Iroquois in the West: 7/16/73; 1/29/74; 3/18/77.

FUNK, ROBERT E., Anthropology Survey, New York State Museum and Science Service, Albany. Post-Pleistocene Adaptations: 4/1/74; 10/28/75; 12/23/76.

GARRAD, CHARLES, Willowdale, Ontario. Khionontateronon (Petun): 7/23/72; 9/1/72; 8/10/76.

GODDARD, IVES, Department of Anthropology, Smithsonian Institution, Washington. Eastern Algonquian Languages: 7/20/72; 4/18/74; 10/11/74. Indians of Southern New England and Long Island: Late Period: 7/31/72; 2/77; 2/11/77. Delaware: 8/23/73; 1/27/75; 9/27/76. Central Algonquian Languages: 8/21/72; 4/22/74; 8/27/74. Mascouten: 8/14/72; 4/17/74; 10/11/74.

GRIFFIN, JAMES B., Museum of Anthropology, University of Michigan, Ann Arbor. Late Prehistory of the Ohio Valley: 5/29/73; 5/10/74; 12/23/76.

HALL, ROBERT L., Department of Anthropology, University of Illinois, Chicago Circle, Chicago. Late Prehistory of the Illinois Area: 9/6/73; 10/2/75; 12/23/76.

HEIDENREICH, CONRAD E., Department of Geography, York University, Downsview, Ontario. Huron: 7/23/72; 2/73; 8/10/76. Khionontateronon (Petun): 7/23/72; 9/1/72; 8/10/76.

HUNTER, WILLIAM A. (retired), Pennsylvania Historical and Museum Commission, Harrisburg. History of the Ohio Valley: 11/7/72; 4/73; 10/29/76.

JENNINGS, FRANCIS, Indian History Program, Newberry Library, Chicago. Susquehannock: 8/1/72; 11/19/72; 4/16/76.

LANDY, DAVID, Department of Anthropology, University of Massachusetts, Boston. Tuscarora Among the Iroquois: 7/20/73; 4/19/76; 1/27/77.

LOUNSBURY, FLOYD G., Department of Anthropology, Yale University, New Haven. Iroquoian Languages: 12/3/76; 3/77; 3/29/77.

LURIE, NANCY OESTREICH, Anthropology Department, Milwaukee Public Museum. Winnebago: 10/3/73; 4/22/74; 10/11/74.

MORISSONNEAU, CHRISTIAN, Centre d'Études nordiques, Université Laval, Québec. Huron of Lorette: 9/21/72; 2/73; 8/11/76.

PENDERGAST, JAMES F., National Museum of Man, Ottawa. Saint Lawrence Iroquoians: 10/16/72; 4/16/74; 10/11/74.

POPE, RICHARD K., Department of Anthropology, University of Saskatchewan, Regina. Kickapoo: 11/16/72; 3/4/75; 11/30/76.

POPE, SUSAN M., Department of Anthropology, University of Saskatchewan, Regina. Kickapoo: 11/16/72; 3/4/75; 11/30/76.

REYNOLDS, BARRIE, Material Culture Research Unit, James Cook University of North Queensland, Townsville, Queensland, Australia. Beothuk: 6/30/75; 8/12/75; 10/13/76.

RITZENTHALER, ROBERT E. (retired), Anthropology Department, Milwaukee Public Museum. Southwestern Chippewa: 1/15/73; 4/30/74; 5/23/77.

ROGERS, E.S., Department of Ethnology, Royal Ontario Museum, Toronto. Southeastern Ojibwa: 6/10/75; 6/19/75; 5/23/77.

SALWEN, BERT, Department of Anthropology, New York University, New York. Indians of Southern New England and Long Island: Early Period: 9/26/73; 9/18/74; 2/11/77.

SIMMONS, WILLIAM S., Department of Anthropology, University of California, Berkeley. Narragansett: 6/8/73; 2/12/75; 2/8/77.

SNOW, DEAN R., Department of Anthropology, State University of New York, Albany. Late Prehistory of the East Coast: 6/23/72; 4/20/74; 12/23/76. Eastern Abenaki: 5/4/72; 4/22/74; 10/11/74.

SPINDLER, LOUISE S., Department of Anthropology, Stanford University, Stanford. Menominee: 11/7/72; 10/12/73; 9/29/76.

STONE, LYLE M., Archaeological Research Services, Tempe, Arizona. History of the Upper Great Lakes Area: 4/20/73; 12/73; 10/29/76.

STURTEVANT, WILLIAM C., Department of Anthropology, Smithsonian Institution, Washington. Oklahoma Seneca-Cayuga: 6/6/77; 6/6/77; 6/16/77.

TOOKER, ELISABETH, Department of Anthropology, Temple University, Philadelphia. History of Research: 6/13/74; 1/17/75; 4/1/77. Wyandot: 7/16/73; 2/15/74; 8/10/76. The League of the Iroquois: Its History, Politics, and Ritual: 7/31/74; 4/16/76; 1/17/77. Iroquois Since 1820: 6/4/73; 9/13/73; 3/2/77. Mohawk: 9/21/73; 4/28/76; 3/23/77. Onondaga: 4/27/72; 7/8/76; 3/2/77. Cayuga: 8/31/74; 6/2/76; 4/15/77. Seneca: 6/14/73; 7/8/76; 4/4/77.

TRIGGER, BRUCE G., Department of Anthropology, McGill University, Montreal. Introduction: 8/17/73; 11/16/73; 1/21/77. Early Iroquoian Contacts with Europeans: 5/2/72; 4/16/74; 10/11/74. Saint Lawrence Iroquoians: 10/16/72; 4/16/74; 10/11/74. Algonquin: 8/2/72; 4/16/74; 10/5/76. Cultural Unity and Diversity: 2/6/74; 7/10/74; 9/29/76.

TUCK, JAMES A., Department of Anthropology, Memorial University, St. John's, Newfoundland. Regional Cultural Development, 3000 to 300 B.C.: 1/25/72; 4/21/74; 12/23/76. Northern Iroquoian Prehistory: 9/26/72; 4/22/74; 12/22/76.

WALLACE, ANTHONY F.C., Department of Anthropology, University of Pennsylvania, Philadelphia. Origins of the Longhouse Religion: 6/30/72; 1/76; 2/25/77.

WASHBURN, WILCOMB E., Office of American Studies, Smithsonian Institution, Washington. Seventeenth-Century Indian Wars: 6/31/73; 10/23/75; 9/13/76.

WEAVER, SALLY M., Department of Anthropology, University of Waterloo, Waterloo, Ontario. Six Nations of the Grand River, Ontario: 8/2/74; 4/23/76; 3/3/77.

WHITE, MARIAN E. (deceased), Department of Anthropology, State University of New York, Buffalo. Neutral and Wenro: 2/12/73; 2/7/74; 8/16/76. Erie: 2/5/73; 1/29/74; 12/30/75. Cayuga: 8/31/74; 6/2/76; 4/15/77.

Bibliography

This list includes all references cited in the volume, arranged in alphabetical order according to the names of the authors as they appear in the citations in the text. Multiple works by the same author are arranged chronologically; second and subsequent titles by the same author in the same year are differentiated by letters added to the dates. Where more than one author with the same surname is cited, one has been arbitrarily selected for text citation by surname alone throughout the volume, while the others are always cited with added initials; the combination of surname with date in text citations should avoid confusion. Where a publication date is different from the series date (as in some annual reports and the like), the former is used. Dates, authors, and titles that do not appear on the original works are enclosed by square brackets. For manuscripts, dates refer to time of composition. For publications reprinted or first published many years after original composition, a bracketed date after the title refers to the time of composition or the date of original publication.

ARCIA = Commissioner of Indian Affairs
1849- Annual Reports to the Secretary of the Interior. Washington: U.S. Government Printing Office. (Reprinted: AMS Press, New York, 1976-1977.)

Abler, Thomas S.
1967 Seneca Nation Factionalism: The First Twenty Years. Pp. 25-26 in Iroquois Culture, History, and Prehistory: Proceedings of the 1965 Conference on Iroquois Research. Elisabeth Tooker, ed. Albany: New York State Museum and Science Service.

———
1969 Factional Dispute and Party Conflict in the Political System of the Seneca Nation (1845-1895): An Ethnohistorical Analysis. (Unpublished Ph.D. Dissertation in Anthropology, University of Toronto, Toronto.)

Abrams, George
1967 Moving of the Fire: A Case of Iroquois Ritual Innovation. Pp. 23-24 in Iroquois Culture, History, and Prehistory: Proceedings of the 1965 Conference on Iroquois Research. Elisabeth Tooker, ed. Albany: New York State Museum and Science Service.

Acrelius, Israel
1912 From the "Account of the Swedish Churches in New Sweden," 1759. Pp. 51-81 in Narratives of Early Pennsylvania, West New Jersey, and Delaware, 1630-1707. Albert C. Myers, ed. New York: Charles Scribner's Sons.

Adair, James
1775 The History of the American Indians. Particularly Those Nations Adjoining the Mississippi, East and West Florida, Georgia, South and North Carolina, and Virginia. London: Printed for Edward and Charles Dilly. (Reprinted as Adair's History of the American Indians. Samuel C. Williams, ed. Watanga Press, Johnson City, Tenn., 1930; Argonaut Press, New York, 1966.)

Adams, D. Warren
1889 Sullivan's Expedition and the Cayugas. Collections of the Cayuga County Historical Society 7:169-193. Auburn, N.Y.

Adams, Richard C.
1901 A Brief Sketch of the Sabine Land Cession in Texas... Made by the Republic of Texas, to the Cherokees, Delawares, Shawnees and Associated Bands, Made by Treaty and Signed... February 23, 1836. Washington: J. Byrne.

———
1905 Legends of the Delaware Indians and Picture Writing. Washington: [no publisher].

———
1906 A Brief History of the Delaware Indians. U.S. Congress. Senate. 59th Cong., 1st sess. Senate Doc. No. 501. (Serial No. 4916) Washington: U.S. Government Printing Office.

Adams, William R.
1949 Archaeological Notes on Posey County, Indiana. Indianapolis: Indiana Historical Bureau.

Adney, Edwin T.
[1887-1950] [Unpublished Manuscripts in the Peabody Museum, Salem, Mass.]

———
1944 The Malecite Indian Names for Native Berries and Fruits, and Their Meanings. Acadian Naturalist 1(3):103-110.

Adney, Edwin T., and Howard I. Chapelle
1964 The Bark Canoes and Skin Boats of North America. U.S. National Museum Bulletin 230. Washington.

Adovasio, James M., Joel D. Gunn, John Donahue, and Robert Stuckenrath
1975 Excavations at Meadowcroft Rockshelter, 1973-1974: A Progress Report. Pennsylvania Archaeologist 45(3):1-30.

Adrien
1956 Conservatisme et changement chez les Indiens Micmacs. Anthropologica 2:1-16. Ottawa.

Ahlgren, I.F., and C.E. Ahlgren
1960 Ecological Effects of Forest Fires. Botanical Review 26(4):483-533.

Alden, Timothy
1827 An Account of Sundry Missions Performed Among the Senecas and Munsees; in a Series of Letters. New York: J. Seymour.

Alexander, Edward P.
1971 An Indian Vocabulary from Fort Christanna, 1716. Virginia Magazine of History and Biography 79(3):303-313.

Alford, Thomas W.
1936 Civilization; As Told to Florence Drake. Norman: University of Oklahoma Press.

Alger, Abby L.
1897 In Indian Tents: Stories Told by Penobscot, Passamaquoddy and Micmac Indians. Boston: Roberts Brothers.

Allen, Charles E.
1870 Report on the Stockbridge Indians to the Legislature. Massachusetts. General Court. House Doc. No. 13. Boston: Wright and Potter.

Allen, John W.
1945 Jackson County Notes. Southern Illinois Normal University, Museum of Natural and Social Sciences Contribution 21. Carbondale.

Allen, Orlando
1903 Personal Recollections of Captains Jones and Parrish, and the Payment of Indian Annuities in Buffalo. Publications of the Buffalo Historical Society 6:539-546. Buffalo.

Allen, Zachariah
1876 Bi-centenary of the Burning of Providence in 1676. Defence of the Rhode Island System of Treatment of the Indians, and of Civil and Religious Liberty. An Address Delivered Before the Rhode Island Historical Society, April 10, 1876. Providence: Providence Press Company.

Allman, John C.
1960 The Erp Bluff-top Site: Notes on the First Season's Work. Ohio Archaeologist 10(2):60-66.

———
1968 The Incinerator Village Site. Ohio Archaeologist 18(2):50-55.

Alsop, George
1666 A Character of the Province of Mary-Land... Also a Small Treatise on the Wilde and Naked Indians (or Susquehanokes) of Mary-Land, Their Customs, Manners, Absurdities, and Religion. London: Peter Dring. (Reprinted: William Gowans, New York, 1869.)

Alvord, Clarence W.
1920   The Illinois Country, 1673-1818. Springfield: Illinois Centennial Commission.

Alvord, Clarence W., and Lee Bidgood
1912   The First Explorations of the Trans-Allegheny Region by the Virginians, 1650-1674. Cleveland: Arthur H. Clark.

Alvord, Clarence W., and Clarence E. Carter, eds.
1915   The Critical Period, 1763-1765. *Collections of the Illinois State Historical Library* 10. Springfield.

_____, eds.
1916   The New Régime, 1765-1767. *Collections of the Illinois State Historical Library* 11. Springfield.

Ames, David W., and Burton R. Fisher
1959   The Menominee Termination Crisis: Barriers in the Way of a Rapid Cultural Transition. *Human Organization* 18(3):101-111.

Ames, Susie M., ed.
1954   County Court Records of Accomack-Northampton, Virginia, 1632-1640. Washington: American Historical Association.

_____, ed.
1973   County Court Records of Accomack-Northampton, Virginia, 1640-1645. (Virginia Historical Society Documents 10) Charlottesville: University of Virginia Press.

Anderson, James E.
1969   A Cahokia Palisade Sequence. Pp. 89-99 in Explorations into Cahokia Archaeology. Melvin L. Fowler, ed. *Illinois Archaeological Survey Bulletin* 7. Urbana.

André, Louis
1688-1715 Préceptes, phrases et mots de la langue algonquine outaouaise pour un missionnaire nouveau. (Manuscript in Jesuit Archives, Montreal.)

Andrews, Charles M.
1934-1938 The Colonial Period of American History. 4 vols. New Haven, Conn.: Yale University Press.

Anonymous
1585   Sketch-map of Raleigh's Virginia. (Manuscript in the Public Record Office, London, Maps and Plans, G.584.) (Printed in The Roanoke Voyages, 1584-1590. David B. Quinn, ed. Vol. 1:215. Cambridge University Press for the Hakluyt Society, London, 1955.)

Anonymous
1645-1651 Northampton County Deeds and Wills, etc., No. 3. (Photostat Copy in Virginia State Library, Richmond.)

1651-1654 Northampton County Deeds and Wills, etc., No. 4. (Photostat Copy in Virginia State Library, Richmond.)

1654-1655 Northampton County Deeds and Wills, etc., No. 5. (Photostat Copy in Virginia State Library, Richmond.)

1657-1664 Northampton County Order Book No. 8. (Photostat Copy in Virginia State Library, Richmond.)

1661   Dictionnaire algonquin, 1661. (Manuscript in the Archives of Notre-Dame de Montréal, Montreal.)

1663-1666 Accomac County Deeds and Wills. (Photostat Copy in Virginia State Library, Richmond.)

1666-1670 Accomac County Order Book No. 9. (Photostat Copy in Virginia State Library, Richmond.)

1671-1673 Accomac County Orders, Wills. (Photostat Copy in Virginia State Library, Richmond.)

1673-1676 Accomac County Wills (Deeds and Orders). (Photostat Copy in Virginia State Library, Richmond.)

1730   Mémoire sur l'état présent du Canada. (Manuscript in Archives de la Guerre, Recueil-Mémoires et Dessins, M.G. 24, B 2, Vol. 3; Copy in Public Archives of Canada, Ottawa.)

1745   [Report of Traders Plundered by Peter Chartier.] *Pennsylvania Gazette* 857, May 16, 1745.

1852   Nanticoke Indians Petitions and Documents. (Manuscript in Vertical Files, Maryland Historical Society, Baltimore.)

1870   The Last of the Narragansetts. *New England Historical and Genealogical Register* 24(2):192.

1874   Report of the Agent of the Passamaquoddy Indians for the Year 1873 and Subsequent Years. Augusta, Me.

[1880]   [Undated, Unsigned Note Naming Surviving Emigrants from Sandusky and Lewistown to Indian Territory.] (Manuscript in Quapaw: Indians, Seneca, Agents' Reports, Indian Archives Division, Oklahoma Historical Society, Oklahoma City.)

1883   The History of the County of Brant, Ontario. Toronto: Warner, Beers.

1887   History of Gallatin, Saline, Hamilton, Franklin, and Williamson Counties, Illinois, from the Earliest Times to the Present.... Chicago: Goodspeed Publishing Company.

1894   Public Officers in Virginia, 1702, 1714. *Virginia Magazine of History and Biography* 1(4):361-377.

1897   Boundary Line Proceedings, 1710. *Virginia Magazine of History and Biography* 4(1):30-42.

1897a   Abstracts of Northampton County (Virginia) Records in the 17th Century. *Virginia Magazine of History and Biography* 4(4):401-410.

1897-1898 [Documents Relating to Early Virginia History.] *Virginia Magazine of History and Biography* 5.

1899-1900 [Documents Relating to Early Virginia History.] *William and Mary College Quarterly* 8(1-4). Williamsburg.

1900   The Indians of Southern Virginia, 1650-1711: Depositions in the Virginia and North Carolina Boundary Case. *Virginia Magazine of History and Biography* 7(4):337-358.

1901   Articles of Peace with the Tuscarora Indians. *North Carolina Historical and Genealogical Register* 2(2):218-219.

1905   The Treaty of Logg's Town, 1752. *Virginia Magazine of History and Biography* 13(2):143-174.

1907   Narrative of a Voyage to Maryland, 1705-1706. *American Historical Review* 12(2):327-340.

1909   Journal of New Netherland, 1647. Pp. 265-284 in Narratives of New Netherland, 1609-1664. J. Franklin Jameson, ed. New York: Charles Scribner's Sons. (Reprinted: Barnes and Noble, New York, 1967.)

1909a   The Representation of New Netherland, 1650. Pp. 285-354 in Narratives of New Netherland, 1609-1664. J. Franklin Jameson, ed. New York: Charles Scribner's Sons. (Reprinted: Barnes and Noble, New York, 1967.)

1910   Nanticoke Manor. *Maryland Historical Magazine* 5(3):252-254.

1910a   A Relation of Maryland [1635]. Pp. 70-112 in Narratives of Early Maryland, 1633-1684. Clayton C. Hall, ed. New York: Charles Scribner's Sons.

1910b   Extracts from the Annual Letters of the English Province of the Society of Jesus, 1634, 1638, 1639, 1640, 1642, 1654, 1656, 1681. Pp. 118-144 in Narratives of Early Maryland, 1633-1684. Clayton C. Hall, ed. New York: Charles Scribner's Sons.

1911   Examination of Indians, 1713(?). *Virginia Magazine of History and Biography* 19(3):272-275.

1924   Mémoire de la dépance faite par le sieur de La Durantaye aux Outaoüacs pour le service du Roy...[1693]. *Bulletin des Recherches Historiques* 30:49.

1937   [Indian Fish Weir at Anthony, R.I.] *Collections of the Rhode Island Historical Society* 30(1):cover photo. Providence.

1970   Activités de la Société d'Archéologie Préhistorique du Québec, 1969. Pointe-aux-Bussons, la Martre, Mandeville, [Montreal.]

1972   The History of the Association of Aroostook Indians. *Agenutemagen* 1(6):2, 6.

1973   Indian Site Added to Historic Register. *The Narragansett Times,* May 24:3B. Wakefield, R.I.

n.d.   Connecticut Archives, Towns and Lands, 1st ser., Vol 1. (Unpublished Documents in Connecticut State Library, Hartford.)

Anson, Bert
1970   The Miami Indians. Norman: University of Oklahoma Press.

Apes, William
1829   A Son of the Forest: The Experience of William Apes, a Native of the Forest. Comprising a Notice of the Pequod Tribe of Indians. New York: William Apes.

1835   Indian Nullification of the Unconstitutional Laws of Massachusetts Relative to the Mashpee Tribe; or, The Pretended Riot Explained. Boston: Jonathan Howe.

Aptheker, Herbert
1939   Maroons Within the Present Limits of the United States. *Journal of Negro History* 24(2):167-184.

Arber, Edward *see* Smith, John

Archer, Gabriel
1607   A Relatyon of the Discovery of Our River. The Discription of the Now Discovered River and Country of Virginia. A Brief Discription of the People. (Manuscript in Public Record Office, London, CO 1:1-56.) (Printed in The Jamestown Voyages. Philip Barbour, ed. Vol. 1:80-104. Cambridge University Press for the Hakluyt Society, London, 1969.)

1906   The Relation of Captaine Gosnols Voyage to the North Part of Virginia, Begunne the Sixe and Twentieth of March, Anno 42. Elizabethae Reginae 1602. and Delivered by Gabriel Archer, a Gentleman in the Said Voyage [1625]. Pp. 302-313 in Vol. 18 of Haklytus Posthumus or Purchas His Pilgrimes, by Samuel Purchas. Glasgow: James MacLehose and Sons.

Armstrong, Benjamin G.
1892   Early Life Among the Indians: Reminiscences from the Life of Benjamin G. Armstrong; Dictated to and Written by Thomas P. Wentworth. Ashland, Wis.: A.W. Bowron.

Armstrong, William
1836   [Letter to Elbert Herring, April 29, 1836.] (Photostat in Western History Collection, Oklahoma University Library, Norman.)

Arnold, Samuel G.
1859-1860 History of the State of Rhode Island and Providence Plantations. 2 vols. New York: D. Appleton.

Asch, Nancy B., Richard I. Ford, and David L. Asch
1972   Paleoethnobotany of the Koster Site: The Archaic Horizons. *Illinois Valley Archaeological Program Research Papers 6, Illinois State Museum Report of Investigations* 24. Springfield.

Ashe, Samuel A'Court
1908-1925 History of North Carolina. 2 vols. Greensboro: C.L. Van Noppen.

Assikinack, Francis
1858   Legends and Traditions of the Odahwah Indians. *Canadian Journal of Industry, Science, and Art* n.s. 3(14):115-125.

1858a   Social and Warlike Customs of the Odahwah Indians. *Canadian Journal of Industry, Science, and Art* n.s. 3(16):297-309.

Association of Iroquois and Allied Indians
1971   The Association of Iroquois and Allied Indians: Position Paper. Brantford, Ont.: Mohawk Institute Woodland Indian Cultural Education Centre.

Atkinson, M.L.
1913   Memories of an Old Settler. *Baraboo Daily News,* April 26, 1913. Baraboo, Wis.

Atwater, Caleb
1820   Description of the Antiquities Discovered in the State of Ohio and Other Western States. *Archaeologia Americana: Transactions and Collections of the American Antiquarian Society* 1:105-267. Worcester, Mass.

[Aubéry, Joseph]
[1715] [Dictionnaire abnaquis-françois.] (Manuscript in the Société Historique d'Odanak, [Pierreville] Que.)

[1715a] Dictionnaire françois-abnaquis. (Manuscript in the Société Historique d'Odanak, [Pierreville] Que.)

Aupaumut, Hendrick
1827   A Narrative of an Embassy to the Western Indians, from the Original Manuscript of Hendrick Aupaumut, with Prefatory Remarks by Dr. B.H. Coates. *Memoirs of the Pennsylvania Historical Society* 2(1):61-131. Philadelphia.

1854   [History of the Muhheakunnuk Indians, 1790.] Pp. 14-23 in Stockbridge Past and Present; or, Records of an Old Mission Station, by Electa F. Jones. Springfield, Mass.: Samuel Bowles.

Babcock, William H.
1899   The Nanticoke Indians of Indian River, Delaware. *American Anthropologist* n.s. 1(2):277-282.

Baby, Raymond S.
1971   Prehistoric Architecture: A Study of House Types in the Ohio Valley. *Ohio Journal of Science* 71(4):193-197.

Baby, Raymond S., and Martha A. Potter
1965   The Cole Complex: A Preliminary Analysis of the Late Woodland Ceramics in Ohio and Their Relationship to the Ohio Hopewell Phase. *Ohio Historical Society Papers in Archaeology* 2. Columbus.

Baby, Raymond S., Martha A. Potter, and Asa Mays, Jr.
1966   Exploration of the O.C. Voss Mound, Big Darby Reservoir Area, Franklin County, Ohio. *Ohio Historical Society Papers in Archaeology* 3. Columbus.

Backus, Isaac
1871   A History of New England with Particular Reference to the Denomination of Christians Called Baptists. 2d ed. Newton, Mass.: Backus Historical Society.

Bacqueville de la Potherie, Claude C. Le Roy
1722   Histoire de l'Amérique septentrionale. 4 vols. Paris: J.L. Nion et F. Didot.

1753   Histoire de l'Amérique septentrionale [1722]. 4 vols. Paris: Nyon.

1911-1912 History of the Savage Peoples Who Are Allies of New France [1753]. Pp. 273-372 in Vol. 1, and pp. 11-136 in Vol. 2 of The Indian Tribes of the Upper Mississippi Valley and Region of the Great Lakes. Emma H. Blair, ed. Cleveland: Arthur H. Clark.

1917   Adventures of Nicolas Perrot, 1665-1670. Pp. 73-92 in Early Narratives of the Northwest, 1634-1699. Louise P. Kellog, ed. New York: Charles Scribner's Sons.

Badin, François-Vincent
1826   Lettre à son frère S.T. Badin, Detroit, 25 décembre 1825. *Annales de la Propagation de la Foi* 2(9):119-138. Lyon.

1830 [Letter from Mission de Saint-Paul.] *Annales de la Propagation de la Foi* 4:534-543. Lyon.

Baerreis, David A.
1973 Chieftainship Among the Potawatomi: An Exploration of Ethnohistoric Methodology. *Wisconsin Archaeologist* 54(3):114-134.

Baerreis, David A., and Reid A. Bryson
1965 Climatic Episodes and the Dating of the Mississippian Cultures. *Wisconsin Archaeologist* 46(4):203-220.

Baerreis, David A., and Joan E. Freeman
1958 Late Woodland Pottery in Wisconsin as Seen from Aztalan. *Wisconsin Archaeologist* 39(1):35-61.

Baerreis, David A., Hiroshi Daifuku, and James E. Lundsted
1954 The Burial Complex of the Reigh Site, Winnebago County, Wisconsin. *Wisconsin Archaeologist* 35(1):1-36.

Bailey, Alfred G.
1933 The Significance of the Identity and the Disappearance of the Laurentian Iroquois. *Transactions of the Royal Society of Canada,* 3d. ser., Vol. 27(2):97-108. Ottawa.

1937 The Conflict of European and Eastern Algonkian Cultures, 1504-1700: A Study in Canadian Civilization. *Publications of the New Brunswick Museum, Monographic Series* 2. Saint John, N.B.

1969 The Conflict of European and Eastern Algonkian Cultures, 1504-1700: A Study in Canadian Civilization. 2d ed. Toronto: University of Toronto Press

Bailey, Paul
1954 Long Island Whalers. Amityville, N.Y.: Long Island Forum.

1962 Early Long Island, its Indians, Whalers, and Folklore Rhymes. Westhampton Beach, N.Y.: Long Island Forum.

Baird, William T.
1890 Seventy Years of New Brunswick Life: Autobiographical Sketches. Saint John, N.B.: George E. Day.

Baldwin, Elizabeth E.
1972 Late Woodland Sites in Southwest Michigan. (Manuscript at Case Western Reserve University, Department of Anthropology, Archaeological Laboratory, Cleveland.)

Baraga, Friedrich
1831-1864 [Briefe an die Zentraldirektion der Leopoldinen-Stiftung und andere Adressaten.] *Berichte der Leopoldinen-Stiftung* 2:10-16, 19-22, 3:30-33, 4:5-16, 5:5-19, 35-37, 7:5-25 8:23-42, 9:44-51, 10:33-37, 30:4-9, 32:40-41, 33:3-6, 34:57-60. Vienna.

1832 Otawa Anamie-Misinaigan. Detroit: George L. Whitney.

1850 A Theoretical and Practical Grammar of the Otchipwe Language, the Language Spoken by the Chippewa Indians: Which Is Also Spoken by the Algonquin, Ottawa and Potawatomi Indians; for the Use of Missionaries and Other Persons Living Among the Indians of the Above Named Tribes. Detroit: Jabez Fox.

1878-1880 A Dictionary of the Otchipwe Language, Explained in English. New ed. 2 vols. Montreal: Beauchemin and Valois. (Reprinted: Ross and Haines, Minneapolis, l973.)

Barbeau, C. Marius
1912 On Huron Work, 1911. *Summary Report of the Geological Survey Branch of the Canadian Department of Mines for the Calendar Year 1911*:381-386. Ottawa.

1912a [Notes on About 15 Days' Ethnographic Fieldwork Among the Oklahoma Seneca-Cayuga.] (Manuscripts in National Museum of Man, Ottawa.)

1914 Supernatural Beings of the Huron and Wyandot. *American Anthropologist* 16(2):288-313.

1914a Cayuga-Seneca Work. Pp. 458-460 in Reports from the Anthropological Division, Summary Report of the Geological Survey for the Calendar Year 1912. *Canada. Department of Mines, Sessional Paper* 26. Ottawa.

1915 Huron and Wyandot Mythology. *Anthropological Series 11, Memoirs of the Canadian Geological Survey* 80. Ottawa.

1915a Classification of Iroquoian Radicals with Subjective Pronominal Prefixes. *Anthropological Series 7, Memoirs of the Canadian Geological Survey* 46. Ottawa.

1940 Indian Trade Silver. *Transactions of the Royal Society of Canada, 3d ser.,* Vol. 34(2):27-41. Ottawa.

1949 How the Huron-Wyandot Language Was Saved from Oblivion. *Proceedings of the American Philosophical Society* 93(3):226-232. Philadelphia.

1950 Indian Captivities. *Proceedings of the American Philosophical Society* 94(6):522-548. Philadelphia.

1960 Huron-Wyandot Traditional Narratives in Translations and Native Texts. *Anthropological Series 47, National Museum of Canada Bulletin* 165. Ottawa.

1961 The Language of Canada in the Voyages of Jacques Cartier (1534-1538). *Anthropological Series 50, National Museum of Canada Bulletin* 173. Ottawa.

Barber, John W.
1838 Connecticut Historical Collections Containing a General Collection of Interesting Facts, Traditions, Biographical Sketches, Anecdotes, etc. Relating to the History and Antiquities of Every Town in Connecticut with Geographical Descriptions. New Haven: Durrie, Peck and J.W. Barber.

Barber, John W., and Henry Howe
1846 Historical Collections of the State of New Jersey Containing a General Collection of the Most Interesting Facts, Traditions, Biographical Sketches, Anecdotes, etc. Relating to its History and Antiquities, with Geographical Descriptions of Every Township in the State. New York: S. Tuttle.

Barbour, Philip L.
1964 The Three Worlds of Captain John Smith. Boston: Houghton Mifflin.

1967 Chickahominy Place Names in Captain John Smith's True Relation. *Names* 15(3):60-71.

———, ed.
1969 The Jamestown Voyages Under the First Charter, 1606-1609: Documents Relating to the Foundation of Jamestown. 2 vols. London: Cambridge University Press for the Hakluyt Society.

1969a Pocahontas and Her World: A Chronicle of America's First Settlement in Which Is Related the Story of the Indians and the Englishmen, Particularly Captain John Smith, Captain Samuel Argall, and Master John Rolfe. Boston: Houghton Mifflin.

1971 The Earliest Reconnaissance of the Chesapeake Bay Area. *Virginia Magazine of History and Biography* 79(3):280-302.

1972 The Earliest Reconnaissance of the Chesapeake Bay Area: Captain John Smith's Map and Indian Vocabulary. Pt. 2. *Virginia Magazine of History and Biography* 80(1):21-51.

Barlowe, Arthur
1589 Arthur Barlowe's Discourse on the First Voyage. Pp. 728-733 in The Principall Navigations, Voiages and Discoveries of the English Nation, by Richard Hakluyt. (Reprinted in the Roanoke Voyages, 1584-1590. David B. Quinn, ed. Vol. 1: 91-116. Cambridge University Press, London, 1955.)

Barnouw, Victor
1950   Acculturation and Personality Among the Wisconsin Chippewa. *Memoirs of the American Anthropological Association* 72(4):5-148. Menasha, Wis.

Barnwell, Joseph, ed.
1908   The Tuscarora Expedition: Letters of Colonel John Barnwell. *South Carolina Historical and Genealogical Magazine* 9(1):28-54.

Barratt, Joseph
1851   The Indian of New-England, and the North-Eastern Provinces; A Sketch of the Life of an Indian Hunter, Ancient Traditions Relating to the Etchemin Tribe, Their Modes of Life, Fishing, Hunting, etc.: With Vocabularies in the Indian and English, Giving the Names of the Animals, Birds, and Fish; the Most Complete that Has Been Given for New-England, in the Languages of the Etchemin and Micmacs. Middleton, Conn.: C.H. Pelton.

Barrett, Samuel A.
1911   The Dream Dance of the Chippewa and Menominee Indians of Northern Wisconsin. *Bulletin of the Public Museum of the City of Milwaukee* 1:251-406. Milwaukee.

1933   Ancient Aztalan. *Bulletin of the Public Museum of the City of Milwaukee* 13. Milwaukee.

Barrett, Samuel A., and E.W. Hawkes
1919   The Kratz Creek Mound Group: A Study in Wisconsin Indian Mounds. *Bulletin of the Public Museum of the City of Milwaukee* 3(1):1-138. Milwaukee.

Barrett, Samuel A., and Alanson B. Skinner
1932   Certain Mounds and Village Sites of Shawano and Oconto Counties, Wisconsin. *Bulletin of the Public Museum of the City of Milwaukee* 10(5):401-552. Milwaukee.

Barth, Fredrik, ed.
1969   Ethnic Groups and Boundaries: The Social Organization of Culture Difference. Boston: Little, Brown; Bergen-Oslo: Universitets Forlaget; London: G. Allen and Unwin.

Barton, Benjamin S.
1787   Observations on Some Parts of Natural History to Which Is Prefixed an Account of Several Remarkable Vestiges of an Ancient Date, Which Have Been Discovered in Different Parts of North America. Pt. 1. London: Printed for the Author.

1798   New Views of the Origin of the Tribes and Nations of America. 2d ed. Philadelphia: Printed for the Author by John Bioren.

Bartram, John
1751   Observations on the Inhabitants, Climate, Soil, Rivers, Productions, Animals, and Other Matters Worthy of Notice, Made by Mr. John Bartram, in His Travels from Pensilvania to Onondago, Oswego and the Lake Ontario, in Canada. London: Printed for J. Whiston and B. White.

Basehart, Harry W.
1953   Historical Changes in the Kinship System of the Oneida Indians. (Unpublished Ph.D. Dissertation in Anthropology, Harvard University, Cambridge, Mass.)

Bastian, Tyler J.
1963   Archaeological Survey of Isle Royale National Park, Michigan, 1960-1962. (Manuscript on File with the National Park Service, Washington.)

Bauman, Robert F.
1949   The Migration of the Ottawa from the Maumee Valley to Walpole Island. *Northwest Ohio Quarterly* 21(2):86-112.

1952   Kansas, Canada, or Starvation. *Michigan History* 36(September):287-299.

1954   Pontiac's Successor. *Northwest Ohio Quarterly* 26(1):8-38.

Bauxar, J. Joseph
1954   Indian Villages of the Illinois Country. (Manuscript in the Illinois State Museum, Springfield.)

1957   Yuchi Ethnoarchaeology. *Ethnohistory* 4(3):279-301, (4):369-464.

Beale, Calvin L.
1957   American Triracial Isolates: Their Status and Pertinence to Genetic Research. *Eugenics Quarterly* 4(4):187-196.

1958   Census Problems of Racial Enumeration. Pp. 537-540 in Race: Individual and Collective Behavior. Edgar T. Thompson and Everett C. Hughes, eds. New York: Free Press of Glencoe.

1972   An Overview of the Phenomenon of Mixed Racial Isolates in the United States. *American Anthropologist* 74(3):704-710.

Beattie, Jessie L.
1960   The Split in the Sky. Toronto: Ryerson Press.

Beatty, Charles
1962   Journals of Charles Beatty, 1762-1769. Guy S. Klett, ed. University Park: Pennsylvania State University Press.

Beauchamp, William M.
1885   The Iroquois White Dog Feast. *American Antiquarian and Oriental Journal* 7(4):235-239.

1886   Permanence of Early Iroquois Clans and Sachemships. *Proceedings of the American Association for the Advancement of Science* 34:381-392. Salem, Mass.

1888   Onondaga Customs. *Journal of American Folk-Lore* 1(3):195-203.

1891   Hi-a-wat-ha. *Journal of American Folk-Lore* 4(15):295-306.

1891a   Iroquois Notes. *Journal of American Folk-Lore* 4(12):39-46.

1892   The Iroquois Trail, or Foot-prints of the Six Nations, in Customs, Traditions, and History, in Which Are Included David Cusick's Sketches of Ancient History of the Six Nations. Fayetteville, N.C.: H.C. Beauchamp.

1893   Notes on Onondaga Dances. *Journal of American Folk-Lore* 6(22):181-184.

1895   An Iroquois Condolence. *Journal of American Folk-Lore* 8(31):313-316.

1895a   Onondaga Notes. *Journal of American Folk-Lore* 8(30):209-216.

1900   Aboriginal Occupation of New York. *New York State Museum Bulletin* 32. Albany.

1901   Wampum and Shell Articles Used by the New York Indians. *New York State Museum Bulletin* 41:319-480. Albany.

1905   A History of the New York Iroquois, Now Commonly Called the Six Nations. *New York State Museum Bulletin* 78. Albany.

1905a   Aboriginal Use of Wood in New York. *New York State Museum Bulletin* 89:87-272. Albany.

1907   Aboriginal Place Names of New York. *New York State Museum Bulletin* 108, *Archaeology* 12. Albany.

1907a   Civil, Religious and Mourning Councils and Ceremonies of Adoption of the New York Indians. *New York State Museum Bulletin* 113:341-451. Albany.

—————, ed.
1916　　Moravian Journals Relating to Central New York, 1745-66. Syracuse, N.Y.: Dehler Press.

1921　　The Founders of the New York Iroquois League and its Probable Date. *Researches and Transactions of the New York State Archaeological Association* 3(1). Rochester.

Beaugrand-Champagne, Aristide
1936　　Les Anciens Iroquois du Québec. *Les Cahiers des Dix* 1:171-199.

1937　　Le Peuple d'Hochelaga. *Les Cahiers des Dix* 2:93-114.

1948　　Les Origines de Montréal. *Les Cahiers des Dix* 13:39-62.

Beaver, R. Pierce
1962　　American Missionary Motivation Before the Revolution. *Church History* 31(2):216-226.

1962a　　Ecumenical Beginnings in Protestant World Mission: A History of Comity. New York: Thomas Nelson.

—————, ed.
1966　　Pioneers in Mission: The Early Missionary Ordination Sermons, Charges, and Instructions; Source Book on the Rise of American Missions to the Heathen. Grand Rapids, Mich.: W.B. Eerdmans Publishing Company.

1966a　　Church, State, and the American Indians: Two and a Half Centuries of Partnership in Missions Between Protestant Churches and Government. St. Louis: Concordia Publishing House.

1968　　Missionary Motivation Through Three Centuries. Pp. 113-151 in Reinterpretation in American Church History. Jerald C. Brauer, ed. (Essays in Divinity 5) Chicago: University of Chicago Press.

1969　　Methods in American Missions to the Indians in the Seventeenth and Eighteenth Centuries: Calvinist Models for Protestant Foreign Missions. *Journal of Presbyterian History* 47(2):124-148.

Becker, Marshall J.
1976　　The Okehocking: A Remnant Band of Delaware Indians. *Pennsylvania Archaeologist* 46(3):24-61.

Bee, Robert L.
1964　　[Fieldnotes, Kansas Potawatomi Study.] (Manuscript in Archives, Wisconsin State Historical Society, Madison.)

Beers, Henry P.
1964　　The French and British in the Old Northwest: A Bibliographical Guide to Archives and Manuscript Sources. Detroit: Wayne State University Press.

Belknap, Jeremy, and Jedidiah Morse
1955　　Report on the Oneida, Stockbridge and Brotherton Indians [1796]. *Museum of the American Indian, Heye Foundation. Indian Notes and Monographs* 54:5-39. New York.

Bell, W.D.
1953　　The MacMurchy Site: A Petun Site in Grey County Ontario. (Manuscript in Library of Ontario Archaeological Society, Toronto.)

Bell, Robert E.
1951　　Dendrochronology at the Kincaid Site. Pp. 233-292 in Kincaid: A Prehistoric Illinois Metropolis, by Fay-Cooper Cole. Chicago: University of Chicago Press.

Belting, Natalia M.
1958　　Illinois Names for Themselves and Other Groups. *Ethnohistory* 5(3):285-291.

Bennett, John W.
1945　　Archaeological Explorations in Jo Daviess County, Illinois: The Work of William Baker Nickerson (1895-1901) and the University of Chicago (1926-1932). Chicago: University of Chicago Press.

1952　　The Prehistory of the Northern Mississippi Valley. Pp. 108-123 in Archeology of Eastern United States. James B. Griffin, ed. Chicago: University of Chicago Press.

Benthall, Joseph, and Ben C. McCary
1973　　The Williamson Site: A New Approach. *Archaeology of Eastern North America* 1(1):127-134. Attleboro, Mass.

Berkeley, Edmund, and Dorothy S. Berkeley, eds.
1968　　Another "Account of Virginia" by the Reverend John Clayton. *Virginia Magazine of History and Biography* 76(4):415-436.

Berkhofer, Robert F., Jr.
1965　　Faith and Factionalism Among the Senecas: Theory and Ethnohistory. *Ethnohistory* 12(2):99-112.

Berlandier, Luis
1969　　The Indians of Texas in 1830. John C. Ewers, ed., Patricia R. Leclercq, trans. Washington: Smithsonian Institution Press.

Bernou, Claude
[1680]　　[Carte du Lac Teiocha—rontiong dit communément Lac Erié.] (Original in Bureau de Service Hydrographique, 4044-B-48, Paris; Copy in Public Archives of Canada, Ottawa.)

Berry, Brewton
1963　　Almost White. New York and London: Macmillan.

1972　　America's Mestizos. Pp. 191-212 in The Blending of Races: Marginality and Identity in World Perspective. Noel P. Gist and A.G. Dworkin, eds. New York: John Wiley.

Bettarel, Robert L.
1970　　The Moccasin Bluff Site and the Woodland Cultures of Southwestern Michigan. 2 vols. (Unpublished Ph.D. Dissertation in Anthropology, University of Michigan, Ann Arbor.)

Beverley, Robert
1705　　The History and Present State of Virginia in Four Parts. London: Printed for R. Parker.

1722　　The History of Virginia. 2d ed. London: Printed for B. and S. Tooke.

1947　　The History and Present State of Virginia [1705]. Louis B. Wright, ed. Chapel Hill: University of North Carolina Press.

Biggar, Henry P., ed.
1911　　The Precursors of Jacques Cartier, 1497-1534: A Collection of Documents Relating to the Early History of the Dominion of Canada. *Publications of the Public Archives of Canada* 5. Ottawa.

—————, ed.
1924　　The Voyages of Jacques Cartier: Published from the Originals with Translations, Notes and Appendices. *Publications of the Public Archives of Canada* 11. Ottawa.

1965　　The Early Trading Companies of New France: A Contribution to the History of Commerce and Discovery in North America [1901]. New York: Argonaut Press.

Bigony, Beatrice A.
1968　　An Archaeological Survey of the South Shore of Lake Superior: Calumet to Naomikong Point. (Manuscript Including Fieldnotes, Maps, and Photographs, Great Lakes Range, Museum of Anthropology, University of Michigan, Ann Arbor.)

1970　　Late Woodland Occupations of the Saginaw Valley. *Michigan Archaeologist* 16(3-4):115-214.

Binford, Lewis R.
1965　　Colonial Period Ceramics of the Nottoway and Weanock Indians of Southeast Virginia. *Quarterly Bulletin of the Archaeological Society of Virginia* 19(4):78-87. Richmond.

1967   An Ethnohistory of the Nottoway, Meherrin and Weanock Indians of Southeastern Virginia. *Ethnohistory* 14(3-4):103-218.

Binford, Lewis R., and Mark L. Papworth
1963   The Eastport Site, Antrim County, Michigan. *University of Michigan Museum of Anthropology, Anthropological Papers* 19:71-123. Ann Arbor.

Binford, Lewis R., and George I. Quimby
1963   Indian Sites and Chipped Stone Materials in the Northern Lake Michigan Area. *Fieldiana: Anthropology* 36(12):277-307. Chicago.

Biörck, Tobias E. *see* Björck, Tobias Er.

Birket-Smith, Kaj
1920   Some Ancient Artifacts from the Eastern United States. *Journal de la Société des Américanistes de Paris* n.s. 12:141-169.

1929   The Caribou Eskimos: Material and Social Life and Their Cultural Position. W.E. Calvert, trans. *Report of the Fifth Thule Expedition 1921-1924*, Vol. 5, Pt. 1. Copenhagen.

Björck, Tobias Er.
1731   ...Dissertatio gradualis, de plantatione ecclesiae svecanae in America, quam, ... in Regio Upsal. atheneo, praesid e, Andrea Bronwall in audit. Gust. maj. d. 14 jun. an. MDCCXXXI. examinandum modeste sistit Tobias E. Biörck, americano-dalekarlus. Uppsala, Sweden: Literis Wernerianus.

Black, Glenn A.
1934   Archaeological Survey of Dearborn and Ohio Counties. *Indiana History Bulletin* 11(7):173-260.

1967   Angel Site: An Archaeological, Historical and Ethnological Study. 2 vols. Indianapolis: Indiana Historical Society.

Black, Meredith
1963   The Distribution and Archaeological Significance of the Marsh Elder *Iva annua* L. *Papers of the Michigan Academy of Science, Arts and Letters* 48:541-547. Ann Arbor.

Blackbird, Andrew J.
1887   History of the Ottawa and Chippewa Indians of Michigan: A Grammar of Their Language, and Personal and Family History of the Author. Ypsilanti, Mich.: The Ypsilantian Job Printing House.

Black Hawk, Sauk Chief
1955   Ma-ka-tai-me-she-kia-kiak, Black Hawk: An Autobiography [1832]. Donald Jackson, ed. Urbana: University of Illinois Press.

Blaeu, Jean
1635   Nova Belgica et Anglia Nova. In Ander Theil Novi Atlantis; Das ist Abbildung und Beschreibung von allen Ländern des Erdreichs. Ganz vernewt und verbessert. Durch Wilhelm und Iohann Blaeu. Amsterdam: Apud Guiljelmum et Johannem Blaeu.

Blair, Emma H., ed.
1911-1912   The Indian Tribes of the Upper Mississippi Valley and Region of the Great Lakes, as Described by Nicolas Perrot, French Commandant in the Northwest; Bacqueville de la Potherie, French Royal Commissioner to Canada; Morrell Marston, American Army Officer; and Thomas Forsyth, United States Agent at Fort Armstrong. 2 vols. Cleveland: Arthur H. Clark.

Bland, Edward
1651   The Discovery of Nevv Brittaine. London: T. Harper for J. Stephenson.

1911   The Discovery of New Brittaine, 1650. Pp. 1-19 in Narratives of Early Carolina, 1650-1708. Alexander S. Salley, ed. New York: Charles Scribner's Sons.

Blau, Harold
1963   Dream Guessing: A Comparative Analysis. *Ethnohistory* 10(3):233-249.

1964   The Iroquois White Dog Sacrifice: Its Evolution and Symbolism. *Ethnohistory* 11(2):97-119.

1966   Function and the False Faces: A Classification of Onondaga Masked Rituals and Themes. *Journal of American Folklore* 79(314):564-580.

1967   Notes on the Onondaga Bowl Game. Pp. 35-49 in Iroquois Culture, History, and Prehistory: Proceedings of the 1965 Conference on Iroquois Research. Elisabeth Tooker, ed. Albany: New York State Museum and Science Service.

Bleed, Peter
1969   The Archaeology of Petaga Point: The Preceramic Component. St. Paul: Minnesota Historical Society.

1970   Notes on Aztalan Shell-tempered Pottery. *Wisconsin Archaeologist* 51(1):1-20.

Bloch, Marc L.B.
1953   The Historian's Craft. Peter Putnam, trans. New York: Alfred A. Knopf.

Bloomfield, Julia K.
1907   The Oneidas. New York: Alden Brothers.

Bloomfield, Leonard
1925   On the Sound System of Central Algonquian. *Language* 1(4):130-156.

1927   Literate and Illiterate Speech. *American Speech* 2:432-439.

1928   Menomini Texts. *Publications of the American Ethnological Society* 12. New York.

1946   Algonquian. Pp. 85-129 in Linguistic Structures of Native America. Harry Hoijer, ed. *Viking Fund Publications in Anthropology* 6. New York.

1957   Eastern Ojibwa: Grammatical Sketch, Texts and Word List. Ann Arbor: University of Michigan Press.

1962   The Menomini Language. New Haven, Conn., and London: Yale University Press.

1975   Menomini Lexicon. Charles F. Hockett, ed. *Milwaukee Public Museum Publications in Anthropology and History* 3. Milwaukee.

Bluhm, Elaine A., and Gloria J. Fenner
1961   The Oak Forest Site. Pp. 138-161 in Chicago Area Archaeology. Elaine A. Bluhm, ed. *Illinois Archaeological Survey Bulletin* 3. Carbondale.

Bluhm, Elaine A., and Allen Liss
1961   The Anker Site. Pp. 89-137 in Chicago Area Archaeology. Elaine A. Bluhm, ed. *Illinois Archaeological Survey Bulletin* 3. Carbondale.

Blume, George W.J.
1951   Present-day Indians of Tidewater Virginia. *Quarterly Bulletin of the Archaeological Society of Virginia* 6(2). Richmond.

Boas, Franz
1887   The Occurrence of Similar Inventions in Areas Widely Apart. *Science* 9(224):485-486.

1887a   Museums of Ethnology and Their Classification. *Science* 9(228):587-589.

1909   Notes on the Iroquois Language. Pp. 427-460 in Putnam Anniversary Volume: Anthropological Essays Presented to F.W. Putnam. New York: G.E. Stechert.

1911   Handbook of American Indian Languages. Pt. 1. *Bureau of American Ethnology Bulletin* 40. Washington.

1911a   The Mind of Primitive Man. New York: Macmillan.

1938   The Mind of Primitive Man. Rev. ed. New York: Macmillan.

Bock, Philip K.
1964   Social Structure and Language Structure. *Southwestern Journal of Anthropology* 20(4):393-403.

1966   The Micmac Indians of Restigouche: History and Contemporary Description. *Anthropological Series 77, National Museum of Canada Bulletin* 213. Ottawa.

1966a   Social Time and Institutional Conflict. *Human Organization* 25(2):96-102.

Boggs, Stephen T.
1958   Culture Change and the Personality of Ojibwa Children. *American Anthropologist* 60(1):47-58.

Boissevain, Ethel (Lesser)
1952   Narragansett Powwow-1951. *Bulletin of the Archeological Society of New Jersey* 5:12-14. Trenton.

1956   The Detribalization of the Narragansett Indians: A Case Study. *Ethnohistory* 3(3):225-245.

1959   Narragansett Survival: A Study of Group Persistence Through Adapted Traits. *Ethnohistory* 6(4):347-362.

1963   Detribalization and Group Identity: The Narragansett Indian Case. *Transactions of the New York Academy of Sciences,* 2d ser., Vol. 25(5):493-502. New York.

1968   From Pagan to Protestant: A Case History and Comparative Analysis of Conversion in Colonial New England. *Bulletin of the New Jersey Academy of Science* 13(1):66-70. Trenton.

1969   Sachems, Kings, Presidents and Chiefs: The Changing Functions and Titles of the Heads of the Narragansett Tribe. (Paper Read at the Northeastern Anthropological Society Meeting, Providence, R.I., April 25, 1969.)

1973   A Week in the Life of a Narragansett Indian in March, 1864. (Paper Read at the Annual Meeting of the American Society for Ethnohistory, Edmond, Okla., October 1973.)

Boissevain, Ethel (Lesser), and Ralph Roberts
1974   The Minutes and Ledgers of the Narragansett Tribe of Indians, 1850-1865: An Intimate Glimpse into the Economic and Social Life of an Acculturated Indian Tribe on the Threshold of Detribalization. *Man in the Northeast* 7:3-28.

Bolt, Robert
1967   Reverend Leonard Slater in the Grand River Valley. *Michigan History* 51(3):241-251.

Bolton, Reginald P.
1909   The Indians of Washington Heights. Pp. 77-109 in The Indians of Greater New York and the Lower Hudson. C. Wissler, ed. *Anthropological Papers of the American Museum of Natural History* 3. New York.

1920   New York City in Indian Possession. *Museum of the American Indian, Heye Foundation. Indian Notes and Monographs* 2(7):223-395. New York.

Bond, C.C.J.
1966   The Hudson's Bay Company in the Ottawa Valley. *The Beaver* (Spring):4-21.

Bond, Beverley W., Jr.
1941-1944   The History of the State of Ohio. Carl Wittke, ed. 2 vols. Columbus: Ohio State Archaeological and Historical Society.

Bond, Richmond P.
1952   Queen Anne's American Kings. Oxford, England: Clarendon Press.

Bonnecamps, Joseph P. de
1749   Carte d'un voyage fait dans la belle rivière en la Nouvelle France. (Original in Bureau de Service Hydrographique 4044-B-21, Paris; Copy in Library of Congress, Washington.)

Bonvillain, Nancy
1973   A Grammar of Akwesasne Mohawk. *Canada. National Museum of Man, Ethnology Division, Mercury Series Paper* 8. Ottawa.

Boucher, Pierre
1664   Histoire véritable et naturelle des moeurs et productions du pays de la Nouvelle France, vulgairement dite le Canada. Paris: F. Lambert.

1881   Canada in the Seventeenth Century [1664]. E.L. Montizambert, trans. Montreal: George E. Desbarats.

Bouchette, Joseph
1832   A Topographical Dictionary of the Province of Lower Canada. London: Longman, Rees, Orme, Brown, Green and Longman.

Boudinot, Elias
1816   A Star in the West; or, A Humble Attempt to Discover the Long Lost Ten Tribes of Israel. Trenton, N.J.: D. Fenton, S. Hutchinson and J. Dunham.

Bougainville, Louis-Antoine de
1924   Le Journal de M. de Bougainville. *Rapport de l'Archiviste de la Province de Québec, 1923-1924*:202-339. Quebec.

1964   Adventure in the Wilderness: The American Journals of Louis Antoine de Bougainville, 1756-1760. Edward P. Hamilton, ed. and trans. Norman: University of Oklahoma Press.

Bourque, Bruce J.
1971   Prehistory of the Central Maine Coast. (Unpublished Ph.D. Dissertation in Anthropology, Harvard University, Cambridge, Mass.)

1975   Comments on the Late Archaic Populations of Central Maine: The View from the Turner Farm. *Arctic Anthropology* 12(2):35-45.

Bouton, Nathaniel
1856   The History of Concord, from its First Grant in 1725, to the Organization of the City Government in 1853, with a History of the Ancient Penacooks, ... Concord, N.H.: B.W. Sanborn.

Boyce, Douglas W.
1971   Notes on Tuscarora Political Organization, 1650-1713. (Unpublished M.A. Thesis in Anthropology, University of North Carolina, Chapel Hill.)

1973   Tuscarora Political Organization, Ethnic Identity, and Sociohistorical Demography, 1711-1825. (Unpublished Ph.D. Dissertation in Anthropology, University of North Carolina, Chapel Hill.)

1973a   A Glimpse of Iroquois Culture History Through the Eyes of Joseph Brant and John Norton. *Proceedings of the American Philosophical Society* 117(4):286-294. Philadelphia.

1975   Did a Tuscarora Confederacy Exist? Pp. 28-45 in Four Centuries of Southern Indians. Charles M. Hudson, ed. Athens: University of Georgia Press.

Boyd, Julian P., ed.
1938   Indian Treaties Printed by Benjamin Franklin, 1736-1762. Philadelphia: Historical Society of Pennsylvania.

Boyle, David
1889   The Land of the Souls. Pp. 4-15 in *Annual Archaeological Report for 1889, Being Part of Appendix to the the Report of the Minister of Education, Ontario.* Toronto.

1898   The Pagan Iroquois. Pp. 54-211 in *Annual Archaeological Report for 1898, Being Part of Appendix to the Report of the Minister of Education, Ontario.* Toronto.

1900   Iroquois Medicine Man's Mask. Pp. 27-30 in *Annual Archaeological Report for 1899, Being Part of the Appendix to the Report of the Minister of Education, Ontario.* Toronto.

1900a   Big Corn Feast (Lower Cayuga). Pp. 34-40 in *Annual Archaeological Report for 1899, Being Part of the Appendix to the Report of the Minister of Education, Ontario.* Toronto.

1900b   On the Paganism of the Civilized Iroquois of Ontario. *Journal of the Royal Anthropological Institute of Great Britain and Ireland* 30:263-273.

1906   The Making of a Cayuga Chief. Pp. 56-59 in *Annual Archaeological Report for 1905, Being Part of the Appendix to the Report of the Minister of Education, Ontario.* Toronto.

Bozman, John L.
1837   A History of Maryland, from its First Settlement, in 1633, to the Restoration in 1660. 2 vols. Baltimore: James Lucas and E.K. Deaver

Brackenridge, Henry M.
1819   [Letter to Thomas Jefferson, July 25, 1813.] P. 89 in Supplement to Volume 16 of *Niles' Weekly Register.* Baltimore.

Brackenridge, Hugh H., ed.
1867   Indian Atrocities: Narratives of the Perils and Sufferings of Dr. Knight and John Slover Among the Indians, During the Revolutionary War. Cincinnati: U.P. James. (Reprinted from the 1843 Nashville Edition.)

Bradford, William
1908   History of Plymouth Plantation, 1606-1646. William T. Davis, ed. New York: Charles Scribner's Sons.

1952   Of Plymouth Plantation, 1620-1647. Samuel E. Morison, ed. New York: Knopf. (Reprinted: Capricorn Books, New York, 1962.)

Bradley, Jim
1976   A Preliminary Report on the Historic Onondaga Sequence. *New York State Archaeological Association Bulletin* 1(1). Albany.

Brainerd, John
1880   The Journal of the Rev. John Brainerd, from January, 1761, to October, 1762. George Macloskie, ed. Toms River, N.J.: The New Jersey Courier.

Brandes, Ray
1962   Don Santiago Kirker, King of the Scalp Hunters. *The Smoke Signal* 6:1-8. Tucson.

Brant-Sero, John O.
1899   The Six Nations Indians in the Province of Ontario, Canada. *Transactions of the Wentworth Historical Society* 2:62-73. Hamilton, Ont.

1899a   Some Descendants of Joseph Brant. *Papers and Records of the Ontario Historical Society* 1:113-117. Toronto.

1901   Dekanawideh: The Law-giver of the Caniengahakas. *Man* n.s. 1(134):166-170.

Brasser, Ted J.C.
1966   Indians of Long Island, 1600-1964. *Monographs on the North American Indians, Publication* 1. Colorado Springs, Colo.

1971   The Coastal Algonkians: People of the First Frontiers. Pp. 64-91 in North American Indians in Historical Perspective. Eleanor B. Leacock and Nancy O. Lurie, eds. New York: Random House.

1975   A Basketful of Indian Culture Change. *Canada. National Museum of Man, Ethnology Division, Mercury Series Paper* 22. Ottawa.

Braun, Emma L.
1950   The Deciduous Forests of Eastern North America. Philadelphia: Blakiston.

Brennan, Louis A.
1962   A Beginning in Chronology for the Croton River Area. *Pennsylvania Archaeologist* 32(3-4):138-156.

1972   The Implications of Two Recent Radiocarbon Dates from Montrose Point on the Lower Hudson River. *Pennsylvania Archaeologist* 42(1-2):1-14.

1974   The Lower Hudson: A Decade of Shell Middens. *Archaeology of Eastern North America* 2(1):81-93. Attleboro, Mass.

Brereton, John
1906   A Briefe and True Relation of the Discoverie of the North Part of Virginia... Made this Present Yeere 1602. Pp. 325-340 in Early English and French Voyages, Chiefly from Hakluyt, 1534-1608. Henry S. Burrage, ed. New York: Charles Scribner's Sons.

Brice, Wallace A.
1868   History of Ft. Wayne, from the Earliest Known Accounts of this Point to the Present Period. Fort Wayne, Ind.: D.W. Jones.

Brickell, John
1737   The Natural History of North Carolina, with an Account of the Trade, Manners, and Customs of the Christian and Indian Inhabitants. Dublin: James Carson. (Reprinted: Johnson Publishing Company, Murfreesboro, N.C., 1968.)

1842   Narrative of John Brickell's Captivity Among the Delaware Indians. *The American Pioneer* 1(2):43-56.

Brinley, Francis
1900   Francis Brinley's Briefe Narrative of the Nanhiganset Countrey. *Publications of the Rhode Island Historical Society* 8(2):69-96. Providence.

Brinton, Daniel G., ed.
1882-1890   Library of Aboriginal American Literature. 8 vols. Philadelphia: D.G. Brinton.

1885   The Lenâpé and Their Legends; with Complete Text and Symbols of the Walam Olum, a New Translation, and an Inquiry into its Authenticity. (Library of Aboriginal American Literature 5) Philadelphia: D.G. Brinton.

1887   On Certain Supposed Nanticoke Words Shown to Be of African Origin. *American Antiquarian and Oriental Journal* 9(6):350-354.

1888   Lenâpé Conversations. *Journal of American Folk-Lore* 1(1):37-43.

Brock, Robert A., ed.
1882-1885   The Official Letters of Alexander Spotswood, Lieutenant-Governor of the Colony of Virginia, 1710-1722. 2 vols. Richmond: Virginia Historical Society.

Brose, David S.
1966   The Valley Sweets Site, 20 SA 24, Saginaw County, Michigan. *Michigan Archaeologist* 12(1):1-21.

1968   The Backlund Mound Group. *Wisconsin Archaeologist* 49(1):34-51.

1970   The Archaeology of Summer Island: Changing Settlement Systems in Northern Lake Michigan. *University of Michigan Museum of Anthropology, Anthropological Papers* 41. Ann Arbor.

1970a The Summer Island Site: A Study of Prehistoric Cultural Ecology and Social Organization in the Northern Lake Michigan Area. *Case Western Reserve University, Studies in Anthropology* 1. Cleveland.

1970b Summer Island III: An Early Historic Site in the Upper Great Lakes. *Historical Archaeology* 4:3-33.

1971 The Direct Historic Approach to Michigan Archaeology. *Ethnohistory* 18(1):51-61.

1971a The Early Historic Indians of Northern Ohio. *The Explorer* 13(1):21-29. Cleveland.

1972 An Initial Summary of the Late Prehistoric Period in Northeastern Ohio. (Paper Read at the Central States Anthropological Association Symposium on Archaeology of Lake Erie, March 1972.)

1973 The Northeastern United States. Pp. 84-115 in The Development of North American Archaeology: Essays in the History of Regional Traditions. James E. Fitting, ed. Garden City, N.Y.: Anchor/Doubleday.

1973a A Preliminary Analysis of Recent Excavations at the South Park Site, Cuyahoga County, Ohio. *Pennsylvania Archaeologist* 43(1):25-42.

———, ed.
[1976] The Late Prehistory of the Lake Erie Drainage Basin: A Symposium. *Scientific Papers of the Cleveland Museum of Natural History*. In Press.

[1976a] The Whittlesey Occupation of Northeast Ohio. In Late Prehistory of the Lake Erie Drainage Basin: A Symposium. David S. Brose, ed. *Scientific Papers of the Cleveland Museum of Natural History*. In Press.

Brose, David S., and Patricia S. Essenpreis
1973 A Report on a Preliminary Archaeological Survey of Monroe County, Michigan. *Michigan Archaeologist* 19(1-2).

Broshar, Helen
1920 The First Push Westward of the Albany Traders. *Mississippi Valley Historical Review* 7(3):228-241.

Brown, Alexander, ed.
1890 The Genesis of the United States. 2 vols. Boston and New York: Houghton Mifflin. (Reprinted: Russell and Russell, New York, 1964.)

Brown, Augustus F.
1950 Structure of Interpersonal Relations in Onondaga Society. (Unpublished M.A. Thesis in Anthropology, University of Pennsylvania, Philadelphia.)

Brown, Charles E.
[1922-1932] [Charles E. Brown Papers.] (Manuscripts in Wisconsin Historical Society, Madison.)

Brown, Ella W.
1971 Love Poems and Songs of a Narragansett Indian. Wakefield, R.I.: Ariosto Press.

Brown, James A.
1964 The Northeastern Extension of the Havana Tradition. *Illinois State Museum Scientific Paper* 12(4):107-122. Springfield.

1965 The Prairie Peninsula: An Interaction Area in the Eastern United States. (Unpublished Ph.D. Dissertation in Anthropology, University of Chicago, Chicago.)

Brown, James A., Roger W. William, Mary A. Barth, and Georg K. Neumann
1967 The Gentleman Farm Site, La Salle County, Illinois. *Illinois State Museum, Report of Investigations* 12. Springfield.

Brown, Raymond H.
1958 The Housatonic Indians: The Aboriginal Inhabitants of Southern Berkshire County. *Bulletin of the Massachusetts Archaeological Society* 19(3):44-50. Attleboro.

Brown, Mrs. W. Wallace
1889 Some Indoor and Outdoor Games of the Wabanaki Indians. *Proceedings and Transactions of the Royal Society of Canada for the Year 1888,* Vol. 6(2):41-96. Montreal.

1892 Chief-making Among the Passamaquoddy Indians. *Journal of American Folk-Lore* 5(16):57-59.

Browne, William H., ed.
1885 Proceedings of the Council of Maryland, 1636-1667. (Archives of Maryland 3) Baltimore: Maryland Historical Society.

Broyles, Bettye J.
1966 Preliminary Report: The St. Albans Site (46Ka 27), Kanawha County, West Virginia. *West Virginia Archaeologist* 19:1-43.

1971 Second Preliminary Report: The St. Albans Site, Kanawha County, West Virginia, 1964-1968. *West Virginia Geological and Economic Survey, Report of Archaeological Investigations* 3. Morgantown.

Bruce, Walter G.
1965 Long Cove: A Maine Shell Deposit Site. *Bulletin of the Massachusetts Archaeological Society* 27(1):8-11. Attleboro.

Brush, Edward H.
1901 Iroquois Past and Present, Including Brief Sketches of Red Jacket, Cornplanter and Mary Jemison, by Edward Dinwoodie Strickland. [Buffalo: Baker, Jones.]

Bruyas, Jacques
1863 Radices verborum iroquaeorum. [Radical Words of the Mohawk Language, with Their Derivatives.] (Shea's Library of American Linguistics 10) New York: Cramoisy Press.

Bry, Theodor de
1590 Merveilleux et estrange rapport, toutesfois fidèle, des commoditez qui se trouvent en Virginia, des façons des naturels habitans dicelle... par Thomas Hariot... Frankfurt: Typis Ioannis Wecheli, sumtibus Vero Theodorij de Bry. [The same plates were used in editions in Latin, English and German, all published by de Bry in 1590.]

Bryson, Reid A., and Wayne M. Wendland
1967 Tentative Climatic Patterns for Some Late Glacial and Post-Glacial Episodes in Central North America. Pp. 271-298 in Life, Land and Water. William J. Mayer-Oakes, ed. (Proceedings of the 1966 Conference on Environmental Studies of the Glacial Lake Agassiz Region) Winnipeg: University of Manitoba Press.

Buchanan, James
1824 Sketches of the History, Manners, and Customs of the North American Indians. London: Black, Young, and Young; New York: W. Borradaile.

Buck, Solon J., and Elizabeth H. Buck
1939 The Planting of Civilization in Western Pennsylvania. Pittsburgh: University of Pittsburgh Press.

Buffinton, Arthur H.
1922 The Policy of Albany and English Westward Expansion. *Mississippi Valley Historical Review* 8(4):327-366.

Buker, William E.
1968 The Archaeology of McKees Rocks Late Prehistoric Village Site. *Pennsylvania Archaeologist* 38(1-4):3-49.

1970 The Drew Site (36-A1-62) Pennsylvania. *Pennsylvania Archaeologist* 40(3-4):21-71.

Bullen, Ripley P., and William J. Bryant
1965 Three Archaic Sites in the Ocala National Forest, Florida. *The William J. Bryant Foundation, American Studies* 6. Orlando, Fla.

Burden, Harold N.
1895   Manitoulin; or Five Years of Church Work Among Ojib-
        way Indians and Lumbermen, Resident Upon that Island
        or in its Vicinity. London: Simpkin, Marshall, Hamilton,
        Kent.

Burggraf, James D.
1938   Some Notes on the Manufacture of Wampum Prior to
        1654. *American Antiquity* 4(1):53-58.

Burke, Charles T.
1967   Puritans at Bay: The War Against King Philip and the
        Squaw Sachems. New York: Exposition Press.

Burlin, Natalie (Curtis), ed.
1907   The Indians' Book: An Offering by the American Indians
        of Indian Lore, Musical and Narrative, to Form a Record
        of the Songs and Legends of Their Race. New York and
        London: Harper Bros. (Reprinted: Dover, New York,
        1968.)

Burnaby, Andrew
1775   Travels Through the Middle Settlements in North Amer-
        ica in the Years 1759 and 1760. London: T. Payne. (Re-
        printed: Cornell University Press, Ithaca, N.Y., 1960.)

Burnell, John P.
1952   The Guineas of West Virginia. (Unpublished M.A. Thesis
        in Sociology, Ohio State University, Columbus.)

Burrage, Henry S., ed.
1906   Early English and French Voyages, Chiefly from Hakluyt,
        1534-1648. New York: Charles Scribner's Sons.

Burton, William, and Richard Lowenthal
1974   The First of the Mohegans. *American Ethnologist*
        1(4):589-599.

Busby, Allie B.
1886   Two Summers Among the Musquakies, Relating to the
        Early History of the Sac and Fox Tribe, Incidents of their
        Noted Chiefs, Location of the Foxes, or Musquakies, in
        Iowa, with a Full Account of Their Traditions, Rites and
        Ceremonies. Vinton, Iowa: Herald Book and Job Rooms.

Bushnell, David I., Jr.
1904   The Cahokia and Surrounding Mound Groups. *Papers of
        the Peabody Museum of American Archaeology and Ethnol-
        ogy, Harvard University* 3(1):5-20. Cambridge, Mass.

1906   The Sloane Collection in the British Museum. *American
        Anthropologist* n.s. 8(4):671-685.

1907   Virginia - From Early Records *American Anthropologist*
        n.s. 9(1):31-44.

1911   New England Names. *American Anthropologist* 13(2):235-
        238.

1919   Native Villages and Village Sites East of the Mississippi
        River. *Bureau of American Ethnology Bulletin* 69. Wash-
        ington.

1927   Drawings by A.B. De Batz in Louisiana, 1732-1735.
        Smithsonian Miscellaneous Collections 80(5). Washington.

Butler, Eva L.
1947   Addendum: Some Early Indian Basket Makers of South-
        ern New England. Pp. 35-54 in Eastern Algonkian Block-
        stamp Decoration: A New World Original or an Accul-
        turated Art, by Frank G. Speck. *Archeological Society of
        New Jersey, Research Series* 1. Trenton.

1948   Algonkian Culture and the Use of Maize in Southern New
        England. *Bulletin of the Archaeological Society of Con-
        necticut* 22:3-39. New Haven.

1953   Notes on Indian Ethnology and History. *Bulletin of the
        Archaeological Society of Connecticut* 27:35-47. New Ha-
        ven.

Butler, Mary
1939   Three Archaeological Sites in Somerset County, Pennsyl-
        vania. *Bulletin of the Pennsylvania Historical and Museum
        Commission* 753. Harrisburg.

Butterfield, Consul W.
1898   History of Brulé's Discoveries and Explorations, 1610-
        1626. Being a Narrative of the Discovery by Stephen
        Brulé of Lakes Huron, Ontario, and Superior, and of His
        Explorations (the First Made by Civilized Man) of Penn-
        sylvania and Western New York, Also of the Province of
        Ontario, Canada. Cleveland: Helman-Taylor.

Butzer, Karl
1971   Environment and Archaeology: An Ecological Approach
        to Prehistory. Chicago: Aldine Press.

Byers, Douglas S.
1954   Bull Brook - A Fluted Point Site in Ipswich, Massachu-
        setts. *American Antiquity* 19(4):343-351.

1955   Additional Information on the Bull Brook Site, Massa-
        chusetts. *American Antiquity* 20(3):274-276.

1956   Ipswich B.C. Essex: Reprinted from the Essex Institute
        Historical Collections.

1959   The Eastern Archaic: Some Problems and Hypotheses.
        American Antiquity 24(3):233-256.

Byers, Douglas S., and Irving Rouse
1960   A Re-examination of the Guida Farm. *Bulletin of the
        Archaeological Society of Connecticut* 30:5-39. New Ha-
        ven.

Byrd, William
1966   Prose Works of William Byrd of Westover: Narratives of
        a Colonial Virginian. Louis B. Wright, ed. Cambridge,
        Mass.: Belknap Press of Harvard University Press.

CDIA = Canada. Department of Indian Affairs
1875-1930 Annual Reports. Ottawa: King's Printer.

Cadillac, Antoine de la Mothe
1930   The Cadillac Memoir on Acadia of 1692. W.F. Ganong,
        ed. (Historical-geographical Documents Relating to New
        Brunswick 8) *Collections of the New Brunswick Historical
        Society* 13:77-97. Saint John, N.B.

Cadzow, Donald A.
1936   Archaeological Studies of the Susquehannock Indians of
        Pennsylvania. *Publications of the Pennsylvania Historical
        Commission* 3. Harrisburg.

Caldwell, Joseph R.
1958   Trend and Tradition in the Prehistory of the Eastern
        United States. *Memoirs of the American Anthropological
        Association* 88. Menasha, Wis.

1964   Interaction Spheres in Prehistory. *Illinois State Museum
        Scientific Paper* 12(6):133-143. Springfield.

Caldwell, Joseph R., and Robert L. Hall, eds.
1964   Hopewellian Studies. *Illinois State Museum Scientific Pa-
        per* 12. Springfield.

Callender, Charles
1955   Changes in Fox Culture Between 1820 and 1955. (Manu-
        script in University of Chicago, Department of Anthro-
        pology, Chicago.

1955a   Fox Genealogies: Charts and Commentaries. (Unpub-
        lished Material in University of Chicago, Department of
        Anthropology, Chicago.)

1962   Social Organization of the Central Algonkian Indians.
        Milwaukee Public Museum Publications in Anthropology 7.
        Milwaukee.

Callender, John
1838   An Historical Discourse, on the Civil and Religious Af-
        fairs of the Colony of Rhode-Island [1739]. Romeo Elton,
        ed. 2d rev. ed. *Collections of the Rhode Island Historical
        Society* 4. Providence.

817

Callihoo, V.
1959   The Iroquois in Alberta. *Alberta Historical Review* 7(2):17-18.

Campanius, Johannes
1696   Lutheri Catechismus; ôfwersatt på American-Virginiske Språket. Stockholm: Burchardi, J.J. Genath. (Reprinted: Ivar Haeggström, and Almqvist and Wiksell, Stockholm and Uppsala, 1937.)

———
1938   Luther's Catechism; Translated into the American-Virginian Language. English Version by Rev. Daniel Nystrom and E.W. Olson. New York: Swedish American Tercentenary Association.

Campbell, Patrick
1937   Travels in North America in the Years 1791 and 1792 [1793]. Toronto: The Champlain Society.

Campisi, Jack
1974   Ethnic Identity and Boundary Maintenance in Three Oneida Communities. (Unpublished Ph.D. Dissertation in Anthropology, State University of New York, Albany.)

Canada
1905   Indian Treaties and Surrenders from 1680 to 1890. 2 vols. Ottawa: Queen's Printer. (Reprinted: Coles, Toronto, 1971.)

Canada (Province) *see* Canada. Parliament. Legislative Assembly

Canada. Department of Indian Affairs
1910   Census of Indians and Eskimos: Religions, Ages, Sexes, Births and Deaths by Provinces up to March 31, 1910. *Annual Report of the Dominion of Canada, Department of Indian Affairs for the Year Ended March 31, 1910.* Appendix. Ottawa.

Canada. Department of Indian Affairs and Northern Development. Indian Affairs Branch
1965   Linguistic and Cultural Affiliations of Canadian Indian Bands. Ottawa: Queen's Printer.

———
1967   Linguistic and Cultural Affiliations of Canadian Indian Bands. Ottawa: Queen's Printer.

———
1970   Linguistic and Cultural Affiliations of Canadian Indian Bands. Ottawa: Queen's Printer.

———
1971   Population Data, File 271/41-3 (A). Fredericton, New Brunswick. Mimeo.

Canada. Department of Indian Affairs. Surveys Branch
1928   Schedule of Indian Reserves in the Dominion of Canada. Ottawa: F.A. Acland.

Canada. House of Commons *see* Canada. Parliament. House of Commons

Canada. Laws, Statutes, etc.
1850   An Act for the Protection of the Indians in Upper Canada from Imposition, and the Property Occupied or Enjoyed by Them from Trespass and Injury. 13-14 Victoria, Chapter 74. Ottawa: Queen's Printer.

———
1869   An Act for the Gradual Enfranchisement of Indians, the Better Management of Indian Affairs, and to Extend the Provisions of the Act. 31 Victoria, Chapter 42. Ottawa: M. Cameron.

Canada. Parliament. House of Commons
1874   Report: The Select Committee Appointed to Inquire into the Conditions and Affairs of the Six Nations Indians in the Counties of Brant and Haldimand, in the Province of Ontario. (Sessional Papers 11) Ottawa: Queen's Printer.

1887   Sessional Papers No. 20B. Ottawa: Queen's Printer.

Canada. Parliament. Legislative Assembly
1844-1845 Report on the Affairs of the Indians in Canada. (Journals of the Legislative Assembly of Canada, 1844-1845, Appendix EEE.) Ottawa: Queen's Printer.

———
1847   Report on the Affairs of the Indians of Canada. (Journals of the Legislative Assembly of Canada, 1847. Appendix T., Section III.) Ottawa: Queen's Printer.

———
1853   Return. (Journals of the Legislative Assembly of Canada, 1853. Appendix EEEE.) Ottawa: Queen's Printer.

Canada. Parliament. Standing Committee on Indian Affairs and Northern Development
1969-1970 Proceedings. Ottawa: Queen's Printer.

Canfield, William W.
1902   The Legends of the Iroquois, Told by "The Cornplanter." New York: A. Wessels.

Cappon, Lester L., ed.
1976   Atlas of Early American History: The Revolutionary Era, 1760-1790. Princeton, N.J.: Princeton University Press.

Carlton, William R.
1940   Overland to Connecticut in 1645: Travel Diary of John Winthrop, Jr. *New England Quarterly* 13:494-510.

Carr, Lloyd G., and Carlos Westez
1945   Surviving Folktales and Herbal Lore Among the Shinnecock Indians of Long Island. *Journal of American Folklore* 58(228):113-123.

Carr, Lucien
1901   The Mascoutins. *Proceedings of the American Antiquarian Society* n.s. 13(3):448-462. Worcester, Mass.

Carrington, Henry B.
1892   Condition of the Six Nations of New York. Pp. 19-83 in The Six Nations of New York, by Thomas Donaldson. Eleventh Census of the United States. Indians. Extra Census Bulletin. Washington: U.S. Government Printing Office.

Carruthers, Peter
1969   The Mikado Earthworks in Alcona County, Michigan. (Unpublished M.A. Thesis in Anthropology, University of Calgary, Calgary, Alberta.)

Carse, Mary (Rowell)
1949   The Mohawk Iroquois. *Bulletin of the Archaeological Society of Connecticut* 23:3-53. New Haven.

Cartier, Jacques
1867   Relation originale du voyage de Jacques Cartier au Canada en 1534. (Documents inédits sur Jacques Cartier et le Canada, nouvelle série) Paris: Tross.

———
1924   The Voyages of Jacques Cartier [1843]. Henry P. Biggar, ed. *Publications of the Public Archives of Canada* 11. Ottawa.

Cartwright, John
1826   Life and Correspondence of Major Cartwright. Francis D. Cartwright, ed. 2 vols. London: H. Colburn.

Carver, Jonathan
[1770] Journals of the Travels of Jona. Carver. (Manuscript, Additional Mss. 8949, 8950, British Library, London.)

———
1778   Travels Through the Interior Parts of North America in the Years 1766, 1767 and 1768. London: Printed for the Author. (Reprinted: Ross and Haines, Minneapolis, 1956.)

Cass, Lewis
1823   Inquiries Respecting the History, Traditions, Languages, Manners, Customs, Religion, etc. of the Indians, Living Within the United States. Detroit: Sheldon and Reed.

Castelnau, Francis de
1842 Vues et souvenirs de l'Amérique du Nord. Paris: Arthus Bertrand.

Catlin, George
1831-1832 Bód-a-sin. (Portrait of Capt. Patterson, a Delaware Chief, Original Catlin No. 274 in National Collection of Fine Arts, Washington.)

1831-1832a Ni-có-man, the Answer. (Portrait of Nahcomin, a Delaware Chief, Original Catlin No. 275 in National Collection of Fine Arts, Washington.)

1848 A Descriptive Catalogue of Catlin's Indian Collection, Containing Portraits, Landscapes, Costumes, etc., and Representations of the Manners and Customs of the American Indians. London: Published by the Author.

1926 North American Indians; Being Letters and Notes on Their Manners, Customs, and Conditions, Written During Eight Years' Travel Amongst the Wildest Tribes of Indians in North America, 1832-1839. 2 vols. Edinburgh: John Grant.

Caudill, William
1949 Psychological Characteristics of Acculturated Wisconsin Ojibwa Children. American Anthropologist 51(3):409-427.

Ceci, Lynn
1975 Fish Fertilizer: A Native North American Practice? Science 188(4183):26-30.

1975a [Reply to Letters on Indian Corn Cultivation.] Science 189(4207):946-949.

Chadwick, Edward M.
1897 The People of the Longhouse. Toronto: The Church of England Publishing Company.

Chafe, Wallace L.
1961 Seneca Thanksgiving Rituals. Bureau of American Ethnology Bulletin 183. Washington.

1962 Estimates Regarding the Present Speakers of North American Indian Languages. International Journal of American Linguistics 28(3):162-171.

1963 Handbook of the Seneca Language. New York State Museum and Science Service Bulletin 388. Albany.

1964 Linguistic Evidence for the Relative Age of Iroquois Religious Practices. Southwestern Journal of Anthropology 20(3):278-285.

1965 Corrected Estimates Regarding Speakers of Indian Languages. International Journal of American Linguistics 31(4):345-346.

1967 Seneca Morphology and Dictionary. Smithsonian Contributions to Anthropology 4. Washington.

1970 A Semantically Based Sketch of Onondaga. Indiana University Publications in Anthropology and Linguistics, Memoir 25. Bloomington.

1973 Siouan, Iroquoian, and Caddoan. Pp. 1164-1209 in Current Trends in Linguistics. Thomas A. Sebeok, ed. Vol. 10: Linguistics in North America. The Hague and Paris: Mouton.

Chalmers, Harvey, with Ethel B. Monture
1955 Joseph Brant: Mohawk. East Lansing: Michigan State University Press.

Chamberlain, Alexander F.
1888 Notes on the History, Customs, and Beliefs of the Mississagua Indians. Journal of American Folk-Lore 1(2):150-160.

1891 The Algonkian Indians of Baptiste Lake. Annual Reports of the Royal Canadian Institute 4:83-89. Ottawa.

1891a Maple Sugar and the Indians. American Anthropologist 4(4):381-383.

1897 In Memoriam: Horatio Hale. Journal of American Folk-Lore 10(36):60-66.

1904 Iroquois in Western Canada. American Anthropologist n.s. 6(4):459-463.

1907 Thomas Jefferson's Ethnological Opinions and Activities. American Anthropologist 9(3):499-509.

Chamberlain, Montague
1898 The Origin of the Maliseets. New Brunswick Magazine 1(1):41-45.

1899 Maliseet Vocabulary. Cambridge, Mass.: Harvard Cooperative Society.

1902 The Primitive Life of the Wapanaki Women. Acadiensis 2(2):75-86.

1904 Indians in New Brunswick in Champlain's Time. Acadiensis 4(3-4):280-295.

Champlain, Samuel de
1613 Les Voyages de sievr de Champlain Xaintongeois, capitaine ordinaire pour le Roy, en la marine... Paris: Jean Berjou.

1619 Voyages et descovvertvres faites en la Nouvelle France depuis l'année 1615 à la fin de l'année 1618. Paris: C. Collet.

1907 Voyages of Samuel de Champlain, 1604-1618. W.L. Grant, ed. New York: Charles Scribner's Sons.

1922-1936 The Works of Samuel de Champlain [1626]. Henry P. Biggar, ed. 6 vols. Toronto: The Champlain Society.

Channing, Edward
1886 The Narragansett Planters: A Study of Causes. Johns Hopkins University Studies in Historical and Political Science, 4th ser., Vol. 3. Baltimore.

1932-1938 A History of the United States. 6 vols. New York: Macmillan. (Reprinted in 1949.)

Chapin, Howard M.
1925 Indian Implements Found in Rhode Island. Collections of the Rhode Island Historical Society 18(1):22-32. Providence.

1926 Unusual Indian Implements Found in Rhode Island. Collections of the Rhode Island Historical Society 19(4):117-128. Providence.

1927 Indian Graves: A Survey of the Indian Graves that Have Been Discovered in Rhode Island. Collections of the Rhode Island Historical Society 20(1):14-32. Providence.

1931 Sachems of the Narragansetts. Providence: Rhode Island Historical Society.

1931a Queen's Fort. Collections of the Rhode Island Historical Society 24(4):141-156. Providence.

Chapin, Israel
1792 Numbers of the Five Nations within the United States. (Manuscript in Henry O'Reilly [O'Rielly] Collection, New-York Historical Society, New York City.)

Chapman, L.J., and D.F. Putnam
1966 The Physiography of Southern Ontario. 2d ed. Toronto: University of Toronto Press.

Chapman, Carl H., and Eleanor F. Chapman
1964 Indians and Archaeology of Missouri. (Missouri Handbook 6) Columbia: University of Missouri Press.

Chard, Chester S.
1961 Invention versus Diffusion: The Burial Mound Complex of the Eastern United States. Southwestern Journal of Anthropology 17(1):21-25.

Charland, Thomas M.
1942   Histoire de Saint-François-du-Lac. Ottawa: Collège Do-
            minicain.

_____
1964   Histoire des Abénakis d'Odanak (1675-1937). Montreal:
            Editions du Lévrier.

Charlevoix, Pierre F.X. de
1744   Histoire et description générale de la Nouvelle France,
            avec le journal historique d'un voyage fait par ordre du roi
            dans l'Amérique septentrionale. 6 vols. Paris: Rollin Fils.

_____
1761   Journal of a Voyage to North America. 2 vols. London:
            Printed for R. and J. Dodsley.

_____
1866-1872   History and General Description of New France [1744].
            John G. Shea, ed. 6 vols. New York: John G. Shea.
            (Reprinted: Loyola University Press, Chicago, 1962.)

_____
1923   Journal of a Voyage to North America [1761]. Louise
            Phelps Kellogg, ed. 2 vols. Chicago: The Caxton Club.

[Chauvinerie, Maray de la]
1928   Dénombrement des nations sauvages qui ont rapport au
            gouvernement de Canada; des guerriers de chaque nation
            avec les armoiries, 1736 [1726]. Bulletin des Recherches
            Historiques 34:541-551.

Chazanof, William
1970   Joseph Ellicott and the Holland Land Company: The
            Opening of Western New York. Syracuse, N.Y.: Syra-
            cuse University Press.

Chazelle, P.
1845   Lettre du R.P. Chazelle, de la Compagnie de Jésus, à MM.
            les Membres du Conseil Central de l'Oeuvre de la Propa-
            gation de la Foi, Sandwich (Haut Canada), 17 avril 1845.
            Annales de la Propagation de la Foi 17(103):449-462.
            Lyon.

Chickasaw and Delaware Chiefs
1853   [Agreement Between the Chickasaw and a Group of Dela-
            wares from Texas, Signed at "Oil Springs, Witchata
            County," June 6, 1853.] (Manuscript, Chickasaw 53:9,
            Indian Archives Division, Oklahoma Historical Society,
            Oklahoma City.)

Chinard, Gilbert
1943   Jefferson and the American Philosophical Society. Pro-
            ceedings of the American Philosophical Society 87(3):263-
            276. Philadelphia.

Choné, P.
1848   Lettre du R.P. Choné, Missionnaire de la Compagnie de
            Jésus dans Haut-Canada, à son Supérieur. Sainte Croix,
            Grande Manitouline, 27 mars 1847. Annales de la Propa-
            gation de la Foi 20(117):140-152. Lyon.

Church, Benjamin
1716   Entertaining Passages Relating to Philip's War, Which
            Began in the Month of June, 1675; as Also of Expeditions
            More Lately Made Against the Common Enemy, and In-
            dian Rebels, in the Eastern Part of New England.
            Thomas Church, comp. Boston: B. Green.

_____
1829   The History of Philip's War, Commonly Called the Great
            Indian War, of 1675 and 1676 [1716], by Thomas Church.
            Samuel G. Drake, ed. 3d ed. Exeter, N.H.: J. and B.
            Williams.

_____
1860   The History of the Great Indian War of 1675 and 1676,
            Commonly Called Philip's War. Also the Old French and
            Indian Wars from 1689 to 1704, by Thomas Church.
            Samuel G. Drake, ed. New York: Dayton.

_____
1867   The History of the Eastern Expeditions of 1689, 1690,
            1692, 1696, and 1704 Against the Indians and French
            [1716]. Boston: J.K. Wiggin and W.P. Lunt.

Clark, A.J., ed.
1932   Earliest Missionary Letters of Rev. John Douse, Written
            from the Salt Springs Mission on the Grand River in 1834
            and 1836. Papers and Records of the Ontario Historical
            Society 28:41-46. Toronto.

Clark, Joshua V.H.
1849   Onondaga; or, Reminiscences of Earlier and Later Times;
            Being a Series of Historical Sketches Relative to Onon-
            daga; with Notes on the Several Towns in the Country,
            and Oswego. 2 vols. Syracuse, N.Y.: Stoddard and Bab-
            cock.

Clark, Robert
1966   A Glimpse of the Past: A Centennial History of Brant-
            ford and Brant County. Brantford, Ont.: Brant Historical
            Society.

[Clark, William]
1942   [Map of 1805]. No. XXXI A-B in Indian Villages of the
            Illinois Country. Sarah Jones Tucker, comp. Illinois State
            Museum Scientific Paper 2(1). Springfield.

Clarke, George F.
1968   Someone Before Us: Our Maritime Indians. Fredericton,
            N.B.: Brunswick Press.

Clarke, Peter D.
1870   Origin and Traditional History of the Wyandotts, and
            Sketches of Other Indian Tribes of North America; True
            Traditional Stories of Tecumseh and His League in the
            Years 1811 and 1812. Toronto: Hunter, Rose.

Clarke, Thomas W.
1940   The Bloody Mohawk. New York: Macmillan.

Claspy, Everett
1966   The Potawatomi Indians of Southwestern Michigan. Do-
            wagiac, Mich.: Braun-Brumfield.

Clayton, John
1965   The Reverend John Clayton, a Parson with a Scientific
            Mind: His Scientific Writings and Other Related Papers.
            Edmund Berkeley and Dorothy S. Berkeley, eds. Char-
            lottesville: University of Virginia Press.

Cleland, Charles E.
1966   The Prehistoric Animal Ecology and Ethnozoology of the
            Upper Great Lakes Region. University of Michigan Mu-
            seum of Anthropology, Anthropological Papers 29. Ann Ar-
            bor.

Cleland, Charles E., and G. Richard Peske
1968   The Spider Cave Site. Pp. 20-60 in The Prehistory of the
            Burnt Bluff Area. James E. Fitting, ed. University of
            Michigan Museum of Anthropology, Anthropological Papers
            34. Ann Arbor.

Clicteur, J.B.
1830   Lettre à M. Fenwick. Cincinnati, 3 juillet 1829. Annales
            de la Propagation de la Foi 4(22):472-485. Lyon.

Clifton, Faye
1964   [Fieldnotes, Kansas Potawatomi Study.] (Manuscript in
            Archives, Wisconsin State Historical Society, Madison.)

Clifton, James A.
1962-1964   [Fieldnotes, Kansas Potawatomi Study.] (Manuscript in
            Archives, Wisconsin Historical Society, Madison.)

_____
1965   Culture Change, Structural Stability and Factionalism in
            the Prairie Potawatomi Reservation Community. Midcon-
            tinent American Studies Journal 6:101-123.

_____
1968   Factional Conflict and the Indian Community: The Prai-
            rie Potawatomi Case. Pp. 115-132 in The American In-
            dian Today. Stuart Levine and Nancy O. Lurie, eds. De-
            land, Fla.: Everett, Edwards.

_____
1969   Sociocultural Dynamics of the Prairie Potawatomi Drum
            Cult. Plains Anthropologist 14(44):85-93.

1970   Chicago Was Theirs. *Chicago History* 1:5-17.

1973   A Report on a Survey of Potawatomi Indian Groups in Canada. Green Bay: University of Wisconsin. Mimeo.

1975   A Place of Refuge for All Time: Migration of the American Potawatomi into Upper Canada, 1830-1850. *Canada. National Museum of Man, Ethnology Division, Mercury Series Paper* 26. Ottawa.

1975a   Applied Anthropology Among Wisconsin's Indians. In The Study of Anthropology. P. Whitten and D. Hunter, eds. New York: Harper and Row.

1977   The Prairie People: Continuity and Change in Potawatomi Culture, 1665-1965. Lawrence: Regents Press of Kansas.

Clifton, James A., and Barry Isaac
1964   The Kansas Prairie Potawatomi: On the Nature of a Contemporary Indian Community. *Transactions of the Kansas Academy of Science* 67(1):1-24. Lawrence.

Clinton, DeWitt
1812   Discourse Delivered Before the New York Historical Society, at Their Anniversary Meeting, 6 December, 1811. New York: James Eastburn.

1849   The Life and Writings of DeWitt Clinton, by William W. Campbell. New York: Baker and Scribner.

Coe, Joffre L.
1964   The Formative Cultures of the Carolina Piedmont. *Transactions of the American Philosophical Society* n.s. 54(5). Philadelphia.

Coe, Michael D.
1960   Archeological Linkages with North and South America at La Victoria, Guatemala. *American Anthropologist* 62(3):363-393.

Cohen, David S.
1974   The Ramapo Mountain People. New Brunswick, N.J.: Rutgers University Press.

Colden, Cadwallader
1747   The History of the Five Indian Nations of Canada, Which Are Dependent on the Province of New-York in America, and Are the Barrier Between the English and French in That Part of the World... 2 vols. London: T. Osborne.

1958   The History of the Five Indian Nations Depending on the Province of New-York in America [1727]. Ithaca, N.Y.: Cornell University Press.

Cole, Douglas
1973   The Origins of Canadian Anthropology, 1850-1910. *Journal of Canadian Studies* 8:33-45.

Cole, Fay-Cooper
1951   Kincaid: A Prehistoric Illinois Metropolis. Chicago: University of Chicago Press.

Cole, Fay-Cooper, and Thorne Deuel
1937   Rediscovering Illinois: Archaeological Explorations in and around Fulton County. Chicago: University of Chicago Press.

Coles, Robert R.
1954   The Long Island Indians. Glen Cove, N.Y.: Little Museum.

Collier, John
1962   John Collier Comments on the Essay of Robert A. Manners: Pluralism and the American Indian. *América Indígena* 22(3):205-208.

Collins, Daniel
1972   The Racially-mixed People of the Ramapos: Undoing the Jackson White Legends. *American Anthropologist* 74(5):1276-1285.

Connecticut (Colony) Laws, Statutes, etc.
1850-1890 The Public Records of the Colony of Connecticut [1636-1776], Transcribed and Published (in Accordance with a Resolution of the General Assembly). 15 vols. Hartford: Case, Lockwood and Brainard.

Connecticut. Commissioners on Distribution of Lands of the Mohegan Indians
1861   Report. Printed by Order of the Legislature. Hartford: J.R. Hawley.

Connecticut. State Department of Environmental Protection. Indian Affairs Council
1975   Report of the Connecticut Indian Affairs Council, 1974. Hartford. (Typed Manuscript.)

Connecticut. State Library
1929   Public Documents of the State of Connecticut. (Its Bulletin 14) 4 vols. Hartford.

1962   Legislative Sessions of Connecticut Colony and State, and the New Haven Colony, 1636-1962. (Its Occasional Research Report 2) Hartford.

Connelley, William E.
1899   Notes on the Folk-Lore of the Wyandots. *Journal of American Folk-Lore* 12(45):116-125.

1899a   The Provisional Government of Nebraska Territory and the Journals of William Walker. *Proceedings and Collections of the Nebraska State Historical Society*, 2d ser., Vol. 3. Lincoln.

1899b   Wyandot Folk-Lore. Topeka, Kans.: Crane.

1900   The First Provisional Constitution of Kansas. *Transactions of the Kansas State Historical Society* 6:97-113. Topeka.

1900a   The Wyandots. Pp. 92-123 in *Annual Archaeological Report for 1899, Being Part of Appendix to the Report of the Minister of Education, Ontario*. Toronto.

1923   Religious Conceptions of the Modern Hurons. *Collections of the Kansas State Historical Society* 15:92-102. Topeka.

1928   History of Kansas, State and People: Kansas at the First Quarter Post of the Twentieth Century. 5 vols. Chicago and New York: American Historical Society.

Conover, George S.
1889   Seneca Villages; Principal Settlements Between Canandaigua and Seneca Lake. Geneva, N.Y.: [no publisher].

Conrad, Lawrence A., and Alan D. Harn
1972   The Spoon River Culture in the Central Illinois River Valley. Mimeo.

Converse, Harriet (Maxwell)
1908   Myths and Legends of the New York State Iroquois. Arthur C. Parker, ed. *New York State Museum Bulletin* 125:5-195. Albany.

Cook, Frederick *see* New York (State) Secretary of State 1881

Cooper, John M.
1938   Snares, Deadfalls and Other Traps of the Northern Algonquians and Northern Athapaskans. *Catholic University of America, Anthropological Series* 5. Washington.

1939   Is the Algonquian Family Hunting Ground System Pre-Columbian? *American Anthropologist* 41(1):66-90.

Cooper John M.
1939a   Truman Michelson. *American Anthropologist* 41(2):281-285.

Cooper, Leland R.
1959   Indian Mounds Park: Archaeological Site, Rice Lake, Wisconsin. *St. Paul Institute Science Museum, Scientific Bulletin* 6. St. Paul.

1965　　Archaeological Survey and Excavation at Mille Lacs-Kathio State Park, 1965. *Minnesota Outdoor Recreation and Resources Commission, Program in Prehistoric Archaeology Report* 1. Minneapolis.

Copway, George
1847　　The Life, History, and Travels of Kah-ge-ga-gah-kowh (George Copway), a Young Indian Chief of the Ojibwa Nation, a Convert to the Christian Faith, and a Missionary to His People for Twelve Years. Philadelphia: James Harmstead.

1850　　The Traditional History and Characteristic Sketches of the Ojibway Nation. London: Charles Gilpin.

Cork, Ella
1962　　"The Worst of the Bargain," Concerning the Dilemmas Inherited from Their Forefathers Along with Their Lands by the Iroquois Nations of the Canadian Grand River Reserve. San Jacinto, Calif.: Foundation for Social Research.

Cormack, W.E.
1829　　Journey in Search of the Red Indians of Newfoundland. *Edinburgh New Philosophical Journal* 6:318-329.

1928　　Narrative of a Journey Across the Island of Newfoundland in 1822. F.A. Bruton, ed. London and New York: Longmans, Green.

Cornelius, Eldon S., and Harold W. Moll
1959　　Locating the Post Molds of Lodges on Sites from Surface Indications. *Michigan Archaeologist* 5(1):1-2.

Corwin, Charles E.
1925　　Efforts of the Dutch-American Colonial Pastors for the Conversion of the Indians. *Journal of the Presbyterian Historical Society* 12(4):225-246.

Council Door (Delaware Indian)
1785　　[Speech at the Treaty of Ft. McIntosh, January 13.] (Wayne Manuscripts, Indian Treaties B., in Historical Society of Pennsylvania, Philadelphia.)

Cowan, William
1973　　Narragansett 126 Years After. *International Journal of American Linguistics* 39(1):7-13.

Coxe, Daniel
1741　　A Description of the English Province of Carolana. London: Oliver Payne.

————, ed.
1741a　　A Collection of Voyages and Travels... to Which Is Added, a Large and Acourate Map of Carolana, and of the River Meschacebe. 3 vols. in 1. London: O. Payne.

Cram, Jacob
1803　　[Extracts from the Rev. Mr. Cram's Journal of 1802 and 1803.] *Massachusetts Missionary Magazine* 1:67-69.

Crane, H.R., and James B. Griffin
1964　　University of Michigan Radiocarbon Dates, IX. *Radiocarbon* 6(1):1-24.

1968　　University of Michigan Radiocarbon Dates, XII. *Radiocarbon* 10(1):61-114.

1972　　University of Michigan Radiocarbon Dates, XV. *Radiocarbon* 14(1):195-222.

Crane, John C.
1898　　The Nipmucks and Their Country. *Collections of the Worcester Society of Antiquity* 16:101-117. Worcester, Mass.

Craven, Wesley F.
1968　　The Colonies in Transition, 1660-1713. New York: Harper and Row.

1971　　White, Red, and Black: The Seventeenth-Century Virginian. Charlottesville: University of Virginia Press.

Cresson, Francis M., Jr.
1942　　Village Sites in Southwestern Pennsylvania. *Pennsylvania Archaeologist* 12(1):16-20.

Crockett, Walter H.
1921　　Vermont: The Green Mountain State. 4 vols. New York: The Century History Company.

Croghan, George
1904　　A Selection of George Croghan's Letters and Journals Relating to Tours into the Western Country-- November 16, 1750 to November, 1765. Pp. 45-173 in Vol. 1 of Early Western Travels, 1748-1846. Reuben G. Thwaites, ed. Cleveland: Arthur H. Clark.

Cross, Dorothy
1941-1956　　Archaeology of New Jersey. 2 vols. Trenton: Archaeological Society of New Jersey and New Jersey State Museum.

Crowell, Samuel P.
1944　　Rites of the Aborigines. *Northwest Ohio Quarterly* 16(3-4):147-157.

Cruickshank, J.G., and Conrad E. Heidenreich
1969　　Pedological Investigations at the Huron Indian Village of Cahiagué. *Canadian Geographer* 13(1):34-46.

Cruikshank, Ernest A., ed.
1902　　Campaigns of 1812-14: Contemporary Narratives by Captain W.H. Merritt, Colonel William Claus, Lieutenant-Colonel Matthew Elliott and Captain John Norton. *Niagara Historical Society Paper* 9:5-46. Niagara-on-the-Lake, Ont.

1930　　The Coming of the Loyalist Mohawks to the Bay of Quinte. *Papers and Records of the Ontario Historical Society* 26(6):390-403. Toronto.

Cumberland, Frederic B.
1904　　Catalogue and Notes of the Oronhyatekha Historical Collection. Toronto: The Supreme Court, Independent Order of Foresters.

Cumming, William P.
1966　　North Carolina in Maps. Raleigh: State Department of Archives and History.

Cumming, William P., R.A. Skelton, and David B. Quinn
1971　　The Discovery of North America. Toronto and New York: American Heritage Press.

Cunningham, Robert E.
1957　　Indian Territory: A Frontier Photographic Record by William S. Prettyman. Norman: University of Oklahoma Press.

Cunningham, Wilbur M.
1948　　A Study of the Glacial Kame Culture in Michigan, Ohio, and Indiana. *University of Michigan Museum of Anthropology, Occasional Contributions* 12:1-51. Ann Arbor.

Cuoq, Jean-André
1869　　Quels étaient les sauvages que rencontre Jacq. Cartier sur les rives du Saint-Laurent. *Annales de Philosophie Chrétienne* 79:198-224.

1872　　Cantique en langue algonquine. Paris: Jouaust.

1882　　Lexique de la langue iroquoise avec notes et appendices. Montreal: J. Chapleau.

1886　　Lexique de la langue algonquine. Montreal: J. Chapleau.

1894　　Anotc Kekon. *Proceedings and Transactions of the Royal Society of Canada for the Year 1893,* Vol. 11(1):137-179. Toronto.

Cushman, Gwynne F.
1968   Arnold Lake Site, Clare County, Michigan. *The Totem Pole* 51(1):13-18. Detroit.

DCB = Brown, George W. et al., eds.
1966   Dictionary of Canadian Biography. -vols. Toronto: University Press.

Dalrymple, Edwin A.
1858   [17-Word Vocabulary Collected from the King William County Pamunkey in 1884.] *Historical Magazine and Notes and Queries Concerning the Antiquities, History and Biography of America,* 1st ser., Vol. 2:182.

Damon, P.E., C.W. Ferguson, A. Long, and E.I. Wallick
1974   Dendrochronologic Calibration of the Radiocarbon Time Scale. *American Antiquity* 39(2):350-366.

Danckaerts, Jasper
1913   Journal of Jasper Danckaerts, 1679-1680. Bartlett B. James and J. Franklin Jameson, eds. New York: C. Scribner's Sons. (Reprinted: Barnes and Noble, New York, 1959.)

Dane, J.K., and B. Eugene Griessman
1972   The Collective Identity of Marginal Peoples: The North Carolina Experience. *American Anthropologist* 74(3):694-704.

Dankers, Jaspar, and Peter Sluyter
1867   Journal of a Voyage to New York and a Tour in Several of the American Colonies in 1679-1680. H.C. Murphy, ed. and trans. *Long Island Historical Society Memoir* 1. Brooklyn, N.Y.

Darnell, Regna
1971   The Powell Classification of American Indian Languages. *Papers in Linguistics* 4(1):71-110.

1971a   The Revision of the Powell Classification. *Papers in Linguistics* 4(2):233-257.

Davidson, Daniel S.
1928   The Family Hunting Territories of the Grand Lake Victoria Indians. Pp. 69-95 in *Proceedings of the 22d International Congress of Americanists.* 2 vols. Rome, 1926.

1937   Snowshoes. *Memoirs of the American Philosophical Society* 6:1-207. Philadelphia.

Dawson, Kenneth C.
1971   Michipicoten Survey 1971, Algoma District, Ontario. *Bulletin of the Canadian Archaeological Association* 3:27-38. Ottawa.

Day, Gordon M.
1953   The Indian as an Ecological Factor in the Northeastern Forest. *Ecology* 34(2):329-346.

1956-1973   [Ethnographic and Linguistic Notes from Fieldwork Among the St. Francis Abenaki.] (Manuscript in Day's Possession.)

1961   A Bibliography of the Saint Francis Dialect. *International Journal of American Linguistics* 27(1):80-85.

1962   English-Indian Contacts in New England. *Ethnohistory* 9(1):24-40.

1964   A St. Francis Abenaki Vocabulary. *International Journal of American Linguistics* 30(4):371-392.

1965   The Identity of the Sokokis. *Ethnohistory* 12(3):237-249.

1967   Historical Notes on New England Languages. Pp. 107-112 in Contributions to Anthropology: Linguistics, I. *Anthropological Series 78, National Museum of Canada Bulletin* 214. Ottawa.

1968   Iroquois: An Etymology. *Ethnohistory* 15(4):389-402.

[1968-1972]   [Ethnographic and Linguistic Notes from 10 Weeks' Fieldwork Among the Algonquins of Golden Lake.] (Manuscripts in Ethnology Archives, National Museum of Man, Ottawa.)

1969   The Indian Languages of the Upper Connecticut Valley. Pp. 74-79 in The Connecticut Valley Indians: An Introduction to Their Archaeology and History. W.R. Young, ed. *Springfield Museum of Science Publications* n.s. 1(1). Springfield, Mass.

1971   The Eastern Boundary of Iroquoia: Abenaki Evidence. *Man in the Northeast* 1(1):7-13.

1972   The Name 'Algonquin'. *International Journal of American Linguistics* 38(4):226-228.

1973   The Problem of the Openangos. *Studies in Linguistics* 23:31-37.

1975   The Mots Loups of Father Mathevet. *Canada. National Museum of Man, Publications in Ethnology* 8. Ottawa.

Deale, Valentine B.
1958   The History of the Potawatomis Before 1722. *Ethnohistory* 5(4):305-360.

Deardorff, Merle H.
1944   Saponi-Tutelo Among the Iroquois: 1792. (Manuscript No. 1638 [Population Statistics] in the American Philosophical Society Library, Philadelphia.)

1946   Zeisberger's Allegheny River Indian Towns: 1767-1770. *Pennsylvania Archaeologist* 16(1):2-19.

1951   The Religion of Handsome Lake: Its Origin and Development. Pp. 77-107 in Symposium on Local Diversity in Iroquois Culture. William N. Fenton, ed. *Bureau of American Ethnology Bulletin* 149. Washington.

De Bry, Theodor *see* Bry, Theodor de

De Cou, George
[1949]   The Historic Rancocas: Sketches of the Towns and Settlers in Rancocas Valley. [Moorestown, N.J.]: [no publisher.]

De Forest, John W.
1851   History of the Indians of Connecticut from the Earliest Known Period to 1850. Hartford, Conn.: W.J. Hamersley. (Reprinted: Shoestring Press, Hamden, Conn., 1964.)

DeJarnette, David L., Edward B. Kurjack, and James A. Cambron
1962   Stanfield-Worley Bluff Shelter Excavations. *Journal of Alabama Archaeology* 8(1-2).

Dejean, Auguste
1828-1831   [Lettres à M., à la Baie-Miamis, Rivière-aux-Hurons, l'Arbre Croche.] *Annales de la Propagation de la Foi* 3(16):306-308, 314-317, 320-325, 4(22):466-469, 491-496, (23):544-546. Lyon.

1831   [Briefe an Bischof Fenwick und Friedrich Rese, 29. März 1829-28. Mai 1830.] *Berichte der Leopoldinen-Stiftung* 1:22-28. Vienna.

De Laet, Joannes *see* Laet, Joannes de

De la Morandière, Charles *see* La Morandière, Charles de

Delanglez, Jean
1938   Some LaSalle Journeys. Chicago: Institute of Jesuit History Publications.

1943   Franquelin, Mapmaker. *Mid-America* 25(1):29-74.

Delaware Annuity Rolls
1858-1898   (Manuscripts in U.S. National Archives, Office of Indian Affairs, Record Group 75. Washington.)

Deliette, Louis
1934   Memoir of De Gannes Concerning the Illinois Country [1702]. T.C. Pease and R.C. Werner, eds. *Collections of the Illinois State Historical Library* 23:302-395. Springfield.

823

Delisle, Guillaume *see* L'Isle, Guillaume de

De Loss Love, William *see* Love, William de Loss

De Mille, Susan
1971   Ethnohistory of Farming: Cape Croker 1820-1930. (Unpublished M. Phil. Thesis in Anthropology, University of Toronto, Toronto.)

Denison, Frederic
1878   Westerly (Rhode Island) and its Witnesses, for Two Hundred and Fifty Years, 1626-1876. Providence, R.I.: J.A. and R.A. Reid.

Denny, Ebenezer
1860   Vocabulary of Words in Use with the Delaware and Shawanee Indians [1785]. *Memoirs of the Pennsylvania Historical Society* 7:478-485. Philadelphia.

Densmore, Frances
1910   Chippewa Music, I. *Bureau of American Ethnology Bulletin* 45. Washington.

————
1913   Chippewa Music, II. *Bureau of American Ethnology Bulletin* 53. Washington.

————
1928   Uses of Plants by the Chippewa Indians. Pp. 275-397 in *44th Annual Report of the Bureau of American Ethnology for the Years 1926-1927*. Washington.

————
1929   Chippewa Customs. *Bureau of American Ethnology Bulletin* 86. Washington.

Denton, Daniel
1845   A Brief Description of New York, Formerly Called New Netherlands, with the Places Thereunto Adjoining. Likewise a Brief Relation of the Customs of the Indians There [1670]. New York: W. Gowans.

Denys, Nicolas
1908   The Description and Natural History of the Coasts of North America (Acadia) [1672]. William F. Ganong, ed. and trans. Toronto: The Champlain Society.

De Rasieres, Isaack *see* Rasieres, Isaack de

Dermer, Thomas
1841   Letter of Thomas Dermer, Describing His Passage from Maine to Virginia, A.D. 1619. *Collections of the New York Historical Society,* 2d ser., Vol. 1(10):343-354. New York.

————
1906   To His Worshipfull Friend M. Samuel Purchas, Preacher of the Word, at the Church a Little Within Ludgate, London. Pp. 129-134 in Vol. 19 of Hakluytus Posthumus or Purchas His Pilgrimes, by Samuel Purchas. Glasgow: James MacLehose and Sons.

De Schweinitz, Edmund A.
1870   The Life and Times of David Zeisberger, the Western Pioneer and Apostle of the Indians. Philadelphia: J.B. Lippincott.

De Smet, Pierre Jean *see* Smet, Pierre Jean de

Desrosiers, Léo-Paul
1947   Iroquoisie. Montreal: Etudes de l'Institut d'Histoire de l'Amérique Française.

Deuel, Thorne, ed.
1952   Hopewellian Communities in Illinois. *Illinois State Museum Scientific Paper* 5. Springfield.

De Valinger, Leon, Jr.
1940-1941 Indian Land Sales in Delaware. *Bulletin of the Archaeological Society of Delaware* 3(3):29-32, (4):25-33. Wilmington.

Devine, Edward J.
1922   Historic Caughnawaga. Montreal: The Messenger Press.

De Vries, David P. *see* Vries, David P. de

Dice, Lee R.
1943   The Biotic Provinces of North America. Ann Arbor: University of Michigan Press.

Dièreville, N. de
1933   Relation of the Voyage to Port Royal in Acadia or New France [1708]. John C. Webster, ed. Toronto: The Champlain Society.

Dillard, Richard
1906   Indian Tribes of Eastern Carolina. *North Carolina Booklet* 6(1). Raleigh.

Dillingham, Betty Ann (Wilder)
1963   The Oklahoma Kickapoo. (Unpublished Ph.D. Dissertation in Anthropology, University of Michigan, Ann Arbor.)

Dillon, John B.
1859   A History of Indiana, from its Earliest Exploration by Europeans to the Close of the Territorial Government, in 1816. Indianapolis: Bingham and Doughty.

Dincauze, Dena F.
1968   Cremation Cemeteries in Eastern Massachusetts. *Papers of the Peabody Museum of American Archaeology and Ethnology, Harvard University* 59(1). Cambridge, Mass.

————
1971   An Archaic Sequence for Southern New England. *American Antiquity* 36(2):194-198.

————
1971a   Population Dynamics in Southeastern New England: An Essay in Prehistory. (Manuscript in Dincauze's Possession.)

Dobbs, Arthur
1744   An Account of the Countries Adjoining to Hudson's Bay, in the North-west Part of America. London: Printed for J. Robinson.

Dobyns, Henry F.
1966   Estimating Aboriginal American Population: An Appraisal of Techniques with a New Hemispheric Estimate. *Current Anthropology* 7(4):395-416.

Dominion of Canada *see* Canada

Donaldson, Thomas
1887   The George Catlin Indian Gallery in the U.S. National Museum (Smithsonian Institution) with Memoir and Statistics. Washington: U.S. Government Printing Office.

Donck, Adriaen van der
1656   Beschryvinge van Nieuvv-Nederlant... Amsterdam: Evert Nieuwenhof.

————
1841   A Description of the New Netherlands... Together with Remarks on the Character and Peculiar Customs of the Savages or Natives of the Land. *Collections of the New York Historical Society,* 2d ser., Vol. 1(5):125-242. New York.

Dorr, Henry C.
1885   The Narragansetts. *Collections of the Rhode Island Historical Society* 7:135-237. Providence.

Dorsey, J. Owen, and Paul Radin
1910   Winnebago. Pp. 958-961 in Vol. 2 of Handbook of American Indians North of Mexico. Frederick W. Hodge, ed. 2 vols. *Bureau of American Ethnology Bulletin* 30. Washington.

Dorwin, John T.
1966   Fluted Points and Late-Pleistocene Geochronology in Indiana. *Indiana Historical Society, Prehistory Research Series* 4(3). Indianapolis.

————
1971   The Bowen Site: An Archaeological Study of Culture Process in the Late Prehistory of Central Indiana. *Indiana Historical Society, Prehistory Research Series* 4(4):195-411. Indianapolis.

Downes, Randolph C.
1940   Council Fires on the Upper Ohio: A Narrative of Indian Affairs in the Upper Ohio Valley Until 1795. Pittsburgh: University of Pittsburgh Press.

Dragoo, Don W.
1955   Excavations at the Johnston Site, Indiana County, Pennsylvania. *Pennsylvania Archaeologist* 25(2):85-141.

1959   Archaic Hunters of the Upper Ohio Valley. *Annals of the Carnegie Museum* 35:139-245. Pittsburgh.

1963   Mounds for the Dead: An Analysis of the Adena Culture. *Annals of the Carnegie Museum* 37. Pittsburgh.

1964   The Development of Adena Culture and its Role in the Formation of Ohio Hopewell. *Illinois State Museum Scientific Paper* 12(1):1-34. Springfield.

1972   Prehistoric Iroquoian Culture in the Upper Ohio Valley. (Paper Read at the Central States Anthropological Association Symposium on Archaeology of Lake Erie, March 1972.)

1973   Wells Creek - An Early Man Site in Stewart County, Tennessee. *Archaeology of Eastern North America* 1(1):1-55. Attleboro, Mass.

Drake, Benjamin
1839   The Life and Adventures of Black Hawk, with Sketches of Keokuk, the Sac and Fox Indians, and the Late Black Hawk War. Cincinnati: G. Conclin.

1841   Life of Tecumseh, and His Brother, the Prophet; with a Historical Sketch of the Shawanoe Indians. Cincinnati: E. Morgan.

Drake, Samuel A.
1897   The Border Wars of New England, Commonly Called King William's and Queen Anne's Wars. New York: Charles Scribner's Sons.

Drake, Samuel G.
1832   Indian Biography Containing the Lives of More than Two Hundred Indian Chiefs: Also Such Others of that Race as Have Rendered Their Names Conspicuous in the History of North America. Boston: J. Drake.

1833   Book of the Indians of North America; Comprising Details in the Lives of About Five Hundred Chiefs and Others. Boston: J. Drake.

1841   The Book of the Indians; or, Biography and History of the Indians of North America, from its First Discovery to the Year 1841. Boston: Antiquarian Bookstore.

1851   Indian Captivities, or Life in the Wigwam; Being the True Narratives of Captives Who Have Been Carried Away by the Indians, from the Frontier Settlements of the U.S., from the Earliest Period to the Present Time. Auburn, N.Y.: Derby and Miller.

Driver, Harold E.
1961   Indians of North America. Chicago: University of Chicago Press.

1967   An Integration of Functional, Evolutionary and Historical Theory by Means of Correlations. Pp. 259-289 in Cross-Cultural Approaches: Readings in Comparative Research. C.S. Ford, ed. New Haven, Conn.: Human Relations Area Files Press.

Driver, Harold E., and William C. Massey
1957   Comparative Studies of North American Indians. *Transactions of the American Philosophical Society* n.s. 47(2). Philadelphia.

Dubuque, Hugo A.
1907   Fall River Indian Reservation. Fall River, Mass.: [no publisher.]

Duchesnay, I. Juchereau
1829   [Letter to Lieutenant-Colonel Couper.] (Manuscript in Public Archives of Canada, C ser., Vol. 268:529-532, Ottawa.)

Du Creux, François
1664   Historiae canadensis, sev Novae - Franciae libri decem, ad annum vsque Christi, MDCLVI. Paris: S. Cramoisy et S. Mabre-Cramoisy.

1951-1952   History of Canada, or New France [1664]. James B. Conacher, ed., Percy J. Robinson, trans. 2 vols. Toronto: The Champlain Society.

Dudley, Joseph
1838   Gov. Thomas Dudley's Letter to the Countess of Lincoln, March, 1631. Pp. 5-19 in Vol. 2 of Tracts and Other Papers Relating Principally to the Origin, Settlement, and Progress of the Colonies in North America from the Discovery of the Country to the Year 1776. Peter Force, ed. 4 vols. Washington: P. Force.

Dumont, Elizabeth
1974   Rockelein I: The Archaic Component. (Report Presented at the 1974 Annual Meeting of the New York State Archeological Association.)

Dumont de Montigny, Jean F.B.
1753   Mémoires historiques sur la Louisiane, contenant ce qui y est arrivé de plus mémorable depuis l'année 1687 jurqu'à présent... 2 vols. Paris: C.J.B. Bauche.

Dunbar, Gary S.
1960   The Hatteras Indians of North Carolina. *Ethnohistory* 7(4):410-418.

Dunbar, Willis F.
1965   Michigan: A History of the Wolverine State. Grand Rapids, Mich.: William B. Eerdmans.

Dunham, Mabel
1945   Grand River. Toronto: McClelland and Stewart.

Dunlap, A.R., and Clinton A. Weslager
1947   Trends in the Naming of Tri-racial Mixed-blood Groups in the Eastern United States. *American Speech* 22(2):81-87.

1958   Toponymy of the Delaware Valley as Revealed by an Early Seventeenth-Century Dutch Map. *Bulletin of the Archeological Society of New Jersey* 15-16:1-13. Trenton.

Dunlap, William
1839-1840   History of the New Netherlands, Province of New York, and State of New York, to the Adoption of the Federal Constitution. 2 vols. New York: Printed for the Author by Carter and Thorp. (Reprinted: Burt Franklin, New York, 1970.)

Dunn, Jacob P.
1908   True Indian Stories, with Glossary of Indiana Indian Names. Indianapolis: Sentinel Printing Company.

Dunnell, Robert C.
1962   The Hughes Farm Site (46-Oh-9) Ohio County, West Virginia. *West Virginia Archaeological Society Publication Series* 7. Moundsville.

Dunnell, Robert C., Lee H. Hanson, Jr., and Donald L. Hardesty
1972   The Woodside Component of the Slone Site, Pike County. *Southeastern Archaeological Conference Bulletin* 14. Morgantown, W. Va.

Dunning, Robert W.
1959   Social and Economic Change Among the Northern Ojibwa. Toronto: University of Toronto Press.

1964   Some Problems of Reserve Indian Communities: A Case Study. *Anthropologica* n.s. 6(1):3-38. Ottawa.

DuPonceau, Peter S.
1819   Report of the Corresponding Secretary to the Committee, of His Progress in the Investigation Committed to Him, and of the General Character and Forms of the Languages of the American Indians. *Transactions of the Com-*

mittee of History, Moral Science and General Literature of the American Philosophical Society 1: xvii-xlvi. Philadelphia.

1838   Mémoire sur le système grammatical des langues de quelques nations indiennes de l'Amérique du Nord. Paris: A. Pihan de La Forest.

Durand, of Dauphiné
1932   Un Français en Virginie: Voyages d'un François exilé pour la religion avec une description de la Virginie et du Marilan dans l'Amérique [1687]. Gilbert Chinard, ed. Paris: E. Droz; Baltimore: Johns Hopkins Press.

Dustin, Fred
1932   Report on Indian Earthworks in Ogemaw County, Michigan. *Cranbrook Institute of Science, Scientific Publication* 1. Bloomfield Hills, Mich.

[Dyer, Daniel B.]
1880   [Undated, Unsigned Note Listing New York Indian Holders of Kansas Allotments.] (Manuscript in Quapaw: Indians, New York, Indian Archives Division, Oklahoma Historical Society, Oklahoma City.)

1884   [Statistical Report of Quapaw Agency Dated July 1, 1884.] (Manuscript in Quapaw: Indians, Seneca, Agents' Reports, Indian Archives Division, Oklahoma Historical Society, Oklahoma City.)

Dyer, Daniel B., Jerry Crow, Joseph Spicer et al.
1881-1882   [Letters to Commissioner of Indian Affairs] (Letters Received, 1881 (Nos. 13349, 21669), 1882 (Nos. 453, 6449, 6840, 7654, 9495, 11031); Record Group 75; National Archives, Washington.)

Easton, John
1858   A Narrative of the Causes Which Led to Philip's Indian War of 1675 and 1676, with Other Documents Concerning this Event in the Office of the Secretary of State of New York. Albany: J. Munsell.

1913   A Relacion of the Indyan Warre, by Mr. Easton, of Roade Isld., 1675. Pp. 7-17 in Narratives of the Indian Wars, 1675-1699. Charles H. Lincoln, ed. New York: Charles Scribner's Sons.

Eccles, William J.
1956   Frontenac's Military Policies, 1689-1698: A Reassessment. *Canadian Historical Review* 37(3):201-224.

1959   Frontenac: The Courtier Governor. Toronto: McClelland and Stewart.

1964   Canada Under Louis XIV, 1663-1701. Toronto: McClelland and Stewart; New York: Oxford University Press.

1969   The Canadian Frontier, 1534-1760. New York: Holt, Rinehart and Winston.

1972   France in America. New York: Harper and Row.

Eckstorm, Fannie (Hardy)
1904   The Penobscot Man. Boston and New York: Houghton Mifflin.

1932   The Handicrafts of the Modern Indians of Maine. *Lafayette National Park Museum Bulletin* 3. Bar Harbor, Me.

1934   The Attack on Norridgewock, 1724. *New England Quarterly* 7(September):541-578.

1936   Pigwacket and Parson Symmes. *New England Quarterly* 9(September):378-403.

1939   Who Was Paugus? *New England Quarterly* 12(June):203-226.

1941   Indian Place-names of the Penobscot Valley and the Maine Coast. *Maine Bulletin 44(4), University of Maine Studies* 2d ser., Vol. 55. Orono.

1945   Old John Neptune and Other Maine Indian Shamans. Portland, Me.: The Southworth-Anthoensen Press.

Edwards, Jonathan
1822   Memoirs of the Rev. David Brainerd, Missionary to the Indians on the Borders of New-York, New Jersey, and Pennsylvania: Chiefly Taken from His Own Diary. Sereno E. Dwight, ed. New Haven, Conn.: S. Converse.

Edwards, Ninian W.
1870   History of Illinois from 1778 to 1833; and Life and Times of Ninian Edwards. Springfield: Illinois State Journal Company.

Eggan, Fred R.
1952   The Ethnological Cultures and Their Archeological Backgrounds. Pp. 35-45 in Archeology of Eastern United States. James B. Griffin, ed. Chicago: University of Chicago Press.

1955   Social Anthropology of North American Tribes. 2d ed. Chicago: University of Chicago Press.

1966   The American Indian: Perspectives for the Study of Social Change. Chicago: Aldine.

Eliot, John
1663   The Holy Bible: Containing the Old Testament and the New. Translated into the Indian Language... by John Eliot. Cambridge, Mass.: Samuel Green and Marmaduke Johnson.

1666   The Indian Grammar Begun; or, An Essay to Bring the Indian Language into Rules for the Help of Such as Desire to Learn the Same for the Furtherance of the Gospel Among Them. Cambridge, Mass.: Marmaduke Johnson. (Reprinted: Old South Leaflets 3(52). Boston, 1896.)

Ellicott, Joseph
1937-1941   Reports of Joseph Ellicott as Chief of Survey (1797-1800) and as Agent (1800-1821) of the Holland Land Company's Purchase in Western New York. Robert W. Bingham, ed. 2 vols. *Buffalo Historical Society Publication* 32-33. Buffalo.

Elliott, Richard R.
1896   The Chippewas of Lake Superior. *American Catholic Quarterly Review* 21(82):354-373.

1898   The Last of the Huron Missions. *American Catholic Quarterly Review* 23(91):526-549.

Ellis, Albert G.
1856   Some Account of the Advent of the New York Indians into Wisconsin. *Collections of the State Historical Society of Wisconsin* 2:415-449. Madison.

Emerson, J. Norman
1954   The Archaeology of the Ontario Iroquois. (Unpublished Ph.D. Dissertation in Anthropology, University of Chicago, Chicago.)

1955   The Kant Site: A Point Peninsula Manifestation in Renfrew County, Ontario. *Transactions of the Royal Canadian Institute* 31(64):24-66. Toronto.

1959   A Rejoinder Upon the MacNeish-Emerson Theory. *Pennsylvania Archaeologist* 29(2):98-107.

1961   Problems of Huron Origins. *Anthropologica* 3(2):181-201. Ottawa.

1968   Understanding Iroquois Pottery in Ontario: A Rethinking. *Ontario Archaeological Society Special Publication.* Toronto.

Emerson, J. Norman, and R.E. Popham
1952   Comments Upon the Huron and Lalonde Occupations of Ontario. *American Antiquity* 18(2):162-164.

Emerson, J. Norman, and W. Russell
1965   The Cahiagué Village Palisade. (Manuscript in Department of Public Records and Archives, Toronto.)

Engberg, Robert M.
1930 Archaeological Work in Westmoreland-Fayette Counties, 1929. *Western Pennsylvania Historical Magazine* 13(2):67-103.

_____
1931 Algonkin Sites of Westmoreland and Fayette Counties, Pennsylvania. *Western Pennsylvania Historical Magazine* 14(3):143-190.

Engelbrecht, William E.
1971 A Stylistic Analysis of New York Iroquois Pottery. (Unpublished Ph.D. Dissertation in Anthropology, University of Michigan, Ann Arbor.)

Erickson, Vincent O.
1966-1974 [Ethnographic and Linguistic Notes from Approximately 4 Years' Fieldwork Among the Maliseet of New Brunswick.] (Manuscript in Erickson's Possession.)

Erickson, Vincent O., and Patricia Hunsley
1970 The Union of New Brunswick Indians. *The Mysterious East* (January):4-6.

Esarey, Logan, ed.
1922 Messages and Letters of William Henry Harrison. 2 vols. Indianapolis: Indiana Historical Commission.

Eshleman, H. Frank
1908 Lancaster County Indians: Annals of the Susquehannocks and Other Indian Tribes of the Susquehanna Territory from About the Year 1500 to 1763, the Date of Their Extinction. Lancaster, Pa.: Express Printing Company.

Evans, Clifford
1955 A Ceramic Study of Virginia Archeology. *Bureau of American Ethnology Bulletin* 160. Washington.

Evans, G. Edward
1961 Ceramic Analysis of the Blackduck Wares and its General Cultural Relationships. *Proceedings of the Minnesota Academy of Science* 29:33-54. Minneapolis.

Evans, Lewis
1755 Geographical, Historical, Political, Philosophical and Mechanical Essays. The First, Containing an Analysis of a General Map of the Middle British Colonies in America; and of the Country of the Confederate Indians. Philadelphia: B. Franklin and D. Hall.

Ewan, Joseph, and Nesta Ewan
1970 John Banister and His Natural History of Virginia, 1678-1692. Urbana: University of Illinois Press.

Ewers, John C.
1948 Gustavus Sohon's Portraits of Flathead and Pend d'Oreille Indians, 1854. *Smithsonian Miscellaneous Collections* 110(7):1-66. Washington.

_____
1963 Iroquois Indians in the Far West. *Montana: The Magazine of Western History* 13(2):2-10.

Ewing, J. Franklin
1953 First Note on the Archaeology of the Mohawk Town of Ossernenon. *American Antiquity* 18(4):389-391.

Eyde, David B., and Paul M. Postal
1961 Avunculocality and Incest: The Development of Unilateral Cross-cousin Marriage and Crow-Omaha Kinship Systems. *American Anthropologist* 63(4):747-771.

Eyman, Frances
1964 Lacrosse and the Cayuga Thunder Rite. *Expedition* 6(4):14-19.

Fabila, Alfonso
1945 La tribu Kikapoo de Coahuila. (Biblioteca Enciclopedica Popular 50) Mexico: Secretaría de Educación Pública.

Fabvre, Bonaventure, comp.
1970 Racines montagnaises [1695]. Gerard E. McNulty, ed. *Centre d'Etudes Nordiques, Travaux Divers* 29. Quebec.

Fadner, Lawrence T., ed.
1966 Fort Wilkins 1844, and the U.S. Mineral Land Agency, 1843, Copper Harbor, Lake Superior, Michigan. New York: Vantage Press.

Faillon, Etienne-Michel
1850-1865 Recherches pour servir à l'histoire du Canada. (Manuscript in Archives of Notre-Dame du Montréal, Montreal.)

Fallers, Lloyd A.
1960 The Role of Factionalism in Fox Acculturation. Pp. 62-86 in Documentary History of the Fox Project, 1948-1959. Frederick O. Gearing, Robert McC. Netting and Lisa R. Peattie, eds. Chicago: University of Chicago Press.

Farber, Joseph C., and Michael Dorris
1975 Native Americans 500 Years After. Photographs by Joseph C. Farber; Text by Michael Dorris. New York: Thomas Y. Crowell.

Faries, Richard, ed.
1938 A Dictionary of the Cree Language as Spoken by the Indians of the Provinces of Quebec, Ontario, Manitoba, Saskatchewan and Alberta. Toronto: The General Synod of the Church of England in Canada.

Farley, Alan W.
1955 The Delaware Indians in Kansas, 1829-1867. Kansas City: Kansas City Posse of the Westerners.

Farnham, Mary F., comp.
1902 The Farnham Papers, 1698-1871. *Documentary History of the State of Maine* 8. Portland.

Farnsworth, Kenneth B.
1973 An Archaeological Survey of the Macoupin Valley. *Research Papers 7, Illinois State Museum Report of Investigations* 26. Springfield.

Faulkner, Charles H.
1960 Walkerton: A Point Peninsula-like Focus in Indiana. *Indiana History Bulletin* 37(10):123-136.

_____
1970 The Late Prehistoric Occupation of Northwestern Indiana: A Study of the Upper Mississippi Culture of Kankakee Valley. (Unpublished Ph.D. Dissertation in Anthropology, Indiana University, Bloomington.)

Feder, Norman
1959 Women's Bow-type Hair Ornaments. *The American Indian Hobbyist* 5(7-8):86-90. Denver.

Feest, Christian F.
1966 Powhatan, a Study in Political Organization. *Wiener Völkerkundliche Mitteilungen* 13:69-83. Vienna.

_____
1966a Virginia Indian Miscellany I. *Archiv für Völkerkunde* 20:1-5. Vienna.

_____
1967 The Virginia Indian in Pictures, 1612-1624. *Smithsonian Journal of History* 2(1):1-30.

_____
1967a Virginia Indian Miscellany II. *Archiv für Völkerkunde* 21:5-25. Vienna.

_____
1968 Indianer Nordamerikas. Vienna: Museum für Völkerkunde.

_____
1969 Virginia Algonkin, 1570-1703: Ethnohistorie und historische Ethnographie. (Unpublished Ph.D. Dissertation in Anthropology, Universität Wien, Austria.)

_____
1972 Virginia Indian Miscellany III. *Archiv für Völkerkunde* 26:1-14. Vienna.

_____
1973 Seventeenth Century Virginia Algonquian Population Estimates. *Quarterly Bulletin of the Archaeological Society of Virginia* 28(2):66-79. Richmond.

_____
1973a Southeastern Algonquian Burial Customs: Ethnohistorical Evidence. *Proceedings of the Fourth Middle Atlantic Archaeological Conference.* Pennsbury, N.J., May, 1973.

1975   Archaeology and Ethnohistory in the Chesapeake Bay Area. *Proceedings of the Annual Meeting of the Archaeological Society of Maryland, Paper* 10. Baltimore.

Feest, Johanna E.
1972   Beiträge zur Ethnographie der Ottawa im nordöstlichen Nordamerika, 1820-1860. (Unpublished Ph.D. Dissertation in Anthropology, Universität Wien, Austria).

Fenner, Gloria J.
1961   The Bowmanville Site. Pp. 37-56 in Chicago Area Archaeology. Elaine A. Bluhm, ed. *Illinois Archaeological Survey Bulletin* 3. Urbana.

Fenton, William N.
1933-1934   [Seneca Fieldnotes.] (Manuscript in Fenton's Possession.)

1936   An Outline of Seneca Ceremonies at Coldspring Longhouse. *Yale University Publications in Anthropology* 9. New Haven, Conn. (Reprinted: Human Relations Area Files Press, New Haven, Conn., 1970.)

1937   The Seneca Society of Faces. *Scientific Monthly* 44(March):215-238.

1940   Problems Arising from the Historic Northeastern Position of the Iroquois. Pp. 159-252 in Essays in Historical Anthropology of North America. *Smithsonian Miscellaneous Collections* 100. Washington.

1940a   A Further Quest for Iroquois Medicines. Pp. 93-96 in *Explorations and Field-work of the Smithsonian Institution in 1939*. Washington.

1940b   An Herbarium from the Allegany Senecas. Pp. 787-796 in The Historic Annals of Southwestern New York. William J. Doty, ed. 3 vols. New York: Lewis Historical Publishing Company.

1941   Tonawanda Longhouse Ceremonies: Ninety Years After Lewis Henry Morgan. *Bureau of American Ethnology Bulletin* 128(15):140-166. Washington.

1941a   Masked Medicine Societies of the Iroquois. Pp. 397-430 in *Annual Report of the Smithsonian Institution for 1940*. Washington.

1942   Fish Drives Among the Cornplanter Senecas. *Pennsylvania Archaeologist* 12(3):48-52.

1942a   Contacts Between Iroquois Herbalism and Colonial Medicine. Pp. 503-526 in *Annual Report of the Smithsonian Institution for 1941*. Washington.

1942b   Songs from the Iroquois Longhouse: Program Notes for an Album of American Indian Music from the Eastern Woodlands. (From Records in The Archives of American Folksongs, Library of Congress.) Washington: Smithsonian Institution.

1944   Simeon Gibson: Iroquois Informant, 1889-1943. *American Anthropologist* 46(2):231-234.

1946   Place Names and Related Activities of the Cornplanter Senecas. *Pennsylvania Archaeologist* 16(2):42-57.

1946a   An Iroquois Condolence Council for Installing Cayuga Chiefs in 1945. *Journal of the Washington Academy of Sciences* 36(4):110-127. Washington.

1947   Seneca Songs from Coldspring Longhouse [Program Notes]. *Library of Congress, Archives of American Folksong, Album* 17. Washington.

1948   The Present Status of Anthropology in Northeastern North America: A Review Article. *American Anthropologist* 50(3):494-515.

1949   Collecting Materials for a Political History of the Six Nations. *Proceedings of the American Philosophical Society* 93(3):233-238. Philadelphia.

1949a   Seth Newhouse's Traditional History and Constitution of the Iroquois Confederacy. *Proceedings of the American Philosophical Society* 93(2):141-158. Philadelphia.

1950   The Roll Call of the Iroquois Chiefs: A Study of a Mnemonic Cane from the Six Nations Reserve. *Smithsonian Miscellaneous Collections* 111(15):1-73. Washington.

1951   Locality as a Basic Factor in the Development of Iroquois Social Structure. *Bureau of American Ethnology Bulletin* 149(3):35-54. Washington.

1953   The Iroquois Eagle Dance: An Offshoot of the Calumet Dance; with An Analysis of the Iroquois Eagle Dance and Songs, by Gertrude P. Kurath. *Bureau of American Ethnology Bulletin* 156. Washington.

1955   Factionalism in American Indian Society. *Actes du IVe Congrès International des Sciences Anthropologiques et Ethnologiques* 2:330-340. Vienna.

1956   Some Questions of Classification, Typology, and Style Raised by Iroquois Masks. *Transactions of the New York Academy of Sciences*, 2d ser., Vol. 18:347-357. New York.

1956a   Toward the Gradual Civilization of the Indian Natives: The Missionary and Linguistic Work of Asher Wright (1803-1875) Among the Senecas of Western New York. *Proceedings of the American Philosophical Society* 100(6):567-581. Philadelphia.

1957   American Indian and White Relations to 1830: Needs and Opportunities for Study. Chapel Hill: University of North Carolina Press.

————, ed.
1957a   Seneca Indians by Asher Wright (1859). *Ethnohistory* 4(3):302-321.

1961   Iroquoian Culture History: A General Evaluation. Pp. 253-277 in Symposium on Cherokee and Iroquois Culture. William N. Fenton and John Gulick, eds. *Bureau of American Ethnology Bulletin* 180. Washington.

1962   This Island, the World on the Turtle's Back. *Journal of American Folklore* 75(298):283-300.

1963   The Seneca Green Corn Ceremony. *New York State Conservationist* 18(October-November):20-22.

————, ed.
1965   The Journal of James Emlen Kept on a Trip to Canandaigua, N.Y., September 15 to October 30, 1794 to Attend the Treaty Between the United States and the Six Nations. *Ethnohistory* 12(4):279-342.

1965a   The Iroquois Confederacy in the Twentieth Century: A Case Study in the Theory of Lewis H. Morgan in "Ancient Society." *Ethnology* 4(3):251-265.

1966   Field Work, Museum Studies, and Ethnohistorical Research. *Ethnohistory* 13(1-2):71-85.

1967   From Longhouse to Ranch-type House: The Second Housing Revolution of the Seneca Nation. Pp. 7-22 in Iroquois Culture, History, and Prehistory: Proceedings of the 1965 Conference on Iroquois Research. Elisabeth Tooker, ed. Albany: New York State Museum and Science Service.

1968   Introduction. Pp. 1-47 in Parker on the Iroquois, W.N. Fenton, ed. Syracuse, N.Y.: University of Syracuse Press.

1971   The Iroquois in History. Pp. 129-168 in North American Indians in Historical Perspective. Eleanor B. Leacock and Nancy O. Lurie, eds. New York: Random House.

1971a   The New York State Wampum Collection: The Case for the Integrity of Cultural Treasures. *Proceedings of the American Philosophical Society* 115(6):437-461. Philadelphia.

1972   Statement of Chief Henan Scrogg on the Six Nations' Meeting of the Handsome Lake Religion at Tonawanda in 1935 [from a Transcript of Fenton's Fieldnotes of September 6, 1935]. (Original Typescript in Fenton's Possession.)

1972a   Howard Sky, 1900-1971: Cayuga Faith-Keeper, Gentleman, and Interpreter of Iroquois Culture. *American Anthropologist* 74(3):758-761.

1972b   Iroquois Masks: A Living Tradition in the Northeast. Pp. 42-47 in American Indian Art: Form and Tradition. An Exhibition Organized by the Walker Art Center, The Indian Art Association, and the Minneapolis Institute of Arts, 22 October-31 December, 1972. [Minneapolis.]

1975   The Lore of the Longhouse: Myth, Ritual and Red Power. *Anthropological Quarterly* 48(3):131-147.

Fenton, William N., and Merle H. Deardorff
1943   The Last Passenger Pigeon Hunts of the Cornplanter Senecas. *Journal of the Washington Academy of Sciences* 33(10):289-315. Washington.

Fenton, William N., and Ernest S. Dodge
1949   An Elm Bark Canoe in the Peabody Museum of Salem. *American Neptune* 9(3):185-206.

Fenton, William N., and Gertrude P. Kurath
1951   The Feast of the Dead, or Ghost Dance, at Six Nations Reserve, Canada. *Bureau of American Ethnology Bulletin* 149(7):139-165. Washington.

Ferguson, Alice L.L.
1940   An Ossuary Near Piscataway Creek, with a Report on the Skeletal Remains, by T.D. Stewart. *American Antiquity* 6(1):4-18.

Fernow, B., ed.
1881   Documents Relating to the History and Settlements of the Towns Along the Hudson and Mohawk Rivers (with the Exception of Albany), from 1630-1684. And Also Illustrating the Relations of the Settlers with the Indians. Albany: Weed, Parsons.

_____, ed.
1883   Documents Relating to the History of the Early Colonial Settlements Principally on Long Island, with a Map of its Western Part, Made in 1666. Albany: Weed, Parsons.

Ferris, Ida M.
1910   The Sauks and Foxes in Franklin and Osage Counties, Kansas. *Collections of the Kansas State Historical Society* 11:333-395. Topeka.

Fewkes, J. Walter
1890   A Contribution to Passamaquoddy Folk-Lore. *Journal of American Folk-Lore* 3(11):257-280.

Finkelstein, J. Joe, and Alice L. Marriott
[1940]   Seneca-Cayuga Ceremonials. (Manuscript in Alice Marriott Collection, Division of Manuscripts, University of Oklahoma Library, Norman.)

Finley, James B.
1840   History of the Wyandott Mission at Upper Sandusky, Ohio, Under the Direction of the Methodist Episcopal Church. Cincinnati: J.F. Wright and L. Swormstedt.

Fisher, George S.
1931   Mr. Fisher's Supplement to R.M. Engberg's Report for Summer of 1930. Pp. 182-190 in Algonkian Sites of Westmoreland and Fayette Counties, Pennsylvania, by Robert M. Engberg. *Western Pennsylvania Historical Magazine* 14(3).

Fisher, Margaret (Welpley)
1939   Preface. Pp.vii-ix in Ethnography of the Fox Indians, by William Jones. *Bureau of American Ethnology Bulletin* 125. Washington.

Fitting, James E.
1963   The Hi-Lo Site: A Late Paleo-Indian Site in Western Michigan. *Wisconsin Archaeologist* 44(2):87-96.

1964   Ceramic Relationships of Four Late Woodland Sites in Northern Ohio. *Wisconsin Archaeologist* 45(4):160-174.

1964a   Bifurcate-stemmed Projectile Points in the Eastern United States. *American Antiquity* 30(1):92-94.

1965   Late Woodland Cultures of Southeastern Michigan. *University of Michigan Museum of Anthropology, Anthropological Papers* 24. Ann Arbor.

_____, ed.
1965a   Observations on Paleo-Indian Adaptive and Settlement Patterns. *Michigan Archaeologist* 11(3-4):103-109.

1966   Edge Area Archaeology. *Michigan Archaeologist* 12(4):143-149.

1968   The Nature and Extent of Havana Influence in the Saginaw Valley of Michigan. (Paper Presented at the Havana Conference in Springfield, Ill., 1968.)

1968a   The Spring Creek Site, 20 MU 3, Muskegon County, Michigan. Pp. 1-78 in Contributions to Michigan Archaeology. J. Fitting, ed. *University of Michigan Museum of Anthropology, Anthropological Papers* 32. Ann Arbor.

1968b   Environmental Potential and the Postglacial Readaptation in Eastern North America. *American Antiquity* 33(4):441-445.

1969   Settlement Analysis in the Great Lakes Region. *Southwestern Journal of Anthropology* 25(4):360-377.

1970   The Archaeology of Michigan: A Guide to the Prehistory of the Great Lakes Region. Garden City, N.Y.: Natural History Press.

1971   Climatic Change and Cultural Frontiers in Eastern North America. (Paper Presented at the Annual Meeting of the Society of American Archaeology. Norman, Okla., May 1971.)

_____, ed.
1972   The Schultz Site at Green Point: A Stratified Occupation Area in the Saginaw Valley of Michigan. *University of Michigan Museum of Anthropology, Memoir* 4. Ann Arbor.

1975   The Archaeology of Michigan: A Guide to the Prehistory of the Great Lakes Region. Bloomfield Hills, Mich.: Cranbrook Institute of Science.

[1976]   The Detroit and St. Clair River Basins. In The Late Prehistory of the Lake Erie Drainage Basin: A Symposium. David S. Brose, ed. *Scientific Papers of the Cleveland Museum of Natural History*. In Press.

Fitting, James E., and David S. Brose
1971   The Northern Periphery of Adena. Pp. 29-55 in Adena: The Seeking of an Identity. B.K. Swartz, ed. Muncie, Ind.: Ball State University Press.

Fitting, James E., and Charles E. Cleland
1969   Late Prehistoric Settlement Patterns in the Upper Great Lakes. *Ethnohistory* 16(4):289-302.

Fitting, James E., Jerry DeVisscher, and Edward J. Wahla
1966   The Paleo-Indian Occupation of the Holcombe Beach. *University of Michigan Museum of Anthropology, Anthropological Papers* 27. Ann Arbor.

Fitting, James E., David S. Brose, Henry T. Wright, and James Dinerstein
1969   The Goodwin-Gresham Site, 20 IS 8, Iosco County, Michigan. *Wisconsin Archaeologist* 50(3):126-183.

Fitzhugh, William W.
1972   Environmental Archaeology and Cultural Systems in Hamilton Inlet, Labrador: A Survey of the Central Labrador Coast from 3000 B.C. to the Present. *Smithsonian Contributions to Anthropology* 16. Washington.

Flanders, Richard E.
1965   A Comparison of Some Middle Woodland Materials from Illinois and Michigan. (Unpublished Ph.D. Dissertation in Anthropology, University of Michigan, Ann Arbor.)

Flannery, Kent V.
1968   Archaeological Systems Theory and Early Mesoamerica. Pp. 67-87 in Anthropological Archaeology in the Americas. Betty J. Meggers, ed. Washington: The Anthropological Society of Washington.

Flannery, Regina
1939   An Analysis of Coastal Algonquian Culture. *Catholic University of America, Anthropological Series* 7. Washington.

————
1940   The Cultural Position of the Spanish River Indians. *Primitive Man* 13(1):1-25.

————
1946   The Culture of the Northeastern Indian Hunters: A Descriptive Survey. Pp. 263-271 in Man in Northeastern North America. Frederick Johnson, ed. *Papers of the Robert S. Peabody Foundation for Archaeology* 3. Andover, Mass.

Fletcher, Alice C.
1888   Indian Education and Civilization; a Report in Answer to Senate Resolution of February 23, 1885, by Alice C. Fletcher Under the Direction of the Commissioner of Education. Washington: U.S. Government Printing Office.

————
1910   War and War Discipline. Pp. 914-915 in Vol. 2 of Handbook of American Indians North of Mexico. Frederick W. Hodge, ed. 2 vols. *Bureau of American Ethnology Bulletin* 30. Washington.

Fletcher, Alice C., and Francis La Flesche
1911   The Omaha Tribe. Pp. 27-672 in *27th Annual Report of the Bureau of American Ethnology for the Years 1905-1906*. Washington.

Flexner, James T.
1959   Mohawk Baronet: Sir William Johnson of New York. New York: Harper and Brothers.

Flint, Timothy
1833   Indian Wars of the West: Containing Biographical Sketches of Those Pioneers Who Headed the Western Settlers in Repelling the Attacks of the Savages, Together with a View of the Character, Manners, Monuments and Antiquities of the Western Indians. Cincinnati: E.H. Flint.

Fontaine, John
1972   The Journal of John Fontaine: An Irish Huguenot Son in Spain and Virginia, 1710-1719. Edward P. Alexander, ed. Williamsburg: Colonial Press of Virginia.

Force, Peter, ed.
1836-1846 Tracts and Other Papers Relating Principally to the Origin, Settlement, and Progress of the Colonies in North America from the Discovery of the Country to the Year 1776. 4 vols. Washington: P. Force. (Reprinted: Peter Smith, Gloucester, Mass., 1947, 1963.)

Ford, James A., and Gordon R. Willey
1941   An Interpretation of the Prehistory of the Eastern United States. *American Anthropologist* 43(3):325-363.

Ford, Percy, and Grace Ford, eds.
1969   Select List of British Parliamentary Papers, 1833-1899. Correspondence and Other Papers Relating to Aboriginal Tribes in British Possessions, 1834. (Anthropology Aborigines 3) Shannon, Ireland: Irish University Press.

Foreman, Carolyn (Thomas)
1946   Black Beaver. *Chronicles of Oklahoma* 24(3):269-292.

Foreman, Grant
1933   Advancing the Frontier, 1830-1860. Norman: University of Oklahoma Press. (Reprinted 1968.)

————
1936   Indians and Pioneers: The Story of the American Southwest before 1830. Rev. ed. Norman: University of Oklahoma Press.

————
1946   The Last Trek of the Indians. Chicago: University of Chicago Press.

Forsyth, Thomas
1822   Letter, May 12, 1822, Thomas Forsyth to Lewis Cass. (Forsyth Papers, Vol. 4, Draper Collection) Madison: State Historical Society of Wisconsin.

————
1827   Letter, May 24, to William Clark. (Forsyth Papers, Vol. 4, Draper Collection) Madison: State Historical Society of Wisconsin.

————
1912   An Account of the Manners and Customs of the Sauk and Fox Nations of Indian Traditions [1827]. Pp. 183-245 in Vol. 2 of The Indian Tribes of the Upper Mississippi Valley and Region of the Great Lakes. Emma H. Blair, ed. 2 vols. Cleveland: Arthur H. Clark.

————
1912a The Kickapoo Prophet. Pp. 280-281 in Vol. 2 of The Indian Tribes of the Upper Mississippi Valley and Region of the Great Lakes. Emma H. Blair, ed. 2 vols. Cleveland: Arthur H. Clark.

Fortier, John, and Donald Chaput
1969   A Historical Reexamination of Juchereau's Illinois Tannery. *Journal of the Illinois State Historical Society* 62(4):385-406. Springfield.

Foster, Michael K.
1972   The Obsequies for Howard Sky, or Cloudy-on-Both Sides. *American Anthropologist* 74(3):762-763.

————
1974   From the Earth to Beyond the Sky: An Ethnographic Approach to Four Longhouse Iroquois Speech Events. *Canada. National Museum of Man, Ethnology Division, Mercury Series Paper* 20. Ottawa.

Fowke, Gerard
1899   Col. Gerrard Fowke and the Indians. *William and Mary College Quarterly Historical Magazine*, 1st ser. Vol. 8(1):23-24. Williamsburg.

Fowler, Melvin L.
1952   The Clear Lake Site: Hopewellian Occupation. *Illinois State Museum Scientific Paper* 5(4):131-174. Springfield.

————
1955   Ware Groupings and Decorations of Woodland Ceramics in Illinois. *American Antiquity* 20(3):213-225.

————
1959   Summary Report of Modoc Rock Shelter, 1952, 1953, 1955, 1956. *Illinois State Museum, Report of Investigations* 8. Springfield.

————
1969   Middle Mississippian Agricultural Fields. *American Antiquity* 34(4):365-375.

————, ed.
1969a Explorations into Cahokia Archaeology. *Illinois Archaeological Survey Bulletin* 7. Urbana.

Fowler, Melvin L., and Robert L. Hall
1972   Archaeological Phases at Cahokia. *Illinois State Museum Research Series, Papers in Anthropology* 1. Springfield.

————
1975   Perspectives in Cahokia Archaeology. *Illinois Archaeological Survey Bulletin* 10:1-14. Urbana.

Fowler, William S.
1966   Ceremonial and Domestic Products of Aboriginal New England. *Bulletin of the Massachusetts Archaeological Society* 27(3-4). Attleboro.

1971-1972   Bone Implements: How They Were Used. *Bulletin of the Massachusetts Archaeological Society* 33(1-2):12-19. Attleboro.

1974-1975   A Pottery Analysis. Bulletin of the Massachusetts Archaeological Society 12(1-2):25-27. Attleboro.

Fox, George R. with Edward J. Wahla, and Harold W. Moll
1959   The Prehistoric Garden Beds of Wisconsin and Michigan and the Fox Indians. *Wisconsin Archaeologist* 40(1):1-19.

Fox, W. Sherwood
1941   St. Ignace, Canadian Altar of Martyrdom. *Transactions of the Royal Society of Canada,* 3d ser., sect. 2, Vol. 35:69-79. Ottawa.

Fox, William A.
1972   Neutral Lithics. (Paper Presented at the Neutral Symposium, Canadian Archaeological Association, St. John's, Newfoundland, 1972.)

Franchère, Gabriel
1969   Journal of a Voyage on the North West Coast of North America During the Years 1811, 1812, 1813, and 1814 [1820]. W. Kaye Lamb, ed. Toronto: The Champlain Society.

Franklin, Benjamin
1764   A Narrative of the Late Massacres, in Lancaster County, of a Number of Indians, Friends of this Province, by Persons Unknown. With Some Observations on the Same. Philadelphia: Anthony Armbruster. (Reprinted in The Papers of Benjamin Franklin. Leonard W. Labaree, ed. Vol. 11:42-69. New Haven and London: Yale University Press, 1959.)

Franquelin, Jean B.L.
1684   Carte de la Louisiane ou des voyages du Sr. de la Salle... (Map). (Manuscript in The Library of Congress, Washington. Reproduced in Hanna 1911, 2:92.)

Franquet, Louis
1889   Voyages et mémoires sur le Canada [1752]. Pp. 29-240 in *Annuaire de l'Institut Canadien de Québec.* Quebec: A. Coté.

Frazier, E. Franklin
1939   The Negro Family in the United States. Chicago: University of Chicago Press.

Freeman, Joan E.
1956   An Analysis of the Point Sauble and Beaumier Farm Sites. (Unpublished M.A. Thesis in Anthropology, University of Wisconsin, Madison.)

Freilich, Morris
1958   Cultural Persistence Among the Modern Iroquois. *Anthropos* 53(3-4):473-483.

Frémiot, N.M.J.
1855   Lettre du R.P. Frémiot, de la Compagnie de Jésus, aux Scolastiques de Laval. Ste. Croix, Grand Manitoulin (lac Huron), 7 août 1853. *Annales de la Propagation de la Foi* 27(163):463-469. Lyon.

French, Goldwin S.
1962   Parsons and Politics: The Rôle of Wesleyan Methodists in Upper Canada and the Maritimes from 1780-1855. Toronto: Ryerson Press.

Frey, S.L.
1898   The Mohawks: An Enquiry into Their Origin, Migrations, and Influence Upon the White Settlers. *Transactions of the Oneida Historical Society* 8:5-41. Utica, N.Y.

Friederici, Georg
1906   Skalpieren und ähnliche Kriegsgebräuche in Amerika. Braunschweig, Germany: F. Vieweg. (Partial translation: Pp. 423-438 in *Annual Report of the Smithsonian Institution for* 1907. Washington.)

Friedl, Ernestine
1956   Persistence in Chippewa Culture and Personality. *American Anthropologist* 58(5):814-825.

Friends, Society of
1840   The Case of the Seneca Indians in the State of New York, Illustrated by Facts. Philadelphia: Merrihew and Thompson.

1857   Documents and Official Reports Illustrating the Causes Which Led to the Revolution in the Government of the Seneca Indians in the Year 1848 and to the Recognition of Their Representative Republican Constitution by the Authorities of the U.S. and the State of New York. Baltimore: W. Woody.

Friends, Society of. London Yearly Meeting
1844   Some Account of the Conduct of the Religious Society of Friends Towards the Indian Tribes in the Settlement of the Colonies of East and West Jersey and Pennsylvania. London: Edward Marsh.

Fries, Adelaide L., ed.
1922   Records of the Moravians in North Carolina. 6 vols. Raleigh: Edwards and Broughton.

Frisch, Jack A.
1970   Revitalization, Nativism and Tribalism Among the St. Regis Mohawks. (Unpublished Ph.D. Dissertation in Anthropology, Indiana University, Bloomington.)

1970a   Tribalism Among the St. Regis Mohawks: A Search for Self-identity. *Anthropologica* n.s. 12(2):207-219. Ottawa.

1976   Some Ethnological and Ethnohistoric Notes on the Iroquois in Alberta. *Man in the Northeast* 12:51-64.

Funk, Robert E.
1965   The Archaic of the Hudson Valley: New Evidence and New Interpretations. *Pennsylvania Archaeologist* 35(3-4):139-160.

1967   Garoga: A Late Prehistoric Iroquois Village in the Mohawk Valley. Pp. 81-84 in Iroquois Culture, History and Prehistory: Proceedings of the 1965 Conference on Iroquois Research. Elisabeth Tooker, ed. Albany: New York State Museum and Science Service.

1967a   A Paleo-Indian Site in the Hudson Valley. *Bulletin of the Eastern States Archaeological Federation* 26:9-10. Lancaster, Pa.

1972   Early Man in the Northeast and the Late-Glacial Environment. *Man in the Northeast* 4:7-39.

1976   Recent Contributions to Hudson Valley Prehistory. *New York State Museum and Science Service Memoir* 22. Albany.

Funk, Robert E., and Howard Hoagland
1972   An Archaic Camp Site in the Upper Susquehanna Drainage. *New York State Archaeological Association Bulletin* 56(November):11-22. Rochester.

Funk, Robert E., and R. Arthur Johnson
1964   A Probable Paleo-Indian Component in Greene County, New York. *Pennsylvania Archaeologist* 34(1):43-46.

Funk, Robert E., and Bruce E. Rippeteau
[1976]   Adaptation, Continuity, and Change in Upper Susquehanna Prehistory. *Occasional Publications in Northeastern Anthropology* 3. In Press.

Funk, Robert E., and Frank F. Schambach
1964   Probable Plano Points in New York State. *Pennsylvania Archaeologist* 34(2):90-93.

Funk, Robert E., Donald W. Fisher, and Edgar M. Reilly, Jr.
1970   Caribou and Paleo-Indian in New York State: A Presumed Association. *American Journal of Science* 268(2):181-186.

Funk, Robert E., George R. Walters, and William F. Ehlers, Jr.
1969   A Radiocarbon Date for Early Man from the Dutchess Quarry Cave. *New York State Archaeological Association Bulletin* 46(July):19-21. Rochester.

Funk, Robert E., Thomas P. Weinman, and Paul L. Weinman
1969   The Kings Road Site: A Recently Discovered Paleo-Indian Manifestation in Greene County, New York. *New York State Archaeological Association Bulletin* 45(March):1-23. Rochester.

Funk, Robert E., George R. Walters, William F. Ehlers, Jr., John E. Guilday, and G. Gordon Connally
1969   The Archeology of Dutchess Quarry Cave, Orange County, New York. *Pennsylvania Archaeologist* 39(1-4):7-22.

Gailland, Maurice
1914-1917   Three Drafts of a Potawatomi Grammar. (From Original Manuscript in St. Mary's College Library, St. Mary's, Kansas; Copy, Manuscript No. 2530 in National Anthropological Archives, Smithsonian Institution, Washington.)

Galinée, René Bréhant de
1903   Exploration of the Great Lakes, 1669-1670, Dollier de Casson and Bréhant de Galinée. Galinée's Narrative and Map. James H. Coyne, ed. Pt. 1. *Papers and Records of the Ontario Historical Society* 4. Toronto.

Galland, Isaac
1869   The Indian Tribes of the West: Their Language, Religion and Traditions. *Annals of Iowa* 7(4):347-366.

Gallatin, Albert
1836   A Synopsis of the Indian Tribes Within the United States East of the Rocky Mountains, and the British and Russian Possessions in North America. Pp. 1-422 in *Archaeologia Americana: Transactions and Collections of the American Antiquarian Society* 2. Cambridge, Mass.

1848   Hale's Indians of North-West America, and Vocabularies of North America. *Transactions of the American Ethnological Society* 2:1-130. New York.

Galloway, William A.
1934   Old Chillicothe; Shawnee and Pioneer History: Conflicts and Romances in the Northwest Territory. Xenia, Ohio: The Buckeye Press.

Ganong, William F.
1899   A Monograph of Historic Sites in the Province of New Brunswick. *Proceedings and Transactions of the Royal Society of Canada*, 2d ser., Vol. 5:213-351. Ottawa.

1964   Crucial Maps in the Early Cartography and Place Nomenclature of the Atlantic Coast of Canada. Toronto: University of Toronto Press.

Gardiner, John L.
1798   A Vocabulary of the Indian Language Spoken by the Montauk Tribe. (Copy, Manuscript No. 22 in National Anthropological Archives, Smithsonian Institution, Washington.)

Gardiner, Lion
1859   Leift Lion Gardener His Relation of the Pequot Warres. Pp. 3-32 in Appendix to the History of the Wars of New-England with the Eastern Indians, by Samuel Penhallow. Cincinnati: Printed for William Dodge by J. Harpel.

Gardner, William M.
1969   The Havana Cultural Tradition Occupation in the Upper Kaskaskia River Valley, Illinois. (Unpublished Ph.D. Dissertation in Anthropology, University of Illinois, Urbana-Champaign.)

1973   Ecological or Historical Determinants in Cultural Patterning Among the Prehistoric Occupants of the Upper Kaskaskia River Valley, Illinois. Pp. 189-197 in Variation in Anthropology: Essays in Honor of John C. McGregor.

Donald W. Lathrap and Jody Douglas, eds. Urbana: Illinois Archaeological Survey.

————, ed.
1974   The Flint Run Paleo-Indian Complex: A Preliminary Report, 1971-1973 Seasons. *Catholic University of America, Department of Anthropology, Archaeology Laboratory Occasional Publication* 1. Washington.

Garfield, James R.
1908   Letter from the Secretary of the Interior, Submitting, in Response to the Direction of Law, a Report of an Investigation of the Claims of the Pottawatomie Indians of Wisconsin. U.S. Congress. House of Representatives. 60th Cong., 1st. sess., House Doc. No. 830. (Serial No. 5374) Washington: U.S. Government Printing Office.

Garrad, Charles
1969   Iron Trade Knives on Historic Petun Sites. *Ontario Archaeology* 13:3-15.

1969a   Bear Jaw Tools from Petun Sites. *Ontario Archaeology* 13:54-60.

1970   A Petun Burial in Nottawasaga Township, Ontario. *Ontario Archaeology* 15:3-15.

1970a   Did Champlain Visit the Bruce Peninsula? An Examination of an Ontario Myth. *Ontario History* 62(4):235-239.

Garraghan, Gilbert J.
1928   New Light on Old Cahokia. *Illinois Historical Catholic Review* 11(2).

Garrett, Thomas
1901   Letter from Thomas Garrett Relating to the Meherrin Indians, October 17, 1706. *North Carolina Historical and Genealogical Register* 2(1):110-111.

Garrow, Patrick H.
1968   An Ethnohistorical Study of Early English Indian Policy. *Working Papers in Sociology and Anthropology* 2(1):35-45.

Gates, Paul W.
1954   Fifty Million Acres: Conflicts Over Kansas Land Policy, 1854-1890. Ithaca, N.Y.: Cornell University Press.

Gatschet, Albert S.
[1877] [Shawnee Grammatical Elements.] (Manuscript No. 2987 in National Anthropological Archives, Smithsonian Institution, Washington.)

————   [Vocabularies, Texts, Notes: Shawnee, Potawatomi, Chippewa, Mainly 1878-1879.] (Manuscript No. 68 in National Anthropological Archives, Smithsonian Institution, Washington.)
[1878-1893]

1881   ["Wandot" (Wyandot) Vocabulary. Wyandot Reserve, Indian Territory, January 8, February 7, March 15, 1881.] (Manuscript No. 1549 in National Anthropological Archives, Smithsonian Institution, Washington.)

————   Linguistic Notes. *American Antiquarian* 4(1):73-77.
1881-1882

[1882-1889]   [Notes and Text on the Fox or Utagami Language; also Earliest Examples of Kickapoo Syllabics.] (Manuscript No. 63 in National Anthropological Archives, Smithsonian Institution, Washington.)

1883-1885   [Tuscarora Notebook Containing Vocabulary, Texts and Miscellaneous Notes from Fieldwork Among the Tuscarora, New York Reservation.] (Manuscript No. 372-b in the J.N.B. Hewitt Papers, National Anthropological Archives, Smithsonian Institution, Washington.)

1885-1890   The Beothuk Indians. *Proceedings of the American Philosophical Society* 22(120):408-424, 23(123):411-432, 28(132):1-16. Philadelphia.

————   Linguistic and Ethnographic Notes. *American Antiquarian* (November):389-393.
1889

1890-1893 [Pamunkey Notebook.] (Manuscript No. 2197 in National Anthropological Archives, Smithsonian Institution, Washington.)

1973 Narragansett Vocabulary Collected in 1879. *International Journal of American Linguistics* 39(1):14.

Gaulein, B.
1840 Lettre de Mgr. Gaulein, coadjuteur de Kingston, à son Evèque. Toronto, 25 septembre 1838. *Annales de la Propagation de la Foi* 12(72):425-432. Lyon.

Gearing, Frederick O.
1970 The Face of the Fox. Chicago: Aldine Press.

Gearing, Frederick O., Robert McC. Netting, and Lisa R. Peattie, eds.
1960 Documentary History of the Fox Project, 1948-1959: A Program in Action Anthropology Directed by Sol Tax. Chicago: University of Chicago, Department of Anthropology.

Geary, James A.
1941 Proto-Algonquian *çk:* Further Examples. *Language* 17(4):304-310.

1953 Strachey's Vocabulary of Indian Words Used in Virginia, 1612. Pp. 208-214 in The Historie of Travell into Virginia Britania [1612]. Louis B. Wright and Virginia Freund, eds. London: Cambridge University Press for the Hakluyt Society.

1955 List of Indian Words Found in the Documents, with Notes on Their Meaning. Pp. 884-900 in Vol. 2 of The Roanoke Voyages, 1584-1590; Documents to Illustrate the English Voyages to North America Under the Patent Granted to Walter Raleigh in 1584. David B. Quinn, ed. 2 vols. London: Cambridge University Press for the Hakluyt Society.

1955a An Introductory Study of the Position of the Indian Language of Virginia and North Carolina in the Algonquian Family. Pp. 873-900 in Vol. 2 of The Roanoke Voyages, 1584-1590; Documents to Illustrate the English Voyages to North America Under the Patent Granted to Walter Raleigh in 1584. David B. Quinn, ed. 2 vols. London: Cambridge University Press for the Hakluyt Society.

Gendron, François
1868 Quelques particularitéz du pays des Hurons en la Nouvelle France, remarquées par le Sieur Gendron, Docteur en Médecine qui a demeuré dans ce pays-là fort longtemps [1660]. I.B. de Rocoles, ed. Albany: J. Munsell.

General Council of the Indian Territory
1873 Journal of the Fourth Annual Session of the General Council of the Indian Territory, Composed of Delegates Duly Elected from the Indian Tribes Legally Resident Therein... Lawrence, Kans.: Journal Steam Book and Job Printing House. (Copy in Indian Archives Division, Oklahoma Historical Society, Oklahoma City.)

1875 Journal of the Sixth Annual Session of the General Council of the Indian Territory, Composed of Delegates Duly Elected from the Indian Tribes Legally Resident Therein... Lawrence, Kans.: Republican Journal Steam Printing Establishment. (Copy in Indian Archives Division, Oklahoma Historical Society, Oklahoma City.)

Gerard, William R.
1907 Virginia's Indian Contributions to English. *American Anthropologist* n.s. 9(1):87-112.

Gérin, Léon
1900 The Hurons of Lorette. Pp. 549-568 in *Report of the British Association for the Advancement of Science for 1900, Committee on the Ethnological Survey of Canada.* London.

Gesner, Abraham
1847 New Brunswick with Notes for Emigrants Comprehending the Early History, an Account of the Indians, Settlement... London: Simmonds and Ward.

1849 The Industrial Resources of Nova Scotia. Halifax, N.S.: Mackinlay.

Gibbon, Guy E.
1969 The Walker-Hooper and Bornick Sites: Two Grand River Phase Oneota Sites in Central Wisconsin. (Unpublished Ph.D. Dissertation in Anthropology, University of Wisconsin, Madison.)

1972 Cultural Dynamics and the Development of the Oneota Life-way in Wisconsin. *American Antiquity* 37(2):166-185.

Gibbs, George
1867 Instructions for Research Relative to the Ethnology and Philology of America. *Smithsonian Miscellaneous Collections* 7(11). Washington.

Gibson, Arrell M.
1963 The Kickapoos: Lords of the Middle Borders. Norman: University of Oklahoma Press.

Gilbert, William H., Jr.
1945 The Wesorts of Southern Maryland: An Outcasted Group. *Journal of the Washington Academy of Sciences* 35(8):237-246. Washington.

1946 Memorandum Concerning the Characteristics of the Larger Mixed-blood Racial Islands of the Eastern United States. *Social Forces* 24(4):438-447.

1946a Mixed Bloods of the Upper Monongahela Valley, West Virginia. *Journal of the Washington Academy of Sciences* 36(1):1-13. Washington.

1948 Surviving Indian Groups of the Eastern United States. Pp. 407-438 in *Annual Report of the Smithsonian Institution for 1948.* Washington.

Gilkison, I.V.
1881 [Letter to "Indian Agent, Tiff City," Mo., Dated Jan. 27, 1881; With Annotations Evidently by Agent D.B. Dyer.] (Manuscript in Quapaw: Indians, Cayuga, Indian Archives Division, Oklahoma Historical Society, Oklahoma City.)

1882 [Letter to D.B. Dyer, Dated Oct. 10, 1882.] (Manuscript in Quapaw: Indians, Cayuga, Indian Archives Division, Oklahoma Historical Society, Oklahoma City.)

Gill, Charles I.
1886 Notes sur de vieux manuscrits Abénakis. Montreal: Eusèbe Senéca et Fils.

Gipson, Lawrence H., ed.
1938 The Moravian Indian Mission on White River: Diaries and Letters, May 5, 1799 to November 12, 1806. *Indiana Historical Collections* 23. Indianapolis.

Giraud, Marcel
1945 Le Métis canadien: Son rôle dans l'histoire des provinces de l'Ouest. *Université de Paris. Institut d'Ethnologie, Travaux et Mémoires* 44. Paris.

Gist, Christopher
1893 Christopher Gist's Journals with Historical, Geographical and Ethnological Notes and Biographies of His Contemporaries [1750-1753]. William M. Darlington, ed. Pittsburgh: J.R. Weldin.

Glover, Thomas
1676 An Account of Virginia, Its Situation, Temperature, Production, Inhabitants and Their Manner of Planting and Ordering of Tobacco, etc. *Philosophical Transactions of the Royal Society of London* 11:623-636. London.

Goddard, Ives
1965 The Eastern Algonquian Intrusive Nasal. *International Journal of American Linguistics* 31(3):206-220.

[1965-1970] [Ethnographic and Linguistic Notes from Approximately 15 Months' Fieldwork Among the Delawares of Ontario and Oklahoma.] (Manuscript in Goddard's Possession.)

1967   The Algonquian Independent Indicative. Pp. 66-106 in Contributions to Anthropology: Linguistics, I (Algonquian). *Anthropological Series 78, National Museum of Canada Bulletin* 214. Ottawa.

1967a   Notes on the Genetic Classification of the Algonquian Languages. Pp. 7-12 in Contributions to Anthropology: Linguistics, I (Algonquian). *Anthropological Series 78, National Museum of Canada Bulletin* 214. Ottawa.

1967b   [Fieldnotes from One Day's Fieldwork on Wyandot at Miami, Okla.] (Manuscript in Goddard's Possession.)

1968   Notes on Delaware Social Organization. (Unpublished Typescript Paper Read at the First Algonquian Conference, St. Pierre de Wakefield, Quebec, 1968.)

1969   Delaware Verbal Morphology: A Descriptive and Comparative Study. (Unpublished Ph.D. Dissertation in Linguistics, Harvard University, Cambridge, Mass.)

1971   More on the Nasalization of PA *a· in Eastern Algonquian. *International Journal of American Linguistics* 37(3):139-145.

1971a   The Ethnohistorical Implications of Early Delaware Linguistic Materials. *Man in the Northeast* 1:14-26.

1972   Historical and Philological Evidence Regarding the Identification of the Mascouten. *Ethnohistory* 19(2):123-134.

1972a   [Note on Alexander 1971.] *International Journal of American Linguistics* 38(3):220.

1973   Proto-Algonquian *nl and *nθ. *International Journal of American Linguistics* 39(1):1-6.

1973a   Delaware Kinship Terminology (with Comparative Notes). *Studies in Linguistics* 23:39-56.

1973b   A Report on Ethnographic and Philosophical Studies of Michelson's Fox Texts. (Paper Read at Algonquian Conference, Green Bay, Wis., April 6, 1973.)

1974   A Further Note on Delaware Clan Names. *Man in the Northeast* 7(Spring):106-109.

1975   The Delaware Language Past and Present. Pp. 103-110 in A Delaware Indian Symposium. Herbert C. Kraft, ed. *Pennsylvania Historical and Museum Commission, Anthropological Series* 4. Harrisburg.

1975a   Fox Social Organization, 1650-1850. Pp. 128-140 in Papers of the 6th Algonquian Conference, 1974. William Cowan, ed. *Canada. National Museum of Man. Ethnology Division, Mercury Series Paper* 23. Ottawa.

Goen, C.C.
1962   Revivalism and Separatism in New England, 1740-1800; Strict Congregationalists and Separate Baptists in the Great Awakening. New Haven, Conn.: Yale University Press.

Goggin, John M.
1949   Cultural Traditions in Florida Prehistory. Pp. 13-44 in The Florida Indian and His Neighbors: Papers Delivered at an Anthropological Conference Held at Rollins College, April 9 and 10, 1949. John W. Griffin, ed. Winter Park, Fla.: Rollins College, Inter-American Center.

1951   The Mexican Kickapoo Indians. *Southwestern Journal of Anthropology* 7(3):314-327.

Goldenweiser, Alexander A.
1912   On Iroquois Work, 1911. Pp. 386-387 in *Summary Report of the Geological Survey Branch of the Canadian Department of Mines for the Calendar Year 1911.* Ottawa.

1912a   The Death of Chief John A. Gibson. *American Anthropologist* 14(4):692-694.

[1912-1914]   [The Separation of the Seneca L.H.] (Fieldnotes, Notebook No. 18 in the Archives of the Ethnology Division, National Museum of Man, Ottawa.)

1912-1914a   [Fieldnotes from the Six Nations Reserve, Ontario.] (Manuscripts in the Archives of the Ethnology Division, National Museum of Man, Ottawa.)

1914   On Iroquois Work, 1912. Pp. 464-475 in *Summary Report of the Geological Survey Branch of the Canadian Department of Mines for the Calendar Year 1912.* Ottawa.

1914a   On Iroquois Work, 1913-1914. Pp. 365-372 in *Summary Report of the Geological Survey Branch of the Canadian Department of Mines for the Calendar Year 1913.* Ottawa.

1915   Functions of Women in Iroquois Society. *American Anthropologist* 17(2):376-377.

1916   [Review of] The Constitution of the Five Nations, by Arthur C. Parker. *American Anthropologist* 18(3):431-436.

Goldschmidt, Walter R., and Robert D. Edgerton
1961   A Picture Technique for the Study of Values. *American Anthropologist* 63(1):24-47.

Gooch, Sir William
1896   Queries from the Lords of Trade to Sir William Gooch Governour of Virginia and His Answers [1735]. *Virginia Magazine of History and Biography* 3:113-123.

Good, Mary E.
1972   Guebert Site: An 18th Century Historic Kaskaskia Indian Village in Randolph County, Illinois. *Memoirs of the Central States Archaeological Societies* 2. Wood River, Ill.

Gookin, Daniel
1836   An Historical Account of the Doings and Sufferings of the Christian Indians in New England in the Years 1675, 1676, 1677. *Archaeologia Americana: Transactions and Collections of the American Antiquarian Society* 2:423-534. Cambridge, Mass.

1854   Indian Children Put to Service [1676]. *New England Historical and Genealogical Register* 8(3):270-273. Boston.

1970   Historical Collections of the Indians in New England [1792]. Jeffrey H. Fiske, ed. [no place]: Towtaid.

Gookin, Warner F.
1958   Massasoit's Domain: Is "Wampanoag" the Correct Designation? *Bulletin of the Massachusetts Archaeological Society* 20(1):12-14. Attleboro.

Gordon, John M.
1959   Michigan Journal [1836]. Douglas H. Gordon and George S. May, eds. *Michigan History* 43(1):10-42, (2):129-149, (3):257-293, (4):433-478.

Gorges, Ferdinando
1890   Sir Ferdinando Gorges and His Province of Maine [1659]. James P. Baxter, ed. Boston: The Prince Society. (Reprinted: Burt Franklin, New York, 1967.)

Gorton, Samuel
1835   Simplicity's Defence Against Seven-headed Policy. *Collections of the Rhode Island Historical Society* 2. Providence.

Gossen, Gary
1964   [Fieldnotes, Kansas Potawatomi Study.] (Manuscript in Archives, Wisconsin State Historical Society, Madison.)

Gowing, Clara
1912   Life Among the Delaware Indians, 1859-1864. *Collections of the Kansas State Historical Society* 12:183-193. Topeka.

Graham, Andrew
1969   Andrew Graham's Observations on Hudson's Bay, 1767-1791. Glyndwr Williams, ed. *Publications of the Hudson's Bay Record Society* 27. London.

Graham, Robert J., and Charles F. Wray
1966   The Boughton Hill Site, Victor, New York. (Mimeographed Report Distributed at the 1966 Annual Meeting

of the New York State Archaeological Association, Rochester, N.Y.)

Graham, William J.
1935   The Indians of Port Tobacco River, Maryland, and Their Burial Places. Washington: Privately Printed.

Grassman, Thomas
1952   The Question of the Locations of Mohawk Indian Village Sites Existing During the Historic Period. *Pennsylvania Archaeologist* 22(3-4):98-111.

———
1952a   The Mohawk-Caughnawaga Excavation. *Pennsylvania Archaeologist* 22(1):33-36.

———, ed.
1969   The Mohawk Indians and Their Valley, Being a Chronological Documentary Record to the End of 1693. Schenectady, N.Y.: Eric Hugo Photography and Printing Company.

Gravier, James
[1700] A Dictionary of the Illinois Language. (Manuscript No. 4871 in National Anthropological Archives, Smithsonian Institution, Washington.)

Gray, Asa, and Merritt L. Fernald
1950   Gray's Manual of Botany: A Handbook of the Flowering Plants and Ferns of the Central and Northeastern United States and Adjacent Canada. 8th ed. New York, Cincinnati, Boston, Atlanta, Dallas, San Francisco: American Book Company.

Gray, Elma E.
1956   Wilderness Christians: The Moravian Mission to the Delaware Indians. Toronto: Macmillan; Ithaca, N.Y.: Cornell University Press.

Graymont, Barbara
1967   Problems of Tuscarora Language Survival. Pp. 27-29 in Iroquois Culture, History, and Prehistory: Proceedings of the 1965 Conference on Iroquois Research. Elisabeth Tooker, ed. Albany: New York State Museum and Science Service.

———
1969   The Tuscarora New Year Festival. *New York History* 50(2):143-163.

———
1972   The Iroquois in the American Revolution. Syracuse, N.Y.: Syracuse University Press.

Greene, Alam
[1971] Forbidden Voice: Reflections of a Mohawk Indian. New York: Hamlyn.

Greenman, Emerson F.
1927   Michigan Mounds, with Special Reference to Two in Missaukee County. *Papers of the Michigan Academy of Science, Arts and Letters* 7:1-9. Ann Arbor.

———
1935   Excavation of the Reeve Village Site, Lake County, Ohio. *Ohio State Archaeological and Historical Quarterly* 44(1):2-64. Columbus.

———
1937   Two Prehistoric Villages Near Cleveland, Ohio. *Ohio State Archaeological and Historical Quarterly* 46(4):305-366. Columbus.

———
1937a   The Younge Site: An Archaeological Record from Michigan. *University of Michigan Museum of Anthropology, Occasional Contributions* 6. Ann Arbor.

———
1939   The Wolf and Furton Sites, Macomb County, Michigan. *University of Michigan Museum of Anthropology, Occasional Contributions* 8. Ann Arbor.

———
1948   The Killarney Sequence and its Old World Connections. *Papers of the Michigan Academy of Science, Arts and Letters* 32:313-332. Ann Arbor.

———
1958   An Early Historic Cemetery at St. Ignace. *Michigan Archaeologist* 4(2):28-35.

———
1961   The Indians of Michigan. *Michigan History* 45:1-33.

Greenman, Emerson F., and George M. Stanley
1940   A Geologically Dated Camp Site, Georgian Bay, Ontario. *American Antiquity* 5(3):194-199.

———
1943   The Archaeology and Geology of Two Early Sites Near Killarney, Ontario. *Papers of the Michigan Academy of Science, Arts and Letters* 28:505-531. Ann Arbor.

Gregg, Michael
1975   A Population Estimate for Cahokia. *Illinois Archaeological Survey Bulletin* 10:126-136. Urbana.

Grenier, Fernand, ed.
1952   Papiers Contrecoeur et autres documents concernant le conflit anglo-français sur l'Ohio de 1745 à 1756. Quebec: Les Presses Universitaires Laval.

Griffin, James B.
1931   Griffin Excavation: Spanish Hill. (Manuscript in Division of Archeology, Pennsylvania Historical and Museum Commission, Harrisburg.)

———
1937   The Archaeological Remains of the Chiwere Sioux. *American Antiquity* 2(3):180-181.

———
1943   The Fort Ancient Aspect, its Cultural and Chronological Position in Mississippi Valley Archaeology. Ann Arbor: University of Michigan Press. (Reprinted: *University of Michigan Museum of Anthropology, Anthropological Papers* 28, Ann Arbor, 1966.)

———
1944   The Iroquois in American Prehistory. *Papers of the Michigan Academy of Science, Arts and Letters* 29:357-374. Ann Arbor.

———
1946   Cultural Change and Continuity in Eastern United States Archaeology. Pp. 37-95 in Man in Northeastern North America. Frederick Johnson, ed. *Papers of the Robert S. Peabody Foundation for Archaeology* 3. Andover, Mass.

———
1949   Meso-America and the Southeast: A Commentary. Pp. 77-99 in The Florida Indian and His Neighbors: Papers Delivered at an Anthropological Conference Held at Rollins College, April 9 and 10, 1949. John W. Griffin, ed. Winter Park, Fla.: Rollins College, Inter-American Center.

———
1952   Culture Periods in Eastern United States Archeology. Pp. 352-364 in Archeology of Eastern United States. James B. Griffin, ed. Chicago: University of Chicago Press.

———
1952a   Some Early and Middle Woodland Pottery Types in Illinois. *Illinois State Museum Scientific Paper* 5(3):93-129, 266-270. Springfield.

———, ed.
1952b   Archeology of Eastern United States. Chicago: University of Chicago Press.

———
1958   The Chronological Position of the Hopewellian Culture in the Eastern United States. *University of Michigan Museum of Anthropology, Anthropological Papers* 12. Ann Arbor.

———
1960   A Hypothesis for the Prehistory of the Winnebago. Pp. 809-865 in Culture in History: Essays in Honor of Paul Radin. Stanley Diamond, ed. New York: Columbia University Press.

———
1960a   Climatic Change: A Contributory Cause of Growth and Decline of Northern Hopewell Culture. *Wisconsin Archaeologist* 41(2):21-33.

———
1960b   Some Prehistoric Connections Between Siberia and America. *Science* 131(3403):801-812.

———
1961   Some Correlations of Climatic and Cultural Change in Eastern North American Prehistory. *Annals of the New York Academy of Sciences* 95:710-717. New York.

1961a   Lake Superior Copper and the Indians: Miscellaneous Studies of Great Lakes Prehistory. *University of Michigan Museum of Anthropology, Anthropological Papers* 17. Ann Arbor.

1961b   [Review of] the Eastern Dispersal of Adena, by William A. Ritchie and Don W. Dragoo. *American Antiquity* 26(4):572-573.

1964   The Northeast Woodlands Area. Pp. 223-258 in Prehistoric Man in the New World. Jesse D. Jennings and Edward Norbeck, eds. Chicago: University of Chicago Press.

1966   Mesoamerica and the Eastern United States in Prehistoric Times. Pp. 111-131 in *Archaeological Frontiers and External Connections.* Vol. 4. Handbook of Middle American Indians. Gordon F. Ekholm and Gordon R. Willey, eds. Austin: University of Texas Press.

1967   Eastern North American Archaeology: A Summary. Prehistoric Cultures Changed from Small Hunting Bands to Well-organized Towns and Tribes. *Science* 156(3772):175-191.

Griffin, James, B., Richard E. Flanders, and Paul F. Titterington
1970   The Burial Complexes of the Knight and Norton Mounds in Illinois and Michigan. *University of Michigan Museum of Anthropology, Memoir* 2. Ann Arbor.

Griffin, James B., A.A. Gordus, and G.A. Wright
1969   Identification of the Sources of Hopewellian Obsidian in the Middle West. *American Antiquity* 34(1):1-14.

Griffin, James B., Frank C. Baker, Richard G. Morgan, Georg K. Neumann, and Jay L.B. Taylor, eds.
1941   Contributions to the Archaeology of the Illinois River Valley. *Transactions of the American Philosophical Society* n.s. 32. Pt. 1. Philadelphia.

Griffin, John W.
1946   The Upper Mississippi Occupation at the Fisher Site, Will County, Illinois. (Unpublished M.A. Thesis in Anthropology, University of Chicago, Chicago.)

Griffin, John W., and Donald E. Wray
1946   Bison in Illinois Archaeology. *Transactions of the Illinois State Academy of Science* 38:21-26. Springfield.

Gros-Louis, Max Oné-Onti, with Marcel Bellier
1971   Le "Premier" des Hurons. Montreal: Editions du Jour.

Guernsey, E.Y.
1939   Relationships Among Various Clark County Sites. *Proceedings of the Indiana Academy of Science* 48:27-32. Indianapolis.

Guilday, John E.
1968   Archaeological Evidence of Caribou from New York and Massachusetts. *Journal of Mammalogy* 49(2):344-345.

1969   A Possible Caribou-Paleo-Indian Association from Dutchess Quarry Cave, Orange County, New York. *New York State Archaeological Association Bulletin* 45(March):24-29. Rochester.

Guilday, John E., and Paul W. Parmalee
1965   Animal Remains from the Sheep Rock Shelter, (36 Hu 1) Huntington County, Pennsylvania. *Pennsylvania Archaeologist* 35(1):34-39.

Guilday, John E., and Donald P. Tanner
1965   Vertebrate Remains from the Kipp Island Site. Pp. 241-242 in The Archaeology of New York State, by William A. Ritchie. Garden City, N.Y.: Natural History Press.

Guthe, Carl E.
1952   Twenty-five Years of Archeology in the Eastern United States. Pp. 1-12 in Archeology of Eastern United States. James B. Griffin, ed. Chicago: University of Chicago Press.

Gyles, John
1851   Memoirs of Odd Adventures, Strange Deliverances, etc., in the Captivity of John Gyles, Esq., Written by Himself [1736]. Pp. 73-109 in Indian Captivities, by Samuel Drake. Auburn, N.Y.: Derby and Miller.

Haag, William G.
1958   The Archeology of Coastal North Carolina. *Louisiana State University Studies, Coastal Studies Series* 2. Baton Rouge.

1961   Twenty-five Years of Eastern Archaeology. *American Antiquity* 27(1):16-23.

Haas, Mary R.
1969   Grammar or Lexicon? The American Indian Side of the Question from Duponceau to Powell. *International Journal of American Linguistics* 35(3):239-255.

1970   [Review of] New Views of the Origin of the Tribes and Nations of North America, by Benjamin S. Barton. *International Journal of American Linguistics* 36(1):68-70.

Habig, Marion A.
1934   The Franciscan Père Marquette: A Critical Biography of Father Zénobe Membré O.F.M., La Salle's Chaplain and Missionary Companion (1645-1689). (Franciscan Studies 13) New York: Joseph F. Wagner.

Hagan, William T.
1958   The Sac and Fox Indians. Norman: University of Oklahoma Press.

Hakluyt, Richard
1589   The Principall Navigations, Voiages and Discoveries of the English Nation. London: George Bishop and Ralph Newberrie.

1965   The Principall Navigations, Voiages and Discoveries of the English Nation [1589]. David B. Quinn and Raleigh A. Skelton, eds. 2 vols. Cambridge, England: University Press.

Hale, Horatio E.
1882   A Lawgiver of the Stone Age. *Proceedings of the American Association for the Advancement of Science* 30:324-341. Salem, Mass. (Also Separately Printed Under the Title "Hiawatha and the Iroquois Confederation," Salem, 1881.)

1883   Indian Migrations, as Evidenced by Language. *American Antiquarian* 5(1):18-28, (2):108-124.

1883a   The Iroquois Book of Rites. (Brinton's Library of Aboriginal American Literature 2) Philadelphia: D.G. Brinton. (Reprinted: University of Toronto Press, Toronto, 1965.)

1883b   The Tutelo Tribe and Language. *Proceedings of the American Philosophical Society* 21(114):1-49. Philadelphia.

1885   Chief George H.M. Johnson, Onwanonsyshon: His Life and Work Among the Six Nations. *Magazine of American History* 8:131-142.

1888   Huron Folk-Lore. *Journal of American Folk-Lore* 1(3):177-183.

1894   The Fall of Hochelaga: A Study of Popular Tradition. *Journal of American Folk-Lore* 7(24):1-14.

1895   An Iroquois Condoling Council. *Proceedings and Transactions of the Royal Society of Canada,* 2d. ser., Vol. 1(2):45-65. Ottawa.

Halkett, John
1825   Historical Notes Respecting the Indians of North America. With Remarks on the Attempts Made to Convert and Civilize Them. London: Printed for A. Constable.

Hall, Clayton C., ed.
1910   Narratives of Early Maryland, 1633-1684. New York: Charles Scribner's Sons.

Hall, Eugene R., and Keith R. Kelson
1959   The Mammals of North America. 2 vols. New York:
           Ronald Press.

Hall, Robert L.
1962   The Archeology of Carcajou Point, with an Interpretation
           of the Development of Oneota Culture in Wisconsin. 2
           vols. Madison: University of Wisconsin Press.

———
1967   Those Late Corn Dates: Isotopic Fractionation as a
           Source of Error in Carbon-14 Dates. *Michigan Archaeolo-
           gist* 1?(4):171-180.

Hall, Wilmer L., ed.
1952   Journals of the Council of the State of Virginia. Vol. 3.
           Richmond: Virginia State Library.

Hallowell, A. Irving
[1918-1932] [Ethnographic and Linguistic Notes from Numerous Vis-
           its to the St. Francis Abenaki.] (Manuscripts in Gordon
           M. Day's Possession.)

———
1926   Bear Ceremonialism in the Northern Hemisphere. *Ameri-
           can Anthropologist* 28(1):1-175.

———
1928   Recent Changes in the Kinship Terminology of the St.
           Francis Abenaki. Pp. 97-145 in *Proceedings of the 22d
           International Congress of Americanists*. 2 vols. Rome,
           1926.

[1932]   The Hunting Grounds and Hunting Customs of the St.
           Francis Abenaki. (Manuscript in Gordon M. Day's Pos-
           session.)

———
1937   Cross-cousin Marriage in the Lake Winnipeg Area. *Publi-
           cations of the Philadelphia Anthropological Society* 1:95-
           110. Philadelphia.

———
1946   Some Psychological Characteristics of the Northeastern
           Indians. Pp. 195-225 in Man in Northeastern North
           America. Frederick Johnson, ed. *Papers of the Robert S.
           Peabody Foundation for Archaeology* 3. Andover Mass.

———
1949   The Size of Algonkian Hunting Territories: A Function
           of Ecological Adjustments. *American Anthropologist*
           51(1):35-45.

———
1951   Frank Gouldsmith Speck, 1881-1950. *American Anthro-
           pologist* 53(1):67-87.

———
1951a   The Use of Projective Techniques in the Study of Socio-
           psychological Aspects of Acculturation. *Journal of Projec-
           tive Techniques* 15:27-44.

———
1952   Ojibwa Personality and Acculturation. Pp. 105-112 in
           Vol. 2 of Acculturation in the Americas: Proceedings and
           Selected Papers of the 29th International Congress of
           Americanists. Sol Tax, ed. 2 vols. Chicago: University of
           Chicago Press.

———
1955   Culture and Experience. *Publications of the Philadelphia
           Anthropological Society* 4. Philadelphia.

———
1957   The Backwash of the Frontier: The Impact of the Indian
           on American Culture. Pp. 229-258 in The Frontier in
           Perspective. Walker D. Wyman and Clifton B. Kroeber,
           eds. Madison: University of Wisconsin Press. (Re-
           printed: Pp. 447-472 in *Annual Report of the Smithsonian
           Institution* for 1958. Washington.)

———
1957a   The Impact of the American Indian on American Culture.
           American Anthropologist 59(2):201-217.

———
1960   The Beginnings of Anthropology in America. Pp. 1-90 in
           Selected Papers from the American Anthropologist, 1888-
           1920. Frederica de Laguna, ed. Evanston and New York:
           Row, Peterson.

Halsey, Francis W.
1901   The Old New York Frontier; Its Wars with Indians and
           Tories; Its Missionary Schools, Pioneers and Land Titles,
           1614-1800. New York: Charles Scribner's Sons.

———, ed.
1906   A Tour of Four Great Rivers: The Hudson, Mohawk,
           Susquehanna and Delaware in 1769; Being the Journal of
           Richard Smith of Burlington, N.J.; With a Short History
           of Pioneer Settlements. New York: C. Scribner's Sons.

Halsey, John R.
1968   The Springwells Mound Group of Wayne County, Michi-
           gan. *University of Michigan Museum of Anthropology, An-
           thropological Papers* 32:79-171. Ann Arbor.

Hamell, George R.
1975   The Boughton Hill Site: An Historical Perspective. (Un-
           published Manuscript in Hamell's Possession.)

Hamilton, Edward P.
1962   The French and Indian Wars: The Story of Battles and
           Forts in the Wilderness. Garden City, N.Y.: Doubleday.

Hamilton, John T.
1900   A History of the Church Known as the Moravian Church,
           or Unitas Fratrum, or the Unity of the Brethren, During
           the Eighteenth and Nineteenth Centuries. *Transactions of
           the Moravian Historical Society* 6. Bethlehem, Pa.

Hamilton-Gordon, Arthur (Lord Stanmore)
1864   Wilderness Journeys in New Brunswick in 1862-1863.
           Saint John, N.B.: J. and A. McMillan.

Hammond, J. Hugh
1905   The Ojibway of Lakes Huron and Simcoe. Pp. 71-73 in
           *Annual Archaeological Report for 1904, Being Part of Ap-
           pendix to the Report of the Minister of Education, Ontario.*
           Toronto.

Hamor, Ralph
1615   A Trve Discovrse of the Present Estate of Virginia, and
           the Successe of the Affaires there till the 18 of June, 1614.
           London: John Beale for W. Welby. (Reprinted: Virginia
           State Library, Richmond, 1957.)

Hamori-Torok, Charles *see* Torok, Charles H.

Handlin, Oscar, and Irving Mark, eds.
1964   Chief Daniel Nimham versus Roger Morris, Beverly Rob-
           inson, and Philip Philipse: An Indian Land Case in Colo-
           nial New York, 1765-1767. *Ethnohistory* 11(3):193-246.

Hanipaux, P.
1846   Lettre du R.P. Hanipaux, Missionnaire apostolique de la
           Société de Jésus, à son Frère. Ste. Croix, Grande Île Mani-
           touline, 14 septembre 1845. *Annales de la Propagation de
           la Foi* 18(108):461-465. Lyon.

Hanna, Charles A.
1911   The Wilderness Trail; or, the Ventures and Adventures of
           the Pennsylvania Traders on the Allegheny Path, with
           Some New Annals of the Old West, and the Records of
           Some Strong Men and Some Bad Ones. 2 vols. New York
           and London: G.P. Putnam's Sons.

Hanson, Lee H., Jr.
1966   The Hardin Village Site. (Studies in Anthropology 4)
           Lexington: University of Kentucky Press.

Hanzeli, Victor E.
1969   Missionary Linguistics in New France: A Study of Seven-
           teenth and Eighteenth Century Descriptions of American
           Indian Languages. *Janua Linguarum, Series Maior* 29.
           The Hague: Mouton.

Hare, Lloyd C.M.
1931   Thomas Mayhew, Patriarch to the Indians. *Americana*
           25(1):1-61, (2):157-219, (3):327-379, (4):486-533.

Hariot, Thomas
1588   A Briefe and True Report of the New Found Land of
           Virginia. London. (Reprinted in The Roanoke Voyages,

1584-1590. D.B. Quinn, ed., Vol. 1:317-387, Cambridge University Press for the Hakluyt Society, London, 1955.)

1590   The True Pictures and Fashions of the People in That Parte of America Now Called Virginia. In America, by Theodor de Bry. Frankfort: T. de Bry. (Reprinted in The Roanoke Voyages, 1584-1590. D.B. Quinn, ed. Vol. 1:399-444, Cambridge University Press for the Hakluyt Society, London, 1955.)

Harn, Alan D.
1970   Notes on the Mississippian Occupation of the Central Illinois River Valley. (Paper Presented at the 69th Annual Meeting of the American Anthropological Association. San Diego, Calif., 1970.)

1971   The Prehistory of the Dickson Mounds: A Preliminary Report. *Dickson Mounds Museum, Anthropological Studies* 1. Springfield, Ill.

1973   Cahokia and the Mississippian Emergence in the Spoon River Area of Illinois. (Paper Presented at the 52d Annual Meeting of the Central States Anthropological Society. St. Louis, 1973.)

Harp, Elmer, Jr., and David R. Hughes
1968   Five Prehistoric Burials from Port-au-Choix, Newfoundland. *Polar Notes* 8(June):1-47.

Harper, J. Russell
1954   Ouigoudi: The Indian Village at the Mouth of the St. John, 1604-1616. Pp. 27-29 in Champlain and the St. John, 1604-1954. George MacBeath, ed. Saint John: New Brunswick Historical Society.

1956   Portland Point, Crossroads of New Brunswick History: Preliminary Report of the 1955 Excavation. *New Brunswick Museum Historical Studies* 9. Saint John.

Harrington, Mark R.
1903   Shinnecock Notes. *Journal of American Folk-Lore* 16(60):37-39.

1908   Vestiges of Material Culture Among the Canadian Delawares. *American Anthropologist* 10(3):408-418.

1913   A Preliminary Sketch of Lenápe Culture. *American Anthropologist* 15(2):208-235.

1914   Sacred Bundles of the Sac and Fox. *University of Pennsylvania Museum, Anthropological Publications* 4(2):125-262. Philadelphia.

1921   Religion and Ceremonies of the Lenape. *Museum of the American Indian, Heye Foundation. Indian Notes and Monographs, Misc. Pub.* 19. New York.

1926   Alanson Skinner. *American Anthropologist* 28(1):275-280.

Harris, R.I.
1949   Osteological Evidence of Disease Amongst the Huron Indians. *University of Toronto Medical Journal* 27(2):71-75.

Harris, William
1902   Harris Papers. *Collections of the Rhode Island Historical Society* 10:11-400. Providence.

1963   A Rhode Islander Reports on King Philip's War: The Second William Harris Letter of August, 1676. Douglas E. Leach, ed. Providence: Rhode Island Historical Society.

Harris, William R.
1896   A Forgotten People: The Flint Workers. *Publications of the Buffalo Historical Society* 4:227-244. Buffalo.

Harrison, Henry
[1633]   [Five Pages of Manuscript Translations of Religious Texts in the Hand of Rev. Andrew White, S.J. on the Front Endpapers of a Copy of a 1610 *Manuale Sacerdotum* Once Owned by Harrison.] (Now in the Special Collections of the Georgetown University Library, Washington.)

Hart, Simon
1959   The Prehistory of the New Netherland Company: Amsterdam Notarial Records of the First Dutch Voyages to the Hudson in the City Archives of Amsterdam. Amsterdam: City of Amsterdam Press.

Harte, Thomas G.
1959   Trends in Mate Selection in a Tri-racial Isolate. *Social Forces* 37(3):215-221.

1963   Social Origins of the Brandywine Population. *Phylon* 24(4):369-378.

Harvey, Henry
1855   History of the Shawnee Indians, from the Year 1681 to 1854, Inclusive. Cincinnati: Ephraim Morgan and Sons. (Reprinted: Kraus Reprint, New York, 1971.)

Hassell, Thomas
1715   [Letter to William Taylor, Dec. 1, St. Thomas, S.C.] (Letter No. 33, Society for the Propagation of the Gospel Records, British Library, London; Microfilm Reel 3, Southern Historical Collection, University of North Carolina, Chapel Hill.)

Hassrick, Royal B., and Edmund Carpenter
1944   Rappahannock Games and Amusements. *Primitive Man* 17(1-2):29-39.

Hatt, Gudmund
1916   Moccasins and Their Relation to Arctic Footwear. *Memoirs of the American Anthropological Association* 3:149-250. Lancaster, Pa.

Hatzan, A. Leon
1925   The True Story of Hiawatha, and History of the Six Nation Indians. Toronto: McClelland and Stewart.

Havard, Verne
1880   The French Half-breeds of the Northwest. Pp. 309-327 in *Annual Report of the Smithsonian Institution for 1879.* Washington.

Haven, Samuel F.
1856   Archaeology of the United States, or Sketches Historical and Bibliographical, of the Progress of Information and Opinion Respecting Vestiges of Antiquity in the United States. *Smithsonian Contributions to Knowledge* 8(2):1-168. Washington.

Hawks, Francis L.
1857-1858 History of North Carolina: With Maps and Illustrations. 2 vols. Fayetteville, N.C.: E.J. Hale and Son. (Reprinted: The Reprint Company, Spartanburg, S.C., 1961.)

Hawley, Charles
1879   Early Chapters of Cayuga History: Jesuit Missions in Goi-o-gouen, 1656-1684. Also an Account of the Sulpitian Mission Among the Emigrant Cayugas, About Quinte Bay, in 1668. Auburn, N.Y.: Knapp and Peck.

1884   Early Chapters of Seneca History: Jesuit Missions in Sonnontouan, 1656-1684. *Collections of the Cayuga County Historical Society* 3:1-89. Auburn, N.Y.

Haycock, Ronald G.
1971   The Image of the Indian. *Waterloo Lutheran University, Monograph Series* 1:1-98. Waterloo, Ont.

Hayes, Charles F.
1967   The Longhouse at the Cornish Site. Pp. 91-97 in Iroquois Culture, History and Prehistory: Proceedings of the 1965 Conference on Iroquois Research. Elisabeth Tooker, ed. Albany: New York State Museum and Science Service.

Hazard, Ebenezer
1792-1794 Historical Collections Consisting of State Papers, and Other Authentic Documents; Intended as Materials for an History of the United States of America. Philadelphia: Printed by T. Dobson.

Heckewelder, John G.E.

1819   An Account of the History, Manners, and Customs of the Indian Nations, Who Once Inhabited Pennsylvania and the Neighbouring States. *Transactions of the Committee of History, Moral Science and General Literature of the American Philosophical Society* 1. Philadelphia.

1820   A Narrative of the Mission of the United Brethren Among the Delaware and Mohegan Indians from its Commencement in the Year 1740 to the Close of the Year 1808. Philadelphia: M'Carty and Davis.

1841   Indian Tradition of the First Arrival of the Dutch at Manhattan Island, 1811-1859. *Collections of the New York Historical Society,* 2d ser., Vol. 1:69-74. New York.

1876   History, Manners, and Customs of the Indian Nations Who Once Inhabited Pennsylvania and the Neighboring States [1818]. Rev. ed. *Memoirs of the Pennsylvania Historical Society* 12. Philadelphia.

Heermans, Augustus

1673   Virginia and Maryland as it is Planted and Inhabited this Present Year 1670, Surveyed and Exactly Drawne by the Only Labour and Endeavour of Augustin Herrman Bohemiensis. London: Sold by J. Seller. (Reprinted: John Carter Brown Library, Providence, R.I., 1963.)

Heidenreich, Conrad E.

1966   Maps Relating to the First Half of the 17th Century and Their Use in Determining the Location of Jesuit Missions in Huronia. *The Cartographer* 3(2):103-126.

1968   A New Location for Carhagouha, Récollect Mission in Huronia. *Ontario Archaeological Society Publication* 11:39-46. Toronto.

1971   Huronia: A History and Geography of the Huron Indians, 1600-1650. Toronto: McClelland and Stewart.

1971a   Soil and Environmental Analysis at the Robitaille Site. Pp. 179-237 in Palaeoecology and Ontario Prehistory. W.M. Hurley and C.E. Heidenreich, eds. *University of Toronto Department of Anthropology, Research Report* 2. Toronto.

1974   A Relict Indian Cornfield Near Creemore, Ontario. *Canadian Geographer* 18(4):379-394.

Heisey, Henry

1971   An Interpretation of Shenk's Ferry Ceramics. *Pennsylvania Archaeologist* 41(4):44-70.

Hemenway, Abby M., ed.

1868-1891   The Vermont Historical Gazetteer: A Magazine, Embracing a History of Each Town, Civil, Ecclesiastical, Biographical and Military. 5 vols. Burlington, Vt.: [no publisher.]

Hening, William W.

1809-1823   The Statutes at Large: Being a Collection of All the Laws of Virginia, from the First Session of the Legislature, in the Year 1619. 13 vols. Richmond: Samuel Pleasants. (Reprinted: University of Virginia Press, Charlottesville, 1969.)

Hennepin, Louis

1880   A Description of Louisiana [1683]. John G. Shea, trans. New York: John G. Shea. (Reprinted: University of Minnesota Press, Minneapolis, 1938.)

1903   A New Discovery of a Vast Country in America [1698]. Reuben G. Thwaites, ed. 2 vols. Chicago: A.C. McClurg.

Henning, Charles L.

1898   The Origin of the Confederacy of the Five Nations. *Proceedings of the American Association for the Advancement of Science* 47:477-480. Salem, Mass.

Henry, Alexander

1901   Travels and Adventures in Canada and the Indian Territories Between the Years 1760 and 1776. James Bain, ed. Boston: Little, Brown.

1969   Travels and Adventures in Canada and in the Indian Territories Between the Years 1760 and 1776. James Bain, ed. Edmonton, Alb.: M.G. Hurtig; New York: B. Franklin.

Henshaw, Henry W.

1890   Indian Origin of Maple Sugar. *American Anthropologist* 3(4):341-352.

Herrick, Ruth

1957   A Report on the Ada Site, Kent County, Michigan. *Michigan Archaeologist* 4(1):1-27.

Herrington, M. Eleanor

1921   Captain John Deserontyou and the Mohawk Settlement at Deseronto. *Bulletin of the Departments of History and Political and Economic Science in Queen's University* 41. Kingston, Ont.

Herrman, Augustine *see* Heermans, Augustus

Hertzberg, Hazel W.

1971   The Search for an American Indian Identity: Modern Pan-Indian Movements. Syracuse, N.Y.: Syracuse University Press.

Hesselius, Gustav

1735   Lapowinsa. (Oil Portrait in the Historical Society of Pennsylvania, Philadelphia.)

1735a   Tishcohan. (Oil Portrait in the Historical Society of Pennsylvania, Philadelphia.)

Hewitt, J.N.B.

1889   [Wyandot Vocabulary Taken from Samuel Rankin, Six Nations Reserve, Ontario.] (Manuscript No. 378 in National Anthropological Archives, Smithsonian Institution, Washington.)

1892   Legend of the Founding of the Iroquois League. *American Anthropologist* 5(2):131-148.

1894   Era of the Formation of the Historic League of the Iroquois. *American Anthropologist* 7(1):61-67.

1895   Tuscarora Customs and Beliefs. (Manuscript in Folder 445, J.N.B. Hewitt Papers, National Anthropological Archives, Smithsonian Institution, Washington.)

1895a   The Iroquoian Concept of the Soul. *Journal of American Folk-Lore* 8(29):107-116.

1902   Orenda and a Definition of Religion. *American Anthropologist* n.s. 4(1):33-46.

1903-1928   Iroquoian Cosmology. Pp. 127-339 in Vol. 21 and pp. 449-819 in Vol. 43 of the *Annual Reports of the Bureau of American Ethnology for the Years 1899-1900* and *1925-1926.* Washington.

1907   Akawenchaka. P. 33 in Vol. 1 of Handbook of American Indians North of Mexico. Frederick W. Hodge, ed. 2 vols. *Bureau of American Ethnology Bulletin* 30. Washington.

1907a   Atrakwaye. Pp. 112-113 in Vol. 1 of Handbook of American Indians North of Mexico. Frederick W. Hodge, ed. 2 vols. *Bureau of American Ethnology Bulletin* 30. Washington.

1907b   Mohawk. Pp. 921-926 in Vol. 1 of Handbook of American Indians North of Mexico. Frederick W. Hodge, ed. 2 vols. *Bureau of American Ethnology Bulletin* 30. Washington.

1907c   Kanagaro. Pp. 649-650 in Vol. 1 of Handbook of American Indians North of Mexico. Frederick W. Hodge, ed. 2 vols. *Bureau of American Ethnology Bulletin* 30. Washington.

1907d   Erie. Pp. 430-432 in Vol. 1 of Handbook of American Indians North of Mexico. Frederick W. Hodge, ed. 2 vols. *Bureau of American Ethnology Bulletin* 30. Washington.

1907e   Ganowarohare. P. 487 in Vol. 1 of Handbook of American Indians North of Mexico. Frederick W. Hodge, ed. 2 vols. *Bureau of American Ethnology Bulletin* 30. Washington.

1907f   Iroquois. Pp. 617-620 in Vol. 1 of Handbook of American Indians North of Mexico. Frederick W. Hodge, ed. 2 vols. *Bureau of American Ethnology Bulletin* 30. Washington.

1907g   Conestoga. Pp. 335-337 in Vol. 1 of Handbook of American Indians North of Mexico. Frederick W. Hodge, ed. 2 vols. *Bureau of American Ethnology Bulletin* 30. Washington.

1910   Sauk. Pp. 471-480 in Vol. 2 of Handbook of American Indians North of Mexico. Frederick W. Hodge, ed. 2 vols. *Bureau of American Ethnology Bulletin* 30. Washington.

1910a   Wenrohronon. Pp. 932-943 in Vol. 2 of Handbook of American Indians North of Mexico. Frederick W. Hodge, ed. 2 vols. *Bureau of American Ethnology Bulletin* 30. Washington.

1910b   Seneca. Pp. 502-508 in Vol. 2 of Handbook of American Indians North of Mexico. Frederick W. Hodge, ed. 2 vols. *Bureau of American Ethnology Bulletin* 30. Washington.

1910c   Tuscarora. Pp. 842-853 in Vol. 2 of Handbook of American Indians North of Mexico. Frederick W. Hodge, ed. 2 vols. *Bureau of American Ethnology Bulletin* 30. Washington.

1910d   Ontarahronon. P. 135 in Vol. 2 of Handbook of American Indians North of Mexico. Frederick W. Hodge, ed. 2 vols. *Bureau of American Ethnology Bulletin* 30. Washington.

1910e   Ontwaganha. P. 136 in Vol. 2 of Handbook of American Indians North of Mexico. Frederick W. Hodge, ed. 2 vols. *Bureau of American Ethnology Bulletin* 30. Washington.

1910f   Squawkihow. Pp. 630-631 in Vol. 2 of Handbook of American Indians North of Mexico. Frederick W. Hodge, ed. 2 vols. *Bureau of American Ethnology Bulletin* 30. Washington.

1910g   Onondaga. Pp. 129-135 in Vol. 2 of Handbook of American Indians North of Mexico. Frederick W. Hodge, ed. 2 vols. *Bureau of American Ethnology Bulletin* 30. Washington.

1910h   Teatontaloga. P. 713 in Vol. 2 of Handbook of American Indians North of Mexico. Frederick W. Hodge, ed. 2 vols. *Bureau of American Ethnology Bulletin* 30. Washington.

1910i   Neutrals. Pp. 60-62 in Vol. 2 of Handbook of American Indians North of Mexico. Frederick W. Hodge, ed. 2 vols. *Bureau of American Ethnology Bulletin* 30. Washington.

1910j   Oneida. Pp. 123-127 in Vol. 2 of Handbook of American Indians North of Mexico. Frederick W. Hodge, ed. 2 vols. *Bureau of American Ethnology Bulletin* 30. Washington.

1916   The Requickening Address of the League of the Iroquois. Pp. 163-179 in Holmes Anniversary Volume: Anthropological Essays Presented to William H. Holmes in Honor of His Seventieth Birthday. Washington: J.W. Bryan Press.

1917   Some Esoteric Aspects of the League of the Iroquois. Pp. 322-326 in *Proceedings of the 19th International Congress of Americanists.* Washington, 1915.

1917a   [Reviews of] The Constitution of the Five Nations, by Arthur C. Parker; Traditional History of the Confederacy of the Six Nations, by Duncan C. Scott; and Civil, Religious and Mourning Councils and Ceremonies of Adoption of the New York Indians, by William Beauchamp. *American Anthropologist* 19(3):429-438.

1920   A Constitutional League of Peace in the Stone Age of America: The League of the Iroquois and its Constitution. Pp. 527-545 in *Annual Report of the Smithsonian Institution for 1918.* Washington.

1927   Ethnological Studies Among the Iroquois Indians. *Smithsonian Miscellaneous Collections* 78(7):237-247. Washington.

1930   The "League of Nations" of the Iroquois Indians in Canada. Pp. 201-206 in *Explorations and Field-work of the Smithsonian Institution in 1929.* Washington.

1933   Field-work Among the Iroquois Indians of New York and Canada. Pp. 81-84 in *Explorations and Field-work of the Smithsonian Institution in 1932.* Washington.

1936   [Munsee Vocabulary from Nicodemus Peters of Six-Nations Reserve, Smoothtown, Grand River Reserve, Ontario, Canada.] (Manuscript No. 3757 in National Anthropological Archives, Smithsonian Institution, Washington.)

Hewitt, J.N.B., and William N. Fenton
1944   The Requickening Address of the Iroquois Condolence Council. *Journal of the Washington Academy of Sciences* 34(3):65-85. Washington.

1945   Some Mnemonic Pictographs Relating to the Iroquois Condolence Council. *Journal of the Washington Academy of Sciences* 35(10):301-315. Washington.

Hewson, John
1968   Beothuk and Algonkian: Evidence Old and New. *International Journal of American Linguistics* 34(2):85-93.

1971   Beothuk Consonant Correspondences. *International Journal of American Linguistics* 37(4):244-249.

Hickerson, Harold
1960   The Feast of the Dead Among the Seventeenth Century Algonkians of the Upper Great Lakes. *American Anthropologist* 62(1):81-107.

1962   The Southwestern Chippewa: An Ethnohistorical Study. *Memoirs of the American Anthropological Association* 92. Menasha, Wis.

1963   The Sociohistorical Significance of Two Chippewa Ceremonials. *American Anthropologist* 65(1):67-85.

1966   The Genesis of Bilaterality Among Two Divisions of Chippewa. *American Anthropologist* 68(1):1-26.

1967   Some Implications of the Theory of the Particularity, or "Atomism" of Northern Algonkians. *Current Anthropology* 8(4):313-343.

1970   The Chippewa and Their Neighbors: A Study in Ethnohistory. New York: Holt, Rinehart and Winston.

Hicks, George L.
1975   The Same North and South: Ethnicity and Change in Two American Indian Groups. Pp. 75-94 in The New Ethnicity: Perspectives from Ethnology. John W. Bennett, ed. *Proceedings of the American Ethnological Society.*

Wrightsville Beach, 1973. St. Paul, New York, Boston, Los Angeles, San Francisco: West Publishing Company.

Hicks, George L., and David I. Kertzer
1972   Making a Middle Way: Problems of Monhegan Identity. *Southwestern Journal of Anthropology* 28(1):1-24.

Hiden, Martha W., and Henry M. Dargan, eds.
1966   John Gibbon's Manuscript Notes Concerning Virginia. *Virginia Magazine of History and Biography* 74(1):3-22.

Hilger, M. Inez
1960   Some Early Customs of the Menomini Indians. *Journal de la Société des Américanistes de Paris* n.s. 49:45-68.

Hill, Asa R.
1922   The Historical Position of the Six Nations. *Papers and Records of the Ontario Historical Society* 19:103-109. Toronto.

Hill, Bruce E.
1964   The Grand River Navigation Company. (Unpublished M.A. Thesis in History, University of Western Ontario, London.)

Hill, George A.
1971   Delaware Ethnobotany. *Newsletter of the Oklahoma Anthropological Society* 19(3):3-18. Norman.

Hill, Leonard U.
1957   John Johnston and the Indians in the Land of the Three Miamis. Columbus, Ohio: Stoneman Press.

Hinsdale, Wilbert B.
1929   Indian Mounds, West Twin Lake, Montmorency County, Michigan. *Papers of the Michigan Academy of Science, Arts and Letters* 10:91-101. Ann Arbor.

Hinsdale, Wilbert B., and Emerson F. Greenman
1936   Perforated Indian Crania in Michigan. *University of Michigan Museum of Anthropology, Occasional Contributions* 5. Ann Arbor.

Hislop, Codman
1948   The Mohawk. New York and Toronto: Rinehart.

Hlady, Walter M., ed.
1970   Ten Thousand Years: Archaeology in Manitoba. [Winipeg]: Manitoba Archaeological Society.

Hockett, Charles F.
1943   The Position of Potawatomi in Central Algonkian. *Papers of the Michigan Academy of Science, Arts and Letters* 28:537-542. Ann Arbor.

_____
1948   Potawatomi. *International Journal of American Linguistics* 14(1):1-10, (2):63-73, (3):139-149, (4):213-225.

_____
1948a   Implications of Bloomfield's Algonquian Studies. *Language* 24(1):117-131.

_____
1957   Central Algonquian Vocabulary: Stems in /k-/. *International Journal of American Linguistics* 23(4):247-268.

_____
1964   The Proto Central Algonquian Kinship System. Pp. 239-257 in Explorations in Cultural Anthropology: Essays in Honor of George P. Murdock. Ward H. Goodenough, ed. New York: McGraw-Hill.

_____, ed.
1970   A Leonard Bloomfield Anthology. Bloomington: Indiana University Press.

Hodge, Frederick W., ed.
1907-1910   Handbook of American Indians North of Mexico. 2 vols. *Bureau of American Ethnology Bulletin* 30. Washington. (Reprinted: Rowman and Littlefield, New York, 1971.)

_____, ed.
1913   Handbook of the Indians of Canada. (Appendix to the 10th Report of the Geographic Board of Canada.) Otta-

wa: The King's Printer. (Reprinted: Coles Publishing Company, Toronto, 1971.)

Hoffman, D.W., R.E. Wiklund, and N.R. Richards
1962   Soil Survey of Simcoe County, Ontario. *Canada. Department of Agriculture and the Ontario Agricultural College, Ontario Soil Survey Report* 29. Guelph.

Hoffman, Bernard G.
1955   The Historical Ethnography of the Micmac of the 16th and 17th Centuries. (Unpublished Ph.D. Dissertation in Anthropology, University of California, Berkeley.)

_____
1955a   The Souriquois, Etechemin and Kwĕdĕch: A Lost Chapter in American Ethnography. *Ethnohistory* 2(1):65-87.

_____
1959   Iroquois Linguistic Classification from Historical Materials. *Ethnohistory* 6(2):160-185.

_____
1961   Cabot to Cartier; Sources for a Historical Ethnography of Northeastern North America, 1497-1550. Toronto: University of Toronto Press.

_____
1964   Observations on Certain Ancient Tribes of the Northern Appalachian Province. *Anthropological Papers 70, Bureau of American Ethnology Bulletin* 191:191-245. Washington.

_____
1967   Ancient Tribes Revisited: A Summary of Indian Distribution and Movement in the Northeastern United States from 1534-1779. 3 Pts. *Ethnohistory* 14(1-2):1-46.

Hoffman, Walter J.
1891   The Midē'wiwin or "Grand Medicine Society" of the Ojibwa. Pp. 143-300 in *7th Annual Report of the Bureau of American Ethnology for the Years 1885-1886*. Washington.

_____
1896   The Menomini Indians. Pp. 3-328 in *14th Annual Report of the Bureau of American Ethnology for the Years 1892-1893*. Pt. 1. Washington.

Hoijer, Harry
1949   An Analytical Dictionary of the Tonkawa Language. *University of California Publications in Linguistics* 5(1):1-174. Berkeley.

Holland, C.G.
1966   Archaeology and Ethnohistory: An Illustration. *Quarterly Bulletin of the Archaeological Society of Virginia* 21(1):2-8. Richmond.

Holm, Thomas Campanius
1834   Description of the Province of New Sweden. Now Called by the English, Pennsylvania, in America. Compiled from the Relations and Writings of Persons Worthy of Credit, and Adorned with Maps and Plates. Peter S. Du Ponceau, ed. Philadelphia: M'Carty and Davis.

Holmes, W.H.
1903   Aboriginal Pottery in the Eastern United States. Pp. 1-201 in *20th Annual Report of the Bureau of American Ethnology for the Years 1898-1899*. Washington.

_____
1914   Areas of American Culture Characterization Tentatively Outlined as an Aid in the Study of Antiquities. *American Anthropologist* 16(3):413-446.

_____
1919   Handbook of Aboriginal American Antiquities. Pt. 1, Introductory: The Lithic Industries. *Bureau of American Ethnology Bulletin* 60. Washington.

Holmes, Elkanah
1903   Letters of the Reverend Elkanah Holmes from Fort Niagara in 1800. *Publications of the Buffalo Historical Society* 6:187-204. Buffalo.

Hooton, Earnest A.
1920   Indian Village Site and Cemetery Near Madisonville, Ohio. *Papers of the Peabody Museum of American Archaeology and Ethnology, Harvard University* 8(1). Cambridge, Mass.

Hopkins, Samuel
1753   Historical Memoirs Relating to the Housatunnuk Indians. Boston: S. Kneeland. (Reprinted: Johnson Reprint Corporation, New York, 1972.)

Horr, David, ed.
1974-   American Indian Ethnohistory. 118 vols. New York and London: Garland.

Houart, Gail L.
1972   Koster: A Stratified Archaic Site in the Illinois Valley. *Illinois State Museum, Report of Investigations* 22. Springfield.

Houck, Louis, ed.
1909   The Spanish Regime in Missouri: A Collection of Papers and Documents Relating to Upper Louisiana Principally Within the Present Limits of Missouri During the Dominion of Spain, from the Archives of the Indies at Seville, etc. 2 vols. Chicago: R.R. Donnelley.

Hough, Franklin B.
1853   A History of St. Lawrence and Franklin Counties, New York, from the Earliest Period to the Present Time. Albany: Little and Company.

————, comp.
1856   Papers Relating to the Island of Nantucket, with Documents Relating to the Original Settlement of that Island, Martha's Vineyard, and Other Islands Adjacent, Known as Duke's County, While Under the Colony of New York. Albany: J. Munsell.

Houghton, Frederick
1912   The Seneca Nation from 1655-1687. *Bulletin of the Buffalo Society of Natural Sciences* 10:363-476. Buffalo.

1920   History of the Buffalo Creek Reservation. *Publications of the Buffalo Historical Society* 24:1-181. Buffalo.

1922   The Archeology of the Genesee Country. *Researches and Transactions of the New York State Archaeological Association* 3(2):39-66. Rochester.

1927   The Migrations of the Seneca Nation. *American Anthropologist* 29(2):241-250.

Howard, James H.
1960   When They Worship the Underwater Panther: A Prairie Potawatomi Bundle Ceremony. *Southwestern Journal of Anthropology* 16(2):217-224.

1961   Cultural Resistance and Cultural Change as Reflected in Oklahoma Seneca-Cayuga Ceremonialism. *Plains Anthropologist* 6(11):21-30.

1965   The Kenakuk Religion: An Early 19th Century Revitalization Movement 140 Years Later. *University of South Dakota, South Dakota Museum News* 26(11-12):1-46. Vermillion.

1970   Environment and Culture: The Case of the Oklahoma Seneca-Cayuga. *Newsletter of the Oklahoma Anthropological Society* 18(6):5-13, (7):5-21. (Reprinted with Revisions from *North Dakota Quarterly* 29(3):66-71, (4):113-122, 1961.)

Howland, Henry R.
1903   The Seneca Mission at Buffalo Creek. *Publications of the Buffalo Historical Society* 6:125-161. Buffalo.

Howley, James P.
1915   The Beothucks, or Red Indians: The Aboriginal Inhabitants of Newfoundland. Cambridge, England: Cambridge University Press. (Facsimile Reprint: Coles Publishing Company, Toronto, 1974.)

Hubbard, Gurdon S.
1911   The Autobiography of Gurdon Saltonstall Hubbard, Papa-ma-ta-be, "The Swift Walker." Chicago: R.R. Donnelley.

Hubbard, Jeremiah
1975   Forty Years Among the Indians [1913]. Knightstown, Ind.: Bookmark.

Hubbard, William
1677   The Present State of New-England. Being a Narrative of the Troubles with the Indians in New-England, from the First Planting Thereof in the Year 1607, to this Present Year 1677. But Chiefly of the Late Troubles in the Two Last Years, 1675 and 1676. To Which is Added a Discourse About the Warre with the Pequods in the Year 1637. London: Printed for Tho. Parkhurst; Boston: John Foster.

1865   The History of the Indian Wars in New England from the First Settlement to the Termination of the War with King Philip, in 1677. Samuel G. Drake, ed. 2 vols. Roxbury, Mass.: W.E. Woodward. (Reprinted: Kraus, New York, 1969.)

Huddleston, Lee E.
1967   Origins of the American Indians: European Concepts, 1492-1729. Austin: University of Texas Press.

Hughes, Thomas A.
1907-1917   History of the Society of Jesus in North America, Colonial and Federal. 3 vols in 4. London, New York: Longmans, Green.

Hulton, Paul H., and David B. Quinn
1964   The American Drawings of John White, 1577-1590. 2 vols. London: Trustees of the British Museum; Chapel Hill: University of North Carolina Press.

Humphrey, Norman B.
1941   The Mock Battle Greeting. *Journal of American Folklore* 54(213-214):186-190.

Humphreys, David
1730   An Historical Account of the Incorporated Society for the Propagation of the Gospel in Foreign Parts. London: Joseph Downing.

Hunt, George T.
1940   The Wars of the Iroquois: A Study in Intertribal Trade Relations. Madison: University of Wisconsin Press.

Hunter, Andrew F.
1890   French Relics from Village Sites of the Hurons. Pp. 42-46 in *Annual Report of the Canadian Institute, Session 1898-1899. Being Part of Appendix to the Report of the Minister of Education, Ontario.* Toronto.

1899   Sites of Huron Villages in the Township of Tiny, Simcoe County and Adjacent Areas. Pp. 5-42 in *Annual Archaeological Report for 1898. Being Part of Appendix to the Report of the Minister of Education, Ontario.* Toronto.

1900   Notes on Sites of Huron Villages in the Township of Tay. Pp. 51-82 in *Annual Archaeological Report for 1899. Being Part of Appendix to the Report of the Minister of Education, Ontario.* Toronto.

1902   Notes on Sites of Huron Villages in the Township of Medonte. Pp. 56-100 in *Annual Archaeological Report for 1901. Being Part of Appendix to the Report of the Minister of Education, Ontario.* Toronto.

1903   Notes on Sites of Huron Villages in the Township of Oro, Simcoe County. Pp. 153-183 in *Annual Archaeological Report for 1902. Being Part of Appendix to the Report of the Minister of Education, Ontario.* Toronto.

1904   Indian Village Sites in North and South Orillia Townships. Pp. 105-125 in *Annual Archaeological Report for 1903. Being Part of Appendix to the Report of the Minister of Education, Ontario.* Toronto.

1907   Survey of Village Sites in the Townships of Flos and Vespra. Pp. 19-56 in *Annual Archaeological Report for 1906. Being Part of Appendix to the Report of the Minister of Education, Ontario.* Toronto.

Hunter, William A.
1951   Provincial Negotiations with the Western Indians, 1754-58. *Pennsylvania History* 18(3):213-219.

——, ed.
1954   John Hays' Diary and Journal of 1760. *Pennsylvania Archaeologist* 24(2):63-84.

1954a   The Ohio, the Indian's Land. *Pennsylvania History* 21(4):338-350.

1956   Refugee Fox Settlements Among the Senecas. *Ethnohistory* 3(1):11-20.

1959   The Historic Role of the Susquehannocks. Pp. 8-18 in Susquehannock Miscellany. John Witthoft and W. Fred Kinsey, III, eds. Harrisburg: Pennsylvania Historical and Museum Commission.

1975   A Note on the Unalachtigo. Pp. 147-152 in A Delaware Indian Symposium. Herbert C. Kraft, ed. *Pennsylvania Historical and Museum Commission, Anthropological Series* 4. Harrisburg.

Hurley, William M.
1966   The Silver Creek Sites: A Complex of Five Woodland Site Localities in Monroe County, Wisconsin. (Unpublished M.A. Thesis in Anthropology, University of Wisconsin, Madison.)

1970   The Wisconsin Effigy Mound Tradition. 2 vols. (Unpublished Ph.D. Dissertation in Anthropology, University of Wisconsin, Madison.)

Hurley, William M., and Conrad E. Heidenreich, eds.
1971   Palaeoecology and Ontario Prehistory, II. *University of Toronto, Department of Anthropology, Research Report* 2. Toronto.

[Hurons of Lorette]
[1678] Vous des Hurons de Lorette en la Nouvelle France à Notre Dame de Chartres. (Manuscript G 445 in Archives d'Eure-et-Loir, Chartres, France.)

Hutton, Elizabeth A.
1963   Indian Affairs in Nova Scotia, 1760-1834. *Collections of the Nova Scotia Historical Society* 34:33-54. Halifax.

Hyde, Jabez B.
1903   A Teacher Among the Senecas: Historical and Personal Narrative of Jabez Backus Hyde, Who Came to the Buffalo Creek Mission in 1811. Written in 1820. *Publications of the Buffalo Historical Society* 6:239-274. Buffalo.

IHC = Illinois State Historical Library
1903-   Collections. —vols. Springfield: Illinois Historical Library.

IHS = Indiana Historical Society
1895   Publications. Indianapolis: Indiana Historical Society.

ISHS = Illinois State Historical Society
1900-1942 Papers in Illinois History and Transactions. 43 vols. Springfield: Illinois State Historical Society.

Imlay, Gilbert
1793   A Topographical Description of the Western Territory of North America. 2d ed. London: Printed for J. Debrett.

1797   A Topographical Description of the Western Territory of North America. 3d ed. London: Printed for J. Debrett.

Ingstad, Helge M.
1969   Westward to Vinland: The Discovery of Pre-Columbian Norse Housesites in North America. Erik J. Friis, trans. New York: St. Martin's Press.

Innis, Harold A.
1940   The Cod Fisheries: The History of an International Economy. New Haven, Conn.: Yale University Press; Toronto: Ryerson Press.

1956   The Fur Trade in Canada: An Introduction to Canadian Economic History [1930]. 2d ed. Toronto: University of Toronto Press.

Irving, Washington
1964   Astoria; or, Anecdotes of an Enterprise Beyond the Rocky Mountains [1836]. E.W. Todd, ed. Norman: University of Oklahoma Press.

Isham, James
1949   Observations on Hudsons Bay, 1743, and Notes on a Book Entitled A Voyage to Hudsons Bay in the Dobbs Galley, 1749. E.E. Rich, ed. Toronto: The Champlain Society.

Ives, Edward D.
1964   Malecite and Passamaquoddy Tales. *Northeast Folklore* 6:5-81.

JR = Thwaites, Reuben G., ed.
1896-1901 The Jesuit Relations and Allied Documents: Travel and Explorations of the Jesuit Missionaries in New France, 1610-1791; the Original French, Latin, and Italian Texts, with English Translations and Notes. 73 vols. Cleveland: Burrows Brothers. (Reprinted: Pageant, New York, 1959.)

Jack, David R.
1901   The Indians of Acadia. *Acadiensis* 1(4):187-201.

Jack, Edward
1881   A Day with the Abenaquis. *The Daily Sun,* July 30:2. Saint John, New Brunswick.

1893   The Abenakis of Saint John River. *Transactions of the Canadian Institute, Session 1891-1892,* Vol. 3:195-205. Toronto.

1895   Maliseet Legends. *Journal of American Folk-Lore* 8(30):193-208.

Jackson, Donald, ed.
1964   Black Hawk, an Autobiography. Urbana: University of Illinois Press.

Jackson, Halliday
1830   Civilization of the Indian Natives. Philadelphia: Marcus T.C. Gould.

1830a   Sketch of the Manners, Customs, Religion, and Government of the Seneca Indians in 1800. Philadelphia: Gould.

Jackson, William H., comp.
1877   Descriptive Catalogue of Photographs of North American Indians. *U.S. Department of the Interior, Geological Survey of the Territories, Miscellaneous Publication* 9. Washington.

Jacobs, Peter
1857-1861 Ojibwa Mission at Manitoulin, Lake Huron. *Mission Field* 2:145-150, 240-246, 3:9-13, 158-161, 4:157-160, 5:232-237, 6:76-79, 259-260.

James, Bernard J.
1961   Social-psychological Dimensions of Ojibwa Acculturation. *American Anthropologist* 63(4):721-746.

James, C[harles] C.
1906   The Downfall of the Huron Nation. *Proceedings and Transactions of the Royal Society of Canada,* 2d ser., sect. 2, Vol. 12:311-346. Ottawa.

James, Edwin, comp.
1905   Account of an Expedition from Pittsburgh to the Rocky Mountains Performed in the Years 1819, 1820; Compiled from the Notes of Major Long, Mr. T. Say, and Other Gentlemen of the Party. Pp. 35-321 in Vol. 14 of Early Western Travels, 1748-1846. Reuben G. Thwaites, ed. 38 vols. Cleveland: Arthur H. Clark.

James, James A., ed.
1912   George Rogers Clark Papers, 1771-1781. *Collections of the Illinois State Historical Library* 8. Springfield.

Jameson, Anna Brownell (Murphy)
1838   Winter Studies and Summer Rambles in Canada. 3 vols. London: Saunders and Otley.

Jameson, J. Franklin, ed.
1909   Narratives of New Netherland, 1609-1664. New York: Charles Scribner's Sons. (Reprinted: Barnes and Noble, New York, 1959.)

Jamieson, Elmer, and Peter Sandiford
1928   The Mental Capacity of Southern Ontario Indians. *Journal of Educational Psychology* 19(5):313-328.

Jamieson, Julia L.
1969   Echoes of the Past: A History of Education from the Time of the Six Nations Settlement on the Banks of the Grand River in 1784 to 1924. Mimeo.

Janzen, Donald E.
1968   Excavations and Survey at Burnt Bluff in 1965. *University of Michigan Museum of Anthropology, Anthropological Papers* 34:61-94. Ann Arbor.

1968a   The Naomikong Point Site and the Dimensions of Laurel in the Lake Superior Region. *University of Michigan Museum of Anthropology, Anthropological Papers* 36. Ann Arbor.

Jefferson, Thomas
1787   Notes on the State of Virginia. London: John Stockdale. (Reprinted: University of North Carolina Press, Chapel Hill, 1955).

1791   [Vocabulary of Unquachog.] (Manuscript No. 1289 in Library of the American Philosophical Society, Philadelphia.)

1801   Notes on the State of Virginia. Philadelphia: R.T. Rawle.

1964   Notes on the State of Virginia [1787]. Thomas P. Abernethy, ed. New York: Harper and Row.

[Jefferys, Thomas]
1757-1772 A Collection of the Dresses of Different Nations, Ancient and Modern; Particularly Old English Dresses. After the Designs of Holbein, Vandyke, Hellar, and Others. With an Account of the Authorities, from Which the Figures Are Taken; and Some Short Historical Remarks on the Subject. To Which Are Added the Habits of the Principal Characters on the English Stage. 4 vols. London: Published by Thomas Jefferys, Geographer to His Majesty in the Strand.

1761   The Natural and Civil History of the French Dominions in North and South America. 2 Pts. in 1. London: Printed for T. Jefferys.

Jenks, Albert E.
1900   The Wild Rice Gatherers of the Upper Lakes: A Study in American Primitive Economics. Pp. 1013-1137 in *19th Annual Report of the Bureau of American Ethnology for the Years 1897-1898.* Washington.

Jenks, William L.
1926   The "Hutchins" Map of Michigan. *Michigan History Magazine* 10(36):358-373.

Jenness, Diamond
1935   The Ojibway Indians of Parry Sound, Their Social and Religious Life. *Anthropological Series 17, National Museum of Canada Bulletin* 78. Ottawa.

Jennings, Francis
1965   The Delaware Interregnum. *Pennsylvania Magazine of History and Biography* 89(2):174-198.

1967   The Indian Trade of the Susquehanna Valley. *Proceedings of the American Philosophical Society* 110(6):406-424. Philadelphia.

1968   Glory, Death, and Transfiguration: The Susquehannock Indians in the Seventeenth Century. *Proceedings of the American Philosophical Society* 112(1):15-53. Philadelphia.

1971   Virgin Land and Savage People. *American Quarterly* 23(4):519-541.

1975   The Invasion of America: Indians, Colonialism, and the Cant of Conquest. Chapel Hill: University of North Carolina Press.

Jeske, John A.
1927   The Grand River Mound Group and Camp Site. *Bulletin of the Public Museum of the City of Milwaukee* 3(2):139-214. Milwaukee.

Joffe, Natalie F.
1940   The Fox of Iowa. Pp. 259-332 in Acculturation in Seven American Indian Tribes. Ralph Linton, ed. New York and London: Appleton-Century.

Johnson, Amandus
1911   The Swedish Settlements on the Delaware; Their History and Relation to the Indians, Dutch and English, 1638-1664, with An Account of the South, the New Sweden, and the American Companies, and the Efforts of Sweden to Regain the Colony. 2 vols. Philadelphia: University of Pennsylvania Press.

————, ed.
1930   The Instruction for Johan Printz, Governor of New Sweden, "the First Constitution or Supreme Law of the States of Pennsylvania and Delaware." Philadelphia: The Swedish Colonial Society.

Johnson, Edward
1910   Johnson's Wonder Working Providence, 1628-1651. J. Franklin Jameson, ed. New York: Charles Scribner's Sons.

Johnson, Elden
1965   The Ojibwa. Pp. 398-401 in The Native Americans. Robert F. Spencer, Jesse D. Jennings et al., eds. New York: Harper and Row.

1969   Preliminary Notes on the Prehistoric Use of Wild Rice. *Minnesota Archaeologist* 30(2):31-43.

1969a   The Prehistoric Peoples of Minnesota. St. Paul: Minnesota Historical Society.

Johnson, Elias
1881   Legends, Traditions and Laws of the Iroquois, or Six Nations, and History of the Tuscarora Indians. Lockport, N.Y.: Union Printing and Publishing.

Johnson, Evelyn H.C.
1913   The Martin Settlement. Pp. 55-64 in Some of the Papers Read During the Years 1908-1911 at Meetings of the Brant Historical Society. Brantford, Ont.

1914   Chief John Smoke Johnson. *Papers and Records of the Ontario Historical Society* 12(9):102-113. Toronto.

1928   Grandfather and Father of E. Pauline Johnson. Pp. 44-47 in *36th Annual Archaeological Report for 1928. Being Part of Appendix to the Report of the Minister of Education, Ontario.* Toronto.

Johnson, Frank R.
1967-1968 The Tuscaroras; Mythology, Medicine, Culture. 2 vols. Murfreesboro, N.C.: Johnson Publishing Company.

Johnson, Frederick
1928   The Algonquin at Golden Lake, Ontario. *Museum of the American Indian, Heye Foundation. Indian Notes* 5(2):173-178. New York.

1929   Notes on the Ojibwa and Potawatomi of the Parry Island Reservation, Ontario. *Museum of the American Indian, Heye Foundation. Indian Notes* 6(3):193-216. New York.

1930   An Algonquin Band at Lac Barrière, Province of Québec. *Museum of the American Indian, Heye Foundation. Indian Notes* 7(1):27-39. New York.

————, ed.
1946   Man in Northeastern North America. *Papers of the Robert S. Peabody Foundation for Archaeology* 3. Andover, Mass.

Johnson, Ida A.
1919   The Michigan Fur Trade. Lansing: Michigan Historical Commission.

Johnson, Laurence A.
1957   The Indian Broom. *The Chronicle of the Early American Industries Association* 10(2):13-14, 24.

Johnson, Sir William
1921-1965 The Papers of Sir William Johnson. James Sullivan et al., eds. 15 vols. Albany: University of the State of New York.

Johnson, William
1972   The Late Woodland Period in Northwestern Pennsylvania: A Preliminary Survey and Analysis. (Paper Read at the Central States Anthropological Association Symposium on Archaeology of Lake Erie, March 1972.)

Johnston, Charles M.
1962   An Outline of Early Settlement in the Grand River Valley. *Ontario History* 54(1):43-67.

1963   Joseph Brant, the Grand River Lands and the Northwest Crisis. *Ontario History* 55(4):267-282.

————, ed.
1964   The Valley of the Six Nations: A Collection of Documents on the Indian Lands of the Grand River. Toronto: University of Toronto Press.

1965   William Claus and John Norton: A Struggle for Power in Old Ontario. *Ontario History* 57(2):101-108.

1967   Brant County: A History, 1784-1945. Toronto: Oxford University Press.

Johnston, James H.
1970   Race Relations in Virginia and Miscegenation in the South, 1776-1860. Amherst: University of Massachusetts Press.

Johnston, John
1820   Account of the Present State of the Indian Tribes Inhabiting Ohio. *Archaeologia Americana: Transactions and Collections of the American Antiquarian Society* 1:269-299. Worcester, Mass. (Reprinted: Pp. 186-192 in John Johnston and the Indians, by Leonard U. Hill, Stoneman Press, Columbus, 1957.)

Johnston, Richard B.
1968   Archaeology of Rice Lake, Ontario. *National Museum of Canada Anthropology Paper* 19. Ottawa.

1968a   The Archaeology of the Serpent Mounds Site. *Royal Ontario Museum, Art and Archaeology Division Occasional Papers* 10. Toronto.

Jones, Arthur E.
1907   The Site of the Mascoutin. *Proceedings of the State Historical Society of Wisconsin* 54:175-182. Madison.

1909   "8Endake Ehen" or Old Huronia. *5th Report of the Bureau of Archives for the Province of Ontario for 1908.* Toronto.

Jones, Augustus
1791   [Map of Grand River Tract.] (Plan No. 2913 in Legal Surveys Division, Department of Energy, Mines and Resources, Ottawa.)

Jones, David
1774   A Journal of Two Visits Made to Some Nations of Indians on the West Side of the River Ohio, in the Years 1772-1773. Burlington, N.J.: Isaac Collins.

Jones, Electa F.
1854   Stockbridge, Past and Present; or, Records of an Old Mission Station. Springfield, Mass.: S. Bowles.

Jones, Hiram W.
1872   Monthly Report of Quapaw Special Agency I.T., 5th March 1872. (Manuscript in Quapaw: Agents' Reports, Indian Archives Division, Oklahoma Historical Society, Oklahoma City.)

1874   [Letters to Enoch Hoag Dated 3/2/1874 and 7/10/1874.] (Manuscripts in Quapaw: Indians, New York, Indian Archives Division, Oklahoma Historical Society, Oklahoma City.)

1875   [Letter to Edward P. Smith, Commissioner of Indian Affairs, Nov. 11, 1875.] (Manuscript in Quapaw: Indians, Cayuga, Indian Archives Division, Oklahoma Historical Society, Oklahoma City.)

1877   [Letter to J.Q. Smith, Commissioner of Indian Affairs, Dated Quapaw Agency, Feb. 1, 1877.] (Manuscript in Quapaw: Agents' Reports, Indian Archives Division, Oklahoma Historical Society, Oklahoma City.)

Jones, Hugh
1700   [Part of a Letter from the Reverend Mr. Hugh Jones to the Reverend Dr. Benjamin Woodroofe, F.R.S. Concerning Several Observables in Maryland.] *Philosophical Transactions of the Royal Society of London for the Year 1699,* Vol. 21:436-442. London.

Jones, Peter
1860   Life and Journals of Kah-ke-wa-quo-nā-by: (Rev. Peter Jones), Wesleyan Missionary. Toronto: A. Green.

1861   History of the Ojebway Indians; with Especial Reference to Their Conversion to Christianity. London: A.W. Bennett.

Jones, Volney H.
1968   Corn from the McKees Rocks Village Site. *Pennsylvania Archaeologist* 38(1-4):81-86.

Jones, William
1907   Fox Texts. *Publications of the American Ethnological Society* 1. Leiden, The Netherlands.

1911   Algonquian (Fox). Pp. 735-873 in Vol. 1 of Handbook of American Indian Languages. Franz Boas, ed. *Bureau of American Ethnology Bulletin* 40. Washington.

1913   Kickapoo Ethnological Notes. *American Anthropologist* 15(2):332-335.

1915   Kickapoo Tales. *Publications of the American Ethnological Society* 9. Leiden, The Netherlands.

1917-1919 Ojibwa Texts. Truman Michelson, ed. 2 vols. *Publications of the American Ethnological Society* 7. Leiden, The Netherlands.

1939   Ethnography of the Fox Indians. Margaret W. Fisher, ed. *Bureau of American Ethnology Bulletin* 125. Washington.

Jordan, Douglas F.
1960   The Bull Brook Site in Relation to "Fluted Point" Manifestations in Eastern North America. (Unpublished Ph.D. Dissertation in Anthropology, Harvard University, Cambridge, Mass.)

Jordan, John W., ed.
1913   Journal of James Kenny, 1761-1763. *Pennsylvania Magazine of History and Biography* 37(1):1-47, (2):152-201.

Josselin de Jong, J.P.B. de
1913   Original Odžibwe-Texts. *Baessler-Archiv*, Beiheft 5:1-54.

Jouve, Odoric Marie
1915   Les Franciscains et le Canada, 1: L'établissement de la foi, 1615-1629. Quebec: Couvent des SS Stigmates.

Juet, Robert
1909   From "The Third Voyage of Master Henry Hudson," 1610. Pp. 11-28 in Narratives of New Netherland, 1609-1664. J. Franklin Jameson, ed. New York: Charles Scribner's Sons. (Reprinted: Barnes and Noble, New York, 1967.)

1910   The Third Voyage of Master Henry Hudson Toward Nova Zembla... [1609]. Edward H. Hall, ed. Pp. 227-346 in *15th Annual Report of the American Scenic and Historic Preservation Society*. Albany, N.Y.

Jukes, Joseph B.
1842   Excursions in and about Newfoundland, during the Years 1839 and 1840. 2 vols. London: J. Murray. (Reprinted: Canadiana House, Toronto.)

Jury, Wilfrid, and W. Sherwood Fox
1947   St. Ignace, Canadian Altar of Martyrdom: Third Campaign of Excavations, 1946. *Transactions of the Royal Society of Canada*, 3d ser., sect. 2, Vol. 41:55-78. Ottawa.

Jury, Wilfrid, and Elsie M. Jury
1954   Sainte-Marie Among the Hurons. Toronto: Oxford University Press.

1955   Saint Louis: Huron Village and Jesuit Mission Site. *University of Western Ontario, Museum of Indian Archaeology Bulletin* 10. London, Ont.

Kalm, Pehr
1935   Pehr Kalm's Description of Maize, How it is Planted and Cultivated in North America, Together with the Many Uses of this Crop Plant [1751-1752]. E. Larsen, trans. *Agricultural History* 9(2):98-117.

1966   The America of 1750: Peter Kalm's Travels in North America; The English Version of 1770. Adolph B. Benson, ed. 2 vols. New York: Dover Publications.

Kane, Paul
1859   Wanderings of an Artist Among the Indians of North America, from Canada to Vancouver's Island and Oregon Through the Hudson's Bay Company's Territory and Back Again. London: Longman, Brown, Green, Longmans and Roberts. (Reprinted: The Radisson Society of Canada, Toronto, 1925; University of Texas, 1971.)

Kappler, Charles J., comp.
1904-1941 Indian Affairs: Laws and Treaties. 5 vols. Washington: U.S. Government Printing Office. (Reprinted: AMS Press, New York, 1971.)

Karpinski, Louis C.
1931   Bibliography of the Printed Maps of Michigan, 1802-1860. Lansing: Michigan Historical Commission.

Keating, William H.
1824   Narrative of an Expedition to the Source of St. Peter's River, Lake Winnepeck, Lake of the Woods, etc. etc. Performed in the Year 1823 Under the Command of Stephen H. Long, Major U.S.T.E. 2 vols. Philadelphia: H.C. Carey and I. Lea.

Keesing, Felix M.
1939   The Menomini Indians of Wisconsin: A Study of Three Centuries of Cultural Contact and Change. *Memoirs of the American Philosophical Society* 10. Philadelphia.

Kehoe, Alice B.
1962   A Hypothesis on the Origin of Northeastern American Pottery. *Southwestern Journal of Anthropology* 18(1):20-29.

1971   Small Boats Upon the North Atlantic. Pp. 275-292 in Man Across the Sea: Problems of Pre-Columbian Contacts. C.L. Riley et al., eds. Austin: University of Texas Press.

Kellar, James H.
1956   An Archaeological Survey of Spencer County. Indianapolis: Indiana Historical Bureau.

1967   Material Remains. Pp. 431-487 in Vol. 2 of Angel Site: Glenn A. Black, ed. 2 vols. Indianapolis: Indiana Historical Society.

Kellaway, William
1961   The New England Company, 1649-1776: Missionary Society to the American Indians. New York: Barnes and Noble.

Kelley, J. Charles
1952   Some Geographic and Cultural Factors Involved in Mexican-Southeastern Contacts. Pp. 139-144 in Vol. 3 of Indian Tribes of Aboriginal America. Sol Tax, ed. Selected Papers of the 29th International Congress of Americanists. 4 vols. Chicago: University of Chicago Press.

1955   Juan Sabeata and Diffusion in Aboriginal Texas. *American Anthropologist* 57(5):981-995.

Kellogg, Louise (Phelps)
1908   The Fox Indians During the French Regime. Pp. 142-188 in *Proceedings of the State Historical Society of Wisconsin for 1907*. Madison.

————, ed.
1916   Frontier Advance on the Upper Ohio, 1778-1779. *Collections of the State Historical Society of Wisconsin 23, Draper Series*, Vol. 4. Madison.

————, ed.
1917   Early Narratives of the Northwest, 1634-1699. New York: Charles Scribner's Sons.

1925   The French Regime in Wisconsin and the Northwest. Madison: The State Historical Society of Wisconsin.

1935   The British Regime in Wisconsin and the Northwest. Madison: The State Historical Society of Wisconsin.

Kelly, G.L.
1954   The History of the St. Ignatius Mission, Montana. (Unpublished M.A. Thesis in History, University of Montana, Missoula.)

Kemper, Charles E., ed.
1921   Documents Relating to Early Projected Swiss Colonies in the Valley of Virginia, 1706-1709. *Virginia Magazine of History and Biography* 29(1):1-17.

Kendall, Edward A.
1809   Travels Through the Northern Parts of the United States, in the Years 1807 and 1808. 3 vols. New York: I. Riley.

Kendall, James
1812   A Sermon, Delivered Before the Society for Propagating the Gospel Among the Indians and Others in North America. Boston: J. Eliot, Jr.

Kendeigh, S. Charles
1961   Animal Ecology. Englewood Cliffs, N.J.: Prentice-Hall.

1974   Ecology with Special Reference to Animals and Man. Englewood Cliffs, N.J.: Prentice-Hall.

Kennedy, Clyde C.
1967   Preliminary Report on the Morrison's Island-6 Site. *Anthropological Series 72, National Museum of Canada Bulletin* 206:100-125. Ottawa.

Kenny, Hamill T.
1961   The Origin and Meaning of the Indian Place Names of Maryland. Baltimore: Waverly Press.

Kent, Barry C., Ira F. Smith, III, and Catherine McCann, eds.
1971   Foundations of Pennsylvania Prehistory. *Pennsylvania Historical and Museum Commission, Anthropological Series* 1. Harrisburg.

846

Kent, Donald H., and Merle H. Deardorff
1960   John Adlum on the Allegheny: Memoirs for the Year 1794. *Pennsylvania Magazine of History and Biography* 84(3):265-324, (4):435-480.

Kenyon, I.T.
1972   Neutral Villages in the Hamilton Region. (Paper Presented at the Neutral Symposium, Canadian Archaeological Association, Saint John's, Newfoundland.)

Kenyon, Walter A.
1961   The Swan Lake Site. *Royal Ontario Museum, Art and Archaeology Division, Occasional Paper* 3:1-36. Toronto.

1966   A Bibliography of Ontario Archaeology. *Ontario Archaeology* 9:35-62.

1968   The Miller Site. *Royal Ontario Museum, Art and Archaeology Division, Occasional Paper* 14. Toronto.

Kidd, Kenneth E.
1949   The Excavation of Ste. Marie I. Toronto: University of Toronto Press.

1951   Burial of an Ojibwa Chief, Muskoka District, Ontario. *Pennsylvania Archaeologist* 21(1-2):3-8.

1952   Sixty Years of Ontario Archeology. Pp. 71-82 in Archeology of Eastern United States. James B. Griffin, ed. Chicago: University of Chicago Press.

1953   The Excavation and Historical Identification of a Huron Ossuary. *American Antiquity* 18(4):359-379.

1969   Historic Site Archaeology in Canada. *National Museum of Canada Anthropology Paper* 22. Ottawa.

Kilby, William H.
1888   The Passamaquoddy Tribe of Indians. Pp. 483-489 in Eastport and Passamaquoddy: A Collection of Historical and Biographical Sketches. William H. Kilby, ed. Eastport, Me.: E.E. Shead.

Kimball, James
1878   The Exploration of the Merrimack River, 1638 by Order of the General Court of Massachusetts, with a Plan of the Same. *Historical Collections of the Essex Institute* 14(3):153-171. Salem, Mass.

King, Joseph B.
1915   The Ottawa Indians in Kansas and Oklahoma. *Collections of the Kansas State Historical Society for 1913-1914,* Vol. 13:373-378. Topeka.

King, Richard
1847   Narrative of a Journey to the Shores of the Arctic Ocean. London: George Routledge.

Kingsbury, Susan M., ed.
1906-1935 The Records of the Virginia Company of London. 4 vols. Washington: U.S. Government Printing Office.

Kinietz, W. Vernon
1940   The Indians of the Western Great Lakes, 1615-1760. *University of Michigan Museum of Anthropology, Occasional Contributions* 10. Ann Arbor.

1946   Delaware Culture Chronology. *Indiana Historical Society, Prehistory Research Series* 3(1):1-143. Indianapolis.

1947   Chippewa Village: The Story of Katikitegon. *Cranbrook Institute of Science Bulletin* 25. Bloomfield Hills, Mich.

Kinnaird, Lawrence, ed.
1946-1949 Spain in the Mississippi Valley, 1765-1794: Translations of Materials from the Spanish Archives in the Bancroft Library. *Annual Report of the American Historical Association for 1945.* Vols. 2-4. Washington: U.S. Government Printing Office.

Kinsey, W. Fred, III
1959   Recent Excavations on Bare Island in Pennsylvania: The Kent-Hally Site. *Pennsylvania Archaeologist* 29(3-4):109-133.

1971   Faucett Site: Chronology and Settlement and its Relationship to the Archaeology of the Northeast. *Bulletin of the Eastern States Archaeological Federation* 30:13. Andover, Mass.

Kinsey, W. Fred, III, and Jeffrey R. Graybill
1971   Murry Site and its Role in Lancaster and Funk Phases of Shenk's Ferry Culture. *Pennsylvania Archaeologist* 41(4):7-43.

Kirkland, Samuel
1764-1804 [Kirkland Papers.] (Manuscripts in Hamilton College Library, Hamilton, N.Y.)

Kittredge, George L., ed.
1913   Letters of Samuel Lee [1690] and Samuel Sewall [1691] Relating to New England and the Indians. *Publications of the Colonial Society of Massachusetts* 14:142-186. Boston.

Klingberg, Frank J., ed.
1956   The Carolina Chronicle of Dr. Francis Le Jau, 1706-1717. *University of California Publications in History* 53. Berkeley.

Klopfenstein, Carl G.
1957   The Removal of the Wyandots from Ohio. *Ohio Historical Quarterly* 66(2):119-136.

Kluckhohn, Clyde
1939   The Place of Theory in Anthropological Studies. *Philosophy of Science* 6(3):328-344.

1944   Navaho Witchcraft. *Papers of the Peabody Museum of American Archaeology and Ethnology, Harvard University* 22(2). Cambridge, Mass.

Kneale, Albert H.
1950   Indian Agent: An Autobiographical Sketch. Caldwell, Ida.: Paxton Printers.

Kneberg, Madeline D.
1956   Some Important Projectile Point Types Found in the Tennessee Area. *Tennessee Archaeologist* 12(1):17-28.

Knowles, Nathaniel
1940   The Torture of Captives by the Indians of Eastern North America. *Proceedings of the American Philosophical Society* 82(2):151-225. Philadelphia.

Kochan, Edward
1961   Riverhaven Sites No. 1 and No. 2, Grand Island, New York. *New York State Archaeological Association Bulletin* 22(13-14). Ossining.

Kohl, Johann G.
1857   Reisen im Nordwesten der Vereinigten Staaten. New York: D. Appleton.

1860   Kitchi-Gami: Wanderings Round Lake Superior. London: Chapman and Hall. (Reprinted: Ross and Haines, Minneapolis, 1956.)

Kraft, Herbert C.
1970   The Miller Field Site, Warren County, N.J.: A Study in Prehistoric Archaeology. South Orange, N.J.: Seton Hall University Press.

1970a   Prehistoric Indian House Patterns in New Jersey. *Bulletin of the Archeological Society of New Jersey* 26:1-11. Trenton.

1974   The Plenge Site: A Paleo-Indian Occupation Site in New Jersey. *Archaeology of Eastern North America* 1(1):56-117. Attleboro, Mass.

1975   The Archaeology of the Tocks Island Area. South Orange, N.J.: Seton Hall University Museum.

847

1975a   The Late Woodland Pottery of the Upper Delaware Valley: A Survey and Reevaluation. *Archaeology of Eastern North America* 3(1):101-140. Attleboro, Mass.

Krauskopf, Frances, ed.
1955   Ouiatanon Documents. *Publications of the Indiana Historical Society* 18(2):[131]-234. Indianapolis.

Kremens, Jack
1940   Pamunkey Animals. Pamunkey Plants and Agriculture. Pamunkey Birds. (Manuscripts 170(21:4F2t, 4F2i, 4F2e) in the Library of the American Philosophical Society, Philadelphia.)

Kroeber, Alfred L.
1939   Cultural and Natural Areas of Native North America. *University of California Publications in American Archaeology and Ethnology* 38. Berkeley.

———, ed.
1953   Anthropology Today: An Encyclopedic Inventory. Chicago: University of Chicago Press.

Kurath, Gertrude (Prokosch)
1951   Local Diversity in Iroquois Music and Dance. *Bureau of American Ethnology Bulletin* 149(6):109-137. Washington.

1953   An Analysis of the Iroquois Eagle Dance and Songs. Pp. 223-306 in The Iroquois Eagle Dance: An Offshoot of the Calumet Dance, by William N. Fenton. *Bureau of American Ethnology Bulletin* 156. Washington.

1954   Onondaga Ritual Parodies. *Journal of American Folklore* 67(266):404-406.

1956   Songs and Dances of Great Lakes Indians. (Ethnic Folkways Records Monograph Series, LP 4003) New York: Folkways Records.

1957   Catholic Hymns of Michigan Indians. *Anthropological Quarterly* 30(2):31-44.

1961   Effects of Environment on Cherokee-Iroquois Ceremonialism, Music and Dance. Pp. 173-195 in Symposium on Cherokee and Iroquois Culture. William N. Fenton and John Gulick, eds. *Bureau of American Ethnology Bulletin* 180. Washington.

1962   The Iroquois Bear Society: Ritual Drama. *American Indian Tradition* 8(2):84-85.

1964   Iroquois Music and Dance: Ceremonial Arts of Two Seneca Longhouses. *Bureau of American Ethnology Bulletin* 187:1-259. Washington.

1966   Michigan Indian Festivals. Ann Arbor, Mich.: Ann Arbor Publishers.

1968   Dance and Song Rituals of Six Nations Reserve, Ontario. *Folklore Series 4, National Museum of Man Bulletin* 220:3-205. Ottawa.

Kurath, Gertrude (Prokosch), and Jane Willets
[1955]   Religious Customs of Modern Michigan Algonquians. (Manuscript No. 104, in Library of the American Philosophical Society, Philadelphia.)

LHC = French, Benjamin F., ed.
1846-1853   Historical Collections of Louisiana, Embracing Translations of Many Rare and Valuable Documents Relating to the Natural, Civil, and Political History of that State. 5 vols. New York: Wiley and Putnam.

Lacombe, Albert
1874   Dictionnaire et grammaire de la langue des Cris. 2 vols. in 1. Montreal: C.O. Beauchemin et Valois.

Laet, Joannes de
1625   Nieuwe Wereldt, ofte Beschrijvinghe van West-Indien. Leiden, The Netherlands: I. Elzevier.

1633   Novus orbis seu descriptionis Indiae occidentalis, libri XVIII. Leiden, The Netherlands: I. Elzevier.

1841   Extracts from the New World, or a Description of the West Indies. *Collections of the New York Historical Society,* 2d ser., Vol. 1:281-316. New York.

1909   From the "New World," by Johan de Laet, 1625, 1630, 1633, 1640. Pp. 29-60 in Narratives of New Netherland, 1609-1664. J. Franklin Jameson, ed. New York: Charles Scribner's Sons. (Reprinted: Barnes and Noble, New York, 1967.)

Lafitau, Joseph-François
1724   Moeurs des sauvages amériquains, comparées aux moeurs des premiers temps. 2 vols in 1. Paris: Saugrain l'aîné.

La Flesche, Francis
1932   A Dictionary of the Osage Language. *Bureau of American Ethnology Bulletin* 109. Washington.

LaFontaine, Urgel
[1866-1907]   Histoire du Lac. (Manuscript in 23 Volumes in the Archives of the Séminaire de Saint-Sulpice of Montréal, Montreal.)

Lahontan, Louis Armand de Lom d'Arce de
1703   Nouveaux voyages de Mr. le baron de Lahontan dans l'Amérique septentrionale. 2 vols. in 1. The Hague: Frères l'Honoré.

1905   New Voyages to North America by the Baron de Lahontan [1703]. Reuben G. Thwaites, ed. 2 vols. Chicago: A.C. McClurg.

1940   Collection Oakes: Nouveaux documents de Lahontan sur le Canada et la Terre-neuve. Gustave Lanctot, ed. Ottawa: J.O. Patenaude.

Laidlaw, George E.
1922   Ojibwa Myths and Tales. Pp. 84-99 in 23d *Annual Archaeological Report for 1921-1922, Being Part of Appendix to the Report of the Minister of Education, Ontario.* Toronto.

Lajeunesse, Ernest J., ed.
1960   The Windsor Border Region, Canada's Southernmost Frontier: A Collection of Documents. Toronto: The Champlain Society.

Lake, Ernest L.
1966   Pioneer Reminiscences of the Upper Ottawa Valley Commemorating Triple Centennial Years of St. John the Evangelist Church, Eganville, Ont. Ottawa: Le Droit.

Lamb, E.E.
1960   [Letter to P.L. Fickinger, Muskogee Area Director, from E.E. Lamb, Supervisory Field Representative, Quapaw Area Field Office, Dated 3 May 1960.] (Manuscript Copy in Quapaw Agency, Bureau of Indian Affairs, Miami, Okla.)

La Morandière, Charles de
1962-1966   Histoire de la pêche française de la morue dans l'Amérique septentrionale. 3 vols. Paris: G.-P. Maisonneuve et Larose.

Landes, Ruth
1937   Ojibwa Sociology. *Columbia University Contributions to Anthropology* 29. New York. (Reprinted 1969.)

1938   The Ojibwa Woman. *Columbia University Contributions to Anthropology* 31. New York.

1963   Potawatomi Medicine. *Transactions of the Kansas Academy of Science* 66(4):553-599. Lawrence.

1968   Ojibwa Religion and the Midéwiwin. Madison: University of Wisconsin Press.

1970   The Prairie Potawatomi: Tradition and Ritual in the Twentieth Century. Madison: University of Wisconsin Press.

Landy, David
[1955]   [Fieldwork Among the Tuscaroras.] (Manuscript in Landy's Possession.)

1955a   Child Training in a Contemporary Iroquois Tribe. *Boston University Graduate Journal* 4(4):59-64.

1958   Tuscarora Tribalism and National Identity. *Ethnohistory* 5(3):250-284.

Lane, Sir Ralph
1589   Ralph Lane's Discourse on the First Colony. Pp. 737-747 in The Principall Navigations, Voiages and Discoveries of the English Nation, by Richard Hakluyt. (Reprinted in The Roanoke Voyages, 1584-1590. D.B. Quinn, ed. Vol. 1:255-294. Cambridge University Press for the Hakluyt Society, London, 1955.)

Lang, R.W.
1968   The Natural Environment and Subsistence Economy of the McKees Rocks Village Site. *Pennsylvania Archaeologist* 38(1-4):50-80.

Lang, William
1880   History of Seneca County, from the Close of the Revolutionary War to July, 1880... Springfield, Ohio: Transcript Printing Company.

Langdon, George D., Jr.
1966   Pilgrim Colony: A History of New Plymouth, 1620-1691. New Haven, Conn.: Yale University Press.

Lanman, James H.
1839   History of Michigan, Civil and Topographical, in a Compendious Form; with a View of the Surrounding Lakes. New York: E. French.

Lapham, Increase A.
1855   The Antiquities of Wisconsin. *Smithsonian Contributions to Knowledge* 7(4):5-95. Washington.

Lapham, Increase A., Levi Blossom, and George G. Dousman
1870   A Paper on the Number, Locality and Times of Removal of the Indians of Wisconsin. Milwaukee: Starr.

Larrabee, Edward McM.
1976   Recurrent Themes and Sequences in North American Indian-European Culture Contact. *Transactions of the American Philosophical Society* 66(7). Philadelphia.

La Salle, Nicolas de
1898   Relation of the Discovery of the Mississippi River; Written from the Narrative of Nicolas de La Salle, Otherwise Known as the Little M. de La Salle. Melville B. Anderson, trans. Chicago: The Caxton Club.

La Salle, Robert Cavelier de
1901   Relation of the Discoveries and Voyages of Cavelier de La Salle from 1679 to 1681, the Official Narrative. Melville B. Anderson, trans. Chicago: The Caxton Club.

1934   La Salle on the Illinois Country, 1680. Pp. 1-16 in The French Foundations, 1680-1693. Theodore C. Pease and Raymond C. Werner, eds. *Collections of the Illinois State Historical Library* 23. Springfield.

Latham, Robert G.
1862   Elements of Comparative Philology. London: Walton and Maberly.

Latorre, Felipe A., and Dolores L. Latorre
1976   The Mexican Kickapoo Indians. Austin and London: University of Texas Press.

Lauber, Almon W.
1913   Indian Slavery in Colonial Times Within the Present Limits of the United States. *Columbia University Studies in History, Economics, and Public Law* 54(3). New York.

Laurent, Joseph
1884   New Familiar Abenakis and English Dialogues, the First Ever Published on the Grammatical System, by Jos. Laurent, Abenakis Chief. Quebec: L. Brousseau.

Lawrence, John, M. Gaviller, and James Morris
1909   Exploration of Petun Village Sites. *Huron Institute Papers and Records* 1:11-18. Collingwood, Ont.

Lawson, John
1709   A New Voyage to Carolina; Containing the Exact Description and Natural History of That Country, Together with the Present State Thereof and a Journal of a Thousand Miles Traveled Through Several Nations of Indians, Giving a Particular Account of Their Customs, Manners, etc. London: [no publisher.]

1952   History of North Carolina... [1714]. Frances L. Harriss, ed. 2d ed. Richmond, Va.: Garrett and Massie.

1967   A New Voyage to Carolina [1709]. Hugh T. Lefler, ed. Chapel Hill: University of North Carolina Press.

Lawson, Publius V.
1900   The Outagamie Village at West Menasha. Pp. 204-211 in *Proceedings of the State Historical Society of Wisconsin for 1899*. Madison.

1907   The Habitat of the Winnebago, 1632-1822. Pp. 144-166 in Proceedings of the State Historical Society of Wisconsin for 1906. Madison.

1920   The Potawatomi. *Wisconsin Archaeologist* 19(2):40-116.

Leach, Douglas E.
1958   Flintlock and Tomahawk: New England in King Philip's War. New York: Macmillan. (Reprinted: W.W. Norton, New York, 1966.)

1966   The Northern Colonial Frontier, 1607-1763. New York: Holt, Rinehart and Winston.

1973   Arms for Empire: A Military History of the British Colonies in North America, 1607-1763. New York: Macmillan.

Leacock, Eleanor B.
1954   The Montagnais "Hunting Territory" and the Fur Trade. *Memoirs of the American Anthropological Association* 78. Menasha, Wis.

Le Boulanger, Jean B. *see* Le Boullenger, Jean B.

[Le Boullenger, Jean B.]
[1725]   [French-Illinois Dictionary.] (Manuscript in the John Carter Brown Library, Brown University, Providence, R.I.; Photostat Copy in Peabody Museum Library, Cambridge, Mass.)

[1740]   [French and Miami-Illinois Dictionary.] (Manuscript in the John Carter Brown Library, Brown University, Providence R.I.; Photostat Copy in Peabody Museum Library, Cambridge, Mass.)

Lechford, Thomas
1642   Plain Dealing: Or, Nevves from New-England: A Short View of New-Englands Present Government... London: Printed by W.E. and I.G. for N. Butter.

1885   Note-book Kept by Thomas Lechford, Esq., Lawyer, in Boston, Massachusetts Bay, from June 27, 1638 to July 29, 1641. Edward E. Hale, ed. *Archaeologia Americana: Transactions and Collections of the American Antiquarian Society* 7. Cambridge, Mass.

Le Clercq, Chrétien
1881   The First Establishment of the Faith in New France [1691]. John G. Shea, trans. 2 vols. New York: J.G. Shea

1910   New Relation of Gaspesia, with the Customs and Religion of the Gaspesian Indians [1691]. W.F. Ganong, ed. and trans. Toronto: The Champlain Society.

Lederer, John
1672 The Discoveries of John Lederer, in Three Several Marches from Virginia, to the West of Carolina, and Other Parts of the Continent, Begun in March 1669, and Ended in September, 1670. Together with a General Map of the Whole Territory Which He Transversed. Sir William Talbot, trans. London: Printed by J.C. for Samuel Heyrick.

1958 The Discoveries of John Lederer, 1669-70. With Unpublished Letters by and about Lederer to Governor John Winthrop, Jr., and an Essay on the Indians of Lederer's Discoveries. William P. Cumming, ed. Charlottesville: University of Virginia Press.

Lee, Chun-fen
1944 Land Utilization in the Middle Grand River Valley of Western Ontario. *Economic Geography* 20(2):130-151.

Lee, Thomas E.
1954 The First Sheguiandah Expedition, Manitoulin Island, Ontario. *American Antiquity* 20(2):101-111.

1956 Position and Meaning of a Radiocarbon Sample from the Sheguiandah Site, Ontario. *American Antiquity* 22(1):79.

1958 The Parker Earthwork, Corunna, Ontario. *Pennsylvania Archaeologist* 28(1):5-32.

1959 An Archaeological Survey of Southwestern Ontario and Manitoulin Island. *Pennsylvania Archaeologist* 29(2):80-92.

Lefler, Hugh T., and William S. Powell
1973 Colonial North Carolina: A History. New York: Charles Scribner's Sons.

Lefroy, J.H.
1853 On the Probable Number of the Native Indian Population of British America. *Canadian Journal of Industry, Science and Art* 1(9):193-198.

Leger, Mary C.
1929 The Catholic Indian Missions of Maine, 1611-1820. *Catholic University of America, Studies in American Church History* 8. Washington.

Lehmann-Hartleben, Karl
1943 Thomas Jefferson, Archaeologist. *American Journal of Archaeology*, 2d ser. Vol. 47(2):161-163.

Leighton, Alexander H.
1937 The Twilight of the Indian Porpoise Hunters. *Natural History* 40(June-December):410-416, 458.

Leland, Charles G.
1884 The Algonquin Legends of New England, or, Myths and Folk-Lore of the Micmac, Passamaquoddy, and Penobscot Tribes. Boston: Houghton Mifflin.

Leland, Charles G., and John D. Prince, trans.
1902 Kuloskap the Master, and Other Algonkin Poems. New York: Funk and Wagnalls.

Leland, Waldo G.
1932 Guide to Materials for American History in the Libraries and Archives of Paris. *Publications of the Carnegie Institution of Washington* 392(1). Washington.

Lemoine, Georges, ed.
1911 Dictionnaire français-algonquin. Quebec: L'Action Sociale. [False Title Page: Chicoatimi: G. Delisle, Bureau du journal "Le Travailleur," 1909.]

Lenig, Donald
1965 The Oak Hill Horizon and its Relation to the Development of Five Nations Iroquois Culture. *Researches and Transactions of the New York State Archaeological Association* 15(1):1-114. Buffalo.

Lescarbot, Marc
1907-1914 The History of New France [1618]. W.L. Grant, trans. 3 vols. Toronto: The Champlain Society.

1928 Nova Francia, or a Description of Acadia [1606]. Henry P. Biggar, ed. London: George Routledge and Sons.

LeSueur, Jacques
1952 History of the Calumet and of the Dance [1864]. *Contributions from the Museum of the American Indian, Heye Foundation* 12(5):1-22. New York.

Levesque, René, F. Fitz Osborne, and James V. Wright
1964 Le gisement de Batiscan: Notes sur des vestiges laissés par une peuplade de culture sylvicole inférieure dans la vallée du Saint-Laurent. *Canada. Musée National Etudes Anthropologiques* 6. Ottawa.

Levinge, Sir Richard G.A.
1846 Echoes from the Backwoods; or, Sketches of Transatlantic Life. London: H. Colburn.

Lewis, Alonzo, and James R. Newhall
1865 History of Lynn, Essex County, Massachusetts: Including Lynnfield, Saugus, Swampscot, and Nahant [1829]. Boston: J.L. Shorey.

Lewis, Cara L.
1971 A Handbook for Delmarva Archaeology. Dover: State of Delaware Office of Archaeology.

Lewis, Clifford M., and Albert J. Loomie
1953 The Spanish Jesuit Mission in Virginia, 1570-1572. Chapel Hill: University of North Carolina Press.

Lewis, Thomas M.N., and Madeline Kneberg
1959 The Archaic Culture in the Middle South. *American Antiquity* 25(2):161-183.

Lewis, Thomas M.N., and Madeline K. Lewis
1961 Eva: An Archaic Site. Knoxville: University of Tennessee Press.

L'Honoré Naber, Samuel P., ed.
1921 Henry Hudson's Reise door Robert Juet. 's-Gravenhage, The Netherlands: Linschoten Vereniging.

Lighthall, W.D.
1932 The False Plan of Hochelaga. *Transactions of the Royal Society of Canada*, 3d ser., Vol. 26(2):181-192. Ottawa.

Lilly, Eli
1937 Prehistoric Antiquities of Indiana: A Description of the More Notable Earthworks, Mounds, Implements, and Ceremonial Objects Left in Indiana by Our Predecessors. Indianapolis: Indiana Historical Society.

Lincoln, Charles H., ed.
1913 Narratives of the Indian Wars, 1675-1699. New York: Charles Scribner's Sons.

Lindeström, Peter
1925 Geographia Americae with an Account of the Delaware Indians Based on Surveys and Notes Made in 1654-1656 [1691]. Amandus Johnson, ed. Philadelphia: The Swedish Colonial Society.

Lindsay, Lionel St-George
1900 Notre Dame de la Jeune-Lorette en la Nouvelle-France. Montreal: La Cie. de Publication de la Revue Canadienne.

Linné, Sigvald
1955 Drei alte Waffen aus Nordamerika im Staatlichen Ethnographischen Museum in Stockholm. *Baessler-Archiv* N.F. 3:85-87.

1958 Three North American Indian Weapons in the Ethnographical Museum of Sweden. *The Connnoisseur* 112(567):34-36.

Lipkind, William
1945 Winnebago Grammar. New York: King's Crown Press.

L'Isle, Guillaume de
1702 Carte du Canada et du Mississipi. (Original in Ministère des Affaires Etrangères, Paris; Copy in Library of Congress, Washington.)

Livermore, Samuel T.
1877   A History of Block Island from its Discovery, in 1514, to the Present Time, 1876. Hartford, Conn.: Case, Lockwood, and Brainard. (Reprinted: Murray Printing Company, Forge Village, Mass., 1961.)

Livingston, Robert
1956   The Livingston Indian Records, 1666-1723. Lawrence H. Leder, ed. Gettysburg: Pennsylvania Historical Association.

Lloyd, T.G.B.
1874   On the "Beothucs," a Tribe of Red Indians, Supposed to Be Extinct, Which Formerly Inhabited Newfoundland. *Journal of the Royal Anthropological Institute of Great Britain and Ireland* 4(1):21-39. London.

Logan, Wilfred D.
1952   Graham Cave, an Archaic Site in Montgomery County, Missouri. *Missouri Archaeological Society Memoir* 2. Columbia.

Long, John
1791   Voyages and Travels of an Indian Interpreter and Trader Describing the Manners and Customs of the North American Indians; with an Account of the Posts Situated on the River Saint Laurence, Lake Ontario, etc. To Which is Added a Vocabulary of the Chippeway Language... a List of the Words in the Iroquois, Mohegan, Shawanee, and Esquimeaux Tongues, and a Table Showing the Analogy Between the Algonkin and Chippeway Languages. London: Printed for the Author.

Longfellow, Samuel, ed.
1886   Life of Henry Wadsworth Longfellow with Extracts from His Journals and Correspondence. 2 vols. Boston: Ticknor and Company.

Lopatin, Ivan A.
1960   Origin of the Native American Steam Bath. *American Anthropologist* 62(6):977-993.

Lopez, Julius
1961   The Areal Distribution and Complexities of "Abbot" Ceramics. *Bulletin of the Archeological Society of New Jersey* 18-19:7-11. Trenton.

Loskiel, George H.
1789   Geschichte der Mission der Evangelischen Brüder unter den Indianern in Nordamerika. Leipzig, Germany: P.G. Kummer.

1794   History of the Mission of the United Brethren Among Indians in North America. Christian Ignatius La Trobe, trans. 3 Pts. London: Printed for the Brethren's Society for the Furtherance of the Gospel.

Lounsbury, Floyd G.
1939-1973   [Fieldnotes on the Oneida, 1939-1940 at Oneida, Wis., and 1972-1973 at Southwold, Ont.; on Onondaga, 1948 at Onondaga Reservation, N.Y.; on Mohawk, Caughnawaga, Que., 1958; on Tuscarora, 1946, 1947, 1952 and 1954 at Lewiston, N.Y.; on Seneca, 1948 at Onondaga Reservation, N.Y.; on Cayuga, 1948, 1960 at Ohsweken; on Cherokee, 1941, at Tahlequah, Okla.] (Manuscripts in Lounsbury's Possession.)

1947   [Fieldnotes from Approximately 10 Days of Fieldwork with William Chew at the Tuscarora Reservation, Lewiston, N.Y.] (Manuscript in Lounsbury's Possession.)

1953   Oneida Verb Morphology. *Yale University Publications in Anthropology* 48. New Haven, Conn.

1960   Iroquois Place-names in the Champlain Valley. (Reprinted from the Report of the New York-Vermont Interstate Commission on the Lake Champlain Basin, 1960, Legislative Document 9:23-66.) Albany: University of the State of New York, State Education Department.

1961   Iroquois-Cherokee Linguistic Relations. (Symposium on Cherokee and Iroquois Culture 2) *Bureau of American Ethnology Bulletin* 180:9-17. Washington.

1964   The Structural Analysis of Kinship Semantics. Pp. 1073-1093 in Proceedings of the 9th International Congress of Linguists. Horace G. Lunt, ed. Cambridge, Mass., 1962. The Hague: Mouton.

1964a   The Formal Analysis of Crow- and Omaha-Type Kinship Terminologies. Pp. 351-393 in Explorations in Cultural Anthropology: Essays in Honor of George P. Murdock. Ward H. Goodenough, ed. New York: McGraw-Hill.

1968   One Hundred Years of Anthropological Linguistics. Pp. 150-225 in One Hundred Years of Anthropology. J.O. Brew, ed. Cambridge, Mass.: Harvard University Press.

1969   [Letter to Gordon M. Day.] (In Day's Possession.)

Love, William De Loss
1899   Samson Occom, and the Christian Indians of New England. Boston and Chicago: Pilgrim Press.

Lowie, Robert H.
1910   Notes Concerning New Collections. *Anthropological Papers of the American Museum of Natural History* 4(2):282. New York.

1954   Indians of the Plains. (American Museum of Natural History, Anthropological Handbook 1) New York: McGraw-Hill.

Luchterhand, Kubet
1970   Early Archaic Projectile Points and Hunting Patterns in the Lower Illinois Valley. *Illinois State Museum, Report of Investigations* 19. Springfield.

Luckenbach, Abraham
1917   Biography of Brother Abraham Luckenbach, Written by Himself and Left for His Dear Children [1850]. Pp. 131-180 in A History of the Moravian Mission Among the Indians on the White River in Indiana, by Harry M. Stocker. Bethlehem, Pa.: Times Publishing Company Printers.

Lucy, Charles L.
1959   Pottery Types of the Upper Susquehanna. *Pennsylvania Archaeologist* 29(1):28-37.

Lurie, Nancy O.
1944-1972   [Ethnographic Notes from Approximately 5 Years' Fieldwork Among the Winnebago of Wisconsin and Nebraska in Rural and Urban Settings.] (Manuscript in Lurie's Possession.)

1952   The Winnebago Indians: A Study in Cultural Change. (Unpublished Ph.D. Dissertation in Anthropology, Northwestern University, Evanston, Ill.)

1953   Winnebago Berdache. *American Anthropologist* 55(4):708-712.

1959   Indian Cultural Adjustment to European Civilization. Pp. 33-60 in Seventeenth-Century America: Essays in Colonial History. James M. Smith, ed. Chapel Hill: University of North Carolina Press. (Reprinted: W.W. Norton, New York, 1972.)

1960   Winnebago Protohistory. Pp. 790-808 in Culture and History: Essays in Honor of Paul Radin. Stanley Diamond, ed. New York: Columbia University Press.

1961   Mountain Wolf Woman: The Autobiography of a Winnebago Indian. Ann Arbor: University of Michigan Press.

1966   A Check List of (Winnebago) Treaty Signers by Clan Affiliation. *Journal of the Wisconsin Indians Research Institute* 2(1):50-73.

1968   Historical Background. Pp. 25-45 in The American Indian Today. Stuart Levine and Nancy O. Lurie, eds. Deland, Fla.: Everett Edwards. (Reprinted: Penguin Books, Baltimore, 1970.)

1972   Menominee Termination: Reservation to Colony. *Human Organization* 31(3):257-270.

Luther, Martin *see* Campanius, Johannes

Lutz, John J.
1906   The Methodist Missions Among the Indian Tribes in Kansas. *Transactions of the Kansas State Historical Society* 9(3):160-230. Topeka.

Lydekker, John W.
1938   The Faithful Mohawks. New York: Macmillan; Cambridge, England: The University Press.

Lyford, Carrie A.
1943   The Crafts of the Ojibwa (Chippewa). Willard W. Beatty, ed. *U.S. Office of Indian Affairs, Indian Handicrafts* 5. Washington.

Md. Arch. = Browne, William H. et al., eds.
1883-1970 Archives of Maryland. 71 vols. Baltimore: Maryland Historical Society.

MeHSC = Maine Historical Society
1831-1887 Collections. 1st ser., Vols. 1-10. Portland: The Society.

MHSC = Massachusetts Historical Society
1792-1915 Collections. 10 series. 70 vols. Cambridge and Boston: The Society.

MPA-F = Rowland, Dunbar, and Albert G. Saunders, eds.
1927-1932 Mississippi Provincial Archives: French Dominion, 1701-1743. 3 vols. Jackson: Mississippi Department of Archives and History.

MPCP = Hazard, Samuel, ed.
1838-1853 Minutes of the Provincial Council of Pennsylvania. 16 vols. Harrisburg: Theophilus Fenn.

MPHC = Michigan Pioneer and Historical Society
1877-1929 Collections and Researches. 40 vols. Lansing: The Society.

Macaulay, J.B.
1839   Report to Sir George Arthur on Indian Affairs. (Manuscript in Public Archives of Canada, Record Group 10, Vol. 718. Ottawa.)

McCallum, James D., ed.
1932   The Letters of Eleazar Wheelock's Indians. Hanover, N.H.: Dartmouth College Publications.

McCary, Ben C.
1950   The Rappahannock Indians. *Quarterly Bulletin of the Archaeological Society of Virginia* 5(1):1-16. Richmond.

1951   A Workshop Site of Early Man in Dinwiddie County, Virginia. *American Antiquity* 17(1):9-17.

1953   The Potts Site, Chickahominy River, New Kent County, Virginia. *Quarterly Bulletin of the Archaeological Society of Virginia* 8(1):1-11. Richmond.

1957   Indians in Seventeenth Century Virginia. (*Jamestown 350th Anniversary Historical Booklet* 18) Williamsburg, Va.: 350th Anniversary Celebration Corporation.

MacCord, Howard A.
1965   The De Shazo Site, King George County, Virginia (44 Kg 3). *Quarterly Bulletin of the Archaeological Society of Virginia* 19(4):98-104. Richmond.

1969   Camden: A Postcontact Indian Site in Caroline County. *Quarterly Bulletin of the Archaeological Society of Virginia* 24(1):1-55. Richmond.

MacCord, Howard A., Karl Schmitt, and Richard G. Slattery
1957   The Shepard Site Study (18 Mo 3) Montgomery County, Md. *Bulletin of the Archeological Society of Maryland* 1. Baltimore.

McCoy, Isaac
1835-1838 The Annual Register of Indian Affairs Within the Indian (or Western) Territory. 4 vols. Shawanoe Mission: J. Meeker.

1840   History of the Baptist Indian Missions: Embracing Remarks on the Former and Present Condition of the Aboriginal Tribes, Their Settlement Within the Indian Territory, and Their Future Prospects. Washington: W.M. Morrison.

MacCurdy, George G.
1899   Extent of Instruction in Anthropology in Europe and the United States. *Science* 10(260):910-917.

McDermott, John F., ed.
1949   Old Cahokia: A Narrative and Documents Illustrating the First Century of its History. J.F. McDermott, with Joseph P. Donnelly et al., eds. St. Louis: St. Louis Historical Documents Foundation.

McDonald, David
1899   Removal of the Potawatomi Indians from Northern Indiana; Embracing Also a Brief Statement of the Indian Policy of the Government and Other Historical Matter Relating to the Indian Question. Plymouth, Ind.: McDonald and Company.

MacDonald, George F.
1966   The Technology and Settlement Pattern of a Paleo-Indian Site at Debert, Nova Scotia. *Quaternaria* 8:59-73. Rome.

1968   Debert: A Paleo-Indian Site in Central Nova Scotia. *National Museum of Canada Anthropology Paper* 16. Ottawa.

McElroy, Ann (Searcy)
1965   [Fieldnotes, Kansas Potawatomi Study.] (Manuscript in Archives, Wisconsin State Historical Society, Madison.)

1965a   Contemporary and Traditional Potawatomi Childlife. (Unpublished B.A. Honors Thesis, Department of Anthropology, University of Kansas, Lawrence.)

McElvain, John
1829   An Abstract Exhibiting the Number of Indians in the Piqua Agency, Ohio... Taken November, 1829. (Manuscript of McElvain to T.L. McKenney in Letters Received by the Office of Indian Affairs, Record Group 75, Microcopy No. M234, Roll 669, Frame 0648, National Archives, Washington.)

McFeat, Tom F.S.
1962   Museum Ethnology and the Algonkian Project. *National Museum of Canada Anthropology Paper* 2. Ottawa.

1962a   Two Malecite Family Industries. *Anthropologica* n.s. 4(2):233-271. Ottawa.

McGee, WJ
1897   The Siouan Indians: A Preliminary Sketch. Pp. 153-204 in *15th Annual Report of the Bureau of American Ethnology for the Years 1893-1894*. Washington.

1897a   The Bureau of American Ethnology. Pp. 367-396 in The Smithsonian Institution, 1846-1896: The History of its First Half Century. George B. Goode, ed. Washington: DeVinne Press.

1898   A Muskwaki Bowl. *American Anthropologist* 11(3):88-91.

McGee, Harold F., Jr.
1972   Windigo Psychosis. *American Anthropologist* 74(1-2):244-246.

McGhee, Robert, and James A. Tuck
1975   An Archaic Sequence from the Strait of Belle Isle, Labrador. *Canada. National Museum of Man, Mercury Series, Archaeological Survey of Canada Paper* 34. Ottawa.

M'Gillivray, Duncan
1929   The Journal of Duncan M'Gillivray of the North West Company at Fort George on the Saskatchewan, 1794-1795. Arthur S. Morton, ed. Toronto: Macmillan.

MacGregor, J.G.
1969   Who Was Yellowhead? *Alberta Historical Review* 17(4):12-13.

McGregor, John C.
1958   The Pool and Irving Villages: A Study of Hopewell Occupation in the Illinois River Valley. Urbana: University of Illinois Press.

_____
1959   The Middle Woodland Period. *Illinois Archaeological Survey Bulletin* 1:21-26. Urbana.

McIlwaine, Henry R., ed.
1918-1919 Legislative Journals of the Council of Colonial Virginia. Richmond: Virginia State Library.

_____, ed.
1924   Minutes of the Council and General Court of Colonial Virginia, 1622-1632, 1670-1676; With Notes and Excerpts from Original Council and General Court Records, into 1683, Now Lost. Richmond: Virginia State Library.

_____, ed.
1925-1945 Executive Journals of the Council of Colonial Virginia. 5 vols. Richmond: Virginia State Library.

McIlwaine, Henry R., and J.P. Kennedy, eds.
1905-1915 Journals of the House of Burgesses of Virginia, 1619-1776. Richmond: Virginia State Library.

McIlwraith, Thomas F.
1947   On the Location of Cahiagué. *Transactions of the Royal Society of Canada*, 3d ser., sect. 2, Vol. 41:99-102. Ottawa.

McKenney, Thomas L., and James Hall
1849-1854 History of the Indian Tribes of North America, with Biographical Sketches and Anecdotes of the Principal Chiefs. 3 vols. Philadelphia: D. Rice and A.N. Hart.

_____
1933-1934 The Indian Tribes of North America, with Biographical Sketches and Anecdotes of the Principal Chiefs. Frederick W. Hodge, ed. 3 vols. Edinburgh: John Grant.

Mackenzie, Sir Alexander
1801   Voyages from Montreal, on the River St. Laurence, Through the Continent of North America, to the Frozen and Pacific Oceans in the Years 1789 and 1793; With a Preliminary Account of the Rise, Progress, and Present State of the Fur Trade of That Country. London: T. Cadell, Jr. and W. Davies.

McKenzie, Douglas H.
1967   The Graham Village Site: A Fort Ancient Settlement in the Hocking Valley, Ohio. Pp. 63-97 in Studies in Ohio Archaeology. Olaf Prufer, and Douglas H. McKenzie, eds. Cleveland: The Press of Western Reserve University.

McKenzie, Douglas H., and John E. Blank
[1976]   The Eiden Site: Late Woodland from the South-central Lake Erie Region. In The Late Prehistory of the Lake Erie Drainage Basin: A Symposium. David S. Brose, ed. *Scientific Papers of the Cleveland Museum of Natural History.* In Press.

Mackenzie, James B.
1882   A Treatise on the Six-Nations Indians. Toronto: Guardian Printing Office.

_____
1896   The Six-Nations Indians in Canada. Toronto: Hunter, Rose.

McKern, William C.
1928   The Neale and McClaughry Mound Groups. *Bulletin of the Public Museum of the City of Milwaukee* 3(3):215-416. Milwaukee.

_____
1930   The Kletzien and Nitschke Mound Groups. *Bulletin of the Public Museum of the City of Milwaukee* 3(4):417-572. Milwaukee.

_____
1937   A Hypothesis for the Asiatic Origin of the Woodland Culture Pattern. *American Antiquity* 3(2):138-143.

_____
1939   The Midwestern Taxonomic Method as an Aid to Archaeological Culture Study. *American Antiquity* 4(4):301-313.

_____
1942   The First Settlers of Wisconsin. *Wisconsin Magazine of History* 26(2):153-169.

_____
1945   Preliminary Report on the Upper Mississippi Phase in Wisconsin. *Bulletin of the Public Museum of the City of Milwaukee* 16(3):109-285. Milwaukee.

_____
1946   Aztalan. *Wisconsin Archaeologist* 27(2):41-52.

_____
1963   The Clam River Focus. *Milwaukee Public Museum Publications in Anthropology* 9. Milwaukee.

McKern, William C., and Robert E. Ritzenthaler
1945   Trait List of the Prehistoric Wisconsin Cultures. *Wisconsin Archaeologist* 26(4):66-79.

McKusick, Marshall B.
1964   Men of Ancient Iowa, as Revealed by Archaeological Discoveries. Ames: Iowa State University Press.

_____
1973   The Grant Oneota Village. *Office of the State Archaeologist of Iowa Report* 4. Iowa City.

McLean, John
1932   John McLean's Notes of a Twenty-five Years' Service in the Hudson Bay Territory [1849]. William S. Wallace, ed. Toronto: The Champlain Society.

MacLeod, William C.
1926   Piscataway Royalty: A Study in Stone Age Government and Inheritance Rulings. *Journal of the Washington Academy of Sciences* 16(11):301-309. Washington.

McMichael, Edward V.
1963   1963 Excavations at the Buffalo Site, 46-Pu-31. *West Virginia Archaeologist* 16:12-23.

_____
1964   1963 Excavations at the Buffalo Site, Putnam County, West Virginia. (Abstract.) *Bulletin of the Eastern States Archaeological Federation* 23(June):9. Andover, Mass.

_____
1966   Three Seasons' Work at the Buffalo Site, Putnam County, West Virginia. *Bulletin of the Eastern States Archaeological Federation* 25(May):11-12. Andover, Mass.

_____
1968   Introduction to West Virginia Archaeology. Morgantown: West Virginia Geological and Economic Survey.

_____
1971   Adena-East, an Appraisal of the More Easterly Extensions of the Spread of the Adena Phenomenon. Pp. 88-89 in Adena: The Seeking of an Identity. B.K. Swartz, ed. Muncie, Ind.: Ball State University Press.

McMurtrie, Douglas C., and Albert H. Allen
1930   Jotham Meeker: Pioneer Printer of Kansas; With a Bibliography of the Known Issues of the Baptist Mission Press at Shawanoe, Stockbridge, and Ottawa, 1834-1854. Chicago: Eyncourt Press.

MacNeish, Richard S.
1944   The Establishment of the Lewis Focus: The Archaeology of Southern Illinois. (Unpublished M.A. Thesis in Anthropology, University of Chicago, Chicago.)

_____
1947   A Preliminary Report on Coastal Tamaulipas, Mexico. *American Antiquity* 13(1):1-15.

_____
1952   Iroquois Pottery Types: A Technique for the Study of Iroquois Prehistory. *Anthropological Series 31, National Museum of Canada Bulletin* 124. Ottawa.

853

1952a The Archeology of the Northeastern United States. Pp. 46-58 in Archeology of the Eastern United States. James B. Griffin, ed. Chicago: University of Chicago Press.

1952b A Possible Early Site in the Thunder Bay District, Ontario. *Anthropological Series 32, National Museum of Canada Bulletin* 126:23-47. Ottawa.

1958 An Introduction to the Archaeology of Southeast Manitoba. *Anthropological Series 44, National Museum of Canada Bulletin* 157. Ottawa.

McNett, Charles, and Barbara McMillan
1974 Initial Season of the Upper Delaware Early Man Project. Washington: The American University. Mimeo.

McPherron, Alan
1967 The Juntunen Site and the Late Woodland Prehistory of the Upper Great Lakes Area. *University of Michigan Museum of Anthropology, Anthropological Papers* 30. Ann Arbor.

McPherson, Elizabeth (Gregory), ed.
1966 Nathaniel Batts, Landholder on Pasquotank River, 1660. *North Carolina Historical Review* 43(1):66-81.

Magnon de Terlaye, François-Auguste
[1755] Langue de[s] Loups. Follows p. 247 in [Dictionnaire onontagué-françois]. (Manuscript in Archives Indiennes, Notre-Dame de Montréal, Montreal.)

Magnusson, Magnus, and Hermann Pálssen, trans.
1965 The Vinland Sagas, the Norse Discovery of America. New York: New York University Press.

Maillard, Antoine S.
1758 An Account of the Customs and Manners of the Micmakis and Maricheets Savage Nations, Now Dependent on the Government of Cape-Breton. London: Printed for S. Hooper and A. Morley.

Maillard, Pierre
1864 Grammar of the Mikmaque Language of Nova Scotia. Joseph M. Bellenger, ed. (Shea's Library of American Linguistics 9) New York: Cramoisy Press.

Maine. Department of Indian Affairs
1970 Census of the Passamaquoddy Tribe, Peter Dana Point, Princeton, Maine, as of January 1, 1970. Augusta.

1971 Census of the Passamaquody Tribe, Pleasant Point, Perry, Maine, as of January 1, 1971. Augusta.

1971a Maine Indians: A Brief Summary. Mimeo.

Maine Historical Society
1869-1916 Documentary History of the State of Maine. 24 vols. Portland: LeFavor-Tower.

1902 Treaty with the Passamaquoddy Tribe of Indians, by the Commonwealth of Massachusetts, September 29, 1794. Pp. 98-102 in Vol. 8 of Documentary History of the State of Maine. 24 vols. Portland: LeFavor-Tower.

Malin, James C.
1921 Indian Policy and Westward Expansion. *Bulletin of the University of Kansas, Humanistic Studies* 2(3). Lawrence.

Malone, Patrick M.
1973 Changing Military Technology Among the Indians of Southern New England, 1600-1677. *American Quarterly* 25(1):48-63.

Mandelbaum, David G.
1940 The Plains Cree. *Anthropological Papers of the American Museum of Natural History* 37(2):155-316. New York.

Mandeville, Sieur de
1740 Carte particulière d'une partie de la belle rivière et de la routte que le détachemt du Canada a tenu.... Relevée à l'estime par le sr Delery fils et dessiné par le sr de Mandeville. (Original in Bureau de Service Hydrographique, 54-C-4044, Paris; Copy in Library of Congress, Washington.)

Mangelsdorf, Paul C., and Carlyle E. Smith, Jr.
1949 New Archaeological Evidence on Evolution in Maize. *Harvard University, Botanical Museum Leaflets* 13(8):213-247.

Mangelsdorf, Paul C., Richard S. MacNeish, and Walton C. Galinat
1956 Archaeological Evidence on the Diffusion and Evolution of Maize in Northwestern Mexico. *Harvard University, Botanical Museum Leaflets* 17(6):151-177.

Manley, Henry S.
1947 Buying Buffalo from the Indians. *Proceedings of the New York State Historical Association 45, New York History* 28:313-329. Cooperstown.

Manners, Robert A.
1962 Pluralism and the American Indian. *América Indígena* 22(1):25-38.

Mansfield, Arthur W.
1963 Seals of Arctic and Eastern Canada. *Bulletin of the Fisheries Research Board of Canada* 137. Ottawa.

Manson, Carl
1948 Marcey Creek Site: An Early Manifestation in the Potomac Valley. *American Antiquity* 13(3):223-227.

Margry, Pierre, ed.
1876-1886 Découvertes et établissements des Français dans l'ouest et dans le sud de l'Amérique septentrionale, 1614-1754. Mémoires et documents originaux. 6 vols. Paris: D. Jouaust.

Marie de l'Incarnation
1967 Word from New France: The Selected Letters of Marie de l'Incarnation, 1633-1671. Joyce Marshall, trans. and ed. Toronto: Oxford University Press.

Marsh, Cutting
1859 [Rev. Cutting Marsh on the Stockbridges.] *Reports and Collections of the State Historical Society of Wisconsin for the Years 1857 and 1858,* Vol. 4:299-301. Madison.

Marshall, Ingebord
1973 A Study of Beothuk Decorated Bone Pieces. *Newfoundland Quarterly* 6(1):17-25.

Marston, Morrell
1912 Letter to Reverend Dr. Jedidiah Morse from Major Marston, U.S.A., Commanding at Ft. Armstrong, Ill., November, 1820. Pp. 137-182 in Vol. 2 of The Indian Tribes of the Upper Mississippi Valley and the Region of the Great Lakes. Emma H. Blair, ed. 2 vols. Cleveland: Arthur H. Clark.

Martijn, Charles A.
1969 Ile aux Basques and the Prehistoric Iroquois Occupation of Southern Quebec. *Cahiers d'Archéologie Québecoise* (mars):55-114.

Martin, Félix
1885 The Life of Father Isaac Jogues, Missionary Priest of the Society of Jesus, Slain by the Mohawk Iroquois, in the Present State of New York, Oct. 18, 1646. New York: Benziger Brothers.

Marye, William B.
1935 Piscattaway. *Maryland Historical Magazine* 30(3):183-240.

1936-1938 Indian Paths of the Delmarva Peninsula. *Bulletin of the Archaeological Society of Delaware* 2(3):5-22, (4):5-27, (5):1-15, app.:1-25, (6):4-11. Wilmington.

1938-1939 The Wicomiss Indians of Maryland. *American Antiquity* 4(2):146-152, 5(1):51-55.

1940 Indian Towns of the Southeastern Part of Sussex County, Delaware. Wilmington: Archaeological Society of Delaware.

Maryland (Colony) Council
1885-1912 Proceedings of the Council of Maryland, 1636-1770. 11 vols. (Archives of Maryland 3) Baltimore: Maryland Historical Society.

Mason, John
1736 A Brief History of the Pequot War: Especially of the Memorable Taking of Their Fort at Mistick in Connecticut in 1637. Boston: S. Kneeland and T. Green. (Reprinted: University Microfilms, Ann Arbor, Mich., 1966.)

Mason, Otis T.
1896 Influence of Environment Upon Human Industries or Arts. Pp. 639-665 in *Annual Report of the Smithsonian Institution for 1895.* Washington.

1907 Environment. Pp. 427-430 in Vol. 1 of Handbook of American Indians North of Mexico. Frederick W. Hodge, ed. 2 vols. *Bureau of American Ethnology Bulletin* 30. Washington.

Mason, Ronald J.
1962 The Paleo-Indian Tradition in Eastern North America. *Current Anthropology* 3(3):227-278.

1966 Two Stratified Sites on the Door Peninsula of Wisconsin. *University of Michigan Museum of Anthropology, Anthropological Papers* 26. Ann Arbor.

1967 The North Bay Component at Porte Des Morts Site, Door County, Wisconsin. *Wisconsin Archaeologist* 48(4):267-345.

1969 Laurel and North Bay: Diffusional Networks in the Upper Great Lakes. *American Antiquity* 34(3):295-302.

1970 Hopewell, Middle Woodland, and the Laurel Culture: A Problem in Archaeological Classification. *American Anthropologist* 72(4):802-815.

1971 Progress Report on Lawrence University Excavation (Third Season) at Rock Island State Park, Door County, Wisconsin: 1971. (Manuscript with Maps and Stratigraphic Profiles in Lawrence College, Appleton, Wis.)

1974 Huron Island and the Island of the Poutouatamis. Pp. 149-156 in Aspects of Upper Great Lake Anthropology: Papers in Honor of Lloyd A. Wilford. Elden Johnson, ed. St. Paul: University of Minnesota Press.

Mason, Ronald J., and Carol Irwin
1960 An Eden-Scottsbluff Burial in Northeastern Wisconsin. *American Antiquity* 26(1):43-57.

Massachusetts (Colony)
1853-1854 Records of the Governor and Company of the Massachusetts Bay in New England. Nathaniel B. Shurtleff, ed. 5 vols. in 6. Boston: William White.

Massachusetts. Commissioners
1849 Report of the Commissioners Relating to the Condition of the Indians in Massachusetts. Massachusetts. General Court. House of Representatives Doc. No. 46. Boston: [no publisher.]

1861 Report to the Governor and Council, Concerning the Indians of the Commonwealth Under the Act of April 6, 1859. John M. Earle, Commissioner. Massachusetts. Senate Document No. 96. Boston: William White.

Masson, Louis F.R.
1889-1890 Les Bourgeois de la Compagnie du Nord-Ouest; récits de voyages, lettres et rapports inédits relatifs au Nord-Ouest canadien. 2 vols. Quebec: A. Coté et Cie.

Mather, Cotton
1702 Magnalia Christi Americana: Or, the Ecclesiastical History of New-England; from its First Planting, in the Year 1620, unto the Year of Our Lord 1698. London: T. Parkhurst.

1913 Decennium Luctuosum: An History of Remarkable Occurrences in the Long War, Which New-England Hath Had with the Indian Savages, from the Year 1688 to the Year 1698. Pp. 169-300 in Narratives of the Indian Wars, 1675-1699. Charles H. Lincoln, ed. New York: Charles Scribner's Sons. (Reprinted in 1952.)

1966 Bonifacius: An Essay Upon the Good [1710]. David Levin, ed. Cambridge, Mass.: Belknap Press of Harvard University Press.

Mather, Increase
1677 A Relation of the Troubles Which Have Hapned in New-England, by Reason of the Indians There. From the Year 1614 to the Year 1675... Boston: John Foster.

Mathevet, Jean-Claude
1750 Mots Loups. (Manuscript in the Archives of Notre-Dame de Montréal, Montreal.)

Mathews, G.H.
1959 Proto-Siouan Kinship Terminology. *American Anthropologist* 61(2):252-278.

Matson, Nehemiah
1874 French and Indians of Illinois River. Princeton, Ill.: Republican Job Printing Establishment.

1878 Memories of Shaubena; With Incidents Relating to the Early Settlement of the West. Chicago: D.B. Cooke.

1882 Pioneers of Illinois, Containing a Series of Sketches Relating to Events That Occurred Previous to 1813. Chicago: Knight and Leonard.

Matthew, George F.
1892 Discoveries at a Village of the Stone Age at Bocabec, N.B. *Bulletin of the Natural History Society of New Brunswick* 2(10):4-29. Saint John.

Matthews, Albert
1913 The Indian Sachem Ninigret. *Publications of the Colonial Society of Massachusetts* 14:187-190. Boston.

Maurault, Joseph P.A.
1866 Histoire des Abenakis, depuis 1605 jusqu'à nos jours. Sorel, Que.: L'Atelier Typographique de la "Gazette de Sorel."

Maurault, Olivier
1930 Oka: Les vicissitudes d'une mission sauvage. *Revue Trimestrielle Canadienne* 16:121-149.

1937 Nos Messieurs. (Collection du Zodiaque 35) Montreal: Les Editions du Zodiaque.

Maxwell, Moreau S.
1950 A Change in the Interpretation of Wisconsin's Prehistory. *Wisconsin Magazine of History* 33(4):427-443.

1951 The Woodland Cultures in Southern Illinois: Archaeological Excavations in the Carbondale Area. *Logan Museum Publications in Anthropology, Bulletin* 7. Beloit, Wis.

1952 The Archeology of the Lower Ohio Valley. Pp. 176-189 in Archeology of Eastern United States. James B. Griffin, ed. Chicago: University of Chicago Press.

1959 The Late Woodland Period. *Illinois Archaeological Survey Bulletin* 1:27-32. Urbana.

1964 Indian Artifacts at Ft. Michilimackinac, Mackinaw City, Michigan. *Michigan Archaeologist* 10(2):23-30.

Mayer-Oakes, William J.
1955 Prehistory of the Upper Ohio Valley: An Introductory Archaeological Study. *Anthropological Series 2, Annals of the Carnegie Museum* 34. Pittsburgh.

1967 Prehistoric Human Population History of the Glacial Lake Agassiz Region. Pp. 339-377 in Life, Land and Water. William J. Mayer-Oakes, ed. (Proceedings of the 1961 Conference on Environmental Studies of the Glacial Lake Agassiz Region) Winnipeg: University of Manitoba Press.

1970   Archaeological Investigations in the Grand Rapids, Manitoba Reservoir, 1961-1962. *University of Manitoba Department of Anthropology, Occasional Papers* 3. Winnipeg.

Mayhew, Experience
1709   Massachuset Psalter. Experience Mayhew, trans. Boston: B. Green and J. Printer.

1727   Indian Converts; or, Some Account of the Lives and Dying Speeches of a Considerable Number of Christianized Indians of Martha's Vineyard... London: J. Osborn and T. Longman; Boston: Samuel Gerrish.

1896   A Brief Journal of My Visitation of the Pequot and Mohegin Indians, at the Desire of the Honourable Commissioners for the Propagation of the Gospel Among the Indians in New England, etc. In, Some Correspondence Between the Governors and Treasurers of the New England Company in London and the Commissioners of the United Colonies in America, the Missionaries of the Company and Others Between the Years 1657 and 1712 to Which Are Added the Journals of the Rev. Experience Mayhew in 1713 and 1714. London: Spottiswoode.

Mead, David
1832   The Last Indians of Virginia. *Atlantic Journal* 1(4):127-128.

Means, Carroll A.
1947   Mohegan-Pequot Relationships, as Indicated by the Events Leading to the Pequot Massacre. *Bulletin of the Archaeological Society of Connecticut* 21:26-33. New Haven.

Mechling, William H.
1913   Maliseet Tales. *Journal of American Folk-Lore* 26(101):219-258.

1914   Malecite Tales. *Anthropological Series 4, Memoirs of the Canadian Geological Survey* 49. Ottawa.

1958-1959   The Malecite Indians, with Notes on the Micmacs, 1916. *Anthropologica* 7:1-160, 8:161-274. Ottawa.

Meeker, Jotham
1850   Ottawa First Book, Containing Lessons for the Learner; Portions of the Gospel by Luke, Omitted by Mathew and John; and the Ottawa Laws. Ottawa Baptist Mission Station [Kan.]: J. Meeker.

1908   [Extract from Manuscript on Ottawas, Sent by Meeker to Rev. I. McCoy, July 18, 1831.] P. 395 in The Shawnee Indians, by J. Spencer. *Collections of the Kansas State Historical Society for 1907-1908,* Vol. 10. Topeka.

Megapolensis, Johannes, Jr.
1909   A Short Account of the Mohawk Indians.... 1644. Pp. 163-180 in Narratives of New Netherland, 1609-1664. J. Franklin Jameson, ed. New York: Charles Scribner's Sons.

Melbye, F. Jerome
1963   The Kane Burial Mounds. *Southern Illinois University Museum, Archaeological Salvage Report* 15. Carbondale.

Menard, M.B.
1836   [Letter to Maj. Gen. Gaines, July 21, 1836.] (Photostat in Western History Collection, Oklahoma University Library, Norman.)

Mereness, Newton D., ed.
1916   Travels in the American Colonies. New York: Macmillan.

Merwin, Bruce W.
1935   An Aboriginal Village Site in Union County. *Journal of the Illinois State Historical Society* 28(1):78-91. Springfield.

Merwin, Ray E.
1906   The Wyandot Indians. *Transactions of the Kansas State Historical Society* 9(1):73-88. Topeka.

Metcalf, Richard P.
1974   Who Should Rule at Home? Native American Politics and Indian-White Relations. *Journal of American History* 61(3):651-665.

Michel, Francis L.
1916   Report of the Journey of Francis Louis Michel from Berne, Switzerland, to Virginia, October 2, 1701- December 1, 1702. William J. Hinke, ed. and trans. *Virginia Magazine of History and Biography* 24(1):1-43, (2):113-141, (3):275-303.

Michels, Joseph W., and James S. Dutt
1968   Archeological Investigations of Sheep Rock Shelter, Huntingdon County, Pennsylvania. Vol. 3. University Park: Pennsylvania State University, Department of Anthropology.

Michels, Joseph W., and Ira F. Smith
1967   Archaeological Investigations of Sheep Rock Shelter, Huntingdon County, Pennsylvania. 2 vols. University Park: Pennsylvania State University, Department of Anthropology.

Michelson, Gunther
1973   A Thousand Words of Mohawk. *Canada. National Museum of Man, Ethnology Division, Mercury Series Paper* 5. Ottawa.

Michelson, Truman
1911   Menominee Tales. *American Anthropologist* 13(1):68-88.

1911a   Note on the Gentes of the Ottawa. *American Anthropologist* 13(2):338.

1912   Preliminary Report on the Linguistic Classification of Algonquian Tribes. Pp. 221-290 in *28th Annual Report of the Bureau of American Ethnology for the Years 1906-1907.* Washington.

[1914]   [Notes on the Stockbridge Language.] (Manuscript No. 2734 in National Anthropological Archives, Smithsonian Institution, Washington.)

[1922]   [Ottawa and Munsee Linguistic and Ethnological Notes.] (Manuscript No. 1635 in National Anthropological Archives, Smithsonian Institution, Washington.)

1923   The Punishment of Impudent Children Among the Kickapoo. *American Anthropologist* 25(2):281-283.

1925   The Traditional Origin of the Fox Society Known as "The Singing Around Rite." Pp. 541-615 in *40th Annual Report of the Bureau of American Ethnology for the Years 1918-1919.* Washington.

1925a   List of [Fox] Stems. Pp. 616-658 in *40th Annual Report of the Bureau of American Ethnology for the Years 1918-1919.* Washington.

1925b   The Autobiography of a Fox Indian Woman. Pp. 291-349 in *40th Annual Report of the Bureau of American Ethnology for the Years 1918-1919.* Washington.

1925c   The Mythical Origin of the White Buffalo Dance of the Fox Indians. Pp. 23-289 in *40th Annual Report of the Bureau of American Ethnology for the Years 1918-1919.* Washington.

1925d   Notes on the Fox Society Known as Those Who Worship the Little Spotted Buffalo. Pp. 497-539 in *40th Annual Report of the Bureau of American Ethnology for the Years 1918-1919.* Washington.

1927   Contributions to Fox Ethnology. *Bureau of American Ethnology Bulletin* 85. Washington.

1929   [Mexican Kickapoo Linguistic Notes.] (Manuscript No. 1329 in National Anthropological Archives, Smithsonian Institution, Washington.)

1930   Contributions to Fox Ethnology, II. *Bureau of American Ethnology Bulletin* 95. Washington.

[1930a]   [List of Tribes Known to Fox Indians.] (Manuscript No. 1222 in National Anthropological Archives, Smithsonian Institution, Washington.)

[1931]   [Fox: Catamenial Society (Ceremony); also Wolf Gens; List of Indian Tribes. Medicine Ceremony at Jim Bear's. Syllabic Text by Harry Lincoln and English Translation of Same.] (Manuscript No. 3217 in National Anthropological Archives, Smithsonian Institution, Washington.)

1932   Three Ottawa Tales. *Journal of American Folk-Lore* 44(172):191-195.

1933   The Linguistic Classification of Powhatan. *American Anthropologist* 35(3):549.

1934   Oüenebigonchelinis Confounded with Winnebago. *American Anthropologist* 36(3):486.

1934a   The Identification of the Mascoutens. *American Anthropologist* 36(2):226-233.

1935   Once More Mascoutens. *American Anthropologist* 37(1):163-164.

1937   A Fox Miscellany. *Bureau of American Ethnology Bulletin* 114. Washington.

1938   Sol Tax on the Social Organization of the Fox Indians. *American Anthropologist* 40(1):177-179.

Miles, Suzanne W.
1951   A Revaluation of the Old Copper Industry. *American Antiquity* 16(3):240-247.

Miller, Helen M., Nancy O. Lurie, and Nadine D. Sieber
1963-1965   Report of Wisconsin Winnebago Project, II. Washington: Privately Printed for the U.S. Department of Health, Education and Welfare, Social Security Administration.

Miller, Jay
1974   The Delaware as Women: A Symbolic Solution. *American Ethnologist* 1(3):507-514.

Miller, Rex K.
1941   McCain Site, Dubois County, Indiana. *Indiana Historical Society, Prehistory Research Series* 2(1). Indianapolis.

Miller, Walter B.
1955   Two Concepts of Authority. *American Anthropologist* 57(2):271-289.

Miller, William D.
1936   The Ancient Paths to Pequot. Providence: Printed for the Rhode Island Historical Society by E.L. Freeman Company.

Milling, Chapman J.
1940   Red Carolinians. Chapel Hill: University of North Carolina Press.

Mills, William C.
1904   Explorations of the Gartner Mound and Village Site. *Ohio State Archaeological and Historical Quarterly* 13(2):128-189. Columbus.

1906   Explorations of the Baum Prehistoric Village Site. *Ohio State Archaeological and Historical Quarterly* 15(1):45-136. Columbus.

1907-1926   Certain Mounds and Village Sites in Ohio. 4 vols. Columbus: Fred J. Heer.

1914   Archaeological Atlas of Ohio, Showing the Distribution of the Various Classes of Prehistoric Remains in the State, with a Map of the Principal Indian Trails and Towns. Columbus: Ohio State Archaeological and Historical Society.

1922   Exploration of the Mound City Group. *Ohio State Archaeological and Historical Quarterly* 31(4):423-584. Columbus.

Mitchell, S.H.
1895   The Indian Chief, Journeycake. Philadelphia: American Baptist Publication Society.

Mitchell, Barry M.
1969   Archaeology of the Petawawa River: The Second Site at Montgomery Lake. *Michigan Archaeologist* 15(1-2):1-53.

Mitchell, Barry M., P. Butler, J. Ford, and J. Lance
1966   The Multi-component Montgomery Lake Site. *Ontario Archaeology* 9:4-24.

Mitchell, Joseph
1960   The Mohawks in High Steel. Pp. 1-36 in Apologies to the Iroquois, by Edmund Wilson. New York: Farrar, Straus and Cudahy.

Mochon, Marion J.
1968   Stockbridge-Munsee Cultural Adaptations: "Assimilated Indians." *Proceedings of the American Philosophical Society* 112(3):182-219. Philadelphia.

Montcalm-Gozon, Louis J. de
1895   Journal du marquis de Montcalm durant ses compagnes en Canada de 1756 à 1759. H.R. Casgrain, ed. Quebec: L.J. Demers.

Montell, Lynwood
1970   The Saga of Coe Ridge: A Study in Oral History. Knoxville: University of Tennessee Press.

1972   The Coe Ridge Colony: A Racial Island Disappears. *American Anthropologist* 74(3):710-719.

Montgomery, Malcolm
1963   The Legal Status of the Six Nations Indians in Canada. *Ontario History* 55(2):93-105.

1965   The Six Nations Indians and the Macdonald Franchise. *Ontario History* 57(1):13-25.

Mook, Maurice A.
1943   The Anthropological Position of the Indian Tribes of Tidewater Virginia. *William and Mary College Quarterly Historical Magazine,* 2d ser., Vol. 23(1):27-40. Williamsburg.

1943a   Virginia Ethnology from an Early Relation. *William and Mary College Quarterly Historical Magazine,* 2d. ser., Vol. 23(2):101-129. Williamsburg.

1943b   The Ethnological Significance of Tindall's Map of Virginia, 1608. *William and Mary College Quarterly Historical Magazine,* 2d. ser., Vol. 23(4):371-408. Williamsburg.

1943c   A Newly Discovered Algonkian Tribe of Carolina. *American Anthropologist* 45(4):635-637.

1944   The Aboriginal Population of Tidewater Virginia. *American Anthropologist* 46(2):193-208.

1944a   Algonkian Ethnohistory of the Carolina Sound. *Journal of the Washington Academy of Sciences* 34(6):181-197, (7):213-228. Washington.

Mooney, James
1890   The Powhatan Indians. *American Anthropologist* 3(2):132.

1894   The Siouan Tribes of the East. *Bureau of American Ethnology Bulletin* 22. Washington.

1896   The Ghost Dance Religion and the Sioux Outbreak of 1890. Pp. 653-1136 in *14th Annual Report of the Bureau of American Ethnology for the Years 1892-1893.* Pt. 1. Washington.

1900   Myths of the Cherokee. Pp. 3-548 in *19th Annual Report of the Bureau of American Ethnology for the Years 1897-1898.* Pt. 1. Washington.

1907   The Powhatan Confederacy, Past and Present. *American Anthropologist* n.s. 9(1):129-152.

1907a   Mingo. Pp. 867-868 in Vol. 1 of Handbook of American Indians North of Mexico. Frederick W. Hodge, ed. 2 vols. *Bureau of American Ethnology Bulletin* 30. Washington.

1907b   Delaware. Pp. 385-387 in Vol. 1 of Handbook of American Indians North of Mexico. Frederick W. Hodge, ed. 2 vols. *Bureau of American Ethnology Bulletin* 30. Washington.

1907c   Munsee. Pp. 957-958 in Vol. 1 of Handbook of American Indians North of Mexico. Frederick W. Hodge, ed. 2 vols. *Bureau of American Ethnology Bulletin* 30. Washington.

1907d   Brotherton. P. 166 in Vol. 1 of Handbook of American Indians North of Mexico. Frederick W. Hodge, ed. 2 vols. *Bureau of American Ethnology Bulletin* 30. Washington.

1907e   Montauk. Pp. 934-935 in Vol. 1 of Handbook of American Indians North of Mexico. Frederick W. Hodge, ed. 2 vols. *Bureau of American Ethnology Bulletin* 30. Washington.

1907f   Mohegan. Pp. 926-927 in Vol. 1 of Handbook of American Indians North of Mexico. Frederick W. Hodge, ed. 2 vols. *Bureau of American Ethnology Bulletin* 30. Washington.

1910   Passamaquoddy. Pp. 207-208 in Vol. 2 of Handbook of American Indians North of Mexico. Frederick W. Hodge, ed. 2 vols. *Bureau of American Ethnology Bulletin* 30. Washington.

1910a   Nottoway. P. 87 in Vol. 2 of Handbook of American Indians North of Mexico. Frederick W. Hodge, ed. 2 vols. *Bureau of American Ethnology Bulletin* 30. Washington.

1910b   Tionontati. Pp. 755-756 in Vol. 2 of Handbook of American Indians North of Mexico. Frederick W. Hodge, ed. 2 vols. *Bureau of American Ethnology Bulletin* 30. Washington.

1910c   Shawnee. Pp. 530-538 in Vol. 2 of Handbook of American Indians North of Mexico. Frederick W. Hodge, ed. 2 vols. *Bureau of American Ethnology Bulletin* 30. Washington.

1910d   Nipissing. Pp. 73-74 in Vol. 2 of Handbook of American Indians North of Mexico. Frederick W. Hodge, ed. 2 vols. *Bureau of American Ethnology Bulletin* 30. Washington.

1910e   Pepikokia. Pp. 228-229 in Vol. 2 of Handbook of American Indians North of Mexico. Frederick W. Hodge, ed. 2 vols. *Bureau of American Ethnology Bulletin* 30. Washington.

1910f   Wappinger. P. 913 in Vol. 2 of Handbook of American Indians North of Mexico. Frederick W. Hodge, ed. 2 vols. *Bureau of American Ethnology Bulletin* 30. Washington.

1910g   Stockbridges. Pp. 637-638 in Vol. 2 of Handbook of American Indians North of Mexico. Frederick W. Hodge, ed. 2 vols. *Bureau of American Ethnology Bulletin* 30. Washington.

1910h   Niantic. Pp. 68-69 in Vol. 2 of Handbook of American Indians North of Mexico. Frederick W. Hodge, ed. 2 vols. *Bureau of American Ethnology Bulletin* 30. Washington.

1910i   Niantic. P. 69 in Vol. 2 of Handbook of American Indians North of Mexico. Frederick W. Hodge, ed. 2 vols. *Bureau of American Ethnology Bulletin* 30. Washington.

1910j   Nipmuc. Pp. 74-75 in Vol. 2 of Handbook of American Indians North of Mexico. Frederick W. Hodge, ed. 2 vols. *Bureau of American Ethnology Bulletin* 30. Washington.

1910k   Quinnipiac. Pp. 344-345 in Vol. 2 of Handbook of American Indians North of Mexico. Frederick W. Hodge, ed. 2 vols. *Bureau of American Ethnology Bulletin* 30. Washington.

1910l   Saint Regis. Pp. 412-413 in Vol. 2 of Handbook of American Indians North of Mexico. 2 vols. *Bureau of American Ethnology Bulletin* 30. Washington.

1911   The Passing of the Delaware Nation. *Proceedings of the Mississippi Valley Historical Association for the Year 1909-1910*, Vol. 3:329-340. Cedar Rapids, Ia..

1928   The Aboriginal Population of America North of Mexico. John R. Swanton, ed. *Smithsonian Miscellaneous Collections* 80(7). Washington.

Mooney, James, and J.N.B. Hewitt
1907   Cayuga. Pp. 223-224 in Vol. 1 of Handbook of American Indians North of Mexico. Frederick W. Hodge, ed. 2 vols. *Bureau of American Ethnology Bulletin* 30. Washington.

1910   Potawatomi. Pp. 289-293 in Vol. 2 of Handbook of American Indians North of Mexico. Frederick W. Hodge, ed. 2 vols. *Bureau of American Ethnology Bulletin* 30. Washington.

1910a   Oka. Pp. 112-113 in Vol. 2 of Handbook of American Indians North of Mexico. Frederick W. Hodge, ed. 2 vols. *Bureau of American Ethnology Bulletin* 30. Washington.

Mooney, James, and William Jones
1907   Kickapoo. Pp. 684-686 in Vol. 1 of Handbook of American Indians North of Mexico. Frederick W. Hodge, ed. 2 vols. *Bureau of American Ethnology Bulletin* 30. Washington.

Mooney, James, and Cyrus Thomas
1907   Menominee. Pp. 842-844 in Vol. 1 of Handbook of American Indians North of Mexico. Frederick W. Hodge, ed. 2 vols. *Bureau of American Ethnology Bulletin* 30. Washington.

1907a   Micmac. Pp. 858-859 in Vol. 1 of Handbook of American Indians North of Mexico. Frederick W. Hodge, ed. 2 vols. *Bureau of American Ethnology Bulletin* 30. Washington.

1907b   Mahican. Pp. 786-789 in Vol. 1 of Handbook of American Indians North of Mexico. Frederick W. Hodge, ed. 2 vols. *Bureau of American Ethnology Bulletin* 30. Washington.

1907c   Conoy. P. 339 in Vol. 1 of Handbook of American Indians North of Mexico. Frederick W. Hodge, ed. 2 vols. *Bureau of American Ethnology Bulletin* 30. Washington.

1907d   Illinois. Pp. 597-599 in Vol. 1 of Handbook of American Indians North of Mexico. Frederick W. Hodge, ed. 2 vols. *Bureau of American Ethnology Bulletin* 30. Washington.

1907e   Miami. Pp. 852-855 in Vol. 1 of Handbook of American Indians North of Mexico. Frederick W. Hodge, ed. 2 vols. *Bureau of American Ethnology Bulletin* 30. Washington.

1907f   Foxes. Pp. 472-474 in Vol. 1 of Handbook of American Indians North of Mexico. Frederick W. Hodge, ed. 2 vols. *Bureau of American Ethnology Bulletin* 30. Washington.

1907g   Chippewa. Pp. 277-281 in Vol. 1 of Handbook of American Indians North of Mexico. Frederick W. Hodge, ed. 2 vols. *Bureau of American Ethnology Bulletin* 30. Washington.

1907h   Missisauga. Pp. 909-910 in Vol. 1 of Handbook of American Indians North of Mexico. Frederick W. Hodge, ed. 2 vols. *Bureau of American Ethnology Bulletin* 30. Washington.

1907i   Massachuset. Pp. 816-817 in Vol. 1 of Handbook of American Indians North of Mexico. Frederick W. Hodge, ed. 2 vols. *Bureau of American Ethnology Bulletin* 30. Washington.

1910   Pennacook. Pp. 225-226 in Vol. 2 of Handbook of American Indians North of Mexico. Frederick W. Hodge, ed. 2 vols. *Bureau of American Ethnology Bulletin* 30. Washington.

1910a   Nauset. Pp. 40-41 in Vol. 2 of Handbook of American Indians North of Mexico. Frederick W. Hodge, ed. 2 vols. *Bureau of American Ethnology Bulletin* 30. Washington.

Moore, John W.
1880   History of North Carolina, from the Earliest Discoveries to the Present Time. 2 vols. Raleigh: A. Williams.

Moore, Winston
1971   The Sand Point Site, Baraga County, Michigan. (Paper Presented at the Annual Meeting of the Midwest Archaeological Conference, Cleveland, 1971.)

Moorehead, Warren K.
1906   A Narrative of Explorations in New Mexico, Arizona, Indiana, etc. *Phillips Academy, Department of Archaeology Bulletin* 3. Andover, Mass.

1910   The Stone Age in North America: An Archaeological Encyclopedia of the Implements, Ornaments, Weapons, Utensils, etc. of the Prehistoric Tribes of North America. Boston and New York: Houghton Mifflin.

1922   A Report on the Archaeology of Maine: Being a Narrative of Explorations in that State, 1912-1920, Together with Work at Lake Champlain, 1917. Andover, Mass.: Phillips Academy, Department of Anthropology.

1929   The Cahokia Mounds. Pt. 1: Explorations of 1922, 1923, 1924 and 1927. *University of Illinois Bulletin* 26(4). Urbana.

Morgan, Arthur E.
1971   Dams and Other Disasters: A Century of the Army Corps of Engineers in Civil Works. Boston: Porter Sargent.

Morgan, Lewis H.
1845   Intelligence Gathered at a Council of the Six Nations of Indians, Held at Tonawanda, Genesee County, New York on the First, Second and Third Days of October, 1845. (Manuscript in Vol. 1, Morgan Manuscript Journals, University of Rochester Library, Rochester, N.Y.)

1847   Letters on the Iroquois, by Skenandoah. *American Review* 5(2):177-190, (3):242-257, (5):447-461, 6(5):477-490, (6):626-633.

1850   Report to the Regents of the University, Upon the Articles Furnished to the Indian Collection. *New York State Cabinet of Antiquities' Annual Report* 3:65-97. Albany.

1851   League of the Ho-dé-no-sau-nee or Iroquois. Rochester, N.Y.: Sage; New York: M.H. Newman. (Reprinted as League of the Iroquois, Corinth Books, New York, 1962.)

1852   Report on the Fabrics, Inventions, Implements, and Utensils of the Iroquois. *New York State Cabinet of Antiquities' Annual Report* 5:66-117. Albany.

1859   Circular Letter in Regard to the Possibility of Identifying the Systems of Consanguinity of the North American Indians with That of Certain Peoples of Asia. Rochester, N.Y.: [no publisher.]

1862   Circular in Reference to the Degrees of Relationship Among Different Nations. *Smithsonian Miscellaneous Collections* 2(10):1-33. Washington.

1871   Systems of Consanguinity and Affinity of the Human Family. *Smithsonian Contributions to Knowledge* 17. Washington.

1877   Ancient Society or Researches in the Lines of Human Progress from Savagery Through Barbarism to Civilization. New York: Henry Holt. (Reprinted: World Publishing Company, Cleveland and New York, 1963; Gordon Press, New York, 1976.)

1881   Houses and House-life of the American Aborigines. (Contributions to North American Ethnology 4.) Washington: U.S. Geological and Geographical Survey of the Rocky Mountain Region.

1901   League of the Ho-dé-no-sau-nee or Iroquois [1851]. Herbert M. Lloyd, ed. 2 vols. New York: Dodd, Mead. (Reprinted: Human Relations Area Files, New Haven, Conn., 1954.)

1959   The Indian Journals 1859-1862. Leslie A. White, ed. Ann Arbor: University of Michigan Press.

1964   Ancient Society [1877]. Leslie A. White, ed. Cambridge, Mass.: Harvard University Press.

Morgan, Richard G.
1952   Outline of Cultures in the Ohio Region. Pp. 83-98 in Archeology of Eastern United States. James B. Griffin, ed. Chicago: University of Chicago Press.

Morison, Samuel E.
1971   The European Discovery of America: The Northern Voyages, A.D. 500-1600. New York: Oxford University Press.

Morris, James L.
1943   Indians of Ontario. Toronto: Ontario Department of Lands and Forests.

Morse, Dan F.
1963   The Steuben Village and Mounds: A Multicomponent Late Hopewell Site in Illinois. *University of Michigan Museum of Anthropology, Anthropological Papers* 21. Ann Arbor.

Morse, Jedidiah
1822   A Report to the Secretary of War of the United States, on Indian Affairs, Comprising a Narrative of a Tour Performed in the Summer of 1820, Under a Commission of the President of the United States, for the Purpose of Ascertaining, for the Use of the Government, the Actual State of the Indian Tribes in Our Country. New Haven, Conn.: S. Converse.

Mortimer, Benjamin
1798   [Diary, August 15 to October 4: Entry of September 22.] (Indian Missions, Box 171, Folder 1, Item 1, Archives of the Moravian Church, Bethlehem, Pa.)

Morton, Nathaniel
1910   New-Englands Memorial [1669]. Pp. 1-224 in Chronicles of the Pilgrim Fathers. John Masefield, ed. New York: E.P. Dutton.

Morton, Richard L.
1960   Colonial Virginia. 2 vols. Chapel Hill: University of North Carolina Press.

Morton, Thomas
1637   The New English Canaan, or New Canaan: Containing an Abstract of New England Composed in Three Books. Amsterdam: J.F. Stam. (Reprinted: Prince Society, Boston, 1883.)

1838   New English Canaan or New Canaan, Containing an Abstract of New England [1637]. (Reprinted: Pp. 1-125 in Vol. 2 of Tracts and Other Papers Relating Principally to the Origin, Settlement, and Progress of the Colonies in North America... Peter Force, ed. 4 vols. Washington: Peter Force.)

Mourt, G.
1963   A Journal of the Pilgrims at Plymouth: Mourt's Relation [1622]. Dwight Heath, ed. New York: Corinth Books.

Mrak, Ignaz
1851   [Brief an den Fürst-Erzbischof in Wien. Lacroix, 20. November 1849.] Berichte der Leopoldinen-Stiftung 23:91-101. Vienna.

Müller, Werner
1956   Die Religionen der Waldlandindianer Nordamerikas. Berlin: Dietrich Reimer.

Munson, Cheryl A., and Patrick J. Munson
1969   Preliminary Report on an Early Historic Site, Cook County, Illinois. Wisconsin Archaeologist 50(3):184-188.

Munson, Patrick J., and Alan D. Harn
1971   Archaeological Surveys of the American Bottoms and Adjacent Bluffs, Illinois. Illinois State Museum, Report of Investigations 21. Springfield.

Munson, Patrick J., Paul W. Parmalee, and Richard A. Yarnell
1971   Subsistence Ecology of Scovill: A Terminal Middle Woodland Village. American Antiquity 36(4):410-431.

Murdock, George P.
1949   Social Structure. New York: Macmillan.

1960   Ethnographic Bibliography of North America. 3d ed. New Haven, Conn.: Human Relations Area Files.

Murdock, George P., and Timothy J. O'Leary
1975   Ethnographic Bibliography of North America. 4th ed. Vol. 2: Arctic and Subarctic; Vol. 4: Eastern United States. New Haven, Conn.: Human Relations Area Files Press.

Murphy, James L.
1971   Whittlesey Ceramic Types. Ohio Archaeologist 21(1):298-303.

Murphy, Joseph F.
1961   Potawatomi Indians of the West: Origins of the Citizen Band. (Unpublished Ph.D. Dissertation in Anthropology, University of Oklahoma, Norman.)

Murray, Florence B., ed.
1963   Muskoka and Haliburton, 1615-1875: A Collection of Documents. (Ontario Series 6) Toronto: The Champlain Society.

Murray, Louise (Welles), ed.
1931   Selected Manuscripts of General John S. Clark Relating to the Aboriginal History of the Susquehanna. Publications of the Society for Pennsylvania Archaeology 1. Athens, Pa.

Murray, William V.
[1792] Vocabulary of the Nanticoke Indians. (Manuscript No. 2366 in the Library of the American Philosophical Society, Philadelphia.)

Myer, William E.
1928   Indian Trails of the Southeast. Pp. 727-857 in 42d Annual Report of the Bureau of American Ethnology for the Years 1924-1925. Washington.

Myers, Albert C., ed.
1937   William Penn: His Own Account of the Lenni Lenape or Delaware Indians, 1683. Moylan, Pa.: A.C. Myers.

Myers, Merlin G.
1962   Household Structure Among the Longhouse Iroquois of the Six Nations Reserve. (Unpublished Ph.D. Dissertation in Anthropology, Cambridge University, Cambridge, England.)

NYCD = O'Callaghan, Edmund B., ed.
1853-1887 Documents Relative to the Colonial History of the State of New York; Procured in Holland, England and France, by John R. Brodhead. 15 vols. Albany: Weed, Parsons.

NYHSC = New-York Historical Society
1868-19ᵣ Collections. John Watts De Peyster Publication Fund Series. New York.

Nagler, Mark
1970   Indians in the City: A Study of the Urbanization of Indians in Toronto. Ottawa: Saint Paul University, Canadian Research Centre for Anthropology.

Nale, Robert F.
1963   The Salvage Excavation of the Boyle Site (36-Wh-19). Pennsylvania Archaeologist 33(4):164-194.

Naroll, Raoul
1956   A Preliminary Index of Social Development. American Anthropologist 58(4):687-715.

The Narragansett Mortgage see Society of Colonial Wars. Rhode Island.

Neill, Edward D.
1876   The Founders of Maryland as Portrayed in Manuscripts, Provincial Records and Early Documents. Albany, N.Y.: J. Munsell.

1886   Virginia Carolorum: The Colony Under the Rule of Charles the First and Second, A.D. 1625 - A.D. 1685, Based Upon Manuscripts of the Period. Albany, N.Y.: J. Munsell's Sons.

Nelson, William
1894   The Indians of New Jersey; Their Origin and Development, Manners and Customs, Language, Religion and Government, with Notices of Some Indian Place Names. Paterson, N.J.: The Press Printing and Publishing Company.

1904   Personal Names of Indians of New Jersey; Being a List of Six Hundred and Fifty Such Names, Gleaned Mostly from Indian Deeds of the Seventeenth Century. Paterson, N.J.: The Paterson History Club.

Neumeyer, Elizabeth
1971   Michigan Indians Battle Against Removal. Michigan History 55(4):275-288.

Newcomb, William W., Jr.
1956   The Culture and Acculturation of the Delaware Indians. University of Michigan Museum of Anthropology, Anthropological Papers 10. Ann Arbor.

1956a   The Peyote Cult of the Delaware Indians. Texas Journal of Science 8(2):202-211.

New Hampshire Historical Society
[1795-1810] Philip's Grant Papers. (One Volume of Manuscripts and Facsimiles in New Hampshire Historical Library, Concord.)

New Haven (Colony)
1857   Records of the Colony and Plantation of New Haven, from 1638 to 1649. Charles J. Hoadly, ed. Hartford: Printed by Case, Tiffany.

Newhouse, Seth
[1885] [Cosmogony of De-ka-na-wi-das' Government of the Iroquois Confederacy: The Original Literal Historical Nar-

ratives of the Iroquois Confederacy.] (Manuscript in Public Archives of Canada, Folder MG 19 F. 26, Ottawa.)

Newnam, Thomas
1722   [Letter to the Secretary of the S.P.G., June 29, N.C.] (Letter no. 9, Society for the Propagation of the Gospel Records, British Library, London; Microfilm Reel 3, Southern Historical Collection, University of North Carolina, Chapel Hill.)

New Plymouth Colony
1855-1861   Records of the Colony of New Plymouth, in New England. Nathaniel B. Shurtleff and David Pulsifer, eds. 12 vols. in 10. Boston: W. White.

New York (State)
1849   Report of the Committee on Indian Affairs on the Memorial of Peter Wilson, a Cayuga Chief, in Respect to the Law of 1848 Providing for the Distribution of the Cayuga Annuities. *New York Senate Report* No. 64. Albany.

New York (State) Commissioners of Indian Affairs
1861   Proceedings of the Commissioners of Indian Affairs, Appointed by Law for the Extinguishment of Indian Titles in the State of New York, by Franklin B. Hough. 2 vols. Albany: J. Munsell.

New York (State) Legislature. Assembly
1889   Report of Special Committee to Investigate the Indian Problem of the State of New York, Appointed by the Assembly of 1888. Albany: The Troy Press.

New York (State) Legislature. Senate. Committee on Indian Affairs
1890   Testimony Taken Before the Senate Committee on Indian Affairs Relative to the Cayuga Indians Under Resolution of May 15, 1889. Transmitted to the Legislature May 9, 1890. (New York State Senate Doc. No. 58.) Albany: J.B. Lyon.

New York (State) Secretary of State
1857   Census of the State of New York for 1855, Prepared by Franklin B. Hough. Albany: Charles Van Benthuysen.

————
1887   Journals of the Military Expedition of Major General John Sullivan Against the Six Nations of Indians in 1779, by Frederick Cook. Auburn, N.Y.: Knapp, Peck and Thomson.

New York State Historical Association
1933-1937   The Sullivan-Clinton Campaign of 1779. Pp. 185-216 in Vol. 4 of History of the State of New York. Alexander C. Flick, ed. 10 vols. New York: Columbia University Press.

Nicholas, Ralph W.
1965   Factions: A Comparative Analysis. Pp. 21-61 in Political Systems and the Distribution of Power. Michael Banton, ed. (A.S.A. Monograph 2) London: Tavistock Publications.

Nichols, John
1974   Potawatomi Orthography. (Manuscript, Wisconsin Native American Languages Project, University of Wisconsin, Milwaukee.)

Nicholson, Francis
1699   [Report on Virginia Indians, April 29-May 15, 1699.] (Manuscript in the Public Record Office, London, Colonial Office 5, Vol. 1310(2): Enclosure xxxviii.)

Nickerson, Horton H.
1953   Variation in Cob Morphology Among Certain Archaeological and Ethnological Races of Maize. *Annals of the Missouri Botanical Garden* 40(2):79-109. St. Louis.

Nicolas, Louis
[1672-1674]   Grammaire de la langue algonquine. (Manuscript in Bibliothèque Nationale, Paris.)

Nieberding, Velma
1954   Chief Splitlog and the Cayuga Mission Church. *Chronicles of Oklahoma* 32(1):18-28.

1956   Seneca-Cayuga Green Corn Ceremonial Feast. *Chronicles of Oklahoma* 34(2):231-234.

Ninegrett, Thomas
1765   [Letter to the Society for the Propagation of the Gospel in New England.] (Manuscript in the Massachusetts Historical Society Library, Boston.)

Nish, Cameron, ed.
1965   The French Régime. (Canadian Historical Documents Series 1) Scarborough, Ont.: Prentice Hall of Canada.

Noble, William C.
1968   Iroquois Archaeology and the Development of Iroquois Social Organization (1000-1650 A.D.): A Study in Culture Change Based on Archaeology, Ethnohistory and Ethnology. (Unpublished Ph.D. Dissertation in Archaeology, University of Calgary, Alberta.)

————
1969   Some Social Implications of the Iroquois 'In Situ' Theory. *Ontario Archaeology* 13:16-28.

————
1970   An Unusual Neutral Iroquois House Structure. *New York State Archaeological Association Bulletin* 48:14-15. Ossining.

————
1971   The Sopher Celt: An Indicator of Early Protohistoric Trade in Huronia. *Ontario Archaeology* 16:43-47.

————
1972   Neutral Settlement Patterns. (Paper Read at the Neutral Symposium, Canadian Archeological Association, St. John's, Newfoundland.)

————
[1974]   Neutral Indians. (Manuscript Submitted for Inclusion Within the Grimsby Historical Society's Centennial Volume. Grimsby, Ont.)

Noon, John A.
1949   Law and Government of the Grand River Iroquois. *Viking Fund Publications in Anthropology* 12. New York.

Norcliffe, G.B., and Conrad E. Heidenreich
1974   The Preferred Orientation of Iroquoian Longhouses in Ontario. *Ontario Archaeology* 23:3-30.

North Carolina (Colony) *see* Saunders, William L.

Norton, John
1970   The Journal of Major John Norton, 1816. Carl F. Klinck, and James J. Talman, eds. Toronto: The Champlain Society.

Norton, Thomas E.
1974   The Fur Trade in Colonial New York, 1686-1776. Madison: University of Wisconsin Press.

Norwood, Henry
1844   A Voyage to Virginia [1650]. *Force's Collection of Historical Tracts* 3(10). Washington. (Reprinted: Peter Smith, New York, 1947.)

Noyes, James
[1690]   Pequot Indian Glossary. (A 27-page Vocabulary; Manuscript Aya 78/B7/Al63 in Beinecke Library, Yale University, New Haven, Conn.)

Nugent, Nell M.
1934   Cavaliers and Pioneers: Abstracts of Virginia Land Patents and Grants, 1623-1666. Vol. 1. Richmond: Dietz. (Reprinted: Genealogical Publishing Company, Baltimore, 1963, 1969.)

Nuttall, Thomas
1821   A Journal of Travels into the Arkansa Territory, During the Year 1819. With Occasional Observations on the Manners of the Aborigines. Philadelphia: T.H. Palmer.

O'Callaghan, Edmund B., ed.
1849-1851   Documentary History of the State of New York. 4 vols. Albany: Weed, Parsons.

———— *see also* NYCD

O'Dowd, Father
1889   Superstitions of the Passamaquoddies. *Journal of American Folk-Lore* 2(6):229-231.

Oehler, Charles M.
1950   Turpin Indians. *Cincinnati Museum of Natural History, Popular Publication Series* 1. Cincinnati.

Oliphant, J. Orin
1947   The Report of the Wyandot Exploring Delegation, 1831. *Kansas Historical Quarterly* 15(3):248-262. Topeka.

O'Meara, Frederick A.
1838-1857 [Letters and Reports to the Society for the Propagation of the Gospel.] (Manuscript C/CAN/503, United Society for the Propagation of the Gospel Archives, London.)

————
1846   Report of a Mission to the Ottahwahs and Ojibwas, on Lake Huron. (Missions to the Heathen 6) London: Society for the Propagation of the Gospel.

————
1846a   Second Report of a Mission to the Ottahwahs and Ojibwas, on Lake Huron. (Missions to the Heathen 13) London: Society for the Propagation of the Gospel.

O'Neill, H.H.
1838-1839 Journal, 1838-1839. (Manuscript C/CAN/491, United Society for the Propagation of the Gospel Archives, London.)

Orchard, William C.
1929   Beads and Beadwork of the American Indians: A Study Based on Specimens in the Museum of the American Indian, Heye Foundation. *Contributions from the Museum of the American Indian, Heye Foundation* 11. New York.

Orcutt, Samuel
1882   The Indians of the Housatonic and Naugatuck Valleys. Hartford, Conn.: Case, Lockwood, and Brainard.

Orfield, Gary
1964   Report on the Termination of the Menominee Reservation. (Unpublished M.A. Thesis in Political Science, University of Chicago, Chicago.)

Orr, R.B.
1915   The Mississaugas. Pp. 7-18 in *27th Annual Archaeological Report for 1915. Being Part of Appendix to the Report of the Minister of Education, Ontario.* Toronto.

Orr, Kenneth G.
1951   Change at Kincaid: A Study of Cultural Dynamics. Pp. 293-359 in Kincaid: A Prehistoric Illinois Metropolis, by Fay-Cooper Cole. Chicago: University of Chicago Press.

Oswalt, Wendell H.
1966   This Land Was Theirs: A Study of the North American Indian. New York: Wiley.

Pa. Arch. = Hazard, Samuel et al., eds.
1852-1949 Pennsylvania Archives. 138 vols. Philadelphia: Joseph Severns; Harrisburg: Commonwealth of Pennsylvania.

Pa. Col. Recs. = Hazard, Samuel, ed.
1838-1853 Minutes of the Provincial Council of Pennsylvania from the Organization to the Termination of the Proprietary Government, March 10, 1683 to September 27, 1775. 16 vols. Harrisburg: Theophilus Fenn.

PAC, Q = Public Archives of Canada, Quebec Series. Manuscript Group 8, Quebec Provincial and Local Records. Quebec.

Pacifique
1934   Le Pays des Micmacs. *Etudes Historiques et Géographiques* 10, 11, and 14. Bonaventure, P.Q., Canada. (Reprinted from *Bulletin de la Société de Géographie de Québec,* Vols. 21, 22, 23, 25, 27, and 28. Montreal.)

————
1939   Leçons grammaticales théoriques et pratiques de la langue micmaque. Sainte Anne de Restigouche, Que.: Bureau du Messager Micmac.

Page and Smith
1972   Illustrated Historical Atlas of Brant County, Ontario [1875]. Belleville, Ont.: Mika Silk Screening.

Painter, Floyd E.
1961   The Last of the Nottoway. *Quarterly Bulletin of the Archaeological Society of Virginia* 15(4):34-38. Richmond.

Palfrey, John G.
1858-1890 History of New England. 5 vols. Boston: Little, Brown.

Palm, Mary (Borgias)
1933   The Jesuit Missions of the Illinois Country, 1673-1763. Cleveland: Privately Printed.

Palmer, William P. et al., eds.
1875-1893 Calendar of Virginia State Papers and Other Manuscripts Preserved in the Capitol at Richmond. Richmond: Virginia State Library.

Papworth, Mark L.
1967   Cultural Traditions in the Lake Forest Region During the Late High-water Stages of the Post-glacial Great Lakes. (Unpublished Ph.D. Dissertation in Anthropology, University of Michigan, Ann Arbor.)

Paquin, Jacques
[1833]   Mémoires sur l'Eglise du Canada. (Manuscript in the Public Archives of Canada, Quebec.)

Parent, Amand
1887   The Life of Rev. Amand Parent, the First French-Canadian Ordained by the Methodist Church. Forty-seven Years' Experience in the Evangelical Work in Canada. Thirty-one Years in Connection with the Conference and Eight Years Among the Oka Indians. Toronto: William Briggs; Montreal: C.W. Coates.

Pargellis, Stanley, ed.
1959   An Account of the Indians in Virginia. *William and Mary College Quarterly Historical Magazine,* 3d. ser. Vol. 16(2):228-243. Williamsburg.

Park, Joseph
1757   [Letter.] (Manuscript in the Massachusetts Historical Society Library, Boston.)

Parker, Arthur C.
1909   Secret Medicine Societies of the Seneca. *American Anthropologist* n.s. 11(2):161-185. (Reprinted in Parker 1913:113-130.)

————
1910   Iroquois Uses of Maize and Other Food Plants. *New York State Museum Bulletin* 144(482):5-113. Albany.

————
1913   The Code of Handsome Lake, the Seneca Prophet. *New York State Museum Bulletin* 163. Albany.

————
1916   The Origin of the Iroquois as Suggested by Their Archaeology. *American Anthropologist* 18(4):479-507.

————
1916a   The Constitution of the Five Nations. *New York State Museum Bulletin* 184:7-158. Albany.

————
1918   A Prehistoric Iroquoian Site on the Reed Farm, Richmond Mills, Ontario County, New York. *Researches and Transactions of the New York State Archaeological Association* 1. Rochester.

————
1919   The Life of General Ely S. Parker: Last Grand Sachem of the Iroquois and General Grant's Military Secretary. *Publications of the Buffalo Historical Society* 23. Buffalo.

————
1922   The Archaeological History of New York. 2 Pts. *New York State Museum Bulletin* 235-238. Albany.

————
1926   An Analytical History of the Seneca Indians. *Researches and Transactions of the New York State Archaeological Association* 6(1-5). Rochester.

1968 Parker on the Iroquois. William N. Fenton, ed. Syracuse, N.Y.: Syracuse University Press.

Parker, Mattie E. (Edwards), ed.
1968 North Carolina Higher-Court Records, 1670-1696; The Colonial Records of North Carolina. Raleigh: State Department of Archives and History.

———, ed.
1971 North Carolina Higher-Court Records, 1697-1701; The Colonial Records of North Carolina. Raleigh: State Department of Archives and History.

Parkman, Francis
1851 History of the Conspiracy of Pontiac, and the War of the North American Tribes Against the English Colonies After the Conquest of Canada. Boston: Little, Brown.

1865 Pioneers of France in the New World. Boston: Little, Brown.

1865-1892 France and England in North America: A Series of Historical Narratives. 9 vols. Boston: Little, Brown.

1867 The Jesuits in North America in the Seventeenth Century. Boston: Little, Brown.

1869 The Discovery of the Great West. Boston: Little, Brown.

1874 The Old Régime in Canada. Boston: Little, Brown.

1883 Count Frontenac and New France Under Louis XIV. 11th ed. Boston: Little, Brown.

1884 Montcalm and Wolfe. 2 vols. Boston: Little, Brown.

1892 A Half-century of Conflict. 2 vols. Boston: Little, Brown.

1897 La Salle and the Discovery of the Great West: France and England in North America. Boston: Little, Brown.

1905 The Conspiracy of Pontiac and the Indian War After the Conquest of Canada. 2 vols. Boston: Little, Brown.

Parsons, Usher, coll.
1861 Indian Names of Places in Rhode-Island. Providence: Knowles, Anthony.

Paschal, Herbert R.
1953 The Tuscarora Indians in North Carolina. (Unpublished M.A. Thesis in History, University of North Carolina, Chapel Hill.)

Pastorius, Francis D.
1912 Circumstantial Geographical Description of Pennsylvania, 1700. Pp. 353-448 in Narratives of Early Pennsylvania, West New Jersey, and Delaware, 1630-1707. Albert C. Myers, ed. New York: Charles Scribner's Sons.

Peale, T.R.
1862 Ancient Mounds at St. Louis, Missouri, in 1819. Pp. 386-391 in *Annual Report of the Smithsonian Institution for 1861*. Washington.

Peale, Arthur L.
1930 Memorials and Pilgrimages in the Mohegan Country. Norwich, Conn.: The Bulletin Company.

Pease, Theodore C., and Ernestine Jenison, eds.
1940 Illinois on the Eve of the Seven Years' War, 1747-1755. *Collections of the Illinois State Historical Library* 29. Springfield.

Pease, Theodore C., and Raymond C. Werner, eds.
1934 The French Foundations, 1680-1693. *Collections of the Illinois State Historical Library* 23. Springfield.

Peattie, Lisa R.
1960 Being a Mesquakie Indian. Pp. 39-62 in Documentary History of the Fox Project, 1948-1959. Frederick O. Gearing, Robert McC. Netting, and Lisa R. Peattie, eds. Chicago: University of Chicago Press.

Peckham, Howard H.
1947 Pontiac and the Indian Uprising. Princeton, N.J.: Princeton University Press. (Reprinted: University of Chicago Press, Chicago, 1961.)

1964 The Colonial Wars, 1689-1762. Chicago: University of Chicago Press.

Peirce, Isaac
1832 The Narraganset Chief; or, The Adventures of a Wanderer. New York: J.K. Porter.

Peirson, Abraham *see* Pierson, Abraham

Pendergast, James F.
1964 Nine Small Sites on Lake St. Francis Representing an Early Iroquois Horizon in the Upper St. Lawrence River Valley. *Anthropologica* n.s. 6(2):183-221. Ottawa.

1966 Three Prehistoric Iroquois Components in Eastern Ontario: The Salem, Grays Creek, and Beckstead Sites. *Anthropological Series 73, National Museum of Canada Bulletin* 208. Ottawa.

1967 The Berry Site V. *Anthropological Series 72, National Museum of Canada Bulletin* 206:26-53. Ottawa.

1972 Archaeological Comparison of Dawson Site with Other Iroquoian Sites in Eastern Ontario. Pp. 267-296 in Cartier's Hochelaga and the Dawson Site. James F. Pendergast and Bruce G. Trigger, eds. Montreal: McGill-Queen's University Press.

Penhallow, Samuel
1726 History of the Wars of New England with the Eastern Indians. Boston: Printed by T. Fleet for S. Gerrish and D. Henchman.

1859 The History of the Wars of New-England with the Eastern Indians [1726]. Cincinnati: For Wm. Dodge by J. Harpel.

1971 Penhallow's Indian Wars: Facsimile Reprint of the First Edition, Printed in Boston in 1726 with the Notes of Earlier Editors and Additions from the Original Manuscript [1924]. Edward Wheelock, ed. Freeport, N.Y.: Books for Libraries Press.

Penn, William
1912 Letter from William Penn to the Committee of the Free Society of Traders, 1683. Pp. 217-244 in Narratives of Early Pennsylvania, West New Jersey and Delaware, 1630-1707. Albert C. Myers, ed. New York: Charles Scribner's Sons.

Penney, Norman, ed.
1912 The Dying Words of Ockanickon. *Journal of the Friends' Historical Society* 9(3):164-166.

Pennsylvania (Colony) Provincial Council *see* Pa. Col. Recs.

Percy, George
1625 Observations Gathered Out of a Discourse of the Plantation of the Southern Colonie in Virginia by the English, 1606. Pp. 1685-1690 in Vol. 4 of Hakluytus Posthumus or Purchas His Pilgrimes, by Samuel Purchas. London: W. Stansby for H. Fetherstone.

1922 A Trewe Relacyon of the Procedeinges and Occurentes of Momente wch have hapned in Virginia from 1609 untill 1612. *Tyler's Quarterly Historical and Genealogical Magazine* 3:259-282. Richmond, Va.

Perley, Moses
1842 Reports on Indian Affairs, 1841. Pp. xcii-cxxvi in the Journal of the House of Assembly of New Brunswick. Fredericton, N.B.

Perrine, Thomas M.
1873 Mounds Near Anna, Union County, Illinois. Pp. 418-420 in *Annual Report of the Smithsonian Institution for 1872*. Washington.

Perrot, Nicolas
1864   Mémoire sur les moeurs, coustumes et relligion des sauvages de l'Amérique septentrionale [1717]. Leipzig and Paris: A. Franck.

———
1911   Memoir on the Manners, Customs, and Religion of the Savages of North America. Pp. 23-272 in Vol. 1 of The Indian Tribes of the Upper Mississippi Valley and Region of the Great Lakes. Emma H. Blair, ed. Cleveland: Arthur H. Clark.

Peske, G. Richard
1966   Oneota Settlement Patterns and Agricultural Patterns in Winnebago County. *Wisconsin Archaeologist* 47(4):188-195.

———
1971   Winnebago Cultural Adaptation to the Fox River Waterway. *Wisconsin Archaeologist* 52(2):62-70.

Petrullo, Vincenzo
1934   The Diabolic Root: A Study of Peyotism, the New Indian Religion Among the Delawares. Philadelphia: University of Pennsylvania Press.

Pierce, Roy G., and Ben C. McCary, comps.
1969   Bibliography of the Virginia Indians. *Archaeological Society of Virginia, Special Publication* 1. Williamsburg.

[Pierson, Abraham] "Abraham Peirson"
1658   Some Helps for the Indians: A Catechism. Cambridge, Mass.: Samuel Green.

Pierz, Franz
1835-1843   [Letters to Various Addresses from Cross Village, Mackinac, Sault Ste. Marie, Arbre Croche.] (Manuscripts in Leopoldinen-Stiftung 3:3.21-24, 3.26, 3.37, 3.40, 3.42. Diözesenarchiv, Erzdiözese Wien, Austria.)

———
1837-1864   Briefe an die Zentraldirektion der Leopoldinenstiftung, Wien, bzw. an den Fürst-Erzbischof in Wien. *Berichte der Leopoldinen-Stiftung* 10:42-47, 11:49-54, 15:62-72, 16:50-53, 17:53-60, 20-64, 21:65-70, 34:43-49. Vienna.

———
1934-1935   Letters of Father Francis Pierz. *Centralblatt and Social Justice* 26:395-396, 27:18-19, 54-56, 91-92, 321-322.

Pike, Albert
[1861]   [Miscellaneous Notes on the Muskogee, Comanche, and Delaware.] (Manuscript No. 593a in National Anthropological Archives, Smithsonian Institution, Washington.)

Pike, Zebulon M.
1811   Exploratory Travels Through the Western Territories of North America Comprising a Voyage from St. Louis, on the Mississippi, to the Source of That River, and a Journey Through the Interior of Louisiana, and the North-Eastern Provinces of New Spain. Performed in the Years 1805, 1806, 1807 by Order of the Government of the United States. Thomas Rees, ed. London: Longman, Hurst, Rees, Orme, and Brown.

Pilling, Arnold R.
1966   Life at Porter Site 8, Midland County, Michigan. *Michigan Archaeologist* 12(4): 235-248.

Pilling, James C.
1880   [Wyandot Vocabulary Taken from John Greyeyes of Indian Territory at Washington, D.C.] (Manuscript No. 398 in National Anthropological Archives, Smithsonian Institution, Washington.)

———
1888   Bibliography of the Iroquoian Languages. *Bureau of American Ethnology Bulletin* 6. Washington.

———
1891   Bibliography of the Algonquian Languages. *Bureau of American Ethnology Bulletin* 13. Washington.

Pitzer, Martin
1854   Verzeichnis der Gegenstände und Arbeiten eines Indianer-Stammes im nördlichsten Amerika nebst einer Charakteristik derselben. Munich, Germany: J.G. Weiss.

Plantagenet, Beauchamp
1648   A Description of the Province of New Albion. (Reprinted: In Tracts and Other Papers, Relating Principally to the Origin, Settlement, and Progress of the Colonies in North America, from the Discovery of the Country to the Year 1776. Peter Force, comp., Vol 2(7), Washington, 1838.)

Polgar, Steven
1960   Biculturation of Mesquakie Teenage Boys. *American Anthropologist* 62(2):217-235.

Pollard, John G.
1894   The Pamunkey Indians of Virginia. *Bureau of American Ethnology Bulletin* 17. Washington.

Pollitzer, William S.
1972   The Physical Anthropology and Genetics of Marginal People of the Southeastern United States. *American Anthropologist* 74(3):719-734.

Pond, Peter
1933   The Narrative of Peter Pond. Pp. 11-59 in Five Fur Traders of the Northwest. Charles M. Gates, ed. Minneapolis: University of Minnesota Press.

Pope, Richard K.
1957   Oklahoma Kickapoo Reactions to Allottment, 1891-1956. (Unpublished Manuscript in Pope's Possession.)

———
1958-1959   The Withdrawal of the Kickapoo. *The American Indian* 8(2):17-27.

Porter, James W.
1969   The Mitchell Site and Prehistoric Exchange Systems at Cahokia: A.D. 1000 ± 300. Pp. 137-164 in Explorations into Cahokia Archaeology. Melvin L. Fowler, ed. *Illinois Archaeological Survey Bulletin* 7. Urbana.

Porter, Kenneth W.
1971   The Negro on the American Frontier. New York: Arno Press and The New York Times.

Postal, Susan (Koessler)
1965   Hoax Nativism at Caughnawaga: A Control Case for the Theory of Revitalization. *Ethnology* 4(3):266-281.

Pote, William
1896   The Journal of Captain William Pote, Jr. During His Captivity in the French-Indian War from May, 1745, to August, 1747. J.F. Hurst, ed. New York: Dodd, Mead.

Potier, Pierre
[1748]   Vocabulaire huron-français. (Manuscript in Collection Gagnon, Montreal Public Library, Montreal.)

———
1920   Elementa grammaticae huronicae [1745]. Pp. 1-157 in *15th Report of the Bureau of Archives for the Province of Ontario for the Years 1918-1919*. Alexander Fraser, ed. Toronto: Clarkson W. James.

———
1920a   Radices huronicae [1751]. Pp. 159-455 in *15th Report of the Bureau of Archives for the Province of Ontario for the Years 1918-1919*. Alexander Fraser, ed. Toronto: Clarkson W. James.

Potter, Elisha R.
1835   The Early History of Narragansett. *Collections of the Rhode Island Historical Society* 3. Providence.

Potter, Martha A.
1968   Ohio's Prehistoric Peoples. Columbus: Ohio Historical Society.

———
1971   Adena Culture Content and Settlement. Pp. 4-11 in Adena: The Seeking of an Identity. B.K. Swartz, Jr., ed. Muncie, Ind.: Ball State University Press.

Potzger, J.E.
1946   Phytosociology of the Primeval Forest in Central-Northern Wisconsin and Upper Michigan, and a Brief Post-Glacial History of the Lake Forest Formation. *Ecological Monographs* 16(3):211-250.

Pound, Arthur
1930 Johnson of the Mohawks: A Biography of Sir William Johnson. New York: Macmillan.

Powell, Bernard W.
1971 First Site Synthesis and Proposed Chronology for the Aborigines of Southwestern Connecticut. *Pennsylvania Archaeologist* 41(1-2):30-37.

Powell, John Wesley
1877 Introduction to the Study of Indian Languages with Words, Phrases and Sentences to Be Collected. Washington: U.S. Government Printing Office.

————
1880 Introduction to the Study of Indian Languages with Words, Phrases and Sentences to Be Collected. 2d ed. Washington: U.S. Government Printing Office.

————
1881 Wyandot Government: A Short Study of Tribal Society. Pp. 57-69 in *1st Annual Report of the Bureau of American Ethnology for the Years 1879-1880.* Washington.

————
1891 Indian Linguistic Families of America North of Mexico. Pp. 1-142 in *7th Annual Report of the Bureau of American Ethnology for the Years 1885-1886.* Washington.

Prahl, Earl J.
1966 The Muskegon River Survey: 1965 and 1966. *Michigan Archaeologist* 12(4):183-209.

————
1968 Archaeological Investigations in the Muskegon River Valley. (Manuscript in Prahl's possession.)

————
1969 Preliminary Comparison of Three Prehistoric Sites in the Vicinity of the Western Lake Erie Shore. *Toledo Area Aboriginal Research Club Bulletin* 1(1):32-63. Toledo, Ohio.

————
1970 The Middle Woodland Period of the Lower Muskegon Valley and the Northern Hopewellian Frontier. (Unpublished Ph.D. Dissertation in Anthropology, University of Michigan, Ann Arbor.)

Prahl, Earl J., and David S. Brose
[1970] The Ekdahl-Goudrean Site, Mackinac County, Michigan. (Manuscript, Fieldnotes, Photographs at the University of Toledo, Department of Sociology and Anthropology, Toledo, Ohio.)

Prahl, Earl J., David S. Brose, and David M. Stothers
[1976] A Preliminary Synthesis of Late Prehistoric Phenomena in the Western Basin of Lake Erie. In The Late Prehistory of the Lake Erie Drainage Basin: A Symposium. David S. Brose, ed. *Scientific Papers of the Cleveland Museum of Natural History.* Cleveland. In Press.

Pratt, Peter P.
1966 Archaeology of the Oneida Iroquois as Related to Early Acculturation and to the Location of the Champlain-Iroquois Battle of 1615. (Unpublished Ph.D. Dissertation in Anthropology, University of Michigan, Ann Arbor.)

————
1976 Archaeology of the Oneida Iroquois. *Occasional Publications in Northeastern Anthropology* 1. George's Mills, N.H.

Price, Edward T.
1950 Mixed-blood Populations of Eastern United States as to Origins, Localizations, and Persistence. (Unpublished Ph.D. Dissertation in Geography, University of California, Berkeley.)

————
1950a The Mixed-blood Racial Strain of Carmel, Ohio, and Magoffin County, Kentucky. *Ohio Journal of Science* 50(6):281-290.

————
1951 The Melungeons: A Mixed-blood Strain of the Southern Appalachians. *Geographical Review* 41(2):256-271.

————
1953 A Geographic Analysis of White-Negro-Indian Racial Mixtures in the Eastern United States. *Annals of the Association of American Geographers* 43(2):138-155.

Prime, Nathaniel S.
1845 A History of Long Island, from its First Settlement by Europeans, to the Year 1845, with Special Reference to its Ecclesiastical Concerns. New York and Pittsburgh: R. Carter.

Prince, J. Dyneley
1897 The Passamaquoddy Wampum Records. *Proceedings of the American Philosophical Society* 36:479-495. Philadelphia.

————
1898 Some Passamaquoddy Documents. *Annals of the New York Academy of Sciences* 11(15):369-377. New York.

————
1899 Some Passamaquoddy Witchcraft Tales. *Proceedings of the American Philosophical Society* 38:181-189. Philadelphia.

————
1901 Notes on Passamaquoddy Literature. *Annals of the New York Academy of Sciences* 13(4):381-386. New York.

————
1902 The Differentiation Between the Penobscot and the Canadian Abenaki Dialects. *American Anthropologist* n.s. 4(1):17-32.

————
1907 Last Living Echoes of the Natick. *American Anthropologist* 9(3):493-498.

————
1909 A Passamaquoddy Aviator. *American Anthropologist* 11(4):628-650.

————
1912 An Ancient New Jersey Indian Jargon. *American Anthropologist* 14(3):508-524.

————
1914 The Morphology of the Passamaquoddy Language of Maine. *Proceedings of the American Philosophical Society* 53:92-117. Philadelphia.

————
1917 A Passamaquoddy Tobacco Famine. *International Journal of American Linguistics* 1(1):58-63.

————
1921 Passamaquoddy Texts. *Publications of the American Ethnological Society* 10. New York.

Prince, J. Dyneley, and Frank G. Speck
1903 The Modern Pequots and Their Language. *American Anthropologist* n.s. 5(2):193-212.

————
1903a Dying American Speech Echoes from Connecticut. *Proceedings of the American Philosophical Society* 42(174):346-352. Philadelphia.

————
1904 Glossary of the Mohegan-Pequot Language. *American Anthropologist* n.s. 6(1):18-45.

Prince, Thomas, ed.
1744-1745 The Christian History Containing Accounts of the Revival and Propagation of Religion in Great Britain and America for the Year 1743. Boston: S. Kneeland and T. Green.

————, ed.
1745 The Christian History Containing Accounts of the Revival and Propagation of Religion in Great Britain and America for the Year 1744. Boston: S. Kneeland and T. Green.

Pring, Martin
1906 A Voyage Set Out from the Citie of Bristoll with a Small Ship and a Barke for the Discouerie of the North Part of Virginia... 1603. Pp. 345-352 in Early English and French Voyages, Chiefly from Hakluyt, 1534-1608. Henry S. Burrage, ed. New York: Charles Scribner's Sons.

Proctor, Thomas
1864-1865 Narrative of Col. Thomas Proctor. Pp. 413-426 in Vol. 1 and pp. 305-318 in Vol. 2 of An Authentic and Comprehensive History of Buffalo, by William Ketchum. 2 vols. Buffalo: Rockwell, Baker and Hill.

Prufer, Olaf H.
1964   The Hopewell Complex of Ohio. *Illinois State Museum Scientific Paper* 12(2):35-83. Springfield.

1964a   The Hopewell Cult. *Scientific American* 211(6):90-102.

1965   The McGraw Site: A Study in Hopewellian Dynamics. *Scientific Publications of the Cleveland Museum of Natural History* n.s. 4(1). Cleveland.

1967   Chesser Cave: A Late Woodland Phase in Southeastern Ohio. Pp. 1-62 in Studies in Ohio Archaeology. Olaf H. Prufer and Douglas H. McKenzie eds., Cleveland: Western Reserve University Press.

1968   Ohio Hopewell Ceramics: An Analysis of the Extant Collections. *University of Michigan Museum of Anthropology, Anthropological Papers* 33. Ann Arbor.

Prufer, Olaf H., and Raymond S. Baby
1963   Paleo-Indians of Ohio. Columbus: Ohio Historical Society.

Prufer, Olaf H., and Douglas McKenzie
1966   Peters Cave: Two Woodland Occupations in Ross County, Ohio. *Ohio Journal of Science* 66(3):233-253.

Prufer, Olaf H., and Orrin C. Shane, III
1970   Blain Village and the Fort Ancient Tradition in Ohio. Kent, Ohio: Kent State University Press.

[1976]   The Portage-Sandusky-Vermilion River Region in Ohio. In The Late Prehistory of the Lake Erie Drainage Basin: A Symposium. David S. Brose, ed. *Scientific Papers of the Cleveland Museum of Natural History*. Cleveland. In Press.

Prufer, Olaf H., Douglas H. McKenzie, Oriol Pi-Sunyer, Hugh C. Cutler, Richard A. Yarnell, Paul W. Parmalee, and David H. Stansbery
1965   The McGraw Site: A Study in Hopewellian Dynamics. *Scientific Publications of the Cleveland Museum of Natural History* n.s. 4(1). Cleveland.

Pryse, J.P.
1963-1964 Pioneer Baptist Missionaries to Upper Canada Tuscaroras. *Canadian Baptist Home Missions Digest* 6:273-282.

Purchas, Samuel
1617   Purchas, His Pilgrimage, or Relations of the Vvorld and the Religions Observed in Al Ages and Places Discouered, from the Creation unto This Present. 3d ed. London: W. Stansby for H. Fetherstone.

1625   Hakluytus Posthumus or Purchas, His Pilgrimes. 4 vols. London: Printed by W. Stansby for Henry Fetherstone. (Reprinted: J. MacLehose and Sons, Glasgow, 1905-1907.)

1625a   The Description of the Countrey of Mawooshen, Discovered by the English in the Yeere 1602.3.4.5.6.7.8. and 9. Pp. 1873-1875 in Vol. 4 of Hakluytus Posthumus or Purchas His Pilgrimes. London: Printed by W. Stansby for Henry Fetherstone. (Reprinted: J. MacLehose and Sons, Glasgow, 1905-1907.)

Putt, Raymond V.
1971   The Role of the Hereditary Chiefs in Contemporary Iroquois Society: A Nativistic Movement on the Six Nations Reserve. *Na'páo* 3(1):11-21.

Quimby, George I.
1938   Dated Indian Burials in Michigan. *Papers of the Michigan Academy of Science, Arts and Letters* 23:63-72. Ann Arbor.

1941   The Goodall Focus: An Analysis of Ten Hopewellian Components in Michigan and Indiana. *Indiana Historical Society, Prehistory Research Series* 2:63-161. Indianapolis.

1952   The Archeology of the Upper Great Lakes Area. Pp. 99-102 in Archeology of Eastern United States. James B. Griffin, ed. Chicago: University of Chicago Press.

1960   Indian Life in the Upper Great Lakes, 11,000 B.C. to A.D. 1800. Chicago: University of Chicago Press.

1961   The Pic River Site. Pp. 83-90 in Lake Superior Copper and the Indians: Miscellaneous Studies of Great Lakes Prehistory. J.B. Griffin, ed. *University of Michigan Museum of Anthropology, Anthropological Papers* 17. Ann Arbor.

1963   The Gros Cap Cemetery in Mackinac County, Michigan. *Michigan Archaeologist* 9(4):50-57.

1964   The Stony Lake Mounds, Oceana County, Michigan. *Michigan Archaeologist* 10(1):11-16.

1965   An Indian Earthwork in Muskegon County, Michigan. Pp. 165-169 in Papers in Honor of Emerson F. Greenman. James E. Fitting, ed. *Michigan Archaeologist* 11(3-4).

1966   Indian Culture and European Trade Goods: The Archaeology of the Historic Period in the Western Great Lakes Region. Madison: University of Wisconsin Press.

1966a   The Dumaw Creek Site: A Seventeenth Century Prehistoric Indian Village and Cemetery in Oceana County, Michigan. *Fieldiana: Anthropology* 56(1):1-91. Chicago.

1972   Hawaiians in the Fur Trade of North-west America, 1785-1820. *Journal of Pacific History* 7:92-103.

Quinn, David B., ed.
1955   The Roanoke Voyages, 1584-1590: Documents to Illustrate the English Voyages to North America Under the Patent Granted to Walter Raleigh in 1584. 2 vols. London: Cambridge University Press for the Hakluyt Society.

1961   Simão Fernandes, a Portugese Pilot in the English Service, Circa 1573-1588. *Congresso Internacional de História dos Descobrimentos, Actas* 3:3-19. Lisbon.

1970   Thomas Hariot and the Virginia Voyages of 1602. *William and Mary College Quarterly*, 3d ser., Vol. 27:273-274. Williamsburg.

Radin, Paul
1909   Winnebago Tales. *Journal of American Folk-Lore* 22(85):288-313.

1915   The Winnebago Myth of the Twins. *Papers of the Southwestern Anthropological Society* 1:1-56.

1920   The Autobiography of a Winnebago Indian. *University of California Publications in American Archaeology and Ethnology* 16(7):381-473. Berkeley.

1923   The Winnebago Tribe. Pp. 33-550 in *37th Annual Report of the Bureau of American Ethnology for the Years 1915-1916*. Washington.

1924   Ojibwa Ethnological Chit-chat. *American Anthropologist* 26(4):491-533.

[1926]   Ottawa-Ojibwa I - VII. (Manuscript 150 (Ott.1-7), in Library of the American Philosophical Society, Philadelphia.)

1926a   Literary Aspects of Winnebago Mythology. *Journal of American Folk-Lore* 39(151):18-52.

1926b   The Trickster Cycle of the Winnebago. *Primitive Culture* 1:8-86.

_____, ed.
1926c   Crashing Thunder: The Autobiography of an American Indian. New York and London: D. Appleton.

1928   Ethnological Notes on the Ojibwa of Southeastern Ontario. *American Anthropologist* 30(4):659-668.

1945   The Road of Life and Death: A Ritual Drama of the American Indians. New York: Pantheon Books.

1948   Winnebago Hero Cycles: A Study in Aboriginal Literature. *Indiana University Publications in Anthropology and Linguistics, Memoir* 1. Bloomington.

1949   The Culture of the Winnebago: As Described by Themselves. *Indiana University Publications in Anthropology and Linguistics, Memoir* 2. Bloomington.

1950   The Origin Myth of the Medicine Rite: Three Versions. *Indiana University Publications in Anthropology and Linguistics, Memoir* 3. Bloomington.

1956   The Trickster: A Study in American Indian Mythology. New York: Philosophical Library.

Radisson, Pierre E.
1885   Voyages of Peter Esprit Radisson, Being an Account of His Travels and Experiences Among the North American Indians, from 1652-1684. Boston: Prince Society.

1967   The Explorations of Pierre Esprit Radisson. Arthur T. Adams, ed. Minneapolis: Ross and Haines.

Rainey, Froelich G.
1936   A Compilation of Historical Data Contributing to the Ethnography of Connecticut and Southern New England Indians. *Bulletin of the Archaeological Society of Connecticut* 3:1-89. New Haven. (Reprinted in 1956.)

[Râle, Sébastien] "Sebastian Rasles"
1833   A Dictionary of the Abnaki Language in North America, [1691-1722]. John Pickering, ed. *Memoirs of the American Academy of Arts and Sciences* n.s. 1:375-565. Cambridge, Mass.

[Ramusio, Giovanni B., ed.]
1556   Terzo volume della navigationi et viaggi. Venice: Stamperia de Givnti.

Rand, Silas T.
1850   A Short Statement of Facts Relating to the History, Manners, Customs, Language, and Literature of the Micmac Tribe of Indians, in Nova-Scotia and P.E. Island. Halifax, N.S.: James Bowes and Son.

1888   Dictionary of the Language of the Micmac Indians Who Reside in Nova Scotia, New Brunswick, Prince Edward Island, Cape Breton and Newfoundland. Halifax, N.S.: Nova Scotia Printing Company.

1894   Legends of the Micmacs. (Wellesley Philological Publications) New York, London: Longmans, Green.

1902   Micmac Dictionary; Prepared from Phonographic Word-lists by S.T. Rand. Transcribed and Alphabetically Arranged by Jeremiah S. Clark. Charlottetown, P.E.I.: Patriot Publishing Company.

Randall, Emilius O., and Daniel J. Ryan
1912   History of Ohio: The Rise and Progress of an American State. 5 vols. New York: Century History Company.

Randle, Martha C.
1951   Iroquois Women, Then and Now. Pp. 167-180 in Symposium on Local Diversity in Iroquois Culture. William N. Fenton, ed. *Bureau of American Ethnology Bulletin* 149. Washington.

Rands, Robert L., and Carroll L. Riley
1958   Diffusion and Discontinuous Distribution. *American Anthropologist* 60(2):274-297.

Rasieres, Isaack de
1909   Letter of Isaack de Rasieres to Samuel Blommaert, 1628. Pp. 97-115 in Narratives of New Netherland, 1609-1664. J. Franklin Jameson, ed. New York: Charles Scribner's Sons. (Reprinted: Barnes and Noble, New York, 1967.)

Rasles, Sebastian *see* Râle, Sébastien

Raudot, Antoine-Denis
1904   Relation par lettres de l'Amérique septentrionale (années 1709-1710). Camille de Rochemonteix, ed. Paris: Letouzey et Ané.

Rawson, Grindal, and Samuel Danforth
1698   The Reverend Mr. Grindal Rawson *Pastor of the Church in* Mendon, *and the Reverend Mr.* Samuel Danforth *Pastor of the Church in* Taunton, *Spent from* May, 30 *to* June 24. 1698 *in Visiting the Several Plantations of the* Indians *within this Province. And the Remainder of this Sheet May Be Well Employed in Giving an Account of it.* Pp. 89-99 in New-Englands Duty and Interest, to Be an Habitation of Justice, and Mountain of Holiness. Boston: Bartholemew Green, and John Allen.

Ray, Margaret
1954   An Indian Mission in Upper Canada. *The Bulletin: Records and Proceedings of the Committee on Archives of the United Church of Canada* 7:10-18. Toronto.

Ray, Verne F.
1971   The Menominee Tribe of Indians, 1940-1970. Escanaba, Mich.: Photo Offset Printing Company.

Raymond, William O.
1910   The River St. John, its Physical Features, Legends and History, from 1604 to 1784. St. John, N.B.: J.A. Bowes. (Reprinted: The Tribune Press, Sackville, N.B., 1950.)

Reaman, George E.
1967   The Trail of the Iroquois Indians: How the Iroquois Nation Saved Canada for the British Empire. London: Muller; New York: Barnes and Noble.

Rebok, Horace M.
1901   The Last of the Mus-qua-kies. *Iowa Historical Record* 17(3):305-335.

Records of Conn. *see* Connecticut (Colony) Laws, Statutes, etc.

Records of Plymouth *see* New Plymouth Colony

Records of R.I. *see* Rhode Island (Colony)

Reed, Nelson A.
1969   Monks and Other Mississippian Mounds. Pp. 31-42 in Explorations into Cahokia Archaeology. Melvin L. Fowler, ed. *Illinois Archaeological Survey Bulletin* 7. Urbana.

Reed, Nelson A., John W. Bennett, and James W. Porter
1968   Solid Core Drilling of Monks Mound: Technique and Findings. *American Antiquity* 33(2):137-148.

Regensburg, R.A.
1970-1971 The Savich Farm Site: A Preliminary Report. *Bulletin of the Massachusetts Archaeological Society* 32(1-2):20-23. Attleboro.

Reichel, William C.
1860   A Memorial of the Dedication of Monuments Erected by the Moravian Historial Society, to Mark the Sites of Ancient Missionary Stations in New York and Connecticut. New York: C.B. Richardson; Philadelphia: J.B. Lippincott.

Renfrew, Colin
1973   Wessex as a Social Question. *Antiquity* 47(187):221-225.

Reports of the Agent to the Passamaquoddy Indians
1876   Report of William T. Hobart for the Year 1876. (Journals of the Legislature of the State of Maine, A.D. 1876.) Augusta: Sprague, Owen and Nash.

Reville, F. Douglas
1920   History of the County of Brant. Brantford, Ont.: Hurley Printing Company.

Rhode Island (Colony)
1856-1865 Records of the Colony of Rhode Island and Providence Plantations, in New England (1636-1792). John R. Bartlett, ed. 10 vols. Providence: A.C. Green and Brothers.

867

Rhode Island. Census Board
1887   Rhode Island State Census, 1885. Providence: E.L. Free-
            man and Son.

Rhode Island. Commissioner on the Narragansett Tribe of Indians
1858   Report of the Commissioner on the Narragansett Tribe of
            Indians, Made to the General Assembly, at its January
            Session, 1858. Providence: Knowles, Anthony.

Rhode Island. General Assembly. Committee on Indian Tribes
1852   Report of the Committee on Indian Tribes, Made to the
            General Assembly, October Session, A.D. 1852... Provi-
            dence: Sayles and Miller.

Rhode Island. General Assembly. House of Representatives
1880   Narragansett Tribe of Indians: Report of the Committee
            of Investigation; a Historical Sketch, and Evidence Taken.
            Made to the House of Representatives at its January Ses-
            sion, A.D. 1880. Providence: E.L. Freeman.

Rhode Island Commission on Affairs of the Narragansett Indians
1881-1884   Annual Reports of the Commission on the Affairs of the
            Narragansett Indians for the Years 1880-1883. 4 vols.
            Providence: E.L. Freeman.

Rhodes, Richard
1976   A Preliminary Report on the Dialects of Eastern Ojibwa-
            Odawa. Pp. 129-156 in Papers of the 7th Algonquian Con-
            ference, 1975. Ottawa: Carleton University.

Ricciardelli, Alex F.
1961   Factionalism at Oneida, an Iroquois Indian Community.
            (Unpublished Ph.D. Dissertation in Anthropology, Uni-
            versity of Pennsylvania, Philadelphia.)

Ricciardelli, Catherine (Hinckle)
1966   Kinship Systems of the Oneida Indians. (Unpublished
            Ph.D. Dissertation in Anthropology, University of Penn-
            sylvania, Philadelphia.)

Richards, Cara E.
1967   Huron and Iroquois Residence Patterns, 1600-1650. Pp.
            51-56 in Iroquois Culture, History and Prehistory: Pro-
            ceedings of the 1965 Conference on Iroquois Research.
            Elisabeth Tooker, ed. Albany: New York State Museum
            and Science Service.

Rickard, Clinton
1973   Fighting Tuscarora: The Autobiography of Chief Clinton
            Rickard. Barbara Graymont, ed. Syracuse, N.Y.: Syra-
            cuse University Press.

Rider, Sidney S.
1904   The Lands of Rhode Island as They Were Known to Cau-
            nounicus and Miantunnomu When Roger Williams Came
            in 1636. Providence: Sidney S. Rider.

Ridley, Frank
1947   A Search for Ossossane and its Environs. Ontario History
            39:7-14.

1952   The Fallis Site, Ontario. American Antiquity 18(1):7-14.

1952a   Huron and Lalonde Occupations of Ontario. American
            Antiquity 17(3):197-210.

1954   The Frank Bay Site, Lake Nipissing, Ontario. American
            Antiquity 20(1):40-50.

1958   Did the Hurons Really Migrate North from the Toronto
            Area? Pennsylvania Archaeologist 28(3-4):143-144.

1961   Archaeology of the Neutral Indians. Port Credit, Ont:
            Etobicoke Historical Society.

1961a   The Lake Superior Site at Michipicoten. Pennsylvania Ar-
            chaeologist 31(3-4):131-147.

1963   The Ontario Iroquoian Controversy. Ontario History
            55(1):49-59.

1966-1968   Report on Archaeological Sites in Huronia. (Manuscript
            in Department of Public Records and Archives, Toronto.)

Rietz, Robert W.
1960   A Discussion of Contemporary Fox Social Organization,
            Together with a Proposal for a Combined Program of So-
            cial Engineering and Social Science Research. Pp. 97-119
            in History of the Fox Project. Frederick O. Gearing, Rob-
            ert McC. Netting, and Lisa R. Peattie, eds. Chicago:
            University of Chicago Press.

Rigaud de Vaudreuil, Phillipe de, and Michel Bégon
1722   [Lettre au Conseil, 17 8bre 1722.] (Manuscript in Archives
            des Colonies, Archives Nationales, Paris; Copy in Public
            Archives of Canada, C11A 46:233-234, Ottawa.)

Riggs, Stephen R., ed.
1852   Grammar and Dictionary of the Dakota Language: Col-
            lected by the Members of the Dakota Mission. Smithso-
            nian Contributions to Knowledge 4. Washington.

1890   A Dakota-English Dictionary. James O. Dorsey, ed.
            (Contributions to North American Ethnology 7) Wash-
            ington: U.S. Geographical and Geological Survey of the
            Rocky Mountain Region.

Rights, Douglas L.
1947   The American Indian in North Carolina. Durham, N.C.:
            Duke University Press.

Rioux, Marcel
1951   Some Medical Beliefs and Practices of the Contemporary
            Iroquois Longhouses of the Six Nations Reserve. Journal
            of the Washington Academy of Sciences 41(5):152-158.
            Washington.

1952   Relations Between Religion and Government Among the
            Longhouse Iroquois of Grand River, Ontario. Anthropo-
            logical Series 32, National Museum of Canada Bulletin
            126:94-98. Ottawa.

Rippeteau, Bruce E.
1973   The Principles and Theory of Radiocarbon Chronology
            and a Radiocarbon Chronology for Lithic Variation in the
            Northeastern United States During 3000 to 500 Calendri-
            cal Years B.C. (Unpublished Ph.D. Dissertation in An-
            thropology, Case Western Reserve University, Cleveland.)

1974   Using C-14 Calendrical Corrections and Conventions. Ar-
            chaeology of Eastern North America 2(1):29-37. Attleboro,
            Mass.

Rising, Johan
1912   Report of Governor Johan Rising [1655]. Pp. 156-165 in
            Narratives of Early Pennsylvania, West New Jersey, and
            Delaware, 1630-1704. Albert C. Myers, ed. New York:
            Charles Scribner's Sons.

Ritchie, William A.
1932   The Lamoka Lake Site: The Type Station of the Archaic
            Algonkin Period in New York. Researches and Transac-
            tions of the New York State Archaeological Association
            7(4). Rochester, N.Y.

1936   A Prehistoric Fortified Village Site at Canandaigua, On-
            tario County, New York. Research Records of the Roches-
            ter Museum of Arts and Sciences 3. Rochester, N.Y.

1940   Two Prehistoric Village Sites at Brewerton, New York:
            Type Components of the Brewerton Focus. Research Rec-
            ords of the Rochester Museum of Arts and Sciences 5.
            Rochester, N.Y.

1944   The Pre-Iroquoian Occupations of New York State. Roch-
            ester Museum of Arts and Sciences Memoir 1. Rochester,
            N.Y.

1946   Archaeological Manifestations and Relative Chronology
            in the Northeast. Pp. 96-105 in Man in Northeastern
            North America. Frederick Johnson, ed. Papers of the Rob-

ert S. Peabody Foundation for Archaeology 3. Andover, Mass.

1949   An Archaeological Survey of the Trent Waterway in Ontario, Canada and its Significance for New York State Prehistory. *Researches and Transactions of the New York State Archaeological Association* 12(1). Rochester, N.Y.

1952   The Chance Horizon: An Early Stage of Mohawk Iroquois Cultural Development. *New York State Museum and Science Service Circular* 29. Albany.

1953   A Probable Paleo-Indian Site in Vermont. *American Antiquity* 18(3):249-258.

1955-1956   The Indian in His Environment. *New York State Conservationist* (December/January):23-27.

1956   Prehistoric Settlement Patterns in Northeastern North America. Pp. 72-80 in Prehistoric Settlement Patterns in the New World. Gordon R. Willey, ed. *Viking Fund Publications in Anthropology* 23. New York.

1957   Traces of Early Man in the Northeast. *New York State Museum and Science Service Bulletin* 358. Albany.

1958   An Introduction to Hudson Valley Prehistory. *New York State Museum and Science Service Bulletin* 367. Albany.

1959   The Stony Brook Site and its Relation to Archaic and Transitional Cultures on Long Island. *New York State Museum and Science Service Bulletin* 372. Albany.

1961   A Typology and Nomenclature for New York Projectile Points. *New York State Museum and Science Service Bulletin* 384. Albany.

1961a   Iroquois Archaeology and Settlement Patterns. Pp. 25-38 in Symposium on Cherokee and Iroquois Culture. William N. Fenton and John Gulick, eds. *Bureau of American Ethnology Bulletin* 180. Washington.

1965   The Archaeology of New York State. Garden City, N.Y.: Natural History Press.

1968   The KI Site, the Vergennes Phase and the Laurentian Tradition. *New York State Archaeological Association Bulletin* 42:1-5. Rochester, N.Y.

1969   The Archaeology of Martha's Vineyard: A Framework for the Prehistory of Southern New England; A Study in Coastal Ecology and Adaptation. Garden City, N.Y.: Natural History Press.

1969a   The Archaeology of New York State. Rev. ed. Garden City, N.Y.: Natural History Press.

1971   The Archaic in New York. *New York State Archaeological Association Bulletin* 52(July):2-12. Rochester, N.Y.

Ritchie, William A., and Don W. Dragoo
1959   The Eastern Dispersal of Adena. *American Antiquity* 25(1):43-50.

Ritchie, William A., and Robert E. Funk
1971   Evidence for Early Archaic Occupations on Staten Island. *Pennsylvania Archaeologist* 41(3):45-59.

1973   Aboriginal Settlement Patterns in the Northeast. *New York State Museum and Science Service Memoir* 20. Albany.

Ritchie, William A., and Richard S. MacNeish
1949   The Pre-Iroquoian Pottery of New York State. *American Antiquity* 15(2):97-124.

Ritchie, William A., Donald Lenig, and P. Schuyler Miller
1953   An Early Owasco Sequence in Eastern New York. *New York State Museum and Science Service Circular* 32. Albany.

Ritzenthaler, Robert E.
1945   Totemic Insult Among the Wisconsin Chippewa. *American Anthropologist* 47(2):322-324.

1946   The Osceola Site, an "Old Copper" Site Near Potosi, Wisconsin. *Wisconsin Archaeologist* 27(3):53-70.

1950   The Oneida Indians of Wisconsin. *Bulletin of the Public Museum of the City of Milwaukee* 19(1). Milwaukee.

1953   The Potawatomi Indians of Wisconsin. *Bulletin of the Public Museum of the City of Milwaukee* 19(3):99-174. Milwaukee.

1953a   Chippewa Preoccupation with Health: Change in a Traditional Attitude Resulting from Modern Health Problems. *Bulletin of the Public Museum of the City of Milwaukee* 19(4):175-257. Milwaukee.

Ritzenthaler, Robert E., and Frederick A. Peterson
1956   The Mexican Kickapoo Indians. *Milwaukee Public Museum Publications in Anthropology* 2. Milwaukee.

Ritzenthaler, Robert E., and Warren L. Wittry
1952   The Oconto Site - an Old Copper Manifestation. *Wisconsin Archaeologist* 33(4):199-223.

Robbins, Louise M., and Georg K. Neumann
1972   The Prehistoric People of the Fort Ancient Culture of the Central Ohio Valley. *University of Michigan Museum of Anthropology, Anthropological Papers* 47. Ann Arbor.

Robbins, Maurice
1960   Wapanucket No. 6: An Archaic Village in Middleboro, Massachusetts. Attleboro: Cohannet Chapter, Massachusetts Archaeological Society.

1968   An Archaic Ceremonial Complex at Assawompsett. Attleboro: Massachusetts Archaeological Society.

Robbins, Maurice, and George A. Agogino
1964   The Wapanucket No. 8 Site: A Clovis-Archaic Site in Massachusetts. *American Antiquity* 29(4):509-513.

Robinson, Percy J.
1942   The Origin of the Name Hochelaga. *Canadian Historical Review* 23(3):295-296.

1945   Some of Cartier's Place-names, 1535-36. *Canadian Historical Review* 26(4):401-405.

1948   The Huron Equivalents of Cartier's Second Vocabulary. *Transactions of the Royal Society of Canada,* 3d ser., sect. 2, Vol. 42:127-146. Ottawa.

1965   Toronto During the French Regime: A History of the Toronto Region from Brûlé to Simcoe, 1615-1793. Toronto: University of Toronto Press.

Robinson, W. Stitt
1959   Tributary Indians in Colonial Virginia. *Virginia Magazine of History and Biography* 67(1):49-64.

Rogers, Edward S.
1962   The Round Lake Ojibwa. *Royal Ontario Museum, Art and Archaeology Division, Occasional Papers* 5. Toronto.

1963   The Hunting Group - Hunting Territory Complex Among the Mistassini Indians. *Anthropological Series 63, National Museum of Canada Bulletin* 195. Ottawa.

1965   The Dugout Canoe in Ontario. *American Antiquity* 30(4):454-459.

1967   Subsistence Areas of the Cree-Ojibwa of the Eastern Subarctic: A Preliminary Study. *Anthropological Series 70, National Museum of Canada Bulletin* 204:59-90. Ottawa.

1967a   [Review of] Some Implications of the Theory of the Particularity, or Atomism' of Northern Algonkians, by Harold Hickerson. *Current Anthropology* 8(4):333-334.

1971   The Indian and Euro-Canadian Society. Pp. 331-350 in Citizen Participation: Canada. Toronto: New Press.

1972-1973   [Fieldnotes from the Northshore Area of Lake Huron.] (Manuscript in Roger's Possession.)

Rogers, Edward S., and Jean Shawana
1974   Programme for Ontario Indians: Action and Reaction. Pp. 565- 577 in Vol. 1 of Proceedings of the 40th International Congress of Americanists. 2 vols. Rome, 1972.

Rogers, Edward S., and Flora Tobobundung
1975   Parry Island Farmers: A Period of Change in the Way of Life of the Algonkians of Southern Ontario. Canada. National Museum of Man, Ethnology Division, Mercury Series Paper 31:247-366. Ottawa.

Rogers, Margaret B.
1972   The 46th Street Site and the Occurrence of Allegan Ware in Southwestern Michigan. Michigan Archaeologist 18(2):47-108.

Rogers, Robert
1961   Journals of Robert Rogers [1765]. Howard H. Peckham, ed. New York: Corinth Books.

Rolingson, Martha A.
1961   The Kirtley Site: A Mississippian Village in McLean County, Kentucky. Transactions of the Kentucky Academy of Science 22(3-4):41-59. Lexington.

Romig, Joseph
1910   The Chippewa and Munsee (or Christian) Indians of Franklin County, Kansas. Collections of the Kansas State Historical Society 11:314-323. Topeka.

Rostlund, Erhard
1952   Freshwater Fish and Fishing in Native North America. University of California Publications in Geography 9. Berkeley.

Roth, Johannes
[1770-1772] Ein Versuch! Der Geschichte unsers Herrn u. Heylandes Jesu Christi. In dass Delawarische übersezt der Unami von der Marter Woche an bis zur Himmelfahrt unsers Herrn. (Manuscript No. 1176 in Library of the American Philosophical Society, Philadelphia.)

Rountree, Helen C.
1972   Being an Indian in Virginia: Four Centuries in Limbo. The Chesopiean 10(1):2-7.

1972a   Powhatan's Descendants in the Modern World: Community Studies of the Two Virginia Indian Reservations, with Notes on Five Non-reservation Enclaves. The Chesopiean 10(3):62-96.

1973   Indian Land Loss in Virginia. (Unpublished Ph.D. Dissertation in Anthropology, University of Wisconsin, Milwaukee.)

1973a   The Termination and Dispersal of the Nottoway Indians of Virginia. (Manuscript in Douglas W. Boyce's Possession.)

Rowe, Chandler W.
1956   The Effigy Mound Culture of Wisconsin. Milwaukee Public Museum Publications in Anthropology 3. Milwaukee.

Rowe, John S.
1959   Forest Regions of Canada. Canada. Department of Northern Affairs and National Resources, Forestry Branch Bulletin 123. Ottawa.

Rowell, Mary K.
1943   Pamunkey Indian Games and Amusements. Journal of American Folklore 56(221):203-207.

Rowlandson, Mary
1913   Narrative of the Captivity of Mrs. Mary Rowlandson [1682]. Pp. 107-167 in Narratives of the Indian Wars 1675-1699. Charles H. Lincoln, ed. New York: C. Scrib-

ner's Sons. (Reprinted: Barnes and Noble, New York, 1941, 1959.)

Royce, Charles C.
1881   An Inquiry into the Identity and History of the Shawnee Indians. American Antiquarian and Oriental Journal 3(3):177-189.

————, comp.
1899   Indian Land Cessions in the United States. Pp. 521-997 in 18th Annual Report of the Bureau of American Ethnology for the Years 1896-1897. Pt. 2. Washington.

Rudes, Blair A.
1976   Historical Phonology and the Development of the Tuscarora Sound System. (Unpublished Ph.D. Dissertation in Linguistics, State University of New York at Buffalo.)

Rupp, Israel D.
1846   Early History of Western Pennsylvania, and of the West, from 1754-1833. Pittsburgh: D.W. Kauffman; Harrisburg: W.O. Hickok.

Ruttenber, Edward M.
1872   History of the Indian Tribes of Hudson's River; Their Origin, Manners and Customs, Tribal and Sub-tribal Organizations, Wars, Treaties, etc., etc. Albany, N.Y.: J. Munsell.

1875   History of the County of Orange; With a History of the Town and City of Newburgh: General, Analytical and Biographical. Newburgh, N.Y.: E.M. Ruttenber and Son, Printers.

Sabine, L.
1852   Indian Tribes of New England. Christian Examiner 52:96-117.

Sady, Rachel R.
1947   The Menominee: Transition from Trusteeship. Applied Anthropology 6(2):1-14.

Saenderl, Simon
1833-1836   [Briefe an Franz Rese und P. Starke, Arbre Croche, Mackinac, Dutch Settlement.] (Manuscripts, Leopoldinen-Stiftung 3: 3.49-50, 3.52-56, 3.60, Diözesenarchiv, Erzdiözese Wien, Austria.)

Sagard-Théodat, Gabriel
1632   Dictionnaire de la langue huronne. Paris: Denys Moreau.

1632a   Le Grand voyage du pays des Hurons, situé en l'Amérique vers la mer douce, ès derniers confins de la Nouvelle France dite Canada. Paris: Denys Moreau.

1636   Histoire du Canada, et voyages que les Frères Mineurs Récollects y ont faicts pour la conversion des infidelles... depuis l'an 1615. 2 vols. Paris: Claude Sonnius.

1865   Le Grand voyage du pays des Hurons situé en l'Amérique vers la mer douce, ès derniers confins de la Nouvelle France dite Canada. 2 vols. Paris: Librairie Tross.

1865a   Dictionnaire de la langue huronne. Paris: Librairie Tross.

1866   Histoire du Canada et voyages que les Frères Mineurs recollects y ont faicts pour la conversion des infidèles depuis l'an 1615. Avec un dictionnaire de la langue huronne. 4 vols. Paris: E. Tross.

1939   Father Gabriel Sagard: The Long Journey to the Country of the Hurons [1632]. George M. Wrong, ed. Toronto: The Champlain Society.

Sahlins, Marshall D.
1968   Tribesmen. Englewood Cliffs, N.J.: Prentice-Hall.

Sainsbury, William N., ed.
1860-1912   Calendar of State Papers, Colonial America and the West Indies, 1574-1702. 20 vols. London: Public Record Office.

St. Cosme, Jean F.B.
1917   The Voyage of St. Cosme, 1698-1699: Letter of M. Jean Frs. Buisson de St. Cosme, Priest of the Seminary of Quebec, 1699. Pp. 342-361 in Early Narratives of the Northwest, 1634-1699. Louise P. Kellogg, ed. New York: Charles Scribner's Sons.

Salley, Alexander S., Jr., ed.
1911   Narratives of Early Carolina, 1650-1708. New York: Charles Scribner's Sons. (Reprinted: Barnes and Noble, New York, 1959.)

Salwen, Bert
1966   European Trade Goods and the Chronology of the Fort Shantok Site. Bulletin of the Archaeological Society of Connecticut 34:5-39. New Haven.

1968   Muskeeta Cove 2: A Stratified Woodland Site on Long Island. American Antiquity 33(3):322-340.

1969   A Tentative "in situ" Solution to the Mohegan-Pequot Problem. Pp. 81-88 in The Connecticut Valley Indians: An Introduction to Their Archaeology and History. William R. Young, ed. Springfield Museum of Science Publication n.s. 1(1). Springfield, Mass.

1970   Cultural Inferences from Faunal Remains: Examples from Three Northeast Coastal Sites. Pennsylvania Archaeologist 40(1-2):1-8.

Salzer, Robert J.
1968   Nakoni's Complex. (Paper Presented at the Meeting of the Central States Anthropological Society. Detroit, 1968.)

1969   An Introduction to the Archaeology of Northern Wisconsin. (Unpublished Ph.D. Dissertation in Anthropology, Southern Illinois University, Carbondale.)

Sample, Katherine A.
1968   Changes in Agriculture on the Six Nations Reserve. (Unpublished M.A. Thesis in Geography, McMaster University, Hamilton, Ont.)

Sanford, Ezekiel
1819   A History of the United States Before the Revolution, with Some Account of the Aborigines. Philadelphia: Anthony Finley.

Sanger, David
1971   Preliminary Report on Excavations at Cow Point, New Brunswick. Man in the Northeast 1:34-47.

1971a   Passamaquoddy Bay Prehistory: A Summary. Bulletin of the Maine Archaeological Society 11:14-19. Castine.

Sanson d'Abbeville, Nicolas see Sanson, Nicolas

Sanson, Guillaume
1692   Atlas nouveau, contenant toutes les parties du monde. Paris. (Copy in Newberry Library, Chicago.)

Sanson, Nicolas
1650   Amérique septentrionale. Paris: Chez l'Auteur et Pierre Mariette.

1656   Le Canada, ou Nouvelle France. Paris. [Map No. 8 in Historical Atlas of the Great Lakes and Michigan; No. 10 in Louis C. Karpinsky, Bibliography of the Printed Maps of Michigan, Lansing, 1931.]

Sapir, Edward
1916   Time Perspective in Aboriginal American Culture: A Study in Method. Anthropological Series 13, Memoirs of the Canadian Geological Survey 90. Ottawa. (Reprinted: Pp. 389-462 in Selected Writings of Edward Sapir in Language, Culture, and Personality. David G. Mandelbaum, ed., University of California Press, Berkeley and Los Angeles, 1949.)

1929   Central and North American Languages. Pp. 138-141 in Vol. 5 of Encyclopedia Britannica (14th ed.) London and New York: Encyclopedia Britannica Company. (Reprinted: Pp. 169-178 in Selected Writings of Edward Sapir in Language, Culture, and Personality. David G. Mandelbaum, ed. University of California Press, Berkeley and Los Angeles, 1949.)

1931   The Concept of Phonetic Law as Tested in Primitive Languages, by Leonard Bloomfield. Pp. 297-306 in Methods in Social Science. Stuart A. Rice, ed. Chicago: University of Chicago Press. (Reprinted: Pp. 73-82 in Selected Writings of Edward Sapir in Language, Culture, and Personality. David G. Mandelbaum, ed., University of California Press, Berkeley and Los Angeles, 1949.)

Sauer, Carl O.
1971   Sixteenth Century North America: The Land and the People as Seen by the Europeans. Berkeley and Los Angeles: University of California Press.

Saunders, William L., ed.
1886-1890   The Colonial Records of North Carolina. 10 vols. Raleigh: P.M. Hale.

Saunders, William L., Walter Clark, and Stephen B. Weeks, eds.
1886-1914   The Colonial and State Records of North Carolina. 30 vols. Raleigh: Printer to the State.

Savage, Howard G.
1971   Faunal Analysis of the Robitaille Site (BeHa-3) and Maurice Site (BeHa-2). Pp. 166-179 in Palaeoecology and Ontario Prehistory. W.M. Hurley and C. E. Heidenreich, eds. University of Toronto Department of Anthropology, Research Report 2. Toronto.

Sayres, William C., ed.
1956   Sammy Louis: The Life History of a Young Micmac. New Haven, Conn.: Compass Publishing Company.

Schaeffer, Claude E.
1942   The Tutelo Indians in Pennsylvania History. Pp. v-xix in The Tutelo Spirit Adoption Ceremony, by Frank G. Speck and George Herzog. Harrisburg: Pennsylvania Historical Commission.

Schafer, Joseph
1937   The Winnebago-Horicon Basin: A Type Study in Western History. Madison: State Historical Society of Wisconsin.

Schambach, Frank F.
1970   Pre-Caddoan Cultures in the Trans-Mississippi South: A Beginning Sequence. (Unpublished Ph.D. Dissertation in Anthropology, Harvard University, Cambridge, Mass.)

Scheffer, Victor B.
1958   Seals, Sea Lions, and Walruses: A Review of the Pinnipedia. Stanford, Calif.: Stanford University Press.

Schlarman, Joseph H.
1929   From Quebec to New Orleans: The Story of the French in America... Belleville, Ill.: Buechler Publishing Company.

Schmitt, Karl, Jr.
1952   Archeological Chronology of the Middle Atlantic States. Pp. 59-70 in Archeology of Eastern United States. James B. Griffin, ed. Chicago: University of Chicago Press.

1965   Patawomeke: An Historic Algonkian Site. Quarterly Bulletin of the Archaeological Society of Virginia 20(1):1-36. Richmond.

Schock, Jack M.
1972   Southwestern New York: The Chautauqua Culture and Other Late Woodland Occupation. (Paper Read at the Central States Anthropological Association Symposium on Archaeology of Lake Erie, March 1972.)

Schoolcraft, Henry R., comp.
1839   Algic Researches, Comprising Inquiries Respecting the Mental Characteristics of the North American Indians. 2 vols. New York: Harper and Brothers.

1846 Notes on the Iroquois; Or, Contributions to the Statistics, Aboriginal History, Antiquities and General Ethnology of Western New York. New York: Bartlett and Welford.

1847 Notes on the Iroquois; Or, Contributions to the Statistics, Aboriginal History, Antiquities, and General Ethnology of Western New York. Albany, N.Y.: Erastus H. Pease.

1851 Personal Memoirs of a Residence of Thirty Years with the Indian Tribes on the American Frontiers: With Brief Notices of Passing Events, Facts, and Opinions, A.D. 1812 to A.D. 1842. Philadelphia: Lippincott, Grambo.

1851a The American Indians, Their History, Condition and Prospects, from Original Notes and Manuscripts. New rev. ed. Rochester, N.Y.: Wanzer, Foot.

1851-1857 Historical and Statistical Information Respecting the History, Condition, and Prospects of the Indian Tribes of the United States. 6 vols. Philadelphia: Lippincott, Grambo.

1856 The Myth of Hiawatha, and Other Oral Legends, Mythologic and Allegoric, of the North American Indians. Philadelphia: J.B. Lippincott.

1956 Schoolcraft's Indian Legends from Algic Researches. Mentor L. Williams, ed. East Lansing: Michigan State University Press.

Schulte-Nordholt, J.W.
1966 Nederlanders in Nieuw Nederland. *Bijdragen en Mededelingen van Historisch Genootschap,* Deel 80. Groningen, The Netherlands.

Schultz, Bernice
1937 Colonial Hempstead. Lynbrook, N.Y.: The Review-Star Press.

Schultz, George A.
1972 An Indian Canaan: Isaac McCoy and the Vision of an Indian State. Norman: University of Oklahoma Press.

Scott, Duncan C., ed.
1912 Traditional History of the Confederacy of the Six Nations, Prepared by a Committee of the Chiefs. *Transactions of the Royal Society of Canada,* 3d ser., Vol. 5(2):195-246. Ottawa.

1919 The Canadian Indians and the Great World War. Pp. 285-328 in Vol. 3 of Canada in the Great World War: An Authentic Account of the Military History of Canada from the Earliest Days to the Close of the War of the Nations, by Various Authorities. 3 vols. Toronto: United Publishers of Canada.

Scully, Edward G.
1951 Some Central Mississippi Valley Projectile Point Types. Ann Arbor: University of Michigan, Museum of Anthropology. Mimeo.

Sears, William H.
1964 The Southeastern United States. Pp. 259-287 in Prehistoric Man in the New World. J.D. Jennings and E. Norbeck, eds. Chicago: University of Chicago Press.

Semmes, Raphael
1929 Aboriginal Maryland, 1608-1689. *Maryland Historical Magazine* 24(2):157-172, (3):195-209.

1937 Captains and Mariners of Early Maryland. Baltimore: Johns Hopkins Press.

Seneca-Cayuga Tribe of Oklahoma
1937 Constitution and By-laws of the Seneca-Cayuga Tribe of Oklahoma, Approved April 26, 1937. Washington: U.S. Government Printing Office.

[Seneca Sachems]
1687 Information Given... to His Excell. Thomas Dongan.... (Penn Manuscripts, Indian Records I:1-5, in Historical Society of Pennsylvania, Philadelphia.)

Sergeant, John
1743 A Letter from the Rev. Mr. Sergeant of Stockbridge, to Dr. Colman of Boston; Containing Mr. Sergeant's Proposal of a More Effectual Method for the Education of Indian Children. Boston: Printed by Rogers and Fowle, for D. Henchman in Cornhill.

[Sergeant, John]
1807 [Report on Rev. John Sergeant's Labours in the Annual Report of the Society for the Propagation of the Gospel Among Indians and Others in North America.] *The Panoplist* 2(January):384-385.

Service, Elman R.
1962 Primitive Social Organization: An Evolutionary Perspective. New York: Random House.

Severance, Frank H., ed.
1903 Narratives of Early Mission Work on the Niagara Frontier and Buffalo Creek. *Buffalo Historical Society Publication* 6:163-380. Buffalo.

1917 An Old Frontier of France: The Niagara Region and Adjacent Lakes Under French Control. 2 vols. New York: Dodd, Mead.

1918 Our Neighbors the Tuscaroras. *Buffalo Historical Society Publication* 22:311-331. Buffalo.

Shalkop, Robert L.
1949 The Jersey Bluff Archaeological Focus. (Unpublished M.A. Thesis in Anthropology, University of Chicago, Chicago.)

Shane, Orrin C., III
1967 The Mixter Site: A Multicomponent Hunting Station in Erie County, Ohio. Pp. 121-186 in Studies in Ohio Archaeology. Olaf H. Prufer and Douglas H. McKenzie, eds. Cleveland: Western Reserve University Press.

1971 The Scioto Hopewell. Pp. 142-157 in Adena: The Seeking of an Identity. B.K. Swartz, Jr., ed. Muncie, Ind.: Ball State University Press.

Shea, John D.G., ed.
1852 Discovery and Exploration of the Mississippi Valley; With the Original Narratives of Marquette, Allouez, Membré, Hennepin, and Anastase Douay. New York: Redfield.

1855 History of the Catholic Missions Among the Indian Tribes of the United States. New York: T.W. Strong.

1857 Journal of an Embassy from Canada to the United Colonies of New England, in 1650, by Father Gabriel Druillettes of the Society of Jesus; Translated from the Original Manuscript, with Notes, etc. *New York Historical Society Collections,* 2d ser., Vol. 3:303-328. Pt. 1. New York.

————, ed.
1857a The Jogues Papers. *New York Historical Society Collections,* 2d ser., Vol. 3:161-229. New York.

————, ed.
1860 A French-Onondaga Dictionary, from a Manuscript of the Seventeenth Century. (Shea's Library of American Linguistics 1) New York: Cramoisy Press.

1861 An Historical Sketch of the Tionontates or Dinondadies, Now Called Wyandots. *Historical Magazine* 5:262-269.

————, ed.
1861a Early Voyages Up and Down the Mississippi, by Cavelier, St. Cosme, Le Sueur, Gravier, and Guignas. Albany, N.Y.: J. Munsell.

————, ed.
1903 Discoveries and Exploration of the Mississippi Valley, with the Original Narratives of Marquette, Allouez,

Membré, Hennepin, and Anastase Douay [1852]. Albany, N.Y.: J. McDonough.

Shetrone, Henry C.
1918   The Indian in Ohio. *Ohio Archaeological and Historical Publication* 27(3):274-510. Columbus.

Shimony, Annemarie A.
1961   Conservatism Among the Iroquois at the Six Nations Reserve. *Yale University Publications in Anthropology* 65. New Haven, Conn.

_____
1961a   The Iroquois Fortunetellers and Their Conservative Influence. Pp. 205-211 in Symposium on Cherokee and Iroquois Culture. William N. Fenton and John Gulick, eds. *Bureau of American Ethnology Bulletin* 180. Washington.

_____
1970   Iroquois Witchcraft at Six Nations. Pp. 239-265 in Systems of North American Witchcraft and Sorcery. Deward E. Walker, Jr., ed. *Anthropological Monographs of the University of Idaho* 1. Moscow.

Shove, Macworth
1866   Two Months on the Tobique, New Brunswick: An Emigrant's Journal, 1851. London: Smith, Elder.

Shurtleff, Mary B.
1963   Old Arbre Croche, a Factual and Comprehensive History of Cross Village, Michigan. [Cross Village.]

Siebert, Frank T., Jr.
1943   [Review of] Indian Place-Names of the Penobscot Valley and the Maine Coast, by Fannie Hardy Eckstorm. *New England Quarterly* 16:503-507.

_____
1967   The Original Home of the Proto-Algonquian People. Pp. 13-47 in Contributions to Anthropology: Linguistics I (Algonquian). *Anthropological Series 78, National Museum of Canada Bulletin* 214. Ottawa.

_____
1967a   Discrepant Consonant Clusters Ending in *-k in Proto-Algonquian, a Proposed Interpretation of Saltatory Sound Changes. Pp. 48-59 in Contributions to Anthropology: Linguistics I (Algonquian). *Anthropological Series 78, National Museum of Canada Bulletin* 214. Ottawa.

_____
[1968-1973] [Unpublished Fieldnotes.] (Manuscripts in Siebert's Possession.)

_____
1973   The Identity of the Tarrantines, with an Etymology. *Studies in Linguistics* 23:69-76.

Silverberg, James
1957   The Kickapoo Indians: First One Hundred Years of White Contact in Wisconsin. *Wisconsin Archaeologist* 38(3):61-181.

Silverberg, Robert
1968   Mound Builders of Ancient America: The Archaeology of a Myth. Greenwich, Conn.: New York Graphic Society.

Simerwell, Robert
1832   Catechism and Hymns Translated into the Potawatomi Language; Preceded by an Alphabet and Notes on Phonetics. (Potawatomi Manuscript No. 6; Ayer Collection Manuscript No. 1668 in Newberry Library, Chicago.)

_____
1834   Wlkr Potrwatome msina'kin; kewrnpinukatr. Shawannoe Mission: J. Meeker.

Simmons, William S.
1970   Cautantowwit's House: An Indian Burial Ground on the Island of Conanicut in Narragansett Bay. Providence, R.I.: Brown University Press.

Simmons, William S., and George F. Aubin
1975   Narragansett Kinship. *Man in the Northeast* 9:21-31.

Simms, Ruthanna M.
1962   A Brief History of Council House Friends Church. Pp. [2-4] in Recipes and Memories of Council House Folks. Wy-

andotte, Okla.: Missionary Society of the Council House Friends Church. Mimeo.

Six Nations
1900   Six Nations Public Health Act: Regulations of the Six Nations Indians of the Grand River. Annex (a) to Privy Council 2050, 25th August, 1900. Ottawa.

_____
1910   Consolidated Regulations of the Six Nations Indians of the Grand River. Ottawa: Government Printing Bureau.

Skelton, Raleigh A., Thomas E. Marston, and George D. Painter
1965   The Vinland Map and the Tartar Relation. New Haven, Conn.: Yale University Press.

Skinner, Alanson B.
1911   Notes on the Eastern Cree and Northern Saulteaux. *Anthropological Papers of the American Museum of Natural History* 9(1):1-179. New York.

_____
1913   Social Life and Ceremonial Bundles of the Menomini Indians. *Anthropological Papers of the American Museum of Natural History* 13(1):1-165. New York.

_____
1915   Associations and Ceremonies of the Menomini Indians. *Anthropological Papers of the American Museum of Natural History* 13(2):167-215. Pt. 2. New York.

_____
1920   Medicine Ceremony of the Menomini, Iowa, and Wahpeton Dakota, with Notes on the Ceremony Among the Ponca, Bungi Ojibwa, and Potawatomi. *Museum of the American Indian, Heye Foundation. Indian Notes and Monographs* 4. New York.

_____
1921   Material Culture of the Menomini. *Museum of the American Indian, Heye Foundation. Indian Notes and Monographs, Misc. ser.* 20(1). New York.

_____
1921a   Notes on Iroquois Archaeology. *Museum of the American Indian, Heye Foundation. Indian Notes and Monographs, Misc. ser.* 18:5-216. New York.

_____
1923-1925 Observations on the Ethnology of the Sauk Indians. *Bulletin of the Public Museum of the City of Milwaukee* 5(1-3). Milwaukee.

_____
1924-1927 The Mascoutens or Prairie Potawatomi Indians. *Bulletin of the Public Museum of the City of Milwaukee* 6(1-3). Milwaukee.

_____
1925   Notes on Mahikan Ethnology. *Bulletin of the Public Museum of the City of Milwaukee* 2(3):87-116. Milwaukee.

_____
1926   An Old Seneca War Club. *Museum of the American Indian, Heye Foundation. Indian Notes* 3(1):45-47. New York.

Skinner, Alanson B., and John V. Satterlee
1915   Folklore of the Menomini Indians. *Anthropological Papers of the American Museum of Natural History* 13(3):217-546. Pt. 3. New York.

Slaymaker, Charles M., III, and Charles M. Slaymaker, Jr.
1971   Au Sagaunashke Village: The Upper Mississippian Occupations of the Knoll Springs Site, Cook County, Illinois. Pp. 192-250 in Mississippian Site Archaeology in Illinois, I; Site Reports from the St. Louis and Chicago Areas. *Illinois Archaeological Survey Bulletin* 8. Urbana.

Slight, Benjamin
1844   Indian Researches; Or, Facts Concerning the North American Indians; Including Notices of Their Present State of Improvement, in Their Social, Civil, and Religious Condition; With Hints for Their Future Advancement. Montreal: Printed for the Author by J.E.L. Miller.

Slotkin, James S.
1952   Menomini Peyotism: A Study of Individual Variation in a Primary Group with a Homogeneous Culture. *Transactions of the American Philosophical Society* n.s. 42(4). Philadelphia.

873

1957   The Menomini Powwow: A Study in Cultural Decay. *Milwaukee Public Museum Publications in Anthropology* 4. Milwaukee.

Slotkin, Richard
1973   Regeneration Through Violence: The Mythology of the American Frontier, 1600-1860. Middletown, Conn.: Wesleyan University Press.

Smet, Pierre Jean de
1905   Life, Letters and Travels of Father Pierre-Jean de Smet, S.J., 1801-1873; Missionary Labors and Adventures Among the Wild Tribes of North American Indians. Hiram M. Chittenden and Alfred T. Richardson, eds. 4 vols. New York: F.P. Harper.

Smith, Carlyle S.
1950   The Archaeology of Coastal New York. *Anthropological Papers of the American Museum of Natural History* 43(2):94-200. New York.

Smith, De Cost
1888   Witchcraft and Demonism of the Modern Iroquois. *Journal of American Folk-Lore* 1(3):184-194.

_____
1889   Additional Notes on Onondaga Witchcraft and Hoⁿ-dó-j̄. *Journal of American Folk-Lore* 2(7):277-281.

_____
1889a   Onondaga Superstitions. *Journal of American Folk-Lore* 2(7):282-283.

Smith, Donald B.
1974   Le Sauvage: The Native People in Quebec Historical Writing on the Heroic Period (1534-1663) of New France. *Canada. National Museum of Man Mercury Series, History Division Paper* 6. Ottawa.

Smith, Dwight L., ed.
1949   An Unsuccessful Negotiation for Removal of the Wyandot Indians from Ohio, 1834. *Ohio State Archaeological and Historical Quarterly* 58(3):305-331. Columbus.

[Smith, Edward P.]
1874   [Letter, Commissioner of Indian Affairs to Enoch Hoag, Dated Jan. 20, 1874.] (Manuscript in Quapaw: Indians, New York, Indian Archives Division, Oklahoma Historical Society, Oklahoma City.)

Smith, Erminnie A.
1883   Myths of the Iroquois. Pp. 47-116 in *2d Annual Report of the Bureau of American Ethnology for the Years 1880-1881.* Washington.

_____
1885   Artificial Wampum. *Science* 5(100):3-4.

Smith, G. Hubert
1931   Noah Webster, the Archaeologist. *American Anthropologist* 33(4):620-624.

Smith, Harlan I.
1910   The Prehistoric Ethnology of a Kentucky Site. *Anthropological Papers of the American Museum of Natural History* 6(2):173-241. New York.

Smith, Harlan I., and W.J. Wintemberg
1929   Some Shell-heaps in Nova Scotia. *Anthropological Series 9, National Museum of Canada Bulletin* 47. Ottawa.

Smith, James
1799   An Account of the Remarkable Occurrences in the Life and Travels of Col. James Smith, During His Captivity with the Indians in the Years 1755, '56, '57, '58, and '59... Lexington, Va.: John Bradford.

_____
1851   An Account of the Remarkable Occurrences in the Life and Travels of Colonel James Smith... Pp. 178-264 in *Indian Captivities, or Life in the Wigwam...*, by Samuel G. Drake. Auburn, N.Y.: Derby and Miller.

Smith, John
1608   A Trve Relation of Such Occurrences and Accidents of Noate as Hath Happened in Virginia Since the First Planting of The Collony. London: Printed for I. Tappe. (Reprinted in The Jamestown Voyages. Philip L. Barbour, ed. Vol. 1:165-208. Cambridge University Press, London, 1969.)

1612   A Map of Virginia, with a Description of the Covntrey, the Commodities, People, Government, and Religion. Oxford: J. Barnes. (Reprinted in The Jamestown Voyages. Philip L. Barbour, ed. Vol. 2:327-464. Cambridge University Press, London, 1969.)

1624   The Generalle Historie of Virginia, New England, and the Summer Isles. London: Printed by I.D. and I.H. for Michael Sparks. (Reprinted: Pp. 273-784 in Captain John Smith, Works, 1608-1631. Edward Arber, ed. Birmingham, England, 1884.)

1884   Capt. John Smith, of Willoughby by Alfoed, Lincolnshire; President of Virginia, and Admiral of New England. Works, 1608-1631. Edward Arber, ed. (The English Scholar's Library 16) Birmingham, England: Unwin.

1910   Travels and Works of Captain John Smith, President of Virginia, and Admiral of New England, 1580-1631. Edward Arber, ed. 2 vols. Edinburgh: John Grant.

1912   The Generalle Historie of Virginia, New-England and the Summer Isles. The Sixth Booke: The Generall Historie of New-England [1624]. Pp. 650-753 in Vol. 2 of Forerunners and Competitors of the Pilgrims and Puritans. Charles H. Levermore, ed. 2 vols. Brooklyn, N.Y.: Published for the New England Society of Brooklyn.

Smith, Nicholas N.
1954   Premonition Spirits Among the Wabanaki. *Bulletin of the Massachusetts Archaeological Society* 15(3):52-56. Attleboro.

_____
1955   Wabanaki Dances. *Bulletin of the Massachusetts Archaeological Society* 16(2):29-37. Attleboro.

_____
1957   Notes on the Malecite of Woodstock, New Brunswick. *Anthropologica* 5:1-39. Ottawa.

1957a   Smoking Habits of the Wabanaki. *Bulletin of the Massachusetts Archaeological Society* 18(4):76-77. Attleboro.

1962   St. Francis Indian Dances - 1960. *Ethnomusicology* 6(1):15-18.

1964   Indian Medicine: Fact or Fiction? *Bulletin of the Massachusetts Archaeological Society* 26(1):13-17. Attleboro.

1966   The Development of Wabanaki Herb Medicines. *Bulletin of the Maine Archaeological Society* 5:1-4. Castine.

Smith, Samuel
1765   The History of the Colony of Nova-Caesaria or New-Jersey: Containing, an Account of its First Settlement, Progressive Improvements, the Original and Present Constitution, and Other Events, to the Year 1721. With Some Particulars Since; and a Short View of its Present State. Burlington, N.J.: James Parker. (Reprinted: William S. Sharp, Trenton, 1877.)

Smith, Wallis M.
1970   A Re-appraisal of the Huron Kinship System. *Anthropologica* n.s. 12(2):191-206. Ottawa.

Smith, William
1765   An Historical Account of the Expedition Against the Ohio Indians, in the Year 1764, Under the Command of Henry Bouquet... Philadelphia: William Bradford. (Reprinted as Expedition Against the Ohio Indians, University Microfilms, Ann Arbor, Mich., 1966.)

Smith, William H., comp.
1882   The St. Clair Papers: The Life and Public Serivce of Arthur St. Clair, Soldier of the Revolutionary War; President of the Continental Congress and Governor of the North West Territories. 2 vols. Cincinnati: R. Clarke.

874

Snow, Dean R.
1968   Wabanaki "Family Hunting Territories." *American Anthropologist* 70(6):1143-1151.

1968a   A Century of Maine Archaeology. *Bulletin of the Maine Archaeological Society* 8. Castine.

1969   A Summary of Excavations at the Hathaway Site in Passadumkeag, Maine, 1912, 1947, and 1968. Orono: University of Maine, Department of Anthropology.

[1971-1973] [Eastern Abenaki Ethnohistory.] (Manuscript in Snow's Possession.)

1972   Rising Sea Level and Prehistoric Cultural Ecology in Northern New England. *American Antiquity* 37(2):211-221.

Snyder, John F.
1894   An Illinois "Teocalli." *The Archaeologist* 2(9):259-264.

1962   Certain Indian Mounds Technically Considered. Pp. 230-273 in John Francis Snyder: Selected Writings. Clyde C. Walton, ed. Springfield: Illinois State Historical Society.

Snyderman, George S.
1948   Behind the Tree of Peace: A Sociological Analysis of Iroquois Warfare. *Pennsylvania Archaeologist* 18(3-4):3-93.

Society of Colonial Wars. Rhode Island
1926   The Narragansett Mortgage: The Documents Concerning the Alien Purchases in Southern Rhode Island. Providence: Society of Colonial Wars in the State of Rhode Island and Providence Plantations.

Society of Friends *see* Friends, Society of

Sockabasin, Allen J., and John G. Stone, comps.
1971   Off-Reservation Indian Survey Me P-74. Augusta: State of Maine Department of Indian Affairs.

Socolofsky, Homer E.
1970   Wyandot Floats. *Kansas Historical Quarterly* 36(3):241-304.

Solecki, Ralph
1950   The Archeological Position of Historic Fort Corchaug, L.I., and its Relation to Contemporary Forts. *Bulletin of the Archaeological Society of Connecticut* 24:3-40. New Haven.

Solenberger, Robert R.
1940   [Rappahannock Fieldnotes.] (Manuscript 170(20:4F3b) in the Library of the American Philosophical Society, Philadelphia.)

Southwell, Sir Robert
1691   The Method the Indians in Virginia and Carolina Use to Dress Buck and Doeskins. *Philosophical Transactions of the Royal Society of London* 17:532-533. London.

Spaulding, Albert C.
1946   Northeastern Archaeology and General Trends in the Northern Forest Zone. Pp. 143-167 in Man in Northeastern North America. Frederick Johnson, ed. *Papers of the Robert S. Peabody Foundation for Archaeology* 3. Andover, Mass.

1952   The Origin of the Adena Culture of the Ohio Valley. *Southwestern Journal of Anthropology* 8(3):260-268.

1955   Prehistoric Cultural Development in the Eastern United States. Pp. 12-27 in New Interpretations of Aboriginal American Culture History. Washington: Anthropological Society of Washington 75th Anniversary Volume.

Speck, Frank G.
1904   A Modern Mohegan-Pequot Text. *American Anthropologist* n.s. 6(4):469-476.

1909   Notes on the Mohegan and Niantic Indians. *Anthropological Papers of the American Museum of Natural History* 3. New York.

1910   Poosepatuck. P. 281 in Vol. 2 of Handbook of American Indians North of Mexico. Frederick W. Hodge, ed. 2 vols. *Bureau of American Ethnology Bulletin* 30. Washington.

1911   Notes on the Material Culture of the Huron. *American Anthropologist* 13(2):208-228.

1911a   Huron Moose Hair Embroidery. *American Anthropologist* 13(1):1-14.

1914   The Family Hunting Band as the Basis of Algonkian Social Organization. *American Anthropologist* 17(2):289-305.

1915   Family Hunting Territories and Social Life of Various Algonkian Bands of the Ottawa Valley. *Anthropological Series 8, Memoirs of the Canadian Geological Survey* 70:1-10. Ottawa.

1915a   Myths and Folk-lore of the Timiskaming Algonquin and Timagami Ojibwa. *Anthropological Series 9, Memoirs of the Canadian Geological Survey* 71:1-27. Ottawa.

1915b   The Nanticoke Community of Delaware. *Contributions from the Museum of the American Indian, Heye Foundation* 2(4). New York.

1915c   The Eastern Algonkian Wabanaki Confederacy. *American Anthropologist* 17(3):492-508.

1915d   The Family Hunting Band as the Basis of Algonkian Social Organization. *American Anthropologist* 17(2):289-305.

1915e   Decorative Art of the Indian Tribes of Connecticut. *Anthropological Series 10, Memoirs of the Canadian Geological Survey* 75. Ottawa.

1916   Remnants of the Machapunga Indians of North Carolina. *American Anthropologist* 18(2):271-276.

1917   Game Totems Among the Northeastern Algonkians. *American Anthropologist* 19(1):9-18.

1917a   The Social Structure of the Northern Algonkian. *Publications of the American Sociological Society* 12:82-100. [Chicago.]

1918   Kinship Terms and the Family Band Among the Northeastern Algonkian. *American Anthropologist* 20(2):143-161.

1918a   Remnants of the Nehantics. *Southern Workman* 47(2):65-69.

1919   Penobscot Shamanism. *Memoirs of the American Anthropological Association* 6:237-288. Lancaster, Pa.

1919-1946 [Manuscripts Relating to the Indians of Eastern Virginia.] (Manuscripts 170(20:4F1, 4F3, 4F4, 4F5, 4F8), 170(21:4F2) in the Library of the American Philosophical Society, Philadelphia.)

1920   Correction to Kinship Terms Among the Northeastern Algonkian. *American Anthropologist* 22(1):85.

1922   Beothuk and Micmac. *Museum of the American Indian, Heye Foundation. Indian Notes and Monographs, Misc. ser.* 22. New York.

1923   Reptile-lore of the Northern Indians. *Journal of American Folk-Lore* 36(141):273-280.

1923a   Algonkian Influence Upon Iroquois Social Organization. *American Anthropologist* 25(2):219-227.

1924   The Ethnic Position of the Southeastern Algonkian. *American Anthropologist* 26(2):184-200.

1925   The Rappahannock Indians of Virginia. *Museum of the American Indian, Heye Foundation. Indian Notes and Monographs* 5(3). New York.

1926   Culture Problems in Northeastern North America. *Proceedings of the American Philosophical Society* 65:272-311. Philadelphia.

1927   The Nanticoke and Conoy Indians with a Review of Linguistic Material from Manuscript and Living Sources: An Historical Study. *Papers of the Historical Society of Delaware* n.s. 1. Wilmington.

1927a   River Desert Indians of Quebec. *Museum of the American Indian, Heye Foundation. Indian Notes* 4(3):240-252. New York.

1927b   Huron Hunting Territories in Quebec. *Museum of the American Indian, Heye Foundation. Indian Notes* 4(1):1-12. New York.

1928   Chapters on the Ethnology of the Powhatan Tribes of Virginia. *Museum of the American Indian, Heye Foundation. Indian Notes and Monographs* 1(5). New York.

1928a   Native Tribes and Dialects of Connecticut: A Mohegan-Pequot Diary. Pp. 199-287 in *43d Annual Report of the Bureau of American Ethnology for the Years 1925-1926.* Washington.

1928b   Wawenock Myth Texts from Maine. Pp. 165-197 in *43d Annual Report of the Bureau of American Ethnology for the Years 1925-1926.* Washington.

1928c   Divination by Scapulimancy Among the Algonquin of River Desert. *Museum of the American Indian, Heye Foundation. Indian Notes* 5(2):167-173. New York.

1928d   Territorial Subdivisions and Boundaries of the Wampanoag, Massachusett, and Nauset Indians. *Museum of the American Indian, Heye Foundation. Indian Notes and Monographs, Misc. ser.* 44. New York.

1928e   Land Ownership Among Hunting Peoples in Primitive America and the World's Marginal Areas. Pp. 323-332 in Vol. 2 of *Proceedings of the 22d International Congress of Americanists.* 2 vols. Rome, 1926.

1929   Boundaries and Hunting Groups of the River Desert Algonquin. *Museum of the American Indian, Heye Foundation. Indian Notes* 6(2):97-120. New York.

1931   A Study of the Delaware Indian Big House Ceremony. *Publications of the Pennsylvania Historical Commission* 2. Harrisburg.

[1931-1946]   [Ethnographic Notes, from Fieldwork Among the Delawares in Ontario and Oklahoma.] (Manuscripts in the Library of the American Philosophical Society, Philadelphia.)

1933   Notes on the Life of John Wilson, the Revealer of Peyote, as Recalled by His Nephew, George Anderson. *General Magazine and Historical Chronicle* 35(4):539-556.

1935   "Abenaki" Clans-Never! *American Anthropologist* 37(3):528-530.

1937   Oklahoma Delaware Ceremonies, Feasts and Dances. *Memoirs of the American Philosophical Society* 7. Philadelphia.

1940   Penobscot Man: The Life History of a Forest Tribe in Maine. Philadelphia: University of Pennsylvania Press. (Reprinted: Octagon Books, New York, 1970.)

1940a   [Notes on Oklahoma Seneca; Notes from Speck Interview, Jan. 3, 1940, with David Whitetree, Oklahoma Seneca-Cayuga.] (Manuscript Box 7, F.G. Speck Collection, American Philosophical Society Library, Philadelphia.)

1942   Back Again to Indian River, Its People and Their Games. *Bulletin of the Archaeological Society of Delaware* 3(5):17-24. Wilmington.

1943   The Frolic Among the Nanticoke of Indian River Hundred, Delaware. *Bulletin of the Archaeological Society of Delaware* 4(1):2-4. Wilmington.

1943a   A Note on the Hassanamisco Band of Nipmuc. *Bulletin of the Massachusetts Archaeological Society* 4(4):49-56. Attleboro.

1945   The Iroquois: A Study in Cultural Evolution. *Cranbrook Institute of Science Bulletin* 23. Bloomfield Hills, Mich.

1946   Cudgelling Rabbits, an Old Nanticoke Hunting Tradition and its Significance. *Bulletin of the Archaeological Society of Delaware* 4(4):9-12. Wilmington.

1946a   Bird Nomenclature and Song Interpretation of the Canadian Delaware: An Essay in Ethno-ornithology. *Journal of the Washington Academy of Sciences* 36(8):249-258. Washington.

1947   Eastern Algonkian Block-stamp Decoration: A New World Original or an Acculturated Art. *Archeological Society of New Jersey, Research Series* 1. Trenton.

1949   A Maker of Eel-pots Among the Nanticokes of Delaware. *Bulletin of the Archaeological Society of Delaware* 4(5):25-27. Wilmington.

1949a   Midwinter Rites of the Cayuga Long House. Philadelphia: University of Pennsylvania Press.

Speck, Frank G., and Ralph W. Dexter
1952   Utilization of Animals and Plants by the Malecite Indians of New Brunswick. *Journal of the Washington Academy of Sciences* 42(1):1-7. Washington.

Speck, Frank G., and Loren C. Eiseley
1939   Significance of Hunting Territory Systems of the Algonkian in Social Theory. *American Anthropologist* 41(2):269-280.

Speck, Frank G., and Wendell S. Hadlock
1946   A Report on Tribal Boundaries and Hunting Areas of the Malecite Indians of New Brunswick. *American Anthropologist* 48(3):355-374.

Speck, Frank G., and Jesse Moses
1945   The Celestial Bear Comes Down to Earth. *Reading Public Museum and Art Gallery, Scientific Publication* 7. Reading, Pa.

Speck, Frank G., and Claude E. Schaeffer
1950   The Deer and the Rabbit Hunting Drive in Virginia and the Southeast. *Southern Indian Studies* 2(1):4-20.

Speck, Frank G., Royal B. Hassrick, and Edmund S. Carpenter
1942   Rappahannock Herbals, Folk-lore and Science of Cures. *Proceedings of the Delaware County Institute of Science* 10(1):7-47. Media, Pa.

1946   Rappahannock Taking Devices: Traps, Hunting and Fishing. *Joint Publication of the Museum of the University of Pennsylvania and Philadelphia Anthropological Society* 1. Philadelphia.

Spelman, Henry
1872   Relation of Virginia, 1609. London: Chiswick Press. (Reprinted: Pp. ci-cxiv in Captain John Smith, Works, 1608-1631. Edward Arber, ed. Birmingham, England, 1884.)

Spence, Michael W.
1967   A Middle Woodland Burial Complex in the St. Lawrence Valley. *National Museum of Canada Anthropology Paper* 14. Ottawa.

Speth, John D.
1966 The Whorley Earthwork. *Michigan Archaeologist* 12(4):211-227.

Spindler, George D.
1955 Sociocultural and Psychological Processes in Menomini Acculturation. *University of California Publications in Culture and Society* 5. Berkeley.

Spindler, George, and Louise S. Spindler
1970 Fieldwork Among the Menomini. Pp. 267-301 in Being an Anthropologist: Fieldwork in Eleven Cultures. G. Spindler, ed. New York: Holt, Rinehart and Winston.

———— 1971 Dreamers Without Power: The Menomini Indians. New York: Holt, Rinehart and Winston.

Spindler, Louise S.
1952 Witchcraft in Menomini Acculturation. *American Anthropologist* 54(4):593-602.

———— 1962 Menomini Women and Culture Change. *Memoirs of the American Anthropological Association* 91. Menasha, Wis.

———— 1971 Menomini Witchcraft. Pp. 183-218 in Systems of North American Witchcraft and Sorcery. D. Walker, ed. *Anthropological Monographs of the University of Idaho* 1. Moscow.

Spindler, Louise S., and George Spindler
1958 Male and Female Adaptations in Culture Change. *American Anthropologist* 60(2):217-233.

Splitlog, Grover C.
1941 The Warriors Come Out with Their Feathers and Paint. *Indians at Work* 8(11):33-34.

Spooner, Harry L.
1931 Indians of Oceana. *Michigan History Magazine* 15(Autumn):654-665. Lansing.

Spragge, William
1865 Comparative Statement of the Population of the Different Indian Bands Throughout Canada, Between the Years 1863 and 1864. P. 22 in *Canada. Indian Affairs. Report for the Half-year Ended June 30th, 1864.* Quebec.

———— 1874 Census Return of the Different Indian Tribes or Bands. Pp. 30-33 in *Report of the Indian Branch of the Department of the Minister of the Interior for the Year Ended June 30, 1873.* Ottawa.

Squier, Ephraim G.
1849 Aboriginal Monuments of the State of New York, Comprising the Results of Original Surveys and Explorations. *Smithsonian Contributions to Knowledge* 2(10):9-188. Washington.

Squier, Ephraim G., and E.H. Davis
1848 Ancient Monuments of the Mississippi Valley, Comprising the Results of Extensive Original Surveys and Explorations. *Smithsonian Contributions to Knowledge* 1. Washington.

Squires, S.K.
[1930] Reminiscences of the St. Marys Indian Reserve, 1880-1890. (Manuscript MYO-H128 in New Brunswick Provincial Archives, Fredericton N.B.)

Squires, Austin
1968 The Great Sagamore of the Maliseets. *Atlantic Advocate* 59(3):49-52.

Stamp, Harley
1915 A Malecite Tale: Adventures of Bukschinskwesk. *Journal of American Folk-Lore* 28(109):243-248.

Stanley, G.F.G.
1963 The Significance of the Six Nations' Participation in the War of 1812. *Ontario History* 55(4):215-232.

Staples, Arthur C., and Roy C. Athearn
1969 The Bear Swamp Site: A Preliminary Report. *Bulletin of the Massachusetts Archaeological Society* 30(3-4):1-9. Attleboro.

Staples, William R.
1843 Annals of the Town of Providence, from its First Settlement, to the Organization of the City Government, in June, 1832. Providence: Knowles and Vose.

Starr, Frederick
1892 Anthropological Work in America. *Popular Science Monthly* 41(3):289-307.

Steiner, Stanley
1968 The New Indians. New York: Harper and Row.

Stephenson, Robert L., and Alice L.L. Ferguson
1963 The Accoceek Site: A Middle Atlantic Seaboard Culture Sequence. *University of Michigan Museum of Anthropology, Anthropological Papers* 20. Ann Arbor.

Stern, Theodore
1951 Pamunkey Pottery Making. *Southern Indian Studies* 3(1):1-78.

———— 1952 Chickahominy: The Changing Culture of a Virginia Indian Community. *Proceedings of the American Philosophical Society* 96(2):157-225. Philadelphia.

Stern, Theodore, and Maurice A. Mook
1941 [Fieldnotes on Western Chickahominy.] (Manuscript 170(20:4F5d) in the Library of the American Philosophical Society, Philadelphia.)

Stevens, Susan (MacCulloch)
[1977] Passamaquoddy Economic Development in Cultural and Historic Perspective. In American Indian Economic Development. Sam Stanley, ed. The Hague: Mouton. In Press.

Stevens, Sylvester K., and Donald H. Kent, eds.
1941 Wilderness Chronicles of Northwestern Pennsylvania. Harrisburg: Pennsylvania Historical Commission.

Steward, Julian H.
1955 Theory of Culture Change: The Methodology of Multilinear Evolution. Urbana: University of Illinois Press.

Steward, William, and T.G. Steward
1913 Gouldtown: A Very Remarkable Settlement of Ancient Date. Philadelphia: Lippincott.

Stewart, T. Dale
1940 The Finding of an Indian Ossuary on the York River in Virginia. *Journal of the Washington Academy of Sciences* 30(8):356-364. Washington.

Stewart, T. Dale, and Waldo R. Wedel
1937 The Finding of Two Ossuaries on the Site of the Indian Village of Nacotchtanke (Anacostia). *Journal of the Washington Academy of Sciences* 27(5):213-219. Washington.

Stewart, Ty
1973 Oklahoma Delaware Women's Dance Clothing. *American Indian Crafts and Culture* 7(6):4-22.

Stiles, Ezra
1755-1794 Itineraries and Memoirs. 6 vols. (Manuscripts in Beinecke Library, Yale University, New Haven, Conn.)

———— 1783 The United States Elevated to Glory and Honor. New Haven, Conn.: Thomas and Samuel Green.

———— 1787 [Vocabulary of Naugatuck (?).] (Manuscript of Words Obtained from Sarah Maweek, in Beinecke Library, Yale University, New Haven, Conn.)

———— 1901 The Literary Diary of Ezra Stiles... [1769-1776]. Franklin B. Dexter, ed. New York: Charles Scribner's Sons.

———— 1916 Extracts from Itineraries and Other Miscellanies of Ezra Stiles, D.D., LL.D., 1755-1794, with a Selection from His Correspondence. Franklin B. Dexter, ed. New Haven, Conn.: Yale University Press.

1973   A Vocabulary of the Pequot Indians, Obtained in 1762 at Groton, Connecticut. Pp. 165-169 in Pequot from Stiles to Speck, by William Cowan. *International Journal of American Linguistics* 39(3):164-172.

1973a   A Narragansett Indian Vocabulary, Dated 6 September 1769. Pp. 8-11 in Narragansett 126 Years After, by William Cowan. *International Journal of American Linguistics* 39(1):7-13.

Stiles, Henry R.
1864   Affairs at Fort Chartres, 1768-1781... Albany, N.Y.: J. Munsell.

Stirling, Thomas
1916   Letter to Gage, December 15, 1765. Pp. 124-127 in The New Regime, 1765-1767. *Collections of the Illinois State Historical Library* 9. Springfield.

Stith, William
1747   The History of the First Discovery and Settlement of Virginia: Being an Essay Towards a General History of this Colony. Williamsburg, Va.: W. Parks.

Stoddard, Solomon
1917   An Answer to Some Cases of Conscience Respecting the Country [1722]. Tarrytown, N.Y.: W. Abbatt.

Stokes, I.N. Phelps
1915-1928   The Iconography of Manhattan Island, 1498-1909. Reproductions of Important Maps, Plans, Views and Documents in Public and Private Collections. 6 vols. New York: R.H. Dodd.

Stoltman, James B.
1962   A Proposed Method for Systematizing the Modal Analysis of Pottery and Its Application to the Laurel Focus. (Unpublished M.A. Thesis in Anthropology, University of Minnesota, St. Paul.)

1973   The Laurel Culture in Minnesota. (Minnesota Prehistoric Archaeological Series 8) St. Paul: Minnesota Historical Society.

1973a   The Southeastern United States. Pp. 116-150 in The Development of North American Archaeology: Essays in the History of Regional Traditions. James E. Fitting, ed. Garden City, N.Y.: Anchor/Doubleday.

Stone, Lyle M.
1967   Michigan State University Museum Field Activities, Summer 1967. *Newsletter of the Michigan Archaeological Society* 674:27-28. Northville.

Stone, William L.
1838   Life of Joseph Brant-Thayendanegea: Including the Border Wars of the American Revolution and Sketches of the Indian Campaigns of Generals Harmer, St. Clair and Wayne; and Other Matters Connected with the Indian Relations of the United States and Great Britain from the Peace of 1783 to the Indian Peace of 1795. 2 vols. New York: A.V. Blake, G. Dearborn and Company. (Reprinted: Kraus Reprint, New York, 1969.)

1841   The Life and Times of Red Jacket, or Sa-go-ye-wat-ha; Being the Sequel to the History of the Six Nations. New York and London: Wiley and Putnam.

1842   Uncas and Miantonomoh. New York: Dayton and Newman.

Story, Thomas
1747   A Journal of the Life of Thomas Story, 1698-1705. James and John Wilson, eds. New Castle upon Tyne, England: Isaac Thompson.

Stothers, David M.
1971   The Princess Point Complex. (Paper Presented at the 4th Annual Meeting of the Canadian Archaeological Association, Calgary, Alberta, February 1971.)

Strachey, William
1906   A True Reportorie of the Wrack, and Redemption of Sir Thomas Gates, Knight, ... July 15, 1610. Pp. 5-72 in Vol. 19 of Hakluytus Posthumus or Purchas His Pilgrimes by Samuel Purchas. Glasgow: James MacLehose and Sons.

1953   The Historie of Travell into Virginia Britania [1612]. Louis B. Wright and Virginia Freund, eds. London: Printed for the Hakluyt Society.

Street, Ida M.
1905   The Simon Cameron Indian Commission of 1838. *Annals of Iowa* 7:115-139, 172-195.

Struever, Stuart
1964   The Hopewell Interaction Sphere in Riverine-western Great Lakes Culture History. *Illinois State Museum Scientific Paper* 12(3):85-106. Springfield.

1965   Middle Woodland Culture History in the Great Lakes Riverine Area. *American Antiquity* 31(2):211-223.

1968   Woodland Subsistence-settlement Systems in the Lower Illinois Valley. Pp. 285-312 in New Perspectives in Archaeology. Sally R. Binford and Lewis R. Binford, eds. Chicago: Aldine.

1968a   A Re-examination of Hopewell in Eastern North America. (Unpublished Ph.D. Dissertation in Anthropology, University of Chicago, Chicago.)

Struever, Stuart, and Kent D. Vickery
1973   The Beginnings of Cultivation in the Midwest-Riverine Area of the United States. *American Anthropologist* 75(5):1197-1220.

Stuart, Charles
1926   The Captivity of Charles Stuart, 1755-57. Beverley W. Bond, Jr., ed. *Mississippi Valley Historical Review* 13(1):58-81.

Stuiver, Minze, and Hans E. Suess
1966   On the Relationship Between Radiocarbon Dates and True Sample Ages. *Radiocarbon* 8:534-540.

Sturtevant, William C.
1957   [Ethnographic Fieldnotes on the Cattaraugus Seneca.] (Manuscript in Sturtevant's Possession.)

1959   Authorship of the Powell Linguistic Classification. *International Journal of American Linguistics* 25(3):196-199.

1961-1962   [Ethnographic Notes from Fieldwork with Oklahoma Seneca-Cayuga, August 5-28, 1961 and July 11-22, 1962.] (Manuscripts in Sturtevant's Possession.)

1965   Historic Carolina Algonkian Cultivation of Chenopodium or Amaranthus. (Proceedings of the 21st Southeastern Archaeological Conference) *Southeastern Archaeological Conference Bulletin* 3:64-65. Cambridge, Mass.

1975   Two 1761 Wigwams at Niantic, Connecticut. *American Antiquity* 40(4):437-444.

Such, Peter
1973   Riverrun. Toronto: Clarke, Irwin.

Sulte, Benjamin
1886   Histoire de Saint-François-du-Lac. Montreal: Impr. de "L'Etendard."

Surtees, Robert J.
1966   Indian Reserve Policy in Upper Canada, 1830-1845. (Unpublished M.A. Thesis in Anthropology, Carleton University, Northfield, Minn.)

Susman, Amelia
1944   The Accentual System of Winnebago. (Unpublished Ph.D. Dissertation in Anthropology, Columbia University, New York.)

Swanton, John R.
1905   The Social Organization of American Tribes. *American Anthropologist* 7(4):663-673.

1922   Early History of the Creek Indians and Their Neighbors. *Bureau of American Ethnology Bulletin* 73. Washington.

1928   Aboriginal Culture of the Southeast. Pp. 673-726 in *42d Annual Report of the Bureau of American Ethnology for the Years 1924-1925.* Washington.

1934   Newly Discovered Powhatan Bird Names. *Journal of the Washington Academy of Sciences* 24(2):96-99. Washington.

1946   The Indians of the Southeastern United States. *Bureau of American Ethnology Bulletin* 137. Washington.

1952   The Indian Tribes of North America. *Bureau of American Ethnology Bulletin* 145. Washington.

Sylvester, Herbert M.
1910   Indian Wars of New England. 3 vols. Boston: W.B. Clarke.

Szabo, Laszlo
[1971]   Malecite Stories. (Xeroxed Manuscript No. 1.6.14 in National Museum of Man, Ottawa.)

TPUS = Carter, Clarence E., comp.
1934-1962   The Territorial Papers of the United States. 26 vols. Washington: U.S. Government Printing Office.

Taft, Grace (Ellis)
1912   The Cayuga Chief, Dr. Peter Wilson. *Records of the Past* 11:261-263.

1912a   Cayuga Notes. *American Antiquarian and Oriental Journal* 34(1):28-33.

1912b   More Cayuga Notes. *American Antiquarian and Oriental Journal* 34(4):295-303.

1913   Cayuga and Seneca as Proprietaries in the Annals of New York. *Records of the Past* 12(3):124-127.

1914   Cayuga Indemnity. *Records of the Past* 13:96-101.

Talbot, George
1910   Report of a Conference Between Coll. Talbot and William Penn [1684]. Pp. 437-448 in Narratives of Early Maryland, 1633-1684. Clayton C. Hall, ed. New York: Charles Scribner's Sons.

Talcott, John
1934   A Letter Written by Maj. John Talcott from Mr. Stanton's at Quonocontaug to Gov. William Leete and the Hon. Council of the Colony of Connecticut. Providence: Society of Colonial Wars in the State of Rhode Island and Providence Plantations.

Talman, James J.
1929   Church of England Missionary Effort in Upper Canada, 1815-1840. *Papers and Records of the Ontario Historical Society* 25:438-449. Toronto.

Tanner, Helen (Hornbeck)
1974   The Chippewa of Eastern Lower Michigan. Pp. 347-374 in Chippewa Indians, V. New York and London: Garland.

Tanner, John
1830   A Narrative of the Captivity and Adventures of John Tanner During Thirty Years' Residence Among the Indians of the Interior of North America. Edwin James, ed. New York: G. and C. and H. Carvill.

1956   A Narrative of the Captivity and Adventures of John Tanner (U.S. Interpreter at Sault Ste. Marie) During Thirty Years' Residence Among the Indians in the Interior of North America. Minneapolis: Ross and Haines.

Tantaquidgeon, Gladys
1928   Mohegan Medicinal Practices, Weather-lore, and Superstition. Pp. 264-279 in *43d Annual Report of the Bureau of American Ethnology for the Years 1925-1926.* Washington.

1930   Notes on the Gay Head Indians of Massachusetts. *Museum of the American Indian, Heye Foundation. Indian Notes* 7(1):1-26. New York.

1930a   Newly Discovered Straw Basketry of the Wampanoag Indians of Massachusetts. *Museum of the American Indian, Heye Foundation. Indian Notes* 7(4):475-484. New York.

1935   Notes on Mohegan-Pequot Basketry Designs. *Indians at Work* 2(17):43-45.

1942   A Study of Delaware Indian Medicine Practice and Folk Beliefs. Harrisburg: Pennsylvania Historical Commission.

1972   Folk Medicine of the Delaware and Related Algonkian Indians. *Pennsylvania Historical and Museum Commission, Anthropological Series* 3. Harrisburg.

Tax, Sol
1932-1934   [Fieldnotes of Investigations Among the Fox.] (Manuscript in University of Chicago, Department of Anthropology, Chicago.)

1955   The Social Organization of the Fox Indians. Pp. 243-282 in Social Anthropology of North American Indian Tribes. Fred Eggan, ed. Enl. ed. Chicago: University of Chicago Press.

Tax, Sol, and Sam Stanley
1960   The North American Indians: 1950 Distribution of Descendants of the Aboriginal Population of Alaska, Canada, and the United States. (Map.) Chicago: University of Chicago, Department of Anthropology.

Taylor, Theodore W.
1972   The States and Their Indian Citizens. Washington: U.S. Government Printing Office.

Teeter, Karl V.
1967   Preliminary Report on Malecite-Passamaquoddy. Pp. 157-162 in Contributions to Anthropology: Linguistics I (Algonquian). *Anthropological Series 78, National Museum of Canada Bulletin* 214. Ottawa.

1971   The Main Features of Malecite-Passamaquoddy Grammar. Pp. 191-250 in Studies in American Indian Languages. Jesse Sawyer, ed. *University of California Publications in Linguistics* 65. Berkeley.

Teit, James A.
1909   The Shuswap. *Memoirs of the American Museum of Natural History* 4(7):443-789. New York.

Temple, Josiah H., and George Sheldon
1875   History of the Town of Northfield, Massachusetts, for 150 Years, with an Account of the Prior Occupation of the Territory by the Squakheags, and with Family Genealogies. Albany, N.Y.: J. Munsell.

Temple, Wayne C.
1958   Indian Villages of the Illinois Country: Historic Tribes. *Illinois State Museum Scientific Paper* 2(2). Springfield.

Thatcher, B.B.
1832   Indian Biography: Or, An Historical Account of Those Individuals Who Have Been Distinguished Among the North American Natives as Orators, Warriors, Statesmen, and Other Remarkable Characters. New York: J. and J. Harper.

Thomas, Cyrus
1887   Burial Mounds of the Northern Sections of the United States. Pp. 3-119 in *5th Annual Report of the Bureau of American Ethnology for the Years 1883-1884.* Washington.

1887a   Work in Mound Exploration of the Bureau of Ethnology. *Bureau of American Ethnology Bulletin* 4. Washington.

1889   The Problem of the Ohio Mounds. *Bureau of American Ethnology Bulletin* 8. Washington.

1891   The Story of a Mound; or, The Shawnees in Pre-Columbian Times. *American Anthropologist* 4(2):109-159, (3):237-273.

1894   Report on the Mound Explorations of the Bureau of Ethnology. Pp. 3-730 in *12th Annual Report of the Bureau of American Ethnology for the Years 1890-1891*. Washington.

1910   Reservations. Pp. 372-391 in Vol. 2 of Handbook of American Indians North of Mexico. Frederick W. Hodge, ed. 2 vols. *Bureau of American Ethnology Bulletin* 30. Washington.

1910a   Pashipaho. Pp. 205-206 in Vol. 2 of Handbook of American Indians North of Mexico. Frederick W. Hodge, ed. 2 vols. *Bureau of American Ethnology Bulletin* 30. Washington.

Thomas, Edward H.
1959   In Search of Etharita or St. Jean. *Pennsylvania Archaeologist* 29(2):93-97.

Thomas, Gabriel
1912   An Historical and Geographical Account of Pennsilvania and of West New Jersey [1698]. Pp. 307-352 in Narratives of Early Pennsylvania, West New Jersey and Delaware, 1630-1707. Albert C. Myers, ed. New York: Charles Scribner's Sons.

Thomas, Peter A.
1971   Middle Connecticut Valley Indian House Types: A Cautionary Note. *Man in the Northeast* 1(1):48-50.

1973   Squakheag Ethnohistory: A Preliminary Study of Culture Conflict on the Seventeenth Century Frontier. *Man in the Northeast* 5:27-36.

Thomas, Ronald A.
1973   Prehistoric Mortuary Complexes of the Delmarva Peninsula. *Proceedings of the Fourth Middle Atlantic Archaeological Conference*. Pennsbury, N.J., May, 1973.

Thomas, Ronald A., and Cara L. Lewis
1966   Archaeological Investigations on Milford Neck. *Delaware Archaeology* 2(4):1-26. Wilmington.

Thomas, Ronald A., and Nancy H. Warren
1970   A Middle Woodland Cemetery in Central Delaware: Excavations at the Island Field Site. *Bulletin of the Archaeological Society of Delaware* n.s. 8:1-33. Dover.

Thompson, Andrew T.
1924   Report by Col. Andrew T. Thompson, Commissioner to Investigate and Enquire into the Affairs of the Six Nations Indians, 1923. Ottawa: King's Printers.

Thompson, Charles N.
1937   Sons of the Wilderness, John and William Conner. *Indiana Historical Society Publication* 12. Indianapolis.

Thompson, David
1916   David Thompson's Narrative of His Explorations in Western America, 1784-1812. J.B. Tyrrell, ed. Toronto: The Champlain Society.

Thompson, Edgar T.
1972   The Little Races. *American Anthropologist* 74(5):1295-1306.

Thompson, Zadock
1842   History of Vermont, Natural, Civil, and Statistical in Three Parts with a Map of the State and 200 Engravings. Burlington, Vt.: C. Goodrich.

[Thomson, Charles]
1759   An Enquiry into the Causes of the Alienation of the Delaware and Shawanese Indians from the British Interest, and into the Measures Taken for Recovering Their Friendship. London: J. Wilkie.

Thornton, Robert J.
1798   Of an Attempt to Make Maple Sugar Above an Hundred Years Ago. *The Philosophical Magazine* 1(June):322. London.

Thorowgood, Thomas
1650   Jewes in America; or, Probabilities That the Americans Are of That Race. With the Removall of Some Contrary Reasonings, and Earnest Desires for Effectuall Endeavours to Make Them Christian. London: W.H. for T. Slater.

Thurman, Melburn D.
1975   Delaware Social Organization. Pp. 111-134 in A Delaware Indian Symposium. Herbert C. Kraft, ed. *Pennsylvania Historical and Museum Commission, Anthropological Series* 4. Harrisburg.

Thwaites, Reuben G., ed.
1904-1907   Early Western Travels, 1748-1846: A Series of Annotated Reprints of Some of the Best and Rarest Contemporary Volumes of Travel, Descriptive of the Aborigines and Social and Economic Conditions in the Middle and Far West, During the Period of Early American Settlement. 38 vols. Cleveland: Arthur H. Clark.

Thwaites, Reuben G., and Louise P. Kellogg, eds.
1908   The Revolution on the Upper Ohio, 1775-1777. Madison: Wisconsin Historical Society.

Thwaites, Reuben G. *see also* JR

Tiedke, Kenneth E.
1951   A Study of the Hannahville Indian Community (Menominee County, Michigan). *Michigan State College, Agricultural Experiment Station Special Bulletin* 369:5-43. East Lansing.

Tindall, Robert
1607   Draughte of Virginia. (Manuscript, Cotton MS, Aug. 1,ii,46 in the British Library, London.) (Printed: P. 105 in Vol. 1 of The Jamestown Voyages, Philip L. Barbour, ed., Cambridge University Press, London, 1969.)

Titterington, Paul F.
1935   Certain Bluff Mounds of Western Jersey County, Illinois. *American Antiquity* 1(1):6-46.

1943   The Jersey County, Illinois, Bluff Focus. *American Antiquity* 9(2):240-245.

1950   Some Non-pottery Sites in the St. Louis Area. *Journal of the Illinois State Archaeological Society* n.s. 1(1):19-30. Springfield.

Todd, Vincent H.
1920   Christoph von Graffenried's Account of the Founding of New Bern. Raleigh, N.C.: Edwards and Broughton.

Tonti, Henri *see* Tonty, Henri de

Tonty, Henri de
1898   Relation of Henri de Tonty Concerning the Explorations of La Salle from 1678 to 1683. Melville B. Anderson, trans. Chicago: The Caxton Club.

1917   Memoir on La Salle's Discoveries, 1678-1690. Pp. 281-322 in Early Narratives of the Northwest, 1634-1699. Louise P. Kellogg, ed. New York: Charles Scribner's Sons.

Tooker, Elisabeth
1960   Three Aspects of Northern Iroquoian Culture Change. *Pennsylvania Archaeologist* 30(2):65-71.

1963   The Iroquois Defeat of the Huron: A Review of Causes. *Pennsylvania Archaeologist* 33(1-2):11-123.

1964   An Ethnography of the Huron Indians, 1615-1649. *Bureau of American Ethnology Bulletin* 190. Washington.

1965   The Iroquois White Dog Sacrifice in the Latter Part of the Eighteenth Century. *Ethnohistory* 12(2):129-140.

1970 Northern Iroquoian Sociopolitical Organization. *American Anthropologist* 72(1):90-97.

1970a The Iroquois Ceremonial of Midwinter. Syracuse, N.Y.: Syracuse University Press.

1971 Clans and Moieties in North America. *Current Anthropology* 12(3):357-376.

[1972] [Notes on Interview with Corbett Sundown, August 6, 1972.] (Manuscript in Tooker's Possession.)

Tooker, William W.
1890 [Montauk Vocabulary Recorded from George Pharoah, March 25, 1798; Copied Feb. 12, 1890 by William W. Tooker from an Old Memorandum Book Belonging to John L. Gardiner.] (Manuscript No. 22 in National Anthropological Archives, Smithsonian Institution, Washington.)

————, ed.
1911 The Indian Place-names on Long Island and Islands Adjacent with Their Probable Significations. New York and London: G.P. Putnam's Sons for the John Jermain Memorial Library.

Torok, Charles H.
1965 The Tyendinaga Mohawks: The Village as a Basic Factor in Mohawk Social Structure. *Ontario History* 57(2):69-77.

1966 The Acculturation of the Mohawks of the Bay of Quinte. (Unpublished Ph.D. Dissertation in Anthropology, University of Toronto, Toronto.)

1967 Tyendinaga Acculturation. Pp. 31-33 in Iroquois Culture, History and Prehistory: Proceedings of the 1965 Conference on Iroquois Research. Elisabeth Tooker, ed. Albany: New York State Museum and Science Service.

Torrence, Clayton
1935 Old Somerset on the Eastern Shore of Maryland: A Study in Foundations and Founders. Richmond, Va.: Whittet and Shepperson.

Towner, Lawrence W.
1955 A Good Master Well-served: A Social History of Servitude in Massachusetts, 1620-1750. (Unpublished Ph.D. Dissertation in History, Northwestern University, Evanston, Ill.)

Townshend, Charles H.
1900 The Quinnipiack Indians and Their Reservation. New Haven, Conn.: Tuttle, Morehouse and Taylor.

Tradescant, John
1656 Musaeum tradescantianum; or, A Collection of Rarities Preserved at South-Lambeth Neer London. London: John Grismond. (Reprinted as Old Ashmolean Reprints 1, Oxford University Press, 1925.)

Travers, Milton A.
1960 The Wampanoag Indian Tribute Tribes of Martha's Vineyard; the Story of the Capowacks of Nope, the Takemmy-Wampanoags, the Nunpaug-Wampanoags, the Aquinnah-Wampanoags, of Catachukutcho (Gay Head Tribe) the Chappaquiddick-Wampanoags. [New Bedford, Mass.]

Trelease, Allen W.
1960 Indian Affairs in Colonial New York: The Seventeenth Century. Ithaca, N.Y.: Cornell University Press.

1962 The Iroquois and the Western Fur Trade: A Problem in Interpretation. *Mississippi Valley Historical Review* 49(1):32-51.

Trent, William
1871 Journal of Captain William Trent from Logstown in Pickawillany, A.D. 1752. Alfred T. Goodman, ed. Cincinnati: R. Clarke.

Trigger, Bruce G.
1960 The Destruction of Huronia: A Study in Economic and Cultural Change, 1609-1650. *Transactions of the Royal Canadian Institute* 33(1):14-45. Ottawa.

1962 The Historic Location of the Hurons. *Ontario History* 54(2):137-148.

1962a Trade and Tribal Warfare on the St. Lawrence in the Sixteenth Century. *Ethnohistory* 9(3):240-256.

1963 Settlement as an Aspect of Iroquoian Adaptation at the Time of Contact. *American Anthropologist* 65(1):86-101.

1968 The French Presence in Huronia: The Structure of Franco-Huron Relations in the First Half of the Seventeenth Century. *Canadian Historical Review* 49(2):107-141.

1968a Archaeological and Other Evidence: A Fresh Look at the "Laurentian Iroquois." *American Antiquity* 33(4):429-440.

1969 The Huron: Farmers of the North. New York, Chicago: Holt, Rinehart and Winston.

1970 The Strategy of Iroquoian Prehistory. *Ontario Archaeology* 14:3-48.

1971 The Mohawk-Mahican War (1624-1628): The Establishment of a Pattern. *Canadian Historical Review* 52(3):276-286.

1971a Champlain Judged by His Indian Policy: A Different View of Early Canadian History. *Anthropologica* n.s. 13(1-2):85-114. Ottawa.

1972 Hochelaga: History and Ethnohistory. Pp. 1-107 in Cartier's Hochelaga and the Dawson Site. James F. Pendergast and Bruce G. Trigger, eds. Montreal: McGill-Queen's University Press.

1976 The Children of Aataentsic: A History of the Huron People to 1660. 2 vols. Montreal: McGill-Queen's University Press.

Trowbridge, Charles C.
1823 Indian Dialect-English Dictionary. (Manuscript in Michigan Historical Collections, University of Michigan, Ann Arbor.)

1823a [Traditions, Manners, and Customs of the Mun-noa'-minnee Nation of Indians.] (Manuscript in Burton Historical Collection. Detroit Public Library, Detroit.)

1824 Traditions of the Lenéé of Lenáúpee or Delawares. (Manuscript in C.C. Trowbridge Papers, Michigan Historical Collections, University of Michigan, Ann Arbor.)

1824a [Delaware Grammar.] (Manuscript in Michigan Historical Collections, University of Michigan, Ann Arbor.)

1938 Meeārmeer Traditions. Vernon Kinietz, ed. *University of Michigan Museum of Anthropology, Occasional Contributions* 7. Ann Arbor.

1939 Shawnese Traditions. Vernon Kinietz and Erminie W. Voegelin, eds. *University of Michigan Museum of Anthropology, Occasional Contributions* 9. Ann Arbor.

1972 Account of Some of the Traditions, Manners and Customs of the Lenēē Lenāūpaa or Delaware Indians. Pp. 473-500 in The Delaware Indans: A History, by C.A. Weslager. New Brunswick, N.J.: Rutgers University Press.

Trudel, Marcel
1963-1966 Histoire de la Nouvelle-France. 2 vols. Montreal: Fides.

Trueman, Stuart
1966 The Ordeal of John Gyles: Being an Account of His Odd Adventures, Strange Deliverances, etc. as a Slave of the Maliseets. Toronto: McClelland and Stuart.

Trumbull, Benjamin
1818   A Complete History of Connecticut, Civil and Ecclesiasti-
            cal, from the Emigration of its First Planters, from Eng-
            land, in the Year 1630, to the Year 1764, and to the Close
            of the Indian Wars. 2 vols. New Haven, Conn.: Malthy,
            Goldsmith.

Trumbull, James Hammond
1873   Notes on Forty Algonkin Versions of the Lord's Prayer.
            Hartford, Conn. (Reprinted from *Transactions of the
            American Philological Association for 1872.* Hartford,
            Conn.)

————, ed.
1873a   Introduction. Pp. 1-11 in Some Help for the Indians: A
            Catechism in the Language of the Quiripi Indians of New
            Haven Colony, by Rev. Abraham Pierson. Hartford,
            Conn.: M. H. Mallory.

1880   The Indian Tongue and Its Literature as Fashioned by
            Eliot and Others. Pp. 465-480 in The Memorial History of
            Boston, Including Suffolk County, Massachusetts, 1630-
            1880. Justin Winsor, ed. Boston: James R. Osgood.

1881   Indian Names of Places etc., in and on the Borders of
            Connecticut: With Interpretations of Some of Them.
            Hartford, Conn.: Case, Lockwood and Brainard. (Re-
            printed: Shoestring Press, Hamden, Conn., 1974.)

Tuck, James A.
1969   Some Recent Work on the Prehistory of the Onondaga
            Nation. *Pennsylvania Archaeologist* 39(1-4):40-52.

1970   An Archaic Indian Cemetery in Newfoundland. *Scientific
            American* 22(6):112-121. New York.

1971   Onondaga Iroquois Prehistory: A Study in Settlement
            Archaeology. Syracuse, N.Y.: Syracuse University Press.

1971a   A Cultural Sequence in Northern Labrador. (Paper Read
            at the Annual Meeting of the Society for American Ar-
            chaeology, Norman, Okla., May 1971.)

1971b   An Archaic Cemetery at Port au Choix, Newfoundland.
            American Antiquity 36(3):343-358.

1971c   The Iroquois Confederacy. *Scientific American* 224(2):32-
            49.

1971d   Newfoundland Prehistory Since 1950: Some Answers and
            More Questions. *Man in the Northeast* 1:27-33.

1971e   A Current Summary of Newfoundland Prehistory. *New-
            foundland Quarterly* 68(2):17-25.

1974   Early Archaic Horizons in Eastern North America. *Ar-
            chaeology of Eastern North America* 2(1):72-80. Attleboro,
            Mass.

[1976]   Newfoundland and Labrador Prehistory. *Canada. Na-
            tional Museum of Man, Mercury Series, Archaeological
            Survey of Canada Paper.* Ottawa. In Press.

1976a   Ancient People of Port au Choix: The Excavation of an
            Archaic Indian Cemetery in Newfoundland. St. John's,
            Newfoundland: Memorial University of Newfoundland,
            Institute of Social and Economic Research.

Tucker, Glenn
1956   Tecumseh: Vision of Glory. Indianapolis: Bobbs-Merrill.

Tucker, Sara (Jones), comp.
1942   Indian Villages of the Illinois Country. *Illinois State Mu-
            seum Scientific Paper* 2(1). Pt. 1. Springfield.

Tucker, William F.
1877   Historical Sketch of the Town of Charlestown, in Rhode
            Island, from 1636-1876. Westerly, R.I.: G.B. and J.H.
            Utter.

Tuckerman, Joseph
1821   A Discourse Preached Before the Society for Propagating
            the Gospel Among the Indians and Others in North
America, November 1, 1821. Cambridge, Mass.: Hilliard
            and Metcalfe.

Tufts, Henry
1807   A Narrative of the Life, Adventures, Travels and Suffer-
            ings of Henry Tufts, Now Residing at Lemington in the
            District of Maine. In Substance, as Compiled from His
            Own Mouth. Dover, N.H.: Samuel Bragg, Jr.

Turner, Katherine C.
1951   Red Men Calling on the Great White Father. Norman:
            University of Oklahoma Press.

[Tuttle, Sarah]
1834   Letters and Conversations on Indian Missions at Seneca,
            Tuscarora, Cattaraugus in the State of New York, and
            Maumee, in the State of Ohio. 2d ed. Boston: T.R. Mar-
            vin for the Sabbath School Society.

Tyler, Lyon G., ed.
1907   Narratives of Early Virginia, 1606-1625. New York: C.
            Scribner's Sons.

Tylor, Edward B.
1888   Notes on Powhatan's Mantle, Preserved in the Ashmolean
            Museum, Oxford. *Internationales Archiv für Ethnographie*
            1:215-217. Leiden, The Netherlands.

Tyyska, A.E.
1972   Huron Sweat-baths: The Prehistory of an Artifact for
            Social Maintenance, Integration and Guidance. (Paper
            Read at the Annual Meeting of the Canadian Archae-
            ological Association, St. John's, Newfoundland, February
            1972.)

USNM = United States National Museum
[1857]   [Delaware Woman's Metal Comb, Collected by Edward
            Palmer.] (Ethnographic Collections, Department of An-
            thropology, Smithsonian Institution.)

Ubelaker, Douglas H.
1974   Reconstruction of Demographic Profiles from Ossuary
            Skeletal Samples: A Case Study from the Tidewater Poto-
            mac. *Smithsonian Contributions to Anthropology* 18.
            Washington.

Underhill, John
1638   Nevvs from America; or, A New and Experimentall Dis-
            coverie of New England; Containing, A Trve Relation of
            Their Warlike Proceedings These Two Years Last Past,
            with a Figure of the Indian Fort, or Palizado... by Cap-
            taine John Underhill, a Commander in the Warres There.
            London: Printed by J.D. for Peter Cole. (Reprinted: Da
            Capo Press, New York, 1971.)

1902   Nevves from America. [Brooklyn, N.Y.]: Underhill Soci-
            ety of America.

U.S. Bureau of the Census
1915   ...Indian Population in the United States and Alaska,
            1910. Washington: U.S. Government Printing Office.

1922   14th Census of the United States Taken in the Year 1920.
            Volume 3: Population. Washington: U.S. Government
            Printing Office.

1937   The Indian Population of the United States and Alaska,
            1930. Washington: U.S. Government Printing Office.

1952   United States Census of Population, 1950. Vol. 2, Pt. 46:
            General Characteristics, Virginia. Washington: U.S. Gov-
            ernment Printing Office.

1963   United States Census of Population, 1960. Vol. 1, Pt. 48:
            Characteristics of Population, Virginia. Washington:
            U.S. Government Printing Office.

1971   United States Census of Population, 1970. Vol. 1, Pt. 48:
            Characteristics of Population, Virginia. Washington:
            U.S. Government Printing Office.

U.S. Census Office *see* U.S. Census Office. 11th Census

U.S. Census Office. 11th Census
1892   ... Indians. The Six Nations of New York, Cayugas, Mohawks (Saint Regis), Oneidas, Onondagas, Senecas, Tuscaroras, by Thomas C. Donaldson. Extra Census Bulletin. Washington: U.S. Government Printing Office.

1894   Report on Indians Taxed and Indians Not Taxed in the United States (Except Alaska) at the Eleventh Census, 1890. Washington: U.S. Government Printing Office.

U.S. Commissioner of Indian Affairs
1837   Treaties Between the United States of America and the Several Indian Tribes, from 1778-1837. Washington: Langtree and O'Sullivan.

U.S. Department of Commerce
1974   Federal and State Indian Reservations and Indian Trust Areas. Washington: U.S. Government Printing Office.

Vail, R.W.G.
1949   The Indians' Captives Relate Their Adventures. Pp. 23-61 in The Voice of the Old Frontier, by R.G.W. Vail. Philadelphia: University of Pennsylvania Press.

[Van den Bogaert, Harmen Meyndertsz]
1909   Narrative of a Journey into the Mohawk and Oneida Country, 1634-1635. Pp. 135-162 in Narratives of New Netherland, 1609-1664. J. Franklin Jameson, ed. New York: Charles Scribner's Sons.

Van der Donck, Adriaen see Donck, Adriaen van der

[Van Dusen, Conrad]
1867   The Indian Chief: An Account of the Labours, Losses, Sufferings, and Oppression of Ke-zig-ko-e-ne-ne (David Sawyer) a Chief of the Ojibway Indians in Canada West, by Enemikeese. London: W. Nichols.

Van Laer, Arnold J.F., ed.
1908   Van Rensselaer Bowier Manuscripts, Being the Letters of Kiliaen Van Rennsselaer, 1630-1643, and Other Documents Relating to the Colony of Rensselaerswyck. Albany: University of the State of New York.

————, ed.
1924   Documents Relating to New Netherland, 1624-1626, in the Henry E. Huntington Library. San Marino, Calif.: The Henry E. Huntington Library.

Van Loon, L.G.
1968   Tawagonshi, Beginning of the Treaty Era. Indian Historian 1(3):23-26.

Van Steen, Marcus
1965   Pauline Johnson: Her Life and Work. Toronto: Musson Book Company.

Van Tassel, Isaac
1826-1836   [Indians in Ohio.] Missionary Herald 22:119-120, 25:32-33, 27:387-388, 28:269, 29:469, 31:29, 32:28. Boston.

Van Wart, Arthur F.
1948   The Indians of the Maritime Provinces: Their Diseases and Native Cures. Canadian Medical Association Journal 59:573-577.

Van Wassenaer, Nicolaes see Wassenaer, Nicolaes van

Vassal, Henri
[1811-1889] Papiers Vassal. (Papers of Several Agents of the St. Francis Abenakis in Archives Séminaire de Nicolet, Nicolet, Que.)

Vaughan, Alden T.
1965   New England Frontier: Puritans and Indians, 1620-1675. Boston: Little, Brown.

1974   "Expulsion of the Savages:" English Attitudes and the Massacre of 1622. (Unpublished Manuscript in Vaughan's Possession.)

Velasco, Alonso de
1611   [Anonymous Map of Virginia, Sent to the King of Spain.] (Manuscript in Archivo General de Simancas, Simancas,

Spain.) (Printed: Facing p. 456 in The Genesis of the United States, by Alexander Brown, Boston, 1890.)

Verill, A. Hyatt
1954   The Real Americans. New York: G.P. Putnam's Sons.

Vetromile, Eugene
1866   The Abenakis and Their History, or Historical Notices on the Aborigines of Acadia. New York: J.B. Kirker.

Virginia (Colony) Council see McIlwaine, Henry R.

Virginia (Colony) County Court (Northampton Co.) see Ames, Susie M.

Virginia. Laws, Statutes, etc. see Hening, William W.

Virginia Company of London see Kingsbury, Susan M., ed.

Voegelin, Charles F.
1935   Shawnee Phonemes. Language 11(1):23-37.

1936   The Shawnee Female Deity. Yale University Publications in Anthropology 10. New Haven, Conn.

1938-1940   Shawnee Stems and the Jacob P. Dunn Dictionary. 5 Pts. Indiana Historical Society, Prehistory Research Series 1(3):63-108, (5):135-167, (8):289-341, (9):345-406, (10):409-476. Indianapolis.

1942   Word Distortions in Delaware Big House and Walam Olum Songs. Proceedings of the Indiana Academy of Science 51:48-54. Indianapolis.

1946   Delaware, an Eastern Algonquian Language. Viking Fund Publications in Anthropology 6:130-157. New York.

1953   From FL (Shawnee) to TL (English). International Journal of American Linguistics 19(1):1-25.

Voegelin, Charles F., and Erminie W. Voegelin
1935   Shawnee Name Groups. American Anthropologist 37(4):617-635.

1944   The Shawnee Female Deity in Historical Perspective. American Anthropologist 46(3):370-375.

1946   Linguistic Considerations of Northeastern North America. Pp. 178-194 in Man in Northeastern North America. Frederick Johnson, ed. Papers of the Robert S. Peabody Foundation for Archaeology 3. Andover, Mass.

Voegelin, Charles F., John F. Yegerlehner, and Florence M. Robinett
1954   Shawnee Laws: Perceptual Statements for the Language and for the Content. Pp. 32-46 in Language in Culture. Harry Hoijer, ed. Chicago: University of Chicago Press. (Also Published as Memoirs of the American Anthropological Association 79.)

Voegelin, Erminie (Wheeler)
1939   Some Possible Sixteenth and Seventeenth Century Locations of the Shawnee. Proceedings of the Indiana Academy of Science 48:13-18. Indianapolis.

1941   The Place of Agriculture in the Subsistence Economy of the Shawnee. Papers of the Michigan Academy of Science, Arts and Letters 24:513-520. Ann Arbor.

1944   Mortuary Customs of the Shawnee and Other Eastern Tribes. Indiana Historical Society, Prehistory Research Series 2(4):227-444. Indianapolis.

1974   Ethnohistorical Report on the Indian Use and Occupancy of Royce Area 53. Docket Nos. 13-E et al. Before the Indian Claims Commission. Pp. 51-315 in Indians of Northern Ohio and Southeastern Michigan. New York: Garland.

1974a   Ethnohistorical Report on the Indian Use and Occupancy of Royce Area 11, Ohio and Indiana. Docket Nos. 13-G

(Chippewa) et al. Before the Indian Claims Commission. Pp. 129-319 in Vol. 1 and pp. 7-468 in Vol. 2 of Indians of Ohio and Indiana Prior to 1795. New York: Garland.

See also Wheeler-Voegelin, Erminie

Vogel, Joseph O.
1975   Trends in Cahokia Ceramics: Preliminary Study of the Collections from Tracts 15A and 15B. *Illinois Archaeological Survey Bulletin* 10:32-71. Urbana.

Vogel, Virgil J.
1967   The Missionary as Acculturation Agent: Peter Dougherty and the Indians of Grand Traverse. *Michigan History* 51(3):185-201.

Voget, Fred W.
1951   Acculturation at Caughnawaga: A Note on the Native-modified Group. *American Anthropologist* 53(2):220-231.

1969   A Six Nations' Diary, 1891-1894. *Ethnohistory* 16(4):345-360.

Volney, Constantin F.C. de
1804   A View of the Soil and Climate of the United States of America. Philadelphia: J. Conrad and Son.

Voorhis, Paul H.
1967   Kickapoo Grammar. (Unpublished Ph.D. Dissertation in Linguistics, Yale University, New Haven, Conn.)

1971   New Notes on the Mesquakie (Fox) Language. *International Journal of American Linguistics* 37(2):63-75.

1971a   Notes on Kickapoo Whistle Speech. *International Journal of American Linguistics* 37(4):238-243.

1974   Introduction to Kickapoo Grammar. (Language Science Monographs 13) Bloomington: Indiana University Press.

Vries, David P. de
1909   From the "Korte Historiael ende journaels aenteyckeninge," 1633-1643 [1655]. Pp. 181-234 in Narratives of New Netherland 1609-1644. J. Franklin Jameson, ed. New York: Charles Scribner's Sons. (Reprinted: Barnes and Noble, New York, 1967.)

1911   Korte historiael ende journaels aenteyckeninge van verscheyden voyagiens in de view deelen des weldtsronde, als Europa, Africa, Asia, ende Amerika [1655]. 'sGravenhage, The Netherlands: M. Nijhoff.

1912   From the "Korte Historiael ende journaels aenteyckeninge," 1630-1633, 1643 [1655]. Pp. 1-29 in Narratives of Early Pennsylvania, West New Jersey and Delaware, 1630-1707. Albert C. Myers, ed. New York: Charles Scribner's Sons.

Vroom, J.
1892-1894   Glimpses of the Past: Contributions to the History of Charlotte County and the Border Towns. St. Stephen, N.B.: St. Croix Courier.

WHC = Draper, Lyman C., and Reuben G. Thwaites, eds.
1855-1911   Collections of the State Historical Society of Wisconsin. 21 vols. Madison: The Society.

Wagner, Norman
1972   A Discriminant Analysis of Three Neutral Sites. (Paper Presented at the Fifth Annual Meeting of the Canadian Archaeological Association. St. John's, Newfoundland, February, 1972.)

Wakefield, Francis
1966   The Elusive Mascoutens. *Michigan History* 50(3):228-234.

Wallace, Anthony F.C.
1947   Woman, Land, and Society: Three Aspects of Aboriginal Delaware Life. *Pennsylvania Archaeologist* 17(1-4):1-35.

1949   King of the Delawares: Teedyuscung, 1700-1763. Philadelphia: University of Pennsylvania Press.

1951   Some Psychological Determinants of Culture Change in an Iroquoian Community. Pp. 55-76 in Symposium on Local Diversity in Iroquois Culture. William N. Fenton, ed. *Bureau of American Ethnology Bulletin* 149(4). Washington.

1952   The Modal Personality Structure of the Tuscarora Indians, as Revealed by the Rorschach Test. *Bureau of American Ethnology Bulletin* 150. Washington.

1956   Revitalization Movements: Some Theoretical Considerations for Their Comparative Study. *American Anthropologist* 58(2):264-281.

1957   Origins of Iroquois Neutrality: The Grand Settlement of 1701. *Pennsylvania History* 24(3):223-235.

1958   The Dekanawideh Myth Analyzed as the Record of a Revitalization Movement. *Ethnohistory* 5(2):118-130.

1958a   Dreams and the Wishes of the Soul: A Type of Psychoanalytic Theory Among the Seventeenth Century Iroquois. *American Anthropologist* 60(2):234-248.

1959   The Institutionalization of Cathartic and Control Strategies in Iroquois Religious Psychotherapy. Pp. 63-96 in Culture and Mental Health. Marvin K. Opler, ed. New York: Macmillan.

1966   Religion: An Anthropological View. New York: Random House.

1969   The Death and Rebirth of the Seneca. New York: Alfred A. Knopf.

1971   Handsome Lake and the Decline of the Iroquois Matriarchate. Pp. 367-376 in Kinship and Culture. Francis L.K. Hsu, ed. Chicago: Aldine.

Wallace, Paul A.W.
1945   Conrad Weiser, 1696-1760, Friend of Colonist and Mohawk. Philadelphia: University of Pennsylvania Press.

1948   The Return of Hiawatha. *New York History* 29(4):385-403.

Waller, Elbert
1928   Waller's History of Illinois. 12th ed. Galesburg, Ill.: Wagoner Printing Company.

Wallis, Wilson D., and Ruth S. Wallis
1955   The Micmac Indians of Eastern Canada. Minneapolis: University of Minnesota Press.

1957   The Malecite Indians of New Brunswick. *Anthropological Series 40, National Museum of Canada Bulletin* 148. Ottawa.

Ward, D.
1906   The Meskwaki People of To-day. *Iowa Journal of History and Politics* 4(2):190-219.

Ward, Harry M.
1961   The United Colonies of New England, 1643-90. New York: Vantage Press.

Warner, Robert A.
1935   The Southern New England Indians, 1725: A Study in Culture Contact. (Unpublished Ph.D. Dissertation in Anthropology, Yale University, New Haven, Conn.)

Warren, William W.
1885   History of the Ojibways, Based Upon Traditions and Oral Statements. *Collections of the Minnesota Historical Society* 5:29-394. St. Paul. (Reprinted as History of the Ojibway Nation, Ross and Haines, Minneapolis, 1957, 1970.)

Washburn, Wilcomb E.
1957   The Governor and the Rebel: A History of Bacon's Rebellion in Virginia. Chapel Hill: University of North Carolina Press.

1957a   Virginia Under Charles I and Cromwell, 1625-1660. *(Jamestown 350th Anniversary Historical Booklets* 7) Williamsburg: Virginia 350th Anniversary Celebration Corporation.

1957b   Governor Berkeley and King Philip's War. *New England Quarterly* 30(September):363-377.

1958   [Review of] Flintlock and Tomahawk: New England in King Philip's War, by Douglas E. Leach. *Pennsylvania Magazine of History and Biography* 82(4):473-474.

1959   The Moral and Legal Justifications for Dispossessing the Indians. Pp. 15-32 in Seventeenth Century America: Essays in Colonial History. James M. Smith, ed. Chapel Hill: University of North Carolina Press.

Wassenaer, Nicolaes van
1622-1635   Historisch verhael alder ghedenckweerdichste geschiedenissen die hier en daer in Europa, etc. voorgevallen syn. 21 vols. in 5. Amsterdam: Ian Evertss.

1909   From the "Historisch Verhael," 1624-1630. Pp. 61-96 in Narratives of New Netherland, 1609-1664. J. Franklin Jameson, ed. New York: Charles Scribner's Sons. (Reprinted: Barnes and Noble, New York, 1967.)

Waters, Joseph H.
1965   Animal Remains from Some New England Woodland Sites. *Bulletin of the Archaeological Society of Connecticut* 33:4-11. New Haven.

Watkins, Frances E.
1935   Ottawa Indian Quill-decorated Birchbark Boxes: The Martha Berry Memorial Collection. *Masterkey* 9(4):123-127.

Watson, Lawrence W.
1907   The Origin of the Melicites. *Journal of American Folk-Lore* 20(77):160-162.

Watson, Patty Jo, and Richard A. Yarnell
1966   Archaeological and Paleoethnobotanical Investigations in Salts Cave, Mammoth Cave National Park, Kentucky. *American Antiquity* 31(6):842-849.

Waugh, Frederick W.
1916   Iroquois Foods and Food Preparation. *Anthropological Series 12, Memoirs of the Canadian Geological Survey* 86. Ottawa.

Weaver, John E., and Frederic E. Clements
1938   Plant Ecology. 2d ed. New York: McGraw Hill

Weaver, Sally M.
[1963-1974] [Ethnographic Notes, from Approximately 3 Years of Fieldwork Among the Grand River Iroquois, Ontario.] (Manuscripts in Weaver's Possession.)

[1970]   Election Behavior Under the Threat of Termination: A Six Nations Example. (Manuscript in Weaver's Possession.)

1971   Smallpox or Chickenpox: An Iroquoian Community's Reaction to Crisis, 1901-1902. *Ethnohistory* 18(4):361-378.

1972   Medicine and Politics Among the Grand River Iroquois: A Study of the Non-conservatives. *Canada. National Museum of Man, Publications in Ethnology* 4. Ottawa.

[1975]   Iroquois Politics: Grand River, 1847-1975. (Manuscript in Weaver's Possession.)

Webb, William S.
1946   Indian Knoll, Site Oh 2, Ohio County, Kentucky. *University of Kentucky Reports in Anthropology and Archaeology* 4(3). Pt. 1. Lexington.

Webb, William S., and Raymond S. Baby
1957   The Adena People, No.2. Columbus: Ohio State University Press.

Webb, William S., and W.G. Haag
1947   Archaic Sites in McLean County, Kentucky. *University of Kentucky Reports in Anthropology and Archaeology* 7(1). Lexington.

Webb, William S., and Charles E. Snow
1945   The Adena People. *University of Kentucky Reports in Anthropology and Archaeology* 6. Lexington.

Weber, Joann Cynthia
1970   Types and Attributes in the Study of Iroquois Pipes. (Unpublished Ph.D. Dissertation in Anthropology, Harvard University, Cambridge, Mass.)

Wedel, Waldo R.
1943   Archeological Investigations in Platte and Clay Counties, Missouri. *U.S. National Museum Bulletin* 183. Washington.

Weeden, William B.
1884   Indian Money as a Factor in New England Civilization. *Johns Hopkins University Studies in Historical and Political Science,* 2d ser., Vol. 8-9. Baltimore.

Weinman, Paul L., and Thomas P. Weinman
1971   Rip Van Winkle Site. *Pennsylvania Archaeologist* 41(1-2):53-60.

Weis, Frederick L.
1959   The New England Company of 1649 and Its Missionary Enterprises. Pp. 134-218 in *Publications of the Colonial Society of Massachusetts* 38. Boston.

Wellman, Beth, and Karen S. Hartgen
1974   Prehistoric Site Survey and Salvage in the Upper Schoharie Valley, New York. (Report on File, New York State Museum and Science Service, Albany.)

Weslager, Clinton A.
1943   Delaware's Forgotten Folk: The Story of the Moors and Nanticoke. Philadelphia: University of Pennsylvania Press.

1943a   The Nanticoke Indians in Early Pennsylvania History. *Pennsylvania Magazine of History and Biography* 67(4):345-355.

1944   Wynicaco - A Choptank Indian Chief. *Proceedings of the American Philosophical Society* 87(5):398-402. Philadelphia.

1944a   The Delaware Indians as Women. *Journal of the Washington Academy of Sciences* 34(12):381-388. Washington.

1946   Susquehannock Indian Religion from an Old Document. *Journal of the Washington Academy of Sciences* 36(9):302-305. Washington.

1947   Further Light on the Delaware Indians as Women. *Journal of the Washington Academy of Sciences* 37(9):298-304. Washington.

1948   The Nanticoke Indians: A Refugee Tribal Group of Pennsylvania. Harrisburg: Pennsylvania Historical and Museum Commission.

1948a   Monongahela Woodland Culture and the Shawnee. *Pennsylvania Archaeologist* 18(1-2):19-22.

1954   Robert Evelyn's Indian Tribes and Place-names of New Albion. *Bulletin of the Archeological Society of New Jersey* 9:1-14. Trenton.

1955   Folklore Among the Nanticokes of Indian River Hundred. *Delaware Folklore Bulletin* 1(5):17-18.

1961   The Accomac and Accohannock Indians from Early Relations. Painter: Eastern Shore of Virginia Historical Society.

[1961a]   Dutch Explorers, Traders and Settlers in the Delaware Valley, 1609-1664. Philadelphia: University of Pennsylvania Press.

1971   Name-giving Among the Delaware Indians. *Names* 19(4):268-283.

1972   The Delaware Indians: A History. New Brunswick, N.J.: Rutgers University Press.

1973   Magic Medicines of the Indians. Somerset, N.J.: Middle Atlantic Press.

1974   Enrollment List of Chippewa and Delaware-Munsies Living in Franklin County, Kansas, May 31, 1900. *Kansas Historical Quarterly* 40(2):234-240. Topeka.

Weslager, Clinton A., with A.R. Dunlap *see* Weslager [1961a]

West, John
1827   The Substance of a Journal During a Residence on the Red River Colony, British North America; and Frequent Excursions Among the North-West American Indians in the Years 1820, 1821, 1822, 1823. 2d ed. London: E.B. Seeley and Son.

Westez, Carlos A.H. (Chief Red Thunder Cloud)
1944   A Study of the Long Island Indian Problem. *Bulletin of the Massachusetts Archaeological Society* 5(2):17-19. Attleboro.

1945   An Ethnological Introduction to the Long Island Indians. *Bulletin of the Massachusetts Archaeological Society* 6(3):39-42. Attleboro.

1958   The Oak Scrub Brush Among the Montauk and Shinnecock. Mimeo.

Westveld, Marinus et al.
1956   Natural Forest Vegetation Zones of New England. *Journal of Forestry* 54(5):332-338.

Wheeler-Voegelin, Erminie
1959   The 19th- and 20th-Century Ethnohistory of Various Groups of Cayuga Indians. (Typescript in Great Lakes-Ohio Valley Ethnohistoric Project, Department of Anthropology Archives, Indiana University, Bloomington; Copy, Manuscript No. 7092 in National Anthropological Archives, Smithsonian Institution, Washington.)

————, ed.
1959a   John Heckewelder to Peter S. Du Ponceau, Bethlehem, 12th Aug. 1818. *Ethnohistory* 6(1):70-81.

[1963]   An Ethnohistorical Report on the Indian Use and Occupancy of Royce Area 87... and Royce Area 88... Defendant's Expert Report, Indian Claims Commission, Docket Nos. 13-F *et al.* Pp. 51-373 in Indians of Northwest Ohio. David Agee Horr, comp. New York and London: Garland, 1974.

[1963a]   An Ethnohistorical Report on the Indian Use and Occupancy of Royce Area 53... [and] Royce Area 54... Defendant's Expert Report, Indian Claims Commission, Docket Nos. 13-E *et al.* Pp. 51-375 in Indians of Northern Ohio and Southwestern Michigan. David Agee Horr, comp. New York and London: Garland, 1974.

[1965]   An Ethnohistorical Report on Indian Use and Occupancy of Royce Area 11, Ohio and Indiana... Defendant's Expert Report, Indian Claims Commission, Docket Nos. 13-G (Chippewa) *et al.* Pp. 129-463 in Vol. 1 and pp. 9-468 in Vol. 2 of Indians of Ohio and Indiana Prior to 1795. David Agee Horr, comp. New York and London: Garland, 1974.

————— *see also* Voegelin, Erminie (Wheeler)

Wheelock, Eleazar
1763   A Plain and Faithful Narrative of the Original Design, Rise, Progress, and Present State of the Indian Charity-School at Lebanon in Connecticut. Boston: Richard and Samuel Draper.

1775   A Continuation of the Narrative of the Indian Charity-School, Begun in Lebanon, Connecticut; Now Incorporated with Dartmouth-College, in Hanover, in the Province of New Hampshire. Hartford, Conn.: E. Watson.

Whipple, Amiel W., Thomas Ewbank, and William W. Turner
1855   Report Upon the Indian Tribes. Part 3 of U.S. War Department Reports of Explorations and Surveys, to Ascertain the Most Practicable and Economical Route for a Railroad from the Mississippi River to the Pacific Ocean. U.S. Congress. Senate. 33d Cong., 2d sess., Senate Executive Doc. No. 78 (Serial No. 752). Washington.

White, John
1585-1586   Map of Eastern North America from Florida to Chesapeake Bay. (Manuscript in the British Museum, Prints and Drawings 1906-5-9-1(2), London.) (Printed in The Roanoke Voyages, 1584-1590, D.B. Quinn, ed. Vol. 1:460, Cambridge University Press for the Hakluyt Society, London, 1955.)

1585-1586a Map of Eastern North America from Cape Lookout to Chespeake Bay. (Manuscript in the British Museum, Prints and Drawings 1906-5-9-1(3). London. Printed in The Roanoke Voyages, 1584-1590, D.B. Quinn, ed. Vol. 1:461, Cambridge University Press for the Hakluyt Society, London, 1955.)

White, Marian E.
1961   Iroquois Culture History in the Niagara Frontier Area of New York State. *University of Michigan Museum of Anthropology, Anthropological Papers* 16. Ann Arbor.

1968   A Re-examination of the Historic Iroquois Van Son Cemetery on Grand Island. *Bulletin of the Buffalo Society of Natural Sciences* 24:7-48. Buffalo.

1971   Ethnic Identification and Iroquois Groups in Western New York and Ontario. *Ethnohistory* 18(1):19-38.

1971a   [Review of] The Bennett Site, by J.V. Wright and J.E. Anderson. *American Antiquity* 36(2):222-223.

1972   On Delineating the Neutral Iroquois of the Eastern Niagara Peninsula of Ontario. *Ontario Archaeology* 17:62-74. Toronto.

Whitetree, John
1873   [Copy of Letter to Hon. C. Delano, Secretary of the Interior, Dated Seneca Nation, Aug. 26, 1873.] (Manuscript in Quapaw: Indians, Seneca, Agents' Reports, Indian Archives Division, Oklahoma Historical Society, Oklahoma City.)

Whittlesey, Charles
1852   Descriptions of Ancient Works in Ohio. *Smithsonian Contributions to Knowledge* 3(7). Washington.

Wild, Isaac
1799   Travels Through the States of North America and the Provinces of Upper and Lower Canada During the Years 1795, 1796, and 1797. London: [no publisher.]

Wilford, Lloyd A.
1941   A Tentative Classification of the Prehistoric Cultures of Minnesota. *American Antiquity* 6(3):231-249.

1950   The Prehistoric Indians of Minnesota: Some Mounds of the Rainy River Aspect. *Minnesota History* 31(3):163-171, (4):231-237.

1955   A Revised Classification of the Prehistoric Cultures of Minnesota. *American Antiquity* 21(2):130-142.

Willets, Jane
[1947]   [Ottawa Indian Manuscripts.] (Manuscript 30(Alg.1) in Library of the American Philosophical Society, Philadelphia.)

1947a   [Ottawa Material.] (Wire, Duplicated on Tape 294 in Library of the American Philosophical Society, Philadelphia.)

1948   Correlated Changes in Ottawa Kinship and Social Organization. (Unpublished M.A. Thesis in Anthropology, University of Pennsylvania, Philadelphia.)

Willey, Gordon R.
1966   An Introduction to American Archaeology. Vol.1: North and Middle America. Englewood Cliffs, N.J.: Prentice-Hall.

Willey, Gordon R., and Philip Phillips
1958   Method and Theory in American Archeology. Chicago: University of Chicago Press.

Willey, Gordon R., and Jeremy A. Sabloff
1974   A History of American Archaeology. San Francisco: W.H. Freeman.

Williams, Eleazer
1832-1840 Papers. (Manuscripts in Neville Public Museum, Green Bay, Wis.)

Williams, Lorraine E.
1972   A Study of Seventeenth Century Culture Contact in the Long Island Sound Area. (Unpublished Ph.D. Dissertation in Anthropology, New York University, New York.)

Williams, Roger
1643   A Key into the Language of America, or an Help to the Language of the Natives in that Part of America Called New-England; Together with Briefe Observations of the Customs, Manners, and Worships, etc. of the Aforesaid Natives, in Peace and Warre, in Life and Death. On all of Which are Added Spiritual Observations Generall and Particular.... London: Gregory Dexter.

1866   A Key into the Language of America [1643]. J. Hammond Trumbull, ed. *Publications of the Narragansett Club* 1(2):1-219. Providence.

1874   The Letters of Roger Williams, 1632-1682. John R. Bartlett, ed. *Publications of the Narragansett Club* 6. Providence. (Reprinted: Massachusetts Historical Society, Boston, 1924; Russell and Russell, New York, 1963.)

1881   Some Letters Written by Roger Williams: Believed to Have Been Hitherto Unpublished. *Rhode Island Historical Tracts* 14:23-62. Providence.

1900   Ten Letters of Roger Williams, 1654-1678. *Publications of the Rhode Island Historical Society* 8(3):141-161. Providence.

1936   A Key into the Language of America [1643]. 5th ed. Providence: The Rhode Island and Providence Plantations Tercentenary Commission. (Reprinted: Wayne State University Press, Detroit, 1973.)

1945   An Answer to a Scandalous Paper Which Came to My Hand from the Massachusetts Clamoring Against the Purchase and Slandering the Purchasers of Qunnunnagut Iland, and Subscribed by John Easton [1658]. Providence, R.I.: The Roger Williams Press.

1963   The Complete Writings of Roger Williams. 7 vols. New York: Russell and Russell.

1971   Copy of a Letter of Roger Williams Telling of the Burning of Providence and of His Conference with the Indians During King Philip's War in 1676. *Publications of the Rhode Island Historical Society* 50. Providence.

Williams, Stephen, and John M. Goggin
1956   The Long-nosed God Mask in Eastern United States. *Missouri Archaeologist* 18(3):1-72.

Williams, Stephen, and James B. Stoltman
1965   An Outline of Southeastern United States Prehistory with Particular Emphasis on the Paleo-Indian Era. Pp. 669-683 in The Quaternary of the United States. Herbert E. Wright, Jr., and David G. Grey, eds. Princeton, N.J.: Princeton University Press.

Williams, Ted C.
1976   The Reservation. Syracuse, N.Y.: Syracuse University Press.

Williamson, James A.
1962   The Cabot Voyages and Bristol Discovery Under Henry VII. Cambridge, England: The University Press.

Williamson, William D.
1832   The History of the State of Maine: From its First Discovery A.D. 1602, to the Separation, A.D. 1820 Inclusive. 2 vols. Hallowell, Me.: Glazier, Masters.

Willoughby, Charles C.
1907   The Virginia Indians in the Seventeenth Century. *American Anthropologist* 9(1):57-86.

1935   Antiquities of the New England Indians with Notes on the Ancient Cultures of the Adjacent Territory. Cambridge, Mass.: Harvard University, Peabody Museum of American Archaeology and Ethnology.

Wilson, Charles Banks
1956   Greencorn, a Ceremony of the Seneca. Pp. 40-42 in Indians of Eastern Oklahoma Including Quapaw Agency Indians. Afton, Okla.: Buffalo Publishing Company.

Wilson, Sir Daniel
1876   Prehistoric Man: Researches into the Origin of Civilization in the Old and the New World. 2 vols. London: Macmillan.

1892   The Lost Atlantis and Other Ethnographic Studies. Edinburgh: D. Douglas; New York: Macmillan.

Wilson, Edmund
1960   Apologies to the Iroquois, with A Study of the Mohawks in High Steel, by Joseph Mitchell. New York: Farrar, Strauss, and Cudahy.

Wilson, Edward F.
1874   Ojebway Language: A Manual for Missionaries and Others Employed Among the Ojebway Indians. 3 Pts. Toronto: Printed by Roswell and Hutchinson for the Society for Promoting Christian Knowledge, London.

Wilson, H. Clyde
1956   A New Interpretation of the Wild Rice District of Wisconsin. *American Anthropologist* 58(6):1059-1064.

Winney, John A.
1880   [Letter to D.B. Dyer, Indian Agent, Quapaw, Dated Aug. 2, 1880.] (Manuscript in Quapaw: Indians, Seneca, Agents' Reports, Indian Archives Division, Oklahoma Historical Society, Oklahoma City.)

1881-1882 [Letters to D.B. Dyer, Indian Agent, Quapaw, Dated Apr. 29 and Nov. 11, 1881, and March 14, 1882.] (Manuscripts in Quapaw: Indians, Seneca, Agents' Reports, and Quapaw: Indians, Cayuga, Indian Archives Division, Oklahoma Historical Society, Oklahoma City.)

1883   [Letter to D.B. Dyer, Quapaw Agency, Dated Mar. 30, 1883.] (Manuscript in Quapaw: Indians, Seneca, Agents' Reports, Indian Archives Division, Oklahoma Historical Society, Oklahoma City.)

1975   Origin of the Seneca Indian Pagan Prophet. Pp. 101-104 in Forty Years Among the Indians, by Jeremiah Hubbard. Knightstown, Ind.: Bookmark.

Winslow, Edward
1910   Winslow's Relation [1624]. Pp. 267-357 in Chronicles of the Pilgrim Fathers. John Masefield, ed. London: J.M. Dent; New York: E.P. Dutton.

Winsor, Justin, ed.
1884-1889   Narrative and Critical History of America. 8 vols. Boston and New York: Houghton Mifflin.

Wintemberg, William J.
1936   The Roebuck Prehistoric Village Site, Grenville County, Ontario. *Anthropological Series 19, National Museum of Canada Bulletin* 83. Ottawa.

[1938]   [Fieldnotes, St. Ignace Excavations.] (In Manuscript Files, Wintemberg Collection, National Museum of Canada, Archaeology Division, Ottawa.)

1946   The Sidey-Mackay Village Site. *American Antiquity* 11(3):154-182.

Winters, Howard D.
1967   An Archaeological Survey of the Wabash Valley in Illinois. Rev. ed. *Illinois State Museum, Report of Investigations* 10. Springfield.

1969   The Riverton Culture: A Second Millenium Occupation in the Central Wabash Valley. *Illinois State Museum, Report of Investigations* 13. Springfield.

Winters, Howard D., and Nancy Hammerslough
1971   The Havana Tradition. Pp. 138-141 in Adena: The Seeking of an Identity. B.K. Swartz, Jr., ed. Muncie, Ind.: Ball State University Press.

Winthrop, John
1825-1826   The History of New England from 1630 to 1649. James Savage, ed. 2 vols. Boston: Phelps and Farnham; Thomas B. Wait and Son.

1853   The History of New England from 1630 to 1649. From His Original Manuscripts. With Notes by James Savage. 2 vols. Boston: Little, Brown.

1908   Winthrop's Journal, "History of New England," [1630-1649]. James K. Hosmer, ed. 2 vols. New York: Charles Scribner's Sons. (Reprinted: Barnes and Noble, New York, 1959.)

Winthrop, John, Jr.
1889   [Letter to Henry Jacie from John Winthrop, Jr.] *Massachusetts Historical Society Collections,* Vol. 3:57-61. Boston.

1929-1947   Winthrop Papers..., 1498-1649. Allyn B. Forbes, ed. 5 vols. Boston: Massachusetts Historical Society.

Winthrop, Wait
1693   The Number of All the Indians: That Belong or Own the Meeting House of Pomppashpissit in Sandwich [.] of the Mr Thomas Tuppur [Tupper] His Teaching House of quâhassit and waweuhtat [Wawayontat]... of manamat bonts [Manomet Ponds]... of manamat [Monument Beach]... Rackoned by Raph Jouns [Rafe Jonus, Ralph Jones], Hope, John putquoi [John Quoi or Quoy], Margestrats. (Manuscript in Pilgrim Hall Museum and Library, Pilgrim Society, Plymouth, Mass.)

Wise, Barton H., ed.
1897   Northhampton County Records in the 17th Century. *Virginia Magazine of History and Biography* 4(4):401-410, 5(1):33-41.

Wissler, Clark
1914   Material Cultures of the North American Indians. *American Anthropologist* 16(3):447-505.

1916   General Discussion of Shamanistic and Dancing Societies. *Anthropological Papers of the American Museum of Natural History* 11(12):855-876. New York.

1917   The American Indian: An Introduction to the Anthropology of the New World. New York: Douglas C. McMurtrie.

1923   Man and Culture. New York: Thomas Y. Crowell.

1926   The Relation of Nature to Man in Aboriginal America. New York and London: Oxford University Press.

Witthoft, John
1949   An Outline of Pennsylvania Indian History. *Pennsylvania History* 16(3):3-15. Harrisburg.

1949a   Green Corn Ceremonialism in the Eastern Woodlands. *University of Michigan Museum of Anthropology, Occasional Contributions* 13. Ann Arbor.

1952   A Paleo-Indian Site in Eastern Pennsylvania: An Early Hunting Culture. *Proceedings of the American Philosophical Society* 96(4):464-495. Lancaster, Pa.

1953   Broad Spearpoints and the Transitional Period Cultures. *Pennsylvania Archaeologist* 23(1):4-31.

1955   [Notes and Reviews.] *Pennsylvania Archaeologist* 25(1):76-77.

1959   Ancestry of the Susquehannocks. Pp. 19-60 in Susquehannock Miscellany. John Witthoft and W. Fred Kinsey, III, eds. Harrisburg: Pennsylvania Historical and Museum Commission.

1959a   Notes on an Indian Burial from North-central Pennsylvania. *Pennsylvania Archaeologist* 29(1):40-48.

Witthoft, John, and William A. Hunter
1955   The Seventeenth-century Origins of the Shawnee. *Ethnohistory* 2(1):42-57.

Witthoft, John, and W. Fred Kinsey, III, eds.
1959   Susquehannock Miscellany. Harrisburg: Pennsylvania Historical and Museum Commission.

Witthoft, John, W. Fred Kinsey, III, and Charles H. Holzinger
1959   A Susquehannock Cemetery: The Ibaugh Site. Pp. 99-119 in Susquehannock Miscellany. John Witthoft and W. Fred Kinsey, III, eds. Harrisburg: Pennsylvania Historical and Museum Commission.

Wittry, Warren L.
1959   The Wakanda Park Mound Group, Dn 1, Menomonie, Wisconsin. *Wisconsin Archaeologist* 40(3):95-115.

1959a   The Raddatz Rockshelter, SK 5, Wisconsin. *Wisconsin Archaeologist* 40(2):33-69.

1959b   Archaeological Studies of Four Wisconsin Rockshelters. *Wisconsin Archaeologist* 40(4):137-267.

1963   The Bell Site, Wn 9: An Early Historic Fox Village. *Wisconsin Archaeologist* 44(1):1-58.

1969   The American Woodhenge. Pp. 43-48 in Explorations into Cahokia Archaeology. Melvin L. Fowler, ed. *Illinois Archaeological Survey Bulletin* 7. Urbana.

Wolley, Charles
1902   A Two Years' Journal in New York and Part of its Territories in America [1701]. Edward G. Bourne, ed. Cleveland: Burrows Brothers.

Wood, John J., Jr.
1907   The Mascoutin Village. *Proceedings of the State Historical Society of Wisconsin* 54:167-174. Madison.

Wood, William
1634   Nevv England's Prospect: A True, Lively and Experi-
           mentall Description of That Part of America, Commonly
           Called Nevv England: Discovering the State of That
           Countrie, Both as it Stands to Our New-Come English
           Planters; and to the Old Native Inhabitants. London:
           Tho. Cotes.

———   1865   Wood's New England's Prospect [1634]. *Publications of
           the Prince Society* 1. Boston. (Reprinted: Burt Franklin,
           New York, 1967.)

Woodson, Carter G.
1918   The Beginnings of Miscegenation of Whites and Blacks.
           Journal of Negro History 3(4):335-353.

Wooster, W.M.
1907   [Census Roll of Wisconsin Potawatomi in Canada and the
           United States.] (Records of the Bureau of Indian Affairs,
           R.G. 75, Wooster Roll (Special Series A, Box 2). National
           Archives and Record Service. Washington.)

Wormington, Hannah M.
1957   Ancient Man in North America. 4th ed. rev. *Museum of
           Natural History Popular Series* 4. Denver.

Wraxall, Peter
1915   An Abridgement of the Indian Affairs Contained in Four-
           folio Volumes, Transacted in the Colony of New York,
           from the Year 1678 to the Year 1751. Charles H. McIl-
           wain, ed. *(Harvard Historical Studies* 21) Cambridge,
           Mass.: Harvard University Press.

Wray, Charles F.
1973   Manual for Seneca Iroquois Archeology. Rochester,
           N.Y.: Cultures Primitive.

Wray, Charles F., and Harry L. Schoff
1953   A Preliminary Report on the Seneca Sequence in Western
           New York, 1550-1687. *Pennsylvania Archaeologist*
           23(2):53-63.

Wray, Donald E.
1952   Archeology of the Illinois Valley: 1950. Pp. 152-164 in
           Archeology of Eastern United States. James B. Griffin,
           ed. Chicago: University of Chicago Press.

Wray, Donald E., and Richard MacNeish
1961   The Hopewellian and Weaver Occupations of the Weaver
           Site, Fulton County, Illinois. Warren L. Wittry, ed. *Illi-
           nois State Museum Scientific Paper* 7(2). Springfield.

Wright, Gary A.
1966   Eastern Edge Survey, 1965 Season. *Michigan Archaeolo-
           gist* 12(4):151-168.

Wright, Gordon K.
1963   The Neutral Indians - a Source Book. *Occasional Papers
           of the New York State Archeological Association* 4. Roch-
           ester, N.Y.

Wright, Harry A., ed.
1905   Indian Deeds of Hampden County: Being Copies of All
           Land Transfers from the Indians Recorded in the County
           of Hampden, Massachusetts, and Some Deeds from Other
           Sources. Springfield, Mass.: [no publisher.]

Wright, Herbert E., Jr.
1971   Late Quaternary Vegetational History of North America.
           Pp. 425-464 in Late Cenozoic Glacial Ages. Karl K. Ture-
           kian, ed. New Haven, Conn.: Yale University Press.

Wright, James V.
1963   An Archaeological Survey Along the North Shore of Lake
           Superior. *National Museum of Canada Anthropology Paper*
           3. Ottawa.

———   1965   A Regional Examination of Ojibwa Culture History.
           Anthropologica n.s. 7(2):189-227. Ottawa.

———   1966   The Ontario Iroquois Tradition. *Anthropological Series 75,
           National Museum of Canada Bulletin* 210. Ottawa.

———   1967   The Laurel Tradition and the Middle Woodland Period.
           *Anthropological Series 79, National Museum of Canada
           Bulletin* 217. Ottawa.

———   1967a   The Pic River Site: A Stratified Late Woodland Site on
           the North Shore of Lake Superior. Pp. 54-99 in Contribu-
           tions to Anthropology, V: Archaeology and Physical An-
           thropology. *Anthropological Series 72, National Museum of
           Canada Bulletin* 206. Pt. 1. Ottawa.

———   1969   The Michipicoten Site. Pp. 1-85 in Contributions to An-
           thropology, VI: Archaeology and Physical Anthropology.
           *Anthropological Series 82, National Museum of Canada
           Bulletin* 224. Ottawa.

———   1971   The Nodwell Site: A Mid-14th Century Iroquois Village.
           Bulletin of the Canadian Archaeological Association 3:1-11.
           Ottawa.

———   1972   Ontario Prehistory: An Eleven-thousand Year Archae-
           ological Outline. Ottawa: National Museum of Man,
           Archaeological Survey of Canada.

———   1974   The Nodwell Site. *Canada. National Museum of Man,
           Mercury Series Archaeological Survey of Canada Paper* 22.
           Ottawa.

Wright, James V., and J.E. Anderson
1963   The Donaldson Site. *Anthropological Series 58, National
           Museum of Canada Bulletin* 184. Ottawa.

Wright, John C.
1917   The Crooked Tree: Indian Legends of Northern Michi-
           gan. 3d ed. Harbor Springs, Mich.: J.C. Wright.

Wright, Muriel H.
1951   A Guide to the Indian Tribes of Oklahoma. Norman:
           University of Oklahoma Press.

Wroth, Lawrence C.
1970   The Voyages of Giovanni da Verrazzano, 1524-1528. New
           Haven, Conn.: Yale University Press.

Wzôkhilain, Peter P.
1830   Wawasi Lagidamwoganek Mdala Chowagidamwoganal
           Tabtagil, Onkawodokodozwal wji Pôbatami Kidwôgan.
           Boston: Crocker and Brewster.

———   1830a   Wôbanaki Kimzowi Awighigan. Boston: Crocker and
           Brewster.

Yarnell, Richard A.
1964   Aboriginal Relationship Between Culture and Plant Life
           in the Upper Great Lakes Region. *University of Michigan
           Museum of Anthropology, Anthropological Papers* 23. Ann
           Arbor.

Yeardley, Francis
1911   Francis Yeardley's Narrative of Excursions into Carolina.
           Pp. 21-29 in Narratives of Early Carolina, 1650-1708.
           Alexander S. Salley, ed. New York: Charles Scribner's
           Sons.

Yegerlehner, John F.
1954   The First Five Minutes of Shawnee Laws in Multiple
           Stage Translation. *International Journal of American Lin-
           guistics* 20(4):281-294.

Young, A.H., ed.
1922   The Rev. Robert Addison: Extracts from the Reports and
           (Manuscript) Journals of the Society for the Propagation
           of the Gospel in Foreign Parts. *Papers and Records of the
           Ontario Historical Society* 19(4):171-191. Toronto.

Young, Egerton R.
1902   An Indian Camp Meeting in Canada. *Missionary Review
           of the World* n.s. 15(1):45-49.

Youse, Hillis J.
1965   Excavation at Rolf Lee Farm Site 46-Ms-51. *West Vir-
           ginia Archaeologist* 18:15-24.

Zeisberger, David
1776   Essay of a Delaware-Indian and English Spelling-Book for the Use of the Schools of the Christian Indians on Muskingum River. Philadelphia: Printed by Henry Miller.

1885   Diary of David Zeisberger, a Moravian Missionary Among the Indians of Ohio, 1781-1798. Eugene F. Bliss, ed., and trans. 2 vols. Cincinnati: Robert Clarke.

1887   Zeisberger's Indian Dictionary; English, German, Iroquois—The Onondaga and Algonquin—The Delaware. Cambridge, Mass.: John Wilson.

1887a   [Vocabularies.] (From the Collection of Manuscripts Presented by Judge Lane to Harvard University, Nos. 1 and 2.) Cambridge, Mass.: E.N. Hartford.

1887-1888   Essay of an Onondaga Grammar, or A Short Introduction to Learn the Onondaga *Al. Maqua Tongue. Pennsylvania Magazine of History and Biography* 11(4):442-453, 12(5):65-75, 233-239, 325-340.

1910   History of the Northern American Indians. Archer B. Hulbert and William N. Schwarze, eds. *Ohio State Archaeological and Historical Quarterly* 19:1-189. Columbus.

1972   Schoenbrunn Story: Excerpts from the Diary of the Reverend David Zeisberger, 1772-1777, at Schoenbrunn in the Ohio Country. August C. Mahr, trans. Excerpted and Introduced by Daniel R. Porter, III. Columbus: The Ohio Historical Society.

Zeisberger, David, and John G. Jungmann
1769-1772   [Diaries of the Moravian Missions in Western Pennsylvania.] Tilde Marx, trans. (Typescript in Merle Deardorff Papers, Warren Historical Society, Warren, Pa.)

Zeisberger, David, and Gottlob Senseman
1912   Diary of David Zeisberger and Gottlob Senseman, 1768-1769. Archer B. Hulbert and William N. Schwarze, eds. *Ohio State Archaeological and Historical Quarterly* 21:42-104. Columbus.

Zúñiga, Pedro de
1608   [Anonymous Map of Virginia, Sent to the King of Spain.] (Manuscript M.P.D., IV-66, XIX-163 in Archivo General de Simancas.) (Printed in the Jamestown Voyages, Philip Barbour, ed. Vol. 1: facing p. 239, Cambridge University Press, London, 1969.)

Index

Mouingouena; synonymy: 680

Mound Builders: 7-8, *7*, 9, 41, 42, 43, 45

Mountain Indians; synonymy: 238

mourning: 114, 130, 156, 219, 231, 374, 428-429, 639, 752-753

Mowacks; synonymy: 478

Mowhakes; synonymy: 478

Moyaon: 240

Moyaoncer; synonymy: 250

Moyowances; synonymy: 250

M'skōā teeau; synonymy: 672

mškwaʔki·θilenawe; synonymy: 646

Mudeater, Mathew: *404*

Muhheakunneuw; synonymy: 211

Muhheakunnuk; synonymy: 211

Muhhekunneyuk; synonymy: 211

Mummapacun; synonymy: 268

Mun-dua; synonymy: 770

Munnoa'min-nee; synonymy: 723

Munnawtawkit; synonymy: 174

Munsee; synonymy: 236. *See also* Delaware

Muns(e)y; synonymy: 236

Murphy complex: 550

Mush-co-desh; synonymy: 672

mush-ko-dains; synonymy: 672

music: 318. instrumental: 133, 262, 757. vocal: 438, *755, 757. See also* ceremonies, dance

musical instruments; drums: *318, 319, 661, 716, 768.* flute: 660. rattles: *318, 319, 461.* tambourine: *756*

Musketoons; synonymy: 672

Muskogean language grouping: 550, 587

Muskogid physical type: 554

Muskotanje; synonymy: 672

Muskrat Indians; synonymy: 135

Muskwaki; synonymy: 646

Musquattamies; synonymy: 672

Musquattimies; synonymy: 646

Musqueto(o)ns; synonymy: 671

Musquitans; synonymy: 672

mùxò·té·nayi·w; synonymy: 499

mwáns·i; synonymy: 236

Myamicks; synonymy: 688

Myamis; synonymy: 688

Mynomanies; synonymy: 723

Mystic Animals, Company of: 460

mythology: *107,* 116, 402, 696, 711, 788. cannibals: 133. creation: 117, 132, 157-158, 220, 319, 372-373, 628, 717-718, 777. culture heroes: 109, 132, 319, 422, 642-643, 661, 717-718, 757, 796. Windigo: 754, 757, 796. *See also* cosmology; supernatural beings

N

Na-a-nos-a-ko-sa: *712*

Nacostines; synonymy: 250

Nacotchtank(e); *241,* 256-257. synonymy: 250. *See also* Anacostank

nad8eia; synonymy: 406

Nahdo(o)ways; synonymy: 406

Nahicans: 168, 172. synonymy: 174

Nahiggonike; synonymy: 174

Nahigonset; synonymy: 174

Nahigonsicks; synonymy: 174

Nahigonsiks; synonymy: 174

nahkawe·wiyiniw; synonymy: 770

nahkawiyiniw; synonymy: 770

Nah-wee-re-coo: *652*

Nai-wah-ro; synonymy: 236

Naiz percez; synonymy: 770

Najack; synonymy: 237

Nakawawuk; synonymy: 770

Nakawewuck; synonymy: 770

Naked Indians: 590. synonymy: 688

Na-ke-wai-mi: *712*

Nalatchwaniak; synonymy: 147

Namatakeeset: 180. synonymy: 188

names; ceremonies for: 236, 454, 615, 626, 638, 658-659, 660, 682-683, 750. chief: 440. clan: 313. lending: 426. personal: 424-426

Namgauck; synonymy: 147

Nanabozho: 422, 717, 757

Nanapeshamet: 166, 170

Nancemondies; synonymy: 268

Nandewy; synonymy: 248

Nandsamund; synonymy: 268

Nandtanghtacund; synonymy: 268

Nandue: *241.* synonymy: 248

Nanduye; synonymy: 248

Nanepashemet: 169

Nangemaick: 247. synonymy: 250

Nangemy; synonymy: 250

Nanhigganĕuck; synonymy: 174

Nanjemy; synonymy: 250

Nanohigganeucks; synonymy: 174

Nanohiggansets; synonymy: 174

Nanrantsoak; synonymy: 147

Nansamund; synonymy: 268

Nansatico; synonymy: 268. *See also* Virginia Algonquians

Nansemond: 95, 96, 256, 262-263, 266, 267, 286. language: 74. population: 257, 263, 267. synonymy: 268. *See also* Indian words

Nansiatico; synonymy: 268

Nansimum; synonymy: 268

Nantansouak; synonymy: 147

Nantaquack: *241.* synonymy: 250

Nantaughs tacum; synonymy: 268

Nantecoke; synonymy: 250

Nantiatico; synonymy: 268

Nanticoke and neighboring tribes: 240-252. Accomac: 73-74, 240-242, 243-244, 245, 248, 251. Acohanock: 73-74, 242, 248. adornment: 244. Assateague: 240-242, 243, 247, 248. ceremonies: 245. Choptank: 240, *241, 241,* 242, 243, 245, 247, 251, 248-249, 250. Choptico: 242, 252. clothing: 244. Conoy: 61, 73, *73,* 85, 224, 240-242, 243, 244-246, 247, 249, 250, 292, 366. death: 245. external relations: 242-243. history: 240-245. language: 71, 73, *73,* 74, 75, 76, 240. marriage: 245, 248. Mattawoman: 242, 243, 247, 250. Nanticoke: 61, 73, 83, 219, 224, 231, 240-252, 292, 366, 525, 528. orthography: 240. Pamunkey: 240, 242, 243, 250. Patuxent: 240, *241,* 242, 243, 244, 251. Pocomoke: 96, 240, *241,* 242, 243, 247, 251. political organization: 240-242, 245, 247, 428. population: 242, 246, 527-528.

puberty: 245. religion: 245. settlement pattern: 244. social organization: *241,* 244-245, 247-248. structures: *247.* subsistence: 244, *247, 249.* synonymy: 248-251. technology: 244, *250.* territory: 240, *241.* Tockwogh: 240, *241,* 242, 249, 251. transport: 244. Wicocomoco: 242, 251. Wicomiss: 240, 242, 243, 251, 363. *See also* Indian words

Nanticoque; synonymy: 250

Nantoüé; synonymy: 770

Nantsattaqunt; synonymy: 268

Nantucket: 169. language: 72. settlement pattern: 188. synonymy: 188

Nanzaticoe; synonymy: 268

Naragooe; synonymy: 147

Naranchouak; synonymy: 147

Narangawock; synonymy: 147

Naraticonck: 215. synonymy: 238

Narautsowak; synonymy: 147

Narauwing; synonymy: 147

Naridgewalk; synonymy: 147

Narragansett: 5, 174, 177, 190-197, 481. ceremonies: 192. clothing: *186.* cosmology: 192. division of labor: 191. education: 195. employment: 195, 196, 197. environment: 190-191. external relations: 65, 171, 174, 193-195, *194.* history: 83, 85, 91-94, *91,* 172, 187, 188, 193-197. kinship: 193. language: 71, 72, 74, 75, 76, 160, 168, 190. orthography: 190. political organization: 167, 168, 181, 190, 193, 195-196. population: 169, 196-197. prehistory: 197. religion: 191-192, 195, *196.* settlement pattern: 190, 191. shamanism: 191-192, *196.* structures: 191, 195, *196.* subsistence: 161, 163, 190-191. synonymy: 174. technology: 166, *192.* territory: *161,* 172, 181, 190-191, *191.* trade: 191, 193. warfare: 90-92, 93-94, 99, 173, 193, *194,* 195. *See also* Indian words

Narragansett Regulation Act: 195-196

Narrigansets; synonymy: 174

Narrow Stemmed Point culture: 35

Nashaway: 148, 170. synonymy: 187

Nashiwaskuk. *See* Davis, Jack

Naskapi: 18, 798. language: 583

Nassauakueton. *See* Ottawa

Nasswatex: 240. synonymy: 251

Natawanute: 173

na·tawɛw; synonymy: 320

natawia; synonymy: 320

Nathattou: 172

Natick: 180, 187, 188

nation. *For French and English names with nation see the main word of the name*

na·towe·(ki); synonymy: 320, 406

na·towe·θaki Wyandots; synonymy: 406

na·towe·w; synonymy: 320

na·towe·wa; synonymy: 289, 320, 406

Nattamonge; synonymy: 268

natuági; synonymy: 321

natwe; synonymy: 406

Naugatuck: 168, 173. language: 72, 76

Naumkeag: 169

Naurantsouak; synonymy: 147

909

912   League of the Iroquois

Prouville de Tracy, Alexandre de: 431, 469, 493, 501
psicania; synonymy: 321
psigania; synonymy: 321
psikania; synonymy: 321
Puan(t)s; synonymy: 706
puberty: 735-736. boys': 129-130, 659, 751, 763. ceremonies: 245, 262, 285, 659, 675, 714, 751. girls': 285, 659, *659*, 751. taboos: 285, 659, *659*. vision quest: 751, 763
Puckanokick; synonymy: 175
Pudaduc; synonymy: 188
Pungotege; synonymy: 248
Pungoteque; synonymy: 248
Punkapoag; synonymy: 187
Punkapog: 170, 180. synonymy: 187
Purchas, Samuel: 137
purification. *See* death practices
Puscattaway; synonymy: 250
Pú-te-wa-ta; synonymy: 741
Putnam, Frederic Ward: 9-10
Puyon; synonymy: 706
Pynchon, William: 150, 174
Pyquans; synonymy: 175
Pyrlaeus, Christopher: 420

Q

Qiuotanck; synonymy: 248
Quackohowaon; synonymy: 269
Quacksis; synonymy: 646
Quacohamaock; population: 257. synonymy: 269
Quadequina: 171
Quaiapan: 99, 193
Quandanquan; synonymy: 251
Quapaw; warfare: 594, 674
Quatoges; synonymy: 405
Quatoghies; synonymy: 405
Quatokeronon; synonymy: 654
Quayoughcohanek; synonymy: 269
Quenongebin: 792
Quequashkecasquick; synonymy: 248
Quieunotatéronon; synonymy: 396
Quillipeage; synonymy: 175
Quillypieck; synonymy: 175
Quinapeake: 168
Quinney, Austin E.: *206*
Quinney, John: 207
Quinney, John W.: *207*, 209, 210
Quinney, Joseph: 209
Quinnipiac: 168. synonymy: 175. *See also* Quiripi
Quinnypiock; synonymy: 175
Quinopiocke; synonymy: 175
Quinté, Bay of; synonymy: 479
Quiocquhannock; synonymy: 269
Quiouhamenec: 167
Quiripey; synonymy: 175
Quiripi: 168, 169, 173. language: 64, 65, 71, 72, 75, 76, 160, 168, 173. settlement pattern: 184. synonymy: 175
Quitways; synonymy: 688
Quiyoughcohannock; population: 257. synonymy: 269
Quinnipiĕuck; synonymy: 175
Quowaughkutt; synonymy: 248

R

Radcliffe-Brown, A.R.: 12
Raddatz culture: 25
radiocarbon dating. *See* archeology
Radisson, Pierre Esprit: 500, 602-603, 786
Raffeix, Pierre: 469
Ragueneau, Paul: 789
Rain Dance. *See* ceremonies
Rakouagega; synonymy: 411
Râle, Sébastien: 143, 794
Raleigh, Walter: 4, 290
Ramapo Mountain People. See marginal groups
Ramcock; synonymy: 238
Ranatshaganha; synonymy: 211
Rancocus; synonymy: 238
Rapahanna; synonymy: 269
Raparouas; synonymy: 680
Rappahannock; synonymy: 269. *See also* Virginia Algonquians
Rappahannocke; synonymy: 269
Rapahanocks; synonymy: 269
Raritan: 213. synonymy: 237
Raritonoos; synonymy: 237
Rariton; synonymy: 238
Rasaouakoueton; synonymy: 730
Rasoughteick; synonymy: 248-249
ratirǫta'kó·wa; synonymy: 490
rattles. *See* musical instruments
rá·waruhki; synonymy: 741
Raymbault, Charles: 602, 789
Rechgawawanc(k); synonymy: 237
Rechgawawank: 214. synonymy: 237
Rechkawyck; synonymy: 237
Rechkewick; synonymy: 237
Recho(u)wacky; synonymy: 237
Rechqua Akie; synonymy: 237
Reckomacki; synonymy: 237
Reckonhacky; synonymy: 237
Reckowacky; synonymy: 237
Red Bird: 697-698
Red Blanket: *749*
Red-Earths; synonymy: 645
Red Eye, Sherman: *462*
Red Jacket: 8, 429, 447, *452*
Red Ocher culture: 41, 43
red ocher use: 42, 103, *103*, 106
Red River Indians; synonymy: 770
re·gáči; synonymy: 769
Régis, Jean François: 473
Registered (Cherokee) Delaware: 224. *See also* Delaware, Unami
religion: 106, 695-696. Drum (Dream) Dance: 716, *716*, 722, 755-756. factionalism: 452, 482-483, 535, 701, 704. Jossakeed: 783. Meta: 783. Peyote: 234, *235*, 542, 701, 704, 717, 721-722, 742, 756-757. souls: 191, 192, 220, 374-375, 696, 777, 783. tobacco use: 643, 754. Wabeno: 783. 1960s: 722, 768. 1970s: 121, 294, 464, 541. *See also* afterlife; ceremonies; Christianity; Handsome Lake, Code of; Longhouse religion; Midewiwin; mythology; shamans; supernatural beings
Remahenoc; synonymy: 237
Remkoke: 215. synonymy: 238
Rémy de Courcelle, Daniel de: 431, 469

Renappi; synonymy: 235
Renards; synonymy: 646
Renarhonon; synonymy: 387
Rencor; synonymy: 646
Requickening Address. *See* Condolence ceremony
reservations and reserves: *178*, 222, 389, 444-445, *450*, 471, 486, 525-536, 608. Algonquin: *793*. Allegany: 436-437, 445, *450*, 509, 511, 512, *512*, *513*, 513-514, 516. administration: 195-196, 210, 487, 526, 540, 645, 701, 721, 723, 738, 745, 785. Anderdon: *398*. Big Spring: *398*. Big Tree: *450*. Broad creek: 297. Brothertown: 222. Buffalo Creek: 435-436, *450-451*, 495-496, 502, 509, 511. Cattaraugus: 436-437, *450*, 503, 509, 511, 512, *512-513*, 516, 539. Caughnawaga: *307*, *308*, *450*, 452, 454, 469-471, *470-471*, 473, 476, 478, 479. Charlestown: 187, 195, 197. Chicacoan: 297. Chippewa: 745-746, *745*. Christiantown: 180. Citizens' band: 737-738. construction on: 196, 197. Cornplanter: 443, 445, *450*, 509, 516. education: 119, 195, 514, 526, 529-530, 532, 731. employment: 195, 463, 498, 531, 535, 720-721. establishment of: 97, 125, 528-530. Fall River: 179-180. Gay Head: 180-181. Gibson: *450*, 471. Golden Hill: 183-184, 187. Grand River: 246, 312, 321, 402, 435-437, *450*, 453-454, *471*, 476, 487-488, 495, 502, 525-536, *526*, *529*, *533*, 539, 542, 778-779. Hassanamisco: 187. Herring Pond: 179. land: 436-437, 450, 453, 502, 525, 526-527, 537-538, 539, 720. Martha's Vineyard: 180. Mashpee: 179. Menominee: 720-723, *720*. Mesquakie Settlement: 645. Mushantuxet: 182, 186. Nebraska: 700-702. Neosho: 538, *538*. Oil Spring: *450*, *512-513*. Ojibwa: 764, *764*. Oka: *450*, *471*, 476, 477, 479, 790. Oneida (Can.): *450*, *486*. Oneida (U.S.): *450*, *486*. Onondaga: *450*, 492, 495-498, 497. Ottawa: *779*. political organization: 119-120, 195-196, 210, 436-437, 487, 498-499, 528, 529, *529*, 531, 532-534, *533*, 535-536, 540, 645, 701, 713-714, 721-722. Poosepatuck: 184, 186. population: 120, 502, 511, 514, 527, 535, 495-496, 720-722. Prairie band: 737-738. religion: 453, 526, 530, 534, 535, 721-722. Restigouche: 119-120. Saint John River: 125, 135. St. Regis: *450*, 469, *471*, 473, 476, 477, 478, 479. sale: 247, 390. Sandusky: 502, 537-538. Schaghticoke: 183, 187. Seneca: *512*, *513*, 539. settlement pattern: 119-120, 123, 173, 179-184, *178*, 186-187, 195, 210-211, 224, *241*, 247, 265, 287-288, 389, *389*, 390-392, 401, 402-404, 435-436, 444-445, *471*, 479, *486*, 492, 495-498, *497*, *508-509*, *512*, 513-514, *513*, 521, *521*, 524, 538, *538*, 654, 664-665, 679, 700-703, 737-738, 745-746, *745*, *764*, 778-780, *779*, 795. settlements: 525-526, 720-722, *720*. Shinnecock: 184, 186. state government: 186. Stockbridge: 181, 210-211, *720*.

283, 428, 519–520, *519, 523*. population: 288, 518, 520, 521, 527. prehistory: 58, 61. puberty: 285. religion: 522. reservation: 287–288, *521, 522*. settlement pattern: 283. social organization: 523–524. structures: 284. subsistence: 283–284, 285, 522. synonymy: 288, 524. territory: 271, 282, *282, 521*. warfare: 273, 279, 285, 481, 518, 520–521. *See also* Indian words; League of the Iroquois

Tuscarorens; synonymy: 524
Tuscarories; synonymy: 524
Tuscaroro(es); synonymy: 524
Tuscorure; synonymy: 524
Tuskarorers; synonymy: 524
Tuskoraries; synonymy: 524
Tuskwawgomeeg; synonymy: 791
Tusquarores; synonymy: 524
Tutelo: 538. language: 9. political organization: 428. population: 502, 527–528. reservations: 502, 528. territory: 246, 501, 525
tuwéhtuwe; synonymy: 688
Twaatwãã; synonymy: 688
twahrò·nǝh; synonymy: 490
Twautwãũ; synonymy: 688
Tweeghtwees; synonymy: 688
Twicktwigs; synonymy: 688
Twightwees; synonymy: 688
Twightwighs; synonymy: 688
Twins. *See* Tharonhiawagon
Tynondady; synonymy: 405
tyonontate⁷ka⁷; synonymy: 405

U

Uchepowuck; synonymy: 769
Uchipweys; synonymy: 769
Umpachenee: 207, 208
Unalâchtgo; synonymy: 236
Unalachtigo; language: 73, 215, 225. synonymy: 236. *See also* Delaware; Indian words
Unalimi; synonymy: 235, 236
Unami; synonymy: 236–237. *See also* Delaware
Unami(e)s; synonymy: 236
Uncas: 8, 90–91, 167, *171,* 172, 173, 185, 194, *194*
Uncas, Ben, II: 181
Unchachage; synonymy: 175
Unchechange; synonymy: 175
Unckachohok; synonymy: 175
Undatomátendi; synonymy: 741
Underhill, John: 90
Unéchtgo; synonymy: 250
Union of New Brunswick Indians: 135
United States government: 515. Indian agent administration: 119–120, 134–135, 145, 608, 664. peacekeeping: 641. relocation program (1950s): 690, 758. reservation policy: 444–445. *See also* Bureau of Indian Affairs; history; land; legislation, United States; reservations and reserves; treaties
universe, concept of. *See* cosmology
Unkechage; synonymy: 175
Unquachack; synonymy: 175

Unquachog: 215. language: 64, 65, 71, 72, 75, 76, 160, 168, 173, 184. synonymy: 175
Unquehiett: 363
Upper Iroquois; synonymy: 320, 515. *See also* League of the Iroquois
Upper Matchotix; synonymy: 268
Upper Mattaponi: 269, 270. population: 267. synonymy: 269
Usququhaga: 363
Utavois; synonymy: 785
Utawawas: 204
Ut-ha-wah. *See* Captain Cold
Uttawaw; synonymy: 785

V

Vanderpool, Anthony: 291
Van Guilders: 209
Van Schaick, Goose: 495, 508
Vassal, Henri: 159
vegetation. *See* environment
Verelst, John: 303, *474*
Vergennes phase: 25–27
Verrazano, Giovanni da: 4, 80, 85, 141, 160, 162, 175, 193, 220, 271
Viele, Aernout: 630
Vignau, Nicolas de: 791
villages: 358–359, *381, 412,* 494, 668, 692. clan: 467. defined: 164. fortified: 218–219, 283, 548, 552, 557. merging: 142, 327–328. multiple: 378. number: 731, 734. palisaded: 123, 166, 198–199, *199,* 244, 259, *278,* 306, 326, 327, 358–359, 375, 377, 481, 564, 578. plan: 276, *358, 400, 491–492, 674, 682, 693, 728*. political organization: 732. population: 166, 306, 358, 359, 377–378, *381,* 395, 595, 693, 734. relocation: 302, 381. settlement pattern: 58, 153, 206, 326, 375, 501. size: 166, 219, 259, 276, 306, 358–359, 377–378, 395, 481, 491, 501, 547, 550, 595, 675, 693. *See also* camps; political organization; praying towns
Village-des-Hurons: 389
Vimont, Barthélemy: 690, 791
Vincennes culture: 550, *561,* 567
Vincent, Phillipe: *390–391*
Vine, Richard: 170
Virginia Algonquians: 6, 13, 58, 61, 62, 244, 253–270, *261,* 271, 273, 279. adornment: 244, 260. Appamatuck I: 254, 257, 262–263, 268. Appamatuck II: 258, 268. ceremonies: 245. Chickahominy: 13, 61, 255–257, 258, 261, 262–263, 265, 266, *266,* 267–268, 270. clothing: 244, 260, *261, 264, 266*. communications: 244, 262. Cuttatawomen I: 258, 268. Cuttatawomen II: 258, 268. death: *62,* 245, 262. division of labor: 259. environment: 253. external relations: 242–243, 254, 256–258, 259, 270. games: 262. history: 240–245, 254–264, 265–268, 269–270. language: 70, 73–74, 75, 240, 253. marriage: 245, 248, 262, 266. Matchotic I: 258, 268. Matchotic II: 257, 268. Moratico: 258, 268. music: 262. Nansatico: 258, 263, 268. Opiscopank: 258, 268. orthography: 253. Pamunkey: 74, 97–98, *98,* 240, 254, 256, 257, 258, 263,

264, 265, 266, 267, 268. Pissasec: 258, 269. political organization: 96, 240–242, 245, 247, 255, 261–262, 266, 804. population: 95, 252, 254, 255–256, 262–263, 265, *265,* 267. Potomac: *97,* 258, 263, 266, 267, 269. Potopaco: 258, 262–263, 269. Powhatan: 1, 70, 73–74, 75, 254, 255–257, 261, 262, 267, 269. prehistory: 58, 253, 269, 270. puberty: 245, 262. racial intermixture: 263. Rappahannock: 96, 258, 262–263, 265, 266, 267, 269, 270. religion: 262, 267–268. Secacawoni: 258, 269. settlement pattern: 58. social organization: *241,* 244–245, 247–248, 261–262, *265.* structures: 58, 259–260. subsistence: 58, 244, 253, 254–255, 258–259. synonymy: 248–251, 268–269. Tauxent: 258, 269. technology: 61, 244, 253, 255, 269, 260–261, 266. territory: 240, 253, *254, 255, 256, 265.* trade: 255, 259. transport: 244. warfare: 96, *97, 98,* 256–257, 259, 262. Wicocomoco: 255, 256–257, 258, 263, 267, 269
Virginia-North Carolina coastal Iroquoians: 282–289. death: 285–286. division of labor: 285. environment: 282–283. external relations: 258, 286. history: 286–288, 289. language: 282–283, 334, 335, 338, 341. marriage: 286–287. Meherrin: 61, 282, *282,* 283–287, 289. Nottaway: 61, 258, 263, 282, *282,* 283, 284, 285–287, 288, 289, 334, 335, 338, 341. orthography: 282, 523. political organization: 283. population: 263, 286, 287. prehistory: 61. puberty: 285. settlement pattern: 283. social organization: 283. structures: 284. subsistence: 283–285. synonymy: 288–289. territory: 282–283, *282*. trade: 284. *See also* Coree; Neusiok; Tuscarora
visions: 231–232, 373, 445–446, 454, 626, 629. dream guardian: 714–715, *715.* guessing rite: 497–498. recitals: 231–232, *232, 234.* revelation: 714. quest: 614, 643, 661, 675, 685, 751, 763, 796
Vnchechange; synonymy: 175
vocabularies. See Indian words; *specific language groupings*
Voegelin, E.: 11
Vosburgh culture: 32

W

waapanahkiiha; synonymy: 236
Wabanaki; synonymy: 137, 147. *See also* confederacies
Wabanaki Confederacy. *See* confederacies
Wabanascum, Pete: *716*
wábaniki; synonymy: 236
wa·bánoxgé; synonymy: 490
Wabemando: 141
Wabnaki; synonymy: 147
Wabokieshiek: 652
Wachetak; synonymy: 248
Waerinnewangh; synonymy: 238
Waganis; synonymy: 785
Wagenhaes; synonymy: 589. *See also* Wagenhanes